EL OCEAN

UNMAPPED
TUNDRA

OAST

SKRAELINGS

GLACIER

ICESCARP
ALPS

SHADOWSWARD
(AVARINHEIM)

SCARP
ARREN

R. NORDRA

FORTRESS

RANGES

WILD DOG
PLAINS

WIDOWMAKER SEA

OLT

IS

NG

HOLDHARD
PASS

R. NORDRA

FORBIDDEN
VALLEY

TAILEM
BEND

SMYRTON

SEAGRASS PLAINS

Literature of the
Western World

LITERATURE OF THE
WESTERN
WORLD

VOLUME II
Neoclassicism Through
The Modern Period

THIRD EDITION

BRIAN WILKIE JAMES HURT

University of Arkansas *University of Illinois*

PRENTICE HALL
Englewood Cliffs, New Jersey 07632

Library of Congress Cataloging-in-Publication Data

Literature of the western world / [compiled] by Brian Wilkie, James
 Hurt.—3rd ed.
 p. cm.
 Includes index.
 Contents: Contents: v. 2. Neoclassicism through the modern period.
 ISBN 0-02-427827-0
 1. Literature—Collections. I. Wilkie, Brian, 1929– .
 II. Hurt, James, 1934– .
PN6104.L615 1992
808.8—dc20
 91-8567
 CIP

Editor: D. Anthony English
Production Supervisor: Charlotte Hyland
Production Manager: Pamela Kennedy Orborski
Cover Designer: Jane Edelstein
Cover Illustration: Edouard Vuillard (1868–1940), "Garden at
Vaucresson."
Tempera on canvas.
H. 59-1/2 in. W. 43-5/8 in. (151.1 x 110.8 cm).
Credit line: The Metropolitan Museum of Art, Wolfe Fund, 1952.
Catharine Lorillard Wolfe Collection. (52.183)

This book was set in Baskerville by York Graphic Services, Inc.

Acknowledgments appear on pages v–viii, which constitute a
continuation of the copyright page.

© 1992 by Prentice-Hall, Inc.
A Simon & Schuster Company
Englewood Cliffs, New Jersey 07632
Earlier editions copyright © 1984 and 1988 by Macmillan Publishing Company

Printed in the United States of America

10 9 8 7

ISBN 0-02-427827-0

Prentice-Hall International (UK) Limited, *London*
Prentice-Hall of Australia Pty. Limited, *Sydney*
Prentice-Hall Canada Inc., *Toronto*
Prentice-Hall Hispanoamericana, S.A., *Mexico*
Prentice-Hall of India Private Limited, *New Delhi*
Prentice-Hall of Japan, Inc., *Tokyo*
Simon & Schuster Asia Pte. Ltd., *Singapore*
Editora Prentice-Hall do Brasil, Ltda., *Rio de Janeiro*

Acknowledgments

APOLLINAIRE, GUILLAUME. "The Mirabeau Bridge," translated by W. S. Merwin, "Annie," translated by Dudley Fitts, "White Snow," translated by Dudley Fitts, "Hills," translated by Dudley Fitts, "Company Commander," translated by Dudley Fitts, and "The Pretty Redhead," translated by Kate Flores. These poems appear in Angel Flores, ed., *An Anthology of French Poetry from Nerval to Valéry in English Translation*, Garden City, N.Y.: Doubleday Anchor Books, 1958. Reprinted by permission of Angel Flores.

BABEL, ISAAC. "The Story of My Dovecot," translated by Walter Morison, reprinted by permission of S. G. Phillips, Inc., from *The Collected Stories of Isaac Babel*. Copyright © 1955 by S. G. Phillips, Inc.

BALDWIN, JAMES. "Sonny's Blues," copyright © 1957 by James Baldwin. From *Going to Meet the Man* by James Baldwin. Used by permission of Doubleday, a division of Bantam Doubleday Dell Publishing Group, Inc.

BEAUMARCHAIS, PIERRE-AUGUSTIN CARON DE. "Figaro's Marriage" by Beaumarchais translated by Jacques Barzun from *Phaedra and Figaro*, translated by Robert Lowell and Jacques Barzun. Copyright © 1961 by Jacques Barzun. Reprinted by permission of Farrar, Straus and Giroux, Inc.

BECKETT, SAMUEL. "Krapp's Last Tape" from *Krapp's Last Tape and Other Dramatic Pieces* by Samuel Beckett. Reprinted by permission of Grove Weidenfeld. Copyright © 1958 by Grove Press, Inc.

BORGES, JORGE LUIS. "Tlön, Uqbar, Orbis Tertius" from *Labyrinths and Other Writings* by Jorge Luis Borges, translated by James E. Irby. Copyright © 1962, 1964 by New Directions Publishing Corporation. Reprinted by permission of New Directions Publishing Corporation.

BORGES, JORGE LUIS. "The Circular Ruins" from *The Aleph and Other Stories* by Jorge Luis Borges. English translation copyright © 1968, 1969, 1970 by Emece Editores, S. A., and Norman Thomas di Giovanni. Copyright © 1970 by Jorge Luis Borges, Adolfo Bioy Casares, and Norman Thomas di Giovanni. All rights reserved. Reprinted by permission of the publisher, Viking Penguin, a division of Penguin Books USA Inc., and by Emece Editores, S. A., and the Estate of Jorge Luis Borges.

BRECHT, BERTOLT. "The Good Woman of Setzuan" from *Parables for the Theatre*. Translated by Eric Bentley. University of Minnesota Press, Minneapolis. Copyright © 1947, 1948, 1956, 1961, 1976 by Eric Bentley; epilogue copyright © 1965 by Eric Bentley. Reprinted by arrangement with the University of Minnesota Press.

BÜCHNER, GEORG. "Woyzeck" from *Georg Büchner: Complete Plays and Prose* translated by Carl Richard Mueller. Translation copyright © 1963 by Carl Richard Mueller. Reprinted by permission of Hill and Wang, a division of Farrar, Straus and Giroux, Inc.

CAMUS, ALBERT. "The Adulterous Woman" from *Exile and the Kingdom*, by Albert Camus, translated by Justin O'Brien. Copyright © 1957, 1958 by Alfred A. Knopf, Inc. Reprinted by permission of the publisher.

CHEKHOV, ANTON. "Gooseberries" from *The Wife and Other Stories* by Anton Chekhov, translated by Constance Garnett. Copyright 1918 by Macmillan Publishing Company, renewed 1946 by Constance Garnett. Reprinted by permission of Macmillan Publishing Company.

CORBIÈRE, TRISTAN. "Oh! That?", "Paris by Night", and "Paris by Day" from *Selections from Les Amours Jaunes*, translated and edited by C. F. MacIntyre. Copyright © 1954 The Regents of the University of California. Reprinted by permission of the publisher, The University of California Press. "The End" translated by Kate Flores. This poem appears in Angel Flores, ed., *An Anthology of French Poetry from Nerval to Valéry in English Translation*, Garden City, N.Y.: Doubleday Anchor Books, 1958. Reprinted by permission of Angel Flores.

DICKINSON, EMILY. "Success is counted sweetest," "I'm 'wife'—I've finished that—," "I taste a liquor never brewed—," "There's a certain Slant of light," "I felt a funeral, in my Brain," "The Soul selects her own Society—," "Before I got my eye put out," "A Bird came down

the Walk—," "After great pain, a formal feeling comes—," "What Soft—Cherubic Creatures," "Much Madness is divinest Sense—," "I heard a Fly buzz—when I died—," "I am alive—I guess—," "I like to see it lap the Miles," "Because I could not stop for Death—," "Presentiment—is that long Shadow—on the Lawn—," "Ample make this Bed—," "Tell all the Truth but tell it slant—," and "My life closed twice before its close—." Reprinted by permission of the publishers and the Trustees of Amherst College from *The Poems of Emily Dickinson,* Thomas H. Johnson, ed., Cambridge, Mass.: The Belknap Press of Harvard University Press, copyright 1951, © 1955, 1979, 1983 by the President and Fellows of Harvard College. "After great pain, a formal feeling comes—" from *The Complete Poems of Emily Dickinson,* edited by Thomas H. Johnson. Copyright 1929 by Martha Dickinson Bianchi. Copyright © renewed 1957 by Mary L. Hamson. By permission of Little, Brown and Company.

Dostoevsky, Fyodor. "The Grand Inquisitor" from *The Brothers Karamazov* by Fyodor Dostoevsky, translated from the Russian by Constance Garnett. Copyright 1923 by Macmillan Publishing Company. Reprinted by permission of Macmillan Publishing Company. "Notes from Underground" from *White Nights and Other Stories* by Fyodor Dostoevsky, translated from the Russian by Constance Garnett. Copyright 1918 by Macmillan Publishing Company. Reprinted by permission of Macmillan Publishing Company.

Eliot, T. S. "Burnt Norton" from *Four Quartets,* copyright 1943 by T. S. Eliot and renewed 1971 by Esme Valerie Eliot, reprinted by permission of Harcourt Brace Jovanovich, Inc. "The Love Song of J. Alfred Prufrock" and "The Waste Land" from *Collected Poems 1909–1962* by T. S. Eliot, copyright 1936 by Harcourt Brace Jovanovich, copyright © 1964, 1963 by T. S. Eliot, reprinted by permission of the publisher.

Faulkner, William. "An Odor of Verbena." Copyright 1938 and renewed 1966 by Estelle Faulkner and Jill Faulkner Summers. Reprinted from *The Faulkner Reader,* by permission of Random House, Inc.

Flaubert, Gustave. "A Simple Heart" from *Three Tales* by Gustave Flaubert, translated by Arthur McDowall. Published 1924 by Alfred A. Knopf, Inc. Reprinted by permission of the publisher.

Freud, Sigmund. Excerpt from "Dora: Fragment of an Analysis of a Case of Hysteria" from *Sigmund Freud: Collected Papers, Volume 3,* by Sigmund Freud. Authorized standard translation by Alix and James Strachey. Published by arrangement with The Hogarth Press Ltd. and the Institute for Psycho-Analysis, London. Reprinted by permission of Basic Books, Inc., Publishers, New York.

Fugard, Athol. "'Master Harold' . . . and the Boys" from *"Master Harold" . . . and the Boys,* by Athol Fugard. Copyright © 1982 by Athol Fugard. Reprinted by permission of Alfred A. Knopf, Inc.

García Márquez, Gabriel. "Big Mama's Funeral," translated by J. S. Bernstein, from *Collected Stories* by Gabriel García Márquez. Copyright © 1984 by Gabriel García Márquez. Reprinted by permission of HarperCollins Publishers.

Ibsen, Henrik. "A Doll House" from *The Complete Major Prose Plays of Henrik Ibsen,* translated by Rolf Fjelde. Copyright © 1965, 1970, 1978 by Rolf Fjelde. Reprinted by permission of the publisher, New American Library, a division of Penguin Books USA Inc.

Joyce, James. "Calypso" from *Ulysses: The Corrected Text* by James Joyce, ed. by Hans Walter Gabler. Copyright © 1986 by Random House, Inc. Reprinted by permission of Random House, Inc. "The Dead" from *Dubliners* by James Joyce. Originally published by B. W. Huebsch in 1916. Definitive text copyright © 1967 by The Estate of James Joyce.

Kafka, Franz. "The Metamorphosis" reprinted from *The Metamorphosis, The Penal Colony, and Other Stories* by Franz Kafka, translated by Willa and Edwin Muir. Published by Schocken Books, reprinted by permission of Pantheon Books, a division of Random House, Inc. Copyright 1948 by Schocken Books Inc. Copyright renewed 1975 by Schocken Books Inc.

Kleist, Heinrich von. "The Marquise of O ———" from *The Marquise of O ——— and Other Stories* by Heinrich von Kleist, translated by Martin Greenberg. Introduction and English translation of stories copyright © 1960 by Martin Greenberg. Reprinted by permission of HarperCollins Publishers.

KUNDERA, MILAN. "Nobody Will Laugh" from *Laughable Loves*, by Milan Kundera, translated by Suzanne Rappaport. Copyright © 1974 by Alfred A. Knopf, Inc. Reprinted by permission of the publisher.

LA FAYETTE, MARIE DE LA VERGNE DE. "The Princesse de Clèves," translated by Nancy Mitford and revised by Leonard Tanock. Copyright 1951 by New Directions Publishing Corporation. Reprinted by permission of New Directions Publishing Corporation.

LAWRENCE, D. H. "The Horse Dealer's Daughter" from *The Complete Short Stories of D. H. Lawrence*. Copyright 1922 by Thomas Seltzer Inc. Copyright renewed 1950 by Frieda Lawrence. Reprinted by permission of the publisher, Viking Penguin, a division of Penguin Books USA Inc. "Odour of Chrysanthemums" from *The Complete Short Stories of D. H. Lawrence*. Copyright 1933 by The Estate of D. H. Lawrence. Copyright © renewed 1961 by Angelo Ravagli and C. M. Weekley, executors of The Estate of Frieda Lawrence Ravagli. Reprinted by permission of the publisher, Viking Penguin, a division of Penguin Books USA Inc.

MACHADO DE ASSIS, JOAQUIM MARIA. "Dona Paula" from *The Devil's Church and Other Stories* by Joaquim Maria Machado de Assis, translated by Jack Schmitt and Lorie Ishimatsu. Translation copyright © 1977 by the University of Texas Press. Reprinted by permission of the University of Texas Press.

MANN, THOMAS. "Disorder and Early Sorrow," translated by H. T. Lowe-Porter. Copyright 1936 and renewed 1964 by Alfred A. Knopf, Inc. Reprinted from *Stories of Three Decades* by Thomas Mann, by permission of the publisher.

MOLIÈRE. "Tartuffe" by Molière, translated by Richard Wilbur, copyright © 1961 and renewed 1989 by Richard Wilbur, reprinted by permission of Harcourt Brace Jovanovich, Inc. *Caution:* All rights, including professional, amateur, motion picture, recitation, lecturing, public readings, radio broadcasting, and television are strictly reserved. Inquiries on all rights should be addressed to Harcourt Brace Jovanovich Inc., Orlando, FL 32887.

OATES, JOYCE CAROL. "Did You Ever Slip on Red Blood?" from *Marriages and Infidelities* by Joyce Carol Oates. Copyright © 1978 by Joyce Carol Oates. Reprinted by permission of John Hawkins & Associates, Inc.

PIRANDELLO, LUIGI. "Six Characters in Search of an Author," translated by Frederick May from *Six Characters in Search of an Author* by Luigi Pirandello. Copyright 1922, renewed 1950 in the names of Stefano, Fausto, and Lietia Pirandello. Reprinted by permission of the publisher, Dutton, an imprint of New American Library, a division of Penguin Books USA Inc.

RACINE, JEAN. "Phaedra" by Racine from *Phaedra and Other Plays* translated by John Cairncross (Penguin Classics, Revised Edition, 1970), copyright © John Cairncross, 1963, 1970.

RICH, ADRIENNE. "Aunt Jennifer's Tigers," "Snapshots of a Daughter-in-Law," "The Burning of Paper Instead of Children," "Diving into the Wreck," "Paula Becker to Clara Westhoff," and "For Julia in Nebraska," from *The Fact of a Doorframe: Poems Selected and New, 1950–1984*, by Adrienne Rich, by permission of W. W. Norton & Company, Inc. Copyright © 1984 by Adrienne Rich. Copyright © 1975, 1978 by W. W. Norton & Company, Inc. Copyright © 1981 by Adrienne Rich. "Look: this January the worst onslaught," "Tearing but not yet torn: this page," "Lately in my dreams I hear long sentences," "I have backroads I take to places," "The Tolstoyans the Afro-American slaves," "This high summer we love will pour its light," and "You who think I find words for everything," from *Your Native Land, Your Life: Poems by Adrienne Rich*, by permission of W. W. Norton & Company, Inc. Copyright © 1986 by Adrienne Rich.

SARTRE, JEAN-PAUL. "The Wall" by Jean-Paul Sartre, translated by Maria Jolas. Copyright 1945 and renewed 1973 by Random House, Inc. Reprinted from *Bedside Book of Famous French Stories*, edited by Belle Becker and Robert N. Linscott, by permission of New Directions Publishing Corp. and Random House, Inc.

TURGENEV, IVAN. "First Love" from *The Borzoi Turgenev* by Ivan Turgenev, translated by Harry Stevens. Copyright 1950 by Alfred A. Knopf, Inc. Reprinted by permission of the publisher.

VERLAINE, PAUL. "My Familiar Dream," translated by C. F. MacIntyre, "Song of the Ingenues,"

translated by C. F. MacIntyre, "Sentimental Conversation," translated by C. F. MacIntyre, "Songs Without Words, VIII," translated by C. F. MacIntyre, and "The Art of Poetry," translated by C. F. MacIntyre: by Paul Verlaine. From Paul Verlaine, *Selected Poems,* translated by C. F. MacIntyre © 1948 The Regents of the University of California, © 1976 Carlyle MacIntyre. "The White Moon," translated by Kate Flores. This poem appears in Angel Flores, ed., *An Anthology of French Poetry from Nerval to Valéry in English Translation,* Garden City, N.Y.: Doubleday Anchor Books, 1958. Reprinted by permission of Angel Flores.

VOLTAIRE. "Candide" from *Candide and Other Tales,* translated by Tobias Smollett and revised by J. C. Thornton. An Everyman's Library Edition, 1937. Reprinted by permission of the publisher in the United States, E. P. Dutton.

WALKER, ALICE. "To Hell With Dying" from *In Love & Trouble: Stories of Black Women,* copyright © 1967 by Alice Walker, reprinted by permission of Harcourt Brace Jovanovich, Inc.

WOOLF, VIRGINIA. "The Mark on the Wall" from *A Haunted House and Other Short Stories* by Virginia Woolf, copyright © 1972 by Harcourt Brace Jovanovich, Inc., reprinted by permission of the publisher. "Shakespeare's Sister" excerpted from *A Room of One's Own* by Virginia Woolf, copyright 1929 by Harcourt Brace Jovanovich, Inc. and renewed 1957 by Leonard Woolf, reprinted by permission of the publisher.

WRIGHT, RICHARD. "Big Boy Leaves Home" from *Uncle Tom's Children* by Richard Wright. Copyright 1936 by Richard Wright; copyright © renewed 1964 by Ellen Wright. Reprinted by permission of HarperCollins Publishers.

YEATS, WILLIAM BUTLER. "The Lake Isle of Innisfree," "To Ireland in the Coming Times," and "He Remembers Forgotten Beauty" by W. B. Yeats, reprinted by permission of Macmillan Publishing Company from *Collected Poems* by W. B. Yeats. Copyright 1956 by Macmillan Publishing Co. Reprinted by permission of Macmillan Publishing Company. "A Coat" by W. B. Yeats, reprinted with permission of Macmillan Publishing Company from *Collected Poems* by W. B. Yeats. Copyright 1916 by Macmillan Publishing Co., Inc., renewed 1944 by Bertha Georgie Yeats. "Easter 1916" and "The Second Coming" by W. B. Yeats, reprinted with permission of Macmillan Publishing Company from *Collected Poems* by W. B. Yeats. Copyright 1924 by Macmillan Publishing Co., Inc., renewed 1952 by Bertha Georgie Yeats. "Sailing to Byzantium," "Two Songs from a Play," "Leda and the Swan," and "Among School Children" by W. B. Yeats, reprinted with permission of Macmillan Publishing Company from *Collected Poems* by W. B. Yeats. Copyright 1928 Macmillan Publishing Co., Inc., renewed 1956 by Georgie Yeats. "Crazy Jane Talks with the Bishop" by W. B. Yeats, reprinted with permission of Macmillan Publishing Co., Inc., renewed 1961 by Bertha Georgie Yeats. "Lapis Lazuli," "The Circus Animals' Desertion," "Under Ben Bulben," and "Deirdre" by W. B. Yeats, reprinted with permission of Macmillan Publishing Company from *Collected Poems* by W. B. Yeats. Copyright 1940 by Georgie Yeats, renewed 1968 by Bertha Georgie Yeats, Michael Butler Yeats, and Anne Yeats.

Preface

The first edition of *Literature of the Western World,* which appeared in 1984, was intended to provide the best possible resource for survey courses in world literature. With this goal in mind, the editors committed themselves to several principles. First, no author was to be represented by a mere snippet. Almost all works were to be presented in their entirety, or—for those few works such as *Don Quixote* too long to be included complete—in substantial and readable abridgments, with omitted parts summarized where summaries were feasible and appropriate. Second, the anthology was to offer a wide range of choices. The book was to be capacious enough to include far more in each volume than would be read in any one version of the course. Whenever possible, more than one selection by an author was to be included so as to offer either a choice or an opportunity to compare and trace common themes through two or three works. This inclusiveness would make it possible for teachers to tailor their assignments to their individual needs and tastes, for students to "read around" the assigned texts and follow up special interests, and for students to take away from the course a basic collection of world literature for their personal libraries. Third, the book was to use the best translations available, the ones that best combined accuracy and sensitivity to the original with readability. This did not always mean—though it frequently did—selecting the most recent or the best-known translations; it did mean choosing the translations that best revealed why the originals were great works of art. Fourth, the anthology was to be timely, presenting works that engage the interest of contemporary experts and general readers alike. Every effort was made to bring alive a work's context, through extensive historical, cultural, and biographical information, along with a few avenues for critical interpretation. Fifth, and most important, the anthology was to be as useful as possible to both teachers and students. Period and author introductions were to be not only informative but also clear in content, style, and format. Notes were to be full and strictly pertinent, and such aids as diagrams, chronologies, and suggestions for further reading were to be provided wherever they would be helpful. The book, in short, was to supply everything needed up to the point where instruction begins without usurping the instructor's responsibility for—and delight in—exploration and interpretation.

The enthusiastic reception given *Literature of the Western World* in its first two editions encouraged the editors to believe that their principles were sound and that they had succeeded in providing the sort of textbook needed for world literature courses. The response to the collection from users of the book throughout the United States did not suggest a need for any basic changes in the conception of the book. Therefore, the underlying

goals of this third edition remain the same as those of the first and second: complete works, a range of choice, the best translations, a contemporary point of view, and ample support material. Within these boundaries, however, a great many changes, both large and small, have been made to keep the book up to date and to bring it even closer to what teachers tell us they would like to have.

In general, our policy in making changes has been to leave the great masterpieces of each period in place while enriching them with other arresting contemporary works, thereby rendering the period in three-dimensional relief or simply fleshing it out. Thus in The Ancient World, we have added the haunting and sensuous *Song of Solomon* to our core selections from the Hebrew Bible; *Philoctetes* to the Sophoclean plays already in the book, *Oedipus the King* and *Antigone;* the witty dialogue *Ion* to the Plato selections; and the complete Gospel According to Saint Luke to the New Testament selections. In The Middle Ages, we have added the Irish "Exile of the Sons of Uisliu," which contains the Deirdre story, and a selection of the *Letters* of Abelard and Heloise. Our most substantial change for the medieval period is an extensive selection of Latin lyrics and English ballads, a mini-anthology of medieval lyric poetry parallel to the groups of Renaissance lyrics and of French Symbolist and Modernist lyrics in the second edition. In Volume II, the Neoclassicism and Romanticism section has been enriched by the inclusion of Beaumarchais's *Figaro's Marriage*, Kleist's "The Marquise of O————," George Sand's "The Marquise," Büchner's *Woyzeck*, Frederick Douglass's *Narrative of the Life of an American Slave*, and a new selection of Whitman's poetry. Turgenev's novella *First Love* and Henry James's complete novel *Daisy Miller* have been added to the Realism and Naturalism section. The most extensive change in the Moderns and Contemporaries section is the addition of Freud's brilliant and much-discussed case study *Dora*. In addition, Yeats's play *Deirdre* has been added as a companion piece to "Exile of the Sons of Uisliu" in Volume I; a selection from *Ulysses* has been added, representing Joyce's later writing as "The Dead" represents his early work; and new works of prose fiction have been added by Richard Wright and Alice Walker.

For the new material, we have been fortunate to obtain translations well up to the high standard set in the first two editions. We have included Robert Fagles's recent brilliant translation of Sophocles' *Antigone; Philoctetes* appears in an eloquent translation by Robert Torrance. The translation of the "Exile of the Sons of Uisliu" is by the distinguished Irish poet Thomas Kinsella, and the *Letters* of Abelard and Heloise, long available in English only in a crude adaptation, appear here in the authoritative translation by Betty Radice. *Figaro's Marriage* is rendered with flair by Jacques Barzun, and *Dora* appears in the standard translation by Alix and James Strachey. The translations of Kleist by Martin Greenberg, of Büchner by Carl Richard Mueller, and of Turgenev by Harry Stevens are notably successful in rendering works that have a particularly elusive tone in their original languages. The translation of Sand's "The Marquise" has been specially revised, corrected, and restored for this book by Kelly Jennings and Sandra Reyes.

Besides major changes in selections, innumerable small changes were

made in presentation. Introductions have been revised, in some cases heavily, and many annotations have been rewritten for thoroughness and clarity. With help from Suzanne McCray and Matthew Conner, we have revised and updated the suggestions for further reading to take into account recent, in some cases major, work on some of our authors in the last few years. We remain, however, deeply indebted to Nancy K. Barry, Frances Stickney Newman, and Willard J. Rusch for the bibliographies they compiled for the first edition and have continued to signal this debt by using their respective initials where appropriate. As in earlier editions, our aim has been to list works that are reliable and authoritative for non-expert readers; many works indispensable to advanced scholarly study have been consciously omitted.

To attempt to represent almost three thousand years of literature within a single book, even a large one, is of course a quixotic undertaking. But we believe that our third-edition changes have moved the book closer to our goals. In any anthology, the part must stand for the whole. We have tried to represent the great national literatures—French, German, Russian, Spanish, English, American—in a balanced if necessarily noncomprehensive way. In the nineteenth and twentieth centuries, especially, we have suggested the riches of literature outside Western Europe and the United States with such writers as Machado de Assis, Babel, Borges, García Márquez, Kundera, and Fugard. We have also been concerned to represent literature by women with an approach to adequacy and to include works by both women and men that explore issues of gender, from Christine de Pizan's *Book of the City of Ladies* and Marguerite de Navarre's *Heptameron* through Mme de La Fayette's *Princesse de Clèves*, Beaumarchais's *Figaro's Marriage*, Austen's *Persuasion*, Ibsen's *A Doll House*, James's *Daisy Miller*, and Chopin's *The Awakening* to Woolf's *A Room of One's Own* and the poetry of Adrienne Rich. Care has also been taken to present a balanced range of genres, from the sweep of epic to the miniature world of the lyric poem. Twenty-two plays are included: a sizable drama anthology within the larger one. The newly added medieval Latin lyrics and English ballads, along with the selections of Renaissance lyric poetry and French Symbolist and Modernist poetry carried over from earlier editions, make up a considerable collection of lyrics. We are especially proud of our representation of prose fiction. Our decision, taken in the early stages of planning the anthology, not to represent the novel by one massive text but rather to enlarge the area of choice has been vindicated by the users of the book. Our five novels—*The Princesse de Clèves, The Sorrows of Young Werther, Persuasion, Daisy Miller,* and *The Awakening*—supplemented by such substantial novellas and other prose narratives as the Gospel of Luke, *Candide, Narrative of the Life of an American Slave, First Love, Notes from Underground, The Death of Ivan Ilyitch, Dora, Heart of Darkness,* and *The Metamorphosis* represent half a dozen national literatures and a wide range of prose forms. We hope that *Literature of the Western World,* third edition, will please its many old friends and win new ones.

Among old friends are a great many who took an active part in planning and advising on this edition. They include: Paul Ady, Assumption College; David Catane, Virginia Commonwealth University; Paula Berg-

gren, Baruch College; William Combs, Western Michigan University; Bill Crider, Alvin Community College; Tom Dasher, Valdosta State College; Kent Forrester, Murray State University; Nicolas P. Gross, University of Delaware; Ruth Hoberman, Eastern Illinois University; Kathleen Holcomb, Angelo State University; Tony Howard, Collin County Community College; Archibald E. Irwin, Indiana University Southeast; Robert K. Johnson, Suffolk University; Craig Kallendorf, Texas A & M University; Rosemary Kenny, Madison Area Technical College; Judith H. McDowell, University of Texas; William R. Mitchell, Oklahoma Baptist University; Charlotte Morse, Virginia Commonwealth University; Michael Palencia-Roth, University of Illinois at Urbana-Champaign; Pamela T. Pittman, Central State University; Jeanne A. Roberts, The American University; Franklin Robinson, Murray State University; Mark Rollins, Ohio University; Gary Russell, Manatee Community College; Talbot Spivak, Edison Community College; Earl E. Stevens, Rhode Island College; Charlotte Templin, University of Indianapolis; Darkebe Unrue, University of Nevada; and Eugene Vecchio, University of Maine. For his detailed suggestions and correction of many typographic errors, we give special thanks to Professor John A. Knapp II of SUNY Oswego.

Consultants for the second edition, whose good influence on the book remains great, include: Anthony W. Annunziata, State University of New York at Oswego; Kenneth Baughman, University of Northern Iowa; Paula Berggren, Baruch College; Ronald Bogue, University of Georgia; Gary Brodsky, Northeastern Illinois University; Robert Burlingame, University of Texas at El Paso; Sondra M. Cooney, Kent State University; Raymond E. Fitch, Ohio University; Earl E. Fitz, Pennsylvania State University; Alan Friedman, University of Texas; Phyllis Goodman, Millersville University; Ervene Gulley, Bloomsburg University; Joseph C. Harrison, Jackson State Community College; Dabney Hart, Georgia State University; Jeffrey D. Hoeper, Arkansas State University; Alfred Kloeckner, Norwich University; Susan M. Levin, Stevens Institute of Technology; Nancy F. Lewis, North Shore Community College; Dean McWilliams, Ohio University; Charles Piltch, John Jay College of Criminal Justice; J. E. Rivers, University of Colorado at Boulder; Roberta Rubenstein, The American University; Evan Seymour, Community College of Philadelphia; Robert L. Stringer, Delaware State University; James Vanden Bosch, Calvin College; and William A. Vincent, Michigan State University.

For advice on particular authors and periods we warmly thank Charles Hansford Adams, Lynn Altenbernd, John Bateman, Barbara Bowen, Vincent Bowen, Edward Brandabur, David Bright, Jackson Campbell, Howard Cole, John Dussinger, Karen Ford, Chester Fontenot, Eva Frayne, John Frayne, John Friedman, Stanley Gray, Achsah Guibbory, Jan Hinely, Bernard Hirsch, Frank Hodgins, Allan Holaday, Anthony Kaufman, David Kay, Keneth Kinnamon, Joan Klein, Dale Kramer, James Marchand, Donald Masterson, Linda Mazer, Michael Mullin, Cary Nelson, John K. Newman, Michael Palencia-Roth, Vernon Robbins, Michael Shapiro, Charles Shattuck, Janet Levarie Smarr, Arnold Stein, Jack Stillinger, Zohreh Sullivan, Benjamin Uroff, Leon Waldoff, Emily Watts, and Richard Wheeler.

For conceiving the idea of this anthology and providing expert guidance throughout the project, we thank D. Anthony English. Our production editors, Charlotte Hyland and Ann-Marie WongSam, performed intelligently and heroically the immense task of guiding the book through the press. The alertness, sensitivity to style, and literary expertise of our copyeditor, Joyce Rappaport, and of Ann Wilkie have been of great value. For further help with copyediting and proofreading, we are deeply indebted to Elisabeth Fleshler and Mary Deeg.

For conceiving the idea of this anthology, and providing expert guidance throughout the project, we thank D. Anthony English. Our production editors, Charlene Hyland and Ann-Marie WongSam, performed brilliantly and heroically the impossible task of guiding the book through the press. The alertness, sensitivity to style, and literary expertise of our copyeditor, Joyce Rappaport, and of Ann Wilkes have been of great value. For further help with copyediting and proofreading, we are deeply indebted to Elisabeth Belfer and Mary Drew.

Contents

❊❊❊❊❊❊

Neoclassicism and Romanticism 1

WILLIAM WORDSWORTH 630
(1770–1850)

SAMUEL TAYLOR COLERIDGE 653
(1772–1834)

Realism and Naturalism 1129

Moderns and Contemporaries 1605

Contents

LUIGI PIRANDELLO 1825
(1867–1936)

THOMAS MANN 1878
(1875–1955)

JAMES JOYCE 1904
(1882–1941)

VIRGINIA WOOLF 1951
(1882–1941)

FRANZ KAFKA 1971
(1883–1924)

D. H. LAWRENCE 2007
(1885–1930)

Contents

Neoclassicism and Romanticism

WESTERN literature from about 1650 to about 1850 was dominated by two impulses: Neoclassicism until about 1760, Romanticism thereafter. The impulses were international, although the typical masterpieces of Neoclassicism were written in French and English. The two labels (imposed, for the most part, after the fact by historians of literature) are not adequate to describe either period comprehensively; many writers and works, novels especially, resist such classification. The term *Neoclassicism* and other related terms into which it blends are applied somewhat differently to different parts of Europe. In France, for example, the purest form of Neoclassicism precedes 1700; the form of aggressive secular French rationalism that dominated the eighteenth century is more properly called the Enlightenment. The entire period from the philosopher René Descartes' *Discourse on Method* (1637) to the outbreak of the French Revolution in 1789 can also be called the Age of Reason, in France and outside it. It is this constellation of roughly allied trends that for the sake of simplicity is called Neoclassicism in the present essay. As for *Romanticism,* the problem has been almost the opposite: not rivalry between competing labels but a proliferation of meanings for the single label *Romanticism,* some of them so wildly unrelated or contradictory that certain historians of literature a few decades ago came to consider the word useless. Attempts at definition since then have produced some hard thinking on the subject. The result has been, if not a generally accepted definition, at least a better understanding of the complex phenomena the word is meant to reflect.

The terms *Neoclassic* and *Romantic,* despite their limitations, are useful in identifying the basic models various artists conformed to or reacted against, each in his or her different way. The periods described by the two terms are generally considered not only as distinct—with some blurring along their mid-eighteenth-century border—but as antithetical. For that very reason, and also because the contrast between the two manners was pressed belligerently by Romantics rebelling against their forebears, it seems useful to consider both together. Another reason for doing so is that the two terms describe not merely historical epochs in the arts and general culture but also recurrent types that have existed in every epoch. A "romantic" person is impulsive (or irresponsible), idealistic (or impractical), imaginative (or unbalanced), and so on. We do not ordinarily apply the word *classic* to persons, but it is widely applied to things, not only books and pieces of music but also automobile designs, sweaters, athletic events (the "Fall Classic"), and almost anything whose appeal is stable, perennial, immune to the whims of fashion. One of the more interesting questions about

1

literary history is how closely the historical senses of the two words correspond to their popular usages.

One feasible way to examine Neoclassicism and Romanticism in literature is to state as baldly as possible the general formulas commonly used to distinguish them and then modify the formulas, as necessary, so as to reflect the truth more closely, if still in a general way. Three such formulas have to do with order, emotion, and nature. As one might expect, the clichés describe the third-rate talents better than the greatest ones, but that does not mean the clichés are useless. All wars are fought partly with slogans, and slogans tell us something, if not the whole truth.

Formula One: Neoclassicism values the orderly, social, and general; Romanticism values the exceptional, individual, and particular.

The Neoclassic age did value order, and it had good reason to do so. The early and middle seventeenth century witnessed an apocalyptic outpouring of hatred, in the form of religious civil wars fought not only between Catholics and Protestants but between factions within Protestantism. The prototype is the great English civil war of the 1640s and 1650s between the Calvinist Puritans, who were both political and religious radicals, and their Anglican-Royalist enemies. In the course of this war King Charles I was beheaded. Theological doctrines and the political philosophies tied up with them were literally fighting words in the hands of partisan pamphleteers such as John Milton. The unrest continued in England even after the Restoration of the monarchy in 1660, culminating in the Glorious Revolution of 1688–89. This reorientation of political power, reducing the stature of the king and elevating the parliament and merchants, cost some people, notably Catholics, civil liberties. But for most people it enlarged these liberties, and it opened the way to a more settled era. Political strife was far from over, but the relative calm was welcomed with relief. (An analogy exists with the 1950s in the United States, when, after two decades when people stood in breadlines and then slept in muddy foxholes, the normal and tranquil seemed to many people heaven itself.) The English began to think of themselves as "Augustans," living in a time like that of Caesar Augustus, Virgil, and Horace after Augustus ended decades of Roman civil war and made civilized life—and civilized art—possible.

Something similar was happening on the European continent. The German states had the terrible Thirty Years War (1618–1648) in their recent past; the French, the bitterly divided period of the Fronde (1648–1653). Political order in the English manner was not possible in Germany, still divided into separate states. In France, the new order meant the triumph of the monarchy, especially under the resplendent "Sun King" Louis XIV and his satellite aristocracy. The middle class, ascendant in England after 1688, had to wait a century to assert itself politically in France. When it did so in the revolution of 1789, which within a few years took a more radical turn toward democracy, the nation and all Europe witnessed the end of eighteenth-century versions of order. A new apocalypse had begun.

Civil disorder in the seventeenth century synchronized ironically with the achievement of a new scientific order, the product of an international synthesis of the kind that ever since has been the rule in scientific advancement. Developing from the discoveries and theories of such astronomer-

2

physicists as Galileo (1564–1642), an Italian, and Johannes Kepler (1571–1630), a German, the Scientific Revolution culminated in the Englishman Isaac Newton's (1642–1727) formulation of the laws of motion and of universal gravitation, describable in terms of a new branch of mathematics, calculus, that Newton himself and the German mathematician Gottfried Wilhelm Leibnitz (1646–1716) invented at about the same time. Newton's astounding achievement, probably the greatest in the history of science, had a historically dramatic timing; his *Principia* was published in 1687, a year before the Glorious Revolution. It was as though the cosmos itself, as revealed in the orderly minds of men intent on natural truth rather than the chimeras of religious "enthusiasm," were giving humankind a broad hint: put your political and cultural house in order too. The ruling model, for government, art, and even human nature, became an inorganic one—sometimes a machine, sometimes an architectural edifice, but at any rate a model articulated by reason, understandable by secular good sense, and governed by widely recognizable rules.

The relationship between the art and science of any period is always a chicken-and-egg problem. The "rules" that came to govern literature and literary theory (especially in France, with its Latinate tradition of the absolute) may have been conditioned by the new science, or it may be that the great seventeenth-century scientific revolution was conditioned by the humanities, specifically the Renaissance adulation of balanced rationality as manifested in ancient literature. At any rate, the Neoclassicists tried to subsume literature under strict rules, infusing rigorous method into the Renaissance version of classicism. As one might expect, the most insistent of the rules governed the most public of the literary genres, the drama, in the form of the three "unities" of action, time, and place. (The first two of these are inferrable from Aristotle's *Poetics;* the third, apparently dictated by pure logic, is found nowhere in his works.) A tragedy had to deal with a single action, its plot had to unfold within twelve (or sometimes twenty-four) hours, and it had to be set in a single place. The most effortlessly perfect realizations of these dramatic rules were the tragedies of Racine, such as his *Phaedra*. Similar rules defined and governed many other genres. A carefully graded scale of diction was elaborated, the loftiest language being reserved for tragedy and the lowest for satire. These rules were to remain in force for a long time. When Victor Hugo's experimental Romantic drama *Hernani* was first staged in 1830, a grand commotion was stirred among Parisian partisans of the old and new by the play's daring opening lines: Hugo had displaced the caesura, or pause, in the twelve-syllable French line from its regular place after the sixth syllable and had actually put in the mouth of a high-born lady the word *escalier,* "stairs."

In doctrinaire Romantics the rules stirred anger; to most people today they seem merely absurd. To keep things in perspective, however, we should stop to consider how many rules still operate, in behavior and the arts—in the popular arts most of all. People dress differently for funerals and for cookouts. One can scan the shelves of a bookstore for a long time before finding on a dust jacket a picture of a novelist who would dare wear a suit and tie. No one would score Dixieland jazz for string quartet or country music for two grand pianos. Much of science fiction observes conventions about how freely scientific laws can be fantasized, and very rigid

3

rules for murder mysteries were codified by Dorothy L. Sayers. A more fundamental modern misunderstanding, however, arises from the inherent ambiguity of the word *rules*. Like its sibling, *laws*, the word can mean either prescriptive, legislated rules, like those of baseball, or rules that purport to describe the nature of reality, like the commutative rule of multiplication (3 times 2 equals 2 times 3). To most Neoclassicists the rules were descriptive, reflecting the almost unalterable conditions necessary for literature to be effective. Thus Pope could write that rules are "Nature methodised; / Nature, like liberty, is but restrained / By the same laws which first herself ordained" (*Essay on Criticism*, I.89–91). To depart from the rules in this sense would cause literature not to work, as on a vaster scale the solar system would not work if the planet Jupiter went its own headstrong way unbeholden to the rules of gravitation. Pope's analogy with liberty is very significant; he and other Neoclassicists wanted literature to be *free* to perform its proper role in the scheme of nature, as environmentalists today want the snail darter to be free to do. (Pope believed, moreover, that there were "nameless graces" beyond the reach of precepts.) But *nature* is a tricky word; about it, more later.

The Romantic penchant for the exceptional and individual needs less explanation, since it accords with twentieth-century attitudes. The audiences for art—"high" art at least—take it for granted that a good artist or work does something not done before, and such originality usually implies novelty of subject matter or artistic method. Here again, however, we can deceive ourselves. Certain stock figures—the alienated hero, for example—can hardly be called original any more, but the alienated hero seems tolerable by modern tastes in almost limitless near-duplication, as his cousin the Byronic hero was for Romantic audiences. Goethe's Werther, that prototype of the misunderstood, eccentric Romantic man of genius and sensibility, was adopted as a blood brother by countless thousands of readers, who felt they understood him perfectly.

The fact is that the best Romantic authors, like their modern counterparts, are not drawn to the eccentric simply for its own sake. To say, in Matthew Arnold's words, "We mortal millions live *alone*" is verbally a paradox, but it is easy enough to understand. A similar paradox—that what all humans share is uniqueness—is fundamental to Romantic literature and thought. Significantly, the French Revolutionists, who in so many ways set the stage for the Romantics, were able to accommodate (along with *equality*) among their three watchwords both *liberty* and *fraternity*, two notions with considerable potential for incompatibility. Wordsworth, following up but modifying Rousseau's choice of "Myself alone" as the subject matter of his *Confessions*, can single himself out in his long autobiographical poem *The Prelude* as a Romantic epic hero exactly because he believes that somehow he can discern and reveal the essence of humanity at large by looking into himself. That is why he continually moves grammatically between *I* and *we*, *my* and *our*, *me* and *us*. That is also why the American arch-Romantic, Walt Whitman, can launch *Song of Myself* with the statement "I celebrate myself" but add almost immediately, "For every atom belonging to me as good belongs to you." The exception, for many Romantics, proves the rule in the relevant sense of *prove*: "put to the test." When human nature is thus "proved" by the seeming uniqueness of the individuals who partake in it,

4

we learn something about the norm of human nature, as the study of abnormal psychology today throws light on what normal behavior is. In a way, then, the Romantics pursued the same objective—the understanding of the universal—that the Neoclassicists pursued. But the Romantics approached this norm by the circuitous paths and side entrances of inference and surprise; the Neoclassicists made frontal assaults on the norm, through explicit generalizations such as Pope utters in almost every couplet.

Romantic individualism marks a real shift from Neoclassicism all the same, and one way to understand the shift is to ask what the alternative to individualism was in each of the two ages. When a person in the early eighteenth century felt threatened *as an individual,* the threat was something localizable, indeed mechanical. It usually operated through the oppressive machinery of the state (sometimes of the church). The threat came from bad laws or the perversion of good laws by identifiable authorities, from the king down, and their official agencies. This kind of mechanical threat to freedom is what the American revolutionists and founding fathers sensed, and against such political malfunctions their safeguard was another machine: the Constitution. It had "checks," "balances," and, one is tempted to add, gears, pulleys, and flywheels.

The Romantics, a generation or two later than the thinkers who influenced James Madison, came to fear something more insidious: the spiritually pervasive, often poisoned atmosphere we have come to call "society." Like its American equivalent, the French Revolution had begun as an attempt to repair or replace political machinery—by reconvening the long-dormant Estates General, for example, and thus renovating the legislative process. But within a few years this daring but still limited rationalist impulse became a total spiritual imperative, exacting allegiance in everything from religion to manners to language to dress. A state had become a society. And the change was permanent, as countless nineteenth-century novels make clear. Ironically, it was Rousseau, himself a patron saint of the Revolution, who first clearly articulated the dangerous pressure exerted on the individual by society so understood. Almost all the Romantics shared this vision. Goethe's Werther, a Romantic in Rousseau's footsteps, is totally unconcerned with governments; the officialdom he tries briefly to become part of and learns to loathe is not a mechanism but a noxious moral atmosphere. It would be ludicrous to imagine Byron's misanthropic heroes voting for a bill or opposing a political party. What these protagonists reject in their environment (apart from certain metaphysical aspects of the human condition in itself) is the deadening spiritual miasma that attacks not one's circumstantial freedom but the integrity of one's psyche, a miasma both omnipresent and intangible. The eighteenth-century mode of establishing freedom was to "charter" a group or corporation, guaranteeing or conceding specified legal rights and immunities. The American Bill of Rights is a charter in this sense. But by the end of the eighteenth century we can also hear voices like that of the speaker in Blake's "London," who almost vomits up the word *chartered* in disgust at the hypocritical mystification implicit in the specious order it expresses. What nauseates him is not merely commercial and other institutionalized mechanisms of oppression but a whole moral complex that, besides corporations, includes poverty, prostitution, loveless marriage, disease, war, and—at the heart of all—the

enslavement of mind by mind. This is no longer political protest but recognizably Romantic—and modern—social protest.

Not incidentally, the social protest in "London" is couched in lyric poetry, uttered by the voice of an individual speaker. The lyric poem is sometimes considered the distinctive Romantic genre. Strictly speaking, this is not true; the lyric is not the form the greatest Romantics consciously chose for their most serious utterances. Goethe's most nearly definitive values are expressed in the two parts of the drama *Faust*. Wordsworth in *The Prelude*, Byron in *Don Juan,* and Blake in *The Four Zoas, Milton,* and *Jerusalem* chose the long verse epic. Victor Hugo (1802–1885) was a great lyricist but is even better known for his novels *Notre Dame de Paris* and *Les Misérables;* Melville brought the novel and the epic together in *Moby-Dick.* But many of these long Romantic works are written in an intensely lyrical vein. Tennyson's *In Memoriam* and Whitman's *Leaves of Grass* are large edifices, but their components are separable lyrics. The quintessence of Romanticism, if not its extended rationale, is isolable in the lyrics, especially the odes, of Keats, despite his heroic attempts to write great long poems. In the last analysis, then, Romanticism is a lyrical impulse, in keeping with its veneration of the individual.

Conversely, Neoclassicism distrusted idiosyncrasy and ranked the lyric rather low in its elaborate hierarchy of literary genres. The loftiest of the genres were tragedy and epic. Theory outstripped achievement here; comedy thrived in Restoration England, and France produced Molière, one of the world's great comic dramatists, but the only really great tragedians were Pierre Corneille (1606–1684) and Racine. The closest approaches to important Neoclassic epic were John Dryden's translation (1697) of Virgil, Pope's of Homer (1715–26), and Voltaire's *Henriade* (1723), an epic that almost no one reads today. The literature of protest took the form of satire, for which the lyric form and voice would have been considered inappropriate and inadequate. Significantly, the great Neoclassic satires do not portray distinctive individuals. Characters have *traits*—Pope's Belinda is charming and vain, Swift's Gulliver is sturdily commonsensical and pragmatic, Voltaire's Candide is resiliently naive and his Pangloss optimistic to the point of lunacy—but they do not have *personalities*. Although they are not allegorical figures like those in the medieval *Everyman,* they are nonetheless generalizations: Candide's name means "open, ingenuous," *Pangloss* means "explainer-away of everything" (the subtitle of the book, "The Optimist," is itself a generalization), *Gulliver* puns on *gull* ("dupe"), *Belinda* puns on *belle,* and her misadventures are further generalized by being filtered through the conventions of classical and Miltonic epic. The typical result of such generalizing is a blend of serious purpose with hilarity, matched in Aristophanes but in scarcely anyone else in the earlier history of literature. Stereotyping can be cruel and unjust in life, but a great deal of humor depends on such reductionism, and satire thrives on it. Like other forms of comedy, comic satire distances us from the intimate personal understanding and empathy that render almost everything tragic or poignant or sentimental. It thus clears the way for the savage moral indignation of a Swift and the keen intellectual indignation of a Voltaire.

Formula Two: Neoclassicism values reason; Romanticism values emotion.

6

On the face of it, this statement seems so indisputably true as to require no further comment, and it is true. But misunderstandings are possible. No one can read Racine's *Phaedra* or Swift's account of the Yahoos without recognizing that the Neoclassicists considered human passion an immensely powerful force. Their very compulsion for order was conditioned by an awareness of its dangerous alternatives, as the seismographic vigilance of Victorian chaperones attested not their undervaluation of sex but their hyperalert awareness of its power. In general, Neoclassicists regarded passion as a threat to health, in the polity and in the individual psyche. It was also an obstacle to clear understanding, an unavoidable but undesirable contaminant of reason. Not all people of the time took that view, however. The optimist followers of the third Earl of Shaftesbury (1671–1713), for example, believed that benevolent feelings were an inherent part of humankind at its best, and this philosophy encouraged a sentimentalizing strain in literature that grew stronger as the eighteenth century progressed. (The middle to late eighteenth century is sometimes called the Age of Sensibility; its preoccupation with tender feelings and the beauties of rustic nature is usually traced to Rousseau, but Shaftesbury was an earlier herald.) Moreover, even for the rationalists reason meant different things. For some of them it meant a severe, secularist intellectuality; this was the basic view of Voltaire and other *philosophes* of the French Enlightenment. For others (Swift, for example), it meant almost the opposite: a pragmatic common sense that rejected fine-spun theorizing as contemptible, immoral, or even insane. This distrust of pure ratiocination harks back to the Renaissance humanists' disdain for cobweb-spinning medieval scholasticism.

Among the Romantics there was unquestionably a cult of feeling. Doubtless some of its initiates indulged their emotions for the simplest of reasons: because feeling strongly felt good. The more one felt, the better; emotion was fine but ecstasy finer still. This deliberate luxuriating in feeling, largely for its own sake, is a charge brought against Goethe's Werther, for example, by readers unsympathetic to him. But it will be immediately obvious that the passion Werther feels is very different from what Pope or Racine or Swift means by passion. In Werther passion has less to do with primal appetites (though there is some evidence that he sublimates these drives) than with softness on one hand and sublimity on the other. Compared with the Neoclassicists' passion, his is both more domestic and more exotic, a combination typical of Romantic sensibility. In other words, the Romantics did not only give emotion a new level of value but also redefined its special quality.

They also redefined the role of emotion in understanding reality. As the philosopher Alfred North Whitehead observed in *Science and the Modern World*, models of reality are constructed by a selective process, and what the models ignore clamors to be readmitted. This, he argued, is what happened in the eighteenth century; understandably, people were so awed by the spectacular success of rationalist science that they excluded from their adopted model something vital and human. The Romantics' task, as the more thoughtful among them saw it, was to rehumanize mankind's sense of itself (and of the cosmos too; we shall get to that later). They envisaged a more comprehensive model of reality, less exclusively ruled by reason. But

7

they knew their new model would be unsatisfactory if it simply substituted feeling for reason; feeling had to ally itself to what is best in the mind, not oppose it. The literary result, especially among the great English Romantics, was a poetry of intense feeling that was also intellectual in an almost unprecedented degree. They were obsessed with the importance of love, for example, but except in Byron and Shelley one would be hard pressed to find many confessional English Romantic love poems, the kind of thing one could include in a letter to one's sweetheart. (Shakespeare, Donne, and other Elizabethan poets are a much more fertile field. The continental Romantics were also more personally amatory, even—in fact, especially— that thinking man's poet, Goethe.) For all his subjectivity, there is scarcely a more intellectual poet than Wordsworth, who wanted not only to reestablish the essential role of human feeling but to redeem poetry from its status as genteel adornment and make it an avenue to truth. The poetry of Blake, the most uncompromising opponent of eighteenth-century rationalism, is as intellectual as that of Dante or Milton, perhaps more so.

The centerpiece of the Romantics' endeavor was a new theory of creative understanding based on the faculty of imagination. This theory, stated by Coleridge in the *Biographia Literaria* (1817) and urged most extravagantly by Blake, was essentially a reaction against John Locke (1632–1704), the philosopher who defined the basic model for eighteenth-century theories of perceiving and knowing (and for much modern thought on these matters as well). Locke held that the human mind begins as a *tabula rasa,* or blank slate. (If he were writing today, one feels sure his metaphor would have been unexposed photographic film.) The blankness is first touched by elementary sense impressions which, subsequently modified and combined in more and more complex overlays (like multi-exposed film), result at last in what we call ideas. The process is essentially passive, positing a reality that exists most fully in material things and agencies outside the mind. What draws human beings together is that their minds respond to things they perceive in common—the same sun, the same trees, and, in well-educated readers, the same great books, poems, and plays. The term *common sense* assumes a new meaning when we interpret it literally as implying sense impressions we have in common.

It is not hard to see how this philosophical model could generate among Neoclassicists a corresponding theory of literature, namely an updated version of the ancient theory of art as imitation, especially imitation of the basic, uneccentric experiences that all human beings share. The Neoclassic term for the creative power was *wit.* The term may surprise us unless we recognize that (1) it goes back to Anglo-Saxon for "reason" or "intelligence"—hence the surviving word *half-wit;* and (2) even today witticisms impress us apparently because of their novelty but basically because behind their cleverness we recognize a familiar truth. ("Punctuality"—not procrastination, as in the proverb—"is the thief of time," says Oscar Wilde; we are startled, and then we remember how much time we have spent waiting for the habitually late.) Hence Pope's famous formula: "True wit is Nature to advantage dressed, / What oft was thought, but ne'er so well expressed" (*Essay on Criticism,* II.297–98). Implicit in this view of mind and of art is a noble ideal of human community, united by collectively endorsed realities as sensed by the best minds from antiquity to the present. The dreadful

alternative was enthrallment by irresponsibly mutant values and quirks of feeling, which in turn could produce a spiritual and social malaise not entirely different from what today is called "the inability to communicate."

This notion of creativity, symbolized as a mirror, was central to Neoclassic art. The alternative Romantic metaphor, as M. H. Abrams has pointed out, was the lamp, which emits light rather than receiving and reflecting it. *Wit* was transformed into *imagination,* which Coleridge defined on two levels. The artist wields the "secondary imagination," becoming a fairly literal creator by shaping and forming the welter of raw experiences, which in themselves are a chaos. In order to do so, he must bring into play all the powers of the psyche, emotion as well as reason, for the goal is an organic integration, not the analytic dissection for which unimpassioned reason alone would suffice. Moreover, underlying the artist's secondary imagination is the primary imagination, an even more basic faculty that Coleridge identifies with all normal human perception. This kind of perception, however, is not to be understood as a receptive act; rather, it is the shaping of chaotic matter into forms such as trees and chairs, which in themselves are a welter of meaningless bits of matter. Both forms of creation are echoes of the ultimate act of creation by God, whose power is manifested less by making matter out of nothing than by giving it living form and order. Coleridge thus achieves a brilliant *tour de force,* asserting the sublime dignity of artistic creation by linking it to the divine, but also defending it on the Lockeans' own ground by linking it with familiar, ordinary sense experiences such as perfectly "unimaginative" people have hundreds of times every minute. Either way, the Coleridgean, Romantic model of creation is a far cry from the undisciplined indulgence of emotion. Wordsworth called imagination "another name for absolute power / And clearest insight, amplitude of mind, / And reason in her most exalted mood" (*The Prelude,* XIV.190–192).

This notion of imagination, and its conflict with Lockean models, is a basic theme on which the Romantics composed countless variations. Wordsworth sounds it continually, now leaning to a Lockean position that nature influences us (as in "Expostulation and Reply"), now in the opposite direction of mind's independence (as in the "Intimations" ode), now toward a compromise according to which we create but half-perceive (as in "Tintern Abbey"). For Blake, his contemporary, there could be no compromise. Oothoon, the rape victim in his *Visions of the Daughters of Albion* (1793), spits out her repeated question "With what sense . . . ?" in a feminist manifesto that is simultaneously an attack on Locke. All animals have senses, she insists, but all animals are different, fulfilling themselves as unique species, not reduced to uniformity by the natural world they experience in common. Analogously, all human beings are unique, each of them being the center of his or her created world. To ignore this fact is to acquiesce in a system which defines people in terms of their sense experience (in Oothoon's case, her history of having been "defiled" by rape) and implicitly to acquiesce in a system of social classification that reduces some classes, such as women and Blacks, to slavery. All this becomes more moving when we understand that Oothoon is in some sense a version of Mary Wollstonecraft, the feminist pioneer whose message in her *Vindication of the Rights of Woman* (1792) strains uneasily, as it probably seemed to Blake, against her

misplaced eighteenth-century faith in the reforming power of reason. Transformed into Oothoon, she sees rationalism as "Urizen" ("your reason"), the "mistaken Demon of Heaven." The explosive anger of the poem is more than a tone, then; it is an assertion of the need for the whole person, not just her reason but her feelings also, to engage the question of what is true and false, right and wrong. Letting off steam is not enough either; one must also *see*. This need explains the poem's form, a debate, which dramatically seems so incongruous with Oothoon's personal crisis. She is the Romantic imagination incarnate, attempting to see life whole if not steadily.

Formula Three: Neoclassicism values _____, *Romanticism values nature.*

The second half of this theorem is the commonest of all generalizations on the subject, but before we go any further the reader is invited to fill in the blank for Neoclassicism by supplying the antonym for *nature*. If one says "indoor scenes," the contrast will make sense and will even be roughly valid. One will search Pope in vain for the mountaintop ecstasies recorded in Wordsworth's *Prelude* and search Wordsworth in vain for anything like Belinda's dressing table in Pope's *Rape of the Lock*. To most Neoclassicists city life did seem the normal human environment; Samuel Johnson, the last great literary voice before the Romantics, equated London with life and sniffed that people who chose to live in the country deserved their fate. This preference for the urban seems to many modern readers, even some confirmed city dwellers, to be a perverse aberration, but one can make a good case for the opposite. Through most of history, cities have been the definitive emblem of the good life, secular and sacred. Socrates envisaged a structured republic, not a pastoral commune. The Lord can be imaged as a shepherd (though even this emblem of nature is half-domesticated), but the basic Christian image of heaven is the City of God. "America the Beautiful" admires "purple mountain majesties," but its highest, futurist vision of America is one wherein "alabaster cities gleam / Undimmed by human tears."

The word *nature* is not so simple, though; in fact, it is one of the most complicated in the language. The range of its meanings is illustrated in Shakespeare's *King Lear*, where the word refers both to the divinely sanctioned human order typified in the loving bond that should unite parent and child and also to the Godless brute creation, so that when Edmund says, "Thou, nature, art my goddess," he is uttering the most blood-curdling blasphemy. C. S. Lewis, in his *Studies in Words*, discusses about twenty senses of *nature*, and even standard collegiate dictionaries record more than a dozen. These are best discriminated by the antonyms for *natural*, which include *artificial* (synthetic vitamins), *man-made* (the Hoover Dam as opposed to a beaver's), *pretentiously affected* (baby talk by an adult), *interfered with* ("don't stunt the child's natural development"), *acquired* ("are males breadwinners by nature or by culture?"), *legislated* (unlike natural laws), *wearing clothes* (au naturel now usually means "nude"), *not pertaining to matter* (social as opposed to natural sciences), *supernatural* (transcending nature, as God does), *magic* ("does demonic possession have a natural explanation?"), *trained* ("did he take lessons or is he just naturally good?"), *socially organized* ("in the state of nature there was no police force"), and many others. The

10

most comprehensive antonym, probably, is *alien to what something, or some-one, really is,* a concept especially useful to people never perplexed by the question of what is real.

All these senses are relevant to Neoclassicism and Romanticism, but to test the two impulses against each of them would take far more space than we have here. Let us say only that some of the meanings support our for-mula, some do not, and some are ambiguous. For example, what it means to *interfere with someone's true nature,* and whether or not it is good to do so, depends on one's premises. One might send children to a *progressive* school because one believes that their natural, good impulses should be unfettered but send them to a progressive *school* because one thinks that what nature has done for their minds must be improved on; whether a Neoclassicist or a Romantic would be the more likely to choose such a school is hard to say. If *nature* means the physical world as illuminated by science, the Neoclassicists probably valued nature even more than the Romantics did. Romantics might value the beaver's dam more than a man-made one, but that man does and should shape his world in a metaphysical sense is a distinctive Romantic idea, as we have seen.

Similar ambiguities cloud the distinctions between Neoclassical and Romantic theories of art and literature. For the Neoclassicists, art was an act of cultivating, but the thing to be cultivated ("to advantage dressed") was nature, understood as the governing reality of the world and life. The complication, as we said earlier, lies in the way one understands reality. Dazzled by the scientifically described cosmic machine, the Neoclassicists naturally (what does the word mean *here,* by the way?) thought of art as having an inorganic order and regularity. As their respect for the rules implies, they saw the literary genres—epic, tragedy, elegy, pastoral, ode, lyric, satire, and so on—as having intrinsic reality as containers, apart from the content poured into them by individual authors. But as the eighteenth century drew to a close and the nineteenth ran its course, scientific models changed. The focus of investigation shifted from astronomy and physics to chemistry to geology (a blend of physical science and history) to the life sciences, culminating in Charles Darwin's (1809–1882) evolutionary theo-ries. An organic model replaced the mechanical one, a shift conditioned by science or conditioning it (another chicken-egg problem). The American founding fathers had invented a machine of government, but by 1863 Abraham Lincoln in the Gettysburg address was describing the origin of the nation in metaphors of conception and childbirth and diagnosing its mid-life crisis. Similarly, the human individual was imaged differently, not as having achieved a definitive human status in being born (*natus*) but as having thus embarked on the evolutionary journey called life. Every stage of life had its own reality and integrity, not excepting childhood. Indeed, childhood had its own special importance, as what Wordsworth called the "seed time" of the soul (note the organic metaphor). The Neoclassicists had internalized nature, modeling the human on an inorganic environment. Conversely, the Romantics projected the life they subjectively experienced onto the cosmos, now seen as vital instead of mechanical.

Two implications of organicism are especially relevant to literature: vital interconnectedness and growth. Both the inorganic models of machines or buildings and the organic models of plants or animals have parts, but in

11

organisms the parts are not discrete and separable as they are in, say, modern component stereo systems. Rather, they are subordinated to a central vital principle, all the parts intimately interdependent, meaningless in isolation, and unable to survive alone. (The validity of this distinction, by the way, is being tested today by surgical organ transplants.) "The spirit of poetry," Coleridge wrote, "like all other living powers . . . must embody in order to reveal itself; but a living body is of necessity an organized one,— and what is organization, but the connection of parts to a whole, so that each part is at once end and means." This implies, first, that every work of art is unique, governed by its own internal ecology; second, that the distinction between form and subject matter is annihilated, because form grows from the essential idea or inspiration of a work as a plant does from its seed; and third, that the process of creation is inseparable from the product created. Perhaps the best example of all three of these implications is Wordsworth's *Prelude*, generating from a literary parentage (not from rules) its unique form of epic, taking the poet's own life as its subject, and incorporating in itself an account of how it was written.

The organicist emphasis on development and growth is even more important for literature. It accounts for the emergence of new forms such as the spiritual autobiography, which is less concerned with circumstances than with the evolution of the author's psyche. The fictional sibling of this form was the "apprenticeship" novel or poem, represented by *The Prelude*, Goethe's *Wilhelm Meister's Apprenticeship* (1795–96), and in our century by James Joyce's *Portrait of the Artist as a Young Man* (1916). This genre, going today as strong as ever, is still the norm for a writer's first novel, frequently combining the autobiographical and fictional impulses. The view of literature as process is reflected also in Tennyson's *In Memoriam*, which grows as naturally but unpredictably as a tree, by way of lyrics we are meant to take as spontaneous records of the passing months and years, from its autobiographical seed in the death of his friend Hallam. Growth and striving became themes also, in innumerable works including Goethe's *Faust.* The medieval romance theme of the quest was revived and adapted to modern subjects, including metaphysical quests for fulfillment. Even the texture of literature became organic for the Romantics; metaphor and symbol, used as in Keats' odes to blend idea and image inseparably, became more typical than the simile, which says only that something is *like* something else. Between Pope's "Bright as the sun, her eyes the gazers strike, / And, like the sun, they shine on all alike" (*The Rape of the Lock*, II.13–14) and Keats' "Thou still unravished bride of quietness" ("Ode on a Grecian Urn," line 1) lies an immense difference in ways of perceiving things. The breathtaking emblems of the spirit that Henry David Thoreau finds in nature (*Walden*, 1854) are climactic expressions of this metaphorical vision.

The Romantic love of nature is more than a taste for pretty scenery; it is an attempt to humanize nature, to replace man's view of himself as part of a machine, however well and benignly made, with a vision of the world as essentially an extension of soul. To call the Romantic view optimistic, as many people do, seems therefore a vast understatement. To other historians of literature and culture, though, there is a darker side to all this. On the simplest level, it is argued, the Romantic celebration of nature is defensive, a reflexive countermovement to the ominous rise of urban industriali-

zation, analogous to modern environmentalist movements inspired not by security but by a sense of danger. On a spiritual level, the Romantics can be seen as claiming kinship to a humanized nature exactly because they feared that that strange phenomenon, human consciousness, is no more than a meaningless freak in a mindless cosmos. This sense of the utter strangeness of consciousness, the fear that, unconcerned with us or anything else, the stars "blindly run," is quite explicit in Tennyson's *In Memoriam* (III.5); compared with that frightening vision, the eighteenth-century deists' vision of a clockwork universe, however impersonal its Designer, seems almost cozy. That Wordsworth, the "worshipper" of nature, should even say "nature never did betray / The heart that loved her" suggests to some readers a fear on his part that she may indeed betray him ("Tintern Abbey," 152, 122–23). Seen in this light, the Byronic hero and his many nineteenth-century progeny are not mere picturesque period types toying with gloom from the security of their spiritual confidence but rather mythic embodiments of a sense of loneliness that dwells at the heart of Romanticism.

Furthermore, it seems inevitable that the Romantics, envisioning themselves and the world in organic terms of growth, should have seen with equal clarity the ultimate implication: that the terminus of organic process in all living things is death. The middle section of Wordsworth's "Intimations" ode traces the human movement toward spiritual as well as physical death; the final intimations—hints, not proofs—of immortality are found not in nature but in the mind's ability to transcend this mere "homely nurse." The implicitness of death in both our ordinary existence and our attempts to escape it is also the central theme of Keats's odes, especially the "Ode to a Nightingale," and it is not coincidental that the poem calls into question the validity of the Romantic imagination in general. Blake saw these negative implications from the beginning of the Romantic age; he may have loved the countryside as much as his brother Romantics, but toward nature as a thing in itself—mechanical or organic, dead or alive— he felt a profound hostility. As a metaphysical entity, it was "satanic," antithetical to the human.

Both Neoclassicists and Romantics, then, in their different ways, revered nature. The Romantics' reverence for it had both bright and dark sides, however. The same is true of their view of human possibilities. The theme of aspiration in their work coexists tensely with their awareness of the limitations imposed on the human spirit by the world, social organization, the mortality of the body, and even certain blocking agents in the psyche itself. These dualities help explain one of the paradoxes of twentieth-century literature. Modern writers rebelled against Romanticism, scorning its moonlit atmosphere, gossamer texture, and spiritual affirmations as unsustaining or irrelevant. On the other hand, they sometimes seem very similar to the Romantics, especially when they turn inward and face up to doubt as the Romantics did in their great crisis lyrics.

A sense of kinship to the Romantics, companionable or hostile, operates also in the many modern readers who find it easier to love or hate the Romantics than to respond in either way to the Neoclassicists. What we owe the latter is best appreciated if we move back from literature and take a wider view. The Neoclassical music of Wolfgang Amadeus Mozart (1756–1791) and of his eighteenth-century Baroque predecessor Johann Sebas-

13

tian Bach (1685–1750), impassioned yet disciplined by formal clarity, has never since been rivaled except by Ludwig van Beethoven (1770–1827), a Romantic with one foot in the age of Neoclassicism. Many of the practical arts of graceful elegance—typified in the furniture designed by Thomas Chippendale (1718–1779)—have advanced little if at all since the eighteenth century. The roots of modern totalitarianism have been traced by some theorists of history to the Puritan regime in seventeenth-century England against which the Neoclassicists reacted and to the French Revolution, which killed Neoclassicism. These allegations have been largely discredited; for example, the nineteenth-century extension of civil and economic rights to the lowest social classes is in the line of descent from the French Revolution. It is significant, however, that such charges could not be brought against the Age of Reason with any plausibility at all. We owe to people of that age—great and ordinary—the theory and much of the machinery in accordance with which most free societies operate to the extent that they are free.

But we should not turn away too fast from literature and language. Besides its imaginative masterpieces, the Neoclassicists excelled in the "nonimaginative" genres dedicated to fact: biography, history, letters, the essay. When the Romantics revived metaphor in literature, they enriched it immeasurably, but the attempt by advocates of science in the latter seventeenth century to kill metaphor were, in the long run, a good thing too. To compare the energy, muscularity, and lucidity of Swift's prose—what in old sexist days was called its virility—with anything written two generations earlier is to recognize that the Neoclassic period created functional modern prose, the syntax and diction of, say, our better magazines. This is also the prose used or aspired to by authors of fiction when clear communication is their main concern. The human spirit needs poetry, both literal poetry and the spiritual adventure symbolized by the word, and these are what the Romantics give us. The spirit also needs Neoclassical prose and the vision of sane order implicit in it.

This distinction, including the poetry-prose metaphor, goes back more than a century, and it is valid enough to be worth preserving. Increasingly, however, students of literature have found it too facile. The Neoclassic and eighteenth-century vision of order seems, on the personal level, to have been more vision that fact; among the English authors alone, Swift, William Collins, Thomas Gray, Samuel Johnson, Christopher Smart, William Cowper, and Robert Burns all suffered from depression, serious mental illness, or the fear of such illness; Thomas Chatterton committed suicide in his teens. In their literary works too there are glimpses of mysterious and irrational psychic depths; for example, that most civilized of poems, Pope's *Rape of the Lock,* includes in its Cave of Spleen a surrealistic fantasy world where, among other things, "Men prove with child, as powerful fancy works, / And maids turned bottles, call aloud for corks" (IV.53–54). The personal lives of the Romantics were, for the most part, not really adventurous, a few such as Byron excepted. Their works, apparently so much closer to wish-fulfillment fantasy than to reality, have come to seem more and more realistic in their depiction of basic truths about the human personality, as depth psychologists have recognized. Behind most human acts and language lies their opposite, according to one maxim of popular psy-

14

chology; the determined life-of-the-party is really shy, the notorious lecher really hates women, and so on. Applying that rule to the periods we are considering, we would conclude that the Neoclassic age was an age of unreason and that the Romantic age was one of sober responsibility. To go that far would surely be perverse and absurd, yet in reading particular works it sometimes helps to keep the theory of opposites and compensations in mind. If we do so, especially when reading the greatest authors, we find that the Neoclassicists and the Romantics are not totally dissimilar, since they are writing about the one world that ultimately all people in all ages inhabit.

The three formulas we have been considering, and modifying, are applicable to prose fiction as well as to other forms of literature, but less pointedly and much less systematically. The emergence over the last three centuries of the novel, and of its more modest sibling the short story, as the most vital and dominant of modern literary forms is one of the more striking phenomena of literary history—especially in connection with the parallel loss of trust, on the part of many readers, in the medium of verse as such. It is hard to generalize, however, about the process of these developments, and to generalize about their cause and meaning would take us into deep waters indeed.

For one thing, it is hard to define what a novel is; there has been some helpful theorizing on the subject, but no real consensus exists. Swift's *Gulliver's Travels* and Voltaire's *Candide* are prose fiction, but one hesitates to call them novels, partly by an evasion: because a handier label for them— satire—suggests itself. To put the point more generally: these works are too patently attempts to manipulate the surface of things in the interests of polemical statement; the true function of novels, according to a common, loose, but perhaps valid assumption, is to portray the world rather than to argue or philosophize. When, in 1945, George Orwell published *Animal Farm*, a barnyard allegory satirizing the Stalinist state, many readers were tacitly reluctant to call the book a novel, not only because it was satire and therefore essentially polemical but also because it drew too exclusively on the conventions of fantasy. Despite the extravagant liberties twentieth-century novelists have been known to take with the genre, the stubborn notion persists that the authentic province of the novel is realism. Whatever views or values the novelist may intend to propagate, one still expects him or her to depict the conditions of mundane life in a recognizable way, to allow us to run our hands over the texture of a world familiar to us.

On the other hand, although the appeal of novels would seem to be grounded somehow in realism, few if any of the notable novels of the last few centuries confine themselves to a textural imitation of the world. The best of them combine with their photographic or otherwise mundane concerns a concern with psychological, sometimes visionary realities, in other words with the spiritual landscape of humankind. One sees this combination at its clearest in the work that is often considered the fountainhead of the modern novel—Cervantes' *Don Quixote* (1615)—a work in which the very point is the tension between the inner visionary world of the Don and the earthy world of his squire, Sancho Panza. Mme de Lafayette's *The Princess de Clèves* is, up to a point, elaborately faithful to its factual and historical setting, but its lasting value is in its fidelity to the elusive psychological

dynamics of its heroine. Much the same thing can be said, after allowing for differences in setting, of Goethe's *The Sorrows of Young Werther* and Austen's *Persuasion*. Balzac's France, Dickens' England, and Pushkin's Russia are unforgettably convincing as places, but what animates them for us is a distinctive spiritual atmosphere that seems to express their essential soul and the souls of their inhabitants. There is no generic reason why such effects cannot be achieved in verse, and of course they were achieved in verse before the mysterious decline in the full-scale verse narrative that gradually occurred in the course of the nineteenth century. The fact remains that this displacement of verse by the novel has occurred. The fascinating thing to watch, as the genre continues to develop, is the way in which its fundamentally realistic method continues, in ever-multiplying ways, to penetrate to the deepest regions of our hearts and minds.

In recent years, some radical innovations have been introduced into the study of literature. On the one hand, certain schools of interpretation, taking as a premise the inherent shiftiness and instability of all language, have questioned whether literature can have any authentic connection with reality outside language and literature themselves. Conversely, other interpreters have begun to insist on the social pertinence of all literary works, regarding them as telltale products of their unique historical circumstances. From both points of view, the very definition of literature becomes more flexible, so that it now takes in not only verse and prose fictions but also factual writings that earlier had been considered marginal at best—for example, Frederick Douglass's narrative of his life.

Roughly speaking, feminist criticism takes the second, more social approach, which can be especially fruitful in connection with eighteenth- and nineteenth-century literature. It was during this period that women first fought in large numbers for the right to a public voice as authors. One of the reasons why novels written by women are particularly difficult to classify by the three formulas cited earlier is that women played a special role in the novel's development and that, even while each of them unmistakably reflects the time when it was written, the novels also form a distinct family tree that flourished in virtual independence of the neoclassical-romantic oppositions. When, in *Northanger Abbey* (published 1818), Jane Austen wrote in angry defense of novel-writing and novel-reading, she was among other things pledging her allegiance to her forerunner Fanny Burney, who in turn was the spiritual heir of women such as those the eighteenth-century novelist Samuel Richardson had gathered around him and inspired to write. Austen's own manner is both Romantic and eighteenth-century. The same can be said of Mary Shelley's *Frankenstein* (1818).

The late eighteenth century and the early nineteenth century were the first consciously feminist age, highlighted by the writings of Mary Shelley's mother, Mary Wollstonecraft, in the 1790s. This meant that social commentary or protest was especially prominent in the works of women writers of the time, but it also meant, paradoxically, that a new kind of realistic and intimate portrayal of private life and private affections became at least equally prominent. Love stories emerged as—and to a large extent have remained—the special province of the novel. From that development, in turn, arose a whole new way of understanding human personality as a complex and subtle essence fully knowable only from within, and best ex-

16

plored in the leisurely, casual detail of prose fiction. A perfect example of this double focus, sociological but also intimately personal, is George Sand's story "The Marquise." It seems entirely fitting that the story has a double setting in time: told in the nineteenth-century Romantic period, set in the neoclassical eighteenth century.

FURTHER READING *(prepared by B. W.)*: Among the words discussed at length in C. S. Lewis's *Studies in Words,* 1960, are *nature, wit,* and *sense,* all key terms in Neoclassicism or Romanticism. The distinguished philosopher-mathematician Alfred North Whitehead, in *Science and the Modern World,* 1925, speculates provocatively and with enduring relevance on the relationship between science, philosophy, and literature since the Renaissance. Martin S. Day's *History of English Literature 1660–1837,* 1963, in the Doubleday College Course Guide series, is an excellent handbook that covers a good deal of ground economically. For a general history of political and many other aspects of eighteenth-century Europe, see Isser Woloch's *Eighteenth-Century Europe, Tradition and Progress 1715–1789,* 1982. Derek Jarrett's *England in the Age of Hogarth,* 1974, is an engrossing, illustrated social history of the eighteenth century. The spirit of the century is also well captured in Peter Gay's *The Enlightenment,* 2 vols., 1966–69. Donald Greene's *The Age of Exuberance,* 1970, is an intellectual and literary history that re-evaluates the adequacy of labels such as *Enlightenment.* On the transition from Neoclassicism to Romanticism many good things have been written. One is Walter Jackson Bate's *From Classic to Romantic,* 1946, which treats the relationship of literature to other currents of thought in the two periods; Basil Willey's *The Eighteenth-Century Background,* 1940, which concentrates chiefly on the idea of nature, is also very good. Two volumes in the Viking Portable series, *The Portable Age of Reason Reader,* ed. Crane Brinton, 1956, and *The Portable Romantic Reader,* ed. Howard E. Hugo, 1957, provide good introductions to the periods and wide samplings of characteristic writings, drawn from several national literatures. On the shift in imagery, the replacement in Romanticism of a God- and nature-centered world view by a human-centered one, and a number of other important issues, see Northrop Frye's *A Study of English Romanticism,* 1968, and "The Imaginative and the Imaginary" in his *Fables of Identity,* 1963. On the transition between Neoclassical models of reality and Romantic organicism, see A. O. Lovejoy's *The Great Chain of Being,* 1936; René Wellek's "The Concept of 'Romanticism' in Literary History" in the 1949 volume of *Comparative Literature;* Morse Peckham's "Toward a Theory of Romanticism" in the 1951 volume of *PMLA;* and Peckham's sequel to that article in the 1961 volume of *Studies in Romanticism.* A variety of essays on the transition to Romanticism are collected in *From Sensibility to Romanticism,* ed. Frederick W. Hilles and Harold Bloom, 1965. On the emergence of the Romantic theory of poetic creation from earlier models, see M. H. Abrams, *The Mirror and the Lamp,* 1953, one of the most highly honored books of modern literary scholarship. For an excellent guide to and description of books and articles on the Romantics, some of which have an international focus, see *The English Romantic Poets: A Review of Research and Criticism,* 4th ed., ed. Frank Jordan, 1985. *Romanticism Reconsidered,* ed. Northrop Frye, 1963, contains appraisals of its subject by four distinguished authorities: Frye, M. H. Abrams, Lionel Trilling, and René Wellek. On the coherence of Romanticism as a movement, see Wellek's broad-ranging second volume, *The Romantic Age,* 1955, in his *History of Modern Criticism 1750–1950.* His "German and English Romanticism: A Confrontation," in the 1964 volume of *Studies in Romanticism,* is valuable on the subject it addresses. An immensely spirited, polemical defense of Romanticism against charges brought against it on political and other grounds is presented by Jacques Barzun in *Classic, Romantic, and Modern,* 1961, a book that also compares "historic" and "perennial" Romanticism. Also lively and penetrating is Harold Bloom's *The Visionary Company;* mainly a series of readings of

individual English Romantic poets, the 2nd edition, 1971, includes also a stimulating general preface on the radical, Protestant political impulse in Romanticism. For a cultural history of the United States in the nineteenth century, see Daniel Boorstin, *The Americans: The National Experience*, 1965. A guide to writings about the major authors is available in *Eight American Authors: A Review of Research and Criticism*, rev. ed., ed. James Woodress, 1971. The central American theme of optimism is explored in R. W. B. Lewis' *The American Adam: Innocence, Tragedy, and Tradition in the Nineteenth Century*, 1955. F. O. Matthiessen's *American Renaissance*, 1941, though in some ways a little outdated, remains one of the classic treatments of nineteenth-century American literature.

Molière

(1622–1673)

Jean-Baptiste Poquelin, whose stage name was Molière, was born in Paris in 1622, into a respectable, well-to-do, middle-class family; his father was an upholsterer who included the king among his customers. Molière was educated at the excellent Collège de Clermont in Paris and then enrolled in a law course in Orléans. At the age of twenty-one, however, he shocked and disappointed his father (his mother had died when he was ten) by abandoning the study of law and becoming an actor. Part of the lure of the theater apparently was the beautiful and talented Madeleine Béjart, six years older than Molière and an experienced actress. Molière joined Madeleine, her brother Joseph, and her sister Genevieve in forming *L'Illustre Théâtre;* upon entering the theater, he took the name of Molière, possibly to spare his father embarrassment. The dozen youthful members of the Illustrious Theater performed sporadically and unsuccessfully for two years in Paris; Molière was twice briefly imprisoned for debt during this time. Finally, Molière and the three Béjarts, with three other loyal members of the company, decided to leave Paris and perform in the provinces. Their tour lasted twelve years, during which the members of the company became seasoned performers and Molière began to write plays.

In 1658, these performers decided to try their luck once more in Paris. They played before the king's brother Philippe (known as "Monsieur"), pleased him, and became established as the "Troupe de Monsieur." During the remaining fifteen years of his life, Molière remained in Paris, writing, directing, and acting in the more than thirty plays upon which his reputation still rests. His career was marked by almost constant intrigue and turmoil, and each major success won him not only admirers but enemies among those his satiric wit had touched. The success of *The Pretentious Young Ladies* in 1659 caused a storm of protest which forced a suspension of the production for two weeks and eventually the closing of the theater in which Molière was then performing, the Petit Bourbon. *The School for Wives* in 1662 launched another series of attacks upon both his art and his character, and *Tartuffe* (1664) provoked such a scandal that public performances were forbidden for five years.

In 1662, at the age of forty, Molière married Armande Béjart, the twenty-year-old youngest sister of his long-time mistress and close friend Madeleine Béjart. Armande was an accomplished actress, specializing in the roles of witty coquettes, many of which Molière wrote for her, such as Eliza in *The School for Wives Criticized* and Célimène in *The Misanthrope*. The couple had three children, two of whom died in infancy, but the marriage was not happy, and they lived separately for several years.

Louis XIV was an enthusiastic though erratic supporter of Molière. In 1665, he conferred upon Molière's company the title of "Troupe of the King," and Molière wrote a number of plays, opera-ballets, and other entertainments for presentation at Versailles and other locations of the court. In 1672, however, the king withdrew his favor from Molière and conferred it upon the devious and manipulative court composer Jean Baptiste Lully.

Hurt by this rejection and by the recent deaths of Madeleine Béjart and of a son and suffering from a worsening of a long-time lung ailment, probably tuberculosis, Molière completed his last play, *The Imaginary Invalid,* paradoxically one of the wittiest and most sparkling of his works. On February 17, 1673, he collapsed, hemorrhaging from the lungs, in the middle of a performance of *The Imaginary Invalid* in which he was playing the role of the hypochondriac Argan. He managed to finish the performance but died later that night in his home. The local priests at first refused to bury him in holy ground, but on the intervention of the king he was finally buried in the Cemetery Saint-Joseph, although his body was taken to the grave in darkness so as to "avoid scandal."

The physical theaters Molière wrote for differed considerably from the theaters of Shakespeare and Calderón. The earliest seventeenth-century French theaters were converted from unused indoor tennis courts, survivals of a short-lived vogue for tennis. These and later theaters were long, narrow rooms with a raised stage at one end and an ornate proscenium arch and a front curtain, much like a modern stage. The stage, unlike Shakespeare's, represented a particular place throughout, depicted in perspective scenery made of wood and canvas. This scenery remained in place throughout the play; because of both the difficulty of shifting scenery and the influence of the idea of "unity of place" (the limitation of a play to one location), no attempt was made to change the set in the course of the action.

All these theatrical conditions affected the form and structure of French neoclassical plays. Molière's casts of characters are small, by Shakespearean standards at least; his plots are comparatively simple and usually confined to domestic, family matters; and the action takes place over a short span of time and in a single place, even when such constriction results in some improbability.

Molière's revolutionary impact upon French drama was in the creation of "character comedy." When he and his company began performing his plays in Paris, the dominant forms of stage comedy were the improvised low comedy of the Italian *commedia dell'arte* and high comedy that depended upon elaborate, complex plots. Molière revived the popular farcical comedy of a quarter-century before, with its preoccupation with cuckoldry and its slapstick devices, and used it to deal with contemporary fashions and customs. The result was a hilarious comedy that shifted the focus from elaborate plotting to character.

In his comedy Molière is recurringly preoccupied with the contrast between *mask* and *face.* His characters are usually drawn from the stock types of popular farce—young lovers, witty servants, tyrannical parents, absurd pedants—but he humanizes these masks by hinting at the psychological forces behind them. His major characters are usually great egotists who disguise their drives to satisfy their appetites behind conventional roles or masks. There is thus frequently a rather infantile quality about Molière's comedy; we sometimes feel that we are watching great babies playing at being fathers, mothers, husbands, wives, or courtiers. Their appetites are frequently so urgent and so all-engulfing that they can be controlled only by theatrical illusion. Tartuffe seems destined to triumph over Orgon and his family up until the very end, when a "messenger from the king" rather improbably reverses the action.

Tartuffe, like all of Molière's greatest plays, comes perilously close to tragedy. Tartuffe is one of dramatic literature's greatest comic creations. Molière daringly delays his entrance until the third act, after he has been discussed thoroughly. When he finally enters, calling with a delicious absurdity for his valet to hang up his hair shirt and his scourge, he fascinates us with his completely amoral and childlike pursuit of his own gratification. But, in many ways, Orgon is even more interesting. Why is he so blind to Tartuffe's true nature? What needs of his own lead him to accept Tartuffe so completely and so self-destructively, while hiding behind his own mask of piety and righteousness? Human beings seem woefully ill-equipped to deal with evil in this play. Cléante, Molière's familiar touchstone character of moderation and the normal, asks his brother-in-law, "Is not a face quite different from a mask? / Cannot sincerity and cunning art, / Reality and semblance, be told apart?" But his good sense cannot prevail against the masked irrational drives of either Orgon or Tartuffe; only the playwright's hand can avert a calamitous ending. The best comedy, Freud told us, has a sting in it; we laugh hardest at things that, if we did not laugh, would make us weep. We laugh all the more at *Tartuffe's* comic masks, perhaps, because we are aware of the tragic faces behind them.

FURTHER READING *(prepared by W. J. R.):* The updated edition of Hallam Walker's *Molière,* 1990, in the Twayne series, is a good introductory overview. D. B. Wyndham Lewis's witty *Molière: The Comic Mask,* 1959, combines biography and criticism of works including *Tartuffe.* Gertrud Mander's *Molière,* trans. by Diana Stone Peters, 1973, begins with a chronology and an essay on Molière's times and then proceeds to introductory discussions of fourteen Molière plays. Reviews of significant modern productions of Molière are collected in the conclusion. Five major plays are discussed in Lionel Gossman's *Men and Masks,* 1963, concluding with an examination of Molière's modern reputation. Nineteen essays on technique, theme, and tradition are collected in *Molière: Stage and Study,* ed. W. D. Howarth and Merlin Thomas, 1973. Gaston Hall's essay on comic images and W. H. Barber's essay on Voltaire and Molière may be of particular interest. W. G. Moore's *Molière: A New Criticism,* 1949, is still an important work in Molière scholarship. Moore identifies several problems in interpreting Molière's drama and analyzes multiple levels of comedy in several major works. An interesting complement to Moore's study is provided in Brian Nicholas's "Is Tartuffe a Comic Character?" *Modern Language Review,* 75 (1980), 753–65. Nicholas responds to Moore's analysis of *Tartuffe* and speculates interestingly on the relationship between comedy and satirical ideas. *Molière: A Collection of Critical Essays,* ed. Jacques Guicharnaud, 1964, contains several fine essays on the art of comedy and on *Dom Juan,* but does not offer essays on *Tartuffe.* Roger W. Herzel provides an interesting essay on a rather neglected topic in "The Decor of Molière's Stage: The Testimony of Brissart and Chauveau," *PMLA,* 93 (1978), 925–54. Using many illustrations, Herzel explains why the stage designs for Molière's comedies may have differed considerably from the barren, static designs used for Racinian tragedies. (See also the bibliography for Racine.)

TARTUFFE

Translated by Richard Wilbur

CHARACTERS

MME. PERNELLE, *Orgon's mother*
ORGON, *Elmire's husband*
ELMIRE, *Orgon's wife*
DAMIS, *Orgon's son, Elmire's stepson*
MARIANE, *Orgon's daughter, Elmire's stepdaughter, in love with Valère*
VALÈRE, *in love with Mariane*
CLÉANTE, *Orgon's brother-in-law*

TARTUFFE, *a hypocrite*
DORINE, *Mariane's lady's-maid*
M. LOYAL, *a bailiff*
A POLICE OFFICER
FLIPOTE, *Mme. Pernelle's maid*

THE SCENE THROUGHOUT:
Orgon's *house in Paris*

ACT I

SCENE 1

MADAME PERNELLE *and* FLIPOTE, *her maid*
ELMIRE DORINE CLÉANTE
MARIANE DAMIS

MADAME PERNELLE. Come, come, Flipote; it's time I left this place.
ELMIRE. I can't keep up, you walk at such a pace.
MADAME PERNELLE. Don't trouble, child; no need to show me out.
 It's not your manners I'm concerned about.
ELMIRE. We merely pay you the respect we owe. 5
 But, Mother, why this hurry? Must you go?
MADAME PERNELLE. I must. This house appalls me. No one in it
 Will pay attention for a single minute.
 Children, I take my leave much vexed in spirit.
 I offer good advice, but you won't hear it. 10
 You all break in and chatter on and on.
 It's like a madhouse with the keeper gone.
DORINE. If . . .
MADAME PERNELLE. Girl, you talk too much, and I'm afraid
 You're far too saucy for a lady's-maid.
 You push in everywhere and have your say. 15
DAMIS. But . . .
MADAME PERNELLE. You, boy, grow more foolish every day.
 To think my grandson should be such a dunce!
 I've said a hundred times, if I've said it once,
 That if you keep the course on which you've started,
 You'll leave your worthy father broken-hearted. 20
MARIANE. I think . . .
MADAME PERNELLE. And you, his sister, seem so pure,
 So shy, so innocent, and so demure.

 But you know what they say about still waters.
 I pity parents with secretive daughters.
ELMIRE. Now, Mother . . .
MADAME PERNELLE. And as for you, child, let me add 25
 That your behavior is extremely bad,
 And a poor example for these children, too.
 Their dear, dead mother did far better than you.
 You're much too free with money, and I'm distressed
 To see you so elaborately dressed. 30
 When it's one's husband that one aims to please,
 One has no need of costly fripperies.
CLÉANTE. Oh, Madame, really . . .
MADAME PERNELLE. You are her brother, Sir,
 And I respect and love you; yet if I were
 My son, this lady's good and pious spouse, 35
 I wouldn't make you welcome in my house.
 You're full of worldly counsels which, I fear,
 Aren't suitable for decent folk to hear.
 I've spoken bluntly, Sir; but it behooves us
 Not to mince words when righteous fervor moves us. 40
DAMIS. Your man Tartuffe is full of holy speeches . . .
MADAME PERNELLE. And practises precisely what he preaches.
 He's a fine man, and should be listened to.
 I will not hear him mocked by fools like you.
DAMIS. Good God! Do you expect me to submit 45
 To the tyranny of that carping hypocrite?
 Must we forgo all joys and satisfactions
 Because that bigot censures all our actions?
DORINE. To hear him talk—and he talks all the time—
 There's nothing one can do that's not a crime. 50
 He rails at everything, your dear Tartuffe.
MADAME PERNELLE. Whatever he reproves deserves reproof.
 He's out to save your souls, and all of you
 Must love him, as my son would have you do.
DAMIS. Ah no, Grandmother, I could never take 55
 To such a rascal, even for my father's sake.
 That's how I feel, and I shall not dissemble.
 His every action makes me seethe and tremble
 With helpless anger, and I have no doubt
 That he and I will shortly have it out. 60
DORINE. Surely it is a shame and a disgrace
 To see this man usurp the master's place—
 To see this beggar who, when first he came,
 Had not a shoe or shoestring to his name
 So far forget himself that he behaves 65
 As if the house were his, and we his slaves.
MADAME PERNELLE. Well, mark my words, your souls would fare
 far better
 If you obeyed his precepts to the letter.
DORINE. You see him as a saint. I'm far less awed;

In fact, I see right through him. He's a fraud. 70
MADAME PERNELLE. Nonsense.
DORINE. His man Laurent's the same, or worse;
 I'd not trust either with a penny purse.
MADAME PERNELLE. I can't say what his servant's morals may be;
 His own great goodness I can guarantee.
 You all regard him with distaste and fear 75
 Because he tells you what you're loath to hear,
 Condemns your sins, points out your moral flaws,
 And humbly strives to further Heaven's cause.
DORINE. If sin is all that bothers him, why is it
 He's so upset when folk drop in to visit? 80
 Is Heaven so outraged by a social call
 That he must prophesy against us all?
 I'll tell you what I think: if you ask me,
 He's jealous of my mistress' company.
MADAME PERNELLE. Rubbish! [*To* ELMIRE.] He's not alone, child, in
 complaining 85
 Of all your promiscuous entertaining.
 Why, the whole neighborhood's upset, I know,
 By all these carriages that come and go,
 With crowds of guests parading in and out
 And noisy servants loitering about. 90
 In all of this, I'm sure there's nothing vicious;
 But why give people cause to be suspicious?
CLÉANTE. They need no cause; they'll talk in any case.
 Madam, this world would be a joyless place
 If, fearing what malicious tongues might say, 95
 We locked our doors and turned our friends away.
 And even if one did so dreary a thing,
 D'you think those tongues would cease their chattering?
 One can't fight slander; it's a losing battle;
 Let us instead ignore their tittle-tattle. 100
 Let's strive to live by conscience's clear decrees,
 And let the gossips gossip as they please.
DORINE. If there is talk against us, I know the source:
 It's Daphne and her little husband, of course.
 Those who have greatest cause for guilt and shame 105
 Are quickest to besmirch a neighbor's name.
 When there's a chance for libel, they never miss it;
 When something can be made to seem illicit
 They're off at once to spread the joyous news,
 Adding to fact what fantasies they choose. 110
 By talking up their neighbor's indiscretions
 They seek to camouflage their own transgressions,
 Hoping that others' innocent affairs
 Will lend a hue of innocence to theirs,
 Or that their own black guilt will come to seem 115
 Part of a general shady color-scheme.
MADAME PERNELLE. All that is quite irrelevant. I doubt

That anyone's more virtuous and devout
Than dear Orante; and I'm informed that she
Condemns your mode of life most vehemently. 120
DORINE. Oh, yes, she's strict, devout, and has no taint
 Of worldliness; in short, she seems a saint.
 But it was time which taught her that disguise;
 She's thus because she can't be otherwise.
 So long as her attractions could enthrall, 125
 She flounced and flirted and enjoyed it all,
 But now that they're no longer what they were
 She quits a world which fast is quitting her,
 And wears a veil of virtue to conceal
 Her bankrupt beauty and her lost appeal. 130
 That's what becomes of old coquettes today:
 Distressed when all their lovers fall away,
 They see no recourse but to play the prude,
 And so confer a style on solitude.
 Thereafter, they're severe with everyone, 135
 Condemning all our actions, pardoning none,
 And claiming to be pure, austere, and zealous
 When, if the truth were known, they're merely jealous,
 And cannot bear to see another know
 The pleasures time has forced them to forgo. 140
MADAME PERNELLE [*initially to* ELMIRE]. That sort of talk is what
 you like to hear,
 Therefore you'd have us all keep still, my dear,
 While Madam rattles on the livelong day.
 Nevertheless, I mean to have my say.
 I tell you that you're blest to have Tartuffe 145
 Dwelling, as my son's guest, beneath this roof;
 That Heaven has sent him to forestall its wrath
 By leading you, once more, to the true path;
 That all he reprehends is reprehensible,
 And that you'd better heed him, and be sensible. 150
 These visits, balls, and parties in which you revel
 Are nothing but inventions of the Devil.
 One never hears a word that's edifying:
 Nothing but chaff and foolishness and lying,
 As well as vicious gossip in which one's neighbor 155
 Is cut to bits with epee, foil, and saber.
 People of sense are driven half-insane
 At such affairs, where noise and folly reign
 And reputations perish thick and fast.
 As a wise preacher said on Sunday last, 160
 Parties are Towers of Babylon, because
 The guests all babble on with never a pause;
 And then he told a story which, I think
 [*To* CLÉANTE.] I heard that laugh, Sir, and I saw that wink!
 Go find your silly friends and laugh some more! 165
 Enough; I'm going; don't show me to the door.

I leave this household much dismayed and vexed;
I cannot say when I shall see you next.
[*Slapping* FLIPOTE.] Wake up, don't stand there gaping into space!
I'll slap some sense into that stupid face. 170
Move, move, you slut.

SCENE 2
CLÉANTE DORINE

CLÉANTE. I think I'll stay behind;
I want no further pieces of her mind.
How that old lady . . .
DORINE. Oh, what wouldn't she say
If she could hear you speak of her that way!
She'd thank you for the *lady,* but I'm sure 5
She'd find the *old* a little premature.
CLÉANTE. My, what a scene she made, and what a din!
And how this man Tartuffe has taken her in!
DORINE. Yes, but her son is even worse deceived;
His folly must be seen to be believed. 10
In the late troubles, he played an able part
And served his king with wise and loyal heart,
But he's quite lost his senses since he fell
Beneath Tartuffe's infatuating spell.
He calls him brother, and loves him as his life, 15
Preferring him to mother, child, or wife.
In him and him alone will he confide;
He's made him his confessor and his guide;
He pets and pampers him with love more tender
Than any pretty mistress could engender, 20
Gives him the place of honor when they dine,
Delights to see him gorging like a swine,
Stuffs him with dainties till his guts distend,
And when he belches, cries "God bless you, friend!"
In short, he's mad; he worships him; he dotes; 25
His deeds he marvels at, his words he quotes,
Thinking each act a miracle, each word
Oracular as those that Moses heard.
Tartuffe, much pleased to find so easy a victim,
Has in a hundred ways beguiled and tricked him, 30
Milked him of money, and with his permission
Established here a sort of Inquisition.
Even Laurent, his lackey, dares to give
Us arrogant advice on how to live;
He sermonizes us in thundering tones 35
And confiscates our ribbons and colognes.
Last week he tore a kerchief into pieces
Because he found it pressed in a *Life of Jesus:*

He said it was a sin to juxtapose
Unholy vanities and holy prose. 40

SCENE 3
ELMIRE DAMIS DORINE
MARIANE CLÉANTE

ELMIRE [*to* CLÉANTE]. You did well not to follow; she stood in the
 door
And said *verbatim* all she'd said before.
I saw my husband coming. I think I'd best
Go upstairs now, and take a little rest.
CLÉANTE. I'll wait and greet him here; then I must go. 5
 I've really only time to say hello.
DAMIS. Sound him about my sister's wedding, please.
 I think Tartuffe's against it, and that he's
 Been urging Father to withdraw his blessing.
 As you well know, I'd find that most distressing. 10
 Unless my sister and Valère can marry,
 My hopes to wed *his* sister will miscarry,
 And I'm determined . . .
DORINE. He's coming.

SCENE 4
ORGON CLÉANTE DORINE

ORGON. Ah, Brother, good-day.
CLÉANTE. Well, welcome back. I'm sorry I can't stay.
 How was the country? Blooming, I trust, and green?
ORGON. Excuse me, Brother; just one moment.
 [*To* DORINE.] Dorine . . .
 [*To* CLÉANTE.] To put my mind at rest, I always learn 5
 The household news the moment I return.
 [*To* DORINE.] Has all been well, these two days I've been gone?
 How are the family? What's been going on?
DORINE. Your wife, two days ago, had a bad fever,
 And a fierce headache which refused to leave her. 10
ORGON. Ah. And Tartuffe?
DORINE. Tartuffe? Why, he's round and red,
 Bursting with health, and excellently fed.
ORGON. Poor fellow!
DORINE. That night, the mistress was unable
 To take a single bite at the dinner-table.
 Her headache-pains, she said, were simply hellish. 15
ORGON. Ah. And Tartuffe?
DORINE. He ate his meal with relish,
 And zealously devoured in her presence

A leg of mutton and a brace of pheasants.
ORGON. Poor fellow!
DORINE. Well, the pains continued strong,
 And so she tossed and tossed the whole night long, 20
 Now icy-cold, now burning like a flame.
 We sat beside her bed till morning came.
ORGON. Ah. And Tartuffe?
DORINE. Why, having eaten, he rose
 And sought his room, already in a doze,
 Got into his warm bed, and snored away 25
 In perfect peace until the break of day.
ORGON. Poor fellow!
DORINE. After much ado, we talked her
 Into dispatching someone for the doctor.
 He bled her, and the fever quickly fell.
ORGON. Ah. And Tartuffe?
DORINE. He bore it very well. 30
 To keep his cheerfulness at any cost,
 And make up for the blood *Madame* had lost,
 He drank, at lunch, four beakers full of port.
ORGON. Poor fellow!
DORINE. Both are doing well, in short.
 I'll go and tell *Madame* that you've expressed 35
 Keen sympathy and anxious interest.

SCENE 5
ORGON CLÉANTE

CLÉANTE. That girl was laughing in your face, and though
 I've no wish to offend you, even so
 I'm bound to say that she had some excuse.
 How can you possibly be such a goose?
 Are you so dazed by this man's hocus-pocus 5
 That all the world, save him, is out of focus?
 You've given him clothing, shelter, food, and care;
 Why must you also . . .
ORGON. Brother, stop right there.
 You do not know the man of whom you speak.
CLÉANTE. I grant you that. But my judgment's not so weak 10
 That I can't tell, by his effect on others . . .
ORGON. Ah, when you meet him, you two will be like brothers!
 There's been no loftier soul since time began.
 He is a man who . . . a man who . . . an excellent man.
 To keep his precepts is to be reborn, 15
 And view this dunghill of a world with scorn.
 Yes, thanks to him I'm a changed man indeed.
 Under his tutelage my soul's been freed

From earthly loves, and every human tie:
My mother, children, brother, and wife could die, 20
And I'd not feel a single moment's pain.
CLÉANTE. That's a fine sentiment, Brother; most humane.
ORGON. Oh, had you seen Tartuffe as I first knew him,
Your heart, like mine, would have surrendered to him.
He used to come into our church each day 25
And humbly kneel nearby, and start to pray.
He'd draw the eyes of everybody there
By the deep fervor of his heartfelt prayer;
He'd sigh and weep, and sometimes with a sound
Of rapture he would bend and kiss the ground; 30
And when I rose to go, he'd run before
To offer me holy-water at the door.
His serving-man, no less devout than he,
Informed me of his master's poverty;
I gave him gifts, but in his humbleness 35
He'd beg me every time to give him less.
"Oh, that's too much," he'd cry, "too much by twice!
I don't deserve it. The half, Sir, would suffice."
And when I wouldn't take it back, he'd share
Half of it with the poor, right then and there. 40
At length, Heaven prompted me to take him in
To dwell with us, and free our souls from sin.
He guides our lives, and to protect my honor
Stays by my wife, and keeps an eye upon her;
He tells me whom she sees, and all she does, 45
And seems more jealous than I ever was!
And how austere he is! Why, he can detect
A mortal sin where you would least suspect;
In smallest trifles, he's extremely strict.
Last week, his conscience was severely pricked 50
Because, while praying, he had caught a flea
And killed it, so he felt, too wrathfully.
CLÉANTE. Good God, man! Have you lost your common sense—
Or is this all some joke at my expense?
How can you stand there and in all sobriety . . . 55
ORGON. Brother, your language savors of impiety.
Too much free-thinking's made your faith unsteady,
And as I've warned you many times already,
'Twill get you into trouble before you're through.
CLÉANTE. So I've been told before by dupes like you: 60
Being blind, you'd have all others blind as well;
The clear-eyed man you call an infidel,
And he who sees through humbug and pretense
Is charged, by you, with want of reverence.
Spare me your warnings, Brother; I have no fear 65
Of speaking out, for you and Heaven to hear,
Against affected zeal and pious knavery.

There's true and false in piety, as in bravery,
And just as those whose courage shines the most
In battle, are the least inclined to boast, 70
So those whose hearts are truly pure and lowly
Don't make a flashy show of being holy.
There's a vast difference, so it seems to me,
Between true piety and hypocrisy:
How do you fail to see it, may I ask? 75
Is not a face quite different from a mask?
Cannot sincerity and cunning art,
Reality and semblance, be told apart?
Are scarecrows just like men, and do you hold
That a false coin is just as good as gold? 80
Ah, Brother, man's a strangely fashioned creature
Who seldom is content to follow Nature,
But recklessly pursues his inclination
Beyond the narrow bounds of moderation,
And often, by transgressing Reason's laws, 85
Perverts a lofty aim or noble cause.
A passing observation, but it applies.
ORGON. I see, dear Brother, that you're profoundly wise;
 You harbor all the insight of the age.
 You are our one clear mind, our only sage, 90
 The era's oracle, its Cato too,
 And all mankind are fools compared to you.
CLÉANTE. Brother, I don't pretend to be a sage,
 Nor have I all the wisdom of the age.
 There's just one insight I would dare to claim: 95
 I know that true and false are not the same;
 And just as there is nothing I more revere
 Than a soul whose faith is steadfast and sincere,
 Nothing that I more cherish and admire
 Than honest zeal and true religious fire, 100
 So there is nothing that I find more base
 Than specious piety's dishonest face—
 Than these bold mountebanks, these histrios
 Whose impious mummeries and hollow shows
 Exploit our love of Heaven, and make a jest 105
 Of all that men think holiest and best;
 These calculating souls who offer prayers
 Not to their Maker, but as public wares,
 And seek to buy respect and reputation
 With lifted eyes and sighs of exaltation; 110
 These charlatans, I say, whose pilgrim souls
 Proceed, by way of Heaven, toward earthly goals,
 Who weep and pray and swindle and extort,
 Who preach the monkish life, but haunt the court,
 Who make their zeal the partner of their vice— 115
 Such men are vengeful, sly, and cold as ice,
 And when there is an enemy to defame

They cloak their spite in fair religion's name,
Their private spleen and malice being made
To seem a high and virtuous crusade, 120
Until, to mankind's reverent applause,
They crucify their foe in Heaven's cause.
Such knaves are all too common; yet, for the wise,
True piety isn't hard to recognize,
And, happily, these present times provide us 125
With bright examples to instruct and guide us.
Consider Ariston and Périandre;
Look at Oronte, Alcidamas, Clitandre;
Their virtue is acknowledged; who could doubt it?
But you won't hear them beat the drum about it. 130
They're never ostentatious, never vain,
And their religion's moderate and humane;
It's not their way to criticize and chide:
They think censoriousness a mark of pride,
And therefore, letting others preach and rave, 135
They show, by deeds, how Christians should behave.
They think no evil of their fellow man,
But judge of him as kindly as they can.
They don't intrigue and wangle and conspire;
To lead a good life is their one desire; 140
The sinner wakes no rancorous hate in them;
It is the sin alone which they condemn;
Nor do they try to show a fiercer zeal
For Heaven's cause than Heaven itself could feel.
These men I honor, these men I advocate 145
As models for us all to emulate.
Your man is not their sort at all, I fear:
And, while your praise of him is quite sincere,
I think that you've been dreadfully deluded.
ORGON. Now then, dear Brother, is your speech concluded? 150
CLÉANTE. Why, yes.
ORGON. Your servant, Sir. [*He turns to go.*]
CLÉANTE. No, Brother; wait.
 There's one more matter. You agreed of late
 That young Valère might have your daughter's hand.
ORGON. I did.
CLÉANTE. And set the date, I understand.
ORGON. Quite so.
CLÉANTE. You've now postponed it; is that true? 155
ORGON. No doubt.
CLÉANTE. The match no longer pleases you?
ORGON. Who knows?
CLÉANTE. D'you mean to go back on your word?
ORGON. I won't say that.
CLÉANTE. Has anything occurred
 Which might entitle you to break your pledge?
ORGON. Perhaps.

CLÉANTE. Why must you hem, and haw, and hedge? 160
 The boy asked me to sound you in this affair . . .
ORGON. It's been a pleasure.
CLÉANTE. But what shall I tell Valère?
ORGON. Whatever you like.
CLÉANTE. But what have you decided?
 What are your plans?
ORGON. I plan, Sir, to be guided
 By Heaven's will.
CLÉANTE. Come, Brother, don't talk rot. 165
 You've given Valère your word; will you keep it, or not?
ORGON. Good day.
CLÉANTE. This looks like poor Valère's undoing;
 I'll go and warn him that there's trouble brewing.

ACT II

SCENE 1
ORGON MARIANE

ORGON. Mariane.
MARIANE. Yes, Father?
ORGON. A word with you; come here.
MARIANE. What are you looking for?
ORGON [*peering into a small closet*]. Eavesdroppers, dear.
 I'm making sure we shan't be overheard.
 Someone in there could catch our every word.
 Ah, good, we're safe. Now, Mariane, my child, 5
 You're a sweet girl who's tractable and mild,
 Whom I hold dear, and think most highly of.
MARIANE. I'm deeply grateful, Father, for your love.
ORGON. That's well said, Daughter; and you can repay me
 If, in all things, you'll cheerfully obey me. 10
MARIANE. To please you, Sir, is what delights me best.
ORGON. Good, good. Now, what d'you think of Tartuffe, our guest?
MARIANE. I, Sir?
ORGON. Yes. Weigh your answer; think it through.
MARIANE. Oh, dear. I'll say whatever you wish me to.
ORGON. That's wisely said, my Daughter. Say of him, then, 15
 That he's the very worthiest of men,
 And that you're fond of him, and would rejoice
 In being his wife, if that should be my choice.
 Well?
MARIANE. What?
ORGON. What's that?
MARIANE. I . . .
ORGON. Well?

MARIANE. Forgive me, pray.
ORGON. Did you not hear me?
MARIANE. Of *whom*, Sir, must I say 20
 That I am fond of him, and would rejoice
 In being his wife, if that should be your choice?
ORGON. Why, of Tartuffe.
MARIANE. But, Father, that's false, you know.
 Why would you have me say what isn't so?
ORGON. Because I am resolved it shall be true. 25
 That it's my wish should be enough for you.
MARIANE. You can't mean, Father . . .
ORGON. Yes, Tartuffe shall be
 Allied by marriage to this family,
 And he's to be your husband, is that clear?
 It's a father's privilege . . . 30

SCENE 2
DORINE ORGON MARIANE

ORGON [*to* DORINE]. What are you doing in here?
 Is curiosity so fierce a passion
 With you, that you must eavesdrop in this fashion?
DORINE. There's lately been a rumor going about—
 Based on some hunch or chance remark, no doubt— 5
 That you mean Mariane to wed Tartuffe.
 I've laughed it off, of course, as just a spoof.
ORGON. You find it so incredible?
DORINE. Yes, I do.
 I won't accept that story, even from you.
ORGON. Well, you'll believe it when the thing is done. 10
DORINE. Yes, yes, of course. Go on and have your fun.
ORGON. I've never been more serious in my life.
DORINE. Ha!
ORGON. Daughter, I mean it; you're to be his wife.
DORINE. No, don't believe your father; it's all a hoax.
ORGON. See here, young woman . . .
DORINE. Come, Sir, no more jokes; 15
 You can't fool us.
ORGON. How dare you talk that way?
DORINE. All right, then: we believe you, sad to say.
 But how a man like you, who looks so wise
 And wears a moustache of such splendid size,
 Can be so foolish as to . . .
ORGON. Silence, please! 20
 My girl, you take too many liberties.
 I'm master here, as you must not forget.
DORINE. Do let's discuss this calmly; don't be upset.
 You can't be serious, Sir, about this plan.
 What should that bigot want with Mariane? 25

Praying and fasting ought to keep him busy.
And then, in terms of wealth and rank, what is he?
Why should a man of property like you
Pick out a beggar son-in-law?
ORGON. That will do.
Speak of his poverty with reverence. 30
His is a pure and saintly indigence
Which far transcends all worldly pride and pelf.
He lost his fortune, as he says himself,
Because he cared for Heaven alone, and so
Was careless of his interests here below. 35
I mean to get him out of his present straits
And help him to recover his estates—
Which, in his part of the world, have no small fame.
Poor though he is, he's a gentleman just the same.
DORINE. Yes, so he tells us; and, Sir, it seems to me 40
Such pride goes very ill with piety.
A man whose spirit spurns this dungy earth
Ought not to brag of lands and noble birth;
Such worldly arrogance will hardly square
With meek devotion and the life of prayer. 45
. . . But this reproach, I see, has drawn a blank;
Let's speak, then, of his person, not his rank.
Doesn't it seem to you a trifle grim
To give a girl like her to a man like him?
When two are so ill-suited, can't you see 50
What the sad consequence is bound to be?
A young girl's virtue is imperilled, Sir,
When such a marriage is imposed on her;
For if one's bridegroom isn't to one's taste,
It's hardly an inducement to be chaste, 55
And many a man with horns upon his brow
Has made his wife the thing that she is now.
It's hard to be a faithful wife, in short,
To certain husbands of a certain sort,
And he who gives his daughter to a man she hates 60
Must answer for her sins at Heaven's gates.
Think, Sir, before you play so risky a role.
ORGON. This servant-girl presumes to save my soul!
DORINE. You would do well to ponder what I've said.
ORGON. Daughter, we'll disregard this dunderhead. 65
Just trust your father's judgment. Oh, I'm aware
That I once promised you to young Valère;
But now I hear he gambles, which greatly shocks me;
What's more, I've doubts about his orthodoxy.
His visits to church, I note, are very few. 70
DORINE. Would you have him go at the same hours as you,
And kneel nearby, to be sure of being seen?
ORGON. I can dispense with such remarks, Dorine.
 [*To* MARIANE.] Tartuffe, however, is sure of Heaven's blessing,

And that's the only treasure worth possessing. 75
This match will bring you joys beyond all measure;
Your cup will overflow with every pleasure;
You two will interchange your faithful loves
Like two sweet cherubs, or two turtle-doves.
No harsh word shall be heard, no frown be seen, 80
And he shall make you happy as a queen.
DORINE. And she'll make him a cuckold, just wait and see.
ORGON. What language!
DORINE. Oh, he's a man of destiny;
 He's *made* for horns, and what the stars demand
 Your daughter's virtue surely can't withstand. 85
ORGON. Don't interrupt me further. Why can't you learn
 That certain things are none of your concern?
DORINE. It's for your own sake that I interfere.

> [*She repeatedly interrupts* ORGON
> *just as he is turning to speak to his*
> *daughter.*]

ORGON. Most kind of you. Now, hold your tongue, d'you hear?
DORINE. If I didn't love you . . .
ORGON. Spare me your affection. 90
DORINE. I love you, Sir, in spite of your objection.
ORGON. Blast!
DORINE. I can't bear, Sir, for your honor's sake,
 To let you make this ludicrous mistake.
ORGON. You mean to go on talking?
DORINE. If I didn't protest
 This sinful marriage, my conscience couldn't rest. 95
ORGON. If you don't hold your tongue, you little shrew . . .
DORINE. What, lost your temper? A pious man like you?
ORGON. Yes! Yes! You talk and talk. I'm maddened by it.
 Once and for all, I tell you to be quiet.
DORINE. Well, I'll be quiet. But I'll be thinking hard. 100
ORGON. Think all you like, but you had better guard
 That saucy tongue of yours, or I'll . . .
 [*Turning back to* MARIANE.] Now, child,
 I've weighed this matter fully.
DORINE [*aside*]. It drives me wild
 That I can't speak.

> [ORGON *turns his head, and she is*
> *silent.*]

ORGON. Tartuffe is no young dandy,
 But, still, his person . . .
DORINE [*aside*]. Is as sweet as candy. 105
ORGON. Is such that, even if you shouldn't care
 For his other merits . . .

> [*He turns and stands facing* DOR-
> INE, *arms crossed.*]

DORINE [*aside*]. They'll make a lovely pair.
 If I were she, no man would marry me

Against my inclination, and go scot-free.
He'd learn, before the wedding-day was over, 110
How readily a wife can find a lover.
ORGON [*to* DORINE]. It seems you treat my orders as a joke.
DORINE. Why, what's the matter? 'Twas not to you I spoke.
ORGON. What *were* you doing?
DORINE. Talking to myself, that's all.
ORGON. Ah! [*Aside.*] One more bit of impudence and gall, 115
And I shall give her a good slap in the face.
 [*He puts himself in position to slap
 her;* DORINE, *whenever he glances
 at her, stands immobile and silent.*]
Daughter, you shall accept, and with good grace,
The husband I've selected . . . Your wedding-day . . .
[*To* DORINE.] Why don't you talk to yourself?
DORINE. I've nothing to say.
ORGON. Come, just one word.
DORINE. No thank you, Sir. I pass. 120
ORGON. Come, speak; I'm waiting.
DORINE. I'd not be such an ass.
ORGON [*turning to* MARIANE]. In short, dear Daughter, I mean to
 be obeyed,
And you must bow to the sound choice I've made.
DORINE [*moving away*]. I'd not wed such a monster, even in jest.
 [ORGON *attempts to slap her, but
 misses.*]
ORGON. Daughter, that maid of yours is a thorough pest; 125
She makes me sinfully annoyed and nettled.
I can't speak further; my nerves are too unsettled.
She's so upset me by her insolent talk,
I'll calm myself by going for a walk.

SCENE 3
DORINE MARIANE

DORINE [*returning*]. Well, have you lost your tongue, girl? Must I play
 Your part, and say the lines you ought to say?
 Faced with a fate so hideous and absurd,
 Can you not utter one dissenting word?
MARIANE. What good would it do? A father's power is great. 5
DORINE. Resist him now, or it will be too late.
MARIANE. But . . .
DORINE. Tell him one cannot love at a father's whim;
 That you shall marry for yourself, not him;
 That since it's you who are to be the bride,
 It's you, not he, who must be satisfied; 10
 And that if his Tartuffe is so sublime,
 He's free to marry him at any time.

MARIANE. I've bowed so long to Father's strict control,
 I couldn't oppose him now, to save my soul.
DORINE. Come, come, Mariane. Do listen to reason, won't you? 15
 Valère has asked your hand. Do you love him, or don't you?
MARIANE. Oh, how unjust of you! What can you mean
 By asking such a question, dear Dorine?
 You know the depth of my affection for him;
 I've told you a hundred times how I adore him. 20
DORINE. I don't believe in everything I hear;
 Who knows if your professions were sincere?
MARIANE. They were, Dorine, and you do me wrong to doubt it;
 Heaven knows that I've been all too frank about it.
DORINE. You love him, then?
MARIANE. Oh, more than I can express. 25
DORINE. And he, I take it, cares for you no less?
MARIANE. I think so.
DORINE. And you both, with equal fire,
 Burn to be married?
MARIANE. That is our one desire.
DORINE. What of Tartuffe, then? What of your father's plan?
MARIANE. I'll kill myself, if I'm forced to wed that man. 30
DORINE. I hadn't thought of that recourse. How splendid!
 Just die, and all your troubles will be ended!
 A fine solution. Oh, it maddens me
 To hear you talk in that self-pitying key.
MARIANE. Dorine, how harsh you are! It's most unfair. 35
 You have no sympathy for my despair.
DORINE. I've none at all for people who talk drivel
 And, faced with difficulties, whine and snivel.
MARIANE. No doubt I'm timid, but it would be wrong . . .
DORINE. True love requires a heart that's firm and strong. 40
MARIANE. I'm strong in my affection for Valère,
 But coping with my father is his affair.
DORINE. But if your father's brain has grown so cracked
 Over his dear Tartuffe that he can retract
 His blessing, though your wedding-day was named, 45
 It's surely not Valère who's to be blamed.
MARIANE. If I defied my father, as you suggest,
 Would it not seem unmaidenly, at best?
 Shall I defend my love at the expense
 Of brazenness and disobedience? 50
 Shall I parade my heart's desires, and flaunt . . .
DORINE. No, I ask nothing of you. Clearly you want
 To be Madame Tartuffe, and I feel bound
 Not to oppose a wish so very sound.
 What right have I to criticize the match? 55
 Indeed, my dear, the man's a brilliant catch.
 Monsieur Tartuffe! Now, there's a man of weight!
 Yes, yes, Monsieur Tartuffe, I'm bound to state,

Is quite a person; that's not to be denied;
'Twill be no little thing to be his bride. 60
The world already rings with his renown;
He's a great noble—in his native town;
His ears are red, he has a pink complexion,
And all in all, he'll suit you to perfection.

MARIANE. Dear God!

DORINE. Oh, how triumphant you will feel 65
At having caught a husband so ideal!

MARIANE. Oh, do stop teasing, and use your cleverness
To get me out of this appalling mess.
Advise me, and I'll do whatever you say.

DORINE. Ah no, a dutiful daughter must obey 70
Her father, even if he weds her to an ape.
You've a bright future; why struggle to escape?
Tartuffe will take you back where his family lives,
To a small town aswarm with relatives—
Uncles and cousins whom you'll be charmed to meet. 75
You'll be received at once by the elite,
Calling upon the bailiff's wife, no less—
Even, perhaps, upon the mayoress,
Who'll sit you down in the *best* kitchen chair.
Then, once a year, you'll dance at the village fair 80
To the drone of bagpipes—two of them, in fact—
And see a puppet-show, or an animal act.
Your husband . . .

MARIANE. Oh, you turn my blood to ice!
Stop torturing me, and give me your advice.

DORINE [*threatening to go*]. Your servant, Madam.

MARIANE. Dorine, I beg of
 you . . . 85

DORINE. No, you deserve it; this marriage must go through.

MARIANE. Dorine!

DORINE. No.

MARIANE. Not Tartuffe! You know I think him . . .

DORINE. Tartuffe's your cup of tea, and you shall drink him.

MARIANE. I've always told you everything, and relied . . .

DORINE. No. You deserve to be tartuffified. 90

MARIANE. Well, since you mock me and refuse to care,
 I'll henceforth seek my solace in despair:
 Despair shall be my counsellor and friend,
 And help me bring my sorrows to an end.

 [*She starts to leave.*]

DORINE. There now, come back; my anger has subsided. 95
 You do deserve some pity, I've decided.

MARIANE. Dorine, if Father makes me undergo
 This dreadful martyrdom, I'll die, I know.

DORINE. Don't fret; it won't be difficult to discover
 Some plan of action . . . But here's Valère, your lover. 100

SCENE 4
VALÈRE MARIANE DORINE

VALÈRE. Madame, I've just received some wondrous news
 Regarding which I'd like to hear your views.
MARIANE. What news?
VALÈRE. You're marrying Tartuffe.
MARIANE. I find
 That Father does have such a match in mind.
VALÈRE. Your father, Madam . . .
MARIANE. . . . has just this minute said 5
 That it's Tartuffe he wishes me to wed.
VALÈRE. Can he be serious?
MARIANE. Oh, indeed he can;
 He's clearly set his heart upon the plan.
VALÈRE. And what position do you propose to take, Madam?
MARIANE. Why—I don't know.
VALÈRE. For heaven's sake— 10
 You don't know?
MARIANE. No.
VALÈRE. Well, well!
MARIANE. Advise me, do.
VALÈRE. Marry the man. That's my advice to you.
MARIANE. That's your advice?
VALÈRE. Yes.
MARIANE. Truly?
VALÈRE. Oh, absolutely.
 You couldn't choose more wisely, more astutely.
MARIANE. Thanks for this counsel; I'll follow it, of course. 15
VALÈRE. Do, do; I'm sure 'twill cost you no remorse.
MARIANE. To give it didn't cause your heart to break.
VALÈRE. I gave it, Madam, only for your sake.
MARIANE. And it's for your sake that I take it, Sir.
DORINE [*withdrawing to the rear of the stage*]. Let's see which fool will
 prove the stubborner. 20
VALÈRE. So! I am nothing to you, and it was flat
 Deception when you . . .
MARIANE. Please, enough of that.
 You've told me plainly that I should agree
 To wed the man my father's chosen for me,
 And since you've designed to counsel me so wisely, 25
 I promise, Sir, to do as you advise me.
VALÈRE. Ah, no, 'twas not by me that you were swayed.
 No, your decision was already made;
 Though now, to save appearances, you protest
 That you're betraying me at my behest. 30
MARIANE. Just as you say.

VALÈRE. Quite so. And I now see
 That you were never truly in love with me.
MARIANE. Alas, you're free to think so if you choose.
VALÈRE. I choose to think so, and here's a bit of news:
 You've spurned my hand, but I know where to turn 35
 For kinder treatment, as you shall quickly learn.
MARIANE. I'm sure you do. Your noble qualities
 Inspire affection . . .
VALÈRE. Forget my qualities, please.
 They don't inspire you overmuch, I find.
 But there's another lady I have in mind 40
 Whose sweet and generous nature will not scorn
 To compensate me for the loss I've borne.
MARIANE. I'm no great loss, and I'm sure that you'll transfer
 Your heart quite painlessly from me to her.
VALÈRE. I'll do my best to take it in my stride. 45
 The pain I feel at being cast aside
 Time and forgetfulness may put an end to.
 Or if I can't forget, I shall pretend to.
 No self-respecting person is expected
 To go on loving once he's been rejected. 50
MARIANE. Now, that's a fine, high-minded sentiment.
VALÈRE. One to which any sane man would assent.
 Would you prefer it if I pined away
 In hopeless passion till my dying day?
 Am I to yield you to a rival's arms 55
 And not console myself with other charms?
MARIANE. Go then: console yourself; don't hesitate.
 I wish you to; indeed, I cannot wait.
VALÈRE. You wish me to?
MARIANE. Yes.
VALÈRE. That's the final straw.
 Madam, farewell. Your wish shall be my law. 60
 [*He starts to leave, and then re-*
 turns: this repeatedly.]
MARIANE. Splendid.
VALÈRE [*coming back again*].
 This breach, remember, is of your making;
 It's you who've driven me to the step I'm taking.
MARIANE. Of course.
VALÈRE [*coming back again*].
 Remember, too, that I am merely
 Following your example.
MARIANE. I see that clearly.
VALÈRE. Enough. I'll go and do your bidding, then. 65
MARIANE. Good.
VALÈRE [*coming back again*].
 You shall never see my face again.
MARIANE. Excellent.

VALÈRE [*walking to the door, then turning about*].

<div align="center">Yes?</div>

MARIANE. What?

VALÈRE. What's that? What did you say?

MARIANE. Nothing. You're dreaming.

VALÈRE. Ah. Well, I'm on my way.
 Farewell, *Madame.*

<div align="right">[*He moves slowly away.*]</div>

MARIANE. Farewell.

DORINE [*to* MARIANE]. If you ask me,
 Both of you are as mad as mad can be. 70
 Do stop this nonsense, now. I've only let you
 Squabble so long to see where it would get you.
 Whoa there, Monsieur Valère!

<div align="right">[*She goes and seizes* VALÈRE *by the
arm; he makes a great show of re-
sistance.*]</div>

VALÈRE. What's this, Dorine?

DORINE. Come here.

VALÈRE. No, no, my heart's too full of spleen.
 Don't hold me back; her wish must be obeyed. 75

DORINE. Stop!

VALÈRE. It's too late now; my decision's made.

DORINE. Oh, pooh!

MARIANE [*aside*]. He hates the sight of me, that's plain.
 I'll go, and so deliver him from pain.

DORINE [*leaving* VALÈRE, *running after* MARIANE].
 And now *you* run away! Come back.

MARIANE. No, no.
 Nothing you say will keep me here. Let go! 80

VALÈRE [*aside*]. She cannot bear my presence, I perceive.
 To spare her further torment, I shall leave.

DORINE [*leaving* MARIANE, *running after* VALÈRE]. Again! You'll not
 escape, Sir; don't you try it.
 Come here, you two. Stop fussing, and be quiet.

<div align="right">[*She takes* VALÈRE *by the hand,
then* MARIANE, *and draws them
together.*]</div>

VALÈRE [*to* DORINE]. What do you want of me?

MARIANE [*to* DORINE]. What is the point of
 this? 85

DORINE. We're going to have a little armistice.
 [*To* VALÈRE.] Now weren't you silly to get so overheated?

VALÈRE. Didn't you see how badly I was treated?

DORINE [*to* MARIANE]. Aren't you a simpleton, to have lost your head?

MARIANE. Didn't you hear the hateful things he said? 90

DORINE [*to* VALÈRE]. You're both great fools. Her sole desire, Valère,
 Is to be yours in marriage. To that I'll swear.
 [*To* MARIANE.] He loves you only, and he wants no wife

But you, Mariane. On that I'll stake my life.

MARIANE [*to* VALÈRE]. Then why you advised me so, I cannot see. 95

VALÈRE [*to* MARIANE]. On such a question, why ask advice of *me?*

DORINE. Oh, you're impossible. Give me your hands, you two.

 [*To* VALÈRE.] Yours first.

VALÈRE [*giving* DORINE *his hand*]. But why?

DORINE [*to* MARIANE]. And now a hand from you.

MARIANE [*also giving* DORINE *her hand*].

 What are you doing?

DORINE. There: a perfect fit.

 You suit each other better than you'll admit. 100

 [VALÈRE *and* MARIANE *hold hands
 for some time without looking at
 each other.*]

VALÈRE [*turning toward* MARIANE]. Ah, come, don't be so haughty.

 Give a man

 A look of kindness, won't you, Mariane?

 [MARIANE *turns toward* VALÈRE
 and smiles.]

DORINE. I tell you, lovers are completely mad!

VALÈRE [*to* MARIANE]. Now come, confess that you were very bad

 To hurt my feelings as you did just now. 105

 I have a just complaint, you must allow.

MARIANE. *You* must allow that you were most unpleasant . . .

DORINE. Let's table that discussion for the present;

 Your father has a plan which must be stopped.

MARIANE. Advise us, then; what means must we adopt? 110

DORINE. We'll use all manner of means, and all at once.

 [*To* MARIANE.] Your father's addled; he's acting like a dunce.

 Therefore you'd better humor the old fossil.

 Pretend to yield to him, be sweet and docile,

 And then postpone, as often as necessary, 115

 The day on which you have agreed to marry.

 You'll thus gain time, and time will turn the trick.

 Sometimes, for instance, you'll be taken sick,

 And that will seem good reason for delay;

 Or some bad omen will make you change the day— 120

 You'll dream of muddy water, or you'll pass

 A dead man's hearse, or break a looking-glass.

 If all else fails, no man can marry you

 Unless you take his ring and say "I do."

 But now, let's separate. If they should find 125

 Us talking here, our plot might be divined.

 [*To* VALÈRE.] Go to your friends, and tell them what's occurred,

 And have them urge her father to keep his word.

 Meanwhile, we'll stir her brother into action,

 And get Elmire, as well, to join our faction. 130

 Good-bye.

VALÈRE [*to* MARIANE]. Though each of us will do his best,

 It's your true heart on which my hopes shall rest.

MARIANE [*to* VALÈRE]. Regardless of what Father may decide,
 None but Valère shall claim me as his bride.
VALÈRE. Oh, how those words content me! Come what will . . . 135
DORINE. Oh, lovers, lovers! Their tongues are never still.
 Be off, now.
VALÈRE [*turning to go, then turning back*].
 One last word . . .
DORINE. No time to chat:
 You leave by this door; and *you* leave by that.
 [DORINE *pushes them, by the shoul-*
 ders, toward opposing doors.]

ACT III

SCENE 1
DAMIS DORINE

DAMIS. May lightning strike me even as I speak,
 May all men call me cowardly and weak,
 If any fear or scruple holds me back
 From settling things, at once, with that great quack!
DORINE. Now, don't give way to violent emotion. 5
 Your father's merely talked about this notion,
 And words and deeds are far from being one.
 Much that is talked about is left undone.
DAMIS. No, I must stop that scoundrel's machinations;
 I'll go and tell him off; I'm out of patience. 10
DORINE. Do calm down and be practical. I had rather
 My mistress dealt with him—and with your father.
 She has some influence with Tartuffe, I've noted.
 He hangs upon her words, seems most devoted,
 And may, indeed, be smitten by her charm. 15
 Pray Heaven it's true! 'Twould do our cause no harm.
 She sent for him, just now, to sound him out
 On this affair you're so incensed about;
 She'll find out where he stands, and tell him, too,
 What dreadful strife and trouble will ensue 20
 If he lends countenance to your father's plan.
 I couldn't get in to see him, but his man
 Says that he's almost finished with his prayers.
 Go, now. I'll catch him when he comes downstairs.
DAMIS. I want to hear this conference, and I will. 25
DORINE. No, they must be alone.
DAMIS. Oh, I'll keep still.
DORINE. Not you. I know your temper. You'd start a brawl,
 And shout and stamp your foot and spoil it all.
 Go on.

DAMIS. I won't; I have a perfect right . . .
DORINE. Lord, you're a nuisance! He's coming; get out of sight. 30

> [DAMIS *conceals himself in a closet*
> *at the rear of the stage.*]

SCENE 2
TARTUFFE DORINE

TARTUFFE [*observing* DORINE, *and calling to his manservant offstage*].
 Hang up my hair-shirt, put my scourge in place,
 And pray, Laurent, for Heaven's perpetual grace.
 I'm going to the prison now, to share
 My last few coins with the poor wretches there.
DORINE [*aside*]. Dear God, what affectation! What a fake! 5
TARTUFFE. You wished to see me?
DORINE. Yes . . .
TARTUFFE [*taking a handkerchief from his pocket*].
 For mercy's sake,
 Please take this handkerchief, before you speak.
DORINE. What?
TARTUFFE. Cover that bosom, girl. The flesh is weak,
 And unclean thoughts are difficult to control.
 Such sights as that can undermine the soul. 10
DORINE. Your soul, it seems, has very poor defenses,
 And flesh makes quite an impact on your senses.
 It's strange that you're so easily excited;
 My own desires are not so soon ignited,
 And if I saw you naked as a beast, 15
 Not all your hide would tempt me in the least.
TARTUFFE. Girl, speak more modestly; unless you do,
 I shall be forced to take my leave of you.
DORINE. Oh, no, it's I who must be on my way;
 I've just one little message to convey. 20
 Madame is coming down, and begs you, Sir,
 To wait and have a word or two with her.
TARTUFFE. Gladly.
DORINE [*aside*]. *That* had a softening effect!
 I think my guess about him was correct.
TARTUFFE. Will she be long?
DORINE. No: that's her step I hear. 25
 Ah, here she is, and I shall disappear.

SCENE 3
ELMIRE TARTUFFE

TARTUFFE. May Heaven, whose infinite goodness we adore,
 Preserve your body and soul forevermore,

And bless your days, and answer thus the plea
Of one who is its humblest votary.
ELMIRE. I thank you for that pious wish. But please, 5
Do take a chair and let's be more at ease.
 [*They sit down.*]
TARTUFFE. I trust that you are once more well and strong?
ELMIRE. Oh, yes: the fever didn't last for long.
TARTUFFE. My prayers are too unworthy, I am sure,
To have gained from Heaven this most gracious cure; 10
But lately, Madam, my every supplication
Has had for object your recuperation.
ELMIRE. You shouldn't have troubled so. I don't deserve it.
TARTUFFE. Your health is priceless, Madam, and to preserve it
I'd gladly give my own, in all sincerity. 15
ELMIRE. Sir, you outdo us all in Christian charity.
You've been most kind. I count myself your debtor.
TARTUFFE. 'Twas nothing, Madam. I long to serve you better.
ELMIRE. There's a private matter I'm anxious to discuss.
I'm glad there's no one here to hinder us. 20
TARTUFFE. I too am glad; it floods my heart with bliss
To find myself alone with you like this.
For just this chance I've prayed with all my power—
But prayed in vain, until this happy hour.
ELMIRE. This won't take long, Sir, and I hope you'll be 25
Entirely frank and unconstrained with me.
TARTUFFE. Indeed, there's nothing I had rather do
Than bare my inmost heart and soul to you.
First, let me say that what remarks I've made
About the constant visits you are paid 30
Were prompted not by any mean emotion,
But rather by a pure and deep devotion,
A fervent zeal . . .
ELMIRE. No need for explanation.
Your sole concern, I'm sure, was my salvation.
TARTUFFE [*taking* ELMIRE's *hand and pressing her fingertips*]. Quite so;
and such great fervor do I feel . . . 35
ELMIRE. Ooh! Please! You're pinching!
TARTUFFE. 'Twas from excess of zeal.
I never meant to cause you pain, I swear.
I'd rather . . .
 [*He places his hand on* ELMIRE's
 knee.]
ELMIRE. What can your hand be doing there?
TARTUFFE. Feeling your gown; what soft, fine-woven stuff!
ELMIRE. Please, I'm extremely ticklish. That's enough. 40
 [*She draws her chair away;* TAR-
 tuffe *pulls his after her.*]
TARTUFFE. [*fondling the lace collar of her gown*]. My, my what lovely
lacework on your dress!

The workmanship's miraculous, no less.
I've not seen anything to equal it.
ELMIRE. Yes, quite. But let's talk business for a bit.
They say my husband means to break his word 45
And give his daughter to you, Sir. Had you heard?
TARTUFFE. He did once mention it. But I confess
I dream of quite a different happiness.
It's elsewhere, Madam, that my eyes discern
The promise of that bliss for which I yearn. 50
ELMIRE. I see: you care for nothing here below.
TARTUFFE. Ah, well—my heart's not made of stone, you
 know.
ELMIRE. All your desires mount heavenward, I'm sure,
In scorn of all that's earthly and impure.
TARTUFFE. A love of heavenly beauty does not preclude 55
A proper love for earthly pulchritude;
Our senses are quite rightly captivated
By perfect works our Maker has created.
Some glory clings to all that Heaven has made;
In you, all Heaven's marvels are displayed. 60
On that fair face, such beauties have been lavished,
The eyes are dazzled and the heart is ravished;
How could I look on you, O flawless creature,
And not adore the Author of all Nature,
Feeling a love both passionate and pure 65
For you, his triumph of self-portraiture?
At first, I trembled lest that love should be
A subtle snare that Hell had laid for me;
I vowed to flee the sight of you, eschewing
A rapture that might prove my soul's undoing; 70
But soon, fair being, I became aware
That my deep passion could be made to square
With rectitude, and with my bounden duty.
I thereupon surrendered to your beauty.
It is, I know, presumptuous on my part 75
To bring you this poor offering of my heart,
And it is not my merit, Heaven knows,
But your compassion on which my hopes repose.
You are my peace, my solace, my salvation;
On you depends my bliss—or desolation; 80
I bide your judgment and, as you think best,
I shall be either miserable or blest.
ELMIRE. Your declaration is most gallant, Sir,
But don't you think it's out of character?
You'd have done better to restrain your passion 85
And think before you spoke in such a fashion.
It ill becomes a pious man like you . . .
TARTUFFE. I may be pious, but I'm human too:
With your celestial charms before his eyes,

A man has not the power to be wise. 90
I know such words sound strangely, coming from me,
But I'm no angel, nor was meant to be,
And if you blame my passion, you must needs
Reproach as well the charms on which it feeds.
Your loveliness I had no sooner seen 95
Than you became my soul's unrivalled queen;
Before your seraph glance, divinely sweet,
My heart's defenses crumbled in defeat,
And nothing fasting, prayer, or tears might do
Could stay my spirit from adoring you. 100
My eyes, my sighs have told you in the past
What now my lips make bold to say at last,
And if, in your great goodness, you will deign
To look upon your slave, and ease his pain,—
If, in compassion for my soul's distress, 105
You'll stoop to comfort my unworthiness,
I'll raise to you, in thanks for that sweet manna,
An endless hymn, an infinite hosanna.
With me, of course, there need be no anxiety,
No fear of scandal or of notoriety. 110
These young court gallants, whom all the ladies fancy,
Are vain in speech, in action rash and chancy;
When they succeed in love, the world soon knows it;
No favor's granted them but they disclose it
And by the looseness of their tongues profane 115
The very altar where their hearts have lain.
Men of my sort, however, love discreetly,
And one may trust our reticence completely.
My keen concern for my good name insures
The absolute security of yours; 120
In short, I offer you, my dear Elmire,
Love without scandal, pleasure without fear.
ELMIRE. I've heard your well-turned speeches to the end,
And what you urge I clearly apprehend.
Aren't you afraid that I may take a notion 125
To tell my husband of your warm devotion,
And that, supposing he were duly told,
His feelings toward you might grow rather cold?
TARTUFFE. I know, dear lady, that your exceeding charity
Will lead your heart to pardon my temerity; 130
That you'll excuse my violent affection
As human weakness, human imperfection;
And that—O fairest!—you will bear in mind
That I'm but flesh and blood, and am not blind.
ELMIRE. Some women might do otherwise, perhaps, 135
But I shall be discreet about your lapse;
I'll tell my husband nothing of what's occurred
If, in return, you'll give your solemn word

To advocate as forcefully as you can
The marriage of Valère and Mariane, 140
Renouncing all desire to dispossess
Another of his rightful happiness,
And . . .

SCENE 4
DAMIS ELMIRE TARTUFFE

DAMIS [*emerging from the closet where he has been hiding*].
 No! We'll not hush up this vile affair;
I heard it all inside that closet there,
Where Heaven, in order to confound the pride
Of this great rascal, prompted me to hide.
Ah, now I have my long-awaited chance 5
To punish his deceit and arrogance,
And give my father clear and shocking proof
Of the black character of his dear Tartuffe.
ELMIRE. Ah no, Damis; I'll be content if he
Will study to deserve my leniency. 10
I've promised silence—don't make me break my word;
To make a scandal would be too absurd.
Good wives laugh off such trifles, and forget them;
Why should they tell their husbands, and upset them?
DAMIS. You have your reasons for taking such a course, 15
And I have reasons, too, of equal force.
To spare him now would be insanely wrong.
I've swallowed my just wrath for far too long
And watched this insolent bigot bringing strife
And bitterness into our family life. 20
Too long he's meddled in my father's affairs,
Thwarting my marriage-hopes, and poor Valère's.
It's high time that my father was undeceived,
And now I've proof that can't be disbelieved—
Proof that was furnished me by Heaven above. 25
It's too good not to take advantage of.
This is my chance, and I deserve to lose it
If, for one moment, I hesitate to use it.
ELMIRE. Damis . . .
DAMIS. No, I must do what I think right.
Madam, my heart is bursting with delight, 30
And, say whatever you will, I'll not consent
To lose the sweet revenge on which I'm bent.
I'll settle matters without more ado;
And here, most opportunely, is my cue.

SCENE 5
Orgon Tartuffe Damis Elmire

DAMIS. Father, I'm glad you've joined us. Let us advise you
Of some fresh news which doubtless will surprise you.
You've just now been repaid with interest
For all your loving-kindness to our guest.
He's proved his warm and grateful feelings toward you; 5
It's with a pair of horns he would reward you.
Yes, I surprised him with your wife, and heard
His whole adulterous offer, every word.
She, with her all too gentle disposition,
Would not have told you of his proposition; 10
But I shall not make terms with brazen lechery,
And feel that not to tell you would be treachery.
ELMIRE. And I hold that one's husband's peace of mind
Should not be spoilt by tattle of this kind.
One's honor doesn't require it: to be proficient 15
In keeping men at bay is quite sufficient.
These are my sentiments, and I wish, Damis,
That you had heeded me and held your peace.

SCENE 6
Orgon Damis Tartuffe

ORGON. Can it be true, this dreadful thing I hear?
TARTUFFE. Yes, Brother, I'm a wicked man, I fear:
A wretched sinner, all depraved and twisted,
The greatest villain that has ever existed.
My life's one heap of crimes, which grows each minute; 5
There's naught but foulness and corruption in it;
And I perceive that Heaven, outraged by me,
Has chosen this occasion to mortify me.
Charge me with any deed you wish to name;
I'll not defend myself, but take the blame. 10
Believe what you are told, and drive Tartuffe
Like some base criminal from beneath your roof;
Yes, drive me hence, and with a parting curse:
I shan't protest, for I deserve far worse.
ORGON [*to* DAMIS]. Ah, you deceitful boy, how dare you try 15
To stain his purity with so foul a lie?
DAMIS. What! Are you taken in by such a bluff?
Did you not hear . . .?
ORGON. Enough, you rogue, enough!
TARTUFFE. Ah, Brother, let him speak: you're being unjust.
Believe his story; the boy deserves your trust. 20
Why, after all, should you have faith in me?
How can you know what I might do, or be?

Is it on my good actions that you base
Your favor? Do you trust my pious face?
Ah, no, don't be deceived by hollow shows; 25
I'm far, alas, from being what men suppose;
Though the world takes me for a man of worth,
I'm truly the most worthless man on earth.
[*To* DAMIS.] Yes, my dear son, speak out now: call me the chief
Of sinners, a wretch, a murderer, a thief; 30
Load me with all the names men most abhor;
I'll not complain; I've earned them all, and more;
I'll kneel here while you pour them on my head
As a just punishment for the life I've led.
ORGON [*to* TARTUFFE]. This is too much, dear Brother.
 [*To* DAMIS.] Have you no
 heart? 35
DAMIS. Are you so hoodwinked by this rascal's art . . . ?
ORGON. Be still, you monster.
 [*To* TARTUFFE.] Brother, I pray you, rise.
 [*To* DAMIS.] Villain!
DAMIS. But . . .
ORGON. Silence!
DAMIS. Can't you realize . . . ?
ORGON. Just one word more, and I'll tear you limb from limb.
TARTUFFE. In God's name, Brother, don't be harsh with him. 40
 I'd rather far be tortured at the stake
 Than see him bear one scratch for my poor sake.
ORGON [*to* DAMIS]. Ingrate!
TARTUFFE. If I must beg you, on bended knee,
 To pardon him . . .
ORGON [*falling to his knees, addressing* TARTUFFE].
 Such goodness cannot be!
 [*To* DAMIS.] Now, *there's* true charity!
DAMIS. What, you . . . ?
ORGON. Villain, be
 still! 45
 I know your motives; I know you wish him ill:
 Yes, all of you—wife, children, servants, all—
 Conspire against him and desire his fall,
 Employing every shameful trick you can
 To alienate me from this saintly man. 50
 Ah, but the more you seek to drive him away,
 The more I'll do to keep him. Without delay,
 I'll spite this household and confound its pride
 By giving him my daughter as his bride.
DAMIS. You're going to force her to accept his hand? 55
ORGON. Yes, and this very night, d'you understand?
 I shall defy you all, and make it clear
 That I'm the one who gives the orders here.
 Come, wretch, kneel down and clasp his blessed feet,
 And ask his pardon for your black deceit. 60

DAMIS. I ask that swindler's pardon? Why, I'd rather . . .
ORGON. So! You insult him, and defy your father!
 A stick! A stick! [*To* TARTUFFE.] No, no—release me, do.
 [*To* DAMIS.] Out of my house this minute! Be off with you,
 And never dare set foot in it again. 65
DAMIS. Well, I shall go, but . . .
ORGON. Well, go quickly, then.
 I disinherit you; an empty purse
 Is all you'll get from me—except my curse!

SCENE 7
ORGON TARTUFFE

ORGON. How he blasphemed your goodness! What a son!
TARTUFFE. Forgive him, Lord, as I've already done.
 [*To* ORGON.] You can't know how it hurts when someone tries
 To blacken me in my dear Brother's eyes.
ORGON. Ahh!
TARTUFFE. The mere thought of such ingratitude 5
 Plunges my soul into so dark a mood . . .
 Such horror grips my heart . . . I gasp for breath,
 And cannot speak, and feel myself near death.
ORGON. [*He runs, in tears, to the door through which he has just driven his
 son.*] You blackguard! Why did I spare you? Why did I not
 Break you in little pieces on the spot? 10
 Compose yourself, and don't be hurt, dear friend.
TARTUFFE. These scenes, these dreadful quarrels, have got to end.
 I've much upset your household, and I perceive
 That the best thing will be for me to leave.
ORGON. What are you saying!
TARTUFFE. They're all against me here; 15
 They'd have you think me false and insincere.
ORGON. Ah, what of that? Have I ceased believing in you?
TARTUFFE. Their adverse talk will certainly continue,
 And charges which you now repudiate
 You may find credible at a later date. 20
ORGON. No, Brother, never.
TARTUFFE. Brother, a wife can sway
 Her husband's mind in many a subtle way.
ORGON. No, no.
TARTUFFE. To leave at once is the solution;
 Thus only can I end their persecution.
ORGON. No, no, I'll not allow it; you shall remain. 25
TARTUFFE. Ah, well; 'twill mean much martyrdom and pain,
 But if you wish it . . .
ORGON. Ah!
TARTUFFE. Enough; so be it.
 But one thing must be settled, as I see it.
 For your dear honor, and for our friendship's sake,

There's one precaution I feel bound to take. 30
I shall avoid your wife, and keep away . . .
ORGON. No, you shall not, whatever they may say.
It pleases me to vex them, and for spite
I'd have them see you with her day and night.
What's more, I'm going to drive them to despair 35
By making you my only son and heir;
This very day, I'll give to you alone
Clear deed and title to everything I own.
A dear, good friend and son-in-law-to-be
Is more than wife, or child, or kin to me. 40
Will you accept my offer, dearest son?
TARTUFFE. In all things, let the will of Heaven be done.
ORGON. Poor fellow! Come, we'll go draw up the deed.
Then let them burst with disappointed greed!

ACT IV

SCENE 1
CLÉANTE TARTUFFE

CLÉANTE. Yes, all the town's discussing it, and truly,
Their comments do not flatter you unduly.
I'm glad we've met, Sir, and I'll give my view
Of this sad matter in a word or two.
As for who's guilty, that I shan't discuss; 5
Let's say it was Damis who caused the fuss;
Assuming, then, that you have been ill-used
By young Damis, and groundlessly accused,
Ought not a Christian to forgive, and ought
He not to stifle every vengeful thought? 10
Should you stand by and watch a father make
His only son an exile for your sake?
Again I tell you frankly, be advised:
The whole town, high and low, is scandalized;
This quarrel must be mended, and my advice is 15
Not to push matters to a further crisis.
No, sacrifice your wrath to God above,
And help Damis regain his father's love.
TARTUFFE. Alas, for my part I should take great joy
In doing so. I've nothing against the boy. 20
I pardon all, I harbor no resentment;
To serve him would afford me much contentment.
But Heaven's interest will not have it so:
If he comes back, then I shall have to go.
After his conduct—so extreme, so vicious— 25
Our further intercourse would look suspicious.
God knows what people would think! Why, they'd describe
My goodness to him as a sort of bribe;

They'd say that out of guilt I made pretense
Of loving-kindness and benevolence— 30
That, fearing my accuser's tongue, I strove
To buy his silence with a show of love.

CLÉANTE. Your reasoning is badly warped and stretched,
And these excuses, Sir, are most far-fetched.
Why put yourself in charge of Heaven's cause? 35
Does Heaven need our help to enforce its laws?
Leave vengeance to the Lord, Sir; while we live,
Our duty's not to punish, but forgive;
And what the Lord commands, we should obey
Without regard to what the world may say. 40
What! Shall the fear of being misunderstood
Prevent our doing what is right and good?
No, no; let's simply do what Heaven ordains,
And let no other thoughts perplex our brains.

TARTUFFE. Again, Sir, let me say that I've forgiven 45
Damis, and thus obeyed the laws of Heaven;
But I am not commanded by the Bible
To live with one who smears my name with libel.

CLÉANTE. Were you commanded, Sir, to indulge the whim
Of poor Orgon, and to encourage him 50
In suddenly transferring to your name
A large estate to which you have no claim?

TARTUFFE. 'Twould never occur to those who know me best
To think I acted from self-interest.
The treasures of this world I quite despise; 55
Their specious glitter does not charm my eyes;
And if I have resigned myself to taking
The gift which my dear Brother insists on making,
I do so only, as he well understands,
Lest so much wealth fall into wicked hands, 60
Lest those to whom it might descend in time
Turn it to purposes of sin and crime,
And not, as I shall do, make use of it
For Heaven's glory and mankind's benefit.

CLÉANTE. Forget these trumped-up fears. Your argument 65
Is one the rightful heir might well resent;
It *is* a moral burden to inherit
Such wealth, but give Damis a chance to bear it.
And would it not be worse to be accused
Of swindling, than to see that wealth misused? 70
I'm shocked that you allowed Orgon to broach
This matter, and that you feel no self-reproach;
Does true religion teach that lawful heirs
May freely be deprived of what is theirs?
And if the Lord has told you in your heart 75
That you and young Damis must dwell apart,
Would it not be the decent thing to beat
A generous and honorable retreat,

Rather than let the son of the house be sent,
For your convenience, into banishment? 80
Sir, if you wish to prove the honesty
Of your intentions . . .
TARTUFFE. Sir, it is half-past three.
I've certain pious duties to attend to,
And hope my prompt departure won't offend you.
CLÉANTE [*alone*]. Damn.

SCENE 2
ELMIRE CLÉANTE MARIANE DORINE

DORINE. Stay, Sir, and help Mariane, for Heaven's sake!
She's suffering so, I fear her heart will break.
Her father's plan to marry her off tonight
Has put the poor child in a desperate plight.
I hear him coming. Let's stand together, now, 5
And see if we can't change his mind, somehow,
About this match we all deplore and fear.

SCENE 3
ORGON MARIANE DORINE
ELMIRE CLÉANTE

ORGON. Hah! Glad to find you all assembled here.
[*To* MARIANE.] This contract, child, contains your happiness,
And what it says I think your heart can guess.
MARIANE [*falling to her knees*]. Sir, by that Heaven which sees me here
distressed,
And by whatever else can move your breast, 5
Do not employ a father's power, I pray you,
To crush my heart and force it to obey you,
Nor by your harsh commands oppress me so
That I'll begrudge the duty which I owe—
And do not so embitter and enslave me 10
That I shall hate the very life you gave me.
If my sweet hopes must perish, if you refuse
To give me to the one I've dared to choose,
Spare me at least—I beg you, I implore—
The pain of wedding one whom I abhor; 15
And do not, by a heartless use of force,
Drive me to contemplate some desperate course.
ORGON [*feeling himself touched by her*]. Be firm, my soul. No human
weakness, now.
MARIANE. I don't resent your love for him. Allow
Your heart free rein, Sir; give him your property, 20
And if that's not enough, take mine from me;
He's welcome to my money; take it, do,

But don't, I pray, include my person too.
Spare me, I beg you; and let me end the tale
Of my sad days behind a convent veil. 25
ORGON. A convent! Hah! When crossed in their amours,
All lovesick girls have the same thought as yours.
Get up! The more you loathe the man, and dread him,
The more ennobling it will be to wed him.
Marry Tartuffe, and mortify your flesh! 30
Enough; don't start that whimpering afresh.
DORINE. But why . . . ?
ORGON. Be still, there. Speak when you're spoken to.
Not one more bit of impudence out of you.
CLÉANTE. If I may offer a word of counsel here . . .
ORGON. Brother, in counseling you have no peer; 35
All your advice is forceful, sound, and clever;
I don't propose to follow it, however.
ELMIRE [*to* ORGON]. I am amazed, and don't know what to say;
Your blindness simply takes my breath away.
You are indeed bewitched, to take no warning 40
From our account of what occurred this morning.
ORGON. Madam, I know a few plain facts, and one
Is that you're partial to my rascal son;
Hence, when he sought to make Tartuffe the victim
Of a base lie, you dared not contradict him. 45
Ah, but you underplayed your part, my pet;
You should have looked more angry, more upset.
ELMIRE. When men make overtures, must we reply
With righteous anger and a battle-cry?
Must we turn back their amorous advances 50
With sharp reproaches and with fiery glances?
Myself, I find such offers merely amusing,
And make no scenes and fusses in refusing;
My taste is for good-natured rectitude,
And I dislike the savage sort of prude 55
Who guards her virtue with her teeth and claws,
And tears men's eyes out for the slightest cause:
The Lord preserve me from such honor as that,
Which bites and scratches like an alley-cat!
I've found that a polite and cool rebuff 60
Discourages a lover quite enough.
ORGON. I know the facts, and I shall not be shaken.
ELMIRE. I marvel at your power to be mistaken.
Would it, I wonder, carry weight with you
If I could *show* you that our tale was true? 65
ORGON. Show me?
ELMIRE. Yes.
ORGON. Rot.
ELMIRE. Come, what if I found a way
To make you see the facts as plain as day?
ORGON. Nonsense.

ELMIRE. Do answer me; don't be absurd.
 I'm not now asking you to trust our word.
 Suppose that from some hiding-place in here 70
 You learned the whole sad truth by eye and ear—
 What would you say of your good friend, after that?
ORGON. Why, I'd say . . . nothing, by Jehoshaphat!
 It can't be true.
ELMIRE. You've been too long deceived,
 And I'm quite tired of being disbelieved. 75
 Come now: let's put my statements to the test,
 And you shall see the truth made manifest.
ORGON. I'll take that challenge. Now do your uttermost.
 We'll see how you make good your empty boast.
ELMIRE [*to* DORINE]. Send him to me.
DORINE. He's crafty; it may be hard 80
 To catch the cunning scoundrel off his guard.
ELMIRE. No, amorous men are gullible. Their conceit
 So blinds them that they're never hard to cheat.
 Have him come down. [*To* CLÉANTE *and* MARIANE.] Please leave us,
 for a bit.

SCENE 4
ELMIRE ORGON

ELMIRE. Pull up this table, and get under it.
ORGON. What?
ELMIRE. It's essential that you be well-hidden.
ORGON. Why there?
ELMIRE. Oh, Heavens! Just do as you are bidden.
 I have my plans; we'll soon see how they fare. 5
 Under the table, now; and once you're there,
 Take care that you are neither seen nor heard.
ORGON. Well, I'll indulge you, since I gave my word
 To see you through this infantile charade.
ELMIRE. Once it is over, you'll be glad we played.
 [*To her husband, who is now under the table.*] I'm going to act quite
 strangely, now, and you
 Must not be shocked at anything I do. 10
 Whatever I may say, you must excuse
 As part of that deceit I'm forced to use.
 I shall employ sweet speeches in the task
 Of making that impostor drop his mask;
 I'll give encouragement to his bold desires, 15
 And furnish fuel to his amorous fires.
 Since it's for your sake, and for his destruction,
 That I shall seem to yield to his seduction,
 I'll gladly stop whenever you decide
 That all your doubts are fully satisfied. 20

I'll count on you, as soon as you have seen
What sort of man he is, to intervene,
And not expose me to his odious lust
One moment longer than you feel you must. 25
Remember: you're to save me from my plight
Whenever . . . He's coming! Hush! Keep out of sight!

SCENE 5
TARTUFFE ELMIRE ORGON

TARTUFFE. You wish to have a word with me, I'm told.
ELMIRE. Yes. I've a little secret to unfold.
 Before I speak, however, it would be wise
 To close that door, and look about for spies.
 [TARTUFFE *goes to the door, closes
 it, and returns.*]
 The very last thing that must happen now 5
 Is a repetition of this morning's row.
 I've never been so badly caught off guard.
 Oh, how I feared for you! You saw how hard
 I tried to make that troublesome Damis
 Control his dreadful temper, and hold his peace. 10
 In my confusion, I didn't have the sense
 Simply to contradict his evidence;
 But as it happened, that was for the best,
 And all has worked out in our interest.
 This storm has only bettered your position; 15
 My husband doesn't have the least suspicion,
 And now, in mockery of those who do,
 He bids me be continually with you.
 And that is why, quite fearless of reproof,
 I now can be alone with my Tartuffe, 20
 And why my heart—perhaps too quick to yield—
 Feels free to let its passion be revealed.
TARTUFFE. Madam, your words confuse me. Not long ago,
 You spoke in quite a different style, you know.
ELMIRE. Ah, Sir, if that refusal made you smart, 25
 It's little that you know of woman's heart,
 Or what that heart is trying to convey
 When it resists in such a feeble way!
 Always, at first, our modesty prevents
 The frank avowal of tender sentiments; 30
 However high the passion which inflames us,
 Still, to confess its power somehow shames us.
 Thus we reluct, at first, yet in a tone
 Which tells you that our heart is overthrown,
 That what our lips deny, our pulse confesses, 35
 And that, in time, all noes will turn to yesses.

I fear my words are all too frank and free,
And a poor proof of woman's modesty;
But since I'm started, tell me, if you will—
Would I have tried to make Damis be still, 40
Would I have listened, calm and unoffended,
Until your lengthy offer of love was ended,
And been so very mild in my reaction,
Had your sweet words not given me satisfaction?
And when I tried to force you to undo 45
The marriage-plans my husband has in view,
What did my urgent pleading signify
If not that I admired you, and that I
Deplored the thought that someone else might own
Part of a heart I wished for mine alone? 50

TARTUFFE. Madam, no happiness is so complete
As when, from lips we love, come words so sweet;
Their nectar floods my every sense, and drains
In honeyed rivulets through all my veins.
To please you is my joy, my only goal; 55
Your love is the restorer of my soul;
And yet I must beg leave, now, to confess
Some lingering doubts as to my happiness.
Might this not be a trick? Might not the catch
Be that you wish me to break off the match 60
With Mariane, and so have feigned to love me?
I shan't quite trust your fond opinion of me
Until the feelings you've expressed so sweetly
Are demonstrated somewhat more concretely,
And you have shown, by certain kind concessions, 65
That I may put my faith in your professions.

ELMIRE. [*She coughs, to warn her husband.*] Why be in such a hurry?
 Must my heart
Exhaust its bounty at the very start?
To make that sweet admission cost me dear,
But you'll not be content, it would appear, 70
Unless my store of favors is disbursed
To the last farthing, and at the very first.

TARTUFFE. The less we merit, the less we dare to hope,
And with our doubts, mere words can never cope.
We trust no promised bliss till we receive it; 75
Not till a joy is ours can we believe it.
I, who so little merit your esteem,
Can't credit this fulfillment of my dream,
And shan't believe it, Madam, until I savor
Some palpable assurance of your favor. 80

ELMIRE. My, how tyrannical your love can be,
And how it flusters and perplexes me!
How furiously you take one's heart in hand,
And make your every wish a fierce command!
Come, must you hound and harry me to death? 85

 Will you not give me time to catch my breath?
 Can it be right to press me with such force,
 Give me no quarter, show me no remorse,
 And take advantage, by your stern insistence,
 Of the fond feelings which weaken my resistance? 90
TARTUFFE. Well, if you look with favor upon my love,
 Why, then, begrudge me some clear proof thereof?
ELMIRE. But how can I consent without offense
 To Heaven, toward which you feel such reverence?
TARTUFFE. If Heaven is all that holds you back, don't worry. 95
 I can remove that hindrance in a hurry.
 Nothing of that sort need obstruct our path.
ELMIRE. Must one not be afraid of Heaven's wrath?
TARTUFFE. Madam, forget such fears, and be my pupil,
 And I shall teach you how to conquer scruple. 100
 Some joys, it's true, are wrong in Heaven's eyes;
 Yet Heaven is not averse to compromise;
 There is a science, lately formulated,
 Whereby one's conscience may be liberated,
 And any wrongful act you care to mention 105
 May be redeemed by purity of intention.
 I'll teach you, Madam, the secrets of that science;
 Meanwhile, just place on me your full reliance.
 Assuage my keen desires, and feel no dread:
 The sin, if any, shall be on my head. 110

 [ELMIRE *coughs, this time more*
 loudly.]
 You've a bad cough.
ELMIRE. Yes, yes. It's bad indeed.
TARTUFFE [*producing a little paper bag*]. A bit of licorice may be what
 you need.
ELMIRE. No, I've a stubborn cold, it seems. I'm sure it
 Will take much more than licorice to cure it.
TARTUFFE. How aggravating.
ELMIRE. Oh, more than I can say. 115
TARTUFFE. If you're still troubled, think of things this way:
 No one shall know our joys, save us alone,
 And there's no evil till the act is known;
 It's scandal, Madam, which makes it an offense,
 And it's no sin to sin in confidence. 120
ELMIRE [*having coughed once more*]. Well, clearly I must do as you re-
 quire,
 And yield to your importunate desire.
 It is apparent, now, that nothing less
 Will satisfy you, and so I acquiesce.
 To go so far is much against my will; 125
 I'm vexed that it should come to this; but still,
 Since you are so determined on it, since you
 Will not allow mere language to convince you,
 And since you ask for concrete evidence, I

See nothing for it, now, but to comply. 130
If this is sinful, if I'm wrong to do it,
So much the worse for him who drove me to it.
The fault can surely not be charged to me.
TARTUFFE. Madam, the fault is mine, if fault there be,
 And . . .
ELMIRE. Open the door a little, and peek out; 135
 I wouldn't want my husband poking about.
TARTUFFE. Why worry about the man? Each day he grows
 More gullible; one can lead him by the nose.
 To find us here would fill him with delight,
 And if he saw the worst, he'd doubt his sight. 140
ELMIRE. Nevertheless, do step out for a minute
 Into the hall, and see that no one's in it.

SCENE 6
ORGON ELMIRE

ORGON [*coming out from under the table*]. That man's a perfect monster,
 I must admit!
 I'm simply stunned. I can't get over it.
ELMIRE. What, coming out so soon? How premature!
 Get back in hiding, and wait until you're sure.
 Stay till the end, and be convinced completely; 5
 We mustn't stop till things are proved concretely.
ORGON. Hell never harbored anything so vicious!
ELMIRE. Tut, don't be hasty. Try to be judicious.
 Wait, and be certain that there's no mistake.
 No jumping to conclusions, for Heaven's sake! 10
 [*She places* ORGON *behind her, as*
 TARTUFFE *re-enters.*]

SCENE 7
TARTUFFE ELMIRE ORGON

TARTUFFE [*not seeing* ORGON]. Madam, all things have worked out to
 perfection;
 I've given the neighboring rooms a full inspection;
 No one's about; and now I may at last . . .
ORGON [*intercepting him*]. Hold on, my passionate fellow, not so fast!
 I should advise a little more restraint. 5
 Well, so you thought you'd fool me, my dear saint!
 How soon you wearied of the saintly life—
 Wedding my daughter, and coveting my wife!
 I've long suspected you, and had a feeling
 That soon I'd catch you at your double-dealing.
 Just now, you've given me evidence galore; 10

It's quite enough; I have no wish for more.

ELMIRE [*to* TARTUFFE]. I'm sorry to have treated you so slyly,
 But circumstances forced me to be wily.

TARTUFFE. Brother, you can't think . . .

ORGON. No more talk from you; 15
 Just leave this household, without more ado.

TARTUFFE. What I intended . . .

ORGON. That seems fairly clear.
 Spare me your falsehoods and get out of here.

TARTUFFE. No, I'm the master, and you're the one to go!
 This house belongs to me, I'll have you know, 20
 And I shall show you that you can't hurt *me*
 By this contemptible conspiracy,
 That those who cross me know not what they do,
 And that I've means to expose and punish you,
 Avenge offended Heaven, and make you grieve 25
 That ever you dared order me to leave.

SCENE 8
ELMIRE ORGON

ELMIRE. What was the point of all that angry chatter?

ORGON. Dear God, I'm worried. This is no laughing matter.

ELMIRE. How so?

ORGON. I fear I understood his drift.
 I'm much disturbed about that deed of gift.

ELMIRE. You gave him . . . ?

ORGON. Yes, it's all been drawn and signed. 5
 But one thing more is weighing on my mind.

ELMIRE. What's that?

ORGON. I'll tell you; but first let's see if there's
 A certain strong-box in his room upstairs.

ACT V

SCENE 1
ORGON CLÉANTE

CLÉANTE. Where are you going so fast?

ORGON. God knows!

CLÉANTE. Then wait;
 Let's have a conference, and deliberate
 On how this situation's to be met.

ORGON. That strong-box has me utterly upset;
 This is the worst of many, many shocks. 5

CLÉANTE. Is there some fearful mystery in that box?

ORGON. My poor friend Argas brought that box to me

With his own hands, in utmost secrecy;
'Twas on the very morning of his flight.
It's full of papers which, if they came to light,
Would ruin him—or such is my impression. 10
CLÉANTE. Then why did you let it out of your possession?
ORGON. Those papers vexed my conscience, and it seemed best
To ask the counsel of my pious guest.
The cunning scoundrel got me to agree 15
To leave the strong-box in his custody,
So that, in case of an investigation,
I could employ a slight equivocation
And swear I didn't have it, and thereby,
At no expense to conscience, tell a lie. 20
CLÉANTE. It looks to me as if you're out on a limb.
Trusting him with that box, and offering him
That deed of gift, were actions of a kind
Which scarcely indicate a prudent mind.
With two such weapons, he has the upper hand, 25
And since you're vulnerable, as matters stand,
You erred once more in bringing him to bay.
You should have acted in some subtler way.
ORGON. Just think of it: behind that fervent face,
A heart so wicked, and a soul so base! 30
I took him in, a hungry beggar, and then . . .
Enough, by God! I'm through with pious men:
Henceforth I'll hate the whole false brotherhood,
And persecute them worse than Satan could.
CLÉANTE. Ah, there you go—extravagant as ever! 35
Why can you not be rational? You never
Manage to take the middle course, it seems,
But jump, instead, between absurd extremes.
You've recognized your recent grave mistake
In falling victim to a pious fake; 40
Now, to correct that error, must you embrace
An even greater error in its place,
And judge our worthy neighbors as a whole
By what you've learned of one corrupted soul?
Come, just because one rascal made you swallow 45
A show of zeal which turned out to be hollow,
Shall you conclude that all men are deceivers,
And that, today, there are no true believers?
Let atheists make that foolish inference;
Learn to distinguish virtue from pretense, 50
Be cautious in bestowing admiration,
And cultivate a sober moderation.
Don't humor fraud, but also don't asperse
True piety; the latter fault is worse,
And it is best to err, if err one must, 55
As you have done, upon the side of trust.

SCENE 2
DAMIS ORGON CLÉANTE

DAMIS. Father, I hear that scoundrel's uttered threats
 Against you; that he pridefully forgets
 How, in his need, he was befriended by you,
 And means to use your gifts to crucify you.
ORGON. It's true, my boy. I'm too distressed for tears. 5
DAMIS. Leave it to me, Sir; let me trim his ears.
 Faced with such insolence, we must not waver.
 I shall rejoice in doing you the favor
 Of cutting short his life, and your distress.
CLÉANTE. What a display of young hotheadedness! 10
 Do learn to moderate your fits of rage.
 In this just kingdom, this enlightened age,
 One does not settle things by violence.

SCENE 3
MADAME PERNELLE DORINE ORGON
MARIANE DAMIS CLÉANTE ELMIRE

MADAME PERNELLE. I hear strange tales of very strange events.
ORGON. Yes, strange events which these two eyes beheld.
 The man's ingratitude is unparalleled.
 I save a wretched pauper from starvation,
 House him, and treat him like a blood relation, 5
 Shower him every day with my largesse,
 Give him my daughter, and all that I possess;
 And meanwhile the unconscionable knave
 Tries to induce my wife to misbehave;
 And not content with such extreme rascality, 10
 Now threatens me with my own liberality,
 And aims, by taking base advantage of
 The gifts I gave him out of Christian love,
 To drive me from my house, a ruined man,
 And make me end a pauper, as he began. 15
DORINE. Poor fellow!
MADAME PERNELLE. No, my son, I'll never bring
 Myself to think him guilty of such a thing.
ORGON. How's that?
MADAME PERNELLE. The righteous always were maligned.
ORGON. Speak clearly, Mother. Say what's on your mind.
MADAME PERNELLE. I mean that I can smell a rat, my dear. 20
 You know how everybody hates him, here.
ORGON. That has no bearing on the case at all.
MADAME PERNELLE. I told you a hundred times, when you were small,
 That virtue in this world is hated ever;

Malicious men may die, but malice never.

ORGON. No doubt that's true, but how does it apply? 25

MADAME PERNELLE. They've turned you against him by a clever lie.

ORGON. I've told you, I was there and saw it done.

MADAME PERNELLE. Ah, slanderers will stop at nothing, Son.

ORGON. Mother, I'll lose my temper . . . For the last time, 30
 I tell you I was witness to the crime.

MADAME PERNELLE. The tongues of spite are busy night and noon,
 And to their venom no man is immune.

ORGON. You're talking nonsense. Can't you realize
 I saw it; saw it; saw it with my eyes?
 Saw, do you understand me? Must I shout it 35
 Into your ears before you'll cease to doubt it?

MADAME PERNELLE. Appearances can deceive, my son. Dear me,
 We cannot always judge by what we see.

ORGON. Drat! Drat!

MADAME PERNELLE. One often interprets things awry; 40
 Good can seem evil to a suspicious eye.

ORGON. Was I to see his pawing at Elmire
 As an act of charity?

MADAME PERNELLE. Till his guilt is clear,
 A man deserves the benefit of the doubt.
 You should have waited, to see how things turned out.

ORGON. Great God in Heaven, what more proof did I need? 45
 Was I to sit there, watching, until he'd . . .
 You drive me to the brink of impropriety.

MADAME PERNELLE. No, no, a man of such surpassing piety
 Could not do such a thing. You cannot shake me. 50
 I don't believe it, and you shall not make me.

ORGON. You vex me so that, if you weren't my mother,
 I'd say to you . . . some dreadful thing or other.

DORINE. It's your turn now, Sir, not to be listened to;
 You'd not trust us, and now she won't trust you. 55

CLÉANTE. My friends, we're wasting time which should be spent
 In facing up to our predicament.
 I fear that scoundrel's threats weren't made in sport.

DAMIS. Do you think he'd have the nerve to go to court?

ELMIRE. I'm sure he won't: they'd find it all too crude 60
 A case of swindling and ingratitude.

CLÉANTE. Don't be too sure. He won't be at a loss
 To give his claims a high and righteous gloss;
 And clever rogues with far less valid cause
 Have trapped their victims in a web of laws.
 I say again that to antagonize 65
 A man so strongly armed was most unwise.

ORGON. I know it; but the man's appalling cheek
 Outraged me so, I couldn't control my pique.

CLÉANTE. I wish to Heaven that we could devise 70
 Some truce between you, or some compromise.

ELMIRE. If I had known what cards he held, I'd not
 Have roused his anger by my little plot.
ORGON [*to* DORINE, *as* M. LOYAL *enters*]. What is that fellow looking
 for? Who is he?
 Go talk to him—and tell him that I'm busy. 75

SCENE 4
MONSIEUR LOYAL DAMIS ELMIRE
MADAME PERNELLE MARIANE CLÉANTE
ORGON DORINE

MONSIEUR LOYAL. Good day, dear sister. Kindly let me see
 Your master.
DORINE. He's involved with company,
 And cannot be disturbed just now, I fear.
MONSIEUR LOYAL. I hate to intrude; but what has brought me here
 Will not disturb your master, in any event. 5
 Indeed, my news will make him most content.
DORINE. Your name?
MONSIEUR LOYAL. Just say that I bring greetings from
 Monsieur Tartuffe, on whose behalf I've come.
DORINE [*to* ORGON]. Sir, he's a very gracious man, and bears
 A message from Tartuffe, which, he declares, 10
 Will make you most content.
CLÉANTE. Upon my word,
 I think this man had best be seen, and heard.
ORGON. Perhaps he has some settlement to suggest.
 How shall I treat him? What manner would be best?
CLÉANTE. Control your anger, and if he should mention 15
 Some fair adjustment, give him your full attention.
MONSIEUR LOYAL. Good health to you, good Sir. May Heaven con-
 found
 Your enemies, and may your joys abound.
ORGON [*aside, to* CLÉANTE]. A gentle salutation: it confirms
 My guess that he is here to offer terms. 20
MONSIEUR LOYAL. I've always held your family most dear;
 I served your father, Sir, for many a year.
ORGON. Sir, I must ask your pardon; to my shame,
 I cannot now recall your face or name.
MONSIEUR LOYAL. Loyal's my name; I come from Normandy, 25
 And I'm a bailiff, in all modesty.
 For forty years, praise God, it's been my boast
 To serve with honor in that vital post,
 And I am here, Sir, if you will permit
 The liberty, to serve you with this writ . . . 30
ORGON. To—*what?*
MONSIEUR LOYAL. Now, please, Sir, let us have no friction:
 It's nothing but an order of eviction.

You are to move your goods and family out
And make way for new occupants, without
Deferment or delay, and give the keys . . . 35
ORGON. I? Leave this house?
MONSIEUR LOYAL. Why yes, Sir, if you please.
This house, Sir, from the cellar to the roof,
Belongs now to the good Monsieur Tartuffe,
And he is lord and master of your estate
By virtue of a deed of present date, 40
Drawn in due form, with clearest legal phrasing . . .
DAMIS. Your insolence is utterly amazing!
MONSIEUR LOYAL. Young man, my business here is not with you,
But with your wise and temperate father, who,
Like every worthy citizen, stands in awe 45
Of justice, and would never obstruct the law.
ORGON. But . . .
MONSIEUR LOYAL. Not for a million, Sir, would you rebel
Against authority; I know that well.
You'll not make trouble, Sir, or interfere
With the execution of my duties here. 50
DAMIS. Someone may execute a smart tattoo
On that black jacket of yours, before you're through.
MONSIEUR LOYAL. Sir, bid your son be silent. I'd much regret
Having to mention such a nasty threat
Of violence, in writing my report. 55
DORINE [*aside*]. This man Loyal's a most disloyal sort!
MONSIEUR LOYAL. I love all men of upright character,
And when I agreed to serve these papers, Sir,
It was your feelings that I had in mind.
I couldn't bear to see the case assigned 60
To someone else, who might esteem you less
And so subject you to unpleasantness.
ORGON. What's more unpleasant than telling a man to leave
His house and home?
MONSIEUR LOYAL. You'd like a short reprieve?
If you desire it, Sir, I shall not press you, 65
But wait until tomorrow to dispossess you.
Splendid. I'll come and spend the night here, then,
Most quietly, with half a score of men.
For form's sake, you might bring me, just before
You go to bed, the keys to the front door. 70
My men, I promise, will be on their best
Behavior, and will not disturb your rest.
But bright and early, Sir, you must be quick
And move out all your furniture, every stick:
The men I've chosen are both young and strong, 75
And with their help it shouldn't take you long.
In short, I'll make things pleasant and convenient,
And since I'm being so extremely lenient,
Please show me, Sir, a like consideration,

And give me your entire cooperation. 80
ORGON [*aside*]. I may be all but bankrupt, but I vow
 I'd give a hundred louis, here and now,
 Just for the pleasure of landing one good clout
 Right on the end of that complacent snout.
CLÉANTE. Careful; don't make things worse.
DAMIS. My bootsole itches 85
 To give that beggar a good kick in the breeches.
DORINE. Monsieur Loyal, I'd love to hear the whack
 Of a stout stick across your fine broad back.
MONSIEUR LOYAL. Take care: a woman too may go to jail if
 She uses threatening language to a bailiff. 90
CLÉANTE. Enough, enough, Sir. This must not go on.
 Give me that paper, please, and then begone.
MONSIEUR LOYAL. Well, *au revoir*. God give you all good cheer!
ORGON. May God confound you, and him who sent you here!

SCENE 5
ORGON ELMIRE DORINE MARIANE
CLÉANTE MADAME PERNELLE DAMIS

ORGON. Now, Mother, was I right or not? This writ
 Should change your notion of Tartuffe a bit.
 Do you perceive his villainy at last?
MADAME PERNELLE. I'm thunderstruck. I'm utterly aghast.
DORINE. Oh, come, be fair. You mustn't take offense 5
 At this new proof of his benevolence.
 He's acting out of selfless love, I know.
 Material things enslave the soul, and so
 He kindly has arranged your liberation
 From all that might endanger your salvation. 10
ORGON. Will you not ever hold your tongue, you dunce?
CLÉANTE. Come, you must take some action, and at once.
ELMIRE. Go tell the world of the low trick he's tried.
 The deed of gift is surely nullified
 By such behavior, and public rage will not 15
 Permit the wretch to carry out his plot.

SCENE 6
VALÈRE ELMIRE
DAMIS ORGON MARIANE
DORINE CLÉANTE MADAME PERNELLE

VALÈRE. Sir, though I hate to bring you more bad news,
 Such is the danger that I cannot choose.
 A friend who is extremely close to me
 And knows my interest in your family
 Has, for my sake, presumed to violate 5

The secrecy that's due to things of state,
And sends me word that you are in a plight
From which your one salvation lies in flight.
That scoundrel who's imposed upon you so
Denounced you to the King an hour ago 10
And, as supporting evidence, displayed
The strong-box of a certain renegade
Whose secret papers, so he testified,
You had disloyally agreed to hide.
I don't know just what charges may be pressed, 15
But there's a warrant out for your arrest;
Tartuffe has been instructed, furthermore,
To guide the arresting officer to your door.
CLÉANTE. He's clearly done this to facilitate
His seizure of your house and your estate. 20
ORGON. That man, I must say, is a vicious beast!
VALÈRE. Quick, Sir; you mustn't tarry in the least.
My carriage is outside, to take you hence;
This thousand louis should cover all expense.
Let's lose no time, or you shall be undone; 25
The sole defense, in this case, is to run.
I shall go with you all the way, and place you
In a safe refuge to which they'll never trace you.
ORGON. Alas, dear boy, I wish that I could show you
My gratitude for everything I owe you. 30
But now is not the time; I pray the Lord
That I may live to give you your reward.
Farewell, my dears; be careful . . .
CLÉANTE. Brother, hurry.
We shall take care of things; you needn't worry.

SCENE 7

THE OFFICER ELMIRE DORINE
TARTUFFE MARIANE CLÉANTE ORGON
VALÈRE MADAME PERNELLE DAMIS

TARTUFFE. Gently, Sir, gently; stay right where you are.
No need for haste; your lodging isn't far.
You're off to prison, by order of the Prince.
ORGON. This is the crowning blow, you wretch; and since
It means my total ruin and defeat, 5
Your villainy is now at last complete.
TARTUFFE. You needn't try to provoke me; it's no use.
Those who serve Heaven must expect abuse.
CLÉANTE. You are indeed most patient, sweet, and blameless.
DORINE. How he exploits the name of Heaven! It's shameless. 10
TARTUFFE. Your taunts and mockeries are all for naught;
To do my duty is my only thought.
MARIANE. Your love of duty is most meritorious,

And what you've done is little short of glorious.
TARTUFFE. All deeds are glorious, Madam, which obey 15
 The sovereign prince who sent me here today.
ORGON. I rescued you when you were destitute;
 Have you forgotten that, you thankless brute?
TARTUFFE. No, no, I well remember everything;
 But my first duty is to serve my King. 20
 That obligation is so paramount
 That other claims, beside it, do not count;
 And for it I would sacrifice my wife,
 My family, my friend, or my own life.
ELMIRE. Hypocrite!
DORINE. All that we most revere, he uses 25
 To cloak his plots and camouflage his ruses.
CLÉANTE. If it is true that you are animated
 By pure and loyal zeal, as you have stated,
 Why was this zeal not roused until you'd sought
 To make Orgon a cuckold, and been caught? 30
 Why weren't you moved to give your evidence
 Until your outraged host had driven you hence?
 I shan't say that the gift of all his treasure
 Ought to have damped your zeal in any measure;
 But if he is a traitor, as you declare, 35
 How could you condescend to be his heir?
TARTUFFE [*to the* OFFICER]. Sir, spare me all this clamor; it's growing
 shrill.
 Please carry out your orders, if you will.
OFFICER. Yes, I've delayed too long, Sir. Thank you kindly.
 You're just the proper person to remind me. 40
 Come, you are off to join the other boarders
 In the King's prison, according to his orders.
TARTUFFE. Who? I, Sir?
OFFICER. Yes.
TARTUFFE. To prison? This can't be true!
OFFICER. I owe an explanation, but not to you.
 [*To* ORGON.] Sir, all is well; rest easy, and be grateful. 45
 We serve a Prince to whom all sham is hateful,
 A Prince who sees into our inmost hearts,
 And can't be fooled by any trickster's arts.
 His royal soul, though generous and human,
 Views all things with discernment and acumen; 50
 His sovereign reason is not lightly swayed,
 And all his judgments are discreetly weighed.
 He honors righteous men of every kind,
 And yet his zeal for virtue is not blind,
 Nor does his love of piety numb his wits 55
 And make him tolerant of hypocrites.
 'Twas hardly likely that this man could cozen
 A King who's foiled such liars by the dozen.
 With one keen glance, the King perceived the whole

Perverseness and corruption of his soul, 60
And thus high Heaven's justice was displayed:
Betraying you, the rogue stood self-betrayed.
The King soon recognized Tartuffe as one
Notorious by another name, who'd done
So many vicious crimes that one could fill 65
Ten volumes with them, and be writing still.
But to be brief: our sovereign was appalled
By this man's treachery toward you, which he called
The last, worst villainy of a vile career,
And bade me follow the impostor here 70
To see how gross his impudence could be,
And force him to restore your property.
Your private papers, by the King's command,
I hereby seize and give into your hand.
The King, by royal order, invalidates 75
The deed which gave this rascal your estates,
And pardons, furthermore, your grave offense
In harboring an exile's documents.
By these decrees, our Prince rewards you for
Your loyal deeds in the late civil war,
And shows how heartfelt is his satisfaction 80
In recompensing any worthy action,
How much he prizes merit, and how he makes
More of men's virtues than of their mistakes.
DORINE. Heaven be praised!
MADAME PERNELLE. I breathe again, at last. 85
ELMIRE. We're safe.
MARIANE. I can't believe the danger's past.
ORGON [*to* TARTUFFE]. Well, traitor, now you see . . .
CLÉANTE. Ah, Brother,
 please,
Let's not descend to such indignities.
Leave the poor wretch to his unhappy fate,
And don't say anything to aggravate 90
His present woes; but rather hope that he
Will soon embrace an honest piety,
And mend his ways, and by a true repentance
Move our just King to moderate his sentence.
Meanwhile, go kneel before your sovereign's throne 95
And thank him for the mercies he has shown.
ORGON. Well said: let's go at once and, gladly kneeling,
Express the gratitude which all are feeling.
Then, when that first great duty has been done,
We'll turn with pleasure to a second one, 100
And give Valère, whose love has proven so true,
The wedded happiness which is his due.

Marie de La Vergne de La Fayette
(1634–1693)

In March, 1678, a slim volume entitled *La Princesse de Clèves*, author not identified, appeared in the Paris bookshops. It caused a sensation with the reading public and came to be recognized as the first classic French novel. In 1942, when the novelist André Maurois looked back across the centuries to the monuments of French culture, then threatened by the occupying Nazis, he singled out *The Princesse de Clèves* for an especially graceful tribute. "This novel," he wrote, "is a kind of miracle because it maintains a perfect equilibrium between the vigor of the passions and the moderation of its tone. . . . If no other language can paint with as delightful exactness as the French the most delicate shades of love, if amorous conversation has become in France the most charming and the most perfect of arts, we owe it in part to the *Précieuses* and even to Mademoiselle de Scudéry, in part to the great moralists, and in part also to Racine; but we also owe it to the woman, so keen, so wise, and so modest, who succeeded, without irony and without excess, in bringing the novel back to the plane of reality and who showed that the beauty of the most ardent sentiments can be painted in the simplest language: I am referring to Madame de La Fayette."

Marie-Madeleine Pioche de La Vergne—the future Mme de La Fayette— was born in Paris in 1634 to parents on the outer fringes of the court. Her father, Marc Pioche, Sieur de La Vergne, was a military engineer with the very minor title of *écuyer* (squire); her mother was simply *demoiselle*. There were two younger daughters; undowried, they entered a convent when their father died.

He died in 1649, when Marie-Madeleine was fifteen. Her mother was remarried a year later to the Chevalier Renaud-René de Sévigné, uncle by marriage to the Marquise de Sévigné. A close friendship sprang up between Marie-Madeleine and the twenty-four-year-old Marquise that was to endure through their lifetimes. The marriage was a step up socially for mother and daughter, and Marie-Madeleine became a member of the court, as a lady-in-waiting to Anne of Austria, widowed queen of Louis XIII and Regent Queen for her son, Louis XIV, who was only five years old when he ascended the throne in 1643. She also began to visit the Convent of the Visitation in Chaillot, where the abbess was Louise-Angélique de La Fayette, Marie-Madeleine's future sister-in-law, and where there lived Henriette-Marie of France, widow of the executed Charles I of England, and her ten-year-old daughter Henriette of England. The young lady-in-waiting and the child became friends; the relationship was later to give Mme de La Fayette access to the court after Henriette married the Duc d'Orléans, the eccentric brother of Louis XIV. Mme de La Fayette also wrote Henriette's biography, taken from her dictation and published long after the deaths of both subject and author.

Meanwhile a marriage was arranged between Marie-Madeleine and the widowed brother of Louise-Angélique de La Fayette. Jean-François Motier, Comte de La Fayette, eighteen years older than his bride, was a provincial nobleman with estates in the Auvergne, a remote and mountainous prov-

ince in central France. These estates, at the time he married, were heavily encumbered with debts and the subject of lawsuits that had been pending for years. The couple were married in 1655 and moved to the Auvergne, where two sons were born, in 1658 and 1659. The La Fayettes visited Paris in 1659; Mme de La Fayette remained there when her husband returned home. She was to live in Paris for the rest of her life, with occasional visits from M. de La Fayette. She looked after her husband's many lawsuits, reared her children, presided over a glittering *salon,* and wrote.

Her first published work (and the only one that appeared under her name during her lifetime) was a portrait of her friend Mme de Sévigné, published in a collection called *Divers Portraits* in 1659. The short novel *La Princesse de Montpensier* appeared anonymously in 1662; set a hundred years earlier in the reign of Charles IX, it reflected Mme de La Fayette's observations of the court of Louis XIV, as did her later works. In 1665, she became a close friend of La Rochefoucauld, who was to collaborate with her on several works. *Zaïde,* a long, rambling novel set in ninth-century Spain, was published in two parts in 1670 and 1671. It was a product of a collaboration with La Rochefoucauld and another close friend, Jean-Regnauld de Segrais, under whose name the novel was published.

In 1672, Mme de La Fayette began research for the historical background of *The Princesse de Clèves,* which was published, anonymously as usual, six years later. The novel caused a great stir. It had already been circulated widely in manuscript, and speculation was high as to its authorship. The Paris journal the *Mercure Galant* invited letters from its readers on the subject of whether the Princess was right or wrong to tell her husband that she loved the Duc de Nemours; by a heavy majority, the correspondents voted against the Princess. Only a few months later, an anonymous critique of the novel appeared in Paris: *Letters to Madame the Marquise of * * * on the Subject of "The Princesse de Clèves."* It was subsequently discovered to be the work of the prominent critic and grammarian Jean de Valincour, a friend of Racine and later the royal historiographer. Valincour did not condemn the novel completely—he said he did not "oppose the deserved admiration of the public" and merely wanted readers "not to admire its faults"—but his strictures were severe and sweeping. Many of his objections were stylistic and grammatical; he cited phrase after phrase "not to be found in the best authors." But he found fault with the content and structure as well, objecting to the digressive episodes, questioning the novel's blending of history and fiction, and finding the famous "confession" scene contrived and incredible. Valincour's *Letters* were widely read and debated, and many readers, including some of Mme de La Fayette's friends, agreed with his criticism.

The following year a reply to Valincour appeared in pamphlet form: *Conversations on the Critique of "The Princesse of Clèves,"* professedly by Jean Antoine, Abbé de Charnes, but certainly commissioned by and probably written by Mme de La Fayette. This rejoinder does not answer Valincour's criticisms very effectively, but it does contain some interesting remarks on fiction that illuminate Mme de La Fayette's intentions and esthetic ideals. The subjects of a work of fiction, she argues, do not have to be flawless, but the writer's responsibility is to "show their beautiful side, remove unpleasant ideas, and show them consonant with nature." She describes with pride

the novel's compression and economy, defends its combination of history and fiction, and asserts its moral soundness; its purpose was to show, she said, that "the most innocent gallantries, between married persons, only cause sorrow." The popularity of the novel was only enhanced by these controversies, the so-called *querelle de "La Princesse de Clèves,"* and they succeeded in articulating, if not resolving, some major issues in the theory and practice of fiction.

The Princesse de Clèves was Mme de La Fayette's last major work published in her lifetime. Her close friend La Rochefoucauld died in 1680, her husband in 1683. She followed them in 1693, leaving three books to be published posthumously: *History of Henriette of England* (1720), a novella, *The Comtesse de Tende* (1724), and *Memoirs of the Court of France During the Years 1688 and 1689* (1731).

One of the most revolutionary features of *The Princesse de Clèves* is its brevity. French fiction in the first half of the seventeenth century had been dominated by historical romances, loosely and episodically constructed and frequently enormously inflated in length. It was common for these *romans romanesques* to run to ten or twelve volumes; *Clélie* (1654–61), by the popular Mlle de Scudéry, was over seven thousand pages long. Already by the time Mme de La Fayette began to write there had been a reaction against these seventeenth-century versions of what Henry James was to call "loose, baggy monsters" in favor of shorter, more tightly constructed works called *nouvelles:* short narratives presumably based on events in the comparatively recent past. It was Mme de La Fayette's distinction to bring this short form to a new height of artistry.

Mme de La Fayette herself, however, called *The Princesse de Clèves* not a *nouvelle* but an *histoire,* taking advantage of the ambiguity of the term, which means both "history" and "story." She placed her work in the French court of a century before and made it an intricate web of fact and fiction; practically everything in the novel is historical except the central character and the central action. By thus embedding her imaginative creation in a detailed matrix of historical fact, Mme de La Fayette hoped to achieve the effect of circumstantial reality while at the same time retaining the freedom to shape her central action as she liked. She also gained the advantage of being able to write about her own society tactfully and with some objective distance. Even its earliest readers recognized that the court of Henri II in the novel in some sense "stands for" the court of Louis XIV, if not in encoded details at least in the general social, moral, and psychological issues raised.

What are these issues? In the most general terms, *The Princesse de Clèves* is a treatment of that favorite seventeenth-century theme: the conflict between love and duty. Mme de Clèves is torn between her love for M. de Nemours and her duty to her husband. But what is so fascinating about the book is that both terms in the equation are so problematical that readers today are as hard put to judge the issue as were those early controversialists in the *querelle de "La Princesse de Clèves."*

A central conflict in the novel is between what things appear to be and what they really are. We are first introduced to the court as it appears to be: "a display of opulence and gallantry such as has never been equalled in France." The men are all handsome and brave, the women charming and

beautiful. But only a few pages into the book, the Princess's mother warns her not to believe everything she sees. "If you judge by appearances in this place," she tells her, "you will go on making mistakes, for things are seldom what they seem." This is good advice for the reader, too, who often must distrust appearances and revise his or her opinion of what has happened.

Not the least ambiguous of the features of the book is the Princess herself, who distinguishes sharply between the "outer" truth of behavior and the "inner" truth of feelings. "You know," she declares late in the book, "that my behavior has never been influenced by my feelings." It is tempting to read this novel by a woman about a woman as a study in feminine issues, and indeed a good gender-based reading would be illuminating. But the reader should be careful not to make hasty judgments based on presumably "universal" gender characteristics. The Princess is very much a woman of her own time—or, perhaps better, of her creator's own time, a hundred years later—and the central issues of that time hinge on hierarchical authority. In the face of the absolute secular authority of the King and the divine authority of God, the individual tends to split experience into an outer show of submissiveness to authority and an inner world of private autonomy. Love, for example, in *The Princesse de Clèves* is split into a publicly accepted "gallantry" (one of the ornaments, we are told in the opening lines, of Henri's court) and private passion, regarded as dangerous and destructive. The moral of the first of the famous "digressions" in the book— Mme de Chartres's account to her daughter of the history of Henri's affair with Diane de Poitiers—seems to be that such irrational passion is destructive both to the individual and to the state. The mother, on her deathbed, warns her daughter that in loving de Nemours she stands "on the edge of a precipice," and as the daughter does stand on the precipice she reflects, "Do I want to expose myself to the cruel remorse, the deadly sadness which love brings in its train?" Such a fear of passionate love makes the Princess sister to Racine's Phaedra.

The dualistic view of love in the novel helps illuminate the famous "confession scene." We may wonder, with those first readers of the novel, whether or not the Princess did the right thing, but we may also wonder why she did it. It is worth noticing that this is not the first confession in the novel. The Princess's first confessor-figure is her mother, who "marvelled at her daughter's candor" in confessing her courtship experiences. It seems that the Princess, in confronting a world of passion she perceives as threatening, may be in the habit of transferring responsibility for moral complexities to an authority figure through confession. It may be significant, too, that the deathbed scenes of the two confessors balance each other in the novel and that both confessors leave deathbed charges to the Princess.

To "gallantry," "passion," and "confession" we may add one final key word in *The Princesse de Clèves:* the French *repos,* which Nancy Mitford renders in English as "peace of mind." The phrase chimes through the text from the beginning, culminating in Mme de Clèves's statement to de Nemours late in the novel: "The duty I owe to M. de Clèves's memory would, in itself, be too weak, were it not reenforced by considerations of my own peace of mind. My peace of mind in its turn needs to be reenforced by duty." "Duty" and "peace of mind" are collaborators here, both opposed to passion. The translation "peace of mind" is particularly felicitous here,

since it reminds us of another kind of "peace": that of the state, shattered by the death of the king and the ensuing struggle for power in the court, a struggle that counterpoints the struggle within the Princess's mind.

Is "peace of mind" too passive and negative a goal to earn the Princess the judgment that she "provided an example of inimitable goodness"? Mme de La Fayette does not say, and we are left to estimate how much irony, if any, there is in that last line of this enigmatic and fascinating novel.

FURTHER READING (*prepared by J. H.*): The last full-scale critical biography of Mme de La Fayette in English is badly outdated: Lilian Rea, *The Life and Times of Marie Madeleine, Countess of La Fayette*, 1908. The best book-length introduction is currently Stirling Haig, *Madame de Lafayette*, 1970. Martin Turnell's "Mme de La Fayette and the *Princesse de Clèves*," in *The Novel in France*, 1950, is a good critical overview of the novel. J. W. Scott's *Madame de La Fayette: "La Princesse de Clèves,"* 1983, in the English series "Critical Guides to French Texts," is an 87-page introduction for students. P. H. Nurse's section on the novel in *Classical Voices*, 1971, is perceptive and illuminating, as is the same author's 40-page introduction to his edition of the French text of the novel in Harrap's French Classics series, 1970. Also highly recommended is Philip Stewart's chapter on *The Princesse de Clèves* in *Rereadings: Eight Early French Novels*, 1984. Some of the best recent criticism of the novel has been from a feminist perspective. Difficult but rewarding are Nancy K. Miller, "Emphasis Added: Plots and Plausibility in Women's Fiction," *PMLA*, 96 (Jan., 1981), 36–48, which examines the "implausible" features of *The Princesse de Clèves* and George Eliot's *The Mill on the Floss* from a feminist point of view, and Marianne Hirsh's "A Mother's Discourse: Incorporation and Repetition in *La Princesse de Clèves*," *Yale French Studies*, 62 (1981), 67–87. A useful guide to criticism, in both French and English, is J. W. Scott's *Madame de Lafayette: A Selective Critical Bibliography*, 1974.

THE PRINCESSE DE CLÈVES

Translated by Nancy Mitford
Revised by Leonard Tancock

PART ONE

The last years of Henri II's reign saw a display of opulence and gallantry such as has never been equalled in France.[1] The King himself, charming to look at, the very flower of his race, was a great lover of women. His passion for Diane de Poitiers, Duchesse de Valentinois,[2] had begun over twenty years before, but it was none the less violent for that, nor were the tokens

[1] Henri II (1519–59) reigned 1547–59. His reign was marked by his continuing struggle against the imperialist ambitions of Charles V, Holy Roman Emperor. Most of the novel takes place in the last year of Henri's reign, in 1558 and 1559. (The editors are indebted, in these notes, to M. Antoine Adam's detailed and perceptive annotations to the Pléiade edition of *La Princesse de Clèves*, 1958.)

[2] Diane de Poitiers (1499–1566), twenty years older than Henri II and formerly mistress to his father, François I, became Henri's mistress while he was still Duc d'Orléans and exercised great power over him throughout his reign.

she received any the less dazzling. He excelled at all forms of sport; much of his time was given up to it; every day there was tilting at the ring,[3] hunting, tennis, ballets, and the like. Madame de Valentinois's colors and ciphers[4] were in evidence, and so was she herself, dressed in a style which would have been more suitable for Mlle de la Marck, her own grand-daughter, who was then just growing up.[5] The presence of the Queen was her warrant. Catherine de Médicis, though no longer in her first youth, was still a beautiful woman; the King had married her when he was Duc d'Or-léans before the death at Tournon of his elder brother the Dauphin;[6] a prince whose birth and great qualities destined him to be a worthy succes-sor to his father François I.

Catherine loved pomp, circumstance, and pleasure; she was ambitious and took great delight in reigning; she hardly seemed to mind the King's attachment to the Duchesse de Valentinois, but then she was a mistress of pretense, her real thoughts never easy to guess. In any case, it was expedi-ent for her to keep the Duchess closely attached to her person, since this also ensured the presence of the King.

The King liked to be surrounded by women even when he was not in love with them, and every day he went to the Queen's apartments at the hour when she was at home, knowing he would find all that was most beautiful and elegant of both sexes. So many lovely women and handsome men have never been gathered together at one court; it seemed as if nature herself had taken a particular delight in bestowing coveted prizes upon the most exalted personages.

Madame Elizabeth of France, who became Queen of Spain, already showed signs of exceptional intelligence and of that incomparable beauty which was to prove so fatal to her happiness.[7] Mary Stuart, the Queen of Scotland, who had just married the Dauphin, and whom they called the Queen-Dauphine, was perfection, both in mind and body.[8] She was brought up at the Court of France, had assimilated all its elegance, and was born with so great a love of beauty that, in spite of her youth, she knew and understood more about art than anybody. The Queen, her mother-in-law, and Madame, the King's sister,[9] also loved poetry, drama, and music; Fran-çois I had made such things the fashion; the taste for them remained, and, since the King, his son, was so fond of outdoor amusements, it can be said that every form of pleasure was to be found at his Court. But its special

[3] In tilting at the ring, horsemen try to carry away a suspended metal ring on the point of their lances.

[4] Court ladies adopted colors which often had a personal symbolism and which were dis-played by their lovers and admirers. "Ciphers" were complex designs made up of initials of the ladies, so interlaced that they could not be read.

[5] Diane de Poitiers was the widow of Louis de Brézé, by whom she had a daughter who married Robert de la Marck, Duc de Bouillon. Their daughter was Antoinette de la Marck; in 1558, she married M. d'Anville, son of the Duc de Montmorency.

[6] Henri's older brother, François de Valois, died in 1539, at the age of 29, thus clearing the way for Henri to inherit the throne.

[7] Elizabeth of France was the daughter of Henri II. She was married in 1559 at the age of fourteen to King Philip II of Spain. She died nine years later; it was rumored, apparently falsely, that she fell in love with her stepson Don Carlos and was poisoned by Philip.

[8] Mary Queen of Scots married François de Valois, son of Henri II and Dauphin (crown-prince) of France, in 1558. He became François II in 1559.

[9] "Madame" was Marguerite de France, Duchesse de Berry.

radiance and magnificence came from the number of princes and great nobles, who adorned their generation, each in his own way.

The King of Navarre was universally respected, both for his rank and for his lofty character.[10] He was a first-rate soldier, and though he was a General he often fought in the thick of the battle like a private, side by side with his rival, the Duc de Guise.[11] This Duke was so brave and successful that the greatest captains of his time felt an admiration not unmixed with envy for him; his courage was only one of many great qualities, since he combined intellect with a noble character and a practical capacity both for war and for politics. The Cardinal of Lorraine, his brother, was overweeningly ambitious, witty, eloquent, and learned; at a time when many new attacks were being launched on the Catholic Church, he used his learning in her defense, and thus added to his own prestige. Another brother, the Chevalier de Guise, later known as the Grand Prior, was a prince whom everybody loved; handsome, witty, clever, and famous throughout Europe for his great courage. The Prince de Condé had an indomitable soul in his small crooked body, and was so amusing that the most beautiful women fell in love with him.[12] The Duc de Nevers,[13] in spite of his advanced age, was an ornament of the Court, and had covered himself with glory both in warfare and in the various high offices which he had held during his lifetime. Of his three handsome sons, the second, known as the Prince de Clèves, had all the qualities necessary to uphold the luster of his name; he was brave, generous, and prudent beyond his years. The Vidame de Chartres[14] was descended from the ancient house of Vendôme, a name famous in love and war which even Princes of the Blood have not been too proud to bear. He was brave and bonny, generous and lively, these qualities were self-evident, and if any human being could be said to be worthy of comparison with the Duc de Nemours,[15] it might be he.

But Nemours was nature's masterpiece. Not only was he the best-looking and the bravest of men, but he had a mental distinction and charm that informed his whole aspect, setting him apart from his fellows. He fascinated both men and women; he excelled at sport; his clothes and the way he wore them set the fashion but were inimitable; there was something about his personality which made it impossible to look at anybody else

[10] Antoine de Bourbon, Duc de Vendôme, took the title King of Navarre in 1555, when he inherited the kingdom of Navarre, in northern Spain, bordering on France.

[11] The brothers François de Lorraine, Duc de Guise (1519–63), Charles de Guise, Cardinal de Lorraine (c. 1525–74), and François de Lorraine, the Chevalier de Guise (1534–63), were a powerful ducal family in conflict with the followers of the Duc de Montmorency, Constable of France, for control of the court. ("Constable" [Fr. *Connétable*] was the title assigned the highest ranking officer of the court.) The Guises, especially the Duc de Guise and the Cardinal of Lorraine, were leaders in the Catholic suppression of Protestants.

[12] Louis I de Bourbon, Prince de Condé (1530–69), was a powerful Protestant leader and general.

[13] François de Clèves, Duc de Nevers (1516–62), actually had three sons: François, Jacques, and Henri. Jacques, whose name Mme de La Fayette found in a genealogy of the period, was only fourteen years old in 1558.

[14] François de Vendôme, Prince de Chabanois, Vidame de Chartres (1524–62). "Vidame" was the title assigned to the lay representative of a bishop and commander of the bishop's troops.

[15] The historical Duc de Nemours was Jacques de Savoie, born in 1531 and married in 1566 to Anne d'Este, widow of François de Lorraine, Duc de Guise.

when he was there. There was not a lady at that Court whose reputation would not have been enhanced had he been in love with her; very few of those to whom he paid attentions could boast of having resisted him; indeed several had loved him without any evidence that they were loved in return. He had such a sweet and affectionate nature, and was so ready to love, that he could never harden his heart against anybody who tried to please him; the result was that he had several mistresses and it would have been difficult to guess which of them he really cared for. He was often to be found in the company of the Queen-Dauphine, and some people thought that he even lifted his eyes to her—quite possible, considering the beauty and sweetness of this lady, her infinite desire to please, and the particular favor she always showed the Duke.

Her uncles, the Guise brothers, had risen in the world by her marriage, and now their ambition was equality with the Princes of the Blood. They also wanted power, the sort of power that was wielded by the Connétable de Montmorency,[16] to whom the King left most of the business of government, the Duc de Guise and the Maréchal de Saint André[17] being merely treated as favorite companions. But whether the King was drawn to people by affection or by interest, they could only maintain their position by deferring to the Duchesse de Valentinois because, though she now had neither youth nor beauty left, she governed the King so completely that she could be said to be mistress both of his person and of the whole realm.

The King had always loved the Constable, and as soon as he succeeded to the throne he recalled him from the exile to which François I had condemned him.[18]

The courtiers were divided; some were for the Guises, and some, among whom were the Princes of the Blood, supported the Constable, and each side was anxious to get the support of the Duchesse de Valentinois. The Duc d'Aumale, brother of the Duc de Guise,[19] had married one of her daughters, and the Constable wanted a similar relationship. It was not enough for him that he had married his eldest son to Diane, daughter of the King by a Piedmontese lady who had gone into a convent as soon as the child was born.[20] The marriage had not been easy to arrange because M. de Montmorency had become involved with a Mademoiselle de Piennes, one of the Queen's ladies, and although the King had arranged matters with the greatest tact and kindness[21] the Constable still felt that he was not quite secure while Madame de Valentinois was so close to the Duc de Guise.

[16] Anne, Duc de Montmorency, Constable of France, was born in 1492 and died in the Battle of Saint-Denis in 1567.

[17] The Maréchal de Saint André was Jacques d'Albon. He became Maréchal (officer of the court) in 1547.

[18] The Duc de Montmorency had been exiled by François I for going over to the side of Charles V, Holy Roman Emperor.

[19] Claude de Lorraine, Duc d'Aumale, was the son of Claude de Lorraine, Duc de Guise, and thus the brother of Duc François de Guise.

[20] François de Montmorency, son of the Constable, married in 1557 Diane, the illegitimate daughter of Henri II.

[21] François de Montmorency secretly married Mlle de Piennes. When the match with Diane was arranged, Mlle de Piennes was asked to renounce her marriage. She agreed, but the Pope, to embarrass the King, refused to approve an annulment.

Now this lady herself was beginning to feel uneasy over the Duke's great ascendancy. She had held up the Queen of Scot's marriage to the Dauphin for as long as possible. The beauty and precocious intelligence of this young Queen, and the prestige which her marriage brought to the Guise family, were more than she could bear. She particularly disliked the Cardinal de Lorraine, who was sarcastic, condescending even, in his attitude towards her, and appeared to be taking the Queen's side. So the Constable found her well disposed towards him and ready to make an alliance by marrying Mlle de la Marck, her granddaughter, to his second son, M. d'Anville (who, later on, in the reign of Charles IX, was to succeed to his office). It never occurred to the Constable that M. d'Anville might be as difficult over this marriage as his brother had been over his, but nevertheless such was the case, though the real reason for it was not disclosed. M. d'Anville was hopelessly in love with the Queen-Dauphine and, though he could expect little enough of this passion, he could not bear to enter upon an engagement which would oblige him to pay attentions to somebody else.

The only courtier who had not taken sides was the Maréchal de Saint André. He was one of the favorites, and owed his position to his personal gifts alone. The King had loved him ever since he was Dauphin, and had made him a Marshal of France at an age when it is most unusual to receive any honors at all. This gave M. de Saint André a prestige which he kept by virtue of his own superiority and charm, the excellence of his table, the taste with which his house was arranged, and by a liberality such as few private people can afford; all made possible by the King's generosity. The King was prodigal with those he loved; though by no means perfect he had many qualities. He was a born soldier, experienced and successful in war; except for the Battle of Saint Quentin[22] his reign was one victory after another. He had won, in person, the battle of Renti,[23] had conquered Piedmont,[24] driven the English from France,[25] and turned the luck of the Emperor Charles V before his very own eyes outside the town of Metz when he was vainly besieging it with all the forces of the Empire and of Spain.[26] Nevertheless, the disaster at Saint Quentin had lowered our hopes of victory, and since the fortunes of war now seemed to be divided between the two Kings, their thoughts turned to peace.

The dowager Duchesse de Lorraine had begun to make overtures at the time of the Dauphin's wedding, and ever since then some secret negotiation or other had been carried on. Finally, Cercamp, in the Artois country, was chosen as a meeting place.[27] The Cardinal de Lorraine, the Connétable de Montmorency, and the Maréchal de Saint André represented the King; the Duke of Alba and the Prince of Orange were there for Philip II, while

[22] The French were badly defeated by the Spanish at Saint-Quentin, in northern France, in 1557.

[23] On the border of Picardy, in northern France, in 1554.

[24] Region in northern Italy, on the French border.

[25] The French army, under the Duc François de Guise, won back the port of Calais from the English, January 6, 1558.

[26] The Duc François de Guise successfully defended Metz, in northeast France, against the Spanish in 1552.

[27] A peace conference between France and Spain took place at Cercamp, in northern France, in 1558.

the Duc and Duchesse de Lorraine acted as mediators. The principal clauses referred to the marriage of Madame Elizabeth of France with Don Carlos, Infante of Spain, and of Madame, the King's sister, with the Duke of Savoy.

Nevertheless, the King did not leave the frontier, and it was here that he heard of the death of Mary Tudor.[28] He sent the Comte de Randan to congratulate Elizabeth upon her succession, and she received him gladly since her rights were not very well established, and it was an advantage to be recognized by the King. The Count discovered that she was well informed about the French court, its personalities and their various merits, and that in particular she knew all about the Duc de Nemours. She spoke to him so often and so earnestly of the Duke that when M. de Randan on his return was giving the King an account of his journey he mentioned the fact that, in his opinion, M. de Nemours could do anything he liked with the Queen, even to marrying her. The King spoke to the Duke about it that very evening, making M. de Randan repeat all the conversations he had had with Elizabeth, and advised him to go and see if he could not win this tremendous prize. At first M. de Nemours hardly believed that the King was serious, but when he saw that he was:

At least Sire, he said, if I do set forth on so extravagant a venture, encouraged by your Majesty and to serve you, I must ask that it may be kept a secret until I have been justified by success, or it will appear that my vanity is such as to make me imagine that a Queen, who has never even set eyes on me, could wish to marry me for love.

The King agreed. He said he would only speak of their plan to the Constable, and in fact he considered that secrecy was an essential of success. M. de Randan advised the Duc de Nemours to go to England as an ordinary traveller, but the Duke could not bring himself to do that. He sent Lignerolles, a clever young man and a favorite of his, to try and establish a relationship with the Queen and to sound her as to her real feelings, and while awaiting the results of this journey he went to Brussels to visit the Duke of Savoy, who was there with the King of Spain. Various obstacles had arisen out of Mary of England's death, the conference broke up at the end of November, and the King returned to Paris.

Now there appeared at the Court a beauty. All eyes were upon her and she must indeed have been a paragon to be so much admired in a place where lovely women were the rule. She belonged to the same family as the Vidame de Chartres, and was one of the greatest heiresses in France. Her father had died young, leaving her to be brought up by his widow, Madame de Chartres, a good, noble, and distinguished person. For some years after her husband's death she left the Court and devoted herself to her daughter's education, not only cultivating her mind and caring for her beauty, but also trying to make her good and give her a real love of virtue. Most mothers think that they can best protect young people by never speaking of love in their presence, but Madame de Chartres had different ideas; she

[28] Mary I of England died in 1558, and her half-sister Elizabeth I ascended the throne. The Comte de Randan was Charles de La Rochefoucauld, ancestor of the seventeenth-century essayist and friend of Mme de La Fayette.

often described it to her daughter, minimizing none of its charm, so that the girl should more readily understand what she told her of its dangers. She told her that men were not very sincere, not very faithful, and not above deceit; she spoke of the unhappiness that love affairs can bring to a family, and then, on the other hand, she showed her the life of a good woman, happy, serene, and enjoying the particular glamour that attaches to noble birth when there is also virtue. She impressed upon her that this virtue can only be kept by extreme mistrust of oneself and by following the one line of conduct which can make a woman happy, that is to say, loving her husband and being loved by him.

The girl was one of the most eligible heiresses in France and, though still extremely young, she had already received several proposals of marriage, but Madame de Chartres, who was inordinately proud, could hardly conceive of anything grand enough for her daughter, and decided, when she was in her sixteenth year, to take her to Court. As soon as she arrived the Vidame called to see her; he was astonished, as well he might be, at the beauty of Mademoiselle de Chartres. She was absolutely dazzling. Indeed there was nobody to touch her, with her white skin, golden hair, classical features, and general aspect of sweetness and charm.

The day after her arrival she went to match some precious stones at the house of an Italian who did a world-wide traffic in such things. This man had come from Florence with the Queen and had waxed so rich that he lived more like a great noble than a merchant. While she was there the Prince de Clèves arrived. He was so obviously astounded by her beauty that Mademoiselle de Chartres, seeing the state into which she had thrown him, could not help blushing. She regained her composure, however, and paid no more attention to the Prince than was demanded by ordinary politeness to a man of quality. M. de Clèves gazed at her with admiration, unable to believe that such a beauty and of the highest rank (as he saw by her manner and her attendants) could exist without his knowing who she was. He thought that she was probably unmarried since she was so young, but she had no mother with her. The Italian, who did not know her, called her Madame. M. de Clèves, very much puzzled, continued to stare, but he noticed that, whereas most young people enjoy seeing the effects of their beauty upon others, it only embarrassed her, and he felt that he was hastening her departure. Soon, indeed, she left. M. de Clèves consoled himself by the thought that now he would find out who she was, but greatly to his surprise, nobody could tell him. An impression of beauty and purity remained with him; he seems then and there to have conceived an overwhelming esteem for her and to have fallen in love.

That evening he went to see Madame, the King's sister, a Princess who was universally courted on account of the influence she had over the King, her brother. This influence was so great that when making peace the King had consented to give up his claim to Piedmont so that she could marry the Duke of Savoy. All her life she had wished to be married, but she would not take any but a sovereign, and for this reason had refused the King of Navarre when he was the Duc de Vendôme. She had hoped to marry the Duke of Savoy, ever since seeing him at Nice during the meeting there between King François I and Pope Paul III. She was a clever woman with a

great love of art; she attracted distinguished people to her, and at certain hours of the day the whole Court could be found in her rooms. M. de Clèves went there as usual, so full of the charm and beauty of Mademoiselle de Chartres that he could speak of nothing else, telling his adventure to all and sundry and singing the praises of this mysterious lady. Madame told him that no such person existed because if she did they would all know her, but Madame de Dampierre, her lady-in-waiting, who was a friend of Madame de Chartres, overheard the conversation, and she whispered to the Princess that it must have been Mademoiselle de Chartres whom the Prince de Clèves had seen. So Madame turned to him and said that if he came the following day she would arrange for him to meet his beauty.

Accordingly, the next day Mademoiselle de Chartres made her first appearance. She was received with the greatest kindness by the two Queens, and with admiration by everybody else; she heard nothing but praise on every hand. This she accepted quite simply as though she hardly noticed it, and it affected her behavior not at all. Next she went to Madame, the King's sister, who complimented her on her beauty and then told her of the bewilderment into which she had thrown M. de Clèves. A moment later the Prince himself appeared.

Come in, she said. Now, have I not kept my word? In showing you Mademoiselle de Chartres am I not showing the very beauty whom you were seeking? And now you may thank me, for I have already told her how much you admire her.

M. de Clèves was overjoyed to find that this lady, who had seemed to him made for love, was as well-born as she was beautiful. He went over to her and begged her never to forget that he had been the first to admire her and that, without knowing who she was, he had all the feelings of respect and admiration that were her due. He and his friend the Chevalier de Guise then went off together, singing the praises of Mademoiselle de Chartres. At last they felt that they must be exaggerating and fell silent, keeping their thoughts to themselves. All the same, whenever they met during the days that followed it was of her that they talked, and, indeed, this new beauty was for a long time the chief subject of every conversation. The Queen was full of her praises and was unusually good to her; the Queen-Dauphine made a favorite of her and begged Madame de Chartres to bring her often. The King's daughters sent for her to join in all their amusements. In fact the whole Court loved her and thought her beautiful; the one exception was Madame de Valentinois—not because she thought that the new beauty would put her in the shade, since by long experience she knew quite well that as far as the King was concerned she had nothing to fear, but because she was on very bad terms with the Vidame de Chartres. She had hoped to get him on her side through the marriage of one of his daughters, but he had preferred to be of the Queen's party. She could not therefore feel favorably disposed towards a lady of his name whom he evidently loved.

The Prince de Clèves, now deeply in love with Mademoiselle de Chartres, longed to marry her, but he was afraid that Madame de Chartres would be too proud to give her daughter to any but the head of a house. Nevertheless, his family was so important (the head of it, the Comte d'Eu,

having recently married a lady nearly connected with the Royal Family)[29] that his fears were hardly reasonable, they came from the natural diffidence of a man in love. He had many rivals; the most dangerous seemed to be the Chevalier de Guise on account of his birth, his qualities, and the royal favor which his family enjoyed.

This Prince had fallen in love with Mademoiselle de Chartres the very first day he saw her. He and M. de Clèves were fully aware of each other's feelings for the lady, their rivalry causing a coolness between them so that they were never able to discuss the matter frankly. M. de Clèves felt it a good omen that he should have been the first to see her—it seemed to give him a start on his rivals—but he foresaw that his father, the Duc de Nevers, would make difficulties. The Duke was hand in glove with Madame de Valentinois, and, since she was at war with the Vidame de Chartres, he was not very likely to allow his son to think of the Vidame's niece.

Madame de Chartres, who had been at such pains to instill virtue into her daughter's character, did not relax her precautions in a place so full of bad examples; indeed they had never been so necessary. The Court gravitated round ambition and love, the chief occupations of men and women alike, for there were so many factions and intrigues, and the women played so large a part in them, that love was always mixed with self-interest, and self-interest with love. Nobody was tranquil or indifferent—everybody was busily trying to better their position by pleasing, by helping, or by hindering somebody else; boredom and idleness were unknown, the occupations of the day were pleasure and plots. The women attached themselves to the Queen, the Queen-Dauphine, the Queen of Navarre, Madame, the King's sister, or the Duchesse de Valentinois, according to inclination, interest, or whim. Those past their first youth, or who professed a certain puritanism, were in the Queen's set. Younger ones, in pursuit of love and happiness, courted the Queen-Dauphine. The Queen of Navarre had her favorites, she was young, and the King, her husband, listened to her; he was attached to the Constable, and this made him influential. Madame, the King's sister, still beautiful, attracted some of the women to her. The Duchesse de Valentinois could have anybody she liked, but she was not fond of women, and, with the exception of a very few intimate friends whose characters suited her, she only received them on those days when it amused her to hold a Court like the Queen's.

All these different cabals vied with each other incessantly, while at the same time the women who composed them had various rivalries among themselves, either for favor or for lovers, so that mixed up with the main objectives of place and promotion were many interests, of lesser importance certainly, but which were no less eagerly canvassed. The result was a discreetly exciting atmosphere which made this Court an agreeable place to live in, though not without its dangers for a young girl. Madame de Chartres was perfectly well aware of these dangers, and her great preoccu-

[29] François de Cléves, Comte d'Eu, was the brother of Jacques de Clèves. He married Anne de Bourbon, daughter of Louis II de Bourbon and Duc de Montpensier. Mme de La Fayette's chronology is off here; the wedding did not take place until 1561, three years later than the novel's setting.

pation was how best to guard her daughter against them. She begged her, not as a mother but rather as a friend, to confide in her whenever words of love were spoken, promising her guidance and support in matters which are often embarrassing when one is young.

The Chevalier de Guise made no secret of his feelings and wishes with regard to Mademoiselle de Chartres—everybody knew of them—but look at it which way he would he saw that what he so much desired was hardly possible. He knew that he was not a suitable husband for Mademoiselle de Chartres, since he had but little means to support his rank, and then his brothers would certainly oppose his marriage, fearing a reduction of power which the marriage of younger sons often brings to great families. The Cardinal de Lorraine, for his part, soon let him see that he was not mistaken, strongly condemning his brother's inclination for Mademoiselle de Chartres, but not giving his real reasons. The Cardinal had a secret hatred for the Vidame which only exploded publicly later on, and he would have preferred any connection for his brother to one with this Vidame. He let it be seen so clearly how much he was opposed to the idea that Madame de Chartres was not a little offended, and was at great pains to put it about that the Cardinal had nothing to fear since she would not even consider this marriage. The Vidame did likewise. He was even more annoyed by the Cardinal's behavior than Madame de Chartres was, since he had a better idea of what caused it.

The Prince de Clèves, unlike the Chevalier de Guise, had not made his feelings public, and it was with dismay that the Duc de Nevers learned of them; he supposed that he would only have to have a word with his son to make him change his mind. He was very much surprised and very disapproving when he found that the Prince was perfectly decided upon marrying Mademoiselle de Chartres. He fell into a rage which he was at so little pains to conceal that the whole Court, including Madame de Chartres, soon knew exactly what was going on. It had not even occurred to her that M. de Nevers could regard his son's marriage with her daughter otherwise than as a great privilege, and she was disagreeably surprised to find that the houses of Clèves and Guise, instead of wishing for the connection, should seem to fear it. Such was her indignation that she now had a mind to marry her daughter to somebody whose rank would put her above those who thought themselves too good for her. After some thought her choice fell upon the son of the Duc de Montpensier, who was just grown up.[30] Nobody at the Court was grander than he. Madame de Chartres was a clever person; she had the Vidame, with all his great prestige, to help her; her daughter was a very considerable heiress; so well did she play her cards that M. de Montpensier was apparently in favor of the marriage and nothing seemed to stand in its way.

Now M. d'Anville was a close friend of the Prince de Montpensier, and the Vidame had the idea of asking the Queen-Dauphine to get him on their side, which she could easily do as he was so deeply in love with her, and ask him to further the cause of Mademoiselle de Chartres with the King and the Prince de Montpensier. So he spoke about it to the Queen-Dauphine, who

[30] François de Bourbon. He was actually only sixteen years old at the time of the action of the novel.

threw herself into the affair, since it was for the sake of Mademoiselle de Chartres, whom she liked so much. She told the Vidame that she would be only too pleased to help, in spite of the fact that she would be crossing her uncle the Cardinal de Lorraine, a consideration that did not weigh heavily with her as he was always taking the Queen's side against her.

Romantic young ladies are always glad of a pretext for talking with those they know are in love with them. As soon as the Vidame had taken his leave of the Queen-Dauphine she told Châtelart, M. d'Anville's friend, who knew of his love for her, to take him a message asking him to go that evening to the Queen's rooms. Châtelart respectfully and gladly undertook this commission. He was a gentleman from Dauphiné, who, though his family was good, had made an even better place for himself by his own qualities and talents. All the great nobles of the Court accepted him and treated him kindly. He was specially attached to M. d'Anville through the patronage of the house of Montmorency. Handsome, good at all sport, he sang charmingly, wrote poetry, and had a passionately sentimental side to his character which so greatly pleased M. d'Anville that he had told him of his love for the Queen-Dauphine. Alas, this confidence was to prove fatal by bringing him within the orbit of that lady; seeing her constantly he could not but fall in love himself and this cost him his reason and eventually his life.[31]

M. d'Anville did not fail to go to the Queen that evening. He was only too happy to have been chosen by Madame la Dauphine to help with something she wanted, and he promised her that he would do exactly as she said. But Madame de Valentinois, having been warned that this marriage was in the air, had taken so much trouble to prevent it, and had so put the King against it, that when M. d'Anville spoke to him he gave him clearly to understand that it would have no support from him, and even commanded him to say so to the Prince de Montpensier.

Madame de Chartres's feelings may be imagined. Not only had her plan failed, but, by its failure, had put her enemies in a better position, while damaging the prospects of her child. The Queen-Dauphine told Mademoiselle de Chartres in a most friendly way that she was very sorry not to have been more helpful.

You see, she said, my power here is but limited. The Queen and Madame de Valentinois both hate me so much that they always manage to prevent me getting my own way, either directly or through their followers. And I have tried so hard to make them like me. They hate me because years ago they were jealous and suspicious of the Queen my mother.[32] The King was in love with her before he was with Madame de Valentinois, and then, during the first childless years of his marriage, he seemed to be thinking of a divorce in order to marry the Queen my mother, although he already loved Madame de Valentinois. She, terrified lest he should marry a woman he had once loved and who was quite beautiful and clever enough

[31] P. de Boscosel de Châtelart loved Mary Stuart and accompanied her to Scotland after the death of her husband, François II. There he was found hiding in her bedchamber and was executed.

[32] The mother of Mary Stuart was Marie de Lorraine, daughter of Claude de Lorraine, Duc de Guise. Her second husband was James V of Scotland. The story Mary tells about her and the future Henri II is true.

to put her in the shade, joined forces with the Constable, who was not at all happy at the idea that the King might marry a sister of the Guises. They won over the late King, in spite of his deadly hatred for Madame de Valentinois, by playing on his love for the Queen his daughter-in-law; they made him work with them against a divorce. In order to get my mother out of the way they married her to the King of Scotland, widower of the King's sister Madame Madeleine, choosing him because it could be done at once.[33] Thus they broke faith with the King of England, with whom there had been an understanding and who greatly wished to marry her. Indeed this nearly caused a quarrel between the two Kings. Henry VIII never got over not having married my mother, and whenever French princesses were offered to him he always said they were no substitute for the one of whom he had been cheated. My mother certainly was a great beauty, and it is a remarkable thing that no fewer than three sovereigns should have wanted to marry the widow of a Duc de Longueville.[34] To her misfortune she married the least important of them, and found herself in a country where there was nothing but trouble. I am said to be like her, and I fear I may resemble her in my unhappy fate, and in spite of the apparent happiness of my lot, I often wonder whether I shall be any luckier than she was.

Mademoiselle de Chartres said that these forebodings were so groundless that they would not last long and begged the Queen-Dauphine not to doubt but that her future would be all it seemed.[35]

After this, none of the men dared to think of marrying Mademoiselle de Chartres. Some feared that by doing so they would annoy the King, and others felt that they were not grand enough for somebody who had hoped for a Prince of the Blood. M. de Clèves alone was influenced by neither of these considerations. The death of his father, the Duc de Nevers, which occurred at this time,[36] left him perfectly free to do as he liked, and as soon as his mourning was over he had but one idea, how best to arrange his marriage with Mademoiselle de Chartres. He thought himself in luck, since at the very time when he wanted to propose, these things had happened to frighten away the other suitors and make it more likely that he would be accepted. His happiness would have been complete had he felt sure of her love, since it was her love he wanted, far more than the certainty of marrying her without it. He had been rather jealous of the Chevalier de Guise, but this jealousy was founded less upon anything he could notice in Mademoiselle de Chartres's manner than upon the qualities of the Prince himself. He longed to know how matters stood for him, and whether she smiled upon his suit, but how to find out? He never saw her except with the two Queens, or at receptions; it was very difficult to speak with her alone. However, he did succeed in doing so, and then, with deep respect, he told her of his love and his hopes for the future, begging her to say what her

[33] James V had been married to Madeleine of France, daughter of François I.

[34] Marie de Lorraine's first husband was the Duc de Longueville. The three kings are Henry VIII of England, Henri II of France, and James V of Scotland.

[35] A bit of irony. François II, Mary's husband, died in 1560 after one year on the throne. She returned to Scotland but was forced to abdicate in 1568. She fled to England where she was imprisoned and finally beheaded by her cousin Queen Elizabeth.

[36] Another minor alteration of chronology. The Duc de Nevers died not in 1558 but in 1562.

feelings were for him. He added that he did not want her to accept him simply in order to please her mother, or from a sense of duty, but that, on the contrary, his feelings for her were such that to do so could only bring him eternal unhappiness.

Since Mademoiselle de Chartres had a charming nature she was touched to the heart, and in her gratitude for M. de Clèves's behavior she answered with a sort of sweetness which was quite enough to raise the hopes of a man so desperately in love. He began to assume that part of his desires had come true.

She reported the conversation to her mother, who told her that she would gladly consent if Mademoiselle de Chartres felt inclined to marry him, enlarging upon his many qualities, noble character, and wisdom beyond his years. Mademoiselle de Chartres replied that she had noticed the same qualities, that she would indeed marry him with less reluctance than another, but that she was not particularly attracted by his person. The next day proposals on behalf of the Prince were made to Madame de Chartres and she accepted them. She felt no qualms; it never even occurred to her that she was perhaps giving her daughter to somebody whom she could not love. The contract was drawn up, the King was informed, and the engagement was then announced.

M. de Clèves was happy without feeling quite satisfied. Mademoiselle de Chartres was grateful to him and had a good opinion of him, but he saw to his sorrow that that was all, and did not flatter himself that there were any hidden depths, because, if there had been, even her extreme modesty would not in their present situation have forbidden her to reveal them. So hardly a day passed but he complained bitterly to her.

How can I not be happy now that I am to marry you? Yet truly I am not. You only have a sort of kindness for me which cannot satisfy me, you have no fever, no longing, none of the agonies of love. In fact I might be marrying you not for yourself but for your money, and my terrible passion seems to pass by you unnoticed.

You are not being fair to me, she replied, what more can you want? I think it would hardly be seemly for me to go any further than I do.

He said, I would be quite contented with your attitude if only I could feel that there was something more, but as for seemliness holding you back I always have the impression that it alone forces you to go as far as you do. I have failed to touch your inclinations or heart, and my presence neither pleases nor disturbs you.

How can you, she said, think that it gives me no pleasure to be with you? As for disturbance, surely you must have noticed how often I blush at the sight of you?

I am not taken in by your blushes, he said, they are simply a sign of modesty and have nothing to do with love. I only take such satisfaction from them as I may.

All these shades of sentiment being above her head Mademoiselle de Chartres had no idea what answer she ought to make; M. de Clèves saw only too well that she could not possibly have the feelings he so longed for her to have, since she did not even understand what they were.

The Chevalier de Guise, who had been away, returned a few days before the wedding. Though he had given up all hope of marrying Mademoi-

selle de Chartres, the difficulties seeming too great, he felt none the less very sad when he saw her about to marry another, and this grief by no means extinguished his passion. He was as much in love as ever. Mademoiselle de Chartres had been in no doubt as to the feelings of the Prince for her. Now that he was back again he gave her to understand that she was the cause of his sad looks; he was so good and charming that she could not but feel compassion for him, especially as she was responsible for his wretchedness. So she pitied him, but this pity did not lead to any other feelings and she confided it to her mother.

Madame de Chartres marvelled at her daughter's candor, as well she might. Nobody ever had a more frank and open nature, and not least was she astonished that her heart had remained untouched, especially as she knew quite well that neither the Prince de Clèves nor anybody else had ever touched it. She took all the more trouble to make her love her husband and to impress upon her how much she owed him for having fallen in love before he even knew who she was, a love to which he had borne witness by choosing her at a time when nobody else dared to think of her.

So this marriage took place. The ceremony was performed at the Louvre,[37] and that evening the King, the Queens, and all the courtiers went to a splendid party given by Madame de Chartres. The Chevalier de Guise dared not make himself conspicuous by staying away from this reception, but he could hardly conceal his misery.

M. de Clèves did not find that Mademoiselle de Chartres had changed her feelings with her name. As a husband he had new privileges but no new place in his wife's heart, so that, always longing for something out of his reach, he continued to behave like a lover. Though her demeanor with him was perfect his passion for her was too violent and agitating for him to be happy. Jealousy did not enter into it; no wife ever gave less cause for that and no husband ever felt it less, in spite of the fact that she was exposed to every temptation. She went each day to the two Queens and to Madame, she met all the young and attractive men in her own rooms and with her brother-in-law the Duc de Nevers, who kept open house, but she had a certain quality which imposed respect and made it impossible to flirt with her. Even the Maréchal de Saint André, though he was nothing if not bold, and furthermore protected by the King's friendship, found himself moved by her beauty without daring to let it be seen that he was. Several others were in the same case, and Madame de Chartres, by her own care for the proprieties combined with her daughter's goodness, managed to give the impression that here indeed was somebody quite out of reach.

The Duchesse de Lorraine, while working in the cause of peace, had also been busy making a match for her son the Duc de Lorraine. It was now settled, the bride being Madame Claude de France, the King's second daughter, and the wedding was to take place in February. Now, all this while, the Duc de Nemours had been living at Brussels, wholly absorbed by his English projects. He spent his time sending and receiving messengers, his hopes rose every day, and at last Lignerolles told him that the moment had come for him to go in person and conclude the matter which had

[37] Now a famous art museum but then a royal residence. In 1558, it was under construction, rebuilding having begun in 1546.

begun so well. He was overjoyed at this news, as any young man would have been at seeing a crown within his grasp, simply on the strength of his own reputation. Though at first he had not believed in such a change of fortune he was now looking upon it as something normal and inevitable. He sent orders to Paris with all speed for a splendid retinue, that he might appear in England suitably equipped. Then he hastened to Paris himself for the wedding of M. de Lorraine. He arrived on the eve of the festivities and went at once to see the King to tell him what progress he had made so far and to ask for advice and instructions for the future. Next he called on the two Queens. Madame de Clèves did not happen to be there, so that she neither saw him nor knew of his arrival. She had heard so much of this Prince, as of the best-looking, most charming man at the Court; Madame la Dauphine in particular was always talking about him, and in such a way as to have aroused her curiosity, so that she was quite impatient to see him.

There was to be a Court ball at the Louvre, and she spent the whole of that day in her own room getting ready for it. When she arrived she was greatly admired, for her clothes, her jewels, and her beauty. The ball opened, and while she was dancing with M. de Guise there was a stir at the entrance to the ballroom, people making way as though for somebody important. Madame de Clèves went on dancing, and while she was considering whom she should take for her next partner the King called to her to take the newcomer. She turned round and saw a man stepping over a seat to get to the dancing-floor; at once she felt that this could be none other than M. de Nemours. The first sight of this handsome Prince, always quite startling, was made more so on this occasion by the trouble he had taken with his appearance, and equally the first sight of Madame de Clèves was an amazement. M. de Nemours was so much struck by her beauty that, as she curtsied to him, he could not conceal his admiration. They began to dance together, and as they did so a murmur of applause ran round the ballroom. The King and Queens reminded each other that these two had never met before, and thought it strange to see them dancing without knowing each other. As soon as the dance was over they called them, giving them no opportunity to speak to anybody else, and asked if they were not dying of curiosity to know who the other was, or whether they had guessed.

For myself, said M. de Nemours, I am not in any doubt, but as Madame de Clèves has not the same reasons for knowing who I am as I had for recognizing her I should be grateful if your Majesty would be good enough to tell her my name.

In my opinion, said the Dauphine, she knows it as well as you know hers.

Madame de Clèves, rather ill at ease, said, I assure you, Madame, that I am not as good at guessing as you seem to think.

You have guessed quite well, and it is very flattering to M. de Nemours, this refusal to admit that, though you have never seen him, you know who he is.

The Queen now broke in, saying that the ball must go on, and M. de Nemours danced with the Queen-Dauphine. This lady had seemed to M. de Nemours perfectly beautiful (as indeed she was) before he went to Flanders, but now he had eyes for nobody but the Princesse de Clèves.

The Chevalier de Guise, who still worshipped her, was at her feet, sad-

dened by what he had just seen. It seemed inevitable, foreordained by fate itself, that M. de Nemours should fall in love with Madame de Clèves. Perhaps there was a shadow on her face, or perhaps the Chevalier, in his jealousy, sensed what was in fact more than the truth. Be that as it may, he thought her deeply affected by M. de Nemours, and could not help saying to her how lucky it was for the Prince to have begun their acquaintance in so strange and romantic a manner.

Madame de Clèves left the ball greatly preoccupied by what had happened. Late as it was, she went to her mother's room to tell her about it, speaking of M. de Nemours in such terms that Madame de Chartres instantly had the same idea as the Chevalier de Guise.

Next day the wedding was solemnized and Madame de Clèves once more thought the charm and good looks of the Duc de Nemours quite extraordinary. During the days which followed she saw him with the Dauphine, she saw him playing tennis with the King, she saw him tilting, and heard him talk. She saw that he was better at games than anybody; so witty and delightful that all conversation centered round him; before long he had made a deep impression on her heart. Since M. de Nemours for his part felt violently attracted to her and, behaving with that slightly fantastic sweetness which often, at first, accompanies a great desire to please, he was even more fascinating than usual. Thus seeing each other all the time, and seeing in each other the very best elements of that Court, they could not but be charmed by what they saw.

The Duchesse de Valentinois was at all the parties, the King showing the same lively affection and paying her the same attentions as when he was first in love. Madame de Clèves, who was at an age when it seems impossible that any woman over twenty-five could be loved, was astonished to see the King's devotion for this grandmother, whose granddaughter had just married. She spoke of this to Madame de Chartres.

How is it possible, she said, that the King can have been in love for so long and how can he have formed this attachment in the first place for a woman, much older than he, who was his father's mistress and who still, from what one hears, has many lovers?

Her mother replied, It is certainly not her merit or faithfulness that has inspired the King's love and kept it alive. I must say that if she had been different, as young, beautiful, and virtuous, for instance, as she was well born, had she loved only the King and loved him for himself alone and not for what he could give her, and had she used her influence for his own good, it would have been impossible not to admire such constancy on his part. If I did not fear that you would say, as people always do of women when they get to be my age, that they tell nothing but old stories of the past, I would tell you how it happened that the King fell in love with this duchess, and many details about the late King's Court besides, which are not unrelated to the present.

If I had a complaint, said the Princess, it would be that you never tell me enough, either about the past or the present. I am so ignorant of the various interests and combinations around me that only a few days ago I still thought the Constable and the Queen were friends.

Yes, indeed, that is very far from being the case, replied Madame de Chartres. The Queen hates M. le Connétable, and if ever she gets any

power into her hands he will be made to feel it. She knows quite well he is for ever telling the King that the only ones of his children who look the least bit like him are the illegitimate ones.

How could I possibly guess at this hatred, interrupted Madame de Clèves, when it is well known that the Queen wrote to M. le Connétable while he was in prison, and seemed overjoyed at his release? Besides which, she, as well as the King, always calls him comrade.

If you judge by appearances in this place, replied Madame de Chartres, you will go on making mistakes, for things here are seldom what they seem. But to go back to Madame de Valentinois, you know, of course, that her real name is Diane de Poitiers and that she comes of an illustrious house, descending from the Dukes of Aquitaine. One of her forebears was an illegitimate daughter of Louis XI—in short, there is nothing mediocre about her birth. Saint Valier, her father, became involved in the affair of the Connétable de Bourbon which you mentioned just now,[38] and was condemned to be beheaded, and even led to the scaffold. But his daughter, who was remarkably beautiful and was already in favor with the late King, succeeded, how I do not know, in obtaining the life of her father. They took his reprieve to him when he had ceased to expect anything but the fatal blow, but he was so terror-struck that he was already unconscious and died a few days later. The daughter then appeared at Court as the King's mistress, but the affair was interrupted by his journey to Italy and his imprisonment.[39] On his return from Spain his mother, the regent, came to Bayonne to meet him, bringing all her ladies, including a Mademoiselle de Pisseleu who has since become Duchesse d'Étampes, and with her the King fell in love. She was neither as well born, as witty, nor as beautiful as Madame de Valentinois, and in fact had only one advantage over her, that of extreme youth. I have heard it said that she was born on the very day that Diane de Poitiers was married, but I think this is a spiteful invention because, if I am not mistaken, the Duchesse de Valentinois married M. de Brèze, high seneschal of Normandy, just about the time when the King was falling in love with Madame d'Étampes. There could be no greater hatred than existed between these two women. The Duchesse de Valentinois never forgave Madame d'Étampes for stealing the title of King's mistress, and Madame d'Étampes was violently jealous of the other because the King never quite dropped her. It was not the habit of this Prince to be faithful to one mistress at a time, he used to have one who enjoyed the title and honors of the position, but his attentions were taken in turns by ladies of what was called the "little set."

It was a terrible blow to the King when his eldest son died at Tournon of suspected poisoning. He was not nearly so fond of his second son, our present King, whom he thought much less brave and vivacious, and he complained about him to the Duchesse de Valentinois. She said that she would make him fall in love with her, that this would liven him up and make him more attractive; as you know, she succeeded perfectly and this

[38] Charles, Duc de Bourbon and Constable of France, betrayed François I in 1523 by joining forces with Emperor Charles V.

[39] Emperor Charles V defeated and imprisoned François I at Pavia, in northern Italy, in 1525.

love has now lasted, unshaken by the passing of time or anything else at all, for twenty long years. The King was against it from the first. He may still have been fond enough of Madame de Valentinois to be jealous, or perhaps the Duchesse d'Étampes, in despair at seeing the Dauphin under the influence of her rival, may have worked on his feelings; in any case he was angry and unhappy about it and made no secret of the fact. However, he did not succeed in intimidating his son, who went on steadily and quite openly with the love affair, so that in the end the King was obliged to put up with it, though it made a breach between him and the Dauphin. The result was that he turned to his third son, the Duc d'Orléans, a handsome, graceful, rather harum-scarum boy, full of fire and ambition, who needed a strong hand but who would have made a very distinguished prince if he had lived long enough to have been ripened by age. The two brothers had been rivals from the nursery, and now that the Dauphin enjoyed the privileges of an eldest son, while the Duc d'Orléans was his father's favorite, their rivalry turned to hatred. When the Emperor passed through France he put the Duc d'Orléans before the Dauphin, who resented it so bitterly that at Chantilly, where the Emperor was, he tried to force the Connétable de Bourbon to arrest him without waiting for orders from the King. The Constable refused, and afterwards found himself blamed by the King for not having listened to his son, and all this had a great deal to do with his being banished from the Court.

Seeing the brothers so much estranged, Madame d'Étampes had the idea of getting the Duc d'Orléans on her side against Madame de Valentinois. She succeeded, and although the Prince was not in love with her he worked almost as much for her interests as the Dauphin did for those of Madame de Valentinois. So you see there were two factions at Court, intriguing away, and not only over the squabbles of women. The Emperor, who remained friendly with M. d'Orléans, more than once offered him the Duchy of Milan, and while proposals for peace were being considered he allowed him to hope for the seventeen provinces and the hand of his daughter. The Dauphin wished neither for peace nor for this marriage, and he made the Constable, whom he had always liked, put it to the King that it would be most unwise to saddle his successor with a brother as powerful as the Duc d'Orléans would become, if related by marriage to the Emperor, and with the seventeen provinces at his back. The Constable agreed with the Dauphin, all the more so because, in this, he was working against his open enemy Madame d'Étampes, who, of course, greatly wished for this aggrandizement of the Duc d'Orléans.

Now the Dauphin was in command of the King's army in Champagne and had so reduced the Imperial forces that they would have been wiped out had not the Duchesse d'Étampes, fearing that, if this happened, we should refuse both to make peace and to allow the Duc d'Orléans's alliance with the Emperor, secretly sent word to the enemy that he would do well to take Épernay and Château Thierry, both of which were filled with provisions. He did so, and by this means saved his army. The Duchess did not enjoy the fruits of her treachery for long. Very soon the Duc d'Orléans died from some sort of contagion at Farmoutier. He had been in love with one of the most beautiful women at the Court and was loved by her in return. I am not going to tell you her name. She has led a good life ever

since, and has been at such pains to conceal the love she had for the Prince that she deserves to keep her reputation. It so happened that she received news of her husband's death on the same day as that of the duke, so that she was not obliged to act a part or to conceal her sorrow.

The King only survived his son by two years. He had strongly recommended to the Dauphin that he should take the Cardinal de Tournon and Admiral d'Annebault as his advisers, saying nothing about the constable, who had been banished to his estates at Chantilly. The first action of the new King, however, was to send for him and put him at the head of the government. Madame d'Étampes was sent away, and was as badly treated as she could have expected to be by an all-powerful enemy. The Duchesse de Valentinois revenged herself to the full, not only on Madame d'Étampes, but on all the people who had earned her displeasure. Her influence over the King was unchallenged, even more complete than it had been when he was Dauphin, and so it is now that he has reigned these twelve years. It is she who makes appointments and disposes of offices; she dismissed the Cardinal de Tournon, Chancelier Olivier, and Villeroy, and whenever anybody has been rash enough to have tried opening the King's eyes to her real conduct they have lost everything as a result. The Comte de Taix, Grandmaster of the Artillery, who did not like her at all, could not resist talking about her love affairs, and especially of that with the Comte de Brissac, of whom the King was already jealous; she managed so well that the Comte de Taix was disgraced, exiled and relieved of his position. Unbelievable as it may seem, this was then bestowed upon Brissac, who was presently made Marshal of France through the efforts of the Duchess. The King's jealousy, however, got so much worse that he could not bear to see the Marshal at Court. Now jealousy, such a bitter and violent emotion with most people, always affects him very mildly because of the awe in which he stands of his mistress, and in this case he dared not exile his rival on some pretext, but made him Governor of Piedmont. M. de Brissac stayed there for several years, coming back last winter, ostensibly to ask for more soldiers and for various things needed by the armies under his command, but perhaps really because he longed to see Madame de Valentinois again, fearing that otherwise she might forget all about him. He was coldly received by the King. The Guises, who hate him but dare not show it because of Madame de Valentinois, used her declared enemy the Vidame to prevent Brissac from obtaining any of the things he wanted. It was not at all difficult to put a spoke in his wheel; the King hated him so much and felt so uneasy in his presence that he was obliged to go away again without anything to show for his journey, unless it was that he had rekindled a spark in Madame de Valentinois's heart which absence had begun to extinguish. These are not the only grounds for jealousy which the King has had, but either he has not known about the others or else he has never dared to complain of them.

Madame de Chartres then added, Perhaps you think I have told you more of these things than you wanted to know.

That, replied Madame de Clèves, is the last complaint I am likely to make, and were I not afraid of being importunate, I should ask about many circumstances of which I am ignorant.

M. de Nemours's love for Madame de Clèves was so violent in its first

stages that he could take no interest in the other women he used to love, with some of whom he had kept in touch while he was away. He did not even bother to find excuses for breaking with them, and could not bring himself to listen to their complaints or answer their reproaches. The Dauphine, with whom formerly he had been rather in love, had no chance against Madame de Clèves, and even his impatience for the English journey began to cool; he was not pressing forward his plans with any of his former enthusiasm.

He saw a good deal of the Queen-Dauphine because Madame de Clèves was constantly there; besides, it suited him perfectly that people should go on thinking he was in love with the Dauphine. He set Madame de Clèves on such a pedestal that he resolved rather to give too few indications of his love than to risk it being made public. He did not even speak of it to his great friend the Vidame de Chartres, from whom he never as a rule kept anything. Altogether he behaved so sensibly that few people had any idea he might be in love with Madame de Clèves; she herself would hardly have been aware of it had her own inclination for him not enhanced her perceptions; as it was, however, she knew quite well how the land lay. But the Chevalier de Guise had guessed everything.

The Princesse de Clèves did not feel inclined to discuss this Prince and his feelings with her mother as she usually did when other people were in love with her. It never occurred to her that she was being underhand in not speaking of him. But Madame de Chartres realized the whole thing only too clearly as well as the inclination her daughter had for him, and it made her wretched. She foresaw terrible rocks ahead for the young woman, loved by such a man as M. de Nemours, if he in his turn attracted her. A few days later she had proof that a mutual attraction did indeed exist.

The Maréchal de Saint André, who was always on the lookout for a chance to show how opulent he was, implored the King to do him the honor of supping with him, bringing the two Queens, on pretext of showing them his newly finished house. He was also not at all unwilling for Madame de Clèves to see what enormous sums he had spent on it. Some days before this supper party was due to take place the King-Dauphin, who was always delicate, became ill and could see nobody, and his wife the Queen spent the whole day with him. Towards evening, feeling better, he sent for the various people who were waiting in his antechamber, and the Queen-Dauphine went back to her own rooms, where she found a few close friends, including Madame de Clèves. As it was already rather late, and she was not dressed, she decided that she would not go to the Queen that evening, but, giving orders that she was at home to nobody, she sent for her jewels. She wanted to choose some for herself to wear at the Maréchal de Saint André's ball and others which she had promised to lend Madame de Clèves, and while they were thus occupied the Prince de Condé came in. Because of his rank no door was shut to him, he could go anywhere. The Queen-Dauphine said that, as he obviously came from the King-Dauphin, he must tell what they were all doing there.

There is a great argument going on, Madame, he replied, the Duc de Nemours against the others. He is sticking to his point so vehemently that I

can see it must apply to himself: probably he has some mistress whom he cannot bear to meet in public, because he says that it is always upsetting to see the person you love at a ball.

What next? said the Dauphine. M. de Nemours doesn't want his lady love to go to parties? I knew that some husbands prefer their wives to stay at home, but it never occurred to me that a lover might feel like that.

Well, replied the Prince de Condé, according to M. de Nemours, there is nothing so unbearable for lovers, whether they are loved in return or not, as going to parties. He says that even if they are loved, when there is a party afoot they must reconcile themselves to taking second place for several days, because the woman doesn't exist who can give her lover a thought during the business of getting a new dress, it is all-absorbing; and then this dressing up is done quite as much to impress the world in general as for the sake of the loved one. Furthermore, at the ball itself it is their idea to be admired by all beholders, and the satisfaction they feel when they are aware of looking beautiful has little or nothing to do with their lover.

Then he goes on to say that of course if love is unrequited it is a torment to see the lady at a party, since the more she is generally admired the more wretched it makes you not to be loved by her, besides which there is always the fear that her beauty will attract some other man who will have better luck with her. In short, he considers that there is only one greater agony than to see your mistress at a ball, and that is to know that she is at one where you yourself are not.

Madame de Clèves pretended that she was paying no attention to what the Prince de Condé said, but she was really listening with all her ears. She knew perfectly well that she was responsible for M. de Nemours's ideas on this subject, and especially for what he said about it being torture to a man if his mistress went to a ball without him, because it so happened that the King was sending him to meet the Duke of Ferrara[40] and he would not be there for the Maréchal de Saint André's ball.

The Queen-Dauphine and the Prince de Condé were laughing together about M. de Nemours, and the Queen-Dauphine said that she did not care for this point of view at all.

He did make one exception, however, ma'am, said M. de Condé, and that in favor of a ball given by the lover himself. He said that last year, when he gave one for your Majesty, his mistress did deign to attend it, although that was apparently on your account. He says that it is always a concession to a lover to go to his own party and that a man naturally likes his mistress to see him on his own ground, entertaining the whole Court, so that he can show her how well he does it.

The Queen-Dauphine said, with a smile, M. de Nemours had every reason to be in favor of his mistress going to that ball, because in those days the title was shared by so many ladies that had they all been absent the attendance would have been rather thin.

As soon as the Prince de Condé began talking about M. de Nemours and his views on parties Madame de Clèves conceived a great wish to stay

[40] Alfonso II d'Este, Duke of Ferrara (Italy), was the grandson of Louis XII and the cousin of Henri II. He spent much of his time in France.

away from the Maréchal de Saint André's ball. She told herself that it really was a mistake to be entertained by a man who loved you; she was delighted to have found such a strict reason for giving pleasure to M. de Nemours. However, she took the jewels which the Queen-Dauphine was lending her to wear, but, when she was showing them to her mother later on in the evening, she mentioned the fact that she had no intention of using them. She explained that the Maréchal de Saint André was always letting it be seen that he was in love with her, that she had no doubt he wanted everybody to know that she would be at his party for the King and she feared that, under pretext of being a good host, he would offer her embarrassing attentions. Madame de Chartres argued for a while with her daughter, who she really thought was being too puritanical, but seeing that her mind was made up she gave in, and said in that case she must pretend to be ill in order to have an excuse for not going, because nobody would approve of her real reason and people must not be allowed to suspect it. Madame de Clèves gladly consented to keep to her room for a few days, if by so doing she could avoid a party where M. de Nemours would not be present. He went away in ignorance of this fact, which would have pleased him so much, and only heard that she had not been there on his return, the day after the ball. Since he had no idea that his conversation at the Dauphin's could have been repeated to her it never even occurred to him that he was lucky enough to have been the cause of her staying home.

Next day, at the Queen's, he was talking to the Queen-Dauphine when Madame de Chartres and Madame de Clèves came in and joined that princess. Madame de Clèves was dressed rather carelessly, like somebody who has been ill, but her face told a different story. The Dauphine said, You are looking so beautiful I find it hard to believe that you have been ill. I believe that when M. de Condé told us what M. de Nemours thinks about parties he put it into your head that by going to his ball you would be conferring a favor on the Marshal, and that this must be your reason for not going.

Madame de Clèves blushed when she realized that Madame la Dauphine had made this lucky guess in front of M. de Nemours, and at that moment Madame de Chartres saw in a flash why it was that her daughter had not wanted to go to the ball. In order to conceal it from M. de Nemours she said, speaking with a great air of sincerity, I can assure you, Madame, that your Majesty is giving my daughter credit for more than she deserves. She really was ill, though indeed, had I not been there to prevent it, I feel sure she would have gone and shown herself, ill as she was, simply for the fun of seeing all those marvels at the ball last night.

The Dauphine quite believed Madame de Chartres, and M. de Nemours, rather put out, thought it sounded true enough, though Madame de Clèves's blushes made him wonder whether there had not been a good deal in what the Dauphine had said after all. As for Madame de Clèves herself, though dreadfully upset at first to think that M. de Nemours should have reason to suppose that he had been the cause of her not going to the Maréchal de Saint André's, she felt a sort of vague disappointment when her mother so firmly disposed of the idea.

The conference at Cercamp had broken up but negotiations for peace still continued, and presently they took such a turn that a new conference,

with the same delegates as before, was convened at Câteau-Cambrésis.[41] The same delegates attended, and with the absence of the Maréchal de Saint André, M. de Nemours's most dangerous rival was out of the way, dangerous rather on account of the close watch he kept over Madame de Clèves and anybody who might approach her than for any progress he himself could make in her affections.

Madame de Chartres was anxious that her daughter should not realize that she knew of her feelings for M. de Nemours, as she wanted to say various things to her without any obvious motive, and one day she began talking about him. She spoke very highly of him, but damned him with faint praise, saying how sensible he was never to fall in love, but to regard all relationships with women simply as pleasure, never allowing them to develop into serious attachments.

Of course, she added, the love of his life is supposed to be the Dauphine, and he certainly does go to her rooms all the time. I think you would be well advised to avoid him as far as possible and on no account to see him alone, because in your position of intimacy with Madame la Dauphine people might say that you were acting as their go-between, and you know what a disagreeable reputation that is. In fact if these rumors continue it might be better for you to see less of Madame la Dauphine rather than become involved in a love affair.

Madame de Clèves had never heard M. de Nemours mentioned in the same breath with the Dauphine; she was so much taken aback by what her mother told her, so positive, now, that she had been mistaken about M. de Nemours and his inclinations, that her face fell, and Madame de Chartres saw this. Just then some people arrived and Madame de Clèves went home and shut herself in her own room.

She was agitated beyond words, her mother having now opened her eyes to the fact that M. de Nemours was much more to her than it was right for him to be. She saw only too clearly that her feelings for him were exactly those which the Prince de Clèves had so often besought her to have for him; she was bitterly ashamed to think that she could have such feelings for one who was not her husband. Also she was wounded to the quick that M. de Nemours should be making use of her to further his affair with the Dauphine. This thought decided her to tell Madame de Chartres her secret.

Accordingly she went to her mother's room in the morning, but finding her unwell, with a little fever, she put off speaking to her, though, as it seemed nothing very much, she went to Madame la Dauphine after dinner as usual. The Dauphine was in her little sitting-room, alone with two or three women, her greatest friends, and when she saw Madame de Clèves she said: We are talking about M. de Nemours, and saying how much he has changed for the better since he got back from Brussels. You know before he went there he had countless mistresses; really one could not approve of it because he was exactly the same to all of them, whether they

[41] Town in northern France. The peace conference between Spain, France, and England ended with the Treaty of Câteau-Cambrésis (1559), which brought to a close the sixty-year struggle between France and Spain over control of Italy. Spain won Milan, Naples, and Sicily. England confirmed French possession of Calais.

were nice or not he made the best of them. Now, since his return, he simply doesn't recognize them. There has never been such a change, and it even seems to me that he is different in himself, less carefree, somehow, than he was.

Madame de Clèves did not reply. She was thinking, with shame, that had her eyes not been opened to the truth about M. de Nemours she would have taken these words as a proof of his love for herself. She felt a certain bitterness towards the Dauphine for pretending to look for reasons and to be surprised when she must have known the truth better than anybody, and could not resist letting her see a part of her thoughts so that, the other women moving away, she said to her quietly, Surely these words cannot have been meant for me? Do you think I don't realize that this change which has come over M. de Nemours is on your account.

Now that's not fair, replied the Dauphine, you know quite well I have no secrets from you. It is true that before M. de Nemours went to Brussels he did perhaps intend me to see that I was not detested by him, but since his return it is clear that he remembers nothing that happened before, and I am bound to confess it intrigues me to know what can have made him so different. I think I shall manage, she went on: the Vidame de Chartres, his greatest friend, is in love with somebody I can influence—I shall find out the reason I'm sure.

Madame la Dauphine's words carried conviction, and Madame de Clèves, in spite of herself, now felt more at peace with the world.

She went back to her mother and saw at once that she had become a good deal worse, that there was much more fever. During the next few days her temperature was so high that she was clearly very ill indeed. Madame de Clèves, terribly worried and unhappy, never left her mother's room, and M. de Clèves also went there nearly every day, partly because he was very fond of his mother-in-law, partly to try and keep his wife from giving way to her sorrow, but chiefly for the pleasure of being with her. He was still passionately in love.

M. de Nemours, who had always liked him very much, had been specially friendly ever since his return from Brussels, and during the illness of Madame de Chartres he made opportunities for seeing Madame de Clèves, going there ostensibly in search of her husband, to take him out, and sometimes going when he knew quite well that he was not there. Then, pretending to wait for him, he would stay in the antechamber, where a few friends were always to be found. Madame de Clèves was in and out most of the time, and her grief made her seem no less beautiful to M. de Nemours. He let her see that he felt for her sorrow, and spoke to her about it in such a way as to make her quite well aware that it was not the Dauphine he loved. She could not suppress an uneasy happiness at the sight of him, but when he was not there the thought that her love had its origins in his physical presence filled her with anguish so that she almost decided that she hated him.

Madame de Chartres now became so ill that they began to despair of her life, and the doctors told her this. She received the news with a courage worthy of her goodness and piety, and when the doctors had gone she sent everybody away, and called Madame de Clèves to her.

My child, she said, holding out her hand, we must now part, and I

grieve the more for the danger in which I see you and the need you have of me now. You are attracted by M. de Nemours—I don't ask you to confess it, I am no longer in a condition to need your confidence in order to be able to guide you. I have seen it for a long time, but hesitated to speak at first for fear of opening your eyes to a fact of which you were, perhaps, not fully aware. Now you know it yourself, only too well. You stand on the edge of a precipice and can only hold back by making a superhuman effort. You must solemnly reflect upon your duty, both to your husband and yourself, remembering that you stand to lose the reputation you have built up and which I have so much desired for you. Be brave my darling, be strong and leave this Court. Force your husband to take you away. Don't be afraid of harsh and difficult measures, for in the end it will be better than the wretchedness of a love affair.

If other reasons than virtue and duty could help you to act as I so pray you will, I would add that if anything could trouble the happiness I hope for on leaving this world it would be the sight of you descending to the level of other women. If this misfortune is to overtake you I am glad to die and avoid seeing such a thing.

Madame de Clèves burst into tears over her mother's hand which she held tightly clasped in both of hers, and Madame de Chartres, herself much moved, said, Farewell my child, we will say no more upon a subject which is affecting us both so deeply, but try and remember all I have told you.

She turned away when she had spoken, telling her daughter to call her women, and refused either to listen or to speak to her any more; it may be imagined in what a state Madame de Clèves left her mother's room. Madame de Chartres was now absorbed in preparations for the end, and during the two days which remained to her she refused to see the only creature in the world whom she loved, her daughter.

Madame de Clèves was terribly unhappy. Her husband never left her, and as soon as Madame de Chartres was no more he took her to the country, away from surroundings which could only intensify her grief. This grief was quite unusual in its intensity because, not only had she loved her mother deeply and felt deeply grateful to her, but just now she felt a particular need for her help to fortify her against M. de Nemours. It seemed dreadful to be left alone at a time when she was so unsure of her own heart and when she so longed for sympathy and strength. The conduct of M. de Clèves made her more than ever anxious not to fail in her duty, and she was sweeter and more friendly to him than she had ever been. She could not bear to have him out of her sight, as it seemed to her that if she clung to him he could protect her against M. de Nemours.

The Duke visited M. de Clèves in the country and made every effort to see Madame de Clèves, but she would not receive him. She knew too well the effect he had upon her, how fatally attractive she found him, and she had resolved never to see him if she could possibly avoid it.

M. de Clèves had to go to Paris to attend Court; he promised his wife that he would return the following day; nevertheless, he only came back the day after that. When she saw him Madame de Clèves said, I was expecting you all day yesterday, and now I must scold you a little bit for not coming as you promised me you would. You must have known that if I

could feel any new grief in my present state it would be at the death of
Madame de Tournon, which I have just heard of this morning. I should
have felt it even if I had not known her, for it is always sad when somebody
young and beautiful, as she was, dies in two days, but she happened to be
one of the people who pleased me most. She always seemed to me as wise as
she was good.

I was very sorry not to come back yesterday, said M. de Clèves, but I was
obliged to stay and do what I could to comfort a very unhappy man. As for
Madame de Tournon, if you really think that you are mourning a wise and
admirable woman I advise you not to feel her death too deeply.

What is this? said Madame de Clèves. Why, I have heard you say over
and over again that there was nobody at Court whom you admired more!

True enough, he replied, but women are quite incomprehensible, and
the more I see of them the more thankful I am to have you. I can hardly
believe my luck.

You put me too high, said Madame de Clèves, sighing, it is not yet
certain that I shall prove worthy of you. But do tell me what it is that has
disillusioned you over Madame de Tournon.

It is not new, he said, for a long time now I have known that she loved
the Comte de Sancerre, even allowing him to hope that she would marry
him.

I can hardly believe it! Do you really mean that Madame de Tournon,
after all her public declarations that she could never marry again, with the
views everybody knows that she has held, since her widowhood, on re-
marriage, has been giving hopes to Sancerre?

If he had been the only one it would not have been so extraordinary,
said M. de Clèves, but at the very same time she was also making promises
to Estouteville. I will now tell you the whole story.

PART TWO

You know what friends I am with Sancerre; nevertheless, he was at great
pains to keep it from me that two years ago he fell in love with Madame de
Tournon, and neither I nor anybody else had an inkling of it.[42] At that
time Madame de Tournon seemed inconsolable for the loss of her husband
and led an austere existence, withdrawn from the world. Almost the only
person she ever visited was Sancerre's sister, and it was there that he fell in
love with her.

One evening, when there was to be a play at the Louvre, we were all
waiting until the King and Madame de Valentinois should come for it to
begin, when we were told that Madame de Valentinois was unwell and that
the King would not be coming. Everybody guessed that this indisposition of

[42] The names Tournon, Sancerre, and Estouteville were well known in sixteenth-century
France, but if Mme de La Fayette had particular historical figures in mind for M. de Clèves'
story, they have not been identified. This seems to be one of the few episodes in the novel,
apart from the central plot, that are purely fictional.

the Duchess was really some squabble with the King. Of course we all knew how dreadfully jealous he had been of M. de Brissac while he was at Court, but it was now several days since he had gone back to Piedmont, so we could not imagine what this was all about. I was discussing it with Sancerre when M. d'Anville appeared and, taking me on one side, told me that the King was in a pitiable state of rage and misery; that when, a few days before, he had made up his quarrel with Madame de Valentinois over M. de Brissac he had given her a ring, begging her to wear it always. Apparently, while she was dressing for this play, the King noticed that she had not got the ring, and asked her why. She seemed surprised not to see it and asked her women, who, most unluckily (or they may not have been warned), said they had not seen it for four or five days. Now that was exactly when M. de Brissac left, so the King had no doubt that she had given him the ring when they said good-bye. His jealousy was revived, he flew into a rage, most unlike him, and reproached her bitterly. He then went back to his own apartments, very miserable, though whether because he thought Madame de Valentinois had sacrificed his ring or because he feared he had annoyed her I do not know.

When M. d'Anville had finished telling me this news I went directly and told Sancerre, saying at the same time that he must keep it to himself because it was a secret somebody had entrusted me with. The next morning rather early I went to my sister-in-law's where I found Madame de Tournon sitting by the bed. She had no love for Madame de Valentinois and she knew that my sister-in-law had not a good word for her either. Sancerre had been to see her after the play and had told her all about the King's quarrel with the Duchess; Madame de Tournon had come round to tell my sister-in-law, without knowing, or having forgotten, that her lover had the story from me. As soon as I appeared my sister-in-law said to Madame de Tournon that I could be trusted with what she had just told her, and, without waiting for Madame de Tournon's permission, recited word for word what I had passed on to Sancerre the evening before. Picture my amazement! I looked at Madame de Tournon, she did seem rather embarrassed and this made me suspicious; I had told nobody but Sancerre, he had gone off and left me at the end of the play without a word of explanation, and I remembered having heard him sing the praises of Madame de Tournon. All these things opened my eyes. I deduced without much difficulty that he was having an affair with her and that it was she whom he had visited when he left me. I felt so much annoyed to think that he had been hiding this affair from me that I said one or two things which must have shown Madame de Tournon that she had been very unwise; I went with her to her carriage and, as we parted, I said how much I envied the luck of whoever it was that had told her of the King's quarrel with Madame de Valentinois.

I then went off at once to find Sancerre and covered him with reproaches. I said I knew now that he loved Madame de Tournon, without saying how it was I had found out. He was obliged to admit it. Then I told him how I knew and he told me all about it, saying that although he was only a younger son and far from being a good match, nevertheless she had made up her mind to marry him. Nobody could be more surprised than I was. I told Sancerre that he had better marry her quickly since he could

expect anything of a woman double-faced enough to have acted such a part in public. He replied that she had really been very miserable until her love for him had cured her, and that she did not want everybody to see how suddenly she had changed.

He gave me several other reasons excusing her behavior, which made me realize how far gone he was in love, and said that he was going to get her consent for me to be in the secret, since it was she who had given it away to me in the first place.

With some difficulty he did obtain her consent, after which I was very much in their confidence.

I have never seen a woman treat her lover better than she did, she was as frank and as delightful with him as she could be, but all the same I could not help feeling shocked at the way she kept up the pretence of being heartbroken. Sancerre was so deeply in love, and so much gratified by her behavior that he hesitated to suggest hurrying on the marriage for fear she might think that his passion was less for herself than for her money. All the same, he did speak to her of it, and she seemed quite decided to marry him; she even relaxed her hermit-like existence and went out a little in the world, going to my sister-in-law at a time of day when some of the Court was likely to be found there. Sancerre hardly ever went, but those who did so every evening, and who often saw her there, thought her charming.

A little while after she had begun to go out like this Sancerre thought he noticed that her love for him was cooling. He said so to me once or twice. I did not take him very seriously, but when he told me that, far from arranging their marriage, she seemed to be putting it off, I began to think he had some grounds for his anxiety. I said it would be hardly surprising if Madame de Tournon's love, having lasted for two years, should have become rather less violent, and that he must not complain if, without its having exactly diminished, it should now no longer be strong enough to make her marry him. This marriage, I pointed out, was going to do him no good in the eyes of the world, because it was a bad match for her and also it would injure her reputation. Under these circumstances he ought merely to wish that she should remain faithful to him without holding out any false hopes.

I also said that supposing she felt she could not marry him or even told him that she loved somebody else, he had no right to be hurt or angry but must respect her and be grateful to her.

I am only telling you to behave as I would myself, I said, because personally I value sincerity so much that though I should be miserable if my mistress, or even my wife, were to come and say frankly that she was attracted by another it would not make me bitter. I would then cast off the role of husband or lover in order to advise and sympathize with her as best I could.

At these words, which seemed to have a bearing upon her own state of mind, Madame de Clèves blushed deeply. Taken by surprise she was very much upset, and it was some time before she recovered her self-possession.

M. de Clèves went on with his story. Sancerre, he said, spoke to Madame de Tournon as I advised him to, but she was at such trouble to reassure him, and seemed, indeed, so much offended by his suspicions, that she completely removed them. It is true that she put off their marriage until after a journey that he was obliged to make and which was going to take

rather long, but she was so nice to him until he went away, and appeared to be so miserable when the time came for his departure, that I thought, quite as much as he did, that she really loved him. It is some three months since he left, and during his absence I was so much taken up with you that I hardly saw Madame de Tournon, I only knew that he was expected back shortly. On arriving in Paris the day before yesterday I heard of her death, so I sent to his house to ask if there were any news of him and was told that he had got back the day before, the very day of Madame de Tournon's death. I immediately went to him, knowing quite well the state I should find him in, but his misery surpassed anything I could have imagined. I have never seen such deep and heartfelt grief. As soon as he saw me he threw himself into my arms and burst into tears.

I shall never see her again, he said, never again. She is dead. I have never been worthy of her and soon I shall follow her.

He fell silent for a while, then wept and moaned. Never, never again, she is dead, and went on in this manner like somebody out of his mind. He told me that he had received very few letters from her while he was away but that this had not surprised him as he knew how much she disliked trusting anybody to take letters for her. He had never doubted that she would marry him on his return, he thought she was the most faithful person in the world and the most worthy of love and supposed himself to be tenderly loved by her. Then, just at the very moment when he thought he was to be joined to her forever he found that he had lost her. All these reflections plunged him into a terrible grief, and I must confess that I was deeply moved to see him in this state. At last I had to leave him in order to go to the King, but I promised to be back very soon.

On my return I was astounded to find him in quite a different mood. He was walking up and down his room as if unable to contain himself for anger—he seemed quite beside himself.

Come in, he said, look at me and see a man in total despair, a thousand times unhappier than I was just now, because I have just found out something about Madame de Tournon which to me is far worse than her death.

As I could imagine nothing worse than the death of an adored and adoring mistress I thought his sorrow must have gone to his head and told him that I could sympathize with him while he kept it within reason but that he really must not allow himself to give way to an insane despair.

I only wish I were mad, he cried, I would welcome it as I would welcome death itself. Madame de Tournon was unfaithful to me. I find out her treachery the day after learning of her death, at a moment when my soul is prostrated with love and grief, at a moment when her memory is enshrined in my heart as perfection, perfect towards me. Now I find that I have made a mistake, that the object of my grief is unworthy—and in spite of everything I mind her death as much as if she had been faithful and her infidelity as much as if she were still alive. Supposing I had found her out before she died I should have been so furious and so jealous that it would have stiffened me to endure her loss, but as it is my state of mind is such that I can neither forget nor hate her.

You can imagine how much these words of Sancerre's amazed me. I asked him how he knew what he had just told me and he said that a moment after I had left his room Estouteville had come to see him. This

Estouteville was one of Sancerre's greatest friends, but he knew nothing
about him and Madame de Tournon. He sat down and began to weep,
saying that Sancerre must forgive him for having kept what he was going to
tell him a secret, imploring his sympathy, since he was going to open his
heart, and then saying that in seeing him Sancerre saw the person whom
the death of Madame de Tournon had afflicted more than anybody in the
world.

Sancerre told me: My instinct was to say that I was more afflicted than
he, but the mention of this name made me quite speechless with surprise.
Estouteville went on, saying that he had been in love with her for six
months, that he had wished me to know it from the first but that she had so
expressly forbidden him to tell me that he had not dared to disobey her. He
said they had both fallen in love simultaneously but had kept it a deadly
secret, he never having been seen at her house. His was the pleasure of
consoling her for the death of her husband, he told me, and they were to
have married just at the very time of her death. She had persuaded her
father to order her to marry Estouteville so that this love match should
seem to be an act of filial duty on the part of one bitterly opposed to
remarriage.

Sancerre went on: While Estouteville was speaking I could not but be-
lieve his words, it all rang too true, and the time when he said he had fallen
in love with Madame de Tournon exactly coincided with the change I my-
self had noticed in her. But a moment later I thought he must be a liar or
a dreamer, and I very nearly said so. Then I thought I would clear the
matter up first so I questioned him further, letting him see that I was not
quite convinced. Finally, when I had done all I could to assure myself of my
own unhappiness, he asked me whether I knew Madame de Tournon's
handwriting, and laid four of her letters and her portrait on my bed. Just
then my brother came in. Estouteville, whose face was bathed in tears, was
obliged to go so as not to be seen, and did so, saying that he would come
back this evening to fetch these things he had left with me. As for me, I sent
my brother away, pretending that I was ill, because I could not wait to look
at the letters, hoping against hope to find a contradiction in them of all that
Estouteville had told me. But alas! what did I not find? What tenderness,
what protestations, what promises of marriage! Oh! those letters—! Never
in her life had she written like that to me. So you see that now I am suffer-
ing from two great sorrows at once, sorrows which have often been com-
pared to each other but which can never have been suffered simultane-
ously by the same person, death and betrayal. I must confess, to my shame,
that I mind her death much more than I do her faithlessness. I cannot feel
that she deserved to die. If she were still here I could have the satisfaction
of reproaching her, of avenging myself by bringing home to her the iniq-
uity of her behavior—but I shall never see her again, he repeated, never,
never again. Nothing can be worse than that, oh would that I could give her
back her life in exchange for mine! And yet, what a wish! If she came back
it would be but to live for Estouteville. How happy was I yesterday, he
moaned, happy! I was sadder than anybody in the world, but it was at least
a reasonable sadness and I found a certain sweetness in the reflection that
nothing would ever be able to console me. Today my feelings are all upside
down; I am paying the same tribute of wretchedness to her sham love for

me as when I thought it was real. It is impossible for me to hate or to love her memory, nor can I grieve, nor can I be consoled. One thing I beg of you, he cried, suddenly turning to me, never, never let me set eyes on Estouteville again, his very name fills me with disgust. I know quite well it was all my own fault, I should never have kept it a secret from him that I loved Madame de Tournon—perhaps, had he realized, he would not have become attached to her, and perhaps she would have remained faithful to me. He came to me with his sorrow and I grieve for him, ah! and with reason since he loved Madame de Tournon, was loved in return, and will never now see her again. All the same I cannot help it, I hate him; so once more I beg of you to take steps so that I may be spared the sight of him.

And upon this Sancerre returned to his tears and lamentations for Madame de Tournon, speaking to her, saying the most loving things imaginable and then passing to reproaches, hatred, and imprecations against her. I saw that he was in such a desperate state that I must find somebody to help me calm him down, so I sent for his brother, whom I had just left with the King. When he arrived I had a word with him in the antechamber, explaining Sancerre's condition. We gave orders that Estouteville was not to be admitted, and then spent a great part of the night trying to make him see reason. This morning I found him more wretched than ever. His brother is with him and I came back to you.

Nobody could be more surprised by all this than I am, said Madame de Clèves, since I thought Madame de Tournon equally incapable of love and of treachery.

It would hardly be possible to have been cleverer or more false than she was, replied her husband. Just consider. At the time when it seemed to Sancerre that she was no longer the same to him he was right, because she had then begun to fall in love with Estouteville. She told Estouteville that he was consoling her for the death of her husband, and was the cause of her coming out of her retreat, while all the time Sancerre thought she was doing so because we had decided that she must stop behaving as if she were heartbroken. She made Estouteville keep their understanding a secret so that she could make it seem as if her father were forcing her to marry him, pretending that all this was due to her care for her reputation, whereas in fact she wanted to be able to drop Sancerre without giving him any cause for complaint. I shall have to go back, M. de Clèves said, to be with this poor fellow, and I think you had better come to Paris with me. It's time you saw some people—and then there are all those visits of condolence which must be got over sooner or later.

Madame de Clèves agreed, and went back the following day. She felt much calmer about M. de Nemours; the dying words of Madame de Chartres and the grief of losing her mother had arrested the course of her feelings for him, so that she was beginning to think that she had quite got over him.

The very evening of her arrival Madame la Dauphine came to see her, and when she had assured her how deeply she shared her sorrow she said, in order to distract her from sad thoughts, that she would tell everything that had happened at the Court during her absence; she then came out with several secrets. But what I am dying to tell you, she went on, is that M. de Nemours is madly in love for certain, though he has not confided in a

single soul and even his best friends cannot find out who the lady is. But this love is strong enough to make him neglect—I should really say give up—the chance of a throne.

Madame la Dauphine told all that had been happening about England. I got it from M. d'Anville, she said; it seems that the King sent yesterday evening for M. de Nemours. Lignerolles has written asking to be recalled because he says he can no longer keep up the Queen of England's interest in view of M. de Nemours's continued delay. She is beginning to be offended by it since, without having actually said yes, she had said enough to have induced him to risk the journey. The King read this letter to M. de Nemours and he, instead of speaking seriously as he had done at first, did nothing but laugh and joke, mocking at Lignerolles's optimism. He said all Europe would blame him for imprudence if he went to England as a suitor for the Queen's hand without being sure of success. Another thing, he added, it seems to me a very bad time to go, just as the King of Spain is making such frenzied efforts to marry this Queen.[43] He might not be a very dangerous rival in a love affair, but surely when it comes to marriage your Majesty would hardly advise me to set myself up against him.

In this case I certainly would advise it, said the King, and it so happens that you would not find yourself against him, because I know he has other ideas. Besides, Queen Mary found the yoke of Spain too disagreeable for her sister to wish it back again or to be dazzled by the prospect of uniting so many kingdoms.

Dazzled or not dazzled, replied M. de Nemours, it seems that she has ideas about being made happy by love. Some years ago she was in love with Lord Courtenay; Queen Mary loved him too, and would have married him had she not realized that the youth and beauty of her sister Elizabeth meant more to him than the hopes of the throne. Your Majesty knows that her jealousy made her clap them both into jail, after which she exiled Lord Courtenay and made up her mind to marry the King of Spain. I feel sure that Elizabeth, now that she is on the throne, will remember this lord, and that her choice is more likely to fall upon a man whom she has already loved, who is very attractive, and who has suffered so much for her, than upon somebody whom she has never even seen.

I should entirely agree with what you say, replied the King, were Courtenay still alive, but I have just heard of his death in Padua, where he was exiled. Well, I can plainly see that we shall be obliged to arrange your wedding as we did with M. le Dauphin, and send ambassadors to marry the Queen of England.

M. d'Anville and M. le Vidame, who were present at the interview, are persuaded that it must be love which has made him change his mind about so great an enterprise. The Vidame, who is closer to him than anybody, told Madame de Martigues that he hardly knows him, he is so much altered. The oddest part of it is that he does not seem to have any special friendship, nor does he disappear at certain hours, in fact he thinks that there can be no understanding with the woman he loves; yet it is most unlike M. de Nemours to suffer from unrequited love.

[43] Philip II of Spain, widower of Queen Mary, proposed marriage to her sister Queen Elizabeth in 1559 and was refused.

Of course these words of Madame la Dauphine were the purest poison to Madame de Clèves. How could she not but recognize this nameless lady? And how not be full of gratitude and tenderness on learning from such a reliable source that this Prince, to whom already she was far from indifferent, was hiding his passion for her from all the world and giving up, for her sake, the chance of a throne?

Impossible to describe her feelings, her very soul was in a turmoil; and if Madame la Dauphine had been watching her carefully she would have seen at once that the subject of this conversation was not indifferent to her, but, as she had no inkling of the truth, she prattled on thoughtlessly enough: M. d'Anville, who, as I said, told me all this, thinks I know more than he does—he puts my attractions so high that he is sure I must be the only person alive who could bring about such a change in M. de Nemours.

These last words threw Madame de Clèves into a new sort of agitation.

I am inclined to agree with M. d'Anville, she said, it seems to ring true. Surely it would require nothing less than a princess, Madame, like yourself, to make the Queen of England seem to be of no account.

Madame la Dauphine replied, If I knew that I would tell you, and furthermore if it were so I should know it. A love of that sort cannot be hidden from the person who is responsible, indeed she would be the first to notice it. M. de Nemours was never specially attentive to me, but even so there is a gulf between his present and his former manner. I can assure you that it is not I who have made him indifferent to the throne of England. But I am gossiping with you and forgetting that I am supposed to go and see Madame now. You know that the peace is practically concluded, but perhaps you do not know that the King of Spain has refused to pass any of its clauses except on condition that Madame[44] should marry him instead of his son Don Carlos. Our King could hardly bring himself to it, but in the end he accepted, and just now he has gone to announce the news to Madame. I think she will be inconsolable; after all it is not a very agreeable prospect, marriage with a man of the King of Spain's age and temperament, especially for one so gay, young, and beautiful, with hopes of marrying a young prince who though she had never seen him, had great attraction for her.

I am not sure the King will find her as accommodating as he hopes; he told me to go and see her, because he knows that she is fond of me and he thinks I might be able to influence her. After that I have a very different visit to pay, since I go to rejoice with Madame the King's sister. All is now arranged for her marriage with the Duke of Savoy; he will be here shortly, and nobody of that Princess's age[45] can ever have been so delighted to marry. This Court is going to be more crowded and more resplendent than we have ever known it, and in spite of your mourning we count on you to show the foreigners that our beauties are by no means to be despised.

On these words the Dauphine left Madame de Clèves, and the next day the whole world knew of Madame's marriage. The day after that the King

[44] Not the King's sister but "the other Madame," his fourteen-year-old daughter, Elizabeth of France.

[45] She was thirty-four when she married the Duke of Savoy, July 9, 1559.

went with the Queens to call on Madame de Clèves. M. de Nemours, who had been awaiting her return with the greatest impatience and who longed to speak with her alone, waited to pay his visit until an hour when it was unlikely that more people would arrive and when, on the contrary, people would be leaving her rooms. His plan succeeded, and just as the last guests were going he arrived. Madame de Clèves lay on her bed; it was very hot weather.[46] The sight of M. de Nemours gave her a color which did not make her less beautiful to look at. He sat facing her in that sort of timidity which betokens a genuine passion and remained for a while unable to utter a word. Madame de Clèves was no less overwhelmed, so that they kept a long silence. At last M. de Nemours spoke, condoling with her in her sorrow. Madame de Clèves, who would have been glad to keep the conversation to that topic, spoke at length of the loss she had sustained, saying that though time might take the edge off her grief such a deep impression had been made on her character that her whole outlook would henceforth be altered.

He replied: Great sorrow can effect great changes in the soul and so can violent passion, and as for me, I don't know myself since I got back from Flanders. Many people have seen this change, and Madame la Dauphine spoke of it again yesterday.

Yes, said Madame de Clèves, I do seem to have heard her mention it.

I am not sorry that she sees it, said M. de Nemours, though I could wish that she were not the only one to do so. There are certain people to whom a man can only express the love he feels by quite indirect methods. Though he may not be brave enough to show it he does at least hope that it may be apparent to his beloved how little he wishes to be loved by anyone else, that no beauty, whatever her rank, can touch his heart, and that even a throne would not tempt him if he could only have it at the price of never seeing her again. Women generally gauge the extent of a man's love by the trouble he takes to seek their company and to please them, but none of that is any trouble if they are the least bit amiable. It is far more difficult to resist the pleasure of being with them and to avoid their company lest the world in general and they themselves should guess the truth. The sign of a real attachment is the change it produces, for instance, if it should make somebody indifferent to ambition and to pleasure who all his life has been given over to these two things.

Madame de Clèves understood perfectly that these words were meant for her. She felt that she ought to make some reply, that she ought to stop him, and yet at the same time she ought not to know what he meant. In short it seemed to her that it was her duty both to speak and to remain silent. She found M. de Nemours's remarks both pleasing and offensive; they confirmed what Madame la Dauphine had put into her head. She found in them a certain chivalry and respect but also too much boldness and frankness. The Prince attracted her so much that she was no longer mistress of her emotions, and the most veiled remarks from a man who exercises such an attraction are more agitating than an open declaration from another. So she did not reply, and M. de Nemours would have noticed her silence, and might have drawn a not unfavorable conclusion from it,

[46] It was not unusual for ladies to receive guests in their bedrooms.

had not the arrival of M. de Clèves put an end both to the conversation and to his visit.

The Prince had come to give his wife news of Sancerre, but she was not really very much interested in the latest installment of that story, and was so entirely absorbed by what had just occurred that she was hardly able to conceal her absence of mind. As soon as she had a chance to think it over quietly she realized how mistaken she had been in supposing that she now felt nothing but indifference towards M. de Nemours. His words had made as deep an impression as he could have hoped, forcing her to believe in his love. Since his actions were suited to his words she was left in no doubt whatever.

Now that she could no longer deceive herself into hoping that she was not in love with him, her only preoccupation was never to give any sign by which he could guess that she was. This would be difficult indeed, how difficult she knew too well already, and she knew that her only chance of success lay in avoiding the Prince.

Owing to her mourning it was quite natural for her to lead a more retired existence than usual, so she made it an excuse never to go where he might see her. She was in very low spirits, but her mother's death seemed to be the reason, and nobody looked for another.

M. de Nemours was in despair at hardly ever seeing her, and when he realized that she was not to be found at assemblies, or at any of the amusements where the whole Court gathered, he could not bring himself to go to them either. He pretended to have a passion for hunting, and arranged hunting parties on those days when the Queens held their receptions. Then he was slightly unwell, and this for a long time gave him an excuse to remain at home and avoid going out to places where he knew he would not find Madame de Clèves.

M. de Clèves fell ill at about the same time, and Madame de Clèves never left his room, but when he was better and beginning to receive visitors, M. de Nemours, under pretext of still feeling weak himself, spent a large part of every day with him. Madame de Clèves felt that she could no longer stay there, although the first few times that he came she had not the strength to leave, it was too long since she had seen him.

The Prince gave her to understand by saying things which seemed meant for everybody, but which she recognized as being on the same lines as what he had told her in her room, that he went hunting to indulge in his dreams, and avoided receptions because she was never there. At last she carried out her resolution of leaving her husband's room whenever he came to it, but only by dint of doing great violence to her feelings; the Prince saw that she fled from him and was deeply affected.

At first M. de Clèves paid no attention to his wife's behavior, but presently he noticed that she refused to stay in his room when he had visitors and he spoke to her about it. She replied that in her opinion it was not seemly for her to spend every evening with the younger members of the Court and begged him to agree that she should lead a more retired life than when her good mother had been there, making it possible, by her presence, for her to do all sorts of things which, at her age, it would be hardly proper for her to do alone. M. de Clèves, who was by nature extremely indulgent to his wife, was not so on this occasion, and he told her

that there could be no question of such a change in her habits. She was on the point of telling him that all the world was saying M. de Nemours was in love with her, but she did not feel able to pronounce his name, and besides she was ashamed to use a false argument and to conceal the truth from a man who valued her so highly.

A few days later, the King being with the Queen at her hour for receiving, the talk was all of horoscopes and prophecies, and opinions were greatly divided as to how much they could be believed. The Queen believed in them, she maintained that it was impossible not to see a great deal of truth in a science which had accurately predicted so many things, while others said that out of an endless number of prophecies very few came true and that it was clearly a question of chance.

I used to be curious about the future, said the King, but I have been told so many lies and improbabilities that now I feel sure one cannot know the truth. Some years ago a man came here with a great reputation as an astrologer. Everybody went to him, I among others, without saying who I was. I took M. de Guise and Descars with me, making them go in first, but it was to me that the astrologer addressed himself, as if he knew that I was their master. Possibly he recognized me, but then he said a thing which could not have applied to me if he had. He told me I should be killed in a duel. Then he told M. de Guise that he would be killed from behind, and Descars that his head would be bashed in by the kick of a horse. M. de Guise was rather angry, as the prophecy seemed to accuse him of running away, nor was Descars exactly pleased to think that he would come to such an unfortunate end. In short, we all left very much dissatisfied with this astrologer. I don't know what may be in store for M. de Guise and Descars, but it seems hardly likely that I shall be killed in a duel. The King of Spain and I have just made peace, but even had we not I doubt whether we would have fought a duel or that I would ever have called him out as my father the King called out Charles V.

Those who had been upholding astrology ceased to do so on hearing of the misfortune which had been foretold for the King, agreeing that it was perfectly incredible.

M. de Nemours said, Nobody could believe less than I do. Then he turned to Madame de Clèves who was beside him and said in a low voice, I have been told that the person for whom I feel the most violent, respectful passion is one day to make me happy by her sweetness to me. So you may well imagine how much I believe in prophecies.

Madame la Dauphine, thinking that, because M. de Nemours's first words were spoken out loud, he was telling some false prophecy that had been made to him, asked what he had said to Madame de Clèves. A man with less presence of mind might have been taken off his guard by this remark, but without a moment's hesitation he replied, I was just saying that once I was told of a tremendous destiny which awaited me, so great that I would not even dare aspire to it.

If you were really told that, Madame la Dauphine said with a smile, thinking of the English affair, you ought not to despise astrology but rather find reasons for supporting it.

Madame de Clèves knew exactly what the Dauphine meant, and she also

knew that the great destiny of which M. de Nemours spoke had nothing to do with being King of England.

Now, quite a long time having elapsed since the death of her mother, she was obliged to begin going out again and take up her duties at the Court. She saw M. de Nemours at Madame la Dauphine's and also at her own house, where he came with other friends of the same age, in order to pass unobserved. She never met him without an agitation of which he was perfectly well aware. However much she sought to avoid his eye, to speak less with him than with others, she gave herself away by something in her first movement, and the Prince felt certain that she was not indifferent to him. A man with less penetration might not have noticed anything, but he had already been loved so many times that he could hardly fail to recognize the symptoms. He knew that the Chevalier de Guise was his rival, and the Chevalier knew that M. de Nemours was his. He was the only man at Court to realize this, his own interest in the matter having made him see more clearly than other people. So the knowledge of each other's feelings introduced a bitterness between them which appeared in everything. Without ever exploding into a quarrel, they always took opposite sides, were it at tilting at the ring or the barrier,[47] or at any of the King's other amusements; their rivalry was so great as to be quite obvious.

The English business was much in Madame de Clèves's thoughts; it seemed to her that M. de Nemours would never be able to hold out against the advice of the King and the representations of Lignerolles. She saw, with some distress, that the latter had not yet returned, and she awaited him impatiently. If she could have known his exact movements they would have indicated how matters stood, but the very reason for her curiosity was also a reason for concealment, so she merely informed herself about the beauty, talents, and character of Queen Elizabeth. Somebody had brought one of her portraits to the King, and Madame de Clèves thought it had more beauty than she had hoped; she could not help remarking that it must flatter the Queen.

I don't think so, said Madame la Dauphine, who was there, they say this Princess is a beauty and that she has a more independent mind than most people; she has been held up to me as an example ever since I can remember. If she is like her mother, Anne Boleyn, she must be charming, for few women have been as attractive in every way as she. I have often heard what a lively and original look she had, nothing in common with other English beauties.

Was she not born in France? said Madame de Clèves, I seem to have heard so.

The people who believe that are wrong, replied Madame la Dauphine, and I will tell you her story in a few words. She came of a good English family; Henry VIII was in love with her sister and her mother, in fact some people think that she was his daughter. She came over here with the sister of Henry VII who married King Louis XII. When her husband died, this Princess, who was young and romantic, was very sad at having to leave the

[47] For tilting at the ring, see footnote 3. The "barrier" was the railing around the tournament ground.

French Court, and Anne Boleyn, who was of the same mind as her mistress, could not decide to go. The late King was in love with her, and she stayed on as lady-in-waiting to Queen Claude. Then the Queen died, and the King's sister Madame Marguerite, Duchesse d'Alençon, afterwards Queen of Navarre, whose stories you have read,[48] took her into her household, when, under the influence of that princess, she became tainted with the new religion. Presently she went back to England, where she charmed everybody with those French manners which other nations find so agreeable; she sang well and danced beautifully. She became lady-in-waiting to Katharine of Aragon; then King Henry VIII fell madly in love with her.

Now Cardinal Wolsey, the King's favorite and chief minister, who had had hopes of the papacy, was dissatisfied with the Emperor for not supporting him in his ambition, so he decided in revenge to make a matrimonial alliance between his King and the King of France. He put it into Henry's head that his marriage with the Emperor's aunt[49] was null and void and proposed to him that he should marry the Duchesse d'Alençon, whose husband had just died. Anne Boleyn, who was ambitious, saw in this divorce the way to a throne. She began by filling the King of England with impressions of Luther's religion, then persuaded our late King to take up the cause of his divorce with Rome, in the hopes of marrying him to the Duchesse d'Alençon. Cardinal Wolsey got himself sent to France, ostensibly on other business but really with a view to negotiating this affair, but his master would not hear of it and sent orders to Calais forbidding him to speak of the marriage. On his return from France, Cardinal Wolsey was received with royal honors; no favorite can ever have carried pride and vanity to such lengths. He brought off a meeting of the two Kings and this took place at Boulogne.[50] François I offered his hand to Henry VIII, who declined to take it. They entertained each other in turn with extraordinary magnificence, exchanging replicas of the suits they had had made for themselves. I remember hearing that the suit our late King sent Henry VIII was of crimson satin trimmed with triangles of pearls and diamonds, and a robe of white velvet embroidered with gold.

After a few days at Boulogne they went on to Calais. Anne Boleyn was lodged with King Henry VIII; she had a queen's retinue and François I gave her presents and honors exactly as if she had been one.

Finally, after having been in love for nine years, Henry married her without waiting for the dissolution of his first marriage, which he had long been demanding from Rome. The Pope immediately pronounced fulminations against him, and Henry was so much irritated by this that he declared himself head of the Church and dragged the whole of England into that unfortunate change of religion in which you see her now. Anne Boleyn did not enjoy her glory for long. The death of Katharine of Aragon having, as she thought, assured her position, she was with the whole Court one day watching her brother, Lord Rochford, tilting at the ring, when the King was suddenly overcome with such an access of jealousy that he left for

[48] Marguerite of Navarre (1492–1549) wrote the *Heptameron*, a collection of seventy stories.
[49] Katherine of Aragon (1485–1536), aunt of Charles V.
[50] In 1532.

London in the middle of the match. Once there he ordered that the Queen, Rochford, and several others whom he suspected of being her confidants or lovers, should be arrested. Although his jealousy seemed to have been born at that very moment it had really been inspired some time since by Lady Rochford, who could not bear the great intimacy between her husband and the Queen, and pretended to the King that it was a guilty passion. The result was that he, already in love with Jane Seymour, soon had but one idea in his head, how best to get rid of Anne Boleyn. In less than three weeks he had caused the Queen and her brother to be tried and executed and had married Jane Seymour. After her he had several more wives, whom he either killed or repudiated, among others Katharine Howard, the confidante of Lady Rochford. They had their heads cut off together, so in the end she was punished for the crimes she had wished on to Anne Boleyn. Henry VIII finally died himself after becoming quite enormous.

All the ladies who were present while Madame la Dauphine told of these events thanked her for teaching them so much about the English Court, and among them was Madame de Clèves, who could not help asking her a few questions about Queen Elizabeth.

The Queen-Dauphine was having miniatures painted of all the Court beauties, to send to her mother the Queen. The day that Madame de Clèves's portrait was finished Madame la Dauphine came to spend the evening with her after dinner. M. de Nemours was there; though he never let it be seen that he sought the company of Madame de Clèves, he never let a chance go by of being with her. That day she was looking so beautiful that he would have fallen in love with her had he not done so already; yet he dared not gaze while her hair was being combed out for fear that people might notice the joy it gave him to look at her. Madame la Dauphine asked M. de Clèves for a miniature he had of his wife, to compare it with that which was just finished, and everybody expressed their opinions on one and the other. Madame de Clèves told the artist to make a little adjustment to the coiffure of the one they had just brought in, and, in order to do so, the artist took it out of its box, worked on it for a while, and then put it back on the table.

Now M. de Nemours had long wished to possess a portrait of Madame de Clèves, and when he saw the one belonging to M. de Clèves he could not resist the temptation of stealing it from a husband whom he thought tenderly loved. It seemed to him that among so many people crowded together suspicion would not fall on him more than on another. The Dauphine was sitting on the bed speaking in a low voice with Madame de Clèves, who stood by her. Madame de Clèves could see M. de Nemours through a curtain which was only half drawn; he had his back to the table at the foot of her bed and she saw how, without turning his head, he deftly picked something off the table. She guessed at once that this must be her portrait and she was very much upset. The Dauphine noticed that she was no longer listening to her and asked out loud what she was looking at. At her words M. de Nemours turned round and met the eyes of Madame de Clèves still upon him, and he thought very likely she had seen what he had just done. Madame de Clèves was not a little embarrassed. It would have been reasonable to ask to have her portrait back again, but if she did so out

loud it would proclaim to everybody there his feelings for her, while to do so when alone with him would have looked like an invitation for him to speak of his love. Finally she judged it best to leave him the portrait, happy to accord him a favor since she could do so without his knowing it. M. de Nemours, noticing her embarrassment and more or less aware of its cause, went up to her and whispered, If you saw what I dared to do, be kind, ignore it. It is all I ask of you. Having said this he left, without waiting for her to reply.

The Dauphine left to go walking, followed by her ladies. M. de Nemours shut himself in his room, for the happiness of owning a portrait of Madame de Clèves was too great to be borne in public. He was enjoying all the most agreeable feelings that love can bring; he loved the most charming woman of the whole Court and was making her love him back whether she would or not; he noticed in everything she did the agitation and shyness which love induces in the innocence of first youth.

That evening they sought the miniature high and low. As the case was still there in its proper place nobody suspected that it might have been stolen but they thought it must have slipped down by accident. M. de Clèves was very sad at his loss and when it had once more been looked for in vain he said to his wife, jokingly, that she must have some secret lover to whom she had given it, or who had stolen it, since none but a lover would want the picture without its case. These words, though he said them laughing, made a deep impression on Madame de Clèves and filled her with remorse. She reflected upon the violence of the inclination which was pushing her towards M. de Nemours. She knew that she could no longer control her words and expression; she knew also that Lignerolles was back, that she no longer feared the English business, that she no longer suspected Madame la Dauphine, in short that her defenses were breaking down and there could be no safety for her except in flight. But since it was not in her power to flee she felt at the end of her tether and ready to fall into what seemed to her the worst wretchedness, that of letting M. de Nemours see what her feelings were for him. She thought of all Madame de Chartres had said when dying and how she had advised her to do anything, resort to any device, however difficult, rather than embark on a love affair. Then she remembered what M. de Clèves had said, when speaking of Madame de Tournon, about sincerity, and she thought it was perhaps her duty to confess to him. She considered this for a long time, then was amazed that she could ever have had such a mad idea, after which she fell back into a state of complete indecision.

Peace was now signed. Madame Elizabeth, in spite of the repugnance she felt, made up her mind to obey the King her father, and the Duke of Alba was nominated to come and marry her as proxy for the Catholic King,[51] and he would soon arrive. The Duke of Savoy was coming to marry Madame, the King's sister, the two weddings were to take place very soon, together, and the King was determined to mark them with a series of entertainments at which his Court should appear to its best advantage. Suggestions were made for everything that was most wonderful in the way of plays

[51] Philip II.

and ballets, but the King considered these amusements too private, and wanted something more spectacular.

So he decided upon a tournament, open to foreigners, at which the people of Paris would be the audience. The Princes and young nobles took up the idea with delight, especially the Duke of Ferrara, M. de Guise, and M. de Nemours, who surpassed all others at this form of sport. The King chose these three to stand with him against all challengers.

It was now proclaimed throughout the kingdom that, on 15 June in the City of Paris, his most Christian Majesty, together with the Princes Alfonso d'Este, Duke of Ferrara, François de Lorraine, Duc de Guise, and Jacques de Savoie, Duc de Nemours, would hold an open tournament against all comers. The first combat to be on horseback in the lists, with double armor, to break four lances and one for the ladies; the second with swords, one against one or two against two, as the judges should direct; and the third on foot, three thrusts of the pike and six of the sword. The champions to provide swords, lances, and pikes as chosen by the combatants. Whoever failed to manage his horse to be put out of the lists. Four judges of the field would give orders, and decide the value of the prize, which would be carried off by whoever performed best and broke most lances. All the combatants, whether French or foreign, to be obliged to touch one, or more if they wished, of the shields which were to hang on a pillar at the bottom of the lists, where a herald at arms should be ready to enroll them, according to their rank and the shields they had touched. The combatants to send a gentleman with their shields to be hung up three days before the tournament, or they would not be admitted without leave of the champions.

Great lists were set up near the Bastille, stretching from the Château des Tournelles, crossing the rue Saint-Antoine, and ending at the royal stables. There were two sides of scaffolding and amphitheaters with covered boxes, forming as it were galleries, very pretty to look at and capable of holding an infinite number of spectators. The Princes and nobles thought of nothing but their accoutrement and how to appear as splendid as possible, also how best they could introduce something charming, and appropriate to the lady of their choice, into mottoes and ciphers.

A few days before the Duke of Alba's arrival, the King played a game of tennis with M. de Nemours, the Chevalier de Guise, and the Vidame de Chartres. The two Queens were there to watch them with all their ladies, including Madame de Clèves. As they were leaving the tennis court, at the end of the game, Châtelart went to the Queen-Dauphine and told her that he had got a love letter which had fallen out of M. de Nemours's pocket. The Dauphine, who was always curious about everything that concerned M. de Nemours, told Châtelart to give it her. She took it and followed the Queen her mother-in-law who had gone with the King to see the work which was being done at the lists. Presently the King sent for some horses which had just come, and in spite of the fact that they were not properly broken in he insisted upon mounting them, giving one to each of his companions. The King and M. de Nemours found themselves on the two wildest, who began trying to hurl themselves at each other. M. de Nemours, fearful of hurting the King, pulled his horse sharply back against a pillar of the riding school, hitting it with such violence that the shock made him sway. They ran to him, thinking he must be badly hurt, and Madame de

Clèves thought him more hurt than anybody else did, owing to the special interest she took in him. She did not think of concealing her agitation, and the expression on her face would have given her away to a man much less in love than the Chevalier de Guise. As it was, he saw only too clearly, being far more interested in the condition of Madame de Clèves than in that of M. de Nemours.

This Prince was completely dazed by the blow, and remained for some time with his head lying limp against those who held him. When at last he lifted it his eyes fell first on Madame de Clèves. He saw, written upon her face, the concern she felt for him and he gave her a look which showed her that he was deeply touched. Then he thanked the Queens for their marks of kindness towards him, excusing himself for having appeared before them in such a condition. The King told him to go away and rest.

Now that Madame de Clèves had got over her fright she began to reflect on the signs of it that had escaped her; nor did the Chevalier de Guise leave her for long in the hope that nothing had been noticed. Giving her his hand to lead her away from the lists he said, I am more deserving of pity than M. de Nemours so you must forgive me if I appear to forget the deep respect I have always had for you and say how sad I am at what I have just seen. This is the first time I have ever been bold enough to speak to you, as it will be the last. I must leave this place, seek death, perpetual exile, anything rather than stay here now that I can no longer even console myself by thinking that all those who lift their eyes to you are as hopeless as I.

Madame de Clèves could only reply to this with a few incoherent words as though she had not quite grasped the Chevalier's meaning. At any other time she would have been angry with him for speaking of his feelings for her, but now she merely felt miserable to think that he had noticed what hers were for M. de Nemours. The Chevalier de Guise was so certain of them, and so penetrated with sadness, that from then on he decided never even to think of being loved by Madame de Clèves. He came back to an idea he had long had in mind, the conquest of Rhodes,[52] which seemed glorious enough to turn his thoughts from the other conquest. When death removed him from this world, in the flower of his age and already famous in his generation, he said that he only had one regret, which was not having been able to carry out such a fine resolution, which he had prepared so carefully that he supposed it to have been infallible.

Madame de Clèves went to the Queen on leaving the lists, much preoccupied by what had just occurred. Presently M. de Nemours came in, splendidly dressed and evidently quite unaffected by his accident, so happy indeed at what he thought he had noticed that he was even gayer and more attractive than usual. Everybody was surprised when he appeared, and all hastened to ask how he felt, except Madame de Clèves, who stood by the chimney piece pretending not to have seen him. The King came in, and seeing him with the others called him over to talk about his accident. M. de Nemours passed by Madame de Clèves and murmured to her, I noticed

[52] Rhodes, an island in the Aegean Sea off Greece, was surrendered by the Christians to the Turkish Suleiman I in 1523. The Chevalier de Guise led an unsuccessful expedition there; he died in 1563.

today that you were concerned about me, but it is not that which I most deserve.

Madame de Clèves had suspected that the Prince must have noticed the weakness she had for him, and his words showed her that she was not mistaken. It was a terrible blow to her to feel that she was now no longer able to hide her feelings and that she had allowed the Chevalier de Guise to become aware of them. She was also displeased that M. de Nemours should know everything, though this displeasure was not unmixed with a sort of sweetness.

The Queen-Dauphine, most impatient to find out what was in the letter which Châtelart had given her, said to Madame de Clèves, Do go and read this letter addressed to M. de Nemours, it looks as if it must be from the new mistress for whose sake he has left all the others. If you can't read it now, keep it and bring it back to me while I am going to bed and tell me if you recognize the writing. Having said this Madame la Dauphine left Madame de Clèves who was so utterly taken aback that for a moment she stood transfixed. She was too impatient and distressed to stay at the Queen's, so went to her own rooms, though it was long before her usual time for retiring. She held the letter in a hand that trembled, her thoughts were confused, nothing seemed clear to her, and she found herself in an agony such as she had never experienced or dreamed of. As soon as she was back in her sitting-room she opened the letter and read as follows:

I have loved you too dearly, I cannot let you go on thinking that the change which you see in me is due to any fickleness of mine and I wish you to know that it is the result of your own unfaithfulness. You may well be surprised that I should speak of this unfaithfulness which you have so cleverly hidden from me, since I also have kept from you the fact that I knew all about it. I am surprised myself that I was able to prevent you from noticing that I knew. Nobody has ever suffered as I do. I thought you were violently in love with me, as I was with you. I made no secret of it, I allowed you to see its full extent, only to find that you were deceiving me and that you loved another; everything goes to show that you are sacrificing me to a new mistress. I knew it the day of the tilting at the ring. I feigned illness to hide my despair, and became ill indeed, for my body was unable to endure the shock. When I began to feel better I went on pretending to be ill in order to have an excuse for neither seeing nor writing to you. I wanted time in order to make up my mind how I ought to behave with you; twenty times I made the same resolutions and twenty times unmade them again; but in the end, thinking you unworthy to witness my misery, I decided to hide it from you. I wanted to wound your vanity by letting you see my love die a natural death, thinking that this would cheapen the sacrifice you were making of it. I had no wish for you to wear my love as an ornament to make you more desirable. I resolved that my letters should be lukewarm and flat, to show her to whom you passed them on that you were no longer loved. I could not bear her to enjoy the delightful knowledge that she had won a victory over me, nor to sweeten her victory with my reproaches and despair. Then I thought that merely to break with you would not punish you enough, that it would be but a slight wound for you if I stopped loving you once you loved me no more. No. You must be forced to love me again if you were to feel the misery, as I was feeling it so bitterly, of being loved no more. If anything could rekindle the feelings you once had for me, I thought, it would be the knowledge that mine for you were dead, especially if I

could make you realize it while pretending to keep it from you as though I was afraid to confess it.

This is what I finally decided, but what a painful decision and, once I had seen you again, how impossible to put into practice! A hundred times I could have burst out with tears and reproaches; only the fact that I was still unwell enabled me to hide my misery from you. After a while the pleasure of deceiving you as you were deceiving me helped me to keep it up; nevertheless, I did myself so much violence in telling and writing my love to you that you noticed a change in me before I meant you to. You were hurt by it, you complained. When I tried to reassure you my manner was so unnatural that you felt more certain than ever that I had stopped loving you; in short I had done exactly what I meant to do. Contrary as ever, you had but to realize that I was putting a distance between us to begin a pursuit. Now I tasted all the joys of vengeance; it seemed to me that you loved me better than you ever had while I let you see that I loved you no more. I had reason to suppose that she for whom you had left me was in her turn abandoned; I also had reasons for thinking that you had never mentioned me to her. Nevertheless, neither your return nor your discretion can make up for your fickleness.

Once your heart has been divided between me and another, once I have been deceived, there is no pleasure left in being loved by you as I felt I deserved to be. So I have made this resolution, which seems to you so surprising, never to see you again.

Madame de Clèves read and re-read this letter many times without even being conscious of having read it at all, conscious indeed of one thing only, that M. de Nemours's love for her was not what she had supposed, that he loved others, and deceived them even as he was deceiving her. This was indeed a sad discovery for one of her temperament, who was madly in love and had allowed not only the object of her love, now shown to have been unworthy, to guess at it, but also somebody else whom she was treating badly on his account. She felt a stinging distress, exacerbated by the events of that day; it even seemed to her that she could have borne M. de Nemours's love for another had she not given him reason to believe that he was possessed of hers, but in this, of course, she was quite mistaken, since the unbearable pain that she was suffering was nothing more nor less than jealousy, accompanied by all its attendant horrors. She understood from this letter that M. de Nemours had a long-standing love affair. The writer of it seemed clever, distinguished, worthy of love, and more controlled, she thought, than she herself could ever be. She envied the courage which had enabled this woman to hide her true feelings from M. de Nemours. By the last words of the letter she saw that the writer thought that she was loved, then it occurred to her that the discretion which the Prince had shown with her, and which she had found so touching, might simply have been due to his passion for this other woman and a fear of displeasing her. So she went on, torturing herself with every fancy which could increase her despair, with self-reproaches and with memories of her mother's advice. Why had she not been quite firm and insisted upon retiring from society, in spite of M. de Clèves, or even followed her impulse of confessing to him that she was attracted by M. de Nemours? She thought now that it would have been far better to have confessed to a husband of whose goodness she was well aware and who had every reason to have kept the secret, than to have had it

discovered by a man unworthy of it, a deceiver who, for all she knew, was only making use of her, only wanted her love out of vanity. The torture she was suffering, even if it drove her to extremities, was nothing to the knowledge that M. de Nemours loved another while she had disclosed her love for him.

She quite forgot that Madame la Dauphine had told her to go there at bedtime; she pretended to feel ill, and went to bed. When M. de Cléves came in from being with the King he was told that she had gone to sleep, but she was really very far indeed from that peaceful state of mind which leads to sleepiness. She read and re-read the letter, working herself into a misery, and so passed the night.

Madame de Cléves was not the only person whose rest had been disturbed by that letter. It was the Vidame de Chartres who had lost it, not M. de Nemours, and he was extremely worried. He had spent the evening with M. de Guise, who gave a big supper party for his brother-in-law the Duke of Ferrara and all the young people of the Court. It so happened that during supper there was talk of letter writing, and the Vidame said that he had on him the most beautifully written letter in the world. They all begged him to show it, but he refused, upon which M. de Nemours said that of course it was non-existent and he had only mentioned it from vanity. The Vidame answered that this was pushing his discretion too far but that all the same he would not show the letter: he would, however, read out certain bits of it which would be enough to show that it was such as few men had ever received. As he spoke he made to bring out the letter, but could not find it; he searched in vain, the others began to taunt him, but he was so evidently upset that they stopped talking of it. He was the first to leave the party, and hurried to his room to see whether he had not left the missing letter there. While he was still hunting for it high and low the Queen's first footman came to him, sent by the Vicomtesse d'Usèz, who thought he should be warned at once of what everybody was saying in the Queen's apartments. It seemed that a love letter had fallen out of his pocket while he was in the tennis court, that most of its contents were already being bandied about, that the Queen was most curious and wanted to read it, and that one of her gentlemen whom she told to get it for her had replied that he had last seen it in the hands of Châtelart.

The first footman told the Vidame de Chartres various other things which made him so uneasy that he went there and then to a great friend of Châtelart and got him out of bed, though it was an extraordinary hour to go asking for letters. He did not even say who wanted the letter or who had lost it. Châtelart, having made up his mind that it was M. de Nemours's letter and that this Prince was in love with Madame la Dauphine, was in no doubts as to who it was that kept asking for it. He answered, with spiteful relish, that he had given the letter to the Queen-Dauphine. His friend went back to the Vidame with this reply, which worried him more than ever. For some time he could not make up his mind what to do, finally he thought that the only person who could help him out of his difficulty was M. de Nemours. He went off to find him and came into his room just as day was breaking. The Prince was in a peaceful sleep, what he had seen of Madame de Cléves the day before having given him none but pleasant thoughts. He was astonished at being woken up by the Vidame de Chartres, and asked

why he had come like that to spoil his sleep. Was it in revenge for the things he had said at supper? But then he saw, from the Vidame's face, that something very serious indeed had brought him there.

I have come to confide in you the most important affair of my life, he said. But you won't be particularly grateful to me. The fact is I need your help, and I know quite well that if I had told you these things without it being absolutely necessary to do so I should have forfeited your esteem. That letter of which I spoke yesterday—it had fallen out of my pocket and it is of the greatest importance that nobody should know it was addressed to me. It fell in the tennis court yesterday, and many of the people who were there have seen it. Now you were there too; I beg and implore of you to say it was you who lost it.

M. de Nemours said, with a smile, It's quite obvious that you think there is nobody with whom I should have a misunderstanding if I allowed it to be supposed that I receive letters of this sort, or you could never make such a proposition.

Please, please listen to me without joking, said the Vidame. If you have a mistress, which I don't doubt, though I have no idea who she may be, you can easily explain everything to her—I will give you all the proofs. Even if you do not explain, the worst that can happen is that you will have a short misunderstanding, whereas I, by this accident, will compromise a woman who has loved me deeply, a really good woman, and besides that I shall draw upon myself an implacable hatred which will cost me my fortune and probably more besides.

I don't understand everything you are saying, said M. de Nemours, but you have opened a peephole and I am beginning to guess that rumors I have heard about a certain great Princess and her interest in yourself are not without foundation.

Indeed they are not, and would to God they were, replied the Vidame, because then I should not find myself in this situation. I had better tell you everything so that you may see how much I have to fear. Ever since I first came to Court the Queen has always been particularly good to me and I have had reason to think that she had a special feeling for me, though there was nothing I could actually lay my finger on and I have never thought of her otherwise than with deep respect. As a matter of fact I was in love with Madame de Thémines, a woman whom you only have to see to realize that love for her, if she returned it, and in my case she did, could be something very deep. Nearly two years ago now, when the Court was at Fontainebleau, it happened several times that I was talking with the Queen at a time of day when there were very few people about. I could see that she found me good company and she entered into everything I said. One day, among other things, we spoke of trusting people. I said that I completely trusted nobody, having found it always led to regrets, and that I knew a great many things which I kept to myself. The Queen remarked that this raised me in her estimation, since she knew nobody in France who could keep a secret, and it was a thing she found particularly thwarting because she could no longer indulge in confidences. She added that it is a necessity for everybody, and especially for people, like her, in high places, to have a person to whom they can speak freely. The next few days she often came back to this

topic, and even told me some rather private things which were happening. I felt that she wanted to be sure of my discretion and to confide in me, and this made me fond of her since I was touched that she should single me out in this way; I became much more attentive to her than I had ever been before. One evening the King and all the ladies went riding in the forest, but she, not feeling very well, stayed behind and I with her. She went down to the lake, leaving her equerries so that she could walk with more freedom. She walked up and down for a while and then, coming to where I was, she told me to follow her, saying, I have something to tell you which will prove that I am your friend.

Having spoken thus she stood still, and looking earnestly at me she continued, You are in love, and since you confide in nobody you imagine, perhaps, that your love is not known. Known it is, however, and by those whom it closely concerns. You are watched, the place where you meet the lady has been noted, and a plan is afoot to surprise you there. I do not know who she is, I only want to protect you from misfortune.

Now just think what a trap the Queen was setting for me, and how difficult it was not to be caught in it. She wanted to know if I really was in love, she asked no questions, she did not appear to be speaking either from curiosity or with some end in view but simply as if it was to please me. All the same I soon got to the bottom of the affair. I was in love, with Madame de Thémines, but although she loved me in return I was not in the happy position of having some special place where I met her and where I might be afraid of discovery, so I knew quite well that the Queen could not be speaking of her. I was also having an affair with another woman, who was less beautiful than Madame de Thémines and less virtuous, and it was not impossible that my meeting place with her had been found out, but as I did not care for her much it was quite easy to protect myself from that danger by not seeing her any more.

So I decided that I would confess nothing to the Queen but on the contrary would assure her that I had long ago given up the sort of women of whom I could have hopes, since they all seemed to me more or less unworthy of an honest man's love, and that nowadays it would take something on a very different plane to compromise me.

You are not telling the truth, said the Queen, the opposite of what you say is really the case and I know it. After the way I have spoken you owe it to me not to conceal anything. I want us to be friends, but in that case you must not hide your affairs from me. That is the price, and you can have two days to think it over, but afterwards be careful what you say to me and remember that if later on I find you have been untruthful I will never forgive you as long as I live.

On these words the Queen left me without waiting for me to answer. You may imagine that I was full of what she had said, and the two days she had given me to make up my mind did not seem any too long for such a decision. I saw that she wanted to find out whether I was in love, and that she was hoping to hear I was not. I foresaw certain consequences of the decision I was to take and was not a little flattered at the idea of a special relationship with the Queen, a Queen, at that, whose physical charms were still considerable. On the other hand I was in love with Madame de

Thémines, and although I was being unfaithful to her in a way with this other woman I mentioned, I really could not decide to break with her altogether. I was clearly exposing myself to danger by deceiving the Queen, and it would be very difficult to take her in successfully, all this I saw, but still could not bring myself to refuse what fortune was offering me. I decided to risk the consequences of my bad behavior. I broke with the woman whose affair with me might have been found out and I hoped that my love for Madame de Thémines could be kept a secret.

At the end of the two days which the Queen had given me I came into her room and, in front of all the women who were there, she said, with a serious look that quite surprised me, Have you seen about the business I wanted you to do for me? What is the truth?

Yes, Madame, I replied, and it is just as I told your Majesty.

Then come this evening at the time when I do my writing, and when I see you I will give you your instructions.

I bowed low, without answering, and did not fail to go at the hour she gave me. I found her in the gallery with her secretary and one of her ladies-in-waiting. When she saw me she took me to the far end of the gallery, saying, So you have nothing to tell me after all these deliberations? I should have thought you might have been frank with me considering my attitude towards you.

Just so, Madame, I replied, and that is why I have nothing to say, and I can answer to your Majesty, with my respectful duty, that I am not in love with any woman of this Court.

I believe you because I wish to do so, said the Queen, and I wish it because I need your undivided allegiance; your friendship would be useless to me if you were in love. Lovers are never trustworthy, you cannot depend upon their discretion, they are too distracted to be wholehearted about anything and their mistress necessarily comes first. None of this fits in with what I want of you. So remember that if I give you all my confidence it is only because I have your word that you are free. I want you to be entirely at my disposal. You must have no friend, either male or female, of whom I do not approve; your only preoccupation must be how to please me. You will lose nothing thereby. I shall watch over your affairs better than you ever could, thinking myself well rewarded for anything I can do if the hopes I place in you are fulfilled. I have singled you out to hear the tale of all my vexations and to help me smooth them over. You have probably guessed that I am not happy, though I may seem to put up with the King's infatuation for Madame de Valentinois without minding very much. The fact is that I find it intolerable. She rules the King; she is unfaithful to him; she despises me, and all my servants are on her side. My daughter-in-law the Queen, proud of her own beauty and of her uncles' prestige, pays me no respect. The Connétable de Montmorency is the real overlord of this King and his kingdom. He hates me and has given evidence of his hatred that I can never forget. The Maréchal de Saint André is as forward as a young favorite can be, and behaves no better to me than the others do. You would be sorry for me if you knew all the details of my misfortune. Up to now I have dared to confide in nobody, but I have faith in you. Please never let me regret it, please be my one consolation.

As she finished speaking the Queen's eyes were quite red, and I was so deeply touched by her confidence that I was ready to throw myself at her feet. Since then I have known all her secrets. She does nothing without consulting me, and the relationship between us exists to this very day.

PART THREE

Now, however preoccupied I may have been by my understanding with the Queen, I was not able to overcome my instinctive inclination for Madame de Thémines and I clung to her very much. I thought that she had begun to love me less, but this fact, instead of curing my love for her, as I should have allowed it to do had I been wise, positively redoubled it, and I behaved so rashly that the Queen got wind of my attachment. People of her race are very prone to jealousy[53]—perhaps, indeed, this Princess has stronger feelings for me than she quite realizes herself. Be this as it may, the rumor that I was in love made her so sad and so uneasy that I thought I was completely finished as far as she was concerned. In the end, however, I managed to reassure her by dancing attendance and uttering many false vows, though I could never have taken her in for long had I not been estranged from Madame de Thémines, in spite of myself, by the great alteration in her. She let me see that she no longer loved me; I felt so sure that this was the truth that I stopped tormenting her and left her in peace.

Some time afterwards she wrote me this letter which I have lost. Then I saw that she had found out the affair I had been having with that other woman I mentioned to you, and that this was the reason for her change of heart.

My affections being no longer divided, the Queen now became quite pleased with me, but, since the feelings I have for her are not such as to make me incapable of any other attachment, and since love cannot be harnessed by will-power, I fell in love again, this time with Madame de Martigues, whom I used to find very attractive in the days when she was a Villemontais[54] and a lady of the Queen-Dauphine. I have reason to suppose that she does not absolutely hate me, and she is pleased by my great discretion in the matter, though she does not know why it is so necessary. The Queen is now assailed by new suspicions, not indeed of Madame de Martigues but very annoying ones all the same. Madame de Martigues is always with the Queen-Dauphine so I go there now much more than I used to and the Queen has got it into her head that I am in love with that Princess. The fact that the Queen-Dauphine is equal in rank with her, while she is infinitely younger and more beautiful, has plunged her into a furious jealousy and hatred of her daughter-in-law which she can no longer conceal.

The Cardinal de Lorraine has now begun to meddle in the affair. He

[53] Catherine was Italian.
[54] Mme de Martigues' maiden name.

has wanted for some time to take my place with the Queen and I have no doubt that, under pretext of bringing her and the Dauphine together again, he has nosed out the truth and is doing me all sorts of harm without the Queen realizing what he is up to.

So this is the present state of affairs. Just imagine the effect of the letter I have lost and which I was unfortunate enough to put in my pocket to return to Madame de Thémines. If the Queen sees this letter she will know I have deceived her and that almost at the very time I was lying to her about Madame de Thémines I was lying to Madame de Thémines about another. Imagine what she will think of me and my trustworthiness. If she does not see this letter what shall I tell her? She knows it has been given to Madame la Dauphine and she will believe that Châtelart has recognized that Queen's writing and that the letter is from her. She will imagine that the person towards whom jealousy was shown is herself. In fact there is nothing she may not be justified in thinking and I may not fear from her thoughts. Add to that the fact that I am very much in love with Madame de Martigues, and Madame la Dauphine is certain to show her the letter which she will suppose to have been written quite recently. And so I shall be in trouble all round, with the person I love most in the world and the person I have most reason to fear. So you see how right I am to beg you to say the letter is yours and to ask you as a favor to get it back from Madame la Dauphine.

Yes, I see plainly, replied M. de Nemours. It would hardly be possible to be in a worse muddle and I am bound to say you deserve it. I have been accused in my time of unfaithfulness and of conducting several affairs at once, but I should never have even dared to consider taking on what you have. How could you have hoped to keep both Madame de Thémines and the Queen? Or have expected to be able to deceive the Queen, an Italian as well as a Queen, that is to say full of suspicions, jealousy, and pride. Then, when by good luck rather than good management you find yourself free from entanglements, what do you do? You take on new ones. How could you possibly have expected to be able to love Madame de Martigues, at this Court, without the Queen noticing anything? Your one idea ought to have been to wipe out the shame she must have felt at taking the first step. Of course she is violently in love with you—this is not a thing for you to say or for me to ask, but it is perfectly obvious. Now she is suspicious, and all the facts are against you.

I don't think it's for you to read me this sermon, the Vidame interrupted him; considering your own experiences you really might be a little more indulgent towards my peccadilloes. I quite admit that I am in the wrong, but now do think of some way out of this horrible situation. All I can think of is that you must go and see the Queen-Dauphine as soon as she is awake and ask for the letter as though you had lost it.

I have already told you that I find this a most peculiar proposition, said M. de Nemours, and one which in my special circumstances is full of difficulties. Furthermore, if the letter was seen falling out of your pocket, it won't be very easy to pretend that it fell out of mine.

I thought I had mentioned that the Queen-Dauphine was told that it fell out of yours, said the Vidame.

M. de Nemours, foreseeing at once in this case a misunderstanding with

Madame de Clèves, said furiously, Do you mean that Madame la Dauphine has been told that I dropped the letter?

Yes, that's it, said the Vidame. When your servants and mine went for our clothes in one of the rooms at the tennis court it happened that several gentlemen of the two Queens were there. The letter fell, the gentlemen picked it up and read it aloud. Some thought it was yours and some thought mine, and Châtelart, who took it and whom I have been asking for it, said that he gave it to the Queen-Dauphine as yours. On the other hand, unfortunately, those who spoke of it to the Queen said that it was mine, so it would be quite easy for you to do as I ask and get me out of this muddle.

M. de Nemours had always been very fond of the Vidame de Chartres, the more so on account of his relationship with Madame de Clèves, but all the same he felt that he could not risk her hearing of this letter in connection with himself. He was deeply considering the whole question when the Vidame, who guessed, more or less, what was on his mind, said: I see what it is, you are afraid of a misunderstanding with your lady love, indeed I could almost suspect that she is none other than Madame la Dauphine, except that you never seem at all jealous of M. d'Anville. But in any case I can't allow my peace of mind to be bought at the expense of yours and I will give you means of proving to the lady that this letter was meant for me and not for you. There. That is a note from Madame d'Amboise, Madame de Thémines's friend, who knows all about her feelings for me and who, in this note, asks me to return the letter I have lost. My name is on it, and the contents prove beyond a shadow of doubt that the letter she is asking for is the one that has been found. I give you this note, you can show it to your mistress and put yourself in the right with her. But please do not lose a single moment, promise me that you will go this very morning and see Madame la Dauphine.

M. de Nemours gave his word and took the note. But before going to see Madame la Dauphine he had something much more urgent to do. He had no doubt but that Madame de Clèves would already have heard about the letter and it was unbearable to him that somebody he loved so deeply should have reason to suppose that he was involved with another woman. He called at her home as soon as he thought she might be awake and sent a message saying that only an affair of great urgency could cause him to ask for the honor of an interview at such an extraordinary hour.

Madame de Clèves was still in bed, bitterly upset by the thoughts which had been tormenting her all night, and great was her surprise when she heard that M. de Nemours was asking for her. She felt so resentful that she did not hesitate to send word that she was unwell and could not see him. The Prince did not find this refusal very upsetting—a little coldness, when it is caused by jealousy, is never a bad sign. He went to M. de Clèves's room, told him that he had called on his wife and that he was particularly sorry that she could not receive him since he had something important to tell her which concerned the Vidame de Chartres. In a few words he gave the gist of the matter to M. de Clèves who then immediately took him into his wife's room. Had she not been in the dark, Madame de Clèves would hardly have been able to conceal her agitation or her great surprise that M. de Nemours should come into the room like this, escorted by her husband. M. de Clèves

told her that it was all about a letter, that her help was wanted in the interests of the Vidame, that he himself had to be off at once as the King had just sent for him, but that he would leave her and M. de Nemours to consider what had best be done.

So M. de Nemours found himself alone with Madame de Clèves just as he had hoped.

I come to ask you whether Madame la Dauphine has spoken to you of a letter which Châtelart put into her hands yesterday?

I believe she did say something about it, replied Madame de Clèves, but I don't see what this letter can have to do with my uncle; I assure you he is not even mentioned in it.

It is quite true that he is not mentioned, said M. de Nemours, nevertheless the letter was written to him and it is of the greatest importance for him that you should get it back from Madame la Dauphine.

Madame de Clèves answered, I don't quite understand. Why should he mind this letter being seen? And why should his name be used for getting it back?

If you would be good enough to give me a few minutes, Madame, I will explain everything and also tell you of certain matters which are so important to the Vidame that I would never even have told M. le Prince de Clèves had I not needed his help to come and see you.

I don't think it's very much good telling me anything, said Madame de Clèves, rather sharply, it would be more to the point to go and see the Queen-Dauphine and tell her without beating about the bush the great interest you take in this letter, because she was given to suppose that it belongs to you.

M. de Nemours had never in his life been so gratified by anything as he was now by the bitterness of Madame de Clèves, so much so that he did not feel in any particular hurry to justify himself.

I have no idea what Madame la Dauphine has been given to suppose, he said, but the letter is absolutely nothing to do with me, it was written to the Vidame.

Very well, replied Madame de Clèves, I believe you, but the Queen-Dauphine happens to have been told a different story, and she may find it hard to see why M. le Vidame's letters should come falling out of your pockets. So unless you have some good reason, of which I know nothing, for lying to the Queen-Dauphine, I think, if I were you, I should confess to her.

There is nothing to confess, he said, it's not my letter, and if I wanted to persuade somebody of this fact that person would not be the Queen-Dauphine. Let that be, however. The point is that M. le Vidame is involved in all this and there are one or two things which I think you ought to know, if you will allow me to tell you of them.

Madame de Clèves said nothing so he assumed that she was willing to listen and went on to tell her, as shortly as possible, what he had learned from the Vidame. She listened to the whole story, which was after all astonishing and worthy of attention, with a coldness that gave the impression either that she had not believed a single word or that she found it perfectly uninteresting. Her attitude did not change until M. de Nemours mentioned Madame d'Amboise's note, addressed to the Vidame de Chartres, which

was to prove that all he had been telling her was true. Madame de Clèves knew that this woman was the friend of Madame de Thémines, and at last she found a semblance of truth in what M. de Nemours was saying which made her think that, after all, it was perhaps not his letter. Suddenly, and in spite of herself, her icy indifference began to melt. M. de Nemours, having read out the contents of the note, handed it to her saying that perhaps she would recognize the writing. She could not help taking it, looking at the superscription to see that it was addressed to the Vidame, and then reading it through to make sure that the letter which was asked for was indeed the one in her own possession. M. de Nemours told her everything he could think of to persuade her, and as it is not difficult to believe what we wish to believe, he ended by convincing Madame de Clèves that the letter had never had anything to do with him.

Now she began to discuss the whole matter with him, the difficult and even dangerous position of the Vidame, the naughtiness of his behavior, and how best he could be helped; she marvelled at the Queen's conduct; she confessed to M. de Nemours that she had the letter all the time—in short now that she believed him innocent she was ready to enter, in an open and happy frame of mind, into an affair to which at first she had hardly deigned to listen. They decided that they must not return the letter to Madame la Dauphine for fear that she might show it to Madame de Martigues, who knew Madame de Thémines's handwriting and whose interest in M. le Vidame would be sure to make her guess that it was addressed to him. They also thought that it would be best not to tell the Queen-Dauphine the part about her mother-in-law the Queen. Madame de Clèves, pretending that this was all for her uncle's sake, was more than ready to keep any secrets told her by M. de Nemours.

The Prince would not have spent the whole time talking about the Vidame and his affairs, indeed the freedom with which they were speaking might have made him bolder than he had ever dared to be hitherto had they not been interrupted by a message from the Dauphine commanding Madame de Clèves's immediate presence. So M. de Nemours had to leave her. He went to find the Vidame to tell him that it had seemed more sensible, on leaving him, to go to Madame de Clèves who was his niece than to go straight to the Queen-Dauphine. He was not at a loss for excellent reasons why the Vidame should approve of this proceeding, and for hoping that all would end well.

Madame de Clèves dressed as quickly as she could to go to the Queen-Dauphine. Hardly had she entered her room than this Princess beckoned her up and said in a low voice, I have been waiting these two hours for you, and never, never have I been so much at a loss how to conceal the truth than I have this morning. The Queen has heard people talking about that letter I gave you yesterday and she imagines that the Vidame de Chartres was the one who dropped it. You know that she takes a good deal of interest in him. So she has been asking for the letter and sent to Châtelart for it; he replied that he had given it to me, then they came to me, explaining that it was a charming example of letter writing and the Queen wanted to see it. I did not dare say that you had it, I was afraid she would think I had given it to you because of the Vidame being your uncle and that there was some understanding between him and me—I have already noticed that she can

hardly bear it when he sees me often. So I said that the letter was in a dress I was wearing yesterday and that whoever has the key of my wardrobe had gone out. Quick now, give me this letter, so that I can send it to her. But first I must read it to see if I know the writing.

Madame de Clèves was even more embarrassed than she had expected to be. I don't know what you can do, Madame, she said, because M. de Clèves, to whom I gave it to read, has given it back to M. de Nemours. He came round this morning imploring him to get it from you, and M. de Clèves was unwise enough to own that he had it and then weak enough to give in to the prayers of M. de Nemours.

You have put me in the most embarrassing situation possible, replied Madame la Dauphine, it was really very wrong of you to give that letter to M. de Nemours without asking my permission, since I was the one who gave it to you. Now what do you suggest for me to say to the Queen, and what is she going to make of all this? She will think, quite naturally, that the letter was to do with me and that there is something between me and the Vidame, and nothing will ever persuade her that this letter really belonged to M. de Nemours.

I am in despair at having caused you this trouble, said Madame de Clèves, but really M. de Clèves is to blame and not me.

Not at all, said the Dauphine. It's your fault for giving him the letter. No other woman in the world runs to her husband with all the things she knows.

Yes, I was in the wrong, said Madame de Clèves, but let us see how the fault can be put right instead of examining whose it was.

At this the Queen-Dauphine asked her if she remembered more or less what there was in the letter and she replied that she knew it well, having read it more than once.

In that case, said the Dauphine, you must go and get it written out in an unknown handwriting and I will send it to the Queen. She won't give it to people who have seen it already, but should she do so I will swear it's the one Châtelart gave me and he won't dare contradict me.

Madame de Clèves agreed to this the more willingly since she thought she would send to M. de Nemours for the real letter so that it could be copied word for word, with a similar handwriting, and then, she thought, the Queen would be quite taken in. As soon as she was back in her own room she told her husband of Madame la Dauphine's predicament and begged him to send for M. de Nemours, which he did, and Nemours came with all haste. Madame de Clèves told him what she had already told her husband and asked for the letter, but M. de Nemours replied that he had already given it back to the Vidame de Chartres, who had been so delighted to have it and to find himself out of danger that he had sent it then and there to Madame de Thémines's friend. Madame de Clèves was now in a new difficulty, but at last, after a great deal of consultation, they decided to write the letter from memory; they shut themselves up to work at it, giving orders that nobody was to be admitted and sending all M. de Nemours's people away. The atmosphere of mystery and secrecy thus created had no little charm for the Prince, and even for Madame de Clèves herself. Her conscience was reassured by the presence of her husband and also the

feeling that all this was in the interests of the Vidame de Chartres, and she was conscious only of the pleasure of seeing M. de Nemours without a qualm; she had never been like this before, in such a state of unclouded happiness, and the joy she was feeling made her more lively and playful than M. de Nemours had ever seen her so that his love for for her was increased a hundredfold. Since he also had never enjoyed himself so much his spirits soared and every time Madame de Clèves began thinking about the letter and how to write it, the Prince, instead of seriously helping her, did nothing but interrupt and make jokes. As Madame de Clèves entered into his mood they had been there a long time and the Queen-Dauphine had sent already twice to hurry up Madame de Clèves before half the letter was written.

M. de Nemours forgot all about his friend's interests and was delighted to spin out the time while he was enjoying himself so much; Madame de Clèves was not exactly bored herself and she also quite forgot the interests of her uncle. By four o'clock the letter was hardly finished, and so badly written, the handwriting so hopelessly different from that which they were supposed to be copying, that the Queen could hardly have failed to guess the truth, and, in fact, she was not the least taken in. In spite of all the trouble that was taken to convince her that the letter was meant for M. de Nemours she remained quite certain in her own mind not only that it belonged to the Vidame de Chartres but also that the Queen-Dauphine had something to do with it, and that these two had an understanding. This idea greatly increased her hatred for the Princess. She never forgave her and persecuted her until the moment when she obliged her to leave France. As for the Vidame de Chartres, he was finished as far as the Queen was concerned. It may be that the Cardinal de Lorraine already had an ascendancy over her, or possibly the affair of the letter, which showed her that she had been deceived, put her in the way of unravelling various other deceptions which the Vidame had already practiced on her; in any case he was never able to make it up with her, their liaison came to an end, and she finally encompassed his ruin at the time of the Amboise conspiracy in which he was involved.[55]

When the letter had gone to Madame la Dauphine, M. de Clèves and M. de Nemours went off together, leaving Madame de Clèves alone. As soon as she no longer felt herself carried away by that special joy of being with the person one loves, she came to her senses, as it were, out of a dream, and began to reflect, with some surprise, on the extraordinary difference between her present state of mind and that of the previous evening. She saw herself as she had been, cold and bitter towards M. de Nemours all the time she supposed that Madame de Thémines's letter had been meant for him, and then, as soon as he had managed to convince her that the letter had nothing to do with him, what a happy calm had replaced her bitterness! When she thought how, only the day before, she felt as if she had committed a crime because she had let him see a solicitude for him which was really

[55] French Huguenots and others plotted in 1560 to abduct François II from the town of Amboise and to arrest Charles and François de Guise. The plot failed and the conspirators were executed.

no more than ordinary compassion, and that now by her bitterness she had made it quite clear that she was jealous as only lovers can be, she hardly recognized herself.

Then she went on to think that M. de Nemours was perfectly well aware that she knew of his love, and he must have noticed how this not only made no difference to her behavior with him, even in the very presence of her husband, but that, on the contrary, she had never been so favorably inclined towards him before and that it was she who had made M. de Clèves send for him so that they could spend an afternoon alone together. She began to feel as if she had an understanding with M. de Nemours, as if she was being unfaithful to a husband who least in the world deserved such behavior, and she was bitterly ashamed. Ashamed, too, at appearing so unworthy in the eyes of her lover. But what seemed to her most unbearable of all was the memory of her state of mind during the night and the agony she had been in when she thought that M. de Nemours was being unfaithful to her and that he loved another.

Up to this time she had been quite ignorant of the deadly anxiety which can be caused by suspicion and jealousy; her only care had been how to prevent herself from falling in love with M. de Nemours and she had not yet begun to fear that he might love another. Now, although the suspicions aroused by the letter had been wiped out, they had given her an idea of what it might be like to be deceived, and gave her feelings of suspicion and jealousy she had never had before. Why, she wondered, had it never occurred to her how unlikely it was that such a man as M. de Nemours, whose dealings with women had always been lighthearted in the extreme, should be capable of a sincere and lasting attachment? She felt that it was nearly impossible for her to be content with any love that he could give her.

But even if I could be, she said to herself, what do I want with it? Do I want to allow it? Do I want to respond? Do I want to enter into a love affair? Do I want to fail M. de Clèves? Do I want to fail myself? And finally, do I want to expose myself to the cruel remorse, the deadly sadness which love brings in its train? I am conquered and overcome by an attraction which is luring me on in spite of myself; vain are my resolutions, I thought yesterday all that I am thinking today but today my actions are the exact contrary of yesterday's resolutions. I must tear myself away from M. de Nemours's presence, I must go to the country; however strange my journey may seem I must go and if M. de Clèves insists upon preventing me, or on knowing my reasons, perhaps I shall be obliged to hurt him and to hurt myself by telling him.

So she made up her mind, and stayed at home the rest of the evening without going to find out from Madame la Dauphine what had become of the forged letter. When M. de Clèves came in she told him that she wished to go to the country, that she was not well and felt the need for fresh air. M. de Clèves, who could see by her radiant looks that there was not much the matter with her, made fun of this journey and said that she must be forgetting the marriages of the Princesses and the great tournament. She had not much time as it was, he said, to see about her clothes if she was to compete with the other women. None of this made her change her mind, and she begged her husband to allow her to go to Coulommiers while he was at

Compiègne with the King.[56] Coulommiers was a beautiful house which they were building with much loving care, about a day's journey from Paris. M. de Clèves consented to this, and she went, planning to stay there longer. The King left for Compiègne, where he was only going to be a few days.

M. de Nemours had felt it deeply that he had not seen Madame de Clèves since the delightful afternoon which he had spent with her and which had greatly raised his hopes. His longing to see her was so great that it gave him no rest, so much so that when the King came back to Paris he decided to go to his sister the Duchesse de Mercoeur, who lived in the country not very far from Coulommiers. He suggested to the Vidame that he might go there with him, thinking that they could then visit Madame de Clèves together, and the Vidame accepted willingly.

Madame de Mercoeur was overjoyed to receive them and her only thought was how they could best be amused. She offered them all the pleasures of the countryside. While they were out stag hunting, M. de Nemours got lost in the forest and when he was asking his way back he discovered that he was quite near Coulommiers. As soon as he heard the word Coulommiers he went off at full gallop in the direction which was shown him, without really knowing what he intended to do when he got there. Presently he found himself in the forest going down well-kept rides at random thinking that they probably led to the house. At the end of these rides he came upon a pavilion consisting of one big room flanked by two closets, of which one opened on a flower garden with only a fence between it and the forest, while the other looked down a great avenue in the park. He went into this pavilion and would have stayed there admiring its beauty had he not seen M. and Madame de Clèves, accompanied by a crowd of servants, coming up the avenue. As he had not expected to see M. de Clèves, whom he had left with the King, his first instinct was to hide, and he went into the closet which gave on to the flower garden, thinking he could get out by a gate he saw open to the forest. But when he realized that Madame de Clèves and her husband had sat down in the pavilion while their servants stayed in the park, unable to get to where he was without going through the place where M. and Madame de Clèves were sitting, he could not resist staying to look at the Princess. The temptation of hearing what she had to say to a husband who made him more jealous than any other rival was too much for him.

He heard M. de Clèves say to his wife: But why don't you want to come back to Paris? What is there to keep you in the country? For some time now you have had a taste for solitude which I find very odd and which makes me unhappy since it separates us. You seem to me rather low, more so than usual, and I am afraid something is worrying you.

No, I have nothing on my mind, she replied, looking rather embarrassed, but there is always so much going on at the Court, and one is always in such a crowd that it cannot but be tiring both for body and soul; I must sometimes have a little rest.

Rest, he replied, is not intended for people of your age. You have no

[56] Compiègne, northeast of Paris, was the site of a royal residence.

cause to be over-tired either at Court or at home, and I am afraid that you must like being separated from me.

If you think that, you are being very unfair to me, she replied, with increasing embarrassment. But I do beg of you to leave me here. If you could live here alone with me, and without the mob which always surrounds you, that would make me very happy.

This look and these words show me only too plainly, cried M. de Clèves, that you have a reason for wishing to be alone. I don't know what it can be and I beg you to tell me.

He went on like this for some time, pressing her to give a reason, but without success, though she defended herself in a way which still further aroused his curiosity, by sitting silent, her eyes on the ground. At last she suddenly looked at him, saying, Do not force me to admit something for which I have not the strength, although several times I have planned to do so. Just reflect however upon one thing. Is it prudent for a woman of my age, mistress of her own behavior, to remain unprotected in the midst of that Court?

What idea are you trying to put into my mind, cried M. de Clèves, something I would not even name, for fear of shocking you.

Madame de Clèves did not answer, and her silence confirmed his suspicions: You say nothing, which is as good as to say that I am right.

Very well, she cried, throwing herself to the ground at his knees, I will make a confession such as no husband has ever heard, which the innocence of my actions and intentions gives me strength to make. It is quite true. I have reasons for leaving the Court. I want to escape the dangers into which people of my age sometimes fall. I have never given any sign of weakness and if you allow me to retire from the Court I have no fear that I shall give any, just as I would have had no fear if Madame de Chartres had still been here to help me. However dangerous the decision, I take it gladly so as to keep myself worthy of you. If my thoughts are displeasing to you I beg you a hundred pardons, and at least I can promise never to displease you by my actions. Consider whether what I am about to do does not indicate a greater love and esteem for a husband than anybody ever had before. Guide me, pity me, and love me still, if you can.

While she spoke, M. de Clèves sat with his head in his hands, quite beside himself and without lifting his wife from her knees, but when she had finished and he saw her there, her face wet with tears, so admirably beautiful, he felt that he could die of grief. He lifted her up and kissed her. Oh, Madame, he said, you must pity me too, I deserve it, and please forgive me if in the first moments of the terrible grief I am feeling I have not responded as I should have to such behavior as yours. You seem to me more worthy of esteem and admiration than any woman, but at the same time I am the saddest man who has ever lived. I loved you from the first moment I set eyes on you; your severity could not quench my love, nor the possession of you, and it is as strong today as ever. But I have never been able to make you love me, and now I see you are afraid of loving somebody else. Who is he, this lucky man who makes you afraid? Since when has he attracted you? What way has he found to your heart? The thought that nobody could touch it consoled me for not having done so myself. Now that another has succeeded where I have failed I am jealous as a husband and as

a lover, but the husband's jealousy can no longer exist after such an action as yours. It is too noble not to reassure me. Even as your lover I feel consoled by it. The faith you have in me is priceless, you think highly enough of me to believe that I will never abuse your confidence and you are right, I will never abuse it and I will love you none the less. You have made me miserable by the greatest proof of fidelity that a woman can give her husband; now, finish the story, tell me who it is you wish to avoid?

I beg of you not to ask me that, she said. I have decided never to tell you, it would not be wise for me to do so.

Have no fear, said M. de Clèves, I know too much of the world to imagine that friendship for a husband has ever prevented anybody from falling in love with a wife. One must hate those who do, but one cannot complain; so once more, Madame, I conjure you to tell me what I want to know.

You can't make me do that, she replied, I am strong enough to keep silent when I think it right. My confession was not made from weakness, it required more courage than would have been needed to keep it to myself.

M. de Nemours did not miss a word of this conversation and what Madame de Clèves said made him hardly less jealous than her husband. He was so madly in love with her that he supposed that everybody else was too, imagining many more rivals than in fact there were, and now he cast about to find whom Madame de Clèves could possibly mean. He had often had the impression that she found him quite attractive, but this was based on such trivialities that it did not even occur to him that this passion, so desperate as to require so desperate a remedy, could have been awakened by him. He was so much carried away that he hardly knew what was happening, and he could not forgive M. de Clèves for not insisting more upon his wife naming the man.

M. de Clèves did make every effort to find out, and after he had tried in vain to make her tell it she said: I think you ought to be satisfied with my frankness without asking anything more. Please do not make me sorry for what I have done, but rest assured that I have never, by any action, disclosed my feelings and nothing has ever been said to me which could offend me.

M. de Clèves suddenly burst out, I can't believe you. I remember how embarrassed you seemed the day your portrait was lost. You gave it away, Madame, you gave the portrait I loved so much and to which I had every right! You have not been able to hide your feelings, you are in love, it is known, only your virtue has so far been your guarantee.

How can you possibly think that there is anything false in a confession such as I have freely made? she cried. You must believe me; I have paid dearly for the confidence I ask of you. Please believe that I never gave my portrait. It is true that I saw somebody take it, but I did not want it known that I saw for fear of having things said to me which up to then the person had not dared to say.

Then how do you know this person loves you? asked M. de Clèves. What signs of love has he given you?

Spare me, she said, from having to tell you certain little things which I am ashamed to have noticed and which made me only too well aware of my own weakness.

You are right, he said, it isn't fair of me. You must always refuse when I ask you things like that, but you must not be angry because I ask.

Just then some of the servants who had been waiting round about in the rides came and told M. de Clèves that a gentleman had just come with a message from the King ordering him to be in Paris that evening. M. de Clèves was obliged to go and could say no more to his wife. He implored her to come the next day and begged her to believe that, although he was very sad, he still loved and admired her and that should satisfy her.

As soon as the Prince had gone, and Madame de Clèves was alone, she began to consider what she had done and she was so appalled by it that she could hardly believe it was true. She thought that by her own action she had thrown away her husband's heart and esteem and had dug herself a pit from which she would never be able to escape. She asked herself how she could have done such a dangerous thing, but she did not know, and she hardly thought that she had meant to. The fact that such a confession was unheard of made her realize all its dangers. But when she thought that, although the remedy was desperate, it was really the only way of defending herself against M. de Nemours, it seemed that she had not taken too great a risk and that she need not be so remorseful. She spent the night full of indecision, worry, and fear, but at last some peace came to her and she even found a certain sweetness in having given proofs of fidelity to a husband who so deeply deserved it, and who had shown his love and confidence by the way in which he had received her confession.

Meanwhile M. de Nemours had left the spot where he had overheard a conversation so closely connected with himself and plunged back into the forest. Madame de Clèves's words about the portrait put new life into him, showing that this man she did not hate was he himself, and for a while he gave himself up to this joy; but the mood did not last long, because he soon realized that the very incident by which he had discovered that it was he who had touched her heart must also prove to him that he could not hope to receive any sign from her, and that he would never have his way with a woman who could do such an extraordinary thing. All the same it pleased him to think that he had reduced her to this extremity and he felt that there was something glorious in having won the love of a woman so different from the rest of her sex. So his great happiness, and his unhappiness, were about equal. He was overtaken by nightfall while yet in the forest and had some trouble in finding his way back to Madame de Mercoeur, only arriving there as day was breaking. It was rather difficult to explain what had delayed him; he got out of this as well as he could and went back to Paris with the Vidame that very day.

M. de Nemours, obsessed with his passion and the surprise of what he had overheard, now fell into a not unusual indiscretion, that of talking in general terms of one's own experience, and narrating one's own adventures with fictitious names. During the journey he brought the conversation round to the subject of love, emphasizing the pleasure of loving a person who was really worthy of it. He spoke of the curious manifestations it sometimes produces and finally, unable to bottle up his amazement at what Madame de Clèves had done, he told the Vidame the whole thing, without mentioning any names or saying that it had anything to do with

him. However, the Vidame guessed this at once from the way in which he spoke and the warm admiration he expressed, and he urged him to own up, saying that he had realized for some time that M. de Nemours was violently in love and that it was hardly fair of him to distrust a man who had entrusted him with all the secrets of his own life. But M. de Nemours was too much in love to be able to confess it, and had always kept it from the Vidame in spite of the fact that he was the greatest friend he had at Court. He replied that one of his friends had told him this story under a vow of secrecy, he begged the Vidame never to repeat it and this the Vidame promised. All the same M. de Nemours now repented of having told him so much.

Meanwhile M. de Clèves had gone back to the King, and he was stricken to his very heart with a mortal sadness. Few husbands can ever have loved their wives so passionately, or felt such admiration for them. He did not admire her any the less for what he had just learned, but in a different way, and he was deeply preoccupied trying to guess who it was who had been able to win her heart. He thought first of M. de Nemours, as the most attractive man at the Court, then of the Chevalier de Guise and the Maréchal de Saint André, both of whom he knew had paid attentions to her and had hoped to please her; he felt sure that it must be one of these three and did not seek any further. When he arrived at the Louvre, the King took him to his study and said that he had chosen him to accompany Madame[57] to Spain as he could think of nobody who would perform this mission so well and nobody who would bring so much credit to France as Madame de Clèves. M. de Clèves received the honor of this choice as he should, and indeed he saw it as something which would take his wife from the Court without any apparent change in her mode of life; nevertheless, the departure was still too far off to provide a way out of his difficulty. He wrote at once to Madame de Clèves, telling her what the King had just said, and repeating that he insisted upon her coming back to Paris. She duly returned. When they saw each other they were both overcome by an extraordinary sadness.

M. de Clèves spoke like the honorable man he was, and worthy of that she had done. I have no misgiving over your conduct, he said, your character and your virtue are stronger than you think, so it is not any fear of the future that makes me so unhappy, but my failure to arouse a feeling in you where another has succeeded.

She replied, What can I say? I feel bitterly ashamed when I talk to you. Please try and spare me these cruel conversations; tell me what I must do, arrange matters so that I see nobody, this is all I ask, but do not make me talk any more about something which puts me in such a shameful light, unworthy of you and of myself.

You are quite right, he answered, I am taking advantage of your sweetness and your trust in me. All the same you must feel sorry for the state of mind into which you have thrown me. Remember that whatever you may have said, what you have not said is a certain name, and I am dying to know it. I am not going to ask, but I cannot help telling you that I believe it is

[57] His daughter, who was to marry Philip II.

either the Maréchal de Saint André, the Duc de Nemours, or the Chevalier de Guise.

She blushed deeply and said, I shall not answer that question or say anything which might increase or decrease your suspicions, and if you try to find out by watching my behavior I shall become so nervous that in the end everybody will notice. For God's sake, therefore, arrange, under some pretext of illness, that I see nobody.

No, Madame, it would soon be known that it was a sham, and furthermore I want to put my trust in you alone; both my heart and my reason approve of this course. In your present state of mind I have you under closer guard by giving you your liberty than in any other way I could imagine.

M. de Clèves was not mistaken. The perfect trust he put in his wife strengthened her defenses against M. de Nemours and made her more strict in her resolutions than any restraint of his could possibly have done. So she went about her ordinary business at the Louvre and with the Queen-Dauphine. She avoided the company and the looks of M. de Nemours so assiduously that she almost killed the joy he had felt at thinking himself loved by her; indeed her every action now persuaded him that she did not. He even began to wonder whether he had not dreamed the whole thing, so unlikely did it seem. Madame de Clèves, however, could not conceal her terrible unhappiness, and this reassured him; all the charm in the world could not have increased his love so much as this austere behavior.

One evening when M. and Madame de Clèves were with the Queen somebody mentioned a rumor that the King was appointing one more great noble of the Court to accompany Madame to Spain, and added that it would probably be either the Maréchal de Saint André or the Chevalier de Guise. M. de Clèves's eyes were upon his wife as these names were mentioned, and he saw that she was quite unaffected by them and by the idea that they would be on the journey with her. This made him think that it was neither of them whose presence she dreaded. To clear up his suspicions he went to the Queen's closet where the King was. He stayed there a little while, and then returned to his wife and whispered in her ear that he had just learned it was M. de Nemours who would go with them.

This name, and the thought that she would be obliged to see him every day of a long journey, in the presence of her husband, threw Madame de Clèves into a state of agitation that she could not conceal, and wishing to put it on to something else she said: I think the choice of this Prince is a very bad one from your point of view, as he will have equal honors with you. You ought to try and arrange for some other person to go, not him.

Your fear of M. de Nemours coming with me has nothing to do with honors, Madame, said M. de Clèves. You mind it for a different reason, and your dejection has shown me something that with any other woman I should have learned from her joy. Have no fear, however, what I have just told you is not true; I invented it to confirm my suspicions.

On these words he left the room. He could see that his wife was deeply embarrassed and had no wish to add to her embarrassment by his presence. At that moment M. de Nemours arrived and saw at once the state Madame de Clèves was in. He went up to her and whispered that his regard for her forbade him to ask why she was so far away, even more than usual.

M. de Nemours's voice brought her back to earth, though she did not take in the sense of what he said. Full as she was of her own thoughts, terrified that her husband might see him with her, she said, Oh! for God's sake leave me alone!

Alas, Madame, he replied, I do nothing but leave you alone, what is your complaint? I do not dare speak with you, hardly even look at you, I tremble to go near you. Do I deserve that you should speak to me like this? And why do you imply that your grief has something to do with me?

Madame de Clèves was very angry with herself for having given M. de Nemours an opening to speak more plainly than ever before. She left him without another word and went back to her own room more agitated than ever. Her husband realized that the moment he saw her; he also realized that she dreaded his mentioning what had happened. He followed her into a little room saying, Don't avoid me, I will say nothing that could displease you; I want you to forgive me for startling you just now—I am punished enough for it by what I found out. Of all men M. de Nemours is the one I was most afraid of, and I see your danger. You must control yourself for your own sake and, if possible, for love of me—I don't ask it as a husband, merely as a man whose happiness depends on you and who loves you even more tenderly and passionately than the man your heart prefers.

As he spoke, M. de Clèves broke down and could hardly finish what he was saying. His wife was penetrated to the heart, and bursting into tears she embraced him with such tender sorrow that his condition became little better than hers. They stayed like this a while and separated without having spoken again, indeed they had no more strength for words.

Everything was now ready for the wedding of Madame. The Duke of Alba arrived to marry her[58] and was given a magnificent reception with all the ceremonies proper to such an occasion. To meet him the King sent the Prince de Condé, the Cardinals of Lorraine and Guise, the Dukes of Lorraine, Ferrara, Aumale, Bouillon, Guise, and Nemours, accompanied by gentlemen and pages dressed in their liveries. The King himself awaited the Duke of Alba at the first gate of the Louvre with two hundred gentlemen in waiting, headed by the Constable. When the Duke came up to the King he would have embraced his knees, but the King prevented him, making him walk at his side to the Queen's apartment and then to Madame's, to whom the Duke of Alba gave a magnificent present on behalf of his master. Next he went to Madame Marguerite, the King's sister, and said many complimentary things about the Duke of Savoy, assuring her that he would be there in a very few days.

Parties were given at the Louvre to show all the Court beauties to the Duke of Alba and the Prince of Orange, who accompanied him. Madame de Clèves did not dare stay away, however much she may have wished to do so, for fear of displeasing her husband, who absolutely ordered her to go to them. What decided her to do so even more than this was the absence of M. de Nemours, who had gone to meet the Duke of Savoy and who, even after the arrival of this prince, was obliged to be with him all the time, helping him with everything to do with the wedding ceremonies. So Madame de

[58] As Philip's stand-in for the ceremony.

Clèves saw him much less than usual, and this gave her some degree of tranquillity.

The Vidame de Chartres had by no means forgotten his conversation with M. de Nemours. He felt sure that the story which the Prince had told him was his own and he watched him so carefully that he would very likely have discovered the truth had not the arrival of the Dukes of Alba and Savoy produced a new bustle in the life at Court which prevented him from seeing what otherwise could have enlightened him. His curiosity, as well as a natural inclination to tell everything to the person one loves, made him tell Madame de Martigues about the extraordinary action of the lady who had confessed her passion for another man to her own husband. He assured her that it was undoubtedly M. de Nemours who had inspired this passion and begged her to help him keep this Prince under observation. Madame de Martigues was enchanted with what the Vidame told her; she had always noticed that the Queen-Dauphine was very curious about everything to do with M. de Nemours, and this made her more anxious than ever to find out the truth of the story.

A few days before that which had been chosen for the wedding the Queen-Dauphine gave a supper party for her father-in-law the King and the Duchesse de Valentinois. Madame de Clèves, who had been busy dressing, went to the Louvre later than usual and on the way she met a gentleman from the Queen-Dauphine coming to fetch her. When she arrived in her room the Princess called to her from the bed, where she lay, that she had been waiting impatiently for her.

Madame de Clèves said, I am not sure that I am going to be grateful for this eagerness, as it no doubt comes from something other than a wish to see me.

Quite right, said the Queen-Dauphine, but all the same you should be grateful because I've got a story for you which I know you'll find fascinating.

Madame de Clèves knelt by the bed, and fortunately for her the light did not fall on her face.

You know, said this Queen, how we have been dying to guess what has made the Duc de Nemours so different. I believe I know it now, and it's something that will amaze you. He is madly in love with one of the beauties here at the Court and she loves him too.

It is easy to imagine the pang these words gave to Madame de Clèves; she could not think that they applied to her, since, as far as she knew, nobody had any idea that she loved M. de Nemours.

This doesn't seem very extraordinary to me, she said, considering M. de Nemours's age and how handsome he is.

That's not the surprise, said Madame la Dauphine. It is that this woman who loves M. de Nemours has never given him any reason to suppose that she does, and furthermore, she is so much afraid that she will not always be able to control her passion that she has told her husband everything so that he shall take her away from the Court. And all this comes straight from M. de Nemours himself.

If Madame de Clèves had begun by feeling hurt that she was not involved in this gossip, Madame la Dauphine's last words involved her a good deal too much and she was plunged into despair by them. She could not

speak, and remained with her forehead leaning against the bed while the Queen prattled on, so much absorbed in what she was saying that she paid no attention to this embarrassment. When Madame de Clèves had recovered herself she said, I don't think all this sounds very probable, Madame, and I should like to know who told it to you?

Madame de Martigues told me, and she got it from the Vidame de Chartres—you know he is in love with her. He confided it to her as a secret, and he had it from the Duc de Nemours himself, though he did not mention the name of the lady, nor did he admit to being the man she loved, but the Vidame doesn't doubt for a moment that he is.

As Madame la Dauphine finished speaking somebody came up to the bed. Madame de Clèves was in such a position that she could not see who it was, but she soon guessed when Madame la Dauphine, with a look of cheerful surprise, cried out, Here's the very person; now I'm going to ask him all about it.

So Madame de Clèves realized that the newcomer was the Duc de Nemours. Without turning towards him she threw herself upon Madame la Dauphine and whispered that on no account must she speak to him about this story which he had confided in the Vidame de Chartres or she might cause a quarrel between them. But the Queen-Dauphine only laughed at her, saying she was too cautious, and turned back to M. de Nemours, who was already dressed for the party. He said, in his usual charming way, It seems to me, Madame, if I might hazard a guess, that you were talking about me when I came in, that you were going to ask me something and that Madame de Clèves was trying to stop you.

Quite right, said Madame la Dauphine, but I am not going to give in to her this time. I want you to tell me if a certain story I heard is true, and if you are not the man who loves and is loved by a lady of the Court who carefully keeps her feelings from you but has confessed them to her husband.

Madame de Clèves's distress and confusion were beyond belief, and if death could have come to her rescue at that moment, she would have welcomed it. As for M. de Nemours he was even more appalled, if possible. That Madame la Dauphine, who, he believed, did not hate him, should speak like this in front of Madame de Clèves, her greatest friend, whom she trusted and who trusted her completely, put so many curious ideas into his head that he really could not control his expression. He saw that Madame de Clèves had been put into a terrible situation, and all through his fault; he thought that now he had done something for which she must loathe him, and he was thunderstruck and speechless.

Madame la Dauphine, seeing that he was fearfully taken aback, said to Madame de Clèves, Just look at him and see if it's not his own story.

However, M. de Nemours, recovering from the first shock and seeing the necessity of doing something quickly which would get them out of this dangerous situation, suddenly regained control of his wits and his expression and said, I must confess, Madame, to a good deal of surprise and distress that the Vidame de Chartres should have been so disloyal as to talk about my friend's affairs, which I had told him as a secret. I could have my revenge, he went on, calmly smiling in a way that almost lulled the suspicions of Madame la Dauphine. He has confided various things in me which

are by no means unimportant to him. But, Madame, he went on, I wonder why you do me the honor of laying all this at my door? The Vidame can hardly have said that I was involved since I had told him precisely the contrary. Perhaps the role of a lover might suit me, but that of a beloved—well, Madame, I should have thought you, of all people, would know better.

The Prince was glad of an opportunity to refer to the past, to a time when he had given the Queen-Dauphine a certain understanding, hoping that like this he would change her ideas. She knew what he meant, or thought she did, but without answering she continued to make sport of his distress.

I have been very uneasy, he went on, over my friend, his interests, and the well-deserved reproaches he will make me for having spoken of something which to him is dearer than life itself. All the same he did not tell me everything, and I don't know the name of the woman he loves; all I know is that nobody is more in love, or more to be pitied.

Why so much to be pitied, said Madame la Dauphine, if he is loved in return?

But do you think he is loved, Madame? Do you think that a woman who was really in love would ever have told her husband? It must be somebody who does not know what love is, she probably felt a sort of gratitude for the passion she had inspired. I don't think my friend can flatter himself that there is much hope for him, but all the same, poor creature, he is happy to think that at least he made her fear that she might love him and he would not change places with the luckiest lover in all the world.

Your friend and his passion are easily satisfied, said Madame la Dauphine, and I am beginning to think you are not talking about yourself; indeed it wouldn't take much to make me think, like Madame de Clèves, that none of this can ever have happened.

No, I really don't think it can have, remarked Madame de Clèves, who so far had not said a word, and if it had, how should we know it? It's not very likely that the sort of woman who could do such an extraordinary thing would be foolish enough to go telling people, and you wouldn't expect the husband to, either—if he did he would be most unworthy of his wife's action.

M. de Nemours, seeing that Madame de Clèves suspected her husband, was only too pleased to increase her suspicions. He knew that M. de Clèves was his most dangerous rival. Ah, he said, a husband can commit many imprudences through jealousy, or a wish, perhaps, to find out more than he has been told.

Madame de Clèves was now at the end of her strength and her courage and, unable to bear this conversation any longer, she was just going to say that she felt ill when, luckily for her, the Duchesse de Valentinois arrived and told the Queen-Dauphine that the King was coming. The Queen-Dauphine went into her dressing room to get ready and as Madame de Clèves was about to follow her M. de Nemours came up and said, I would give my life to have a word with you, but of all the many important things I want to say, the most urgent is this. I beg you to believe that if I said anything which the Dauphine might take to herself I did so for reasons far removed from her.

Madame de Clèves pretended not to have heard; she left M. de Nemours without so much as a glance and followed the King who had just appeared. There were a great many people; she got caught up in her train; slipped and fell, and then made this accident an excuse to leave. She pretended that she could not go on, and went home. In truth she was not equal to staying there.

M. de Clèves came to the Louvre and was surprised not to find his wife until they told him of her accident. He went at once to see how she was, found her in bed, and learned that there was nothing much wrong with her. He had not been with her for long before he realized that she was feeling desperately sad and he wondered why.

What's the matter? he said. You seem to have something besides the pain that you speak of.

I have the deepest affliction I could ever have, she replied. What use have you made of the extraordinary, even mad, trust I had in you? Surely I deserved that you should keep the secret, and even had I not deserved it, was it not in your own interest to have kept it? Were you obliged, in your curiosity to know a name I must not tell you, to confide in somebody else so as to find it out? Nothing but this curiosity could have made you commit such a cruel indiscretion, the results of which could hardly be more grievous. The whole story has come out, people have just been telling me about it without knowing that I was the principal party concerned.

What is this, Madame, you accuse me of having repeated something that passed between you and me, you tell me that all is known! I am not going to justify myself, you would not believe me if I did, but of course you must have taken somebody else's story for your own.

But there could not be another story like mine, no other woman would be capable of such a thing! It cannot have been invented or imagined by chance, nobody but me has ever conceived of such a thing. Madame la Dauphine has just told it to me word for word, she got it from the Vidame de Chartres and he from M. de Nemours.

M. de Nemours! cried M. de Clèves, with a despairing gesture. So M. de Nemours knows that you love him and that I know it.

You always pick on M. de Nemours, she replied, and I tell you again that I am not going to make any remark upon your suspicions. I have no idea whether M. de Nemours knows that I figure in this story or that you have allotted him the other character; be that as it may, he told it to the Vidame de Chartres, saying that it had happened to a friend of his who had kept back the lady's name. I suppose this friend of M. de Nemours is also a friend of yours, and that you put yourself in his hands in the hopes of being enlightened.

Is there a friend in all the world to whom one would make such a confidence? said M. de Clèves. It would be a heavy price to pay for enlightenment, to tell a thing one is trying to hide, even from oneself. I think, Madame, that it is rather for you to ask yourself whom you have told, since the secret is more likely to have got out through you than through me. Your burden became too heavy for you, you could no longer bear it alone, and you sought relief in wailing to some confidante who has betrayed you.

You want to crush me to earth, she cried, by accusing me of something you yourself have done, and it is very cruel of you. How can you suspect

me? I was brave enough to speak to you, how can you think I would breathe a word to anybody else?

Indeed, Madame de Clèves, by the confession to her husband, had given such absolute proof of sincerity, and she denied having told anybody else with such vehemence, that M. de Clèves hardly knew what to think. He knew that he had not told anybody and yet a thing which could not possibly be guessed at was now known, and could only be known through one or the other of them. But to him what mattered most was that somebody was now in possession of this secret, and that soon it must become common knowledge.

These selfsame thoughts were also passing through the mind of Madame de Clèves. She found it equally impossible to believe that her husband had, or had not, talked, though M. de Nemours's words about the indiscretion of husbands seemed so directly related to M. de Clèves's state of mind that she could hardly believe it was said by accident and they made her think that M. de Clèves must have abused her trust in him. They were both so much absorbed that they remained a long while without saying a word, only breaking this silence to repeat what had already been said several times; finally they were more estranged in heart and soul than they had ever been.

It is not difficult to imagine what sort of a night each of them spent. M. de Clèves's reserves of fortitude were already exhausted by his efforts to endure the agonizing spectacle of his adored wife in love with somebody else. He could bear it no more, and indeed felt that he ought not to bear something so prejudicial to his good name. He no longer knew what to think of his wife, he no longer knew what he ought to make her do or how he himself ought to behave; on every hand he saw some deadly peril. Finally, after much painful indecision, he made up his mind, in view of the Spanish journey, to do nothing which might increase suspicion or knowledge of his unhappy state. He went to find Madame de Clèves, and told her that it was no longer a question of finding out which of them had given away the secret but of making it quite obvious that the story was a fable and nothing to do with her, that he relied on her to persuade M. de Nemours and the others of this, by treating him with all the coldness and strictness due to a man who was letting her see that he loved her; thus she would easily disabuse him of the idea that she had a fancy for him; there was no point in worrying about what he might be thinking because, so long as she did not weaken, these thoughts would disappear of their own accord. Above all, he said, it was absolutely essential for her to go in the ordinary way to the Louvre and to all the parties.

Then M. de Clèves left his wife without waiting for an answer.

She thought there was a great deal in what he said, and that her anger with M. de Nemours would make it quite easy for her to carry out his wishes, though she knew it would not be easy to look happy and carefree at the wedding ceremonies. Since, however, she had been chosen from among many ladies to carry the Dauphine's train she could hardly have got out of doing so without causing a great deal of gossip and curiosity as to what her reason might be. So she made up her mind to a tremendous effort, and, taking the whole of the day to prepare for it, she retired alone to her closet and gave herself over to her worries. What seemed to her the

worst feature of the whole affair was that she now had this cause for anger against M. de Nemours, for whom, try as she might, she could find no justification. She could not doubt that he had told the story to the Vidame de Chartres (he had owned as much); neither could she doubt, from the way in which he had spoken, that he knew it had to do with her. How could she forgive such an indiscretion? And what could have come over this Prince, whose discretion hitherto had so touched her heart? She said to herself, he was discreet enough while he thought he had nothing to hope for, but the mere hint of success, even if very uncertain, quite changed his outlook. As soon as he thought himself beloved he wanted everybody to know it and said as much as he could; I never admitted to loving him, he guessed it, and let it be seen that he had guessed. Had he been certain he would have acted in the same way. How mistaken I was when I thought there existed a man capable of hiding anything which flattered his own vanity! And it is for the sake of this man, who seemed to me so different, that I find myself on a level with other women, I, who used to be different indeed; I have thrown away the love and esteem of a husband who should have been my joy and soon everybody will know that I am the victim of a wild and uncontrollable passion—M. de Nemours knows it already. Yet it was in order to avoid these very misfortunes that I risked my peace of mind, perhaps even life itself.

These sad thoughts called forth a torrent of tears; but in her heart she knew quite well that she could have borne anything had she been satisfied with M. de Nemours's behavior.

This Prince, on his side, was in no better case. The thought of his indiscretion in having spoken to the Vidame de Chartres, and its cruel consequences, tormented him, he could hardly bear to think of the embarrassment and misery he had seen on Madame de Clèves's face; he was inconsolable at some of the things he had said to her about this affair which, though they may have been romantic in themselves, seemed to him now both coarse and rude, since they showed that he knew she was the lady in love and that he was the object of that love. He only longed to speak with her, though feeling that he ought to dread this rather than wish for it.

What could I say to her? Underline what I have already said too definitely? Force her to see that I know she loves me—I who have never even dared to tell her of my love? Should I begin by speaking openly about my passion for her like a man emboldened by hope? How can I even think of approaching her? The very sight of me must upset her now. I cannot justify myself, I have no excuse, I am quite simply unworthy that she should look at me and I cannot hope that she ever will again. She sought a defense against me, and might never have found one had I myself not put it into her hands. By my imprudence I have thrown away the distinction and happiness of being loved by this good and exquisite woman. I would not even have minded that so much had I not dealt her such a blow at the same time. It is for the harm I have done her that I am suffering, even more than for that I have done myself in her eyes.

These thoughts went round and round in M. de Nemours's brain, he was tormented by them, and all the time he was longing to speak to Madame de Clèves. He considered how he could manage this, he thought of writing to her, but at last decided that, having put himself in the wrong,

and taking her present mood into account, the best would be to show his deep respect by keeping a sorrowful silence, to let her see that he did not dare to approach her, and to trust that time, luck, and her inclination would do something for him. He resolved not to reproach the Vidame de Chartres for his breach of confidence, for fear of strengthening his suspicions.

Madame's betrothal took place the next day, and her wedding the day after that, and these ceremonies kept the whole Court so busy that it was not difficult for Madame de Clèves and M. de Nemours to conceal their agitation. Madame la Dauphine hardly mentioned the conversation with M. de Nemours to Madame de Clèves, and M. de Clèves made a point of only speaking to her about current events, so that she was not nearly as much embarrassed as she had expected to be.

The engagement took place at the Louvre, and after a banquet and a ball the whole of the royal household went to sleep, as was the custom, at the Bishop's Palace. Next morning the Duke of Alba, who usually dressed with great simplicity, wore a coat of cloth of gold shot with flame, yellow, and black, all embroidered with precious stones, and on his head a closed crown. The Prince of Orange, magnificent, followed by the servants in his livery and all the other Spaniards followed by theirs, came for the Duke of Alba at the Hôtel de Villeroi where he was staying, and then all advanced upon the Bishop's Palace, marching in fours. As soon as he had arrived there was a procession to the Church, the King leading Madame, who also had a closed crown. Her train was carried by Mesdemoiselles de Montpensier and Longueville. The Queen came next, without a crown, and after her the Queen-Dauphine, Madame the King's sister, Madame de Lorraine, and the Queen of Navarre, all of whom had their trains carried by Princesses. The attendants of the Queens and the Princesses were magnificently dressed in the same colors as themselves, so that one could see which their ladies were by the colors of their gowns. A platform had been specially built inside the Church; they all mounted on to this and the marriage ceremonies were then performed. Afterwards they dined at the Bishop's Palace, leaving at about five o'clock to go to the palace where a banquet was given for members of the parliament, the royal households, and dignitaries of the town. The King, the Queens, the Princes and Princesses, ate from the marble table in the great hall of the palace, the Duke of Alba sitting next the new Queen of Spain. A step or two below the marble table, on the King's right hand, was a table for ambassadors, archbishops, and knights of the various orders, while on the other side was a table for members of the parliament.

The Duc de Guise, dressed in gold frieze, served the King as Great Chamberlain, M. le Prince de Condé as Steward of the Household, and the Duc de Nemours as Cup-bearer. When the tables had been removed the ball began, with interludes consisting of ballets and wonderful theatrical machinery. Finally, after midnight, the King and the whole Court went back to the Louvre. Sad though Madame de Clèves might have been feeling, her beauty was unaffected, in the eyes of the world and above all in those of M. de Nemours it seemed incomparable. He did not venture to speak to her, though he could easily have done so during the ceremonies, but let her see how subdued he was and how respectfully aloof, so much so

that she began to think him less to blame although he had not said anything which could justify his behavior. For the next few days his conduct was the same and it made the same impression upon Madame de Clèves.

At last the day of the tournament arrived. The Queens went to their places in the galleries and on the platforms specially built for them.

The four champions appeared at the ends of the lists, with a number of horses and men in livery, the most magnificent sight that had ever been seen in France.

The King always had the same colors, white and black, which he wore in honor of Madame de Valentinois, who was a widow. The Duke of Ferrara and his retinue were in yellow and red. M. de Guise appeared in flesh-pink and white, and everybody wondered why he had chosen these colors until it was remembered that they were those of a certain beauty he had loved before her marriage, and whom he still loved though he no longer dared allow her to see it. M. de Nemours had yellow and black and the reason for this was sought in vain by all but Madame de Clèves, who guessed it without difficulty, remembering that she had once said in front of him that she loved yellow and was sorry that being so fair it did not suit her. The Prince therefore felt he could take it without indiscretion; Madame de Clèves never wore it and nobody could think that it was her color.

The champions now performed unheard-of prodigies of skill; the King was the best horseman in the land, yet it was difficult to choose between them. M. de Nemours showed a grace in all his movements that might have inclined in his favor ladies less interested than Madame de Clèves. As soon as she saw him appear at the end of the lists she felt an extraordinary emotion, and she could scarcely conceal her joy each time he won a heat. Towards evening, when it was nearly over and everybody was getting ready to go home, the King, most unluckily for his country, decided to break one more lance. He sent for the Comte de Montgomery, who was very skilled, to come into the lists. The Count begged the King to be let off, making all the excuses he could think of, but the King, almost angrily, insisted.

Then the Queen sent a message to the King begging him to give over, to be content with his great success and come and join her.

He replied that it was in her honor that he was going to fight once more, and entered the ring. She sent the Duke of Savoy to beg him a second time, but to no avail. He fought, the lances were shattered, and a splinter from that of M. de Montgomery lodged in his eye. He at once fell from his horse, his equerries and M. de Montmorency, one of the marshals, ran to him, thunderstruck to see him wounded. But the King was perfectly calm, saying that it was very slight and that he forgave the Comte de Montgomery. So this day, which was to have been so delightful, ended in a dire calamity causing an agitation and sorrow which can easily be imagined.

As soon as the King had been put to bed the surgeons who examined his wound pronounced it to be very serious, and now the Constable remembered the prophecy which had been made to the King that he would be killed in single combat, and he felt sure that this prophecy was about to be fulfilled. The King of Spain, who was at Brussels, was informed of the accident and immediately sent his own doctor, a man of great reputation, but he considered that there was no hope for the King.

A Court, divided as this one was and full of opposing interests, would

naturally be thrown into a fever of agitation on the eve of so momentous an
event; nevertheless, all the intrigues went on behind closed doors and ap-
parently there was only one absorbing preoccupation, the King's health.
The Queens, the Princes and Princesses hardly left his antechamber.

Madame de Clèves was supposed to be there too. But so, she knew,
would M. de Nemours and then she would never be able to hide her em-
barrassment from the eyes of her husband; she realized, too, that the mere
presence of this Prince justified him in her eyes and melted her resolutions.
She therefore pretended to be ill. The Court had other things to think of
than her behavior and whether she was really ill or not; her husband was
the only person who knew the truth, and she did not mind his knowing it.
So she remained at home, indifferent to the great change there was going
to be and free to think at leisure of her own affairs.

Everybody was with the King. M. de Clèves came back from time to time
with the latest bulletin. He was exactly the same as he had always been with
her except that when they were alone together he was a little cooler and
more reserved. He never spoke of what had passed between them and she,
even had she thought it wise, did not feel strong enough to broach the
subject.

M. de Nemours, who had expected a chance of speaking with Madame
de Clèves, was surprised and upset not even to have the joy of seeing her.

The King's wound was so serious that on the seventh day the doctors
gave him up. He showed great fortitude in the face of death, all the more
creditable considering that he was losing his life through a miserable acci-
dent, dying in his prime, happy, adored by his people, and loved by a
mistress with whom he was madly in love. On the eve of his death he had
Madame, his sister, married to the Duke of Savoy without any ceremony.

The Duchesse de Valentinois's state of mind can be imagined. The
Queen would not allow her to see the King, and sent to her for the seals of
this Prince and the crown jewels which she always kept. The Duchess asked
whether the King were dead, and on being told that he was not she said, In
that case I own no other master and nobody can make me give up what he
confided to me.

As soon as he had expired, at the Château de Tournelles, the Dukes of
Ferrara, Guise, and Nemours conducted the Queen-Mother, the new King,
and the Queen, his wife, to the Louvre. The Queen-Mother was led by M.
de Nemours. As they started she went back a few steps and told her
daughter-in-law the Queen that now it was her place to go first, but it was
easy to see that these fair words were spoken with more bitterness than
courtesy.

PART FOUR

The Cardinal de Lorraine's influence with the Queen-Mother was now
paramount and the Vidame de Chartres was quite out of favor. He did not
mind this as much as he ought to have; he was glad to be free to indulge in
his love for Madame de Martigues. The Cardinal had had plenty of time,

during the ten days of the King's illness, to lay his schemes and to make the Queen take decisions which would further them. Thus, as soon as the King was dead the Queen ordered the Constable to remain with his body at Tournelles for the usual ceremonies, a task which separated him from all that was going on and took away his liberty of action. He sent a messenger to the King of Navarre urging him to come with all speed so that together they might make a stand against great acquisition of power by the Guise brothers.

The Duc de Guise was given command of the army and the Cardinal de Lorraine put in charge of finance. The Duchesse de Valentinois was driven from the Court, the Cardinal de Tournon, an open enemy of the Constable, was recalled as was the Chancelier Olivier, open enemy of the Duchesse de Valentinois; in short the whole aspect of the Court was changed. The Duc de Guise carried the King's mantle during the funeral ceremonies exactly as if he had been a Prince of the Blood; he and his brothers ruled supreme, not only because of the Cardinal's influence over the Queen but because this Princess supposed that she would be able to get rid of them if they displeased her, which she could never have done with the Constable, supported as he was by Princes of the Blood.

When the mourning ceremonies were over the Constable went to the Louvre and was coldly received by the new King. He had hoped to see him alone, but the King sent for the Guises and said, in front of them, that he advised him to take a rest, that the army and finances had been disposed of, and that he would send for him if he ever needed him. The Queen-Mother showed him even less favor than had her son; she reproached him for having told the late King that his children did not look like him.

The King of Navarre arrived and his reception was no better. The Prince de Condé, who had less self-control than his brother, complained to everybody, to no avail however; he was simply removed from the Court and sent to Flanders to sign the ratification of the peace treaty. The King of Navarre was shown a forged letter, purporting to come from the King of Spain, accusing him of having designs on his fortresses; it was suggested to him that his land was in danger and that he had better go back to Béarn.[59] The Queen provided him with the means of doing so, putting Madame Elizabeth in his charge and even making him go ahead of this Princess. Thus there was not a single person left at the Court who could balance the power of the House of Guise.

Although M. de Clèves was annoyed at not going with Madame Elizabeth he could not say anything in view of the importance of the substitute, and indeed it was not so much for the honors which the mission would have brought that he regretted it as the fact that it would have been a way of removing his wife from the Court without its looking as if he wanted to do so.

A few days after the King's death it was decided to go to Rheims for the Coronation.[60] As soon as this journey was mooted Madame de Clèves, who still kept to her room, pretended to be ill and begged her husband to let her

[59] Region in southwest France adjoining the Basque province of Navarre.
[60] Kings of France were traditionally crowned in the great cathedral at Rheims.

off following the Court and to allow her to go, for a change of air, to Coulommiers. He replied that he had no wish to find out whether it was really her health which prevented her from going to Rheims, but that in any case he gave his consent. It was no trouble to him, he had already come to the same decision. Highly though he rated his wife's virtue he saw that it would not be prudent to expose it any longer to the sight of the man she loved.

M. de Nemours soon found out that Madame de Clèves was not going with the Court, and unable to bear going without having seen her he went to call on the eve of his departure, as late as he decently could, in the hopes of finding her alone. Luck was with him. As he came into the courtyard he found Madame de Nevers and Madame de Martigues, who were leaving and who told him that she was alone. He went upstairs in a state of agitation which was nothing compared with that of Madame de Clèves when she heard that M. de Nemours was there to see her.

Fears that he might speak of his passion, of giving too favorable a reply, of the anxiety this visit would cause her husband, of giving an account of it to her husband or of hiding it from him, assailed her and threw her into such a fever of embarrassment that she resolved to avoid the one thing that perhaps she longed for most in the world. She sent one of her maids to M. de Nemours, who was in her antechamber, to say that she had been taken ill and regretted that she must decline the honor he wished to do her. What sorrow for this Prince, not only not to have seen Madame de Clèves but that this should have been so by her own wish. He left the next day feeling that there was now nothing to hope for; he had not spoken to her since the conversation with Madame la Dauphine and he had reason to suppose that he had ruined his own chances of success by what he had told the Vidame. In short, as he left his pain was deeply tinged with bitterness.

As soon as Madame de Clèves had recovered from her first emotion at the idea of a visit from the Duke, all the reasons for not seeing him melted away and she even thought she had been in the wrong. Had she dared to do so, had there still been time, she would have called him back.

Meanwhile, Mesdames de Nevers and Martigues went on to the Queen-Dauphine and there they found M. de Clèves. This Princess asked where they had been and they said they had just come from Madame de Clèves where they had spent the afternoon with quite a lot of people but that only M. de Nemours was there when they left.

These words, which seemed harmless to them, were not so to M. de Clèves. Although he must have realized that M. de Nemours had numerous opportunities of speaking with his wife, the idea of him alone with her, able to tell her of his love, suddenly came upon him with all the force of novelty, and he was more violently jealous than he had ever been. He could not stay at the Queen's and went home hardly knowing why he went or whether he intended to interrupt M. de Nemours. When he came to his house he looked for signs that M. de Nemours was still there, was relieved to see that he was not, and comforted to think that he could not have stayed very long.

Then he imagined that perhaps it was not of M. de Nemours that he ought to be jealous, and although he had no real doubts he tried to make

himself doubt it; but so many things pointed to him that this mood of willful indecision did not last long. He went straight to his wife's room, and after having spoken awhile on trivial subjects he could not resist asking what she had done and whom she had seen, and she gave him an account of everything. When she did not mention M. de Nemours he asked her, trembling with emotion, if that was everybody she had seen, so as to give her the opportunity to name this Prince and thus spare him the sorrow of feeling that she was not being quite frank with him. As she had not seen him she did not name him, and M. de Clèves then spoke in a voice which betrayed his anguish. And what about M. de Nemours? Have you not seen him? Perhaps you have forgotten?

No, she replied, I didn't see him. I felt unwell and sent him one of my maids to make my excuses.

You only felt ill for him, said M. de Clèves. You saw everybody else. Why this special behavior for M. de Nemours? Why is he not the same as anyone else to you? Why let him see that he frightens you, making use of the power his love gives you over him? Would you dare refuse to see him if he did not know quite well that there is more than mere incivility behind your refusal? Why must you be so severe with him? From somebody like you everything counts as a favor except indifference.

I never thought, suspicious though you may be of M. de Nemours, that you could reproach me with not having seen him, said Madame de Clèves.

Yes, I do reproach you, and with reason. Why refuse to see him if he has never said anything to you? The answer is that he has spoken, if his silence had been sole witness to his passion it could never have affected you so deeply. You have not been able to tell me the whole truth, you have hidden the greater part of it from me, repenting even of the little you did tell and having no strength to go on. I am more wretched than I thought, the most wretched of all men. You are my wife, I love you like a mistress, I know you are in love with another, and he is the most fascinating man at Court who sees you every day and is aware that you love him—I must have been mad to think that you would be able to overcome your passion for him.

Madame de Clèves replied sadly, I do not know whether you were wrong when you approved of an action as extraordinary as mine, but I cannot help wondering whether I was right in thinking that you would treat me with fairness.

Then stop wondering, he answered, because I can tell you. You were not right. What you expected from me was as impossible as what I expected from you. How could you hope that I should be reasonable? I suppose you forgot that I loved you madly and that I was your husband? One or other might drive a man to extremities, but what about both together? Alas, how else do they affect me? I have violent and wavering emotions which I cannot control—I feel myself no longer worthy of you, and you no longer worthy of me. I adore and hate you; I offend you and ask your forgiveness; I admire you and am ashamed to do so. There is no peace in me nor any reason either. I don't know how I have survived the words you spoke at Coulommiers, or the day you heard from Madame la Dauphine that your story was public property. I have no means of guessing how it came out, or what may have passed on the subject between yourself and M. de

Nemours—you will never explain this nor do I ask that you should, I only ask you to bear in mind that you have made me the unhappiest man in the world.

On these words M. de Clèves left his wife's room, and went off the next day without seeing her again, but he wrote her a letter full of affliction, courtesy, and affection. Her reply was so touching, so reassuring as to her past and future conduct, that, since all this was founded upon truth and she really meant what she wrote, it made a great impression on M. de Clèves. He felt more easy in his mind, especially as M. de Nemours was also with the King, and no longer in the same place as Madame de Clèves. When this Princess was with her husband, his love for her, her candid behavior, her friendship for him, and her duty towards him were enough to drive the image of M. de Nemours out of his heart, but these impressions only lasted a little while and then he reverted to his original idea which was becoming more and more real to him.

For a day or two after the Duc de Nemours had left the Court Madame de Clèves hardly noticed his absence; soon, however, she began to feel it cruelly. Since the beginning of her love for him not a day had passed but she could look for a meeting with alternate longing and apprehension, and she suffered to think that chance could no longer bring them face to face. She went to Coulommiers, taking with her two big pictures which had been copied for her from originals painted for Madame de Valentinois's beautiful house at Anet and which represented all the outstanding events of the King's reign. Among others there was the siege of Metz, with portraits of all those who had distinguished themselves there; M. de Nemours was one of these and perhaps that may have been the reason why Madame de Clèves was so anxious to own these paintings.

Madame de Martigues, who had been unable to leave with the Court, promised her to spend a few days at Coulommiers. The fact that they were both in such favor with the Queen had never caused any jealousy between them and they were friends, though they did not confide all their emotions to each other. Madame de Clèves knew that Madame de Martigues loved the Vidame but Madame de Martigues did not know that Madame de Clèves loved and was loved by M. de Nemours. Madame de Clèves, as niece of the Vidame, was doubly dear to Madame de Martigues, and she loved her in return the more so for knowing that she was also somebody with a passion, and that for an intimate friend of her own beloved.

So Madame de Martigues came, as she had promised, to Coulommiers, and there she found her friend leading a very solitary existence; indeed she took special steps to be left quite alone so that she could spend her evenings, without any servants, in the garden.

She would go to the pavilion where M. de Nemours had heard her speak, into the room that opened on the garden, while her women and servants stayed in the other small room or in the pavilion, only going to her if she called them. Madame de Martigues had never seen Coulommiers and was amazed by all its many beauties, above all the charm of this pavilion; she and Madame de Clèves sat there every evening. These two young women, both passionately in love, alone together in such a beautiful spot, could never come to the end of all they had to say and though they made no confidences they took great pleasure in each other's company.

Madame de Martigues would have been sorry to leave Coulommiers had she not been going to a place where she was to find the Vidame. She left for Chambord,[61] where the Court then was.

The Coronation had been celebrated at Rheims, by the Cardinal de Lorraine, and the rest of the summer was to be spent at Chambord, which had just been built. The Queen was very happy to see Madame de Martigues again and asked her to tell about Madame de Clèves and what she did with herself in the country. M. de Nemours and M. de Clèves were both in the Queen's room at the time. Madame de Martigues, who had thought Coulommiers delightful, told of all its beauties and extended herself in a description of the forest pavilion, describing how Madame de Clèves loved to spend part of the night there alone. M. de Nemours, knowing the spot well enough to understand what she was talking about, thought it not impossible that he could see Madame de Clèves there without her seeing him. He asked Madame de Martigues some questions to make more certain, and M. de Clèves, who had been watching him all the time she was speaking and thought he could guess exactly what was passing through his mind, was confirmed in his thought when he heard these questions. He felt sure that this Prince was planning to go and see his wife, nor was he mistaken. M. de Nemours was so much taken up with the idea that, after thinking all night how it could be put into practice, next morning he asked the King's permission, on some pretext or other which he invented, to take leave and go to Paris.

M. de Clèves had no doubts as to the motive of this departure, and he now decided that he would find out once and for all how his wife behaved, and put an end to the cruel suspense in which he lived. He would have liked to leave at the same time as M. de Nemours, and to see for himself, from some hiding place, whether this journey was successful, but he was afraid that his departure might seem rather odd, and that M. de Nemours, hearing of it, would change his plans. So he decided to trust one of his gentlemen, upon whose fidelity and good sense he could rely. He told him everything, of his own dilemma and of the virtuous conduct till then of Madame de Clèves, and ordered him to follow M. de Nemours, keep him under observation, and see whether he was not bound for Coulommiers and did not go into the garden after nightfall.

The gentleman, who was quite competent to handle an affair of this sort, did so with the greatest exactness. He followed M. de Nemours to a village half a league from Coulommiers where the Prince settled down, no doubt, he thought, to wait for the night. The gentleman decided not to stay with him; he pushed on to a spot in the forest where it seemed that M. de Nemours would be likely to pass by. He was perfectly right in all his conjectures. As soon as night fell he heard footsteps, and, though it was very dark, he easily recognized M. de Nemours. He saw him walk round the garden as though listening if anybody was there and seeking a place by which he could easily enter it. The fence was high; beyond that there was another to keep people out. It was quite difficult to get over them.

However, M. de Nemours managed somehow, and once in the garden he easily discovered the whereabouts of Madame de Clèves. He saw lights

[61] Village in north-central France, site of a large palace built by François I.

in the little room; all its windows were wide open; in a state of mind which can be imagined, he stole along the fence and placed himself behind one of the french windows to see what she was doing. She was alone and looking so beautiful that he could hardly control his emotion at the sight of her. It was a hot evening and she wore nothing over her head and bosom but her hair, which hung loose. She lay on a day-bed and on a table beside her there were several baskets full of ribbons. She was picking over these ribbons and choosing out certain ones, and M. de Nemours saw that these were of the very colors he had carried at the tournament, and then he saw that she was making knots and bows to go on an unusual malacca cane which, having used it for some time, he had given to his sister. Madame de Clèves had taken it from her without seeming to recognize it as having once been his. She worked away with a grace and a look of pure goodness which reflected the state of her soul; then, when she had finished, she took a candlestick and went up to a big table which stood before the picture of the siege of Metz in which was a portrait of M. de Nemours. She sat down and gazed at this portrait with a far-away look that only love can give.

How to express the feelings of M. de Nemours at this moment? What lover can ever have seen, at night, in the most perfect spot imaginable, the person he adored, have seen her without her knowing it and have seen that she was only occupied with things which had to do with himself and the love she kept hidden from him? Such things had never been enjoyed or imagined by any other lover. The Prince was beside himself, so much so that he forgot the precious minutes were ticking away as he stood there looking at Madame de Clèves. When he was a little more himself again he thought he had better wait to speak to her until she went into the garden— it seemed the safest plan as then she would be further from her women; but then, seeing that she stayed where she was, he decided to go in. Just as he was about to do so, however, he was seized with misgivings; she might, he thought, be furious with him, and he could not bear the idea that that sweet expression might change to one of anger on his account. He began to think that he had been incredibly foolish, not in having come to see Madame de Clèves, but to have considered for a moment letting her see him. It would clearly be the height of extravagance to take by surprise, in the middle of the night, a lady to whom he had never yet spoken of love. He also thought there was little hope that she would listen to him, and that, on the contrary, she would very rightly be angry at the dangerous position he was putting her in. His courage failed him, and several times he was on the point of going away without showing himself. Finally, driven by his intense longing to speak to her, and reassured by the hopeful signs he had just seen, he did advance a few steps. He was so much agitated that a scarf he was wearing caught in the window and he made a little noise. Madame de Clèves turned her head; and it may have been her obsession with this Prince, or perhaps enough light fell upon him for her to see who it was, in any case she thought she recognized him, and without a moment's hesitation, without another look towards him, she went back to her women. She was extremely agitated and, in order to hide the fact, she pretended to be ill, thinking that this would give her people something to occupy them and that M. de Nemours would have more time to escape.

On further reflection, however, she felt that she must have made a

mistake and that she had only fancied it was M. de Nemours whom she had seen. She knew him to be at Chambord, and it seemed most unlikely that he would attempt anything so dangerous. Several times she thought of going back to the little room and looking into the garden to see if anyone was there, and very likely hoped quite as much as she feared to find M. de Nemours, but in the end prudence prevailed and she decided it was better to stay in doubt as she was, rather than risk trying to find out. All the same, it was a long time before she could bring herself to leave a spot so near, perhaps, to this Prince, and when at last she got back to the house day had nearly dawned.

M. de Nemours had remained in the garden and while lights were still burning he did not despair of seeing Madame de Clèves again, although he felt sure she had recognized him and had gone away in order to avoid him; but when he saw the doors being shut he realized that he had no more to hope for and went to find his horse, quite near to the place where M. de Clèves's gentleman was waiting. The gentleman then followed him back to the village he had set out from the previous evening.

M. de Nemours decided to spend the day there so that he could go back that night to Coulommiers and see whether Madame de Clèves would be cruel enough to run away again, or even to keep herself hidden from him. Although it was a joy to have seen her so deeply absorbed in thoughts of him, he was very much cast down that her first instinct should have been to escape.

Never has there been a passion so tender and so ardent as then possessed this Prince. Behind the house where he was hiding there ran a little willow-bordered stream; here he wandered, and, going as far as he could so that nobody should see or hear him, he gave way to transports of love. His heart was so full that he even wept a little, tears which had nothing to do with grief but were really a distillation of love's sweet charm. He passed in review all Madame de Clèves's actions since first he had fallen in love with her, remembering how perfectly correct she had always been, in spite of her love for him. For after all, he said, she does love me, she does love me, there can be no doubt of that, pledges and promises, favors and indulgences, could not make me more certain of it than what I have seen with my own eyes. Yet I am treated as if I were loathed; I had hoped that time would be on my side, but no! The defense against me and against herself goes on. If I were not loved I could think how best to make her fall in love, but I do attract her, I am loved, and it is concealed from me. What have I to hope for and what change of fortune can there ever be for me? I am loved by this most adorable creature, and if this brings happiness it also brings agony. Beautiful Princess, he cried, show me your true feelings! Show them to me once, but one little moment and then I can bear your severity for evermore. Only look at me as you looked this night at my portrait—how could you look so sweetly at my portrait and then so cruelly fly from my presence? What is it? Why do you fear my love? You love me, useless to try and conceal the fact, you have given me absolute proofs, in spite of yourself. Allow me to enjoy this happiness and stop cutting me to the heart. Is it possible that Madame de Clèves loves me and even so I am unhappy? How beautiful she looked in the night! How could I have resisted throwing myself at her feet? If I had done so perhaps I might have

stopped her from running away by assuring her of my deep respect. All the same it is possible that she did not recognize me; perhaps I am torturing myself unnecessarily and it was simply the sight of a man, at so strange an hour, that terrified her.

All day these thoughts turned round in M. de Nemours's head. He could hardly wait for night to fall and as soon as it did he made for Coulommiers. M. de Clèves's gentleman, who had now assumed a disguise to make himself more unobtrusive, followed him to the same spot as the night before and once more saw him enter the garden. The Prince soon realized that Madame de Clèves had not wanted to risk his trying to see her again, every door was shut; he went all round the building looking for lights but there was nothing.

Madame de Clèves, guessing that M. de Nemours would probably come back, had stayed in her own room. She feared that another time she might not have the strength to run away and she would not put herself in a position in which she might be unable to keep up the standard of behavior she had set herself.

M. de Nemours, although he had no longer the slightest hope of seeking her, could not bring himself to leave a place to which she so often came, and spent the whole night in the garden, finding a certain consolation in the sight of objects on which her eyes rested every day. The sun rose before he thought of going away, but at last fear of being discovered obliged him to do so.

He could not bear to leave for good without seeing Madame le Clèves at all, so he went to Madame de Mercoeur, who was at her house in the neighborhood. She was extremely surprised to see her brother but he invented a reason for his journey, plausible enough to take her in, and very cleverly got her to suggest, herself, that they should go and call on Madame de Clèves. This plan was executed the very same day, M. de Nemours telling his sister that he would have to part from her at Coulommiers to hurry back to the King, thinking that he could let her be the first to leave and thus make certain of being able to speak with Madame de Clèves.

When they arrived she was out walking in a great avenue which bordered the garden. The sight of M. de Nemours upset her terribly, and left her in no doubt that it was he whom she had seen two nights before, and she felt furious with him for behaving so rashly.

The Prince saw a certain coldness in her look; it hurt him bitterly. They talked of nothing in particular, but he did so with such wit, and in such obvious admiration of Madame de Clèves, that she could not help thawing a little under his charm. As soon as he felt sure of his ground he asked to go and see the pavilion in the forest, speaking of it as the most delicious spot imaginable and describing it in such detail that Madame de Mercoeur said he must often have been there as he seemed to know it so well. But Madame de Clèves remarked that it was only just finished and she was sure M. de Nemours had never been there.

On the contrary, said M. de Nemours, with a meaning look in her direction, I was there a short time ago and it is not very flattering that you should already have forgotten seeing me.

Madame de Mercoeur, who was admiring the garden, was not listening

to her brother. Madame de Clèves blushed, lowered her eyes, and without looking at M. de Nemours she said,

I don't in the least remember having seen you there, indeed if you have been there it must have been without my knowledge.

It is quite true that you never invited me, said M. de Nemours, all the same there I was, and there I experienced the sweetest, cruellest moments I have ever known.

Madame de Clèves understood only too well what he meant, but she said nothing. She wanted to prevent Madame de Mercoeur from going into the little room of the pavilion, not wishing her to see the portrait of M. de Nemours hanging there, and she managed so well that time went on; at last Madame de Mercoeur spoke of going home. But when Madame de Clèves realized that M. de Nemours and his sister were not leaving together, she saw what was coming and that she would be in the same embarrassing situation as she had been once before in Paris, and, as before, was afraid that such a visit would confirm her husband's suspicions. So she took the same line of action, and, in order to avoid being left alone with M. de Nemours, she told Madame de Mercoeur that she would accompany her to the edge of the forest, ordering her own carriage to follow them. The Prince, in despair at seeing that Madame de Clèves still kept up her attitude of terrible strictness, became so pale that Madame de Mercoeur asked him if he felt ill. He threw a look at Madame de Clèves, which nobody else saw, but which plainly told her that what ailed him was simply despair. There was nothing for it but to let them go without following them, and as, after what he had just said, he could hardly have returned with his sister, he went to Paris and spent the night there.

M. de Clèves's gentleman, who had kept him under observation all this time, also went back to Paris, and, seeing that M. de Nemours had left for Chambord, he took the post so as to get there first and give an account of his journey. His master was awaiting his return as though his whole future depended upon it, but as soon as he set eyes upon him he realized, from his look and from his silence, that he had nothing agreeable to tell. The Prince remained awhile, his head bowed, speechless with misery, and at last signed to him to go away, saying, I see how it is but I cannot bear you to tell me.

I have no proof of anything, replied the gentleman, though M. de Nemours did go into the forest garden two nights running and then the day after went to Coulommiers with Madame de Mercoeur.

Enough, said M. de Clèves, dismissing him with a gesture, that is all I want to know.

The gentleman was obliged to leave his master plunged in utter despair. Seldom can any man with the qualities of heart and mind that distinguished M. de Clèves have suffered at one and the same time the pain caused by a mistress's infidelity and the shame of being betrayed by a wife. It was too much for him, and he succumbed that very night to a high fever, with such complications that he was at once pronounced dangerously ill. Madame de Clèves was sent for and came without delay, to find that he was already much worse. She was amazed and very much upset by the coldness of his manner towards her; he seemed hardly able to bear her to do anything for him; however, she thought that this must be a result of his illness.

When she first arrived at Blois, where the Court now was, M. de Nemours could not help feeling very happy to think that she was so near. He tried to see her, going every day to M. de Clèves's house on pretext of hearing how he was, but all in vain. She never left her husband's bedside, and was distracted with worry. M. de Nemours was in despair, realizing that her affection for M. de Clèves was being renewed and that this must be a dangerous diversion to the other love in her heart. For a time this caused him extreme pain. Presently, however, the extremity of M. de Clèves's illness gave rise to new hopes. He saw that soon Madame de Clèves might be free to follow her own inclinations and that the future might then open a vista of eternal happiness for him. He dared not dwell upon this idea for it filled him with so much anxiety and emotion that he put it out of his mind for fear of being too distressed if his hopes came to nought.

Meanwhile the doctors had all but given up hope. On one of the last days of his illness, the morning after a bad night, M. de Clèves said that he wanted to sleep, and everybody but Madame de Clèves left his room. It seemed to her that he was not only not sleeping, but was exceedingly restless; she went over and knelt by his bed, her face wet with tears. M. de Clèves had made up his mind that she should never know the grievance he had against her, but now he could control himself no more. The loving care that she had showered on him since his illness, her sorrow, which at times he felt to be perfectly genuine and at others the height of hypocrisy, so that he hardly knew what to believe, had thrown him off his balance.

All these tears, he said, are for a death of which you yourself are the cause and which can hardly grieve you as much as you pretend it does. I am in no condition to upbraid you, he went on, his voice weakened by illness and sorrow, but the fact is that I am dying of grief because of what you have done. Your courage in speaking to me at Coulommiers has had but a sorry sequel. Why tell me of your passion for M. de Nemours at all if your virtue was not strong enough to resist him? I am ashamed to say my love for you is such that I would far rather have gone on in that state of ignorance out of which you elected to shake me. Why not leave me in my false Paradise—it is a condition common, I believe, to husbands, and I might never have realized, to the end of my life, that you loved M. de Nemours.

Now I am dying, and I should like you to know that, thanks to you, I welcome death. Life would have been odious to me now that I can no longer love and believe in you. Indeed what can life hold for me? The choice between living with her I loved so deeply and who has so cruelly disappointed me, or living apart from her, thus coming to open quarrels so contrary to my whole nature and to my passionate feelings. I must tell you that these feelings greatly surpassed anything you could have guessed at, since, not wishing to annoy you or to lessen your regard for me by behavior which you might have thought unsuitable in a husband, I kept them hidden from you to a certain extent. I did deserve your love, and as I cannot have it and can no longer wish for it now, I repeat that death means nothing to me. Farewell. Maybe one day you will regret a man whose love for you was just and true, a relationship between two reasonable people, and you will then see a difference between such love as mine and that which merely aims at having the honor of seducing you. But my death will leave you free to make M. de Nemours happy without committing a sin. Not that

I care what happens after I am gone, he added, it is a weakness in me to think of it.

Madame de Clèves, who had no idea at all that her husband had any reason to suspect her, listened to these words without understanding what they could mean, unless they were a reproach for loving M. de Nemours. Suddenly, however, the scales fell from her eyes.

Committing a sin! she cried, me? Why, such a thought has never entered my head. Virtue herself could not have been more strict than I—I have done nothing behind your back that I would not have done had you been present.

M. de Clèves looked at her with deep contempt and said, Then you would gladly have had me present during those nights you spent with M. de Nemours? I can hardly even now believe it is of you I speak when I speak of a woman spending nights with a man.

But it is not, she cried, I have spent neither nights nor minutes with M. de Nemours—he has never seen me alone—I have never listened to what he had to say—I swear, I swear—

M. de Clèves interrupted her. Enough, he said, false vows might hurt me as much as a confession.

Madame de Clèves could not answer for tears, but at last she made a great effort and said, You must at least look at me and hear what I have to say. For myself I could bear these reproaches, but is a question of your life, so for your own sake you must listen. I must be able to convince you of my innocence, with so much right on my side.

I would to God you could, he said, but what can you say? Was not M. de Nemours at Coulommiers with his sister? And did he not spend the previous two nights with you in the forest garden?

If this is my crime, she replied, I can easily clear myself. I don't ask you to believe me, but you must believe the testimony of all your own servants. Find out from them if I went into the forest garden the night before M. de Nemours came to Coulommiers and whether I did not leave it two hours earlier than I usually do, the night before that.

She went on to tell him how she thought she had seen somebody in the garden, admitting that she had an idea it might be M. de Nemours and speaking with great conviction. Her manner, combined with the fact that truth, even an unlikely truth, is always self-evident, did much to convince M. de Clèves of her innocence.

He said, I don't know whether I ought to let myself believe you, I feel so near death that I would almost prefer not to have a reason for wishing to live. This explanation has come too late, though I am glad to depart in the knowledge that you were worthy of my perfect confidence. I should like also to be able to think that you will cherish my memory and that you wanted to feel for me what you felt for that other.

He tried to go on, but he was too weak to say another word. Madame de Clèves sent for the doctors and they found that life was almost extinct; he lingered, however, a few more days, dying with an admirable firmness of spirit.

Madame de Clèves was almost out of her mind with sorrow. The Queen was very good to her, came to see her, and took her to a convent. She went without having any idea where she was, then her sisters-in-law brought her

back to Paris before the full force of her grief had broken. But when she was stronger and began to see things more clearly it was borne in upon her what a husband she had lost, and then, realizing that her love for another had killed him, she was seized with an indescribable loathing for herself and for M. de Nemours.

This Prince, in the first stages, did not dare go beyond the usual politeness, knowing Madame de Clèves quite well enough to know that she would be displeased by any special attentions, but presently he heard something which showed him that he would have to be extremely circumspect for a long time to come. One of his equerries told him that he was great friends with M. de Clèves's gentleman who, distracted with grief, said that his master's death was the direct result of M. de Nemours's visit to Coulommiers. At first this amazed M. de Nemours, but, on thinking it over he guessed more or less what had happened and then he saw exactly what Madame de Clèves's first reactions would be and what a distance there would be between her and him if she really supposed her husband's illness to have been brought on by jealousy. He decided it would be better not even to bring his name to her attention and followed this course, painful though it was to him.

When he went to Paris, however, he could not resist going to her door and asking for news of her. He was told that she saw nobody and her orders were that she was not to be given the names of her callers, very precise directions which may have been issued with a view to the Prince, so that she should not even hear his name. Now M. de Nemours was far too much in love to be capable of living absolutely starved of the sight of Madame de Clèves, and he resolved to find a way, however difficult it might be, of putting an end to this unbearable situation.

The Princess's grief went beyond the bounds of reason. Her husband's death-bed preyed on her mind, how he had died because of her and all the time behaving so tenderly to her. She remembered everything she owed him, going over it again and again, and making a crime of not having been passionately in love with him, as though it were a thing she could have helped. Her only consolation was in the thought that she wept for him as he deserved, and in resolving to behave, for the rest of her life, as he would have wished had he still been there. She sometimes wondered how it was he knew that M. de Nemours had been to Coulommiers. She did not suspect this Prince of having told it to anybody, but she thought herself so completely cured of love for him that the whole thing now seemed a matter of supreme indifference. All the same it grieved her that he should have been the cause of her husband's death and she remembered with sorrow how much M. de Clèves, on his death-bed, had worried lest she should marry him. All these things, however, were engulfed in the great sorrow of losing her husband, and she thought that nothing else mattered to her.

Several months went by during which her violent grief gave way to a more passive condition, though she was still very sad. Madame de Martigues, on a visit to Paris, tried to be kind to her, telling all the news from the Court, and though Madame de Clèves seemed quite uninterested she persevered in the hopes of distracting her. She gossiped away about the Vidame, M. de Guise, and everybody of interest. And as for M. de Nemours, she said, I can't make out whether it is that politics have taken

the place of love affairs, but he certainly is very much less happy than he used to be and seems quite indifferent to women. He comes a great deal to Paris, in fact I believe he is here now.

At the mention of M. de Nemours Madame de Clèves felt a shock. She blushed and changed the subject without Madame de Martigues noticing her agitation.

The next day the Princess, who was always looking out for some suitable occupation, went to see a man in her own neighborhood who did a special kind of work in silk; she thought she could perhaps have something similar done for herself. After she had been shown everything she noticed a door leading to a room where she thought there might be some more, and asked to have it opened. The owner replied that he had not got the key, that the room was occupied by a man who came from time to time, during daylight, to paint the beautiful houses and gardens which could be seen from the windows.

You never saw such a distinguished man, he went on, never would one think that he would be obliged to earn a livelihood. He comes here, and I see him gazing at the houses and gardens, but I have never once seen him at work.

Madame de Clèves listened to him with all her ears. The words of Madame de Martigues about M. de Nemours and how he was often in Paris seemed to have a link in her imagination with this handsome man who came to her own neighborhood. A mental picture of M. de Nemours, determined to see her, rose before her eyes and threw her into an agitation which she could not understand. She went to the windows to see what the view from them might be; it was her own garden and the windows of her own rooms. Back at home again she easily recognized the window to which, she had been told, the unknown man often came. The thought that this might be M. de Nemours changed her whole outlook upon life; she was shaken from a sort of peaceful melancholy, that she was beginning to find pleasant, into the throes of restlessness and agitation until, unable to stay quiet any longer, she went out to walk in a garden outside the city where she thought she would be alone. She believed this was so when she got there, and seeing no sign of life she walked about for quite a long time. Presently she went through a little wood and noticed that in the remotest part of the garden there was a kind of summerhouse, open at the sides, at the end of an alley, towards which she directed her steps. When she was quite near it she suddenly saw that there was a man, apparently deep in reverie, stretched upon one of the benches, and that this man was M. de Nemours. She stopped dead at the sight of him, but the people who were with her made some noise which aroused M. de Nemours from his thoughts. Without looking to see who it was that had made the noise, he got up to avoid the people who were approaching and with a low bow, which prevented him from seeing whom he thus saluted, turned up another alley. If only he had known who it was that he avoided how gladly would he have gone back! But he followed the alley until Madame de Clèves saw him leave by a side entrance where his coach awaited him. The effect which this glimpse of him produced upon Madame de Clèves may well be imagined—her sleeping passion had a violent reawakening. She went to the place where M. de Nemours had been and sat like one who has been stunned.

She suddenly saw the Prince in a new light, as an adorable being who had loved her long and faithfully, respecting her grief, only wishing to see her without being seen, giving up everything, even a Court of which he was the darling, in order to gaze at the walls of her home and to come and dream in a place where he could hardly hope to meet her, in short as a man worthy to reign alone in her heart, whom she loved and would have loved even had there been no return; all this, and a person of her own high rank into the bargain. Duty and virtue no longer presented an obstacle to her feelings, nothing that was past could count any more except the love which she and M. de Nemours had for each other.

Such ideas were a novelty to Madame de Clèves, grief over her husband's death having engrossed her whole being until then, but at the sight of M. de Nemours they came over her in force, filling her imagination. But when she had let her imagination dwell on these ideas she reminded herself that this man whom she was considering as a possible husband was the cause of her own husband's death, that she had loved him during M. de Clèves's lifetime, and that M. de Clèves on his very death-bed had expressed his anxiety lest she should marry him, and all this, so painful to a woman of her strict virtue, made her feel that it would be almost as much of a crime to marry M. de Nemours now as it had been to love him during the life of her husband. She fervently embraced these ideas, though they were a death-knell to her happiness, bolstering them up with considerations of her own peace of mind and the various evils which might result from her marriage with this Prince. After spending two hours in that place she went home, firmly convinced that it was her duty to shun him for ever.

But this conviction, child of her reason and her virtue, left M. de Nemours in complete possession of her heart, so much so that she was really to be pitied. Sleep was out of the question, and she spent one of the most horrible nights that she had ever known. In the morning her first instinct was to go and see if there was anybody at the window which overlooked her house, and there she saw M. de Nemours. Greatly startled, she withdrew so quickly that the Prince guessed he had been recognized, as indeed he had longed to be ever since his great love had driven him to find this way of seeing Madame de Clèves. When he gave up hope of seeing her there he used to go and dream in the garden where she had found him.

At last, tired of this sad and unsatisfactory condition, he decided that he must take steps to find out what was to be his fate.

After all, he thought, what am I waiting for? I have known for a long time that she loves me; she is free; it is no longer her duty to keep me at arm's length; why should I be reduced to seeing her like this, without being seen and without speaking to her? Is it possible that I have taken leave of my senses, and lost all initiative? Love has never done that to me before. It was right to respect her grief, but I have respected it for too long altogether, and if I am not careful her feelings for me will begin to fade.

He now began to think how best to approach her, and it occurred to him that as there was no longer any reason for hiding his love from the Vidame de Chartres it would be best to tell him the whole thing, and that he hoped to marry his niece. The Vidame was in Paris, where all the world was, preparing carriages and clothes to follow the King, who was to escort

the Queen of Spain. So M. de Nemours went to see the Vidame and confessed everything which he had hitherto kept so secret except that he did not admit his knowledge of Madame de Clèves's feelings for him. The Vidame was overjoyed and said that, though he had no idea M. de Nemours loved her, he had often, since she had become a widow, thought that she was really the only one good enough to marry him. M. de Nemours asked if he could arrange a meeting and find out whether she was well disposed towards him. The Vidame then suggested taking him to see her, but M. de Nemours thought she might be shocked by this because she still received nobody. They decided that the Vidame should ask her to go to him, on some pretext or other, and that M. de Nemours should join them secretly, by a special staircase. It all happened as they had planned: Madame de Clèves arrived, the Vidame went to receive her and took her to a large room at the end of his apartment. Presently M. de Nemours came in, as though by chance. Madame de Clèves was very much startled to see him; she turned scarlet and tried to conceal the fact. The Vidame chatted away on different subjects and then left them, saying he must give some orders. He asked Madame de Clèves if she would be good enough to act as hostess for him and added that he would be back very soon.

So, at long last, M. de Nemours and Madame de Clèves found themselves alone and able to speak openly, and their state of mind can be imagined better than it can be described. They said nothing for a while, but at last M. de Nemours broke the silence. You must forgive M. de Chartres, he said, for letting me have an opportunity of seeing you, which you yourself have always so cruelly denied me.

She replied, No, I must not forgive him. He forgets my present situation and that he is endangering my good name. And she made as if to go away. But M. de Nemours prevented her, saying, You have nothing to fear, Madame, nobody knows that I am here and no mischance is to be feared. I implore you to hear what I have to say, if not out of kindness to me then for your own sake, to protect yourself from the follies to which I shall surely be driven by this love I can no longer control.

For the first time Madame de Clèves gave way to her feelings for M. de Nemours and looked at him with a sweet and charming expression.

But what have you to hope for if I consent? she said. You may regret it and I certainly shall. You deserve a happier fate than you have had up to now and than you will have in future unless you look elsewhere for it.

Look elsewhere for happiness? he cried. What other happiness can there be except in being loved by you? Although I have never spoken to you, I think you cannot be unaware that my love is true and strong. Heaven knows it has been put to the proof, by you, with your terrible strictness, and by other things you would not understand.

Very well, said Madame de Clèves, sitting down, since you wish me to speak and since I myself have decided to do so I will be perfectly frank with you, more than is usual in a woman. I will not pretend not to have seen that you were deeply attached to me, and perhaps you won't believe me when I say that not only did I see it, but I saw it in the light in which you wanted me to.

He interrupted her to say, And if you really saw it were you not touched? May I ask whether it did not make some impression on your heart?

That you must have judged from my behavior, she replied, and I would be glad to know what you did think of it.

I would not dare speak of that until I am in a happier situation, he said, it has nothing to do with the future. But I am bound to say I could have wished that instead of telling M. de Clèves what you kept from me, you had kept it from him and allowed me to know it.

She blushed and asked him how it was that he knew of her confession to M. de Clèves.

I heard it from your own lips, he replied, but before you condemn my boldness you must consider whether I abused the knowledge in any way, whether it raised my hopes and whether it made me less discreet in my approach. And he began telling her how it was that he had overheard her conversation with M. de Clèves, but she soon interrupted him. Don't go on, she said, I see now why it was that you knew so much—I thought you seemed to be very well informed that day with Madame la Dauphine who had the whole story from the people to whom you had told it.

M. de Nemours told her how this had happened, but she said, You need not make these excuses, I have long ago forgiven you without them. Since you heard from me myself what I meant to keep from you all my life I will now confess that you inspired me with feelings which were not only unknown to me before I saw you but of which I had not even guessed the existence, so that the agitation which they always bring was in my case exacerbated by my great astonishment. I can tell you all this without much shame because it is no longer a crime for me to do so and you know that my behavior has never been influenced by my feelings.

M. de Nemours threw himself at her feet, saying, How can I survive this happiness?

She smiled, and said, I am not telling you anything that you do not already know too well.

Ah! but there is a difference between finding out by an accident and being told by you yourself, of your own free will, glad that I should know.

Quite true, she said, I am glad that you should know and there is a certain sweetness in telling you, so much so that perhaps I do it more for my own sake than for yours. When all's said and done, this confession will be without consequences, and I shall follow the lines, austere though they be, laid down by my duty.

But you surely forget that you are free now, cried M. de Nemours, duty no longer enters into the question—indeed if I might make so bold I would ask you to put yourself in a position in which your first duty would be to cherish these feelings for me.

My duty, she replied, forbids me ever to think of any man, and of you less than anybody in the world, for reasons which are unknown to you.

Perhaps not entirely unknown, but your reasons are not valid. It would seem that M. de Clèves supposed me luckier than in fact I was and imagined that you had approved of certain extravagances which I committed, driven to them by my great love and without knowing whether or not it was requited.

Don't, please, remind me of that episode, she said, I only want to forget it—I can't think of it without shame and deepest grief for the consequences. The plain truth is that the suspicions you aroused by your utterly irresponsible behavior caused my husband's death as surely as if you had killed him with your own hands. Supposing you had done so, you know what my duty would be—oh, in the eyes of the world it is not the same, I am quite well aware of that, but to me there is no difference at all, since I know that his death was caused by you and because of me.

Alas, said M. de Nemours, what is this phantom of duty which you are placing between me and my happiness? A vain thought with no foundation is to keep you from making the man you love happy. I have been able to entertain the hope of spending my life with you, my destiny has led me to love the most estimable person in the world, I have found in her everything that can make a perfect mistress, she loves me and I have found in her behavior everything that could be desired in a perfect wife. Indeed, Madame, you are perhaps the only person who has ever so completely combined the qualities necessary to both. Those who marry the mistresses by whom they are loved do so in fear and trembling, measuring their possible behavior with other men in terms of their relationship with themselves. But in your case there is nothing to fear since whichever way one looks at your behavior the causes for admiration can only be multiplied. Must such great felicity lie within my grasp and must I then see you yourself raising these obstacles? Ah, Madame, you forget that you distinguished me above all other men, or rather you did not, but were mistaken and I flattered myself.

You did not flatter yourself at all, she replied, and it is quite possible that the reasons for what seems to be my duty would not be so insuperable were it not that I do so distinguish you. That is what makes me feel that loving you can only end in unhappiness for me.

Now what can I say? So unhappiness is all you anticipate? I had hardly expected to have such a cruel reason put forward after all you have been good enough to tell me.

And yet there is nothing offensive to you in it, replied Madame de Clèves, so much the contrary that I find it quite difficult to explain what I mean.

Indeed! And what is this thing that you are so afraid is too flattering after what you have just told me?

I shall go on speaking quite openly, she said, and without the shades of reserve that I ought perhaps to maintain during our very first conversation, so please to listen without interrupting me. Your love for me seems to deserve that I should let you see my own feelings exactly as they are; it is the least that I can do. I suppose that this is the only time in my life when I shall allow myself to show you what I feel; nevertheless, it is not without shame that I make this confession. The fact is that I dare not expose myself to the misery of seeing your present love grow cold. It is sure to happen, it seems to me the most terrible of fates, and, since it is not my duty to risk it, I feel that I cannot do so. You are free, I am free, people may not have any reasons for censuring either of us if we decide to spend the rest of our days together, but in these eternal relationships does any man preserve his original passion? Can I expect a miracle in my case? And dare I put myself in a position whence I shall be obliged to witness the inevitable death of a love

in which lies all my joy? There was perhaps one man and one man only capable of remaining in love with his wife, and that was M. de Clèves. It was my bad luck that this brought me no happiness—possibly this passion of his would not have continued so strong if I had requited it, but I cannot use that means for keeping yours. Then I have an idea that it was the obstacles which kept you so true to me; there were enough of them to rouse your mettle, while my involuntary actions and the various things you found out by chance gave you the necessary amount of hope to sustain you.

Really I cannot keep silent any longer, said M. de Nemours. You are being too unfair to me and showing only too plainly that you are very far from being predisposed in my favor.

I confess, she said, that I can be led by my passions, but they have never blinded me and I cannot help knowing that you are a born lover, with every attribute that makes for success; you have already been in love several times and will be again. I should not make you happy, I should see you with somebody else as you had been with me, and it would strike me to the heart, defenseless as I am against jealousy. I have said too much to conceal from you that I've felt this jealousy already, indeed I suffered so terribly the evening when the Queen gave me Madame de Thémines's letter, which was supposed to be yours, that I know it for the worst of all evils.

Every woman alive, whether from love or vanity, longs to make a conquest of you; there are very few who do not feel your charm, indeed it seems to me, from my own experience, that you can attract whom you please. I should always imagine you as loved and loving, and should seldom be mistaken, and then there would be nothing for me to do but suffer; I should not even dare to complain. A lover can be reproached, but what can be said to a husband whose only fault is having ceased to love? I might get used to it, I suppose, but could I ever get used to thinking I see M. de Clèves accusing you of having killed him, reproaching me for loving and having married you, and making me feel the difference between his love and yours? Here are reasons which admit of no argument and I am resolved to go on as I am now for ever and ever.

Yes, but will you be able to? cried M. de Nemours. Do you really think such resolutions are much good against a man who worships you and who is fortunate enough to attract you? It is perhaps more difficult than you know to put up a resistance to love. So far you have succeeded by means of an unexampled virtue, but your present feelings have nothing to do with virtue and I am hoping that, in spite of yourself, they will win the day.

I realize that nothing could be more difficult than to carry out my decision, said Madame de Clèves, and I mistrust my strength in the midst of my reasoning. The duty I owe to M. de Clèves's memory would, in itself, be too weak, were it not re-enforced by considerations of my own peace of mind. My peace of mind in its turn needs to be re-inforced by duty. I may be unsure of myself but I think my scruples are invincible for, though never shall I be able to overcome my inclination for you, I know that to indulge it would end in too much unhappiness. So I am not going to see you again, whatever it costs me, and I conjure you by all the power I have over you not to try and see me. In my present state of mind things which would ordinarily seem permissible become magnified into crimes, and propriety forbids that we should see each other.

Now M. de Nemours lost all his self-control. He threw himself at her feet and bore witness by his words and his tears to as lively and tender a passion as has ever been felt by human heart. That of Madame de Clèves being not quite insensitive, she said, as she looked at the Prince, her eyes all swollen with tears, Oh why am I obliged to lay my husband's death at your door? Why could I not have met you since I have been free or before I became engaged? Why must there be so insurmountable a barrier between us?

There is no such barrier, replied M. de Nemours. You alone have put yourself between me and my happiness, inventing a law which neither virtue nor sense would have imposed upon you.

Yes, I am indeed sacrificing much to a duty which only exists in my own imagination, she said, wait a little, see what time may do. M. de Clèves has only just died, all this is too near for me to see it in a proper perspective. Take what pleasure you can in the thought that you have awakened love in one who would never have known what it meant had she never seen you. You must believe that the feelings I have for you will never change whatever my actions may be. Adieu. I am ashamed of this conversation but please give an account of it to M. le Vidame. I allow you to, I even ask you to do so.

On these words she left M. de Nemours, he could not stop her. She found M. le Vidame in the next room; he saw that she was deeply upset, and did not dare speak, but accompanied her to her carriage in silence. He went back to M. de Nemours, whom he found out of his mind with joy, misery, and an amazed admiration, in short all the feelings that there are in a passion which knows not whether to hope or to fear. It was a long time before the Vidame could make head or tail of the conversation they had had; but when finally he understood everything he felt, though not in love with her, as much admiration for Madame de Clèves, for her virtue, her spirit, and her general worth, as M. de Nemours did himself. They talked the matter over, weighing M. de Nemours's chances of success, and he, in spite of an anxiety which really came from being so much in love, agreed with M. le Vidame that Madame de Clèves would never be able to keep to her resolution. They decided, however, that he had better do as she wished lest people should notice his feelings for her and that she, fearing that it would be said she had loved him during her husband's life, should take a certain line of action which later on she might feel obliged to maintain.

M. de Nemours decided to travel with the King, since in any case it would have been difficult for him to get out of that journey, and to go without attempting to see Madame de Clèves again, even from the place where he had sometimes watched her. He asked the Vidame to speak to her for him, pouring out a hundred things which he was to say, a hundred reasons why she must overcome her scruples, indeed the night was well advanced before it occurred to him that his friend might want to go to bed.

There was no peace for Madame de Clèves that night either. After all, this had been the first time she had abandoned her self-imposed restraint as well as the first time she had ever allowed anybody to make a declaration of love to her, added to which she herself had now admitted to being in love. She did not recognize herself any more. She was amazed to think what she had done, and, not knowing whether to be glad or sorry, her mind was

filled with a passionate restlessness. She went over the reasons which duty seemed to put between her and her happiness, and found, to her sorrow, that they were very powerful; she wished now that she had not described them so lucidly to M. de Nemours. Although she had conceived the idea of marrying him as soon as she saw him in the garden it was not brought home to her as strongly as after their conversation. Now she had moments when she found it hard to believe that such a marriage would make her unhappy, so much did she long to be able to think that this idea was founded on a misapprehension of past scruples and fears for the future. Duty and good sense suggested at other times quite different courses, but all paths led to a final resolution not to remarry and never to see M. de Nemours again. It was not easy to reconcile her heart to this, deeply affected as it was and given over for the first time to the delights of love; so, seeking a little respite, she told herself that she need not force herself just yet to a final decision, since the very proprieties demanded that she should take her time; but she was perfectly decided to be firm about not seeing M. de Nemours.

The Vidame came to see her and did what he could for M. de Nemours, putting his heart and soul into the matter, but without success. She would not relax either her own behavior or that which she had imposed upon M. de Nemours. She told the Vidame that she intended to remain as she was, that she knew this would be far from easy but that she hoped to find the strength for it. He realized now her certitude of M. de Nemours's responsibility for her husband's death and that it was her absolute duty not to marry him, so much so that he saw it would be very difficult to remove this conviction.

However, when repeating the talk he had had with her to the Duke he did not add his own reflections but left him in the not unreasonable optimism of a man who knows himself beloved.

Next day they went off to join the King. M. le Vidame wrote to Madame de Clèves, at the request of M. de Nemours, speaking of this Prince, and to a second letter, which quickly followed the first, M. de Nemours added a few lines in his own hand. But Madame de Clèves, who was determined to keep to the rules she herself had laid down and who dreaded the various mishaps which letters can bring in their train, sent word to the Vidame that she could not receive any more from him if he continued to speak of M. de Nemours. She made such a point of this that M. de Nemours himself asked the Vidame not to mention him again.

The Court accompanied the Queen of Spain as far as Poitou. During this absence Madame de Clèves was left to herself and the further removed she felt from M. de Nemours and all the things which could remind her of him the more she made it a point of honor to cherish the memory of M. de Clèves. Her reasons against marrying M. de Nemours now seemed insurmountable both with regard to her duty and her peace of mind. She thought it quite sure that marriage would put an end to his love and expose her to all the horrors of jealousy and that she would therefore be delivering herself up to certain unhappiness if she married him, but she also realized that if she went on seeing him it would be impossible to resist this charming man she loved so much and who loved her, especially as neither virtue nor decency demanded that she should do so. She saw that absence and dis-

tance alone could fortify her, she needed it, not only if she were to keep her resolution to enter into no engagement, but also to prevent her from meeting M. de Nemours; she therefore decided upon a fairly long journey so that she could be quite alone for the rest of the time she was in mourning. A large estate she owned near the Pyrenees seemed the best place, and a few days before the Court was due back she started off. Before leaving she wrote and begged M. le Vidame that nobody should write to her or try to have news of her.

M. de Nemours felt this journey as another might feel the death of his mistress. Having had the happiness of seeing Madame de Clèves and of knowing that his love had affected her, it was a great blow to be deprived of her presence for so long. There was nothing to be done but grieve, and his grief was greater than ever. As for Madame de Clèves, the stresses and strains were too much for her and as soon as she arrived at her house she became very ill. This news duly reached the Court; M. de Nemours could not be consoled, his grief became quite exaggerated, and the Vidame had all the trouble in the world to prevent him from parading it in front of everybody and from going himself to find out how she was. As M. le Vidame was a relation and close friend it was natural for him to send messengers; at last they heard that the immediate danger was over but she had gone into a decline and there was not much hope that she would live.

With death so near her for so long Madame de Clèves's ideas had changed very much and she saw the world and all that pertains to it with an eye which can never be the same as that of good health. Feeling sure that she would die she became perfectly detached, a state of mind which the length of her illness turned into a habit. Later on, when she was more herself again, she found that though the image of M. de Nemours had by no means faded in her heart, the arguments against the marriage now seemed conclusive, and after an inner struggle of some violence she succeeded in smothering the remains of her passion that had been weakened by her reflections during her illness. Thoughts of death had brought back memories of M. de Clèves, and those memories, which coincided with her duty, made a strong impression on her heart. The passions and entanglements of the world now appeared to her as they do to people with higher and more detached vision. Her health, which remained very delicate, helped her to preserve these sentiments, but as she well knew the power of sheer chance over the wisest resolutions, she was determined not to risk destroying her own by returning to places frequented by the man she had loved. Alleging the need for a change of air she retired to a convent, but gave no hint of any fixed intention of leaving Court.

As soon as M. de Nemours heard of this he saw that it was an important move. In fact it now seemed to him that he had no more to hope for, though this presentiment did not stop him from doing his utmost to bring back Madame de Clèves. He made the Queen write to her, he made the Vidame write, and go and see her, in vain. When the Vidame saw her she did not mention that she had quite made up her mind, but all the same he felt sure that she would never come back. Finally M. de Nemours went himself under pretext of taking the waters.[62] She was deeply troubled and

[62] That is, bathing in medicinal waters at a spa.

surprised to hear that he had arrived. She had with her a superior person whom she loved, and sent word by her that she begged him not to think it strange of her if she did not expose herself to the danger of seeing him and of having her present state of mind, which seemed right to her, destroyed by his presence. She wanted him to know that, since to give way to her feeling for him would be fatal to her inward peace, as well as contrary to her duty (as she had renounced the world, which no longer held anything for her, and had fixed her thoughts upon the world to come) her only wish now was to see him in the same state.

M. de Nemours thought he would die of grief in the presence of the woman who told him all this. Twenty times he besought her to go back to Madame de Clèves and arrange somehow for him to see her, but she told him that Madame de Clèves had not only forbidden her to bring any message from him but even to give her any account of their conversation. So at last this Prince was obliged to go away, overcome with sorrow, as indeed well he might be, he who could never again hope to see the lady he loved with the most violent, the most natural, and the best founded passion that ever was. Even now he would not give up, and did everything imaginable to make her change her mind. At last, after the passage of whole years, time and absence healed his grief and his passion died away. Madame de Clèves gave no sign of ever returning to the world. She spent a part of each year in the convent and the rest of it at home but living in an even greater austerity, with even more saintly occupations than in the strictest of orders. Indeed her life, which was not a long one, provided an example of inimitable goodness.

Jean Racine
(1639–1699)

Of all the drama of Western literature, the Neoclassic drama of seventeenth-century France seems the most remote from modern tastes, which are likely to find the moral values, revolving around a rigid view of honor, and the stage practice, shackled by a strict observance of the unities, both impossibly narrow and artificial. This is a pity, because at its best the drama of seventeenth-century France turns its limitations into virtues and uses its concentration to deal with depths of the human mind rarely plumbed elsewhere. What it sacrifices in breadth it compensates for in intensity and penetration. What Molière is to French Neoclassic comedy, Racine is to Neoclassic tragedy. Both are poets of obsession, of the manias that flourish in the human mind in narrow, repressive societies. But where Molière reaps laughter from man's obsessive delusions, Racine explores their tragic implications.

Jean Racine was born in 1639, seventeen years after Molière, in La Ferté-Milon, about fifty miles northeast of Paris. Orphaned at the age of four, he

was taken in by the nuns of Port-Royal, an abbey which was a center of Jansenism, a strict and austere Catholic sect that had much in common with Calvinism in its belief in predestination and emphasis upon divine grace, personal holiness, and austerity. All his life, Racine was to be torn between Jansenist ideas and contrary worldly impulses. He remained at Port-Royal until he was nineteen, when he enrolled in the Collège d'Harcourt in the University of Paris. There he fell under the influence of the literary and theatrical life of the capital and won some notice as a poet. His progress was briefly interrupted when his family removed him to the provincial town of Uzès, where his uncle, a canon of the church, was to prepare him for the priesthood. He returned to Paris after two years, however, and committed himself to a literary career.

The critic Nicolas Boileau, at the threshold of his own career, befriended him and gave him valuable direction, as did Jean de La Fontaine, then at work on the *Fables* which were to make him famous. Molière, who was at the height of his career, helped the ambitious young playwright, read and criticized his work, and finally accepted Racine's fourth play, *The Theban Brothers* (1664), for production at the Théâtre du Palais-Royal. The play was a modest success, and Molière also accepted Racine's next play, *Alexander the Great* (1665). Racine, however, turned against his benefactor and, while Molière was performing the play, turned it over to the rival theater of the Hôtel de Bourgogne. The breach between the two playwrights was further widened two years later when Racine persuaded his mistress Thérèse du Parc, one of Molière's leading actresses, to quit Molière's troupe and join that of the Hôtel du Bourgogne. Racine at the age of twenty-eight began the series of seven tragedies that were to establish him as the master of French tragedy: *Andromache* (1667), *Brittanicus* (1668), *Berenice* (1670), *Bajazet* (1672), *Mithridates* (1673), *Iphigenia* (1674), and *Phaedra* (1677).

During the years of his theatrical triumphs, Racine was a familiar figure at the court of Louis XIV, the "Sun King," and gained an apparently well-deserved reputation for unscrupulous ambition and intrigue, often using his influence at court to gain the upper hand over his theatrical rivals, especially the elderly Pierre Corneille. He had quarreled bitterly with his Jansenist friends, who disapproved strongly of the theater, in 1665. But in 1677, soon after the production of *Phaedra*, he suddenly renounced the theater, married, was reconciled with the Jansenists, and was appointed royal historiographer. The last twenty-two years of his life were spent in chronicling the activities of the king, in religious studies, and in rearing his seven children. He returned to dramatic writing twice during these latter years, composing the religious plays *Esther* (1689) and *Athalie* (1691), at the request of the king's wife, Mme. de Maintenon, who wanted plays to be performed in her school at Saint-Cyr. Racine fell from the king's favor in 1698 and died the following year.

The physical theater for which Racine wrote was the same one Molière wrote for: a long, narrow room with a raised stage at one end, a proscenium arch, a front curtain, and painted scenery representing a particular place, often "a room in the palace," a theater very different from the spacious, open, and indeterminate space of Shakespeare's stage. The unities were insisted upon even more in tragedy than in comedy: the unity of time,

requiring that the plot cover no more than twelve or at most twenty-four hours; the unity of place, dictating that the action take place in one location; and the unity of action, demanding that every speech and every action bear upon the main plot. A number of subordinate rules, or proprieties, were to be observed: the characters should be noble, their language should be appropriate to their rank, they should never touch each other, either in anger or in love, and no violence should be directly depicted.

It is Racine's triumph that he turned these seeming shackles into dramatic tools, accepting their limitations, and using them to create a drama of intense inner action, as if the violent action proscribed in the outer world found its alternative outlet in the psychological conflicts of the characters.

Racine's source for *Phaedra* is Euripides' *Hippolytus* (428 B.C.). The change of title is significant. Euripides' drama places the ascetic and virginal Hippolytus at center stage, and Phaedra's suffering is only incidental to the main action of Aphrodite's punishing an arrogant rebel against her power. In Euripides' play, when Hippolytus learns of Phaedra's helpless love, he lashes out in a vicious attack on all womankind. Phaedra hangs herself but leaves a letter accusing Hippolytus of raping her. Theseus condemns his son, who is attacked by the monster from the sea and dies, but not before a final deathbed scene with his father, whom he forgives.

Racine is rather disingenuous in his "Preface to *Phaedra*" when he says that he "followed a slightly different route from Euripides." It is true that he follows the main outline of the plot fairly closely, but the emphases, the motivations, and the meanings of the story are more than "slightly" changed. Phaedra, strictly a secondary character in Euripides, dominates Racine's play. Hippolytus, far from being a woman-hater, is a rather tediously normal young man, in love with the insipid Aricia. He is shocked by his stepmother's profession of love, but hardly rabid; he would prefer to forget it, to "consign this shameful secret to oblivion." Phaedra's decision to allow Oenone to tell the fatal lie to Theseus is motivated only by Hippolytus's "bold gaze"; one critic has pointed out that this is the only tragedy in history whose climax rests upon the misinterpretation of a look. Thus the focus stays firmly upon Phaedra and her thought processes. Her passion, explained in Euripides as the result of Aphrodite's curse, is here presented in wholly naturalistic terms, as a result of her heredity (her mother Pasiphae was also given to monstrous love, having copulated with a bull and given birth to the Minotaur) and her thoroughly human subjection to the arbitrary forces of uncontrollable passion. The lesson of Euripides' play seems to be that the forces of life and fertility must be acknowledged along with the complementary human impulses toward purity and isolation. The vision of passionate love in Racine's play is very nearly the opposite; it seems to be a curse which can lead only to destruction.

If the classical gods have no place in the action of *Phaedra*, the stern God of the Jansenists may. There is none of the "joy of sex" in *Phaedra;* the queen, from the moment she enters, supported in her agony by Oenone, is devoured by the most wrenching guilt and self-hate. She never wavers in her conviction that her love is wholly loathsome, not only hopeless but adulterous and incestuous as well. She does not even like the object of her obsession: Hippolytus is a "fearful monster" in her eyes. How are we to

explain this strange fixation? In his Preface, Racine says that her passion is "a punishment of the gods rather than an urge flowing from her own will." In the absence of the classical gods, we may suspect that "the gods" are the wrathful God of the Jansenists and that Phaedra, as the Jansenist theologian Arnauld is said to have believed, is "one of the just to whom grace was not vouchsafed." The two gods who figure in the play—Phaedra's grandfather, the Sun, and her father, Minos, now god of the underworld—sound suspiciously like the Jansenist God, who like the Sun sees every human action and who like Minos prepares a punishment in the afterlife below.

Whatever its explanation, the fatal passion of Phaedra is one of the givens in the play, and the real power of the tragedy is in the human reactions to this passion. Phaedra is on the rack, and in her great scenes she reveals all the twistings and turnings of the human mind in conflict with itself. Everything else in the drama is subordinated to this inner struggle. Racine has taken the story of Phaedra as it came down to him and wrought his play so that every detail serves his central action on some level or another. The monstrous story of Phaedra's family on Crete serves as a frightful analogue of her own state of mind. (The word *monster* chimes like a bell throughout the play.) Theseus's double career as monster-killer and amorous adventurer and his son's prowess with horses and his pallid love affair with Aricia stand as ironic commentaries on Phaedra's suffering. Even the setting, the claustrophobic backwater town of Troezen, echoes the theme of Phaedra's entrapment. No finer achievement exists in the narrowly circumscribed but emotionally concentrated drama of Neoclassicism.

FURTHER READING *(prepared by W. J. R.):* A fine account of Racine's life and works is Geoffrey Brereton's *Jean Racine, A Critical Biography,* 1951, which includes good general discussions of *Phèdre, Andromaque,* and other plays. A good recent introduction is Michael Wood's essay on Racine in *European Writers: The Age of Reason and the Enlightenment,* Vol. 3, ed. George Stade, 1984. Two enduring general works on the period of Racine and Molière are C. H. C. Wright's *French Classicism,* 1920, and Martin Turnell's *The Classical Moment,* 1946. Both discuss in detail the seventeenth-century French artistic environment. Fine background information on the French theater of Racine's day is available in P. J. Yarrow's *Racine,* 1978. The concluding chapters of this work discuss tragedy and style and offer new theories on Racine's artistry. Bernard Weinberg's *The Art of Jean Racine,* 1963, discusses eleven of the later plays in separate chapters. Weinberg's work is of particular value for acquainting the new reader of Racine with less famous works, such as *Bajazet* and *Athalie.* A chronology of Racine's life and fourteen critical essays are offered in *Racine: Modern Judgments,* ed. R. C. Knight, 1969. The introduction surveys the development of Racine's modern reputation.

PHAEDRA

A TRAGEDY

Translated by John Cairncross

RACINE'S PREFACE TO *PHAEDRA*

Here is another tragedy of which I have borrowed the subject from Euripides. Although I have followed a slightly different route from that author as regards the plot, I have not failed to enrich my play with everything which seemed to me to be most striking in his. Even if I owed him only the idea of Phaedra's character, I should be justified in saying that I owe him what is probably the clearest and most closely-knit play I have written. I am not surprised that this character should have met with such a favourable reception in Euripides' day and that it should still be so successful in our time, since it possesses all the qualities required by Aristotle in a tragic hero, that is, the ability to arouse pity and terror. For Phaedra is neither entirely guilty nor altogether innocent. She is involved by her destiny, and by the anger of the gods, in an unlawful passion at which she is the very first to be horrified. She makes every effort to overcome it. She prefers to let herself die rather than declare it to anyone. And, when she is forced to disclose it, she speaks with such embarrassment that it is clear that her crime is a punishment of the gods rather than an urge flowing from her own will.

I have even been at pains to make her slightly less odious than in the tragedies of the ancients, where she resolves of her own accord to accuse Hippolytus. I felt that calumny was somewhat too low and foul to be put in the mouth of a princess whose sentiments were otherwise so noble and virtuous. This baseness seemed to me to be more appropriate to a nurse, who could well have more slave-like inclinations, and who nevertheless launches this false accusation only in order to save the life and honour of her mistress. Phaedra consents to it only because she is in such a state of excitement as to be out of her mind, and she appears a moment later in order to exculpate her innocent victim and declare the truth.

In Euripides and Seneca, Hippolytus is accused of having violated his stepmother: *Vim corpus tulit.* But here he is only accused of having intended to do so. I wished to spare Theseus a degree of agitation which could have detracted from the sympathy aroused by him among the spectators.

As regards the role of Hippolytus, I had noticed that the ancients reproached Euripides with having portrayed him as a sage free from any imperfection. As a result, the young prince's death caused much more indignation than pity. I felt obliged to leave him one weakness which would make him slightly guilty towards his father, without however depriving him in any way of the nobility with which he spares Phaedra's honour and allows himself to be mistreated without accusing her. I regard as a weakness the passion he feels in spite of himself for Aricia, who is the daughter and sister of his father's mortal enemies.

This character—Aricia—was not invented by me. Virgil says that Hippolytus married her, and had a son by her, after Aesculapius had brought him back to life. And I have also read in certain authors that Hippolytus married and took to Italy a young Athenian lady of high birth who was called Aricia and who gave her name to a small Italian town.

I cite these authorities, because I have been very scrupulous in trying to follow the classical account. I have even been faithful to the story of Theseus as recounted by Plutarch.

It was in this historian that I found that what gave rise to the belief that Theseus

172

went down to the underworld to abduct Proserpine was a journey by this prince in Epirus towards the source of the Acheron to a king whose wife Pirithous wished to carry off and who kept Theseus prisoner after having put Pirithous to death.[1] In this way, I have endeavoured to retain the credibility of the story without losing anything of the ornaments of the legend which constitutes a rich source of poetry. And the rumour of Theseus' death, based on this legendary journey, gives rise to Phaedra's profession of love which becomes one of the main causes of her downfall, since she would never have dared to speak had she believed that her husband was alive.

For the rest, I do not as yet dare to affirm that this play is my best tragedy. I leave it to the readers and to time to decide as to its real value. What I can affirm is that in no other play of mine is virtue given greater prominence. The slightest transgressions are severely punished. The very thought of crime is regarded with as much horror as crime itself. Weaknesses caused by love are treated as real weaknesses. The passions are portrayed merely in order to show the aberrations to which they give rise; and vice is painted throughout in colours which bring out its hideousness and hatefulness. That is really the objective which everyone working for the public should have in mind. And it is what the tragedians of early times aimed at above all else. Their theatre was a school in which virtue was taught not less well than in the schools of the philosophers. Hence it was that Aristotle was prepared to lay down rules for drama; and Socrates, the wisest of philosophers, did not disdain to lend a hand to the composition of Euripides' tragedies. It would be greatly to be desired that modern writings were as sound and full of useful precepts as the works of these poets. This might perhaps provide a means of reconciling to tragedy a host of people famous for their piety and their doctrine who have recently condemned it and who would no doubt pass a more favourable judgement on it if writers were as keen to edify their spectators as to amuse them, thereby complying with the real purpose of tragedy.

PHAEDRA

CAST

THESEUS,[2] *son of Aegeus,*
 King of Athens
PHAEDRA, *wife of Theseus,*
 daughter of Minos and Pasiphae
HIPPOLYTUS, *son of Theseus and*
 Antiope, Queen of the Amazons
ARICIA,[3] *princess of the blood*
 royal of Athens
THERAMENES, *Hippolytus's*
 governor

OENONE, *Phaedra's nurse and*
 confidante
ISMENE, *Aricia's confidante*
PANOPE, *a woman of Phaedra's*
 retinue

THE SCENE *is in Troezen, a town*
 in the Peloponnese

[1] This sentence is neither more nor less involved than in the original. (All notes to *Phaedra* are by the translator, John Cairncross.)
[2] Pronounced as two syllables. [3] Pronounced as four syllables.

ACT ONE

SCENE ONE
HIPPOLYTUS THERAMENES

HIPPOLYTUS. It is resolved, Theramenes. I go.
 I will depart from Troezen's pleasant land.
 Torn by uncertainty about the King,
 I am ashamed of standing idly by.
 For over half a year I have not heard
 Of my dear father Theseus' destiny
 Nor even by what far sky he is concealed.
THERAMENES. And, where, my lord, would you make search for him?
 Already, to allay your rightful fears,
 I have scoured both the seas that Corinth joins; 10
 I have sought news of Theseus on the shores
 Of Acheron, the river of the dead;
 Elis I searched, then sailed past Tenaros
 On to the sea where Icarus came down.[4]
 What makes you hope that you may find his trace
 In some more favoured region of the world?
 Who knows indeed if it is his desire
 To have the secret of his absence known?
 And whether, as we tremble for his life,
 He is not tasting all the joys of love, 20
 And soon the outraged victim of his wiles. . . .
HIPPOLYTUS. No more of this, Theramenes. The King
 Has seen the errors of his amorous youth.
 He is above unworthy dalliance,
 And, stronger than his old inconstancy,
 Phaedra has in his heart long reigned alone.
 But, to be brief, I must make search for him
 Far from this city where I dare not stay.
THERAMENES. Since when do you, my lord, fear to frequent
 These peaceful haunts you cherished as a boy, 30
 Which I have seen you many a time prefer
 To the loud pomp of Athens and the court?
 What peril, or what trouble, drives you hence?
HIPPOLYTUS. Those happy days are gone, and all is changed,
 Since to these shores the mighty gods have sent
 The child of Minos and Pasiphae.[5]

[4] The isthmus of Corinth links the main part of Greece with the peninsula of the Peloponnese. The two seas are the Ionian and the Aegean. The River Acheron has its source in the mountains of Epirus in northwest Greece. Theramenes' wanderings took him from there southward to Elis, a province on the western shore of the Peloponnese, then to Tenaros on its southern tip, and finally to the Aegean Sea on the east side of Greece.

[5] Minos was King of Crete, and later judge in Hades. Pasiphae was the daughter of the Sun. She had two daughters by Minos—Ariadne and Phaedra (the latter being the one that Hippolytus has in mind). Aphrodite, the goddess of love, inspired Pasiphae with a monstrous passion for a bull, and from this union there was born the Minotaur, half man, half bull. Theseus brought back Phaedra from Crete after killing the monster in its labyrinth.

THERAMENES. I understand. The cause of your distress
 Is known. The sight of Phaedra vexes you.
 Theseus' new wife had scarcely seen you than
 Your exile gave the measure of her power. 40
 But now her hate that never let you be
 Has vanished or is greatly on the wane.
 Besides what perils threaten you from her—
 A woman dying or who seeks to die?
 Racked by a malady she will not name,
 Tired of herself and of the light of day,
 Phaedra has not the strength to do you ill.
HIPPOLYTUS. I do not fear her vain hostility.
 If I go hence, I flee, let me confess,
 Another enemy . . . Aricia,
 Last of a line that plotted Theseus' death. 50
THERAMENES. What! Would you stoop to persecute her too?
 Though she is sprung of Pallas' cruel race,
 She never joined in her false brothers' schemes.[6]
 Why hate her then if she is innocent?
HIPPOLYTUS. I would not flee her if I hated her.
THERAMENES. My lord, may I explain your sudden flight?
 Are you no more the man that once you were,
 Relentless foe of all the laws of love
 And of a yoke Theseus himself has borne?
 Will Venus whom you haughtily disdained 60
 Vindicate Theseus after all these years
 By forcing you to worship with the throng
 Of ordinary mortals at her shrine?
 Are you in love?
HIPPOLYTUS.

 My friend, what have you said?
 You who have known me since I first drew breath,
 You ask me shamefully to disavow
 The feelings of a proud disdainful heart?
 The Amazon, my mother,[7] with her milk
 Suckled me on that pride you wonder at.
 And I myself, on reaching man's estate, 70
 Approved my nature when I knew myself.
 Serving me with unfeignéd loyalty,
 You would relate my father's history.
 You know how, as I hung upon your words,
 My heart would glow at tales of his exploits
 When you portrayed Theseus, that demi-god,
 Consoling mortals for Alcides'[8] loss,
 Monsters suppressed and brigands brought to book—

[6] Pallas was descended from Erechtheus, the original King of Athens and son of the earth god. Aegeus, Theseus's father, had obtained the throne by adoption. Aricia's brothers plotted Theseus's downfall, but were discovered and put to death.
[7] Antiope (Hippolyta). [8] Hercules.

Procrustes, Sciron, Sinis, Cercyon; 80
The giants' bones in Epidaurus strewn
And Crete red with the slaughtered Minotaur.
But, when you told me of less glorious deeds,
His word pledged and believed in countless lands:
Helen in Sparta ravished from her home,
Salamis, scene of Periboea's tears;
Others whose very names he has forgot,
Too trusting spirits all deceived by him;
Wronged Ariadne[9] crying to the winds;
Phaedra abducted, though for lawful ends; 90
You know how, loath to hear this sorry tale,
I often urged you quickly to conclude,
Happy could I have kept the shameful half
Of these adventures from posterity.
And am I to be vanquished in my turn?
And can the gods have humbled me so far?
In base defeat the more despicable
Since countless exploits plead on his behalf,
Whereas no monsters overcome by me
Have given me the right to err like him. 100
And, even if I were fated to succumb,
Should I have chosen to love Aricia?
Should not my wayward feelings have recalled
That she is barred from me eternally?
King Theseus frowns upon her and decrees
That she shall not prolong her brothers' line:
He fears this guilty stock will blossom forth,
And, to ensure her name shall end with her,
Condemns her to be single till she dies—
No marriage torch shall ever blaze for her. 110
Should I espouse her cause and brave his wrath?
Set an example to foolhardiness?
And, on a foolish passion launched, my youth. . .
THERAMENES. Ah! when your hour has once but struck, my lord,
Heaven of our reasons takes but little heed.
Theseus opens your eyes despite yourself.
His hatred of Aricia has fanned
Your passion and has lent her added grace.
Besides, my lord, why fear a worthy love?
If it is sweet, will you not dare to taste? 120
Will you be always ruled by modesty?
Can you go wrong where Hercules has trod?
What hearts has Venus' power not subdued?
Where would you be yourself, who fight her now,
If, combating her love, Antiope

[9] Minos' daughter, Phaedra's sister, who led Theseus through the labyrinth and thus enabled him to kill the Minotaur; she eloped with Theseus, and was abandoned by him on the island of Naxos.

Had never been consumed for Theseus?
However, what avails this haughty tone?
Confess it, all is changed; for some days past
You are less often seen, aloof and proud,
Speeding your chariot along the shore, 130
Or, skilful in the seagod Neptune's art,
Bending an untamed courser to the curb.
The woods less often to your cries resound;
Your eyes grow heavier with secret fire.
There is no doubt, you are consumed with love.
You perish from a malady you hide.
Has fair Aricia enraptured you?
HIPPOLYTUS. Theramenes, I go to seek the King.
THERAMENES. And will you see Phaedra before you leave,
 My lord?
HIPPOLYTUS.

 I mean to. You may tell her so. 140
See her I must, since duty so commands.
But what new burden weighs Oenone down?

SCENE TWO
HIPPOLYTUS OENONE THERAMENES

OENONE. Alas, my lord, what cares can equal mine?
 The Queen is almost at her destined end.
 In vain I watch over her night and day.
 She's dying from a hidden malady;
 Eternal discord reigns within her mind.
 Her restless anguish tears her from her bed.
 She longs to see the light, and yet, distraught
 With pain, she bids me banish everyone. . .
 But here she comes.
HIPPOLYTUS.

 Enough. I'll take my leave
And will not show her my detested face. 10

SCENE THREE
PHAEDRA OENONE

PHAEDRA. No further. Here, Oenone, let us stay.
 I faint, I fall; my strength abandons me.
 My eyes are dazzled by the daylight's glare,
 And my knees, trembling, give beneath my weight.
 Alas!
OENONE.

 May our tears move you, mighty gods!
PHAEDRA. How these vain jewels, these veils weigh on me!
 What meddling hand has sought to re-arrange

My hair, by braiding it across my brow?
All things contrive to grieve and thwart me, all.

OENONE. How all her wishes war among themselves! 10
Yourself, condemning your unlawful plans,
A moment past, bade us adorn your brow;
Yourself, summoning up your former strength,
Wished to come forth and see the light again.
Scarce have you seen it than you long to hide,
You hate the daylight you came forth to see.

PHAEDRA. O shining founder of an ill-starred line,
You, whom my mother dared to boast her sire,[10]
Who blush perhaps to see me thus distraught,
Sungod, for the last time, I look on you. 20

OENONE. What? you will not give up this fell desire?
And will you, always saying no to life,
Make mournful preparation for your death?

PHAEDRA. Would I were seated in the forest's shade!
When can I follow through the swirling dust
The lordly chariot's flight along the course?

OENONE. What?

PHAEDRA.
 Madness! Where am I, what have I said?
Whither have my desires, my reason strayed?
Lost, lost, the gods have carried it away.
Oenone, blushes sweep across my face; 30
My grievous shame stands all too clear revealed,
And tears despite me fill my aching eyes.

OENONE. If you must blush, blush for your silence, for
It but inflames the fury of your ills.
Deaf to our wild entreaties, pitiless,
Will you allow yourself to perish thus?
What madness cuts you off in mid career?
What spell, what poison, has dried up the source?
Thrice have the shades of night darkened the skies
Since sleep last made its entry in your eyes, 40
And thrice the day has driven forth dim night
Since last your fainting lips took nourishment.
What dark temptation lures you to your doom?
What right have you to plot to end your life?
In this you wrong the gods from whom you spring,
You are unfaithful to your wedded lord;
Unfaithful also to your hapless sons,
Whom you would thrust beneath a heavy yoke.
Remember, that same day their mother dies,
Hope for the alien woman's son revives, 50
For that fierce enemy of you and yours,
That youth whose mother was an Amazon,
Hippolytus . . .

[10] The Sun was Pasiphae's father and hence Phaedra's grandfather.

PHAEDRA.
 God!
OENONE.
 That reproach struck home.
PHAEDRA. Ah! wretched woman, what name crossed your lips?
OENONE. Your anger now bursts forth, and rightly so.
 I love to see you shudder at the name.
 Live then. Let love and duty spur you on.
 Live on. Do not allow a Scythian's son
 To lord it with his harsh and odious rule
 Over the pride of Greece and of the gods. 60
 Do not delay! for every moment kills.
 Haste to replenish your enfeebled strength
 While yet the fires of life, though all but spent,
 Are burning and can still flame bright again.
PHAEDRA. I have prolonged my guilty days too far.
OENONE. What, are you harried by some keen remorse?
 What crime could ever bring you to this pass?
 Your hands were never stained with guiltless blood.
PHAEDRA. Thanks be to heaven, my hands have done no wrong.
 Would God my heart were innocent as they! 70
OENONE. What fearful project then have you conceived
 Which strikes such terror deep into my heart?
PHAEDRA. I have revealed enough. Spare me the rest.
 I die, and my grim secret dies with me.
OENONE. Keep silence then, inhuman one, and die;
 But seek some other hand to close your eyes.
 Although the candle of your life burns low,
 I will go down before you to the dead.
 Thither a thousand different roads converge,
 My misery will choose the shortest one. 80
 When have I ever failed you, cruel one?
 Remember, you were born into my arms.
 For you I have lost country, children, all.[11]
 Is this how you reward fidelity?
PHAEDRA. What do you hope to gain by violence?
 If I should speak, you would be thunderstruck.
OENONE. And what, ye gods, could be more terrible
 Than seeing you expire before my eyes?
PHAEDRA. Even when you know my crime and cruel fate,
 I yet will die, and die the guiltier. 90
OENONE. By all the tears that I have shed for you,
 And by your faltering knees I hold entwined,
 Deliver me from dire uncertainty.
PHAEDRA. You wish it. Rise.
OENONE.
 Speak. I await your words.
PHAEDRA. What shall I say to her and where begin?

[11] The nurse had accompanied Phaedra from her native Crete to Athens.

OENONE. Wound me no longer by such vain affrights!
PHAEDRA. Oh hate of Venus! Anger-laden doom!
 Into what dark abyss love hurled my mother![12]
OENONE. Ah, Queen, forget; and for all time to come
 Eternal silence seal this memory. 100
PHAEDRA. Oh sister Ariadne, from what love
 You died deserted on a barren shore!
OENONE. What ails you, and what mortal agony
 Drives you to fury against all your race?
PHAEDRA. Since Venus wills it, of this unblest line
 I perish, I, the last and wretchedest.
OENONE. You are in love?
PHAEDRA.
 Love's furies rage in me.
OENONE. For whom?
PHAEDRA.
 Prepare to hear the crowning woe.
 I love . . . I tremble, shudder at the name;
 I love . . .
 [OENONE *leans forward.*]
PHAEDRA.
 You know that prince whom I myself 110
 So long oppressed, son of the Amazon?
OENONE. Hippolytus?
PHAEDRA.
 You have pronounced his name.
OENONE. Merciful heavens! My blood chills in my veins.
 O grief! O crime! O lamentable race!
 Ill-fated journey and thrice ill-starred coast!
 Would we had never neared your dangerous shores!
PHAEDRA. My malady goes further back. I scarce
 Was bound by marriage to Aegeus' son;[13]
 My peace of mind, my happiness seemed sure—
 Athens revealed to me my haughty foe. 120
 As I beheld, I reddened, I turned pale.
 A tempest raged in my distracted mind.
 My eyes no longer saw. I could not speak.
 I felt my body freezing, burning; knew
 Venus was on me with her dreaded flames,
 The fatal torments of a race she loathes.
 By sleepless vows, I thought to ward her off.
 I built a temple to her, rich and fair.
 No hour went by but I made sacrifice,
 Seeking my reason in the victims' flanks. 130
 Weak remedies for love incurable!
 In vain my hand burned incense on the shrine.
 Even when my lips invoked the goddess' name,
 I worshipped *him*. His image followed me.

[12] An allusion to Pasiphae's monstrous passion for the bull. [13] Theseus.

Even on the altar's steps, my offerings
Were only to the god I dared not name.
I shunned him everywhere. O crowning woe!
I found him mirrored in his father's face!
Against myself at last I dared revolt.
I spurred my feelings on to harass him.
To banish my adoréd enemy, 140
I feigned a spite against this stepson, kept
Urging his exile, and my ceaseless cries
Wrested him from a father's loving arms.
I breathed more freely since I knew him gone.
The days flowed by, untroubled, innocent.
Faithful to Theseus, hiding my distress,
I nursed the issue of our ill-starred bed.
Ah vain precautions! Cruel destiny!
Brought by my lord himself to Troezen's shores, 150
I saw once more the foe I had expelled.
My open wound at once poured blood again.
The fire no longer slumbers in the veins.
All Venus' might has fastened on her prey.
I have a fitting horror for my crime;
I hate this passion and I loathe my life.
Dying, I could have kept my name unstained,
And my dark passion from the light of day;
Your tears, your pleas have forced me to confess,
And I shall not regret what I have done, 160
If you, respecting the approach of death,
Will cease to vex me with reproaches, and
Your vain assistance will not try to fan
The last faint flicker still alight in me.

SCENE FOUR
PHAEDRA OENONE PANOPE

PANOPE. Would I could hide from you the grievous news,
 My lady, but I cannot hold it back.
 Death has abducted your unconquered lord
 And this mischance is known to all but you.
OENONE. What, Panope?
PANOPE.

 The Queen in vain, alas!
 Importunes heaven for Theseus' safe return,
 For, from the vessels just arrived in port,
 Hippolytus, his son, has learned his death.
PHAEDRA. God!
PANOPE.

 Athens is divided in its choice
 Of master. Some favor the prince, your son, 10

Others, forgetful of the State's decrees,[14]
Dare to support the foreign woman's son.
Rumour even has it that a bold intrigue
Wishes to give Aricia the throne.
I deemed it right to warn you of this threat.
Hippolytus is ready to set sail,
And in this turmoil it is to be feared
He may win fickle Athens to his cause.

OENONE. Panope, cease! You may be sure the Queen
Will give due heed to this important news. 20

SCENE FIVE
PHAEDRA OENONE

OENONE. Ah, Queen, I had relinquished you to death
And thought to follow you down to the tomb.
I had no longer words to turn you back;
But this news bids you steer another course.
Now all is changed, and fortune smiles on you.
The King is dead, and you must take his place.
He leaves a son with whom your duty lies:
A slave without you; if you live, a king.
On whom in his misfortune can he lean?
If you are dead, no hand will dry his tears; 10
And his fond cries, borne upwards to the gods,
Will bring his forebears' anger down on you.
Live then, no longer tortured by reproach.
Your love becomes like any other love.
Theseus, in dying, has dissolved the bonds
Which made your love a crime to be abhorred.
You need no longer dread Hippolytus,
And you may see him and be guiltless still.
Perhaps, convinced of your hostility,
He is prepared to captain the revolt. 20
Quick, undeceive him; bend him to your will.
King of these fertile shores, Troezen is his.
But well he knows the laws assign your son
The soaring ramparts that Minerva built.[15]
Both of you have a common enemy.
Join forces then against Aricia.

PHAEDRA. Then be it so. Your counsels have prevailed.
I'll live, if I can be recalled to life,
And if the love I bear my son can still
In this grim hour revive my failing strength. 30

[14] Which ruled out the succession of anyone even partly of non-Greek blood.
[15] Athens.

ACT TWO

SCENE ONE
Aricia Ismene

Aricia. Hippolytus has asked to see me here?
 Hippolytus wishes to say farewell?
 Ismene, are you not mistaken?
Ismene.
 No.
 This is the first result of Theseus' death.
 Make ready to receive from every side
 Allegiances that Theseus filched from you.
 Aricia is mistress of her fate,
 And soon all Greece will bow the knee to her.
Aricia. This was no rumour then, Ismene. Now
 My enemy, my tyrant is no more. 10
Ismene. Indeed. The gods no longer frown on you,
 And Theseus wanders with your brothers' shades.
Aricia. By what adventure did he meet his end?
Ismene. The tales told of his death are past belief.
 They say that in some amorous escapade
 The waters closed over his faithless head.
 The thousand tongues of rumour even assert
 That with Pirithous he went down to Hell,
 Beheld Cocytus[16] and the sombre shores,
 Showed himself living to the shades below, 20
 But that he could not, from the house of death,
 Recross the river whence is no return.
Aricia. Can mortal man, before he breathes his last,
 Descend into the kingdom of the dead?
 What magic lured him to that dreaded shore?
Ismene. You alone doubt it. Theseus is no more.
 Athens is stricken; Troezen knows the news,
 And now pays tribute to Hippolytus.
 Here in this palace, trembling for her son,
 Phaedra takes counsel with her anxious friends. 30
Aricia. But will Hippolytus be kinder than
 His father was to me, loosen my chains,
 And pity my mishaps?
Ismene.
 I think he will.
Aricia. Do you not know severe Hippolytus?
 How can you hope that he will pity me,
 Honouring in me alone a sex he spurns?
 How constantly he has avoided us,
 Haunting those places which he knows we shun!

[16] The river of the underworld.

ISMENE. I know the tales of his unfeelingness;
 But I have seen him in your presence, and 40
 The legend of Hippolytus' reserve
 Doubled my curiosity in him.
 His aspect did not tally with his fame;
 At the first glance from you he grew confused.
 His eyes, seeking in vain to shun your gaze,
 Brimming with languor, took their fill of you.
 Although the name of lover wounds his pride,
 He has a lover's eye, if not his tongue.
ARICIA. How avidly, Ismene, does my heart
 Drink in these sweet, perhaps unfounded words! 50
 O you who know me, can it be believed
 That the sad plaything of a ruthless fate,
 A heart that always fed on bitterness,
 Should ever know the frenzied pangs of love?
 Last of the issue of Earth's royal son,[17]
 I only have escaped the scourge of war.
 I lost, all in their springtime's flowering,
 Six brothers, pride of an illustrious line.
 The sword swept all away and drenched the earth,
 Which drank, unwillingly, Erechtheus' blood. 60
 You know that, since their death, a cruel law
 Forbids all Greeks to seek me as their wife,
 Since it was feared my marriage might some day
 Kindle my brothers' ashes into life.
 But you recall with what disdain I viewed
 These moves of a suspicious conqueror,
 For, as a lifelong enemy of love,
 I rendered thanks to Theseus' tyranny,
 Which merely helped to keep me fancy free.
 My eyes had not yet lighted on his son. 70
 Not that my eyes alone yield to the charm
 Of his much vaunted grace, his handsomeness,
 Bestowed by nature, but which he disdains,
 And seems not even to realize he owns.
 I love and prize in him far nobler gifts—
 His father's virtues, not his weaknesses.
 I love, let me confess, that manly pride,
 Which never yet has bowed beneath love's yoke.
 Phaedra in vain gloried in Theseus' sighs.
 I am more proud, and spurn the easy prize 80
 Of homage to a thousand others paid
 And of a heart accessible to all.
 But to bring an unbending spirit down,
 To cause an aching where no feeling was,
 To stun a conqueror with his defeat,
 In vain revolt against a yoke he loves:

[17] Erechtheus.

That rouses my ambition, my desire.
Even Hercules was easier to disarm.
Vanquished more often than Hippolytus,
He yielded a less glorious victory. 90
But, dear Ismene, what rash hopes are these?
For his resistance will be all too strong.
You yet may hear me, humble in my grief,
Bewail the very pride I now admire.
Hippolytus in love? By what excess
Of fortune could I . . .

ISMENE.
 You yourself will hear.
Hither he comes.

SCENE TWO
HIPPOLYTUS ARICIA ISMENE

HIPPOLYTUS.
 Princess, before I go,
I deemed it right to let you know your fate.
My father is no more. My fears divined
The secret of his lengthy absence. Death,
Death only, ending his illustrious deeds,
Could hide him from the universe so long.
The gods at last deliver to the Fates
Alcides' friend, companion, and his heir.
I feel that, silencing your hate, even you
Hear in good part the honours due to him.
One hope alone tempers my mortal grief. 10
I can release you from a stern control,
Revoking laws whose harshness I deplore.
Yourself, your heart, do with them what you will;
And in this Troezen, now assigned to me
As my sage grandsire Pittheus' heritage,
Which with a single voice proclaimed me king,
I leave you free as I am; nay, more free.
ARICIA. Limit your boundless generosity.
By honouring me, despite adversity,
My lord, you place me, more than you believe, 20
Beneath those laws from which you set me free.
HIPPOLYTUS. Athens, uncertain whom to choose as heir,
Talks of yourself, of me, and the Queen's son.
ARICIA. Me?
HIPPOLYTUS.
 I would not wish to deceive myself.
My claim appears to be annulled by law
Because my mother was an Amazon.
But, if my only rival for the throne
Were Phaedra's son, my stepbrother, I could

Protect my rights against the law's caprice.
If I do not assert my claim, it is 30
To hand, or rather to return, to you
A sceptre given to your ancestors
By that great mortal whom the earth begot.
Adoption placed it in Aegeus' hands.
Theseus, his son, defended and enlarged
The bounds of Athens, which proclaimed him king
And left your brothers in oblivion.
Athens recalls you now within her walls.
Too long has she deplored this endless feud;
Too long your noble kinsmen's blood has flown, 40
Drenching the very fields from which it sprang.
If Troezen falls to me, the lands of Crete
Offer a rich domain to Phaedra's son.
But Attica is yours. And I go hence
To unify our votes on your behalf.

ARICIA. At all I hear, astounded and amazed,
 I almost fear a dream deceives my ears.
 Am I awake? Is it to be believed?
 What god, my lord, inspired you with the thought?
 How rightly is your glory spread abroad! 50
 And how the truth surpasses your renown!
 You in my favour will renounce your claim?
 Surely it was enough to keep your heart
 So long free from that hatred of my line,
 That enmity . . .

HIPPOLYTUS.
 I hate you, Princess? No.
However my aloofness be decried,
Do you believe a monster gave me birth?
What churlish breeding, what unbending hate
Would not have melted at the sight of you?
Could I resist the soft beguiling spell . . . 60

ARICIA. What! My lord . . .

HIPPOLYTUS.
 No, I cannot now draw back!
Reason, I see, gives way to violence.
And, since I have begun to speak my mind,
Princess, I must go on: I must reveal
A secret that my heart can not conceal.
Before you stands a pitiable prince,
Signal example of rash arrogance.
I who, in proud rebellion against love,
Have long mocked other captives' sufferings,
Who, pitying the shipwrecks of the weak, 70
Had thought to watch them always from the shore,
Am now, in bondage to the common law,
Cut from my moorings by a surging swell.
A single blow has quelled my recklessness:

My haughty spirit is at last in thrall.
For six long months ashamed and in despair,
Pierced by the shaft implanted in my side,
I battle with myself, with you, in vain.
Present I flee you; absent, you are near.
Deep in the woods, your image follows me. 80
The light of day, the shadows of the night,
Everything conjures up the charms I flee;
Each single thing delivers up my heart.
And, sole reward for all my fruitless care,
I seek but cannot find myself again.
Bow, chariot, javelins, all importune me;
The lessons Neptune taught me are forgot.[18]
My idle steeds no longer know my voice,
And only to my cries the woods resound.
Perhaps the tale of so uncouth a love 90
Brings, as you listen, blushes to your face.
What words with which to offer you a heart!
How strange a conquest for so fair a maid!
But you should prize the offering the more.
Remember that I speak an unknown tongue,
And do not scorn my clumsy gallantry,
Which, but for you, I never would have known.

SCENE THREE
Hippolytus Aricia
Theramenes Ismene

THERAMENES. The Queen is coming, Prince. She looks for you.
HIPPOLYTUS. For me?
THERAMENES.
 I do not know what she intends.
You have been sent for by her messenger.
Before you leave, Phaedra would speak with you.
HIPPOLYTUS. What can I say? And what can she expect . . .
ARICIA. Consent at least, my lord, to hear her speak.
Although she was your bitter enemy,
You owe some shade of pity to her tears.
HIPPOLYTUS. Meanwhile you go. I leave, and am in doubt
Whether I have offended my beloved, 10
Or if my heart that I commit to you . . .
ARICIA. Go, Prince. Pursue your generous designs.
Make Athens' State pay homage to me. All
The gifts you offer to me I accept.
But Athens' empire, glorious though it be,
Is not your most endearing offering.

[18] The seagod was also the god of horses.

SCENE FOUR
HIPPOLYTUS THERAMENES

HIPPOLYTUS. Are you all ready? But here comes the Queen.
Let everyone prepare with all despatch
To sail. Go, give the signal; hasten back,
And free me from a tedious interview.

SCENE FIVE
PHAEDRA HIPPOLYTUS OENONE

PHAEDRA [*to* OENONE *at the back of the stage*].
He comes . . . My blood sweeps back into my heart.
Forgotten are the words I had prepared.
OENONE. Think of your son, who hopes in you alone.
PHAEDRA. They say that you are leaving us at once,
My lord. I come to join my tears to yours.
I come to tell you of a mother's fears.
My son is fatherless, and soon, too soon,
He must behold my death as well. Even now,
Numberless enemies beset his youth.
You, only you, can see to his defence. 10
But I am harried by remorse within.
I fear lest you refuse to hear his cries.
I tremble lest you visit on a son
Your righteous anger at a mother's crimes.
HIPPOLYTUS. How could I ever be so infamous?
PHAEDRA. If you should hate me, I would not complain,
For I appeared resolved to do you ill.
Deep in my inmost heart you could not read.
I drew upon myself your enmity,
And where I dwelt, I would not suffer you. 20
With unrelenting hate, I sought to be
Divided from you by a waste of seas.
I even ordained by an express decree
That in my presence none should speak your name.
But, if the punishment should fit the crime,
If hate alone could bring your hate on me,
Never did woman merit pity more
And less, my lord, deserve your enmity.
HIPPOLYTUS. A mother jealous of her children's rights
Rarely forgives another woman's son, 30
I realize; and from a second bed
Awkward suspicion all too often springs.
Another would have taken like offence,
And at her hands I might have suffered more.
PHAEDRA. Ah! My lord, heaven, I dare here attest,

Has quite dispensed me from the common rule.
Far other is the care that weighs on me.
HIPPOLYTUS. Lady, it is too early yet to grieve.
Who knows, your husband may be still alive.
Heaven may vouchsafe him to your tears again. 40
Protected by the seagod, not in vain
Will Theseus call on mighty Neptune's aid.
PHAEDRA. No mortal visits twice the house of death.
Since Theseus has beheld the sombre shores,
In vain you hope a god will send him back,
And hungry Acheron holds fast his prey.
But no, he is not dead; he lives, in you.
Always I think I see my husband's face.
I see him, speak to him, and my fond heart . . .
My frenzied love bursts forth in spite of me. 50
HIPPOLYTUS. In this I see the wonder of your love.
Dead as he is, Theseus still lives for you.
Still does his memory inflame your heart.
PHAEDRA. Yes, Prince, I pine, I am on fire for him.
I love King Theseus, not as once he was,
The fickle worshipper at countless shrines,
Dishonouring the couch of Hades' god;[19]
But constant, proud, and even a little shy;
Enchanting, young, the darling of all hearts,
Fair as the gods; or fair as you are now. 60
He had your eyes, your bearing, and your speech.
His face flushed with your noble modesty.
When towards my native Crete he cleft the waves,[20]
Well might the hearts of Minos' daughters burn!
What were you doing then? Why without you
Did he assemble all the flower of Greece?
Why could you not, too young, alas, have fared
Forth with the ship that brought him to our shores?
You would have slain the monstrous Cretan bull
Despite the windings of his endless lair. 70
My sister[21] would have armed you with the thread
To lead you through the dark entangled maze—
No. *I* would have forestalled her. For my love
Would instantly have fired me with the thought.
I, only I, would have revealed to you
The subtle windings of the labyrinth.
What care I would have lavished on your head!
A thread would not have reassured my fears.
Affronting danger side by side with you,
I would myself have wished to lead the way, 80

[19] Pluto, King of the underworld.
[20] On the expedition to Crete against the Minotaur. [21] Ariadne.

And Phaedra, with you in the labyrinth,
Would have returned with you or met her doom.
HIPPOLYTUS. What do I hear? Have you forgotten that
 King Theseus is my father, you his wife?
PHAEDRA. What makes you think, my lord, I have forgot,
 Or am no longer mindful of my name?
HIPPOLYTUS. Forgive me. Blushing, I confess your words
 Were innocent, and I misunderstood.
 For very shame I cannot bear your gaze.
 I go . . .
PHAEDRA.
 Ah, cruel, you have understood 90
 Only too well. I have revealed enough.
 Know Phaedra then, and all her wild desires.
 I burn with love. Yet, even as I speak,
 Do not imagine I feel innocent,
 Nor think that my complacency has fed
 The poison of the love that clouds my mind.
 The hapless victim of heaven's vengeances,
 I loathe myself more than you ever will.
 The gods are witness, they who in my breast
 Have lit the fire fatal to all my line; 100
 Those gods whose cruel glory it has been
 To lead astray a feeble mortal's heart.
 Yourself recall to mind the past, and how
 I shunned you, cruel one, nay, drove you forth.
 I strove to seem to you inhuman, vile;
 The better to resist, I sought your hate.
 But what availed my needless sufferings?
 You hated me the more, I loved not less.
 Even your misfortunes lent you added charms.
 I pined, I drooped, in torments and in tears. 110
 Your eyes alone could see that it is so,
 If for a moment they could look at me.
 Nay, this confession to you, ah! the shame,
 Think you I made it of my own free will?
 I meant to beg you, trembling, not to hate
 My helpless children, whom I dared not fail.
 My foolish heart, alas, too full of you,
 Could talk to you of nothing but yourself.
 Take vengeance. Punish me for loving you.
 Come, prove yourself your father's worthy son, 120
 And of a vicious monster rid the world.
 I, Theseus' widow, dare to love his son!
 This frightful monster must not now escape.
 Here is my heart. Here must your blow strike home.
 Impatient to atone for its offence,
 I feel it strain to meet your mighty arm.
 Strike. Or if it's unworthy of your blows,
 Or such a death too mild for my deserts,

Or if you deem my blood too vile to stain
Your hand, lend me, if not your arm, your sword. 130
Give me it!
OENONE.
 Ah! What are you doing? God!
Someone is coming. You must not be seen.
Come let's go in, quick, to avoid disgrace.

SCENE SIX
HIPPOLYTUS THERAMENES

THERAMENES. Can that be Phaedra who was dragged away?
Why, my lord, why this sudden, sharp dismay?
I find you without sword, aghast and pale.
HIPPOLYTUS. Flee, flee, Theramenes. I cannot speak,
Nor without horror look upon myself.
Phaedra. . . . No, mighty gods, let us consign
This shameful secret to oblivion.
THERAMENES. If you will leave, the sails are all unfurled.
But Athens has already made her choice.
Her chieftains have consulted all the tribes. 10
Your brother rules;[22] and Phaedra wins the day.
HIPPOLYTUS. Phaedra?
THERAMENES.
 A herald speaking Athens' will
Into her hands conveyed the reins of state.
Her son is king, my lord.
HIPPOLYTUS.
 Oh God, who knows
Her heart, is it her virtue you reward?
THERAMENES. Meanwhile, vague rumours say the King still lives,
And even that in Epirus he was seen.
But I, who sought him there, my lord, I know . . .
HIPPOLYTUS. No matter. Let us study every clue.
Have this new rumour traced back to its source. 20
But, if it does not then prove credible,
Let us depart and, at whatever cost,[23]
Replace the sceptre in more worthy hands.

ACT THREE

SCENE ONE
PHAEDRA OENONE

PHAEDRA. Ah, take away those royal honours. How
Can you importune me to show myself?

[22] i.e., half-brother, son of Theseus and Phaedra, whereas Hippolytus' mother was Antiope
(Hippolyta).
[23] That is, even at the cost of a rebellion.

And why seek to beguile my grieving heart?
Rather conceal me. I have said too much.
My frantic passion has revealed itself.
I have said what should never have been heard.
God! how he listened to me. By what shifts
He long pretended not to understand.
How his whole being hankered to be gone.
And how his blushes added to my shame. 10
Why did you ever thwart my baneful plan?
Ah! when his sword was pointed at my breast,
Did he turn pale for me, or did he wrench
It from me? I had but to touch it once
To make it horrible for him, and for
The wretched sword to soil his cruel hands.

OENONE. Thus your misfortunes breed self-pity, and
Only inflame a fire you ought to quench.
Daughter of Minos, should you not aspire
To seek your peace of mind in nobler cares? 20
Resort to flight from an ungrateful youth,
Reign, and assume the guidance of the State?

PHAEDRA. *I* reign? *I* bring a State beneath my rule,
When reason reigns no longer over me;
When I have lost my self-dominion; when
Beneath a shameful sway I scarcely breathe;
When I am dying?

OENONE.
 Flee.

PHAEDRA.
 I cannot go.

OENONE. You sent him into exile. Shun him now.

PHAEDRA. Too late, too late. He knows my mad desires.
I have transgressed the bounds of modesty. 30
I to Hippolytus have bared my shame,
And hope, despite me, has seduced my heart.
You yourself, rallying my failing strength
When on my lips my soul was hovering,
By guileful counsels brought me back to life.
You gave me glimpses of a sinless love.

OENONE. Alas! guilty or no of your mishaps,
What would I not have done to save your life?
But, if by insults you were ever stung,
Can you forget a haughty youth's disdain? 40
God! with what cruel, stern, unfeeling heart
He left you well-nigh prostrate at his feet!
How hateful was his virtuous haughtiness!
Why did not Phaedra see him with my eyes?

PHAEDRA. He may discard this pride that angers you.
Bred in the forests, he is wild like them.
Hardened by rude upbringing, he perhaps
For the first time listens to words of love.

Perhaps his silence mirrors his surprise,
And our reproaches are too violent. 50
OENONE. An Amazon, forget not, gave him birth.
PHAEDRA. Though a barbarian, yet did she love.
OENONE. He hates all women with a deadly hate.
PHAEDRA. No rival, then, will triumph over me.
 In short, the time for good advice is past.
 Serve my wild heart, Oenone, not my head.
 If he is inaccessible to love,
 Let us attack him at some weaker point.
 He seemed attracted by an empire's rule.
 He could not hide it; Athens beckoned him. 60
 Thither his vessels' prows were headed, and
 The white sails fluttered, streaming in the wind.
 Oenone, play on his ambition. Go,
 Dazzle him with the glitter of the crown.
 Let him assume the sacred diadem.
 Myself to bind it on is all I ask,
 Yielding to him the power I cannot hold.
 He will instruct my son how to command;
 Perhaps he will be father to the boy.
 Mother and son I will commit to him. 70
 In short, try every means to win him round.
 Your words will find a readier ear than mine.
 Urge! Weep! Paint Phaedra at death's door.
 You may assume a supplicating tone.
 I will endorse it, whatsoe'er you do.
 Go. Upon your success depends my fate.

SCENE TWO
PHAEDRA [*alone*]

PHAEDRA. O you who see the depths of this my shame,
 Relentless Venus, is my fall complete?
 Your cruelty could go no further. Now
 You triumph. All your arrows have struck home.
 O cruel goddess! if you seek new fame,
 Attack a more rebellious enemy.
 Frigid Hippolytus, flouting your wrath,
 Has at your altars never bowed the knee.
 Your name seems to offend his haughty ear.
 Goddess, avenge yourself. Our cause is one. 10
 Make him love . . . but Oenone, you are back.
 Did he not listen? Does he loathe me still?

SCENE THREE
PHAEDRA OENONE

OENONE. Your love is vain and you must stifle it,
 O Queen, and summon up your former strength.

The King we thought was dead will soon be here;
Theseus is come; Theseus is on his way.
Headlong, the crowd rushes to welcome him.
I had gone out to seek Hippolytus
When, swelling to the heavens, a thousand cries . . .

PHAEDRA. My husband lives. Oenone, say no more.
 I have confessed a love that soils his name.
 He is alive, and more I will not know. 10

OENONE. What?

PHAEDRA.
 I foretold it but you would not hear.
 Your tears prevailed over my keen remorse.
 I died this morning worthy to be mourned;
 I took your counsel and dishonoured die.

OENONE. You mean to die?

PHAEDRA.
 Great God, what have I done?
 My husband and his son are on their way.
 I will behold the witness of my guilt
 Observe me as I dare approach the King,
 My heart heavy with sighs he heard unmoved,
 My eyes wet with tears the wretch disdained. 20
 Mindful of Theseus' honour, as he is,
 Will he conceal from him my fierce desires?
 Will he be false to father and to king,
 Restrain the horror that he feels for me?
 His silence would be vain, Oenone, for
 I know my baseness, and do not belong
 To those bold wretches who with brazen front
 Can revel in their crimes unblushingly.
 I know my transports and recall them all.
 Even now I feel these very walls, these vaults, 30
 Will soon give tongue and, with accusing voice,
 Await my husband to reveal the truth.
 Then, death, come free me from so many woes.
 Is it so terrible to cease to live?
 Death holds no terrors for the wretched. No.
 I fear only the name I leave behind,
 For my poor children what a heritage.
 The blood of Jove should make their spirit swell;[24]
 But, whatsoever pride that blood inspires,
 A mother's crime lies heavy on her sons. 40
 I tremble lest reports, alas, too true,
 One day upbraid them with a mother's guilt.
 I tremble lest, crushed by this odious weight,
 Neither will ever dare hold up his head.

OENONE. Ah! do not doubt it. Pity both of them.
 Never was fear more justified than yours.

[24] Jove (Zeus) was father to Minos and grandfather to Phaedra.

But why expose them to such base affronts?
And why bear witness now against yourself?
That way lies ruin. Phaedra, they will say,
Fled from the dreaded aspect of her lord. 50
Hippolytus is fortunate indeed.
By laying down your life, you prove him right.
How can I answer your accuser's charge?
I shall be all too easy to confound.
I shall behold his hideous triumph as
He tells your shame to all who care to hear.
Ah! sooner let the flames of heaven descend.
But tell me frankly, do you love him still?
How do you view this overweening prince?
PHAEDRA. He is a fearful monster in my eyes. 60
OENONE. Then why concede him such a victory?
You fear him. Dare then to accuse him first
Of the offence he soon may charge you with.
Nothing is in his favour; all is yours—
His sword, left by good fortune in your hands,
Your present agitation, your past grief,
His father, turned against him by your cries,
And, last, his exile you yourself obtained.
PHAEDRA. Should I oppress and blacken innocence?
OENONE. All I need is your silence to succeed. 70
Like you I tremble and I feel remorse.
Sooner would I affront a thousand deaths,
But, since without this remedy you die,
For me your life must come before all else.
Therefore I'll speak. Despite his wrath, the King
Will do naught to his son but banish him.
A father when he punishes is still
A father, and his judgement will be mild.
But, even if guiltless blood must still be shed,
What does your threatened honour not demand? 80
It is too precious to be compromised.
Its dictates, all of them, must be obeyed.
And, to safeguard your honour, everything,
Yes, even virtue, must be sacrificed.
But who comes here? Theseus!
PHAEDRA.
 Hippolytus!
In his bold gaze my ruin is writ large.
Do as you will. My fate is in your hands.
My whirling mind has left me powerless.

SCENE FOUR
THESEUS HIPPOLYTUS PHAEDRA
OENONE THERAMENES

THESEUS. Fortune at last ceases to frown on me,
O Queen, and in your arms again . . .

PHAEDRA.
 No more.
Do not profane your transports of delight.
No more do I deserve this tenderness.
You have been outraged. Jealous fortune's blows
During your absence have not spared your wife.
I am unworthy to approach you, and
Henceforth my only thought must be to hide.

SCENE FIVE
THESEUS HIPPOLYTUS THERAMENES

THESEUS. Why this cold welcome to your father?
HIPPOLYTUS.
 Sire,
Phaedra alone can solve this mystery.
But, if my ardent wish can move you still,
Allow me never to set eyes on her.
Suffer your trembling son to disappear
For ever from the place where Phaedra dwells.
THESEUS. You, my son, leave me?
HIPPOLYTUS.
 Yes. It was not I
Who sought her. You, my lord, you brought her here.
For you, on leaving, brought Aricia
And your Queen, Phaedra, here to Troezen's shore. 10
You even committed them into my care.
But, since your safe return, why should I stay?
Long have I squandered in the woods of Greece
My manhood's skill on paltry enemies.
Should not I, fleeing shameful idleness,
Redden my javelins in more glorious blood?
Before you had attained my present years,
More than one tyrant, monsters more than one,
Had felt the might of your unconquered arm;
Even then, you were the scourge of insolence. 20
You had cleared all the shores of both the seas.
The traveller now fares freely through the land.
Hercules, resting on his laurels' fame,
Already for his labours looked to you.
And I, a glorious father's unknown son,
Lag far behind even my mother's deeds.
Let me at least show you my mettle and,
If some fell monster has escaped your sword,
Place at your feet its honourable spoils.
Or let the memory of a glorious death, 30
Engraving in eternity my life,
Prove to the universe I was your son.
THESEUS. What do I see? What horror spread around

Drives back from me, distraught, my family?
If I return, so feared, so undesired,
O heaven! why did you free me from my gaol?
I had one friend alone.[25] He rashly tried
To seize the consort of Epirus' King.
I served his amorous plan reluctantly;
But fate in anger blinded both of us. 40
The tyrant took me by surprise unarmed.
Pirithous I beheld, a woeful sight,
Thrown to fierce monsters by the barbarous king,
Who fed them on the blood of helpless men.
Me he confined in sombre caves profound
Nearby the shadowy kingdom of the dead.
The gods at last relented towards me and
Allowed me to outwit my guardian.
I purged the world of a perfidious knave,
And his own monsters battened on his flesh. 50
But when I joyfully prepare to meet
My dearest ones, all that the gods have spared,
Nay, when my soul, that is its own again,
Would feast itself upon so dear a sight,
Only with shudders am I welcomed home;
Everyone flees, rejecting my embrace.
Myself, filled with the horror I inspire,
Would I were prisoner in Epirus still.
Speak! Phaedra tells of outrage done to me.
Who played me false? Why am I unavenged? 60
Has Greece, so often guarded by my arm,
Afforded shelter to the criminal?
You do not answer. Is my son, my own
Dear son, in league, then, with my enemies?
Let us go in and end this grim suspense.
Let us discover criminal and crime,
And Phaedra tell us why she is distraught.

SCENE SIX
HIPPOLYTUS THERAMENES

HIPPOLYTUS. What meant these words that made my blood run cold?
 Will Phaedra, still in her delirium,
 Denounce herself, bring ruin on her head?
 O God! What will the King say then? How love
 Has spread its baleful poison through the house!
 Myself, full of a passion he condemns,
 As once he knew me, so he finds me still.
 Gloomy forebodings terrify my soul.
 But innocence has surely naught to fear.

[25] Pirithous.

Come, let me with some new and happier 10
Approach revive my father's tenderness,
And tell him of a love he may oppose
But which it is not in his power to change.

ACT FOUR

SCENE ONE
THESEUS OENONE

THESEUS. What do I hear? A reckless libertine
 Conceived this outrage on his father's name?
 How harshly you pursue me, destiny.
 I know not where I am, whither I go.
 O son! O ill-rewarded tenderness!
 Daring the scheme, detestable the thought.
 To gain his lustful and nefarious ends,
 The shameless villain had resort to force.
 I recognized the sword he drew on her,
 That sword I gave him for a nobler use. 10
 Could all the ties of blood not hold him back?
 Phaedra was slow in bringing him to book?
 In keeping silent, Phaedra spared the knave?
OENONE. Rather did Phaedra spare a father's tears.
 Ashamed of a distracted lover's suit,
 And of the vicious passion she had caused,
 Phaedra, my lord, was dying and her hand
 Was on the point of cutting short her days.
 I saw her raise her arm, I ran to her.
 I, only I, preserved her for your love, 20
 And, pitying her distress and your alarm,
 Reluctantly I lent her tears a voice.
THESEUS. The criminal! He blenched despite himself.
 As I drew near, I saw him start with fear.
 I was astonished by his joyless mien;
 His cold embraces froze my tenderness.
 But had this guilty love that eats him up
 Already, even in Athens, shown itself?
OENONE. My lord, recall how oft the Queen complained.
 Infamous love gave rise to all her hate. 30
THESEUS. And here in Troezen this flamed up again?
OENONE. My lord, I have related all I know.
 The grieving Queen too long remains alone;
 Allow me to withdraw and go to her.

SCENE TWO
THESEUS HIPPOLYTUS

THESEUS. Ah, it is he. Great gods! what eye would not
 Be duped like mine by such nobility?

Must needs the brow of an adulterer
Be bright with virtue's sacred character?
And ought we not by fixed certain signs
To see into perfidious mortals' hearts?

HIPPOLYTUS. May I inquire of you what baleful cloud
Has overcast, my lord, your regal brow?
Will you not venture to confide in me?

THESEUS. Villain! How dare you come before me now? 10
Monster, the thunderbolt too long has spared!
Last of the brigands whom I swept away!
After the frenzy of your wicked lust
Has driven you to assault your father's bed,
You dare to show your hateful face to me,
Here in this place full of your infamy,
And seek not out, under an unknown sky,
Countries to which your fame has never spread.
Flee, villain, flee. Brave not my hatred here
Nor tempt my anger that I scarce restrain. 20
I have my portion of eternal shame
To have begot so criminal a son,
Without his death, disgrace to my renown,
Soiling the glory of my labours past.
Flee, and if you desire not to be joined
To all the villains fallen by my hand,
Take care that never does the shining sun
Behold you in these palaces again.
Flee then, and never more return;
And of your hideous presence purge my realm. 30
And, Neptune, in time past if my strong hand
Of infamous assassins cleared your shores,
Remember that, to recompense my deeds,
You swore to grant the first of my desires.
In the long hardships of a cruel gaol
I did not call on your immortal power;
With miser's care I put aside your aid,
Holding it in reserve for greater needs.
I call upon you now. Revenge my wrong.
I give this villain over to your wrath; 40
Drown in his blood his shameless foul desires.
Your favours will be measured by your rage.

HIPPOLYTUS. Phaedra accuses me of sinful love?
So infinite a horror numbs my soul,
So many unforeseen and heavy blows
Rain down upon me that I cannot speak.

THESEUS. Villain, you thought that Phaedra would conceal
In craven silence your vile insolence.
You should not, as you fled, have dropped the sword
That, in her hands, establishes your guilt. 50
Rather should you have crowned your perfidy
And at one stroke robbed her of speech and life.

HIPPOLYTUS. Rightly indignant at so black a lie,
 I ought, my lord, to let the truth speak out,
 But I will not resolve this mystery
 Out of the deep respect that seals my lips.
 And, if you will not deepen your distress,
 Look at my life; remember who I am.
 Some little crimes lead up to greater crimes.
 Whoever goes beyond the bounds of law 60
 Can in the end flout the most sacred rules.
 No less than virtue, crime has its degrees,
 And innocence has never yet been known
 To swing at once to licence's extreme.
 A single day cannot change virtuous men
 To craven and incestuous murderers.
 Reared by a virtuous Amazon from birth,
 I never have belied my mother's blood.
 Pittheus, esteemed the wisest far of men,
 Instructed me after I left her hands. 70
 I do not seek to paint myself too fair;
 But, if one virtue is my birthright, that
 Is above all, my lord, as I have shown,
 Hate of the crime that they accuse me of.
 That is what I am famous for in Greece.
 I carried virtue to the sternest lengths,
 My obdurate austerity is known;
 The daylight is not purer than my heart.
 Yet I, they say, fired by unholy love . . .
THESEUS. Yes, by that very pride you stand condemned. 80
 The reason why you were so cold is clear;
 Phaedra alone entranced your lustful eyes.
 And, by all other charms unmoved, your heart
 Disdained to glow with innocent desire.
HIPPOLYTUS. No, father, for this may not be concealed,
 I have not scorned to glow with virtuous love,
 And at your feet confess my real offence.
 I am in love; in love despite your ban.
 Aricia is mistress of my heart
 And Pallas' daughter has subdued your son. 90
 I worship her and, flouting your command,
 For her alone I pine, I am consumed.
THESEUS. You love her? God! The ruse is gross indeed!
 You feign to err to justify yourself.
HIPPOLYTUS. For half a year I have been deep in love.
 Trembling, I came to tell you so myself.
 What! Can no word of mine unseal your eyes?
 What fearful oath, to move you, must I swear?
 May heaven and earth and everything that is . . .
THESEUS. Foulness goes hand in hand with perjury. 100
 Cease! Spare me an importunate harangue,
 If your false virtue has no other stay.

HIPPOLYTUS. To you I may seem false and full of guile.
 Phaedra does justice to me in her heart.
THESEUS. Ah! how my wrath grows at your shamelessness.
HIPPOLYTUS. What time and what the place of banishment?
THESEUS. Were you beyond Alcides' pillars,[26] still
 Would I believe your villainy too near.
HIPPOLYTUS. Crushed by the crime that you suspect me of,
 If you desert me who will pity me? 110
THESEUS. Go seek out friends who in their viciousness
 Applaud adultery and incest. These
 Villains and ingrates, lawless, honourless,
 Will shelter evildoers such as you.
HIPPOLYTUS. You harp on incest and adultery.
 I will say nought; but Phaedra, as you know,
 My lord, is of a mother, of a line,
 Richer in all these horrors than my own.
THESEUS. What! are there no bounds to your frantic rage?
 For the last time, begone from out my sight. 120
 Go, libertine, before a father's wrath
 Has you with ignominy torn from hence.

SCENE THREE
THESEUS [*alone*]

THESEUS. Unhappy youth! Haste to your certain doom.
 By the stream dreaded even of the gods
 Neptune has given and will fulfill his word.
 A god of vengeance follows hard on you.
 I loved you and, in spite of your offence,
 My heart is stirred for you forebodingly.
 But you have forced me to pronounce your doom.
 Was ever wretched father outraged so?
 O God who sees my overwhelming grief,
 How could I have begot so foul a child? 10

SCENE FOUR
PHAEDRA THESEUS

PHAEDRA. My Lord, I come stricken with terror, for
 Your dreaded voice has reached me and I fear
 Your menace may be given prompt effect.
 If it is not too late, then spare your son.
 Respect your flesh and blood, I beg of you,
 And save me from the horror of his cries.

[26] The Pillars of Hercules, at the western end of the Mediterranean; hence any extremely remote locality.

Do not lay up for me the endless grief
Of causing bloodshed by a father's hand.
THESEUS. No, Queen, my hand has not bathed in his blood,
But still the villain will not now escape. 10
Immortal hands are with his ruin charged.
This Neptune owes me. You will be avenged.
PHAEDRA. This Neptune owes you. What? Your anger calls . . .
THESEUS. How! You already fear I may be heard?
Rather unite your wishes with my own.
In all their heinousness depict his crimes;
Stir up my sluggish cold resentment, for
You do not know the measure of his crimes.
His fury showers affronts upon your name.
Your mouth, he says, speaks nothing but deceit; 20
He swears Aricia has won his heart,
And that he loves her.
PHAEDRA.
 What!
THESEUS.
 Those were his words.
But I am not the dupe of vain pretence.
Let us expect swift justice from the god.
I shall myself to Neptune's altars, there
To urge fulfilment of immortal oaths.

SCENE FIVE
PHAEDRA [*alone*]

PHAEDRA. He's gone. What tidings have assailed my ears!
What smouldering fire awakens in my heart!
God! What a thunderbolt! What baleful news!
Flying with but one thought to aid his son,
I tore myself from pale Oenone's arms,
Yielding to the remorse that tortured me.
Who knows how far repentance would have gone?
Perhaps I might even have accused myself?
Perhaps, had not my voice died in my throat,
The frightful truth would have escaped my lips. 10
Hippolytus can love but loves not me.
Aricia has won his heart, his troth.
Ah! when, inexorable to my pleas,
Hippolytus put on a front of steel,
I thought his heart for ever closed to love,
And against women all alike was armed.
Another none the less has conquered him.
She has found favour in his cruel eyes.
Perhaps he has a heart easy to move.
Alone of women me he cannot bear. 20
And I was hastening to his defence!

SCENE SIX
PHAEDRA OENONE

PHAEDRA. Oenone, do you know what I have heard?
OENONE. No, but I still am trembling, to be frank.
 As you rushed forth, I blenched at your intent.
 I was afraid you would destroy yourself.
PHAEDRA. Who would have thought it? There was someone else.
OENONE. What!
PHAEDRA.

 Yes. Hippolytus is deep in love.
 This shy, invincible antagonist,
 Whom my respect displeased, my tears annoyed,
 Whom I could never speak to unafraid,
 Submissive, tamed, proclaims his own defeat. 10
 Aricia is mistress of his heart.
OENONE. Aricia?
PHAEDRA.

 Ah! unplumbed depths of woe!
 For what new torments have I spared myself?
 All I have suffered, jealous torments, fears,
 Raging desire, the horror of remorse,
 A cruel, harsh, intolerable slight,
 Were a mere foretaste of my torments now.
 They love each other. By what spell did they
 Deceive me? How, where did they meet, since when?
 You knew. Why did you let me be misled? 20
 Why did you keep from me their stealthy love?
 Were they seen oft exchanging looks and words?
 Deep in the forests were they wont to hide?
 Alas! They had the utmost liberty.
 Heaven smiled upon their innocent desires.
 They followed where love led them, conscience free.
 For them the dawn rose shining and serene.
 And I, rejected by all living things,
 I hid myself from day, I shunned the light;
 Death was the only god I dared invoke. 30
 I waited for the moment of my end,
 Feeding on gall and drinking deep of tears.
 Too closely watched, I did not even dare
 Give myself up in freedom to my grief.
 Trembling, this baleful pleasure I enjoyed
 And, cloaking with a feignéd calm my woes,
 Was often driven to forego my tears.
OENONE. What good will their love do them? Never will
 They meet again.
PHAEDRA.

 Their love will always live.
 Even as I speak, ah cruel, deadly thought! 40

They flout the fury of my insane rage.
Despite this exile which will sever them
They swear a thousand oaths never to part.
No. No. Their happiness is gall to me.
Oenone, pity my wild jealousy.
Aricia must perish, and the King
Be stirred to wrath against her odious race.
No trifling retribution will suffice.
The sister has outdone her brothers' crime.
I will implore him in my jealous rage. 50
What am I doing? I have lost my mind!
I, jealous? and 'tis Theseus I implore!
My husband is alive and yet I pine.
For whom? Whose heart have I been coveting?
At every word my hair stands up on end.
Henceforth the measure of my crimes is full.
I reek with foulest incest and deceit.
My hands, that strain for murder and revenge,
Burn with desire to plunge in guiltless blood.
Wretch! and I live and can endure the gaze 60
Of the most sacred sun from which I spring.
My grandsire is the lord of all the gods;
My forebears fill the sky, the universe.
Where can I hide? In dark infernal night?
No, there my father holds the urn of doom.
Destiny placed it in his ruthless hands.
Minos judges in hell the trembling dead.
Ah! how his horror-stricken shade will start
To see before him his own daughter stand,
Forced to admit to such a host of sins 70
And some, perhaps, unknown even in hell!
What, father, will you say to that dread sight?
I see your hand slip from the fateful urn;
I see you searching for new punishments,
Yourself your own kin's executioner.
Forgive me. Venus' wrath has doomed your race.
Your daughter's frenzy shows that vengeance forth.
Alas, my sad heart never has enjoyed
The fruits of crimes whose dark shame follows me.
Dogged by misfortune to my dying breath, 80
I end upon the rack a life of pain.

OENONE. Ah, Queen! dismiss these unbecoming fears,
And of your error take a different view.
You are in love. We cannot change our fate.
By destined magic you were swept along.
Is that so strange or so miraculous?
Has love then triumphed only over you?
Frailty is human and but natural.
Mortal, you must a mortal's lot endure.
This thraldom was imposed long, long ago. 90

The gods themselves that in Olympus dwell,
Who smite the evildoer with their bolt,
Have sometimes felt unlawful passions' fire.
PHAEDRA. Great gods! What counsels dare you offer me?
Even to the last you seek to poison me.
Wretch! Thus it is that you have caused my doom.
You, when I fled from life, you called me back;
At your entreaties duty was forgot;
It was *you* made me see Hippolytus.
You meddling fool. Why did your impious lips, 100
Falsely accusing him, besmirch his life?
You may have killed him, if the gods have heard
A maddened father's sacrilegious wish.
I'll hear no more. Hence, loathsome monster, hence.
Go, leave me to my pitiable fate.
May the just heavens reward you fittingly,
And may your punishment forever fright
All who, as you have done, by base deceit,
Pander to ill-starred princes' weaknesses,
Urging them on to yield to their desires, 110
And dare to smooth the path of crime for them,
Vile flatterers, the most ill-fated boon
The anger of the gods can make to kings!
OENONE. Ah God! to save her what have I not done;
But this is the reward I have deserved.

ACT FIVE

SCENE ONE
HIPPOLYTUS ARICIA

ARICIA. What, in this peril you refuse to speak?
You leave a loving father undeceived?
Cruel one, can you, by my tears unmoved,
Consent without a sigh to part from me?
Go hence and leave me to my grieving heart.
But, if you go, at least preserve your life.
Defend your honour from a foul reproach
And force your father to revoke your doom.
There still is time. Wherefore, from what caprice,
Will you let Phaedra's slander hold the field? 10
Tell Theseus all.
HIPPOLYTUS.
 Ah, what have I not said?
Should I make known the outrage to his bed
And by an all too frank relation bring
Over my father's brow a blush of shame?
This odious secret you alone have pierced.
My sole confidants are the gods and you.

Judge of my love, I have not hid from you
All I desired to hide even from myself.
But, since you have been sworn to secrecy,
Forget, if it be possible, my words. 20
And never may your pure unsullied lips
Recount the details of this horrid scene.
Let's trust the justice of the gods above.
Their interest lies in vindicating me.
Sooner or later Phaedra will be brought
To book and meet an ignominious doom.
That is the only boon I ask of you.
My anger takes all other liberties.
Reject the bondage under which you pine;
Dare to accompany me in my flight. 30
Tear yourself free from an unhallowed spot
Where virtue breathes a foul, polluted air.
Let us to cover our escape exploit
The wild confusion that my downfall spreads.
I can provide you with the means for flight.
The only guards controlling you are mine.
Mighty defenders will take up our cause.
Argos awaits us; Sparta summons us.
Let's bear our grievance to our new allies.
Phaedra must never profit from our fall[27] 40
And drive us both from off my father's throne,
Making her son the heir to our estates.
Now is our chance. We must lay hands on it.
What holds you back? You seem to hesitate.
Only your interest thus emboldens me.
When I am ardent, why are you so cold?
Are you afraid to share an exile's lot?
ARICIA. Alas! How pleasant to be banished thus!
With what delight, linking my fate with yours,
By all the world forgotten I would live! 50
But, since we are not joined by that sweet bond,
Could I in honour flee from here with you?
I know that, even by the strictest code,
I may throw off your father's tutelage.
No bond of home or parents holds me back,
And flight from tyrants is permissible.
You love me, though, my lord, and my good name . . .
HIPPOLYTUS. No. No. Your honour is too dear to me.
I come before you with a nobler plan. 60
Flee from my foes. Flee as my wedded wife.
Alone in exile, since heaven wills it so,
We need no man's consent to pledge our faith.
Not always torches blaze for Hymen's rites.

[27] i.e., profit by obtaining the kingdom which normally would have gone to Hippolytus and Aricia.

Not far from Troezen's gates, among these tombs,
My princely forebears' ancient burial place,
There stands a shrine dreaded of perjurers.
There mortals never swear an oath in vain.
Who breaks his word is punished instantly,
And men forsworn, afraid of certain death, 70
Are held in check by this most dreaded threat.
There, if you trust me, we will ratify
By solemn oath our everlasting love,
Taking to witness this old temple's god.
We'll pray him to be father to us both.
I'll call to witness the most sacred gods,
And chaste Diana, Juno the august,
And all the gods, witnesses of my love,
Will lend their blessing to my holy vows.
ARICIA. The King is coming. Flee, make haste. To cloak 80
My own departure, I will stay awhile.
Go now, but leave me someone I can trust
To lead my steps to the appointed place.

SCENE TWO
THESEUS ARICIA ISMENE

THESEUS. O God! lighten the darkness of my mind.
 Show me the truth that I am searching for.
ARICIA. Make ready, dear Ismene, for our flight.

SCENE THREE
THESEUS ARICIA

THESEUS. Your colour changes and you seem aghast,
 Lady. What was the young prince doing here?
ARICIA. My lord, he took eternal leave of me.
THESEUS. You have subdued that proud rebellious heart,
 And his first raptures were inspired by you.
ARICIA. My lord, I cannot well deny the truth.
 Your unjust hatred is not shared by him.
 He did not treat me like a criminal.
THESEUS. I know. He swore eternal love to you.
 Do not rely on that inconstant heart, 10
 For he to others swore the self same oaths.
ARICIA. He, Sire?
THESEUS.
 You ought to have restrained him. How
 Could you endure to share his fickle heart?
ARICIA. And how could you allow such calumny
 To tarnish the bright glory of his life?
 Have you so little knowledge of his heart?

Can you not tell baseness from innocence?
Must from your eyes alone an odious cloud
Conceal his virtues which shine bright to all?
I cannot let him further be maligned. 20
Stop and repent of your assassin's prayer.
Fear, my lord, fear lest the unbending heavens
Hate you enough to grant you your desire.
Oft in their wrath they take our sacrifice.
Often their gifts are sent to scourge our sins.

THESEUS. In vain you seek to cover his offence.
Your passion blinds you to his faults. But I
Have faith in sure, trustworthy witnesses.
I have seen tears which surely were not feigned.

ARICIA. Take care, my lord. Invincible, your hands 30
Have freed the world from monsters numberless;
But all are not destroyed. You still let live
One . . . But your son forbids me to proceed.
Knowing his wishes, I respect you still.
I would but grieve him if I dared to speak.
Following his restraint, I will withdraw
Rather than let the truth escape my lips.

SCENE FOUR
THESEUS [alone]

THESEUS. What does she mean, and what do these words hide,
Begun and broken off, begun again?
Is it their aim to trick me by a feint?
Are they in league to put me on the rack?
But I myself, despite my stern resolve,
What plaintive voice cries in my inmost heart?
A lurking flash of pity harrows me.
I'll have Oenone questioned once again;
I must have more light thrown upon the crime.
Guards, bring Oenone out to me alone. 10

SCENE FIVE
THESEUS PANOPE

PANOPE. I do not know what the Queen purposes,
But her distraction is a fearful sight.
Mortal despair cries from her haggard face,
And death has laid its paleness on her cheeks.
Oenone, driven out with shame, has plunged
Already into the unsounded sea.
We do not know what led her to this death;
The waves have closed for ever over her.

THESEUS. What?

PANOPE.
 This dark action did not calm the Queen.
Distraction seems to swell her wavering heart. 10
Sometimes, to soothe her secret sufferings,
She takes her children, bathes them in her tears;
Then, suddenly, renouncing mother's love,
Shuddering with horror, will have none of them.
This way and that, she wanders aimlessly;
Wildly she looks at us, but knows us not.
She thrice has written, then has changed her mind,
And thrice torn up the letter she began.
See her, we beg you. We implore your help.
THESEUS. Oenone's dead, and Phaedra seeks to die. 20
Call back my son, let him defend himself
And speak to me! I'll lend a willing ear.
 [*Alone.*]
Do not be overhasty with your gifts,
Neptune! I wish my prayer may not be heard.
Perhaps I have believed false witnesses,
Lifting too soon my cruel hand to you.
Ah! if you act, what will be my despair!

 SCENE SIX
 THESEUS THERAMENES

THESEUS. What have you done with him, Theramenes?
I put him as a boy into your hands.
But why the tears that trickle down your cheeks?
What of my son?
THERAMENES.
 O tardy vain concern!
O unavailing love! Your son's no more.
THESEUS. God!
THERAMENES.
 I have seen the best of mortals die,
And the most innocent, I dare to add.
THESEUS. Dead? When I open wide my arms to him,
The gods, impatient, hasten on his death?
What blow, what thunderbolt snatched him away? 10
THERAMENES. Scarce were we issuing from Troezen's gates;
He drove his chariot; round about him ranged,
Copying his silence, were his cheerless guards.
Pensive, he followed the Mycenae road,
And let the reins hang loose upon his steeds.
These haughty steeds, that once upon a time,
Noble, high-spirited, obeyed his voice,
Now dull of eye and with dejected air
Seemed to conform to his despondent thoughts.
A ghastly cry from out the water's depths 20

That moment rent the quiet of the air.
From the earth's entrails then a fearful voice
Made answer with a groan to that dread cry.
Deep in our hearts our blood with horror froze.
The coursers' manes, on hearing, stood erect.
And now, there rose upon the liquid plain
A watery mountain seething furiously.
The surge drew near, dissolved and vomited
A raging monster from among the foam.
His forehead huge was armed with fearsome horns 30
And his whole body sheathed in yellow scales,
Half bull, half dragon, wild, impetuous.
His crupper curved in many a winding fold.
The shore quaked with his long-drawn bellowings.
The heavens beheld the monster, horror-struck;
It poisoned all the air; it rocked the earth.
The wave that brought it in recoiled aghast.
Everyone, throwing courage to the winds,
Took refuge in the temple near at hand.
Hippolytus alone, undaunted, stayed, 40
Reined in his steeds and seized his javelins,
Had at the monster and, with sure-flung dart,
Dealt him a gaping wound deep in his flank.
With rage and pain the monster, starting up,
Collapsed and, falling at the horses' feet,
Rolled over, opening wide his flaming jaws,
And covered them with smoke and blood and fire.
Carried away by terror, deaf, the steeds
No more responded to his curb or voice.
Their master spent his efforts all in vain. 50
They stained the bridle with their bloody foam.
In this wild tumult, it is even said,
A god appeared, goading their dusty flanks.
Over the rocks fear drove them headlong on;
The axle groaned and broke. Hippolytus
Saw his whole chariot shattered into bits.
He fell at last, entangled in the reins.
Forgive my grief. For me this picture spells
Eternal sorrow and perpetual tears.
I have beheld, my lord, your ill-starred son 60
Dragged by the horses that his hand had fed.
His voice that called them merely frightened them.
Onward they flew—his body one whole wound.
The plain resounded with our cries of woe.
At last they slackened their impetuous course.
They halted near the old ancestral tombs
Where all his royal forebears lie in state.
I and his guards hastened to him in tears.
The traces of his blood showed us the way.
The rocks were stained with it, the cruel thorns 70

Dripped with the bleeding remnants of his hair.
I saw him, called him; giving me his hand,
He opened, then that moment closed, his eyes.
"Heaven takes my life, though innocent," he cried.
"When I am dead, protect Aricia.
Friend, if my father ever learns the truth,
And pities the misfortunes of his son,
And would appease me in the life to come,
Tell him to show that princess clemency,
To give her back. . . ." And then he passed away, 80
And in my arms lay a disfigured corpse,
A tribute to the anger of the gods
That even his father would not recognize.
THESEUS. My son, fond hope I have myself destroyed!
Inexorable, all too helpful gods!
What keen remorse will haunt me all my life!
THERAMENES. Aricia then came upon the scene.
She came, my lord, fleeing your royal wrath,
Before the gods to pledge her faith to him.
As she drew near, she saw the reeking grass. 90
She saw, a grim sight for a lover's eyes,
Hippolytus, disfigured, deadly pale.
A while she tried to doubt her evil fate.
She sees the body of Hippolytus,
Yet still pursues the quest for her beloved.
But, in the end, only too sure 'tis he,
With one sad look, accusing heaven's spite,
Cold, moaning, and well nigh inanimate,
She falls, unconscious, at her sweetheart's feet.
Ismene, bending over her, in tears, 100
Summons her back to life, a life of pain.
And I have come, my lord, hating the world,
To tell you of Hippolytus' last wish
And to discharge the bitter embassy
Which he entrusted to me as he died.
But hither comes his deadly enemy.

SCENE SEVEN
THESEUS PHAEDRA THERAMENES
PANOPE GUARDS

THESEUS. Well, then, you triumph and my son's no more.
What grounds I have for fear! What cruel doubt
Gnaws at my heart, pleading his innocence!
But he is dead. Accept your victim. Joy
In his undoing, justified or no,
For I am willing to deceive myself.
Since you accuse him, I accept his guilt.
His death will make my tears flow fast enough

Without my seeking for enlightenment
Which could not ever bring him back to me 10
And might perhaps but sharpen my distress.
Let me flee, far from you and from these shores,
The bloody vision of my mangled son.
Stunned and pursued by this grim memory,
Would I were in another universe!
Everything seems to brand my wicked wrath.
My very name increases my despair.
Less known of mortals, I could hide myself.
I hate even the favours of the gods.
And now I must bewail their murderous gifts, 20
No longer tiring them with fruitless prayers.
Whatever they have done for me, their aid
Cannot give back what they have robbed me of.

PHAEDRA. No, Theseus. No, I must at last speak out.
I must redress the wrong I did your son,
For he was innocent,

THESEUS.
 Wretch that I am!
If I condemned him, it was on your word.
Cruel one, do you hope to be forgiven . . .

PHAEDRA. Each moment's precious. Listen. It was I,
Theseus, who on your virtuous, filial son 30
Made bold to cast a lewd, incestuous eye.
Heaven in my heart lit an ill-omened fire.
Detestable Oenone did the rest.
She feared your son, knowing my frenzy, might
Reveal a guilty passion he abhorred.
The wretch, exploiting my enfeebled state,
Rushed to denounce Hippolytus to you.
She has exacted justice on herself
And found beneath the waves too mild a death.
By now I would have perished by the sword, 40
But first I wished to clear my victim's name.
I wished, revealing my remorse to you,
To choose a slower road down to the dead.
I have instilled into my burning veins
A poison that Medea brought to Greece.[28]
Already it has reached my heart and spread
A strange chill through my body. Even now
Only as through a cloud I see the bright
Heaven and the husband whom I still defile.
But death, robbing my eyes of light, will give 50
Back to the sun its tarnished purity.

[28] Medea, princess of Colchis, helped Jason win the Golden Fleece and fled with him.
When Jason lost interest in her and wanted to marry Creusa, Medea, who had powers of
sorcery, sent her a gown that burned her to death. She then killed her own children and
escaped to Athens.

PANOPE. Ah! she is dying.
THESEUS.
 Would the memory
Of her appalling misdeeds die with her!
Let us, now that my error's all too clear,
Go out and mourn over my ill-starred son.
Let us embrace my cherished son's remains
And expiate my mad atrocious wish,
Rendering him the honours he deserves,
And, to appease the anger of his shade,
Let his beloved, despite her brothers' crime, 60
Be as a daughter to me from this day.

Jonathan Swift
(1667–1745)

The most powerful English satirist in an age of great satire, Jonathan Swift
was also a dedicated clergyman, a political journalist, an accomplished poet,
and a master of English prose style whose interest in language reflects his
attitude toward the integrity or corruption of society. He was born in 1667
in Dublin, a descendant of a family that had supported the monarchy in the
English civil wars of the mid-seventeenth century. His father died before
Jonathan was born. Supported by uncles, he attended Kilkenny, an excel-
lent school, and then Trinity College, Dublin, where he had a mediocre
career as a student. Because of the disturbances in Ireland following on the
English revolution of 1688, Swift emigrated to England, where in 1689 he
became secretary in the household of Sir William Temple, a writer and
retired diplomat, with whom Swift spent the greater part of the next ten
years. There Swift met a young girl named Esther Johnson (the "Stella" to
whom he later wrote a series of engrossing letters). Swift's subsequent rela-
tionship with her is still mysterious. He may have married her, but if so the
marriage was not consummated, possibly (to cite one of several specula-
tions on the matter) because of a blood kinship between the two. In 1692
Swift took a master's degree from Oxford, and in 1695 he was ordained a
priest of the Anglican church of Ireland. He read a good deal while he was
with Temple and embarked there on his literary career. After some early
experiments in the Pindaric ode, which were discouraged by the poet John
Dryden, he adopted a drier and more direct poetic style closer to the mor-
dant prose that would become characteristic of him.

During this decade he also began work on two early satiric masterpieces
in prose: A Tale of a Tub and The Battle of the Books. These works, published
together in 1704, illustrate the conservative bent that Swift shares with
many other great satirists. The former is a dazzling, difficult, kaleidoscopic
work attacking religious, scientific, and scholarly corruptions, including
what seemed to Swift an illusory theory of human progress and modernist
forms of rationalism. (Swift believed strongly in the value of reason, but he
hated abstract and metaphysical systems.) The Battle of the Books is a mock

epic in which Swift sides with the "ancients," who favored the "old" learning and especially the classics, in a contemporary debate between them and the "moderns," who resisted intellectual authority and tended to champion the new science. A famous passage in *The Battle* compares the moderns to the spider, absorbed in itself and producing only excrement and venom, whereas the ancients are like the bee, bringing home from its wide-ranging flights honey and wax and thus producing "the two noblest of things, which are sweetness and light."

After Temple's death, Swift went through several years of unsettledness. He lived partly in Ireland and partly in England, where he began to acquire some prestige and fame, although his hopes for a high appointment in the Church were frustrated. He associated with prominent Whigs including the essayists Addison and Steele and the playwright Congreve. But, although Swift was still a Whig and supported the Whig position that royal power must be balanced by parliament, he was uncomfortable with that party's encouragement of religious Dissenters. In 1710 he shifted his allegiance to the Tories, who were then in power. Swift soon became their foremost political journalist. He also became part of the "Scriblerus Club," a group of brilliant Tory wits that included Alexander Pope and the dramatist John Gay. Some years later, in 1728, Swift helped inspire Pope's satire *The Dunciad* and Gay's *The Beggar's Opera*.

This period, the height of Swift's political influence, ended in 1714 with the death of Queen Anne and the overthrow of the Tories. Although disappointed in his desire for a deanery in England, Swift was named in 1713 dean of St. Patrick's Cathedral in Dublin. He spent most of the rest of his life in Ireland. There, after a period of discouragement, he resumed his political writing, attacking the Whigs and defending the Irish against oppressive English economic policy. His *Drapier's Letters* (1724–25) brought charges of sedition against him, but he was now a hero of the Irish and, although known to have written the work, was not prosecuted. The best known today of his pieces about the Irish is the brief, brilliant tract *A Modest Proposal* (1729), a parody of social scientism that turns on its head the economic theory that the wealth of a nation lies in its population. Swift's calculating, "public-spirited" persona recommends a scheme of cannibalism of Irish children that is symbolically the equivalent of what was actually happening to them and their parents.

Despite a fallacious tradition that Swift was uncontrollably irascible and even mad, his mental powers remained firm until his very last years, and he received public honors in Ireland as late as 1739. He later suffered a stroke, and in 1742 he had to be entrusted to guardians. He died in Dublin in 1745. The epitaph he composed for himself was later rendered as follows by the great modern AngloIrishman William Butler Yeats:

> Swift has sailed into his rest;
> Savage indignation there
> Cannot lacerate his breast.
> Imitate him if you dare,
> World-besotted traveller; he
> Served human liberty.

Gulliver's Travels, Swift's greatest work, was begun around 1720 and published in 1726. It was brought out anonymously, or rather as the work of Lemuel Gulliver himself. It was an immediate success with all manner of readers. A famous anecdote cites an Irish bishop who declared that it was "full of improbable lies, and for his part he hardly believed a word of it"—a strangely oblique acknowledgment of an ingenious circumstantial realism in the book that has made it popular as early science fiction and (in cut versions) as a children's fantasy. Its meticulous factuality owes something to the many travel books that, among other things, it satirizes. It also owes something to the genres of allegory and beast fable; "philosophical voyages" that took an admiring primitivist view of non-European peoples; utopias; and sermon literature of the day that dwelt on the fallen corruption of mankind. The rhetorical forms of irony—understatement, exaggeration, sarcasm, the bland utterance of shocking statements, the assumption that the reasonable is outrageous or vice versa—succeed one another, often without transition, so that the reader's mental nimbleness is continually tested. The satiric strategy, even when it springs from essentially simple devices, is equally versatile. Size, in itself and as a metaphor, is used tellingly in Parts I and II, the visits to Lilliput and Brobdingnag, realizing in literal terms psychological associations with size that are half-latent in our vocabulary ("magnanimous," "small-minded"). Thus, the literally petite Lilliputians often (though not always) seem mentally petty too, whereas the big Brobdingnagians often (though not always) seem broad-minded. Physically, on the other hand, the Lilliputians, who can be seen only from a "distance," are more attractive than the giants, whose coarse skin and body hairs (our own, of course) can be seen "close up." The metaphor of seeing is, in fact, used repeatedly and intricately. The slipperiness of the satire can be seen also in the episode of the Grand Academy of Lagado in Part III, where we are first drawn into feeling contempt for the scientists' insane experiments and immediately afterward see their colleagues pursuing even more ludicrous schemes such as rewarding integrity and altruism in politics.

Much of the book's satire reaches us indirectly, through the medium of Gulliver's mind and personality. An avidly curious observer and a dutiful reporter of what he encounters, Gulliver remains essentially impressionable and naive in his value judgments. But that general fact about him does not by any means solve all our problems with the satire, for he is just as protean as everything else in the book. At times he merely reports without reaction what ought to stir a strong response in him, and when he does respond he is frequently out of phase (though in unpredictable ways) with the moral judgment expected of the reader. He can accept enormities without blinking and can defend the indefensible. He is especially good at missing connections. The unbending dogmatist whom we see after his return from Houyhnhnmland is the same man who can say of the ill-fated Captain Pocock: "He was an honest man, and a good sailor, but a little too positive in his own opinions, which was the cause of his destruction, as it hath been of several others" (IV, Chapter I). Lest we miss this irony, we have Gulliver's letter to Cousin Sympson in which Gulliver complains that even "after above six months' warning" the evils of the human race have not

been totally cured by his book. Perhaps more than anything else, it is the distance between Gulliver's judgment (or his failure to make one) and our own that marks the effect and intensity of the satire.

It is ironic, then, and an index to fluctuations in senses of humor, that for the better part of two centuries readers have often identified Gulliver's judgment of the Houyhnhnms and yahoos with Swift's. Although no reader could have missed the satiric intent of at least parts of *Gulliver's Travels*, it was first enjoyed largely for its wit and inventiveness. Before long, though, readers began to find in the book a repellent misanthropy (an especially serious evil by the standards of Swift's contemporaries) and later the signs of a seriously deranged mind. The most extreme formulation of this judgment on Swift was that of the Victorian novelist Thackeray: "a monster gibbering shrieks and gnashing imprecations against mankind—tearing down all shreds of modesty, past all sense of manliness and shame; filthy in word, filthy in thought, furious, raging, obscene." The occasions for charges in this vein include occasional ribaldry and misogyny, as well as Swift's so-called "excremental vision"; but the crux of the matter is his treatment of the yahoos and Houyhnhnms. The nauseating yahoos, it is assumed, are Swift's considered picture of humanity, set off by the sober, reasonable, and admirable horses. In the last fifty years or so, most authorities on Swift have repudiated this view as wrong or at best simplistic. They point to the book's comic tone and to the character Gulliver's limitations and errors—for example, his condescension toward the humane captain Don Pedro de Mendez, the obtuseness of the final, prideful attack on pride, and ludicrous details such as Gulliver's acquired habit of conversing with his horses.

This corrective view of the book has been widely, if not universally, accepted. But no one wants to deny that Part IV is satire, like the earlier parts, and the question is "On what?" One possibility is to see the yahoos as a symbolic extreme, derived partly from the tradition of Christian sermons on fallen man, representing the bestiality and decay of reason in the fallen state, and the Houyhnhnms as equally extreme in their rationalism without Christian charity, the real human being lying somewhere between and possibly above both. The comic touches in the descriptions of the Houyhnhnms—their threading of needles, for example—may hint at a deeper critique of them: in their coldness and rigidity they may be a hostile caricature of the thoroughgoing rationalistic ideal of benevolent natural mankind espoused by deists and freethinkers. Or the Houyhnhnms may be a positive but still limited ideal, implying that if human beings were truly rational and not merely *capable* of reason they might be imperfect but would at least avoid the worst excesses of their passions (the yahoos) and of their perversions of reason (European man). And many other readings are possible.

Welcome though such corrective modern interpretations are, it can be objected that they tend to make Swift seem too blandly normal. Granted that *Gulliver's Travels* is funny, it still seems impossible to regard the fourth part as primarily comedy. And the explanations of his satire as fundamentally an expression of values current in his time may seem to deny the unique energy, passion, and urgency that make *Gulliver's Travels* so powerful a work. It seems certain that the debate about it, and especially about Part IV, will continue.

FURTHER READING *(prepared by J. H.):* The authoritative critical life of Swift is Irvin Ehrenpreis's monumental *Swift: The Man, His Works, and the Age,* 3 vols., 1962–1983. A shorter treatment is David Nokes's *Jonathan Swift: A Hypocrite Reversed,* 1985. Claude J. Rawson's *Gulliver and the Gentle Reader: Studies in Swift and Our Time,* 1973, is a provocative study emphasizing analogies between Swift and modern writers. Rawson also edited a good collection of essays, *The Character of Swift's Satire,* 1983, which contains general essays on Swift's work and three good essays on *Gulliver's Travels.* For treatments of Swift's politics and his comedy, see J. A. Downie, *Jonathan Swift: Political Writer,* 1984; and Allan Ingram, *Intricate Laughter in the Satire of Swift and Pope,* 1986.

GULLIVER'S TRAVELS

SUMMARY OF PARTS I, II, AND III

PART I. *Lemuel Gulliver is an English physician who, after unsuccessful attempts to practice medicine at home, sails as a ship's doctor. A storm destroys his ship, and Gulliver has to swim for his life to a nearby coast, where he falls asleep in exhaustion. When he awakes, he finds himself surrounded by the Lilliputians, people six inches tall, who have tied him down with ropes, which to Gulliver are threads. Given drugged wine, Gulliver falls asleep again, after which the little people load him onto a platform and with 1,500 tiny horses haul him to the capital. There he is lodged snugly in what for Lilliput is a vast building. Gulliver learns the language, becomes more at home, and is allowed some freedom to move about in a country that proves to have many similarities (which Swift exploits for satiric purposes) to England, especially in politics and religion. The effect is to make the supposedly momentous events of European history seem trivial. In some respects, however, the Lilliputian ways and institutions seem admirable.*

Gulliver aids the Lilliputians in their war with the neighboring island of Blefuscu (representing France), wading across the intervening channel and single-handedly towing away the enemy fleet of tiny ships. Gulliver is honored by the Lilliputian emperor but later falls out with him over Gulliver's unwillingness to destroy and enslave Blefuscu. Amid much court intrigue, Gulliver is charged with treason and threatened with the loss of his eyesight. He goes to Blefuscu and is received cordially. While there, he finds a human-size small boat that has been washed ashore. Aided by a vast number of Blefuscu craftsmen, he refits the boat, sets out to sea, and is picked up by an English ship, which takes him home. Gulliver is able to vouch for and profit from his amazing adventure through displaying some tiny cattle he has brought away with him.

PART II. *After two months at home, Gulliver goes to sea again. A storm takes the ship far off its course. Gulliver goes ashore with a foraging party in a land we later learn is called Brobdingnag. He strays from his comrades and is abandoned by them when they have to row for safety from a gigantic human being who pursues them. Gulliver hides like a small insect in a giant-scale wheat field but is discovered by a sixty-foot-tall farm laborer, who carries him to the landowner's house. Gulliver becomes a kind of toy there and is entrusted to the care of the farmer's nine-year-old daughter. He learns the giants' language. The farmer makes money by displaying his tiny curiosity, taking him to the metropolis for this purpose. After Gulliver's health begins to suffer, the farmer sells him to the queen, the farmer's daughter being retained as his guardian and nurse. He finds himself constantly beset with dangers from normally small creatures like wasps*

*that in Brobdingnag are enormous. Conversing with the king, Gulliver loyally
and proudly describes civilization and what we know to be its evils. The king,
representing in his size a moral perspective larger than Gulliver's, concludes that
Gulliver's race are "the most pernicious race of little odious vermin that nature
ever suffered to crawl upon the surface of the earth."*

*A "little" box is constructed in which Gulliver can be carried around. During
a visit to the seacoast, he and his box are carried off by a giant bird, which later
drops them into the ocean. Gulliver is rescued by a ship bound for England; there
he finds it hard to adjust to life among such "tiny" men as his countrymen.*

*PART III. Bored in England, Gulliver once more goes to sea, this time to
Indo-China. From there he sets out on a trading excursion to the nearby islands.
He is captured by pirates who then abandon him in a small boat, in which he
reaches an uninhabited island. One day he sights overhead the flying island
named Laputa; the inhabitants spot Gulliver and draw him aboard. The ruling-
class men of Laputa (unlike the servants and women, who are much earthier and
more normal) are an excessively intellectual people, interested only in the theoret-
ical subtleties of mathematics, science, and music. They are so absent-minded that
they must have their servants cue them when it is their turn to reply in a conversa-
tion with one another. They also terrorize the regions they control on the earth
below by hurling down large stones or threatening to let the island drop on them.*

*When the flying island reaches the country of Balnibarbi, Gulliver gets per-
mission to visit it. There he inspects the Grand Academy of Lagado, a parody of
the Royal Society, an association of English scientists. The experimenters in the
Academy are engaged in such lunatic schemes as trying to extract sunbeams from
cucumbers and to construct buildings from the top down. At the same time the
social scientists are engaged in equally "absurd" schemes—for example, choosing
political leaders on the basis of their devotion to the public good.*

*Gulliver visits Glubbdubdrib, a land of magicians. The ghosts of the illustri-
ous dead are conjured up, and Gulliver learns from them, among other things,
how false and flattering history books are. Moving on to Luggnagg, he is shown
the struldbruggs, who will never die. Gulliver's admiration and enthusiasm over
these immortals cease when he finds that they nevertheless continue to age
throughout their endless lives.*

*Finally, Gulliver arrives in Japan, where he finds a ship to take him back to
England.*

PART IV: A VOYAGE TO THE
COUNTRY OF THE HOUYHNHNMS.

CHAPTER I

*The author sets out as captain of a ship. His men conspire against him, confine
him a long time to his cabin, set him on shore in an unknown land. He travels up
in the country. The yahoos, a strange sort of animal, described. The author meets
two Houyhnhnms.*

I continued at home with my wife and children about five months in a very
happy condition, if I could have learned the lesson of knowing when I was
well. I left my poor wife big with child, and accepted an advantageous offer
made me to be captain of the *Adventure*, a stout merchantman of 350 tons:
for I understood navigation well, and being grown weary of a surgeon's

employment at sea, which however I could exercise upon occasion, I took a skilful young man of that calling, one Robert Purefoy, into my ship. We set sail from Portsmouth[1] upon the 7th day of September, 1710;[2] on the 14th, we met with Captain Pocock of Bristol, at Tenariff, who was going to the bay of Campechy, to cut logwood.[3] On the 16th, he was parted from us by a storm; I heard since my return that his ship foundered, and none escaped, but one cabin-boy. He was an honest man, and a good sailor, but a little too positive in his own opinions, which was the cause of his destruction, as it hath been of several others. For if he had followed my advice, he might at this time have been safe at home with his family as well as myself.

I had several men died in my ship of calentures,[4] so that I was forced to get recruits out of Barbadoes, and the Leeward Islands,[5] where I touched by the direction of the merchants who employed me, which I had soon too much cause to repent; for I found afterwards that most of them had been buccaneers.[6] I had fifty hands on board, and my orders were, that I should trade with the Indians in the South Sea, and make what discoveries I could. These rogues whom I had picked up debauched my other men, and they all formed a conspiracy to seize the ship and secure me; which they did one morning, rushing into my cabin, and binding me hand and foot, threatening to throw me overboard, if I offered to stir. I told them, I was their prisoner, and would submit. This they made me swear to do, and then unbound me, only fastening one of my legs with a chain near my bed, and placed a sentry at my door with his piece[7] charged, who was commanded to shoot me dead if I attempted my liberty. They sent me down victuals and drink, and took the government of the ship to themselves. Their design was to turn pirates, and plunder the Spaniards, which they could not do till they got more men. But first they resolved to sell the goods in the ship, and then go to Madagascar[8] for recruits, several among them having died since my confinement. They sailed many weeks, and traded with the Indians, but I knew not what course they took, being kept close prisoner in my cabin, and expecting nothing less than to be murdered, as they often threatened me.

Upon the 9th day of May, 1711, one James Welch came down to my cabin; and said he had orders from the captain to set me ashore. I expostulated with him, but in vain; neither would he so much as tell me who their new captain was. They forced me into the long-boat, letting me put on my best suit of clothes, which were as good as new, and a small bundle of linen, but no arms except my hanger;[9] and they were so civil as not to search my pockets, into which I conveyed what money I had, with some other little necessaries. They rowed about a league, and then set me down on a

[1] A port on the south coast of England. [2] Gulliver's age is now forty-nine.
[3] Tenariff is the largest of the Canary Islands, off northwest Africa. The bay of Campechy is the southern part of the Gulf of Mexico, off Yucatan. Logwood is a Central American tree from which a dye is derived.
[4] Delirious tropical fever or sunstroke. [5] Islands in the West Indies.
[6] Seventeenth-century pirates frequenting the West Indies. The occasions for Gulliver's adventures are progressively more evil in the four Parts: in I he was shipwrecked; in II he was left behind when his shipmates had to flee to save themselves; in III he was captured by pirates; in IV he is the victim of treachery.
[7] Firearm. [8] A large island off southeastern Africa, now the Malagasy Republic.
[9] A small sword hanging from the belt.

strand.[10] I desired them to tell me what country it was. They all swore, they knew no more than myself, but said, that the captain (as they called him) was resolved, after they had sold the lading,[11] to get rid of me in the first place where they discovered land. They pushed off immediately, advising me to make haste, for fear of being overtaken by the tide, and bade me farewell.

In this desolate condition I advanced forward, and soon got upon firm ground, where I sat down on a bank to rest myself, and consider what I had best to do. When I was a little refreshed I went up into the country, resolving to deliver myself to the first savages I should meet, and purchase my life from them by some bracelets, glass rings, and other toys, which sailors usually provide themselves with in those voyages, and whereof I had some about me: the land was divided by long rows of trees, not regularly planted, but naturally growing; there was great plenty of grass, and several fields of oats. I walked very circumspectly for fear of being surprised, or suddenly shot with an arrow from behind or on either side. I fell into a beaten road, where I saw many tracks of human feet, and some of cows, but most of horses. At last I beheld several animals in a field, and one or two of the same kind sitting in trees. Their shape was very singular, and deformed, which a little discomposed me, so that I lay down behind a thicket to observe them better. Some of them coming forward near the place where I lay, gave me an opportunity of distinctly marking their form. Their heads and breasts were covered with a thick hair, some frizzled and others lank; they had beards like goats, and a long ridge of hair down their backs, and the foreparts of their legs and feet, but the rest of their bodies were bare, so that I might see their skins, which were of a brown buff colour. They had no tails, nor any hair at all on their buttocks, except about the anus; which, I presume, nature had placed there to defend them as they sat on the ground; for this posture they used, as well as lying down, and often stood on their hind feet. They climbed high trees, as nimbly as a squirrel, for they had strong extended claws before and behind, terminating in sharp points, and hooked. They would often spring, and bound, and leap with prodigious agility. The females were not so large as the males; they had long lank hair on their heads, and only a sort of down on the rest of their bodies, except about the anus, and pudenda. Their dugs[12] hung between their fore-feet, and often reached almost to the ground as they walked. The hair of both sexes was of several colours, brown, red, black, and yellow. Upon the whole, I never beheld in all my travels so disagreeable an animal, or one against which I naturally conceived so strong antipathy. So that thinking I had seen enough, full of contempt and aversion, I got up and pursued the beaten road, hoping it might direct me to the cabin of some Indian. I had not gone far when I met one of these creatures full in my way, and coming up directly to me. The ugly monster, when he saw me, distorted several ways every feature of his visage, and stared as at an object he had never seen before; then approaching nearer, lifted up his forepaw, whether out of curiosity or mischief, I could not tell. But I drew my hanger, and gave him a good blow with the flat side of it, for I durst not strike him with the edge, fearing the inhabitants might be provoked against me, if they should

[10]Beach. [11]Cargo. [12]Breasts.

come to know that I had killed or maimed any of their cattle. When the beast felt the smart, he drew back, and roared so loud, that a herd of at least forty came flocking about me from the next field, howling and making odious faces; but I ran to the body of a tree, and leaning my back against it, kept them off, by waving my hanger. Several of this cursed brood getting hold of the branches behind leaped up into the tree, from whence they began to discharge their excrements on my head: however, I escaped pretty well, by sticking close to the stem of a tree, but was almost stifled with the filth, which fell about me on every side.

In the midst of this distress, I observed them all to run away on a sudden as fast as they could, at which I ventured to leave the tree, and pursue the road, wondering what it was that could put them into this fright. But looking on my left hand, I saw a horse walking softly in the field, which my persecutors having sooner discovered, was the cause of their flight. The horse started a little when he came near me, but soon recovering himself, looked full in my face with manifest tokens of wonder: he viewed my hands and feet, walking round me several times. I would have pursued my journey, but he placed himself directly in the way, yet looking with a very mild aspect, never offering the least violence. We stood gazing at each other for some time; at last I took the boldness to reach my hand towards his neck, with a design to stroke it, using the common style and whistle of jockeys when they are going to handle a strange horse. But this animal, seeming to receive my civilities with disdain, shook his head, and bent his brows, softly raising up his left forefoot to remove my hand. Then he neighed three or four times, but in so different a cadence, that I almost began to think he was speaking to himself in some language of his own.

While he and I were thus employed, another horse came up; who applying himself to the first in a very formal manner, they gently struck each other's right hoof before, neighing several times by turns, and varying the sound, which seemed to be almost articulate. They went some paces off, as if it were to confer together, walking side by side, backward and forward, like persons deliberating upon some affair of weight, but often turning their eyes towards me, as it were to watch that I might not escape. I was amazed to see such actions and behaviour in brute beasts, and concluded with myself, that if the inhabitants of this country were endued with a proportionable degree of reason, they must needs be the wisest people upon earth. This thought gave me so much comfort, that I resolved to go forward until I could discover some house or village, or meet with any of the natives, leaving the two horses to discourse together as they pleased. But the first, who was a dapple grey, observing me to steal off, neighed after me in so expressive a tone, that I fancied myself to understand what he meant; whereupon I turned back, and came near him, to expect[13] his farther commands. But concealing my fear as much as I could, for I began to be in some pain, how this adventure might terminate; and the reader will easily believe I did not much like my present situation.

The two horses came up close to me, looking with great earnestness upon my face and hands. The grey steed rubbed my hat all round with his right fore-hoof, and discomposed it so much, that I was forced to adjust it

[13] Wait for.

better, by taking it off, and settling it again; whereat both he and his companion (who was a brown bay) appeared to be much surprised; the latter felt the lappet[14] of my coat, and finding it to hang loose about me, they both looked with new signs of wonder. He stroked my right hand, seeming to admire[15] the softness, and colour; but he squeezed it so hard between his hoof and his pastern,[16] that I was forced to roar; after which they both touched me with all possible tenderness. They were under great perplexity about my shoes and stockings, which they felt very often, neighing to each other, and using various gestures, not unlike those of a philosopher, when he would attempt to solve some new and difficult phenomenon.

Upon the whole, the behaviour of these animals was so orderly and rational, so acute and judicious, that I at last concluded, they must needs be magicians, who had thus metamorphosed themselves upon some design,[17] and seeing a stranger in the way, were resolved to divert themselves with him; or perhaps were really amazed at the sight of a man so very different in habit, feature, and complexion from those who might probably live in so remote a climate. Upon the strength of this reasoning, I ventured to address them in the following manner: Gentlemen, if you be conjurers, as I have good cause to believe, you can understand any language; therefore I make bold to let your Worships know, that I am a poor distressed English man, driven by his misfortunes upon your coast, and I entreat one of you, to let me ride upon his back, as if he were a real horse, to some house or village, where I can be relieved. In return of which favour, I will make you a present of this knife and bracelet (taking them out of my pocket). The two creatures stood silent while I spoke, seeming to listen with great attention; and when I had ended, they neighed frequently towards each other, as if they were engaged in serious conversation. I plainly observed, that their language expressed the passions very well, and the words might with little pains be resolved into an alphabet more easily than the Chinese.

I could frequently distinguish the word *yahoo*, which was repeated by each of them several times; and although it was impossible for me to conjecture what it meant, yet while the two horses were busy in conversation, I endeavoured to practice this word upon my tongue; and as soon as they were silent, I boldly pronounced *yahoo* in a loud voice, imitating, at the same time, as near as I could, the neighing of a horse; at which they were both visibly surprised, and the grey repeated the same word twice, as if he meant to teach me the right accent, wherein I spoke after him as well as I could, and found myself perceivably to improve every time, although very far from any degree of perfection. Then the bay tried me with a second word, much harder to be pronounced; but reducing it to the English orthography, may be spelt thus, *Houyhnhnm*.[18] I did not succeed in this so well as the former, but after two or three farther trials, I had better fortune; and they both appeared amazed at my capacity.

After some farther discourse, which I then conjectured might relate to me, the two friends took their leaves, with the same compliment of striking

[14] Lapel. [15] Wonder at. [16] The back of a horse's foot, just above the hoof.
[17] For some purpose.
[18] Imitative of the whinnying of a horse; probably pronounced *hwinnum*.

each other's hoof; and the grey made me signs that I should walk before him, wherein I thought it prudent to comply, till I could find a better director. When I offered to slacken my pace, he would cry *hhuun, hhuun;* I guessed his meaning, and gave him to understand, as well as I could, that I was weary, and not able to walk faster; upon which he would stand a while to let me rest.

CHAPTER II

The author conducted by a Houyhnhnm to his house. The house described. The author's reception. The food of the Houyhnhnms. The author in distress for want of meat, is at last relieved. His manner of feeding in that country.

Having travelled about three miles, we came to a long kind of building, made of timber stuck in the ground, and wattled[1] across; the roof was low, and covered with straw. I now began to be a little comforted, and took out some toys, which travellers usually carry for presents to the savage Indians of America and other parts, in hopes the people of the house would be thereby encouraged to receive me kindly. The horse made me a sign to go in first; it was a large room with a smooth clay floor, and a rack and manger extending the whole length on one side. There were three nags, and two mares, not eating, but some of them sitting down upon their hams,[2] which I very much wondered at; but wondered more to see the rest employed in domestic business. They seemed but ordinary cattle; however, this confirmed my first opinion, that a people who could so far civilize brute animals must needs excel in wisdom all the nations of the world. The grey came in just after, and thereby prevented any ill treatment which the others might have given me. He neighed to them several times in a style of authority, and received answers.

Beyond this room there were three others, reaching the length of the house, to which you passed through three doors, opposite to each other, in the manner of a vista;[3] we went through the second room towards the third; here the grey walked in first, beckoning me to attend:[4] I waited in the second room, and got ready my presents for the master and mistress of the house: they were two knives, three bracelets of false pearl, a small looking-glass and a bead necklace. The horse neighed three or four times, and I waited to hear some answers in a human voice, but I heard no other returns than in the same dialect, only one or two a little shriller than his. I began to think that this house must belong to some person of great note among them, because there appeared so much ceremony before I could gain admittance. But that a man of quality should be served all by horses was beyond my comprehension. I feared my brain was disturbed by my sufferings and misfortunes: I roused myself, and looked about me in the

[1] Made of intertwined reeds or twigs. [2] Buttocks.
[3] A long view; the doorways are so arranged that one can see through them the length of the building.
[4] Wait.

room where I was left alone; this was furnished as the first, only after a more elegant manner. I rubbed my eyes often, but the same objects still occurred. I pinched my arms and sides, to awake myself, hoping I might be in a dream. I then absolutely concluded, that all these appearances could be nothing else but necromancy and magic. But I had no time to pursue these reflections; for the grey horse came to the door, and made me a sign to follow him into the third room, where I saw a very comely mare, together with a colt and foal, sitting on their haunches, upon mats of straw, not unartfully made, and perfectly neat and clean.

The mare, soon after my entrance, rose from her mat, and coming up close, after having nicely[5] observed my hands and face, gave me a most contemptuous look; then turning to the horse, I heard the word *yahoo* often repeated betwixt them; the meaning of which word I could not then comprehend, although it were the first I had learned to pronounce; but I was soon better informed, to my everlasting mortification: for the horse beckoning to me with his head, and repeating the word *hhuun, hhuun,* as he did upon the road, which I understood was to attend him, led me out into a kind of court, where was another building at some distance from the house. Here we entered, and I saw three of those detestable creatures, which I first met after my landing, feeding upon roots, and the flesh of some animals, which I afterwards found to be that of asses and dogs, and now and then a cow dead by accident or disease. They were all tied by the neck with strong withes,[6] fastened to a beam; they held their food between the claws of their forefeet, and tore it with their teeth.

The master horse ordered a sorrel nag, one of his servants, to untie the largest of these animals, and take him into the yard. The beast and I were brought close together, and our countenances diligently compared, both by master and servant, who thereupon repeated several times the word *yahoo.* My horror and astonishment are not to be described, when I observed, in this abominable animal, a perfect human figure; the face of it indeed was flat and broad, the nose depressed, the lips large, and the mouth wide. But these differences are common to all savage nations, where the lineaments of the countenance are distorted by the natives suffering their infants to lie grovelling on the earth, or by carrying them on their backs, nuzzling with their face against the mother's shoulders. The forefeet of the yahoo differed from my hands in nothing else but the length of the nails, the coarseness and brownness of the palms, and the hairiness on the backs. There was the same resemblance between our feet, with the same differences, which I knew very well, although the horses did not, because of my shoes and stockings; the same in every part of our bodies, except as to hairiness and colour, which I have already described.

The great difficulty that seemed to stick with the two horses, was to see the rest of my body so very different from that of a yahoo, for which I was obliged to my clothes, whereof they had no conception: the sorrel nag offered me a root, which he held (after their manner, as we shall describe in its proper place) between his hoof and pastern; I took it in my hand, and having smelt it, returned it to him as civilly as I could. He brought out of

[5] Carefully and fastidiously. [6] Flexible willow twigs.

the yahoo's kennel a piece of ass's flesh, but it smelt so offensively that I turned from it with loathing: he then threw it to the yahoo, by whom it was greedily devoured. He afterwards showed me a wisp of hay, and a fetlock[7] full of oats; but I shook my head, to signify, that neither of these were food for me. And indeed, I now apprehended, that I must absolutely starve, if I did not get to some of my own species: for as to those filthy yahoos, although there were few greater lovers of mankind, at that time, than myself, yet I confess I never saw any sensitive[8] being so detestable on all accounts; and the more I came near them, the more hateful they grew, while I stayed in that country. This the master horse observed by my behaviour, and therefore sent the yahoo back to his kennel. He then put his fore-hoof to his mouth, at which I was much surprised, although he did it with ease, and with a motion that appeared perfectly natural, and made other signs to know what I would eat; but I could not return him such an answer as he was able to apprehend; and if he had understood me, I did not see how it was possible to contrive any way for finding myself nourishment. While we were thus engaged, I observed a cow passing by, whereupon I pointed to her, and expressed a desire to let me go and milk her. This had its effect; for he led me back into the house, and ordered a mare-servant to open a room, where a good store of milk lay in earthen and wooden vessels, after a very orderly and cleanly manner. She gave me a large bowl full, of which I drank very heartily, and found myself well refreshed.

About noon I saw coming towards the house a kind of vehicle drawn like a sledge by four yahoos. There was in it an old steed, who seemed to be of quality; he alighted with his hind feet forward, having by accident got a hurt in his left forefoot. He came to dine with our horse, who received him with great civility. They dined in the best room, and had oats boiled in milk for the second course, which the old horse eat[9] warm, but the rest cold. Their mangers were placed circular in the middle of the room, and divided into several partitions, round which they sat on their haunches upon bosses[10] of straw. In the middle was a large rack with angles answering to every partition of the manger. So that each horse and mare eat their own hay, and their own mash of oats and milk, with much decency and regularity. The behaviour of the young colt and foal appeared very modest, and that of the master and mistress extremely cheerful and complaisant to their guest. The grey ordered me to stand by him, and much discourse passed between him and his friend concerning me, as I found by the stranger's often looking on me, and the frequent repetition of the word *yahoo*.

I happened to wear my gloves, which the master grey observing, seemed perplexed, discovering[11] signs of wonder what I had done to my forefeet; he put his hoof three or four times to them, as if he would signify, that I should reduce them to their former shape, which I presently did, pulling off both my gloves, and putting them into my pocket. This occasioned farther talk, and I saw the company was pleased with my behaviour, whereof I soon found the good effects. I was ordered to speak the few

[7] A projection above and behind the hoof. [8] Sentient. [9] Ate.
[10] Hassocks. [11] Revealing.

words I understood, and while they were at dinner, the master taught me the names for oats, milk, fire, water, and some others: which I could readily pronounce after him, having from my youth a great facility in learning languages.

When dinner was done, the master horse took me aside, and by signs and words made me understand the concern he was in, that I had nothing to eat. Oats in their tongue are called *hlunnh*. This word I pronounced two or three times; for although I had refused them at first, yet upon second thoughts, I considered that I could contrive to make of them a kind of bread, which might be sufficient with milk to keep me alive, till I could make my escape to some other country, and to creatures of my own species. The horse immediately ordered a white mare-servant of his family to bring me a good quantity of oats in a sort of wooden tray. These I heated before the fire as well as I could, and rubbed them till the husks came off, which I made a shift[12] to winnow from the grain; I ground and beat them between two stones, then took water, and made them into a paste or cake, which I toasted at the fire, and eat warm with milk. It was at first a very insipid[13] diet, although common enough in many parts of Europe, but grew tolerable by time; and having been often reduced to hard fare in my life, this was not the first experiment I had made how easily nature is satisfied. And I cannot but observe, that I never had one hour's sickness, while I stayed in this island. It is true, I sometimes made a shift to catch a rabbit, or bird, by springes[14] made of yahoos' hairs, and I often gathered wholesome herbs, which I boiled, or eat as salads with my bread, and now and then, for a rarity, I made a little butter, and drank the whey.[15] I was at first at a great loss for salt; but custom soon reconciled the want of it; and I am confident that the frequent use of salt among us is an effect of luxury, and was first introduced only as a provocative to drink; except where it is necessary for preserving of flesh in long voyages, or in places remote from great markets. For we observe no animal to be fond of it but man:[16] and as to myself, when I left this country, it was a great while before I could endure the taste of it in anything that I eat.

This is enough to say upon the subject of my diet, wherewith other travellers fill their books, as if the readers were personally concerned whether we fared well or ill. However, it was necessary to mention this matter, lest the world should think it impossible that I could find sustenance for three years in such a country, and among such inhabitants.

When it grew towards evening, the master horse ordered a place for me to lodge in; it was but six yards from the house, and separated from the stable of the yahoos. Here I got some straw, and covering myself with my own clothes, slept very sound. But I was in a short time better accommodated, as the reader shall know hereafter, when I come to treat more particularly about my way of living.

[12]Managed. [13]Lacking flavor. [14]Snares. [15]The watery ingredient in milk.
[16]An error (by Swift or Gulliver); many animals like and need salt, especially herbivorous ones.

CHAPTER III

The author studious to learn the language, the Houyhnhnm his master assists in teaching him. The language described. Several Houyhnhnms of quality come out of curiosity to see the author. He gives his master a short account of his voyage.

My principal endeavour was to learn the language, which my master (for so I shall henceforth call him) and his children and every servant of his house were desirous to teach me. For they looked upon it as a prodigy that a brute animal should discover[1] such marks of a rational creature. I pointed to every thing, and enquired the name of it, which I wrote down in my journal-book when I was alone, and corrected my bad accent, by desiring those of the family to pronounce it often. In this employment, a sorrel nag, one of the under servants, was very ready to assist me.

In speaking, they pronounce through the nose and throat, and their language approaches nearest to the High Dutch or German, of any I know in Europe; but is much more graceful and significant. The Emperor Charles V made almost the same observation, when he said, that if he were to speak to his horse, it should be in High Dutch.[2]

The curiosity and impatience of my master were so great, that he spent many hours of his leisure to instruct me. He was convinced (as he afterwards told me) that I must be a yahoo, but my teachableness, civility and cleanliness astonished him; which were qualities altogether so opposite to those animals. He was most perplexed about my clothes, reasoning sometimes with himself, whether they were a part of my body; for I never pulled them off till the family were asleep, and got them on before they waked in the morning. My master was eager to learn from whence I came, how I acquired those appearances of reason which I discovered in all my actions, and to know my story from my own mouth, which he hoped he should soon do by the great proficiency I made in learning and pronouncing their words and sentences. To help my memory, I formed all I learned into the English alphabet, and writ the words down with the translations. This last, after some time, I ventured to do in my master's presence. It cost me much trouble to explain to him what I was doing; for the inhabitants have not the least idea of books or literature.

In about ten weeks time I was able to understand most of his questions, and in three months could give him some tolerable answers. He was extremely curious to know from what part of the country I came, and how I was taught to imitate a rational creature, because the yahoos (whom he saw I exactly resembled in my head, hands and face, that were only visible), with some appearance of cunning, and the strongest disposition to mischief, were observed to be the most unteachable of all brutes. I answered, that I came over the sea, from a far place, with many others of my own

[1] Reveal; evince.

[2] Charles V was Holy Roman Emperor and king of Spain. He is said to have remarked that he would address his God in Spanish, his mistress in Italian, and his horse in German. The German (Hanoverian) kings who, beginning with George I in 1714, had become rulers of England were not popular with the Tories.

kind, in a great hollow vessel made of the bodies of trees. That my companions forced me to land on this coast, and then left me to shift for myself. It was with some difficulty, and by the help of many signs, that I brought him to understand me. He replied, that I must needs be mistaken, or that I "said the thing which was not." (For they have no words in their language to express lying or falsehood.) He knew it was impossible that there could be a country beyond the sea, or that a parcel of brutes could move a wooden vessel whither they pleased upon water. He was sure no Houyhnhnm alive could make such a vessel, or would trust yahoos to manage it.

The word *Houyhnhnm*, in their tongue, signifies a *horse*, and in its etymology, *the perfection of nature.* I told my master, that I was at a loss for expression, but would improve as fast as I could; and hoped in a short time I should be able to tell him wonders: he was pleased to direct his own mare, his colt and foal, and the servants of the family to take all opportunities of instructing me, and every day for two or three hours he was at the same pains himself: several horses and mares of quality in the neighbourhood came often to our house upon the report spread of a wonderful yahoo, that could speak like a Houyhnhnm, and seemed in his words and actions to discover some glimmerings of reason. These delighted to converse with me; they put many questions, and received such answers as I was able to return. By all which advantages, I made so great a progress, that in five months from my arrival I understood whatever was spoke, and could express myself tolerably well.

The Houyhnhnms who came to visit my master, out of a design of seeing and talking with me, could hardly believe me to be a right[3] yahoo, because my body had a different covering from others of my kind. They were astonished to observe me without the usual hair or skin except on my head, face, and hands; but I discovered that secret to my master, upon an accident, which happened about a fortnight before.

I have already told the reader, that every night, when the family were gone to bed, it was my custom to strip and cover myself with my clothes: it happened one morning early, that my master sent for me, by the sorrel nag, who was his valet; when he came, I was fast asleep, my clothes fallen off on one side, and my shirt above my waist. I awaked at the noise he made, and observed him to deliver his message in some disorder; after which he went to my master, and in a great fright gave him a very confused account of what he had seen: this I presently discovered; for going, as soon as I was dresssed, to pay my attendance upon his Honour, he asked me the meaning of what his servant had reported, that I was not the same thing when I slept as I appeared to be at other times; that his valet assured him, some part of me was white, some yellow, at least not so white, and some brown.

I had hitherto concealed the secret of my dress, in order to distinguish myself as much as possible from that cursed race of yahoos; but now I found it in vain to do so any longer. Besides, I considered that my clothes and shoes would soon wear out, which already were in a declining condition, and must be supplied by some contrivance from the hides of yahoos

[3] True; genuine.

or other brutes; whereby the whole secret would be known: I therefore told my master, that in the country from whence I came those of my kind always covered their bodies with the hairs of certain animals prepared by art, as well for decency, as to avoid inclemencies of air both hot and cold; of which, as to my own person, I would give him immediate conviction, if he pleased to command me; only desiring his excuse, if I did not expose those parts that nature taught us to conceal. He said my discourse was all very strange, but especially the last part; for he could not understand why nature should teach us to conceal what nature had given. That neither himself nor family were ashamed of any parts of their bodies; but however I might do as I pleased. Whereupon, I first unbuttoned my coat, and pulled it off. I did the same with my waistcoat; I drew off my shoes, stockings, and breeches. I let my shirt down to my waist, and drew up the bottom, fastening it like a girdle about my middle to hide my nakedness.

My master observed the whole performance with great signs of curiosity and admiration.[4] He took up all my clothes in his pastern, one piece after another, and examined them diligently; he then stroked my body very gently and looked round me several times, after which he said, it was plain I must be a perfect yahoo; but that I differed very much from the rest of my species, in the whiteness and smoothness of my skin, my want of hair in several parts of my body, the shape and shortness of my claws behind and before, and my affectation of walking continually on my two hinder feet. He desired to see no more, and gave me leave to put on my clothes again, for I was shuddering with cold.

I expressed my uneasiness at his giving me so often the appellation of *yahoo*, an odious animal, for which I had so utter an hatred and contempt; I begged he would forbear applying that word to me, and take the same order in his family, and among his friends whom he suffered[5] to see me. I requested likewise, that the secret of my having a false covering to my body might be known to none but himself, at least as long as my present clothing should last; for as to what the sorrel nag his valet had observed, his Honour might command him to conceal it.

All this my master very graciously consented to, and thus the secret was kept till my clothes began to wear out, which I was forced to supply by several contrivances, that shall hereafter be mentioned. In the mean time, he desired I would go on with my utmost diligence to learn their language, because he was more astonished at my capacity for speech and reason than at the figure of my body, whether it were covered or no; adding, that he waited with some impatience to hear the wonders which I promised to tell him.

From thenceforward he doubled the pains he had been at to instruct me; he brought me into all company, and made them treat me with civility, because, as he told them privately, this would put me into good humour, and make me more diverting.

Every day when I waited on him, beside the trouble he was at in teaching, he would ask me several questions concerning myself, which I answered as well as I could; and by those means he had already received some general ideas, although very imperfect. It would be tedious to relate the

[4] Wonder. [5] Permitted.

several steps by which I advanced to a more regular conversation: but the first account I gave of myself in any order and length, was to this purpose:

That I came from a very far country, as I already had attempted to tell him, with about fifty more of my own species; that we travelled upon the seas, in a great hollow vessel made of wood, and larger than his Honour's house. I described the ship to him in the best terms I could, and explained by the help of my handkerchief displayed, how it was driven forward by the wind. That upon a quarrel among us, I was set on shore on this coast, where I walked forward without knowing whither, till he delivered me from the persecution of those execrable yahoos. He asked me, who made the ship, and how it was possible that the Houyhnhnms of my country would leave it to the management of brutes? My answer was, that I durst proceed no farther in my relation, unless he would give me his word and honour that he would not be offended, and then I would tell him the wonders I had so often promised. He agreed; and I went on by assuring him, that the ship was made by creatures like myself, who in all the countries I had travelled, as well as in my own, were the only governing, rational animals; and that upon my arrival hither, I was as much astonished to see the Houyhnhnms act like rational beings, as he or his friends could be in finding some marks of reason in a creature he was pleased to call a yahoo, to which I owned[6] my resemblance in every part, but could not account for their degenerate and brutal nature. I said farther, that if good fortune ever restored me to my native country, to relate my travels hither, as I resolved to do, everybody would believe that I "said the thing which was not"; that I invented the story out of my own head; and with all possible respect to himself, his family and friends, and under his promise of not being offended, our countrymen would hardly think it probable, that a Houyhnhnm should be the presiding creature of a nation, and a yahoo the brute.

CHAPTER IV

The Houyhnhnms' notion of truth and falsehood. The author's discourse disapproved by his master. The author gives a more particular account of himself, and the accidents of his voyage.

My master heard me with great appearances of uneasiness in his countenance, because *doubting* or *not believing,* are so little known in this country, that the inhabitants cannot tell how to behave themselves under such circumstances. And I remember in frequent discourses with my master concerning the nature of manhood,[1] in other parts of the world, having occasion to talk of *lying* and *false representation,* it was with much difficulty that he comprehended what I meant, although he had otherwise a most acute judgment. For he argued thus; that the use of speech was to make us understand one another, and to receive information of facts; now if any one *said the thing which was not,* these ends were defeated; because I cannot properly be said to understand him, and I am so far from receiving infor-

[6] Admitted; acknowledged. [1] Humanity.

mation, that he leaves me worse than in ignorance, for I am led to believe a thing black when it is white, and short when it is long. And these were all the notions he had concerning that faculty of lying, so perfectly well understood, and so universally practised among human creatures.

To return from this digression; when I asserted that the yahoos were the only governing animals in my country, which my master said was altogether past his conception, he desired to know, whether we had Houyhnhnms among us, and what was their employment: I told him, we had great numbers, that in summer they grazed in the fields, and in winter were kept in houses, with hay and oats, where yahoo servants were employed to rub their skins smooth, comb their manes, pick their feet, serve them with food, and make their beds. I understand you well, said my master, it is now very plain, from all you have spoken, that whatever share of reason the yahoos pretend to, the Houyhnhnms are your masters; I heartily wish our yahoos would be so tractable.[2] I begged his Honour would please to excuse me from proceeding any farther, because I was very certain that the account he expected from me would be highly displeasing. But he insisted in commanding me to let him know the best and the worst: I told him, he should be obeyed. I owned, that the Houyhnhnms among us, whom we called horses, were the most generous[3] and comely animal we had, that they excelled in strength and swiftness; and when they belonged to persons of quality, employed in travelling, racing, and drawing chariots, they were treated with much kindness and care, till they fell into diseases, or became foundered[4] in the feet; but then they were sold, and used to all kind of drudgery till they died; after which their skins were stripped and sold for what they were worth, and their bodies left to be devoured by dogs and birds of prey. But the common race of horses had not so good fortune, being kept by farmers and carriers and other mean people,[5] who put them to greater labour, and feed them worse. I described, as well as I could, our way of riding, the shape and use of a bridle, a saddle, a spur, and a whip, of harness and wheels. I added, that we fastened plates of a certain hard substance called "iron" at the bottom of their feet, to preserve their hoofs from being broken by the stony ways on which we often travelled.

My master, after some expressions of great indignation, wondered how we dared to venture upon a Houyhnhnm's back, for he was sure that the weakest servant in his house would be able to shake off the strongest yahoo, or by lying down, and rolling upon his back, squeeze the brute to death. I answered, that our horses were trained up from three or four years old to the several uses we intended them for; that if any of them proved intolerably vicious, they were employed for carriages; that they were severely beaten while they were young, for any mischievous tricks; that the males, designed for the common use of riding or draught,[6] were generally castrated about two years after their birth, to take down their spirits, and make them more tame and gentle; that they were indeed sensible[7] of rewards and punishments; but his Honour would please to consider, that they had not the least tincture of reason any more than the yahoos in this country.

[2] Easily controlled. [3] Noble. [4] Lamed. [5] People of the lower classes.
[6] Hauling of heavy loads. [7] Aware.

It put me to the pains of many circumlocutions to give my master a right idea of what I spoke; for their language doth not abound in variety of words, because their wants and passions are fewer than among us. But it is impossible to express his noble resentment at our savage treatment of the Houyhnhnm race, particularly after I had explained the manner and use of castrating horses among us, to hinder them from propagating their kind, and to render them more servile. He said, if it were possible there could be any country where yahoos alone were endued with reason, they certainly must be the governing animal, because reason will in time always prevail against brutal strength. But, considering the frame of our bodies, and especially of mine, he thought no creature of equal bulk was so ill contrived for employing that reason in the common offices of life; whereupon he desired to know whether those among whom I lived resembled me or the yahoos of his country. I assured him, that I was as well shaped as most of my age: but the younger and the females were much more soft and tender, and the skins of the latter generally as white as milk. He said, I differed indeed from other yahoos, being much more cleanly, and not altogether so deformed, but in point of real advantage he thought I differed for the worse. That my nails were of no use either to my fore or hinder feet; as to my forefeet, he could not properly call them by that name, for he never observed me to walk upon them; that they were too soft to bear the ground; that I generally went with them uncovered, neither was the covering I sometimes wore on them of the same shape or so strong as that on my feet behind. That I could not walk with any security, for if either of my hinder feet slipped, I must inevitably fall. He then began to find fault with other parts of my body, the flatness of my face, the prominence of my nose, my eyes placed directly in front, so that I could not look on either side without turning my head: that I was not able to feed myself without lifting one of my forefeet to my mouth: and therefore nature had placed those joints to answer that necessity. He knew not what could be the use of those several clefts and divisions in my feet behind; that these were too soft to bear the hardness and sharpness of stones without a covering made from the skin of some other brute; that my whole body wanted a fence[8] against heat and cold, which I was forced to put on and off every day with tediousness and trouble. And lastly, that he observed every animal in this country naturally to abhor the yahoos, whom the weaker avoided, and the stronger drove from them. So that supposing us to have the gift of reason, he could not see how it were possible to cure that natural antipathy which every creature discovered against us; nor consequently, how we could tame and render them serviceable. However, he would (as he said) debate the matter no farther, because he was more desirous to know my own story, the country where I was born, and the several actions and events of my life before I came hither.

I assured him how extremely desirous I was that he should be satisfied in every point; but I doubted much, whether it would be possible for me to explain myself on several subjects whereof his Honour could have no con-

[8] Defense.

ception, because I saw nothing in his country to which I could resemble them. That however, I would do my best, and strive to express myself by similitudes, humbly desiring his assistance when I wanted proper words; which he was pleased to promise me.

I said, my birth was of honest parents, in an island called England, which was remote from this country as many days' journey as the strongest of his Honour's servants could travel in the annual course of the sun. That I was bred a surgeon, whose trade is to cure wounds and hurts in the body, got by accident or violence; that my country was governed by a female man, whom we called *queen*.[9] That I left it to get riches, whereby I might maintain myself and family when I should return. That in my last voyage I was commander of the ship, and had about fifty yahoos under me, many of which died at sea, and I was forced to supply them by others picked out from several nations. That our ship was twice in danger of being sunk; the first time by a great storm, and the second, by striking against a rock. Here my master interposed, by asking me, how I could persuade strangers out of different countries to venture with me, after the losses I had sustained, and the hazards I had run. I said, they were fellows of desperate fortunes, forced to fly from the places of their birth, on account of their poverty or their crimes. Some were undone by lawsuits; others spent all they had in drinking, whoring, and gaming; others fled for treason; many for murder, theft, poisoning, robbery, perjury, forgery, coining false money, for committing rapes or sodomy, for flying from their colours, or deserting to the enemy, and most of them had broken prison; none of these durst return to their native countries for fear of being hanged, or of starving in a jail; and therefore were under a necessity of seeking a livelihood in other places.

During this discourse, my master was pleased often to interrupt me; I had made use of many circumlocutions in describing to him the nature of the several crimes, for which most of our crew had been forced to fly their country. This labour took up several days' conversation before he was able to comprehend me. He was wholly at a loss to know what could be the use or necessity of practising those vices. To clear up which I endeavoured to give him some ideas of the desire of power and riches, of the terrible effects of lust, intemperance, malice and envy. All this I was forced to define and describe by putting of cases, and making suppositions. After which, like one whose imagination was struck with something never seen or heard of before, he would lift up his eyes with amazement and indignation. Power, government, war, law, punishment, and a thousand other things had no terms wherein that language could express them, which made the difficulty almost insuperable to give my master any conception of what I meant. But being of an excellent understanding, much improved by contemplation and converse, he at last arrived at a competent knowledge of what human nature in our parts of the world is capable to perform, and desired I would give him some particular account of that land which we call Europe, especially of my own country.

[9] At the time of this voyage, England was ruled by Queen Anne (reigned 1702–14), daughter of James II and last of the Stuart rulers.

<center>CHAPTER V</center>

The author, at his master's commands, informs him of the state of England. The causes of war among the princes of Europe. The author begins to explain the English constitution.

The reader may please to observe, that the following extract of many conversations I had with my master contains a summary of the most material points which were discoursed at several times for above two years; his Honour often desiring fuller satisfaction as I farther improved in the Houyhnhnm tongue. I laid before him, as well as I could, the whole state of Europe; I discoursed of trade and manufactures, of arts and sciences; and the answers I gave to all the questions he made, as they arose upon several subjects, were a fund of conversation not to be exhausted. But I shall here only set down the substance of what passed between us concerning my own country, reducing it into order as well as I can, without any regard to time or other circumstances, while I strictly adhere to truth. My only concern is, that I shall hardly be able to do justice to my master's arguments and expressions, which must needs suffer by my want of capacity, as well as by a translation into our barbarous English.

In obedience therefore to his Honour's commands, I related to him the Revolution under the Prince of Orange; the long war with France entered into by the said prince, and renewed by his successor the present queen, wherein the greatest powers of Christendom were engaged, and which still continued: I computed, at his request, that about a million of yahoos might have been killed in the whole progress of it, and perhaps a hundred or more cities taken, and five times as many ships burnt or sunk.[1]

He asked me what were the usual causes or motives that made one country go to war with another. I answered they were innumerable, but I should only mention a few of the chief. Sometimes the ambition of princes, who never think they have land or people enough to govern: sometimes the corruption of ministers, who engage their master in a war in order to stifle or divert the clamour of the subjects against their evil administration. Difference in opinions hath cost many millions of lives: for instance, whether flesh be bread, or bread be flesh; whether the juice of a certain berry be blood or wine; whether whistling be a vice or a virtue; whether it be better to kiss a post, or throw it into the fire; what is the best colour for a coat, whether black, white, red, or grey; and whether it should be long or

[1] In the "Glorious Revolution" of 1688, King James II, a Catholic and an unpopular ruler, was dethroned in favor of his Protestant daughter, who then became Mary II and ruled jointly with her Dutch husband and cousin William of Orange, who became William III. James fled to France, and the "Declaration of Rights" of 1689 made Parliament the supreme power in England. Wars with France followed, including (after Anne came to the throne in 1702) the War of the Spanish Succession, in which many European nations were involved and which was still continuing when Gulliver arrived in the Houyhnhnms' land. Swift exaggerates the number of casualties.

short, narrow or wide, dirty or clean, with many more.[2] Neither are any wars so furious and bloody, or of so long continuance, as those occasioned by difference in opinion, especially if it be in things indifferent.[3]

Sometimes the quarrel between two princes is to decide which of them shall dispossess a third of his dominions, where neither of them pretend to any right. Sometimes one prince quarrelleth with another, for fear the other should quarrel with him. Sometimes a war is entered upon, because the enemy is too strong, and sometimes because he is too weak. Sometimes our neighbours want the things which we have, or have the things which we want; and we both fight, till they take ours or give us theirs. It is a very justifiable cause of war to invade a country after the people have been wasted by famine, destroyed by pestilence, or embroiled by factions amongst themselves. It is justifiable to enter into a war against our nearest ally, when one of his towns lies convenient for us, or a territory of land, that would render our dominions round and compact. If a prince send forces into a nation where the people are poor and ignorant, he may lawfully put half of them to death, and make slaves of the rest, in order to civilize and reduce them from their barbarous way of living. It is a very kingly, honourable, and frequent practice, when one prince desires the assistance of another to secure him against an invasion, that the assistant, when he hath driven out the invader, should seize on the dominions himself, and kill, imprison or banish the prince he came to relieve. Alliance by blood or marriage is a sufficient cause of war between princes, and the nearer the kindred is, the greater is their disposition to quarrel: poor nations are hungry, and rich nations are proud, and pride and hunger will ever be at variance. For these reasons, the trade of a soldier is held the most honourable of all others: because a soldier is a yahoo hired to kill in cold blood as many of his own species, who have never offended him, as possibly he can.

There is likewise a kind of beggarly princes in Europe, not able to make war by themselves, who hire out their troops to richer nations, for so much a day to each man; of which they keep three fourths to themselves, and it is the best part of their maintenance; such are those in Germany[4] and many northern parts of Europe.

What you have told me (said my master) upon the subject of war, does indeed discover most admirably the effects of that reason you pretend to: however, it is happy that the shame is greater than the danger; and that nature hath left you utterly uncapable of doing much mischief. For your mouths lying flat with your faces, you can hardly bite each other to any purpose, unless by consent. Then as to the claws upon your feet before and behind, they are so short and tender, that one of our yahoos would drive a

[2] The references are to divisions among Protestants and between them and Catholics over the doctrine of transubstantiation (the changing of bread and wine into Christ's body and blood), the proper use of music in church, the veneration of images and particularly of the crucifix, and liturgical vestments.

[3] Unimportant.

[4] King George I, while he was Elector of Hanover, had been involved in this trade in mercenaries. The early editions of *Gulliver's Travels* omit the provocative reference to Germany.

dozen of yours before him. And therefore in recounting the numbers of those who have been killed in battle, I cannot but think that you have *said the thing which is not.*

I could not forbear shaking my head and smiling a little at his ignorance. And being no stranger to the art of war, I gave him a description of cannons, culverins,[5] muskets, carabines, pistols, bullets, powder, swords, bayonets, battles, sieges, retreats, attacks, undermines, countermines, bombardments, sea-fights; ships sunk with a thousand men, twenty thousand killed on each side; dying groans, limbs flying in the air, smoke, noise, confusion, trampling to death under horses' feet; flight, pursuit, victory; fields strewed with carcases left for food to dogs, and wolves, and birds of prey; plundering, stripping, ravishing, burning and destroying. And to set forth the valour of my own dear countrymen, I assured him, that I had seen them blow up a hundred enemies at once in a siege, and as many in a ship, and beheld the dead bodies drop down in pieces from the clouds, to the great diversion of all the spectators.

I was going on to more particulars, when my master commanded me silence. He said, whoever understood the nature of yahoos might easily believe it possible for so vile an animal to be capable of every action I had named, if their strength and cunning equalled their malice. But as my discourse had increased his abhorrence of the whole species, so he found it gave him a disturbance in his mind, to which he was wholly a stranger before. He thought his ears being used to such abominable words, might by degrees admit them with less detestation. That although he hated the yahoos of this country, yet he no more blamed them for their odious qualities, than he did a *gnnayh* (a bird of prey) for its cruelty, or a sharp stone for cutting his hoof. But when a creature pretending to reason could be capable of such enormities, he dreaded lest the corruption of that faculty might be worse than brutality itself. He seemed therefore confident, that instead of reason, we were only possessed of some quality fitted to increase our natural vices; as the reflection from a troubled stream returns the image of an ill-shapen body, not only larger, but more distorted.

He added, that he had heard too much upon the subject of war, both in this and some former discourses. There was another point which a little perplexed him at present. I had said, that some of our crew left their country on account of being ruined by *law;* that I had already explained the meaning of the word; but he was at a loss how it should come to pass, that the *law* which was intended for every man's preservation, should be any man's ruin. Therefore he desired to be farther satisfied what I meant by *law,* and the dispensers thereof according to the present practice in my own country; because he thought nature and reason were sufficient guides for a reasonable animal, as we pretended to be, in showing us what we ought to do, and what to avoid.

I assured his Honour, that law was a science wherein I had not much conversed, further than by employing advocates in vain, upon some injustices that had been done me. However, I would give him all the satisfaction I was able.

I said there was a society of men among us, bred up from their youth in

[5] Thin-barreled cannons.

the art of proving by words multiplied for the purpose, that white is black, and black is white, according as they are paid. To this society all the rest of the people are slaves.

For example, if my neighbour hath a mind to my cow, he hires a lawyer to prove that he ought to have my cow from me. I must then hire another to defend my right, it being against all rules of law that any man should be allowed to speak for himself. Now in this case, I who am the true owner lie under two great disadvantages. First, my lawyer, being practiced almost from his cradle in defending falsehood, is quite out of his element when he would be an advocate for justice, which as an office unnatural, he always attempts with great awkwardness, if not with ill will. The second disadvantage is, that my lawyer must proceed with great caution, or else he will be reprimanded by the judges, and abhorred by his brethren, as one who would lessen the practice of the law. And therefore I have but two methods to preserve my cow. The first is to gain over my adversary's lawyer with a double fee, who will then betray his client by insinuating that he hath justice on his side. The second way is for my lawyer to make my cause appear as unjust as he can, by allowing the cow to belong to my adversary; and this if it be skilfully done will certainly bespeak the favour of the bench.

Now, your Honour is to know that these judges are persons appointed to decide all controversies of property, as well as for the trial of criminals, and picked out from the most dextrous lawyers who are grown old or lazy, and having been biassed all their lives against truth and equity, lie under such a fatal necessity of favouring fraud, perjury, and oppression, that I have known several of them refuse a large bribe from the side where justice lay, rather than injure the faculty[6] by doing any thing unbecoming their nature or their office.

It is a maxim among these lawyers, that whatever hath been done before may legally be done again: and therefore they take special care to record all the decisions formerly made against common justice and the general reason of mankind. These, under the name of *precedents*, they produce as authorities, to justify the most iniquitous opinions; and the judges never fail of decreeing accordingly.

In pleading, they studiously avoid entering into the merits of the cause, but are loud, violent, and tedious in dwelling upon all circumstances which are not to the purpose. For instance, in the case already mentioned; they never desire to know what claim or title my adversary hath to my cow, but whether the said cow were red or black, her horns long or short; whether the field I graze her in be round or square, whether she was milked at home or abroad, what diseases she is subject to, and the like; after which they consult precedents, adjourn the cause from time to time, and in ten, twenty, or thirty years come to an issue.

It is likewise to be observed that this society hath a peculiar cant and jargon of their own, that no other mortal can understand, and wherein all their laws are written, which they take special care to multiply; whereby they have wholly confounded the very essence of truth and falsehood, of right and wrong; so that it will take thirty years to decide whether the field

[6] The legal profession.

left me by my ancestors for six generations belongs to me or to a stranger three hundred miles off.

In the trial of persons accused for crimes against the state the method is much more short and commendable: the judge first sends to sound the disposition of those in power, after which he can easily hang or save the criminal, strictly preserving all due forms of law.

Here my master, interposing, said it was a pity, that creatures endowed with such prodigious abilities of mind as these lawyers, by the description I gave of them, must certainly be, were not rather encouraged to be instructors of others in wisdom and knowledge. In answer to which I assured his Honour, that in all points out of their own trade they were usually the most ignorant and stupid generation among us, the most despicable in common conversation, avowed enemies to all knowledge and learning, and equally disposed to pervert the general reason of mankind in every other subject of discourse, as in that of their own profession.

CHAPTER VI

A continuation of the state of England under Queen Anne. The character of a first minister in the courts of Europe.

My master was yet wholly at a loss to understand what motives could incite this race of lawyers to perplex, disquiet, and weary themselves by engaging in a confederacy of injustice, merely for the sake of injuring their fellow-animals; neither could he comprehend what I meant in saying they did it for hire. Whereupon I was at much pains to describe to him the use of money, the materials it was made of, and the value of the metals; that when a yahoo had got a great store of this precious substance, he was able to purchase whatever he had a mind to, the finest clothing, the noblest houses, great tracts of land, the most costly meats and drinks, and have his choice of the most beautiful females. Therefore since money alone was able to perform all these feats, our yahoos thought they could never have enough of it to spend or to save, as they found themselves inclined from their natural bent either to profusion or avarice. That the rich man enjoyed the fruit of the poor man's labour, and the latter were a thousand to one in proportion to the former. That the bulk of our people were forced to live miserably, by labouring every day for small wages to make a few live plentifully. I enlarged myself much on these and many other particulars to the same purpose: but his Honour was still to seek,[1] for he went upon a supposition that all animals had a title to their share in the productions of the earth, and especially those[2] who presided over the rest. Therefore he desired I would let him know what these costly meats were, and how any of us happened to want[3] them. Whereupon I enumerated as many sorts as came into my head, with the various methods of dressing them, which could not be done without sending vessels by sea to every part of the world, as well for liquors to drink, as for sauces, and innumerable other conveniencies. I assured him, that this whole globe of earth must be at least three times gone

[1] Unable to understand. [2] That species. [3] Lack.

round, before one of our better female yahoos could get her breakfast, or a cup to put it in. He said, that must needs be a miserable country which cannot furnish food for its own inhabitants. But what he chiefly wondered at was how such vast tracts of ground as I described should be wholly without fresh water, and the people put to the necessity of sending over the sea for drink. I replied, that England (the dear place of my nativity) was computed to produce three times the quantity of food more than its inhabitants are able to consume, as well as liquors extracted from grain, or pressed out of the fruit of certain trees, which made excellent drink, and the same proportion in every other convenience of life. But in order to feed the luxury and intemperance of the males, and the vanity of the females, we sent away the greatest part of our necessary things to other countries, from whence in return we brought the materials of diseases, folly, and vice, to spend among ourselves. Hence it follows of necessity that vast numbers of our people are compelled to seek their livelihood by begging, robbing, stealing, cheating, pimping, forswearing, flattering, suborning,[4] forging, gaming, lying, fawning, hectoring,[5] voting, scribbling, star-gazing,[6] poisoning, whoring, canting,[7] libelling, free-thinking,[8] and the like occupations: every one of which terms, I was at much pains to make him understand.

That wine was not imported among us from foreign countries to supply the want of water or other drinks, but because it was a sort of liquid which made us merry, by putting us out of our senses; diverted all melancholy thoughts, begat wild extravagant imaginations in the brain, raised our hopes, and banished our fears, suspended every office of reason for a time, and deprived us of the use of our limbs, until we fell into a profound sleep; although it must be confessed, that we always awaked sick and dispirited, and that the use of this liquor filled us with diseases, which made our lives uncomfortable and short.

But beside all this, the bulk of our people supported themselves by furnishing the necessities or conveniencies of life to the rich, and to each other. For instance, when I am at home and dressed as I ought to be, I carry on my body the workmanship of an hundred tradesmen; the building and furniture of my house employ as many more, and five times the number to adorn my wife.

I was going on to tell him of another sort of people, who get their livelihood by attending the sick, having upon some occasions informed his Honour that many of my crew had died of diseases. But here it was with the utmost difficulty that I brought him to apprehend what I meant. He could easily conceive that a Houyhnhnm grew weak and heavy[9] a few days before his death, or by some accident might hurt a limb. But that Nature, who works all things to perfection, should suffer any pains to breed in our bodies, he thought impossible, and desired to know the reason of so unaccountable an evil. I told him, we fed on a thousand things which operated contrary to each other; that we eat when we were not hungry, and drank without the provocation of thirst; that we sat whole nights drinking strong

[4] Inducing a person to do wrong, especially commit perjury.
[5] Threatening.　　[6] Using astrology.　　[7] Using jargon, especially of piety.
[8] Rationalist rejection of religious doctrine.　　[9] Weary.

liquors without eating a bit, which disposed us to sloth, enflamed our bod-
ies, and precipitated or prevented digestion. That prostitute female yahoos
acquired a certain malady, which bred rottenness in the bones of those who
fell into their embraces; that this and many other diseases were propagated
from father to son, so that great numbers come into the world with compli-
cated maladies upon them; that it would be endless to give him a catalogue
of all diseases incident to human bodies; for they could not be fewer than
five or six hundred, spread over every limb and joint; in short, every part,
external and intestine,[10] having diseases appropriated to each. To remedy
which, there was a sort of people bred up among us, in the profession or
pretence of curing the sick. And because I had some skill in the faculty, I
would, in gratitude to his Honour, let him know the whole mystery and
method by which they proceed.

Their fundamental is, that all diseases arise from repletion,[11] from
whence they conclude that a great evacuation of the body is necessary,
either through the natural passage, or upwards at the mouth. Their next
business is, from herbs, minerals, gums, oils, shells, salts, juices, seaweed,
excrements, barks of trees, serpents, toads, frogs, spiders, dead men's flesh
and bones, birds, beasts and fishes, to form a composition for smell and
taste the most abominable, nauseous and detestable that they can possibly
contrive, which the stomach immediately rejects with loathing; and this
they call a vomit; or else from the same storehouse, with some other poi-
sonous additions, they command us to take in at the orifice above or below
(just as the physician then happens to be disposed) a medicine equally an-
noying and disgustful to the bowels, which, relaxing the belly, drives down
all before it, and this they call a purge or a clyster.[12] For nature (as the
physicians allege) having intended the superior anterior orifice only for the
intromission of solids and liquids, and the inferior posterior for ejection,
these artists ingeniously considering that in all diseases Nature is forced out
of her seat, therefore to replace her in it, the body must be treated in a
manner directly contrary, by interchanging the use of each orifice, forcing
solids and liquids in at the anus, and making evacuations at the mouth.

But besides real diseases we are subject to many that are only imaginary,
for which the physicians have invented imaginary cures; these have their
several names, and so have the drugs that are proper for them, and with
these our female yahoos are always infested.

One great excellency in this tribe is their skill at prognostics, wherein
they seldom fail; their predictions in real diseases, when they rise to any
degree of malignity, generally portending death, which is always in their
power, when recovery is not: and therefore, upon any unexpected signs of
amendment, after they have pronounced their sentence, rather than be
accused as false prophets, they know how to approve[13] their sagacity to the
world by a seasonable dose.

They are likewise of special use to husbands and wives who are grown
weary of their mates, to eldest sons, to great ministers of state, and often to
princes.

I had formerly upon occasion discoursed with my master upon the na-
ture of our government in general, and particularly of our own excellent

[10] Internal. [11] Fullness. [12] Enema. [13] Prove.

constitution, deservedly the wonder and envy of the whole world. But having here accidentally mentioned a "minister of state," he commanded me some time after to inform him, what species of yahoo I particularly meant by that appellation.

I told him that a first or chief minister[14] of state, who was the person I intended to describe, was a creature wholly exempt from joy and grief, love and hatred, pity and anger; at least makes use of no other passions but a violent desire of wealth, power, and titles; that he applies his words to all uses, except to the indication of his mind; that he never tells a truth, but with an intent that you should take it for a lie; nor a lie, but with a design that you should take it for a truth; that those he speaks worst of behind their backs are in the surest way to preferment;[15] and whenever he begins to praise you to others or to yourself, you are from that day forlorn. The worst mark you can receive is a promise, especially when it is confirmed with an oath; after which every wise man retires, and gives over all hopes.

There are three methods by which a man may rise to be chief minister: the first is, by knowing how with prudence to dispose of a wife, a daughter, or a sister: the second, by betraying or undermining his predecessor: and the third is, by a furious zeal in public assemblies against the corruptions of the court. But a wise prince would rather choose to employ those who practise the last of these methods; because such zealots prove always the most obsequious and subservient to the will and passions of their master. That these "ministers" having all employments at their disposal, preserve themselves in power by bribing the majority of a senate or great council; and at last, by an expedient called an "act of indemnity"[16] (whereof I described the nature to him) they secure themselves from after reckonings, and retire from the public, laden with the spoils of the nation.

The palace of a chief minister is a seminary to breed up others in his own trade; the pages, lackeys, and porter, by imitating their master, become ministers of state in their several districts, and learn to excel in the three principal ingredients, of insolence, lying, and bribery. Accordingly, they have a subaltern[17] court paid to them by persons of the best rank, and sometimes by the force of dexterity and impudence arrive through several gradations to be successors to their lord.

He is usually governed by a decayed wench or favourite footman, who are the tunnels through which all graces are conveyed, and may properly be called, in the last resort, the governors of the kingdom.

One day my master, having heard me mention the nobility of my country, was pleased to make me a compliment which I could not pretend to deserve: that he was sure I must have been born of some noble family, because I far exceeded in shape, colour, and cleanliness, all the yahoos of his nation, although I seemed to fail in strength and agility, which must be imputed to my different way of living from those other brutes, and besides, I was not only endowed with the faculty of speech, but likewise with some rudiments of reason, to a degree that with all his acquaintance I passed for a prodigy.

He made me observe, that among the Houyhnhnms, the white, the

[14] Prime Minister. [15] Promotion.

[16] A law exempting an official from punishment for illegal acts. [17] Subordinate.

sorrel, and the iron-grey were not so exactly shaped as the bay, the dapple-grey, and the black; nor born with equal talents of the mind, or a capacity to improve them; and therefore continued always in the condition of servants, without ever aspiring to match out of their own race, which in that country would be reckoned monstrous and unnatural.

I made his Honour my most humble acknowledgments for the good opinion he was pleased to conceive of me; but assured him at the same time that my birth was of the lower sort, having been born of plain honest parents, who were just able to give me a tolerable education: that nobility among us was altogether a different thing from the idea he had of it; that our young noblemen are bred from their childhood in idleness and luxury; that as soon as years will permit, they consume their vigor and contract odious diseases among lewd females; and when their fortunes are almost ruined, they marry some woman of mean birth, disagreeable person, and unsound constitution, merely for the sake of money, whom they hate and despise. That the productions of such marriages are generally scrofulous, ricketty, or deformed children, by which means the family seldom continues above three generations, unless the wife takes care to provide a healthy father among her neighbours or domestics, in order to improve and continue the breed. That a weak diseased body, a meager countenance, and sallow complexion are the true marks of noble blood; and a healthy robust appearance is so disgraceful in a man of quality, that the world concludes his real father to have been a groom, or a coachman. The imperfections of his mind run parallel with those of his body, being a composition of spleen,[18] dulness, ignorance, caprice, sensuality, and pride.

Without the consent of this illustrious body[19] no law can be enacted, repealed, or altered, and these nobles have likewise the decision of all our possessions without appeal.

CHAPTER VII

The author's great love of his native country. His master's observations upon the constitution and administration of England, as described by the author, with parallel cases and comparisons. His master's observations upon human nature.

The reader may be disposed to wonder how I could prevail on myself to give so free a representation of my own species, among a race of mortals who were already too apt to conceive the vilest opinion of human kind from that entire congruity betwixt me and their yahoos. But I must freely confess, that the many virtues of those excellent quadrupeds, placed in opposite view to human corruptions, had so far opened my eyes and enlarged my understanding, that I began to view the actions and passions of man in a very different light, and to think the honour of my own kind not worth managing;[1] which, besides, it was impossible for me to do before a person of so acute a judgment as my master, who daily convinced me of a

[18] A vague malady characterized by ill temper, gloom, outbursts of passion, and melancholy.

[19] The House of Lords. [1] Carefully protecting.

thousand faults in myself, whereof I had not the least perception before, and which with us would never be numbered even among human infirmities: I had likewise learned from his example an utter detestation of all falsehood or disguise; and truth appeared so amiable to me, that I determined upon sacrificing every thing to it.

Let me deal so candidly with the reader as to confess, that there was yet a much stronger motive for the freedom I took in my representation of things. I had not been a year in this country before I contracted such a love and veneration for the inhabitants, that I entered on a firm resolution never to return to human kind, but to pass the rest of my life among these admirable Houyhnhnms in the contemplation and practice of every virtue; where I could have no example or incitement to vice. But it was decreed by Fortune, my perpetual enemy, that so great a felicity should not fall to my share. However, it is now some comfort to reflect, that in what I said of my countrymen I extenuated their faults as much as I durst before so strict an examiner, and upon every article gave as favourable a turn as the matter would bear. For, indeed, who is there alive that will not be swayed by his bias and partiality to the place of his birth?

I have related the substance of several conversations I had with my master, during the greatest part of the time I had the honour to be in his service, but have indeed for brevity sake omitted much more than is here set down.

When I had answered all his questions, and his curiosity seemed to be fully satisfied, he sent for me one morning early, and commanding me to sit down at some distance (an honour which he had never before conferred upon me), he said he had been very seriously considering my whole story, as far as it related both to myself and my country: that he looked upon us as a sort of animals to whose share, by what accident he could not conjecture, some small pittance of reason had fallen, whereof we made no other use than by its assistance to aggravate our natural corruptions, and to acquire new ones which Nature had not given us. That we disarmed ourselves of the few abilities she had bestowed, had been very successful in multiplying our original wants, and seemed to spend our whole lives in vain endeavours to supply them by our own inventions. That as to myself, it was manifest I had neither the strength or agility of a common yahoo, that I walked infirmly on my hinder feet, had found out a contrivance to make my claws of no use or defence, and to remove the hair from my chin, which was intended as a shelter from the sun and the weather. Lastly, that I could neither run with speed, nor climb trees like my brethren (as he called them) the yahoos in this country.

That our institutions of government and law were plainly owing to our gross defects in reason, and by consequence, in virtue; because reason alone is sufficient to govern a rational creature; which was therefore a character we had no pretence to challenge,[2] even from the account I had given of my own people, although he manifestly perceived, that in order to favour them I had concealed many particulars, and often *said the thing which was not.*

He was the more confirmed in this opinion, because he observed, that

[2] A title we had no right to claim.

as I agreed in every feature of my body with other yahoos, except where it was to my real disadvantage in point of strength, speed, and activity, the shortness of my claws, and some other particulars where nature had no part; so from the representation I had given him of our lives, our manners, and our actions, he found as near a resemblance in the disposition of our minds. He said the yahoos were known to hate one another more than they did any different species of animals; and the reason usually assigned was the odiousness of their own shapes, which all could see in the rest, but not in themselves. He had therefore begun to think it not unwise in us to cover our bodies, and, by that invention, conceal many of our deformities from each other, which would else be hardly supportable. But he now found he had been mistaken, and that the dissensions of those brutes in his country were owing to the same cause with ours, as I had described them. For if (said he) you throw among five yahoos as much food as would be sufficient for fifty, they will, instead of eating peaceably, fall together by the ears, each single one impatient to have all to itself, and therefore a servant was usually employed to stand by while they were feeding abroad, and those kept at home were tied at a distance from each other; that if a cow died of age or accident, before a Houyhnhnm could secure it for his own yahoos, those in the neighbourhood would come in herds to seize it, and then would ensue such a battle as I had described, with terrible wounds made by their claws on both sides, although they seldom were able to kill one another, for want of such convenient instruments of death as we had invented. At other times the like battles have been fought between the yahoos of several neighbourhoods without any visible cause; those of one district watching all opportunities to surprise the next before they are prepared. But if they find their project hath miscarried, they return home, and, for want of enemies, engage in what I call a civil war among themselves.

That in some fields of his country there are certain shining stones of several colours, whereof the yahoos are violently fond, and when part of these stones are fixed in the earth, as it sometimes happeneth, they will dig with their claws for whole days to get them out, carry them away, and hide them by heaps in their kennels; but still looking round with great caution, for fear their comrades should find out their treasure. My master said, he could never discover the reason of this unnatural appetite, or how these stones could be of any use to a yahoo; but now he believed it might proceed from the same principle of avarice which I had ascribed to mankind; that he had once, by way of experiment, privately removed a heap of these stones from the place where one of his yahoos had buried it: whereupon the sordid animal, missing his treasure, by his loud lamenting brought the whole herd to the place, there miserably howled, then fell to biting and tearing the rest, began to pine away, would neither eat, nor sleep, nor work, till he ordered a servant privately to convey the stones into the same hole and hide them as before; which when his yahoo had found, he presently recovered his spirits and good humour, but took care to remove them to a better hiding-place, and hath ever since been a very serviceable brute.

My master farther assured me, which I also observed myself, that in the fields where these shining stones abound, the fiercest and most frequent battles are fought, occasioned by perpetual inroads of the neighbouring yahoos.

He said, it was common, when two yahoos discovered such a stone in a field, and were contending which of them should be the proprietor, a third would take the advantage, and carry it away from them both; which my master would needs contend to have some resemblance with our suits at law; wherein I thought it for our credit not to undeceive him; since the decision he mentioned was much more equitable than many decrees among us: because the plaintiff and defendant there lost nothing beside the stone they contended for, whereas our courts of equity would never have dismissed the cause while either of them had any thing left.

My master, continuing his discourse, said, there was nothing that rendered the yahoos more odious than their undistinguishing[3] appetite to devour every thing that came in their way, whether herbs, roots, berries, corrupted flesh of animals, or all mingled together: and it was peculiar in their temper, that they were fonder of what they could get by rapine or stealth at a greater distance, than much better food provided for them at home. If their prey held out, they would eat till they were ready to burst, after which Nature had pointed out to them a certain root that gave them a general evacuation.

There was also another kind of root very juicy, but somewhat rare and difficult to be found, which the yahoos sought for with much eagerness, and would suck it with great delight; and it produced in them the same effects that wine hath upon us. It would make them sometimes hug, and sometimes tear one another; they would howl and grin, and chatter, and reel, and tumble, and then fall asleep in the mud.

I did indeed observe, that the yahoos were the only animals in this country subject to any diseases; which, however, were much fewer than horses have among us, and contracted not by any ill treatment they meet with, but by the nastiness and greediness of that sordid brute. Neither has their language any more than a general appellation for those maladies, which is borrowed from the name of the beast, and called *hnea-yahoo*, or the *yahoo's-evil*, and the cure prescribed is a mixture of their own dung and urine forcibly put down the yahoo's throat. This I have since often known to have been taken with success, and do here freely recommend it to my countrymen, for the public good, as an admirable specific[4] against all diseases produced by repletion.

As to learning, government, arts, manufactures, and the like, my master he could find little or no resemblance between the yahoos of that country and those in ours. For he only meant to observe what parity[5] there was in our natures. He had heard indeed some curious[6] Houyhnhnms observe, that in most herds there was a sort of ruling yahoo (as among us there is generally some leading or principal stag in a park), who was always more deformed in body, and mischievous in disposition, than any of the rest. That this leader had usually a favourite as like himself as he could get, whose employment was to lick his master's feet and posteriors, and drive the female yahoos to his kennel; for which he was now and then rewarded with a piece of ass's flesh. This favourite is hated by the whole herd, and therefore, to protect himself, keeps always near the person of his leader.

[3] Undiscriminating. [4] Medication; remedy. [5] Resemblance.
[6] Carefully observant.

He usually continues in office till a worse can be found; but the very moment he is discarded, his successor, at the head of all the yahoos in that district, young and old, male and female, come in a body, and discharge their excrements upon him from head to foot. But how far this might be applicable to our courts and favourites, and ministers of state, my master said I could best determine.

I durst make no return to this malicious insinuation, which debased human understanding below the sagacity of a common hound, who has judgment enough to distinguish and follow the cry of the ablest dog in the pack, without being ever mistaken.

My master told me, there were some qualities remarkable in the yahoos, which he had not observed me to mention, or at least very slightly, in the accounts I had given him of human kind; he said, those animals, like other brutes, had their females in common; but in this they differed, that the she-yahoo would admit the male while she was pregnant, and that the hees would quarrel and fight with the females as fiercely as with each other. Both which practices were such degrees of infamous brutality, that no other sensitive creature ever arrived at.

Another thing he wondered at in the yahoos was their strange disposition to nastiness and dirt, whereas there appears to be a natural love of cleanliness in all other animals. As to the two former accusations, I was glad to let them pass without any reply, because I had not a word to offer upon them in defence of my species, which otherwise I certainly had done from my own inclinations. But I could have easily vindicated human kind from the imputation of singularity upon the last article, if there had been any swine in that country (as unluckily for me there were not), which, although it may be a sweeter quadruped than a yahoo, cannot, I humbly conceive, in justice pretend to more cleanliness; and so his Honour himself must have owned, if he had seen their filthy way of feeding, and their custom of wallowing and sleeping in the mud.

My master likewise mentioned another quality which his servants had discovered in several yahoos, and to him was wholly unaccountable. He said, a fancy would sometimes take a yahoo to retire into a corner, to lie down and howl, and groan, and spurn away all that came near him, although he were young and fat, and wanted neither food nor water; nor did the servants imagine what could possibly ail him. And the only remedy they found was to set him to hard work, after which he would infallibly come to himself. To this I was silent out of partiality to my own kind; yet here I could plainly discover the true seeds of spleen, which only seizeth on the lazy, the luxurious, and the rich; who, if they were forced to undergo the same regimen, I would undertake for the cure.

His Honour had farther observed, that a female yahoo would often stand behind a bank or a bush, to gaze on the young males passing by, and then appear, and hide, using many antic gestures and grimaces, at which time it was observed, that she had a most offensive smell; and when any of the males advanced, would slowly retire, looking often back, and with a counterfeit show of fear, run off into some convenient place where she knew the male would follow her.

At other times if a female stranger came among them, three or four of her own sex would get about her, and stare and chatter, and grin, and smell

her all over, and then turn off with gestures that seemed to express contempt and disdain.

Perhaps my master might refine[7] a little in these speculations, which he had drawn from what he observed himself, or had been told him by others: however, I could not reflect without some amazement, and much sorrow, that the rudiments of lewdness, coquetry, censure, and scandal, should have place by instinct in womankind.

I expected every moment that my master would accuse the yahoos of those unnatural appetites[8] in both sexes, so common among us. But Nature, it seems, hath not been so expert a school-mistress; and these politer pleasures are entirely the productions of art and reason, on our side of the globe.

CHAPTER VIII

The author relates several particulars of the yahoos. The great virtues of the Houyhnhnms. The education and exercise of their youth. Their general assembly.

As I ought to have understood human nature much better than I supposed it possible for my master to do, so it was easy to apply the character[1] he gave of the yahoos to myself and my countrymen, and I believed I could yet make farther discoveries from my own observation. I therefore often begged his Honour to let me go among the herds of yahoos in the neighbourhood, to which he always very graciously consented, being perfectly convinced that the hatred I bore those brutes would never suffer me to be corrupted by them; and his Honour ordered one of his servants, a strong sorrel nag, very honest and good-natured, to be my guard, without whose protection I durst not undertake such adventures. For I have already told the reader how much I was pestered by those odious animals upon my first arrival. And I afterwards failed very narrowly three or four times of falling into their clutches, when I happened to stray at any distance without my hanger. And I have reason to believe they had some imagination that I was of their own species, which I often assisted myself, by stripping up my sleeves, and showing my naked arms and breast in their sight, when my protector was with me. At which times they would approach as near as they durst, and imitate my actions after the manner of monkeys, but ever with great signs of hatred, as a tame jackdaw,[2] with cap and stockings, is always persecuted by the wild ones, when he happens to be got among them.

They are prodigiously nimble from their infancy; however, I once caught a young male of three years old, and endeavoured by all marks of tenderness to make it quiet; but the little imp fell a squalling, and scratching, and biting with such violence, that I was forced to let it go, and it was high time, for a whole troop of old ones came about us at the noise, but finding the cub was safe (for away it ran), and my sorrel nag being by, they durst not venture near us. I observed the young animal's flesh to smell very

[7] Be excessively subtle. [8] Sodomy, presumably. [1] Description; sketch.
[2] A bird resembling a crow.

rank, and the stink was somewhat between a weasel and a fox, but much more disagreeable. I forgot another circumstance (and perhaps I might have the reader's pardon if it were wholly omitted) that while I held the odious vermin in my hands, it voided its filthy excrements of a yellow liquid substance all over my clothes; but by good fortune there was a small brook hard by, where I washed myself as clean as I could, although I durst not come into my master's presence, until I were sufficiently aired.

By what I could discover, the yahoos appear to be the most unteachable of all animals, their capacities never reaching higher than to draw or carry burthens. Yet I am of opinion this defect ariseth chiefly from a perverse, restive disposition. For they are cunning, malicious, treacherous and revengeful. They are strong and hardy, but of a cowardly spirit, and by consequence insolent, abject, and cruel. It is observed, that the redhaired of both sexes are more libidinous and mischievous than the rest, whom yet they much exceed in strength and activity.

The Houyhnhnms keep the yahoos for present use in huts not far from the house; but the rest are sent abroad to certain fields, where they dig up roots, eat several kinds of herbs, and search about for carrion,[3] or sometimes catch weasels and *luhimuhs* (a sort of wild rat), which they greedily devour. Nature hath taught them to dig deep holes with their nails on the side of a rising ground, wherein they lie by themselves, only the kennels of the females are larger, sufficient to hold two or three cubs.

They swim from their infancy like frogs, and are able to continue long under water, where they often take fish, which the females carry home to their young. And upon this occasion, I hope the reader will pardon my relating an odd adventure.

Being one day abroad with my protector the sorrel nag, and the weather exceeding hot, I entreated him to let me bathe in a river that was near. He consented, and I immediately stripped myself stark naked, and went down softly into the stream. It happened that a young female yahoo, standing behind a bank, saw the whole proceeding, and inflamed by desire, as the nag and I conjectured, came running with all speed, and leaped into the water within five yards of the place where I bathed. I was never in my life so terribly frighted; the nag was grazing at some distance, not suspecting any harm. She embraced me after a most fulsome manner; I roared as loud as I could, and the nag came galloping towards me, whereupon she quitted her grasp, with the utmost reluctancy, and leaped upon the opposite bank, where she stood gazing and howling all the time I was putting on my clothes.

This was matter of diversion to my master and his family, as well as of mortification to myself. For now I could no longer deny that I was a real yahoo in every limb and feature, since the females had a natural propensity to me as one of their own species: neither was the hair of this brute of a red colour (which might have been some excuse for an appetite a little irregular) but black as a sloe,[4] and her countenance did not make an appearance altogether so hideous as the rest of the kind; for, I think, she could not be above eleven years old.

Having already lived three years in this country, the reader I suppose

[3] The flesh of dead animals. [4] A blue-black fruit.

will expect that I should, like other travellers, give him some account of the manners and customs of its inhabitants, which it was indeed my principal study to learn.

As these noble Houyhnhnms are endowed by nature with a general disposition to all virtues, and have no conceptions or ideas of what is evil in a rational creature, so their grand maxim is, to cultivate reason, and to be wholly governed by it. Neither is reason among them a point problematical as with us, where men can argue with plausibility on both sides of a question; but strikes you with immediate conviction; as it must needs do where it is not mingled, obscured, or discoloured by passion and interest. I remember it was with extreme difficulty that I could bring my master to understand the meaning of the word *opinion*, or how a point could be disputable; because reason taught us to affirm or deny only where we are certain; and beyond our knowledge we cannot do either. So that controversies, wranglings, disputes, and positiveness in false or dubious propositions are evils unknown among the Houyhnhnms. In the like manner, when I used to explain to him our several systems of natural philosophy,[5] he would laugh that a creature pretending to reason should value itself upon the knowledge of other people's conjectures, and in things where that knowledge, if it were certain, could be of no use. Wherein he agreed entirely with the sentiments of Socrates, as Plato delivers them;[6] which I mention as the highest honour I can do that prince of philosophers. I have often since reflected what destruction such a doctrine would make in the libraries of Europe, and how many paths to fame would be then shut up in the learned world.

Friendship and benevolence are the two principal virtues among the Houyhnhnms, and these not confined to particular objects, but universal to the whole race. For a stranger from the remotest part is equally treated with the nearest neighbour, and wherever he goes, looks upon himself as at home. They preserve decency and civility in the highest degrees, but are altogether ignorant of ceremony. They have no fondness[7] for their colts or foals, but the care they take in educating them proceeds entirely from the dictates of reason. And I observed my master to show the same affection to his neighbour's issue that he had for his own. They will have it that nature teaches them to love the whole species, and it is reason only that maketh a distinction of persons, where there is a superior degree of virtue.

When the matron Houyhnhnms have produced one of each sex, they no longer accompany with their consorts, except they lose one of their issue by some casualty, which very seldom happens: but in such a case they meet again, or when the like accident befalls a person whose wife is past bearing, some other couple bestows on him one of their own colts, and then go together a second time till the mother be pregnant. This caution is necessary to prevent the country from being overburthened with numbers. But the race of inferior Houyhnhnms bred up to be servants is not so strictly limited upon this article; these are allowed to produce three of each sex, to be domestics in the noble families.

[5] Physical science.
[6] In Book V of Plato's *Republic*, Socrates distinguishes between vague opinion and true (therefore morally useful) knowledge.
[7] Doting affection.

In their marriages they are exactly careful to choose such colours as will not make any disagreeable mixture in the breed. Strength is chiefly valued in the male, and comeliness in the female, not upon the account of love, but to preserve the race from degenerating; for where a female happens to excel in strength, a consort is chosen with regard to comeliness. Courtship, love, presents, jointures, settlements,[8] have no place in their thoughts, or terms whereby to express them in their language. The young couple meet and are joined, merely because it is the determination of their parents and friends: it is what they see done every day, and they look upon it as one of the necessary actions in a reasonable being. But the violation of marriage, or any other unchastity, was never heard of: and the married pair pass their lives with the same friendship and mutual benevolence that they bear to all others of the same species who come in their way; without jealousy, fondness, quarrelling, or discontent.

In educating the youth of both sexes, their method is admirable, and highly deserves our imitation. These are not suffered to taste a grain of oats, except upon certain days, till eighteen years old; nor milk, but very rarely; and in summer they graze two hours in the morning, and as many in the evening, which their parents likewise observe, but the servants are not allowed above half that time, and a great part of the grass is brought home, which they eat at the most convenient hours, when they can be best spared from work.

Temperance, industry, exercise and cleanliness, are the lessons equally enjoined to the young ones of both sexes: and my master thought it monstrous in us to give the females a different kind of education from the males, except in some articles of domestic management; whereby, as he truly observed, one half of our natives were good for nothing but bringing children into the world: and to trust the care of their children to such useless animals, he said, was yet a greater instance of brutality.

But the Houyhnhnms train up their youth to strength, speed, and hardiness, by exercising them in running races up and down steep hills, or over hard stony grounds, and when they are all in a sweat, they are ordered to leap over head and ears into a pond or a river. Four times a year the youth of certain districts meet to show their proficiency in running and leaping, and other feats of strength or agility, where the victor is rewarded with a song made in his or her praise. On this festival the servants drive a herd of yahoos into the field, laden with hay, and oats, and milk for a repast to the Houyhnhnms; after which these brutes are immediately driven back again, for fear of being noisome[9] to the assembly.

Every fourth year, at the vernal equinox, there is a representative council of the whole nation, which meets in a plain about twenty miles from our house, and continues about five or six days. Here they inquire into the state and condition of the several districts; whether they abound or be deficient in hay or oats, or cows or yahoos. And wherever there is any want (which is but seldom) it is immediately supplied by unanimous consent and contribution. Here likewise the regulation of children is settled: as for instance, if a

[8] Jointures and settlements are property and money legally apportioned to a woman upon her marriage.
[9] Offensive, especially in odor.

Houyhnhnm hath two males, he changeth one of them with another who hath two females: and when a child hath been lost by any casualty, where the mother is past breeding, it is determined what family in the district shall breed another to supply the loss.

CHAPTER IX

A grand debate at the general assembly of the Houyhnhnms, and how it was determined. The learning of the Houyhnhnms. Their buildings. Their manner of burials. The defectiveness of their language.

One of these grand assemblies was held in my time, about three months before my departure, whither my master went as the representative of our district. In this council was resumed their old debate, and indeed, the only debate that ever happened in their country; whereof my master after his return gave me a very particular account.

The question to be debated was, whether the yahoos should be exterminated from the face of the earth. One of the members for the affirmative offered several arguments of great strength and weight, alleging, that as the yahoos were the most filthy, noisome, and deformed animal which nature ever produced, so they were the most restive and indocible,[1] mischievous and malicious: they would privately suck the teats of the Houyhnhnms' cows, kill and devour their cats, trample down their oats and grass, if they were not continually watched, and commit a thousand other extravagancies. He took notice of a general tradition, that yahoos had not been always in their country: but that many ages ago two of these brutes appeared together upon a mountain, whether produced by the heat of the sun upon corrupted mud and slime, or from the ooze and froth of the sea, was never known. That these yahoos engendered, and their brood in a short time grew so numerous as to overrun and infest the whole nation. That the Houyhnhnms, to get rid of this evil, made a general hunting, and at last enclosed the whole herd; and destroying the older, every Houyhnhnm kept two young ones in a kennel, and brought them to such a degree of tameness, as an animal so savage by nature can be capable of acquiring; using them for draught and carriage. That there seemed to be much truth in this tradition, and that those creatures could not be *ylnhniamshy* (or *aborigines* of the land) because of the violent hatred the Houyhnhnms, as well as all other animals, bore them; which although their evil disposition sufficiently deserved, could never have arrived at so high a degree, if they had been aborigines, or else they would have long since been rooted out. That the inhabitants taking a fancy to use the service of the yahoos, had very imprudently neglected to cultivate the breed of asses, which were a comely animal, easily kept, more tame and orderly, without any offensive smell, strong enough for labour, although they yield to the other in agility of body; and if their braying be no agreeable sound, it is far preferable to the horrible howlings of the yahoos.

Several others declared their sentiments to the same purpose, when my

[1] Restless and unteachable.

master proposed an expedient to the assembly, whereof he had indeed borrowed the hint from me. He approved of the tradition, mentioned by the "honourable member" who spoke before, and affirmed, that the two yahoos said to be first seen among them had been driven thither over the sea; that coming to land, and being forsaken by their companions, they retired to the mountains, and degenerating by degrees, became in process of time much more savage than those of their own species in the country from whence these two originals came. The reason of his assertion was, that he had now in his possession a certain wonderful yahoo (meaning myself) which most of them had heard of, and many of them had seen. He then related to them how he first found me; that my body was all covered with an artificial composure of the skins and hairs of other animals: that I spoke in a language of my own, and had thoroughly learned theirs: that I had related to him the accidents which brought me thither: that when he saw me without my covering, I was an exact yahoo in every part, only of a whiter colour, less hairy, and with shorter claws. He added, how I had endeavoured to persuade him, that in my own and other countries the yahoos acted as the governing, rational animal, and held the Houyhnhnms in servitude: that he observed in me all the qualities of a yahoo, only a little more civilized by some tincture of reason, which however was in a degree as far inferior to the Houyhnhnm race as the yahoos of their country were to me: that, among other things, I mentioned a custom we had of castrating Houyhnhnms when they were young, in order to render them tame; that the operation was easy and safe; that it was no shame to learn wisdom from brutes, as industry is taught by the ant, and building by the swallow. (For so I translate the word *lyhannh,* although it be a much larger fowl.) That this invention might be practised upon the younger yahoos here, which, besides rendering them tractable and fitter for use, would in an age put an end to the whole species without destroying life. That in the mean time the Houyhnhnms should be exhorted to cultivate the breed of asses, which, as they are in all respects more valuable brutes, so they have this advantage, to be fit for service at five years old, which the others are not till twelve.

This was all my master thought fit to tell me at that time of what passed in the grand council. But he was pleased to conceal one particular, which related personally to myself, whereof I soon felt the unhappy effect, as the reader will know in its proper place, and from whence I date all the succeeding misfortunes of my life.

The Houyhnhnms have no letters,[2] and consequently their knowledge is all traditional. But there happening few events of any moment among a people so well united, naturally disposed to every virtue, wholly governed by reason, and cut off from all commerce with other nations, the historical part is easily preserved without burthening their memories. I have already observed, that they are subject to no diseases, and therefore can have no need of physicians. However, they have excellent medicines composed of herbs, to cure accidental bruises and cuts in the pastern or frog[3] of the foot by sharp stones, as well as other maims and hurts in the several parts of the body.

They calculate the year by the revolution of the sun and the moon, but

[2] Writings. [3] Part of the sole of the hoof.

use no subdivisions into weeks. They are well enough acquainted with the motions of those two luminaries, and understand the nature of eclipses; and this is the utmost progress of their astronomy.

In poetry they must be allowed to excel all other mortals; wherein the justness of their similes, and the minuteness, as well as exactness of their descriptions, are indeed inimitable. Their verses abound very much in both of these, and usually contain either some exalted notions of friendship and benevolence, or the praises of those who were victors in races and other bodily exercises. Their buildings, although very rude and simple, are not inconvenient, but well contrived to defend them from all injuries of cold and heat. They have a kind of tree, which at forty years old loosens in the root, and falls with the first storm; it grows very straight, and being pointed like stakes with a sharp stone (for the Houyhnhnms know not the use of iron), they stick them erect in the ground about ten inches asunder, and then weave in oat-straw, or sometimes wattles betwixt them. The roof is made after the same manner, and so are the doors.

The Houyhnhnms use the hollow part between the pastern and the hoof of their forefeet as we do our hands, and this with greater dexterity than I could at first imagine. I have seen a white mare of our family thread a needle (which I lent her on purpose) with that joint. They milk their cows, reap their oats, and do all the work which requires hands, in the same manner. They have a kind of hard flints, which, by grinding against other stones, they form into instruments, that serve instead of wedges, axes, and hammers. With tools made of these flints they likewise cut their hay, and reap their oats, which there groweth naturally in several fields: the yahoos draw home the sheaves in carriages, and the servants tread them in certain covered huts, to get out the grain, which is kept in stores. They make a rude kind of earthen and wooden vessels, and bake the former in the sun.

If they can avoid casualties, they die only of old age, and are buried in the obscurest places that can be found, their friends and relations expressing neither joy nor grief at their departure; nor does the dying person discover the least regret that he is leaving the world, any more than if he were upon[4] returning home from a visit to one of his neighbours; I remember my master having once made an appointment with a friend and his family to come to his house upon some affair of importance; on the day fixed, the mistress and her two children came very late; she made two excuses, first for her husband, who, as she said, happened that very morning to *lhnuwnh*. The word is strongly expressive in their language, but not easily rendered into English; it signifies, "to retire to his first mother." Her excuse for not coming sooner was, that her husband dying late in the morning, she was a good while consulting her servants about a convenient place where his body should be laid; and I observed she behaved herself at our house as cheerfully as the rest: she died about three months after.

They live generally to seventy or seventy-five years, very seldom to fourscore: some weeks before their death they feel a gradual decay, but without pain. During this time they are much visited by their friends, because they cannot go abroad[5] with their usual ease and satisfaction. However, about ten days before their death, which they seldom fail in comput-

[4] On the point of. [5] Away from home.

ing, they return the visits that have been made them by those who are nearest in the neighbourhood, being carried in a convenient sledge drawn by yahoos, which vehicle they use, not only upon this occasion, but when they grow old, upon long journeys, or when they are lamed by any accident. And therefore when the dying Houyhnhnms return those visits, they take a solemn leave of their friends, as if they were going to some remote part of the country, where they designed to pass the rest of their lives.

I know not whether it may be worth observing, that the Houyhnhnms have no word in their language to express any thing that is evil, except what they borrow from the deformities or ill qualities of the yahoos. Thus they denote the folly of a servant, an omission of a child, a stone that cuts their feet, a continuance of foul or unseasonable weather, and the like, by adding to each the epithet of *yahoo*. For instance, *hhnm yahoo, whnaholm yahoo, ynlhnmawihlma yahoo*, and an ill-contrived house *ynholmhnmrohlnw yahoo*.

I could with great pleasure enlarge farther upon the manners and virtues of this excellent people; but intending in a short time to publish a volume by itself expressly upon that subject, I refer the reader thither. And in the mean time, proceed to relate my own sad catastrophe.[6]

CHAPTER X

The author's economy[1] and happy life among the Houyhnhnms. His great improvement in virtue, by conversing with them. Their conversations. The author has notice given him by his master that he must depart from the country. He falls into a swoon for grief, but submits. He contrives and finishes a canoe, by the help of a fellow-servant, and puts to sea at a venture.[2]

I had settled my little economy to my own heart's content. My master had ordered a room to be made for me after their manner, about six yards from the house, the sides and floors of which I plastered with clay, and covered with rush mats of my own contriving; I had beaten hemp, which there grows wild, and made of it a sort of ticking: this I filled with the feathers of several birds I had taken with springes made of yahoos' hairs, and were excellent food. I had worked two chairs with my knife, the sorrel nag helping me in the grosser and more laborious part. When my clothes were worn to rags, I made myself others with the skins of rabbits, and of a certain beautiful animal about the same size, called *nnuhnoh*, the skin of which is covered with a fine down. Of these I likewise made very tolerable stockings. I soled my shoes with wood which I cut from a tree, and fitted to the upper leather, and when this was worn out, I supplied it with the skins of yahoos dried in the sun. I often got honey out of hollow trees, which I mingled with water, or eat it with my bread. No man could more verify the truth of these two maxims, *That nature is very easily satisfied;* and *That necessity is the mother of invention.* I enjoyed perfect health of body and tranquillity of mind; I did not feel the treachery or inconstancy of a friend, nor the injuries of a secret or open enemy. I had no occasion of bribing, flattering or

[6]Conclusion (as of a play). [1]Living arrangements. [2]At random.

pimping to procure the favour of any great man or of his minion.[3] I wanted no fence against fraud or oppression; here was neither physician to destroy my body, nor lawyer to ruin my fortune; no informer to watch my words and actions, or forge accusations against me for hire: here were no gibers, censurers, backbiters, pickpockets, highwaymen, housebreakers, attorneys, bawds, buffoons, gamesters, politicans, wits, splenetics,[4] tedious talkers, controvertists,[5] ravishers, murderers, robbers, virtuosos: no leaders or followers of party and faction: no encouragers to vice, by seducement or examples: no dungeon, axes, gibbets, whipping-posts, or pillories: no cheating shopkeepers or mechanics:[6] no pride, vanity, or affectation: no fops, bullies, drunkards, strolling whores, or poxes:[7] no ranting, lewd, expensive wives: no stupid, proud pedants: no importunate, overbearing, quarrelsome, noisy, roaring, empty, conceited, swearing companions: no scoundrels, raised from the dust upon the merit of their vices, or nobility thrown into it on account of their virtues: no lords, fiddlers, judges or dancing-masters.

I had the favour of being admitted to several Houyhnhnms, who came to visit or dine with my master; where his Honour graciously suffered me to wait in the room, and listen to their discourse. Both he and his company would often descend to ask me questions, and receive my answers. I had also sometimes the honour of attending my master in his visits to others. I never presumed to speak, except in answer to a question, and then I did it with inward regret, because it was a loss of so much time for improving myself: but I was infinitely delighted with the station of an humble auditor in such conversations, where nothing passed but what was useful, expressed in the fewest and most significant words: where (as I have already said) the greatest decency was observed, without the least degree of ceremony; where no person spoke without being pleased himself, and pleasing his companions; where there was no interruptions, tediousness, heat, or difference of sentiments. They have a notion, that when people are met together, a short silence doth much improve conversation: this I found to be true; for during those little intermissions of talk, new ideas would arise in their minds, which very much enlivened the discourse. Their subjects are generally on friendship and benevolence, or order and economy, sometimes upon the visible operations of nature, or ancient traditions, upon the bounds and limits of virtue, upon the unerring rules of reason, or upon some determinations to be taken at the next great assembly, and often upon the various excellencies of poetry. I may add without vanity, that my presence often gave them sufficient matter for discourse, because it afforded my master an occasion of letting his friends into the history of me and my country, upon which they were all pleased to descant[8] in a manner not very advantageous to human kind; and for that reason I shall not repeat what they said: only I may be allowed to observe, that his Honour, to my great admiration, appeared to understand the nature of yahoos much better than myself. He went through all our vices and follies, and discovered many which I had never mentioned to him, by only supposing what

[3] Obsequious favorite. [4] People suffering from spleen.
[5] Disputers; controversialists. [6] Craftsmen; low fellows.
[7] Skin diseases, especially syphilis. [8] Discourse.

qualities a yahoo of their country, with a small proportion of reason, might be capable of exerting; and concluded, with too much probability, how vile as well as miserable such a creature must be.

I freely confess, that all the little knowledge I have of any value was acquired by the lectures I received from my master, and from hearing the discourses of him and his friends; to which I should be prouder to listen, than to dictate to the greatest and wisest assembly in Europe. I admired the strength, comeliness, and speed of the inhabitants; and such a constellation of virtues in such amiable persons produced in me the highest veneration. At first, indeed, I did not feel that natural awe which the yahoos and all other animals bear towards them; but it grew upon me by degrees, much sooner than I imagined, and was mingled with a respectful love and gratitude, that they would condescend to distinguish me from the rest of my species.

When I thought of my family, my friends, my countrymen, or human race in general, I considered them as they really were, yahoos in shape and disposition, only a little more civilized, and qualified with the gift of speech, but making no other use of reason than to improve and multiply those vices whereof their brethren in this country had only the share that nature allotted them. When I happened to behold the reflection of my own form in a lake or fountain, I turned away my face in horror and detestation of myself, and could better endure the sight of a common yahoo, than of my own person. By conversing with the Houyhnhnms, and looking upon them with delight, I fell to imitate their gait and gesture, which is now grown into a habit, and my friends often tell me in a blunt way that I "trot like a horse"; which, however, I take for a great compliment: neither shall I disown, that in speaking I am apt to fall into the voice and manner of the Houyhnhnms, and hear myself ridiculed on that account without the least mortification.

In the midst of all this happiness, when I looked upon myself to be fully settled for life, my master sent for me one morning a little earlier than his usual hour. I observed by his countenance that he was in some perplexity, and at a loss how to begin what he had to speak. After a short silence, he told me, he did not know how I would take what he was going to say; that in the last general assembly, when the affair of the yahoos was entered upon, the representatives had taken offence at his keeping a yahoo (meaning myself) in his family more like a Houyhnhnm than a brute animal. That he was known frequently to converse with me, as if he could receive some advantage or pleasure in my company: that such a practice was not agreeable to reason or nature, or a thing ever heard of before among them. The assembly did therefore exhort him, either to employ me like the rest of my species, or command me to swim back to the place from whence I came. That the first of these expedients was utterly rejected by all the Houyhnhnms who had ever seen me at his house or their own: for they alleged, that because I had some rudiments of reason, added to the natural pravity[9] of those animals, it was to be feared, I might be able to seduce them into the woody and mountainous parts of the country, and bring them in troops by night to destroy the Houyhnhnms' cattle, as being naturally of the ravenous kind, and averse from labour.

[9] Depravity.

My master added, that he was daily pressed by the Houyhnhnms of the neighbourhood to have the assembly's exhortation executed, which he could not put off much longer. He doubted[10] it would be impossible for me to swim to another country, and therefore wished I would contrive some sort of vehicle resembling those I had described to him, that might carry me on the sea, in which work I should have the assistance of his own servants, as well as those of his neighbours. He concluded, that for his own part he could have been content to keep me in his service as long as I lived, because he found I had cured myself of some bad habits and dispositions, by endeavouring, as far as my inferior nature was capable, to imitate the Houyhnhnms.

I should here observe to the reader, that a decree of the general assembly in this country is expressed by the word *hnhloayn*, which signifies an *exhortation*, as near as I can render it: for they have no conception how a rational creature can be compelled, but only advised or exhorted, because no person can disobey reason, without giving up his claim to be a rational creature.

I was struck with the utmost grief and despair at my master's discourse, and being unable to support the agonies I was under, I fell into a swoon at his feet; when I came to myself he told me that he concluded I had been dead. (For these people are subject to no such imbecilities of nature.) I answered, in a faint voice, that death would have been too great an happiness; that although I could not blame the assembly's exhortation, or the urgency of his friends, yet, in my weak and corrupt judgment, I thought it might consist with reason to have been less rigorous. That I could not swim a league, and probably the nearest land to theirs might be distant above an hundred; that many materials, necessary for making a small vessel to carry me off, were wholly wanting in this country, which, however, I would attempt in obedience and gratitude to his Honour, although I concluded the thing to be impossible, and therefore looked on my self as already devoted[11] to destruction. That the certain prospect of an unnatural death was the least of my evils: for, supposing I should escape with life by some strange adventure, how could I think with temper[12] of passing my days among yahoos, and relapsing into my old corruptions, for want of examples to lead and keep me within the paths of virtue? That I knew too well upon what solid reasons all the determinations of the wise Houyhnhnms were founded, not to be shaken by arguments of mine, a miserable yahoo; and therefore, after presenting him with my humble thanks for the offer of his servants' assistance in making a vessel, and desiring a reasonable time for so difficult a work, I told him I would endeavour to preserve a wretched being; and, if ever I returned to England, was not without hopes of being useful to my own species, by celebrating the praises of the renowned Houyhnhnms, and proposing their virtues to the imitation of mankind.

My master in a few words made me a very gracious reply, allowed me the space of two months to finish my boat; and ordered the sorrel nag, my fellow-servant (for so at this distance I may presume to call him) to follow

[10] Suspected. [11] Doomed. [12] Calmness.

my instructions, because I told my master, that his help would be sufficient, and I knew he had a tenderness for me.

In his company my first business was to go to that part of the coast where my rebellious crew had ordered me to be set on shore. I got upon a height, and looking on every side into the sea, fancied I saw a small island, towards the northeast: I took out my pocket-glass, and could then clearly distinguish it about five leagues off, as I computed; but it appeared to the sorrel nag to be only a blue cloud: for as he had no conception of any country beside his own, so he could not be as expert in distinguishing remote objects at sea as we who so much converse in[13] that element.

After I had discovered this island, I considered no farther; but resolved it should, if possible, be the first place of my banishment, leaving the consequence to fortune.

I returned home, and consulting with the sorrel nag, we went into a copse at some distance, where I with my knife, and he with a sharp flint fastened very artificially[14] after their manner, to a wooden handle, cut down several oak wattles about the thickness of a walking-staff, and some larger pieces. But I shall not trouble the reader with a particular description of my own mechanics; let it suffice to say that in six weeks' time, with the help of the sorrel nag, who performed the parts that required most labour, I finished a sort of Indian canoe, but much larger, covering it with the skins of yahoos well stitched together, with hempen threads of my own making. My sail was likewise composed of the skins of the same animal; but I made use of the youngest I could get, the older being too tough and thick, and I likewise provided myself with four paddles. I laid in a stock of boiled flesh, of rabbits and fowls, and took with me two vessels, one filled with milk, and the other with water.

I tried my canoe in a large pond near my master's house, and then corrected in it what was amiss; stopping all the chinks with yahoos' tallow, till I found it staunch, and able to bear me and my freight. And when it was as complete as I could possibly make it, I had it drawn on a carriage very gently by yahoos to the seaside, under the conduct of the sorrel nag and another servant.

When all was ready, and the day came for my departure, I took leave of my master and lady, and the whole family, my eyes flowing with tears, and my heart quite sunk with grief. But his Honour, out of curiosity, and perhaps (if I may speak it without vanity) partly out of kindness, was determined to see me in my canoe, and got several of his neighbouring friends to accompany him. I was forced to wait above an hour for the tide, and then observing the wind very fortunately bearing towards the island, to which I intended to steer my course, I took a second leave of my master: but as I was going to prostrate myself to kiss his hoof, he did me the honour to raise it gently to my mouth. I am not ignorant how much I have been censured for mentioning this last particular. Detractors are pleased to think it improbable, that so illustrious a person should descend to give so great a mark of distinction to a creature so inferior as I. Neither have I forgot how apt some travellers are to boast of extraordinary favours they have received. But if these censurers were better acquainted with the noble

[13] Are familiar with. [14] Ingeniously.

and courteous disposition of the Houyhnhnms, they would soon change their opinion.

I paid my respects to the rest of the Houyhnhnms in his Honour's company; then getting into my canoe, I pushed off from shore.

CHAPTER XI

The author's dangerous voyage. He arrives at New Holland,[1] hoping to settle there. Is wounded with an arrow by one of the natives. Is seized and carried by force into a Portuguese ship. The great civilities of the captain. The author arrives at England.

I began this desperate voyage on February 15, 1714–5,[2] at 9 o'clock in the morning. The wind was very favourable; however, I made use at first only of my paddles, but considering I should soon be weary, and that the wind might probably chop about, I ventured to set up my little sail; and thus with the help of the tide I went at the rate of a league and a half an hour, as near as I could guess. My master and his friends continued on the shore till I was almost out of sight; and I often heard the sorrel nag (who always loved me) crying out, *Hnuy illa nyha maiah yahoo,* Take care of thyself, gentle yahoo.

My design was, if possible, to discover some small island uninhabited, yet sufficient by my labour to furnish me with the necessaries of life, which I would have thought a greater happiness than to be first minister in the politest court of Europe; so horrible was the idea I conceived of returning to live in the society and under the government of yahoos. For in such a solitude as I desired, I could at least enjoy my own thoughts, and reflect with delight on the virtues of those inimitable Houyhnhnms, without any opportunity of degenerating into the vices and corruptions of my own species.

The reader may remember what I related when my crew conspired against me, and confined me to my cabin. How I continued there several weeks, without knowing what course we took, and when I was put ashore in the long-boat, how the sailors told me with oaths, whether true or false, that they knew not in what part of the world we were. However, I did then believe us to be about ten degrees southward of the Cape of Good Hope, or about 45 degrees southern latitude, as I gathered from some general words I overheard among them, being I supposed to the southeast in their intended voyage to Madagascar. And although this were but little better than conjecture, yet I resolved to steer my course eastward, hoping to reach the southwest coast of New Holland,[3] and perhaps some such island as I desired, lying westward of it. The wind was full west, and by six in the evening I computed I had gone eastward at least eighteen leagues, when I spied a

[1] The coast of Australia.

[2] That is, 1714 in England (which, still using the old calendar, dated the new year from March 25), but 1715 elsewhere in Europe. England did not adopt the new calendar until 1752.

[3] Swift or Gulliver is in error; the western coast of Australia, or New Holland, is thousands of miles from Africa.

very small island about half a league off, which I soon reached.[4] It was
nothing but a rock, with one creek, naturally arched by the force of
tempests. Here I put in my canoe, and climbing a part of the rock, I could
plainly discover land to the east, extending from south to north. I lay all
night in my canoe, and repeating my voyage early in the morning, I arrived
in seven hours to the southeast point of New Holland. This confirmed me
in the opinion I have long entertained, that the maps and charts place this
country at least three degrees more to the east than it really is; which
thought I communicated many years ago to my worthy friend Mr. Herman
Moll,[5] and gave him my reasons for it, although he hath rather chosen to
follow other authors.

I saw no inhabitants in the place where I landed, and being unarmed, I
was afraid of venturing far into the country. I found some shellfish on the
shore, and eat them raw, not daring to kindle a fire, for fear of being
discovered by the natives. I continued three days feeding on oysters and
limpets,[6] to save my own provisions, and I fortunately found a brook of
excellent water, which gave me great relief.

On the fourth day, venturing out early a little too far, I saw twenty or
thirty natives upon a height, not above five hundred yards from me. They
were stark naked, men, women, and children, round a fire, as I could
discover by the smoke. One of them spied me, and gave notice to the rest;
five of them advanced towards me, leaving the women and children at the
fire. I made what haste I could to the shore, and getting into my canoe,
shoved off: the savages observing me retreat, ran after me; and before I
could get far enough into the sea, discharged an arrow, which wounded me
deeply on the inside of my left knee (I shall carry the mark to my grave). I
apprehended the arrow might be poisoned, and paddling out of the reach
of their darts (being a calm day), I made a shift to suck the wound, and
dress it as well as I could.

I was at a loss what to do, for I durst not return to the same landing-
place, but stood to the north, and was forced to paddle; for the wind,
although very gentle, was against me, blowing northwest.[7] As I was looking
about for a secure landing-place, I saw a sail to the north-northeast, which
appearing every minute more visible, I was in some doubt, whether I
should wait for them or no; but at last my detestation of the yahoo race
prevailed, and turning my canoe, I sailed and paddled together to the
south, and got into the same creek from whence I set out in the morning,
choosing rather to trust myself among these barbarians, than live with Eu-
ropean yahoos. I drew up my canoe as close as I could to the shore, and hid
myself behind a stone by the little brook, which, as I have already said, was
excellent water.

The ship came within a half a league of this creek, and sent out her
long-boat with vessels to take in fresh water (for the place it seems was very
well known) but I did not observe it until the boat was almost on shore, and
it was too late to seek another hiding-place. The seamen at their landing
observed my canoe, and rummaging it all over, easily conjectured that the

[4] Another lapse; in Book X the plan had been to sail to an island five leagues (15 miles)
from Houyhnhnmland.

[5] A Dutch-English mapmaker. [6] A kind of shellfish. [7] Out of the northwest.

owner could not be far off. Four of them well armed searched every cranny and lurking-hole, till at last they found me flat on my face behind the stone. They gazed a while in admiration[8] at my strange uncouth dress, my coat made of skins, my wooden-soled shoes, and my furred stockings; from whence, however, they concluded I was not a native of the place, who all go naked. One of the seamen in Portuguese bid me rise, and asked who I was. I understood that language very well, and getting upon my feet, said, I was a poor yahoo, banished from the Houyhnhnms, and desired they would please to let me depart. They admired to hear me answer them in their own tongue, and saw by my complexion I must be an European; but were at loss to know what I meant by yahoos and Houyhnhnms, and at the same time fell a laughing at my strange tone in speaking, which resembled the neighing of a horse. I trembled all the while betwixt fear and hatred: I again desired leave to depart, and was gently moving to my canoe; but they laid hold on me, desiring to know, what country I was of, whence I came, with many other questions. I told them I was born in England, from whence I came about five years ago, and then their country and ours were at peace. I therefore hoped they would not treat me as an enemy, since I meant them no harm, but was a poor yahoo, seeking some desolate place where to pass the remainder of his unfortunate life.

When they began to talk, I thought I never heard or saw any thing so unnatural; for it appeared to me as monstrous as if a dog or a cow should speak in England, or a yahoo in Houyhnhnmland. The honest[9] Portuguese were equally amazed at my strange dress, and the odd manner of delivering my words, which however they understood very well. They spoke to me with great humanity, and said they were sure their captain would carry me *gratis* to Lisbon, from whence I might return to my own country; that two of the seamen would go back to the ship, inform the captain of what they had seen, and receive his orders; in the mean time, unless I would give my solemn oath not to fly, they would secure me by force. I thought it best to comply with their proposal. They were very curious to know my story, but I gave them very little satisfaction; and they all conjectured that my misfortunes had impaired my reason. In two hours the boat, which went loaden with vessels of water, returned with the captain's commands to fetch me on board. I fell on my knees to preserve my liberty; but all was in vain, and the men having tied me with cords, heaved me into the boat, from whence I was taken into the ship, and from thence into the captain's cabin.

His name was Pedro de Mendez; he was a very courteous and generous person; he entreated me to give some account of my self, and desired to know what I would eat or drink; said, I should be used as well as himself, and spoke so many obliging things, that I wondered to find such civilities from a yahoo. However, I remained silent and sullen; I was ready to faint at the very smell of him and his men. At last I desired something to eat out of my own canoe; but he ordered me a chicken and some excellent wine, and then directed that I should be put to bed in a very clean cabin. I would not undress myself, but lay on the bed-clothes, and in half an hour stole out, when I thought the crew was at dinner, and getting to the side of the ship was going to leap into the sea, and swim for my life, rather than

[8] Wonder. [9] Unpretentious; ingenuous.

continue among yahoos. But one of the seamen prevented me, and having informed the captain, I was chained to my cabin.

After dinner Don Pedro came to me, and desired to know my reason for so desperate an attempt: assured me he only meant to do me all the service he was able, and spoke so very movingly, that at last I descended[10] to treat him like an animal which had some little portion of reason. I gave him a very short relation of my voyage, of the conspiracy against me by my own men, of the country where they set me on shore, and of my three years' residence there. All which he looked upon as if it were a dream or a vision; whereat I took great offence; for I had quite forgot the faculty of lying, so peculiar to yahoos in all countries where they preside, and, consequently, the disposition of suspecting truth in others of their own species. I asked him, whether it were the custom of his country to *say the thing that was not*. I assured him I had almost forgot what he meant by falsehood, and if I had lived a thousand years in Houyhnhnmland, I should never have heard a lie from the meanest servant; that I was altogether indifferent whether he believed me or no; but however, in return for his favours, I would give so much allowance to the corruption of his nature as to answer any objection he would please to make, and he might easily discover the truth.

The captain, a wise man, after many endeavours to catch me tripping in some part of my story, at last began to have a better opinion of my veracity. But he added, that since I professed so inviolable an attachment to truth, I must give him my word of honour to bear him company in this voyage without attempting anything against my life, or else he would continue me a prisoner till we arrived in Lisbon. I gave him the promise he required; but at the same time protested that I would suffer the greatest hardships rather than return to live among yahoos.

Our voyage passed without any considerable accident.[11] In gratitude to the captain I sometimes sat with him at his earnest request, and strove to conceal my antipathy to human kind, although it often broke out, which he suffered to pass without observation. But the greatest part of the day, I confined myself to my cabin, to avoid seeing any of the crew. The captain had often entreated me to strip myself of my savage dress, and offered to lend me the best suit of clothes he had. This I would not be prevailed on to accept, abhorring to cover myself with anything that had been on the back of a yahoo. I only desired he would lend me two clean shirts, which having been washed since he wore them, I believed would not so much defile me. These I changed every second day, and washed them myself.

We arrived at Lisbon, Nov. 5, 1715. At our landing the captain forced me to cover myself with his cloak, to prevent the rabble from crowding about me. I was conveyed to his own house, and, at my earnest request, he led me up to the highest room backwards.[12] I conjured him to conceal from all persons what I had told him of the Houyhnhnms, because the least hint of such a story would not only draw numbers of people to see me, but probably put me in danger of being imprisoned, or burnt by the Inquisi-

[10] Condescended. [11] Incident. [12] In the rear (of the house).

tion.[13] The captain persuaded me to accept a suit of clothes newly made, but I would not suffer the tailor to take my measure; however, Don Pedro being almost of my size, they fitted me well enough. He accoutred me with other necessaries all new, which I aired for twenty-four hours before I would use them.

The captain had no wife, nor above three servants, none of which were suffered to attend at meals, and his whole deportment was so obliging, added to very good *human* understanding, that I really began to tolerate his company. He gained so far upon me, that I ventured to look out of the back window. By degrees I was brought into another room, from whence I peeped into the street, but drew my head back in a fright. In a week's time he seduced me down to the door. I found my terror gradually lessened, but my hatred and contempt seemed to increase. I was at last bold enough to walk the street in his company, but kept my nose well stopped with rue,[14] or sometimes with tobacco.

In ten days Don Pedro, to whom I had given some account of my domestic affairs, put it upon me as a point of honour and conscience, that I ought to return to my native country, and live at home with my wife and children. He told me, there was an English ship in the port just ready to sail, and he would furnish me with all things necessary. It would be tedious to repeat his arguments, and my contradictions. He said it was altogether impossible to find such a solitary island as I had desired to live in; but I might command in my own house, and pass my time in a manner as recluse as I pleased.

I complied at last, finding I could not do better. I left Lisbon the 24th day of November, in an English merchantman, but who was the master I never inquired. Don Pedro accompanied me to the ship, and lent me twenty pounds. He took kind leave of me, and embraced me at parting, which I bore as well as I could. During this last voyage I had no commerce[15] with the master or any of his men, but pretending I was sick kept close in my cabin. On the fifth of December, 1715, we cast anchor in the Downs[16] about nine in the morning, and at three in the afternoon I got safe to my house at Redriff.[17]

My wife and family received me with great surprise and joy, because they concluded me certainly dead; but I must freely confess the sight of them filled me only with hatred, disgust and contempt, and the more by reflecting on the near alliance I had to them. For although, since my unfortunate exile from the Houyhnhnm country, I had compelled myself to tolerate the sight of yahoos, and to converse with Don Pedro de Mendez, yet my memory and imaginations were perpetually filled with the virtues and ideas of those exalted Houyhnhnms. And when I began to consider, that by copulating with one of the yahoo species I had become a parent of more, it struck me with the utmost shame, confusion, and horror.

[13] The Roman Catholic court designed to prosecute heresy. (To claim that horses were superior to humans in rationality would be heretical.)
[14] An aromatic herb. [15] Social contact.
[16] An anchorage area in the English Channel, off the coast of Kent in southeast England.
[17] A district in south London.

As soon as I entered the house, my wife took me in her arms, and kissed me, at which, having not been used to the touch of that odious animal[18] for so many years, I fell in a swoon for almost an hour. At the time I am writing it is five years since my last return to England: during the first year I could not endure my wife or children in my presence, the very smell of them was intolerable, much less could I suffer them to eat in the same room. To this hour they dare not presume to touch my bread, or drink out of the same cup, neither was I ever able to let one of them take me by the hand. The first money I laid out was to buy two young stone-horses,[19] which I keep in a good stable, and next to them the groom is my greatest favourite; for I feel my spirits revived by the smell he contracts in the stable. My horses understand me tolerably well; I converse with them at least four hours every day. They are strangers to bridle or saddle; they live in great amity with me, and friendship to each other.

CHAPTER XII

The author's veracity. His design in publishing this work. His censure of those travellers who swerve from the truth. The author clears himself from any sinister ends in writing. An objection answered. The method of planting colonies. His native country commended. The right of the crown to those countries described by the author is justified. The difficulty of conquering them. The author takes his last leave of the reader, proposeth his manner of living for the future, gives good advice, and concludes.

Thus, gentle reader, I have given thee a faithful history of my travels for sixteen years, and above seven months, wherein I have not been so studious of[1] ornament as of truth. I could perhaps like others have astonished thee with strange improbable tales; but I rather chose to relate plain matter of fact in the simplest manner and style, because my principal design was to inform, and not to amuse thee.

It is easy for us who travel into remote countries, which are seldom visited by Englishmen or other Europeans, to form descriptions of wonderful animals both at sea and land. Whereas a traveller's chief aim should be to make men wiser and better, and to improve their minds by the bad as well as good example of what they deliver concerning foreign places.

I could heartily wish a law were enacted, that every traveller, before he were permitted to publish his voyages, should be obliged to make oath before the Lord High Chancellor that all he intended to print was absolutely true to the best of his knowledge; for then the world would no longer be deceived as it usually is, while some writers, to make their works pass the better upon the public, impose the grossest falsities on the unwary reader. I have perused several books of travels with great delight in my younger days; but having since gone over most parts of the globe, and been able to contradict many fabulous accounts from my own observation, it hath given

[18] This may refer to the yahoo species rather than to the wife personally.
[19] Ungelded horses; stallions. [1] Zealous for.

me a great disgust against this part of reading, and some indignation to see the credulity of mankind so impudently abused. Therefore since my acquaintance were pleased to think my poor endeavours might not be unacceptable to my country, I imposed on myself as a maxim, never to be swerved from, that I would *strictly adhere to truth;* neither indeed can I be ever under the least temptation to vary from it, while I retain in my mind the lectures and example of my noble master, and the other illustrious Houyhnhnms, of whom I had so long the honour to be an humble hearer.

> —*Nec si miserum Fortuna Sinonem*
> *Finxit, vanum etiam mendacemque improba finget.*[2]

I know very well how little reputation is to be got by writings which require neither genius nor learning, nor indeed any other talent, except a good memory or an exact journal. I know likewise, that writers of travels, like dictionary-makers, are sunk into oblivion by the weight and bulk of those who come after, and therefore lie uppermost. And it is highly probable, that such travellers who shall hereafter visit the countries described in this work of mine, may, by detecting my errors (if there be any), and adding many new discoveries of their own, jostle me out of vogue, and stand in my place, making the world forget that ever I was an author. This indeed would be too great a mortification if I wrote for fame: but, as my sole intention was the PUBLIC GOOD, I cannot be altogether disappointed. For who can read of the virtues I have mentioned in the glorious Houyhnhnms, without being ashamed of his own vices, when he considers himself as the reasoning, governing animal of his country? I shall say nothing of those remote nations where yahoos preside, amongst which the least corrupted are the Brobdingnagians,[3] whose wise maxims in morality and government it would be our happiness to observe. But I forbear descanting further, and rather leave the judicious reader to his own remarks and applications.

I am not a little pleased that this work of mine can possibly meet with no censurers: for what objections can be made against a writer who relates only plain facts that happened in such distant countries, where we have not the least interest with respect either to trade or negotiations? I have carefully avoided every fault with which common writers of travels are often too justly charged. Besides, I meddle not the least with any *party,*[4] but write without passion, prejudice, or ill-will against any man or number of men whatsover. I write for the noblest end, to inform and instruct mankind, over whom I may, without breach of modesty, pretend to some superiority from the advantages I received by conversing so long among the most accomplished Houyhnhnms. I write without any view towards profit or

[2] From Virgil's *Aeneid*, Book II: "Sinon is wretched, / Fortune has made him so, but she will never / Make him a liar" (Rolfe Humphries translation). This is a literary joke, because Sinon is indeed a liar who hoodwinks the Trojans into harboring the wooden horse inside which are concealed the Greek soldiers who will sack Troy. For Sinon, see also Dante, *Inferno*, XXX.98 ff.

[3] Giants whose land Gulliver visited in Part II.

[4] The earlier parts of *Gulliver's Travels* are actually full of political gibes, especially against the Whig party in England.

praise. I never suffer a word to pass that may look like reflection,[5] or possibly give the least offence even to those who are most ready to take it. So that I hope I may with justice pronounce myself an author perfectly blameless, against whom the tribe of answerers, considerers, observers, reflecters, detecters, remarkers, will never be able to find matter for exercising their talents.

I confess, it was whispered to me that I was bound in duty, as a subject of England, to have given in a memorial to a secretary of state, at my first coming over; because, whatever lands are discovered by a subject belong to the crown. But I doubt whether our conquests in the countries I treat of would be as easy as those of Ferdinando Cortez over the naked Americans.[6] The Lilliputians,[7] I think, are hardly worth the charge of a fleet and army to reduce them, and I question whether it might be prudent or safe to attempt the Brobdingnagians. Or whether an English army would be much at their ease with the Flying Island[8] over their heads. The Houyhnhnms, indeed, appear not to be so well prepared for war, a science to which they are perfect strangers, and especially against missive weapons.[9] However, supposing myself to be a minister of state, I could never give my advice for invading them. Their prudence, unanimity, unacquaintedness with fear, and their love of their country would amply supply all defects in the military art. Imagine twenty thousand of them breaking into the midst of an European army, confounding the ranks, overturning the carriages,[10] battering the warriors' faces into mummy,[11] by terrible yerks[12] from their hinder hoofs. For they would well deserve the character given to Augustus; *Recalcitrat undique tutus.*[13] But instead of proposals for conquering that magnanimous nation, I rather wish they were in a capacity or disposition to send a sufficient number of their inhabitants for civilizing Europe, by teaching us the first principles of honour, justice, truth, temperance, public spirit, fortitude, chastity, friendship, benevolence, and fidelity. The names of all which virtues are still retained among us in most languages, and are to be met with in modern as well as ancient authors; which I am able to assert from my own small reading.

But I had another reason which made me less forward to enlarge his Majesty's dominions by my discoveries. To say the truth, I had conceived a few scruples with relation to the distributive justice[14] of princes upon those occasions. For instance, a crew of pirates are driven by a storm they know not whither, at length a boy discovers land from the topmast, they go on shore to rob and plunder, they see an harmless people, are entertained with kindness, they give the country a new name, they take formal possession of it for the king, they set up a rotten plank or a stone for a memorial,

[5] Censure.
[6] The Spanish explorer Cortez conquered the Aztecs of Mexico in 1521 with only a small force of men.
[7] The tiny humans visited by Gulliver in Part I.
[8] The flying island of Laputa, described in Part III, can crush the towns underneath it by descending on them.
[9] Weapons hurled or shot. [10] Gun carriages. [11] Pulp. [12] Kicks.
[13] From Horace's *Satires*, II: "He kicks on all sides with safety."
[14] The branch of justice concerned with giving to different people their proper shares.

they murder two or three dozen of the natives, bring away a couple more by force for a sample, return home, and get their pardon. Here commences a new dominion acquired with a title by *divine right*. Ships are sent with the first opportunity, the natives driven out or destroyed, their princes tortured to discover their gold, a free license given to all acts of inhumanity and lust, the earth reeking with the blood of its inhabitants: and this execrable crew of butchers employed in so pious an expedition, is a modern colony sent to convert and civilize an idolatrous and barbarous people.

But this description, I confess, doth by no means affect the British nation, who may be an example to the whole world for their wisdom, care, and justice in planting colonies; their liberal endowments for the advancement of religion and learning; their choice of devout and able pastors to propagate Christianity; their caution in stocking their provinces with people of sober lives and conversations[15] from this the mother kingdom; their strict regard to the distribution of justice, in supplying the civil administration through all their colonies with officers of the greatest abilities, utter strangers to corruption; and to crown all, by sending the most vigilant and virtuous governors, who have no other views than the happiness of the people over whom they preside, and the honour of the king their master.

But as those countries which I have described do not appear to have any desire of being conquered, and enslaved, murdered or driven out by colonies, nor abound either in gold, silver, sugar or tobacco; I did humbly conceive they were by no means proper objects of our zeal, our valour, or our interest. However, if those whom it may concern think fit to be of another opinion, I am ready to depose, when I shall be lawfully called, that no European did ever visit these countries before me. I mean, if the inhabitants ought to be believed; unless a dispute may arise about the two yahoos, said to have been seen many ages ago on a mountain in Houyhnhnmland, from whence the opinion is, that the race of those brutes hath descended; and these, for any thing I know, may have been English, which indeed I was apt to suspect from the lineaments of their posterity's countenances, although very much defaced. But, how far that will go to make out a title, I leave to the learned in colony-law.

But as to the formality of taking possession in my sovereign's name, it never came once into my thoughts; and if it had, yet as my affairs then stood, I should perhaps, in point of prudence and self-preservation, have put it off to a better opportunity.

Having thus answered the *only* objection that can ever be raised against me as a traveller, I here take a final leave of my courteous readers, and return to enjoy my own speculations in my little garden at Redriff, to apply those excellent lessons of virtue which I learned among the Houyhnhnms, to instruct the yahoos of my own family as far as I shall find them docible[16] animals, to behold my figure often in a glass, and thus if possible habituate myself by time to tolerate the sight of a human creature; to lament the brutality[17] of Houyhnhnms in my own country, but always treat their persons with respect, for the sake of my noble master, his family, his friends,

[15] Way of living; behavior. Some of the British colonists were, in fact, convicted felons.
[16] Teachable. [17] Brutalization.

and the whole Houyhnhnm race, whom these of ours have the honour to resemble in all their lineaments, however their intellectuals[18] came to degenerate.

I began last week to permit my wife to sit at dinner with me, at the farthest end of a long table, and to answer (but with the utmost brevity) the few questions I ask her. Yet the smell of a yahoo continuing very offensive, I always keep my nose well stopped with rue, lavender, or tobacco leaves. And although it be hard for a man late in life to remove old habits, I am not altogether out of hopes in some time to suffer a neighbour yahoo in my company without the apprehensions I am yet under of his teeth or his claws.

My reconcilement to the yahoo-kind in general might not be so difficult if they would be content with those vices and follies only which nature hath entitled them to. I am not in the least provoked at the sight of a lawyer, a pickpocket, a colonel, a fool, a lord, a gamester, a politician, a whore-monger, a physician, an evidence,[19] a suborner, an attorney, a traitor, or the like; this is all according to the due course of things: but when I behold a lump of deformity and diseases both in body and mind, smitten with pride, it immediately breaks all the measures of my patience; neither shall I be ever able to comprehend how such an animal and such a vice could tally together. The wise and virtuous Houyhnhnms, who abound in all excellencies that can adorn a rational creature, have no name for this vice in their language, which hath no terms to express any thing that is evil, except those whereby they describe the detestable qualities of their yahoos, among which they were not able to distinguish this of pride, for want of thoroughly understanding human nature, as it showeth itself in other countries, where that animal presides. But I, who had more experience, could plainly observe some rudiments of it among the wild yahoos.

But the Houyhnhnms, who live under the government of reason, are no more proud of the good qualities they possess, than I should be for not wanting a leg or an arm, which no man in his wits would boast of, although he must be miserable without them. I dwell the longer upon this subject from the desire I have to make the society of an English yahoo by any means not insupportable, and therefore I here entreat those who have any tincture of this absurd vice, that they will not presume to appear in my sight.

FINIS

A LETTER FROM CAPT. GULLIVER
TO HIS COUSIN SYMPSON.[1]

I hope you will be ready to own publicly, whenever you shall be called to it, that by your great and frequent urgency you prevailed on me to publish a very loose and uncorrect account of my travels; with direction to hire some young gentlemen of either university to put them in order, and correct the

[18] Intellects. [19] Paid false witness.

[1] A fictitious person. The present letter first appeared in the 1735 edition, nine years after the first edition. Although the letter is largely a spoof, it expresses Swift's genuine resentment about changes in the text made by the publisher in the interests of political safety.

style, as my cousin Dampier[2] did by my advice, in his book called *A Voyage round the World*. But I do not remember I gave you power to consent, that any thing should be omitted, and much less that any thing should be inserted: therefore, as to the latter, I do here renounce every thing of that kind; particularly a paragraph about her Majesty the late Queen Anne,[3] of most pious and glorious memory; although I did reverence and esteem her more than any of human species. But you, or your interpolator, ought to have considered, that as it was not my inclination, so was it not decent to praise any animal of our composition[4] before my master Houyhnhnm: and besides, the fact was altogether false; for to my knowledge, being in England during some part of her Majesty's reign, she did govern by a chief minister; nay, even by two successively; the first whereof was the Lord of Godolphin, and the second the Lord of Oxford; so that you have made me *say the thing that was not.* Likewise, in the account of the Academy of Projectors,[5] and several passages of my discourse to my master Houyhnhnm, you have either omitted some material circumstances, or minced or changed them in such a manner, that I do hardly know mine own work. When I formerly hinted to you something of this in a letter, you were pleased to answer, that you were afraid of giving offence; that people in power were very watchful over the press, and apt not only to interpret, but to punish every thing which looked like an *innuendo* (as I think you called it). But pray, how could that which I spoke so many years ago, and at above five thousand leagues distance, in another reign, be applied to any of the yahoos who now are said to govern the herd; especially at a time when I little thought on or feared the unhappiness of living under them? Have not I the most reason to complain, when I see these very yahoos carried by Houyhnhnms in a vehicle, as if these were brutes, and those the rational creatures? And, indeed, to avoid so monstrous and detestable a sight was one principal motive of my retirement hither.[6]

Thus much I thought proper to tell you in relation to your self, and to the trust I reposed in you.

I do in the next place complain of my own great want of judgment, in being prevailed upon by the intreaties and false reasonings of you and some others, very much against mine own opinion, to suffer my travels to be published. Pray bring to your mind how often I desired you to consider, when you insisted on the motive of public good, that the yahoos were a species of animals utterly incapable of amendment by precepts or examples, and so it hath proved; for instead of seeing a full stop put to all abuses and corruptions, at least in this little island, as I had reason to expect: behold, after above six months' warning, I cannot learn that my book hath produced one single effect according to mine intentions: I desired you

[2] William Dampier (1652–1715), a well known buccaneer, explorer, and adventurer. He rescued the castaway Alexander Selkirk, the model for Daniel Defoe's *Robinson Crusoe*.

[3] This passage, inserted in Part IV, chapter 6, was removed in later editions.

[4] Make-up.

[5] An organization of scientists, portrayed in Part III, engaged in ingenious but insane experiments.

[6] Gulliver is supposed to have retired from London to Nottinghamshire, in central England.

would let me know by a letter, when party and faction were extinguished; judges learned and upright; pleaders honest and modest, with some tincture of common sense; and Smithfield[7] blazing with pyramids of lawbooks; the young nobility's education entirely changed; the physicians banished; the female yahoos abounding in virtue, honour, truth and good sense; courts and levees[8] of great ministers thoroughly weeded and swept; wit, merit and learning rewarded; all disgracers of the press in prose and verse condemned to eat nothing but their own cotton,[9] and quench their thirst with their own ink. These, and a thousand other reformations, I firmly counted upon by your encouragement; as indeed they were plainly deducible from the precepts delivered in my book. And, it must be owned, that seven months were a sufficient time to correct every vice and folly to which yahoos are subject, if their natures had been capable of the least disposition to virtue or wisdom; yet so far have you been from answering mine expectation in any of your letters, that on the contrary you are loading our carrier every week with libels, and keys, and reflections, and memoirs, and second parts;[10] wherein I see myself accused of reflecting upon great states-folk; of degrading human nature (for so they have still the confidence to style it), and of abusing the female sex. I find likewise, that the writers of those bundles are not agreed among themselves; for some of them will not allow me to be author of mine own travels; and others make me author of books to which I am wholly a stranger.

I find likewise that your printer hath been so careless as to confound the times, and mistake the dates of my several voyages and returns, neither assigning the true year, or the true month, or day of the month; and I hear the original manuscript is all destroyed since the publication of my book. Neither have I any copy left; however, I have sent you some corrections, which you may insert if ever there should be a second edition: and yet I cannot stand to[11] them, but shall leave that matter to my judicious and candid readers, to adjust it as they please.

I hear some of our sea-yahoos find fault with my sea-language, as not proper in many parts, nor now in use. I cannot help it. In my first voyages, while I was young, I was instructed by the oldest mariners, and learned to speak as they did. But I have since found that the sea-yahoos are apt, like the land ones, to become new-fangled in their words; which the latter change every year, insomuch as I remember upon each return to mine own country, their old dialect was so altered that I could hardly understand the new. And I observe, when any yahoo comes from London out of curiosity to visit me at mine own house, we neither of us are able to deliver our conceptions in a manner intelligible to the other.

If the censure of yahoos could any way affect me, I should have great reason to complain that some of them are so bold as to think my book of travels a mere fiction out of mine own brain; and have gone so far as to

[7] An area of London where alleged heretics and criminals had formerly been burned.
[8] Receptions held in the morning. [9] Used to make paper and to clean type.
[10] Spurious commentaries on and continuations of *Gulliver's Travels* began to appear immediately after its first publication.
[11] Stand behind.

drop hints that the Houyhnhnms and yahoos have no more existence than the inhabitants of Utopia.[12]

Indeed I must confess, that as to the people of Lilliput, Brobdingrag (for so the word should have been spelt, and not erroneously 'Brobdingnag') and Laputa, I have never yet heard of any yahoo so presumptuous as to dispute their being, or the facts I have related concerning them; because the truth immediately strikes every reader with conviction. And is there less probability in my account of the Houyhnhnms or yahoos, when it is manifest as to the latter, there are so many thousands even in this city,[13] who only differ from their brother brutes in Houyhnhnmland, because they use a sort of a jabber, and do not go naked? I wrote for their amendment, and not their approbation. The united praise of the whole race would be of less consequence to me than the neighing of those two degenerate Houyhnhnms I keep in my stable; because from these, degenerate as they are, I still improve in some virtues, without any mixture of vice.

Do these miserable animals presume to think that I am so far degenerated as to defend my veracity? Yahoo as I am, it is well known through all Houyhnhnmland, that by the instructions and example of my illustrious master, I was able in the compass of two years (although I confess with the utmost difficulty) to remove that infernal habit of lying, shuffling,[14] deceiving, and equivocating, so deeply rooted in the very souls of all my species, especially the Europeans.

I have other complaints to make upon this vexatious occasion; but I forbear troubling myself or you any further. I must freely confess, that since my last return some corruptions of my yahoo nature have revived in me by conversing with a few of your species, and particularly those of mine own family, by an unavoidable necessity; else I should never have attempted so absurd a project as that of reforming the yahoo race in this kingdom; but I have now done with all such visionary schemes for ever.
April 2, 1727

A MODEST PROPOSAL

FOR

PREVENTING THE CHILDREN OF POOR PEOPLE IN IRELAND FROM BEING A BURDEN TO THEIR PARENTS OR COUNTRY, AND FOR MAKING THEM BENEFICIAL TO THE PUBLIC

It is a melancholy object to those who walk through this great town,[1] or travel in the country, when they see the streets, the roads and cabin-doors crowded with beggars of the female sex, followed by three, four, or six

[12] Thomas More's great satire *Utopia* (1516) depicts an ideal state flourishing in a far-away part of the world.
[13] London, apparently, although Gulliver is supposed to have moved away.
[14] Acting deceitfully; equivocating. [1] Dublin.

children, all in rags, and importuning every passenger for an alms. These mothers, instead of being able to work for their honest livelihood, are forced to employ all their time in strolling, to beg sustenance for their helpless infants, who, as they grow up, either turn thieves for want of work, or leave their dear native country to fight for the Pretender[2] in Spain, or sell themselves to the Barbadoes.[3]

I think it is agreed by all parties that this prodigious number of children, in the arms, or on the backs, or at the heels of their mothers, and frequently of their fathers, is in the present deplorable state of the kingdom a very great additional grievance; and therefore whoever could find out a fair, cheap, and easy method of making these children sound and useful members of the commonwealth would deserve so well of the public as to have his statue set up for a preserver of the nation.

But my intention is very far from being confined to provide only for the children of professed beggars; it is of a much greater extent, and shall take in the whole number of infants at a certain age who are born of parents in effect as little able to support them as those who demand our charity in the streets.

As to my own part, having turned my thoughts for many years upon this important subject, and maturely weighed the several schemes of other projectors,[4] I have always found them grossly mistaken in their computation. It is true a child just dropped from its dam may be supported by her milk for a solar year with little other nourishment, at most not above the value of two shillings, which the mother may certainly get, or the value in scraps, by her lawful occupation of begging, and it is exactly at one year old that I propose to provide for them, in such a manner as, instead of being a charge[5] upon their parents, or the parish, or wanting food and raiment for the rest of their lives, they shall, on the contrary, contribute to the feeding and partly to the clothing of many thousands.

There is likewise another great advantage in my scheme, that it will prevent those voluntary abortions, and that horrid practice of women murdering their bastard children, alas, too frequent among us, sacrificing the poor innocent babes, I doubt,[6] more to avoid the expense than the shame, which would move tears and pity in the most savage and inhuman breast.

The number of souls in Ireland being usually reckoned one million and a half, of these I calculate there may be about two hundred thousand couples whose wives are breeders, from which number I subtract thirty thousand couples who are able to maintain their own children, although I apprehend there cannot be so many under the present distresses of the kingdom, but this being granted, there will remain an hundred and seventy thousand breeders. I again subtract fifty thousand for those women who miscarry, or whose children die by accident or disease within the year.

[2] The Stuart claimant of the English throne; the exiled family had been deposed and succeeded by the house of Hanover (George I and his descendants). The Old Pretender was James Francis Edward Stuart (1688–1766), son of James II; his son Charles Edward ("Bonnie Prince Charlie," 1720–1788) was the Young Pretender.
[3] Barbados, in the West Indies. Emigrants agreed to work for a period in return for the cost of their transportation.
[4] Experimental reformers; a pejorative term for Swift.
[5] Financial burden. [6] Suspect.

There only remain an hundred and twenty thousand children of poor parents annually born: the question therefore is, how this number shall be reared, and provided for, which, as I have already said, under the present situation of affairs is utterly impossible by all the methods hitherto proposed, for we can neither employ them in handicraft or agriculture; we neither build houses (I mean in the country), nor cultivate land: they can very seldom pick up a livelihood by stealing until they arrive at six years old, except where they are of towardly parts,[7] although I confess they learn the rudiments much earlier, during which time they can however be properly looked upon only as probationers,[8] as I have been informed by a principal gentleman in the County of Cavan, who protested to me that he never knew above one or two instances under the age of six, even in a part of the kingdom so renowned for the quickest proficiency in that art.

I am assured by our merchants that a boy or a girl before twelve years old, is no saleable commodity, and even when they come to this age, they will not yield above three pounds, or three pounds and half-a-crown at most on the Exchange, which cannot turn to account either to the parents or the kingdom, the charge of nutriment and rags having been at least four times that value.

I shall now therefore humbly propose my own thoughts, which I hope will not be liable to the least objection.

I have been assured by a very knowing American of my acquaintance in London, that a young healthy child well nursed is at a year old a most delicious, nourishing and wholesome food, whether stewed, roasted, baked, or boiled, and I make no doubt that it will equally serve in a fricassee, or a ragout.

I do therefore humbly offer it to public consideration, that of the hundred and twenty thousand children already computed, twenty thousand may be reserved for breed, whereof only one fourth part to be males, which is more than we allow to sheep, black-cattle, or swine, and my reason is that these children are seldom the fruits of marriage, a circumstance not much regarded by our savages, therefore one male will be sufficient to serve four females. That the remaining hundred thousand may at a year old be offered in sale to the persons of quality, and fortune, through the kingdom, always advising the mother to let them suck plentifully in the last month, so as to render them plump, and fat for a good table. A child will make two dishes at an entertainment for friends, and when the family dines alone, the fore or hind quarter will make a reasonable dish, and seasoned with a little pepper or salt will be very good boiled on the fourth day, especially in winter.

I have reckoned upon a medium,[9] that a child just born will weigh twelve pounds, and in a solar year if tolerably nursed increaseth to twenty-eight pounds.

I grant this food will be somewhat dear, and therefore very proper for landlords, who, as they have already devoured most of the parents, seem to have the best title to the children.

Infant's flesh will be in season throughout the year, but more plentiful

[7] Precocious talents. [8] Persons undergoing a trial period; apprentices.
[9] On the average.

in March, and a little before and after, for we are told by a grave author, an eminent French physician,[10] that fish being a prolific diet, there are more children born in Roman Catholic countries about nine months after Lent[11] than at any other season; therefore reckoning a year after Lent, the markets will be more glutted than usual, because the number of Popish infants is at least three to one in this kingdom, and therefore it will have one other collateral advantage by lessening the number of Papists[12] among us.

I have already computed the charge of nursing a beggar's child (in which list I reckon all cottagers, labourers, and four-fifths of the farmers) to be about two shillings *per annum*, rags included, and I believe no gentleman would repine to give ten shillings for the carcass of a good fat child, which, as I have said, will make four dishes of excellent nutritive meat, when he hath only some particular friend or his own family to dine with him. Thus the Squire will learn to be a good landlord and grow popular among his tenants, the mother will have eight shillings net profit, and be fit for work until she produces another child.

Those who are more thrifty (as I must confess the times require) may flay the carcass; the skin of which artificially[13] dressed, will make admirable gloves for ladies, and summer boots for fine gentlemen.

As to our city of Dublin, shambles[14] may be appointed for this purpose, in the most convenient parts of it, and butchers we may be assured will not be wanting, although I rather recommend buying the children alive, and dressing them hot from the knife, as we do roasting pigs.

A very worthy person, a true lover of his country, and whose virtues I highly esteem, was lately pleased, in discoursing on this matter to offer a refinement upon my scheme. He said that many gentlemen of this kingdom, having of late destroyed their deer, he conceived that the want of venison might be well supplied by the bodies of young lads and maidens, not exceeding fourteen years of age, nor under twelve, so great a number of both sexes in every county being now ready to starve, for want of work and service: and these to be disposed of by their parents if alive, or otherwise by their nearest relations. But with due deference to so excellent a friend, and so deserving a patriot, I cannot be altogether in his sentiments. For as to the males, my American acquaintance assured me from frequent experience that their flesh was generally tough and lean, like that of our schoolboys, by continual exercise, and their taste disagreeable, and to fatten them would not answer the charge. Then as to the females, it would, I think with humble submission, be a loss to the public, because they soon would become breeders themselves: and besides, it is not improbable that some scrupulous people might be apt to censure such a practice (although indeed very unjustly) as a little bordering upon cruelty, which I confess, hath always been with me the strongest objection against any project, howsoever well intended.

But in order to justify my friend, he confessed that this expedient was

[10] François Rabelais, author of *Gargantua and Pantagruel*.
[11] Abstention from meat was practiced in Lent by Catholics.
[12] This term for Catholics, like "Popish," was a pejorative one. [13] Skillfully.
[14] Slaughterhouses.

put into his head by the famous Psalmanazar,[15] a native of the island For-
mosa, who came from thence to London, above twenty years ago, and in
conversation told my friend that in his country when any young person
happened to be put to death, the executioner sold the carcass to persons of
quality, as a prime dainty, and that, in his time, the body of a plump girl of
fifteen, who was crucified for an attempt to poison the emperor, was sold to
his Imperial Majesty's Prime Minister of State, and other great Mandarins
of the Court, in joints from the gibbet, at four hundred crowns. Neither
indeed can I deny that if the same use were made of several plump young
girls in this town who, without one single groat to their fortunes, cannot stir
abroad without a chair,[16] and appear at the playhouse and assemblies in
foreign fineries, which they never will pay for, the kingdom would not be
the worse.

Some persons of a desponding spirit are in great concern about that
vast number of poor people, who are aged, diseased, or maimed, and I have
been desired to employ my thoughts what course may be taken to ease the
nation of so grievous an encumbrance. But I am not in the least pain upon
that matter, because it is very well known that they are every day dying, and
rotting, by cold, and famine, and filth, and vermin, as fast as can be reasonably
expected. And as to the younger labourers they are now in almost as hopeful a
condition. They cannot get work, and consequently pine away from want of
nourishment, to a degree that if at any time they are accidentally hired to
common labour, they have not strength to perform it; and thus the country
and themselves are in a fair way of being soon delivered from the evils to
come.

I have too long digressed, and therefore shall return to my subject. I
think the advantages by the proposal which I have made are obvious and
many, as well as of the highest importance.

For first, as I have already observed, it would greatly lessen the number
of Papists, with whom we are yearly over-run, being the principal breeders
of the nation, as well as our most dangerous enemies, and who stay at home
on purpose with a design to deliver the kingdom to the Pretender, hoping
to take their advantage by the absence of so many good Protestants, who
have chosen rather to leave their country than stay at home and pay tithes[17]
against their conscience to an idolatrous Episcopal curate.

Secondly, the poorer tenants will have something valuable of their own,
which by law may be made liable to distress,[18] and help to pay their land-
lord's rent, their corn and cattle being already seized, and money a thing
unknown.

Thirdly, whereas the maintenance of an hundred thousand children,
from two years old, and upwards, cannot be computed at less than ten
shillings a piece *per annum,* the nation's stock will be thereby increased fifty
thousand pounds *per annum,* besides the profit of a new dish, introduced to
the tables of all gentlemen of fortune in the kingdom, who have any refine-

[15] A literary fraud who published a fictitious description of Formosa.
[16] Sedan chair.
[17] Contributions of a tenth of one's income for the support of the church.
[18] Seizure of goods for the payment of debt.

ment in taste, and the money will circulate among ourselves, the goods being entirely of our own growth and manufacture.

Fourthly, the constant breeders, besides the gain of eight shillings sterling *per annum*, by the sale of their children, will be rid of the charge of maintaining them after the first year.

Fifthly, this food would likewise bring great custom to taverns, where the vintners will certainly be so prudent as to procure the best receipts[19] for dressing it to perfection, and consequently have their houses frequented by all the fine gentlemen, who justly value themselves upon their knowledge in good eating; and a skilful cook, who understands how to oblige his guests, will contrive to make it as expensive as they please.

Sixthly, this would be a great inducement to marriage, which all wise nations have either encouraged by rewards, or enforced by laws and penalties. It would increase the care and tenderness of mothers towards their children, when they were sure of a settlement for life, to the poor babes, provided in some sort by the public to their annual profit instead of expense. We should soon see an honest emulation[20] among the married women, which of them could bring the fattest child to the market. Men would become as fond of their wives, during the time of their pregnancy, as they are now of their mares in foal, their cows in calf, or sows when they are ready to farrow, nor offer to beat or kick them (as it is too frequent a practice) for fear of a miscarriage.

Many other advantages might be enumerated. For instance, the addition of some thousand carcasses in our exportation of barrelled beef; the propagation of swine's flesh, and improvement in the art of making good bacon, so much wanted among us by the great destruction of pigs, too frequent at our tables, which are no way comparable in taste or magnificence to a well-grown, fat yearling child, which roasted whole will make a considerable figure at a Lord Mayor's feast, or any other public entertainment. But this and many others I omit, being studious of brevity.

Supposing that one thousand families in this city would be constant customers for infants' flesh, besides others who might have it at merry meetings, particularly weddings and christenings; I compute that Dublin would take off annually about twenty thousand carcasses, and the rest of the kingdom (where probably they will be sold somewhat cheaper) the remaining eighty thousand.

I can think of no one objection that will possibly be raised against this proposal, unless it should be urged that the number of people will be thereby much lessened in the kingdom. This I freely own,[21] and it was indeed one principal design in offering it to the world. I desire the reader will observe, that I calculate my remedy *for this one individual Kingdom of Ireland, and for no other that ever was, is, or, I think, ever can be upon earth. Therefore let no man talk to me of other expedients: Of taxing our absentees at five shillings a pound: Of using neither clothes, nor household furniture, except what is of our own growth and manufacture: Of utterly rejecting the materials and instruments that promote foreign luxury: Of curing the expensiveness of pride, vanity, idleness, and gaming in our women: Of introducing a vein of parsimony, prudence, and temperance: Of learning to love our country, wherein we differ even*

[19] Recipes. [20] Rivalry. [21] Admit.

from Laplanders, *and the inhabitants of* Topinamboo:[22] *Of quitting our animosities and factions, nor act any longer like the* Jews, *who were murdering one another at the very moment their city was taken: Of being a little cautious not to sell our country and consciences for nothing: Of teaching landlords to have at least one degree of mercy towards their tenants.* Lastly, *of putting a spirit of honesty, industry, and skill into our shopkeepers, who, if a resolution could now be taken to buy only our native goods, would immediately unite to cheat and exact upon us in the price, the measure and the goodness, nor could ever yet be brought to make one fair proposal of just dealing, though often and earnestly invited to it.*

Therefore I repeat, let no man talk to me of these and the like expedients, till he hath at least a glimpse of hope that there will ever be some hearty and sincere attempt to put them in practice.

But as to myself, having been wearied out for many years with offering vain, idle, visionary thoughts, and at length utterly despairing of success, I fortunately fell upon this proposal, which as it is wholly new, so it hath something solid and real, of no expense and little trouble, full in our own power, and whereby we can incur no danger in disobliging England. For this kind of commodity will not bear exportation, the flesh being of too tender a consistence to admit a long continuance in salt, *although perhaps I could name a country*[23] *which would be glad to eat up our whole nation without it.*

After all I am not so violently bent upon my own opinion as to reject any offer, proposed by wise men, which shall be found equally innocent, cheap, easy and effectual. But before some thing of that kind shall be advanced in contradiction to my scheme, and offering a better, I desire the author, or authors, will be pleased maturely to consider two points. First, as things now stand, how they will be able to find food and raiment for a hundred thousand useless mouths and backs? And secondly, there being a round million of creatures in human figure, throughout this kingdom, whose whole subsistence put into a common stock would leave them in debt two millions of pounds sterling; adding those who are beggars by profession, to the bulk of farmers, cottagers, and labourers with their wives and children, who are beggars in effect; I desire those politicians who dislike my overture, and may perhaps be so bold to attempt an answer, that they will first ask the parents of these mortals whether they would not at this day think it a great happiness to have been sold for food at a year old, in the manner I prescribe, and thereby have avoided such a perpetual scene of misfortunes as they have since gone through, by the oppression of landlords, the impossibility of paying rent without money or trade, the want of common sustenance, with neither house nor clothes to cover them from the inclemencies of weather, and the most inevitable prospect of entailing the like, or greater miseries upon their breed for ever.

I profess in the sincerity of my heart that I have not the least personal interest in endeavouring to promote this necessary work, having no other motive than the *public good of my country, by advancing our trade, providing for infants, relieving the poor, and giving some pleasure to the rich.* I have no children by which I can propose to get a single penny; the youngest being nine years old, and my wife past child-bearing.

[22] An area of Brazil. [23] England.

Alexander Pope
(1688–1744)

Perhaps the quintessential writer of the Neoclassic period in Europe was the English poet Alexander Pope. Pope was born in 1688 into a middle-class Roman Catholic family in London. In the same year, the Glorious Revolution deposed the Catholic James II and placed the Protestant William and Mary on the English throne; Pope suffered all his life from the anti-Catholicism of the strongly Protestant age that followed. Barred as a Catholic from universities, he was educated by tutors and at small private schools and by his own reading and study. When he was twelve, his family moved to a country house in Windsor Forest, in an area more tolerant of Catholics. He contracted tuberculosis in childhood; it left him with a curved spine, a stunted, twisted body only four feet, six inches tall, and a lifetime of recurring pain.

Publication of his *Pastorals* in 1709 and of the *Essay on Criticism* in 1711 catapulted him at the age of twenty-one into the exciting but sometimes cut-throat life of literary London. He met the magisterial Joseph Addison and was briefly a member of the group of young Whig writers who gathered around Addison at Button's Coffeehouse. He soon gravitated, however, to the more congenial circle of the Tory satirists Jonathan Swift, John Arbuthnot, Thomas Parnell, and John Gay. Together, these five made up the "Scriblerus Club," which met regularly at the apartments of Arbuthnot, a court physician, to compose the *Memoirs of Martinus Scriblerus*, a burlesque of all the kinds of pedantry and literary folly that fell under their scrutiny. The *Memoirs* did not see the light of publication until 1741, when Pope published them, much rewritten, long after the deaths of Arbuthnot, Parnell, and Gay. But the spirit of the group inspired a number of satirical works, most notably Swift's *Gulliver's Travels*, Pope's *Dunciad*, and perhaps Gay's *Beggar's Opera*.

In 1717, Pope's father died, and a few months later, Pope leased the villa of Twickenham on the Thames, near Richmond, and moved there with his mother. Here he lived the rest of his life, moving in a glittering social circle and participating vigorously in London artistic life and controversy. Among his friends were the philosopher George Berkeley, the composer Handel, and a number of painters (Pope himself was an accomplished amateur): William Kent, Charles Jervas, Sir Godfrey Kneller, and the two Jonathan Richardsons.

Pope's literary career consists of three clearly marked periods. The first, from the beginning to 1717, Pope described in the *Epistle to Dr. Arbuthnot* as devoted to noncontroversial topics: "a painted mistress or a purling stream." The 1717 collected *Poems*, which brought together his early work, contained the *Pastorals* and the bucolic *Windsor Forest;* a number of imitations and translations of Virgil, Ovid, and Chaucer; the highly emotional *Verses to the Memory of an Unfortunate Lady* and *Eloisa to Abelard;* the *Essay on Criticism;* and *The Rape of the Lock.*

After the appearance of the 1717 *Poems,* Pope turned to ten years of editing and translating in a successful attempt to gain financial security.

The first volume of his translation of Homer's *Iliad,* in a deluxe edition for advance subscribers, appeared in 1715. It involved Pope in the first of many literary wars, since Addison, no longer friendly, had arranged for a rival translation by Thomas Tickell to appear at the same time. Pope's translation was a great success, however, and he followed it by a translation of the *Odyssey;* his income from the two translations has been estimated at the considerable sum of £9,000. His fortune was further augmented by his six-volume edition of Shakespeare, which appeared in 1725.

When Pope returned to original composition in 1727, he, as he wrote, "stooped to truth, and moralized his song": that is, he became a satirist. This third period produced the *Dunciad,* the *Moral Essays,* the imitations of Horace, and other satires. The *Dunciad,* originally conceived as a project of the Scriblerus Club, was a mock epic devoted to counterattacks on all Pope's literary enemies, especially the Shakespearian scholar and editor Lewis Theobald, who had attacked Pope's Shakespeare edition, and Colley Cibber, actor, playwright, and poet laureate. Pope continued to revise the *Dunciad* for the rest of his life to accommodate new enemies, and it appeared in three distinct versions over a period of fifteen years. The *Moral Essays,* which included the *Essay on Man,* were part of a large plan for a series of poems which would comprise a complete ethical system. The first part was to consist of the four epistles of the *Essay on Man;* the second was to consist of nine further epistles. Of this second group, four were actually written: *Of the Knowledge and Characters of Men, Of the Characters of Women,* and two both called *Of the Use of Riches.* During the years in which the ethical poems were appearing, Pope continued to publish a number of satires in which he was able to attack the policies of George II and his Whig prime minister Robert Walpole under the guise of Horace's satires on the court of the Emperor Augustus.

Pope's pen was often dipped in acid, and during the nineteenth-century Romantic reaction to Neoclassicism, it was common to think of him only as a shallow and spiteful controversialist, the "wasp of Twickenham." More recent readers have recognized the consistent and thoughtful morality of his satire. Deeply conservative by temperament and background, Pope lived at a time when economic and political power in England was passing from the established landed aristocracy to a new commercial class. Pope, like his fellow Tory Swift, saw this shift as threatening a general deterioration of the quality of English life, in public and private morality, in intellectual life, and in art. Pope's "dunces" matched Swift's "yahoos" as images of a rising tide of vulgarity, opportunism, and "dullness," which the two writers thought they saw in the Whig ascendancy, Pope stressing the corruption of civilized man as Swift satirized the debasement of brute human nature. But Pope's vision is not wholly negative, any more than Swift's is, as the *Epistle to Dr. Arbuthnot* makes clear. He measured contemporary life against a generous and humane standard of honesty, charity, and selflessness, qualities that he found both in his parents and in his friend John Arbuthnot. Pope's celebration of the individual, his reverence for the classics, his keen appreciation of nature, and his vision of a humane and ordered society all identify him as a true heir of English Renaissance thought.

The masterwork of the 1717 volume of Pope's poems was *The Rape of the Lock,* which he had written in a short first version in 1711. In Pope's home

village of Binfield, a certain Lord Petre had cut off one of Miss Arabella Fermor's curls without her consent. The incident provoked a quarrel and a serious breach between the two families. Pope's friend John Caryll, who knew both families, suggested that he write a poem to reconcile them. The result was a delightful, miniature mock epic, which Pope expanded in 1714 by adding the Rosicrucian "supernatural machinery" of sylphs and gnomes. Every convention of the epic finds its diminished echo in *The Rape of the Lock*. The epic hero becomes a fashionable belle, the epic battle is a game of cards, the journey to the underworld becomes Belinda pouting in the "Cave of Spleen," the arming of the hero is a scene at a dressing table, and the gods and goddesses who oversee the epic action become Rosicrucian sylphs and gnomes. In addition, the poem is an intricate web of verbal echoes from the *Iliad*, the *Odyssey*, the *Aeneid*, and most of all *Paradise Lost*. The basis of *The Rape of the Lock* is a trick of perspective; Pope tries to bring the real-life participants in the incident of the lock back to common sense and good humor by showing how trivial the incident was in the context of greater things. But on another level, *The Rape of the Lock* is not trivial at all; it takes on some of the seriousness of its heroic models as it traces Belinda's Eve-like fall from innocence to experience, delicately articulated in the poem's recurring imagery of broken china.

As an aside, one might add that Pope's attempt at peace-making was not an unqualified success. He sent advance copies of the poem to both Lord Petre and Miss Fermor, and both seemed pleased. But when the poem appeared and friends commented on the strong sexual undercurrent of the poem, they began to have doubts. Pope, however, restored good relations by dedicating the final version of the poem to Miss Fermor, with a warm introductory letter.

An Essay on Man was intended as the cornerstone of the ethical system that Pope developed in a series of poems late in his life. The *Moral Epistles* were to explore particular problems of human life; the *Essay* was to present an overview of the human condition, "a *general Map* of MAN." Pope quite deliberately invites comparison with Milton when he declares that his purpose is to "vindicate the ways of God to Man," but a comparison suggests more differences than similarities. Milton's orientation is thoroughly religious; Pope is attempting to construct an ethical system independent of religion, although not necessarily incompatible with it. There is nothing particularly original in this system; here, as in the *Essay on Criticism*, Pope is merely attempting to say "what oft was thought, but ne'er so well expressed." Readers of *Candide* may be tempted, especially when they read the famous line "Whatever is, is right," to identify Pope's position with the Leibnitzian Optimism of Dr. Pangloss. But none of the ideas in the poem can be traced to a single source. Rather the poem is an attempt to weave commonplace, well-established ideas of Pope's day into an orderly and coherent whole: the hierarchical conception of the universe as organized in a Great Chain of Being, with man in the middle of the Chain; the view of evil as a good viewed from a partial perspective; a theory of human character as defined by "humors" and organized by a "ruling passion"; the conception of society as having declined from an earlier "Golden Age," and several other such familiar ideas.

But the *Essay on Man* is memorable not as philosophy but as art. Pope

chose verse instead of prose for the *Essay*, he said, not only because it was more concise but also because it could capture better the "force" and "grace" of arguments. What the reader takes away from the *Essay on Man* is not so much a body of doctrine as the sense of a lively and orderly mind "expatiating free" over received ideas and communicating vividly and movingly what it feels like to hold such ideas.

The *Epistle to Dr. Arbuthnot* is perhaps the most brilliant of the Horatian satires that Pope wrote in his later years. Unlike many of the others, it is not based on a specific original in Horace but is rather an original composition in the general style of Horace. Its immediate occasion Pope himself explained in a 1734 letter to Arbuthnot. Arbuthnot, terminally ill, had written to his old friend urging him, while preserving Pope's "noble disdain and abhorrence of vice," to moderate his satire in the interests of his own safety. Pope replied: "I took very kindly your advice concerning avoiding ill will from writing satire, and it has worked so much upon me (considering the time and state you gave it in) that I determine to address to you one of my epistles, written by piecemeal many years, and which I have now made haste to put together, wherein the question is stated, what were and are, my motives of writing, the objections to them, and my answers."

Pope had a further motive in rushing the Epistle into print when he did. Lady Mary Wortley Montagu, an old friend from whom he had become estranged, had taken offense at Pope's references to her as "Sappho" in his recent *Imitation of the First Satire of the Second Book of Horace* and had enlisted the aid of Lord Hervey, another of Pope's victims ("Lord Fanny" in the First Satire) to help her write a fierce reply to Pope called "Verses Addressed to the Imitator of Horace." Hervey went on to write a separate attack of his own called "An Epistle to a Doctor of Divinity from a Nobleman at Hampton court." The *Epistle to Dr. Arbuthnot* is, on one level, a continuation of Pope's paper battle with Lady Mary and Lord Hervey.

Pope, however, dismisses his immediate enemies fairly quickly (though not without dealing with them in some of the most acid satire he ever wrote) and moves to the large questions he had broached to Dr. Arbuthnot: his "motives of writing" and his defense of them. The *Epistle* thus becomes a capsule account of Pope's career and a passionate defense of the moral basis of his art.

FURTHER READING *(prepared by W. J. R.):* The long-time lack of a full biography of Pope has recently been magnificently filled by Maynard Mack's *Alexander Pope: A Life*, 1986. Two recent works provide fine introductions to Pope's poetry for the general reader: Pat Rogers' *Introduction to Pope*, 1976, considers Pope's work poem by poem and surveys earlier scholarship; I. R. F. Gordon's *A Preface to Pope*, 1976, contains a lengthy biographical section and surveys the major works more briefly. Frederick M. Keener's *An Essay on Pope*, 1974, studies eight poems, including *The Rape of the Lock*. Keener discusses Pope's life in relation to his work and concludes with a discussion of how to read Pope. Reuben Arthur Brower's important *Alexander Pope: The Poetry of Allusion*, 1959, traces Pope's development in terms of his use of allusion. Laura Brown's *Alexander Pope*, 1985, is a provocative rethinking of Pope in terms of contemporary literary theory. *Alexander Pope: Essays for the Tercentenary*, ed. C. E. Nicholson, 1988, includes several good essays on historical and political contexts. Major critical trends in Pope criticism are discussed in Ralph Cohen's "Pope's Meanings and the Strategies of Interrelation," in *English Literature in the Age*

of Disguise, ed. Maximilian Novak, 1977. A superlative collection of critical essays is *Pope: Recent Essays by Several Hands,* ed. Maynard Mack and James A. Winn, 1980. This extensive collection covers all of Pope's writings and represents a great variety of critical approaches.

THE RAPE OF THE LOCK

AN HEROI-COMICAL POEM

> *Nolueram, Belinda, tuos violare capillos;*
> *Sed juvat, hoc precibus me tribuisse tuis.*
> MART. *Epigr.* XII. 84.[1]

To Mrs. Arabella Fermor

CANTO I

What dire offence from am'rous causes springs,
What mighty contests rise from trivial things,
I sing—This verse to CARYLL,[2] Muse! is due:
This, even Belinda may vouchsafe to view:
Slight is the subject, but not so the praise, 5
If She inspire, and He approve my lays.
 Say what strange motive, Goddess! could compel
A well-bred Lord t' assault a gentle Belle?
O say what stranger cause, yet unexplored,
Could make a gentle Belle reject a Lord? 10
In tasks so bold, can little men engage,
And in soft bosoms dwells such mighty Rage?
 Sol through white curtains shot a tim'rous ray,
And oped those eyes that must eclipse the day:
Now lap-dogs give themselves the rousing shake, 15
And sleepless lovers, just at twelve, awake:
Thrice rung the bell, the slipper knocked the ground,[3]
And the pressed watch returned a silver sound.[4]
Belinda still her downy pillow prest,

[1] "I was unwilling, Belinda, to ravish your locks; but I rejoice to have conceded this to your prayers." (Pope changes Martial's "Polytimus" to "Belinda.")
[2] John Caryll, the friend who suggested the poem. The beginning is a mock epic invocation.
[3] Since her bell was not answered, she knocked on the floor with her slipper.
[4] A "repeater" watch that sounded the hours and the quarters when a pin was pushed.

Her guardian SYLPH[5] prolonged the balmy rest: 20
'Twas He had summoned to her silent bed
The morning-dream that hovered o'er her head;
A Youth more glitt'ring than a Birth-night Beau,[6]
(That even in slumber caused her cheek to glow)
Seemed to her ear his winning lips to lay, 25
And thus in whispers said, or seemed to say.
 "Fairest of mortals, thou distinguished care
Of thousand bright Inhabitants of Air!
If e'er one vision touched thy infant thought,
Of all the Nurse and all the Priest have taught; 30
Of airy Elves by moonlight shadows seen,
The silver token, and the circled green,[7]
Or virgins visited by Angel-powers,
With golden crowns and wreaths of heav'nly flowers;
Hear and believe! thy own importance know, 35
Nor bound thy narrow views to things below.
Some secret truths, from learnéd pride concealed,
To Maids alone and Children are revealed:
What though no credit doubting Wits may give?
The Fair and Innocent shall still believe. 40
Know, then, unnumbered Spirits round thee fly,
The light Militia of the lower sky:
These, though unseen, are ever on the wing,
Hang o'er the Box, and hover round the Ring.[8]
Think what an equipage thou hast in Air, 45
And view with scorn two Pages and a Chair.
As now your own, our beings were of old,
And once inclosed in Woman's beauteous mould;
Thence, by a soft transition, we repair
From earthly Vehicles to these of air. 50
Think not, when Woman's transient breath is fled,
That all her vanities at once are dead;
Succeeding vanities she still regards,
And though she plays no more, o'erlooks the cards.
Her joy in gilded Chariots, when alive, 55

[5] This is the first reference to the "supernatural machinery" of the poem. As Pope explained in his introductory letter to Arabella Fermor, the spirits are borrowed from Rosicrucian lore: "According to these Gentlemen [the Rosicrucians], the four Elements are inhabited by Spirits, which they call *Sylphs, Gnomes, Nymphs,* and *Salamanders.* The *Gnomes,* or Daemons of Earth, delight in Mischief; but the *Sylphs,* whose Habitation is in the Air, are the best-condition'd Creatures imaginable. For they say, any Mortals may enjoy the most intimate Familiarities with these gentle Spirits, upon a Condition very easie to all true *Adepts,* an inviolate Preservation of Chastity." In epics, the gods often communicate with the hero through apparitions during sleep.
[6] Beaux dressed with particular splendor for the royal birthday celebrations.
[7] Fairies were supposed to leave coins (the "silver token") and rings of green grass, where they held fairy dances.
[8] That is, a theater box and the fashionable circular drive for coaches in Hyde Park.

And love of Ombre,[9] after death survive.
For when the Fair in all their pride expire,
To their first Elements their Souls retire:
The Sprites of fiery Termagants[10] in Flame
Mount up, and take a Salamander's name. 60
Soft yielding minds to Water glide away,
And sip, with Nymphs, their elemental Tea.
The graver Prude sinks downward to a Gnome,
In search of mischief still on Earth to roam.
The light Coquettes in Sylphs aloft repair, 65
And sport and flutter in the fields of Air.
 "Know further yet; whoever fair and chaste
Rejects mankind, is by some Sylph embraced:
For Spirits, freed from mortal laws, with ease
Assume what sexes and what shapes they please. 70
What guards the purity of melting Maids,
In courtly balls, and midnight masquerades,
Safe from the treach'rous friend, the daring spark,[11]
The glance by day, the whisper in the dark,
When kind occasion prompts their warm desires, 75
When music softens, and when dancing fires?
'Tis but their Sylph, the wise Celestials know,
Though Honour is the word with Men below.
 "Some nymphs there are, too conscious of their face,[12]
For life predestined to the Gnomes' embrace. 80
These swell their prospects and exalt their pride,
When offers are disdained, and love denied:
Then gay Ideas crowd the vacant brain,
While Peers, and Dukes, and all their sweeping train,
And Garters, Stars, and Coronets appear, 85
And in soft sounds, Your Grace salutes their ear.
'Tis these that early taint the female soul,
Instruct the eyes of young Coquettes to roll,
Teach Infant-cheeks a bidden blush to know,
And little hearts to flutter at a Beau. 90
 "Oft, when the world imagine women stray,
The Sylphs through mystic mazes guide their way,
Through all the giddy circle they pursue,
And old impertinence[13] expel by new.
What tender maid but must a victim fall 95
To one man's treat, but for another's ball?
When Florio speaks what virgin could withstand,
If gentle Damon did not squeeze her hand?
With varying vanities, from every part,
They shift the moving Toyshop[14] of their heart; 100
Where wigs with wigs, with sword-knots sword-knots strive,[15]

[9] A popular card game. See III.27–104. [10] Scolding, bad-tempered women.
[11] A fashionable, foppish man. [12] Too aware of their beauty.
[13] A trifling bauble. [14] A shop for trinkets and baubles.
[15] "Sword-knots" were ribbons tied to the hilts of ornamental swords.

Beaux banish beaux, and coaches coaches drive.
This erring mortals Levity may call;
Oh blind to truth! the Sylphs contrive it all.
 "Of these am I, who thy protection claim,
A watchful sprite, and Ariel is my name. 105
Late, as I ranged the crystal wilds of air,
In the clear Mirror of thy ruling Star
I saw, alas! some dread event impend,
Ere to the main this morning sun descend,
But heaven reveals not what, or how, or where: 110
Warned by the Sylph, oh pious maid, beware!
This to disclose is all thy guardian can:
Beware of all, but most beware of Man!"
 He said; when Shock,[16] who thought she slept too long,
Leaped up, and waked his mistress with his tongue. 115
'Twas then, Belinda, if report say true,
Thy eyes first opened on a Billet-doux;[17]
Wounds, Charms, and Ardors were no sooner read,
But all the Vision vanished from thy head.
 And now, unveiled, the Toilet stands displayed,[18] 120
Each silver Vase in mystic order laid.
First, robed in white, the Nymph intent adores,
With head uncovered, the Cosmetic powers.
A heav'nly image in the glass appears,
To that she bends, to that her eyes she rears; 125
Th' inferior Priestess, at her altar's side,
Trembling begins the sacred rites of Pride.
Unnumbered treasures ope at once, and here
The various off'rings of the world appear;
From each she nicely culls with curious toil, 130
And decks the Goddess with the glitt'ring spoil.
This casket India's glowing gems unlocks,
And all Arabia breathes from yonder box.
The Tortoise here and Elephant unite,
Transformed to combs, the speckled, and the white. 135
Here files of pins extend their shining rows,
Puffs, Powders, Patches, Bibles, Billet-doux.
Now awful Beauty puts on all its arms;
The fair each moment rises in her charms,
Repairs her smiles, awakens every grace, 140
And calls forth all the wonders of her face;
Sees by degrees a purer blush arise,
And keener lightnings quicken in her eyes.
The busy Sylphs surround their darling care, 145

[16] Belinda's lapdog. A "shock" or "shough" was a breed of small dog. [17] Love letter.
[18] The following passage parodies an epic ceremonial worship of a goddess. Belinda is the
chief priestess, and the goddess is her own image in the mirror. The passage also parodies the
arming of the epic hero.

These set the head, and those divide the hair,
Some fold the sleeve, whilst others plait the gown;
And Betty's[19] praised for labours not her own.

CANTO II

Not with more glories, in th' etherial plain,
The Sun first rises o'er the purpled main,
Than, issuing forth, the rival of his beams
Launched on the bosom of the silver Thames.
Fair Nymphs, and well-drest Youths around her shone, 5
But every eye was fixed on her alone.
On her white breast a sparkling Cross she wore,
Which Jews might kiss, and Infidels adore.
Her lively looks a sprightly mind disclose,
Quick as her eyes, and as unfixed as those: 10
Favours to none, to all she smiles extends;
Oft she rejects, but never once offends.
Bright as the sun, her eyes the gazers strike,
And, like the sun, they shine on all alike.
Yet graceful ease, and sweetness void of pride, 15
Might hide her faults, if Belles had faults to hide:
If to her share some female errors fall,
Look on her face, and you'll forget 'em all.
 This Nymph, to the destruction of mankind,
Nourished two Locks, which graceful hung behind 20
In equal curls, and well conspired to deck
With shining ringlets the smooth iv'ry neck.
Love in these labyrinths his slaves detains,
And mighty hearts are held in slender chains.
With hairy springes[20] we the birds betray, 25
Slight lines of hair surprise the finny prey,
Fair tresses man's imperial race ensnare,
And beauty draws us with a single hair.
 Th' advent'rous Baron the bright locks admired;
He saw, he wished, and to the prize aspired. 30
Resolved to win, he meditates the way,
By force to ravish, or by fraud betray;
For when success a Lover's toil attends,
Few ask, if fraud or force attained his ends.
 For this, ere Phoebus rose, he had implored 35
Propitious heaven, and every power adored,
But chiefly Love—to Love an Altar built,
Of twelve vast French Romances, neatly gilt.
There lay three garters, half a pair of gloves;
And all the trophies of his former loves; 40
With tender Billet-doux he lights the pyre,

[19]"Betty" was a generic term for a lady's maid. [20]Snares.

And breathes three am'rous sighs to raise the fire.
Then prostrate falls, and begs with ardent eyes
Soon to obtain, and long possess the prize:
The powers gave ear, and granted half his prayer, 45
The rest, the winds dispersed in empty air.
 But now secure the painted vessel glides,
The sun-beams trembling on the floating tides:
While melting music steals upon the sky,
And softened sounds along the waters die; 50
Smooth flow the waves, the Zephyrs gently play,
Belinda smiled, and all the world was gay.
All but the Sylph—with careful thoughts opprest,
Th' impending woe sat heavy on his breast.
He summons strait his Denizens of air; 55
The lucid squadrons round the sails repair:
Soft o'er the shrouds aërial whispers breathe,
That seemed but Zephyrs to the train beneath.
Some to the sun their insect-wings unfold,
Waft on the breeze, or sink in clouds of gold; 60
Transparent forms, too fine for mortal sight,
Their fluid bodies half dissolved in light,
Loose to the wind their airy garments flew,
Thin glitt'ring textures of the filmy dew,
Dipt in the richest tincture of the skies, 65
Where light disports in ever-mingling dyes,
While every beam new transient colours flings,
Colours that change whene'er they wave their wings.
Amid the circle, on the gilded mast,
Superior by the head, was Ariel placed; 70
His purple pinions opening to the sun,
He raised his azure wand, and thus begun.
 "Ye Sylphs and Sylphids, to your chief give ear!
Fays, Fairies, Genii, Elves, and Daemons, hear!
Ye know the spheres and various tasks assigned 75
By laws eternal to th' aërial kind.
Some in the fields of purest Aether play,
And bask and whiten in the blaze of day.
Some guide the course of wand'ring orbs on high,
Or roll the planets through the boundless sky. 80
Some less refined, beneath the moon's pale light
Pursue the stars that shoot athwart the night,
Or suck the mists in grosser air below,
Or dip their pinions in the painted bow,
Or brew fierce tempests on the wintry main, 85
Or o'er the glebe[21] distil the kindly rain.
Others on earth o'er human race preside,
Watch all their ways, and all their actions guide:

[21] Cultivated field.

Of these the chief the care of Nations own,
And guard with Arms divine the British Throne. 90
"Our humbler province is to tend the Fair,
Not a less pleasing, though less glorious care;
To save the powder from too rude a gale,
Nor let th' imprisoned essences exhale;
To draw fresh colours from the vernal flowers; 95
To steal from rainbows e'er they drop in showers
A brighter wash; to curl their waving hairs,
Assist their blushes, and inspire their airs;
Nay oft, in dreams, invention we bestow,
To change a Flounce, or add a Furbelow. 100
"This day, black Omens threat the brightest Fair,
That e'er deserved a watchful spirit's care;
Some dire disaster, or by force, or slight;
But what, or where, the fates have wrapt in night.
Whether the nymph shall break Diana's law,22 105
Or some frail China jar receive a flaw;
Or stain her honour or her new brocade;
Forget her prayers, or miss a masquerade;
Or lose her heart, or necklace, at a ball;
Or whether Heaven has doomed that Shock must fall. 110
Haste, then, ye spirits! to your charge repair:
The flutt'ring fan be Zephyretta's care;
The drops to thee, Brillante, we consign;
And, Momentilla, let the watch be thine;
Do thou, Crispissa,23 tend her fav'rite Lock; 115
Ariel himself shall be the guard of Shock.
"To fifty chosen Sylphs, of special note,
We trust th' important charge, the Petticoat:24
Oft have we known that seven-fold fence to fail,
Though stiff with hoops, and armed with ribs of whale; 120
Form a strong line about the silver bound,
And guard the wide circumference around.
"Whatever spirit, careless of his charge,
His post neglects, or leaves the fair at large,
Shall feel sharp vengeance soon o'ertake his sins, 125
Be stopped in vials, or transfixed with pins;
Or plunged in lakes of bitter washes lie,
Or wedged whole ages in a bodkin's eye:25
Gums and Pomatums shall his flight restrain,
While clogged he beats his silken wings in vain; 130
Or Alum styptics with contracting power

22 That is, the law of chastity.
23 "Crispissa" is derived from the Latin *crispere*, to curl.
24 Pope is parodying epic descriptions of the hero's shield.
25 Here "bodkin" means a blunt-pointed needle. Later (IV.98 and V.95) it means a hair
ornament, and (V.55 and 88), a dagger. Pope plays on these various meanings.

Shrink his thin essence like a rivelled[26] flower:
Or, as Ixion[27] fixed, the wretch shall feel
The giddy motion of the whirling Mill,
In fumes of burning Chocolate shall glow,
And tremble at the sea that froths below!" 135
 He spoke; the spirits from the sails descend;
Some, orb in orb, around the nymph extend;
Some thrid the mazy ringlets of her hair;
Some hang upon the pendants of her ear:
With beating hearts the dire event they wait, 140
Anxious, and trembling for the birth of Fate.

CANTO III

Close by those meads, forever crowned with flowers,
Where Thames with pride surveys his rising towers,
There stands a structure of majestic frame,
Which from the neighb'ring Hampton[28] takes its name.
Here Britain's statesmen oft the fall foredoom 5
Of foreign Tyrants and of Nymphs at home;
Here thou, great ANNA![29] whom three realms obey,
Dost sometimes counsel take—and sometimes Tea.
 Hither the heroes and the nymphs resort,
To taste awhile the pleasures of a Court;
In various talk th' instructive hours they past, 10
Who gave the ball, or paid the visit last;
One speaks the glory of the British Queen,
And one describes a charming Indian screen;
A third interprets motions, looks, and eyes;
At every word a reputation dies. 15
Snuff, or the fan, supply each pause of chat,
With singing, laughing, ogling, *and all that.*
 Meanwhile, declining from the noon of day,
The sun obliquely shoots his burning ray;
The hungry Judges soon the sentence sign, 20
And wretches hang that jury-men may dine;
The merchant from th' Exchange returns in peace,
And the long labours of the Toilet cease.
Belinda now, whom thirst of fame invites,
Burns to encounter two advent'rous Knights, 25

[26] Wrinkled, shrunken.
[27] In Greek mythology, Ixion was punished by being tied to an everturning wheel in the underworld.
[28] Hampton Court is the royal palace about fifteen miles up the Thames from London.
[29] Queen Anne. The "three realms" are England, Scotland, and Wales.

At Ombre[30] singly to decide their doom;
And swells her breast with conquests yet to come.
Straight the three bands prepare in arms to join,
Each band the number of the sacred nine. 30
Soon as she spreads her hand, th' aërial guard
Descend, and sit on each important card:
First Ariel perched upon a Matadore,
Then each, according to the rank they bore;
For Sylphs, yet mindful of their ancient race, 35
Are, as when women, wondrous fond of place.
 Behold, four Kings in majesty revered,
With hoary whiskers and a forky beard;
And four fair Queens whose hands sustain a flower,
Th' expressive emblem of their softer power; 40
Four Knaves in garbs succinct, a trusty band,
Caps on their heads, and halberts in their hand;
And particoloured troops, a shining train,
Draw forth to combat on the velvet plain.
 The skilful Nymph reviews her force with care: 45
Let Spades be trumps! she said, and trumps they were.
 Now move to war her sable Matadores,
In show like leaders of the swarthy Moors.
Spadillio first, unconquerable Lord!
Led off two captive trumps, and swept the board. 50
As many more Manillio forced to yield,
And marched a victor from the verdant field.
Him Basto followed, but his fate more hard
Gained but one trump and one Plebeian card.
With his broad sabre next, a chief in years, 55
The hoary Majesty of Spades appears,
Puts forth one manly leg, to sight revealed,
The rest, his many-coloured robe concealed.
The rebel Knave, who dares his prince engage,
Proves the just victim of his royal rage. 60
Even mighty Pam, that Kings and Queens o'erthrew
And mowed down armies in the fights of Lu,[31]
Sad chance of war! now destitute of aid,
Falls undistinguished by the victor spade!
 Thus far both armies to Belinda yield; 65
Now to the Baron fate inclines the field.
His warlike Amazon her host invades,

[30] The epic battle is the card game of ombre. Ombre was a Spanish game (Spanish *hombre*, man), somewhat like bridge or whist. It was played with a pack of forty cards; the 8's, 9's and 10's were not used. The "Matadores" were the Ace of Spades ("Spadillio"), the Ace of Clubs ("Basto"), and one other card ("Manillio"), in this case the two of spades. The principal player was the Ombre; if one of the other players won the game, he was said to "give Codille" to the Ombre. Pope describes a real game so precisely that it is possible to reconstruct it and replay it. Belinda is the Ombre and wins by a narrow margin. The Baron has a strong hand, but the third player (never directly mentioned) has a weak one.
[31] "Pam" is the knave of clubs, the highest trump in the game of loo.

Th' imperial consort of the crown of Spades.
The Club's black Tyrant first her victim dyed,
Spite of his haughty mien, and barb'rous pride:
What boots the regal circle on his head, 70
His giant limbs, in state unwieldy spread;
That long behind he trails his pompous robe,
And, of all monarchs, only grasps the globe?
 The Baron now his Diamonds pours apace;
Th' embroidered King who shows but half his face, 75
And his refulgent Queen, with powers combined
Of broken troops an easy conquest find.
Clubs, Diamonds, Hearts, in wild disorder seen,
With throngs promiscuous strew the level green.
Thus when dispersed a routed army runs, 80
Of Asia's troops, and Afric's sable sons,
With like confusion different nations fly,
Of various habit, and of various dye,
The pierced battalions dis-united fall,
In heaps on heaps; one fate o'erwhelms them all. 85
 The Knave of Diamonds tries his wily arts,
And wins (oh shameful chance!) the Queen of Hearts.
At this, the blood the virgin's cheek forsook,
A livid paleness spreads o'er all her look;
She sees, and trembles at th' approaching ill, 90
Just in the jaws of ruin, and Codille.
And now (as oft in some distempered State)
On one nice Trick depends the general fate.
An Ace of Hearts steps forth: The King unseen
Lurked in her hand, and mourned his captive Queen: 95
He springs to Vengeance with an eager pace,
And falls like thunder on the prostrate Ace.
The nymph exulting fills with shouts the sky;
The walls, the woods, and long canals reply.
 Oh thoughtless mortals! ever blind to fate, 100
Too soon dejected, and too soon elate.
Sudden, these honours shall be snatched away,
And cursed for ever this victorious day.
 For lo! the board with cups and spoons is crowned,
The berries crackle, and the mill turns round; 105
On shining Altars of Japan[32] they raise
The silver lamp; the fiery spirits blaze:
From silver spouts the grateful liquors glide,
While China's earth receives the smoking tide:
At once they gratify their scent and taste, 110
And frequent cups prolong the rich repast.
Straight hover round the Fair her airy band;
Some, as she sipped, the fuming liquor fanned,

[32] The mill is a coffee mill and the "shining Altars of Japan" are lacquered oriental coffee tables. Pope is parodying epic feasts.

Some o'er her lap their careful plumes displayed, 115
Trembling, and conscious of the rich brocade.
Coffee, (which makes the politician wise,
And see through all things with his half-shut eyes)
Sent up in vapours to the Baron's brain
New Stratagems, the radiant Lock to gain. 120
Ah cease, rash youth! desist ere 'tis too late,
Fear the just Gods, and think of Scylla's Fate!
Changed to a bird, and sent to flit in air,
She dearly pays for Nisus' injured hair![33]
　　But when to mischief mortals bend their will, 125
How soon they find fit instruments of ill!
Just then, Clarissa drew with tempting grace
A two-edged weapon[34] from her shining case:
So Ladies in Romance assist their Knight,
Present the spear, and arm him for the fight. 130
He takes the gift with rev'rence, and extends
The little engine on his fingers' ends;
This just behind Belinda's neck he spread,
As o'er the fragrant steams she bends her head.
Swift to the Lock a thousand Sprites repair, 135
A thousand wings, by turns, blow back the hair;
And thrice they twitched the diamond in her ear;
Thrice she looked back, and thrice the foe drew near.
Just in that instant, anxious Ariel sought
The close recesses of the Virgin's thought; 140
As on the nosegay in her breast reclined,
He watched th' Ideas rising in her mind,
Sudden he viewed, in spite of all her art,
An earthly Lover lurking at her heart.
Amazed, confused, he found his power expired, 145
Resigned to fate, and with a sigh retired.
　　The Peer now spreads the glitt'ring Forfex wide,
T' inclose the Lock; now joins it, to divide.
Even then, before the fatal engine closed,
A wretched Sylph too fondly interposed; 150
Fate urged the shears, and cut the Sylph in twain,
(But airy substance soon unites again)
The meeting points the sacred hair dissever
From the fair head, forever, and forever!
　　Then flashed the living lightning from her eyes, 155
And screams of horror rend th' affrighted skies.
Not louder shrieks to pitying heaven are cast,
When husbands, or when lap-dogs breathe their last;
Or when rich China vessels fall'n from high,
In glitt'ring dust and painted fragments lie! 160

[33] Scylla, daughter of King Nisus, fell in love with King Minos and cut off for him a purple
hair from her father's head, upon which the safety of his kingdom depended. She was pun-
ished by being turned into a bird. The story appears in Ovid's *Metamorphoses*.
[34] Scissors.

Let wreaths of triumph now my temples twine,
(The victor cried) the glorious Prize is mine!
While fish in streams, or birds delight in air,
Or in a coach and six the British Fair,
As long as Atalantis[35] shall be read, 165
Or the small pillow grace a Lady's bed,
While visits shall be paid on solemn days,
When num'rous wax-lights in bright order blaze,
While nymphs take treats, or assignations give,
So long my honour, name, and praise shall live! 170
What Time would spare, from Steel receives its date,
And monuments, like men, submit to fate!
Steel could the labour of the Gods destroy,
And strike to dust th' imperial towers of Troy;
Steel could the works of mortal pride confound, 175
And hew triumphal arches to the ground.
What wonder then, fair nymph! thy hairs should feel,
The conq'ring force of unresisted steel?

CANTO IV

But anxious cares the pensive nymph oppressed,
And secret passions laboured in her breast.
Not youthful kings in battle seized alive,
Not scornful virgins who their charms survive,
Not ardent lovers robbed of all their bliss,
Not ancient ladies when refused a kiss, 5
Not tyrants fierce that unrepenting die,
Not Cynthia when her manteau's[36] pinned awry,
E'er felt such rage, resentment, and despair,
As thou, sad Virgin! for thy ravished Hair.
 For, that sad moment, when the Sylphs withdrew 10
And Ariel weeping from Belinda flew,
Umbriel,[37] a dusky, melancholy sprite,
As ever sullied the fair face of light,
Down to the central earth, his proper scene,
Repaired to search the gloomy Cave of Spleen. 15
 Swift on his sooty pinions flits the Gnome,
And in a vapour[38] reached the dismal dome.
No cheerful breeze this sullen region knows,
The dreaded East is all the wind that blows. 20

[35] Mrs. Manley's *Secret Memories and Manners of several Persons of Quality, of Both Sexes. From the New Atalantis, an Island in the Mediterranean* (1709) was a fashionable book of thinly veiled allusions to current scandals.

[36] A loose robe.

[37] The name Umbriel suggests shadows and darkness. The episode of the Cave of Spleen (ill-humor) represents Belinda's sulking and parodies the epic visit to the underworld.

[38] Here and later, Pope puns on "vapour," which is both mist and the fashionable feminine malady of the "vapours."

Here in a grotto, sheltered close from air,
And screened in shades from day's detested glare,
She sighs for ever on her pensive bed,
Pain at her side, and Megrim[39] at her head.
 Two handmaids wait the throne: alike in place, 25
But diff'ring far in figure and in face.
Here stood Ill-nature like an ancient maid,
Her wrinkled form in black and white arrayed;
With store of prayers, for mornings, nights, and noons,
Her hand is filled; her bosom with lampoons. 30
 There Affectation, with a sickly mien,
Shows in her cheek the roses of eighteen,
Practised to lisp, and hang the head aside,
Faints into airs, and languishes with pride,
On the rich quilt sinks with becoming woe, 35
Wrapt in a gown, for sickness, and for show.
The fair ones feel such maladies as these,
When each new night-dress gives a new disease.
 A constant Vapour o'er the palace flies;
Strange phantoms rising as the mists arise; 40
Dreadful, as hermit's dreams in haunted shades,
Or bright, as visions of expiring maids.
Now glaring fiends, and snakes on rolling spires,
Pale spectres, gaping tombs, and purple fires:
Now lakes of liquid gold, Elysian scenes, 45
And crystal domes, and angels in machines.[40]
 Unnumbered throngs on every side are seen,
Of bodies changed to various forms by Spleen.
Here living Tea-pots stand, one arm held out,
One bent; the handle this, and that the spout: 50
A Pipkin there, like Homer's Tripod[41] walks;
Here sighs a Jar, and there a Goose-pie talks;
Men prove with child, as powerful fancy works,
And maids turned bottles, call aloud for corks.
 Safe past the Gnome through this fantastic band, 55
A branch of healing Spleenwort[42] in his hand.
Then thus addressed the power: "Hail, wayward Queen!
Who rule the sex to fifty from fifteen:
Parent of vapours and of female wit,
Who give th' hysteric or poetic fit, 60
On various tempers act by various ways,
Make some take physic, others scribble plays;
Who cause the proud their visits to delay,

[39] Headache. The organ called the spleen is on the left side of the body; therefore Pain is at Spleen's side and Megrim at her head.
 [40] These are both splenetic hallucinations and, satirically, scenic effects in contemporary opera and pantomime.
 [41] A pipkin is an earthenware pot. According to Homer, Vulcan made self-propelling tripods, or stools, for the gods.
 [42] An herb, so called because it was supposed to cure the spleen.

And send the godly in a pet to pray.
A nymph there is, that all thy power disdains, 65
And thousands more in equal mirth maintains.
But oh! if e'er thy Gnome could spoil a grace,
Or raise a pimple on a beauteous face,
Like Citron-waters[43] matrons' cheeks inflame,
Or change complexions at a losing game; 70
If e'er with airy horns[44] I planted heads,
Or rumpled petticoats, or tumbled beds,
Or caus'd suspicion when no soul was rude,
Or discomposed the head-dress of a Prude,
Or e'er to costive lap-dog gave disease, 75
Which not the tears of brightest eyes could ease:
Hear me, and touch Belinda with chagrin,
That single act gives half the world the spleen."
 The Goddess with a discontented air
Seems to reject him, though she grants his prayer. 80
A wondrous Bag with both her hands she binds,
Like that where once Ulysses held the winds;[45]
There she collects the force of female lungs,
Sighs, sobs, and passions, and the war of tongues.
A Vial next she fills with fainting fears, 85
Soft sorrows, melting griefs, and flowing tears.
The Gnome rejoicing bears her gifts away,
Spreads his black wings, and slowly mounts to day.
 Sunk in Thalestris'[46] arms the nymph he found,
Her eyes dejected and her hair unbound. 90
Full o'er their heads the swelling bag he rent,
And all the Furies issued at the vent.
Belinda burns with more than mortal ire,
And fierce Thalestris fans the rising fire.
"Oh wretched maid!" she spread her hands, and cried, 95
(While Hampton's echoes, "Wretched maid!" replied)
"Was it for this you took such constant care
The bodkin, comb, and essence to prepare?
For this your locks in paper durance bound,
For this with torturing irons wreathed around? 100
For this with fillets strained your tender head,
And bravely bore the double loads of lead?[47]
Gods! shall the ravisher display your hair,
While the Fops envy, and the Ladies stare!
Honour forbid! at whose unrivalled shrine 105
Ease, pleasure, virtue, all our sex resign.

[43] Brandy distilled with the rind of citrons.
[44] Suspicions of adultery, "airy" because the horns exist only in the jealous husband's mind.
[45] Aeolus, god of the winds, gave Ulysses a bag containing all the winds that would hamper his voyage home. See the *Odyssey*, Book X.
[46] Queen of the Amazons. Belinda is being comforted by a rather intimidating matron.
[47] The torturing irons are curling irons. Curl papers were fastened with flexible strips of lead.

Methinks already I your tears survey,
Already hear the horrid things they say,
Already see you a degraded toast,
And all your honour in a whisper lost! 110
How shall I, then, your helpless fame defend?
'Twill then be infamy to seem your friend!
And shall this prize, th' inestimable prize,
Exposed through crystal to the gazing eyes,
And heightened by the diamond's circling rays, 115
On that rapacious hand for ever blaze?
Sooner shall grass in Hyde-park Circus grow,
And wits take lodgings in the sound of Bow;[48]
Sooner let earth, air, sea, to Chaos fall,
Men, monkeys, lap-dogs, parrots, perish all!" 120
 She said; then raging to Sir Plume repairs,
And bids her Beau demand the precious hairs:
(Sir Plume of amber snuff-box justly vain,
And the nice conduct of a clouded cane)
With earnest eyes, and round unthinking face, 125
He first the snuff-box opened, then the case,
And thus broke out—"My Lord, why, what the devil?
Z—ds! damn the lock! 'fore Gad, you must be civil!
Plague on't! 'tis past a jest—nay prithee, pox!
Give her the hair"—he spoke, and rapped his box. 130
 "It grieves me much" (replied the Peer again)
"Who speaks so well should ever speak in vain.
But by this Lock, this sacred Lock I swear,
(Which never more shall join its parted hair;
Which never more its honours shall renew, 135
Clipped from the lovely head where late it grew)
That while my nostrils draw the vital air,
This hand, which won it, shall for ever wear."
He spoke, and speaking, in proud triumph spread
The long-contended honours of her head. 140
 But Umbriel, hateful Gnome! forbears not so;
He breaks the Vial whence the sorrows flow.
Then see! the nymph in beauteous grief appears,
Her eyes half-languishing, half-drowned in tears;
On her heaved bosom hung her drooping head, 145
Which, with a sigh, she raised; and thus she said.
 "For ever cursed be this detested day,
Which snatched my best, my fav'rite curl away!
Happy! ah, ten times happy had I been,
If Hampton-Court these eyes had never seen! 150
Yet am not I the first mistaken maid,
By love of Courts to numerous ills betrayed.
Oh had I rather un-admired remained

[48] An unfashionable neighborhood in the City of London proper, within sound of the bells of St. Mary-le-Bow in Cheapside.

In some lone isle, or distant Northern land;
Where the gilt Chariot never marks the way, 155
Where none learn Ombre, none e'er taste Bohea![49]
There kept my charms concealed from mortal eye,
Like roses, that in deserts bloom and die.
What moved my mind with youthful Lords to roam?
Oh had I stayed, and said my prayers at home! 160
'Twas this, the morning omens seemed to tell,
Thrice from my trembling hand the patch-box[50] fell;
The tott'ring China shook without a wind,
Nay, Poll sat mute, and Shock was most unkind!
A Sylph too warned me of the threats of fate, 165
In mystic visions, now believed too late!
See the poor remnants of these slighted hairs!
My hands shall rend what even thy rapine spares:
These in two sable ringlets taught to break,
Once gave new beauties to the snowy neck; 170
The sister-lock now sits uncouth, alone,
And in its fellow's fate foresees its own;
Uncurled it hangs, the fatal shears demands,
And tempts once more, thy sacrilegious hands.
Oh hadst thou, cruel! been content to seize 175
Hairs less in sight, or any hairs but these!"

CANTO V

She said: the pitying audience melt in tears.
But Fate and Jove had stopped the Baron's ears.
In vain Thalestris with reproach assails,
For who can move when fair Belinda fails?
Not half so fixed the Trojan could remain, 5
While Anna begged and Dido raged in vain.[51]
Then grave Clarissa graceful waved her fan;
Silence ensued, and thus the nymph began.
 "Say why are Beauties praised and honoured most,
The wise man's passion, and the vain man's toast? 10
Why decked with all that land and sea afford,
Why Angels called, and Angel-like adored?
Why round our coaches crowd the white-gloved Beaux,
Why bows the side-box[52] from its inmost rows;
How vain are all these glories, all our pains, 15
Unless good sense preserve what beauty gains:
That men may say, when we the front-box grace:
'Behold the first in virtue as in face!'

[49] An expensive and fashionable kind of tea.
[50] A box to hold "beauty-patches" of court plaster.
[51] The Trojan is Aeneas, who abandoned Dido despite her anger and the pleas of her sister Anna.
[52] The "side-box" and the "front-box" are theater boxes.

Oh! if to dance all night, and dress all day,
Charmed the small-pox, or chased old-age away; 20
Who would not scorn what housewife's cares produce,
Or who would learn one earthly thing of use?
To patch, nay ogle, might become a Saint,
Nor could it sure be such a sin to paint.
But since, alas! frail beauty must decay, 25
Curled or uncurled, since Locks will turn to grey;
Since painted, or not painted, all shall fade,
And she who scorns a man, must die a maid;
What then remains but well our power to use,
And keep good-humour still whate'er we lose? 30
And trust me, dear! good-humour can prevail,
When airs, and flights, and screams, and scolding fail.
Beauties in vain their pretty eyes may roll;
Charms strike the sight, but merit wins the soul."[53]
 So spoke the Dame, but no applause ensued; 35
Belinda frowned, Thalestris called her Prude.
"To arms, to arms!" the fierce Virago cries,
And swift as lightning to the combat flies.
All side in parties, and begin th' attack;
Fans clap, silks rustle, and tough whalebones crack; 40
Heroes' and Heroines' shouts confus'dly rise,
And bass and treble voices strike the skies.
No common weapons in their hands are found,
Like Gods they fight, nor dread a mortal wound.
 So when bold Homer makes the Gods engage, 45
And heavenly breasts with human passions rage;
'Gainst Pallas, Mars; Latona, Hermes arms;
And all Olympus rings with loud alarms:
Jove's thunder roars, heaven trembles all around,
Blue Neptune storms, the bellowing deeps resound: 50
Earth shakes her nodding towers, the ground gives way,
And the pale ghosts start at the flash of day!
 Triumphant Umbriel on a sconce's[54] height
Clapped his glad wings, and sat to view the fight:
Propped on their bodkin spears, the Sprites survey 55
The growing combat, or assist the fray.
 While through the press enraged Thalestris flies,
And scatters death around from both her eyes,
A Beau and Witling perished in the throng,
One died in metaphor, and one in song. 60
"O cruel nymph! a living death I bear,"
Cried Dapperwit, and sunk beside his chair.
A mournful glance Sir Fopling upwards cast,
"Those eyes are made so killing"—was his last.[55]

[53] Clarissa's speech is a parody of the speech of Sarpedon to Glaucus in the *Iliad*.
[54] A wall bracket for a candlestick.
[55] Pope pointed out that Sir Fopling's last words are from the fashionable opera *Camilla*, by Buononcini.

Thus on Meander's flowery margin lies 65
Th' expiring Swan, and as he sings he dies.
 When bold Sir Plume had drawn Clarissa down,
Chloe stepped in, and killed him with a frown;
She smiled to see the doughty hero slain,
But, at her smile, the Beau revived again. 70
 Now Jove suspends his golden scales in air,
Weighs the Men's wits against the Lady's hair;
The doubtful beam long nods from side to side;
At length the wits mount up, the hairs subside.
 See, fierce Belinda on the Baron flies, 75
With more than usual lightning in her eyes:
Nor feared the Chief th' unequal fight to try,
Who sought no more than on his foe to die.
But this bold Lord with manly strength endued,
She with one finger and a thumb subdued: 80
Just where the breath of life his nostrils drew,
A charge of Snuff the wily virgin threw;
The Gnomes direct, to every atom just,
The pungent grains of titillating dust.
Sudden, with starting tears each eye o'erflows, 85
And the high dome re-echoes to his nose.
 "Now meet thy fate," incensed Belinda cried,
And drew a deadly bodkin from her side,
(The same, his ancient personage to deck,
Her great great grandsire wore about his neck, 90
In three seal-rings; which after, melted down,
Formed a vast buckle for his widow's gown:
Her infant grandame's whistle next it grew,
The bells she jingled, and the whistle blew;
Then in a bodkin graced her mother's hairs, 95
Which long she wore, and now Belinda wears.)
 "Boast not my fall" (he cried) "insulting foe!
Thou by some other shalt be laid as low,
Nor think, to die dejects my lofty mind:
All that I dread is leaving you behind! 100
Rather than so, ah let me still survive,
And burn in Cupid's flames—but burn alive."
 "Restore the Lock!" she cries; and all around
"Restore the Lock!" the vaulted roofs rebound.
Not fierce Othello in so loud a strain 105
Roared for the handkerchief that caused his pain.[56]
But see how oft ambitious aims are crossed,
And chiefs contend 'till all the prize is lost!
The Lock, obtained with guilt, and kept with pain,
In every place is sought, but sought in vain: 110

[56] In Shakespeare's *Othello*, Iago steals a handkerchief decorated with strawberries from Desdemona, gives it to Cassio, and leads Othello to believe that Desdemona has given it to Cassio as a love gift. Othello confronts Desdemona and "roars for the handkerchief" in Act III, Scene iv.

With such a prize no mortal must be blest,
So heaven decrees! with heaven who can contest?
Some thought it mounted to the Lunar sphere,
Since all things lost on earth are treasured there.
There Heroes' wits are kept in pond'rous vases, 115
And beaux's in snuff-boxes and tweezer-cases.
There broken vows and death-bed alms are found,
And lovers' hearts with ends of riband bound,
The courtier's promises, and sick man's prayers,
The smiles of harlots, and the tears of heirs, 120
Cages for gnats, and chains to yoke a flea,
Dried butterflies, and tomes of casuistry.
But trust the Muse—she saw it upward rise,
Though marked by none but quick, poetic eyes:
(So Rome's great founder to the heavens withdrew,[57] 125
To Proculus alone confessed in view.)
A sudden Star, it shot through liquid air,
And drew behind a radiant trail of hair.
Not Berenice's Locks first rose so bright,[58]
The heavens bespangling with dishevelled light. 130
The Sylphs behold it kindling as it flies,
And pleased pursue its progress through the skies.
This the Beau monde shall from the Mall[59] survey,
And hail with music its propitious ray.
This the blest Lover shall for Venus take, 135
And send up vows from Rosamonda's lake.[60]
This Partridge[61] soon shall view in cloudless skies,
When next he looks through Galileo's eyes;[62]
And hence th' egregious wizard shall foredoom
The fate of Louis, and the fall of Rome. 140
Then cease, bright Nymph! to mourn thy ravished hair,
Which adds new glory to the shining sphere!
Not all the tresses that fair head can boast,
Shall draw such envy as the Lock you lost.
For, after all the murders of your eye, 145
When, after millions slain, yourself shall die:
When those fair suns shall set, as set they must,
And all those tresses shall be laid in dust,
This Lock, the Muse shall consecrate to fame,
And 'midst the stars inscribe Belinda's name. 150

[57] Romulus, legendary founder of Rome, was said to have been carried to heaven in a storm cloud.
[58] Berenice dedicated a lock of her hair to the gods for the safe return from war of her husband Ptolemy III. It became a constellation.
[59] An enclosed walk in St. James' Park. [60] A pond in St. James' Park.
[61] "John Partridge was a ridiculous star-gazer, who in his Almanacs every year never failed to predict the downfall of the Pope and the King of France, then at war with the English" (Pope).
[62] That is, a telescope.

from *AN ESSAY ON MAN*

To Henry St. John, Lord Bolingbroke

THE DESIGN

Having proposed to write some pieces on Human Life and Manners, such as (to use my Lord Bacon's expression) *come home to Men's Business and Bosoms,* I thought it more satisfactory to begin with considering *Man* in the abstract, his *Nature* and his *State;* since, to prove any moral duty, to enforce any moral precept, or to examine the perfection or imperfection of any creature whatsoever, it is necessary first to know what *condition* and *relation* it is placed in, and what is the proper *end* and *purpose* of its *being.*

The science of Human Nature is, like all other sciences, reduced to a *few clear points:* There are not *many certain truths* in this world. It is therefore in the Anatomy of the mind as in that of the Body; more good will accrue to mankind by attending to the large, open, and perceptible parts, than by studying too much such finer nerves and vessels, the conformations and uses of which will forever escape our observation. The *disputes* are all upon these last, and, I will venture to say, they have less sharpened the *wits* than the *hearts* of men against each other, and have diminished the practice, more than advanced the theory of Morality. If I could flatter myself that this Essay has any merit, it is in steering betwixt the extremes of doctrines seemingly opposite, in passing over terms utterly unintelligible, and in forming a *temperate* yet not *inconsistent,* and a *short* yet not *imperfect* system of Ethics.

This I might have done in prose, but I chose verse, and even rhyme, for two reasons. The one will appear obvious; that principles, maxims, or precepts so written, both strike the reader more strongly at first, and are more easily retained by him afterwards: The other may seem odd, but is true, I found I could express them more *shortly* this way than in prose itself; and nothing is more certain, than that much of the *force* as well as *grace* of arguments or instructions, depends on their *conciseness.* I was unable to treat this part of my subject more in *detail,* without becoming dry and tedious; or more *poetically,* without sacrificing perspicuity to ornament, without wandering from the precision, or breaking the chain of reasoning: If any man can unite all these without diminution of any of them, I freely confess he will compass a thing above my capacity.

What is now published, is only to be considered as a *general Map of* MAN, marking out no more than the *greater parts,* their *extent,* their *limits,* and their *connection,* and leaving the particular to be more fully delineated in the charts which are to follow. Consequently, these Epistles in their progress (if I have health and leisure to make any progress) will be less dry, and more susceptible of poetical ornament. I am here only opening the *fountains,* and clearing the passage. To deduce the *rivers,* to follow them in their course, and to observe their effects, may be a task more agreeable.

EPISTLE I

Of the Nature and State of Man, with respect to the Universe

Awake, my ST. JOHN![1] leave all meaner things
To low ambition, and the pride of Kings.
Let us (since Life can little more supply

[1] Pope's friend, Henry St. John, Viscount Bolingbroke.

Than just to look about us and to die)
Expatiate[2] free o'er all this scene of Man; 5
A mighty maze! but not without a plan;
A Wild, where weeds and flowers promiscuous shoot;
Or Garden, tempting with forbidden fruit.
Together let us beat this ample field,
Try what the open, what the covert yield; 10
The latent tracts, the giddy heights, explore
Of all who blindly creep, or sightless soar;
Eye Nature's walks, shoot Folly as it flies,
And catch the Manners living as they rise;
Laugh where we must, be candid[3] where we can; 15
But vindicate the ways of God to Man.[4]
 I. Say first, of God above, or Man below,
What can we reason, but from what we know?
Of Man, what see we but his station here,
From which to reason, or to which refer? 20
Through worlds unnumbered though the God be known,
'Tis ours to trace him only in our own.
He, who through vast immensity can pierce,
See worlds on worlds compose one universe,
Observe how system into system runs, 25
What other planets circle other suns,
What varied Being peoples every star,
May tell why Heaven has made us as we are.
But of this frame the bearings, and the ties,
The strong connexions, nice dependencies, 30
Gradations[5] just, has thy pervading soul
Looked through? or can a part contain the whole?
 Is the great chain,[6] that draws all to agree,
And drawn supports, upheld by God, or thee?
 II. Presumptuous Man! the reason wouldst thou find, 35
Why formed so weak, so little, and so blind?
First, if thou canst, the harder reason guess,
Why formed no weaker, blinder, and no less?
Ask of thy mother earth, why oaks are made
Taller or stronger than the weeds they shade? 40
Or ask of yonder argent fields above,
Why JOVE's satellites are less than JOVE?
 Of Systems possible, if 'tis confest
That Wisdom infinite must form the best,
Where all must full or not coherent be, 45
And all that rises, rise in due degree;
Then, in the scale of reas'ning life, 'tis plain,

[2] Wander at will. [3] Kindly or benign.
[4] An allusion to Milton's *Paradise Lost*, I.26: "And justify the ways of God to men."
[5] "Connexions," "dependencies," and "gradations" were technical astronomical terms relating to the hierarchies of the stellar systems.
[6] The Great Chain of Being, the traditional expression of the hierarchical arrangement of the universe.

There must be, somewhere, such a rank as Man:
And all the question (wrangle e'er so long)
Is only this, if God has placed him wrong? 50
 Respecting Man, whatever wrong we call,
May, must be right, as relative to all.
In human works, though labored on with pain,
A thousand movements scarce one purpose gain;
In God's, one single can its end produce; 55
Yet serves to second too some other use.
So Man, who here seems principal alone,
Perhaps acts second to some sphere unknown,
Touches some wheel, or verges to some goal;
'Tis but a part we see, and not a whole. 60
 When the proud steed shall know why Man restrains
His fiery course, or drives him o'er the plains:
When the dull Ox, why now he breaks the clod,
Is now a victim, and now Egypt's God:
Then shall Man's pride and dulness comprehend 65
His actions', passions', being's, use and end;
Why doing, suffering, checked, impelled; and why
This hour a slave, the next a deity.
 Then say not Man's imperfect, Heaven in fault;
Say rather, Man's as perfect as he ought: 70
His knowledge measured to his state and place;
His time a moment and a point his space.
If to be perfect in a certain sphere,
What matter, soon or late, or here or there?
The blest today is as completely so, 75
As who began a thousand years ago.
 III. Heaven from all creatures hides the book of Fate,
All but the page prescribed, their present state:
From brutes what men, from men what spirits know:
Or who could suffer Being here below? 80
The lamb thy riot dooms to bleed today,
Had he thy Reason, would he skip and play?
Pleased to the last, he crops the flowery food,
And licks the hand just raised to shed his blood.
Oh blindness to the future! kindly given, 85
That each may fill the circle marked by Heaven:
Who sees with equal eye, as God of all,
A hero perish, or a sparrow fall,
Atoms or systems[7] into ruin hurled,
And now a bubble burst, and now a world. 90
 Hope humbly then; with trembling pinions soar;
Wait the great teacher Death; and God adore.
What future bliss, he gives not thee to know,
But gives that Hope to be thy blessing now.
Hope springs eternal in the human breast: 95

[7] Solar systems.

Man never Is, but always To be blest:
The soul, uneasy and confined from home,
Rests and expatiates in a life to come.
 Lo, the poor Indian! whose untutored mind
Sees God in clouds, or hears him in the wind; 100
His soul, proud Science never taught to stray
Far as the solar walk, or milky way;
Yet simple Nature to his hope has given,
Behind the cloud-topt hill, an humbler heaven;
Some safer world in depth of woods embraced, 105
Some happier island in the watery waste,
Where slaves once more their native land behold,
No fiends torment, no Christians thirst for gold.
To Be, contents his natural desire,
He asks no Angel's wing, no Seraph's fire; 110
But thinks, admitted to that equal sky,
His faithful dog shall bear him company.
 IV. Go, wiser thou! and, in thy scale of sense,
Weigh thy Opinion against Providence;
Call imperfection what thou fanciest such, 115
Say, here he gives too little, there too much:
Destroy all Creatures for thy sport or gust,[8]
Yet cry, If Man's unhappy, God's unjust;
If Man alone engross not Heaven's high care,
Alone made perfect here, immortal there: 120
Snatch from his hand the balance and the rod,
Re-judge his justice, be the GOD of GOD.
In Pride, in reas'ning Pride, our error lies;
All quit their sphere, and rush into the skies.
Pride still is aiming at the blest abodes, 125
Men would be Angels, Angels would be Gods.
Aspiring to be Gods, if Angels fell,
Aspiring to be Angels, Men rebel:
And who but wishes to invert the laws
Of ORDER, sins against th' Eternal Cause. 130
 V. Ask for what end the heavenly bodies shine,
Earth for whose use? Pride answers, "'Tis for mine:
For me kind Nature wakes her genial[9] Power,
Suckles each herb, and spreads out every flower;
Annual for me, the grape, the rose renew 135
The juice nectareous, and the balmy dew;
For me, the mine a thousand treasures brings;
For me, health gushes from a thousand springs;
Seas roll to waft me, suns to light me rise;
My foot-stool earth, my canopy the skies." 140
 But errs not Nature from this gracious end,
From burning suns when livid deaths[10] descend,
When earthquakes swallow, or when tempests sweep

[8]Taste or appetite. [9]Generative. [10]Plague victims had a gray or bluish color.

Towns to one grave, whole nations to the deep?
"No, ('tis replied) the first Almighty Cause 145
Acts not by partial, but by gen'ral laws;
Th' exceptions few; some change since all began:
And what created perfect?"—Why then Man?
If the great end be human Happiness,
Then Nature deviates; and can Man do less? 150
As much that end a constant course requires
Of showers and sun-shine, as of Man's desires;
As much eternal springs and cloudless skies,
As Men for ever temp'rate, calm, and wise.
If plagues or earthquakes break not Heaven's design, 155
Why then a Borgia, or a Catiline?[11]
Who knows but he, whose hand the lightning forms,
Who heaves old Ocean, and who wings the storms;
Pours fierce Ambition in a Caesar's mind,
Or turns young Ammon[12] loose to scourge mankind? 160
From pride, from pride, our very reasoning springs;
Account for moral, as for natural things:
Why charge we Heaven in those, in these acquit?
In both, to reason right is to submit.
 Better for Us, perhaps, it might appear, 165
Were there all harmony, all virtue here;
That never air or ocean felt the wind;
That never passion discomposed the mind.
But ALL subsists by elemental strife;
And Passions are the elements of Life. 170
The gen'ral ORDER, since the whole began,
Is kept in Nature, and is kept in Man.
 VI. What would this Man? Now upward will he soar,
And little less than Angel, would be more;
Now looking downwards, just as grieved appears 175
To want the strength of bulls, the fur of bears.
Made for his use all creatures if he call,
Say what their use, had he the powers of all?
Nature to these, without profusion, kind,
The proper organs, proper powers assigned; 180
Each seeming want compensated of course,[13]
Here with degrees of swiftness, there of force;
All in exact proportion to the state;
Nothing to add, and nothing to abate.
Each beast, each insect, happy in its own: 185
Is heaven unkind to Man, and Man alone?
Shall he alone, whom rational we call,
Be pleased with nothing, if not blessed with all?
 The bliss of Man (could Pride that blessing find)

[11] The Borgia family of Renaissance Italy was famous for its cruelty. Catiline led a first-century B.C. revolt against the Roman consuls.
[12] Alexander the Great. [13] In the normal course of events.

Is not to act or think beyond mankind; 190
No powers of body or of soul to share,
But what his nature and his state can bear.
Why has not Man a microscopic eye?
For this plain reason, Man is not a Fly.[14]
Say what the use, were finer optics given, 195
T' inspect a mite, not comprehend the heaven?
Or touch, if tremblingly alive all o'er,
To smart and agonize at every pore?
Or quick effluvia[15] darting through the brain,
Die of a rose in aromatic pain? 200
If nature thundered in his opening ears,
And stunned him with the music of the spheres,
How would he wish that Heaven had left him still
The whisp'ring Zephyr, and the purling rill?
Who finds not Providence all good and wise, 205
Alike in what it gives, and what denies?
 VII. Far as Creation's ample range extends,
The scale of sensual, mental powers ascends:
Mark how it mounts, to Man's imperial race,
From the green myriads in the peopled grass: 210
What modes of sight betwixt each wide extreme,
The mole's dim curtain, and the lynx's beam:[16]
Of smell, the headlong lioness between,
And hound sagacious[17] on the tainted green:
Of hearing, from the life that fills the Flood, 215
To that which warbles through the vernal wood:
The spider's touch, how exquisitely fine!
Feels at each thread, and lives along the line:
In the nice[18] bee, what sense so subtly true
From pois'nous herbs extracts the healing dew?[19] 220
How Instinct varies in the grov'lling swine,
Compared, half-reas'ning elephant, with thine!
'Twixt that, and Reason, what a nice barrier,
For ever sep'rate, yet for ever near![20]
Remembrance and Reflection how allied; 225
What thin partitions Sense from Thought divide:
And Middle natures, how they long to join,
Yet never pass th' insuperable line!
Without this just gradation, could they be
Subjected, these to those, or all to thee? 230

[14] Flies were thought to have eyes with microscopic powers.
[15] Epicurus believed that odors were communicated to the brain by means of streams of invisible particles or "effluvia."
[16] Sight was thought to involve an emission of rays from the eye.
[17] Acute in the senses, especially that of smell. [18] Accurate, precise.
[19] Honey was used medicinally in Pope's day.
[20] Pope expresses the orthodox view, opposed by Montaigne and others, that man differs from animals in kind, not merely in degree.

The powers of all subdued by thee alone,
Is not thy Reason all these powers in one?
 VIII. See, through this air, this ocean, and this earth,
All matter quick, and bursting into birth.
Above, how high, progressive life may go! 235
Around, how wide! how deep extend below!
Vast chain of Being! which from God began,
Natures ethereal, human, angel, man,
Beast, bird, fish, insect, what no eye can see,
No glass can reach; from Infinite to thee, 240
From thee to Nothing.—On superior powers
Were we to press, inferior might on ours:
Or in the full creation leave a void,
Where, one step broken, the great scale's destroyed:
From Nature's chain whatever link you strike, 245
Tenth or ten thousandth, breaks the chain alike.
 And, if each system in gradation roll
Alike essential to th' amazing Whole,
The least confusion but in one, not all
That system only, but the Whole must fall. 250
Let Earth unbalanced from her orbit fly,
Planets and Suns run lawless through the sky;
Let ruling Angels from their spheres be hurled,
Being on Being wrecked, and world on world;
Heaven's whole foundations to their centre nod, 255
And Nature tremble to the throne of God.
All this dread ORDER break—for whom? for thee?
Vile worm!—Oh Madness! Pride! Impiety!
 IX. What if the foot, ordained the dust to tread,
Or hand, to toil, aspired to be the head? 260
What if the head, the eye, or ear repined
To serve mere engines²¹ to the ruling Mind?
Just as absurd, for any part to claim
To be another, in this gen'ral frame:
Just as absurd, to mourn the tasks or pains, 265
The great directing MIND of ALL ordains.
 All are but parts of one stupendous whole,
Whose body Nature is, and God the soul;
That, changed through all, and yet in all the same;
Great in the earth, as in th' ethereal frame; 270
Warms in the sun, refreshes in the breeze,
Glows in the stars, and blossoms in the trees,
Lives through all life, extends through all extent,
Spreads undivided, operates unspent;
Breathes in our soul, informs our mortal part, 275
As full, as perfect, in a hair as heart:
As full, as perfect, in vile Man that mourns,

²¹ Tools or instruments.

As the rapt Seraph that adores and burns:[22]
To him no high, no low, no great, no small;
He fills, he bounds, connects, and equals all. 280
 X. Cease then, nor ORDER Imperfection name:
Our proper bliss depends on what we blame.
Know thy own point: this kind, this due degree
Of blindness, weakness, Heaven bestows on thee.
Submit.—In this, or any other sphere, 285
Secure to be as blest as thou canst bear:
Safe in the hand of one disposing Power,
Or in the natal, or the mortal hour.
All Nature is but Art, unknown to thee;
All Chance, Direction, which thou canst not see; 290
All Discord, Harmony not understood;
All partial Evil, universal Good:
And, spite of Pride, in erring Reason's spite,
One truth is clear, WHATEVER IS, IS RIGHT.

EPISTLE II

Of the Nature and State of Man with respect to HIMSELF,
as an Individual

I. Know then thyself, presume not God to scan;
The proper study of Mankind is Man.
Placed on this isthmus of a middle state,
A Being darkly wise, and rudely great:
With too much knowledge for the Sceptic side, 5
With too much weakness for the Stoic's pride,[23]
He hangs between; in doubt to act, or rest;
In doubt to deem himself a God, or Beast;
In doubt his Mind or Body to prefer;
Born but to die, and reas'ning but to err; 10
Alike in ignorance, his reason such,
Whether he thinks too little, or too much:
Chaos of Thought and Passion, all confused;
Still by himself abused, or disabused;
Created half to rise, and half to fall; 15
Great lord of all things, yet a prey to all;
Sole judge of Truth, in endless Error hurled:
The glory, jest, and riddle of the world!
 Go, wondrous creature! mount where Science guides.
Go, measure earth, weigh air, and state the tides; 20
Instruct the planets in what orbs to run,

[22] The Seraphim, the highest order of angels, were said to be pure flame. Cf. l. 110 preceding.

[23] The Skeptics maintained that real knowledge of things was impossible. The Stoics were said to be "proud" because they believed that men could escape their passions and achieve the serenity of God.

Correct old Time, and regulate the Sun;
Go, soar with Plato to th' empyreal sphere,[24]
To the first good, first perfect, and first fair;
Or tread the mazy round his follow'rs trod, 25
And quitting sense[25] call imitating God;
As Eastern priests in giddy circles run,
And turn their heads to imitate the Sun.
Go, teach Eternal Wisdom how to rule—
Then drop into thyself, and be a fool! 30
 Superior beings, when of late they saw
A mortal Man unfold all Nature's law,
Admired such wisdom in an earthly shape,
And shewed a NEWTON as we shew an Ape.[26]
 Could he, whose rules the rapid Comet bind, 35
Describe or fix one movement of his Mind?
Who saw its fires here rise, and there descend,
Explain his own beginning, or his end?
Alas what wonder! Man's superior part
Unchecked may rise, and climb from art to art; 40
But when his own great work is but begun,
What Reason weaves, by Passion is undone.
 Trace Science then, with Modesty thy guide;
First strip off all her equipage of Pride;
Deduct what is but Vanity, or Dress, 45
Or Learning's Luxury, or Idleness;
Or tricks to shew the stretch of human brain,
Mere curious pleasure, or ingenious pain;
Expunge the whole, or lop th' excrescent parts
Of all, our Vices have created Arts; 50
Then see how little the remaining sum,
Which served the past, and must the times to come!
 II. Two Principles in human nature reign;
Self-love,[27] to urge, and Reason, to restrain;
Nor this a good, nor that a bad we call, 55
Each works its end, to move or govern all:
And to their proper operation still,
Ascribe all Good; to their improper, Ill.
 Self-love, the spring of motion, acts[28] the soul;
Reason's comparing balance rules the whole. 60
Man, but for that, no action could attend,
And but for this, were active to no end:
Fixed like a plant on his peculiar spot,
To draw nutrition, propagate, and rot;
Or, meteor-like, flame lawless through the void, 65
Destroying others, by himself destroyed.

[24] The empyreal sphere was the outermost sphere of the Ptolemaic universe, the abode of God. Pope thinks of it as also the location of Plato's archetypes or Ideas.
[25] Neoplatonic trances.
[26] The English translation of Sir Isaac Newton's *Principia* had been published in 1729.
[27] Self-preservation; maintenance of life. [28] Activates.

Most strength the moving principle requires;
Active its task, it prompts, impels, inspires.
Sedate and quiet the comparing lies,
Formed but to check, delib'rate, and advise. 70
Self-love still stronger, as its objects nigh;
Reason's at distance, and in prospect lie:
That sees immediate good by present sense;
Reason, the future and the consequence.
Thicker than arguments, temptations throng, 75
At best more watchful this, but that more strong.
The action of the stronger to suspend,
Reason still use, to Reason still attend.
Attention, habit and experience gains;
Each strengthens Reason, and Self-love restrains. 80
 Let subtle schoolmen teach these friends to fight,
More studious to divide than to unite;
And Grace and Virtue, Sense and Reason split,
With all the rash dexterity of wit.
Wits, just like Fools, at war about a name, 85
Have full as oft no meaning, or the same.
Self-love and Reason to one end aspire,
Pain their aversion, Pleasure their desire;
But greedy That, its object would devour,
This taste the honey, and not wound the flower: 90
Pleasure, or wrong or rightly understood,
Our greatest evil, or our greatest good.
 III. Modes of Self-love the Passions we may call:
'Tis real good, or seeming, moves them all:
But since not every good we can divide, 95
And Reason bids us for our own provide;
Passions, though selfish, if their means be fair,
List[29] under Reason, and deserve her care;
Those, that imparted,[30] court a nobler aim,
Exalt their kind, and take some Virtue's name. 100
 In lazy Apathy let Stoics boast
Their Virtue fixed; 'tis fixed as in a frost;
Contracted all, retiring to the breast;
But strength of mind is Exercise, not Rest:
The rising tempest puts in act the soul, 105
Parts it may ravage, but preserves the whole.
On life's vast ocean diversely we sail,
Reason the card,[31] but Passion is the gale;
Nor God alone in the still calm we find,
He mounts the storm, and walks upon the wind. 110
 Passions, like Elements, though born to fight,
Yet, mixed and softened, in his work unite:

[29] Enlist. [30] That is, the passions when reason is imparted to them.
[31] A mariner's chart or map.

These 'tis enough to temper and employ;
But what composes Man, can Man destroy?
Suffice that Reason keep to Nature's road, 115
Subject, compound them, follow her and God.
Love, Hope, and Joy, fair pleasure's smiling train,
Hate, Fear, and Grief, the family of pain,
These mixed with art, and to due bounds confined,
Make and maintain the balance of the mind: 120
The lights and shades, whose well accorded strife
Gives all the strength and colour of our life.
 Pleasures are ever in our hands or eyes;
And when in act they cease, in prospect rise:
Present to grasp, and future still to find, 125
The whole employ of body and of mind.
All spread their charms, but charm not all alike;
On diff'rent senses diff'rent objects strike;
Hence diff'rent Passions more or less inflame,
As strong or weak, the organs of the frame; 130
And hence one MASTER PASSION in the breast,
Like Aaron's serpent, swallows up the rest.[32]
 As Man, perhaps, the moment of his breath,
Receives the lurking principle of death;
The young disease, that must subdue at length, 135
Grows with his growth, and strengthens with his strength:
So, cast and mingled with his very frame,
The Mind's disease, its RULING PASSION came;
Each vital humour[33] which should feed the whole,
Soon flows to this, in body and in soul: 140
Whatever warms the heart, or fills the head,
As the mind opens, and its functions spread,
Imagination plies her dang'rous art,
And pours it all upon the peccant[34] part.
 Nature its mother, Habit is its nurse; 145
Wit, Spirit, Faculties, but make it worse;
Reason itself but gives it edge and power;
As Heaven's blest beam turns vinegar more sour.
 We, wretched subjects, though to lawful sway,
In this weak queen some fav'rite still obey: 150
Ah! if she lend not arms, as well as rules,
What can she more than tell us we are fools?
Teach us to mourn our Nature, not to mend,
A sharp accuser, but a helpless friend!
Or from a judge turn pleader, to persuade 155
The choice we make, or justify it made;

[32] Aaron was Moses' brother. In a miracle before the Pharaoh's court, Aaron's rod became a serpent. When the Egyptian magicians turned their own rods into serpents, Aaron's serpent swallowed them. See Exodus 7:8–13.
[33] The fluids or "spirits" that were thought to govern physical and mental functions.
[34] "Peccant" humours were either diseased or too abundant.

Proud of an easy conquest all along,
She but removes weak passions for the strong:
So, when small humours gather to a gout,[35]
The doctor fancies he has driven them out. 160
 Yes, Nature's road must ever be preferred;
Reason is here no guide, but still a guard:
'Tis hers to rectify, not overthrow,
And treat this passion more as friend than foe:
A mightier Power the strong direction sends, 165
And several Men impels to several ends:
Like varying winds, by other passions tossed,
This drives them constant to a certain coast.
Let power or knowledge, gold, or glory, please,
Or (oft more strong than all) the love of ease; 170
Through life 'tis followed, even at life's expense;
The merchant's toil, the sage's indolence,
The monk's humility, the hero's pride,
All, all alike find Reason on their side.
 Th' Eternal Art educing good from ill, 175
Grafts on this Passion our best principle:
'Tis thus the Mercury of Man is fixed,[36]
Strong grows the Virtue with his nature mixed;
The dross cements what else were too refined,
And in one interest body acts with mind. 180
 As fruits, ungrateful to the planter's care,
On savage stocks inserted, learn to bear;
The surest Virtues thus from Passions shoot,
Wild Nature's vigor working at the root.
What crops of wit and honesty appear 185
From spleen, from obstinacy, hate, or fear!
See anger, zeal and fortitude supply;
Even av'rice, prudence; sloth, philosophy;
Lust, through some certain strainers well refined,
Is gentle love, and charms all womankind; 190
Envy, to which th' ignoble mind's a slave,
Is emulation in the learned or brave;
Nor Virtue, male or female, can we name,
But what will grow on Pride, or grow on Shame.
 Thus Nature gives us (let it check our pride) 195
The virtue nearest to our vice allied:
Reason the bias turns to good from ill,
And Nero reigns a Titus, if he will.

[35] Gout was thought to be caused by the body driving diseased humours into the extremities.

[36] A metallurgical metaphor. "Primal mercury" was thought to be the basis of all metals, which were "fixed" in different forms by different "sulphurs." Pope is saying that the ruling passion "sets" one's personality.

The fiery soul abhorred in Catiline,
In Decius charms, in Curtius is divine:[37] 200
The same ambition can destroy or save,
And makes a patriot as it makes a knave.
 IV. This light and darkness in our chaos joined,
What shall divide? The God within the mind:
 Extremes in Nature equal ends produce, 205
In Man they join to some mysterious use;
Though each by turns the other's bound invade,
As, in some well-wrought picture, light and shade,
And oft so mix, the diff'rence is too nice
Where ends the Virtue, or begins the Vice. 210
 Fools! who from hence into the notion fall,
That Vice or Virtue there is none at all.
If white and black blend, soften, and unite
A thousand ways, is there no black or white?
Ask your own heart, and nothing is so plain; 215
'Tis to mistake them, costs the time and pain.
 V. Vice is a monster of so frightful mien,
As, to be hated, needs but to be seen;
Yet seen too oft, familiar with her face,
We first endure, then pity, then embrace. 220
But where th' Extreme of Vice, was ne'er agreed:
Ask where's the North? at York, 'tis on the Tweed;
In Scotland, at the Orcades; and there,
At Greenland, Zembla, or the Lord knows where.
No creature owns it in the first degree, 225
But thinks his neighbour further gone than he;
Even those who dwell beneath its very zone,
Or never feel the rage, or never own;
What happier natures shrink at with affright,
The hard inhabitant contends is right. 230
 VI. Virtuous and vicious every Man must be,
Few in th' extreme, but all in the degree;
The rogue and fool by fits is fair and wise;
And even the best, by fits, what they despise.
'Tis but by parts we follow good or ill; 235
For, Vice or Virtue, Self directs it still;
Each individual seeks a sev'ral goal;
But HEAVEN's great view is One, and that the Whole.
That counter-works each folly and caprice;
That disappoints th' effect of every vice; 240
That, happy frailties to all ranks applied,
Shame to the virgin, to the matron pride,

[37] Nero was a "bad" emperor of Rome, Titus a "good" one. Catiline was a famous rebel against Rome; Decius and Curtius performed acts of patriotic self-sacrifice described by the Roman historian Livy.

Fear to the statesman, rashness to the chief,
To kings presumption, and to crowds belief:
That, Virtue's ends from Vanity can raise, 245
Which seeks no int'rest, no reward but praise;
And build on wants, and on defects of mind,
The joy, the peace, the glory of Mankind.
　　Heaven forming each on other to depend,
A master, or a servant, or a friend, 250
Bids each on other for assistance call,
Till one Man's weakness grows the strength of all.
Wants, frailties, passions, closer still ally
The common int'rest, or endear the tie.
To these we owe true friendship, love sincere, 255
Each home-felt joy that life inherits here;
Yet from the same we learn, in its decline,
Those joys, those loves, those int'rests to resign;
Taught half by Reason, half by mere decay,
To welcome death, and calmly pass away. 260
　　Whate'er the Passion, knowledge, fame, or pelf,
Not one will change his neighbour with himself.
The learned is happy nature to explore,
The fool is happy that he knows no more;
The rich is happy in the plenty given, 265
The poor contents him with the care of Heaven.
See the blind beggar dance, the cripple sing,
The sot a hero, lunatic a king;
The starving chemist in his golden views
Supremely blest, the poet in his Muse. 270
　　See some strange comfort every state attend,
And Pride bestowed on all, a common friend;
See some fit Passion every age supply,
Hope travels through, nor quits us when we die.
　　Behold the child, by Nature's kindly law, 275
Pleased with a rattle, tickled with a straw:
Some livelier play-thing gives his youth delight,
A little louder, but as empty quite:
Scarfs,[38] garters, gold, amuse his riper stage,
And beads and prayer-books are the toys of age: 280
Pleased with this bauble still, as that before;
'Til tired he sleeps, and Life's poor play is o'er.
　　Meanwhile Opinion gilds with varying rays
Those painted clouds that beautify our days;
Each want of happiness by hope supplied, 285
And each vacuity of sense by Pride:
These build as fast as knowledge can destroy;
In Folly's cup still laughs the bubble, joy;
One prospect lost, another still we gain;
And not a vanity is given in vain; 290

[38] The traditional badge of doctors of divinity.

Even mean Self-love becomes, by force divine,
The scale to measure others' wants by thine.
See! and confess, one comfort still must rise,
'Tis this, Though Man's a fool, yet GOD IS WISE.

EPISTLE TO DR. ARBUTHNOT

ADVERTISEMENT

This paper is a sort of bill of complaint, begun many years since, and drawn up by snatches, as the several occasions offered. I had no thoughts of publishing it, till it pleased some persons of rank and fortune (the authors of *Verses to the Imitator of Horace,* and of an *Epistle to a Doctor of Divinity from a Nobleman at Hampton Court*)[1] to attack, in a very extraordinary manner, not only my writings (of which, being public, the public is judge), but my person, morals, and family, whereof, to those who know me not, a truer information may be requisite. Being divided between the necessity to say something of myself, and my own laziness to undertake so awkward a task, I thought it the shortest way to put the last hand to this Epistle. If it have anything pleasing, it will be that by which I am most desirous to please, the truth and the sentiment; and if anything offensive, it will be only to those I am least sorry to offend, the vicious or the ungenerous.

Many will know their own pictures in it, there being not a circumstance but what is true; but I have, for the most part, spared their names, and they may escape being laughed at, if they please.

I would have some of them know, it was owing to the request of the learned and candid friend to whom it is inscribed,[2] that I make not as free use of theirs as they have done of mine. However, I shall have this advantage, and honor, on my side, that whereas, by their proceeding, any abuse may be directed at any man, no injury can possibly be done by mine, since a nameless character can never be found out, but by its truth and likeness.—POPE

P. SHUT, shut the door, good John![3] fatigued, I said,
Tie up the knocker, say I'm sick, I'm dead.
The Dog Star rages![4] nay 'tis past a doubt,
All Bedlam, or Parnassus,[5] is let out:
Fire in each eye, and papers in each hand, 5
They rave, recite, and madden round the land.
 What walls can guard me, or what shades can hide?

[1] Lord Hervey and Lady Mary Wortley Montagu. See introduction to Pope.
[2] Dr. Arbuthnot had written to Pope, advising him to temper his satire. See introduction to Pope.
[3] Pope's servant, John Serle.
[4] The Dog Star is Sirius, which is associated with both madness and poetry, because it appears in August, a time of maddening heat, and because August, in ancient Rome, was the season for reciting poetry. Pope did the final revisions on the *Epistle to Dr. Arbuthnot* in August 1734.
[5] Bedlam was the London insane asylum, Parnassus the mountain sacred to poetry, art, and culture in ancient Greece.

They pierce my thickets, through my grot[6] they glide,
By land, by water, they renew the charge,
They stop the chariot, and they board the barge.[7] 10
No place is sacred, not the church is free,
Even Sunday shines no sabbath-day to me:
Then from the Mint[8] walks forth the man of rhyme,
Happy! to catch me, just at dinner-time.

 Is there a parson, much bemused in beer, 15
A maudlin poetess, a rhyming peer,
A clerk, foredoomed his father's soul to cross,
Who pens a stanza, when he should engross?[9]
Is there, who, locked from ink and paper, scrawls
With desperate charcoal round his darkened walls? 20
All fly to Twit'nam,[10] and in humble strain
Apply to me, to keep them mad or vain.
Arthur, whose giddy son neglects the laws,[11]
Imputes to me and my damned works the cause:
Poor Cornus[12] sees his frantic wife elope, 25
And curses wit, and poetry, and Pope.

 Friend to my life! (which did not you prolong,
The world had wanted many an idle song)
What drop[13] or nostrum can this plague remove?
Or which must end me, a fool's wrath or love? 30
A dire dilemma! either way I'm sped,
If foes, they write, if friends, they read me dead.
Seized and tied down to judge,[14] how wretched I!
Who can't be silent, and who will not lie:
To laugh, were want of goodness and of grace, 35
And to be grave, exceeds all power of face.
I sit with sad civility, I read
With honest anguish, and an aching head;
And drop at last, but in unwilling ears,
This saving counsel, "Keep your piece nine years." 40

 "Nine years!" cries he, who, high in Drury Lane,[15]
Lulled by soft zephyrs through the broken pane,

[6] Pope, a notable gardener, had an ornamental grotto on the grounds of his home at Twickenham.

[7] Pope had a private barge to convey him between Twickenham and London.

[8] An area in Southwark that served as a sanctuary for debtors (who could not be arrested anywhere on Sundays).

[9] Copy business or legal documents. [10] Twickenham, Pope's estate.

[11] Arthur Moore was a businessman and member of Parliament for Grimsby. He and his "giddy" son James earned Pope's enmity when James incorporated some of Pope's lines, with Pope's permission, into his comedy *The Rival Modes* and then, when Pope withdrew his permission, refused to remove the lines.

[12] "Cornus" comes from Latin *cornu*, horn, and thus means "cuckold."

[13] "Ward's drop" was a worthless patent medicine sold by a quack doctor named Joshua Ward. It was notorious in the summer of 1734 because Ward had succeeded in winning the patronage of King George.

[14] In a scene in William Wycherley's comedy *The Plain Dealer* (1676), Oldfox ties down Widow Blackacre and makes her listen to his verses.

[15] That is, in a garret in Drury Lane, a disreputable area in Pope's time.

Rhymes ere he wakes, and prints before Term ends,[16]
Obliged by hunger, and request of friends:[17]
"The piece, you think, is incorrect? why, take it,
I'm all submission; what you'd have it, make it." 45
 Three things another's modest wishes bound,
My friendship, and a prologue, and ten pound.
 Pitholeon[18] sends to me: "You know his Grace,
I want a patron; ask him for a place."
Pitholeon libelled me—"But here's a letter 50
Informs you, Sir, 'twas when he knew no better.
Dare you refuse him? Curll[19] invites to dine,
He'll write a journal, or he'll turn divine."[20]
 Bless me! a packet. " 'Tis a stranger sues,
A virgin tragedy, an orphan Muse." 55
If I dislike it, "Furies, death and rage!"
If I approve, "Commend it to the stage."
There (thank my stars) my whole commission ends,
The players and I are, luckily, no friends.
Fired that the house reject him, " 'Sdeath! I'll print it, 60
And shame the fools—Your interest, Sir, with Lintot."[21]
Lintot, dull rogue! will think your price too much:
"Not, Sir, if you revise it, and retouch."
All my demurs but double his attacks;
At last he whispers, "Do; and we go snacks."[22] 65
Glad of a quarrel, straight I clap the door,
"Sir, let me see your works and you no more."
 'Tis sung, when Midas' ears began to spring,
(Midas, a sacred person and a king),
His very minister who spied them first, 70
(Some say his queen) was forced to speak, or burst.[23]
And is not mine, my friend, a sorer case,
When every coxcomb perks them in my face?
 A. Good friend, forbear! you deal in dangerous things. 75

[16] The publishing seasons coincided with the legal terms, when the courts were sitting, possibly because a great many potential book-buyers were in the city then.

[17] Pope is satirizing the cliché in prefaces that the author is presenting his work only because of the urging of his friends.

[18] Pope, as one version of the manuscript shows, was thinking of Leonard Welsted, a government clerk and minor poet who had collaborated with James Moore Smythe (see l.24) on a satire called "One Epistle to Mr. Pope" (1730) in which they implied that Pope had caused the death of the lady he mourned in his "Elegy to the Memory of an Unfortunate Lady." Pope returns to Welsted in l.375.

[19] Edmund Curll was a notorious publisher and bookseller of pirated books and pornography.

[20] Leonard Welsted both attacked Pope in the *London Journal* and wrote a treatise on theology.

[21] Bernard Lintot, Pope's publisher. [22] Divide the profits.

[23] The story of King Midas, upon whom Apollo bestowed ass's ears when Midas preferred Pan's flute-playing to Apollo's, is told in Ovid's *Metamorphoses*, where, however, it is his barber, rather than his minister or queen, who first sees the ears.

I'd never name queens, ministers, or kings;[24]
Keep close to ears, and those let asses prick,
'Tis nothing—— *P*. Nothing? if they bite and kick?
Out with it, DUNCIAD! let the secret pass,
That secret to each fool, that he's an ass: 80
The truth once told (and wherefore should we lie?)
The Queen of Midas slept, and so may I.
 You think this cruel? Take it for a rule,
No creature smarts so little as a fool.
Let peals of laughter, Codrus! round thee break, 85
Thou unconcerned canst hear the mighty crack:
Pit, box, and gallery in convulsions hurled,
Thou standst unshook amidst a bursting world.[25]
Who shames a scribbler? break one cobweb through,
He spins the slight, self-pleasing thread anew:[26] 90
Destroy his fib or sophistry, in vain,
The creature's at his dirty work again,
Throned in the center of his thin designs,
Proud of a vast extent of flimsy lines!
Whom have I hurt? has poet yet, or peer, 95
Lost the arched eyebrow, or Parnassian sneer?
And has not Colley[27] still his lord, and whore?
His butchers Henley,[28] his Freemasons Moore?[29]
Does not one table Bavius[30] still admit?
Still to one bishop Philips[31] seem a wit? 100
Still Sappho[32]—— *A*. Hold! for God's sake—you'll offend,
No names—be calm—learn prudence of a friend:
I too could write, and I am twice as tall;
But foes like these—— *P*. One flatterer's worse than all.
Of all mad creatures, if the learned are right, 105
It is the slaver kills, and not the bite.
A fool quite angry is quite innocent:
Alas! 'tis ten times worse when they repent.

[24] Arbuthnot recognizes that Pope's version of the story of Midas alludes to King George, Queen Caroline, and the Prime Minister, Robert Walpole.

[25] Pope is quoting and comically reapplying a line from Joseph Addison's translation of Horace's Ode III.3: "Should the whole frame of nature round him break, / In ruine and confusion hurl'd, / He, unconcern'd, would hear the mighty crack, / And stand secure amidst a falling world." Pope had already made fun of the third line in *Peri Bathous*, as an illustration of how a single word ("crack") can "vulgarize a poetical idea."

[26] Swift, in *The Battle of the Books*, had also compared hack writers to spiders.

[27] Colley Cibber, the Poet Laureate and a favorite target of Pope's satire.

[28] John Henley, an eccentric preacher, delivered a "Butcher's Lecture" at Newport Market in 1729, the purpose of which was "to display the religious history and use of the butcher's calling . . . and to plan the theology of this vocation."

[29] James Moore Smythe (see l.23) was a Freemason and often marched in their processions.

[30] Bavius is the bad poet in Virgil's *Eclogues III*.

[31] Ambrose Philips, an early rival of Pope's in the writing of pastorals. His insipid, sentimental style earned him the nickname of "Namby-Pamby Philips." The bishop is Hugh Boulter, bishop of Armagh in Ireland, who once employed Philips as his secretary.

[32] Lady Mary Wortley Montagu.

One dedicates in high heroic prose,
And ridicules beyond a hundred foes: 110
One from all Grub Street[33] will my fame defend,
And, more abusive, calls himself my friend.
This prints my letters,[34] that expects a bribe,
And others roar aloud, "Subscribe, subscribe."[35]
 There are, who to my person pay their court: 115
I cough like Horace, and, though lean, am short,
Ammon's great son[36] one shoulder had too high,
Such Ovid's nose, and "Sir! you have an eye"—
Go on, obliging creatures, make me see
All that disgraced my betters, met in me. 120
Say for my comfort, languishing in bed,
"Just so immortal Maro[37] held his head":
And when I die, be sure you let me know
Great Homer died three thousand years ago.
 Why did I write? what sin to me unknown
Dipped me in ink, my parents', or my own? 125
As yet a child, nor yet a fool to fame,
I lisped in numbers,[38] for the numbers came.
I left no calling for this idle trade,
No duty broke, no father disobeyed. 130
The Muse but served to ease some friend, not wife,
To help me through this long disease, my life,
To second, ARBUTHNOT! thy art and care,
And teach the being you preserved, to bear.
 But why then publish? Granville the polite,[39] 135
And knowing Walsh, would tell me I could write;
Well-natured Garth inflamed with early praise;
And Congreve loved, and Swift endured my lays;
The courtly Talbot, Somers, Sheffield read,
Even mitred Rochester would nod the head, 140
And St. John's self (great Dryden's friends before)
With open arms received one poet more.
Happy my studies, when by these approved!
Happier their author, when by these beloved!

[33] A general term for the whole group of contemporary hack writers.

[34] Edmund Curll (see l.53 and note) had printed some letters from Pope to Henry Cromwell without permission in 1726.

[35] That is, to a forthcoming book. Publishers often tried to ensure the success of a book by requiring a certain number of "subscriptions" or advance orders before publication.

[36] Alexander the Great. Plutarch said that he leaned his head toward his left shoulder.
[37] Virgil. [38] Metrical feet; verse.

[39] Pope's note to this list of early friends reads, "These are the persons to whose account the author charges the publication of his first writings. The catalogue might have been extended very much to his honor but that he confined it to friends of that early date." George Granville, William Walsh, and Samuel Garth were poets, William Congreve was a playwright, the "courtly" Charles Talbot, Duke of Shrewsbury, Lord Sommers, and John Sheffield, Duke of Buckinghamshire, were titled statesmen, and Francis Atterbury was Bishop of Rochester. All had been friends of Dryden, to whom Pope is heir, as he implies.

From these the world will judge of men and books, 145
Not from the Burnets, Oldmixons, and Cookes.[40]
Soft were my numbers; who could take offense
While pure description held the place of sense?
Like gentle Fanny's[41] was my flowery theme,
A painted mistress, or a purling stream. 150
Yet then did Gildon[42] draw his venal quill;
I wished the man a dinner, and sat still.
Yet then did Dennis[43] rave in furious fret;
I never answered—I was not in debt.
If want provoked, or madness made them print, 155
I waged no war with Bedlam or the Mint.
 Did some more sober critic come abroad?
If wrong, I smiled; if right, I kissed the rod.
Pains, reading, study, are their just pretense,
And all they want is spirit, taste, and sense. 160
Commas and points they set exactly right,
And 'twere a sin to rob them of their mite.
Yet ne'er one sprig of laurel graced these ribalds,
From slashing Bentley[44] down to piddling Tibbalds:[45]
Each wight, who reads not, and but scans and spells, 165
Each word-catcher, that lives on syllables,
Even such small critics some regard may claim,
Preserved in Milton's or in Shakespeare's name.
Pretty! in amber to observe the forms
Of hairs, or straws, or dirt, or grubs, or worms! 170
The things, we know, are neither rich nor rare,
But wonder how the devil they got there.
 Were others angry: I excused them too;
Well might they rage, I gave them but their due.
A man's true merit 'tis not hard to find; 175
But each man's secret standard in his mind,
That casting-weight[46] pride adds to emptiness,
This, who can gratify? for who can guess?
The bard whom pilfered Pastorals renown,

[40] Thomas Burnet, John Oldmixon, and Thomas Cooke. Pope, in his note, calls these men "authors of secret and scandalous history." He is contrasting the distinction of his supporters with the meanness of his detractors.

[41] Lord Hervey had written a number of sentimental poems in the form of epistles from forsaken mistresses.

[42] Charles Gildon, a mediocre poet and critic who had attacked *The Rape of the Lock* and *Windsor Forest,* at, Pope believed, Addison's instigation.

[43] John Dennis, a well-known critic and long-time foe of Pope. He had collaborated with Gildon in his attacks on Pope as well as writing several hostile reviews of his own.

[44] Richard Bentley, a prominent classical scholar, had criticized Pope's translation of Homer ("a pretty poem, Mr. Pope, but you must not call it Homer"). Pope calls him "slashing Bentley" because in Bentley's edition of *Paradise Lost* he had put slash marks around passages he didn't like. He also "slashes" the laurels of the preceding line, of course.

[45] Lewis Theobald, a scholar of Elizabethan literature, attacked Pope's edition of Shakespeare; Pope made him King of the Dunces in the *Dunciad* of 1728.

[46] The weight that tips a scale; thus, the deciding factor.

Who turns a Persian tale for half-a-crown,[47] 180
Just writes to make his barrenness appear,
And strains, from hard-bound brains, eight lines a year;
He, who still wanting, though he lives on theft,
Steals much, spends little, yet has nothing left:
And he, who now to sense, now nonsense leaning, 185
Means not, but blunders round about a meaning:
And he, whose fustian's so sublimely bad,
It is not poetry, but prose run mad:
All these, my modest satire bade translate,
And owned that nine such poets made a Tate.[48] 190
How did they fume, and stamp, and roar, and chafe!
And swear, not Addison himself was safe.
 Peace to all such! but were there one whose fires[49]
True genius kindles, and fair fame inspires;
Blest with each talent and each art to please, 195
And born to write, converse, and live with ease:
Should such a man, too fond to rule alone,
Bear, like the Turk, no brother near the throne,
View him with scornful, yet with jealous eyes,
And hate for arts that caused himself to rise; 200
Damn with faint praise, assent with civil leer,
And, without sneering, teach the rest to sneer;
Willing to wound, and yet afraid to strike,
Just hint a fault, and hesitate dislike;
Alike reserved to blame, or to commend, 205
A timorous foe, and a suspicious friend;
Dreading even fools, by flatterers besieged,
And so obliging, that he ne'er obliged;
Like Cato,[50] give his little senate laws,
And sit attentive to his own applause; 210
While wits and Templars[51] every sentence raise,
And wonder with a foolish face of praise—
Who but must laugh, if such a man there be?
Who would not weep, if Atticus were he?
 What though my name stood rubric[52] on the walls, 215
Or plastered posts, with claps,[53] in capitals?
Or smoking forth, a hundred hawkers' load,
On wings of winds came flying all abroad?

[47] Ambrose Philips (see l.100 and note). Philips had published a book of translations of Persian tales, for which he received half-a-crown for each tale. Dr. Johnson commented that this was liberal pay, but "half-a-crown had a mean sound."
[48] Nahum Tate was poet laureate from 1692 until his death in 1715. Pope is alluding to the old saying that it takes nine tailors to make one man.
[49] The portrait of Atticus in this section is based on Joseph Addison.
[50] In his prologue to Addison's tragedy *Cato*, Pope had written, "While Cato gives his little Senate laws."
[51] Law students.
[52] Bernard Lintot, Pope's publisher, advertised his books by posting red-letter titlepages outside his office in Fleet Street.
[53] Posters.

I sought no homage from the race that write;
I kept, like Asian monarchs, from their sight: 220
Poems I heeded (now be-rhymed so long)
No more than thou, great George! a birthday song.
I ne'er with wits or witlings passed my days,
To spread about the itch of verse and praise;
Nor like a puppy, daggled[54] through the town, 225
To fetch and carry sing-song up and down;
Nor at rehearsals sweat, and mouthed, and cried,
With handkerchief and orange at my side;
But sick of fops, and poetry, and prate,
To Bufo left the whole Castalian state.[55] 230
 Proud as Apollo on his forkèd hill,[56]
Sate full-blown Bufo,[57] puffed by every quill;
Fed with soft dedication all day long,
Horace and he went hand in hand in song.
His library (where busts of poets dead 235
And a true Pindar stood without a head[58])
Received of wits an undistinguished race,
Who first his judgment asked, and then a place:
Much they extolled his pictures, much his seat,[59]
And flattered every day, and some days eat: 240
Till grown more frugal in his riper days,
He paid some bards with port, and some with praise;
To some a dry rehearsal was assigned,
And others (harder still) he paid in kind.
Dryden alone (what wonder?) came not nigh, 245
Dryden alone escaped this judging eye:
But still the great have kindness in reserve,
He helped to bury whom he helped to starve.[60]
 May some choice patron bless each gray goose quill!
May every Bavius have his Bufo still! 250
So when a statesman wants a day's defense,
Or envy holds a whole week's war with sense,
Or simple pride for flattery makes demands,

[54] Trailed through dirt and mud.

[55] The Castalian spring on Mount Parnassus was sacred to Apollo and the Muses.

[56] Mount Parnassus was "forked" becasue it had two peaks, one sacred to Apollo, the other to Dionysus.

[57] The characterization of Bufo is a generalized portrait of a tasteless patron of the arts, though apparently Pope had the Earl of Halifax and George Bubb Dodington, Baron Melcombe, in mind. Halifax, First Lord of the Treasury, had supported Pope's translation of the *Iliad.* Dodington was a wealthy, ostentatious man who exercised considerable political power through his control of several parliamentary boroughs; Pope had no personal contact with him, as far as is known.

[58] Pope's note: "ridicules the affectation of antiquaries, who frequently exhibit the headless trunks and terms of statues for Plato, Homer, Pindar, etc."

[59] Estate. "Seat" was pronounced "sate" in the eighteenth century and would thus rhyme with "eat" (pronounced "ate") in the following line; "eat" was a common past tense form in Pope's time.

[60] Halifax, although he did not contribute to Dryden's funeral expenses, proposed to donate a monument to him in Westminister Abbey, a plan which was not carried out.

May dunce by dunce be whistled off my hands!
Blessed be the great! for those they take away, 255
And those they left me; for they left me GAY;[61]
Left me to see neglected genius bloom,
Neglected die, and tell it on his tomb:
Of all thy blameless life the sole return
My verse, and QUEENSBERRY[62] weeping o'er thy urn! 260
 Oh let me live my own, and die so too!
("To live and die is all I have to do:")[63]
Maintain a poet's dignity and ease,
And see what friends, and read what books I please;
Above a patron, though I condescend 265
Sometimes to call a minister my friend.
I was not born for courts or great affairs:
I pay my debts, believe, and say my prayers;
Can sleep without a poem in my head,
Nor know, if Dennis be alive or dead. 270
 Why am I asked what next shall see the light?
Heavens! was I born for nothing but to write?
Has life no joys for me? or (to be grave)
Have I no friend to serve, no soul to save?
"I found him close with Swift"—"Indeed? no doubt," 275
(Cries prating Balbus[64]) "something will come out."
'Tis all in vain, deny it as I will.
"No, such a genius never can lie still";
And then for mine obligingly mistakes
The first lampoon Sir Will. or Bubo[65] makes. 280
Poor guiltless I! and can I choose but smile,
When every coxcomb knows me by my style?
 Cursed be the verse, how well soe'er it flow,
That tends to make one worthy man my foe,
Give virtue scandal, innocence a fear, 285
Or from the soft-eyed virgin steal a tear!
But he who hurts a harmless neighbor's peace,
Insults fallen worth, or beauty in distress,
Who loves a lie, lame slander helps about,
Who writes a libel, or who copies out: 290
That fop, whose pride affects a patron's name,
Yet absent, wounds an author's honest fame:
Who can your merit selfishly approve,
And show the sense of it without the love;
Who has the vanity to call you friend, 295

[61] John Gay, poet and playwright and close friend of Pope and Swift.
[62] Gay's patrons were the Duke and Duchess of Queensberry.
[63] Slightly paraphrased from Sir John Denham's poem "Of Prudence": "To live and die is all we have to do."
[64] "Balbus" seems to be Viscount Dupplin, a member of Parliament noted for his "incessant small talk."
[65] Sir William Yonge, a Whig politician and minor poet. "Bubo" is George Bubb Dodington (see l.232 and note).

Yet wants the honor, injured, to defend;
Who tells whate'er you think, whate'er you say,
And if he lie not, must at least betray:
Who to the dean, and silver bell can swear,
And sees at Cannons what was never there;[66] 300
Who reads, but with a lust to misapply,
Make satire a lampoon, and fiction, lie.
A lash like mine no honest man shall dread,
But all such babbling blockheads in his stead.
 Let Sporus[67] tremble—— A. What? that thing of silk, 305
Sporus, that mere white curd of ass's milk?[68]
Satire or sense, alas! can Sporus feel?
Who breaks a butterfly upon a wheel?
 P. Yet let me flap this bug with gilded wings,
This painted child of dirt, that stinks and stings; 310
Whose buzz the witty and the fair annoys,
Yet wit ne'er tastes, and beauty ne'er enjoys:
So well-bred spaniels civilly delight
In mumbling of the game they dare not bite.
Eternal smiles his emptiness betray, 315
As shallow streams run dimpling all the way.
Whether in florid impotence he speaks,
And, as the prompter breathes, the puppet squeaks;
Or at the ear of Eve,[69] familiar toad,
Half froth, half venom, spits himself abroad, 320
In puns, or politics, or tales, or lies,
Or spite, or smut, or rhymes, or blasphemies.
His wit all see-saw, between that and this,
Now high, now low, now master up, now miss,
And he himself one vile antithesis. 325
Amphibious thing! that acting either part,
The trifling head, or the corrupted heart,
Fop at the toilet, flatterer at the board,
Now trips a lady, and now struts a lord.
Eve's tempter thus the rabbins[70] have expressed, 330
A cherub's face, a reptile all the rest;
Beauty that shocks you, parts that none will trust,
Wit that can creep, and pride that licks the dust.
 Not fortune's worshiper, nor fashion's fool,
Not lucre's madman, nor ambition's tool, 335

[66] Cannons was the estate of the Duke of Chandos. Pope's enemies accused him of satirizing it as Timon's villa in the *Epistle to Burlington*. Pope denied it, pointing out that Cannons had no dean or silver bell, as Timon's villa did.

[67] Sporus is Lord Hervey. Pope got the name from Roman history; the emperor Nero publicly married a boy named Sporus.

[68] Ass's milk was frequently prescribed as a diet for invalids.

[69] Pope, in his note to this line, identifies the allusion to Eve and the serpent in *Paradise Lost* but does not make the further identification of Eve with Queen Caroline, to whom Lord Hervey was a close advisor.

[70] Rabbis; interpreters and commentators on Jewish sacred texts.

Not proud, nor servile; be one poet's praise,
That, if he pleased, he pleased by manly ways:
That flattery, even to kings, he held a shame,
And thought a lie in verse or prose the same.
That not in fancy's maze he wandered long, 340
But stooped[71] to truth, and moralized his song:
That not for fame, but virtue's better end,
He stood the furious foe, the timid friend,
The damning critic, half-approving wit,
The coxcomb hit, or fearing to be hit; 345
Laughed at the loss of friends he never had,
The dull, the proud, the wicked, and the mad;
The distant threats of vengeance on his head,
The blow unfelt, the tear he never shed;
The tale revived, the lie so oft o'erthrown, 350
The imputed trash,[72] and dullness not his own;
The morals blackened when the writings 'scape,
The libelled person, and the pictured shape;[73]
Abuse, on all he loved, or loved him, spread,
A friend in exile,[74] or a father, dead; 355
The whisper, that to greatness still too near,[75]
Perhaps, yet vibrates on his sovereign's ear—
Welcome for thee, fair Virtue! all the past:
For thee, fair Virtue! welcome even the last!
 A. But why insult the poor, affront the great? 360
 P. A knave's a knave, to me, in every state:
Alike my scorn, if he succeed or fail,
Sporus at court, or Japhet[76] in a jail,
A hireling scribbler, or a hireling peer,
Knight of the post[77] corrupt, or of the shire; 365
If on a pillory, or near a throne,
He gain his prince's ear, or lose his own.[78]
 Yet soft by nature, more a dupe than wit,
Sappho can tell you how this man was bit:
This dreaded satirist Dennis will confess 370
Foe to his pride, but friend to his distress:[79]
So humble, he has knocked at Tibbald's door,

[71] In falconry, the hawk "stoops" when it dives on its prey.
[72] Edmund Curll had printed a number of blasphemous and libelous poems falsely attributed to Pope.
[73] Pope's deformed body was frequently the target of his enemies' tasteless attacks.
[74] Pope's friend Francis Atterbury, Bishop of Rochester, was tried in the House of Lords in 1723 on charges of complicity in a plot to restore the Pretender to the throne. He was found guilty and banished.
[75] The whisperer is Lord Hervey, who is "too near" to greatness (Queen Caroline).
[76] Japhet Crook was a famous forger convicted in 1731.
[77] A "knight of the post" was someone who made his living by giving false evidence.
[78] Japhet Crook's punishment included having his ears cut off.
[79] Pope had been "friend to [Dennis's] distress" by writing a prologue to Colley Cibber's play *The Provoked Husband,* performed as a benefit for Dennis in 1733.

Has drunk with Cibber, nay has rhymed for Moore.[80]
Full ten years slandered, did he once reply?
Three thousand suns went down on Welsted's lie.[81] 375
To please a mistress one aspersed his life;
He lashed him not, but let her be his wife:
Let Budgell charge low Grub Street on his quill,[82]
And write whate'er he pleased, except his will;
Let the two Curlls of town and court,[83] abuse 380
His father, mother, body, soul, and Muse.
Yet why? that father held it for a rule,
It was a sin to call our neighbor fool:
That harmless mother thought no wife a whore:
Hear this, and spare his family, James Moore! 385
Unspotted names, and memorable long!
If there be force in virtue, or in song.
 Of gentle blood (part shed in honor's cause,
While yet in Britain honor had applause)
Each parent sprung—— *A.* What fortune, pray?——
 P. Their own, 390
And better got, than Bestia's[84] from the throne.
Born to no pride, inheriting no strife,
Nor marrying discord in a noble wife,
Stranger to civil and religious rage,
The good man walked innoxious through his age. 395
No courts he saw, no suits would ever try,
Nor dared an oath,[85] nor hazarded a lie.
Unlearned, he knew no schoolman's subtle art,
No language, but the language of the heart.
By nature honest, by experience wise, 400
Healthy by temperance, and by exercise;
His life, though long, to sickness passed unknown,
His death was instant, and without a groan.
O grant me thus to live, and thus to die!
Who sprung from kings shall know less joy than I. 405
 O friend! may each domestic bliss be thine!
Be no unpleasing melancholy mine:
Me, let the tender office long engage,
To rock the cradle of reposing age,

[80] Pope, despite his satirical attacks on Cibber, was personally friendly with him. He had allowed James Moore Smythe to use some of his lines for Smythe's play *The Rival Modes* (see l.23 and note).

[81] Welsted's lie, told ten years ("three thousand suns") before, was that Pope had caused the death of the young woman in the "Elegy to the Memory of an Unfortunate Lady" (see l.49 and note).

[82] Eustace Budgell was a hack writer and minor government official who accused Pope (apparently mistakenly) of having accused him of forgery in the *Grubstreet Journal*.

[83] Edmund Curll was the Curll of the town, Lord Hervey that of the court.

[84] Bestia seems to be the Duke of Marlborough, who got his fortune through the favor of Queen Anne. Pope got the name from Calpurnius Bestia, a corrupt Roman consul.

[85] Pope's father refused to take the oaths of allegiance required of Catholics.

With lenient arts extend a mother's breath, 410
Make languor smile, and smooth the bed of death.
Explore the thought, explain the asking eye,
And keep awhile one parent from the sky![86]
On cares like these if length of days attend,
May Heaven, to bless those days, preserve my friend, 415
Preserve him social, cheerful, and serene,
And just as rich as when he served a queen.[87]
 A. Whether that blessing be denied or given,
Thus far was right, the rest belongs to heaven.

Voltaire
(*1694–1778*)

Perhaps no single figure better embodies what is meant by the "Enlightenment," in all its many senses, than the French *philosophe*, playwright, historian, novelist, and poet François-Marie Arouet, who wrote under the pen name Voltaire. During a career that spanned six decades, from 1718 to 1778, he poured out an astonishing number of plays, poems, historical works, polemical pamphlets and essays, satires, and philosophical tales; his collected works run to fifty-two volumes. The recurring rallying cry through all these works is *Écrasez l'infâme!* or "Crush infamy." By infamy, he seems to have meant all forms of intolerance and dogmatism, especially religious, but political, social, artistic, and moral as well, all forms of "darkness" that oppress mankind.

Voltaire was born in 1694 into a prosperous middle-class family in Paris. He was educated at the Jesuit Collège Louis-le-Grand, studied law, and became a member of a circle of Paris wits and free-thinkers who jibed at the intellectual stagnation of the court of Louis XIV. When he was twenty-two, Voltaire was exiled to Sully-sur-Loire for political satires, and a year later he was imprisoned in the Bastille for a similar offense. During the eleven months he spent in prison, he wrote a tragedy, *Oedipus*, which was produced upon his release and made a great success. When it was printed a year later, he took the name Voltaire, a rough anagram of "Arouet," by which he was known for the rest of his life.

Voltaire's long career was marked by enormous energy and productiv-

[86] Pope first drafted these lines in 1731, when he was nursing his mother through a serious illness; she died in 1733.

[87] Dr. Arbuthnot had been physician to Queen Anne; the point of the line is that Arbuthnot had not taken unfair advantage of his position.

ity and by continual political and religious controversy. In 1726, he was again imprisoned in the Bastille and then exiled to England, where he learned English, studied English literature, and became the friend of Pope, Swift, and other prominent English writers of the time. By the age of thirty, he had become wealthy as a result of shrewd speculations; his fortune increased rapidly for the rest of his life, making him one of the richest writers of all time. His wealth gave him a certain measure of independence and allowed him to maintain a series of lavish establishments, where he entertained distinguished visitors from all over the world. During the five years that followed his return from England in 1729, he wrote voluminously, producing a number of successful plays and satiric poems, as well as a history of Charles XII which has been called the first modern history.

In 1734, Voltaire was forced to flee Paris again as the result of the publication of the daring *Philosophical Letters.* He took up residence with the brilliant Madame du Châtelet, at Cirey, in the region of Lorraine in eastern France. Although he was allowed to return to Paris in 1735, he made his home at Cirey during ten years of vigorous literary activity, during which he continued to write tragedies, as well as satires and philosophical and scientific works. After 1743, he recovered some measure of favor at court and was made official Historiographer of France and elected to the French Academy.

In 1749, Madame du Châtelet died; she and Voltaire had continued on good terms, although she had ceased to be his mistress some time before and he had become involved with his niece, the vulgar and ugly Madame Denis. In 1750, he accepted an invitation from Frederick II to take up residence in Prussia, where he remained for three years, until he quarreled with Frederick and was forced to leave. Voltaire then resettled in Switzerland, where he purchased an estate named *Les Délices* (The Delights). Controversy still followed him, especially over the publication of a sardonic article on Geneva in the French *Encyclopedia,* and he left Switzerland after three years to purchase his great estate Ferney, in France near the Swiss frontier. He spent the rest of his life there. Voltaire wrote *Candide* in 1758, the same year he bought Ferney.

During Voltaire's last twenty years, the years at Ferney, he devoted more of his time to political, philosophical, and religious controversy than to literature. He continued to propagandize vigorously in a steady stream of essays, pamphlets, satirical dialogues, didactic tales, and a massive number of private letters. (Voltaire's published correspondence fills 107 volumes.) He was also closely involved in the operation of Ferney, carrying out a number of agricultural experiments and projects to employ the poor. He also took an active part in defenses of a number of people persecuted for their beliefs, including campaigns to rehabilitate the memories of the Huguenots Jean Calas and Sirven, both executed on false charges of murder; La Barre, a youth beheaded on a minor religious charge; and the comte de Lally, governor-general of the French posts in India, who was executed after their loss. In 1778, Voltaire, aged and ill, returned to Paris for the first time in twenty-eight years to be lionized with wild enthusiasm. He witnessed a performance of his last tragedy, *Irene,* at the Comédie-Française and was crowned with a wreath of laurel. The celebration weakened

him, and he died a few weeks later. He had to be buried secretly, the Church having refused him burial; thirteen years later, his body was exhumed and triumphantly reinterred in the Pantheon.

Even after two centuries, the meaning and significance of Voltaire's work remain controversial. The French critic Faguet wittily summed up one view of his work in the famous phrase, "a chaos of clear ideas." Voltaire was often inconsistent in a body of work that was voluminous, produced over a long period of time, and often inspired by immediate circumstances. But certain ideas remain consistent throughout his work, especially his hostility toward all extremes and all forms of absolutism and fanaticism, whether religious, political, or social. In general, Voltaire moved from a rather optimistic rationalism in his early life to a period of comparative pessimism in the early 1750s, a response, perhaps, to a number of personal misfortunes as well as such external events as the Seven Years' War and the Lisbon earthquake, which inspired the despairing "Poem on the Disaster of Lisbon" (1756). In his later years, he turned to a modestly melioristic position, in which he largely abandoned abstract speculation in favor of an emphasis upon small, immediate reforms, expressed in his various crusades and by his work on the *Encyclopedia*, as well as by his reforming projects in his own "garden" of Ferney.

As a writer, Voltaire is one of those men for whom no single masterpiece or handful of major works seems to sum up their total achievement or impact. In his own day, Voltaire was regarded as a great dramatist, historian, and philosopher, as well as a controversialist and general man of letters. Our own perspective has shifted; his tragedies, his epic *The Henriad*, and his massive histories are not much read, and he is valued primarily for his work in minor forms—epigrams, satiric verse, letters, and especially philosophic tales—as well as for the record of his vigorous personality.

Candide is the single work for which Voltaire is now most widely known, and it contains an excellent sampling of Voltaire's sardonic wit as well as many of his most fundamental ideas. Much of the humor is very broad. Candide, Dr. Pangloss, and Cunegund are two-dimensional characters; we could hardly bear the sadism of their horrifying mishaps in this ultimate hard-luck story if they were more real and if we did not know that, even after each apparent death, ravishing, or mutilation, they would pop up again, marvelously and comically restored, like characters in a film cartoon.

Voltaire's satiric point is aimed at a larger target than the ostensible one of Leibnitz's philosophy of Optimism. (The subtitle refers not just to a general attitude but to a formal philosophical concept.) His subject is the problem of how one should live one's life in the face of the pervasive evil of the world, both physical and social, and his satire is directed against all the various dogmas and fanaticisms which man uses to shield himself against reality and to veil his naked self-interest. The various episodes of the book read like a catalogue of the ills flesh is heir to: uncontrollable natural calamities such as tempests and earthquakes, great human disasters that transcend any individual human responsibility such as syphilis and the plague, and calamities in which the innocent suffer along with the guilty such as the naval battle in Chapter 20. But Voltaire saves his most sardonic anger for those evils that have their origin in human illusions: war, the Inquisition,

colonialism and proselytizing by the sword, rabid nationalism, and all the other manifestations of man's cruelty, hypocrisy, and greed.

The comically naive Candide wanders through all these woes, spiritually girded up by the wonderfully absurd Dr. Pangloss, encountering as he goes a great range of possible worlds or human societies. Westphalia, the garden from which he is expelled to begin his wanderings, is a false paradise in the grip of Panglossian self-delusion and petty aristocratic tyranny. Bulgaria, Paraguay, and Holland are ruled by various sorts of military, religious, and economic despotisms, and Lisbon is the seat of religious fanaticism and sadism. The primitive society of the Oreillons represents Voltaire's sardonic commentary on the idealization of the Noble Savage, such as Montaigne's in his essay "Of Cannibals." The world of cities is no better: Paris is a viper's nest of venom and intrigue, and the palace of Pococurante is a place of purposelessness and decadent boredom. Among all these possible worlds, one impossible one stands out as a sort of utopian dream of human happiness, that of El Dorado.

The famous ending of the tale, in which Candide resolves to "take care of his garden," deserves close attention. Candide has remained unshaken in his Panglossian optimism and idealization until the episode in Surinam, when "the villainy of mankind presented itself to his mind in all its deformity, and his soul was a prey to the most gloomy ideas." His drift toward pessimism is spurred by the arrival on the scene of Martin, the "Manichaean" pessimist to balance the optimistic Pangloss. Candide never quite comes to accept Martin's "detestable principles," however, and at the end of the book, he becomes the center of a modest micro-society devoted neither to optimism nor to pessimism but to a meliorism based on honest labor, cooperation, and a realistic view of the possible. This conclusion may sum up the final wisdom of Voltaire, who wrote in his old age: "I have done a bit of good; that is my finest work."

FURTHER READING *(prepared by W. J. R.):* Theodore Besterman's *Voltaire,* 3rd ed. 1976, is a massive and excellent biography, which utilizes a great deal of new information. An appendix offers a long excerpt from Voltaire's autobiography. A less ambitious, introductory work is Wayne Andrews's *Voltaire,* 1981. An even briefer but reliable introduction is Jean Sareil's "Voltaire," in *European Writers: The Age of Reason and the Enlightenment,* Vol. 4, ed. George Stade, 1984. Voltaire is admirably portrayed in the context of his own times in Owen Aldridge's *Voltaire and the Century of Light,* 1975. Aldridge uses the methods of comparative literature to present Voltaire's eighteenth-century France. See also A. J. Ayer's *Voltaire,* 1986. Haydn Mason's *Voltaire,* 1975, attempts to make the writer more accessible to the general public. Mason's work is organized according to significant aspects of Voltaire's career, such as his work as historian and as poet. Ira O. Wade's *Voltaire and "Candide,"* 1959, is an important work in *Candide* criticism, divided into sections on the philosophical background, genesis, publication, and meaning. Ten essays, mostly on topics related to Voltaire as philosopher, are collected in *Voltaire: A Collection of Critical Essays,* ed. William F. Bottiglia, 1968.

CANDIDE

OR

THE OPTIMIST

Translated from the German of Doctor Ralph

With the additions which were found in the Doctor's pocket
when he died at Minden, in the year of grace 1759.[1]

Translated by Tobias Smollett and revised by J. C. Thornton

CHAPTER I

*How Candide was brought up in a magnificent castle, and how he was driven
from thence.*

In the country of Westphalia, in the castle of the most noble Baron of
Thunder-ten-tronckh,[2] lived a youth whom nature had endowed with a
most sweet disposition. His face was the true index of mind. He had a solid
judgment joined to the most unaffected simplicity; and hence, I presume,
he had his name of Candide. The old servants of the house suspected him
to have been the son of the Baron's sister, by a mighty good sort of a
gentleman of the neighborhood, whom that young lady refused to marry,
because he could produce no more than threescore and eleven quarterings
in his arms;[3] the rest of the genealogical tree belonging to the family having
been lost through the injuries of time.

The Baron was one of the most powerful lords in Westphalia; for his
castle had not only a gate, but even windows; and his great hall was hung
with tapestry. He used to hunt with his mastiffs and spaniels instead of
greyhounds; his groom served him for huntsman; and the parson of the
parish officiated as grand almoner.[4] He was called "My Lord" by all his
people, and he never told a story but every one laughed at it.

My lady Baroness weighed three hundred and fifty pounds, conse-
quently was a person of no small consideration; and then she did the hon-
ors of the house with a dignity that commanded universal respect. Her
daughter Cunegund was about seventeen years of age, fresh colored,
comely, plump, and desirable.[5] The Baron's son seemed to be a youth in

[1] "Doctor Ralph" is, of course, a fiction. The battle of Minden, in Westphalia, was an
episode in the Seven Years' War (1756–1763).
[2] Westphalia is a region in northwest Germany. The castle of "Thunder-ten-tronckh" is
fictitious, Voltaire's idea of an absurd German name.
[3] "Quarterings" are groupings of coats of arms upon one shield, to indicate family alli-
ances. Seventy-one quarterings is an absurdly high number.
[4] Dispenser of alms, or charity.
[5] Cunegund is apparently a namesake of Queen Kunigunda, who walked barefoot on red-
hot irons to prove her faithfulness to her husband, Emperor Henry II. The name is somewhat
inappropriate in the light of Cunegund's later sexual career.

every respect worthy of his father. Pangloss the preceptor was the oracle of the family, and little Candide listened to his instructions with all the simplicity natural to his age and disposition.[6]

Master Pangloss taught the metaphysico-theologo-cosmolo-nigology. He could prove to admiration that there is no effect without a cause; and that, in this best of all possible worlds, the Baron's castle was the most magnificent of all castles, and my lady the best of all possible baronesses.[7]

"It is demonstrable," said he, "that things cannot be otherwise than they are; for as all things have been created for some end, they must necessarily be created for the best end. Observe, for instance, the nose is formed for spectacles, therefore we wear spectacles. The legs are visibly designed for stockings, accordingly we wear stockings. Stones were made to be hewn, and to construct castles, therefore my lord has a magnificent castle; for the greatest baron in the province ought to be the best lodged. Swine were intended to be eaten; therefore we eat pork all the year round: and they who assert that everything is right do not express themselves correctly; they should say, that everything is best."[8]

Candide listened attentively, and believed implicitly; for he thought Miss Cunegund excessively handsome, though he never had the courage to tell her so. He concluded that next to the happiness of being Baron of Thunder-ten-tronckh, the next was that of being Miss Cunegund, the next that of seeing her every day, and the last that of hearing the doctrine of Master Pangloss, the greatest philosopher of the whole province, and consequently of the whole world.

One day, when Miss Cunegund went to take a walk in a little neighboring wood, which was called a park, she saw, through the bushes, the sage Doctor Pangloss giving a lecture in experimental physics to her mother's chambermaid, a little brown wench, very pretty, and very tractable. As Miss Cunegund had a great disposition for the sciences, she observed with the utmost attention the experiments which were repeated before her eyes; she perfectly well understood the force of the doctor's reasoning upon causes and effects. She retired greatly flurried, quite pensive, and filled with the desire of knowledge, imagining that she might be a sufficing reason for young Candide, and he for her.

On her way back she happened to meet Candide; she blushed, he blushed also: she wished him a good morning in a faltering tone; he returned the salute, without knowing what he said. The next day, as they were rising from dinner, Cunegund and Candide slipped behind the screen; she dropped her handkerchief, the young man picked it up. She innocently took hold of his hand, and he as innocently kissed hers with a warmth, a sensibility, a grace—all very extraordinary; their lips met; their eyes sparkled; their knees trembled; their hands strayed. The Baron of Thunder-ten-tronckh chanced to come by; he beheld the cause and effect,

[6] Pangloss means "all-tongue," or "explainer-away of everything." Candide suggests "candid" or the French *candide* (ingenuous or artless).

[7] Master Pangloss is a follower of the German philosopher and mathematician Leibnitz (1646–1716), who viewed the world as a hierarchical system of "monads," or units of spiritual force or matter, rising up to the supreme monad, God. His system emphasized strict cause-and-effect relationships and regarded God as allowing freedom of the will while still shaping the world as the best of all possible worlds.

[8] Voltaire is here reducing to absurdity the philosophical "argument from design."

and, without hesitation, saluted Candide with some notable kicks on the breech, and drove him out of doors. Miss Cunegund fainted away, and, as soon as she came to herself, the Baroness boxed her ears. Thus a general consternation was spread over this most magnificent and most agreeable of all possible castles.

CHAPTER II

What befell Candide among the Bulgarians.[9]

Candide, thus driven out of this terrestrial paradise, wandered a long time, without knowing where he went; sometimes he raised his eyes, all bedewed with tears, towards heaven, and sometimes he cast a melancholy look towards the magnificent castle where dwelt the fairest of young baronesses. He laid himself down to sleep in a furrow, heartbroken and supperless. The snow fell in great flakes, and, in the morning when he awoke, he was almost frozen to death; however, he made shift to crawl to the next town, which was called Waldberghoff-trarbkdikdorff, without a penny in his pocket, and half dead with hunger and fatigue. He took up his stand at the door of an inn. He had not been long there, before two men dressed in blue[10] fixed their eyes steadfastly upon him.

"Faith, comrade," said one of them to the other, "yonder is a well-made young fellow, and of the right size."

Thereupon they made up to Candide, and with the greatest civility and politeness invited him to dine with them.

"Gentlemen," replied Candide, with a most engaging modesty, "you do me much honor, but, upon my word, I have no money."

"Money, Sir!" said one of the men in blue to him, "young persons of your appearance and merit never pay anything; why, are not you five feet five inches high?"

"Yes, gentlemen, that is really my size," replied he, with a low bow.

"Come then, Sir, sit down along with us; we will not only pay your reckoning, but will never suffer such a clever young fellow as you to want money. Mankind were born to assist one another."

"You are perfectly right, gentlemen," said Candide; "that is precisely the doctrine of Master Pangloss; and I am convinced that everything is for the best."

His generous companions next entreated him to accept of a few crowns, which he readily complied with, at the same time offering them his note for payment, which they refused, and sat down to table.

"Have you not a great affection for—"

"O yes!" he replied, "I have a great affection for the lovely Miss Cunegund."

"Maybe so," replied one of the men, "but that is not the question! We

[9] The "Bulgarians" are the Prussian troops of Frederick the Great. Voltaire chose the name to suggest sodomy (compare French *bougre* and English "buggery").

[10] Frederick the Great's recruiting officers wore blue uniforms. The recruiters are tall and regard Candide as "the right size" in reference to Prussian regiments that would accept only men over six feet tall.

are asking you whether you have not a great affection for the King of the Bulgarians?"

"For the King of the Bulgarians?" said Candide. "Not at all. Why, I never saw him in my life."

"Is it possible! Oh, he is a most charming king! Come, we must drink his health."

"With all my heart, gentlemen," Candide said, and he tossed off his glass.

"Bravo!" cried the blues; "you are now the support, the defender, the hero of the Bulgarians; your fortune is made; you are on the high road to glory."

So saying, they put him in irons, and carried him away to the regiment. There he was made to wheel about to the right, to the left, to draw his ramrod, to return his ramrod, to present, to fire, to march, and they gave him thirty blows with a cane; the next day he performed his exercise a little better, and they gave him but twenty; the day following he came off with ten, and was looked upon as a young fellow of surprising genius by all his comrades.

Candide was struck with amazement, and could not for the soul of him conceive how he came to be a hero. One fine spring morning, he took it into his head to take a walk, and he marched straight forward, conceiving it to be a privilege of the human species, as well as of the brute creation, to make use of their legs how and when they pleased. He had not gone above two leagues when he was overtaken by four other heroes, six feet high, who bound him neck and heels, and carried him to a dungeon. A court-martial sat upon him, and he was asked which he liked best, either to run the gauntlet six and thirty times through the whole regiment, or to have his brains blown out with a dozen musket-balls. In vain did he remonstrate to them that the human will is free, and that he chose neither; they obliged him to make a choice, and he determined, in virtue of that divine gift called free will, to run the gauntlet six and thirty times. He had gone through his discipline twice, and the regiment being composed of two thousand men, they composed for him exactly four thousand strokes, which laid bare all his muscles and nerves, from the nape of his neck to his rump. As they were preparing to make him set out the third time, our young hero, unable to support it any longer, begged as a favor they would be so obliging as to shoot him through the head. The favor being granted, a bandage was tied over his eyes, and he was made to kneel down. At that very instant, his Bulgarian Majesty, happening to pass by, inquired into the delinquent's crime, and being a prince of great penetration, he found, from what he heard of Candide, that he was a young metaphysician, entirely ignorant of the world; and therefore, out of his great clemency, he condescended to pardon him, for which his name will be celebrated in every journal, and in every age.[11] A skillful surgeon made a cure of Candide in three weeks, by means of emollient unguents prescribed by Dioscorides.[12] His sores were

[11] The incident of Candide's desertion is based on an episode in which Voltaire intervened with Frederick the Great for the release of a French deserter. Leibnitz's doctrine of free will was said to encourage soldiers to desert.

[12] Dioscorides was a first-century A.D. Greek physician and author of a textbook on medicines.

now skinned over, and he was able to march, when the King of the Bulgarians gave battle to the King of the Abares.[13]

CHAPTER III

How Candide escaped from the Bulgarians. And what befell him afterwards.

Never was anything so gallant, so well accoutred, so brilliant, and so finely disposed as the two armies. The trumpets, fifes, hautboys, drums, and cannon, made such harmony as never was heard in hell itself. The entertainment began by a discharge of cannon, which, in the twinkling of an eye, laid flat about six thousand men on each side. The musket bullets swept away, out of the best of all possible worlds, nine or ten thousand scoundrels that infested its surface. The bayonet was next the sufficient reason for the deaths of several thousands. The whole might amount to thirty thousand souls. Candide trembled like a philosopher, and concealed himself as well as he could during this heroic butchery.

At length, while the two kings were causing *Te Deum*[14] to be sung in each of their camps, Candide took a resolution to go and reason somewhere else upon causes and effects. After passing over heaps of dead or dying men, the first place he came to was a neighboring village, in the Abarian territories, which had been burned to the ground by the Bulgarians in accordance with international law. Here lay a number of old men covered with wounds, who beheld their wives dying with their throats cut, and hugging their children to their breasts all stained with blood. There several young virgins, whose bellies had been ripped open after they had satisfied the natural necessities of the Bulgarian heroes, breathed their last; while others, half burned in the flames, begged to be dispatched out of the world. The ground about them was covered with the brains, arms, and legs of dead men.

Candide made all the haste he could to another village, which belonged to the Bulgarians, and there he found that the heroic Abares had enacted the same tragedy. From thence continuing to walk over palpitating limbs, or through ruined buildings, at length he arrived beyond the theater of war, with a little provision in his pouch, and Miss Cunegund's image in his heart. When he arrived in Holland his provisions failed him; but having heard that the inhabitants of that country were all rich and Christians, he made himself sure of being treated by them in the same manner as at the Baron's castle, before he had been driven from thence through the power of Miss Cunegund's bright eyes.

He asked charity of several grave-looking people, who one and all answered him that if he continued to follow this trade, they would have him sent to the house of correction, where he should be taught to earn his bread.

He next addressed himself to a person who had just been haranguing a

[13] There was actually a barbaric tribe named the Abares, but here the name is used for the French, opponents of the Prussians in the Seven Years' War.
[14] An ancient Latin hymn of praise and thanksgiving for victory.

numerous assembly for a whole hour on the subject of charity. The orator, squinting at him under his broad-brimmed hat, asked him sternly, what brought him thither? and whether he was for the good cause?

"Sir," said Candide, in a submissive manner, "I conceive there can be no effect without a cause; everything is necessarily concatenated and arranged for the best. It was necessary that I should be banished from the presence of Miss Cunegund; that I should afterwards run the gauntlet; and it is necessary I should beg my bread, till I am able to earn it: all this could not have been otherwise."

"Hark ye, friend," said the orator, "do you hold the Pope to be Antichrist?"

"Truly, I never heard anything about it," said Candide; "but whether he is or not, I am in want of something to eat."

"Thou deservest not to eat or to drink," replied the orator, "wretch, monster that thou art! hence! avoid my sight, nor ever come near me again while thou livest."

The orator's wife happened to put her head out of the window at that instant, when, seeing a man who doubted whether the Pope was Antichrist, she discharged upon his head a chamber-pot full of ——. Good heavens, to what excess does religious zeal transport the female kind!

A man who had never been christened, an honest Anabaptist, named James, was witness to the cruel and ignominious treatment showed to one of his brethren, to a rational, two-footed, unfledged being.[15] Moved with pity, he carried him to his own house, cleaned him up, gave him meat and drink, and made him a present of two florins, at the same time proposing to instruct him in his own trade of weaving Persian silks which are fabricated in Holland. Candide threw himself at his feet, crying:

"Now I am convinced that Master Pangloss told me truth, when he said that everything was for the best in this world; for I am infinitely more affected by your extraordinary generosity than by the inhumanity of that gentleman in the black cloak and his wife."

The next day, as Candide was walking out, he met a beggar all covered with scabs, his eyes were sunk in his head, the end of his nose was eaten off, his mouth drawn on one side, his teeth as black as coal, snuffling and coughing most violently, and every time he attempted to spit, out dropped a tooth.

CHAPTER IV

How Candide found his old master in philosophy, Dr. Pangloss, again, and what happened to them.

Candide, divided between compassion and horror, but giving way to the former, bestowed on this shocking figure the two florins which the honest Anabaptist James had just before given to him. The spectre looked at him

[15] "Anabaptist" was the scornful name applied to certain sixteenth-century sects who opposed infant baptism; Voltaire respected a number of contemporary Anabaptists. "A rational, two-footed, unfledged (or unfeathered) being" is Plato's definition of man.

very earnestly, shed tears, and threw his arms about his neck. Candide started back aghast.

"Alas!" said the one wretch to the other, "don't you know your dear Pangloss?"

"What do I hear? Is it you, my dear master! you I behold in this piteous plight? What dreadful misfortune has befallen you? What has made you leave the most magnificent and delightful of all castles? What is become of Miss Cunegund, the mirror of young ladies, and nature's masterpiece?"

"Oh Lord!" cried Pangloss, "I am so weak I cannot stand."

Thereupon Candide instantly led him to the Anabaptist's stable, and procured him something to eat. As soon as Pangloss had a little refreshed himself, Candide began to repeat his inquiries concerning Miss Cunegund.

"She is dead," replied the other.

Candide immediately fainted away: his friend recovered him by the help of a little bad vinegar which he found by chance in the stable. Candide opened his eyes.

"Dead! Miss Cunegund dead!" he said. "Ah, where is the best of worlds now? But of what illness did she die? Was it for grief upon seeing her father kick me out of his magnificent castle?"

"No," replied Pangloss; "her belly was ripped open by the Bulgarian soldiers, after they had ravished her as much as it was possible for a damsel to be ravished: they knocked the Baron her father on the head for attempting to defend her; my lady her mother was cut in pieces; my poor pupil was served just in the same manner as his sister;[16] and as for the castle, they have not left one stone upon another; they have destroyed all the ducks, and the sheep, the barns, and the trees: but we have had our revenge, for the Abares have done the very same thing in a neighboring barony, which belonged to a Bulgarian lord."

At hearing this, Candide fainted away a second time; but, having come to himself again, he said all that it became him to say; he inquired into the cause and effect, as well as into the sufficing reason, that had reduced Pangloss to so miserable a condition.

"Alas!" replied the other, "it was love: love, the comfort of the human species; love, the preserver of the universe, the soul of all sensible beings; love! tender love!"

"Alas," replied Candide, "I have had some knowledge of love myself, this sovereign of hearts, this soul of souls; yet it never cost me more than a kiss, and twenty kicks on the backside. But how could this beautiful cause produce in you so hideous an effect?"

Pangloss made answer in these terms: "O my dear Candide, you must remember Pacquette, that pretty wench, who waited on our noble Baroness; in her arms I tasted the pleasures of paradise, which produced these hell-torments with which you see me devoured. She was infected with the disease, and perhaps is since dead of it; she received this present of a learned cordelier,[17] who derived it from the fountain-head; he was indebted for it to an old countess, who had it of a captain of horse, who had

[16] Voltaire slyly associates Cunegund's brother with homosexuality throughout.
[17] A cordelier is a Franciscan friar, so called because of his girtle of knotted cord.

it of a marchioness, who had it of a page; the page had it of a Jesuit, who, during his novitiate, had it in a direct line from one of the fellow-adventurers of Christopher Columbus;[18] for my part I shall give it to nobody, I am a dying man."

"O Pangloss," cried Candide, "what a strange genealogy is this! Is not the devil the root of it?"

"Not at all," replied the great man, "it was a thing unavoidable, a necessary ingredient in the best of worlds; for if Columbus had not, in an island of America, caught this disease, which contaminates the source of generation, and frequently impedes propagation itself, and is evidently opposite to the great end of nature, we should have had neither chocolate nor cochineal. It is also to be observed that, even to the present time, in this continent of ours, this malady, like our religious controversies, is peculiar to ourselves. The Turks, the Indians, the Persians, the Chinese, the Siamese, and the Japanese are entirely unacquainted with it; but there is a sufficing reason for them to know it in a few centuries. In the meantime, it is making prodigious progress among us, especially in those armies composed of well-disciplined hirelings, who determine the fate of nations; for we may safely affirm that, when an army of thirty thousand men fights another equal in number, there are about twenty thousand of them poxed on each side."

"Very surprising, indeed," said Candide, "but you must get cured."

"How can I?" said Pangloss: "My dear friend, I have not a penny in the world; and you know one cannot be bled, or have a clyster,[19] without a fee."

This last speech had its effect on Candide; he flew to the charitable Anabaptist James, he flung himself at his feet, and gave him so touching a picture of the miserable situation of his friend, that the good man, without any further hesitation, agreed to take Dr. Pangloss into his house, and to pay for his cure. The cure was effected with only the loss of one eye and an ear. As he wrote a good hand and understood accounts tolerably well, the Anabaptist made him his book-keeper. At the expiration of two months, being obliged to go to Lisbon, about some mercantile affairs, he took the two philosophers with him in the same ship; Pangloss, during the voyage, explained to him how everything was so constituted that it could not be better. James did not quite agree with him on this point.

"Mankind," said he, "must, in some things, have deviated from their original innocence; for they were not born wolves, and yet they worry one another like those beasts of prey. God never gave them twenty-four pounders nor bayonets, and yet they have made cannon and bayonets to destroy one another. To this account I might add, not only bankruptcies, but the law, which seizes on the effects of bankrupts, only to cheat the creditors."

"All this was indispensably necessary," replied the one-eyed doctor; "for private misfortunes are public benefits; so that the more private misfortunes there are, the greater is the general good."

While he was arguing in this manner, the sky was overcast, the winds

[18] Voltaire is reflecting the belief that syphilis came to Europe from America.
[19] An enema.

blew from the four quarters of the compass, and the ship was assailed by a most terrible tempest, within sight of the port of Lisbon.

CHAPTER V

A tempest, a shipwreck, an earthquake; and what else befell Dr. Pangloss, Candide, and James the Anabaptist.

One half of the passengers, weakened and half dead with the inconceivable anguish which the rolling of a vessel at sea occasions to the nerves and all the humors of the body, tossed about in opposite directions, were lost to all sense of the danger that surrounded them. The other made loud outcries, or betook themselves to their prayers; the sails were blown into shivers, and the masts were brought by the board. The vessel leaked. Every one was busily employed, but nobody could be either heard or obeyed. The Anabaptist, being upon deck, lent a helping hand as well as the rest, when a brutish sailor gave him a blow, and laid him speechless; but, with the violence of the blow, the tar himself tumbled head foremost overboard, and fell upon a piece of the broken mast, which he immediately grasped. Honest James flew to his assistance, and hauled him in again, but, in the attempt, was thrown overboard himself in sight of the sailor, who left him to perish without taking the least notice of him. Candide, who beheld all that passed, and saw his benefactor one moment rising above water, and the next swallowed up by the merciless waves, was preparing to jump after him; but was prevented by the philosopher Pangloss, who demonstrated to him that the coast of Lisbon had been made on purpose for the Anabaptist to be drowned there. While he was proving his argument *à priori,*[20] the ship foundered, and the whole crew perished, except Pangloss, Candide, and the brute of a sailor who had been the means of drowning the good Anabaptist. The villain swam ashore; but Pangloss and Candide got to land upon a plank.

As soon as they had recovered a little, they walked towards Lisbon; with what little money they had left they thought to save themselves from starving after having escaped drowning.

Scarce had they done lamenting the loss of their benefactor and set foot in the city, when they perceived the earth to tremble under their feet, and the sea, swelling and foaming in the harbor, dash in pieces the vessels that were riding at anchor. Large sheets of flames and cinders covered the streets and public places; the houses tottered, and were tumbled topsy-turvy, even to their foundations, which were themselves destroyed, and thirty thousand inhabitants of both sexes, young and old, were buried beneath the ruins.[21]

The sailor, whistling and swearing, cried, "Damn it, there's something to be got here."

[20] An *a priori* argument is independent of factual support.
[21] Lisbon was destroyed by a major earthquake and fire on November 1, 1755. Voltaire wrote a long poem on the subject, "Poem on the Disaster of Lisbon" (1756), in which he used the incident to attack the idea of a benevolent Providence.

"What can be the sufficing reason of this phenomenon?" said Pangloss.

"It is certainly the day of judgment," said Candide.

The sailor, defying death in the pursuit of plunder, rushed into the midst of the ruin, where he found some money, with which he got drunk, and after he had slept himself sober, he purchased the favors of the first good-natured wench that came his way, amidst the ruins of demolished houses, and the groans of half-buried and expiring persons. Pangloss pulled him by the sleeve.

"Friend," said he, "this is not right, you trespass against the universal reason, and have mistaken your time."

"Death and zounds!" answered the other, "I am a sailor, and born at Batavia, and have trampled four times upon the crucifix in as many voyages to Japan:[22] you are come to a good hand with your universal reason."

Candide, who had been wounded by some pieces of stone that fell from the houses, lay stretched in the street, almost covered with rubbish.

"For God's sake," said he to Pangloss, "get me a little wine and oil. I am dying."

"This concussion of the earth is no new thing," replied Pangloss, "the city of Lima, in America, experienced the same last year; the same cause, the same effects: there is certainly a train of sulphur all the way under ground from Lima to Lisbon."

"Nothing more probable," said Candide; "but, for the love of God, a little oil and wine."

"Probable!" replied the philosopher, "I maintain that the thing is demonstrable."

Candide fainted away, and Pangloss fetched him some water from a neighboring spring.

The next day, in searching among the ruins, they found some eatables with which they repaired their exhausted strength. After this, they assisted the inhabitants in relieving the distressed and wounded. Some, whom they had humanely assisted, gave them as good a dinner as could be expected under such terrible circumstances. The repast, indeed, was mournful, and the company moistened their bread with their tears; but Pangloss endeavored to comfort them under this affliction by affirming that things could not be otherwise than they were.

"For," said he, "all this is for the very best end; for if there is a volcano at Lisbon, it could be on no other spot; for it is impossible for things not to be as they are, for everything is for the best."

By his side sat a little man dressed in black, who was one of the familiars of the Inquisition.[23] This person, taking him up with great politeness, said, "Possibly, my good Sir, you do not believe in original sin; for if everything is best, there could have been no such thing as the fall or punishment of man."

"I humbly ask your Excellency's pardon," answered Pangloss, still more

[22] Batavia is the former Dutch name for Djakarta, in Java. The Dutch were the only Europeans allowed into Japan in the seventeenth century. The belief that they had to trample on the crucifix to gain entry was a widespread slander.

[23] A familiar was an undercover agent of the Inquisition.

politely; "for the fall of man, and the curse consequent thereupon necessarily entered into the system of the best of worlds."

"That is as much as to say, Sir," rejoined the familiar, "you do not believe in free will."

"Your Excellency will be so good as to excuse me," said Pangloss; "free will is consistent with absolute necessity; for it was necessary we should be free, for in that the will——"

Pangloss was in the midst of his proposition, when the familiar made a sign to the attendant who was helping him to a glass of port wine.

CHAPTER VI

How the Portuguese made a superb auto-da-fé to prevent any future earthquakes, and how Candide underwent public flagellation.

After the earthquake which had destroyed three-quarters of the city of Lisbon, the sages of that country could think of no means more effectual to preserve the kingdom from utter ruin, than to entertain the people with an *auto-da-fé*,[24] it having been decided by the University of Coimbra that burning a few people alive by a slow fire, and with great ceremony, is an infallible secret to prevent earthquakes.

In consequence thereof they had seized on a Biscayan for marrying his godmother, and on two Portuguese for taking out the bacon of a larded pullet they were eating.[25] After dinner they came and secured Dr. Pangloss, and his pupil Candide; the one for speaking his mind, and the other for seeming to approve what he had said. They were conducted to separate apartments, extremely cool, where they were never incommoded with the sun. Eight days afterwards they were each dressed in a *fanbenito*,[26] and their heads were adorned with paper mitres. The mitre and *fanbenito* worn by Candide were painted with flames reversed, and with devils that had neither tails nor claws; but Dr. Pangloss's devils had both tails and claws, and his flames were upright. In these habits they marched in procession, and heard a very pathetic sermon, which was followed by a chant, beautifully intoned. Candide was flogged in regular cadence, while the chant was being sung; the Biscayan, and the two men who would not eat bacon, were burnt, and Pangloss was hanged, although this is not a common custom at these solemnities. The same day there was another earthquake, which made most dreadful havoc.[27]

Candide, amazed, terrified, confounded, astonished, and trembling from head to foot, said to himself, "If this is the best of all possible worlds, what are the others? If I had only been whipped, I could have put up with it, as I did among the Bulgarians; but, O my dear Pangloss! thou greatest of

[24] An *auto de fé* (literally "act of faith") was the public announcement of a judgment of the Inquisition, followed by execution of the judgment.
[25] The Biscayan is accused of violating the ecclesiastical laws against spiritual incest. The Portuguese are suspected of being Jews.
[26] A *fanbenito* was a long yellow cape worn by prisoners of the Inquisition.
[27] Lisbon experienced a second earthquake on December 21, 1755.

philosophers! that ever I should live to see thee hanged, without knowing for what! O my dear Anabaptist, thou best of men, that it should be thy fate to be drowned in the very harbor! O Miss Cunegund, you mirror of young ladies! that it should be your fate to have your belly ripped open."

He was making the best of his way from the place where he had been preached to, whipped, absolved, and received benediction, when he was accosted by an old woman, who said to him, "Take courage, my son, and follow me."

CHAPTER VII

How the old woman took care of Candide, and how he found the object of his love.

Candide followed the old woman, though without taking courage, to a decayed house where she gave him a pot of pomatum to anoint his sores, showed him a very neat bed, with a suit of clothes hanging up by it; and set victuals and drink before him.

"There," said she, "eat, drink, and sleep, and may our blessed Lady of Atocha, and the great St. Anthony of Padua, and the illustrious St. James of Compostella, take you under their protection. I shall be back to-morrow."

Candide, struck with amazement at what he had seen, at what he had suffered, and still more with the charity of the old woman, would have shown his acknowledgment by kissing her hand.

"It is not my hand you ought to kiss," said the old woman, "I shall be back to-morrow. Anoint your back, eat, and take your rest."

Candide, notwithstanding so many disasters, ate and slept. The next morning, the old woman brought him his breakfast; examined his back, and rubbed it herself with another ointment. She returned at the proper time, and brought him his dinner; and at night she visited him again with his supper. The next day she observed the same ceremonies.

"Who are you?" said Candide to her. "What god has inspired you with so much goodness? What return can I ever make you?"

The good old beldame kept a profound silence. In the evening she returned, but without his supper.

"Come along with me," said she, "but do not speak a word."

She took him by the arm, and walked with him about a quarter of a mile into the country, till they came to a lonely house surrounded with moats and gardens. The old woman knocked at a little door, which was immediately opened, and she showed him up a pair of back stairs into a small, but richly furnished apartment. There she made him sit down on a brocaded sofa, shut the door upon him, and left him. Candide thought himself in a trance; he looked upon his whole life hitherto as a frightful dream, and the present moment as a very agreeable one.

The old woman soon returned, supporting with great difficulty a young lady, who appeared scarce able to stand. She was of a majestic mien and stature; her dress was rich, and glittering with diamonds, and her face was covered with a veil.

"Take off that veil," said the old woman to Candide.

The young man approached, and, with a trembling hand, took off her veil. What a happy moment! What surprise! He thought he beheld Miss Cunegund; he did behold her, it was she herself. His strength failed him, he could not utter a word, he fell at her feet. Cunegund fainted upon the sofa. The old woman bedewed them with spirits; they recovered; they began to speak. At first they could express themselves only in broken accents; their questions and answers were alternately interrupted with sighs, tears, and exclamations. The old woman desired them to make less noise; and left them together.

"Good heavens!" cried Candide, "is it you? Is it Miss Cunegund I behold, and alive? Do I find you again in Portugal? Then you have not been ravished? They did not rip open your belly, as the philosopher Pangloss informed me?"

"Indeed but they did," replied Miss Cunegund; "but these two accidents do not always prove mortal."

"But were your father and mother killed?"

"Alas!" answered she, "it is but too true!" and she wept.

"And your brother?"

"And my brother also."

"And how did you come to Portugal? And how did you know of my being here? And by what strange adventure did you contrive to have me brought into this house?"

"I will tell you all," replied the lady, "but first you must acquaint me with all that has befallen you since the innocent kiss you gave me, and the rude kicking you received."

Candide, with the greatest submission, obeyed her, and though he was still wrapped in amazement, though his voice was low and tremulous, though his back pained him, yet he gave her a most ingenuous account of everything that had befallen him since the moment of their separation. Cunegund, with her eyes uplifted to heaven, shed tears when he related the death of the good Anabaptist James, and of Pangloss; after which, she thus related her adventures to Candide, who lost not one syllable she uttered, and seemed to devour her with his eyes all the time she was speaking.

CHAPTER VIII

The history of Cunegund.

"I was in bed and fast asleep, when it pleased heaven to send the Bulgarians to our delightful castle of Thunder-ten-tronckh, where they murdered my father and brother, and cut my mother in pieces. A tall Bulgarian soldier, six feet high, perceiving that I had fainted away at this sight, attempted to ravish me; the operation brought me to my senses. I cried, I struggled, I bit, I scratched, I would have torn the tall Bulgarian's eyes out, not knowing that what had happened at my father's castle was a customary thing. The brutal soldier gave me a cut in the left groin with his hanger,[28] the mark of which I still carry."

[28] A light sabre.

"I hope I shall see it," said Candide, with all imaginable simplicity. "You shall," said Cunegund; "but let me proceed."

"Pray do," replied Candide.

She continued. "A Bulgarian captain came in and saw me weltering in my blood, and the soldier still as busy as if no one had been present. The officer, enraged at the fellow's want of respect to him, killed him with one stroke of his sabre as he lay upon me. This captain took care of me, had me cured, and carried me prisoner of war to his quarters. I washed what little linen he was master of, and dressed his victuals: he thought me very pretty, it must be confessed; neither can I deny that he was well made, and had a white soft skin, but he was very stupid, and knew nothing of philosophy: it might plainly be perceived that he had not been educated under Doctor Pangloss. In three months' time, having gamed away all his money, and being grown tired of me, he sold me to a Jew, named Don Issachar, who traded in Holland and Portugal, and was passionately fond of women. This Jew showed me great kindness in hopes to gain my favors; but he never could prevail on me. A modest woman may be once ravished; but her virtue is greatly strengthened thereby. In order to make sure of me, he brought me to this country house you now see. I had hitherto believed that nothing could equal the beauty of the castle of Thunder-ten-tronckh; but I found I was mistaken.

"The Grand Inquisitor saw me one day at mass, ogled me all the time of service, and, when it was over, sent to let me know he wanted to speak with me about some private business. I was conducted to his palace, where I told him of my parentage: he represented to me how much it was beneath a person of my birth to belong to an Israelite. He caused a proposal to be made to Don Issachar that he should resign me to his lordship. Don Issachar, being the court banker, and a man of credit, was not easily to be prevailed upon. His lordship threatened him with an *auto-da-fé;* in short, my Jew was frightened into a compromise, and it was agreed between them that the house and myself should belong to both in common; that the Jew should have Monday, Wednesday, and the Sabbath to himself; and the Inquisitor the other days of the week. This agreement has lasted almost six months; but not without several disputes, whether the space from Saturday night to Sunday morning belonged to the old or the new law.[29] For my part, I have hitherto withstood them both, and truly I believe this is the very reason why they both still love me.

"At length, to turn aside the scourge of earthquakes, and to intimidate Don Issachar, my lord Inquisitor was pleased to celebrate an *auto-da-fé.* He did me the honor to invite me to the ceremony. I had a very good seat; and refreshments were offered the ladies between mass and the execution. I was dreadfully shocked at the burning of the two Jews, and the honest Biscayan who married his godmother; but how great was my surprise, my consternation, and concern, when I beheld a figure so like Pangloss, dressed in a *sanbenito* and mitre! I rubbed my eyes, I looked at him attentively. I saw him hanged, and I fainted away: scarce had I recovered my senses, when I beheld you stark naked; this was the height of horror, grief,

[29]The "old law" is that of the Old Testament, hence of the Jew; the "new law" that of the New Testament, or the Christian.

and despair. I must confess to you for a truth, that your skin is far whiter and more blooming than that of the Bulgarian captain. This spectacle worked me up to a pitch of distraction. I screamed out, and would have said, 'Hold, barbarians!' but my voice failed me; and indeed my cries would have been useless. After you had been severely whipped I said to myself, 'How is it possible that the lovely Candide and the sage Pangloss should be at Lisbon, the one to receive a hundred lashes, and the other to be hanged by order of my lord Inquisitor, of whom I am so great a favorite? Pangloss deceived me most cruelly, in saying that everything is fittest and best.'

"Thus agitated and perplexed, now distracted and lost, now half dead with grief, I revolved in my mind the murder of my father, mother, and brother; the insolence of the rascally Bulgarian soldier; the wound he gave me in the groin; my servitude; my being a cook wench to my Bulgarian captain; my subjection to the villainous Don Issachar, and my cruel Inquisitor; the hanging of Doctor Pangloss; the *Miserere*[30] sung while you were whipped; and particularly the kiss I gave you behind the screen the last day I ever beheld you. I returned thanks to God for having brought you to the place where I was, after so many trials. I charged the old woman who attends me to bring you hither, as soon as possible. She has carried out my orders well, and I now enjoy the inexpressible satisfaction of seeing you, hearing you, and speaking to you. But you must certainly be half dead with hunger; I myself have got a good appetite, and so let us sit down to supper."

Upon this the two lovers immediately placed themselves at table, and, after having supped they returned to seat themselves again on the magnificent sofa already mentioned; they were there when Signor Don Issachar, one of the masters of the house, entered unexpectedly; it was the Sabbath day, and he came to enjoy his privilege, and sigh forth his tender passion.

CHAPTER IX

What happened to Cunegund, Candide, the Grand Inquisitor, and the Jew.

This same Issachar was the most choleric little Hebrew that had ever been in Israel since the captivity in Babylon.

"What," said he, "you Galilean bitch, my lord Inquisitor was not enough for thee, but this rascal must come in for a share with me?"

Uttering these words, he drew out a long poniard[31] which he always carried about him, and never dreaming that his adversary had any arms, he attacked him most furiously; but our honest Westphalian had received a handsome sword from the old woman with the suit of clothes. Candide drew his rapier; and though he was the most gentle, sweet-tempered young man breathing, he whipped it into the Israelite and laid him sprawling on the floor at the fair Cunegund's feet.

"Holy Virgin!" cried she, "what will become of us? A man killed in my apartment! If the peace-officers come, we are undone."

"Had not Pangloss been hanged," replied Candide, "he would have

[30] The *Miserere* ("have pity") is the 51st Psalm, a penitential hymn. [31] Dagger.

given us most excellent advice in this emergency, for he was a profound philosopher. But, since he is not here, let us consult the old woman."

She was very intelligent, and was beginning to give her advice when another door opened suddenly. It was now one o'clock in the morning, and of course the beginning of Sunday, which, by agreement, fell to the lot of my lord Inquisitor. Entering, he discovered the flagellated Candide with his drawn sword in his hand, a dead body stretched on the floor, Cunegund frightened out of her wits, and the old woman giving advice.

At that very moment a sudden thought came into Candide's head.

"If this holy man," thought he, "should call assistance, I shall most undoubtedly be consigned to the flames, and Miss Cunegund may perhaps meet with no better treatment; besides, he was the cause of my being so cruelly whipped; he is my rival; and I have now begun to dip my hands in blood; there is no time to hesitate."

This whole train of reasoning was clear and instantaneous; so that, without giving time to the Inquisitor to recover from his surprise, he ran him through the body, and laid him by the side of the Jew.

"Good God!" cried Cunegund, "here's another fine piece of work! now there can be no mercy for us, we are excommunicated; our last hour is come. But how in the name of wonder could you, who are of so mild a temper, dispatch a Jew and a prelate in two minutes' time?"

"Beautiful lady," answered Candide, "when a man is in love, is jealous, and has been flogged by the Inquisition, he becomes lost to all reflection."

The old woman then put in her word.

"There are three Andalusian horses in the stable," said she, "with as many bridles and saddles; let the brave Candide get them ready; madam has moidores[32] and jewels; let us mount immediately, though I have only one buttock to sit upon; let us set out for Cadiz; it is the finest weather in the world, and there is great pleasure in travelling in the cool of the night."

Candide, without any further hesitation, saddled the three horses; and Miss Cunegund, the old woman, and he set out, and travelled thirty miles without once stopping. While they were making the best of their way, the Holy Brotherhood[33] entered the house. My Lord the Inquisitor was interred in a magnificent manner, and Issachar's body was thrown upon a dunghill.

Candide, Cunegund, and the old woman had, by this time, reached the little town of Aracena, in the midst of the mountains of Sierra Morena, and were engaged in the following conversation in an inn.

CHAPTER X

In what distress Candide, Cunegund, and the old woman arrive at Cadiz; and of their embarkation.

"Who could it be who has robbed me of my moidores and jewels?" exclaimed Miss Cunegund, all bathed in tears. "How shall we live? What shall we do? Where shall I find Inquisitors and Jews who can give me more?"

[32] Portuguese and Brazilian coins.
[33] The "Holy Brotherhood" was a Spanish semi-religious order with police powers.

"Alas!" said the old woman, "I have a shrewd suspicion of a reverend father cordelier, who lay last night in the same inn with us at Badajoz: God forbid I should condemn any one wrongfully, but he came into our room twice, and he set off in the morning long before us."

"Alas!" said Candide, "Pangloss has often demonstrated to me that the goods of this world are common to all men, and that every one has an equal right to the enjoyment of them; but, according to these principles, the cordelier ought to have left us enough to carry us to the end of our journey. Have you nothing at all left, my beautiful Cunegund?"

"Not a sou," replied she.

"What is to be done then?" said Candide.

"Sell one of the horses," replied the old woman, "I will get behind my young lady though I have only one buttock to ride on, and we shall reach Cadiz, never fear."

In the same inn there was a Benedictine prior who bought the horse very cheap. Candide, Cunegund, and the old woman, after passing through Lucena, Chellas, and Lebrija, arrived at length at Cadiz. A fleet was then getting ready, and troops were assembling in order to reduce the reverend fathers, the Jesuits of Paraguay, who were accused of having excited one of the Indian tribes, in the neighborhood of the town of the Holy Sacrament,[34] to revolt against the Kings of Spain and Portugal. Candide, having been in the Bulgarian service, performed the military exercise of that nation before the general of this little army with so intrepid an air, and with such agility and expedition that he gave him the command of a company of foot. Being now made a captain, he embarked with Miss Cunegund, the old woman, two valets, and the two Andalusian horses which had belonged to the Grand Inquisitor of Portugal.

During their voyage they amused themselves with many profound reasonings on poor Pangloss's philosophy.

"We are now going into another world," said Candide, "and surely it must be there that everything is best; for I must confess that we have had some little reason to complain of what passes in ours, both as to the physical and moral part."

"Though I have a sincere love for you," said Miss Cunegund, "yet I still shudder at the reflection of what I have seen and experienced."

"All will be well," replied Candide, "the sea of this new world is already better than our European seas: it is smoother, and the winds blow more regularly."

"God grant it," said Cunegund; "but I have met with such terrible treatment in this that I have almost lost all hopes of a better."

"What murmuring and complaining is here indeed!" cried the old woman. "If you had suffered half what I have done, there might be some reason for it."

Miss Cunegund could scarcely refrain from laughing at the good old woman, and thought it droll enough to pretend to a greater share of misfortunes than herself.

"Alas! my good dame," said she, "unless you have been ravished by two Bulgarians, have received two deep wounds in your belly, have seen two of

[34] Colonia del Sacramento, in Paraguay.

your own castles demolished, and beheld two fathers and two mothers barbarously murdered before your eyes, and, to sum up all, have had two lovers whipped at an *auto-da-fé,* I cannot see how you could be more unfortunate than me. Add to this, though born a baroness and bearing seventy-two quarterings, I have been reduced to a cook-wench."

"Miss," replied the old woman, "you do not know my family as yet; but if I were to show you my backside, you would not talk in this manner, but suspend your judgment."

This speech raised a high curiosity in Candide and Cunegund; and the old woman continued as follows.

CHAPTER XI

The history of the old woman.

"I have not always been blear-eyed. My nose did not always touch my chin, nor was I always a servant. You must know that I am the daughter of Pope Urban X,[35] and of the Princess of Palestrina. Up to the age of fourteen I was brought up in a castle, compared with which all the castles of the German barons would not have been fit for stabling, and one of my robes would have bought half the province of Westphalia. I grew in beauty, in wit, and in every graceful accomplishment, in the midst of pleasures, homage, and the highest expectations. I already began to inspire the men with love: my breast began to take its right form; and such a breast! white, firm, and formed like that of Venus of Medici: my eyebrows were as black as jet; and as for my eyes, they darted flames, and eclipsed the lustre of the stars, as I was told by the poets of our part of the world. My maids, when they dressed and undressed me, used to fall into an ecstasy in viewing me before and behind: and all the men longed to be in their places.

"I was contracted to a sovereign prince of Massa-Carrara. Such a prince! as handsome as myself, sweet-tempered, agreeable, of brilliant wit, and in love with me over head and ears. I loved him too, as our sex generally do for the first time, with transport and idolatry. The nuptials were prepared with surprising pomp and magnificence; the ceremony was attended with a succession of feasts, carousals, and burlesques: all Italy composed sonnets in my praise, though not one of them was tolerable. I was on the point of reaching the summit of bliss, when an old marchioness who had been mistress to the Prince my husband invited him to drink chocolate. In less than two hours after he returned from the visit he died of most terrible convulsions: but this is a mere trifle. My mother, in despair, and yet less afflicted than me, determined to absent herself for some time from so fatal a place. As she had a very fine estate in the neighborhood of Gaeta, we embarked on board a galley which was gilded like the high altar of St. Peter's at Rome. In our passage we were boarded by a Sallee corsair. Our men defended themselves like true Pope's soldiers; they flung themselves

[35] As Voltaire pointed out in a note, there was never a pope named Urban X.

upon their knees, laid down their arms and begged the corsair to give them absolution *in articulo mortis.*[36]

"The Moors presently stripped us as bare as monkeys. My mother, my maids of honor, and myself, were served all in the same manner. It is amazing how quick these gentry are at undressing people. But what surprised me most was that they thrust their fingers into that part of our bodies where we women seldom permit anything but enemas to enter. I thought it a very strange kind of ceremony; for thus we are generally apt to judge of things when we have not seen the world. I afterwards learnt that it was to discover if we had any diamonds concealed. This practice has been established since time immemorial among those civilized nations that scour the seas. I was informed that the religious Knights of Malta never fail to make this search, whenever any Moors of either sex fall into their hands. It is a part of the law of nations from which they never deviate.

"I need not tell you how great a hardship it was for a young princess and her mother to be made slaves and carried to Morocco. You may easily imagine what we must have suffered on board a corsair. My mother was still extremely handsome, our maids of honor, and even our common waiting-women, had more charms than were to be found in all Africa. As to myself, I was enchanting; I was beauty itself, and then I had my virginity. But, alas! I did not retain it long; this precious flower, which was reserved for the lovely Prince of Massa-Carrara, was cropped by the captain of the Moorish vessel, who was a hideous negro, and thought he did me infinite honor. Indeed, both the Princess of Palestrina and myself must have had very strong constitutions to undergo all the hardships and violences we suffered till our arrival at Morocco. But I will not detain you any longer with such common things; they are hardly worth mentioning.

"Upon our arrival at Morocco, we found that kingdom bathed in blood. Fifty sons of the Emperor Muley Ishmael[37] were each at the head of a party. This produced fifty civil wars of blacks against blacks, of blacks against tawnies, of tawnies against tawnies, and of mulattoes against mulattoes. In short, the whole empire was one continual scene of carnage.

"No sooner were we landed than a party of blacks, of a contrary faction to that of my captain, came to rob him of his booty. Next to the money and jewels, we were the most valuable things he had. I was witness on this occasion to such a battle as you never beheld in your cold European climates. The northern nations have not that fermentation in their blood, nor that raging lust for women that is so common in Africa. The natives of Europe seem to have their veins filled with milk only; but fire and vitriol circulate in those of the inhabitants of Mount Atlas and the neighboring provinces. They fought with the fury of the lions, tigers, and serpents of their country, to know who should have us. A Moor seized my mother by the right arm, while my captain's lieutenant held her by the left; another Moor laid hold of her by one leg, and one of our corsairs held her by the other. In this manner were almost every one of our women dragged between soldiers. My captain kept me concealed behind him, and with his

[36] "At the point of death."
[37] Muley Ishmael was a real Sultan of Morocco (1646?–1727).

drawn scimitar cut down every one who opposed him; at length I saw all our Italian women and my mother mangled and torn in pieces by the monsters who contended for them. The captives, my companions, the Moors who had taken them, the soldiers, the sailors, the blacks, the tawnies, the whites, the mulattoes, and lastly my captain himself, were all slain, and I remained alone expiring upon a heap of dead bodies. The like barbarous scenes were enacted every day over the whole country, which is an extent of three hundred leagues, and yet they never missed the five stated times of prayer enjoined by their prophet Mahomet.

"I disentangled myself with great difficulty from such a heap of slaughtered bodies, and made shift to crawl to a large orange tree that stood on the bank of a neighboring rivulet, where I fell down exhausted with terror, and overwhelmed with horror, despair, and hunger. My senses being overpowered, I fell asleep, or rather seemed to be in a trance. Thus I lay in a state of weakness and insensibility between life and death, when I felt myself pressed by something that moved up and down upon my body. This brought me to myself; I opened my eyes, and saw a pretty fair-faced man, who sighed and muttered these words between his teeth, '*O che sciagura d'essere senza coglioni!*' "[38]

CHAPTER XII

The adventures of the old woman continued.

"Astonished and delighted to hear my native language, and no less surprised at the young man's words, I told him that there were far greater misfortunes in the world than what he complained of. And to convince him of it, I gave him a short history of the horrible disasters that had befallen me; and again fell into a swoon. He carried me in his arms to a neighboring cottage, where he had me put to bed, procured me something to eat, waited on me, comforted me, caressed me, told me that he had never seen anything so perfectly beautiful as myself, and that he had never so much regretted the loss of what no one could restore to him."

" 'I was born at Naples,' said he, 'where they caponize[39] two or three thousand children every year: several die of the operation; some acquire voices far beyond the most tuneful of your ladies; and others are sent to govern states and empires. I underwent this operation very happily, and was one of the singers in the Princess of Palestrina's chapel.'

" 'How,' cried I, 'in my mother's chapel!'

" 'The Princess of Palestrina, your mother!' cried he, bursting into a flood of tears, 'is it possible you should be the beautiful young princess whom I had the care of bringing up till she was six years old, and who, at that tender age, promised to be as fair as I now behold you?'

" 'I am the same,' I replied. 'My mother lies about a hundred yards from here, cut in pieces, and buried under a heap of dead bodies.'

"I then related to him all that had befallen me, and he in return acquainted me with all his adventures, and how he had been sent to the court

[38] "Oh, what a misfortune to have no testicles!" [39] Castrate.

of the King of Morocco by a Christian prince to conclude a treaty with that monarch; in consequence of which he was to be furnished with military stores, and ships to enable him to destroy the commerce of other Christian governments.

" 'I have executed my commission,' said the eunuch; 'I am going to take shipping at Ceuta, and I'll take you along with me to Italy. *Ma che sciagura d'essere senza coglioni!'*

"I thanked him with tears of joy; but, instead of taking me with him into Italy, he carried me to Algiers, and sold me to the dey of that province. I had not been long a slave when the plague, which had made the tour of Africa, Asia, and Europe, broke out at Algiers with redoubled fury. You have seen an earthquake; but tell me, miss, had you ever the plague?"

"Never," answered the young Baroness.

"If you ever had," continued the old woman, "you would own an earthquake was a trifle to it. It is very common in Africa; I was seized with it. Figure to yourself the situation of the daughter of a pope, only fifteen years old, and who in less than three months had felt the miseries of poverty and slavery; had been ravished almost every day; had beheld her mother cut into four quarters; had experienced the scourges of famine and war, and was now dying of the plague at Algiers. I did not, however, die of it; but my eunuch, and the dey, and almost the whole seraglio of Algiers, were swept off.

"As soon as the first fury of this dreadful pestilence was over, a sale was made of the dey's slaves. I was purchased by a merchant, who carried me to Tunis. This man sold me to another merchant, who sold me again to another at Tripoli; from Tripoli I was sold to Alexandria, from Alexandria to Smyrna, and from Smyrna to Constantinople. After many changes, I at length became the property of an aga of the janissaries, who, soon after I came into his possession, was ordered away to the defence of Azov, then besieged by the Russians.[40]

"The aga being fond of women, took his whole seraglio with him, and lodged us in a small fort on Lake Maeotis, with two black eunuchs and twenty soldiers for our guard. Our army made a great slaughter among the Russians, but they soon returned us the compliment. Azov was taken by storm, and the enemy spared neither age nor sex, but put all to the sword, and laid the city in ashes. Our little fort alone held out; they resolved to reduce us by famine. The twenty janissaries had bound themselves by an oath never to surrender the place. Being reduced to the extremity of famine, they found themselves obliged to eat two eunuchs rather than violate their oath. After a few days they determined to devour the women.

"We had a very pious and humane imam,[41] who made them a most excellent sermon on this occasion, exhorting them not to kill us all at once.

" 'Only cut off one of the buttocks of each of those ladies,' said he, 'and you will fare extremely well; if ye are still under the necessity of having recourse to the same expedient again, ye will find the like supply a few days

[40] The Crimean town of Azov was besieged by Russia in 1696. A janissary is an elite Turkish soldier.
[41] Moslem priest.

hence. Heaven will approve of so charitable an action, and work your deliverance.'

"By the force of this eloquence he easily persuaded them, and all underwent the operation. The imam applied the same balsam as they do to children after circumcision. We were all ready to give up the ghost.

"The janissaries had scarcely time to finish the repast with which we had supplied them, when the Russians attacked the place by means of flat-bottomed boats, and not a single janissary escaped. The Russians paid no regard to the condition we were in; but as there are French surgeons in all parts of the world, a skillful operator took us under his care, and made a cure of us; and I shall never forget, while I live, that as soon as my wounds were perfectly healed, he made me certain proposals. In general, he desired us all to have a good heart, assuring us that the like had happened in many sieges; and that it was the law of war.

"As soon as my companions were in a condition to walk, they were sent to Moscow. As for me, I fell to the lot of a boyard,[42] who put me to work in his garden, and gave me twenty lashes a-day. But this nobleman having, in about two years afterwards, been broken alive upon the wheel, with about thirty others, for some court intrigues,[43] I took advantage of the event, and made my escape. I travelled over a great part of Russia. I was a long time an innkeeper's servant at Riga, then at Rostock, Wismar, Leipsic, Cassel, Utrecht, Leyden, The Hague, and Rotterdam: I have grown old in misery and disgrace, living with only one buttock, and in the perpetual remembrance that I was a pope's daughter. I have been an hundred times upon the point of killing myself, but still was fond of life. This ridiculous weakness is, perhaps, one of the dangerous principles implanted in our nature. For what can be more absurd than to persist in carrying a burden of which we wish to be eased? to detest, and yet to strive to preserve our existence? In a word, to caress the serpent that devours us, and hug him close to our bosoms till he has gnawed into our hearts?

"In the different countries which it has been my fate to traverse, and the many inns where I have been a servant, I have observed a prodigious number of people who held their existence in abhorrence, and yet I never knew more than twelve who voluntarily put an end to their misery; namely, three negroes, four Englishmen, as many Genoese, and a German professor named Robek.[44] My last place was with the Jew, Don Issachar, who placed me near your person, my fair lady; to your fortunes I have attached myself, and have been more affected by your adventures than my own. I should never have even mentioned the latter to you, had you not a little piqued me on the head of sufferings; and if it were not customary to tell stories on board a ship in order to pass away the time. In short, my dear miss, I have a great deal of knowledge and experience of the world, therefore take my advice; divert yourself, and prevail upon each passenger to tell his story, and if there is one of them all that has not cursed his existence many times,

[42] Russian nobleman.
[43] Voltaire is referring to an abortive revolt against Peter the Great in 1698.
[44] Johann Robeck (1672–1739) wrote a treatise advocating suicide and actually drowned himself.

and said to himself over and over again, that he was the most wretched of mortals, I give you leave to throw me headforemost into the sea."

CHAPTER XIII

How Candide was obliged to leave the fair Cunegund and the old woman.

The fair Cunegund, being thus made acquainted with the history of the old woman's life and adventures, paid her all the respect and civility due to a person of her rank and merit. She very readily came into her proposal of engaging every one of the passengers to relate their adventures in their turns, and was at length, as well as Candide, compelled to acknowledge that the old woman was in the right.

"It is a thousand pities," said Candide, "that the sage Pangloss should have been hanged contrary to the custom of an *auto-da-fé*, for he would have read us a most admirable lecture on the moral and physical evil which overspreads the earth and sea; and I think I should have courage enough to presume to offer (with all due respect) some few objections."

While everyone was reciting his adventures, the ship continued her way, and at length arrived at Buenos Ayres, where Cunegund, Captain Candide, and the old woman landed and went to wait upon the Governor Don Fernando d'Ibaraa y Figueora y Mascarenas y Lampourdos y Souza. This nobleman carried himself with a haughtiness suitable to a person who bore so many names. He spoke with the most noble disdain to every one, carried his nose so high, strained his voice to such a pitch, assumed so imperious an air, and stalked with so much loftiness and pride, that everyone who had the honor of conversing with him was violently tempted to bastinade[45] his Excellency. He was immoderately fond of women, and Cunegund appeared in his eyes a paragon of beauty. The first thing he did was to ask her if she was the captain's wife. The air with which he made this demand alarmed Candide; he did not dare to say he was married to her, because, indeed, he was not; neither durst he say she was his sister, because she was not that either: and though a lie of this nature proved of great service to one of the ancients,[46] and might possibly be useful to some of the moderns, yet the purity of his heart would not permit him to violate the truth.

"Miss Cunegund," replied he, "is to do me the honor of marrying me, and we humbly beseech your Excellency to condescend to grace the ceremony with your presence."

Don Fernando d'Ibaraa y Figueora y Mascarenas y Lampourdos y Souza, twirling his mustachio, and putting on a sarcastic smile, ordered Captain Candide to go and review his company. Candide obeyed, and the Governor was left with Miss Cunegund. He made her a strong declaration of love, protesting that he was ready on the morrow to give her his hand in the face of the Church, or otherwise, as should appear most agreeable to a young lady of her prodigious beauty. Cunegund desired leave to retire a quarter of an hour to consult the old woman, and determine how she should proceed.

[45] Beat with a stick. [46] See the story of Abraham and Sarah, Genesis, chapter 12.

The old woman gave her the following counsel: "Miss, you have seventy-two quarterings in your arms, it is true, but you have not a penny to bless yourself with: it is your own fault if you are not wife to one of the greatest noblemen in South America, with an exceeding fine mustachio. What business have you to pride yourself upon an unshaken constancy? You have been ravished by a Bulgarian soldier; a Jew and an Inquisitor have both tasted of your favors. People take advantage of misfortunes. I must confess, were I in your place, I should, without the least scruple, give my hand to the Governor, and thereby make the fortune of the brave Captain Candide."

While the old woman was thus haranguing, with all the prudence that old age and experience furnish, a small bark entered the harbor, in which was a magistrate and his alguazils.[47] Matters had fallen out as follows.

The old woman rightly guessed that the cordelier with the long sleeves was the person who had taken Cunegund's money and jewels while they and Candide were at Badajoz, in their hasty flight from Lisbon. This same friar attempted to sell some of the diamonds to a jeweller, who at once knew them to have belonged to the Grand Inquisitor. The cordelier, before he was hanged, confessed that he had stolen them, and described the persons, and the road they had taken. The flight of Cunegund and Candide was already the town-talk. They sent in pursuit of them to Cadiz; and the vessel which had been sent, to make the greater dispatch, had now reached the port of Buenos Ayres. A report was spread that a magistrate was going to land, and that he was in pursuit of the murderers of my lord the Grand Inquisitor. The wise old woman immediately saw what was to be done.

"You cannot run away," said she to Cunegund; "but you have nothing to fear; it was not you who killed my lord Inquisitor: besides, as the Governor is in love with you, he will not suffer you to be ill-treated; therefore stand your ground."

Then hurrying away to Candide, "Be gone," said she, "from hence this instant, or you will be burned alive."

Candide found there was no time to be lost; but how could he part from Cunegund, and whither must he fly for shelter?

CHAPTER XIV

The reception Candide and Cacambo met with among the Jesuits in Paraguay.

Candide had brought with him from Cadiz such a footman as one often meets with on the coasts of Spain and in the colonies. He was the fourth part of a Spaniard, of a mongrel breed, and born in Tucuman.[48] He had successively gone through the profession of a choirboy, sexton, sailor, monk, peddler, soldier, and lackey. His name was Cacambo; he had a great affection for his master because his master was a mighty good man. He immediately saddled the two Andalusian horses.

"Come, my good master," he said, "let us follow the old woman's advice,

[47] Police officers. [48] A province in Argentina.

and make all the haste we can from this place, without staying to look behind us."

Candide burst into a flood of tears.

"O my dear Cunegund, must I then be compelled to quit you, just as the Governor was going to honor us with his presence at our wedding! Cunegund, so long lost, and found again, what will become of you?"

"Lord!" said Cacambo, "she must do as well as she can; women are never at a loss. God takes care of them, and so let us make the best of our way."

"But whither wilt thou carry me? Where can we go? What can we do without Cunegund?" cried the disconsolate Candide.

"By St. James of Compostella," said Cacambo, "you were going to fight against the Jesuits of Paraguay; now, let us go and fight for them: I know the road perfectly well; I'll conduct you to their kingdom; they will be delighted with a captain that understands the Bulgarian exercise; you will certainly make a prodigious fortune. If we cannot find our account in one world, we may in another. It is a great pleasure to see new objects, and perform new exploits."

"Then you have been in Paraguay?" said Candide.

"Ay, marry, have I," replied Cacambo: "I was a scout in the College of the Assumption, and I am as well acquainted with the new government of Los Padres[49] as I am with the streets of Cadiz. Oh, it is an admirable government, that is most certain! The kingdom is at present upwards of three hundred leagues in diameter, and divided into thirty provinces; the fathers are there masters of everything, and the people have no money at all; this is the masterpiece of justice and reason. For my part, I see nothing so divine as the good fathers, who wage war in this part of the world against the King of Spain and the King of Portugal, at the same time they hear the confessions of those very princes in Europe; who kill Spaniards in America, and send them to Heaven in Madrid. This pleases me exceedingly, but let us push forward; you are going to be the most fortunate of all mortals. How charmed will those fathers be to hear that a captain who understands the Bulgarian exercise is coming among them!"

As soon as they reached the first barrier, Cacambo called to the advance guard, and told them that a captain wanted to speak to my Lord the General. Notice was given to the main guard, and immediately a Paraguayan officer ran to throw himself at the feet of the Commandant to impart this news to him. Candide and Cacambo were immediately disarmed, and their two Andalusian horses were seized. The two strangers were now conducted between two files of musketeers, the Commandant was at the farther end with a three-cornered cap on his head, his gown tucked up, a sword by his side, and a half-pike in his hand; he made a sign, and instantly four-and-twenty soldiers drew up round the newcomers. A sergeant told them that they must wait, the Commandant could not speak to them; and that the Reverend Father Provincial did not suffer any Spaniard to open his mouth but in his presence, or to stay above three hours in the province.

"And where is the Reverend Father Provincial?" said Cacambo.

"He is just come from mass, and is at the parade," replied the sergeant,

[49] "Los Padres" were the Jesuit fathers.

"and in about three hours' time, you may possibly have the honor to kiss his spurs."

"But," said Cacambo, "the captain, who, as well as myself, is perishing with hunger, is no Spaniard, but a German; therefore, pray, might we not be permitted to break our fast till we can be introduced to his Reverence?"

The sergeant immediately went, and acquainted the Commandant with what he heard.

"God be praised," said the Reverend Commandant, "since he is a German, I will hear what he has to say; let him be brought to my arbor."

Immediately they conducted Candide to a beautiful pavilion, adorned with a colonnade of green and gold marble, and with trellises of vines, which served as a kind of cage for parrots, humming-birds, fly-birds, guinea-hens, and all other curious kinds of birds. An excellent breakfast was provided in vessels of gold; and while the Paraguayans were eating coarse Indian corn out of wooden dishes in the open air, and exposed to the burning heat of the sun, the Reverend Father Commandant retired to his cool arbor.

He was a very handsome young man, round-faced, fair, and fresh-colored, his eyebrows were finely arched, he had a piercing eye, the tips of his ears were red, his lips vermilion, and he had a bold and commanding air; but such a boldness as neither resembled that of a Spaniard nor of a Jesuit. He ordered Candide and Cacambo to have their arms restored to them, together with their two Andalusian horses. Cacambo gave the poor beasts some oats to eat close by the arbor, keeping a strict eye upon them all the while for fear of surprise.

Candide having kissed the hem of the Commandant's robe, they sat down to table.

"It seems you are a German?" said the Jesuit to him in that language.

"Yes, Reverend Father," answered Candide.

As they pronounced these words, they looked at each other with great amazement, and with an emotion that neither could conceal.

"From what part of Germany do you come?" said the Jesuit.

"From the dirty province of Westphalia," answered Candide: "I was born in the castle of Thunder-ten-tronckh."

"Oh heavens! is it possible?" said the Commandant.

"What a miracle!" cried Candide.

"Can it be you?" said the Commandant.

On this they both retired a few steps backwards, then embraced, and let fall a shower of tears.

"Is it you then, Reverend Father? You are the brother of the fair Cunegund? you who were slain by the Bulgarians! you the Baron's son! you a Jesuit in Paraguay! I must confess this is a strange world we live in. O Pangloss! Pangloss! what joy would this have given you, if you had not been hanged."

The Commandant dismissed the negro slaves, and the Paraguayans who were presenting them with liquor in crystal goblets. He returned thanks to God and St. Ignatius a thousand times; he clasped Candide in his arms, and both their faces were bathed in tears.

"You will be more surprised, more affected, more transported," said

Candide, "when I tell you that Miss Cunegund, your sister, whose belly was supposed to have been ripped open, is in perfect health."

"Where?"

"In your neighborhood, with the Governor of Buenos Ayres; and I myself was going to fight against you."

Every word they uttered during this long conversation was productive of some new matter of astonishment. Their souls fluttered on their tongues, listened in their ears, and sparkled in their eyes. Like true Germans, they continued a long time at table, waiting for the Reverend Father Provincial; and the Commandant spoke to his dear Candide as follows:

CHAPTER XV

How Candide killed the brother of his dear Cunegund.

"Never while I live shall I lose the remembrance of that horrible day on which I saw my father and mother barbarously butchered before my eyes, and my sister ravished. When the Bulgarians retired, we found no sign of my dear sister; but the bodies of my father, mother, and myself, with two servant maids, and three little boys with their throats cut, were thrown into a cart, to be buried in a chapel belonging to the Jesuits, within two leagues of our family seat. A Jesuit sprinkled us with some holy water, which was confoundedly salt, and a few drops of it went into my eyes; the father perceived that my eyelids stirred a little; he put his hand on my breast, and felt my heart beat; upon which he gave me proper assistance, and at the end of three weeks I was perfectly recovered. You know, my dear Candide, I was very handsome; I became still more so, and the Reverend Father Croust,[50] Superior of the House, took a great fancy to me; he gave me a novice's habit, and some years afterwards I was sent to Rome. Our general stood in need of new levies of young German Jesuits. The sovereigns of Paraguay admit as few Spanish Jesuits as possible; they prefer those of other nations, as being more obedient to command. The Reverend Father General looked upon me as a proper person to work in that vineyard. I set out in company with a Pole and a Tyrolese. Upon my arrival, I was honored with a subdeaconship and a lieutenancy. Now I am colonel and priest. We shall give a warm reception to the King of Spain's troops; I can assure you, they will be well excommunicated and beaten. Providence has sent you hither to assist us. But is it true that my dear sister Cunegund is in the neighborhood with the Governor of Buenos Ayres?"

Candide swore that nothing could be more true; and the tears began again to trickle down their cheeks.

The Baron knew no end of embracing Candide: he called him his brother, his deliverer.

"Perhaps," said he, "my dear Candide, we shall be fortunate enough to enter the town sword in hand, and rescue my sister Cunegund."

[50] There really was a Father Croust, a French Jesuit with whom Voltaire had quarreled. Voltaire is, of course, implying a homosexual relationship.

"Ah! that would crown my wishes," replied Candide, "for I intended to marry her; and I hope I shall still be able to do so."

"Insolent fellow!" replied the Baron. "You! you have the impudence to marry my sister, who bears seventy-two quarterings! I think you have an insufferable degree of assurance to dare so much as to mention such an audacious design to me."

Candide, thunder-struck at the oddness of this speech, answered, "Reverend Father, all the quarterings in the world are of no significance. I have delivered your sister from a Jew and an Inquisitor; she is under many obligations to me, and she is resolved to give me her hand. Master Pangloss always told me that mankind are by nature equal. Therefore, you may depend upon it, that I will marry your sister."

"We shall see about that, villain!" said the Jesuit Baron of Thunder-ten-tronckh, and struck him across the face with the flat side of his sword.

Candide, in an instant, drew his rapier, and plunged it up to the hilt in the Jesuit's body; but, in pulling it out reeking hot, he burst into tears.

"Good God!" cried he, "I have killed my old master, my friend, my brother-in-law; I am the mildest man in the world, and yet I have already killed three men; and of these three two were priests."

Cacambo, standing sentry near the door of the arbor, instantly ran up.

"Nothing remains," said his master, "but to sell our lives as dearly as possible; they will undoubtedly look into the arbor; we must die sword in hand."

Cacambo, who had seen many of these kind of adventures, was not discouraged! He stripped the Baron of his Jesuit's habit, and put it upon Candide, then gave him the dead man's three-cornered cap, and made him mount on horseback. All this was done as quick as thought.

"Gallop, master," cried Cacambo; "everybody will take you for a Jesuit going to give orders; and we shall have passed the frontiers before they are able to overtake us."

He flew as he spoke these words, crying out aloud in Spanish, "Make way, make way for the Reverend Father Colonel."

CHAPTER XVI

What happened to our two travellers with two girls, two monkeys, and the savages, called Oreillons.

Candide and his servant had already passed the frontiers before it was known that the German Jesuit was dead. The wary Cacambo had taken care to fill his wallet with bread, chocolate, ham, fruit, and a few bottles of wine. They penetrated with their Andalusian horses into a strange country where they could discover no beaten path. At length, a beautiful meadow, intersected with streams, opened to their view. Our two travellers allowed their steeds to graze. Cacambo urged his master to take some food, and he set him an example.

"How can you desire me to eat ham, when I have killed the son of my Lord the Baron, and am doomed never more to see the beautiful Cunegund? What will it avail me to prolong a wretched life that might be

spent far from her in remorse and despair; and then, what will the *Journal of Trevoux* say?"[51]

While he was making these reflections, he still continued eating. The sun was now on the point of setting, when the ears of our two were assailed with cries which seemed to be uttered by a female voice. They could not tell whether these were cries of grief or joy: however, they instantly started up, full of that uneasiness and apprehension which a strange place inspires. The cries proceeded from two young women who were tripping stark naked on the edge of the prairie, while two monkeys followed close at their heels biting their buttocks. Candide was touched with compassion; he had learned to shoot while he was among the Bulgarians, and he could hit a filbert in a hedge without touching a leaf. Accordingly, he took up his double-barrelled Spanish musket, pulled the trigger, and laid the two monkeys lifeless on the ground.

"God be praised, my dear Cacambo, I have rescued two poor girls from a most perilous situation: if I have committed a sin in killing an Inquisitor and a Jesuit, I made ample amends by saving the lives of these two girls. Who knows but they may be young ladies of a good family, and that this assistance I have been so happy to give them may procure great advantage in this country."

He was about to continue, when he felt himself struck speechless at seeing the two girls embracing the dead bodies of the monkeys in the tenderest manner, bathing their wounds with their tears, and rending the air with the most doleful lamentations.

"Really," said he to Cacambo, "I should not have expected to see such a prodigious share of good nature."

"Master," replied Cacambo, "you have made a precious piece of work of it; do you know that you have killed the lovers of these two ladies!"

"Their lovers! Cacambo, you are jesting! it cannot be! I can never believe it!"

"Dear Sir," replied Cacambo, "you are surprised at everything; why should you think it so strange that there should be a country where monkeys insinuate themselves into the good graces of the ladies? They are the fourth part of a man as I am the fourth part of a Spaniard."

"Alas!" replied Candide, "I remember to have heard Master Pangloss say that such accidents as these frequently came to pass in former times, and that these commixtures are productive of centaurs, fauns, and satyrs; and that many of the ancients had seen such monsters: but I looked upon the whole as fabulous."

"Now you are convinced," said Cacambo, "that it is very true, and you see what use is made of those creatures by persons who have not had a proper education: all I am afraid of is that these same ladies will play us some ugly trick."

These judicious reflections operated so far on Candide, as to make him quit the meadow and strike into a thicket. There he and Cacambo supped, and after heartily cursing the Grand Inquisitor, the Governor of Buenos Ayres, and the Baron, they fell asleep on the ground. When they awoke, they were surprised to find that they could not move; the reason was that

[51] The *Journal of Trevoux* was a Jesuit journal which regularly attacked Voltaire.

the Oreillons[52] who inhabit that country, and to whom the two girls had denounced them, had bound them with cords made of the bark of trees. They were surrounded by fifty naked Oreillons armed with bows and arrows, clubs, and hatchets of flint; some were making a fire under a large cauldron; and others were preparing spits, crying out one and all, "A Jesuit! a Jesuit! We shall be revenged; we shall have excellent cheer; let us eat this Jesuit; let us eat him up."

"I told you, master," cried Cacambo mournfully, "that those two wenches would play us some scurvy trick."

Candide seeing the cauldron and the spits, cried out, "I suppose they are going either to boil or roast us. Ah! what would Master Pangloss say if he were to see how pure nature is formed! Everything is right: it may be so: but I must confess it is something hard to be bereft of Miss Cunegund, and to be spitted by these Oreillons."

Cacambo, who never lost his presence of mind in distress, said to the disconsolate Candide, "Do not despair; I understand a little of the jargon of these people; I will speak to them."

"Ay, pray do," said Candide, "and be sure you make them sensible of the horrid barbarity of boiling and roasting human creatures, and how little of Christianity there is in such practices."

"Gentlemen," said Cacambo, "you think perhaps you are going to feast upon a Jesuit; if so, it is mighty well; nothing can be more agreeable to justice than thus to treat your enemies. Indeed, the law of nature teaches us to kill our neighbor, and accordingly we find this practiced all over the world; and if we do not indulge ourselves in eating human flesh, it is because we have much better fare; but you have not such resources as we have; it is certainly much better judged to feast upon your enemies than to abandon to the fowls of the air the fruits of your victory. But surely, gentlemen, you would not choose to eat your friends. You imagine you are going to roast a Jesuit, whereas my master is your friend, your defender, and you are going to spit the very man who has been destroying your enemies: as to myself, I am your countryman; this gentleman is my master, and so far from being a Jesuit, he has very lately killed one of that order, whose spoils he now wears, and which have probably occasioned your mistake. To convince you of the truth of what I say, take the habit he now has on, and carry it to the first barrier of the Jesuits' kingdom, and inquire whether my master did not kill one of their officers. There will be little or no time lost by this, and you may still reserve our bodies in your power to feast on, if you should find what we have told you to be false. But, on the contrary, if you find it to be true, I am persuaded you are too well acquainted with the principles of the laws of society, humanity, and justice, not to use us courteously."

This speech appeared very reasonable to the Oreillons; they deputed two of their people with all expedition to inquire into the truth of this affair. The two delegates acquitted themselves of their commission like men of sense, and soon returned with good tidings. Upon this the Oreillons

[52] The name "Oreillons" is an attempt to render the American-Spanish *Orejones* ("long-eared," "unbranded," or "wild"). Voltaire got the name and a number of other details from a 1609 book on Peru by Garcilaso de Vega.

released their two prisoners, showed them all sorts of civilities, offered them girls, gave them refreshments, and reconducted them to the confines of their country, crying before them all the way, in token of joy, "He is no Jesuit, he is no Jesuit."

Candide could not help admiring the cause of his deliverance.

"What men! what manners!" cried he: "if I had not fortunately run my sword up to the hilt in the body of Miss Cunegund's brother, I should have infallibly been eaten alive. But, after all, pure nature is an excellent thing; since these people, instead of eating me, showed me a thousand civilities, as soon as they knew I was not a Jesuit."

CHAPTER XVII

Candide and his servant arrive in the country of El Dorado. What they saw there.

When they got to the frontiers of the Oreillons, Cacambo said to Candide, "You see, this hemisphere is no better than the other: take my advice, and let us return to Europe by the shortest way possible."

"But how can we get back?" said Candide; "and whither shall we go? To my own country? the Bulgarians and the Abares are laying that waste with fire and sword. Or shall we go to Portugal? there I shall be burned; and if we abide here, we are every moment in danger of being spitted. But how can I bring myself to quit that part of the world where Miss Cunegund has her residence?"

"Let us turn towards Cayenne," said Cacambo; "there we shall meet with some Frenchmen; for you know those gentry ramble all over the world; perhaps they will assist us, and God will look with pity on our distress."

It was not so easy to get to Cayenne. They knew pretty nearly whereabouts it lay; but the mountains, rivers, precipices, robbers, savages, were dreadful obstacles in the way. Their horses died with fatigue, and their provisions were at an end. They subsisted a whole month upon wild fruit, till at length they came to a little river bordered with cocoa-nut palms, the sight of which at once sustained life and hope.

Cacambo, who was always giving as good advice as the old woman herself, said to Candide, "You see there is no holding out any longer; we travelled enough on foot. I see an empty canoe near the river-side; let us fill it with cocoa-nuts, get into it, and go down with the stream; a river always leads to some inhabited place. If we do not meet with agreeable things, we shall at least meet with something new."

"Agreed," replied Candide; "let us recommend ourselves to Providence."

They rowed a few leagues down the river, the banks of which were in some places covered with flowers; in others barren; in some parts smooth and level, and in others steep and rugged. The stream widened as they went further on, till at length it passed under one of the frightful rocks whose summits seemed to reach the clouds. Here our two travellers had the courage to commit themselves to the stream beneath this vault, which, contracting in this part, hurried them along with a dreadful noise and rapidity.

At the end of four-and-twenty hours, they saw daylight again; but their canoe was dashed to pieces against the rocks. They were obliged to creep along, from rock to rock, for the space of a league, till at last a spacious plain presented itself to their sight, bound by inaccessible mountains. The country appeared cultivated equally for pleasure, and to produce the necessaries of life. The useful and agreeable were here equally blended. The roads were covered, or rather adorned, with carriages formed of glittering materials, in which were men and women of a surprising beauty, drawn with great rapidity by red sheep of a very large size, which far surpassed in speed the finest coursers of Andalusia, Tetuan, or Mequinez.

"Here is a country, however," said Candide, "preferable to Westphalia."

He and Cacambo landed near the first village they saw, at the entrance of which they perceived some children covered with tattered garments of the richest brocade, playing at quoits. Our two inhabitants of the other hemisphere amused themselves greatly with what they saw. The quoits were large round pieces, yellow, red, and green, which cast a most glorious lustre. Our travellers picked some of them up, and they proved to be gold, emeralds, rubies, and diamonds, the least of which would have been the greatest ornament to the superb throne of the great Mogul.

"Without doubt," said Cacambo, "those children must be the king's sons, that are playing at quoits."

As he was uttering those words, the schoolmaster of the village appeared, who came to call them to school.

"There," said Candide, "is the preceptor of the royal family."

The little ragamuffins immediately quitted their game, leaving the quoits on the ground with all their other playthings. Candide gathered them up, ran to the schoolmaster, and, with a most respectful bow, presented them to him, giving him to understand by signs that their Royal Highnesses had forgotten their gold and precious stones. The schoolmaster, with a smile, flung them upon the ground, then having examined Candide from head to foot with an air of great surprise, went on his way.

Our travellers took care, however, to gather up the gold, the rubies, and the emeralds.

"Where are we?" cried Candide. "The king's children in this country must have an excellent education, since they are taught to show such a contempt for gold and precious stones."

Cacambo was as much surprised as his master.

They at length drew near the first house in the village, which was built after the manner of a European palace. There was a crowd of people round the door, and a still greater number in the house. The sound of the most delightful musical instruments was heard, and the most agreeable smell came from the kitchen. Cacambo went up to the door, and heard those within talking in the Peruvian language, which was his mother tongue; for every one knows that Cacambo was born in a village of Tucuman where no other language is spoken.

"I will be your interpreter here," said he to Candide, "let us go in; this is an eating-house."

Immediately two waiters, and two servant-girls, dressed in cloth of gold, and their hair braided with ribbons of tissue, accosted the strangers, and invited them to sit down to the ordinary. Their dinner consisted of four

dishes of different soups, each garnished with two young paroquets, a large dish of bouille[53] that weighed two hundredweight, two roasted monkeys of a delicious flavor, three hundred humming-birds in one dish, and six hundred fly-birds in another; some excellent ragouts, delicate tarts, and the whole served up in dishes of rock-crystal. Several sorts of liquors, extracted from the sugar-cane, were handed about by the servants who attended.

Most of the company were chapmen and wagoners,[54] all extremely polite: they asked Cacambo a few questions, with the utmost discretion and circumspection; and replied to his in a most obliging and satisfactory manner.

As soon as dinner was over, both Candide and Cacambo thought they would pay very handsomely for their entertainment by laying down two of those large gold pieces which they had picked off the ground; but the landlord and landlady burst into a fit of laughing and held their sides for some time before they were able to speak.

"Gentlemen," said the landlord, "I plainly perceive you are strangers, and such we are not accustomed to see; pardon us, therefore, for laughing when you offered us the common pebbles of our highways for payment of your reckoning. To be sure, you have none of the coin of this kingdom; but there is no necessity to have any money at all to dine in this house. All the inns, which are established for the convenience of those who carry on the trade of this nation, are maintained by the government. You have found but very indifferent entertainment here, because this is only a poor village; but in almost every other of these public houses you will meet with a reception worthy of persons of your merit."

Cacambo explained the whole of this speech of the landlord to Candide, who listened to it with the same astonishment with which his friend communicated it.

"What sort of a country is this," said the one to the other, "that is unknown to all the world, and in which Nature has everywhere so different an appearance from what she has in ours? Possibly this is that part of the globe where everything is right, for there must certainly be some such place; and, for all that Master Pangloss could say, I often perceived that things went very ill in Westphalia."

CHAPTER XVIII

What they saw in the country of El Dorado.

Cacambo vented all his curiosity upon the landlord by a thousand different questions.

The honest man answered him thus: "I am very ignorant, Sir, but I am contented with my ignorance; however, we have in this neighborhood an old man retired from court, who is the most learned and communicative person in the whole kingdom."

He then directed Cacambo to the old man; Candide acted now only a second character, and attended his servant. They entered a quite plain house, for the door was nothing but silver, and the ceiling was only of

[53] Stew. [54] Merchants and wagondrivers.

beaten gold, but wrought in so elegant a taste as to vie with the richest. The antechamber, indeed, was only encrusted with rubies and emeralds; but the order in which everything was disposed made amends for this great simplicity.

The old man received the strangers on a sofa, which was stuffed with humming-birds' feathers; and ordered his servants to present them with liquors in golden goblets, after which he satisfied their curiosity in the following terms:

"I am now one hundred and seventy-two years old; and I learned of my late father who was equerry to the king the amazing revolutions of Peru, to which he had been an eye-witness. This kingdom is the ancient patrimony of the Incas, who very imprudently quitted it to conquer another part of the world, and were at length conquered and destroyed themselves by the Spaniards.

"Those princes of their family who remained in their native country acted more wisely. They ordained, with the consent of their whole nation, that none of the inhabitants of our little kingdom should ever quit it; and to this wise ordinance we owe the preservation of our innocence and happiness. The Spaniards had some confused notion of this country, to which they gave the name of El Dorado; and Sir Walter Raleigh, an Englishman, actually came very near it, about a hundred years ago:[55] but the inaccessible rocks and precipices with which our country is surrounded on all sides have hitherto secured us from the rapacious fury of the people of Europe, who have an unaccountable fondness for the pebbles and dirt of our land, for the sake of which they would murder us all to the very last man."

The conversation lasted some time and turned chiefly on the form of government, the customs, the women, the public diversions, and the arts. At length, Candide, who had always had a taste for metaphysics, asked whether the people of that country had any religion.

The old man reddened a little at this question.

"Can you doubt it?" said he. "Do you take us for wretches lost to all sense of gratitude?"

Cacambo asked in a respectful manner what was the established religion of El Dorado. The old man blushed again.

"Can there be two religions then?" he said. "Ours, I apprehend, is the religion of the whole world; we worship God from morning till night."

"Do you worship but one God?" said Cacambo, who still acted as the interpreter of Candide's doubts.

"Certainly," said the old man; "there are not two, nor three, nor four Gods. I must confess the people of your world ask very extraordinary questions."

However, Candide could not refrain from making many more inquiries of the old man; he wanted to know in what manner they prayed to God in El Dorado.

"We do not pray to him at all," said the reverend sage; "we have nothing

[55] The myth of El Dorado, the land of gold, was very widespread. Sir Walter Raleigh explored the Orinoco River in 1595 and again in 1616, in search of this mythical land.

to ask of him, he has given us all we want, and we give him thanks incessantly."

Candide had a curiosity to see some of their priests, and desired Cacambo to ask the old man where they were.

At this he, smiling, said, "My friends, we are all of us priests; the King and all the heads of families sing solemn hymns of thanksgiving every morning, accompanied by five or six thousand musicians."

"What!" said Cacambo, "have you no monks among you, to dispute, to govern, to intrigue, and to burn people who are not of the same opinion with themselves?"

"Do you take us for fools?" said the old man. "Here we are all of one opinion, and know not what you mean by your monks."

During the whole of this discourse Candide was in raptures, and he said to himself:

"What a prodigious difference is there between this place and Westphalia, and this house and the Baron's castle! If our friend Pangloss had seen El Dorado, he would no longer have said that the castle of Thunderten-Tronckh was the finest of all possible edifices: there is nothing like seeing the world, that's certain."

This long conversation being ended, the old man ordered six sheep to be harnessed, and put to the coach, and sent twelve of his servants to escort the travellers to Court.

"Excuse me," said he, "for not waiting on you in person; my age deprives me of that honor. The King will receive you in such a manner that you will have no reason to complain; and doubtless you will make a proper allowance for the customs of the country, if they should not happen altogether to please you."

Candide and Cacambo got into the coach, the six sheep flew, and in less than a quarter of an hour they arrived at the King's palace, which was situated at the further end of the capital. At the entrance was a portal two hundred and twenty feet high, and one hundred wide; but it is impossible for words to express the materials of which it was built. The reader, however, will readily conceive they must have a prodigious superiority over the pebbles and sand which we call gold and precious stones.

Twenty beautiful young virgins-in-waiting received Candide and Cacambo at their alighting from the coach, conducted them to the bath, and clad them in robes woven of the down of humming-birds; after this they were introduced by the great officers of the crown of both sexes to the King's apartment, between two files of musicians, each file consisting of a thousand, according to the custom of the country. When they drew near to the presence chamber, Cacambo asked one of the officers in what manner they were to pay their obeisance to his Majesty: whether it was the custom to fall upon their knees, or to prostrate themselves upon the ground? whether they were to put their hands upon their heads, or behind their backs? whether they were to lick the dust off the floor? in short, what was the ceremony usual on such occasions?

"The custom," said the great officer, "is to embrace the King, and kiss him on each cheek."

Candide and Cacambo accordingly threw their arms round his Majes-

ty's neck; and he received them in the most gracious manner imaginable, and very politely asked them to sup with him.

While supper was preparing, orders were given to show them the city, where they saw public structures that reared their lofty heads to the clouds; the market-places decorated with a thousand columns; fountains of spring water, besides others of rose water, and of liquors drawn from the sugar-cane, incessantly flowing in the great squares; these were paved with a kind of precious stone that emitted an odor like that of cloves and cinnamon. Candide asked to see the high court of justice, the parliament; but was answered that they have none in that country, being utter strangers to lawsuits. He then inquired if they had any prisons; they replied, "None." But what gave him at once the greatest surprise and pleasure was the Palace of Sciences, where he saw a gallery two thousand feet long, filled with the various apparatus of mathematics and natural philosophy.

After having spent the whole afternoon in seeing only about the thousandth part of the city, they were brought back to the King's palace. Candide sat down at the table with his Majesty, his servant Cacambo, and several ladies of the Court. Never was entertainment more elegant, nor could any one possibly show more wit than his Majesty displayed while they were at supper. Cacambo explained all the King's *bons mots*[56] to Candide, and although they were translated they still appeared to be *bons mots*. Of all the things that surprised Candide, this was not the least. They spent a whole month in this hospitable place, during which time Candide was continually saying to Cacambo:

"I own, my friend, once more, that the castle where I was born is a mere nothing in comparison with the place where we now are; but still Miss Cunegund is not here, and you yourself have doubtless some mistress in Europe. If we remain here, we shall only be as others are: whereas, if we return to our own world with only a dozen of El Dorado sheep, loaded with the pebbles of this country, we shall be richer than all the kings in Europe; we shall no longer need to stand in awe of the Inquisitors; and we may easily recover Miss Cunegund."

This speech pleased Cacambo. A fondness for roving, for making a figure in their own country, and for boasting of what they had seen in their travels, was so strong in our two wanderers that they resolved to be no longer happy; and demanded permission of his Majesty to quit the country.

"You are about to do a rash and silly action," said the King; "I am sensible my kingdom is an inconsiderable spot; but when people are tolerably at their ease in any place, I should think it would be their interest to remain there. Most assuredly, I have no right to detain you or any strangers against your wills; this is an act of tyranny to which our manners and our laws are equally repugnant: all men are free; you have an undoubted liberty to depart whenever you please, but you will have many difficulties in passing the frontiers. It is impossible to ascend that rapid river which runs under high and vaulted rocks, and by which you were conveyed hither by a miracle. The mountains by which my kingdom is hemmed in on all sides

[56] Witticisms.

are ten thousand feet high, and perfectly perpendicular; they are above ten leagues over each, and the descent from them is one continued precipice. However, since you are determined to leave us, I will immediately give orders to the superintendent of machines to cause one to be made that will convey you safely. When they have conducted you to the back of the mountains, nobody can attend you further; for my subjects have made a vow never to quit the kingdom, and they are too prudent to break it. Ask me whatever else you please."

"All we shall ask of your Majesty," said Cacambo, "is a few sheep laden with provisions, pebbles, and the clay of your country."

The King smiled at the request, and said, "I cannot imagine what pleasure you Europeans find in our yellow clay; but take away as much of it as you will, and much good may it do you."

He immediately gave orders to his engineers to make a machine to hoist these two extraordinary men out of the kingdom. Three thousand good mathematicians went to work and finished it in about fifteen days; and it did not cost more than twenty millions sterling of that country's money. Candide and Cacambo were placed on this machine, and they took with them two large red sheep, bridled and saddled, to ride upon when they got on the other side of the mountains; twenty others to serve as pack-horses for carrying provisions; thirty laden with presents of whatever was most curious in the country; and fifty with gold, diamonds, and other precious stones. The King embraced the two wanderers with the greatest cordiality.

It was a curious sight to behold the manner of their setting off, and the ingenious method by which they and their sheep were hoisted to the top of the mountains. The mathematicians and engineers took leave of them as soon as they had conveyed them to a place of safety, and Candide was wholly occupied with the thoughts of presenting his sheep to Miss Cunegund.

"Now," said he, "thanks to heaven, we have more than sufficient to pay the Governor of Buenos Ayres for Miss Cunegund, if she is redeemable. Let us make the best of our way to Cayenne, where we will take ship, and then we may at leisure think of what kingdom we shall purchase."

CHAPTER XIX

What happened to them at Surinam, and how Candide became acquainted with Martin.

Our travellers' first day's journey was very pleasant; they were elated with the prospect of possessing more riches than were to be found in Europe, Asia, and Africa together. Candide, in amorous transports, cut the name of Miss Cunegund on the trees. The second day, two of their sheep sank into a morass, and were swallowed up with their loads; two more died of fatigue some few days afterwards; seven or eight perished with hunger in a desert, and others, at different times, tumbled down precipices; so that, after travelling about a hundred days, they had only two sheep left.

Said Candide to Cacambo, "You see, my dear friend, how perishable the riches of this world are; there is nothing solid but virtue and the joy of seeing Miss Cunegund again."

"Very true," said Cacambo; "but we have still two sheep remaining, with more treasure than ever the King of Spain will be possessed of; and I espy a town at a distance, which I take to be Surinam, a town belonging to the Dutch. We are now at the end of our troubles, and at the beginning of happiness."

As they drew near the town, they saw a negro stretched on the ground with only one half of his habit, which was a pair of blue cotton drawers; for the poor man had lost his left leg, and his right hand.

"Good God," said Candide in Dutch, "what dost thou here, friend, in this deplorable condition?"

"I am waiting for my master Mynheer Vanderdendur, the famous trader," answered the negro.

"Was it Mynheer Vanderdendur that used you in this cruel manner?"

"Yes, Sir," said the negro; "it is the custom here. They give a pair of cotton drawers twice a year, and that is all our covering. When we labor in the sugar-works, and the mill happens to snatch hold of a finger, they instantly chop off our hand; and when we attempt to run away, they cut off a leg. Both these cases have happened to me, and it is at this expense that you eat sugar in Europe; and yet when my mother sold me for ten pattacoons on the coast of Guinea, she said to me, "My dear child, bless our fetishes;[57] adore them for ever; they will make thee live happy; thou hast the honor to be a slave to our lords the whites, by which thou wilt make the fortune of us thy parents." Alas! I know not whether I have made their fortunes; but they have not made mine: dogs, monkeys, and parrots, are a thousand times less wretched than me. The Dutch fetishes who converted me tell me every Sunday that, blacks and whites, we are all children of Adam. As for me, I do not understand anything of genealogies; but if what these preachers say is true, we are all second cousins; and you must allow, that it is impossible to be worse treated by our relations than we are."

"O Pangloss!" cried out Candide, "such horrid doings never entered thy imagination. Here is an end of the matter; I find myself, after all, obliged to renounce thy Optimism."

"Optimism!" said Cacambo, "what is that?"

"Alas!" replied Candide, "it is the obstinacy of maintaining that everything is best when it is worst": and so saying, he turned his eyes towards the poor negro, and shed a flood of tears; and in this weeping mood he entered the town of Surinam.

Immediately upon their arrival, our travellers inquired if there was any vessel in the harbor which they might send to Buenos Ayres. The person they addressed themselves to happened to be the master of a Spanish bark, who offered to agree with them on moderate terms, and appointed them a meeting at a public-house. Thither Candide and his faithful Cacambo went to wait for him, taking with them their two sheep.

Candide, who was all frankness and sincerity, made an ingenuous re-

[57] Priests.

cital of his adventures to the Spaniard, declaring to him at the same time his resolution of carrying off Miss Cunegund.

"In that case," said the shipmaster, "I'll take good care not to take you to Bueno Ayres. It would prove a hanging matter to us all. The fair Cunegund is the Governor's favorite mistress."

These words were like a clap of thunder to Candide; he wept bitterly for a long time, and, taking Cacambo aside, he said to him:

"I'll tell you, my dear friend, what you must do. We have each of us in our pockets to the value of five or six millions in diamonds; you are cleverer at these matters than I; you must go to Buenos Ayres and bring off Miss Cunegund. If the Governor makes any difficulty, give him a million; if he holds out, give him two; as you have not killed an Inquisitor, they will have no suspicion of you: I'll fit out another ship and go to Venice, where I will wait for you. Venice is a free country, where we shall have nothing to fear from Bulgarians, Abares, Jews, or Inquisitors."

Cacambo greatly applauded this wise resolution. He was inconsolable at the thought of parting with so good a master, who treated him more like an intimate friend than a servant; but the pleasure of being able to do him a service soon got the better of his sorrow. They embraced each other with a flood of tears. Candide charged him not to forget the old woman. Cacambo set out the same day. This Cacambo was a very honest fellow.

Candide continued some days longer at Surinam, waiting for any captain to carry him and his two remaining sheep to Italy. He hired domestics and purchased many things necessary for a long voyage; at length, Mynheer Vanderdendur, skipper of a large Dutch vessel, came and offered his service.

"What will you take," said Candide, "to carry me, my servants, my baggage, and these two sheep you see here, direct to Venice?"

The skipper asked ten thousand piastres; and Candide agreed to his demand without hesitation.

"Oh, ho!" said the cunning Vanderdendur to himself, "this stranger must be very rich; he agrees to give me ten thousand piastres without hesitation."

Returning a little while after, he told Candide that upon second consideration he could not undertake the voyage for less than twenty thousand.

"Very well, you shall have them," said Candide.

"Zounds!" said the skipper to himself, "this man agrees to pay twenty thousand piastres with as much ease as ten."

Accordingly he went back again, and told him roundly that he would not carry him to Venice for less than thirty thousand piastres.

"Then you shall have thirty thousand," said Candide.

"Odso!" said the Dutchman once more to himself, "thirty thousand piastres seem a trifle to this man. Those sheep must certainly be laden with an immense treasure. I'll stop here and ask no more; but make him pay down the thirty thousand piastres, and then we shall see."

Candide sold two small diamonds, the least of which was worth more than all the skipper asked. He paid him before-hand, and the two sheep were put on board, and Candide followed in a small boat to join the vessel in the road. The skipper took his opportunity, hoisted his sails, and put out

to sea with a favorable wind. Candide, confounded and amazed, soon lost sight of the ship.

"Alas!" said he, "this is a trick like those in our old world!"

He returned back to the shore overwhelmed with grief; and, indeed, he had lost what would have been the fortune of twenty monarchs.

Immediately upon his landing, he applied to the Dutch magistrate: being transported with passion, he thundered at the door; which being opened, he went in, told his case, and talked a little louder than necessary. The magistrate began with fining him ten thousand piastres for his petulance, and then listened very patiently to what he had to say, promised to examine into the affair at the skipper's return, and ordered him to pay ten thousand piastres more for the fees of the court.

This treatment put Candide out of all patience: it is true, he had suffered misfortunes a thousand times more grievous; but the cool insolence of the judge and of the skipper who robbed him raised his choler and threw him into a deep melancholy. The villainy of mankind presented itself to his mind in all its deformity, and his soul was a prey to the most gloomy ideas. After some time, hearing that the captain of a French ship was ready to set sail for Bordeaux, as he had no more sheep loaded with diamonds to put on board, he hired the cabin at the usual price; and made it known in the town that he would pay the passage and board of any honest man who would give him his company during the voyage; besides making him a present of ten thousand piastres, on condition that such person was the most dissatisfied with his condition and the most unfortunate in the whole province.

Upon this there appeared such a crowd of candidates that a large fleet could not have contained them. Candide, willing to choose from among those who appeared most likely to answer his intention, selected twenty, who seemed to him the most sociable, and who all pretended to merit the preference. He invited them to his inn, and promised to treat them with a supper, on condition that every man should bind himself by an oath to relate his own history. He declared at the same time that he would make choice of that person who should appear to him the most deserving of compassion, and the most justly dissatisfied with his condition of life; and that he would make a present to the rest.

This extraordinary assembly continued sitting till four in the morning. Candide, while he was listening to their adventures, called to mind what the old woman had said to him on their voyage to Buenos Ayres, and the wager she had laid that there was not a person on board the ship but had met with some great misfortune. Every story he heard put him in mind of Pangloss.

"My old master," said he, "would be confoundedly put to it to demonstrate his favorite system. Would he were here! Certainly if everything is for the best, it is in El Dorado, and not in the other parts of the world."

At length he determined in favor of a poor scholar who had labored ten years for the booksellers at Amsterdam, being of opinion that no employment could be more detestable.

This scholar, who was in fact a very honest man, had been robbed by his wife, beaten by his son, and forsaken by his daughter, who had run away

with a Portuguese. He had been likewise deprived of a small employment on which he subsisted, and he was persecuted by the clergy of Surinam, who took him for a Socinian.[58] It must be acknowledged that the other competitors were, at least, as wretched as he; but Candide was in hopes that the company of a man of letters would relieve the tediousness of the voyage. All the other candidates complained that Candide had done them great injustice; but he stopped their mouths by a present of a hundred piastres to each.

CHAPTER XX

What befell Candide and Martin on their voyage.

The old scholar, whose name was Martin, took shipping with Candide for Bordeaux. They both had seen and suffered a great deal; and if the ship had been destined to sail from Surinam to Japan round the Cape of Good Hope, they could have found sufficient entertainment for each other during the whole voyage in discoursing upon moral and natural evil.

Candide, however, had one advantage over Martin: he lived in the pleasing hopes of seeing Miss Cunegund once more; whereas the poor philosopher had nothing to hope for. Besides, Candide had money and jewels, and, notwithstanding he had lost a hundred red sheep, laden with the greatest treasure on the earth, and though he still smarted from the reflection of the Dutch skipper's knavery, yet when he considered what he had still left, and repeated the name of Cunegund, especially after mealtimes, he inclined to Pangloss's doctrine.

"And pray," said he to Martin, "what is your opinion of the whole of this system? What notion have you of moral and natural evil?"

"Sir," replied Martin, "our priests accused me of being a Socinian; but the real truth is, I am a Manichaean."[59]

"Nay, now you are jesting," said Candide; "there are no Manichaeans existing at present in the world."

"And yet I am one," said Martin; "but I cannot help it; I cannot for the soul of me think otherwise."

"Surely the devil must be in you," said Candide.

"He concerns himself so much," replied Martin, "in the affairs of this world that it is very probable he may be in me as well as everywhere else; but I must confess, when I cast my eye on this globe, or rather globule, I cannot help thinking that God has abandoned it to some malignant being. I always except El Dorado. I scarce ever knew a city that did not wish the destruction of its neighboring city; nor a family that did not desire to exterminate some other family. The poor, in all parts of the world, bear an

[58] Follower of a rationalist, anti-Trinitarian religious system, founded by the sixteenth-century Polish reformers Laelius and Faustus Socinus.

[59] Manichaeanism was a religion founded by a third-century Persian named Mani, who taught that the world was ruled by two powers, one good and one evil.

inveterate hatred to the rich, even while they creep and cringe to them; and the rich treat the poor like sheep, whose wool and flesh they barter for money: a million of regimented assassins traverse Europe from one end to the other to get their bread by regular depredation and murder, because it is the most gentleman-like profession. Even in those cities which seem to enjoy the blessings of peace, and where the arts flourish, the inhabitants are devoured with envy, care, and anxiety, which are greater plagues than any experienced in a town besieged. Private chagrins are still more dreadful than public calamities. In a word, I have seen and suffered so much, that I am a Manichaean."

"And yet there is some good in the world," replied Candide.

"May be," said Martin, "but it has escaped my knowledge."

While they were deeply engaged in this dispute they heard the report of cannon, which redoubled every moment. Each took out his glass, and they espied two ships warmly engaged at the distance of about three miles. The wind brought them both so near the French ship that those on board her had the pleasure of seeing the fight with great ease. At last one of the two vessels gave the other a shot between wind and water, which sank her outright. Then could Candide and Martin plainly perceive a hundred men on the deck of the vessel which was sinking, who, with hands uplifted to heaven, sent forth piercing cries, and were in a moment swallowed up by the waves.

"Well," said Martin, "you now see in what manner mankind treat each other."

"It is certain," said Candide, "that there is something diabolical in this affair."

As he was speaking thus, he saw something of a shining red hue, which swam close to the vessel. The boat was hoisted out to see what it might be, when it proved to be one of his sheep. Candide felt more joy at the recovery of this one animal than he did grief when he lost the other hundred, though laden with the large diamonds of El Dorado.

The French captain quickly perceived that the victorious ship belonged to the crown of Spain; that the other which sank was a Dutch pirate, and the very same captain who had robbed Candide. The immense riches which this villain had amassed were buried with him in the deep, and only this one sheep saved out of the whole.

"You see," said Candide to Martin, "that vice is sometimes punished: this villain, the Dutch skipper, has met with the fate he deserved."

"Very true," said Martin; "but why should the passengers be doomed also to destruction? God has punished the knave, and the devil has drowned the rest."

The French and Spanish ships continued their cruise, and Candide and Martin their conversation. They disputed fourteen days successively, at the end of which they were just as far advanced as the first moment they began. However, they had the satisfaction of disputing, of communicating their ideas, and of mutually comforting each other. Candide embraced his sheep.

"Since I have found thee again," said he, "I may possibly find my Cunegund once more."

CHAPTER XXI

Candide and Martin, while thus reasoning with each other, draw near to the coast of France.

At length they sighted the coast of France.

"Pray, Mr. Martin," said Candide, "have you ever been in France?"

"Yes, Sir," said Martin, "I have been in several provinces of that kingdom. In some, one half of the people are madmen; in some, they are too artful; in others, again, they are in general either very good-natured or very brutal; while in others, they affect to be witty, and in all, their ruling passion is love, the next is slander, and the last is to talk nonsense."

"But pray, Mr. Martin, were you ever in Paris?"

"Yes, Sir, I have been in that city, and it is a place that contains the several species just described; it is a chaos, a confused multitude, where everyone seeks for pleasure without being able to find it; at least, as far as I have observed during my short stay in that city. At my arrival, I was robbed of all I had in the world by pickpockets and sharpers, at the fair of St. Germain. I was taken up myself for a robber, and confined in prison a whole week; after that I hired myself as corrector to a press in order to get a little money towards defraying my expenses back to Holland on foot. I knew the whole tribe of scribblers, malcontents, and religious convulsionaries.[60] It is said the people of that city are very polite; I believe that may be so."

"For my part, I have no curiosity to see France," said Candide, "you may easily conceive, my friend, that, after spending a month at El Dorado, I can desire to behold nothing upon earth but Miss Cunegund; I am going to wait for her at Venice; I intend to pass through France on my way to Italy; will you not bear me company?"

"With all my heart," said Martin: "they say Venice is agreeable to none but noble Venetians; but that, nevertheless, strangers are well received there when they have plenty of money; now I have none, but you have, therefore I will attend you wherever you please."

"Now we are upon this subject," said Candide, "do you think that the earth was originally sea, as we read in that great book[61] which belongs to the captain of the ship?"

"I believe nothing of it," replied Martin, "any more than I do of the many other chimeras which have been related to us for some time past."

"But then, to what end," said Candide, "was the world formed?"

"To make us mad," said Martin.

"Are you not surprised," continued Candide, "at the love which the two girls in the country of the Oreillons had for those two monkeys?—You know I have told you the story."

"Surprised!" replied Martin, "not in the least; I see nothing strange in

[60] The "religious convulsionaries" were Jansenists, a conservative Catholic sect whose members made public display of their spiritual ecstasies.

[61] The "great book" is the Bible, which in Genesis describes the earth as originally covered with water.

this passion. I have seen so many extraordinary things, that there is nothing extraordinary to me now."

"Do you think," said Candide, "that mankind always massacred each other as they do now? Were they always guilty of lies, fraud, treachery, ingratitude, inconstancy, envy, ambition, and cruelty? Were they always thieves, fools, cowards, gluttons, drunkards, misers, calumniators, debauchees, fanatics, and hypocrites?"

"Do you believe," said Martin, "that hawks have always been accustomed to eat pigeons when they came in their way?"

"Doubtless," said Candide.

"Well, then," replied Martin, "if hawks have always had the same nature, why should you pretend that mankind change theirs?"

"Oh!" said Candide, "there is a great deal of difference, for free will . . ."

Reasoning thus, they arrived at Bordeaux.

CHAPTER XXII

What happened to Candide and Martin in France.

Candide stayed no longer at Bordeaux than was necessary to dispose of a few of the pebbles he had brought from El Dorado, and to provide himself with a post-chaise for two persons, for he could no longer stir a step without his philosopher Martin. The only thing that gave him concern was the being obliged to leave his sheep behind him, which he entrusted to the care of the Academy of Sciences at Bordeaux. The academicians proposed, as a prize-subject for the year, to prove why the wool of this sheep was red; and the prize was adjudged to a northern sage,[62] who demonstrated by A plus B, minus C, divided by Z, that the sheep must necessarily be red, and die of the rot.

In the meantime, all the travellers whom Candide met with in the inns, or on the road, told him to a man that they were going to Paris. This general eagerness gave him likewise a great desire to see this capital, and it was not much out of his way to Venice.

He entered the city by the suburbs of St. Marceau, and thought himself in one of the vilest hamlets in all Westphalia.

Candide had not been long at his inn before he was seized with a slight disorder owing to the fatigue he had undergone. As he wore a diamond of an enormous size on his finger, and had, among the rest of his equipage, a strong box that seemed very weighty, he soon found himself between two physicians whom he had not sent for, a number of intimate friends whom he had never seen, and who would not quit his bedside, and two female devotees who warmed his soup for him.

"I remember," said Martin to him, "that the first time I came to Paris I was likewise taken ill; I was very poor, and, accordingly, I had neither friends, nurses, nor physicians, and yet I did very well."

[62] The "northern sage" is Maupertius Le Lapon, who was said to prove the existence of God by mathematics.

However, by dint of purging and bleeding Candide's disorder became very serious. The priest of the parish came with all imaginable politeness to desire a note of him, payable to the bearer in the other world.[63] Candide refused to comply with his request; but the two devotees assured him that it was a new fashion. Candide replied that he was not one that followed the fashion. Martin was for throwing the priest out of the window. The clerk swore Candide should not have Christian burial. Martin swore in turn that he would bury the clerk alive, if he continued to plague them any longer. The dispute grew warm; Martin took him by the shoulders, and turned him out of the room, which gave great scandal, and occasioned a lawsuit.

Candide recovered; and, till he was in a condition to go abroad, had a great deal of very good company to pass the evenings with him in his chamber. They played deep.[64] Candide was surprised to find he could never turn a trick; and Martin was not at all surprised at the matter.

Among those who did him the honors of the place was a little spruce Abbé from Périgord, one of those insinuating, busy, fawning, impudent, accommodating fellows that lie in wait for strangers at their arrival, tell them all the scandal of the town, and offer to minister to their pleasures at various prices. This man conducted Candide and Martin to the playhouse: they were acting a new tragedy. Candide found himself placed near a cluster of wits: this, however, did not prevent him from shedding tears at some scenes which were perfectly acted. One of these talkers said to him between the acts:

"You are greatly to blame in shedding tears; that actress plays horribly, and the man that plays with her still worse, and the piece itself is still more execrable than the representation. The author does not understand a word of Arabic, and yet he has laid his scene in Arabia; and what is more, he is a fellow who does not believe in innate ideas.[65] To-morrow I will bring you a score of pamphlets that have been written against him."

"Pray, Sir," said Candide to the Abbé, "how many theatrical pieces have you in France?"

"Five or six thousand," replied the other.

"Indeed! that is a great number," said Candide: "but how many good ones may there be?"

"About fifteen or sixteen."

"Oh! that is a great number," said Martin.

Candide was greatly taken with an actress who performed the part of Queen Elizabeth in a dull kind of tragedy that is played sometimes.[66]

"That actress," said he to Martin, "pleases me greatly; she has some sort of resemblance to Miss Cunegund. I should be very glad to pay my respects to her."

The Abbé of Périgord offered his services to introduce him to her at her own house. Candide, who was brought up in Germany, desired to

[63] *Billets de confession* were required of seriously ill persons in eighteenth-century France. These authorized a priest to give such persons the last rites and bury them in consecrated ground.

[64] A card game.

[65] Descartes believed that certain ideas were innate rather than acquired; Locke denied that any ideas were innate. Neither theory, of course, has anything to do with tragedy.

[66] Thomas Corneille's *The Earl of Essex* (1678).

know what might be the ceremonial used on those occasions, and how a Queen of England was treated in France.

"There is a necessary distinction to be observed in these matters," said the Abbé. "In a country town we take them to a tavern; here in Paris, they are treated with great respect during their lifetime, provided they are handsome, and when they die, we throw their bodies upon a dunghill."[67]

"How," said Candide, "throw a queen's body upon a dunghill!"

"The gentleman is quite right," said Martin; "he tells you nothing but the truth. I happened to be in Paris when Mlle. Monime made her exit, as one may say, out of this world into another.[68] She was refused what they call here the rights of sepulture; that is to say, she was denied the privilege of rotting in a churchyard by the side of all the beggars in the parish. She was buried alone by her troupe at the corner of Burgundy Street, which must certainly have shocked her extremely, as she had very exalted notions of things."

"This is acting very impolitely," said Candide.

"Lord!" said Martin, "what can be said to it? It is the way of these people. Figure to yourself all the contradictions, all the inconsistencies possible, and you may meet with them in the government, the courts of justice, the churches, and the public spectacles of this odd nation."

"Is it true," said Candide, "that the people of Paris are always laughing?"

"Yes," replied the Abbé, "but it is with anger in their hearts; they express all their complaints by loud bursts of laughter, and commit the most detestable crimes with a smile on their faces."

"Who was that great overgrown beast," said Candide, "who spoke so ill to me of the piece with which I was so much affected, and of the players who gave me so much pleasure?"

"A good-for-nothing sort of a man," answered the Abbé, "one who gets his livelihood by abusing every new book and play; he abominates to see anyone meet with success, like eunuchs, who detest every one that possesses those powers they are deprived of; he is one of those vipers in literature who nourish themselves with their own venom; a pamphlet-monger."

"A pamphlet-monger!" said Candide, "what is that?"

"Why, a pamphlet-monger," replied the Abbé, "is a writer of pamphlets, a Fréron."[69]

Candide, Martin, and the Abbé of Périgord argued thus on the staircase, while they stood to see people go out of the playhouse.

"Though I am very earnest to see Miss Cunegund again," said Candide, "yet I have a great inclination to sup with Mlle. Clairon,[70] for I am really much taken with her."

[67] Voltaire campaigned vigorously against the ban on burying actors and actresses in consecrated ground.

[68] "Mlle. Monime" was Adrienne Lecouvreur (1690–1730), who made her debut as Monime in Racine's *Mithridate* and became the greatest tragic actress of her age. Voltaire's "Ode on the death of Mlle. Lecouvreur" protests the Church's refusal to allow her to be buried in holy ground; he was present at her secret, midnight funeral.

[69] Fréron was a journalist who had attacked Voltaire's plays.

[70] Mlle. Clairon was Claire Leris, an actress who had performed in Voltaire's plays.

The Abbé was not a person to show his face at this lady's house, which was frequented by none but the best company.

"She is engaged this evening," said he; "but I will do myself the honor of introducing you to a lady of quality of my acquaintance, at whose house you will see as much of the manners of Paris as if you had lived here for four years."

Candide, who was naturally curious, suffered himself to be conducted to this lady's house, which was in the suburb of St. Honoré. The company were engaged at faro;[71] twelve melancholy punters held each in his hand a small pack of cards, the corners of which doubled down were so many registers of their ill-fortune. A profound silence reigned throughout the assembly, a pallid dread was in the countenances of the punters, and restless anxiety in the face of him who kept the bank; and the lady of the house, who was seated next to him, observed pitilessly with lynx's eyes every parole, and sept-et-la-va as they were going, as likewise those who tallied, and made them undouble their cards with a severe exactness, though mixed with a politeness which she thought necessary not to frighten away her customers. This lady assumed the title of Marchioness of Parolignac. Her daughter, a girl of about fifteen years of age, was one of the punters, and took care to give her mamma an item, by signs, when any one of them attempted to repair the rigor of their ill fortune by a little innocent deception. The company were thus occupied, when Candide, Martin, and the Abbé made their entrance: not a creature rose to salute them, or indeed took the least notice of them, being wholly intent upon the business in hand.

"Ah!" said Candide, "my lady Baroness of Thunder-ten-tronckh would have behaved more civilly."

However, the Abbé whispered in the ear of the marchioness, who half rose, and honored Candide with a gracious smile and Martin with a dignified inclination of her head. She then ordered a seat for Candide and a hand of cards. He lost fifty thousand francs in two rounds. After that, they supped very elegantly, and every one was astounded that Candide was not disturbed at his loss. The servants said to each other in their servants' language:

"This must be some English lord!"

Supper was like most others of this kind in Paris; at first there was silence, then there was an indistinguishable babel of words, then jokes, most of them insipid, false reports, bad reasonings, a little political talk, and much scandal. They spoke also of new books.

"Have you seen," said the Abbé of Périgord, "the romance written by Monsieur Gauchat, the doctor of theology?"[72]

"Yes," replied one of the guests, "but I had not the patience to go through it. We have a throng of impertinent writers, but all of them together do not approach Gauchat, the doctor of theology, in impertinence. I am so sated with reading these piles of vile stuff that flood upon us that I even resolved to come here and make a party at faro."

[71] A card game. The players are called "punters" and they bet against the banker. A "parole" is an illegal doubling of one's bet. (Hence the lady's title of "Marchioness of Parolignac.") A "sept-et-la-va" is a bet at high odds, and "tallying" is folding down a card as a signal.
[72] Another literary enemy of Voltaire's.

"But what say you to Archdeacon Trublet's miscellanies?"[73] said the Abbé.

"Oh," cried the Marchioness of Parolignac, "tedious creature. What pains he is at to tell one things that all the world knows. How he labors an argument that is hardly the slightest consideration! How absurdly he makes use of other people's wit! How he mangles what he pilfers from them! How he disgusts me! But he will disgust me no more. It is enough to have read a few pages of the Archdeacon."

There was at the table a person of learning and taste, who supported what the Marchioness had advanced. They next began to talk of tragedies. The lady desired to know how it came about that there were several tragedies which still continued to be played, but which were unreadable. The man of taste explained very clearly how a piece may be in some manner interesting, without having a grain of merit. He showed, in a few words, that it is not sufficient to throw together a few incidents that are to be met with in every romance, and that dazzle the spectator; the thoughts should be new without being far-fetched; frequently sublime, but always natural; the author should have a thorough knowledge of the human heart and make it speak properly. He should be a complete poet, without showing an affectation of it in any of the characters of his piece; he should be a perfect master of his language, speak it with all its purity, and with the utmost harmony, and yet not so as to make the sense a slave to the rhyme.

"Whoever," added he, "neglects any of these rules, though he may write two or three tragedies with tolerable success, will never be reckoned in the number of good authors. There are a few good tragedies, some are idylls, in well-written and harmonious dialogue, and others a chain of political reasonings that send one to sleep, or else pompous and high-flown amplifications that disgust rather than please. Others again are the ravings of a madman, in an uncouth style, with unmeaning flights, or long apostrophes, to the deities, for want of knowing how to address mankind; in a word, a collection of false maxims and dull commonplaces."

Candide listened to this discourse with great attention, and conceived a high opinion for the person who delivered it; and as the Marchioness had taken care to place him at her side, he took the liberty to whisper softly in her ear and ask who this person was who spoke so well.

"It is a man of letters," replied her ladyship, "who never plays and whom the Abbé brings with him to my house sometimes to spend an evening. He is a great judge of writing, especially in tragedy; he has composed one himself which was damned, and has written a book which was never seen out of his bookseller's shop, excepting only one copy, which he sent me with a dedication."

"What a great man," cried Candide, "he is a second Pangloss."

Then, turning towards him, "Sir," said he, "you are doubtless of the opinion that everything is for the best in the physical and moral world and that nothing could be otherwise than it is?"

"I, Sir," replied the man of letters, "I think no such thing, I assure you. I find that all in this world is set the wrong end uppermost. No one knows what is his rank, his office, nor what he does, nor what he should do; and

[73] Trublet had also attacked Voltaire's writing.

that except for our evenings which we generally pass tolerably merrily, the rest of our time is spent in idle disputes and quarrels, Jansenists against Molinists,[74] the Parliament against the Church, men of letters against men of letters, countries against countries, financiers against the people, wives against husbands, relations against relations. In short, there is eternal warfare."

"Yes," said Candide, "and I have seen worse than all that; and yet a learned man, who had the misfortune to be hanged, taught me that everything was marvellously well, and that these evils you are speaking of were only so many shadows in a beautiful picture."

"Your hempen sage," said Martin, "laughed at you. These shadows as you call them are most horrible blemishes."

"It is men who make these blemishes," rejoined Candide, "and they cannot do otherwise."

"Then it is not their fault," added Martin.

The great part of the gamesters, who did not understand a syllable of this discourse, continued to drink, while Martin reasoned with the learned gentleman, and Candide recounted some of his adventures to the lady of the house.

After supper, the Marchioness conducted Candide into her dressing-room, and made him sit down on a sofa.

"Well," said she, "are you still so violently fond of Miss Cunegund of Thunder-ten-tronckh?"

"Yes, Madam," replied Candide.

The Marchioness said to him with a tender smile, "You answer like a young man from Westphalia. A Frenchman would have said, 'It is true, Madam, I had a great passion for Miss Cunegund, but since I have seen you, I fear I can no longer love her as I did.'"

"Alas! Madam," replied Candide, "I'll make you what answer you please."

"You fell in love with her, I find, in picking up her handkerchief. You shall pick up my garter."

"With all my heart," said Candide.

"But you must tie it on," said the lady; and Candide tied it on.

"Look you," said the lady, "you are a stranger. I make some of my lovers here in Paris languish for me a fortnight, but I surrender to you the first night, because I am willing to do the honors of my country to a young Westphalian."

The fair one having cast her eye on two large diamonds on the young stranger's finger, praised them in so earnest a manner that they passed from Candide's fingers to those of the Marchioness.

As Candide was going home with the Abbé, he felt some qualms of conscience for having been guilty of infidelity to Miss Cunegund. The Abbé shared with him in his uneasiness; he had but an inconsiderable share in the fifty thousand francs that Candide had lost at play, and in the value of the two jewels, half given, half extorted from him. His plan was to profit as much as he could from the advantages which his acquaintance with Can-

[74] For the Jansenists, see footnote 60. The Molinists were the Jesuit party. They differed on the issue of grace and good works in attaining salvation.

dide could procure for him. He spoke to him much of Miss Cunegund, and Candide assured him that he would heartily ask pardon of that fair one for his infidelity to her, when he saw her at Venice.

The Abbé redoubled his civilities and seemed to interest himself warmly in everything that Candide said, did, or seemed inclined to do.

"And so, Sir, you have a *rendez-vous* at Venice?"

"Yes, Monsieur l'Abbé," answered Candide. "I must indeed go and find Miss Cunegund."

Then the pleasure he took in talking about the object he loved led him insensibly to relate, according to custom, part of his adventures with the illustrious Westphalian beauty.

"I fancy," said the Abbé, "Miss Cunegund has a great deal of wit, and that her letters must be very entertaining."

"I never received any from her," said Candide, "for you are to consider that being kicked out of the castle on her account, I could not write to her; especially as, soon after my departure, I heard she was dead; that though I found her again, I lost her, and that I have sent a messenger to her two thousand five hundred leagues from here, and I wait here for his return with an answer from her."

The Abbé listened attentively—and seemed a little thoughtful. He soon took leave of the two strangers, after having embraced them tenderly. The next day, immediately on waking, Candide received a letter couched in these terms:

"My dearest lover, I have been ill in this city these eight days. I have heard of your arrival and should fly to your arms, were I able to move a limb of me. I was informed of your procedure at Bordeaux. I left there the faithful Cacambo and the old woman who will soon follow me. The Governor of Buenos Ayres has taken everything from me; but I still have your heart. Come. Your presence will restore me to life or will make me die with pleasure."

At the receipt of this charming, this unexpected letter, Candide felt the utmost joy, though the malady of his beloved Cunegund overwhelmed him with grief. Distracted between these two passions, he took his gold and his diamonds and procured a person to direct him with Martin to the house where Miss Cunegund lodged. He entered, trembling with emotion, his heart fluttered, his tongue faltered. He attempted to draw the curtain apart, and called for a light to the bedside.

"Take care," said the servant, "the light is unbearable to her"; and immediately she closed the curtains again.

"My beloved," said Candide, weeping, "how are you? If you cannot see me, at least speak to me."

"She cannot speak," said the servant. The lady then put from the bed a plump hand which Candide bathed with his tears; then filled with diamonds, leaving a purse full of gold on the arm-chair.

In the midst of his transports there arrived an officer, followed by the Abbé of Périgord and a file of musketeers.

"There," said he, "are the two suspected foreigners."

He had them seized forthwith and bade the soldiers carry them off to prison.

"Travellers are not treated in this manner in El Dorado," said Candide.

"I am more of a Manichaean now than ever," said Martin.

"But pray, good Sir, where are you taking us?" asked Candide.

"To a dungeon," said the officer.

Martin having recovered his calm judged that the lady who pretended to be Cunegund was a cheat, that the Abbé of Périgord was a sharper, who had imposed upon Candide's simplicity so quickly as he could, and the officer another knave whom they might easily get rid of.

Candide, following the advice of his friend Martin, and burning with impatience to see the real Cunegund, rather than be obliged to appear at a court of justice, proposed to the officer to make him a present of three small diamonds, each of them worth three thousand pistoles.

"Ah, Sir," said this understrapper of justice, "had you committed ever so much villainy, this would render you the honestest man living in my eyes. Three diamonds, worth three thousand pistoles. Why, my dear Sir, so far from leading you to jail, I would lose my life to serve you. There are orders to arrest all strangers, but leave it to me. I have a brother at Dieppe in Normandy. I myself will conduct you thither, and if you have a diamond left to give him, he will take as much care of you as I myself should."

"But why," said Candide, "do they arrest all strangers?"

The Abbé of Périgord answered that it was because a poor devil of the province of Atrébatie heard somebody tell foolish stories, and this induced him to commit a parricide; not such a one as that in the month of May, 1610, but such as that in the month of December in the year 1594, and such as many that have been perpetrated in other months and years by other poor devils who had heard foolish stories.[75]

The officer then explained to them what the Abbé meant.

"Monsters," exclaimed Candide. "Is it possible that such horrors should pass among a people who are continually singing and dancing? Is there no immediate means of flying this abominable country, where monkeys provoke tigers? I have seen bears in my country, but men I have beheld nowhere but in El Dorado. In the name of God, Sir," said he to the officer, "do me the kindness to conduct me to Venice, where I am to wait upon Miss Cunegund."

"I cannot conduct you further than Lower Normandy," said the officer.

So saying, he ordered Candide's irons to be struck off and sent his followers about their business, after which he conducted Candide and Martin to Dieppe, and left them to the care of his brother. There happened just then to be a small Dutch ship in the roads. The Norman, whom the other three diamonds had converted into the most obliging, serviceable being that ever breathed, took care to see Candide and his attendants safe on board the vessel, that was just ready to sail for Portsmouth in England. This was not the nearest way to Venice indeed; but Candide thought himself escaped out of hell, and did not in the least doubt but he should quickly find an opportunity of resuming his voyage to Venice.

[75] Atrébatie is the Latin name for the district of Artois, the home of a man who attempted to assassinate Louis XV in 1757. The years 1594 and 1610 were the dates of attempted assassinations of Henry IV (Henry of Navarre), the second one successful.

CHAPTER XXIII

Candide and Martin touch upon the English coast; what they saw there.

"Ah Pangloss! Pangloss! Ah, Martin! Martin! Ah, my dear Miss Cunegund! What sort of a world is this?" Thus exclaimed Candide, as soon as he had got on board the Dutch ship.

"Why, something very foolish, and very abominable," said Martin.

"You are acquainted with England," said Candide; "are they as great fools in that country, as in France?"

"Yes, but in a different manner," answered Martin. "You know that these two nations are at war about a few acres of snow in the neighborhood of Canada, and that they have expended much greater sums in the contest than all Canada is worth.[76] To say exactly whether there are a greater number fit to be inhabitants of a mad-house in the one country than the other, exceeds the limits of my imperfect capacity; I know, in general, that the people we are going to visit are of a very dark and gloomy disposition."

As they were chatting thus together, they arrived at Portsmouth. The shore, on each side of the harbor, was lined with a multitude of people, whose eyes were steadfastly fixed on a lusty man, who was kneeling down on the deck of one of the men of war, with his eyes bound. Opposite to this personage stood four soldiers, each of whom shot three bullets into his skull, with all the composure imaginable; and when it was done, the whole company went away perfectly well satisfied.[77]

"What the devil is all this for?" said Candide; "and what demon lords it thus over all the world?"

He then asked who was that lusty man who had been sent out of the world with so much ceremony, and he received for answer, that it was an admiral.

"And, pray," he said, "why do you put your admiral to death?"

"Because he did not put a sufficient number of his fellow creatures to death. You must know, he had an engagement with a French admiral, and it has been proved against him that he was not near enough to his antagonist."

"But," replied Candide, "the French admiral must have been as far from him."

"There is no doubt of that; but in this country it is found requisite, now and then, to put one admiral to death, in order to spirit up the others."

Candide was so shocked at what he saw and heard that he would not set foot on shore, but made a bargain with the Dutch skipper (were he even to rob him like the captain of Surinam) to carry him directly to Venice.

The skipper was ready in two days. They sailed along the coast of France, and passed within sight of Lisbon, at which Candide trembled. From thence they proceeded to the straits, entered the Mediterranean, and at length arrived at Venice.

[76] The wars of the French and English over Canada lasted until 1763.
[77] Voltaire based this incident on the execution of the English admiral John Byng, in 1757.

"God be praised," said Candide, embracing Martin, "this is the place where I am to behold my beloved Cunegund once again. I can rely on Cacambo, like another self. All is well, all very well, all as well as possible."

CHAPTER XXIV

Of Pacquette and Friar Giroflée.

Upon their arrival at Venice, he went in search of Cacambo at every inn and coffee-house, and among all the ladies of pleasure; but could hear nothing of him. He sent every day to inquire of every ship and every vessel that came in: still no news of Cacambo.

"It is strange!" said he to Martin, "very strange! that I should have had time to sail from Surinam to Bordeaux; to travel from thence to Paris, to Dieppe, to Portsmouth; to sail along the coast of Portugal and Spain, and up the Mediterranean, to spend some months in Venice; and that my lovely Cunegund should not have arrived. Instead of her, I only met with a Parisian impostor, and a rascally Abbé of Périgord. Cunegund is actually dead, and I have nothing to do but to follow her. Alas! how much better would it have been for me to have remained in the paradise of El Dorado than to have returned to this cursed Europe! You are in the right, my dear Martin; you are certainly in the right; all is misery and deceit."

He fell into a deep melancholy, and neither went to the opera in vogue, nor partook of any of the diversions of the Carnival; not a woman caused him even a moment's temptation.

Martin said to him, "Upon my word, I think you are very simple to imagine that a rascally valet, with five or six millions in his pocket, would go in search of your mistress to the further end of the world, and bring her to Venice to meet you. If he finds her, he will take her for himself; if he does not, he will take another. Let me advise you to forget your valet Cacambo, and your mistress Cunegund."

Martin's speech was not consoling. Candide's melancholy increased, and Martin never left proving to him that there is very little virtue or happiness in this world; except, perhaps, in El Dorado where hardly anybody can gain admittance.

While they were disputing on this important subject, and still expecting Miss Cunegund, Candide perceived a young Theatine friar[78] in St. Mark's Place, with a girl under his arm. The Theatine looked fresh-colored, plump, and vigorous; his eyes sparkled; his air and gait were bold and lofty. The girl was very pretty, and was singing a song; and every now and then gave her Theatine an amorous ogle and wantonly pinched his ruddy cheeks.

"You will at least allow," said Candide to Martin, "that these two are happy. Hitherto I have met with none but unfortunate people in the whole habitable globe, except in El Dorado; but, as to this couple, I would venture to lay a wager they are happy."

[78] Member of a Catholic order founded in 1524.

"Done," said Martin; "they are not, for what you will."

"Well, we have only to ask them to dine with us," said Candide, "and you will see whether I am mistaken or not."

Thereupon he accosted them, and with great politeness invited them to his inn to eat some macaroni, with Lombard partridges and caviar, and to drink a bottle of Montepulciano, Lacrima Christi, Cyprus and Samos wine. The girl blushed; the Theatine accepted the invitation, and she followed him, eyeing Candide every now and then with a mixture of surprise and confusion, while the tears stole down her cheeks. No sooner did she enter his apartment than she cried out:

"How, Mr. Candide, have you quite forgotten poor Pacquette? Do you not know her again?"

Candide, who had not regarded her with any degree of attention before, being wholly occupied with the thoughts of his dear Cunegund, exclaimed:

"Ah! is it you, child? Was it you that reduced Dr. Pangloss to that fine condition I saw him in?"

"Alas! Sir," answered Pacquette, "it was I, indeed. I find you are acquainted with everything; and I have been informed of all the misfortunes that happened to the whole family of my lady Baroness and the fair Cunegund. But I can safely swear to you that my lot was no less deplorable; I was innocence itself when you saw me last. A cordelier, who was my confessor, easily seduced me; the consequences proved terrible. I was obliged to leave the castle some time after the Baron kicked you out by the backside from there; and if a famous surgeon had not taken compassion on me, I had been a dead woman. Gratitude obliged me to live with him some time as a mistress: his wife, who was a very devil for jealousy, beat me unmercifully every day. Oh! she was a perfect fury. The doctor himself was the most ugly of all mortals, and I the most wretched creature existing, to be continually beaten for a man whom I did not love. You are sensible, Sir, how dangerous it was for an ill-natured woman to be married to a physician. Incensed at the behavior of his wife, he one day gave her so affectionate a remedy for a slight cold she had caught, that she died in less than two hours in most dreadful convulsions. Her relations prosecuted the husband, who was obliged to fly, and I was sent to prison. My innocence would not have saved me, if I had not been tolerably handsome. The judge gave me my liberty on condition he should succeed the doctor. However, I was soon supplanted by a rival, turned off without a farthing, and obliged to continue the abominable trade which you men think so pleasing, but which to us unhappy creatures is the most dreadful of all sufferings. At length I came to follow the business at Venice. Ah! Sir, did you but know what it is to be obliged to lie indifferently with old tradesmen, with counsellors, with monks, gondoliers, and abbés; to be exposed to all their insolence and abuse; to find it often necessary to borrow a petticoat, only that it may be taken up by some disagreeable wretch; to be robbed by one gallant of what we get from another; to be subject to the extortions of civil magistrates; and to have for ever before one's eyes the prospect of old age, a hospital, or a dunghill, you would conclude that I am one of the most unhappy wretches breathing."

Thus did Pacquette unbosom herself to honest Candide in his closet, in the presence of Martin, who took occasion to say to him:

"You see I have half won the wager already."

Friar Giroflée[79] was all this time in the parlor refreshing himself with a glass or two of wine till dinner was ready.

"But," said Candide to Pacquette, "you looked so gay and content, when I met you, you were singing, and caressing the Theatine with so much fondness that I absolutely thought you as happy as you say you are now miserable."

"Ah! dear Sir," said Pacquette, "this is one of the miseries of the trade; yesterday I was stripped and beaten by an officer; yet to-day I must appear good-humored and gay to please a friar."

Candide was convinced, and acknowledged that Martin was in the right. They sat down to table with Pacquette and the Theatine; the entertainment was very agreeable, and towards the end they began to converse together with some freedom.

"Father," said Candide, to the friar, "you seem to me to enjoy a state of happiness that even kings might envy; joy and health are painted in your countenance. You have a tight pretty wench to divert you; and you seem to be perfectly well contented with your condition as a Theatine."

"Faith, Sir," said Friar Giroflée, "I wish with all my soul the Theatines were every one of them at the bottom of the sea. I have been tempted a thousand times to set fire to the convent and go and turn Turk. My parents obliged me, at the age of fifteen, to put on this detestable habit only to increase the fortune of an elder brother of mine, whom God confound! Jealousy, discord, and fury reside in our convent. It is true, I have preached some paltry sermons, by which I have got a little money, half of which the prior robs me of, and the remainder helps to pay my girls; but, at night, when I go hence to my convent, I am ready to dash my brains against the walls of the dormitory; and this is the case with all the rest of our fraternity."

Martin, turning towards Candide, with his usual indifference, said, "Well, what think you now? Have I won the wager entirely?"

Candide gave two thousand piastres to Pacquette, and a thousand to Friar Giroflée, saying, "I will answer that this will make them happy."

"I am not of your opinion," said Martin; "perhaps this money will only make them much more wretched."

"Be that as it may," said Candide, "one thing comforts me; I see that one often meets with those whom we expected never to see again; so that, perhaps, as I have found my red sheep and Pacquette, I may be lucky enough to find Miss Cunegund also."

"I wish," said Martin, "she one day may make you happy, but I doubt it much."

"You are very hard of belief," said Candide.

"It is because," said Martin, "I have seen the world."

"Observe those gondoliers," said Candide; "are they not perpetually singing?"

[79] Giroflée means "gillyflower," and Paquette means "daisy."

"You do not see them," answered Martin, "at home with their wives and brats. The doge[80] has his chagrin, gondoliers theirs. Nevertheless, in the main, I look upon the gondolier's life as preferable to that of the doge; but the difference is so trifling that it is not worth the trouble of examining into."

"I have heard great talk," said Candide, "of the senator Pococurante,[81] who lives in that fine house at the Brenta, where, they say, he entertains foreigners in the most polite manner. They claim that this man is a perfect stranger to uneasiness."

"I should be glad to see so extraordinary a being," said Martin.

Candide thereupon sent a messenger to Signor Pococurante, desiring permission to wait on him the next day.

CHAPTER XXV

Candide and Martin pay a visit to Signor Pococurante, a noble Venetian.

Candide and his friend Martin went in a gondola on the Brenta, and arrived at the palace of the noble Pococurante: the gardens were laid out in an elegant taste, and adorned with beautiful marble statues; his palace was architecturally magnificent. The master of the house, who was a man of sixty, and very rich, received our two travellers with great politeness, but without much ceremony, which somewhat disconcerted Candide, but was not at all displeasing to Martin.

First, two very pretty girls, neatly dressed, brought in chocolate, which was extremely well frothed. Candide could not help praising their beauty and graceful carriage.

"The creatures are well enough," said the senator; "I make them lie with me sometimes, for I am heartily tired of the women of the town, their coquetry, their jealousy, their quarrels, their humors, their meannesses, their pride, and their folly; I am weary of making sonnets, or of paying for sonnets to be made on them; but, after all, these two girls begin to grow very indifferent to me."

After having refreshed himself, Candide walked into a large gallery, where he was struck with the sight of a fine collection of paintings. He asked what master had painted the two first.

"They are Raphael's," answered the senator. "I gave a great deal of money for them some years ago, purely out of conceit, as they were said to be the finest pieces in Italy; but I cannot say they please me: the coloring is dark and heavy; the figures do not swell nor come out enough, and the drapery has no resemblance to the actual material. In short, notwithstanding the encomiums lavished upon them, they are not, in my opinion, a true representation of nature. I approve of no paintings but where I think I behold nature herself; and there are none of that kind to be met with. I have what is called a fine collection, but I take no manner of delight in them."

[80]Chief magistrate of Venice. [81]Pococurante means "small care."

While dinner was getting ready, Pococurante ordered a concert. Candide praised the music to the skies.

"This noise," said the noble Venetian, "may amuse one for a little time, but if it was to last above half an hour, it would grow tiresome to everybody, though perhaps no one would care to own it. Music is become the art of executing what is difficult; now, whatever is difficult cannot be long pleasing. I believe I might take more pleasure in an opera, if they had not made such a monster of it as perfectly shocks me; and I am amazed how people can bear to see wretched tragedies set to music; where the scenes are contrived for no other purpose than to lug in, as it were by the ears, three or four ridiculous songs, to give a favorite actress an opportunity of exhibiting her pipe. Let who will, or can, die away in raptures at the trills of an eunuch quavering the majestic part of Caesar or Cato, and strutting in a foolish manner upon the stage; for my part, I have long ago renounced these paltry entertainments which constitute the glory of modern Italy, and are so dearly purchased by crowned heads."

Candide opposed these sentiments; but he did it in a discreet manner; as for Martin, he was entirely of the old senator's opinion.

Dinner being served they sat down to table, and after a very hearty repast returned to the library. Candide, observing Homer richly bound, commended the noble Venetian's taste.

"This," said he, "is a book that was once the delight of the great Pangloss, the best philosopher in Germany."

"Homer is no favorite of mine," answered Pococurante, very coolly: "I was made to believe once that I took a pleasure in reading him; but his continual repetitions of battles have all such a resemblance with each other; his gods that are for ever in a hurry and bustle, without ever doing anything; his Helen, that is the cause of the war, and yet hardly acts in the whole performance; his Troy, that holds out so long, without being taken: in short, all these things together make the poem very insipid to me. I have asked some learned men, whether they are not in reality as much tired as myself with reading this poet: those who were sincere assured me that he had made them fall asleep; and yet, that they could not well avoid giving him a place in their libraries as a monument of antiquity or like those rusty medals which are of no use in commerce."

"But your Excellency does not surely form the same opinion of Virgil?" said Candide.

"Why, I grant," replied Pococurante, "that the second, third, fourth, and sixth book of his *Aeneid* are excellent; but as for his pious Aeneas, his strong Cloanthus, his friendly Achates, his boy Ascanius, his silly king Latinus, his ill-bred Amata, his insipid Lavinia, I think there cannot in nature be anything more flat and disagreeable. I must confess, I prefer Tasso far beyond him; nay, even that sleepy tale-teller Ariosto."

"May I take the liberty to ask if you do not receive great pleasure from reading Horace?" said Candide.

"There are maxims in this writer," replied Pococurante, "from whence a man of the world may reap some benefit; and the short and forceful measure of the verse makes them more easily to be retained in the memory. But I see nothing extraordinary in his journey to Brundisium, and his account of his bad dinner; nor in his dirty low quarrel between one

Rupilius, whose words, as he expresses it, were full of poisonous filth, and another, whose language was dipped in vinegar. His indelicate verses against old women and witches have frequently given me great offense; nor can I discover the great merit of his telling his friend Maecenas that if he will but rank him in the class of lyric poets, his lofty head shall touch the stars. Ignorant readers are apt to praise everything by the lump in a writer of reputation. For my part, I read only to please myself. I like nothing but what makes for my purpose."

Candide, who had been brought up with a notion of never making use of his own judgment, was astonished at what he had heard; but Martin found there was a good deal of reason in the senator's remarks.

"Oh! here is a Cicero," said Candide: "this great man, I fancy, you are never tired of reading?"

"Indeed, I never read him at all," replied Pococurante. "What a deuce is it to me whether he pleads for Rabirius or Cluentius? I try causes enough myself. I had once some liking for his philosophical works; but when I found he doubted of everything, I thought I knew as much as he, and had no need of a guide to learn ignorance."

"Ha!" cried Martin, "here are fourscore volumes of the memoirs of the Academy of Science; perhaps there may be something valuable in them."

"Yes," answered Pococurante; "so there might if any one of the compilers of this rubbish had only invented the art of pin-making: but all these volumes are filled with mere chimerical systems without one single article conducive to real utility."

"I see a prodigious number of plays," said Candide, "in Italian, Spanish, and French."

"Yes," replied the Venetian; "there are I think three thousand, and not three dozen of them good for anything. As to these huge volumes of divinity, and those enormous collections of sermons, they are altogether not worth one single page in Seneca; and I fancy you will readily believe that neither myself, nor any one else, ever looks into them."

Martin noticed some shelves filled with English books.

"I fancy," he said, "that a republican must be highly delighted with those books, which are most of them written with a noble spirit of freedom."

"It is noble to write as we think," said Pococurante; "it is the privilege of humanity. Throughout Italy we write only what we do not think; and the present inhabitants of the country of the Caesars and Antoninuses dare not acquire a single idea without the permission of a Dominican friar. I should be enamored of the spirit of the English nation, did it not utterly frustrate the good effects it would produce, by passion and the spirit of party."

Candide, seeing a Milton, asked the senator if he did not think that author a great man.

"Who?" said Pococurante sharply; "that barbarian who writes a tedious commentary in ten books of rumbling verse, on the first chapter of Genesis? that slovenly imitator of the Greeks, who disfigures the creation, by making the Messiah take a pair of compasses from heaven's armory to plan the world; whereas Moses represented the Deity as producing the whole universe by his fiat? Can I, think you, have any esteem for a writer who has spoiled Tasso's hell and the devil? who transforms Lucifer sometimes into a toad, and, at others, into a pigmy? who makes him say the same thing over

again a hundred times? who metamorphoses him into a school-divine? and who, by an absurdly serious imitation of Ariosto's comic invention of fire-arms, represents the devils and angels cannonading each other in heaven? Neither I nor any other Italian can possibly take pleasure in such melancholy reveries; but the marriage of Sin and Death, and snakes issuing from the womb of the former, are enough to make any person sick that is not lost to all sense of delicacy, while his long description of a lazar-house is fit only for a gravedigger. This obscene, whimsical and disagreeable poem met with neglect at its first publication; and I only treat the author now as he was treated in his own country by his contemporaries."

Candide was sensibly grieved at this speech, as he had a great respect for Homer and was very fond of Milton.

"Alas!" said he softly to Martin, "I am afraid this man holds our German poets in great contempt."

"There would be no such great harm in that," said Martin.

"O what a surprising man!" said Candide, still to himself; "what a prodigious genius is this Pococurante! Nothing can please him."

After finishing their survey of the library, they went down into the garden, when Candide commended the several beauties that offered themselves to his view.

"I know nothing upon earth laid out in such bad taste," said Pococurante; "everything about it is childish and trifling; but I shall have another laid out to-morrow upon a nobler plan."

As soon as our two travellers had taken leave of his Excellency, Candide said to Martin:

"I hope you will own that this man is the happiest of all mortals, for he is above everything he possesses."

"But do not you see," answered Martin, "that he likewise dislikes everything he possesses? It was an observation of Plato, long since, that those are not the best stomachs that reject, without distinction, all sorts of aliments."

"True," said Candide, "but still there must certainly be a pleasure in criticizing everything, and in perceiving faults where others think they see beauties."

"That is," replied Martin, "there is a pleasure in having no pleasure."

"Well, well," said Candide, "I find that I shall be the only happy man at last, when I am blessed with the sight of my dear Cunegund."

"It is good to hope," said Martin.

In the meanwhile, days and weeks passed away, and no news of Cacambo. Candide was so overwhelmed with grief, that he did not reflect on the behavior of Pacquette and Friar Giroflée, who never stayed to return him thanks for the presents he had so generously made them.

CHAPTER XXVI

Candide and Martin sup with six strangers; and who they were.

One evening when Candide, with his attendant Martin, were going to sit down to supper with some foreigners who lodged in the same inn, a man,

with a face the color of soot, came behind him, and taking him by the arm, said:

"Hold yourself in readiness to go along with us, be sure you do not fail."

He turned and beheld Cacambo. Nothing but the sight of Cunegund could have given greater joy and surprise. He was almost beside himself with joy. After embracing this dear friend, he said:

"Cunegund must be here? Where, where is she? Carry me to her this instant, that I may die with joy in her presence."

"Cunegund is not here," answered Cacambo; "she is at Constantinople."

"Good heavens, at Constantinople! but no matter if she was in China, I would fly thither. Let us be gone."

"We depart after supper," said Cacambo. "I cannot at present stay to say anything more to you; I am a slave, and my master waits for me; I must go and attend him at table: but say not a word, only get your supper, and hold yourself in readiness."

Candide, divided between joy and grief, charmed to have thus met with his faithful agent again, and surprised to hear he was a slave, his heart palpitating, his senses confused, but full of the hopes of recovering his mistress, sat down to table with Martin, who beheld all these scenes with great unconcern, and with six strangers who had come to spend the carnival at Venice.

Cacambo waited at table upon one of these strangers. When supper was nearly over, he drew near to his master, and whispered him in the ear:

"Sire, your Majesty may go when you please, the ship is ready."

Having said these words, he left the room. The guests, surprised at what they had heard, looked at each other without speaking a word; when another servant drawing near to his master, in like manner said:

"Sire, your Majesty's post-chaise is at Padua, and the bark is ready."

His master made him a sign, and he instantly withdrew. The company all stared at each other again, and the general astonishment was increased. A third servant then approached another of the strangers, and said:

"Sire, if your Majesty will be advised by me, you will not stay any longer in this place; I will go and get everything ready"—and he instantly disappeared.

Candide and Martin then took it for granted that this was some of the diversions of the carnival, and that these were characters in masquerade. Then a fourth domestic said to the fourth stranger:

"Your Majesty may set out when you please." Saying this, he went away like the rest.

A fifth valet said the same to a fifth master. But the sixth domestic spoke in a different style to the person on whom he waited, and who sat next to Candide.

"Troth, Sir," said he, "they will trust your Majesty no longer, nor myself neither; and we may both of us chance to be sent to jail this very night; and therefore I shall take care of myself, and so adieu."

The servants being all gone, the six strangers, with Candide and Martin, remained in a profound silence. At length Candide broke it by saying:

"Gentlemen, this is a very singular joke, upon my word; why, how came you all to be kings? For my part, I own frankly, that neither my friend Martin here nor myself have any claim to royalty."

Cacambo's master then began, with great gravity, to deliver himself thus in Italian:

"I am not joking in the least, my name is Achmet III. I was Grand Sultan for many years; I dethroned my brother, my nephew dethroned me, my viziers lost their heads, and I am condemned to end my days in the old seraglio. My nephew, the Grand Sultan Mahmud, gives me permission to travel sometimes for my health, and I am come to spend the carnival at Venice."

A young man who sat by Achmet spoke next, and said:

"My name is Ivan. I was once Emperor of all the Russias, but was dethroned in my cradle. My parents were confined, and I was brought up in a prison; yet I am sometimes allowed to travel, though always with persons to keep a guard over me, and I am come to spend the carnival at Venice."

The third said:

"I am Charles Edward, King of England; my father has renounced his right to the throne in my favor. I have fought in defense of my rights, and eight hundred of my followers have had their hearts taken out of their bodies alive and thrown in their faces. I have myself been confined in a prison. I am going to Rome to visit the King my father, who was dethroned as well as myself and my grandfather; and I am come to spend the carnival at Venice."

The fourth spoke thus:

"I am the King of Poland; the fortune of war has stripped me of my hereditary dominions. My father experienced the same vicissitudes of fate. I resign myself to the will of Providence, in the same manner as Sultan Achmet, the Emperor Ivan, and King Charles Edward, whom God long preserve; and I am come to spend the carnival at Venice."

The fifth said:

"I am King of Poland also. I have twice lost my kingdom; but Providence has given me other dominions, where I have done more good than all the Sarmatian kings put together were ever able to do on the banks of the Vistula: I resign myself likewise to Providence; and am come to spend the carnival at Venice."

It now came to the sixth monarch's turn to speak.

"Gentlemen," said he, "I am not so great a prince as the rest of you, it is true; but I am, however, a crowned head. I am Theodore, elected King of Corsica. I have had the title of Majesty, and am now hardly treated with common civility. I have coined money, and am not now worth a single ducat. I have had two secretaries of state, and am now without a valet. I was once seated on a throne, and since that have lain upon a truss of straw in a common jail in London, and I very much fear I shall meet with the same fate here in Venice, where I come, like your Majesties, to divert myself at the carnival."[82]

The other five kings listened to this speech with great attention; it excited their compassion; each of them made the unhappy Theodore a pres-

[82] The six kings are real historical figures: Achmet III of Turkey (1673–1736); Ivan VI of Russia (1740–1764); Charles Edward of England, "Bonnie Prince Charlie" (1720–1788); Augustus III of Poland (1696–1763); Stanislas Leczinski of Poland (1677–1766); and Theodore von Neuhof (1690–1756), who served as elected king of Corsica for about eight months.

ent of twenty sequins to get clothes and shirts, and Candide gave him a diamond worth just an hundred times that sum.

"Who can this private person be," said the five kings, "who is able to give, and has actually given, a hundred times as much as any of us? Are you, Sir, also a king?"

"No, gentlemen, and I have no wish to be one."

Just as they rose from table, in came four Serene Highnesses who had also been stripped of their territories by the fortune of war, and were come to spend the remainder of the carnival at Venice. Candide took no manner of notice of them; for his thoughts were wholly employed on his voyage to Constantinople, whither he intended to go in search of his beloved Cunegund.

CHAPTER XXVII

Candide's voyage to Constantinople.

The trusty Cacambo had already engaged the captain of the Turkish ship that was to carry Sultan Achmet back to Constantinople, to take Candide and Martin on board. Accordingly, they both embarked, after paying their obeisance to his miserable Highness. As they were going on board, Candide said to Martin:

"You see we supped in company with six dethroned kings, and to one of them I gave charity. Perhaps there may be a great many other princes still more unfortunate. For my part, I have lost only a hundred sheep, and am now going to fly to the arms of Cunegund. My dear Martin, I must insist on it, that Pangloss was in the right. All is for the best."

"I wish it may be," said Martin.

"But this was an odd adventure we met with at Venice. I do not think there ever was an instance before, of six dethroned monarchs supping together at a public inn."

"This is no more extraordinary," said Martin, "than most of what has happened to us. It is a very common thing for kings to be dethroned; and as for our having the honor to sup with six of them, it is a mere accident, not deserving our attention. What does it matter with whom one sups, provided one has good fare?"

As soon as Candide set his foot on board the vessel, he flew to his old friend and servant Cacambo; and throwing his arms about his neck, embraced him with transports of joy.

"Well," said he, "what news of Cunegund? Does she still continue the paragon of beauty? Does she love me still? How is she? You have, doubtless, purchased a palace for her at Constantinople?"

"My dear master," replied Cacambo, "Cunegund washes dishes on the banks of the Propontis, in the house of a prince who has very few to wash. She is at present a slave in the family of an ancient sovereign, named Ragotsky,[83] whom the Grand Turk allows three crowns a day

[83] Or Rakoczy, briefly king of Transylvania, later interned in Turkey from 1720 to 1735.

to maintain him in his exile; but the most melancholy circumstance of all is, that she has lost her beauty and turned horribly ugly."

"Ugly or handsome," said Candide, "I am a man of honor; and, as such, am obliged to love her still. But how could she possibly have been reduced to so abject a condition, when I sent five or six millions to her by you?"

"Lord bless me," said Cacambo, "was not I obliged to give two millions to Señor Don Fernando d'Ibaraa y Figueora y Mascarenas y Lampourdos y Souza, Governor of Buenos Ayres, for liberty to take Miss Cunegund away with me? and then did not a brave fellow of a pirate very gallantly strip us of all the rest? and then did not this same pirate carry us with him to Cape Matapan, to Milo, to Nicaria, to Samos, to Petra, to the Dardanelles, to Marmora, to Scutari? Cunegund and the old woman are now servants to the prince I have told you of; and I myself am slave to the dethroned Sultan."

"What a chain of terrible calamities!" exclaimed Candide. "But, after all, I have still some diamonds left, with which I can easily procure Cunegund's liberty. It is a pity she is grown so very ugly."

Then turning to Martin, "What think you, friend," said he, "whose condition is most to be pitied, the Emperor Achmet's, the Emperor Ivan's, King Charles Edward's, or mine?"

"Faith, I cannot resolve your question," said Martin, "unless I had been in the breasts of you all."

"Ah!" cried Candide, "was Pangloss here now, he would have known, and satisfied me at once."

"I know not," said Martin, "in what balance your Pangloss could have weighed the misfortunes of mankind, and have set a just estimation on their sufferings. All that I pretend to know of the matter is that there are millions of men on the earth whose conditions are an hundred times more pitiable than those of King Charles Edward, the Emperor Ivan, or Sultan Achmet."

"Why, that may be," answered Candide.

In a few days they reached the Bosphorus; and the first thing Candide did was to pay a high ransom for Cacambo: then, without losing time, he and his companions went on board a galley, in order to search for his Cunegund, on the banks of the Propontis, notwithstanding she was grown so ugly.

There were two slaves among the crew of the galley, who rowed very ill, and to whose bare backs the master of the vessel frequently applied a lash of oxhide. Candide, from natural sympathy, looked at these two slaves more attentively than at any of the rest, and drew near them with a look of pity. Their features, though greatly disfigured, appeared to him to bear a strong resemblance with those of Pangloss and the unhappy Baron Jesuit, Miss Cunegund's brother. This idea affected him with grief and compassion: he examined them more attentively than before.

"In troth," said he, turning to Martin, "if I had not seen my master Pangloss fairly hanged, and had not myself been unlucky enough to run the Baron through the body, I could believe these are they rowing in the galley."

No sooner had Candide uttered the names of the Baron and Pangloss

than the two slaves gave a great cry, ceased rowing, and let fall their oars out of their hands. The master of the vessel, seeing this, ran up to them, and redoubled the discipline of the lash.

"Hold, hold," cried Candide, "I will give you what money you ask for these two persons."

"Good heavens! it is Candide," said one of the men.

"Candide!" cried the other.

"Do I dream," said Candide, "or am I awake? Am I actually on board this galley? Is this my lord Baron, whom I killed? and that my master Pangloss, whom I saw hanged?"

"It is I! it is I!" cried they both together.

"What! is this your great philosopher?" said Martin.

"My dear Sir," said Candide to the master of the galley, "how much do you ask for the ransom of the Baron of Thunder-ten-tronckh, who is one of the first barons of the empire, and of Mr. Pangloss, the most profound metaphysician in Germany?"

"Why then, Christian cur," replied the Turkish captain, "since these two dogs of Christian slaves are barons and metaphysicians, who no doubt are of high rank in their own country, thou shalt give me fifty thousand sequins."

"You shall have them, Sir: carry me back as quick as thought to Constantinople, and you shall receive the money immediately. No! carry me first to Miss Cunegund."

The captain, upon Candide's first proposal, had already tacked about, and he made the crew apply their oars so effectively that the vessel flew through the water quicker than a bird cleaves the air.

Candide bestowed a thousand embraces on the Baron and Pangloss. "And so then, my dear Baron, I did not kill you? and you, my dear Pangloss, are come to life again after your hanging? But how came you slaves on board a Turkish galley?"

"And is it true that my dear sister is in this country?" said the Baron.

"Yes," said Cacambo.

"And do I once again behold my dear Candide?" said Pangloss.

Candide presented Martin and Cacambo to them; they embraced each other, and all spoke together. The galley flew like lightning, and now they were got back to the port. Candide instantly sent for a Jew, to whom he sold for fifty thousand sequins a diamond richly worth one hundred thousand, though the fellow swore to him all the time, by Abraham, that he gave him the most he could possibly afford. He no sooner got the money into his hands than he paid it down for the ransom of the Baron and Pangloss. The latter flung himself at the feet of his deliverer, and bathed him with his tears: the former thanked him with a gracious nod, and promised to return him the money at the first opportunity.

"But is it possible," said he, "that my sister should be in Turkey?"

"Nothing is more possible," answered Cacambo; "for she scours the dishes in the house of a Transylvanian prince."

Candide sent directly for two Jews, and sold more diamonds to them; and then he set out with his companions in another galley, to deliver Cunegund from slavery.

CHAPTER XXVIII

What befell Candide, Cunegund, Pangloss, Martin, & c.

"Pardon," said Candide to the Baron; "once more let me entreat your pardon, Reverend Father, for running you through the body."

"Say no more about it," replied the Baron; "I was a little too hasty I must own: but as you seem to be anxious to know by what accident I came to be a slave on board the galley where you saw me, I will inform you. After I had been cured of the wound you gave me, by the apothecary of the College, I was attacked and carried off by a party of Spanish troops, who clapped me up in prison in Buenos Ayres, at the very time my sister was setting out from there. I asked leave to return to Rome, to the general of my Order, who appointed me chaplain to the French Ambassador at Constantinople. I had not been a week in my new office, when I happened to meet one evening with a young icoglan;[84] extremely handsome and well made. The weather was very hot; the young man had an inclination to bathe. I took the opportunity to bathe likewise. I did not know it was a crime for a Christian to be found naked in company with a young Turk. A cadi ordered me to receive a hundred blows on the soles of my feet, and sent me to the galleys. I do not believe that there was ever an act of more flagrant injustice. But I would fain know how my sister came to be a scullion to a Transylvanian prince who has taken refuge among the Turks?"

"But how happens it that I behold you again, my dear Pangloss?" said Candide.

"It is true," answered Pangloss, "you saw me hanged, though I ought properly to have been burned; but you may remember that it rained extremely hard when they were going to roast me. The storm was so violent that they found it impossible to light the fire; so they hanged me because they could do no better. A surgeon purchased my body, carried it home, and prepared to dissect me. He began by making a crucial incision from my navel to the clavicle. It is impossible for any one to have been more lamely hanged than I had been. The executioner of the Holy Inquisition was a subdeacon, and knew how to burn people very well, but as for hanging, he was a novice at it, being quite out of the way of his practice; the cord being wet, and not slipping properly, the noose did not join. In short, I still continued to breathe; the crucial incision made me scream to such a degree that my surgeon fell flat upon his back; and imagining it was the devil he was dissecting, ran away, and in his fright tumbled downstairs. His wife hearing the noise flew from the next room, and, seeing me stretched upon the table with my crucial incision, was still more terrified than her husband. She took to her heels and fell over him. When they had a little recovered themselves, I heard her say to her husband, 'My dear, how could you think of dissecting an heretic? Don't you know that the devil is always in them? I'll run directly to a priest to come and drive the evil spirit out.' I trembled from head to foot at hearing her talk in this manner, and exerted what little strength I had left to cry out, 'Have mercy on me!' At length the Portu-

[84] Page to the sultan. The Baron is again presented, by implication, as homosexual.

guese barber took courage, sewed up my wound, and his wife nursed me; and I was upon my legs in a fortnight's time. The barber got me a place as lackey to a Knight of Malta who was going to Venice; but finding my master had no money to pay me my wages, I entered into the service of a Venetian merchant, and went with him to Constantinople.

"One day I happened to enter a mosque, where I saw no one but an old imam and a very pretty young female devotee, who was saying her prayers; her neck was quite bare, and in her bosom she had a beautiful nosegay of tulips, roses, anemones, ranunculuses, hyacinths, and auriculas. She let fall her nosegay. I ran immediately to take it up, and presented it to her with a most respectful bow. I was so long in delivering it, that the imam began to be angry; and, perceiving I was a Christian, he cried out for help; they carried me before the cadi, who ordered me to receive one hundred bastinadoes, and sent me to the galleys. I was chained in the very galley, and to the very same bench with my lord the Baron. On board this galley there were four young men belonging to Marseilles, five Neapolitan priests, and two monks of Corfu, who told us that the like adventures happened every day. The Baron pretended that he had been worse used than myself; and I insisted that there was far less harm in taking up a nosegay, and putting it into a woman's bosom, than to be found stark naked with a young icoglan. We were continually in dispute, and received twenty lashes a-day with a thong, when the concatenation of sublunary events brought you on board our galley to ransom us from slavery."

"Well, my dear Pangloss," said Candide to him, "when you were hanged, dissected, whipped, and tugging at the oar, did you continue to think that every thing in this world happens for the best?"

"I have always abided by my first opinion," answered Pangloss; "for, after all, I am a philosopher; and it would not become me to retract my sentiments; especially, as Leibnitz could not be in the wrong; and that pre-established harmony is the finest thing in the world, as well as the *plenum* and the *materia subtilis.*"[85]

CHAPTER XXIX

In what manner Candide found Cunegund and the old woman again.

While Candide, the Baron, Pangloss, Martin, and Cacambo were relating their several adventures, and reasoning on the contingent or non-contingent events of this world; while they were disputing on causes and effects, on moral and physical evil, on free will and necessity, and on the consolation that may be felt by a person when a slave and chained to an oar in a Turkish galley, they arrived at the house of the Transylvanian prince on the coasts of the Propontis. The first objects they beheld there were Miss Cunegund and the old woman, who were hanging some table-cloths on a line to dry.

The Baron turned pale at the sight. Even the tender Candide, that

[85] "Pre-established harmony," the *plenum* (matter presumed to fill all space), and the *materia subtilis* (all spiritual agencies) are terms and concepts in Leibnitz's system.

affectionate lover, upon seeing his fair Cunegund all sun-burned, with blear eyes, a withered neck, wrinkled face and arms, all covered with a red scurf,[86] started back with horror; but, recovering himself, he advanced towards her out of good manners. She embraced Candide and her brother; they embraced the old woman, and Candide ransomed them both.

There was a small farm in the neighborhood, which the old woman proposed to Candide to make a shift with till the company should meet with a more favorable destiny. Cunegund, not knowing that she was grown ugly, as no one had informed her of it, reminded Candide of his promise in so peremptory a manner that the simple lad did not dare to refuse her; he then acquainted the Baron that he was going to marry his sister.

"I will never suffer," said the Baron, "my sister to be guilty of an action so derogatory to her birth and family; nor will I bear this insolence on your part: no, I never will be reproached that my nephews are not qualified for the first ecclesiastical dignities in Germany; nor shall a sister of mine ever be the wife of any person below the rank of a baron of the Empire."

Cunegund flung herself at her brother's feet, and bedewed them with her tears, but he still continued inflexible.

"Thou foolish fellow," said Candide, "have I not delivered thee from the galleys, paid thy ransom, and thy sister's too who was a scullion, and is very ugly, and yet I condescend to marry her? and shalt thou make claim to oppose the match? If I were to listen only to the dictates of my anger, I should kill thee again."

"Thou mayest kill me again," said the Baron, "but thou shalt not marry my sister while I am living."

CHAPTER XXX

Conclusion.

Candide had, in truth, no great inclination to marry Cunegund; but the extreme impertinence of the baron determined him to conclude the match; and Cunegund pressed him so warmly that he could not recant. He consulted Pangloss, Martin, and the faithful Cacambo. Pangloss composed a fine memorial, by which he proved that the Baron had no right over his sister; and that she might, according to all the laws of the Empire, marry Candide with the left hand.[87] Martin concluded that they should throw the Baron into the sea: Cacambo decided that he must be delivered to the Turkish captain and sent to the galleys; after which he should be conveyed by the first ship to the Father General at Rome. This advice was found to be very good; the old woman approved of it, and not a syllable was said to his sister; the business was executed for a little money: and they had the pleasure of tricking a Jesuit and punishing the pride of a German baron.

It was altogether natural to imagine that after undergoing so many

[86] Scales.
[87] A marriage "with the left hand" is a morganatic marriage, one in which the partner of lower rank relinquishes any claim to rank or property.

disasters, Candide married to his mistress, and living with the philosopher Pangloss, the philosopher Martin, the prudent Cacambo, and the old woman, having besides brought home so many diamonds from the country of the ancient Incas, would lead the most agreeable life in the world. But he had been so much cheated by the Jews that he had nothing else left but his little farm; his wife, every day growing more and more ugly, became ill-natured and insupportable; the old woman was infirm, and more bad-tempered yet than Cunegund. Cacambo, who worked in the garden, and carried the produce of it to sell at Constantinople, was past his labor, and cursed his fate. Pangloss despaired of making a figure in any of the German universities. And as to Martin, he was firmly persuaded that a person is equally ill-situated everywhere. He took things with patience. Candide, Martin, and Pangloss disputed sometimes about metaphysics and morality. Boats were often seen passing under the windows of the farm fraught with effendis, pashas, and cadis, that were going into banishment to Lemnos, Mytilene, and Erzeroum. And other cadis, pashas, and effendis were seen coming back to succeed the place of the exiles, and were driven out in their turns. They saw several heads very curiously stuffed with straw, being carried as presents to the Sublime Porte. Such sights gave occasion to frequent dissertations; and when no disputes were carried on, the irksomeness was so excessive that the old woman ventured one day to say to them:

"I would be glad to know which is worst, to be ravished a hundred times by negro pirates, to have one buttock cut off, to run the gauntlet among the Bulgarians, to be whipped and hanged at an *auto-da-fé*, to be dissected, to be chained to an oar in a galley, and in short to experience all the miseries through which every one of us hath passed,—or to remain here doing nothing?"

"This," said Candide, "is a big question."

This discourse gave birth to new reflections, and Martin especially concluded that man was born to live in the convulsions of disquiet, or in the lethargy of idleness. Though Candide did not absolutely agree to this; yet he was sure of nothing. Pangloss avowed that he had undergone dreadful sufferings; but having once maintained that everything went on as well as possible, he still maintained it, and at the same time believed nothing of it.

There was one thing which, more than ever, confirmed Martin in his detestable principles, made Candide hesitate, and embarrassed Pangloss. This was the arrival of Pacquette and Friar Giroflée one day at their farm. This couple had been in the utmost distress; they had very speedily made away with their three thousand piastres; they had parted, been reconciled; quarrelled again, been thrown into prison; had made their escape, and at last Brother Giroflée turned Turk. Pacquette still continued to follow her trade wherever she came; but she got little or nothing by it.

"I foresaw very well," said Martin to Candide, "that your presents would soon be squandered, and only make them more miserable. You and Cacambo have spent millions of piastres, and yet you are not more happy than Brother Giroflée and Pacquette."

"Ah!" said Pangloss to Pacquette. "It is heaven who has brought you here among us, my poor child! Do you know that you have cost me the tip of my nose, one eye, and one ear? What a handsome shape is here! and what is this world!"

This new adventure engaged them more deeply than ever in philosophical disputations.

In the neighborhood lived a very famous dervish,[88] who passed for the best philosopher in Turkey; him they went to consult: Pangloss, who was their spokesman, addressed him thus:

"Master, we come to entreat you to tell us why so strange an animal as man has been formed."

"Why do you trouble your head about it?" said the dervish. "Is it any business of yours?"

"But, my Reverend Father," said Candide, "there is a horrible deal of evil on the earth."

"What signifies it," said the dervish, "whether there is evil or good? When his Highness sends a ship to Egypt, does he trouble his head whether the rats in the vessel are at their ease or not?"

"What must then be done?" said Pangloss.

"Be silent," answered the dervish.

"I flattered myself," replied Pangloss, "that we should have the pleasure of arguing with you on causes and effects, on the best of possible worlds, the origin of evil, the nature of the soul, and the pre-established harmony."

At these words the dervish shut the door in their faces.

During this conversation, news was spread abroad that two viziers of the bench and the mufti[89] had just been strangled at Constantinople, and several of their friends impaled. This catastrophe made a great noise for some hours. Pangloss, Candide, and Martin, as they were returning to the little farm, met with a good-looking old man, who was taking the air at his door, under an alcove formed of orange-trees. Pangloss, who was as inquisitive as he was argumentative, asked him what was the name of the mufti who was lately strangled.

"I cannot tell," answered the good old man; "I never knew the name of any mufti or vizier breathing. I am entirely ignorant of the event you speak of; I presume that, in general, such as are concerned in public affairs sometimes come to a miserable end; and that they deserve it: but I never inquire what is happening at Constantinople; I am content with sending thither the produce of the garden which I cultivate."

After saying these words, he invited the strangers to come into his house. His two daughters and two sons presented them with diverse sorts of iced sherbet of their own making; besides *caymac*,[90] heightened with the peel of candied citrons, oranges, lemons, pine-apples, pistachio-nuts, and Mocha coffee unadulterated with the bad coffee of Batavia or the West Indies. After which the two daughters of this good Mussulman perfumed the beards of Candide, Pangloss, and Martin.

"You must certainly have a vast estate," said Candide to the Turk.

"I have no more than twenty acres of ground," he replied, "the whole of which I cultivate myself with the help of my children; and our labor keeps off from us three great evils, idleness, vice, and want."

Candide, as he was returning home, made profound reflections on the Turk's discourse.

[88] Member of a Moslem ascetic order. [89] A Moslem advisor on religious law.
[90] A Turkish dessert.

"This good old man," he said to Pangloss and Martin, "appears to me to have chosen for himself a lot much preferable to that of the six kings with whom we had the honor to sup."

"Human grandeur," said Pangloss, "is very dangerous, if we believe the testimonies of almost all philosophers; for we find Eglon, King of the Moabites, was assassinated by Ehud; Absalom was hanged by the hair of his head, and run through with three darts; King Nadab, son of Jeroboam, was slain by Baasha; King Elah by Zimri; Ahaziah by Jehu; Athaliah by Jehoiada; the Kings Jehoiakim, Jechoniah, and Zedekiah were led into captivity: I need not tell you what was the fate of Croesus, Astyages, Darius, Dionysius of Syracuse, Pyrrhus, Perseus, Hannibal, Jugurtha, Ariovistus, Caesar, Pompey, Nero, Otho, Vitellius, Domitian, Richard III of England, Edward II, Henry VI, Richard II, Mary Stuart, Charles I, the three Henrys of France, and the Emperor Henry IV."

"Neither need you tell me," said Candide, "that we must take care of our garden."

"You are in the right," said Pangloss; "for when man was put into the Garden of Eden, it was with an intent to dress it: and this proves that man was not born to be idle."

"Work then without disputing," said Martin; "it is the only way to render life supportable."

The little society, one and all, entered into this laudable design; and set themselves to exert their different talents. The little piece of ground yielded them a plentiful crop. Cunegund indeed was very ugly, but she became an excellent hand at pastry-work; Pacquette embroidered; the old woman had the care of the linen. There was none, down to Brother Giroflée, but did some service; he was a very good carpenter, and became an honest man. Pangloss used now and then to say to Candide:

"There is a concatenation of all events in the best of possible worlds; for, in short, had you not been kicked out of a fine castle by the backside for the love of Miss Cunegund, had you not been put into the Inquisition, had you not travelled over America on foot, had you not run the Baron through the body, and had you not lost all your sheep which you brought from the good country of El Dorado, you would not have been here to eat preserved citrons and pistachio-nuts."

"Excellently observed," answered Candide; "but let us take care of our garden."

Pierre-Augustin Caron de Beaumarchais
(1732–1799)

Collectors of trivia may note that George Washington and the French satirist and playwright Beaumarchais were born in the same year (just a few weeks apart) and also died in the same year. On second thought, the coincidence seems a little less trivial, since each man played a part in a momentous political revolution, in America or France. (Indeed, Beaumarchais had

a hand in both.) There the resemblance ends, however; Beaumarchais led a dizzying eventful life, almost to the point where his life overshadows his literary achievement, but personally he was not cut from the cloth of lofty heroic legend. He was a man of vision, of sorts, a prototypical representative of his rapidly changing times, but he was also an opportunist and a trafficker in his own personality and image. Like Figaro, the most memorable character in his plays, he was a jack of many trades whose career included a violent succession of ups and downs. His two greatest plays, *The Barber of Seville* and *Figaro's Marriage*, have the frenzied pace and the mercurial spirits we might have expected from such an author. What we had no right to expect is that Beaumarchais could sometimes blend with his highly topical and often farcical dramatic material, full of brashness and high jinks, a sensitive insight into human psychology, along with tenderness and pathos.

At his birth in 1732, in Paris, he was simply Pierre-Augustin Caron, the son of a Parisian *horloger*, or clock- and watch-maker; the aristocratic amplification *de Beaumarchais* came later, as a result of marriage. It has been suggested that his penchant for intricate dramatic plots, after he started writing plays, may be connected with his early familiarity with timepieces. The inventive streak in him showed up early, by way of an improved watch-escapement mechanism he invented. He soon got into a complicated legal squabble with another man who claimed to have invented the mechanism—a portent of things to come. The young Caron won his case, but not before the matter had cost him a great deal of trouble. This pattern would be repeated in several later legal imbroglios.

Soon after this decision was rendered, he began to rise rapidly in the social scale. The first step was an appointment as *horloger* to the king. Since the young Beaumarchais was also a highly skilled musician, that appointment led in turn to a post as music teacher (of the harp) to the king's daughters. At the age of twenty-four, he married a well-heeled widow, Madeleine-Catherine Franquet, acquiring the title *de Beaumarchais* by virtue of a property she owned, and acquiring also the office at the royal court formerly held by Mme Franquet's late husband. She herself died ten months after the marriage. (It almost goes without saying that Beaumarchais had to fight off a lawsuit brought by her other heirs.) Something similar was to happen about ten years later: he married the wealthy Geneviève-Madeleine Lévêque, but she too died, after two years, as did also, a year or two after that, the son she had borne him. All this caused some dark suspicions and accusations, especially among people envious of Beaumarchais's rapid social climb, and although there had in fact been no dirty work it is nevertheless typical that the ever-embattled Beaumarchais should have had to defend himself. This was something he was very good at. On one occasion a foppish young courtier, out to remind him of his lowly origins, asked Beaumarchais to repair the courtier's new watch. After confessing apologetically that he had become rusty at the trade, Beaumarchais took the very costly watch, examined it, "accidentally" dropped it on the stone floor (ruining it), bowed, and made his exit. That was his style.

His connections at the royal court also opened the door for Beaumarchais to the world of big money, by bringing him into contact with a financier, fifty years his senior, named Pâris-Duverney, a man who specialized in

enterprises ranging from speculation to military supply (and was not above trying to break into the slave trade). Beaumarchais acquired a fortune, which enabled him—as was common practice at the time—to buy high office and a title, Secretary to the King, that conferred noble status. It was to do business for Pâris-Duverney that Beaumarchais traveled to Spain in 1764, though by his own account he went there to vindicate the honor of his jilted sister. In Spain he absorbed local color—observing especially abuses by the government and the aristocracy—that he would later infuse into his two dramatic masterpieces. When Pâris-Duverney died, another legal contest ensued, brought by his heir to contest the portion Beaumarchais claimed of his late associate's assets.

While that dispute was being adjudicated, Beaumarchais went to prison on still another matter, arising out of a quarrel with the Duc de Chaulnes, whose abused mistress had become attracted to Beaumarchais. The only way out of this morass for Beaumarchais was to grease the palms of a dishonest official named Goezman, of Goezman's wife, and of his secretary. This time Beaumarchais was outbid by the other side. After losing his case and being threatened with the additional charge of corrupting a judge, Beaumarchais decided to go public in his own defense. The result was a series of published *Mémoires* attacking Goezman (1773–74) that for their polemical brilliance have been acclaimed as masterpieces of French literature. Goezman was dismissed, though Beaumarchais also suffered for a time the revocation of his rights as a citizen. After another legal struggle, and aided by the accession of King Louis XVI in 1774, he was vindicated in the Goezman affair.

Beaumarchais also served with great zest as a foreign envoy on some delicate and important missions, including one to England in 1774 to deal with a prospective blackmailer of Louis XV's mistress, Madame Du Barry. A little later he undertook to deal with another blackmailer intent on publishing a libelous account of the alleged sterility of Louis XVI and his queen Marie Antoinette; this adventure led Beaumarchais to several European countries and to the Viennese court of the queen's mother, the Austrian empress Marie-Thérèse. Still another attempt to stem the flood of royal scandal took him to England in 1775, where he successfully negotiated with a mysterious former French ambassador, now living as a transvestite and therefore of uncertain sex. (He turned out to be a man, but Beaumarchais claimed he was a woman, and in love with Beaumarchais at that! That was also Beaumarchais's style.)

Still more important to political history than these quixotic—and, by Beaumarchais, much melodramatized—services to the French royal families was his active intrigue in support of England's American colonies, which were in the process of declaring themselves independent. In this connection he belabored the French government with reasons why it would be politic to assist the Americans. He was successful in getting covert French financial backing for a trading company, Rodrigue Hortalez and Co., that he had volunteered to set up to channel aid to these transatlantic contras. Although there was much of Beaumarchais's usual love of intrigue for its own sake in all this, and although his efforts were hampered by counter-intrigues at home and some standoffishness on the part of the

Americans, there is no doubt that he was a wholehearted supporter of the American revolution and played a key role in winning French diplomatic recognition of the new country in 1778.

In the years between the American revolution and the French one that broke out in 1789, Beaumarchais continued to hatch new schemes, with his usual abandon and gusto. These included an ambitious project to publish the works of the renowned but subversive Voltaire. Understandably, it got only cool support from the French authorities; the edition, a financial disaster to Beaumarchais, was brought out in Germany, after Beaumarchais stoutly resisted an attempt by the authorities there to cut out the offensive parts. Still another of his projects was the formation of a Parisian company to supply the city with river water. After the Revolution erupted, Beaumarchais had the satisfaction of seeing an earlier effort of his crowned with success: authors of plays, as distinguished from the acting companies, were given ownership of the dramatic rights. Beaumarchais's status as a wealthy aristocrat put him in peril. All the same, he continued to offer his services as man of enterprise. He agreed to negotiate the purchase for the French revolutionary regime of a large cache of guns in the Netherlands. In this complicated project he was double-crossed by dishonest French officials, so that he barely avoided being executed and had to flee to England. At great risk, he returned to Paris to plead still one more case in his own defense, this time before the revolutionary National Assembly. After enormous complications and reverses, of the kind that had always set the pattern in his life, he was acquitted of wrongdoing still one more time. The matter did not end there, however. Commissioned once again to buy the Dutch guns, under much the same crippling limitations as the first time, he again went abroad and, as a result, came under proscription by the Revolutionary government as an "emigrant," a status that meant perpetual banishment as an enemy of the state. He remained abroad until 1796, by which time the Revolutionary storm had largely abated. Deaf in his last years, he died suddenly in Paris, of apoplexy, in 1799.

Beaumarchais lived the most public of lives, and it is appropriate that his most important literary work should also have been in the most public, extroverted of modes: satirical pamphleteering and playmaking. Early in his life he wrote a number of short plays of the kind called *parades*, and subsequently, in *Eugénie* (1767) and *The Two Friends* (1770), he tried his hand at the new genre called *drame*, which Beaumarchais considered to be the theatrical form of the future. This kind of play was a deliberate hybrid, written in a domestic or realistic vein between comedy and tragedy and using less artificial language than the French stage was used to; in short, the *drame* was an attempt to escape the rigid, rule-bound structure of seventeenth-century French neoclassic comedy and tragedy as practiced by Molière and Racine. In the *drame* it was common for the characters to put forward moral or philosophical ideas, often on social issues.

Beaumarchais did his greatest work, however, in a vein influenced by *drame* but more exuberant: a pair of fast-paced comedies, *The Barber of Seville* (1775) and *Figaro's Marriage* (1783), notable for their wit, sparkle, freshness, and impudence. Both plays center on Figaro, a barber and later a steward. Figaro can do just about anything, or thinks he can, which in

some ways amounts to the same thing. In both plays Figaro is matched, as accomplice or rival, with the Count Almaviva, to whom Figaro is technically an inferior or servant but really at least an equal. In *The Barber of Seville* Figaro helps Almaviva in his comic, romantic, and finally successful quest for the lovely Rosine, who is under the thumb of a guardian who plans to marry her himself.

Figaro's Marriage takes place several years later. The Count's romantic passion for Rosine, now his Countess, has dulled to indifference (though he can still be fiercely jealous) and has been replaced by a desperate, restless womanizing. The skies have darkened since *The Barber of Seville*, a darkening reflected not only in the Count's character but, even more, in that of the Countess, whose distress arises from the very persistence of her love for her husband and from the still agonizingly vivid memory of their romantic feelings for each other. Indeed, the Count's own lusts are perhaps not merely that; his pursuit of Suzanne, the Countess's personal maid and Figaro's fiancée, almost seems to be a sorry and joyless travesty of his earlier love for Rosine.

Against this pathos, *Figaro's Marriage* counterpoints a vein of gleeful, madcap merriment, not only in Figaro but even more markedly in two newly invented characters: Suzanne, who is every bit Figaro's equal in wit, vivacity, and enterprise; and the adolescent boy Cherubino (cast, however, in a stroke of genius, for an actress). Cherubino's omnivorous love for everything female has all the freshness and innocence so conspicuously absent from the Count's parallel version of promiscuous skirt-chasing. In this intricately plotted play, Cherubino is remarkable for being, as regards plot, almost dispensable. Yet he (she?) contributes immensely to the play and provides several links between the pathetic and farcical plot strands. Not only, in his eager appetites and love-drunk idealism, does he contrast with the Count's jadedness, but he also brings out several sides of the Countess. Cherubino's worship of her above all other women is a constant reminder to her that she is beautiful and desirable. Moreover, she is in a peculiar way strongly attracted to him. Why? Out of angry resentment of her husband and an accompanying half-defiant impulse—all the more defiant because she would almost be robbing the cradle—to take a lover herself? Or is it that she sees in Cherubino a reflection of the Count's former devotion to her, so that in Cherubino she loves an image of the husband she still hopes to win back? Or is it that in Cherubino she can visualize an almost abstract ideal of love that she herself, in the teeth of her experience, still believes in?

That *The Barber of Seville* and especially *Figaro's Marriage* were blowings in the wind that, a few years later, became the French Revolution is one of the commonplaces of literary history. Significantly, both plays, and especially *Figaro*, ran into serious trouble with the censors. Figaro's long monologue in the last act says some mordant things about the organization of society, and Marceline's speech on the condition of women (cut from the acted version but printed by Beaumarchais in his Preface) does the same thing from a specifically feminist point of view. The entire plot turns on the Count's attempt to revive the infamous sexual *droit de seigneur* ("lord's right"), an abuse that, whether or not it was historically legal or commonly

practiced, had become a propagandizing symbol of the evils of the *ancien régime*. King Louis XVI is said to have decried the play's mocking of the government and to have linked the play's subversive potential to the destruction of the Bastille, before the fact.

On the other hand: Authorities on the eighteenth century are generally agreed that the actual ideas introduced in *Figaro's Marriage* had already been familiar, in the literature of reform, for several decades. Aristocrats seem not to have felt sorely threatened by the play; in fact, they loved it, as they had loved *The Barber of Seville*, which as late as 1785 was acted by the royal court with Queen Marie-Antoinette playing Rosine, the female lead. As for the character of Figaro, he does not exactly embody an efficient incendiary radicalism; despite his reputation for cleverness, his plans to hoodwink the Count turn out not to work, the women are left to hatch their own alternative scheme (which does work), and Figaro himself is made to look pretty silly in the last act before he catches on to what is happening.

What is most novel about *Figaro's Marriage* is not a set of revolutionary tenets but rather a set of assumptions about the autonomy of the individual human personality. In this play, the value of personality is inherent rather than conditioned by categories—of rank, profession, or gender. Implicit in what Figaro and Suzanne say to one another, and to other people of whatever rank, and in how they say it, is their confident assumption that as people they are at least as valuable, complex, and interesting as anyone else. The page Cherubino, for example, is a youngster of good birth, but fundamentally he is a youngster, and Suzanne unselfconsciously treats him like any other likable young pest. The Count is a nobleman, but the more pertinent fact is that he is a man on the make and has to be handled by Suzanne much as she would handle any other such man. If underneath Suzanne's familiarity toward the Countess lies a deep respect such as most people in the play feel toward that great lady, the respect is owing not so much to the Countess's rank as to her inherent personal and moral stature.

Figaro's Marriage is one of those great comedies that manage to combine vivacity with tenderness; it is as fast-paced, farcical, and dependent on tricky stage business as a Marx brothers movie, but it also moves toward the more rarefied condition of music. This musical dimension is entirely in character for Beaumarchais; he originally wrote *The Barber of Seville* as an opera, and in 1787 he collaborated with the composer Antonio Salieri on an undistinguished but commercially successful opera called *Tarare*. His two masterpieces, *The Barber* and *Figaro,* are now probably better known (outside France, at least) in operatic versions, with music by Gioacchino Rossini and Wolfgang Amadeus Mozart respectively. Rossini's *Barber of Seville* (1816,—one of at least eleven operatic versions of the play—is an appropriately irrepressible romp. Mozart's *Marriage of Figaro* (1786), however, though equally fun-filled, is also a work of such radiant beauty and emotional resonance as to place it among the world's supreme works of art. Much has been said about the changes Mozart, with his librettist Lorenzo Da Ponte, made in the play, but in fact they adopted Beaumarchais's plot and language with rather remarkable exactness. They edited out Figaro's monologue and the "vaudeville" songs in the last act and gave Cherubino a different ballad to sing in Act Two, but in almost every way they remained

faithful to the double mood, of exuberance and muted sadness, that make Beaumarchais's *Figaro* an enduring masterpiece in its own right.

FURTHER READING (*prepared by S. M.*): Georges Lemaitre's *Beaumarchais*, 1949, though somewhat dated, is a readable and informative full-length biography; readers on the run can get a good introductory overview of Beaumarchais's career in the eight pages devoted to him in Volume 3 (Robert Niklaus, *The Eighteenth Century: 1715–1789*, 1970) of *A Literary History of France*, ed. P. E. Charvet. Joseph Sungolowsky's *Beaumarchais*, 1974, in the Twayne's World Authors Series, is a medium-length biographical and critical overview, good on several matters including the humor in *Figaro's Marriage*. Cynthia Fox's *The Real Figaro: The Extraordinary Career of Caron de Beaumarchais*, 1962, examines Beaumarchais's many social and legal difficulties. Useful on his historic place in French drama is Julie Hayes, "Rewriting Bourgeois Drama: Beaumarchais's Double Plan," in *The Age of Theatre in France*, 1988, ed. Nicole Boursier. In a long and insightful preface, in English, to the French text of *Le Marriage de Figaro*, 1983, Louis Allen marks the similarities between Figaro and Beaumarchais. For further analysis of characters in the play, see Ralph Nablow, "Figaro's Monologue and Voltaire's Pauvre Diable," *Romance Notes*, vol. 28 (Winter, 1987), and Jack Udank's "Beaumarchais' Transformations," in *Modern Language Notes*, vol. 100 (1985).

FIGARO'S MARRIAGE

Translated by Jacques Barzun

CHARACTERS AND COSTUMING

COUNT ALMAVIVA (Governor of Andalusia)[1] must be played with nobility of mien, but also with lightness and ease. The corruption of his heart must not diminish the perfect good form of his manners. In keeping with the morals *of those days*, the great regarded the conquest of women as a frolic. This role is an uncomfortable one in that its grandeur is invariably brought down and sacrificed to the other characters. But in the hands of a good actor the role can bring out all the others and insure the success of the piece.

In the first and second acts the Count wears a hunting costume in the old Spanish style with half-length boots. In the remaining acts he wears a more gorgeous version of the same costume.

COUNTESS ALMAVIVA, who is moved by two opposite feelings, must show only a restrained tenderness and a moderate anger. Nothing must lower in the spectator's eyes her virtuous and lovable character. This role is one of the most difficult in the play.

The Countess's costume in the first, second, third, and fourth acts consists of a comfortable house coat of straight and simple lines. She wears no ornament on her head. She is supposed to be indisposed and keeping to her room. In the fifth act she wears Suzanne's clothes and the high hairdress that goes with them.

[1] An old region of southern Spain.

FIGARO (valet to the Count and steward of the castle). The actor who plays this role cannot be too strongly urged to study and make prevail at all times the true spirit of the character. If the actor finds in the part nothing but argumentativeness spiced with gaiety and wit; or even worse, if he allows himself any burlesquing, he will debase a role with which the greatest comedian can do himself honor by seizing upon its many nuances and sustaining the highest possibilities of its conception.

Figaro's clothes are the same as in the *The Barber of Seville*,[2] that is, the suit of a Spanish majordomo.[3] On his hair he wears a net; his hat is white and has a colored ribbon around the crown. A silk scarf is loosely tied around his neck. His vest and breeches are of satin with buttons and buttonholes finished in silver. His silk sash is very broad, his garters tied with cord and tassels which hang down on the leg. His coat must be of a color contrasting with the vest, but the lapels match the latter. White stockings and gray shoes.

SUZANNE (chief chambermaid to the Countess). A clever girl, full of wit and laughter, but displaying nothing of the impudent frivolity of our corruptive chambermaids. In her role, though it is nearly the longest in the play, there is not a word that is not inspired by goodness and devotion to her duty. The only trickery she allows herself is in behalf of her mistress, who relies on Suzanne's attachment and who has herself none but honorable thoughts.

Suzanne's costume in the first four acts is a tight bodice with flounced skirt, elegant though modeled on the peasant style. Her hat is a high toque (later called in France *à la Suzanne*). In the festivities of Act IV, the Count places on her head a white toque adorned with a long veil, tall feathers, and ribbons. In Act V she wears the Countess's house coat and nothing on her head.

MARCELINE (housekeeper in the castle) is an intelligent woman with lively instincts, whose experiences and mistakes have amended her character. If the actress who plays the role can rise with a certain judicious pride to the high morality that follows the recognition scene in Act III, it will add greatly to the interest of the play.

Her costume is that of the Spanish duenna,[4] modest in color, a black bonnet on the head.

ANTONIO (a gardener, uncle of Suzanne and father of Fanchette) must display only a half-tipsy condition, which gradually wears off, so that by Act V it is almost unnoticeable.

His clothes are those of a Spanish peasant; the sleeves hang down behind; a hat and white shoes.

[2] A play (1775) by Beaumarchais, to which *Figaro's Marriage* is a sequel. The barber of the earlier play was Figaro, whose clever resourcefulness helped Count Almaviva woo and win the beautiful young Rosine, ward of Doctor Bartholo. Rosine is now the Countess Almaviva.
[3] Steward; principal servant. [4] An older woman who chaperones a younger one.

FANCHETTE (the daughter of Antonio) is a girl of twelve[5] and very naïve. Her costume has a tight-fitting bodice, peasant style, brown with silver buttons. The skirt is of contrasting color. She wears a black toque with feathers. The other girls in the wedding party are dressed like her.

CHERUBINO (chief page to the Count). This role cannot be properly played except by a young and very pretty woman. There is no young man on our stage who is sufficiently educated to feel the subtleties of the part. Excessively shy before the Countess, he is elsewhere a charmingly naughty boy. A vague restless desire is at the root of his character. He is rushing headlong through adolescence, but aimlessly and without worldly knowledge; he is the plaything of each passing event. In short, he is probably what every mother would like her son to be, even when she knows she will suffer for it.

In the first and second acts, Cherubino's costume is the rich court dress of a Spanish page, white trimmed with silver lace. He wears a light blue cloak off the shoulder and a hat with large plumes. In Act IV, he wears the bodice, skirt and toque of the peasant girls; in Act V, an officer's uniform, a sword, and a cockade.

BARTHOLO (a doctor from Seville). His character and costume are the same as in the *Barber of Seville,* that is, a short, black gown, buttoned up to the neck, and a large wig. The collar and cuffs are turned back and the belt is black. Outdoors he wears a long scarlet coat. In the present play, his role is secondary.

BASIL (the Countess's music master). Also secondary, Basil's character and costume are the same as in *The Barber,* which is to say: a black hat with hanging brim, a gown like a cassock[6] and a long coat without turned-up collar or cuffs.

DON GUZMAN BRIDLEGOOSE (Associate Justice of the district). He must have the open and easy self-assurance of an animal that has overcome its shyness. His stammer is only an additional charm, scarcely noticeable though it is. The performer would make a grave mistake to stress the ludicrous in this part, for the principle of it is the natural contrast between the solemnity of his office and the absurdity of his person. Therefore the less the actor burlesques the man, the more truly will the character appear and the actor's talent shine.

The costume is the robe of a Spanish judge, but less full than that of our state's attorneys—it is almost a cassock. He wears a great wig and a neckband Spanish style, and he carries a long white wand.

DOUBLEFIST (clerk and secretary to Bridlegoose). He is dressed like the justice, but carries a shorter wand.

[5] It is sometimes suggested that, in more modern terms, Fanchette should be understood to be about thirteen or fourteen.

[6] A full-length, close-fitting garment, of the kind worn by priests.

THE BEADLE or alguazil[7] wears a coat and carries at his side a sword with a leather guard, but without a leather belt. Not boots but shoes, which are black. A white curly wig and a short white wand.

SUNSTRUCK (a young shepherd) wears peasant clothes, sleeves hanging down, bright colored coat, white hat.

A YOUNG SHEPHERDESS—dressed like Fanchette.

PETER (the Count's postilion). Short belted coat over a vest, a courier's boots, hat and whip, a net over his hair.

Walk-on Parts (valets and peasants)—Some in judge's costume, others dressed as peasants, the rest in livery.

ACT 1

The scene is a half-furnished room. An invalid chair is in the middle. FIGARO *is measuring the floor with a yardstick.* SUZANNE, *in front of a mirror, is fixing in her hair the sprig of orange blossoms commonly called "the bride's bonnet."*

FIGARO. Nineteen feet by twenty-six.
SUZANNE. Look, Figaro—my bonnet. Do you like it better now?
FIGARO [*taking both her hands in his*]. Infinitely better, my sweet. My, what that bunch of flowers—so pretty, so virginal, so suited to the head of a lovely girl—does to a lover on the morning of his wedding!
SUZANNE [*leaving*]. What are you measuring there, my lad?
FIGARO. I am finding out, dear Suzy, whether the beautiful big bed that his lordship is giving us will fit into this room.
SUZANNE. *This* room?
FIGARO. He's letting us have it.
SUZANNE. But I don't want it.
FIGARO. Why not?
SUZANNE. I don't want it.
FIGARO. But tell me why.
SUZANNE. I don't like it.
FIGARO. You might give a reason.
SUZANNE. And supposing I don't?
FIGARO. Women! As soon as they have us tied down—
SUZANNE. To give a reason would imply that I might be unreasonable. Are you with me or against me?
FIGARO. You are turning down the most convenient room in the castle. It connects with both suites. At night, if my lady is unwell and wants you, she rings—and crack! there you are in two hops. Is it something that my lord requires? a tinkle from his side, and zing! I am at the ready in three strides.

[7] Constable; police officer.

SUZANNE. Right enough! But when he's tinkled in the morning and given you a good long errand, zing! in three strides he is at my door, and crack! in two hops he—

FIGARO. What do you mean by those words?

SUZANNE. You'd better listen to me carefully.

FIGARO. What the devil is going on?

SUZANNE. What is going on is that his lordship Count Almaviva is tired of pursuing the beauties of the neighborhood and is heading for home— not to *his* wife, you understand, but to yours. *She* is the one he has his eye on, and he hopes this apartment will favor his plans. And that is what the faithful Basil, the trusted agent of the Count's pleasures, and my noble singing master as well, tells me every day during my lesson.

FIGARO. Basil, my boy, if ever the application of green birch to an ailing back has helped to correct curvature of the spine, I will—

SUZANNE. So in your innocence you thought that this dowry the Count is giving me was for your beaux yeux[8] and your high merit?

FIGARO. I've done enough to hope it was.

SUZANNE. How stupid bright people are!

FIGARO. So they say.

SUZANNE. But *they* won't believe it!

FIGARO. *They* are wrong.

SUZANNE. Get it into your head that the dowry is to get from me, privately, a certain privilege which formerly was the right of the lord of the manor—you know what a grievous right it was.[9]

FIGARO. I know it so well that if the Count had not abolished its shameful exercise when he himself was married, I should never have planned to marry you on his lands.

SUZANNE. He abolished it right enough, but he has had second thoughts. And he's thinking your fiancée is the one to restore it to him.

FIGARO [*rubbing his forehead*]. My head grows mushy with surprise and my sprouting forehead—[10]

SUZANNE. Please don't rub it.

FIGARO. What's the harm?

SUZANNE. If you brought on a little pimple, superstitious people might—

FIGARO. You're laughing at me, you slut. Now if I could think of some way to catch out this professional deceiver, turn the tables on him and pocket his money—

SUZANNE. Plotting and pocketing—you're in your element.

FIGARO. It certainly isn't shame that holds me back.

SUZANNE. Fear, then?

FIGARO. It's no great feat to start on a dangerous undertaking; the thing is to succeed and avoid trouble. Any knavish fool can go into a man's house at night, enjoy his wife, and get a beating for his pains—nothing is easier. But—[*a bell rings*]

[8] (French:) Good looks; literally, "beautiful eyes."

[9] The *droit de seigneur* ("lord's right"), the supposed privilege of the feudal lord to sexually enjoy any woman on his estate on her wedding night. That such a custom really did exist has been disputed.

[10] An allusion to the popular myth that a cuckolded husband grew horns on his forehead.

SUZANNE. My lady is awake. She wanted me to be sure and be the first to talk to her this morning about the wedding.

FIGARO. Some more goings-on?

SUZANNE. The almanac says it brings good luck to forsaken wives. Goodbye Fi-fi-garo, darling; think about ways and means.

FIGARO. To prime my brains give a little kiss.

SUZANNE. To a lover, today? No sir! What would my husband say tomorrow?

<div align="center">[FIGARO kisses her.]</div>

SUZANNE. Now, now!

FIGARO. You don't know how much I love you.

SUZANNE [*adjusting her dress*]. When will you learn not to bore me with it from morning till night?

FIGARO [*as if telling a secret*]. Why, when I can prove it to you from night till morning.

<div align="center">[The bell rings again.]</div>

SUZANNE [*blowing him a kiss from the door*]. There's your kiss, sir, I have nothing else of yours to return.

FIGARO [*running after her*]. But you didn't receive mine across the void like this.

<div align="center">[Exit SUZANNE.]</div>

FIGARO [*alone*]. What a ravishing girl! Always gay, laughing, full of sap, wit, love, joy—and how well-behaved! [*He walks about briskly, rubbing his hands*]. Ah, my lord, my dear lord! You want to give me—something to remember? I was wondering, too, why I am first made Steward, and then supposed to become part of the embassy and serve as King's Messenger. Now I understand, Your Excellency: three promotions at one stroke—you as envoy plenipotentiary;[11] myself as political lightning-rod; and Suzy as lady in residence, as private ambassadress—and then, Sir Messenger, be off! While I gallop in one direction, you will drive my girl a long way in the other. While I wade through mud and break my neck for the glory of your family, you will collaborate in the increase of mine. What sweet reciprocity! But, my lord, there is excess in this. To carry on in London the business at once of the King your master and of your humble servant, to represent in a foreign court both him and me—that is too much by half, much too much. As for you, Basil, my pretty scoundrel, I will teach you to limp with the halt[12] and the lame. I will—no! We must play up to both of them if we are to knock their heads together. Now Figaro, concentrate on today. First, move ahead the time for the wedding, so as to make sure the knot is tied; then distract old Marceline, who is too fond of you; pick up whatever money and gifts there may be; mislead the Count and his little appetites; give a sound drubbing to Mister Basil, and—well, well, well, here is the fat doctor! The party is complete. [*Enter* BARTHOLO *and* MARCELINE.] Good-morning, dear doctor of my heart. Is it my wedding with Suzy that brings you to the house?

BARTHOLO [*disdainful*]. Not at all, my dear sir.

FIGARO. It would indeed be a generous act.

[11] A diplomat having full authority to conclude agreements. [12] Crippled.

BARTHOLO. Exactly, and therefore inconceivably stupid.

FIGARO. It was my bad luck that I had to thwart your designs.[13]

BARTHOLO. Haven't you anything else to say?

FIGARO. Perhaps your mule hasn't been looked after?[14]

BARTHOLO [*furious*]. Confounded babbler, leave us alone!

FIGARO. You are angry, doctor? Yours is a cruel profession: no more kindness to animals than if they were men. Farewell, Marceline, are you still thinking of suing me at law? "Though thou love not, must thou therefore hate?"[15] I put it to the doctor.

BARTHOLO. What is all this about?

FIGARO [*leaving*]. She will tell you. [*Exit.*]

BARTHOLO [*looking at the departing* FIGARO]. The fellow never improves. If someone doesn't flog him alive he will die inside the skin of the most conceited ass I know.

MARCELINE [*attracting his attention*]. Well, here you are at last, Doctor Ubiquitous,—you always so grave and respectable that one could die waiting for your help, just as some time back someone got married despite your efforts.

BARTHOLO. And you—always bitter and provoking. But why am I needed here so urgently? Has the Count met with an accident?

MARCELINE. No, doctor.

BARTHOLO. And Rosine, his conspiring countess, could she be—God be praised—unwell?

MARCELINE. She is pining away.

BARTHOLO. What about?

MARCELINE. Her husband neglects her.

BARTHOLO [*with great satisfaction*]. Ah, worthy husband, my avenger!

MARCELINE. It is hard to make out the Count: at once jealous and a philanderer.

BARTHOLO. A philanderer from boredom and jealous from vanity—it's clear as day.

MARCELINE. Today, for example, he is marrying off our Suzanne to Figaro, on whom he lavishes gifts in honor of this union . . .

BARTHOLO. Which His Excellency has made necessary?

MARCELINE. Not quite; but which His Excellency would like to celebrate in secret with the bride . . .

BARTHOLO. Of Mr. Figaro? That's an arrangement the latter is surely willing to enter into.

MARCELINE. Basil is sure it is not so.

BARTHOLO. That other lout lives here too? It's a regular den. What does he do?

MARCELINE. All the evil he can. The worst is the hopeless passion he has so long nursed for me.

BARTHOLO. In your place I should have disposed of that for good.

MARCELINE. How?

BARTHOLO. By marrying him.

[13] In *The Barber of Seville*, Bartholo had planned to marry his ward Rosine himself.
[14] A reference to a stratagem used by Figaro in *The Barber of Seville*.
[15] A line from *Nanine*, a comedy by Voltaire.

MARCELINE. Tiresome, brutish wit! Why don't you dispose of mine in the same way? You're in honor bound—remember all your promises—and also our little Emmanuel, the offspring of a forgotten love, who was to lead us to the altar.

BARTHOLO. Was it to listen to this rigmarole that you had me come from Seville?—What is this fit of marrying you've suddenly fallen into?

MARCELINE. We'll say no more about it. But at least help me to marry someone else.

BARTHOLO. Gladly. But what mortal, bereft of heaven and women's favors, would . . .

MARCELINE. Now, who *could* it be, doctor, but the gay, handsome, lovable Figaro!

BARTHOLO. That good-for-nothing?

MARCELINE. Never cross, always good-humored, always ready to enjoy the passing moment, worrying as little about the future as about the past—attractive, generous, oh generous! . . .

BARTHOLO. . . . as a scamp . . .

MARCELINE. . . . as a lord. Delightful, in short. But he is a monster too.

BARTHOLO. What about his Suzanne?

MARCELINE. She'd never get him, clever as she is, if you would help me, dear doctor, and hold him to a promissory note of his that I have.

BARTHOLO. On his wedding day?

MARCELINE. Weddings have gone farther than this and been broken off. If I didn't mind giving away a feminine secret—

BARTHOLO. There aren't any secrets for a physician.

MARCELINE. You know very well I have no secrets from you. Well, our sex is ardent but shy. A certain attraction may draw us toward pleasure, yet the most adventurous woman will say to herself—"Be beautiful if you can, sensible if you will, but stay respectable: you must!" Now since every woman knows what reputation is worth, we can scare off Suzanne by threatening to expose the offers that are being made to her.

BARTHOLO. What will that accomplish?

MARCELINE. Just this: ashamed and apprehensive, she will keep on refusing the Count. He, from spite, will support my opposition to her marriage, and hence mine will become a certainty.

BARTHOLO. She's right, by God! It's an excellent trick to marry off my old housekeeper to the scoundrel who pinched my young protégée . . .

MARCELINE [*quickly*]. . . . the man who plans to serve his pleasure and disappoint my hopes . . .

BARTHOLO. . . . the man who once upon a time swindled me out of a hundred pounds that I haven't forgotten.

MARCELINE. Ah what bliss!—

BARTHOLO. To punish a swindler!—

MARCELINE. To marry him, doctor, to marry him!

[*Enter* SUZANNE.]

SUZANNE [*holding a bonnet with large ribbons and a woman's dress over her arm*]. To marry? To marry whom? My Figaro?

MARCELINE [*sourly*]. Why not? Aren't you thinking of it yourself?

BARTHOLO [*laughing*]. An angry woman's typical argument! We were speaking, Suzanne my dear, of his happiness in possessing you.

MARCELINE. To say nothing of my lord besides.

SUZANNE [*with a curtsy*]. Your servant, madam. There is always a touch of gall in your remarks.

MARCELINE [*curtsying*]. Your servant as well, madam. Where is the gall? Isn't it justice that a free-handed nobleman share a little in the good things he procures for his people?

SUZANNE. He procures?

MARCELINE. Yes, madam.

SUZANNE. Fortunately, your jealousy is as well known as your claims on Figaro are slight.

MARCELINE. They could have been strengthened by the same means that you chose to use.

SUZANNE. But those means, madam, are open only to learned ladies.

MARCELINE. And this poor child is all innocence—like an old judge!

BARTHOLO [*pulling* MARCELINE *away*]. Goodbye, little bride of Figaro!

MARCELINE [*curtsying*]. Also promised to the Count.

SUZANNE [*curtsying*]. She gives you best regards, madam.

MARCELINE [*curtsying*]. Will she also love me a little, madame?

SUZANNE [*curtsying*]. As to that, pray have no fears.

MARCELINE [*curtsying*]. Madam is as kind as she is pretty.

SUZANNE [*curtsying*]. Enough, perhaps, to disconcert madam.

MARCELINE [*curtsying*]. And above all, respectable.

SUZANNE [*curtsying*]. That's a monopoly of dowagers.

MARCELINE [*outraged*]. Dowagers, dowagers!

BARTHOLO [*interrupting her*]. Marceline!

MARCELINE. Let's go, doctor, or I shan't be able to restrain myself. Goodbye, madam. [*Curtsy*]

[*Exeunt.*]

SUZANNE. Go, madam; go, pedant. I am as little afraid of your plots as I am of your insults. Look at the old Sibyl![16] Because she has a little learning and used it to torment my lady in her youth,[17] she wants to rule the castle. [*Throws the dress from her arm to a chair*] I've forgotten what I came for.

[*Enter* CHERUBINO.]

CHERUBINO [*running in*]. Suzy, I've been waiting two hours to catch you alone. I'm miserable: you're getting married and I'm going away.

SUZANNE. How does my getting married cause the departure of his lordship's favorite page?

CHERUBINO [*piteously*]. Suzanne: he's dismissed me!

SUZANNE [*mimicking him*]. Cherubino: what nonsense!

CHERUBINO. He found me yesterday at your cousin's, at Fanchette's. I was rehearsing her ingenue[18] part in tonight's show and he flew into a rage on seeing me. "Get out," he said, "you little—" I don't dare repeat the bad word he used. "Get out! Tonight is your last night in this house!" If

[16] Prophetess of doom; witch.

[17] Marceline had been governess to Rosine (the Countess) when Rosine was Bartholo's ward.

[18] A stage term for a standard role: an innocent girl or young woman.

my lady, my dear godmother, doesn't calm him down about this, it's all over with me, Suzy; I'll never lay eyes on you again.

SUZANNE. On *me*? It's my turn, is it? So you don't go sighing around my lady anymore?

CHERUBINO. Oh, Suzy. She is beautiful, majestic, but so—imposing!

SUZANNE. That is to say, *I* am not and you can take liberties.

CHERUBINO. You're mean! You know perfectly well I never dare take anything. How lucky you are, seeing her all the time, talking to her, dressing her in the morning, undressing her at night, unpinning each pin— oh, Suzy, I'd give anything—what's that in your hand?

SUZANNE [*mockingly*]. It's the blissful bonnet and the fortunate ribbon which enclose, at night, the hair of your beautiful godmother. . . .

CHERUBINO. Her ribbon—at night! Give it to me, be a dear, my love.

SUZANNE [*pulling it away*]. Not so fast. "His love!" What familiarity! If you weren't just a whippersnapper—[CHERUBINO *seizes the ribbon.*] Oh, the ribbon!

CHERUBINO [*going behind and around the invalid chair*]. You can say you mislaid it, ruined it, lost it. Say anything you like.

SUZANNE [*chases after him around the chair*]. I promise you that in three or four years you will be the biggest little miscreant on earth! Give me back that ribbon! [*She snatches at it.*]

CHERUBINO [*drawing a paper from his pocket*]. Let me, do let me have it, Suzy. I'll give you my song here, and while the memory of my beautiful mistress will sadden all my days, the thought of you will bring me the only ray of joy that could lighten my heart.

SUZANNE [*tears the song out of his grasp*]. "Lighten his heart!" the little scoundrel! Do you think you are talking to your Fanchette? My lord finds you with her; you breathe vows in secret to my lady; and on top of that you make me declarations to my face!

CHERUBINO [*excited*]. It's true, on my honor! I don't know who I am or what I'm doing, but just lately, at the mere sight of a woman I've felt my breath come in gasps and my heart beat fast. The words "love" and "bliss" arouse and upset me. In short, the need to say to someone "I love you" has become so compelling that I say it to myself when I cross the park, I say it to our lady and to you, to the clouds and the wind that carries my useless words away. Yesterday I ran into Marceline—

SUZANNE [*laughing*]. Ahahaha!

CHERUBINO. Why not? She's a woman! She's a maid! A maid! A woman! Oh what sweet words are those—and how interesting![19]

SUZANNE. He is losing his mind.

CHERUBINO. Fanchette is very sweet: at least she listens to me and you don't.

SUZANNE. What a pity! Let us listen to the gentleman. [*She snatches again at the ribbon.*]

CHERUBINO [*turns and runs*]. Not on your life! No once can take it, you see, except with *my* life. But if the price does not suit you, I'll increase it by a thousand kisses. [*He starts chasing her around the chair.*]

[19] *Interesting* has an old sense here, suggesting deep emotional involvement.

SUZANNE [*turning on him as she flies*]. A thousand slaps in the face if you come near me. I'll complain to my lady, and far from interceding for you I'll go to my lord and say: "Send back that petty thief to his parents. He is a good-for-nothing who puts on airs about being in love with Madam, and on the rebound tries to kiss me."

CHERUBINO [*sees the Count entering and hides behind the armchair*]. That's the end of me!

SUZANNE. Coward![20] [*intercepts the Count and helps to conceal the page.*]

COUNT [*coming forward*]. You are upset, Suzette, you were talking to yourself. Your little heart seems to me full of agitation—understandably enough on a day like this.

SUZANNE [*embarrassed*]. My lord, what do you want with me? If someone saw us . . .

COUNT. I should hate to be surprised here. But you know the interest I take in you. Basil must have told you I love you. I have only a moment to tell you so myself. Listen—[*he sits in the armchair.*]

SUZANNE. I will not listen.

COUNT [*taking her hand*]. Just one word. You know the King has made me ambassador to London. I am taking Figaro with me, giving him an excellent post. Now since it is a wife's duty to follow her husband—

SUZANNE. Oh, if I had the courage to speak—

COUNT [*drawing her to him*]. Don't hesitate, speak, my dear. Assume a privilege which you may use with me for life.

SUZANNE [*frightened*]. I don't want to, my lord, I don't want to. Please leave me.

COUNT. But first tell me.

SUZANNE [*angrily*]. I don't know what I was saying.

COUNT. Something about a wife's duty.

SUZANNE. Very well. When you, my lord, eloped with your lady from the doctor's house and married her for love, and when in her honor you abolished that dreadful right of the lord of the manor—

COUNT. Which annoyed the girls so much, no doubt! Look, Suzette, it was a charming right and if you'll come and prattle with me about it this evening in the garden, I'll rate that little favor so high—

BASIL [*speaking from without*]. He is not at home, my lord.

COUNT [*rising*]. Whose voice is that?

SUZANNE. This is dreadful!

COUNT. Go out so that nobody comes in.

SUZANNE [*upset*]. And leave you here?

BASIL [*from outside*]. His lordship was with my lady, then he left; I'll go look for him.

COUNT. No spot where I can hide. Yes, behind that chair. It's not very good but—send him packing.

> [SUZANNE *bars his way; he gently pushes*
> *her; she retreats and thus comes between*
> *him and the page. But while the* COUNT

[20] Suzanne, who does not see the Count until after Cherubino does, thinks that Cherubino's last words refer to her threat to denounce him.

stoops and takes CHERUBINO'S *place, the latter throws himself kneeling on the seat and clings to the cushions.* SUZANNE *picks up the dress she formerly carried, drapes it over the page, and takes her stand in front of the chair].*

BASIL [*entering*]. Did you by any chance see the Count, Miss?

SUZANNE [*brusquely*]. How could I? Please go.

BASIL [*coming nearer*]. If you only think a little you will see there was nothing surprising about my question. Figaro is looking for him.

SUZANNE. So he's looking for the man who is his worst enemy after yourself.

COUNT [*aside*]. Let's see how he takes my part.

BASIL. Is it being a man's enemy to wish his wife well?

SUZANNE. Not in your book of rules, you vile corrupter.

BASIL. What does anyone ask of you that you aren't going to bestow on another? Thanks to a lovely ceremony, the things that were forbidden yesterday will be required tomorrow.

SUZANNE. Disgusting wretch!

BASIL. Marriage being the most comic of all serious things, I had thought—

SUZANNE [*outraged*]. Contemptible thought! Who gave you leave to come in here!

BASIL. There, there, naughty girl. God grant you peace! You'll do just as you like. But don't go thinking that I regard Mister Figaro as an impediment to my lord—and if it weren't for the little page . . .

SUZANNE [*shyly*]. Don Cherubino?

BASIL [*mimicking her*]. *Cherubino diamore,*[21] yes. He's always buzzing about you and this morning again was at this door when I left you: say it isn't true.

SUZANNE. What lies! Slanderer! Go away!

BASIL. A slanderer because I see things as they are. Isn't it also for you the page has a song he carries mysteriously about him?

SUZANNE [*angrily*]. For me indeed!

BASIL. Unless he made it up for her ladyship. Truth to tell, when he serves at table, they say that he cannot take his eyes off her. But let him look out: my lord is a brute upon that point.

SUZANNE [*outraged*]. And you are a scoundrel, going about spreading gossip and ruining a wretched child who is already in disgrace with his master.

BASIL. Did I make it up? I say these things because everybody says them.

COUNT [*rising*]. Who, everybody?

SUZANNE. Heavens!

BASIL. Ha ha!

COUNT. Run along, Basil, and see that the boy is sent away.

BASIL. I am truly sorry that I came in here.

SUZANNE [*upset*]. Oh dear, oh dear!

[21] (Italian:) Cherub, or lovely child, of love. The music master Basil sarcastically adopts the hackneyed language of Italian love songs.

COUNT. She is faint, help her into the chair.

SUZANNE [*fending him off energetically*]. I don't want to sit. To walk in here without leave is an outrage.

COUNT. But there are two of us with you, my dear. There's not the slightest danger.

BASIL. For my part, I deeply regret having made light of the page—since you overheard me. I was using it to ascertain her feelings, because essentially—

COUNT. Fifty pounds, a horse, and back to his parents.

BASIL. My lord, it was frivolous gossip.

COUNT. A young libertine whom I found only yesterday with the gardener's daughter.

BASIL. With Fanchette?

COUNT. In her room.

SUZANNE [*outraged*]. Where my lord had business also?

COUNT [*cheerfully*]. That's an idea!

BASIL. It is of good omen.

COUNT [*still cheerful*]. Of course not. I was looking for your uncle Antonio, my drunken gardener, to give him some instructions. I knock. No one opens for quite a while. Your little cousin looks embarrassed. I grow suspicious while I talk to her and as I do so I cast an eye about. Behind the door there was a curtain of sorts, a wardrobe, something for old clothes. Without seeming to, I gently, slowly lift the curtain [*he illustrates by lifting the dress off the armchair*] and I see—[*he catches sight of* CHERUBINO]—I say!

BASIL. Ha ha!

COUNT. This is as good as before.

BASIL. It's better.

COUNT [*to* SUZANNE]. Congratulations, dear lady: hardly engaged to be married and yet able to manage such tricks! Was it to entertain my page that you wished to be alone? As for you, sir, whose behavior never varies, the only lack of respect for your godmother you had so far overlooked was to pay your addresses to her maid, who is the bride of your friend. But I will not allow Figaro, a man I love and esteem, to be the victim of this deception. Was he with you, Basil?

SUZANNE [*indignant*]. There is no deception and no victim. [*pointing*] He was here while you were talking to me.

COUNT [*carried away*]. I hope you lie when you say so. His worst enemy could wish him nothing worse.

SUZANNE. He was asking me to beseech my lady to obtain his pardon from you. Your coming in upset him so much that he hid in the chair.

COUNT [*angrily*]. Infernal cleverness! But I sat in that chair the moment I arrived.

CHERUBINO. Alas, my lord, I was shaking in my shoes behind it.

COUNT. Another trick! I stood there myself just now.

CHERUBINO. Forgive me, but that is when I came around and crouched inside.

COUNT. This young snake in the grass must be a—poisonous adder: he heard what we said?

CHERUBINO. On the contrary, my lord, I did my best to hear nothing at all.

COUNT. O treachery! [*To* SUZANNE] You shan't marry Figaro!

BASIL. Moderation, if you please: someone's coming.

COUNT [*pulling* CHERUBINO *out of the armchair and setting him on his feet*]. He
would stay there in front of the whole world!

> [*Enter* FIGARO, *the* COUNTESS, FAN-
> CHETTE, *with several footmen and coun-
> try people dressed in white.*]

FIGARO [*holding a woman's hat covered with white feathers and ribbons and speak-
ing to the* COUNTESS]. Only you, my lady, can obtain this favor for us.

COUNTESS. You hear him, Count? They imagine that I wield an influence I
do not in fact possess. Still, as their request is not unreasonable—

COUNT [*embarrassed*]. It would indeed have to be very much so—

FIGARO [*speaking low to* SUZANNE]. Back up my attempt—

SUZANNE [*the same to* FIGARO]. Which won't help any.

FIGARO [*in low voice*]. Never mind, do it.

COUNT [*to* FIGARO]. What is it you want?

FIGARO. My lord, your vassals, who are deeply touched by the abolition of a
certain regrettable right that you gave up out of love for my lady—

COUNT. Well, the right *is* abolished; what are you getting at?

FIGARO. Only that it is high time the virtue of so good a master should be
manifest. I myself stand to gain so much from it today that I want to be
the first to glorify it at our wedding.

COUNT [*still more embarrassed*]. You can't be serious. The abolition of a
shameful right is only the payment of a debt to decency. A Spaniard
may want to conquer beauty by devotion, but to be the first to exact the
sweetest of rewards as if it were a servile due—why, that's the tyrannical
violence of a Vandal,[22] not the acknowledged right of a Castilian[23] no-
bleman!

FIGARO [*holding* SUZANNE'S *hand*]. Then deign that this young creature,
whose honor has been preserved by your noble reason, receive from
your hand the virgin's coif[24] of white feathers and ribbons as a symbol
of the purity of your intentions. Have this ceremony become a custom
at all weddings and let an appropriate chorus be sung each time to
commemorate the event.

COUNT [*embarrassed*]. If I did not know that to be a lover, a poet, and a
musician excused every kind of folly—

FIGARO. Join with me, my friends.

ALL [*together*]. My lord! my lord!

SUZANNE [*to the* COUNT]. Why brush aside an honor you so much deserve?

COUNT [*aside*]. Deceitful wretch!

FIGARO. Look at her, my lord: no prettier face will ever signalize the extent
of your sacrifice.

SUZANNE. Leave my face out of it and let us only praise his virtue.

[22] In the fifth century A.D. the east-Germanic Vandals ravaged Gaul (France), Spain, north
Africa, and Rome.

[23] Of Castile, a former kingdom making up much of what is now Spain.

[24] Headdress.

COUNT [*aside*]. The whole thing is a plot.

COUNTESS. I too join with them, Count, knowing as I do that this cere-
mony, ever to be cherished, owes its being to the gracious love you used
to have for me.

COUNT. Which I still have, madam, and because of which I now yield.

ALL [*together*]. Bravo!

COUNT [*aside*]. I've been had. [*Aloud*] In order to give the ceremony yet
more splendor, I should like to see it postponed till somewhat later.
[*Aside*] Quick, let us get hold of Marceline!

FIGARO [*to* CHERUBINO]. What about you, my lad, you don't applaud?

SUZANNE. He is in despair; his lordship is sending him home.

COUNTESS. Ah, my lord, I ask for his pardon.

COUNT. He doesn't deserve it.

COUNTESS. The poor boy is so young.

COUNT. Not so young as you think.

CHERUBINO [*trembling*]. Clemency is not the lordly right you gave up when
you married my lady.

COUNTESS. He only gave up the one that afflicted you all.

SUZANNE. If my lord had abandoned the right to pardon, it would surely
be the first right he would want to restore in secret.

COUNT [*embarrassed*]. Oh, quite.

COUNTESS. So what need to restore it?

CHERUBINO [*to the* COUNT]. I was giddy in my actions, my lord, that is true.
But there never was the least impropriety in my words.

COUNT [*embarrassed*]. All right, that's enough.

FIGARO. What does he mean?

COUNT [*sharply*]. Enough, enough! Everybody wants him pardoned: I so
order it. I'll do more: I'll give him a company in my regiment.

ALL [*together*]. Bravo!

COUNT. But on one condition—that he leave at once to join up in Catalo-
nia.

FIGARO. Oh, my lord, make it tomorrow.

COUNT. I have given an order.

CHERUBINO. And I obey.

COUNT. Salute your godmother and entreat her protection.

[CHERUBINO *kneels on one knee before
the* COUNTESS, *unable to utter a word.*]

COUNTESS [*much moved*]. Since you cannot stay even for today, young man,
go. New duties call you: fulfill them worthily. Honor your benefactor.
Remember this house where your youth was so leniently treated. Be
upright, obedient, and brave. We shall all share in the pleasure of your
success.

[CHERUBINO *gets up and goes to where he
stood before.*]

COUNT. You seem deeply moved, madam.

COUNTESS. I do not apologize for it. Who knows what fate is in store for a
child thrown into such a dangerous career? He is related to my family,
as well as being my godson.

COUNT [*aside*]. Basil was evidently right. [*Aloud*] Young man, give a kiss to
Suzanne, for the last time.

FIGARO. Why the last, my lord? He'll come and spend the winters with us.[25]
Give me a kiss too, captain. [*They embrace.*] Goodbye, Cherubino. You
are going to lead a very different life, my child. Thus: no more hanging
about the women's quarters the livelong day, no more sweet drinks and
pastries, no more blindman's buff and spinning the bottle. Just veteran
soldiers, by God, weatherbeaten and dressed in rags, a huge musket
that weighs a ton—Right! turn! Left! turn! Forward! march! To glory—
and don't you go stumbling on the way—unless a well-placed shot—

SUZANNE. Horrors! be quiet!

COUNTESS. What a send-off!

COUNT. Where can Marceline be? Isn't it odd that she isn't with the rest of
you?

FANCHETTE. My lord, she went walking to town, by the lane along the farm.

COUNT. And she is coming back?

BASIL. When it may please God.

FIGARO. May it please Him never to please . . .

FANCHETTE. The gentleman doctor was giving her his arm.

COUNT [*quickly*]. The doctor is here?

BASIL. She fastened upon him at once.

COUNT [*aside*]. He could not come at a better time.

FANCHETTE. She was all excited. She spoke very loud and paced back and
forth and stopped and did like this with her arms. And the gentleman
doctor, he did like this with his hand, to calm her down. She mentioned
my cousin Figaro.

COUNT [*taking her chin in his hand*]. Cousin . . . yet to be.[26]

FANCHETTE [*pointing to* CHERUBINO]. My lord, have you forgiven us for
yesterday?

COUNT [*interrupting*]. Good day, good day, my dear.

FIGARO. It's her confounded love that keeps her obsessed.[27] She would
have spoiled our party.

COUNT [*aside*]. She will spoil it yet, I promise you. [*Aloud*] Come, madam,
let us go in. Basil, please stop in to see me.

SUZANNE [*to* FIGARO]. You'll be joining me, sonny?

FIGARO [*in low voice to* SUZANNE]. Wasn't he properly stuck?

SUZANNE [*low*]. Delightful character![28] [*Exeunt all but* FIGARO, CHERUBINO,
and BASIL.]

FIGARO. By the way, you fellows: the new ceremony having been adopted,
the show tonight becomes a sequel to it. We mustn't forget our lines.
Let's not be like those players who never act so poorly as on the night
when the critics are wide awake. We haven't any tomorrow to recoup
ourselves, so let's learn our parts today.

BASIL [*maliciously*]. Mine is more difficult than you think.

FIGARO [*in pantomime, unseen by* BASIL, *pretends to give him a beating*]. But you
don't suspect the ovation you will get.

CHERUBINO. Dear friend, you forget that I am leaving—

FIGARO. —when you would like to stay.

[25] Military campaigns were rarely waged in winter.
[26] Cousin by marriage, if and when Figaro marries Fanchette's cousin Suzanne.
[27] Figaro is talking about Marceline. [28] Suzanne means Figaro.

CHERUBINO. Oh, if I only could!

FIGARO. Then, we must have a scheme. Not a murmur against your leaving. Traveling cloak on your shoulders. Make a show of packing, your horse at the gates, a brief gallop as far as the farm and come back on foot by the back way. My lord will think you gone: just keep out of his sight. I undertake to calm him down after the wedding party.

CHERUBINO. But Fanchette does not know her role.

BASIL. What the dickens were you teaching her this last week when you've hardly been away from her?

FIGARO. You have nothing to do today—for heaven's sake coach her in her lines.

BASIL. Be careful, young man, be careful! Her father is suspicious; the girl has been slapped and hasn't learned her lines—Cherubino, Cherubino, she will be sorry—the pot that goes once too often to the well . . .

FIGARO. Ah, there's our curmudgeon with his old proverbs. Tell us, you old pedant, what the wisdom of nations has to say about the pot that goes to the well.

BASIL. It gets filled.

FIGARO [*leaving*]. Not so dumb as I thought.

ACT 2

A magnificent bedroom with a large bed in an alcove and a platform in front. The main door is upstage to the right, the dressing-room door downstage to the left. A third door, at the back, leads to the women's quarters. The window is on the opposite side.

SUZANNE *and the* COUNTESS *enter Right.*

COUNTESS [*throws herself into a wing chair*]. Shut the door, Suzanne, and tell me everything in detail.

SUZANNE. I do not mean to hold back anything, my lady.

COUNTESS. And so he wanted to seduce you?

SUZANNE. Certainly not! My lord does not take that much trouble with servants: he wanted to buy me.

COUNTESS. And the little page was there all the while?

SUZANNE. Yes, that is to say he was hidden behind the big armchair. He had come to ask me to intercede with you for his pardon.

COUNTESS. Why not come to me direct? Do you suppose I would have refused him, Suzy?

SUZANNE. That's what I told him, but his sadness at leaving, especially at leaving you—"Ah, Suzy," he said, "how noble and beautiful she is, but how imposing!"

COUNTESS. Do I really look that way, Suzy, I who have always stood up for him?

SUZANNE. Then he saw the ribbon of your nightdress, which I had in my hand, and he jumped and grabbed it.

COUNTESS [*smiling*]. My ribbon? What a child!

SUZANNE. I tried to take it from him, madam, but he was like a wild beast,

his eyes shone: "You'll get it only with my life," he said, and his voice cracked.

COUNTESS [*dreamily*]. And then, Suzy?

SUZANNE. Well madam, how can one put a stop to it? The little devil! "My godmother," he says, and "I wish I could," says he. And just because he wouldn't even dare kiss the hem of your gown, my lady, he always wants to be kissing me in earnest.

COUNTESS [*still dreaming*]. Enough . . . enough nonsense. At last, then, my husband came to the point and told you . . .

SUZANNE. . . . that if I refused to listen to him, he would use his influence in behalf of Marceline.

COUNTESS [*rising, pacing, and fanning herself vigorously*]. He does not love me at all any more.

SUZANNE. Why then is he so jealous?

COUNTESS. Like every husband, my dear—it is pride. Ah, I loved him too much. I wearied him with my caresses, bored him with my love. That is my chief wrong in relation to him. But I do not intend that his charming thoughts should bring you harm; you shall marry Figaro. He alone can help us: is he going to join us?

SUZANNE. As soon as the hunt is on its way.

COUNTESS [*using her fan again*]. Open the window on the garden a bit. It's exceedingly warm in here.

SUZANNE. That is because your ladyship has been talking and walking so actively. [*She opens the window at the back.*]

COUNTESS [*absentmindedly*]. In avoiding me of set purpose . . . men are creatures full of guilt.

SUZANNE [*shouting from the window*]. There is my lord riding through the big field. Peter is with him and one, two, three, four—setters.

COUNTESS. That gives us plenty of time. [*She sits.*] Someone is knocking, Suzy.

SUZANNE [*runs singing to the door*]. Why, it's my Figaro, it's my Figaro!
 [*Enter* FIGARO.]

SUZANNE. Dear friend, come in. My lady can hardly wait.

FIGARO. And what about you, little Sue? Her ladyship must not take on so. After all, what is all this fuss about?—a trifle. My lord Count finds our young lady charming and would like to make her his mistress— perfectly natural.

SUZANNE. Natural?

FIGARO. Then he appointed me king's messenger and my Suzy—er— attachée to the Embassy. No mental confusion there.

SUZANNE. Are you through?

FIGARO. And because Suzanne, my bride, declines the post and privileges, he wants to promote the plans of Marceline. Could anything be more simple? To seek revenge on those who thwart our purpose by interfering with theirs is what everybody does, it's what we ourselves are about to do. And that, so to speak, is that.

COUNTESS. Figaro, how can you joke about a project that will rob us all of happiness?

FIGARO. Who says it will, my lady?

SUZANNE. Instead of sharing our grief, you—

FIGARO. Isn't it enough that I am busy about it? No, no, let us be as methodical as he, and cool his desire for our belongings by arousing in him an apprehension for his own.

COUNTESS. A good idea, but how?

FIGARO. It is all done, madam. A piece of false information about you—

COUNTESS. About me! You are out of your mind!

FIGARO. No: it is he who must be driven out of his.

COUNTESS. A man as jealous as he—

FIGARO. So much the better. To make the most out of people like him, all you have to do is to whip up their blood—a device all women use. As soon as a man of his type is red hot with passion, the most trifling subterfuge enables one to lead him by the nose into the nearest fishpond. I have used Basil to deliver an anonymous note which informs his lordship that tonight a gallant will try to approach you during the ball.

COUNTESS. You play fast and loose with the truth about a woman of honor?

FIGARO. There are but few I would have dared to risk it with, madam, for fear of stating no more than the facts.

COUNTESS. And now you'll expect me to thank you!

FIGARO. Honestly, isn't it delightful to have cut out his work for him so that he will be prowling around his lady and swearing under his breath during the time that he counted on for dallying with mine? Already he is bewildered: will he gallop over this one, shall he mount guard over that one? [*At the window*] In his disturbed state of mind—look, look, how he races across the meadow after a poor hare who can't help himself! The hour of the wedding hastens on, but he won't be able to decide against it: he will never dare oppose it to my lady's face.

SUZANNE. No, but Marceline, that *grande dame*, will not hesitate to dare.

FIGARO. Ah! That doesn't worry me. Just let my lord know that you will meet him at dusk in the garden.

SUZANNE. So that's your great device—to rely on him?

FIGARO. See here: people who don't want to do anything about anything never achieve anything and aren't good for anything. That's my last word.

SUZANNE. A pleasant one!

COUNTESS. And so is her question: you really would let her meet him in the garden?

FIGARO. Not at all. I'll arrange for someone to put on one of Suzy's dresses. Taken in the act, how can he get out of it?

SUZANNE. Who will wear my dress?

FIGARO. Cherubino.

COUNTESS. He's gone.

FIGARO. Not as far as I'm concerned. Will the ladies allow me?

SUZANNE. One can always trust this fellow to hatch a scheme.

FIGARO. A scheme! Two, three or four at once, well scrambled and working from both ends against the middle: I was born to be a courtier.

SUZANNE. They say it's a difficult profession.

FIGARO. Accept, take, and ask—that's the secret in three words.

COUNTESS. He has so much self-confidence it rubs off on one!

FIGARO. That was my idea.

SUZANNE. You were saying?

Figaro. That during the Count's absence I will send you Cherubino. Dress
 him up and do his hair and I'll conceal and indoctrinate him. After
 which, my lord, how you will dance! [*Exit*]
Countess [*holding her box of patches*[29]]. Heavens, Suzy, I look a sight, and
 this young man is coming in!
Suzanne. Don't you want him to get over it?
Countess [*gazing in the mirror*]. I? You'll see how I'm going to scold him!
Suzanne. Let's get him to sing his romance. [*She lays it on the* Countess's
 lap]
Countess. But really my hair is in a state—
Suzanne. I'll just roll up these two curls; they will help your ladyship to
 scold him.
Countess [*returning to reality*]. What are you saying, Missy?
Suzanne. Come in, officer. We are visible.
 [*Enter* Cherubino].
Cherubino [*trembling*]. Oh how that title distresses me, madam. It tells me
 I must leave a place . . . a godmother . . . so good to me.
Suzanne. And so beautiful.
Cherubino [*with a sigh*]. Oh, yes.
Suzanne [*mimicking him*]. "Oh, yes." The nice young man, with his long,
 hypocritical lashes. Come, bluebird, sing us a song for my lady.
Countess [*unfolding the paper*]. Whose is it?
Suzanne. See the guilty blush: it's a foot deep on his face.
Cherubino. Is it forbidden to—cherish?
Suzanne [*shaking her fist in his face*]. I am going to tell on you, ne'er-do-well!
Countess. Enough. Does he sing?
Cherubino. Please, madam, I am shaking all over.
Suzanne [*laughing and mimicking*]. Nya, nya, nya, nya, nya, nya, nya. As
 soon as madam wishes. These modest authors! I'll accompany him.
Countess. Take my guitar. [*Seated, she holds the paper to follow the words.*
 Suzanne, *behind her armchair, begins the introduction, reading the notes over
 her mistress's head. The page stands in front, his eyes lowered. The scene dupli-
 cates the beautiful print made from Vanloo's painting entitled "Conversation in
 Spain."*]

 [*To the tune of Malbrouck*]
 My weary steed astride
 (Oh my heart, oh my heart, it is breaking)
 Uncaring where, I ride
 The solitary plain.

 Uncaring where I ride,
 No squire[30] is at my side,
 (Oh my heart, oh my heart, it is breaking)
 For my godmother I pine,
 And weep for her in vain.

[29] Small pieces of black cloth, worn cosmetically to emphasize a fair complexion.
[30] A candidate for knighthood, in the service of another knight.

For her I weep in vain,
And as the fates decree,
I carve upon a tree
(Oh my heart, oh my heart, it is breaking)
The letters of her name—
The king that moment came.

The king that moment came,
His bishops and his peers.
"Sweet page," spoke up the Queen,
(Oh my heart, oh my heart, it is breaking)
"'Tis sore distress, I ween,[31]
"That draws from you these tears.

"What draws from you these tears,
"Declare to us, poor lad."
"My lady Queen, my lord,
(Oh my heart, oh my heart, it is breaking)
"A godmother I had,
"Whom always I adored—

"Whom always I adored
"And I'll die dreaming of."
"Sweet page," the Queen implored,
(Oh my heart, oh my heart, it is breaking)
"That godmother you love,
"Pray let me take her place.

"Yes, let me take her place,
"And give you, page of mine,
"A maiden fair of face
(Oh my heart, oh my heart, it is breaking)
"A captain's daughter true,
"To whom I'll marry you."

"To whom I'll marry you!
"Those words I must deny,
"And for one favor sue:
(Oh my heart, oh my heart, it is breaking)
"To let me live in grief,
"And from my grieving die."

COUNTESS. It is full of naïve simplicity,[32] and even of true sentiment.

SUZANNE [*laying the guitar on a chair*]. Oh, as far as sentiment goes, this
young man is—But say, officer, have you been told that to enliven this
evening's party we need to know whether one of my gowns will more or
less fit you?

[31] Think.
[32] The Countess is praising the song as a good attempt at a folk ballad—a genre becoming
popular in the late eighteenth century.

COUNTESS. I'm afraid it won't.

SUZANNE [*comparing their statures*]. He's about my size. Let's take off the coat. [*She takes it off him.*]

COUNTESS. What if someone comes in?

SUZANNE. We're not doing anything wrong. I'll shut the door. [*She runs.*] But it's the hair I want to see.

COUNTESS. In my dressing room, a wrapper of mine.

[SUZANNE *goes into the dressing room.*]

COUNTESS. Until the ball opens, the Count will not know that you are still in the castle. We shall tell him afterwards that the time required to prepare your commission gave us the idea of—

CHERUBINO [*showing her the paper*]. Unfortunately, madam, my commission is here, signed. Basil gave it to me from my lord.

COUNTESS. Already! Not a minute lost. [*She reads*] In so much of a hurry that he forgot to affix the seal. [*She hands it back*]

SUZANNE [*carrying also a wide brimmed hat*]. The seal to what?

COUNTESS. His commission.

SUZANNE. Already?

COUNTESS. That's what I was saying. Is that the wrapper?

SUZANNE [*seated near the* COUNTESS]. The handsomest of all. [*She sings with pins in her mouth.*]

> Turn your head, oh Johnny my dear,
> Turn, my handsome cavalier.

[CHERUBINO *kneels beside her to have his hair dressed.*]

Madam, he is sweet!

COUNTESS. Pull his collar more like a woman.

SUZANNE. There—look at that ragamuffin, what a pretty girl he makes. I'm jealous. [*She takes his chin in her hand.*] Will you please not be so pretty as you are?

COUNTESS. Silly girl! You must turn back the cuff so that the undersleeve shows up better. [*She lifts the sleeve.*] What has he put on his arm?—a ribbon!

SUZANNE. *Your* ribbon. I am glad madam saw it. I warned him I would tell on him. I swear, if my lord had not come in, I would have got the ribbon back. I'm almost as strong as he is.

COUNTESS. I see blood. [*She takes off the ribbon.*]

CHERUBINO [*shamefaced*]. This morning, when I knew I had to leave, I was adjusting the snaffle[33] on my horse. He tossed his head and the boss on the bit scratched my arm.

COUNTESS. But why put a ribbon—

SUZANNE. A *stolen* ribbon at that! Just imagine what the baffle—the snaffle— the raffle—I can't keep those things straight—look at that white skin! It's a woman's arm, whiter than mine, see? [*She compares.*]

COUNTESS [*freezingly*]. Kindly get me some court plaster[34] from my dress-

[33] A bit with rings to which the reins are attached.

[34] An adhesive fabric, cut into pieces either to treat cuts or to make cosmetic "beauty spots."

ing table. [SUZANNE *gives* CHERUBINO *a shove, he falls forward on his hands. She goes into the dressing room. The* COUNTESS *remains silent a moment, her eyes on the ribbon.* CHERUBINO *gazes at her intently.*] As to my ribbon, sir— it's the color I find most becoming to me—I was very much annoyed to be without it.

SUZANNE [*returning*]. The bandage for his arm. [*She gives the* COUNTESS *the plaster and a pair of scissors.*]

COUNTESS. When you go for your dress, bring back the ribbon from some other bonnet. [SUZANNE *leaves by the center door, taking the page's coat with her.*]

CHERUBINO [*eyes lowered*]. The ribbon you're taking from me would have cured me in no time.

COUNTESS. Owing to what specific virtue?[35] [*Pointing to the plaster*] That is so much better.

CHERUBINO [*hesitating*]. When a ribbon . . . has bound the head . . . or touched the skin . . . of a person . . .

COUNTESS [*breaking in*]. of a stranger, it cures wounds? That is news to me. I will test it by keeping the one you put around your arm. At the first scratch—on one of my maids—I shall try it out.

CHERUBINO [*deeply moved*]. You are keeping it—but I'm leaving!

COUNTESS. But not forever.

CHERUBINO. I'm so unhappy!

COUNTESS [*moved*]. Now he is weeping. It's Figaro's fault for prophesying—

CHERUBINO. Oh how I wish the time had come that he spoke about! If I were sure of dying at once, perhaps my lips would dare—

COUNTESS [*interrupts by wiping his eyes with her handkerchief*]. Be quiet, child, be quiet. There isn't a grain of sense in what you're saying. [*A knock at the door; she raises her voice.*] Who is it?

COUNT [*outside*]. Why are you locked in?

COUNTESS [*upset*]. It's my husband. Heavens! . . . [*To* CHERUBINO, *who has also got up*] You, without your coat, your collar open and your arms bare—alone with me—the general disarray—the anonymous letter he received, his jealousy—

COUNT [*outside*]. You won't open?

COUNTESS. The fact is . . . I am alone.

COUNT. Alone? With whom are you talking, then?

COUNTESS [*fumbling*]. With you, I should think.

CHERUBINO [*aside*]. After those scenes of yesterday and this morning he would kill me on the spot. [*He runs into the dressing room and shuts the door.*]

COUNTESS [*removes the key and opens the other door to admit the* COUNT]. What a dreadful mistake!

COUNT [*somewhat severe*]. You are not in the habit of shutting yourself up.

COUNTESS [*upset*]. I was trying on—yes—odds and ends—with Suzanne. She went for a minute to her room.

COUNT. You look and sound quite strange.

[35] Medicinal potency.

COUNTESS. It's not surprising, not surprising at all, I assure you. We were speaking about you. She just left, as I said—

COUNT. You were speaking about me? Well, here I am. I've come back much disturbed. On setting out, I was handed a note—though I take no stock in it—it upset me.

COUNTESS. How so, what note, sir?

COUNT. You must admit, madam, that you or I must be surrounded by people who are—uncommonly wicked. Someone informs me that a person, whom I falsely suppose to be absent, will attempt to approach you.

COUNTESS. Whoever this rash being may be, he will have to make his way to this very spot, for I do not intend to stir for the rest of the day.

COUNT. What about tonight, for Suzanne's wedding?

COUNTESS. Not at any price; I am quite indisposed.

COUNT. Fortunately the doctor is here. [*The page overturns a chair in the dressing room.*] What noise was that?

COUNTESS [*distraught*]. Noise?

COUNT. Someone in there upset a piece of furniture.

COUNTESS. I—I heard nothing.

COUNT. You must be powerfully preoccupied.

COUNTESS. Preoccupied? What about?

COUNT. Madam: there is someone in that dressing room!

COUNTESS. Indeed, who could there be, sir?

COUNT. It is for me to ask that question: I have just arrived.

COUNTESS. It must be Suzanne putting things away.

COUNT. You told me she had gone to her room.

COUNTESS. Gone there—or here—I don't know which.

COUNT. If it is Suzanne, why your evident distress?

COUNTESS. Distress—over my maid?

COUNT. Over your maid it may be, but distress without a doubt.

COUNTESS. Without a doubt, sir, that girl concerns and occupies your mind much more than I.

COUNT. She concerns me so much that I want to see her at once.

COUNTESS. I readily believe that this is what you often want. But your ill-founded suspicions—

[SUZANNE *enters at the back, unseen, with clothes in her arms.*]

COUNT. If so, they will be easily dispelled. [*He speaks through the dressing-room door.*] Come out, Suzanne, I order you to. [SUZANNE *stops near the alcove at the back.*]

COUNTESS. She is almost naked, sir. How can you intrude in this way on women in their apartments? She was trying on some old things I am giving her on the occasion of her wedding. She fled when she heard you.

COUNT. If she is afraid to show herself, she can at least speak. [*He turns again to the closed door.*] Answer me, Suzanne: are you in the dressing room? [SUZANNE, *still at the back of the alcove, hides behind the bed.*]

COUNTESS [*quickly, to the closed door*]. Suzy, I forbid you to answer. [*To the* COUNT] No one has ever carried tyranny so far!

COUNT [*turning again*]. If she won't speak, dressed or undressed I shall see her.

COUNTESS [*intercepting him*]. Anywhere else I can't prevent you, but I trust that in my own room—

COUNT. And I trust that in one minute I shall know who this mysterious Suzanne is. I can see it is useless to ask you for the key, but it is not hard to break down this trumpery[36] door. Ho, there, anybody!

COUNTESS. You would bring in your people, create a public scandal—all on the strength of a vague suspicion!—We'll be the talk of the castle.

COUNT. An excellent point, madam, I can do without help. This instant I go to my rooms and return with what I need. [*He starts to go and turns back*] But in order that everything shall remain as it is, will you kindly accompany me, quietly and decently—since scandal displeases you so? My simple request will surely not be denied?

COUNTESS [*upset*]. Sir, who would dream of crossing you?

COUNT. Oh, I was forgetting: the door which leads to your maids' quarters. I must also shut it so that you may be fully vindicated. [*He shuts the center door and takes the key.*]

COUNTESS [*aside*]. Oh what a fateful whim!

COUNT [*returning*]. Now that this chamber is sealed, I beg you to accept my arm. [*He raises his voice.*] As for the Suzanne in the dressing room, she will have the goodness to await my return. The least of the evils that may befall her then is—

COUNTESS. Really, sir, this is the most odious performance—

 [*The* COUNT *leads her out and locks the
 door.*]

SUZANNE [*runs from the alcove to the dressing-room door and speaks through the keyhole*]. Open up, Cherubino, open, quick, it's Suzanne, open and hurry out.

CHERUBINO [*coming out*]. Oh, Suzy, what a dreadful mess!

SUZANNE. Go, go, you haven't a minute to lose.

CHERUBINO [*frightened*]. How can I get out?

SUZANNE. Don't ask me, just go.

CHERUBINO. But I can't if I'm locked in.

SUZANNE. After this afternoon's encounter he would break you, and she and I would be doomed. Go tell Figaro—

CHERUBINO. Maybe the window over the garden isn't too high up. [*He runs to see.*]

SUZANNE [*frightened*]. A whole story—you can't do it! Oh my poor lady! And my marriage, dear God!

CHERUBINO [*coming back*]. It overlooks the melon patch. All it would spoil is a couple of beds.

SUZANNE [*holding him back and crying out*]. You will kill yourself!

CHERUBINO [*excited*]. I'd throw myself into an open furnace—I would, Suzy—rather than cause her harm. And a kiss from you will bring me luck. [*Kisses her, runs toward the window, and leaps out*]

SUZANNE [*again cries out; then, overcome, falls into a chair; finally drags herself to the window and comes back*]. He's off and away, the young devil!! As light

[36] Trashy; trifling.

on his feet as he's pretty to look at. He'll have all the women he wants, I bet. Now to take his place, quick! [*Goes into the dressing room*] From here on, my lord, you can tear down the wall if it gives you pleasure, you don't get a word out of me. [*Shuts the door*]

> [*The* COUNT *and* COUNTESS *return. He holds a pair of pliers which he soon throws upon a chair.*]

COUNT. Everything is as I left it. Madam, if you compel me to break down that door you must think of the consequences: once again, will you open it yourself?

COUNTESS. But sir, what singular ill-temper can so destroy considerateness between husband and wife? If it were love that possessed you to the point of causing this fury, I could excuse it, however demented. The motive could make me forget the offense. But how can mere vanity move a well-bred man to such excesses?

COUNT. Love or vanity, you open that door or I do it on the spot.

COUNTESS [*before the door*]. My lord, please desist! Can you think me capable of forgetting what I owe to my self-respect?

COUNT. Put it any way you like, madam, I mean to see who is in that dressing room.

COUNTESS [*frightened*]. Very well, you shall see. But first listen to me quietly.

COUNT. So it isn't Suzanne?

COUNTESS [*embarrassed*]. At least it isn't a person . . . about whom you should have any . . . we were bent on a practical joke . . . quite harmless, really, for this evening . . . and I swear to you . . .

COUNT. You swear to me—what?

COUNTESS. That neither he nor I meant to offend you.

COUNT. He—it is a man, then?

COUNTESS. A child, dear sir.

COUNT. And who, pray tell?

COUNTESS. I hardly dare give his name.

COUNT [*furious*]. I'll kill him!

COUNTESS. Merciful powers!

COUNT. Speak up!

COUNTESS. The young . . . Cherubino.

COUNT. That impudent whelp! That explains my suspicions—and the anonymous note.

COUNTESS [*her hands palm to palm in prayer*]. Oh, sir, do not allow yourself to suppose—

COUNT [*stamping his foot and speaking aside*]. That accursèd page turns up wherever I go. [*Aloud*] Come, madam, now that I know everything, open up. You would not have been so moved saying goodbye to him this morning, you would not have used such elaborate lies in your tale of Suzanne, and he would not have hidden so quickly and for so long, unless misconduct and guilt were the reason.

COUNTESS. He was afraid of irritating you by showing himself.

COUNT [*beside himself, shouting at the dressing-room door*]. Come out of there, you little scrub!

COUNTESS [*seizing the* COUNT *with both arms and thrusting him aside*]. My dear

sir, my dear sir, your anger makes me afraid for him. Don't, I beg, trust your own suspicions, which are unjust, and don't let his disheveled state—

COUNT. Disheveled!

COUNTESS. Alas, you will see—one of my bonnets on his head, without his coat, his neckband open and arms bare, ready to dress up as a woman. He was going to try to—

COUNT. And you wanted to stay all day in his room! Worthless woman! You *shall* keep to your room—I'll see to it—and for a long time! But first I must kick out that insolent stripling that I may never come upon him again.

COUNTESS [*on her knees, arms uplifted*]. Count, you must spare a mere child. I shall never forgive myself for being the cause of—

COUNT. Your fears deepen his guilt.

COUNTESS. He is not guilty—he was leaving. It is I who had him fetched.

COUNT [*in anger*]. Get up. Remove yourself—shameless woman, to dare entreat me in behalf of another.

COUNTESS. Very well. I will remove myself, I will get up and give you the key to the door, but in the name of your love—

COUNT. My love, hypocrite!

COUNTESS [*gets up and gives him the key*]. Promise that you will let the child go harmless—and may you vent your fury on me later if I do not convince you that—

COUNT [*taking the key*]. I'm no longer listening.

COUNTESS [*throws herself into an armchair, her handkerchief over her face*]. God, oh God, he will be killed!

COUNT [*opens the door*]. You!

SUZANNE [*comes out laughing*]. "I will kill him—I will kill him!" Why *don't* you kill him, your villainous page?

COUNT [*aside*]. Lord! What a lesson! [*Looking at the* COUNTESS, *who is stupefied*] And you pretend to be surprised, too? But perhaps Suzanne wasn't alone. [*He goes in.*]

SUZANNE [*going to* COUNTESS]. Recover yourself, madam, he's nowhere near—he jumped [*gesture*].

COUNTESS. Oh, Suzy, I am all in.

COUNT [*emerges, vexed and silent*]. There's no one else and this time I was wrong. Madam, you are a good actress—

SUZANNE. What about me, my lord? [COUNTESS *holds her handkerchief to her mouth and says nothing, to regain her composure.*]

COUNT [*approaching*]. And so, madam, you were joking?

COUNTESS [*recovering*]. And why not, sir?

COUNT. An absurd practical joke, and for what reason, tell me?

COUNTESS. Does your outrageous behavior deserve consideration?

COUNT. Do you call outrageous what relates to honor?

COUNTESS [*gradually herself again*]. Did I join my life to yours only to be a perpetual victim of your neglect and your jealousy, two things which only you can reconcile?

COUNT. Ah, madam, you spare me nothing—

SUZANNE. She did! My lady had only to let you call the servants—

COUNT. You are right and I abase myself. Forgive me. I am discomfited.[37]

SUZANNE. And deserve to be, you must admit.

COUNT. But why wouldn't you come out when I called to you?

SUZANNE. I was putting on some clothes as well as I could, with a multitude of pins: my lady's forbidding me to stir was for a good reason.

COUNT. Instead of reminding me of my error, help me to soothe her.

COUNTESS. No, my lord, an offense such as this is not to be palliated. I am about to retire to a convent. It is high time I did.

COUNT. Shall you be without regrets?

SUZANNE. For my part, I am sure the day you leave will be the beginning of endless grief.

COUNTESS. Even if it is, Suzy, I'd rather miss him than basely forgive him. He has wounded me too deeply.

COUNT. Rosine!

COUNTESS. I am Rosine no longer, the Rosine you so tenaciously pursued. I am the poor Countess Almaviva, the sad forsaken wife you no longer love.

SUZANNE. Oh, madam!

COUNT [*suppliant*]. For charity's sake!

COUNTESS. When have you ever shown me any?

COUNT. But that anonymous letter—it curdled my blood.

COUNTESS. I did not agree to its being written.

COUNT. You knew about it?

COUNTESS. It was that harebrained Figaro—

COUNT. He was party to it?

COUNTESS. —who gave it to Basil—

COUNT. —who told me he had it from a peasant. Oh, sinister singing-master, two-faced underling: you shall pay for everybody's crimes!

COUNTESS. How like a man! You beg for yourself a forgiveness you deny to others. Let me tell you: if ever I consent to pardon you for the error you committed on the strength of that note, I shall demand that the amnesty be general.

COUNT. With all my heart, Countess. But how can I ever make up for so humiliating a blunder?

COUNTESS [*rising*]. It humiliated us both.

COUNT. No, no, only myself, believe me. But I am still amazed at the ease with which you women take on the proper look and tone of each circumstance. You were flushed, crying, your face was working—I assure you, you still look undone.

COUNTESS [*trying to smile*]. I was flushing with resentment against your suspiciousness. But men are not delicate enough creatures to distinguish between the indignation of an honorable person suffering outrage and the confusion produced by a justified accusation.

COUNT [*smiling*]. What about the disheveled page, coatless and half naked?

COUNTESS [*pointing to* SUZANNE]. There he is. Aren't you glad to have caught this one instead of the other? Generally speaking, you do not hate to catch this one.

[37] A strong word: "utterly routed."

COUNT [*laughing*]. And your entreaties and simulated tears?

COUNTESS. You make me laugh and I do not feel like it.

COUNT. We men think we are practiced in the art of politics, but we are children. It is you, you, madam, whom the King should appoint ambassador to London! Your sex must have made a deep study of the art of controlling the countenance to succeed as you did today.

COUNTESS. We are forced into it—and always by men.

SUZANNE. But put us on parole and you will see what honorable beings we are.

COUNTESS. Enough for the moment, Count. Possibly I went too far, but my leniency in so grave a case must be matched by yours.

COUNT. Do say again that you forgive me.

COUNTESS. Have I said it at all, Suzy?

SUZANNE. I did not hear it, madam.

COUNT. Well then, let the words slip out.

COUNTESS. You think you deserve it, you ungrateful man?

COUNT. I do, I do—because I repent.

SUZANNE. To suspect a man in my lady's dressing room!

COUNT. She has already punished me so severely!

SUZANNE. Not to believe her when she says it is her chambermaid!

COUNT. Rosine, are you unrelenting?

COUNTESS. Oh, Suzy, how weak I am! What a poor example I give you! [*Holding out her hand to the* COUNT] No one will ever believe again in a woman's anger.

SUZANNE. It's all right, madam. One always comes to this with men. [*The* COUNT *ardently kisses his wife's hand.*]

FIGARO [*enters breathless*]. I heard that madam was seriously unwell. I've been running. I see there is no truth in the report.

COUNT [*drily*]. You are most attentive.

FIGARO. It is my duty. But since there is nothing in it, my lord, let me say that all your younger vassals of either sex are downstairs with their violins and pipes, awaiting the moment when you will allow me to bring my bride, so that they may accompany—

COUNT. And who will look after the Countess indoors?

FIGARO. Look after her—but she's not ill?

COUNT. No, but there is a mysterious stranger who will try to approach her.

FIGARO. What stranger?

COUNT. The man in the note that you gave to Basil.

FIGARO. Who said I gave him a note?

COUNT. Even if I hadn't been told, rascal, I could read it in your lying face.

FIGARO. Then it's my face deceiving you, not I.

SUZANNE. Figaro, my poor darling, don't waste your eloquence in defeat: we told his lordship everything.

FIGARO. Told what? You treat me as if I were Basil!

SUZANNE. Told him you had written a note to make my lord believe that when he came in here he would find the young page in the dressing room where I shut myself up.

COUNT. What have you to say to that?

COUNTESS. There's no further need to conceal anything, Figaro, the joke is over.

Figaro [*trying to guess*]. The joke is over?

Count. Yes, over, consummated: what do you say to that?

Figaro. Consummated? I say that—that I wish I could say the same about my marriage. You have only to give the word—

Count. You admit the anonymous note?

Figaro. Since my lady wants it so, and Suzanne wants it so, and you want it so, I can't help wanting it too. But if I were you, my lord, really, I wouldn't believe a word of anything we are telling you.

Count. You're always telling lies and always in the teeth of evidence; it's beginning to get on my nerves.

Countess [*laughing*]. The poor fellow! Why should you expect, sir, that he would tell the truth even once?

Figaro [*low to* Suzanne]. I've warned him of the danger ahead—that's all a gentleman can do.

Suzanne [*low*]. Did you see the page?

Figaro [*low*]. Yes, all rumpled.

Suzanne [*low*]. Oh, wretched!

Countess. Look, my dear Count, they long to be united. Their impatience is understandable: let us go and celebrate the wedding.

Count [*aside*]. But Marceline . . . where is Marceline? [*Aloud*] I'd like a moment to dress.

Countess. To be with our own people? You see what I have on.

Antonio [*enters half tipsy, holding a pot of partly crushed flowers*]. My lord, my lord!

Count. What do you want with me, Antonio?

Antonio. I wish you'd have the windows over my beds fitted with bars. They throw every kind of thing out of those windows, a while back they threw out a man.

Count. Out of these windows?

Antonio. Just look at my gillyflowers!

Suzanne [*low to* Figaro]. Look out, Figaro, on your toes!

Figaro. My lord, he gets drunk every day from the crack of dawn.

Antonio. You're wrong—with me there's always a little leftover from the day before. But that's how people judge you—in the dark.

Count [*breathing fire*]. The man, what man, where is he?

Antonio. Where he is?

Count. Yes, where?

Antonio. That's what *I* say. I want to have him found. I'm your servant. There's only me takes real care of your garden. Man falls on it—you can't help . . . appreciating . . . my reputation is . . . uprooted.

Suzanne [*low to* Figaro]. Change the subject, hurry!

Figaro. Won't you ever give up drinking?

Antonio. If I didn't drink I'd go out of my mind.

Countess. But to drink as you do, without thirst . . .

Antonio. To drink without thirst and make love at any time, my lady, 'swhat distinguishes us from the other animals.

Count [*fiercely*]. Answer me or I'll have you thrown on the parish.[38]

Antonio. I wouldn't go.

[38] Dismissed and put on welfare.

COUNT. What's that?

ANTONIO [*touching his forehead*]. If *that* isn't enough to make you keep a good servant, on my side I'm not so dumb as to get rid of a good master.

COUNT [*shaking him violently*]. You say they threw a man out the window.

ANTONIO. Yes, excellency, just a while back, in a white vest, and he picked himself up and ran away.

COUNT [*impatient*]. And then?

ANTONIO. I tried to run after him, but I bumped into the fence so hard my finger [*he shows which*] is still numb. It can't move hand or foot of itself.

COUNT. But you'd recognize the man?

ANTONIO. That I could if I had seen him, as you might say.

SUZANNE [*low to* FIGARO]. He never saw him.

FIGARO. What a pother about a pot! How long do you mean to carry on about your bluebells, you old watering jug? No use asking, my lord, it was I who jumped down.

COUNT. You? Why?

ANTONIO. "How long I carry on," eh? Why, you must have grown since I saw you jump, 'cause you were smaller and thinner at the time.

FIGARO. Naturally: when one jumps one gathers oneself together.

ANTONIO. Methought 'twas rather the whippersnapper I saw—the page.

COUNT. Cherubino, you mean?

FIGARO. Of course, having come back—he and his horse—from the gates of Seville, where he probably is now.

ANTONIO. I didn't say that, I didn't say that! I didn't see a horse jump, or I'd say so.

COUNT. Oh to be patient!

FIGARO. I was in the women's quarters in my white vest—terribly hot day. I was waiting there for Suzanette, when suddenly I heard your voice, my lord, and a great noise going on. I don't know why, I was seized with fear—perhaps about the anonymous note. . . . To make a clean breast of it, I lost my head and jumped down on the flowers, spraining my ankle for my pains. [*he rubs his foot*]

ANTONIO. As it's you, then I've got to give you back this bit of paper that fell out of your vest when you landed.

COUNT [*snatching it*]. Give it to me. [*He unfolds the paper and folds it again*]

FIGARO [*aside*]. This is the end.

COUNT [*to* FIGARO]. Your great fright has surely not made you forget the contents of this paper, nor how it got into your pocket?

FIGARO [*embarrassed, looks into all his pockets, bringing out letters and papers*]. Oh certainly not—but I carry so many about me—every one has to be answered. [*He looks at a paper.*] This, for instance, what's—? ah, yes, a letter from Marceline, four pages, a beautiful letter. Could that other one be the petition from that poacher[39] who is in prison? No—here it is. I also had a list of the furniture in the pavilion, in my other pocket— (*The* COUNT *reopens the paper in his hand.*)

COUNTESS [*low to* SUZANNE]. Heavens, Suzy, it's the officer's commission.

SUZANNE [*low to* FIGARO]. We're undone: it's the commission!

COUNT [*folding the paper*]. Well, resourceful sir, you can't guess?

[39] A trespasser who filches a property-owner's game animals or fish.

ANTONIO [*going toward* FIGARO]. My lord says as how you can't guess?
FIGARO [*pushing him away*]. Hence, varlet,[40] and don't speak into my nose!
COUNT. You cannot recall for me what the paper might be?
FIGARO. Ah, ah, ah! I have it!—the poor boy! It must be Cherubino's com-
 mission, which the dear child showed me and I forgot to give back.
 What a scatterbrain I am! But how can he manage without his commis-
 sion? We must go after him—
COUNT. Why should he have given it to you?
FIGARO [*embarrassed*]. He wanted—something done to it.
COUNT [*looks at paper*]. There's nothing needs doing.
COUNTESS [*low to* SUZANNE]. The seal.
SUZANNE [*low to* FIGARO]. The seal's not on it.
COUNT [*to* FIGARO]. You have nothing to say?
FIGARO. Yes, the fact is . . . something *is* missing. He says it is customary.
COUNT. Customary? What is customary?
FIGARO. To affix the seal showing your coat of arms. But perhaps it isn't
 worth the trouble.
COUNT [*reopens the paper and crumples it up angrily*]. Confound it! My fate
 decrees that I'm to be kept in the dark. [*Aside*] This—this Figaro is the
 master mind, and I—I should keep from striking back! [*He starts to stalk
 out.*]
FIGARO [*stopping him*]. You're not going without giving the word about my
 wedding?

 [*Enter* BASIL, BARTHOLO, MARCELINE,
 and SUNSTRUCK.]

MARCELINE [*to the* COUNT]. Don't give the word, my lord. Before you do
 him a favor, you must do me justice. He has obligations toward me.
COUNT [*aside*]. My revenge at last!
FIGARO. Obligations? Of what sort? Please explain.
MARCELINE. Of course I shall explain, false knave! [COUNTESS *sits in an
 armchair,* SUZANNE *behind her.*]
COUNT. What is it you are referring to, Marceline?
MARCELINE. A promise of marriage.
FIGARO. A promissory note for money I borrowed, nothing more.
MARCELINE [*to* COUNT]. But with the forfeit of marrying me. You are a
 great lord, the highest judge in the province . . .
COUNT. Come to the assizes.[41] I will give everybody justice.
BASIL [*pointing to* MARCELINE]. In that case, Your Worship will permit me
 to put in evidence my claims on Marceline?[42]
COUNT [*aside*]. This is the scoundrel of the anonymous note.
FIGARO. As mad as she is—birds of a feather!
COUNT [*to* BASIL, *angrily*]. Your claims, your claims! What right have you to
 speak up in my presence, master fool?
ANTONIO [*striking his fist into the palm of his other hand*]. Got it the first time: it
 sure is his right name!

[40] An archaic term: "worthless person."
[41] Court sessions. (The Count is a judge by virtue of his position as nobleman and lord of
the manor.)
[42] What these claims are we learn in the fourth act.

COUNT. Marceline, everything is recessed until the public hearing of your
 plea, which shall take place in the large reception room. You, wise Basil,
 as my faithful and reliable agent, shall go into town and summon the
 bench.
BASIL. For her case?
COUNT. And bring along the peasant who gave you the note.
BASIL. How shall I know him?
COUNT. You object?
BASIL. I did not enter your service to run errands.
COUNT. What's that?
BASIL. A talented performer on the parish organ, I teach my lady the
 keyboard, coach her women in singing and your pages on the mando-
 lin. But my chief employment is to entertain your company on the gui-
 tar, when it pleases you to command me.
SUNSTRUCK [*coming forward*]. I'll go, your lordsy, if they's what you want.
COUNT. What is your name and your employment?
SUNSTRUCK. My name is Sunstruck, good lordsy. I watch the goats, and bin
 asked in for the fireworks. It's holiday today for all us herds. But I know
 where's the roaring big trial-shop in town.
COUNT. Your gumption pleases me, go do my errand. As for you, [*to*
 BASIL] go along with the gentleman, singing and playing the guitar to
 entertain him on the way, for he is of my company.
SUNSTRUCK [*elated*]. I—I'm of the—[SUZANNE *calms him down by pointing to*
 the COUNTESS.]
BASIL [*taken aback*]. Go along with Sunstruck while playing the guitar?
COUNT. It is your profession: off you go, you're dismissed. [*Exit*]
BASIL [*to himself*]. I'm certainly not going to fight the iron pot, I who am—
FIGARO. —already cracked.
BASIL [*aside*]. Instead of furthering their wedding, I am going to insure
 Marceline's and mine. [*To* FIGARO] Don't sign anything, I warn you,
 until I come back. [*He picks up his guitar from a chair at the back*]
FIGARO [*following him*]. Sign anything? Don't worry! I shan't, even if you
 never come back. But you don't seem in the mood for song. Would you
 like me to begin? Come on, a smile, and the high *la-mi-la* for my bride.
 [*He walks backward and dances the following Seguidilla.*[43] BASIL *accompanies*
 him and everyone joins in]

> Better than riches, I love
> The goodness of
> My Suzanne,
> Zann, zann, zann,
> Zann, zann, zann,
> Zann, zann, zann
>
> Always on her I'll depend
> And madly end
> As I began
> Gan, gan, gan,

[43] A fast-paced Spanish dance, in triple time.

> Gan, gan, gan,
> Gan, gan, gan.

[Exeunt singing and dancing.]

COUNTESS *[in the wing chair]*. You see, Suzanne, the ordeal I had to go through, thanks to your wild friend's anonymous note?

SUZANNE. Oh, madam, if you could have seen your face when I came out of the dressing room—you lost all your color, but only for an instant, then you grew red—oh so red!

COUNTESS. And he jumped out of the window?

SUZANNE. Without a moment's hesitation, the dear child—light as a bird.

COUNTESS. That deplorable gardener! The whole thing made me so dizzy I couldn't keep two ideas together in my mind.

SUZANNE. Not at all, my lady, on the contrary. I saw at once what facility the habit of high society confers on respectable ladies who have to tell lies.

COUNTESS. Do you think the Count was taken in? What if he finds the poor child in the castle?

SUZANNE. I'm going to make sure he is well hidden.

COUNTESS. He must go away. After what happened, you can imagine I'm not tempted to send him into the garden dressed like you.

SUZANNE. And I shan't go either, so once again my wedding is—

COUNTESS. Wait! What if in your place, or another's—why shouldn't *I* go?

SUZANNE. You, madam?

COUNTESS. No one could be reprimanded—and the Count couldn't explain the facts away. First to have punished jealousy, and then to demonstrate his infidelity—it would be . . . ! Come, our luck in the first adventure encourages me to try a second. Let him know quickly that you will go into the garden. But be sure no one knows—

SUZANNE. Not Figaro?

COUNTESS. No, no. He would want to contribute ideas . . . Fetch me my stick and my velvet mask. I'll go out on the terrace and daydream. *[SUZANNE *goes into the dressing room.*]*

COUNTESS. My scheme is surely brash enough. *[turns around]* Ah, my ribbon, my pretty ribbon, I had forgotten you. *[She takes it, sits, and rolls it up.]* Henceforth you will be with me always, you will remind me of the scene in which that poor boy . . . Oh, Count, what have you done!—and what am *I* doing right now? *[SUZANNE *re-enters; the* COUNTESS *furtively slips the ribbon into her bosom.*]*

SUZANNE. Here is the stick and your mask.

COUNTESS. Remember, I forbid you to say one word to Figaro.

SUZANNE *[joyful]*. Your plan is delightful, my lady. I've been thinking about it. It brings everything together, concludes everything, embraces everything. Whatever comes of it, my marriage is now assured. *[She kisses the* COUNTESS's *hand. Exeunt.]*

During the intermission, the courtroom is prepared. Two settees are brought in for counsel, one on each side of the stage, but allowing free passage behind. In the center, toward the back, a raised platform with two steps, on which is put the COUNT'S *chair of state. The clerk's table and his stool are to one side downstage; seats for* BRID-LEGOOSE *and the other judges are placed alongside the* COUNT'S *platform.*

ACT 3

A room in the castle, known as the throne room and used as a reception room. To one side a canopy over a monumental chair, and on the wall, a portrait of the King. The COUNT *with* PETER, *who is wearing coat and boots and is holding a sealed package.*

COUNT [*speaking fast*]. It's clearly understood?
PETER. Yes, your Excellency. [*Exit*]
COUNT [*shouting*]. Peter!
PETER [*returning*]. Excellency?
COUNT. No one saw you?
PETER. Not a soul.
COUNT. Take the arab.
PETER. He's at the garden gate saddled and ready.
COUNT. Straight to Seville without a stop.
PETER. It's only ten miles and a fair road.
COUNT. As soon as you arrive, find out if the page is there.
PETER. At the house?
COUNT. Yes, and how long he's been there.
PETER. I understand.
COUNT. Give him his commission and come back as fast as you can.
PETER. What if he isn't there?
COUNT. Come back even faster. Tell me at once. Quick, be off!
[*Exit* PETER.]
COUNT [*pacing and meditating*]. It was clumsy of me to send Basil away . . . Anger is a bad counselor . . . That note he gave me telling of an attempt to approach the Countess . . . The chambermaid locked in that room when I come back . . . Her mistress making believe she was a prey to terror, or really terrified. . . . A man jumps out of the window and the other, later, owns up to it, or pretends it was he. There is a link missing. Something devious is going on. A certain license among my vassals— what can it matter? But the Countess, if some upstart dared! . . . my mind wanders. Truly, when anger rules, the most controlled imagination runs wild, as in a dream. She was laughing—I heard her smothered giggles, their ill-concealed amusement. But she has self-respect . . . and my honor—in whose keeping is it? As to the other affair, where do I stand? Did that rascally Suzanne give me away?—seeing it isn't *her* secret yet.[44] Why am I so bent on having her? A dozen times, I've thought of giving her up. The results of indecision are certainly strange: if I wanted her without hesitation, I shouldn't feel nearly so much desire. Figaro is behind time as usual: I must deftly plumb his thoughts. [FIGARO *enters upstage and stops.*] At any rate I must find out from his replies to what I shall put to him casually whether or not he knows I'm in love with Suzanne.
FIGARO [*aside*]. Here it comes.
COUNT. That is, if she has dropped a hint.
FIGARO. [*aside*]. I guessed it, I guess.

[44] The Count means that, because Suzanne has not yet acquiesced in his attempt to seduce her, she feels no need so far to keep the matter a secret.

COUNT. Next, I marry him off to the old girl . . .

FIGARO. [*aside*]. Mister Basil's belovèd?

COUNT. And then see what I can do with the young one.

FIGARO. [*aside*]. With my wife, if you please.

COUNT. [*turning around*]. Eh, what ? Who is it?

FIGARO. Me, at your service.

COUNT. What were you saying?

FIGARO. I haven't breathed a word.

COUNT. "My wife, if you please."

FIGARO. Oh that!—That is the conclusion of a reply I was making: "Go and tell my wife, if you please."

COUNT [*pacing*]. His wife! I am curious to know what business can detain your lordship when I have you called.

FIGARO [*pretending to adjust his clothing*]. I'd got dirty falling on that flower-bed, so I changed.

COUNT. Does it take an hour?

FIGARO. It takes the time it takes.

COUNT. The servants here need longer to dress than the masters.

FIGARO. That's because they have no valets to help them.

COUNT. I didn't quite understand what compelled you a moment ago to risk your life for nothing by jumping—

FIGARO. Risk my life! One would suppose I had leaped into a bottomless pit!

COUNT. Don't try to put me off the point by pretending you missed it yourself, you devious lackey. You understand very well that it isn't the danger to your life that concerns me, but your motive.

FIGARO. On the strength of a false alarm you came rushing in furiously, overturning everything like a mountain torrent. You're looking for a man: you have to find one or you will break down the doors and splinter the walls! I happen to be in your way—how am I to know that in your wrath—

COUNT. You could have escaped by the stairs—

FIGARO. And you'd catch me in the hall.

COUNT [*angry*]. In the hall! [*Aside*] I'm getting the worst of it, and no nearer finding out what I am after.

FIGARO [*aside*]. Let us see his game and match him trick for trick.

COUNT [*softening his tone*]. That isn't what I wanted to tell you. Let's drop the subject. I thought—as a matter of fact, I did think of taking you with me to London, as King's Messenger, but on second thoughts—

FIGARO. Your lordship has changed his mind?

COUNT. In the first place you don't know English.

FIGARO. I know "God damn!"

COUNT. I don't follow you.

FIGARO. I say that I know "God damn!"

COUNT. What about it?

FIGARO. I mean, English is a wonderful language—it takes but a few words to cover a lot of ground. With "God damn," in English, a man need lack for nothing. Do you want to sink your teeth into a nice juicy fowl? Go into a tavern and make this gesture [*turning a spit*] and say "God damn!" The waiter brings you a joint of salt beef with no bread—it's marvelous!

Do you want a good glass of burgundy or claret—just do this [*drawing a cork*] "God damn!" and they bring you a foaming tankard of beer—it's perfectly wonderful! Should you meet one of those attractive ladies who go trotting about with their elbows pulled back and their hips swinging a bit, just put your four fingers delicately on your lips—"God damn!"— and you get slapped as by a stevedore. That proves they get your meaning. The English people, it is true, use a word or two more, here and there in conversation, but it is clear that "God damn" is the core of the language—so if your only reason for leaving me behind in Spain is—

COUNT [*aside*]. He wants to go to London: she hasn't told him.

FIGARO [*aside*]. He thinks I know nothing. Let's encourage his delusion.

COUNT. What motive did the Countess have for playing that trick on me?

FIGARO. Really, my lord, you know the reason better than I.

COUNT. I anticipate all her wishes and smother her with gifts.

FIGARO. You give but you aren't faithful: would anyone be grateful for luxuries who is starved of necessities?

COUNT. You used to tell me everything.

FIGARO. And now I keep nothing from you.

COUNT. How much did the Countess give you for being in league with her?

FIGARO. How much did you give me to extricate her from Bartholo's hands?[45] Look here, my lord, it's best not to humiliate a man who serves you well, for fear he may turn into a nasty underling.

COUNT. Why is there something shady about everything you do?

FIGARO. Things always look bad when someone's bent on finding fault.

COUNT. You have a hateful reputation!

FIGARO. Maybe it's undeserved: how many noblemen can say as much?

COUNT. Time and again I've seen you on the path to fame and fortune— you always go astray.

FIGARO. What do you expect? The mob is all around, pushing, struggling, crowding, using their elbows, knocking you down. Survive who can; the rest are crushed. And so my mind's made up: I'm through.

COUNT. Through with success? [*Aside*] That's news.

FIGARO [*aside*]. My turn now. [*Aloud*] Your excellency favored me with the stewardship of the castle: my lot is a happy one. True, I shan't be King's Messenger and be the first to hear interesting news; but by way of compensation, I'll enjoy wedded bliss here in the heart of Andalusia.

COUNT. Why not take your wife to London?

FIGARO. I'd have to leave her so often[46] I'd soon find marriage a bore.

COUNT. With your brains and character, you could make your way in the administration.

FIGARO. Make your way with brains? You must think mine are addled: be dull and obsequious if you want to succeed.

COUNT. All you'd have to do is to learn statecraft under me.

FIGARO. I know all about it.

COUNT. As you do English—the basic tongue?

FIGARO. Yes—and it's nothing to boast about. Only pretend not to know

[45] Figaro is referring to his role in helping the Count outwit the watchful Bartholo and thus woo Bartholo's young ward Rosine. The implication here is that Figaro's help went unrewarded financially.

[46] That is, to carry dispatches and run other errands for the Count.

what you do know and vice versa; understand what's unintelligible and
fail to take in what is clear; above all, put forth more strength than you
possess; make a secret, often, of what no one is hiding; shut yourself up
and trim goosequills[47] so as to seem deep when you are only, as they say,
a stuffed shirt; play a part well or ill, send out spies and hire informers,
tamper with seals and intercept letters, and try to make ignoble tricks
look noble in the light of important ends—that's all of statecraft or God
strike me dead!

COUNT. But that's mere intrigue you're describing.

FIGARO. Statecraft, intrigue—as you like. To me, they're kith and kin, and
the world is welcome to them. "I'd rather have my own best girl" as the
man told the king in the ballad.[48]

COUNT [*aside*]. He wants to stay. I see . . . : Suzanne gave me away.

FIGARO [*aside*]. I've scored and paid him back in his own coin.

COUNT. And so you hope to win your case against Marceline?

FIGARO. Do you impute it to me as a crime that I refuse an old maid when
Your Excellency feels free to snatch all the young ones?

COUNT [*bantering*]. On the bench the judge will put self aside and heed
nothing but the law.

FIGARO. The law!—lenient to the great, harsh to the humble.

COUNT. Do you think I am joking?

FIGARO. Who knows, my lord? But *Tempo è galant'uomo,*[49] as the Italian
proverb says. Time always tells the truth—that's how I'll learn what
good or ill is to befall me.

COUNT [*aside*]. I can see she's told him everything; he's got to marry the
duenna.

FIGARO [*aside*]. He thinks he has me fooled. Actually, what has he found
out?

[*Enter* FOOTMAN].

FOOTMAN [*announcing*]. Don Guzman Bridlegoose.

COUNT. Bridlegoose?

FIGARO. Of course! the associate justice, your understudy and right-hand
man.

COUNT. Let him wait. [*Exit* FOOTMAN.]

FIGARO [*waiting a moment longer while the* COUNT *is abstracted*]. What else did
your lordship require?

COUNT [*wide awake*]. I? I was saying this room should be prepared for the
public hearing.

FIGARO. It's all set: the big chair for you, pretty good chairs for the justices,
the clerk's stool, benches for the lawyers, the foreground for the quality
and the rest of the floor for the groundlings.[50] I shall dismiss the clean-
ing women. [*Exit*]

COUNT [*to himself*]. That upstart is becoming a nuisance. When he argues
he gets the best of me. He presses in and corners you. Oh fox and vixen!
You have combined to take me in. Well, be friends, be lovers, be what
you will—I don't care. But when it comes to marrying—

[47] Used as writing instruments.
[48] An old song used in Molière's famous comedy *The Misanthrope* (1666).
[49] "Time is an honorable gentleman." [50] The more common spectators.

[*Enter* SUZANNE.]

SUZANNE [*breathless*]. My lord, forgive me, my lord.

COUNT [*crossly*]. What is it, miss?

SUZANNE. You are angry?

COUNT. I take it there is something you want?

SUZANNE [*shyly*]. It's because my lady has the vapors.[51] I ran to ask you to
lend us your bottle of ether. I'll bring it back immediately.

COUNT [*giving it to her*]. Never mind. Keep it for yourself: you'll soon need
it.

SUZANNE. Do women of my sort have vapors too? Isn't it a class disease,
which is caught only in boudoirs?

COUNT. Well, a girl who is in love and engaged and who loses her in-
tended—

SUZANNE. But if he pays Marceline out of the dowry you promised me—

COUNT. *I* promised you?

SUZANNE [*lowering her eyes*]. Sir, I believe I heard you say so.

COUNT. You did, but only if on your side you were willing to listen to me.

SUZANNE [*eyes still lowered*]. Isn't it my duty to listen to you?

COUNT. Then, cruel girl, why didn't you tell me sooner?

SUZANNE. It's never too late to tell the truth.

COUNT. You'll come into the garden tonight?

SUZANNE. As if I didn't go walking there every evening.

COUNT. This morning you behaved very harshly to me.

SUZANNE. This morning, yes, with the page behind the armchair.

COUNT. You are right. I forgot. But why your stubbornness before, when
Basil spoke to you on my behalf?

SUZANNE. Why should someone like Basil—

COUNT. You are *always* right. Still, there is a certain Figaro to whom I think
you have told everything.

SUZANNE. To be sure: I tell him everything . . . except what need never be
told.

COUNT [*laughing*]. You darling! You promise, then? If you break your
word—let's be clear about it, sweetheart—no dowry, no marriage.

SUZANNE [*curtsying*]. By the same token, my lord, no marriage, no right of
the lord of the manor.

COUNT. Where does she learn this repartee? I swear, I'm crazy about her—
but your mistress is waiting for the ether.

SUZANNE [*laughing and giving back the bottle*]. How could I have talked to you
without a pretext?

COUNT [*trying to kiss her*]. Lovely creature!

SUZANNE [*running off*]. People are coming.

COUNT [*aside*]. She is mine! [*He runs off.*]

SUZANNE. Quick, now to report to my lady.

FIGARO [*enters*]. Suzanne, Suzanne, where are you off to in such a hurry
after leaving my lord?

SUZANNE. You can go to court now, you've just won your suit. [*Running
offstage*]

[51] A kind of lowness of spirits supposed to be suffered mainly by fashionable, hypochon-
driacal ladies, as Suzanne goes on to imply. It was attributed to vapors rising to the brain.

Figaro [*following*]. See here—[*Exit*]

Count [*returning*]. "You've just won your suit"! So I was pitching headlong
into a trap! O my dear damnable schemers, you will rue the day! . . . a
sound, solid decision from the bench . . . of course, he might pay off the
duenna . . . but what with? If he should pay. . . . Ah, ah, I have the
proud Antonio, whose worthy ambition looks down on Figaro as root-
less and unworthy of his niece. By nursing this idée fixe[52] —and why
not? In the field of intrigue one must cultivate everything, even the
vanity of fools. [*He starts to call.*] Anto—[*sees* Marceline *and others, exits.*]

[*Enter* Marceline, Bartholo, *and*
Bridlegoose.]

Marceline *to* Bridlegoose. Sir, pray listen to my case.

Bridlegoose [*gowned and stammering slightly*]. Very well, let us s-s-speak of
it verbally.

Bartholo. It's a promise of marriage—

Marceline. Linked with a loan of money.

Bridlegoose. I und-derstand, etcetera and the rest.

Marceline. No sir, no etcetera.

Bridlegoose. I und-derstand: you have the money?

Marceline. No sir, it was I who lent it.

Bridlegoose. I quite und-derstand: you want the money back.

Marceline. No sir, I want him to marry me.

Bridlegoose. I told you I und-derstood. But he—does he want to
m-marry you?

Marceline. No sir, that is the point of the case.

Bridlegoose. Do you mean to imply that I do not und-derstand the case?

Marceline. No sir, [*to* Bartholo] What a spot we're in! [*To* Bridlegoose]
You say you are going to decide the case?

Bridlegoose. Why else would I have bought my j-judgeship?[53]

Marceline [*sighing*]. It seems to me a great wrong to sell them.

Bridlegoose. True, it would be better to g-give them to us for n-nothing.
Whom are you suing?

[*Enter* Figaro *rubbing his hands.*]

Marceline [*pointing*]. That unscrupulous man!

Figaro [*cheerfully to* Marceline]. Perhaps I'm in your way? My lord will be
back in a moment, Your Worship.

Bridlegoose. I've seen that fellow somewhere.

Figaro. In the house of your lady wife, at Seville, and in her service, coun-
selor.

Bridlegoose. In what year?

Figaro. A little less than a year before the birth of your younger son, who
is a very pretty child if I do say so myself.

Bridlegoose. Yes, he is the b-best-looking of them all. They tell me here
that you are up to your old tricks.

Figaro. You flatter me, sir. It's only a trifle.

Bridlegoose. A promise of marriage! What a booby it is!

Figaro. Sir!

[52] Fixed idea; obsession. [53] Actually, the count will judge the case.

BRIDLEGOOSE. Have you seen my secretary, a very nice chap?[54]

FIGARO. You mean Doublefist, the clerk?

BRIDLEGOOSE. Yes, I do. He feeds in two places, too.

FIGARO. Feeds! I'll swear he wolfs. Yes indeed, I saw him about the writ, and then again about the supplement to the writ, as is customary.

BRIDLEGOOSE. Forms must be observed.

FIGARO. Unquestionably. Just as the cause of the suit belongs to the parties, so the forms are the property of the court.

BRIDLEGOOSE. The lad is not so stupid as I thought at first. Well, friend, since you know so much, we'll t-take care of you in court.

FIGARO. Sir, I rely on your sense of equity even though you are one of our justices.

BRIDLEGOOSE. What? . . . It's true I am a j-justice. But what if you owe and don't pay?

FIGARO. Surely you can see it comes out exactly as if I didn't owe.

BRIDLEGOOSE. No d-doubt . . . what? What? What did he say?

> [*Enter the* COUNT *and a beadle, who walks ahead of him shouting for silence.*]

COUNT. Gown and bands in this place, Master Bridlegoose? For a hearing in camera,[55] ordinary clothes are good enough.

BRIDLEGOOSE. 'Tis you are good enough, my lord. But I never go out ung-gowned, don't you see, it is a matter of f-form. A man will laugh at a judge in a short coat but tremble at the sight of an attorney in a g-gown, thanks to the f-form, the f-form.

COUNT. Let the court convene.

BEADLE [*croaking as he opens the doors*]. The court! The court!

> [*Enter* ANTONIO, *the Count's servants and his tenants, men and women, who are dressed for the wedding. The* COUNT *sits in the big chair,* BRIDLEGOOSE *to one side, the clerk on his stool. The justices and counsel on the benches,* MARCELINE *next to* BARTHOLO, FIGARO *on another bench, the servants and tenants behind them.*]

BRIDLEGOOSE [*to the clerk*]. Doublefist, call up the cases.

DOUBLEFIST [*reading from a paper*]. The noble, high, and puissant Don Pedro George, Hidalgo and Baron de los Altos y Montes Fieros y otros montes[56] v. Alonzo Calderón, a young playwright, in the matter of a stillborn play, which each disowns and attributes to the other.

COUNT. They are both right. With a view to insuring public attention if they write another work together, it is ordered that the nobleman shall contribute his name and the poet his talent. Case dismissed.

DOUBLEFIST [*from another paper*]. Andrea Petrucchio, farmer, v. the tax collector, in the matter of an arbitrary foreclosure.

[54] A personal satiric allusion to some serious legal trouble Beaumarchais got into in 1773–74, involving a corrupt official named Goezman, his wife, and his secretary. (Earlier in Act III Bridlegoose's first name was identified as Guzman.)

[55] In private chambers rather than the public court.

[56] An exaggeratedly aristocratic string of Spanish titles: "Nobleman and Baron of the Heights and of the Fierce Mountains and of other mountains." The nobleman's contribution is merely to allow his name to appear as co-author.

COUNT. Not within my jurisdiction. I shall serve my vassals[57] best by spon-
soring them at the King's court. Next.

DOUBLEFIST [*reading a third paper.* BARTHOLO *and* FIGARO *rise*]. Barbara
Hagar Rahab Magdeleine Nicola Marceline Greenleaf spinster of age
[MARCELINE *rises and bows*] *v.* Figaro, first name missing—

FIGARO. Anonymous.

BRIDLEGOOSE. Anonymous? What patron s-saint is that?

FIGARO. Mine.

DOUBLEFIST [*writing*]. "*versus*—Anonymous Figaro." Profession?

FIGARO. Gentleman.

COUNT. You a gentleman? [*The clerk is still writing.*]

FIGARO. God willing, I should have been the son of a prince.

COUNT [*to the clerk*]. Go on.

BEADLE [*croaking*]. Silence in court!

DOUBLEFIST [*reading*]. . . . in the matter of a dispute about the marriage of
the said Figaro by the said Greenleaf, the learned doctor Bartholo ap-
pearing for the plaintiff and the said Figaro for himself—provided the
Court allows it against the tenor of custom and the rules of the bench.

FIGARO. Custom, Mister Doublefist, is often mere corruption. A party to a
suit always knows his case better than some barrister who sweats without
conviction and shouts his head off about everything he knows, except
the facts, and who does not mind ruining the suitor, boring the court,
and putting the jury to sleep. And afterwards he is as puffed up as if he
had written Cicero's[58] orations. I can put my case in two words. Gen-
tlemen—

DOUBLEFIST. Those you've uttered so far are wasted, for you are not the
plaintiff. You can only defend. Come forward, doctor, and read into the
evidence the promise of marriage.

FIGARO. Yes, the promise.

BARTHOLO [*putting on his glasses*]. It is explicit.

BRIDLEGOOSE. We have to see.

DOUBLEFIST. Gentlemen, please be quiet.

BEADLE [*croaking*]. Silence in court!

BARTHOLO. "I, the undersigned, acknowledge having received from the
Damozel, etcetera, Marceline Greenleaf, of the manor of Aguas-Fres-
cas, the sum of two thousand piastres, which sum I shall repay on her
demand and in the said manor,—er—and shall marry her as a token of
gratitude, etcetera, signed: Figaro—er—just Figaro. My client asks for
the payment of the note and the execution of the promise, with costs.
[*Pleading*] Gentlemen! Never was a more moving request brought to the
bar of a Court. Since the case of Alexander the Great,[59] who promised
marriage to the beautiful Thalestris—

COUNT [*interrupting*]. Before you go farther, counsel, is the genuineness of
the document stipulated?

BRIDLEGOOSE [*to* FIGARO]. What do you say to the f-f-facts just read into the
evidence?

[57] Feudal dependents. [58] The greatest of the Roman orators, first century B.C.

[59] Macedonian king of the fourth century B.C., who conquered Greece and much of Asia.
The original French in the ensuing episode of legal quibbling plays on the French words *ou*
("or," "either," "else") and *où* ("where").

FIGARO. I say there is malice, error, or inadvertence in the manner in which the document was read. For the statement does not say: "Which sum I shall repay *and* I shall marry her;" it says: "Which sum I shall repay *or* I shall marry her," which is very different.

COUNT. Does the document say *and* or does it say *or*?

BARTHOLO. It says *and*.

FIGARO. It says *or*.

BRIDLEGOOSE. Doublefist, you read it.

DOUBLEFIST [*taking the paper*]. That's always wise, because the parties twist things as they read. Er—er—er—"Damozel—er—Greenleaf—er— Ha! Which sum I shall repay on her demand, and in the said manor,— er—shall marry—and . . . or . . . there's *and* after demand and *or* at the end of man*or*, but after that it's hard to make out—there is a blot.

BRIDLEGOOSE. A b-blot? Ah, I und-derstand!

BARTHOLO [*pleading again*]. I submit, my lord and gentlemen, that the decisive word is the copulative conjunction *and* which links the correlative members of the sentence: "I shall pay the Damozel, etcetera, *and* I shall marry her."

FIGARO [*in the same tone*]. And I maintain that it is the alternative conjunction *or*, which separates the said members: "I shall pay the damsel *or* I shall marry her." To his pedantry I oppose my superpedantry: if he drops into Latin, I come up with Greek and exterminate him.

COUNT. How am I to adjudicate such a question?

BARTHOLO. To settle it and no longer quibble over a syllable, we stipulate the absence of the second *and,* after *manor.*

FIGARO. I ask for an affidavit to that effect.

BARTHOLO. We stand by our stipulation. But it affords no escape for the guilty, for let us examine the document with the stipulation in mind: "Which sum I shall repay on demand—and in the said manor shall marry her . . . " It is as if one said: "I shall have myself bled in this room—and in this bed will remain until I feel better." Or again: "He will take a dose of calomel[60] tonight—and in the morning will experience the good effect." Thus, my lord and gentlemen, "he will repay on demand—and in the said manor will marry. . . . "

FIGARO. Nothing of the kind! There is a word under the blot and it is *or*, as thus: "Either illness carries you off, OR your physician will see to it." That is irrefutable. Another example: "Either you write wretched stuff, OR all the fools will mark you down." Does Dr. Bartholo think that I have forgotten my grammar? "I shall repay, on her demand and in the said manor COMMA or I shall marry her."

BARTHOLO [*quickly*]. There's no comma.

FIGARO [*just as quickly*]. There is. It goes:"Comma, or I shall marry her."

BARTHOLO [*glancing at the paper*]. It's without a comma.

FIGARO. It was there, my lord and gentlemen, before the blot. Besides, does a man who marries have to pay the debt as well?

BARTHOLO [*instantly*]. Yes, because we marry under a separate property agreement.

FIGARO [*just as fast*]. If marriage does not cancel the debt, we insist on the separation of persons *and* property!

[60] A laxative.

[*The Judges rise and confer.*]

BARTHOLO. A rewarding cancellation!

DOUBLEFIST. Silence, gentlemen!

BEADLE [*croaking*]. Silence in court!

BARTHOLO. Scoundrels of this stripe call it paying their debts!

FIGARO. Are you speaking now on your own behalf?

BARTHOLO. I am defending this lady.

FIGARO. You may go on raving, but please stop casting aspersions. When the law, fearing the passions of the interested parties, allowed the intervention of counsel, it did not mean to permit these temperate defenders to become privileged slanderers. That would have been to degrade the noblest of institutions.

[*The judges are still conferring.*]

ANTONIO [*to* MARCELINE *and pointing to the judges*]. Why must they palaverate so long?

MARCELINE. They got at the chief justice, he is getting around the other one, and I am about to lose the case.

BARTHOLO [*somberly*]. I am afraid so.

FIGARO [*gaily*]. Cheer up, Marceline!

DOUBLEFIST [*jumping up and addressing* MARCELINE]. That's too much! I denounce you, and for the honor of the Court I ask that before the other case is settled you be tried for contempt!

COUNT [*sitting down*]. No, master clerk. I shall not judge in my own case for an insult to my person. No Spanish judge will have to blush for such an abuse of power, worthy only of an oriental despot. We commit enough wrongs as it is. I am now going to correct one of these by stating the reasons for my decision. Any judge who rules and gives no reason is an enemy of the law. What does the plaintiff ask? Marriage failing payment. Both together would be contradictory.

DOUBLEFIST. Silence, gentlemen!

BEADLE [*croaking*]. Silence in court!

COUNT. What does the defendant rejoin? That he wants to retain possession of his person. Permission is granted.

FIGARO. I've won!

COUNT. But since the text says: Which sum I shall repay on the first demand *or* I shall marry, etc., the Court orders the defendant to pay the plaintiff two thousand piastres *or* to marry her within the day. [*Rises*]

FIGARO [*petrified*]. I've lost!

ANTONIO [*delighted*]. A magnificent decision!

FIGARO. How, magnificent?

ANTONIO. On account of how you aren't no longer my nephew-in-law, thank the lord!

BEADLE [*croaking*]. Move along, gem'mun. [*Exeunt*]

ANTONIO. I'm off to tell all about it to my niece.

MARCELINE [*sitting down*]. Now I can breathe freely.

FIGARO. But I am suffocating.

COUNT [*aside*]. And I am avenged; it's very soothing.

FIGARO [*aside*]. Where's Basil, who was supposed to prevent Marceline's marriage—he's back in good time, I don't think! [*To the* COUNT *on his way out*] Leaving us, my lord?

COUNT. There's nothing more to judge.

FIGARO [*looking at* BRIDLEGOOSE]. If it weren't for that fathead—

BRIDLEGOOSE. Me, a fathead?

FIGARO. Who can doubt it? And I shan't marry her: I am a gentleman after all. [*The* COUNT *stops.*]

BARTHOLO. You will marry her.

FIGARO. Without my noble progenitors'[61] consent?

BARTHOLO. Give us their name, exhibit them.

FIGARO. Give me a little time. I must be close to finding them, I've been looking for fifteen years.

BARTHOLO. Conceited ass! A foundling![62]

FIGARO. Not found, doctor, lost, or rather, stolen.

COUNT [*returning*]. Stolen, lost—where's the proof? Otherwise he'll cry out that he's being cheated.

FIGARO. My lord, even if the lace on my baby clothes, and the embroidered coverlet, and the gold and jewels I wore when the brigands[63] snatched me, did not suffice to prove my high birth, the care that had been taken to put distinctive marks on me would show that I was a valuable off-spring. I have hieroglyphics on my arm . . . [*He starts to roll up his right sleeve.*]

MARCELINE [*rising quickly*]. You have a mark like a spatula[64] on your right arm?

FIGARO. How do you know I have?

MARCELINE. Good God, it's he!

FIGARO. Of course it's me.

BARTHOLO [*to* MARCELINE]. Who?

MARCELINE [*quickly*]. It's Emmanuel!

BARTHOLO [*to* FIGARO]. You were kidnapped by gypsies?

FIGARO [*excited*]. Near a castle, yes. My good doctor, if you restore me to my noble family, set a high price on your services. Gold and treasure are trifles to my illustrious parents.

BARTHOLO [*pointing to* MARCELINE]. There is your mother.

FIGARO. Foster mother?

BARTHOLO. Your own mother.

COUNT. His mother?

FIGARO. Explain.

MARCELINE [*pointing to* BARTHOLO]. There is your father.

FIGARO [*in distress*]. Ah, oh, woe is me!

MARCELINE. Didn't the voice of nature tell you so again and again?

FIGARO. Not once.

COUNT [*aside*]. His mother!

BRIDLEGOOSE. One thing is c-c-clear: he won't marry her.[65]

[61] Ancestors'.

[62] A child of unknown parentage, abandoned and found by strangers.

[63] Robber bandits.

[64] A flattened blade or scoop, round at one end, used at the time mainly by pharmacists.

[65] At this point there was originally a passage in which Marceline angrily protests against the treatment of women at the time. Beaumarchais reluctantly cut the passage from the per-formance version at the request of the actors, who thought it would dampen the play's high spirits. He supplied the passage in his printed Preface, however, and it can be found in this volume as an Appendix at the end of the play, in a translation by the editors of the anthology.

COUNT. Stupid turn of events—most annoying!

BRIDLEGOOSE [*to* FIGARO]. And your nobility? Your castle? You would hoodwink the law with false pretenses?

FIGARO. The law! It nearly made me commit a prize blunder, the law did— on top of the fact that for those accursèd hundred pounds,[66] many is the time I almost beat up this gentleman who turns out to be my father. But since heaven has saved my virtue from these temptations, father of mine, please accept my apologies . . . And you, mother mine, fold me in your arms—as maternally as you can.

[MARCELINE *clasps him about the neck*].

SUZANNE [*running with a purse in her hand*]. My lord, stop everything! Do not marry them: I've come to pay this lady with the dowry madam has given me.

COUNT [*aside*]. The devil take the countess! It is as if everything conspired . . . [*Exit*]

ANTONIO [*seeing* FIGARO *embracing his mother, addresses* SUZANNE]. Payment, eh? I see, I see.

SUZANNE [*turning her back*]. I've seen enough; let's go, uncle.

FIGARO. Please don't! What is it you've seen enough?

SUZANNE. My weakness of mind and your lack of integrity—

FIGARO. Neither of them a fact.

SUZANNE [*angrily*].—and your willingness to marry her and caress her.

FIGARO [*gaily*]. I caress but don't marry. [SUZANNE *tries to leave;* FIGARO *prevents her;* SUZANNE *slaps him.*]

SUZANNE. You are impertinent and rude, let me go!

FIGARO [*to the company*]. That's love for you! Before you go, though, I beg you take a good look at the dear woman in front of you.

SUZANNE. I'm looking.

FIGARO. How does she strike you?

SUZANNE. Horrible!

FIGARO. Long live jealousy! No half measures about it.

MARCELINE [*arms open to* SUZANNE]. Come kiss your mother, my pretty Suzanette. The naughty boy who is tormenting you is my son.

SUZANNE [*running to her*]. You—his mother! [*They stay clasped in each other's arms.*]

ANTONIO. It must have just happened.

FIGARO. No, only just disclosed.

MARCELINE [*with fervor*]. My heart was right to be so strongly drawn to him, though mistaking its reason. Blood was speaking to me.

FIGARO. And good sense to me, which worked like instinct, to make me refuse you. For I was far from hating you, witness the money. . . .

MARCELINE [*handing him a paper*]. The money is yours: take back your note. It is your dowry.

SUZANNE [*throwing the purse to him*]. And take this too!

FIGARO. Many thanks!

MARCELINE [*excited*]. I was unfortunate as a girl, and just now was about to become the most wretched of wives; I am now the happiest of mothers. Come kiss me, children: all my feelings of love are centered upon you. I

am as happy as anyone can be and—oh, children, how I am going to love you!

FIGARO [*moved and speaking with vehemence*]. Please stop, dearest mother, or you will see my eyes dissolve away in the first tears I have ever shed. They are tears of joy—but what a fool I am: I nearly felt ashamed of myself as I felt the drops on my hands. [*He shows his hands, fingers outspread.*] I stupidly tried to hold them back. Away, false shame! I want to laugh and cry all at once. What I now feel does not come to a man twice in a lifetime. [*He kisses his mother to one side of him,* SUZANNE *on the other.*]

MARCELINE. Oh, my dear!

SUZANNE. My very dear!

BRIDLEGOOSE [*wiping his eyes*]. It seems I am a f-fool also!

FIGARO [*excited*]. Grief! I can now defy you: afflict me if you can, between these two women I love.

ANTONIO [*to* FIGARO]. Not so many pretty speeches, if you please. Apropos of marriage, in good families, that of the parents is supposed to precede. Do your parents ask each other's hand?

BARTHOLO. May my hand rot and fall off if I ever offer it to the mother of such a character!

ANTONIO [*to* BARTHOLO]. In other words you're nothing but an unnatural father? [*To* FIGARO] In that case, Lothario,[67] the bargain's off.

SUZANNE. Oh, uncle!

ANTONIO. D'you think I'll give my sister's child to this here who's no one's child?

BRIDLEGOOSE. How do you make that out, idiot? Everyone is somebody's child!

ANTONIO. Yah, yah: he shan't have her nohow. [*Exit*]

BARTHOLO [*to* FIGARO]. Better look for somebody to adopt you.

 [*He tries to go, but* MARCELINE *seizes him
 around the middle and pulls him back*].

MARCELINE. One moment, doctor, don't go.

FIGARO [*aside*]. It's incredible but all the fools in Andalusia are rabid against my poor desire to get married.

SUZANNE [*to* BARTHOLO]. Dear little father, he is your son.

MARCELINE. He has wit, talent, and presence.

FIGARO. And he never cost you a penny.

BARTHOLO. What about the hundred pounds he robbed me of?

MARCELINE [*cuddling him*]. We'll take such good care of you, papa![68]

SUZANNE [*cuddling*]. We'll love you so much, dear little papa!

BARTHOLO [*yielding*]. "Papa, papa, dear papa—" Now I'm going to be as big a fool as this gentleman [*pointing to* BRIDLEGOOSE]. I'm being led like a child. [MARCELINE *and* SUZANNE *kiss him.*] Now, now, I haven't said Yes. [*Turning around*] What's become of his lordship?

FIGARO. Let's join him, quick, and force a decision from him. If he were to think up some new scheme, we'd have to start all over again.

ALL TOGETHER. Let's go, let's go! [*They drag* BARTHOLO *outside.*]

[67] Equivalent to "Lover-boy"; from the name of a character in Nicholas Rowe's play *The Fair Penitent* (1703).

[68] Accent on the second syllable, as in mamma later. (Translator's note.)

Bridlegoose [*left alone*]. "As big a fool as this gentleman." A man can say
 that sort of thing about himself, but . . . they're not at all p-polite in this
 p-place. [*Exit*]

ACT 4

*A large room with candelabra all lighted, floral decorations, and other ornaments
indicative of preparations for a party. Downstage right stands a table and on it a
writing case. Behind the table is an armchair.*

Figaro [*hugging* Suzanne]. Well, love, are you happy? She got round the
 doctor, didn't she, my silver-tongued mother? Despite his distaste he is
 marrying her, and your curmudgeon[69] of an uncle can't help himself.
 That leaves only my lord in a rage; for after all, our marriage is the
 upshot of theirs. What a happy ending! Aren't you inclined to laugh?
Suzanne. I never knew anything so odd.
Figaro. Say rather so jolly. All we wanted was a dowry, squeezed out of his
 Excellency. Now we have two which owe nothing to him. A relentless
 rival was hounding you and I was bedeviled by a fury. That trouble has
 for us both taken the form of a loving mother. Yesterday I was, so to
 speak, alone in the world; today I have all my relatives complete about
 me. True, they're not so resplendent as if I had designed them myself,
 but good enough for us who haven't the ambition to be rich.
Suzanne. And yet none of the things that you planned and we expected
 came through.
Figaro. Chance did a better job, my sweet. That's the way of the world.
 You toil, you scheme, you make projects, all in your own corner; For-
 tune works in another. From the insatiable conqueror who would like to
 swallow the globe to the peaceable blind man led by his dog, all human
 beings are the playthings of fate. Indeed, the blind man is often better
 served by his dog, less deceived in his opinions, than some other self-
 blinded man with his retinue.[70] As for that delightful blind fellow called
 Love . . . [*He again embraces her tenderly.*]
Suzanne. He's the only one I care about.
Figaro. Well then, let me be the serviceable dog in folly's employ, who
 makes it his job to lead him to your charming little door.[71] And there
 we'll be cozy for the rest of our lives.
Suzanne [*laughing*]. Love and you?
Figaro. I and Love.
Suzanne. And you won't look for other lodgings?
Figaro. If you catch me at it, I'm willing to have a hundred million philan-
 derers—
Suzanne. You're going to say more than you mean: tell me the honest
 truth.
Figaro. My truest truth?
Suzanne. Shame on you, rascal! Is there more than one?

[69] Cantankerous person. [70] Train of attendants.
[71] Proverbially, blind Love is led and guided by Folly.

FIGARO. I should say so! Ever since it has been observed that with the passage of time old follies turn into wisdom, and that early little lies, even though poorly planted, bloom into great big truths—ever since then, there have been endless species of truths. There are those one dare not utter, for not every truth is fit to say; there are those one flaunts without putting faith in them, for not every truth is fit to believe. And then there are the passionate promises, the parental threats, the resolutions of drinkers, the assurances of office holders, the "positively final offers" of business men—there's no end to them. Only my love for Suzy is true coin.

SUZANNE. I love your gaiety because it is wild. It shows you are happy. But let's talk about meeting the Count in the garden.

FIGARO. Far better never speak of that again. It nearly cost me my Sue.

SUZANNE. You don't want me to go through with it?

FIGARO. If you love me, Suzy, give me your word on this. Let him eat his heart out—it'll be his punishment.

SUZANNE. I found it harder at first to agree to it than now to give it up—I'll never mention it again.

FIGARO. That's your truest truth?

SUZANNE. I'm not like you learned people. I have only one truth.

FIGARO. And you'll love me a little?

SUZANNE. Much.

FIGARO. That isn't much.

SUZANNE. What do you mean?

FIGARO. Why, in love, don't you see, too much is barely enough.

SUZANNE. Your subtleties are beyond me, but I intend to love only my husband.

FIGARO. Stick to it and you will represent a remarkable exception to the rule. [*Starts to kiss her. Enter* COUNTESS.]

COUNTESS. I was just saying: wherever they happen to be, you may be sure they're together. I really think, Figaro, that each time you indulge in a tête-à-tête[72] you are living off the future, drawing on wedded bliss, and robbing yourself. People look for you and get impatient.

FIGARO. You are right, madam. I was forgetting myself. I will show them my excuse. [*He tries to take* SUZANNE *with him.*]

COUNTESS [*holding her back*]. She'll follow later. [*He goes.* COUNTESS *to* SUZANNE] Have you got what's needed to change clothes with me?

SUZANNE. Nothing is needed, madam. The assignation is off.

COUNTESS. You have changed your mind?

SUZANNE. It's Figaro—

COUNTESS. You are deceiving me.

SUZANNE. God is my witness!

COUNTESS. Figaro is not a man to let a dowry slip from his grasp.

SUZANNE. Oh, madam, what can you be thinking?

COUNTESS. Why, that in concert with the Count, you are now sorry you made me privy to his plans. I can read you like a book. Leave me to myself. [*She starts to leave.*]

SUZANNE [*on her knees*]. In the name of heaven which is our hope, you

[72] Two persons alone together.

cannot know the wrong you do me. When you have been so endlessly good to me, after the dowry you've given me, how could I—

COUNTESS [*lifting her up*]. But—of course! I must have been out of my mind. Since you are changing places with me, dear heart, you won't be going into the garden. You'll be keeping your word to your husband and helping me recapture mine.

SUZANNE. Oh how you upset me!

COUNTESS. I've been terribly scatterbrained. [*Kisses* SUZANNE, *on the forehead*] Where is the meeting place?

SUZANNE [*kissing the* COUNTESS's *hand*]. All I heard was "garden."

COUNTESS [*motioning* SUZANNE *to the table*]. Take that pen and we will name a spot.

SUZANNE. I, write to him?

COUNTESS. You must.

SUZANNE. But at least, madam, you—

COUNTESS. I'll take the responsibility for everything.

[SUZANNE *sits at the table.*]

COUNTESS [*dictating*]. "A new song to the tune of . . . : 'How lovely under the elms at night, How lovely . . . '"

SUZANNE [*writing*]. ". . . under the elms" Yes, nothing else?

COUNTESS. Have you the slightest fear that he won't understand?

SUZANNE. You're right. [*She folds the note.*] What sort of seal?

COUNTESS. A pin, quick—it will serve to reply with. Write on the back: "Please return the seal."

SUZANNE [*laughing*]. Ho! the seal! This seal, my lady, is a funnier joke than the one on the officer's commission.

COUNTESS [*in painful recollection*]. Oh!

SUZANNE [*looking on her person*]. I haven't a pin on me.

COUNTESS [*unpinning her collar*]. Take this. [*The page's ribbon falls from her bosom.*] Oh, my ribbon!

SUZANNE [*picking it up*]. Ah, the little thief's property . . . and you were cruel enough to—

COUNTESS. Could I let him wear it on his arm? A fine spectacle! Give it back to me.

SUZANNE. Your ladyship cannot wear it: it is spotted with the young man's blood.

COUNTESS. It will be just right for Fanchette . . . when she next brings me flowers.

[*Enter a young shepherdess,* CHERUBINO *dressed as a girl,* FANCHETTE *and other girls dressed like her and carrying bouquets.*]

FANCHETTE. My lady, these girls from the village bring you flowers.

COUNTESS [*quickly hides the ribbon again*]. They are delightful. It grieves me, dears, not to know you all by name. [*Pointing to* CHERUBINO] But who is this lovely child who seems so shy?

SHEPHERDESS. A cousin of mine, ma'am, come to visit for the wedding.

COUNTESS. So pretty! Since I can't wear all twenty of your posies, I'll honor the stranger. [*She takes* CHERUBINO's *bouquet and kisses him on the forehead.*] She's blushing. Suzy, don't you think she looks like someone we know?

SUZANNE. So much so I can hardly tell them apart.

CHERUBINO [*aside, both hands on his heart*]. Oh, that kiss went right through me!

ANTONIO [*entering with the* COUNT]. And I tell you he's here somewhere. They dressed him at my daughter's, all the clothes are still around, and here's his regulation hat, which I picked out of the lot. [*Steps forward, scans the girls' faces and recognizes* CHERUBINO, *whose female bonnet he pulls off. As* CHERUBINO's *long hair falls in ringlets,* ANTONIO *tosses the military hat on top*] By gum, there's your officer!

COUNTESS [*stepping back*]. Heavens!

SUZANNE. The rapscallion![73]

ANTONIO. I was telling you upstairs it was him.

COUNT [*angry*]. Well, madam?

COUNTESS. Well, sir, you find me as surprised as you and equally angry.

COUNT. It may be, but what about this morning?

COUNTESS. I should be guilty indeed if I kept up the deception any longer. He had dropped in to see me, and it was then we undertook the practical joke which these children have completed. You discovered Suzanne and me dressing him up. You are so quick to anger that he ran away, I lost my good judgment, and general dismay did the rest.

COUNT [*disgruntled*]. Why haven't you left?

CHERUBINO [*flinging off the hat*]. My lord—

COUNT. I shall punish you for disobeying.

FANCHETTE [*thoughtlessly*]. Oh, my lord, please listen to me: every time you come by and kiss me you always say: "Fanchette, dear, if you will love me, I'll give you anything you want."

COUNT [*flushing*]. I have said that?

FANCHETTE. Yes, my lord. Well, instead of punishing Cherubino, give him to me for a husband, and then I'll love you madly.

COUNT [*aside*]. Diddled by a page!

COUNTESS. Count, it is your turn now. This child's naïve confession, as innocent as mine, bears witness to a double truth, which is that when I cause you anguish it is always unintentionally, whereas you do your utmost to increase and justify my own.

ANTONIO. You too my lord? By gum, I'm going to get after that chit as I did after her mother, now gathered. . . . Not that it's of consequence, but as my lady knows, these little girls when they grow up. . . .

COUNT [*discomfited, aside*]. There is an evil genius[74] in this place who turns everything against me.

FIGARO [*entering*]. My lord, if you detain the young ladies, the party can't begin, or the dance either.

COUNT. You want to dance? Have you forgotten how you fell this morning and sprained your right foot?

FIGARO [*swinging his leg*]. It's still a trifle sore, but it's nothing. [*To the girls*] Come along, darlings, come.

COUNT [*turning* FIGARO *about*]. You were lucky the flowerbed was soft earth.

FIGARO. Very lucky—otherwise . . .

[73] Rascal. [74] Spirit.

ANTONIO [*twists him the other way*]. Besides he "gathered himself together" as he fell all the way to the bottom.

FIGARO. A really clever man would have stopped halfway down. [*To the girls*] Are you coming, ladies?

ANTONIO [*twisting* FIGARO *again*]. All the while the little page was galloping on his horse toward Seville.

FIGARO. Galloping, or maybe sauntering. . . .

COUNT [*twists* FIGARO *the other way*]. And his commission was in your pocket.

FIGARO [*somewhat surprised*]. Undoubtedly, but why this examination? [*To the girls*] Now come on, girls!

ANTONIO [*pulling* CHERUBINO *by the arm*]. Here's one who says my future nephew is a liar.

FIGARO [*taken aback*]. Cherubino! [*Aside*] Blast the little braggart!

ANTONIO. Have you got it now?

FIGARO. Got it, got it! . . . By the by, what's his story?

COUNT [*drily*]. Hardly a story, he says it was he who jumped into the gillyflowers.

FIGARO [*abstracted*]. Hm, if he says so . . . it may well be. I don't argue about what I don't know.

COUNT. So both you and he . . .

FIGARO. Why not? The jumping fever is catching—just think of sheep over a fence.[75] And when my lord is angry, anyone would prefer to risk his neck—

COUNT. Now really, two by two?

FIGARO. We'd have done it by the dozen—and why should you care, my lord, seeing no one was hurt? [*To the girls*] I say, are you coming in or aren't you?

COUNT [*outraged*]. Is it a farce we're playing together, you and I?

[*Music begins offstage*]

FIGARO. There's the opening march. Fall in, my beauties, fall in. Here, Suzanne, give me your arm.

[*Exeunt except* CHERUBINO *who stays behind, his head hung down.*]

COUNT [*gazing at Figaro's back*]. Did you ever see greater nerve? [*To* CHERUBINO] As for you, sly boots who now pretend to be ashamed, go dress yourself properly and let me not see your face for the rest of the evening.

COUNTESS. He will be terribly bored.

CHERUBINO [*thoughtlessly*]. Bored? I carry on my brow enough happiness to outweigh a hundred years in jail! [*He puts on his hat and leaves.*]

COUNTESS [*fans herself violently*].

COUNT. What is so happy about his brow?

COUNTESS [*embarrassed*]. His first military hat, I suppose. With children any novelty is like a toy. [*She starts to leave.*]

COUNT. You won't stay, Countess?

COUNTESS. I told you I did not feel well.

[75] In the original Beaumarchais refers to the sheep in Rabelais which Panurge induced to jump overboard by throwing over the first one. (Translator's note.)

458 Neoclassicism

COUNT. One moment more for the sake of your protégée[76]—or I'll think you are cross.

COUNTESS. Here come the two wedding processions. Let us sit and receive them.

COUNT [*aside*]. The wedding! . . . Well, what can't be cured must be endured. [COUNT *and* COUNTESS *sit to one side of the room. Enter the processions to a march based on the* FOLIES D'ESPAGNE:[77]

> *A gamekeeper, a musket on his shoulder*
> *The mayor, the aldermen,* BRIDLEGOOSE
> *Peasants and their women in party dress*
> *Two young girls carrying the virgin's bonnet*
> *Two others in white veils*
> *Two others, wearing gloves and a corsage at the waist*
> ANTONIO *holding* SUZANNE'S *hand to give her away to* FIGARO
> *Other girls with other types of bonnets and veils*
> MARCELINE *wearing a white veil and bonnet similar to the first*
> FIGARO *holding* MARCELINE'S *hand to give her away to:*
> *The doctor, who brings up the rear of the procession, wearing a large boutonniere.*
> *The girls, as they pass in front of the* COUNT, *deliver to his footmen the paraphernalia for* SUZANNE *and* MARCELINE.
> *The peasants, men and women, in two lines, dance the fandango[78] to an accompaniment of castanets. Then the orchestra plays the introduction of the duet, during which* ANTONIO *takes* SUZANNE *to the* COUNT. *She kneels before him, he puts the virgin's bonnet on her head, and gives her a bouquet. During this ceremony the girls sing the following duet:*

> Sing, young bride, the grateful benefaction!
> Your master has his selfish lust displaced:
> He gives up pleasure for a noble action,
> And to your husband hands you pure and chaste.

As the duet concludes, SUZANNE, *still kneeling, tugs at the* COUNT'S *cloak and shows him the note she has for him. She then puts her hand to her hair and he takes the note while seeming to adjust her bonnet. He puts the note inside his coat, the duet ends,* SUZANNE *rises and makes a low curtsy.* FIGARO *receives* SUZANNE *from the hand of the* COUNT *and steps back with her to the other end of the room, near* MARCELINE. *There is meanwhile a reprise[79] of the fandango. The* COUNT, *being in a hurry to read his note, comes downstage and pulls the paper from his pocket. The pin evidently pricks him, for he shakes his finger, squeezes it, and licks it. He looks at the folded paper and speaks.*

COUNT. The devil take all women! They stick pins into everything.
> [*He throws the pin on the ground, reads the note and kisses it. While he and* FIG-

[76] Person in whom one takes a benevolent interest—here, Suzanne.
[77] An old Spanish dance tune.
[78] A Spanish dance in triple time, in which the two partners accompany themselves on castanets.
[79] A repetition, in a stage show, of music heard earlier.

ARO *speak, the orchestra plays pianissimo.*
FIGARO, *who has seen the by-play, speaks*
to SUZANNE *and his mother*].

FIGARO. It must be a billet-doux[80] some little wench slipped into his hand
as she walked by. It was sealed with a pin which impudently pricked
him.

[*The dance resumes. The* COUNT *turns
the note over and sees the request to return
the pin. He looks for it on the ground,
finds it, and sticks it in his sleeve*].

FIGARO [*to* SUZANNE *and* MARCELINE). From the beloved any object is dear,
so he's retrieved the pin. What a harlequin[81] he is!

[*Meanwhile,* SUZANNE *and the* COUNT-
ESS *have been exchanging signals. The
dance concludes and the introduction of
the duet is played again.* FIGARO *takes*
MARCELINE *to the* COUNT, *and the cere-
mony repeats. But just as the* COUNT *lifts
the bonnet and as the duet strikes up, the
proceedings are interrupted by a great
noise at the door*].

FOOTMAN. Keep back, keep back, gentlemen, you can't all get in together.
Help here! the guards! [*Guards step quickly toward the door.*]
COUNT [*rising*]. What is the matter there?
FOOTMAN. My lord, it is Mister Basil who is followed by the whole township
because he sings as he walks.
COUNT. Admit him alone.
COUNTESS. Please command me to withdraw.
COUNT. I shan't forget your obliging me.
COUNTESS. Suzanne! . . . [*To the* COUNT] She will be back at once. [*Aside, to*
SUZANNE] Let's go change our clothes.
[*Exeunt*].
MARCELINE. He never shows up but to do harm.
FIGARO. You see if I don't change his tune.
[*Enter* BASIL, *guitar in hand, followed by*
SUNSTRUCK].
BASIL [*sings to the music of the final song of the play*].

Faithful, tender, loving hearts
Who condemn love's wanderings,
Do not launch your angry darts;
It is not a crime to change,
For if Cupid carries wings
It must be to flit and range!
It must be to flit and range!

FIGARO [*going toward* BASIL]. Yes, that's the reason precisely why Love has
wings on his back. Friend, what do you mean by your song?

[80] Love letter. [81] Clown.

BASIL [*pointing to* SUNSTRUCK]. I mean that after showing submissiveness to my lord and entertaining this gentleman, who is of my lord's company, I want to claim my lord's justice.

SUNSTRUCK. Pah, your lordsy, he didn't entertain me at all—he just had fits of yodeling!

COUNT. What is it you want, Basil?

BASIL. That which already belongs to me, my lord—the hand of Marceline.

FIGARO [*drawing near*]. How long has it been since you saw the face of a lunatic?

BASIL. My good sir, I see one right now.

FIGARO. Since you use my eyes as a mirror, study the effect therein of the prophecy I am about to make: if you so much as seem to gravitate toward madame—

BARTHOLO [*laughing*]. But why? Let him speak.

BRIDLEGOOSE [*coming forward*]. Is it n-necessary for two old f-friends . . .

FIGARO. He and I friends?

BASIL. Absurd!

FIGARO [*setting a rapid pace for the ensuing dialogue*]. Friends because he writes the dullest church music?

BASIL. While he writes newspaper verse?

FIGARO. A tavern musician!

BASIL. A penny-a-liner!

FIGARO. An oratorio-monger!

BASIL. A diplomatic nag!

COUNT [*seated*]. Vulgarians both!

BASIL. He's failed me at every turn.

FIGARO. That's an idea I wish were true.

BASIL. He goes round calling me an ass.

FIGARO. Don't mistake me for public opinion.

BASIL. Whereas there's hardly a talented singer I haven't trained.

FIGARO. Strained!

BASIL. He persists!

FIGARO. And why shouldn't I, if I speak the truth? Are you a prince that you should be flattered? Learn to live with the truth, faker! It's certain no liar could make much of you. Perhaps you're afraid the truth will come out of our mouths? If so, why did you interrupt our nuptials?

BASIL [*to* MARCELINE]. Did you or did you not promise me that if you weren't provided for within four years, you would give me your hand?

MARCELINE. Under what condition did I promise this?

BASIL. That if you found your lost child, I would adopt him out of kindness to you.

ALL [*together*]. He's been found!

BASIL. All right, I'm ready.

ALL [*together, pointing to* FIGARO]. There he is!

BASIL [*shrinking back*]. Get thee behind me!

BRIDLEGOOSE. That means you g-give up his d-dear mother?

BASIL. What could be worse than to be thought the father of such a fellow?

FIGARO. Why, to be thought your son! You're pulling my leg!

BASIL [*pointing to* FIGARO]. The moment this character is somebody in this house, I want everyone to know that I am nobody. [*Exit*]

BARTHOLO [*laughing*]. Hahahaha!

FIGARO [*leaping with joy*]. At last, at last, I'll have my bride!

COUNT [*aside*]. And I my mistress. [*He rises*]

BRIDLEGOOSE [*to* MARCELINE]. With everybody s-satisfied.

COUNT. Let the two marriage contracts be drawn up. I shall sign them.

ALL [*together*]. Bravo!

COUNT. I need time to myself. [*He starts to leave with the others.*]

SUNSTRUCK [*to* FIGARO]. Now I'm going to set up the fireworks under the
 elms as I was told.

COUNT [*coming back*]. What idiot gave you that order?

FIGARO. What's wrong with it?

COUNT. Why, the Countess is indisposed. How can she see the display from
 indoors unless it's on the terrace, below her room?

FIGARO. You heard him, Sunstruck? On the terrace.

COUNT. Under the elms, the idea! [*Leaving, aside*] They were going to set
 fire to my tête-à-tête.

FIGARO. What considerateness for his wife! [*Starts to leave*]

MARCELINE [*stopping him*]. A word with you, my son. I owe you an apology.
 Mistaken feeling for you made me unjust to your wife: I thought her in
 league with the Count, even though Basil had told me she always re-
 jected his advances.

FIGARO. You don't know your son if you think that female whims and wiles
 can shake him. I challenge the cleverest to upset me.

MARCELINE. It's nice to feel that way, at any rate, because jealousy—

FIGARO. Is but a stupid child of pride, or else it's a madman's disease. I
 assure you, mother, on this point I'm a philosopher—unshakable. So if
 Suzanne ever deceives me, I forgive her in advance, for she will have
 worked hard and long to do it.[82] [*He turns and sees* FANCHETTE *who is
 looking everywhere for someone.*]

FIGARO. So-o, little cousin! Getting an earful?

FANCHETTE. Oh, no! I was brought up to think it's not nice.

FIGARO. True enough, but since it's useful, it's often considered worth the
 trouble.

FANCHETTE. I was finding out if somebody was here.

FIGARO. So young and so full of guile! You know perfectly well he can't be
 here.

FANCHETTE. Who's that?

FIGARO. Cherubino.

FANCHETTE. It isn't he I'm after. I know where *he* is. It's cousin Sue.

FIGARO. And what do you want with her?

FANCHETTE. I can tell *you*, because you're my cousin now. It's about a pin
 I'm supposed to give her.

FIGARO [*startled*]. A pin? A pin did you say? And from whom, you little
 hussy? At your age you're already in the business of—[*He catches himself
 and goes on gently.*] You're already pretty good at whatever you do,
 Fanchette; and my pretty cousin is so obliging that—

FANCHETTE. What did I do to make you cross with me? I'm going . . .

FIGARO. Don't. I was only teasing. I'll tell you: that pin of yours is one that

[82] Suzanne, Figaro implies, will have found it hard to trick a master of trickery like himself.

my lord told you to give to Suzanne. It's the one that fastened the paper
he had in his hand: you see I know what I'm talking about.

FANCHETTE. Why ask me if you know?

FIGARO [*fumbling*]. Oh . . . because it's fun to know how his lordship went
about sending you on your errand.

FANCHETTE [*with naïveté*]. Well, he did it almost as you say: "Here,
Fanchette," he said, "give back this pin to your beautiful cousin; just tell
her it's the seal for the big elms."

FIGARO. "The big—?

FANCHETTE. "—elms." Oh, yes, and he added: "Be sure no one sees you."

FIGARO. Well, cousin, you must do as you're told and it's lucky no one *has*
seen you. Run your pretty errand and don't tell Suzanne a word more
than his lordship told you.

FANCHETTE. Why should I say more, cousin? He takes me for a child. [*She
goes out skipping.*]

FIGARO. Well, mother?

MARCELINE. Well, my son?

FIGARO [*choking*]. That cursèd clown! Really some things are too much!

MARCELINE. Some things, what things?

FIGARO [*hands on his breast*]. What I've just learned, mother, weighs on me
like lead—here.

MARCELINE [*laughing*]. It would seem that your assured countenance of a
while ago was only an inflated bag of wind—a pin has made it collapse.

FIGARO [*furious*]. But that pin, mother, that pin was the one he picked up!

MARCELINE [*recalling his words*]. "As for jealousy, I am a philosopher—
unshakable: if Suzanne deceives me, I forgive her . . . "

FIGARO. Oh, mother, a man speaks as he feels at the time. Let the coolest
judge on the bench plead his own case and see how he explains the
law.[83] I understand now why he was annoyed about the fireworks. As
for my darling and her subtlety with pins, she hasn't got where she
thinks she is, elms or no elms. It's true my marriage is enough to war-
rant my anger, but it isn't enough to keep me from dropping one wife
and wedding another.

MARCELINE. A splendid conclusion! Let's wreck everything on a mere sus-
picion. How do you know it's you she's deceiving and not the Count?
Have you studied her thoroughly that you condemn her without ap-
peal? Do you know for a fact that she is going under those trees, or what
her intention is, or what she will say and do if she goes there? I thought
you had more judgment!

FIGARO [*kissing her hand*]. A mother is always right, mother, and you are
right, entirely right! But make allowance, dear mamma, for natural
impulse. One feels better after giving way to it. Now let us weigh before
accusing and acting. I know where the assignation is to be. Farewell,
mother. [*Exit*]

MARCELINE. Farewell. And I too know where it is. Now that I've stopped
him, I'd better look after Suzanne—or rather, give her warning. She is
such a pretty creature! I must say, when our own interest does not
divide us, we women are all inclined to make common cause in defense

[83] That is, see how impassioned he becomes, how he loses his cool.

of our downtrodden sex against this proud, terrifying [*laughing*] and somewhat slow-witted masculine sex. [*Exit*]

ACT 5

A stand of elms in the park. Two pavilions, kiosks,[84] or garden temples occupy respectively the right and left middle ground. Behind is a clearing hung with decorations; in front a lawn with seats. The scene is dark.

FANCHETTE [*alone and carrying in one hand two small cakes and an orange; in the other, a lighted paper lantern*]. He said the pavilion on the left. It must be this one. But what if my fine fellow doesn't show up? They wouldn't even give me an orange and two cookies, those kitchen people. "But for whom, miss?" "Why, sir, it's for somebody." "We thought as much, miss." Supposing the worst—just because my lord doesn't want to set eyes on him, that's no reason he should starve. All the same, it cost me a big kiss on the cheek. Who knows, maybe he'll pay me back for it in kind. [*She catches sight of* FIGARO *who comes forward to identify her. She cries out*] Ah! . . . [*Runs away and enters pavilion at left*]

FIGARO [*in a large cloak, alone at first*]. It's Fanchette! [*He scans the others as they arrive and speaks roughly to them.*] Good day, gentlemen, good evening. Are you all here?

BASIL. All those you asked to come.

FIGARO. What time is it, about?

ANTONIO [*nose in the air*]. The moon should be up.

BARTHOLO. What black arts are you getting ready for? He looks like a conspirator.

FIGARO. Isn't it for a wedding that you're gathered at the castle?

BRIDLEGOOSE. C-certainly.

ANTONIO. We were going over yonder, in the park, and wait for the signal to start the festivities.

FIGARO. You shan't go a step farther. It's here, under the elms, that we're going to celebrate the faithful bride I am marrying and the faithful lord who has reassigned her to himself.

BASIL [*recalling the day's events*]. Ah, yes. I know all about it. Let's remove ourselves, if you please. It's a matter of a rendezvous. I'll tell you about it later.

BRIDLEGOOSE [*to* FIGARO]. We'll c-come back.

FIGARO. When you hear me call, don't fail to appear. You can curse me if I don't provide you with a fine spectacle.

BARTHOLO. Remember that a wise man does not start a quarrel with the great and powerful.

FIGARO. I'll remember.

BARTHOLO. They begin with a score of forty-love against us, thanks to their rank.

FIGARO. To say nothing of their capacity for hard work, which you're forgetting. But remember also that once a man is known to be scared, he's at the mercy of every scoundrel.

[84] Small, open-sided garden pavilions.

BARTHOLO. Well said.

FIGARO. And among my names is Greenleaf, from my mother's side.

BARTHOLO. He is full of the devil.

BRIDLEGOOSE. He y-y-is.

BASIL [*aside*]. The Count and Suzanne planned this without me—I'm rather glad of this ambush.

FIGARO [*to the footmen*]. You fellows do as I told you—light up all around here, or in the name of Death, which I'd like to throttle, when I grab the arm of one of you—[*He grabs* SUNSTRUCK.]

SUNSTRUCK [*goes off crying*]. Ah, oh, ah, perish the brute!

BASIL [*leaving*]. God give you joy, young newlywed!

FIGARO [*pacing up and down alone in the dark and speaking in sombre tones*]. Oh, woman, woman, woman! weak and deceitful creature! No animal on earth can go against instinct; is it yours to deceive? After refusing me stubbornly when I begged her in front of her mistress—in the very instant of plighting her troth to me, in the middle of the ceremony—He was laughing as he read, the traitor! And I like a poor booby . . . No, my lord Count, you shan't have her, you shan't! Because you are a great lord you think you are a great genius. Nobility, wealth, honors, emoluments[85]—it all makes a man so proud! What have you done to earn so many advantages? You took the trouble to be born, nothing more. Apart from that, you're a rather common type. Whereas I—by God!—lost in the nameless herd, I had to exert more strategy and skill merely to survive than has been spent for a hundred years in governing the Spanish Empire. . . . And you want to tangle with me!

Someone's coming—it is she—no, it's nobody. The night is dark as pitch and here am I plying the silly trade of husband, even though I'm only half of one. [*He sits on a bench.*] Can anything be stranger than my career? The son of God knows whom, stolen by bandits and reared in their ways, I become disgusted and try to lead an honest life. Everywhere I am repulsed. I learn chemistry, pharmacy, surgery,[86] yet the whole influence of a great lord hardly succeeds in securing me the practice of a veterinary. Tired of pestering sick animals, hoping in fact to do just the opposite, I go headlong for the stage. Far better have hung a millstone around my neck! I write a play satirizing life in the harem: being a Spanish author I thought I could make fun of Mohammed without fear. At once, an emissary from God knows where complains that my verses offend the Sublime Porte,[87] Persia, part of the Indian peninsula, all of Egypt, the kingdoms of Barca, Tripoli, Tunis, Algiers, and Morocco[88]—and there goes my play up the spout, to please the Mohammedan princes, not one of whom (I believe) can read, and all of whom brand us on the shoulder and call us Christian dogs. Whoever fails to degrade the mind avenges himself by insulting it. My cheeks were growing hollow, my lodging was unpaid, I could see from afar the

[85] Income from offices held.
[86] In the eighteenth century, a "surgeon" was a kind of paramedic who specialized in incisions; barbers commonly served the purpose.
[87] The "Sublime Gate," a name for the former Turkish government.
[88] Mohammedan countries in north Africa.

threatening bailiff[89] with a pen stuck in his wig, so I shudder and exert myself afresh. A public debate starts up about the nature of wealth, and since one needn't own something in order to argue about it, being in fact penniless, I write on the value of money and interest. Immediately, I find myself inside a coach looking at the drawbridge of a prison and leaving hope and freedom behind. [*He gets up.*] How I should like to hold in the hollow of my hand one of these potentates who last four days in office and are ready to ordain punishments! When a healthy fall from grace had sobered his pride, I'd let him know that printed nonsense is dangerous only in countries where its free circulation is hampered; that without the right to criticize, praise and approval are worthless, and that only petty men fear petty writings. [*Sits down*] One day, tired of feeding an obscure guest, they threw me out into the street, and since a man must eat even when out of jail, I sharpen my quill once more and ask people what is in the news. I am told that during my retreat at public expense, free trade and a free press have been established in Madrid,[90] so that, provided I do not write about the government, or about religion, or politics, or morals, or those in power, or public bodies, or the Opera, or the other state theatres, or about anybody who is active in anything, I can print whatever I want with perfect freedom under the supervision of two or three censors. To take advantage of such sweet liberty, I let it be known that I am starting a periodical, and to make sure that I am not treading on anybody's heels, I call it *The Useless Journal.* Mercy! No sooner done than I see a thousand poor devils of subsidized hacks in arms against me. I am put down and once again unemployed. Despair nearly had me by the throat when someone thought of me for a vacant place. Unfortunately I was qualified for it. They needed an accountant and put in a dancer. The only way out was to turn thief. I set up as croupier[91] of a gambling den. Ah, then, my dears, I was in the swim! I dine out and people known as respectable courteously open their houses to me, keeping for themselves only three quarters of the take. I could have recouped all my losses—I had even begun to understand that to grow rich, know-how is better than knowledge, but since everyone around me was robbing the till while requiring that I stay honest, I went under for the third time.

I'd had enough and meant to break with the world—five fathoms of water would suffice, and nearly did, when my guardian angel recalled me to my original trade. I take up my razors and lancet[92] and leave glory to the fools who feed on its aroma. With it also, I leave behind dishonor, which is too heavy a load for a pedestrian. Hiking from town to town, shaving as I go, I live at last a life without care. But a great lord passing through Seville recognizes me. I get him married off,[93] and as a reward for my helping him secure a wife, he now wants to intercept mine. Thereupon, storms and intrigues. I am on the edge of an abyss,

[89] The official who arrested people for debt.

[90] The reference is to the modernizing economic reforms sponsored by Turgot, French comptroller-general of finance under Louis XVI during the 1770's. As often in this play, Spanish references really apply to France.

[91] Table operator or dealer. [92] Surgeon's knife.

[93] This happens in Beaumarchais's *Barber of Seville.*

nearly wedded to my own mother, when lo! my relatives materialize, Indian file. [*He gets up and grows vehement.*] Follows a regular scrimmage— "it's he, it's you, it's I. No, it isn't, not I." Well, who then? [*He falls back into the seat.*] What an incredible series of events! How did it happen to *me*? Why these things and not others? Who drew them down on my head? Forcibly set on the road of life, not knowing where it leads, and bound to leave it against my will, I've tried to keep it as rosy as my natural cheerfulness permits. Here again I say *my* cheerfulness without knowing if it belongs to me any more than those other things; nor do I know who this *I* may be with which I am so concerned—it's first a shapeless collection of unknown parts, then a helpless puny thing, then a lively little animal, then a young man thirsting for pleasure, with a full capacity to enjoy and ready to use any shifts[94] to live—master here and valet there, at the whim of fortune; ambitious from vanity, industrious from need—and lazy . . . with delight! An orator in tight spots, a poet for relaxation, a musician from time to time, a lover in hot fits: I have seen everything, done everything, worn out everything. At last my illusion is shattered and I'm now wholly disabused . . . blasé, . . . Oh Suzy! Suzy! my Suzy, what torments you are putting me through! I hear footsteps . . . someone's coming . . . This is the crisis. [*He retires into the downstage wing on his right.*]

> [*Enter the* Countess *dressed as* Suzanne, Suzanne *dressed as the* Countess, *and* Marceline.]

Suzanne [*speaking low to the* Countess]. Yes, Marceline said Figaro would be here.

Marceline. And so he is; be quiet.

Suzanne. I see; the one's eavesdropping, the other's coming to fetch me— let the show begin.

Marceline. I don't want to miss a word; I'm going to hide in the pavilion. [*Enters the same pavilion as* Fanchette]

Suzanne [*aloud*]. You're trembling, madam: are you cold?

Countess [*aloud*]. The evening is damp, I am going in.

Suzanne [*aloud*]. If my lady does not need me, I should like to take the air a little while under the trees.

Countess [*aloud*]. Take the air! catch your death, you mean.

Suzanne. I'm used to it.

Figaro [*aside*]. Her death, my eye! [Suzanne *retreats to a spot near the wings, on the opposite side from* Figaro.]

Cherubino [*dressed as an officer, comes on singing the words of his song*]. "Tra-la-la-la-la, A godmother I had, Whom always I adored!"

Countess [*aside*]. The little page!

Cherubino. People are walking about. I must take to my refuge, where Fanchette is—oh, it's a woman!

Countess. Oh, mercy!

Cherubino [*stooping and peering*]. Am I mistaken? That hat I see with feathers outlined against the sky looks to me like Suzy.

Countess. Oh, if the Count were to appear! [*The* Count *enters from the back.*]

[94] Tricks; strategems.

CHERUBINO [*goes up to* COUNTESS *and takes her hand, she pulls away*]. I'm right, it's that adorable girl named Sue! How could I mistake this soft hand, or that slight trembling . . . or the beating of my own heart! [*He tries to put the* COUNTESS's *hand against his heart.*]

COUNTESS [*whispering*]. Go away!

CHERUBINO. Could it be that you took pity on my lot and came here where I have been hiding since afternoon?

COUNTESS. Figaro is coming.

COUNT [*stepping forward, aside*]. Isn't that Suzanne I see?

CHERUBINO [*to* COUNTESS]. I'm not afraid of Figaro and it's not him you're waiting for.

COUNTESS. Who then?

COUNT [*aside*]. Somebody is with her.

CHERUBINO. It's my lord, hussy, who asked you out here this morning when I hid behind the chair.

COUNT [*aside, furious*]. It's that infernal page again!

FIGARO [*aside*]. And they say it isn't nice to eavesdrop!

SUZANNE [*aside*]. The little chatterbox!

COUNTESS [*to* CHERUBINO]. Do me the kindness to go away.

CHERUBINO. Not without a reward for my compliance.

COUNTESS [*frightened*]. You claim—?

CHERUBINO [*with heat*]. Twenty kisses on your account first; then a hundred for your fair mistress.

COUNTESS. You would not dare!

CHERUBINO. Yes, I would! You're taking her place with my lord, I take his with you. The one who gets left is Figaro.

FIGARO [*aside*]. The rapscallion!

SUZANNE [*aside*]. Brash as a little page! [CHERUBINO *tries to kiss the* COUNTESS; *the* COUNT *comes between them and receives the kiss.*]

COUNTESS [*retreating*]. Dear God!

FIGARO [*aside, hearing the sound of the kiss*]. It's a pretty baggage I'm marrying! [*Listens intently*]

CHERUBINO [*feeling the* COUNT's *clothes; aside*]. It's my lord! [*He flees into the pavilion where* FANCHETTE *and* MARCELINE *are hiding.*]

FIGARO [*approaching*]. I'm going to—

COUNT [*thinking the page still there*]. Since you don't repeat the kiss . . . [*lashes out with his hand*]

FIGARO [*coming within range, gets the slap*]. Ow!

COUNT. That's one paid off, anyhow.

FIGARO [*retreating and rubbing his cheek*]. This eavesdropping business isn't all pure gain.

SUZANNE [*laughing*]. Hahahaha!

COUNT [*to* COUNTESS *whom he mistakes for* SUZANNE]. That page is beyond belief—he gets slapped full in the face and goes off laughing.

FIGARO [*aside*]. He should be grieving for me!

COUNT. And he's intolerable: I can't take a step—But let's forget the puzzle or it will spoil the delight I feel in finding you here.

COUNTESS [*imitating* SUZANNE's *voice*]. Were you expecting me?

COUNT. What do you think, after your clever note? [*He takes her hand.*] You're trembling.

COUNTESS. I've been frightened.

COUNT. It wasn't to deprive you of a kiss that I took his. [*Kisses her on the forehead*]

COUNTESS. Such liberties!

FIGARO [*aside*]. The trollop![95]

SUZANNE [*aside*]. The darling!

COUNT [*takes* COUNTESS's *hand*]. How fine and soft your skin is! Your hand is more lovely than the Countess's.

COUNTESS [*aside*]. What preconception will do!

COUNT. And this little arm, how firm and round . . . these pretty fingers full of grace and mischief!

COUNTESS [*speaking like* SUZANNE]. And what of love . . . ?

COUNT. Love . . . is the fiction of the heart. Its history is pleasure, and hence you find me at your feet.

COUNTESS. You do not love her any more?

COUNT. I love her very much, but three years make marriage so respectable.

COUNTESS. What did you want from her?

COUNT [*caressing her*]. What I find in you, my sweet.

COUNTESS. But tell me what . . .

COUNT. I don't know . . . Less sameness, perhaps; more spice in your manner—something, I don't know what, which makes for charm; it's because you deny me sometimes, I don't know. Our wives think they can't do better than to love us. They take this for granted and love us and love us—if they love us—and they are so compliant and constant, always and without stint, that suddenly one day one finds satiety where one looked for happiness.

COUNTESS [*aside*]. What a lesson to me!

COUNT. To tell the truth, Suzy, I have often thought that when we seek elsewhere the pleasure we miss in them, it is because they make no effort to sustain our interest, to renew their attractions in love, to resurrect—so to speak—the delight of possession by affording that of variety.

COUNTESS [*vexed*]. And so theirs is the whole responsibility?

COUNT [*laughing*]. And the man has none, you mean? Well, can we change nature? Our task is to obtain . . .

COUNTESS. Yes, and theirs—?

COUNT. Is to . . . retain . . . That's generally overlooked.

COUNTESS. Not by me.

COUNT. Nor me.

FIGARO [*aside*]. Nor me.

SUZANNE [*aside*]. Nor me.

COUNT [*taking* COUNTESS's *hand again*). There's an echo hereabouts; let's lower our voices. You for one needn't worry about holding a man! Love has fashioned you so fair and sprightly. Add a touch of caprice and you would be the most titillating mistress. [*Kisses her forehead*] My Suzy, a Castilian has nothing but his word of honor. I give you the ransom I promised, to redeem that old claim I no longer have upon the sweet concession you are about to make me.

[95] Immoral woman; slut.

COUNTESS [*curtsying*]. Your Suzanne accepts everything.

FIGARO [*aside*]. They don't exist more wanton than that.

SUZANNE [*aside*]. It means good money in our pockets.

COUNT [*aside*]. She's mercenary—all the better!

COUNTESS [*turning toward the back*]. I see torches.

COUNT. That's for your wedding. Let's go into the pavilion until they're by.

COUNTESS. Without a light?

COUNT [*pulling her gently*]. Why a light! We don't intend to read.

FIGARO [*aside*]. She's going in, the drab![96] I thought so. [*He steps forward.*]

COUNT [*turning around, in a voice of command*]. Who's wandering around, there?

FIGARO [*angry*]. Nobody's wandering; I'm coming on purpose!

COUNT [*to* COUNTESS]. It's Figaro. [*He runs away*]

COUNTESS. I'll follow you. [*She enters the pavilion on the right while the* COUNT *hides in the wood at the back.*]

FIGARO [*trying to find them both*]. I don't hear anything. They must have gone in. So here we are. [*In a changed voice*] Oh, you clumsy husbands who hire spies and toy with suspicion for months without confirming it, why not take your cue from me? I shadow my wife from the beginning, the first day. I listen secretly, and in a twinkling I know everything: it's enchanting—no doubts left, all is known. [*Pacing briskly*] Lucky that it doesn't bother me and that I'm no longer upset by her treachery. I've got them at last.

SUZANNE [*creeping up behind him; aside*]. You're going to pay for those fine suspicions! [*Imitating the* COUNTESS] Who goes there?

FIGARO [*wildly*]. "Who goes there?" A man who thinks the plague should have taken—

SUZANNE. Why, it's Figaro!

FIGARO [*quickly*]. My lady Countess!

SUZANNE. Speak low!

FIGARO [*quickly*]. Ah madam, how fortunate that you should have come. Where do you think my lord may be?

SUZANNE. What does an ungrateful husband matter to me? Tell me rather—

FIGARO [*speaking still more rapidly*]. And Suzanne, my bride, where do you imagine she might be?

SUZANNE. *Please* lower your voice!

FIGARO. Suzanne, my Suzy whom everybody thought so virtuous, who acted so modest! Well, they're locked up in there. I'm going to call out.

SUZANNE. [*putting her hand on his mouth and forgetting to disguise her voice*]. Don't call out!

FIGARO [*aside*]. *This* is Suzy! God damn!

SUZANNE [*imitating the* COUNTESS]. You seem upset.

FIGARO [*aside*]. The minx! Trying to catch me!

SUZANNE. We must avenge ourselves, Figaro.

FIGARO. Do you feel a pressing need of it?

SUZANNE. Am I not a woman? Men, though, have better means.

FIGARO [*confiding*]. Madam, your presence is as necessary as mine. And women's means . . . are the best.

[96] Slut; whore.

SUZANNE [*aside*]. I'd like to slap the lout!

FIGARO [*aside*]. Wouldn't it be fun if even before we're married . . .

SUZANNE. But what kind of revenge is it that lacks the spice of love?

FIGARO. If you see no signs of love, you may be sure I am only restrained by deference.

SUZANNE [*nettled*]. I can't tell whether you mean that honestly, but you certainly don't say it gracefully.

FIGARO [*with comical fervor, kneeling*]. Oh, madam, I worship you. But consider the time, the place, the circumstance, and let your anger supply the fire which my entreaty lacks.

SUZANNE [*aside*]. My hand is itching.

FIGARO [*aside*]. My heart is beating.

SUZANNE. But, sir, have you reflected?

FIGARO. Oh, yes, madam, yes indeed, I have reflected.

SUZANNE. In anger and in love—

FIGARO. Delay is fatal, I know. Your hand, madam.

SUZANNE [*in her own voice and slapping him*]. Here it is.

FIGARO. Lucifer, what a fist!

SUZANNE. What fist?—is this the one? [*Slaps him again*]

FIGARO. Now, what the devil? Are you playing windmill?

SUZANNE [*slapping him with each phrase*]. "Ah, Lucifer, Suzanne!" Take *that* for your suspicion, and *that* for your revenge, and *that* for your schemes, and your insults, and your double dealing. Then you can say as you did this morning: "That's love for you!"

FIGARO [*laughing as he gets up*]. By all the saints, it is!—pure love! What happiness, what bliss! Thrice-blessed Figaro! Hit me, belovèd, again and again. Only, when you're through painting me black and blue, Suzy, look kindly upon the luckiest man ever beaten by a woman.

SUZANNE. The luckiest, you scoundrel? As if you weren't busy seducing the Countess with your pretty turns of phrase, to the point where I was forgetting myself and yielding in her place!

FIGARO. As if I had mistaken the sound of your lovely voice!

SUZANNE [*laughing*]. You recognized me, did you? I'll take my toll for that too.

FIGARO. Just like a woman to beat a body and bear a grudge besides. But tell me by what good fortune I find you here when I thought you there. And these clothes, which fooled me at first, and now prove you innocent . . .

SUZANNE. *You* are the innocent, to walk into a trap laid for someone else. Is it our fault if in trying to catch a fox we catch two?

FIGARO. Who's catching the other?

SUZANNE. His wife.

FIGARO. His wife?

SUZANNE. His wife.

FIGARO [*wildly*]. Ah Figaro, go hang yourself on the nearest tree. You never guessed! His wife! Oh, clever, clever, clever women. So all those resounding kisses . . .

SUZANNE. Fell on my lady.

FIGARO. And the one from the page?

SUZANNE. On my lord.

FIGARO. And this morning, behind the chair?

SUZANNE. On nobody.

FIGARO. Are you sure?

SUZANNE [*laughing*]. Figaro! You know how fists fly about at dusk!

FIGARO [*seizes her hand and kisses it*]. Yours are jewels to me. But the Count's in my face was fair enough.

SUZANNE. Come, proud one, abase yourself.

FIGARO [*acting as he speaks*]. Fair enough: on my knees, bowed low, prone and flat on the ground.

SUZANNE [*laughing*]. The poor Count! What trouble he's gone to . . .

FIGARO [*rising and kneeling*]. . . . to seduce his wife.

→ COUNT [*entering from the back and going straight to the pavilion on the right; aside*]. I can't find her in the wood; perhaps she's stepped in here.

SUZANNE [*whispering to* FIGARO]. There he goes.

COUNT [*at the open door of the pavilion*]. Suzanne, are you there?

FIGARO [*low*]. He's looking for her. I thought . . .

SUZANNE [*low*]. He never recognized her.

FIGARO. Let's finish him off, shall we? [*Kisses her hand noisily*]

COUNT [*turning around*]. A man kneeling before the Countess . . . And I'm unarmed. [*He comes forward.*]

FIGARO [*rising and disguising his voice*]. Forgive me, madam, if I did not realize that this meeting place would be in the path of the festivities.

COUNT [*aside*]. That's the man of this morning in the dressing room. [*He strikes his forehead.*]

FIGARO. But such a silly interference shan't postpone our pleasure.

COUNT [*aside*]. Death and damnation!

FIGARO [*leading* SUZANNE *to the pavilion; aside*]. He's cursing. [*Aloud*] Let us hasten, madam, and repair the misfortune we suffered earlier when I jumped out of the window.

COUNT [*aside*]. Now I see it all!

SUZANNE [*near the pavilion on the left*]. Before we go in, make sure nobody is following. [*He kisses her forehead.*]

COUNT [*shouting*]. Revenge! [SUZANNE *flees into the pavilion where* MARCELINE, FANCHETTE, *AND* CHERUBINO *already are. The* COUNT *seizes* FIGARO *by the arm.*]

FIGARO [*pretending great fright*]. It's the master!

COUNT. Ah, villain, it's you! Ho, somebody, come at once!

[*Enter* PETER, *booted and spurred*].

PETER. So there you are, my lord, at last.

COUNT. Good! Are you alone, Peter?

PETER. Back from Seville, hell for leather.

COUNT. Come close to me and shout very loud.

PETER [*at the top of his lungs*]. No more page in Seville than on the back of my hand—and that's a fact!

COUNT [*pushing him away*]. Stupid oaf!

PETER. Your lordship said I must shout aloud.

COUNT [*holding* FIGARO]. It was to call for help. Ho, there, somebody! Whoever hears me, come quick!

PETER. Figaro's here with me: what are you afraid of?

[*Enter* BRIDLEGOOSE, BARTHOLO,

BASIL, ANTONIO, *and* SUNSTRUCK, *followed by the wedding party carrying torches*].

BARTHOLO [*to* FIGARO]. You see: we came as soon as we heard you.

COUNT [*pointing to the pavilion on the left*]. Peter, guard that door. [PETER *goes.*]

BASIL [*low to* FIGARO]. You caught him with Suzanne?

COUNT [*pointing to* FIGARO]. You, vassals, surround this man and answer for him with your lives.

BASIL. Oh, oh!

COUNT [*angry*]. Be quiet. [*To* FIGARO, *freezingly*] Sir Knight, will you answer a few questions?

FIGARO [*coolly*]. Who indeed could give me leave not to? You have command of everybody here except yourself.

COUNT [*mastering his fury*]. Except myself?

ANTONIO. That's the way to talk!

COUNT [*giving way to his anger*]. If anything could make me angrier, it's the air of calmness he puts on.

FIGARO. Are we like soldiers, killing and being killed for reasons they know nothing of? For my part, I always like to know what I'm angry about.

COUNT [*beside himself*]. Murder! [*controlling himself*] Man of gentle birth who pretend not to know my reasons, would you at least do us the favor of telling us what lady you have brought into this pavilion?

FIGARO [*mischievously pointing to the other*]. Into that one?

COUNT [*quickly*]. Into this.

FIGARO [*coldly*]. That's different. It's a young lady who honors me with her favors.

BASIL [*surprised*]. Oh?

COUNT [*quickly*]. You heard him, gentlemen?

BARTHOLO [*surprised*]. We heard him.

COUNT. And this young person is otherwise unattached?

FIGARO [*coldly*]. I know that a great lord paid her some attentions for a while. But whether it be that he neglected her or that she likes me better, I am the one preferred.

COUNT [*quickly*]. The one pref- [*restraining himself*] At least he is candid. What he has just admitted, I myself have seen and heard, gentlemen, from the mouth of his accomplice. I give you my word on it.

BRIDLEGOOSE [*petrified*]. His ac-complice!

COUNT [*in fury*]. Now, when dishonor is public, so must be the revenge! [*He goes into the pavilion.*]

ANTONIO. He's right.

BRIDLEGOOSE. [*to* FIGARO]. Who took who-o-o's wife?

FIGARO [*laughing*]. No one had that special satisfaction.

COUNT [*speaking from inside the pavilion and tugging at someone not yet identifiable*]. It is no use, madam, the hour has struck and you are doomed. [*He comes out and turns to the rest without looking.*] How fortunate that there lives no pledge of our hateful union—!

FIGARO [*calling out*]. Cherubino!

COUNT. The page!

BASIL. Haha!

COUNT. Always the damned page! What were you doing in that room?

CHERUBINO [*shyly*]. I was hiding, as you ordered me to do.

PETER. What use was it to nearly kill a horse![97]

COUNT. Go in there, Antonio, and bring before her judge the criminal who has dishonored me.

BRIDLEGOOSE. Is it my lady that you are l-looking for?

ANTONIO. 'Tis Providence, by gum, for your carryings-on all over the countryside.

COUNT [*furious*]. Get in there! [ANTONIO *goes in*]

COUNT. You shall see, gentlemen, that the page was not alone.

CHERUBINO [*shyly*]. It would have been hard on me if a gentle soul had not sweetened the bitter pill.

ANTONIO [*pulling out someone not recognizable at first*]. Come, my lady, don't make me coax you, everybody knows you went in.

FIGARO [*calling out*]. My little cousin!

BASIL. Haha!

COUNT. Fanchette!

ANTONIO [*turns around*]. By jiminy 'twas right smart, my lord, to pick on me to show the company it's my daughter caused all the randan, now wasn't it?

COUNT [*indignant*]. Who could suppose she was in there? [*He tries to go in.*]

BARTHOLO [*interposing*]. Allow me, my lord. All this is far too upsetting for you; but perhaps I can deal with it in cold blood. [*He goes in.*]

BRIDLEGOOSE. It's certainly too confusing for me.

BARTHOLO [*speaking from inside and coming out.*] Do not be afraid, madam, no one will hurt you, I promise you. [*He turns around and cries out.*] Marceline!

BASIL. Haha!

FIGARO [*laughing*]. A madhouse! My mother in it too!

ANTONIO. The jades[98] are playing who can be the worst.

COUNT [*outraged*]. What is that to me? It's the Countess . . . [SUZANNE *comes out, her face behind a fan.*] Ah, there she is at last, gentlemen. [*He takes her violently by the arm.*] What does such an odious woman deserve, gentlemen—?

> [SUZANNE *falls on her knees, bowing her head.*]

COUNT. Never, never! [FIGARO *kneels next to her.*]

COUNT [*louder*]. Never! [MARCELINE *kneels beside the others.*]

COUNT [*still louder*]. Never, never! [*They all kneel.*]

COUNT [*beside himself*]. Never, not if there were a hundred of you!

COUNTESS [*coming out of the other pavilion*]. At least, I can make one more.

COUNT [*looking alternately at* SUZANNE *and the* COUNTESS]. What do I see?

BRIDLEGOOSE [*laughing*]. What d'you kn-n-know, it's my lady!

COUNT [*trying to lift her up*]. It was you, Countess? [*In a supplicating tone*] Only the most generous forgiveness . . .

COUNTESS [*laughing*]. In my place, you would say "Never, never!" whereas I, for the third time today, forgive you unconditionally. [*She gets up.*]

[97] By riding to and from Seville, at top speed, to look for Cherubino.
[98] Loose women.

SUZANNE [*getting up*]. And so do I.

MARCELINE [*getting up*]. And I.

FIGARO [*getting up*]. And I. There's an echo hereabouts.

[*All get up.*]

COUNT. An echo! I tried to outsmart them and they fooled me like a child.

COUNTESS [*laughing*]. Don't act as if you were sorry, my lord.

FIGARO [*brushing off his knees with his hat*]. A day like today is ideal training for an ambassador.

COUNT [*to* SUZANNE]. That note sealed with a pin? . . .

SUZANNE. Madam dictated it.

COUNT. The answer is overdue. [*He kisses the* COUNTESS's *hand.*]

COUNTESS. Each will regain his own. [*She gives the purse to* FIGARO *and the diamond to* SUZANNE.]

SUZANNE [*to* FIGARO]. Still another dowry!

FIGARO [*striking the purse*]. That makes three. But this one took some contriving.

SUZANNE. Like our marriage.

SUNSTRUCK. What about the bride's garter? Can I have it?

COUNTESS [*taking out the ribbon from her bosom*]. The garter? It was in her clothes. Here you are. [*She throws the ribbon; the boys try to scramble for it.*]

CHERUBINO [*swiftly picking it up*]. Try and get it!

COUNT [*laughing*]. Since you're so touchy a gentleman, what made you laugh so hard when I boxed your ear?

CHERUBINO [*taking a step backward and half drawing his sword*[99]]. My ear, colonel?

FIGARO [*comically angry*]. He got it on *my* cheek, as always happens when lords mete out justice.

COUNT [*laughing*]. On your cheek, ha, ha, ha, isn't that good, what do you say, dear Countess?

COUNTESS [*abstracted and returning to reality*]. Indeed, dear Count, I do—for life, unswervingly, I swear it.

COUNT [*slapping* BRIDLEGOOSE *on the shoulder*]. And you, Bridlegoose, let us have your opinion.

BRIDLEGOOSE. On what has taken p-place, my lord? Well, my opinion is that I d-don't know what to think, and that's my opinion.

ALL [*together*]. A very sound judgment!

FIGARO. I was poor and despised. When I showed a little cleverness, hatred dogged me. Now with a pretty girl and some money . . .

BARTHOLO [*laughing*]. Everybody will crowd around you!

FIGARO. Do you think so?

BARTHOLO. I know my kind.

FIGARO [*bowing to the spectators*]. Aside from my wife and my goods, you are welcome to all I have. [*The orchestra plays the introduction to the entertainment.*]

BASIL.

Triple dowry, handsome wife—
To a husband, what largesse!

[99] A box on the ears is the kind of insult that can provoke a duel, and Cherubino is of a high social rank.

'Gainst a lord or beardless page
Only fools feel jealous rage.
Let the Latin proverb bless
Man's incalculable life:

FIGARO. Don't I know that proverb! [*sings*] "Happy those of noble birth!"
BASIL. No you *don't* know it! [*sings*] "Happy those who own the earth!"

SUZANNE.

Let a man his wife betray
He is boastful, all are gay;
Let his wife indulge her whim
She is punished, unlike him.
If you ask why this is so,
'Tis the stronger's wicked law.

MARCELINE.

Every man his mother knows,
Her who'd give her life for him.
But beyond this all is dim—
How explain love's secret lure?

FIGARO (*breaking in*). Secret, though the end disclose
That the offspring of a boor
May turn out a gentleman.

FIGARO.

By the accident of birth,
One is shepherd, t'other king.
Chance made lord and underling,
Only genius threads the maze:
Twenty kings are fed on praise
Who in death are common earth,
While Voltaire[1] immortal stays.

CHERUBINO.

Flighty sex we all adore,
You who torment all our days,
Everyone complains of you;
In the end we kneel and sue.
To the pit[2] thus players do:
Such a one professes scorn
Who would crawl to earn your bays.[3]

FIGARO.

Jack McJohn, the jealous lout,
Hoped to have both wife and peace;
Hired a dog to roam about
In the garden, fierce and free;

[1] The famous French satirist Voltaire (1694–1778) was idolized by Beaumarchais.
[2] The ground level of theater seats; the spectators.
[3] Wreath of bay-leaves; a symbol of honor and triumph.

Barks as claimed in guaranty;
All are bitten by the beast,
Save the lover from whom leased.

COUNTESS.

There's a wife who's proudly prude
Though she loves her husband not;
There's another, nearly lewd,
Swears she loveth none but he;
Now the worthiest is she,
Never swearing this or that,
Who but strives for honesty.

COUNT.

Any woman far from Court
Who believes in duty strict
In romance falls somewhat short.
I prefer the derelict:
Like a piece of currency,
Stamped with one man's effigy,
She can serve the needs of all.

SUZANNE.

If there should a moral lurk
In this mad yet cheerful work,
For the sake of gaiety,
Pray accept it as a whole.
Thus does Nature, sensibly,
Using pleasures we pursue,
Lead up gently to her goal.

BRIDLEGOOSE.

Now dear sirs, the c-comic art,
Which you shortly mean to j-judge,
Apes the l-life of all of you
Sitting there and taking p-part.
When annoyed you bear a g-grudge
But although you grumble l-long,
All our d-doings end in song.

APPENDIX:
MARCELINE ON THE CONDITION OF WOMEN

The following passage, part of the episode in Act Three wherein Figaro discovers who his parents are, was deleted from the staged version of *Figaro's Marriage* at the request of the actors at the Comédie Française but was included in Beaumarchais' Preface to the printed text of the play. The translation of this passage is by the editors of *Literature of the Western World*.

[BRIDLEGOOSE. One thing is c-c-clear; he won't marry her.]

BARTHOLO. Nor will I.

MARCELINE. Nor will you? What about your son? You often used to swear to me . . .

BARTHOLO. I was out of my mind. If such memories of the past were binding on people, everybody would have to marry everybody.

BRIDLEGOOSE. A-and if people examined things so closely, n-nobody would ever marry anybody.

BARTHOLO. All these things coming out in public! A lamentable youth!

MARCELINE [*getting more and more worked up*]. Yes, lamentable, and more lamentable than people realize! I'm not denying my own sins; this day has brought them to light all too clearly! But it's cruel to have to go on living them down after thirty years of leading a decent life! By my nature I was cut out to be sensible and good, and as soon as I was allowed to use my mind I did become sensible and good. But at an age when all a girl knows is illusions, inexperience, and poverty, when she is besieged by seducers at the very time when misfortune is holding a knife to her throat, what resistance can she offer—a mere child—to enemies all lined up against her? Why should a man judge her so severely when chances are that he himself has ruined ten unfortunate creatures like her?

FIGARO. The guiltiest people are the least forgiving; that's the way it goes.

MARCELINE [*with passion*]. Oh, you men who are worse than ingrates, who feel withering scorn for the toys of your own passions, for your own victims! You are the ones who should have to pay the price for the errors of our youth—you and your public officials, so stupidly puffed up with your authority to judge us, you who with criminal negligence take away from us every honest means of earning a living. Is there just one way for women to support themselves? Making women's clothing is something they're by nature good at, and you go to the trouble of training a thousand male workers to do that kind of work.

FIGARO [*angrily*]. Even soldiers are required to do embroidery!

MARCELINE [*almost beside herself*]. Even at the highest levels of society, your attentions to women are a mere mockery; women are lured into a state of servitude with the bait of "respect"; in matters of property you treat them as children, but in matters of misbehavior you treat them as grown-ups! From every point of view, the way you treat us should arouse horror and pity!

FIGARO. She's right!

COUNT [*aside*]. All too right!

BRIDLEGOOSE. B-by God, she is right.

MARCELINE. Still, my son, what if an unjust man refuses to give us justice? Don't look at where you have been, look at where you're going; that's the only really important thing for all of us. In a few months your fiancée will be of legal age to make decisions on her own, and I guarantee that she will accept you. From now on you will live with a loving wife and a loving mother who will try to outdo each other in their affection toward you. Be kind to them for their sakes, be happy for your own sake, be cheerful, open, and good for everybody's sake; your mother will have everything she wants and needs.

FIGARO. Those are golden words, Mother, and I intend to stick to them. Really, what fools we are! For thousands and thousands of years the world has been spinning around; from this ocean of time I happen to have been able to snatch thirty puny years that are now gone forever, and then I go beating my brains out wondering to whom I am indebted for those thirty years! People who go making all that trouble for themselves deserve what they get! To spend your life wrangling with people is to have a heavy yoke around your neck all the time, like those poor horses who drag loads upriver, who never rest even when they stop, who are always pulling even when they aren't on the move. We'll just let time take its course.
[COUNT. Stupid turn of events—most annoying!]

Jean-Jacques Rousseau
(1712–1778)

It might be argued that, compared with the eighteenth century, the nineteenth and twentieth centuries produced more striking and widespread changes in the outward conditions of life, especially in technology and social organization. But it is at least tenable that the eighteenth century witnessed a greater intellectual ferment, especially in new ethical norms, in new images of human nature, and in new views of the relationship between human beings and their natural and social surroundings. To single out any one person, therefore, as the central figure of the century is to put a heavy weight of responsibility on him, for better or worse. But many people would so identify Jean-Jacques Rousseau. His most immediate, verifiable impact was on the democratic political theory that strongly influenced the direction of the American and especially the French Revolution. His ideas on education have come into their own in the twentieth century, in now orthodox theories of learning and even more clearly in the movements loosely summarized as "progressive education"; even earlier, though, these ideas produced a new view of the nature of childhood. In literature, he propagated the vogues of sentiment and reverence for natural scenery, and he pioneered a new kind of spiritual autobiography centered on the psychological development and personal uniqueness of the author, a confessional mode that influenced poetry and fiction as well; in these respects, and others, he is clearly a founding father of Romanticism. Perhaps the most comprehensive of his achievements was to familiarize the intellectual world with a new model of innate human goodness and dignity.

Rousseau was born in 1712 in Geneva, the son of a Swiss watchmaker. He grew up in an atmosphere in which democratic workers' associations helped instill in him the egalitarian principles he was to preach later in his life, the more persuasively for the working-class origins that distinguished him from the typically aristocratic radicals of his time. In his childhood and boyhood, described in Book I of his *Confessions,* he had a passion for read-

ing but got little formal education; Rousseau is one of the prototypes of the self-taught genius. The youthful personality he recalls was a curious mixture of mental sordidness and dreaming idealism. Not surprisingly, his revelations—about the effects upon him and his father of his mother's death in giving birth to him, and about the lasting effect of spankings upon his personality, especially his sexual urges—have intrigued psychoanalytic interpreters and biographers, especially because Rousseau explicitly articulates ideas resembling Freud's on the lasting effect of childhood experiences.

After being unhappily apprenticed to an engraver, he ran away in 1728, fearful of punishment for having been stranded outside the city walls one night. He found refuge with a Madame de Warens, who for several years thereafter was a mother figure to him. Under her influence he was converted from his Genevan Calvinism to Catholicism, and at twenty-one he became her lover. During the next two decades he was a vagabond, geographically and vocationally; in Paris and many other parts of Europe, he was at different times a lackey, an engraver, a seminarian for the Catholic priesthood, a census clerk, a tutor (unsuccessful), and a secretary to the French ambassador in Venice. For a time he read intensively, becoming an admirer of Voltaire (later his bitter enemy). More than anything else, he defined his vocation as music; he tried to win Parisian recognition for a new system of musical notation and later was to write an opera performed before the king. In 1745 he entered into a liaison with a servant named Thérèse Le Vasseur, by whom he had five children, all consigned to a home for foundlings. (More than twenty years later, in 1768, he married her.) He met several of the French "Encyclopedists," the rationalist radicals of the time, including D'Alembert and Diderot. The latter became a close friend of Rousseau's.

In 1749, while walking to Vincennes to visit Diderot, who had been imprisoned there for violating the press laws, Rousseau came upon an announcement in a French journal of an essay contest, sponsored by the Academy of Dijon, on the question of whether the arts and sciences had improved human morals. Rousseau, feverishly excited and feeling that he had struck upon the ideas that would define his role in life, began immediately a prize-winning essay, published the following year, arguing that the arts and sciences had corrupted the primitive virtues of mankind and were tools by which the wealthy and powerful enslaved others. In this rather extreme form appeared Rousseau's first important statement of his lifelong theme: the conflict between corrupting civilization and natural virtue. In the following years he wrote articles on music and other subjects for the *Encyclopedia*. Although courted by the fashionable world, Rousseau chose to live a life of sturdy independence and poverty, eking out a small income as a music copyist. By 1753 he was notorious enough to have come under police scrutiny.

In an essay written that year for another Dijon contest, on the question of inequality, Rousseau posited and praised a former golden age of human existence when man, having moved from his first natural condition into a healthy communal one, lived still uncorrupted by private property and oppressive laws. In 1754 he revisited Geneva, reconverting to Protestantism. His theistic convictions, although unorthodox in some important re-

spects, were emerging as one source of increasing friction between him and the anti-religious Encyclopedists, and he made a sharp break with them when, in 1758, he opposed a scheme favored by Voltaire to introduce a theater in Geneva. Rousseau argued, in a long *Letter to D'Alembert on Plays,* that the introduction in Geneva of aristocratic dramas such as those of Molière and Voltaire himself would corrupt a still healthy community. Rousseau had now forfeited his standing in both the conservative and radical camps; increasingly thereafter his life was to be a series of persecutions, some real and many imaginary, culminating in the mental derangement of his very last years.

Rousseau never felt comfortable in the refined and structured social life of Paris, and he left the city in 1756, settling near the wood of Montmorency. In 1761 and 1762, after a few years of intense productivity, he published the three works that, along with the *Confessions,* are his greatest: the novel *Julie, or The New Heloise; The Social Contract;* and *Emile, or Education. The New Heloise* was one of the most spectacularly popular novels of the century, going through fifty editions; for a time it was rented out by lending libraries for ten sous per hour. Influenced by Rousseau's platonic but intense love for the Countess d'Houdetot, the book is a triangular love story, a sentimental novel of passion set in simple rustic surroundings and saturated by a deep feeling for nature. One of its incidental but not insignificant effects was to make Swiss scenery a poetic symbol for such poets as Byron and Shelley and a tourist mecca for them and for thousands of lesser devotees through the eighteenth and nineteenth centuries.

The same concern with nature, in a somewhat different sense, pervades *Emile,* a combination of tract and narrative outlining Rousseau's ideas on education. One of the book's basic themes is Rousseau's familiar premise that human nature is originally good; the child will be corrupted only if outside, alien forces of social evil are allowed to infect his world. For this reason, much of the pupil Emile's early education is "negative," a guarding against pernicious outside influences; that is why he is reared in the country. Moreover, childhood is defined as a period with its own autonomy; it is not merely potential adulthood: "Nature wants children to be children before being men." Because the faculty of reason develops late, children in their early years should learn not through precepts or books but by doing and experiencing *things,* things they recognize as useful and interesting. Memorization has no place in this regime. Each child must be led to discover his real self and to express it. An atmosphere of trust should exist between the adolescent pupil and the teacher, the two linked by an unforced mutual contract. Parental affection is important; therefore, for instance, mothers should breast-feed their children instead of relegating them to wet-nurses, but, far from being coddled, the children should be inured to natural physical rigors. The last goal should be the introduction of the child into the responsibilities of mature adult social relations.

This goal of humane socialization is one of the links between Rousseau's ideas of education and his political theory as expressed in *The Social Contract.* There may seem to be a conflict between such socialization and Rousseau's view of society as an evil force, but he was realist enough to recognize that civilization could not just return to its primitive forms of organization.

The challenge for him was to envision a principle (not necessarily concrete institutions) of social order that would enhance human freedom to the greatest possible extent. Building on but transforming ideas of earlier political theorists, including Hobbes and Locke, Rousseau posited an implicit agreement, or contract, made freely among free citizens, to yield their absolute individualism to a state in which the "general will" would represent their own best interests. The state exists, then, as the creation of its subjects, *all* its subjects, who in renouncing the right to indulge their own individual impulses fulfill their higher needs. Similarly, because the citizens are sovereign, they may undo the contract (a notion also stated in the opening sentences of the American Declaration of Independence). It is not surprising that the leaders of the French Revolution hailed Rousseau as its sacred prophet.

The publication of these definitive works so nearly at the same time marked another epoch in Rousseau's life. Alienated from the intellectual left, he also suffered now a rapid series of blows from the political and religious right: the Catholic hierarchy, the French royal court, the Parlement of Paris, the city council of Geneva, and Protestant ministers. (*Emile* contained a section arguing that the child's education in Christianity could be accomplished through nature rather than revelation.) *Emile* and *The Social Contract* were condemned and burned in Paris and Geneva, and an order was issued in Paris for Rousseau's arrest. As if these real persecutions were not enough, Rousseau developed strong delusions of persecution that remained with him to the end of his life. The man who had felt ready to retire, his great work accomplished, now found that he had to move repeatedly from one refuge to another, all over western Europe.

In 1766, at the invitation of the philosopher David Hume, he went to England, where he worked on his *Confessions,* but he came to believe that Hume too was involved in a conspiracy against him and fled the country in 1767. In 1770, the *Confessions* completed (though not published until two years after his death), Rousseau returned to Paris, where in 1775 there occurred an incident characteristic of his last years: convinced that all human beings were against him, he tried to deposit one of his autobiographical works on the altar of Notre Dame Cathedral but found the altar barred by an iron grille, so that even God seemed to have disowned him. In the last two years of his life, he wrote his *Reveries of a Solitary Walker,* a work of tranquil charm that shows once more Rousseau's intense feeling for nature. He died in 1778, of an apoplectic stroke, in Ermenonville, a town near Paris. (Voltaire had died a month earlier.) Soon after Rousseau's death came the universal acclaim and affection he had despaired of before he died. Among his worshipers were Robespierre and the other men who, a few years later, directed the French Revolution—not to mention many of the great Romantic poets of the next generation.

The *Confessions* has been vastly influential. The first paragraph reveals Rousseau's purported intention, which he claims was unprecedented: total self-revelation for its own sake. (This goal will seem somewhat less egoistic if we recall Rousseau's premise in works such as *Emile* that every individual is unique.) The book is more concerned with Rousseau's private self than with public events. "Myself alone!"—that is its theme. Perhaps only in

Montaigne had anyone attempted the like before, since the one earlier great *Confessions,* that of St. Augustine, was written not so much to reveal its author as to praise and help reveal God.

Rousseau's *Confessions* is a spiritual autobiography, but that label is misleading if it obscures Rousseau's emphasis that in him spirit was indissociably attached to an animal nature. The combination of high idealism with sleaziness in Rousseau's character can be unedifying to some readers; others, however, recognizing in themselves traits and impulses that are less than noble, will be comforted to recognize that such faults do not necessarily exclude one from sympathy and understanding. For Rousseau in Book I, embarrassing self-revelation is the voucher for his honesty, since, as he asserts in connection with his "spankings" fetish, it is easier to acknowledge criminal faults than ridiculous ones. Even granting Rousseau's honesty, though, there remain questions about the quality of that honesty; for example, is the revelation of one's petty vices a sign of humility or of a perverse pride? However we answer such questions, we can see in the stated aim of the *Confessions* an early milestone in the evolution of "sincerity," one of the great, almost mythic watchwords of the modern personality, a characteristically modern measure of value in personal relationships and literature alike.

In many other respects too Rousseau was one of the great mythmakers of modern times, if we take "myth" to mean a deep-seated image or belief that governs a culture's ideas, ideals, values, premises, and behavior. Rousseau held some views that make modernists uneasy: his view of female education in *Emile* is very conservative, and some people detect a disturbingly statist mystique in his political theory of the "general will" (something different from the sum of individual wills) and in his insistence that religious tolerance coexist with certain articles of civic religion. But in many more respects Rousseau was the spokesman, supremely eloquent, for ideas accepted by many people today so unselfconsciously that they are hardly aware of them as distinct beliefs open to challenge: that man is naturally good; that crime and vice are extrinsic evils curable by education and by adjustments in the political and economic environment; that the innocence and integrity of childhood are not merely negative conditions of inexperience but an idyll that later life in the world tragically shatters; that education ought not to be the bending and beating of resistant iron in a smithy but the nurturing of a plant; that the tendency of complex civilization is to corrupt the hardy virtues of earlier times; that city life is not the normal milieu for human beings; that what is artificial is inferior, and that intellect is more artificial than instinctual feeling; that each of us must labor to discern and realize the elusive, unique, inner being whose enemy is conformity and convention, in short, to "be ourselves"; that autobiography (like first novels) should tell, in effect, "how I got to be me." The most fundamental myth of all (in the sense defined earlier) is the existence of something called "society," understood not merely as a convenient term for statistical tendencies in the human world around us but as an organized, almost conscious force against which our aspirations and needs bruise themselves. Stated so, these are simplifications of what Rousseau wrote, as most myths are simplifications. And some of these notions go back to earlier writers and ages. But that they are often attributed to Rousseau is itself

revelatory of the impact of his dynamic literary personality; he is a good person to pin things on, from Romanticism to the totalitarian state to modern radicalism. If he did not in fact create all the myths associated with him, for many of them he is at least the accredited mythographer.

FURTHER READING (*prepared by W. J. R.*): Frances Winwar's *Jean-Jacques Rousseau: Conscience of an Era*, 1961, is a thorough biography written with sympathy for Rousseau's theories. A good brief introduction is Paul H. Fry's "Jean-Jacques Rousseau," in *European Writers: The Age of Reason and the Enlightenment*, Vol. 4, ed. George Stade, 1984. See also Ronald Grimsley, *Jean-Jacques Rousseau*, 1983. N. J. H. Dent's *Rousseau*, 1989, is a helpful short book on Rousseau's ideas. C. H. Dobinson's *Jean-Jacques Rousseau: His Thought and Its Relevance Today*, 1969, examines Rousseau's views of education and discusses his life and intellectual development. The coherence of Rousseau's thought, a disputed subject, is defended in Ernst Cassirer's *The Question of Jean-Jacques Rousseau*, 1932, trans. and ed. Peter Gay, 1954, which attempts a comprehensive interpretation. Judith N. Shklar's *Men and Citizens: A Study of Rousseau's Social Theory*, 1969, contains interesting chapters on Rousseau and utopias and on his theories of authority. Several excellent essays on Rousseau's politics, relationships with other writers, and other topics are collected in *Reappraisals of Rousseau*, ed. Simon Harvey, Marian Hobson, David Kelley, and others, 1980 (French articles are not translated into English).

CONFESSIONS*

BOOK I

[1712–1719.]—I am commencing an undertaking, hitherto without precedent, and which will never find an imitator. I desire to set before my fellows the likeness of a man in all the truth of nature, and that man myself.

Myself alone! I know the feelings of my heart, and I know men. I am not made like any of those I have seen; I venture to believe that I am not made like any of those who are in existence. If I am not better, at least I am different. Whether Nature has acted rightly or wrongly in destroying the mold in which she cast me, can only be decided after I have been read.

Let the trumpet of the Day of Judgment sound when it will, I will present myself before the Sovereign Judge with this book in my hand. I will say boldly: "This is what I have done, what I have thought, what I was. I have told the good and the bad with equal frankness. I have neither omitted anything bad, nor interpolated anything good. If I have occasionally made use of some immaterial embellishments, this has only been in order to fill a gap caused by lack of memory. I may have assumed the truth of that which I knew might have been true, never of that which I knew to be false. I have shown myself as I was: mean and contemptible, good, high-minded and sublime, according as I was one or the other. I have unveiled my inmost self even as Thou hast seen it, O Eternal Being. Gather round me the countless host of my fellow-men; let them hear my confessions, lament for my un-

*Translator anonymous. Reprinted from *The Confessions of Jean-Jacques Rousseau*, Modern Library, Random House, Inc., New York, 1945.

worthiness, and blush for my imperfections. Then let each of them in turn reveal, with the same frankness, the secrets of his heart at the foot of the Throne, and say, if he dare, '*I was better than that man!*'"

I was born at Geneva, in the year 1712, and was the son of Isaac Rousseau and Susanne Bernard, citizens. The distribution of a very moderate inheritance amongst fifteen children had reduced my father's portion almost to nothing; and his only means of livelihood was his trade of watchmaker, in which he was really very clever. My mother, a daughter of the Protestant minister[1] Bernard, was better off. She was clever and beautiful, and my father had found difficulty in obtaining her hand. Their affection for each other had commenced almost as soon as they were born. When only eight years old, they walked every evening upon the Treille;[2] at ten, they were inseparable. Sympathy and union of soul strengthened in them the feeling produced by intimacy. Both, naturally full of tender sensibility, only waited for the moment when they should find the same disposition in another—or, rather, this moment waited for them, and each abandoned his heart to the first which opened to receive it. Destiny, which appeared to oppose their passion, only encouraged it. The young lover, unable to obtain possession of his mistress, was consumed by grief. She advised him to travel, and endeavor to forget her. He travelled, but without result, and returned more in love than ever. He found her whom he loved still faithful and true. After this trial of affection, nothing was left for them but to love each other all their lives. This they swore to do, and Heaven blessed their oath.

Gabriel Bernard, my mother's brother, fell in love with one of my father's sisters, who only consented to accept the hand of the brother, on condition that her own brother married the sister. Love arranged everything, and the two marriages took place on the same day.[3] Thus my uncle became the husband of my aunt, and their children were doubly my first cousins. At the end of a year, a child was born to both, after which they were again obliged to separate.

My uncle Bernard was an engineer. He took service in the Empire[4] and in Hungary, under Prince Eugène. He distinguished himself at the siege and battle of Belgrade. My father, after the birth of my only brother, set out for Constantinople, whither he was summoned to undertake the post of watchmaker to the Sultan. During his absence, my mother's beauty, intellect and talents gained for her the devotion of numerous admirers.[5] M. de la Closure, the French Resident, was one of the most eager to offer his. His passion must have been great, for, thirty years later, I saw him greatly

[1] Susanne was actually the daughter of a clockmaker, although she was reared by a minister uncle after her father died when she was nine. Rousseau is not always exact in his facts and dates.

[2] A public walk on the Geneva city walls.

[3] The two marriages were really five years apart. This statement, like some other errors early in the book, may either be deliberate poeticizing or represent family traditions Rousseau believed were true.

[4] The Austrian empire; Prince Eugène was an Austrian general.

[5] "Her talents were too brilliant for her position, since her father, the minister, who worshipped her, had educated her with great care. She drew, sang, accompanied herself on the téorbe [a stringed instrument, resembling a lute]; she read much, and wrote tolerable verses. . . ." [Rousseau's note.]

affected when speaking to me of her. To enable her to resist such advances, my mother had more than her virtue: she loved her husband tenderly. She pressed him to return; he left all, and returned. I was the unhappy fruit of this return. Ten months later I was born, a weak and ailing child; I cost my mother her life, and my birth was the first of my misfortunes.

I have never heard how my father bore this loss, but I know that he was inconsolable. He believed that he saw his wife again in me, without being able to forget that it was I who had robbed him of her; he never embraced me without my perceiving, by his sighs and the convulsive manner in which he clasped me to his breast, that a bitter regret was mingled with his caresses, which were on that account only the more tender. When he said to me, "Jean-Jacques, let us talk of your mother," I used to answer, "Well, then, my father, we will weep!"—and this word alone was sufficient to move him to tears. "Ah!" said he, with a sigh, "give her back to me, console me for her loss, fill the void which she has left in my soul. Should I love you as I do, if you were only my son?" Forty years after he had lost her, he died in the arms of a second wife, but the name of the first was on his lips and her image at the bottom of his heart.

Such were the authors of my existence. Of all the gifts which Heaven had bestowed upon them, a sensitive heart is the only one they bequeathed to me; it had been the source of their happiness, but for me it proved the source of all the misfortunes of my life.

I was brought into the world in an almost dying condition; little hope was entertained of saving my life. I carried within me the germs of a complaint[6] which the course of time has strengthened, and which at times allows me a respite only to make me suffer more cruelly in another manner. One of my father's sisters, an amiable and virtuous young woman, took such care of me that she saved my life. At this moment, while I am writing, she is still alive, at the age of eighty, nursing a husband younger than herself, but exhausted by excessive drinking. Dear aunt, I forgive you for having preserved my life; and I deeply regret that, at the end of your days, I am unable to repay the tender care which you lavished upon me at the beginning of my own.[7] My dear old nurse Jacqueline is also still alive, healthy and robust. The hands which opened my eyes at my birth will be able to close them for me at my death.

I felt before I thought: this is the common lot of humanity. I experienced it more than others. I do not know what I did until I was five or six years old. I do not know how I learned to read; I only remember my earliest reading, and the effect it had upon me; from that time I date my uninterrupted self-consciousness. My mother had left some romances behind her, which my father and I began to read after supper. At first it was only a question of practicing me in reading by the aid of amusing books; but soon the interest became so lively, that we used to read in turns without stopping, and spent whole nights in this occupation. We were unable to leave off until the volume was finished. Sometimes, my father, hearing the

[6] Probably uremia, a symptom of kidney disease accompanied by nausea, headache, and coma.

[7] "The name of this aunt was Madame Gonceru. In March, 1767, Rousseau settled upon her an income of one hundred livres, and, even in the time of his greatest distress, always paid it with scrupulous exactitude." [Translator's note.]

swallows begin to twitter in the early morning, would say, quite ashamed, "Let us go to bed; I am more of a child than yourself."

In a short time I acquired, by this dangerous method, not only extreme facility in reading and understanding what I read, but a knowledge of the passions that was unique in a child of my age. I had no idea of things in themselves, although all the feelings of actual life were already known to me. I had conceived nothing, but felt everything. These confused emotions which I felt one after the other, certainly did not warp the reasoning powers which I did not as yet possess; but they shaped them in me of a peculiar stamp, and gave me odd and romantic notions of human life, of which experience and reflection have never been able wholly to cure me.

[1719–1723.]—The romances came to an end in the summer of 1719. The following winter brought us something different. My mother's library being exhausted, we had recourse to the share of her father's which had fallen to us. Luckily, there were some good books in it; in fact, it could hardly have been otherwise, for the library had been collected by a minister, who was even a learned man according to the fashion of the day, and was at the same time a man of taste and intellect. The "History of the Empire and the Church," by Le Sueur; Bossuet's "Treatise upon Universal History"; Plutarch's "Lives of Famous Men"; Nani's "History of Venice"; Ovid's "Metamorphoses"; La Bruyère; Fontenelle's "Worlds"; his "Dialogues of the Dead"; and some volumes of Molière—all these were brought over into my father's room, and I read to him out of them while he worked. I conceived a taste for them that was rare and perhaps unique at my age. Plutarch, especially, became my favorite author. The pleasure I took in reading him over and over again cured me a little of my taste for romance, and I soon preferred Agesilaus, Brutus, and Aristides to Orondates, Artamenes, and Juba.[8] This interesting reading, and the conversations between my father and myself to which it gave rise, formed in me the free and republican spirit, the proud and indomitable character unable to endure slavery or servitude, which has tormented me throughout my life in situations the least fitted to afford it scope. Unceasingly occupied with thoughts of Rome and Athens, living as it were amongst their great men, myself by birth the citizen of a republic and the son of a father whose patriotism was his strongest passion, I was fired by his example; I believed myself a Greek or a Roman; I lost my identity in that of the individual whose life I was reading; the recitals of the qualities of endurance and intrepidity which arrested my attention made my eyes glisten and strengthened my voice. One day, while I was relating the history of Scaevola at table, those present were alarmed to see me come forward and hold my hand over a chafing-dish, to illustrate his action.[9]

I had a brother seven years older than myself, who was learning my father's trade. The excessive affection which was lavished upon myself caused him to be somewhat neglected, which treatment I cannot approve of. His education felt the consequences of this neglect. He took to evil

[8] The first three are among the heroes in the *Parallel Lives* of the ancient Greeks and Romans by Plutarch (c. A.D. 46–120), a lifelong favorite author of Rousseau's; the last three are heroes of romances.

[9] Scaevola was an ancient Roman who put his hand on a brazier to dramatize an oath to kill the king of the Etruscan enemies.

courses before he was old enough to be a regular profligate. He was put with another master, from whom he was continually running away, as he had done from home. I hardly ever saw him; I can scarcely say that I knew him; but I never ceased to love him tenderly, and he loved me as much as a vagabond can love anything. I remember that, on one occasion, when my father was chastising him harshly and in anger, I threw myself impetuously between them and embraced him closely. In this manner I covered his body with mine, and received the blows which were aimed at him; I so obstinately maintained my position that at last my father was obliged to leave off, being either disarmed by my cries and tears, or afraid of hurting me more than him. At last, my brother turned out so badly that he ran away and disappeared altogether. Sometime afterwards we heard that he was in Germany. He never once wrote to us. From that time nothing more has been heard of him, and thus I have remained an only son.

If this poor boy was carelessly brought up, this was not the case with his brother; the children of kings could not be more carefully looked after than I was during my early years—worshipped by all around me, and, which is far less common, treated as a beloved, never as a spoiled child. Till I left my father's house, I was never once allowed to run about the streets by myself with the other children; in my case no one ever had to satisfy or check any of those fantastic whims which are attributed to Nature, but are all in reality the result of education. I had the faults of my age: I was a chatterbox, a glutton, and, sometimes, a liar. I would have stolen fruits, bonbons, or eatables; but I have never found pleasure in doing harm or damage, in accusing others, or in tormenting poor dumb animals. I remember, however, that I once made water[10] in a saucepan belonging to one of our neighbors, Madame Clot, while she was at church. I declare that, even now, the recollection of this makes me laugh, because Madame Clot, a good woman in other respects, was the most confirmed old grumbler I have ever known. Such is the brief and true story of all my childish offenses.

How could I become wicked, when I had nothing but examples of gentleness before my eyes, and none around me but the best people in the world? My father, my aunt, my nurse, my relations, our friends, our neighbors, all who surrounded me, did not, it is true, obey me, but they loved me; and I loved them in return. My wishes were so little excited and so little opposed, that it did not occur to me to have any. I can swear that, until I served under a master, I never knew what a fancy was. Except during the time I spent in reading or writing in my father's company, or when my nurse took me for a walk, I was always with my aunt, sitting or standing by her side, watching her at her embroidery or listening to her singing; and I was content. Her cheerfulness, her gentleness and her pleasant face have stamped so deep and lively an impression on my mind that I can still see her manner, look, and attitude; I remember her affectionate language: I could describe what clothes she wore and how her head was dressed, not forgetting the two little curls of black hair on her temples, which she wore in accordance with the fashion of the time.

I am convinced that it is to her I owe the taste, or rather passion, for

[10] Urinated.

music, which only became fully developed in me a long time afterwards.
She knew a prodigious number of tunes and songs which she used to sing
in a very thin, gentle voice. This excellent woman's cheerfulness of soul
banished dreaminess and melancholy from herself and all around her. The
attraction which her singing possessed for me was so great that not only
have several of her songs always remained in my memory, but even now,
when I have lost her, and as I grew older, many of them, totally forgotten
since the days of my childhood, return to my mind with inexpressible
charm. Would anyone believe that I, an old dotard, eaten up by cares and
troubles, sometimes find myself weeping like a child, when I mumble one of
those little airs in a voice already broken and trembling? One of them,
especially, has come back to me completely, as far as the tune is concerned;
the second half of the words, however, has obstinately resisted all my ef-
forts to recall it, although I have an indistinct recollection of the rhymes.
Here is the beginning, and all that I can remember of the rest:

> Tircis, je n'ose
> Écouter ton chalumeau
> Sous l'ormeau:
> Car on en cause
> Déjà dans notre hameau.
>
> un berger
> s'engager
> sans danger
> Et toujours l'épine est sous la rose.[11]

I ask, where is the affecting charm which my heart finds in this song? it
is a whim, which I am quite unable to understand; but, be that as it may, it
is absolutely impossible for me to sing it through without being interrupted
by my tears. I have intended, times without number, to write to Paris to
make inquiries concerning the remainder of the words, in case anyone
should happen to know them; but I am almost certain that the pleasure
which I feel in recalling the air would partly disappear, if it should be
proved that others besides my poor aunt Susan have sung it.

Such were my earliest emotions on my entry into life; thus began to
form or display itself in me that heart at once so proud and tender, that
character so effeminate but yet indomitable, which, ever wavering between
timidity and courage, weakness and self-control, has throughout my life
made me inconsistent, and has caused abstinence and enjoyment, pleasure
and prudence equally to elude my grasp.

This course of education was interrupted by an accident, the conse-
quences of which have exercised an influence upon the remainder of my
life. My father had a quarrel with a captain in the French army, named
Gautier, who was connected with some of the members of the Common

[11] Including the words Rousseau could not remember, the song goes: "Tircis, I dare not
listen to your pipe under the elm; people are beginning to talk about it in the village. It is
dangerous for a heart to have too much to do with a shepherd; there is no rose without its
thorn."

Council. This Gautier, a cowardly and insolent fellow (whose nose happened to bleed during the affray), in order to avenge himself, accused my father of having drawn his sword within the city walls. My father, whom they wanted to send to prison, persisted that, in accordance with the law, the accuser ought to be imprisoned as well as himself. Being unable to have his way in this, he preferred to quit Geneva and expatriate himself for the rest of his life, than to give way on a point in which honor and liberty appeared to him to be compromised.

I remained under the care of my uncle Bernard, who was at the time employed upon the fortifications of Geneva. His eldest daughter was dead, but he had a son of the same age as myself. We were sent together to Bossey,[12] to board with the Protestant minister Lambercier, in order to learn, together with Latin, all the sorry trash which is included under the name of education.

Two years spent in the village in some degree softened my Roman roughness and made me a child again. At Geneva, where no tasks were imposed upon me, I loved reading and study, which were almost my only amusements; at Bossey, my tasks made me love the games which formed a break in them. The country was so new to me, that my enjoyment of it never palled. I conceived so lively an affection for it, that it has never since died out. The remembrance of the happy days I have spent there filled me with regretful longing for its pleasures, at all periods of my life, until the day which has brought me back to it. M. Lambercier was a very intelligent person, who, without neglecting our education, never imposed excessive tasks upon us. The fact that, in spite of my dislike of restraint, I have never recalled my hours of study with any feeling of disgust—and also that, even if I did not learn much from him, I learnt without difficulty what I did learn and never forgot it—is sufficient proof that his system of instruction was a good one.

The simplicity of this country life was of inestimable value to me, in that it opened my heart to friendship. Up to that time I had only known lofty but imaginary sentiments. The habit of living peacefully together with my cousin Bernard drew us together in tender bonds of union. In a short time, my feelings towards him became more affectionate than those with which I had regarded my brother, and they have never been effaced. He was a tall, lanky, weakly boy, as gentle in disposition as he was feeble in body, who never abused the preference which was shown to him in the house as the son of my guardian. Our tasks, our amusements, our tastes were the same: we were alone, we were of the same age, each of us needed a companion: separation was to us, in a manner, annihilation. Although we had few opportunities of proving our mutual attachment, it was very great; not only were we unable to live an instant apart, but we did not imagine it possible that we could ever be separated. Being, both of us, ready to yield to tenderness, and docile, provided compulsion was not used, we always agreed in everything. If, in the presence of those who looked after us, he had some advantage over me in consequence of the favor with which they regarded him, when we were alone I had an advantage over him which restored the equilibrium. When we were saying our lessons, I prompted him if he hesi-

[12] A village about three miles from Geneva.

tated; when I had finished my exercise, I helped him with his; and in our amusements, my more active mind always led the way. In short, our two characters harmonized so well, and the friendship which united us was so sincere, that, in the five years and more, during which, whether at Bossey or Geneva, we were almost inseparable, although I confess that we often fought, it was never necessary to separate us, none of our quarrels ever lasted longer than a quarter of an hour, and neither of us ever made any accusation against the other. These observations are, if you will, childish, but they furnish an example which, since the time that there have been children, is perhaps unique.

The life which I led at Bossey suited me so well that, had it only lasted longer, it would have completely decided my character. Tender, affectionate and gentle feelings formed its foundation. I believe that no individual of our species was naturally more free from vanity than myself. I raised myself by fits and starts to lofty flights, but immediately fell down again into my natural languor. My liveliest desire was to be loved by all who came near me. I was of a gentle disposition; my cousin and our guardians were the same. During two whole years I was neither the witness nor the victim of any violent feeling. Everything nourished in my heart those tendencies which it received from Nature. I knew no higher happiness than to see all the world satisfied with me and with everything. I shall never forget how, if I happened to hesitate when saying my catechism in church, nothing troubled me more than to observe signs of restlessness and dissatisfaction on Mademoiselle Lambercier's face. That alone troubled me more than the disgrace of failing in public, which, nevertheless, affected me greatly: for, although little susceptible to praise, I felt shame keenly; and I may say here that the thought of Mademoiselle's reproaches caused me less uneasiness than the fear of offending her.

When it was necessary, however, neither she nor her brother were wanting in severity; but, since this severity was nearly always just, and never passionate, it pained me without making me insubordinate. Failure to please grieved me more than punishment, and signs of dissatisfaction hurt me more than corporal chastisement. It is somewhat embarrassing to explain myself more clearly, but, nevertheless, I must do so. How differently would one deal with youth, if one could more clearly see the remote effects of the usual method of treatment, which is employed always without discrimination, frequently without discretion! The important lesson which may be drawn from an example as common as it is fatal makes me decide to mention it.

As Mademoiselle Lambercier had the affection of a mother for us, she also exercised the authority of one, and sometimes carried it so far as to inflict upon us the punishment of children when we had deserved it. For some time she was content with threats, and this threat of a punishment that was quite new to me appeared very terrible; but, after it had been carried out, I found the reality less terrible than the expectation; and, what was still more strange, this chastisement made me still more devoted to her who had inflicted it. It needed all the strength of this devotion and all my natural docility to keep myself from doing something which would have deservedly brought upon me a repetition of it; for I had found in the pain, even in the disgrace, a mixture of sensuality which had left me less afraid

than desirous of experiencing it again from the same hand. No doubt some precocious sexual instinct was mingled with this feeling, for the same chastisement inflicted by her brother would not have seemed to me at all pleasant. But, considering his disposition, there was little cause to fear the substitution; and if I kept myself from deserving punishment, it was solely for fear of displeasing Mademoiselle Lambercier; for, so great is the power exercised over me by kindness, even by that which is due to the senses, that it has always controlled the latter in my heart.

The repetition of the offense, which I avoided without being afraid of it, occurred without any fault of mine, that is to say, of my will, and I may say that I profited by it without any qualm of conscience. But this second time was also the last; for Mademoiselle Lambercier, who had no doubt noticed something which convinced her that the punishment did not have the desired effect, declared that it tired her too much, and that she would abandon it. Until then we had slept in her room, sometimes even in her bed during the winter. Two days afterwards we were put to sleep in another room, and from that time I had the honor, which I would gladly have dispensed with, of being treated by her as a big boy.

Who would believe that this childish punishment, inflicted upon me when only eight years old by a young woman of thirty,[13] disposed of my tastes, my desires, my passions, and my own self for the remainder of my life, and that in a manner exactly contrary to that which should have been the natural result? When my feelings were once inflamed, my desires so went astray that, limited to what I had already felt, they did not trouble themselves to look for anything else. In spite of my hot blood, which has been inflamed with sensuality almost from my birth, I kept myself free from every taint until the age when the coldest and most sluggish temperaments begin to develop. In torments for a long time, without knowing why, I devoured with burning glances all the pretty women I met; my imagination unceasingly recalled them to me, only to make use of them in my own fashion, and to make of them so many Mlles. Lambercier.

Even after I had reached years of maturity, this curious taste, always abiding with me and carried to depravity and even frenzy, preserved my morality, which it might naturally have been expected to destroy. If ever a bringing-up was chaste and modest, assuredly mine was. My three aunts were not only models of propriety, but reserved to a degree which has long since been unknown amongst women. My father, a man of pleasure, but a gallant of the old school, never said a word, even in the presence of women whom he loved more than others, which would have brought a blush to a maiden's cheek; and the respect due to children has never been so much insisted upon as in my family and in my presence. In this respect I found M. Lambercier equally careful; and an excellent servant was dismissed for having used a somewhat too free expression in our presence. Until I was a young man, I not only had no distinct idea of the union of the sexes, but the confused notion which I had regarding it never presented itself to me except in a hateful and disgusting form. For common prostitutes I felt a loathing which has never been effaced: the sight of a profligate always filled me with contempt, even with affright. My horror of debauchery

[13] Actually, at the time described, Mlle. Lambercier was about 38 and Rousseau about 11.

became thus pronounced ever since the day when, walking to Little Sacconex[14] by a hollow way, I saw on both sides holes in the ground, where I was told that these creatures carried on their intercourse. The thought of the one always brought back to my mind the copulation of dogs, and the bare recollection was sufficient to disgust me.

This tendency of my bringing-up, in itself adapted to delay the first outbreaks of an inflammable temperament, was assisted, as I have already said, by the direction which the first indications of sensuality took in my case. Only busying my imagination with what I had actually felt, in spite of most uncomfortable effervescence of blood, I only knew how to turn my desires in the direction of that kind of pleasure with which I was acquainted, without ever going as far as that which had been made hateful to me, and which, without my having the least suspicion of it, was so closely related to the other. In my foolish fancies, in my erotic frenzies, in the extravagant acts to which they sometimes led me, I had recourse in my imagination to the assistance of the other sex, without ever thinking that it was serviceable for any purpose than that for which I was burning to make use of it.

In this manner, then, in spite of an ardent, lascivious and precocious temperament, I passed the age of puberty without desiring, even without knowing of any other sensual pleasures than those of which Mademoiselle Lambercier had most innocently given me the idea; and when, in course of time, I became a man, that which should have destroyed me again preserved me. My old childish taste, instead of disappearing, became so associated with the other, that I could never banish it from the desires kindled by my senses; and this madness, joined to my natural shyness, has always made me very unenterprising with women, for want of courage to say all or power to do all. The kind of enjoyment, of which the other was only for me the final consummation, could neither be appropriated by him who longed for it, nor guessed by her who was able to bestow it. Thus I have spent my life in idle longing, without saying a word, in the presence of those whom I loved most. Too bashful to declare my taste, I at least satisfied it in situations which had reference to it and kept up the idea of it. To lie at the feet of an imperious mistress, to obey her commands, to ask her forgiveness— this was for me a sweet enjoyment; and, the more my lively imagination heated my blood, the more I presented the appearance of a bashful lover. It may be easily imagined that this manner of making love does not lead to very speedy results, and is not very dangerous to the virtue of those who are its object. For this reason I have rarely possessed, but have none the less enjoyed myself in my own way—that is to say, in imagination. Thus it has happened that my senses, in harmony with my timid disposition and my romantic spirit, have kept my sentiments pure and my morals blameless, owing to the very tastes which, combined with a little more impudence, might have plunged me into the most brutal sensuality.

I have taken the first and most difficult step in the dark and dirty labyrinth of my confessions. It is easier to admit that which is criminal than that which is ridiculous and makes a man feel ashamed. Henceforth I am sure of myself; after having ventured to say so much, I can shrink from noth-

[14] A village on the outskirts of Geneva.

ing. One may judge what such confessions have cost me, from the fact that, during the whole course of my life, I have never dared to declare my folly to those whom I loved with the frenzy of a passion which deprived me of sight and hearing, which robbed me of my senses and caused me to tremble all over with a convulsive movement. I have never brought myself, even when on most intimate terms, to ask women to grant me the only favor of all which was wanting. This never happened to me but once—in my childhood, with a girl of my own age;[15] even then, it was she who first proposed it.

While thus going back to the first traces of my inner life, I find elements which sometimes appear incompatible, and yet have united in order to produce with vigor a simple and uniform effect; and I find others which, although apparently the same, have formed combinations so different, owing to the co-operation of certain circumstances, that one would never imagine that these elements were in any way connected. Who, for instance, would believe that one of the most powerful movements of my soul was tempered in the same spring from which a stream of sensuality and effeminacy has entered my blood? Without leaving the subject of which I have just spoken, I shall produce by means of it a very different impression.

One day I was learning my lesson by myself in the room next to the kitchen. The servant had put Mademoiselle Lambercier's combs in front of the fire-place to dry. When she came back to fetch them, she found one with a whole row of teeth broken. Who was to blame for the damage? No one except myself had entered the room. On being questioned, I denied that I had touched the comb. M. and Mademoiselle Lambercier both began to admonish, to press, and to threaten me; I obstinately persisted in my denial; but the evidence was too strong, and outweighed all my protestations, although it was the first time that I had been found to lie so boldly. The matter was regarded as serious, as in fact it deserved to be. The mischievousness, the falsehood, the obstinacy appeared equally deserving of punishment; but this time it was not by Mademoiselle Lambercier that chastisement was inflicted. My uncle Bernard was written to, and he came. My poor cousin was accused of another equally grave offense; we were involved in the same punishment. It was terrible. Had they wished to look for the remedy in the evil itself and to deaden for ever my depraved senses, they could not have set to work better, and for a long time my senses left me undisturbed.

They could not draw from me the desired confession. Although I was several times brought up before them and reduced to a pitiable condition, I remained unshaken. I would have endured death, and made up my mind to do so. Force was obliged to yield to the diabolical obstinacy of a child—as they called my firmness. At last I emerged from this cruel trial, utterly broken, but triumphant.

It is now nearly fifty years since this incident took place, and I have no fear of being punished again for the same thing. Well, then, I declare in the sight of heaven that I was innocent of the offense, that I neither broke nor touched the comb, that I never went near the fire-place, and had never

[15] A Mlle. Goton, described later in Book I.

even thought of doing so. It would be useless to ask me how the damage was done: I do not know, and I cannot understand; all that I know for certain is that I had nothing to do with it.

Imagine a child, shy and obedient in ordinary life, but fiery, proud, and unruly in his passions: a child who had always been led by the voice of reason and always treated with gentleness, justice, and consideration, who had not even a notion of injustice, and who for the first time becomes acquainted with so terrible an example of it on the part of the very people whom he most loves and respects! What an upset of ideas! what a disturbance of feelings! what revolution in his heart, in his brain, in the whole of his little intellectual and moral being! Imagine all this, I say, if possible. As for myself, I feel incapable of disentangling and following up the least trace of what then took place within me.

I had not yet sense enough to feel how much appearances were against me, and to put myself in the place of the others. I kept to my own place, and all that I felt was the harshness of a frightful punishment for an offense which I had not committed. The bodily pain, although severe, I felt but little: all I felt was indignation, rage, despair. My cousin, whose case was almost the same, and who had been punished for an involuntary mistake as if it had been a premeditated act, following my example, flew into a rage, and worked himself up to the same pitch of excitement as myself. Both in the same bed, we embraced each other with convulsive transports: we felt suffocated; and when at length our young hearts, somewhat relieved, were able to vent their wrath, we sat upright in bed and began to shout, times without number, with all our might: *Carnifex! carnifex! carnifex!* [16]

While I write these words, I feel that my pulse beats faster; those moments will always be present to me though I should live a hundred thousand years. That first feeling of violence and injustice has remained so deeply graven on my soul, that all the ideas connected with it bring back to me my first emotion; and this feeling, which, in its origin, had reference only to myself, has become so strong in itself and so completely detached from all personal interest, that, when I see or hear of any act of injustice— whoever is the victim of it, and wherever it is committed—my heart kindles with rage, as if the effect of it recoiled upon myself. When I read of the cruelties of a ferocious tyrant, the crafty atrocities of a rascally priest, I would gladly set out to plunge a dagger into the heart of such wretches, although I had to die for it a hundred times. I have often put myself in a perspiration, pursuing or stoning a cock, a cow, a dog, or any animal which I saw tormenting another merely because it felt itself the stronger. This impulse may be natural to me, and I believe that it is; but the profound impression left upon me by the first injustice I suffered was too long and too strongly connected with it, not to have greatly strengthened it.

With the above incident the tranquillity of my childish life was over. From that moment I ceased to enjoy a pure happiness, and even at the present day I feel that the recollection of the charms of my childhood ceases there. We remained a few months longer at Bossey. We were there, as the first man is represented to us—still in the earthly paradise, but we no

[16] Executioner; tormentor (Latin).

longer enjoyed it; in appearance our condition was the same, in reality it was quite a different manner of existence. Attachment, respect, intimacy, and confidence no longer united pupils and guides: we no longer regarded them as gods, who were able to read in our hearts; we became less ashamed of doing wrong and more afraid of being accused; we began to dissemble, to be insubordinate, to lie. All the vices of our age corrupted our innocence and threw a veil of ugliness over our amusements. Even the country lost in our eyes that charm of gentleness and simplicity which goes to the heart. It appeared to us lonely and somber: it seemed as it were covered with a veil which concealed its beauties from our eyes. We ceased to cultivate our little gardens, our plants, our flowers. We no longer scratched up the ground gently, or cried with joy when we saw the seed which we had sown beginning to sprout. We were disgusted with the life, and others were disgusted with us; my uncle took us away, and we separated from M. and Mademoiselle Lambercier, having had enough of each other, and feeling but little regret at the separation.

Nearly thirty years have passed since I left Bossey, without my recalling to mind my stay there with any connected and pleasurable recollections; but, now that I have passed the prime of life and am approaching old age, I feel these same recollections springing up again while others disappear; they stamp themselves upon my memory with features, the charm and strength of which increase daily, as if, feeling life already slipping away, I were endeavoring to grasp it again by its commencement. The most trifling incidents of that time please me, simply because they belong to that period. I remember all the details of place, persons, and time. I see the maid or the manservant busy in the room, a swallow darting through the window, a fly settling on my hand while I was saying my lesson: I see the whole arrangement of the room in which we used to live; M. Lambercier's study on the right, a copperplate engraving of all the Popes, a barometer, a large almanac hanging on the wall, the raspberry bushes which, growing in a garden situated on very high ground facing the back of the house, shaded the window and sometimes forced their way through it. I am quite aware that the reader does not want to know all this; but I am bound to tell him. Why have I not the courage to relate to him in like manner all the trifling anecdotes of that happy time, which still make me tremble with joy when I recall them? Five or six in particular—but let us make a bargain. I will let you off five, but I wish to tell you one, only one, provided that you will permit me to tell it in as much detail as possible, in order to prolong my enjoyment.

If I only had your pleasure in view, I might choose the story of Mademoiselle Lambercier's backside, which, owing to an unfortunate somersault at the bottom of the meadow, was exhibited in full view to the King of Sardinia, who happened to be passing by;[17] but that of the walnut-tree on the terrace is more amusing for me who took an active part in it, whereas I was merely a spectator of the somersault; besides, I declare that I found absolutely nothing to laugh at in an accident which, although comic in itself, alarmed me for the safety of a person whom I loved as a mother and, perhaps, even more.

[17] This royal procession passed through in August 1724.

Now, O curious readers of the important history of the walnut-tree on the terrace, listen to the horrible tragedy, and keep from shuddering if you can!

Outside the gate of the court, on the left of the entrance, there was a terrace, where we often went to sit in the afternoon. As it was entirely unprotected from the sun, M. Lambercier had a walnut-tree planted there. The process of planting was carried out with the greatest solemnity. The two boarders were its godfathers; and, while the hole was being filled up, we each of us held the tree with one hand and sang songs of triumph. In order to water it, a kind of basin was made round the foot. Every day, eager spectators of this watering, my cousin and I became more strongly convinced, as was natural, that it was a finer thing to plant a tree on a terrace than a flag upon a breach, and we resolved to win this glory for ourselves without sharing it with anyone.

With this object, we proceeded to cut a slip from a young willow, and planted it on the terrace, at a distance of about eight or ten feet from the august walnut-tree. We did not forget to dig a similar trench round our tree; the difficulty was how to fill it, for the water came from some distance, and we were not allowed to run and fetch it. However, it was absolutely necessary to have some for our willow. For a few days, we had recourse to all kinds of devices to get some, and we succeeded so well that we saw it bud and put forth little leaves, the growth of which we measured every hour, convinced that, although not yet a foot high, it would soon afford us a shade.

As our tree so completely claimed our attention that we were quite incapable of attending to or learning anything else, and were in a sort of delirium: as our guardians, not knowing what was the matter with us, kept a tighter hand upon us, we saw the fatal moment approaching when we should be without water, and were inconsolable at the thought of seeing our tree perish from drought. At length necessity, the mother of invention, suggested to us how to save ourselves from grief and the tree from certain death; this was, to make a channel underground, which should secretly conduct part of the water intended for the walnut-tree to our willow. This undertaking was at first unsuccessful, in spite of the eagerness with which it was carried out. We had made the incline so clumsily that the water did not run at all. The earth fell in and stopped up the channel; the entrance was filled with mud; everything went wrong. But nothing disheartened us: *Labor omnia vincit improbus.*[18] We dug our basin deeper, in order to allow the water to run; we cut some bottoms of boxes into small narrow planks, some of which were laid flat, one after the other, and others set up on both sides of these at an angle, thus forming a triangular canal for our conduit. At the entrance we stuck small pieces of wood, some little distance apart, which, forming a kind of grating or lattice-work, kept back the mud and stones, without stopping the passage of the water. We carefully covered our work with well-trodden earth; and when all was ready, we awaited, in the greatest excitement of hope and fear, the time of watering. After centuries of waiting, the hour at length arrived; M. Lambercier came as usual to assist at

[18]"Tenacious work overcomes all obstacles" (from Virgil's *Georgics*, I. 145–146).

the operation, during which we both kept behind him, in order to conceal our tree, to which very luckily he turned his back.

No sooner had the first pail of water been poured out, than we saw some of it running into our basin. At this sight, our prudence deserted us: we began to utter cries of joy which made M. Lambercier turn round; this was a pity, for he took great delight in seeing how good the soil of the walnut-tree was, and how greedily it absorbed the water. Astonished at seeing it distribute itself into two basins, he cried out in his turn, looked, perceived the trick, ordered a pickaxe to be brought, and, with one blow, broke off two or three pieces from our planks; then, crying loudly, "An aqueduct, an aqueduct!" he dealt merciless blows in every direction, each of which went straight to our hearts. In a moment planks, conduit, basin, willow, everything was destroyed and uprooted, without his having uttered a single word, during this terrible work of destruction, except the exclamation which he incessantly repeated. "An aqueduct!" he cried, while demolishing everything, "an aqueduct, an aqueduct!"

It will naturally be imagined that the adventure turned out badly for the little architects: that would be a mistake: it was all over. M. Lambercier never uttered a single word of reproach, or looked upon us with displeasure, and said nothing more about it; shortly afterwards, we even heard him laughing loudly with his sister, for his laughter could be heard a long way off; and what was still more astonishing, when the first fright was over, we ourselves were not much troubled about the matter. We planted another tree somewhere else, and often reminded ourselves of the disaster that overtook the first, by repeating with emphasis, "An aqueduct, an aqueduct!" Hitherto I had had intermittent attacks of pride, when I was Aristides or Brutus;[19] then it was that I felt the first well-defined promptings of vanity. To have been able to construct an aqueduct with our own hands, to have put a cutting in competition with a large tree, appeared to me the height of glory. At ten years of age I was a better judge on this point than Caesar at thirty.

The thought of this walnut-tree and the little history connected with it has remained so vivid in my memory, or returned to it, that one of the plans which gave me the greatest pleasure, on my journey to Geneva, in 1754, was to go to Bossey and revisit the memorials of my boyish amusements, above all, the dear walnut-tree, which by that time must have been a third of a century old; but I was so continually occupied, so little my own master, that I could never find the moment to afford myself this satisfaction. There is little prospect of the opportunity ever occurring again; yet the wish has not disappeared with the hope; and I am almost certain that, if ever I should return to those beloved spots and find my dear walnut-tree still alive, I should water it with my tears.

After my return to Geneva, I lived for two or three years[20] with my uncle, waiting until my friends had decided what was to be done with me. As he intended his own son to be an engineer, he made him learn a little drawing and taught him the elements of Euclid.[21] I learned these subjects

[19] Ancient heroes, mentioned earlier, whom Rousseau had read about in Plutarch.
[20] Actually, this period lasted only about eight months.
[21] Greek author, third century B.C., of the ancient classic on geometry.

together with him, and acquired a taste for them, especially for drawing. In the meantime, it was debated whether I should be a watchmaker, an attorney, or a minister. My own preference was for the last, for preaching seemed to me to be a very fine thing; but the small income from my mother's property, which had to be divided between my brother and myself, was not sufficient to allow me to prosecute my studies. As, considering my age at that time, there was no immediate need to decide, I remained for the present with my uncle, making little use of my time and, in addition, as was only fair, paying a tolerably large sum for my board. My uncle, a man of pleasure like my father, was unable, like him, to tie himself down to his duties, and troubled himself little enough about us. My aunt was somewhat of a pietist, and preferred to sing psalms rather than attend to our education. We were allowed almost absolute freedom, which we never abused. Always inseparable, we were quite contented with our own society; and, having no temptation to make companions of the street boys of our own age, we learned none of the dissolute habits into which idleness might have led us. I am even wrong in saying that we were idle, for we were never less so in our lives; and the most fortunate thing was that all the ways of amusing ourselves, with which we successively became infatuated, kept us together busy in the house, without our being even tempted to go out into the street. We made cages, flutes, shuttlecocks, drums, houses, squirts,[22] and cross-bows. We spoilt my good old grandfather's tools in trying to make watches as he did. We had a special taste for wasting paper, drawing, painting in water-colors, illuminating, and spoiling colors. An Italian showman, named Gamba-Corta, came to Geneva; we went to see him once and never wanted to go again. But he had a marionette-show, and we proceeded to make marionettes; his marionettes played comedies and we composed comedies for ours. For want of a squeaker, we imitated Punch's[23] voice in our throat, in order to play the charming comedies, which our poor and kind relations had the patience to sit and listen to. But, my uncle Bernard having one day read aloud in the family circle a very fine sermon which he had composed himself, we abandoned comedy and began to write sermons. These details are not very interesting, I confess, but they show how exceedingly well-conducted our early education must have been, seeing that we, almost masters of our time and ourselves at so tender an age, were so little tempted to abuse our opportunities. We had so little need of making companions, that we even neglected the chances of doing so. When we went for a walk, we looked at their amusements as we passed by without the slightest desire, or even the idea of taking part in them. Our friendship so completely filled our hearts, that it was enough for us to be together to make the simplest amusements a delight.

Being thus inseparable, we began to attract attention: the more so as, my cousin being very tall while I was very short, we made an oddly-assorted couple. His long, slim figure, his little face like a boiled apple, his gentle manner, and his slovenly walk excited the children's ridicule. In the *patois*[24]

[22] Toy pistols.
[23] Punch and Judy are characters in an old tradition of slapstick puppet shows; they make raucous sounds but don't utter words.
[24] Dialect; slang (French).

of the district he was nicknamed Barna Bredanna,[25] and, directly we went out, we heard nothing but "Barna Bredanna!" all round us. He endured it more quietly than I did: I lost my temper and wanted to fight. This was just what the little rascals desired. I fought and was beaten. My poor cousin helped me as well as he could; but he was weak, and a single blow of the fist knocked him down. Then I became furious. However, although I received blows in abundance, I was not the real object of attack, but Barna Bredanna; but my obstinate anger made matters so much worse, that, in future, we only ventured to go out during school-hours, for fear of being hooted and followed.

Behold me already a redresser of wrongs! In order to be a regular Paladin[26] I only wanted a lady; I had two. From time to time I went to see my father at Nyon, a little town in the Vaud[27] country, where he had settled. He was very much liked, and his son felt the effects of his popularity. During the short time I stayed with him, friends vied with each other in making me welcome. A certain Madame de Vulson, especially, bestowed a thousand caresses upon me, and, to crown all, her daughter took me for her lover. It is easy to understand the meaning of a lover eleven years old[28] for a girl of twenty-two. But all these roguish young women are so ready to put little puppets in front in order to hide larger ones, or to tempt them with the idea of an amusement which they know how to render attractive! As for myself, I saw no incongruity between us and took the matter seriously; I abandoned myself with all my heart, or rather with all my head— for it was only in that part of me that I was in love, although madly—and my transports, excitement and frenzy produced scenes enough to make anyone split his sides with laughing.

I am acquainted with two very distinct and very real kinds of love, which have scarcely anything in common, although both are very fervent, and which both differ from tender friendship. The whole course of my life has been divided between these two kinds of love, essentially so different, and I have even felt them both at the same time; for instance, at the time of which I am speaking, while I took possession of Mademoiselle de Vulson so openly and so tyrannically that I could not endure that any man should approach her, I had several meetings, brief but lively, with a certain little Mademoiselle Goton, in which she deigned to play the schoolmistress,[29] and that was all; but this all, which was really all for me, seemed to me the height of happiness; and, already feeling the value of the mystery, although I only knew how to make use of it as a child, I paid Mademoiselle de Vulson, who had scarcely any suspicion of it, in the same coin for the assiduity with which she made use of me to conceal other amours. But, to my great regret, my secret was discovered, or not so well kept on the part of my little schoolmistress as on my own; we were soon separated; and, some time

[25] A regional term equivalent to "bridled or saddled donkey," or "ignorant lout."
[26] A hero of chivalry (originally, one of Charlemagne's twelve nobles, as in *The Song of Roland*).
[27] A region of western Switzerland northeast of Geneva.
[28] To be exact, Rousseau was 12 at the time.
[29] That is, spank him. This is the "girl of my own age" mentioned earlier as having performed this service for Rousseau.

afterwards, on my return to Geneva, while passing through Coutance, I heard some little girls cry, in an undertone, "Goton tic-tac[30] Rousseau!"

This little Mademoiselle Goton was really a singular person. Without being pretty, she had a face which was not easy to forget, and which I still recall to mind, often too tenderly for an old fool. Neither her form, nor her manner, nor, above all, her eyes were in keeping with her age. She had a proud and commanding air, which suited her part admirably, and which in fact had suggested the first idea of it to us. But the oddest thing about her was a mixture of impudence and reserve which it was difficult to comprehend. She took the greatest liberties with me, but never allowed me to take any with her. She treated me just like a child, which makes me believe, either that she was no longer one herself, or that, on the contrary, she was still childish enough to see nothing but an amusement in the danger to which she exposed herself.

I belonged entirely, so to say, to each of these two persons, and so completely, that, when I was with one, I never thought of the other. In other respects, there was not the slightest similarity between the feelings with which they inspired me. I could have spent all my life with Mademoiselle de Vulson, without ever thinking of leaving her; but, when I approached her, my joy was tranquil and free from emotion. I loved her above all in fashionable society; the witty sallies, railleries, and even the petty jealousies attracted and interested me; I felt a pride and glory in the marks of preference she bestowed upon me in the presence of grown-up rivals whom she appeared to treat with disdain. I was tormented, but I loved the torment. The applause, encouragement, and laughter warmed and inspirited me. I had fits of passion and broke out into audacious sallies. In society, I was transported with love; in a *tête-à-tête*[31] I should have been constrained, cold, perhaps wearied. However, I felt a real tenderness for her; I suffered when she was ill; I would have given my own health to restore her own, and, observe! I knew very well from experience the meaning of illness and health. When absent from her, I thought of her and missed her; when I was by her side, her caresses reached my heart—not my senses. I was intimate with her with impunity; my imagination demanded no more than she granted; yet I could not have endured to see her do even as much for others. I loved her as a brother, but I was as jealous of her as a lover.

I should have been as jealous of Mademoiselle Goton as a Turk, a madman, or a tiger, if I had once imagined that she could accord the same treatment to another as to myself; for even that was a favor which I had to ask on my knees. I approached Mademoiselle de Vulson with lively pleasure, but without emotion; whereas, if I only saw Mademoiselle Goton, I saw nothing else, all my senses were bewildered. With the former I was familiar without familiarity; while on the contrary, in the presence of the latter, I was as bashful as I was excited, even in the midst of our greatest familiarities. I believe that, if I had remained with her long, I should have died; the throbbings of my heart would have suffocated me. I was equally

[30] Either "has come to blows with" or "is in love with." Coutance is a neighborhood in Geneva where Rousseau's family lived after 1718.
[31] Private conversation.

afraid of displeasing either; but I was more attentive to the one and more obedient to the other. Nothing in the world would have made me annoy Mademoiselle de Vulson; but if Mademoiselle Goton had ordered me to throw myself into the flames, I believe I should have obeyed her immediately.

My amour, or rather my meetings, with the latter, continued only for a short time—happily for both of us. Although my relations with Mademoiselle de Vulson had not the same danger, they were not without their catastrophe, after they had lasted a little longer. The end of all such connections should always be somewhat romantic, and furnish occasion for exclamations of sorrow. Although my connection with Mademoiselle de Vulson was less lively, it was perhaps closer. We never separated without tears, and it is remarkable into what an overwhelming void I felt myself plunged as soon as I had left her. I could speak and think of nothing but her; my regret was genuine and lively; but I believe that, at bottom, this heroic regret was not felt altogether for her, and that, without my perceiving it, the amusements, of which she was the center, played their part in it. To moderate the pangs of absence, we wrote letters to each other, pathetic enough to melt the heart of a stone. At last I triumphed; she could endure it no longer, and came to Geneva to see me. This time my head was completely turned; I was drunk and mad during the two days she remained. When she left I wanted to throw myself in the water after her, and the air resounded with my screams. Eight days afterwards she sent me some bonbons and gloves, which I should have considered a great compliment, if I had not learnt at the same time that she was married, and that the visit with which she had been pleased to honor me was really made in order to buy her weddingdress. I will not attempt to describe my fury; it may be imagined. In my noble rage I swore that I would never see the faithless one again, being unable to imagine a more terrible punishment for her. She did not, however, die of it; for, twenty years afterwards, when on a visit to my father, while rowing with him on the lake, I asked who the ladies were whom I saw in a boat not far from ours. "What!" said my father with a smile, "does not your heart tell you? it is your old love, Mademoiselle de Vulson that was, now Madame Cristin." I started at the almost forgotten name, but I told the boatmen to change their course. Although I had a fine opportunity of avenging myself at that moment, I did not think it worth while to perjure myself and to renew a quarrel, twenty years old, with a woman of forty.

[1723–1728.]—Thus the most valuable time of my boyhood was wasted in follies, before my future career had been decided upon. After long deliberation as to the bent of my natural inclination, a profession was determined upon for which I had the least taste; I was put with M. Masseron, the town clerk, in order to learn, under his tuition, the useful trade of a *fee-grabber*.[32] This nickname was extremely distasteful to me; the hope of gaining a number of crowns in a somewhat sordid business by no means flattered my pride; the occupation itself appeared to me wearisome and unendurable; the constant application, the feeling of servitude completed my dislike, and I never entered the office without a feeling of horror, which

[32] Disparaging term for "lawyer."

daily increased in intensity. M. Masseron, on his part, was ill-satisfied with me, and treated me with contempt; he continually reproached me with my dullness and stupidity, dinning into my ears every day that my uncle had told him that I knew something, whereas, in reality, I knew nothing; that he had promised him a sharp lad, and had given him a jackass. At last I was dismissed from the office in disgrace as being utterly incapable, and M. Masseron's clerks declared that I was good for nothing except to handle a file.

My calling being thus settled, I was apprenticed, not, however, to a watchmaker, but to an engraver. The contempt with which I had been treated by M. Masseron had made me very humble, and I obeyed without a murmur. My new master, M. Ducommun, was a rough and violent young man, who in a short time succeeded in tarnishing all the brightness of my childhood, stupefying my loving and lively nature, and reducing me, in mind as well as in position, to a real state of apprenticeship. My Latin, my antiquities, my history, were all for a long time forgotten; I did not even remember that there had ever been any Romans in the world. My father, when I went to see him, no longer found in me his idol; for the ladies I was no longer the gallant Jean Jacques; and I felt so certain myself that the Lamberciers would not have recognised their pupil in me, that I was ashamed to pay them a visit, and have never seen them since. The vilest tastes, the lowest street-blackguardism took the place of my simple amusements and effaced even the remembrance of them. I must, in spite of a most upright training, have had a great propensity to degenerate; for the change took place with great rapidity, without the least trouble, and never did so precocious a Caesar so rapidly become a Laridon.[33]

The trade in itself was not disagreeable to me; I had a decided taste for drawing; the handling of a graving-tool amused me; and as the claims upon the skill of a watchmaker's engraver were limited, I hoped to attain perfection. I should, perhaps, have done so, had not my master's brutality and excessive restraint disgusted me with my work. I stole some of my working hours to devote to similar occupations, but which had for me the charm of freedom. I engraved medals for an order of knighthood for myself and my companions. My master surprised me at this contraband occupation, and gave me a sound thrashing, declaring that I was training for a coiner, because our medals bore the arms of the Republic. I can swear that I had no idea at all of bad, and only a very faint one of good, money. I knew better how the Roman *As*[34] was made than our three-sou pieces.

My master's tyranny at length made the work, of which I should have been very fond, altogether unbearable, and filled me with vices which I should otherwise have hated, such as lying, idleness and thieving. The recollection of the alteration produced in me by that period of my life has taught me, better than anything else, the difference between filial dependence and abject servitude. Naturally shy and timid, no fault was more foreign to my disposition than impudence; but I had enjoyed an honorable liberty, which hitherto had only been gradually restrained, and at length disappeared altogether. I was bold with my father, unrestrained with

[33] In one of La Fontaine's fables, a name for degenerate dogs.
[34] A Roman unit of weight and money.

M. Lambercier, and modest with my uncle; I became timid with my master, and from that moment I was a lost child. Accustomed to perfect equality in my intercourse with my superiors, knowing no pleasure which was not within my reach, seeing no dish of which I could not have a share, having no desire which I could not have openly expressed, and carrying my heart upon my lips—it is easy to judge what I was bound to become, in a house in which I did not venture to open my mouth, where I was obliged to leave the table before the meal was half over, and the room as soon as I had nothing more to do there; where, incessantly fettered to my work, I saw only objects of enjoyment for others and of privation for myself; where the sight of the liberty enjoyed by my master and companions increased the weight of my servitude; where, in disputes about matters as to which I was best informed, I did not venture to open my mouth; where, in short, everything that I saw became for my heart an object of longing, simply because I was deprived of all. From that time my ease of manner, my gaiety, the happy expressions which, in former times, when I had done something wrong, had gained me immunity from punishment—all were gone. I cannot help laughing when I remember how, one evening, at my father's house, having been sent to bed without any supper for some piece of roguery, I passed through the kitchen with my melancholy piece of bread, and, seeing the joint turning on the spit, sniffed at it. All the household was standing round the hearth, and, in passing, I was obliged to say good-night to everybody. When I had gone the round, I winked at the joint, which looked so nice and smelt so good, and could not help bowing to it as well, and saying in a mournful voice, "Good-night, roast beef!" This naïve sally amused them so much that they made me stop to supper. Perhaps it might have had the same effect with my master, but I am sure that it would never have occurred to me, and that I should not have had the courage to say it in his presence.

In this manner I learnt to covet in silence, to dissemble, to lie, and, lastly, to steal—an idea which, up to that time, had never even entered my mind, and of which since then I have never been able to cure myself completely. Covetousness and weakness always lead in that direction. This explains why all servants are rogues, and why all apprentices ought to be; but the latter, in a peaceful state of equality, where all that they see is within their reach, lose, as they grow up, this disgraceful propensity. Not having had the same advantages, I have not been able to reap the same benefits.

It is nearly always good, but badly-directed principles, that make a child take the first step towards evil. In spite of continual privations and temptations, I had been more than a year with my master without being able to make up my mind to take anything, even eatables. My first theft was a matter of obliging some one else, but it opened the door to others, the motive of which was not so praiseworthy.

My master had a journeyman,[35] named M. Verrat, whose house was in the neighborhood, and had a garden some way off which produced very fine asparagus. M. Verrat, who was not too well supplied with money, conceived the idea of stealing some of his mother's young asparagus and sell-

[35] A person who has completed his apprenticeship but is not yet an independent master craftsman.

ing it in order to provide himself with two or three good breakfasts. As he was unwilling to run the risk himself, and was not very active, he selected me for the expedition. After some preliminary cajoleries, which the more easily succeeded with me as I did not see their aim, he proposed it to me as an idea that had struck him on the spur of the moment. I strongly opposed it; he persisted. I have never been able to resist flattery: I gave in. I went every morning to gather a crop of the finest asparagus, and carried it to the Molard, where some good woman, who saw that I had just stolen it, told me so to my face in order to get it cheaper. In my fright I took whatever she chose to offer me, and took it to Verrat. The amount was immediately converted into a breakfast, of which I was the purveyor, and which he shared with another companion; I myself was quite satisfied with a few scraps, and never even touched their wine.

This little arrangement continued several days, without its even occurring to me to rob the robber, and to levy my tithe[36] of the proceeds of M. Verrat's asparagus. I performed my part in the transaction with the greatest loyalty; my only motive was to please him who prompted me to carry it out. And yet, if I had been caught, what blows, abuse, and cruel treatment should I have had to endure, while the wretch, who would have been sure to give me the lie, would have been believed on his word, and I should have suffered double punishment for having had the impudence to accuse him, seeing that he was a journeyman, while I was only an apprentice! So true it is that, in every condition of life, the strong man who is guilty saves himself at the expense of the innocent who is weak.

In this manner I learned that stealing was not so terrible a thing as I had imagined, and I soon knew how to make such good use of my discovery, that nothing I desired, if it was within my reach, was safe from me. I was not absolutely ill-fed, and abstinence was only rendered difficult to me from seeing that my master observed it so ill himself. The custom of sending young people from the table when the most appetizing dishes are brought on appears to me admirably adapted to make them gluttons as well as thieves. In a short time I became both the one and the other; and, as a rule, I came off very well; occasionally, when I was caught, very badly.

I shudder, and at the same time laugh, when I remember an apple hunt which cost me dear. These apples were at the bottom of a store-room, which was lighted from the kitchen by means of a high grating. One day, when I was alone in the house, I climbed upon the kneading-trough, in order to look at the precious fruit in the garden of the Hesperides,[37] which was out of my reach. I went to fetch the spit[38] to see if I could touch the apples; it was too short. To make it longer, I tied on to it another little spit which was used for small game, for my master was very fond of sport. I thrust several times without success; at last, to my great delight, I felt that I had secured an apple. I pulled very gently; the apple was close to the grating; I was ready to catch hold of it. But who can describe my grief,

[36] Small share (literally, one-tenth of one's goods contributed to the church).

[37] In Greek myth, nymphs who, along with a dragon, guarded a tree with golden apples in the western Isles of the Blest.

[38] A sharpened rod or stick used to support meat cooked over a fire.

when I found that it was too large to pass through the bars? How many expedients I tried, to get it through! I had to find supports to keep the spit in its place, a knife long enough to divide the apple, a lath to hold it up. At last I managed to divide it, and hoped to be able to pull the pieces towards me one after the other; but no sooner were they separated than they both fell into the store-room. Compassionate reader, share my affliction!

I by no means lost courage; but I had lost considerable time. I was afraid of being surprised. I put off a more lucky attempt till the following day, and returned to my work as quietly as if I had done nothing, without thinking of the two tell-tale witnesses in the store-room.

The next day, finding the opportunity favorable, I made a fresh attempt. I climbed upon my stool, lengthened the spit, adjusted it, and was ready to make a lunge. . . . but, unfortunately, the dragon was not asleep; all at once the door of the store-room opened, my master came out, folded his arms, looked at me, and said, "Courage!". . . . the pen falls from my hand.

In consequence of continuous ill-treatment I soon became less sensitive to it, and regarded it as a kind of compensation for theft, which gave me the right to continue the latter. Instead of looking back and considering the punishment, I looked forward and thought of revenge. I considered that, if I were beaten as a rogue, I was entitled to behave like one. I found that stealing and a flogging went together, and constituted a sort of bargain, and that, if I performed my part, I could safely leave my master to carry out his own. With this idea, I began to steal more quietly than before. I said to myself: "What will be the result? I shall be flogged. Never mind; I am made to be flogged."

I am fond of eating, but am not greedy; I am sensual, but not a gourmand;[39] too many other tastes prevent that. I have never troubled myself about my food except when my heart has been unoccupied: and that has so seldom been the case during my life that I have scarcely had time to think about dainties. For this reason I did not long confine my thievish propensities to eatables, but soon extended them to everything which tempted me; and, if I did not become a regular thief, it was because I have never been much tempted by money. Leading out of the common workshop was a private room belonging to my master, the door of which I found means to open and shut without being noticed. There I laid under contribution his best tools, drawings, proofs—in fact, everything which attracted me and which he purposely kept out of my reach. At bottom, these thefts were quite innocent, being only committed to serve him; but I was transported with joy at having these trifles in my power; I thought that I was robbing him of his talent together with its productions. Besides, I found boxes containing gold and silver filings, little trinkets, valuables and coins. When I had four or five sous[40] in my pocket, I thought I was rich; and yet, far from touching anything of what I found there, I do not even remember that I ever cast longing eyes upon it. I looked upon it with more affright than pleasure. I believe that this horror of stealing money and valuables was in great part the result of my bringing-up. With it were combined secret thoughts of disgrace, prison, punishment and the gallows,

[39] A person passionately fond of eating. [40] Coins of very small value.

which would have made me shudder if I had been tempted; whereas my tricks only appeared to me in the light of pieces of mischief, and in fact were nothing else. They could lead to nothing but a sound flogging from my master, and I prepared myself for that beforehand.

But, I repeat, I never felt sufficient longing to need to control myself; I had nothing to contend with. A single sheet of fine drawing-paper tempted me more than money enough to buy a ream of it. This singularity is connected with one of the peculiarities of my character; it has exercised such great influence upon my conduct that it is worthwhile to explain it.

I am a man of very strong passions, and, while I am stirred by them, nothing can equal my impetuosity; I forget all discretion, all feelings of respect, fear and decency; I am cynical, impudent, violent and fearless; no feeling of shame keeps me back, no danger frightens me; with the exception of the single object which occupies my thoughts, the universe is nothing to me. But all this lasts only for a moment, and the following moment plunges me into complete annihilation. In my calmer moments I am indolence and timidity itself; everything frightens and discourages me; a fly, buzzing past, alarms me; a word which I have to say, a gesture which I have to make, terrifies my idleness; fear and shame overpower me to such an extent that I would gladly hide myself from the sight of my fellow-creatures. If I have to act, I do not know what to do; if I have to speak, I do not know what to say; if anyone looks at me, I am put out of countenance. When I am strongly moved I sometimes know how to find the right words, but in ordinary conversation I can find absolutely nothing, and my condition is unbearable for the simple reason that I am obliged to speak.

Add to this, that none of my prevailing tastes center in things that can be bought. I want nothing but unadulterated pleasures, and money poisons all. For instance, I am fond of the pleasures of the table; but, as I cannot endure either the constraint of good society or the drunkenness of the tavern, I can only enjoy them with a friend; alone, I cannot do so, for my imagination then occupies itself with other things, and eating affords me no pleasure. If my heated blood longs for women, my excited heart longs still more for affection. Women who could be bought for money would lose for me all their charms; I even doubt whether it would be in me to make use of them. I find it the same with all pleasures within my reach; unless they cost me nothing, I find them insipid. I only love those enjoyments which belong to no one but the first man who knows how to enjoy them.

Money has never appeared to me as valuable as it is generally considered. More than that, it has never even appeared to me particularly convenient. It is good for nothing in itself; it has to be changed before it can be enjoyed; one is obliged to buy, to bargain, to be often cheated, to pay dearly, to be badly served. I should like something which is good in quality; with my money I am sure to get it bad. If I pay a high price for a fresh egg, it is stale; for a nice piece of fruit, it is unripe; for a girl, she is spoilt. I am fond of good wine, but where am I to get it? At a wine merchant's? Whatever I do, he is sure to poison me. If I really wish to be well served, what trouble and embarrassment it entails! I must have friends, correspondents, give commissions, write, go backwards and forwards, wait, and in the end be often deceived! What trouble with my money! my fear of it is greater than my fondness for good wine.

Times without number, during my apprenticeship and afterwards, I have gone out with the intention of buying some delicacy. Coming to a pastrycook's shop, I notice some women at the counter; I think I can already see them laughing amongst themselves at the little glutton. I go on to a fruiterer's; I eye the fine pears; their smell tempts me. Two or three young people close by me look at me; a man who knows me is standing in front of his shop; I see a girl approaching in the distance: is it the housemaid? My short-sightedness causes all kinds of illusions. I take all the passers-by for acquaintances; everywhere I am intimidated, restrained by some obstacle; my desire increases with my shame, and at last I return home like a fool, consumed with longing, having in my pocket the means of satisfying it, and yet not having had the courage to buy anything.

I should enter into the most insipid details if, in relating how my money was spent by myself or others, I were to describe the embarrassment, the shame, the repugnance, the inconvenience, the annoyances of all kinds which I have always experienced. In proportion as the reader, following the course of my life, becomes acquainted with my real temperament, he will understand all this, without my taking the trouble to tell him.

This being understood, it will be easy to comprehend one of my apparent inconsistencies—the union of an almost sordid avarice with the greatest contempt for money. It is a piece of furniture in which I find so little convenience, that it never enters my mind to long for it when I have not got it, and that, when I have got it, I keep it for a long time without spending it, for want of knowing how to make use of it in a way to please myself; but if a convenient and agreeable opportunity presents itself, I make such good use of it that my purse is empty before I know it. Besides this, one need not expect to find in me that curious characteristic of misers—that of spending for the sake of ostentation; on the contrary, I spend in secret for the sake of enjoyment; far from glorying in my expenditure, I conceal it. I feel so strongly that money is of no use to me, that I am almost ashamed to have any, still more to make use of it. If I had ever had an income sufficient to live comfortably upon, I am certain that I should never have been tempted to be a miser. I should have spent it all, without attempting to increase it; but my precarious circumstances make me careful. I worship freedom; I abhor restraint, trouble, dependence. As long as the money in my purse lasts, it assures my independence; it relieves me of the trouble of finding expedients to replenish it, a necessity which always inspired me with dread; but the fear of seeing it exhausted makes me hoard it carefully. The money which a man possesses is the instrument of freedom; that which we eagerly pursue is the instrument of slavery. Therefore I hold fast to that which I have, and desire nothing.

My disinterestedness is, therefore, nothing but idleness; the pleasure of possession is not worth the trouble of acquisition. In like manner, my extravagance is nothing but idleness; when the opportunity of spending agreeably presents itself, it cannot be too profitably employed. Money tempts me less than things, because between money and the possession of the desired object there is always an intermediary, whereas between the thing itself and the enjoyment of it there is none. If I see the thing, it tempts me; if I only see the means of gaining possession of it, it does not. For this reason I have committed thefts, and even now I sometimes pilfer

trifles which tempt me, and which I prefer to take rather than to ask for; but neither when a child nor a grown-up man do I ever remember to have robbed anyone of a farthing,[41] except on one occasion, fifteen years ago, when I stole seven *livres* ten *sous*. The incident is worth recording, for it contains a most extraordinary mixture of folly and impudence, which I should have found difficulty in believing if it concerned anyone but myself.

It took place at Paris, I was walking with M. de Franceuil in the Palais-Royal about five o'clock. He pulled out his watch, looked at it, and said: "Let us go to the Opera." I agreed; we went. He took two tickets for the amphitheater,[42] gave me one, and went on in front with the other. I followed him; he went in. Entering after him, I found the door blocked. I looked, and seeing everybody standing up, thought it would be easy to lose myself in the crowd, or at any rate to make M. de Franceuil believe that I had lost myself. I went out, took back my check,[43] then my money, and went off, without thinking that as soon as I had reached the door everybody had taken their seats, and that M. de Franceuil clearly saw that I was no longer there.

As nothing was ever more foreign to my disposition than such behavior, I mention it in order to show that there are moments of semi-delirium during which men must not be judged by their actions. I did not exactly want to steal the money, I wanted to steal the employment of it; the less of a theft it was, the greater its disgracefulness.

I should never finish these details if I were to follow all the paths along which, during my apprenticeship, I descended from the sublimity of heroism to the depths of worthlessness. And yet, although I adopted the vices of my position, I could not altogether acquire a taste for them. I wearied of the amusements of my companions; and when excessive restraint had rendered work unendurable to me, I grew tired of everything. This renewed my taste for reading, which I had for some time lost. This reading, for which I stole time from my work, became a new offense which brought new punishment upon me. The taste for it, provoked by constraint, became a passion, and soon a regular madness. La Tribu, a well-known lender of books, provided me with all kinds of literature. Good or bad, all were alike to me; I had no choice, and read everything with equal avidity. I read at the worktable, I read on my errands, I read in the wardrobe, and forgot myself for hours together; my head became giddy with reading; I could do nothing else. My master watched me, surprised me, beat me, took away my books. How many volumes were torn, burnt, and thrown out of the window! how many works were left in odd volumes in La Tribu's stock! When I had no more money to pay her, I gave her my shirts, neckties and clothes; my three sous of pocket-money were regularly taken to her every Sunday.

Well, then, I shall be told, money had become necessary to me. That is true; but it was not until my passion for reading had deprived me of all activity. Completely devoted to my new hobby, I did nothing but read, and no longer stole. Here again is one of my characteristic peculiarities. In the midst of a certain attachment to any manner of life, a mere trifle distracts

[41] One-fourth of a British penny. [42] Gallery; balcony.
[43] A ticket given to theatergoers allowing them to leave and then re-enter. In the present instance, Rousseau uses it to get a refund, which he keeps, of money his friend has paid.

me, alters me, rivets my attention, and finally becomes a passion. Then everything is forgotten; I no longer think of anything except the new object which engrosses my attention. My heart beat with impatience to turn over the leaves of the new book which I had in my pocket; I pulled it out as soon as I was alone, and thought no more of rummaging my master's workroom. I can hardly believe that I should have stolen even if I had had more expensive tastes. Limited to the present, it was not in my way to make preparations in this manner for the future. La Tribu gave me credit, the payments on account were small, and, as soon as I had my book in my pocket, I forgot everything else. The money which came to me honestly passed in the same manner into the hands of this woman; and, when she pressed me, nothing was easier to dispose of than my own property. It required too much foresight to steal in advance, and I was not even tempted to steal in order to pay.

In consequence of quarrels, blows, and secret and ill-chosen reading, my disposition became savage and taciturn; my mind became altogether perverted, and I lived like a misanthrope. However, if my good taste did not keep me from silly and insipid books, my good fortune preserved me from such as were filthy and licentious; not that La Tribu, a woman in all respects most accommodating, would have made any scruple about lending them to me; but, in order to increase their importance, she always mentioned them to me with an air of mystery which had just the effect of making me refuse them, as much from disgust as from shame; and chance aided my modest disposition so well that I was more than thirty years old before I set eyes upon any of those dangerous books which a fine lady finds inconvenient because they can only be read with one hand.

In less than a year I exhausted La Tribu's little stock, and want of occupation, during my spare time, became painful to me. I had been cured of my childish and knavish propensities by my passion for reading, and even by the books I read, which, although ill-chosen and frequently bad, filled my heart with nobler sentiments than those with which my sphere of life had inspired me. Disgusted with everything that was within my reach, and feeling that everything which might have tempted me was too far removed from me, I saw nothing possible which might have flattered my heart. My excited senses had long clamored for an enjoyment, the object of which I could not even imagine. I was as far removed from actual enjoyment as if I had been sexless; and, already fully developed and sensitive, I sometimes thought of my crazes, but saw nothing beyond them. In this strange situation, my restless imagination entered upon an occupation which saved me from myself and calmed my growing sensuality. This consisted in feeding myself upon the situations which had interested me in the course of my reading, in recalling them, in varying them, in combining them, in making them so truly my own that I became one of the persons who filled my imagination, and always saw myself in the situations most agreeable to my taste; and that, finally, the fictitious state in which I succeeded in putting myself made me forget my actual state with which I was so dissatisfied. This love of imaginary objects, and the readiness with which I occupied myself with them, ended by disgusting me with everything around me, and decided that liking for solitude which has never left me. In the sequel we shall see more than once the curious effects of this disposition, apparently so

gloomy and misanthropic, but which is really due to a too affectionate, too loving and too tender heart, which, being unable to find any in existence resembling it, is obliged to nourish itself with fancies. For the present, it is sufficient for me to have defined the origin and first cause of a propensity which has modified all my passions, and which, restraining them by means of themselves, has always made me slow to act, owing to my excessive impetuosity in desire.

In this manner I reached my sixteenth year, restless, dissatisfied with myself and everything, without any of the tastes of my condition of life, without any of the pleasures of my age, consumed by desires of the object of which I was ignorant, weeping without any cause for tears, sighing without knowing why—in short, tenderly caressing my chimeras,[44] since I saw nothing around me which counterbalanced them. On Sundays, my fellow-apprentices came to fetch me after service to go and amuse myself with them. I would gladly have escaped from them if I had been able; but, once engaged in their amusements, I became more excited and went further than any of them; it was as difficult to set me going as to stop me. Such was always my disposition. During our walks outside the city I always went further than any of them without thinking about my return, unless others thought of it for me. Twice I was caught: the gates[45] were shut before I could get back. The next day I was treated as may be imagined; the second time I was promised such a reception if it ever happened again that I resolved not to run the risk of it; yet this third time, so dreaded, came to pass. My watchfulness was rendered useless by a confounded Captain Minutoli, who always shut the gate at which he was on guard half-an-hour before the others. I was returning with two companions. About half a league from the city I heard the retreat sounded: I doubled my pace: I heard the tattoo[46] beat, and ran with all my might. I arrived out of breath and bathed in perspiration; my heart beat; from a distance I saw the soldiers at their posts; I rushed up and cried out with a voice half-choked. It was too late! Twenty paces from the outposts, I saw the first bridge raised. I shuddered when I saw those terrible horns rising in the air—a sinister and fatal omen of the destiny which that moment was opening for me.

In the first violence of my grief I threw myself on the *glacis*[47] and bit the ground. My companions, laughing at their misfortune, immediately made up their minds what to do. I did the same, but my resolution was different from theirs. On the spot I swore never to return to my master; and the next morning, when they entered the city after the gates were opened, I said good-bye to them for ever, only begging them secretly to inform my cousin Bernard of the resolution I had taken, and of the place where he might be able to see me once more.

After I had entered upon my apprenticeship I saw less of him. For some time we used to meet on Sunday, but gradually each of us adopted other habits, and we saw one another less frequently. I am convinced that his mother had much to do with this change. He was a child of the upper city;

[44] Unreal products of the imagination. [45] The gates of the city.
[46] Military signals sounded at the end of the day. This decisive event in Rousseau's life took place on March 14, 1728, a few months before his sixteenth birthday.
[47] A slope in front of a military fortification.

I, a poor apprentice, was only a child of Saint-Gervais.[48] In spite of our relationship, there was no longer any equality between us; it was derogatory to him to associate with me. However, relations were not entirely broken off between us, and, as he was a good-natured lad, he sometimes followed the dictates of his heart instead of his mother's instructions. When he was informed of my resolution, he hastened to me, not to try and dissuade me from it or to share it, but to lessen the inconveniences of my flight by some small presents, since my own resources could not take me very far. Amongst other things he gave me a small sword, which had taken my fancy exceedingly, and which I carried as far as Turin, where necessity obliged me to dispose of it, and where, as the saying is, I passed it through my body.[49] The more I have since reflected upon the manner in which he behaved towards me at this critical moment, the more I have felt convinced that he followed the instructions of his mother, and perhaps of his father; for it is inconceivable that, left to himself, he would not have made some effort to keep me back, or would not have been tempted to follow; but, no! he rather encouraged me in my plan than tried to dissuade me; and, when he saw me quite determined, he left me without shedding many tears. We have never corresponded or seen each other since. It is a pity; his character was essentially good; we were made to love each other.

Before I abandon myself to the fatality of my lot, allow me to turn my eyes for a moment upon the destiny which, in the nature of things, would have awaited me if I had fallen into the hands of a better master. Nothing was more suitable to my disposition or better adapted to make me happy than the quiet and obscure lot of a respectable artisan,[50] especially of a certain class such as that of the engravers of Geneva. Such a position, sufficiently lucrative to afford a comfortable livelihood, but not sufficiently so to lead to fortune, would have limited my ambition for the rest of my days, and, leaving me an honorable leisure to cultivate modest tastes, would have confined me within my own sphere, without offering me the means of getting out of it. My imaginative powers were rich enough to beautify all callings with their chimeras, and strong enough to transport me, so to speak, at will from one to another; so it would have been immaterial to me in what position I actually found myself. It could not have been so far from the place where I was to my first castle in the air, that I could not have taken up my abode there without any difficulty. From this alone it followed that the simplest vocation, that which involved the least trouble and anxiety, that which allowed the greatest mental freedom, was the one which suited me best: and that was exactly my own. I should have passed a peaceful and quiet life, such as my disposition required, in the bosom of my religion, my country, my family and my friends, in the monotony of a profession that suited my taste, and in a society after my own heart. I should have been a good Christian, a good citizen, a good father of a family, a good friend, a good workman, a good man in every relation of life. I should have loved my position in life, perhaps honored it; and, having spent a life—simple, indeed, and obscure, but calm and serene—I should

[48] Part of the lower-class section of Geneva.
[49] Said of a poor soldier who sells his arms for food.
[50] A person skilled in a manual craft.

have died peacefully in the bosom of my family. Though, doubtless, soon forgotten, I should at least have been regretted as long as anyone remembered me.

Instead of that—what picture am I going to draw? Let us not anticipate the sorrows of my life; I shall occupy my readers more than enough with this melancholy subject.

Johann Wolfgang von Goethe
(*1749–1832*)

Johann Wolfgang von Goethe, supreme in German literature, is also one of the titans of world literature, not only because of the international fame of his works but also because he was interested in many national literatures and was one of the first men to conceive of them as an organic global entity. Beginning in childhood, he wrote almost continuously throughout his long life, so that—even discounting work he was dissatisfied with and destroyed—we have an enormous body of writing, in virtually every literary genre: short poems including ballads and some of the world's most beautiful lyrics, in many modes and meters; prose fiction of several different types; dramas in both prose and verse treating historical, classical, and mythical subjects; and a considerable amount of autobiographical writing. Nor did he limit himself to imaginative literature; he studied and wrote extensively on science, especially botany, zoology, geology, anatomy, optics, the history of science, and the psychology of scientific research. He was a painter of significant if limited gifts and a practical man of the theater. He was trained as a lawyer, and his official profession was that of a public statesman, concerned with matters ranging from diplomacy to technology. He had many love affairs, as one might expect of a man who made the "eternal feminine," as he called it, a symbol and vehicle of spiritual salvation. Although he was one of the great romanticists, his work is also profoundly classical. In short, he transcends and redefines the categories we usually use to classify human beings and their achievements.

Goethe was born in 1749 (on August 28, the birthday he assigns to Werther), in Frankfurt-am-Main in western Germany, the son of a lawyer. His early years were happy ones, and he mixed easily with people. His cultured parents provided him with a good education that fostered both his intellectual and esthetic gifts. From 1765 to 1768 he was a law student at the University of Leipzig, a sophisticated city he later dubbed the Paris of Germany. There he continued to write, especially in established eighteenth-century modes of drama and light poetry, besides occupying himself with music, medicine, and the visual arts. His first published book was the anonymous *New Songs*, which appeared in 1769.

Illness forced Goethe to leave Leipzig and ushered in a darker and more intense period of his life. When he resumed his law studies in Stras-

bourg (where he took his degree in 1771), he was ready to indulge a new kind of sensibility, expressed in the *Sturm und Drang* (Storm and Stress) movement of which J. G. Herder was the principal apologist. This intensely emotional literary vogue, a herald of Romanticism, rebelled against Enlightenment rationalism and the art associated with it, calling instead for a more organically natural literature freed from formal rules, a more direct link between experience and expression, a new mystique of external nature as a model for art and human conduct, the use of national subjects and folk forms, and the celebration of the unaffectedly spontaneous, represented in life by children and the lower classes and in literature by "primitive" or "natural" poets like Homer and Shakespeare. (Some of these goals were clearly influenced by Rousseau.) Goethe's first great contribution to the Storm and Stress movement was the rousing historical drama *Götz von Berlichingen* (1773), which made him a name in Germany. He became an international name the following year, with *The Sorrows of Young Werther,* one of the most popular and influential books ever written. Like much of Goethe's work, it drew largely on his life, specifically an intense, hopeless love he felt, while living in the town of Wetzlar in 1772, for Charlotte Buff, a young woman engaged to Goethe's friend Johann Kestner. With this autobiographical experience Goethe united another source from life, the suicide of his acquaintance Karl Jerusalem, an embassy secretary snubbed by the aristocracy and hopelessly in love with another man's wife. From these events Goethe fashioned not merely a voguish period piece from the Age of Sensibility (Werther's dress, ideas, and even his unhappy exit from the world were aped) but a work of enduring eloquence and artistry, one of literature's best specimens of the psychological novel and a milestone in the development of Romanticism.

In 1775 Goethe entered into an engagement, soon broken off, with Lili Schönemann, the fashionable daughter of a banker. The same year he entered the service of his admirer Duke Karl August of Saxe-Weimar, and the east-central German city of Weimar was to be his home during most of the remainder of his life. He soon was a member of the cabinet, and he became a noble in 1782. His social and civic duties were to occupy a good deal of his time at Weimar; he supervised activities ranging from theatricals to finance to mining to military recruiting. Goethe was a good administrator, but he did not sell his independence. Although his duties slowed him, he continued to write (his Storm-and-Stress mood having calmed considerably) and to immerse himself in scientific subjects; among other achievements he discovered the intermaxillary bone. A close attachment to Charlotte von Stein, a woman of great intelligence and gifts but, once more, another man's wife, evoked some of his finest lyrics. The counter-Romantic strain in him was reinforced by a trip to Italy in 1786–1788. There, while experimenting with a career as painter and sculptor and (as always) writing, he immeasurably deepened his commitment to classical art and its values of order, harmony, and proportion. Thereafter one finds in his work a fruitful tension between romantic individualism and classical discipline and universality. In 1787 two of his dramatic masterpieces were published: *Egmont* is a treatment of the theme of freedom based on the struggle for Dutch independence from Spain, building to a musical ending for which Beethoven later wrote incidental music; *Iphigenia in Tauris* is a re-

shaping of the Orestes myth that supremely illustrates Goethe's vision of woman as redeemer. Three years later, another great play appeared: *Torquato Tasso,* at once a penetrating psychological study of the Italian Renaissance poet and an examination of the nature of poetry.

After returning from Italy in 1788, Goethe took as his mistress Christiane Vulpius, a woman of modest social station by whom he had several children and whom he married eighteen years later. She helped inspire the sensuous *Roman Elegies,* one of Goethe's lyrical triumphs. The next years, until 1794, were a time of relative retirement and spiritual unsettledness. Although still supported by the Duke, Goethe had few state duties. The French Revolution erupted, and Goethe accompanied the Duke's army on an ill-fated campaign against France. One literary offshoot of the Revolutionary experience was to be *Hermann and Dorothea* (1797), an experiment in the adaptation of the ancient epic manner and meter to a modern love story in a setting of war.

In 1794 Goethe began a new phase of productivity enhanced by his friendship and collaboration with the poet Friedrich Schiller, a cross-fertilization of minds comparable to what was happening at the same time in England between Wordsworth and Coleridge. In 1796 Goethe published *Wilhelm Meister's Apprenticeship,* which he had started some years earlier; this work is one of the central models for the *Bildungsroman,* or "apprenticeship novel," which relates fictionally the process through which a young person is educated for living. One of Goethe's most popular works, it was extended three decades later by a sequel, *Wilhelm Meister's Travels,* which tried to bring the earlier work into line with the much changed world of the Industrial Revolution.

The greatest result of this productive decade, however, was *Faust,* the First Part of which (following on earlier fragmentary versions) was published in 1808. This was Goethe's supreme work, ranking with the world's greatest dramas. The despair of translators because of its many intricate verse forms and the mixture of tones including the sublime, lyrically melodious, grotesque, and farcical, it nevertheless enjoys a worldwide eminence. It expresses one of the most deep-seated myths of modern consciousness: the highly gifted man who contracts with the Devil in return for fuller existence and self-realization. Goethe gives the issue an even more cosmic setting by placing the story in the framework of a bet, like that in the Book of Job, between God and the Devil over the redemption of Faust, whose identity is the arena for a struggle between good and evil. Part One leaves the outcome unresolved, and not until more than twenty years later did Goethe complete the drama in Part Two, which he reserved for publication after his death. Part Two is far-ranging symbolism that takes Faust from the smaller world he had encountered in Margarete, the heroine of Part One, into the larger public world where he meets his ultimate test and—in some sense about which interpreters differ—triumphs.

Schiller died in 1805, a loss Goethe felt keenly. He found some compensation, however, in the society of the young Romantics of the day, whose values he shared in many ways although he felt they were insufficiently respectful of the ideal of form. In 1809 he published *Elective Affinities,* a complex psychological novel on the issue of marriage and divorce, and in

1808–1810 one of his major scientific works, *On the Theory of Colors*, a study he ranked high among his achievements. He embarked on serious study of non-Western literatures, stirred by an ideal of world literature as an agency for international understanding and universal culture. The culmination of these studies in his own creative work was the Persian-inspired *West-Easterly Divan* (1819), a collection that includes some of his most beautiful poems. Much of his very last writing was autobiographical.

Goethe's international stature, well established by the turn of the century, grew ever greater in his last decades; great public figures, including Napoleon, paid him homage. Thomas Mann created an interesting imaginative picture of Goethe's late years of fame in *Lotte in Weimar*, a novel about a visit to Goethe some forty years after *Werther* by the real-life prototype of Lotte. A celebrity's celebrity, his status late in life was that of a godlike sage. He remained concerned to the end with new currents of events and social tendencies, especially the problems and promise of technology. And, one hardly needs to add, he wrote until the end, completing the aforementioned sequel to *Wilhelm Meister* and Second Part of *Faust*, which was published a year after his death in 1832.

The Sorrows of Young Werther, the selection from Goethe that follows in this book, has been in some ways the victim of its own notoriety. Safely pigeonholed as part of Storm-and-Stress (and therefore "low") Romanticism, as a representation in caricature of a passing mood in the history of taste, it invites new readers to be tolerantly amused at best by things that people once, inexplicably, took seriously. This misjudgment seldom survives an actual reading of the novel. To be sure, some things in it are dated—most obviously, the vogue of "Ossian's" poetry, which Werther reads to Lotte near the end with such cyclonic effect. Even things like this, however, are often redeemed by the narrative context; certainly that final scene gives the murky gloom of Ossianic poetry a power the poetry does not possess in itself. *Werther* is, in fact, by no means low Romanticism; in its treatment of nature as half the creation of the human mind, in its exploration of the conflict between the quest for absolutes and the confinements of the actual, in its examination of the role of work and social convention in the life of the idealist, in its treatment of love as both spiritual and fleshy desire, and above all in the acuity of its psychological analysis of the relationship between neurosis (if that is the right word) and genius, *Werther* is very near in sophistication to high Romanticism at its best.

These great themes are half-concealed by the realistic, seemingly effortless flow of the epistolary novel form. But it would be a mistake, the protagonist's penchant for artlessness notwithstanding, to underestimate Goethe's artistry in *Werther*. Enough eloquence survives translation to make the book linguistically impressive. Its general movement, modulating skillfully between calm and storm (both literally in nature and psychologically), shows firm control of form. The themes are introduced early and deftly; this is most obviously true in the lengthy discussion of suicide, but there are subtler touches too, including the irony of Werther's tirade against the poisoning effect of ill-humor (1 July 1771) and the still more subtle irony—a mere suggestion—in Werther's very first letter, in which he shows concern over having broken a woman's heart. Expressive threads of imagery weave their

patterns throughout. For example, Werther's outrage at the chopping down of the walnut trees is more than tenderness toward flora; significantly, it blends in his mind with the perpetrator's rationalist modern theology and the sleaziness of commerce. The large patterns are hard to miss, like those sustained in the Biblical references, but even the smallest details can pull their weight, as in the two acts of gathering flowers described on 10 August 1771 and 30 November 1772.

The abiding challenge in reading *Werther* is to understand the psychology of its hero (to some extent, Lotte and Albert too) and to evaluate him. A distinguishing quality of certain great books is that they evoke widely different responses, all of which can be plausibly defended. This is certainly true of *Werther*. To some readers its hero is the man described in the opening paragraph as certain to win our "admiration and love," a noble victim either of hopeless passion for a woman or of the more metaphysical doom that sent him with an unquenchable thirst for being into a world that ultimately reveals itself as a parched wasteland. To some readers he is exasperating, perversely ignoring not only the sensible advice of other people but his own best wisdom, including his conviction, already mentioned, that we need to control our ill-humor in the interests of our friends' happiness. Some readers find in him a case study of morbid, pathological neurosis and then go on (somewhat inconsistently, since they are talking about a man they define as sick) to condemn him roundly not just as contemptible but even as cruel. These wildly varying interpretations of him suggest that, however Goethe wanted us to respond to it, *Werther* is a touchstone by which readers reveal certain of their fundamental values—the degree of their idealism and realism (and how they understand those problematical terms), the importance they attribute to love as an emotional experience, and—in the psychologist's phrase—their "threshold of pain interpretation" (a matter Werther and Albert explicitly address; see the letter of 12 August 1771). That a book which engages our interest so intensely as sheer story can do all this is surely a sign that its author, even at twenty-five, was a man of extraordinary vision and intelligence.

FURTHER READING *(prepared by W. J. R.):* An introductory overview of Goethe's life and work is Terence J. Reed's *Goethe*, 1984. A fine introduction to *The Sorrows of Young Werther* can be found in the Bantam bilingual edition of the work, with introduction by Harry Steinhauer, 1962. Steinhauer sketches Goethe's life, discusses *Werther* as a drama, and considers controversial interpretations of Werther himself. On *Werther*, Martin Swales's *Goethe: "The Sorrows of Young Werther,"* 1987, in the Landmarks of World Literature series, can be recommended. Critical surveys of Goethe's total output are legion; Barker Fairley's *A Study of Goethe*, 1947, is probably still the best one available in English. Fairley provides fine biographical information and discusses the writing of *Faust* at particular length. Liselotte Dieckmann's *Johann Wolfgang Goethe*, 1974, is also a good introductory piece, taking a traditional approach. Ronald Gray's *Goethe: A Critical Introduction*, 1967, can also be highly recommended; Gray's biographical account is particularly useful for the influences on Goethe's development. On a more advanced critical level, Ilse Graham's *Goethe: Portrait of the Artist*, 1977, takes a thematic approach to the problem of defining what constitutes a "Goethean" work.

THE SORROWS OF YOUNG WERTHER

(1774 VERSION)[1]

Translated by William Rose

Whatever I have been able to discover of the story of poor Werther I have industriously collected, and put it now before you, and I know that you will thank me for it. You will not be able to withhold your admiration and love for his mind and character or your tears for his fate.

And you, good soul, who are laboring under the same distress as he, draw consolation from his sufferings and, if you should be prevented by fate or your own fault from finding one more intimate, let this little book be your friend.

PART ONE

4 MAY, 1771.

How glad I am to have got away! My dear friend, what a thing is the heart of man! To leave you whom I love so much, from whom I was inseparable—and yet be cheerful! I know you will forgive me. Were not all my other friendships veritably chosen by Fate to oppress a heart like mine? Poor Leonore! And yet the blame was not mine! Could I help it if her poor heart conceived a passion for me while the capricious charms of her sister afforded me agreeable entertainment! And yet—am I altogether blameless? Did I not feed her emotions? Did I not myself find pleasure in the sincere manifestations of Nature which so often made us laugh, however little conducive they were to laughter? Did I not—Oh! what is man, that he may bewail his lot?—I will, dear friend, I promise you, I will mend my ways; I will no longer chew the cud of misfortune that Fate ekes out to us, as I have always done. I will enjoy the present, and the past shall be done with. You are surely right, my best of friends. The sufferings of men would be less if they did not so busily engage their imagination—God knows why they are so constituted—in recalling the memory of bygone ills, rather than bear an indifferent present.

Will you be so good as to tell my mother that I shall look after her business as well as I can and that I shall write to her about it in a day or two? I called on my aunt and did not by any means find the ill-tempered woman that they make her out to be at home. She is lively, impetuous and very

[1] Goethe revised *Werther* in 1786. In the later version, the fictional editor, after he steps in to tell the story near the end, portrays Albert more sympathetically than in the present version. The other most significant difference is the insertion of a brief episode of tragic love, summarized in the footnote to Werther's letter of 6 December 1772. Stylistically, the second version is smoother, the first more colloquial and closer to the mood of the Storm-and-Stress period.

warm-hearted. I explained to her my mother's grievances about the legacy that had been held back. She told me the reasons that had impelled her to do it and the terms under which she would be ready to hand everything over—more, in fact, than we asked.—In short, I don't want to write about it now, but tell my mother everything will be all right. And in dealing with this little matter I have again found that misunderstandings and indolence are perhaps the cause of more disturbance in the world than cunning or malice. At any rate the last two are certainly more rare.

For the rest, I am quite happy here. Solitude is delicious balm to my heart in this heavenly spot, and this youthful season pours the fulness of its warmth into my oft-shivering heart. Every tree, every hedge is a nosegay, and one would like to turn into a cockchafer[2] to float in a sea of fragrance and find in it all the nourishment one needs.

The town itself is not very agreeable, but it lies amidst the most inexpressible natural beauty, which led the late Count von M. to lay out a garden on one of the intersecting hills which form the most charming valleys in the loveliest diversity of Nature. The garden is simple, and one feels as soon as one enters that it was planned not by a scientific gardener but by an impressionable soul that wanted here to take its pleasure. I have shed many a tear for the departed owner in the crumbling arbor which was his favorite sojourn, and is also mine. Soon I shall be the master of the garden. The gardener has become devoted to me during the few days I have been here, and he will not do at all badly by it.

10 MAY.

My whole soul is imbued with a wondrous serenity, like the pleasant spring mornings which I enjoy with all my heart. I am completely alone and find life so enjoyable in this spot which was created for souls like mine. I am so happy, so absorbed in the sensation of a tranquil existence, that my art is suffering. I could not draw a line at this moment, and yet I have never been more of a painter than I am now. When the mist is rising from the lovely valley and the sun is high above the impenetrable shade of my wood, so that only now and then a ray steals into the inner sanctuary, and I lie in the tall grass by the falling brook, and discover a thousand different grasses on the surface of the earth; when I feel nearer to my heart the teeming little world among the blades, the innumerable, unfathomable creatures in the shape of worms and insects, and when I feel the presence of the Almighty Spirit Who created us all in His image, the breath of the All-loving One who sustains us as we float in illimitable bliss—Oh! friend, when the world then grows dim before my eyes and earth and sky are absorbed into my soul like the form of a beloved, I am often consumed with longing and think, ah! would that I could express it, would that I could breathe on to paper that which lives so warm and full within me, so that it might become the mirror of my soul as my soul is the mirror of the eternal God! My friend—

[2] A beetle.

but it is beyond my power, and I succumb to the splendor of what lies before me.

12 MAY.

I know not whether deluding spirits are hovering round this spot, or whether it is the divine and ardent fancy of my heart which turns everything around me into a Paradise. Right in front of the gate is a spring, a spring by which I am enchanted like Melusine[3] and her sisters. On descending a small hill you come to an arch, with about twenty steps going down to where the clearest of water gushes from the marble rock. The little wall above which encloses it, the tall trees all round, the coolness of the place—there is something so attractive, so awesome about it all. Hardly a day passes without my sitting there for an hour. Then the girls come from the town to fetch water, the most innocent and necessary of services which once even the daughters of kings performed. As I sit there I am reminded vividly of the days of the patriarchs,[4] all striking up acquaintance or plighting their troth at the well, and kindly spirits hovering round the springs and fountains. Oh! he can never have refreshed himself at the coolness of a spring, after a hard walk on a summer's day, who is unable to sympathize with my emotion.

13 MAY.

You ask whether you are to send my books along? I entreat you, for the Lord's sake, do not bother me with books. I no longer want to be guided, enlivened or excited. This heart is in sufficient of a ferment without their help. I need lullabies and I have found them in abundance in my Homer. How often do I lull my stormy spirit, for never have you seen anything so restless, so changeable as this heart. Dear friend! do I need to tell *you* who have so often borne the burden of my transition from grief to excessive joy, from gentle melancholy to devastating passion? I treat my heart like a sick child and gratify its every whim. Don't repeat this, there are people who would take it amiss.

15 MAY.

The poor folk here know me already and have an affection for me, especially the children. I have noticed something which saddens me. When I first mixed with them and asked in a friendly manner about one thing or another, some of them thought I wanted to scoff, and they put me off very rudely. I did not take offense, but I felt very keenly, what I have often noticed, that people in a better position always keep coldly aloof from the common folk as though they feared to lose something by proximity, and there are even heedless, mischievous wags who appear to act condescend-

[3] A mermaid.
[4] Abraham, Isaac, and Jacob. Episodes at wells led to the betrothals of Isaac to Rebekah and of Jacob to Rachel (Genesis, chs. 24, 29).

ingly in order to make poor people all the more sensitive to their arro-
gance. I know quite well that we are not all equal, and that we never can be
so. But I maintain that anyone who thinks it necessary to hold himself aloof
from the so-called rabble, in order to keep its respect, is quite as blame-
worthy as a coward who hides from the enemy because he is afraid of
defeat.

A little while ago I came to the spring and found a young maidservant
who had put her pitcher on the lowest step and was looking round for one
of her friends to help her lift it on to her head. I went down and looked at
her. "Shall I help you, young woman?" I asked. She blushed to the roots of
her hair. "Oh no, sir!" she said. "Come, don't stand on ceremony."—She
adjusted her headpiece and I helped her. She thanked me and went up the
steps.

17 MAY.
I have made all sorts of acquaintances but have not yet got into any circle. I
do not know what there is about me that attracts people, so many like me
and become attached to me, and it always grieves me when our paths are
the same for only such a very short distance. When you ask what the people
here are like, I must reply, like everywhere else. The human race does not
vary much. Most people pass the greater part of their lives in work, in
order to live, and the modicum of free time they have to themselves makes
them so uneasy that they seek every means they can to kill it. Alas, the
destiny of man!

But they are a very worthy type of folk! When I on occasion forget
myself, and am able to enjoy with them the pleasures that still remain to
man, to exchange jests in all candor and sincerity at a well-set board, to
arrange a walk or a dance at the proper time and so on, it has a good effect
on me, so long as I do not remember all the other forces lying dormant in
me, all untried and becoming atrophied, which I must carefully conceal.
Oh! all this clutches at my heart—and yet! It is the fate of a man like me to
be misunderstood.

Alas! that the friend of my youth is gone, alas! that I ever knew her! I
would say to myself "You are a fool! You are seeking what does not exist
down here." But she was mine, I felt the heart, the great soul in whose
presence I seemed to myself to be more than I really was, since I was
everything that I could be. God! was there a single force in my soul that
remained untried, was I not able to develop in her presence all the won-
drous perception with which my heart embraces Nature, was not our inter-
course an endless weaving of the most delicate feeling, the keenest wit,
whose variations were all stamped, even to the extent of extravagance, with
the impress of genius? And now—Alas! she descended before me to the
grave, for she had the advantage in years. Never shall I forget her, never
shall I cease to recall her steadfast mind and divine fortitude.

A few days ago I met a young man named V., a straightforward youth
with very pleasing features. He has just come down from the University,
does not exactly consider himself a sage but yet thinks he knows more than
other people. He was very diligent, as I can tell from various signs, in short,
he is pretty well informed. As he had heard that I draw a great deal and

know Greek (two unusual phenomena in these parts) he came to me and dug out his store of learning, from Batteux to Wood, from de Piles to Winckelmann, assuring me that he had read right through the first part of Sulzer's *Theory* and possessed a manuscript of Heyne's about the study of antiquity.[5] I did not pursue the subject.

I have made the acquaintance of another very worthy fellow, the prince's bailiff.[6] A straightforward, simple man. They say it does one's heart good to see him among his children, of whom he has nine. In particular they talk a great deal about his eldest daughter. He has invited me to come and see him, and I am going to call on him very soon. He lives in one of the prince's hunting lodges, an hour and a half from here, to which he received permission to move after the death of his wife, since he found staying here in the town, in the bailiff's lodge, too painful.

In addition I have come across a few eccentric oddities whom I find quite insufferable, most insupportable of all being their attestations of friendship.

Farewell! you will like this letter, it is all about things that have happened.

22 MAY.

That the life of man is only a dream has already occurred to many, and I also am always haunted by this feeling. When I see the restrictions by which the active, speculative powers of man are hemmed in, when I see how all activity is directed toward the satisfaction of needs which themselves have no other purpose than to prolong our wretched existence, and that the only way to meet certain speculations is by a dreamy resignation, in which we paint the walls of our prison with colored figures and bright prospects—all this, Wilhelm, makes me dumb. I turn in upon myself and find a world! But again more with presentiment and obscure craving than plastic[7] power and vital force. Everything swims before my senses and i continue on my way through the world with a dreamy smile.

All learned teachers and instructors are agreed that children do not know the reason for their desires. But nobody likes to believe that grown-ups are also walking unsteadily upon this earth, that, like children, they do not know whence they come nor whither they are going, that their actions are equally devoid of true purpose, that they are ruled in the same way by the promise of biscuits, cake or the birch,[8] and yet it seems to me the thing is evident.

I willingly admit, for I know what your reply will be, that the happiest mortals are those who, like children, live for the day, drag about their dolls, don and doff their clothes, creep respectfully round the cupboard where mother keeps the tarts and, when they at last snatch what they are after, stuff their cheeks and cry for more.—Such beings are happy. And they also are well-off who give high-sounding names to their miserable pursuits, or even their passions, and attribute to them a colossal influence on the welfare and prosperity of the human race. He is lucky who can do so! But

[5] The six men named were authorities on esthetics, archeology, and language.
[6] Manager of an estate. [7] Shaping. [8] Rod for punishing children.

whoever in his humbleness recognizes what all this leads to, who sees how neatly every contented citizen trims his little garden into an Eden, and how even unhappy mortals pant along patiently under their heavy load and everybody alike is eager to see the light of the sun for another minute— such a man is tranquil and likewise creates his world out of his own soul, happy because he is a human being. And then, circumscribed as he is, he yet always preserves in his heart the sweet feeling of freedom and the thought that he can leave this prison when he will.

26 MAY.

You know of old the way I settle down, build myself a cabin in some intimate spot and take up my modest quarters there. I have again found a corner that attracts me.

About an hour's journey from the town lies a hamlet called Wahlheim.[9] It is very interestingly situated on a hill and, when you walk out of the village by the footpath above, you see the whole valley spread out at your feet. A kindly landlady, obliging and cheerful in her old age, dispenses wine, beer and coffee and, what is most delightful of all, there are two limes whose spreading branches cast their shade over the little open space in front of the church, which is closed in on all sides by the cottages of the peasants, their barns and farmyards. I have rarely found a spot more intimate or cozy, and I have my little table and chair brought out from the inn, drink my coffee and read my Homer. The first time I came by accident upon the limes one fine afternoon, the place was a solitude. Everybody was in the fields. Only one little boy about four years of age was sitting on the ground, holding a child of about six months between his feet, clasping him with both arms to his breast so that he formed a kind of armchair for him and, in spite of the vivacity which sparkled in his black eyes, he was quite still. The sight pleased me and, sitting down on a plow opposite them, I amused myself by drawing their brotherly attitude, including the neighboring hedge, the doorway of a threshing-floor and some broken cartwheels, just as they all stood, so that in an hour I had made a well-grouped and very interesting sketch without adding anything at all that was not in my model. This strengthened my resolution to keep to Nature in the future. Nature alone is infinitely rich, and Nature alone forms the great artist. Much can be adduced in favor of rules that can be applied with more or less equal justice in praise of middle-class society. The man who models himself on them will never produce anything inferior or in bad taste, just as one who allows his life to be fashioned by precepts and the laws of propriety will never become a disagreeable neighbor or a remarkable villain; on the other hand, whatever people may say, rules destroy the true feeling for Nature and its true expression. You will say, "That is too severe! they only act as a check, prune the rank[10] tendrils, and so on." My good friend, shall I submit a parable to you? It is like love. A youth cleaves wholly to a maid, passes all

[9] "The reader need not exert himself to find out which are the places referred to here, as it has been necessary to change the names mentioned in the original letters."—Note in original German text.

[10] Growing wild; overfertile.

his hours in her company, expends all his forces, all his fortune, to express to her at every moment that he is completely devoted to her. And then there comes a Philistine,[11] a man engaged in a public office, who says to him, "Young Man, to love is human, only you must love in a human way! Divide up your hours, giving some to work, and your hours of recreation you may dedicate to your maid; calculate your fortune, and from whatever you have beyond your needs you may offer her a gift, say on her birth or name day,[12] only not too often, and so on." If he obeys, he will become an efficient young man and I would advise any prince to give him a post in the government service; but there will be an end to his love and, if he is an artist, to his art. Oh my friends! Why does the stream of genius break forth so rarely, so rarely roar down in a raging torrent, mountain high, to convulse your wondering souls? My friends, there are tranquil fellows dwelling on both banks whose arbors, tulip-beds and cabbage-plots would be devastated, and so they are able to ward off the threatening danger by timely damming and draining.

27 MAY.

I see that I have lapsed into parable and ecstatic declamation, and have quite forgotten to tell you the sequel to my adventure with the children. I had been sitting on my plow for about two hours entirely absorbed in perceptions of the picturesque which my letter of yesterday will have transmitted to you in a very fragmentary manner. Towards evening a young woman comes up to the children, who during all this time had not moved, with a little basket on her arm, and calls out when she is still some distance away, "Philip, you are a very good boy." She greeted me, I thanked her, stood up, went up to her and inquired whether she was the mother of the children. She said she was and, giving the older one half a roll, she picked up the baby and kissed it with every sign of maternal affection. "I gave my Philip the baby to hold," she said, "and went into the town with my eldest boy to buy white bread and sugar and an earthenware saucepan for porridge." I saw all this in the basket from which the lid had fallen off. "I want to cook Hans (that was the name of the baby) some broth before he goes to bed; my scamp of an eldest broke my saucepan yesterday as he was quarrelling with Philip over what was left of the porridge." I inquired about the eldest boy, and she had hardly told me that he was chasing a couple of geese on the common when he came running up with a hazel switch for Philip. In further conversation with the mother I learned that she was the daughter of the schoolmaster, and that her husband was on his way to Switzerland to fetch a legacy that had been left him by a cousin. "They tried to cheat him out of it," she said, "and did not answer his letters, so he has gone there himself. I hope nothing has happened to him, as I have not heard from him since." I found it difficult to tear myself away. I gave each of the children a *Kreuzer*,[13] including one for the baby which I gave to the mother to buy him a roll for his broth when she went into the town, and so I left them.

[11] An insensitive middle-class opponent of culture.
[12] Feast day of the saint whose name one bears. [13] Small coin.

I tell you, my dear fellow, when my mind is all a riot, it is soothed by the sight of such a mortal pursuing in tranquil contentment the narrow round of her existence, making both ends meet from day to day, and with no other thought, when she sees the leaves falling, but that winter is near.

I have often gone out since, and the children have become quite used to me. When I drink my coffee they have their share of the sugar, and they share my bread and butter and sour milk in the evening. On Sundays they never fail to receive their *Kreuzer*, and if I am not there after the hour of prayer the landlady has orders to pay it to them.

I have won their confidence and they tell me all sorts of things. I find it particularly delightful to watch them vent their passions and express their desires so naïvely when a number of children from the village are collected together.

I had a lot of trouble to relieve the mother of her apprehension lest they might "incommode the gentleman."

16 JUNE.

Why don't I write to you? You ask me that though you are also numbered among the scholars! You should be able to divine that I am well, and indeed—in short, I have met someone in whom my heart is interested. I have—I do not know.

To tell you in proper order how it happened that I made the acquaintance of one of the most charming of beings will be no easy matter; I am content and happy, so am not likely to be a satisfactory narrator.

An angel! By Heaven, everybody says that of his mistress! Doesn't he? And yet I am incapable of telling you how perfect she is, or why she is perfect, enough, she has taken complete possession of my mind.

So much naïveté combined with such intelligence, such kindness and such resolve, such tranquillity of soul in such an active life.

This is all hopeless twaddle that I am saying about her, mere abstractions which fail to express a single feature of her real self. Another time—No, not another time, I will tell you now, immediately. If I don't do it now, I never shall. For, between ourselves, since I began this letter I have been three times on the verge of laying down my pen, saddling my horse and riding off though I vowed early this morning that I would not—and yet every minute I go to the window to see how high the sun stands. . . .

I could not help it, I had to go out to her. I am back once more, Wilhelm, and will eat my supper and finish this letter. How it enraptures my soul to see her among the dear happy children, her eight brothers and sisters.

If I continue like this, you will be no wiser at the end than you were at the beginning, so listen, I will force myself to give you details.

I wrote to you recently that I had made the acquaintance of the bailiff S., and that he had invited me to come and visit him soon at his hermitage, or rather his little kingdom. I neglected to do so and would perhaps never have gone, if there had not been revealed to me by accident the treasure concealed in that tranquil spot.

The young people here had arranged a ball in the country, and I gladly agreed to go. I offered my escort to a nice, good-looking, but not otherwise

interesting girl in this town, and it was settled that I was to hire a coach to drive out to the scene of the festivities with my partner and her cousin, and that we were to pick up Charlotte S. on the way. "You will make the acquaintance of a beautiful girl," my partner said, as we drove through a broad avenue in the wood towards the hunting lodge. "Take care," her cousin added, "that you don't fall in love." "What do you mean?" I asked. "She is already betrothed," the former replied, "to a very worthy man who has gone to put his affairs in order after his father's death and to apply for an important post." The information did not interest me particularly.

The sun was still a quarter of an hour from the hilltop when we reached the lodge gate; it was very sultry and the ladies expressed their anxiety lest we should be overtaken by a storm which we could see gathering in heavy, whitish-gray little clouds round the horizon. I relieved their fears by pretending to a knowledge of the weather, though I began myself to have a foreboding that our festivities would be interrupted.

I had alighted, and a maid who came to the gate begged us to wait a moment, Mamselle Lottchen[14] would be with us straightway. I went across the courtyard to the well-built house and, when I had ascended the steps in front and entered at the door, I caught sight of the most charming scene that I have ever witnessed. In the entrance hall there swarmed six children, from two to eleven years of age, round a handsome girl of middle height, who wore a simple white frock with pink bows on the breast and arms. She was holding a loaf of black bread and cutting a slice for each of the children round her in proportion to its age and appetite, offering it with such an amiable air and each one crying "Thank you!" so artlessly, after he had stretched his little hands up as high as he could before his slice was cut, and then springing away contentedly with his supper or, if he was of a quieter nature, walking tranquilly towards the gate to see the strangers and the coach in which their Lotte was to drive away.—"I beg your pardon," she said, "for giving you the trouble of coming in and making the ladies wait. While I was dressing and making all sorts of arrangements for the house in my absence, I forgot to give my children their supper, and they won't have their bread cut by anyone but me." I paid her some harmless compliment while my whole soul was absorbed in the contemplation of her figure, her voice, her bearing, and I had just time to recover from my surprise when she ran into the room to fetch her gloves and fan. The children kept at a little distance, casting sidelong glances at me, and I went up to the youngest who was a most pleasant-looking child. He had just drawn back when Lotte appeared in the doorway and said, "Louis, shake hands with your cousin." The boy did so with a very frank air, and I could not refrain from kissing him heartily in spite of his dirty little nose. "Cousin?" I said, as I offered her my hand. "Do you consider that I deserve the happiness of being related to you?" "Oh!" she said, with a roguish smile, "our circle of cousins is very extensive, and I should be very sorry if you were the least worthy among them." As we went she ordered Sophie, the next oldest sister to herself, a girl of about eleven, to keep an eye on the little ones, and greet their father when he came back from his ride. The little ones she admonished to obey their sister Sophie as they would herself,

[14] Diminutive form of *Charlotte*.

and some of them expressly promised to do so. A pert little blonde, however, of about six years, said, "But it isn't you, after all, Lottchen! we like you better." The two eldest boys had climbed up behind the coach, and at my request she allowed them to travel with us until we reached the edge of the wood, so long as they promised not to tease each other and to hold on firmly.

Hardly had we fitted ourselves in and the ladies greeted one another, each in turn expressing her views about the others' costumes, particularly bonnets, and duly passing in review the company that they expected to meet, when Lotte stopped the coach for her brothers to descend; they asked to kiss her hand once more, and the older one did so with all the delicacy that could be expected of a boy of fifteen, the other with impetuousness and levity. She bade them give her love once more to the little ones, and the coach rolled on.

The cousin inquired whether she had finished the book she had recently sent her. "No," said Lotte. "I do not like it; you can have it back. The one you sent me before was no better." When I asked what the books were, I was amazed at her reply.[15] There was so much character in all she said, and with every word I discovered fresh charms, saw new flashes of intelligence lighting up her features, which appeared gradually to brighten with pleasure because she felt that I understood her.

"When I was younger," she said, "I liked nothing so much as novels. Heaven knows I felt happy when I could sit in some corner on Sundays and share with my whole heart the fortune or distress of some Miss Jenny. Nor do I deny that this kind of romance still has some charm for me. But since I now so seldom have time for a book, it must be suited to my taste. And the author I most prefer is the one in whom I find my own world again, who describes happenings such as I see around me and yet whose story I find as interesting, as sympathetic as my own domestic existence, which is, to be sure, not a Paradise, but nevertheless on the whole a source of inexpressible bliss."

I did my best to conceal my emotions at these words. I was not, it is true, very successful, for when I heard her speak incidentally, but with such truth, about the Vicar of Wakefield and about[16]—, I lost my control and told her everything that forced itself to my lips, and only noticed after some time, when Lotte directed her remarks to the others, that these had been sitting there the whole time with wide-open eyes, as though they were not there at all. The cousin looked at me more than once with a mocking air, which however was of little consequence to me.

The conversation turned upon the pleasure of dancing. "If this passion is a fault," said Lotte, "I willingly confess I know nothing that excels danc-

[15] "It has been thought necessary to suppress this passage in the manuscript so as not to afford anyone grounds for complaint. Although, as a matter of fact, no author can be much concerned at the judgment of a single girl and an unbalanced young man."—Note in original German text.

[16] "The names of some of our native authors have been omitted here also. Whoever shares Lotte's appreciation will certainly feel in his own heart who they are, if he should read these lines. And there is no necessity for anybody else to know."—Note in original German text. Oliver Goldsmith's sentimental novel *The Vicar of Wakefield* (1766) enjoyed a considerable popularity.

ing. And when I have something on my mind and drum out a quadrille on my squeaky old harpsichord, then everything is all right again."

How I gazed into her black eyes as she spoke, how her vivacious lips and her fresh, lively mien drew my whole soul on, how totally absorbed I became in the glorious feeling of listening to her, so that I often did not even hear the words by which she expressed herself!—Of this you can have some idea, since you know me. In short, I descended from the coach as though in a dream when we came to a halt in front of the summer house, and I was still so immersed in dreams amid the darkling world around me that I hardly noticed the music which was wafted down to us from the brightly lit hall.

Two gentlemen named Audran and a certain N.N.—who can remember everybody's name!—who were the partners of Lotte and the cousin, met us at the coach door, took charge of their ladies, and I escorted mine upstairs.

We glided round one another in minuets, I engaged one lady after another, and it was just the least attractive ones who could not manage to change hands and end the figure. Lotte and her partner began an English quadrille,[17] and you can imagine how happy I was when the turn came for her to begin the figure with us. You should see her dance! She is so absorbed in it, heart and soul, her whole body *one* harmony, as care-free, as unaffected, as though nothing else mattered, as though she thought or felt nothing else, and it is certain that at such moments everything else has ceased to exist for her.

I asked her for the second quadrille, but she promised me the third, and with the most charming ingenuousness in the world she assured me that she was very fond of dancing in the German way. "It is the fashion here," she continued, "that each couple who are together remain together in the German dance, but my partner is an indifferent waltzer and he will be grateful if I relieve him of the labor. Your lady can't waltz either and doesn't like it, and I saw during the quadrille that you waltz well; if you care to be my partner for the German dance, go and ask leave of my partner while I go and ask your lady." I agreed, and it was soon arranged that her partner should sit out the waltz with mine.

We then began, and took delight in interlacing our arms in diverse ways. What charm, what fleetness of movement! And when we came to the waltz, and the dancers revolved round each other like planets, there was at first a certain amount of confusion since very few are expert at it. We were prudent and let them wear themselves out, and when the clumsiest couples had left the floor we joined in and held out valiantly to the end together with another pair, Audran and his partner. Never have I danced so easily. I was no longer a mortal. To have the most charming creature in the world in my arms and to fly around with her like lightning, so that everything round about ceased to exist and—Wilhelm, to be candid, I *did* vow that the girl I loved, on whom I had claims, should never waltz with another, even if it meant the end of me. You understand!

We took a turn or two round the room after the dance in order to recover our breath. Then she sat down, and the lemons I had stolen when

[17] A square dance involving four couples and five "figures," or patterns of steps.

the punch was being brewed, which were now the only ones left and which I brought her cut into slices with sugar, had an excellent refreshing effect, except that with every slice the lady sitting next to her took out of the cup a stab went through my heart, though for the sake of decency I had to offer it to her also.

In the third quadrille we were the second couple. As we danced through the ranks and I, God knows with what rapture, kept my eyes, as she hung upon my arm, fixed upon hers, in which shone the sincerest expression of frank and pure enjoyment, we reached a lady who had attracted my attention on account of her sympathetic mien, though her face was no longer exactly young. She looked at Lotte with a smile, lifted a minatory[18] finger, and mentioned the name Albert twice with considerable emphasis as she whirled past.

"Who is Albert," I asked Lotte, "if it is not presumption on my part?" She was about to reply when we had to separate to make the figure of eight, and it seemed to me that I saw a certain pensiveness shade her brow as we crossed in front of each other. "Why should I keep it from you?" she said, as she gave me her hand for the promenade. "Albert is a worthy man to whom I am as good as betrothed." This was not news to me, for the girls had told me in the carriage, and yet it *was* entirely new to me, since I had not thought of it in connection with her who had come to mean so much to me in such a short time. Enough—I became confused, forgot the steps, and danced in between the wrong couple so that everything became mixed up and Lotte's whole presence of mind and pulling and tugging were necessary to restore order.

The dance had not yet come to an end when the flashes of lightning, which we had for some time seen gleaming on the horizon and which I had pretended were sheet lightning, began to grow more pronounced and the thunder drowned the music. Three ladies ran out of the ranks, followed by their partners, confusion became general, and the music ceased. It is natural, when our pleasure is interrupted by an accident or something terrifying, that the impression made upon us should be stronger than usual, partly because of the contrast which is felt so vividly, partly and even more because our senses are susceptible and receive an impression all the more quickly. To these causes must be attributed the wondrous grimaces which I saw appear on the faces of several ladies. The wisest of them sat down in a corner with her back to the window and held her hands over her ears, another knelt down and buried her face in the lap of the first one, a third pushed her way in between them both and clasped her little sisters to her with a thousand tears. Some wanted to drive home, others, who were even less aware what they were doing, had not sufficient presence of mind to avoid the impertinences of some of the young gentlemen who had had a little to drink, and who appeared to be busily engaged in capturing from the lips of the beauties in distress the timorous prayers which were meant for Heaven. Some of the gentlemen had gone downstairs to smoke a quiet pipe, and the rest of the company did not refuse when the hostess hit upon the clever idea of showing us into a room which had curtains and shutters.

[18] Of warning disapproval.

Hardly had we entered when Lotte began to arrange chairs in a circle, to seat the guests and suggest a game.

I saw more than one gentleman purse his lips and stretch his limbs in expectation of a luscious forfeit.[19] "We are going to play at Counting," she said, "so pay attention. I am going round in a circle from right to left, and each of you must also count round the number that comes to him, but it must go like wildfire, and whoever hesitates or makes a mistake receives a box on the ears, and so on to a thousand."—It was a merry sight. She went round the circle with her arm stretched out. "One," cried the first, his neighbor "two," "three" the next and so on. Then she began to go more quickly, more and more quickly. One man missed his number, *smack!* a box on the ears; the next man laughed so much that he also missed, *smack!* And more and more quickly. I received two slaps on the face myself, and with secret pleasure I thought I felt that they were harder than those she gave the others. A general uproar and outburst of laughter brought the game to an end before the thousand was counted. Those who were most intimate with each other drew aside, the storm was over, and I followed Lotte into the ballroom. On the way she said, "During the ear-boxing they forgot the weather and everything!" I did not know what to reply. "I was one of the most timorous," she said, "and by pretending to be brave in order to give the others courage I became courageous myself." We stepped to the window, the thunder could be heard away to the side, and the glorious rain was pattering down on to the earth, while the most refreshing fragrance rose up to us in a full, warm vapor. She stood leaning on her elbow, her gaze searching the landscape; she looked up to the heavens and then at me, I saw her eyes fill with tears, she put her hand on mine and murmured— *Klopstock!*[20] I became submerged in the flood of emotions which this name let loose upon me. I could not bear it, I bent over her hand and kissed it amidst the most ecstatic tears. And looked up again into her eyes—Noble Poet! would that thou hadst seen thy apotheosis[21] in that gaze, and would that I might never hear again thy so oft desecrated name!

19 JUNE.

I no longer know where I broke off my story. All I know is that it was two o'clock in the morning when I went to bed, and that if, instead of writing, I had been able to babble to you, I should probably have kept you up till daybreak.

I have not yet told you what happened on our way home from the ball and I haven't time to tell you to-day either.

There was a lovely sunrise. The dripping wood and the freshened fields round about! Our companions in the coach were nodding off. She asked if I did not want to join them, as far as she was concerned I need not be embarrassed. "As long as I see your eyes open," I said, looking at her

[19] Penalty, in a parlor game.
[20] German poet (1724–1803); Charlotte is thinking of an emotional description of a thunderstorm in his ode "The Rite of Spring."
[21] Transformation into a god.

firmly, "there is no danger of that." And we both held out until we reached the gates of her home, when the maid opened gently and assured her, in answer to her inquiries, that her father and the little ones were all right and were still asleep. Then I took leave with the protestation that I would see her that same day, and I kept my promise; and since that time sun, moon and stars can journey calmly on their round, I know not whether it is night or day and the whole world about me has ceased to have any existence.

21 JUNE.
My days are as happy as those God allots to His saints; and whatever the future may have in store for me, I shall not be able to say that I have not experienced the joys, the purest joys of life. You know my Wahlheim. I am quite settled there. It is only half an hour away from Lotte, and there I feel I am myself and possess all the happiness that is granted to mankind.

Had I but thought, when I selected Wahlheim as the goal of my walks, that it lies so near to Heaven! How often in the course of my long wanderings did I see the hunting lodge, which now encompasses all my desires, either from the hill or in the plain across the river.

Dear Wilhelm, I have pondered over so many things, man's craving to extend, to make new discoveries, to rove about; and then again his inward urge to submit willingly to his limitations, to travel along the path of custom and have no thought for the right hand or the left.

It is wonderful how I came here and gazed down from the hilltop into the lovely valley, how I was enchanted by everything round about. There the little wood! Oh could you but mingle in its shade! There the summit of the mount! Oh could you but survey from there the broad landscape! The chain of hills and intimate valleys! Oh could I but lose myself in them! I hurried thither and returned, and had not found that which I sought. Oh! distant vistas are like the distant future! A vast darkling whole lies before our soul, our emotions merge into it, like our gaze, and we yearn to surrender our entire being, to be filled with all the rapture of a single great glorious feeling.—And oh! when we rush up to it, when the distant *there* becomes *here*, everything is as it was before, and we stand hemmed in by our poverty, while our soul pants for the draft that is beyond its reach.

And so even the most restless wanderer longs at last for his native land, and finds in his poor cabin, at the breast of his wife, amidst his children and the occupations necessary for their sustenance, all the rapture which he sought in vain in the wide and dreary world.

When I set out at daybreak to walk to my Wahlheim and pick peas for myself in the garden of the inn, and sit down and shell them while I read my Homer; when I then go into the little kitchen to find a pot, cut off a piece of butter, put my peas on the fire, cover the pot and sit down to keep turning them—then I feel so vividly how the glorious haughty suitors of Penelope[22] slaughtered oxen and swine, cut them up and roasted them. Nothing so fills me with a sincere, calm emotion as the features of patriar-

[22] The wife of Odysseus in Homer's *Odyssey;* during the ten years it took him to return from the Trojan war, Penelope was courted by princes who fed off Odysseus' stock.

chal life which I, thanks be to God, am able without affectation to weave into my mode of living.

How happy I am that my heart can feel the simple, innocent joy of the man who brings to his table a cabbage that he has grown himself, and enjoys at the same moment not only the cabbage but also all the fine days, the beautiful morning when he planted it, the pleasant evenings when he watered it and when he rejoiced in its increasing size.

29 JUNE.

The physician came here from the town the day before yesterday to visit the bailiff and found me on the floor among Lotte's children, some crawling over me and the others teasing me while I was tickling them, and we all made a great uproar. The doctor, who is a very dogmatic puppet and arranges the folds of his cuffs while he is discoursing and pulls out his frill as far as his navel, thought this beneath the dignity of an intelligent person, as I could see by the way he turned up his nose. I did not let myself be put out, however, but let him pursue his wise disquisition, and continued to rebuild a house of cards that the children had knocked down. He afterwards went about the town complaining that the bailiff's children were sufficiently badly brought up without that fellow Werther spoiling them completely.

Yes, Wilhelm, children are nearer to my heart than anything else on earth. When I watch them and see in the little creatures the germs of all the virtues and all the powers that they will one day find so indispensable, when I see in their obstinacy all the future constancy and firmness of character, in their wantonness all the future good humor and facility in gliding over the hazards of life, all so unspoilt, so undiminished—I always, always repeat the golden words of the Teacher of men, "Unless ye become even as one of these!"[23] And yet we treat them, who are such as we, whom we should look upon as our models, after the manner of inferior beings. They are said to be lacking in will!—Have we then none? And in what lies our superiority? In our age and maturer wisdom? God in Heaven, Thou seest old children and young children, and that is all, and Thy Son has long since proclaimed in which Thou findest greater joy. But they do not believe in Him and do not hear Him—that is also out of fashion!—and they model their children upon themselves, and —Adieu, Wilhelm, I have no wish to continue this idle talk.

1 JULY.

What Lotte must be to a sick man I feel in my own poor heart, which is worse off than many a one which is languishing on a bed of sickness. She is to pass some days in the town at the bedside of an honest woman who, so the doctors say, is nearing her end, and who wishes to have Lotte near her in her last moments. I went with her last week to visit the pastor of St., a

[23] "Except ye be converted, and become as little children, ye shall not enter into the kingdom of heaven."—Matthew 18:3.

hamlet an hour's journey away in the mountains. We arrived about four. Lotte had brought her second sister with her. When we entered the court-yard of the parsonage, which is shaded by two tall walnut trees, we found the good old man sitting on a bench before the house door, and when he saw Lotte it was as though he were imbued with new life. He forgot his knotted stick and made an effort to rise and come towards her. She ran towards him and made him sit down, while she took a seat at his side, gave him her father's best greetings, and embraced his youngest child, an un-clean, ugly lad but the darling of his father's old age. You ought to have seen her occupying the old man's attention, raising her voice to reach his half-deaf ears, telling him about robust young people who had unexpect-edly died, how excellent Karlsbad[24] was and praising his resolve to go there next summer, and how she thought that he looked much better and more cheerful than the last time she had seen him. I had meantime paid my respects to the pastor's wife. The old man became quite cheerful, and since I could not help praising the handsome walnut trees that shaded us so pleasantly, he began, though with a little difficulty, to tell us their history. "The old one," he said, "we don't know who planted that, some say one pastor, some say another. But the young one over there is the same age as my wife, fifty years next October. Her father planted it the morning of the day she was born. He was my predecessor in the living,[25] and I cannot tell you how much he loved that tree; it is in truth no less dear to me. My wife was seated beneath it on a log with her knitting when I first entered this courtyard as a poor student seven and twenty years ago." Lotte inquired after his daughter, and he told her that she had gone out to the workmen in the meadow with Mr. Schmidt; then, continuing his narrative, he ex-plained how his predecessor had grown fond of him, and the daughter as well, and how he had first become his curate and then his successor. He had hardly finished his story when his daughter came through the garden with the said Mr. Schmidt. She welcomed Lotte with considerable warmth, and I must admit that I found her by no means unattractive. A lively bru-nette with a good figure, who would have been quite entertaining company during a short stay in the country. Her suitor, for as such Mr. Schmidt soon presented himself, was a cultivated but reserved individual, who did not show any desire to join in our conversation, although Lotte kept turning to him, and what most depressed me was that I thought I could gather from his expression that it was caprice and ill-humor rather than limited intelli-gence which prevented him from being more communicative. In the sequel this unfortunately grew only too evident, for when Friederike, as we walked along, kept to the side of Lotte or occasionally came over to me, the gentleman's face, which was in any case of a brownish hue, darkened so visibly that it was time for Lotte to tug me by the sleeve and advise me to refrain from making myself agreeable to Friederike. Now nothing aggra-vates me more than when people torment each other, especially when young couples, who might be most receptive to all the joys that come in the prime of life, spoil the few days that might be so pleasant with crotchets,[26] and only realize when it is too late that they have wasted what cannot be

[24] City in what is now Czechoslovakia; site of medicinal baths.
[25] Appointment as pastor to a church. [26] Ill-natured whims.

recovered. It vexed me mightily, and when we returned to the parsonage towards evening and were supping at a table in the courtyard on bread dipped in milk, I could not help taking up the subject when the conversation turned on the joys and sorrows of this world, and attacking most heartily the vice of ill-humor. "We mortals frequently complain," I began, "that the days of our happiness are too few and those of our sorrow too many, and I think we are generally wrong. If our hearts were always open to enjoy the good which God gives us each day, then we should also have sufficient strength to bear misfortune when it comes." "But we have not control over our natures," replied the pastor's wife. "How much depends on our bodies! When we feel unwell, everything seems wrong." I admitted that. "Then let us regard it as a disease and inquire whether there is no remedy for it." "That is worth considering," said Lotte. "I believe at least that much depends on ourselves. I know it from my own nature. When anything worries me and is inclined to make me depressed, I jump up and sing a couple of quadrille airs up and down the garden, and it goes immediately." "That is just what I wanted to say," I rejoined. "Ill-humor is like laziness, for it is a kind of laziness; our natures are strongly inclined that way, and yet, when we only have the strength to assume control of ourselves, our tasks are done with no difficulty and we find a real pleasure in activity." Friederike was very attentive, and her young suitor objected that man is not his own master, having control least of all over his emotions. "We are referring here to a disagreeable emotion," I replied. "Everyone is anxious to get rid of it, and nobody knows the extent of his strength until he has tried. A sick man will certainly consult all the physicians and will not reject the greatest trials, the bitterest medicines, in order to win back the health he desires." I noticed that the worthy old man was straining his hearing to take part in the conversation, and I raised my voice as I directed my remarks to him. "People preach against so many vices," I said, "but I have never heard anyone denouncing ill-humor from the pulpit."[27] "The pastors in the towns ought to do that," he answered; "the peasants are never ill-tempered. Though it would not hurt occasionally and would at least be a lesson to our wives—to say nothing of the bailiff." Everybody burst out laughing, and he joined in heartily until he fell into a fit of coughing, which interrupted the conversation for a time, before the young man again took up the thread. "You called ill-humor a vice. I think that is an exaggeration." "Not at all," I declared, "if that which harms oneself and one's dear ones deserves the name. Is it not enough that we cannot make each other happy; must we in addition deprive each other of the pleasure that each heart is able at times to afford itself? And I should like to know the name of the man who is in an ill-humor and yet has the virtue to conceal it, to bear it alone without destroying the happiness of those around him. Is it not rather an inward displeasure at our own unworthiness, a dissatisfaction with ourselves which is always combined with an envy that a foolish conceit has incited? We see happy people whose happiness has not been caused by *us,* and we cannot bear it." Lotte smiled at me when she saw the vehemence with which I

[27]"We now possess an excellent sermon by Lavater on this text, among those on the Book of Jonah."—Note in original German text. Johann Kaspar Lavater (1741–1801) was a Swiss thinker whom Goethe highly admired.

spoke, and a tear in the eye of Friederike spurred me on to continue. "Woe be to those," I said, "who abuse their power over the heart of another to deprive it of the simplest joys that spring up in it. All the gifts, all the good-will in the world, cannot replace a moment of pure pleasure which the envious constraint of a tyrant has embittered."

My whole heart was full at this moment, the memory of so much that had happened in the past rushed into my soul, and my eyes filled with tears.

"If people would only think to themselves every day," I cried, "that you can do nothing for your friends save leave them their pleasure and augment their happiness by enjoying it with them. Have you the power, when their inmost soul is tortured by an agony of passion, torn with grief, to offer them a drop of comfort? And when the last fatal sickness overtakes the being whom you helped to wear away in the days of her youth, and she lies there in pitiable exhaustion, her eyes raised unseeingly to Heaven, the death-sweat coming and going on her brow, and you stand at the bedside like one of the damned, with the feeling in your inmost soul that with all your power you can do nothing, you are inwardly convulsed with the agonizing thought that you would give your all to be able to instill into the dying being a particle of vigor, a spark of courage."

The memory of such a scene, at which I had been present, took possession of me with undiminished force as I uttered these words. I put my handkerchief to my eyes and left the company. Only the voice of Lotte, who called to me that it was time to go, brought me to myself. And how she scolded me on the way home for taking too warm an interest in everything, declaring that it would be my ruin, that I should spare myself!—Oh angel! For thy sake I must live!

6 JULY.

She is still looking after her dying friend and is always the same, always the devoted, lovely creature who soothes pain and spreads happiness wherever she goes. She went for a walk yesterday evening with Marianne and little Amalie. I knew of this and went to meet them. After an hour and a half we had come back to the town and the spring which is so precious to me, and which became a thousand times more precious when Lotte sat down on the wall beside it. I gazed around, and alas! the time when my heart was so solitary again came vividly into my mind. "Beloved spring," I said, "I have not rested since then in thy cool shade, and often have I hastened past thee without a glance." I looked down and saw that Amalie was ascending the steps with a glass of water. I looked at Lotte and felt all that she means to me. Amalie meanwhile approached with the glass and Marianne wanted to take it from her, but "No!" cried the child with the sweetest expression, "no, you shall drink first, Lotte!" I was so enraptured with the sincerity, the goodness with which she said this, that I found no other way to express my emotion but to take the child up in my arms and kiss her so violently that she straightway began to scream and weep. "That was wrong of you," said Lotte. I was disconcerted. "Come, Amy," she continued, taking the child by the hand and leading her down the steps, "quick, wash your face in the

running water and it won't hurt you." As I stood there and watched the child busily rubbing her cheeks with her wet hands; when I saw the faith she had that the miraculous spring would wash away all defilement and prevent the disgrace of growing an ugly beard; how she even continued to wash away after Lotte had said, "It's enough!", as though too much was better than too little—I tell you, Wilhelm, I have never felt more reverent at a baptism. And when Lotte came up, I would have liked to cast myself at her feet as before a prophet who has washed away in consecrated water the sins of a nation.

That evening I could not help, in the happiness of my heart, relating the incident to a man from whom I expected human understanding, since he is a man of common sense. But what did I find! He said it was very wrong of Lotte, that children should not be told such stories, since they gave rise to all sorts of misconceptions and superstitions, against which children should be guarded at an early age. It occurred to me, however, that he had had a child of his own baptized a week previously, so I said nothing and silently kept to my conviction that we ought to treat children as God treats us.—He makes us happiest when He lets us wander on under the intoxication of agreeable illusions.

8 JULY.

What children we are! How we crave a glance! What children we are! We had gone to Wahlheim. The ladies were driving out, and during our walks I thought I could see in Lotte's black eyes—I am foolish, forgive me, but you should see these eyes. In short, for I can hardly keep my eyes open, the ladies were getting into the coach round which young W., Selstadt, Audran and I were standing. They were talking through the window to the fellows who were, to be sure, pretty thoughtless and frivolous. I sought Lotte's eyes! Alas! they were glancing from one to the other! But on me! me! me! who stood there absorbed in her alone, they did not fall! My heart bade her a thousand adieux! And she did not see me! The coach drove past and a tear stood in my eye. I gazed after her! And I saw Lotte's coiffure leaning out of the window as she turned to look back. Oh! at me?—It is in this uncertainty that I hover! It is this which is my consolation. Perhaps it was I at whom she turned to look. Perhaps—good night! Oh! how childish I am!

10 JULY.

You should see what a foolish figure I make when she is spoken of in company. And when I am asked how I like her—like! I hate the word. What sort of a fellow must he be who likes Lotte and whose whole mind, whose whole heart is not entirely absorbed by her. Like! The other day someone asked me how I liked Ossian![28]

[28] In one of the great literary frauds of the century, James Macpherson published in the 1760s supposed translations of a legendary third-century Gaelic poet named Ossian. Goethe shared the widespread craze over these works. A passage from Macpherson-Ossian appears later in *Werther*.

11 JULY.

Mrs. M. is very ill. I pray for her, for I suffer with Lotte. I see her rarely at a friend's, and to-day she told me of a marvelous happening. Old M. is a miserly curmudgeon who has curbed and harassed his wife pretty well during her life, though she has always been able to manage tolerably. A few days ago, when the doctor said there was no hope for her, she sent for her husband while Lotte was in the room and spoke to him thus: "I must confess something that might cause you confusion and vexation after my death. Hitherto I have kept house in as orderly and economical a manner as possible, but you will forgive me for having deceived you these thirty years. When we first married, you allowed me a trifling sum for food and other domestic expenses. When our household became larger and our business grew, I could not move you to increase my weekly allowance to meet the altered circumstances. In short, you know that when our expenses were greatest I had to manage with seven florins a week. I accepted this amount without protest and abstracted the remainder from the receipts every week, since no one had any suspicion that your wife would steal from the till. I have never been extravagant and would have gone tranquilly to my eternal rest without confessing this, if it were not that the one who follows me in keeping house for you will not know how to make both ends meet, and yet you might still insist that your first wife had been able to manage."

I talked with Lotte concerning the incredible delusion of the human mind, which can prevent a man from suspecting that there is something wrong when seven florins suffice to cover an obvious outlay of possibly twice as much. I have, however, myself known people who would not have been surprised at the presence in their house of the widow's inexhaustible cruse.[29]

13 JULY.

No, I am not deceiving myself! I can read in her black eyes a real interest in me and my destiny. Yes, I feel (and in this matter I can trust my heart) that she—Oh! may I, can I express the Paradise that lies in these words?— that she loves me.

Loves me! How the thought exalts me in my own eyes! How I—I may tell you, perhaps, for you can sympathize with such an emotion—how I worship myself since she loves me.

And be it presumption or perception of the true state of affairs—I do not know the man whose rivalry I would have to fear in Lotte's heart. And yet—when she speaks of her betrothed with such warmth, with such affection, I feel like one who has been deprived of all his honors and dignities and has had to yield up his sword.

16 JULY.

Oh! how the blood rushes through my veins when my finger accidentally touches hers, when our feet meet under the table. I draw back as from a

[29] Jar. God sustained the prophet Elijah during a drought and famine by having him lodge with a widow whose store of food was miraculously replenished. 1 Kings 17:1–16.

flame, and a secret force thrusts me forward again. All my senses swim. And oh! her innocence, her pure soul, does not feel the torment which these little intimacies occasion me. When she lays her hand on mine as we converse, and moves nearer to me as she grows more interested, so that her divine breath is wafted to my lips—I feel that I am about to sink to the ground as though struck by lightning. And, Wilhelm, if I should ever dare to—but no, my heart is not so depraved! Weak! weak enough! Is that not depravity?

She is sacred to me. All lust ceases in her presence. I am never aware what I feel when I am with her; it is as though my soul were revolving in all my nerves. There is a melody which she plays on the harpsichord with the touch of an angel, so simple and spiritual. It is her favorite song, and I am cured of all my harassing bewilderment and melancholy so soon as she strikes the first note.

I do not find it difficult to believe the stories of the magic power of music in ancient times. How this simple song fascinates me! And how well she knows when to play it, often at a time when I feel like putting a bullet in my brain! All the confusion and gloom in my soul are dispersed, and I breathe more freely again.

18 JULY.

What meaning has the world for our souls without love, Wilhelm? It is a magic lantern[30] without its lamp. Hardly have you inserted the lamp when the most colorful pictures appear on the white screen. And even if that were all there is, nothing but passing phantoms, yet it makes us happy when we stand in front like simple children and are enraptured by the wonderful pictures. I was unable to visit Lotte to-day, being detained by an unavoidable engagement. What could I do? I sent my lad out, just to have somebody about me who had been in her presence to-day. How impatiently I awaited his return, how glad I was to see him again! I would have liked to take him in my arms and embrace him, had I not been ashamed to do so.

It is said of the Bologna stone that when it is placed in the sun it attracts the rays, and is luminous for a time by night. So it was with the lad. The feeling that her eyes had rested on his face, his cheeks, his coat buttons, the collar of his surtout,[31] made them all so sacred and precious to me that I would not at that moment have exchanged the lad for a thousand *Talers*.[32] I felt so happy in his presence.—May God preserve you from laughing at this. Can these be phantoms, Wilhelm, that make us so happy?

19 JULY.

"I am going to see her!" I cry aloud every morning, when I am aroused and gaze happily at the glorious sun. "I am going to see her!" And I have no further wish for the rest of the day. Everything, everything is absorbed in this prospect.

[30] An early form of the slide projector. [31] Long, close-fitting coat.
[32] German silver coins.

20 JULY.

I cannot yet accept your suggestion that I should accompany the ambassador to * * *. I am not fond of discipline, and we all know that he is, in any case, a disagreeable fellow. You write that my mother would like to see me occupied? It makes me laugh. Am I not now occupied? And is it not, at bottom, a matter of indifference whether I count peas or lentils? Everything in this world ends in nothingness, after all, and a fellow who wears himself out for somebody else's sake, without its being his own ambition, in order to achieve wealth or dignity or anything else, is simply a fool.

24 JULY.

Since you are so anxious that I should not neglect my drawing, I would rather say nothing about it than confess that hitherto I have done little.

I was never happier, never has my sympathy with Nature down to the stones and blades of grass been fuller and more ardent, and yet—I know not how to express myself, but my powers of perception are so weak, everything swims and trembles before my soul so that I cannot seize the outline; but I think, if I had clay or wax, I could probably fashion it out. If this lasts much longer I shall procure some clay and mold it, even if all I can make is cakes.

I have begun Lotte's portrait three times, and each time I have made a mess of it, which vexes me all the more since I got it quite successfully some time ago. Then I cut out her silhouette, and that will have to suffice.

26 JULY.

I have often made up my mind not to see her so frequently. If I could only keep to my resolution! Every day I succumb to temptation and promise myself sacredly that I will stay away next day, and when the morning comes I again discover some irresistible reason and find myself there before I am aware of it. Either she has said the evening before, "You will come tomorrow, won't you?" (who could remain away under such circumstances?)—or the day is so very lovely, I walk to Wahlheim, and when I am there it is only half an hour to her. I am too near to her presence—in a trice I am there. My grandmother used to tell me a story of a magnetic mountain. The ships which approached too closely to it were suddenly deprived of all their ironwork, the nails shot towards the mountain, and the poor wretches sank amidst the collapsing planks.

30 JULY.

Albert has arrived, and I shall go. Even if he were the best, the most noble of men, to whom I were prepared in every respect to give way, it would be intolerable to see him before my eyes in possession of so many perfections. Possession!—Enough, Wilhelm, her betrothed has arrived. A worthy, agreeable fellow, whom one cannot help liking. Luckily, I was not present when she welcomed him. It would have torn my heartstrings. He is so honorable and has never even kissed Lotte when I was there. May God reward him for it! I must love him for the respect with which he treats the

girl. He is well-intentioned towards me, but I suspect that is due to Lotte more than to his own disposition, for in this matter women are delicate, and rightly so. If they can keep two admirers on good terms with each other, the advantage is always theirs, though it is seldom practicable.

Meanwhile I cannot deny Albert my esteem. His outward calm is in very vivid contrast to the restlessness of my character, which I am unable to conceal. He is a man of feeling and knows what he possesses in Lotte. He appears rarely to be in an ill-humor and, as you know, that is the sin I hate more than any other.

He considers me a man of intellect, and my attachment to Lotte, with the ardent pleasure I take in all her actions, increases his triumph, and he loves me all the more. Whether he does not sometimes plague her privately with petty jealousy is a matter about which I will offer no opinion. At any rate, I should not in his place be altogether free from the demon.

Be that as it may, my pleasure in Lotte's company is gone. Am I to call it foolishness or infatuation? What do names matter? The thing itself is evident. I knew everything that I know now before Albert came. I knew that I could have no claim on her, nor did I make any, that is to say, as far as it is possible to be without desire in the case of so many charms. And the ridiculous fellow opens his eyes wide now that the other man has arrived and takes the girl away.

I grit my teeth and mock at my wretchedness, and mock doubly and trebly at those who might say I should be resigned, since it cannot be helped.—Rid me of these fellows!—I wander about in the woods, and when I come to Lotte's and Albert is sitting with her in the summer house in the garden, and I can get no further, I behave in an extravagant manner, practice all sorts of crazy buffoonery. "For Heaven's sake," Lotte said to me to-day, "I beg of you! no more scenes like that of yesterday evening! You are dreadful when you act so wildly." Between ourselves, I wait till he is occupied elsewhere; *presto!* I am there in a trice, and I am always happy when I find her alone.

8 AUGUST.

Please, Wilhelm, I did not mean you when I wrote, "Rid me of the fellows who say I ought to be resigned." I really did not think that you could be of that opinion. And at bottom you are right. Only one thing, my dear friend! In this world it is rarely possible to settle matters with an "either, or," since there are as many gradations of emotion and conduct as there are stages between a hooked nose and one that turns up.

So you will not take it amiss if I grant you your whole argument and nevertheless try to steal my way between your "either, or."

Either I have hopes of Lotte, you say, or I have not. Good! In the former case I must seek to realize them, seek to achieve the fulfilment of my desires; in the latter case I must pull myself together and try to rid myself of a wretched emotion which is bound to consume all my energies. That is well said, my friend, and—soon said.

Can you demand of the unhappy man whose life is gradually and irremediably ebbing under the influence of an insidious malady, can you demand of him that he should put an end to his torture with a dagger? Does

not the disease which is consuming his energies at the same time rob him of the courage to procure his own deliverance?

You can of course answer me with a similar allegory—who would not rather submit to the amputation of an arm than risk his life by doubts and hesitations? I do not know. And we will not attack each other with allegories. Enough . . . Yes, Wilhelm, I often have such moments of bounding, vehement courage, and then, if I only knew whither, I would probably go.

10 AUGUST.

I could lead the happiest and best of lives were I not a fool. Such a combination of favorable circumstances is rarely found for the delight of a man's heart as that in which I am now placed. Alas! how true it is that our heart is alone responsible for its own happiness. To be a member of this charming family, loved by the old man like a son, by the little ones like a father, and by Lotte . . . and now this worthy Albert, who never disturbs my happiness by any display of ill-humor, who regards me with sincere friendship, who, next to Lotte, loves me more than anything in the world. Wilhelm, it is a joy to hear us on our walks, when we talk about Lotte. There has never been anything more ridiculous than this relationship, and yet it often brings the tears to my eyes.

When he tells me about her righteous mother, how she entrusted her house and children to Lotte on her deathbed and confided Lotte to his care, how since then Lotte has been imbued with a new spirit, how in her concern for the household she has really become a mother, how not a moment of her time but has been occupied or absorbed in some task of affection, and yet she has not lost her cheerful lightheartedness. I walk along beside him and pluck flowers by the wayside, bind them very carefully into a nosegay and—cast them into the brook that flows past to watch them gently float along. I do not know whether I have written to you that Albert is to remain here and receive a post at a handsome salary from the Court,[33] where he is in very good favor. I have rarely seen his equal for regularity and diligence at his occupation.

12 AUGUST.

Albert is certainly the most excellent of men. There was an extraordinary scene between us yesterday. I went to his house to take leave of him, for I had conceived a desire to ride into the hills, whence I am now writing to you, and as I was walking up and down the room I caught sight of a pair of pistols. "Lend me your pistols," I said, "for my journey." "Certainly," he replied, "if you will take the trouble to load them; I only keep them here *pro forma*."[34] I took one of them down, and he continued, "Since my prudence played me such a scurvy trick, I don't like having anything more to do with the things." I was curious to hear the story. "When I was staying with a friend in the country for about three months," he told me, "I had a brace of unloaded pocket-pistols with me and slept unperturbed. One rainy after-

[33] The sovereign or the people around him. [34] As a matter of form (Latin).

noon, as I was sitting idly thinking, it occurred to me for some reason or other that we might be attacked, that we might have need of the pistols and—you know the sort of thing I mean. I gave them to the servant to clean and load. He dallies with the maidservants, tries to frighten them, and, the Lord knows how, the pistol goes off with the ramrod still in it, and shoots the latter through the ball of the thumb of the right hand of one of the girls, smashing it. I had to bear the lamentation and pay the surgeon into the bargain, and since that time I leave my pistols unloaded. My dear fellow, what's the use of precautions? One cannot guard against every peril. To be sure. . . ." Now, you know, I am very fond of the man until he says "To be sure . . ."; for is it not a matter of course that every general proposition is subject to exceptions? But he is so anxious to justify his opinion, that when he thinks he has said anything rash, made a general statement, or uttered a half-truth, he never ceases to qualify, modify, add to, or subtract from what he has said, until finally there is nothing left of his original assertion. On this occasion he dilated at great length on the subject, till I at last ceased to listen to him, subsided into a state of melancholy, and pressed the mouth of the pistol with a flourish to my forehead above the right eye. "Come!" said Albert, snatching at the pistol. "What is the meaning of this?" "It is not loaded," I said. "And even so, what is the meaning of it?" he asked impatiently. "I cannot imagine how a man can be so foolish as to shoot himself. The very thought is repellent."

"Why do you people," I cried, "when you speak of anything, declare immediately 'this is foolish, this is wise, this is good, this is bad!' What is the meaning of it all? Have you discovered the inward circumstances of an action? Can you determine exactly why it happened, why it was bound to happen? Had you done that, you would be less hasty in your judgments."

"You will admit," said Albert, "that certain actions are vicious from whatever motive they may occur."

I shrugged my shoulders and granted him that. "But, my dear fellow," I continued, "even in that case there are exceptions. It is true that thieving is a vice, but does a man who sets out to steal in order to preserve himself and his family from a miserable death by starvation, deserve punishment or sympathy? Who will be the first to cast a stone at the man who sacrifices an unfaithful wife and her worthless seducer to his righteous wrath? Against the girl who in a moment of rapture loses herself amid the impetuous joys of love? Even our laws, those cold-blooded pedants, are not insensible, and refrain from punishment."

"That is a very different matter," Albert replied, "because a man who is swept away by passion is deprived of all power of reflection and is in the same category as a drunkard or a madman."—"Oh you men of reason!" I cried with a smile. "Passion! Drunkenness! Madness! You stand there so calmly, you moral creatures, so unsympathetic, scolding the drunkard, abhorring the lack of reason, passing by like the priest and thanking your God like the Pharisee that he has not made you like one of these.[35] I have been drunk more than once, my passions were never far from madness,

[35] In the parable of the Good Samaritan, the priest passes by the man in distress without helping him; Luke 10:31. For the Pharisee's self-righteous boast of superiority to sinners, see Luke 18:11.

and for neither do I feel remorse, for I have learned in my own measure to understand that all men above the ordinary who have done anything great or seemingly impossible have invariably been decried as drunkards or madmen.

"But even in our daily life it is intolerable to hear it said of a man who has done anything at all generous, noble or unexpected, 'The fellow is crazy,' or 'The fellow is drunk.' Shame upon you sober beings! Shame upon you sages!"

"This is another of your crotchets," said Albert. "You exaggerate everything, and here at least you are certainly wrong in comparing suicide, which we are now discussing, with exalted actions, since it is not possible to regard it as anything but a weakness, for it is surely easier to die than to bear a life of agony without flinching."

I was about to break off, for no argument in the world so disconcerts me as when a fellow comes out with some insignificant platitude when I am speaking with my whole heart. But I contained myself, for it had often occurred to me and I had often been vexed at it, and rejoined with some heat, "You call that weakness? I beg of you not to be deceived by appearances. When a nation is groaning under the intolerable yoke of a tyrant, can you term it weak if it finally rises up and bursts its fetters? When a man, under the influence of horror at seeing his house break out in flames, is able to put forth all his strength and bear with ease burdens which in a calmer mood he can scarcely move—when a man, in a rage at some injury, attacks half a dozen foes single-handed and conquers them—are these to be called weak? And, my friend, if exertion is strength, why should over-tension be the reverse?"

Albert looked at me and said, "Do not take it amiss, but the instances you quote appear to me to be quite inapplicable." "It may be so," I replied. "I have often been informed that my method of argument verges on the absurd. Let us see then whether we can in any other way depict the state of mind of a man who has resolved to cast off the burden of life, which is generally so agreeable, for only in so far as we experience his emotions can we have the right to discuss the matter."

"Human nature," I continued, "has its limits; it can bear joy, sorrow and pain to a certain degree, but it succumbs when this is exceeded.

"The question, therefore, is not whether a man is strong or weak, but whether he can endure the measure of his suffering, moral or physical, and I find it just as extraordinary to say that a man is a coward who takes his own life, as it would be improper to call a man a coward who dies of a virulent fever."

"Paradoxical, very paradoxical," cried Albert. "Not so much as you imagine," I replied. "You will admit we call it a mortal disease when nature is so seriously affected that its forces are partly consumed, partly so put out of action that it cannot be set right, that the ordinary course of life can not by any happy transformation be restored.

"Well, let us apply this to the mind. Let us see how man is circumscribed, how he is affected by impressions, obsessed by ideas, until finally a growing passion robs him of the power of calm reflection and brings him to grief.

"It is in vain that a cool, reasoning individual perceives the unhappy

man's condition and talks to him in a persuasive manner, just as a healthy man is unable to inspire an invalid with even a modicum of his own vigor."

This was speaking in terms too general for Albert. I reminded him of a girl who had been found dead in the water some time previously, and recapitulated her story. "A respectable young creature, who had grown up within the restricted sphere of her domestic occupations, with no other prospect of amusement than being able to walk out on a Sunday in the best clothes which she had gradually accumulated, her companions being girls in a similar situation to herself, with an occasional dance on the chief holidays, or the opportunity of whiling away an hour or two by a lively chat with a neighbor about the cause of a quarrel or some scandalous rumor; whose ardent nature eventually felt more inward cravings, which were intensified by the flatteries of men. All her former pleasures gradually grew insipid, till she finally met a man to whom she was irresistibly attracted by some hitherto unknown emotion, on whom she cast all her hopes, forgetting the world about her, hearing nothing, seeing nothing, sensing nothing but him alone, longing for nothing but him alone. Unspoilt by the empty pleasures of an inconstant vanity, her desire marches straight to its fulfilment; she wants to be his, to find in an indissoluble union all the happiness which she has missed, to experience all the combined joys for which she has longed. Reiterated promises, which seal the certainty of all her hopes, bold caresses, which intensify her cravings, encompass her whole being; she hovers in a semi-conscious state of bliss, with the premonitory feeling of supreme rapture, worked up to the highest pitch, until at last she stretches forth her arms to embrace her desires—and is abandoned by her lover. Stupefied, out of her mind, she stands on the verge of an abyss, everything is dark around her, with no hope for the future, no solace, since he has left her with whom alone her existence was bound up. She is blind to the world which lies before her, to those who could replace what she has lost, she feels herself alone, abandoned by all the world. And unseeingly, oppressed by the dreadful agony in her soul, she hurls herself down to still her torment in an encircling death.—That, Albert, is the story of so many mortals, and tell me, is it not analogous to the condition of an invalid? Nature can find no way out of the entangled labyrinth of confused and contradictory instincts, and the mortal must die.

"Woe to him who would say, 'Foolish woman! Had she but waited till time had exerted its healing effect, her despair would have abated and another would have come to give her solace.' That is as though one would say, 'The fool! to die of a fever! Had he but waited till his strength was restored, his humors were adjusted, the tumult of his blood had subsided, all would have been well and he would still be alive to-day!'"

Albert, who was still unwilling to accept my analogy, continued to put forward objections, among others, that I had only adduced the case of a simple girl; and he wanted to know what excuse could be found for a reasoning being who was not so circumscribed and understood better the connections of things.

"My friend," I cried, "a man is a man, and the little reasoning power he may possess is of small advantage, or of none at all, when passion rages and he is oppressed by the limits of humanity. Much rather—but another time," I said, and seized my hat. Oh! my heart was so full. And we parted,

without having understood each other. How difficult it is for one to understand the other in this world!

15 AUGUST.
It is, after all, certain that nothing in the world renders a man indispensable save love. I feel that Lotte would not willingly lose me, and the children have no other notion but that I shall return every morning. I went out to-day to tune Lotte's harpsichord, but I was unable to set to work at it, for the children besought me to tell them a fairy tale, and then Lotte herself asked me to comply with their wish. I cut the bread for their supper, which they now accept almost as eagerly from me as from Lotte, and told them their favorite tale of the princess who was served by hands. It teaches me a great deal, I assure you, and I am amazed at the impression it makes on them. Since I often have to invent an episode, which on the next occasion I forget, they tell me at once that it was different at the previous telling, so that I now practice reciting it mechanically in a sort of chant. This has taught me that an author must necessarily spoil his book when he alters the story for a second edition, however much it may be improved from the artistic point of view. The first impression finds us receptive, and man is so constituted that he can be convinced of the most extravagant incidents; these, however, are immediately embedded in his mind, and woe to him who attempts to erase and obliterate them.

18 AUGUST.
Was it ordained by Fate that that which renders a man happy becomes later the source of his misery?

My heart's full and ardent sympathy with Nature, which flooded me with such bliss and made the world round about into a Paradise, has now become an unbearable torment, a torturing spirit which pursues me everywhere. When I used to stand upon the rock and survey the fertile valley across the river as far as the distant hills, when I saw everything about me surge forth and germinate, the mountains clad thickly from foot to summit with tall trees, all the vales in their manifold windings shaded by the most delightful forests, with the river gently flowing among the whispering reeds, mirroring the clouds which were wafted along by the gentle evening breeze; when I heard the birds awakening the forest and the myriad swarms of midges danced merrily in the red rays of the setting sun, whose last quivering glance roused the humming chafer from his grassy bed, while the whirring life about me drew my attention to the ground, where the moss, which wrests its nourishment from the hard rock, and the broom, which grows down the arid sandhill, revealed to me the inward, fervent, sacred life of Nature—how I took all this into my ardent heart, lost myself in its unending abundance, while the glorious forms of the unending world stirred within my animated soul. Vast mountains surrounded me, precipices lay at my feet, torrents poured down, rivers streamed below me, and forest and hills resounded. I saw all the unfathomable forces at their interweaving work of creation in the depths of the earth. Above the earth and below the sky there swarm the innumerable species of creatures. Everything, every-

thing populated with a thousand kinds of shapes, and mankind secures itself in little houses and settles down and rules in its own way over the wide world. Poor fool! you who deem everything of little significance because you are yourself so small. From the inaccessible mountain, across the wilderness which no foot has ever trod, to the end of the unknown ocean there breathes the spirit of the Eternal Creator Who rejoices at every speck of dust that receives it and lives. How often have I longed to be borne on the wings of the crane which flew above my head to the shores of the immeasurable ocean, to quaff the swelling rapture of life from the foaming goblet of the infinite, and to feel for but a moment the curbed forces of my soul extended by one drop of the bliss of that Being Who brings forth all things in and through Himself.

Brother, it is only the memory of those hours that gives me ease. Even the exertion of recalling and again clothing in words those inexpressible emotions, exalts my soul above itself, only to let me feel in double measure the anguish of my condition.

It is as though a curtain has been drawn from before my soul, and the scene of eternal life is being transformed before my eyes into the abyss of the ever open grave. Can you say *This is,* when everything is transitory, everything rolls past with the speed of lightning, only rarely endures till its life force is spent, but is carried away by the current, submerged and smashed against the rocks? Not a moment but consumes you and yours, not a moment when you do not yourself destroy something, and inevitably so. The most innocent stroll costs a myriad tiny creatures their lives, one step annihilates the laborious construction of a nation of ants and crushes a world in little to ignominious ruin. It is not the great occasional catastrophes of the world, the floods that sweep away your villages, the earthquakes that devour your cities, by which I am moved. It is the consuming force latent in universal Nature, that has formed nothing that has not destroyed its neighbor and itself, which saps my soul. And so I reel along in anguish, surrounded by earth and sky and all the weaving forces of Nature. I see nothing but a monster, eternally devouring, eternally chewing the cud.

21 AUGUST.

In vain I stretch out my arms towards her in the morning when I wake from troubled dreams. In vain I seek her at night in my bed when an innocent dream has made me happy with the illusion that I am sitting beside her in the meadow, holding her hand and covering it with a thousand kisses. Oh! when I put out my hand to touch her, still drunk with sleep, and rouse myself by doing so, a stream of tears wells up from my oppressed heart, and I weep for the hopelessness of the gloomy future.

22 AUGUST.

My condition is wretched, Wilhelm! All my energies are reduced to a restless inactivity. I cannot be idle, and yet I am unable to take up any task. I have no power of imagination, no interest in Nature, and my books all repel me. When we lose ourselves, we have lost everything. I vow I could

sometimes wish to be a laborer, so as to have every morning, when I awake, some prospect for the ensuing day, some urge, some hope. I often envy Albert, whom I see buried to the ears in his documents, and pretend to myself that I should like to be in his place. More than once it has suddenly occurred to me to write to you and the minister in order to apply for the post at the legation which you assure me I should not fail to obtain. I believe so too. The minister has long been fond of me, and used frequently to urge me to take up some profession. For an hour or so I occupy myself with the notion, but later, when I think about it again, I remember the fable of the horse that was tired of its freedom, allowed itself to be saddled and bridled, and was ridden to death. I do not know what to do, and is not perhaps my longing for a change in my situation a deep-seated, uneasy impatience which will pursue me wherever I may go?

28 AUGUST.

Truly, if my malady could be cured, these people would do it. It is my birthday to-day, and very early this morning I received a packet from Albert. As soon as I opened it I caught sight of one of the pink bows that Lotte was wearing on her bosom when I first met her, and which I had since then more than once asked her for. There were also two little books in duodecimo[36] in the packet, the Wetstein edition of Homer, which I had so often wanted to possess so as not to have to drag about the edition of Ernesti on my walks. You see! that is how they anticipate my desires, how they think of all the small friendly services which are a thousand times more appreciated than the brilliant presents that humiliate us and are due to the vanity of the giver. I kiss the bow a thousand times, and with every breath I drink in the memory of the rapture which more than filled those few happy days that can return no more. The blossoms of life are only a mirage. It is so, Wilhelm, and I do not complain. How many fade and do not leave a trace behind; how few bear fruit, and how little of the fruit reaches maturity! And yet sufficient remain, but—Oh my brother! can we neglect, despise the ripened fruit, let it wither and rot without having been enjoyed?

Farewell! The summer is glorious and I often sit in the fruit trees in Lotte's orchard, picking pears from the highest branches with a long rod. She stands below and receives them when I reach them down.

30 AUGUST.

Foolish wretch that I am! Do I not deceive myself? What is the purpose of all this endless raging passion? I offer no prayers now save to her; no form appears before my mind save hers; and everything in the world about me I see only in relation to her. And this affords me so many happy hours—till I must again tear myself away from her. Oh! Wilhelm, whither does my heart so often urge me! When I have sat with her thus for two hours or three, feasting my eyes on her form, her bearing, listening to the divine

[36] Pocket-size book format.

words that come from her lips, and then gradually all my senses become taut, my eyes grow dim, I hardly hear what is said, and I feel as though some assassin were gripping me by the throat, while my heart beats wildly in the endeavor to free my oppressed senses but only increases their confusion—Wilhelm, I am scarcely aware at such times whether I am in this world! And often, if melancholy does not gain the ascendancy and Lotte offer me the wretched solace of pouring forth my anguish in tears upon her hand, I am compelled to rush away, out into the fields where I rove about, or to find pleasure in climbing a steep hill, thrusting my way through a trackless wood, being wounded by hedges and torn by thorns. Then I feel somewhat relieved. Somewhat! And when I sometimes sink down on the way, overcome with weariness and thirst, in the dead of night when the full moon is floating above my head, or sit on a crooked tree in the lonely forest to rest the aching soles of my feet, and fall asleep in the lulling stillness of the half light. . . . Oh! Wilhelm, a solitary cell, a hair-shirt[37] and a belt of thorns were the relief for which my soul is languishing. Adieu! I see no end to all this misery but the grave.

3 SEPTEMBER.
I must away. I thank you, Wilhelm, that you have confirmed my wavering resolve. For a fortnight I have been trying to make up my mind to leave her. I must. She is again in the town on a visit to a friend. And Albert—and—I must away.

10 SEPTEMBER.
What a night that was! Now, Wilhelm, I can surmount anything. I shall not see her again. Oh! that I cannot fly to your breast, tell you amid a thousand tears and transports all the emotions which are assailing my heart. Here I sit and gasp for air, try to calm myself, and await the morning. The horses are to be ready at dawn.

She sleeps peacefully and does not think that she will never see me again. I have torn myself away, was strong enough, during a conversation lasting two hours, not to reveal my purpose. And God! what a conversation!

Albert had promised me that he would be in the garden with Lotte immediately after supper. I stood on the terrace beneath the tall chestnuts and gazed at the sun, which I saw for the last time sinking over the lovely valley and the gentle stream. How often I had stood with her at this spot watching the same glorious scene, and now. . . . I walked to and fro along the avenue which was so dear to me; I had so often been bound here by some mysterious, sympathetic attraction before ever I knew Lotte—and how we rejoiced when we discovered, at the beginning of our friendship, our mutual inclination for the place, which is really one of the most romantic productions of art that I have ever seen.

First, you have the broad prospect between the chestnut trees—Oh! I

[37] A painfully rough undergarment worn by religious ascetics.

remember I have, I think, already written you a lot about how one is finally closed in by a high rampart of beeches and the avenue grows darker and darker on account of a plantation[38] that adjoins it, until one at last emerges into a confined clearing over which there hovers the awe of solitude. I can still feel the queer emotion by which I was stirred when I first entered it one high noon; I had a faint presentiment of all the pain and bliss of which it was to be the scene.

I had been revelling for about half an hour in the sweet languishing thoughts of parting and seeing her again, when I heard them coming up the terrace, ran towards them, seized her hand with an inward shudder and kissed it. We had just reached the top when the moon rose behind the tree-clad hill; we spoke of a diversity of things and approached imperceptibly the gloomy recess. Lotte entered and sat down, Albert at her side, and I also seated myself, but my restlessness soon made me start up again; I stood in front of her, walked to and fro, sat down again and was most distressed. She drew our attention to the beautiful effect of the moonlight which illuminated the whole terrace at the end of the rampart of beeches, a glorious sight which was rendered all the more striking by the deep twilight which closed us in all round. We were silent, and after a time she said, "I never go for a walk in the moonlight without being accompanied by the thought of my dead ones, without being oppressed by the feeling of death, of what is to come. We shall exist, Werther," she continued with the most exalted emotion in her voice, "but shall we meet again? and recognize one another? What do you surmise, what do you say?"

"Lotte," I replied, giving her my hand, my eyes filling with tears, "we shall meet again! Here and beyond!"—I could say no more. . . . Wilhelm, why did she have to ask me that, at the moment when I bore the anguish of this parting in my heart?

"And do our dear departed ones know anything about us?" she continued. "Do they feel, when it fares well with us, that we remember them with warm affection? Oh! my mother's form is always hovering about me, in the quiet evenings when I am sitting among her children, my children, and they are gathered round me as they were once gathered round her. When I gaze yearningly up to Heaven with tears in my eyes and wish that she might for a moment be able to look down and see how I am keeping the promise I gave on her deathbed to be a mother to her children. A hundred times I cry out, 'Forgive me, dearest one, if I am not to them what you were. Oh! I do whate'er I can, they are clad, fed, and oh! what is more than all, cared for and loved. Could you but see the harmony in which we live, dear saint! You would glorify with the most fervent gratitude the God Whom you entreated with your last bitter tears to protect your children!'"

That is what she said. Oh! Wilhelm! who can repeat her words, how can the dead cold letter depict the divine efflorescence of her spirit? Albert broke in gently, "It affects you too deeply, dear Lotte; I know your soul clings strongly to these notions, but I beg of you . . ." "Oh! Albert!" she said, "I know you do not forget the evenings when we sat together at the

[38] Grove of cultivated trees.

small round table, when father was away on a journey and we had sent the little ones to bed. You often had a good book with you, but you seldom succeeded in reading anything. Was not intercourse with this splendid soul more than all else? The beautiful, gentle, cheerful, ever busy woman! God knows with what tears I often cast myself before Him as I lay in bed, and entreated Him to make me as she was."

"Lotte!" I cried, throwing myself at her feet and seizing her hands, which I moistened with a thousand tears. "Lotte! the blessing of God and the spirit of your mother rest upon you." "If you had known her," she said, pressing my hand, "she was worthy to be known by you." I thought I should swoon. Never had anything so exalted, so proud been said in my praise. She continued, "And this woman was taken away in the prime of her life, when her youngest son was not yet six months old. Her illness did not last long, she was tranquil, resigned, regretting only her children, especially the babe. As the end drew near she said to me, 'Let them come up to me,' and I brought them in, the little ones who did not understand, and the older ones who were beside themselves; they stood round the bed and she raised her hands and prayed over them, and kissed them one after the other and sent them away, and said to me, 'Be a mother to them!' I gave her my hand as I made the vow. 'It is no little thing which you are promising, my daughter,' she said, 'the heart of a mother and the eye of a mother. I have often seen by your grateful tears that you know what that means. Let your brothers and sisters find them in you, and show to your father the faithfulness and obedience of a wife. You will afford him consolation.' She asked after him, but he had gone out to conceal from us the unbearable grief he felt. His heart was lacerated.

"You were in the room, Albert! She heard someone walking, inquired who it was, and asked you to approach. And as she gazed at you and at me, with a tranquil look, confident that we should be happy, happy together. . . ." Albert fell on her neck and kissed her, and cried, "We are! we shall be!" The usually serene Albert had entirely lost his self-possession, and I myself was on the verge of losing consciousness.

"Werther," she began, "this is the woman that we have lost! God! when I think, as I so often do, how we thus let the dearest thing in our life be taken away, and no one feels it so keenly as the children; who long continued to complain that the black men had carried away their mama."

She rose, but I was agitated and shaken and remained seated, holding her hand. "We must go," she said; "it is growing late." She wished to withdraw her hand, but I held it more firmly. "We shall meet again," I cried. "We shall come together, under whatever form we shall recognize one another. I go, I go willingly, and yet, if I had to say 'for ever,' I could not bear it. Farewell, Lotte! Farewell, Albert! We shall meet again." "To-morrow, I think," she replied jestingly. I was affected by this "to-morrow." Oh! she did not know as she withdrew her hand from mine . . . They went out along the avenue, I stood, looked after them in the moonlight, then threw myself on the earth and wept my fill, sprang up, ran out on to the terrace and could still perceive below, in the shadow of the tall limes, her white frock gleaming on the way to the garden door, I stretched out my arms, and it disappeared.

PART TWO

20 OCTOBER.
We arrived at this place yesterday. The ambassador is unwell, & will there-
fore keep to the house for some days. If only he were not so ungracious, all
would be well. I perceive, I perceive that Fate has hard trials in store for
me. But I must be of good courage! A light heart can bear everything. A
light heart! I cannot help laughing as the word falls from my pen. A little
more lightness of heart would make me the happiest being under the sun.
What! where other men, with their modicum of energy and talent, are
strutting around me in complacent self-assurance, do I despair of my en-
ergy, of my talents? God in Heaven, Who didst endow me with all this, why
didst Thou not withhold the half and give me instead self-confidence and
contentment!

Patience! Patience! Things will mend. For I tell you my friend, you are
right. Since I have been compelled to move about among the people like
this every day, and see what they do and how they go about things, I am on
much better terms with myself. To be sure, since we are, after all, so consti-
tuted that we compare everything with ourselves and ourselves with every-
thing, happiness or misery lies in the things with which we establish the
analogy, and so nothing is more dangerous than solitude. Our power of
imagination, forced by its nature to assert itself, nourished by the fantastic
visions of poetry, raises for itself a series of beings of which we are the
lowest, and where everything that is external to ourselves appears more
splendid, everyone else more perfect. And the process is quite natural. We
feel so often that there is something lacking in us, and it is just what we lack
that often appears to us to be possessed by someone else, to whom we then
impute, in addition, everything that we have ourselves and a certain ideal
ease to boot. And so the happy being is perfect, the creature of our own
imagination.

When, on the other hand, weak as we are, we only continue laboriously
with our work, we very often find that with all our dawdling and tacking[39]
we get further than others with their sails and oars—and—it does impart a
feeling of self-confidence when one keeps up with or even outstrips others.

10 NOVEMBER.
I am beginning to settle down tolerably well here so far. The best of it is
that there is enough to do, and then the various kinds of people, the diver-
sity of new faces, present a motley scene to my soul. I have made the
acquaintance of Count C., a man whom I learn to esteem more every day.
A broad and lofty mind, making allowances for much and therefore by no
means unsympathetic. One's connection with him is illumined by such feel-
ing for friendship and affection. He took an interest in me when I had
some business to arrange with him, and he perceived at the opening of our
conversation that we understood one another, that he could talk to me as

[39] Laborious zigzag sailing into the wind.

he could not talk to everybody. And I cannot sufficiently praise his frank bearing towards me. There is no real ardent pleasure to equal that of being given access to a great soul.

24 DECEMBER.
The ambassador causes me much chagrin, as I anticipated. He is the most meticulous fool that can be imagined. He proceeds step by step and is as fussy as an old woman. A man who is never satisfied with himself and whom therefore nobody can please. I like to work quickly, and as a thing turns out so I leave it, but he is capable of giving me back a memorandum and saying, "It is good, but look through it again, there is always a better word, a more precise particle." It is enough to drive me crazy. No "and" or other conjunction may be omitted, and he is a mortal enemy of all the inversions which occasionally escape me. If one's periods[40] are not ground out in accordance with the time-honored rhythm, he is unable to understand them. It is a penance to have to deal with such a man.

The confidence of Count von C. is the only thing which compensates me. He confessed to me quite openly the other day how dissatisfied he is with the dull-witted scrupulousness of my ambassador. Such people make things more difficult for themselves and for others. "But," he said, "we must be resigned, like a traveller who has a mountain to cross. Of course, if the mountain weren't there, the way would be easier and shorter, but it *is* there and it has to be got over."

My chief probably feels, also, the preference the Count gives me over him, and that vexes him, so that he seizes every opportunity to speak ill of the Count to me. I oppose him, of course, and thereby only render matters worse. Yesterday he even made me fly into a passion, for he included me in his remarks—that the Count was quite good for affairs of the world, being a very quick worker and having a facile pen, but he was lacking in solid erudition, like all literary folk. I would have liked to thrash him for this, for there is no other way of reasoning with such fellows, but since this was not possible, I disputed with some heat and told him that the Count was a man who inspires esteem not only on account of his character but also of his knowledge. "I have never known anyone," I said, "who has so succeeded in enlarging his mind, to embrace matters innumerable, without surrendering his activity in ordinary life." This was all Greek to his brain, and I took my leave to avoid having to choke down more choler at further nonsensical talk.

You are all responsible for this, who talked me into assuming the yoke and prated so much of "activity." Activity! If the man who plants potatoes and rides to town to sell his corn, is not doing more than I, then I will wear myself out for another ten years in the galley to which I am now fettered.

And the gilded misery, the boredom among the loathsome people who are assembled here! Their love of rank, the way they keep watch and guard to steal the smallest march[41] upon each other, their most wretched and pitiable passions which they make no attempt to conceal. There is a woman, for instance, who tells everybody about her noble birth and her country, so

[40] Sentence constructions. [41] Stealthily gain the slightest advantage.

that every stranger must think, "What a fool she is with her conceited notions of her trivial patent of nobility and the fame of her country." That isn't the worst of it, however, for this very woman is the daughter of a district clerk in these parts. I cannot understand the human race that has so little sense as to make such a downright fool of itself.

To be sure, I perceive more clearly every day how foolish it is to judge others by oneself . . . And since I have so much to occupy me in myself, and my heart and mind are so tempestuous—oh! I would gladly let the others go their way, if they could only let me go my way too.

What irritates me most of all is the odious social conditions. To be sure, I am as well aware as anybody of the necessity for class distinctions and of the advantages that I myself receive from them; but they ought not to stand in my way just when I could enjoy a little pleasure, a gleam of happiness on this earth. During one of my walks recently I made the acquaintance of a Fräulein von B., a charming creature, who has preserved considerable naturalness in spite of the stiff conventional life here. We found one another's conversation agreeable and, when we parted, I asked permission to call upon her. This she granted with such frankness, that I could hardly await the appropriate hour to go to her. She does not come from this part, and is staying with an aunt, an old maid whose physiognomy was displeasing to me. I paid the latter much attention, applied my conversation mostly to her, and in less than half an hour I had pretty well conjectured what the young lady herself afterwards admitted to me—that the aunt, lacking everything, with neither a respectable fortune nor qualities of mind, has no support in her old age other than her ancestral tree, no protection other than the rank behind which she barricades herself, and no pleasure except to look down from her height and ignore the middle classes. She is said to have been beautiful in her youth and to have trifled away her life, first tormenting many a poor young man with her capriciousness, and in later years bowing to the domination of an elderly officer, who, in return for this and a passable income, passed the brass age[42] with her and then died. And now she has reached the iron age, she is alone, and would not receive any consideration, if her niece were not so charming.

8 JANUARY, 1772.

What creatures they are whose whole soul is bound up with ceremonial, whose thoughts and aims are for years directed towards the means of worming their way on to a chair which is one move higher up the table! And it is not as though the fellows had no other opportunities. No! there is work in abundance, for the very reason that the petty vexations hinder the progress of the important matters. Last week there was a quarrel during a sledge drive and all the fun was spoilt.

Fools, not to see that the place does not really matter at all, and that he who occupies the first very rarely plays the chief part! How many kings are ruled by their ministers, and how many ministers by their secretaries! And who is then the first? The one, it seems to me, who can take in the others at

[42] According to myth, the human race degenerated from golden to silver to bronze (or brass) to iron ages.

a glance, and has sufficient power or cunning to harness their energies and passions to the execution of his plans.

20 JANUARY.
I must write to you, dear Lotte, here in the taproom of a poor rustic inn where I have taken refuge from a heavy storm. Since I have been moving about in that wretched hole of a town, among strangers, complete strangers to my heart, there has not been a moment, not a single one, when my heart bade me write to you. And now in this hut, in this solitude, where I am so hemmed in, and snow and hail are beating furiously against the window panes, here my first thought was of you. As I entered, your form appeared before my mind. Oh, Lotte! with such sacred fervor! God! the first happy moment recaptured!

If you could see me now, in this deluge of distraction! How dried up my senses are becoming, not one moment when I can allow my heart full play, not one single hour of tearful bliss! Nothing! Nothing! It is as though I am standing in front of a raree-show,[43] watching the mannikins and the little horses moving about, and I often ask myself whether it is not an optical illusion. I join in the general movement, or rather I am moved like a marionette, and often seize the wooden hand of my neighbor and start back with a shudder.

I have only discovered a single feminine being here. A Fräulein von B. She resembles you, Lotte, if it is possible for anyone to resemble you. "Ah!" you will say, "the fellow is paying compliments!" There is some truth in that. For some time I have been very well-mannered, since, after all, I cannot help myself. I have a ready wit, and the ladies say nobody utters such delicate compliments as I do (and lies, you will add, for otherwise they cannot be successful, do you follow me?). I was speaking about Fräulein B. She has much soul which shines from her blue eyes, and is oppressed by her rank which does not satisfy any of her heart's desires. She longs to escape from the turmoil, and we pass many an hour in fanciful conversation about rural scenes of unalloyed happiness—and about you. How often does she have to pay you homage! There is no "must," she does it with all her heart, likes so much to hear about you, loves you.

Oh! would that I were sitting at your feet in the dear familiar room, and our little ones were tumbling about around me, and when they grew too noisy for you I would collect them round me and quieten them with a weird fairy tale. The sun is setting gloriously over a gleaming, snow-white earth, and the storm has passed on. And I—must again shut myself up in my cage. Adieu! Is Albert with you! And how—? God forgive me the question!

17 FEBRUARY.
I fear that my ambassador and I will not stay together much longer. The fellow is perfectly unbearable. His way of working and doing business is so ridiculous, that I cannot refrain from contradicting him and frequently doing a thing in my own way and to my own mind, which, of course, then

[43] Exhibition viewed through a small peephole.

never suits him. He recently complained of me at Court on this account, and the minister reproved me, mildly to be sure, but nevertheless it was a reproof, and I was about to send in my resignation when I received a private letter[44] from him, a letter before which I sank on my knees and worshipped the lofty, wise and noble mind that knows so well how to correct my too great sensitiveness, respecting, indeed, my exaggerated notions of activity, of influence over others, of getting the mastery in affairs, as a praiseworthy, youthful spirit, trying not to eradicate them, but only to temper them and guide them to where they can have full scope and achieve their most useful purpose. I am now fortified for a week, and in harmony with myself. Tranquillity of soul is a glorious thing, and joy in oneself. Dear friend, if only the thing were not just as fragile as it is beautiful and precious.

20 FEBRUARY.

God bless you, my dear ones, and grant you all the happy days that He takes from me.

I thank you, Albert, for deceiving me; I was awaiting news when your wedding day was to be, and had intended on that day solemnly to take down Lotte's silhouette from the wall and bury it under other papers. Now you are married, and her portrait is still here! Well, it shall stay! Why not? I know that I am also with you, that I am in Lotte's heart, without prejudice to you. I have, yes, I have the second place in it, and will and must retain it. Oh! I would go mad, if she were able to forget. . . . Albert, hell lies in the thought. Albert, farewell! Farewell, angel from heaven, farewell, Lotte!

15 MARCH.

I have been subjected to a mortification that will drive me away from here, and makes me gnash my teeth. The Devil! It cannot be made good, and the whole fault is yours, all of you who spurred me on, and drove me and worried me to accept a post that was not to my mind. Well, here I am! You have got your way! And in order that you may not tell me again that my exaggerated notions spoil everything—here, my dear Sir, is a story, clear and simple, as a chronicler would record it.

Count von C. is fond of me, pays me special attention, that is well known and I have already told you so a hundred times. I was dining with him yesterday, on the particular day when the aristocratic company of ladies and gentlemen assembles at his house in the evening. I had forgotten this, and it never occurred to me that we of inferior rank are not acceptable on such occasions. Good. I dine with the Count, and after table we walk up and down the great hall, I converse with him and with Colonel B. who puts in an appearance, and thus the hour for the party approaches. God knows, I suspect nothing. Then there enters the more-than-gracious Madame von S. with her consort and her nobly hatched little goose of a flat-chested,

[44] "This letter, together with another which is referred to later on, has been withdrawn from this collection out of respect for this excellent man, as it was not thought that such boldness could be excused by the gratitude, however warm, of the public."—Note in original German text.

tight-laced daughter. They widen their eyes and nostrils in the traditional, highly-aristocratic manner *en passant*,[45] and, as I loathe the herd with all my heart, I was about to take my leave, waiting only until the Count should be free from the exchange of dreadful twaddle, when suddenly my Fräulein von B. entered. Since it always raises my spirits a little when I see her, I remained, took my place behind her chair, and only noticed after some time that she was talking to me with less frankness than usual, indeed with some embarrassment. I was struck by this. If she is like all these people, I thought to myself, may the Devil take her! I was irritated and wanted to depart, and yet remained, for I was intrigued and wished for more light on the matter. Meanwhile the room was filling up. Baron F., wearing his whole wardrobe dating from the coronation of the Emperor Francis the First,[46] Hofrat[47] R., here called *in qualitate* Herr *von* R.,[48] with his deaf wife etc., to say nothing of J., who is badly off, his antiquated garments contrasting strangely with the fashionable oddments he wore with them—all these were arriving, and I was conversing with some of the people I knew, who were all very laconic.[49] I was occupied with my thoughts, and only concerned with my Fräulein B. I did not notice that the women were whispering to each other at the end of the room, that this infected the men, that Frau von S. was talking to the Count (Fräulein B. told me all this afterwards), until finally the Count came up to me and led me to a window. "You are aware," he said, "of our odd conventions. The company, I observe, is displeased to see you here. I would not for anything in the world. . . ." "Your Excellency," I interrupted, "I beg a thousand pardons. I should have thought of it before, but I know you will forgive my *faux pas*.[50] I was about to take my leave some time ago, but," I added with a smile as I bowed, "an evil genius held me back." The Count pressed my hand with a sympathy which said more than words. I made my bow to the distinguished company, and took a coach as far as M. to see the sun setting from the top of the hill, and read in my Homer the glorious canto where Ulysses is entertained by the worthy swineherd.[51] This was all delightful.

In the evening I returned home to sup. There were only a few people left in the coffee-room, and they had turned back the table cloth and were throwing dice in a corner. Then Adelin came in, put down his hat, as he glanced at me, came up and said softly, "You were rebuffed?" "*I* was?" I said. "The Count asked you to leave the company." "The Devil take them," I said. "I was glad to get out into the fresh air." "Good," he said, "that you treat it lightly. But I am annoyed. Everybody is talking about it." Now for the first time the matter began to vex me. I thought everyone who looked at me at table did so because he knew about it. This began to rouse my choler.[52]

[45] In passing (French).
[46] Holy Roman Emperor from 1745 to 1765. The present date is 1772.
[47] Court Councillor.
[48] Given the aristocratic preposition *von* ("of"), since he has been accepted in aristocratic company.
[49] Abrupt in speech. [50] Social blunder.
[51] In Homer's *Odyssey*, the disguised Odysseus, after returning to Ithaca, enjoys the hospitality of his faithful old swineherd Eumaeus.
[52] Anger.

And now, when I am pitied wherever I go, when I hear those who are jealous of me exclaiming triumphantly that one could see what happened to arrogant fellows who boasted of their modicum of intellect and thought it gave them a right to set themselves above all conventions, and that sort of twaddle—it is enough to make a man stick a knife in his heart. For whatever people may say about independence, I would like to see who can bear scoundrels talking about him when they have him at a disadvantage. If it is only empty talk, oh! then one can easily ignore them.

16 MARCH.

Everything is combining to provoke me! Today I met Fräulein B. in the avenue. I could not refrain from addressing her, and showing her, as soon as we were some distance from the rest of the company, that I was hurt at her recent behavior. "Oh! Werther!" she said, in a tone of deep sincerity, "could you thus interpret my confusion, knowing my heart as you do? How I suffered for your sake, from the moment when I entered the room! I foresaw everything, a hundred times it was on the tip of my tongue to warn you, I knew that Madame von S. and Madame von T., together with their husbands, would rather take their departure than stay in your company, I knew that the Count would not venture to fall out with them—and now all this fuss . . ." "What do you mean?" I asked, and concealed my dismay, for everything that Adelin had told me the day before yesterday coursed through my veins like boiling water at this moment. "How much it has already cost me!" said the sweet creature, with tears in her eyes. I could no longer control myself, was about to throw myself at her feet. "Tell me what you mean," I cried. The tears ran down her cheeks. I was beside myself. She dried them without any attempt at concealment. "You know my aunt," she began. "She was there, and oh! how she opened her eyes! Werther, I endured last night and this morning a sermon about my intercourse with you, and had to listen to you being disparaged, degraded, and was only half able to defend you."

Every word she uttered pierced my heart like a sword. She did not see what a mercy it would have been to hide all this from me, and she now told me all the further gossip there would be, how all the malicious fellows would be triumphant. How from now on they would proclaim that my arrogance and disdain of others, which they had long blamed in me, was now punished and humbled. To hear all this from her lips, Wilhelm, in a tone of sincerest sympathy—I was overcome, and am still raging inwardly. I wish someone would dare to cast it in my teeth,[53] that I might thrust my sword through his body! If I were to see blood I should feel better. Oh! I have taken up a knife a hundred times to let air into my suffocating heart. It is related of a noble species of horses that, when they are frightfully heated and at their last gasp, they instinctively bite open a vein to help them to breathe. I often feel like that. I would like to open a vein and achieve eternal freedom.

[53] Reproach me (and thus provoke a duel).

24 MARCH.
I have handed in my resignation at Court and hope it will be accepted. You will forgive me for not asking your permission first. I *had* to go away, and I already know everything you would say to persuade me to stay, so—sugar the pill for my mother. I cannot help myself so she must put up with it, though I cannot help her either. It will certainly grieve her. To see the brilliant career which was leading her son to a privy councillorship or an embassy suddenly interrupted and the horse put back in its stable! Make of it what you will and add up the possible eventualities which might have made it possible for me to stay, or obliged me to do so. Enough, I am going. And that you may know whither I am going, Prince ***, who relishes my society, is here, and asked me, when he heard of my intention, to accompany him to his estates and spend the beautiful spring there. He has promised that I shall be left entirely to myself and, since we understand each other up to a certain point, I will try my luck and go with him.

19 APRIL.
For your Information.
I thank you for your two letters. I did not reply, since I was leaving this letter until my resignation had been accepted at Court, for I feared my mother might apply to the minister and render my purpose difficult. Now, however, it is all over, and I have my discharge. I hardly like to tell you how unwillingly they gave it me, and what the minister has written; you would break out into fresh lamentations. The hereditary prince has sent me a parting gift of twenty-five ducats, with a letter that moved me to tears. So my mother need not send me the money I wrote for recently.

5 MAY.
I leave here to-morrow, and since the place where I was born is only a few miles away, I would like to see it again, and recall the happy days I used to dream away. I will enter by the very gate from which I drove out with my mother when she left the dear, familiar spot after my father's death, to shut herself up in her unbearable town. Adieu, Wilhelm, you shall have news of my progress.

9 MAY.
I have fulfilled the pilgrimage to my home with a pilgrim's reverence and have been affected by many an unexpected emotion. I stopped at the great lime tree, a quarter of an hour's journey outside the town on the way to S. I alighted and bade the postillion[54] take the coach on, that I might go on foot to savor each memory anew, vividly, and in my own way. There I stood beneath the lime which used to be the goal and boundary of my walks as a boy. How different the circumstances! Then, in my blissful ignorance, I had yearned to go out into the unknown world, where my heart hoped to

[54]Coachman.

find all the nourishment, all the enjoyment of which I so often felt the lack
in my bosom. Now I was coming back from the wide world—with oh! how
many hopes miscarried, how many plans shattered!—I saw the range of
mountains in front of me, that had times without number been the object
of my desires. I had sat here for hours at a time, yearning to be there,
fervently absorbed in the woods and valleys which appeared before me in
an intimate halflight—and then, when the time came to return home, how
unwillingly I left the beloved spot! I approached the town, greeted all the
old familiar summer-houses, and disliked the new ones as well as all the
other changes which had taken place. I went in through the gate and there
I found myself again completely. I will not give you all the details, for,
charming as they were to me, the record would only be monotonous. I had
made up my mind to take a lodging in the market-place, next door to our
old house. As I walked along I noticed that the little school, where our
childhood had been penned up by an honest old dame, was turned into a
shop. I recalled the restlessness, the tears, the mental apathy and heart-
aches I had endured in that den.—Every step I took was fraught with
interest. No pilgrim in the Holy Land comes across so many shrines of
pious memory, and the souls of few are so filled with sacred emotion. One
more detail that must suffice for a thousand. I went down the river to a
certain farm, which used also to be one of my walks, and looked at the
places where we boys tried who could make the flat stones rebound most
often as we skimmed them along the surface of the water. I remember most
vividly how I often stood there and gazed at the stream, the wondrous
presentiments with which I followed it, how romantic the country ap-
peared to me to which it was flowing, how I soon found that there were
limits to my imagination and yet I had to penetrate further, ever further,
until I had completely lost myself in the illimitable distance. Is that not just
what the glorious patriarchs felt! When Ulysses[55] speaks of the immeasura-
ble ocean and the unbounded earth, is not that more true, more human,
more fervent, than nowadays when every schoolboy thinks himself a mira-
cle of wisdom because he can repeat that the world is round?

Here I am in the Prince's hunting-box.[56] He is quite agreeable to live
with, being simple and sincere. I am often pained, however, when he talks
about things that he only knows from hearsay or reading, and always from
a second-hand point of view.

And he has more understanding for my intellect and talents than for
my heart, which is, after all, my only pride, the sole source of everything, all
vigor, all bliss and all misery. Oh! anyone can know what I know.—My
heart is my own.

25 MAY.

I had something in my mind about which I was unwilling to tell you any-
thing until it had been put into execution but, now that it has come to
nothing, I may just as well do so. I wanted to go to the wars! My heart was
long intent on it. It was the chief reason why I came here with the Prince,
who is a general in the *** service. I revealed my intention to him during

[55] Homer's Odysseus. [56] Hunting lodge.

one of our walks, he dissuaded me, and it would have had to be a passion rather than a whim to prevent me listening to his arguments.

11 JUNE.
Say what you will, I cannot stay any longer. What is the use? I am finding it tedious. The Prince treats me as an equal and yet I do not feel at home. And we have not really anything in common. He is a man of intellect, but of a low order, and I find his conversation no more entertaining than a well-written book. I shall stay another week and then resume my wanderings. The best thing I have done here is my sketching. The Prince has a feeling for art, though this would be deeper if he were not limited by the abominations of science and the usual terminology. It often makes me gnash my teeth when, upon my introducing with warmth and imagination topics of nature and art, he thinks he is doing quite well as he suddenly blunders in with some conventional technical term.

18 JUNE.
Where am I going? I will tell you in confidence. I have to remain here another fortnight after all, and then I pretend to myself that I am going to visit the mines in ***. Nothing of the sort, however. I only want to see Lotte again. That is all. And I ridicule my own heart—but shall do what it demands.

29 JULY.
No, it is all right! Everything is all right! I—her husband! Oh! God, Who made me, if Thou hadst granted me that bliss, my whole life would be one continual prayer. I will not complain, and crave pardon for these tears, pardon for my vain desires.—She—my wife! If I had the dearest being under the sun enfolded in my arms—a shudder goes through my whole body, Wilhelm, when Albert embraces her slender waist.

And—ought I to say it? Why not, Wilhelm? She would have been happier with me than with him! Oh! he is not the man to fulfill all the longings of that heart. A certain lack of delicacy, a lack—take it as you will, that his heart does not beat in sympathy at—oh!—at a passage in a beloved book where my heart and Lotte's meet as one. In a hundred other cases, when it happens that we express our feelings at the action of someone else. Dear Wilhelm!—He *does* love her with his whole soul, and what is such a love not worth. . . .

I have been interrupted by an insupportable fellow. My tears are dried. I am distracted. Adieu, dear friend!

4 AUGUST.
I am not the only one to suffer thus. All men find their hopes deceived, their expectations betrayed. I visited the good woman who lives by the lime tree. Her eldest boy ran towards me, and his shouts of joy attracted his mother, who looked very downcast. Her first words were, "Good Sir! Alas,

my Hans is dead."—He was the youngest of her sons. I was silent.—"And my husband," she continued, "has returned from Switzerland with empty hands, and were it not for some kind people he would have had to go a-begging. He fell ill of a fever on the way." I knew not what to say to her, and gave something to the little one. She asked me to accept some apples, which I did and left the place of melancholy memory.

21 AUGUST.

I change in a flash. Sometimes I find a gleam of joy in life once more, but alas! only for a moment. When I thus lose myself in my dreams, I cannot avoid the thought—"What if Albert were to die! You would, she would—," and then I pursue the will o' the wisp till it leads me to the verge of abysses before which I shudder back.

When I go out at the town gate, the way I first went when I fetched Lotte to the ball—how different it all was! All, all is over. Not a vestige of the former world, not a throb of the emotion I then felt. I feel like a ghost that has returned to the burnt-out castle which it once built in its princely glory and bequeathed on its death-bed, splendidly furnished, to a beloved son.

3 SEPTEMBER.

I am sometimes unable to comprehend how another can, or may love her, when I love her so singleheartedly, so fervently, so completely, and know nothing, am aware of nothing, have nothing but her.

6 SEPTEMBER.

I had a difficult struggle before I was able to make up my mind to put aside the simple blue coat in which I first danced with Lotte, but it grew at last too shabby. I have had a new one made, just like the last, with collar and facings, and another yellow waistcoat and pair of breeches.

But it has not quite the same effect. I do not know—perhaps, with time, I shall grow to like it more.

15 SEPTEMBER.

It is enough to make one resign oneself to the Devil to see all the hounds that God tolerates on this earth, without sense or feeling for what little there is of value on it. You know the walnut trees beneath which I sat with Lotte at the honest old clergyman's in St., the glorious walnut trees which, God knows, always filled my soul with the greatest content. How intimate and cool they made the courtyard, how glorious their branches were. And the memories they held, back to the good clergymen who had planted them so many years ago. The schoolmaster often mentioned the name of one of them, which he had learned from his grandfather. He is said to have been such a worthy man and his memory was always sacred to me under the trees. I tell you there were tears in the schoolmaster's eyes yesterday when

we discussed their having been cut down.—Cut down! The thought makes me frenzied, I could murder the hound who struck the first blow. I, who could pine away with grief if a few trees stood in my courtyard and one of them withered with age—I have to look on at this. But there is one point worth mentioning. What a thing is human feeling! The whole village is muttering, and I hope the minister's wife will feel the difference in the way of butter, eggs and other presents, to show how she has wounded the villagers. For it is she who is to blame, the wife of the new minister (the old one is dead), a scraggy, sickly brute with very good cause to take no interest in the world, since no one takes any in her. An ugly creature who puts forth pretensions to learning, takes a hand in the examination of the canon,[57] works a great deal at the new-fangled, critico-moral reformation of Christianity and shrugs her shoulders at the enthusiasms of Lavater, is quite shattered in health and therefore without joy on God's earth. Only such a creature could find it possible to cut down my walnut trees. I cannot keep cool! Just imagine, the falling leaves make the courtyard dank and dirty, the trees take away the light and, when the nuts are ripe, the boys throw stones at them and that jars her nerves, disturbs the profundity of her meditations when she is pondering the differing views of Kennicott, Semler and Michaelis.[58] When I saw how discontented the villagers were, especially the old ones, I asked why they had suffered it. "When the mayor wants a thing hereabouts," they replied, "what can we do?" But one justice was done at least. The mayor and the parson, who at any rate wanted to make something out of his wife's whims, which don't bring him in much profit, thought of sharing the proceeds, but the revenue-office heard of it and said, "This way please!", and sold the trees to the highest bidder. There they lie! Oh if I were but a Prince! The parson's wife, the mayor and the revenue-office would be—Prince!—Well, if I were a Prince, would I worry about the trees in my country!

10 OCTOBER.

If I only look into her black eyes, I am already cured! And what mortifies me is that Albert does not appear to be as happy as he—expected—as I—thought I would be—if—I am not fond of dashes, but it is the only way I can express myself here—and I think it is clear enough.

12 OCTOBER.

Ossian has crowded Homer out of my heart. To what a world this glorious poet has introduced me! To wander over the heath, with the storm wind howling round me, carrying along in the steaming mists the ghosts of ancestors under the light of the moon. To hear from the mountains, amid the roaring of the forest river, the fading groans of spirits in their caves and the laments of the maiden pining with grief by the four moss-covered, grass-grown stones that mark the grave of her noble lover. Then when I find him, the wandering gray bard, who seeks on the broad heath the

[57] Of the authenticity of books of the Bible. [58] Biblical scholars.

foot-steps of his fathers, and finds alas! their tombstones, and then gazes lamenting at the evening star which is hiding in the rolling ocean, and ages long gone by re-awaken in the soul of the hero, when the friendly beam shed its light upon the perils of the brave ones and the moon illumined their ship returning wreathed in victory; when I read the deep sorrow on his brow, see the last forlorn hero tottering exhausted to the grave, drinking in ever fresh, grievously glowing joys in the impotent presence of the shades of his departed ones, and looking down on the cold earth and the high waving grass, crying out: "The traveller will come, will come, who knew me in my beauty and will ask, 'Where is the minstrel, Fingal's worthy son?'[59] His foot-step will pass over my grave and he will ask for me upon the earth in vain."—Oh Friend! I would like to draw my sword like a noble armor-bearer[60] and free my lord with one blow from the quivering torment of this slowly receding life, and send my soul to follow the freed demi-god.

19 OCTOBER.

Oh! this void, this dreadful void within my breast. I often think—if you could but press her once, only once, to your heart, the void would all be filled.

26 OCTOBER.

Yes, I am growing certain, friend, certain and ever more certain, that the existence of any creature matters little, very little. One of Lotte's friends came to see her, and I went into the next room to find a book, but could not read, so took up a pen to write. I heard them speaking softly, exchanging trifling gossip, news of the town, how one girl had married, another was very sick. "She has a dry cough, the bones are sticking out of her face, she gets fainting fits, I wouldn't give a penny for her life," said the friend. "So and so is also in a bad way," said Lotte. "He has swollen up already," said the other. My vivid imagination set me at the bedsides of these poor people, I saw how reluctantly they turned their backs on this life, how they—and Wilhelm, these ladies were discussing the matter in the way we usually discuss a stranger's death. And when I look round, and see the room, with Lotte's clothes lying about, her ear-rings here on the table, and Albert's papers and the furniture with which I am so familiar, even this ink-pot, and think to myself, "See what you are to this house! All in all. Your friends esteem you. You often make them happy and your heart feels that it could not exist without them; and yet—if you were to go? if you were to leave this circle? would they, and for how long, feel the void which your loss would make in their lot? for how long?"—Oh! man is so transitory that even where he finds the actual certainty of his existence, where he leaves the only true impress of his presence, in the memory, in the soul of those he loves—even there he must be extinguished, must disappear, and oh! how soon!

[59] Fingal was the legendary Ossian's father.
[60] Warrior who carried his ruler's weapons.

27 OCTOBER.

I would often like to tear my breast and dash out my brains at the thought that two mortals can be so little to one another. The love, the joy, the ardor, the rapture that do not come from myself will not be given me by another, and though my whole heart be full of bliss I cannot make another happy if he stands before me cold and limp.

30 OCTOBER.

If I have not a hundred times been on the verge of embracing her! The great God knows what it feels like to see so much charm about one and not be able to grasp it. And that is yet the most natural of human instincts. Do not children grasp at everything they see?—And I?

3 NOVEMBER.

God knows, I lie down to sleep so often with the wish, sometimes with the hope, that I shall not wake again; and in the morning I open my eyes, see the sun again and am wretched. Oh! that I could be peevish, could shift the blame to the weather, to a third party, to an unsuccessful venture; the intolerable burden of ill-humor would then only half rest upon myself. Woe is me, I feel only too truly that the whole fault is mine alone—not fault! Enough that the source of all my misery lies concealed within myself, as formerly was the source of all my happiness. Am I not still the same who formerly hovered amidst all the abundance of emotion, with a Paradise following on every step, with a heart able to embrace a whole world with love? And this heart is now dead, no more delights flow from it, my eyes are dry, and my faculties, no longer revived by refreshing tears, draw uneasy furrows across my brow. I am suffering much, because I have lost what was the sole delight of my life, the holy vivifying power with which I created worlds around me. It has gone!—When I look out of my window at the distant hill, as the morning sun pierces the mist above it and illumines the tranquil meadows in the valley, and the gentle stream winds towards me between its leafless willows—oh! when this glorious scene appears before me as fixed as a varnished picture and all this rapture is incapable of pumping a single drop of happiness from my heart up into my brain, and my whole churlish self stands before the face of God like a dried-up spring, like a cracked pitcher! I have so often cast myself upon the ground and implored God to send me tears as a husbandman[61] prays for rain, when the sky is brazen[62] overhead and the earth about him is parched.

But oh! I feel that God does not send rain and sunshine at our impetuous bidding, and those times, the memory of which torments me, why were they so happy if not because I patiently awaited His spirit and received with a grateful fervent heart the rapture which He caused to descend upon me!

8 NOVEMBER.

She has reproached me with my lack of control, and oh! so gently! That I sometimes allow myself to be seduced by a glass of wine into drinking the

[61] Farmer. [62] Like brass.

whole bottle. "Don't do it," she said, "think of Lotte!" "Think!" I said. "Do you need to bid me do that? I think!—or do not think! You are always present to my soul. I sat to-day at the spot where you alighted lately from the coach. . . ." She changed the topic, to stop me pursuing the subject further. Friend, I am lost! She can do with me what she will.

15 NOVEMBER.

I am grateful to you, Wilhelm, for your sincere sympathy, for your well-meant advice, and would beg you to be tranquil. Let me endure it to the end; with all my lassitude I have strength enough to see it out. I have respect for religion, as you know, I feel that it is a staff for many a weary soul, refreshment for many who are faint. But—can it, must it then be for everyone? When you look at the great world, you see thousands for whom it has not been, thousands for whom it will not be—preached or not preached—must it then be for me? Does not even the Son of God say that those would be about Him whom His Father has given to Him?[63] Supposing our Father wishes to keep me for Himself, as my heart tells me? I beg you, do not interpret this falsely, do not look for mockery in these innocent words; it is my whole soul that I am baring to you. Otherwise I would rather have remained silent, for I do not willingly waste words about things of which no one knows any more than I do. What is it but the fate of man to endure his lot, to drain his cup?—And if the cup was too bitter for the human lips of the God Who came from Heaven,[64] why should I brag and pretend it tastes sweet to me? And why should I be ashamed, in the dread moment when my whole existence is trembling between being and not being, when the past is gleaming like lightning over the dark abyss of the future, when everything around me is falling away and the world crashing to ruin over my head?—Is it not the voice of the mortal who is thrust wholly in upon himself, insufficient unto himself, plunging headlong into the chasm, which grates from the secret recesses of his vainly upward-striving soul: "My God, My God, why hast Thou forsaken me?"[65] And should I be ashamed to say this, should I stand in dread of the moment when even He did not escape it Who rolls the Heavens together like a cloth?

21 NOVEMBER.

She does not see, she does not feel that she is preparing a poison which will bring us both to grief. And I am voluptuously draining the cup that she is handing me for my destruction. What is the meaning of the kindly glance with which she often—often?—no, not often, but nevertheless sometimes looks at me, the favor with which she receives an involuntary expression of my feeling, the sympathy with my suffering that I see on her brow?

Yesterday, as I was leaving, she gave me her hand and said, "Adieu,

[63] John 6:37, 17:24.

[64] The reference is to Jesus' prayer in Gethsemane on the night before the Crucifixion: "O my Father, if it be possible, let this cup pass from me: nevertheless, not as I will, but as thou wilt" (Matthew 26:39; compare also Mark 14:36 and Luke 22:42).

[65] Jesus' words on the cross (Matthew 27:46; Mark 15:34), quoted from Psalms 22:1.

dear Werther!" Dear Werther! It was the first time that she called me "dear," and it penetrated to my very marrow. I repeated it to myself a hundred times, and last night, as I was going to bed, as I was chattering to myself about nothing in particular, I suddenly said, "Good night, dear Werther!" and had to laugh at myself afterwards.

24 NOVEMBER.
She feels what I am suffering. Her gaze went deep into my heart to-day. I found her alone. I said nothing, and she looked at me. And I no longer saw in her the charming beauty, no longer saw the shining of her fine spirit; all that disappeared from before my eyes. The gaze which affected me was far more glorious, full of an expression of the most ardent interest, the sweetest sympathy. Why could I not cast myself at her feet? Why could I not embrace her in reply with a thousand kisses?—She took refuge at the harpsichord, and in a sweet, soft voice breathed harmonious sounds to accompany her playing. Never have I seen her lips so alluring; it was as though they opened thirstily to drink in the sweet tones that welled forth from the instrument, and only the secret echo was returning from her sweet mouth—if I could only tell you what it was like! I no longer resisted; I bowed my head and vowed that I would never venture to imprint a kiss on those lips on which the spirits of Heaven are hovering. And yet—I will—Ha! you see, it stands like a barrier before my soul—this bliss—and then to go down to do penance for my sin—sin?

30 NOVEMBER.
I cannot, I cannot regain command of myself. Wherever I go I encounter an apparition which totally deranges me. To-day! Oh fate! Oh humanity!

At noon I went down to the river, I had no desire for food. Everything was so dreary. A damp, cold west wind was blowing from the mountains and the gray storm clouds were being wafted along the valley. From a distance I saw a man in a shabby green coat crawling about among the rocks and appearing to search for herbs. When I came close to him, and the noise I made caused him to turn round, I saw a very interesting physiognomy of which the chief feature was a quiet melancholy, but which otherwise expressed only a good and frank disposition; his black hair was held in two coils by pins, and the rest woven into a thick plait which hung down his back. Since his dress seemed to me to denote a man of inferior rank, I thought he would not take it amiss if I betrayed an interest in his occupation, so I asked him what he was looking for. "I am looking for flowers," he replied with a deep sigh, "and can find none." "This is not the season for them," I said with a smile. "There are so many flowers," he said, coming down towards me. "In my garden there are roses and two kinds of honeysuckle, one of which my father gave me; they grow like weeds; I have been searching for two days and cannot find any. Out there also there are always flowers, yellow and blue and red, and the centaury has a beautiful flower. I cannot find any at all." There seemed to be something queer about this, so I asked him in a roundabout way, "What do you want the flowers for then?" His mouth twitched with an odd wry smile. "If you will not give me

away," he said, pressing his finger to his lips, "I have promised to take a nosegay to my sweetheart." "That is fine," I said. "Oh!" he replied, "She has a lot of other things, she is rich." "And yet she would like your nosegay," I said. "Oh!" he continued, "she has jewels and a crown." "What is her name?" "If the States General[66] were to pay me," he replied, "I should be another man. Yes, there was once a time when I was so well off. Now it is all over with me, now I am. . . ."—a tearful gaze at the heavens expressed everything. "So you were happy?" I asked. "Oh! I wish I were so again!" he said, "then I was so well off, so gay, as happy as a fish in water." "Heinrich!" cried an old woman who came along the path, "Heinrich, where have you been? We have looked for you everywhere. Come and eat." "Is he your son?" I asked, going up to her. "Yes, my poor son," she replied. "God has given me a heavy cross to bear." "How long has he been like this?" I asked. "He has been as quiet as this for half a year now. Thank God he has got so far! Before that he was in a frenzy for a whole year, and he lay in chains in the madhouse. Now he would not harm anybody, and is only occupied with kings and emperors. He was such a good quiet boy, who helped to keep me and wrote a good hand; but suddenly he grew melancholy, fell into a violent fever, then into a frenzy, and now he is as you see him. If I were to tell you, Sir . . ." I broke in upon her stream of reminiscences by asking what he meant by the time when he was so happy and well off. "The crazy fellow," she cried with a smile of compassion. "He means the time when he was out of his mind; he always praises it. That was when he was in the madhouse, when he was unaware of his condition."—I was thunderstruck. I pressed a piece of money in her hand and rushed away.

"When you were happy!" I cried aloud, as I hastened towards the town. "Happy as a fish in water.—God in Heaven! hast Thou made it the fate of man that he is only to be happy when he has come to his senses and when he loses them again! Poor fellow! yet how I envy your melancholy, the confusion of mind in which you are languishing! You set out hopefully to pluck flowers for your queen—in Winter—and are sad that you can find none, and cannot comprehend why you can find none. And I—and I set out without hope or purpose, and return home as I came. You indulge your fancy of what you would do if the States General were to pay you. Blissful being, who can impute his lack of happiness to an earthly obstacle. You do not feel! you do not feel that your misery springs from your ravaged heart, from your unhinged brain, and that all the kings on earth cannot help you."

He should perish without hope who mocks a sick man for traveling to the furthermost spring that will only intensify his malady and render his death more painful, who assumes himself superior to an oppressed being when the latter, to rid himself of remorse and the sufferings of the spirit, makes a pilgrimage to the Holy Tomb. Every footprint on an untrodden path is a drop of balsam for the anguished soul, and with every day's toilsome journey he lies down relieved of so much affliction. And can you call that madness—you armchair windbags?—Madness!—Oh God! Thou seest my tears! Why didst Thou, Who createdst man in wretchedness enough, put brothers at his side to rob him of his morsel of wretchedness, the mor-

[66] The Dutch government, a symbol of great wealth.

sel of trust he has in Thee, in Thee, Thou All-loving One? For what is trust in a healing root, in the tears of the vine,[67] but trust in Thee, that Thou hast laid in all the things about us the power to heal and soothe which we need at every step? Father, Whom I do not know! Father, Who didst formerly fill my whole soul and now hast turned away Thy face from me! Call me to Thee! Break Thy silence! Thy silence cannot sustain this thirsting soul—and could a man, a father, be angry whose son returned before his time and fell upon his neck and cried, "I am returned, my father. Be not angry that I have broken off my journey which, according to thy will, I should have prolonged. The world is everywhere the same, for work and toil, reward and joy, but what is that to me? I am only well where thou art, and in thy presence I will suffer and rejoice."—And Thou, dear Heavenly Father, wouldst *Thou* turn him from Thee?

1 DECEMBER.
Wilhelm! the man I wrote to you about, the happy unhappy one, was a clerk in the employ of Lotte's father, and an unhappy passion for her which he nourished, concealed, and then revealed, so that he was dismissed from his office, sent him mad. Feel, fellow, at these dry words, the distraction with which I listened to this story when Albert related it as calmly as you, perhaps, will read it.

4 DECEMBER.
I beg of you—you see, it is all over with me—I can bear it all no longer. I sat by her to-day—sat, she played on the harpsichord, various melodies, with such expression! such expression!—what will you?—her little sister sat on my knee and dressed her doll. Tears came into my eyes. I bent my head and caught sight of her wedding ring.—My tears flowed.—And suddenly she played the divine old melody, suddenly, and through my soul there coursed a feeling of solace and memory of all the past, all the occasions when I had heard the song, all the dismal intervals of chagrin and hopes miscarried, and then—I walked up and down the room, my heart suffocating under it all. "For God's sake," I said, going up to her in a violent outburst. "For God's sake, stop!" She ceased playing and gazed at me fixedly. "Werther," she said, with a smile that went to my soul, "Werther, you are very ill, you have taken a dislike to your favorite dishes. Go, I beg you! Calm yourself!" I tore myself away, and—God! Thou seest my misery and wilt put an end to it.

6 DECEMBER.
How her form pursues me! Waking and dreaming she absorbs my soul. Here, when I close my eyes, here in my forehead, at the focus of inward vision, are her black eyes. Here! I cannot explain it to you. When I close my eyes, they are there, like an ocean, like an abyss they lie before me, in me, absorb my mental faculties.

[67] Wine.

What is man? The lauded demi-god! Are not his powers deficient just when he has most need of them? And when he soars up in bliss or sinks down in suffering, is he not held back, is he not again restored to cold dull consciousness, just at the moment when he longed to lose himself in the fullness of the infinite?[68]

8 DECEMBER.

Dear Wilhelm, my condition is that in which those unhappy beings must have been who were believed to be driven about by evil spirits. I am often possessed by something which is not fear, not craving. It is an unknown inward raging that threatens to tear my breast, that clutches my throat. I am wretched! wretched! And then I wander about the dread nocturnal countryside of this inhuman season.

Last night I was impelled to go out. I had heard in the evening that the stream had overflowed, and all the brooks, and that the whole of my dear valley, from Wahlheim downwards, was inundated. At night, some time after eleven, I hastened out. A dreadful scene. To see the turbulent flood whirling down from the rock in the moonlight over fields, meadows and hedges, and up and down the broad valley a raging sea lashed by the howling wind. When the moon came out again and illumined the black clouds and the booming flood rolled out in front of me in the dreadful glorious reflection, I was overcome by awe and longing. Oh! I faced the abyss with widespread arms and breathed, "Down! down!", and was immersed in the rapture of hurling down there all my torment and all my suffering, to rage along like the torrent. And oh! I was incapable of raising my foot from the ground to put an end to all my affliction!—My clock has not yet run down—I feel it! Oh Wilhelm! how willingly would I have surrendered all my humanity to tear the clouds apart with the storm wind, to embrace the flood. Ha! Will not perhaps the prisoner one day share this rapture?—

And as I gazed down pensively at a spot where I had rested with Lotte beneath a willow when we were heated with our walk, it was also submerged, and I could hardly make out where the willow was. And I thought of her meadows, and the whole region round her hunting-lodge! how our summer-house was now scattered by the raging stream! And a sunbeam from the past gleamed out as when a captive dreams of herds, meadows and

[68] The fictional editor begins his narrative at this point in the later, 1786 version. Besides commenting on Werther's situation and state of mind, he relates an episode for which that version has prepared us through two earlier letters by Werther. In May of 1771 he had described meeting a peasant servant who loved his mistress, a widow, purely but passionately, and Werther had entered sympathetically into the man's feelings. Later, about three months before the present date in December 1772, he learned that the servant, who had previously received some encouragement from the widow, had lost control of himself, tried to force himself on her, and been dismissed from her service, partly at the insistence of her brother, who feared that her money would be lost to his children if she remarried. Now Werther learns that the desperately jealous peasant, determined that no one else shall have the widow, has murdered the man who has replaced him both as servant and in her affections. Although Werther knows the man committed the murder, he believes in his essential guiltlessness and pleads fervently for him before the bailiff, who insists that the law must take its course. Albert sides with the bailiff. After this last fruitless burst of quixotic energy, Werther's depression sets in once more.

cornfields. I stayed.—I do not blame myself, for I have the courage to die.—I should have. . . . Now I am sitting here like an old woman gleaning wood from hedges and begging bread at doors to prolong and alleviate her wasting, joyless life for yet another moment.

17 DECEMBER.
What is this, my friend? I start back in terror from myself! Is not my love for her the holiest, purest, most brotherly love? Have I ever borne in my soul a culpable desire?—I will not maintain. . . . And now—dreams! Oh! how true a perception they had when they ascribed such contradictory effects to strange forces! Last night, I shudder to say it, I held her in my arms, clasped her tightly to my bosom and covered her love-lisping lips with unending kisses. My eyes swam in the intoxication of hers. God! am I to blame that I even yet feel an ecstasy in recalling with all their fervor these glowing joys? Lotte! Lotte!—And it is all over with me! My senses are confused. For a week I have lost my powers of deliberation, my eyes have been filled with tears. I am at ease nowhere and everywhere. I desire nothing, require nothing. It is better that I should go.

THE EDITOR

To The Reader

In order to supply the detailed story of our friend's last remarkable days, I am compelled to interrupt his letters by a narration, the material for which I gathered from the mouth of Lotte, Albert, his servant and other witnesses.

Werther's passion had gradually undermined the peace of Albert and his wife. The latter loved her with the tranquil faithfulness of an honorable man, and his amiable intercourse with her was in time subordinated more and more to his profession. To be sure, he did not want to admit to himself the difference which distinguished the present situation from the days when they were betrothed, but he felt a certain inward resentment at Werther's attentions to Lotte, which must have seemed both an interference with his privileges and a silent reproach. This increased the ill-humor which was often generated by overwork in his hampered and badly-paid profession, and, since Werther's situation made him also a depressing companion, the anguish of his heart having consumed his remaining spiritual faculties, his vivacity and his acumen, it was unavoidable that at last Lotte should also be infected and that she fell into a kind of melancholy in which Albert thought he could perceive a growing passion for the lover, and Werther a deep chagrin at the changed demeanor of her husband. The distrust with which the two friends regarded one another rendered their mutual presence very embarrassing to them. Albert avoided his wife's room when Werther was with her, and the latter, noticing it, after some fruitless attempts to keep away from her altogether, seized the opportunity of visiting her when her husband was detained at his office. This gave cause for fresh discontent, their tempers grew more and more exasperated, until

at last Albert said rather curtly to his wife that she should at least for people's sake give a different turn to her relations to Werther, and put an end to his too-frequent visits.

It was about this time that the resolve to quit the world had taken shape in the poor youth's soul. It had always been a favorite idea of his, which had occupied him particularly since his return to Lotte.

It was, however, to be no precipitate, rash act; he wanted to take the step with the firmest conviction, with the most tranquil resolution.

His doubts, his struggle with himself, can be seen in a note that is probably the beginning of a letter to Wilhelm, and was found undated among his papers.

Her presence, her fate, her sympathy with mine, press the last tears from my parched brain.

To raise the curtain and step behind, that is all! So why this fear and hesitation?—Because we do not know what it is like behind?—And because there is no return?—And because it is the quality of our mind to forebode confusion and darkness where we know nothing definite.

He could not forget the rebuff at the embassy. He rarely mentioned it, but one could feel imperceptibly that he considered his honor irretrievably outraged, and that the episode had inspired him with a dislike for a profession or political activity. He therefore resigned himself totally to the odd emotional and mental idiosyncrasies with which we are acquainted from his letters, and to a bottomless passion which was bound to cause the eventual extinction of all his vital energies. The eternal monotony of a melancholy attachment to the charming and beloved being whose peace of mind he was upsetting, the tempestuous wearing down of his vitality, without hope or purpose, drove him at last to the dreadful act.

20 DECEMBER.

I am grateful, Wilhelm, for the affection that has prompted you to accept my remark as you have. Yes, you are right, it is better that I should go. Your suggestion that I should return to you does not please me altogether; at least, I would like to come by a roundabout way, especially as it is to be expected that the frost will last and the roads be good. I am glad that you will come to fetch me, but postpone it for a fortnight until you have received a letter from me with further news. Nothing should be plucked until it is ripe. And a fortnight more or less can do much. Ask my mother to pray for her son, and to forgive all the trouble I have caused her. It was my fate to sadden those to whom I owed happiness. Farewell, my dearest friend. All the blessing of Heaven be upon you! Farewell!

On that very day—it was the Sunday before Christmas—he came to Lotte in the evening, and found her alone. She was occupied in arranging some toys that she had prepared as Christmas presents for her little brothers and sisters. He talked about the pleasure the little ones would experience, and about the times when the unexpected opening of the door and the appearance of a decorated Christmas tree with wax candles, sweetmeats & apples inspired a heavenly ecstasy. "You also," said Lotte, concealing her embarrassment with a sweet smile, "you also are to receive Christmas pres-

ents, if you behave properly, a little roll of wax tapers and something else."
"And what do you call behaving properly?" he cried. "What am I to do,
what can I do, dearest Lotte?" "Thursday evening," she said, "is Christmas
Eve, when the children are coming, and my father also, then everyone will
receive his present, and you are to come as well—but not before." Werther
was taken aback. "I beg of you," she continued, "that is how things are, and
I beg you for the sake of my peace of mind, we cannot, we cannot continue
like this!"—He turned his eyes away from her, went up and down the
room, and muttered, "we cannot continue like this!" between his teeth.
Lotte, who perceived the terrible state these words had put him in, tried to
divert his thoughts by asking him all manner of questions, but without
avail. "No, Lotte," he cried, "I shall not see you again!"—"Why?" she re-
joined, "you can, you must see us again, only control yourself. Oh! why
were you born with this impetuosity, this persistent passion for everything
that you once touch! I beg of you," she continued, taking his hand, "control
yourself. Your intellect, your knowledge, your talents—what diverse enjoy-
ments do these not offer you! Be a man. Rid yourself of this melancholy
attachment to a person who can do nought but pity you." He grated his
teeth and looked at her gloomily. She held his hand. "Only one moment of
calm thinking, Werther," she said. "Do you not perceive that you are de-
ceiving yourself, that you are the voluntary cause of your own undoing?
Why me, Werther? Just me, who belong to another? Just this? I fear, I fear
it is only the impossibility of possessing me that makes this desire so allur-
ing." He withdrew his hand from hers, gazing at her with a fixed and
angry look. "Clever!" he cried. "Very clever! Did Albert say that, I wonder?
Subtle! Very subtle!"—"Anyone might say it," she replied. "Is there then
no maiden in the wide world who could fulfil the desires of your heart?
Bring yourself to look for her, and I swear to you that you will find her. For
a long time I have feared for you and for us the restriction you have im-
posed upon yourself. Bring yourself to it! A journey will and must distract
you! Seek and find a worthy object for all your love, then return and let us
enjoy together the happiness of a true friendship."

"That ought to be printed," he said with a cold laugh, "and recom-
mended to all tutors. Dear Lotte, let me have just a little repose, and every-
thing will be all right."—"Only this, Werther! that you do not come back till
Christmas Eve."—He was about to reply, when Albert entered the room.
They bade one another a frigid good evening, and walked up and down
the room together with some embarrassment. Werther began some trifling
conversation, which soon petered out. Albert did the same and then asked
his wife about some commissions and, when he heard that they had not yet
been carried out, returned a sharp answer that cut Werther to the heart.
He wanted to go, could not, and delayed till eight o'clock. Their irritation
and ill-humor with one another increased more and more until the table
was laid and he took his hat and stick, when Albert, with conventional
politeness, invited him to take pot-luck with them.

He arrived at his lodging, took the candle from his servant who wanted
to light him on his way, and went alone to his room, where he wept aloud,
spoke in an excited manner to himself, strode violently up and down, and
finally threw himself, fully clad, on his bed, where he was found by his man
who ventured about eleven o'clock to go in and ask whether he should take

off his master's boots. This he let him do, and then ordered him not to come into the room the next morning until he was called.

On Monday morning, the twenty-first of December, he wrote the following letter to Lotte, which was found sealed on his writing-desk after his death and brought to her. I will insert it here at intervals, just as—and this is evident from what happened—he wrote it.

My mind is made up, Lotte. I intend to die, and I am writing you this calmly, without romantic exaltation, on the morning of the day when I shall see you for the last time. When you read this, my dearest, the cool grave will already cover the stiffened remains of the restless, unhappy man who knows no sweeter bliss in the last moments of his life than to converse with you. I have had a terrible night, which has strengthened, has fixed my wavering resolve. I intend to die. When I tore myself away from you yesterday, with my senses in a state of fearful excitement, when it all rushed in upon my heart, and the thought of my hopeless, joyless existence at your side seized hold of me with chill horror—I was hardly able to reach my room, beside myself I fell upon my knees, and oh! God! Thou didst grant me the final boon of bitter tears! A thousand plans, a thousand possibilities coursed through my brain, and at last it was there, firmly, wholly, the one ultimate thought—I intend to die!—I lay down, and this morning, in all the tranquillity of my awakening, it is still firm, still strong in my heart—I intend to die!—It is not despair, but the certainty that I have reached the end, and that I am sacrificing myself for you. Yes, Lotte! Why should I not say it? One of us three must go, and I will be the one. Oh! my dearest, the frenzy has often crept through my torn heart, often—to murder your husband!—You!—Myself! So let it be then!—When you climb up the hill, on a beautiful summer evening, remember me, how I often came thus up the valley, and then gaze across at the churchyard to my grave, as the wind gently waves the grass to and fro in the rays of the setting sun.—I was calm when I began, and now I am weeping like a child when I see it all so vividly.

Towards ten o'clock Werther called his servant, and said to him as he dressed that he was going away in a few days, and his clothes should therefore be turned out and made ready for packing. He also ordered him to ask everywhere for bills to be sent in, to collect some books that had been lent, and to pay two months advance to some poor people to whom he was accustomed to give something every week.

He had his meal brought to his room, and rode out afterwards to the bailiff, whom he did not find at home. He walked pensively up and down the garden, and appeared to want to bury himself at the last moment under all his melancholy memories.

The little ones did not long leave him in peace, but pursued him, sprang up at him, told him that when tomorrow had come, and then another day, and another day after that, they were going to Lotte's to fetch their Christmas presents, and spoke of the wonders that their little imaginations promised them. "Tomorrow!" he cried, "and then another day, and another day after that!" And he kissed them all affectionately, and was about to go when the smallest one tried to whisper something in his ear. He confided to him that his big brothers had written beautiful New Year greetings, so big! one for papa, one for Albert and Lotte, and also one for Herr Werther. They were going to hand them over early on New Year's Day.

This overcame him. He gave each one something, mounted his horse, asked them to give his regards to the old man, and rode away with tears in his eyes.

He reached home towards five, ordered the maid to see to the fire and to keep it going till night time. He told his servant to pack his books and linen in his trunk downstairs and to sew his clothes up in a bale. Then he probably wrote the following passage in his last letter to Lotte.

You do not expect me. You think I shall obey you and not see you again till Christmas Eve. Oh, Lotte! To-day or never again. On Christmas Eve you will hold this letter in your hand and tremble as you moisten it with your sweet tears. I will, I must! Oh! how glad I am that I have made up my mind!

At half past six he went to Albert's house, and found Lotte alone, very alarmed at his visit. She had told her husband in the course of conversation that Werther would not return until Christmas Eve. Soon after he had had his horse saddled, saying he was riding to an official in the neighborhood with whom he had some business to settle, and had gone out in spite of the inclement weather. Lotte, who knew quite well that he had long postponed this matter and that it would keep him from home all night, understood the pantomime only too well, and was very depressed. She sat alone, her heart was touched, she thought of the past, feeling how precious it had been, and her love for her husband, who now, instead of the promised happiness, was beginning to make her life wretched. Her thoughts came back to Werther. She blamed him, but could not hate him. A mysterious trait had attracted her to him from the beginning of their friendship and now, after so long, after having lived through so many experiences, the impression on her heart was bound to be inextinguishable. Her oppressed heart at last found relief in tears, and she fell into a quiet melancholy in which she became more and more deeply immersed. But how her heart hammered when she heard Werther ascending the steps and asking for her outside! It was too late to say she was not at home, and she had only half recovered from her confusion when he entered the room. "You have not kept your word!" she cried. "I made no promise," was his answer. "Then you should at least have acceded to my request," she said, "it was for both our sakes." As she spoke, she made up her mind to send for some girl friends. These should be witnesses to her conversation with Werther and, since he would have to see them home, she would be able to get rid of him early. He had brought her back some books, and she inquired about some others, trying to keep the conversation on a general level until her friends arrived, when the maid returned and informed her that they both begged to be excused, one of them having some relations visiting her whom she could not send away, and the other not wanting to dress and go out in such wretched weather.

This made her ponder for a few minutes, until the feeling of her innocence roused her pride. She decided to defy Albert's crotchets, and the purity of her heart fortified her, so that she did not, as she at first intended, call her maid into the room but, after she had played a number of minuets on the harpsichord to recover herself and allay the confusion of her heart, sat down calmly on the sofa at Werther's side. "Have you nothing to read?" she said. He had nothing. "In my drawer there," she began, "is your trans-

lation of some of the songs of Ossian. I have not read them yet, for I hoped to hear you recite them, but ever since you haven't been fit for anything." He smiled, fetched the songs, a tremor ran through him as he took them in his hand, and his eyes filled with tears as he looked at them. He sat down and read:[69]

"Star of descending night! fair is thy light in the west! thou liftest thy unshorn head from thy cloud: thy steps are stately on thy hill. What dost thou behold in the plain? The stormy winds are laid. The murmur of the torrent comes from afar. Roaring waves climb the distant rock. The flies of evening are on their feeble wings; the hum of their course is on the field. What dost thou behold, fair light? But thou dost smile and depart. The waves come with joy around thee: they bathe thy lovely hair. Farewell, thou silent beam! Let the light of Ossian's soul arise!

"And it does arise in its strength! I behold my departed friends. Their gathering is on Lora, as in the days of other years. Fingal comes like a watry column of mist! his heroes are around: and see the bards of song, grey-haired Ullin! stately Ryno! Alpin, with the tuneful voice! the soft complaint of Minona! How are ye changed, my friends, since the days of Selma's feast? when we contended, like gales of spring, as they fly along the hill, and bend by turns the feebly-whistling grass.

"Minona[70] came forth in her beauty; with down-cast look and tearful eye. Her hair flew slowly on the blast, that rushed unfrequent from the hill. The souls of the heroes were sad when she raised the tuneful voice. Often had they seen the grave of Salgar, the dark dwelling of white-bosomed Colma. Colma left alone on the hill, with all her voice of song! Salgar promised to come:[71] but the night descended around. Hear the voice of Colma, when she sat alone on the hill!

COLMA

"It is night; I am alone, forlorn on the hill of storms. The wind is heard on the mountain. The torrent pours down the rock. No hut receives me from the rain; forlorn on the hill of winds!

"Rise, moon! from behind thy clouds. Stars of the night, arise! Lead me, some light, to the place, where my love rests from the chase alone! his bow near him, unstrung: his dogs panting around him. But here I must sit alone, by the rock of the mossy stream. The stream and the wind roar aloud. I hear not the voice of my love! Why delays my Salgar, why the chief of the hill, his promise? Here is the rock, and here the tree! here is the roaring stream! Thou didst promise with night to be here. Ah! whither is my Salgar gone? With thee I would fly, from my father; with thee, from my brother of pride. Our races have long been foes; we are not foes, O Salgar!

"Cease a little while, O wind! stream, be thou silent a while! let my voice be heard around. Let my wanderer hear me! Salgar! it is Colma who calls. Here is the tree,

[69]"This extract from Ossian's *The Songs of Selma* is here reproduced in the original." —Translator's note. On Ossian, see the note to Werther's letter of 10 July 1771. The excerpt that follows begins with a passage about the evening star by the bard Ossian. He then relates three stories he heard in the past at the feast of Selma, in Lora, the palace of his father Fingal, a Scottish king.

[70]Minona was the first of the bards to sing at the feast. She told of the death at each other's hands of Colma's lover Salgar and her brother.

[71]To keep a lovers' tryst with Colma.

and the rock. Salgar, my love! I am here. Why delayest thou thy coming? Lo! the calm moon comes forth. The flood is bright in the vale. The rocks are grey on the steep. I see him not on the brow. His dogs come not before him, with tidings of his near approach. Here I must sit alone!

"Who lie on the heath beside me? Are they my love and my brother? Speak to me, O my friends! To Colma they give no reply. Speak to me: I am alone! My soul is tormented with fears! Ah! they are dead! Their swords are red from the fight. O my brother! my brother! why hast thou slain my Salgar? why, O Salgar! hast thou slain my brother? Dear were ye both to me! what shall I say in your praise? Thou wert fair on the hill among thousands! he was terrible in fight. Speak to me; hear my voice; hear me, sons of my love! They are silent; silent for ever! Cold, cold are their breasts of clay! Oh! from the rock on the hill; from the top of the windy steep, speak, ye ghosts of the dead! speak, I will not be afraid! Whither are ye gone to rest? In what cave of the hill shall I find the departed? No feeble voice is on the gale: no answer half-drowned in the storm!

"I sit in my grief; I wait for morning in my tears! Rear the tomb, ye friends of the dead. Close it not till Colma come. My life flies away like a dream: why should I stay behind? Here shall I rest with my friends, by the stream of the sounding rock. When night comes on the hill; when the loud winds arise; my ghost shall stand in the blast, and mourn the death of my friends. The hunter shall hear from his booth. He shall fear but love my voice! For sweet shall my voice be for my friends: pleasant were her friends to Colma!

"Such was thy song, Minona, softly-blushing daughter of Torman. Our tears descended for Colma, and our souls were sad! Ullin[72] came with his harp! he gave the song of Alpin. The voice of Alpin was pleasant: the soul of Ryno was a beam of fire! But they had rested in the narrow house: their voice had ceased in Selma. Ullin had returned, one day, from the chase, before the heroes fell. He heard their strife[73] on the hill; their song was soft but sad! They mourned the fall of Morar, first of mortal men! His soul was like the soul of Fingal; his sword like the sword of Oscar.[74] But he fell, and his father mourned: his sister's eyes were full of tears, Minona's eyes were full of tears, the sister of car-borne Morar. She retired from the song of Ullin, like the moon in the west, when she foresees the shower, and hides her fair head in a cloud. I touched the harp with Ullin; the song of mourning rose!

RYNO

"The wind and the rain are past: calm is the noon of day. The clouds are divided in heaven. Over the green hills flies the inconstant sun. Red through the stony vale comes down the stream of the hill. Sweet are thy murmurs, O stream! but more sweet is the voice I hear. It is the voice of Alpin, the son of song, mourning for the dead! Bent is his head of age; red his tearful eye. Alpin, thou son of song, why alone on the silent hill? why complainest thou, as a blast in the wood; as a wave on the lonely shore?

[72] Another bard who sang at the remembered feast. He mourned Morar, brother to the Minona who had just sung, by way of repeating a dialogue between Ryno and Alpin, who were both dead at the time of the feast. Ullin sang the part of Alpin and Ossian himself the part of Ryno.
[73] The strife of the dead heroes Ryno and Alpin, contending with each other in song.
[74] Ossian's son.

ALPIN

"My tears, O Ryno! are for the dead; my voice for those that have passed away. Tall thou art on the hill; fair among the sons of the vale. But thou shalt fall like Morar; the mourner shall sit on thy tomb. The hills shall know thee no more; thy bow shall lie in thy hall unstrung!

"Thou wert swift, O Morar! as a roe on the desert; terrible as a meteor of fire. Thy wrath was as the storm. Thy sword in battle, as lightning in the field. Thy voice was a stream after rain; like thunder on distant hills. Many fell by thy arm; they were consumed in the flames of thy wrath. But when thou didst return from war, how peaceful was thy brow! Thy face was like the sun after rain; like the moon in the silence of night; calm as the breast of the lake when the loud wind is laid.

"Narrow is thy dwelling now! dark the place of thine abode! With three steps I compass thy grave, O thou who wast so great before! Four stones, with their heads of moss, are the only memorial of thee. A tree with scarce a leaf, long grass, which whistles in the wind, mark to the hunter's eye the grave of the mighty Morar. Morar! thou art low indeed. Thou hast no mother to mourn thee; no maid with her tears of love. Dead is she that brought thee forth. Fallen is the daughter of Morglan.

"Who on his staff is this? who is this, whose head is white with age? whose eyes are red with tears? who quakes at every step? It is thy father, O Morar! the father of no son but thee. He heard of thy fame in war; he heard of foes dispersed. He heard of Morar's renown; why did he not hear of his wound? Weep, thou father of Morar! weep; but thy son heareth thee not. Deep is the sleep of the dead; low their pillow of dust. No more shall he hear thy voice; no more awake at thy call. When shall it be morn in the grave, to bid the slumberer awake? Farewell, thou bravest of men! thou conqueror in the field! but the field shall see thee no more; nor the dark wood be lightened with the splendour of thy steel. Thou hast left no son. The song shall preserve thy name. Future times shall hear of thee; they shall hear of the fallen Morar!

"The grief of all arose, but most the bursting sigh of Armin.[75] He remembers the death of his son, who fell in the days of his youth. Carmor was near the hero, the chief of the echoing Galmal. Why bursts the sigh of Armin? he said. Is there a cause to mourn? The song comes, with its music, to melt and please the soul. It is like soft mist, that, rising from a lake, pours on the silent vale; the green flowers are filled with dew, but the sun returns in his strength, and the mist is gone. Why art thou sad, O Armin, chief of sea-surrounded Gorma?

"Sad! I am! nor small is my cause of woe! Carmor, thou hast lost no son; thou hast lost no daughter of beauty. Colgar the valiant lives; and Annira fairest maid. The boughs of thy house ascend, O Carmor! but Armin is the last of his race. Dark is thy bed, O Daura! deep thy sleep in the tomb! When shalt thou awake with thy songs? with all thy voice of music?

"Arise, winds of autumn, arise; blow along the heath! streams of the mountains, roar! roar, tempests, in the groves of my oaks! walk through broken clouds, O moon! show thy pale face, at intervals! bring to my mind the night, when all my children fell; when Arindal the mighty fell; when Daura the lovely failed! Daura, my daughter! thou wert fair; fair as the moon on Fura; white as the driven snow; sweet as the breathing gale. Arindal, thy bow was strong. Thy spear was swift in the

[75] One of the guests at the feast. The mourning song he had just heard reminded him of the deaths of his son Arindal, his daughter Daura, and Daura's betrothed Armar, because of the treachery of Erath, Armar's enemy.

field. Thy look was like mist on the wave: thy shield, a red cloud in a storm. Armar, renowned in war, came, and sought Daura's love. He was not long refused: fair was the hope of their friends!

"Erath, son of Odgal, repined: his brother had been slain by Armar. He came disguised like a son of the sea: fair was his skiff on the wave; white his locks of age; calm his serious brow. Fairest of women, he said, lovely daughter of Armin! a rock not distant in the sea, bears a tree on its side; red shines the fruit afar! There Armar waits for Daura. I come to carry his love! She went; she called on Armar. Nought answered, but the son of the rock, Armar, my love! my love! why tormentest thou me with fear? hear, son of Arnart, hear: it is Daura who calleth thee! Erath the traitor fled laughing to the land. She lifted up her voice; she called for her brother and her father. Arindal! Armin! none to relieve your Daura!

"Her voice came over the sea. Arindal my son descended from the hill; rough in the spoils of the chase. His arrows rattled by his side; his bow was in his hand: five dark grey dogs attend his steps. He saw fierce Erath on the shore: he seized and bound him to an oak. Thick wind the thongs of the hide around his limbs; he loads the wind with his groans. Arindal ascends the deep in his boat, to bring Daura to land. Armar came in his wrath, and let fly the grey-feathered shaft.[76] It sung; it sunk in thy heart, O Arindal my son! for Erath the traitor thou diedst. The oar is stopped at once; he panted on the rock and expired. What is thy grief, O Daura, when round thy feet is poured thy brother's blood! The boat is broken in twain. Armar plunges into the sea, to rescue his Daura, or die. Sudden a blast from the hill came over the waves. He sunk, and he rose no more.

"Alone, on the sea-beat rock, my daughter was heard to complain. Frequent and loud were her cries. What could her father do? All night I stood on the shore. I saw her by the faint beam of the moon. All night I heard her cries. Loud was the wind; the rain beat hard on the hill. Before morning appeared, her voice was weak. It died away, like the evening-breeze among the grass of the rocks. Spent with grief she expired; and left thee, Armin, alone. Gone is my strength in war! fallen my pride among women![77] When the storms aloft arise; when the north lifts the wave on high; I sit by the sounding shore, and look on the fatal rock. Often by the setting moon, I see the ghost of my children. Half-viewless,[78] they walk in mournful conference together."

A stream of tears, which gushed from Lotte's eyes and afforded relief to her oppressed heart, interrupted Werther's reading. He threw down the sheets, seized her hand and wept bitterly. Lotte supported herself on her other arm and hid her eyes in her handkerchief. The agitation of both of them was terrible. They felt their own misery in the fate of those noble ones, felt it together, and their tears mingled. Werther's lips and eyes burned on Lotte's arms, a tremor ran through her, she tried to withdraw, and all her grief, all her pity lay heavy as lead upon her. She took a deep breath to recover herself and begged him with a sob to continue, begged him with the whole voice of Heaven. Werther trembled, his heart felt as though it would burst, he picked up the sheet and read in a broken voice:[79]

[76] He thinks Arindal is Erath.
[77] His "strength" and "pride" are his son and daughter. [78] Half invisible.
[79] "From Ossian's *Berrathon*."—Translator's note.

"Why dost thou awake me, O breath of Spring, thou dost woo me and say: 'I cover thee with the drops of heaven.' But the time of my fading is near, the blast that shall scatter my leaves. To-morrow shall the traveller come; he that saw me in my beauty shall come. His eyes will search the field, but they will not find me."

The whole force of these words deprived the unhappy man of his self-possession. He threw himself at Lotte's feet in utter despair, seized her hands, pressed them against his eyes, against his forehead, and a foreboding of his dreadful intention appeared to flash through her soul. Her mind grew confused, she clasped his hands, pressed them against her breast, bent over him with a sorrowful air, and their burning cheeks touched. They were lost to the world, he twined his arms round her, pressed her to his breast, and covered her trembling, stammering lips with frenzied kisses. "Werther!" she cried in a suffocating voice, turning away her face, "Werther!", and she thrust him away from her breast with a nerveless hand. "Werther!" she cried in a calm tone with noble dignity. He did not resist, released her from his embrace, and threw himself madly at her feet. She got up hastily and, in nervous confusion, trembling between love and anger, she said, "This is the last time, Werther! You shall not see me again." With a look, fraught with love, at the unhappy man, she rushed into the next room and locked the door behind her. Werther stretched his arms out towards her, not daring to hold her back. He lay on the ground, his head on the sofa, and in this attitude he remained for half an hour, until a sound recalled him to himself. It was the maid who wanted to lay the table. He walked up and down the room and, when he saw that he was alone again, went to the door of the cabinet and called gently, "Lotte! Lotte! only one word more, in farewell!"—She was silent, he waited—and begged—and waited, then tore himself away and cried, "Farewell, Lotte! Farewell for ever!"

He came to the town gate. The watchmen, who were used to him, let him out without a word. There was a drizzle, half rain half snow, and it was getting on for eleven when he knocked at the gate again. His servant noticed, when Werther returned home, that he was without his hat. He did not venture to say anything and undressed him. Everything was wet. The hat was found afterwards on a rock, on the slope of the hill towards the valley, and it is inconceivable how he managed to climb up there on a wet dark night without falling headlong.

He lay down in bed and slept for many hours. His servant found him writing, when, at his call, he brought in his coffee next morning. He added the following to the letter to Lotte:

For the last time then, for the last time I open these eyes. They are alas! to see the sun no more; it is hidden by a dark and misty day. Mourn then, Nature! thy son, thy friend, thy lover nears his end. Lotte, it is a feeling without compare, and yet it is most akin to a twilight dream, to say to oneself, 'This is the last morning.' The last! Lotte, I have no conception of the word—the last! Do I not stand here in all my strength, and to-morrow I shall lie stretched out and inert on the ground! Die! What does that mean? We are dreaming when we speak of death. I have seen many people die, yet humanity is so limited that it has no conception of the beginning and

end of its existence. Still mine, thine! thine! beloved, and the next moment—separated, parted—perhaps for ever.—No, Lotte, no.—How can I pass away, how can you pass away, do we not exist!—Pass away!—What does that mean? It is again a word! an empty sound, that awakes no echo in my heart.—Dead, Lotte! Interred in the cold earth, so narrow, so dark!—There was a girl who was everything to me in my helpless youth; she died, and I followed her corpse and stood beside her grave. As they let down the coffin and pulled up the whirring ropes again from under it, as the first shovelful of earth thudded down and the fearful shell gave back a muffled sound, becoming more and more muffled till it was at last entirely covered—I sank down beside the grave—moved, shaken, in anguish, my soul torn, but I knew not what had happened to me—what will happen to me—Death! The grave! I do not understand the words!

Oh, forgive me! Yesterday! It should have been the last hour of my life. Oh, you angel! for the first time, for the first time there glowed through the depths of my soul, without room for doubt, the feeling of rapture: She loves me! She loves me! The sacred fire that streamed from your lips still burns on mine, a fresh rapturous warmth is in my heart. Forgive me, forgive me.

Oh, I knew that you loved me, knew from the first soulful glances, the first hand pressure, and yet when I went away again, when I saw Albert at your side, I again despaired with feverish doubtings.

Do you remember the flowers you sent me, when you were unable to say a word to me, or give me your hand, at that odious party? Oh! I have knelt in front of them half the night and they put the seal on your love for me. But alas! these impressions faded, as the believer gradually loses the sense of his God's loving kindness which was accorded him with all Heaven's abundance in sacred and visible symbols.

All this is transitory, but no eternity can extinguish the glowing essence that I imbibed yesterday from your lips, that I feel within me. She loves me! This arm has embraced her, these lips have trembled on her lips, this mouth has stammered against hers. She is mine! You are mine! Yes, Lotte, for ever!

And what does it mean, that Albert is your husband? Husband!—That is to say in this world—and in this world it is a sin that I love you, that I would like to snatch you from his arms into mine? A sin? Good! I am punishing myself for it. I have tasted this sin in all its divine rapture, have drunk restoring balsam and strength into my heart. From that moment you were mine! mine, Lotte! I go ahead! to my Father and to yours. To Him I will bring my plaint, and He will solace me till you come and I can fly to you, clasp you, stay with you before the face of the Infinite in an eternal embrace.

This is no dream, no delusion! On the verge of the grave I saw more clearly. We *shall* exist! We shall see one another again! See your mother! I shall see her, find her, and oh! pour out all my heart before her. Your mother, bearing the semblance of yourself.

Towards eleven o'clock Werther inquired of his servant whether Albert had yet returned. The servant said that he had, for he had seen his horse being led. His master then gave him an unsealed note with the following contents:

Would you lend me your pistols for a journey I am about to undertake? Farewell.

Lotte had slept little that night; she was in a state of feverish agitation, and her heart was ravaged with a thousand emotions. In spite of herself, she felt deep within her breast the passion of Werther's embraces, and at the same time she saw with double beauty the days of her artless innocence, of her care-free confidence in herself. She already feared beforehand her husband's gaze and his half-vexed, half-mocking questions, when he should hear of Werther's visit. She had never dissembled, she had never lied, and now she was faced, for the first time, with the unavoidable necessity of doing so. The reluctance, the embarrassment she felt, made the fault all the greater in her eyes, and yet she could neither hate him who was the cause of it nor promise herself never to see him again. She wept till morning, when she sank into a sleep of exhaustion, from which she had hardly risen and dressed when her husband returned, whose presence for the first time she found quite unbearable. For she trembled lest he should discover in her the traces of a sleepless night spent in tears, and this increased her confusion, so that she greeted him with an impetuous embrace which was more expressive of consternation and remorse than passionate delight, thereby attracting the attention of Albert, who asked her curtly, after he had opened some letters and packets, whether anything had happened, whether any one had called. She answered hesitatingly that Werther had been there for an hour on the previous day.—"He chooses his time well," he replied, and went to his study. Lotte remained alone for a quarter of an hour. The presence of her husband, whom she loved and honored, had made a fresh impression on her heart. She remembered all his kindness, generosity and affection, and reproached herself for having so ill requited them. An obscure impulse made her follow him; she took her work, as she was sometimes wont to do, and went to his room. She asked him whether he needed anything, but he said that he did not and sat down at his desk to write, while she sat down to do her knitting. They had been together for an hour in this way, when Albert began to walk up and down the room. Lotte spoke to him, but he made little or no reply, only sitting down at his desk again, and she fell into a train of melancholy thoughts which were all the more distressing since she tried to hide them and to stay her tears.

The appearance of Werther's boy plunged her in the greatest embarrassment. He handed the note to Albert, who turned coldly to his wife and said, "Give him the pistols."—"I wish him a good journey," he said to the youth. This was like a thunderclap to her. She faltered in an attempt to rise. She could not understand her feelings. Slowly she went to the wall, took them down trembling, wiped off the dust and hesitated, and would have delayed still more if Albert's inquiring glance had not impelled her. She gave the fatal weapons to the boy, without being able to utter a word, and when he had gone she gathered her work together and went to her room in a state of the most inexpressible anguish. Her heart prophesied all sorts of catastrophes. At first she was on the verge of throwing herself at her husband's feet and revealing everything—what had happened on the previous evening, her own fault and forebodings. Then she could not see what would be the advantage of such a step. Least of all could she hope to persuade her husband to go to Werther. The table was laid, and a friend of Lotte's, who only came to make some inquiry but was not allowed by Lotte

to leave, made conversation bearable during the meal. They constrained themselves, discussed sundry matters, and were able to forget.

The boy brought the pistols to Werther, who took them from him in a transport of delight when he heard that they had been handed to him by Lotte. He had bread and wine brought in, told the boy to go and have his dinner, and sat down to write.

They have passed through your hands, you have wiped the dust from them, I kiss them a thousand times for you have touched them. Thou, Spirit of Heaven, dost favor my resolve! And you, Lotte, offer me the weapon, you, at whose hands I wished to encounter death and alas! now encounter it! Oh! I made my servant tell me everything—you trembled when you handed them to him, you bade me no farewell!—Alas! Alas!—no farewell! Is it possible that you have closed your heart to me on account of the moment which sealed me to you for ever? Lotte, a thousand years cannot wipe out the impress! And I feel that you cannot hate him who burns for you thus.

After the meal he ordered his boy to finish packing everything, destroyed a number of papers, and went out to settle some small debts. He returned home, went out again beyond the gate, in spite of the rain, as far as the Count's garden, roved about the neighborhood, came back as night fell, and wrote:

I have seen field, wood and sky for the last time, Wilhelm. I bid you farewell, also! Forgive me, mother! Console her, Wilhelm. God bless you both! My affairs are all in order. Farewell! We shall meet again in happier circumstances.

I have ill rewarded you, Albert, but you will forgive me. I have ruined the peace of your house and sowed distrust between you. Farewell, I am about to make an end. Oh! that my death might restore your happiness! Albert! Albert! Make the angel happy. And may God's blessing rest upon you!

He spent much time turning out his papers during the evening, tore many of them up and threw them in the stove, and sealed a number of packages which he addressed to Wilhelm. They contained small essays and disconnected ideas, several of which I have seen. After having the fire made up and a flask of wine brought in, he sent his servant, who slept some distance away, as did the other domestics, to bed. The boy lay down in his clothes in order to be at hand at an early hour, for his master had told him that the coach horses would be at the door before six.

AFTER ELEVEN.

All is so still around me and my soul so calm. I thank thee, Lord, for these last moments of strength and ardor.

I step to the window, my dearest, and still see some stars shining through the fleeting storm-clouds. No, you will not fall! The Eternal One bears you at his heart, and me. I saw the wheeler stars of Charles's Wain,[80] the loveliest of all the constellations. When I left you at night, as I went out at the gate, it was in front of me. With

[80] The Big Dipper; located in the north, it wheels around the North Star as the night passes.

what intoxication have I so often gazed at it, raised aloft my hands and made it a symbol, a sacred token of the bliss I felt, and still—Oh! Lotte, what is there that does not remind me of you! Are you not about me always! And have I not always, like a child, insatiably, seized every trifle that your saintly hands had touched!

Beloved silhouette! I now return it to you at my death, Lotte, and beg you to hold it in honor. I have pressed a thousand, thousand kisses on it, waved a thousand greetings to it when I went out or returned.

I have left a note for your father entreating him to protect my body. In the churchyard there are two lime trees, at the back in a corner, towards the field, and there I wish to lie. He can and will do this for his friend. Add your entreaties to mine. I will not ask pious Christians to allow their bodies to rest beside that of a poor wretch. Oh! I could wish to be buried by the wayside, or in the lonely valley, that priest and Levite might cross themselves as they passed by the stone which marked the spot, and the Samaritan shed a tear.[81]

Here, Lotte! I do not shudder to take the dread cold cup from which I am to drink the ecstasy of death! It is you who have handed it to me, and I do not fear. All! All! thus are the desires and hopes of my life fulfilled! To knock so cold, so stiff, at the brazen gate of death.

That I might have been granted the happiness to die for you! To sacrifice myself for you, Lotte! I would die with a stout heart, I would die gladly, if I could restore the tranquillity, the rapture of your life. But alas! it was granted to but few noble souls to shed their blood for those they loved, and by their deaths to kindle for them a new life enhanced a hundredfold.

I wish to be buried in these clothes, Lotte. You have touched and sanctified them. I have asked your father to grant me this favor. My soul will hover over my coffin. Let them not search my pockets. This pink bow which you wore on your bosom, when I met you first among your children—Oh! kiss them a thousand times and tell them the fate of their unhappy friend. The darlings, how they swarm about me. Oh! how I attached myself to you, could not keep away from you from the first moment! Let this bow be buried with me. You gave it me on my birthday! How eagerly I accepted it all!—Alas, I did not think that the way would lead to this!—Be calm! I beg you, be calm!—

They are loaded—it is striking twelve!—So be it then—Lotte! Lotte, farewell! Farewell!

A neighbor saw the flash of the powder and heard the shot, but as everything remained still he paid no more attention.

At six next morning the servant entered with a candle and found his master stretched on the floor, with blood about and the pistol by him. He called to him, seized hold of him, but there was no answer, only a rattling in the throat. He ran for a doctor, for Albert. Lotte heard the bell, all her limbs began to tremble. She woke her husband, they got up, the servant stammered the news amid sobs, Lotte sank to the ground in a swoon in front of Albert.

When the physician arrived, he found the unhappy youth on the floor beyond all hope; his pulse was still beating but all his limbs were paralyzed. He had shot himself through the head above the right eye, and his brains

[81] A despised Samaritan helped the man in distress, while the conventionally pious priest and Levite passed him by. Luke 10:31–33.

were protruding. He was bled[82] in the arm, the blood flowed and he still breathed.

From the blood on the arm of his chair it was concluded that he had committed the deed sitting at his desk. He had then sunk down and twisted convulsively round the chair. He lay on his back in the direction of the window, deprived of strength, fully dressed in boots, blue coat and yellow waistcoat.

The house, the neighbors, the whole town were in a turmoil. Albert entered. Werther had been laid on the bed, his forehead tied up, his face already like that of a dead man, without moving a limb. A dreadful rattling noise still came from his lungs, now faintly, now more loudly; the end was near.

He had only drunk one glass of the wine. *Emilia Galotti*[83] lay open on his desk.

I cannot describe Albert's dismay, Lotte's grief.

The old bailiff came galloping up at the news, and he kissed the dying youth as the hot tears coursed down his cheeks. His eldest sons arrived soon afterwards on foot and sank beside the bed with expressions of the most unrestrained sorrow, kissed his hands and mouth, and the eldest, of whom he had been the most fond, clung to his lips and had to be torn away by force. He died at noon. The presence of the bailiff and the arrangements he made prevented a crowd from assembling. He had him buried towards eleven o'clock at night at the spot that he had chosen. The old man and his sons followed the body. Albert could not. Lotte's life was in danger. He was carried by workmen. There was no pastor present.

William Blake
(1757–1827)

The number of spiritually lonely artists neglected in their time and canonized by posterity only after their deaths is not as great as popular imagination conceives, but there have been some, and William Blake was among them. His writings (he was also a great painter) reached only a tiny audience during his life. For forty years after he died almost none of his work was known, and then for another sixty it was very imperfectly understood. The fault did not lie entirely with a blind and unfeeling world. Most of Blake's literary work was issued in a format that—contrary to his hopes and intentions—precluded wide readership, and his last, longest poems are forbiddingly complex to the point of seeming incoherent. Those who have committed their minds and imaginative energies to Blake's kaleidoscopic, mythic epics have been rewarded with an awed exhilaration comparable to what James Joyce's devotees get from *Finnegans Wake*, but there are still

[82] To draw blood from the sick was a standard medical treatment.
[83] A tragedy by Gotthold Ephraim Lessing (1729–1781).

people who doubt that the effort (for either writer) is worth it. Whoever is right, there is a strong irony here, for in lyrics like *Songs of Innocence and of Experience,* most of *The Marriage of Heaven and Hell,* the wonderful marginalia he recorded in books he owned, and notebook epigrams, Blake proves that he can say things with an almost unique gnomic economy and bluntness. He hated "mystery"—religious or scientifically rationalist—with his whole soul and mind. The crowning irony is that there is far greater agreement, among those who have studied them, about the meaning of his "incomprehensible" poems than about the more accessible ones such as *Thel* and the *Songs,* which have been read in wildly different ways.

The intensity of Blake's work contrasts with the tenor of his life, in which there were few dramatic peaks. The son of a hosier and haberdasher, he was born in 1757, in London, where except for three years he spent his whole life. He was endowed with hyperacute visual powers, from boyhood onward seeing and imagining things with a preternatural clarity that must be distinguished from the mystic's sensory blackout where, in Wordsworth's phrase, "we are laid asleep in body and become a living soul." At ten Blake began formal study of drawing (of conventional education he had none), and by twenty-one he had completed a seven-year apprenticeship as an engraver, which thereafter was his bread-and-butter occupation. He also studied for a time at the Royal Academy of Art, developing an antipathy to its eminent president, Sir Joshua Reynolds, and his approved style of painting. Blake believed that the line was everything in artistic technique and despised painters like Rembrandt who produced murky "blurs." This principle remained with him, his passion for clarity of outline in art, and for watercolors instead of oils, coalescing with his philosophical detestation of "mystery." In 1782 he married the illiterate Catherine Boucher, who seems to have fallen in love with him at first sight; Blake taught her to write, and she became a valuable collaborator in his artistic work. In 1787 he lost a beloved younger brother, Robert, who according to Blake remained a source of visionary inspiration to him thereafter.

In 1783 Blake's only conventionally printed book appeared, a collection of youthful poems and other pieces called *Poetical Sketches.* In 1789 he produced *Songs of Innocence,* his first important volume in the unique format of illuminated etching he continued to use, with some variation, in his literary work from then on. The method was to compose a design, usually a combination of text and picture, transfer it to a copper plate in an acid-resistant medium, etch away the remaining surface, make inked impressions on good paper, and then hand-color each page of each work. This process was not only an effort by a man uniquely gifted as both great poet and painter to exercise both his talents; it was also symptomatic of a synthesizing impulse in Blake's mind as a whole, a physical emblem of the unification of the powers of the human psyche whose division from one another, he believed, is reflected in the personal and political distresses of the world. The relationship of picture to text is sometimes straightforward, but more often it is indirect, and frequently it is ironical. The text of the last plate of *The Book of Thel,* for example, dramatizes a world of tortured sexuality, but the picture shows three naked children of both sexes—true innocents—riding a phallic serpent-monster with blithe nonchalance.

Between 1789 and 1795 Blake created a number of relatively short volumes by this method. (Their dates overlap somewhat.) Two of them—*Thel* and *Visions of the Daughters of Albion*—explore the theme of human growth in connection with sexual repression and freedom, *Visions* extending the theme to include the status of women and black slavery. This poem was written under the influence of Mary Wollstonecraft, author of *A Vindication of the Rights of Woman* (1792), who along with Blake and other radicals gathered around the leftist publisher Joseph Johnson in the revolutionary 1790s. *The Marriage of Heaven and Hell*, written in reaction against the Swedish mystic Emanuel Swedenborg whom Blake had once admired, is a titanically impudent satire calling for the release of creative "infernal" energies from the control imposed by an "angelic" Establishment in state, church, and personal morality. Three works—*America, Europe,* and *The Song of Los*—make up a political trilogy, in the vein of the "Song of Liberty" which concludes *The Marriage,* placing the American and French Revolutions in the context of a long-range myth going back beyond the time of Christ but also presenting historical protagonists. George III, Washington, Paine, Franklin, Hancock, and the others are cast in colossal molds, like Greek titans or Norse gods; these for Blake were truer portraits than "realistic" depictions of bewigged, bespectacled Enlightenment colonists. Another trilogy—the Books of *Urizen, Ahania,* and *Los*—is psychological, tracing the causes of the fallen—that is, crippled—human psyche in terms of a secession by Urizen ("your reason") from the primal unity of the human faculties. In 1794 Blake issued *Songs of Experience,* combining it pointedly with the earlier *Innocence* to produce one of the world's greatest volumes of lyric poetry.

In several of these works, especially the political and psychological trilogies, Blake was working toward a grander mythic vision that after 1795 absorbed his energies as poet. The first epic was *The Four Zoas* (about 1795 to 1803; left in manuscript), in which Blake personified in Zoas—"living creatures"—the four basic faculties in man—reason, passion, imagination, and instinct—whose strife with one another and alienation from what is best in themselves (personified in female "Emanations") are the root of both individual neurosis and social evil. As in *Visions of the Daughters of Albion,* the vehicle for these themes is "the torments of love and jealousy." His next epic, *Milton* (about 1800 to 1810), arose in part from personal frictions. William Hayley, a prominent if undistinguished poet and man of letters, invited Blake to join him in the country at Felpham on the coast south of London, where Blake lived from 1800 to 1803. Despite Hayley's sincere wish to help him, Blake came to see Hayley as a spiritual enemy, threatening to lead Blake from his true vocation as poet-prophet into the byways of genteel art. *Milton* allegorizes this test of artistic integrity as part of its larger story, in which the great poet, admired by Blake above all others except the biblical authors, renounces his place in Heaven and goes back to earth so that, reincarnated in Blake, he may fulfill his revolutionary, visionary potential and redeem his Puritan errors. This concept, outrageous on its face, was typical of Blake's attitude toward writers of the past; in his book illustrations he treated them not as having had their final say but rather as still-living presences continually striving to correct and per-

fect their prophetic visions with the collaboration of their fellow-prophet
Blake. While he was at Felpham, the most dramatic incident in Blake's life
occurred when he expelled a soldier from his garden and in turn was
charged with, then tried for, treason. He was acquitted, but the episode
helped shape the symbolism of Blake's final epic, *Jerusalem: The Emanation
of the Giant Albion* (about 1804 to 1820). It was the culmination of his many
attempts to fuse the themes of personal and social redemption. The title
epitomizes Blake's view of his place in the tradition of biblical prophecy:
Albion is England and also mankind; Jerusalem—a city and a woman—is
the holy city of the biblical Jews and also man's exiled spiritual freedom,
enslaved as the Jews were by Babylon. The symbolic juxtapositions reflect
Blake's conviction that he must be to his own nation what prophets like
Ezekiel were to theirs. It is these three epics especially that have earned
Blake his reputation for obscurity. They are unquestionably difficult, but
also sublime; in their combination of intensity of feeling, extravagance of
thematic elaboration, boldness of formal innovation, and sheer mental
power, they have a close analogue in the late music of Beethoven (which, in
fact, was written at the same time).

In 1809 Blake gave a public exhibition of his paintings, partly to pro-
mote his idea for the use of portable frescos in public buildings, but he won
no converts. The next decade of his life was an unhappy one about which
we do not know a great deal. But in his last years Blake was discovered
admiringly by a band of gifted young artists, and he responded with some
of his best pictorial work, including illustrations to the Book of Job and
Dante, where his reinterpretations of his sources merged their visions with
his own in the way typical of him. He died—while singing, it is said—in
August, 1827 (four months after Beethoven).

Those who regret Blake's turn from lyric to epic prophecy may have a
case, but to see it as simply a move from clarity to obscurity is misleading.
The *Songs* are plain in their language and rather conventional in symbol-
ism, but the impression of forthright directness one gets from a first read-
ing does not survive re-readings. Actually, they are enormously complex.
"My Pretty Rose Tree," for example, obviously portrays a man whose mari-
tal fidelity goes unappreciated by his wife, but a half dozen other possible
scenarios gradually emerge, some of them very different in their implica-
tions. And if this richness is discernible within individual poems, it is fur-
ther enhanced when one reads the *Songs* complete, as one should, and
listens for the powerful resonances between them. They are most patent in
the explicitly contrasting poems with identical or parallel titles, but in fact
they pulsate throughout. The relation of the black "little black boy" in the
poem so named and the white little black boy of the "Chimney Sweeper"
poems is synergistic.

The *Songs* make one of the most powerful statements ever of social
protest; yet, in Blake's characteristic way, they simultaneously explore the
intimate recesses of individual minds. "London" is a howl of anger over the
tyranny of institutions, but, like all the *Songs*, it also reveals the speaker's
attitudes; one notes the intention stated in the volume's subtitle to show
"the two contrary states of the human *soul*." He is a sensitive and acute
social critic, but his repeated "every" may suggest his own victimization by

"mind-forged manacles" that blind him to everything except horror. If that is true, it by no means lets the world's tyrants off the hook; damaged psyches are as tragic as damaged bodies. The problem that challenges him and the other speakers is how to integrate the innocent's trust with experience, love with knowledge, in a vision that transcends half-truths.

The same challenge is dramatized in the *Experience* songs about love, which provide another arena where the "torments of love and jealousy" are enacted, again with a multiple vision of the evils of society and of the evils of damaged souls. "Earth's Answer," "The Clod & the Pebble," "The Garden of Love," "The Sick Rose," "The Angel," and several other poems invite both rage at an era when "Love! sweet Love! was thought a crime" and understanding of the mental damage—cynicism, suspiciousness, paranoia—evident in the souls of the speakers, even those most sensitive, who sometimes seem perversely acquiescent in the very evils they deplore.

These harsh tones—of rage, cynicism, desperation—seem worlds removed from the delicate little tone poem *The Book of Thel*, yet with closer reading we find in the poem's "pensive queen" the same struggle with sex and love, the same ambivalent attraction and repulsion toward them. Some readers have taken *Thel* to be a metaphysical allegory—about, for example, the descent of the soul into the material world—but the poem can be read more literally, as depicting a crisis of female adolescence. Thel's initial seeking-out of death as an escape from mortality (a paradox that Keats too will explore, in certain of his great odes) leads her through a series of encounters that culminate in an encounter with herself and a recognition that the themes of mortality and of sexual growth are intimately connected. The question raised in the last plate, and debated endlessly by interpreters of Blake, is whether her shrieking flight at the finale is or is not an act of emotional suicide, a cowardly refusal to grow.

Visions of the Daughters of Albion was clearly intended as an antithetical twin to *The Book of Thel*; the parallels between the two poems, beginning with the opening dialogues with flowers, are almost countless. Oothoon, faced with the same challenge of growth and sexuality as Thel, rushes boldly to embrace them. The upshot, it would seem, is that she suffers in her person but, ultimately, liberates her spirit (though one must also wonder why she remains attached to the despicable Theotormon). In trying to counter Theotormon's diseased mentality, she achieves a rhetorical power and prophetic insight that seem irresistible. Yet, as with many of the speakers in *Songs of Experience*, we may wonder whether she is not still suffering from deep psychic damage. For example, are we to regard her sordid vision of marriage as necessarily more valid than what the Clod of Clay has to say about it in *The Book of Thel*?

Probably the most vexing problems for new readers of Blake (and some more seasoned ones) arise from his views of religion and of the relationship between nature, mind, and the senses. The key to both problems is Blake's belief in the literal divinity of humankind. The fundamental reality for Blake is the human imagination, which is almost identical with one's identity and consciousness. He therefore believed in the divine inspiration of the Old Testament, with its fundamental premise that man is God's image (Genesis 1:26–27; and see Blake's "The Divine Image") and its history of

intimacy between man and God. (He rejected the complementary Jewish idea that God is unapproachably Other.) Even more emphatically, Blake was a Christian, believing that the New Testament shows the literal union, in time and eternity, of the divine and human in the person of Jesus. (Blake's Christianity is most evident in his later works, but it is implicit from the beginning.) He believed that most of the evils in the world are actually parodies of the true and good; war between nations, for example, is an appallingly twisted version of the life-giving war of contraries that energizes the healthy human mind and ought to operate in society. Christianity as the churches teach it is for Blake one of these demonic parodies, turning the doctrine of the Incarnation into a one-way avenue by which a suprahuman and infinitely superior God descends to a lesser human condition, patiently tolerating in his human disguise the misconception that he is one of us. Blake believed in the Incarnation too, literally, but he reversed the direction of its thrust, seeing Jesus as achieving the Godhood latent but paralyzed in other human beings. This view is not to be confused with that of certain nineteenth-century religious liberals who saw in Jesus an incomparable ethical model on the plane of mere nature. Blake's view of the divine humanity in Jesus is just as supernatural as that of the theologians: Jesus transcended nature, among other things through his miracles (*if* the subject believed), and so can we all. In fact, Blake believed we all do so in the imaginative act of perception, which creates nature in as real a sense as that ascribed to the God of Genesis.

To Blake nature has no true existence in itself if by existence we understand meaningful form. For all Blake cares, there may well exist "out there" a cloud of atoms or other particles bumping one another around into blobs, some of which are denser than others. But to mistake that for reality would be false, and in extreme cases it would be mental derangement. Fortunately, most people escape this insanity; for example, to save them from their "rational" conviction that immaterial mind cannot possibly affect the behavior of matter in the form of human bodies and speedily approaching automobiles, imagination intervenes with the happy "illusion" that people have the freedom to jump back and avoid getting run over. Even the most casual acts of perception are acts of imaginative sculpture; when we see a desk or refrigerator or tree we mentally carve it out of space, giving it significant reality in the only way possible. If, rising to a higher level, we bring the entire force of our imaginations to these acts, giving vital intensity to what we see, as an inspired painter observes his subject or a lover his beloved, we create an even fuller reality, because we have made it more fully human. And in these acts our sense organs are not causes but apertures allowing creative energy to move freely. The "doors of perception" are to be cleansed, as *The Marriage* stipulates, not to let objects penetrate to our passive minds but to let our mental and spiritual powers move out and create. For Blake this freedom of and from the senses, so that we use them rather than the other way around, has ethical and political implications. We can be as free from the tyrannical forms of God, neurotic conscience, and institutions as we can from the mere machinery of our sense organs. For Blake this truth applies to all kinds of sense experience, but he dwells most emphatically on vision and the sexual sense of touch. And so,

although Blake could and did love the world of outdoors, he would have no part of Wordsworthian "guidance" by nature, or of its indirect deification by scientists implicitly worshipping its "laws," and least of all of deism, a religion whose remote, clockwork God combines the worst of both religious orthodoxy and of fallen science.

What makes Blake exciting, though at times difficult, is his organic vision of things: the cross-fertilization of words and images in different works, the fusion of the personal and public, the ultimate unity of his religious, psychological, and political mythology, his marriage of the arts, his annihilation of the barrier between feeling and intelligence. As one might expect, then, his influence today is very great not only in literature but in other fields including psychology, theology, and politics. His vision is also organic in endowing everything, from stars to grains of sand, with an intense life both vast and intimately human. In his essay on his painting *The Vision of the Last Judgment,* he exhorts his public to "enter into these images in . . . imagination, approaching them on the fiery chariot of . . . contemplative thought," making "a friend and companion of . . . these images of wonder." He calls for the same vivifying effort by his readers.

The text in the selections that follow is as edited by David V. Erdman, except for a few slight changes.

FURTHER READING *(prepared by B. W.):* Good introductory books on Blake include Max Plowman's *An Introduction to the Study of Blake,* 1927; H. M. Margoliouth's *William Blake,* 1950; and J. Middleton Murry's *William Blake,* 1933. Murry's is the most detailed and takes a somewhat personal approach. David Lindsay's *Blake,* 1989, in the Critics Debate series, is also helpful. Very possibly the best study of Blake is Northrop Frye's *Fearful Symmetry,* 1947; most of it is for advanced students, but the first two chapters, on Blake's ideas of imagination, mind, perception, and religion, make an exciting introduction for any reader. Good biographies that also give some attention to Blake's individual works include Mona Wilson's *The Life of William Blake,* 1927, 1971 ed. by Geoffrey Keynes; and Michael Davis's *William Blake: A New Kind of Man,* 1977. Stimulating explications of a variety of works by Blake appear in Harold Bloom's *Blake's Apocalypse,* 1963, and the Blake section of Bloom's *The Visionary Company,* 1961. For the *Songs,* including their designs, Joseph H. Wicksteed's *Blake's Innocence and Experience,* 1928, can still be recommended; more modern, and more controversial, readings appear in D. G. Gillham's *Blake's Contrary States,* 1966, in which the *Songs* are treated as "dramatic poems." Zachary Leader, in *Reading Blake's "Songs,"* 1981, explicates the *Songs* and their pictorial designs in detail, while arguing that in them Blake confronted central problems in his art and thought. Brian Wilkie, *Blake's Thel and Oothoon,* 1990, a monograph-length discussion of *Thel* and *Visions,* discusses the poems as psychological dramas. On sexual and feminist themes in Blake, see Diana Hume George's eloquent, even-handed study, *Blake and Freud,* 1980. David V. Erdman's *The Illuminated Blake,* 1974, contains black-and-white reproductions of all the plates in Blake's illuminated poetry, along with commentary on each plate. Inexpensive color reproductions of various Blake works appear from time to time, from various publishers. Those who wish to read further in Blake, with good help, are directed to *Blake's Poetry and Designs,* ed. Mary Lynn Johnson and John E. Grant, 1979, which includes good annotations, selected color illustrations, and a sampling of critical essays. Nelson Hilton, *Literal Imagination: Blake's Vision of Words,* 1983, is an exciting study, from a recent critical perspective, of Blake's style and wordplay.

SONGS OF INNOCENCE AND OF EXPERIENCE

Shewing the Two Contrary States of the Human Soul

Songs of Innocence

INTRODUCTION

Piping down the valleys wild
Piping songs of pleasant glee
On a cloud I saw a child.
And he laughing said to me.[1]

Pipe a song about a Lamb; 5
So I piped with merry chear,
Piper pipe that song again—
So I piped, he wept to hear.

Drop thy pipe thy happy pipe
Sing thy songs of happy chear, 10
So I sung the same again
While he wept with joy to hear

Piper sit thee down and write
In a book that all may read—
So he vanish'd from my sight. 15
And I pluck'd a hollow reed.

And I made a rural pen,
And I stain'd the water clear,
And I wrote my happy songs
Every child may joy to hear 20

THE SHEPHERD

How sweet is the Shepherds sweet lot,
From the morn to the evening he strays:
He shall follow his sheep all the day
And his tongue shall be filled with praise.

[1] Blake's eccentric punctuation and capitalization have been left as in the text he engraved, because he probably intended them to affect the rhetorical rhythms and meaning, as with the dashes in Emily Dickinson's poems. Quotation marks sometimes supplied by editors have been avoided because (as in "Infant Joy" of *Innocence* and "The Chimney Sweeper" of *Experience*) they can do away with ambiguities Blake almost certainly intended.

For he hears the lambs innocent call, 5
And he hears the ewes tender reply,
He is watchful while they are in peace,
For they know when their Shepherd is nigh.

THE ECCHOING GREEN

The Sun does arise,
And make happy the skies.
The merry bells ring
To welcome the Spring.
The sky-lark and thrush, 5
The birds of the bush,
Sing louder around,
To the bells chearful sound.
While our sports shall be seen
On the Ecchoing Green. 10

Old John with white hair
Does laugh away care,
Sitting under the oak,
Among the old folk,
They laugh at our play, 15
And soon they all say.
Such such were the joys.
When we all girls & boys,
In our youth-time were seen,
On the Ecchoing Green. 20

Till the little ones weary
No more can be merry
The sun does descend,
And our sports have an end:
Round the laps of their mothers, 25
Many sisters and brothers,
Like birds in their nest,
Are ready for rest;
And sport no more seen,
On the darkening Green. 30

THE LAMB

Little Lamb who made thee
Dost thou know who made thee
Gave thee life & bid thee feed.

By the stream & o'er the mead;[1]
Gave thee clothing of delight, 5
Softest clothing wooly bright;
Gave thee such a tender voice,
Making all the vales rejoice!
 Little Lamb who made thee
 Dost thou know who made thee 10

 Little Lamb I'll tell thee,
 Little Lamb I'll tell thee!
He is called by thy name,
For he calls himself a Lamb:
He is meek & he is mild, 15
He became a little child:
I a child & thou a lamb,
We are called by his name.
 Little Lamb God bless thee.
 Little Lamb God bless thee. 20

THE LITTLE BLACK BOY

My mother bore me in the southern wild,
And I am black, but O! my soul is white;
White as an angel is the English child:
But I am black as if bereav'd[1] of light.

My mother taught me underneath a tree 5
And sitting down before the heat of day,
She took me on her lap and kissed me,
And pointing to the east began to say.

Look on the rising sun: there God does live
And gives his light, and gives his heat away. 10
And flowers and trees and beasts and men recieve
Comfort in morning joy in the noon day.

And we are put on earth a little space,[2]
That we may learn to bear the beams of love,
And these black bodies and this sun-burnt face 15
Is but a cloud, and like a shady grove.

For when our souls have learn'd the heat to bear
The cloud will vanish we shall hear his voice.
Saying: come out from the grove my love & care,
And round my golden tent like lambs rejoice. 20

[1] Meadow. [1] Deprived. [2] Period of time.

Thus did my mother say and kissed me,
And thus I say to little English boy.
When I from black and he from white cloud free,
And round the tent of God like lambs we joy:

Ill shade him from the heat till he can bear, 25
To lean in joy upon our fathers knee.
And then I'll stand and stroke his silver hair,
And be like him and he will then love me.

THE BLOSSOM

Merry Merry Sparrow
Under leaves so green
A happy Blossom
Sees you swift as arrow
Seek your cradle narrow 5
Near my Bosom.

Pretty Pretty Robin
Under leaves so green
A happy Blossom
Hears you sobbing sobbing 10
Pretty Pretty Robin
Near my Bosom.

THE CHIMNEY SWEEPER

When my mother died I was very young,
And my father sold me[1] while yet my tongue,
Could scarcely cry weep weep weep weep.[2]
So your chimneys I sweep & in soot I sleep.

Theres little Tom Dacre, who cried when his head 5
That curl'd like a lambs back, was shav'd,[3] so I said.
Hush Tom never mind it, for when your head's bare,
You know that the soot cannot spoil your white hair.

[1] "Sold" is a more accurate word than "apprenticed" would be. A 1788 law prohibited the use of children under eight years old as sweeps, but it was not enforced. The sweeps' plight was even worse than Blake paints it in the poem.
[2] The boys' slurred street-cry, for "Sweep."
[3] The shaving was for streamlining in crawling into chimneys. The sweeps worked naked in them.

And so he was quiet, & that very night,
As Tom was a sleeping he had such a sight,
That thousands of sweepers Dick, Joe Ned & Jack 10
Were all of them lock'd up in coffins of black

And by came an Angel who had a bright key,
And he open'd the coffins & set them all free.
Then down a green plain leaping laughing they run 15
And wash in a river and shine in the Sun.

Then naked & white, all their bags[4] left behind,
They rise upon clouds, and sport in the wind.
And the Angel told Tom if he'd be a good boy,
He'd have God for his father & never want joy. 20

And so Tom awoke and we rose in the dark
And got with our bags & our brushes to work.
Tho' the morning was cold, Tom was happy & warm,
So if all do their duty, they need not fear harm.

THE LITTLE BOY LOST

Father, father, where are you going
O do not walk so fast.
Speak father, speak to your little boy
Or else I shall be lost,

The night was dark no father was there 5
The child was wet with dew.
The mire was deep, & the child did weep
And away the vapour flew.

THE LITTLE BOY FOUND

The little boy lost in the lonely fen,[1]
Led by the wand'ring light,
Began to cry, but God ever nigh,
Appeard like his father in white.

He kissed the child & by the hand led 5
And to his mother brought,
Who in sorrow pale, thro' the lonely dale
Her little boy weeping sought.

[4] Bags for hauling soot. [1] Marsh.

LAUGHING SONG

When the green woods laugh, with the voice of joy
And the dimpling stream runs laughing by,
When the air does laugh with our merry wit,
And the green hill laughs with the noise of it.

When the meadows laugh with lively green 5
And the grasshopper laughs in the merry scene,
When Mary and Susan and Emily,
With their sweet round mouths sing Ha, Ha, He.

When the painted[1] birds laugh in the shade
Where our table with cherries and nuts is spread 10
Come live & be merry and join with me,
To sing the sweet chorus of Ha, Ha, He.

A CRADLE SONG

Sweet dreams form a shade,
O'er my lovely infants head.
Sweet dreams of pleasant streams,
By happy silent moony beams.

Sweet sleep with soft down, 5
Weave thy brows an infant crown.
Sweet sleep Angel mild,
Hover o'er my happy child.

Sweet smiles in the night,
Hover over my delight. 10
Sweet smiles Mothers smiles
All the livelong night beguiles.

Sweet moans, dovelike sighs,
Chase not slumber from thy eyes.
Sweet moans, sweeter smiles, 15
All the dovelike moans beguiles.

Sleep sleep happy child.
All creation slept and smil'd.

[1] Variously colored.

Sleep sleep, happy sleep,
While o'er thee thy mother weep. 20

Sweet babe in thy face,
Holy image I can trace.
Sweet babe once like thee,
Thy maker lay and wept for me

Wept for me for thee for all, 25
When he was an infant small.
Thou his image ever see,
Heavenly face that smiles on thee.

Smiles on thee on me on all,
Who became an infant small, 30
Infant smiles are his own smiles.
Heaven & earth to peace beguiles.

THE DIVINE IMAGE

To Mercy Pity Peace and Love,
All pray in their distress:
And to these virtues of delight
Return their thankfulness.

For Mercy Pity Peace and Love, 5
Is God our father dear:
And Mercy Pity Peace and Love,
Is Man his child and care.

For Mercy has a human heart
Pity, a human face: 10
And Love, the human form divine,
And Peace, the human dress.

Then every man of every clime,
That prays in his distress,
Prays to the human form divine 15
Love Mercy Pity Peace.

And all must love the human form,
In heathen, turk or jew.
Where Mercy, Love & Pity dwell
There God is dwelling too. 20

HOLY THURSDAY[1]

Twas on a Holy Thursday their innocent faces clean
The children walking two & two in red & blue & green
Grey headed beadles[2] walkd before with wands as white as snow
Till into the high dome of Pauls they like Thames waters flow

O what a multitude they seemd these flowers of London town 5
Seated in companies they sit with radiance all their own
The hum of multitudes was there but multitudes of lambs
Thousands of little boys & girls raising their innocent hands

Now like a mighty wind they raise to heaven the voice of song
Or like harmonious thunderings the seats of heaven among 10
Beneath them[3] sit the aged men wise guardians of the poor
Then cherish pity, lest you drive an angel from your door

NIGHT

The sun descending in the west
The evening star does shine.
The birds are silent in their nest,
And I must seek for mine,
The moon like a flower, 5
In heavens high bower;
With silent delight,
Sits and smiles on the night.

Farewell green fields and happy groves,
Where flocks have took delight; 10
Where lambs have nibbled, silent moves
The feet of angels bright;
Unseen they pour blessing,
And joy without ceasing,
On each bud and blossom, 15
And each sleeping bosom.

They look in every thoughtless nest,
Where birds are coverd warm;
They visit caves of every beast,

[1] The poor children of London's charity schools attended a service at St. Paul's Cathedral on the first Thursday in May.
[2] Minor church officers. [3] The children sat in temporary grandstands.

To keep them all from harm; 20
If they see any weeping,
That should have been sleeping
They pour sleep on their head
And sit down by their bed.

When wolves and tygers howl for prey 25
They pitying stand and weep;
Seeking to drive their thirst away,
And keep them from the sheep.
But if they rush dreadful;
The angels most heedful, 30
Recieve each mild spirit,
New worlds to inherit.

And there the lions ruddy eyes,
Shall flow with tears of gold:
And pitying the tender cries, 35
And walking round the fold:
Saying: wrath by his meekness
And by his health, sickness,
Is driven away,
From our immortal day. 40

And now beside thee bleating lamb,
I can lie down and sleep;
Or think on him who bore thy name,
Grase after thee and weep.
For wash'd in lifes river, 45
My bright mane for ever,
Shall shine like the gold,
As I guard o'er the fold.

SPRING

Sound the Flute!
Now it's mute.
Birds delight
Day and Night.
Nightingale 5
In the dale
Lark in Sky
Merrily
Merrily Merrily to welcome in the Year

Little Boy
Full of joy. 10

Little Girl
Sweet and small,
Cock does crow
So do you. 15
Merry voice
Infant noise
Merrily Merrily to welcome in the Year.

Little Lamb
Here I am, 20
Come and lick
My white neck.
Let me pull
Your soft Wool.
Let me kiss 25
Your soft face.
Merrily Merrily we welcome in the Year

NURSE'S SONG

When the voices of children are heard on the green
And laughing is heard on the hill,
My heart is at rest within my breast
And every thing else is still

Then come home my children, the sun is gone down 5
And the dews of night arise
Come come leave off play, and let us away
Till the morning appears in the skies

No no let us play, for it is yet day
And we cannot go to sleep 10
Besides in the sky, the little birds fly
And the hills are all coverd with sheep

Well well go & play till the light fades away
And then go home to bed
The little ones leaped & shouted & laugh'd 15
And all the hills ecchoed

INFANT JOY

I have no name
I am but two days old.—
What shall I call thee?

I happy am
Joy is my name,— 5
Sweet joy befall thee!

Pretty joy!
Sweet joy but two days old.
Sweet joy I call thee:
Thou dost smile. 10
I sing the while
Sweet joy befall thee.

A DREAM

Once a dream did weave a shade,
O'er my Angel-guarded bed,
That an Emmet[1] lost it's way
Where on grass methought I lay.

Troubled wilderd[2] and folorn 5
Dark benighted travel-worn,
Over many a tangled spray
All heart-broke I heard her say.

O my children! do they cry
Do they hear their father sigh. 10
Now they look abroad to see,
Now return and weep for me.

Pitying I drop'd a tear:
But I saw a glow-worm near:
Who replied. What wailing wight[3] 15
Calls the watchman of the night.

I am set to light the ground,
While the beetle goes his round:
Follow now the beetles hum,
Little wanderer hie[4] thee home. 20

ON ANOTHERS SORROW

Can I see anothers woe,
And not be in sorrow too.
Can I see anothers grief,
And not seek for kind relief.

[1] Ant. [2] Lost. [3] Creature. [4] Hurry.

Can I see a falling tear, 5
And not feel my sorrows share,
Can a father see his child,
Weep, nor be with sorrow fill'd.

Can a mother sit and hear,
An infant groan an infant fear— 10
No no never can it be.
Never never can it be.

And can he who smiles on all
Hear the wren with sorrows small,
Hear the small birds grief & care 15
Hear the woes that infants bear—

And not sit beside the nest
Pouring pity in their breast,
And not sit the cradle near
Weeping tear on infants tear. 20

And not sit both night & day,
Wiping all our tears away.
O! no never can it be.
Never never can it be.

He doth give his joy to all. 25
He becomes an infant small.
He becomes a man of woe
He doth feel the sorrow too.

Think not, thou canst sigh a sigh,
And thy maker is not by. 30
Think not, thou canst weep a tear,
And thy maker is not near.

O! he gives to us his joy,
That our grief he may destroy
Till our grief is fled & gone 35
He doth sit by us and moan

Songs of Experience

INTRODUCTION

Hear the voice of the Bard![1]
Who Present, Past, & Future sees

[1] Inspired poet.

Whose ears have heard,
The Holy Word,
That walk'd among the ancient trees. 5

Calling the lapsed Soul
And weeping in the evening dew;[2]
That might controll,
The starry pole;
And fallen fallen light renew! 10

O Earth O Earth return!
Arise from out the dewy grass;
Night is worn,
And the morn
Rises from the slumberous mass. 15

Turn away no more:
Why wilt thou turn away
The starry floor
The watry shore[3]
Is giv'n thee till the break of day. 20

EARTH'S ANSWER

Earth rais'd up her head,
From the darkness dread & drear.
Her light fled:
Stony dread!
And her locks cover'd with grey despair. 5

Prison'd on watry shore
Starry Jealousy does keep my den
Cold and hoar
Weeping o'er
I hear the Father of the ancient men[1] 10

Selfish father of men
Cruel jealous selfish fear
Can delight

[2] In Genesis 3:8–19 God appears to the fallen ("lapsed") Adam and Eve in the evening, condemning them to death. Blake substitutes "Holy Word"—the Son of God—for God. Antecedents and pronoun references in lines 1–8 are ambiguous, and several readings are possible.

[3] *Starry floor* and *watry shore* are paradoxical symbols in Blake, both for humanity's fallen condition and for a saving limit that preserves it from a final, irreversible fallenness.

[1] The Father is in pointed parallel-contrast with "Holy Word" in the "Introduction."

Chain'd in night
The virgins of youth and morning bear.[2] 15

Does spring hide its joy
When buds and blossoms grow?
Does the sower?
Sow by night?
Or the plowman in darkness plow? 20

Break this heavy chain,
That does freeze my bones around
Selfish! vain,
Eternal bane![3]
That free Love with bondage bound. 25

THE CLOD & THE PEBBLE

Love seeketh not Itself to please,
Nor for itself hath any care;
But for another gives its ease,
And builds a Heaven in Hells despair.

So sang a little Clod of Clay, 5
Trodden with the cattles feet:
But a Pebble of the brook,
Warbled out these metres meet.[1]

Love seeketh only Self to please,
To bind another to its delight; 10
Joys in anothers loss of ease,
And builds a Hell in Heavens despite.[2]

HOLY THURSDAY[1]

Is this a holy thing to see,
In a rich and fruitful land,
Babes reducd to misery,
Fed with cold and usurous hand?

[2] Probably "If they are chained in night, can the virgins of youth and morning bear de-
light?", but the word order is ambiguous.
[3] Ruin. [1] Appropriate. [2] Spiteful defiance.
[1] For the situation described, see note to title of "Holy Thursday" in *Innocence*.

Is that trembling cry a song? 5
Can it be a song of joy?
And so many children poor?
It is a land of poverty!

And their sun does never shine.
And their fields are bleak & bare. 10
And their ways are fill'd with thorns.
It is eternal winter there.

For where-e'er the sun does shine,
And where-e'er the rain does fall:
Babe can never hunger there, 15
Nor poverty the mind appall.

THE LITTLE GIRL LOST[1]

In futurity
I prophetic see,
That the earth from sleep,
(Grave the sentence[2] deep)

Shall arise and seek 5
For her maker meek:
And the desart wild
Become a garden mild.

In the southern clime,
Where the summers prime, 10
Never fades away;
Lovely Lyca lay.

Seven summers old
Lovely Lyca told,[3]
She had wanderd long, 15
Hearing wild birds song.

Sweet sleep come to me
Underneath this tree;
Do father, mother weep.—
"Where can Lyca sleep". 20

Lost in desart wild
Is your little child.

[1] This poem and its "Found" sequel were originally in *Songs of Innocence.*
[2] A complex pun; "grave" includes the meaning "engrave." [3] Numbered.

How can Lyca sleep,
If her mother weep.

If her heart does ake, 25
Then let Lyca wake;
If my mother sleep,
Lyca shall not weep.

Frowning frowning night,
O'er this desart bright, 30
Let thy moon arise,
While I close my eyes.

Sleeping Lyca lay;
While the beasts of prey,
Come from caverns deep, 35
View'd the maid asleep

The kingly lion stood
And the virgin view'd,
Then he gambold⁴ round
O'er the hallowd ground: 40

Leopards, tygers play,
Round her as she lay;
While the lion old,
Bow'd his mane of gold.

And her bosom lick, 45
And upon her neck,
From his eyes of flame,
Ruby tears there came;

While the lioness,
Loos'd her slender dress, 50
And naked they convey'd
To caves the sleeping maid.

THE LITTLE GIRL FOUND

All the night in woe
Lyca's parents go:
Over vallies deep,
While the desarts weep.

⁴ Skipped playfully.

Tired and woe-begone, 5
Hoarse with making moan:
Arm in arm seven days,
They trac'd the desart ways.

Seven nights they sleep,
Among shadows deep: 10
And dream they see their child
Starv'd in desart wild.

Pale thro pathless ways
The fancied image strays,
Famish'd, weeping, weak 15
With hollow piteous shriek

Rising from unrest,
The trembling woman prest,
With feet of weary woe;
She could no further go. 20

In his arms he bore,
Her arm'd with sorrow sore;
Till before their way,
A couching lion lay.

Turning back was vain, 25
Soon his heavy mane,
Bore them to the ground;
Then he stalk'd around,

Smelling to his prey.
But their fears allay, 30
When he licks their hands;
And silent by them stands.

They look upon his eyes
Fill'd with deep surprise:
And wondering behold, 35
A spirit arm'd in gold.

On his head a crown
On his shoulders down,
Flow'd his golden hair.
Gone was all their care. 40

Follow me he said,
Weep not for the maid;
In my palace deep,
Lyca lies asleep.

Then they followed, 45
Where the vision led:
And saw their sleeping child,
Among tygers wild.

To this day they dwell
In a lonely dell 50
Nor fear the wolvish howl,
Nor the lions growl.

THE CHIMNEY SWEEPER[1]

A little black thing among the snow:
Crying weep, weep, in notes of woe!
Where are thy father & mother? say?
They are both gone up to the church to pray.

Because I was happy upon the heath, 5
And smil'd among the winters snow:
They clothed me in the clothes of death,
And taught me to sing the notes of woe.

And because I am happy, & dance & sing,
They think they have done me no injury: 10
And are gone to praise God & his Priest & King
Who make up a heaven of our misery.

NURSE'S SONG

When the voices of children, are heard on the green
And whisprings are in the dale:
The days of my youth rise fresh in my mind,
My face turns green and pale.

Then come home my children, the sun is gone down 5
And the dews of night arise
Your spring & your day, are wasted in play
And your winter and night in disguise.

[1] See notes to "The Chimney Sweeper" in *Innocence*.

THE SICK ROSE

O Rose thou art sick.
The invisible worm,
That flies in the night
In the howling storm:

Has found out thy bed 5
Of crimson joy:
And his dark secret love
Does thy life destroy.

THE FLY

Little Fly
Thy summers play,
My thoughtless hand
Has brush'd away.

Am not I 5
A fly like thee?
Or art not thou
A man like me?

For I dance
And drink & sing; 10
Till some blind hand
Shall brush my wing.

If thought is life
And strength & breath;
And the want 15
Of thought is death;

Then am I
A happy fly,
If I live,
Or if I die. 20

THE ANGEL

I Dreamt a Dream! what can it mean?
And that I was a maiden Queen:

Guarded by an Angel mild;
Witless[1] woe, was ne'er beguil'd![2]

And I wept both night and day　　　　　　　　　　　　　5
And he wip'd my tears away
And I wept both day and night
And hid from him my hearts delight

So he took his wings and fled:
Then the morn blush'd rosy red:　　　　　　　　　　　　10
I dried my tears & armd my fears,
With ten thousand shields and spears.

Soon my Angel came again:
I was arm'd, he came in vain:
For the time of youth was fled　　　　　　　　　　　　15
And grey hairs were on my head.

THE TYGER

Tyger Tyger, burning bright,
In the forests of the night;
What immortal hand or eye,
Could frame[1] thy fearful symmetry?

In what distant deeps or skies　　　　　　　　　　　　5
Burnt the fire of thine eyes!
On what wings dare he aspire?
What the hand, dare sieze the fire?

And what shoulder, & what art,
Could twist the sinews of thy heart?　　　　　　　　　10
And when thy heart began to beat,
What dread hand? & what dread feet?

What the hammer? what the chain,
In what furnace was thy brain?
What the anvil? what dread grasp,　　　　　　　　　15
Dare its deadly terrors clasp?

[1] Possibly "unwitting"—unaware, naive. The word also means "stupid."
[2] Taken in by guile.
[1] If there is also a pun on picture-framing here, line 20 refers not only to the creation of the world but also to the artist's creative process. Blake's works contain many symbols based on his graphic methods.

When the stars threw down their spears
And water'd heaven with their tears:[2]
Did he smile his work to see?
Did he who made the Lamb make thee? 20

Tyger, Tyger burning bright,
In the forests of the night:
What immortal hand or eye,
Dare frame thy fearful symmetry?

MY PRETTY ROSE TREE[1]

A flower was offerd to me;
Such a flower as May never bore.
But I said I've a Pretty Rose-tree,
And I passed the sweet flower o'er.

Then I went to my Pretty Rose-tree; 5
To tend her by day and by night.
But my Rose turnd away with jealousy:
And her thorns were my only delight.

AH! SUN-FLOWER

Ah Sun-flower! weary of time,
Who countest the steps of the Sun:
Seeking after that sweet golden clime
Where the travellers journey is done.

Where the Youth pined away with desire, 5
And the pale Virgin shrouded in snow:
Arise from their graves and aspire,
Where my Sun-flower wishes to go.

THE LILLY

The modest Rose puts forth a thorn:
The humble Sheep, a threatning horn:

[2] These words recur in a passage in Blake's *Four Zoas*, V, in which Urizen, fallen reason, marshals forces (called "stars") to rebel against his creator, as Satan did against God. The present line therefore probably refers to a primordial time just before the creation of the world and man.
[1] This and the following two poems, all of them about passivity versus activity in love, form a single plate.

While the Lilly white, shall in Love delight,
Nor a thorn nor a threat stain her beauty bright

THE GARDEN OF LOVE

I went to the Garden of Love,
And saw what I never had seen:
A Chapel was built in the midst,
Where I used to play on the green.

And the gates of this Chapel were shut, 5
And Thou shalt not. writ over the door;
So I turn'd to the Garden of Love,
That so many sweet flowers bore,

And I saw it was filled with graves,
And tomb-stones where flowers should be: 10
And Priests in black gowns, were walking their rounds,
And binding with briars, my joys & desires.

THE LITTLE VAGABOND

Dear Mother, dear Mother, the Church is cold.
But the Ale-house is healthy & pleasant & warm;
Besides I can tell where I am use'd well,
Such usage in heaven will never do well.

But if at the Church they would give us some Ale. 5
And a pleasant fire, our souls to regale;
We'd sing and we'd pray, all the live-long day;
Nor ever once wish from the Church to stray,

Then the Parson might preach & drink & sing.
And we'd be as happy as birds in the spring: 10
And modest dame Lurch, who is always at Church,
Wou'ld not have bandy[1] children nor fasting nor birch.[2]

And God like a father rejoicing to see,
His children as pleasant and happy as he:
Would have no more quarrel with the Devil or the Barrel 15
But kiss him & give him both drink and apparel.

[1] Bent like a bow. [2] Stick for punishing children.

LONDON

I wander thro' each charter'd[1] street,
Near where the charter'd Thames does flow.
And mark in every face I meet
Marks of weakness, marks of woe.

In every cry of every Man, 5
In every Infants cry of fear,
In every voice: in every ban,[2]
The mind-forg'd manacles I hear

How the Chimney-sweepers cry
Every blackning Church appalls, 10
And the hapless Soldiers sigh,
Runs in blood down Palace walls

But most thro' midnight streets I hear
How the youthful Harlots curse
Blasts the new-born Infants tear[3] 15
And blights with plagues the Marriage hearse

THE HUMAN ABSTRACT

Pity would be no more,
If we did not make somebody Poor:
And Mercy no more could be,
If all were as happy as we;

And mutual fear brings peace; 5
Till the selfish loves increase.
Then Cruelty knits a snare,
And spreads his baits with care.

He sits down with holy fears,
And waters the ground with tears: 10
Then Humility takes its root
Underneath his foot.

[1] Rented out; also, given prerogatives by charter. In the latter sense the word was part of the jargon of patriotism, as in "the chartered rights of Englishmen."
[2] Decree of prohibition; also curse; possibly also a pun on "banns (announcement) of marriage."
[3] Produces congenital blindness through venereal disease.

Soon spreads the dismal shade
Of Mystery[1] over his head;
And the Catterpiller and Fly, 15
Feed on the Mystery.

And it bears the fruit of Deceit,
Ruddy and sweet to eat;
And the Raven his nest has made
In its thickest shade. 20

The Gods of the earth and sea,
Sought thro' Nature to find this Tree
But their search was all in vain:
There grows one in the Human Brain

INFANT SORROW

My mother groand! my father wept.
Into the dangerous world I leapt:
Helpless, naked, piping loud;
Like a fiend hid in a cloud.

Struggling in my fathers hands: 5
Striving against my swadling bands:[1]
Bound and weary I thought best
To sulk upon my mothers breast.

A POISON TREE[1]

I was angry with my friend;
I told my wrath, my wrath did end.
I was angry with my foe:
I told it not, my wrath did grow.

And I waterd it in fears, 5
Night & morning with my tears:
And I sunned it with smiles,
And with soft deceitful wiles.

[1] In Blake's myth, Mystery (often in the form of a tree) represents the counter-human tendencies of both religious worship of a remote God and of scientific rationalism implicitly worshipping the hidden god Nature. Blake regarded the churches and the rationalists, apparent enemies of each other, as merely different forms of the same thing, although the attack on religious hypocrisy is the more explicit in this poem.
[1] Cloths wound restrictively around infants.
[1] In Blake's notebook draft entitled "Christian Forbearance."

And it grew both day and night.
Till it bore an apple bright. 10
And my foe beheld it shine.
And he knew that it was mine.

And into my garden stole,
When the night had veild the pole;
In the morning glad I see; 15
My foe outstretchd beneath the tree.

A LITTLE BOY LOST

Nought loves another as itself
Nor venerates another so.
Nor is it possible to Thought
A greater than itself to know:

And Father, how can I love you, 5
Or any of my brothers more?
I love you like the little bird
That picks up crumbs around the door.

The Priest sat by and heard the child.
In trembling zeal he siez'd his hair: 10
He led him by his little coat:
And all admir'd the Priestly care.

And standing on the altar high,
Lo what a fiend is here! said he:
One who sets reason up for judge 15
Of our most holy Mystery.[1]

The weeping child could not be heard.
The weeping parents wept in vain:
They strip'd him to his little shirt.
And bound him in an iron chain. 20

And burn'd him in a holy place,
Where many had been burn'd before:
The weeping parents wept in vain.
Are such things done on Albions[2] shore.

[1] See note to "The Human Abstract," line 14.
[2] England's. The literal answer to the question is no.

A LITTLE GIRL LOST

Children of the future Age,
Reading this indignant page:
Know that in a former time,
Love! sweet Love! was thought a crime.

In the Age of Gold, 5
Free from winters cold:
Youth and maiden bright,
To the holy light,
Naked in the sunny beams delight.

Once a youthful pair 10
Fill'd with softest care:
Met in garden bright,
Where the holy light,
Had just removd the curtains of the night.

There in rising day, 15
On the grass they play:
Parents were afar:
Strangers came not near:
And the maiden soon forgot her fear.

Tired with kisses sweet 20
They agree to meet,
When the silent sleep
Waves o'er heavens deep;
And the weary tired wanderers weep.

To her father white 25
Came the maiden bright:
But his loving look,
Like the holy book,
All her tender limbs with terror shook.

Ona! pale and weak! 30
To thy father speak:
O the trembling fear!
O the dismal care!
That shakes the blossoms of my hoary[1] hair

[1] White with age.

TO TIRZAH[1]

Whate'er is Born of Mortal Birth,
Must be consumed with the Earth
To rise from Generation[2] free;
Then what have I to do with thee?[3]

The Sexes sprung from Shame & Pride 5
Blow'd[4] in the morn: in evening died
But Mercy changd Death into Sleep;
The Sexes rose to work & weep.[5]

Thou Mother of my Mortal part
With cruelty didst mould my Heart, 10
And with false self-decieving tears,
Didst bind my Nostrils Eyes & Ears.

Didst close my Tongue in senseless clay
And me to Mortal Life betray:
The Death of Jesus set me free, 15
Then what have I to do with thee?

THE SCHOOL BOY[1]

I love to rise in a summer morn,
When the birds sing on every tree;
The distant huntsman winds his horn,
And the sky-lark sings with me.
O! what sweet company. 5

[1] This poem was written some years after the other *Songs* and appears only in late copies of the volume. It reflects Blake's later myth, where Tirzah appears as a demonic female who tortures men sexually. Here she is Nature seen as the mother of what is perishable rather than immortal in us, a connection Blake made clear in a text from I Corinthians 15:44, "it is raised a spiritual body," engraved on the pictorial plate.

[2] The life of material and temporal flux; also, the world of Experience, where our souls can succumb or win their freedom.

[3] Jesus' words to his mother, in John 2:4, in apparent resistance to her plea for his help when the wine runs out at the wedding at Cana; he nevertheless goes on to change water into wine, his first miracle.

[4] Blossomed. Tradition held that Adam and Eve sinned on the same day they were created.

[5] After the fall, Eve was cursed with pain in childbirth, Adam with painfully hard labor, and both with death (Genesis 3:16–19), but Christianity changed death into sleep through the doctrine of the resurrection of the body.

[1] Blake sometimes placed this poem in *Innocence*.

But to go to school in a summer morn
O! it drives all joy away;
Under a cruel eye outworn,
The little ones spend the day,
In sighing and dismay. 10

Ah! then at times I drooping sit,
And spend many an anxious hour.
Nor in my book can I take delight,
Nor sit in learnings bower,
Worn thro' with the dreary shower 15

How can the bird that is born for joy,
Sit in a cage and sing.
How can a child when fears annoy,[2]
But droop his tender wing,
And forget his youthful spring. 20

O! father & mother, if buds are nip'd,
And blossoms blown away,
And if the tender plants are strip'd
Of their joy in the springing day,
By sorrow and cares dismay, 25

How shall the summer arise in joy
Or the summer fruits appear
Or how shall we gather what griefs destroy
Or bless the mellowing year,
When the blasts of winter appear. 30

THE VOICE OF THE ANCIENT BARD[1]

Youth of delight come hither:
And see the opening morn,
Image of truth new born
Doubt is fled & clouds of reason
Dark disputes & artful teazing. 5
Folly is an endless maze,
Tangled roots perplex her ways,
How many have fallen there!
They stumble all night over bones of the dead;
And feel they know not what but care; 10
And wish to lead others when they should be led.

[2] Harm (a stronger word than it is today).
[1] Another poem sometimes placed in *Innocence*.

A DIVINE IMAGE[1]

[A rejected Song of Experience]

Cruelty has a Human Heart
And Jealousy a Human Face
Terror, the Human Form Divine
And Secrecy, the Human Dress

The Human Dress, is forged Iron 5
The Human Form, a fiery Forge.
The Human Face, a Furnace seal'd
The Human Heart, its hungry Gorge.[2]

THE BOOK OF THEL[1]

PLATE i

THEL'S MOTTO

Does the Eagle know what is in the pit?
Or wilt thou go ask the Mole:
Can Wisdom be put in a silver rod?
Or Love in a golden bowl?[2]

PLATE 1

THEL

I

The daughters of Mne Seraphim[3] led round their sunny flocks,
All but the youngest. she in paleness sought the secret air.
To fade away like morning beauty from her mortal day:
Down by the river of Adona[4] her soft voice is heard:
And thus her gentle lamentation falls like morning dew. 5

[1] Blake substituted "The Human Abstract" for this poem. [2] Gullet.
[1] The name Thel comes from the Greek for "wish" or "will." The poem is an illuminated engraving and thus is divided into "plates"; see the Introduction to Blake.
[2] The silver rod and golden bowl are male and female sexual symbols and also recall a description in Ecclesiastes 12:5–6 of a time when "desire shall fail because man goeth to his long home . . . or ever the . . . golden bowl be broken."
[3] "Mne" is the root of the Greek word for "memory," which in Blake has sinister associations with living in the past; yoked here with "Seraphim," the order of angels associated with love, it suggests the division within Thel.
[4] Derived from Adonis, the personification in myth of fertility arising from death.

O life of this our spring! why fades the lotus of the water?
Why fade these children of the spring? born but to smile & fall.
Ah! Thel is like a watry bow, and like a parting cloud,
Like a reflection in a glass. like shadows in the water.
Like dreams of infants. like a smile upon an infants face, 10
Like the doves voice, like transient day, like music in the air;
Ah! gentle may I lay me down, and gentle rest my head.
And gentle sleep the sleep of death. and gentle hear the voice
Of him that walketh in the garden in the evening time.[5]

The Lilly of the valley breathing in the humble grass 15
Answer'd the lovely maid and said; I am a watry weed,
And I am very small, and love to dwell in lowly vales;
So weak, the gilded butterfly scarce perches on my head
Yet I am visited from heaven and he that smiles on all.
Walks in the valley. and each morn over me spreads his hand 20
Saying, rejoice thou humble grass, thou new-born lilly flower,
Thou gentle maid of silent valleys. and of modest brooks;
For thou shalt be clothed in light, and fed with morning manna:[6]
Till summers heat melts thee beside the fountains and the springs
To flourish in eternal vales: then why should Thel complain, 25

PLATE 2
Why should the mistress of the vales of Har,[7] utter a sigh.

She ceasd & smild in tears, then sat down in her silver shrine.

Thel answerd. O thou little virgin of the peaceful valley.
Giving to those that cannot crave, the voiceless, the o'ertired.
Thy breath doth nourish the innocent lamb, he smells thy milky
 garments, 5
He crops thy flowers. while thou sittest smiling in his face,
Wiping his mild and meekin[8] mouth from all contagious taints.
Thy wine doth purify the golden honey, thy perfume,
Which thou dost scatter on every little blade of grass that springs
Revives the milked cow, & tames the fire-breathing steed. 10
But Thel is like a faint cloud kindled at the rising sun:
I vanish from my pearly throne, and who shall find my place.

Queen of the vales the Lilly answerd, ask the tender cloud,
And it shall tell thee why it glitters in the morning sky,
And why it scatters its bright beauty thro' the humid air. 15
Descend O little cloud & hover before the eyes of Thel.

[5] God, declaring the sentence of death to Adam and Eve after their fall (Genesis 3:8–19).
[6] In Exodus 16:14–21, the miraculous but highly perishable food (the sun melted it) provided by God to the Israelites in the wilderness.
[7] In Blake's *Tiriel*, an Adam-figure who lives with his mate Heva ("Eve") in childish senility in an artificially preserved paradise.
[8] Meek.

The Cloud descended, and the Lilly bowd her modest head:
And went to mind her numerous charge[9] among the verdant grass.

PLATE 3
 II
O little Cloud the virgin said, I charge thee tell to me,
Why thou complainest not when in one hour thou fade away:
Then we shall seek thee but not find; ah Thel is like to Thee.
I pass away. yet I complain, and no one hears my voice.

The Cloud then shew'd his golden head & his bright form emerg'd, 5
Hovering and glittering on the air before the face of Thel.

O virgin know'st thou not. our steeds drink of the golden springs
Where Luvah[10] doth renew his horses: look'st thou on my youth,
And fearest thou because I vanish and am seen no more.
Nothing remains; O maid I tell thee, when I pass away, 10
It is to tenfold life, to love, to peace, and raptures holy:
Unseen descending, weigh my light wings upon balmy flowers;
And court the fair eyed dew. to take me to her shining tent;[11]
The weeping virgin, trembling kneels before the risen sun,
Till we arise link'd in a golden band, and never part; 15
But walk united, bearing food to all our tender flowers

Dost thou O little Cloud? I fear that I am not like thee;
For I walk through the vales of Har. and smell the sweetest flowers;
But I feed not the little flowers: I hear the warbling birds,
But I feed not the warbling birds. they fly and seek their food; 20
But Thel delights in these no more because I fade away,
And all shall say, without a use this shining woman liv'd,
Or did she only live. to be at death the food of worms.

The Cloud reclind upon his airy throne and answer'd thus.

Then if thou art the food of worms. O virgin of the skies, 25
How great thy use. how great thy blessing; every thing that lives,
Lives not alone, nor for itself: fear not and I will call
The weak worm from its lowly bed, and thou shalt hear its voice.
Come forth worm of the silent valley, to thy pensive queen.

The helpless worm arose, and sat upon the Lillys leaf, 30
And the bright Cloud saild on, to find his partner in the vale.

[9] Those in her custody.
[10] A pun on "love"; in Blake's later myth, the representative of passion.
[11] Biblical image for consummation of marriage.

PLATE 4

III

Then Thel astonish'd view'd the Worm upon its dewy bed.

Art thou a Worm? image of weakness. art thou but a Worm?
I see thee like an infant wrapped in the Lillys leaf:
Ah weep not little voice, thou can'st not speak. but thou can'st weep;
Is this a Worm? I see thee lay helpless & naked: weeping, 5
And none to answer, none to cherish thee with mothers smiles.
The Clod of Clay[12] heard the Worms voice, & raisd her pitying
 head;
She bow'd over the weeping infant, and her life exhal'd
In milky fondness, then on Thel she fix'd her humble eyes.

O beauty of the vales of Har. we live not for ourselves, 10
Thou seest me the meanest thing, and so I am indeed;
My bosom of itself is cold. and of itself is dark,

PLATE 5

But he that loves the lowly, pours his oil upon my head.
And kisses me, and binds his nuptial bands around my breast,
And says; Thou mother of my children, I have loved thee.
And I have given thee a crown that none can take away
But how this is sweet maid, I know not, and I cannot know, 5
I ponder, and I cannot ponder; yet I live and love.

The daughter of beauty wip'd her pitying tears with her white veil,
And said. Alas! I knew not this, and therefore did I weep:
That God would love a Worm I knew, and punish the evil foot
That wilful, bruis'd its helpless form: but that he cherish'd it 10
With milk and oil. I never knew; and therefore did I weep,
And I complaind in the mild air, because I fade away,
And lay me down in thy cold bed, and leave my shining lot.

Queen of the vales, the matron Clay answerd; I heard thy sighs.
And all thy moans flew o'er my roof. but I have call'd them down: 15
Wilt thou O Queen enter my house. 'tis given thee to enter,
And to return; fear nothing. enter with thy virgin feet.

PLATE 6

IV

The eternal gates terrific porter lifted the northern bar:[13]
Thel enter'd in & saw the secrets of the land unknown;

[12] Compare Blake's "The Clod and the Pebble," in *Songs of Experience*. Here the Clod is a
version of Mother Earth.

[13] In Homer's *Odyssey*, Book XIII, mortals enter the cave of the Naiads (sea nymphs) by the
northern gate, deities by the southern gate. This sixth plate, with its account of a subterranean
descent, was composed later than the rest of the poem.

She saw the couches of the dead, & where the fibrous roots
Of every heart on earth infixes deep its restless twists:
A land of sorrows & of tears where never smile was seen. 5

She wanderd in the land of clouds thro' valleys dark, listning
Dolours & lamentations: waiting oft beside a dewy grave
She stood in silence. listning to the voices of the ground,
Till to her own grave plot she came, & there she sat down.
And heard this voice of sorrow breathed from the hollow pit. 10

Why cannot the Ear be closed to its own destruction?
Or the glistning Eye to the poison of a smile!
Why are Eyelids stord with arrows ready drawn,
Where a thousand fighting men in ambush lie?
Or an Eye of gifts & graces, show'ring fruits & coined gold! 15
Why a Tongue impress'd with honey from every wind?
Why an Ear, a whirlpool fierce to draw creations in?
Why a Nostril wide inhaling terror trembling & affright
Why a tender curb upon the youthful burning boy!
Why a little curtain of flesh on the bed of our desire?[14] 20

The Virgin started from her seat, & with a shriek.
Fled back unhinderd till she came into the vales of Har

<div align="center">The End</div>

VISIONS OF THE DAUGHTERS OF ALBION

<div align="center">The Eye sees more than the Heart knows.</div>

This poem is an antithetical twin to *The Book of Thel.* There are many parallels and contrasts in structure and imagery (for example, the opening dialogues with flowers, one a retiring lily, the other a bold marigold). The most obvious parallel-contrast is in the situations and actions of the two heroines. Both begin in a state of virginity and longing, but Oothoon passes almost at the outset from a Thel-like hesitancy to decisive action. She loves Theotormon (whose name, from Greek, suggests that he is "tormented by God"). Her plucking of the marigold is symbolic of a conversion in her psyche, through which she accepts sexuality and growth. Then tragedy strikes: while winging her way to join Theotormon, she is raped by Bromion (a thunder-titan whose name suggests the Greek for "roarer"). After a period of shame, penitence, and attempted atonement, she suddenly has a breakthrough, in a way the poem does not explicitly describe, recognizing that shame in her situation is absurd and is born of false values that the two men still share (despite the superficial difference between the introvert Theotormon and the brute Bromion).

[14]The boy is probably Cupid, god of love; the curtain is the hymen, or "maidenhead." These two lines protest against the restraint of the sexual sense (touch); the preceding lines protest against the hyperactivity of the other four senses.

The poem is also sociology. "Albion" means England, and in that context his "Daughters" are Englishwomen, the potential recipients of a message of liberation sent from the New World of America, of which Oothoon is the "soft soul." In Blake's later myth Albion is also humanity; his daughters, then, would be all womankind, the audience for the message on a more universal level. Bromion is identified as a slave trader, so that America, the land of freedom darkened by slavery, suffers from a moral cancer. This concern with racial slavery blends with the more obvious feminist theme, derived in part from Blake's acquaintance with Mary Wollstonecraft, author of *A Vindication of the Rights of Woman* (1792), who probably provided one model for Oothoon. With all these themes Blake interweaves his ideas about the proper use of the senses (tyrannously hyperactive in Bromion, repressed in Theotormon) and about jealousy, the psychological analogue in Blake for all forms of tyranny. [*Editors' headnote.*]

PLATE iii[1]

THE ARGUMENT[2]
I loved Theotormon
And I was not ashamed
I trembled in my virgin fears
And I hid in Leutha's[3] vale!

I plucked Leutha's flower, 5
And I rose up from the vale;
But the terrible thunders[4] tore
My virgin mantle in twain.

PLATE I

Visions
Enslav'd, the Daughters of Albion weep: a trembling lamentation
Upon their mountains; in their valleys.[5] sighs toward America.

For the soft soul of America, Oothoon[6] wanderd in woe,
Along the vales of Leutha seeking flowers to comfort her;
And thus she spoke to the bright Marygold of Leutha's vale 5

Art thou a flower! art thou a nymph! I see thee now a flower;
Now a nymph! I dare not pluck thee from thy dewy bed?

The Golden nymph replied; pluck thou my flower Oothoon the
 mild
Another flower shall spring, because the soul of sweet delight
Can never pass away. she ceas'd & closd her golden shrine. 10

[1] For Blake's method of engraved illuminations, see the Introduction to Blake. Plates i and ii are a pictorial frontispiece and the title page.
[2] Subject matter.
[3] In Blake's larger myth, a female embodiment of sexual repression and guilt.
[4] Bromion. (See Headnote.)
[5] On Blake's punctuation, see note to "Introduction" to *Songs of Innocence.*
[6] Oothoon's name derives ironically from a character in Ossian (see Goethe's *Werther,* note to letter of 10 July 1771) who is suicidally gloomy over a sexual abduction.

Then Oothoon pluck'd the flower saying, I pluck thee from thy bed
Sweet flower. and put thee here to glow between my breasts
And thus I turn my face to where my whole soul seeks.

Over the waves she went in wing'd exulting swift delight;
And over Theotormons reign,[7] took her impetuous course. 15

Bromion rent her with his thunders. on his stormy bed
Lay the faint maid, and soon her woes appalld his thunders hoarse

Bromion spoke. behold this harlot here on Bromions bed,
And let the jealous dolphins sport around the lovely maid;
Thy soft American plains are mine, and mine thy north & south: 20
Stampt with my signet are the swarthy children of the sun:[8]
They are obedient, they resist not, they obey the scourge:
Their daughters worship terrors and obey the violent:

PLATE 2
Now thou maist marry Bromions harlot, and protect the child
Of Bromions rage, that Oothoon shall put forth in nine moons time

Then storms rent Theotormons limbs; he rolld his waves around.
And folded his black jealous waters round the adulterate pair
Bound back to back in Bromions caves terror & meekness dwell 5

At entrance Theotormon sits wearing the threshold hard
With secret tears; beneath him sound like waves on a desart shore
The voice of slaves beneath the sun, and children bought with
 money.[9]
That shiver in religious caves beneath the burning fires
Of lust, that belch incessant from the summits of the earth 10

Oothoon weeps not: she cannot weep! her tears are locked up;
But she can howl incessant writhing her soft snowy limbs.
And calling Theotormons Eagles to prey upon her flesh.

I call with holy voice! kings of the sounding air,
Rend away this defiled bosom that I may reflect. 15
The image of Theotormon on my pure transparent breast.

The Eagles at her call descend & rend their bleeding prey;
Theotormon severely smiles. her soul reflects the smile;
As the clear spring mudded with feet of beasts grows pure &
 smiles.

The Daughters of Albion hear her woes. & eccho back her sighs. 20

[7] Over the Atlantic ocean. [8] A reference to the branding of slaves.
[9] Exploited child labor blends with the other forms of oppression.

Why does my Theotormon sit weeping upon the threshold;[10]
And Oothoon hovers by his side, perswading him in vain:
I cry arise O Theotormon for the village dog
Barks at the breaking day. the nightingale has done lamenting.
The lark does rustle in the ripe corn, and the Eagle returns 25
From nightly prey, and lifts his golden beak to the pure east;
Shaking the dust from his immortal pinions[11] to awake
The sun that sleeps too long. Arise my Theotormon I am pure.
Because the night is gone that clos'd me in its deadly black.
They told me that the night & day were all that I could see; 30
They told me that I had five senses[12] to inclose me up.
And they inclos'd my infinite brain into a narrow circle.
And sunk my heart into the Abyss, a red round globe hot burning
Till all from life I was obliterated and erased.
Instead of morn arises a bright shadow, like an eye 35
In the eastern cloud: instead of night a sickly charnel house;[13]
That Theotormon hears me not! to him the night and morn
Are both alike: a night of sighs, a morning of fresh tears;

PLATE 3
And none but Bromion can hear my lamentations.

With what sense[14] is it that the chicken shuns the ravenous hawk?
With what sense does the tame pigeon measure out the expanse?
With what sense does the bee form cells? have not the mouse & frog
Eyes and ears and sense of touch? yet are their habitations. 5
And their pursuits, as different as their forms and as their joys:
Ask the wild ass why he refuses burdens: and the meek camel
Why he loves man: is it because of eye ear mouth or skin
Or breathing nostrils? No. for these the wolf and tyger have.
Ask the blind worm the secrets of the grave, and why her spires 10
Love to curl round the bones of death; and ask the rav'nous snake
Where she gets poison: & the wing'd eagle why he loves the sun
And then tell me the thoughts of man, that have been hid of old.

Silent I hover all the night, and all day could be silent.
If Theotormon once would turn his loved eyes upon me; 15
How can I be defild when I reflect thy image pure?
Sweetest the fruit that the worm feeds on. & the soul prey'd on
 by woe

[10] We get no explanation of the transition to the new Oothoon we hear from this point on.
[11] Wings.
[12] For Blake, the senses can be either avenues to spiritual freedom or a form of imprisonment; see the Introduction to Blake.
[13] Tomb.
[14] Oothoon's speech, like the following ones by Theotormon and Bromion, explores the relationship between inner mental or spiritual realities and their physical embodiments in sense experience. Implicit in the debate are the questions whether virginity is a condition of the soul or a matter of physical intactness and whether universal laws rather than the uniqueness of each individual should govern values and one's sense of reality.

The new wash'd lamb ting'd with the village smoke & the bright
 swan
By the red earth of our immortal river: I bathe my wings.
And I am white and pure to hover round Theotormons breast. 20

Then Theotormon broke his silence. and he answered.

Tell me what is the night or day to one o'erflowd with woe?
Tell me what is a thought? & of what substance is it made?
Tell me what is a joy? & in what gardens do joys grow?
And in what rivers swim the sorrows? and upon what mountains 25

PLATE 4
Wave shadows of discontent? and in what houses dwell the wretched
Drunken with woe forgotten. and shut up from cold despair.

Tell me where dwell the thoughts forgotten till thou call them forth
Tell me where dwell the joys of old! & where the ancient loves?
And when will they renew again & the night of oblivion past? 5
That I might traverse times & spaces far remote and bring
Comforts into a present sorrow and a night of pain
Where goest thou O thought? to what remote land is thy flight?
If thou returnest to the present moment of affliction
Wilt thou bring comforts on thy wings. and dews and honey and
 balm; 10
Or poison from the desart wilds, from the eyes of the envier.

Then Bromion said: and shook the cavern with his lamentation

Thou knowest that the ancient trees seen by thine eyes have fruit;
But knowest thou that trees and fruits flourish upon the earth
To gratify senses unknown? trees beasts and birds unknown: 15
Unknown, not unpercievd, spread in the infinite microscope,
In places yet unvisited by the voyager. and in worlds
Over another kind of seas, and in atmospheres unknown:
Ah! are there other wars, beside the wars of sword and fire!
And are there other sorrows, beside the sorrows of poverty! 20
And are there other joys, beside the joys of riches and ease?
And is there not one law for both the lion and the ox?
And is there not eternal fire, and eternal chains?
To bind the phantoms of existence from eternal life?

Then Oothoon waited silent all the day. and all the night, 25

PLATE 5
But when the morn arose, her lamentation renewd,
The Daughters of Albion hear her woes, & eccho back her sighs.

O Urizen![15] Creator of men! mistaken Demon of heaven:
Thy joys are tears! thy labour vain, to form men to thine image.
How can one joy absorb another? are not different joys 5
Holy, eternal, infinite! and each joy is a Love.

Does not the great mouth laugh at a gift? & the narrow eyelids
 mock
At the labour that is above payment, and wilt thou take the ape
For thy councellor? or the dog, for a schoolmaster to thy children?
Does he who contemns poverty,[16] and he who turns with abhorrence 10
From usury: feel the same passion or are they moved alike?
How can the giver of gifts experience the delights of the merchant?
How the industrious citizen the pains of the husbandman.[17]
How different far the fat fed hireling with hollow drum;
Who buys whole corn fields into wastes, and sings upon the heath:[18] 15
How different their eye and ear! how different the world to them!
With what sense does the parson claim the labour of the farmer?[19]
What are his nets & gins & traps. & how does he surround him
With cold floods of abstraction, and with forests of solitude,
To build him castles and high spires. where kings & priests may
 dwell. 20
Till she who burns with youth. and knows no fixed lot; is bound
In spells of law to one she loaths: and must she drag the chain
Of life, in weary lust! must chilling murderous thoughts. obscure
The clear heaven of her eternal spring? to bear the wintry rage
Of a harsh terror driv'n to madness, bound to hold a rod 25
Over her shrinking shoulders all the day; & all the night
To turn the wheel of false desire: and longings that wake her womb
To the abhorred birth of cherubs in the human form
That live a pestilence & die a meteor & are no more.
Till the child dwell with one he hates. and do the deed he loaths 30
And the impure scourge force his seed into its unripe birth
E'er yet his eyelids can behold the arrows of the day.[20]

Does the whale worship at thy footsteps as the hungry dog?
Or does he scent the mountain prey, because his nostrils wide
Draw in the ocean? does his eye discern the flying cloud 35
As the ravens eye? or does he measure the expanse like the vulture?
Does the still spider view the cliffs where eagles hide their young?

[15] The name ("your reason," with a further pun on "horizon," a circular limit) refers to a
figure in Blake's later myth who embodies reason (usually in its familiar "fallen" or corrupted
form), God seen as a remote but vindictive tyrant, political tyranny, and compulsively rigid
conscience.
[16] Feels contempt for the poor. [17] Farmer. (The "citizen" is the city-dweller.)
[18] The servant of the rich landowner and the military recruiter, who turn farmland into
hunting land and conscript farm workers.
[19] The parson forces the payment of tithes, taxes to support the church.
[20] As often in Blake, the transitions are breathless, here moving rapidly from marriage to
parenthood to children in a catalogue of the ills resulting from marriage understood as slavery
to law.

Or does the fly rejoice. because the harvest is brought in?
Does not the eagle scorn the earth & despise the treasures beneath?
But the mole[21] knoweth what is there, & the worm shall tell it thee. 40
Does not the worm erect a pillar in the mouldering church yard?

PLATE 6

And a palace of eternity in the jaws of the hungry grave
Over his porch these words are written. Take thy bliss O Man!
And sweet shall be thy taste & sweet thy infant joys renew!

Infancy, fearless, lustful, happy! nestling for delight
In laps of pleasure; Innocence! honest, open, seeking 5
The vigorous joys of morning light; open to virgin bliss,
Who taught thee modesty, subtil modesty! child of night & sleep
When thou awakest. wilt thou dissemble[22] all thy secret joys
Or wert thou not, awake when all this mystery was disclos'd!
Then com'st thou forth a modest virgin knowing to dissemble 10
With nets found under thy night pillow, to catch virgin joy,
And brand it with the name of whore; & sell it in the night,
In silence. ev'n without a whisper, and in seeming sleep:
Religious dreams and holy vespers,[23] light thy smoky fires:
Once were thy fires lighted by the eyes of honest morn 15
And does my Theotormon seek this hypocrite modesty!
This knowing, artful, secret, fearful, cautious, trembling hypocrite.
Then is Oothoon a whore indeed! and all the virgin joys
Of life are harlots: and Theotormon is a sick mans dream
And Oothoon is the crafty slave of selfish holiness. 20

But Oothoon is not so, a virgin fill'd with virgin fancies
Open to joy and to delight where ever beauty appears
If in the morning sun I find it: there my eyes are fix'd

PLATE 7

In happy copulation;[24] if in evening mild. wearied with work;
Sit on a bank and draw the pleasures of this free born joy.

 The moment of desire! the moment of desire! The virgin
That pines for man; shall awaken her womb to enormous joys
In the secret shadows of her chamber; the youth shut up from
The lustful joy. shall forget to generate. & create an amorous image 5
In the shadows of his curtains and in the folds of his silent pillow.
Are not these the places of religion? the rewards of continence?
The self enjoyings of self denial? Why dost thou seek religion?

[21] Compare the eagle and mole in "Thel's Motto" in *The Book of Thel*—one of hundreds of such interconnections between Blake's works.

[22] Conceal one's true nature. [23] Evening prayers.

[24] The act of seeing is described as a sexual union.

Is it because acts are not lovely, that thou seekest solitude, 10
Where the horrible darkness is impressed with reflections of desire.

Father of Jealousy.[25] be thou accursed from the earth!
Why hast thou taught my Theotormon this accursed thing?
Till beauty fades from off my shoulders darken'd and cast out,
A solitary shadow wailing on the margin of non-entity.[26] 15

I cry, Love! Love! Love! happy happy Love! free as the mountain
 wind!
Can that be Love, that drinks another as a sponge drinks water?
That clouds with jealousy his nights, with weepings all the day:
To spin a web of age around him. grey and hoary! dark!
Till his eyes sicken at the fruit that hangs before his sight. 20
Such is self-love that envies all! a creeping skeleton
With lamplike eyes watching around the frozen marriage bed.

But silken nets and traps of adamant[27] will Oothoon spread,
And catch for thee girls of mild silver, or of furious gold;
I'll lie beside thee on a bank & view their wanton play 25
In lovely copulation bliss on bliss with Theotormon:
Red as the rosy morning, lustful as the first born beam,
Oothoon shall view his dear delight, nor e'er with jealous cloud
Come in the heaven of generous love; nor selfish blightings bring.

Does the sun walk in glorious raiment. on the secret floor 30

PLATE 8
Where the cold miser spreads his gold? or does the bright cloud drop
On his stone threshold? does his eye behold the beam that brings
Expansion to the eye of pity? or will he bind himself
Beside the ox to thy hard furrow? does not that mild beam blot
The bat, the owl, the glowing tyger, and the king of night. 5
The sea fowl takes the wintry blast. for a cov'ring to her limbs:
And the wild snake, the pestilence to adorn him with gems & gold.
And trees. & birds. & beasts. & men. behold their eternal joy.
Arise you little glancing wings, and sing your infant joy!
Arise and drink your bliss, for every thing that lives is holy! 10

Thus every morning wails Oothoon. but Theotormon sits
Upon the margind ocean conversing with shadows dire.

The Daughters of Albion hear her woes, & eccho back her sighs.

The End

[25] Urizen. [26] A state described elsewhere in Blake as psychic disintegration.
[27] A very hard stone or other substance. The nets and traps are Oothoon's ironic reversal
of the nets used by hypocritical modesty in 6:10–11.

William Wordsworth

(1770–1850)

Like several other Romantic poets, William Wordsworth is a paradox. In much of his best poetry his aim was to celebrate the changeless things in nature and man. Yet his contemporaries sensed in his work a strangeness and bold originality that were bracing or unsettling depending on how willing they were to accept a new kind of poetry. In retrospect, we can see still more clearly how original he was, and if he no longer startles us that is partly because so many later poets—Matthew Arnold and Robert Frost, to name just two—have made his strategies familiar, especially his habit of philosophizing from natural emblems. Wordsworth embarked on his most creative period by trying to chasten and chastise eighteenth-century poetry, using a language of limpid, plate-glass purity freed from mannered artifice. Yet his own manner was so distinctive that he is among the most parodied of poets. His plainness of diction, along with the unpretentious, aggressively banal subjects he sometimes wrote on, earned him the dubious epithet "the simple Wordsworth." Yet much of his work was and still is difficult, groping as it does toward the expression of elusive states of the mind and soul. (In *Don Juan*, I.xc, a clowning Byron calls him "unintelligible," which would hardly be funny if no one else agreed.) In his lifetime, Wordsworth was rightly considered, along with Byron, one of the two pivotal figures of English Romanticism, and this despite the fact that his greatest, most characteristic, and in some respects most revolutionary work remained unpublished until after his death.

Wordsworth once defined the imagination, which he considered the highest faculty of the creative mind, as something which "produces impressive effects out of simple elements." We could apply this phrase to his life, which was outwardly rather uneventful except for a few years in his early twenties that we don't know much about. He was born in 1770 in Cockermouth, in northwest England, the scenic "Lake District" he was to make famous. His father was business agent to Sir James Lowther, a tightfisted man whose failure to repay a debt to his agent created money problems for the five Wordsworth children until his heir finally made amends in 1802. Wordsworth's mother, the daughter of a linen draper, died when the poet was eight, his father five years later. (As they also do with the nature-loving, motherless Rousseau, critics with a psychoanalytic bent make much of the maternal and nurse images the orphaned Wordsworth applies to nature; see, for example, "Ode: Intimations of Immortality," lines 77–84.) When he was nine Wordsworth was sent to a very good school at Hawkshead, about thirty miles from home, where for eight years he boarded during school terms with a townswoman. Hawkshead was the center of the intense boyhood experiences in nature he describes in the early books of *The Prelude*—a discipline in both "beauty" and "fear" to which he later ascribed the formation of his character. When he was seventeen he enrolled in St. John's College, Cambridge. The uncles who had become his guardians expected him to win a fellowship and become a clergyman, but that career

had no appeal for Wordsworth, and for several years his worldly prospects were to be perilous and indeterminate.

In his third year at Cambridge he took the walking tour to the Alps described in Book VI of *The Prelude*. After returning to Cambridge and taking an undistinguished degree in 1791, he spent some time in London; according to *The Prelude*, he found the metropolis a phantasmagoria, the antithesis of the stable grandeur and dignity of his native hills. In late 1791 he went to France again, this time for a year. The French Revolution was moving toward its critical phase, and Wordsworth learned to understand what it was about from a French officer named Michael Beaupuy. In France Wordsworth also fell in love with a surgeon's daughter named Annette Vallon, by whom he had an illegitimate child—a well-kept secret until the twentieth century. Forced by lack of money to come back to England, Wordsworth was prevented by the outbreak of war from seeing mother or child for ten years, and he never married Annette as they had once intended. (In 1802, during a brief peace just before his marriage to Mary Hutchinson, Wordsworth did revisit Annette and their daughter Caroline, to whose support he later contributed.) And another, mental crisis emerged from the war. As an Englishman, Wordsworth felt guilty about his French sympathies, which in themselves became a source of anguish when the Revolution turned more violently bloody and France turned from self-defense to military aggression. Taking psychological refuge in the uncompromising rationalism of the London radicals only made things worse, and he reached a state he called "despair." At this dark moment a modest but sufficient bequest from Raisley Calvert, whom Wordsworth had helped care for before his death in 1795, allowed Wordsworth and his adoring and loved sister Dorothy to establish a home in Dorsetshire, in southern England. She helped restore his mental health and remained with him through old age, her journals providing Wordsworth with material for his poems and us with valuable insights into his creative methods.

In 1797 they cemented a recent friendship with Samuel Taylor Coleridge and moved again in order to be near his home in Somerset, in the southwest. The friendship between the two men, like that between Goethe and Schiller at the same time, was one of the most fruitful relationships in literary history. In 1793 Wordsworth had published two long poems *(An Evening Walk* and *Descriptive Sketches)* more or less in the prevailing eighteenth-century style, and Coleridge's poetry too had been derivative. Now they conceived together both a new poetic style and a whole new rationale of what poetry should do. It was to be an agency not of mere diversion but of the profoundest truth, truth uniting the best insights of mind and heart in an imaginative union that would enlighten and help heal a spiritually ailing world. According to Coleridge's account some years later, their division of labor called for him to treat supernatural or exotic subjects with psychological realism and for Wordsworth to treat everyday subjects in such a way as to give them the novelty and excitement we normally expect only from the supernatural. The medium would be an honest language really spoken by men, cleansed of unfunctional conventionality. This program produced their epoch-making volume *Lyrical Ballads,* first published in 1798. Its rationale was expressed in the famous Preface of 1800 (revised

in 1802), written by Wordsworth and traditionally considered the manifesto of English Romanticism. Of the poems themselves, Coleridge contributed only four, but they included his masterpiece "The Rime of the Ancient Mariner." Wordsworth contributed nineteen, adding many more in the new editions that followed in the next few years. A few (including "Tintern Abbey") are not ballads at all but elevated blank-verse meditations. Wordsworth's ballads in the volume fell, roughly speaking, into two groups: 1) treatments of almost absurdly "unpoetic" subjects like that of "The Idiot Boy," expressed in aggressively commonplace language; and 2) certain quintessentially Wordsworthian poems about simple situations, written in a chaste basic English—neither lofty nor low. (The first four poems that follow in this anthology belong to this second set.) However simple-minded or disarming they may seem, all the poems have, in Wordsworth's portentous phrase, "a worthy *purpose*" (the emphasis is his). These "purposes" are easy to miss or mistake, but almost always they have to do with the way our minds work. For example, it may well be valid and in keeping with the Wordsworthian spirit to read "We Are Seven" as a poem illustrating the child's higher religious insight (though this presents problems, for the child apparently does not have any notion of an afterlife, while the adult does speak of heaven); what emerges from a closer reading is the pattern of differences between the mental mechanics of adult and child. Oddly, one of the things that obscure the "purposes" in many of Wordsworth's poems is the very simplicity of the language; one of the hardest things in reading his works is to concentrate on the behavior of words that seem not to be doing anything special at all. For example: "Come forth into the light of things" ("The Tables Turned," line 15), where *things* is emphatic, in contrast with the light of *books*. Or, from the same poem: "She [nature] has a world of ready wealth" (line 17), where "ready wealth" is a financial metaphor equivalent to "liquid assets"; in other words, nature gives us something we can use immediately, like money in our pockets, while books represent an investment tied up and transferable into profit only at some time in the future.

In 1799, after a winter in Germany, Wordsworth and his sister moved back permanently to the northern Lake District where they had been children. The friendship with Coleridge continued, interrupted by an estrangement in 1810–1812 that was later healed but not completely. Under Coleridge's influence, Wordsworth had early projected a monumental "philosophical poem" on no less a subject than man, nature, and society. Understandably, he found this a heavy task. More congenial was the poem on his own life which for a long time he considered as an appendage to the projected philosophical work. The poetic autobiography grew from a two-book version completed in the late 1790's to a five-book version in 1804 to the full-scale epic *Prelude* he completed in 1804–1805. This work tells the story of his life from infancy to the era of *Lyrical Ballads*. The philosophical poem, to be called *The Recluse*, remained unwritten except for an opening passage and the entire second part (of three parts planned), which appeared in 1814 as *The Excursion*. That poem was, and is, a disappointment, at least when compared with Wordsworth's earlier poetry. Wordsworth was uneasy about publishing so apparently self-centered a work as *The Prelude*, but it meant much to him and he carefully revised it several times over the

next decades. It was published after his death, his wife providing the now familiar title (Wordsworth had never given it one). As for the unrealized philosophical poem, there is probably no cause to grieve, since it is hard to believe that Wordsworth had much more to say than he said in *The Prelude*.

With the magnificent *Poems in Two Volumes* of 1807—which included the "Intimations" ode, some sonnets unsurpassed in English, and other fine lyrics— Wordsworth's "great decade" ended. Thereafter, although his discriminating critical sense helped him to clarify the form and (some believe) to improve the style of *The Prelude,* his new poems suddenly and mysteriously declined in quality. There have been innumerable guesses about why this happened, the most common ones having to do with his growing conservatism in politics and especially in religion. But that is only a guess, and it begs many questions about the relationship between creativity and belief. At any rate, the most salient fact about Wordsworth's last four decades is the growth in his reputation. At first the object of enthusiasm by a cult, he became better known when Coleridge wrote a brilliant assessment of his friend in the *Biographia Literaria* (1817), and by 1843 he was well enough known and accepted to be named Poet Laureate. He died in 1850. In that year Matthew Arnold wrote the poem "Memorial Verses," in which he mourns Goethe, Byron, and Wordsworth. The first two, long dead, had taught us "how to dare, / And against fear our breast to steel; / Others will strengthen us to bear." But, now that Wordsworth is dead, "who, ah! who, will make us feel?"

The typical movement of Wordsworth's major works is oscillation— between observation of the external scene and introspective analysis of feelings, between experiences and the ideas they generate, between the remembered past and present circumstances, between personal confession *(I)* and universal truths *(We)*. He himself called attention to this movement in connection with "Tintern Abbey," but it is discernible also in the "Intimations" ode and it governs the narrative ebb and flow in *The Prelude*. (If the poem were an automobile, we could say that it has a lot of play in the steering.) Sometimes the juxtapositions are sharply dramatic, as in the "Intimations" ode, but more often they are leisurely, producing the characteristic Wordsworthian hovering effect, by which ideas seem to grow unforcedly and organically from the scene or incident described.

We need to keep this back-and-forth movement in mind when we call Wordsworth a "nature poet." Though it is everywhere in his work, nature rarely appears simply for its own sake, and there are not many sharp-focused close-ups. Rather, nature is a mythic emblem—of a mysterious, perhaps divine "presence" (to use one of Wordsworth's typical soft-focus nouns), of a dynamic of steady order in the universe, and especially of the meaningful development and spiritual experience of individual persons. Moreover, nature can cut two ways. It is beauty, but it is also fear—the salutary fear that comes as a vivid aftermath to transgressions, the soul-ennobling fear inherent in the sublime, the chilling fear that, while nature remains the same, we human beings perish, bodily and emotionally. This last fear is at the heart of "Tintern Abbey" and the "Intimations" ode, which present almost the same problem of the loss of inner vitality but offer very different answers, one naturalistic and the other metaphysical. (Some readers, satisfied with the answers given, regard Wordsworth as a

poet of joy; others, more skeptical, find in him the deepest anxiety.) In these poems, as in many others, Wordsworth's subject is not ultimately nature but the psyche.

That does not mean that the psyche can ever be sufficient unto itself; it needs a "nurse" or "anchor" in the "mighty world / Of eye and ear" ("Tintern Abbey," lines 105–109). This last phrase is justly famous, since it leads us toward the center of Wordsworth's poetry. On the simplest level, it helps us focus on what he is saying; in the "Intimations" ode, for example, patterns of sight- and sound-imagery parallel the movements between hope and fear, reality and self-delusion. More important, by pointing at once to the world "out there" and the organic human instruments necessary for communication with that world, the phrase hints at an "ennobling interchange / Of action from without and from within"—still another form of oscillation—that ensures "spiritual dignity" (*Prelude,* XIII.373–376). If we need nature, it is equally true that nature needs us.

FURTHER READING (*prepared by B. W.*): Since Wordsworth's poetry is uneven, a selection is advisable for new readers; a good choice is the Riverside edition *Selected Poems and Prefaces,* ed. by Jack Stillinger, 1965, which is well annotated and includes the entire 1850 *Prelude.* The three main versions of *The Prelude*—1799, 1805, and 1850—with good notes and a selection of critical essays are accessible in a format that facilitates comparison in the Norton Critical Edition of *The Prelude,* ed. Jonathan Wordsworth, M. H. Abrams, and Stephen Gill, 1979. An excellent biography is Stephen Gill, *William Wordsworth: A Life,* 1989. An excellent general work on Wordsworth, usable as an introduction but intelligently meaty, is Carl Woodring's *Wordsworth,* 1965; Helen Darbishire's *The Poet Wordsworth,* 1949, and John Williams, *Wordsworth,* 1989, can also be recommended. Lionel Trilling has an exciting essay (first published in 1942) on the "Intimations" ode in *The Liberal Imagination,* 1950; Cleanth Brooks gives the poem a close reading in *The Well Wrought Urn,* 1947, especially good on imagery. Geoffrey H. Hartman, in *The Unmediated Vision,* 1954, has an excellent section on Wordsworth, especially on "Tintern Abbey" and the conflicts in it. This essay, along with Basil Willey's "On Wordsworth and the Locke Tradition" in *The Seventeenth-Century Background,* 1934, depicts a Wordsworth struggling to find value in a world vacated of older forms of supernatural certainty. The tensions between Wordsworth's faith in nature and his faith in human mind-imagination-spirit are explored in John Jones's *The Egotistical Sublime,* 1954; David Perkins's *The Quest for Permanence,* 1959; David Ferry's *The Limits of Mortality,* 1959; and Geoffrey H. Hartman's *Wordsworth's Poetry 1787–1814,* 1964. Robert Rehder's *Wordsworth and the Beginnings of Modern Poetry,* 1981, discusses the poet in the context of European literature, focusing particularly on the theme of consciousness. *Discussions of William Wordsworth,* ed. by Jack Davis, 1964, begins with classic evaluations of the poet by Coleridge and Matthew Arnold and moves to important modern critics. Both classic essays and new ones are included in *Critical Essays on William Wordsworth,* ed. George H. Gilpin, 1990.

ANECDOTE FOR FATHERS[1]

I have a boy of five years old;
His face is fair and fresh to see;
His limbs are cast in beauty's mould,
And dearly he loves me.

One morn we strolled on our dry walk,
Our quiet home all full in view,
And held such intermitted talk
As we are wont to do.

My thoughts on former pleasures ran;
I thought of Kilve's delightful shore, 10
Our pleasant home when spring began,
A long, long year before.

A day it was when I could bear
Some fond regrets to entertain;
With so much happiness to spare,
I could not feel a pain.

The green earth echoed to the feet
Of lambs that bounded through the glade,
From shade to sunshine, and as fleet
From sunshine back to shade. 20

Birds warbled round me—and each trace
Of inward sadness had its charm;
Kilve, thought I, was a favoured place,
And so is Liswyn farm.

My boy beside me tripped, so slim
And graceful in his rustic dress!
And, as we talked, I questioned him,
In very idleness.

"Now tell me, had you rather be,"
I said, and took him by the arm, 30
"On Kilve's smooth shore, by the green sea,
Or here at Liswyn farm?"

In careless mood he looked at me,
While still I held him by the arm,

[1] In the first edition of 1798, this poem had the subtitle "Showing How the Art of Lying May be Taught." In 1845 Wordsworth gave the poem a Latin epigraph which may be translated "Restrain your force or else you will make me tell lies."

And said, "At Kilve I'd rather be
Than here at Liswyn farm."

"Now, little Edward, say why so:
My little Edward, tell me why."—
"I cannot tell, I do not know."—
"Why, this is strange," said I; 40

"For here are woods, hills smooth and warm:
There surely must some reason be
Why you would change sweet Liswyn farm
For Kilve by the green sea."

At this my boy hung down his head,
He blushed with shame, nor made reply;
And three times to the child I said,
"Why, Edward, tell me why?"

His head he raised—there was in sight
It caught his eye, he saw it plain— 50
Upon the house-top, glittering bright,
A broad and gilded vane.

Then did the boy his tongue unlock,
And eased his mind with this reply:
"At Kilve there was no weather-cock;[2]
And that's the reason why."

O dearest, dearest boy! my heart
For better lore would seldom yearn,
Could I but teach the hundredth part
Of what from thee I learn. 60

WE ARE SEVEN

—A simple child,
That lightly draws its breath,
And feels its life in every limb,
What should it know of death?[1]

I met a little cottage girl:
She was eight years old, she said;

[2] Weather vane in the shape of a rooster. [1] Lines 1–4 were supplied by Coleridge.

Her hair was thick with many a curl
That clustered round her head.

She had a rustic, woodland air,
And she was wildly clad:
Her eyes were fair, and very fair;
—Her beauty made me glad.

"Sisters and brothers, little maid,
How many may you be?"
"How many? Seven in all," she said,
And wondering looked at me.

"And where are they? I pray you tell."
She answered, "Seven are we;
And two of us at Conway dwell,
And two are gone to sea.

"Two of us in the church-yard lie,
My sister and my brother;
And, in the church-yard cottage, I
Dwell near them with my mother."

"You say that two at Conway dwell,
And two are gone to sea,
Yet ye are seven! I pray you tell,
Sweet maid, how this may be."

Then did the little maid reply,
"Seven boys and girls are we;
Two of us in the church-yard lie,
Beneath the church-yard tree."

"You run about, my little maid,
Your limbs they are alive;
If two are in the church-yard laid,
Then ye are only five."

"Their graves are green, they may be seen,"
The little maid replied,
"Twelve steps or more from my mother's door,
And they are side by side.

"My stockings there I often knit,
My kerchief there I hem;
And there upon the ground I sit,
And sing a song to them.

"And often after sun-set, sir,
When it is light and fair,

10

20

30

40

I take my little porringer,[2]
And eat my supper there.

"The first that died was sister Jane;
In bed she moaning lay,
Till God released her of her pain; 50
And then she went away.

"So in the church-yard she was laid;
And, when the grass was dry,
Together round her grave we played,
My brother John and I.

"And when the ground was white with snow,
And I could run and slide,
My brother John was forced to go,
And he lies by her side." 60

"How many are you, then," said I,
"If they two are in heaven?"
Quick was the little maid's reply,
"O master! we are seven."

"But they are dead; those two are dead!
Their spirits are in heaven!"
'Twas throwing words away; for still
The little maid would have her will,
And said, "Nay, we are seven!"

EXPOSTULATION AND REPLY

"Why, William, on that old grey stone,
Thus for the length of half a day,
Why, William, sit you thus alone,
And dream your time away?

"Where are your books?—that light bequeathed
To beings else forlorn and blind!
Up! up! and drink the spirit breathed
From dead men to their kind.[1]

"You look round on your Mother Earth,
As if she for no purpose bore you; 10
As if you were her first-born birth,
And none had lived before you!"

[2] Bowl with a handle. [1] Their species, with a pun on "those like them."

One morning thus, by Esthwaite lake,
When life was sweet, I knew not why,
To me my good friend Matthew spake,
And thus I made reply:

"The eye—it cannot choose but see;
We cannot bid the ear be still;
Our bodies feel, where'er they be,
Against or with our will. 20

"Nor less I deem that there are powers
Which of themselves our minds impress;
That we can feed this mind of ours
In a wise passiveness.

"Think you, 'mid all this mighty sum
Of things for ever speaking,
That nothing of itself will come,
But we must still be seeking?

"—Then ask not wherefore, here, alone,
Conversing² as I may, 30
I sit upon this old grey stone,
And dream my time away."

THE TABLES TURNED

AN EVENING SCENE
ON THE SAME SUBJECT

Up! up! my friend, and quit your books;
Or surely you'll grow double:
Up! up! my friend, and clear your looks;
Why all this toil and trouble?

The sun, above the mountain's head,
A freshening lustre mellow
Through all the long green fields has spread,
His first sweet evening yellow.

Books! 'tis a dull and endless strife:
Come, hear the woodland linnet, 10
How sweet his music! on my life,
There's more of wisdom in it.

² Associating with others.

And hark! how blithe the throstle[1] sings!
He, too, is no mean preacher:
Come forth into the light of things,
Let nature be your teacher.

She has a world of ready wealth,
Our minds and hearts to bless—
Spontaneous wisdom breathed by health,
Truth breathed by cheerfulness. 20

One impulse from a vernal wood
May teach you more of man,
Of moral evil and of good,
Than all the sages can.

Sweet is the lore which nature brings;
Our meddling intellect
Mis-shapes the beauteous forms of things:—
We murder to dissect.

Enough of science and of art;
Close up those barren leaves; 30
Come forth, and bring with you a heart
That watches and receives.

LINES

COMPOSED A FEW MILES ABOVE TINTERN ABBEY ON REVISITING THE BANKS OF THE WYE[1] DURING A TOUR, JULY 13, 1798

Five years have past; five summers, with[2] the length
Of five long winters! and again I hear
These waters, rolling from their mountain-springs
With a soft inland murmur.—Once again
Do I behold these steep and lofty cliffs,
That on a wild secluded scene impress
Thoughts of more deep seclusion; and connect
The landscape with the quiet of the sky.
The day is come when I again repose
Here, under this dark sycamore, and view 10
These plots of cottage-ground, these orchard-tufts,
Which at this season, with their unripe fruits,

[1] Thrush.
[1] A river in Wales and western England flowing into the Severn. Tintern Abbey is an old ruined monastery.
[2] And also.

Are clad in one green hue, and lose themselves
'Mid groves and copses. Once again I see
These hedge-rows, hardly hedge-rows, little lines
Of sportive wood run wild: these pastoral farms,
Green to the very door; and wreaths of smoke
Sent up, in silence, from among the trees!
With some uncertain notice, as might seem
Of vagrant dwellers in the houseless woods, 20
Or of some hermit's cave, where by his fire
The hermit sits alone.

 These beauteous forms,
Through a long absence, have not been to me
As is a landscape to a blind man's eye:
But oft, in lonely rooms, and 'mid the din
Of towns and cities, I have owed to them
In hours of weariness, sensations sweet,
Felt in the blood, and felt along the heart;
And passing even into my purer mind,
With tranquil restoration:—feelings too 30
Of unremembered pleasure: such, perhaps,
As have no slight or trivial influence
On that best portion of a good man's life,
His little, nameless, unremembered, acts
Of kindness and of love. Nor less, I trust,
To them I may have owed another gift,
Of aspect more sublime; that blessed mood,
In which the burthen[3] of the mystery,
In which the heavy and the weary weight
Of all this unintelligible world, 40
Is lightened:—that serene and blessed mood,
In which the affections gently lead us on,—
Until, the breath of this corporeal frame
And even the motion of our human blood
Almost suspended, we are laid asleep
In body, and become a living soul:
While with an eye made quiet by the power
Of harmony, and the deep power of joy,
We see into the life of things.
 If this
Be but a vain belief, yet, oh! how oft— 50
In darkness and amid the many shapes
Of joyless daylight; when the fretful stir
Unprofitable, and the fever of the world,
Having hung upon the beatings of my heart—
How oft, in spirit, have I turned to thee,
O sylvan Wye! thou wanderer thro' the woods,
How often has my spirit turned to thee!

[3] Burden.

And now, with gleams of half-extinguished thought,
With many recognitions dim and faint,
And somewhat of a sad perplexity, 60
The picture of the mind revives again:
While here I stand, not only with the sense
Of present pleasure, but with pleasing thoughts
That in this moment there is life and food
For future years. And so I dare to hope,
Though changed, no doubt, from what I was when first
I came among these hills; when like a roe
I bounded o'er the mountains, by the sides
Of the deep rivers, and the lonely streams,
Wherever nature led: more like a man 70
Flying from something that he dreads, than one
Who sought the thing he loved. For nature then
(The coarser pleasures of my boyish days,
And their glad animal movements all gone by)
To me was all in all.—I cannot paint
What then I was. The sounding cataract
Haunted me like a passion: the tall rock,
The mountain, and the deep and gloomy wood,
Their colours and their forms, were then to me
An appetite; a feeling and a love, 80
That had no need of a remoter charm,
By thought supplied, nor any interest
Unborrowed from the eye.—That time is past,
And all its aching joys are now no more,
And all its dizzy raptures. Not for this
Faint[4] I, nor mourn nor murmur;[5] other gifts
Have followed; for such loss, I would believe,
Abundant recompense. For I have learned
To look on nature, not as in the hour
Of thoughtless youth; but hearing oftentimes 90
The still, sad music of humanity,
Nor harsh nor grating, though of ample power
To chasten and subdue. And I have felt
A presence that disturbs me with the joy
Of elevated thoughts; a sense sublime
Of something far more deeply interfused,
Whose dwelling is the light of setting suns,
And the round ocean and the living air,
And the blue sky, and in the mind of man:
A motion and a spirit, that impels 100
All thinking things, all objects of all thought,
And rolls through all things. Therefore am I still
A lover of the meadows and the woods,
And mountains; and of all that we behold
From this green earth; of all the mighty world

[4] Grow weak in spirit. [5] Complain.

Of eye, and ear,—both what they half create,
And what perceive; well pleased to recognise
In nature and the language of the sense
The anchor of my purest thoughts, the nurse,
The guide, the guardian of my heart, and soul 110
Of all my moral being.
 Nor perchance,
If I were not thus taught, should I the more
Suffer my genial[6] spirits to decay:
For thou art with me here upon the banks
Of this fair river; thou my dearest friend,
My dear, dear friend; and in thy voice I catch
The language of my former heart,[7] and read
My former pleasures in the shooting lights
Of thy wild eyes. Oh! yet a little while
May I behold in thee what I was once, 120
My dear, dear sister! and this prayer I make,
Knowing that nature never did betray
The heart that loved her; 'tis her privilege,
Through all the years of this our life, to lead
From joy to joy: for she can so inform[8]
The mind that is within us, so impress
With quietness and beauty, and so feed
With lofty thoughts, that neither evil tongues,
Rash judgments, nor the sneers of selfish men,
Nor greetings where no kindness is, nor all 130
The dreary intercourse of daily life,
Shall e'er prevail against us, or disturb
Our cheerful faith, that all which we behold
Is full of blessings. Therefore let the moon
Shine on thee in thy solitary walk;
And let the misty mountain-winds be free
To blow against thee: and, in after years,
When these wild ecstasies shall be matured
Into a sober pleasure; when thy mind
Shall be a mansion for all lovely forms, 140
Thy memory be as a dwelling-place
For all sweet sounds and harmonies; oh! then,
If solitude, or fear, or pain, or grief,
Should be thy portion, with what healing thoughts
Of tender joy wilt thou remember me,
And these my exhortations! Nor, perchance—
If I should be where I no more can hear

[6] A key word in Romantic poetry, *genial* can mean "innate," "sociable," "creative," "life-giving," or "pertaining to genius"; the meanings often overlap in any specific usage and have to be determined by the context. Compare Coleridge's "Dejection: An Ode," line 39.

[7] Wordsworth's sister Dorothy, to whom he was very close, was only a year and a half younger than he, but in this poem he suggests that she is in the stage he went through five years earlier.

[8] Mold.

Thy voice, nor catch from thy wild eyes these gleams
Of past existence—wilt thou then forget
That on the banks of this delightful stream 150
We stood together; and that I, so long
A worshipper of nature, hither came
Unwearied in that service: rather say
With warmer love—oh! with far deeper zeal
Of holier love. Nor wilt thou then forget
That after many wanderings, many years
Of absence, these steep woods and lofty cliffs,
And this green pastoral landscape, were to me
More dear, both for themselves and for thy sake!

A SLUMBER DID MY SPIRIT SEAL

A slumber did my spirit seal;
 I had no human fears:
She seemed a thing that could not feel
 The touch of earthly years.

No motion has she now, no force;
 She neither hears nor sees;
Rolled round in earth's diurnal course,
 With rocks, and stones, and trees.

COMPOSED UPON WESTMINSTER BRIDGE,[1]
SEPTEMBER 3, 1802

Earth has not any thing to show more fair:
Dull would he be of soul who could pass by
A sight so touching in its majesty:
This City now doth, like a garment, wear
The beauty of the morning; silent, bare,
Ships, towers, domes, theatres, and temples lie
Open unto the fields, and to the sky;
All bright and glittering in the smokeless air.
Never did sun more beautifully steep
In his first splendour, valley, rock, or hill; 10
Ne'er saw I, never felt, a calm so deep!
The river glideth at his own sweet will:
Dear God! the very houses seem asleep;
And all that mighty heart is lying still!

[1] A bridge over the river Thames, in London.

IT IS A BEAUTEOUS EVENING, CALM AND FREE

It is a beauteous evening, calm and free,
The holy time is quiet as a Nun
Breathless with adoration; the broad sun
Is sinking down in its tranquillity;
The gentleness of heaven broods o'er the Sea:
Listen! the mighty Being is awake,
And doth with his eternal motion make
A sound like thunder—everlastingly.
Dear Child! dear Girl![1] that walkest with me here,
If thou appear untouched by solemn thought, 10
Thy nature is not therefore less divine:
Thou liest in Abraham's bosom[2] all the year;
And worshipp'st at the Temple's inner shrine,
God being with thee when we know it not.

LONDON, 1802

Milton! thou should'st be living at this hour:[1]
England hath need of thee: she is a fen
Of stagnant waters: altar, sword, and pen,
Fireside, the heroic wealth of hall and bower,
Have forfeited their ancient English dower
Of inward happiness. We are selfish men;
Oh! raise us up, return to us again;
And give us manners, virtue, freedom, power.
Thy soul was like a Star, and dwelt apart:
Thou hadst a voice whose sound was like the sea: 10
Pure as the naked heavens, majestic, free,
So didst thou travel on life's common way,
In cheerful godliness; and yet thy heart
The lowliest duties on herself did lay.

THE WORLD IS TOO MUCH WITH US

The world is too much with us; late and soon,
Getting and spending, we lay waste our powers:
Little we see in Nature that is ours;
We have given our hearts away, a sordid boon!

[1] The girl is probably Caroline, Wordsworth's ten-year-old illegitimate French daughter. Wordsworth visited her in 1802, during a lull in the war with France. The setting here is the French coast of the English Channel.
[2] In heaven. The phrase is from Luke 16:22.
[1] Besides having enormous influence as the epic poet of England, John Milton (1608–74) was a symbol to many Englishmen of incorruptible integrity and public service.

This Sea that bares her bosom to the moon;
The winds that will be howling at all hours,
And are up-gathered now like sleeping flowers;
For this, for every thing, we are out of tune;
It moves us not.—Great God! I'd rather be
A Pagan suckled in a creed outworn; 10
So might I, standing on this pleasant lea,
Have glimpses that would make me less forlorn;
Have sight of Proteus rising from the sea;
Or hear old Triton[1] blow his wreathèd horn.

I WANDERED LONELY AS A CLOUD

I wandered lonely as a cloud
That floats on high o'er vales and hills,
When all at once I saw a crowd,
A host, of golden daffodils;
Beside the lake, beneath the trees,
Fluttering and dancing in the breeze.

Continuous as the stars that shine
And twinkle on the milky way,
They stretched in never-ending line
Along the margin of a bay: 10
Ten thousand saw I at a glance,
Tossing their heads in sprightly dance.

The waves beside them danced; but they
Out-did the sparkling waves in glee:
A poet could not but be gay,
In such a jocund company:
I gazed—and gazed—but little thought
What wealth the show to me had brought:

For oft, when on my couch I lie
In vacant or in pensive mood, 20
They flash upon that inward eye
Which is the bliss of solitude;
And then my heart with pleasure fills,
And dances with the daffodils.

[1] In ancient mythology, Proteus and Triton were sea-gods. Triton was commonly represented as blowing a conch-shell trumpet.

THE SOLITARY REAPER

Behold her, single in the field,
Yon solitary Highland[1] Lass!
Reaping and singing by herself;
Stop here, or gently pass!
Alone she cuts and binds the grain,
And sings a melancholy strain;
O listen! for the Vale profound
Is overflowing with the sound.

No Nightingale did ever chaunt
More welcome notes to weary bands 10
Of travellers in some shady haunt,
Among Arabian sands:
A voice so thrilling ne'er was heard
In spring-time from the Cuckoo-bird,
Breaking the silence of the seas
Among the farthest Hebrides.[2]

Will no one tell me what she sings?—
Perhaps the plaintive numbers flow
For old, unhappy, far-off things,
And battles long ago: 20
Or is it some more humble lay,[3]
Familiar matter of to-day?
Some natural sorrow, loss, or pain,
That has been, and may be again?

Whate'er the theme, the Maiden sang
As if her song could have no ending;
I saw her singing at her work,
And o'er the sickle bending;—
I listened, motionless and still;
And, as I mounted up the hill, 30
The music in my heart I bore,
Long after it was heard no more.

MY HEART LEAPS UP
WHEN I BEHOLD

My heart leaps up when I behold
A rainbow in the sky:

[1] The Highlands of northern Scotland. The girl is singing in Erse, the Gaelic language.
[2] Islands off the west coast of Scotland. [3] Song; poem.

So was it when my life began;
So is it now I am a man;
So be it when I shall grow old,
 Or let me die!
The child is father of the man;
And I could wish my days to be
Bound each to each by natural piety.

ODE

INTIMATIONS OF IMMORTALITY
FROM RECOLLECTIONS OF EARLY CHILDHOOD

The child is father of the man;
And I could wish my days to be
Bound each to each by natural piety.[1]

I

There was a time when meadow, grove, and stream,
The earth, and every common sight,
 To me did seem
 Apparelled in celestial light,
The glory[2] and the freshness of a dream.
It is not now as it hath been of yore;—
 Turn wheresoe'er I may,
 By night or day,
The things which I have seen I now can see no more.

II

 The Rainbow comes and goes,
 And lovely is the rose, 10
 The moon doth with delight
Look round her when the heavens are bare,
 Waters on a starry night
 Are beautiful and fair;
The sunshine is a glorious birth;
 But yet I know, where'er I go,
That there hath past away a glory from the earth.

III

Now, while the birds thus sing a joyous song,
 And while the young lambs bound 20

[1] These three lines are from "My Heart Leaps Up When I Behold." The theme of human continuity in that poem makes it an appropriate epigraph for the ode.
[2] Here and later in the poem, the concrete meaning of the word is "halo" or "nimbus of light," as also in "glorious " and "glories."

As to the tabor's[3] sound,
To me alone there came a thought of grief:
A timely utterance gave that thought relief,
 And I again am strong:
The cataracts blow their trumpets from the steep;
No more shall grief of mine the season wrong;
I hear the echoes through the mountains throng,
The winds come to me from the fields of sleep,[4]
 And all the earth is gay;
 Land and sea 30
 Give themselves up to jollity,
 And with the heart of May
 Doth every beast keep holiday;—
 Thou child of joy,
Shout round me, let me hear thy shouts, thou happy
 shepherd-boy!

 IV

Ye blessèd creatures, I have heard the call
 Ye to each other make; I see
The heavens laugh with you in your jubilee;
 My heart is at your festival,
 My head hath its coronal, 40
The fulness of your bliss, I feel—I feel it all.
 Oh evil day! if I were sullen
 While earth herself is adorning,
 This sweet May-morning,
 And the children are culling
 On every side,
 In a thousand valleys far and wide,
 Fresh flowers; while the sun shines warm,
And the babe leaps up on his mother's arm:—
 I hear, I hear, with joy I hear! 50
 —But there's a tree, of many, one,[5]
A single field which I have looked upon,
Both of them speak of something that is gone:
 The pansy at my feet
 Doth the same tale repeat:
Whither is fled the visionary gleam?
Where is it now, the glory and the dream?

 V

Our birth is but a sleep and a forgetting:
The soul that rises with us, our life's star,

[3] Small drum. Strophes III and IV combine realism with the conventional imagery of
classical pastoral—e.g., the "coronal" (wreath of flowers) of line 40.

[4] *fields of sleep.* An obscure phrase; the meaning may be that the winds of morning seem to
be blowing out of the night (fields of sleep) that has just ended.

[5] *of many, one.* An individual tree singled out from many around it because it is associated
with something that happened in the past. What the memory is we are not told.

Hath had elsewhere its setting, 60
 And cometh from afar:
Not in entire forgetfulness,
 And not in utter nakedness,
But trailing clouds of glory do we come
 From God, who is our home:
Heaven lies about us in our infancy!
Shades of the prison-house begin to close
 Upon the growing boy,
But he beholds the light, and whence it flows,
 He sees it in his joy; 70
The youth, who daily farther from the east
 Must travel, still is nature's priest,
 And by the vision splendid
 Is on his way attended;
At length the man perceives it die away,
And fade into the light of common day.

VI

Earth fills her lap with pleasures of her own;
Yearnings she hath in her own natural kind,[6]
And, even with something of a mother's mind,
 And no unworthy aim, 80
 The homely nurse doth all she can
To make her foster-child, her inmate man,
 Forget the glories he hath known,
And that imperial palace whence he came.

VII

Behold the child among his new-born blisses,
A six years' darling of a pigmy size!
See, where 'mid work of his own hand he lies,
Fretted by sallies[7] of his mother's kisses,
With light upon him from his father's eyes!
See, at his feet, some little plan or chart, 90
Some fragment from his dream of human life,
Shaped by himself with newly-learned art;
 A wedding or a festival,
 A mourning or a funeral;
 And this hath now his heart,
 And unto this he frames his song:
 Then will he fit his tongue
To dialogues of business, love, or strife;
 But it will not be long
 Ere this be thrown aside, 100
 And with new joy and pride
The little actor cons[8] another part;

[6]Mode; way. [7]Attacked by (almost military) raids. [8]Memorizes.

Filling from time to time his "humorous stage"[9]
With all the persons, down to palsied age,
That life brings with her in her equipage;[10]
 As if his whole vocation
 Were endless imitation.

VIII

Thou, whose exterior semblance doth belie
 Thy soul's immensity;
Thou best philosopher, who yet dost keep 110
Thy heritage, thou eye among the blind,
That, deaf and silent, read'st the eternal deep,[11]
Haunted for ever by the eternal mind,—
 Mighty prophet! Seer blest!
 On whom those truths do rest,
Which we are toiling all our lives to find,
In darkness lost, the darkness of the grave;
Thou, over whom thy immortality
Broods like the day, a master o'er a slave,
A presence which is not to be put by;[12] 120
Thou little child, yet glorious in the might
Of heaven-born freedom on thy being's height,
Why with such earnest pains dost thou provoke
The years to bring the inevitable yoke,
Thus blindly with thy blessedness at strife?
Full soon thy soul shall have her earthly freight,
And custom lie upon thee with a weight,
Heavy as frost, and deep almost as life!

IX

 O joy! that in our embers
 Is something that doth live, 130
 That nature yet remembers
 What was so fugitive!
The thought of our past years in me doth breed
Perpetual benediction: not indeed
For that which is most[13] worthy to be blest;
Delight and liberty, the simple creed
Of childhood, whether busy or at rest,
With new-fledged hope still fluttering in his breast:—
 Not for these I raise
 The song of thanks and praise; 140
 But for those obstinate questionings
 Of sense and outward things,
 Fallings from us, vanishings;

[9] Quoted from the dedicatory sonnet of Samuel Daniel's *Musophilus* (1599). There is probably also an allusion to Jaques' speech describing the "seven ages" of human life ("All the world's a stage . . ."), in Shakespeare's *As You Like It,* II.vii.139–166.
[10] Ceremonial procession. [11] Ocean. [12] Got rid of. [13] Very.

Blank misgivings of a creature
Moving about in worlds not realised,[14]
High instincts before which our mortal nature
Did tremble like a guilty thing surprised:[15]
But for those first affections,
Those shadowy recollections,
Which, be they what they may,[16] 150
Are yet the fountain-light of all our day,
Are yet a master-light of all our seeing;
Uphold us, cherish, and have power to make
Our noisy years seem moments in the being
Of the eternal silence: truths that wake,
To perish never:
Which neither listlessness, nor mad endeavour,
Nor man nor boy,
Nor all that is at enmity with joy,
Can utterly abolish or destroy. 160
Hence in a season of calm weather
Though inland far we be,
Our souls have sight of that immortal sea
Which brought us hither,
Can in a moment travel thither,
And see the children sport upon the shore,
And hear the mighty waters rolling evermore.

 x
Then sing, ye birds, sing, sing a joyous song!
And let the young lambs bound
As to the tabor's sound!
We in thought will join your throng, 170
Ye that pipe and ye that play,
Ye that through your hearts to-day
Feel the gladness of the May!
What though the radiance which was once so bright
Be now for ever taken from my sight,
Though nothing can bring back the hour
Of splendour in the grass, of glory in the flower;
We will grieve not, rather find
Strength in what remains behind; 180
In the primal sympathy
Which having been must ever be;
In the soothing thoughts that spring
Out of human suffering;

[14] Made real.
[15] Like a supernatural spirit taken by surprise. (The words "guilty thing" are a quotation from Shakespeare's *Hamlet*, I.i.148, where they refer to the ghost of Hamlet's father.)
[16] *lines 141–150*. This groping passage, according to statements Wordsworth made later in life, is based on his memory from childhood of feeling an immunity to death and an "abyss of idealism" in which physical objects seemed merely the emanations of his inner self.

In the faith that looks through death,
In years that bring the philosophic mind.

XI

And O, ye fountains, meadows, hills, and groves,
Forebode not any severing of our loves!
Yet in my heart of hearts I feel your might;
I only have relinquished one delight 190
To live beneath your more habitual sway.
I love the brooks which down their channels fret,
Even more than when I tripped lightly as they;
The innocent brightness of a new-born day
 Is lovely yet;
The clouds that gather round the setting sun
Do take a sober colouring from an eye
That hath kept watch o'er man's mortality;
Another race hath been, and other palms[17] are won.
Thanks to the human heart by which we live, 200
Thanks to its tenderness, its joys, and fears,
To me the meanest flower that blows[18] can give
Thoughts that do often lie too deep for tears.

Samuel Taylor Coleridge
(1772–1834)

"Dejection: An Ode" is inserted here for comparison with Wordsworth's
"Ode: Intimations of Immortality," which it sometimes echoes. In 1802
Coleridge heard recited the opening four strophes of his friend
Wordsworth's poem (all that Wordsworth had then written), and in reply
Coleridge wrote "Dejection." The unhappiness the poem expresses arose
from Coleridge's ill health, his unhappy marriage to Sara Fricker, and his
hopeless love for Sara Hutchinson, sister of the Mary Hutchinson whom
Wordsworth married later in 1802. The first version of "Dejection," ad-
dressed to "Sara" (Hutchinson), ran 340 lines; in later versions Coleridge
changed the addressee to "William," then to "Edmund," and finally to
"Lady." He published an early version in a newspaper on Wordsworth's
wedding day, which was also Coleridge's wedding anniversary. The version
printed here is the final one, published in 1817.
 "Kubla Khan" illustrates the exotic side of Coleridge's poetic imagina-
tion. He claimed that the poem was written under the influence of opium,
that afterward he wrote down part of what he had composed, and that the

[17] Emblems of victories. [18] *meanest . . . blows.* Most lowly flower that blooms.

rest was permanently driven from his memory by the arrival of a visitor.
(The accuracy of his account has been challenged, however.)

 Besides being a poet, Coleridge was the foremost English literary critic
and theorist of his time. For more about his relationship with Wordsworth,
see the Introduction to Wordsworth. Walter Jackson Bate, in *Coleridge*,
1968, provides a very good account of his life, works, and ideas.

DEJECTION: AN ODE

Late, late yestreen I saw the new moon,
With the old moon in her arms;[1]
And I fear, I fear, my master dear!
We shall have a deadly storm.

—*Ballad of* SIR PATRICK SPENCE

I

Well! If the bard was weather-wise, who made
 The grand old ballad of Sir Patrick Spence,
 This night, so tranquil now, will not go hence
Unroused by winds, that ply a busier trade
Than those which mould yon cloud in lazy flakes,
Or the dull sobbing draft, that moans and rakes
Upon the strings of this Aeolian lute,[2]
 Which better far were mute.
 For lo! the new-moon winter-bright!
 And overspread with phantom light, 10
 (With swimming phantom light o'erspread
 But rimmed and circled by a silver thread)
I see the old moon in her lap, foretelling
 The coming-on of rain and squally blast.
And oh! that even now the gust were swelling,
 And the slant night-shower driving loud and fast!
Those sounds which oft have raised me, whilst they awed,
 And sent my soul abroad,
Might now perhaps their wonted[3] impulse give,
Might startle this dull pain, and make it move and live! 20

 [1] *new moon . . . arms.* Coleridge gives a visual description of this phenomenon in lines 9–13
below. Astronomers call it the "ashen light"—a grayish light covering the whole disc of the
very new moon and caused by sunlight reflected off the earth. (When it is new moon on Earth,
it is "full Earth" on the moon.) Almost wholly back-lighted, the moon has a fine bright line
around the entire disc. The phenomenon is especially noticeable in April, the setting for
"Dejection." According to the old ballad Coleridge quotes, the ashen light is a sign of a coming
storm.
 [2] An Aeolian lute is an instrument that produces music when the wind blows over it. Sev-
eral of the Romantics used it as a symbol of inspiration.
 [3] Usual.

II

A grief without a pang, void, dark, and drear,
 A stifled, drowsy, unimpassioned grief,
 Which finds no natural outlet, no relief,
 In word, or sigh, or tear—
O lady! in this wan and heartless mood,
To other thoughts by yonder throstle[4] woo'd,
 All this long eve, so balmy and serene,
Have I been gazing on the western sky,
 And its peculiar tint of yellow green:
And still I gaze—and with how blank an eye! 30
And those thin clouds above, in flakes and bars,
That give away their motion to the stars;
Those stars, that glide behind them or between,
Now sparkling, now bedimmed, but always seen:
Yon crescent moon, as fixed as if it grew
In its own cloudless, starless lake of blue;
I see them all so excellently fair,
I see, not feel, how beautiful they are!

III

 My genial[5] spirits fail;
 And what can these[6] avail 40
To lift the smothering weight from off my breast?
 It were a vain endeavour,
 Though I should gaze for ever
On that green light that lingers in the west:
I may not hope from outward forms to win
The passion and the life, whose fountains are within.

IV

O lady! we receive but what we give,
And in our life alone does nature live:
Ours is her wedding garment, ours her shroud!
 And would we aught behold, of higher worth, 50
Than that inanimate cold world allowed
To the poor loveless ever-anxious crowd,
 Ah! from the soul itself must issue forth
A light, a glory, a fair luminous cloud
 Enveloping the Earth—
And from the soul itself must there be sent
 A sweet and potent voice, of its own birth,
Of all sweet sounds the life and element!

[4] Thrush.
[5] A key word for the Romantics; see note to Wordsworth's "Lines Composed a Few Miles Above Tintern Abbey," line 113.
[6] The natural objects described above.

V

O pure of heart! thou need'st not ask of me
What this strong music in the soul may be! 60
What, and wherein it doth exist,
This light, this glory, this fair luminous mist,
This beautiful and beauty-making power.
 Joy, virtuous lady! Joy that ne'er was given,
Save to the pure, and in their purest hour,
Life, and life's effluence,[7] cloud at once and shower,
Joy, lady! is the spirit and the power,
Which wedding nature to us gives in dower
 A new Earth and new Heaven,[8]
Undreamt of by the sensual and the proud— 70
Joy is the sweet voice, joy the luminous cloud—
 We in ourselves rejoice!
And thence flows all that charms or ear or[9] sight,
 All melodies the echoes of that voice,
All colours a suffusion[10] from that light.

VI

There was a time when, though my path was rough,
 This joy within me dallied with distress,
And all misfortunes were but as the stuff[11]
 Whence fancy made me dreams of happiness:
For hope grew round me, like the twining vine, 80
And fruits, and foliage, not my own, seemed mine.
But now afflictions bow me down to earth:
Nor care I that they rob me of my mirth;
 But oh! each visitation
Suspends what nature gave me at my birth,
 My shaping spirit of imagination.
For not to think of what I needs must feel,
 But to be still and patient, all I can;
And haply[12] by abstruse research to steal
 From my own nature all the natural man— 90
 This was my sole resource, my only plan:
Till that which suits a part infects the whole,
And now is almost grown the habit of my soul.

VII

Hence, viper thoughts, that coil around my mind,
 Reality's dark dream!
I turn from you, and listen to the wind,

[7] Something that flows out.
[8] Joy achieves a wedding between the bride nature and us, giving as the bride's dowry a new earth and new heaven. (The reader should mentally supply commas after "Which" and "us" in line 68.)
[9] *or ear or.* Either ear or. [10] Something that spreads. [11] Material. [12] Perhaps.

Which long has raved unnoticed. What a scream
Of agony by torture lengthened out
That lute sent forth! Thou wind, that rav'st without,[13]
 Bare crag, or mountain-tairn,[14] or blasted tree, 100
Or pine-grove whither woodman never clomb,
Or lonely house, long held the witches' home,
 Methinks were fitter instruments for thee,
Mad lutanist! who in this month of showers,
Of dark-brown gardens, and of peeping flowers,
Mak'st devils' yule, with worse than wintry song,
The blossoms, buds, and timorous leaves among.
 Thou actor, perfect in all tragic sounds!
Thou mighty poet, e'en to frenzy bold!
 What tell'st thou now about? 110
 'Tis of the rushing of an host in rout,
With groans, of trampled men, with smarting wounds—
At once they groan with pain, and shudder with the cold!
But hush! there is a pause of deepest silence!
 And all that noise, as of a rushing crowd,
With groans, and tremulous shudderings—all is over—
 It tells another tale, with sounds less deep and loud!
 A tale of less affright,
 And tempered with delight,
As Otway's[15] self had framed the tender lay,— 120
 'Tis of a little child
 Upon a lonesome wild,
Not far from home, but she hath lost her way:
And now moans low in bitter grief and fear,
And now screams loud, and hopes to make her mother hear.

VIII

'Tis midnight, but small thoughts have I of sleep:
Full seldom may my friend such vigils keep!
Visit her, gentle sleep! with wings of healing,
 And may this storm be but a mountain-birth,
May all the stars hang bright above her dwelling, 130
 Silent as though they watched the sleeping Earth!
 With light heart may she rise,
 Gay fancy, cheerful eyes,
Joy lift her spirit, joy attune her voice;
To her may all things live, from pole to pole,
Their life the eddying of her living soul!
 O simple spirit, guided from above,
Dear lady! friend devoutest of my choice,
 Thus mayest thou ever, evermore rejoice.

[13]Outdoors. [14]Small lake.
[15]Thomas Otway (1652–1685), dramatist known for pathetic effects. Coleridge's original
version read "William's."

KUBLA KHAN

OR, A VISION IN A DREAM

A FRAGMENT

In Xanadu did Kubla Khan
A stately pleasure-dome decree:
Where Alph, the sacred river, ran
Through caverns measureless to man
 Down to a sunless sea.
So twice five miles of fertile ground
With walls and towers were girdled round:
And there were gardens bright with sinuous rills,
Where blossomed many an incense-bearing tree;
And here were forests ancient as the hills, 10
Enfolding sunny spots of greenery.

But oh! that deep romantic chasm which slanted
Down the green hill athwart a cedarn cover!
A savage place! as holy and enchanted
As e'er beneath a waning moon was haunted
By woman wailing for her demon-lover!
And from this chasm, with ceaseless turmoil seething,
As if this earth in fast thick pants were breathing,
A mighty fountain momently was forced:
Amid whose swift half-intermitted burst 20
Huge fragments vaulted like rebounding hail,
Or chaffy grain beneath the thresher's flail:
And 'mid these dancing rocks at once and ever
It flung up momently the sacred river.
Five miles meandering with a mazy motion
Through wood and dale the sacred river ran,
Then reached the caverns measureless to man,
And sank in tumult to a lifeless ocean:
And 'mid this tumult Kubla heard from far
Ancestral voices prophesying war! 30
 The shadow of the dome of pleasure
 Floated midway on the waves;
 Where was heard the mingled measure
 From the fountain and the caves.
It was a miracle of rare device,
A sunny pleasure-dome with caves of ice!

 A damsel with a dulcimer
 In a vision once I saw:
 It was an Abyssinian maid,
 And on her dulcimer she played, 40
 Singing of Mount Abora.

Could I revive within me
Her symphony and song,
To such a deep delight 'twould win me,
That with music loud and long,
I would build that dome in air,
That sunny dome! those caves of ice!
And all who heard should see them there,
And all should cry, Beware! Beware!
His flashing eyes, his floating hair! 50
Weave a circle round him thrice,
And close your eyes with holy dread,
For he on honey-dew hath fed,
And drunk the milk of Paradise.

Jane Austen
(1775–1817)

If Greatest English Novelist were an electoral office, Jane Austen might not win the election, though she would get a healthy share of the votes. Election analysts, in any case, would be hard-pressed to say on what platform, or even on what ticket, she had run. Chronologically, she lived and wrote at the very center of the English Romantic period, yet there has been an almost official conspiracy by literary historians to regard her as a non-Romantic, even an anti-Romantic. Her novels, sometimes regarded as fare for connoisseurs or as sermons on moderation, have also, for generations, been read avidly by ingenuous teenagers and immoderately celebrated by an adoring cult of "Janeites." To some people she is a model of decorousness, yet she is one of the great comic writers and can be wickedly funny in a number of veins. Although the human heart has seldom been revealed more sensitively than in her novels, and although she was a major force in making love stories the staple subject of that genre, her narrating voice is noted for its frequently cool, ironic detachment toward life and her characters. (This voice, incidentally, may or may not be Austen's own.) The novelist Charlotte Brontë said of Austen that "The Passions are perfectly unknown to her; even to the Feelings she vouchsafes no more than an occasional graceful but distant recognition," yet it can be cogently argued that such human emotions are the very bread and butter of Austen's works.

Her life has been described as geographically limited, having been confined to the south of England. To call this a limitation is about as true—and as untrue—as to make such a statement today about a woman who had spent her whole life in the region between Massachusetts and Virginia. (Europe was off limits, a war zone, from the time Austen was fourteen until two years before she died.) Her life has also been described, only half accurately, as uneventful. In some ways, that judgment is a slightly disguised way of saying that her life was a happy one—which seems to have been largely the case, though we cannot be quite sure. Austen lived from her birth to her death in the friendly bosom of her family, studiously avoid-

ing, for example, the society of other authors. (Her novels were published anonymously.) Her surviving relatives, who destroyed many of her letters, may have painted over some dark patches in her experience and some complexities in her character.

Austen was born in 1775, the seventh child (and second daughter) of eight children born to the Reverend George Austen, rector of Steventon in the southern English county of Hampshire, and his wife, née Cassandra Leigh. Both sides of the family had interesting histories. George had risen from poverty to make a noteworthy academic career at Oxford. Cassandra too had ties to Oxford, including an uncle who was Master of Balliol College; she also had titled connections and could trace her family line to the Norman Conquest in the eleventh century. Both George and Cassandra were good-looking, cultivated in an unpretentious way, literary, and kindly. The atmosphere of their household was genteel but also down-to-earth—literally so, in fact, since George doubled as a farmer. Relationships among their children were cordial and gregarious; characteristically, they were fond of putting on plays at home. Several of the children, besides Jane, were to have noteworthy futures: one brother inherited a considerable estate from a family connection and was knighted in Jane's lifetime; another (Jane's favorite brother, Henry, who managed her affairs as an author) was in turn a soldier, a banker, and a clergyman; two others distinguished themselves in the Royal Navy and, after Jane's death, rose to be high-ranking Admirals. Jane's interest in the navy is reflected in two of her novels, *Mansfield Park* and *Persuasion*.

Her only sister, Cassandra, who was two years older, was Jane's lifelong companion, confidante, and (when they were apart) correspondent. As young children the two girls attended schools at Oxford, Southampton (where Jane came close to dying of a fever), and Reading, but after Jane reached the age of ten the sisters were educated, expertly, at home. In subsequent years, Jane acquired her share of the conventional "female accomplishments," including playing the piano, respectable skill in foreign languages, and dancing (which she loved). Above all, she read hungrily from an early age, especially in the great and the popular eighteenth-century writers. (*Northanger Abbey* contains a spirited passage in defense of reading novels.) It is not coincidental that Samuel Richardson, the groundbreaking psychological novelist who had written *Pamela* and *Clarissa* and during his life had gathered around him an admiring circle of women and aspiring women writers, was among Austen's favorite authors.

She began writing even more precociously; her juvenile efforts (most of them comic and satiric), which were warmly encouraged by the rest of the family, date from when she was twelve. Her early works are more than commonly interesting and significant, since the line between them and her mature works is somewhat blurred. Her first published novels, *Sense and Sensibility* in 1811 and *Pride and Prejudice* in 1813, along with *Northanger Abbey*, published shortly after she died, were the culmination, after several revisions, of works she had begun and, in a sense, completed in the 1790s.

Austen confessed to having been shy as a young girl, but she must have outgrown that stage; she attended and apparently enjoyed thoroughly her share of parties and balls, up into her thirties. Though she was never to marry, and her nephews and nieces, as she acquired them, came to dote on

her, there was nothing "spinsterish" about her; her personality was warm, and she was good-looking in figure and face. The evidence is fairly strong, though not very concrete, that she fell in love at least once, in her mid-twenties, with a man who died shortly thereafter—not to mention a rather bizarre incident, a little later, in which she accepted a proposal of marriage one day and retracted her acceptance the next morning.

Although Austen lived at the center of a close-knit family, she was anything but a stay-at-home; it is quite wrong to think of her as a kind of English Emily Dickinson. She visited extensively among friends and relatives in various counties of southern England. Nor was her life free of trauma and grief. The French husband of her cousin (and future sister-in-law) Elizabeth was guillotined in 1794 by the French Revolutionists for alleged disloyal activities; the impeachment trial in Parliament of the eminent and controversial colonial governor Warren Hastings (a family connection) ran for seven years before it concluded with his acquittal in 1795; in 1797 Austen shared her sister Cassandra's grief over the death in the West Indies of Cassandra's fiancé; in the following year, a cousin was killed in a horse-traffic accident; a few years after that, Austen and her sister contemplated going to assist their uncle and aunt, the latter having been imprisoned for seven months on a capital charge of shoplifting (a frame-up, which resulted in acquittal); Austen's dearest friend died in 1804. These incidents, added to the perils her brothers in the Navy were undergoing in the wars with France, belie the notion that Austen led a totally sheltered and tranquil life. The point is worth emphasizing because critics so often marvel at what they consider the unruffled, ahistorical texture of her novels (as though all novelists were obligated to chronicle their eras as Tolstoy did in *War and Peace*). *Persuasion,* which does include some references to events in the great world, shows that Austen was not averse on principle to mentioning them.

Austen left Steventon and accompanied her parents when her father retired in 1801 and moved to the resort city of Bath (a place she was not overly fond of), which she described extensively in her two posthumous novels *Northanger Abbey* and *Persuasion.* The move represented a step downward for the family, and Austen saw her piano sold, along with many of her books. During part of 1804 the family stayed at Lyme Regis, on the English Channel, the setting of Louisa Musgrove's accident in *Persuasion*—a town, as the novel implies, that Austen liked very much. After her father died in 1805, an unsettled period of four years ensued, after which the sisters and their mother moved back to Chawton, near the old home town of Steventon. This was Austen's residence during the six years of life that remained for her, though she continued to travel frequently, on family matters and on those connected with her publishing. By 1817, however, it had become apparent that she was suffering from what is now called Addison's disease, a failure of the adrenal glands. After two months in Winchester, where she moved with Cassandra to be near her doctor, she died in July. She is buried in the great cathedral there.

These last six years at Chawton, when Austen settled down to serious writing again after four nomadic years, witnessed one of the great miracles of literary history: the composition of most of her six mature works and the publication of all of them. Though often occupied with family responsibili-

ties, she managed to produce some of the most moving, witty, beautifully crafted novels in the English language. They brought her no fame, since they were published anonymously, but they were fairly well received by the public, and the last ones were brought out by John Murray, one of the most eminent London publishers. Walter Scott, in reviewing her, praised her highly. Some of her novels were translated into French.

Austen's novels defy description; certainly no plot summary could even begin to suggest their richness, interest, and polished workmanship. The variety they represent is often underestimated; no two of them are alike, despite the rough similarity of their genteel settings. *Northanger Abbey*, begun early but published posthumously (1818), and *Sense and Sensibility* (1811) are the two most deeply rooted in the eighteenth-century manner and themes usually associated with Austen. The former begins as an affectionate satire on the young heroine's love for the gothic melodramas popular at the turn of the century and earlier, but the novel transcends this topical satire to tell a moving love story that, in its way, is just as exotic as any of the gothic romances that have addled the young heroine's brain. *Sense and Sensibility* also reads at first as a topical satire, on the romantic cult of intense feeling and its esthetic clichés. Elinor, the older of the two heroines, represents "sense" and self-control, while her younger sister Marianne represents self-indulgent "sensibility." The novel seems to come down, though ambiguously, on the side of Elinor's less extravagant values, but in the meantime we get, in Marianne, a case history in the pathology of unhappy love that, in its way, is as frightening and powerful as anything the Brontë sisters were to portray. In the presence of Marianne's agony, moralizing about sense and sensibility seems almost an impertinence. *Pride and Prejudice* (1813) is another "theme" novel, as its title suggests, but this book moves away from timely topicality and instead concentrates on the love-duel between two proud and prejudiced persons: the saturnine Fitzwilliam Darcy and the ebullient Elizabeth Bennet, a character in the tradition of Shakespeare's great comic heroines.

The three novels just named were revisions of earlier ones. In *Mansfield Park* (1814), the first of three entirely new ones, Austen deliberately forsook the brightness and sparkle of *Pride and Prejudice* to present the poor, devout, even mousy Fanny Price, who is taken from the squalor of her parents' home in Portsmouth to be reared at the country estate of her rich uncle. This relatively somber novel, with its air of unworldly religiosity, has puzzled many of Austen's admirers and sometimes even embarrassed them. Its power and fascination, for some readers, lie in the combination of two story-threads, one showing the vindication of Fanny's moral and religious principles, the other showing—in a way that is essentially unconnected with morality or religion—her growth into health, beauty, self-assurance, and happiness. In her next novel, *Emma* (1816), Austen reverted to something like her earlier comic manner and also achieved a *tour de force*, creating in Emma Woodhouse one of her most irresistible heroines despite the fact that Emma is a thorough snob and busybody who wreaks havoc in the love-lives of her acquaintances. In her last completed book, *Persuasion* (published 1818), Austen achieved a remarkable blend of autumnal melancholy and of hopeful, springtime freshness—"purification and perfume," to borrow a phrase from the novel (Chapter 21). If one agrees with the

common judgment that it is the most romantic of Austen's novels, one is tempted to see in it her retraction of the (alleged) anti-Romanticism of *Sense and Sensibility;* Anne Elliott of *Persuasion,* talked into renouncing her early love, "had been forced into prudence in her youth, she learned romance as she grew older—the natural sequel of an unnatural beginning" (Chapter 4). When she died, Austen left behind her a partially written novel called *Sanditon* that, intriguingly, shows her as embarking on a new and earthier kind of comic satire. This new direction seems less surprising, however, when one remembers that in each of her completed books the author struck out in directions she had not explored earlier.

New readers of Jane Austen are invited to consider two generalizations about her that are widespread but challengeable. One of these maintains that her world is entirely and exclusively a woman's world. In a sense, that is obviously true; the day-to-day, chapter-to-chapter doings of her novels are relentlessly feminine, and all her point-of-view characters are women. For some readers, the most striking evidence of Austen's feminine slant is the often-noted fact that she never composed an episode (other than off-stage events rendered indirectly, in the third person) in which at least one woman is not present. But this fact need mean no more than that she refused to attempt dialogue of a kind that, by definition, she could never have heard. To draw the broader inference, as certain readers do, that Austen was interested only in women's doings and feelings, and only in feminine psychology (whatever that may be), is quite another matter. Our access to the minds of her male characters is usually more indirect than with her women, but a good case can be made that Austen understood her male characters very sensitively. We get glimpses—sometimes much more than that—of complex crises of personal growth in Willoughby of *Sense and Sensibility,* Darcy of *Pride and Prejudice,* Captain Wentworth of *Persuasion,* and some of her other fictional men.

The other common but dubious generalization maintains that Austen speaks for the necessity of limitations: reasonable people settle sensibly for a kind of fulfillment strictly bounded by unextravagant levelheadedness, decorum, moderation—in short, a conditioned life. But the opposite might well be argued: that in most, perhaps all, of her novels the central characters attain a kind of fulfillment that levelheaded probability has given them no right to expect. Austen's heroines (not to mention her heroes), the argument might run, are in fact obstinate idealists who seek nothing short of radical freedom, a kind of amplitude of being that their limited horizons would seem to rule out as impossible. It is a curious fact that near the end of almost all her novels—*Persuasion* included—the narrator or one of the main characters jokes breezily about the "bad morality" of the conclusion and makes it clear that the protagonists are receiving, not what they deserve, but rather (it is implied) a kind of grace that makes a joyful mockery of merit and probability.

This, of course, is what everyone feels who is happily in love—that some kind of miracle has occurred. The fairy-tale, or Cinderella, motif often discerned in Austen's novels is therefore, simply, a proof that she knew what a love story—any love story—is all about. The kind of triviality, domesticity, and prosaicness through which she leads her protagonists—the style of living, for example, of Anne Elliott in the first half of *Persuasion,*

from which escape seems now a permanently closed door—is in effect an emblem of the flat, conditioned world before it is transformed by the spiritual liberation of happy love. The long months, after Wentworth's reappearance, during which Anne can do nothing but passively wait and observe—this added to the eight preceding hopeless years—are an especially protracted example of the kind of agonizing, helpless ordeal of waiting that the leading characters in all of Austen's books have to undergo in one way or another. To understand these ordeals of passivity as a reflection of the female condition in a man's world is not beside the point; in her tender and unreproaching way, Anne addresses this very point in her crucial conversation with Captain Harville near the end of *Persuasion*. But the ordeal of waiting is not limited in Austen's novels to the women; several of her male protagonists, Wentworth included, have to undergo a near equivalent of it. The waiting is, rather, another emblem, like the empty triviality of Sir Walter's and Elizabeth's drawing-rooms, of the desperate emptiness of the conditioned life, from which love, not mere effort or good sense, effects the only complete deliverance.

The title of *Persuasion* invites us to consider it as, like some of Austen's earlier books, a theme-novel. To read it as such provides a fruitful entry into its world, values, and workmanship. In addition to the one major act of persuasion the novel is concerned with, the dissuasion of the younger Anne Elliott from marrying Wentworth, the novel provides countless examples, major and minor, of persuasion, including self-persuasion. (Consider, to take just one minor example, the incident at Lyme in which Henrietta Musgrove tries to enlist Anne's moral support in her self-serving rationalizations about Dr. Shirley's retirement—Chapter 12.) The danger in the theme-novel approach, however, is that it invites us to define Austen simply as a moralist arguing a position, in this case the relative desirability of docility and decisiveness. Even in *Sense and Sensibility*, where Austen had apparently set out to moralize in this way, the judgmental scaffolding falls away, so that the themes announced in the title are not so much abstract values as keys to personality. This is even more true in *Persuasion*, where the motif announced in the title is less a debate topic than a reminder of the anxieties inherent in free human choice and in the timing of the pursuit of happiness.

FURTHER READING *(prepared by B. W.):* The authoritative six-volume illustrated Oxford edition *The Novels of Jane Austen*, ed. R. W. Chapman, 1933–69 (including dates of revised editions), contains useful notes on all of Austen's novels and many valuable appendices—on her vocabulary, the topography of Bath, etc. (*Persuasion* is in Volume 5, with revisions and additions by Mary Lascelles.) Chapman also edited what remains of Austen's interesting correspondence in *Jane Austen's Letters*, rev. ed. 1959. Although other biographies have since appeared, the most generally satisfactory one is probably still Elizabeth Jenkins' *Jane Austen: A Biography*, rev. ed. 1956, which also contains valuable discussions of the novels. A more compact biography, enlivened by good illustrations, is Marghanita Laski's *Jane Austen and Her World*, 1969. B. C. Southam's lucid and stimulating pamphlet *Jane Austen*, 1975, in the series Writers & Their Work, constitutes an excellent general introduction to Austen's work; longer and more ambitious, though still of manageable size, are Christopher Gillie's *A Preface to Jane Austen*, rev. ed., 1985; and F. B. Pinion's *A Jane Austen Companion*, 1973. Mary Lascelles, *Jane Austen and Her Art*, 1939, is an outstanding

general critical study; also very good are W. A. Craik, *Jane Austen: The Six Novels,* 1965; A. Walton Litz, *Jane Austen: A Study of Her Artistic Development,* 1965; Darrel Mansell, *The Novels of Jane Austen: An Interpretation,* 1973; Barbara Hardy, *A Reading of Jane Austen,* 1976 (organized topically, not by separate novels); Susan Morgan, *In the Meantime: Character and Perception in Jane Austen's Fiction,* 1980; David Monaghan, *Jane Austen: Structure and Social Vision,* 1980; and P. J. M. Scott, *Jane Austen: A Reassessment,* 1982. On Austen's language and style, see Norman Page, *The Language of Jane Austen,* 1972; and Kenneth C. Phillipps, *Jane Austen's English,* 1970. Notable collections of essays on Austen include Ian Watt, ed., *Jane Austen: A Collection of Critical Essays,* 1963; B. C. Southam, ed., *Critical Essays on Jane Austen,* 1968; J. O'Neill, ed., *Critics on Jane Austen,* 1970; and (largely true to its title) Janet Todd, ed., *Jane Austen: New Perspectives,* 1983. Almost all the books mentioned above are valuable on *Persuasion.* Recent perspectives on feminist issues in Austen are provided in Claudia Johnson, *Jane Austen: Women, Politics, and the Novel,* 1988; and Margaret Kirkham, *Jane Austen, Feminism and Fiction,* 1983. John Dussinger's *In the Pride of the Moment: Encounters in Jane Austen's World,* 1990, is a fresh and perceptive book. See also Tony Tanner's *Jane Austen,* 1986; and Michael J. Williams' *Jane Austen: Six Novels and Their Methods,* 1985.

PERSUASION

CHAPTER 1

Sir Walter Elliot, of Kellynch-hall, in Somersetshire, was a man who, for his own amusement, never took up any book but the Baronetage;[1] there he found occupation for an idle hour, and consolation in a distressed one; there his faculties were roused into admiration and respect, by contemplating the limited remnant of the earliest patents;[2] there any unwelcome sensations, arising from domestic affairs, changed naturally into pity and contempt, as he turned over the almost endless creations[3] of the last century— and there, if every other leaf were powerless, he could read his own history with an interest which never failed—this was the page at which the favourite volume always opened:

ELLIOT OF KELLYNCH-HALL

Walter Elliot, born March 1, 1760, married, July 15, 1784, Elizabeth, daughter of James Stevenson, Esq. of South Park, in the county of Gloucester;[4] by which lady (who died 1800) he has issue Elizabeth, born June 1, 1785; Anne, born August 9, 1787; a still-born son, Nov. 5, 1789; Mary, born Nov. 20, 1791.

Precisely such had the paragraph originally stood from the printer's hands; but Sir Walter had improved it by adding, for the information of

[1] *Somersetshire:* the county of Somerset, in southwestern England. *the Baronetage:* J. Debrett's *Baronetage of England,* a periodically updated who's-who of the lower-ranking titled British families.

[2] Patents (grants) of titles by the sovereign. [3] Newly appointed baronets.

[4] In south-central England.

himself and his family, these words, after the date of Mary's birth—
"married, Dec. 16, 1810, Charles, son and heir of Charles Musgrove, Esq.
of Uppercross, in the county of Somerset,"—and by inserting most accu-
rately the day of the month on which he had lost his wife.

Then followed the history and rise of the ancient and respectable fam-
ily, in the usual terms: how it had been first settled in Cheshire; how men-
tioned in Dugdale[5]—serving the office of High Sheriff, representing a
borough in three successive parliaments, exertions of loyalty, and dignity
of baronet, in the first year of Charles II.,[6] with all the Marys and Eliza-
beths they had married; forming altogether two handsome duodecimo
pages,[7] and concluding with the arms and motto: "Principal seat, Kellynch-
hall, in the county of Somerset," and Sir Walter's hand-writing again in this
finale:

"Heir presumptive,[8] William Walter Elliot, Esq., great grandson of the
second Sir Walter."

Vanity was the beginning and the end of Sir Walter Elliot's character:
vanity of person[9] and of situation. He had been remarkably handsome in
his youth; and, at fifty-four, was still a very fine man. Few women could
think more of their personal appearance than he did; nor could the valet of
any new made lord be more delighted with the place he held in society. He
considered the blessing of beauty as inferior only to the blessing of a
baronetcy; and the Sir Walter Elliot, who united these gifts, was the con-
stant object of his warmest respect and devotion.

His good looks and his rank had one fair claim on his attachment; since
to them he must have owed a wife of very superior character to any thing
deserved by his own. Lady Elliot had been an excellent woman, sensible
and amiable; whose judgment and conduct, if they might be pardoned the
youthful infatuation which made her Lady Elliot, had never required in-
dulgence afterwards.—She had humoured, or softened, or concealed his
failings, and promoted his real respectability for seventeen years; and
though not the very happiest being in the world herself, had found enough
in her duties, her friends, and her children, to attach her to life, and make
it no matter of indifference to her when she was called on to quit them.
—Three girls, the two eldest sixteen and fourteen, was an awful legacy for
a mother to bequeath; an awful charge rather, to confide to the authority
and guidance of a conceited, silly father. She had, however, one very inti-
mate friend, a sensible, deserving woman, who had been brought, by
strong attachment to herself, to settle close by her, in the village of Kel-
lynch; and on her kindness and advice, Lady Elliot mainly relied for the
best help and maintenance of the good principles and instruction which
she had been anxiously giving her daughters.

This friend, and Sir Walter, did *not* marry, whatever might have been
anticipated on that head by their acquaintance.—Thirteen years had

[5] *Cheshire:* a county in northwest England. *Dugdale:* the author of a book (1682) on the
coats-of-arms of old families.

[6] King Charles II, son of the deposed and beheaded (1649) Charles I, restored the mon-
archy in England (1660) after the Puritan revolution of the mid-seventeenth century.

[7] Duodecimo was a small page-size, about five by eight inches.

[8] The expected successor to the title, by the male line. [9] Physical appearance.

passed away since Lady Elliot's death, and they were still near neighbours and intimate friends; and one remained a widower, the other a widow.

That Lady Russell, of steady age and character, and extremely well provided for, should have no thought of a second marriage, needs no apology to the public, which is rather apt to be unreasonably discontented when a woman *does* marry again, than when she does *not*; but Sir Walter's continuing in singleness requires explanation.—Be it known then, that Sir Walter, like a good father, (having met with one or two private disappointments in very unreasonable applications) prided himself on remaining single for his dear daughter's sake. For one daughter, his eldest, he would really have given up any thing, which he had not been very tempted to do. Elizabeth had succeeded, at sixteen, to all that was possible, of her mother's rights and consequence;[10] and being very handsome, and very like himself, her influence had always been great, and they had gone on together most happily. His two other children were of very inferior value. Mary had acquired a little artificial importance, by becoming Mrs. Charles Musgrove; but Anne, with an elegance of mind and sweetness of character, which must have placed her high with any people of real understanding, was nobody with either father or sister: her word had no weight; her convenience was always to give way;—she was only Anne.

To Lady Russell, indeed, she was a most dear and highly valued god-daughter, favourite and friend. Lady Russell loved them all; but it was only in Anne that she could fancy the mother to revive again.

A few years before, Anne Elliot had been a very pretty girl, but her bloom had vanished early; and as even in its height, her father had found little to admire in her, (so totally different were her delicate features and mild dark eyes from his own); there could be nothing in them now that she was faded and thin, to excite his esteem. He had never indulged much hope, he had now none, of ever reading her name in any other page of his favourite work. All equality of alliance must rest with Elizabeth; for Mary had merely connected herself with an old country family of respectability and large fortune, and had therefore *given* all the honour, and received none: Elizabeth would, one day or other, marry suitably.

It sometimes happens, that a woman is handsomer at twenty-nine than she was ten years before; and, generally speaking, if there has been neither ill health nor anxiety, it is a time of life at which scarcely any charm is lost. It was so with Elizabeth; still the same handsome Miss Elliot that she had begun to be thirteen years ago; and Sir Walter might be excused, therefore, in forgetting her age, or, at least, be deemed only half a fool, for thinking himself and Elizabeth as blooming as ever, amidst the wreck of the good looks of every body else; for he could plainly see how old all the rest of his family and acquaintance were growing. Anne haggard, Mary coarse, every face in the neighbourhood worsting; and the rapid increase of the crow's foot about Lady Russell's temples had long been a distress to him.

Elizabeth did not quite equal her father in personal contentment. Thirteen years had seen her mistress of Kellynch-hall, presiding and directing with a self-possession and decision which could never have given the idea of her being younger than she was. For thirteen years had she been doing

[10] Prestige; importance.

the honours, and laying down the domestic law at home, and leading the way to the chaise and four,[11] and walking immediately after Lady Russell out of all the drawing-rooms and dining-rooms in the country. Thirteen winters' revolving frosts had seen her opening every ball of credit which a scanty neighbourhood afforded; and thirteen springs shewn their blossoms, as she travelled up to London with her father, for a few weeks annual enjoyment of the great world. She had the remembrance of all this; she had the consciousness of being nine-and-twenty, to give her some regrets and some apprehensions. She was fully satisfied of being still quite as handsome as ever; but she felt her approach to the years of danger, and would have rejoiced to be certain of being properly solicited by baronet-blood within the next twelvemonth or two. Then might she again take up the book of books with as much enjoyment as in her early youth; but now she liked it not. Always to be presented with the date of her own birth, and see no marriage follow but that of a youngest sister, made the book an evil; and more than once, when her father had left it open on the table near her, had she closed it, with averted eyes, and pushed it away.

She had had a disappointment, moreover, which that book, and especially the history of her own family, must ever present the remembrance of. The heir presumptive, the very William Walter Elliot, Esq. whose rights had been so generously supported by her father, had disappointed her.

She had, while a very young girl, as soon as she had known him to be, in the event of her having no brother, the future baronet, meant to marry him; and her father had always meant that she should. He had not been known to them as a boy, but soon after Lady Elliot's death Sir Walter had sought the acquaintance, and though his overtures had not been met with any warmth, he had persevered in seeking it, making allowance for the modest drawing back of youth; and in one of their spring excursions to London, when Elizabeth was in her first bloom, Mr. Elliot had been forced into the introduction.

He was at that time a very young man, just engaged in the study of the law; and Elizabeth found him extremely agreeable, and every plan in his favour was confirmed. He was invited to Kellynch-hall; he was talked of and expected all the rest of the year; but he never came. The following spring he was seen again in town, found equally agreeable, again encouraged, invited and expected, and again he did not come; and the next tidings were that he was married. Instead of pushing his fortune in the line marked out for the heir of the house of Elliot, he had purchased independence by uniting himself to a rich woman of inferior birth.

Sir Walter had resented it. As the head of the house, he felt that he ought to have been consulted, especially after taking the young man so publicly by the hand: "For they must have been seen together," he observed, "once at Tattersal's,[12] and twice in the lobby of the House of Commons." His disapprobation was expressed, but apparently very little regarded. Mr. Elliot had attempted no apology, and shewn himself as unsolicitous of being longer noticed by the family, as Sir Wal-

[11] Carriage drawn by four horses.
[12] Auction rooms in London frequented by men interested in horses and horseracing.

ter considered him unworthy of it: all acquaintance between them had ceased.

This very awkward history of Mr. Elliot, was still, after an interval of several years, felt with anger by Elizabeth, who had liked the man for himself, and still more for being her father's heir, and whose strong family pride could see only in *him*, a proper match for Sir Walter Elliot's eldest daughter. There was not a baronet from A to Z, whom her feelings could have so willingly acknowledged as an equal. Yet so miserably had he conducted himself, that though she was at this present time, (the summer of 1814,) wearing black ribbons for his wife,[13] she could not admit him to be worth thinking of again. The disgrace of his first marriage might, perhaps, as there was no reason to suppose it perpetuated by offspring, have been got over, had he not done worse; but he had, as by the accustomary intervention of kind friends they had been informed, spoken most disrespectfully of them all, most slightingly and contemptuously of the very blood he belonged to, and the honours which were hereafter to be his own. This could not be pardoned.

Such were Elizabeth Elliot's sentiments and sensations; such the cares to alloy, the agitations to vary, the sameness and the elegance, the prosperity and the nothingness, of her scene of life—such the feelings to give interest to a long, uneventful residence in one country circle, to fill the vacancies which there were no habits of utility abroad, no talents or accomplishments for home, to occupy.

But now, another occupation and solicitude of mind was beginning to be added to these. Her father was growing distressed for money. She knew, that when he now took up the Baronetage, it was to drive the heavy bills of his tradespeople, and the unwelcome hints of Mr. Shepherd, his agent, from his thoughts. The Kellynch property was good, but not equal to Sir Walter's apprehension of the state required in its possessor. While Lady Elliot lived, there had been method, moderation, and economy, which had just kept him within his income; but with her had died all such rightmindedness, and from that period he had been constantly exceeding it. It had not been possible for him to spend less; he had done nothing but what Sir Walter Elliot was imperiously called on to do; but blameless as he was, he was not only growing dreadfully in debt, but was hearing of it so often, that it became vain to attempt concealing it longer, even partially, from his daughter. He had given her some hints of it last spring in town; he had gone so far even as to say, "Can we retrench? does it occur to you that there is any one article in which we can retrench?"—and Elizabeth, to do her justice, had, in the first ardour of female alarm, set seriously to think what could be done, and had finally proposed these two branches of economy: to cut off some unnecessary charities, and to refrain from new-furnishing the drawing-room; to which expedients she afterwards added the happy thought of their taking no present down to Anne, as had been the usual yearly custom. But these measures, however good in themselves, were insufficient for the real extent of the evil, the whole of which Sir Walter found himself obliged to confess to her soon afterwards. Elizabeth had

[13] Mourning the wife's death.

nothing to propose of deeper efficacy. She felt herself ill-used and unfortu-
nate, as did her father; and they were neither of them able to devise any
means of lessening their expenses without compromising their dignity, or
relinquishing their comforts in a way not to be borne.

There was only a small part of his estate that Sir Walter could dispose of;
but had every acre been alienable,[14] it would have made no difference. He
had condescended to mortgage as far as he had the power, but he would
never condescend to sell. No; he would never disgrace his name so far. The
Kellynch estate should be transmitted whole and entire, as he had received it.

Their two confidential friends, Mr. Shepherd, who lived in the neigh-
bouring market town, and Lady Russell, were called on to advise them; and
both father and daughter seemed to expect that something should be
struck out by one or the other to remove their embarrassments and reduce
their expenditure, without involving the loss of any indulgence of taste or
pride.

CHAPTER 2

Mr. Shepherd, a civil, cautious lawyer, who, whatever might be his hold or
his views on Sir Walter, would rather have the *disagreeable* prompted by any
body else, excused himself from offering the slightest hint, and only
begged leave to recommend an implicit deference to the excellent judg-
ment of Lady Russell,—from whose known good sense he fully expected to
have just such resolute measures advised, as he meant to see finally
adopted.

Lady Russell was most anxiously zealous on the subject, and gave it
much serious consideration. She was a woman rather of sound than of
quick abilities, whose difficulties in coming to any decision in this instance
were great, from the opposition of two leading principles. She was of strict
integrity herself, with a delicate sense of honour; but she was as desirous of
saving Sir Walter's feelings, as solicitous for the credit of the family, as
aristocratic in her ideas of what was due to them, as any body of sense and
honesty could well be. She was a benevolent, charitable, good woman, and
capable of strong attachments; most correct in her conduct, strict in her
notions of decorum, and with manners that were held a standard of good-
breeding. She had a cultivated mind, and was, generally speaking, rational
and consistent—but she had prejudices on the side of ancestry; she had a
value for rank and consequence, which blinded her a little to the faults of
those who possessed them. Herself, the widow of only a knight, she gave
the dignity of a baronet all its due; and Sir Walter, independent of his
claims as an old acquaintance, an attentive neighbour, an obliging landlord,
the husband of her very dear friend, the father of Anne and her sisters,
was, as being Sir Walter, in her apprehension entitled to a great deal of
compassion and consideration under his present difficulties.

They must retrench; that did not admit of a doubt. But she was very
anxious to have it done with the least possible pain to him and Elizabeth.
She drew up plans of economy, she made exact calculations, and she did,

[14] Legally transferrable to another person.

what nobody else thought of doing, she consulted Anne, who never seemed considered by the others as having any interest[15] in the question. She consulted, and in a degree was influenced by her, in marking out the scheme of retrenchment, which was at last submitted to Sir Walter. Every emendation of Anne's had been on the side of honesty against importance. She wanted more vigorous measures, a more complete reformation, a quicker release from debt, a much higher tone of indifference for every thing but justice and equity.

"If we can persuade your father to all this," said Lady Russell, looking over her paper, "much may be done. If he will adopt these regulations, in seven years he will be clear; and I hope we may be able to convince him and Elizabeth, that Kellynch-hall has a respectability in itself, which cannot be affected by these reductions; and that the true dignity of Sir Walter Elliot will be very far from lessened, in the eyes of sensible people, by his acting like a man of principle. What will he be doing, in fact, but what very many of out first families have done,—or ought to do?—There will be nothing singular[16] in his case; and it is singularity which often makes the worst part of our suffering, as it always does of our conduct. I have great hope of our prevailing. We must be serious and decided—for, after all, the person who has contracted debts must pay them; and though a great deal is due to the feelings of the gentleman, and the head of a house, like your father, there is still more due to the character of an honest man."

This was the principle on which Anne wanted her father to be proceeding, his friends to be urging him. She considered it as an act of indispensable duty to clear away the claims of creditors, with all the expedition which the most comprehensive retrenchments could secure, and saw no dignity in any thing short of it. She wanted it to be prescribed, and felt as a duty. She rated Lady Russell's influence highly, and as to the severe degree of self-denial, which her own conscience prompted, she believed there might be little more difficulty in persuading them to a complete, than to half a reformation. Her knowledge of her father and Elizabeth, inclined her to think that the sacrifice of one pair of horses would be hardly less painful than of both, and so on, through the whole list of Lady Russell's too gentle reductions.

How Anne's more rigid requisitions might have been taken, is of little consequence. Lady Russell's had no success at all—could not be put up with—were not to be borne. "What! Every comfort of life knocked off! Journeys, London, servants, horses, table,—contractions and restrictions every where. To live no longer with the decencies even of a private gentleman! No, he would sooner quit Kellynch-hall at once, than remain in it on such disgraceful terms."

"Quit Kellynch-hall." The hint was immediately taken up by Mr. Shepherd, whose interest was involved in the reality of Sir Walter's retrenching, and who was perfectly persuaded that nothing would be done without a change of abode.—"Since the idea had been started in the very quarter which ought to dictate, he had no scruple," he said, "in confessing his judgment to be entirely on that side. It did not appear to him that Sir

[15] Anything at stake; any right to be involved.
[16] Departing from the customary norm.

Walter could materially alter his style of living in a house which had such a character of hospitality and ancient dignity to support.—In any other place, Sir Walter might judge for himself; and would be looked up to, as regulating the modes of life, in whatever way he might choose to model his household."

Sir Walter would quit Kellynch-hall;—and after a very few days more of doubt and indecision, the great question of whither he should go, was settled, and the first outline of this important change made out.

There had been three alternatives, London, Bath,[17] or another house in the country. All Anne's wishes had been for the latter. A small house in their own neighbourhood, where they might still have Lady Russell's society, still be near Mary, and still have the pleasure of sometimes seeing the lawns and groves of Kellynch, was the object of her ambition. But the usual fate of Anne attended her, in having something very opposite from her inclination fixed on. She disliked Bath, and did not think it agreed with her—and Bath was to be her home.

Sir Walter had at first thought more of London, but Mr. Shepherd felt that he could not be trusted in London, and had been skillful enough to dissuade him from it, and make Bath preferred. It was a much safer place for a gentleman in his predicament:—he might there be important at comparatively little expense.—Two material advantages of Bath over London had of course been given all their weight, its more convenient distance from Kellynch, only fifty miles, and Lady Russell's spending some part of every winter there; and to the very great satisfaction of Lady Russell, whose first views on the projected change had been for Bath, Sir Walter and Elizabeth were induced to believe that they should lose neither consequence nor enjoyment by settling there.

Lady Russell felt obliged to oppose her dear Anne's known wishes. It would be too much to expect Sir Walter to descend into a small house in his own neighborhood. Anne herself would have found the mortifications of it more than she foresaw, and to Sir Walter's feelings they must have been dreadful. And with regard to Anne's dislike of Bath, she considered it as a prejudice and mistake, arising first from the circumstance of her having been three years at school there, after her mother's death, and secondly, from her happening to be not in perfectly good spirits the only winter which she had afterwards spent there with herself.

Lady Russell was fond of Bath in short, and disposed to think it must suit them all; and as to her young friend's health, by passing all the warm months with her at Kellynch-lodge, every danger would be avoided; and it was, in fact, a change which must do both health and spirits good. Anne had been too little from home, too little seen. Her spirits were not high. A larger society would improve them. She wanted her to be more known.

The undesirableness of any other house in the same neighbourhood for Sir Walter, was certainly much strengthened by one part, and a very material part of the scheme, which had been happily engrafted on the beginning. He was not only to quit his home, but to see it in the hands of others; a trial of fortitude, which stronger heads than Sir Walter's have found too

[17] An ancient city in Somersetshire dating from Roman times, Bath was a fashionable and elegant resort famous for its medicinal springs.

much.—Kellynch-hall was to be let. This, however, was a profound secret; not to be breathed beyond their own circle.

Sir Walter could not have borne the degradation of being known to design letting his house.—Mr. Shepherd had once mentioned the word, "advertise;"—but never dared approach it again; Sir Walter spurned the idea of its being offered in any manner; forbad the slightest hint being dropped of his having such an intention; and it was only on the supposition of his being spontaneously solicited by some most unexceptionable applicant, on his own terms, and as a great favour, that he would let it at all.

How quick come the reasons for approving what we like!—Lady Russell had another excellent one at hand, for being extremely glad that Sir Walter and his family were to remove from the country. Elizabeth had been lately forming an intimacy, which she wished to see interrupted. It was with a daughter of Mr. Shepherd, who had returned, after an unprosperous marriage, to her father's house, with the additional burthen of two children. She was a clever young woman, who understood the art of pleasing; the art of pleasing, at least, at Kellynch-hall; and who had made herself so acceptable to Miss Elliot,[18] as to have been already staying there more than once, in spite of all that Lady Russell, who thought it a friendship quite out of place, could hint of caution and reserve.

Lady Russell, indeed, had scarcely any influence with Elizabeth, and seemed to love her, rather because she would love her, than because Elizabeth deserved it. She had never received from her more than outward attention, nothing beyond the observances of complaisance;[19] had never succeeded in any point which she wanted to carry, against previous inclination. She had been repeatedly very earnest in trying to get Anne included in the visit to London, sensibly open to all the injustice and all the discredit of the selfish arrangements which shut her out, and on many lesser occasions had endeavoured to give Elizabeth the advantage of her own better judgment and experience—but always in vain; Elizabeth would go her own way—and never had she pursued it in more decided opposition to Lady Russell, than in this selection of Mrs. Clay; turning from the society of so deserving a sister to bestow her affection and confidence on one who ought to have been nothing to her but the object of distant civility.

From situation, Mrs. Clay was, in Lady Russell's estimate, a very unequal, and in her character she believed a very dangerous companion—and a removal that would leave Mrs. Clay behind, and bring a choice of more suitable intimates within Miss Elliot's reach, was therefore an object of first-rate importance.

CHAPTER 3

"I must take leave to observe, Sir Walter," said Mr. Shepherd one morning at Kellynch-hall, as he laid down the newspaper, "that the present juncture is much in our favour. This peace will be turning all our rich Navy Officers

[18] In Jane Austen's day, the title *Miss* used without a first name referred to the eldest unmarried daughter.
[19] Politeness.

ashore. They will be all wanting a home. Could not be a better time, Sir Walter, for having a choice of tenants, very responsible tenants. Many a noble fortune has been made during the war.[20] If a rich Admiral were to come in our way, Sir Walter—"

"He would be a very lucky man, Shepherd," replied Sir Walter, "that's all I have to remark. A prize indeed would Kellynch-hall be to him; rather the greatest prize of all, let him have taken ever so many before—hey, Shepherd?"

Mr. Shepherd laughed, as he knew he must, at this wit, and then added,

"I presume to observe, Sir Walter, that, in the way of business, gentlemen of the navy are well to deal with. I have had a little knowledge of their methods of doing business, and I am free to confess that they have very liberal[21] notions, and are as likely to make desirable tenants as any set of people one should meet with. Therefore, Sir Walter, what I would take leave to suggest is, that if in consequence of any rumours getting abroad of your intention—which must be contemplated as a possible thing, because we know how difficult it is to keep the actions and designs of one part of the world from the notice and curiosity of the other,—consequence has its tax—I, John Shepherd, might conceal any family-matters that I chose, for nobody would think it worth their while to observe me, but Sir Walter Elliot has eyes upon him which it may be very difficult to elude—and therefore, thus much I venture upon, that it will not greatly surprise me if, with all our caution, some rumour of the truth should get abroad—in the supposition of which, as I was going to observe, since applications will unquestionably follow, I should think any from our wealthy naval commanders particularly worth attending to—and beg leave to add, that two hours will bring me over at any time, to save you the trouble of replying."

Sir Walter only nodded. But soon afterwards, rising and pacing the room, he observed sarcastically,

"There are few among the gentlemen of the navy, I imagine, who would not be surprised to find themselves in a house of this description."

"They would look around them, no doubt, and bless their good fortune," said Mrs. Clay, for Mrs. Clay was present; her father had driven her over, nothing being of so much use to Mrs. Clay's health as a drive to Kellynch: "but I quite agree with my father in thinking a sailor might be a very desirable tenant. I have known a good deal of the profession; and besides their liberality, they are so neat and careful in all their ways! These valuable pictures of yours, Sir Walter, if you chose to leave them, would be perfectly safe. Every thing in and about the house would be taken such excellent care of! the gardens and shrubberies would be kept in almost as high order as they are now. You need not be afraid, Miss Elliot, of your own sweet flower-garden's being neglected."

"As to all that," rejoined Sir Walter coolly, "supposing I were induced to let my house, I have by no means made up my mind as to the privileges to be annexed to it. I am not particularly disposed to favour a tenant. The

[20] During the quarter-century preceding 1814, the present date in the novel, England had been almost continuously at war with France, in consequence of the French Revolution, which began in 1789, and the subsequent rule and military adventures of Napoleon Bonaparte. Naval officers often got rich by capturing enemy ships ("prizes") along with their cargoes.
[21] Generous; free-spending.

park[22] would be open to him of course, and few navy officers, or men of any other description, can have had such a range; but what restrictions I might impose on the use of the pleasure-grounds, is another thing. I am not fond of the idea of my shrubberies being always approachable; and I should recommend Miss Elliot to be on her guard with respect to her flower-garden. I am very little disposed to grant a tenant of Kellynch-hall any extraordinary favour, I assure you, be he sailor or soldier."

After a short pause, Mr. Shepherd presumed to say,

"In all these cases, there are established usages which make every thing plain and easy between landlord and tenant. Your interest, Sir Walter, is in pretty safe hands. Depend upon me for taking care that no tenant has more than his just rights. I venture to hint, that Sir Walter Elliot cannot be half so jealous for his own, as John Shepherd will be for him."

Here Anne spoke,—

"The navy, I think, who have done so much for us, have at least an equal claim with any other set of men, for all the comforts and all the privileges which any home can give. Sailors work hard enough for their comforts, we must all allow."

"Very true, very true. What Miss Anne says, is very true," was Mr. Shepherd's rejoinder, and "Oh! certainly," was his daughter's; but Sir Walter's remark was, soon afterwards—

"The profession has its utility, but I should be sorry to see any friend of mine belonging to it."

"Indeed!" was the reply, and with a look of surprise.

"Yes; it is in two points offensive to me; I have two strong grounds of objection to it. First, as being the means of bringing persons of obscure birth into undue distinction, and raising men to honours which their fathers and grandfathers never dreamt of; and secondly, as it cuts up a man's youth and vigour most horribly; a sailor grows old sooner than any other man; I have observed it all my life. A man is in greater danger in the navy of being insulted by the rise of one whose father, his father might have disdained to speak to, and of becoming prematurely an object of disgust[23] himself, than in any other line. One day last spring, in town, I was in company with two men, striking instances of what I am talking of, Lord St. Ives, whose father we all know to have been a country curate, without bread to eat; I was to give place to Lord St. Ives, and a certain Admiral Baldwin, the most deplorable looking personage you can imagine, his face the colour of mahogany, rough and rugged to the last degree, all lines and wrinkles, nine grey hairs of a side, and nothing but a dab of powder at top.—'In the name of heaven, who is that old fellow?' said I, to a friend of mine who was standing near, (Sir Basil Morley.) 'Old fellow!' cried Sir Basil, 'it is Admiral Baldwin. What do you take his age to be?' 'Sixty,' said I, 'or perhaps sixty-two.' 'Forty,' replied Sir Basil, 'forty, and no more.' Picture to yourselves my amazement; I shall not easily forget Admiral Baldwin. I never saw quite so wretched an example of what a seafaring life can do; but to a degree, I know it is the same with them all: they are all knocked about, and exposed to every climate, and every weather, till they are not fit to be

[22] The fields and woods belonging to the estate.
[23] Distaste. (The word was milder than it is today.)

seen. It is a pity they are not knocked on the head at once, before they reach Admiral Baldwin's age."

"Nay, Sir Walter," cried Mrs. Clay, "this is being severe indeed. Have a little mercy on the poor men. We are not all born to be handsome. The sea is no beautifier, certainly; sailors do grow old betimes; I have often observed it; they soon lose the look of youth. But then, is not it the same with many other professions, perhaps most other? Soldiers, in active service, are not at all better off: and even in the quieter professions, there is a toil and a labour of the mind, if not of the body, which seldom leaves a man's looks to the natural effect of time. The lawyer plods, quite care-worn; the physician is up at all hours, and travelling in all weather; and even the clergyman—" she stopt a moment to consider what might do for the clergyman;—"and even the clergyman, you know, is obliged to go into infected rooms, and expose his health and looks to all the injury of a poisonous atmosphere. In fact, as I have long been convinced, though every profession is necessary and honourable in its turn, it is only the lot of those who are not obliged to follow any, who can live in a regular way, in the country, choosing their own hours, following their own pursuits, and living on their own property, without the torment of trying for more; it is only *their* lot, I say, to hold the blessings of health and a good appearance to the utmost: I know no other set of men but what lose something of their personableness[24] when they cease to be quite young."

It seemed as if Mr. Shepherd, in this anxiety to bespeak Sir Walter's goodwill towards a naval officer as tenant, had been gifted with foresight; for the very first application for the house was from an Admiral Croft, with whom he shortly afterwards fell into company in attending the quarter sessions[25] at Taunton; and indeed, he had received a hint of the admiral from a London correspondent. By the report which he hastened over to Kellynch to make, Admiral Croft was a native of Somersetshire, who having acquired a very handsome fortune, was wishing to settle in his own country, and had come down to Taunton in order to look at some advertised places in that immediate neighbourhood, which, however, had not suited him; that accidentally hearing—(it was just as he had foretold, Mr. Shepherd observed, Sir Walter's concerns could not be kept a secret,)— accidentally hearing of the possibility of Kellynch-hall being to let, and understanding his (Mr. Shepherd's) connection with the owner, he had introduced himself to him in order to make particular inquiries, and had, in the course of a pretty long conference, expressed as strong an inclination for the place as a man who knew it only by description, could feel; and given Mr. Shepherd, in his explicit account of himself, every proof of his being a most responsible, eligible tenant.

"And who is Admiral Croft?" was Sir Walter's cold suspicious inquiry.

Mr. Shepherd answered for his being of a gentleman's family, and mentioned a place; and Anne, after the little pause which followed, added—

"He is rear admiral of the white.[26] He was in the Trafalgar action,[27] and

[24] Handsomeness. [25] Court sessions held every three months.

[26] The White squadron, one of the divisions of the British fleet.

[27] Trafalgar, a Spanish cape on the Atlantic, was the site of the famous naval battle (1805) in which the British fleet, commanded by the heroic Admiral Horatio Nelson, defeated the fleets of France and Spain. Nelson was killed in the battle.

has been in the East Indies since; he has been stationed there, I believe, several years."

"Then I take it for granted," observed Sir Walter, "that his face is about as orange as the cuffs and capes of my livery."

Mr. Shepherd hastened to assure him, that Admiral Croft was a very hale, hearty, well-looking man, a little weather-beaten, to be sure, but not much; and quite the gentleman in all his notions and behaviour;—not likely to make the smallest difficulty about terms;—only wanted a comfortable home, and to get into it as soon as possible;—knew he must pay for his convenience;—knew what rent a ready-furnished house of that consequence might fetch;—should not have been surprised if Sir Walter had asked more;—had inquired about the manor;—would be glad of the deputation,[28] certainly, but made no great point of it;—said he sometimes took out a gun, but never killed;—quite the gentleman.

Mr. Shepherd was eloquent on the subject; pointing out all the circumstances of the admiral's family, which made him peculiarly desirable as a tenant. He was a married man, and without children; the very state to be wished for. A house was never taken good care of, Mr. Shepherd observed, without a lady: he did not know whether furniture might not be in danger of suffering as much where there was no lady, as where there were many children. A lady, without a family, was the very best preserver of furniture in the world. He had seen Mrs. Croft, too; she was at Taunton with the admiral, and had been present almost all the time they were talking the matter over.

"And a very well-spoken, genteel, shrewd lady, she seemed to be," continued he; "asked more questions about the house, and terms, and taxes, than the admiral himself, and seemed more conversant with business. And moreover, Sir Walter, I found she was not quite unconnected in this country, any more than her husband; that is to say, she is sister to a gentleman who did live amongst us once; she told me so herself: sister to the gentleman who lived a few years back, at Monkford. Bless me! what was his name? At this moment I cannot recollect his name, though I have heard it so lately. Penelope, my dear, can you help me to the name of the gentleman who lived at Monkford—Mrs. Croft's brother?"

But Mrs. Clay was talking so eagerly with Miss Elliot, that she did not hear the appeal.

"I have no conception whom you can mean, Shepherd; I remember no gentleman resident at Monkford since the time of old Governor Trent."

"Bless me! how very odd! I shall forget my own name soon, I suppose. A name that I am so very well acquainted with; knew the gentleman so well by sight; seen him a hundred times; came to consult me once, I remember, about a trespass of one of his neighbours; farmer's man breaking into his orchard—wall torn down—apples stolen—caught in the fact; and afterwards, contrary to my judgment, submitted to an amicable compromise. Very odd indeed!"

After waiting another moment—

"You mean Mr. Wentworth, I suppose," said Anne.

Mr. Shepherd was all gratitude.

[28] The delegated right to kill game animals.

"Wentworth was the very name! Mr. Wentworth was the very man. He had the curacy of Monkford, you know, Sir Walter, some time back, for two or three years. Came there about the year—5, I take it. You remember him, I am sure."

"Wentworth? Oh! ay,—Mr. Wentworth, the curate of Monkford. You misled me by the term *gentleman.* I thought you were speaking of some man of property: Mr. Wentworth was nobody, I remember; quite unconnected; nothing to do with the Strafford family. One wonders how the names of many of our nobility become so common."

As Mr. Shepherd perceived that this connexion of the Crofts did them no service with Sir Walter, he mentioned it no more; returning, with all his zeal, to dwell on the circumstances more indisputably in their favour; their age, and number, and fortune; the high idea they had formed of Kellynch-hall, and extreme solicitude for the advantage of renting it; making it appear as if they ranked nothing beyond the happiness of being the tenants of Sir Walter Elliot: an extraordinary taste, certainly, could they have been supposed in the secret of Sir Walter's estimate of the dues of a tenant.

It succeeded, however; and though Sir Walter must ever look with an evil eye on any one intending to inhabit that house, and think them infinitely too well off in being permitted to rent it on the highest terms, he was talked into allowing Mr. Shepherd to proceed in the treaty, and authorising him to wait on Admiral Croft, who still remained at Taunton, and fix a day for the house being seen.

Sir Walter was not very wise; but still he had experience enough of the world to feel, that a more unobjectionable tenant, in all essentials, than Admiral Croft bid fair to be, could hardly offer. So far went his understanding; and his vanity supplied a little additional soothing, in the admiral's situation in life, which was just high enough, and not too high. "I have let my house to Admiral Croft," would sound extremely well; very much better than to any mere *Mr.*——; a *Mr.* (save, perhaps, some half dozen in the nation,) always needs a note of explanation. An admiral speaks his own consequence, and, at the same time, can never make a baronet look small. In all their dealings and intercourse, Sir Walter Elliot must ever have the precedence.

Nothing could be done without a reference to Elizabeth; but her inclination was growing so strong for a removal, that she was happy to have it fixed and expedited by a tenant at hand; and not a word to suspend decision was uttered by her.

Mr. Shepherd was completely empowered to act; and no sooner had such an end been reached, than Anne, who had been a most attentive listener to the whole, left the room, to seek the comfort of cool air for her flushed cheeks; and as she walked along a favourite grove, said, with a gentle sigh, "a few months more, and *he,* perhaps, may be walking here."

CHAPTER 4

He was not Mr. Wentworth, the former curate of Monkford, however suspicious appearances may be, but a captain Frederick Wentworth, his brother, who being made commander in consequence of the action off St.

Domingo,[29] and not immediately employed, had come into Somersetshire, in the summer of 1806; and having no parent living, found a home for half a year, at Monkford. He was, at that time, a remarkably fine young man, with a great deal of intelligence, spirit and brilliancy; and Anne an extremely pretty girl, with gentleness, modesty, taste, and feeling.—Half the sum of attraction, on either side, might have been enough, for he had nothing to do, and she had hardly any body to love; but the encounter of such lavish recommendations could not fail. They were gradually acquainted, and when acquainted, rapidly and deeply in love. It would be difficult to say which had seen highest perfection in the other, or which had been the happiest; she, in receiving his declarations and proposals, or he in having them accepted.

A short period of exquisite felicity followed, and but a short one.—Troubles soon arose. Sir Walter, on being applied to, without actually withholding his consent, or saying it should never be, gave it all the negative of great astonishment, great coldness, great silence, and a professed resolution of doing nothing for his daughter. He thought it a very degrading alliance; and Lady Russell, though with more tempered and pardonable pride, received it as a most unfortunate one.

Anne Elliot, with all her claims of birth, beauty, and mind, to throw herself away at nineteen; involve herself at nineteen in an engagement with a young man, who had nothing but himself to recommend him, and no hopes of attaining affluence, but in the chances of a most uncertain profession, and no connexions to secure even his farther rise in that profession; would be, indeed, a throwing away, which she grieved to think of! Anne Elliot, so young; known to so few, to be snatched off by a stranger without alliance or fortune; or rather sunk by him into a state of most wearing, anxious, youth-killing dependence! It must not be, if by any fair interference of friendship, any representations from one who had almost a mother's love, and mother's rights, it would be prevented.

Captain Wentworth had no fortune. He had been lucky in his profession, but spending freely, what had come freely, had realized nothing. But, he was confident that he should soon be rich;—full of life and ardour, he knew that he should soon have a ship, and soon be on a station that would lead to every thing he wanted. He had always been lucky; he knew he should be so still.—Such confidence, powerful in its own warmth, and bewitching in the wit which often expressed it, must have been enough for Anne; but Lady Russell saw it very differently.—His sanguine temper, and fearlessness of mind, operated very differently on her. She saw in it but an aggravation of the evil. It only added a dangerous character to himself. He was brilliant, he was headstrong.—Lady Russell had little taste for wit; and of any thing approaching to imprudence a horror. She deprecated the connexion in every light.

Such opposition, as these feelings produced, was more than Anne could combat. Young and gentle as she was, it might yet have been possible to withstand her father's ill-will, though unsoftened by one kind word or look on the part of her sister;—but Lady Russell, whom she had always loved and relied on, could not, with such steadiness of opinion, and such tender-

[29] A British naval victory, in 1806, over a French squadron.

ness of manner, be continually advising her in vain. She was persuaded to believe the engagement a wrong thing—indiscreet, improper, hardly capable of success, and not deserving it. But it was not a merely selfish caution, under which she acted, in putting an end to it. Had she not imagined herself consulting his good, even more than her own, she could hardly have given him up.—The belief of being prudent, and self-denying principally for *his* advantage, was her chief consolation, under the misery of a parting—a final parting; and every consolation was required, for she had to encounter all the additional pain of opinions, on his side, totally unconvinced and unbending, and of his feeling himself ill-used by so forced a relinquishment.—He had left the country in consequence.

A few months had seen the beginning and the end of their acquaintance; but, not with a few months ended Anne's share of suffering from it. Her attachment and regrets had, for a long time, clouded every enjoyment of youth; and an early loss of bloom and spirits had been their lasting effect.

More than seven years were gone since this little history of sorrowful interest had reached its close; and time had softened down much, perhaps nearly all of peculiar attachment to him,—but she had been too dependent on time alone; no aid had been given in change of place, (except in one visit to Bath soon after the rupture,) or in any novelty or enlargement of society.—No one had ever come within the Kellynch circle, who could bear a comparison with Frederick Wentworth, as he stood in her memory. No second attachment, the only thoroughly natural, happy, and sufficient cure, at her time of life, had been possible to the nice tone of her mind, the fastidiousness of her taste, in the small limits of the society around them. She had been solicited, when about two-and-twenty, to change her name, by the young man, who not long afterwards found a more willing mind in her younger sister; and Lady Russell had lamented her refusal; for Charles Musgrove was the eldest son of a man, whose landed property and general importance, were second, in that country, only to Sir Walter's, and of good character and appearance; and however Lady Russell might have asked yet for something more, while Anne was nineteen, she would have rejoiced to see her at twenty-two, so respectably removed from the partialities and injustice of her father's house, and settled so permanently near herself. But in this case, Anne had left nothing for advice to do; and though Lady Russell, as satisfied as ever with her own discretion, never wished the past undone, she began now to have the anxiety which borders on hopelessness for Anne's being tempted, by some man of talents and independence, to enter a state for which she held her to be peculiarly fitted by her warm affections and domestic habits.

They knew not each other's opinion, either its constancy or its change, on the one leading point of Anne's conduct, for the subject was never alluded to,—but Anne, at seven and twenty, thought very differently from what she had been made to think at nineteen.—She did not blame Lady Russell, she did not blame herself for having been guided by her; but she felt that were any young person, in similar circumstances, to apply to her for counsel, they would never receive any of such certain immediate wretchedness, such uncertain future good.—She was persuaded that under every disadvantage of disapprobation at home, and every anxiety

attending his profession, all their probable fears, delays and disappointments, she should yet have been a happier woman in maintaining the engagement than she had been in the sacrifice of it; and this, she fully believed, had the usual share, had even more than a usual share of all such solicitudes and suspense been theirs, without reference to the actual results of their case, which, as it happened, would have bestowed earlier prosperity than could be reasonably calculated on. All his sanguine expectations, all his confidence had been justified. His genius and ardour had seemed to foresee and to command his prosperous path. He had, very soon after their engagement ceased, got employ; and all that he had told her would follow, had taken place. He had distinguished himself, and early gained the other step in rank—and must now, by successive captures, have made a handsome fortune. She had only navy lists and newspapers for her authority, but she could not doubt his being rich;—and, in favour of his constancy, she had no reason to believe him married.

How eloquent could Anne Elliot have been,—how eloquent, at least, were her wishes on the side of early warm attachment, and a cheerful confidence in futurity, against that over-anxious caution which seems to insult exertion and distrust Providence!—She had been forced into prudence in her youth, she learned romance as she grew older—the natural sequel of an unnatural beginning.

With all these circumstances, recollections and feelings, she could not hear that Captain Wentworth's sister was likely to live at Kellynch, without a revival of former pain; and many a stroll and many a sigh were necessary to dispel the agitation of the idea. She often told herself it was folly, before she could harden her nerves sufficiently to feel the continual discussion of the Crofts and their business no evil. She was assisted, however, by that perfect indifference and apparent unconsciousness, among the only three of her own friends in the secret of the past, which seemed almost to deny any recollection of it. She could do justice to the superiority of Lady Russell's motives in this, over those of her father and Elizabeth; she could honour all the better feelings of her calmness—but the general air of oblivion among them was highly important, from whatever it sprung; and in the event of Admiral Croft's really taking Kellynch-hall, she rejoiced anew over the conviction which had always been most grateful to her, of the past being known to those three only among her connexions, by whom no syllable, she believed, would ever be whispered, and in the trust that among his, the brother only with whom he had been residing, had received any information of their short-lived engagement.—That brother had been long removed from the country—and being a sensible man, and, moreover, a single man at the time, she had a fond dependence on no human creature's having heard of it from him.

The sister, Mrs. Croft, had then been out of England, accompanying her husband on a foreign station, and her own sister, Mary, had been at school while it all occurred—and never admitted by the pride of some, and the delicacy of others, to the smallest knowledge of it afterwards.

With these supports, she hoped that the acquaintance between herself and the Crofts, which, with Lady Russell still resident in Kellynch, and Mary fixed only three miles off, must be anticipated, need not involve any particular awkwardness.

<div align="center">CHAPTER 5</div>

On the morning appointed for Admiral and Mrs. Croft's seeing Kellynch-hall, Anne found it most natural to take her almost daily walk to Lady Russell's, and keep out of the way till all was over; when she found it most natural to be sorry that she had missed the opportunity of seeing them.

This meeting of the two parties proved highly satisfactory, and decided the whole business at once. Each lady was previously well disposed for an agreement, and saw nothing, therefore, but good manners in the other; and, with regard to the gentlemen, there was such an hearty good humour, such an open, trusting liberality on the Admiral's side, as could not but influence Sir Walter, who had besides been flattered into his very best and most polished behaviour by Mr. Shepherd's assurances of his being known, by report, to the Admiral, as a model of good breeding.

The house and grounds, and furniture, were approved, the Crofts were approved, terms, time, every thing, and every body, was right; and Mr. Shepherd's clerks were set to work, without there having been a single preliminary difference to modify of all that "This indenture sheweth."

Sir Walter, without hesitation, declared the Admiral to be the best-looking sailor he had ever met with, and went so far as to say, that, if his own man might have had the arranging of his hair, he should not be ashamed of being seen with him any where; and the Admiral, with sympathetic cordiality, observed to his wife as they drove back through the Park, "I thought we should soon come to a deal, my dear, in spite of what they told us at Taunton. The baronet will never set the Thames on fire, but there seems no harm in him:"—reciprocal compliments, which would have been esteemed about equal.

The Crofts were to have possession at Michaelmas,[30] and as Sir Walter proposed removing to Bath in the course of the preceding month, there was no time to be lost in making every dependent arrangement.

Lady Russell, convinced that Anne would not be allowed to be of any use, or any importance, in the choice of the house which they were going to secure, was very unwilling to have her hurried away so soon, and wanted to make it possible for her to stay behind, till she might convey her to Bath herself after Christmas; but having engagements of her own, which must take her from Kellynch for several weeks, she was unable to give the full invitation she wished; and Anne, though dreading the possible heats of September in all the white glare of Bath, and grieving to forego all the influence so sweet and so sad of the autumnal months in the country, did not think that, every thing considered, she wished to remain. It would be most right, and most wise, and, therefore, must involve least suffering, to go with the others.

Something occurred, however, to give her a different duty. Mary, often a little unwell, and always thinking a great deal of her own complaints, and always in the habit of claiming Anne when any thing was the matter, was indisposed; and foreseeing that she should not have a day's health all the autumn, entreated, or rather required her, for it was hardly entreaty, to

[30] The feast of St. Michael, September 29.

come to Uppercross Cottage, and bear her company as long as she should want her, instead of going to Bath.

"I cannot possibly do without Anne," was Mary's reasoning; and Elizabeth's reply was, "Then I am sure Anne had better stay, for nobody will want her in Bath."

To be claimed as a good, though in an improper style, is at least better than being rejected as no good at all; and Anne, glad to be thought of some use, glad to have any thing marked out as a duty, and certainly not sorry to have the scene of it in the country, and her own dear country, readily agreed to stay.

This invitation of Mary's removed all Lady Russell's difficulties, and it was consequently soon settled that Anne should not go to Bath till Lady Russell took her, and that all the intervening time should be divided between Uppercross Cottage and Kellynch-lodge.

So far all was perfectly right; but Lady Russell was almost startled by the wrong of one part of the Kellynch-hall plan, when it burst on her, which was, Mrs. Clay's being engaged to go to Bath with Sir Walter and Elizabeth, as a most important and valuable assistant to the latter in all the business before her. Lady Russell was extremely sorry that such a measure should have been resorted to at all—wondered, grieved, and feared—and the affront it contained to Anne, in Mrs. Clay's being of so much use, while Anne could be of none, was a very sore aggravation.

Anne herself was become hardened to such affronts; but she felt the imprudence of the arrangement quite as keenly as Lady Russell. With a great deal of quiet observation, and a knowledge, which she often wished less, of her father's character, she was sensible that results the most serious to his family from the intimacy, were more than possible. She did not imagine that her father had at present an idea of the kind. Mrs. Clay had freckles, and a projecting tooth, and a clumsy wrist, which he was continually making severe remarks upon, in her absence; but she was young, and certainly altogether well-looking, and possessed, in an acute mind and assiduous pleasing manners, infinitely more dangerous attractions than any merely personal might have been. Anne was so impressed by the degree of their danger, that she could not excuse herself from trying to make it perceptible to her sister. She had little hope of success; but Elizabeth, who in the event of such a reverse would be so much more to be pitied than herself, should never, she thought, have reason to reproach her for giving no warning.

She spoke, and seemed only to offend. Elizabeth could not conceive how such an absurd suspicion should occur to her; and indignantly answered for each party's perfectly knowing their situation.

"Mrs. Clay," she said warmly, "never forgets who she is; and as I am rather better acquainted with her sentiments than you can be, I can assure you, that upon the subject of marriage they are particularly nice;[31] and that she reprobates all inequality of condition and rank more strongly than most people. And as to my father, I really should not have thought that he, who has kept himself single so long for our sakes, need be suspected now.

[31] Delicate; scrupulous.

If Mrs. Clay were a very beautiful woman, I grant you, it might be wrong to have her so much with me; not that any thing in the world, I am sure, would induce my father to make a degrading match; but he might be rendered unhappy. But poor Mrs. Clay, who, with all her merits, can never have been reckoned tolerably pretty! I really think poor Mrs. Clay may be staying here in perfect safety. One would imagine you had never heard my father speak of her personal misfortunes, though I know you must fifty times. That tooth of hers! and those freckles! Freckles do not disgust me so very much as they do him: I have known a face not materially disfigured by a few, but he abominates them. You must have heard him notice Mrs. Clay's freckles."

"There is hardly any personal defect," replied Anne, "which an agreeable manner might not gradually reconcile one to."

"I think very differently," answered Elizabeth, shortly; "an agreeable manner may set off handsome features, but can never alter plain ones. However, at any rate, as I have a great deal more at stake on this point than any body else can have, I think it rather unnecessary in you to be advising me."

Anne had done—glad that it was over, and not absolutely hopeless of doing good. Elizabeth, though resenting the suspicion, might yet be made observant by it.

The last office of the four carriage-horses was to draw Sir Walter, Miss Elliot, and Mrs. Clay to Bath. The party drove off in very good spirits; Sir Walter prepared with condescending bows for all the afflicted tenantry and cottagers who might have had a hint to shew themselves; and Anne walked up at the same time, in a sort of desolate tranquillity, to the Lodge, where she was to spend the first week.

Her friend was not in better spirits than herself. Lady Russell felt this break-up of the family exceedingly. Their respectability was as dear to her as her own; and a daily intercourse had become precious by habit. It was painful to look upon their deserted grounds, and still worse to anticipate the new hands they were to fall into; and to escape the solitariness and the melancholy of so altered a village, and be out of the way when Admiral and Mrs. Croft first arrived, she had determined to make her own absence from home begin when she must give up Anne. Accordingly their removal was made together, and Anne was set down at Uppercross Cottage, in the first stage of Lady Russell's journey.

Uppercross was a moderate-sized village, which a few years back had been completely in the old English style; containing only two houses superior in appearance to those of the yeomen[32] and labourers,—the mansion of the 'squire, with its high walls, great gates, and old trees, substantial and unmodernized—and the compact, tight parsonage, enclosed in its own neat garden, with a vine and a pear-tree trained round its casements; but upon the marriage of the young 'squire, it had received the improvement of a farmhouse elevated into a cottage for his residence; and Uppercross Cottage, with its veranda, French windows, and other prettinesses, was quite as likely to catch the traveller's eye, as the more consistent and consid-

[32] Independent small farmers.

erable aspect and premises of the Great House, about a quarter of a mile farther on.

Here, Anne had often been staying. She knew the ways of Uppercross as well as those of Kellynch. The two families were so continually meeting, so much in the habit of running in and out of each other's house at all hours, that it was rather a surprise to her to find Mary alone; but being alone, her being unwell and out of spirits, was almost a matter of course. Though better endowed than the elder sister, Mary had not Anne's understanding or temper. While well, and happy, and properly attended to, she had great good humour and excellent spirits; but any indisposition sunk her completely; she had no resources for solitude; and inheriting a considerable share of the Elliot self-importance, was very prone to add to every other distress that of fancying herself neglected and ill-used. In person, she was inferior to both sisters, and had, even in her bloom, only reached the dignity of being "a fine girl." She was now lying on the faded sofa of the pretty little drawing-room, the once elegant furniture of which had been gradually growing shabby, under the influence of four summers and two children; and, on Anne's appearing, greeted her with,

"So, you are come at last! I began to think I should never see you. I am so ill I can hardly speak. I have not seen a creature the whole morning!"

"I am sorry to find you unwell," replied Anne. "You sent me such a good account of yourself on Thursday!"

"Yes, I made the best of it; I always do; but I was very far from well at the time; and I do not think I ever was so ill in my life as I have been all this morning—very unfit to be left alone, I am sure. Suppose I were to be seized of a sudden in some dreadful way, and not able to ring the bell! So, Lady Russell would not get out. I do not think she has been in this house three times this summer."

Anne said what was proper, and enquired after her husband. "Oh! Charles is out shooting. I have not seen him since seven o'clock. He would go, though I told him how ill I was. He said he should not stay out long; but he has never come back, and now it is almost one. I assure you, I have not seen a soul this whole long morning."

"You have had your little boys with you?"

"Yes, as long as I could bear their noise; but they are so unmanageable that they do me more harm than good. Little Charles does not mind a word I say, and Walter is growing quite as bad."

"Well, you will soon be better now," replied Anne, cheerfully. "You know I always cure you when I come. How are your neighbours at the Great House?"

"I can give you no account of them. I have not seen one of them to-day, except Mr. Musgrove, who just stopped and spoke through the window, but without getting off his horse; and though I told him how ill I was, not one of them have been near me. It did not happen to suit the Miss Musgroves, I suppose, and they never put themselves out of their way."

"You will see them yet, perhaps, before the morning is gone. It is early."

"I never want them, I assure you. They talk and laugh a great deal too much for me. Oh! Anne, I am so very unwell! It was quite unkind of you not to come on Thursday."

"My dear Mary, recollect what a comfortable account you sent me of

yourself! You wrote in the cheerfullest manner, and said you were per-
fectly well, and in no hurry for me; and that being the case, you must be
aware that my wish would be to remain with Lady Russell to the last; and
besides what I felt on her account, I have really been so busy, have had so
much to do, that I could not very conveniently have left Kellynch sooner."

"Dear me! what can *you* possibly have to do?"

"A great many things, I assure you. More than I can recollect in a mo-
ment; but I can tell you some. I have been making a duplicate of the cata-
logue of my father's books and pictures. I have been several times in the
garden with Mackenzie, trying to understand, and make him understand,
which of Elizabeth's plants are for Lady Russell. I have had all my own little
concerns to arrange—books and music to divide, and all my trunks to
repack, from not having understood in time what was intended as to the
waggons. And one thing I have had to do, Mary, of a more trying nature;
going to almost every house in the parish, as a sort of take-leave. I was told
that they wished it. But all these things took up a great deal of time."

"Oh! well;"—and after a moment's pause, "But you have never asked
me one word about our dinner at the Pooles yesterday."

"Did you go then? I have made no enquiries, because I concluded you
must have been obliged to give up the party."

"Oh! yes, I went. I was very well yesterday; nothing at all the matter
with me till this morning. It would have been strange if I had not gone."

"I am very glad you were well enough, and I hope you had a pleasant
party."

"Nothing remarkable. One always knows beforehand what the dinner
will be, and who will be there. And it is so very uncomfortable, not having a
carriage of one's own. Mr. and Mrs. Musgrove took me, and we were so
crowded! They are both so very large, and take up so much room! And Mr.
Musgrove always sits forward. So, there was I, crowded into the back seat
with Henrietta and Louisa. And I think it very likely that my illness to-day
may be owing to it."

A little farther perseverance in patience, and forced cheerfulness on
Anne's side, produced nearly a cure on Mary's. She could soon sit upright
on the sofa, and began to hope she might be able to leave it by dinner-time.
Then, forgetting to think of it, she was at the other end of the room,
beautifying a nosegay; then, she ate her cold meat; and then she was well
enough to propose a little walk.

"Where shall we go?" said she, when they were ready. "I suppose you
will not like to call at the Great House before they have been to see you?"

"I have not the smallest objection on that account," replied Anne. "I
should never think of standing on such ceremony with people I know so
well as Mrs. and the Miss Musgroves."

"Oh! but they ought to call upon you as soon as possible. They ought to
feel what is due to you as *my* sister. However, we may as well go and sit with
them a little while, and when we have got that over, we can enjoy our walk."

Anne had always thought such a style of intercourse highly imprudent;
but she had ceased to endeavour to check it, from believing that, though
there were on each side continual subjects of offence, neither family could
now do without it. To the Great House accordingly they went, to sit the full
half hour in the old-fashioned square parlour, with a small carpet and

shining floor, to which the present daughters of the house were gradually giving the proper air of confusion by a grand piano forte and a harp, flower-stands and little tables placed in every direction. Oh! could the originals of the portraits against the wainscot, could the gentlemen in brown velvet and the ladies in blue satin have seen what was going on, have been conscious of such an overthrow of all order and neatness! The portraits themselves seemed to be staring in astonishment.

The Musgroves, like their houses, were in a state of alteration, perhaps of improvement. The father and mother were in the old English style, and the young people in the new. Mr. and Mrs. Musgrove, were a very good sort of people; friendly and hospitable, not much educated, and not at all elegant. Their children had more modern minds and manners. There was a numerous family; but the only two grown up, excepting Charles, were Henrietta and Louisa, young ladies of nineteen and twenty, who had brought from a school at Exeter[33] all the usual stock of accomplishments, and were now, like thousands of other young ladies, living to be fashionable, happy, and merry. Their dress had every advantage, their faces were rather pretty, their spirits extremely good, their manners unembarrassed and pleasant; they were of consequence at home, and favourites abroad. Anne always contemplated them as some of the happiest creatures of her acquaintance; but still, saved as we all are by some comfortable feeling of superiority from wishing for the possibility of exchange, she would not have given up her own more elegant and cultivated mind for all their enjoyments; and envied them nothing but that seemingly perfect good understanding and agreement together, that good-humoured mutual affection, of which she had known so little herself with either of her sisters.

They were received with great cordiality. Nothing seemed amiss on the side of the Great House family, which was generally, as Anne very well knew, the least to blame. The half hour was chatted away pleasantly enough; and she was not at all surprised, at the end of it, to have their walking party joined by both the Miss Musgroves, at Mary's particular invitation.

CHAPTER 6

Anne had not wanted this visit to Uppercross, to learn that a removal from one set of people to another, though at a distance of only three miles, will often include a total change of conversation, opinion, and idea. She had never been staying there before, without being struck by it, or without wishing that other Elliots could have her advantage in seeing how unknown, or unconsidered there, were the affairs which at Kellynch-hall were treated as of such general publicity and pervading interest; yet, with all this experience, she believed she must now submit to feel that another lesson, in the art of knowing our own nothingness beyond our own circle, was become necessary for her;—for certainly, coming as she did, with a heart full of the subject which had been completely occupying both houses in Kellynch for many weeks, she had expected rather more curiosity and sympa-

[33] A good-sized town in Devonshire, in southwest England.

thy than she found in the separate, but very similar remark of Mr. and Mrs. Musgrove—"So, Miss Anne, Sir Walter and your sister are gone; and what part of Bath do you think they will settle in?" and this, without much waiting for an answer;—or in the young ladies' addition of, "I hope *we* shall be in Bath in the winter; but remember, papa, if we do go, we must be in a good situation[34]—none of your Queen-squares for us!" or in the anxious supplement from Mary, of "Upon my word, I shall be pretty well off, when you are all gone away to be happy at Bath!"

She could only resolve to avoid such self-delusion in future, and think with heightened gratitude of the extraordinary blessing of having one such truly sympathising friend as Lady Russell.

The Mr. Musgroves had their own game to guard, and to destroy; their own horses, dogs, and newspapers to engage them; and the females were fully occupied in all the other common subjects of house-keeping, neighbours, dress, dancing, and music. She acknowledged it to be very fitting, that every little social commonwealth should dictate its own matters of discourse; and hoped, ere long, to become a not unworthy member of the one she was now transplanted into.—With the prospect of spending at least two months at Uppercross, it was highly incumbent on her to clothe her imagination, her memory, and all her ideas in as much of Uppercross as possible.

She had no dread of these two months. Mary was not so repulsive[35] and unsisterly as Elizabeth, nor so inaccessible to all influence of hers; neither was there any thing among the other component parts of the cottage inimical to comfort.—She was always on friendly terms with her brother-in-law; and in the children, who loved her nearly as well, and respected her a great deal more than their mother, she had an object of interest, amusement, and wholesome exertion.

Charles Musgrove was civil and agreeable; in sense and temper he was undoubtedly superior to his wife; but not of powers, or conversation, or grace, to make the past, as they were connected together, at all a dangerous contemplation; though, at the same time, Anne could believe, with Lady Russell, that a more equal match might have greatly improved him; and that a woman of real understanding might have given more consequence to his character, and more usefulness, rationality, and elegance to his habits and pursuits. As it was, he did nothing with much zeal, but sport; and his time was otherwise trifled away, without benefit from books, or any thing else. He had very good spirits, which never seemed much affected by his wife's occasional lowness; bore with her unreasonableness sometimes to Anne's admiration; and, upon the whole, though there was very often a little disagreement, (in which she had sometimes more share than she wished, being appealed to by both parties) they might pass for a happy couple. They were always perfectly agreed in the want of more money, and a strong inclination for a handsome present from his father; but here, as on most topics, he had the superiority, for while Mary thought it a great shame that such a present was not made, he always contended for his father's having many other uses for his money, and a right to spend it as he liked.

[34] Location. [35] Cold; forbidding.

As to the management of their children, his theory was much better than his wife's, and his practice not so bad.—"I could manage them very well, if it were not for Mary's interference,"—was what Anne often heard him say, and had a good deal of faith in; but when listening in turn to Mary's reproach of "Charles spoils the children so that I cannot get them into any order,"—she never had the smallest temptation to say, "Very true."

One of the least agreeable circumstances of her residence there, was her being treated with too much confidence by all parties, and being too much in the secret of the complaints of each house. Known to have some influence with her sister, she was continually requested, or at least receiving hints to exert it, beyond what was practicable. "I wish you could persuade Mary not to be always fancying herself ill," was Charles's language; and, in an unhappy mood, thus spoke Mary;—"I do believe if Charles were to see me dying, he would not think there was any thing the matter with me. I am sure, Anne, if you would, you might persuade him that I really am very ill—a great deal worse than I ever own."

Mary's declaration was, "I hate sending the children to the Great House, though their grandmamma is always wanting to see them, for she humours and indulges them to such a degree, and gives them so much trash and sweet things, that they are sure to come back sick and cross for the rest of the day."—And Mrs. Musgrove took the first opportunity of being alone with Anne, to say, "Oh! Miss Anne, I cannot help wishing Mrs. Charles had a little of your method with those children. They are quite different creatures with you! But to be sure, in general they are so spoilt! It is a pity you cannot put your sister in the way of managing them. They are as fine healthy children as ever were seen, poor little dears, without partiality; but Mrs. Charles knows no more how they should be treated!—Bless me, how troublesome they are sometimes!—I assure you, Miss Anne, it prevents my wishing to see them at our house so often as I otherwise should. I believe Mrs. Charles is not quite pleased with my not inviting them oftener; but you know it is very bad to have children with one, that one is obliged to be checking every moment; 'don't do this, and don't do that;'—or that one can only keep in tolerable order by more cake than is good for them."

She had this communication, moreover, from Mary. "Mrs. Musgrove thinks all her servants so steady, that it would be high treason to call it in question; but I am sure, without exaggeration, that her upper house-maid and laundry-maid, instead of being in their business, are gadding about the village, all day long. I meet them wherever I go; and I declare, I never go twice into my nursery without seeing something of them. If Jemima were not the trustiest, steadiest creature in the world, it would be enough to spoil her; for she tells me, they are always tempting her to take a walk with them." And on Mrs. Musgrove's side, it was—"I make a rule of never interfering in any of my daughter-in-law's concerns, for I know it would not do; but I shall tell *you*, Miss Anne, because you may be able to set things to rights, that I have no very good opinion of Mrs. Charles's nursery-maid; I hear strange stories of her; she is always upon the gad: and from my own knowledge, I can declare, she is such a fine-dressing lady, that she is

enough to ruin any servants she comes near. Mrs. Charles quite swears by her, I know; but I just give you this hint, that you may be upon the watch; because, if you see any thing amiss, you need not be afraid of mentioning it."

Again; it was Mary's complaint, that Mrs. Musgrove was very apt not to give her the precedence that was her due, when they dined at the Great House with other families; and she did not see any reason why she was to be considered so much at home as to lose her place. And one day, when Anne was walking with only the Miss Musgroves, one of them, after talking of rank, people of rank, and jealousy of rank, said, "I have no scruple of observing to *you,* how nonsensical some persons are about their place, because, all the world knows how easy and indifferent you are about it: but I wish any body could give Mary a hint that it would be a great deal better if she were not so very tenacious; especially, if she would not be always putting herself forward to take place of mamma. Nobody doubts her right to have precedence of mamma, but it would be more becoming in her not to be always insisting on it. It is not that mamma cares about it the least in the world, but I know it is taken notice of by many persons."

How was Anne to set all these matters to rights? She could do little more than listen patiently, soften every grievance, and excuse each to the other; give them all hints of the forbearance necessary between such near neighbours, and make those hints broadeast which were meant for her sister's benefit.

In all other respects, her visit began and proceeded very well. Her own spirits improved by change of place and subject, by being removed three miles from Kellynch; Mary's ailments, lessened by having a constant companion; and their daily intercourse with the other family, since there was neither superior affection, confidence, nor employment in the cottage, to be interrupted by it, was rather an advantage. It was certainly carried nearly as far as possible, for they met every morning, and hardly ever spent an evening asunder; but she believed they should not have done so well without the sight of Mr. and Mrs. Musgrove's respectable forms in the usual places, or without the talking, laughing, and singing of their daughters.

She played a great deal better than either of the Miss Musgroves; but having no voice, no knowledge of the harp, and no fond parents to sit by and fancy themselves delighted, her performance was little thought of, only out of civility, or to refresh the others, as she was well aware. She knew that when she played she was giving pleasure only to herself; but this was no new sensation: excepting one short period of her life, she had never, since the age of fourteen, never since the loss of her dear mother, known the happiness of being listened to, or encouraged by any just appreciation or real taste. In music she had been always used to feel alone in the world; and Mr. and Mrs. Musgrove's fond partiality for their own daughters' performance, and total indifference to any other person's, gave her much more pleasure for their sakes, than mortification for her own.

The party at the Great House was sometimes increased by other company. The neighbourhood was not large, but the Musgroves were visited by

every body, and had more dinner parties, and more callers, more visitors by invitation and by chance, than any other family. They were more completely popular.

The girls were wild for dancing; and the evenings ended, occasionally, in an unpremeditated little ball. There was a family of cousins within a walk of Uppercross, in less affluent circumstances, who depended on the Musgroves for all their pleasures: they would come at any time, and help play at any thing, or dance any where; and Anne, very much preferring the office of musician to a more active post, played country dances to them by the hour together; a kindness which always recommended her musical powers to the notice of Mr. and Mrs. Musgrove more than any thing else, and often drew this compliment; —"Well done, Miss Anne! very well done indeed! Lord bless me! how those little fingers of yours fly about!"

So passed the first three weeks. Michaelmas came; and now Anne's heart must be in Kellynch again. A beloved home made over to others; all the precious rooms and furniture, groves, and prospects, beginning to own other eyes and other limbs! She could not think of much else on the 29th of September; and she had this sympathetic touch in the evening, from Mary, who, on having occasion to note down the day of the month, exclaimed, "Dear me! is not this the day the Crofts were to come to Kellynch? I am glad I did not think of it before. How low it makes me!"

The Crofts took possession with true naval alertness, and were to be visited. Mary deplored the necessity for herself. "Nobody knew how much she should suffer. She should put it off as long as she could." But was not easy till she had talked Charles into driving her over on an early day; and was in a very animated, comfortable state of imaginary agitation, when she came back. Anne had very sincerely rejoiced in there being no means of her going. She wished, however, to see the Crofts, and was glad to be within when the visit was returned. They came; the master of the house was not at home, but the two sisters were together; and as it chanced that Mrs. Croft fell to the share of Anne, while the admiral sat by Mary, and made himself very agreeable by his good-humoured notice of her little boys, she was well able to watch for a likeness, and if it failed her in the features, to catch it in the voice, or in the turn of sentiment and expression.

Mrs. Croft, though neither tall nor fat, had a squareness, uprightness, and vigour of form, which gave importance to her person. She had bright dark eyes, good teeth, and altogether an agreeable face; though her reddened and weather-beaten complexion, the consequence of her having been almost as much at sea as her husband, made her seem to have lived some years longer in the world than her real eight and thirty. Her manners were open, easy, and decided, like one who had no distrust of herself, and no doubts of what to do; without any approach to coarseness, however, or any want of good humour. Anne gave her credit, indeed, for feelings of great consideration towards herself, in all that related to Kellynch; and it pleased her: especially, as she had satisfied herself in the very first half minute, in the instant even of introduction, that there was not the smallest symptom of any knowledge or suspicion on Mrs. Croft's side, to give a bias of any sort. She was quite easy on that head, and consequently full of

strength and courage, till for a moment electrified by Mrs. Croft's suddenly saying,—

"It was you, and not your sister, I find, that my brother had the pleasure of being acquainted with, when he was in this country."

Anne hoped she had outlived the age of blushing; but the age of emotion she certainly had not.

"Perhaps you may not have heard that he is married," added Mrs. Croft.

She could now answer as she ought; and was happy to feel, when Mrs. Croft's next words explained it to be Mr. Wentworth of whom she spoke, that she had said nothing which might not do for either brother. She immediately felt how reasonable it was, that Mrs. Croft should be thinking and speaking of Edward, and not of Frederick; and with shame at her own forgetfulness, applied herself to the knowledge of their former neighbour's present state, with proper interest.

The rest was all tranquillity; till just as they were moving, she heard the admiral say to Mary,

"We are expecting a brother of Mrs. Croft's here soon; I dare say you know him by name."

He was cut short by the eager attacks of the little boys, clinging to him like an old friend, and declaring he should not go; and being too much engrossed by proposals of carrying them away in his coat pocket, &c. to have another moment for finishing or recollecting what he had begun, Anne was left to persuade herself, as well as she could, that the same brother must still be in question. She could not, however, reach such a degree of certainty, as not to be anxious to hear whether any thing had been said on the subject at the other house, where the Crofts had previously been calling.

The folks of Great House were to spend the evening of this day at the Cottage; and it being now too late in the year for such visits to be made on foot, the coach was beginning to be listened for, when the youngest Miss Musgrove walked in. That she was coming to apologize, and that they should have to spend the evening by themselves, was the first black idea; and Mary was quite ready to be affronted, when Louisa made all right by saying, that she only came on foot, to leave more room for the harp, which was bringing in the carriage.

"And I will tell you our reason," she added, "and all about it. I am come on to give you notice, that papa and mamma are out of spirits this evening, especially mamma; she is thinking so much of poor Richard! And we agreed it would be best to have the harp, for it seems to amuse her more than the piano-forte. I will tell you why she is out of spirits. When the Crofts called this morning, (they called here afterwards, did not they?) they happened to say, that her brother, Captain Wentworth, is just returned to England, or paid off, or something, and is coming to see them almost directly; and most unluckily it came into mamma's head, when they were gone, that Wentworth, or something very like it, was the name of poor Richard's captain, at one time, I do not know when or where, but a great while before he died, poor fellow! And upon looking over his letters and things, she found it was so; and is perfectly sure that this must be the very

man, and her head is quite full of it, and of poor Richard! So we must all be as merry as we can, that she may not be dwelling upon such gloomy things."

The real circumstances of this pathetic piece of family history were, that the Musgroves had had the ill fortune of a very troublesome, hopeless son; and the good fortune to lose him before he reached his twentieth year; that he had been sent to sea, because he was stupid and unmanageable on shore; that he had been very little cared for at any time by his family, though quite as much as he deserved; seldom heard of, and scarcely at all regretted, when the intelligence of his death abroad had worked its way to Uppercross, two years before.

He had, in fact, though his sisters were now doing all they could for him, by calling him "poor Richard," been nothing better than a thick-headed, unfeeling, unprofitable Dick Musgrove, who had never done any thing to entitle himself to more than the abbreviation of his name, living or dead.

He had been several years at sea, and had, in the course of those removals to which all midshipmen are liable, and especially such midshipmen as every captain wishes to get rid of, been six months on board Captain Frederick Wentworth's frigate, the Laconia; and from the Laconia he had, under the influence of his captain, written the only two letters which his father and mother had ever received from him during the whole of his absence; that is to say, the only two disinterested[36] letters; all the rest had been mere applications for money.

In each letter he had spoken well of his captain; but yet, so little were they in the habit of attending to such matters, so unobservant and incurious were they as to the names of men or ships, that it had made scarcely any impression at the time; and that Mrs. Musgrove should have been suddenly struck, this very day, with a recollection of the name of Wentworth, as connected with her son, seemed one of those extraordinary bursts of mind which do sometimes occur.

She had gone to her letters, and found it all as she supposed; and the reperusal of these letters, after so long an interval, her poor son gone for ever, and all the strength of his faults forgotten, had affected her spirits exceedingly, and thrown her into greater grief for him than she had known on first hearing of his death. Mr. Musgrove was, in a lesser degree, affected likewise; and when they reached the cottage, they were evidently in want, first, of being listened to anew on this subject, and afterwards, of all the relief which cheerful companions could give.

To hear them talking so much of Captain Wentworth, repeating his name so often, puzzling over past years, and at last ascertaining that it *might*, that it probably *would*, turn out to be the very same Captain Wentworth whom they recollected meeting, once or twice, after their coming back from Clifton;[37]—a very fine young man; but they could not say whether it was seven or eight years ago,—was a new sort of trial to Anne's nerves. She found, however, that it was one to which she must enure herself. Since he actually was expected in the country, she must teach herself to be insensible on such points. And not only did it appear that he was ex-

[36] Without a selfish motive. [37] A resort spa in southwest England.

pected, and speedily, but the Musgroves, in their warm gratitude for the kindness he had shewn poor Dick, and very high respect for his character, stamped as it was by poor Dick's having been six months under his care, and mentioning him in strong, though not perfectly well spelt praise, as "a fine dashing felow, only two perticular about the school-master,"[38] were bent on introducing themselves, and seeking his acquaintance, as soon as they could hear of his arrival.

The resolution of doing so helped to form the comfort of their evening.

CHAPTER 7

A very few days more, and Captain Wentworth was known to be at Kellynch, and Mr. Musgrove had called on him, and come back warm in his praise, and he was engaged with the Crofts to dine at Uppercross, by the end of another week. It had been a great disappointment to Mr. Musgrove, to find that no earlier day could be fixed, so impatient was he to shew his gratitude, by seeing Captain Wentworth under his own roof, and welcoming him to all that was strongest and best in his cellars. But a week must pass; only a week, in Anne's reckoning, and then, she supposed, they must meet; and soon she began to wish that she could feel secure even for a week.

Captain Wentworth made a very early return to Mr. Musgrove's civility, and she was all but calling there in the same half hour!—She and Mary were actually setting forward for the great house, where, as she afterwards learnt, they must inevitably have found him, when they were stopped by the eldest boy's being at that moment brought home in consequence of a bad fall. The child's situation put the visit entirely aside, but she could not hear of her escape with indifference, even in the midst of the serious anxiety which they afterwards felt on his account.

His collar-bone was found to be dislocated, and such injury received in the back, as roused the most alarming ideas. It was an afternoon of distress, and Anne had every thing to do at once—the apothecary[39] to send for—the father to have pursued and informed—the mother to support and keep from hysterics—the servants to control—the youngest child to banish, and the poor suffering one to attend and soothe;—besides sending, as soon as she recollected it, proper notice to the other house, which brought her an accession rather of frightened, enquiring companions, than of very useful assistants.

Her brother's return was the first comfort; he could take best care of his wife, and the second blessing was the arrival of the apothecary. Till he came and had examined the child, their apprehensions were the worse for being vague;—they suspected great injury, but knew not where; but now the collar-bone was soon replaced, and though Mr. Robinson felt and felt, and rubbed, and looked grave, and spoke low words both to the father and

[38]Too strict in making the ship's schoolmaster perform his duties. Midshipmen (apprentice officers), such as Dick Musgrove, were often teenagers still getting their education.

[39]Apothecaries were persons who prepared and sold medicines; they also served as general medical practitioners.

the aunt, still they were all to hope the best, and to be able to part and eat their dinner in tolerable ease of mind; and then it was, just before they parted, that the two young aunts were able so far to digress from their nephew's state, as to give the information of Captain Wentworth's visit;—staying five minutes behind their father and mother, to endeavour to express how perfectly delighted they were with him, how much handsomer, how infinitely more agreeable they thought him than any individual among their male acquaintance, who had been at all a favourite before—how glad they had been to hear papa invite him to stay dinner—how sorry when he said it was quite out of his power—and how glad again, when he had promised in reply to papa and mamma's farther pressing invitations, to come and dine with them on the morrow, actually on the morrow!—And he had promised it in so pleasant a manner, as if he felt all the motive of their attention just as he ought!—And, in short, he had looked and said every thing with such exquisite grace, that they could assure them all, their heads were both turned by him!—And off they ran, quite as full of glee as of love, and apparently more full of Captain Wentworth than of little Charles.

The same story and the same raptures were repeated, when the two girls came with their father, through the gloom of the evening, to make enquiries; and Mr. Musgrove, no longer under the first uneasiness about his heir, could add his confirmation and praise, and hope there would be now no occasion for putting Captain Wentworth off, and only be sorry to think that the cottage party, probably, would not like to leave the little boy, to give him the meeting.—"Oh, no! as to leaving the little boy!"—both father and mother were in much too strong and recent alarm to bear the thought; and Anne, in the joy of the escape, could not help adding her warm protestations to theirs.

Charles Musgrove, indeed, afterwards shewed more of inclination; "the child was going on so well—and he wished so much to be introduced to Captain Wentworth, that, perhaps, he might join them in the evening; he would not dine from home, but he might walk in for half an hour." But in this he was eagerly opposed by his wife, with "Oh, no! indeed, Charles, I cannot bear to have you go away. Only think, if any thing should happen!"

The child had a good night, and was going on well the next day. It must be a work of time to ascertain that no injury had been done to the spine, but Mr. Robinson found nothing to increase alarm, and Charles Musgrove began consequently to feel no necessity for longer confinement. The child was to be kept in bed, and amused as quietly as possible; but what was there for a father to do? This was quite a female case, and it would be highly absurd in him, who could be of no use at home, to shut himself up. His father very much wished him to meet Captain Wentworth, and there being no sufficient reason against it, he ought to go; and it ended in his making a bold public declaration, when he came in from shooting, of his meaning to dress directly, and dine at the other house.

"Nothing can be going on better than the child," said he, "so I told my father just now that I would come, and he thought me quite right. Your sister being with you, my love, I have no scruple at all. You would not like to leave him yourself, but you see I can be of no use. Anne will send for me if any thing is the matter."

Husbands and wives generally understand when opposition will be vain.

Mary knew, from Charles's manner of speaking, that he was quite deter-
mined on going, and that it would be of no use to teaze him.[40] She said
nothing, therefore, till he was out of the room, but as soon as there was only
Anne to hear,

"So! You and I are to be left to shift by ourselves, with this poor sick
child—and not a creature coming near us all the evening! I knew how it
would be. This is always my luck! If there is any thing disagreeable going
on, men are always sure to get out of it, and Charles is as bad as any of
them. Very unfeeling! I must say it is very unfeeling of him, to be running
away from his poor little boy; talks of his being going on so well! How does
he know that he is going on well, or that there may not be a sudden change
half an hour hence? I did not think Charles would have been so unfeeling.
So, here he is to go away and enjoy himself, and because I am the poor
mother, I am not to be allowed to stir;—and yet, I am sure, I am more unfit
than any body else to be about the child. My being the mother is the very
reason why my feelings should not be tried. I am not at all equal to it. You
saw how hysterical I was yesterday."

"But that was only the effect of the suddenness of your alarm—of the
shock. You will not be hysterical again. I dare say we shall have nothing to
distress us. I perfectly understand Mr. Robinson's directions, and have no
fears; and indeed, Mary, I cannot wonder at your husband. Nursing does
not belong to a man, it is not his province. A sick child is always the moth-
er's property, her own feelings generally make it so."

"I hope I am as fond of my child as any mother—but I do not know that
I am of any more use in the sick-room than Charles, for I cannot be always
scolding and teazing a poor child when it is ill; and you saw, this morning,
that if I told him to keep quiet, he was sure to begin kicking about. I have
not nerves for the sort of thing."

"But, could you be comfortable yourself, to be spending the whole eve-
ning away from the poor boy?"

"Yes; you see his papa can, and why should not I?—Jemima is so care-
ful! And she could send us word every hour how he was. I really think
Charles might as well have told his father we would all come. I am not more
alarmed about little Charles now than he is. I was dreadfully alarmed yes-
terday, but the case is very different to-day."

"Well—if you do not think it too late to give notice for yourself, suppose
you were to go, as well as your husband. Leave little Charles to my care. Mr.
and Mrs. Musgrove cannot think it wrong, while I remain with him."

"Are you serious?" cried Mary, her eyes brightening. "Dear me! that's a
very good thought, very good indeed. To be sure I may just as well go as
not, for I am of no use at home—am I? and it only harasses me. You, who
have not a mother's feelings, are a great deal the properest person. You can
make little Charles do any thing; he always minds you at a word. It will be
a great deal better than leaving him with only Jemima. Oh! I will certainly
go; I am sure I ought if I can, quite as much as Charles, for they want me
excessively to be acquainted with Captain Wentworth, and I know you do
not mind being left alone. An excellent thought of yours, indeed, Anne! I
will go and tell Charles, and get ready directly. You can send for us, you

[40] Provoke him by opposition.

know, at a moment's notice, if any thing is the matter; but I dare say there will be nothing to alarm you. I should not go, you may be sure, if I did not feel quite at ease about my dear child."

The next moment she was tapping at her husband's dressing-room door, and as Anne followed her up stairs, she was in time for the whole conversation, which began with Mary's saying, in a tone of great exultation,

"I mean to go with you, Charles, for I am of no more use at home than you are. If I were to shut myself up for ever with the child, I should not be able to persuade him to do any thing he did not like. Anne will stay; Anne undertakes to stay at home and take care of him. It is Anne's own proposal, and so I shall go with you, which will be a great deal better, for I have not dined at the other house since Tuesday."

"This is very kind of Anne," was her husband's answer, "and I should be very glad to have you go; but it seems rather hard that she should be left at home by herself, to nurse our sick child."

Anne was now at hand to take up her own cause, and the sincerity of her manner being soon sufficient to convince him, where conviction was at least very agreeable, he had no farther scruples as to her being left to dine alone, though he still wanted her to join them in the evening, when the child might be at rest for the night, and kindly urged her to let him come and fetch her; but she was quite unpersuadable; and this being the case, she had ere long the pleasure of seeing them set off together in high spirits. They were gone, she hoped, to be happy, however oddly constructed such happiness might seem; as for herself, she was left with as many sensations of comfort, as were, perhaps, ever likely to be hers. She knew herself to be of the first utility to the child; and what was it to her, if Frederick Wentworth were only half a mile distant, making himself agreeable to others!

She would have liked to know how he felt as to a meeting. Perhaps indifferent, if indifference could exist under such circumstances. He must be either indifferent or unwilling. Had he wished ever to see her again, he need not have waited till this time; he would have done what she could not but believe that in his place she should have done long ago, when events had been early giving him the independence which alone had been wanting.

Her brother and sister came back delighted with their new acquaintance, and their visit in general. There had been music, singing, talking, laughing, all that was most agreeable; charming manners in Captain Wentworth, no shyness or reserve; they seemed all to know each other perfectly, and he was coming the very next morning to shoot with Charles. He was to come to breakfast, but not at the Cottage, though that had been proposed at first; but then he had been pressed to come to the Great House instead, and he seemed afraid of being in Mrs. Charles Musgrove's way, on account of the child; and therefore, somehow, they hardly knew how, it ended in Charles's being to meet him to breakfast at his father's.

Anne understood it. He wished to avoid seeing her. He had enquired after her, she found, slightly, as might suit a former slight acquaintance, seeming to acknowledge such as she had acknowledged, actuated, perhaps, by the same view of escaping introduction when they were to meet.

The morning hours of the Cottage were always later than those of the other house; and on the morrow the difference was so great, that Mary and

Anne were not more than beginning breakfast when Charles came in to say
that they were just setting off, that he was come for his dogs, that his sisters
were following with Captain Wentworth, his sisters meaning to visit Mary
and the child, and Captain Wentworth proposing also to wait on her for a
few minutes, if not inconvenient; and though Charles had answered for the
child's being in no such state as could make it inconvenient, Captain Went-
worth would not be satisfied without his running on to give notice.

Mary, very much gratified by this attention, was delighted to receive
him; while a thousand feelings rushed on Anne, of which this was the most
consoling, that it would soon be over. And it was soon over. In two minutes
after Charles's preparation, the others appeared; they were in the drawing-
room. Her eye half met Captain Wentworth's; a bow, a curtsey passed; she
heard his voice—he talked to Mary, said all that was right; said something
to the Miss Musgroves, enough to mark an easy footing: the room seemed
full—full of persons and voices—but a few minutes ended it. Charles
shewed himself at the window, all was ready, their visitor had bowed and
was gone; the Miss Musgroves were gone too, suddenly resolving to walk to
the end of the village with the sportsmen: the room was cleared, and Anne
might finish her breakfast as she could.

"It is over! it is over!" she repeated to herself again, and again, in ner-
vous gratitude. "The worst is over!"

Mary talked, but she could not attend. She had seen him. They had met.
They had been once more in the same room!

Soon, however, she began to reason with herself, and try to be feeling
less. Eight years, almost eight years had passed, since all had been given up.
How absurd to be resuming the agitation which such an interval had ban-
ished into distance and indistinctness! What might not eight years do?
Events of every description, changes, alienations, removals,—all, all must
be comprised in it; and oblivion of the past—how natural, how certain too!
It included nearly a third part of her own life.

Alas! with all her reasonings, she found, that to retentive feelings eight
years may be little more than nothing.

Now, how were his sentiments to be read? Was this like wishing to avoid
her? And the next moment she was hating herself for the folly which asked
the question.

On one other question, which perhaps her utmost wisdom might not
have prevented, she was soon spared all suspense; for after the Miss
Musgroves had returned and finished their visit at the Cottage, she had this
spontaneous information from Mary:

"Captain Wentworth is not very gallant by you, Anne, though he was so
attentive to me. Henrietta asked him what he thought of you, when they
went away; and he said, You were so altered he should not have known you
again."

Mary had no feelings to make her respect her sister's in a common
way; but she was perfectly unsuspicious of inflicting any peculiar wound.

"Altered beyond his knowledge!" Anne fully submitted, in silent, deep
mortification. Doubtless it was so; and she could take no revenge, for he
was not altered, or not for the worse. She had already acknowledged it to
herself, and she could not think differently, let him think of her as he
would. No; the years which had destroyed her youth and bloom had only

given him a more glowing, manly, open look, in no respect lessening his personal advantages. She had seen the same Frederick Wentworth.

"So altered that he should not have known her again!" These were words which could not but dwell with her. Yet she soon began to rejoice that she had heard them. They were of sobering tendency; they allayed agitation; they composed, and consequently must make her happier.

Frederick Wentworth had used such words, or something like them, but without an idea that they would be carried round to her. He had thought her wretchedly altered, and, in the first moment of appeal, had spoken as he felt. He had not forgiven Anne Elliot. She had used him ill; deserted and disappointed him; and worse, she had shewn a feebleness of character in doing so, which his own decided, confident temper could not endure. She had given him up to oblige others. It had been the effect of over-persuasion. It had been weakness and timidity.

He had been most warmly attached to her, and had never seen a woman since whom he thought her equal; but, except from some natural sensation of curiosity, he had no desire of meeting her again. Her power with him was gone for ever.

It was now his object to marry. He was rich, and being turned on shore, fully intended to settle as soon as he could be properly tempted; actually looking round, ready to fall in love with all the speed which a clear head and quick taste could allow. He had a heart for either of the Miss Musgroves, if they could catch it; a heart, in short, for any pleasing young woman who came in his way, excepting Anne Elliot. This was his only secret exception, when he said to his sister, in answer to her suppositions,

"Yes, here I am, Sophia, quite ready to make a foolish match. Any body between fifteen and thirty may have me for asking. A little beauty, and a few smiles, and a few compliments to the navy, and I am a lost man. Should not this be enough for a sailor, who has had no society among women to make him nice?"[41]

He said it, she knew, to be contradicted. His bright, proud eye spoke the happy conviction that he was nice; and Anne Elliot was not out of his thoughts, when he more seriously described the woman he should wish to meet with. "A strong mind, with sweetness of manner," made the first and the last of the description.

"This is the woman I want, said he. Something a little inferior I shall of course put up with, but it must not be much. If I am a fool, I shall be a fool indeed, for I have thought on the subject more than most men."

CHAPTER 8

From this time Captain Wentworth and Anne Elliot were repeatedly in the same circle. They were soon dining in company together at Mr. Musgrove's, for the little boy's state could no longer supply his aunt with a pretence for absenting herself; and this was but the beginning of other dinings and other meetings.

[41] Choosy; hard to please.

Whether former feelings were to be renewed, must be brought to the proof; former times must undoubtedly be brought to the recollection of each; *they* could not but be reverted to; the year of their engagement could not but be named by him, in the little narratives or descriptions which conversation called forth. His profession qualified him, his disposition led him, to talk; and "*That* was in the year six;" "*That* happened before I went to sea in the year six," occurred in the course of the first evening they spent together: and though his voice did not falter, and though she had no reason to suppose his eye wandering towards her while he spoke, Anne felt the utter impossibility, from her knowledge of his mind, that he could be unvisited by remembrance any more than herself. There must be the same immediate association of thought, though she was very far from conceiving it to be of equal pain.

They had no conversation together, no intercourse but what the commonest civility required. Once so much to each other! Now nothing! There *had* been a time, when of all the large party now filling the drawing-room at Uppercross, they would have found it most difficult to cease to speak to one another. With the exception, perhaps, of Admiral and Mrs. Croft, who seemed particularly attached and happy, (Anne could allow no other exception even among the married couples) there could have been no two hearts so open, no tastes so similar, no feelings so in unison, no countenances so beloved. Now they were as strangers; nay, worse than strangers, for they could never become acquainted. It was a perpetual estrangement.

When he talked, she heard the same voice, and discerned the same mind. There was a very general ignorance of all naval matters throughout the party; and he was very much questioned, and especially by the two Miss Musgroves, who seemed hardly to have any eyes but for him, as to the manner of living on board, daily regulations, food, hours, &c.; and their surprise at his accounts, at learning the degree of accommodation and arrangement which was practicable, drew from him some pleasant ridicule, which reminded Anne of the early days when she too had been ignorant, and she too had been accused of supposing sailors to be living on board without any thing to eat, or any cook to dress it if there were, or any servant to wait, or any knife and fork to use.

From thus listening and thinking, she was roused by a whisper of Mrs. Musgrove's, who, overcome by fond regrets, could not help saying,

"Ah! Miss Anne, if it had pleased Heaven to spare my poor son, I dare say he would have been just such another by this time."

Anne suppressed a smile, and listened kindly, while Mrs. Musgrove relieved her heart a little more; and for a few minutes, therefore, could not keep pace with the conversation of the others.—When she could let her attention take its natural course again, she found the Miss Musgroves just fetching the navy-list,—(their own navy list, the first that had ever been at Uppercross); and sitting down together to pore over it, with the professed view of finding out the ships which Captain Wentworth had commanded.

"Your first was the Asp, I remember; we will look for the Asp."

"You will not find her there.—Quite worn out and broken up. I was the last man who commanded her.—Hardly fit for service then.—Reported fit for home service for a year or two,—and so I was sent off to the West Indies."

The girls looked all amazement.

"The admiralty," he continued, "entertain themselves now and then, with sending a few hundred men to sea, in a ship not fit to be employed. But they have a great many to provide for; and among the thousands that may just as well go to the bottom as not, it is impossible for them to distinguish the very set who may be least missed."

"Phoo! phoo!" cried the admiral, "what stuff these young fellows talk! Never was a better sloop[42] than the Asp in her day.—For an old built sloop, you would not see her equal. Lucky fellow to get her!—He knows there must have been twenty better men than himself applying for her at the same time. Lucky fellow to get any thing so soon, with no more interest[43] than his."

"I felt my luck, admiral, I assure you;" replied Captain Wentworth, seriously.—"I was as well satisfied with my appointment as you can desire. It was a great object with me, at that time, to be at sea,—a very great object. I wanted to be doing something."

"To be sure you did.—What should a young fellow, like you, do ashore, for half a year together?—If a man has not a wife, he soon wants to be afloat again."

"But, Captain Wentworth," cried Louisa, "how vexed you must have been when you came to the Asp, to see what an old thing they had given you."

"I knew pretty well what she was, before that day;" said he, smiling. "I had no more discoveries to make, than you would have as to the fashion and strength of any old pelisse,[44] which you had seen lent about among half your acquaintance, ever since you could remember, and which at last, on some very wet day, is lent to yourself.—Ah! she was a dear old Asp to me. She did all that I wanted. I knew she would.—I knew that we should either go to the bottom together, or that she would be the making of me; and I never had two days of foul weather all the time I was at sea in her; and after taking privateers[45] enough to be very entertaining, I had the good luck, in my passage home the next autumn, to fall in with the very French frigate[46] I wanted.—I brought her into Plymouth;[47] and here was another instance of luck. We had not been six hours in the Sound, when a gale came on, which lasted four days and nights, and which would have done for poor old Asp, in half the time; our touch with the Great Nation not having much improved our condition. Four-and-twenty hours later, and I should only have been a gallant Captain Wentworth, in a small paragraph at one corner of the newspapers; and being lost in only a sloop, nobody would have thought about me."

Anne's shudderings were to herself, alone: but the Miss Musgroves could be as open as they were sincere, in their exclamations of pity and horror.

"And so then, I suppose," said Mrs. Musgrove, in a low voice, as if thinking aloud, "so then he went away to the Laconia, and there he met with our poor boy.—Charles, my dear," (beckoning him to her), "do ask

[42] A small ship, armed with guns on only one deck. [43] Influential connections.
[44] A loose cloak worn by women. [45] Privately owned enemy ships.
[46] A fast, medium-sized naval vessel.
[47] A seaport in Devonshire, in southwest England, on the English Channel.

Captain Wentworth where it was he first met with your poor brother. I
always forget."

"It was at Gibraltar, mother, I know. Dick had been left ill at Gibraltar,
with a recommendation from his former captain to Captain Wentworth."

"Oh!—but, Charles, tell Captain Wentworth, he need not be afraid of
mentioning poor Dick before me, for it would be rather a pleasure to hear
him talked of, by such a good friend."

Charles, being somewhat more mindful of the probabilities of the case,
only nodded in reply, and walked away.

The girls were now hunting for the *Laconia*; and Captain Wentworth
could not deny himself the pleasure of taking the precious volume into his
own hands to save them the trouble, and once more read aloud the little
statement of her name and rate,[48] and present non-commissioned class,
observing over it, that she too had been one of the best friends man ever
had.

"Ah! those were pleasant days when I had the *Laconia*! How fast I made
money in her.—A friend of mine, and I, had such a lovely cruise together
off the Western Islands.—Poor Harville, sister! You know how much he
wanted[49] money—worse than myself. He had a wife.—Excellent fellow! I
shall never forget his happiness. He felt it all, so much for her sake.—I
wished for him again the next summer, when I had still the same luck in
the Mediterranean."

"And I am sure, Sir," said Mrs. Musgrove, "it was a lucky day for *us*,
when you were put captain into that ship. *We* shall never forget what you
did."

Her feelings made her speak low; and Captain Wentworth, hearing
only in part, and probably not having Dick Musgrove at all near his
thoughts, looked rather in suspense, and as if waiting for more.

"My brother," whispered one of the girls; "mamma is thinking of poor
Richard."

"Poor dear fellow!" continued Mrs. Musgrove; "he was grown so steady,
and such an excellent correspondent, while he was under your care! Ah! it
would have been a happy thing, if he had never left you. I assure you,
Captain Wentworth, we are very sorry he ever left you."

There was a momentary expression in Captain Wentworth's face at this
speech, a certain glance of his bright eye, and curl of his handsome mouth,
which convinced Anne, that instead of sharing in Mrs. Musgrove's kind
wishes, as to her son, he had probably been at some pains to get rid of him;
but it was too transient an indulgence of self-amusement to be detected by
any who understood him less than herself; in another moment he was
perfectly collected and serious; and almost instantly afterwards coming up
to the sofa, on which she and Mrs. Musgrove were sitting, took a place by
the latter, and entered into conversation with her, in a low voice, about her
son, doing it with so much sympathy and natural grace, as shewed the
kindest consideration for all that was real and unabsurd in the parent's
feelings.

They were actually on the same sofa, for Mrs. Musgrove had most read-
ily made room for him;—they were divided only by Mrs. Musgrove. It was

[48] Class, as reflected by size and power. [49] Needed.

no insignificant barrier indeed. Mrs. Musgrove was of a comfortable substantial size, infinitely more fitted by nature to express good cheer and good humour, than tenderness and sentiment; and while the agitations of Anne's slender form, and pensive face, may be considered as very completely screened, Captain Wentworth should be allowed some credit for the self-command with which he attended to her large fat sighings over the destiny of a son, whom alive nobody had cared for.

Personal size and mental sorrow have certainly no necessary proportions. A large bulky figure has as good a right to be in deep affliction, as the most graceful set of limbs in the world. But, fair or not fair, there are unbecoming conjunctions, which reason will patronize in vain,—which taste cannot tolerate,—which ridicule will seize.

The admiral, after taking two or three refreshing turns about the room with his hands behind him, being called to order by his wife, now came up to Captain Wentworth, and without any observation of what he might be interrupting, thinking only of his own thoughts, began with,

"If you had been a week later at Lisbon, last spring, Frederick, you would have been asked to give a passage to Lady Mary Grierson and her daughters."

"Should I? I am glad I was not a week later then."

The admiral abused him for his want of gallantry. He defended himself; though professing that he would never willingly admit any ladies on board a ship of his, excepting for a ball, or a visit, which a few hours might comprehend.

"But, if I know myself," said he, "this is from no want of gallantry towards them. It is rather from feeling how impossible it is, with all one's efforts, and all one's sacrifices, to make the accommodations on board, such as women ought to have. There can be no want of gallantry, admiral, in rating the claims of women to every personal comfort *high*—and this is what I do. I hate to hear of women on board, or to see them on board; and no ship, under my command, shall ever convey a family of ladies any where, if I can help it."

This brought his sister upon him.

"Oh Frederick!—But I cannot believe it of you.—All idle refinement!—Women may be as comfortable on board, as in the best house in England. I believe I have lived as much on board as most women, and I know nothing superior to the accommodations of a man of war.[50] I declare I have not a comfort or an indulgence about me, even at Kellynch-hall," (with a kind bow to Anne) "beyond what I always had in most of the ships I have lived in; and they have been five altogether."

"Nothing to the purpose," replied her brother. "You were living with your husband; and were the only woman on board."

"But you, yourself, brought Mrs. Harville, her sister, her cousin, and the three children, round from Portsmouth[51] to Plymouth. Where was this superfine, extraordinary sort of gallantry of yours, then?"

"All merged in my friendship, Sophia. I would assist any brother offi-

[50] Warship.

[51] The main base of the Royal Navy, on the south-central coast of England about 120 miles east of Plymouth.

cer's wife that I could, and I would bring any thing of Harville's from the world's end, if he wanted it. But do not imagine that I did not feel it an evil in itself."

"Depend upon it they were all perfectly comfortable."

"I might not like them the better for that, perhaps. Such a number of women and children have no *right* to be comfortable on board."

"My dear Frederick, you are talking quite idly. Pray, what would become of us poor sailors' wives, who often want to be conveyed to one port or another, after our husbands, if every body had your feelings?"

"My feelings, you see, did not prevent my taking Mrs. Harville, and all her family, to Plymouth."

"But I hate to hear you talking so, like a fine gentleman, and as if women were all fine ladies, instead of rational creatures. We none of us expect to be in smooth water all our days."

"Ah! my dear," said the admiral, "when he has got a wife, he will sing a different tune. When he is married, if we have the good luck to live to another war, we shall see him do as you and I, and a great many others, have done. We shall have him very thankful to any body that will bring him his wife."

"Ay, that we shall."

"Now I have done," cried Captain Wentworth—"When once married people begin to attack me with, 'Oh! you will think very differently, when you are married.' I can only say, 'No, I shall not;' and then they say again, 'Yes, you will,' and there is an end of it."

He got up and moved away.

"What a great traveller you must have been, ma'am!" said Mrs. Musgrove to Mrs. Croft.

"Pretty well, ma'am, in the fifteen years of my marriage; though many women have done more. I have crossed the Atlantic four times, and have been once to the East Indies, and back again; and only once, besides being in different places about home—Cork, and Lisbon, and Gibraltar. But I never went beyond the Streights[52]—and never was in the West Indies. We do not call Bermuda or Bahama, you know, the West Indies."

Mrs. Musgrove had not a word to say in dissent; she could not accuse herself of having ever called them any thing in the whole course of her life.

"And I do assure you, ma'am," pursued Mrs. Croft, "that nothing can exceed the accommodations of a man of war; I speak, you know, of the higher rates. When you come to a frigate, of course, you are more confined—though any reasonable woman may be perfectly happy in one of them; and I can safely say, that the happiest part of my life has been spent on board a ship. While we were together, you know, there was nothing to be feared. Thank God! I have always been blessed with excellent health, and no climate disagrees with me. A little disordered always the first twenty-four hours of going to sea, but never knew what sickness was afterwards. The only time that I ever really suffered in body or mind, the only time that I ever fancied myself unwell, or had any ideas of danger, was the winter I passed by myself at Deal,[53] when the Admiral (*Captain* Croft then)

[52] The Straits of Magellan, at the southern tip of South America.
[53] A town at the southeastern tip of England, near Dover.

was in the North Seas. I lived in perpetual fright at that time, and had all manner of imaginary complaints from not knowing what to do with myself, or when I should hear from him next; but as long as we could be together, nothing ever ailed me, and I never met with the smallest inconvenience."

"Ay, to be sure.—Yes, indeed, oh yes, I am quite of your opinion, Mrs. Croft," was Mrs. Musgrove's hearty answer. "There is nothing so bad as a separation. I am quite of your opinion. *I* know what it is, for Mr. Musgrove always attends the assizes,[54] and I am so glad when they are over, and he is safe back again."

The evening ended with dancing. On its being proposed, Anne offered her services, as usual, and though her eyes would sometimes fill with tears as she sat at the instrument, she was extremely glad to be employed, and desired nothing in return but to be unobserved.

It was a merry, joyous party, and no one seemed in higher spirits than Captain Wentworth. She felt that he had every thing to elevate him, which general attention and deference, and especially the attention of all the young women could do. The Miss Hayters, the females of the family of cousins already mentioned, were apparently admitted to the honour of being in love with him; and as for Henrietta and Louisa, they both seemed so entirely occupied by him, that nothing but the continued appearance of the most perfect good-will between themselves, could have made it credible that they were not decided rivals. If he were a little spoilt by such universal, such eager admiration, who could wonder?

These were some of the thoughts which occupied Anne, while her fingers were mechanically at work, proceeding for half an hour together, equally without error, and without consciousness. *Once* she felt that he was looking at herself—observing her altered features, perhaps, trying to trace in them the ruins of the face which had once charmed him; and *once* she knew that he must have spoken of her;—she was hardly aware of it, till she heard the answer; but then she was sure of his having asked his partner whether Miss Elliot never danced? The answer was, "Oh! no, never; she has quite given up dancing. She had rather play. She is never tired of playing." Once, too, he spoke to her. She had left the instrument on the dancing being over, and he had sat down to try to make out an air which he wished to give the Miss Musgroves an idea of. Unintentionally she returned to that part of the room; he saw her, and, instantly rising, said, with studied politeness,

"I beg your pardon, madam, this is your seat;" and though she immediately drew back with a decided negative, he was not to be induced to sit down again.

Anne did not wish for more of such looks and speeches. His cold politeness, his ceremonious grace, were worse than any thing.

CHAPTER 9

Captain Wentworth was come to Kellynch as to a home, to stay as long as he liked, being as thoroughly the object of the Admiral's fraternal kindness as

[54] The county court sessions, held periodically.

of his wife's. He had intended, on first arriving, to proceed very soon into Shropshire,[55] and visit the brother settled in that county, but the attractions of Uppercross induced him to put this off. There was so much of friendliness, and of flattery, and of every thing most bewitching in his reception there; the old were so hospitable, the young so agreeable, that he could not but resolve to remain where he was, and take all the charms and perfections of Edward's wife upon credit a little longer.

It was soon Uppercross with him almost every day. The Musgroves could hardly be more ready to invite than he to come, particularly in the morning, when he had no companion at home, for the Admiral and Mrs. Croft were generally out of doors together, interesting themselves in their new possessions, their grass, and their sheep, and dawdling about in a way not endurable to a third person, or driving out in a gig, lately added to their establishment.

Hitherto there had been but one opinion of Captain Wentworth, among the Musgroves and their dependencies. It was unvarying, warm admiration every where. But this intimate footing was not more than established, when a certain Charles Hayter returned among them, to be a good deal disturbed by it, and to think Captain Wentworth very much in the way.

Charles Hayter was the eldest of all the cousins, and a very amiable, pleasing young man, between whom and Henrietta there had been a considerable appearance of attachment previous to Captain Wentworth's introduction. He was in orders,[56] and having a curacy in the neighbourhood where residence was not required, lived at his father's house, only two miles from Uppercross. A short absence from home had left his fair one unguarded by his attentions at this critical period, and when he came back he had the pain of finding very altered manners, and of seeing Captain Wentworth.

Mrs. Musgrove and Mrs. Hayter were sisters. They had each had money, but their marriages had made a material difference in their degree of consequence. Mr. Hayter had some property of his own, but it was insignificant compared with Mr. Musgrove's; and while the Musgroves were in the first class of society in the country, the young Hayters would, from their parents' inferior, retired, and unpolished way of living, and their own defective education, have been hardly in any class at all, but for their connexion with Uppercross; this eldest son of course excepted, who had chosen to be a scholar and a gentleman, and who was very superior in cultivation and manners to all the rest.

The two families had always been on excellent terms, there being no pride on one side, and no envy on the other, and only such a consciousness of superiority in the Miss Musgroves, as made them pleased to improve their cousins.—Charles's attentions to Henrietta had been observed by her father and mother without any disapprobation. "It would not be a great match for her; but if Henrietta liked him,—and Henrietta *did* seem to like him."

Henrietta fully thought so herself, before Captain Wentworth came; but from that time Cousin Charles had been very much forgotten.

[55] A county in west-central England, on the Welsh border.
[56] In holy orders; a clergyman.

Which of the two sisters was preferred by Captain Wentworth was as yet quite doubtful, as far as Anne's observation reached. Henrietta was perhaps the prettiest, Louisa had the higher spirits; and she knew not *now*, whether the more gentle or the more lively character were most likely to attract him.

Mr. and Mrs. Musgrove, either from seeing little, or from an entire confidence in the discretion of both their daughters, and of all the young men who came near them, seemed to leave every thing to take its chance. There was not the smallest appearance of solicitude or remark about them, in the Mansion-house; but it was different at the Cottage; the young couple there were more disposed to speculate and wonder; and Captain Wentworth had not been above four or five times in the Miss Musgroves' company, and Charles Hayter had but just reappeared, when Anne had to listen to the opinions of her brother and sister, as to *which* was the one liked best. Charles gave it for Louisa, Mary for Henrietta, but quite agreeing that to have him marry either would be extremely delightful.

Charles "had never seen a pleasanter man in his life; and from what he had once heard Captain Wentworth himself say, was very sure that he had not made less than twenty thousand pounds by the war. Here was a fortune at once; besides which, there would be the chance of what might be done in any future war; and he was sure Captain Wentworth was as likely a man to distinguish himself as any officer in the navy. Oh! it would be a capital match for either of his sisters."

"Upon my word it would," replied Mary. "Dear me! If he should rise to any very great honours! If he should ever be made a Baronet! 'Lady Wentworth' sounds very well. That would be a noble thing, indeed, for Henrietta! She would take place of me then, and Henrietta would not dislike that. Sir Frederick and Lady Wentworth! It would be but a new creation, however, and I never think much of your new creations."

It suited Mary best to think Henrietta the one preferred, on the very account of Charles Hayter, whose pretensions she wished to see put an end to. She looked down very decidedly upon the Hayters, and thought it would be quite a misfortune to have the existing connection between the families renewed—very sad for herself and her children.

"You know," said she, "I cannot think him at all a fit match for Henrietta; and considering the alliances which the Musgroves have made, she has no right to throw herself away. I do not think any young woman has a right to make a choice that may be disagreeable and inconvenient to the *principal* part of her family, and be giving bad connections to those who have not been used to them. And, pray, who is Charles Hayter? Nothing but a country curate. A most improper match for Miss Musgrove, of Uppercross."

Her husband, however, would not agree with her here; for besides having a regard for his cousin, Charles Hayter was an eldest son, and he saw things as an eldest son himself.

"Now you are talking nonsense, Mary," was therefore his answer. "It would not be a *great* match for Henrietta, but Charles has a very fair chance, through the Spicers, of getting something from the Bishop in the course of a year or two; and you will please to remember, that he is the eldest son; whenever my uncle dies, he steps into very pretty property. The estate at Winthrop is not less than two hundred and fifty acres, besides the

farm near Taunton, which is some of the best land in the country. I grant you, that any of them but Charles would be a very shocking match for Henrietta, and indeed it could not be; he is the only one that could be possible; but he is a very good-natured, good sort of a fellow; and whenever Winthrop comes into his hands, he will make a different sort of place of it, and live in a very different sort of way; and with that property, he will never be a contemptible man. Good, freehold property. No, no; Henrietta might do worse than marry Charles Hayter; and if she has him, and Louisa can get Captain Wentworth, I shall be very well satisfied."

"Charles may say what he pleases," cried Mary to Anne, as soon as he was out of the room, "but it would be shocking to have Henrietta marry Charles Hayter; a very bad thing for *her,* and still worse for *me;* and therefore it is very much to be wished that Captain Wentworth may soon put him quite out of her head, and I have very little doubt that he has. She took hardly any notice of Charles Hayter yesterday. I wish you had been there to see her behaviour. And as to Captain Wentworth's liking Louisa as well as Henrietta, it is nonsense to say so; for he certainly *does* like Henrietta a great deal the best. But Charles is so positive![57] I wish you had been with us yesterday, for then you might have decided between us; and I am sure you would have thought as I did, unless you had been determined to give it against me."

A dinner at Mr. Musgrove's had been the occasion, when all these things should have been seen by Anne; but she had staid at home, under the mixed plea of a headache of her own, and some return of indisposition in little Charles. She had thought only of avoiding Captain Wentworth; but an escape from being appealed to as umpire, was now added to the advantages of a quiet evening.

As to Captain Wentworth's views, she deemed it of more consequence that he should know his own mind, early enough not to be endangering the happiness of either sister, or impeaching his own honour, than that he should prefer Henrietta to Louisa, or Louisa to Henrietta. Either of them would, in all probability, make him an affectionate, good-humoured wife. With regard to Charles Hayter, she had delicacy which must be pained by any lightness of conduct in a well-meaning young woman, and a heart to sympathize in any of the sufferings it occasioned; but if Henrietta found herself mistaken in the nature of her feelings, the alteration could not be understood too soon.

Charles Hayter had met with much to disquiet and mortify him in his cousin's behaviour. She had too old a regard for him to be so wholly estranged, as might in two meetings extinguish every past hope, and leave him nothing to do but to keep away from Uppercross; but there was such a change as became very alarming, when such a man as Captain Wentworth was to be regarded as the probable cause. He had been absent only two Sundays; and when they parted, had left her interested even to the height of his wishes, in his prospect of soon quitting his present curacy, and obtaining that of Uppercross instead. It had then seemed the object nearest her heart, that Dr. Shirley, the rector, who for more than forty years had been zealously discharging all the duties of his office, but was now growing

[57] Dogmatic.

too infirm for many of them, should be quite fixed on engaging a curate; should make his curacy quite as good as he could afford, and should give Charles Hayter the promise of it. The advantage of his having to come only to Uppercross, instead of going six miles another way; of his having, in every respect, a better curacy; of his belonging to their dear Dr. Shirley, and of dear, good Dr. Shirley's being relieved from the duty which he could no longer get through without most injurious fatigue, had been a great deal, even to Louisa, but had been almost every thing to Henrietta. When he came back, alas! the zeal of the business was gone by. Louisa could not listen at all to his account of a conversation which he had just held with Dr. Shirley: she was at window, looking out for Captain Wentworth; and even Henrietta had at best only a divided attention to give, and seemed to have forgotten all the former doubt and solicitude of the negociation.

"Well, I am very glad indeed, but I always thought you would have it; I always thought you sure. It did not appear to me that—In short, you know Dr. Shirley *must* have a curate, and you had secured his promise. Is he coming, Louisa?"

One morning, very soon after the dinner at the Musgroves, at which Anne had not been present, Captain Wentworth walked in to the drawing-room at the Cottage, where were only herself and the little invalid Charles, who was lying on the sofa.

The surprise of finding himself almost alone with Anne Elliot, deprived his manners of their usual composure: he started, and could only say, "I thought the Miss Musgroves had been here—Mrs. Musgrove told me I should find them here," before he walked to the window to recollect himself, and feel how he ought to behave.

"They are up stairs with my sister—they will be down in a few moments, I dare say,"—had been Anne's reply, in all the confusion that was natural; and if the child had not called her to come and do something for him, she would have been out of the room the next moment, and released Captain Wentworth as well as herself.

He continued at the window; and after calmly and politely saying, "I hope the little boy is better," was silent.

She was obliged to kneel down by the sofa, and remain there to satisfy her patient; and thus they continued a few minutes, when, to her very great satisfaction, she heard some other person crossing the little vestibule. She hoped, on turning her head, to see the master of the house; but it proved to be one much less calculated for making matters easy—Charles Hayter, probably not at all better pleased by the sight of Captain Wentworth, than Captain Wentworth had been by the sight of Anne.

She only attempted to say, "How do you do? Will not you sit down? The others will be here presently."

Captain Wentworth, however, came from his window, apparently not ill-disposed for conversation; but Charles Hayter soon put an end to his attempts, by seating himself near the table, and taking up the newspaper; and Captain Wentworth returned to his window.

Another minute brought another addition. The younger boy, a remarkable stout, forward child,[58] of two years old, having got the door opened

[58] *stout:* strong. *forward:* precocious.

for him by some one without, made his determined appearance among them, and went straight to the sofa to see what was going on, and put in his claim to any thing good that might be giving away.

There being nothing to be eat, he could only have some play; and as his aunt would not let him teaze his sick brother, he began to fasten himself upon her, as she knelt, in such a way that, busy as she was about Charles, she could not shake him off. She spoke to him—ordered, intreated, and insisted in vain. Once she did contrive to push him away, but the boy had the greater pleasure in getting upon her back again directly.

"Walter," said she, "get down this moment. You are extremely troublesome. I am very angry with you."

"Walter," cried Charles Hayter, "why do you not do as you are bid? Do not you hear your aunt speak? Come to me, Walter, come to cousin Charles."

But not a bit did Walter stir.

In another moment, however, she found herself in the state of being released from him; some one was taking him from her, though he had bent down her head so much, that his little sturdy hands were unfastened from around her neck, and he was resolutely borne away, before she knew that Captain Wentworth had done it.

Her sensations on the discovery made her perfectly speechless. She could not even thank him. She could only hang over little Charles, with most disordered feelings. His kindness in stepping forward to her relief—the manner—the silence in which it had passed—the little particulars of the circumstance—with the conviction soon forced on her by the noise he was studiously making with the child, that he meant to avoid hearing her thanks, and rather sought to testify that her conversation was the last of his wants, produced such a confusion of varying, but very painful agitation, as she could not recover from, till enabled by the entrance of Mary and the Miss Musgroves to make over her little patient to their cares, and leave the room. She could not stay. It might have been an opportunity of watching the loves and jealousies of the four; they were now all together, but she could stay for none of it. It was evident that Charles Hayter was not well inclined towards Captain Wentworth. She had a strong impression of his having said, in a vexed tone of voice, after Captain Wentworth's interference, "You ought to have minded *me*, Walter; I told you not to teaze your aunt;" and could comprehend his regretting that Captain Wentworth should do what he ought to have done himself. But neither Charles Hayter's feelings, nor any body's feelings, could interest her, till she had a little better arranged her own. She was so ashamed of herself, quite ashamed of being so nervous, so overcome by such a trifle; but so it was; and it required a long application of solitude and reflection to recover her.

CHAPTER 10

Other opportunities of making her observations could not fail to occur. Anne had soon been in company with all the four together often enough to have an opinion, though too wise to acknowledge as much at home, where she knew it would have satisfied neither husband nor wife; for while she

considered Louisa to be rather the favourite, she could not but think, as far as she might dare to judge from memory and experience, that Captain Wentworth was not in love with either. They were more in love with him; yet there it was not love. It was a little fever of admiration; but it might, probably must, end in love with some. Charles Hayter seemed aware of being slighted, and yet Henrietta had sometimes the air of being divided between them. Anne longed for the power of representing to them all what they were about, and of pointing out some of the evils they were exposing themselves to. She did not attribute guile to any. It was the highest satisfaction to her, to believe Captain Wentworth not in the least aware of the pain he was occasioning. There was no triumph, no pitiful triumph in his manner. He had, probably, never heard, and never thought of any claims of Charles Hayter. He was only wrong in accepting the attentions—(for accepting must be the word) of two young women at once.

After a short struggle, however, Charles Hayter seemed to quit the field. Three days had passed without his coming once to Uppercross; a most decided change. He had even refused one regular invitation to dinner; and having been found on the occasion by Mr. Musgrove with some large books before him, Mr. and Mrs. Musgrove were sure all could not be right, and talked, with grave faces, of his studying himself to death. It was Mary's hope and belief, that he had received a positive dismissal from Henrietta, and her husband lived under the constant dependance of seeing him to-morrow. Anne could only feel that Charles Hayter was wise.

One morning, about this time, Charles Musgrove and Captain Wentworth being gone a shooting together, as the sisters in the cottage were sitting quietly at work, they were visited at the window by the sisters from the mansion-house.

It was a very fine November day, and the Miss Musgroves came through the little grounds, and stopped for no other purpose than to say, that they were going to take a *long* walk, and, therefore, concluded Mary could not like to go with them; and when Mary immediately replied, with some jealousy, at not being supposed a good walker, "Oh, yes, I should like to join you very much, I am very fond of a long walk," Anne felt persuaded, by the looks of the two girls, that it was precisely what they did not wish, and admired[59] again the sort of necessity which the family-habits seemed to produce, of every thing being to be communicated, and every thing being to be done together, however undesired and inconvenient. She tried to dissuade Mary from going, but in vain; and that being the case, thought it best to accept the Miss Musgroves' much more cordial invitation to herself to go likewise, as she might be useful in turning back with her sister, and lessening the interference in any plan of their own.

"I cannot imagine why they should suppose I should not like a long walk!" said Mary, as she went up stairs. "Every body is always supposing that I am not a good walker! And yet they would not have been pleased, if we had refused to join them. When people come in this manner on purpose to ask us, how can one say no?"

Just as they were setting off, the gentlemen returned. They had taken out a young dog, who had spoilt their sport, and sent them back early.

[59] Wondered at.

Their time and strength, and spirits, were, therefore, exactly ready for this walk, and they entered into it with pleasure. Could Anne have foreseen such a junction, she would have staid at home; but, from some feelings of interest and curiosity, she fancied now that it was too late to retract, and the whole six set forward together in the direction chosen by the Miss Musgroves, who evidently considered the walk as under their guidance.

Anne's object was, not to be in the way of any body, and where the narrow paths across the fields made many separations necessary, to keep with her brother and sister. Her *pleasure* in the walk must arise from the exercise and the day, from the view of the last smiles of the year upon the tawny leaves and withered hedges, and from repeating to herself some few of the thousand poetical descriptions extant of autumn, that season of peculiar and inexhaustible influence on the mind of taste and tenderness, that season which has drawn from every poet, worthy of being read, some attempt at description, or some lines of feeling. She occupied her mind as much as possible in such like musings and quotations; but it was not possible, that when within reach of Captain Wentworth's conversation with either of the Miss Musgroves, she should not try to hear it; yet she caught little very remarkable. It was mere lively chat,—such as any young persons, on an intimate footing, might fall into. He was more engaged with Louisa than with Henrietta. Louisa certainly put more forward for his notice than her sister. This distinction appeared to increase, and there was one speech of Louisa's which struck her. After one of the many praises of the day, which were continually bursting forth, Captain Wentworth added,

"What glorious weather for the Admiral and my sister! They meant to take a long drive this morning; perhaps we may hail them from some of these hills. They talked of coming into this side of the country. I wonder whereabouts they will upset to-day. Oh! it does happen very often, I assure you—but my sister makes nothing of it—she would as lieve be tossed out as not."

"Ah! You make the most of it, I know," cried Louisa, "but if it were really so, I should do just the same in her place. If I loved a man, as she loves the Admiral, I would be always with him, nothing should ever separate us, and I would rather be overturned by him, than driven safely by anybody else."

It was spoken with enthusiasm.

"Had you?" cried he, catching the same tone; "I honour you!" And there was silence between them for a little while.

Anne could not immediately fall into a quotation again. The sweet scenes of autumn were for a while put by—unless some tender sonnet, fraught with the apt analogy of the declining year, with declining happiness, and the images of youth and hope, and spring, all gone together, blessed her memory. She roused herself to say, as they struck by order into another path, "Is not this one of the ways to Winthrop?" But nobody heard, or, at least, nobody answered her.

Winthrop, however, or its environs—for young men are, sometimes, to be met with, strolling about near home, was their destination; and after another half mile of gradual ascent through large enclosures, where the ploughs at work, and the fresh-made path spoke the farmer, counteracting the sweets of poetical despondence, and meaning to have spring again,

they gained the summit of the most considerable hill, which parted Uppercross and Winthrop, and soon commanded a full view of the latter, at the foot of the hill on the other side.

Winthrop, without beauty and without dignity, was stretched before them; an indifferent house, standing low, and hemmed in by the barns and buildings of a farm-yard.

Mary exclaimed, "Bless me! here is Winthrop—I declare I had no idea!—well, now I think we had better turn back; I am excessively tired."

Henrietta, conscious[60] and ashamed, and seeing no cousin Charles walking along any path, or leaning against any gate, was ready to do as Mary wished; but "No," said Charles Musgrove, and "No, no," cried Louisa more eagerly, and taking her sister aside, seemed t be arguing the matter warmly.

Charles, in the meanwhile, was very decidedly declaring his resolution of calling on his aunt, now that he was so near; and very evidently, though more fearfully, trying to induce his wife to go too. But this was one of the points on which the lady shewed her strength, and when he recommended the advantage of resting herself a quarter of an hour at Winthrop, as she felt so tired, she resolutely answered, "Oh! no, indeed!—walking up that hill again would do her more harm than any sitting down could do her good;"—and, in short, her look and manner declared, that go she would not.

After a little succession of these sort of debates and consultations, it was settled between Charles and his two sisters, that he, and Henrietta, should just run down for a few minutes, to see their aunt and cousins, while the rest of the party waited for them at the top of the hill. Louisa seemed the principal arranger of the plan; and, as she went a little way with them, down the hill, still talking to Henrietta, Mary took the opportunity of looking scornfully around her, and saying to Captain Wentworth,

"It is very unpleasant, having such connexions! But I assure you, I have never been in the house above twice in my life."

She received no other answer, than an artificial, assenting smile, followed by a contemptuous glance, as he turned away, which Anne perfectly knew the meaning of.

The brow of the hill, where they remained, was a cheerful spot; Louisa returned, and Mary finding a comfortable seat for herself, on the step of a stile,[61] was very well satisfied so long as the others all stood about her; but when Louisa drew Captain Wentworth away, to try for a gleaning of nuts in an adjoining hedge-row, and they were gone by degrees quite out of sight and sound, Mary was happy no longer, she quarrelled with her own seat,—was sure Louisa had got a much better somewhere,—and nothing could prevent her from going to look for a better also. She turned through the same gate,—but could not see them.—Anne found a nice seat for her, on a dry sunny bank, under the hedge-row, in which she had no doubt of their still being—in some spot or other. Mary sat down for a moment, but it would not do; she was sure Louisa had found a better seat somewhere else, and she would go on, till she overtook her.

Anne, really tired herself, was glad to sit down; and she very soon heard

[60] Feeling guilty and self-conscious. [61] Steps leading over a fence.

Captain Wentworth and Louisa in the hedge-row, behind her, as if making their way back, along the rough, wild sort of channel, down the centre. They were speaking as they drew near. Louisa's voice was the first distinguished. She seemed to be in the middle of some eager speech. What Anne first heard was,

"And so, I made her go. I could not bear that she should be frightened from the visit by such nonsense. What!—would I be turned back from doing a thing that I had determined to do, and that I knew to be right, by the airs and interference of such a person?—or, of any person I may say. No,—I have no idea of being so easily persuaded. When I have made up my mind, I have made it. And Henrietta seemed entirely to have made up hers to call at Winthrop to-day—and yet, she was as near giving it up, out of nonsensical complaisance!"[62]

"She would have turned back then, but for you?"

"She would indeed. I am almost ashamed to say it."

"Happy for her, to have such a mind as yours at hand!—After the hints you gave just now, which did but confirm my own observations, the last time I was in company with him, I need not affect to have no comprehension of what is going on. I see that more than a mere dutiful morning-visit to your aunt was in question;—and woe betide him, and her too, when it comes to things of consequence, when they are placed in circumstances, requiring fortitude and strength of mind, if she have not resolution enough to resist idle interference in such a trifle as this. Your sister is an amiable creature; but *yours* is the character of decision and firmness, I see. If you value her conduct or happiness, infuse as much of your own spirit into her, as you can. But this, no doubt, you have been always doing. It is the worst evil of too yielding and indecisive a character, that no influence over it can be depended on.—You are never sure of a good impression being durable. Every body may sway it; let those who would be happy be firm.—Here is a nut," said he, catching one down from an upper bough. "To exemplify,—a beautiful glossy nut, which, blessed with original strength, has outlived all the storms of autumn. Not a puncture, not a weak spot any where.—This nut," he continued, with playful solemnity,—"while so many of its brethren have fallen and been trodden under foot, is still in possession of all the happiness that a hazel-nut can be supposed capable of." Then, returning to his former earnest tone: "My first wish for all, whom I am interested in, is that they should be firm. If Louisa Musgrove would be beautiful and happy in her November of life, she will cherish all her present powers of mind."

He had done,—and was unanswered. It would have surprised Anne, if Louisa could have readily answered such a speech—words of such interest, spoken with such serious warmth!—she could imagine what Louisa was feeling. For herself—she feared to move, lest she should be seen. While she remained, a bush of low rambling holly protected her, and they were moving on. Before they were beyond her hearing, however, Louisa spoke again.

"Mary is good-natured enough in many respects," said she; "but she does sometimes provoke me excessively, by her nonsense and her pride;

[62] Submissiveness to another person.

the Elliot pride. She has a great deal too much of the Elliot pride.—We do so wish that Charles had married Anne instead.—I suppose you know he wanted to marry Anne?"

After a moment's pause, Captain Wentworth said,

"Do you mean that she refused him?"

"Oh! yes, certainly."

"When did that happen?"

"I do not exactly know, for Henrietta and I were at school at the time; but I believe about a year before he married Mary. I wish she had accepted him. We should all have liked her a great deal better; and papa and mamma always think it was her great friend Lady Russell's doing, that she did not.—They think Charles might not be learned and bookish enough to please Lady Russell, and that therefore, she persuaded Anne to refuse him."

The sounds were retreating, and Anne distinguished no more. Her own emotions still kept her fixed. She had much to recover from, before she could move. The listener's proverbial fate was not absolutely hers; she had heard no evil of herself,—but she had heard a great deal of very painful import. She saw how her own character was considered by Captain Wentworth; and there had been just that degree of feeling and curiosity about her in his manner, which must give her extreme agitation.

As soon as she could, she went after Mary, and having found, and walked back with her to their former station, by the stile, felt some comfort in their whole party being immediately afterwards collected, and once more in motion together. Her spirits wanted the solitude and silence which only numbers could give.

Charles and Henrietta returned, bringing, as may be conjectured, Charles Hayter with them. The minutiae of the business Anne could not attempt to understand; even Captain Wentworth did not seem admitted to perfect confidence here; but that there had been a withdrawing on the gentleman's side, and a relenting on the lady's, and that they were now very glad to be together again, did not admit a doubt, Henrietta looked a little ashamed, but very well pleased;—Charles Hayter exceedingly happy, and they were devoted to each other almost from the first instant of their all setting forward for Uppercross.

Every thing now marked out Louisa for Captain Wentworth; nothing could be plainer; and where many divisions were necessary, or even where they were not, they walked side by side, nearly as much as the other two. In a long strip of meadow-land, where there was ample space for all, they were thus divided—forming three distinct parties; and to that party of the three which boasted least animation, and least complaisance,[63] Anne necessarily belonged. She joined Charles and Mary, and was tired enough to be very glad of Charles's other arm;—but Charles, though in very good humour with her, was out of temper with his wife. Mary had shewn herself disobliging to him, and was now to reap the consequence, which consequence was his dropping her arm almost every moment, to cut off the heads of some nettles in the hedge with his switch; and when Mary began to complain of it, and lament her being ill-used, according to custom, in being

[63] Desire to please.

on the hedge side, while Anne was never incommoded on the other, he dropped the arms of both to hunt after a weasel which he had a momentary glance of; and they could hardly get him along at all.

This long meadow bordered a lane, which their footpath, at the end of it, was to cross; and when the party had all reached the gate of exit, the carriage advancing in the same direction, which had been some time heard, was just coming up, and proved to be Admiral Croft's gig.—He and his wife had taken their intended drive, and were returning home. Upon hearing how long a walk the young people had engaged in, they kindly offered a seat to any lady who might be particularly tired; it would save her full a mile, and they were going through Uppercross. The invitation was general, and generally declined. The Miss Musgroves were not at all tired, and Mary was either offended, by not being asked before any of the others, or what Louisa called the Elliot pride could not endure to make a third in a one horse chaise.

The walking-party had crossed the lane, and were surmounting an opposite stile; and the admiral was putting his horse into motion again, when Captain Wentworth cleared the hedge in a moment to say something to his sister.—The something might be guessed by its effects.

"Miss Elliot, I am sure *you* are tired," cried Mrs. Croft. "Do let us have the pleasure of taking you home. Here is excellent room for three, I assure you. If we were all like you, I believe we might sit four.—You must, indeed, you must."

Anne was still in the lane; and though instinctively beginning to decline, she was not allowed to proceed. The admiral's kind urgency came in support of his wife's; they would not be refused; they compressed themselves into the smallest possible space to leave her a corner, and Captain Wentworth, without saying a word, turned to her, and quietly obliged her to be assisted into the carriage.

Yes,—he had done it. She was in the carriage, and felt that he had placed her there, that his will and his hands had done it, that she owed it to his perception of her fatigue, and his resolution to give her rest. She was very much affected by the view of his disposition towards her which all these things made apparent. This little circumstance seemed the completion of all that had gone before. She understood him. He could not forgive her,—but he could not be unfeeling. Though condemning her for the past, and considering it with high and unjust resentment, though perfectly careless of her, and though becoming attached to another, still he could not see her suffer, without the desire of giving her relief. It was a remainder of former sentiment; it was an impulse of pure, though unacknowledged friendship; it was a proof of his own warm and amiable heart, which she could not contemplate without emotions so compounded of pleasure and pain, that she knew not which prevailed.

Her answers to the kindness and the remarks of her companions were at first unconsciously given. They had travelled half their way along the rough lane, before she was quite awake to what they said. She then found them talking of "Frederick."

"He certainly means to have one or other of those two girls, Sophy," said the admiral;—"but there is no saying which. He has been running after them, too, long enough, one would think, to make up his mind. Ay,

this comes of the peace. If it were war, now, he would have settled it long ago.—We sailors, Miss Elliot, cannot afford to make long courtships in time of war. How many days was it, my dear, between the first time of my seeing you, and our sitting down together in our lodgings at North Yarmouth?"[64]

"We had better not talk about it, my dear," replied Mrs. Croft, pleasantly; "for if Miss Elliot were to hear how soon we came to an understanding, she would never be persuaded that we could be happy together. I had known you by character, however, long before."

"Well, and I had heard of you as a very pretty girl; and what were we to wait for besides?—I do not like having such things so long in hand. I wish Frederick would spread a little more canvas, and bring us home one of these young ladies to Kellynch. Then, there would always be company for them.—And very nice young ladies they both are; I hardly know one from the other."

"Very good humoured, unaffected girls, indeed," said Mrs. Croft, in a tone of calmer praise, such as made Anne suspect that her keener powers might not consider either of them as quite worthy of her brother; "and a very respectable family. One could not be connected with better people.— My dear admiral, that post!—we shall certainly take that post."

But by coolly giving the reins a better direction herself, they happily passed the danger; and by once afterwards judiciously putting out her hand, they neither fell into a rut, nor ran foul of a dung-cart; and Anne, with some amusement at their style of driving, which she imagined no bad representation of the general guidance of their affairs, found herself safely deposited by them at the cottage.

CHAPTER 11

The time now approached for Lady Russell's return; the day was even fixed, and Anne, being engaged to join her as soon as she was resettled, was looking forward to an early removal to Kellynch, and beginning to think how her own comfort was likely to be affected by it.

It would place her in the same village with Captain Wentworth, within half a mile of him; they would have to frequent the same church, and there must be intercourse between the two families. This was against her; but, on the other hand, he spent so much of his time at Uppercross, that in removing thence she might be considered rather as leaving him behind, than as going towards him; and, upon the whole, she believed she must, on this interesting question, be the gainer, almost as certainly as in her change of domestic society, in leaving poor Mary for Lady Russell.

She wished it might be possible for her to avoid ever seeing Captain Wentworth at the hall;—those rooms had witnessed former meetings which would be brought too painfully before her; but she was yet more anxious for the possibility of Lady Russell and Captain Wentworth never meeting any where. They did not like each other, and no renewal of acquaintance now could do any good; and were Lady Russell to see them

[64] A town on the east-central coast of England.

together, she might think that he had too much self-possession, and she too little.

These points formed her chief solicitude in anticipating her removal from Uppercross, where she felt she had been stationed quite long enough. Her usefulness to little Charles would always give some sweetness to the memory of her two months visit there, but he was gaining strength apace, and she had nothing else to stay for.

The conclusion of her visit, however, was diversified in a way which she had not at all imagined. Captain Wentworth, after being unseen and unheard of at Uppercross for two whole days, appeared again among them to justify himself by a relation of what had kept him away.

A letter from his friend, Captain Harville, having found him out at last, had brought intelligence of Captain Harville's being settled with his family at Lyme for the winter;[65] of their being, therefore, quite unknowingly, within twenty miles of each other. Captain Harville had never been in good health since a severe wound which he received two years before, and Captain Wentworth's anxiety to see him had determined him to go immediately to Lyme. He had been there for four-and-twenty hours. His acquittal was complete, his friendship warmly honoured, a lively interest excited for his friend, and his description of the fine country about Lyme so feelingly attended to by the party, that an earnest desire to see Lyme themselves, and a project for going thither was the consequence.

The young people were all wild to see Lyme. Captain Wentworth talked of going there again himself; it was only seventeen miles from Uppercross; though November, the weather was by no means bad; and, in short, Louisa, who was the most eager of the eager, having formed the resolution to go, and besides the pleasure of doing as she liked, being now armed with the idea of merit in maintaining her own way, bore down all the wishes of her father and mother for putting it off till summer; and to Lyme they were to go—Charles, Mary, Anne, Henrietta, Louisa, and Captain Wentworth.

The first heedless scheme had been to go in the morning and return at night, but to this Mr. Musgrove, for the sake of his horses, would not consent; and when it came to be rationally considered, a day in the middle of November would not leave much time for seeing a new place, after deducting seven hours, as the nature of the country required, for going and returning. They were consequently to stay the night there, and not to be expected back till the next day's dinner. This was felt to be a considerable amendment; and though they all met at the Great House at rather an early breakfast hour, and set off very punctually, it was so much past noon before the two carriages, Mr. Musgrove's coach containing the four ladies, and Charles's curricle, in which he drove Captain Wentworth, were descending the long hill into Lyme, and entering upon the still steeper street of the town itself, that it was very evident they would not have more than time for looking about them, before the light and warmth of the day were gone.

[65] Lyme, or Lyme Regis, is a small town on the southern coast of England, about halfway between Plymouth and Portsmouth. The most striking feature of its oceanfront is the Cobb, a massive stone breakwater, topped by a walkway, extending in a curve across the beach and into the English Channel.

After securing accommodations, and ordering a dinner at one of the inns, the next thing to be done was unquestionably to walk directly down to the sea. They were come too late in the year for any amusement or variety which Lyme, as a public place, might offer; the rooms[66] were shut up, the lodgers almost all gone, scarcely any family but of the residents left—and, as there is nothing to admire in the buildings themselves, the remarkable situation of the town, the principal street almost hurrying into the water, the walk to the Cobb, skirting round the pleasant little bay, which in the season is animated with bathing machines and company, the Cobb itself, its old wonders and new improvements, with the very beautiful line of cliffs stretching out to the east of the town, are what the stranger's eye will seek; and a very strange stranger it must be, who does not see charms in the immediate environs of Lyme, to make him wish to know it better. The scenes in its neighbourhood, Charmouth, with its high grounds and extensive sweeps of country, and still more its sweet retired bay, backed by dark cliffs, where fragments of low rock among the sands make it the happiest spot for watching the flow of the tide, for sitting in unwearied contemplation;—the woody varieties of the cheerful village of Up Lyme, and, above all, Pinny, with its green chasms between romantic rocks, where the scattered forest trees and orchards of luxuriant growth declare that many a generation must have passed away since the first partial falling of the cliff prepared the ground for such a state, where a scene so wonderful and so lovely is exhibited, as may more than equal any of the resembling scenes of the far-famed Isle of Wight:[67] these places must be visited, and visited again, to make the worth of Lyme understood.

The party from Uppercross passing down by the now deserted and melancholy–looking rooms, and still descending, soon found themselves on the sea shore, and lingering only, as all must linger and gaze on a first return to the sea, who ever deserve to look on it at all, proceeded toward the Cobb, equally their object in itself and on Captain Wentworth's account; for in a small house, near the foot of an old pier of unknown date, were the Harvilles settled. Captain Wentworth turned in to call on his friend; the others walked on, and he was to join them on the Cobb.

They were by no means tired of wondering and admiring; and not even Louisa seemed to feel that they had parted with Captain Wentworth long, when they saw him coming after them, with three companions, all well known already by description to be Captain and Mrs Harville, and a Captain Benwick, who was staying with them.

Captain Benwick had some time ago been first lieutenant of the Laconia; and the account which Captain Wentworth had given of him, on his return from Lyme before; his warm praise of him as an excellent young man and an officer, whom he had always valued highly, which must have stamped him well in the esteem of every listener, had been followed by a little history of his private life, which rendered him perfectly interesting[68]

[66] The public assembly-rooms.

[67] A good-sized island and resort in the English Channel, just off the coast near Portsmouth.

[68] The word was much stronger than it is today, meaning "of intense human or emotional interest."

in the eyes of all the ladies. He had been engaged to Captain Harville's sister, and was now mourning her loss. They had been a year or two waiting for fortune and promotion. Fortune came, his prize-money as lieutenant being great,—promotion, too, came at *last*; but Fanny Harville did not live to know it. She had died the preceding summer, while he was at sea. Captain Wentworth believed it impossible for man to be more attached to woman than poor Benwick had been to Fanny Harville, or to be more deeply afflicted under the dreadful change. He considered his disposition as of the sort which must suffer heavily, uniting very strong feelings with quiet, serious, and retiring manners, and a decided taste for reading, and sedentary pursuits. To finish the interest of the story, the friendship between him and the Harvilles seemed, if possible, augmented by the event which closed all their views of alliance, and Captain Benwick was now living with them entirely. Captain Harville had taken his present house for half a year, his taste, and his health, and his fortune all directing him to a residence unexpensive, and by the sea; and the grandeur of the country, and the retirement of Lyme in the winter, appeared exactly adapted to Captain Benwick's state of mind. The sympathy and good-will excited towards Captain Benwick was very great.

"And yet," said Anne to herself, as they now moved forward to meet the party, "he has not, perhaps, a more sorrowing heart than I have. I cannot believe his prospects so blighted for ever. He is younger than I am; younger in feeling, if not in fact; younger as a man. He will rally again, and be happy with another."

They all met, and were introduced. Captain Harville was a tall, dark man, with a sensible, benevolent countenance; a little lame; and from strong features, and want of health, looking much older than Captain Wentworth. Captain Benwick looked and was the youngest of the three, and, compared with either of them, a little man. He had a pleasing face and a melancholy air, just as he ought to have, and drew back from conversation.

Captain Harville, though not equalling Captain Wentworth in manners, was a perfect gentleman, unaffected, warm, and obliging. Mrs. Harville, a degree less polished than her husband, seemed however to have the same good feelings; and nothing could be more pleasant than their desire of considering the whole party as friends of their own, because the friends of Captain Wentworth, or more kindly hospitable than their entreaties for their all promising to dine with them. The dinner, already ordered at the inn, was at last, though unwillingly, accepted as an excuse; but they seemed almost hurt that Captain Wentworth should have brought any such party to Lyme, without considering it as a thing of course that they should dine with them.

There was so much attachment to Captain Wentworth in all this, and such a bewitching charm in a degree of hospitality so uncommon, so unlike the usual style of give-and-take invitations, and dinners of formality and display, that Anne felt her spirits not likely to be benefited by an increasing acquaintance among his brother-officers. "These would have been all my friends," was her thought; and she had to struggle against a great tendency to lowness.

On quitting the Cobb, they all went indoors with their new friends, and

found rooms so small as none but those who invite from the heart could think capable of accommodating so many. Anne had a moment's astonishment on the subject herself; but it was soon lost in the pleasanter feelings which sprang from the sight of all the ingenious contrivances and nice arrangements of Captain Harville, to turn the actual space to the best possible account, to supply the deficiencies of lodging-house furniture, and defend the windows and doors against the winter storms to be expected. The varieties in the fitting-up of the rooms, where the common necessaries provided by the owner, in the common indifferent plight, were contrasted with some few articles of a rare species of wood, excellently worked up, and with something curious and valuable from all the distant countries Captain Harville had visited, were more than amusing to Anne: connected as it all was with his profession, the fruit of its labours, the effect of its influence on his habits, the picture of repose and domestic happiness it presented, made it to her a something more, or less, than gratification.

Captain Harville was no reader; but he had contrived excellent accommodations, and fashioned very pretty shelves, for a tolerable collection of well-bound volumes, the property of Captain Benwick. His lameness prevented him from taking much exercise; but a mind of usefulness and ingenuity seemed to furnish him with constant employment within. He drew, he varnished, he carpentered, he glued; he made toys for the children, he fashioned new netting-needles and pins with improvements; and if everything else was done, sat down to his large fishing-net at one corner of the room.

Anne thought she left great happiness behind her when they quitted the house; and Louisa, by whom she found herself walking, burst forth into raptures of admiration and delight on the character of the navy—their friendliness, their brotherliness, their openness, their uprightness; protesting that she was convinced of sailors having more worth and warmth than any other set of men in England; that they only knew how to live, and they only deserved to be respected and loved.

They went back to dress and dine; and so well had the scheme answered already, that nothing was found amiss; though its being "so entirely out of the season," and the "no-thorough-fare of Lyme," and the "no expectation of company," had brought many apologies from the heads of the inn.

Anne found herself by this time growing so much more hardened to being in Captain Wentworth's company than she had at first imagined could ever be, that the sitting down to the same table with him now, and the interchange of the common civilities attending on it—(they never got beyond) was become a mere nothing.

The nights were too dark for the ladies to meet again till the morrow, but Captain Harville had promised them a visit in the evening; and he came, bringing his friend also, which was more than had been expected, it having been agreed that Captain Benwick had all the appearance of being oppressed by the presence of so many strangers. He ventured among them again, however, though his spirits certainly did not seem fit for the mirth of the party in general.

While Captains Wentworth and Harville led the talk on one side of the room, and, by recurring to former days, supplied anecdotes in abundance to occupy and entertain the others, it fell to Anne's lot to be placed rather

apart with Captain Benwick; and a very good impulse of her nature obliged her to begin an acquaintance with him. He was shy, and disposed to abstraction; but the engaging mildness of her countenance, and gentleness of her manners, soon had their effect; and Anne was well repaid the first trouble of exertion. He was evidently a young man of considerable taste in reading, though principally in poetry; and besides the persuasion of having given him at least an evening's indulgence in the discussion of subjects, which his usual companions had probably no concern in, she had the hope of being of real use to him in some suggestions as to the duty and benefit of struggling against affliction, which had naturally grown out of their conversation. For, though shy, he did not seem reserved; it had rather the appearance of feelings glad to burst their usual restraints; and having talked of poetry, the richness of the present age, and gone through a brief comparison of opinion as to the first-rate poets, trying to ascertain whether *Marmion* or *The Lady of the Lake* were to be preferred, and how ranked the *Giaour* and *The Bride of Abydos;* and moreover, how the *Giaour* was to be pronounced,[69] he shewed himself so intimately acquainted with all the tenderest songs of the one poet, and all the impassioned descriptions of hopeless agony of the other;[70] he repeated, with such tremulous feeling, the various lines which imaged a broken heart, or a mind destroyed by wretchedness, and looked so entirely as if he meant to be understood, that she ventured to hope he did not always read only poetry; and to say, that she thought it was the misfortune of poetry, to be seldom safely enjoyed by those who enjoyed it completely; and that the strong feelings which alone could estimate it truly, were the very feelings which ought to taste it but sparingly.

His looks shewing him not pained, but pleased with this allusion to his situation, she was emboldened to go on; and feeling in herself the right of seniority of mind, she ventured to recommend a larger allowance of prose in his daily study; and on being requested to particularize, mentioned such works of our best moralists, such collections of the finest letters, such memoirs of characters of worth and suffering, as occurred to her at the moment as calculated to rouse and fortify the mind by the highest precepts, and the strongest examples of moral and religious endurances.

Captain Benwick listened attentively, and seemed grateful for the interest implied; and though with a shake of the head, and sighs which declared his little faith in the efficacy of any books on grief like his, noted down the names of those she recommended, and promised to procure and read them.

When the evening was over, Anne could not but be amused at the idea of her coming to Lyme, to preach patience and resignation to a young man whom she had never seen before; nor could she help fearing, on more serious reflection, that, like many other great moralists and preachers, she

[69] Walter Scott, author of *Marmion* (1808) and *The Lady of the Lake* (1810), and Lord Byron, author of *The Giaour* and *The Bride of Abydos* (both 1813), were incredibly popular best-selling poets of the time. Both wrote on highly romantic subjects, Scott specializing in medieval and Scottish tales, Byron in tales of the eastern Mediterranean. *Giaour* is a Muslim term meaning "infidel Christian" and is pronounced JOW-er.

[70] The tender songs are Scott's, the descriptions of agony are Byron's.

had been eloquent on a point in which her own conduct would ill bear examination.

CHAPTER 12

Anne and Henrietta, finding themselves the earliest of the party the next morning, agreed to stroll down to the sea before breakfast.—They went to the sands, to watch the flowing of the tide, which a fine south-easterly breeze was bringing in with all the grandeur which so flat a shore admitted. They praised the morning; gloried in the sea; sympathized in the delight of the fresh-feeling breeze—and were silent; till Henrietta suddenly began again, with,

"Oh! yes,—I am quite convinced that, with very few exceptions, the sea-air always does good. There can be no doubt of its having been of the greatest service to Dr. Shirley, after his illness, last spring twelvemonth. He declares himself, that coming to Lyme for a month, did him more good than all the medicine he took; and, that being by the sea, always makes him feel young again. Now, I cannot help thinking it a pity that he does not live entirely by the sea. I do think he had better leave Uppercross entirely, and fix at Lyme.—Do not you, Anne?—Do not you agree with me, that it is the best thing he could do, both for himself and Mrs. Shirley?—She has cousins here, you know, and many acquaintance, which would make it cheerful for her,—and I am sure she would be glad to get to a place where she could have medical attendance at hand, in case of his having another seizure. Indeed I think it quite melancholy to have such excellent people as Dr. and Mrs. Shirley, who have been doing good all their lives, wearing out their last days in a place like Uppercross, where, excepting our family, they seem shut out from all the world. I wish his friends would propose it to him. I really think they ought. And, as to procuring a dispensation, there could be no difficulty at his time of life, and with his character. My only doubt is, whether any thing could persuade him to leave his parish. He is so very strict and scrupulous in his notions; over-scrupulous, I must say. Do not you think, Anne, it is being over-scrupulous? Do not you think it is quite a mistaken point of conscience, when a clergyman sacrifices his health for the sake of duties, which may be just as well performed by another person?— And at Lyme too,—only seventeen miles off,—he would be near enough to hear, if people thought there was any thing to complain of."

Anne smiled more than once to herself during this speech, and entered into the subject, as ready to do good by entering into the feelings of a young lady as of a young man,—though here it was good of a lower standard, for what could be offered but general acquiescence?—She said all that was reasonable and proper on the business; felt the claims of Dr. Shirley to repose, as she ought; saw how very desirable it was that he should have some active, respectable young man, as a resident curate, and was even courteous enough to hint at the advantage of such resident curate's being married.

"I wish," said Henrietta, very well pleased with her companion, " I wish Lady Russell lived at Uppercross, and were intimate with Dr. Shirley. I have always heard of Lady Russell, as a woman of the greatest influence

with every body! I always look upon her as able to persuade a person to any thing! I am afraid of her, as I have told you before, quite afraid of her, because she is so very clever; but I respect her amazingly, and wish we had such a neighbour at Uppercross."

Anne was amused by Henrietta's manner of being grateful, and amused also, that the course of events and the new interests of Henrietta's views should have placed her friend at all in favour with any of the Musgrove family; she had only time, however, for a general answer, and a wish that such another woman were at Uppercross, before all subjects suddenly ceased, on seeing Louisa and Captain Wentworth coming towards them. They came also for a stroll till breakfast was likely to be ready; but Louisa recollecting, immediately afterwards, that she had something to procure at a shop, invited them all to go back with her into the town. They were all at her disposal.

When they came to the steps, leading upwards from the beach, a gentle-man at the same moment preparing to come down, politely drew back, and stopped to give them way. They ascended and passed him; and as they passed, Anne's face caught his eye, and he looked at her with a degree of earnest admiration, which she could not be insensible of. She was looking remarkably well; her very regular, very pretty features, having the bloom and freshness of youth restored by the fine wind which had been blowing on her complexion, and by the animation of eye which it had also pro-duced. It was evident that the gentleman, (completely a gentleman in man-ner) admired her exceedingly. Captain Wentworth looked round at her instantly in a way which shewed his noticing of it. He gave her a momentary glance,—a glance of brightness, which seemed to say, "That man is struck with you,—and even I, at this moment, see something like Anne Elliot again."

After attending Louisa through her business, and loitering about a little longer, they returned to the inn; and Anne in passing afterwards quickly from her own chamber to their dining-room, had nearly run against the very same gentleman, as he came out of an adjoining apartment. She had before conjectured him to be a stranger like themselves, and determined that a well-looking groom, who was strolling about near the two inns as they came back, should be his servant. Both master and man being in mourning, assisted the idea. It was now proved that he belonged to the same inn as themselves; and this second meeting, short as it was, also proved again by the gentleman's looks, that he thought hers very lovely, and by the readi-ness and propriety of his apologies, that he was a man of exceedingly good manners. He seemed about thirty, and, though not handsome, had an agreeable person. Anne felt that she should like to know who he was.

They had nearly done breakfast, when the sound of a carriage, (almost the first they had heard since entering Lyme) drew half the party to the window. "It was a gentleman's carriage—a curricle—but only coming round from the stable-yard to the front door—Somebody must be going away.—It was driven by a servant in mourning."

The word curricle made Charles Musgrove jump up, that he might compare it with his own, the servant in mourning roused Anne's curiosity, and the whole six were collected to look, by the time the owner of the

curricle was to be seen issuing from the door amidst the bows and civilities of the household, and taking his seat, to drive off.

"Ah!" cried Captain Wentworth, instantly, and with half a glance at Anne; "it is the very man we passed."

The Miss Musgroves agreed to it; and having all kindly watched him as far up the hill as they could, they returned to the breakfast-table. The waiter came into the room soon afterwards.

"Pray," said Captain Wentworth, immediately, "can you tell us the name of the gentleman who is just gone away?"

"Yes, Sir, a Mr. Elliot; a gentleman of large fortune,—came in last night from Sidmouth,—dare say you heard the carriage, Sir, while you were at dinner; and going on now for Crewkherne, in his way to Bath and London."

"Elliot!"—Many had looked on each other, and many had repeated the name, before all this had been got through, even by the smart rapidity of a waiter.

"Bless me!" cried Mary; "It must be our cousin;—it must be our Mr. Elliot, it must, indeed!—Charles, Anne, must not it? In mourning, you see, just as our Mr. Elliot must be. How very extraordinary! In the very same inn with us! Anne, must not it be our Mr. Elliot; my father's next heir? Pray Sir," (turning to the waiter), "did not you hear,—did not his servant say whether he belonged to the Kellynch family?"

"No, ma'am,—he did not mention no particular family; but he said his master was a very rich gentleman, and would be a baronight some day."

"There! you see!" cried Mary, in an ecstacy, "Just as I said! Heir to Sir Walter Elliot!—I was sure that would come out, if it was so. Depend upon it, that is a circumstance which his servants take care to publish wherever he goes. But, Anne, only conceive how extraordinary! I wish I had looked at him more. I wish we had been aware in time, who it was, that he might have been introduced to us. What a pity that we should not have been introduced to each other!—Do you think he had the Elliot countenance? I hardly looked at him, I was looking at the horses; but I think he had something of the Elliot countenance. I wonder the arms[71] did not strike me! Oh!—the great-coat was hanging over the panel, and hid the arms; so it did, otherwise, I am sure, I should have observed them, and the livery too; if the servant had not been in mourning, one should have known him by the livery."

"Putting all these very extraordinary circumstances together," said Captain Wentworth, "we must consider it to be the arrangement of Providence, that you should not be introduced to your cousin."

When she could command Mary's attention, Anne quietly tried to convince her that their father and Mr. Elliot had not, for many years, been on such terms as to make the power of attempting an introduction at all desirable.

At the same time, however, it was a secret gratification to herself to have seen her cousin, and to know that the future owner of Kellynch was undoubtedly a gentleman, and had an air of good sense. She would not, upon

[71] Coat of arms.

any account, mention her having met with him the second time; luckily Mary did not much attend to their having passed close by him in their early walk, but she would have felt quite ill-used by Anne's having actually run against him in the passage, and received his very polite excuses, while she had never been near him at all; no, that cousinly little interview must remain a perfect secret.

"Of course," said Mary, "you will mention our seeing Mr. Elliot, the next time you write to Bath. I think my father certainly ought to hear of it; do mention all about him."

Anne avoided a direct reply, but it was just the circumstance which she considered as not merely unnecessary to be communicated, but as what ought to be suppressed. The offence which had been given her father, many years back, she knew; Elizabeth's particular share in it she suspected; and that Mr. Elliot's idea always produced irritation in both, was beyond a doubt. Mary never wrote to Bath herself; all the toil of keeping up a slow and unsatisfactory correspondence with Elizabeth fell on Anne.

Breakfast had not been long over, when they were joined by Captain and Mrs. Harville, and Captain Benwick, with whom they had appointed to take their last walk about Lyme. They ought to be setting off for Uppercross by one, and in the meanwhile were to be all together, and out of doors as long as they could.

Anne found Captain Benwick getting near her, as soon as they were all fairly in the street. Their conversation, the preceding evening, did not disincline him to seek her again; and they walked together some time, talking as before of Mr. Scott and Lord Byron, and still as unable, as before, and as unable as any other two readers, to think exactly alike of the merits of either, till something occasioned an almost general change amongst their party, and instead of Captain Benwick, she had Captain Harville by her side.

"Miss Elliot," said he, speaking rather low, "you have done a good deed in making that poor fellow talk so much. I wish he could have such company oftener. It is bad for him, I know, to be shut up as he is; but what can we do? we cannot part."

"No," said Anne, "that I can easily believe to be impossible; but in time, perhaps—we know what time does in every case of affliction, and you must remember, Captain Harville, that your friend may yet be called a young mourner—Only last summer, I understand."

"Ay, true enough," (with a deep sigh) "only June."

"And not known to him, perhaps, so soon."

"Not till the first week in August, when he came home from the Cape,—just made[72] into the Grappler. I was at Plymouth, dreading to hear of him; he sent in letters, but the Grappler was under orders for Portsmouth. There the news must follow him, but who was to tell it? not I. I would as soon have been run up to the yard-arm. Nobody could do it, but that good fellow, (pointing to Captain Wentworth.) The Laconia had come into Plymouth the week before; no danger of her being sent to sea again. He stood his chance for the rest—wrote up for leave of absence, but without waiting the return, travelled night and day till he got to Portsmouth, rowed off to

[72] Promoted.

the Grappler that instant, and never left the poor fellow for a week; that's what he did, and nobody else could have saved poor James. You may think, Miss Elliot, whether he is dear to us!"

Anne did think on the question with perfect decision, and said as much in reply as her own feelings could accomplish, or as his seemed able to bear, for he was too much affected to renew the subject—and when he spoke again, it was of something totally different.

Mrs. Harville's giving it as her opinion that her husband would have quite walking enough by the time he reached home, determined the direction of all the party in what was to be their last walk; they would accompany them to their door, and then return and set off themselves. By all their calculations there was just time for this; but as they drew near the Cobb, there was such a general wish to walk along it once more, all were so inclined, and Louisa soon grew so determined, that the difference of a quarter of an hour, it was found, would be no difference at all, so with all the kind leave-taking, and all the kind interchange of invitations and promises which may be imagined, they parted from Captain and Mrs. Harville at their own door, and still accompanied by Captain Benwick, who seemed to cling to them to the last, proceeded to make the proper adieus to the Cobb.

Anne found Captain Benwick again drawing near her. Lord Byron's "dark blue seas"[73] could not fail of being brought forward by their present view, and she gladly gave him all her attention as long as attention was possible. It was soon drawn perforce another way.

There was too much wind to make the high part of the new Cobb pleasant for the ladies, and they agreed to get down the steps to the lower, and all were contented to pass quietly and carefully down the steep flight, excepting Louisa; she must be jumped down them by Captain Wentworth. In all their walks, he had had to jump her from the stiles; the sensation was delightful to her. The hardness of the pavement for her feet, made him less willing upon the present occasion; he did it, however; she was safely down, and instantly, to shew her enjoyment, ran up the steps to be jumped down again. He advised her against it, thought the jar too great; but no, he reasoned and talked in vain; she smiled and said, "I am determined I will:" he put out his hands; she was too precipitate by half a second, she fell on the pavement on the Lower Cobb, and was taken up lifeless!

There was no wound, no blood, no visible bruise; but her eyes were closed, she breathed not, her face was like death.—The horror of that moment to all who stood around!

Captain Wentworth, who had caught her up, knelt with her in his arms, looking on her with a face as pallid as her own, in an agony of silence. "She is dead! she is dead!" screamed Mary, catching hold of her husband, and contributing with his own horror to make him immoveable; and in another moment, Henrietta, sinking under the conviction, lost her senses[74] too, and would have fallen on the steps, but for Captain Benwick and Anne, who caught and supported her between them.

"Is there no one to help me?" were the first words which burst from Captain Wentworth, in a tone of despair, and as if all his own strength were gone.

[73] From *The Corsair* (1814), line 1. [74] Fainted.

"Go to him, go to him," cried Anne, "for heaven's sake go to him. I can support her myself. Leave me, and go to him. Rub her hands, rub her temples; here are salts,—take them, take them."

Captain Benwick obeyed, and Charles at the same moment, disengaging himself from his wife, they were both with him; and Louisa was raised up and supported more firmly between them, and every thing was done that Anne had prompted, but in vain; while Captain Wentworth, staggering against the wall for his support, exclaimed in the bitterest agony,

"Oh God! her father and mother!"

"A surgeon!" said Anne.

He caught the word; it seemed to rouse him at once, and saying only "True, true, a surgeon this instant," was darting away; when Anne eagerly suggested,

"Captain Benwick, would not it be better for Captain Benwick? He knows where a surgeon is to be found."

Every one capable of thinking felt the advantage of the idea, and in a moment (it was all done in rapid moments) Captain Benwick had resigned the poor corpse-like figure entirely to the brother's care, and was off for the town with the utmost rapidity.

As to the wretched party left behind, it could scarcely be said which of the three, who were completely rational, was suffering most, Captain Wentworth, Anne, or Charles, who, really a very affectionate brother, hung over Louisa with sobs of grief, and could only turn his eyes from one sister, to see the other in a state as insensible, or to witness the hysterical agitations of his wife, calling on him for help which he could not give.

Anne, attending with all the strength and zeal, and thought, which instinct supplied, to Henrietta, still tried, at intervals, to suggest comfort to the others, tried to quiet Mary, to animate Charles, to assuage the feelings of Captain Wentworth. Both seemed to look to her for directions.

"Anne, Anne," cried Charles, "what is to be done next? What, in heaven's name, is to be done next?"

Captain Wentworth's eyes were also turned towards her.

"Had not she better be carried to the inn? Yes, I am sure, carry her gently to the inn."

"Yes, yes, to the inn," repeated Captain Wentworth, comparatively collected, and eager to be doing something. "I will carry her myself. Musgrove, take care of the others."

By this time the report of the accident had spread among the workmen and boatmen about the Cobb, and many were collected near them, to be useful if wanted, at any rate, to enjoy the sight of a dead young lady, nay, two dead young ladies, for it proved twice as fine as the first report. To some of the best-looking of these good people Henrietta was consigned, for, though partially revived, she was quite helpless; and in this manner, Anne walking by her side, and Charles attending to his wife, they set forward, treading back with feelings unutterable, the ground which so lately, so very lately, and so light of heart, they had passed along.

They were not off the Cobb, before the Harvilles met them. Captain Benwick had been seen flying by their house, with a countenance which shewed something to be wrong; and they had set off immediately, informed and directed, as they passed, towards the spot. Shocked as Captain

Harville was, he brought senses and nerves that could be instantly useful; and a look between him and his wife decided what was to be done. She must be taken to their house—all must go to their house—and wait the surgeon's arrival there. They would not listen to scruples: he was obeyed; they were all beneath his roof; and while Louisa, under Mrs. Harville's direction, was conveyed up stairs, and given possession of her own bed, assistance, cordials, restoratives were supplied by her husband to all who needed them.

Louisa had once opened her eyes, but soon closed them again, without apparent consciousness. This had been a proof of life, however, of service to her sister; and Henrietta, though perfectly incapable of being in the same room with Louisa, was kept, by the agitation of hope and fear, from a return of her own insensibility. Mary, too, was growing calmer.

The surgeon was with them almost before it had seemed possible. They were sick with horror while he examined; but he was not hopeless. The head had received a severe contusion, but he had seen greater injuries recovered from: he was by no means hopeless; he spoke cheerfully.

That he did not regard it as a desperate case—that he did not say a few hours must end it—was at first felt, beyond the hope of most; and the ecstasy of such a reprieve, the rejoicing, deep and silent, after a few fervent ejaculations of gratitude to Heaven had been offered, may be conceived.

The tone, the look, with which "Thank God!" was uttered by Captain Wentworth, Anne was sure could never be forgotten by her; nor the sight of him afterwards, as he sat near a table, leaning over it with folded arms, and face concealed, as if overpowered by the various feelings of his soul, and trying by prayer and reflection to calm them.

Louisa's limbs had escaped. There was no injury but to the head.

It now became necessary for the party to consider what was best to be done, as to their general situation. They were now able to speak to each other, and consult. That Louisa must remain where she was, however distressing to her friends to be involving the Harvilles in such trouble, did not admit a doubt. Her removal was impossible. The Harvilles silenced all scruples; and, as much as they could, all gratitude. They had looked forward and arranged every thing, before the others began to reflect. Captain Benwick must give up his room to them, and get a bed elsewhere—and the whole was settled. They were only concerned that the house could accommodate no more; and yet perhaps by "putting the children away in the maids' room, or swinging a cot somewhere," they could hardly bear to think of not finding room for two or three besides, supposing they might wish to stay; though, with regard to any attendance on Miss Musgrove, there need not be the least uneasiness in leaving her to Mrs. Harville's care entirely. Mrs. Harville was a very experienced nurse; and her nursery-maid, who had lived with her long and gone about with her every where, was just such another. Between those two, she could want no possible attendance by day or night. And all this was said with a truth and sincerity of feeling irresistible.

Charles, Henrietta, and Captain Wentworth were the three in consultation, and for a little while it was only an interchange of perplexity and terror. "Uppercross,—the necessity of some one's going to Uppercross,—the news to be conveyed—how it could be broken to Mr. and Mrs. Mus-

grove—the lateness of the morning,—an hour already gone since they ought to have been off,—the impossibility of being in tolerable time. At first, they were capable of nothing more to the purpose than such exclamations; but, after a while, Captain Wentworth, exerting himself, said,

"We must be decided, and without the loss of another minute. Every minute is valuable. Some must resolve on being off for Uppercross instantly. Musgrove, either you or I must go."

Charles agreed; but declared his resolution of not going away. He would be as little incumbrance as possible to Captain and Mrs. Harville; but as to leaving his sister in such a state, he neither ought, nor would. So far it was decided; and Henrietta at first declared the same. She, however, was soon persuaded to think differently. The usefulness of her staying!—She, who had not been able to remain in Louisa's room, or to look at her, without sufferings which made her worse than helpless! She was forced to acknowledge that she could do no good; yet was still unwilling to be away, till touched by the thought of her father and mother, she gave it up; she consented, she was anxious to be at home.

The plan had reached this point, when Anne, coming quietly down from Louisa's room, could not but hear what followed, for the parlour door was open.

"Then it is settled, Musgrove," cried Captain Wentworth, "that you stay, and that I take care of your sister home. But as to the rest;—as to the others;—If one stays to assist Mrs. Harville, I think it need be only one.—Mrs. Charles Musgrove will, of course, wish to get back to her children; but, if Anne will stay, no one so proper, so capable as Anne!"

She paused a moment to recover from the emotion of hearing herself so spoken of. The other two warmly agreed to what he said, and she then appeared.

"You will stay, I am sure; you will stay and nurse her;" cried he, turning to her and speaking with a glow, and yet a gentleness, which seemed almost restoring the past.—She coloured deeply; and he recollected himself, and moved away.—She expressed herself most willing, ready, happy to remain. "It was what she had been thinking of, and wishing to be allowed to do.—A bed on the floor in Louisa's room would be sufficient for her, if Mrs. Harville would but think so."

One thing more, and all seemed arranged. Though it was rather desirable that Mr. and Mrs. Musgrove should be previously alarmed by some share of delay; yet the time required by the Uppercross horses to take them back, would be a dreadful extension of suspense; and Captain Wentworth proposed, and Charles Musgrove agreed, that it would be much better for him to take a chaise from the inn, and leave Mr. Musgrove's carriage and horses to be sent home the next morning early, when there would be the farther advantage of sending an account of Louisa's night.

Captain Wentworth now hurried off to get every thing ready on his part, and to be soon followed by the two ladies. When the plan was made known to Mary, however, there was an end of all peace in it. She was so wretched, and so vehement, complained so much of injustice in being expected to go away, instead of Anne;—Anne, who was nothing to Louisa, while she was her sister, and had the best right to stay in Henrietta's stead! Why was not she to be as useful as Anne? And to go home without Charles,

too—without her husband! No, it was too unkind! And, in short, she said more than her husband could long withstand; and as none of the others could oppose when he gave way, there was no help for it: the change of Mary for Anne was inevitable.

Anne had never submitted more reluctantly to the jealous and ill-judging claims of Mary; but so it must be, and they set off for the town, Charles taking care of his sister, and Captain Benwick attending to her. She gave a moment's recollection, as they hurried along, to the little circumstances which the same spots had witnessed earlier in the morning. There she had listened to Henrietta's schemes for Dr. Shirley's leaving Uppercross; farther on, she had first seen Mr. Elliot; a moment seemed all that could now be given to any one but Louisa, or those who were wrapt up in her welfare.

Captain Benwick was most considerately attentive to her; and, united as they all seemed by the distress of the day, she felt an increasing degree of good-will towards him, and a pleasure even in thinking that it might, perhaps, be the occasion of continuing their acquaintance.

Captain Wentworth was on the watch for them, and a chaise and four in waiting, stationed for their convenience in the lowest part of the street; but his evident surprise and vexation, at the substitution of one sister for the other—the change of his countenance—the astonishment—the expressions begun and suppressed, with which Charles was listened to, made but a mortifying reception of Anne; or must at least convince her that she was valued only as she could be useful to Louisa.

She endeavoured to be composed, and to be just. Without emulating the feelings of an Emma towards her Henry,[75] she would have attended on Louisa with a zeal above the common claims of regard, for his sake; and she hoped he would not long be so unjust as to suppose she would shrink unnecessarily from the office of a friend.

In the meanwhile she was in the carriage. He had handed them both in, and placed himself between them; and in this manner, under these circumstances full of astonishment and emotion to Anne, she quitted Lyme. How the long stage would pass; how it was to affect their manners; what was to be their sort of intercourse, she could not foresee. It was all quite natural, however. He was devoted to Henrietta; always turning towards her; and when he spoke at all, always with the view of supporting her hopes and raising her spirits. In general, his voice and manner were studiously calm. To spare Henrietta from agitation seemed the governing principle. Once only, when she had been grieving over the last ill-judged, ill-fated walk to the Cobb, bitterly lamenting that it ever had been thought of, he burst forth, as if wholly overcome—

"Don't talk of it, don't talk of it," he cried. "Oh God! that I had not given way to her at the fatal moment! Had I done as I ought! But so eager and so resolute! Dear, sweet Louisa!"

Anne wondered whether it ever occurred to him now, to question the justness of his own previous opinion as to the universal felicity and advantage of firmness of character; and whether it might not strike him, that, like all other qualities of the mind, it should have its proportions and limits. She

[75] In the poem *Henry and Emma,* by Matthew Prior (1644–1721), Emma offers to serve the woman who is her rival for Henry's love.

thought it could scarcely escape him to feel, that a persuadable temper might sometimes be as much in favour of happiness, as a very resolute character.

They got on fast. Anne was astonished to recognise the same hills and the same objects so soon. Their actual speed, heightened by some dread of the conclusion, made the road appear but half as long as on the day before. It was growing quite dusk, however, before they were in the neighbourhood of Uppercross, and there had been total silence among them for some time, Henrietta leaning back in the corner, with a shawl over her face, giving the hope of her having cried herself to sleep; when, as they were going up their last hill, Anne found herself all at once addressed by Captain Wentworth. In a low, cautious voice, he said,

"I have been considering what we had best do. She must not appear at first. She could not stand it. I have been thinking whether you had not better remain in the carriage with her, while I go in and break it to Mr. and Mrs. Musgrove. Do you think this a good plan?"

She did: he was satisfied, and said no more. But the remembrance of the appeal remained a pleasure to her—as a proof of friendship, and of deference for her judgment, a great pleasure; and when it became a sort of parting proof, its value did not lessen.

When the distressing communication at Uppercross was over, and he had seen the father and mother quite as composed as could be hoped, and the daughter all the better for being with them, he announced his intention of returning in the same carriage to Lyme; and when the horses were baited,[76] he was off.

CHAPTER 13[77]

The remainder of Anne's time at Uppercross, comprehending only two days, was spent entirely at the mansion-house, and she had the satisfaction of knowing herself extremely useful there, both as an immediate companion, and as assisting in all those arrangements for the future, which, in Mr. and Mrs. Musgrove's distressed state of spirits, would have been difficulties.

They had an early account from Lyme the next morning. Louisa was much the same. No symptoms worse than before had appeared. Charles came a few hours afterwards, to bring a later and more particular account. He was tolerably cheerful. A speedy cure must not be hoped, but every thing was going on as well as the nature of the case admitted. In speaking of the Harvilles, he seemed unable to satisfy his own sense of their kindness, especially of Mrs. Harville's exertions as a nurse. "She really left nothing for Mary to do. He and Mary had been persuaded to go early to their inn last night. Mary had been hysterical again this morning. When he came away, she was going to walk out with Captain Benwick, which, he hoped, would do her good. He almost wished she had been prevailed on to come

[76] Rested and fed.

[77] *Persuasion* was originally published in two volumes, the second one beginning here, with chapter numbers reverting to 1.

home the day before; but the truth was, that Mrs. Harville left nothing for any body to do."

Charles was to return to Lyme the same afternoon, and his father had at first half a mind to go with him, but the ladies could not consent. It would be going only to multiply trouble to the others, and increase his own distress; and a much better scheme followed and was acted upon. A chaise was sent for from Crewkherne, and Charles conveyed back a far more useful person in the old nursery-maid of the family, one who having brought up all the children, and seen the very last, the lingering and long-petted master Harry, sent to school after his brothers, was now living in her deserted nursery to mend stockings, and dress all the blains[78] and bruises she could get near her, and who, consequently, was only too happy in being allowed to go and help dear Miss Louisa. Vague wishes of getting Sarah thither, had occurred before to Mrs. Musgrove and Henrietta; but without Anne, it would hardly have been resolved on, and found practicable so soon.

They were indebted, the next day, to Charles Hayter for all the minute knowledge of Louisa, which it was so essential to obtain every twenty-four hours. He made it his business to go to Lyme, and his account was still encouraging. The intervals of sense and consciousness were believed to be stronger. Every report agreed in Captain Wentworth's appearing fixed in Lyme.

Anne was to leave them on the morrow, an event which they all dreaded. "What should they do without her? They were wretched comforters for one another!" And so much was said in this way, that Anne thought she could not do better than impart among them the general inclination to which she was privy, and persuade them all to go to Lyme at once. She had little difficulty; it was soon determined that they would go, go to-morrow, fix themselves at the inn, or get into lodgings, as it suited, and there remain till dear Louisa could be moved. They must be taking off some trouble from the good people she was with; they might at least relieve Mrs. Harville from the care of her own children; and in short they were so happy in the decision, that Anne was delighted with what she had done, and felt that she could not spend her last morning at Uppercross better than in assisting their preparations, and sending them off at an early hour, though her being left to the solitary range of the house was the consequence.

She was the last, excepting the little boys at the cottage, she was the very last, the only remaining one of all that had filled and animated both houses, of all that had given Uppercross its cheerful character. A few days had made a change indeed!

If Louisa recovered, it would all be well again. More than former happiness would be restored. There could not be a doubt, to her mind there was none, of what would follow her recovery. A few months hence, and the room now so deserted, occupied but by her silent, pensive self, might be filled again with all that was happy and gay, all that was glowing and bright in prosperous love, all that was most unlike Anne Elliot!

An hour's complete leisure for such reflections as these, on a dark November day, a small thick rain almost blotting out the very few objects ever to be discerned from the windows, was enough to make the sound of Lady

[78] Sores.

Russell's carriage exceedingly welcome; and yet, though desirous to be gone, she could not quit the mansion-house, or look an adieu to the cottage, with its black, dripping, and comfortless veranda, or even notice through the misty glasses the last humble tenements of the village, without a saddened heart.—Scenes had passed in Uppercross, which made it precious. It stood the record of many sensations of pain, once severe, but now softened; and of some instances of relenting feeling, some breathings of friendship and reconciliation, which could never be looked for again, and which could never cease to be dear. She left it all behind her; all but the recollection that such things had been.

Anne had never entered Kellynch since her quitting Lady Russell's house, in September. It had not been necessary, and the few occasions of its being possible for her to go to the hall she had contrived to evade and escape from. Her first return, was to resume her place in the modern and elegant apartments of the lodge, and to gladden the eyes of its mistress.

There was some anxiety mixed with Lady Russell's joy in meeting her. She knew who had been frequenting Uppercross. But happily, either Anne was improved in plumpness and looks, or Lady Russell fancied her so; and Anne, in receiving her compliments on the occasion, had the amusement of connecting them with the silent admiration of her cousin, and of hoping that she was to be blessed with a second spring of youth and beauty.

When they came to converse, she was soon sensible of some mental change. The subjects of which her heart had been full on leaving Kellynch, and which she had felt slighted, and been compelled to smother among the Musgroves, were now become but of secondary interest. She had lately lost sight even of her father and sister and Bath. Their concerns had been sunk under those of Uppercross, and when Lady Russell reverted to their former hopes and fears, and spoke her satisfaction in the house in Camden-place, which had been taken, and her regret that Mrs. Clay should still be with them, Anne would have been ashamed to have it known, how much more she was thinking of Lyme, and Louisa Musgrove, and all her acquaintance there; how much more interesting to her was the home and the friendship of the Harvilles and Captain Benwick, than her own father's house in Camden-place, or her own sister's intimacy with Mrs. Clay. She was actually forced to exert herself, to meet Lady Russell with any thing like the appearance of equal solicitude, on topics which had by nature the first claim on her.

There was a little awkwardness at first in their discourse on another subject. They must speak of the accident at Lyme. Lady Russell had not been arrived five minutes the day before, when a full account of the whole had burst on her; but still it must be talked of, she must make enquiries, she must regret the imprudence, lament the result, and Captain Wentworth's name must be mentioned by both. Anne was conscious of not doing it so well as Lady Russell. She could not speak the name, and look straight forward to Lady Russell's eye, till she had adopted the expedient of telling her briefly what she thought of the attachment between him and Louisa. When this was told, his name distressed her no longer.

Lady Russell had only to listen composedly, and wish them happy; but internally her heart revelled in angry pleasure, in pleased contempt, that the man who at twenty-three had seemed to understand somewhat of the

value of an Anne Elliot, should, eight years afterwards, be charmed by a Louisa Musgrove.

The first three or four days passed most quietly, with no circumstance to mark them excepting the receipt of a note or two from Lyme, which found their way to Anne, she could not tell how, and brought a rather improving account of Louisa. At the end of that period, Lady Russell's politeness could repose no longer, and the fainter self-threatenings of the past, became in a decided tone, "I must call on Mrs. Croft; I really must call upon her soon. Anne, have you courage to go with me, and pay a visit in that house? It will be some trial to us both."

Anne did not shrink from it; on the contrary, she truly felt as she said, in observing,

"I think you are very likely to suffer the most of the two; your feelings are less reconciled to the change than mine. By remaining in the neighbourhood, I am become inured to it."

She could have said more on the subject; for she had in fact so high an opinion of the Crofts, and considered her father so very fortunate in his tenants, felt the parish to be so sure of a good example, and the poor of the best attention and relief, that however sorry and ashamed for the necessity of the removal, she could not but in conscience feel that they were gone who deserved not to stay, and that Kellynch-hall had passed into better hands than its owners'. These convictions must unquestionably have their own pain, and severe was its kind; but they precluded that pain which Lady Russell would suffer in entering the house again, and returning through the well-known apartments.

In such moments Anne had no power of saying to herself, "These rooms ought to belong only to us. Oh, how fallen in their destination! How unworthily occupied! An ancient family to be so driven away! Strangers filling their place!" No, except when she thought of her mother, and remembered where she had been used to sit and preside, she had no sigh of that description to heave.

Mrs. Croft always met her with a kindness which gave her the pleasure of fancying herself a favourite; and on the present occasion, receiving her in that house, there was particular attention.

The sad accident at Lyme was soon the prevailing topic; and on comparing their latest accounts of the invalid, it appeared that each lady dated her intelligence from the same hour of yester morn, that Captain Wentworth had been in Kellynch yesterday—(the first time since the accident) had brought Anne the last note, which she had not been able to trace the exact steps of, had staid a few hours and then returned again to Lyme—and without any present intention of quitting it any more.—He had enquired after her, she found, particularly;—had expressed his hope of Miss Elliot's not being the worse for her exertions, and had spoken of those exertions as great.—This was handsome,—and gave her more pleasure than almost any thing else could have done.

As to the sad catastrophe itself, it could be canvassed only in one style by a couple of steady, sensible women, whose judgments had to work on ascertained events; and it was perfectly decided that it had been the consequence of much thoughtlessness and much imprudence; that its effects were most alarming, and that it was frightful to think, how long Miss

Musgrove's recovery might yet be doubtful, and how liable she would still remain to suffer from the concussion hereafter!—The Admiral wound it all up summarily by exclaiming,

"Ay, a very bad business indeed.—A new sort of way this, for a young fellow to be making love, by breaking his mistress's head!—is not it, Miss Elliot?—This is breaking a head and giving a plaister truly!"

Admiral Croft's manners were not quite of the tone to suit Lady Russell, but they delighted Anne. His goodness of heart and simplicity of character were irresistible.

"Now, this must be very bad for you," said he, suddenly rousing from a little reverie, "to be coming and finding us here.—I had not recollected it before, I declare,—but it must be very bad.—But now, do not stand upon ceremony.—Get up and go over all the rooms in the house if you like it."

"Another time, Sir, I thank you, not now."

"Well, whenever it suits you.—You can slip in from the shrubbery at any time. And there you will find we keep our umbrellas, hanging up by that door. A good place, is not it? But" (checking himself) "you will not think it a good place, for yours were always kept in the butler's room. Ay, so it always is, I believe. One man's ways may be as good as another's, but we all like our own best. And so you must judge for yourself, whether it would be better for you to go about the house or not."

Anne, finding she might decline it, did so, very gratefully.

"We have made very few changes either!" continued the Admiral, after thinking a moment. "Very few.—We told you about the laundry-door, at Uppercross. That has been a very great improvement. The wonder was, how any family upon earth could bear with the inconvenience of its opening as it did, so long!—You will tell Sir Walter what we have done, and that Mr. Shepherd thinks it the greatest improvement the house ever had. Indeed, I must do ourselves the justice to say, that the few alterations we have made have been all very much for the better. My wife should have the credit of them, however. I have done very little besides sending away some of the large looking-glasses from my dressing-room, which was your father's. A very good man, and very much the gentleman I am sure—but I should think, Miss Elliot" (looking with serious reflection) "I should think he must be rather a dressy man for his time of life.—Such a number of looking-glasses! oh Lord! there was no getting away from oneself. So I got Sophy to lend me a hand, and we soon shifted their quarters; and now I am quite snug, with my little shaving glass[79] in one corner, and another great thing that I never go near."

Anne, amused in spite of herself, was rather distressed for an answer, and the Admiral, fearing he might not have been civil enough, took up the subject again, to say,

"The next time you write to your good father, Miss Elliot, pray give my compliments and Mrs. Croft's, and say that we are settled here quite to our liking, and have no fault at all to find with the place. The breakfast-room chimney smokes a little, I grant you, but it is only when the wind is due north and blows hard, which may not happen three times a winter. And take it altogether, now that we have been into most of the houses here-

[79]Mirror.

abouts and can judge, there is not one that we like better than this. Pray say so, with my compliments. He will be glad to hear it."

Lady Russell and Mrs. Croft were very well pleased with each other; but the acquaintance which this visit began, was fated not to proceed far at present; for when it was returned, the Crofts announced themselves to be going away for a few weeks, to visit their connexions in the north of the county, and probably might not be at home again before Lady Russell would be removing to Bath.

So ended all danger to Anne of meeting Captain Wentworth at Kellynch-hall, or of seeing him in company with her friend. Every thing was safe enough, and she smiled over the many anxious feelings she had wasted on the subject.

CHAPTER 14

Though Charles and Mary had remained at Lyme much longer after Mr. and Mrs. Musgrove's going, than Anne conceived they could have been at all wanted, they were yet the first of the family to be at home again, and as soon as possible after their return to Uppercross, they drove over to the lodge.—They had left Louisa beginning to sit up; but her head, though clear, was exceedingly weak, and her nerves susceptible to the highest extreme of tenderness; and though she might be pronounced to be altogether doing very well, it was still impossible to say when she might be able to bear the removal home; and her father and mother, who must return in time to receive their younger children for the Christmas holidays, had hardly a hope of being allowed to bring her with them.

They had been all in lodgings together. Mrs. Musgrove had got Mrs. Harville's children away as much as she could, every possible supply from Uppercross had been furnished, to lighten the inconvenience to the Harvilles, while the Harvilles had been wanting them to come to dinner every day; and in short, it seemed to have been only a struggle on each side as to which should be most disinterested[80] and hospitable.

Mary had had her evils; but upon the whole, as was evident by her staying so long, she had found more to enjoy than to suffer.—Charles Hayter had been at Lyme oftener than suited her, and when they dined with the Harvilles there had been only a maid-servant to wait, and at first, Mrs. Harville had always given Mrs. Musgrove precedence; but then, she had received so very handsome an apology from her on finding out whose daughter she was, and there had been so much going on every day, there had been so many walks between their lodgings and the Harvilles, and she had got books from the library and changed them so often, that the balance had certainly been much in favour of Lyme. She had been taken to Charmouth too, and she had bathed, and she had gone to church, and there were a great many more people to look at in the church at Lyme than at Uppercross,—and all this, joined to the sense of being so very useful, had made really an agreeable fortnight.

[80] Unselfish.

Anne enquired after Captain Benwick. Mary's face was clouded directly. Charles laughed.

"Oh! Captain Benwick is very well, I believe, but he is a very odd young man. I do not know what he would be at. We asked him to come home with us for a day or two; Charles undertook to give him some shooting, and he seemed quite delighted, and for my part, I thought it was all settled; when behold! on Tuesday night, he made a very awkward sort of excuse; 'he never shot' and he had 'been quite misunderstood,'—and he had promised this and he had promised that, and the end of it was, I found, that he did not mean to come. I suppose he was afraid of finding it dull; but upon my word I should have thought we were lively enough at the Cottage for such a heartbroken man as Captain Benwick."

Charles laughed again and said, "Now Mary, you know very well how it really was.—It was all your doing," (turning to Anne.) "He fancied that if he went with us, he should find you close by; he fancied every body to be living in Uppercross; and when he discovered that Lady Russell lived three miles off, his heart failed him, and he had not courage to come. That is the fact, upon my honour. Mary knows it is."

But Mary did not give into it very graciously; whether from not considering Captain Benwick entitled by birth and situation to be in love with an Elliot, or from not wanting to believe Anne a greater attraction to Uppercross than herself, must be left to be guessed. Anne's good-will, however, was not to be lessened by what she heard. She boldly acknowledged herself flattered, and continued her enquiries.

"Oh! he talks of you." cried Charles, "in such terms,"—Mary interrupted him. "I declare, Charles, I never heard him mention Anne twice all the time I was there. I declare, Anne, he never talks of you at all."

"No," admitted Charles, "I do not know that he ever does, in a general way—but however, it is a very clear thing that he admires you exceedingly.— His head is full of some books that he is reading upon your recommendation, and he wants to talk to you about them; he has found out something or other in one of them which he thinks—Oh! I cannot pretend to remember it, but it was something very fine—I overheard him telling Henrietta all about it—and then 'Miss Elliot' was spoken of in the highest terms!—Now Mary, I declare it was so, I heard it myself, and you were in the other room,—'Elegance, sweetness, beauty,' Oh! there was no end of Miss Elliot's charms."

"And I am sure," cried Mary warmly, "it was very little to his credit, if he did. Miss Harville only died last June. Such a heart is very little worth having; is it, Lady Russell? I am sure you will agree with me."

"I must see Captain Benwick before I decide," said Lady Russell, smiling.

"And that you are very likely to do very soon, I can tell you, ma'am," said Charles. "Though he had not nerves for coming away with us and setting off again afterwards to pay a formal visit here, he will make his way over to Kellynch one day by himself, you may depend on it. I told him the distance and the road, and I told him of the church's being so very well worth seeing, for as he has a taste for those sort of things, I thought that would be a good excuse, and he listened with all his understanding and

soul; and I am sure from his manner that you will have him calling here soon. So, I give you notice, Lady Russell."

"Any acquaintance of Anne's will always be welcome to me," was Lady Russell's kind answer.

"Oh! as to being Anne's acquaintance," said Mary, "I think he is rather my acquaintance, for I have been seeing him every day this last fortnight."

"Well, as your joint acquaintance, then, I shall be very happy to see Captain Benwick."

"You will not find any thing very agreeable in him, I assure you, ma'am. He is one of the dullest young men that ever lived. He has walked with me, sometimes, from one end of the sands to the other, without saying a word. He is not at all a well-bred young man. I am sure you will not like him."

"There we differ, Mary," said Anne. "I think Lady Russell would like him. I think she would be so much pleased with his mind, that she would very soon see no deficiency in his manner."

"So do I, Anne," said Charles. "I am sure Lady Russell would like him. He is just Lady Russell's sort. Give him a book, and he will read all day long."

"Yes, that he will!" exclaimed Mary, tauntingly. "He will sit poring over his book, and not know when a person speaks to him, or when one drops one's scissors, or anything that happens. Do you think Lady Russell would like that?"

Lady Russell could not help laughing. "Upon my word," said she, "I should not have supposed that my opinion of any one could have admitted of such difference of conjecture, steady and matter of fact as I may call myself. I have really a curiosity to see the person who can give occasion to such directly opposite notions. I wish he may be induced to call here. And when he does, Mary, you may depend upon hearing my opinion; but I am determined not to judge him before-hand."

"You will not like him, I will answer for it."

Lady Russell began talking of something else. Mary spoke with animation of their meeting with, or rather missing, Mr. Elliot so extraordinarily.

"He is a man," said Lady Russell, "whom I have no wish to see. His declining to be on cordial terms with the head of his family, has left a very strong impression in his disfavour with me."

This decision checked Mary's eagerness, and stopped her short in the midst of the Elliot countenance.

With regard to Captain Wentworth, though Anne hazarded no enquiries, there was voluntary communication sufficient. His spirits had been greatly recovering lately, as might be expected. As Louisa improved, he had improved; and he was now quite a different creature from what he had been the first week. He had not seen Louisa; and was so extremely fearful of any ill consequence to her from an interview, that he did not press for it at all; and, on the contrary, seemed to have a plan of going away for a week or ten days, till her head were stronger. He had talked of going down to Plymouth for a week, and wanted to persuade Captain Benwick to go with him; but, as Charles maintained to the last, Captain Benwick seemed much more disposed to ride over to Kellynch.

There can be no doubt that Lady Russell and Anne were both occasion-

ally thinking of Captain Benwick, from this time. Lady Russell could not hear the door-bell without feeling that it might be his herald; nor could Anne return from any stroll of solitary indulgence in her father's grounds, or any visit of charity in the village, without wondering whether she might see him or hear of him. Captain Benwick came not, however. He was either less disposed for it than Charles had imagined, or he was too shy; and after giving him a week's indulgence, Lady Russell determined him to be unworthy of the interest which he had been beginning to excite.

The Musgroves came back to receive their happy boys and girls from school, bringing with them Mrs. Harville's little children, to improve the noise of Uppercross, and lessen that of Lyme. Henrietta remained with Louisa; but all the rest of the family were again in their usual quarters.

Lady Russell and Anne paid their compliments to them once, when Anne could not but feel that Uppercross was already quite alive again. Though neither Henrietta, nor Louisa, nor Charles Hayter, nor Captain Wentworth were there, the room presented as strong a contrast as could be wished, to the last state she had seen it in.

Immediately surrounding Mrs. Musgrove were the little Harvilles, whom she was sedulously guarding from the tyranny of the two children from the Cottage, expressly arrived to amuse them. On one side was a table, occupied by some chattering girls, cutting up silk and gold paper; and on the other were tressels and trays, bending under the weight of brawn[81] and cold pies, where riotous boys were holding high revel; the whole completed by a roaring Christmas fire, which seemed determined to be heard, in spite of all the noise of the others. Charles and Mary also came in, of course, during their visit; and Mr. Musgrove made a point of paying his respects to Lady Russell, and sat down close to her for ten minutes, talking with a very raised voice, but, from the clamour of the children on his knees, generally in vain. It was a fine family-piece.

Anne, judging from her own temperament, would have deemed such a domestic hurricane a bad restorative of the nerves, which Louisa's illness must have so greatly shaken; but Mrs. Musgrove, who got Anne near her on purpose to thank her most cordially, again and again, for all her attentions to them, concluded a short recapitulation of what she had suffered herself, by observing, with a happy glance round the room, that after all she had gone through, nothing was so likely to do her good as a little quiet cheerfulness at home.

Louisa was now recovering apace. Her mother could even think of her being able to join their party at home, before her brothers and sisters went to school again. The Harvilles had promised to come with her and stay at Uppercross, whenever she returned. Captain Wentworth was gone, for the present, to see his brother in Shropshire.

"I hope I shall remember, in future," said Lady Russell, as soon as they were reseated in the carriage, "not to call at Uppercross in the Christmas holidays."

Every body has their taste in noises as well as in other matters; and sounds are quite innoxious, or most distressing, by their sort rather than their quantity. When Lady Russell, not long afterwards, was entering Bath

[81] Pickled pigs' feet and similar meats.

on a wet afternoon, and driving through the long course of streets from the Old Bridge to Camden-place, amidst the dash of other carriages, the heavy rumble of carts and drays, the bawling of newsmen, muffin-men and milk-men, and the ceaseless clink of pattens,[82] she made no complaint. No, these were noises which belonged to the winter pleasures; her spirits rose under their influence; and, like Mrs. Musgrove, she was feeling, though not say-ing, that, after being long in the country, nothing could be so good for her as a little quiet cheerfulness.

Anne did not share these feelings. She persisted in a very determined, though very silent, disinclination for Bath; caught the first dim view of the extensive buildings, smoking in rain, without any wish of seeing them bet-ter; felt their progress through the streets to be, however disagreeable, yet too rapid; for who would be glad to see her when she arrived? And looked back, with fond regret, to the bustles of Uppercross and the seclusion of Kellynch.

Elizabeth's last letter had communicated a piece of news of some inter-est. Mr. Elliot was in Bath. He had called in Camden-place; had called a second time, a third; had been pointedly attentive: if Elizabeth and her father did not deceive themselves, had been taking as much pains to seek the acquaintance, and proclaim the value of the connection, as he had formerly taken pains to shew neglect. This was very wonderful,[83] if it were true; and Lady Russell was in a state of very agreeable curiosity and per-plexity about Mr. Elliot, already recanting the sentiment she had so lately expressed to Mary, of his being "a man whom she had no wish to see." She had a great wish to see him. If he really sought to reconcile himself like a dutiful branch, he must be forgiven for having dismembered himself from the paternal tree.

Anne was not animated to an equal pitch by the circumstance; but she felt that she would rather see Mr. Elliot again than not, which was more than she could say for many other persons in Bath.

She was put down in Camden-place; and Lady Russell then drove to her own lodgings, in Rivers-street.

CHAPTER 15

Sir Walter had taken a very good house in Camden-place, a lofty, dignified situation, such as becomes a man of consequence; and both he and Eliza-beth were settled there, much to their satisfaction.

Anne entered it with a sinking heart, anticipating an imprisonment of many months, and anxiously saying to herself, "Oh! when shall I leave you again?" A degree of unexpected cordiality, however, in the welcome she received, did her good. Her father and sister were glad to see her, for the sake of shewing her the house and furniture, and met her with kindness. Her making a fourth, when they sat down to dinner, was noticed as an advantage.

Mrs. Clay was very pleasant, and very smiling; but her courtesies and smiles were more a matter of course. Anne had always felt that she would

[82]Wooden shoes or clogs. [83]Amazing.

pretend what was proper on her arrival; but the complaisance of the others was unlooked for. They were evidently in excellent spirits, and she was soon to listen to the causes. They had no inclination to listen to her. After laying out for some compliments of being deeply regretted in their old neighbourhood, which Anne could not pay, they had only a few faint enquiries to make, before the talk must be all their own. Uppercross excited no interest, Kellynch very little, it was all Bath.

They had the pleasure of assuring her that Bath more than answered their expectations in every respect. Their house was undoubtedly the best in Camden-place; their drawing-rooms had many decided advantages over all the others which they had either seen or heard of; and the superiority was not less in the style of the fitting-up, or the taste of the furniture. Their acquaintance was exceedingly sought after. Every body was wanting to visit them. They had drawn back from many introductions, and still were perpetually having cards left by people of whom they knew nothing.

Here were funds of enjoyment! Could Anne wonder that her father and sister were happy? She might not wonder, but she might sigh that her father should feel no degradation in his change; should see nothing to regret in the duties and dignity of the resident land-holder; should find so much to be vain of in the littlenesses of a town; and she must sigh, and smile, and wonder too, as Elizabeth threw open the folding-doors, and walked with exultation from one drawing-room to the other, boasting of their space, at the possibility of that woman, who had been mistress of Kellynch—hall, finding extent to be proud of between two walls, perhaps thirty feet asunder.

But this was not all which they had to make them happy. They had Mr. Elliot, too. Anne had a great deal to hear of Mr. Elliot. He was not only pardoned, they were delighted with him. He had been in Bath about a fortnight; (he had passed through Bath in November, in his way to London, when the intelligence of Sir Walter's being settled there had of course reached him, though only twenty-four hours in the place, but he had not been able to avail himself of it): but he had now been a fortnight in Bath, and his first object, on arriving, had been to leave his card in Camden-place, following it up by such assiduous endeavours to meet, and, when they did meet, by such great openness of conduct, such readiness to apologize for the past, such solicitude to be received as a relation again, that their former good understanding was completely re-established.

They had not a fault to find in him. He had explained away all the appearance of neglect on his own side. It had originated in misapprehension entirely. He had never had an idea of throwing himself off; he had feared that he was thrown off, but knew not why; and delicacy had kept him silent. Upon the hint of having spoken disrespectfully or carelessly of the family, and the family honours, he was quite indignant. He, who had ever boasted of being an Elliot, and whose feelings, as to connection, were only too strict to suit the unfeudal tone of the present day! He was astonished, indeed! But his character and general conduct must refute it. He could refer Sir Walter to all who knew him; and, certainly, the pains he had been taking on this, the first opportunity of reconciliation, to be restored to the footing of a relation and heir-presumptive, was a strong proof of his opinions on the subject.

The circumstances of his marriage too were found to admit of much extenuation. This was an article not to be entered on by himself; but a very intimate friend of his, a Colonel Wallis, a highly respectable man, perfectly the gentleman, (and not an ill-looking man, Sir Walter added) who was living in very good style in Marlborough Buildings, and had, at his own particular request, been admitted to their acquaintance through Mr. Elliot, had mentioned one or two things relative to the marriage, which made a material difference in the discredit of it.

Colonel Wallis had known Mr. Elliot long, had been well acquainted also with his wife, had perfectly understood the whole story. She was certainly not a woman of family, but well educated, accomplished, rich, and excessively in love with his friend. There had been the charm. She had sought him. Without that attraction, not all her money would have tempted Elliot, and Sir Walter was, moreover, assured of her having been a very fine woman. Here was a great deal to soften the business. A very fine woman, with a large fortune, in love with him! Sir Walter seemed to admit it as complete apology, and though Elizabeth could not see the circumstance in quite so favourable a light, she allowed it be a great extenuation.

Mr. Elliot had called repeatedly, had dined with them once, evidently delighted by the distinction of being asked, for they gave no dinners in general; delighted, in short, by every proof of cousinly notice, and placing his whole happiness in being on intimate terms in Camden-place.

Anne listened, but without quite understanding it. Allowances, large allowances, she knew, must be made for the ideas of those who spoke. She heard it all under embellishment. All that sounded extravagant or irrational in the progress of the reconciliation might have no origin but in the language of the relators. Still, however, she had the sensation of there being something more than immediately appeared, in Mr. Elliot's wishing, after an interval of so many years, to be well received by them. In a worldly view, he had nothing to gain by being on terms with Sir Walter, nothing to risk by a state of variance. In all probability he was already the richer of the two, and the Kellynch estate would as surely be his hereafter as the title. A sensible man! and he had looked like a *very* sensible man, why should it be an object to him? She could only offer one solution; it was, perhaps, for Elizabeth's sake. There might really have been a liking formerly, though convenience and accident had drawn him a different way, and now that he could afford to please himself, he might mean to pay his addresses to her. Elizabeth was certainly very handsome, with well-bred, elegant manners, and her character might never have been penetrated by Mr. Elliot, knowing her but in public, and when very young himself. How her temper and understanding might bear the investigation of his present keener time of life was another concern, and rather a fearful one. Most earnestly did she wish that he might not be too nice,[84] or too observant, if Elizabeth were his object; and that Elizabeth was disposed to believe herself so, and that her friend Mrs. Clay was encouraging the idea, seemed apparent by a glance or two between them, while Mr. Elliot's frequent visits were talked of.

Anne mentioned the glimpses she had had of him at Lyme, but without being much attended to. "Oh! yes, perhaps, it had been Mr. Elliot. They

[84] Fastidious; finicky.

did not know. It might be him, perhaps." They could not listen to her description of him. They were describing him themselves; Sir Walter especially. He did justice to his very gentleman-like appearance, his air of elegance and fashion, his good shaped face, his sensible eye, but, at the same time, "must lament his being very much under-hung,[85] a defect which time seemed to have increased; nor could he pretend to say that ten years had not altered almost every feature for the worse. Mr. Elliot appeared to think that he (Sir Walter) was looking exactly as he had done when they last parted;" but Sir Walter had "not been able to return the compliment entirely, which had embarrassed him. He did not mean to complain, however. Mr. Elliot was better to look at than most men, and he had no objection to being seen with him any where."

Mr. Elliot, and his friends in Marlborough Buildings, were talked of the whole evening. "Colonel Wallis had been so impatient to be introduced to them! and Mr. Elliot so anxious that he should!" And there was a Mrs. Wallis, at present only known to them by description, as she was in daily expectation of her confinement;[86] but Mr. Elliot spoke of her as "a most charming woman, quite worthy of being known in Camden-place," and as soon as she recovered, they were to be acquainted. Sir Walter thought much of Mrs. Wallis; she was said to be an excessively pretty woman, beautiful. "He longed to see her. He hoped she might make some amends for the many very plain faces he was continually passing in the streets. The worst of Bath was, the number of its plain women. He did not mean to say that there were no pretty women, but the number of the plain was out of all proportion. He had frequently observed, as he walked, that one handsome face would be followed by thirty, or five and thirty frights; and once, as he had stood in a shop in Bond-street, he had counted eighty-seven women go by, one after another, without there being a tolerable face among them. It had been a frosty morning, to be sure, a sharp frost, which hardly one woman in a thousand could stand the test of. But still, there certainly were a dreadful multitude of ugly women in Bath; and as for the men! they were infinitely worse. Such scare-crows as the streets were full of! It was evident how little the women were used to the sight of any thing tolerable, by the effect which a man of decent appearance produced. He had never walked any where arm in arm with Colonel Walis, (who was a fine military figure, though sandy-haired) without observing that every woman's eye was upon him; every woman's eye was sure to be upon Colonel Wallis." Modest Sir Walter! He was not allowed to escape, however. His daughter and Mrs. Clay united in hinting that Colonel Wallis's companion might have as good a figure as Colonel Wallis, and certainly was not sandy-haired.

"How is Mary looking?" said Sir Walter, in the height of his good humour. "The last time I saw her, she had a red nose, but I hope that may not happen every day."

"Oh! no, that must have been quite accidental. In general she has been in very good health, and very good looks since Michaelmas."

"If I thought it would not tempt her to go out in sharp winds, and grow coarse, I would send her a new hat and pelisse."

[85] Having a jutting chin and jaw. [86] Time of giving birth.

Anne was considering whether she should venture to suggest that a gown, or a cap, would not be liable to any such misuse, when a knock at the door suspended every thing. "A knock at the door! and so late! It was ten o'clock. Could it be Mr. Elliot? They knew he was to dine in Lansdown Crescent. It was possible that he might stop in his way home, to ask them how they did. They could think of no one else. Mrs. Clay decidedly thought it Mr. Elliot's knock." Mrs. Clay was right. With all the state which a butler and foot-boy could give, Mr. Elliot was ushered into the room.

It was the same, the very same man, with no difference but of dress. Anne drew a little back, while the others received his compliments, and her sister his apologies for calling at so unusual an hour, but "he could not be so near without wishing to know that neither she nor her friend had taken cold the day before, &c. &c." which was all as politely done, and as politely taken as possible, but her part must follow then. Sir Walter talked of his youngest daughter; "Mr. Elliot must give him leave to present him to his youngest daughter"—(there was no occasion for remembering Mary) and Anne, smiling and blushing, very becomingly shewed to Mr. Elliot the pretty features which he had by no means forgotten, and instantly saw, with amusement at his little start of surprise, that he had not been at all aware of who she was. He looked completely astonished, but not more astonished than pleased; his eyes brightened, and with the most perfect alacrity he welcomed the relationship, alluded to the past, and entreated to be received as an acquaintance already. He was quite as good-looking as he had appeared at Lyme, his countenance improved by speaking, and his manners were so exactly what they ought to be, so polished, so easy, so particularly agreeable, that she could compare them in excellence to only one person's manners. They were not the same, but they were, perhaps, equally good.

He sat down with them, and improved their conversation very much. There could be no doubt of his being a sensible man. Ten minutes were enough to certify that. His tone, his expressions, his choice of subject, his knowing where to stop,—it was all the operation of a sensible, discerning mind. As soon as he could, he began to talk to her of Lyme, wanting to compare opinions respecting the place, but especially wanting to speak of the circumstance of their happening to be guests in the same inn at the same time, to give his own route, understand something of hers, and regret that he should have lost such an opportunity of paying his respects to her. She gave him a short account of her party, and business at Lyme. His regret increased as he listened. He had spent his whole solitary evening in the room adjoining theirs; had heard voices—mirth continually; thought they must be a most delightful set of people—longed to be with them; but certainly without the smallest suspicion of his possessing the shadow of a right to introduce himself. If he had but asked who the party were! The name of Musgrove would have told him enough. "Well, it would serve to cure him of an absurd practice of never asking a question at an inn, which he had adopted, when quite a young man, on the principle of its being very ungenteel to be curious.

"The notions of a young man of one or two and twenty," said he, " as to what is necessary in manners to make him quite the thing, are more absurd,

I believe, than those of any other set of beings in the world. The folly of the means they often employ is only to be equalled by the folly of what they have in view."

But he must not be addressing his reflections to Anne alone; he knew it; he was soon diffused again among the others, and it was only at intervals that he could return to Lyme.

His enquiries, however, produced at length an account of the scene she had been engaged in there, soon after his leaving the place. Having alluded to "an accident," he must hear the whole. When he questioned, Sir Walter and Elizabeth began to question also; but the difference in their manner of doing it could not be unfelt. She could only compare Mr. Elliot to Lady Russell, in the wish of really comprehending what had passed, and in the degree of concern for what she must have suffered in witnessing it.

He staid an hour with them. The elegant little clock on the mantle-piece had struck "eleven with its silver sounds,"[87] and the watchman was beginning to be heard at a distance telling the same tale, before Mr. Elliot or any of them seemed to feel that he had been there long.

Anne could not have supposed it possible that her first evening in Camden-place could have passed so well!

<div align="center">

CHAPTER 16

</div>

There was one point which Anne, on returning to her family, would have been more thankful to ascertain, even than Mr. Elliot's being in love with Elizabeth, which was, her father's not being in love with Mrs. Clay; and she was very far from easy about it, when she had been at home a few hours. On going down to breakfast the next morning, she found there had just been a decent pretence on the lady's side of meaning to leave them. She could imagine Mrs. Clay to have said, that "now Miss Anne was come, she could not suppose herself at all wanted;" for Elizabeth was replying, in a sort of whisper, "That must not be any reason, indeed. I assure you I feel it none. She is nothing to me, compared with you;" and she was in full time to hear her father say, "My dear Madam, this must not be. As yet, you have seen nothing of Bath. You have been here only to be useful. You must not run away from us now. You must stay to be acquainted with Mrs. Wallis, the beautiful Mrs. Wallis. To your fine mind, I well know the sight of beauty is a real gratification."

He spoke and looked so much in earnest, that Anne was not surprised to see Mrs. Clay stealing a glance at Elizabeth and herself. Her countenance, perhaps, might express some watchfulness; but the praise of the fine mind did not appear to excite a thought in her sister. The lady could not but yield to such joint entreaties, and promise to stay.

In the course of the same morning, Anne and her father chancing to be alone together, he began to compliment her on her improved looks; he thought her "less thin in her person, in her cheeks; her skin, her complexion, greatly improved—clearer, fresher. Had she been using any thing in

[87] A loose quotation of Alexander Pope's *The Rape of the Lock*, I.18.

particular?" "No, nothing." "Merely Gowland,"[88] he supposed. "No, nothing at all." "Ha! he was surprised at that;" and added, "Certainly you cannot do better than continue as you are; you cannot be better than well; or I should recommend Gowland, the constant use of Gowland, during the spring months. Mrs. Clay has been using it at my recommendation, and you see what it has done for her. You see how it has carried away her freckles."

If Elizabeth could but have heard this! Such personal praise might have struck her, especially as it did not appear to Anne that the freckles were at all lessened. But every thing must take its chance. The evil of the marriage would be much diminished, if Elizabeth were also to marry. As for herself, she might always command a home with Lady Russell.

Lady Russell's composed mind and polite manners were put to some trial on this point, in her intercourse in Camden-place. The sight of Mrs. Clay in such favour, and of Anne so overlooked, was a perpetual provocation to her there; and vexed her as much when she was away, as a person in Bath who drinks the water,[89] gets all the new publications, and has a very large acquaintance, has time to be vexed.

As Mr. Elliot became known to her, she grew more charitable, or more indifferent, towards the others. His manners were an immediate recommendation; and on conversing with him she found the solid so fully supporting the superficial, that she was at first, as she told Anne, almost ready to exclaim, "Can this be Mr. Elliot?" and could not seriously picture to herself a more agreeable or estimable man. Every thing united in him; good understanding, correct opinions, knowledge of the world, and a warm heart. He had strong feelings of family-attachment and family-honour, without pride or weakness; he lived with the liberality of a man of fortune, without display; he judged for himself in every thing essential, without defying public opinion in any point of worldly decorum. He was steady, observant, moderate, candid;[90] never run away with by spirits or by selfishness, which fancied itself strong feeling; and yet, with a sensibility to what was amiable and lovely, and a value for all the felicities of domestic life, which characters of fancied enthusiasm and violent agitation seldom really possess. She was sure that he had not been happy in marriage. Colonel Wallis said it, and Lady Russell saw it; but it had been no unhappiness to sour his mind, nor (she began pretty soon to suspect) to prevent his thinking of a second choice. Her satisfaction in Mr. Elliot outweighed all the plague of Mrs. Clay.

It was now some years since Anne had begun to learn that she and her excellent friend could sometimes think differently; and it did not surprise her, therefore, that Lady Russell should see nothing suspicious or inconsistent, nothing to require more motives than appeared, in Mr. Elliot's great desire of a reconciliation. In Lady Russell's view, it was perfectly natural that Mr. Elliot, at a mature time of life, should feel it a most desirable object, and what would very generally recommend him, among all sensible people, to be on good terms with the head of his family; the simplest

[88] A patent skin-lotion. [89] The mineral-spring water.
[90] Generous in judging other people. (The word means nearly the opposite of what it means today.)

process in the world of time upon a head naturally clear, and only erring in the heyday of youth. Anne presumed, however, still to smile about it; and at last to mention "Elizabeth." Lady Russell listened, and looked, and made only this cautious reply: "Elizabeth! Very well. Time will explain."

It was a reference to the future, which Anne, after a little observation, felt she must submit to. She could determine nothing at present. In that house Elizabeth must be first; and she was in the habit of such general observance as "Miss Elliot," that any particularity of attention seemed almost impossible. Mr. Elliot, too, it must be remembered, had not been a widower seven months. A little delay on his side might be very excusable. In fact, Anne could never see the crape round his hat, without fearing that she was the inexcusable one, in attributing to him such imaginations; for though his marriage had not been very happy, still it had existed so many years that she could not comprehend a very rapid recovery from the awful impression of its being dissolved.

However it might end, he was without any question their pleasantest acquaintance in Bath; she saw nobody equal to him; and it was a great indulgence now and then to talk to him about Lyme, which he seemed to have as lively a wish to see again, and to see more of, as herself. They went through the particulars of their first meeting a great many times. He gave her to understand that he had looked at her with some earnestness. She knew it well; and she remembered another person's look also.

They did not always think alike. His value for rank and connexion she perceived to be greater than hers. It was not merely complaisance, it must be a liking to the cause, which made him enter warmly into her father and sister's solicitudes on a subject which she thought unworthy to excite them. The Bath paper one morning announced the arrival of the Dowager Viscountess Dalrymple, and her daughter, the Honourable Miss Carteret; and all the comfort of No.—, Camden-place, was swept away for many days; for the Dalrymples (in Anne's opinion, most unfortunately) were cousins of the Elliots; and the agony was, how to introduce themselves properly.

Anne had never seen her father and sister before in contact with nobility, and she must acknowledge herself disappointed. She had hoped better things from their high ideas of their own situation in life, and was reduced to form a wish which she had never foreseen—a wish that they had more pride; for "our cousins Lady Dalrymple and Miss Carteret;" "our cousins, the Dalrymples," sounded in her ears all day long.

Sir Walter had once been in company with the late Viscount, but had never seen any of the rest of the family, and the difficulties of the case arose from there having been a suspension of all intercourse by letters of ceremony, ever since the death of that said late Viscount, when, in consequence of a dangerous illness of Sir Walter's at the same time, there had been an unlucky omission at Kellynch. No letter of condolence had been sent to Ireland. The neglect had been visited on the head of the sinner, for when poor Lady Elliot died herself, no letter of condolence was received at Kellynch, and, consequently, there was but too much reason to apprehend that the Dalrymples considered the relationship as closed. How to have this anxious business set to rights, and be admitted as cousins again, was the question; and it was a question which, in a more rational manner, neither Lady Russell nor Mr. Elliot thought unimportant. "Family connexions were

always worth preserving, good company always worth seeking; Lady Dalrymple had taken a house, for three months, in Laura-place, and would be living in style. She had been at Bath the year before, and Lady Russell had heard her spoken of as a charming woman. It was very desirable that the connexion should be renewed, if it could be done, without any compromise of propriety on the side of the Elliots."

Sir Walter, however, would choose his own means, and at last wrote a very fine letter of ample explanation, regret and entreaty, to his right honourable cousin. Neither Lady Russell nor Mr. Elliot could admire the letter; but it did all that was wanted, in bringing three lines of scrawl from the Dowager Viscountess. "She was very much honoured, and should be happy in their acquaintance." The toils of the business were over, the sweets began. They visited in Laura-place, they had the cards of Dowager Viscountess Dalrymple, and the Hon. Miss Carteret, to be arranged wherever they might be most visible; and "Our cousins in Laura-place,"—"Our cousins, Lady Dalrymple and Miss Carteret," were talked of to every body.

Anne was ashamed. Had Lady Dalrymple and her daughter even been very agreeable, she would still have been ashamed of the agitation they created, but they were nothing. There was no superiority of manner, accomplishment, or understanding. Lady Dalrymple had acquired the name of "a charming woman," because she had a smile and a civil answer for every body. Miss Carteret, with still less to say, was so plain and so awkward, that she would never have been tolerated in Camden-place but for her birth.

Lady Russell confessed that she had expected something better; but yet "it was an acquaintance worth having," and when Anne ventured to speak her opinion of them to Mr. Elliot, he agreed to their being nothing in themselves, but still maintained that as a family connexion, as good company, as those who would collect good company around them, they had their value. Anne smiled and said,

"My idea of good company, Mr. Elliot, is the company of clever, well-informed people, who have a great deal of conversation; that is what I call good company."

"You are mistaken," said he gently, "that is not good company, that is the best. Good company requires only birth, education and manners, and with regard to education is not very nice. Birth and good manners are essential; but a little learning is by no means a dangerous thing[91] in good company, on the contrary, it will do very well. My cousin, Anne, shakes her head. She is not satisfied. She is fastidious. My dear cousin, (sitting down by her) you have a better right to be fastidious than almost any other woman I know; but will it answer? Will it make you happy? Will it not be wiser to accept the society of these good ladies in Laura-place, and enjoy all the advantages of the connexion as far as possible? You may depend upon it, that they will move in the first set in Bath this winter, and as rank is rank, your being known to be related to them will have its use in fixing your family (our family let me say) in that degree of consideration which we must all wish for."

[91] An allusion to Alexander Pope's *An Essay on Criticism*, 215–16: "A little learning is a dang'rous thing; / Drink deep, or taste not the Pierian spring."

"Yes," sighed Anne, "we shall, indeed, be known to be related to them!"—then recollecting herself, and not wishing to be answered, she added, "I certainly do think there has been by far too much trouble taken to procure the acquaintance. I suppose (smiling) I have more pride than any of you; but I confess it does vex me, that we should be so solicitous to have the relationship acknowledged, which we may be very sure is a matter of perfect indifference to them."

"Pardon me, my dear cousin, you are unjust to your own claims. In London, perhaps, in your present quiet style of living, it might be as you say; but in Bath, Sir Walter Elliot and his family will always be worth knowing, always acceptable as acquaintance."

"Well," said Anne, "I certainly am proud, too proud to enjoy a welcome which depends so entirely upon place."

"I love your indignation," said he; "it is very natural. But here you are in Bath, and the object is to be established here with all the credit and dignity which ought to belong to Sir Walter Elliot. You talk of being proud, I am called proud I know, and I shall not wish to believe myself otherwise, for our pride, if investigated, would have the same object, I have no doubt, though the kind may seem a little different. In one point, I am sure, my dear cousin, (he continued, speaking lower, though there was no one else in the room) in one point, I am sure, we must feel alike. We must feel that every addition to your father's society, among his equals or superiors, may be of use in diverting his thoughts from those who are beneath him."

He looked, as he spoke, to the seat which Mrs. Clay had been lately occupying, a sufficient explanation of what he particularly meant; and though Anne could not believe in their having the same sort of pride, she was pleased with him for not liking Mrs. Clay; and her conscience admitted that his wishing to promote her father's getting great acquaintance, was more than excusable in the view of defeating her.

CHAPTER 17

While Sir Walter and Elizabeth were assiduously pushing their good fortune in Laura-place, Anne was renewing an acquaintance of a very different description.

She had called on her former governess, and had heard from her of there being an old school-fellow in Bath, who had the two strong claims on her attention, of past kindness and present suffering. Miss Hamilton, now Mrs. Smith, had shewn her kindness in one of those periods of her life when it had been most valuable. Anne had gone unhappy to school, grieving for the loss of a mother whom she had dearly loved, feeling her separation from home, and suffering as a girl of fourteen, of strong sensibility and not high spirits, must suffer at such a time; and Miss Hamilton, three years older than herself, but still from the want of near relations and a settled home, remaining another year at school, had been useful and good to her in a way which had considerably lessened her misery, and could never be remembered with indifference.

Miss Hamilton had left school, had married not long afterwards, was said to have married a man of fortune, and this was all that Anne had

known of her, till now that their governess's account brought her situation forward in a more decided but very different form.

She was a widow, and poor. Her husband had been extravagant; and at his death, about two years before, had left his affairs dreadfully involved. She had had difficulties of every sort to contend with, and in addition to these distresses, had been afflicted with a severe rheumatic fever, which finally settling in her legs, had made her for the present a cripple. She had come to Bath on that account, and was now in lodgings near the hotbaths,[92] living in a very humble way, unable even to afford herself the comfort of a servant, and of course almost excluded from society.

Their mutual friend answered for the satisfaction which a visit from Miss Elliot would give Mrs. Smith, and Anne therefore lost no time in going. She mentioned nothing of what she had heard, or what she intended, at home. It would excite no proper interest there. She only consulted Lady Russell, who entered thoroughly into her sentiments, and was most happy to convey her as near to Mrs. Smith's lodgings in Westgate-buildings, as Anne chose to be taken.

The visit was paid, their acquaintance re-established, their interest in each other more than re-kindled. The first ten minutes had its awkwardness and its emotion. Twelve years were gone since they had parted, and each presented a somewhat different person from what the other had imagined. Twelve years had changed Anne from the blooming, silent, unformed girl of fifteen, to the elegant little woman of seven and twenty, with every beauty excepting bloom, and with manners as consciously right as they were invariably gentle; and twelve years had transformed the fine-looking, well-grown Miss Hamilton, in all the glow of health and confidence of superiority, into a poor, infirm, helpless widow, receiving the visit of her former protegeé as a favour; but all that was uncomfortable in the meeting had soon passed away, and left only the interesting charm of remembering former partialities and talking over old times.

Anne found in Mrs. Smith the good sense and agreeable manners which she had almost ventured to depend on, and a disposition to converse and be cheerful beyond her expectation. Neither the dissipations of the past—and she had lived very much in the world, nor the restrictions of the present; neither sickness nor sorrow seemed to have closed her heart or ruined her spirits.

In the course of a second visit she talked with great openness, and Anne's astonishment increased. She could scarcely imagine a more cheerless situation in itself than Mrs. Smith's. She had been very fond of her husband,—she had buried him. She had been used to affluence,—it was gone. She had no child to connect her with life and happiness again, no relations to assist in the arrangement of perplexed affairs, no health to make all the rest supportable. Her accommodations were limited to a noisy parlour, and a dark bed-room behind, with no possibility of moving from one to the other without assistance, which there was only one servant in the house to afford, and she never quitted the house but to be conveyed into the warm bath.—Yet, in spite of all this, Anne had reason to believe that she had moments only of languor and depression, to hours of occupation

[92] The natural hot springs for which the city was named.

and enjoyment. How could it be?—She watched—observed—reflected—
and finally determined that this was not a case of fortitude or of resignation
only.—A submissive spirit might be patient, a strong understanding would
supply resolution, but here was something more; here was that elasticity of
mind, that disposition to be comforted, that power of turning readily from
evil to good, and of finding employment which carried her out of herself,
which was from Nature alone. It was the choicest gift of Heaven; and Anne
viewed her friend as one of those instances in which, by a merciful appoint-
ment,[93] it seems designed to counter-balance almost every other want.

There had been a time, Mrs. Smith told her, when her spirits had nearly
failed. She could not call herself an invalid now, compared with her state
on first reaching Bath. Then, she had indeed been a pitiable object—for
she had caught cold on the journey, and had hardly taken possession of her
lodgings, before she was again confined to her bed, and suffering under
severe and constant pain; and all this among strangers—with the absolute
necessity of having a regular nurse, and finances at that moment particu-
larly unfit to meet any extraordinary expense. She had weathered it how-
ever, and could truly say that it had done her good. It had increased her
comforts by making her feel herself to be in good hands. She had seen too
much of the world, to expect sudden or disinterested attachment any
where, but her illness had proved to her that her landlady had a charac-
ter[94] to preserve, and would not use her ill; and she had been particularly
fortunate in her nurse, as a sister of her landlady, a nurse by profession,
and who had always a home in that house when unemployed, chanced to be
at liberty just in time to attend her.—"And she," said Mrs. Smith, "besides
nursing me most admirably, has really proved an invaluable acquaintance.—
As soon as I could use my hands, she taught me to knit, which has been a
great amusement; and she put me in the way of making these little thread-
cases, pin-cushions, and card-racks, which you always find me so busy
about, and which supply me with the means of doing a little good to one or
two very poor families in this neighbourhood. She has a large acquaint-
ance, of course professionally, among those who can afford to buy, and she
disposes of my merchandize. She always takes the right time for applying.
Every body's heart is open, you know, when they have recently escaped
from severe pain, or are recovering the blessing of health, and nurse Rooke
thoroughly understands when to speak. She is a shrewd, intelligent, sensi-
ble woman. Hers is a line for seeing human nature; and she has a fund of
good sense and observation which, as a companion, make her infinitely
superior to thousands of those who having only received 'the best educa-
tion in the world,' know nothing worth attending to. Call it gossip if you
will; but when nurse Rooke has half an hour's leisure to bestow on me, she
is sure to have something to relate that is entertaining and profitable, some-
thing that makes one know one's species better. One likes to hear what is
going on, to be *au fait*[95] as to the newest modes of being trifling and silly.
To me, who live so much alone, her conversation I assure you is a treat."

Anne, far from wishing to cavil at the pleasure, replied, "I can easily
believe it. Women of that class have great opportunities, and if they are
intelligent may be well worth listening to. Such varieties of human nature

[93] Dispensation (of Providence). [94] Reputation. [95] Knowledgeable (French).

as they are in the habit of witnessing! And it is not merely in its follies, that
they are well read; for they see it occasionally under every circumstance
that can be most interesting or affecting. What instances must pass before
them of ardent, disinterested, self-denying attachment, of heroism, forti-
tude, patience, resignation—of all the conflicts and all the sacrifices that
ennoble us most. A sick chamber may often furnish the worth of volumes."

"Yes," said Mrs. Smith more doubtingly, "sometimes it may, though I
fear its lessons are not often in the elevated style you describe. Here and
there, human nature may be great in times of trial, but generally speaking
it is its weakness and not its strength that appears in a sick chamber; it is
selfishness and impatience rather than generosity and fortitude, that one
hears of. There is so little real friendship in the world!—and unfortu-
nately" (speaking low and tremulously) "there are so many who forget to
think seriously till it is almost too late."

Anne saw the misery of such feelings. The husband had not been what
he ought, and the wife had been led among the part of mankind which
made her think worse of the world, than she hoped it deserved. It was but a
passing emotion however with Mrs. Smith, she shook it off, and soon added
in a different tone,

"I do not suppose the situation my friend Mrs. Rooke is in at present,
will furnish much either to interest or edify me.—She is only nursing Mrs.
Wallis of Marlborough-buildings—a mere pretty, silly, expensive, fashiona-
ble woman, I believe—and of course will have nothing to report but of lace
and finery.—I mean to make my profit of Mrs. Wallis, however. She has
plenty of money, and I intend she shall buy all the high-priced things I
have in hand now."

Anne had called several times on her friend, before the existence of
such a person was known in Camden-place. At last, it became necessary to
speak of her.—Sir Walter, Elizabeth and Mrs. Clay returned one morning
from Laura-place, with a sudden invitation from Lady Dalrymple for the
same evening, and Anne was already engaged, to spend that evening in
Westgate-buildings. She was not sorry for the excuse. They were only
asked, she was sure, because Lady Dalrymple being kept at home by a bad
cold, was glad to make use of the relationship which had been so pressed on
her,—and she declined on her own account with great alacrity—"She was
engaged to spend the evening with an old schoolfellow." They were not
much interested in any thing relative to Anne, but still there were questions
enough asked, to make it understood what this old schoolfellow was; and
Elizabeth was disdainful, and Sir Walter severe.

"Westgate-buildings!" said he; "and who is Miss Anne Elliot to be visit-
ing in Westgate-buildings?—A Mrs. Smith. A widow Mrs. Smith,—and
who was her husband? One of the five thousand Mr. Smiths whose names
are to be met with every where. And what is her attraction? That she is old
and sickly.—Upon my word, Miss Anne Elliot, you have the most extraor-
dinary taste! Every thing that revolts other people, low company, paltry
rooms, foul air, disgusting associations are inviting to you. But surely, you
may put off this old lady till to-morrow. She is not so near her end, I
presume, but that she may hope to see another day. What is her age?
Forty?"

"No, Sir, she is not one and thirty; but I do not think I can put off my

engagement, because it is the only evening for some time which will at once
suit her and myself.—She goes into the warm bath to-morrow, and for the
rest of the week you know we are engaged."

"But what does Lady Russell think of this acquaintance?" asked Elizabeth.

"She sees nothing to blame in it," replied Anne; "on the contrary, she
approves it; and has generally taken me, when I have called on Mrs.
Smith."

"Westgate-buildings must have been rather surprised by the appear-
ance of a carriage drawn up near its pavement!" observed Sir Walter.—"Sir
Henry Russell's widow, indeed, has no honours to distinguish her arms;
but still, it is a handsome equipage, and no doubt is well known to convey a
Miss Elliot.—A widow Mrs. Smith, lodging in Westgate-buildings!—A poor
widow, barely able to live, between thirty and forty—a mere Mrs. Smith, an
every day Mrs. Smith, of all people and all names in the world, to be the
chosen friend of Miss Anne Elliot, and to be preferred by her, to her own
family connections among the nobility of England and Ireland! Mrs. Smith,
such a name!"

Mrs. Clay, who had been present while all this passed, now thought it
advisable to leave the room, and Anne could have said much and did long
to say a little, in defence of *her* friend's not very dissimilar claims to theirs,
but her sense of personal respect to her father prevented her. She made no
reply. She left it to himself to recollect, that Mrs. Smith was not the only
widow in Bath between thirty and forty, with little to live on, and no sur-
name of dignity.

Anne kept her appointment; the others kept theirs, and of course she
heard the next morning that they had a delightful evening.—She had been
the only one of the set absent; for Sir Walter and Elizabeth had not only
been quite at her ladyship's service themselves, but had actually been happy
to be employed by her in collecting others, and had been at the trouble of
inviting both Lady Russell and Mr. Elliot; and Mr. Elliot had made a point
of leaving Colonel Wallis early, and Lady Russell had fresh arranged all her
evening engagements in order to wait on her. Anne had the whole history
of all that such an evening could supply, from Lady Russell. To her, its
greatest interest must be, in having been very much talked of between her
friend and Mr. Elliot, in having been wished for, regretted, and at the same
time honoured for staying away in such a cause.—Her kind, compassionate
visits to this old schoolfellow, sick and reduced, seemed to have quite de-
lighted Mr. Elliot. He thought her a most extraordinary young woman; in
her temper, manners, mind, a model of female excellence. He could meet
even Lady Russell in a discussion of her merits; and Anne could not be
given to understand so much by her friend, could not know herself to be so
highly rated by a sensible man, without many of those agreeable sensations
which her friend meant to create.

Lady Russell was now perfectly decided in her opinion of Mr. Elliot. She
was as much convinced of his meaning to gain Anne in time, as of his
deserving her; and was beginning to calculate the number of weeks which
would free him from all the remaining restraints of widowhood, and leave
him at liberty to exert his most open powers of pleasing. She would not
speak to Anne with half the certainty she felt on the subject, she would
venture on little more than hints of what might be hereafter, of a possible

attachment on his side, of the desirableness of the alliance, supposing such attachment to be real, and returned. Anne heard her, and made no violent exclamations. She only smiled, blushed, and gently shook her head.

"I am no match-maker, as you well know," said Lady Russell, "being much too well aware of the uncertainty of all human events and calculations. I only mean that if Mr. Elliot should some time hence pay his addresses to you, and if you should be disposed to accept him, I think there would be every possibility of your being happy together. A most suitable connection every body must consider it—but I think it might be a very happy one."

"Mr. Elliot is an exceedingly agreeable man, and in many respects I think highly of him," said Anne; "but we should not suit."

Lady Russell let this pass, and only said in rejoinder, "I own that to be able to regard you as the future mistress of Kellynch, the future Lady Elliot—to look forward and see you occupying your dear mother's place, succeeding to all her rights, and all her popularity, as well as to all her virtues, would be the highest possible gratification to me.—You are your mother's self in countenance and disposition; and if I might be allowed to fancy you such as she was, in situation, and name, and home, presiding and blessing in the same spot, and only superior to her in being more highly valued! My dearest Anne, it would give me more delight than is often felt at my time of life!"

Anne was obliged to turn away, to rise, to walk to a distant table, and, leaning there in pretended employment, try to subdue the feelings this picture excited. For a few moments her imagination and her heart were bewitched. The idea of becoming what her mother had been; of having the precious name of "Lady Elliot" first revived in herself; of being restored to Kellynch, calling it her home again, her home for ever, was a charm which she could not immediately resist. Lady Russell said not another word, willing to leave the matter to its own operation; and believing that, could Mr. Elliot at that moment with propriety have spoken for himself!—She believed, in short, what Anne did not believe. The same image of Mr. Elliot speaking for himself, brought Anne to composure again. The charm of Kellynch and of "Lady Elliot" all faded away. She never could accept him. And it was not only that her feelings were still adverse to any man save one; her judgment, on a serious consideration of the possibilities of such a case, was against Mr. Elliot.

Though they had now been acquainted a month, she could not be satisfied that she really knew his character. That he was a sensible man, an agreeable man,—that he talked well, professed good opinions, seemed to judge properly and as a man of principle,—this was all clear enough. He certainly knew what was right, nor could she fix on any one article of moral duty evidently transgressed; but yet she would have been afraid to answer for his conduct. She distrusted the past, if not the present. The names which occasionally dropt of former associates, the allusions to former practices and pursuits, suggested suspicions not favourable of what he had been. She saw that there had been bad habits; that Sunday-travelling had been a common thing; that there had been a period of his life (and probably not a short one) when he had been, at least, careless on all serious matters; and, though he might now think very differently, who could an-

swer for the true sentiments of a clever, cautious man, grown old enough to appreciate a fair character?[96] How could it ever be ascertained that his mind was truly cleansed?

Mr. Elliot was rational, discreet, polished,—but he was not open. There was never any burst of feeling, any warmth of indignation or delight, at the evil or good of others. This, to Anne, was a decided imperfection. Her early impressions were incurable. She prized the frank, the open-hearted, the eager character beyond all others. Warmth and enthusiasm did captivate her still. She felt that she could so much more depend upon the sincerity of those who sometimes looked or said a careless or a hasty thing, than of those whose presence of mind never varied, whose tongue never slipped.

Mr. Elliot was too generally agreeable. Various as were the tempers in her father's house, he pleased them all. He endured too well,—stood too well with everybody. He had spoken to her with some degree of openness of Mrs. Clay; had appeared completely to see what Mrs. Clay was about, and to hold her in contempt; and yet Mrs. Clay found him as agreeable as anybody.

Lady Russell saw either less or more than her young friend, for she saw nothing to excite distrust. She could not imagine a man more exactly what he ought to be than Mr. Elliot; nor did she ever enjoy a sweeter feeling than the hope of seeing him receive the hand of her beloved Anne in Kellynch church, in the course of the following autumn.

CHAPTER 18

It was the beginning of February; and Anne, having been a month in Bath, was growing very eager for news from Uppercross and Lyme. She wanted to hear much more than Mary communicated. It was three weeks since she had heard at all. She only knew that Henrietta was at home again; and that Louisa, though considered to be recovering fast, was still at Lyme; and she was thinking of them all very intently one evening, when a thicker letter than usual from Mary was delivered to her, and, to quicken the pleasure and surprise, with Admiral and Mrs. Croft's compliments.

The Crofts must be in Bath! A circumstance to interest her. They were people whom her heart turned to very naturally.

"What is this?" cried Sir Walter. "The Crofts arrived in Bath? The Crofts who rent Kellynch? What have they brought you?"

"A letter from Uppercross Cottage, Sir."

"Oh! those letters are convenient passports. They secure an introduction. I should have visited Admiral Croft, however, at any rate. I know what is due to my tenant."

Anne could listen no longer; she could not even have told how the poor Admiral's complexion escaped; her letter engrossed her. It had been begun several days back.

[96]Reputation for uprightness; good name.

February 1st, ——.

My Dear Anne,

I make no apology for my silence, because I know how little people think of letters in such a place as Bath. You must be a great deal too happy to care for Uppercross, which, as you well know, affords little to write about. We have had a very dull Christmas; Mr. and Mrs. Musgrove have not had one dinner-party all the holidays. I do not reckon the Hayters as any body. The holidays, however, are over at last: I believe no children ever had such long ones. I am sure I had not. The house was cleared yesterday, except of the little Harvilles; but you will be surprised to hear that they have never gone home. Mrs. Harville must be an odd mother to part with them so long. I do not understand it. They are not at all nice children, in my opinion; but Mrs. Musgrove seems to like them quite as well, if not better, than her grand-children. What dreadful weather we have had! It may not be felt in Bath, with your nice pavements; but in the country it is of some consequence. I have not had a creature call on me since the second week in January, except Charles Hayter, who has been calling much oftener than was welcome. Between ourselves, I think it a great pity Henrietta did not remain at Lyme as long as Louisa; it would have kept her a little out of his way. The carriage is gone to-day, to bring Louisa and the Harvilles to-morrow. We are not asked to dine with them, however, till the day after, Mrs. Musgrove is so afraid of her being fatigued by the journey, which is not very likely, considering the care that will be taken of her; and it would be much more convenient to me to dine there to-morrow. I am glad you find Mr. Elliot so agreeable, and wish I could be acquainted with him too; but I have my usual luck, I am always out of the way when any thing desirable is going on; always the last of my family to be noticed. What an immense time Mrs. Clay has been staying with Elizabeth! Does she never mean to go away? But perhaps if she were to leave the room vacant we might not be invited. Let me know what you think of this. I do not expect my children to be asked, you know. I can leave them at the Great House very well, for a month or six weeks. I have this moment heard that the Crofts are going to Bath almost immediately; they think the admiral gouty. Charles heard it quite by chance: they have not had the civility to give me any notice, or offer to take any thing. I do not think they improve at all as neighbours. We see nothing of them, and this is really an instance of gross inattention. Charles joins me in love, and every thing proper. Yours, affectionately,

Mary M——.

I am sorry to say that I am very far from well; and Jemima has just told me that the butcher says there is a bad sore-throat very much about. I dare say I shall catch it; and my sore-throats, you know, are always worse than anybody's.

So ended the first part, which had been afterwards put into an envelope, containing nearly as much more.

I kept my letter open, that I might send you word how Louisa bore her journey, and now I am extremely glad I did, having a great deal to add. In the first place, I had a note from Mrs. Croft yesterday, offering to convey any thing to you; a very kind, friendly note indeed, addressed to me, just as it ought; I shall therefore be able to make my letter as long as I like.[97] The admiral does not seem very ill, and I sincerely hope Bath will do him all the good he wants. I shall be truly glad to have them back again. Our neighbourhood cannot spare such a pleasant family. But now for Louisa. I have something to communicate that will astonish you not a little. She and the Harvilles came on Tuesday very safely, and in the evening we went to ask her how she did, when we were rather surprised not to find Captain Benwick of the party, for he had been invited as well as the Harvilles; and what do you think was the reason? Neither more nor less than his being in love with Louisa, and not choosing to venture to Uppercross till he had had an answer from Mr. Musgrove; for it was all settled between him and her before she came away, and he had written to her father by Captain Harville. True, upon my honour. Are not you astonished? I shall be surprised at least if you ever received a hint of it, for I never did. Mrs. Musgrove protests solemnly that she knew nothing of the matter. We are all very well pleased, however; for though it is not equal to her marrying Captain Wentworth, it is infinitely better than Charles Hayter; and Mr. Musgrove has written his consent, and Captain Benwick is expected to-day. Mrs. Harville says her husband feels a good deal on his poor sister's account; but, however, Louisa is a great favourite with both. Indeed Mrs. Harville and I quite agree that we love her the better for having nursed her. Charles wonders what Captain Wentworth will say; but if you remember, I never thought him attached to Louisa; I never could see any thing of it. And this is the end, you see, of Captain Benwick's being supposed to be an admirer of yours. How Charles could take such a thing into his head was always incomprehensible to me. I hope he will be more agreeable now. Certainly not a great match for Louisa Musgrove; but a million times better than marrying among the Hayters.

Mary need not have feared her sister's being in any degree prepared for the news. She had never in her life been more astonished. Captain Benwick and Louisa Musgrove! It was almost too wonderful[98] for belief; and it was with the greatest effort that she could remain in the room, preserve an air of calmness, and answer the common questions of the moment. Happily for her, they were not many. Sir Walter wanted to know whether the Crofts travelled with four horses, and whether they were likely to be situated in such a part of Bath as it might suit Miss Elliot and himself to visit in; but had little curiosity beyond.

"How is Mary?" said Elizabeth; and without waiting for an answer, "And pray what brings the Crofts to Bath?"

"They come on the Admiral's account. He is thought to be gouty."

"Gout and decrepitude!" said Sir Walter. "Poor old gentleman."

[97] Since the letter is to be delivered personally by the Crofts, Mary can avoid paying postage (which was expensive).

[98] Amazing.

"Have they any acquaintance here?" asked Elizabeth.

"I do not know; but I can hardly suppose that, at Admiral Croft's time of life, and in his profession, he should not have many acquaintance in such a place as this."

"I suspect," said Sir Walter coolly, "that Admiral Croft will be best known in Bath as the renter of Kellynch-hall. Elizabeth, may we venture to present him and his wife in Laura-place?"

"Oh! no, I think not. Situated as we are with Lady Dalrymple, cousins, we ought to be very careful not to embarrass her with acquaintance she might not approve. If we were not related, it would not signify; but as cousins, she would feel scrupulous as to any proposal of ours. We had better leave the Crofts to find their own level. There are several odd-looking men walking about here, who, I am told, are sailors. The Crofts will associate with them!"

This was Sir Walter and Elizabeth's share of interest in the letter; when Mrs. Clay had paid her tribute of more decent attention, in an enquiry after Mrs. Charles Musgrove, and her fine little boys, Anne was at liberty.

In her own room she tried to comprehend it. Well might Charles wonder how Captain Wentworth would feel! Perhaps he had quitted the field, had given Louisa up, had ceased to love, had found he did not love her. She could not endure the idea of treachery or levity, or any thing akin to ill-usage between him and his friend. She could not endure that such a friendship as theirs should be severed unfairly.

Captain Benwick and Louisa Musgrove! The high-spirited, joyous, talking Louisa Musgrove, and the dejected, thinking, feeling, reading Captain Benwick, seemed each of them every thing that would not suit the other. Their minds most dissimilar! Where could have been the attraction? The answer soon presented itself. It had been in situation. They had been thrown together several weeks; they had been living in the same small family party; since Henrietta's coming away, they must have been depending almost entirely on each other, and Louisa, just recovering from illness, had been in an interesting state, and Captain Benwick was not inconsolable. That was a point which Anne had not been able to avoid suspecting before; and instead of drawing the same conclusion as Mary, from the present course of events, they served only to confirm the idea of his having felt some dawning of tenderness toward herself. She did not mean, however, to derive much more from it to gratify her vanity, than Mary might have allowed. She was persuaded that any tolerably pleasing young woman who had listened and seemed to feel for him, would have received the same compliment. He had an affectionate heart. He must love somebody.

She saw no reason against their being happy. Louisa had fine naval fervour to begin with, and they would soon grow more alike. He would gain cheerfulness, and she would learn to be an enthusiast for Scott and Lord Byron; nay, that was probably learnt already; of course they had fallen in love over poetry. The idea of Louisa Musgrove turned into a person of literary taste, and sentimental reflection, was amusing, but she had no doubt of its being so. The day at Lyme, the fall from the Cobb, might influence her health, her nerves, her courage, her character to the end of her life, as thoroughly as it appeared to have influenced her fate.

The conclusion of the whole was, that if the woman who had been

sensible of Captain Wentworth's merits could be allowed to prefer another man, there was nothing in the engagement to excite lasting wonder; and if Captain Wentworth lost no friend by it, certainly nothing to be regretted. No, it was not regret which made Anne's heart beat in spite of herself, and brought the colour into her cheeks when she thought of Captain Wentworth unshackled and free. She had some feelings which she was ashamed to investigate. They were too much like joy, senseless joy!

She longed to see the Crofts, but when the meeting took place, it was evident that no rumour of the news had yet reached them. The visit of ceremony was paid and returned, and Louisa Musgrove was mentioned, and Captain Benwick too, without even half a smile.

The Crofts had placed themselves in lodgings in Gay-street, perfectly to Sir Walter's satisfaction. He was not at all ashamed of the acquaintance, and did, in fact, think and talk a great deal more about the Admiral, than the Admiral ever thought or talked about him.

The Crofts knew quite as many people in Bath as they wished for, and considered their intercourse with the Elliots as a mere matter of form, and not in the least likely to afford them any pleasure. They brought with them their country habit of being almost always together. He was ordered to walk, to keep off the gout, and Mrs. Croft seemed to go shares with him in every thing, and to walk for her life, to do him good. Anne saw them wherever she went. Lady Russell took her out in her carriage almost every morning, and she never failed to think of them, and never failed to see them. Knowing their feelings as she did, it was a most attractive picture of happiness to her. She always watched them as long as she could; delighted to fancy she understood what they might be talking of, as they walked along in happy independence, or equally delighted to see the Admiral's hearty shake of the hand when he encountered an old friend, and observe their eagerness of conversation when occasionally forming into a little knot of the navy, Mrs. Croft looking as intelligent and keen as any of the officers around her.

Anne was too much engaged with Lady Russell to be often walking herself, but it so happened that one morning, about a week or ten days after the Crofts' arrival, it suited her best to leave her friend, or her friend's carriage, in the lower part of town, and return alone to Camden-place; and in walking up Milsom-street, she had the good fortune to meet with the Admiral. He was standing by himself, at a printshop window, with his hands behind him, in earnest contemplation of some print, and she not only might have passed him unseen, but was obliged to touch as well as address him before she could catch his notice. When he did perceive and acknowledge her, however, it was done with all his usual frankness and good humour. "Ha! is it you? Thank you, thank you. This is treating me like a friend. Here I am, you see, staring at a picture. I can never get by this shop without stopping. But what a thing here is, by way of a boat. Do look at it. Did you ever see the like? What queer fellows your fine painters must be, to think that any body would venture their lives in such a shapeless old cockleshell as that. And yet, here are two gentlemen stuck up in it mightily at their ease, and looking about them at the rocks and mountains, as if they were not to be upset the next moment, which they certainly must be. I wonder where that boat was built!" (laughing heartily) "I would not ven-

ture over a horsepond in it. Well," (turning away) "now, where are you bound? Can I go any where for you, or with you? Can I be of any use?"

"None, I thank you, unless you will give me the pleasure of your company the little way our road lies together. I am going home."

"That I will, with all my heart, and farther too. Yes, yes, we will have a snug walk together; and I have something to tell you as we go along. There, take my arm; that's right; I do not feel comfortable if I have not a woman there. Lord! what a boat it is!" taking a last look at the picture, as they began to be in motion.

"Did you say that you had something to tell me, sir?"

"Yes, I have. Presently. But here comes a friend, Captain Brigden; I shall only say, 'How d'ye do,' as we pass, however. I shall not stop. 'How d'ye do.' Brigden stares to see anybody with me but my wife. She, poor soul, is tied by the leg. She has a blister on one of her heels, as large as a three shilling piece.[99] If you look across the street, you will see Admiral Brand coming down and his brother. Shabby fellows, both of them! I am glad they are not on this side of the way. Sophy cannot bear them. They played me a pitiful trick once—got away some of my best men. I will tell you the whole story another time. There comes old Sir Archibald Drew and his grandson. Look, he sees us; he kisses his hand to you; he takes you for my wife. Ah! the peace has come too soon for that younker.[1] Poor old Sir Archibald! How do you like Bath, Miss Elliot? It suits us very well. We are always meeting with some old friend or other; the streets full of them every morning; sure to have plenty of chat; and then we get away from them all, and shut ourselves into our lodgings, and draw in our chairs, and are as snug as if we were at Kellynch, ay, or as we used to be even at North Yarmouth and Deal. We do not like our lodgings here the worse, I can tell you, for putting us in mind of those we first had at North Yarmouth. The wind blows through one of the cupboards just in the same way."

When they were got a little farther, Anne ventured to press again for what he had to communicate. She had hoped, when clear of Milsom-street, to have her curiosity gratified; but she was still obliged to wait, for the Admiral had made up his mind not to begin, till they had gained the greater space and quiet of Belmont, and as she was not really Mrs. Croft, she must let him have his own way. As soon as they were fairly ascending Belmont, he began,

"Well, now you shall hear something that will surprise you. But first of all, you must tell me the name of the young lady I am going to talk about. That young lady, you know, that we have all been so concerned for. The Miss Musgrove, that all this has been happening to. Her christian name—I always forget her christian name."

Anne had been ashamed to appear to comprehend so soon as she really did; but now she could safely suggest the name of "Louisa."

"Ay, ay, Miss Louisa Musgrove, that is the name. I wish young ladies had not such a number of fine christian names. I should never be out, if they were all Sophys, or something of that sort. Well, this Miss Louisa, we all thought, you know, was to marry Frederick. He was courting her week

[99] At the time, the Bank of England issued large token coins of this denomination.
[1] Youngster; a midshipman.

after week. The only wonder was, what they could be waiting for, till the business at Lyme came; then, indeed, it was clear enough that they must wait till her brain was set to right. But even then, there was something odd in their way of going on. Instead of staying at Lyme, he went off to Plymouth, and then he went off to see Edward. When we came back from Minehead,[2] he was gone down to Edward's, and there he has been ever since. We have seen nothing of him since November. Even Sophy could not understand it. But now, the matter has taken the strangest turn of all; for this young lady, this same Miss Musgrove, instead of being to marry Frederick, is to marry James Benwick. You know James Benwick."

"A little. I am a little acquainted with Captain Benwick."

"Well, she is to marry him. Nay, most likely they are married already, for I do not know what they should wait for."

"I thought Captain Benwick a very pleasing young man," said Anne, "and I understand that he bears an excellent character."

"Oh! yes, yes, there is not a word to be said against James Benwick. He is only a commander, it is true, made last summer, and these are bad times for getting on, but he has not another fault that I know of. An excellent, good-hearted fellow, I assure you, a very active, zealous officer too, which is more than you would think for, perhaps, for that soft sort of manner does not do him justice."

"Indeed you are mistaken there, sir. I should never augur want of spirit from Captain Benwick's manners. I thought them particularly pleasing, and I will answer for it they would generally please."

"Well, well, ladies are the best judges; but James Benwick is rather too piano[3] for me, and though very likely it is all our partiality, Sophy and I cannot help thinking Frederick's manners better than his. There is something about Frederick more to our taste."

Anne was caught. She had only meant to oppose the too-common idea of spirit and gentleness being incompatible with each other, not at all to represent Captain Benwick's manners as the very best that could possibly be, and, after a little hesitation, she was beginning to say, "I was not entering into any comparison of the two friends," but the Admiral interrupted her with,

"And the thing is certainly true. It is not a mere bit of gossip. We have it from Frederick himself. His sister had a letter from him yesterday, in which he tells us of it, and he had just had it in a letter from Harville, written upon the spot, from Uppercross. I fancy they are all at Uppercross."

This was an opportunity which Anne could not resist; she said, therefore, "I hope, Admiral, I hope there is nothing in the style of Captain Wentworth's letter to make you and Mrs. Croft particularly uneasy. It did certainly seem, last autumn, as if there were an attachment between him and Louisa Musgrove; but I hope it may be understood to have worn out on each side equally, and without violence. I hope his letter does not breathe the spirit of an ill-used man."

[2] A town on the north coast of Somersetshire, on the Bristol Channel.
[3] Italian for "quiet."

"Not at all, not at all; there is not an oath or a murmur from beginning to end."

Anne looked down to hide her smile.

"No, no; Frederick is not a man to whine and complain; he has too much spirit for that. If the girl likes another man better, it is very fit she should have him."

"Certainly. But what I mean is, that I hope there is nothing in Captain Wentworth's manner of writing to make you suppose he thinks himself ill-used by his friend, which might appear, you know, without its being absolutely said. I should be very sorry that such a friendship as has subsisted between him and Captain Benwick should be destroyed, or even wounded, by a circumstance of this sort."

"Yes, yes, I understand you. But there is nothing at all of that nature in the letter. He does not give the least fling at Benwick; does not so much as say, 'I wonder at it, I have a reason of my own for wondering at it.' No, you would not guess, from his way of writing, that he had ever thought of this Miss (what's her name?) for himself. He very handsomely hopes they will be happy together, and there is nothing very unforgiving in that, I think."

Anne did not receive the perfect conviction which the Admiral meant to convey, but it would have been useless to press the enquiry farther. She, therefore, satisfied herself with common-place remarks, or quiet attention, and the Admiral had it all his own way.

"Poor Frederick!" said he at last. "Now he must begin all over again with somebody else. I think we must get him to Bath. Sophy must write, and beg him to come to Bath. Here are pretty girls enough, I am sure. It would be of no use to go to Uppercross again, for that other Miss Musgrove, I find, is bespoke by her cousin, the young parson. Do not you think, Miss Elliot, we had better try to get him to Bath?"

CHAPTER 19

While Admiral Croft was taking this walk with Anne, and expressing his wish of getting Captain Wentworth to Bath, Captain Wentworth was already on his way thither. Before Mrs. Croft had written, he was arrived; and the very next time Anne walked out, she saw him.

Mr. Elliot was attending his two cousins and Mrs. Clay. They were in Milsom-street. It began to rain, not much, but enough to make shelter desirable for women, and quite enough to make it very desirable for Miss Elliot to have the advantage of being conveyed home in Lady Dalrymple's carriage, which was seen waiting at a little distance; she, Anne, and Mrs. Clay, therefore, turned into Molland's,[4] while Mr. Elliot stepped to Lady Dalrymple, to request her assistance. He soon joined them again, successful, of course; Lady Dalrymple would be most happy to take them home, and would call for them in a few minutes.

Her ladyship's carriage was a barouche,[5] and did not hold more than four with any comfort. Miss Carteret was with her mother; consequently it

[4] A confectioner's shop. [5] A carriage with a collapsible top.

was not reasonable to expect accommodation for all the three Camden-place ladies. There could be no doubt as to Miss Elliot. Whoever suffered inconvenience, she must suffer none, but it occupied a little time to settle the point of civility between the other two. The rain was a mere trifle, and Anne was most sincere in preferring a walk with Mr. Elliot. But the rain was also a mere trifle to Mrs. Clay; she would hardly allow it even to drop at all, and her boots were so thick! much thicker than Miss Anne's; and, in short, her civility rendered her quite as anxious to be left to walk with Mr. Elliot, as Anne could be, and it was discussed between them with a generosity so polite and so determined, that the others were obliged to settle it for them; Miss Elliot maintaining that Mrs. Clay had a little cold already, and Mr. Elliot deciding on appeal, that his cousin Anne's boots were rather the thickest.

It was fixed accordingly that Mrs. Clay should be of the party in the carriage; and they had just reached this point when Anne, as she sat near the window, descried, most decidedly and distinctly, Captain Wentworth walking down the street.

Her start was perceptible only to herself; but she instantly felt that she was the greatest simpleton in the world, the most unaccountable and absurd! For a few minutes she saw nothing before her. It was all confusion. She was lost; and when she had scolded back her senses, she found the others still waiting for the carriage, and Mr. Elliot (always obliging) just setting off for Union-street on a commission of Mrs. Clay's.

She now felt a great inclination to go to the outer door; she wanted to see if it rained. Why was she to suspect herself of another motive? Captain Wentworth must be out of sight. She left her seat, she would go, one half of her should not be always so much wiser than the other half, or always suspecting the other of being worse than it was. She would see if it rained. She was sent back, however, in a moment by the entrance of Captain Wentworth himself, among a party of gentlemen and ladies, evidently his acquaintance, and whom he must have joined a little below Milsom-street. He was more obviously struck and confused by the sight of her, than she had ever observed before; he looked quite red. For the first time, since their renewed acquaintance, she felt that she was betraying the least sensibility of the two. She had the advantage of him, in the preparation of the last few moments. All the overpowering, blinding, bewildering, first effects of strong surprise were over with her. Still, however, she had enough to feel! It was agitation, pain, pleasure, a something between delight and misery.

He spoke to her, and then turned away. The character of his manner was embarrassment. She could not have called it either cold or friendly, or any thing so certainly as embarrassed.

After a short interval, however, he came towards her and spoke again. Mutual enquiries on common subjects passed; neither of them, probably, much the wiser for what they heard, and Anne continuing fully sensible of his being less at ease than formerly. They had, by dint of being so very much together, got to speak to each other with a considerable portion of apparent indifference and calmness; but he could not do it now. Time had changed him, or Louisa had changed him. There was consciousness of some sort or other. He looked very well, not as if he had been suffering in

health or spirits, and he talked of Uppercross, of the Musgroves, nay, even of Louisa, and had even a momentary look of his own arch significance as he named her; but yet it was Captain Wentworth not comfortable, not easy, not able to feign that he was.

It did not surprise, but it grieved Anne to observe that Elizabeth would not know him. She saw that he saw Elizabeth, that Elizabeth saw him, that there was complete internal recognition on each side; she was convinced that he was ready to be acknowledged as an acquaintance, expecting it, and she had the pain of seeing her sister turn away with unalterable coldness.

Lady Dalrymple's carriage, for which Miss Elliot was growing very impatient, now drew up; the servant came in to announce it. It was beginning to rain again, and altogether there was a delay, and a bustle, and a talking, which must make all the little crowd in the shop understand that Lady Dalrymple was calling to convey Miss Elliot. At last Miss Elliot and her friend, unattended but by the servant (for there was no cousin returned) were walking off; and Captain Wentworth, watching them, turned again to Anne, and by manner, rather than words, was offering his services to her.

"I am much obliged to you," was her answer, "but I am not going with them. The carriage would not accommodate so many. I walk. I prefer walking."

"But it rains."

"Oh! very little. Nothing that I regard."

After a moment's pause he said, "Though I came only yesterday, I have equipped myself properly for Bath already, you see," (pointing to a new umbrella) "I wish you would make use of it, if you are determined to walk; though, I think, it would be more prudent to let me get you a chair."[6]

She was very much obliged to him, but declined it all, repeating her conviction, that the rain would come to nothing at present, and adding, "I am only waiting for Mr. Elliot. He will be here in a moment, I am sure."

She had hardly spoken the words, when Mr. Elliot walked in. Captain Wentworth recollected him perfectly. There was no difference between him and the man who had stood on the steps at Lyme, admiring Anne as she passed, except in the air and look and manner of the privileged relation and friend. He came in with eagerness, appeared to see and think only of her, apologised for his stay, was grieved to have kept her waiting, and anxious to get her away without further loss of time, and before the rain increased; and in another moment they walked off together, her arm under his, a gentle and embarrassed glance, and a "good morning to you" being all that she had time for, as she passed away.

As soon as they were out of sight, the ladies of Captain Wentworth's party began talking of them.

"Mr. Elliot does not dislike his cousin, I fancy?"

"Oh! no, that is clear enough. One can guess what will happen there. He is always with them; half lives in the family, I believe. What a good-looking man!"

"Yes, and Miss Atkinson, who dined with him once at the Wallises, says he is the most agreeable man she ever was in company with."

[6] A sedan chair (carried on poles).

"She is pretty, I think; Anne Elliot; very pretty, when one comes to look at her. It is not the fashion to say so, but I confess I admire her more than her sister."

"Oh! so do I."

"And so do I. No comparison. But the men are all wild after Miss Elliot. Anne is too delicate for them."

Anne would have been particularly obliged to her cousin, if he would have walked by her side all the way to Camden-place, without saying a word. She had never found it so difficult to listen to him, though nothing could exceed his solicitude and care, and though his subjects were principally such as were wont to be always interesting—praise, warm, just, and discriminating, of Lady Russell, and insinuations highly rational against Mrs. Clay. But just now she could think only of Captain Wentworth. She could not understand his present feelings, whether he were really suffering much from disappointment or not; and till that point were settled, she could not be quite herself.

She hoped to be wise and reasonable in time; but alas! alas! she must confess to herself that she was not wise yet.

Another circumstance very essential for her to know, was how long he meant to be in Bath; he had not mentioned it, or she could not recollect it. He might be only passing through. But it was more probable that he should be come to stay. In that case, so liable as every body was to meet every body in Bath, Lady Russell would in all likelihood see him somewhere.—Would she recollect him? How would it all be?

She had already been obliged to tell Lady Russell that Louisa Musgrove was to marry Captain Benwick. It had cost her something to encounter Lady Russell's surprise; and now, if she were by any chance to be thrown into company with Captain Wentworth, her imperfect knowledge of the matter might add another shade of prejudice against him.

The following morning Anne was out with her friend, and for the first hour, in an incessant and fearful sort of watch for him in vain; but at last, in returning down Pulteney-street, she distinguished him on the right hand pavement at such a distance as to have him in view the greater part of the street. There were many other men about him, many groups walking the same way, but there was no mistaking him. She looked instinctively at Lady Russell; but not from any mad idea of her recognising him so soon as she did herself. No, it was not to be supposed that Lady Russell would perceive him till they were nearly opposite. She looked at her however, from time to time, anxiously; and when the moment approached which must point him out, though not daring to look again (for her own countenance she knew was unfit to be seen), she was yet perfectly conscious of Lady Russell's eyes being turned exactly in the direction for him, of her being in short intently observing him. She could thoroughly comprehend the sort of fascination he must possess over Lady Russell's mind, the difficulty it must be for her to withdraw her eyes, the astonishment she must be feeling that eight or nine years should have passed over him, and in foreign climes and in active service too, without robbing him of one personal grace!

At last, Lady Russell drew back her head.—"Now, how would she speak of him?"

"You will wonder," said she, "what has been fixing my eye so long; but I

was looking after some window-curtains, which Lady Alicia and Mrs. Frankland were telling me of last night. They described the drawing-room window-curtains of one of the houses on this side of the way, and this part of the street, as being the handsomest and best hung of any in Bath, but could not recollect the exact number, and I have been trying to find out which it could be; but I confess I can see no curtains hereabouts that answer their description."

Anne sighed and blushed and smiled, in pity and disdain, either at her friend or herself.—The part which provoked her most, was that in all this waste of foresight and caution, she should have lost the right moment for seeing whether he saw them.

A day or two passed without producing any thing.—The theatre or the rooms, where he was most likely to be, were not fashionable enough for the Elliots, whose evening amusements were solely in the elegant stupidity of private parties, in which they were getting more and more engaged; and Anne, wearied of such a state of stagnation, sick of knowing nothing, and fancying herself stronger because her strength was not tried, was quite impatient for the concert evening. It was a concert for the benefit of a person patronised by Lady Dalrymple. Of course they must attend. It was really expected to be a good one, and Captain Wentworth was very fond of music. If she could only have a few minutes conversation with him again, she fancied she should be satisfied; and as to the power of addressing him she felt all over courage if the opportunity occurred. Elizabeth had turned from him, Lady Russell overlooked him; her nerves were strengthened by these circumstances; she felt that she owed him attention.

She had once partly promised Mrs. Smith to spend the evening with her; but in a short hurried call she excused herself and put it off, with the more decided promise of a longer visit on the morrow. Mrs. Smith gave a most good-humoured acquiescence.

"By all means," said she; "only tell me all about it, when you do come. Who is your party?"

Anne named them all. Mrs. Smith made no reply; but when she was leaving her, said, and with an expression half serious, half arch, "Well, I heartily wish your concert may answer; and do not fail me to-morrow if you can come; for I begin to have a foreboding that I may not have many more visits from you."

Anne was startled and confused, but after standing in a moment's suspense, was obliged, and not sorry to be obliged, to hurry away.

CHAPTER 20

Sir Walter, his two daughters, and Mrs. Clay, were the earliest of all their party, at the rooms in the evening; and as Lady Dalrymple must be waited for, they took their station by one of the fires in the octagon room. But hardly were they so settled, when the door opened again, and Captain Wentworth walked in alone. Anne was the nearest to him, and making yet a little advance, she instantly spoke. He was preparing only to bow and pass on, but her gentle "How do you do?" brought him out of the straight line to stand near her, and make enquiries in return, in spite of the formidable

father and sister in the back ground. Their being in the back ground was a
support to Anne; she knew nothing of their looks, and felt equal to every-
thing which she believed right to be done.

While they were speaking, a whispering between her father and Eliza-
beth caught her ear. She could not distinguish, but she must guess the
subject; and on Captain Wentworth's making a distant bow, she compre-
hended that her father had judged so well as to give him that simple ac-
knowledgment of acquaintance, and she was just in time by a side glance to
see a slight curtsey from Elizabeth herself. This, though late and reluctant
and ungracious, was yet better than nothing, and her spirits improved.

After talking however of the weather and Bath and the concert, their
conversation began to flag, and so little was said at last, that she was expect-
ing him to go every moment; but he did not; he seemed in no hurry to
leave her; and presently with renewed spirit, with a little smile, a little glow,
he said,

"I have hardly seen you since our day at Lyme. I am afraid you must
have suffered from the shock, and the more from its not overpowering you
at the time."

She assured him that she had not.

"It was a frightful hour," said he, "a frightful day!" and he passed his
hand across his eyes, as if the remembrance were still too painful; but in a
moment half smiling again, added, "The day has produced some effects
however—has had some consequences which must be considered as the
very reverse of frightful.—When you had the presence of mind to suggest
that Benwick would be the properest person to fetch a surgeon, you could
have little idea of his being eventually one of those most concerned in her
recovery."

"Certainly I could have none. But it appears—I should hope it would be
a very happy match. There are on both sides good principles and good
temper."

"Yes," said he, looking not exactly forward—"but there I think ends the
resemblance. With all my soul I wish them happy, and rejoice over every
circumstance in favour of it. They have no difficulties to contend with at
home, no opposition, no caprice, no delays.—The Musgroves are behaving
like themselves, most honourably and kindly, only anxious with true paren-
tal hearts to promote their daughter's comfort. All this is much, very much
in favour of their happiness; more than perhaps—"

He stopped. A sudden recollection seemed to occur, and to give him
some taste of that emotion which was reddening Anne's cheeks and fixing
her eyes on the ground.—After clearing his throat, however, he proceeded
thus,

"I confess that I do think there is a disparity, too great a disparity, and
in a point no less essential than mind.—I regard Louisa Musgrove as a very
amiable, sweet-tempered girl, and not deficient in understanding; but Ben-
wick is something more. He is a clever man, a reading man—and I confess
that I do consider his attaching himself to her, with some surprise. Had it
been the effect of gratitude, had he learnt to love her, because he believed
her to be preferring him, it would have been another thing. But I have no
reason to suppose it so. It seems, on the contrary, to have been a perfectly

spontaneous, untaught feeling on his side, and this surprises me. A man like him, in his situation! With a heart pierced, wounded, almost broken! Fanny Harville was a very superior creature; and his attachment to her was indeed attachment. A man does not recover from such a devotion of the heart to such a woman!—He ought not—he does not."

Either from the consciousness, however, that his friend had recovered, or from some other consciousness, he went no farther; and Anne, who, in spite of the agitated voice in which the latter part had been uttered, and in spite of all the various noises of the room, the almost ceaseless slam of the door, and ceaseless buzz of persons walking through, had distinguished every word, was struck, gratified, confused, and beginning to breathe very quick, and feel an hundred things in a moment. It was impossible for her to enter on such a subject; and yet, after a pause, feeling the necessity of speaking, and having not the smallest wish for a total change, she only deviated so far as to say,

"You were a good while at Lyme, I think?"

"About a fortnight. I could not leave it till Louisa's doing well was quite ascertained. I had been too deeply concerned in the mischief to be soon at peace. It had been my doing—solely mine. She would not have been obstinate if I had not been weak. The country round Lyme is very fine. I walked and rode a great deal; and the more I saw, the more I found to admire."

"I should very much like to see Lyme again," said Anne.

"Indeed! I should not have supposed that you could have found any thing in Lyme to inspire such a feeling. The horror and distress you were involved in—the stretch of mind, the wear of spirits!—I should have thought your last impressions of Lyme must have been strong disgust."

"The last few hours were certainly very painful," replied Anne: "but when pain is over, the remembrance of it often becomes a pleasure. One does not love a place the less for having suffered in it, unless it has been all suffering, nothing but suffering—which was by no means the case at Lyme. We were only in anxiety and distress during the last two hours; and, previously, there had been a great deal of enjoyment. So much novelty and beauty! I have travelled so little, that every fresh place would be interesting to me—but there is real beauty at Lyme: and in short" (with a faint blush at some recollections) "altogether my impressions of the place are very agreeable."

As she ceased, the entrance door opened again, and the very party appeared for whom they were waiting. "Lady Dalrymple, Lady Dalrymple," was the rejoicing sound; and with all the eagerness compatible with anxious elegance, Sir Walter and his two ladies stepped forward to meet her. Lady Dalrymple and Miss Carteret, escorted by Mr. Elliot and Colonel Wallis, who had happened to arrive nearly at the same instant, advanced into the room. The others joined them, and it was a group in which Anne found herself also necessarily included. She was divided from Captain Wentworth. Their interesting, almost too interesting conversation must be broken up for a time; but slight was the penance compared with the happiness which brought it on! She had learnt, in the last ten minutes, more of his feelings towards Louisa, more of all his feelings, than she dared to think of! and she gave herself up to the demands of the party, to the needful

civilities of the moment, with exquisite, though agitated sensations. She was in good humour with all. She had received ideas which disposed her to be courteous and kind to all, and to pity every one, as being less happy than herself.

The delightful emotions were a little subdued, when, on stepping back from the group, to be joined again by Captain Wentworth, she saw that he was gone. She was just in time to see him turn into the concert room. He was gone—he had disappeared: she felt a moment's regret. But "they should meet again. He would look for her—he would find her out long before the evening were over—and at present, perhaps, it was as well to be asunder. She was in need of a little interval for recollection."

Upon Lady Russell's appearance soon afterwards, the whole party was collected, and all that remained, was to marshal themselves, and proceed into the concert room; and be of all the consequence in their power, draw as many eyes, excite as many whispers, and disturb as many people as they could.

Very, very happy were both Elizabeth and Anne Elliot as they walked in. Elizabeth, arm in arm with Miss Carteret, and looking on the broad back of the dowager Viscountess Dalrymple before her, had nothing to wish for which did not seem within her reach; and Anne—but it would be an insult to the nature of Anne's felicity, to draw any comparison between it and her sister's; the origin of one all selfish vanity, of the other all generous attachment.

Anne saw nothing, thought nothing of the brilliancy of the room. Her happiness was from within. Her eyes were bright, and her cheeks glowed,—but she knew nothing about it. She was thinking only of the last half hour, and as they passed to their seats, her mind took a hasty range over it. His choice of subjects, his expressions, and still more his manner and look, had been such as she could see in only one light. His opinion of Louisa Musgrove's inferiority, an opinion which he had seemed solicitous to give, his wonder at Captain Benwick, his feelings as to a first, strong attachment,—sentences begun which he could not finish—his half averted eyes, and more than half expressive glance,—all, all declared that he had a heart returning to her at last; that anger, resentment, avoidance, were no more; and that they were succeeded, not merely by friendship and regard, but by the tenderness of the past; yes, some share of the tenderness of the past. She could not contemplate the change as implying less.—He must love her.

These were thoughts, with their attendant visions, which occupied and flurried her too much to leave her any power of observation; and she passed along the room without having a glimpse of him, without even trying to discern him. When their places were determined on, and they were all properly arranged, she looked round to see if he should happen to be in the same part of the room, but he was not, her eye could not reach him; and the concert being just opening, she must consent for a time to be happy in an humbler way.

The party was divided, and disposed of on two contiguous benches: Anne was among those on the foremost, and Mr. Elliot had manoeuvred so well, with the assistance of his friend Colonel Wallis, as to have a seat by her. Miss Elliot, surrounded by her cousins, and the principal object of Colonel Wallis's gallantry, was quite contented.

Anne's mind was in a most favourable state for the entertainment of the evening: it was just occupation enough: she had feelings for the tender, spirits for the gay, attention for the scientific,[7] and patience for the wearisome; and had never liked a concert better, at least during the first act. Towards the close of it, in the interval succeeding an Italian song, she explained the words of the song to Mr. Elliot.—They had a concert bill between them.

"This," said she, "is nearly the sense, or rather the meaning of the words, for certainly the sense of an Italian love-song must not be talked of,—but it is as nearly the meaning as I can give; for I do not pretend to understand the language. I am a very poor Italian scholar."

"Yes, yes, I see you are. I see you know nothing of the matter. You have only knowledge enough of the language, to translate at sight these inverted, transposed, curtailed Italian lines, into clear, comprehensible, elegant English. You need not say anything more of your ignorance.—Here is complete proof."

"I will not oppose such kind politeness; but I should be sorry to be examined by a real proficient."

"I have not had the pleasure of visiting in Camden-place so long," replied he, "without knowing something of Miss Anne Elliot; and I do regard her as one who is too modest, for the world in general to be aware of half her accomplishments, and too highly accomplished for modesty to be natural in any other woman."

"For shame! for shame!—this is too much of flattery. I forget what we are to have next," turning to the bill.

"Perhaps," said Mr. Elliot, speaking low, "I have had a longer acquaintance with your character than you are aware of."

"Indeed!—How so? You can have been acquainted with it only since I came to Bath, excepting as you might hear me previously spoken of in my own family."

"I knew you by report long before you came to Bath. I had heard you described by those who knew you intimately. I have been acquainted with you by character many years. Your person, your disposition, accomplishments, manner—they were all described, they were all present to me."

Mr. Elliot was not disappointed in the interest he hoped to raise. No one can withstand the charm of such a mystery. To have been described long ago to a recent acquaintance, by nameless people, is irresistible; and Anne was all curiosity. She wondered, and questioned him eagerly—but in vain. He delighted in being asked, but he would not tell.

"No, no—some time or other perhaps, but not now. He would mention no names now; but such, he could assure her, had been the fact. He had many years ago received such a description of Miss Anne Elliot, as had inspired him with the highest idea of her merit, and excited the warmest curiosity to know her."

Anne could think of no one so likely to have spoken with partiality of her many years ago, as the Mr. Wentworth, of Monkford, Captain

[7] Intellectual or technical.

Wentworth's brother. He might have been in Mr. Elliot's company, but she had not courage to ask the question.

"The name of Anne Elliot," said he, "has long had an interesting sound to me. Very long has it possessed a charm over my fancy; and, if I dared, I would breathe my wishes that the name might never change."

Such she believed were his words; but scarcely had she received their sound, than her attention was caught by other sounds immediately behind her, which rendered every thing else trivial. Her father and Lady Dalrymple were speaking.

"A well-looking man," said Sir Walter, "a very well-looking man."

"A very fine young man indeed!" said Lady Dalrymple. "More air than one often sees in Bath.—Irish, I dare say."

"No, I just know his name. A bowing acquaintance. Wentworth—Captain Wentworth of the navy. His sister married my tenant in Somersetshire,—the Croft, who rents Kellynch."

Before Sir Walter had reached this point, Anne's eyes had caught the right direction, and distinguished Captain Wentworth, standing among a cluster of men at a little distance. As her eyes fell on him, his seemed to be withdrawn from her. It had that appearance. It seemed as if she had been one moment too late; and as long as she dared observe, he did not look again: but the performance was re-commencing, and she was forced to seem to restore her attention to the orchestra, and look straight forward.

When she could give another glance, he had moved away. He could not have come nearer to her if he would; she was so surrounded and shut in: but she would rather have caught his eye.

Mr. Elliot's speech too distressed her. She had no longer any inclination to talk to him. She wished him not so near her.

The first act was over. Now she hoped for some beneficial change; and, after a period of nothing-saying amongst the party, some of them did decide on going in quest of tea. Anne was one of the few who did not choose to move. She remained in her seat, and so did Lady Russell; but she had the pleasure of getting rid of Mr. Elliot; and she did not mean, whatever she might feel on Lady Russell's account, to shrink from conversation with Captain Wentworth, if he gave her the opportunity. She was persuaded by Lady Russell's countenance that she had seen him.

He did not come however. Anne sometimes fancied she discerned him at a distance, but he never came. The anxious interval wore away unproductively. The others returned, the room filled again, benches were re-claimed and re-possessed, and another hour of pleasure or of penance was to be set out, another hour of music was to give delight or the gapes, as real or affected taste for it prevailed. To Anne, it chiefly wore the prospect of an hour of agitation. She could not quit that room in peace without seeing Captain Wentworth once more, without the interchange of one friendly look.

In re-settling themselves, there were now many changes, the result of which was favourable for her. Colonel Wallis declined sitting down again, and Mr. Elliot was invited by Elizabeth and Miss Carteret, in a manner not to be refused, to sit between them; and by some other removals, and a little

scheming of her own, Anne was enabled to place herself much nearer the end of the bench than she had been before, much more within reach of a passer-by. She could not do so, without comparing herself with Miss Larolles,[8] the inimitable Miss Larolles,—but still she did it, and not with much happier effect; though by what seemed prosperity in the shape of an early abdication in her next neighbours, she found herself at the very end of the bench before the concert closed.

Such was her situation, with a vacant space at hand, when Captain Wentworth was again in sight. She saw him not far off. He saw her too; yet he looked grave, and seemed irresolute, and only by very slow degrees came at last near enough to speak to her. She felt that something must be the matter. The change was indubitable. The difference between his present air and what it had been in the octagon room was strikingly great.— Why was it? She thought of her father—of Lady Russell. Could there have been any unpleasant glances? He began by speaking of the concert, gravely; more like the Captain Wentworth of Uppercross; owned himself disappointed, had expected better singing; and, in short, must confess that he should not be sorry when it was over. Anne replied, and spoke in defence of the performance so well, and yet in allowance for his feelings, so pleasantly, that his countenance improved, and he replied again with almost a smile. They talked for a few minutes more; the improvement held; he even looked down towards the bench, as if he saw a place on it well worth occupying; when, at that moment, a touch on her shoulder obliged Anne to turn round.—It came from Mr. Elliot. He begged her pardon, but she must be applied to, to explain Italian again. Miss Carteret was very anxious to have a general idea of what was next to be sung. Anne could not refuse; but never had she sacrificed to politeness with a more suffering spirit.

A few minutes, though as few as possible, were inevitably consumed; and when her own mistress again, when able to turn and look as she had done before, she found herself accosted by Captain Wentworth, in a reserved yet hurried sort of farewell. "He must wish her good night. He was going—he should get home as fast as he could."

"Is not this song worth staying for?" said Anne, suddenly struck by an idea which made her yet more anxious to be encouraging.

"No!" he replied impressively, "there is nothing worth my staying for;" and he was gone directly.

Jealousy of Mr. Elliot! It was the only intelligible motive. Captain Wentworth jealous of her affection! Could she have believed it a week ago— three hours ago! For a moment the gratification was exquisite. But alas! there were very different thoughts to succeed. How was such jealousy to be quieted? How was the truth to reach him? How, in all the peculiar disadvantages of their respective situations, would he ever learn her real sentiments? It was misery to think of Mr. Elliot's attentions.—Their evil was incalculable.

[8] A character, in Fanny Burney's novel *Cecilia* (1782), who similarly sits on the aisle to make herself approachable.

CHAPTER 21

Anne recollected with pleasure the next morning her promise of going to Mrs. Smith; meaning that it should engage her from home at the time when Mr. Elliot would be most likely to call; for to avoid Mr. Elliot was almost a first object.

She felt a great deal of good will towards him. In spite of the mischief of his attentions, she owed him gratitude and regard, perhaps compassion. She could not help thinking much of the extraordinary circumstances attending their acquaintance; of the right which he seemed to have to interest her, by every thing in situation, by his own sentiments, by his early prepossession. It was altogether very extraordinary.—Flattering, but painful. There was much to regret. How she might have felt, had there been no Captain Wentworth in the case, was not worth enquiry; for there was a Captain Wentworth: and be the conclusion of the present suspense good or bad, her affection would be his for ever. Their union, she believed, could not divide her more from other men, than their final separation.

Prettier musings of high-wrought love and eternal constancy, could never have passed along the streets of Bath, than Anne was sporting with from Camden-place to Westgate-buildings. It was almost enough to spread purification and perfume all the way.

She was sure of a pleasant reception; and her friend seemed this morning particularly obliged to her for coming, seemed hardly to have expected her, though it had been an appointment.

An account of the concert was immediately claimed; and Anne's recollections of the concert were quite happy enough to animate her features, and make her rejoice to talk of it. All that she could tell, she told most gladly; but the all was little for one who had been there, and unsatisfactory for such an enquirer as Mrs. Smith, who had already heard, through the short cut of a laundress and a waiter, rather more of the general success and produce[9] of the evening than Anne could relate; and who now asked in vain for several particulars of the company. Every body of any consequence or notoriety in Bath was well known by name to Mrs. Smith.

"The little Durands were there, I conclude," said she, "with their mouths open to catch the music; like unfledged sparrows ready to be fed. They never miss a concert."

"Yes. I did not see them myself, but I heard Mr. Elliot say they were in the room."

"The Ibbotsons—were they there? and the two new beauties, with the tall Irish officer, who is talked of for one of them."

"I do not know.—I do not think they were."

"Old Lady Mary Maclean? I need not ask after her. She never misses, I know; and you must have seen her. She must have been in your own circle, for as you went with Lady Dalrymple, you were in the seats of grandeur; round the orchestra, of course."

"No, that was what I dreaded. It would have been very unpleasant to me in every respect. But happily Lady Dalrymple always chooses to be farther

[9] *success and produce:* upshot, consequences.

off; and we were exceedingly well placed—that is for hearing; I must not say for seeing, because I appear to have seen very little."

"Oh! you saw enough for your own amusement.—I can understand. There is a sort of domestic enjoyment to be known even in a crowd, and this you had. You were a large party in yourselves, and you wanted nothing beyond."

"But I ought to have looked about me more," said Anne, conscious while she spoke, that there had in fact been no want of looking about; that the object only had been deficient.

"No, no—you were better employed. You need not tell me that you had a pleasant evening. I see it in your eye. I perfectly see how the hours passed—that you had always something agreeable to listen to. In the intervals of the concert, it was conversation."

Anne half smiled and said, "Do you see that in my eye?"

"Yes, I do. Your countenance perfectly informs me that you were in company last night with the person, whom you think the most agreeable in the world, the person who interests you at this present time, more than all the rest of the world put together."

A blush overspread Anne's cheeks. She could say nothing.

"And such being the case," continued Mrs. Smith, after a short pause, "I hope you believe that I do know how to value your kindness in coming to me this morning. It is really very good of you to come and sit with me, when you must have so many pleasanter demands upon your time."

Anne heard nothing of this. She was still in the astonishment and confusion excited by her friend's penetration, unable to imagine how any report of Captain Wentworth could have reached her. After another short silence—

"Pray," said Mrs. Smith, "is Mr. Elliot aware of your acquaintance with me? Does he know that I am in Bath?"

"Mr. Elliot!" repeated Anne, looking up surprised. A moment's reflection shewed her the mistake she had been under. She caught it instantaneously; and, recovering courage with the feeling of safety, soon added, more composedly, "are you acquainted with Mr. Elliot?"

"I have been a good deal acquainted with him," replied Mrs. Smith, gravely, "but it seems worn out now. It is a great while since we met."

"I was not at all aware of this. You never mentioned it before. Had I known it, I would have had the pleasure of talking to him about you."

"To confess the truth," said Mrs. Smith, assuming her usual air of cheerfulness, "that is exactly the pleasure I want you to have. I want you to talk about me to Mr. Elliot. I want your interest[10] with him. He can be of essential service to me; and if you would have the goodness, my dear Miss Elliot, to make it an object to yourself, of course it is done."

"I should be extremely happy—I hope you cannot doubt my willingness to be of even the slightest use to you," replied Anne; "but I suspect that you are considering me as having a higher claim on Mr. Elliot—a greater right to influence him, than is really the case. I am sure you have, somehow or other, imbibed such a notion. You must consider me only as Mr. Elliot's

[10] Influence.

relation. If in that light, if there is any thing which you suppose his cousin might fairly ask of him, I beg you would not hesitate to employ me."

Mrs. Smith gave her a penetrating glance, and then, smiling, said,

"I have been a little premature, I perceive. I beg your pardon. I ought to have waited for official information. But now, my dear Miss Elliot, as an old friend, do give me a hint as to when I may speak. Next week? To be sure by next week I may be allowed to think it all settled, and build my own selfish schemes on Mr. Elliot's good fortune."

"No," replied Anne, "nor next week, nor next, nor next. I assure you that nothing of the sort you are thinking of will be settled any week. I am not going to marry Mr. Elliot. I should like to know why you imagine I am."

Mrs. Smith looked at her again, looked earnestly, smiled, shook her head, and exclaimed,

"Now, how I do wish I understood you! How I do wish I knew what you were at! I have a great idea that you do not design to be cruel, when the right moment comes. Till it does come, you know, we women never mean to have any body. It is a thing of course among us, that every man is refused—till he offers. But why should you be cruel? Let me plead for my—present friend I cannot call him—but for my former friend. Where can you look for a more suitable match? Where could you expect a more gentlemanlike, agreeable man? Let me recommend Mr. Elliot. I am sure you hear nothing but good of him from Colonel Wallis; and who can know him better than Colonel Wallis?"

"My dear Mrs. Smith, Mr. Elliot's wife has not been dead much above half a year. He ought not to be supposed to be paying his addresses to any one."

"Oh! if these are your only objections," cried Mrs. Smith, archly, "Mr. Elliot is safe, and I shall give myself no more trouble about him. Do not forget me when you are married, that's all. Let him know me to be a friend of yours, and then he will think little of the trouble required, which it is very natural for him now, with so many affairs and engagements of his own, to avoid and get rid of as he can—very natural, perhaps. Ninety-nine out of a hundred would do the same. Of course, he cannot be aware of the importance to me. Well, my dear Miss Elliot, I hope and trust you will be very happy. Mr. Elliot has sense to understand the value of such a woman. Your peace will not be shipwrecked as mine has been. You are safe in all worldly matters, and safe in his character. He will not be led astray, he will not be misled by others to his ruin."

"No," said Anne, "I can readily believe all that of my cousin. He seems to have a calm, decided temper, not at all open to dangerous impressions. I consider him with great respect. I have no reason, from any thing that has fallen within my observation, to do otherwise. But I have not known him long; and he is not a man, I think, to be known intimately soon. Will not this manner of speaking of him, Mrs. Smith, convince you that he is nothing to me? Surely, this must be calm enough. And, upon my word, he is nothing to me. Should he ever propose to me (which I have very little reason to imagine he has any thought of doing), I shall not accept him. I assure you I shall not. I assure you Mr. Elliot had not the share which you have been supposing, in whatever pleasure the concert of last night might afford:—not Mr. Elliot; it is not Mr. Elliot that—"

She stopped, regretting with a deep blush that she had implied so much; but less would hardly have been sufficient. Mrs. Smith would hardly have believed so soon in Mr. Elliot's failure, but from the perception of there being a somebody else. As it was, she instantly submitted, and with all the semblance of seeing nothing beyond; and Anne, eager to escape farther notice, was impatient to know why Mrs. Smith should have fancied she was to marry Mr. Elliot, where she could have received the idea, or from whom she could have heard it.

"Do tell me how it first came into your head."

"It first came into my head," replied Mrs. Smith, "upon finding how much you were together, and feeling it to be the most probable thing in the world to be wished for by everybody belonging to either of you; and you may depend upon it that all your acquaintance have disposed of you in the same way. But I never heard it spoken of till two days ago."

"And has it indeed been spoken of?"

"Did you observe the woman who opened the door to you, when you called yesterday?"

"No. Was not it Mrs. Speed, as usual, or the maid? I observed no one in particular."

"It was my friend, Mrs. Rooke—Nurse Rooke, who, by the by, had a great curiosity to see you, and was delighted to be in the way to let you in. She came away from Marlborough-buildings only on Sunday; and she it was who told me you were to marry Mr. Elliot. She had had it from Mrs. Wallis herself, which did not seem bad authority. She sat an hour with me on Monday evening, and gave me the whole history."

"The whole history!" repeated Anne, laughing. "She could not make a very long history, I think, of one such little article of unfounded news."

Mrs. Smith said nothing.

"But," continued Anne, presently, "though there is no truth in my having this claim on Mr. Elliot, I should be extremely happy to be of use to you, in any way that I could. Shall I mention to him your being in Bath? Shall I take any message?"

"No, I thank you: no, certainly not. In the warmth of the moment, and under a mistaken impression, I might, perhaps, have endeavoured to interest you in some circumstances. But not now: no, I thank you, I have nothing to trouble you with."

"I think you spoke of having known Mr. Elliot many years?"

"I did."

"Not before he married, I suppose?"

"Yes; he was not married when I knew him first."

"And—were you much acquainted?"

"Intimately."

"Indeed! Then do tell me what he was at that time of life. I have a great curiosity to know what Mr. Elliot was as a very young man. Was he at all such as he appears now?"

"I have not seen Mr. Elliot these three years," was Mrs. Smith's answer, given so gravely that it was impossible to pursue the subject farther; and Anne felt that she had gained nothing but an increase of curiosity. They were both silent—Mrs. Smith very thoughtful. At last,

"I beg your pardon, my dear Miss Elliot," she cried, in her natural tone

of cordiality, "I beg your pardon for the short answers I have been giving you, but I have been uncertain what I ought to do. I have been doubting and considering as to what I ought to tell you. There were many things to be taken into the account. One hates to be officious, to be giving bad impressions, making mischief. Even the smooth surface of family-union seems worth preserving, though there may be nothing durable beneath. However, I have determined; I think I am right; I think you ought to be made acquainted with Mr. Elliot's real character. Though I fully believe that, at present, you have not the smallest intention of accepting him, there is no saying what may happen. You might, some time or other, be differently affected towards him. Hear the truth, therefore, now, while you are unprejudiced. Mr. Elliot is a man without heart or conscience; a designing, wary, cold-blooded being, who thinks only of himself; who, for his own interest or ease, would be guilty of any cruelty, or any treachery, that could be perpetrated without risk of his general character. He has no feeling for others. Those whom he has been the chief cause of leading into ruin, he can neglect and desert without the smallest compunction. He is totally beyond the reach of any sentiment of justice or compassion. Oh! he is black at heart, hollow and black!"

Anne's astonished air, and exclamation of wonder, made her pause, and in a calmer manner she added,

"My expressions startle you. You must allow for an injured, angry woman. But I will try to command myself. I will not abuse him. I will only tell you what I have found him. Facts shall speak. He was the intimate friend of my dear husband, who trusted and loved him, and thought him as good as himself. The intimacy had been formed before our marriage. I found them most intimate friends; and I, too, became excessively pleased with Mr. Elliot, and entertained the highest opinion of him. At nineteen, you know, one does not think very seriously, but Mr. Elliot appeared to me quite as good as others, and much more agreeable than most others, and we were almost always together. We were principally in town,[11] living in very good style. He was then the inferior in circumstances, he was then the poor one; he had chambers in the Temple,[12] and it was as much as he could do to support the appearance of a gentleman. He had always a home with us whenever he chose it; he was always welcome; he was like a brother. My poor Charles, who had the finest, most generous spirit in the world, would have divided his last farthing with him; and I know that his purse was open to him; I know that he often assisted him."

"This must have been about that very period of Mr. Elliot's life," said Anne, "which has always excited my particular curiosity. It must have been about the same time that he became known to my father and sister. I never knew him myself, I only heard of him, but there was a something in his conduct then with regard to my father and sister, and afterwards in the circumstances of his marriage, which I never could quite reconcile with present times. It seemed to announce a different sort of man."

"I know it all, I know it all," cried Mrs. Smith. "He had been introduced to Sir Walter and your sister before I was acquainted with him, but I heard him speak of them for ever. I know he was invited and encouraged, and I

[11] In London. [12] The center, in London, for the study and practice of law.

know he did not choose to go. I can satisfy you, perhaps, on points which you would little expect; and as to his marriage, I knew all about it at the time. I was privy to all the fors and againsts, I was the friend to whom he confided his hopes and plans, and though I did not know his wife previously, (her inferior situation in society, indeed, rendered that impossible) yet I knew her all her life afterwards, or, at least, till within the last two years of her life, and can answer any question you wish to put."

"Nay," said Anne, "I have no particular enquiry to make about her. I have always understood they were not a happy couple. But I should like to know why, at that time of his life, he should slight my father's acquaintance as he did. My father was certainly disposed to take very kind and proper notice of him. Why did Mr. Elliot draw back?"

"Mr. Elliot," replied Mrs. Smith, "at that period of his life, had one object in view—to make his fortune, and by a rather quicker process than the law. He was determined to make it by marriage. He was determined, at least, not to mar it by an imprudent marriage; and I know it was his belief, (whether justly or not, of course I cannot decide) that your father and sister, in their civilities and invitations, were designing a match between the heir and the young lady; and it was impossible that such a match should have answered his ideas of wealth and independence. That was his motive for drawing back, I can assure you. He told me the whole story. He had no concealments with me. It was curious, that having just left you behind me in Bath, my first and principal acquaintance on marrying, should be your cousin; and that, through him, I should be continually hearing of your father and sister. He described one Miss Elliot, and I thought very affectionately of the other."

"Perhaps," cried Anne, struck by a sudden idea, "you sometimes spoke of me to Mr. Elliot?"

"To be sure I did, very often. I used to boast of my own Anne Elliot, and vouch for your being a very different creature from——"

She checked herself just in time.

"This accounts for something which Mr. Elliot said last night," cried Anne. "This explains it. I found he had been used to hear of me. I could not comprehend how. What wild imaginations one forms, where dear self is concerned! How sure to be mistaken! But I beg your pardon; I have interrupted you. Mr. Elliot married, then, completely for money? The circumstance, probably, which first opened your eyes to his character."

Mrs. Smith hesitated a little here. "Oh! those things are too common. When one lives in the world, a man or woman's marrying for money is too common to strike one as it ought. I was very young, and associated only with the young, and we were a thoughtless, gay set, without any strict rules of conduct. We lived for enjoyment. I think differently now; time and sickness, and sorrow, have given me other notions; but, at that period, I must own I saw nothing reprehensible in what Mr. Elliot was doing. 'To do the best for himself,' passed as a duty."

"But was not she a very low woman?"

"Yes; which I objected to, but he would not regard. Money, money, was all that he wanted. Her father was a grazier,[13] her grandfather had been a

[13] One who grazes cattle.

butcher, but that was all nothing. She was a fine[14] woman, had had a decent education, was brought forward by some cousins, thrown by chance into Mr. Elliot's company, and fell in love with him; and not a difficulty or a scruple was there on his side, with respect to her birth. All his caution was spent in being secured of the real amount of her fortune, before he committed himself. Depend upon it, whatever esteem Mr. Elliot may have for his own situation in life now, as a young man he had not the smallest value for it. His chance of the Kellynch estate was something, but all the honour of the family he held as cheap as dirt. I have often heard him declare, that if baronetcies were saleable, any body should have his for fifty pounds, arms and motto, name and livery included; but I will not pretend to repeat half that I used to hear him say on that subject. It would not be fair. And yet you ought to have proof; for what is all this but assertion? and you shall have proof."

"Indeed, my dear Mrs. Smith, I want[15] none," cried Anne. "You have asserted nothing contradictory to what Mr. Elliot appeared to be some years ago. This is all in confirmation, rather, of what we used to hear and believe. I am more curious to know why he should be so different now?"

"But for my satisfaction; if you will have the goodness to ring for Mary—stay, I am sure you will have the still greater goodness of going yourself into my bed-room, and bringing me the small inlaid box which you will find on the upper shelf of the closet."

Anne, seeing her friend to be earnestly bent on it, did as she was desired. The box was brought and placed before her, and Mrs. Smith, sighing over it as she unlocked it, said,

"This is full of papers belonging to him, to my husband, a small portion only of what I had to look over when I lost him. The letter I am looking for, was one written by Mr. Elliot to him before our marriage, and happened to be saved; why, one can hardly imagine. But he was careless and immethodical, like other men, about those things; and when I came to examine his papers, I found it with others still more trivial from different people scattered here and there, while many letters and memorandums of real importance had been destroyed. Here it is. I would not burn it, because being even then very little satisfied with Mr. Elliot, I was determined to preserve every document of former intimacy. I have now another motive for being glad that I can produce it."

This was the letter, directed to "Charles Smith, Esq. Tunbridge Wells,"[16] and dated from London, as far back as July, 1803.

Dear Smith,

I have received yours. Your kindness almost overpowers me. I wish nature had made such hearts as yours more common, but I have lived three and twenty years in the world, and have seen none like it. At present, believe me, I have no need of your services, being in cash again. Give me joy: I have got rid of Sir Walter and Miss. They are gone back to Kellynch, and almost made me swear to visit them this summer, but my first visit to Kellynch will be with a surveyor, to tell me how to bring it with best advan-

[14] Of striking dress and appearance. [15] Need.
[16] A fashionable resort about twenty miles southeast of London.

tage to the hammer.[17] The baronet, nevertheless, is not unlikely to marry again; he is quite fool enough. If he does, however, they will leave me in peace, which may be a decent equivalent for the reversion.[18] He is worse than last year.

I wish I had any name but Elliot. I am sick of it. The name of Walter I can drop, thank God! and I desire you will never insult me with my second W. again, meaning, for the rest of my life, to be only yours truly,

<div align="right">Wm. Elliot.</div>

Such a letter could not be read without putting Anne in a glow; and Mrs. Smith, observing the high colour in her face, said,

"The language, I know, is highly disrespectful. Though I have forgot the exact terms, I have a perfect impression of the general meaning. But it shews you the man. Mark his professions to my poor husband. Can any thing be stronger?"

Anne could not immediately get over the shock and mortification of finding such words applied to her father. She was obliged to recollect that her seeing the letter was a violation of the laws of honour, that no one ought to be judged or to be known by such testimonies, that no private correspondence could bear the eye of others, before she could recover calmness enough to return the letter which she had been meditating over, and say,

"Thank you. This is full proof undoubtedly, proof of every thing you were saying. But why be acquainted with us now?"

"I can explain this too," cried Mrs. Smith, smiling.

"Can you really?"

"Yes. I have shewn you Mr. Elliot, as he was a dozen years ago, and I will shew him as he is now. I cannot produce written proof again, but I can give as authentic oral testimony as you can desire, of what he is now wanting, and what he is now doing. He is no hypocrite now. He truly wants to marry you. His present attentions to your family are very sincere, quite from the heart. I will give you my authority; his friend Colonel Wallis."

"Colonel Wallis! are you acquainted with him?"

"No. It does not come to me in quite so direct a line as that; it takes a bend or two, but nothing of consequence. The stream is as good as at first; the little rubbish it collects in the turnings, is easily moved away. Mr. Elliot talks unreservedly to Colonel Wallis of his views on you—which said Colonel Wallis I imagine to be in himself a sensible, careful, discerning sort of character; but Colonel Wallis has a very pretty silly wife, to whom he tells things which he had better not, and he repeats it all to her. She, in the overflowing spirits of her recovery, repeats it all to her nurse; and the nurse, knowing my acquaintance with you, very naturally brings it all to me. On Monday evening my good friend Mrs. Rooke let me thus much into the secrets of Marlborough-buildings. When I talked of a whole history therefore, you see, I was not romancing so much as you supposed."

"My dear Mrs. Smith, your authority is deficient. This will not do. Mr. Elliot's having any views on me will not in the least account for the efforts

[17] The auctioneer's gavel. [18] Inheritance of the title and estate.

he made towards a reconciliation with my father. That was all prior to my coming to Bath. I found them on the most friendly terms when I arrived."

"I know you did; I know it all perfectly, but"—

"Indeed, Mrs. Smith, we must not expect to get real information in such a line. Facts or opinions which are to pass through the hands of so many, to be misconceived by folly in one, and ignorance in another, can hardly have much truth left."

"Only give me a hearing. You will soon be able to judge of the general credit due, by listening to some particulars which you can yourself immediately contradict or confirm. Nobody supposes that you were his first inducement. He had seen you indeed, before he came to Bath and admired you, but without knowing it to be you. So says my historian at least. Is this true? Did he see you last summer or autumn, 'somewhere down in the west,' to use her own words, without knowing it to be you?"

"He certainly did. So far it is very true. At Lyme; I happened to be at Lyme."

"Well," continued Mrs. Smith triumphantly, "grant my friend the credit due to the establishment of the first point asserted. He saw you then at Lyme, and liked you so well as to be exceedingly pleased to meet with you again in Camden-place, as Miss Anne Elliot, and from that moment, I have no doubt, had a double motive in his visits there. But there was another, and an earlier; which I will now explain. If there is any thing in my story which you know to be either false or improbable, stop me. My account states, that your sister's friend, the lady now staying with you, whom I have heard you mention, came to Bath with Miss Elliot and Sir Walter as long ago as September, (in short when they first came themselves) and has been staying there ever since; that she is a clever, insinuating, handsome woman, poor and plausible, and altogether such in situation and manner, as to give a general idea among Sir Walter's acquaintance, of her meaning to be Lady Elliot, and as general a surprise that Miss Elliot should be apparently blind to the danger."

Here Mrs. Smith paused a moment; but Anne had not a word to say, and she continued,

"This was the light in which it appeared to those who knew the family, long before your return to it; and Colonel Wallis had his eye upon your father enough to be sensible of it, though he did not then visit in Camden-place; but his regard for Mr. Elliot gave him an interest in watching all that was going on there, and when Mr. Elliot came to Bath for a day or two, as he happened to do a little before Christmas, Colonel Wallis made him acquainted with the appearance of things, and the reports beginning to prevail.—Now you are to understand that time had worked a very material change in Mr. Elliot's opinions as to the value of a baronetcy. Upon all points of blood and connexion, he is a completely altered man. Having long had as much money as he could spend, nothing to wish for on the side of avarice or indulgence, he has been gradually learning to pin his happiness upon the consequence he is heir to. I thought it coming on, before our acquaintance ceased, but it is now a confirmed feeling. He cannot bear the idea of not being Sir William. You may guess therefore that the news he heard from his friend, could not be very agreeable, and you may guess what it produced; the resolution of coming back to Bath as soon as possible,

and of fixing himself here for a time, with the view of renewing his former acquaintance and recovering such a footing in the family, as might give him the means of ascertaining the degree of his danger, and of circumventing the lady if he found it material. This was agreed upon between the two friends, as the only thing to be done; and Colonel Wallis was to assist in every way that he could. He was to be introduced, and Mrs. Wallis was to be introduced, and every body was to be introduced. Mr. Elliot came back accordingly; and on application was forgiven, as you know, and re-admitted into the family; and there it was his constant object, and his only object (till your arrival added another motive) to watch Sir Walter and Mrs. Clay. He omitted no opportunity of being with them, threw himself in their way, called at all hours—but I need not be particular on this subject. You can imagine what an artful man would do; and with this guide, perhaps, may recollect what you have seen him do."

"Yes," said Anne, "you tell me nothing which does not accord with what I have known, or could imagine. There is always something offensive in the details of cunning. The manoeuvres of selfishness and duplicity must ever be revolting, but I have heard nothing which really surprises me. I know those who would be shocked by such a representation of Mr. Elliot, who would have difficulty in believing it; but I have never been satisfied. I have always wanted some other motive for his conduct than appeared.—I should like to know his present opinion, as to the probability of the event he has been in dread of; whether he considers the danger to be lessening or not."

"Lessening, I understand," replied Mrs. Smith. "He thinks Mrs. Clay afraid of him, aware that he sees through her, and not daring to proceed as she might do in his absence. But since he must be absent some time or other, I do not perceive how he can ever be secure, while she holds her present influence. Mrs. Wallis has an amusing idea, as nurse tells me, that it is to be put into the marriage articles when you and Mr. Elliot marry, that your father is not to marry Mrs. Clay. A scheme, worthy of Mrs. Wallis's understanding, by all accounts; but my sensible nurse Rooke sees the absurdity of it.—'Why, to be sure, ma'am,' said she, 'it would not prevent his marrying any body else.' And indeed, to own the truth, I do not think nurse in her heart is a very strenuous opposer of Sir Walter's making a second match. She must be allowed to be a favourer of matrimony you know, and (since self will intrude) who can say that she may not have some flying visions of attending the next Lady Elliot, through Mrs. Wallis's recommendation?"

"I am very glad to know all this," said Anne, after a little thoughtfulness. "It will be more painful to me in some respects to be in company with him, but I shall know better what to do. My line of conduct will be more direct. Mr. Elliot is evidently a disingenuous, artificial,[19] worldly man, who has never had any better principle to guide him than selfishness."

But Mr. Elliot was not yet done with. Mrs. Smith had been carried away from her first direction, and Anne had forgotten, in the interest of her own family concerns, how much had been originally implied against him; but her attention was now called to the explanation of those first hints, and she

[19] Using artifice; methodically scheming.

listened to a recital which, if it did not perfectly justify the unqualified bitterness of Mrs. Smith, proved him to have been very unfeeling in his conduct towards her, very deficient both in justice and compassion.

She learned that (the intimacy between them continuing unimpaired by Mr. Elliot's marriage) they had been as before always together, and Mr. Elliot had led his friend into expenses much beyond his fortune. Mrs. Smith did not want to take blame to herself, and was most tender of throwing any on her husband; but Anne could collect that their income had never been equal to their style of living, and that from the first, there had been a great deal of general and joint extravagance. From his wife's account of him, she could discern Mr. Smith to have been a man of warm feelings, easy temper, careless habits, and not strong understanding, much more amiable than his friend, and very unlike him—led by him, and probably despised by him. Mr. Elliot, raised by his marriage to great affluence, and disposed to every gratification of pleasure and vanity which could be commanded without involving himself, (for with all his self-indulgence he had become a prudent man) and beginning to be rich, just as his friend ought to have found himself to be poor, seemed to have had no concern at all for that friend's probable finances, but, on the contrary, had been prompting and encouraging expenses, which could end only in ruin. And the Smiths accordingly had been ruined.

The husband had died just in time to be spared the full knowledge of it. They had previously known embarrassments enough to try the friendship of their friends, and to prove that Mr. Elliot's had better not be tried; but it was not till his death that the wretched state of his affairs was fully known. With a confidence in Mr. Elliot's regard, more creditable to his feelings than his judgment, Mr. Smith had appointed him the executor of his will; but Mr. Elliot would not act, and the difficulties and distresses which this refusal had heaped on her, in addition to the inevitable sufferings of her situation, had been such as could not be related without anguish of spirit, or listened to without corresponding indignation.

Anne was shewn some letters of his on the occasion, answers to urgent applications from Mrs. Smith, which all breathed the same stern resolution of not engaging in a fruitless trouble, and, under a cold civility, the same hard-hearted indifference to any of the evils it might bring on her. It was a dreadful picture of ingratitude and inhumanity; and Anne felt at some moments, that no flagrant open crime could have been worse. She had a great deal to listen to; all the particulars of past sad scenes, all the minutiae of distress upon distress, which in former conversations had been merely hinted at, were dwelt on now with a natural indulgence. Anne could perfectly comprehend the exquisite relief, and was only the more inclined to wonder at the composure of her friend's usual state of mind.

There was one circumstance in the history of her grievances of particular irritation. She had good reason to believe that some property of her husband in the West Indies, which had been for many years under a sort of sequestration[20] for the payment of its own incumbrances, might be recoverable by proper measures; and this property, though not large, would be enough to make her comparatively rich. But there was nobody to stir in it.

[20] The reservation of income from a property to satisfy incumbrances (liens against it).

Mr. Elliot would do nothing, and she could do nothing herself, equally disabled from personal exertion by her state of bodily weakness, and from employing others by her want of money. She had no natural connexions to assist her even with their counsel, and she could not afford to purchase the assistance of the law. This was a cruel aggravation of actually streightened means. To feel that she ought to be in better circumstances, that a little trouble in the right place might do it, and to fear that delay might be even weakening her claims, was hard to bear!

It was on this point that she had hoped to engage Anne's good offices with Mr. Elliot. She had previously, in the anticipation of their marriage, been very apprehensive of losing her friend by it; but on being assured that he could have made no attempt of that nature, since he did not even know her to be in Bath, it immediately occurred, that something might be done in her favour by the influence of the woman he loved, and she had been hastily preparing to interest Anne's feelings, as far as the observances due to Mr. Elliot's character would allow, when Anne's refutation of the supposed engagement changed the face of every thing, and while it took from her the new-formed hope of succeeding in the object of her first anxiety, left her at least the comfort of telling the whole story her own way.

After listening to this full description of Mr. Elliot, Anne could not but express some surprise at Mrs. Smith's having spoken of him so favourably in the beginning of their conversation. "She had seemed to recommend and praise him!"

"My dear," was Mrs. Smith's reply, "there was nothing else to be done. I considered your marrying him as certain, though he might not yet have made the offer, and I could no more speak the truth of him, than if he had been your husband. My heart bled for you, as I talked of happiness. And yet, he is sensible, he is agreeable, and with such a woman as you, it was not absolutely hopeless. He was very unkind to his first wife. They were wretched together. But she was too ignorant and giddy for respect, and he had never loved her. I was willing to hope that you must fare better."

Anne could just acknowledge within herself such a possibility of having been induced to marry him, as made her shudder at the idea of the misery which must have followed. It was just possible that she might have been persuaded by Lady Russell! And under such a supposition, which would have been most miserable, when time had disclosed all, too late?

It was very desirable that Lady Russell should be no longer deceived; and one of the concluding arrangements of this important conference, which carried them through the greater part of the morning, was, that Anne had full liberty to communicate to her friend every thing relative to Mrs. Smith, in which his conduct was involved.

CHAPTER 22

Anne went home to think over all that she had heard. In one point, her feelings were relieved by this knowledge of Mr. Elliot. There was no longer any thing of tenderness due to him. He stood, as opposed to Captain Wentworth, in all his own unwelcome obtrusiveness; and the evil of his attentions last night, the irremediable mischief he might have done, was consid-

ered with sensations unqualified, unperplexed.—Pity for him was all over. But this was the only point of relief. In every other respect, in looking around her, or penetrating forward, she saw more to distrust and to apprehend. She was concerned for the disappointment and pain Lady Russell would be feeling, for the mortifications which must be hanging over her father and sister, and had all the distress of foreseeing many evils, without knowing how to avert any one of them.—She was most thankful for her own knowledge of him. She had never considered herself as entitled to reward for not slighting an old friend like Mrs. Smith, but here was a reward indeed springing from it!—Mrs. Smith had been able to tell her what no one else could have done. Could the knowledge have been extended through her family!—But this was a vain idea. She must talk to Lady Russell, tell her, consult with her, and having done her best, wait the event[21] with as much composure as possible; and after all, her greatest want of composure would be in that quarter of the mind which could not be opened to Lady Russell, in that flow of anxieties and fears which must be all to herself.

She found, on reaching home, that she had, as she intended, escaped seeing Mr. Elliot; that he had called and paid them a long morning visit; but hardly had she congratulated herself, and felt safe till to-morrow, when she heard that he was coming again in the evening.

"I had not the smallest intention of asking him," said Elizabeth, with affected carelessness, "but he gave so many hints; so Mrs. Clay says, at least."

"Indeed I do say it. I never saw any body in my life spell[22] harder for an invitation. Poor man! I was really in pain for him; for your hard-hearted sister, Miss Anne, seems bent on cruelty."

"Oh!" cried Elizabeth, "I have been rather too much used to the game to be soon overcome by a gentleman's hints. However, when I found how excessively he was regretting that he should miss my father this morning, I gave way immediately, for I would never really omit an opportunity of bringing him and Sir Walter together. They appear to so much advantage in company with each other! Each behaving so pleasantly! Mr. Elliot looking up with so much respect!"

"Quite delightful!" cried Mrs. Clay, not daring, however, to turn her eyes towards Anne. "Exactly like father and son! Dear Miss Elliot, may I not say father and son?"

"Oh! I lay no embargo on any body's words. If you will have such ideas! But, upon my word, I am scarcely sensible of his attentions being beyond those of other men."

"My dear Miss Elliot!" exclaimed Mrs. Clay, lifting up her hands and eyes, and sinking all the rest of her astonishment in a convenient silence.

"Well, my dear Penelope, you need not be so alarmed about him. I did invite him, you know. I sent him away with smiles. When I found he was really going to his friends at Thornberry-park for the whole day to-morrow, I had compassion on him."

Anne admired the good acting of the friend, in being able to shew such pleasure as she did, in the expectation, and in the actual arrival of the very

[21] Eventual outcome. [22] Ask, by hinting.

person whose presence must really be interfering with her prime object. It was impossible but that Mrs. Clay must hate the sight of Mr. Elliot; and yet she could assume a most obliging, placid look, and appear quite satisfied with the curtailed license of devoting herself only half as much to Sir Walter as she would have done otherwise.

To Anne herself it was most distressing to see Mr. Elliot enter the room; and quite painful to have him approach and speak to her. She had been used before to feel that he could not be always quite sincere, but now she saw insincerity in every thing. His attentive deference to her father, contrasted with his former language, was odious; and when she thought of his cruel conduct towards Mrs. Smith, she could hardly bear the sight of his present smiles and mildness, or the sound of his artificial good sentiments. She meant to avoid any such alteration of manners as might provoke a remonstrance on his side. It was a great object with her to escape all enquiry or eclat;[23] but it was her intention to be as decidedly cool to him as might be compatible with their relationship, and to retrace, as quietly as she could, the few steps of unnecessary intimacy she had been gradually led along. She was accordingly more guarded, and more cool, than she had been the night before.

He wanted to animate her curiosity again as to how and where he could have heard her formerly praised; wanted very much to be gratified by more solicitation; but the charm was broken: he found that the heat and animation of a public room were necessary to kindle his modest cousin's vanity; he found, at least, that it was not to be done now, by any of those attempts which he could hazard among the too-commanding claims of the others. He little surmised that it was a subject acting now exactly against his interest, bringing immediately into her thoughts all those parts of his conduct which were least excusable.

She had some satisfaction in finding that he was really going out of Bath the next morning, going early, and that he would be gone the greater part of two days. He was invited again to Camden-place the very evening of his return; but from Thursday to Saturday evening his absence was certain. It was bad enough that a Mrs. Clay should be always before her; but that a deeper hypocrite should be added to their party, seemed the destruction of every thing like peace and comfort. It was so humiliating to reflect on the constant deception practised on her father and Elizabeth; to consider the various sources of mortification preparing for them! Mrs. Clay's selfishness was not so complicate nor so revolting as his; and Anne would have compounded for the marriage at once, with all its evils, to be clear of Mr. Elliot's subtleties, in endeavouring to prevent it.

On Friday morning she meant to go very early to Lady Russell, and accomplish the necessary communication; and she would have gone directly after breakfast but that Mrs. Clay was also going out on some obliging purpose of saving her sister trouble, which determined her to wait till she might be safe from such a companion. She saw Mrs. Clay fairly off, therefore, before she began to talk of spending the morning in Riversstreet.

"Very well," said Elizabeth, "I have nothing to send but my love. Oh!

[23] Sensational scene.

you may as well take back that tiresome book she would lend me, and pretend I have read it through. I really cannot be plaguing myself for ever with all the new poems and states of the nation that come out. Lady Russell quite bores one with her new publications. You need not tell her so, but I thought her dress hideous the other night. I used to think she had some taste in dress, but I was ashamed of her at the concert. Something so formal and *arrangé* in her air! and she sits so upright! My best love, of course."

"And mine," added Sir Walter. "Kindest regards. And you may say, that I mean to call upon her soon. Make a civil message. But I shall only leave my card. Morning visits are never fair by women at her time of life, who make themselves up so little. If she would only wear rouge, she would not be afraid of being seen; but last time I called, I observed the blinds were let down immediately."

While her father spoke, there was a knock at the door. Who could it be? Anne, remembering the preconcerted visits, at all hours, of Mr. Elliot, would have expected him, but for his known engagement seven miles off. After the usual period of suspense, the usual sounds of approach were heard, and "Mr. and Mrs. Charles Musgrove" were ushered into the room.

Surprise was the strongest emotion raised by their appearance; but Anne was really glad to see them; and the others were not so sorry but that they could put on a decent air of welcome; and as soon as it became clear that these, their nearest relations, were not arrived with any views of accommodation in that house, Sir Walter and Elizabeth were able to rise in cordiality, and do the honours of it very well. They were come to Bath for a few days with Mrs. Musgrove, and were at the White Hart. So much was pretty soon understood; but till Sir Walter and Elizabeth were walking Mary into the other drawing-room, and regaling themselves with her admiration, Anne could not draw upon Charles's brain for a regular history of their coming, or an explanation of some smiling hints of particular business, which had been ostentatiously dropped by Mary, as well as of some apparent confusion as to whom their party consisted of.

She then found that it consisted of Mrs. Musgrove, Henrietta, and Captain Harville, beside their two selves. He gave her a very plain, intelligible account of the whole; a narration in which she saw a great deal of most characteristic proceeding. The scheme had received its first impulse by Captain Harville's wanting to come to Bath on business. He had begun to talk of it a week ago; and by way of doing something, as shooting was over, Charles had proposed coming with him, and Mrs. Harville had seemed to like the idea of it very much, as an advantage to her husband; but Mary could not bear to be left, and had made herself so unhappy about it that, for a day or two, every thing seemed to be in suspense, or at an end. But then, it had been taken up by his father and mother. His mother had some old friends in Bath, whom she wanted to see; it was thought a good opportunity for Henrietta to come and buy wedding-clothes for herself and her sister; and, in short, it ended in being his mother's party, that every thing might be comfortable and easy to Captain Harville; and he and Mary were included in it, by way of general convenience. They had arrived late the night before. Mrs. Harville, her children, and Captain Benwick, remained with Mr. Musgrove and Louisa at Uppercross.

Anne's only surprise was, that affairs should be in forwardness enough

for Henrietta's wedding-clothes to be talked of; she had imagined such difficulties of fortune to exist there as must prevent the marriage from being near at hand; but she learned from Charles that, very recently, (since Mary's last letter to herself) Charles Hayter had been applied to by a friend to hold a living[24] for a youth who could not possibly claim it under many years; and that, on the strength of this present income, with almost a certainty of something more permanent long before the term in question, the two families had consented to the young people's wishes, and that their marriage was likely to take place in a few months, quite as soon as Louisa's. "And a very good living it was," Charles added, "only five-and-twenty miles from Uppercross, and in a very fine country—fine part of Dorsetshire. In the centre of some of the best preserves[25] in the kingdom, surrounded by three great proprietors, each more careful and jealous[26] than the other; and to two of the three, at least, Charles Hayter might get a special recommendation. Not that he will value it as he ought," he observed, "Charles is too cool about sporting. That's the worst of him."

"I am extremely glad, indeed," cried Anne, "particularly glad that this should happen: and that of two sisters, who both deserve equally well, and who have always been such good friends, the pleasant prospects of one should not be dimming those of the other—that they should be so equal in their prosperity and comfort. I hope your father and mother are quite happy with regard to both."

"Oh! yes. My father would be as well pleased if the gentlemen were richer, but he has no other fault to find. Money, you know, coming down with money—two daughters at once—it cannot be a very agreeable operation, and it streightens him as to many things. However, I do not mean to say they have not a right to it. It is very fit they should have daughters' shares; and I am sure he has always been a very kind, liberal father to me. Mary does not above half like Henrietta's match. She never did, you know. But she does not do him justice, nor think enough about Winthrop. I cannot make her attend to the value of the property. It is a very fair match, as times go; and I have liked Charles Hayter all my life, and I shall not leave off now."

"Such excellent parents as Mr. and Mrs. Musgrove," exclaimed Anne, "should be happy in their children's marriages. They do every thing to confer happiness, I am sure. What a blessing to young people to be in such hands! Your father and mother seem so totally free from all those ambitious feelings which have led to so much misconduct and misery, both in young and old! I hope you think Louisa perfectly recovered now?"

He answered rather hesitatingly, "Yes, I believe I do—very much recovered; but she is altered: there is no running or jumping about, no laughing or dancing; it is quite different. If one happens only to shut the door a little hard, she starts and wriggles like a young dab chick[27] in the water; and Benwick sits at her elbow, reading verses, or whispering to her, all day long."

[24] Appointment to a church as clergyman, with the attendant revenue.
[25] Game-preserves. [26] Eager (to exclude poachers).
[27] A small, diving water bird.

Anne could not help laughing. "That cannot be much to your taste, I know," said she; "but I do believe him to be an excellent young man."

"To be sure he is. Nobody doubts it; and I hope you do not think I am so illiberal as to want every man to have the same objects and pleasures as myself. I have a great value for Benwick; and when one can but get him to talk, he has plenty to say. His reading has done him no harm, for he has fought as well as read. He is a brave fellow. I got more acquainted with him last Monday than ever I did before. We had a famous set-to at rat-hunting all the morning, in my father's great barns; and he played his part so well, that I have liked him the better ever since."

Here they were interrupted by the absolute necessity of Charles's following the others to admire mirrors and china; but Anne had heard enough to understand the present state of Uppercross, and rejoice in its happiness; and though she sighed as she rejoiced, her sigh had none of the ill-will of envy in it. She would certainly have risen to their blessings if she could, but she did not want to lessen theirs.

The visit passed off altogether in high good humour. Mary was in excellent spirits, enjoying the gaiety and the change; and so well satisfied with the journey in her mother-in-law's carriage with four horses, and with her own complete independence of Camden-place, that she was exactly in a temper to admire every thing as she ought, and enter most readily into all the superiorities of the house, as they were detailed to her. She had no demands on her father or sister, and her consequence was just enough increased by their handsome drawing-rooms.

Elizabeth was, for a short time, suffering a good deal. She felt that Mrs. Musgrove and all her party ought to be asked to dine with them, but she could not bear to have the difference of style, the reduction of servants, which a dinner must betray, witnessed by those who had been always so inferior to the Elliots of Kellynch. It was a struggle between propriety and vanity; but vanity got the better, and then Elizabeth was happy again. These were her internal persuasions.—"Old fashioned notions—country hospitality—we do not profess to give dinners—few people in Bath do— Lady Alicia never does; did not even ask her own sister's family, though they were here a month: and I dare say it would be very inconvenient to Mrs. Musgrove—put her quite out of her way. I am sure she would rather not come— she cannot feel easy with us. I will ask them all for an evening; that will be much better—that will be a novelty and a treat. They have not seen two such drawing rooms before. They will be delighted to come to-morrow evening. It shall be a regular party—small, but most elegant." And this satisfied Elizabeth: and when the invitation was given to the two present, and promised for the absent, Mary was as completely satisfied. She was particularly asked to meet Mr. Elliot, and be introduced to Lady Dalrymple and Miss Carteret, who were fortunately already engaged to come; and she could not have received a more gratifying attention. Miss Elliot was to have the honour of calling on Mrs. Musgrove in the course of the morning, and Anne walked off with Charles and Mary, to go and see her and Henrietta directly.

Her plan of sitting with Lady Russell must give way for the present. They all three called in Rivers-street for a couple of minutes; but Anne convinced herself that a day's delay of the intended communication could

be of no consequence, and hastened forward to the White Hart, to see again the friends and companions of the last autumn, with an eagerness of good will which many associations contributed to form.

They found Mrs. Musgrove and her daughter within, and by themselves, and Anne had the kindest welcome from each. Henrietta was exactly in that state of recently-improved views, of fresh-formed happiness, which made her full of regard and interest for every body she had ever liked before at all; and Mrs. Musgrove's real affection had been won by her usefulness when they were in distress. It was a heartiness, and a warmth, and a sincerity which Anne delighted in the more, from the sad want of such blessings at home. She was intreated to give them as much of her time as possible, invited for every day and all day long, or rather claimed as a part of the family; and in return, she naturally fell into all her wonted ways of attention and assistance, and on Charles's leaving them together, was listening to Mrs. Musgrove's history of Louisa, and to Henrietta's of herself, giving opinions on business, and recommendations to shops; with intervals of every help which Mary required, from altering her ribbon to settling her accounts, from finding her keys, and assorting her trinkets, to trying to convince her that she was not ill used by any body; which Mary, well amused as she generally was in her station at a window overlooking the entrance to the pump-room,[28] could not but have her moments of imagining.

A morning of thorough confusion was to be expected. A large party in an hotel ensured a quick-changing, unsettled scene. One five minutes brought a note, the next a parcel, and Anne had not been there half an hour, when their dining-room, spacious as it was, seemed more than half filled: a party of steady old friends were seated round Mrs. Musgrove, and Charles came back with Captains Harville and Wentworth. The appearance of the latter could not be more than the surprise of the moment. It was impossible for her to have forgotten to feel, that this arrival of their common friends must be soon bringing them together again. Their last meeting had been most important in opening his feelings; she had derived from it a delightful conviction; but she feared from his looks, that the same unfortunate persuasion, which had hastened him away from the concert room, still governed. He did not seem to want to be near enough for conversation.

She tried to be calm, and leave things to take their course; and tried to dwell much on this argument of rational dependence—"Surely, if there be constant attachment on each side, our hearts must understand each other ere long. We are not boy and girl, to be captiously irritable, misled by every moment's inadvertence, and wantonly playing with our own happiness." And yet, a few minutes afterwards, she felt as if their being in company with each other, under their present circumstances, could only be exposing them to inadvertencies and misconstructions of the most mischievous kind.

"Anne," cried Mary, still at her window, "there is Mrs. Clay, I am sure, standing under the colonnade, and a gentleman with her. I saw them turn the corner from Bath-street just now. They seem deep in talk. Who is it?—Come, and tell me. Good heavens! I recollect.—It is Mr. Elliot himself."

[28] A fashionable assembly-room that contained a mineral-water fountain.

"No," cried Anne quickly, "it cannot be Mr. Elliot, I assure you. He was to leave Bath at nine this morning, and does not come back till to-morrow."

As she spoke, she felt that Captain Wentworth was looking at her; the consciousness of which vexed and embarrassed her, and made her regret that she had said so much, simple as it was.

Mary, resenting that she should be supposed not to know her own cousin, began talking very warmly about the family features, and protesting still more positively that it was Mr. Elliot, calling again upon Anne to come and look herself; but Anne did not mean to stir, and tried to be cool and unconcerned. Her distress returned, however, on perceiving smiles and intelligent glances pass between two or three of the lady visitors, as if they believed themselves quite in the secret. It was evident that the report concerning her had spread; and a short pause succeeded, which seemed to ensure that it would now spread farther.

"Do come, Anne," cried Mary, "come and look yourself. You will be too late, if you do not make haste. They are parting, they are shaking hands. He is turning away. Not know Mr. Elliot indeed!—You seem to have forgot all about Lyme."

To pacify Mary, and perhaps screen her own embarrassment, Anne did move quietly to the window. She was just in time to ascertain that it really was Mr. Elliot (which she had never believed), before he disappeared on one side, as Mrs. Clay walked quickly off on the other; and checking the surprise which she could not but feel at such an appearance of friendly conference between two persons of totally opposite interests, she calmly said, "Yes, it is Mr. Elliot certainly. He has changed his hour of going, I suppose, that is all—or I may be mistaken; I might not attend;" and walked back to her chair, recomposed, and with the comfortable hope of having acquitted herself well.

The visitors took their leave; and Charles, having civilly seen them off, and then made a face at them, and abused them for coming, began with—

"Well, mother, I have done something for you that you will like. I have been to the theatre, and secured a box for to-morrow night. A'n't I a good boy? I know you love a play; and there is room for us all. It holds nine. I have engaged Captain Wentworth. Anne will not be sorry to join us, I am sure. We all like a play. Have not I done well, mother?"

Mrs. Musgrove was good humouredly beginning to express her perfect readiness for the play, if Henrietta and all the others liked it, when Mary eagerly interrupted her by exclaiming,

"Good heavens, Charles! how can you think of such a thing? Take a box for to-morrow night! Have you forgot that we are engaged to Camden-place to-morrow night? and that we were most particularly asked on purpose to meet Lady Dalrymple and her daughter and Mr. Elliot—all the principal family connexions—on purpose to be introduced to them? How can you be so forgetful?"

"Phoo! phoo!" replied Charles, "what's an evening party? Never worth remembering. Your father might have asked us to dinner, I think, if he had wanted to see us. You may do as you like, but I shall go to the play."

"Oh! Charles, I declare it will be too abominable if you do! when you promised to go."

"No, I did not promise. I only smirked and bowed, and said the word 'happy.' There was no promise."

"But you must go, Charles. It would be unpardonable to fail. We were asked on purpose to be introduced. There was always such a great connexion between the Dalrymples and ourselves. Nothing ever happened on either side that was not announced immediately. We are quite near relations, you know: and Mr. Elliot too, whom you ought so particularly to be acquainted with! Every attention is due to Mr. Elliot. Consider, my father's heir—the future representative of the family."

"Don't talk to me about heirs and representatives," cried Charles. "I am not one of those who neglect the reigning power to bow to the rising sun. If I would not go for the sake of your father, I should think it scandalous to go for the sake of his heir. What is Mr. Elliot to me?"

The careless expression was life to Anne, who saw that Captain Wentworth was all attention, looking and listening with his whole soul; and that the last words brought his enquiring eyes from Charles to herself.

Charles and Mary still talked on in the same style; he, half serious and half jesting, maintaining the scheme for the play; and she, invariably serious, most warmly opposing it, and not omitting to make it known, that however determined to go to Camden-place herself, she should not think herself very well used, if they went to the play without her. Mrs. Musgrove interposed.

"We had better put it off. Charles, you had better go back and change the box for Tuesday. It would be a pity to be divided, and we should be losing Miss Anne too, if there is a party at her father's; and I am sure neither Henrietta nor I should care at all for the play, if Miss Anne could not be with us."

Anne felt truly obliged to her for such kindness; and quite as much so, moreover, for the opportunity it gave her of decidedly saying—

"If it depended only on my inclination, ma'am, the party at home (excepting on Mary's account) would not be the smallest impediment. I have no pleasure in the sort of meeting, and should be too happy to change it for a play, and with you. But, it had better not be attempted, perhaps."

She had spoken it; but she trembled when it was done, conscious that her words were listened to, and daring not even to try to observe their effect.

It was soon generally agreed that Tuesday should be the day, Charles only reserving the advantage of still teasing his wife, by persisting that he would go to the play to-morrow, if nobody else would.

Captain Wentworth left his seat, and walked to the fire-place; probably for the sake of walking away from it soon afterwards, and taking a station, with less barefaced design, by Anne.

"You have not been long enough in Bath," said he, "to enjoy the evening parties of the place."

"Oh! no. The usual character of them has nothing for me. I am no card-player."

"You were not formerly, I know. You did not use to like cards; but time makes many changes."

"I am not yet so much changed," cried Anne, and stopped, fearing she

hardly knew what misconstruction. After waiting a few moments he said—and as if it were the result of immediate feeling—"It is a period, indeed! Eight years and a half is a period!"

Whether he would have proceeded farther was left to Anne's imagination to ponder over in a calmer hour; for while still hearing the sounds he had uttered, she was startled to other subjects by Henrietta, eager to make use of the present leisure for getting out, and calling on her companions to lose no time, lest somebody else should come in.

They were obliged to move. Anne talked of being perfectly ready, and tried to look it; but she felt that could Henrietta have known the regret and reluctance of her heart in quitting that chair, in preparing to quit the room, she would have found, in all her own sensations for her cousin, in the very security of his affection, wherewith to pity her.

Their preparations, however, were stopped short. Alarming sounds were heard; other visitors approached, and the door was thrown open for Sir Walter and Miss Elliot, whose entrance seemed to give a general chill. Anne felt an instant oppression, and, wherever she looked, saw symptoms of the same. The comfort, the freedom, the gaiety of the room was over, hushed into cold composure, determined silence, or insipid talk, to meet the heartless elegance of her father and sister. How mortifying to feel that it was so!

Her jealous eye was satisfied in one particular. Captain Wentworth was acknowledged again by each, by Elizabeth more graciously than before. She even addressed him once, and looked at him more than once. Elizabeth was, in fact, revolving a great measure. The sequel explained it. After the waste of a few minutes in saying the proper nothings, she began to give the invitation which was to comprise all the remaining dues of the Musgroves. "To-morrow evening, to meet a few friends, no formal party." It was all said very gracefully, and the cards with which she had provided herself, the "Miss Elliot at home," were laid on the table, with a courteous, comprehensive smile to all; and one smile and one card more decidedly for Captain Wentworth. The truth was, that Elizabeth had been long enough in Bath, to understand the importance of a man of such an air and appearance as his. The past was nothing. The present was that Captain Wentworth would move about well in her drawing-room. The card was pointedly given, and Sir Walter and Elizabeth arose and disappeared.

The interruption had been short, though severe; and ease and animation returned to most of those they left, as the door shut them out, but not to Anne. She could think only of the invitation she had with such astonishment witnessed; and of the manner in which it had been received, a manner of doubtful meaning, of surprise rather than gratification, of polite acknowledgement rather than acceptance. She knew him; she saw disdain in his eye, and could not venture to believe that he had determined to accept such an offering, as atonement for all the insolence of the past. Her spirits sank. He held the card in his hand after they were gone, as if deeply considering it.

"Only think of Elizabeth's including every body!" whispered Mary very audibly. "I do not wonder Captain Wentworth is delighted! You see he cannot put the card out of his hand."

Anne caught his eye, saw his cheeks glow, and his mouth form itself into

a momentary expression of contempt, and turned away, that she might neither see nor hear more to vex her.

The party separated. The gentlemen had their own pursuits, the ladies proceeded on their own business, and they met no more while Anne belonged to them. She was earnestly begged to return and dine, and give them all the rest of the day; but her spirits had been so long exerted, that at present she felt unequal to more, and fit only for home, where she might be sure of being as silent as she chose.

Promising to be with them the whole of the following morning, therefore, she closed the fatigues of the present, by a toilsome walk to Camden-place, there to spend the evening chiefly in listening to the busy arrangements of Elizabeth and Mrs. Clay for the morrow's party, the frequent enumeration of the persons invited, and the continually improving detail of all the embellishments which were to make it the most completely elegant of its kind in Bath, while harassing herself in secret with the never-ending question, of whether Captain Wentworth would come or not? They were reckoning him as certain, but, with her, it was a gnawing solicitude never appeased for five minutes together. She generally thought he would come, because she generally thought he ought; but it was a case which she could not so shape into any positive act of duty or discretion, as inevitably to defy the suggestions of very opposite feelings.

She only roused herself from the broodings of this restless agitation, to let Mrs. Clay know that she had been seen with Mr. Elliot three hours after his being supposed to be out of Bath; for having watched in vain for some intimation of the interview from the lady herself, she determined to mention it; and it seemed to her that there was guilt in Mrs. Clay's face as she listened. It was transient, cleared away in an instant, but Anne could imagine she read there the consciousness of having, by some complication of mutual trick, or some overbearing authority of his, been obliged to attend (perhaps for half an hour) to his lectures and restrictions on her designs on Sir Walter. She exclaimed, however, with a very tolerable imitation of nature,

"Oh dear! very true. Only think, Miss Elliot, to my great surprise I met with Mr. Elliot in Bath-street! I was never more astonished. He turned back and walked with me to the Pump-yard. He had been prevented setting off for Thornberry, but I really forget by what—for I was in a hurry, and could not much attend, and I can only answer for his being determined not to be delayed in his return. He wanted to know how early he might be admitted to-morrow. He was full of "to-morrow;" and it is very evident that I have been full of it too ever since I entered the house, and learnt the extension of your plan, and all that had happened, or my seeing him could never have gone so entirely out of my head."

CHAPTER 23

One day only had passed since Anne's conversation with Mrs. Smith; but a keener interest had succeeded, and she was now so little touched by Mr. Elliot's conduct, except by its effects in one quarter, that it became a matter of course the next morning, still to defer her explanatory visit in Rivers-

street. She had promised to be with the Musgroves from breakfast to dinner. Her faith was plighted, and Mr. Elliot's character, like the Sultaness Scheherazade's head, must live another day.[29]

She could not keep her appointment punctually, however; the weather was unfavourable, and she had grieved over the rain on her friends' account, and felt it very much on her own, before she was able to attempt the walk. When she reached the White Hart, and made her way to the proper apartment, she found herself neither arriving quite in time, nor the first to arrive. The party before her were Mrs. Musgrove, talking to Mrs. Croft, and Captain Harville to Captain Wentworth, and she immediately heard that Mary and Henrietta, too impatient to wait, had gone out the moment it had cleared, but would be back again soon, and that the strictest injunctions had been left with Mrs. Musgrove, to keep her there till they returned. She had only to submit, sit down, be outwardly composed, and feel herself plunged at once in all the agitations which she had merely laid her account of tasting a little before the morning closed. There was no delay, no waste of time. She was deep in the happiness of such misery, or the misery of such happiness, instantly. Two minutes after her entering the room, Captain Wentworth said,

"We will write the letter we were talking of, Harville, now, if you will give me the materials."

Materials were all at hand, on a separate table; he went to it, and nearly turning his back on them all, was engrossed by writing.

Mrs. Musgrove was giving Mrs. Croft the history of her eldest daughter's engagement, and just in that inconvenient tone of voice which was perfectly audible while it pretended to be a whisper. Anne felt that she did not belong to the conversation, and yet, as Captain Harville seemed thoughtful and not disposed to talk, she could not avoid hearing many undesirable particulars, such as "how Mr. Musgrove and my brother Hayter had met again and again to talk it over; what my brother Hayter had said one day, and what Mr. Musgrove had proposed the next, and what had occurred to my sister Hayter, and what the young people had wished, and what I said at first I never could consent to, but was afterwards persuaded to think might do very well," and a great deal in the same style of open-hearted communication—Minutiae which, even with every advantage of taste and delicacy which good Mrs. Musgrove could not give, could be properly interesting only to the principals. Mrs. Croft was attending with great good humour, and whenever she spoke at all, it was very sensibly. Anne hoped the gentlemen might each be too much self-occupied to hear.

"And so, ma'am, all these things considered," said Mrs. Musgrove in her powerful whisper, "though we could have wished it different, yet altogether we did not think it fair to stand out any longer; for Charles Hayter was quite wild about it, and Henrietta was pretty near as bad; and so we thought they had better marry at once, and make the best of it, as many others have done before them. At any rate, said I, it will be better than a long engagement."

[29]Scheherazade was the spellbinding storyteller of *The Arabian Nights Entertainments;* her skill enabled her, one night at a time, to avoid being executed like the Sultan's earlier wives.

"That is precisely what I was going to observe," cried Mrs. Croft. "I would rather have young people settle on a small income at once, and have to struggle with a few difficulties together, than be involved in a long engagement. I always think that no mutual—"

"Oh! dear Mrs. Croft," cried Mrs. Musgrove, unable to let her finish her speech, "there is nothing I so abominate for young people as a long engagement. It is what I always protested against for my children. It is all very well, I used to say, for young people to be engaged, if there is a certainty of their being able to marry in six months, or even twelve, but a long engagement!"

"Yes, dear ma'am," said Mrs. Croft, "or an uncertain engagement; an engagement which may be long. To begin without knowing that at such a time there will be the means of marrying, I hold to be very unsafe and unwise, and what, I think, all parents should prevent as far as they can."

Anne found an unexpected interest here. She felt its application to herself, felt it in a nervous thrill all over her, and at the same moment that her eyes instinctively glanced towards the distant table, Captain Wentworth's pen ceased to move, his head was raised, pausing, listening, and he turned round the next instant to give a look—one quick, conscious look at her.

The two ladies continued to talk, to re-urge the same admitted truths, and enforce them with such examples of the ill effect of a contrary practice, as had fallen within their observation, but Anne heard nothing distinctly; it was only a buzz of words in her ear, her mind was in confusion.

Captain Harville, who had in truth been hearing none of it, now left his seat, and moved to a window; and Anne seeming to watch him, though it was from thorough absence of mind, became gradually sensible that he was inviting her to join him where he stood. He looked at her with a smile, and a little motion of the head, which expressed, "Come to me, I have something to say;" and the unaffected, easy kindness of manner which denoted the feelings of an older acquaintance than he really was, strongly enforced the invitation. She roused herself and went to him. The window at which he stood, was at the other end of the room from where the two ladies were sitting, and though nearer to Captain Wentworth's table, not very near. As she joined him, Captain Harville's countenance reassumed the serious, thoughtful expression which seemed its natural character.

"Look here," said he, unfolding a parcel in his hand, and displaying a small miniature painting, "do you know who that is?"

"Certainly, Captain Benwick."

"Yes, and you may guess who it is for. But (in a deep tone) it was not done for her. Miss Elliot, do you remember our walking together at Lyme, and grieving for him? I little thought then—but no matter. This was drawn at the Cape. He met with a clever young German artist at the Cape, and in compliance with a promise to my poor sister, sat to him, and was bringing it home for her. And I have now the charge of getting it properly set for another! It was a commission to me! But who else was there to employ? I hope I can allow for him. I am not sorry, indeed, to make it over to another. He undertakes it—(looking towards Captain Wentworth) he is writing about it now." And with a quivering lip he wound up the whole by adding, "Poor Fanny! she would not have forgotten him so soon!"

"No," replied Anne, in a low feeling voice. "That, I can easily believe."
"It was not in her nature. She doated on him."

"It would not be the nature of any woman who truly loved."

Captain Harville smiled, as much as to say, "Do you claim that for your sex?" and she answered the question, smiling also, "Yes. We certainly do not forget you, so soon as you forget us. It is, perhaps, our fate rather than our merit. We cannot help ourselves. We live at home, quiet, confined, and our feelings prey upon us. You are forced on exertion. You have always a profession, pursuits, business of some sort or other, to take you back into the world immediately, and continual occupation and change soon weaken impressions."

"Granting your assertion that the world does all this so soon for men, (which, however, I do not think I shall grant) it does not apply to Benwick. He has not been forced upon any exertion. The peace turned him on shore at the very moment, and he has been living with us, in our little family-circle, ever since."

"True," said Anne, "very true; I did not recollect; but what shall we say now, Captain Harville? If the change be not from outward circumstances, it must be from within; it must be nature, man's nature, which has done the business for Captain Benwick."

"No, no, it is not man's nature. I will not allow it to be more man's nature than woman's to be inconstant and forget those they do love, or have loved. I believe the reverse. I believe in a true analogy between our bodily frames and our mental; and that as our bodies are the strongest, so are our feelings; capable of bearing most rough usage, and riding out the heaviest weather."

"Your feelings may be the strongest," replied Anne, "but the same spirit of analogy will authorise me to assert that ours are the most tender. Man is more robust than woman, but he is not longer-lived; which exactly explains my view of the nature of their attachments. Nay, it would be too hard upon you, if it were otherwise. You have difficulties, and privations, and dangers enough to struggle with. You are always labouring and toiling, exposed to every risk and hardship. Your home, country, friends, all quitted. Neither time, nor health, nor life, to be called your own. It would be too hard indeed" (with a faltering voice) "if woman's feelings were to be added to all this."

"We shall never agree upon this question"—Captain Harville was beginning to say, when a slight noise called their attention to Captain Wentworth's hitherto perfectly quiet division of the room. It was nothing more than that his pen had fallen down, but Anne was startled at finding him nearer than she had supposed, and half inclined to suspect that the pen had only fallen, because he had been occupied by them, striving to catch sounds, which yet she did not think he could have caught.

"Have you finished your letter?" said Captain Harville.

"Not quite, a few lines more. I shall have done in five minutes."

"There is no hurry on my side. I am only ready whenever you are.—I am in very good anchorage here," (smiling at Anne) "well supplied, and want for nothing.—No hurry for a signal at all.—Well, Miss Elliot," (lowering his voice) "as I was saying, we shall never agree I suppose upon this point. No man and woman would, probably. But let me observe that all

histories are against you, all stories, prose and verse. If I had such a memory as Benwick, I could bring you fifty quotations in a moment on my side the argument, and I do not think I ever opened a book in my life which had not something to say upon woman's inconstancy. Songs and proverbs, all talk of woman's fickleness. But perhaps you will say, these were all written by men."

"Perhaps I shall.—Yes, yes, if you please, no reference to examples in books. Men have had every advantage of us in telling their own story. Education has been theirs in so much higher a degree; the pen has been in their hands. I will not allow books to prove any thing."

"But how shall we prove any thing?"

"We never shall. We never can expect to prove any thing upon such a point. It is a difference of opinion which does not admit of proof. We each begin probably with a little bias towards our own sex, and upon that bias build every circumstance in favour of it which has occurred within our own circle; many of which circumstances (perhaps those very cases which strike us the most) may be precisely such as cannot be brought forward without betraying a confidence, or in some respect saying what should not be said."

"Ah!" cried Captain Harville, in a tone of strong feeling, "if I could but make you comprehend what a man suffers when he takes a last look at his wife and children, and watches the boat that he has sent them off in, as long as it is in sight, and then turns away and says, 'God knows whether we ever meet again!' And then, if I could convey to you the glow of his soul when he does see them again; when, coming back after a twelvemonth's absence perhaps, and obliged to put into another port, he calculates how soon it be possible to get them there, pretending to deceive himself, and saying, 'They cannot be here till such a day,' but all the while hoping for them twelve hours sooner, and seeing them arrive at last, as if Heaven had given them wings, by many hours sooner still! If I could explain to you all this, and all that a man can bear and do, and glories to do for the sake of these treasures of his existence! I speak, you know, only of such men as have hearts!" pressing his own with emotion.

"Oh!" cried Anne eagerly, "I hope I do justice to all that is felt by you, and by those who resemble you. God forbid that I should undervalue the warm and faithful feelings of any of my fellow-creatures. I should deserve utter contempt if I dared to suppose that true attachment and constancy were known only by woman. No, I believe you capable of every thing great and good in your married lives. I believe you equal to every important exertion, and to every domestic forbearance, so long as—if I may be allowed the expression, so long as you have an object. I mean, while the woman you love lives, and lives for you. All the privilege I claim for my own sex (it is not a very enviable one, you need not covet it) is that of loving longest, when existence or when hope is gone."

She could not immediately have uttered another sentence; her heart was too full, her breath too much oppressed.

"You are a good soul," cried Captain Harville, putting his hand on her arm quite affectionately. "There is no quarrelling with you.—And when I think of Benwick, my tongue is tied."

Their attention was called towards the others.—Mrs. Croft was taking leave.

"Here, Frederick, you and I part company, I believe," said she. "I am going home, and you have an engagement with your friend.—To-night we may have the pleasure of all meeting again, at your party," (turning to Anne.) "We had your sister's card yesterday, and I understood Frederick had a card too, though I did not see it— and you are disengaged, Frederick, are you not, as well as ourselves?"

Captain Wentworth was folding up a letter in great haste, and either could not or would not answer fully.

"Yes," said he, "very true; here we separate, but Harville and I shall soon be after you, that is, Harville, if you are ready, I am in half a minute. I know you will not be sorry to be off. I shall be at your service in half a minute."

Mrs. Croft left them, and Captain Wentworth, having sealed his letter with great rapidity, was indeed ready, and had even a hurried, agitated air, which shewed impatience to be gone. Anne knew not how to understand it. She had the kindest "Good morning, God bless you," from Captain Harville, but from him not a word, nor a look. He had passed out of the room without a look!

She had only time, however, to move closer to the table where he had been writing, when footsteps were heard returning; the door opened; it was himself. He begged their pardon, but he had forgotten his gloves, and instantly crossing the room to the writing table, and standing with his back towards Mrs. Musgrove, he drew out a letter from under the scattered paper, placed it before Anne with eyes of glowing entreaty fixed on her for a moment, and hastily collecting his gloves, was again out of the room, almost before Mrs. Musgrove was aware of his being in it—the work of an instant!

The revolution which one instant had made in Anne, was almost beyond expression. The letter, with a direction hardly legible, to "Miss A. E.—." was evidently the one which he had been folding so hastily. While supposed to be writing only to Captain Benwick, he had been also addressing her! On the contents of that letter depended all which this world could do for her! Any thing was possible, any thing might be defied rather than suspense. Mrs. Musgrove had little arrangements of her own at her own table; to their protection she must trust, and sinking into the chair which he had occupied, succeeding to the very spot where he had leaned and written, her eyes devoured the following words:

I can listen no longer in silence. I must speak to you by such means as are within my reach. You pierce my soul. I am half agony, half hope. Tell me not that I am too late, that such precious feelings are gone for ever. I offer myself to you again with a heart even more your own, than when you almost broke it eight years and a half ago. Dare not say that man forgets sooner than woman, that his love has an earlier death. I have loved none but you. Unjust I may have been, weak and resentful I have been, but never inconstant. You alone have brought me to Bath. For you alone I think and plan.—Have you not seen this? Can you fail to have understood my wishes?—I had not waited even these ten days, could I have read your feelings, as I think you must have penetrated mine. I can hardly write. I am every instant hearing something which overpowers me. You sink your

voice, but I can distinguish the tones of that voice, when they would be lost on others.—Too good, too excellent creature! You do us justice indeed. You do believe that there is true attachment and constancy among men. Believe it to be most fervent, most undeviating in

<div align="right">F. W.</div>

I must go, uncertain of my fate; but I shall return hither, or follow your party, as soon as possible. A word, a look will be enough to decide whether I enter your father's house this evening, or never.

Such a letter was not to be soon recovered from. Half an hour's solitude and reflection might have tranquillized her; but the ten minutes only, which now passed before she was interrupted, with all the restraints of her situation, could do nothing towards tranquillity. Every moment rather brought fresh agitation. It was an overpowering happiness. And before she was beyond the first stage of full sensation, Charles, Mary, and Henrietta all came in.

The absolute necessity of seeming like herself produced then an immediate struggle; but after a while she could do no more. She began not to understand a word they said, and was obliged to plead indisposition and excuse herself. They could then see that she looked very ill—were shocked and concerned—and would not stir without her for the world. This was dreadful! Would they only have gone away, and left her in the quiet possession of that room, it would have been her cure; but to have them all standing or waiting around her was distracting, and, in desperation, she said she would go home.

"By all means, my dear," cried Mrs. Musgrove, "go home directly and take care of yourself, that you may be fit for the evening. I wish Sarah was here to doctor you, but I am no doctor myself. Charles, ring and order a chair. She must not walk."

But the chair would never do. Worse than all! To lose the possibility of speaking two words to Captain Wentworth in the course of her quiet, solitary progress up the town (and she felt almost certain of meeting him) could not be borne. The chair was earnestly protested against; and Mrs. Musgrove, who thought only of one sort of illness, having assured herself, with some anxiety, that there had been no fall in the case; that Anne had not, at any time lately, slipped down, and got a blow on her head; that she was perfectly convinced of having had no fall, could part with her cheerfully, and depend on finding her better at night.

Anxious to omit no possible precaution, Anne struggled, and said,

"I am afraid, ma'am, that it is not perfectly understood. Pray be so good as to mention to the other gentlemen that we hope to see your whole party this evening. I am afraid there has been some mistake; and I wish you particularly to assure Captain Harville, and Captain Wentworth, that we hope to see them both."

"Oh! my dear, it is quite understood, I give you my word. Captain Harville has no thought but of going."

"Do you think so? But I am afraid; and I should be so very sorry! Will you promise me to mention it, when you see them again? You will see them both again this morning, I dare say. Do promise me."

"To be sure I will, if you wish it. Charles, if you see Captain Harville any where, remember to give Miss Anne's message. But indeed, my dear, you need not be uneasy. Captain Harville holds himself quite engaged, I'll answer for it; and Captain Wentworth the same, I dare say."

Anne could do no more; but her heart prophesied some mischance, to damp the perfection of her felicity. It could not be very lasting, however. Even if he did not come to Camden-place himself, it would be in her power to send an intelligible sentence by Captain Harville.

Another momentary vexation occurred. Charles, in his real concern and good-nature, would go home with her; there was no preventing him. This was almost cruel! But she could not be long ungrateful; he was sacrificing an engagement at a gunsmith's to be of use to her; and she set off with him, with no feeling but gratitude apparent.

They were in Union-street, when a quicker step behind, a something of familiar sound, gave her two moments preparation for the sight of Captain Wentworth. He joined them; but, as if irresolute whether to join or to pass on, said nothing—only looked. Anne could command herself enough to receive that look, and not repulsively. The cheeks which had been pale now glowed, and the movements which had hesitated were decided. He walked by her side. Presently, struck by a sudden thought, Charles said,

"Captain Wentworth, which way are you going? only to Gay-street, or farther up the town?"

"I hardly know," replied Captain Wentworth, surprised.

"Are you going as high as Belmont? Are you going near Camden-place? Because if you are, I shall have no scruple in asking you to take my place, and give Anne your arm to her father's door. She is rather done for this morning, and must not go so far without help. And I ought to be at that fellow's in the market-place. He promised me the sight of a capital gun he is just going to send off; said he would keep it unpacked to the last possible moment, that I might see it; and if I do not turn back now, I have no chance. By his description, a good deal like the second-sized double-barrel of mine, which you shot with one day, round Winthrop."

There could not be an objection. There could be only a most proper alacrity, a most obliging compliance for public view; and smiles reined in and spirits dancing in private rapture. In half a minute, Charles was at the bottom of Union-street again, and the other two proceeding together; and soon words enough had passed between them to decide their direction towards the comparatively quiet and retired gravel-walk, where the power of conversation would make the present hour a blessing indeed; and prepare for it all the immortality which the happiest recollections of their own future lives could bestow. There they exchanged again those feelings and those promises which had once before seemed to secure every thing, but which had been followed by so many, many years of division and estrangement. There they returned again into the past, more exquisitely happy, perhaps, in their re-union, than when it had been first projected; more tender, more tried, more fixed in a knowledge of each other's character, truth, and attachment; more equal to act, more justified in acting. And there, as they slowly paced the gradual ascent, heedless of every group around them, seeing neither sauntering politicians, bustling house-keepers, flirting girls, nor nursery-maids and children, they could indulge in

those retrospections and acknowledgments, and especially in those explanations of what had directly preceded the present moment, which were so poignant and so ceaseless in interest. All the little variations of the last week were gone through; and of yesterday and to-day there could scarcely be an end.

She had not mistaken him. Jealousy of Mr. Elliot had been the retarding weight, the doubt, the torment. That had begun to operate in the very hour of first meeting her in Bath; that had returned, after a short suspension, to ruin the concert; and that had influenced him in every thing he had said and done, or omitted to say and do, in the last four-and-twenty hours. It had been gradually yielding to the better hopes which her looks, or words, or actions occasionally encouraged; it had been vanquished at last by those sentiments and those tones which had reached him while she talked with Captain Harville; and under the irresistible governance of which he had seized a sheet of paper, and poured out his feelings.

Of what he had then written, nothing was to be retracted or qualified. He persisted in having loved none but her. She had never been supplanted. He never even believed himself to see her equal. Thus much indeed he was obliged to acknowledge—that he had been constant unconsciously, nay unintentionally; that he had meant to forget her, and believed it to be done. He had imagined himself indifferent, when he had only been angry; and he had been unjust to her merits, because he had been a sufferer from them. Her character was now fixed on his mind as perfection itself, maintaining the loveliest medium of fortitude and gentleness; but he was obliged to acknowledge that only at Uppercross had he learnt to do her justice, and only at Lyme had he begun to understand himself.

At Lyme, he had received lessons of more than one sort. The passing admiration of Mr. Elliot had at least roused him, and the scenes on the Cobb, and at Captain Harville's, had fixed her superiority.

In his preceding attempts to attach himself to Louisa Musgrove (the attempts of angry pride), he protested that he had for ever felt it to be impossible; that he had not cared, could not care for Louisa; though, till that day, till the leisure for reflection which followed it, he had not understood the perfect excellence of the mind with which Louisa's could so ill bear a comparison; or the perfect, unrivalled hold it possessed over his own. There, he had learnt to distinguish between the steadiness of principle and the obstinacy of self-will, between the darings of heedlessness and the resolution of a collected mind. There, he had seen every thing to exalt in his estimation the woman he had lost, and there begun to deplore the pride, the folly, the madness of resentment, which had kept him from trying to regain her when thrown in his way.

From that period his penance had become severe. He had no sooner been free from the horror and remorse attending the first few days of Louisa's accident, no sooner begun to feel himself alive again, than he had begun to feel himself, though alive, not at liberty.

"I found," said he, "that I was considered by Harville an engaged man! That neither Harville nor his wife entertained a doubt of our mutual attachment. I was startled and shocked. To a degree, I could contradict this instantly; but, when I began to reflect that others might have felt the same— her own family, nay, perhaps herself, I was no longer at my own disposal. I

was hers in honour if she wished it. I had been unguarded. I had not thought seriously on this subject before. I had not considered that my excessive intimacy must have its danger of ill consequence in many ways; and that I had no right to be trying whether I could attach myself to either of the girls, at the risk of raising even an unpleasant report, were there no other ill effects. I had been grossly wrong, and must abide the consequences."

He found too late, in short, that he had entangled himself; and that precisely as he became fully satisfied of his not caring for Louisa at all, he must regard himself as bound to her, if her sentiments for him were what the Harvilles supposed. It determined him to leave Lyme, and await her complete recovery elsewhere. He would gladly weaken, by any fair means, whatever feelings or speculations concerning him might exist; and he went, therefore, to his brother's, meaning after a while to return to Kellynch, and act as circumstances might require.

"I was six weeks with Edward," said he, "and saw him happy. I could have no other pleasure. I deserved none. He enquired after you very particularly; asked even if you were personally altered, little suspecting that to my eye you could never alter."

Anne smiled, and let it pass. It was too pleasing a blunder for a reproach. It is something for a woman to be assured, in her eight-and-twentieth year, that she has not lost one charm of earlier youth: but the value of such homage was inexpressibly increased to Anne, by comparing it with former words, and feeling it to be the result, not the cause of a revival of his warm attachment.

He had remained in Shropshire, lamenting the blindness of his own pride, and the blunders of his own calculations, till at once released from Louisa by the astonishing and felicitous intelligence of her engagement with Benwick.

"Here," said he, "ended the worst of my state; for now I could at least put myself in the way of happiness, I could exert myself, I could do something. But to be waiting so long in inaction, and waiting only for evil, had been dreadful. Within the first five minutes I said, 'I will be at Bath on Wednesday,' and I was. Was it unpardonable to think it worth my while to come? and to arrive with some degree of hope? You were single. It was possible that you might retain the feelings of the past, as I did; and one encouragement happened to be mine. I could never doubt that you would be loved and sought by others, but I knew to a certainty that you had refused one man at least, of better pretensions than myself: and I could not help often saying, Was this for me?"

Their first meeting in Milsom-street afforded much to be said, but the concert still more. That evening seemed to be made up of exquisite moments. The moment of her stepping forward in the octagon-room to speak to him, the moment of Mr. Elliot's appearing and tearing her away, and one or two subsequent moments, marked by returning hope or increasing despondence, were dwelt on with energy.

"To see you," cried he, "in the midst of those who could not be my well-wishers, to see your cousin close by you, conversing and smiling, and feel all the horrible eligibilities and proprieties of the match! To consider it

as the certain wish of every being who could hope to influence you! Even, if your own feelings were reluctant or indifferent, to consider what powerful supports would be his! Was it not enough to make the fool of me which I appeared? How could I look on without agony? Was not the very sight of the friend who sat behind you, was not the recollection of what had been, the knowledge of her influence, the indelible, immoveable impression of what persuasion had once done—was it not all against me?"

"You should have distinguished," replied Anne. "You should not have suspected me now; the case so different, and my age so different. If I was wrong in yielding to persuasion once, remember that it was to persuasion exerted on the side of safety, not of risk. When I yielded, I thought it was to duty; but no duty could be called in aid here. In marrying a man indifferent to me, all risk would have been incurred, and all duty violated."

"Perhaps I ought to have reasoned thus," he replied, "but I could not. I could not derive benefit from the late knowledge I had acquired of your character. I could not bring it into play: it was overwhelmed, buried, lost in those earlier feelings which I had been smarting under year after year. I could think of you only as one who had yielded, who had given me up, who had been influenced by any one rather than by me. I saw you with the very person who had guided you in that year of misery. I had no reason to believe her of less authority now.—The force of habit was to be added."

"I should have thought," said Anne, "that my manner to yourself might have spared you much or all of this."

"No, no! your manner might be only the ease which your engagement to another man would give. I left you in this belief; and yet—I was determined to see you again. My spirits rallied with the morning, and I felt that I had still a motive for remaining here."

At last Anne was at home again, and happier than any one in that house could have conceived. All the surprise and suspense, and every other painful part of the morning dissipated by this conversation, she re-entered the house so happy as to be obliged to find an alloy in some momentary apprehensions of its being impossible to last. An interval of meditation, serious and grateful, was the best corrective of every thing dangerous in such high-wrought felicity; and she went to her room, and grew steadfast and fearless in the thankfulness of her enjoyment.

The evening came, the drawing-rooms were lighted up, the company assembled. It was but a card-party, it was but a mixture of those who had never met before, and those who met too often—a common-place business, too numerous for intimacy, too small for variety; but Anne had never found an evening shorter. Glowing and lovely in sensibility and happiness, and more generally admired than she thought about or cared for, she had cheerful or forbearing feelings for every creature around her. Mr. Elliot was there; she avoided, but she could pity him. The Wallises; she had amusement in understanding them. Lady Dalrymple and Miss Carteret; they would soon be innoxious cousins to her. She cared not for Mrs. Clay, and had nothing to blush for in the public manners of her father and sister. With the Musgroves, there was the happy chat of perfect ease; with Captain Harville, the kind-hearted intercourse of brother and sister; with Lady

Russell, attempts at conversation, which a delicious consciousness cut short; with Admiral and Mrs. Croft, every thing of peculiar cordiality and fervent interest, which the same consciousness sought to conceal;—and with Captain Wentworth, some moments of communication continually occurring, and always the hope of more, and always the knowledge of his being there!

It was in one of these short meetings, each apparently occupied in admiring a fine display of green-house plants, that she said—

"I have been thinking over the past, and trying impartially to judge of the right and wrong, I mean with regard to myself; and I must believe that I was right, much as I suffered from it, that I was perfectly right in being guided by the friend whom you will love better than you do now. To me, she was in the place of a parent. Do not mistake me, however. I am not saying that she did not err in her advice. It was, perhaps, one of those cases in which advice is good or bad only as the event[30] decides; and for myself, I certainly never should, in any circumstance of tolerable similarity, give such advice. But I mean, that I was right in submitting to her, and that if I had done otherwise, I should have suffered more in continuing the engagement that I did even in giving it up, because I should have suffered in my conscience. I have now, as far as such a sentiment is allowable in human nature, nothing to reproach myself with; and if I mistake not, a strong sense of duty is no bad part of a woman's portion."[31]

He looked at her, looked at Lady Russell, and looking again at her, replied, as if in cool deliberation,

"Not yet. But there are hopes of her being forgiven in time. I trust to being in charity with her soon. But I too have been thinking over the past, and a question has suggested itself, whether there may not have been one person more my enemy even than that lady? My own self. Tell me if, when I returned to England in the year eight, with a few thousand pounds, and was posted[32] into the Laconia, if I had then written to you, would you have answered my letter? would you, in short, have renewed the engagement then?"

"Would I!" was all her answer; but the accent was decisive enough.

"Good God!" he cried, "you would! It is not that I did not think of it, or desire it, as what could alone crown all my other success. But I was proud, too proud to ask again. I did not understand you. I shut my eyes, and would not understand you, or do you justice. This is a recollection which ought to make me forgive every one sooner than myself. Six years of separation and suffering might have been spared. It is a sort of pain, too, which is new to me. I have been used to the gratification of believing myself to earn every blessing that I enjoyed. I have valued myself on honourable toils and just rewards. Like other great men under reverses," he added with a smile, "I must endeavour to subdue my mind to my fortune. I must learn to brook being happier than I deserve."

[30] Outcome; result. [31] Dowry.

[32] Promoted to post-captain; as Chapter 4 implies, he was later promoted again, to commander.

CHAPTER 24

Who can be in doubt of what followed? When any two young people take it into their heads to marry, they are pretty sure by perseverance to carry their point, be they ever so poor, or ever so imprudent, or ever so little likely to be necessary to each other's ultimate comfort. This may be bad morality to conclude with, but I believe it to be truth; and if such parties succeed, how should a Captain Wentworth and an Anne Elliot, with the advantage of maturity of mind, consciousness of right, and one independent fortune between them, fail of bearing down every opposition? They might in fact have borne down a great deal more than they met with, for there was little to distress them beyond the want of graciousness and warmth.—Sir Walter made no objection, and Elizabeth did nothing worse than look cold and unconcerned. Captain Wentworth, with five-and-twenty thousand pounds, and as high in his profession as merit and activity could place him, was no longer nobody. He was now esteemed quite worthy to address the daughter of a foolish, spendthrift baronet, who had not had principle or sense enough to maintain himself in the situation in which Providence had placed him, and who could give his daughter at present but a small part of the share of ten thousand pounds which must be hers hereafter.

Sir Walter indeed, though he had no affection for Anne, and no vanity flattered, to make him really happy on the occasion, was very far from thinking it a bad match for her. On the contrary, when he saw more of Captain Wentworth, saw him repeatedly by daylight and eyed him well, he was very much struck by his personal claims, and felt that his superiority of appearance might be not unfairly balanced against her superiority of rank; and all this, assisted by his well-sounding name, enabled Sir Walter at last to prepare his pen with a very good grace for the insertion of the marriage in the volume of honour.

The only one among them, whose opposition of feeling could excite any serious anxiety, was Lady Russell. Anne knew that Lady Russell must be suffering some pain in understanding and relinquishing Mr. Elliot, and be making some struggles to become truly acquainted with, and do justice to Captain Wentworth. This however was what Lady Russell had now to do. She must learn to feel that she had been mistaken with regard to both; that she had been unfairly influenced by appearances in each; that because Captain Wentworth's manners had not suited her own ideas, she had been too quick in suspecting them to indicate a character of dangerous impetuosity; and that because Mr. Elliot's manners had precisely pleased her in their propriety and correctness, their general politeness and suavity, she had been too quick in receiving them as the certain result of the most correct opinions and well regulated mind. There was nothing less for Lady Russell to do, than to admit that she had been pretty completely wrong, and to take up a new set of opinions and of hopes.

There is a quickness of perception in some, a nicety in the discernment of character, a natural penetration, in short, which no experience in others can equal, and Lady Russell had been less gifted in this part of understanding than her young friend. But she was a very good woman, and if her

second object was to be sensible and well-judging, her first was to see Anne happy. She loved Anne better than she loved her own abilities; and when the awkwardness of the beginning was over, found little hardship in attaching herself as a mother to the man who was securing the happiness of her other child.

Of all the family, Mary was probably the one most immediately gratified by the circumstance. It was creditable to have a sister married, and she might flatter herself with having been greatly instrumental to the connexion, by keeping Anne with her in the autumn; and as her own sister must be better than her husband's sisters; it was very agreeable that Captain Wentworth should be a richer man than either Captain Benwick or Charles Hayter.—She had something to suffer perhaps when they came into contact again, in seeing Anne restored to the rights of seniority, and the mistress of a very pretty landaulette;[33] but she had a future to look forward to, of powerful consolation. Anne had no Uppercross-hall before her, no landed estate, no headship of a family; and if they could but keep Captain Wentworth from being made a baronet, she would not change situations with Anne.

It would be well for the eldest sister if she were equally satisfied with her situation, for a change is not very probable there. She had soon the mortification of seeing Mr. Elliot withdraw; and no one of proper condition has since presented himself to raise even the unfounded hopes which sunk with him.

The news of his cousin Anne's engagement burst on Mr. Elliot most unexpectedly. It deranged his best plan of domestic happiness, his best hope of keeping Sir Walter single by the watchfulness which a son-in-law's rights would have given. But, though discomfited and disappointed, he could still do something for his own interest and his own enjoyment. He soon quitted Bath; and on Mrs. Clay's quitting it likewise soon afterwards, and being next heard of as established under his protection in London, it was evident how double a game he had been playing, and how determined he was to save himself from being cut out by one artful woman, at least.

Mrs. Clay's affections had overpowered her interest, and she had sacrificed, for the young man's sake, the possibility of scheming longer for Sir Walter. She has abilities, however, as well as affections; and it is now a doubtful point whether his cunning, or hers, may finally carry the day; whether, after preventing her from being the wife of Sir Walter, he may not be wheedled and caressed at last into making her the wife of Sir William.

It cannot be doubted that Sir Walter and Elizabeth were shocked and mortified by the loss of their companion, and the discovery of their deception in her. They had their great cousins, to be sure, to resort to for comfort; but they must long feel that to flatter and follow others, without being flattered and followed in turn, is but a state of half enjoyment.

Anne, satisfied at a very early period of Lady Russell's meaning to love Captain Wentworth as she ought, had no other alloy to the happiness of her prospects than what arose from the consciousness of having no rela-

[33] A small carriage with a detachable roof.

tions to bestow on him which a man of sense could value. There she felt her own inferiority keenly. The disproportion in their fortune was nothing; it did not give her a moment's regret; but to have no family to receive and estimate him properly; nothing of respectability, of harmony, of good-will to offer in return for all the worth and all the prompt welcome which met her in his brothers and sisters, was a source of as lively pain as her mind could well be sensible of, under circumstances of otherwise strong felicity. She had but two friends in the world to add to his list, Lady Russell and Mrs. Smith. To those, however, he was very well disposed to attach himself. Lady Russell, in spite of all her former transgressions, he could now value from his heart. While he was not obliged to say that he believed her to have been right in originally dividing them, he was ready to say almost every thing else in her favour; and as for Mrs. Smith, she had claims of various kinds to recommend her quickly and permanently.

Her recent good offices by Anne had been enough in themselves; and their marriage, instead of depriving her of one friend, secured her two. She was their earliest visitor in their settled life; and Captain Wentworth, by putting her in the way of recovering her husband's property in the West Indies; by writing for her, acting for her, and seeing her through all the petty difficulties of the case, with the activity and exertion of a fearless man and a determined friend, fully requited the services which she had rendered, or ever meant to render, to his wife.

Mrs. Smith's enjoyments were not spoiled by this improvement of income, with some improvement of health, and the acquisition of such friends to be often with, for her cheerfulness and mental alacrity did not fail her; and while these prime supplies of good remained, she might have bid defiance even to greater accessions of worldly prosperity. She might have been absolutely rich and perfectly healthy, and yet be happy. Her spring of felicity was in the glow of her spirits, as her friend Anne's was in the warmth of her heart. Anne was tenderness itself, and she had the full worth of it in Captain Wentworth's affection. His profession was all that could ever make her friends wish that tenderness less; the dread of a future war all that could dim her sunshine. She gloried in being a sailor's wife, but she must pay the tax of quick alarm for belonging to that profession which is, if possible, more distinguished in its domestic virtues than in its national importance.

Heinrich von Kleist
(1777–1811)

The labels most often used to docket eighteenth- and nineteenth-century literature—classicism, Romanticism, and realism—often seem least useful in connection with the most powerful authors and their work. Heinrich von Kleist, whom many authorities would call the greatest German master of

short fiction and some would even call the greatest German dramatist, is a good case in point. He had the classicist's objectivity of manner and concern with literary form. He had the Romantic's interest in the aberrations of human psychology, especially as called forth by bizarre, extreme circumstances, and an equally Romantic interest in the conflict between human individuals and social institutions. He had the realist's matter-of-factness and authorial self-effacement; although his work can be highly rhetorical and poetic, his is not the lyric voice of individual self-expression. The least inadequate way to categorize Kleist, it could be argued, is to move him a century out of his time and call him a twentieth-century modernist. Kleist has been repeatedly compared to Franz Kafka (who admired him enthusiastically), not only because both Kleist and Kafka lived much the same kind of emotionally tortured life but also because both created in their fiction an eerily dislocated world, in which appearances are unreliable, the core of human personality is inchoate, and meaning is at best elusive.

Kleist was born in 1777, in Frankfurt-on-the-Oder (one of the two German cities named Frankfurt). Like Kafka a century later, he inherited a family tradition—in Kleist's case that of the Prussian military—not very hospitable to artistic types, and, again like Kafka, Kleist never achieved emotional independence from these family bonds. Though orphaned early—losing his father when he was ten and his mother when he was fifteen—he followed in the career marked out for him, joining the army in his early teens. Almost immediately, in 1793, he saw action in the war waged unsuccessfully by the European powers to overwhelm revolutionary France. For some years thereafter he lived an army garrison life, which he came to hate. The result was his first major break with family tradition: he resigned in 1799 and, under the influence of eighteenth-century Enlightenment rationalism, enrolled at the local university in Frankfurt. His academic interests were primarily science, mathematics, and philosophy. But he stayed there only a year (in fact, he would never thereafter stay anywhere very long); having become engaged to a young woman from another military family, he left the university with the intent of getting a post in the government bureaucracy—another parallel with Kafka—that would enable him to support a wife and family. To the end of his life money would remain a problem for him.

Two key events in Kleist's life took place around this time. One was a series of journeys he took to Würzburg (apparently to be treated for a sexual dysfunction), then to Dresden, Paris, and Switzerland. This contact with a larger world than he had hitherto known persuaded him that the civil service was not for him, led him to postpone his marriage, and prompted him to try a literary career. Soon thereafter, the engagement was permanently broken off. (One thinks of Kafka's several abortive relationships; neither man ever married.) The other key event was his reading of the philosophy of Immanuel Kant, which Kleist interpreted (not very accurately) as proving the impossibility of reliable knowledge and thus as delivering a death-blow to his Enlightenment belief that the world is rational, ordered, and comprehensible. Literature, it seemed, could do better justice to the confusion, richness, and inscrutableness of experience.

His first major work was the play *The Feud of the Schroffensteins* (1803), a tragedy of passion modeled on Shakespeare's *Romeo and Juliet* but exhibit-

ing, even so early in his career, Kleist's distinctive note of consuming erotic passion, along with an equally characteristic uncertainty about motivation, felt not only by the characters but also by the audience. On a far more ambitious level, he undertook a historical tragedy of the Crusades, *Robert Guiskard, Duke of the Normans,* an opus that, as a test of his powers, would bring him close to despair. Immensely admired by good judges to whom he showed or read portions of it, the play remains a fragment; Kleist destroyed much of the manuscript and later reconstructed it only in part. His desperate attempts to complete it were punctuated by a number of bizarre episodes: a sojourn with Wieland, the famous German poet, was cut short when Wieland's daughter fell in love with Kleist, and a little later Kleist tried to enlist, for deliberately suicidal purposes, in the Napoleonic army poised to cross the English Channel from Normandy. This latter escapade by Kleist was foiled; he was sternly rebuked for attempting to enlist under an enemy nation and was ordered by the Prussian ambassador to return to Germany.

In Berlin and Königsberg, in 1804–05, Kleist once more tried a civil service career and once more, this time under cover of sick leave, abandoned it for literature. In the meantime, France defeated the Prussians at the great battle of Jena in 1806 and took possession of Berlin. Plagued by his habitual bad luck, Kleist was arrested during a trip through the capital and, suspected of anti-French activities because he had been a Prussian officer, was imprisoned for the first six months of 1807. At this time was published his earlier-written play *Amphitryon* (1805), a re-doing of Molière's classic comedy, now transformed into the mode of Kleistian sublimity. Goethe, although impressed by the new work, ascribed to it a "confusion of feelings" (or "confounding of affects"), a phrase that, now construed to indicate power rather than weakness, has become a keynote in interpretations of many other works by Kleist as well.

A peace treaty having been signed and Kleist released from prison, things began to look up for him. Goethe, director of the court theater at Weimar, agreed to stage another play by Kleist, *The Broken Pitcher: A Comedy* (written in 1805). This work, concerning a trial in which the judge is himself the guilty party, again typified the author's blend of sexuality with psychological insight. Together with some friends, Kleist also formed his own publishing company in Dresden, which among other things launched a magazine called *Phoebus.* The play failed to interest its audience, however (the production, Kleist complained with entire justice, was botched by Goethe), and the journal also foundered, after a short life beset with difficulties, its lasting achievement having been to publish a number of key works by Kleist himself. One of these was a fragment of his problematical great play *Robert Guiskard.* Another was an excerpt from the tragedy *Penthesilea* (1808), Kleist's most sensational and in some ways most powerful play. In this grotesque and disturbing work "confusion of feelings" receives its ultimate expression as the heroine, queen of the female-warrior Amazons fighting in the Trojan War, tries both to overcome the enemy Achilles in war and to win his love. The rawness of female erotic passion in *Penthesilea,* culminating in cannibalism, proved too much for Kleist's public, and also for Goethe, who after his initial interest in Kleist had begun to think of the young man as psychologically sick.

Kleist had also begun to write the first of his eight prose stories and novellas. (They would be collected and published, in two volumes, in the last year of Kleist's life.) One of the earliest of these, first published in the short-lived *Phoebus,* was "The Marquise of O———," the subject of which created a great scandal: a woman of high rank, heretofore regarded as wholly virtuous, publishes in a newspaper an advertisement for the unknown father of a child she is about to bear, agreeing in advance to marry him. As happened often with Kleist, the shocking material, chronicled without authorial comment or judgment, blocked out for most readers the artistry, intricate psychological subtlety, and magnanimous spirituality of the story, which required some time after Kleist's death to make themselves felt. Kleist's unconventional prose style, which was rather difficult and at times seemed ungainly, was also a problem. Some of these eight prose masterpieces, including "The Marquise of O———," were up-to-date in setting. Others were set in the distant past, including "The Duel," another story about female sexual virtue. Here a noble and pious lady, accused of fornication, confidently invites her innocence to be vindicated by God in a medieval trial by combat, only to see her champion apparently defeated—a defeat that seems to force on everyone, including the heroine, a choice between belief in her truth and belief in God's. The longest of the novellas, and the one often regarded as Kleist's greatest achievement in the form, is *Michael Kohlhaas,* a Kleistian reworking of a sixteenth-century chronicle about a man who becomes a kind of anarchist crusader against governments exactly because he believes so strongly in the sanctity of the law and the advantages of a comprehensive world order.

Kleist continued in the meantime to write plays, including *Katie of Heilbronn* (first performed in 1810 but written in 1808), a work in a milder vein than was usual for Kleist. The aim was to have this play staged in Vienna; Kleist had become a fervent supporter of Austria and Germany in their struggle against France. This struggle—ill-fated, like most things Kleist got involved in—seemed to have failed when France defeated the Austrians in 1809. In Berlin in 1810, Kleist's effort to have the history play *Prince Frederick of Homburg* produced was unsuccessful, owing to what was considered unheroic behavior in its protagonist, a Prussian officer. Kleist's other main project in Berlin in this twilight of his short life was to help edit a daily newspaper, but, like his earlier effort in journalism, this one failed after some months. One of the issues of the journal contained a striking essay contributed by Kleist in 1810, "On the Marionette Theater," which is often taken as a key to Kleist's theory of fiction and of human nature. In the essay (more exactly, a dialogue), a prominent dancer argues that utter gracefulness is possible only to beings who are either gods, with comprehensive consciousness, or to beings such as puppets who wholly lack consciousness (and therefore self-consciousness also). Humankind must therefore eat again of the Tree of Knowledge if it is to achieve again the state of innocence.

Kleist felt increasingly alone and depressed during the last months of his life. His poverty, for one thing, was a sore problem—despite his early experiences, he even contemplated rejoining the army—and he seems to have felt that he had exhausted the world's spiritual resources as well. Late in 1811, at the age of thirty-four and reduced to hopelessness, he arranged

a suicide pact with a woman acquaintance, Henriette Vogel, who was suffering from terminal cancer of the uterus. Kleist shot her in the chest, then himself in the mouth. They were buried on the spot, just outside Berlin, where the shootings occurred. Shortly before he died, Kleist destroyed a number of his papers, including letters and manuscripts of his literary works, as Kafka after him would ask that his writings be destroyed. Fortunately, Kafka's instructions were disobeyed. Kleist, however, left no such room for disobedience. We are thus left with an incomplete knowledge of his work to match our uncertainties about important parts of his life, the many uncertainties felt by his fictional characters in their efforts to understand their lives, and the uncertainties felt by readers who try to understand those characters.

Readers of "The Marquise of O——," as of most novellas by Kleist, are likely to be struck first by the audacity of the subject matter in itself, which is immediately heralded in the story's famous opening sentence. Few writers know better than Kleist how to get off to a fast start. Before reading very much farther, though, the reader is apt to feel somewhat disturbed by the narrative method, as though the breathless author were one of those people who, in telling a story, feel they have to give us every last detail but still wind up not telling us what we most need to know. Did the author, for example, expect us to understand from the very beginning who the father is of the Marquise's expected baby? If so—we may initially feel—he could have given us the kind of hint that a smoothly professional storyteller knows how to insert. If, on the other hand, the father's identity is supposed to be as much a mystery to us as it is to the Marquise, is not the later revelation of his identity an anticlimactic retreat to the obvious? When, near the end, the Marquise learns who the father is, one may wonder why she reacts so negatively at first to a man who, it would seem, will at least make a better husband than some of the unknown persons she has declared herself ready to marry. And why do we never learn anything about the state of mind that could impel the father, a high-minded man, to commit an especially appalling form of rape?

As we become better acquainted with Kleist, we get used to these feelings that either we are off balance or the narrator is. We are inundated with factual information, yet we are left groping for the formula needed to give it shape and meaning. Eventually, we come to recognize that Kleist's method is a very precise one, and that the effect of unsettledness is at the very heart of what his stories are doing. And the unsettledness is even more profound when we turn from matters of storytelling technique to the moral or political or psychological issues his stories raise. What, for example, are we to make of the highly erotic rendering of the reconciliation between the Marquise and her father? Is the brief allusion to the virgin birth of Jesus a mere passing detail or should we give it heavier weight? How is it possible that, as in this story, a man can be capable of the highest reaches of chivalry and courtesy and also of the most unnerving brutality?

For many readers, the ultimate effect of such bewilderment is a kind of existential fear. As Thomas Mann wrote in his Preface to the Martin Greenberg translation of Kleist's stories, "the suspense [Kleist's] stories create has a specificity, a concreteness, that is positively alarming. We are filled with anxiety and terror, shudder in the face of mystery, doubt in the pow-

ers of reason and, indeed, in the power of God himself—all our 'affects are confounded.'" Nor do the "happy endings" that—as often as not—Kleist gives us do much to alleviate our sense of fear. The world being as inscrutable as it is, things could as easily have turned out very differently.

FURTHER READING *(prepared by S.M.):* Kleist's complete prose fiction fits handily into a single medium-length volume; all of his stories are collected and well translated by Martin Greenberg in *The Marquise of O—— and Other Stories,* 1960, which also contains stimulating introductory essays by Thomas Mann and by Greenberg. Joachim Maass's *Kleist,* 1983, is a good biography (and includes some discussion of "The Marquise of O——"). An excellent brief account of Kleist's life and artistry is James M. McGlathery's chapter in *German Writers in the Age of Goethe, 1789–1832,* 1989, ed. James Hardin and Christoph E. Schweitzer, which is volume 90 in the *Dictionary of Literary Biography.* Another brief introduction is the pamphlet-length overview in Richard March's *Heinrich von Kleist,* 1954, in the series Studies in Modern European Literature and Thought. McGlathery's book *Desire's Sway,* 1983, which examines love stories centering on sexual guilt or sublimation, provides still another excellent discussion of plays and stories by Kleist including "The Marquise of O——," "Michael Kohlhaas," and "The Earthquake in Chile." Again because Kleist wrote so little fiction, most books on him other than those concerned entirely with his plays can linger in some detail over the stories, including "The Marquise of O——"; see, for example, John Gearey, *Heinrich von Kleist: A Study in Tragedy and Anxiety,* 1968; Robert E. Helbling, *The Major Works of Heinrich von Kleist,* 1975; Denys Dyer, *The Stories of Kleist: A Critical Study,* 1977; and John M. Ellis, *Heinrich von Kleist: Studies in the Character and Meaning of His Writings,* 1979. Noteworthy also, on religious meaning, is Steven R. Huff's essay "Kleist and Expectant Virgins: The Meaning of 'O' in *Die Marquise von O . . . ,*" *JEGP,* vol. 81 (1982).

THE MARQUISE OF O——

Translated by Martin Greenberg

In M——, a large town in northern Italy, the widowed Marquise of O——, a lady of unblemished reputation and the mother of several well-bred children, published the following notice in the newspapers: that, without her knowing how, she was in the family way; that she would like the father of the child she was going to bear to report himself; and that her mind was made up, out of consideration for her people, to marry him. The lady whom unalterable circumstances forced to take this unusual step, which she did so bravely in the face of the derision it was bound to excite in the world, was the daughter of Colonel G——, Commandant of the citadel of M——. Three years or so previously, her husband, the Marquis of O——, to whom she had been devoted heart and soul, had died during a trip to Paris on family business. After his death, yielding to the wishes of Madam G——, her worthy mother, she left the estate near V—— where she had lived until then and returned to the Commandant's house with her two children. There she spent the following years in strict seclusion, occupying her time with painting, reading, educating her children, and caring for her parents: until the —— War suddenly filled the neighborhood with troops

of nearly all the powers, including those of Russia.[1] Colonel G——, who
was under orders to defend the fortress, urged his wife and daughter to
retire to the latter's estate near V—— or to his son's place. But before the
ladies could make up their minds as between the hardships of a siege or the
horrors they might be exposed to in the open country, the citadel was
invested[2] by Russian troops and commanded to surrender. Announcing to
his family that he would carry on as if they were not there, the Colonel
retorted with shot and shell. The enemy in turn bombarded the fortress.
He set the magazines[3] ablaze, captured an outworks, and, when the Colo-
nel delayed to answer a second summons to surrender, ordered a night
assault and carried the fort by storm.

Just as the Russian troops, supported by a violent cannonade, were
breaking into the citadel, the left wing of the Commandant's residence
caught fire and the women were forced to flee. The Colonel's wife panted
after her daughter, who was flying down the stairs with her children, and
shouted for them all to keep together and take refuge in the cellars; but a
shell exploding in the house at that very moment made the confusion there
complete. The Marquise, flinging open a door, found herself in the citadel
square, where the flashing of the cannon in violent action lit up the night
and drove her, helpless to know where she should turn, back inside the
burning building. Here, unluckily, just as she was about to escape by the
back door, she ran into a troop of enemy sharpshooters who fell silent the
instant they laid eyes on her, slung their muskets, and, gesturing obscenely,
marched her off with them. In vain the Marquise screamed for help to her
terror-stricken women fleeing through the back gate as she was flung back
and forth among the horrible gang of quarreling soldiers. They dragged
her to the rear castle yard, where she was on the point of collapsing to the
ground under the filthy abuse inflicted on her when a Russian officer,
hearing her screams, came running up and began to lay about him with
furious strokes, scattering the dogs panting after their prey. To the Mar-
quise he seemed a very angel from heaven. He smashed the last of the
murderous brutes, whose arms were wound about her slender figure, in
the face with the hilt of his sword and made him reel back with the blood
gushing from his mouth; then, saluting her courteously in French, he of-
fered her his arm and led her, speechless from all she had gone through, to
the other wing of the residence, which had not caught fire yet, where she
fainted dead away. A little while after, when her terrified women ap-
peared, he told them to call a doctor; promised them, as he put his hat on,
that she would soon recover; and returned to the fray.

In a short time the square was entirely in the hands of the Russians, and
the Commandant, who kept up a resistance only because no quarter[4] was
offered him, was just falling back with his dwindling force on the entrance
door to the residence when the Russian officer, with a heated face, came
out of that very door and called on him to surrender. The Commandant

[1] In 1799, in the wake of the French Revolution and just before Napoleon seized power in
France, Russia was allied with Great Britain, Austria, and other European powers in an at-
tempt to defeat France. The strategy called for Russia and Austria to recapture the Italian
states conquered by the French or allied with them.
[2] Surrounded. [3] Storehouses, especially for ammunition and explosives.
[4] Mercy; sparing of life on condition of surrender.

answered that that was just what he had been waiting for, handed him his sword, and asked permission to go into the castle and look for his family. The Russian officer who, judging by his actions, was one of the leaders of the assault, granted his request on condition that he was accompanied by a guard; he placed himself hurriedly at the head of a detachment, threw his force into the fighting wherever it was still in doubt, and posted men as fast as possible at all the strong points of the fort. No sooner was this done than he ran back to the drill square and ordered his men to battle the roaring flames which were threatening to spread in every direction, himself performing prodigies of exertion when his orders were not carried out with the necessary zeal. One minute he was scrambling among the burning gables, hose in hand, aiming the stream of water at the flames, the next minute he had darted into the magazines and, striking terror to the souls of his fellow Asiatics, was rolling out powder kegs and live grenades. Meanwhile the Commandant had passed inside the house and was horrified to learn about the misfortune that had befallen his daughter. The Marquise, however, who had entirely recovered without the help of any doctor, just as the Russian officer said she would, and who was overjoyed to find all her people safe and sound and stayed in bed only to allay their extreme anxiety about her, assured him that her one wish was to get up and tell her rescuer how grateful she was to him. She already knew that he was Count F——, Lieutenant-Colonel of the T——th Rifle Corps and Knight of the Order of Merit and of several others. She asked her father to beg him not to leave the citadel before he had made an appearance, if only for a minute or so, at the residence. The Commandant, who respected his daughter's feeling, returned without delay to the fort, where he found the Count on the ramparts, going up and down among his battered troops and issuing an uninterrupted stream of orders; and, no better opportunity offering, he then and there conveyed his grateful daughter's wish to him. The Count promised him that he was only waiting to snatch a moment from his duties to pay her his respects. He had been anxious all along to hear how the Marquise was, but the reports of some of his officers had drawn him back into the thick of the fighting.

At daybreak the Commanding General of the Russian forces arrived to inspect the fort. He paid his respects to the Commandant, regretted that his bravery had not been helped by better luck, and gave him leave to go wherever he liked on his parole.[5] The Commandant thanked him earnestly and said how much this day had put him in debt to the Russians in general and to the young Count F——, Lieutenant-Colonel of the T——th Rifle Corps, in particular. The General asked what had happened; when he was told the story of the criminal attack on the Commandant's daughter, he became furious. Calling the Count forward by name, he praised his noble-spirited conduct in a short speech, which caused the officer to blush furiously, and ended his words by ordering the villains who had dishonored the Czar's name to be shot; would he tell him who they were? Count F—— gave a confused reply, in which he said that he could not give the General their names because it had been impossible to recognize their faces by the feeble glimmer of the castle-yard lamps. The General, who had heard that

[5] Word of honor (that he will not try to escape or take up arms again).

the castle was already in flames at the time of the episode, looked surprised; it was possible, he remarked, to recognize people one knew well by their voices in the dark; and ordered him, when the Count shrugged his shoulders with an embarrassed air, to investigate the matter at once. But just then somebody pressed forward from the back of the circle and reported that one of the villains whom the Count had wounded had fallen in the corridor and that the Commandant's people had lugged him into a closet where he still was. The General sent a guard to fetch the man; questioned him briefly; and, when he had revealed the names of the others, had the whole crew, five all told, shot. When this was done, the General posted a small garrison in the fort and issued marching orders to the rest of his troops; the officers scattered on the double to their different corps; the Count made his way through the crowd of hurrying soldiers to the Commandant and said how very sorry he was, but under the circumstances he could only send his warmest regards to the Marquise; and in less than an hour the entire fort was clear of Russians again.

The family now began to think how they might find some occasion in the future to tell the Count how grateful they felt toward him; imagine their horror, then, when they learned that he had been killed in a skirmish on the very same day that he had marched away from the fort. The messenger who brought this news to M—— had with his own eyes seen him carried off, mortally wounded in the chest, toward P——, where he had died, according to a reliable report, at the very moment when the bearers were lifting him from their shoulders. The Commandant went in person to the post-house[6] to see if he could learn anything more about the Russian's death. He discovered that when the Count was hit on the battlefield he had cried out, "Julietta, with this shot you are avenged!" and after that had never opened his lips again. The Marquise was inconsolable for having let the chance slip to throw herself at his feet. She made the most violent accusations against herself for not having gone to him in the fort when he declined (probably, as she thought, from modesty) to come to her in the castle; pitied the unfortunate lady, with the same name as her own, whom he had been thinking about even as he was dying; tried in vain to learn her whereabouts so as to tell her the unhappy news; and could not get the thought of him out of her mind until several months had passed.

At this time the family were obliged to move out of the Commandant's residence to make room for the Russian commander. At first they thought of going to Colonel G——'s estate, which was very much the Marquise's inclination; but as the Colonel had no liking for country life, they ended by taking a house in town and fixing it up to live there permanently. Their life now flowed back into its accustomed channels. The Marquise had resumed the long-interrupted education of her children, and in her leisure hours turned to her easel[7] and her books, when, quite unaccountably for someone who had always been a paragon of good health, she found herself troubled by a persistent indisposition that made it impossible for her to see anyone for weeks on end. She suffered from nausea, dizziness, and fainting spells, and was at a loss to explain her strange condition. One morning,

[6] Station where express travelers changed horses.
[7] Painting or drawing (literally, the stand that holds the picture being worked on).

as the family sat at tea and her father had gone out of the room for a
moment, the Marquise, rousing herself from a lengthy fit of abstraction,
said to her mother, "If a woman were to tell me that she felt the way I did
just now when I picked up the cup, I should certainly think to myself that
she was pregnant." Madam G—— said she didn't know what her daughter
meant. The Marquise explained that she had just felt the same sort of
twinge she had had when she was carrying her second child. Madam G——
said it was perhaps the spirit of fantasy that her daughter was going to be
delivered of, and laughed. Yes, the Marquise replied in the same humorous
spirit, and Morpheus[8] was the father or one of his attendant dreams. But
then the Colonel came back, the conversation was interrupted, and when
the Marquise recovered a few days later the whole thing was forgotten.

Not long after this, just when the Commandant's son, who was Forest
Warden, happened to be at home, the family were frightened out of their
wits to hear a servant enter the room and announce that Count F—— was
there. "Count F——!" gasped father and daughter together, and they all
fell speechless. The servant swore that his eyes and ears had not deceived
him and that the visitor was already waiting in the anteroom. The Com-
mandant immediately jumped up to open the door himself, and the Count
entered, handsome as a young god, even if his face was rather pale. After
they had gotten over their surprise and the Count had assured the parents—
who said no, it couldn't be, he must be dead—that he was very much alive,
he turned, with an expression of great tenderness on his face, to the daugh-
ter; and the very first thing he asked her was, how did she feel? Very well,
the Marquise said, she only wanted to know how he had come back from
the dead. But he would not let his question drop and said she was not
telling him the truth; her face showed signs of unusual fatigue; unless he
was much mistaken, she was feeling ill. The Marquise, softened by the
warmth with which he spoke, replied: very well, her fatigue, since he would
have it so, was perhaps the last trace of an indisposition that had troubled
her several weeks ago; she did not think that anything more would come of
it. To which he replied, with an outburst of delight: nor did he!—and he
asked her if she would marry him. The Marquise did not know what to
make of such behavior. Blushing deeply, she looked at her mother who, in
turn, was staring in embarrassment at her husband and son; whereupon
the Count went up to the Marquise and, taking her hand as if to kiss it,
asked her if she had understood him. The Commandant inquired if he
would not like to sit down; and with elaborate courtesy, touched neverthe-
less with some solemnity, he drew a chair up for the Count.

"Indeed," said the Colonel's wife, "we shall go on thinking you are a
ghost until you've told us how you rose up out of the grave in which they
buried you at P——." Letting go the lady's hand, the Count sat down and
said that he was forced to be very brief: he had been wounded mortally in
the breast and carried to P——; for months there he had despaired of his
life; during this time his only thoughts had been for the Marquise; he could
not describe the pleasure and the pain that coupled together in his image
of her; after his recovery, he had returned to the army, where he had felt a
terrible restlessness; more than once he had reached for a pen to pour his

[8] In classical mythology, the god of dreams.

heart out to the Colonel and the Marquise; but unexpectedly he was sent to Naples with dispatches; he could not be sure that he wouldn't be sent from there to Constantinople—he might even have to go to St. Petersburg;[9] meanwhile it was impossible for him to go on living any longer without a clear understanding about something that was absolutely necessary for his soul's peace; he had not been able to resist taking a few steps in that direction while passing through M——; in short, he cherished the hope of obtaining the Marquise's hand, and he implored them as earnestly as he knew how to give his suit an immediate answer.

After a long pause, the Commandant replied that the offer, if seriously intended, as he did not doubt it was, was a very flattering one. But his daughter had made up her mind, after the death of her husband, the Marquis of O——, never to marry again. However, as the Count had recently laid so great an obligation on her, it was not impossible that this should sway her from her resolution; he asked him to allow her a little time to think the matter over quietly. The Count assured him that his friendly answer was a great encouragement to his hopes; that in other circumstances it would have made him perfectly content; that he appreciated fully how boorish it seemed for him to ask for more; but that compelling reasons, into which it was impossible for him to go, made a definite answer extremely desirable; that the horses which were to take him to Naples were already hitched to his carriage; and that he implored them with all his heart and soul, if there was anybody in that house to take his part—here he shot a look at the Marquise—not to let him ride away without a more favorable reply. The Colonel, rather taken aback by such insistence, said that although the gratitude his daughter felt for him justified his assuming a great deal, it did not justify his assuming so much; she could not take a step on which the happiness of her life depended without giving it prudent consideration beforehand. It was absolutely necessary for his daughter to enjoy the pleasure of his closer acquaintance before declaring herself. He invited him to return to M—— after his trip was done and be their guest for a while. If after that—but not before—the Marquise thought that she could find her happiness with him, he would be only too happy to hear that she had given him the answer he wanted. The Count blushed and said that during the whole trip he had foreseen that his impatient desires would meet with this fate; that he looked forward to being utterly miserable during the interim period; that although he could hardly like the unhappy part he was now compelled to play, he would not deny that a closer acquaintance was all to the good; that he believed he could answer for his reputation, although it was a question whether any consideration should be given to that most deceptive of all things; that the only dishonorable act he had ever committed was a secret from the world and he was already on the way to making it good—in short, that he was an honorable man, and he begged the Commandant to accept his assurance of the truthfulness of all he said. The Commandant smiled faintly, though without a trace of irony,

[9] A struggle against the French took place in Naples, in southern Italy; a puppet republic was first proclaimed there by France and then overthrown in 1799. Constantinople (modern Istanbul) was the capital of the Ottoman Empire, which was part of the anti-French coalition. St. Petersburg (modern Leningrad) was the principal city of Russia.

and said that he quite agreed with everything the Count had said. He had
never come across a young man who in so short a time had revealed so
many superior traits of character. He was pretty well convinced that a brief
period of reflection would overcome all present hesitation; but before he
talked things over with his own family as well as with the Count's, no other
course was possible. At this, the Count announced that his parents were
dead and he was his own master. His uncle was General K——, on whose
assent to the marriage he could rely. He added that he possessed consider-
able means and would be able to make Italy his home.

The Commandant bowed politely, explained his wishes once again, and
requested him not to press his suit any further until he returned from his
trip. The Count, after a short pause in which he showed every sign of
extreme uneasiness, turned to the Marquise's mother and said that he had
done everything possible to get out of having to make the trip; that he had
gone as far as he dared in importuning the Commanding General and
General K——, his uncle, to be relieved of the mission, but that they hoped
that the journey would rouse him out of the melancholy still weighing on
him from his illness; and that, for this reason, he was now completely mis-
erable.

The family did not know what to say to this. The Count rubbed his
forehead and went on, saying that if there were any hope of his coming
nearer the goal he sought, he would put off his departure for a day or even
more. And he looked in turn at the Commandant, the Marquise, and her
mother. The Commandant stared at the floor with an expression of dis-
pleasure and did not speak. His wife said, "Go along, why don't you, and
make your trip to Naples; then come back to M—— and give us the plea-
sure of your company for a while; we'll see about everything else after
that."

The Count sat where he was for a minute and seemed to be trying to
decide what he should do. Then, getting up and putting his chair aside, he
said that since he was forced to recognize that the hopes with which he had
entered their house were premature, and since the family insisted on a
closer acquaintance, which he was far from blaming them for, he would
send his dispatches back to the headquarters at Z——, for them to be for-
warded by some other means, and accept their kind invitation to be a guest
in their house for a few weeks. Then he paused for a moment, standing by
the wall with his hand on the chair, and gazed at the Commandant. The
latter replied that he would feel extremely sorry if the passion that the
Count seemed to cherish for his daughter should get him into serious trou-
ble; right now the Count must know what he absolutely had to do and what
he didn't, and whether he could send the dispatches back and occupy the
room they had for him. At these words they saw the Count change color;
he kissed Madam G——'s hand, bowed to the others, and withdrew.

The family did not know what to make of such behavior. The mother
said that surely it was not possible that he should think of sending the
dispatches he was carrying to Naples back to Z—— simply because he had
not been able, on his way through M——, during a five minutes' conversa-
tion, to persuade a lady whom he did not know at all to consent to his
proposal of marriage. The Forest Warden exclaimed that such reckless
behavior would certainly be punished by nothing less than imprisonment

in a fortress! And such a man would be dismissed into the bargain, added the Commandant. However, the latter continued, there was no danger of that. The Count had only been talking wildly; he would think twice before returning the dispatches. But the mother, when she learned about this danger, was extremely apprehensive that he would send them back. His headstrong, single-minded nature, she thought, was capable of just such a deed. She begged her son to run after him and dissuade him from a step that promised nothing but disaster. The Forest Warden replied that his interfering in that way would have the opposite effect and only encourage the Count to hope that he could gain his purpose by this stratagem. The Marquise thought the same thing, although she was convinced that, unless her brother did something, the Count would certainly send the dispatches back; he would rather bring disaster on himself than show himself up for an empty talker. All were agreed that his behavior was extraordinary and that he seemed accustomed to capturing ladies' hearts, like fortresses, by storm.

At this moment the Commandant noticed that the Count's coach was standing ready before the door. He called his family to the window and asked a servant, who came into the room just then, whether the Count was still in the house. The servant said that he was below in the servants' hall, in the company of an adjutant,[10] writing letters and sealing packets. The Commandant, repressing his dismay, hurried downstairs with his son and asked the Count, whom he found conducting his business at a most unsuitable table, if he didn't care to step into his own room, and if there was not anything else he might do for him. The Count's pen continued to dash across the paper as he said no, thank you, his business was already done; he asked the Commandant what the time was as he sealed the letter, and, after giving the adjutant the whole portfolio, wished the latter a pleasant journey. The Commandant, who could not believe his eyes, said to the Count, as the adjutant left the house, "Sir, unless you have very weighty reasons——"

"The most compelling reasons," the Count interrupted, and walked with the adjutant to the carriage and opened the door for him.

"In that case," the Commandant continued, "I would at least send along the dispatches——"

"Impossible," the Count retorted as he helped the adjutant to his seat. "The dispatches wouldn't do any good in Naples without me. I thought of that too. Drive on!"

"And your uncle's letters?" called the adjutant, leaning out of the coach door.

"They can reach me," replied the Count, "at M——."

"Drive on!" the adjutant called, and away went the carriage.

Count F—— now turned to the Commandant and asked him if he would be good enough to have somebody show him to his room. He would have the honor of doing that himself, the disconcerted Colonel replied; he called to the Count's servants and his own to look after the luggage, and conducted him to the guest room; after which he stiffly said good day. The Count dressed; left the house to report to the military governor of the

[10] A military aide.

place; and for the rest of the day was nowhere to be seen, only returning to the house just before dinner.

Meanwhile the family were feeling extremely upset. The Forest Warden described how peremptorily the Count had answered the Commandant's questions; said his returning the dispatches looked to him quite deliberately done; and asked what on earth could be the reason for wooing at a post-horse gallop. The Commandant said that he could not make head or tail of the business and ordered his family not to mention it again in his presence. The mother kept peering out of the window from one minute to the next to see if the Count had not come back regretting his hasty decision and wanting to undo it. Finally when it got dark she sat down next to the Marquise, who was working busily at a table and seemed to shun conversation, and asked her in an undertone, while the father was pacing up and down the room, what she made of the whole thing. Looking hesitantly toward the Commandant, the Marquise said that if her father had prevailed on him to go to Naples, everything would have been all right. "To Naples!" exclaimed the Commandant, who had overheard what she said. "Should I have had the priest sent for? Or should I have had him locked up and sent to Naples under guard?"

"No, no," the Marquise said. "But a real effort to remonstrate with him would have had an effect." And she bent down, a trifle unwillingly, over her work again.

At last, toward evening, the Count appeared. They were only waiting for the matter to come up again, after the first greetings were over, so as to attack him with their combined force and get him to retrieve what he had done, if that was still possible. But they waited in vain. During the entire dinner he carefully skirted everything that might have touched on the subject and talked instead to the Commandant about the war and to the Forest Warden about hunting. When he happened to mention the skirmish at P—— in which he had been wounded, the mother drew him into an account of his illness, asking him how it had been in the little town and if he had had everything he needed there. In the course of this conversation he told them a number of things that were interesting for what they revealed about his passion for the Marquise: how she had seemed always to be at his bedside during his illness; how in his feverish delirium he kept confusing her image with that of a swan that he had seen as a boy on his uncle's estate; how he was especially moved by the recollection of a time when he had spattered the swan with mud and it had dived silently under the water to rise up pure and shining again; how the Marquise, in the shape of the swan, was always swimming about on a flaming flood and he had called out Thinka, which was the name of the swan from his boyhood, but had not been able to make her come to him, for all her pleasure lay in gliding up and down and haughtily puffing out her breast—suddenly he said, with a deep blush, that he was terribly in love with her; looked down at his plate again, and was silent. At last it was time to get up from the table; the Count, after a few words with the mother, bowed to the company and retired to his room, leaving them standing there in complete perplexity again. The Commandant thought that they should let matters take their course. In doing what he did, the Count was probably counting on the influence of his relatives, for otherwise he would be ignominiously dismissed. Madam

G—— asked her daughter what she thought of him after all this, and whether she could find it in her to say something to him that would avert a catastrophe. "Mother dear," replied the Marquise, "I am afraid I can't. I am sorry that my gratitude should be put to such a hard test. But I had made up my mind not to remarry; I really shouldn't want to put my happiness at stake a second time, and certainly not without giving the whole matter a lot of thought." The Forest Warden said that if that was her firm resolve, it would be a help to the Count, even so, to know it; it seemed evident to him that he needed to be given some sort of definite answer. The Colonel's wife replied that since this young man, who was the possessor of so many unusual qualities, had said that he was willing to live in Italy, she thought it was only fair to give his offer some consideration and to test the Marquise's determination not to remarry. The Forest Warden dropped into a chair next to his sister and asked her if she liked the way the Count looked. The Marquise answered with some embarrassment, "I like him and I don't like him," and appealed to the way the others felt.

"Supposing," said Madam G——, "that nothing that we are able to learn about him while he is away in Naples contradicts the general impression you have of him now, and supposing he renews his offer on his return, what answer would you give him then?"

"In that case," replied the Marquise, "since in fact his desire to marry me seems so strong—" she hesitated at this point and her eyes glistened— "in that case I would be ready to satisfy it for the sake of what I owe him."

Her mother, who had always wished her daughter to remarry, was hard put to it to conceal the joy this declaration gave her, and wondered what it would lead to. The Forest Warden got up restlessly from his chair and said that if the Marquise thought there was any possibility of her favoring the Count with her hand, then something ought to be said to him right away which would make it possible to avert the consequences of the crazy thing he had done. His mother thought so too. After all, she said, with a man like that there was no great risk, since one need hardly fear that the rest of his life would not be in keeping with all those superior qualities he had demonstrated on the night the Russians stormed the fortress. The Marquise looked down at the ground with a tense and nervous expression. "Perhaps he might be told," her mother went on, as she took her hand, "something to the effect that until he returns from Naples, you won't enter into any other engagement."

"I can promise him that," the Marquise said. "Only I am afraid that it won't be enough for him and will get us all embroiled."

"Let me worry about that!" her mother said with elation, and turned her head to look for the Commandant. "Lorenzo," she asked "what do you think?" and she began to rise from her chair. The Commandant, who had heard everything, continued standing at the window and looking out into the street without saying anything. The Forest Warden promised them that with this harmless assurance he would guarantee to get the Count out of the house.

"Well, go ahead and do it! Do it right now!" his father exclaimed, turning away from the window. "Here I am, surrendering to this Russian a second time!"

His wife jumped up at these words, kissed him and her daughter, and,

while her husband smiled at her bustling energy, wanted to know how they could tell the Count about it right away. It was decided, at the Forest Warden's suggestion, to ask him if he would not care to join the family for a moment if he were still dressed. The Count sent back the answer that he would be honored to join them at once, and hardly had the valet returned with this message than he himself burst into the room, with great strides of joy, and threw himself down at the Marquise's feet in a state of intense emotion. The Commandant was about to speak when the Count, springing to his feet, said that he knew everything that he needed to know, kissed his hand and that of his wife, hugged the Marquise's brother, and asked them if they would do him the favor of helping him to find a traveling coach. The Marquise, though her feelings had been stirred by this scene, said, "I really am afraid, Count F——, lest your impetuous hopes——"

"Not at all! Not at all!" replied the Count. "You've agreed to nothing, if the reports you get about me should clash with the feeling that moved you to call me back into this room." On hearing this, the Commandant gave him a hearty hug, the Forest Warden offered him his own carriage on the spot, a soldier was sent running to the posthouse to hire horses, and, all in all, his leaving occasioned more rejoicing than ever they had known at anybody's coming. He hoped, said the Count, to overtake the adjutant with the dispatches at B——, from where he would go on to Naples by a shorter way than through M——; in Naples he would do everything possible to get out of having to make the trip to Constantinople; and since his mind was made up, if the worst came to worst, to sham illness, he promised them that, unless he ran into unavoidable delays, he would be back in M—— without fail in about four to six weeks. Just then his orderly reported that the horses were harnessed and everything was ready for his departure. The Count picked up his hat, went up to the Marquise, and took her hand. "Well, Julietta," he said, "I feel a great deal easier now,"—and he put his hand in hers—"although it was my dearest wish to marry you before I left."

"Marry her!" they all exclaimed.

"Marry her," the Count reiterated, kissed the Marquise's hand, and assured her, when she asked him if he had taken leave of his senses, that a day would come when she would understand his meaning. The family were ready to get angry; but he immediately bade goodbye to them all very warmly, begged them not to bother their heads about what he had just said, and took his departure.

Several weeks passed, during which the family anxiously awaited, with very different feelings, the outcome of this strange affair. The Commandant received a polite letter from General K——, the Count's uncle; the Count himself wrote from Naples; the answers the family received to their inquiries spoke quite well of him; in short, the engagement seemed as good as concluded when the Marquise's indisposition came back again stronger then ever. And for the first time she noticed an inexplicable change in her figure. She spoke frankly to her mother about her condition and said she did not know what to make of it. Her mother, who felt very anxious about her daughter's health because of these strange attacks, wanted her to call a doctor in for consultation. But the Marquise was against the idea and hoped that her natural vigor would prevail; she suffered the sharpest pains for several days without following her mother's advice, until recurrent sen-

sations of so unusual a kind filled her with such alarm that she had the doctor called; he was a man who enjoyed her father's fullest confidence. Inviting him to sit down on the divan—her mother was away just then—after a brief introduction she told him jokingly what her condition looked like to her. The doctor gave her a searching look; deliberated a while after he had finished his careful examination; and then said, with an expression of great earnestness, that the Marquise's diagnosis was perfectly correct. When she asked him what he meant and he had explained himself quite clearly, observing with a smile he was unable to repress that she was in perfect health and needed no physician, the Marquise tugged the bell cord while she looked at him very hard from the side, and asked him to leave. Speaking under her breath as if he were not worth bothering about, she muttered that it was no pleasure for her to joke with him about such things. The doctor testily replied that he wished she had always been as little inclined to joking as she was now, took his hat and stick, and got up to go. The Marquise promised him that she would report his insults to her father. The physician retorted that he would swear to his opinion in a court of law, opened the door, bowed, and began to leave the room. As he stooped to pick up a glove that he had dropped, the Marquise asked, "But how is it possible, Doctor?" The doctor said he didn't really see any need for him to tell her about the ultimate causes of things, bowed once more, and left.

The Marquise stood there as if thunderstruck. Then she pulled herself together and was about to run to her father when she recalled the intensely serious manner of the man who she thought had insulted her, and her limbs were paralyzed. She threw herself down on the couch in a state of violent agitation. Mistrusting herself, she reviewed every minute of the past year, and decided she had gone mad when she thought about what had just happened. At last her mother came in; when she asked her in alarm why she was so upset, her daughter told her what the physician had said. Madam G—— unhesitatingly called him a shameless, frivolous quack and encouraged her daughter in her determination to tell her father how the doctor had insulted her. The Marquise assured her that the doctor had spoken in deadly earnest and that he seemed perfectly prepared to repeat his mad opinion to her father's face. Madam G——, now more than a little frightened, wanted to know if she thought there was any possibility of her being in such a condition.

"Graves would start to teem first," the Marquise said, "and the womb of a corpse give birth!"

"You are a strange child," her mother said, giving her a tight hug. "Why are you so upset then? If you *know* that it isn't so, why should a doctor's opinion, even the opinion of a whole panel of doctors, bother you? He either made a mistake or he was being malicious, but what difference does it make to you? I think, however, that the right thing for us to do is to tell your father."

"Oh my God!" exclaimed the Marquise, with a convulsive start. "How can I feel calm about it? Don't my own internal sensations, which I am only too familiar with, argue against me? If I knew that somebody else had these symptoms, wouldn't I myself think that she was pregnant?"

"Oh, how awful!" the Colonel's wife replied.

"Malice or mistake!" the Marquise continued. "Why should a man who

seemed to deserve our respect until today try to hurt me in such a mean and wanton way? Me, who never once offended him? Who received him with absolute confidence, anticipating in advance the gratitude I would feel toward him? And whose own wish, as his first words showed, seemed an honest and straightforward one to help, not to cause me greater pain than I have ever felt before? But if, since a choice has to be made," she went on, while her mother steadily regarded her, "I conclude that he made a mistake, how is it possible for me to believe that a physician, even a mediocre one, could err in such a matter?"

Her mother said, with a touch of sharpness, "And yet it has to be one or the other."

"Yes indeed, Mother dear," the Marquise replied, her face reddening with an expression of injured innocence as she kissed her hand, "so it does. Although my condition is such an enigma that you must allow me to have my doubts. I swear, for such an assurance is needed, that I am as innocent as my own children; your own conscience cannot be clearer, more honorable. Nevertheless, I must ask you to send for a midwife; I need to convince myself about the way things really are with me and, whatever the result, find some peace of mind."

"A midwife!" Madam G—— cried in a shocked voice. "A clear conscience and a midwife!" And she was unable to speak.

"A midwife, Mother dear," the Marquise repeated, falling on her knees before her, "and this very instant, or I'll go mad."

"Very well," the Colonel's wife replied, "But please make sure you don't have the confinement under my roof." And she got up to leave the room. The Marquise, following her with outstretched arms, prostrated herself on the ground and embraced her knees. "If a life against which it was impossible to level one reproach," she cried with the eloquence of grief, "a life that followed your example, gives me a right to your respect, if any maternal feeling still pleads for me in your heart as long as my guilt is still not absolutely clear, please don't forsake me at this terrible time!"

"Please tell me why you are so upset," her mother said. "Is it just because of what the doctor said? Just because of those internal sensations you have?"

"Yes, Mother," the Marquise said, with her hand on her heart. "There is no other reason."

"No other, Julietta?" her mother asked. "Think a moment. A misstep, as unspeakably painful as it would be to me, does, well, sometimes happen, and in the end I should have to forgive you; but if you went and invented some fairy tale about a revolution in nature in order to escape your mother's censure, and piled one blasphemous oath on another so as to impose on a heart that is only too ready to believe everything you say, that would be more shameful than I know how to say; I could never love you again."

"May the kingdom of heaven lie as open to me some day as my heart is open to you now," cried the Marquise. "I have concealed nothing from you, Mother."

This exclamation, which was uttered with so much pathos, shook her mother deeply. "Oh heavens!" she cried. "My darling child, how sorry I am for you!" And she raised her daughter up, kissed her, and held her in her

arms. "What in the world are you afraid of, then? Come, you look quite ill to me." And she wanted to take her to her bed. But the Marquise, whose tears were flowing copious and fast, protested that she was very well and that there was nothing wrong with her except for that strange and inexplicable condition.

"Condition!" her mother burst out again. "What condition? If you are so sure about your memory, isn't it madness to be so terribly afraid? Can't these vague internal sensations of yours have deceived you?"

"No, no!" the Marquise said. "I haven't deceived myself! If you'll just call the midwife in, you will see that this dreadful thing which is destroying me is true."

"Come, my darling," said Madam G——, who was beginning to fear for her reason. "Come along with me and lie down. Whatever was it that you think the doctor told you? How flushed your face is! All your limbs are trembling! What could the doctor have told you?"—and now completely skeptical of what the Marquise said had passed between her and the doctor, she drew her daughter away with her.

"Dear, best Mother!" the Marquise said, smiling through her tears. "I've not gone out of my mind. The doctor told me that I was pregnant. Send for the midwife and, the instant she says it isn't so, I'll feel easy again."

"Good, fine," the Colonel's wife said, stifling her fear. "She'll come right away; since you are absolutely set on having her laugh in your face, I'll get her in right away so she can tell you what a dreamer you are, and not quite right in the head." And she pulled the bell cord and immediately sent one of her people to fetch the midwife.

The Marquise was still lying in her mother's arms, her breast heaving apprehensively, when the woman appeared and heard Madam G——'s explanation of the strange idea that was making her daughter ill: the Marquise swore that her behavior had always been virtuous and yet, deluded by some kind of mysterious sensations, she insisted on being examined by an experienced woman. The midwife, as she probed the Marquise, gabbled about young blood and the cunning of the world; when she finished, she said she had had to do with similar cases in the past; all the young widows who found themselves in her predicament would absolutely have it that they had been living on a desert island; at the same time she spoke soothingly to the Marquise and promised her that the lighthearted buccaneer who had landed in the night would soon come back to her. When the Marquise heard this, she fainted dead away. The Colonel's wife could not subdue her motherly feelings and, with the help of the midwife, labored to revive her; but her anger got the better of her when her daughter came to. "Julietta!" she cried, in accents of intense suffering, "Won't you please, please tell me the truth and say who the father is?" She still seemed ready to forgive her. But when the Marquise said she would lose her mind, her mother got up from the couch and shouted, "Go on, then! You are a contemptible creature! I curse the hour I bore you!" and she ran out of the room.

The Marquise, who was about to swoon again, drew the midwife down to her and laid her violently trembling head on her breast. In a faltering voice she asked her how inflexible the laws of nature were: was it possible to

conceive without one's knowing it? The midwife smiled, undid the Marquise's dress, and said that that was not the present case. No, no, of course not, the Marquise hastened to say, she had known when she conceived, she only wanted to know in general whether such an occurrence was possible in nature. The midwife answered that, with the exception of the Holy Virgin, no such thing had ever happened to any woman on this earth. The Marquise trembled more and more violently. Fearing that she was going to give birth any minute, she clutched the midwife in terror and begged her not to leave her. The woman tried to reassure her, telling her that her confinement was still a long way off, advising her how in such cases one could escape the cackling of the world, and promising her that everything would turn out all right. But as these words, which were meant to comfort her, only pierced her bosom like so many knife thrusts, the Marquise managed to get a grip on herself, announced that she was feeling better, and asked her companion to leave.

Hardly was the midwife out of the room when the Marquise received a note from her mother that read as follows: "It is Colonel G——'s wish that in view of the existing circumstances the Marquise should leave his house. He sends her herewith all the papers concerning her property, and trusts that God will spare him the misery of ever seeing her again."

The letter, however, was wet with tears and in one corner a word— "dictated"—had been erased. The Marquise burst into tears. Weeping over her parents' mistake and the injustice into which these good people were led, she stumbled to her mother's apartment. Madam G—— was with her father, she was told; she tottered to her father's apartment. When she found the door shut against her, she sank to the ground in front of it and in a pitiable voice called all the saints to witness that she was innocent. She must have been there for several minutes or so before the Forest Warden came out and, with an inflamed face, said that the Commandant refused to see her. The Marquise, sobbing brokenly, exclaimed, "Dear brother!" pushed against him into the room, cried, "My beloved father!" and stretched her arms out to the Commandant. He turned his back on her and hurried into his bedroom. When she followed him there he shouted, "Go away!" and tried to slam the door; but she wailed and pleaded and would not let him do it, until he suddenly gave up and retreated, pursued by the Marquise, to the far wall of the room, where he stood with his back to her. Just as she threw herself at his feet and hugged his knees in her trembling arms, a pistol that he had snatched from the wall went off and the shot crashed into the ceiling.

"Dear God!" cried the Marquise, got up from her knees as white as a corpse, and ran from her father's apartment. "Order the carriage for me," she shouted as she came into her apartment; dropped into a chair deathly tired; dressed her children as fast as possible; and had her things packed. Just as she was holding her younger child between her knees and wrapping a last shawl around him before getting into the coach, the Forest Warden entered and said that her father had ordered her to leave the children behind in his care.

"My children!" she exclaimed, and stood up. "Go and tell that unnatural father of yours that he can come and put a pistol bullet through me, but that he won't take my children away from me!" And with all the pride of

innocence she picked her two children up in her arms, carried them into the coach without her brother's daring to stop her, and drove away.

Having learned how strong she was through this courageous effort, she was suddenly able to raise herself, as if by her own bootstraps, out of the depths into which fate had cast her. The turmoil in her breast quieted as soon as she was on the open road, she kissed her children, the precious spoils of her struggle, over and over again, and felt quite pleased with herself when she thought about the victory she had won over her brother, thanks to the strength of her unspotted conscience. Her reason, which had been strong enough not to crack under the strain of her uncanny situation, now bowed before the great, holy and inscrutable scheme of things. She saw the impossibility of persuading her family of her innocence, understood that she must accept that fact if she did not want to be destroyed, and in a matter of days after her arrival at V—— her grief had given way to a heroic resolution to arm herself with pride against the onslaughts of the world. She decided to withdraw into herself entirely, to concentrate all her energies on the education of the two children she already possessed, and to lavish all her mother love on the third that God had made her a gift of. She made plans for restoring her beautiful estate, which, owing to her long absence, had fallen a little into disrepair, once she was over her confinement; sat in the summerhouse and knitted little caps and stockings for little limbs, while she thought about a comfortable arrangement of the rooms; and also which one she would fill with books and which would be best to put her easel in. And so, before the date of Count F——'s return from Naples arrived, she had become quite reconciled to living a life of ever greater seclusion. The porter was given orders to let nobody into the house. One thought only she could not endure, that the young being whom she had conceived in the purest innocence and whose origin seemed more divine to her than other people's just because it was more mysterious, should bear a stigma in society. An unusual means to discover its father occurred to her, a means that, when she first thought of it, made her start in pure terror and drop her knitting. Tossing restlessly through long sleepless nights, she kept turning the idea, which wounded her in her most sensitive feelings, over in her mind so as to accustom herself to it. Meanwhile she tried repeatedly to get in touch with the man who had deceived her so, even though she had made up her mind that he must belong beyond all redemption to the scum of his sex, and could only have sprung from the blackest and filthiest mire, whatever one might think of the place he now occupied in the world. But as her own feelings of independence grew stronger and stronger, and as she reflected that a gem keeps its value regardless of how it is mounted, she plucked up her courage, one morning when the new life stirred inside her, and had inserted in the newspapers of M—— that extraordinary appeal of which the reader was apprised at the beginning of this story.

Count F——, whom unavoidable business detained in Naples, had meanwhile written to the Marquise a second time to say that other circumstances might arise which would make it desirable for her to keep the tacit promise she had given him. As soon as he could get excused from making the trip to Constantinople, and his other obligations permitted, he left Naples and came right to M——, arriving only a few days after the time he

had said he would. The Commandant received him with an embarrassed expression, said that urgent business called him away from the house, and asked the Forest Warden to entertain the guest in the meantime. The Forest Warden led him to his room and, after a brief exchange of greetings, inquired if he knew anything about what had occurred in the Commandant's house during his absence. The Count paled and answered, "No." Whereupon the Forest Warden told him about the shame that the Marquise had brought upon the family, recounting the whole story that our readers have just heard. The Count struck his forehead. "Why were so many obstacles put in my way!" he cried, forgetting himself. "If the marriage had taken place, we should have been spared all this shame and suffering!" The Forest Warden gaped at him and asked whether he was crazy enough to want to marry someone so contemptible. The Count retorted that she was worth more than the whole world that condemned her; that he had absolute confidence in her innocence, and that he would go to V—— today and renew his marriage proposal. At once he picked up his hat, said goodbye to the Forest Warden, who thought he had taken leave of his senses, and left.

Jumping on a horse, he galloped off to V——. When he dismounted at the gate and tried to enter the hall, the porter told him that the Marquise would not see anyone. The Count asked him whether this ban applied to a friend of the house as well as to strangers, to which the porter replied that there were no exceptions he knew of, and right after inquired with a doubtful air if he were not Count F——. "No," replied the Count, after looking at him sharply, and, turning to his servant and speaking loud enough for the porter to hear, he said that in that case they would stop at an inn and he would announce himself to the Marquise in writing. As soon as he was out of the porter's sight, he turned a corner and slipped along the wall of a great garden that stretched behind the house. Entering the garden through an open gate that he discovered, he walked up a path and was just about to climb the slope at the rear of the house when he caught sight, in a summerhouse off to one side, of the charming and mysterious figure of the Marquise, who was busily working at a small table. He walked silently toward her and stood in the entrance to the summerhouse before she noticed him, three short steps away from her.

"Count F——!" exclaimed the Marquise, looking up in surprise and blushing. The Count smiled, stood for a moment in the entrance without moving, then sat down next to her with such modest importunity[11] that it was impossible for her to take alarm, and slipped his arm around her waist before she could think what to do. "Where did you come from, Count, how is it possible——?" the Marquise asked, and looked shyly at the ground.

"From M——," the Count replied, pressing her gently to him, "through a back gate that I found standing open. I was sure you would forgive me if I came in."

"Didn't they say anything to you in M—— about ——?" she said, without moving in his arms, and stopped.

"They told me everything, dear Lady," replied the Count. "But as I am absolutely convinced of your innocence——"

[11] Pleading insistence.

"What!" exclaimed the Marquise, standing up and trying to free herself from his embrace. "In spite of that you are willing to come here——!"

"In spite of the world," he said, holding her fast, "in spite of your family, even in spite of your own lovely self," and he kissed her fervently on the breast.

"Please go away!" the Marquise cried.

"As convinced," he said, "my darling Julietta, as if I were omniscient, as if my own soul lived in your bosom."

"Let me go!" she cried.

"I've come here," he said—and he would not let her go—"to repeat my proposal and receive my happiness from your hand if you will hear my suit."

"Let me go this instant! I order you to!" And she wrenched herself from his arms and started from the summerhouse.

"Darling! Paragon!"[12] he whispered, getting up and reaching out to hold her.

"Did you hear me!" the Marquise panted, turning and eluding his grasp.

"Only let me whisper one secret to you!" begged the Count as he grabbed clumsily at the smooth arm slipping through his hands.

"I won't hear a word," the Marquise retorted, gave him a push against his chest, fled up the slope, and disappeared.

He was halfway up the slope in pursuit, determined to make her listen to him at whatever cost, when the door banged shut in front of him and he heard the bolt shoot home in rattling haste. He stopped short, not knowing what to do and wondering if he should climb through an open window at the side of the house and keep on until he reached his goal; but as hard as it was for him in every way to give up, he saw no help for it now. Angry with himself for letting her get away from him, he stole down the slope and left the garden to look for his horses. He felt that his attempt to explain himself to her directly had irretrievably failed, and, going at a slow walk back toward M——, he revolved in his mind the letter he now saw himself condemned to write. But in the evening, when he was in the blackest mood possible, whom should he run into at the common table of an inn but the Forest Warden, who immediately wanted to know if his suit had succeeded at V——. The Count answered with a short "No" and was tempted to say something nasty and snubbing; but for the sake of courtesy, he added after a while that he had decided to write to her and would shortly have the whole thing cleared up. The Forest Warden said that he was sorry that the Count's passion for the Marquise had robbed him of his senses. He had to tell him, however, that she was already getting ready to make another choice; he rang for the latest papers and handed the Count the sheet that contained her appeal to the father of her child. The blood rushed to his face as the Count read it through. His mood changed abruptly. The Forest Warden asked him whether he thought the man the Marquise was looking for would appear? "Without a doubt!" the Count retorted as he bent over the paper and greedily devoured what it said. Then, after going to the window for a moment while folding up the paper, he said, "Now every-

[12] Model of perfection.

thing is all right! Now I know what I have to do!" He turned around and courteously asked the Forest Warden if he would see him again soon; said goodbye, and went away fully reconciled to his fate.

Meanwhile some lively scenes had taken place at the Commandant's house. The Colonel's wife was very angry at her husband's violent rage and at her own weakness in tamely submitting to the tyrannical expulsion of her daughter from her home. When the shot had sounded in the Commandant's bedroom and her daughter had come rushing out, she had fainted away; true, she had recovered at once, but all the Commandant had said when she awoke was that he was sorry she had been frightened for nothing, and he had tossed the discharged pistol on a table. Later, when they were talking about demanding the children from the Marquise, she had timidly remarked that they had no right to take such a step; she pleaded, in a voice still weak and pathetic from the fainting fit, that there should be no more violent scenes in the house; but the Commandant had only turned to the Forest Warden and, livid with rage, had said, "Go and bring them here!" When Count F——'s second letter arrived, the Commandant ordered it sent to the Marquise at V——; she, as they learned later from the messenger, merely laid it aside and said thank you. The Colonel's wife, who was in the dark about so many things in the whole affair, and especially about her daughter's intention to enter into a new marriage for which she had not the slightest desire, vainly tried to bring the subject of the Count's proposal up again. But the Colonel always asked her, in a way that resembled an order more than a request, not to speak to him about it; on one such occasion, when he happened to be taking down a portrait of his daughter that still hung on the wall, he told his wife that he wanted to wipe the Marquise out of his memory completely, and that he no longer had a daughter. It was at this point that the Marquise's extraordinary appeal appeared in the newspapers. Madam G——, absolutely dazed by it, went holding the newspaper, which her husband had given her, into his room, where she found him working at a table, and asked him what in the world he thought about it all? The Commandant, without looking up from his writing, said, "Oh, of course, she's innocent."

"What!" Madam G—— burst out in complete astonishment; "Innocent?"

"She did it in her sleep," the Commandant said, without looking up.

"In her sleep!" Madam G—— replied; "Such a terrible thing could——?"

"Idiot!" shouted the Commandant, pushed his papers into a heap, and left the room.

The next time the newspapers appeared, the Colonel's wife read the following reply, the ink of which was still wet, in one of them, as she and her husband were sitting at breakfast: "If the Marquise of O—— will come to the house of her father, Colonel G——, at eleven o'clock in the morning on the 3rd of——, the person whom she is looking for will appear there to throw himself at her feet."

Before she had read halfway through the announcement, the Colonel's wife was struck speechless; hastily glancing at the end, she handed the paper to the Commandant. The Colonel read it through three times, as if

he could not believe his eyes. "Now for heaven's sake, Lorenzo," exclaimed his wife, "tell me what you think about it!"

"The vile creature!" replied the Commandant and stood up. "The cunning impostor! Ten times the shamelessness of a bitch joined to ten times the slyness of a fox would not equal hers! What a face! Did you ever see two such eyes? A cherub's look is no truer!" And he went on in this vein and could not calm himself.

"But if it is a trick," his wife asked, "what in the world can she hope to gain by it?"

"What does she hope to gain by it? She wants to carry her contemptible pretense to the bitter end," the Colonel replied. "She has already learned by heart the story that the two of them, he and she, intend to tell us here at eleven o'clock in the morning of the third. 'My dear little daughter,' I am supposed to say, 'I didn't realize that, who could have believed it, I beg your pardon, receive my blessing, all is forgiven.' But there is a bullet here for the man who crosses my threshold on the morning of the third! I think, therefore, that it would be better to have the servants put him out of the house."

After reading the newspaper notice over again, Madam G—— said that, if it were a choice between two incredibilities, she would rather believe in some mysterious action of fate than in the infamy of a daughter otherwise so excellent. But before she had a chance to finish what she was saying, the Commandant shouted, "Do me the favor of keeping still! I can't stand hearing one more word about it!" and he left the room.

A few days later the Commandant received a letter from the Marquise in which she asked him, with the most touching respect, to have the goodness to send on to her at V——, since she was denied the favor of being allowed to enter her father's house, the man who would appear on the morning of the third. The Colonel's wife happened to be there when he received the letter; and, noticing the confusion of feelings plainly reflected in his face—for if the whole thing were a deception, what motive could he impute to his daughter now that she did not seem to be asking for his forgiveness—she was emboldened to propose a plan to him that she had been nursing for some time in her troubled breast. While the Colonel continued to stare vacuously at the newspaper, she said that a notion had occurred to her: would he allow her to visit V—— for a day or so? If the Marquise really knew the man who had published the reply to her appeal and he was only pretending to be a stranger to her, she knew how to put her in a position where she would have to betray herself even though she were the most cunning dissembler in the world. The Commandant answered her by tearing the letter to bits with sudden violence: she knew very well that he wanted to have nothing to do with the Marquise, and he forbade her to communicate with her in any way. He sealed the torn pieces in an envelope, addressed it to the Marquise, and gave it back to the messenger; that was his answer. Hiding the exasperation she felt at his crazy obstinacy, which destroyed any possibility of getting to the bottom of the business, his wife decided to carry out her plan in spite of him. The following morning, taking one of the Commandant's soldiers with her, she rode over to V—— while her husband was still in bed. When her carriage drew up

before the gates of the estate, the porter told her that nobody was allowed to see the Marquise. Madam G—— said that she had been told that that was so, but asked him nevertheless to go in and announce that Madam G—— was there. He said it would not do any good, since there was not a person in the world that the Marquise would speak to. Madam G—— replied that the Marquise must certainly have mentioned her, as she was her mother, and that he was not to dawdle any longer but to do his duty. It was hardly a moment between the porter's going into the house on what he considered to be a useless errand and the Marquise's bursting out of the door, running toward the gate, and falling on her knees before the coach. Madam G—— got out of the carriage with the help of the soldier and, more than a little moved, lifted her daughter from the ground. Overcome with emotion, the Marquise bent over her mother's hand and, while the tears streamed down her face, she led her, with great deference, into the house.

"Dear, dear Mother," she said, after showing her to the couch but remaining standing herself and drying her eyes, "what happy chance must I thank for your coming to visit me?" Madam G—— gave her daughter an affectionate hug and said she simply had to come to see her to beg her pardon for the brutal way in which she had been turned out of her father's house.

"Pardon!" the Marquise broke in, and wanted to kiss her hands. But her mother would not let her and went on, "Not only did the answer that just appeared in the newspapers to your advertisement convince me as well as your father that you are innocent; I also have to tell you that the man himself appeared in person at the house, to our great and pleasant surprise."

"Who appeared——?" the Marquise exclaimed, sitting down beside her mother; "which man appeared in person?"—and her face was tense with expectation.

"The one who wrote that answer," Madam G—— replied, "the very man you addressed your appeal to, he himself in person."

"Then for goodness' sake," the Marquise said, her breast heaving violently, "who is he?" And again, "Who is he?"

"That," Madam G—— replied, "I would rather let you guess. Just imagine it—yesterday when we were having tea, right in the middle of our reading the answer in the newspaper, a man whom all of us know very well rushed into the room in wild despair and fell at your father's feet and, a moment after, at mine. We didn't know what to make of it all and asked him to explain himself. His conscience, he said, left him no peace, he was the scoundrel who had deceived the Marquise; he must know how his crime was judged and, if vengeance on him was demanded, he came himself to satisfy that demand."

"But who is he? Who? Who?" the Marquise cried.

"As I have said," continued Madam G——, "a young and otherwise well-bred man whom we should never have thought capable of such a despicable act. But I hope, my daughter, that you won't be horrified to learn that he is of humble station and lacks all those qualities which we should otherwise require of a husband for you."

"Just the same, Mother dear," the Marquise said, "he can't be entirely

unworthy, since he threw himself at your feet before mine. But who is he, won't you please tell me who he is?"

"Well," her mother replied, "he is Leopardo, the chasseur,[13] whom your father had come from the Tyrol[14] not long ago and whom I have brought along with me, as you may have noticed, to introduce to you as your bridegroom."

"Leopardo, the chasseur!" cried the Marquise, clapping her hand to her forehead in despair.

"What are you afraid of?" the Colonel's wife asked. "Have you any reason to doubt he is the one?"

"How? Where? When?" the Marquise asked in bewilderment.

"He will only tell you that," she said. "Shame and love, he says, make it impossible for him to talk to anyone else but you. But, if you like, we can open the door to the anteroom where he is waiting with a beating heart, and while I go off somewhere you can see if you can get him to tell his secret."

"Oh, my God!" the Marquise exclaimed. "I once dozed off on the couch in the midday heat and when I woke up I saw him slinking away!" And she hid her shame-reddened face in her small hands.

Her mother dropped on her knees in front of her. "Oh my daughter!" she cried. "Oh my wonderful daughter!" and she threw her arms around her. "And oh your contemptible mother!" she said, burying her face in her daughter's lap.

"What's the matter, Mother?" the Marquise asked in dismay.

"I want you to know," her mother continued, "you who are purer than the angels, that there is not a word of truth in anything I said; that my soul is so corrupt that I could not believe in such radiant innocence as yours; and that I needed to play this shameful trick in order to convince myself."

"My darling mother," said the Marquise, and full of joy she bent down to lift her up.

"No," she said, "I won't budge from here, you marvelous, saintly girl, until you say you can forgive my vicious behavior."

"I forgive you, Mother, oh I do! Stand up," cried the Marquise. "Oh please do!"

"First tell me," said Madam G——, "if you can ever love and respect me as you used to."

"My adored mother!" the Marquise said, and also went down on her knees. "I never lost the reverence and love I feel for you. How could anybody have believed me when the circumstances were so queer? I am so happy that you don't blame me."

"From now on," Madam G—— said, getting to her feet with the help of her daughter, "I will wait upon you hand and foot, my darling child. You shall have your confinement in my house; if the circumstances were different and I were expecting you to present me with a young prince, I shouldn't take care of you with greater tenderness and consideration. I'll not budge from your side again the rest of my days. I defy the whole world;

[13] Uniformed servant.
[14] An Alpine region of northernmost Italy and western Austria.

from now on your shame is the only glory I wish, if only you will think well of me again and forget the cruel way in which I repudiated you." The Marquise tried to comfort her with endless caresses and reassurances, but the evening came, and then midnight, before she succeeded. The following day, when the old lady's excitement, which gave her a fever during the night, had somewhat abated, mother, daughter, and grandchildren drove back to M——. The journey was like a triumph. They were as jolly as they could be and joked about Leopardo, the chasseur, who was sitting up front in the coachman's box; her mother said to the Marquise that she saw her blush every time she looked at his broad back. The Marquise responded to this with something between a sigh and a smile. "Who knows," she said, "who will finally show up at eleven o'clock on the morning of the third!"

Thereafter, the closer they drew to M——, the more serious they became, in anticipation of the fateful scene that was about to take place. When they alighted in front of the house, Madam G——, saying not a word about her plans, took her daughter to her old rooms, told her to make herself at home, and, declaring that she would be back shortly, slipped away. An hour later she returned, her face quite flushed. "Did you ever see such a fellow?" she said, secretly pleased nevertheless. "Such a doubting Thomas! It took me a whole hour to convince him, and now of course he is sitting there and crying!"

"Who?" the Marquise asked.

"Who else but the one who has the most reason to cry."

"You don't mean Father?" the Marquise said.

"Like a baby!" her mother said. "If I hadn't had to wipe the tears out of my own eyes, I would have burst out laughing as soon as I was out of the room."

"And all because of me?" the Marquise asked, getting up. "And I sit here——?"

"Don't you budge!" Madam G—— exclaimed. "Why did he dictate that letter to me? Let him come looking for you here if he ever wants to see me again."

"Mother dear!" begged the Marquise.

"I won't relent!" her mother interrupted. "Why did he reach for that pistol!"

"I implore you!"

"No, you won't," Madam G—— replied, pushing her daughter back into her chair. "And if he doesn't come here by this evening, you and I will go away tomorrow." The Marquise said it would be cruel and unjust to do that. But her mother said: "Be quiet"—for just then she heard a sound of sobbing drawing near; "Here he is now!"

"Where?" the Marquise asked, and listened. "Can that be someone at the door, that terrible——?"

"Of course," Madam G—— replied. "He wants us to let him in."

"Let me go!" cried the Marquise and jumped out of her chair.

"If you love me, Julietta," replied the Colonel's wife, "then stay where you are." And at that very instant the Commandant entered, holding his handkerchief to his eyes. Madam G—— took up a position in front of her daughter, as if to protect her, and turned her back to the Colonel.

"Dear, dear Father," cried the Marquise and stretched her arms out to him.

"Don't you budge!" commanded her mother. "Do you hear?" The Commandant stood in the middle of the room and wept. "Let him apologize to you," continued Madam G——. "Why must he be so violent! And why must he be so obstinate! I love him, but I love you too; I honor him, but you too. And if I must make a choice, then I'll stay with you because you are the better one." The Commandant bent down until he was almost doubled over and roared so loudly that the walls rang.

"Oh my God!" exclaimed the Marquise, gave in to her mother all at once, reached for her handkerchief, and let her own tears flow.

Madam G—— said, "He can't even speak," and moved a little to one side. At which her daughter got up, put her arms around the Commandant, and begged him to calm himself. She herself was weeping furiously. She asked him if he would not sit down; she tried to persuade him to sit down; she pushed a chair toward him for him to sit on; but he would not say one word; there was no budging him from where he was, and yet he would not take a seat, just stood there in the center of the room, his head bowed to the ground, and cried. The Marquise turned halfway toward her mother as she held him up and said that he would get ill; even her mother seemed to waver in her firmness when she saw how convulsed he was. But when the Commandant yielded to the incessant pleadings of his daughter and finally sat down, and she crouched at his feet and caressed and comforted him incessantly, the mother started talking again, said that it served him right and that perhaps he would now come back to his senses, walked out of the room and left them alone.

Once outside, she wiped her own tears away, and wondered if the violent agitation of feeling to which she had exposed him might not be a danger to his health and if it were perhaps advisable to send for a doctor. For the evening meal, she prepared everything that she could think of that had a fortifying and soothing effect, turned back the coverlets of his bed and warmed the sheets so that she could tuck him in as soon as he appeared on his daughter's arm, and, when he still did not come and the table was already laid, tiptoed to the Marquise's room to hear what was going on. As she listened with her ear against the door, she heard a soft whisper that subsided into silence at that very moment; it seemed to have come from the Marquise; and as she was able to see through the keyhole, her daughter was sitting on the Commandant's lap, something he never in his life had allowed her to do. Finally she opened the door and peered in—and her heart leaped for joy: her daughter lay motionless in her father's arms, her head thrown back and her eyes closed, while he sat in the armchair, with tear-choked, glistening eyes, and pressed long, warm and avid kisses on her mouth: just as if he were her lover! Her daughter did not speak, her husband did not speak; he hung over her as if she were his first love and held her mouth and kissed it. The mother's delight was indescribable; standing unobserved behind the chair, she hesitated to disturb the joy of reconciliation that had come to her home. At last she moved nearer and, peering around one side of the chair, she saw her husband again take his daughter's face between his hands and with unspeakable delight bend down and press

his lips against her mouth. On catching sight of her, the Commandant looked away with a frown and was about to say something; but calling out, "Oh, what a face!" she kissed him in her turn so that his frown went away, and with a joke dispelled the intense emotion filling the hushed room. She invited them both to supper, and they followed her to the table like a pair of newlyweds; the Commandant, to be sure, seemed quite cheerful during the meal, but he ate and spoke little, from time to time a sob escaped him, and he stared down at his plate and played with his daughter's hand.

Next day the great question was, who would appear at eleven o'clock of the following morning, for it was now the eve of the dreaded third. Father and mother, and the brother as well—for he too had made it up with his sister—were all agreed that, if the man were at all passable, the Marquise should marry him; everything that could possibly make the Marquise's position a happy one should be done. But if his circumstances were such that even with their help a marked discrepancy would still exist between his position and the Marquise's, then her parents were against the marriage; the Marquise could stay with them as before and they would adopt the child. She, however, seemed inclined to stick to her promise, providing the man was not an out-and-out scoundrel, and to give her child a father at whatever cost to herself. In the evening the mother asked how they should receive the visitor. The Commandant thought the best thing would be to leave the Marquise alone around eleven o'clock. But the Marquise insisted that she wanted her two parents present, and her brother too, since she had no wish to share any kind of secrets with the person. Also she thought that their visitor's answer to her advertisement, in which he proposed the Commandant's house as the meeting place, suggested that he too wished to have her family present—a fact about the reply, she had to confess, that had won her good opinion. Madam G—— pointed out that her father and her brother would have very awkward parts indeed to play in the proceeding, and asked her daughter to excuse the men; but she was perfectly agreeable to being present herself. After a moment's reflection her daughter accepted this suggestion.

And finally, after a night of the most anxious suspense, the morning of the dreaded third arrived. As the clock struck eleven, the two women were sitting in the reception room, dressed as if for a betrothal; you could have heard the pounding of their hearts if the clatter of the morning had been hushed. The eleventh stroke was still shivering in the air when the door opened to admit Leopardo, the chasseur, whom their father had sent to the Tyrol for. The women paled when they saw him. "Count F——'s carriage," he announced, "is at the door and he begs to be received."

"Count F——!" the two exclaimed together, in utter consternation. The Marquise shouted, "Bolt the door! We are not at home to him," jumped up and was about to push the chasseur, who was standing in her way, out of the room and bar the door herself when the Count entered, wearing the same uniform, plus his decorations and sword, that he had worn during the capture of the fortress. The Marquise felt like sinking into the ground with confusion; she snatched up a handkerchief she had left on the chair and meant to fly into a neighboring room; but Madam G—— caught hold of her hand, cried, "Julietta!"—and as if choking on her own thoughts, her voice failed her. Riveting her eyes on the Count, Madam G—— repeated,

"Julietta, please!" and tried to pull her daughter back. "After all, whom were we waiting for—?"

"Oh no, surely not for him!" she cried, suddenly turning around and shooting the Count a look that crackled like lightning while a deathlike pallor spread across her face. The Count went down on one knee to her; his right hand was pressed against his heart, his head hung down on his breast, and he stared with burning intensity in front of him, saying nothing.

"Whom else!" gasped the Colonel's wife. "We are such idiots—whom else but him——?"

The Marquise stood stiffly erect over him and said, "I am going out of my mind, Mother."

"You goose!" her mother retorted, pulled her to her and whispered something in her ear. The Marquise turned away and, hiding her face in her hands, went and fell on the sofa. "What's the matter with you!" her mother cried. "What has happened that you weren't expecting?" The Count did not move from the mother's side; still kneeling, he caught up the hem of her dress and kissed it. "Dear, kind, gracious lady!" he whispered and a tear rolled down his cheek.

"Get up, Count, please get up!" the Colonel's wife said. "Go over there and make her feel better; that way we shall all be reconciled and everything will be forgiven and forgotten." The Count stood up, crying. Getting down again before the Marquise, he took her hand as delicately as if it were made of gold that his slightest touch would tarnish. But she stood erect, crying, "Go away! Go away! Go away! I was ready for some villain of a fellow, but not—not—not the devil!" and, walking around him as if he had the plague, she opened the door and said, "Call the Colonel!"

"Julietta!" her mother panted. The Marquise looked with murderous fierceness first at the Count and then at her mother; her breast heaved, her eyes blazed; one of the Furies[15] could not have looked more terrible. The Colonel and the Forest Warden entered. "Father," she called out before he had even come through the doorway, "I can't marry this man!" thrust her hand into a vessel of holy water fastened behind the door, with a sweep of her arm sprinkled her father, mother and brother with the water, and disappeared.[16]

The Commandant looked surprised and asked what had happened; his face went white when he saw Count F—— in the room. The mother took the Count's hand and said, "Don't ask any questions. This young man is sincerely sorry for what he has done; give him your blessing, come, give it to him, and all will end well." The Count looked completely crushed. The Commandant laid his hand on him; his eyelids twitched, his lips were as white as chalk. "May God's curse avoid this head!" he cried. "When do you mean to get married?"

"Tomorrow," the mother answered for him, for he was absolutely speechless. "Tomorrow or today. Whatever you wish; the Count, who has

[15] In classical mythology, terrifying goddesses who punished the wicked.

[16] One of the uses of holy water, blessed by the Church, was to ward off Satan and other evil spirits.

shown such praiseworthy eagerness to redeem his offense, will certainly prefer the earliest possible date."

"Then I shall have the pleasure of meeting you tomorrow morning at eleven at St. Augustine's Church," the Commandant said, bowed to him, asked his wife and son to accompany him to the Marquise's room, and left the Count standing there.

They tried in vain to get the Marquise to explain her strange behavior; she was in a violent fever, would not hear of the marriage, and begged them to leave her alone. When they asked her why she had suddenly changed her mind and what made the Count more obnoxious to her than somebody else, she stared blankly at her father and did not answer. Madam G—— asked her if she had forgotten that she was going to be a mother; she said that in this case she had to think of herself more than of her child and, calling on all the angels and saints as witnesses, she swore again that she would never marry. Her father, seeing that she was extremely over-wrought, said that she must keep her word, left the room, and, after duly exchanging notes with the Count, gave all the necessary orders for the wedding. He also submitted a marriage contract to the Count in which the latter renounced all his rights as a husband, at the same time that he agreed to do anything and everything that might be required of him. The Count signed the paper and sent it back moistened with his tears. The next morning, when the Commandant brought the contract to the Marquise, he found her somewhat more composed. Sitting up in bed, she read it over several times, folded it up reflectively, unfolded it, and read it over again; and then announced that she would be at St. Augustine's Church at eleven o'clock.

She got up, dressed herself without a word, got into the coach with all her family when the hour sounded, and drove to the church.

The Count was not allowed to join them until they were at the church door. During the entire ceremony the Marquise stared straight ahead at the altar painting; she did not even vouchsafe the man with whom she exchanged rings a passing glance. After the service the Count gave her his arm; but as soon as they were out of the church the Countess bowed to him; the Commandant asked him if he might have the honor of seeing him occasionally in his daughter's apartment, to which the Count stammered something in reply that nobody could understand, pulled his hat off to the company, and went away. He took a place in M—— and several months went by without his so much as setting foot in the Commandant's house, where the Countess continued to stay.

Thanks only to the delicate, honorable, and exemplary way he behaved whenever he encountered the family, he was invited, after the Countess was duly delivered of a son, to the latter's baptism. The Countess, sitting up in bed with rugs around her shoulders, saw him only for a moment as he stood in the doorway and bowed respectfully to her from the distance. Into the cradle among the gifts with which the guests welcomed the newborn child he tossed two papers, one of which, as it turned out when he departed, was a gift of 20,000 rubles[17] to the boy, the other a will making the mother, in case he died, the heiress of everything he owned. From that day

[17] Russian units of money.

on, thanks to Madam G——'s management, he was invited to the house more often; he was free to come and go, and soon no evening passed in which he did not appear there. When his feelings told him that everybody, seeing what an imperfect place the world in general was, had pardoned him, he began to court his wife the Countess anew. After a year she consented for the second time, and a second marriage was celebrated, happier than the first, after which the whole family moved to V——. A whole line of young Russians now followed the first; and when the Count once asked his wife, in a happy moment, why on that terrible third of the month, when she seemed ready to accept any villain of a fellow that came along, she had fled from him as if from the Devil, she threw her arms around his neck and said: he wouldn't have looked like a devil to her then if he had not seemed like an angel to her at his first appearance.

John Keats
(1795–1821)

The world could ill spare *Adonais,* Percy Bysshe Shelley's great funeral elegy for John Keats, but it could easily spare the myth that sprang from the poem and long persisted among its readers: that Keats was a hypersensitively vulnerable flower nipped in its early bud by a cold world personified in a hostile literary critic. That picturesque image is a sad one, but the truth about Keats is different and infinitely sadder. The blows life dealt him were less airily abstract and until near the end of his short life were borne bravely, almost uncomplainingly, by a young man with guts and a tough mind, not to mention a thoroughly engaging, vital personality. Posterity's loss is almost equally painful to contemplate. Had disease and then death not cut short his career at the height of his powers, he almost certainly would have reached even greater heights, for, like certain other great artists who died young—including Mozart, Schubert, and Shelley himself— he was driven by a dynamic of experiment and growth. It is hard to imagine him outliving his genius as, say, Wordsworth did.

Keats was born in London in 1795. His mother's father owned a livery stable that Keats's father eventually took over. The latter was killed in an accident when John was not quite nine, the first of a series of deaths in the family that would shadow the poet's life. His mother remarried some two months later and then separated from her second husband. Keats and his three younger siblings lived with their grandmother for much of this unsettled time, and Keats had to learn early the role of surrogate parent, especially after his mother died of tuberculosis, which ran in the family, when he was fourteen. One finds in Keats's mature personality a combination of dependence on others and self-reliance shaped by these early years.

Keats went to a good school and was a good student, but he showed no precocious talent for, or even deep interest in, literature. He was more

conspicuous for getting into fights; one of his schoolmates recalled years later that Keats seemed cut out more for a military career than for poetry. At sixteen he began a four-year apprenticeship as a "surgeon," a term that in Keats's day described a kind of skilled paramedic, after which he spent a year in training at Guy's Hospital. This medical background—in the days before anesthesia—is significant, showing that the unparalleled concrete sensuousness of his later poetry was grounded in an intimate knowledge of the brute facts of pain.

In the meantime, Keats had been converted (in the strongest sense of the word) to poetry, largely through the influence of Charles Cowden Clarke, his schoolmaster's son. Keats soon abandoned his medical prospects. His first enthusiasm was Spenser, whose *Faerie Queene* made a striking impact on him. Spenser (whose stanza Keats later used in *The Eve of St. Agnes*) pointed the young poet toward romance, a genre that, whether indulged for its own sake or as a vehicle of serious themes, took Keats's imagination into exotic settings far removed in time and place from familiar scenes. This side of Keats persisted through his last poetry, but increasingly it came into conflict with a sterner ambition to face and explore poetically the harsher side of life, the side most people (however simplistically) call "reality." He half-foresaw, half-willed this progression in himself in his early "Sleep and Poetry." The thirst for sternness he came to associate with epic rather than romance. The polarity was to take many other forms for Keats in his never-ceasing attempt to see life in its wholeness: the value of thought versus feeling; philosophy versus art (including poetry); active striving versus passive, open receptivity; waking versus sleep; humanity versus deity; earth versus the sky.

Spenser was also the first of a line of poets Keats learned from over the next five years, quickly bleeding them white, one after another, of everything he felt he could assimilate to himself from their minds and styles. One early, and unfortunate, model was Leigh Hunt, a prominent man of letters who in 1816 made a protégé of Keats, introduced him to a public circle of writers and artists (including Shelley), and instilled in the impressionable young poet the stylistic principles of an undiscriminating reaction against Pope and the other neoclassicists. The result in Keats's early poems was the substitution for eighteenth-century aphoristic tightness of a limp, simpering softness that helped conceal his real promise and did his reputation no good at the time. The worst excesses of this style emerge in Keats's first published volume, the *Poems* of 1817. They reappear in his next published work, the long romance *Endymion* (1818) about the love of a mortal for the goddess of the moon, where they mar an ambitious and interesting work that, in its tension between the demands of earthly life and aspiration to the heavens, foreshadows the greater poetry to come. One dwells on these shortcomings in a novice poet only because they illustrate tendencies he later turned to good account. The "luxuries" he loved to dwell on in his early poems would be transformed into the powerful symbols of rich imaginative experience in the great odes, and his early fumblings with new-coined words and the romance mode were the matrix from which emerged the magical language and atmosphere of *The Eve of St. Agnes*.

The bad reception his work got from influential literary journals (inspired partly by opposition to Hunt's leftist politics and social snobbery that

contemptuously relegated Keats to a "Cockney" school of poetry) did not devastate Keats as legend was to assert but rather confirmed in part his own dissatisfaction with his poetry and turned him toward models he could profit from. Shakespeare (especially as interpreted in the lectures of William Hazlitt) had already begun to teach Keats the value of the poet's self-less impersonality and empathy with his creations; from the other direction, Wordsworth had made him see the possibilities of making high poetry from inner, subjective experience. This dialectic, over the next year or two, would coalesce with influences from Milton, for his Latinate grandeur of tone and the serious universality of his public themes; Dryden, for his lithe, energetic versification; and Dante, for his directness of diction and image and his allegorical sure-footedness.

The growth in Keats's poetic powers was also shaped by two key events in his private life. One was the death, in December 1818, of his younger brother Tom (again, from tuberculosis). In nursing him over the last months of his life, Keats sharpened his awareness of pain and death in the most vivid way possible while also learning to appreciate by contrast the beauty of life, its claims all the more urgent for its perishability. A similar clash of feelings arose from his love for Fanny Brawne, a young woman Keats met some time in 1818 and became engaged to late in 1819. His consuming love for her was dashed with intense anxieties and insecurities about their relationship. The paradoxical feelings generated by these experiences of death and love, blending with other paradoxes that had always obsessed Keats and with his rapidly developed craftsmanship, gave birth to a miraculous year. Between September 1818 and September 1819 Keats produced the Miltonic epic fragment *Hyperion; The Eve of St. Agnes;* the five great odes on Psyche, the nightingale, the Grecian urn, melancholy, and autumn; *Lamia; The Fall of Hyperion* (a more personal reworking of his epic); and such great lyrics as "La Belle Dame Sans Merci" and the sonnet "To Sleep." No poet ever produced a richer variety of great poems in twelve months. Most of these poems appeared in Keats's third volume, *Lamia, Isabella, The Eve of St. Agnes, and Other Poems,* published in 1820.

But that marked the end. Early in 1820 the symptoms of tuberculosis had become unmistakable, and the last year of Keats's life makes an almost unbearable story. Suffering agonies over his approaching death and, with it, his loss of Fanny and the failure, as he thought, of his poetic ambitions, Keats left England in September 1820, on money his friends had raised, and sailed for Italy, where it was hoped the climate would help him. It did not. Nursed by a friend, the young painter Joseph Severn, Keats lingered on for a few months in pain, then died in Rome in February 1821, at the age of twenty-five, and was buried there. The mood of his last days is captured in the epitaph he devised for himself: "Here lies one whose name was writ in water."

Keats's development can be seen in cameo form by comparing the sonnets "On First Looking into Chapman's Homer" (1816), his first really fine poem, and "To Sleep" (1819). Apart from their themes, which illustrate respectively the exuberance of Keats's love of poetry and his heavily freighted recurring symbol of sleep, the two poems reflect opposite strategies. "Chapman's Homer" is the work of a young poet at play, a tour de force that cleverly separates the sustained image of geographical explora-

tion from the exploration of literature it allegorizes. The geographical met-
aphor can stand on its own, and our pleasure in the poem comes partly
from solving a puzzle by matching its details, one by one, with what they
stand for. "To Sleep" typifies the way in which Keats, three years later, had
learned to *interfuse* meaning and metaphor, the hymn to sleep and its image
of death blending inseparably and mysteriously to produce an effect both
morbid and, somehow, sensuously vital.

The Eve of St. Agnes illustrates most of Keats's characteristic themes and
techniques. Its movement is like that of many poems by Keats, which in
time, space, or intensity of emotion penetrate and then withdraw, or rise
and then descend, or move from *now* to *then* back to *now*. Its imagery is
typically Keatsian in exploiting not only the Wordsworthian "mighty world
of eye and ear" but also the earthier senses—smell, taste, touch—that de-
pend on physical contact. Thematically, the gorgeousness of the love story
and of the cozy but fragile shelteredness of the lovers from a world of
danger and death reflects Keats's recurrent concern with "luxury" versus
pain. It also examines, not discursively but in the symbolic and dramatic
manner of Keats at his best, the validity of imaginative experience, asking
in effect whether or not dreams come true, and if so how and with what
result.

This testing of imagination is also the theme of the great odes, which
have been called the "essence"—idea, distillation, and perfume—of Ro-
manticism. They cap the Romantic tradition of "crisis" lyric that includes
Wordsworth's "Tintern Abbey" and "Intimations" ode and Coleridge's
"Dejection." Keats's odes, like the others, are compressed dramas in which
the self confronts the threats to it, from the world and from within. They
image a state of ecstatic bliss and at the same time the perils of achieving or
even aspiring to it. If bliss is by definition free from the threat of change,
under what conditions, if at all, can it exist in a world where change seems
to be the only certainty? On the other hand, can anything really be called
happiness that does *not* change, grow, even die? One way to appreciate
Keats is to compare the abstractions in those last two sentences with the
concreteness of the odes. Keats creates symbols—the nightingale, the urn,
and the others—of almost inexhaustible implications, rendered in words
whose meanings seem to open like doors, revealing an endless series of
other doors. We approach the core of the poems as we approach a limit in
calculus, always getting closer but never quite reaching it. At the same time,
Keats wholly engages our senses as always, often in a peculiarly kinesthetic
way typical of him, balancing motion against frozen stillness so that we feel
an almost literal muscular tension, as if we were the figures on the Grecian
urn.

Like some other poets (and unlike some), Keats had both intelligence
and imagination. Perhaps what makes him unique is his almost unparal-
leled honesty. This was part of his personal character, as we learn from his
matchless letters, many of which rival the poems by combining opalescent
brilliance with rich suggestiveness, but always with an eye to what is really
true, about the world and the author himself. Both the letters and the
poems are full of tensions and contradictions, showing a man willing to
entertain almost all possibilities but finally endorsing no axiom until, in his
own words, it has "been proved on the pulses" of both mind and heart. In

the odes especially, he shows the need both to explore and to verify, so that many readers feel they can profitably retrace his steps in exploring for their own forms of truth. Victorian poets like Tennyson learned a great deal from Keats. His kinship with poets—and many other people—of our century is even stronger, if less obvious, providing a model for their own efforts to affirm life in the teeth of doubt.

FURTHER READING (*prepared by B. W.*): The moving story of Keats's brief life is told in Walter Jackson Bate's superb biography *John Keats*, 1963, which also includes sensitive criticism of the poetry. Sophisticated knowledge about Keats is combined with detailed close readings of key poems in Earl Wasserman's *The Finer Tone*, 1953. David Perkins's *The Quest for Permanence*, 1959, approaches Keats's meaning by way of his symbolism, stressing the tension between flux and permanence. The close readings in Stuart Sperry's *Keats the Poet*, 1973, are both searching and cogently argued. See also Helen Vendler's *The Odes of John Keats*, 1983; and Leon Waldoff's *Keats and the Silent Work of Imagination*, 1985. *Keats: A Collection of Critical Essays*, ed. Walter Jackson Bate, 1964, includes several important essays, including a highly original and somewhat controversial one by Jack Stillinger on *The Eve of St. Agnes* ("The Hoodwinking of Madeline," included also in his book so named, 1971). Stillinger also is the editor of the collection *Twentieth Century Interpretations of Keats's Odes*, 1968. Harold Bloom, in *The Visionary Company*, rev. ed. 1971, is at his brilliant best in his brief readings of key poems by Keats. Bloom has also edited *John Keats*, 1985, a volume of critical essays in the Modern Critical Views series.

ON FIRST LOOKING INTO CHAPMAN'S HOMER[1]

Much have I travell'd in the realms of gold,
 And many goodly states and kingdoms seen;
 Round many western islands have I been
Which bards in fealty to Apollo[2] hold.
Oft of one wide expanse had I been told 5
 That deep-brow'd Homer ruled as his demesne;[3]
 Yet did I never breathe its pure serene[4]
Till I heard Chapman speak out loud and bold:
Then felt I like some watcher of the skies
 When a new planet swims into his ken;[5] 10
Or like stout Cortez when with eagle eyes
 He star'd at the Pacific—and all his men
Look'd at each other with a wild surmise—
 Silent, upon a peak in Darien.[6]

[1] George Chapman (1559?–1634) published his translations of Homer's *Iliad* and *Odyssey* between 1598 and 1616.
[2] *Bards* are poets. *Fealty* is the allegiance of a feudal underlord to his lord. *Apollo* is the god of poetry.
[3] Domain. [4] Clear sky or air.
[5] View. Uranus was discovered by F. W. (later Sir William) Herschel in 1781; the planets out through Saturn had been known to antiquity.
[6] Panama. The Pacific was actually discovered by Balboa (1475–1517), not by Cortez.

THE EVE OF ST. AGNES[1]

I

St. Agnes' Eve—Ah, bitter chill it was!
The owl, for all his feathers, was a-cold;
The hare limped trembling through the frozen grass,
And silent was the flock in woolly fold:
Numb were the beadsman's[2] fingers, while he told[3] 5
His rosary, and while his frosted breath,
Like pious incense from a censer old,
Seemed taking flight for Heaven, without a death,
Past the sweet Virgin's picture, while his prayer he saith.

II

His prayer he saith, this patient, holy man; 10
Then takes his lamp, and riseth from his knees,
And back returneth, meagre, barefoot, wan,
Along the chapel aisle by slow degrees:
The sculptured dead on each side seem to freeze,
Imprisoned in black, purgatorial rails: 15
Knights, ladies, praying in dumb orat'ries,[4]
He passeth by; and his weak spirit fails
To think how they may ache in icy hoods and mails.[5]

III

Northward he turneth through a little door,
And scarce three steps, ere music's golden tongue 20
Flattered to tears this agéd man and poor;
But no—already had his deathbell rung:
The joys of all his life were said and sung:
His was harsh penance on St. Agnes' Eve:
Another way he went, and soon among 25
Rough ashes sat he for his soul's reprieve,
And all night kept awake, for sinners' sake to grieve.

IV

That ancient beadsman heard the prelude soft;
And so it chanced, for many a door was wide,
From hurry to and fro. Soon, up aloft, 30
The silver, snarling trumpets 'gan to chide:[6]
The level chambers, ready with their pride,[7]
Were glowing to receive a thousand guests:

[1] Third-century patron saint of virgins. Her feast day is January 21.
[2] A religious man supported by a family in return for his prayers for them.
[3] Counted. [4] Oratories; side-chapels. [5] Coats of armor. [6] Scold.
[7] Gorgeousness.

 The carvéd angels, ever eager-eyed,
 Stared, where upon their heads the cornice[8] rests, 35
With hair blown back, and wings put crosswise on their breasts.

V

 At length burst in the argent revelry,[9]
 With plume, tiara, and all rich array,
 Numerous as shadows haunting faerily
 The brain, new stuffed in youth, with triumphs gay 40
 Of old romance. These let us wish away,
 And turn, sole-thoughted, to one lady there,
 Whose heart had brooded, all that wintry day,
 On love, and winged St. Agnes' saintly care,
As she had heard old dames full many times declare. 45

VI

 They told her how, upon St. Agnes' Eve,
 Young virgins might have visions of delight,
 And soft adorings from their loves receive
 Upon the honeyed middle of the night,
 If ceremonies due they did aright; 50
 As, supperless to bed they must retire,
 And couch supine their beauties, lily white;
 Nor look behind, nor sideways, but require[10]
Of Heaven with upward eyes for all that they desire.

VII

 Full of this whim was thoughtful Madeline: 55
 The music, yearning like a god in pain,
 She scarcely heard: her maiden eyes divine,
 Fixed on the floor, saw many a sweeping train[11]
 Pass by—she heeded not at all: in vain
 Came many a tiptoe, amorous cavalier, 60
 And back retired; not cooled by high disdain,
 But she saw not: her heart was otherwhere:
She sighed for Agnes' dreams, the sweetest of the year.

VIII

 She danced along with vague, regardless eyes,
 Anxious her lips, her breathing quick and short: 65
 The hallowed hour was near at hand: she sighs
 Amid the timbrels,[12] and the thronged resort
 Of whisperers in anger, or in sport;
 'Mid looks of love, defiance, hate, and scorn,

[8] Horizontal top supported by columns.
[9] Revelers. "Argent" is the term for "silver" in heraldry (the study of coats of arms).
[10] Ask. [11] Of skirts (Keats's explanation). [12] Tambourines.

Hoodwinked with faery fancy; all amort,[13] 70
Save to St. Agnes and her lambs unshorn,[14]
And all the bliss to be before tomorrow morn.

 IX

So, purposing each moment to retire,
She lingered still. Meantime, across the moors,
Had come young Porphyro, with heart on fire 75
For Madeline. Beside the portal doors,
Buttressed[15] from moonlight, stands he, and implores
All saints to give him sight of Madeline
But for one moment in the tedious hours,
That he might gaze and worship all unseen; 80
Perchance speak, kneel, touch, kiss—in sooth[16] such things have been.

 X

He ventures in: let no buzzed whisper tell:
All eyes be muffled, or a hundred swords
Will storm his heart, love's fev'rous citadel:
For him, those chambers held barbarian hordes, 85
Hyena foemen, and hot-blooded lords,
Whose very dogs would execrations[17] howl
Against his lineage: not one breast affords
Him any mercy, in that mansion foul,
Save one old beldame,[18] weak in body and in soul. 90

 XI

Ah, happy chance! the agéd creature came,
Shuffling along with ivory-headed wand,
To where he stood, hid from the torch's flame,
Behind a broad hall-pillar, far beyond
The sound of merriment and chorus bland: 95
He startled her; but soon she knew his face,
And grasped his fingers in her palsied hand,
Saying, "Mercy, Porphyro! hie thee from this place:
They are all here to-night, the whole blood-thirsty race!

 XII

"Get hence! get hence! there's dwarfish Hildebrand; 100
He had a fever late, and in the fit
He curséd thee and thine, both house and land:
Then there's that old Lord Maurice, not a whit
More tame for his gray hairs—Alas me! flit!
Flit like a ghost away."—"Ah, gossip[19] dear, 105

[13] Equivalent of "dead to the world."
[14] At the "Agnus Dei" ("Lamb of God") prayer in the Mass on St. Agnes' feast day, lambs
with virgin wool were presented at the altar. ("Agnes" also derives from "lamb.")
[15] In the shadow of a buttress, a massive stone support for a wall. [16] Truly.
[17] Curses. [18] Old woman. [19] Archaic term for a female crony.

We're safe enough; here in this arm chair sit,
And tell me how"—"Good saints! not here, not here;
Follow me, child, or else these stones will be thy bier."

XIII

He followed through a lowly archéd way,
Brushing the cobwebs with his lofty plume,
And as she muttered "Well-a—well-a-day!" 110
He found him in a little moonlight room,
Pale, latticed, chill, and silent as a tomb.
"Now tell me where is Madeline," said he,
"Oh tell me, Angela, by the holy loom 115
Which none but secret sisterhood²⁰ may see,
When they St. Agnes' wool are weaving piously."

XIV

"St. Agnes! Ah! it is St. Agnes' Eve—
Yet men will murder upon holy days:
Thou must hold water in a witch's sieve,
And be liege-lord of all the elves and fays,²¹ 120
To venture so: it fills me with amaze
To see thee, Porphyro!—St. Agnes' Eve!
God's help! my lady fair the conjuror²² plays
This very night: good angels her deceive! 125
But let me laugh awhile, I've mickle²³ time to grieve."

XV

Feebly she laugheth in the languid moon
While Porphyro upon her face doth look,
Like puzzled urchin on an agéd crone
Who keepeth closed a wond'rous riddle-book,
As spectacled she sits in chimney nook. 130
But soon his eyes grew brilliant, when she told
His lady's purpose; and he scarce could brook²⁴
Tears, at the thought of those enchantments cold,
And Madeline asleep in lap of legends old. 135

XVI

Sudden a thought came like a full-blown²⁵ rose,
Flushing his brow, and in his painéd heart
Made purple riot: then doth he propose
A stratagem, that makes the beldame start:
"A cruel man and impious thou art: 140
Sweet lady, let her pray, and sleep, and dream
Alone with her good angels, far apart
From wicked men like thee. Go, go!—I deem
Thou canst not surely be the same that thou didst seem."

²⁰ See note to line 71. After the ceremony, nuns spun the wool. ²¹ Fairies.
²² Summoner of spirits. ²³ Much. ²⁴ Hold back. ²⁵ Full-blossomed.

XVII

"I will not harm her, by all saints I swear," 145
Quoth Porphyro: "O may I ne'er find grace
When my weak voice shall whisper its last prayer,
If one of her soft ringlets I displace,
Or look with ruffian passion in her face:
Good Angela, believe me by these tears; 150
Or I will, even in a moment's space,
 Awake, with horrid shout, my foemen's ears,
And beard them, though they be more fanged than wolves and bears."

XVIII

"Ah! why wilt thou affright a feeble soul?
A poor, weak, palsy-stricken, churchyard thing, 155
Whose passing-bell[26] may ere the midnight toll;
Whose prayers for thee, each morn and evening,
Were never missed."—Thus plaining,[27] doth she bring
A gentler speech from burning Porphyro;
So woful, and of such deep sorrowing, 160
That Angela gives promise she will do
Whatever he shall wish, betide her weal or woe.[28]

XIX

Which was, to lead him, in close secrecy,
Even to Madeline's chamber, and there hide
Him in a closet,[29] of such privacy 165
That he might see her beauty unespied,
And win perhaps that night a peerless bride,
While legioned faeries paced the coverlet,
And pale enchantment held her sleepy-eyed.
Never on such a night have lovers met, 170
Since Merlin paid his demon all the monstrous debt.[30]

XX

"It shall be as thou wishest," said the Dame:
"All cates[31] and dainties shall be storéd there
Quickly on this feast-night: by the tambour frame[32]
Her own lute thou wilt see: no time to spare, 175
For I am slow and feeble, and scarce dare
On such a catering trust my dizzy head.
Wait here, my child, with patience; kneel in prayer
The while: Ah! thou must needs the lady wed,
Or may I never leave my grave among the dead." 180

[26] Bell tolled for the dead. [27] Complaining.
[28] *betide . . . woe.* Whatever happens to her, good or bad. [29] Small room.
[30] *Merlin . . . debt.* Merlin was a magician in the King Arthur legends. The obscure reference to paying a debt may refer to his dying, on a stormy and magic-filled night.
[31] Delicate foods. [32] Embroidery frame.

XXI

So saying, she hobbled off with busy fear.
The lover's endless minutes slowly passed;
The dame returned, and whispered in his ear
To follow her, with agéd eyes aghast
From fright of dim espial. Safe at last, 185
Through many a dusky gallery, they gain
The maiden's chamber, silken, hushed, and chaste;
Where Porphyro took covert, pleased amain.[33]
His poor guide hurried back with agues[34] in her brain.

XXII

Her faltering hand upon the balustrade, 190
Old Angela was feeling for the stair,
When Madeline, St. Agnes' charméd maid,
Rose, like a missioned spirit, unaware:
With silver taper's[35] light, and pious care,
She turned, and down the agéd gossip led 195
To a safe level matting. Now prepare,
Young Porphyro, for gazing on that bed;
She comes, she comes again, like ring-dove frayed[36] and fled.

XXIII

Out went the taper as she hurried in;
Its little smoke, in pallid moonshine, died: 200
She closed the door, she panted, all akin
To spirits of the air, and visions wide:
No uttered syllable, or, woe betide!
But to her heart, her heart was voluble,[37]
Paining with eloquence her balmy side; 205
As though a tongueless nightingale should swell
Her throat in vain, and die, heart-stifled, in her dell.

XXIV

A casement high and triple-arched there was,
All garlanded with carven imag'ries
Of fruits, and flowers, and bunches of knot-grass, 210
And diamonded with panes of quaint device,
Innumerable of stains and splendid dyes,
As are the tiger-moth's deep-damasked wings;
And in the midst, 'mong thousand heraldries,
And twilight saints, and dim emblazonings,[38] 215
A shielded scutcheon blushed with blood of queens and kings.[39]

[33] Greatly. [34] Fevers; chills. [35] Candle's. [36] Frightened.
[37] Speaking fluently. [38] Ornamentations from heraldry.
[39] *shielded . . . kings.* The description is of a red coat of arms, in the shape of a shield,
showing the family's royal connections.

XXV

Full on this casement shone the wintry moon,
And threw warm gules[40] on Madeline's fair breast,
As down she knelt for heaven's grace and boon;[41]
Rose-bloom fell on her hands, together prest, 220
And on her silver cross soft amethyst,
And on her hair a glory,[42] like a saint:
She seemed a splendid angel, newly drest,
 Save wings, for heaven:—Porphyro grew faint:
She knelt, so pure a thing, so free from mortal taint. 225

XXVI

Anon his heart revives: her vespers[43] done,
Of all its wreathèd pearls her hair she frees;
Unclasps her warmèd jewels one by one;
Loosens her fragrant bodice; by degrees
Her rich attire creeps rustling to her knees: 230
Half-hidden like a mermaid in sea-weed,
Pensive awhile she dreams awake, and sees,
 In fancy, fair St. Agnes in her bed,
But dares not look behind, or all the charm is fled.

XXVII

Soon trembling in her soft and chilly nest, 235
In sort of wakeful swoon, perplexed she lay,
Until the poppied warmth of sleep oppressed
Her soothèd limbs, and soul fatigued away;
Flown, like a thought, until the morrow day;
Blissfully havened both from joy and pain; 240
Clasped like a missal where swart Paynims pray;[44]
 Blinded alike from sunshine and from rain,
As though a rose should shut, and be a bud again.

XXVIII

Stolen to this paradise, and so entranced,
Porphyro gazed upon her empty dress, 245
And listened to her breathing, if it chanced
To wake into a slumberous tenderness;
Which when he heard, that minute did he bless,
And breathed himself: then from the closet crept,
Noiseless as fear in a wide wilderness, 250
 And over the hushed carpet, silent stept,
And 'tween the curtains peeped, where lo!—how fast she slept.

[40] Red (in heraldry). [41] Blessing; favor. [42] Halo. [43] Evening prayers.
[44] *Clasped . . . pray.* Either locked with a clasp or grasped protectively, like a Catholic Mass-book in a land of dark-skinned ("swart") pagans.

XXIX

Then by the bedside, where the faded moon
Made a dim, silver twilight, soft he set
A table, and, half anguished, threw thereon 255
A cloth of woven crimson, gold, and jet:—
O for some drowsy Morphean amulet![45]
The boisterous, midnight, festive clarion,[46]
The kettle-drum, and far-heard clarinet,
Affray[47] his ears, though but in dying tone:— 260
The hall door shuts again, and all the noise is gone.

XXX

And still she slept an azure-lidded sleep,
In blanchéd[48] linen, smooth, and lavendered,
While he from forth the closet brought a heap
Of candied apple, quince, and plum, and gourd; 265
With jellies soother[49] than the creamy curd,
And lucent syrups, tinct[50] with cinnamon;
Manna and dates, in argosy[51] transferred
From Fez; and spicéd dainties, every one,
From silken Samarcand[52] to cedared Lebanon. 270

XXXI

These delicates he heaped with glowing hand
On golden dishes and in baskets bright
Of wreathéd silver: sumptuous they stand
In the retiréd quiet of the night,
Filling the chilly room with perfume light.— 275
"And now, my love, my seraph fair, awake!
Thou art my heaven, and I thine eremite:[53]
Open thine eyes for meek St. Agnes' sake,
Or I shall drowse beside thee, so my soul doth ache."

XXXII

Thus whispering, his warm, unnervéd[54] arm 280
Sank in her pillow. Shaded was her dream
By the dusk curtains:—'twas a midnight charm
Impossible to melt as icéd stream:
The lustrous salvers in the moonlight gleam;
Broad golden fringe upon the carpet lies: 285

[45] Charm inducing sleep (from Morpheus, god of sleep).
[46] Trumpet with a piercing sound. [47] Frighten. [48] Bleached. [49] Smoother.
[50] *lucent.* Translucent. *tinct.* Tinctured; containing a touch of.
[51] *Manna.* Delicious fruit. *argosy.* Trading ship.
[52] *Fez, Samarcand.* Cities in, respectively, Morocco and Persia, the latter noted for its silk.
[53] Religious hermit. [54] Nerveless; inert.

It seemed he never, never could redeem
From such a steadfast spell his lady's eyes;
So mused awhile, entoiled in wooféd phantasies.[55]

XXXIII
Awakening up, he took her hollow lute,—
Tumultuous,—and, in chords that tenderest be, 290
He played an ancient ditty, long since mute,
In Provence called, "La belle dame sans mercy":[56]
Close to her ear touching the melody;—
Wherewith disturbed, she uttered a soft moan:
He ceased—she panted quick—and suddenly 295
Her blue affrayéd eyes wide open shone:
Upon his knees he sank, pale as smooth-sculptured stone.

XXXIV
Her eyes were open, but she still beheld,
Now wide awake, the vision of her sleep:
There was a painful change, that nigh expelled 300
The blisses of her dream so pure and deep;
At which fair Madeline began to weep,
And moan forth witless[57] words with many a sigh;
While still her gaze on Porphyro would keep;
Who knelt, with joinéd hands and piteous eye, 305
Fearing to move or speak, she looked so dreamingly.

XXXV
"Ah, Porphyro!" said she, "but even now
Thy voice was at sweet tremble in mine ear,
Made tuneable with every sweetest vow;
And those sad eyes were spiritual and clear: 310
How changed thou art! how pallid, chill, and drear!
Give me that voice again, my Porphyro,
Those looks immortal, those complainings dear!
Oh leave me not in this eternal woe,
For if thou diest, my love, I know not where to go." 315

XXXVI
Beyond a mortal man impassioned far
At these voluptuous accents, he arose,
Ethereal, flushed, and like a throbbing star
Seen mid the sapphire heaven's deep repose;
Into her dream he melted, as the rose 320
Blendeth its odour with the violet,—

[55] *entoiled . . . phantasies.* Ensnared in woven fantasies.
[56] *"La belle . . . mercy."* "The beautiful lady without pity." Provence was the land of the troubadour poets, in southern France.
[57] Unwitting; unaware or unintentional.

Solution sweet: meantime the frost-wind blows
Like love's alarum[58] pattering the sharp sleet
Against the window-panes; St. Agnes' moon hath set.

XXXVII

'Tis dark: quick pattereth the flaw-blown[59] sleet: 325
"This is no dream, my bride, my Madeline!"
'Tis dark: the icéd gusts still rave and beat:
"No dream, alas! alas! and woe is mine!
Porphyro will leave me here to fade and pine,—
Cruel! what traitor could thee hither bring? 330
I curse not, for my heart is lost in thine,
Though thou forsakest a deceivéd thing;—
A dove forlorn and lost with sick unprunéd[60] wing."

XXXVIII

"My Madeline! sweet dreamer! lovely bride!
Say, may I be for ay thy vassal[61] blest? 335
Thy beauty's shield, heart-shaped and vermeil[62] dyed?
Ah, silver shrine, here will I take my rest
After so many hours of toil and quest,
A famished pilgrim,—saved by miracle.
Though I have found, I will not rob thy nest 340
Saving of thy sweet self; if thou think'st well
To trust, fair Madeline, to no rude infidel.

XXXIX

"Hark! 'tis an elfin-storm from faery land,
Of haggard[63] seeming, but a boon indeed:
Arise—arise! the morning is at hand;— 345
The bloated wassailers[64] will never heed:—
Let us away, my love, with happy speed;
There are no ears to hear, or eyes to see,—
Drowned all in Rhenish and the sleepy mead:[65]
Awake! arise! my love, and fearless be, 350
For o'er the southern moors I have a home for thee."

XL

She hurried at his words, beset with fears,
For there were sleeping dragons all around,
At glaring watch, perhaps, with ready spears—
Down the wide stairs a darkling way they found.— 355
In all the house was heard no human sound.
A chain-drooped lamp was flickering by each door;

[58] Warning. [59] Squall-blown. [60] Unpreened; disheveled. [61] Bondman.
[62] Vermilion. [63] Wild. [64] Drunken carousers.
[65] *Rhenish.* Rhine wine. *mead.* Fermented beverage made from honey.

The arras,[66] rich with horseman, hawk, and hound,
Fluttered in the besieging wind's uproar;
And the long carpets rose along the gusty floor. 360

XLI

They glide, like phantoms, into the wide hall;
Like phantoms, to the iron porch they glide;
Where lay the porter, in uneasy sprawl,
With a huge empty flagon by his side:
The wakeful bloodhound rose, and shook his hide, 365
But his sagacious eye an inmate owns:[67]
By one, and one, the bolts full easy slide:—
The chains lie silent on the footworn stones;—
The key turns, and the door upon its hinges groans.

XLII

And they are gone: aye, ages long ago 370
These lovers fled away into the storm.
That night the Baron dreamt of many a woe,
And all his warrior-guests, with shade and form
Of witch, and demon, and large coffin-worm
Were long be-nightmared. Angela the old 375
Died palsy-twitched, with meagre face deform;
The beadsman, after thousand aves[68] told,
For ay unsought for slept among his ashes cold.

LA BELLE DAME SANS MERCI[1]

I

O what can ail thee, knight-at-arms,
 Alone and palely loitering?
The sedge[2] has withered from the lake,
 And no birds sing.

II

O what can ail thee, knight-at-arms, 5
 So haggard and so woe-begone?
The squirrel's granary is full,
 And the harvest's done.

III

I see a lily on thy brow,
 With anguish moist and fever dew, 10

[66] Tapestry. [67] Acknowledges.
[68] Prayers beginning "Hail, Mary," part of the rosary (line 6).
[1] *La Belle . . . Merci.* Keats got the title, which means "The beautiful lady without pity,"
from a medieval poem by Alain Chartier.
[2] Grasslike plant.

And on thy cheek a fading rose
Fast withereth too.

IV

"I met a lady in the meads,[3]
 Full beautiful—a faery's child,
Her hair was long, her foot was light,
 And her eyes were wild. 15

V

"I made a garland for her head,
 And bracelets too, and fragrant zone;[4]
She looked at me as she did love,
 And made sweet moan. 20

VI

"I set her on my pacing steed,
 And nothing else saw all day long,
For sidelong would she bend and sing
 A faery's song.

VII

"She found me roots of relish sweet, 25
 And honey wild, and manna dew,[5]
And sure in language strange she said
 'I love thee true.'

VIII

"She took me to her elfin grot,[6]
 And there she wept and sighed full sore, 30
And there I shut her wild wild eyes
 With kisses four.

IX

"And there she lullèd me asleep,
 And there I dreamed—Ah! woe betide!
The latest dream I ever dreamt 35
 On the cold hill side.

X

"I saw pale kings and princes too,
 Pale warriors, death-pale were they all;
They cried, 'La Belle Dame sans Merci
 Hath thee in thrall!'[7] 40

[3] Meadows. [4] Belt of flowers. [5] The juice of an exotic fruit. [6] Grotto; cave.
[7] Bondage.

XI

"I saw their starved lips in the gloom[8]
 With horrid warning gapéd wide,
And I awoke, and found me here,
 On the cold hill's side.

XII

"And this is why I sojourn here, 45
 Alone and palely loitering,
Though the sedge is withered from the lake,
 And no birds sing."

TO SLEEP

O soft embalmer of the still midnight,
 Shutting, with careful fingers and benign,
Our gloom-pleas'd eyes, embower'd from the light,
 Enshaded in forgetfulness divine:
O soothest[1] Sleep! if so it please thee, close 5
 In midst of this thine hymn my willing eyes,
Or wait the "Amen," ere thy poppy throws
 Around my bed its lulling charities.
Then save me, or the passéd day will shine
Upon my pillow, breeding many woes,— 10
 Save me from curious[2] conscience, that still lords[3]
Its strength for darkness, burrowing like a mole;
 Turn the key deftly in the oiléd wards,[4]
And seal the hushéd casket[5] of my soul.

ODE TO PSYCHE[1]

O Goddess! hear these tuneless numbers, wrung
 By sweet enforcement and remembrance dear,
And pardon that thy secrets should be sung
 Even into thine own soft-conchéd[2] ear:
Surely I dreamt to-day, or did I see 5

[8]Twilight. [1]Most soothing.
[2]Besides its ordinary meaning, this may have the Latinate sense of scrupulously careful, painstaking. "Conscience" may include its older meaning of consciousness.
[3]Proudly assembles. Some editions have "hoards" instead of "lords."
[4]Ridges inside a lock.
[5]Small box for precious objects. (The meaning "coffin" is an Americanism.)
[1]Goddess of the mind, or soul, described by Keats as a latecomer among the classical deities and therefore never properly worshiped by the ancients. Cupid, or Eros, god of love, fell in love with her.
[2]Like a conch shell, which is spiral-shaped.

The wingéd Psyche with awaken'd eyes?
I wander'd in a forest thoughtlessly,
 And, on the sudden, fainting with surprise,
Saw two fair creatures, couchéd side by side
 In deepest grass, beneath the whisp'ring roof 10
 Of leaves and trembled blossoms, where there ran
 A brooklet, scarce espied:
'Mid hush'd, cool-rooted flowers, fragrant-eyed,
 Blue, silver-white, and budded Tyrian,[3]
They lay calm-breathing on the bedded grass; 15
 Their arms embracéd, and their pinions[4] too;
 Their lips touch'd not, but had not bade adieu,
As if disjoinéd by soft-handed slumber,
And ready still past kisses to outnumber
 At tender eye-dawn of aurorean[5] love: 20
 The wingéd boy[6] I knew;
 But who wast thou, O happy, happy dove?
 His Psyche true!

O latest born and loveliest vision far
 Of all Olympus'[7] faded hierarchy! 25
Fairer than Phoebe's sapphire-region'd star,[8]
 Or Vesper,[9] amorous glow-worm of the sky;
Fairer than these, though temple thou hast none,
 Nor altar heap'd with flowers;
Nor virgin-choir to make delicious moan 30
 Upon the midnight hours;
No voice, no lute, no pipe, no incense sweet
 From chain-swung censer teeming;
No shrine, no grove, no oracle,[10] no heat
 Of pale-mouth'd prophet dreaming. 35

O brightest! though too late for antique vows,
 Too, too late for the fond believing lyre,[11]
When holy were the haunted forest boughs,
 Holy the air, the water, and the fire;
Yet even in these days so far retir'd 40
 From happy pieties, thy lucent fans,[12]
 Fluttering among the faint Olympians,
I see, and sing, by my own eyes inspir'd.
So let me be thy choir, and make a moan
 Upon the midnight hours; 45
Thy voice, thy lute, thy pipe, thy incense sweet

[3] Purple (from the dye made in ancient Tyre). [4] Wings.
[5] Awakening (from Aurora, goddess of the dawn). [6] Cupid.
[7] Mountain-home of the classical gods.
[8] *Phoebe's . . . star.* The moon, of which Phoebe (Artemis, Diana) was the virgin goddess.
[9] The evening star; Venus (Aphrodite).
[10] Priest who is the earthly spokesman of the goddess.
[11] Harp (of worshipers and of poets). [12] Luminous wings.

From swingéd censer teeming;
Thy shrine, thy grove, thy oracle, thy heat
 Of pale-mouth'd prophet dreaming.

Yes, I will be thy priest, and build a fane[13] 50
 In some untrodden region of my mind,
Where branchéd thoughts, new grown with pleasant pain,
 Instead of pines shall murmur in the wind:
Far, far around shall those dark-cluster'd trees
 Fledge[14] the wild-ridgéd mountains steep by steep; 55
And there by zephyrs,[15] streams, and birds, and bees,
 The moss-lain Dryads[16] shall be lull'd to sleep;
And in the midst of this wide quietness
A rosy sanctuary will I dress
With the wreath'd trellis of a working brain, 60
 With buds, and bells, and stars without a name,
With all the gardener Fancy e'er could feign,
 Who breeding flowers, will never breed the same:
And there shall be for thee all soft delight
 That shadowy thought can win, 65
A bright torch, and a casement ope at night,
 To let the warm Love[17] in!

ODE TO A NIGHTINGALE

I

My heart aches, and a drowsy numbness pains
 My sense, as though of hemlock[1] I had drunk,
Or emptied some dull opiate to the drains
 One minute past, and Lethe-wards[2] had sunk:
'Tis not through envy of thy happy lot, 5
 But being too happy in thine happiness,—
 That thou, light-wingéd Dryad[3] of the trees,
 In some melodious plot
Of beechen green, and shadows numberless,
 Singest of summer in full-throated ease. 10

II

O, for a draught of vintage! that hath been
 Cool'd a long age in the deep-delvéd earth,
Tasting of Flora[4] and the country green,
 Dance, and Provençal[5] song, and sunburnt mirth!
O for a beaker full of the warm South, 15

[13] Temple. [14] Fringe. [15] Soft breezes. [16] Tree-nymphs. [17] Cupid.
[1] A poison; usable also as a sedative.
[2] Toward Lethe, in ancient myth the river of forgetfulness in the underworld.
[3] Tree-nymph. [4] Roman goddess of flowers. [5] Of Provence, in southern France.

Full of the true, the blushful Hippocrene,[6]
 With beaded bubbles winking at the brim,
 And purple-stainéd mouth;
That I might drink, and leave the world unseen,
 And with thee fade away into the forest dim: 20

III

Fade far away, dissolve, and quite forget
 What thou among the leaves hast never known,
The weariness, the fever, and the fret
 Here, where men sit and hear each other groan;
 Where palsy shakes a few, sad, last gray hairs, 25
 Where youth grows pale, and spectre-thin, and dies;[7]
 Where but to think is to be full of sorrow
 And leaden-eyed despairs,
 Where Beauty cannot keep her lustrous eyes,
 Or new Love pine at them beyond to-morrow. 30

IV

Away! away! for I will fly to thee,
 Not charioted by Bacchus and his pards,[8]
But on the viewless[9] wings of Poesy,
 Though the dull brain perplexes and retards:
Already with thee! tender is the night, 35
 And haply[10] the Queen-Moon is on her throne,
 Cluster'd around by all her starry Fays;[11]
 But here there is no light,
 Save what from heaven is with the breezes blown
 Through verdurous glooms and winding mossy ways. 40

V

I cannot see what flowers are at my feet,
 Nor what soft incense hangs upon the boughs,
But, in embalméd darkness, guess each sweet
 Wherewith the seasonable month endows
The grass, the thicket, and the fruit-tree wild; 45
 White hawthorn, and the pastoral eglantine;
 Fast fading violets cover'd up in leaves;
 And mid-May's eldest child,
 The coming musk-rose, full of dewy wine,
 The murmurous haunt of flies on summer eves. 50

VI

Darkling[12] I listen; and, for many a time
 I have been half in love with easeful Death,

[6] In Greek myth, the fountain of poetic inspiration.
[7] *youth . . . dies.* Keats's brother Tom had died in December, 1818, about five months before this poem was written.
[8] *Bacchus . . . pards.* The god of wine and the leopards who drew his chariot.
[9] Invisible; also, unseeing. [10] Perhaps. [11] Fairies. [12] In the dark.

Call'd him soft names in many a muséd rhyme,
 To take into the air my quiet breath;
Now more than ever seems it rich to die, 55
 To cease upon the midnight with no pain,
 While thou art pouring forth thy soul abroad
 In such an ecstasy!
 Still wouldst thou sing, and I have ears in vain—
 To thy high requiem[13] become a sod. 60

VII

Thou wast not born for death, immortal Bird!
 No hungry generations tread thee down;
The voice I hear this passing night was heard
 In ancient days by emperor and clown:[14]
Perhaps the self-same song that found a path 65
 Through the sad heart of Ruth,[15] when, sick for home,
 She stood in tears amid the alien corn;
 The same that oft-times hath
 Charm'd magic casements, opening on the foam
 Of perilous seas, in faery lands forlorn. 70

VIII

Forlorn! the very word is like a bell
 To toll me back from thee to my sole self!
Adieu! the fancy cannot cheat so well
 As she is fam'd to do, deceiving elf.
Adieu! adieu! thy plaintive anthem fades 75
 Past the near meadows, over the still stream,
 Up the hill-side; and now 'tis buried deep
 In the next valley-glades:
 Was it a vision, or a waking dream?
 Fled is that music:—Do I wake or sleep? 80

ODE ON A GRECIAN URN

I

Thou still unravish'd[1] bride of quietness,
 Thou foster-child of silence and slow time,
Sylvan[2] historian, who canst thus express
 A flowery tale more sweetly than our rhyme:
What leaf-fring'd legend haunts about thy shape 5
 Of deities or mortals, or of both,

[13] A high requiem (Mass for the dead) is one with music. [14] Peasant.
[15] In the Old Testament book of Ruth, chapter 2, Ruth works in the fields while exiled from her homeland. "Corn" means "barley," not what Americans call corn.
[1] Virginal. [2] Of forests.

In Tempe or the dales of Arcady?[3]
What men or gods are these? What maidens loth?[4]
What mad pursuit? What struggle to escape?
What pipes and timbrels?[5] What wild ecstasy? 10

II

Heard melodies are sweet, but those unheard
Are sweeter; therefore, ye soft pipes, play on;
Not to the sensual[6] ear, but, more endear'd,
Pipe to the spirit ditties of no tone:
Fair youth, beneath the trees, thou canst not leave 15
Thy song, nor ever can those trees be bare;
Bold lover, never, never canst thou kiss,
Though winning near the goal—yet, do not grieve;
She cannot fade, though thou hast not thy bliss,
For ever wilt thou love, and she be fair! 20

III

Ah, happy, happy boughs! that cannot shed
Your leaves, nor ever bid the spring adieu;
And, happy melodist, unwearied,
For ever piping songs for ever new:
More happy love! more happy, happy love! 25
For ever warm and still to be enjoy'd,
For ever panting, and for ever young;
All breathing human passion far above,[7]
That leaves a heart high-sorrowful and cloy'd,
A burning forehead, and a parching tongue. 30

IV

Who are these coming to the sacrifice?
To what green altar, O mysterious priest,
Lead'st thou that heifer lowing at the skies,
And all her silken flanks with garlands drest?
What little town by river or sea shore, 35
Or mountain-built with peaceful citadel,
Is emptied of this folk, this pious morn?
And, little town, thy streets for evermore
Will silent be; and not a soul to tell
Why thou art desolate, can e'er return. 40

V

O Attic shape! Fair attitude! with brede[8]
Of marble men and maidens overwrought,[9]

[3] *Tempe, Arcady.* Sites associated with ancient Greek pastoral. Tempe (a valley) was also sacred to Apollo, god of poetry.
[4] Reluctant. [5] Tambourines. [6] Sensory.
[7] *All . . . above.* Normal word order would be "Far above all breathing human passion."
[8] *Attic.* Greek. *attitude.* Pose (as of an artist's model). *brede.* Embroidery.
[9] Covered with (artistic) work.

With forest branches and the trodden weed;
 Thou, silent form, dost tease us out of thought
As doth eternity: Cold pastoral! 45
 When old age shall this generation waste,
 Thou shalt remain, in midst of other woe
 Than ours, a friend to man, to whom thou say'st,
 "Beauty is truth, truth beauty,"—that is all
 Ye know on earth, and all ye need to know.[10] 50

ODE ON MELANCHOLY

I

No, no, go not to Lethe, neither twist
 Wolf's bane, tight-rooted, for its poisonous wine;
Nor suffer thy pale forehead to be kiss'd
 By nightshade, ruby grape of Proserpine;
Make not your rosary of yew-berries, 5
 Nor let the beetle, nor the death-moth be
 Your mournful Psyche, nor the downy owl[1]
A partner in your sorrow's mysteries;[2]
 For shade to shade will come too drowsily,
 And drown the wakeful anguish of the soul. 10

II

But when the melancholy fit shall fall
 Sudden from heaven like a weeping cloud,
That fosters the droop-headed flowers all,
 And hides the green hill in an April shroud;
Then glut thy sorrow on a morning rose, 15
 Or on the rainbow of the salt sand-wave,[3]
 Or on the wealth of globéd peonies;
Or if thy mistress some rich anger shows,
 Emprison her soft hand, and let her rave,
 And feed deep, deep upon her peerless eyes. 20

[10]*Beauty . . . know.* Possibly the two lines in English poetry most discussed and debated, on the scores of meaning, appropriateness to the poem, and punctuation. Punctuated as here, there is more than one possible answer to the question who is addressing whom, and the possibilities are multiplied if, like many critics and editors, one puts the entire last two lines in quotation marks.
[1]*lines 1-7.* Keats piles up images of gloom and oblivion. Lethe is the river of forgetfulness in the mythological underworld; wolfsbane is a poisonous plant; nightshade is another, with red berries here associated with Proserpine, the queen of the dead; yew-berries are also poisonous; the "beetle" is the Egyptian scarab, buried with the dead; the death moth has markings resembling a skull (and contrasts with the butterfly that often symbolizes Psyche, the living soul); the owl is a nocturnal bird.
[2]Secret rituals of a pagan religious cult.
[3]*rainbow . . . wave.* Rainbow effects seen in the moisture on beaches.

III

She dwells with Beauty—Beauty that must die;
And Joy, whose hand is ever at his lips
Bidding adieu; and aching Pleasure nigh,
Turning to poison while the bee-mouth sips:
Ay, in the very temple of delight 25
Veil'd Melancholy has her sovran[4] shrine,
Though seen of none save him whose strenuous tongue
Can burst Joy's grape against his palate fine;
His soul shall taste the sadness of her might,
And be among her cloudy trophies hung.[5] 30

TO AUTUMN

I

Season of mists and mellow fruitfulness,
Close bosom-friend of the maturing sun;
Conspiring with him how to load and bless
With fruit the vines that round the thatch-eves[1] run;
To bend with apples the moss'd cottage-trees, 5
And fill all fruit with ripeness to the core;
To swell the gourd, and plump the hazel shells
With a sweet kernel; to set budding more,
And still more, later flowers for the bees,
Until they think warm days will never cease, 10
For Summer has o'er-brimm'd their clammy cells.

II

Who hath not seen thee oft amid thy store?[2]
Sometimes whoever seeks abroad[3] may find
Thee sitting careless on a granary floor,
Thy hair soft-lifted by the winnowing[4] wind; 15
Or on a half-reap'd furrow sound asleep,
Drows'd with the fume of poppies, while thy hook
Spares the next swath[5] and all its twinéd flowers:
And sometimes like a gleaner[6] thou dost keep
Steady thy laden head across a brook; 20
Or by a cyder-press, with patient look,
Thou watchest the last oozings hours by hours.

[4] *sovran.* Supreme. (Apollo, for example, had many lesser temples, but his "sovran" one was at Delphi.)
[5] *among . . . hung.* Trophies, or spoils, of victory were often hung on the walls of ancient temples and thus dedicated to their deities.
[1] Eaves of thatched roofs. [2] Abundance. [3] Outdoors.
[4] Separating grain from chaff by air currents. [5] Amount of crop cut by one stroke.
[6] One who gathers grain the reapers missed.

III
Where are the songs of Spring? Ay, where are they?
 Think not of them, thou hast thy music too,—
While barréd clouds bloom the soft-dying day, 25
 And touch the stubble-plains with rosy hue;
Then in a wailful choir the small gnats mourn
 Among the river sallows,[7] borne aloft
 Or sinking as the light wind lives or dies;
And full-grown lambs loud bleat from hilly bourn;[8] 30
 Hedge-crickets sing; and now with treble soft
 The red-breast whistles from a garden-croft;[9]
 And gathering swallows twitter in the skies.

Alexander Pushkin
(1799–1837)

Alexander Pushkin occupies a place in Russian literature roughly compara-
ble to those of Dante in Italian, Shakespeare in English, and Goethe in
German literature, in that his works are celebrated not only for their own
excellence but also as groundbreaking explorations of the literary possibili-
ties of their language and culture. Pushkin's efforts to forge a literary lan-
guage from Russian, his probings into Russian themes and subjects, and his
naturalization of formal models from other literatures laid down the terms,
in a sense, along which modern Russian literature would develop. For Rus-
sia, he was, in Maxim Gorky's words, "the beginning of beginnings."
 Pushkin was born in Moscow in 1799. He always prided himself on his
aristocratic antecedents—he could trace, he said, his family back six hun-
dred years—but by the time he was born his family had lost most of its
fortune and lived in comparatively straitened circumstances. His father,
Sergey Pushkin, was a minor writer who had a good library of French
classics and regularly played host to the most prominent writers of the day.
His mother was part black; she was the granddaughter of Abram Hannibal,
an Abyssinian slave whom Peter the Great bought in Constantinople and
who later rose to prominence in Peter's court. (Pushkin commemorated
this great-grandfather in his unfinished historical novel *The Negro of Peter
the Great* [1837]). Pushkin's parents were, like most early nineteenth-
century Russian aristocrats, thoroughly oriented toward French culture,
and Alexander and his brother and sister spoke and read French from
childhood. The family was not close, however, and Alexander was left for
long periods of time in the care of his maternal grandmother and his
nurse, both of whom told him stories in Russian, sources at least in spirit of
many of his most famous works. The tension between an adopted French

[7] Willow trees. [8] Boundary between fields. [9] Small plot.

culture and an indigenous Russian one, which was to run throughout Push-
kin's artistic life, thus perhaps had its origins in his childhood.

When he was twelve, Pushkin entered the Imperial Lyceum at
Tsarskoye Selo, a school designed to provide an education for boys des-
tined for government service. Three years later, at the age of fifteen, he
published his first work, a verse epistle called "To My Friend, the Poet,"
and by the time he left school, when he was eighteen, he already had some-
thing of a reputation among the leading writers and critics of the day.

After graduation, Pushkin accepted a post in the foreign office in St.
Petersburg, although by this time he was personally committed to a literary
career. St. Petersburg at this time was a hotbed of clandestine liberal agita-
tion, especially among young aristocrats. This agitation was to culminate in
the ill-fated Decembrist Revolt of 1825. Pushkin, through a series of
poems, unpublishable but circulated in manuscript, quickly became known
as the literary spokesman for the liberals. In 1820, after the especially out-
spoken "Ode to Freedom" came to the attention of the authorities, it was
arranged that Pushkin be transferred out of the capital to a remote south-
ern province and placed under the close supervision of the military com-
mander there. Thus began a program of surveillance and control under
which Pushkin was to chafe for the rest of his life, which profoundly af-
fected his work as well as his personal life, and which was to lead indirectly
to his early death.

Pushkin's banishment from St. Petersburg coincided with the comple-
tion of his first major work, *Ruslan and Lyudmila* (1820). This fanciful tale of
the pursuit by Ruslan, with three companions, of his bride Lyudmila, spir-
ited away on their wedding day by an evil magician, is in the comic epic
tradition of Pope's *Rape of the Lock* and Voltaire's *La Pucelle*. But its materi-
als are drawn from Russian fairy tales, treated with an urbane irony. This
mediation between Western literary traditions and Russian ones was to be
repeated, in a variety of ways, throughout Pushkin's career.

Pushkin's exile lasted for six years, first in Kishinyov (1820–23), then in
Odessa (1823–24), and finally, after dismissal from the foreign service, on
his mother's estate of Mikhaylovskoye (1824–26). Pushkin spent the first
four years of this exile living the violent, hard-drinking, amorous life of a
young aristocrat; he fought several duels and was dismissed from the ser-
vice not only for an indiscreet letter to a friend in which he said he was
taking "lessons in pure atheism" but, less directly, for passionately and
openly courting the wife of his superior officer in Odessa. He also contin-
ued to write fluently and brilliantly. While traveling in the Caucasus in
1821, he read Byron for the first time and under his spell wrote his "south-
ern cycle" of Byronic narrative poems: *The Prisoner of the Caucasus* (1822),
The Robber Brothers (1821–22), and *The Fountain of Bakchisaray* (1821–23).
When these poems were published, they catapulted Pushkin into the posi-
tion of the most famous poet in Russia and the acknowledged spokesman
of the romantic, freedom-loving generation of the 1820s.

During this period, too, Pushkin began work on his masterpiece, a
"novel in verse" named *Evgeny Onegin* which was to occupy him for eight
years, finally appearing in 1833. *Evgeny Onegin* was an ambitious attempt to
expand the Romantic Byronic verse narrative (one of its models was By-
ron's *Don Juan*) to encompass the realistic, panoramic qualities of the social

novel. The story is set in contemporary Russia, moving from St. Petersburg to a provincial estate, Moscow, and St. Petersburg again. Onegin himself is presented not as an idealized Byronic hero but as a realistic portrait of a contemporary Russian, shaped by the forces of Russian life.

The other masterpiece of the years of banishment was the verse tragedy *Boris Gudunov*, written at Mikhaylovskoye in 1824–25. Boris Gudunov was a nobleman who briefly became Czar in 1598 during the chaos that followed the death of Fyodor, son of Ivan the Terrible and the last of the Ryurik dynasty. Boris ruled for only seven years, dying in 1605 on the threshold of defeat by a rival who claimed to be the true heir Dimitry (whom Boris had murdered). *Boris Gudunov* is Pushkin's attempt to claim Shakespeare as a significant model for the development of Russian drama. "I am firmly convinced," he wrote, "that the *popular* rules of Shakespearean drama are better suited to our theater than the courtly customs of Racine's tragedy." Here he is alluding to the pervasive influence of French neoclassic models upon the Russian theater. *Boris Gudunov* follows Shakespeare's open, fluid construction with its twenty-three scenes, his verse form with its unrhymed iambic pentameters, and his freedom from the French "unities" with its loose treatment of time and place. A permanent classic of the Russian theater, it exercised a major influence over the course of later Russian drama.

Czar Alexander I died in 1825, and Pushkin seized the opportunity to appeal to the new Czar Nicholas I for release from his exile. This was granted, and Pushkin left Mikhaylovskoye for Moscow. There he had an interview with the new Czar in which he complained about the censorship to which he was subjected, whereupon Nicholas told him to submit his work directly to the Czar, claiming, "I will be your censor." In practice, however, Nicholas delegated his censorship to the chief of his security police, Count Benkendorf, with whom Pushkin remained in constant conflict.

Despite these constraints, however, the decade following Pushkin's return from exile saw the full flowering of his genius. A remarkable three months in the autumn of 1830 produced the four "little tragedies," experiments in highly compressed psychological dramas: *The Covetous Knight, Mozart and Salieri, The Stone Guest,* and *The Feast During the Plague;* the five brilliant short stories that make up *Tales of the Late I. P. Belkin;* and the comic poem of lower-class life *A Small House in Kolomna,* as well as a number of lyric poems, essays, and other material. The year 1831 saw the completion of *Evgeny Onegin* (published 1833). The narrative poem *The Bronze Horseman,* generally regarded as second only to *Evgeny Onegin* among Pushkin's works, was written in 1833, "The Queen of Spades" in 1834, and the important historical novel *The Captain's Daughter* between 1833 and 1836.

In 1831, Pushkin married Natalia Nikolaevna Goncharova, a young and impoverished but strikingly beautiful and socially ambitious woman. Pushkin seems to have hoped that his marriage would bring stability to his rather disordered life, and in some respects it did; the marriage produced four children. But the expense of Natalia Nikolaevna's society life put a considerable strain on Pushkin, as did the attentions of other men to his wife, which were not always rejected. Even the Czar was attracted, and in 1833 he humiliatingly appointed the distinguished poet to the post of *Kam-*

merjunker (gentleman of the bedchamber), a post generally given to young aristocratic nonentities and obviously designed to keep Pushkin and his beautiful wife in close attendance on the court. It was not the Czar, however, who was to be Pushkin's nemesis but a young man named George d'Anthès, the adopted son of the ambassador to Russia from the Netherlands. D'Anthès met Natalia Nikolaevna in 1834 and quickly embarked on a scandalously open affair with her. By 1836, Pushkin's position was very difficult; he was deeply in debt, his wife's affair with d'Anthès made him a figure of ridicule, and he himself was involved in an embarrassing affair with Natalia Nikolaevna's sister. In January of 1837, Pushkin wrote a deliberately insulting letter to d'Anthès' adoptive father, and the following day d'Anthès challenged him to a duel. The meeting took place on January 27 on the outskirts of Petersburg; Pushkin was mortally wounded and died two days later at the age of thirty-seven.

It is as a poet, and especially as the poet of *Evgeny Onegin* and *The Bronze Horseman,* that Pushkin reigns supreme. His stature must therefore be taken partially on faith by readers who do not know Russian (though Vladimir Nabokov's brilliant, if controversial, translation of *Evgeny Onegin* [1964] has done much to make his poetic masterpiece accessible to English speakers). But Pushkin's contributions to Russian prose fiction, though overshadowed by his poetry, were considerable. Pushkin's ideals of prose style, like his poetic goals, were well thought out and consciously directed toward the reform of Russian literature. Russian prose, he believed, was undisciplined and weakened by a tendency toward a Romantic excess. "Precision, tidiness: these are the prime matters of prose," he wrote. "It demands thought and more thought; brilliant expressions are of no use."

These qualities are apparent, even in translation, in the brilliant short story "The Queen of Spades." "Tidiness" and "precision" characterize not only the prose style but the narrative structure as well. The world of the story—the world of impoverished young aristocrats on the fringes of the court and "on the make"—is swiftly and economically evoked by the first sentence: "Card-playing was going on in the quarters of Narumov, an officer in the Horse Guards." But the surface simplicity of the style and structure of the story conceals great depths of suggestiveness. Superficially, the story is a "society tale," a titillating tale of high life of the sort popular in Russia when it was written. But Pushkin deepens and enriches the stereotype. The central character, Hermann, is at first glance a Byronic cliché: "a most romantic individual" with "the profile of a Napoleon and the soul of a Mephistopheles." But this romantic persona is largely a construct of Lisaveta, helped along by Tomsky. Tomsky's description "coincided with the image she had herself formed, and this type which the latest novels have made a commonplace at once alarmed and captivated her imagination." Hermann is both more ordinary and more interesting than Lisaveta's image; he fascinated Dostoevsky, who used him as the model for both Aleksei Ivanovich in *The Gambler* (1866) and Raskolnikov in *Crime and Punishment* (1866). The minor characters are equally interesting, especially the antithetical sepulchral old Countess and the vital, if oppressed, Lisaveta—powerful embodiments of the dualities of ethical values, existential realities, and historical forces that play upon the ambitious Hermann.

"The Queen of Spades" created a sensation when it was first published in 1834 in St. Petersburg. There were a number of stage adaptations of it, culminating in Tchaikovsky's operatic version (1890). Its influence even reached the gambling tables, where, as Pushkin recorded in his diary, the favorite bet for a time was the three, the seven, and the ace. (Pushkin, it is only fair to report, did not note how often this combination won!)

FURTHER READING *(prepared by J. H.):* Reliable critical biographies of Pushkin in English include those by Ernest J. Simmons, 1937; Henri Troyat, 1936, English translation 1950; and David Magarshack, 1967. Edmund Wilson's classic essay "In Honor of Pushkin," in *The Triple Thinkers*, 1952, gives English-speakers a good sense of Pushkin, though Wilson deals only with *Evgeny Onegin* and *The Bronze Horseman*, not with "The Queen of Spades." William M. Todd's entry on Pushkin in *Handbook of Russian Literature*, ed. Victor Terras, 1985, is also an excellent starting point for the critical study of Pushkin. Walter N. Vickery's *Alexander Pushkin*, 1970, offers a brief biography and balanced introductory accounts of Pushkin's major works. Pushkin's own criticism is collected in *Pushkin on Literature*, trans. and ed. by Tatiana Wolff, rev. ed. 1986. John Bayley's *Pushkin: A Comparative Commentary*, 1971, includes fine readings of the individual works, including "The Queen of Spades." By far the most detailed critical account in English of "The Queen of Spades" is Paul Debreczeny's chapter in *The Other Pushkin: A Study of Alexander Pushkin's Prose Fiction*, 1983, which also has the advantage of providing summaries of the major criticism in Russian. *Alexander Pushkin*, ed. Harold Bloom, 1987, in the Modern Critical Interpretations series, can also be recommended.

THE QUEEN OF SPADES

Translated by Ivy and Tatiana Litvinov

The Queen of Spades stands for secret enmity.

Latest Fortunetelling Book

I

> *On a cold winter day*
> *They would gather and play,*
> *Smoking,*
>
> *And many a stake*
> *Those youngsters would make,*
> *Joking.*
>
> *Of the stakes that they won*
> *They chalked up every one*
> *Paying,*
>
> *And so, many a day*
> *They would squander away,*
> *Playing.*[1]

[1] This is Pushkin's own poem, written five years before the story.

Card-playing was going on in the quarters of Narumov, an officer in the Horse Guards. The long winter night passed imperceptible; it was five in the morning when they sat down to supper. Those who had won, plied their forks eagerly; the rest sat in front of their empty plates with an air of abstraction. But champagne was set on the table, the talk became lively, and all took part in it.

"How did you get on, Surin?" asked the host.

"Lost as usual. It must be admitted that I am unlucky. I play for low stakes, I never get excited, always keep my head, and yet I lose all the time."

"And are you never tempted? Don't you ever long to raise the stakes on a card? Your firmness amazes me."

"Look at Hermann!" said one of the guests, pointing to a young officer from an engineer regiment. "Never picked up a card in his whole life, never doubled a stake, and sits beside us till five o'clock, watching us play!"

"I take a great interest in cards," said Hermann, "but I am not in a position to sacrifice what is necessary in the hope of gaining what is superfluous."

"Hermann's a Teuton, and therefore cautious—that's all!" remarked Tomsky. "Now, my grandmother, Countess Anna Fedotovna—she's an enigma, if there ever was one."

"What? What's that?" cried the guests.

"I can't understand," continued Tomsky, "how it is that my grandmother never gambles."

"What is there remarkable about an eighty-year-old woman not wanting to gamble?" said Narumov.

"D'you mean to say you don't know anything about her?"

"Nothing whatsoever. Upon my word!"

"Then let me tell you.

"You must know that my grandmother, sixty years ago, visited Paris and was all the fashion there. People followed her about to have a look at *la Vénus moscovite;*[2] Richelieu[3] paid her court, and my grandmother vows that her cruelty almost drove him to suicide.

"In those days ladies used to play faro.[4] One day, while playing cards at court, she incurred a debt of honor for a great sum of money to the Duc d'Orléans. When she got home, my grandmother, while removing the patches from her face, and undoing her panniers,[5] recounted her losses to my grandfather, and ordered him to pay up.

[2] "The Venus from Moscow."

[3] Not the famous seventeenth-century Cardinal Richelieu, but his great-nephew, Armand de la Porte, duc de Richelieu (1696–1788). He was prominent in the courts of Louis XIV, the Regent, and Louis XV.

[4] Faro was a gambling game imported into Russia from the French court. A player took a card from his deck and placed it face down on the table. The dealer, or "banker," then dealt cards from his deck placing them alternately on his right and left. If the player's card matched in rank the card on the banker's left, the player won whatever sum he had placed on the card. If his card matched that on the banker's right, the banker won.

[5] The "patches" are beauty patches: small bits of cloth attached to the face with adhesive to show off the complexion by contrast, fashionable in the eighteenth century. "Panniers" are puffed draperies or covered, basket-like frames used to distend a woman's skirts at the hips, another eighteenth-century fashion.

"My late grandfather, as far as I can remember, was a kind of steward to my grandmother. He feared her like the plague; but when he heard of such appalling losses he flew into a rage, took up the abacus and proved to her that they had spent half a million during the last six months, that they had no Moscow or Saratov estates in the neighborhood of Paris, and flatly refused to pay. My grandmother gave him a box on the ear, and banished him from her bedroom, as a token of her disfavor.

"The next day she sent for her husband, hoping that the domestic chastisement would have had its effect on him, but she found him adamant. For the first time in their married life she condescended to argument and explanations. She tried to shame him by pointing out condescendingly that there were debts and debts, and that there was a difference between a prince and a coachmaker. Useless! My grandfather rebelled. He said no, and that his 'no' was final. My grandmother was at her wits' end.

"Among her intimates was a very remarkable individual. You have heard of Comte Saint-Germain, of whom such extraordinary tales are told. You know he gave himself out to be the Eternal Jew,[6] the discoverer of the elixir of life and the philosopher's stone, and so on. People laughed at him as a charlatan, and Casanova[7] wrote in his memoirs that he was a spy; despite his mysterious reputation, however, Germain had a most respectable appearance and knew how to make himself agreeable in society. My grandmother loves him to distraction to this day, and will not allow him to be spoken of disrespectfully. She knew Germain had a great amount of money at his disposal, and, deciding to have recourse to his aid, sent him a note asking him to come to her at once.

"The old eccentric responded to her summons immediately and found my grandmother overcome with grief. She painted in the darkest colors her husband's cruelty, and ended by declaring that her only hope was in Germain's friendship and chivalry.

"Germain pondered. 'I could let you have this sum,' he said, 'but I know you would never have any peace until you had paid me back, and I should not like to cause you fresh cares. There is another means—you can win it back.'

"'But my dear Count,' replied my grandmother, 'I tell you we have no money at all.' 'You will not need money,' said the Count. 'Be so kind as to hear me out.' And he told her a secret which any one of us would pay dear to know . . . "

The youthful gamblers redoubled their attention. Tomsky lit his pipe, inhaled the smoke, and continued:

"That same night my grandmother appeared at Versailles, *au jeu de la Reine*.[8] The Duc d'Orléans dealt. My grandmother gave some slight apology for not having brought the money for her debt, inventing a little story in her justification, and began playing against him. She selected three

[6] The Wandering Jew; according to medieval legend, a Jew who mocked Christ on the way to the Cross and was condemned to wander the earth until the Last Judgment.

[7] Giovanni Giacomo Casanova de Seingalt, a famous eighteenth-century Venetian adventurer, whose famous *Memoirs* (1826–38) emphasized his amorous exploits. He was the model for the Comte Saint–Germain.

[8] "At the Queen's card party."

cards, which she played one after another—all three proved to be winning cards, and my grandmother won back the whole of her debt."

"A mere fluke!" said one of the guests.

"A fairy-tale," said Hermann.

"Perhaps the cards were marked," put in another.

"Hardly," replied Tomsky with dignity.

"What!" said Narumov. "You have a grandmother who can play three winning cards running, and you have not yet been able to discover the secret of these cabalistics!"

"It's not so simple, devil take it!" replied Tomsky. "She had four sons, of whom one was my father. All four were desperate gamblers, and she did not disclose her secret to any of them, although this would have been no bad thing for them—nor for me either, for that matter. But this is what my uncle, Count Ivan Ilyich, told me, on his word of honor. The late Chaplitsky, that same Chaplitsky who died in poverty, having squandered millions, once lost about three hundred thousand rubles in his youth—to Zorich, I think. He was in despair. My grandmother, who was always very hard on the vagaries of young men, for some reason took pity on Chaplitsky. She named three cards to him, which he was to play in succession, but extorted from him the promise, on his word of honor, never to gamble any more. Chaplitsky went to the rooms of his fortunate opponent, and they sat down to the gaming table. Chaplitsky staked fifty thousand on the first card and won, then he doubled and redoubled the stake, and won back his losses, with a generous margin . . .

"But it's time to go to bed—it's a quarter to six." Indeed it was getting light already—the young men finished what was in their glasses and dispersed.

II

*"Il paraît que monsieur est
décidément pour les suivantes."
"Que voulez-vous, madame?
Elles sont plus fraîches."*[9]

Society talk

The old Countess was sitting in her dressing-room in front of her mirror. Three serving-maids hovered around her. One held a pot of rouge, another a box of hairpins, and the third a high cap with flame-colored ribbons. The Countess, who had not the slightest pretensions to beauty, which had long faded, nevertheless preserved all the habits of her youth, adhering strictly to the fashions of the 1770s, and spending as much time and energy over her toilet as she had done sixty years before. Seated before

[9] "It appears that monsieur decidedly prefers waiting–maids." "What do you expect, madame? They are fresher." This is an actual snatch of conversation overheard by the poet D. V. Davydov and reported to Pushkin.

a tambour[10] at the window was a young lady, the Countess' companion.

"Good morning, Grand'maman!" said a young officer who had just come into the room. *"Bonjour, Mademoiselle Lise.* I have come to ask a favor of you, Grand'maman."

"What is it, Paul?"

"Permit me to introduce a friend of mine to you, and to bring him to your ball on Friday."

"Bring him straight to the ball, you can introduce him to me there. Were you at the ***'s yesterday?"

"Oh, yes! It was very gay. We danced till five. Eletskaya was exquisite."

"Eh, my dear! What can you see in her? You should have seen her grandmother, the Princess Darya Petrovna! She must be very old now, I suppose—the Princess Darya Petrovna."

"Old?" replied Tomsky absently. "She's been dead these seven years."

The young lady at the window raised her head and made a sign to the young man. He remembered that the death of her contemporaries was always kept from the old Countess, and bit his lip. But the Countess received this information, which was news to her, with the utmost indifference.

"Dead!" she repeated. "And I did not know! We became maids of honor at the same time, and when we were presented, the Empress . . . "

And the Countess told her story to her grandson for the hundredth time.

"Well, Paul," she said, after a pause. "Now help me to get up. Lise, where's my snuff-box?"

And the Countess retired behind a screen, accompanied by her maids, to finish her toilet. Tomsky remained with the young lady.

"Whom do you wish to introduce to her?" asked Lisaveta Ivanovna in low tones.

"Narumov. Do you know him?"

"No. Is he a military or a civilian?"

"Military."

"An engineer?"

"No. A cavalryman. What made you think he was an engineer?"

The girl gave a short laugh, but answered not a word.

"Paul!" cried the Countess from behind the screen. "Send me a new novel, but not a modern one, if you please."

"What do you mean, Grand'maman?"

"I mean a novel in which the hero strangles neither his father nor his mother, and in which there are no drowned bodies. I have a perfect horror of drowned bodies!"

"There are no such novels nowadays. Unless, of course, you would like a Russian novel."

"Are there any Russian novels? Send me one, Sir, by all means, send me one!"

"I must say good-bye to you, Grand'maman. I am pressed for time.

[10] An embroidery frame mounted on a floor stand.

Good-bye, Lisaveta Ivanovna. What made you think Narumov was an engineer?"

And Tomsky went out of the dressing-room.

Lisaveta Ivanovna remained alone—she turned from her embroidery and began looking out of the window. Very soon a young officer made his appearance round the corner on the other side of the street. A blush covered her cheeks; she took up her work again, bending her head low over the canvas. Just then the Countess reappeared, fully dressed.

"Order the carriage, Lisanka," she said. "We'll go for a drive."

Lise rose from the embroidery frame and began putting away her work.

"Are you deaf, Child?" cried the Countess. "Order the carriage instantly!"

"Yes, Grand'maman," said the girl softly, and went quickly into the entrance hall.

A servant entered with some books for the Countess from Prince Pavel Alexandrovich.

"Very good. Give him my thanks," said the Countess. "Lise! Lise! Where are you going?"

"To dress."

"There's plenty of time, Child! Stay where you are! Open the first volume. Read to me . . . "

The girl picked up the book and read a few lines.

"Louder!" said the Countess. "What's the matter with you, my dear? Have you lost your voice? Wait a minute—give me a footstool. Nearer, can't you?"

Lisaveta Ivanovna read two more pages. The Countess yawned.

"Put the book down," she said. "A lot of nonsense! Send it back to Prince Pavel with my thanks. Well, where's the carriage?"

"The carriage is ready," said Lisaveta Ivanovna, glancing out of the window.

"And why aren't you dressed?" said the Countess. "You always keep me waiting. It's intolerable, my dear!"

Lise ran to her room. Before two minutes had passed the Countess began ringing her bell with all her might. The three maids came running in at one door, and the footman at the other.

"Can't you come when you're called?" exclaimed the Countess. "Tell Lisaveta Ivanovna I'm waiting for her."

Lisaveta Ivanovana came in, in her cloak and hat.

"At last!" said the Countess. "How you're dressed up! What for, I wonder? Whom do you want to conquer? What's the weather like? It seems to be windy."

"Not at all, Your Highness. It's very still weather," replied the footman.

"You always say the first thing that comes into your head. Open the *fortochka*.[11] There, I knew there was a wind, and a very cold one, too! Send away the carriage. We're not going, Lise. You needn't have dressed yourself up."

"And this is my life!" thought Lisaveta Ivanovna.

[11] Small ventilation pane in window.

Indeed, Lisaveta Ivanovna was a most unhappy creature. The bread of charity is bitter, said Dante, and the steps to a stranger's house are steep,[12] and who knows that bitterness so well as a poor girl dependent on an aristocratic old dame? The Countess did not really have a bad disposition, but she was capricious, like all women who have once been the spoiled darlings of society, and she was stingy, completely absorbed in her cold selfishness, like all old people who, having expended their tenderer emotions during a long lifetime, feel that they do not belong to the present. She participated in all the vanities of high society, dragging herself to balls, where, seated in a corner, rouged and dressed according to the fashion of ancient days, she was the hideous and essential ornament of the ballroom; newly-arrived guests went up to her and bowed low, as though in obedience to an established ritual, after which nobody took any notice of her. In her own home she received the whole town, observing the strictest etiquette, though she did not recognize any of her guests. Her innumerable household, growing fat and gray in her service, did whatever they liked and vied with one another in plundering the dying old woman. Lisaveta Ivanovna was a domestic martyr. She poured out tea and was scolded for the waste of sugar; she read novels aloud and was held guilty for all the author's shortcomings; she accompanied the old lady on her drives, and had to answer for the weather and the state of the road. She was allotted a salary which she never received in full; and was expected to be dressed like everyone else, which is to say like very few. In society she played the most pitiable role. Everyone knew her and no one took any notice of her; at balls, she only danced when a *vis-à-vis*[13] was needed, and the ladies took her arm whenever they had to retire in order to set to rights some detail of their toilet. Sensitive and therefore fully alive to her position, she was always on the lookout for a deliverer. But the young men, vain and calculating, did not honor her with their attention, although Lisaveta Ivanovna was infinitely more attractive than the cold, arrogant maidens upon whom they danced attendance. How many times, noiselessly departing from the dull, luxurious drawing-room, did she retire to weep in her humble chamber, with its wall-papered screen, its chest of drawers, its little mirror and painted bedstead, where a tallow candle in a brass candlestick burned dimly.

Once—a day or two after the evening described in the beginning of this tale, and a week before the scene just enacted—Lisaveta Ivanovna, seated before her tambour at the window, happened to glance into the street, and caught sight of a young man in the uniform of an engineer regiment standing motionless, his eyes fixed on her window. She lowered her head and resumed her work; five minutes later she looked out again—the young officer was still there. Not being in the habit of flirting with passing officers, she stopped looking out of the window and went on stitching for another two hours or so without raising her head. Dinner was served. Rising, she began to put away her tambour and, glancing out of the window, observed that the officer was still there. This struck her as somewhat

[12] These lines appear in a brief autobiographical passage in the *Divine Comedy: Paradiso*, canto 17.

[13] A partner for a *vis à vis*, a group ballroom dance like a quadrille.

strange. After dinner she went to the window with uneasy feelings, but the officer was no longer there—and she forgot about him . . .

Two days later, while going out with the Countess to get into the carriage, she saw him again. He was standing right at the porch, his beaver collar turned up to hide his face—a pair of black eyes gleamed from beneath his cap. Lisaveta Ivanovna was alarmed, she knew not why, and seated herself in the carriage with inexplicable trepidation.

As soon as she returned home she ran to the window—the officer was standing in his former place, his eyes fixed on her; she moved away, tortured by curiosity and an agitation which was quite new to her.

From that time, not a day passed without the young man appearing beneath the windows of their house at a certain hour. A curious relationship sprang up between them. While seated at her work she would feel his approach and raise her head, her glance resting on him for a longer space of time every day. The young man seemed to be beholden to her for this; with the keen sight of youth, she saw the instant blush which covered his pale cheeks whenever their eyes met. A week later, and she was greeting him with a smile . . .

When Tomsky asked permission to introduce his friend to the Countess, the poor girl's heart began to beat. But when she learned that Narumov was not an engineer but a horse-guardsman she regretted that, by her indiscreet question, she had given away her secret to the volatile Tomsky.

Hermann was the son of a Russianized German who had left him a very small fortune. Firmly convinced of the necessity of consolidating his independence, Hermann did not even touch the interest from it, and lived exclusively on his pay, never allowing himself the slightest indulgences. He was, however, reserved and ambitious, and his comrades seldom had occasion to laugh at his excessive thriftiness. He was a man of strong passions and a fiery imagination, but his firmness of character saved him from the usual errors of youth. Thus, while by nature a gambler, he never played cards, calculating that his fortune was not such as to allow him (to use his own words) *to sacrifice the necessary in the hope of gaining the superfluous,* and yet he would sit beside the gaming tables all night long, following with feverish excitement the vicissitudes of the game.

The story of the three cards affected his imagination powerfully, and he could not get it out of his head all night. "Supposing," he said to himself, roaming the streets of Petersburg the next night, "supposing the old Countess were to reveal her secret to me? Supposing she were to tell me the names of those three infallible cards? Why should I not try my luck? Present myself to her, get into her favor—perhaps become her lover . . . but all this would take time, and she is eighty-seven, she might die next week, the day after tomorrow! And the story itself—is it to be believed? No! Caution, moderation and diligence—these are my three faithful cards, with these I will treble my fortune, increase it seven-fold, achieve tranquillity and independence."

Thus meditating, he found himself in one of the principal streets of Petersburg, before a house of ancient architecture. The street was thronged with carriages, which were still rolling up one after another to the

brilliantly lighted porch. The slender foot of some young belle, a jackboot with jingling spurs, the striped stocking and the slipper of an ambassador, were thrust in rapid succession from the carriage doors. Furred mantles and cloaks flashed past the majestic footman. Hermann came to a standstill.

"Whose house is this?" Hermann asked the gendarme at the corner.

"The Countess'," replied the latter.

Hermann was thrown into trepidation. The marvellous story again rose before the eye of his fancy. He began walking up and down in front of the house, thinking of its mistress and her miraculous power. It was late when he returned to his humble dwelling; he lay awake a long time, and when sleep overcame him he dreamed of cards, the baize-covered table, heaps of notes, piles of golden coins. He staked one card after another, firmly doubled the stakes, won repeatedly, scraped the gold towards him, pocketed the notes. He awoke late, sighing for the loss of his fantastic riches, and once more went to the city, once more found himself in front of the Countess' mansion. It was as if some mysterious force had drawn him to it. He stood still and looked up at the windows. Behind one of them he saw a dark head bent either over a book or work. The head was lifted. Hermann saw a youthful face and black eyes. This moment decided his fate.

III

*Vous m'écrivez, mon ange, des
lettres de quatre pages plus vite
que je ne puis les lire.*[14]

Correspondence

Hardly had Lisaveta Ivanovna taken off her cloak and hat, when the Countess sent for her and ordered the carriage to be brought round again. And so they went out of the house to get into it. Just at the moment when two footmen were half-lifting, half-pushing the old dame through the carriage door, Lisaveta Ivanovna saw her engineer standing close to the wheels. He seized her hand; she was almost stupefied with terror; the young man vanished—a letter remained in her hand. She hid it inside her glove and neither saw nor heard anything during the whole drive. It was the Countess' habit to fire off question after question when in the carriage—Who's that, just gone by? What bridge is that? What's written on that sign? This time Lisaveta Ivanovna answered at random, and her meaningless remarks angered the Countess.

"What's come over you, my dear? Don't you hear me, or is it that you don't understand what I say? . . . I don't lisp, thank the Lord, and I am still in possession of my wits!"

Lisaveta Ivanovna in very truth was not listening. As soon as she got

[14]"You write, my angel, four–page letters more quickly than I can read them." Pushkin also used this fragment in his story "In the Corner of a Small Square"; its source is unknown.

back she hastened to her room and drew the missive out of her glove—it was unsealed. Lisaveta Ivanovna ran her eyes over it. The letter contained professions of love: it was tender and respectful, copied word-for-word from a German novel. But Lisaveta Ivanovna, who did not know German, was enchanted with the letter.

The letter she had received nevertheless caused her excessive agitation. It was the first time she had entered upon secret, intimate relations with a young man. His audacity appalled her. She reproached herself with indiscreet behavior, and could not make up her mind what to do. Should she stop sitting at the window and cool the officer's desire for further pursuit by displaying indifference? Ought she to send him back his letter, or, perhaps, answer it coldly and decisively? There was no one for her to consult— she had neither friends nor counsellors. Lisaveta Ivanovna made up her mind to reply.

She sat down at her little writing-table, got out pen and paper, and fell to musing. She began her letter several times, tearing it up each time—her words seemed to her either too indulgent, or too severe. At last she succeeded in writing a few lines with which she was satisfied: "I am confident," she wrote, "that your intentions are honorable, and that you would not wish to insult me by a thoughtless act; but our acquaintance must not begin in this wise. I return you your letter and trust that in future I shall have no cause to complain of unmerited disrespect."

The next day, as soon as she saw Hermann approaching, Lisaveta Ivanovna rose from her tambour, went into the adjoining room, opened the *fortochka* and tossed her letter out of the window, relying on the young officer's dexterity. Hermann ran to the spot where the letter had fallen, picked it up and entered the shop of a pastry cook. Breaking the seal, he found his own letter and the reply of Lisaveta Ivanovna. It was what he had expected and he went home deeply absorbed in his intrigue.

Three days after this, a sharp-eyed girl from a milliner's shop brought Lisaveta Ivanovna a note.

Lisaveta Ivanovna opened it anxiously, fearing it might be a dun, when she suddenly recognised Hermann's handwriting.

"You've made a mistake, child," she said. "This note is not for me."

"It is, it is! It's for you," answered the bold girl, not troubling to conceal a sly smile. "Be so good as to read it."

Lisaveta Ivanovna ran her eye hastily over the note. Hermann demanded a rendez-vous.

"You must be mistaken, my girl," said Lisaveta Ivanovna, alarmed both by the precipitancy of the demand, and the means employed by Hermann. "This letter is probably not intended for me." And she tore it into fragments.

"If it's not for you then why did you tear it up?" said the shop-girl. "I could have given it back to the person who sent it."

"I would ask you not to bring me any more notes in the future, child," said Lisaveta Ivanovna, flushing at the girl's remark. "And tell the person who sent you that he ought to be ashamed of himself . . . "

But Hermann did not desist from his efforts. Lisaveta Ivanovna received letters from him daily, through various channels. They were no longer translated from German. Hermann wrote them under the inspira-

tion of passion, and used language which was natural to him—his letters expressed both his unwavering desire and the chaos of his unbridled imagination. Lisaveta Ivanovna no longer attempted to return them to him, she revelled in them; she began answering them, and her notes became longer and more tender with every day. At last she threw the following letter out of the window to him:

"There is a ball at the Embassy tonight. The Countess will be there. We shall be there till two o'clock. This would be your chance to see me alone. As soon as the Countess leaves, her servants are sure to go away; there will be only the doorman in the porch, and he usually goes into his own little room. Come at half past eleven. Go straight upstairs. If you find anyone in the hall, ask for the Countess. They'll tell you she isn't at home, and there will be nothing for you to do, but go. But you will probably meet no one. The maids stay in their own room, all together. From the hall, turn to the left and go straight on till you get to the Countess' bedroom. There you will see a screen in front of two little doors. The one on the right leads to the study, where the Countess never goes. The one on the left leads to a passage, from which there is a narrow spiral staircase to my room."

Hermann awaited the appointed time, like a tiger ready to pounce. By ten o'clock he had already taken up position in front of the Countess' house. The weather was atrocious, the wind howled and snow fell in moist flakes. The lamps burned dimly, the streets were deserted. Every now and then a cabby drove his lean hack by, in the hope of picking up a belated wayfarer. Hermann had nothing on over his frock-coat, but was conscious neither of wind nor snow. At last the Countess' carriage was brought round. Hermann saw the footmen come out, supporting on either side the bowed form of the old woman in her sable cloak, and her youthful companion slip by after her, in her thin wrap, with flowers in her hair. The carriage door slammed. The carriage rolled heavily over the loose snow. The doorman closed the front door. The windows went dark. Hermann began walking up and down in front of the deserted mansion. When he got to a street lamp he glanced at his watch—it was twenty minutes past eleven. He stood in the light of the lamp, his eyes fixed on the hands of his watch, waiting for the remaining minutes to pass. Precisely at half past eleven he stepped on to the Countess' porch and into the brightly lit entrance. The doorman was not there. Hermann ran up the stairs, opened the door into the hall, and saw a serving-man asleep beneath a lamp, in an ancient, greasy arm-chair. Hermann passed him with a light, firm tread. The ballroom and drawing-room were dark. The lamp in the hall shed a dim light on them. Hermann entered the bedroom. A gilded lamp swung in front of an iconostasis[15] filled with ancient icons. Arm-chairs upholstered in faded damask, and downstuffed sofas, with the gilt wearing off in patches, stood in mournful symmetry along the walls, which were hung with Chinese wallpaper. There were two portraits painted in Paris by Madame Lebrun[16] on the walls. One was the likeness of a man of some forty years, rosy-cheeked and stout, in a bright-green uniform with a star on his breast; the other

[15] A screen or partition for the exhibition of icons: religious images, usually painted on small wooden panels.

[16] Elisabeth Vigée–Lebrun (1755–1842) was a fashionable Parisian portrait painter.

showed a young belle with an aquiline nose, her powdered locks, brushed up from the temples, adorned with a rose. In every corner could be seen porcelain shepherdesses, clocks made by the skilled hand of Leroy,[17] ornamental boxes, tops, fans, and various toys invented for the amusement of ladies in the end of the previous century, along with Montgolfier's balloon and Mesmer's magnetism.[18] Hermann went behind the screen. There stood a small iron bedstead; on the right was the door of the study, on the left the door into the passage. Hermann opened it, and saw the narrow spiral staircase leading to the poor young lady's room. But he turned back and entered the dark study.

The hours passed slowly. All was quiet. The clock in the drawing-room struck midnight. Clocks in all the other rooms chimed in one after the other. And all was quiet again. Hermann stood leaning against the cold stove. He was quite calm; his heart beat regularly, like that of one who has resolved upon what was dangerous, but inevitable. The clocks struck one, and then two—and he heard the distant sound of carriage wheels. He was thrown into a state of agitation. The carriage drove up and came to a stop. He could hear the clatter of the steps being let down. There were sounds of bustle in the house. People came running, voices were heard, and the house lit up. Three elderly lady's maids hastened into the bedroom, and the Countess, more dead than alive, entered and sank into the high-backed arm-chair. Hermann peeped through a crack in the door. Lisaveta Ivanovna passed close to him. He could hear her hurried footsteps ascending her staircase. He felt something like a pang of remorse, but it died down at once. He stood as if turned to stone.

The Countess began undressing in front of the mirror. Her maids unpinned her rose-trimmed cap, removed the powdered wig from her gray, closely cropped head. Pins fell from her in showers. The yellow dress embroidered in silver dropped to her swollen feet. Hermann was a witness of the horrid secrets of her toilet. At last the Countess was clad in nothing but a night-gown and night-cap—in this attire, more appropriate to her age, she was not so sinister and hideous.

Like all old people, the Countess suffered from insomnia. When her maids had undressed her she sat down near the window in the high-backed arm-chair and dismissed them. The candles were carried out, and once more the only light in the room came from the icon lamp. Her face a bilious yellow, her drooping lips twitching, the Countess swayed from left to right in her chair. Utter absence of thought could be seen in her dim eyes. Looking at her, one might have supposed that the terrible old woman swayed from side to side, not of her own accord, but under the influence of some concealed galvanic force.

Suddenly an indescribable change came over her death-like countenance. Her lips ceased their twitching, and a light came into her eyes. A strange man stood before the Countess.

"Do not be afraid, for God's sake, do not be afraid!" he was saying in

[17] The Leroys, Julien and his son Pierre, were famous eighteenth–century French watchmakers.

[18] Eighteenth–century fads. The Montgolfier brothers, Joseph and Jacques, invented the first practical balloon (first demonstrated in 1783). Friedrich Anton Mesmer (1733?–1815), a German physician, developed a system of hypnosis known as mesmerism.

low, clear tones. "I have no intention of harming you—I have come to beg a single favor of you."

The old woman gazed at him in silence, but seemed not to have heard him. Hermann, supposing her to be deaf, bent right over her ear and repeated his words. The old woman was as silent as ever.

"You can make me happy for life," continued Hermann, "and it will cost you nothing. I know that you are able to guess three cards to be played in succession. . ."

Hermann broke off. Evidently the Countess understood what was wanted of her, and was searching for words to answer him with.

"It was only a jest," she said at last. "I swear to you! It was a jest!"

"This is no jesting matter," replied Hermann sternly. "Remember Chaplitsky whom you helped to win back his losses."

The Countess was visibly embarrassed. Some powerful emotion showed itself on her face, but very soon she sank back into her former apathy.

"Can you name me these three infallible cards?" continued Hermann.

The Countess remained silent. Hermann continued:

"For whom are you treasuring your secret? For your grandchildren? They are rich, as it is; they do not understand the value of money. Your three cards will not help a spendthrift. He who allows a father's legacy to slip through his fingers will die in poverty, despite any diabolical efforts. I am no spendthrift. I know the value of money. Your three cards will not be wasted on me. Come, now! .."

He ceased speaking, and waited anxiously for her reply. The countess remained silent. Hermann fell on his knees.

"If your heart ever knew the feeling of love," he said, "if you remember its ecstasies, if you have only once smiled to hear the crying of a new-born son, if anything human ever beat in your bosom, I appeal to you as wife, mistress, mother, by all that is sacred in life, do not refuse my request! Reveal your secret to me! Perchance it may be linked with some terrible sin, with the forfeiture of eternal bliss, a pact with the devil. Bethink yourself that you are old, you have not long to live, I am ready to take your sins on myself. Only reveal to me your secret. Bethink yourself that the happiness of a human being is in your hands. That not only I, but my children, grandchildren and great-grandchildren will bless your memory, and hold it sacred. . ."

The old woman did not say a word.

Hermann rose.

"Old witch!" he said, clenching his teeth. "Then I will make you answer me!"

With these words he drew a pistol from his pocket.

At the sight of the pistol the Countess again showed signs of powerful emotion. She jerked back her head and raised her hand, as if to ward off a shot. . . Then she fell against the back of her chair. . . and remained motionless.

"Come, you are not a child!" said Hermann, taking her hand. "I ask you for the last time—do you intend to tell me what these three cards are? Yes or no?"

The Countess made no answer. Hermann saw that she was dead.

IV

7 Mai. . .
Homme sans moeurs et sans religion![19]
Correspondence

Lisaveta Ivanovna was seated in her room, still in her ball dress, absorbed in profound meditation. As soon as she got home she hastily dismissed her drowsy maid, who offered her services reluctantly, and said she would undress herself. Then she went up to her own room with a fluttering heart, hoping to find Hermann there, and desiring not to find him. She saw at a glance that he was not there, and thanked her stars for the obstacle in the way of their rendez-vous. She sat down without taking off her clothes and began to go over in her mind all the circumstances which had carried her so far in such a short space of time. Three weeks had not yet elapsed since the day she had first seen the young man beneath her window—and she was already corresponding with him, while he had wrung from her the promise of a nocturnal rendez-vous. If she knew his name, it was only because some of his letters had been signed. She had never spoken to him, never heard his voice, never heard anything about him—till this very evening. And strange to say, at the ball, Tomsky, vexed with the youthful Princess Pauline—for flirting with someone else for a change—wished to revenge himself and show his indifference. He invited Lisaveta Ivanovna to dance with him, and went through the endless mazes of the mazurka with her. He had jested the whole time about her partiality for engineers, assuring her that he knew a great deal more than she could possibly imagine, and some of his jests so nearly hit the mark that Lisaveta Ivanovna could not help thinking, more than once, that he knew her secret.

"Who told you all this?" she asked him, laughing.

"A friend of a certain person whom you know," replied Tomsky. "A most remarkable man."

"And who is this remarkable person?"

"His name is Hermann."

Lisaveta Ivanovna made no reply, but her hands and feet turned cold as ice.

"This Hermann," continued Tomsky, "is a most romantic individual. He has the profile of a Napoleon, and the soul of a Mephistopheles. I believe he has at least three crimes on his conscience. How pale you are! .."

"My head aches. . . What did that, what's his name—Hermann—tell you?"

"Hermann is greatly displeased with his friend. He says he would have acted quite differently. . . I'm inclined to think that Hermann has an eye on you himself, for he listens with great interest to the enamoured exclamations of his friend."

"But where can he have seen me?"

[19]"May 7. A man without morals and without religion!" The phrase is Pushkin's own.

"At church, perhaps, or out driving. . . God knows—perhaps in your room, while you were asleep. Anything may be expected of him."

Three ladies came up to them with the question: "*oubli ou regret?*"[20] and the conversation, of such agonizing interest for Lisaveta Ivanovna, had to be interrupted.

The lady whom Tomsky chose was the Princess herself. During one round of the ball-room and a turn in front of her chair they had come to an understanding, and by the time Tomsky got back to his place he was no longer interested either in Hermann or in Lisaveta Ivanovna. She was longing to revive the interrupted conversation; but the mazurka came to an end, and soon after the old Countess took her departure.

Tomsky's words had been nothing but ball-room small talk, but they had sunk deep into the soul of the romantic girl. The portrait sketched by Tomsky coincided with the image she had herself formed, and this type which the latest novels have made a commonplace at once alarmed and captivated her imagination. She sat with her bare arms folded, her head, with the flowers still in her hair, drooping over her half-exposed breast. . . Suddenly the door opened and Hermann entered. She felt a profound thrill. . .

"Where have you been?" she asked in a frightened whisper.

"In the old Countess' bedroom," replied Hermann. "I've just come from her. The Countess is dead."

"Dear God! What d'you mean?"

"And it seems," continued Hermann, "that it was I who caused her death."

Lisaveta Ivanovna glanced at him, and Tomsky's words echoed in her heart: *that man has at least three crimes on his conscience.* Hermann seated himself on the window-sill next to her and told her all.

Lisaveta Ivanovna heard him with horror. And so it was not love that had inspired all those passionate letters, those ardent requests, that audacious, stubborn pursuit! Money—that was what his soul thirsted after. It was not she who could quench his desires and make him happy. The poor companion had been nothing but the blind accomplice of a criminal, the murderer of her old benefactress. She wept bitterly, in her belated, anguished repentance. Hermann looked at her in silence—he, too, felt a pang, but it was not the poor girl's tears, nor the exquisite beauty of her grief which stirred his hard heart. He felt no remorse at the thought of the old woman who was dead. Only one thing appalled him—the irretrievable loss of the secret which he had hoped would enrich him.

"You are a monster," said Lisaveta Ivanovna at last.

"I did not desire her death," replied Hermann. "My pistol was not loaded."

They were both silent.

Day began to break. Lisaveta Ivanovna extinguished the dying candle—a pale light crept into the room. She dried her eyes, which were red with weeping, and raised them to Hermann's face: he was sitting on the window-

[20]"Oblivion or regret." A playful invitation to dance. The person so addressed by two ladies had to choose one of the words and dance with the lady it stood for. The third lady is probably a chaperone.

sill with his arms crossed, frowning ominously. In this pose he strikingly resembled a portrait of Napoleon. Even Lisaveta Ivanovna was impressed by the likeness.

"How are you to get out of the house?" she said, after a pause. "I had intended to take you by a concealed stairway, but we should have to go past her bedroom, and I am afraid."

"Tell me how I can find this concealed stairway. I will go."

Lisaveta Ivanovna rose, went to her chest of drawers and took out a key which she handed to Hermann, giving him full instructions. Hermann pressed her cold, passive hand, kissed the top of her bent head, and went away.

He descended the spiral staircase and once more entered the bedroom of the old Countess. The dead old woman sat there as if turned to stone; there was an expression of profound calm on her features. Hermann stood before her, gazed long at her, as if desirous of confirming to himself the appalling truth. At last he went into the study, felt for the papered door in the wall, and began descending the dark staircase, a prey to the strangest sensations. By this very staircase, he told himself, sixty years ago into this very bedroom, at this very hour, in a long embroidered coat, his hair brushed *à l'oiseau royal*,[21] his three-cornered hat pressed to his heart, may have stolen a young fortunate, now long moldering in the grave, while the heart of his aged mistress had this day ceased to beat. . .

At the foot of the staircase Hermann found a door, which he unlocked with the same key, and emerged in a passage leading right through the house to the street.

V

The late Baroness von V. appeared to me that night. She was attired in white and said to me: "Greetings, Mr. Privy Councillor."

Swedenborg[22]

Three days after the fatal night Hermann went to the monastery, where a service was to be held over the remains of the deceased Countess. While he felt no remorse he could not, however, quite silence the voice of conscience, which told him: it is you who murdered the old woman. He had little true faith, but many superstitious beliefs. He believed that the dead Countess might have an injurious influence on his life—and resolved to attend her funeral in order to beg her forgiveness.

The church was full. Hermann could hardly push his way through the crowd of mourners. The coffin stood on a rich bier beneath a velvet pall. The dead woman lay with hands folded on her breast, clad in a lace cap and

[21] "Like a royal bird": fashionable eighteenth–century male hair style.
[22] Emanuel Swedenborg (1688–1772) was a Swedish theologian and mystic who believed that God had spoken directly to him, revealing the inner truth of His doctrines. This passage has not been found in his voluminous writings; it is probably Pushkin's original parody of Swedenborg's style.

white satin dress. Around the coffin stood her household—the servants in
black liveries, with crested ribbons on their shoulders, holding candles, the
relatives—her children, grandchildren and great-grandchildren—in deep
mourning. No one wept; tears would have been *une affectation*. The Count-
ess had been so old that her death caused no surprise to anyone, and her
relatives had long regarded her as one who had outlived her time. A youth-
ful priest preached the funeral sermon. He described in simple and touch-
ing phrases the peaceful end of the pious lady, for whom the long years
had been a calm, affecting preparation for a Christian death. "The angel of
death," said the preacher, "found her watchful, in the midst of holy medi-
tations, awaiting the midnight bridegroom." The service was accomplished
with mournful propriety. The relatives went first to bid farewell to the
body. After them, the innumerable guests, who had come to pay obeisance
to her who had so long been a participator in their vain festivities, moved
towards the coffin. Then came the members of the household. And finally
there approached an ancient serving-maid, who was the same age as her
mistress. Two youthful serving-maids held her up by her arms. She had no
strength to bow down to the ground, and, alone of them all, shed a few
tears as she kissed the cold hand of her late mistress. After her, Hermann
ventured to approach the coffin. He bowed to the ground, prostrating
himself for a few moments on the cold pavingstones, strewn with branches
of fir. Then he rose, as white as the corpse itself, ascended the steps of the
bier, and bent down. . . It seemed to him that the dead woman looked at
him quizzically, and winked. Retreating hastily, he missed the step, and fell
flat on the ground. He was picked up. At that very moment Lisaveta
Ivanovna was carried out to the porch of the church in a swoon. This
incident disturbed for a few moments the solemnity of the gloomy ritual. A
hollow murmur arose from the crowd and a lean courtier, a near relation
to the deceased, whispered in the ear of an Englishman standing beside
him that the young officer was her natural son, to which the Englishman
replied with a dry: "Oh?"

Hermann was in a state of excessive agitation all day. He dined in a
lonely tavern and, contrary to his custom, drank a great deal, in the hope of
drowning his anxiety. But the wine only inflamed his imagination still
more. As soon as he got home he threw himself down on his bed in his
clothes, and fell sound asleep.

When he woke up it was night; the moon lit up his room. He glanced at
his watch—it was a quarter to three. He no longer wanted to sleep, and sat
up in bed, thinking about the old Countess' funeral.

Just then someone in the street looked at him through the window, and
immediately stepped back. Hermann paid no attention to this. A minute
later he heard the front door being opened. He thought it was his orderly,
drunk as usual, returning from his nocturnal revelries. But he heard unfa-
miliar footsteps: someone approached with softly shuffling slippers. The
door of his room opened and a woman in a white dress entered. Hermann
took her for his old nurse and wondered what could have brought her
there at such a time. But the white woman glided forward, and was sud-
denly quite close to him—and Hermann recognized the Countess.

"I have come to you against my will," she said in firm tones. "I have
been bidden to fulfill your request. A Three, a Seven and an Ace in

succession are your winning cards, but only on condition that you do not stake more than one card a day, and after that never again play your whole life long. I forgive you my death, on condition that you marry my protégée Lisaveta Ivanovna. . ."

With these words she turned softly towards the door, and shuffled out. Hermann heard the door in the porch bang, and saw someone peer through the window into his room again.

It was a long time before he could recover his senses. He went into the next room. The orderly was asleep on the floor. Hermann roused him with great difficulty. He was drunk as usual, and Hermann could get nothing out of him. The door to the porch was bolted. Hermann went back to his room, lit a candle and wrote an account of the vision he had seen.

VI

> *"Attendez!"*
> *"How dare you tell me* attendez?"
> *"I said* 'attendez-vous', *Your Excellency."*[23]

Two fixed ideas cannot exist simultaneously in our moral nature, any more than two bodies can occupy one and the same place in the physical world. The Three, the Seven, the Ace soon blurred the image of the dead old woman in Hermann's imagination. The Three, the Seven, the Ace were continually in his mind, and hovered on his lips. When he caught sight of a young girl he said: "How graceful she is—a regular Three of Hearts!" When asked what the time was, he answered five minutes to the Seven. Every paunchy man he came across reminded him of the Ace. The Three, the Seven, the Ace haunted his dreams, assuming all sorts of forms. The Three blossomed out before his eyes in the image of an enormous flower, the Seven was represented by Gothic portals, the Ace by a huge spider. All his thoughts were merged in a single one—to profit by the secret which had cost him so dear. He began thinking of retiring and travelling. He longed to wrench the treasure from enchanted Fortune in the public gambling salons of Paris. Chance relieved him of these cares.

At that time there was a society of wealthy gamblers in Moscow presided over by the renowned Chekalinsky, whose whole life had been spent playing cards, and who had accumulated millions, winning promissory notes, and losing ready cash. His experience and wisdom had earned him the confidence of his comrades, and his hospitality, famous chef, kindliness and cheerfulness had gained him the esteem of the public. He came to Petersburg. The young men flocked to him, neglecting balls for card-playing and preferring the seductions of faro to the sweets of courting. Narumov brought Hermann to his house.

They passed through a suite of resplendent rooms lined with respectful

[23] In faro, the player shouted *"Attendez"* ("wait") when he wanted to make or change a bet. This could sound rude (in contrast to the politer *Attendez–vous*), especially if the banker were an older man.

men-servants. A few generals and privy councillors were playing whist. Young men sprawled on the damask sofas, eating ices and smoking pipes. The host was keeping the bank at a long table in the drawing-room, around which crowded some twenty gamblers. He was a man of about sixty of the most genteel appearance. His hair was a silvery gray; his plump, fresh-colored countenance expressed good humor; his eyes shone, lit up by a continual smile. Narumov introduced Hermann to him. Chekalinsky pressed his hand cordially, asked him not to stand upon ceremony, and went on playing.

The game was a long one. There were over thirty cards on the table. Chekalinsky paused after every deal in order to give the players time to look over their hands, jotted down losses, lent a courteous ear to all demands, and still more courteously smoothed back the corner of a card bent over by a careless hand. At last the game came to an end. Chekalinsky shuffled the cards and prepared to begin another.

"I would like to stake a card, if you please," said Hermann, stretching out his hand from behind a fat gentleman at the card-table. Chekalinsky smiled and bowed silently, in token of submissive consent. Narumov laughingly congratulated Hermann on the breaking of his long fast, and wished him good luck.

"I am ready!" said Hermann, chalking in the sum above his card.

"What's that?" asked the holder of the bank, screwing up his eyes. "I am not sure that I read your sum right."

"Forty-seven thousand," replied Hermann.

At the sound of these words all heads were turned immediately, and all eyes were fixed on Hermann.

"He's gone mad," thought Narumov.

"Allow me to remark," said Chekalinsky, with his habitual smile, "that your stake is high. No one has ever staked more than two hundred and seventy-five *simple*[24] here."

"Well?" replied Hermann. "Will you play?"

Chekalinsky bowed with his usual air of submission.

"I only wished to inform you," he said, "that, since I am honored with the confidence of my friends, I am obliged to play for cash only. For my part, I am, of course, willing to rely on your word, but for form's sake and to avoid misunderstanding I would ask you to place your money on the table."

Hermann took a bank-note from his pocket and handed it to Chekalinsky, who, glancing rapidly at it, placed it on Hermann's card.

He began dealing. On the right lay a nine, on the left a three.

"Mine!" said Hermann, showing his card.

A murmur rose from the players. Chekalinsky frowned, but the smile returned immediately to his face.

"Shall I give it to you now?" he asked Hermann.

"If it's no trouble."

Chekalinsky drew a bundle of bank-notes from his pocket and counted out the required sum. Hermann took his winning and retired from the

[24] The *simple* ("single") was the first bet in faro.

table. Narumov was almost beside himself. Hermann drank a glass of lemonade and went home.

On the evening of the next day he repaired to Chekalinsky's again. The host was dealing. Hermann went up to the table; the other players immediately made room for him. Chekalinsky bowed to him urbanely.

Hermann waited for a fresh deal, and laid down a card, on which he placed his forty-seven thousand, and his winnings of the previous night.

Chekalinsky began dealing. A knave was on the right, a seven on the left.

Hermann turned up a seven.

Everyone gasped. Chekalinsky was visibly disconcerted. He counted out ninety-four thousand in notes and handed them to Hermann. Hermann received them with the utmost sang-froid and immediately withdrew.

On the following evening Hermann was again at the table. Everyone was expecting him. The generals and privy councillors abandoned their rubber of whist to watch the unusual play. The young officers sprang up from the sofas. All the men-servants were gathered in the drawing-room. Everyone pressed round Hermann. The other players did not put down their stakes, but waited eagerly to see how the game would go. Hermann stood at the table, ready to play against the pale, but ever-smiling Chekalinsky. Each unsealed a new pack of cards. Chekalinsky shuffled. Hermann cut and laid down his card, covering it with a heap of bank-notes. It was like a duel. Profound silence reigned in the room.

Chekalinsky began to deal with an unsteady hand. On the right he turned up a queen, on the left, an ace.

"The ace wins," said Hermann, and showed his card.

"Your queen is covered," said Chekalinsky urbanely.

Hermann started: it was true—instead of an ace there lay the Queen of Spades. He could hardly believe his eyes, and wondered how he could have made such a blunder.

And all of a sudden it seemed to him that the Queen of Spades was narrowing her eyes and laughing at him. He was struck by an extraordinary likeness.

"The old woman!" he cried in horror.

Chekalinsky drew his winnings towards him. Hermann stood motionless. When he went away from the table everyone started talking loudly. "What a game!" exclaimed the players. Chekalinsky again shuffled the cards: the game went on as usual.

CONCLUSION

Hermann has gone mad. He is in ward Number 17 of the Obukhov Hospital, and never answers when he is spoken to, only muttering over and over again with extraordinary rapidity: "Three, seven, ace. . . three, seven, queen! . ."

Lisaveta Ivanovna married a very well-bred young man; he works in a government office and is the possessor of a considerable fortune. He is the

son of the old Countess' former steward. Lisaveta Ivanovna is bringing up an impoverished female relative.

Tomsky has been promoted to a captaincy and is going to marry the Princess Pauline.

George Sand
(1804–1876)

In her own lifetime, George Sand—to give her the pen name she adopted in her late twenties—was among the best-known people in France, as both author and newsworthy personality. Her seventy or so novels, not to mention short stories, plays (many of them staged), travel books, autobiographical writings, children's classics, literary criticism, and correspondence—all produced, to use her own metaphor, like water pouring from a faucet—brought her a wide readership and an international influence. The youthful Fyodor Dostoevsky and Ivan Turgenev, for example, treasured her books as a principal source through which censored Russia could stay abreast of new ideas. Among French fiction-writers Sand was the preeminent Romantic "idealist" and voice of reformist hope, on the same level of prestige with her opposite number, the equally prolific, cynically disillusioned Romantic "realist" Honoré de Balzac. Yet by the early twentieth century Sand's reputation had precipitously declined. She continued to get high marks, unanimously, for her storytelling gifts, and almost equally high marks for her elegantly expressive prose style, but—barring a series of pastoral novels she wrote in her middle age—her fiction seemed to have failed the test of time. For many people it was Sand the personality who survived, in lurid caricature: the bohemian Parisian dandy, wearer of men's clothes and smoker of cigars, the "infamous woman" best known for her sensational liaisons with great men such as the poet-dramatist Alfred de Musset and the composer Frédéric Chopin, besides an indeterminate number of other lovers. Today, however, there are signs that the wheel is coming full circle and restoring Sand to her former place as a great writer, indeed, as some have asserted, the greatest woman writer France has produced. This rehabilitation is closely tied to efforts over the last two decades to reform the "canon," the quasi-official membership roll of great authors and books. The case of George Sand illustrates a number of key issues in that connection.

Even the name Sand was given at her birth (in Paris, in 1804) varies with almost every account of her, but in her autobiography she calls herself Amantine-Lucile-Aurore Dupin; she was Aurore for short. On her father's side her lineage had luster; he was descended from the distinguished eighteenth-century military commander Maurice de Saxe and in his own person had served as aide-de-camp to Murat, one of Napoleon Bonaparte's right-hand marshals. Aurore's mother, on the other hand, was a mere Pari-

sian dressmaker. Socially speaking, Sand felt comfortable with both blood-lines; as she wrote in her autobiography, "one is not only Papa's child, one is Mama's too [Although] I have some illegitimate cousinage with Louis XVIII [the king restored after Napoleon's downfall], it is just as true that the People's blood runs in my veins; and besides, there is no bastardy on that side." As a result, she explained, she learned to think hard about class origins, and indeed throughout her later career as a writer she was to explore the possibilities and difficulties of love between high- and low-born persons.

The young girl's education was a contrasting mix of easygoing Rous-seauvian permissiveness and convent-school training. At the convent school, in her early teens, Aurore went through a stage of religious enthusi-asm that tempted her to become a nun, but her freethinking grandmother, sensing the danger, squelched the temptation by withdrawing Aurore from the school, after which the girl's religious faith withered away in any case as she read some of the more extravagantly Romantic authors such as Byron. Her religious fervor did not disappear, however; it was merely diverted into more secular channels, particularly as she read Rousseau and eagerly drank in his ideas about the primacy of the heart's affections.

At the age of eighteen, this ardent young enthusiast made the bad mis-take of marrying a retired army officer named Dudevant, a rough-hewn and insensitive country squire with whom she had little if anything in com-mon. The union lasted eight years, during which Aurore bore two chil-dren, to whom she remained devoted throughout her life. In 1830, the marriage having broken up, Aurore took off for Paris, where she soon began to eke out her meager funds by writing. (Years later the separation became a legal one.) In collaboration with Jules Sandeau, she produced the book *Rose et Blanche* (1831), but the most permanent effect of this venture was to coin Aurore's new identity as George Sand. Under this name she published, on her own, the novel *Indiana* (1832), which made her famous and also notorious, for the book was an impassioned protest, in the name of human dignity and free love, against the spiritual crippling of human be-ings, especially women, in institutionalized marriage. For all the later turns, twists, and occasional quirks in Sand's philosophy, her concern with the lot of women and the sacred rights of untrammeled love remained pretty much a constant. A number of other novels followed in a similarly passion-ate vein, including *Valentine* (1832), *Lélia* (1833), and *Mauprat* (1837; "high in the class of readable bad books," says the 1966 printing of *The Oxford Companion to French Literature*). The attitudes expressed in these novels clearly owed much to Sand's own experience; even more than most Ro-mantic writers she invested a good deal of herself in her works. She came to specialize in a distinctive type of protagonist: *la femme incomprise*, or "misun-derstood woman."

The decade of the 1840's, leading up to the momentous but early-aborted revolutions that swept through Europe in 1848 (the year when Marx and Engels published *The Communist Manifesto*), was a time of kaleido-scopic ideological ferment, alive with new notions ranging from the silliest crackpot fantasies to the noblest humanitarian visions. Sand was caught up in a number of them—often those espoused by her lovers or friends—including reincarnation and the new political idea called socialism. Detrac-

tors tend to consider her impressionableness a sign that Sand had no real mind of her own; admirers tend to find her openness valuable exactly because, in so many ways, she reflected the characteristic currents of her time. It should be added that Sand often played the role of mentor herself. Later in her life the younger novelist Gustave Flaubert, a great writer and a painstaking perfectionist as unfaucetlike as anyone could be, regarded Sand as his "old master," valued her advice, and profited from it, notably in his novella *A Simple Heart*, where he followed Sand's counsel and created an unironic portrait of goodness. Influence could be a two-way street between her and some of her more eminent contemporaries: the composer Franz Liszt, Balzac, the elder Alexandre Dumas, and others. In any case, Sand's novels of the 1840's tend to be activist, reforming works, often enforcing a thesis about the evils of the class system; *The Journeyman on the Tour of France* (1840), *Consuelo* (1842), and *The Miller from Angibault* (1845) are examples.

Sand was a zealous political journalist during the crisis of '48, but when the brief era of reform and revolution ended she moved away from politics in sadness and disillusionment, concentrating now on a series of novels about ordinary, mostly admirable country people, in a vein that she had already in fact begun to work: *The Devil's Pool* (1846); *Little Fadette*, or *Fanchon the Cricket* (1849); *François le Champi* (1850); and *The Bagpipers* (1853). These works, which kept Sand's fame alive during the twentieth-century twilight of her reputation, are a kind of French rendering of Wordsworthian pastoral, treating rural men and women in a somewhat idealized but clear-sighted way. Finally, in Sand's last phase, she returned to the romantic love story but in a voice less extravagant and revolutionary than that of her earliest novels. She spent most of the latter part of her life at the estate, once her grandmother's, where Sand had spent much of her girlhood and where, in her last years, her benevolence and popularity earned her the sobriquet "the good lady of Nohant." She died there in 1876.

The case for reinstating George Sand in the canon, or elevating her place in it, is based partly on arguments having to do with her individually. Her image as a cigar-smoking transvestite, which has sometimes tended to block out or trivialize her achievements as a literary artist, can in a feminist age be taken more seriously as political statement, not mere eccentricity, or as sheer practicality (male disguise allowed her to buy the cheaper theater seats reserved for men). Her openness to new ideas in her activist period need no longer be dismissed, as it often has been, as merely passive ("feminine") dependence on the views held by Sand's changing cast of friends and lovers. Did all these men themselves, feminists are apt to ask, arrive at their ideas wholly on their own, without external influence? Why should a woman's openness to influence somehow confirm her status as intellectually inferior when the history of art is replete with examples of men— Keats, Shelley, Hugo, and countless others—who fruitfully and laudably derived ideas and values from other people, from books, and from the general culture of their times?

Other, even broader and more controversial, considerations also come into play. Recent revisionists of literary history have argued that the criterion of "universality" invoked to canonize great books and authors has been used, consciously or not, as an ideological filter that eliminates works

and authors concerned with the concrete social issues of their time—as, for example, Harriet Beecher Stowe was concerned with slavery in *Uncle Tom's Cabin* (1852)—and that these works of more immediate social pertinence are exactly those that tend to have been written by women or members of socially marginal groups. By this reasoning, it would seem inevitable that George Sand's more "thesis-ridden" works should be those that have fallen into disrepute while her ideologically milder bucolic novels ("pastels," as they have been called) have rated higher with the authorities who define the literary canon. Indeed, it has even been argued—by Naomi Schor, for example, in *A New History of French Literature* (1989)—that the mode of "realism" is psychologically a manifestation of a male-oriented and middle-class acquiescence in the status quo, and that as such it has tended to pre-empt the mode of nonrealistic, visionary, reforming idealism that is most characteristic of early works by Sand such as *Lélia*. If that is a valid argument, however, some ironies emerge, for Sand's idealism is not merely a program designed to inspire readers by portraying good people but also an attempt to get at the *essence* of certain human types—in short, to depict and achieve "universality."

The small-scale psychological masterpiece "The Marquise" (1832), one of Sand's early stories, is explicitly concerned with various kinds of idealism. Near the end, the protagonist challenges the narrator to believe in "the ideality of the eighteenth century," an ironic twist in view of the typical and complacent Romantic claim to have reached a higher spiritual level than existed in that allegedly coarser age. Moreover, the Marquise's love for the actor Lelio depends heavily on her preserving a clear distinction between the spiritually elevated characters the actor brings to life behind the footlights and the commonplace vulgarity she has discovered in him as a man. Sand's lifelong interest in the barriers of social class also helps inform the story. Yet these two themes—idealism and the arbitrariness of class distinctions—play against each other throughout, in disturbing tension with each other. The Marquise is an idealist, a rebel, in many ways an unconventional person, a transvestite like George Sand, and Lelio too is all of these things in his own different way. Yet neither of them thinks seriously of violating or challenging the social taboo that separates them. It is this psychological puzzle—along with the philosophical questions the story raises about the relation of art to life—that cries out to be understood and explained.

FURTHER READING (*prepared by S.M.*): Although Sand's stature as a literary artist is being recognized again after a period of eclipse, biographical approaches to her continue to share center stage—sometimes with new emphases arising from the current feminist movement. Curtis Cate's *George Sand: A Biography*, 1975, and Joseph Barry's *Infamous Woman: The Life of George Sand*, 1977, can be recommended. Readable also, though lacking in documentation, is Renee Winegarten's *The Double Life of George Sand, Woman and Writer*, 1978. David A. Powell's general survey *George Sand*, 1990, contains some brief but interesting discussion of "The Marquise." Kathryn J. Crecilius's *Family Romances: George Sand's Early Novels*, 1987, is good on such novels as *Indiana* and *Valentine*. Interesting essays (a few of them in French) are brought together in *George Sand: Collected Essays*, ed. Janis Glasgow, 1987. Paul Blount's *George Sand and the Victorian World*, 1979, locates Sand's work in her time. Donna Dickenson, *George Sand: A Brave Man—The Most Womanly Woman*, 1988, is a feminist-based attempt to clear away the legendary biographical scandals and ap-

proach Sand as a professional. Naomi Schor's essays in *A New History of French Literature*, 1989, mentioned in the present introduction, on Sand's relationship to the fictional modes of her time, are particularly provocative.

THE MARQUISE

Translated by Kelly Jennings and Sandra Reyes[1]

I

The Marquise de R—— never said brilliant things, although it is the fashion in French fiction to make every old woman sparkle with wit. Her ignorance was extreme in all matters which contact with the world had not taught her, and she had none of that nicety of expression, that exquisite penetration, that marvelous tact, which belong, it is said, to women who have seen all the different phases of life and society; she was blunt, heedless, and sometimes very cynical. She put to flight every idea I had formed concerning the noble ladies of the olden times, yet she was a genuine Marquise and had seen the court of Louis XV.[2] But she was not a typical character, and you should not expect to find in her story a serious study of the manners and customs of her time. The society of any era seems to me so difficult to understand and depict well that I will not get involved in any such attempt. Instead, I will recount certain events that testify to an unimpeachable bond of sympathy among people of all societies and eras.

I had never found the Marquise's company very fascinating. She seemed to me remarkable for nothing much except her prodigious memory for the events of her youth and the masculine lucidity with which she expressed her reminiscences. For the rest, she was, like all aged persons, forgetful of recent events and indifferent to everything in which she had not any present personal concern.

She had never been one of those provocative charmers who, for want of striking physical attractions, must get by on wit instead. By using their minds, women like that can outshine those far lovelier. No, the Marquise had had the misfortune to be incontrovertibly beautiful. I have seen her portrait, for, like all old women, she was vain enough to hang it up for inspection in her apartments. She was represented in the character of a huntress nymph,[3] with a low satin waist painted to imitate tiger-skin, sleeves of antique lace, bow of sandal-wood, and a crescent of pearl lighting up her hair. It was an admirable painting, and, above all, an admirable woman—tall, slender, dark, with black eyes, austere and noble features,

[1] Revised from the anonymous, abridged translation in *The Blue Flower: Best Stories of the Romanticists*, ed. Hermann Kesten, Roy Publishers, New York, 1946. The omissions are here restored.

[2] The court of Louis XV (reigned 1715–74) was proverbial for its dissipation and corruption. It was during the reign of his grandson and successor, Louis XVI, that the French Revolution erupted.

[3] Stylized, fashionable portraits were often painted of aristocratic women in the innocent guise of shepherdesses or of followers of Diana, virgin goddess of the hunt.

unsmiling, deep red lips, and hands which, it was said, had thrown the Princess de Lamballe[4] into despair. Without lace, satin, or powder, she might indeed have seemed one of those beautiful, proud nymphs fabled to appear to mortals in the depth of the forest or upon the solitary mountainsides, only to drive them mad with passion and regret.

And yet the Marquise had made few conquests. She told me herself that people had considered her dull. In her time *roués*[5] were more taken by charm and wit than by beauty, and women infinitely less admired than she had robbed her of all her adorers. Strangely enough, she seemed indifferent to her fate. What she told me of her life, in bits and snatches, seemed to reveal a woman whose heart had never been young, one whose whole being had been dominated by a cold selfishness. On the other hand, I saw in her many signs of kindness remarkable in one so elderly; her grandchildren were warmly attached to her, and she gave alms without ostentation. But, since she made no pretense to be high-principled and freely confessed that she had never loved her admirer the Vicomte de Larrieux, I did not know what to make of her.

One evening I found her even more communicative than usual; there was much of sadness in her voice. "My child," she said, "the Vicomte de Larrieux has just died of the gout. It is a great sorrow to me, for I have been his friend these sixty years. It's frightening, how people die. In his case it's not surprising, of course; he was so old!"

"What was his age?" I asked.

"Eighty-four. I am eighty, but not so infirm as he was, and I can hope to live longer. *N'importe!*[6] Several of my friends have gone this year, and although I tell myself that I am younger and stronger than any of them, I can not help being frightened when I see my contemporaries dropping off around me."

"And these," said I, "are the only regrets you feel for poor Larrieux, a man who worshipped you for sixty years, who never ceased to complain of your cruelty, yet never revolted from his allegiance? He was a model lover: there are no more such men."

"Oh, enough," she said, smiling coldly. "All that man did was complain and call himself unhappy—which he was not, as everyone knows."

Since my Marquise seemed to feel like talking, I pressed her with questions about the Vicomte de Larrieux and herself. This is the odd response I got:

"My dear child, you seem to find me heartless. Well, you may be right: judge for yourself. I will give you the whole story, I will confess to you things I have never told a soul. You, a young man of these unprejudiced times, may find me less culpable than I seem to myself; but, whatever you think, at least I will not die without having shown someone what I was really like. Maybe you will even feel some pangs of compassion—that would sweeten the sadness of my memories.

"I was brought up at Saint-Cyr, where the brilliant education I got did me very little good. At sixteen, I left to marry the Marquis of R——, who

[4] A famous beauty, friend of Louis XVI's wife Marie Antoinette.
[5] Dissipated men; rakes. [6] "Never mind."

was fifty years old. I dared not complain; everyone was congratulating me on my wonderful match, and my poorer classmates envied my good luck.

"I was never very bright, and at that time I was positively stupid; the education of the cloister had completely benumbed my faculties. I left the convent with a romantic idea of life and of the world, stupidly considered a merit in young girls, but which often results in the misery of their whole lives. As a natural consequence, the experience brought me by my brief married life was lodged in so narrow a mind that it was of no use to me. I learned, not to understand life, but to doubt myself. I went out into the world with ideas that were wholly false, with prejudices that would influence the whole course of my life.

"At sixteen and a half I was already a widow, and my mother-in-law, who had taken a liking to me because I was a perfect little ninny, urged me to remarry. Of course, it was also true that I was pregnant, and the meager dowry my husband had left me would go back to his family if I managed to acquire a stepfather for his heir. At any rate, as soon as my mourning was over I was presented to society again and found suitors swarming all around me. I was then in all the splendor of my beauty, and it was generally admitted that there was neither face nor figure that could compare with mine; but my husband, an old, worn-out, dissipated man, who had never shown me anything but irony and disdain, and had married me only to secure an office promised with my hand, had left me such an aversion to marriage that I could never be brought to contract new ties. In my ignorance of life I fancied that all men resembled him, and that in a second husband I should find M. de R——'s hard heart, his pitiless irony, and that insulting coldness which had so deeply humiliated me. Shallow and ignorant though I was, I recognized that his rare fits of transport had no real feeling behind them and were merely directed at a beautiful woman—after which I could go back to being a simpleton, to be ridiculed and disowned in public.

"This terrible entrance into life left me permanently disillusioned. My heart, perhaps not originally cold, retreated into itself and hardened with distrust. I looked at all men with aversion and disgust. Their homage I took as an affront: pretending to be my slaves, their real aim was to tyrannize over me.

"When we don't need virtue, we don't have it. That is why, though austerely moral, I had no virtue at all. And how I regretted that! How I longed for virtue, for that moral and religious strength that struggles against passion and thus gives intensity to existence! My inner powers were so frozen, so futile! What would I not have given to have passions to subdue, to have to fight battles, to go down on my knees like the young girls I saw, fresh from the convent, praying for fervid strength and will power so that they might remain virtuous in the world for a few years! But me? Alas, what had I to do in the world? Nothing but to adorn myself, put myself on display, and be bored. I had no heart, no regrets, no terrors; instead of watching over me, my guardian angel slept. The Virgin with her chaste mysteries afforded me neither comfort nor poetic daydreams. I had no need of such heavenly protection; dangers were not for me. I scorned myself for a condition I should have gloried in.

"Yet, let me assure you, I encountered reproaches, not only from myself

but also from other people, when I found that my unwillingness to love had become an inability to love. For when women pressed me to choose this husband or that lover, I often confided in them, telling them of my distaste, the coldness that had been instilled into me by men's selfishness and brutality. When I said such things they laughed in my face, assuring me that all men were not my late husband and that men had secret ways which made up for their flaws and vices. Such gross assurances were revolting to me; it made me ashamed to be a woman, listening to other women talk so, hearing them laugh idiotically at the indignation that showed in my face. There were times when I felt I was worth the whole pack of them.

"And then I would retreat into myself. Boredom ate away at me. Those others had full lives; mine was empty and idle. I began to think that I was foolish and overweening, I began to believe what I had heard from those laughing female philosophers who accepted so effortlessly the times they lived in. I told myself that I had been the victim of my own ignorance, that I had deluded myself with chimerical hopes, that I had dreamed foolishly of perfect and devoted men such as had no existence on earth. In a word, I began to accept every accusation that had been leveled against me.

"As long as these women believed that I was on the way to being converted by their maxims—what they called their 'wisdom'—they stood by me. Oh, there was more than one who invested in me all her need for self-justification, more than one who had made the transition from exaggerated protestations of fierce virtue to loose behavior and counted on me to sanction her fall by a similar fall of my own.

"But when, finally, they saw that I was incorruptible, that I had reached the age of twenty without anything coming of their efforts, they recoiled from me in horror: they began to see me as their critic incarnate, their living judge. They ridiculed me to their lovers, and the idea of conquering me inspired in people the most outrageous schemes and scurrilous projects. Women of even the highest rank did not blush to contrive, gleefully, the most infamous plots against me, and as for those of country morals, by them I was attacked with an obsessiveness akin to hatred. Men would vow to their mistresses to break and tame me, and these women would give them full permission to try. Hostesses would offer to ply me with too much wine so as to addle my brains. Friends and relations would 'tempt' me with men no better than coachmen. Since I had been naive enough to open my soul to them, they all knew quite well that it was not piety or honor or a former love that fenced me round but simply mistrust and an involuntary feeling of repulsion, and they did not hesitate to share this knowledge. Taking no account of the uncertainties and anguish that filled my soul, they eagerly spread it about that I hated all men. No attitude wounds men more keenly than that; they find it easier to pardon debauchery or contempt. Sharing the aversion women felt for me, they wooed me with the sole purpose of taking vengeance on me and then making a jest of the matter thereafter. As for me, I found irony and deceit written clearly in their faces, and my misanthropy thus grew from day to day.

"Of course, any woman of spirit and wit would have risen to meet all this. She would have relished the resistance, if for no better reason than to enrage her adversaries. She would have made a public show of piety, so as to unite around her the women (there were a few, even back then) who

were models of virtue. But I had not the strength of character to stand against that storm. I felt myself to be abandoned, misunderstood, hated, accused of the most hideous or bizarre perversions. There were women wholly given over to the most abandoned debauchery who pretended to find my company dangerous.

II

"About this time there came to Paris from the provinces a man who had neither talent, strength, nor fascination, but who possessed a frankness and uprightness of feeling very rare among the people with whom I had lived. I began to believe that here at last was someone whom I could, as my acquaintances put it, 'choose.' I could not, as a mother, bring myself to marry, and I did not think it right in any case, doubting as I did that any man could be truly good. It was as a lover that I would have to take him, so as to live at the level of people I knew. I made up my mind, then, to accept this provincial gentleman; his name and his place in the world would protect me very nicely. He was the Vicomte de Larrieux.

"He, poor fellow, loved me sincerely in his soul. His soul! Had he a soul? He was one of those hard, prosaic men who have not even the elegance of vice or the glitter of falsehood. I suppose he loved me in his ordinary way, as my husband had sometimes loved me. He was struck only by my beauty; he took no pains to discover my heart. This was not disdain on his part, it was incapacity. Had he found in me the power of loving, he would not have known how to respond to it.

"I do not think there ever lived a man more wedded to material things than poor Larrieux. He ate with delight, and fell asleep in all the armchairs; the remainder of the time he took snuff. He was always occupied in satisfying some appetite. I do not think he had one idea a day.

"I waited; I did not bring our relationship to the level of intimacy until I had begun to feel some friendship toward him. I found in him no greatness, but I found no meanness either, and that in itself made him superior to everyone else around me. So I flattered myself: I thought that if I indulged his gallantries he would help reconcile me to human nature. I trusted myself to his sense of fealty. But no sooner had I granted him those privileges that weak women can never take back than he came after me with intolerable obsessiveness, reducing his entire apparatus of affection to that one way of displaying it that he was fitted to understand.

"As you can see, my dear friend, I had gone from Charybdis to Scylla.[7] This man, with his enormous appetites and his constant napping, this man whom I had believed to be so cool-blooded, did not understand even in theory the kind of strong friendship I had hoped to find. He used to say with a laugh that no one could feel friendship toward a beautiful woman. And if you only knew what his idea of love was——!

"I don't pretend to have been 'molded from a finer clay' than other human beings. At my present stage of life, I don't really belong to one sex

[7] Two equally repellent alternatives (from the monsters who, in mythology, guarded either side of the strait between Italy and Sicily).

or the other, but at that time I believe I had my full share of womanliness. But my development was stunted: I never met a man whom I could love so as to instill some poetry into the brute facts of animal life. But this is beside the point. You are a man, and therefore you may be less delicate on this matter of sentiment, but surely you can understand the heart's disgust when one has to submit to the demands of love without the comprehension of its real needs . . . In three days the Vicomte de Larrieux became intolerable to me.

"And yet, my dear friend, would you believe it? I never had the energy to get rid of him; for sixty years he was my torment. Constantly offended by my repulses, yet constantly drawn to me by the very obstacles I placed in the way of his passion, he had for me the most faithful, the most undying, the most wearisome love that ever man felt for woman.

"And, of course, once I had accepted a protector for myself, my life became infinitely less disagreeable. Men no longer dared come after me, for the Vicomte was a formidable swordsman and was also atrociously jealous. The women who had predicted that I would be unable to get and hold a man were stung by the sight of the Vicomte chained to my chariot wheel. And it may be that mixed with my patience toward him was a certain amount of woman's vanity in not wanting to be abandoned. Poor Larrieux— he was not the kind of prize I could be very vain about. Still, he was a good-looking man, he had courage, he knew when to hold his tongue, he knew how to live well, and he had a touch of that modest fatuity that makes a woman's good points stand out by contrast. And, finally, apart from the fact that women didn't at all look down their noses at the Vicomte's rather fussy good looks (which, in my eyes, were his weakest point), they were struck with his faithful devotion to me, so that they held him up as an example to their lovers. In short, I found myself in an enviable position— though that, I can assure you, was poor payment for the tedious duties of our intimate relationships. But I put up with them stoically, and I remained scrupulously faithful to Larrieux. So judge, then, my dear boy: am I as blamable as you thought toward him?"

"I understand you perfectly," I said. "I feel both sympathy and respect for you. You were acting as your time and society demanded, and you were sacrificed to them. Being better than your time, you were persecuted. Still, with a greater moral effort you might have found in virtue all the happiness you did not find in a liaison. But one thing surprises me—have you never found anywhere, through all your life, even one man capable of understanding you and converting you to real love? Must we conclude that the men of today are superior to those of other times?"

"That would be a great piece of vanity on your part," she answered, smiling. "I have little reason to speak well of the men of my own time; yet I doubt, too, whether you have made much progress; but I will not moralize. The cause of my misfortune was entirely within myself. I had no tact, no judgment. A woman as proud as I was should have possessed a superior character, and should have been able to distinguish at a glance many of the insipid, false, insignificant men who surrounded me. I was too ignorant, too narrow-minded for this. As I lived on I acquired more judgment and have learned that several of the objects of my hatred deserved far other feelings."

"And while you were young," I rejoined, "were you never tempted to make a second trial? Was this deep-rooted aversion never shaken off? It is strange."

III

The Marquise was silent, then hastily laying her gold snuffbox on the table— "I have begun my confession," said she, "and I will acknowledge everything. Listen. Once, and only once, I have loved, with a love as passionate and indomitable as it was imaginative and ideal. For you see, my child, you young men think you understand women, but you know nothing about them. If many old women of eighty were occasionally to tell you the history of their loves, you would perhaps find that the feminine soul contains sources of good and evil of which you have no idea. And now, guess what was the rank of the man for whom I entirely lost my head—I, a Marquise, and prouder and haughtier than any other."

"The King of France, or the Dauphin, Louis XVI."

"Oh, if you go on in that manner, it will be three hours before you come to my lover. I prefer to tell you at once—he was an actor."

"A king, notwithstanding, I imagine."

"The noblest, the most elegant that ever trod the boards. You are not amazed?"

"Not much. I have heard that such ill-sorted passions were not rare, even when the prejudices of caste in France were more powerful than they are today. Which one of those friends of Madame d'Epinay was it who lived with Jeliotte?"

"So you do know something about our time, then. Ah, that was a pity. But surely you can see that, precisely because such things are reported in memoirs and mentioned with astonishment, they happened rarely and were inconsistent with the mores of the times. Rest assured, those things were great scandals in their time; and whenever you hear about horrible depravity, or about the Duc de Guiche and Manicamp, or about Madame de Lionne and her daughter, you can be certain that the affairs seemed every bit as shocking when they happened as they do to you reading about them today. Do you really believe that the indignant authors who handed down accounts of such things were the only upright people in France?"

I did not dare contradict the Marquise, since I was not sure either of us was competent to settle the dispute. I brought her back to her own story. She went on:

"To show you how little that sort of thing was tolerated then: The first time I saw him I expressed my admiration to the Comtesse de Ferrières, who happened to be beside me, and she answered: 'Do not speak so warmly to anyone but me. You would be cruelly taunted were you suspected of forgetting that in the eyes of a woman of rank an actor can never be a man.'

"Madame de Ferrières' words remained in my mind, I know not why. At the time this contemptuous tone of hers seemed to me absurd, and this fear of committing myself a piece of malicious hypocrisy.

"His name was Lelio; he was by birth an Italian, but spoke French admirably. He may have been thirty-five, although on the stage he often seemed

less than twenty. He played Corneille; after this he played Racine, and in both he was admirable."[8]

"I am surprised," said I, interrupting the Marquise, "that his name does not appear in the annals of dramatic talent."

"He was never famous,"she answered, "and was appreciated neither by the court nor the town. I have heard that he was outrageously hissed when he first appeared. Afterward he was valued for his feeling, his fire, and his efforts at correct elocution. He was tolerated and sometimes applauded, but, on the whole, he was always considered an actor without taste.

"He was a man who in his art belonged to another century, just as I did in my values and behavior. This was perhaps the intangible, all-powerful bond which, despite our positions at opposite ends of the social chain, drew us spiritually together. The public understood and judged him no better than it did me.

"'That man puts on too much,' they used to say about him. 'He forces it; he feels nothing.' And of me they said: 'That woman is spiteful and cold; she has no heart.' And yet who knows but that we felt more intensely than any two people of our era?

"In those days tragedy was played 'properly': it was necessary to die with taste, to fall gracefully, and to have an air of good breeding, even in the case of a blow. Dramatic art was modeled upon the usage of good society, and the diction and gestures of the actors were in harmony with the hoops and hair powder, which even then disfigured 'Phèdre.'[9] I have never appreciated the defects of this school of art. I bravely endured it twice in the week, for it was the fashion to like it; but I listened with so cold and constrained an air that it was generally said I was insensible to the charms of fine poetry.

"One evening, after a rather long absence from Paris, I went to the Comédie Française to see 'Le Cid.'[10] Lelio had been admitted to this theater during my stay in the country, and I saw him for the first time. He played Rodrique. I was deeply moved by the very first tone of his voice. It was penetrating rather than sonorous, but vibrating and strongly accentuated. His voice was much criticized. That of the Cid was supposed to be deep and powerful, just as all the heroes of antiquity were supposed to be tall and strong. A king who was but five feet six inches could not wear the diadem; it would have been contrary to the decrees of taste. Lelio was small and slender. His beauty lay not in the features, but in the nobleness of his forehead, the irresistible grace of his attitude,[11] the careless ease of his movements, the proud but melancholy expression of his face. The word charm should have been invented for him; it belonged to all his words, to all his glances, to all his motions. It was indeed a charm which he threw around me. This man, who stepped, spoke, moved without system or affectation, who sobbed with his heart as much as with his voice, who forgot

[8] Pierre Corneille (1606–84) and Jean Racine (1639–99) were the two preeminent French tragic dramatists of the neoclassical period.

[9] A tragedy by Racine (1677).

[10] A tragedy by Corneille (1637), about the legendary eleventh-century Spanish hero Rodrigo Diaz de Bivar. The Comédie Française, founded in 1680, is the national theater of France.

[11] Physical bearing; carriage.

himself to become identified with his passion; this man in whom the body seemed wasted and shattered by the soul, and a single one of whose glances contained all the life I failed to find in real life, exercised over me a really magnetic power. I alone could follow and understand him, and he was for five years my king, my life, my love.

"I could no longer live without seeing him. He controlled me, he owned me, he was more than a man—as I, far better than Madame de Ferrières, understood: he was a moral force, an intellectual master whose soul molded mine at will. Soon I was unable to conceal the impression he made on me. I gave up my box at the Comédie Française in order not to betray myself. I pretended I had become pious, and in the evening I went to pray in the churches; instead of that I dressed myself as a working woman and mingled with the common people that I might listen to him unconstrained. At last I bribed one of the employees of the theater to let me occupy a little corner where no one could see me and which I reached by a side corridor. As an additional precaution, I dressed myself as a schoolboy. These follies, committed for the sake of a man with whom I had never exchanged so much as a glance or word, had for me all the allure of the mysterious, spiced with an illusion of total happiness. When the hour for the theater sounded from the large clock in my drawing-room I was seized with violent palpitations. While my carriage was getting ready I tried to control myself; and if Larrieux happened to be with me I was rude to him, and threatened to send him away. I must have had great dissimulation and great tact to have hidden all this for five years from Larrieux, the most jealous of men, and from all the malicious people about me.

"I must tell you that instead of struggling against this passion I yielded to it with eagerness, with delight. It was so pure! Why should I have blushed for it? It gave me new life; it initiated me into all the feelings I had wished to experience; it almost made me a woman. I was proud to feel myself thrill and tremble. The first time my dormant heart beat aloud, I was as proud as a young mother the first time her baby nestles against her breast. I grew moody with this passion, jocular, kittenish, unpredictable. Larrieux attributed these strange whims to my new interest in religion. People began to say that I grew more beautiful every day, that my dark eyes softened, that my smile was more expressive, that what I said was truer and had more meaning than they would have expected of me. The credit for all this went to Larrieux, though of course he was entirely innocent in the matter.

"I have begun to ramble, but that is because my memories of that time wash over me like waves. In telling you these things I seem to have become young again: the name Lelio makes my heart beat wildly as it did then. But, as I was saying: When the clock struck, I used to tremble with joy and eagerness. I seem to experience again, even now, that delicious feeling that took hold of me, as if I could hardly breathe. Since then, through the vicissitudes of fortune, I have come to find myself very happy in the possession of a few small rooms in the Marais.[12] Well, of all my magnificent

[12] A historic district in east-central Paris that in the nineteenth century had lost much of its prestige.

house, my aristocratic *faubourg*,[13] and my past splendor I regret only that which could have recalled to me those days of love and dreams. I have saved from the general ruin a few pieces of furniture which I look upon with as much emotion as if the hour for the theater were about to strike now, and my horses were pawing at the door. Oh! my child, never love as I loved; it is a storm which death alone can quell.

"Then I learned to take pleasure in being young, wealthy, and beautiful. Seated in my coach, my feet buried in furs, I could see myself reflected in the mirror in front of me. The dress of that time, which has since been so laughed at, was of extraordinary richness and splendor. When arranged with taste and modified in its exaggeration, it endowed a beautiful woman with dignity, with a softness the grace of which the portraits of that time could give you no idea. A woman, clothed in its panoply of feathers, of silks, and flowers, was obliged to move slowly. I have seen very fair women in white robes with long trains of watered silk, their hair powdered and dressed with white plumes, who might without exaggeration have been compared to swans. Despite all Rousseau[14] has said, those enormous folds of satin, that profusion of muslin which enveloped a slender little body as down envelops a dove, made us resemble birds, rather than wasps. Long wings of lace fell from our arms, and our ribbons, purses, and jewels were variegated with the most brilliant colors. Balancing ourselves in our little high-heeled shoes, we seemed to fear to touch the earth and walked with the disdainful circumspection of a little bird on the edge of a brook.

"At the time of which I am speaking blonde powder began to be worn and gave the hair a light and soft color. This method of modifying the crude shades of the hair gave softness to the face, and an extraordinary brilliance to the eyes. The forehead was completely uncovered, its outline melted insensibly into the pale shades of the hair. It thus appeared higher and prouder, and gave all women a majestic air. It was the fashion, too, to dress the hair low, with large curls thrown back and falling on the neck. This was very becoming to me, and I was celebrated for the taste and magnificence of my dress. I sometimes wore red velvet with grebe-skin, sometimes white satin edged with tiger-skin, sometimes lilac damask shot with silver, with white feathers and pearls in my hair. Thus attired I would pay a few visits until the hour for the second piece at the theater, for Lelio never came on in the first. I created a sensation wherever I appeared, and, when I again found myself in my carriage, I contemplated with much pleasure the reflected image of the woman who loved Lelio, and might have been loved by him. Until then, the only pleasure I had found in being beautiful lay in the jealousy I excited. But from the moment that I loved I began to enjoy my beauty for its own sake. It was all I had to offer Lelio as a compensation for the triumphs which were denied him in Paris, and I loved to think of the pride and joy this poor actor, so misjudged, so laughed at, would feel were he told that the Marquise de R—— had dedicated her heart to him. These dreams, however, were as brief as they were

[13] District on the outer edge of the city.
[14] Jean-Jacques Rousseau (1712-78), French author who advocated natural simplicity as opposed to artifice.

beautiful. As soon as my thoughts assumed some consistency, as soon as they took the form of any plan whatever, I had the fortitude to suppress them, and all the pride of rank reasserted its empire over my soul. You seem surprised at this. I will explain it by and by.

"About eight o'clock my carriage stopped at the little Church of the Carmelites near the Luxembourg,[15] and I sent it away, for I was supposed to be attending the religious lectures which were given there at that hour. But I only crossed the church and the garden and came out on the other street. I went to the garret of a young needlewoman named Florence, who was devoted to me. I locked myself up in her room, and joyfully laid aside all my adornments to don the black square-cut coat, the sword and wig of a young college professor. Tall, with my dark complexion and inoffensive glances, I really had the awkward hypocritical look of a little priestling who had stolen in to see the play. I took a hackney coach,[16] and hastened to hide myself in my little box at the theater. Then my joy, my terror, my trembling ceased. A profound calm came upon me and I remained until the raising of the curtain as if absorbed in expectation of some great solemnity.

"As the vulture in his hypnotic circling surrounds the partridge and holds him panting and motionless, so did the soul of Lelio, that great soul of a poet and tragedian, envelop all my faculties, and plunge me into a torpor of admiration. I listened, my hands clasped upon my knees and my chin upon the front of the box, and my forehead bathed in perspiration; I hardly breathed; the crude light of the lamps tortured my eyes, which, tired and burning, were fastened on his every gesture, his every step. His feigned emotions, his simulated misfortune, impressed me as if they were real. I could hardly distinguish between truth and illusion. To me, Lelio was indeed Rodrique, Bajazet, Hippolyte.[17] I hated his enemies. I trembled at his dangers; his sorrows drew from me floods of tears, and when he died I was compelled to stifle my emotions in my handkerchief.

"Between the acts I sat down at the back of my box; I was as one dead until the sour tones of the orchestra warned me that the curtain was about to rise again. Then I sprang up, full of strength and ardor, the power to feel, to weep. How much freshness, poetry, and youth there was in that man's talent! That whole generation must have been of ice not to have fallen at his feet.

"And yet, although he offended every conventional idea, although he could not adapt his taste to that silly public, although he scandalized the women by the carelessness of his dress and deportment, and displeased the men by his contempt for their foolish actions, there were moments when, by an irresistible fascination, by the power of his eye and his voice, he held the whole of this ungrateful public as if in the hollow of his hand, and compelled it to applaud and tremble. This happened but seldom, for the entire spirit of the age can not be suddenly changed; but when it did happen, the applause was frantic. It seemed as if the Parisians, subjugated by

[15] A seventeenth-century palace originally built for Marie de' Medici, widow of the French king Henri IV; today the seat of the French Senate.
[16] Horse-drawn taxi.
[17] Heroes of, respectively, Corneille's *Le Cid*, Racine's *Bajazet* (1672), and Racine's *Phèdre*.

his genius, wished to atone for all their injustice. As for me, I believed that this man had at such times a supernatural power, and that those who most bitterly despised him were compelled to swell his triumph in spite of themselves. In truth, at such times the Comédie Française seemed smitten with madness, and the spectators, on leaving the theater, were amazed to remember that they had applauded Lelio. As for me, I seized the opportunity to give full play to my emotion; I shouted, I wept, I passionately called his name. Happily for me, my weak voice was drowned in the storm which raged about me.

"At other times he was hissed when he seemed to me to be sublime, and then I left the theater, my heart full of rage. Those nights were the most dangerous for me. I was violently tempted to seek him out, to weep with him, to curse the age in which we lived, and to console him by offering him my enthusiasm and love.

"One evening as I left the theater by the side passage which led to my box, a small, slender man passed in front of me, and turned into the street. One of the stage-carpenters took off his hat and said: 'Good evening, Monsieur Lelio.' Eager to obtain a nearer view of this extraordinary man, I ran after him, crossed the street and, forgetting the danger to which I exposed myself, followed him into a café. Fortunately, it was not one in which I was likely to meet anyone of my own rank.

"When, by the light of the smoky lamp, I looked at Lelio, I thought I had been mistaken, and had followed another man. He was at least thirty-five, sallow, withered, and worn out. He was badly dressed, he looked vulgar, spoke in a hoarse, broken voice, shook hands with the meanest wretches, drank brandy, and swore horribly. It was not until I had heard his name repeated several times that I felt sure that this was the divinity of the theater, interpreter of the great Corneille. I could recognize none of those charms which had so fascinated me, not even his glance, so bright, so ardent, and so sad. His eyes were dull, dead, almost stupid; his strongly accentuated pronunciation seemed ignoble when he called to the waiter, or talked of gambling and taverns. He walked badly, he looked vulgar, and the paint was only half wiped from his cheeks. It was no longer Hippolyte—it was Lelio. The temple was empty; the oracle was dumb; the divinity had become a man, not even a man—an actor.

"He went out, and I sat stupefied without even presence of mind to drink the hot spiced wine I had called for. When I remembered where I was, and perceived the insulting stares which were aimed at me, I became frightened. It was the first time I had ever found myself in such an equivocal position, and in such immediate contact with people of that class.

"I rose and tried to escape, but forgot to pay my reckoning. The waiter ran after me; I was terribly ashamed; I was obliged to return, enter into explanations at the desk, and endure all the mocking and suspicious looks which were turned upon me. When I left I thought I was followed. In vain I looked for a hackney-coach; there were none remaining in front of the theater. I constantly heard heavy steps echoing my own. Trembling, I turned my head, and recognized a tall, ill-looking fellow whom I had noticed in one corner of the café, and who had very much the air of a spy or something worse. He spoke to me; I do not know what he said; I was too

much frightened to hear, but I had still presence of mind enough to rid myself of him. I struck him in the face with my cane, and, leaving him stunned at my audacity, I shot away swift as an arrow, and did not stop till I reached Florence's little garret. When I awoke the next morning in my own bed with its wadded curtains and coronal of pink feathers, I almost thought I had dreamed, and felt greatly mortified when I recollected the disillusions of the previous night. I thought myself thoroughly cured of my love, and I tried to rejoice at it, but in vain. I was filled with a mortal regret, the weariness of life again entered my heart, the world had not a pleasure which could charm me. That day I sent Larrieux away.

"Evening came, but it brought no more magnanimous feelings. Society seemed to me stupid. I went to church and listened to the evening lecture with a determination of becoming pious; I caught cold, and came home quite ill. I remained in bed several days. The Comtesse de Ferrières came to see me, assured me that I had no fever, that lying still made me ill, that I must amuse myself, go out, go to the theater. She compelled me to go with her to see 'Cinna.'[18] 'You no longer go to the theater,' said she to me; 'your health is undermined by your piety, and the dullness of your life. You have not seen Lelio for some time; he has improved, and he is now sometimes applauded. I think he may some day become very tolerable.'

"I do not know why I allowed myself to be persuaded. However, as I was completely disenchanted with Lelio, I thought I no longer ran any risk in braving his fascinations in public. I dressed myself with excessive brilliance, and, in a court proscenium box,[19] fronted a danger in which I no longer believed.

"But the danger was never more imminent. Lelio was sublime, and I had never been more in love with him. My recent adventure seemed but a dream. I could not believe that Lelio was other than he seemed upon the stage. In spite of myself, I yielded to the terrible agitations into which he had the power of throwing me. My face was bathed in tears, and I was compelled to cover it with my handkerchief. In the disorder of my mind I wiped off my rouge and my patches,[20] and the Comtesse de Ferrières advised me to retire to the back of my box, for my emotion was creating a sensation in the house. I fortunately had had the skill to make everyone believe it was the acting of Mlle. Hippolyte Clairon which affected me so deeply. She was, in my own opinion, a very cold and formal actress, too superior perhaps for her profession, as it was then understood; but her manner of saying 'Tout beau,'[21] in 'Cinna,' had given her a great reputation. It must be said, however, that when she played with Lelio she outdid herself. Although she took pains to proclaim her share in the fashionable contempt for his method of acting, she assuredly felt the influence of his genius.

"That evening Lelio noticed me, either on account of my dress or my emotion; for I saw him, when he was not acting, bend over one of the spectators, who, at that epoch, sat upon the stage, and inquire my name. I

[18] A tragedy by Corneille (1640). [19] A box immediately beside the stage.
[20] "Beauty spots," small black patches worn cosmetically to emphasize the fairness of the skin.
[21] "Gently," "Not so fast."

guessed his question by the way both looked at me. My heart beat almost to suffocation, and I noticed during the play that Lelio's eyes turned several times toward me. What would I not have given to hear what the Chevalier de Bretillac, whom he had questioned, had said to him about me! Lelio's face did not indicate the nature of the information he had received, for he was obliged to retain the expression suited to his part. I knew this Bretillac very slightly, and I could not imagine whether he would speak well or ill of me.

"That night I understood for the first time the nature of the passion which enchained me to Lelio. It was a passion purely intellectual, purely ideal. It was not he I loved, but those heroes of ancient times whose sincerity, whose fidelity, whose tenderness he knew how to portray; with him and by him I was carried back to an epoch of forgotten virtues. I was proud enough to think that in those days I should not have been misjudged and hated, and that I should not have been reduced to loving a phantom of the footlights. Lelio was to me but the shadow of the Cid, the representative of that antique chivalric love now ridiculed in France. The man, the actor— no longer need I feel anxiety about him. I had seen that person. I could love Lelio in his public guise only. The Lelio who belonged to me was a fictitious being who had no existence outside the theater. To exist as an object of my love he needed the illusion of the stage, the reflection of the footlights, make-up, costume. Divested of those trappings he faded into nothingness, as a star fades at break of day. Off the boards[22] I had not the slightest desire to see him; indeed, I felt that to do so would plunge me into the deepest despondency, as though I were seeing a funerary urn containing the little bit of dust that had once been a great man.

"My frequent absence at the times when Larrieux usually visited, and especially my explicit refusal, from that time on, to continue our relationship on a footing other than friendship, provoked in him a fit of jealousy— one better founded, I can assure you, than those he had felt before. One evening as I was going to the Carmelite church with the intention of leaving it by the passage door, I perceived that he was following me. Convinced that henceforth it would be almost impossible to conceal the object of my nocturnal expeditions, I decided to go publicly to the theater. I became more adeptly hypocritical in hiding my feelings, and moreover, as a way of putting people off the scent, I professed everywhere my admiration for Mlle. Hippolyte Clairon. All this was a great encumbrance: I was now forced to keep a strict watch over myself, and so my pleasure became less keen and profound. But from this situation arose another that soon compensated for it: Lelio began to pay close attention to me. My beauty had struck him, my sensibility flattered him. His attention sometimes wandered so much as to displease the public. Soon I could no longer doubt. He was madly in love with me.

"My box had provoked the envy of the Princess de Vaudemont. I gave it up to her, and took for myself a smaller one, less in view of the house and better situated. I was almost upon the stage, I did not lose one of Lelio's glances; and he could look at me without it being seen by the public. But I no longer needed to catch his eye in order to understand all his feelings.

[22] Stage.

The sound of his voice, his sighs, the expression which he gave to certain verses, certain words, told me that he was speaking to me. I was the happiest and proudest of women, for then it was the hero, not the actor, who loved me.

"Well, after two years of feeding my love secretly, in the depths of my soul, I spent three more winters like this. My love was now shared by Lelio, but never by looks did I encourage him to hope for anything more than this mysterious and intimate closeness. I have since heard that Lelio often followed me in my walks and drives; so little did I desire to see him outside of the theater that I never perceived it. Of the eighty years I have passed in this world, those five are the only ones in which I really lived.

"One day I read in the *Mercure de France*[23] the name of a new actor engaged at the Comédie Française to replace Lelio, who was about to leave France.

"This announcement was a mortal blow to me. I could not conceive how I should exist when deprived of these emotions, this life of passion and storm. This event gave an immense development to my love, and was wellnigh my ruin.

"I no longer struggled with myself; I no longer sought to stifle all thoughts contrary to my rank. No longer was it enough to rejoice in Lelio as he was. I regretted that he was not what he appeared on the stage; I wished him as young and handsome as he seemed each night before the footlights, that I might sacrifice to him all my pride, all my prejudices. Now that I was about to lose this ideal being who had long filled my soul, the desire seized me to give my dream world a factual existence, even if the ultimate price of doing so might be hatred for life, for Lelio, and for my very self.

"While I was in this state of irresolution, I received a letter in an unknown hand. It is the only love letter I have ever kept. Though Larrieux has written me innumerable protestations, and I have received a thousand perfumed declarations from a hundred others, it is the only real love letter that was ever sent me."

The Marquise rose, opened with a steady hand an inlaid casket,[24] and took from it a crumpled, worn-out letter, which I read with difficulty.

"Madame—I am certain you will feel nothing but contempt for this letter, you will not even deem it worthy of your anger. But, to a man falling into an abyss, what matters one more stone at the bottom? You will think me mad, and you will be right. You will perhaps pity me, for you will not doubt my sincerity. However humble your piety may have made you, you will understand the extent of my despair; you must already know how much evil and how much good your eyes can do.

"If I note in you a single mark of compassion, if this evening at the eagerly awaited hour when, as every evening, I come again to life, I see in your face even a suggestion of pity, then I will leave less miserable; I will carry from France a memory that may strengthen me to go on living and following my thankless and burdensome career.

"You must know this already, madame; it is impossible that the violent emotions I have portrayed upon the stage, my cries of wrath and despair,

[23] "The Messenger [literally, Mercury] of France"; a newspaper.
[24] A box for holding jewels or other valuable objects.

have not twenty times revealed to you my passion. You can not have lighted all these flames without being conscious of what you did. Perhaps you played with me as a tiger with his prey; perhaps the spectacle of my folly and my tortures was your pastime. But no; to think so were to presume too much. No, madame, I do not believe it; you never thought of me. You felt the verses of the great Corneille, you identified these with the noble passions of tragedy; that was all. And I, madman that I was, I dared to think that my voice alone sometimes awoke your sympathies, that my heart echoed in yours, that between you and me there was something more than between me and the public. Oh, my madness was arrant, but it was sweet! Leave me my illusions, madame; what are they to you? Do you fear that I should boast of them? By what right should I do so, and who would believe me? I should only make myself a laughing-stock among sensible people. Leave me this conviction; it has given me more joy than the severity of the public has caused me sorrow. Let me bless you, let me thank you upon my knees, for the sensibility which I have discovered in your soul, and which no one else has ever shown me; for the tears which I have seen you shed for my fictitious sorrows, and which have often raised my inspiration almost to delirium; for the timid glances which sought, at least it seemed so, to console me for the coldness of my audience.

"Oh, why were you born to pomp and splendor! Why am I an obscure and nameless artist! Why have I not riches and the favor of the public, that I might exchange them for a name, for one of those titles which I have hitherto disdained, and which, perhaps, would permit me to aspire as high as you are placed! Once I deemed the distinctions conferred upon talent superior to all others. To what purpose, thought I, is a man a Chevalier or a Marquis but to be the sillier, the vainer, and the more insolent? I hated the pride of men of rank, and thought that I should be sufficiently avenged for their disdain if my genius raised me above them.

"Dreams and delusions all! My strength has not equalled my mad ambition. I have remained obscure; I have done worse—I have touched success, and allowed it to escape me. I thought myself great, and I was cast down to the dust; I imagined that I was almost sublime, and I was condemned to be ridiculous. Fate took me—me and my audacious dreams—and crushed me as if I had been a reed. I am a most wretched man!

"But I committed my greatest folly when I cast my eyes beyond that row of lights which marked between me and the rest of society an invisible line of separation. It is to me a circle of Popilius.[25] I, an actor, I dared to raise my eyes and fasten them upon a beautiful woman—upon a woman, you, lovely, and of high rank; for you are all this, madame, and I know it. The world accuses you of coldness and of exaggerated piety. I alone understand you. Your first smile, your first tear, sufficiently disproved the absurd fable which the Chevalier de Bretillac repeated against you.

"But then what a destiny is yours! What fatality weighs upon you as upon me, that in the midst of society so brilliant, which calls itself so enlightened, you should have found only the heart of a poor actor to do you

[25] A Roman envoy of the second century B.C who, in a humiliating way, forced the invading king Antiochus Epiphanes to withdraw from Egypt: the king was required to accept the terms before stepping outside a circle that Popilius had drawn.

justice. Nothing will deprive me of the sad and consoling thought that, had we been born in the same rank, you would have been mine in spite of my rivals, in spite of my inferiority. You would have been compelled to acknowledge that there is in me something greater than their wealth, and their titles—the power of loving you.

<div align="right">Lelio."</div>

"This letter," continued the Marquise, "was of a character very unusual at the time it was written, and seemed to me, notwithstanding some passages of theatrical declamation at the beginning, so powerful, so true, so full of bold passion, that I was overwhelmed by it. The pride which still struggled within me faded away. I would have given all the remaining days I had to live for one hour of such love.

"I won't describe to you all my anxieties, my fantasies and terrors; indeed, I wouldn't be able to sort them out even in my own mind. But I responded with these words, as nearly as I can recall:

"'I do not accuse you, Lelio; I accuse destiny. I do not pity you alone; I pity myself also. Neither pride nor prudence shall make me deny you the consolation of believing that I have felt a preference for you. Keep it, for it is the only one I can offer you. I can never consent to see you.'

"Next day I received a note which I hastily read and threw into the fire, to prevent Larrieux from seeing it, for he came suddenly upon me while I was reading it. It read thus:

"'Madame—I must see you or I must die. Once—once only, but for a single hour, if such is your will. Why should you fear an interview since you trust my honor and my prudence? Madame, I know who you are; I am well aware of your piety and of the austerity of your life. I am not fool enough to hope for anything but a word of compassion, but it must fall from your own lips. My heart must receive it and bear it away, or my heart must break. Lelio.'

"I will say, to my glory—for all noble and courageous trust is glorious in the face of danger—that I never thought for a moment I might be part of some shameless libertine's game. I believed implicitly in the humility, in the sincerity of Lelio. Besides, I had ample reason to trust my own strength. I resolved to see him. I had completely forgotten his faded features, his low-bred manners, his vulgar aspect; I recollected only the fascination of his genius, his letters, and his love. I answered:

"'I will see you. Find some secure place, but hope for nothing but for what you have asked. Should you seek to abuse my trust, you would be a villain, and I should not fear you.'

"Answer:

"'Your trust would save you from the basest of villains. You will see, Madame, that Lelio is not unworthy of it. Duke ——— has often been good enough to offer me the use of his house in the Rue de Valois. What use could it serve me? Over the last three years there has only been one woman in the world as far as I was concerned. Deign to meet me there after the play.'

"Some explanations and directions as to the locality of the house fol-

lowed. I received this note at four o'clock. The whole negotiation had occupied but a day. I had spent it in wandering through the house like one distracted; I was in a fever. This rapid succession of events bore me along as in a dream.

"When I had made the final decision, when it was impossible to draw back, I sank down upon my ottoman,[26] breathless and dizzy.

"I was really ill. A surgeon was sent for; I was bled. I told my servants not to mention my indisposition to any one; I dreaded the intrusion of officious advisers, and was determined not to be prevented from going out that night.

"I threw myself upon my bed to await the appointed hour, and gave orders that no visitors should be admitted, even M. Larrieux.

"The blood-letting had relieved and weakened me; I sank into a great depression of spirits. All my illusions vanished with the excitement which had accompanied my fever. Reason and memory returned; I remembered my disenchantment in the coffee-house, and Lelio's wretched appearance there; I prepared to blush for my folly, and to fall from the height of my deceitful visions to a bare and despicable reality. I no longer understood how it had been possible for me to consent to exchange my heroic and romantic tenderness for the revulsion of feeling which awaited me, and the sense of shame which would henceforth poison all my recollections. I bitterly regretted what I had done; I wept for my illusions, my love, and that future of pure and secret joys which I was about to forfeit. Above all, I mourned for Lelio, whom in seeing I should forever lose, in whose love I had found five years of happiness, and for whom in a few hours I should feel nothing but indifference.

"In the paroxysm of my grief I violently wrung my arms; the vein reopened, and I had barely time to ring for my maid, who found me in a swoon in my bed. A deep and heavy sleep, against which I struggled in vain, seized me. I neither dreamed nor suffered; I was as one dead for several hours. When I again opened my eyes my room was almost dark, my house silent; my waiting-woman was asleep in a chair at the foot of my bed. I remained for some time in such a state of numbness and weakness that I recollected nothing. Suddenly my memory returned, and I asked myself whether the hour and the day of rendezvous were passed, whether I had slept an hour or a century; whether I had killed Lelio by breaking my word. Was there yet time? I tried to rise, but my strength failed me. I struggled for some moments as if in a nightmare. At last I summoned all the forces of my will. I sprang to the floor, opened the curtains, and saw the moon shining upon the trees of my garden. I ran to the clock; the hands marked ten. I seized my maid and waked her: 'Quinette, what day of the week is it?' She sprang from her chair, screaming, and tried to escape from me, for she thought me delirious; I reassured her and learned that I had only slept three hours. I thanked God. I asked for a hackney-coach. Quinette looked at me in amazement. At last she became convinced that I had the full use of my senses, transmitted my order, and began to dress me.

"I asked for my simplest dress; I put no ornaments in my hair, I refused to wear my rouge. I wished above all things for Lelio's esteem and respect,

[26] Sofa.

for they were far more precious to me than his love. Nevertheless, I was pleased when Quinette, who was much surprised at this new caprice, said, examining me from head to foot: 'Truly, madame, I know not how you manage it. You are dressed in a plain white robe, without either train or pannier;[27] you are ill and as pale as death; you have not even put on a patch; yet I never saw you so beautiful as tonight. I pity the men who will look upon you!' 'Do you think me so very austere, my poor Quinette?' 'Alas, madame, every day I pray Heaven to make me like you; but up to this time—' 'Come, simpleton, give me my mantle and muff.'

"At midnight I was at the house in the Rue de Valois. I was carefully veiled, a sort of valet de chambre[28] received me; he was the only human being to be seen in this mysterious dwelling. He led me through the windings of a dark garden to a pavilion buried in silence and shadow. Depositing his green silk lantern in the vestibule, he opened the door of a large dusky room, showed me by a respectful gesture and with a most impassive face a ray of light proceeding from the other extremity, and said, in a tone so low that it seemed as if he feared to awaken the sleeping echoes: 'Your ladyship is alone, no one else has yet come. Your ladyship will find in the summer parlor a bell which I will answer if you need anything.' He disappeared as if by enchantment, shutting the door upon me.

"I was terribly frightened; I thought I had fallen into some trap. I called him back. He instantly reappeared, and his air of stupid solemnity reassured me. I asked him what time it was, although I knew perfectly well, for I had sounded my watch twenty times in the carriage.[29]

"'It is midnight,' answered he, without raising his eyes.

"I saw that he was a man perfectly instructed in the business at hand. I now resolutely entered the summer parlor, and I realized how unfounded were my fears when I saw that the doors which opened upon the garden were only of painted silk. Nothing could be more charming than this boudoir; it was fitted up as a concert-room. The walls were of stucco as white as snow, and the mirrors were framed in unpolished silver. Musical instruments of unusually rich material were scattered about, upon seats of white velvet, trimmed with pearls. The light came from above through leaves of alabaster,[30] which formed a dome. This soft, even light might have been mistaken for that of the moon. I examined with curiosity, with fascination, the furnishings of this little retreat, which was unlike anything I could remember. This was the first time in my life I had set foot in such a nest; but, either because this was not the actual room designed for the celebration of the rites of love or because Lelio had removed everything that might give me offense or make me ill at ease, I was able to dismiss the forebodings I had felt on first entering. A single statue of white marble stood in the middle of the room; it was an antique and represented Isis[31] veiled, with her finger upon her lips. The mirrors which reflected us, both pale and draped in white, produced such an illusion that I could scarcely distinguish my figure from hers.

[27] A device for distending or puffing out a skirt at the hips. [28] Personal manservant.
[29] The watch is a "repeater" that, when a button is pressed in the dark, strikes the hours and quarters.
[30] A white, translucent ceramic material. [31] An ancient Egyptian fertility goddess.

"Suddenly the silence was interrupted; the door was opened and closed, and light footsteps sounded upon the floor. I sank into a chair more dead than alive, for I was about to see Lelio shorn of the illusions of the stage. I closed my eyes, and inwardly bade them farewell before I reopened them.

"But how much was I surprised! Lelio was beautiful as an angel. He had not taken off his stage dress, and it was the most elegant I had ever seen him wear. His Spanish doublet was of white satin, his shoulder and garter knots of cherry ribbons, and a short cloak of the same color was thrown over his shoulder. He wore an immense ruff of English lace; his hair was short and unpowdered, partially covered by a cap of white feathers and a diamond rose. In this costume he had just played Don Juan in 'Festin de Pierre.'[32] Never had I seen him so beautiful, so young, so poetical, as at that moment. Velasquez[33] would have worshipped such a model.

"He knelt before me. I could not help stretching out my hand to him, he seemed so submissive, so fearful of displeasing me. A man sufficiently in love to tremble before a woman was rare in those times, and this one was thirty-five and an actor.

"It seemed to me then, it seems to me still, that he was in the first bloom of youth. In his white dress he looked like a young page; his forehead had all the purity, his heart all the ardor of a first love. He took my hands and covered them with kisses. And then I lost control of myself: I drew his head onto my lap, I caressed his burning forehead, his stiff black hair, and the brown neck which disappeared in the soft whiteness of his collar. But Lelio did not press me; all his ardor was concentrated in his heart. He wept like a woman. I was overwhelmed with surprise.

"I wept delicious tears. I compelled him to raise his head and look at me. How splendid, how tender were his eyes! How much fascination his warm, true soul communicated to the very defects of his face, and the scars left upon it by time and toil! Ah, the mightiness of the soul! Whoever does not understand the miracles it works has never been in love! When I saw the premature wrinkles upon his beautiful forehead, when I saw the pallor of his lips, the languor of his smile, my heart was melted. I felt that I must needs weep for his griefs, his disappointments, the labors of his life. I identified myself with him in all his sorrows, even that of his long, hopeless love for me, and I had but one wish—to compensate him for the ills he had suffered.

"'My dear Lelio, my great Rodrique, my beautiful Don Juan!' I said to him distractedly.

"His eyes seared me. He spoke to me, he told me how from a dissipated actor I had made him a man full of life and ardor; how I had raised him in his own eyes, and restored to him the illusions of his youth; he spoke of his respect, his veneration for me, of his contempt for the species of love which was then in fashion. He told me that he would sacrifice all the remaining days of his life in return for one hour in my arms, but that he would sacrifice that hour and all those days together rather than offend me in the slightest way. Never did a man with more penetrating eloquence speak to

[32] "The Stone Guest," a 1665 dramatization of the Don Juan legend by Molière (1622–73), another great French dramatist of the neoclassic period.

[33] Velasquez (1599–1660) was official portrait-painter to the court of Phillip IV of Spain.

the heart of a woman; never did Racine make love utter itself with such conviction of its own truth, such poetry, such strength. Everything elevated and profound, everything sweet and fiery which passion can inspire, lay in his words, his face, his eyes, his caresses. Alas! did he deceive himself? Was he playing a part?"

"I certainly do not think so," I cried, looking at the Marquise. She seemed to grow young as she spoke; and, like the fairy Urgela, to cast off her hundred years. I know not who has said that a woman's heart has no wrinkles.

"Listen to the end," said she. "I threw my arms around his neck; I shivered as I touched the satin of his coat, as I breathed the perfume of his hair. My emotion was too violent and I fainted.

"He recalled me to myself by his prompt assistance. I found him still kneeling at my feet. 'Pity me, kill me,' cried he. He was paler and far more ill than I.

"But all the violent nervous turmoil I had gone through in the course of that long, tempestuous day was driving me emotionally from pillar to post. The quick bright light that had revealed to me a new mode of existence faded, and my blood grew calm. The refinement and delicacy of real love regained the upper hand.

"'Listen to me, Lelio,' I said. 'It is not haughty disdain that tears me away from the rapture you are feeling. I might have within me all the touch-me-not oversensitivity that is drilled into us from our earliest days, so that it becomes second nature, but I could forget all that now, for my nature has been utterly transformed into a new one that I never was aware of before. If you love me, help me to resist you. Let me carry away from this place the delicious satisfaction of having loved you with my heart only. Perhaps if I had never belonged to anyone else I would be able to give myself to you, and joyfully. But you need to know that Larrieux has defiled me. You need to know that, swept along by the horrible necessity of doing what everyone else does, I have submitted to the caresses of a man I never loved. You need to know that the loathing I feel as a result has stunted my imagination, to the point where, if I had given myself to you just now, I might well have come to hate you afterwards. Oh, let us not put ourselves to so fearful a test! Let me keep you in my heart and memory as something untainted! Here we part forever, but let us carry from this place a whole future of blissful thoughts and adored memories. I swear, Lelio, to love you till my death. I swear it without fear, for I feel that the snows of age will not have the power to extinguish this ardent flame.' Lelio knelt before me; he did not implore me, he did not reproach me; he said that he had not hoped for so much happiness as I had given him, and that he had no right to ask for more. Nevertheless, as he bade me farewell, his despair, the emotion which trembled in his face, terrified me. I asked him if he would not find happiness in thinking of me, if the ecstasy of our meeting would not lend its charm to all the days of his life, if his past and future sorrows would not be softened each time he recalled it. He roused himself to promise, to swear all I asked. He again fell at my feet and passionately kissed my dress. I felt a great unsteadiness: I made a sign to him and he left me. The carriage I had sent for came.

"The automaton servant of the house knocked three times outside to

warn me. Lelio despairingly threw himself in front of the door; he looked like a specter. I gently repulsed him and he yielded. I crossed the threshold, and as he attempted to follow me, I showed him a chair in the middle of the room, underneath the statue of Isis. He sat down in it. A passionate smile wandered over his lips, his eyes sent out one more flash of gratitude and love. He was still beautiful, still young, still a grandee[34] of Spain. After a few steps, when I was about to lose him forever, I turned back and looked at him once more. Despair had crushed him. He was old, altered, frightful. His body seemed paralyzed. His stiffened lips attempted an unmeaning smile. His eyes were glassy and dim; he was now only Lelio, the shadow of a lover and a prince."

The Marquise paused; then, with a somber smile, her whole face breaking up like a building falling into ruins, she added: "Since then I have not heard him mentioned."

The Marquise made a second and a longer pause; then, with the terrible fortitude which comes with length of years, which springs from the persistent love of life or the near hope of death, she said with a smile: "Well, do you not now believe in the ideality of the eighteenth century?"

"Madame," I answered, "I am not inclined to question it. All the same, were I not so touched, perhaps I might tell you that you were well-advised to let yourself be bled that day."

"Wretched men!" said the Marquise; "In matters of the heart, you understand nothing at all!"

Alfred, Lord Tennyson
(1809–1892)

The long and prolific career of Alfred Tennyson (Lord Tennyson after 1883) marks the road from Romantic to modern poetry. It winds gently forth from Wordsworth, Byron, Shelley, and Keats at the earlier end but meets roadblocks and S-curves at the later one. In many ways, Tennyson represented—or at least seemed to— everything turn-of-the-century modernism wanted to free itself from: a high-ceremonial style at odds with the idiom of familiar life; a tendency to subordinate literary art to statement, and complacent statement at that; an ideal of beauty too nearly synonymous with exoticism and mere prettiness; the imposition of a false vision of order on a fragmented world; cozy domestic sentimentalism; an obsessive Victorian need to resolve the darkness of life into light. These identifications with Tennyson—some of them anticipated by his own younger contemporaries—range between quarter- and half-truths. No reader of *In Memoriam* can deny that Tennyson gives darkness its due. The tension between the public and private roles of poetry was something he felt keenly,

[34] Eminent nobleman.

and he was as much a harsh critic of Victorian society as its spokesman. Indeed, much of the early twentieth-century reaction to him amounts to a tribute to his stature; rebels rebel against what is there, and what was there at the turn of the century was, to a great extent, Tennyson. Even they could not convincingly deny Tennyson's mastery of language and technique, in a broad range of styles and forms. It is true that he did not always find matter adequate to his gifts, but one can say the same thing of most other great artists who were unstintingly prolific, like Mozart or Bach. In his best work, though, of which there is a considerable quantity, Tennyson did find apt matter, and then the result was great poetry.

Tennyson's life is mainly the story of his poetry; he never had another profession. He was born in 1809, the third of eleven children, in Lincoln-shire, a county in east-central England where some of the early lyrics in *In Memoriam* are set. His father, a clergyman, was a devoted parent in most ways but was subject to drunken outbursts that provoked severe melan-choly in the young Tennyson, foreshadowing a note of poignant Virgilian sadness that would later mix with optimism in his work—not to mention mental health problems in his real life. Enormously precocious, he wrote poems from the time he was five and by his mid-teens was producing ambi-tious, skillfully crafted poems. In 1828, at Cambridge, he met Arthur Henry Hallam, the central figure in his life. The two were members of the "Apostles," a society at Cambridge that met regularly to discuss directions in various branches of thought as well as politics and literature. The keen-minded and personally appealing Hallam was at the center of this brilliant group of young men, and Tennyson came to depend on him not only as a friend (they traveled together to Spain and to the Rhine) but also as his inspiration and guide in poetry. Hallam and the Apostles had discovered Keats and Shelley, and when in 1831 Hallam reviewed Tennyson's *Poems, Chiefly Lyrical* (1830) he saw and encouraged the sensuousness that in much of Tennyson's work, as in Keats's, is posed against a sterner acceptance of duty, social responsibility, and pain. Hallam's review (a remarkable literary essay, incidentally, for a twenty-year-old) also asserted the sufficiency and integrity of the poetic calling, the need for the artist to fix his attention on his feelings and art rather than on what distracts from them, however lofty these distractions might be. In some of Tennyson's early work we find him exploring this question of the poet's role and balancing, like Keats, the imagery of static quietude ("The Lotos-Eaters," for example), escape, and death against the need to act, suffer, immerse oneself in the life of the world. Tennyson's delicately beautiful "The Lady of Shalott" is among the poems that explore this conflict.

Reviews of Tennyson's next volume, the *Poems* of 1832, were mixed, but they included a devastating one by John Wilson Croker—appropriately, since Croker is best known today for a similar savaging of Keats. Poetically speaking, the sensitive Tennyson withdrew into himself, writing and revis-ing but publishing almost nothing for ten years. But the review was a tri-fling blow compared with another one, the crucial event in Tennyson's life: Hallam died suddenly in 1833 in Vienna, at the age of twenty-two. Tenny-son's grief over his lost friend and counsellor was profound, his individual loss aggravated by a further personal bond in Hallam's engagement to Tennyson's sister Emily and the public loss of a man whom his friends had

believed destined to become a national leader. The poem "Tithonus," with its death-wish theme and despair over irrecoverable youth, was one response to Hallam's death, as in a different way was "Ulysses," with its contrasting heroic resolve to act and endure even though youth is gone. (We note in passing that "Ulysses" is sometimes read very differently: as a condemnation of the protagonist's escapist irresponsibility.) But the main record of Tennyson's grief, and of the troubling ideas it gave rise to, was a series of tender, pensive, anguished, speculative brief lyrics ("short swallow-flights of song"—XLVIII.15) that, written randomly at first like a diary, were later gathered, ordered, and published (anonymously) in 1850 as *In Memoriam.*

The compelling private and public themes of *In Memoriam* challenged the highest reaches of Tennyson's imagination and artistry, and the result is one of the centerpieces of Victorian culture. Growing from an expression of personal bereavement, it becomes also a way of exploring religious, philosophical, and social issues including the compatibility of science with faith and of spiritual with intellectual progress. Considered in its broadest aspect, the poem is a wrestling with the problem of evil and suffering, in the line of the Book of Job. What distinguishes *In Memoriam* from many other treatments of this formidable question is its nakedness and personal immediacy; written originally without any large formal or public purpose in mind, each poem is free to record honestly a passing mood or address a concrete philosophical issue, in the context not of fiction but of real life, and without subordination to an artificial consistency of plan or attitude. The result, thematically, is a work both universal (as Tennyson put it, "the voice of the human race" speaking through the poet) and personal— personal not only from the poet's viewpoint but also from that of many modern readers for whom the problem of belief takes the same form, science versus religion, that it takes in *In Memoriam.* For such readers, therefore, the poem requires little or no conversion by analogy into their own dilemmas. As art, the result is a prime example of nineteenth-century organicism: a poem that, like Wordsworth's *Prelude,* has to evolve its own themes, purpose, and organization through the process of being written and records that artistic evolution in parallel with the evolution from chaotic grief to ordered affirmation. And, again like *The Prelude, In Memoriam* emerges as a work with its own unique kind of developmental unity organically inseparable from the experiences recorded. Both art and life, at first apparently random, ultimately have pattern.

In the year when *In Memoriam* was published, a long-lapsed engagement between Tennyson, now forty-one, and Emily Sellwood was revived, and the two were married. (The obstacles had included differences in religious belief and Tennyson's unsettled financial prospects; it has been suggested that Tennyson's hauntedness with Hallam also played a part.) Still another milestone in 1850 was the death of Wordsworth and the naming of Tennyson as the new poet laureate of England. The great success of *In Memoriam* had paved the way, following on the impressive 1842 volume of poems and *The Princess* (1847), a curiously ambivalent but lyrically glorious examination of the role and education of women. Thereafter Tennyson was an institution, like Dickens. His volumes were immensely popular best sellers. Some were comfortably sentimental, like *Enoch Arden* (1864), a work about

the return of a supposedly dead spouse that is remembered today mainly because its title is used to describe laws governing the subject of presumed but unproved death. Tennyson did not, however, simply become the voice of complacency. In the Byronic "Locksley Hall" (1842) Tennyson's protagonist had greeted the new age in the bracing words "Forward, forward let us range, / Let the great world spin for ever down the ringing grooves of change," but the poem had also indicted the materialism of the age, and this critique was sustained in the experimental *Maud; A Monodrama* (1855) and in the series *Idylls of the King,* Tennyson's equivalent of epic. Published over three decades beginning in 1859, this retelling of the King Arthur story emerges as a societal *memento mori* reminding the reader of how a noble civilization can undergo moral decay. In the 1870s and 1880s Tennyson wrote several plays, most of which were staged. He was made a baron in 1883. In 1892 he died, aged eighty-three, and was buried with much ceremony in Westminster Abbey.

Tennyson's recognized poetic craftsmanship has many sides. To begin with, he is a master of what in modern filmmaking are called "special effects," though in his best poems these cannot be isolated from creative imaginative vision. A good example is lines 34–39 of "Tithonus," which simultaneously describe the goddess's body and the coming of dawn on earth; this is certainly virtuoso work, but it is also authentic mythmaking. The sustaining of a single sentence through all sixteen lines of *In Memoriam* LXXXVI is a technical feat, but the technique is functional, reinforcing the theme of wind and breath that runs through the whole. Tennyson's skill in using the distant mythical past to explore contemporary, immediately personal, or universal themes (as in "The Lotos-Eaters," "Ulysses," and "Tithonus") can rightly be praised as a technique, but it represents also a remarkable act of imaginative fusion. (Hallam's review recognized this power of Tennyson's, of "embodying himself in ideal characters, or rather moods of character, with such extreme accuracy of adjustment, that the circumstances of the narration seem to have a natural correspondence with the predominant feeling, and, as it were, to be evolved from it by assimilative force.") Tennyson excels in meticulous description, though this too is often much more than mannerism. The description of the high waterfall in lines 8–9 of "The Lotos-Eaters" that "like a downward smoke . . . Along the cliff to fall and pause and fall did seem" is not mere backdrop, nor is it simply acute sensory psychology, registering the common optical illusion that the water alternately falls and is arrested; the lines also evoke the poem's theme of rest versus action. Tennyson can also create mood masterfully through sound, meter, and imagery. Like Keats, he is a master of vowel and consonant interplay—a "miser of sound and syllable," to borrow a phrase from Keats himself. ("The shallop flitteth silken-sail'd / Skimming down to Camelot"— "The Lady of Shallot.") He prided himself on knowing the quantity—that is, the temporal duration of the syllables—of every English word except "scissors." The range of his voice is almost unparalleled; we remember best his high sonorities, but he can also achieve a studied plainness ("He is not here; but far away / The noise of life begins again"—*In Memoriam*, VII.9–10) and even write dialect. His public rhetorical voice can be exhilarating, as in the famous New-Year's poem (*In Memoriam*, CVI), but the voice of private intimacy is equally moving, as in

the lyrics about Hallam's house (VII, CXIX). Perhaps the best way to summarize Tennyson's style is to draw a negative comparison. Someone once defined poetry whimsically as language that, when printed, leaves an uneven right margin, and there are indeed poems so unassumingly prosaic as to be unrecognizable as poems without this typographic help. Tennyson's poetry is the antithesis of that. He is sometimes criticized for overpoeticizing, as in the notorious example from the epilogue to *In Memoriam* where he calls champagne "the foaming grape of eastern France" (line 80). But such excesses, if they can be called that, are a small price to pay for the verbal magic of passages like this one:

> And suck'd from out the distant gloom
> A breeze began to tremble o'er
> The large leaves of the sycamore,
> And fluctuate all the still perfume,
>
> And gathering freshlier overhead
> Rock'd the full-foliaged elms, and swung
> The heavy-folded rose, and flung
> The lilies to and fro, and said,
>
> "The dawn, the dawn," and died away;
> And East and West, without a breath,
> Mixt their dim lights, like life and death,
> To broaden into boundless day.
> [*In Memoriam*, XCV.53–64]

FURTHER READING (*prepared by W. J. R.*): The most complete life is Sir Charles Tennyson's *Alfred Tennyson*, 1949, which draws heavily on the correspondence. James D. Kissane's *Alfred Tennyson*, 1970, is a particularly good survey of the poet's life, works, and modern reputation. Paul Turner's *Tennyson*, 1976, is another critical survey, especially good on *Idylls of the King* and *In Memoriam*. F. B. Pinion's *A Tennyson Companion: Life and Works*, 1984, is an authoritative handbook. Andrew Cecil Bradley's *A Commentary on Tennyson's "In Memoriam,"* 1901, rev. 1910, is still a valuable work, with an interpretation of the poem which has become fairly standard. *Tennyson: A Collection of Critical Essays*, ed. Elizabeth A. Francis, 1980, contains twelve essays by T. S. Eliot, Douglas Bush, and others, and is intended for the general reader. Alan Sinfield's *Alfred Tennyson*, 1986, and Daniel Albright's *Tennyson: The Muse's Tug-of-War*, 1986, are stimulating contemporary reconsiderations. W. David Shaw's *Tennyson's Style*, 1976, analyzes carefully stylistic developments in Tennyson's artistry and discusses *In Memoriam, Maud,* and *Idylls* in detail.

THE LOTOS-EATERS[1]

"Courage!" he[2] said, and pointed toward the land,
"This mounting wave will roll us shoreward soon."

[1] This poem was suggested by an episode in Homer's *Odyssey*, Book IX. After the ten-years' war against Troy, Odysseus (in Latin, "Ulysses") and his men underwent many perils while trying to return to Ithaca, their island home. At one point they reached the island of the lotos. When tasted, the fruit of this plant sapped the crew's willpower to continue their journey.
[2] Odysseus.

In the afternoon they came unto a land
In which it seemed always afternoon.
All round the coast the languid air did swoon,
Breathing like one that hath a weary dream.
Full-faced above the valley stood the moon;
And, like a downward smoke, the slender stream
Along the cliff to fall and pause and fall did seem.

A land of streams! some, like a downward smoke, 10
Slow-dropping veils of thinnest lawn,[3] did go;
And some thro' wavering lights and shadows broke,
Rolling a slumbrous sheet of foam below.
They saw the gleaming river seaward flow
From the inner land; far off, three mountain-tops,
Three silent pinnacles of aged snow,
Stood sunset-flush'd; and, dew'd with showery drops,
Up-clomb the shadowy pine above the woven copse.[4]

The charmed[5] sunset linger'd low adown
In the red West; thro' mountain clefts the dale 20
Was seen far inland, and the yellow down[6]
Border'd with palm, and many a winding vale
And meadow, set with slender galingale;[7]
A land where all things always seem'd the same!
And round about the keel[8] with faces pale,
Dark faces pale against that rosy flame,
The mild-eyed melancholy Lotos-eaters came.

Branches they bore of that enchanted stem,
Laden with flower and fruit, whereof they gave
To each, but whoso did receive of them 30
And taste, to him the gushing of the wave
Far far away did seem to mourn and rave
On alien shores; and if his fellow spake,
His voice was thin, as voices from the grave;
And deep-asleep he seem'd, yet all awake,
And music in his ears his beating heart did make.

They sat them down upon the yellow sand,
Between the sun and moon upon the shore;
And sweet it was to dream of Fatherland,
Of child, and wife, and slave; but evermore 40
Most weary seem'd the sea, weary the oar,
Weary the wandering fields of barren foam.
Then some one said, "We will return no more;"
And all at once they sang, "Our island home
Is far beyond the wave; we will no longer roam."

[3] A thin fabric. [4] Dense shrubbery. [5] Under a magic spell. [6] Rolling upland.
[7] An herb. [8] The center beam of the ship.

<div align="center">

CHORIC SONG

I

</div>

There is sweet music here that softer falls
Than petals from blown[9] roses on the grass,
Or night-dews on still waters between walls
Of shadowy granite, in a gleaming pass;
Music that gentlier on the spirit lies,
Than tired eyelids upon tired eyes;
Music that brings sweet sleep down from the blissful skies.
Here are cool mosses deep,
And thro' the moss the ivies creep,
And in the stream the long-leaved flowers weep, 10
And from the craggy ledge the poppy hangs in sleep.

<div align="center">

II

</div>

Why are we weigh'd upon with heaviness,
And utterly consumed with sharp distress,
While all things else have rest from weariness?
All things have rest: why should we toil alone,
We only toil, who are the first of things,
And make perpetual moan,
Still from one sorrow to another thrown;
Nor ever fold our wings,
And cease from wanderings, 20
Nor steep our brows in slumber's holy balm;
Nor harken what the inner spirit sings,
"There is no joy but calm!"—
Why should we only toil, the roof and crown of things?

<div align="center">

III

</div>

Lo! in the middle of the wood,
The folded leaf is woo'd from out the bud
With winds upon the branch, and there
Grows green and broad, and takes no care,
Sun-steep'd at noon, and in the moon
Nightly dew-fed; and turning yellow 30
Falls, and floats adown the air.
Lo! sweeten'd with the summer light,
The full-juiced apple, waxing over-mellow,
Drops in a silent autumn night.
All its allotted length of days
The flower ripens in its place,
Ripens and fades, and falls, and hath no toil,
Fast-rooted in the fruitful soil.

<div align="center">

IV

</div>

Hateful is the dark-blue sky,
Vaulted o'er the dark-blue sea. 40

[9] Past their bloom.

Death is the end of life; ah, why
Should life all labor be?
Let us alone. Time driveth onward fast,
And in a little while our lips are dumb.
Let us alone. What is it that will last?
All things are taken from us, and become
Portions and parcels of the dreadful past.
Let us alone. What pleasure can we have
To war with evil? Is there any peace
In ever climbing up the climbing wave? 50
All things have rest, and ripen toward the grave
In silence—ripen, fall, and cease:
Give us long rest or death, dark death, or dreamful ease.

V

How sweet it were, hearing the downward stream,
With half-shut eyes ever to seem
Falling asleep in a half-dream!
To dream and dream, like yonder amber light,
Which will not leave the myrrh-bush on the height;
To hear each other's whisper'd speech;
Eating the Lotos day by day, 60
To watch the crisping[10] ripples on the beach,
And tender curving lines of creamy spray;
To lend our hearts and spirits wholly
To the influence of mild-minded melancholy;
To muse and brood and live again in memory,
With those old faces of our infancy
Heap'd over with a mound of grass,
Two handfuls of white dust, shut in an urn of brass!

VI

Dear is the memory of our wedded lives,
And dear the last embraces of our wives 70
And their warm tears; but all hath suffer'd change;
For surely now our household hearths are cold,
Our sons inherit us, our looks are strange,
And we should come like ghosts to trouble joy.
Or else the island princes[11] over-bold
Have eat our substance, and the minstrel sings
Before them of the ten years' war in Troy,
And our great deeds, as half-forgotten things.
Is there confusion in the little isle?
Let what is broken so remain. 80
The Gods are hard to reconcile;
'T is hard to settle order once again.

[10] Curling.
[11] In the *Odyssey,* men from neighboring islands woo Odysseus' wife, the presumed widow
Penelope, while living off his land and goods.

There *is* confusion worse than death,
Trouble on trouble, pain on pain,
Long labor unto aged breath,
Sore task to hearts worn out by many wars
And eyes grown dim with gazing on the pilot-stars.[12]

VII

But, propt on beds of amaranth and moly,[13]
How sweet—while warm airs lull us, blowing lowly—
With half-dropt eyelid still, 90
Beneath a heaven dark and holy,
To watch the long bright river drawing slowly
His waters from the purple hill—
To hear the dewy echoes calling
From cave to cave thro' the thick-twined vine—
To watch the emerald-color'd water falling
Thro' many a woven acanthus-wreath[14] divine!
Only to hear and see the far-off sparkling brine,
Only to hear were sweet, stretch'd out beneath the pine.

VIII

The Lotos blooms below the barren peak, 100
The Lotos blows by every winding creek;
All day the wind breathes low with mellower tone;
Thro' every hollow cave and alley lone
Round and round the spicy downs the yellow Lotos-dust is blown.
We have had enough of action, and of motion we,
Roll'd to starboard, roll'd to larboard, when the surge was seething
 free,
Where the wallowing monster[15] spouted his foam-fountains in the
 sea.
Let us swear an oath, and keep it with an equal mind,
In the hollow Lotos-land to live and lie reclined
On the hills like Gods together, careless of mankind. 110
For they lie beside their nectar,[16] and the bolts are hurl'd
Far below them in the valleys, and the clouds are lightly curl'd
Round their golden houses, girdled with the gleaming world;
Where they smile in secret, looking over wasted[17] lands,
Blight and famine, plague and earthquake, roaring deeps and fiery
 sands,
Clanging fights, and flaming towns, and sinking ships, and praying
 hands.
But they smile, they find a music centred in a doleful song
Steaming up, a lamentation and an ancient tale of wrong,
Like a tale of little meaning tho' the words are strong;

[12] Stars that are used in navigation.
[13] Respectively, a flower that does not fade and a magical herb.
[14] A plant sacred to the ancient gods. [15] Whale.
[16] The drink of the gods. [17] Laid waste.

Chanted from an ill-used race of men that cleave the soil, 120
Sow the seed, and reap the harvest with enduring toil,
Storing yearly little dues of wheat, and wine and oil;
Till they perish and they suffer—some, 't is whisper'd—down in
 hell
Suffer endless anguish, others in Elysian valleys dwell,
Resting weary limbs at last on beds of asphodel.[18]
Surely, surely, slumber is more sweet than toil, the shore
Than labor in the deep mid-ocean, wind and wave and oar;
O, rest ye, brother mariners, we will not wander more.

ULYSSES[1]

It little profits that an idle king,
By this still hearth, among these barren crags,
Match'd with an aged wife, I mete and dole[2]
Unequal laws unto a savage race,
That hoard, and sleep, and feed, and know not me.
I cannot rest from travel; I will drink
Life to the lees.[3] All times I have enjoy'd
Greatly, have suffer'd greatly, both with those
That loved me, and alone; on shore, and when
Thro' scudding drifts the rainy Hyades[4] 10
Vext the dim sea. I am become a name;
For always roaming with a hungry heart
Much have I seen and known,—cities of men
And manners, climates, councils, governments,
Myself not least, but honor'd of them all,—
And drunk delight of battle with my peers,
Far on the ringing plains of windy Troy.
I am a part of all that I have met;
Yet all experience is an arch wherethro'
Gleams that untravell'd world whose margin fades 20
For ever and for ever when I move.
How dull it is to pause, to make an end,
To rust unburnish'd,[5] not to shine in use!
As tho' to breathe were life! Life piled on life
Were all too little, and of one to me
Little remains; but every hour is saved
From that eternal silence, something more,

[18] A yellow flower supposed to grow in the Elysian Fields, the Greek equivalent of Paradise.
[1] See notes 1 and 11 to "The Lotos-Eaters." Ulysses-Odysseus has come home to Ithaca and
defeated the suitors but is now restless with his life there. Developing a hint from Homer's
Odyssey, Book XI, Tennyson in "Ulysses" builds mainly on Dante's account of the hero's last
voyage (*Inferno*, XXVI.90–142), in which he sails boldly westward past Gibraltar to his death.
[2] Give out in small measured quantities. [3] Dregs.
[4] Stars associated with rain and storm. [5] Unpolished.

A bringer of new things; and vile it were
For some three suns[6] to store and hoard myself,
And this gray spirit yearning in desire 30
To follow knowledge like a sinking star,
Beyond the utmost bound of human thought.
 This is my son, mine own Telemachus,
To whom I leave the sceptre and the isle,—
Well-loved of me, discerning to fulfil
This labor, by slow prudence to make mild
A rugged people, and thro' soft degrees[7]
Subdue them to the useful and the good.
Most blameless is he, centred in the sphere
Of common duties, decent not to fail 40
In offices of tenderness, and pay
Meet adoration to my household gods,
When I am gone. He works his work, I mine.
 There lies the port; the vessel puffs her sail;
There gloom the dark, broad seas. My mariners,
Souls that have toil'd, and wrought, and thought with me,—
That ever with a frolic welcome took
The thunder and the sunshine, and opposed
Free hearts, free foreheads,—you and I are old;
Old age hath yet his honor and his toil. 50
Death closes all; but something ere the end,
Some work of noble note, may yet be done,
Not unbecoming men that strove with Gods.[8]
The lights begin to twinkle from the rocks;
The long day wanes; the slow moon climbs; the deep
Moans round with many voices. Come, my friends.
'T is not too late to seek a newer world.
Push off, and sitting well in order smite
The sounding furrows; for my purpose holds
To sail beyond the sunset, and the baths 60
Of all the western stars, until I die.
It may be that the gulfs will wash us down;
It may be we shall touch the Happy Isles,
And see the great Achilles,[9] whom we knew.
Tho' much is taken, much abides; and tho'
We are not now that strength which in old days
Moved earth and heaven, that which we are, we are,—
One equal temper[10] of heroic hearts,
Made weak by time and fate, but strong in will
To strive, to seek, to find, and not to yield. 70

[6] Three years. [7] Gradual steps.
[8] In Homer's *Iliad*, gods fight on both sides in the Trojan war.
[9] The hero of the *Iliad*, foremost of the Greek warriors against Troy. After their death, heroes dwelt in the Happy Isles, located in the Atlantic.
[10] Possibly "consistent strength" (like that of a well-tempered sword), possibly "well-matched personal characters."

TITHONUS[1]

The woods decay, the woods decay and fall,
The vapors weep their burthen[2] to the ground,
Man comes and tills the field and lies beneath,
And after many a summer dies the swan.
Me only cruel immortality
Consumes; I wither slowly in thine arms,
Here at the quiet limit[3] of the world,
A white-hair'd shadow roaming like a dream
The ever-silent spaces of the East,
Far-folded mists, and gleaming halls of morn. 10
 Alas! for this gray shadow, once a man—
So glorious in his beauty and thy choice,
Who madest him thy chosen, that he seem'd
To his great heart none other than a God!
I ask'd thee, "Give me immortality."
Then didst thou grant mine asking with a smile,
Like wealthy men who care not how they give.
But thy strong Hours indignant work'd their wills,
And beat me down and marr'd and wasted me,
And tho' they could not end me, left me maim'd 20
To dwell in presence of immortal youth,
Immortal age beside immortal youth,
And all I was in ashes. Can thy love,
Thy beauty, make amends, tho' even now,
Close over us, the silver star,[4] thy guide,
Shines in those tremulous eyes that fill with tears
To hear me? Let me go; take back thy gift.
Why should a man desire in any way
To vary from the kindly[5] race of men,
Or pass beyond the goal of ordinance[6] 30
Where all should pause, as is most meet[7] for all?
 A soft air fans the cloud apart; there comes
A glimpse of that dark world where I was born.
Once more the old mysterious glimmer steals
From thy pure brows, and from thy shoulders pure,
And bosom beating with a heart renew'd.
Thy cheek begins to redden thro' the gloom,
Thy sweet eyes brighten slowly close to mine,
Ere yet they blind the stars, and the wild team[8]
Which love thee, yearning for thy yoke, arise, 40
And shake the darkness from their loosen'd manes,

[1] A Trojan prince; Eos, the goddess of the dawn, loved him and persuaded Zeus to grant him immortality. She forgot, however, to ask that he be given eternal youth.
[2] Burden. [3] Eastern edge. [4] The morning star.
[5] In accordance with one's kind (species). [6] Limit set by established custom or law.
[7] Fitting. [8] Horses that draw the dawn's chariot.

And beat the twilight into flakes of fire.
 Lo! ever thus thou growest beautiful
In silence, then before thine answer given
Departest, and thy tears are on my cheek.
 Why wilt thou ever scare me with thy tears,
And make me tremble lest a saying learnt,
In days far-off, on that dark earth, be true?
"The Gods themselves cannot recall their gifts."
 Ay me! ay me! with what another heart 50
In days far-off, and with what other eyes
I used to watch—if I be he that watch'd—
The lucid outline forming round thee; saw
The dim curls kindle into sunny rings;
Changed with thy mystic change, and felt my blood
Glow with the glow that slowly crimson'd all
Thy presence and thy portals, while I lay,
Mouth, forehead, eyelids, growing dewy-warm
With kisses balmier than half-opening buds
Of April, and could hear the lips that kiss'd 60
Whispering I knew not what of wild and sweet,
Like that strange song I heard Apollo sing,
While Ilion like a mist rose into towers.[9]
 Yet hold me not for ever in thine East;
How can my nature longer mix with thine?
Coldly thy rosy shadows bathe me, cold
Are all thy lights, and cold my wrinkled feet
Upon thy glimmering thresholds, when the steam
Floats up from those dim fields about the homes
Of happy men that have the power to die, 70
And grassy barrows[10] of the happier dead.
Release me, and restore me to the ground.
Thou seest all things, thou wilt see my grave;
Thou wilt renew thy beauty morn by morn,
I earth in earth forget these empty courts,
And thee returning on thy silver wheels.

IN MEMORIAM A. H. H.

OBIIT[1] MDCCCXXXIII

Arthur Henry Hallam, Tennyson's best friend and his sister Emily's fiancé, died
unexpectedly in Vienna in 1833 when he was twenty-two and Tennyson twenty-
four years old. The two men had known each other well at Cambridge University,

[9] Troy (Ilion) was built by the song of Apollo, god of music, poetry, and the sun.
[10] Grave mounds.
[1] Died (Latin). The prefatory poem, written shortly before the publication of *In Memoriam,*
is a retrospect on the work as a whole.

where Hallam had been highly regarded as a thinker and a potential public figure. Over the next sixteen years Tennyson expressed his grief, its phases, and related speculations in brief lyrics, not originally intended for publication or collection together. He gave them their present sequence in 1849, a year before they were published, anonymously, as *In Memoriam*. Tennyson remarked that he intended the work as "a kind of Divine Commedia" in which grief yields ultimately to joy. He also explained that the "I" in the poems is not always Tennyson personally but "the voice of the human race speaking through him."

> Strong Son of God, immortal Love,
> Whom we, that have not seen thy face,
> By faith, and faith alone, embrace,
> Believing where we cannot prove;
>
> Thine are these orbs of light and shade;[2]
> Thou madest Life in man and brute;
> Thou madest Death; and lo, thy foot
> Is on the skull which thou hast made.
>
> Thou wilt not leave us in the dust:
> Thou madest man, he knows not why, 10
> He thinks he was not made to die;
> And thou hast made him: thou art just.
>
> Thou seemest human and divine,
> The highest, holiest manhood, thou.
> Our wills are ours, we know not how;
> Our wills are ours, to make them thine.
>
> Our little systems[3] have their day;
> They have their day and cease to be;
> They are but broken[4] lights of thee,
> And thou, O Lord, art more than they. 20
>
> We have but faith: we cannot know,
> For knowledge is of things we see;
> And yet we trust it comes from thee,
> A beam in darkness: let it grow.
>
> Let knowledge grow from more to more,
> But more of reverence in us dwell;
> That mind and soul, according well,
> May make one music as before,[5]
>
> But vaster. We are fools and slight;
> We mock thee when we do not fear: 30

[2] *orbs . . . shade.* The moon and planets. [3] Philosophical systems.
[4] Refracted. [5] As in past ages of faith.

But help thy foolish ones to bear;
Help thy vain worlds to bear thy light.

Forgive what seem'd my sin in me,
 What seem'd my worth since I began;
 For merit lives from man to man,
And not from man, O Lord, to thee.

Forgive my grief for one removed,
 Thy creature, whom I found so fair.
 I trust he lives in thee, and there
I find him worthier to be loved. 40

Forgive these wild and wandering cries,
 Confusions of a wasted[6] youth;
 Forgive them where they fail in truth,
And in thy wisdom make me wise.
1849

I

I held it truth, with him[7] who sings
 To one clear harp in divers tones,[8]
 That men may rise on stepping-stones
Of their dead selves to higher things.

But who shall so forecast the years
 And find in loss a gain to match?
 Or reach a hand thro' time to catch
The far-off interest[9] of tears?

Let Love clasp Grief[10] lest both be drown'd,
 Let darkness keep her raven gloss. 10
 Ah, sweeter to be drunk with loss,
To dance with Death, to beat the ground,

Than that the victor Hours should scorn
 The long result of love, and boast,
 "Behold the man that loved and lost,
But all he was is overworn."[11]

II

Old yew,[12] which graspest at the stones
 That name the underlying dead,

[6] Laid waste; desolated. [7] Goethe, according to Tennyson's explanation.
[8] Various literary styles. [9] A commercial metaphor: like profit on an investment.
[10] Let love cling to grief so that recovery from grief will not show that the love was weak.
[11] Worn away.
[12] A yew tree in a church graveyard. The yew's leaves are less sensitive to seasonal changes than those of other trees, and it can reach a very old age.

Thy fibres net the dreamless head,
Thy roots are wrapt about the bones.

The seasons bring the flower again,
 And bring the firstling[13] to the flock;
 And in the dusk of thee the clock
Beats out the little lives of men.

O, not for thee the glow, the bloom,
 Who changest not in any gale, 10
 Nor branding[14] summer suns avail
To touch thy thousand years of gloom;

And gazing on thee, sullen tree,
 Sick for thy stubborn hardihood,
 I seem to fail from out my blood
And grow incorporate into thee.

III

O Sorrow, cruel fellowship,
 O Priestess in the vaults of Death,
 O sweet and bitter in a breath,
What whispers from thy lying lip?

"The stars," she whispers, "blindly run;
 A web is woven across the sky;
 From out waste places comes a cry,
And murmurs from the dying sun;[15]

"And all the phantom, Nature, stands—
 With all the music in her tone, 10
 A hollow echo[16] of my own,—
A hollow form with empty hands."

And shall I take a thing[17] so blind,
 Embrace her as my natural good;
 Or crush her, like a vice of blood,
Upon the threshold of the mind?

V

I sometimes hold it half a sin
 To put in words the grief I feel:
 For words, like Nature, half reveal
And half conceal the Soul within.

[13] First-born. [14] "Burning," probably.
[15] *Lines 5–8.* Sorrow, personified, says that nature is blind, mechanical, and dying. The implication is that in such a world man has no special importance.
[16] Nature's voice echoes the mournful tone of Sorrow. [17] Sorrow.

But, for the unquiet heart and brain,
　　A use in measured language[18] lies;
　　The sad mechanic exercise,
Like dull narcotics, numbing pain.

In words, like weeds,[19] I'll wrap me o'er,
　　Like coarsest clothes against the cold;
　　But that large grief which these enfold
Is given in outline and no more.

VII

Dark house,[20] by which once more I stand
　　Here in the long unlovely street,
　　Doors, where my heart was used to beat
So quickly, waiting for a hand,

A hand that can be clasp'd no more—
　　Behold me, for I cannot sleep,
　　And like a guilty thing[21] I creep
At earliest morning to the door.

He is not here; but far away
　　The noise of life begins again,
　　And ghastly thro' the drizzling rain
On the bald street breaks the blank day.

IX

Fair ship, that from the Italian shore[22]
　　Sailest the placid ocean-plains
　　With my lost Arthur's loved remains,
Spread thy full wings, and waft[23] him o'er.

So draw him home to those that mourn
　　In vain; a favorable speed
　　Ruffle thy mirror'd mast, and lead
Thro' prosperous floods[24] his holy urn.

All night no ruder air perplex
　　Thy sliding keel, till Phosphor,[25] bright
　　As our pure love, thro' early light
Shall glimmer on the dewy decks.

Sphere all your lights around, above;[26]
　　Sleep, gentle heavens, before the prow;

[18] Language in poetic meter.　　[19] Garments.
[20] Hallam's house in London. With this poem compare CXIX.
[21] "Guilty thing" is quoted from Shakespeare's *Hamlet*, where the phrase refers to the ghost of Hamlet's father.
[22] The ship bearing Hallam's body home sailed from Trieste.　　[23] Carry gently.
[24] Favorable seas.　　[25] The morning star.　　[26] This is addressed to the heavens.

Sleep, gentle winds, as he sleeps now,
My friend, the brother of my love;

My Arthur, whom I shall not see
 Till all my widow'd race be run;
 Dear as the mother to the son,
More than my brothers are to me. 20

<div align="center">X</div>

I hear the noise about thy keel;
 I hear the bell struck in the night;
 I see the cabin-window bright;
I see the sailor at the wheel.

Thou bring'st the sailor to his wife,
 And travell'd men from foreign lands;
 And letters unto trembling hands;
And, thy dark freight, a vanish'd life.

So bring him; we have idle dreams;
 This look of quiet flatters thus 10
 Our home-bred fancies.[27] O, to us,
The fools of habit, sweeter seems

To rest beneath the clover sod,
 That takes the sunshine and the rains,
 Or where the kneeling hamlet drains
The chalice of the grapes of God;[28]

Than if with thee the roaring wells
 Should gulf him fathom-deep in brine,
 And hands so often clasp'd in mine,
Should toss with tangle[29] and with shells. 20

<div align="center">XI</div>

Calm is the morn without a sound,
 Calm as to suit a calmer grief,
 And only thro' the faded leaf
The chestnut pattering to the ground;

Calm and deep peace on this high wold,[30]
 And on these dews that drench the furze,[31]
 And all the silvery gossamers[32]
That twinkle into green and gold;

Calm and still light on yon great plain
 That sweeps with all its autumn bowers, 10

[27] Our simple tastes (which prefer that loved ones be buried on land rather than at sea).
[28] *chalice . . . God.* The Communion chalice. [29] Seaweed. [30] Undulating plain.
[31] Shrubs. [32] Cobwebs with dew reflecting the sunlight.

And crowded farms and lessening[33] towers,
To mingle with the bounding main;[34]

Calm and deep peace in this wide air,
 These leaves that redden to the fall,
 And in my heart, if calm at all,
If any calm, a calm despair;

Calm on the seas, and silver sleep,
 And waves that sway themselves in rest,
 And dead calm in that noble breast
Which heaves but with the heaving deep. 20

XV

To-night the winds begin to rise
 And roar from yonder dropping day;
 The last red leaf is whirl'd away,
The rooks[35] are blown about the skies;

The forest crack'd, the waters curl'd,
 The cattle huddled on the lea;
 And wildly dash'd on tower and tree
The sunbeam strikes along the world:

And but for fancies, which aver
 That all thy motions[36] gently pass 10
 Athwart a plane of molten glass,
I scarce could brook the strain and stir

That makes the barren branches loud;
 And but for fear it is not so,[37]
 The wild unrest that lives in woe
Would dote and pore on yonder cloud

That rises upward always higher,
 And onward drags a laboring breast,
 And topples round the dreary west,
A looming bastion fringed with fire. 20

XVI

What words are these have fallen from me?
 Can calm despair and wild unrest
 Be tenants of a single breast,
Or Sorrow such a changeling[38] be?

[33] Seeming to diminish in the distance. [34] Bordering ocean.
[35] Crowlike birds. [36] The motions of the ship carrying Hallam's body.
[37] *fear it is not so.* Fear that in fact the ship is storm-tossed. If it were not for this fear, the speaker could identify sympathetically with the storm cloud he is looking at.
[38] Fickle person.

Or doth she only seem to take
 The touch of change in calm or storm,
 But knows no more of transient form
In her deep self, than some dead lake

That holds the shadow of a lark
 Hung in the shadow of a heaven? 10
 Or has the shock, so harshly given,
Confused me like the unhappy bark[39]

That strikes by night a craggy shelf,
 And staggers blindly ere she sink?
 And stunn'd me from my power to think
And all my knowledge of myself;

And made me that delirious man
 Whose fancy fuses old and new,
 And flashes into false and true,
And mingles all without a plan? 20

XVIII

'T is well; 't is something; we may stand
 Where he in English earth[40] is laid,
 And from his ashes may be made
The violet of his native land.

'T is little; but it looks in truth
 As if the quiet bones were blest
 Among familiar names to rest
And in the places of his youth.

Come then, pure hands, and bear the head
 That sleeps or wears the mask of sleep, 10
 And come, whatever loves to weep,
And hear the ritual of the dead.

Ah yet, even yet, if this might be,
 I, falling on his faithful heart,
 Would breathing thro' his lips impart
The life that almost dies in me;[41]

That dies not, but endures with pain,
 And slowly forms the firmer mind,
 Treasuring the look it cannot find,
The words that are not heard again. 20

[39] Ship.

[40] Tennyson was not actually present at Hallam's funeral, nor did he visit the burial place until many years later.

[41] *breathing . . . me.* The identification of life and spirit with the physical breath is an ancient and widespread metaphor. Compare LVI.7.

XIX

The Danube to the Severn[42] gave
 The darken'd heart that beat no more;
 They laid him by the pleasant shore,
And in the hearing of the wave.

There twice a day the Severn fills;
 The salt sea-water passes by,
 And hushes half the babbling Wye,[43]
And makes a silence in the hills.

The Wye is hush'd nor moved along,
 And hush'd my deepest grief of all, 10
 When fill'd with tears that cannot fall,
I brim with sorrow drowning song.

The tide flows down, the wave again
 Is vocal in its wooded walls;
 My deeper anguish also falls,
And I can speak a little then.

XXI

I sing to him that rests below,
 And, since the grasses round me wave,
 I take the grasses of the grave,
And make them pipes whereon to blow.[44]

The traveller hears me now and then,
 And sometimes harshly will he speak:
 "This fellow would make weakness weak,
And melt the waxen hearts of men."

Another answers: "Let him be,
 He loves to make parade of pain, 10
 That with his piping he may gain
The praise that comes to constancy."

A third is wroth:[45] "Is this an hour
 For private sorrow's barren song,
 When more and more the people throng
The chairs and thrones of civil power?[46]

[42] *Danube, Severn.* Vienna, where Hallam died, is on the Danube River; he was buried near the Severn, a river in western England that, like the Thames in the east, widens into a very broad tidal estuary.

[43] The Wye river flows into the Severn; when the tide backs it up, the sound of its flow ceases.

[44] *pipes . . . blow.* The poet compares his verses to the pipings of the conventional shepherd of ancient pastoral poetry.

[45] Angry.

[46] *people . . . power.* A reference to social unrest in England and perhaps the revolutions in France since 1789.

"A time to sicken and to swoon,
 When Science reaches forth her arms
 To feel from world to world, and charms
Her secret from the latest moon?"[47] 20

Behold, ye speak an idle thing;
 Ye never knew the sacred dust.
 I do but sing because I must,
And pipe but as the linnets[48] sing;

And one is glad; her note is gay,
 For now her little ones have ranged;
 And one is sad; her note is changed,
Because her brood is stolen away.

XXII

The path by which we twain did go,
 Which led by tracts that pleased us well,
 Thro' four sweet years[49] arose and fell,
From flower to flower, from snow to snow;

And we with singing cheer'd the way,
 And, crown'd with all the season lent,
 From April on to April went,
And glad at heart from May to May.

But where the path we walk'd began
 To slant the fifth autumnal slope, 10
 As we descended following Hope,
There sat the Shadow fear'd of man;

Who broke our fair companionship,
 And spread his mantle dark and cold,
 And wrapt thee formless in the fold,
And dull'd the murmur on thy lip,

And bore thee where I could not see
 Nor follow, tho' I walk in haste,
 And think that somewhere in the waste[50]
The Shadow sits and waits for me. 20

XXIII

Now, sometimes in my sorrow shut,
 Or breaking into song by fits,
 Alone, alone, to where he sits,[51]
The Shadow cloak'd from head to foot,

[47] The planet Neptune and its satellite were discovered in 1846. [48] Songbirds.
[49] Tennyson met Hallam in 1828. [50] Wasteland.
[51] The main verb is "wander" in line 6: "I wander . . . to where he (the Shadow, death) sits."

Who keeps the keys of all the creeds,[52]
 I wander, often falling lame,
 And looking back to whence I came,
Or on to where the pathway leads;

And crying, How changed from where it ran
 Thro' lands where not a leaf was dumb,
 But all the lavish hills would hum 10
The murmur of a happy Pan;[53]

When each by turns was guide to each,
 And Fancy light from Fancy caught,
 And Thought leapt out to wed with Thought
Ere Thought could wed itself with Speech;[54]

And all we met was fair and good,
 And all was good that Time could bring,
 And all the secret of the Spring
Moved in the chambers of the blood; 20

And many an old philosophy
 On Argive[55] heights divinely sang,
 And round us all the thicket rang
To many a flute of Arcady.[56]

XXIV

And was the day of my delight
 As pure and perfect as I say?
 The very source and fount of day
Is dash'd with wandering isles of night.[57]

If all was good and fair we met,
 This earth had been[58] the Paradise
 It never look'd to human eyes
Since our first sun arose and set.

And is it that the haze of grief
 Makes former gladness loom so great?
 The lowness of the present state, 10
That sets the past in this relief?

Or that the past will always win
 A glory from its being far,
 And orb into the perfect star
We saw not when we moved therein?[59]

[52]*keeps . . . creeds.* Reveals what is true about religious beliefs. [53]God of nature.
[54]*Lines 15–16.* Where communication preceded words. [55]Ancient Greek.
[56]In Greece, the setting for pastoral poetry.
[57]*Lines 3–4.* There are spots even in the sun. [58]Would have been.
[59]*Lines 15–16.* Become a perfect circle only when seen from a distance (like the earth to an outbound astronaut). "Orb" is a verb.

XXVI

Still onward winds the dreary way;
 I with it, for I long to prove
 No lapse of moons[60] can canker Love,
Whatever fickle tongues may say.

And if that eye which watches guilt
 And goodness, and hath power[61] to see
 Within the green the moulder'd tree,
And towers fallen as soon as built—

O, if indeed that eye foresee
 Or see—in Him is no before— 10
 In more of life true life no more
And Love the indifference to be,[62]

Then might I find, ere yet the morn
 Breaks hither over Indian seas,
 That Shadow waiting with the keys,
To shroud me from my proper scorn.[63]

XXVII

I envy not in any moods
 The captive void of noble rage,
 The linnet born within the cage,
That never knew the summer woods;

I envy not the beast that takes
 His license in the field of time,[64]
 Unfetter'd by the sense of crime,
To whom a conscience never wakes;

Nor, what may count itself as blest,
 The heart that never plighted troth[65] 10
 But stagnates in the weeds of sloth:
Nor any want-begotten rest.[66]

I hold it true, whate'er befall;
 I feel it, when I sorrow most;
 'T is better to have loved and lost
Than never to have loved at all.

[60] Passage of months, that is, of time.
[61] The power of the deity to see the future hidden within the present.
[62] *And Love . . . be.* And can see love turning to indifference in the future.
[63] My scorn of myself. [64] *takes . . . time.* Follows its amoral natural impulses in life.
[65] Never became engaged, that is, never made an emotional commitment to someone or something.
[66] Quiet life resulting from the lack of qualities like imagination or initiative.

<div align="center">XXVIII</div>

The time draws near the birth of Christ.
 The moon is hid, the night is still;
 The Christmas bells from hill to hill
Answer each other in the mist.

Four voices of four hamlets round,
 From far and near, on mead[67] and moor,
 Swell out and fail, as if a door
Were shut between me and the sound;

Each voice four changes[68] on the wind,
 That now dilate, and now decrease, 10
 Peace and goodwill, goodwill and peace,
Peace and goodwill, to all mankind.

This year[69] I slept and woke with pain,
 I almost wish'd no more to wake,
 And that my hold on life would break
Before I heard those bells again;

But they my troubled spirit rule,
 For they controll'd me when a boy;
 They bring me sorrow touch'd with joy,
The merry, merry bells of Yule. 20

<div align="center">XXIX</div>

With such compelling cause to grieve
 As daily vexes household peace,
 And chains regret to his decease,
How dare we keep our Christmas-eve,

Which brings no more a welcome guest
 To enrich the threshold of the night
 With shower'd largess[70] of delight
In dance and song and game and jest?

Yet go, and while the holly boughs
 Entwine the cold baptismal font,[71] 10
 Make one wreath more for Use and Wont,[72]
That guard the portals of the house;

Old sisters of a day gone by,
 Gray nurses, loving nothing new—

[67] Meadow.
[68] Combinations of tones in different orders, as in the familiar "Westminster chime." The sound is imitated in lines 11–12.
[69] 1833, the year of Hallam's death. [70] Generosity in giving.
[71] Sculptured basin (in the church). [72] *Use and Wont*. Traditional custom.

Why should they miss their yearly due
Before their time? They too will die.

<div align="center">xxx</div>

With trembling fingers[73] did we weave
 The holly round the Christmas hearth;
 A rainy cloud possess'd the earth,
And sadly fell our Christmas-eve.

At our old pastimes in the hall
 We gamboll'd,[74] making vain pretence
 Of gladness, with an awful sense
Of one mute Shadow watching all.

We paused: the winds were in the beech;
 We heard them sweep the winter land; 10
 And in a circle hand-in-hand
Sat silent, looking each at each.

Then echo-like our voices rang;
 We sung, tho' every eye was dim,
 A merry song we sang with him
Last year; impetuously we sang.

We ceased; a gentler feeling crept
 Upon us: surely rest is meet.[75]
 "They rest," we said, "their sleep is sweet,"
And silence follow'd, and we wept. 20

Our voices took a higher range;
 Once more we sang: "They do not die
 Nor lose their mortal sympathy,
Nor change to us, although they change;

"Rapt[76] from the fickle and the frail
 With gather'd power, yet the same,
 Pierces the keen seraphic flame[77]
From orb to orb, from veil to veil."[78]

Rise, happy morn, rise, holy morn,
 Draw forth the cheerful day from night: 30
 O Father, touch the east, and light
The light that shone when Hope was born.

[73] *With trembling fingers, etc.* This is the first of three Christmas poems that, according to many interpreters, divide *In Memoriam* into four parts. Compare the ideas and tones in LXXVIII and CV.
[74] Behaved merrily. [75] Appropriate. [76] Carried away.
[77] "Seraphic flame"—i.e., the soul—is the subject of "pierces."
[78] *From . . . veil.* Through different states of existence.

XXXIV

My own dim life should teach me this,
 That life shall live for evermore,
 Else earth is darkness at the core,
And dust and ashes all that is;

This round of green, this orb of flame,[79]
 Fantastic beauty; such as lurks
 In some wild poet, when he works
Without a conscience or an aim.

What then were God to such as I?
 'T were hardly worth my while to choose 10
 Of things all mortal, or to use
A little patience ere I die;

'T were best at once to sink to peace,
 Like birds the charming[80] serpent draws,
 To drop head-foremost in the jaws
Of vacant darkness and to cease.

XXXV

Yet if some voice that man could trust
 Should murmur from the narrow house,[81]
 "The cheeks drop in, the body bows;
Man dies, nor is there hope in dust;"

Might I not say? "Yet even here,
 But for one hour, O Love, I strive
 To keep so sweet a thing alive."
But I should turn mine ears and hear

The moanings of the homeless sea,
 The sound of streams that swift or slow 10
 Draw down Aeonian[82] hills, and sow
The dust of continents to be;

And Love would answer with a sigh,
 "The sound of that forgetful shore[83]
 Will change my sweetness more and more,
Half-dead to know that I shall die."

O me, what profits it to put
 An idle case?[84] If Death were seen

[79] *round . . . flame.* The earth and sun. [80] Casting a hypnotizing spell.
[81] The grave.
[82] Lasting through vast geological ages; Charles Lyell's geological theories, which Tennyson knew, held that the earth evolved gradually.
[83] *sound . . . shore.* The voice from the grave denying life after death; "forgetful shore" refers to Lethe, the river of forgetfulness in the land of the dead.
[84] *put . . . case.* Imagine a merely hypothetical case.

At first as Death, Love had not been,
Or been in narrowest working shut, 20

Mere fellowship of sluggish moods,
 Or in his coarsest Satyr-shape
 Had bruised the herb and crush'd the grape,
And bask'd and batten'd[85] in the woods.[86]

XLVII

That each, who seems a separate whole,
 Should move his rounds, and fusing all
 The skirts of self again, should fall
Remerging in the general Soul,

Is faith as vague as all unsweet.[87]
 Eternal form shall still divide
 The eternal soul from all beside;
And I shall know him when we meet;

And we shall sit at endless feast,
 Enjoying each the other's good. 10
 What vaster dream can hit the mood
Of Love on earth? He seeks at least

Upon the last and sharpest height,
 Before the spirits fade away,
 Some landing-place, to clasp and say,
"Farewell! We lose ourselves in light."[88]

XLVIII

If these brief lays,[89] of Sorrow born,
 Were taken to be such as closed[90]
 Grave doubts and answers here proposed,
Then these were such as men might scorn.

Her care is not to part[91] and prove;
 She takes, when harsher moods remit,
 What slender shade of doubt may flit,
And makes it vassal unto love;

And hence, indeed, she sports with words,
 But better serves a wholesome law, 10

[85] Gorged oneself like an animal.
[86] *Lines 18–24.* If we knew from the beginning that death would be final, we would never have loved or else love would have been merely sensual (like that of Satyrs, lecherous mythological creatures).
[87] *Lines 1–5.* It is comfortless to imagine human individuality lost by absorption into an impersonal cosmic soul.
[88] *Lines 12–16.* "If we are to be finally merged into the Universal Soul, Love asks to have at least one more parting before we lose ourselves."—Tennyson's note.
[89] Poems. [90] Resolved finally. [91] Intellectually classify and analyze.

And holds it sin and shame to draw
The deepest measure from the chords;

Nor dare she trust a larger lay,
 But rather loosens from the lip
 Short swallow-flights of song, that dip
Their wings in tears, and skim away.

L

Be near me[92] when my light is low,
 When the blood creeps, and the nerves prick
 And tingle; and the heart is sick,
And all the wheels of being slow.

Be near me when the sensuous frame
 Is rack'd with pangs that conquer trust;
 And Time, a maniac scattering dust,
And Life, a Fury[93] slinging flame.

Be near me when my faith is dry,
 And men[94] the flies of latter spring,
 That lay their eggs, and sting and sing 10
And weave their petty cells and die.

Be near me when I fade away,
 To point the term of human strife,[95]
 And on the low dark verge of life
The twilight of eternal day.

LIV

O, yet we trust that somehow good
 Will be the final goal of ill,
 To pangs of nature, sins of will,
Defects of doubt, and taints of blood;

That nothing walks with aimless feet;
 That not one life shall be destroy'd,
 Or cast as rubbish to the void,
When God hath made the pile[96] complete;

That not a worm is cloven in vain;
 That not a moth with vain desire 10

[92] The speaker addresses Hallam.
[93] The terrifying Furies of Greek mythology were sometimes imagined as carrying torches.
[94] Men seem.
[95] *point . . . strife.* Show the final goal of human life—that is, the "twilight of eternal day" mentioned two lines later.
[96] Building; edifice.

Is shrivell'd in a fruitless fire,
Or but subserves another's gain.[97]

Behold, we know not anything;
 I can but trust that good shall fall
 At last—far off—at last, to all,
And every winter change to spring.

So runs my dream; but what am I?
 An infant crying in the night;
 An infant crying for the light,
And with no language but a cry. 20

LV

The wish, that of the living whole
 No life may fail beyond the grave,
 Derives it not from what we have
The likest God within the soul?[98]

Are God and Nature then at strife,
 That Nature lends such evil dreams?
 So careful of the type[99] she seems,
So careless of the single life,

That I, considering everywhere
 Her secret meaning in her deeds,
 And finding that of fifty seeds 10
She often brings but one to bear,

I falter where I firmly trod,
 And falling with my weight of cares
 Upon the great world's altar-stairs
That slope thro' darkness up to God,

I stretch lame hands of faith, and grope,
 And gather dust and chaff, and call
 To what I feel is Lord of all,
And faintly trust the larger hope.[1] 20

LVI

"So careful of the type?" but no.
 From scarped cliff and quarried stone

[97] *but . . . gain.* The speaker finds no comfort in the idea of ecological cycles in which some creatures exist to be the prey of others.

[98] *Lines 3–4.* Does it not spring from what is most Godlike in us? Tennyson defined this as the "inner consciousness."

[99] Species, as opposed to any individual member of the species.

[1] According to Tennyson's son, this hope was "that the whole human race would through, perhaps, ages of suffering, be at length purified and saved." Or perhaps the hope is the wish stated in lines 1–2.

She cries, "A thousand types are gone;
I care for nothing, all shall go.²

"Thou makest thine appeal to me;
 I bring to life, I bring to death;
 The spirit does but mean the breath:³
I know no more." And he, shall he,

Man, her last work, who seem'd so fair,
 Such splendid purpose in his eyes,
 Who roll'd the psalm to wintry skies, 10
Who built him fanes of fruitless prayer,⁴

Who trusted God was love indeed
 And love Creation's final law—
 Tho' Nature, red in tooth and claw
With ravine,⁵ shriek'd against his creed—

Who loved, who suffer'd countless ills,
 Who battled for the True, the Just,
 Be blown about the desert dust,
Or seal'd within the iron hills?⁶ 20

No more? A monster then, a dream,
 A discord. Dragons of the prime,
 That tare each other⁷ in their slime,
Were mellow music match'd with him.⁸

O life as futile, then, as frail!
 O for thy⁹ voice to soothe and bless!
 What hope of answer, or redress?
Behind the veil, behind the veil.

LVII

Peace; come away: the song of woe
 Is after all an earthly song.

²*Lines 1–4.* Nature (the "She" of line 3) is not concerned for species either, as shown by fossil evidence of extinct species found in quarries and the rock layers in vertically cut ("scarped") cliffs. Tennyson was influenced by Lyell's writings on geology; Darwin's account of evolution in *The Origin of Species* was not published until 1859, nine years after *In Memoriam* was completed.

³*spirit . . . breath.* See note on XVIII.15–16. Here Nature says that breath is not a metaphor for something higher that we call spirit (as in Latin, where *spiritus* means "breath"); rather, physical acts like breathing are all there is to life.

⁴*fanes . . . prayer.* Temples where deluded man prayed to the nonexistent God of a meaningless universe.

⁵Ravin; predatory fierceness.

⁶*seal'd . . . hills.* Become a buried fossil, like other species.

⁷*Dragons . . . other.* Primeval monsters that tore each other.

⁸*Lines 22–24.* Because at least the monsters did not suffer from a "discord" in their natures whereby, like man, they aspired to an illusory immortality.

⁹Hallam's.

Peace; come away: we do him wrong
To sing so wildly: let us go.

Come; let us go: your cheeks[10] are pale;
But half my life I leave behind.
Methinks my friend is richly shrined;[11]
But I shall pass, my work will fail.

Yet in these ears, till hearing dies,
One set slow bell will seem to toll 10
The passing of the sweetest soul
That ever look'd with human eyes.

I hear it now, and o'er and o'er,
Eternal greetings to the dead;
And "Ave, Ave, Ave," said,
"Adieu, adieu," for evermore.[12]

LXX

I cannot see the features right,
When on the gloom[13] I strive to paint
The face I know; the hues are faint
And mix with hollow masks of night;

Cloud-towers by ghostly masons wrought,
A gulf that ever shuts and gapes,
A hand that points, and palled shapes[14]
In shadowy thoroughfares of thought;

And crowds that stream from yawning doors,
And shoals of pucker'd faces drive; 10
Dark bulks that tumble half alive,
And lazy lengths on boundless shores;

Till all at once beyond the will[15]
I hear a wizard music roll,
And thro' a lattice on the soul
Looks thy fair face and makes it still.

LXXVIII

Again at Christmas[16] did we weave
The holly round the Christmas hearth;

[10] Perhaps the cheeks of Tennyson's sister Emily (Hallam's fiancée), perhaps those of all mourners for Hallam.

[11] That is, shrined in these poems.

[12] *Ave, Adieu.* Hail and farewell. Tennyson alludes to the last words of Catullus's poem 101, the elegy for his dead brother.

[13] The darkness, as he is falling asleep. [14] Veiled figures.

[15] As he falls asleep and the will becomes powerless.

[16] The second of the Christmas poems; compare XXX and CV.

The silent snow possess'd the earth,
And calmly fell our Christmas-eve.

The yule-clog[17] sparkled keen with frost,
 No wing of wind the region swept,
 But over all things brooding slept
The quiet sense of something lost.

As in the winters left behind,
 Again our ancient games had place,
 The mimic picture's[18] breathing grace,
And dance and song and hoodman-blind.[19]

Who show'd a token of distress?
 No single tear, no mark of pain—
 O sorrow, then can sorrow wane?
O grief, can grief be changed to less?

O last regret, regret can die!
 No—mixt with all this mystic frame,
 Her deep relations are the same,
But with long use her tears are dry.

LXXXVI

Sweet after showers, ambrosial[20] air,
 That rollest from the gorgeous gloom
 Of evening over brake[21] and bloom
And meadow, slowly breathing bare

The round of space, and rapt below
 Thro' all the dewy tassell'd wood,
 And shadowing down the horned flood[22]
In ripples, fan my brows and blow

The fever from my cheek, and sigh
 The full new life that feeds thy breath
 Throughout my frame, till Doubt and Death,
Ill brethren, let the fancy fly

From belt to belt of crimson seas[23]
 On leagues of odor streaming far,
 To where in yonder orient[24] star
A hundred spirits whisper "Peace."

[17] Log. [18] A game, resembling charades, in which famous paintings were acted out.
[19] Blind man's buff.
[20] Like ambrosia, the food of the gods; fragrant. This poem, a single sentence, describes a west wind at sundown, according to Tennyson.
[21] Fern. [22] An inlet of the ocean winding between two promontories.
[23] *belt . . . seas.* The streaks of red in the sunset. [24] Rising.

LXXXVII

I past beside the reverend walls
 In which of old I wore the gown;[25]
 I roved at random thro' the town,
And saw the tumult of the halls;

And heard once more in college fanes[26]
 The storm their high-built organs make,
 And thunder-music, rolling, shake
The prophet blazon'd on the panes;

And caught once more the distant shout,
 The measured pulse of racing oars
 Among the willows; paced the shores
And many a bridge, and all about

The same gray flats again, and felt
 The same, but not the same; and last
 Up that long walk of limes I past
To see the rooms in which he dwelt.

Another name was on the door.
 I linger'd; all within was noise
 Of songs, and clapping hands, and boys
That crash'd the glass and beat the floor;

Where once we held debate, a band[27]
 Of youthful friends, on mind and art,
 And labor, and the changing mart,
And all the framework of the land;

When one would aim an arrow fair,
 But send it slackly from the string;[28]
 And one would pierce an outer ring,
And one an inner, here and there;

And last the master-bowman, he,[29]
 Would cleave the mark. A willing ear
 We lent him. Who but hung to hear
The rapt oration flowing free

From point to point, with power and grace
 And music in the bounds of law,
 To those conclusions when we saw
The God within him light his face,

[25] The gown of a student—at Trinity College, Cambridge. [26] Chapels.
[27] "The Apostles," a discussion group that Hallam and Tennyson belonged to.
[28] *aim . . . string.* Try to make a good point but express it poorly. [29] Hallam.

And seem to lift the form, and glow
 In azure orbits heavenly-wise;
 And over those ethereal eyes
The bar of Michael Angelo?[30] 40

XCV

By night[31] we linger'd on the lawn,
 For underfoot the herb was dry;
 And genial warmth; and o'er the sky
The silvery haze of summer drawn;

And calm that let the tapers[32] burn
 Unwavering: not a cricket chirr'd;
 The brook alone far-off was heard,
And on the board the fluttering urn.[33]

And bats went round in fragrant skies,
 And wheel'd or lit the filmy shapes[34] 10
 That haunt the dusk, with ermine capes
And woolly breasts and beaded eyes;

While now we sang old songs that peal'd
 From knoll to knoll, where, couch'd at ease,
 The white kine[35] glimmer'd, and the trees
Laid their dark arms about the field.

But when those others, one by one,
 Withdrew themselves from me and night,
 And in the house light after light
Went out, and I was all alone, 20

A hunger seized my heart; I read
 Of that glad year which once had been,
 In those fallen leaves which kept their green,
The noble letters of the dead.

And strangely on the silence broke
 The silent-speaking words, and strange
 Was love's dumb cry defying change
To test his worth; and strangely spoke

The faith, the vigor, bold to dwell
 On doubts that drive the coward back, 30
 And keen thro' wordy snares to track
Suggestion to her inmost cell.

[30] *bar . . . Angelo.* Hallam himself once remarked that both he and Michelangelo had a ridge over the eyebrows.
[31] *By night, etc.* This poem is often considered the heart of the whole work.
[32] Candles. [33] Tea-urn, over a flame. [34] Moths. [35] Cows.

So word by word, and line by line,
 The dead man touch'd me from the past,
 And all at once it seem'd at last
The living soul was flash'd on mine,

And mine in this was wound, and whirl'd[36]
 About empyreal[37] heights of thought,
 And came on that which is, and caught
The deep pulsations of the world, 40

Aeonian[38] music measuring out
 The steps of Time—the shocks of Chance—
 The blows of Death. At length my trance
Was cancell'd, stricken thro' with doubt.

Vague words! but ah, how hard to frame
 In matter-moulded forms of speech,
 Or even for intellect to reach
Thro' memory that which I became;[39]

Till now the doubtful dusk reveal'd
 The knolls once more where, couch'd at ease, 50
 The white kine glimmer'd, and the trees
Laid their dark arms about the field;

And suck'd from out the distant gloom
 A breeze began to tremble o'er
 The large leaves of the sycamore,
And fluctuate all the still perfume,

And gathering freshlier overhead,
 Rock'd the full-foliaged elms, and swung
 The heavy-folded rose, and flung
The lilies to and fro, and said, 60

"The dawn, the dawn," and died away;
 And East and West, without a breath,
 Mixt their dim lights, like life and death,
To broaden into boundless day.

XCVI
You say, but with no touch of scorn,
 Sweet-hearted, you,[40] whose light-blue eyes

[36] *Lines 36, 37.* Tennyson's original published text read "His living soul" and "mine in his." His intention in the revision was apparently to suggest the cosmic or divine soul as including Hallam's.
[37] Heavenly. [38] Enduring for ages.
[39] *Lines 45–48.* Probably an echo of the end of Dante's *Paradise*, especially XXXIII. 121–123.
[40] A woman of simple piety.

Are tender over drowning flies,
You tell me, doubt is Devil-born.

I know not: one indeed I knew
 In many a subtle question versed,
 Who touch'd a jarring lyre at first,
But ever strove to make it true;

Perplext in faith, but pure in deeds,
 At last he beat his music out. 10
There lives more faith in honest doubt,
Believe me, than in half the creeds.

He fought his doubts and gather'd strength,
 He would not make his judgment blind,
 He faced the spectres of the mind
And laid[41] them; thus he came at length

To find a stronger faith his own,
 And Power was with him in the night,
 Which makes the darkness and the light,
And dwells not in the light alone, 20

But in the darkness and the cloud,
 As over Sinaï's peaks of old,
 While Israel made their gods of gold,
Altho' the trumpet blew so loud.[42]

 CIV
The time draws near the birth of Christ;
 The moon is hid, the night is still;
 A single church below the hill
Is pealing, folded in the mist.

A single peal of bells below,
 That wakens at this hour of rest
 A single murmur in the breast,
That these are not the bells I know.[43]

Like strangers' voices here they sound,
 In lands where not a memory strays, 10
 Nor landmark breathes of other days,
But all is new unhallow'd ground.

[41] To lay a ghost is to exorcise or overcome it.
[42] *Lines 21–24.* God appeared to Moses on Mount Sinai in a dark cloud while the Israelites below were worshiping their golden calf; Exodus, chapters 19, 32. Hallam, like Moses, found truth by exploring the darkness, unlike facile but materialistic "believers."
[43] *not . . . know.* The Tennyson family had moved from their old home at Somersby in east central England to a new one in Epping Forest, north of London.

CV

To-night[44] ungather'd let us leave
 This laurel, let this holly stand:
 We live within the stranger's land,
And strangely falls our Christmas-eve.

Our father's dust[45] is left alone
 And silent under other snows:
 There in due time the woodbine blows,[46]
The violet comes, but we are gone.

No more shall wayward grief abuse[47]
 The genial hour with mask and mime; 10
 For change of place, like growth of time,
Has broke the bond of dying use.[48]

Let cares that petty shadows cast,
 By which our lives are chiefly proved,[49]
 A little spare the night I loved,
And hold it solemn to the past.

But let no footstep beat the floor,
 Nor bowl of wassail mantle[50] warm;
 For who would keep an ancient form
Thro' which the spirit breathes no more? 20

Be neither song, nor game, nor feast;
 Nor harp be touch'd, nor flute be blown;
 No dance, no motion, save alone
What lightens in the lucid East

Of rising worlds by yonder wood.
 Long sleeps the summer in the seed;
 Run out your measured arcs, and lead
The closing cycle[51] rich in good.

CVI

Ring out, wild bells, to the wild sky,
 The flying cloud, the frosty light:
 The year is dying in the night;[52]
Ring out, wild bells, and let him die.

Ring out the old, ring in the new,
 Ring, happy bells, across the snow:
 The year is going, let him go;
Ring out the false, ring in the true.

[44] *Tonight, etc.* The third of the Christmas poems; compare XXX and LXXVIII.
[45] Body in his grave. [46] Blossoms. [47] Do wrong to. [48] Custom; tradition.
[49] Tested. [50] Become frothy. [51] Final era.
[52] *year . . . night.* A week has passed; it is New Year's Eve.

Ring out the grief that saps the mind,
 For those that here we see no more;
 Ring out the feud of rich and poor,
Ring in redress[53] to all mankind.

Ring out a slowly dying cause,
 And ancient forms of party strife;
 Ring in the nobler modes of life,
With sweeter manners, purer laws.

Ring out the want, the care, the sin,
 The faithless coldness of the times;
 Ring out, ring out my mournful rhymes,
But ring the fuller minstrel[54] in.

Ring out false pride in place and blood,[55]
 The civic slander and the spite;
 Ring in the love of truth and right,
Ring in the common love of good.

Ring out old shapes of foul disease;
 Ring out the narrowing lust of gold;
 Ring out the thousand wars of old,
Ring in the thousand years of peace.

Ring in the valiant man and free,
 The larger heart, the kindlier hand;
 Ring out the darkness of the land,
Ring in the Christ that is to be.[56]

CXIV

Who loves not Knowledge? Who shall rail
 Against her beauty? May she mix
 With men and prosper! Who shall fix
Her pillars?[57] Let her work prevail.

But on her forehead sits a fire;
 She sets her forward countenance
 And leaps into the future chance,
Submitting all things to desire.

Half-grown as yet, a child, and vain—
 She cannot fight the fear of death.

[53] Remedy for wrongs. [54] Singer; poet. [55] High office and aristocratic lineage.
[56] *Christ . . . be.* According to Tennyson, a nobler Christianity of the future, free from bigotry and sectarian controversy.
[57] Possibly an analogy to the seven pillars of Wisdom's house (Proverbs 9:1); possibly limits (from the Pillars of Hercules, or strait of Gibraltar, considered by the ancients as the limit of the world).

What is she, cut from love and faith,
But some wild Pallas[58] from the brain

Of demons? fiery-hot to burst
 All barriers in her onward race
 For power. Let her know her place;
She is the second, not the first.

A higher hand must make her mild,
 If all be not in vain, and guide
 Her footsteps, moving side by side
With Wisdom, like the younger child; 20

For she is earthly of the mind,
 But Wisdom heavenly of the soul.
 O friend, who camest to thy goal
So early, leaving me behind,

I would the great world grew like thee,
 Who grewest not alone in power
 And knowledge, but by year and hour
In reverence and in charity.

CXV

Now fades the last long streak of snow,
 Now burgeons every maze of quick[59]
 About the flowering squares,[60] and thick
By ashen roots[61] the violets blow.

Now rings the woodland loud and long,
 The distance takes a lovelier hue,
 And drown'd in yonder living blue
The lark becomes a sightless[62] song.

Now dance the lights on lawn and lea,
 The flocks are whiter down the vale, 10
 And milkier every milky sail
On winding stream or distant sea;

Where now the seamew pipes, or dives
 In yonder greening gleam,[63] and fly
 The happy birds, that change their sky
To build and brood, that live their lives

From land to land; and in my breast
 Spring wakens too, and my regret

[58] Athene, the Greek goddess of knowledge, wisdom, and manual crafts, born from the head of Zeus, the king of the gods.
[59] *burgeons . . . quick.* Every hedge brings forth buds. [60] Fields.
[61] Roots of ash trees. [62] Invisible. [63] The ocean.

Becomes an April violet,
And buds and blossoms like the rest. 20

CXVIII

Contemplate all this work of Time,
 The giant laboring in his youth;
 Nor dream of human love and truth,
As dying Nature's earth and lime;[64]

But trust that those we call the dead
 Are breathers of an ampler day
 For ever nobler ends. They say,
The solid earth whereon we tread

In tracts of fluent[65] heat began,
 And grew to seeming-random forms, 10
 The seeming prey of cyclic storms,
Till at the last arose the man;

Who throve and branch'd from clime to clime,
 The herald of a higher race,
 And of himself in higher place,[66]
If so he type this work of time

Within himself,[67] from more to more;
 Or, crown'd with attributes of woe
 Like glories,[68] move his course, and show
That life is not as idle ore, 20

But iron dug from central gloom,
 And heated hot with burning fears,
 And dipt in baths of hissing tears,
And batter'd[69] with the shocks of doom

To shape and use. Arise and fly
 The reeling Faun,[70] the sensual feast;
 Move upward, working out the beast,
And let the ape and tiger die.

CXIX

Doors,[71] where my heart was used to beat
 So quickly, not as one that weeps

[64] *Lines 3–4.* Do not imagine that love and truth disappear as rotted physical bodies do; the "lime" is the calcium compounds in decayed bones.
[65] Flowing; that is, gaseous. [66] The afterlife, probably.
[67] *If . . . himself.* If he follows the pattern of development in his moral nature that time followed in physical evolution.
[68] Halos.
[69] Hammered; the whole figure of speech is from the shaping of metal by a blacksmith.
[70] In mythology, a creature half man and half goat.
[71] The doors of Hallam's house in London; compare poem VII.

I come once more; the city sleeps;
I smell the meadow in the street;

I hear a chirp of birds; I see
 Betwixt the black fronts long-withdrawn
 A light-blue lane of early dawn,
And think of early days and thee,

And bless thee, for thy lips are bland,
 And bright the friendship of thine eye; 10
 And in my thoughts with scarce a sigh
I take the pressure of thine hand.

CXXI

Sad Hesper[72] o'er the buried sun
 And ready, thou, to die with him,
 Thou watchest all things ever dim
And dimmer, and a glory done.

The team is loosen'd from the wain,[73]
 The boat is drawn upon the shore;
 Thou listenest to the closing door,
And life is darken'd in the brain.

Bright Phosphor,[74] fresher for the night,
 By thee the world's great work is heard 10
 Beginning, and the wakeful bird;
Behind thee comes the greater light.

The market boat is on the stream,
 And voices hail it from the brink;
 Thou hear'st the village hammer clink,
And see'st the moving of the team.

Sweet Hesper-Phosphor, double name
 For what is one,[75] the first, the last,
 Thou, like my present and my past,
Thy place is changed; thou art the same. 20

CXXIII

There rolls the deep where grew the tree.
 O earth, what changes hast thou seen!
 There where the long street roars hath been
The stillness of the central sea.

[72] The evening star. [73] Farm wagon. [74] The morning star.
[75] The same planet (usually Venus) serves at different times as either morning or evening star.

The hills are shadows, and they flow
 From form to form, and nothing stands;
 They melt like mist, the solid lands,
Like clouds they shape themselves and go.

But in my spirit will I dwell,
 And dream my dream, and hold it true; 10
 For tho' my lips may breathe adieu,
I cannot think the thing farewell.

CXXIV

That which we dare invoke to bless;
 Our dearest faith; our ghastliest doubt;[76]
 He, They, One, All; within, without;
The Power in darkness whom we guess,—

I found Him not in world or sun,
 Or eagle's wing, or insect's eye,[77]
 Nor thro' the questions men may try,
The petty cobwebs we have spun.

If e'er when faith had fallen asleep,
 I heard a voice, "believe no more," 10
 And heard an ever-breaking shore
That tumbled in the Godless deep,

A warmth within the breast would melt
 The freezing reason's colder part,
 And like a man in wrath the heart
Stood up and answer'd, "I have felt."

No, like a child[78] in doubt and fear:
 But that blind clamor made me wise;
 Then was I as a child that cries,
But, crying, knows his father near; 20

And what I am beheld again
 What is, and no man understands;[79]
 And out of darkness came the hands
That reach thro' nature, moulding men.

CXXVI

Love is and was my lord and king,
 And in his presence I attend

[76] *Our . . . doubt.* That is, our thoughts about God inspire extremes of both faith and doubt.

[77] *Lines 5–6.* I did not find faith through the argument from design, namely that intricately functioning creatures must have had a conscious designer.

[78] See poem LIV.17–20.

[79] *What is . . . understands.* God, whom no man can understand.

To hear the tidings of my friend,
Which every hour his couriers bring.

Love is and was my king and lord,
 And will be, tho' as yet I keep
 Within the court[80] on earth, and sleep
Encompass'd by his faithful guard,

And hear at times a sentinel
 Who moves about from place to place,
 And whispers to the worlds of space, 10
In the deep night, that all is well.

<div align="center">

EPILOGUE

</div>

O true and tried, so well and long,
 Demand not thou a marriage lay;[81]
 In that it is thy marriage day
Is music more than any song.

Nor have I felt so much of bliss
 Since first he told me that he loved
 A daughter of our house,[82] nor proved
Since that dark day[83] a day like this;

Tho' I since then have number'd o'er
 Some thrice three years; they went and came, 10
 Remade the blood and changed the frame,
And yet is love not less, but more;

No longer caring to embalm
 In dying songs a dead regret,
 But like a statue solid-set,
And moulded in colossal calm.

Regret is dead, but love is more
 Than in the summers that are flown,
 For I myself with these have grown
To something greater than before; 20

Which makes appear the songs I made
 As echoes out of weaker times,

[80] The court of Love the king.

[81] *Demand . . . lay.* Do not ask for an epithalamium, or formal wedding poem. This epilogue describes the wedding of Tennyson's sister Cecilia with Edmund Lushington in 1842, nine years after Hallam's death.

[82] *he told . . . house.* The "he" is Hallam, the "daughter" is Emily, another of Tennyson's sisters, who had been engaged to Hallam.

[83] The day of Hallam's death.

As half but idle brawling rhymes,
The sport of random sun and shade.

But where is she, the bridal flower,
 That must be made a wife ere noon?
 She enters, glowing like the moon
Of Eden on its bridal bower.

On me she bends her blissful eyes
 And then on thee; they meet thy look 30
 And brighten like the star that shook
Betwixt the palms of Paradise.

O, when her life was yet in bud,
 He too foretold the perfect rose.[84]
 For thee she grew, for thee she grows
For ever, and as fair as good.

And thou art worthy, full of power;
 As gentle; liberal-minded, great,
 Consistent; wearing all that weight
Of learning[85] lightly like a flower. 40

But now set out: the noon is near,
 And I must give away the bride;
 She fears not, or with thee beside
And me behind her, will not fear.

For I that danced her on my knee,[86]
 That watch'd her on her nurse's arm,
 That shielded all her life from harm,
At last must part with her to thee;

Now waiting to be made a wife,
 Her feet, my darling, on the dead; 50
 Their pensive tablets round her head,[87]
And the most living words of life

Breathed in her ear. The ring is on,
 The "Wilt thou?" answer'd, and again
 The "Wilt thou?" ask'd, till out of twain
Her sweet "I will" has made you one.

Now sign your names, which shall be read,
 Mute symbols of a joyful morn,

[84] *Lines 33–34*. Hallam had predicted Cecilia's beauty when she was still a child.
[85] Lushington was a professor of Greek.
[86] Cecilia was eight years younger than Tennyson.
[87] *Lines 50–51*. There are graves under the church and commemorative tablets on the wall.

By village eyes as yet unborn.
The names are sign'd, and overhead 60

Begins the clash and clang that tells
　　The joy to every wandering breeze;
　　The blind wall rocks, and on the trees
The dead leaf trembles to the bells.

O happy hour, and happier hours
　　Await them. Many a merry face
　　Salutes them—maidens of the place,
That pelt us in the porch with flowers.

O happy hour, behold the bride
　　With him to whom her hand I gave.
　　They leave the porch, they pass the grave 70
That has to-day its sunny side.

To-day the grave is bright for me,
　　For them the light of life increased,
　　Who stay to share the morning feast,
Who rest to-night beside the sea.

Let all my genial spirits advance
　　To meet and greet a whiter sun;
　　My drooping memory will not shun
The foaming grape of eastern France.[88] 80

It circles round, and fancy plays.
　　And hearts are warm'd and faces bloom,
　　As drinking health to bride and groom
We wish them store of happy days.

Nor count me all to blame if I
　　Conjecture of a stiller guest,[89]
　　Perchance, perchance, among the rest,
And, tho' in silence, wishing joy.

But they must go, the time draws on,
　　And those white-favor'd[90] horses wait:
　　They rise, but linger; it is late; 90
Farewell, we kiss, and they are gone.

A shade falls on us like the dark
　　From little cloudlets on the grass,
　　But sweeps away as out we pass
To range the woods, to roam the park,

[88] *foaming . . . France.* Champagne.　　　[89] Hallam.　　　[90] Decorated with white.

Discussing how their courtship grew,
 And talk of others that are wed,
 And how she look'd, and what he said,
And back we come at fall of dew. 100

Again the feast, the speech, the glee,[91]
 The shade of passing thought, the wealth
 Of words and wit, the double health,
The crowning cup, the three-times-three,[92]

And last the dance;—till I retire.
 Dumb is that tower which spake so loud,
 And high in heaven the streaming cloud,
And on the downs[93] a rising fire:

And rise, O moon, from yonder down,
 Till over down and over dale 110
 All night the shining vapor sail
And pass the silent-lighted town,

The white-faced halls, the glancing rills,
 And catch at every mountain head.
 And o'er the friths[94] that branch and spread
Their sleeping silver thro' the hills;

And touch with shade the bridal doors,
 With tender gloom the roof, the wall;
 And breaking let the splendor fall
To spangle all the happy shores 120

By which they rest, and ocean sounds,
 And, star and system rolling past,
 A soul shall draw from out the vast
And strike his being into bounds,

And, moved thro' life of lower phase,[95]
 Result in man, be born and think,
 And act and love, a closer link
Betwixt us and the crowning race

Of those that, eye to eye, shall look
 On knowledge; under whose command 130
 Is Earth and Earth's, and in their hand
Is Nature like an open book;

[91] Song sung in harmony (as in "glee club"). [92] Cheer. [93] Rolling pastures.
[94] Elongated bays at the mouths of rivers; fjords. (Variant of "firths.")
[95] *Lines 123–125*. The newlyweds will conceive a child that, in the womb, will pass through stages corresponding to lower animal forms.

No longer half-akin to brute,
 For all we thought and loved and did,
 And hoped, and suffer'd, is but seed
Of what in them is flower and fruit;

Whereof the man that with me trod
 This planet was a noble type[96]
 Appearing ere the times were ripe,
That friend of mine who lives in God, 140

That God, which ever lives and loves,
 One God, one law, one element,
 And one far-off divine event,[97]
To which the whole creation moves.
1833–1849 (1850)

Robert Browning
(1812–1889)

Robert Browning ranks with Tennyson as one of the two greatest English Victorian poets. Like Tennyson, he had an idealistic creed to express, and both his wife and his reading public encouraged him to express it. But there was also another side of Browning that made him struggle to detach himself from the men and women of his poems, presenting them as what they are in themselves, tantalizing quirky fragments of a total truth comprehensible only by God. This dialogue between the preacher and dramatic painter in Browning informs his work from beginning to end. Browning the sage did not outlast the Victorian period, but the verse dramatist in him had a strong influence on a number of modern poets.

 Browning was born in 1812, near London, the son of a clerk who worked for the Bank of England. He got a spotty formal education, but he read exhaustively in the six thousand books his father had collected, and from them he derived much of the widely varied factual information he later drew on in his poems. Headstrong in his youth, he early discovered Shelley and decided to be a poet—against all financial practicalities but with the support of his family. Response to his anonymous, Shelleyan poem *Pauline* (1833) brought home to him that, contrary to his intentions, he had revealed a good deal of himself in the poem, in a not very attractive light. Thereafter he made a stronger effort to efface his own personality in his work. One of the two options he explored was writing stage plays, but the convoluted self-examinations of his characters were not good theater, and those of his plays that were produced failed. The other, much more fruitful, option was the dramatic monologue; this was to be the vehicle of his

[96] Symbolic model. [97] Final result.

most characteristic poems, long and short (though he wrote fine lyrics too). *Dramatic Lyrics* (1842) included his first triumph in the dramatic monologue, "My Last Duchess," along with other notable works like "Porphyria's Lover," "Soliloquy of the Spanish Cloister," and "The Pied Piper of Hamelin," a children's classic. *Dramatic Romances and Lyrics*, in which "The Bishop Orders His Tomb at St. Praxed's Church" appeared, was published in 1845. Neither volume sold well.

Browning did not invent the dramatic monologue, but he perfected a distinctive form of it. The requirements of the genre (not all of them observed in every Browning monologue) call for a single speaker, addressing a silent listener or one whose words must be imagined, in a concrete situation that either represents a crisis in the speaker's life or brings out through the circumstantial setting his or her personality and values. The persons portrayed often reveal more about themselves than they are aware of doing, and they sometimes touch on ideas Browning himself felt strongly about. Much of the fascination of the dramatic monologues arises from our sense of tension between different sides of the protagonist, between his or her values and Browning's, and between the characters' limited visions and implicit fuller visions of reality. The monologues make stringent demands on the reader, who is expected to know a good deal about history and special subjects (about statuary stone, for example, in "The Bishop Orders His Tomb") and to have the mental acuity to piece out what is happening— not to mention sensing the psychological implications and appreciating the artistry. Browning developed in his own time, and has still not entirely shed, a reputation for composing difficult puzzles. But to many readers the experience of discovery in reading his poems and the need to complete the poems' meaning in their minds are part of the excitement.

In 1845 Browning met Elizabeth Barrett; the result was one of the famous love stories of the century. She was then (and remained throughout her life) much the more popular poet of the two, but she was an invalid recluse dominated by a possessive father. She and Browning, against the father's wishes, married secretly in 1846 and eloped to Italy, where they spent most of the next fifteen years, her health substantially restored. There Browning absorbed the Italian lore that he used in many of his best poems. In 1855 he published *Men and Women,* one of the most marvelous poetic volumes of the century, including such masterpieces as "Andrea del Sarto," "Love Among the Ruins," "Fra Lippo Lippi," "A Toccata of Galuppi's," and the eerie "Childe Roland to the Dark Tower Came."

After Elizabeth died in 1861, Browning, now near fifty, left Italy and returned with their son to England where Browning prepared an edition of his wife's poems. His own fame was now to arrive. In 1864 he published *Dramatis Personae,* a less impressive volume than *Men and Women* but Browning's first popular success. This was crowned by *The Ring and the Book* (1868–1869), a 21,000-line poem in four volumes about a seventeenth-century murder trial in Rome. Divided into sections told from the particular, limited perspectives of the people involved, the poem uses the dramatic monologue on an epic scale. In its exploration of point-of-view storytelling it anticipates an important later novelistic technique. During the rest of his life, Browning continued to write prolifically, especially on modern themes. His public image as a genial dinner guest of his friends

made a strange contrast to the imaginatively rich, often bizarre work that is typical of him. Much honored in his last years, he died in 1889, in Venice, and was buried in Westminster Abbey.

Browning has perhaps a wider range of voices than even Tennyson; for example, the sinister haughtiness of the Duke of Ferrara, the fevered incoherencies of the dying Bishop, and the limp musings and entreaties of Andrea del Sarto could hardly be more dissimilar. The three monologues are typical of Browning in their creation of distinctive speakers in concrete situations, in their Italian settings, and in their concern with sensuousness, idealism, and other aspects of art. "My Last Duchess" and "The Bishop Orders His Tomb" are typical in their focus on climactic moments (a marriage negotiation, the approach of death), "Andrea del Sarto" in its focus on a characteristic scene and episode (Andrea's deference to but resentment of his wife, who has her own reasons for enduring his long speech). "Andrea" further explores a theme central in Browning: the relationship between a noble if impossible quest for achievement and an ignoble if understandable refusal of the challenge.

Some Victorians found in Browning's earthier form of idealism a bracing alternative to the magisterial Tennysonian manner. Early twentieth-century English and American poets, in the act of rejecting him along with the other Victorians, also found some of their paths cleared by Browning's use of "undignified" and racy language, his zest for gnarled cacaphonies ("Shrewd was that snatch from out the corner south / He graced his carrion with, God curse the same!"—"The Bishop Orders His Tomb," lines 18–19), his admiration of Donne, his concern with modern subjects, his tolerance of unedifying or grotesque characters, his interest in the vagaries of human psychology, and of course his development of the dramatic monologue, with its transitionless stream of consciousness. Poets like Ezra Pound and the T. S. Eliot who wrote "Prufrock" owe him a considerable debt.

FURTHER READING *(prepared by W. J. R.):* W. Hall Griffin's *The Life of Robert Browning,* completed and ed. by H. C. Minchin, 1938, is still the most valuable single biography; to this volume may be added John Maynard's *Browning's Youth,* 1977, an excellent study of the poet's education and the artistic climate of his day. Robert Brainard Pearsall's *Robert Browning,* 1976, surveys Browning's entire poetic career and contains extensive discussions of major themes and works. Twenty-three of the lyric poems are given individual attention in Norton B. Crowell's *A Reader's Guide to Robert Browning,* 1972, which also provides a biographical sketch. Leonard Burrows's *Browning the Poet: An Introductory Study,* 1969, contains analyses of some thirty poems. A detailed treatment of Browning's development as a poet is included in William Clyde DeVane's *A Browning Handbook,* 1935, 2nd ed. 1955, which combines factual information with excellent analyses of Browning's poetic methods and styles. A good discussion of the technique of Browning's dramatic monologues, including "Andrea del Sarto," "Fra Lippo Lippi," and "The Bishop Orders His Tomb," is Roma A. King, Jr.'s *The Bow and the Lyre,* 1957. E. Warwick Slinn's *Browning and the Fictions of Identity,* 1982, discusses Browning as a psychological dramatist in the monologues, emphasizing the tension between concerns with the self and with other people. William O. Raymond's *The Infinite Moment and Other Essays in Robert Browning,* 1950, explains the genesis and composition of *The Ring and the Book.* Eleven essays on Browning by prominent scholars are collected in *Browning's Mind and Art,* ed. by Clarence Tracy, 1968.

MY LAST DUCHESS

FERRARA[1]

That's my last Duchess painted on the wall,
Looking as if she were alive; I call
That piece a wonder, now: Frà Pandolf's[2] hands
Worked busily a day, and there she stands.
Will't please you sit and look at her? I said 5
'Frà Pandolf' by design, for never read
Strangers like you that pictured countenance,
The depth and passion of its earnest glance,
But to myself they turned (since none puts by
The curtain I have drawn for you, but I) 10
And seemed as they would ask me, if they durst,[3]
How such a glance came there; so, not the first
Are you to turn and ask thus. Sir, 'twas not
Her husband's presence only, called that spot
Of joy into the Duchess' cheek: perhaps 15
Frà Pandolf chanced to say 'Her mantle laps
Over my Lady's wrist too much,' or 'Paint
Must never hope to reproduce the faint
Half-flush that dies along her throat;' such stuff
Was courtesy, she thought, and cause enough 20
For calling up that spot of joy. She had
A heart . . . how shall I say? . . . too soon made glad,
Too easily impressed; she liked whate'er
She looked on, and her looks went everywhere.
Sir, 'twas all one! My favour[4] at her breast, 25
The dropping of the daylight in the West,
The bough of cherries some officious fool
Broke in the orchard for her, the white mule
She rode with round the terrace—all and each
Would draw from her alike the approving speech, 30
Or blush, at least. She thanked men,—good; but thanked
Somehow . . . I know not how . . . as if she ranked
My gift of a nine-hundred-years-old name
With anybody's gift. Who'd stoop to blame
This sort of trifling? Even had you skill 35
In speech—(which I have not)—to make your will
Quite clear to such an one, and say 'Just this
Or that in you disgusts me; here you miss,
Or there exceed the mark'[5]—and if she let
Herself be lessoned so, nor plainly set 40
Her wits to yours, forsooth, and made excuse,

[1] City in northern Italy. [2] Brother Pandolf, a fictitious monk and painter.
[3] Dared. [4] Gift. [5] Standard; criterion.

—E'en then would be some stooping, and I choose
Never to stoop. Oh, Sir, she smiled, no doubt,
Whene'er I passed her; but who passed without
Much the same smile? This grew; I gave commands; 45
Then all smiles stopped together. There she stands
As if alive. Will't please you rise? We'll meet
The company below, then. I repeat,
The Count your Master's known munificence
Is ample warrant that no just pretence 50
Of mine for dowry will be disallowed;
Though his fair daughter's self, as I avowed
At starting, is my object. Nay, we'll go
Together down, Sir! Notice Neptune, though,
Taming a sea-horse, thought a rarity, 55
Which Claus of Innsbruck[6] cast in bronze for me.

THE BISHOP ORDERS HIS TOMB AT
SAINT PRAXED'S CHURCH[1]

ROME, 15—

Vanity, saith the preacher, vanity![2]
Draw round my bed: is Anselm keeping back?
Nephews[3]—sons mine . . . ah God, I know not! Well—
She, men would have to be your mother once,
Old Gandolf[4] envied me, so fair she was! 5
What's done is done, and she is dead beside,
Dead long ago, and I am Bishop since,
And as she died so must we die ourselves,
And thence ye may perceive the world's a dream.
Life, how and what is it? As here I lie 10
In this state-chamber, dying by degrees,
Hours and long hours in the dead night, I ask
"Do I live, am I dead?" Peace, peace seems all.
Saint Praxed's ever was the church for peace;
And so, about this tomb of mine. I fought 15
With tooth and nail to save my niche, ye know:
—Old Gandolf cozened[5] me, despite my care;
Shrewd was that snatch from out the corner south
He graced his carrion[6] with, God curse the same!

[6] Another fictitious artist. Neptune, god of the ocean, was a standard subject of Renaissance art.

[1] A church in Rome, named for a second-century Roman virgin-martyr converted to Christianity and noted for giving her goods to the poor. The characters in the poem are fictional.

[2] "Vanity of vanities, says the Preacher, . . . All is vanity." Ecclesiastes 1:2.

[3] In reality, illegitimate sons. He is now ready to call them that.

[4] His predecessor as bishop. [5] Cheated. [6] Rotten flesh.

Yet still my niche is not so cramped but thence 20
One sees the pulpit o' the epistle-side,[7]
And somewhat of the choir, those silent seats,
And up into the aëry dome where live
The angels, and a sunbeam's sure to lurk.
And I shall fill my slab of basalt[8] there, 25
And 'neath my tabernacle[9] take my rest,
With those nine columns round me, two and two,
The odd one at my feet where Anselm stands,
Peach-blossom marble all, the rare, the ripe,
As fresh-poured red wine of a mighty pulse.[10] 30
—Old Gandolf with his paltry onion-stone,[11]
Put me where I may look at him! True peach,
Rosy and flawless; how I earned the prize!
Draw close. That conflagration of my church
—What then? So much was saved if aught were missed! 35
My sons, ye would not be my death? Go dig
The white-grape vineyard where the oil-press stood,
Drop water gently till the surface sinks,
And if ye find . . . ah God, I know not, I! . . .
Bedded in store of rotten fig-leaves soft, 40
And corded up in a tight olive-frail,[12]
Some lump, ah God, of *lapis lazuli*,[13]
Big as a Jew's head cut off at the nape,
Blue as a vein o'er the Madonna's breast—
Sons, all have I bequeathed you, villas, all, 45
That brave Frascati[14] villa with its bath—
So, let the blue lump poise between my knees,
Like God the Father's globe on both his hands
Ye worship in the Jesu Church so gay,
For Gandolf shall not choose but see and burst! 50
Swift as a weaver's shuttle fleet our years;[15]
Man goeth to the grave, and where is he?
Did I say basalt for my slab, sons? Black—
'Twas ever antique-black[16] I meant! How else
Shall ye contrast my frieze[17] to come beneath? 55
The bas-relief in bronze ye promised me,
Those Pans and Nymphs ye wot of, and perchance
Some tripod, thyrsus,[18] with a vase or so,
The Saviour at his sermon on the mount,
St. Praxed in a glory,[19] and one Pan 60
Ready to twitch the Nymph's last garment off,

[7] In the Mass, excerpts from the biblical Epistles were read at the right-hand side of the altar, from the Gospels at the left.
[8] Hard, dark-colored rock. [9] Canopy. [10] Strength.
[11] Cheap marble that peeled like an onion. [12] Basket.
[13] High-quality blue stone. [14] Fashionable area near Rome.
[15] *Swift . . . years.* Loosely quoted from Job 7:6. [16] A finer marble.
[17] Decorated horizontal surface. [18] Wand carried by Bacchus, god of wine.
[19] Halo.

And Moses with the tables . . . but I know
Ye mark me not! What do they whisper thee,
Child of my bowels, Anselm? Ah, ye hope
To revel down my villas while I gasp 65
Bricked o'er with beggar's moldy travertine[20]
Which Gandolf from his tomb-top chuckles at!
Nay, boys, ye love me—all of jasper,[21] then!
'Tis jasper ye stand pledged to, lest I grieve
My bath must needs be left behind, alas! 70
One block, pure green as a pistachio-nut,
There's plenty jasper somewhere in the world—
And have I not St. Praxed's ear to pray
Horses for ye, and brown Greek manuscripts,
And mistresses with great smooth marbly limbs? 75
—That's if ye carve my epitaph aright,
Choice Latin, picked phrase, Tully's every word,
No gaudy ware like Gandolf's second line—
Tully, my masters? Ulpian[22] serves his need!
And then how I shall lie through centuries, 80
And hear the blessed mutter of the Mass,
And see God made and eaten all day long,
And feel the steady candle-flame, and taste
Good strong, thick, stupefying incense-smoke!
For as I lie here, hours of the dead night, 85
Dying in state and by such slow degrees,
I fold my arms as if they clasped a crook,[23]
And stretch my feet forth straight as stone can point,
And let the bedclothes for a mort-cloth[24] drop
Into great laps and folds of sculptor's-work. 90
And as yon tapers[25] dwindle, and strange thoughts
Grow, with a certain humming in my ears,
About the life before I lived this life,
And this life too, popes, cardinals, and priests,
St. Praxed at his sermon on the mount, 95
Your tall pale mother with her talking eyes,
And new-found agate urns as fresh as day,
And marble's language, Latin pure, discreet,
—Aha, ELUCESCEBAT[26] quoth our friend?
No Tully, said I, Ulpian at the best! 100
Evil and brief hath been my pilgrimage.
All *lapis*, all, sons! Else I give the Pope
My villas. Will ye ever eat my heart?
Ever your eyes were as a lizard's quick;
They glitter like your mother's for my soul, 105
Or ye would heighten my impoverished frieze,

[20] Inferior stone. [21] A variety of quartz.
[22] *Tully, Ulpian.* Tully (Cicero) was a model for excellent and Ulpian for poor Latin style.
[23] The crozier, a bishop's symbolic staff shaped like a shepherd's crook.
[24] Funeral drapery. [25] Candles.
[26] "He was glorious." This verb form is inferior Latin; "elucebat" is purer.

Piece out its starved design, and fill my vase
With grapes, and add a vizor and a term,[27]
And to the tripod ye would tie a lynx
That in his struggle throws the thyrsus down, 110
To comfort me on my entablature[28]
Whereon I am to lie till I must ask
"Do I live, am I dead?" There, leave me, there!
For ye have stabbed me with ingratitude
To death—ye wish it—God, ye wish it! Stone— 115
Gritstone,[29] a-crumble! Clammy squares which sweat
As if the corpse they keep were oozing through—
And no more *lapis* to delight the world!
Well, go! I bless ye. Fewer tapers there,
But in a row. And, going, turn your backs 120
—Aye, like departing altar-ministrants,
And leave me in my church, the church for peace,
That I may watch at leisure if he leers—
Old Gandolf—at me, from his onion-stone,
As still he envied me, so fair she was. 125

ANDREA DEL SARTO[1]

CALLED "THE FAULTLESS PAINTER"

But do not let us quarrel any more,
No, my Lucrezia! bear with me for once:
Sit down and all shall happen as you wish.
You turn your face, but does it bring your heart?
I'll work then for your friend's friend,[2] never fear, 5
Treat his own subject after his own way,
Fix his own time, accept too his own price,
And shut the money into this small hand
When next it takes mine. Will it? tenderly?
Oh, I'll content him,—but to-morrow, Love! 10
I often am much wearier than you think,
This evening more than usual: and it seems
As if—forgive now—should you let me sit
Here by the window, with your hand in mine,
And look a half hour forth on Fiesolè,[3] 15
Both of one mind, as married people use,
Quietly, quietly the evening through,

[27] A vizor is a mask, a term is a bust on a pedestal.
[28] Horizontal part of a classical structure. [29] Cheap sandstone.
[1] Florentine painter; he was born in 1486 and died of the plague in 1531. Browning's account of him here is based largely on the *Lives of the Painters* by Giorgio Vasari, the famous art historian, who was a pupil of Andrea's.
[2] Some friend of Lucrezia's so-called "cousin" mentioned later in the poem.
[3] A town near Florence.

I might get up to-morrow to my work
Cheerful and fresh as ever. Let us try.
To-morrow, how you shall be glad for this! 20
Your soft hand is a woman of itself,
And mine, the man's bared breast she curls inside.
Don't count the time lost, neither; you must serve
For each of the five pictures we require:
It saves a model. So! keep looking so— 25
My serpentining beauty, rounds on rounds!
—How could you ever prick those perfect ears,
Even to put the pearl there! oh, so sweet—
My face, my moon, my everybody's moon,
Which everybody looks on and calls his, 30
And, I suppose, is looked on by in turn,
While she looks—no one's: very dear, no less.
You smile? why, there's my picture ready made,
There's what we painters call our harmony!
A common grayness silvers everything,— 35
All in a twilight, you and I alike
—You, at the point of your first pride in me
(That's gone you know),—but I, at every point;
My youth, my hope, my art, being all toned down
To yonder sober pleasant Fiesolè. 40
There's the bell clinking from the chapel-top;
That length of convent-wall across the way
Holds the trees safer, huddled more inside;
The last monk leaves the garden; days decrease,
And autumn grows, autumn in everything. 45
Eh? the whole seems to fall into a shape
As if I saw alike my work and self
And all that I was born to be and do,
A twilight-piece. Love, we are in God's hand.
How strange now looks the life he makes us lead; 50
So free we seem, so fettered fast we are!
I feel he laid the fetter: let it lie!
This chamber for example—turn your head—
All that's behind us! You don't understand,
Nor care to understand, about my art, 55
But you can hear at least when people speak:
And that cartoon,[4] the second from the door
—It is the thing, Love! so such things should be—
Behold Madonna!—I am bold to say.
I can do with my pencil what I know, 60
What I see, what at bottom of my heart
I wish for, if I ever wish so deep—
Do easily, too—when I say, perfectly,
I do not boast, perhaps: yourself are judge,
Who listened to the Legate's[5] talk last week, 65

[4] Sketch drawn as preliminary to a painting. [5] Diplomatic envoy of the Pope.

And just as much they used to say in France.
At any rate, 'tis easy, all of it!
No sketches first, no studies, that's long past:
I do what many dream of all their lives,
—Dream? strive to do, and agonize to do, 70
And fail in doing. I could count twenty such
On twice your fingers, and not leave this town,
Who strive—you don't know how the others strive
To paint a little thing like that you smeared
Carelessly passing with your robes afloat,— 75
Yet do much less, so much less, Someone[6] says,
(I know his name, no matter)—so much less!
Well, less is more, Lucrezia: I am judged.
There burns a truer light of God in them,
In their vexed, beating, stuffed, and stopped-up brain, 80
Heart, or whate'er else, than goes on to prompt
This low-pulsed forthright craftsman's hand of mine.
Their works drop groundward, but themselves, I know,
Reach many a time a heaven that's shut to me,
Enter and take their place there sure enough, 85
Though they come back and cannot tell the world.
My works are nearer heaven, but I sit here.
The sudden blood of these men! at a word—
Praise them, it boils, or blame them, it boils too.
I, painting from myself and to myself, 90
Know what I do, am unmoved by men's blame
Or their praise either. Somebody remarks
Morello's[7] outline there is wrongly traced,
His hue mistaken; what of that? or else,
Rightly traced and well ordered; what of that? 95
Speak as they please, what does the mountain care?
Ah, but a man's reach should exceed his grasp,
Or what's a heaven for? All is silver-gray,
Placid and perfect with my art: the worse!
I know both what I want and what might gain; 100
And yet how profitless to know, to sigh
"Had I been two, another and myself,
Our head would have o'erlooked the world!" No doubt.
Yonder's a work now, of that famous youth
The Urbinate[8] who died five years ago. 105
('Tis copied, George Vasari sent it me.)
Well, I can fancy how he did it all,
Pouring his soul, with kings and popes to see,
Reaching, that heaven might so replenish him,
Above and through his art—for it gives way; 110
That arm is wrongly put—and there again—
A fault to pardon in the drawing's lines,

[6]Michelangelo (1475–1564); he is referred to later in the poem. [7]A mountain.
[8]Native of Urbino—that is, Raphael (1483–1520), who executed work for Pope Julius II.

Its body, so to speak: its soul is right,
He means right—that, a child may understand.
Still, what an arm! and I could alter it; 115
But all the play, the insight and the stretch—
Out of me, out of me! And wherefore out?
Had you enjoined them on me, given me soul,
We might have risen to Rafael, I and you.
Nay, Love, you did give all I asked, I think— 120
More than I merit, yes, by many times.
But had you—oh, with the same perfect brow,
And perfect eyes, and more than perfect mouth,
And the low voice my soul hears, as a bird
The fowler's[9] pipe, and follows to the snare— 125
Had you, with these the same, but brought a mind!
Some women do so. Had the mouth there urged
"God and the glory! never care for gain.
The present by the future, what is that?
Live for fame, side by side with Agnolo![10] 130
Rafael is waiting: up to God, all three!"
I might have done it for you. So it seems:
Perhaps not. All is as God overrules.
Beside, incentives come from the soul's self;
The rest avail not. Why do I need you? 135
What wife had Rafael, or has Agnolo?
In this world, who can do a thing, will not;
And who would[11] do it, cannot, I perceive:
Yet the will's somewhat—somewhat, too, the power—
And thus we half-men struggle. At the end, 140
God, I conclude, compensates, punishes.
'Tis safer for me, if the award be strict,
That I am something underrated here,
Poor this long while, despised, to speak the truth.
I dared not, do you know, leave home all day, 145
For fear of chancing on the Paris lords.[12]
The best is when they pass and look aside;
But they speak sometimes; I must bear it all.
Well may they speak! That Francis, that first time,
And that long festal year at Fontainebleau! 150
I surely then could sometimes leave the ground,
Put on the glory, Rafael's daily wear,
In that humane great monarch's golden look,—
One finger in his beard or twisted curl
Over his mouth's good mark that made the smile, 155
One arm about my shoulder, round my neck,
The jingle of his gold chain in my ear,

[9] Hunter of birds. [10] Michelangelo. [11] Desires to.

[12] Andrea had worked in 1518 for King Francis I of France at his palace in Fontainebleau, near Paris. According to the story, now questioned, Lucrezia got Andrea to return to Florence, where she induced him to spend on a new house money entrusted to him so that he might buy paintings for the king.

I painting proudly with his breath on me,
All his court round him, seeing with his eyes,
Such frank French eyes, and such a fire of souls 160
Profuse, my hand kept plying by those hearts,—
And, best of all, this, this, this face beyond,
This in the background, waiting on my work,
To crown the issue with a last reward!
A good time, was it not, my kingly days? 165
And had you not grown restless . . . but I know—
'Tis done and past; 'twas right, my instinct said;
Too live the life grew, golden and not gray,
And I'm the weak-eyed bat no sun should tempt
Out of his grange[13] whose four walls make his world. 170
How could it end in any other way?
You called me, and I came home to your heart.
The triumph was—to reach and stay there; since
I reached it ere the triumph, what is lost?
Let my hands frame your face in your hair's gold, 175
You beautiful Lucrezia that are mine!
"Rafael did this, Andrea painted that;
The Roman's[14] is the better when you pray,
But still the other's Virgin was his wife—"
Men will excuse me. I am glad to judge 180
Both pictures in your presence; clearer grows
My better fortune, I resolve to think.
For, do you know, Lucrezia, as God lives,
Said one day Agnolo, his very self,
To Rafael . . . I have known it all these years . . . 185
 (When the young man was flaming out his thoughts
Upon a palace-wall for Rome to see,
Too lifted up in heart because of it)
"Friend, there's a certain sorry little scrub
Goes up and down our Florence, none cares how, 190
Who, were he set to plan and execute
As you are, pricked on by your popes and kings,
Would bring the sweat into that brow of yours!"
To Rafael's!—And indeed the arm is wrong.
I hardly dare . . . yet, only you to see, 195
Give the chalk here—quick, thus the line should go!
Ay, but the soul! he's Rafael! rub it out!
Still, all I care for, if he spoke the truth,
(What he? why, who but Michel Agnolo?
Do you forget already words like those?) 200
If really there was such a chance so lost,—
Is, whether you're—not grateful—but more pleased.
Well, let me think so. And you smile indeed!
This hour has been an hour! Another smile?
If you would sit thus by me every night 205

[13] Barn. [14] Raphael, who painted in St. Peter's.

I should work better, do you comprehend?
I mean that I should earn more, give you more.
See, it is settled dusk now; there's a star;
Morello's gone, the watch-lights show the wall,
The cue-owls speak the name we call them by. 210
Come from the window, love,—come in, at last,
Inside the melancholy little house
We built to be so gay with. God is just.
King Francis may forgive me: oft at nights
When I look up from painting, eyes tired out, 215
The walls become illumined, brick from brick
Distinct, instead of mortar, fierce bright gold,
That gold of his I did cement them with!
Let us but love each other. Must you go?
That cousin here again? he waits outside? 220
Must see you—you, and not with me? Those loans?
More gaming[15] debts to pay? you smiled for that?
Well, let smiles buy me! have you more to spend?
While hand and eye and something of a heart
Are left me, work's my ware, and what's it worth? 225
I'll pay my fancy. Only let me sit
The gray remainder of the evening out,
Idle, you call it, and muse perfectly
How I could paint, were I but back in France,
One picture, just one more—the Virgin's face, 230
Not yours this time! I want you at my side
To hear them—that is, Michel Agnolo—
Judge all I do and tell you of its worth.
Will you? To-morrow, satisfy your friend.
I take the subjects for his corridor, 235
Finish the portrait out of hand—there, there,
And throw him in another thing or two
If he demurs;[16] the whole should prove enough
To pay for this same cousin's freak. Beside,
What's better and what's all I care about, 240
Get you the thirteen scudi[17] for the ruff!
Love, does that please you? Ah, but what does he,
The cousin! what does he to please you more?
 I am grown peaceful as old age to-night.
I regret little, I would change still less. 245
Since there my past life lies, why alter it?
The very wrong to Francis!—it is true
I took his coin, was tempted and complied,
And built this house and sinned, and all is said.
My father and my mother died of want. 250
Well, had I riches of my own? you see
How one gets rich! Let each one bear his lot.
They were born poor, lived poor, and poor they died:

[15] Gambling. [16] Is not satisfied. [17] Italian coins.

And I have labored somewhat in my time
And not been paid profusely. Some good son 255
Paint my two hundred pictures—let him try!
No doubt, there's something strikes a balance. Yes,
You loved me quite enough, it seems to-night.
This must suffice me here. What would one have?
In heaven, perhaps, new chances, one more chance— 260
Four great walls in the New Jerusalem[18]
Meted on each side by the angel's reed,[19]
For Leonard,[20] Rafael, Agnolo and me
To cover—the three first without a wife,
While I have mine! So—still they overcome 265
Because there's still Lucrezia,—as I choose.
Again the cousin's whistle! Go, my Love.

Georg Büchner
(1813–1837)

Georg Büchner found his place in the first rank of German writers by one of the strangest routes imaginable. A student of zoology and comparative anatomy, he wrote his first play, *Danton's Death,* when he was twenty-one. Two years later, he was dead of typhoid fever, leaving behind only two more plays, a comedy named *Leonce and Lena* and an unfinished play named *Woyzeck,* and a brief, fragmentary narrative named *Lenz.* Thirteen years later, in 1850, Ludwig Büchner, a prominent physician and writer, edited and published the pitifully small *Collected Works* of his dead brother; these were greeted with indifference. And then in 1879, a scholar named Karl Emil Fronzos became interested in Büchner and published a new "critical edition" of his work. Interest in Büchner's work began to grow. The plays were performed for the first time: *Leonce and Lena* in 1895, *Danton's Death* in 1902, and finally *Wozzeck* (as it was then called) in 1913. Then the greatest German stage director of the time, Max Reinhardt, staged Büchner's plays in Berlin: *Danton's Death* in 1916 and *Wozzeck* in 1921, and his productions established Büchner's plays as classics of the European theater.

Or perhaps we should say more precisely that they are classics of the *modern* European theater. Their long delay in becoming known meant that they began to have an impact only in the 1880's, at a time of rapid change in the theater. One of the most striking features of Büchner's plays is the fact that they have been a major influence on every important movement in the modern theater. The German Naturalistic playwrights Gerhart Hauptmann and Frank Wedekind, responding to the blunt realism of the plays, made a cult of Büchner and made pilgrimages to his grave. The Expressionists, perhaps emphasizing the eerie intensity of the atmosphere of

[18] Heaven. [19] *Meted . . . reed.* Measured by the angel's yardstick.
[20] Leonardo da Vinci (1452–1519).

Büchner's work, equally found him an inspiration. Bertolt Brecht found in Büchner's brief, staccato scenes a model for his own "epic theater," while Antonin Artaud, prophet of a very different, ecstatic, ritualistic "theater of cruelty," could admire Büchner for his emotionalism; he planned a never-realized production of *Woyzeck*. And, finally, Büchner, with his sense of the meaninglessness underlying human life, has been claimed as an important precursor of the modern existentialist playwrights and of Samuel Beckett. No wonder that the contemporary Büchner critic Reinhold Grimm imagines Büchner's plays at the center of a great web: "a veritable center, or hub, around which all kinds of connections radiate."

Büchner was born in 1813 in Goddelau, a small town in Hesse-Darmstadt, a ducal state in southern Germany. His father was a physician in the service of the Grand Duke; his mother also came from a family of physicians. There were six other children; one died in infancy, but several of the others had distinguished careers, especially Ludwig, a doctor and materialist philosopher who wrote an influential book called *Power and Matter* (1855), and Luise, a leader of the German feminist movement and the author of *Women and Their Profession* (also 1855).

Büchner was educated first at home and at a private school and then at the Darmstadt high school, where he did excellently in his studies. He also became increasingly radical in his politics. The German states were then in the grip of a wave of repression in the wake of the French Revolution. Büchner read intensively about the Revolution and began to greet his classmates with a subversive "Bonjours, citoyens!"

At the age of eighteen, Büchner enrolled as a student of medicine and science at the University of Strasbourg, in the comparatively liberal French province of Alsace. Here he spent perhaps the happiest two years of his life, revelling in the atmosphere of freedom, roaming the beautiful countryside, and falling in love with (and becoming secretly engaged to) Wilhelmine Jaeglé, the daughter of the Protestant minister in whose house he roomed. In 1831, however, Büchner's permission from the German authorities to study abroad ran out, and he was forced to return home to continue his academic work at the inferior University of Giessen. Here he became increasingly depressed by the brutal political repression he witnessed around him and took up revolutionary activity, forming a secret "Society for Human Rights" and writing a revolutionary pamphlet, *The Hessian Courier*. When this pamphlet fell into the hands of the police, they began a round-up of those responsible, aided by an informer. Büchner's collaborator on the pamphlet, a radical pastor named Ludwig Weidig, was arrested, held in prison, and periodically tortured for two years until he died in 1837, an apparent suicide. Büchner's rooms were searched, but fortunately no incriminating evidence was found, and he was safe, temporarily. He returned to his family home in Darmstadt, and it was here, hiding in an upstairs room with a younger brother watching for the police, that he wrote, in a frantic five weeks, *Danton's Death*, in order to make money to finance a flight from the country. The editor Karl Gutzkow agreed to publish the play in his journal *Phoenix*, and Büchner, with a warrant hanging over his head, fled to France.

Back in Strasbourg, Büchner plunged into a punishing regime of work, leading one of his friends to call him "the proletarian of intellectual labor." He carried on a full program of anatomical studies and was awarded the degree of Doctor of Philosophy from the newly founded University of

Zurich in September, 1836, and, after a demonstration lecture on the nerves in the heads of fish, was appointed Lecturer in Natural Sciences. Meanwhile, he also translated two plays by Victor Hugo into German; wrote his novella *Lenz*, based on the diaries of Jean-Frédéric Oberlin, who had treated the poet and playwright Jakob Michael Reinhold Lenz as Lenz slowly succumbed to schizophrenia; wrote his comedy *Leonce and Lena* for a literary competition (but submitted it too late); wrote another play, *Pietro Aretino* (now lost); and nearly completed *Woyzeck*. (In addition, he taught himself English and Italian!) On February 2, 1837, he developed symptoms of typhoid fever, and after seventeen days of illness, he died. His friends suspected, probably rightly, that he had weakened himself through over-work; one said that Büchner had "worked himself smilingly to death."

As *Danton's Death* is based closely on historical accounts of the French Revolution, so *Woyzeck* is based on an actual incident: the murder in 1821 of a woman in Leipzig by her lover, a man named Johann Christian Woyzeck. The case came to Büchner's attention through an article in a medical journal by a Dr. J. C. A. Clarus. Woyzeck had been convicted and sentenced to death for the murder. The defense requested a reprieve on grounds of insanity, and Dr. Clarus was called on to make a psychological examination. Woyzeck, he reported, was orphaned as a child. He had drifted around Europe as a youth, trying to pursue a trade as a barber and wigmaker. He had eventually become a soldier, serving in a series of armies. He had fallen in love with a Swedish girl and had a child by her but, unable to marry her because his papers were not in order, had abandoned her. In Leipzig, he drifted into a relationship with a widow named Frau Woost, who tormented him by continuing to prostitute herself with soldiers. He gradually became a derelict, supporting himself by begging, and sleeping in open fields. He also began to develop psychotic symptoms, including irrational fears (especially of Freemasons) and visual and auditory hallucinations. Finally, stung by Frau Woost's failing to meet him because she had gone off with a soldier, Woyzeck stabbed her to death.

Despite the clear evidence of psychosis, Clarus concluded that Woyzeck should be held responsible. His only problem was alcoholism, he said, holding that the paranoia and hallucinations had developed only after the murder. Accordingly, Woyzeck was executed by beheading in the Leipzig market square on August 27, 1824. The case attracted wide interest and continued to be debated in the press for several years after Woyzeck's death. (Büchner seems to have drawn for minor details on two other cases of men murdering their mistresses, those of Daniel Schmolling in 1817 and Johann Diess in 1830. Büchner may even have participated in an autopsy of Diess's body; it was taken to the University of Giessen for dissection while Büchner was a medical student there.)

Shortly before he died, Büchner wrote to his fiancée that *Woyzeck* would be completed "in a week at most." So it is clear that he did not plan any major additions to the play. But the manuscripts he left are far from clear as to his final intentions. One manuscript seems to have been intended as the final version (though it is incomplete). Three other manuscripts contain numerous scenes, out of order, some of which may have been discarded, others of which seem to have been intended for insertion into the final version. Scholars, in attempting to work out Büchner's intentions, have arrived at radically different conclusions. The first editor, in 1879 (*Woyzeck* was omitted from Ludwig Büchner's 1850 edition), misread the

protagonist's name as "Wozzeck" and made many mistakes in transcription. (Alban Berg's 1925 opera is based on this edition and thus is entitled *Wozzeck*.) To make matters worse, the editor painted the manuscript with acid to make the ink more readable, a process that caused the manuscript to gradually turn black over the subsequent years. It was only with the development of modern photographic techniques that the manuscripts could be reexamined and the transcriptions corrected. The problem of the order of the scenes remains, however, and different solutions to the problem have resulted in editions and productions of the play that differ wildly from one another.

The textual uncertainties of *Woyzeck* could be taken as a metaphor for larger indeterminacies about the play's meaning. In *Woyzeck*, Büchner explores, for the first time in dramatic history, the consciousness of an ordinary man, or perhaps a less than ordinary man, for Woyzeck, marginalized by society and tormented by his own inner demons, is less able than most of us to control his own life. Why does Woyzeck murder Marie? Many answers are possible, whether social, political, or psychological, but none seems quite adequate. Underlying them all is the frightening suggestion of a world without meaning, in which all such answers are merely feeble attempts to fend off our acknowledgment of that meaninglessness.

FURTHER READING *(prepared by J. H.):* Julian Hilton's *Georg Büchner*, 1982, in the Grove Press Modern Dramatists series, is a short, useful introductory account of Büchner's work, with good readings of the plays. *Büchner: The Complete Plays*, edited and introduced by Michael Patterson, 1987, in the Methuen World Dramatists series, has useful introductions and commentaries, especially strong on the stage histories of the plays. Patterson reprints *The Hessian Courier*, a selection of letters, and even part of Büchner's lecture "On Cranial Nerves," which throws some unexpected light on his themes. Longer critical surveys include A. H. J. Knight, *Georg Büchner*, 1951; Herbert Lindenberger, *Georg Büchner*, 1964; Maurice B. Benn, *The Drama of Revolt: A Critical Study of Georg Büchner*, 1976; and David G. Richards, *Georg Büchner and the Birth of Modern Drama*, 1977. The periodical *Yale/Theatre* ran a special issue on Büchner (Winter 1972), which includes illuminating essays by Robert Brustein, Richard Gilman, Timothy Wiles, and others, as well as a useful Büchner bibliography.

WOYZECK

Translated by Carl Richard Mueller

CHARACTERS

WOYZECK	JEW
MARIE	INNKEEPER
CAPTAIN	APPRENTICES
DOCTOR	KATHY
DRUM MAJOR	KARL THE TOWN IDIOT
SERGEANT	GRANDMOTHER
ANDRES	POLICEMAN
MARGRET	SOLDIERS, STUDENTS, YOUNG MEN
PROPRIETOR OF THE BOOTH	AND GIRLS, CHILDREN, JUDGE,
CHARLATAN	COURT CLERK, PEOPLE
OLD MAN WITH BARREL-ORGAN	

SCENE 1

[*At the* CAPTAIN'*s. The* CAPTAIN *in a chair.* WOYZECK *shaving him.*]

CAPTAIN. Not so fast, Woyzeck, not so fast! One thing at a time! You're making me dizzy. What am I to do with the ten extra minutes that you'll finish early today? Just think, Woyzeck: you still have thirty beautiful years to live! Thirty years! That makes three hundred and sixty months! And days! Hours! Minutes! What do you think you'll do with all that horrible stretch of time? Have you ever thought about it, Woyzeck?

WOYZECK. Yes, sir, Captain.

CAPTAIN. It frightens me when I think about the world . . . when I think about eternity. Busyness, Woyzeck, busyness! There's the eternal: that's eternal, that is eternal. That you can understand. But then again it's not eternal. It's only a moment. A mere moment. Woyzeck, it makes me shudder when I think that the earth turns itself about in a single day! What a waste of time! Where will it all end? Woyzeck, I can't even look at a mill wheel any more without becoming melancholy.

WOYZECK. Yes, sir, Captain.

CAPTAIN. Woyzeck, you always seem so exasperated! A good man isn't like that. A good man with a good conscience, that is. Well, say something, Woyzeck! What's the weather like today?

WOYZECK. Bad, Captain, sir, bad: wind!

CAPTAIN. I feel it already. Sounds like a real storm out there. A wind like that has the same effect on me as a mouse. [*Cunningly.*] I think it must be something out of the north-south.

WOYZECK. Yes, sir, Captain.

CAPTAIN. Ha! Ha! Ha! North-south! Ha! Ha! Ha! Oh, he's a stupid one! Horribly stupid! [*Moved.*] Woyzeck, you're a good man, but [*with dignity*] Woyzeck, you have no morality! Morality, that's when you have morals, you understand. It's a good word. You have a child without the blessings of the Church, just like our Right Reverend Garrison Chaplain says: "Without the blessings of the Church." It's not *my* phrase.

WOYZECK. Captain, sir, the good Lord's not going to look at a poor worm just because they said Amen over it before they went at it. The Lord said: "Suffer little children to come unto me."[1]

CAPTAIN. What's that you said? What kind of strange answer's that? You're confusing me with your answers!

WOYZECK. It's us poor people that . . . You see, Captain, sir . . . Money, money! Whoever hasn't got money . . . Well, who's got morals when he's bringing something like me into the world? We're flesh and blood, too. Our kind is miserable only once: in this world and in the next. I think if we ever got to Heaven we'd have to help with the thunder.

CAPTAIN. Woyzeck, you have no virtue! You're not a virtuous human being! Flesh and blood? Whenever I rest at the window, when it's finished raining, and my eyes follow the white stockings along as they hurry across the street . . . Damnation, Woyzeck, I know what love is, too, then! I'm made of flesh and blood, too. But, Woyzeck: Virtue!

[1] Words of Jesus, in Luke 18:16, Mark 10:14, Matthew 19:14.

Virtue! How was I to get rid of the time? I always say to myself: "You're a virtuous man [*moved*], a good man, a good man."

WOYZECK. Yes, Captain, sir: Virtue. I haven't got much of that. You see, us common people, we haven't got virtue. That's the way it's got to be. But if I could be a gentleman, and if I could have a hat and a watch and a cane, and if I could talk refined, I'd want to be virtuous, all right. There must be something beautiful in virtue, Captain, sir. But I'm just a poor good-for-nothing!

CAPTAIN. Good, Woyzeck. You're a good man, a good man. But you think too much. It eats at you. You always seem so exasperated. Our discussion has affected me deeply. You can go now. And don't run so! Slowly! Nice and slowly down the street!

SCENE 2

[*An open field. The town in the distance.* WOYZECK *and* ANDRES *cut twigs from the bushes.* ANDRES *whistles.*]

WOYZECK. Andres? You know this place is cursed? Look at that light streak over there on the grass. There where the toadstools grow up. That's where the head rolls every night. One time somebody picked it up. He thought it was a hedgehog. Three days and three nights and he was in a box. [*Low.*] Andres, it was the Freemasons, don't you see, it was the Freemasons!

ANDRES [*sings*].

Two little rabbits sat on a lawn
Eating, oh, eating the green green grass . . .[2]

WOYZECK. Quiet! Can you hear it, Andres? Can you hear it? Something moving!

ANDRES [*sings*].

Eating, oh, eating the green green grass
Till all the grass was gone.

WOYZECK. It's moving behind me! Under me! [*Stamps on the ground.*] Listen! Hollow! It's all hollow down there! It's the Freemasons!

ANDRES. I'm afraid.

WOYZECK. Strange how still it is. You almost want to hold your breath. Andres!

ANDRES. What?

WOYZECK. Say something! [*Looks about fixedly.*] Andres! How bright it is! It's all glowing over the town! A fire's sailing around the sky and a noise coming down like trumpets. It's coming closer! Let's get out of here! Don't look back! [*Drags him into the bushes.*]

ANDRES [*after a pause*]. Woyzeck? Do you still hear it?

[2] This, like most of the other songs in *Woyzeck*, is part of a German folk song.

WOYZECK. It's quiet now. So quiet. Like the world's dead.
ANDRES. Listen! I can hear the drums inside. We've got to go!

SCENE 3

[*The town.* MARIE *with her* CHILD *at the window.* MARGRET. *The Retreat[3] passes,* THE DRUM MAJOR *at its head.*]

MARIE [*rocking* THE CHILD *in her arms*]. Ho, boy! Da-da-da-da! Can you hear? They're coming! There!
MARGRET. What a man! Built like a tree!
MARIE. He walks like a lion.

[THE DRUM MAJOR *salutes* MARIE.]

MARGRET. Oh, what a look he threw you, neighbor! We're not used to such things from you.
MARIE [*sings*].

Soldiers, oh, you pretty lads . . .

MARGRET. Your eyes are still shining.
MARIE. And if they are? Take *your* eyes to the Jew's and let him clean them for you. Maybe he can shine them so you can sell them for a pair of buttons!
MARGRET. Look who's talking! Just look who's talking! If it isn't the Virgin herself! I'm a respectable person. But you! Everyone knows you could stare your way through seven layers of leather pants!
MARIE. Slut! [*Slams the window shut.*] Come, boy! What's it to them, anyway! Even if you are just a poor whore's baby, your dishonorable little face still makes your mother happy! [*Sings.*]

I have my trouble and bother
But, baby dear, where is your father?
Why should I worry and fight?
I'll hold you and sing through the night:
Heio popeio, my baby, my dove
What do I want now with love?

[*A knock at the window.*]

Who's there? Is it you, Franz? Come in!
WOYZECK. Can't. There's roll call.
MARIE. Did you cut wood for the Captain?
WOYZECK. Yes, Marie.
MARIE. What is it, Franz? You look so troubled.
WOYZECK. Marie, it happened again, only there was more. Isn't it written: "And there arose a smoke out of the pit, as the smoke of a great furnace"?[4]

[3] Formation or ceremony at the end of the military day.
[4] Revelation 9:2, where the smoke is rising from "the bottomless pit."

MARIE. Oh, Franz!

WOYZECK. Shh! Quiet! I've got it! The Freemasons! There was a terrible
noise in the sky and everything was on fire! I'm on the trail of some-
thing, something big. It followed me all the way to the town. Something
that I can't put my hands on, or understand. Something that drives us
mad. What'll come of it all?

MARIE. Franz!

WOYZECK. Don't you see? Look around you! Everything hard and fixed, so
gloomy. What's moving back there? When God goes, everything goes.
I've got to get back.

MARIE. And the child?

WOYZECK. My God, the boy!—Tonight at the fair! I've saved something
again. [*He leaves.*]

MARIE. That man! Seeing things like that! He'll go mad if he keeps think-
ing that way! He frightened me! It's so gloomy here. Why are you so
quiet, boy? Are you afraid? It's growing so dark. As if we were going
blind. Only that street lamp shining in from outside. [*Sings.*]

> And what if your cradle is bad?
> Sleep tight, my lovey, my lad.

I can't stand it! It makes me shiver! [*She goes out.*]

SCENE 4

> [*Fair booths. Lights. People. OLD MAN
> with a CHILD, WOYZECK, MARIE,
> CHARLATAN, WIFE, DRUM MAJOR, and
> SERGEANT.*]

OLD MAN [*sings while THE CHILD dances to the barrel-organ*].

> There's nothing on this earth will last,
> Our lives are as the fields of grass,
> Soon all is past, is past.

WOYZECK. Ho! Hip-hop there, boy! Hip-hop! Poor man, old man! Poor
child, young child! Trouble and happiness!

MARIE. My God, when fools still have their senses, then we're all fools. Oh,
what a mad world! What a beautiful world!

> [*They go over to THE CHARLATAN who
> stands in front of a booth, his WIFE in
> trousers, and a monkey in costume.*]

CHARLATAN. Gentlemen, gentlemen! You see here before you a creature as
God created it! Yet it is nothing this way! Absolutely nothing! But now
look at what Art can do. It walks upright. Wears coat and pants. And
even carries a saber. This monkey here is a regular soldier. So what if he
isn't much different! So what if he *is* still on the bottom rung of the
human ladder! Hey there, take a bow! That's the way! Now you're a
baron, at least. Give us a kiss!

[*The monkey trumpets.*]
This little customer's musical, too. And, gentlemen, in here you will see
the astronomical horse and the little lovebirds. Favorites of all the
crowned heads of Europe. They'll tell you anything: how old you are,
how many children you have, what your ailments are. The performance
is about to begin. And at the beginning. The beginning of the begin-
ning!

WOYZECK. You know, I had a little dog once who kept sniffing around the
rim of a big hat, and I thought I'd be good to him and make it easier for
him and sat him on top of it. And all the people stood around and
clapped.

GENTLEMEN. Oh, grotesque! How really grotesque!

WOYZECK. Don't you believe in God either? It's an honest fact I don't be-
lieve in God.—You call that grotesque? I like what's grotesque. See that?
That grotesque enough for you?—[*To* MARIE.] You want to go in?

MARIE. Sure. That must be nice in there. Look at the tassels on him! And
his wife's got pants on!

[*They go inside.*]

DRUM MAJOR. Wait a minute! Did you see her? What a piece!

SERGEANT. Hell, she could whelp a couple regiments of cavalry!

DRUM MAJOR. *And* breed drum majors!

SERGEANT. Look at the way she carries that head! You'd think all that black
hair would pull her down like a weight. And those eyes!

DRUM MAJOR. Like looking down a well . . . or up a chimney. Come on,
let's go after her!

SCENE 5

[*Interior of the brightly lighted booth.*
MARIE, WOYZECK, PROPRIETOR OF THE
BOOTH, SERGEANT, *and* DRUM
MAJOR.]

MARIE. All these lights!

WOYZECK. Sure, Marie. Black cats with fiery eyes.

PROPRIETOR OF THE BOOTH [*bringing forward a horse*]. Show your talent!
Show your brute reason! Put human society to shame! Gentlemen, this
animal you see here, with a tail on its torso, and standing on its four
hoofs, is a member of all the learned societies—as well as a professor at
our university where he teaches students how to ride and fight. But that
requires simple intelligence. Now think with your double reason! What
do you do when you think with your double reason? Is there a jackass in
this learned assembly?

[*The nag shakes its head.*]

How's that for double reasoning? That's physiognomy[5] for you. This is
no dumb animal. This is a person! A human being! But still an animal.
A beast.

[5] Facial features as a reflection of personality. In the German the word translated (*Vieh-
sionomik*) is a pun, *Vieh* meaning "dumb animal."

[*The nag conducts itself indecently.*]
That's right, put society to shame. As you can see, this animal is still in a
state of Nature. Not ideal Nature, of course! Take a lesson from him!
But ask your doctor first, it may prove highly dangerous! What we have
been told by this is: Man must be natural! You are created of dust, sand,
and dung. Why must you be more than dust, sand, and dung? Look
there at his reason. He can figure even if he can't count it off on his
fingers. And why? Because he cannot express himself, can't explain. A
metamorphosed human being. Tell the gentlemen what time it is!
Which of you ladies and gentlemen has a watch? A watch?

SERGEANT. A watch? [*He pulls a watch imposingly and measuredly from his
pocket.*] There you are, my good man!

MARIE. I want to see this. [*She clambers down to the first row of seats;* THE
SERGEANT *helps her.*]

DRUM MAJOR. What a piece!

SCENE 6

[MARIE'S *room.* MARIE *with her* CHILD.]

MARIE [*sitting, her* CHILD *on her lap, a piece of mirror in her hand*]. He told
Franz to get the hell out, so what could he do! [*Looks at herself in the
mirror.*] Look how the stones shine! What kind are they, I wonder? What
kind did he say they were? Sleep, boy! Close your eyes! Tight! Stay that
way now. Don't move or he'll get you! [*Sings.*]

> Hurry, lady, close up tight
> A gypsy lad is out tonight
> And he will take you by the hand
> And lead you into gypsyland.

[*Continues to look at herself in the mirror.*] They must be gold! I wonder
how they'll look on me at the dance? Our kind's got only a little corner
in the world and a piece of broken mirror. But my mouth is just as red
as any of the fine ladies with their mirrors from top to bottom, and their
handsome gentlemen that kiss their hands for them! I'm just a poor
common piece!

[THE CHILD *sits up.*]
Quiet, boy! Close your eyes! There's the sandman! Look at him run
across the wall! [*She flashes with the mirror.*] Eyes tight! Or he'll look into
them and make you blind!

[WOYZECK *enters behind her. She jumps
up, her hands at her ears.*]

WOYZECK. What's that?

MARIE. Nothing.

WOYZECK. There's something shiny in your hands.

MARIE. An earring. I found it.

WOYZECK. I never have luck like that! Two at a time!

MARIE. Am I human or not?

WOYZECK. I'm sorry, Marie.—Look at the boy asleep. Lift his arm, the
chair's hurting him. Look at the shiny drops on his forehead. Every-

thing under the sun works! We even sweat in our sleep. Us poor people! Here's some money again, Marie. My pay and something from the Captain.

MARIE. God bless you, Franz.

WOYZECK. I've got to get back. Tonight, Marie! I'll see you tonight! [*He goes off.*]

MARIE [*alone, after a pause*]. I *am* bad, I *am!* I could run myself through with a knife! Oh, what a life, what a life! We'll all end up in hell, anyway, in the end: man, woman, and child!

SCENE 7

[*At the* DOCTOR's. THE DOCTOR *and* WOYZECK.]

DOCTOR. I don't believe it, Woyzeck! And a man of your word!

WOYZECK. What's that, Doctor, sir?

DOCTOR. I saw it all, Woyzeck. You pissed on the street! You were pissing on the wall like a dog! And here I'm giving you three groschen a day plus board! That's terrible, Woyzeck! The world's becoming a terrible place, a terrible place!

WOYZECK. But, Doctor, sir, when Nature . . .

DOCTOR. When Nature? When Nature? What has Nature to do with it? Did I or did I not prove to you that the *musculus constrictor vesicae*[6] is controlled by your will? Nature! Woyzeck, man is free! In Mankind alone we see glorified the individual's will to freedom! And you couldn't hold your water! [*Shakes his head, places his hands behind the small of his back, and walks back and forth.*] Have you eaten your peas today, Woyzeck? Nothing but peas! *Cruciferae!*[7] Remember that! There's going to be a revolution in science! I'm going to blow it sky-high! *Urea*[8] *Oxygen.* Ammonium hydrochloratem hyperoxidic. Woyzeck, couldn't you just *try* to piss again? Go in the other room there and make another try.

WOYZECK. Doctor, sir, I can't.

DOCTOR [*disturbed*]. But you could piss on the wall. I have it here in black and white. Our contract is right here! I saw it. I saw it with these very eyes. I had just stuck my head out the window, opening it to let in the rays of the sun, so as to execute the process of sneezing. [*Going toward him.*] No, Woyzeck, I'm not going to vex myself. Vexation is unhealthy. Unscientific. I'm calm now, completely calm. My pulse is beating at its accustomed sixty, and I am speaking to you in utmost cold-bloodedness. Why should I vex myself over a man, God forbid! A man! Now if he were a Proteus,[9] it would be worth the vexation! But, Woyzeck, you really shouldn't have pissed on the wall.

WOYZECK. You see, Doctor, sir, sometimes a person's got a certain kind of character, like when he's made a certain way. But with Nature it's not the same, you see. With Nature [*he snaps his fingers*], it's like *that!* How should I explain, it's like——

[6] Latin: the constrictor muscle of the bladder.
[7] A botanical category of plants (literally, in Latin, "cross-bearing" ones).
[8] A chemical constituent of urine.
[9] In classical mythology, a sea god who could assume many shapes.

DOCTOR. Woyzeck, you're philosophizing again.

WOYZECK [*confidingly*]. Doctor, sir, did you ever see anything with double nature? Like when the sun stops at noon, and it's like the world was going up in fire? That's when I hear a terrible voice saying things to me!

DOCTOR. Woyzeck, you have an *aberratio!*[10]

WOYZECK [*places his finger at his nose*]. It's in the toadstools, Doctor, sir, that's where it is. Did you ever see the shapes the toadstools make when they grow up out of the earth? If only somebody could read what they say!

DOCTOR. Woyzeck, you have a most beautiful *aberratio mentalis partialis* of a secondary order! And so wonderfully developed! Woyzeck, your salary is increased! *Idée fixe*[11] of a secondary order, and with a generally rational state. You go about your business normally? Still shaving the Captain?

WOYZECK. Yes, sir.

DOCTOR. You eat your peas?

WOYZECK. Just as always, Doctor, sir. My wife gets the money for the household.

DOCTOR. Still in the army?

WOYZECK. Yes, sir, Doctor.

DOCTOR. You're an interesting case. Patient Woyzeck, you're to have an increase in salary. So behave yourself! Let's feel the pulse. Ah yes.

SCENE 8

[MARIE'S *room*. DRUM MAJOR *and* MARIE.]

DRUM MAJOR. Marie!

MARIE [*looking at him, with expression*]. Go on, show me how you march!— Chest broad as a bull's and a beard like a lion! There's not another man in the world like that! And there's not a prouder woman than me!

DRUM MAJOR. Wait till Sunday when I wear my helmet with the plume and my white gloves! Damn, that'll be a sight for you! The Prince always says: "My God, there goes a real man!"

MARIE [*scoffing*]. Ha! [*Goes toward him.*] A man?

DRUM MAJOR. You're not such a bad piece yourself! Hell, we'll plot a whole brood of drum majors! Right? [*He puts his arm around her.*]

MARIE [*annoyed*]. Let go!

DRUM MAJOR. Bitch!

MARIE [*fiercely*]. You just touch me!

DRUM MAJOR. There's devils in your eyes.

MARIE. Let there be, for all I care! What's the difference!

SCENE 9

[*Street.* CAPTAIN *and* DOCTOR. THE CAPTAIN *comes panting along the street, stops; pants, looks about.*]

CAPTAIN. Ho, Doctor, don't run so fast! Don't paddle the air so with your

[10]Latin: derangement. [11]French: fixed idea; obsession.

stick! You're only courting death that way! A good man with a good conscience never walks as fast as that. A good man . . . [*He catches him by the coat.*] Doctor, permit me to save a human life!

DOCTOR. I'm in a hurry, Captain, I'm in a hurry!

CAPTAIN. Doctor, I'm so melancholy. I have such fantasies. I start to cry every time I see my coat hanging on the wall.

DOCTOR. Hm! Bloated, fat, thick neck: apoplectic constitution. Yes, Captain, you'll be having *apoplexia cerebria*[12] any time now. Of course you could have it on only one side. In which case you'll be paralyzed down that one side. Or if things go really well you'll be mentally disabled so that you can vegetate away for the rest of your days. You may look forward to something approximately like that within the next four weeks! And, furthermore, I can assure you that you give promise of being a most interesting case. And if it is God's will that only one half of your tongue become paralyzed, then we will conduct the most immortal of experiments.

CAPTAIN. Doctor, you mustn't scare me that way! People are said to have died of fright. Of pure, sheer fright. I can see them now with lemons in their hands. But they'll say: "He was a good man, a good man." You devil's coffinnail maker!

DOCTOR [*extending his hat toward him*]. Do you know who this is, Captain? This is Sir Hollowhead, my most honorable Captain Drilltheirassesoff!

CAPTAIN [*makes a series of folds in his sleeve*]. And do you know who this is, Doctor? This is Sir Manifold, my dear devil's coffinnail maker! Ha! Ha! Ha! But no harm meant! I'm a good man, but I can play, too, when I want to, Doctor, when I want to . . .

> [WOYZECK *comes toward them and tries to pass in a hurry.*]

Ho! Woyzeck! Where are you off to in such a hurry? Stay awhile, Woyzeck! Running through the world like an open razor, you're liable to cut someone. He runs as if he had to shave a castrated regiment and would be hung before he discovered and cut the longest hair that wasn't there. But on the subject of long beards . . . What was it I wanted to say? Woyzeck, why was I thinking about beards?

DOCTOR. The wearing of long beards on the chin, remarks Pliny,[13] is a habit of which soldiers must be broken——

CAPTAIN [*continues*]. Ah, yes, this thing about beards! Tell me, Woyzeck, have you found any long hairs from beards in your soup bowl lately? Ho, I don't think he understands! A hair from a human face, from the beard of an engineer, a sergeant, a . . . a drum major? Well, Woyzeck? But then he's got a good woman. It's not the same with the others.

WOYZECK. Yes, sir, Captain! What was it you wanted to say to me, Captain, sir?

CAPTAIN. What a face he's making! Well, maybe not in his soup, but if he hurries home around the corner I'll wager he might still find one on a certain pair of lips. A pair of lips, Woyzeck. I know what love is, too, Woyzeck. Look at him, he's white as chalk!

[12] Latin: stroke.
[13] Pliny the Elder, a first-century A.D. Roman writer on a variety of subjects.

WOYZECK. Captain, sir, I'm just a poor devil. And there's nothing else I've got in the world but her. Captain, sir, if you're just making a fool of me . . .

CAPTAIN. A fool? Me? Making a fool of you, Woyzeck?

DOCTOR. Your pulse, Woyzeck, your pulse! Short, hard, skipping, irregular.

WOYZECK. Captain, sir, the earth's hot as coals in hell. But I'm cold as ice, cold as ice. Hell is cold, I'll bet you. I don't believe it! God! God! I don't believe it!

CAPTAIN. Look here, you, how would you . . . how'd you like a pair of bullets in your skull? You keep stabbing at me with those eyes of yours, and I'm only trying to help. Because you're a good man, Woyzeck, a good man.

DOCTOR. Facial muscles rigid, taut, occasional twitches. Condition strained, excitable.

WOYZECK. I'm going. Anything's possible. The bitch! Anything's possible. —— The weather's nice, Captain, sir. Look, a beautiful, hard, gray sky. You'd almost like to pound a nail in up there and hang yourself on it. And only because of that little dash between Yes and Yes again . . . and No. Captain, sir: Yes and No: did No make Yes or Yes make No? I must think about that. [*He goes off with long strides, slowly at first, then faster and faster.*]

DOCTOR [*shouting after him*]. Phenomenon! Woyzeck, you get a raise!

CAPTAIN. I get so dizzy around such people. Look at him go! Long-legged rascals like him step out like a shadow running away from its own spider. But short ones only dawdle along. The long-legged ones are the lightning, the short ones the thunder. Haha . . . Grotesque! Grotesque!

SCENE 10

[MARIE's *room.* WOYZECK *and* MARIE.]

WOYZECK [*looks fixedly at her and shakes his head*]. Hm! I don't see it! I don't see it! My God, why can't I see it, why can't I take it in my fists!

MARIE [*frightened*]. Franz, what is it?—You're raving, Franz.

WOYZECK. A sin so swollen and big—it stinks to smoke the angels out of Heaven! You have a red mouth, Marie! No blisters on it? Marie, you're beautiful as sin. How can mortal sin be so beautiful?

MARIE. Franz, it's your fever making you talk this way!

WOYZECK. Damn you! Is this where he stood? Like this? Like this?

MARIE. While the day's long and the world's old a lot of people can stand in one spot, one right after the other.—Why are you looking at me so strange, Franz! I'm afraid!

WOYZECK. It's a nice street for walking, uh? You could walk corns on your feet! It's nice walking on the street, going around in society.

MARIE. Society?

WOYZECK. A lot of people pass through this street here, don't they! And you talk to them—to whoever you want—but that's not my business!— Why wasn't it me!

MARIE. You expect me to tell people to keep off the streets—and take their mouths with them when they leave?

WOYZECK. And don't you ever leave your lips at home, they're too beautiful, it would be a sin! But then I guess the wasps like to light on them, uh?

MARIE. And what wasp stung you! You're like a cow chased by hornets!

WOYZECK. I saw him!

MARIE. You can see a lot with two eyes while the sun shines!

WOYZECK. Whore! [*He goes after her.*]

MARIE. Don't you touch me, Franz! I'd rather have a knife in my body than your hands touch me. When I looked at him, my father didn't dare lay a hand on me from the time I was ten.

WOYZECK. Whore! No, it should show on you! Something! Every man's a chasm. It makes you dizzy when you look down in. It's got to show! And she looks like innocence itself. So, innocence, there's a spot on you. But I can't prove it—can't prove it! Who can prove it? [*He goes off.*]

SCENE 11

[*The guardhouse.* WOYZECK *and* AN-DRES.]

ANDRES [*sings*].

> Our hostess she has a pretty maid
> She sits in her garden night and day
> She sits within her garden . . .

WOYZECK. Andres!

ANDRES. Hm?

WOYZECK. Nice weather.

ANDRES. Sunday weather.—They're playing music tonight outside the town. All the whores are already there. The men stinking and sweating. Wonderful, uh?

WOYZECK [*restlessly*]. They're dancing, Andres, they're dancing!

ANDRES. Sure. So what? [*Sings.*]

> She sits within her garden
> But when the bells have tollèd late
> Then she waits at her garden gate
> Or so the soldiers say.

WOYZECK. Andres, I can't keep quiet.

ANDRES. You're a fool!

WOYZECK. I've got to go out there. It keeps turning and turning in my head. They're dancing, dancing! Will she have hot hands, Andres? God damn her, Andres! God damn her!

ANDRES. What do you want?

WOYZECK. I've got to go out there. I've got to see them.

ANDRES. Aren't you ever satisfied? What's all this for a whore?
WOYZECK. I've got to get out of here! I can't stand the heat!

SCENE 12

> [*The inn. The windows are open. Danc-
> ing. Benches in front of the inn.* AP-
> PRENTICES.]

FIRST APPRENTICE [*sings*].
 This shirt I wear, it is not mine
 And my soul stinketh of brandywine . . .
SECOND APPRENTICE. Brother, let me be a real friend and knock a hole in
 your nature! Forward! I'll knock a hole in his nature! Hell, I'm as good
 a man as he is; I'll kill every flea on his body!
FIRST APPRENTICE. My soul, my soul stinketh of brandywine!—And even
 money passeth into decay! Forget me not, but the world's a beautiful
 place! Brother, my sadness could fill a barrel with tears! I wish our
 noses were two bottles so we could pour them down one another's
 throats.
THE OTHERS [*in chorus*].

 A hunter from the Rhine
 Once rode through a forest so fine
 Hallei-hallo, he called to me
 From high on a meadow, open and free
 A hunter's life for me.

> [WOYZECK *stands at the window.* MARIE
> *and* THE DRUM MAJOR *dance past with-
> out noticing him.*]

WOYZECK. Both of them! God damn her!
MARIE [*dancing past*]. Don't stop! Don't stop!
WOYZECK [*seats himself on the bench, trembling, as he looks from there through the
 window*]. Listen! Listen! Ha, roll on each other, roll and turn! Don't stop,
 don't stop, she says!
IDIOT. Pah! It stinks!
WOYZECK. Yes, it stinks! Her cheeks are red, red, why should she stink
 already? Karl, what is it you smell?
IDIOT. I smell, I smell blood.
WOYZECK. Blood? Why are all things red that I look at now? Why are they
 all rolling in a sea of blood, one on top of the other, tumbling, tumbling!
 Ha, the sea is red!—Don't stop! Don't stop! [*He starts up passionately, then
 sinks down again onto the bench.*] Don't stop! Don't stop! [*Beating his hands
 together.*] Turn and roll and roll and turn! God, blow out the sun and let
 them roll on each other in their lechery! Man and woman and man and
 beast! They'll do it in the light of the sun! They'll do it in the palm of
 your hand like flies! Whore! That whore's red as coals, red as coals!
 Don't stop! Don't stop! [*Jumps up.*] Watch how the bastard takes hold of

her! Touching her body! He's holding her now, holding her . . . the way I held her once. [*He slumps down in a stupor.*]

FIRST APPRENTICE [*preaching from a table*]. I say unto you, forget not the wanderer who standeth leaning against the stream of time, and who giveth himself answer with the wisdom of God, and saith: What is Man? What is Man? Yea, verily I say unto you: How should the farmer, the cooper, the shoemaker, the doctor, live, had not God created Man for their use? How should the tailor live, had not God implanted in Man his sense of shame? And the soldier, had not God endowed Man with the need to slaughter himself? And therefore doubt ye not, for all things are lovely and sweet! Yet the world with all its things is an evil place, and even money passeth into decay. In conclusion, my beloved brethren, let us piss once more upon the Cross so that somewhere a Jew will die!

[*Amid the general shouting and laughing*
WOYZECK *wakens.* PEOPLE *are leaving the inn.*]

ANDRES. What are you doing there?

WOYZECK. What time is it?

ANDRES. Ten.

WOYZECK. Is that all it is? I think it should go faster—I want to think about it before night.

ANDRES. Why?

WOYZECK. So it'll be over.

ANDRES. What?

WOYZECK. The fun.

ANDRES. Why are you sitting here by the door?

WOYZECK. Because it feels good, and because I know—a lot of people sit by doors, but they don't know—they don't know till they're dragged out feet first.

ANDRES. Come with me!

WOYZECK. It feels good here like this—and even better if I laid myself down . . .

ANDRES. There's blood on your head.

WOYZECK. *In* my head, maybe.—If they all knew what time it was they'd strip themselves naked and put on a silk shirt and let the carpenter make their bed out of wood shavings.

ANDRES. He's drunk. [*Goes off with the others.*]

WOYZECK. The world is out of order! Why did the street-lamp cleaner forget to wipe my eyes—everything's dark. Devil damn you, God! I lay in my own way: jump over myself. Where's my shadow gone? There's no safety in the kennels any more. Shine the moon through my legs again to see if my shadow's here. [*Sings.*]

Eating, oh, eating the green green grass
Eating, oh, eating the green green grass
Till all the grass was go-o-one.

What's that lying over there? Shining like that? It's making me look. How it sparkles. I've got to have it. [*He rushes off.*]

SCENE 13

[An open field. WOYZECK.]

WOYZECK. Don't stop! Don't stop! Hishh! Hashh! That's how the fiddles
and pipes go.—Don't stop! Don't stop!—Stop your playing! What's that
talking down there? [He stretches out on the ground.] What? What are you
saying? What? Louder! Louder! Stab? Stab the goat-bitch dead? Stab?
Stab her? The goat-bitch dead? Should I? Must I? Do I hear it there,
too? Does the wind say so, too? Won't it ever stop, ever stop? Stab her!
Stab her! Dead! Dead!

SCENE 14

[A room in the barracks. Night. ANDRES
and WOYZECK in a bed.]

WOYZECK [softly]. Andres! [ANDRES murmurs in his sleep. Shakes ANDRES.]
Andres! Hey, Andres!

ANDRES. Mmmmm! What do you want?

WOYZECK. I can't sleep! When I close my eyes everything turns and turns. I
hear voices in the fiddles: Don't stop! Don't stop! And then the walls
start to talk. Can't you hear it?

ANDRES. Sure. Let them dance! I'm tired. God bless us all. Amen.

WOYZECK. It's always saying: Stab! Stab! And then when I close my eyes it
keeps shining there, a big, broad knife, on a table by a window in a
narrow, dark street, and an old man sitting behind it. And the knife is
always in front of my eyes.

ANDRES. Go to sleep, you fool!

WOYZECK. Andres! There's something outside. In the ground. They're al-
ways pointing to it. Don't you hear them now, listen, now, knocking on
the walls? Somebody must have seen me out the window. Don't you
hear? I hear it all day long. Don't stop. Stab! Stab the——

ANDRES. Lay down. You ought to go to the hospital. They'll give you a
schnapps[14] with a powder in it. It'll cut your fever.

WOYZECK. Don't stop! Don't stop!

ANDRES. Go to sleep! [He goes back to sleep.]

SCENE 15

[THE DOCTOR'S courtyard. STUDENTS
and WOYZECK below, THE DOCTOR in
the attic window.]

DOCTOR. Gentlemen, I find myself on the roof like David when he beheld
Bathsheba.[15] But all I see are the Parisian panties of the girls' boarding
school drying in the garden. Gentlemen, we are concerned with the
weighty question of the relationship of the subject to the object. If, for

[14] A strong alcoholic drink.
[15] David first glimpsed the beautiful Bathsheba, his adulterous lover and later his wife,
from the roof of his palace, while she was washing herself; 2 Samuel 11:2.

example, we were to take one of those innumerable things in which we see the highest manifestation of the self-affirmation of the Godhead, and examine its relationship to space, to the earth, and to the planetary constellations . . . Gentlemen, if we were to take this cat and toss it out the window: how would this object conduct itself in conformity with its own instincts towards its *centrum gravitationis?*[16] Well, Woyzeck? [*Roars.*] Woyzeck!

WOYZECK [*picks up the cat*]. Doctor, sir, she's biting me!

DOCTOR. Damn, why do you handle the beast so tenderly! It's not your grandmother! [*He descends.*]

WOYZECK. Doctor, I'm shaking.

DOCTOR [*utterly delighted*]. Excellent, Woyzeck, excellent! [*Rubs his hands, takes the cat.*] What's this, gentlemen? The new species of rabbit louse! A beautiful species . . . [*He pulls out a magnifying glass; the cat runs off.*] Animals, gentlemen, simply have no scientific instincts. But in its place you may see something else. Now, observe: for three months this man has eaten nothing but peas. Notice the effect. Feel how irregularly his pulse beats! And look at his eyes!

WOYZECK. Doctor, sir, everything's going dark! [*He sits down.*]

DOCTOR. Courage, Woyzeck! A few more days and then it will all be over with. Feel, gentlemen, feel!

> [*They fumble over his temples, pulse, and chest.*]

DOCTOR. Apropos,[17] Woyzeck, wiggle your ears for the gentlemen! I've meant to show you this before. He uses only two muscles. Let's go, let's go! You stupid animal, shall I wiggle them for you? Trying to run out on us like the cat? There you are, gentlemen! Here you see an example of the transition into a donkey: frequently the result of being raised by women and of a persistent usage of the Germanic language. How much hair has your mother pulled out recently for sentimental remembrances of you? It's become so thin these last few days. It's the peas, gentlemen, the peas!

SCENE 16

[*The inn.* WOYZECK. THE SERGEANT.]

WOYZECK [*sings*].

> Oh, daughter, my daughter
> And didn't you know
> That sleeping with coachmen
> Would bring you low?

What is it that our Good Lord God cannot do? What? He cannot make what is done undone. Ha! Ha! Ha!——But that's the way it is, and that's the way it should be. But to make things better is to make things better. And a respectable man loves his life, and a man who loves his life has no

[16] Latin: Center of gravity. [17] By the way.

courage, and a virtuous man has no courage. A man with courage is a dirty dog.

SERGEANT [*with dignity*]. You're forgetting yourself in the presence of a brave man.

WOYZECK. I wasn't talking about anybody, I wasn't talking about anything, not like the Frenchmen do when they talk, but it was good of you.—But a man with courage is a dirty dog.

SERGEANT. Damn you! You broken mustache cup! You watch or I'll see you drink a pot of your own piss and swallow your own razor!

WOYZECK. Sir, you do yourself an injustice! Was it *you* I talked about? Did I say *you* had courage? Don't torment me, sir! My name is Science. Every week for my scientific career I get half a guilder.[18] You mustn't cut me in two or I'll go hungry. I'm a *Spinosa pericyclia;* I have a Latin behind. I am a living skeleton. All Mankind studies me. —What is Man? Bones! Dust, sand, dung. What is Nature? Dust, sand, dung. But poor, stupid Man, stupid Man! We must be friends. If only you had no courage, there would be no science. Only Nature, no amputation, no articulation. What is this? Woyzeck's arm: flesh, bones, veins. What is this? Dung. Why is it rooted in dung? Must I cut off my arm? No, Man is selfish, he beats, shoots, stabs his own kind. [*He sobs.*] We must be friends. I wish our noses were two bottles that we could pour down each other's throats. What a beautiful place the world is! Friend! My friend! The world! [*Moved.*] Look! The sun coming through the clouds—like God emptying His bedpan on the world. [*He cries.*]

SCENE 17

[*The barracks yard.* WOYZECK. AN-
DRES.]

WOYZECK. What have you heard?

ANDRES. He's still inside with a friend.

WOYZECK. He said something.

ANDRES. How do you know? Why do I have to be the one to tell you? Well, he laughed and then he said she was some piece. And then something or other about her thighs—and that she was hot as a red poker.

WOYZECK [*quite coldly*]. So, he said that? What was that I dreamed about last night? About a knife? What stupid dreams we get!

ANDRES. Hey, friend! Where you off to?

WOYZECK. Get some wine for the Captain. Andres, you know something? There aren't many girls like she was.

ANDRES. Like who was?

WOYZECK. Nothing. I'll see you. [*Goes off.*]

SCENE 18

[*The inn.* DRUM MAJOR, WOYZECK, *and*
PEOPLE.]

DRUM MAJOR. I'm a man! [*He pounds his chest.*] A man, you hear? Anybody

[18] A coin.

say different? Anybody who's not as crocked as the Lord God Himself better keep off. I'll screw his nose up his own ass! I'll . . . [*To* WOYZECK.] You there, get drunk! I wish the world was a schnapps, schnapps! You better start drinking! [WOYZECK *whistles.*] Son-of-a-bitch, you want me to pull your tongue out and wrap it around your middle?

[*They wrestle;* WOYZECK *loses.*]

You want I should leave enough wind in you for a good old lady's fart? Uh!

[*Exhausted and trembling,* WOYZECK *seats himself on the bench.*]

The son-of-a-bitch can whistle himself blue in the face for all I care. [*Sings.*]

> Brandy's all my life, my life
> Brandy gives me courage!

A MAN. He sure got more than he asked for.
ANOTHER. He's bleeding.
WOYZECK. One thing after another.

SCENE 19

[*Pawnbroker's shop.* WOYZECK *and* THE JEW.]

WOYZECK. The pistol costs too much.
JEW. So you want it or not? Make up your mind.
WOYZECK. How much was the knife?
JEW. It's straight and sharp. What do you want it for? To cut your throat? So what's the matter? You get it as cheap here as anywhere else. You'll die cheap enough, but not for nothing. What's the matter? It'll be a cheap death.
WOYZECK. This'll cut more than bread.
JEW. Two groschen.
WOYZECK. There! [*He goes out.*]
JEW. There, he says! Like it was nothing! And it's real money! —Dog!

SCENE 20

[MARIE's *room.* THE IDIOT. THE CHILD. MARIE.]

IDIOT [*lying down, telling fairy tales on his fingers*]. This one has the golden crown. He's the Lord King. Tomorrow I'll bring the Lady Queen her child. Bloodsausage says: Come, Liversausage . . .
MARIE [*paging through her Bible*]. "And no guile is found in his mouth."[19] Lord God, Lord God! Don't look at me! [*Paging further.*] "And the Scribes and Pharisees brought unto him a woman taken in adultery, and set her in the midst . . . And Jesus said unto her: Neither do I condemn

[19] In 1 Peter 2:22 these words are applied to Christ.

thee; go, and sin no more."²⁰ [*Striking her hands together.*] Lord God! Lord God! I can't. Lord God, give me only so much strength that I may pray.

[THE CHILD *presses himself close to her.*]
The child is a sword in my heart. [*To* THE IDIOT.] Karl!—I've strutted it in the light of the sun, like the whore I am—my sin, my sin!

[THE IDIOT *takes* THE CHILD *and grows quiet.*]
Franz hasn't come. Not yesterday. Not today. It's getting hot in here! [*She opens the window and reads further.*] "And stood at his feet weeping, and began to wash his feet with tears, and did wipe them with the hairs of her head, and anointed them with ointment."²¹ [*Striking her breast.*] Everything dead! Saviour! Saviour! If only I might anoint Your feet!

SCENE 21

[*An open field.* WOYZECK.]

WOYZECK [*buries the knife in a hole*]. Thou shalt not kill. Lay here! I can't stay here! [*He rushes off.*]

SCENE 22

[*The barracks.* ANDRES. WOYZECK *rummages through his belongings.*]

WOYZECK. Andres, this jacket's not part of the uniform, but you can use it, Andres.

ANDRES [*replies numbly to almost everything with*] Sure.

WOYZECK. The cross is my sister's. And the ring.

ANDRES. Sure.

WOYZECK. I've got a Holy Picture, too; two hearts—they're real gold. I found it in my mother's Bible, and it said:

> O Lord with wounded head so sore
> So may my heart be evermore.

My mother only feels now when the sun shines on her hands . . . that doesn't matter.

ANDRES. Sure.

WOYZECK [*pulls out a paper*]. Friedrich Johann Franz Woyzeck. Soldier, Rifleman, Second Regiment, Second Battalion, Fourth Company. Born: the Feast of the Annunciation, twentieth of July.²² Today I'm thirty years old, seven months and twelve days.

²⁰ John 8:3–11.
²¹ Luke 7:38. The woman in the episode is a sinner, and her attentions to Jesus scandalize his host, a Pharisee, but Jesus defends the woman and declares her sins forgiven, "for she loved much." Luke 7:36–48.
²² The feast of the Annunciation is actually March 25.

ANDRES. Go to the hospital, Franz. Poor guy, you've got to drink some schnapps with a powder in it. It'll kill the fever.

WOYZECK. You know, Andres—when the carpenter puts those boards together, nobody knows who it's made for.

SCENE 23

> [*The street.* MARIE *with little* GIRLS *in front of the house door.* GRANDMOTHER. *Later* WOYZECK.]

GIRLS [*singing*].

> The sun shone bright on Candlemas Day[23]
> And the corn was all in bloom
> And they marched along the meadow way
> They marched by two and two.
> The pipers marched ahead
> The fiddlers followed through
> And their socks were scarlet red . . .

FIRST CHILD. I don't like that one.

SECOND CHILD. Why do you always want to be different?

FIRST CHILD. *You* sing for us, Marie!

MARIE. I can't.

SECOND CHILD. Why?

MARIE. Because.

SECOND CHILD. But *why* because?

THIRD CHILD. Grandmother, *you* tell us a story!

GRANDMOTHER. All right, you little crab apples! Once upon a time there was a poor little girl who had no father and no mother. Everyone was dead, and there was no one left in the whole wide world. Everyone was dead. And the little girl went out and looked for someone night and day. And because there was no one left on the earth, she wanted to go to Heaven. And the moon looked down so friendly at her. And when she finally got to the moon, it was a piece of rotten wood. And so she went to the sun, and it was a faded sunflower. And when she got to the stars, they were little golden flies, stuck up there as if they were caught in a spider's web. And when she wanted to go back to earth, the earth was an upside-down pot. And she was all alone. And she sat down there and she cried. And she sits there to this day, all, all alone.

WOYZECK [*appears*]. Marie!

MARIE [*startled*]. What!

WOYZECK. Let's go. It's getting time.

MARIE. Where to?

WOYZECK. How should I know?

[23] The feast of the Purification of the Virgin Mary after giving birth to Jesus, celebrated on February 2. The feast includes the blessing of candles.

SCENE 24

[*A pond by the edge of the woods.* MARIE *and* WOYZECK.]

MARIE. Then the town must be out that way. It's so dark.

WOYZECK. You can't go yet. Come, sit down.

MARIE. But I've got to get back.

WOYZECK. You don't want to run your feet sore.

MARIE. What's happened to you?

WOYZECK. You know how long it's been, Marie?

MARIE. Two years from Pentecost.[24]

WOYZECK. You know how much longer it'll last?

MARIE. I've got to get back. Supper's not made yet.

WOYZECK. Are you freezing, Marie? And still you're so warm. Your lips are hot as coals! Hot as coals, the hot breath of a whore! And still I'd give up Heaven just to kiss them again. Are you freezing? When you're cold through, you won't freeze any more. The morning dew won't freeze you.

MARIE. What are you talking about?

WOYZECK. Nothing. [*Silence.*]

MARIE. Look how red the moon is! It's rising.

WOYZECK. Like a knife washed in blood.

MARIE. What are you going to do? Franz, you're so pale.

[*He raises the knife.*]

MARIE. Franz! Stop! For Heaven's sake! Help me! Help me!

WOYZECK [*stabbing madly*]. There! There! Why can't you die? There! There! Ha, she's still shivering! Still not dead? Still not dead? Still shivering? [*Stabbing at her again.*] Are you dead? Dead! Dead! [*He drops the knife and runs away.*]

[*Two* MEN *approach.*]

FIRST MAN. Wait!

SECOND MAN. You hear something? Shh! Over there!

FIRST MAN. Whhh! There! What a sound!

SECOND MAN. It's the water, it's calling. It's a long time since anyone drowned here. Let's go! I don't like hearing such sounds!

FIRST MAN. Whhh! There it is again! Like a person, dying!

SECOND MAN. It's uncanny! So foggy, nothing but gray mist as far as you can see—and the hum of beetles like broken bells. Let's get out of here!

FIRST MAN. No, it's too clear, it's too loud! Let's go up this way! Come on!

[*They hurry on.*]

SCENE 25

[*The inn.* WOYZECK, KATHY, INN-KEEPER, IDIOT, *and* PEOPLE.]

WOYZECK. Dance! Everybody! Don't stop! Sweat and stink! He'll get you all in the end. [*Sings.*]

[24] The feast, seven Sundays after Easter, commemorating the descent of the Holy Ghost upon the Apostles after Jesus' ascension into heaven.

> Oh, daughter, my daughter
> And didn't you know
> That sleeping with coachmen
> Would bring you low?

[*He dances.*] Ho, Kathy! Sit down! I'm so hot, so hot! [*Takes off his coat.*] That's the way it is: the devil takes one and lets the other get away. Kathy, you're hot as coals! Why, tell me why? Kathy, you'll be cold one day, too. Be reasonable. —Can't you sing something?

KATHY [*sings*].

> That Swabian[25] land I cannot bear
> And dresses long I will not wear
> For dresses long and pointed shoes
> Are clothes a chambermaid never should choose.

WOYZECK. No shoes, no shoes! We can get to hell without shoes.

KATHY [*sings*].

> To such and like I'll not be prone
> Take back your gold and sleep alone.

WOYZECK. Sure, sure! What do I want to get all bloody for?

KATHY. Then what's that on your hand?

WOYZECK. Me? Me?

KATHY. Red! It's blood!

[PEOPLE *gather round him.*]

WOYZECK. Blood? Blood?

INNKEEPER. Blood!

WOYZECK. I think I cut myself. Here, on my right hand.

INNKEEPER. Then why is there blood on your elbow?

WOYZECK. I wiped it off.

INNKEEPER. Your right hand and you wiped it on your right elbow? You're a smart one!

IDIOT. And then the giant said: "I smell, I smell the flesh of man."[26] Pew, it stinks already!

WOYZECK. What do you want from me? Is it your business? Out of my way or the first one who . . . Damn you! Do I look like I murdered somebody? Do I look like a murderer? What are you looking at? Look at yourselves! Look! Out of my way! [*He runs off.*]

SCENE 26

[*At the pond.* WOYZECK, *alone.*]

WOYZECK. The knife! Where's the knife? I left it here. It'll give me away! Closer! And closer! What is this place? What's that noise? Something's

[25] Swabia was a region of southwest Germany, approximately modern Bavaria.
[26] A line from an old folk or nursery rhyme.

moving! It's quiet now.—It's got to be here, close to her. Marie? Ha, Marie! Quiet. Everything's quiet! Why are you so pale, Marie? Why are you wearing those red beads around your neck? Who was it gave you that necklace for sinning with him? Your sins made you black, Marie, they made you black! Did I make you so pale? Why is your hair uncombed? Did you forget to twist your braids today? The knife, the knife! I've got it! There! [*He runs toward the water.*] There, into the water! [*He throws the knife into the water.*] It dives like a stone into the black water. No, it's not out far enough for when they swim! [*He wades into the pond and throws it out farther.*] There! Now! But in the summer when they dive for mussels? Ha, it'll get rusty, who'll ever notice it! Why didn't I break it first! Am I still bloody? I've got to wash myself. There, there's a spot, and there's another . . . [*He goes farther out into the water.*]

SCENE 27

[*The street.* CHILDREN.]

FIRST CHILD. Let's go find Marie!
SECOND CHILD. What happened?
FIRST CHILD. Don't you know? Everybody's out there. They found a body!
SECOND CHILD. Where?
FIRST CHILD. By the pond, out in the woods.
SECOND CHILD. Hurry, so we can still see something. Before they bring it back. [*They rush off.*]

SCENE 28

[*In front of* MARIE's *house.* IDIOT, CHILD, WOYZECK.]

IDIOT [*holding* THE CHILD *on his knee, points to* WOYZECK *as he enters*]. Looky there, he fell in the water, he fell in the water, he fell in the water!
WOYZECK. Boy! Christian!
IDIOT [*looks at him fixedly*]. He fell in the water.
WOYZECK [*wanting to embrace* THE CHILD *tenderly, but it turns from him and screams*]. My God! My God!
IDIOT. He fell in the water.
WOYZECK. I'll buy you a horsey, Christian. There, there. [THE CHILD *pulls away. To* THE IDIOT]. Here, buy the boy a horsey!
[THE IDIOT *stares at him.*]
Hop! Hop! Hip-hop, horsey!
IDIOT [*shouting joyously*]. Hop! Hop! Hip-hop horsey! Hip-hop horsey!
[*He runs off with* THE CHILD. WOYZECK *is alone.*]

SCENE 29

[*The morgue.* JUDGE, COURT CLERK, POLICEMAN, CAPTAIN, DOCTOR, DRUM MAJOR, SERGEANT, IDIOT, *and others.* WOYZECK.]

POLICEMAN. What a murder! A good, genuine, beautiful murder! Beautiful a murder as you could hope for! It's been a long time since we had a murder like this!

[WOYZECK *stands in their midst, dumbly looking at the body of* MARIE; *he is bound, the dogmatic atheist, tall, haggard, timid, good-natured, scientific.*]

Frederick Douglass
(1818–1895)

Slave narratives loom large in American literature, in both number and significance. Ex-slaves left over six thousand accounts of their experiences; many were in the form of interviews or essays, but over a hundred were book-length narratives. Of these, the generally acknowledged masterpiece is the *Narrative of the Life of Frederick Douglass, An American Slave, Written by Himself* (1845), a book that not only captures the horrors of slavery that formed the chief appeal of many of these narratives but also offers a subtle and powerful spiritual autobiography, the story of the successive unmaking and remaking of a human being. The result is, on the one hand, a troubling indictment of the human capacity to become inhuman, as well as, on the other, a moving exploration of the power to make oneself fully human, in the face of the most daunting odds.

Douglass's life down to the age of twenty-three is covered thoroughly in the *Narrative:* his birth into slavery in rural Maryland, his being sent at the age of eight to Baltimore, where he secretly taught himself to read and write, his return to field work when he was sixteen, his experiences while being hired out to a brutal slave-breaker, a failed attempt at escape, a return to Baltimore where he learned the craft of ship-calking, and his eventual flight to freedom. Douglass escaped from slavery when he was twenty; the events of his later life were covered in two subsequent autobiographies: *My Bondage and My Freedom* (1855) and *The Life and Times of Frederick Douglass* (1892). As recounted in the last lines of the *Narrative*, Douglass became an agent and speaker for the Massachusetts Anti-Slavery Society after a stirring speech to an Abolitionist convention in 1841. After the publication of his *Narrative,* fearing recapture and return to slavery under the Fugitive

Slave Act, he traveled to England and Ireland for a two-year speaking tour. He returned in 1847 with enough money to both purchase his freedom and found a black-oriented antislavery newspaper, *The North Star,* in Rochester, New York. The establishment of *The North Star* was part of a bitter break with William Lloyd Garrison, leader of the white Abolitionist establishment, over the need for an autonomous black Abolitionist movement. *The North Star,* renamed *Frederick Douglass' Paper* in 1851, continued publication until 1859. It was succeeded by *Douglass' Monthly* (1859–63) and *The New National Era* (1870–73). Douglass thus spent the major part of his career as a pioneer black journalist.

During the Civil War, Douglass was a forceful and eloquent spokesperson for blacks, urging Lincoln and the federal government to make emancipation the explicit central aim of the war and arguing, successfully, for the enlistment of black troops in the Union Army. After the war, he was frequently urged to run for elective office, but he decided to remain an independent voice, accepting only a few minor appointive posts: assistant secretary to the Santo Domingo Commission (1871), marshal (1877–81) and recorder of deeds (1881–86) for the District of Columbia, and U.S. minister and consul general to Haiti (1889–91). He continued to represent blacks forcefully through the Reconstruction era, campaigning for their full civil rights, combating the pervasive racism in American life that persisted after emancipation, and taking an active part in the women's rights movement. When he died, in 1895, Douglass had been the most prominent voice for African-Americans for close to fifty years; significantly, in the same year, Booker T. Washington delivered his famous Atlanta Exposition address and moved into the role of black leadership passed down from his heroic predecessor.

Douglass incorporated the materials of his 1845 *Narrative* into both *My Bondage and My Freedom* and the *Life and Times.* Nevertheless, most readers have found his first telling of his story the best. The later books, though more inclusive, lack the lean, terse style, the polemical urgency, and the symbolic richness of the early *Narrative.* The later books are fuller, but they are more loosely constructed, and too often, when Douglass is retelling a story from the earlier book, he weakens it through cluttering detail and stylistic elaboration.

Autobiography has comparatively recently come to be recognized as a form of literary art, and many of its features are beautifully illustrated by Douglass's *Narrative:* the double presence of the self acting in the past and of the self writing in the present; the process of selection and emphasis needed to make one's life into a coherent, shapely story; and the role of implicit and explicit metaphors in both creating and expressing the meaning of one's life. Douglass's account of his early life is both a maturation narrative, a story of growing up, and the kind of autobiography we call a conversion narrative, an account of a transforming experience that gives life meaning. The maturation narrative is bitterly ironic; to be born into slavery is to be born not into life but into death, as Douglass's first clear memory, the whipping of Aunt Hester, makes clear: "It was the blood-stained gate, the entrance to the hell of slavery, through which I was about to pass." The conversion narrative, which opposes this bleak vision, gives

the book a two-part structure. The central line of the book appears in Chapter 10 in Douglass's account of his year with Covey the slave-breaker: "You have seen how a man was made a slave; you shall see how a slave was made a man." The movement of the story downward to the point where Douglass feels "broken in body, soul, and spirit" is now reversed, and Douglass moves steadily toward both an inner and an outer freedom through the rest of the book.

Douglass's account of his self-liberation is enriched by several powerful recurring images. Animal imagery is used for both slaves (pigs, dogs, oxen) and for masters (snakes, tigers, wolves); inevitably it keeps before us the definition of what is human and of the boundary between the human and the less-than-human. Ships, too, take on more than their literal meaning, from the first time they are mentioned in Chapter 5, when the eight-year-old Frederick on the way to Baltimore by ship plants himself in the bow and spends the journey "in looking ahead, interesting myself in what was in the distance rather than in things near by or behind."

Even more central to the *Narrative* than animals or ships is mastery of language. The odd "written by himself" on the original title page was intended to counter charges of Abolitionist ghost-writing, but it also names an important theme in the book. How a slave, deliberately kept illiterate, came to be able to write his own story so eloquently is an important part of the process of a slave becoming a man which the book chronicles. If we include the original preface by William Lloyd Garrison as an integral part of the book (the preface and the letter from Wendell Phillips were part of the process of white sponsorship by which black authors were customarily presented to the public), the book begins and ends with the same scene: the act of verbal mastery by which Douglass overcame his reticence to hold a large audience spellbound. "The truth was, I felt myself a slave, and the idea of speaking to white people weighed me down. I spoke but a few moments, when I felt a degree of freedom, and said what I desired with considerable ease." How Douglass acquired mastery of language and with it a sense of his own identity and thus "a degree of freedom" is at the center of this short autobiographical masterpiece.

FURTHER READING (*prepared by J. H.*): The authoritative biography is William S. McFeely's *Frederick Douglass*, 1991. Benjamin Quarles has edited a collection of essays in the Twentieth Century Views series: *Frederick Douglass*, 1968. An important study upon which many later studies have drawn is Albert E. Stone's "Identity and Art in Frederick Douglass's *Narrative*," *CLA Journal* 17 (1973), 192–213. More recent criticism includes Donald B. Gibson, "Reconciling Public and Private in Frederick Douglass's *Narrative*," *American Literature* 57:4 (1985), 549–69; Ann Kibbey, "Language in Slavery: Frederick Douglass's *Narrative*," *Prospects* 8 (1983), 163–82; Peter Ripley, "The Autobiographical Writings of Frederick Douglass," *Southern Studies* 24:1 (1985), 5–29; John Sekora, "Comprehending Slavery: Language and Personal History in Douglass's *Narrative* of 1845," *CLA Journal* 29:2 (1985), 157–70; and Eric J. Sundquist, "Slavery, Revolution, and the American Renaissance," in *The American Renaissance Reconsidered*, ed. W. B. Michaels and Donald E. Pease, 1985, pp. 1–33.

NARRATIVE OF THE LIFE OF FREDERICK DOUGLASS, AN AMERICAN SLAVE

PREFACE[1]

In the month of August, 1841, I attended an anti-slavery convention in Nantucket, at which it was my happiness to become acquainted with FREDERICK DOUGLASS, the writer of the following Narrative. He was a stranger to nearly every member of that body; but, having recently made his escape from the southern prison-house of bondage, and feeling his curiosity excited to ascertain the principles and measures of the abolitionists,—of whom he had heard a somewhat vague description while he was a slave,— he was induced to give his attendance, on the occasion alluded to, though at that time a resident in New Bedford.

Fortunate, most fortunate occurrence!—fortunate for the millions of his manacled brethren, yet panting for deliverance from their awful thraldom!—fortunate for the cause of negro emancipation, and of universal liberty!—fortunate for the land of his birth, which he has already done so much to save and bless!—fortunate for a large circle of friends and acquaintances, whose sympathy and affection he has strongly secured by the many sufferings he has endured, by his virtuous traits of character, by his ever-abiding remembrance of those who are in bonds, as being bound with them!—fortunate for the multitudes, in various parts of our republic, whose mind he has enlightened on the subject of slavery, and who have been melted to tears by his pathos, or roused to virtuous indignation by his stirring eloquence against the enslavers of men!—fortunate for himself, as it at once brought him into the field of public usefulness, "gave the world assurance of a MAN," quickened the slumbering energies of his soul, and consecrated him to the great work of breaking the rod of the oppressor, and letting the oppressed go free!

I shall never forget his first speech at the convention—the extraordinary emotion it excited in my own mind—the powerful impression it created upon a crowded auditory, completely taken by surprise—the applause which followed from the beginning to the end of his felicitous remarks. I think I never hated slavery so intensely as at that moment; certainly, my perception of the enormous outrage which is inflicted by it, on the godlike nature of its victims, was rendered far more clear than ever. There stood one, in physical proportion and stature commanding and exact—in intellect richly endowed—in natural eloquence a prodigy—in soul manifestly "created but a little lower than the angels"[2]—yet a slave, ay, a fugitive slave,—trembling for his safety, hardly daring to believe that on the American soil, a single white person could be found who would befriend him at all hazards, for the love of God and humanity! Capable of high attainments

[1] The preface is by William Lloyd Garrison (1805–79), founder of both the abolitionist newspaper *The Liberator* and the American Anti-Slavery Society and one of the most outspoken abolitionists in America.
[2] Psalm 8:5.

as an intellectual and moral being—needing nothing but a comparatively small amount of cultivation to make him an ornament to society and a blessing to his race—by the law of the land, by the voice of the people, by the terms of the slave code, he was only a piece of property, a beast of burden, a chattel personal, nevertheless!

A beloved friend from New Bedford prevailed on Mr. Douglass to address the convention. He came forward to the platform with a hesitancy and embarrassment, necessarily the attendants of a sensitive mind in such a novel position. After apologizing for his ignorance, and reminding the audience that slavery was a poor school for the human intellect and heart, he proceeded to narrate some of the facts in his own history as a slave, and in the course of his speech gave utterance to many noble thoughts and thrilling reflections. As soon as he had taken his seat, filled with hope and admiration, I rose, and declared that PATRICK HENRY,[3] of revolutionary fame, never made a speech more eloquent in the cause of liberty, than the one we had just listened to from the lips of that hunted fugitive. So I believed at that time—such is my belief now. I reminded the audience of the peril which surrounded this self-emancipated young man in the North—even in Massachusetts, on the soil of the Pilgrim Fathers, among the descendants of revolutionary sires; and I appealed to them, whether they would ever allow him to be carried back into slavery,—law or no law, constitution or no constitution. The response was unanimous and in thunder-tones—"NO!" "Will you succor and protect him as a brother-man—a resident of the Bay State?" "YES!" shouted the whole mass, with an energy so startling, that the ruthless tyrants south of Mason and Dixon's line[4] might almost have heard the mighty burst of feeling, and recognized it as the pledge of an invincible determination, on the part of those who gave it, never to betray him that wanders, but to hide the outcast, and firmly to abide the consequences.

It was at once deeply impressed upon my mind, that, if Mr. Douglass could be persuaded to consecrate his time and talents to the promotion of the anti-slavery enterprise, a powerful impetus would be given to it, and a stunning blow at the same time inflicted on northern prejudice against a colored complexion. I therefore endeavored to instill hope and courage into his mind, in order that he might dare to engage in a vocation so anomalous and responsible for a person in his situation; and I was seconded in this effort by warm-hearted friends, especially by the late General Agent of the Massachusetts Anti-Slavery Society, Mr. JOHN A. COLLINS, whose judgment in this instance entirely coincided with my own. At first, he could give no encouragement; with unfeigned diffidence, he expressed his conviction that he was not adequate to the performance of so great a task; the path marked out was wholly an untrodden one; he was sincerely apprehensive that he should do more harm than good. After much deliberation, however, he consented to make a trial; and ever since that period, he has acted

[3] Patrick Henry (1736–99), who served in the Continental Congress and as governor of Virginia, was renowned as an orator.

[4] The Mason-Dixon line is the boundary between Pennsylvania and Maryland, extended to present-day West Virginia. It marked the boundary between free and slave states before the Civil War.

as a lecturing agent, under the auspices either of the American or the Massachusetts Anti-Slavery Society. In labors he has been most abundant; and his success in combating prejudice, in gaining proselytes, in agitating the public mind, has far surpassed the most sanguine expectations that were raised at the commencement of his brilliant career. He has borne himself with gentleness and meekness, yet with true manliness of character. As a public speaker, he excels in pathos, wit, comparison, imitation, strength of reasoning, and fluency of language. There is in him that union of head and heart, which is indispensable to an enlightenment of the heads and a winning of the hearts of others. May his strength continue to be equal to his day! May he continue to "grow in grace, and in the knowledge of God," that he may be increasingly serviceable in the cause of bleeding humanity, whether at home or abroad!

It is certainly a very remarkable fact, that one of the most efficient advocates of the slave population, now before the public, is a fugitive slave, in the person of FREDERICK DOUGLASS; and that the free colored population of the United States are as ably represented by one of their own number, in the person of CHARLES LENOX REMOND,[5] whose eloquent appeals have extorted the highest applause of multitudes on both sides of the Atlantic. Let the calumniators of the colored race despise themselves for their baseness and illiberality of spirit, and henceforth cease to talk of the natural inferiority of those who require nothing but time and opportunity to attain to the highest point of human excellence.

It may, perhaps, be fairly questioned, whether any other portion of the population of the earth could have endured the privations, sufferings and horrors of slavery, without having become more degraded in the scale of humanity than the slaves of African descent. Nothing has been left undone to cripple their intellects, darken their minds, debase their moral nature, obliterate all traces of their relationship to mankind; and yet how wonderfully they have sustained the mighty load of a most frightful bondage, under which they have been groaning for centuries! To illustrate the effect of slavery on the white man,—to show that he has no powers of endurance, in such a condition, superior to those of his black brother,—DANIEL O'CONNELL, the distinguished advocate of universal emancipation, and the mightiest champion of prostrate but not conquered Ireland,[6] relates the following anecdote in a speech delivered by him in the Conciliation Hall, Dublin, before the Loyal National Repeal Association, March 31, 1845. "No matter," said Mr. O'CONNELL, "under what specious term it may disguise itself, slavery is still hideous. *It has a natural, an inevitable tendency to brutalize every noble faculty of man.* An American sailor, who was cast away on the shore of Africa, where he was kept in slavery for three years, was at the expiration of that period, found to be imbruted and stultified—he had lost all reasoning power; and having forgotten his native language, could only utter some savage gibberish between Arabic and English, which nobody could understand, and which even he himself found difficulty in pronouncing. So

[5] Charles Lenox Remond (1810–73), the son of a former slave, became a prominent anti-slavery advocate and orator.
[6] The Irish political leader Daniel O'Connell (1775–1847), "The Liberator," led the campaign against the disenfranchisement of Irish Catholics. His efforts led to the Catholic Emancipation Act of 1829.

much for the humanizing influence of THE DOMESTIC INSTITUTION!" Admitting this to have been an extraordinary case of mental deterioration, it proves at least that the white slave can sink as low in the scale of humanity as the black one.

Mr. DOUGLASS has very properly chosen to write his own Narrative, in his own style, and according to the best of his ability, rather than to employ some one else. It is, therefore, entirely his own production; and, considering how long and dark was the career he had to run as a slave,—how few have been his opportunities to improve his mind since he broke his iron fetters,—it is, in my judgment, highly creditable to his head and heart. He who can peruse it without a tearful eye, a heaving breast, an afflicted spirit,—without being filled with an unutterable abhorrence of slavery and all its abettors, and animated with a determination to seek the immediate overthrow of that execrable system,—without trembling for the fate of this country in the hands of a righteous God, who is ever on the side of the oppressed, and whose arm is not shortened that it cannot save,—must have a flinty heart, and be qualified to act the part of a trafficker "in slaves and the souls of men." I am confident that it is essentially true in all its statements; that nothing has been set down in malice, nothing exaggerated, nothing drawn from the imagination; that it comes short of the reality, rather than overstates a single fact in regard to SLAVERY AS IT IS. The experience of FREDERICK DOUGLASS, as a slave, was not a peculiar one; his lot was not especially a hard one; his case may be regarded as a very fair specimen of the treatment of slaves in Maryland, in which State it is conceded that they are better fed and less cruelly treated than in Georgia, Alabama, and Louisiana. Many have suffered incomparably more, while very few on the plantations have suffered less, than himself. Yet how deplorable was his situation! what terrible chastisements were inflicted upon his person! what still more shocking outrages were perpetrated upon his mind! with all his noble powers and sublime aspirations, how like a brute was he treated, even by those professing to have the same mind in them that was in Christ Jesus! to what dreadful liabilities was he continually subjected! how destitute of friendly counsel and aid, even in his greatest extremities! how heavy was the midnight of woe which shrouded in blackness the last ray of hope, and filled the future with terror and gloom! what longings after freedom took possession of his breast, and how his misery augmented, in proportion as he grew reflective and intelligent,—thus demonstrating that a happy slave is an extinct man! how he thought, reasoned, felt, under the lash of the driver, with the chains upon his limbs! what perils he encountered in his endeavors to escape from his horrible doom! and how signal have been his deliverance and preservation in the midst of a nation of pitiless enemies!

This Narrative contains many affecting incidents, many passages of great eloquence and power; but I think the most thrilling one of them all is the description DOUGLASS gives of his feelings, as he stood soliloquizing respecting his fate, and the chances of his one day being a freeman, on the banks of the Chesapeake Bay—viewing the receding vessels as they flew with their white wings before the breeze, and apostrophizing them as animated by the living spirit of freedom. Who can read that passage, and be insensible to its pathos and sublimity? Compressed into it is a whole Alex-

andrian library[7] of thought, feeling, and sentiment—all that can, all that need be, urged, in the form of expostulation, entreaty, rebuke, against that crime of crimes,—making man the property of his fellow-man! O, how accursed is that system, which entombs the godlike mind of man, defaces the divine image, reduces those who by creation were crowned with glory and honor to a level with four-footed beasts, and exalts the dealer in human flesh above all that is called God! Why should its existence be prolonged one hour? Is it not evil, only evil, and that continually? What does its presence imply but the absence of all fear of God, all regard for man, on the part of the people of the United States? Heaven speed its eternal overthrow!

So profoundly ignorant of the nature of slavery are many persons, that they are stubbornly incredulous whenever they read or listen to any recital of the cruelties which are daily inflicted on its victims. They do not deny that the slaves are held as property; but that terrible fact seems to convey to their minds no idea of injustice, exposure to outrage, or savage barbarity. Tell them of cruel scourgings, of mutilations and brandings, of scenes of pollution and blood, of the banishment of all light and knowledge, and they affect to be greatly indignant at such enormous exaggerations, such wholesale misstatements, such abominable libels on the character of the southern planters! As if all these direful outrages were not the natural results of slavery! As if it were less cruel to reduce a human being to the condition of a thing, than to give him a severe flagellation, or to deprive him of necessary food and clothing! As if whips, chains, thumb-screws, paddles, bloodhounds, overseers, drivers, patrols, were not all indispensable to keep the slaves down, and to give protection to their ruthless oppressors! As if, when the marriage institution is abolished, concubinage, adultery, and incest, must not necessarily abound; when all the rights of humanity are annihilated, any barrier remains to protect the victim from the fury of the spoiler; when absolute power is assumed over life and liberty, it will not be wielded with destructive sway! Skeptics of this character abound in society. In some few instances, their incredulity arises from a want of reflection; but, generally, it indicates a hatred of the light, a desire to shield slavery from the assaults of its foes, a contempt of the colored race, whether bond or free. Such will try to discredit the shocking tales of slaveholding cruelty which are recorded in this truthful Narrative; but they will labor in vain. Mr. Douglass has frankly disclosed the place of his birth, the names of those who claimed ownership in his body and soul, and the names also of those who committed the crimes which he has alleged against them. His statements, therefore, may easily be disproved, if they are untrue.

In the course of his Narrative, he relates two instances of murderous cruelty,—in one of which a planter deliberately shot a slave belonging to a neighboring plantation, who had unintentionally gotten within his lordly domain in quest of fish; and in the other, an overseer blew out the brains of a slave who had fled to a stream of water to escape a bloody scourging. Mr. Douglass states that in neither of these instances was any thing done by way of legal arrest or judicial investigation. The Baltimore American, of

[7]The library at Alexandria, in Egypt, was the greatest in the classical world.

March 17, 1845, relates a similar case of atrocity, perpetrated with similar impunity—as follows:—"*Shooting a Slave.*—We learn, upon the authority of a letter from Charles county, Maryland, received by a gentleman of this city, that a young man, named Matthews, a nephew of General Matthews, and whose father, it is believed, holds an office at Washington, killed one of the slaves upon his father's farm by shooting him. The letter states that young Matthews had been left in charge of the farm; that he gave an order to the servant, which was disobeyed, when he proceeded to the house, *obtained a gun, and, returning, shot the servant.* He immediately, the letter continues, fled to his father's residence, where he still remains unmolested."—Let it never be forgotten, that no slaveholder or overseer can be convicted of any outrage perpetrated on the person of a slave, however diabolical it may be, on the testimony of colored witnesses, whether bond or free. By the slave code, they are adjudged to be as incompetent to testify against a white man, as though they were indeed a part of the brute creation. Hence, there is no legal protection in fact, whatever there may be in form, for the slave population; and any amount of cruelty may be inflicted on them with impunity. Is it possible for the human mind to conceive of a more horrible state of society?

The effect of a religious profession on the conduct of southern masters is vividly described in the following Narrative, and shown to be any thing but salutary. In the nature of the case, it must be in the highest degree pernicious. The testimony of Mr. DOUGLASS, on this point, is sustained by a cloud of witnesses, whose veracity is unimpeachable. "A slaveholder's profession of Christianity is a palpable imposture. He is a felon of the highest grade. He is a man-stealer. It is of no importance what you put in the other scale."

Reader! are you with the man-stealers in sympathy and purpose, or on the side of their down-trodden victims? If with the former, then are you the foe of God and man. If with the latter, what are you prepared to do and dare in their behalf? Be faithful, be vigilant, be untiring in your efforts to break every yoke, and let the oppressed go free. Come what may—cost what it may—inscribe on the banner which you unfurl to the breeze, as your religious and political motto—" NO COMPROMISE WITH SLAVERY! NO UNION WITH SLAVEHOLDERS!"

<div align="right">WM. LLOYD GARRISON.</div>

Boston, *May* 1, 1845.

LETTER
FROM WENDELL PHILLIPS, ESQ.[8]

<div align="right">Boston, *April* 22, 1845.</div>

My Dear Friend:

You remember the old fable of "The Man and the Lion," where the lion complained that he should not be so misrepresented "when the lions wrote history."

[8] Wendell Phillips (1811–84) was a well-known Boston reformer and orator. He vehemently agitated for the abolition of slavery, as well as for Prohibition, women's suffrage, and the abolition of capital punishment.

I am glad the time has come when the "lions write history." We have been left long enough to gather the character of slavery from the involuntary evidence of the masters. One might, indeed, rest sufficiently satisfied with what, it is evident, must be, in general, the results of such a relation, without seeking farther to find whether they have followed in every instance. Indeed, those who stare at the half-peck of corn a week, and love to count the lashes on the slave's back, are seldom the "stuff" out of which reformers and abolitionists are to be made. I remember that, in 1838, many were waiting for the results of the West India experiment,[9] before they could come into our ranks. Those "results" have come long ago; but, alas! few of that number have come with them, as converts. A man must be disposed to judge of emancipation by other tests than whether it has increased the produce of sugar,—and to hate slavery for other reasons than because it starves men and whips women,—before he is ready to lay the first stone of his anti-slavery life.

I was glad to learn, in your story, how early the most neglected of God's children waken to a sense of their rights, and of the injustice done them. Experience is a keen teacher; and long before you had mastered your A B C, or knew where the "white sails" of the Chesapeake were bound, you began, I see, to gauge the wretchedness of the slave, not by his hunger and want, not by his lashes and toil, but by the cruel and blighting death which gathers over his soul.

In connection with this, there is one circumstance which makes your recollections peculiarly valuable, and renders your early insight the more remarkable. You come from that part of the country where we are told slavery appears with its fairest features. Let us hear, then, what it is at its best estate—gaze on its bright side, if it has one; and then imagination may task her powers to add dark lines to the picture, as she travels southward to that (for the colored man) Valley of the Shadow of Death,[10] where the Mississippi sweeps along.

Again, we have known you long, and can put the most entire confidence in your truth, candor, and sincerity. Every one who has heard you speak has felt, and, I am confident, every one who reads your book will feel, persuaded that you give them a fair specimen of the whole truth. No one-sided portrait,—no wholesale complaints,—but strict justice done, whenever individual kindliness has neutralized, for a moment, the deadly system with which it was strangely allied. You have been with us, too, some years, and can fairly compare the twilight of rights, which your race enjoy at the North, with that "noon of night" under which they labor south of Mason and Dixon's line. Tell us whether, after all, the half-free colored man of Massachusetts is worse off than the pampered slave of the rice swamps!

In reading your life, no one can say that we have unfairly picked out some rare specimens of cruelty. We know that the bitter drops, which even you have drained from the cup, are no incidental aggravations, no individual ills, but such as must mingle always and necessarily in the lot of every slave. They are the essential ingredients, not the occasional results, of the system.

[9] The emancipation of slaves in British Caribbean colonies which began in 1834.
[10] Psalm 23:4: "Yea, though I walk through the valley of the shadow of death. . . ."

After all, I shall read your book with trembling for you. Some years ago, when you were beginning to tell me your real name and birthplace, you may remember I stopped you, and preferred to remain ignorant of all. With the exception of a vague description, so I continued, till the other day, when you read me your memoirs. I hardly knew, at the time, whether to thank you or not for the sight of them, when I reflected that it was still dangerous, in Massachusetts, for honest men to tell their names! They say the fathers, in 1776, signed the Declaration of Independence with the halter about their necks. You, too, publish your declaration of freedom with danger compassing you around. In all the broad lands which the Constitution of the United States overshadows, there is no single spot,—however narrow or desolate,—where a fugitive slave can plant himself and say, "I am safe." The whole armory of Northern Law has no shield for you. I am free to say that, in your place, I should throw the MS. into the fire.

You, perhaps, may tell your story in safety, endeared as you are to so many warm hearts by rare gifts, and a still rarer devotion of them to the service of others. But it will be owing only to your labors, and the fearless efforts of those who, trampling the laws and Constitution of the country under their feet, are determined that they will "hide the outcast," and that their hearths shall be, spite of the law, an asylum for the oppressed, if, some time or other, the humblest may stand in our streets, and bear witness in safety against the cruelties of which he has been the victim.

Yet it is sad to think, that these very throbbing hearts which welcome your story, and form your best safeguard in telling it, are all beating contrary to the "statute in such case made and provided." Go on, my dear friend, till you, and those who, like you, have been saved, so as by fire, from the dark prison-house, shall stereotype these free, illegal pulses into statutes; and New England, cutting loose from a blood-stained Union, shall glory in being the house of refuge for the oppressed;—till we no longer merely "*hide* the outcast," or make a merit of standing idly by while he is hunted in our midst; but, consecrating anew the soil of the Pilgrims as an asylum for the oppressed, proclaim our *welcome* to the slave so loudly, that the tones shall reach every hut in the Carolinas, and make the broken-hearted bondman leap up at the thought of old Massachusetts.

God Speed the day!

Till then, and ever,

Yours truly,

WENDELL PHILLIPS.

FREDERICK DOUGLASS.

CHAPTER I.

I was born in Tuckahoe, near Hillsborough, and about twelve miles from Easton, in Talbot county, Maryland. I have no accurate knowledge of my

age, never having seen any authentic record containing it. By far the larger part of the slaves know as little of their ages as horses know of theirs, and it is the wish of most masters within my knowledge to keep their slaves thus ignorant. I do not remember to have ever met a slave who could tell of his birthday. They seldom come nearer to it than planting-time, harvest-time, cherry-time, spring-time, or fall-time. A want of information concerning my own was a source of unhappiness to me even during childhood. The white children could tell their ages. I could not tell why I ought to be deprived of the same privilege. I was not allowed to make any inquiries of my master concerning it. He deemed all such inquiries on the part of a slave improper and impertinent, and evidence of a restless spirit. The nearest estimate I can give makes me now between twenty-seven and twenty-eight years of age. I come to this, from hearing my master say, some time during 1835, I was about seventeen years old.

My mother was named Harriet Bailey. She was the daughter of Isaac and Betsey Bailey, both colored, and quite dark. My mother was of a darker complexion than either my grandmother or grandfather.

My father was a white man. He was admitted to be such by all I ever heard speak of my parentage. The opinion was also whispered that my master was my father; but of the correctness of this opinion, I know nothing; the means of knowing was withheld from me. My mother and I were separated when I was but an infant—before I knew her as my mother. It is a common custom, in the part of Maryland from which I ran away, to part children from their mothers at a very early age. Frequently, before the child has reached its twelfth month, its mother is taken from it, and hired out on some farm a considerable distance off, and the child is placed under the care of an old woman, too old for field labor. For what this separation is done, I do not know, unless it be to hinder the development of the child's affection toward its mother, and to blunt and destroy the natural affection of the mother for the child. This is the inevitable result.

I never saw my mother, to know her as such, more than four or five times in my life; and each of these times was very short in duration, and at night. She was hired by a Mr. Stewart, who lived about twelve miles from my home. She made her journeys to see me in the night, travelling the whole distance on foot, after the performance of her day's work. She was a field hand, and a whipping is the penalty of not being in the field at sunrise, unless a slave has special permission from his or her master to the contrary—a permission which they seldom get, and one that gives to him that gives it the proud name of being a kind master. I do not recollect of ever seeing my mother by the light of day. She was with me in the night. She would lie down with me, and get me to sleep, but long before I waked she was gone. Very little communication ever took place between us. Death soon ended what little we could have while she lived, and with it her hardships and suffering. She died when I was about seven years old, on one of my master's farms, near Lee's Mill. I was not allowed to be present during her illness, at her death, or burial. She was gone long before I knew any thing about it. Never having enjoyed, to any considerable extent, her soothing presence, her tender and watchful care, I received the tidings of her death with much the same emotions I should have probably felt at the death of a stranger.

Called thus suddenly away, she left me without the slightest intimation of who my father was. The whisper that my master was my father, may or may not be true; and, true or false, it is of but little consequence to my purpose whilst the fact remains, in all its glaring odiousness, that slaveholders have ordained, and by law established, that the children of slave women shall in all cases follow the condition of their mothers, and this is done too obviously to administer to their own lusts, and make a gratification of their wicked desires profitable as well as pleasurable; for by this cunning arrangement, the slaveholder, in cases not a few, sustains to his slaves the double relation of master and father.

I know of such cases; and it is worthy of remark that such slaves invariably suffer greater hardships, and have more to contend with, than others. They are, in the first place, a constant offence to their mistress. She is ever disposed to find fault with them; they can seldom do any thing to please her; she is never better pleased than when she sees them under the lash, especially when she suspects her husband of showing to his mulatto children favors which he withholds from his black slaves. The master is frequently compelled to sell this class of his slaves, out of deference to the feelings of his white wife; and, cruel as the deed may strike any one to be, for a man to sell his own children to human flesh-mongers, it is often the dictate of humanity for him to do so; for, unless he does this, he must not only whip them himself, but must stand by and see one white son tie up his brother, of but few shades darker complexion than himself, and ply the gory lash to his naked back; and if he lisp one word of disapproval, it is set down to his parental partiality, and only makes a bad matter worse, both for himself and the slave whom he would protect and defend.

Every year brings with it multitudes of this class of slaves. It was doubtless in consequence of a knowledge of this fact, that one great statesman of the south predicted the downfall of slavery by the inevitable laws of population. Whether this prophecy is ever fulfilled or not, it is nevertheless plain that a very different-looking class of people are springing up at the south, and are now held in slavery, from those originally brought to this country from Africa; and if their increase will do no other good, it will do away the force of the argument, that God cursed Ham, and therefore American slavery is right. If the lineal descendants of Ham are alone to be scripturally enslaved,[11] it is certain that slavery at the south must soon become unscriptural; for thousands are ushered into the world, annually, who, like myself, owe their existence to white fathers, and those fathers most frequently their own masters.

I have had two masters. My first master's name was Anthony. I do not remember his first name. He was generally called Captain Anthony—a title which, I presume, he acquired by sailing a craft on the Chesapeake Bay. He was not considered a rich slaveholder. He owned two or three farms, and about thirty slaves. His farms and slaves were under the care of an overseer. The overseer's name was Plummer. Mr. Plummer was a miserable drunkard, a profane swearer, and a savage monster. He always went armed

[11] Noah cursed his son Ham, telling him that he would be "a servant of servants." The story was used as a specious biblical authority for slavery. See Genesis 9:21–25.

Romanticism

with a cowskin[12] and a heavy cudgel. I have known him to cut and slash the women's heads so horribly, that even master would be enraged at his cruelty, and would threaten to whip him if he did not mind himself. It required extraordinary barbarity on the part of an overseer to affect him. He was a cruel man, hardened by a long life of slaveholding. He would at times seem to take great pleasure in whipping a slave. I have often been awakened at the dawn of day by the most heart-rending shrieks of an own aunt of mine, whom he used to tie up to a joist, and whip upon her naked back till she was literally covered with blood. No words, no tears, no prayers, from his gory victim, seemed to move his iron heart from its bloody purpose. The louder she screamed, the harder he whipped; and where the blood ran fastest, there he whipped longest. He would whip her to make her scream, and whip her to make her hush; and not until overcome by fatigue, would he cease to swing the blood-clotted cowskin. I remember the first time I ever witnessed this horrible exhibition. I was quite a child, but I well remember it. I never shall forget it whilst I remember any thing. It was the first of a long series of such outrages, of which I was doomed to be a witness and a participant. It struck me with awful force. It was the blood-stained gate, the entrance to the hell of slavery, though which I was about to pass. It was a most terrible spectacle. I wish I could commit to paper the feelings with which I beheld it.

This occurrence took place very soon after I went to live with my old master, and under the following circumstances. Aunt Hester went out one night,—where or for what I do not know,—and happened to be absent when my master desired her presence. He had ordered her not to go out evenings, and warned her that she must never let him catch her in company with a young man, who was paying attention to her, belonging to Colonel Lloyd. The young man's name was Ned Roberts, generally called Lloyd's Ned. Why master was so careful of her, may be safely left to conjecture. She was a woman of noble form, and of graceful proportions, having very few equals, and fewer superiors, in personal appearance, among the colored or white women of our neighborhood.

Aunt Hester had not only disobeyed his orders in going out, but had been found in company with Lloyd's Ned; which circumstance, I found, from what he said while whipping her, was the chief offence. Had he been a man of pure morals himself, he might have been thought interested in protecting the innocence of my aunt; but those who knew him will not suspect him of any such virtue. Before he commenced whipping Aunt Hester, he took her into the kitchen, and stripped her from neck to waist, leaving her neck, shoulders, and back, entirely naked. He then told her to cross her hands, calling her at the same time a d——d b——h. After crossing her hands, he tied them with a strong rope, and led her to a stool under a large hook in the joist, put in for the purpose. He made her get upon the stool, and tied her hands to the hook. She now stood fair for his infernal purpose. Her arms were stretched up at their full length, so that she stood upon the ends of her toes. He then said to her, "Now, you d——d b——h,

[12] A "cowskin" was an especially brutal whip made of rawhide, or untanned ox hide, designed to cut the skin.

I'll learn you how to disobey my orders!" and after rolling up his sleeves, he commenced to lay on the heavy cowskin, and soon the warm, red blood (amid heart-rending shrieks from her, and horrid oaths from him) came dripping to the floor. I was so terrified and horror-stricken at the sight, that I hid myself in a closet, and dared not venture out till long after the bloody transaction was over. I expected it would be my turn next. It was all new to me. I had never seen anything like it before. I had always lived with my grandmother on the outskirts of the plantation, where she was put to raise the children of the younger women. I had therefore been, until now, out of the way of the bloody scenes that often occurred on the plantation.

CHAPTER II.

My master's family consisted of two sons, Andrew and Richard, one daughter, Lucretia, and her husband, Captain Thomas Auld. They lived in one house, upon the home plantation of Colonel Edward Lloyd. My master was Colonel Lloyd's clerk and superintendent. He was what might be called the overseer of the overseers. I spent two years of childhood on this plantation in my old master's family. It was here that I witnessed the bloody transaction recorded in the first chapter; and as I received my first impressions of slavery on this plantation, I will give some description of it, and of slavery as it there existed. The plantation is about twelve miles north of Easton, in Talbot county, and is situated on the border of Miles River. The principal products raised upon it were tobacco, corn, and wheat. These were raised in great abundance; so that, with the products of this and the other farms belonging to him, he was able to keep in almost constant employment a large sloop, in carrying them to market at Baltimore. This sloop was named Sally Lloyd, in honor of one of the colonel's daughters. My master's son-in-law, Captain Auld, was master of the vessel; she was otherwise manned by the colonel's own slaves. Their names were Peter, Isaac, Rich, and Jake. These were esteemed very highly by the other slaves, and looked upon as the privileged ones of the plantation; for it was no small affair, in the eyes of the slaves, to be allowed to see Baltimore.

Colonel Lloyd kept from three to four hundred slaves on his home plantation, and owned a large number more on the neighboring farms belonging to him. The names of the farms nearest to the home plantation were Wye Town and New Design. "Wye Town" was under the overseership of a man named Noah Willis. New Design was under the overseership of a Mr. Townsend. The overseers of these, and all the rest of the farms, numbering over twenty, received advice and direction from the managers of the home plantation. This was the great business place. It was the seat of government for the whole twenty farms. All disputes among the overseers were settled here. If a slave was convicted of any high misdemeanor, became unmanageable, or evinced a determination to run away, he was brought immediately here, severely whipped, put on board the sloop, carried to Baltimore, and sold to Austin Woolfolk, or some other slave-trader, as a warning to the slaves remaining.

Here, too, the slaves of all the other farms received their monthly allowance of food, and their yearly clothing. The men and women slaves received, as their monthly allowance of food, eight pounds of pork, or its equivalent in fish, and one bushel of corn meal. Their yearly clothing consisted of two coarse linen shirts, one pair of linen trousers, like the shirts, one jacket, one pair of trousers for winter, made of coarse negro cloth, one pair of stockings, and one pair of shoes; the whole of which could not have cost more than seven dollars. The allowance of the slave children was given to their mothers, or the old women having the care of them. The children unable to work in the field had neither shoes, stockings, jackets, nor trousers, given to them; their clothing consisted of two coarse linen shirts per year. When these failed them, they went naked until the next allowance-day. Children from seven to ten years old, of both sexes, almost naked, might be seen at all seasons of the year.

There were no beds given the slaves, unless one coarse blanket be considered such, and none but the men and women had these. This, however, is not considered a very great privation. They find less difficulty from the want of beds, than from the want of time to sleep; for when their day's work in the field is done, the most of them having their washing, mending, and cooking to do, and having few or none of the ordinary facilities for doing either of these, very many of their sleeping hours are consumed in preparing for the field the coming day; and when this is done, old and young, male and female, married and single, drop down side by side, on one common bed,—the cold, damp floor,—each covering himself or herself with their miserable blankets; and here they sleep till they are summoned to the field by the driver's horn. At the sound of this, all must rise, and be off to the field. There must be no halting; every one must be at his or her post; and woe betides them who hear not this morning summons to the field; for if they are not awakened by the sense of hearing, they are by the sense of feeling: no age nor sex finds any favor. Mr. Severe, the overseer, used to stand by the door of the quarter, armed with a large hickory stick and heavy cowskin, ready to whip any one who was so unfortunate as not to hear, or, from any other cause, was prevented from being ready to start for the field at the sound of the horn.

Mr. Severe was rightly named: he was a cruel man. I have seen him whip a woman, causing the blood to run half an hour at the time; and this, too, in the midst of her crying children, pleading for their mother's release. He seemed to take pleasure in manifesting his fiendish barbarity. Added to his cruelty, he was a profane swearer. It was enough to chill the blood and stiffen the hair of an ordinary man to hear him talk. Scarce a sentence escaped him but that was commenced or concluded by some horrid oath. The field was the place to witness his cruelty and profanity. His presence made it both the field of blood and blasphemy. From the rising till the going down of the sun, he was cursing, raving, cutting, and slashing among the slaves of the field, in the most frightful manner. His career was short. He died very soon after I went to Colonel Lloyd's; and he died as he lived, uttering, with his dying groans, bitter curses and horrid oaths. His death was regarded by the slaves as the result of a merciful providence.

Mr. Severe's place was filled by a Mr. Hopkins. He was a very different man. He was less cruel, less profane, and made less noise, than Mr. Severe.

His course was characterized by no extraordinary demonstrations of cruelty. He whipped, but seemed to take no pleasure in it. He was called by the slaves a good overseer.

The home plantation of Colonel Lloyd wore the appearance of a country village. All the mechanical operations for all the farms were performed here. The shoemaking and mending, the blacksmithing, cartwrighting, coopering, weaving, and grain-grinding, were all performed by the slaves on the home plantation. The whole place wore a business-like aspect very unlike the neighboring farms. The number of houses, too, conspired to give it advantage over the neighboring farms. It was called by the slaves the *Great House Farm.* Few privileges were esteemed higher, by the slaves of the out-farms, than that of being selected to do errands at the Great House Farm. It was associated in their minds with greatness. A representative could not be prouder of his election to a seat in the American Congress, than a slave on one of the out-farms would be of his election to do errands at the Great House Farm. They regarded it as evidence of great confidence reposed in them by their overseers; and it was on this account, as well as a constant desire to be out of the field from under the driver's lash, that they esteemed it a high privilege, one worth careful living for. He was called the smartest and most trusty fellow, who had this honor conferred upon him the most frequently. The competitors for this office sought as diligently to please their overseers, as the office-seekers in the political parties seek to please and deceive the people. The same traits of character might be seen in Colonel Lloyd's slaves, as are seen in the slaves of the political parties.

The slaves selected to go to the Great House Farm, for the monthly allowance for themselves and their fellow-slaves, were peculiarly enthusiastic. While on their way, they would make the dense old woods, for miles around, reverberate with their wild songs, revealing at once the highest joy and the deepest sadness. They would compose and sing as they went along, consulting neither time nor tune. The thought that came up, came out—if not in the word, in the sound;—and as frequently in the one as in the other. They would sometimes sing the most pathetic sentiment in the most rapturous tone, and the most rapturous sentiment in the most pathetic tones. Into all of their songs they would manage to weave something of the Great House Farm. Especially would they do this, when leaving home. They would then sing most exultingly the following words:—

> I am going away to the Great House Farm!
> O, yea! O, yea! O!

This they would sing, as a chorus, to words which to many would seem unmeaning jargon, but which, nevertheless, were full of meaning to themselves. I have sometimes thought that the mere hearing of those songs would do more to impress some minds with the horrible character of slavery, than the reading of whole volumes of philosophy on the subject could do.

I did not, when a slave, understand the deep meaning of those rude and apparently incoherent songs. I was myself within the circle; so that I neither saw nor heard as those without might see and hear. They told a tale of woe which was then altogether beyond my feeble comprehension; they

were tones loud, long, and deep; they breathed the prayer and complaint of souls boiling over with the bitterest anguish. Every tone was a testimony against slavery, and a prayer to God for deliverance from chains. The hearing of those wild notes always depressed my spirit, and filled me with ineffable sadness. I have frequently found myself in tears while hearing them. The mere recurrence to those songs, even now, afflicts me; and while I am writing these lines, an expression of feeling has already found its way down my cheek. To those songs I trace my first glimmering conception of the dehumanizing character of slavery. I can never get rid of that conception. Those songs still follow me, to deepen my hatred of slavery, and quicken my sympathies for my brethren in bonds. If any one wishes to be impressed with the soul-killing effects of slavery, let him go to Colonel Lloyd's plantation, and, on allowance-day, place himself in the deep pine woods, and there let him, in silence, analyze the sounds that shall pass through the chambers of his soul,—and if he is not thus impressed, it will only be because "there is no flesh in his obdurate heart."

I have often been utterly astonished, since I came to the north, to find persons who could speak of the singing, among slaves, as evidence of their contentment and happiness. It is impossible to conceive of a greater mistake. Slaves sing most when they are most unhappy. The songs of the slave represent the sorrows of his heart; and he is relieved by them, only as an aching heart is relieved by its tears. At least, such is my experience. I have often sung to drown my sorrow, but seldom to express my happiness. Crying for joy, and singing for joy, were alike uncommon to me while in the jaws of slavery. The singing of a man cast away upon a desolate island might be as appropriately considered as evidence of contentment and happiness, as the singing of a slave; the songs of the one and of the other are prompted by the same emotion.

CHAPTER III.

Colonel Lloyd kept a large and finely cultivated garden, which afforded almost constant employment for four men, besides the chief gardener, (Mr. M'Durmond.) This garden was probably the greatest attraction of the place. During the summer months, people came from far and near—from Baltimore, Easton, and Annapolis—to see it. It abounded in fruits of almost every description, from the hardy apple of the north to the delicate orange of the south. This garden was not the least source of trouble on the plantation. Its excellent fruit was quite a temptation to the hungry swarms of boys, as well as the older slaves, belonging to the colonel, few of whom had the virtue or the vice to resist it. Scarcely a day passed, during the summer, but that some slave had to take the lash for stealing fruit. The colonel had to resort to all kinds of stratagems to keep his slaves out of the garden. The last and most successful one was that of tarring his fence all around; after which, if a slave was caught with any tar upon his person, it was deemed sufficient proof that he had either been into the garden, or had tried to get in. In either case, he was severely whipped by the chief

gardener. This plan worked well; the slaves became as fearful of tar as of the lash. They seemed to realize the impossibility of touching *tar* without being defiled.[13]

The colonel also kept a splendid riding equipage. His stable and carriage-house presented the appearance of some of our large city livery establishments. His horses were of the finest form and noblest blood. His carriage-house contained three splendid coaches, three or four gigs, besides dearborns and barouches of the most fashionable style.

This establishment was under the care of two slaves—old Barney and young Barney—father and son. To attend to this establishment was their sole work. But it was by no means an easy employment; for in nothing was Colonel Lloyd more particular than in the management of his horses. The slightest inattention to these was unpardonable, and was visited upon those, under whose care they were placed, with the severest punishment; no excuse could shield them, if the colonel only suspected any want of attention to his horses—a supposition which he frequently indulged, and one which, of course, made the office of old and young Barney a very trying one. They never knew when they were safe from punishment. They were frequently whipped when least deserving, and escaped whipping when most deserving it. Every thing depended upon the looks of the horses, and the state of Colonel Lloyd's own mind when his horses were brought to him for use. If a horse did not move fast enough, or hold his head high enough, it was owing to some fault of his keepers. It was painful to stand near the stable-door, and hear the various complaints against the keepers when a horse was taken out for use. "This horse has not had proper attention. He has not been sufficiently rubbed and curried, or he has not been properly fed; his food was too wet or too dry; he got it too soon or too late; he was too hot or too cold; he had too much hay, and not enough of grain; or he had too much grain, and not enough of hay; instead of old Barney's attending to the horse, he had very improperly left it to his son." To all these complaints, no matter how unjust, the slave must answer never a word. Colonel Lloyd could not brook any contradiction from a slave. When he spoke, a slave must stand, listen, and tremble; and such was literally the case. I have seen Colonel Lloyd make old Barney, a man between fifty and sixty years of age, uncover his bald head, kneel down upon the cold, damp ground, and receive upon his naked and toil-worn shoulders more than thirty lashes at the time. Colonel Lloyd had three sons—Edward, Murray, and Daniel,—and three sons-in-law, Mr. Winder, Mr. Nicholson, and Mr. Lowndes. All of these lived at the Great House Farm, and enjoyed the luxury of whipping the servants when they pleased, from old Barney down to William Wilkes, the coach-driver. I have seen Winder make one of the house-servants stand off from him a suitable distance to be touched with the end of his whip, and at every stroke raise great ridges upon his back.

To describe the wealth of Colonel Lloyd would be almost equal to describing the riches of Job. He kept from ten to fifteen house-servants. He was said to own a thousand slaves, and I think this estimate quite within the truth. Colonel Lloyd owned so many that he did not know them when he

[13] A play on the proverb "He who touches pitch shall be defiled."

saw them; nor did all the slaves of the out-farms know him. It is reported of him, that, while riding along the road one day, he met a colored man, and addressed him in the usual manner of speaking to colored people on the public highways of the south: "Well, boy, whom do you belong to?" "To Colonel Lloyd," replied the slave. "Well, does the colonel treat you well?" "No sir," was the ready reply. "What, does he work you too hard?" "Yes, sir." "Well, don't he give you enough to eat?" "Yes, sir, he gives me enough, such as it is."

The colonel, after ascertaining where the slave belonged, rode on; the man also went on about his business, not dreaming that he had been conversing with his master. He thought, said, and heard nothing more of the matter, until two or three weeks afterwards. The poor man was then informed by his overseer that, for having found fault with his master, he was now to be sold to a Georgia trader. He was immediately chained and handcuffed; and thus, without a moment's warning, he was snatched away, and forever sundered, from his family and friends, by a hand more unrelenting than death. This is the penalty of telling the truth, of telling the simple truth, in answer to a series of plain questions.

It is partly in consequence of such facts, that slaves, when inquired of as to their condition and the character of their masters, almost universally say they are contented, and that their masters are kind. The slaveholders have been known to send in spies among their slaves, to ascertain their views and feelings in regard to their condition. The frequency of this has had the effect to establish among the slaves the maxim, that a still tongue makes a wise head. They suppress the truth rather than take the consequences of telling it, and in so doing prove themselves a part of the human family. If they have any thing to say of their masters, it is generally in their masters' favor, especially when speaking to an untried man. I have been frequently asked, when a slave, if I had a kind master, and do not remember ever to have given a negative answer; nor did I, in pursuing this course, consider myself as uttering what was absolutely false; for I always measured the kindness of my master by the standard of kindness set up among slaveholders around us. Moreover, slaves are like other people, and imbibe prejudices quite common to others. They think their own better than that of others. Many, under the influence of this prejudice, think their own masters are better than the masters of other slaves; and this, too, in some cases, when the very reverse is true. Indeed, it is not uncommon for slaves even to fall out and quarrel among themselves about the relative goodness of their masters, each contending for the superior goodness of his own over that of the others. At the very same time, they mutually execrate their masters when viewed separately. It was so on our plantation. When Colonel Lloyd's slaves met the slaves of Jacob Jepson, they seldom parted without a quarrel about their masters; Colonel Lloyd's slaves contending that he was the richest, and Mr. Jepson's slaves that he was the smartest, and most of a man. Colonel Lloyd's slaves would boast his ability to buy and sell Jacob Jepson. Mr. Jepson's slaves would boast his ability to whip Colonel Lloyd. These quarrels would almost always end in a fight between the parties, and those that whipped were supposed to have gained the point at issue. They seemed to think that the greatness of their masters was transferable to

themselves. It was considered as being bad enough to be a slave; but to be a poor man's slave was deemed a disgrace indeed!

CHAPTER IV.

Mr. Hopkins remained but a short time in the office of overseer. Why his career was so short, I do not know, but suppose he lacked the necessary severity to suit Colonel Lloyd. Mr. Hopkins was succeeded by Mr. Austin Gore, a man possessing, in an eminent degree, all those traits of character indispensable to what is called a first-rate overseer. Mr. Gore had served Colonel Lloyd, in the capacity of overseer, upon one of the out-farms, and had shown himself worthy of the high station of overseer upon the home or Great House Farm.

Mr. Gore was proud, ambitious, and persevering. He was artful, cruel, and obdurate. He was just the man for such a place, and it was just the place for such a man. It afforded scope for the full exercise of all his powers, and he seemed to be perfectly at home in it. He was one of those who could torture the slightest look, word, or gesture, on the part of the slave, into impudence, and would treat it accordingly. There must be no answering back to him; no explanation was allowed a slave, showing himself to have been wrongfully accused. Mr. Gore acted fully up to the maxim laid down by slaveholders—"It is better that a dozen slaves suffer under the lash, than that the overseer should be convicted, in the presence of the slaves, of having been at fault." No matter how innocent a slave might be—it availed him nothing, when accused by Mr. Gore of any misdemeanor. To be accused was to be convicted, and to be convicted was to be punished; the one always following the other with immutable certainty. To escape punishment was to escape accusation; and few slaves had the fortune to do either, under the overseership of Mr. Gore. He was just proud enough to demand the most debasing homage of the slave, and quite servile enough to crouch, himself, at the feet of the master. He was ambitious enough to be contented with nothing short of the highest rank of overseers, and persevering enough to reach the height of his ambition. He was cruel enough to inflict the severest punishment, artful enough to descend to the lowest trickery, and obdurate enough to be insensible to the voice of a reproving conscience. He was, of all the overseers, the most dreaded by the slaves. His presence was painful; his eye flashed confusion; and seldom was his sharp, shrill voice heard, without producing horror and trembling in their ranks.

Mr. Gore was a grave man, and, though a young man, he indulged in no jokes, said no funny words, seldom smiled. His words were in perfect keeping with his looks, and his looks were in perfect keeping with his words. Overseers will sometimes indulge in a witty word, even with the slaves; not so with Mr. Gore. He spoke but to command, and commanded but to be obeyed; he dealt sparingly with his words, and bountifully with his whip, never using the former where the latter would answer as well. When he whipped, he seemed to do so from a sense of duty, and feared no conse-

quences. He did nothing reluctantly, no matter how disagreeable; always at his post, never inconsistent. He never promised but to fulfill. He was, in a word, a man of the most inflexible firmness and stone-like coolness.

His savage barbarity was equalled only by the consummate coolness with which he committed the grossest and most savage deeds upon the slaves under his charge. Mr. Gore once undertook to whip one of Colonel Lloyd's slaves, by the name of Demby. He had given Demby but few stripes, when, to get rid of the scourging, he ran and plunged himself into a creek, and stood there at the depth of his shoulders, refusing to come out. Mr. Gore told him that he would give him three calls, and that, if he did not come out at the third call, he would shoot him. The first call was given. Demby made no response, but stood his ground. The second and third calls were given with the same result. Mr. Gore then, without consultation or deliberation with any one, not even giving Demby an additional call, raised his musket to his face, taking deadly aim at his victim, and in an instant poor Demby was no more. His mangled body sank out of sight, and blood and brains marked the water where he had stood.

A thrill of horror flashed through every soul upon the plantation, excepting Mr. Gore. He alone seemed cool and collected. He was asked by Colonel Lloyd and my old master, why he resorted to this extraordinary expedient. His reply was, (as well as I can remember,) that Demby had become unmanageable. He was setting a dangerous example to the other slaves,—one which, if suffered to pass without some such demonstration on his part, would finally lead to the total subversion of all rule and order upon the plantation. He argued that if one slave refused to be corrected, and escaped with his life, the other slaves would soon copy the example; the result of which would be, the freedom of the slaves, and the enslavement of the whites. Mr. Gore's defence was satisfactory. He was continued in his station as overseer upon the home plantation. His fame as an overseer went abroad. His horrid crime was not even submitted to judicial investigation. It was committed in the presence of slaves, and they of course could neither institute a suit, nor testify against him; and thus the guilty perpetrator of one of the bloodiest and most foul murders goes unwhipped of justice, and uncensured by the community in which he lives. Mr. Gore lived in St. Michael's, Talbot county, Maryland, when I left there; and if he is still alive, he very probably lives there now; and if so, he is now, as he was then, as highly esteemed and as much respected as though his guilty soul had not been stained with his brother's blood.

I speak advisedly when I say this,—that killing a slave, or any colored person, in Talbot county, Maryland, is not treated as a crime, either by the courts or the community. Mr. Thomas Lanman, of St. Michael's, killed two slaves, one of whom he killed with a hatchet, by knocking his brains out. He used to boast of the commission of the awful and bloody deed. I have heard him do so laughingly, saying, among other things, that he was the only benefactor of his country in the company, and that when others would do as much as he had done, we should be relieved of "the d——d niggers."

The wife of Mr. Giles Hicks, living but a short distance from where I used to live, murdered my wife's cousin, a young girl between fifteen and sixteen years of age, mangling her person in the most horrible manner, breaking her nose and breastbone with a stick, so that the poor girl expired

in a few hours afterward. She was immediately buried, but had not been in her untimely grave but a few hours before she was taken up and examined by the coroner, who decided that she had come to her death by severe beating. The offence for which this girl was thus murdered was this:—She had been set that night to mind Mrs. Hicks's baby, and during the night she fell asleep, and the baby cried. She, having lost her rest for several nights previous, did not hear the crying. They were both in the room with Mrs. Hicks. Mrs. Hicks, finding the girl slow to move, jumped from her bed, seized an oak stick of wood by the fireplace, and with it broke the girl's nose and breastbone, and thus ended her life. I will not say that this most horrid murder produced no sensation in the community. It did produce sensation, but not enough to bring the murderess to punishment. There was a warrant issued for her arrest, but it was never served. Thus she escaped not only punishment, but even the pain of being arraigned before a court for her horrid crime.

Whilst I am detailing bloody deeds which took place during my stay on Colonel Lloyd's plantation, I will briefly narrate another, which occurred about the same time as the murder of Demby by Mr. Gore.

Colonel Lloyd's slaves were in the habit of spending a part of their nights and Sundays in fishing for oysters, and in this way made up the deficiency of their scanty allowance. An old man belonging to Colonel Lloyd, while thus engaged, happened to get beyond the limits of Colonel Lloyd's, and on the premises of Mr. Beal Bondly. At this trespass, Mr. Bondly took offence, and with his musket came down to the shore, and blew its deadly contents into the poor old man.

Mr. Bondly came over to see Colonel Lloyd the next day, whether to pay him for his property, or to justify himself in what he had done, I know not. At any rate, this whole fiendish transaction was soon hushed up. There was very little said about it at all, and nothing done. It was a common saying, even among little white boys, that it was worth a half-cent to kill a "nigger," and a half-cent to bury one.

CHAPTER V.

As to my own treatment while I lived on Colonel Lloyd's plantation, it was very similar to that of the other slave children. I was not old enough to work in the field, and there being little else than field work to do, I had a great deal of leisure time. The most I had to do was to drive up the cows at evening, keep the fowls out of the garden, keep the front yard clean, and run off errands for my old master's daughter, Mrs. Lucretia Auld. The most of my leisure time I spent in helping Master Daniel Lloyd in finding his birds, after he had shot them. My connection with Master Daniel was of some advantage to me. He became quite attached to me, and was a sort of protector of me. He would not allow the older boys to impose upon me, and would divide his cakes with me.

I was seldom whipped by my old master, and suffered little from any thing else than hunger and cold. I suffered much from hunger, but much more from cold. In hottest summer and coldest winter, I was kept almost

naked—no shoes, no stockings, no jacket, no trousers, nothing on but a
coarse tow linen shirt, reaching only to my knees. I had no bed. I must have
perished with cold, but that, the coldest nights, I used to steal a bag which
was used for carrying corn to the mill. I would crawl into this bag, and
there sleep on the cold, damp, clay floor, with my head in and feet out. My
feet have been so cracked with the frost, that the pen with which I am
writing might be laid in the gashes.

We were not regularly allowanced. Our food was coarse corn meal
boiled. This was called *mush*. It was put into a large wooden tray or trough,
and set down upon the ground. The children were then called, like so
many pigs, and like so many pigs they would come and devour the mush;
some with oystershells, others with pieces of shingle, some with naked
hands, and none with spoons. He that ate fastest got most; he that was
strongest secured the best place; and few left the trough satisfied.

I was probably between seven and eight years old when I left Colonel
Lloyd's plantation. I left it with joy. I shall never forget the ecstasy with
which I received the intelligence that my old master (Anthony) had deter-
mined to let me go to Baltimore, to live with Mr. Hugh Auld, brother to my
old master's son-in-law, Captain Thomas Auld. I received this information
about three days before my departure. They were three of the happiest
days I ever enjoyed. I spent the most part of all these three days in the
creek, washing off the plantation scurf, and preparing myself for my de-
parture.

The pride of appearance which this would indicate was not my own. I
spent the time in washing, not so much because I wished to, but because
Mrs. Lucretia had told me I must get all the dead skin off my feet and
knees before I could go to Baltimore; for the people in Baltimore were very
cleanly, and would laugh at me if I looked dirty. Besides, she was going to
give me a pair of trousers, which I should not put on unless I got all the dirt
off me. The thought of owning a pair of trousers was great indeed! It was
almost a sufficient motive, not only to make me take off what would be
called by pig-drovers the mange, but the skin itself. I went at it in good
earnest, working for the first time with the hope of reward.

The ties that ordinarily bind children to their homes were all suspended
in my case. I found no severe trial in my departure. My home was charm-
less; it was not home to me; on parting from it, I could not feel that I was
leaving any thing which I could have enjoyed by staying. My mother was
dead, my grandmother lived far off, so that I seldom saw her. I had two
sisters and one brother, that lived in the same house with me; but the early
separation of us from our mother had well nigh blotted the fact of our
relationship from our memories. I looked for home elsewhere, and was
confident of finding none which I should relish less than the one which I
was leaving. If, however, I found in my new home hardship, hunger, whip-
ping, and nakedness, I had the consolation that I should not have escaped
any one of them by staying. Having already had more than a taste of them
in the house of my old master, and having endured them there, I very
naturally inferred my ability to endure them elsewhere, and especially at
Baltimore; for I had something of the feeling about Baltimore that is ex-
pressed in the proverb, that "being hanged in England is preferable to

dying a natural death in Ireland." I had the strongest desire to see Baltimore. Cousin Tom, though not fluent in speech, had inspired me with that desire by his eloquent description of the place. I could never point out any thing at the Great House, no matter how beautiful or powerful, but that he had seen something at Baltimore far exceeding, both in beauty and strength, the object which I pointed out to him. Even the Great House itself, with all its pictures, was far inferior to many buildings in Baltimore. So strong was my desire, that I thought a gratification of it would fully compensate for whatever loss of comforts I should sustain by the exchange. I left without a regret, and with the highest hopes of future happiness.

We sailed out of Miles River for Baltimore on a Saturday morning. I remember only the day of the week, for at that time I had no knowledge of the days of the month, nor the months of the year. On setting sail, I walked aft, and gave to Colonel Lloyd's plantation what I hoped would be the last look. I then placed myself in the bows of the sloop, and there spent the remainder of the day in looking ahead, interesting myself in what was in the distance rather than in things near by or behind.

In the afternoon of that day, we reached Annapolis, the capital of the State. We stopped but a few moments, so that I had no time to go on shore. It was the first large town that I had ever seen, and though it would look small compared with some of our New England factory villages, I thought it a wonderful place for its size—more imposing even than the Great House Farm!

We arrived at Baltimore early on Sunday morning, landing at Smith's Wharf, not far from Bowley's Wharf. We had on board the sloop a large flock of sheep; and after aiding in driving them to the slaughterhouse of Mr. Curtis on Louden Slater's Hill, I was conducted by Rich, one of the hands belonging on board of the sloop, to my new home in Alliciana Street, near Mr. Gardner's ship-yard, on Fells Point.

Mr. and Mrs. Auld were both at home, and met me at the door with their little son Thomas, to take care of whom I had been given. And here I saw what I had never seen before; it was a white face beaming with the most kindly emotions; it was the face of my new mistress, Sophia Auld. I wish I could describe the rapture that flashed through my soul as I beheld it. It was a new and strange sight to me, brightening up my pathway with the light of happiness. Little Thomas was told, there was his Freddy,—and I was told to take care of little Thomas; and thus I entered upon the duties of my new home with the most cheering prospect ahead.

I look upon my departure from Colonel Lloyd's plantation as one of the most interesting events of my life. It is possible, and even quite probable, that but for the mere circumstance of being removed from that plantation to Baltimore, I should have to-day, instead of being here seated by my own table, in the enjoyment of freedom and the happiness of home, writing this Narrative, been confined in the galling chains of slavery. Going to live at Baltimore laid the foundation, and opened the gateway, to all my subsequent prosperity. I have ever regarded it as the first plain manifestation of that kind providence which has ever since attended me, and marked my life with so many favors. I regarded the selection of myself as being somewhat remarkable. There were a number of slave children that might have

been sent from the plantation to Baltimore. There were those younger, those older, and those of the same age. I was chosen from among them all, and was the first, last, and only choice.

I may be deemed superstitious, and even egotistical, in regarding this event as a special interposition of divine Providence in my favor. But I should be false to the earliest sentiments of my soul, if I suppressed the opinion. I prefer to be true to myself, even at the hazard of incurring the ridicule of others, rather than to be false, and incur my own abhorrence. From my earliest recollection, I date the entertainment of a deep conviction that slavery would not always be able to hold me within its foul embrace; and in the darkest hours of my career in slavery, this living word of faith and spirit of hope departed not from me, but remained like ministering angels to cheer me through the gloom. This good spirit was from God, and to him I offer thanksgiving and praise.

CHAPTER VI.

My new mistress proved to be all she appeared when I first met her at the door,—a woman of the kindest heart and finest feelings. She had never had a slave under her control previously to myself, and prior to her marriage she had been dependent upon her own industry for a living. She was by trade a weaver; and by constant application to her business, she had been in a good degree preserved from the blighting and dehumanizing effects of slavery. I was utterly astonished at her goodness. I scarcely knew how to behave towards her. She was entirely unlike any other white woman I had ever seen. I could not approach her as I was accustomed to approach other white ladies. My early instruction was all out of place. The crouching servility, usually so acceptable a quality in a slave, did not answer when manifested toward her. Her favor was not gained by it; she seemed to be disturbed by it. She did not deem it impudent or unmannerly for a slave to look her in the face. The meanest slave was put fully at ease in her presence, and none left without feeling better for having seen her. Her face was made of heavenly smiles, and her voice of tranquil music.

But, alas! this kind heart had but a short time to remain such. The fatal poison of irresponsible power was already in her hands, and soon commenced its infernal work. That cheerful eye, under the influence of slavery, soon became red with rage; that voice, made all of sweet accord, changed to one of harsh and horrid discord; and that angelic face gave place to that of a demon.

Very soon after I went to live with Mr. and Mrs. Auld, she very kindly commenced to teach me the A, B, C. After I had learned this, she assisted me in learning to spell words of three or four letters. Just at this point of my progress, Mr. Auld found out what was going on, and at once forbade Mrs. Auld to instruct me further, telling her, among other things, that it was unlawful, as well as unsafe, to teach a slave to read. To use his own words, further, he said, "If you give a nigger an inch, he will take an ell. A nigger should know nothing but to obey his master—to do as he is told to

do. Learning would *spoil* the best nigger in the world. Now," said he, "if you teach that nigger (speaking of myself) how to read, there would be no keeping him. It would forever unfit him to be a slave. He would at once become unmanageable, and of no value to his master. As to himself, it could do him no good, but a great deal of harm. It would make him discontented and unhappy." These words sank deep into my heart, stirred up sentiments within that lay slumbering, and called into existence an entirely new train of thought. It was a new and special revelation, explaining dark and mysterious things, with which my youthful understanding had struggled, but struggled in vain. I now understood what had been to me a most perplexing difficulty—to wit, the white man's power to enslave the black man. It was a grand achievement, and I prized it highly. From that moment, I understood the pathway from slavery to freedom. It was just what I wanted, and I got it at a time when I the least expected it. Whilst I was saddened by the thought of losing the aid of my kind mistress, I was gladdened by the invaluable instruction which, by the merest accident, I had gained from my master. Though conscious of the difficulty of learning without a teacher, I set out with high hope, and a fixed purpose, at whatever cost of trouble, to learn how to read. The very decided manner with which he spoke, and strove to impress his wife with the evil consequences of giving me instruction, served to convince me that he was deeply sensible of the truths he was uttering. It gave me the best assurance that I might rely with the utmost confidence on the results which, he said, would flow from teaching me to read. What he most dreaded, that I most desired. What he most loved, that I most hated. That which to him was a great evil, to be carefully shunned, was to me a great good, to be diligently sought; and the argument which he so warmly urged, against my learning to read, only served to inspire me with a desire and determination to learn. In learning to read, I owe almost as much to the bitter opposition of my master, as to the kindly aid of my mistress. I acknowledge the benefit of both.

I had resided but a short time in Baltimore before I observed a marked difference, in the treatment of slaves, from that which I had witnessed in the country. A city slave is almost a freeman, compared with a slave on the plantation. He is much better fed and clothed, and enjoys privileges altogether unknown to the slave on the plantation. There is a vestige of decency, a sense of shame, that does much to curb and check those outbreaks of atrocious cruelty so commonly enacted upon the plantation. He is a desperate slaveholder, who will shock the humanity of his nonslaveholding neighbors with the cries of his lacerated slave. Few are willing to incur the odium attaching to the reputation of being a cruel master; and above all things, they would not be known as not giving a slave enough to eat. Every city slaveholder is anxious to have it known of him, that he feeds his slaves well; and it is due to them to say, that most of them do give their slaves enough to eat. There are, however, some painful exceptions to this rule. Directly opposite to us, on Philpot Street, lived Mr. Thomas Hamilton. He owned two slaves. Their names were Henrietta and Mary. Henrietta was about twenty-two years of age, Mary was about fourteen; and of all the mangled and emaciated creatures I ever looked upon, these two were the most so. His heart must be harder than stone, that could look upon these unmoved. The head, neck, and shoulders of Mary were literally cut to

pieces. I have frequently felt her head, and found it nearly covered with festering sores, caused by the lash of her cruel mistress. I do not know that her master ever whipped her, but I have been an eye-witness to the cruelty of Mrs. Hamilton. I used to be in Mr. Hamilton's house nearly every day. Mrs. Hamilton used to sit in a large chair in the middle of the room, with a heavy cowskin always by her side, and scarce an hour passed during the day but was marked by the blood of one of these slaves. The girls seldom passed her without her saying, "Move faster, you *black gip!*"[14] at the same time giving them a blow with the cowskin over the head or shoulders, often drawing the blood. She would then say, "Take that, you *black gip!*"— continuing, "If you don't move faster, I'll move you!" Added to the cruel lashings to which these slaves were subjected, they were kept nearly half-starved. They seldom knew what it was to eat a full meal. I have seen Mary contending with the pigs for the offal thrown into the street. So much was Mary kicked and cut to pieces, that she was often called "*pecked*" than by her name.

CHAPTER VII.

I lived in Master Hugh's family about seven years. During this time, I succeeded in learning to read and write. In accomplishing this, I was compelled to resort to various stratagems. I had no regular teacher. My mistress, who had kindly commenced to instruct me, had, in compliance with the advice and direction of her husband, not only ceased to instruct, but had set her face against my being instructed by any one else. It is due, however, to my mistress to say of her, that she did not adopt this course of treatment immediately. She at first lacked the depravity indispensable to shutting me up in mental darkness. It was at least necessary for her to have some training in the exercise of irresponsible power, to make her equal to the task of treating me as though I were a brute.

My mistress was, as I have said, a kind and tender-hearted woman; and in the simplicity of her soul she commenced, when I first went to live with her, to treat me as she supposed one human being ought to treat another. In entering upon the duties of a slaveholder, she did not seem to perceive that I sustained to her the relation of a mere chattel, and that for her to treat me as a human being was not only wrong, but dangerously so. Slavery proved as injurious to her as it did to me. When I went there, she was a pious, warm, and tender-hearted woman. There was no sorrow or suffering for which she had not a tear. She had bread for the hungry, clothes for the naked, and comfort for every mourner that came within her reach. Slavery soon proved its ability to divest her of these heavenly qualities. Under its influence, the tender heart became stone, and the lamblike disposition gave way to one of tiger-like fierceness. The first step in her downward course was in her ceasing to instruct me. She now commenced to practice her husband's precepts. She finally became even more violent in her opposition than her husband himself. She was not satisfied with simply

[14] A cheat, a worthless person.

doing as well as he had commanded; she seemed anxious to do better. Nothing seemed to make her more angry than to see me with a newspaper. She seemed to think that here lay the danger. I have had her rush at me with a face made all up of fury, and snatch from me a newspaper, in a manner that fully revealed her apprehension. She was an apt woman; and a little experience soon demonstrated, to her satisfaction, that education and slavery were incompatible with each other.

From this time I was most narrowly watched. If I was in a separate room any considerable length of time, I was sure to be suspected of having a book, and was at once called to give an account of myself. All this, however, was too late. The first step had been taken. Mistress, in teaching me the alphabet, had given me the *inch*, and no precaution could prevent me from taking the *ell*.

The plan which I adopted, and the one by which I was most successful, was that of making friends of all the little white boys whom I met in the street. As many of these as I could, I converted into teachers. With their kindly aid, obtained at different times and in different places, I finally succeeded in learning to read. When I was sent of errands, I always took my book with me, and by going one part of my errand quickly, I found time to get a lesson before my return. I used also to carry bread with me, enough of which was always in the house, and to which I was always welcome; for I was much better off in this regard than many of the poor white children in our neighborhood. This bread I used to bestow upon the hungry little urchins, who, in return, would give me that more valuable bread of knowledge. I am strongly tempted to give the names of two or three of those little boys, as a testimonial of the gratitude and affection I bear them; but prudence forbids;—not that it would injure me, but it might embarrass them; for it is almost an unpardonable offense to teach slaves to read in this Christian country. It is enough to say of the dear little fellows, that they lived on Philpot Street, very near Durgin and Bailey's ship-yard. I used to talk this matter of slavery over with them. I would sometimes say to them, I wished I could be as free as they would be when they got to be men. "You will be free as soon as you are twenty-one, *but I am a slave for life!* Have not I as good a right to be free as you have?" These words used to trouble them; they would express for me the liveliest sympathy, and console me with the hope that something would occur by which I might be free.

I was now about twelve years old, and the thought of being *a slave for life* began to bear heavily upon my heart. Just about this time, I got hold of a book entitled "The Columbian Orator."[15] Every opportunity I got, I used to read this book. Among much of other interesting matter, I found in it a dialogue between a master and his slave. The slave was represented as having run away from his master three times. The dialogue represented the conversation which took place between them, when the slave was re-taken the third time. In this dialogue, the whole argument in behalf of slavery was brought forward by the master, all of which was disposed of by the slave. The slave was made to say some very smart as well as impressive things in reply to his master—things which had the desired though unex-

[15] *The Columbian Orator,* edited by Caleb Bingham, was a popular 1807 anthology of poems, plays, and speeches.

pected effect; for the conversation resulted in the voluntary emancipation of the slave on the part of the master.

In the same book, I met with one of Sheridan's[16] mighty speeches on and in behalf of Catholic emancipation. These were choice documents to me. I read them over and over again with unabated interest. They gave tongue to interesting thoughts of my own soul, which had frequently flashed through my mind, and died away for want of utterance. The moral which I gained from the dialogue was the power of truth over the conscience of even a slaveholder. What I got from Sheridan was a bold denunciation of slavery, and a powerful vindication of human rights. The reading of these documents enabled me to utter my thoughts, and to meet the arguments brought forward to sustain slavery; but while they relieved me of one difficulty, they brought on another even more painful than the one of which I was relieved. The more I read, the more I was led to abhor and detest my enslavers. I could regard them in no other light than a band of successful robbers, who had left their homes, and gone to Africa, and stolen us from our homes, and in a strange land reduced us to slavery. I loathed them as being the meanest as well as the most wicked of men. As I read and contemplated the subject, behold! that very discontentment which Master Hugh had predicted would follow my learning to read had already come, to torment and sting my soul to unutterable anguish. As I writhed under it, I would at times feel that learning to read had been a curse rather than a blessing. It had given me a view of my wretched condition, without the remedy. It opened my eyes to the horrible pit, but to no ladder upon which to get out. In moments of agony, I envied my fellow-slaves for their stupidity. I have often wished myself a beast. I preferred the condition of the meanest reptile to my own. Any thing, no matter what, to get rid of thinking! It was this everlasting thinking of my condition that tormented me. There was no getting rid of it. It was pressed upon me by every object within sight or hearing, animate or inanimate. The silver trump of freedom had roused my soul to eternal wakefulness. Freedom now appeared, to disappear no more forever. It was heard in every sound, and seen in every thing. It was ever present to torment me with a sense of my wretched condition. I saw nothing without seeing it, I heard nothing without hearing it, and felt nothing without feeling it. It looked from every star, it smiled in every calm, breathed in every wind, and moved in every storm.

I often found myself regretting my own existence, and wishing myself dead; and but for the hope of being free, I have no doubt but that I should have killed myself, or done something for which I should have been killed. While in this state of mind, I was eager to hear any one speak of slavery. I was a ready listener. Every little while, I could hear something about the abolitionists. It was some time before I found what the word meant. It was always used in such connections as to make it an interesting word to me. If a slave ran away and succeeded in getting clear, or if a slave killed his master, set fire to a barn, or did any thing very wrong in the mind of a

[16] Richard Brinsley Sheridan (1751–1816) was a noted Irish playwright and statesman. Author of *The Rivals* and *The School for Scandal*, he entered Parliament in 1780 and became noted as an orator.

slaveholder, it was spoken of as the fruit of *abolition.* Hearing the word in this connection very often, I set about learning what it meant. The dictionary afforded me little or no help. I found it was "the act of abolishing," but then I did not know what was to be abolished. Here I was perplexed. I did not dare to ask any one about its meaning, for I was satisfied that it was something they wanted me to know very little about. After a patient waiting, I got one of our city papers, containing an account of the number of petitions from the north, praying for the abolition of slavery in the District of Columbia, and of the slave trade between the States. From this time I understood the words *abolition* and *abolitionist,* and always drew near when that word was spoken, expecting to hear something of importance to myself and fellow-slaves. The light broke in upon me by degrees. I went one day down on the wharf of Mr. Waters; and seeing two Irishmen unloading a scow of stone, I went, unasked, and helped them. When we had finished, one of them came to me and asked me if I were a slave. I told him I was. He asked, "Are ye a slave for life?" I told him that I was. The good Irishman seemed to be deeply affected by the statement. He said to the other that it was a pity so fine a little fellow as myself should be a slave for life. He said it was a shame to hold me. They both advised me to run away to the north; that I should find friends there, and that I should be free. I pretended not to be interested in what they said, and treated them as if I did not understand them; for I feared they might be treacherous. White men have been known to encourage slaves to escape, and then, to get the reward, catch them and return them to their masters. I was afraid that these seemingly good men might use me so; but I nevertheless remembered their advice, and from that time I resolved to run away. I looked forward to a time at which it would be safe for me to escape. I was too young to think of doing so immediately; besides, I wished to learn how to write, as I might have occasion to write my own pass. I consoled myself with the hope that I should one day find a good chance. Meanwhile, I would learn to write.

The idea as to how I might learn to write was suggested to me by being in Durgin and Bailey's shipyard, and frequently seeing the ship carpenters, after hewing, and getting a piece of timber ready for use, write on the timber the name of that part of the ship for which it was intended. When a piece of timber was intended for the larboard side, it would be marked thus—"L." When a piece was for the starboard side, it would be marked thus—"S." A piece for the larboard side forward, would be marked thus—"L. F." When a piece was for starboard side forward, it would be marked thus—"S. F." For larboard aft, it would be marked thus—"L. A." For starboard aft, it would be marked thus—"S. A." I soon learned the names of these letters, and for what they were intended when placed upon a piece of timber in the ship-yard. I immediately commenced copying them, and in a short time was able to make the four letters named. After that, when I met with any boy who I knew could write, I would tell him I could write as well as he. The next word would be, "I don't believe you. Let me see you try it." I would then make the letters which I had been so fortunate as to learn, and ask him to beat that. In this way I got a good many lessons in writing, which it is quite possible I should never have gotten in any other way. During this time, my copy-book was the board fence, brick wall, and pavement; my pen and ink was a lump of chalk. With these, I learned mainly

how to write. I then commenced and continued copying the Italics in Web-
ster's Spelling Book, until I could make them all without looking on the
book. By this time, my little Master Thomas had gone to school, and
learned how to write, and had written over a number of copy-books. These
had been brought home, and shown to some of our near neighbors, and
then laid aside. My mistress used to go to class meeting at the Wilk Street
meeting-house every Monday afternoon, and leave me to take care of the
house. When left thus, I used to spend the time in writing in the spaces left
in master Thomas's copy-book, copying what he had written. I continued
to do this until I could write a hand very similar to that of Master Thomas.
Thus, after a long, tedious effort for years, I finally succeeded in learning
how to write.

CHAPTER VIII.

In a very short time after I went to live at Baltimore, my old master's
youngest son Richard died; and in about three years and six months after
his death, my old master, Captain Anthony, died, leaving only his son,
Andrew, and daughter, Lucretia, to share his estate. He died while on a
visit to see his daughter at Hillsborough. Cut off thus unexpectedly, he left
no will as to the disposal of his property. It was therefore necessary to have
a valuation of the property, that it might be equally divided between Mrs.
Lucretia and Master Andrew. I was immediately sent for, to be valued with
the other property. Here again my feelings rose up in detestation of slav-
ery. I had now a new conception of my degraded condition. Prior to this, I
had become, if not insensible to my lot, at least partly so. I left Baltimore
with a young heart overborne with sadness, and a soul full of apprehen-
sion. I took passage with Captain Rowe, in the schooner Wild Cat, and,
after a sail of about twenty-four hours, I found myself near the place of my
birth. I had now been absent from it almost, if not quite, five years. I,
however, remembered the place very well. I was only about five years old
when I left it, to go and live with my old master on Colonel Lloyd's planta-
tion; so that I was now between ten and eleven years old.
 We were all ranked together at the valuation. Men and women, old and
young, married and single, were ranked with horses, sheep, and swine.
There were horses and men, cattle and women, pigs and children, all hold-
ing the same rank in the scale of being, and were all subjected to the same
narrow examination. Silvery-headed age and sprightly youth, maids and
matrons, had to undergo the same indelicate inspection. At this moment, I
saw more clearly than ever the brutalizing effects of slavery upon both slave
and slaveholder.
 After the valuation, then came the division. I have no language to ex-
press the high excitement and deep anxiety which were felt among us poor
slaves during this time. Our fate for life was now to be decided. We had no
more voice in that decision than the brutes among whom we were ranked.
A single word from the white men was enough—against all our wishes,
prayers, and entreaties—to sunder forever the dearest friends, dearest kin-
dred, and strongest ties known to human beings. In addition to the pain of

separation, there was the horrid dread of falling into the hands of Master Andrew. He was known to us all as being a most cruel wretch,—a common drunkard, who had, by his reckless mismanagement and profligate dissipation, already wasted a large portion of his father's property. We all felt that we might as well be sold at once to the Georgia traders, as to pass into his hands; for we knew that that would be our inevitable condition,—a condition held by us all in the utmost horror and dread.

I suffered more anxiety than most of my fellow-slaves. I had known what it was to be kindly treated; they had known nothing of the kind. They had seen little or nothing of the world. They were in very deed men and women of sorrow, and acquainted with grief.[17] Their backs had been made familiar with the bloody lash, so that they had become callous; mine was yet tender; for while at Baltimore I got few whippings, and few slaves could boast of a kinder master and mistress than myself; and the thought of passing out of their hands into those of Master Andrew—a man who, but a few days before, to give me a sample of his bloody disposition, took my little brother by the throat, threw him on the ground, and with the heel of his boot stamped upon his head till the blood gushed from his nose and ears— was well calculated to make me anxious as to my fate. After he had committed this savage outrage upon my brother, he turned to me, and said that was the way he meant to serve me one of these days,—meaning, I suppose, when I came into his possession.

Thanks to a kind Providence, I fell to the portion of Mrs. Lucretia, and was sent immediately back to Baltimore, to live again in the family of Master Hugh. Their joy at my return equalled their sorrow at my departure. It was a glad day to me. I had escaped a worse than lion's jaws. I was absent from Baltimore, for the purpose of valuation and division, just about one month, and it seemed to have been six.

Very soon after my return to Baltimore, my mistress, Lucretia, died, leaving her husband and one child, Amanda; and in a very short time after her death, Master Andrew died. Now all the property of my old master, slaves included, was in the hands of strangers,—strangers who had had nothing to do with accumulating it. Not a slave was left free. All remained slaves, from the youngest to the oldest. If any one thing in my experience, more than another, served to deepen my conviction of the infernal character of slavery, and to fill me with unutterable loathing of slaveholders, it was their base ingratitude to my poor old grandmother. She had served my old master faithfully from youth to old age. She had been the source of all his wealth; she had peopled his plantation with slaves; she had become a great grandmother in his service. She had rocked him in infancy, attended him in childhood, served him through life, and at his death wiped from his icy brow the cold death-sweat, and closed his eyes forever. She was nevertheless left a slave—a slave for life—a slave in the hands of strangers; and in their hands she saw her children, her grandchildren, and her great-grandchildren, divided, like so many sheep, without being gratified with the small privilege of a single word, as to their or her own destiny. And, to cap the climax of their base ingratitude and fiendish barbarity, my grand-

[17] Isaiah 53:3: The servant of the Lord is "despised and rejected of men; a man of sorrows, and acquainted with grief."

mother, who was now very old, having outlived my old master and all his
children, having seen the beginning and end of all of them, and her pres-
ent owners finding she was of but little value, her frame already racked
with the pains of old age, and complete helplessness fast stealing over her
once active limbs, they took her to the woods, built her a little hut, put up a
little mud-chimney, and then made her welcome to the privilege of sup-
porting herself there in perfect loneliness; thus virtually turning her out to
die! If my poor old grandmother now lives, she lives to suffer in utter
loneliness; she lives to remember and mourn over the loss of children, the
loss of grandchildren, and the loss of great-grandchildren. They are, in the
language of the slave's poet, Whittier,—

> Gone, gone, sold and gone
> To the rice swamp dank and lone,
> Where the slave-whip ceaseless swings,
> Where the noisome insect stings,
> Where the fever-demon strews
> Poison with the falling dews,
> Where the sickly sunbeams glare
> Through the hot and misty air:—
> > Gone, gone, sold and gone
> > To the rice swamp dank and lone,
> > From Virginia hills and waters—
> > Woe is me, my stolen daughters![18]

The hearth is desolate. The children, the unconscious children, who
once sang and danced in her presence, are gone. She gropes her way, in the
darkness of age, for a drink of water. Instead of the voices of her children,
she hears by day the moans of the dove, and by night the screams of the
hideous owl. All is gloom. The grave is at the door. And now, when
weighed down by the pains and aches of old age, when the head inclines to
the feet, when the beginning and ending of human existence meet, and
helpless infancy and painful old age combine together—at this time, this
most needful time, the time for the exercise of that tenderness and affec-
tion which children only can exercise towards a declining parent—my poor
old grandmother, the devoted mother of twelve children, is left all alone, in
yonder little hut, before a few dim embers. She stands—she sits—she stag-
gers—she falls—she groans—she dies—and there are none of her chil-
dren or grandchildren present, to wipe from her wrinkled brow the cold
sweat of death, or to place beneath the sod her fallen remains. Will not a
righteous God visit for these things?

In about two years after the death of Mrs. Lucretia, Master Thomas
married his second wife. Her name was Rowena Hamilton. She was the
eldest daughter of Mr. William Hamilton. Master now lived in St. Mi-
chael's. Not long after his marriage, a misunderstanding took place be-
tween himself and Master Hugh; and as a means of punishing his brother,
he took me from him to live with himself at St. Michael's. Here I underwent

[18] John Greenleaf Whittier, "The Farewell of a Virginia Slave Mother to her Daughters
Sold into Southern Bondage" (1838).

another most painful separation. It, however, was not so severe as the one I dreaded at the division of property; for, during this interval, a great change had taken place in Master Hugh and his once kind and affectionate wife. The influence of brandy upon him, and of slavery upon her, had effected a disastrous change in the characters of both; so that, as far as they were concerned, I thought I had little to lose by the change. But it was not to them that I was attached. It was to those little Baltimore boys that I felt the strongest attachment. I had received many good lessons from them, and was still receiving them, and the thought of leaving them was painful indeed. I was leaving, too, without the hope of ever being allowed to return. Master Thomas had said he would never let me return again. The barrier betwixt himself and brother he considered impassable.

I then had to regret that I did not at least make the attempt to carry out my resolution to run away; for the chances of success are tenfold greater from the city than from the country.

I sailed from Baltimore for St. Michael's in the sloop Amanda, Captain Edward Dodson. On my passage, I paid particular attention to the direction which the steamboats took to go to Philadelphia. I found, instead of going down, on reaching North Point they went up the bay, in a north-easterly direction. I deemed this knowledge of the utmost importance. My determination to run away was again revived. I resolved to wait only so long as the offering of a favorable opportunity. When that came, I was determined to be off.

CHAPTER IX.

I have now reached a period of my life when I can give dates. I left Baltimore, and went to live with Master Thomas Auld, at St. Michael's, in March, 1832. It was now more than seven years since I lived with him in the family of my old master, on Colonel Lloyd's plantation. We of course were now almost entire strangers to each other. He was to me a new master, and I to him a new slave. I was ignorant of his temper and disposition; he was equally so of mine. A very short time, however, brought us into full acquaintance with each other. I was made acquainted with his wife not less than with himself. They were well matched, being equally mean and cruel. I was now, for the first time during a space of more than seven years, made to feel the painful gnawings of hunger—a something which I had not experienced before since I left Colonel Lloyd's plantation. It went hard enough with me then, when I could look back to no period at which I had enjoyed a sufficiency. It was tenfold harder after living in Master Hugh's family, where I had always had enough to eat, and of that which was good. I have said Master Thomas was a mean man. He was so. Not to give a slave enough to eat, is regarded as the most aggravated development of meanness even among slaveholders. The rule is, no matter how coarse the food, only let there be enough of it. This is the theory; and in the part of Maryland from which I came, it is the general practice,—though there are many exceptions. Master Thomas gave us enough of neither coarse nor fine food. There were four slaves of us in the kitchen—my sister Eliza, my aunt

Priscilla, Henny, and myself; and we were allowed less than a half of a bushel of corn-meal per week, and very little else, either in the shape of meat or vegetables. It was not enough for us to subsist upon. We were therefore reduced to the wretched necessity of living at the expense of our neighbors. This we did by begging and stealing, whichever came handy in the time of need, the one being considered as legitimate as the other. A great many times have we poor creatures been nearly perishing with hunger, when food in abundance lay mouldering in the safe and smoke-house,[19] and our pious mistress was aware of the fact; and yet that mistress and her husband would kneel every morning, and pray that God would bless them in basket and store!

Bad as all slaveholders are, we seldom meet one destitute of every element of character commanding respect. My master was one of this rare sort. I do not know of one single noble act ever performed by him. The leading trait in his character was meanness; and if there were any other element in his nature, it was made subject to this. He was mean; and, like most other mean men, he lacked the ability to conceal his meanness. Captain Auld was not born a slaveholder. He had been a poor man, master only of a Bay craft. He came into possession of all his slaves by marriage; and of all men, adopted slaveholders are the worst. He was cruel, but cowardly. He commanded without firmness. In the enforcement of his rules, he was at times rigid, and at times lax. At times, he spoke to his slaves with the firmness of Napoleon and the fury of a demon; at other times, he might well be mistaken for an inquirer who had lost his way. He did nothing of himself. He might have passed for a lion, but for his ears.[20] In all things noble which he attempted, his own meanness shone most conspicuous. His airs, words, and actions, were the airs, words, and actions of born slaveholders, and, being assumed, were awkward enough. He was not even a good imitator. He possessed all the disposition to deceive, but wanted the power. Having no resources within himself, he was compelled to be the copyist of many, and being such, he was forever the victim of inconsistency; and of consequence he was an object of contempt, and was held as such even by his slaves. The luxury of having slaves of his own to wait upon him was something new and unprepared for. He was a slaveholder without the ability to hold slaves. He found himself incapable of managing his slaves either by force, fear, or fraud. We seldom called him "master;" we generally called him "Captain Auld," and were hardly disposed to title him at all. I doubt not that our conduct had much to do with making him appear awkward, and of consequence fretful. Our want of reverence for him must have perplexed him greatly. He wished to have us call him master, but lacked the firmness necessary to command us to do so. His wife used to insist upon our calling him so, but to no purpose. In August, 1832, my master attended a Methodist camp-meeting held in the Bay-side, Talbot county, and there experienced religion. I indulged a faint hope that his conversion would lead him to emancipate his slaves, and that, if he did not

[19] A meat safe was a cabinet used to store food; a smokehouse is used both to cure and to store pork.

[20] Apparently a reference to Aesop's fable "The Fox and the Ass," in which an ass disguises himself in a lion's skin. A fox tells him, "If you had held your tongue I might have taken you for a lion, but now that you bray, I know who you are."

do this, it would, at any rate, make him more kind and humane. I was disappointed in both these respects. It neither made him to be humane to his slaves, nor to emancipate them. If it had any effect on his character, it made him more cruel and hateful in all his ways; for I believe him to have been a much worse man after his conversion than before. Prior to his conversion, he relied upon his own depravity to shield and sustain him in his savage barbarity; but after his conversion, he found religious sanction and support for his slaveholding cruelty. He made the greatest pretensions to piety. His house was the house of prayer. He prayed morning, noon, and night. He very soon distinguished himself among his brethren, and was soon made a class-leader and exhorter. His activity in revivals was great, and he proved himself an instrument in the hands of the church in converting many souls. His house was the preachers' home. They used to take great pleasure in coming there to put up; for while he starved us, he stuffed them. We have had three or four preachers there at a time. The names of those who used to come most frequently while I lived there, were Mr. Storks, Mr. Ewery, Mr. Humphry, and Mr. Hickey. I have also seen Mr. George Cookman at our house. We slaves loved Mr. Cookman. We believed him to be a good man. We thought him instrumental in getting Mr. Samuel Harrison, a very rich slaveholder, to emancipate his slaves; and by some means got the impression that he was laboring to effect the emancipation of all the slaves. When he was at our house, we were sure to be called in to prayers. When the others were there, we were sometimes called in and sometimes not. Mr. Cookman took more notice of us than either of the other ministers. He could not come among us without betraying his sympathy for us, and, stupid as we were, we had the sagacity to see it.

While I lived with my master in St. Michael's, there was a white young man, a Mr. Wilson, who proposed to keep a Sabbath school for the instruction of such slaves as might be disposed to learn to read the New Testament. We met but three times, when Mr. West and Mr. Fairbanks, both class-leaders, with many others, came upon us with sticks and other missiles, drove us off, and forbade us to meet again. Thus ended our little Sabbath school in the pious town of St. Michael's.

I have said my master found religious sanction for his cruelty. As an example, I will state one of many facts going to prove the charge. I have seen him tie up a lame young woman, and whip her with a heavy cowskin upon her naked shoulders, causing the warm red blood to drip; and, in justification of the bloody deed, he would quote this passage of Scripture— "He that knoweth his master's will, and doeth it not, shall be beaten with many stripes."[21]

Master would keep this lacerated young woman tied up in this horrid situation four or five hours at a time. I have known him to tie her up early in the morning, and whip her before breakfast; leave her, go to his store, return at dinner, and whip her again, cutting her in the places already made raw with his cruel lash. The secret of master's cruelty toward "Henny" is found in the fact of her being almost helpless. When quite a child, she fell into the fire, and burned herself horribly. Her hands were so

[21]Luke 12:47. The passage has nothing to do with slavery but appears in one of Jesus' parables about the relationship between God and humanity.

burnt that she never got the use of them. She could do very little but bear heavy burdens. She was to master a bill of expense; and as he was a mean man, she was a constant offense to him. He seemed desirous of getting the poor girl out of existence. He gave her away once to his sister; but, being a poor gift, she was not disposed to keep her. Finally, my benevolent master, to use his own words, "set her adrift to take care of herself." Here was a recently-converted man, holding on upon the mother, and at the same time turning out her helpless child, to starve and die! Master Thomas was one of the many pious slaveholders who hold slaves for the very charitable purpose of taking care of them.

My master and myself had quite a number of differences. He found me unsuitable to his purpose. My city life, he said, had had a very pernicious effect upon me. It had almost ruined me for every good purpose, and fitted me for every thing which was bad. One of my greatest faults was that of letting his horse run away, and go down to his father-in-law's farm, which was about five miles from St. Michael's. I would then have to go after it. My reason for this kind of carelessness, or carefulness, was, that I could always get something to eat when I went there. Master William Hamilton, my master's father-in-law, always gave his slaves enough to eat. I never left there hungry, no matter how great the need of my speedy return. Master Thomas at length said he would stand it no longer. I had lived with him nine months, during which time he had given me a number of severe whippings, all to no good purpose. He resolved to put me out, as he said, to be broken; and, for this purpose, he let me for one year to a man named Edward Covey. Mr. Covey was a poor man, a farm-renter. He rented the place upon which he lived, as also the hands with which he tilled it. Mr. Covey had acquired a very high reputation for breaking young slaves, and this reputation was of immense value to him. It enabled him to get his farm tilled with much less expense to himself than he could have had it done without such a reputation. Some slaveholders thought it not much loss to allow Mr. Covey to have their slaves one year, for the sake of the training to which they were subjected, without any other compensation. He could hire young help with great ease, in consequence of this reputation. Added to the natural good qualities of Mr. Covey, he was a professor of religion—a pious soul—a member and a class-leader in the Methodist church. All of this added weight to his reputation as a "nigger-breaker." I was aware of all the facts, having been acquainted with them by a young man who had lived there. I nevertheless made the change gladly; for I was sure of getting enough to eat, which is not the smallest consideration to a hungry man.

CHAPTER X.

I left Master Thomas's house, and went to live with Mr. Covey, on the 1st of January, 1833. I was now, for the first time in my life, a field hand. In my new employment, I found myself even more awkward than a country boy appeared to be in a large city. I had been at my new home but one week before Mr. Covey gave me a very severe whipping, cutting my back, causing the blood to run, and raising ridges on my flesh as large as my little

finger. The details of this affair are as follows: Mr. Covey sent me, very early in the morning of one of our coldest days in the month of January, to the woods, to get a load of wood. He gave me a team of unbroken oxen. He told me which was the in-hand ox, and which the off-hand one.[22] He then tied the end of a large rope around the horns of the in-hand ox, and gave me the other end if it, and told me, if the oxen started to run, that I must hold on upon the rope. I had never driven oxen before, and of course I was very awkward. I, however, succeeded in getting to the edge of the woods with little difficulty; but I had got a very few rods into the woods, when the oxen took fright, and started full tilt, carrying the cart against trees, and over stumps, in the most frightful manner. I expected every moment that my brains would be dashed out against the trees. After running thus for a considerable distance, they finally upset the cart, dashing it with great force against a tree, and threw themselves into a dense thicket. How I escaped death, I do not know. There I was, entirely alone, in a thick wood, in a place new to me. My cart was upset and shattered; my oxen were entangled among the young trees, and there was none to help me. After a long spell of effort, I succeeded in getting my cart righted, my oxen disentangled, and again yoked to the cart. I now proceeded with my team to the place where I had, the day before, been chopping wood, and loaded my cart pretty heavily, thinking in this way to tame my oxen. I then proceeded on my way home. I had now consumed one half of the day. I got out of the woods safely, and now felt out of danger. I stopped my oxen to open the woods gate; and just as I did so, before I could get hold of my ox-rope, the oxen again started, rushed through the gate, catching it between the wheel and the body of the cart, tearing it to pieces, and coming within a few inches of crushing me against the gate-post. Thus twice, in one short day, I escaped death by the merest chance. On my return, I told Mr. Covey what had happened, and how it happened. He ordered me to return to the woods again immediately. I did so, and he followed in after me. Just as I got into the woods, he came up and told me to stop my cart, and that he would teach me how to trifle away my time, and break gates. He then went to a large gum tree, and with his axe cut three large switches, and, after trimming them up neatly with his pocket-knife, he ordered me to take off my clothes. I made him no answer, but stood with my clothes on. He repeated his order. I still made him no answer, nor did I move to strip myself. Upon this he rushed at me with the fierceness of a tiger, tore off my clothes, and lashed me till he had worn out his switches, cutting me so savagely as to leave the marks visible for a long time after. This whipping was the first of a number just like it, and for similar offenses.

I lived with Mr. Covey one year. During the first six months, of that year, scarce a week passed without his whipping me. I was seldom free from a sore back. My awkwardness was almost always his excuse for whipping me. We were worked fully up to the point of endurance. Long before day we were up, our horses fed, and by the first approach of day we were off to the field with our hoes and ploughing teams. Mr. Covey gave us enough to eat, but scarce time to eat it. We were often less than five minutes taking our meals. We were often in the field from the first approach of day

[22] The in-hand ox is on the left in a team, the off-hand one on the right.

till its last lingering ray had left us; and at saving-fodder time, midnight often caught us in the field binding blades.[23]

Covey would be out with us. The way he used to stand it, was this. He would spend the most of his afternoons in bed. He would then come out fresh in the evening, ready to urge us on with his words, example, and frequently with the whip. Mr. Covey was one of the few slaveholders who could and did work with his hands. He was a hard-working man. He knew by himself just what a man or a boy could do. There was no deceiving him. His work went on in his absence almost as well as in his presence; and he had the faculty of making us feel that he was ever present with us. This he did by surprising us. He seldom approached the spot where we were at work openly, if he could do it secretly. He always aimed at taking us by surprise. Such was his cunning, that we used to call him, among ourselves, "the snake." When we were at work in the cornfield, he would sometimes crawl on his hands and knees to avoid detection, and all at once he would rise nearly in our midst, and scream out, "Ha, ha! Come, come! Dash on, dash on!" This being his mode of attack, it was never safe to stop a single minute. His comings were like a thief in the night. He appeared to us as being ever at hand. He was under every tree, behind every stump, in every bush, and at every window, on the plantation. He would sometimes mount his horse, as if bound to St. Michael's, a distance of seven miles, and in half an hour afterwards you would see him coiled up in the corner of the wood-fence, watching every motion of the slaves. He would, for this purpose, leave his horse tied up in the woods. Again, he would sometimes walk up to us, and give us orders as though he was upon the point of starting on a long journey, turn his back upon us, and make as though he was going to the house to get ready; and, before he would get half way thither, he would turn short and crawl into a fence-corner, or behind some tree, and there watch us till the going down of the sun.

Mr. Covey's *forte* consisted in his power to deceive. His life was devoted to planning and perpetrating the grossest deceptions. Every thing he possessed in the shape of learning or religion, he made conform to his disposition to deceive. He seemed to think himself equal to deceiving the Almighty. He would make a short prayer in the morning, and a long prayer at night; and, strange as it may seem, few men would at times appear more devotional than he. The exercises of his family devotions were always commenced with singing; and, as he was a very poor singer himself, the duty of raising the hymn generally came upon me. He would read his hymn, and nod at me to commence. I would at times do so; at others, I would not. My non-compliance would almost always produce much confusion. To show himself independent of me, he would start and stagger through with his hymn in the most discordant manner. In this state of mind, he prayed with more than ordinary spirit. Poor man! such was his disposition, and success at deceiving, I do verily believe that he sometimes deceived himself into the solemn belief, that he was a sincere worshipper of the most high God; and this, too, at a time when he may be said to have been guilty of compelling his woman slave to commit the sin of adultery. The facts in the case are

[23] "Saving-fodder time" is the fall corn harvest; "binding blades" is tying up sheaves of cornstalks and leaves to feed to stock.

these: Mr. Covey was a poor man; he was just commencing in life; he was only able to buy one slave; and, shocking as is the fact, he bought her, as he said, for *a breeder*. This woman was named Caroline. Mr. Covey bought her from Mr. Thomas Lowe, about six miles from St. Michael's. She was a large, able-bodied woman, about twenty years old. She had already given birth to one child, which proved her to be just what he wanted. After buying her, he hired a married man of Mr. Samuel Harrison, to live with him one year; and him he used to fasten up with her every night! The result was, that, at the end of the year, the miserable woman gave birth to twins. At this result Mr. Covey seemed to be highly pleased, both with the man and the wretched woman. Such was his joy, and that of his wife, that nothing they could do for Caroline during her confinement was too good, or too hard, to be done. The children were regarded as being quite an addition to his wealth.

If at any one time of my life more than another, I was made to drink the bitterest dregs of slavery, that time was during the first six months of my stay with Mr. Covey. We were worked in all weathers. It was never too hot or too cold; it could never rain, blow, hail, or snow, too hard for us to work in the field. Work, work, work, was scarcely more the order of the day than of the night. The longest days were too short for him, and the shortest nights too long for him. I was somewhat unmanageable when I first went there, but a few months of this discipline tamed me. Mr. Covey succeeded in breaking me: I was broken in body, soul, and spirit. My natural elasticity was crushed, my intellect languished, the disposition to read departed, the cheerful spark that lingered about my eye died; the dark night of slavery closed in upon me; and behold a man transformed into a brute!

Sunday was my only leisure time. I spent this in a sort of beast-like stupor, between sleep and wake, under some large tree. At times I would rise up, a flash of energetic freedom would dart through my soul, accompanied with a faint beam of hope, that flickered for a moment, and then vanished. I sank down again, mourning over my wretched condition. I was sometimes prompted to take my life, and that of Covey, but was prevented by a combination of hope and fear. My sufferings on this plantation seem now like a dream rather than a stern reality.

Our house stood within a few rods of the Chesapeake Bay, whose broad bosom was ever white with sails from every quarter of the habitable globe. Those beautiful vessels, robed in purest white, so delightful to the eye of freemen, were to me so many shrouded ghosts, to terrify and torment me with thoughts of my wretched condition. I have often, in the deep stillness of a summer's Sabbath, stood all alone upon the lofty banks of that noble bay, and traced, with saddened heart and tearful eye, the countless number of sails moving off to the mighty ocean. The sight of these always affected me powerfully. My thoughts would compel utterance; and there, with no audience but the Almighty, I would pour out my soul's complaint, in my rude way, with an apostrophe to the moving multitude of ships:—

"You are loosed from your moorings, and are free; I am fast in my chains, and am a slave! You move merrily before the gentle gale, and I sadly before the bloody whip! You are freedom's swift-winged angels, that fly around the world; I am confined in bands of iron! O that I were free! O, that I were on one of your gallant decks, and under your protecting wing!

Alas! betwixt me and you, the turbid waters roll. Go on, go on. O that I could also go! Could I but swim! If I could fly! O, why was I born a man, of whom to make a brute! The glad ship is gone; she hides in the dim distance. I am left in the hottest hell of unending slavery. O God, save me! God, deliver me! Let me be free! Is there any God? Why am I a slave? I will run away. I will not stand it. Get caught, or get clear, I'll try it. I had as well die with ague as the fever. I have only one life to lose. I had as well be killed running as die standing. Only think if it; one hundred miles straight north, and I am free! Try it? Yes! God helping me, I will. It cannot be that I shall live and die a slave. I will take to the water. This very bay shall yet bear me into freedom. The steamboats steered in a north-east course from North Point. I will do the same; and when I get to the head of the bay, I will turn my canoe adrift, and walk straight through Delaware into Pennsylvania. When I get there, I shall not be required to have a pass; I can travel without being disturbed. Let but the first opportunity offer, and, come what will, I am off. Meanwhile, I will try to bear up under the yoke. I am not the only slave in the world. Why should I fret? I can bear as much as any of them. Besides, I am but a boy, and all boys are bound to some one. It may be that my misery in slavery will only increase my happiness when I get free. There is a better day coming."

Thus I used to think, and thus I used to speak to myself; goaded almost to madness at one moment, and at the next reconciling myself to my wretched lot.

I have already intimated that my condition was much worse, during the first six months of my stay at Mr. Covey's, than in the last six. The circumstances leading to the change in Mr. Covey's course toward me form an epoch in my humble history. You have seen how a man was made a slave; you shall see how a slave was made a man. On one of the hottest days of the month of August, 1833, Bill Smith, William Hughes, a slave named Eli, and myself, were engaged in fanning wheat.[24] Hughes was clearing the fanned wheat from before the fan, Eli was turning, Smith was feeding, and I was carrying wheat to the fan. The work was simple, requiring strength rather than intellect; yet, to one entirely unused to such work, it came very hard. About three o'clock of that day, I broke down; my strength failed me; I was seized with a violent aching of the head, attended with extreme dizziness; I trembled in every limb. Finding what was coming, I nerved myself up, feeling it would never do to stop work. I stood as long as I could stagger to the hopper with grain. When I could stand no longer, I fell, and felt as if held down by an immense weight. The fan of course stopped; every one had his own work to do; and no one could do the work of the other, and have his own go on at the same time.

Mr. Covey was at the house, about one hundred yards from the treading-yard where we were fanning. On hearing the fan stop, he left immediately, and came to the spot where we were. He hastily inquired what the matter was. Bill answered that I was sick, and there was no one to bring wheat to the fan. I had by this time crawled away under the side of the post and rail-fence by which the yard was enclosed, hoping to find relief by getting out of the sun. He then asked where I was. He was told by one of

[24] A method of separating the seed from the straw by means of a fan operated by a crank.

the hands. He came to the spot, and, after looking at me awhile, asked me what was the matter. I told him as well as I could, for I scarce had strength to speak. He then gave me a savage kick in the side, and told me to get up. I tried to do so, but fell back in the attempt. He gave me another kick, and again told me to rise. I again tried, and succeeded in gaining my feet; but, stooping to get the tub with which I was feeding the fan, I again staggered and fell. While down in this situation, Mr. Covey took up the hickory slat with which Hughes had been striking off the half-bushel measure, and with it gave me a heavy blow upon the head, making a large wound, and the blood ran freely; and with this again told me to get up. I made no effort to comply, having now make up my mind to let him do his worst. In a short time after receiving this blow, my head grew better. Mr. Covey had now left me to my fate. At this moment I resolved, for the first time, to go to my master, enter a complaint, and ask his protection. In order to do this, I must that afternoon walk seven miles; and this, under the circumstances, was truly a severe undertaking. I was exceedingly feeble; made so as much by the kicks and blows which I received, as by the severe fit of sickness to which I had been subjected. I, however, watched my chance, while Covey was looking in an opposite direction, and started for St. Michael's. I succeeded in getting a considerable distance on my way to the woods, when Covey discovered me, and called after me to come back, threatening what he would do if I did not come. I disregarded both his calls and his threats, and made my way to the woods as fast as my feeble state would allow; and thinking I might be overhauled by him if I kept the road, I walked through the woods, keeping far enough from the road to avoid detection, and near enough to prevent losing my way. I had not gone far before my little strength again failed me. I could go no farther. I fell down, and lay for a considerable time. The blood was yet oozing from the wound on my head. For a time I thought I should bleed to death; and think now that I should have done so, but that the blood so matted my hair as to stop the wound. After lying there about three quarters of an hour, I nerved myself up again, and started on my way, through bogs and briers, barefooted and bareheaded, tearing my feet sometimes at nearly every step; and after a journey of about seven miles, occupying some five hours to perform it, I arrived at master's store. I then presented an appearance enough to affect any but a heart of iron. From the crown of my head to my feet, I was covered with blood. My hair was all clotted with dust and blood; my shirt was stiff with blood. My legs and feet were torn in sundry places with briers and thorns, and were also covered with blood. I suppose I looked like a man who had escaped a den of wild beasts, and barely escaped them. In this state I appeared before my master, humbly entreating him to interpose his authority for my protection. I told him all the circumstances as well as I could, and it seemed, as I spoke, at times to affect him. He would then walk the floor, and seek to justify Covey by saying he expected I deserved it. He asked me what I wanted. I told him, to let me get a new home; that as sure as I lived with Mr. Covey again, I should live with but to die with him; that Covey would surely kill me; he was in a fair way for it. Master Thomas ridiculed the idea that there was any danger of Mr. Covey's killing me, and said that he knew Mr. Covey; that he was a good man, and that he could not think of taking me from him; that, should he do so, he would lose the

whole year's wages; that I belonged to Mr. Covey for one year, and that I must go back to him, come what might; and that I must not trouble him with any more stories, or that he would himself *get hold of me*. After threatening me thus, he gave me a very large dose of salts, telling me that I might remain in St. Michael's that night, (it being quite late,) but that I must be off back to Mr. Covey's early in the morning; and that if I did not, he would *get hold of me*, which meant that he would whip me. I remained all night, and, according to his orders, I started off to Covey's in the morning, (Saturday morning,) wearied in body and broken in spirit. I got no supper that night, or breakfast that morning. I reached Covey's about nine o'clock; and just as I was getting over the fence that divided Mrs. Kemp's fields from ours, out ran Covey with his cowskin, to give me another whipping. Before he could reach me, I succeeded in getting to the cornfield; and as the corn was very high, it afforded me the means of hiding. He seemed very angry, and searched for me a long time. My behavior was altogether unaccountable. He finally gave up the chase, thinking, I suppose, that I must come home for something to eat; he would give himself no further trouble in looking for me. I spent that day mostly in the woods, having the alternative before me,—to go home and be whipped to death, or stay in the woods and be starved to death. That night, I fell in with Sandy Jenkins, a slave with whom I was somewhat acquainted. Sandy had a free wife who lived about four miles from Mr. Covey's; and it being Saturday, he was on his way to see her. I told him my circumstances, and he very kindly invited me to go home with him. I went home with him, and talked this whole matter over, and got his advice as to what course it was best for me to pursue. I found Sandy an old adviser. He told me, with great solemnity, I must go back to Covey; but that before I went, I must go with him into another part of the woods, where there was a certain *root*, which, if I would take some of it with me, carrying it *always on my right side*, would render it impossible for Mr. Covey, or any other white man, to whip me. He said he had carried it for years; and since he had done so, he had never received a blow, and never expected to while he carried it. I at first rejected the idea, that the simple carrying of a root in my pocket would have any such effect as he had said, and was not disposed to take it; but Sandy impressed the necessity with much earnestness, telling me it could do no harm, if it did no good. To please him, I at length took the root, and, according to his direction, carried it upon my right side. This was Sunday morning. I immediately started for home; and upon entering the yard gate, out came Mr. Covey on his way to meeting. He spoke to me very kindly, bade me drive the pigs from a lot near by, and passed on towards the church. Now, this singular conduct of Mr. Covey really made me begin to think that there was something in the *root* which Sandy had given me; and had it been on any other day than Sunday, I could have attributed the conduct to no other cause than the influence of that root; and as it was, I was half inclined to think the *root* to be something more than I at first had taken it to be. All went well till Monday morning. On this morning, the virtue of the *root* was fully tested. Long before daylight, I was called to go and rub, curry, and feed, the horses. I obeyed, and was glad to obey. But whilst thus engaged, whilst in the act of throwing down some blades from the loft, Mr. Covey entered the

stable with a long rope; and just as I was half out of the loft, he caught hold of my legs, and was about tying me. As soon as I found what he was up to, I gave a sudden spring, and as I did so, he holding to my legs, I was brought sprawling on the stable floor. Mr. Covey seemed now to think he had me, and could do what he pleased; but at this moment—from whence came the spirit I don't know—I resolved to fight; and, suiting my action to the resolution, I seized Covey hard by the throat; and as I did so, I rose. He held on to me, and I to him. My resistance was so entirely unexpected, that Covey seemed taken all aback. He trembled like a leaf. This gave me assurance, and I held him uneasy, causing the blood to run where I touched him with the ends of my fingers. Mr. Covey soon called out to Hughes for help. Hughes came, and, while Covey held me, attempted to tie my right hand. While he was in the act of doing so, I watched my chance, and gave him a heavy kick close under the ribs. This kick fairly sickened Hughes, so that he left me in the hands of Mr. Covey. This kick had the effect of not only weakening Hughes, but Covey also. When he saw Hughes bending over with pain, his courage quailed. He asked me if I meant to persist in my resistance. I told him I did, come what might; that he had used me like a brute for six months, and that I was determined to be used so no longer. With that, he strove to drag me to a stick that was lying just out of the stable door. He meant to knock me down. But just as he was leaning over to get the stick, I seized him with both hands by his collar, and brought him by a sudden snatch to the ground. By this time, Bill came. Covey called upon him for assistance. Bill wanted to know what he could do. Covey said, "Take hold of him, take hold of him!" Bill said his master hired him out to work, and not to help to whip me; so he left Covey and myself to fight our own battle out. We were at it for nearly two hours. Covey at length let me go, puffing and blowing at a great rate, saying that if I had not resisted, he would not have whipped me half so much. The truth was, that he had not whipped me at all. I considered him as getting entirely the worst end of the bargain; for he had drawn no blood from me, but I had from him. The whole six months afterwards, that I spent with Mr. Covey, he never laid the weight of his finger upon me in anger. He would occasionally say, he didn't want to get hold of me again. "No," thought I, "you need not; for you will come off worse than you did before."

This battle with Mr. Covey was the turning-point in my career as a slave. It rekindled the few expiring embers of freedom, and revived within me a sense of my own manhood. It recalled the departed self-confidence, and inspired me again with a determination to be free. The gratification afforded by the triumph was a full compensation for whatever else might follow, even death itself. He only can understand the deep satisfaction which I experienced, who has himself repelled by force the bloody arm of slavery. I felt as I never felt before. It was a glorious resurrection, from the tomb of slavery, to the heaven of freedom. My long-crushed spirit rose, cowardice departed, bold defiance took its place; and I now resolved that, however long I might remain a slave in form, the day had passed forever when I could be a slave in fact. I did not hesitate to let it be known of me, that the white man who expected to succeed in whipping, must also succeed in killing me.

From this time I was never again what might be called fairly whipped, though I remained a slave four years afterwards. I had several fights, but was never whipped.

It was for a long time a matter of surprise to me why Mr. Covey did not immediately have me taken by the constable to the whipping-post, and there regularly whipped for the crime of raising my hand against a white man in defense of myself. And the only explanation I can now think of does not entirely satisfy me; but such as it is, I will give it. Mr. Covey enjoyed the most unbounded reputation for being a first-rate overseer and negro-breaker. It was of considerable importance to him. That reputation was at stake; and had he sent me—a boy about sixteen years old—to the public whipping-post, his reputation would have been lost; so, to save his reputation, he suffered me to go unpunished.

My term of actual service to Mr. Edward Covey ended on Christmas day, 1833. The days between Christmas and New Year's day are allowed as holidays; and, accordingly, we were not required to perform any labor, more than to feed and take care of the stock. This time we regarded as our own, by the grace of our masters; and we therefore used or abused it nearly as we pleased. Those of us who had families at a distance, were generally allowed to spend the whole six days in their society. This time, however, was spent in various ways. The staid, sober, thinking and industrious ones of our number would employ themselves in making corn-brooms, mats, horse-collars, and baskets; and another class of us would spend the time in hunting opossums, hares, and coons. But by far the larger part engaged in such sports and merriments as playing ball, wrestling, running foot-races, fiddling, dancing, and drinking whisky; and this latter mode of spending the time was by far the most agreeable to the feelings of our masters. A slave who would work during the holidays was considered by our masters as scarcely deserving them. He was regarded as one who rejected the favor of his master. It was deemed a disgrace not to get drunk at Christmas; and he was regarded as lazy indeed, who had not provided himself with the necessary means, during the year, to get whisky enough to last him through Christmas.

From what I know of the effect of these holidays upon the slave, I believe them to be among the most effective means in the hands of the slaveholder in keeping down the spirit of insurrection. Were the slaveholders at once to abandon this practice, I have not the slightest doubt it would lead to an immediate insurrection among the slaves. These holidays serve as conductors, or safety-valves, to carry off the rebellious spirit of enslaved humanity. But for these, the slave would be forced up to the wildest desperation; and woe betide the slaveholder, the day he ventures to remove or hinder the operation of those conductors! I warn him that, in such an event, a spirit will go forth in their midst, more to be dreaded than the most appalling earthquake.

The holidays are part and parcel of the gross fraud, wrong, and inhumanity of slavery. They are professedly a custom established by the benevolence of the slaveholders; but I undertake to say, it is the result of selfishness, and one of the grossest frauds committed upon the down-trodden slave. They do not give the slaves this time because they would not like to have their work during its continuance, but because they know it would be

unsafe to deprive them of it. This will be seen by the fact, that the slave-holders like to have their slaves spend those days just in such a manner as to make them as glad of their ending as of their beginning. Their object seems to be, to disgust their slaves with freedom, by plunging them into the lowest depths of dissipation. For instance, the slaveholders not only like to see the slave drink of his own accord, but will adopt various plans to make him drunk. One plan is, to make bets on their slaves, as to who can drink the most whisky without getting drunk; and in this way they succeed in getting whole multitudes to drink to excess. Thus, when the slave asks for virtuous freedom, the cunning slaveholder, knowing his ignorance, cheats him with a dose of vicious dissipation, artfully labelled with the name of liberty. The most of us used to drink it down, and the result was just what might be supposed: many of us were led to think that there was little to choose between liberty and slavery. We felt, and very properly too, that we had almost as well be slaves to man as to rum. So, when the holidays ended, we staggered up from the filth of our wallowing, took a long breath, and marched to the field,—feeling, upon the whole, rather glad to go, from what our master had deceived us into a belief was freedom, back to the arms of slavery.

I have said that this mode of treatment is a part of the whole system of fraud and inhumanity of slavery. It is so. The mode here adopted to dis-gust the slave with freedom, by allowing him to see only the abuse of it, is carried out in other things. For instance, a slave loves molasses; he steals some. His master, in many cases, goes off to town, and buys a large quan-tity; he returns, takes his whip, and commands the slave to eat the molasses, until the poor fellow is made sick at the very mention of it. The same mode is sometimes adopted to make the slaves refrain from asking for more food than their regular allowance. A slave runs through his allowance, and ap-plies for more. His master is enraged at him; but, not willing to send him off without food, gives him more than is necessary, and compels him to eat it within a given time. Then, if he complains that he cannot eat it, he is said to be satisfied neither full nor fasting, and is whipped for being hard to please! I have an abundance of such illustrations of the same principle, drawn from my own observation, but think the cases I have cited sufficient. The practice is a very common one.

On the first of January, 1834, I left Mr. Covey, and went to live with Mr. William Freeland, who lived about three miles from St. Michael's. I soon found Mr. Freeland a very different man from Mr. Covey. Though not rich, he was what would be called an educated southern gentleman. Mr. Covey, as I have shown, was a well-trained negro-breaker and slave-driver. The former (slaveholder though he was) seemed to possess some regard for honor, some reverence for justice, and some respect for humanity. The latter seemed totally insensible to all such sentiments. Mr. Freeland had many of the faults peculiar to slaveholders, such as being very passionate and fretful; but I must do him the justice to say, that he was exceedingly free from those degrading vices to which Mr. Covey was constantly ad-dicted. The one was open and frank, and we always knew where to find him. The other was a most artful deceiver, and could be understood only by such as were skillful enough to detect his cunningly-devised frauds. Another advantage I gained in my new master was, he made no preten-

sions to, or profession of, religion; and this, in my opinion, was truly a great advantage. I assert most unhesitatingly, that the religion of the south is a mere covering for the most horrid crimes,—a justifier of the most appalling barbarity,—a sanctifier of the most hateful frauds,—and a dark shelter under which the darkest, foulest, grossest, and most infernal deeds of slaveholders find the strongest protection. Were I to be again reduced to the chains of slavery, next to that enslavement, I should regard being the slave of a religious master the greatest calamity that could befall me. For of all slaveholders with whom I have ever met, religious slaveholders are the worst. I have ever found them the meanest and basest, the most cruel and cowardly, of all others. It was my unhappy lot not only to belong to a religious slaveholder, but to live in a community of such religionists. Very near Mr. Freeland lived the Rev. Daniel Weeden, and in the same neighborhood lived the Rev. Rigby Hopkins. These were members and ministers in the Reformed Methodist Church. Mr. Weeden owned, among others, a woman slave, whose name I have forgotten. This woman's back, for weeks, was kept literally raw, made so by the lash of this merciless, *religious* wretch. He used to hire hands. His maxim was, Behave well or behave ill, it is the duty of a master occasionally to whip a slave, to remind him of his master's authority. Such was his theory, and such his practice.

 Mr. Hopkins was even worse than Mr. Weeden. His chief boast was his ability to manage slaves. The peculiar feature of his government was that of whipping slaves in advance of deserving it. He always managed to have one or more of his slaves to whip every Monday morning. He did this to alarm their fears, and strike terror into those who escaped. His plan was to whip for the smallest offences, to prevent the commission of large ones. Mr. Hopkins could always find some excuse for whipping a slave. It would astonish one, unaccustomed to a slaveholding life, to see with what wonderful ease a slaveholder can find things, of which to make occasion to whip a slave. A mere look, word, or motion,—a mistake, accident, or want of power,—are all matters for which a slave may be whipped at any time. Does a slave look dissatisfied? It is said, he has the devil in him, and it must be whipped out. Does he speak loudly when spoken to by his master? Then he is getting high-minded, and should be taken down a button-hole lower. Does he forget to pull off his hat at the approach of a white person? Then he is wanting in reverence, and should be whipped for it. Does he ever venture to vindicate his conduct, when censured for it? Then he is guilty of impudence,—one of the greatest crimes for which a slave can be guilty. Does he ever venture to suggest a different mode of doing things from that pointed out by his master? He is indeed presumptuous, and getting above himself; and nothing less than a flogging will do for him. Does he, while ploughing, break a plough,—or, while hoeing, break a hoe? It is owing to his carelessness, and for it a slave must always be whipped. Mr. Hopkins could always find something of this sort to justify the use of the lash, and he seldom failed to embrace such opportunities. There was not a man in the whole county, with whom the slaves who had the getting their own home, would not prefer to live, rather than with this Rev. Mr. Hopkins. And yet there was not a man any where round, who made higher professions of religion, or was more active in revivals—more attentive to the class, love-feast, prayer and preaching meetings, or more devotional in his family,—

that prayed earlier, later, louder, and longer,—than this same reverend slave-driver, Rigby Hopkins.

But to return to Mr. Freeland, and to my experience while in his employment. He, like Mr. Covey, gave us enough to eat; but, unlike Mr. Covey, he also gave us sufficient time to take our meals. He worked us hard, but always between sunrise and sunset. He required a good deal of work to be done, but gave us good tools with which to work. His farm was large, but he employed hands enough to work it, and with ease, compared with many of his neighbors. My treatment, while in his employment, was heavenly, compared with what I experienced at the hands of Mr. Edward Covey.

Mr. Freeland was himself the owner of but two slaves. Their names were Henry Harris and John Harris. The rest of his hands he hired. These consisted of myself, Sandy Jenkins,[25] and Handy Caldwell. Henry and John were quite intelligent, and in a very little while after I went there, I succeeded in creating in them a strong desire to learn how to read. This desire soon sprang up in the others also. They very soon mustered up some old spelling-books, and nothing would do but that I must keep a Sabbath school. I agreed to do so, and accordingly devoted my Sundays to teaching these my loved fellow-slaves how to read. Neither of them knew his letters when I went there. Some of the slaves of the neighboring farms found what was going on, and also availed themselves of this little opportunity to learn to read. It was understood, among all who came, that there must be as little display about it as possible. It was necessary to keep our religious masters at St. Michael's unacquainted with the fact, that, instead of spending the Sabbath in wrestling, boxing, and drinking whisky, we were trying to learn how to read the will of God; for they had much rather see us engaged in those degrading sports, than to see us behaving like intellectual, moral, and accountable beings. My blood boils as I think of the bloody manner in which Messrs. Wright Fairbanks and Garrison West, both class-leaders, in connection with many others, rushed in upon us with sticks and stones, and broke up our virtuous little Sabbath school, at St. Michael's—all calling themselves Christians! humble followers of the Lord Jesus Christ! But I am again digressing.

I held my Sabbath school at the house of a free colored man, whose name I deem it imprudent to mention; for should it be known, it might embarrass him greatly, though the crime of holding the school was committed ten years ago. I had at one time over forty scholars, and those of the right sort, ardently desiring to learn. They were of all ages, though mostly men and women. I look back to those Sundays with an amount of pleasure not to be expressed. They were great days to my soul. The work of instructing my dear fellow-slaves was the sweetest engagement with which I was ever blessed. We loved each other, and to leave them at the close of the Sabbath was a severe cross indeed. When I think that these precious souls are to-day shut up in the prison-house of slavery, my feelings overcome

[25] "This is the same man who gave me the roots to prevent my being whipped by Mr. Covey. He was 'a clever soul.' We used frequently to talk about the fight with Covey, and as often as we did so, he would claim my success as the result of the roots which he gave me. This superstition is very common among the more ignorant slaves. A slave seldom dies but that his death is attributed to trickery" [Douglass's note].

me, and I am almost ready to ask, "Does a righteous God govern the universe? and for what does he hold the thunders in his right hand, if not to smite the oppressor, and deliver the spoiled out of the hand of the spoiler?" These dear souls came not to Sabbath school because it was popular to do so, nor did I teach them because it was reputable to be thus engaged. Every moment they spent in that school, they were liable to be taken up, and given thirty-nine lashes. They came because they wished to learn. Their minds had been starved by their cruel masters. They had been shut up in mental darkness. I taught them, because it was the delight of my soul to be doing something that looked like bettering the condition of my race. I kept up my school nearly the whole year I lived with Mr. Freeland; and, beside my Sabbath school, I devoted three evenings in the week, during the winter, to teaching the slaves at home. And I have the happiness to know, that several of those who came to Sabbath school learned how to read; and that one, at least, is now free through my agency.

The year passed off smoothly. It seemed only about half as long as the year which preceded it. I went through it without receiving a single blow. I will give Mr. Freeland the credit of being the best master I ever had, *till I became my own master.* For the ease with which I passed the year, I was, however, somewhat indebted to the society of my fellow-slaves. They were noble souls; they not only possessed loving hearts, but brave ones. We were linked and inter-linked with each other. I loved them with a love stronger than any thing I have experienced since. It is sometimes said that we slaves do not love and confide in each other. In answer to this assertion, I can say, I never loved any or confided in any people more than my fellow-slaves, and especially those with whom I lived at Mr. Freeland's. I believe we would have died for each other. We never undertook to do any thing, of any importance, without a mutual consultation. We never moved separately. We were one; and as much so by our tempers and dispositions, as by the mutual hardships to which we were necessarily subjected by our condition as slaves.

At the close of the year 1834, Mr. Freeland again hired me of my master, for the year of 1835. But, by this time, I began to want to live *upon free land* as well as *with Freeland;* and I was no longer content, therefore, to live with him or any other slaveholder. I began, with the commencement of the year, to prepare myself for a final struggle, which should decide my fate one way or the other. My tendency was upward. I was fast approaching manhood, and year after year had passed, and I was still a slave. These thoughts roused me—I must do something. I therefore resolved that 1835 should not pass without witnessing an attempt, on my part, to secure my liberty. But I was not willing to cherish this determination alone. My fellow-slaves were dear to me. I was anxious to have them participate with me in this, my life-giving determination. I therefore, though with great prudence, commenced early to ascertain their views and feelings in regard to their condition, and to imbue their minds with thoughts of freedom. I bent myself to devising ways and means for our escape, and meanwhile strove, on all fitting occasions, to impress them with the gross fraud and inhumanity of slavery. I went first to Henry, next to John, then to the others. I found, in them all, warm hearts and noble spirits. They were ready to hear, and ready to act when a feasible plan should be proposed. This was what I

wanted. I talked to them of our want of manhood, if we submitted to our enslavement without at least one noble effort to be free. We met often, and consulted frequently, and told our hopes and fears, recounted the difficulties, real and imagined, which we should be called on to meet. At times we were almost disposed to give up, and try to content ourselves with our wretched lot; at others, we were firm and unbending in our determination to go. Whenever we suggested any plan, there was shrinking—the odds were fearful. Our path was beset with the greatest obstacles; and if we succeeded in gaining the end of it, our right to be free was yet questionable—we were yet liable to be returned to bondage. We could see no spot, this side of the ocean, where we could be free. We knew nothing about Canada. Our knowledge of the north did not extend farther than New York; and to go there, and be forever harassed with the frightful liability of being returned to slavery—with the certainty of being treated tenfold worse than before—the thought was truly a horrible one, and one which it was not easy to overcome. The case sometimes stood thus: At every gate through which we were to pass, we saw a watchman—at every ferry a guard—on every bridge a sentinel—and in every wood a patrol. We were hemmed in upon every side. Here were the difficulties, real or imagined— the good to be sought, and the evil to be shunned. On the one hand, there stood slavery, a stern reality, glaring frightfully upon us,—its robes already crimsoned with the blood of millions, and even now feasting itself greedily upon our own flesh. On the other hand, away back in the dim distance, under the flickering light of the north star, behind some craggy hill or snow-covered mountain, stood a doubtful freedom—half frozen— beckoning us to come and share its hospitality. This in itself was sometimes enough to stagger us; but when we permitted ourselves to survey the road, we were frequently appalled. Upon either side we saw grim death, assuming the most horrid shapes. Now it was starvation, causing us to eat our own flesh;—now we were contending with the waves, and were drowned;—now we were overtaken, and torn to pieces by the fangs of the terrible bloodhound. We were stung by scorpions, chased by wild beasts, bitten by snakes, and finally, after having nearly reached the desired spot,—after swimming rivers, encountering wild beasts, sleeping in the woods, suffering hunger and nakedness,—we were overtaken by our pursuers, and, in our resistance, we were shot dead upon the spot! I say, this picture sometimes appalled us, and made us

> rather bear those ills we had,
> Than fly to others, that we knew not of.[26]

In coming to a fixed determination to run away, we did more than Patrick Henry, when he resolved upon liberty or death. With us it was a doubtful liberty at most, and almost certain death if we failed. For my part, I should prefer death to hopeless bondage.

Sandy, one of our number, gave up the notion, but still encouraged us. Our company then consisted of Henry Harris, John Harris, Henry Bailey, Charles Roberts, and myself. Henry Bailey was my uncle, and belonged to

[26] *Hamlet* III.i.81–82.

my master. Charles married my aunt: he belonged to my master's father-in-law, Mr. William Hamilton.

The plan we finally concluded upon was, to get a large canoe belonging to Mr. Hamilton, and upon the Saturday night previous to Easter holidays, paddle directly up the Chesapeake Bay. On our arrival at the head of the bay, a distance of seventy or eighty miles from where we lived, it was our purpose to turn our canoe adrift, and follow the guidance of the north star till we got beyond the limits of Maryland. Our reason for taking the water route was, that we were less liable to be suspected as runaways; we hoped to be regarded as fishermen; whereas, if we should take the land route, we should be subjected to interruptions of almost every kind. Any one having a white face, and being so disposed, could stop us, and subject us to examination.

The week before our intended start, I wrote several protections, one for each of us. As well as I can remember, they were in the following words, to wit:—

This is to certify that I, the undersigned, have given the bearer, my servant, full liberty to go to Baltimore, and spend the Easter holidays. Written with mine own hand, &c., 1835.

WILLIAM HAMILTON,
Near St. Michael's, in Talbot county, Maryland.

We were not going to Baltimore; but, in going up the bay, we went toward Baltimore, and these protections were only intended to protect us while on the bay.

As the time drew near for our departure, our anxiety became more and more intense. It was truly a matter of life and death with us. The strength of our determination was about to be fully tested. At this time, I was very active in explaining every difficulty, removing every doubt, dispelling every fear, and inspiring all with the firmness indispensable to success in our undertaking; assuring them that half was gained the instant we made the move; we had talked long enough; we were now ready to move; if not now, we never should be; and if we did not intend to move now, we had as well fold our arms, sit down, and acknowledge ourselves fit only to be slaves. This, none of us were prepared to acknowledge. Every man stood firm; and at our last meeting, we pledged ourselves afresh, in the most solemn manner, that, at the time appointed, we would certainly start in pursuit of freedom. This was in the middle of the week, at the end of which we were to be off. We went, as usual, to our several fields of labor, but with bosoms highly agitated with thoughts of our truly hazardous undertaking. We tried to conceal our feelings as much as possible; and I think we succeeded very well.

After a painful waiting, the Saturday morning, whose night was to witness our departure, came. I hailed it with joy, bring what of sadness it might. Friday night was a sleepless one for me. I probably felt more anxious than the rest, because I was, by common consent, at the head of the whole affair. The responsibility of success or failure lay heavily upon me. The glory of the one, and the confusion of the other, were alike mine. The first two hours of that morning were such as I never experienced before,

and hope never to again. Early in the morning, we went, as usual, to the field. We were spreading manure; and all at once, while thus engaged, I was overwhelmed with an indescribable feeling, in the fulness of which I turned to Sandy, who was near by, and said, "We are betrayed!" "Well," said he, "that thought has this moment struck me." We said no more. I was never more certain of any thing.

The horn was blown as usual, and we went up from the field to the house for breakfast. I went for the form, more than for want of any thing to eat that morning. Just as I got to the house, in looking out at the lane gate, I saw four white men, with two colored men. The white men were on horseback, and the colored ones were walking behind, as if tied. I watched them a few moments till they got up to our lane gate. Here they halted, and tied the colored men to the gate-post. I was not yet certain as to what the matter was. In a few moments, in rode Mr. Hamilton, with a speed betokening great excitement. He came to the door, and inquired if Master William was in. He was told he was at the barn. Mr. Hamilton, without dismounting, rode up to the barn with extraordinary speed. In a few moments, he and Mr. Freeland returned to the house. By this time, the three constables rode up and in great haste dismounted, tied their horses, and met Master William and Mr. Hamilton returning from the barn; and after talking awhile, they all walked up to the kitchen door. There was no one in the kitchen but myself and John. Henry and Sandy were up at the barn. Mr. Freeland put his head in at the door, and called me by name, saying, there were some gentlemen at the door who wished to see me. I stepped to the door, and inquired what they wanted. They at once seized me, and, without giving me any satisfaction, tied me—lashing my hands closely together. I insisted upon knowing what the matter was. They at length said, that they had learned I had been in a "scrape," and that I was to be examined before my master; and if their information proved false, I should not be hurt.

In a few moments, they succeeded in tying John. They then turned to Henry, who had by this time returned, and commanded him to cross his hands. "I won't!" said Henry, in a firm tone, indicating his readiness to meet the consequences of his refusal. "Won't you?" said Tom Graham, the constable. "No, I won't!" said Henry, in a still stronger tone. With this, two of the constables pulled out their shining pistols, and swore, by their Creator, that they would make him cross his hands or kill him. Each cocked his pistol, and, with fingers on the trigger, walked up to Henry, saying, at the same time, if he did not cross his hands, they would blow his damned heart out. "Shoot me, shoot me!" said Henry; "you can't kill me but once. Shoot, shoot,—and be damned! *I won't be tied!*" This he said in a tone of loud defiance; and at the same time, with a motion as quick as lightning, he with one single stroke dashed the pistols from the hand of each constable. As he did this, all hands fell upon him, and, after beating him some time, they finally overpowered him, and got him tied.

During the scuffle, I managed, I know not how, to get my pass out, and, without being discovered, put it into the fire. We were all now tied; and just as we were to leave for Easton jail, Betsy Freeland, mother of William Freeland, came to the door with her hands full of biscuits, and divided them between Henry and John. She then delivered herself of a speech, to

the following effect:—addressing herself to me, she said, *"You devil! You yellow devil!* it was you that put it into the heads of Henry and John to run away. But for you, you long-legged mulatto devil! Henry nor John would never have thought of such a thing." I made no reply, and was immediately hurried off towards St. Michael's. Just a moment previous to the scuffle with Henry, Mr. Hamilton suggested the propriety of making a search for the protections which he had understood Frederick had written for himself and the rest. But, just at the moment he was about carrying his proposal into effect, his aid was needed in helping to tie Henry; and the excitement attending the scuffle caused them either to forget, or to deem it unsafe, under the circumstances, to search. So we were not yet convicted of the intention to run away.

When we got about half way to St. Michael's, while the constables having us in charge were looking ahead, Henry inquired of me what he should do with his pass. I told him to eat it with his biscuit, and own nothing; and we passed the word around, *"Own nothing;"* and *"Own nothing!"* said we all. Our confidence in each other was unshaken. We were resolved to succeed or fail together, after the calamity had befallen us as much as before. We were now prepared for any thing. We were to be dragged that morning fifteen miles behind horses, and then to be placed in the Easton jail. When we reached St. Michael's, we underwent a sort of examination. We all denied that we ever intended to run away. We did this more to bring out the evidence against us, than from any hope of getting clear of being sold; for, as I have said, we were ready for that. The fact was, we cared but little where we went, so we went together. Our greatest concern was about separation. We dreaded that more than any thing this side of death. We found the evidence against us to be the testimony of one person; our master would not tell who it was; but we came to a unanimous decision among ourselves as to who their informant was. We were sent off to the jail at Easton. When we got there, we were delivered up to the sheriff, Mr. Joseph Graham, and by him placed in jail. Henry, John, and myself, were placed in one room together—Charles, and Henry Bailey, in another. Their object in separating us was to hinder concert.

We had been in jail scarcely twenty minutes, when a swarm of slave traders, and agents for slave traders, flocked into jail to look at us, and to ascertain if we were for sale. Such a set of beings I never saw before! I felt myself surrounded by so many fiends from perdition. A band of pirates never looked more like their father, the devil. They laughed and grinned over us, saying, "Ah, my boys! we have got you, haven't we?" And after taunting us in various ways, they one by one went into an examination of us, with intent to ascertain our value. They would impudently ask us if we would not like to have them for our masters. We would make them no answer, and leave them to find out as best they could. Then they would curse and swear at us, telling us that they could take the devil out of us in a very little while, if we were only in their hands.

While in jail, we found ourselves in much more comfortable quarters than we expected when we went there. We did not get much to eat, nor that which was very good; but we had a good clean room, from the windows of which we could see what was going on in the street, which was very much

better than though we had been placed in one of the dark, damp cells. Upon the whole, we got along very well, so far as the jail and its keeper were concerned. Immediately after the holidays were over, contrary to all our expectations, Mr. Hamilton and Mr. Freeland came up to Easton, and took Charles, the two Henrys, and John, out of jail, and carried them home, leaving me alone. I regarded this separation as a final one. It caused me more pain than any thing else in the whole transaction. I was ready for any thing rather than separation. I supposed that they had consulted together, and had decided that, as I was the whole cause of the intention of the others to run away, it was hard to make the innocent suffer with the guilty; and that they had, therefore, concluded to take the others home, and sell me, as a warning to the others that remained. It is due to the noble Henry to say, he seemed almost as reluctant at leaving the prison as at leaving home to come to the prison. But we knew we should, in all probability, be separated, if we were sold; and since he was in their hands, he concluded to go peaceably home.

I was now left to my fate. I was all alone, and within the walls of a stone prison. But a few days before, and I was full of hope. I expected to have been safe in a land of freedom; but now I was covered with gloom, sunk down to the utmost despair. I thought the possibility of freedom was gone. I was kept in this way about one week, at the end of which, Captain Auld, my master, to my surprise and utter astonishment, came up, and took me out, with the intention of sending me, with a gentleman of his acquaintance, into Alabama. But, from some cause or other, he did not send me to Alabama, but concluded to send me back to Baltimore, to live again with his brother Hugh, and to learn a trade.

Thus, after an absence of three years and one month, I was once more permitted to return to my old home at Baltimore. My master sent me away, because there existed against me a very great prejudice in the community, and he feared I might be killed.

In a few weeks after I went to Baltimore, Master Hugh hired me to Mr. William Gardner, an extensive ship-builder, on Fell's Point. I was put there to learn how to calk. It, however, proved a very unfavorable place for the accomplishment of this object. Mr. Gardner was engaged that spring in building two large man-of-war brigs, professedly for the Mexican government. The vessels were to be launched in the July of that year, and in failure thereof, Mr. Gardner was to lose a considerable sum; so that when I entered, all was hurry. There was no time to learn any thing. Every man had to do that which he knew how to do. In entering the ship-yard, my orders from Mr. Gardner were, to do whatever the carpenters commanded me to do. This was placing me at the beck and call of about seventy-five men. I was to regard all these as masters. Their word was to be my law. My situation was a most trying one. At times I needed a dozen pairs of hands. I was called a dozen ways in the space of a single minute. Three or four voices would strike my ear at the same moment. It was—"Fred., come help me to cant this timber here."—"Fred., come carry this timber yonder."— "Fred., bring that roller here."—"Fred., go get a fresh can of water."— "Fred., come help saw off the end of this timber."—"Fred., go quick, and get the crowbar."—"Fred., hold on the end of this fall."—"Fred., go to the

blacksmith's shop, and get a new punch."—"Hurra,[27] Fred.! run and bring me a cold chisel."—"I say, Fred., bear a hand, and get up a fire as quick as lightning under that steam-box."—"Halloo, nigger! come, turn this grindstone."—"Come, come! move, move! and *bowse*[28] this timber forward."—"I say, darky, blast your eyes, why don't you heat up some pitch?"—"Halloo! halloo! halloo!" (Three voices at the same time.) "Come here!—Go there!—Hold on where you are! Damn you, if you move, I'll knock your brains out!"

This was my school for eight months; and I might have remained there longer, but for a most horrid fight I had with four of the white apprentices, in which my left eye was nearly knocked out, and I was horribly mangled in other respects. The facts in the case were these: Until a very little while after I went there, white and black ship-carpenters worked side by side, and no one seemed to see any impropriety in it. All hands seemed to be well satisfied. Many of the black carpenters were freemen. Things seemed to be going on very well. All at once, the white carpenters knocked off, and said they would not work with free colored workmen. Their reason for this, as alleged, was, that if free colored carpenters were encouraged, they would soon take the trade into their own hands, and poor white men would be thrown out of employment. They therefore felt called upon at once to put a stop to it. And, taking advantage of Mr. Gardner's necessities, they broke off, swearing they would work no longer, unless he would discharge his black carpenters. Now, though this did not extend to me in form, it did reach me in fact. My fellow-apprentices very soon began to feel it degrading to them to work with me. They began to put on airs, and talk about the "niggers" taking the country, saying we all ought to be killed; and, being encouraged by the journeymen, they commenced making my condition as hard as they could, by hectoring me around, and sometimes striking me. I, of course, kept the vow I made after the fight with Mr. Covey, and struck back again, regardless of consequences; and while I kept them from combining, I succeeded very well; for I could whip the whole of them, taking them separately. They, however, at length combined, and came upon me, armed with sticks, stones, and heavy handspikes. One came in front with a half brick. There was one at each side of me, and one behind me. While I was attending to those in front, and on either side, the one behind ran up with the handspike, and struck me a heavy blow upon the head. It stunned me. I fell, and with this they all ran upon me, and fell to beating me with their fists. I let them lay on for a while, gathering strength. In an instant, I gave a sudden surge, and rose to my hands and knees. Just as I did that, one of their number gave me, with his heavy boot, a powerful kick in the left eye. My eyeball seemed to have burst. When they saw my eye closed, and badly swollen, they left me. With this I seized the handspike, and for a time pursued them. But here the carpenters interfered, and I thought I might as well give it up. It was impossible to stand my hand against so many. All this took place in sight of not less than fifty white ship-carpenters, and not one interposed a friendly word; but some cried, "Kill the damned nigger! Kill him! kill him! He struck a white person." I found my only chance for life was in flight. I succeeded in getting away without an

[27] "Hurry." [28] Haul by means of a tackle.

additional blow, and barely so; for to strike a white man is death by Lynch law,—and that was the law in Mr. Gardner's ship-yard; nor is there much of any other out of Mr. Gardner's ship-yard.

I went directly home, and told the story of my wrong to Master Hugh; and I am happy to say of him, irreligious as he was, his conduct was heavenly, compared with that of his brother Thomas under similar circumstances. He listened attentively to my narration of the circumstances leading to the savage outrage, and gave many proofs of his strong indignation at it. The heart of my once overkind mistress was again melted into pity. My puffed-out eye and blood-covered face moved her to tears. She took a chair by me, washed the blood from my face, and, with a mother's tenderness, bound up my head, covering the wounded eye with a lean piece of fresh beef. It was almost compensation for my suffering to witness, once more, a manifestation of kindness from this, my once affectionate old mistress. Master Hugh was very much enraged. He gave expression to his feelings by pouring out curses upon the heads of those who did the deed. As soon as I got a little the better of my bruises, he took me with him to Esquire Watson's, on Bond Street, to see what could be done about the matter. Mr. Watson inquired who saw the assault committed. Master Hugh told him it was done in Mr. Gardner's ship-yard, at midday, where there were a large company of men at work. "As to that," he said, "the deed was done, and there was no question as to who did it." His answer was, he could do nothing in the case, unless some white man would come forward and testify. He could issue no warrant on my word. If I had been killed in the presence of a thousand colored people, their testimony combined would have been insufficient to have arrested one of the murderers. Master Hugh, for once, was compelled to say this state of things was too bad. Of course, it was impossible to get any white man to volunteer his testimony in my behalf, and against the white young men. Even those who may have sympathized with me were not prepared to do this. It required a degree of courage unknown to them to do so; for just at that time, the slightest manifestation of humanity toward a colored person was denounced as abolitionism, and that name subjected its bearer to frightful liabilities. The watchwords of the bloody-minded in that region, and in those days, were, "Damn the abolitionists!" and "Damn the niggers!" There was nothing done, and probably nothing would have been done if I had been killed. Such was, and such remains, the state of things in the Christian city of Baltimore.

Master Hugh, finding he could get no redress, refused to let me go back again to Mr. Gardner. He kept me himself, and his wife dressed my wound till I was again restored to health. He then took me into the ship-yard of which he was foreman, in the employment of Mr. Walter Price. There I was immediately set to calking, and very soon learned the art of using my mallet and irons. In the course of one year from the time I left Mr. Gardner's, I was able to command the highest wages given to the most experienced calkers. I was now of some importance to my master. I was bringing him from six to seven dollars per week. I sometimes brought him nine dollars per week: my wages were a dollar and a half a day. After learning how to calk, I sought my own employment, made my own contracts, and collected the money which I earned. My pathway became much more smooth than before; my condition was now much more comfortable. When I could get

no calking to do, I did nothing. During these leisure times, those old no-
tions about freedom would steal over me again. When in Mr. Gardner's
employment, I was kept in such a perpetual whirl of excitement, I could
think of nothing, scarcely, but my life; and in thinking of my life, I almost
forgot my liberty. I have observed this in my experience of slavery,—that
whenever my condition was improved, instead of its increasing my content-
ment, it only increased my desire to be free, and set me to thinking of plans
to gain my freedom. I have found that, to make a contented slave, it is
necessary to make a thoughtless one. It is necessary to darken his moral
and mental vision, and, as far as possible, to annihilate the power of reason.
He must be able to detect no inconsistencies in slavery; he must be made to
feel that slavery is right; and he can be brought to that only when he ceases
to be a man.

I was now getting, as I have said, one dollar and fifty cents per day. I
contracted for it; I earned it; it was paid to me; it was rightfully my own;
yet, upon each returning Saturday night, I was compelled to deliver every
cent of that money to Master Hugh. And why? Not because he earned
it,—not because he had any hand in earning it,—not because I owed it to
him,—nor because he possessed the slightest shadow of a right to it; but
solely because he had the power to compel me to give it up. The right of the
grim-visaged pirate upon the high seas is exactly the same.

CHAPTER XI.

I now come to that part of my life during which I planned, and finally
succeeded in making my escape from slavery. But before narrating any of
the peculiar circumstances, I deem it proper to make known my intention
not to state all the facts connected with the transaction. My reasons for
pursuing this course may be understood from the following: First, were I
to give a minute statement of all the facts, it is not only possible, but quite
probable, that others would thereby be involved in the most embarrassing
difficulties. Secondly, such a statement would most undoubtedly induce
greater vigilance on the part of slaveholders than has existed heretofore
among them; which would, of course, be the means of guarding a door
whereby some dear brother bondman might escape his galling chains. I
deeply regret the necessity that impels me to suppress any thing of impor-
tance connected with my experience in slavery. It would afford me great
pleasure indeed, as well as materially add to the interest of my narrative,
were I at liberty to gratify a curiosity, which I know exists in the minds of
many, by an accurate statement of all the facts pertaining to my most fortu-
nate escape. But I must deprive myself of this pleasure, and the curious of
the gratification which such a statement would afford. I would allow myself
to suffer under the greatest imputations which evil-minded men might
suggest, rather than exculpate myself, and thereby run the hazard of clos-
ing the slightest avenue by which a brother slave might clear himself of the
chains and fetters of slavery.

I have never approved of the very public manner in which some of our

western friends have conducted what they call the *underground railroad*,[29] but which, I think, by their open declarations, has been made most emphatically the *upperground railroad.* I honor those good men and women for their noble daring, and applaud them for willingly subjecting themselves to bloody persecution, by openly avowing their participation in the escape of slaves. I, however, can see very little good resulting from such a course, either to themselves or the slaves escaping; while, upon the other hand, I see and feel assured that those open declarations are a positive evil to the slaves remaining, who are seeking to escape. They do nothing towards enlightening the slave, whilst they do much towards enlightening the master. They stimulate him to greater watchfulness, and enhance his power to capture his slave. We owe something to the slaves south of the line[30] as well as to those north of it; and in aiding the latter on their way to freedom, we should be careful to do nothing which would be likely to hinder the former from escaping from slavery. I would keep the merciless slaveholder profoundly ignorant of the means of flight adopted by the slave. I would leave him to imagine himself surrounded by myriads of invisible tormentors, ever ready to snatch from his infernal grasp his trembling prey. Let him be left to feel his way in the dark; let darkness commensurate with his crime hover over him; and let him feel that at every step he takes, in pursuit of the flying bondman, he is running the frightful risk of having his hot brains dashed out by an invisible agency. Let us render the tyrant no aid; let us not hold the light by which he can trace the footprints of our flying brother. But enough of this. I will now proceed to the statement of those facts, connected with my escape, for which I am alone responsible, and for which no one can be made to suffer but myself.

In the early part of the year 1838, I became quite restless. I could see no reason why I should, at the end of each week, pour the reward of my toil into the purse of my master. When I carried to him my weekly wages, he would, after counting the money, look me in the face with a robber-like fierceness, and ask, "Is this all?" He was satisfied with nothing less than the last cent. He would, however, when I made him six dollars, sometimes give me six cents, to encourage me. It had the opposite effect. I regarded it as a sort of admission of my right to the whole. The fact that he gave me any part of my wages was proof, to my mind, that he believed me entitled to the whole of them. I always felt worse for having received any thing; for I feared that the giving me a few cents would ease his conscience, and make him feel himself to be a pretty honorable sort of robber. My discontent grew upon me. I was ever on the look-out for means of escape; and, finding no direct means, I determined to try to hire my time, with a view of getting money with which to make my escape. In the spring of 1838, when Master Thomas came to Baltimore to purchase his spring goods, I got an opportunity, and applied to him to allow me to hire my time. He unhesitatingly refused my request, and told me this was another stratagem by which to escape. He told me I could go nowhere but that he could get me; and that, in the event of my running away, he should spare no pains in his

[29] A loosely organized system for helping fugitive slaves escape into free territory.
[30] The Mason-Dixon line.

efforts to catch me. He exhorted me to content myself, and be obedient. He told me, if I would be happy, I must lay out no plans for the future. He said, if I behaved myself properly, he would take care of me. Indeed, he advised me to complete thoughtlessness of the future, and taught me to depend solely upon him for happiness. He seemed to see fully the pressing necessity of setting aside my intellectual nature, in order to [attain] contentment in slavery. But in spite of him, and even in spite of myself, I continued to think, and to think about the injustice of my enslavement, and the means of escape.

About two months after this, I applied to Master Hugh for the privilege of hiring my time. He was not acquainted with the fact that I had applied to Master Thomas, and had been refused. He too, at first, seemed disposed to refuse; but, after some reflection, he granted me the privilege, and proposed the following terms: I was to be allowed all my time, make all contracts with those for whom I worked, and find my own employment; and, in return for this liberty, I was to pay him three dollars at the end of each week; find myself in calking tools, and in board and clothing. My board was two dollars and a half per week. This, with the wear and tear of clothing and calking tools, made my regular expenses about six dollars per week. This amount I was compelled to make up, or relinquish the privilege of hiring my time. Rain or shine, work or no work, at the end of each week the money must be forthcoming, or I must give up my privilege. This arrangement, it will be perceived, was decidedly in my master's favor. It relieved him of all need of looking after me. His money was sure. He received all the benefits of slaveholding without its evils; while I endured all the evils of a slave, and suffered all the care and anxiety of a freeman. I found it a hard bargain. But, hard as it was, I thought it better than the old mode of getting along. It was a step towards freedom to be allowed to bear the responsibilities of a freeman, and I was determined to hold on upon it. I bent myself to the work of making money. I was ready to work at night as well as day, and by the most untiring perseverance and industry, I made enough to meet my expenses, and lay up a little money every week. I went on thus from May till August. Master Hugh then refused to allow me to hire my time longer. The ground for his refusal was a failure on my part, one Saturday night, to pay him for my week's time. This failure was occasioned by my attending a camp meeting about ten miles from Baltimore. During the week, I had entered into an engagement with a number of young friends to start from Baltimore to the camp ground early Saturday evening; and being detained by my employer, I was unable to get down to master Hugh's without disappointing the company. I knew that master Hugh was in no special need of the money that night. I therefore decided to go to the camp meeting, and upon my return pay him the three dollars. I staid at the camp meeting one day longer than I intended when I left. But as soon as I returned, I called upon him to pay him what he considered his due. I found him very angry; he could scarce restrain his wrath. He said he had a great mind to give me a severe whipping. He wished to know how I dared go out of the city without asking his permission. I told him I hired my time, and while I paid him the price which he asked for it, I did not know that I was bound to ask him when and where I should go. This reply troubled him; and, after reflecting a few moments, he turned to me, and said I

should hire my time no longer; that the next thing he should know of, I would be running away. Upon the same plea, he told me to bring my tools and clothing home forthwith. I did so; but instead of seeking work, as I had been accustomed to do previously to hiring my time, I spent the whole week without the performance of a single stroke of work. I did this in retaliation. Saturday night, he called upon me as usual for my week's wages. I told him I had no wages; I had done no work that week. Here we were upon the point of coming to blows. He raved, and swore his determination to get hold of me. I did not allow myself a single word; but was resolved, if he laid the weight of his hand upon me, it should be blow for blow. He did not strike me, but told me that he would find me in constant employment in future. I thought the matter over during the next day, Sunday, and finally resolved upon the third day of September, as the day upon which I would make a second attempt to secure my freedom. I now had three weeks during which to prepare for my journey. Early on Monday morning, before Master Hugh had time to make any engagement for me, I went out and got employment of Mr. Butler, at his ship-yard near the drawbridge, upon what is called the City Block, thus making it unnecessary for him to seek employment for me. At the end of the week, I brought him between eight and nine dollars. He seemed very well pleased, and asked me why I did not do the same the week before. He little knew what my plans were. My object in working steadily was to remove any suspicion he might entertain of my intent to run away; and in this I succeeded admirably. I suppose he thought I was never better satisfied with my condition than at the very time during which I was planning my escape. The second week passed, and again I carried him my full wages; and so well pleased was he, that he gave me twenty-five cents, (quite a large sum for a slaveholder to give a slave) and bade me to make a good use of it. I told him I would.

Things went on without very smoothly indeed, but within there was trouble. It is impossible for me to describe my feelings as the time of my contemplated start drew near. I had a number of warm-hearted friends in Baltimore,—friends that I loved almost as I did my life,—and the thought of being separated from them forever was painful beyond expression. It is my opinion that thousands would escape from slavery, who now remain, but for the strong cords of affection that bind them to their friends. The thought of leaving my friends was decidedly the most painful thought with which I had to contend. The love of them was my tender point, and shook my decision more than all things else. Besides the pain of separation, the dread and apprehension of a failure exceeded what I had experienced at my first attempt. The appalling defeat I then sustained returned to torment me. I felt assured that, if I failed in this attempt, my case would be a hopeless one—it would seal my fate as a slave forever. I could not hope to get off with any thing less than the severest punishment, and being placed beyond the means of escape. It required no very vivid imagination to depict the most frightful scenes through which I should have to pass, in case I failed. The wretchedness of slavery, and the blessedness of freedom, were perpetually before me. It was life and death with me. But I remained firm, and, according to my resolution, on the third day of September, 1838, I left my chains, and succeeded in reaching New York without the slightest interruption of any kind. How I did so,—what means I adopted,—what direc-

tion I travelled, and by what mode of conveyance—I must leave unexplained, for the reasons before mentioned.[31]

I have been frequently asked how I felt when I found myself in a free State. I have never been able to answer the question with any satisfaction to myself. It was a moment of the highest excitement I ever experienced. I suppose I felt as one may imagine the unarmed mariner to feel when he is rescued by a friendly man-of-war from the pursuit of a pirate. In writing to a dear friend, immediately after my arrival at New York, I said I felt like one who had escaped a den of hungry lions. This state of mind, however, very soon subsided; and I was again seized with a feeling of great insecurity and loneliness. I was yet liable to be taken back, and subjected to all the tortures of slavery. This in itself was enough to damp the ardor of my enthusiasm. But the loneliness overcame me. There I was in the midst of thousands, and yet a perfect stranger; without home and without friends, in the midst of thousands of my own brethren—children of a common Father, and yet I dared not to unfold to any one of them my sad condition. I was afraid to speak to any one for fear of speaking to the wrong one, and thereby falling into the hands of money-loving kidnappers, whose business it was to lie in wait for the panting fugitive, as the ferocious beasts of the forest lie in wait for their prey. The motto which I adopted when I started from slavery was this—"Trust no man!" I saw in every white man an enemy, and in almost every colored man cause for distrust. It was a most painful situation; and, to understand it, one must needs experience it, or imagine himself in similar circumstances. Let him be a fugitive slave in a strange land—a land given up to be the hunting-ground for slaveholders—whose inhabitants are legalized kidnappers—where he is every moment subjected to the terrible liability of being seized upon by his fellowmen, as the hideous crocodile seizes upon his prey!—I say, let him place himself in my situation—without home or friends—without money or credit—wanting shelter, and no one to give it—wanting bread, and no money to buy it,—and at the same time let him feel that he is pursued by merciless menhunters, and in total darkness as to what to do, where to go, or where to stay,—perfectly helpless both as to the means of defence and means of escape,—in the midst of plenty, yet suffering the terrible gnawings of hunger,—in the midst of houses, yet having no home,—among fellowmen, yet feeling as if in the midst of wild beasts, whose greediness to swallow up the trembling and half-famished fugitive is only equalled by that with which the monsters of the deep swallow up the helpless fish upon which they subsist,—I say, let him be placed in this most trying situation,—the situation in which I was placed,—then, and not till then, will he fully appreciate the hardships of, and know how to sympathize with, the toilworn and whip-scarred fugitive slave.

Thank Heaven, I remained but a short time in this distressed situation. I was relieved from it by the humane hand of Mr. DAVID RUGGLES, whose vigilance, kindness, and perseverance, I shall never forget. I am glad of an

[31] Douglass was later able to reveal his method of escape. Dressed as a sailor and carrying borrowed papers, he took the train from Baltimore to the Susquehanna River. He crossed by ferry to Wilmington, Delaware, took a steamboat to Philadelphia, and then took the train to New York.

opportunity to express, as far as words can, the love and gratitude I bear him. Mr. Ruggles is now afflicted with blindness, and is himself in need of the same kind offices which he was once so forward in the performance of toward others. I had been in New York but a few days, when Mr. Ruggles sought me out, and very kindly took me to his boarding-house at the corner of Church and Lespenard Streets. Mr. Ruggles was then very deeply engaged in the memorable *Darg* case, as well as attending to a number of other fugitive slaves, devising ways and means for their successful escape; and, though watched and hemmed in on almost every side, he seemed to be more than a match for his enemies.[32]

Very soon after I went to Mr. Ruggles, he wished to know of me where I wanted to go; as he deemed it unsafe for me to remain in New York. I told him I was a calker, and should like to go where I could get work. I thought of going to Canada; but he decided against it, and in favor of my going to New Bedford, thinking I should be able to get work there at my trade. At this time, Anna,[33] my intended wife, came on; for I wrote to her immediately after my arrival at New York, (notwithstanding my homeless, houseless, and helpless condition,) informing her of my successful flight, and wishing her to come on forthwith. In a few days after her arrival, Mr. Ruggles called in the Rev. J. W. C. Pennington, who, in the presence of Mr. Ruggles, Mrs. Michaels, and two or three others, performed the marriage ceremony, and gave us a certificate, of which the following is an exact copy;—

This may certify, that I joined together in holy matrimony Frederick Johnson[34] and Anna Murray, as man and wife, in the presence of Mr. David Ruggles and Mrs. Michaels.

<div align="right">JAMES W. C. PENNINGTON.</div>

New York, Sept. 15, 1838.

Upon receiving this certificate, and a five-dollar bill from Mr. Ruggles, I shouldered one part of our baggage, and Anna took up the other, and we set out forthwith to take passage on board of the steamboat John W. Richmond for Newport, on our way to New Bedford. Mr. Ruggles gave me a letter to a Mr. Shaw in Newport, and told me, in case my money did not serve me to New Bedford, to stop in Newport and obtain further assistance; but upon our arrival at Newport, we were so anxious to get to a place of safety, that, notwithstanding we lacked the necessary money to pay our fare, we decided to take seats in the stage, and promise to pay when we got to New Bedford. We were encouraged to do this by two excellent gentlemen, residents of New Bedford, whose names I afterward ascertained to be Joseph Ricketson and William C. Taber. They seemed at once to understand our circumstances, and gave us such assurance of their friendliness as put us fully at ease in their presence. It was good indeed to meet with such friends, at such a time. Upon reaching New Bedford, we were directed to the house of Mr. Nathan Johnson, by whom we were kindly received, and

[32] David Ruggles (1810–49) was a black New York journalist and reformer. The Darg case was a slavery case called after the plaintiff, a slaveowner named John P. Darg.

[33] "She was free" [Douglass's note].

[34] "I had changed my name from Frederick Bailey to that of Johnson" [Douglass's note].

hospitably provided for. Both Mr. and Mrs. Johnson took a deep and lively interest in our welfare. They proved themselves quite worthy of the name of abolitionists. When the stage-driver found us unable to pay our fare, he held on upon our baggage as security for the debt. I had but to mention the fact to Mr. Johnson, and he forthwith advanced the money.

We now began to feel a degree of safety, and to prepare ourselves for the duties and responsibilities of a life of freedom. On the morning after our arrival at New Bedford, while at the breakfast-table, the question arose as to what name I should be called by. The name given me by my mother was, "Frederick Augustus Washington Bailey." I, however, had dispensed with the two middle names long before I left Maryland so that I was generally known by the name of "Frederick Bailey." I started from Baltimore bearing the name of "Stanley." When I got to New York, I again changed my name to "Frederick Johnson," and thought that would be the last change. But when I got to New Bedford, I found it necessary again to change my name. The reason of this necessity was, that there were so many Johnsons in New Bedford, it was already quite difficult to distinguish between them. I gave Mr. Johnson the privilege of choosing me a name, but told him he must not take from me the name of "Frederick." I must hold on to that, to preserve a sense of my identity. Mr. Johnson had just been reading the "Lady of the Lake," and at once suggested that my name be "Douglass."[35] From that time until now I have been called "Frederick Douglass;" and as I am more widely known by that name than by either of the others, I shall continue to use it as my own.

I was quite disappointed at the general appearance of things in New Bedford. The impression which I had received respecting the character and condition of the people of the north, I found to be singularly erroneous. I had very strangely supposed, while in slavery, that few of the comforts, and scarcely any of the luxuries, of life were enjoyed at the north, compared with what were enjoyed by the slaveholders of the south. I probably came to this conclusion from the fact that northern people owned no slaves. I supposed that they were about upon a level with the non-slaveholding population of the south. I knew *they* were exceedingly poor, and I had been accustomed to regard their poverty as the necessary consequence of their being non-slaveholders. I had somehow imbibed the opinion that, in the absence of slaves, there could be no wealth, and very little refinement. And upon coming to the north, I expected to meet with a rough, hard-handed, and uncultivated population, living in the most Spartanlike simplicity, knowing nothing of the ease, luxury, pomp, and grandeur of southern slaveholders. Such being my conjectures, any one acquainted with the appearance of New Bedford may very readily infer how palpably I must have seen my mistake.

In the afternoon of the day when I reached New Bedford, I visited the wharves, to take a view of the shipping. Here I found myself surrounded with the strongest proofs of wealth. Lying at the wharves, and riding in the stream, I saw many ships of the finest model, in the best order, and of the largest size. Upon the right and left, I was walled in by granite warehouses

[35] Sir Walter Scott's narrative poem *The Lady of the Lake* concerns the Douglas clan in Scotland.

of the widest dimensions, stowed to their utmost capacity with the necessaries and comforts of life. Added to this, almost every body seemed to be at work, but noiselessly so, compared with what I had been accustomed to in Baltimore. There were no loud songs heard from those engaged in loading and unloading ships. I heard no deep oaths or horrid curses on the laborer. I saw no whipping of men; but all seemed to go smoothly on. Every man appeared to understand his work, and went at it with a sober, yet cheerful earnestness, which betokened the deep interest which he felt in what he was doing, as well as a sense of his own dignity as a man. To me this looked exceedingly strange. From the wharves I strolled around and over the town, gazing with wonder and admiration at the splendid churches, beautiful dwellings, and finely-cultivated gardens; evincing an amount of wealth, comfort, taste, and refinement, such as I had never seen in any part of slaveholding Maryland.

Every thing looked clean, new, and beautiful. I saw few or no dilapidated houses, with poverty-stricken inmates; no half-naked children and barefooted women, such as I had been accustomed to see in Hillsborough, Easton, St. Michael's, and Baltimore. The people looked more able, stronger, healthier, and happier, than those of Maryland. I was for once made glad by a view of extreme wealth, without being saddened by seeing extreme poverty. But the most astonishing as well as the most interesting thing to me was the condition of the colored people, a great many of whom, like myself, had escaped thither as a refuge from the hunters of men. I found many, who had not been seven years out of their chains, living in finer houses, and evidently enjoying more of the comforts of life, than the average slaveholders in Maryland. I will venture to assert that my friend Mr. Nathan Johnson (of whom I can say with a grateful heart, "I was hungry, and he gave me meat; I was thirsty, and he gave me drink; I was a stranger, and he took me in"[36]) lived in a neater house; dined at a better table; took, paid for, and read, more newspapers; better understood the moral, religious, and political character of the nation,—than nine tenths of the slaveholders in Talbot county, Maryland. Yet Mr. Johnson was a working man. His hands were hardened by toil, and not his alone, but those also of Mrs. Johnson. I found the colored people much more spirited than I had supposed they would be. I found among them a determination to protect each other from the blood-thirsty kidnapper, at all hazards. Soon after my arrival, I was told of a circumstance which illustrated their spirit. A colored man and a fugitive slave were on unfriendly terms. The former was heard to threaten the latter with informing his master of his whereabouts. Straightway a meeting was called among the colored people, under the stereotyped notice, "Business of importance!" The betrayer was invited to attend. The people came at the appointed hour, and organized the meeting by appointing a very religious old gentleman as president, who, I believe, made a prayer, after which he addressed the meeting as follows: *"Friends, we have got him here, and I would recommend that you young men just take him outside the door, and kill him!"* With this, a number of them bolted at him; but they were intercepted by some more timid than themselves, and the betrayer escaped their vengeance, and has not been seen in New Bed-

[36] Matthew 25:35.

ford since. I believe there have been no more such threats, and should there be hereafter, I doubt not that death would be the consequence.

I found employment, the third day after my arrival, in stowing a sloop with a load of oil. It was new, dirty, and hard work for me; but I went at it with a glad heart and a willing hand. I was now my own master. It was a happy moment, the rapture of which can be understood only by those who have been slaves. It was the first work, the reward of which was to be entirely my own. There was no Master Hugh standing ready, the moment I earned the money, to rob me of it. I worked that day with a pleasure I had never before experienced. I was at work for myself and newly-married wife. It was to me the starting-point of a new existence. When I got through with that job, I went in pursuit of a job of calking; but such was the strength of prejudice against color, among the white calkers, that they refused to work with me, and of course I could get no employment.[37] Finding my trade of no immediate benefit, I threw off my calking habiliments, and prepared myself to do any kind of work I could get to do. Mr. Johnson kindly let me have his wood-horse and saw, and I very soon found myself plenty of work. There was no work too hard—none too dirty. I was ready to saw wood, shovel coal, carry the hod, sweep the chimney, or roll oil casks,—all of which I did for nearly three years in New Bedford, before I became known to the anti-slavery world.

In about four months after I went to New Bedford, there came a young man to me, and inquired if I did not wish to take the "Liberator."[38] I told him I did; but, just having made my escape from slavery, I remarked that I was unable to pay for it then. I, however, finally became a subscriber to it. The paper came, and I read it from week to week with such feelings as it would be quite idle for me to attempt to describe. The paper became my meat and my drink. My soul was set all on fire. Its sympathy for my brethren in bonds—its scathing denunciations of slaveholders—its faithful exposures of slavery—and its powerful attacks upon the upholders of the institution—sent a thrill of joy through my soul, such as I had never felt before!

I had not long been a reader of the "Liberator," before I got a pretty correct idea of the principles, measures, and spirit of the anti-slavery reform. I took right hold of the cause. I could do but little; but what I could, I did with a joyful heart, and never felt happier than when in an anti-slavery meeting. I seldom had much to say at the meetings, because what I wanted to say was said so much better by others. But, while attending an antislavery convention at Nantucket, on the 11th of August, 1841, I felt strongly moved to speak, and was at the same time much urged to do so by Mr. William C. Coffin, a gentleman who had heard me speak in the colored people's meeting at New Bedford. It was a severe cross, and I took it up reluctantly. The truth was, I felt myself a slave, and the idea of speaking to white people weighed me down. I spoke but a few moments, when I felt a degree of freedom, and said what I desired with considerable ease. From that time until now, I have been engaged in pleading the cause of my

[37] "I am told that colored persons can now get employment at calking in New Bedford—a result of anti-slavery effort" [Douglass's note].

[38] William Lloyd Garrison's abolitionist newspaper.

brethren—with what success, and with what devotion, I leave those acquainted with my labors to decide.

APPENDIX.

I find, since reading over the foregoing Narrative that I have, in several instances, spoken in such a tone and manner, respecting religion, as may possibly lead those unacquainted with my religious views to suppose me an opponent of all religion. To remove the liability of such misapprehension, I deem it proper to append the following brief explanation. What I have said respecting and against religion, I mean strictly to apply to the *slaveholding religion* of this land, and with no possible reference to Christianity proper; for, between the Christianity of this land, and the Christianity of Christ, I recognize the widest possible difference—so wide, that to receive the one as good, pure, and holy, is of necessity to reject the other as bad, corrupt, and wicked. To be the friend of the one, is of necessity to be the enemy of the other. I love the pure, peaceable, and impartial Christianity of Christ: I therefore hate the corrupt, slaveholding, women-whipping, cradle-plundering, partial and hypocritical Christianity of this land. Indeed, I can see no reason, but the most deceitful one, for calling the religion of this land Christianity. I look upon it as the climax of all misnomers, the boldest of all frauds, and the grossest of all libels. Never was there a clearer case of "stealing the livery of the court of heaven to serve the devil in." I am filled with unutterable loathing when I contemplate the religious pomp and show, together with the horrible inconsistencies, which every where surround me. We have men-stealers for ministers, women-whippers for missionaries, and cradle-plunderers for church members. The man who wields the blood-clotted cowskin during the week fills the pulpit on Sunday, and claims to be a minister of the meek and lowly Jesus. The man who robs me of my earnings at the end of each week meets me as a class-leader on Sunday morning, to show me the way of life, and the path of salvation. He who sells my sister, for purposes of prostitution, stands forth as the pious advocate of purity. He who proclaims it a religious duty to read the Bible denies me the right of learning to read the name of the God who made me. He who is the religious advocate of marriage robs whole millions of its sacred influence, and leaves them to the ravages of wholesale pollution. The warm defender of the sacredness of the family relation is the same that scatters whole families,—sundering husbands and wives, parents and children, sisters and brothers,—leaving the hut vacant, and the hearth desolate. We see the thief preaching against theft, and the adulterer against adultery. We have men sold to build churches, women sold to support the gospel, and babes sold to purchase Bibles for the *poor heathen! all for the glory of God and the good of souls!* The slave auctioneer's bell and the church-going bell chime in with each other, and the bitter cries of the heart-broken slave are drowned in the religious shouts of his pious master. Revivals of religion and revivals in the slave-trade go hand in hand together. The slave prison and the church stand near each other. The clanking of fetters and the rattling of chains in the prison, and the pious psalm and solemn prayer in

the church, may be heard at the same time. The dealers in the bodies and souls of men erect their stand in the presence of the pulpit, and they mutually help each other. The dealer gives his blood-stained gold to support the pulpit, and the pulpit, in return, covers his infernal business with the garb of Christianity. Here we have religion and robbery the allies of each other—devils dressed in angels' robes, and hell presenting the semblance of paradise.

> Just God! and these are they,
> Who minister at thine altar, God of right!
> Men who their hands, with prayer and blessing, lay
> On Israel's ark of light.
>
> What! preach, and kidnap men?
> Give thanks, and rob thy own afflicted poor?
> Talk of thy glorious liberty, and then
> Bolt hard the captive's door?
>
> What! servants of thy own
> Merciful Son, who came to seek and save
> The homeless and the outcast, fettering down
> The tasked and plundered slave!
>
> Pilate and Herod friends!
> Chief priests and rulers, as of old, combine!
> Just God and holy! is that church which lends
> Strength to the spoiler thine?[39]

The Christianity of America is a Christianity, of whose votaries it may be as truly said, as it was of the ancient scribes and Pharisees, "They bind heavy burdens, and grievous to be borne, and lay them on men's shoulders, but they themselves will not move them with one of their fingers. All their works they do for to be seen of men.—They love the uppermost rooms at feasts, and the chief seats in the synagogues, and to be called of men, Rabbi, Rabbi.—But woe unto you, scribes and Pharisees, hypocrites! for ye shut up the kingdom of heaven against men; for ye neither go in yourselves, neither suffer ye them that are entering to go in. Ye devour widows' houses, and for a pretence make long prayers; therefore ye shall receive the greater damnation. Ye compass sea and land to make one proselyte, and when he is made, ye make him twofold more the child of hell than yourselves.—Woe unto you, scribes and Pharisees, hypocrites! for ye pay tithe of mint, and anise, and cumin, and have omitted the weightier matters of the law, judgment, mercy, and faith; these ought ye to have done, and not to leave the other undone. Ye blind guides! which strain at a gnat, and swallow a camel. Woe unto you, scribes and Pharisees, hypocrites! for ye make clean the outside of the cup and of the platter; but within, they are full of extortion and excess.—Woe unto you, scribes and Pharisees, hypocrites! for ye are like unto whited sepulchres, which indeed appear

[39] John Greenleaf Whittier, "Clerical Oppressors" (1835).

beautiful outward, but are within full of dead men's bones, and of all un-
cleanness. Even so ye also outwardly appear righteous unto men, but
within ye are full of hypocrisy and iniquity."[40]

Dark and terrible as is this picture, I hold it to be strictly true of the
overwhelming mass of professed Christians in America. They strain at a
gnat, and swallow a camel. Could any thing be more true of our churches?
They would be shocked at the proposition of fellowshipping a *sheep*-stealer;
and at the same time they hug to their communion a *man*-stealer, and
brand me with being an infidel, if I find fault with them for it. They attend
with Pharisaical strictness to the outward forms of religion, and at the same
time neglect the weightier matters of the law, judgment, mercy, and faith.
They are always ready to sacrifice, but seldom to show mercy. They are
they who are represented as professing to love God whom they have not
seen, whilst they hate their brother whom they have seen. They love the
heathen on the other side of the globe. They can pray for him, pay money
to have the Bible put into his hand, and missionaries to instruct him; while
they despise and totally neglect the heathen at their own doors.

Such is, very briefly, my view of the religion of this land; and to avoid
any misunderstanding, growing out of the use of general terms, I mean, by
the religion of this land, that which is revealed in the words, deeds, and
actions, of those bodies, north and south, calling themselves Christian
churches, and yet in union with slaveholders. It is against religion, as pre-
sented by these bodies, that I have felt it my duty to testify.

I conclude these remarks by copying the following portrait of the reli-
gion of the south, (which is, by communion and fellowship, the religion of
the north,) which I soberly affirm is "true to the life," and without carica-
ture or the slightest exaggeration. It is said to have been drawn, several
years before the present anti-slavery agitation began, by a northern Meth-
odist preacher, who, while residing at the south, had an opportunity to see
slaveholding morals, manners, and piety, with his own eyes. "Shall I not
visit these things? saith the Lord. Shall not my soul be avenged on such a
nation as this?"[41]

A Parody[42]

Come, saints and sinners, hear me tell
How pious priests whip Jack and Nell,
And women buy and children sell,
And preach all sinners down to hell,
 And sing of heavenly union.

They'll bleat and baa, dona[43] like goats,
Gorge down black sheep, and strain at motes,

[40] Jesus' denunciation of the Scribes and Pharisees in Matthew 23. The Scribes were ex-
perts in Jewish law, the Pharisees a party within Judaism represented—with questionable
accuracy—in the Gospels and later Christian tradition as emphasizing strict adherence to law.
Douglass is suggesting a comparison with Southern slaveholders who observe the forms of
religion but not its spirit.
[41] Jeremiah 5:9. [42] The parody is of a southern hymn called "Heavenly Union."
[43] "Make noise," "resound" (obsolete).

Array their backs in fine black coats,
Then seize their negroes by their throats,
 And choke, for heavenly union.

They'll church you if you sip a dram,
And damn you if you steal a lamb;
Yet rob old Tony, Doll, and Sam,
Of human rights, and bread and ham;
 Kidnapper's heavenly union.

They'll loudly talk of Christ's reward,
And bind his image with a cord,
And scold, and swing the lash abhorred,
And sell their brother in the Lord
 To handcuffed heavenly union.

They'll read and sing a sacred song,
And make a prayer both loud and long,
And teach the right and do the wrong,
Hailing the brother, sister throng,
 With words of heavenly union.

We wonder how such saints can sing,
Or praise the Lord upon the wing,
Who roar, and scold, and whip, and sting,
And to their slaves and mammon cling,
 In guilty conscience union.

They'll raise tobacco, corn, and rye,
And drive, and thieve, and cheat, and lie,
And lay up treasures in the sky,
By making switch and cowskin fly,
 In hope of heavenly union.

They'll crack old Tony on the skull,
And preach and roar like Bashan bull,[44]
Or braying ass, of mischief full,
Then seize old Jacob by the wool,
 And pull for heavenly union.

A roaring, ranting, sleek man-thief,
Who lived on mutton, veal, and beef,
Yet never would afford relief
To needy, sable sons of grief,
 Was big with heavenly union.

'Love not the world,' the preacher said,
And winked his eye, and shook his head;

[44] A bull from Bashan, in Palestine, as mentioned occasionally in the Old Testament. See, for example, Psalm 22:12.

He seized on Tom, and Dick, and Ned,
Cut short their meat, and clothes, and bread,
 Yet still loved heavenly union.

Another preacher whining spoke
Of One whose heart for sinners broke:
He tied old Nanny to an oak,
And drew the blood at every stroke,
 And prayed for heavenly union.

Two others oped their iron jaws,
And waved their children-stealing paws;
There sat their children in gewgaws;
By stinting negroes' backs and maws,
 They kept up heavenly union.

All good from Jack another takes,
And entertains their flirts and rakes,
Who dress as sleek as glossy snakes,
And cram their mouths with sweetened cakes;
 And this goes down for union.

Sincerely and earnestly hoping that this little book may do something toward throwing light on the American slave system, and hastening the glad day of deliverance to the millions of my brethren in bonds—faithfully relying upon the power of truth, love, and justice, for success in my humble efforts—and solemnly pledging my self anew to the sacred cause,—I subscribe myself,

FREDERICK DOUGLASS.

Lynn, *Mass., April* 28, 1845.

THE END.

Walt Whitman
(*1819–1892*)

Among the great archetypal heroes of nineteenth-century Romanticism— Blake's Albion, Goethe's Faust, Byron's haunted protagonists—surely one of the most appealing and suggestive embodies both the exuberant individualism of Romanticism in general and the optimistic expansionism of America's Westward Movement in particular. His name was "Walt," and he was the self-conscious and deliberate creation of a New York printer and journalist named Walt Whitman. Whitman's literary persona—"an Ameri-

can, one of the roughs, a kosmos"—first appeared in 1855 with the initial publication of *Leaves of Grass* and continued to develop over the next four decades, through eight more editions, as Whitman amplified and refined the book that was "an attempt . . . of a naïve, masculine, affectionate, contemplative, sensual, imperious person to cast into literature not only his own grit and arrogance, but his own flesh and form, undraped, regardless of all models, regardless of modesty or law; and ignorant, as at first it appears, of . . . all outside of the fiercely loved land of his birth."

The Brooklyn of the 1830's and 1840's is preserved in Whitman's poetry as the Dublin of 1904 is preserved in Joyce's work or rural Mississippi is in Faulkner's. "Remember," Whitman told a friend late in life, "the book arose out of my life in Brooklyn and New York from 1838 to 1853, absorbing a million people, for fifteen years, with an intimacy, an eagerness, an abandon, probably never equalled."

Whitman was born on Long Island in 1819; when he was not quite five, the family moved to what was then the small town of Brooklyn, where the father set up a carpentry shop. The peaceful woods and beaches of Long Island and the hustle and bustle of Brooklyn and of New York, just up the bay, were to figure equally in Whitman's memories of his youth and in his poetry. He left school when he was eleven and became an office boy for a lawyer and a doctor and then an apprentice to a printer. By the time he was seventeen, he was a fully qualified compositor, also working from time to time as a country schoolteacher. Printing led into journalism, and for about twelve years, from the time he was nineteen until he was thirty-one, he was caught up in the daily pressures of newspaper work, churning out news stories, editorials, some rather conventional poetry and fictional sketches, and even a hack-work temperance novel named *Franklin Evans* (1842). Whitman's journalism culminated in his two-year editorship (1846–48) of the prosperous Brooklyn *Daily Eagle*, a job he lost because of his liberal politics. When the job on the *Eagle* ended, he made a three-month trip to New Orleans as an editor of the *Daily Crescent;* on the way, he also visited Chicago and the Midwest.

The trip to New Orleans coincided with, if it did not trigger, a remarkable change in Whitman's personality and public identity. Until then, he had been something of a dandy in his dress; he had led the life of a city newspaperman on the fringes of the bohemian artistic circles of New York; and his style had been slick, conventional, and journalistic. Now, at the age of thirty-one, he began to wear workman's clothes, he grew a full beard, and, as his notebooks show, he began to conceive of himself as a potential bard and prophet of an ideal America and to forge a new poetic style to express this role. Over the next few years, he accepted some journalistic assignments, but his main energies went into the preparation of the first edition of *Leaves of Grass,* which he published himself in 1855.

The first, 1855 version of *Leaves of Grass* contained a long preface in which Whitman proclaimed that "The United States themselves are essentially the greatest poem," and called for a new race of poets and a new kind of poetry adequate to express the inherent poetic content of America. It also contained "Song of Myself" and eleven shorter poems. The initial impact of the book did not appear in sales, which were very small, but in a series of reviews, which Whitman carefully arranged. A few reviewers were

shocked and repelled by the unconventionality of the poetry and the book's frank egotism and explicit sexuality. But there were also some reviews, in both America and England, which recognized the book's importance. The Concord transcendentalists, especially, praised the book, and Emerson, to whom Whitman sent a copy, responded quickly with a remarkable letter to Whitman in which he said, "I give you joy of your free & brave thought. I have great joy in it. I find incomparable things said incomparably well, as they must be. . . . I greet you at the beginning of a great career, which yet must have had a long foreground somewhere, for such a start." Henry David Thoreau and Bronson Alcott, too, liked the book and made pilgrimages to Brooklyn to visit Whitman later that year; Emerson followed in 1856.

The rest of Whitman's life was devoted primarily to producing further editions of *Leaves of Grass,* each with added poems and revisions and rearrangements of earlier ones. The book thus took on a living, organic quality, as its title suggested, growing and evolving along with its creator. A second edition appeared quickly, in 1856, and eight further editions were printed at regular intervals until Whitman's death in 1892. The general direction of the revisions of *Leaves of Grass* was away from the immediate, personal, erotic emphasis of the first edition and toward the development of the "Walt" figure as a more generalized, sage-like, public embodiment of democratic man. The Civil War poems called "Drum Taps" were added in the 1867 edition, and the long "Passage to India," which used the opening of the Suez Canal as the occasion to celebrate both scientific progress and a spiritual progress to "more than India," first appeared in the edition of 1876.

The Civil War affected Whitman deeply. His initial response was exhilaration, as in the poem "Beat! Beat! Drums!" But as the war wore on, he became more and more touched by the personal suffering of the soldiers. In 1862, he went to the front in Virginia to seek his brother George, who had been reported wounded. He remained in Washington for the rest of the war, working as a volunteer among the wounded in military hospitals, raising money for his efforts by writing war correspondence for New York and Brooklyn papers. Both his experiences with the casualties of the war and the assassination of Lincoln perhaps are responsible for a richer, more tragic tone which enters his later poetry.

After the war, Whitman worked as a clerk in government offices in Washington, first in the Department of the Interior, from which he was dismissed when it was discovered that he had written an "indecent book," and later in the office of the Attorney General. He suffered a serious paralytic stroke in 1873 and left Washington for Camden, New Jersey, where he remained, with some intervals away, for the rest of his life, frail and in ill health but revered by what amounted to a cult of worldwide admirers and followers. He died in 1892.

As Emerson shrewdly surmised in 1855, what at first seemed like a startling new voice in American poetry had "a long foreground." Part of that foreground was Emerson himself. Whitman's intensive self-education during his newspaper years had included a close reading of Emerson's essays, and the 1855 *Leaves of Grass* was a "transcendental" work, in the broadest sense of that term. For Whitman, as for Emerson, the individual

stood at the center of his own universe and he arrived at understanding not through received doctrines but through ecstatic and intuitive communion with a universe harmonious with his own soul. Whitman's Walt, like Emerson's American scholar, celebrates the continuous re-creation of the world in the imagination of each individual, the intuition of "a world primal again." There were other roots, too, for Whitman's joyous and genial individualism, including the Jacksonian political ideas of his carpenter father and the Quakerism of his mother's family.

But Whitman was not just putting new American wine into old Romantic bottles. His vision of America grew less out of tradition than out of "loafing" and "inviting his soul," as he contemplated himself and his relation to the restless, hustling, westward-moving America in which he grew up. For all his kinship with the New England transcendentalists, he is as different from them as New York is from Concord. For all their love of the natural world, Emerson and Thoreau were both nervous about the flesh; the carnal was always a steppingstone to the spiritual. Whitman had no such nervousness: "I find no sweeter fat than sticks to my own bones," he declared. And while the transcendentalists were at best ambivalent about the crude energies of a rapidly expanding America, Whitman embraced them without reserve, loving "the blab of the pave" and America at work as much as the ponds and woods and America in contemplation.

"Walt," in *Leaves of Grass,* is an infinitely protean character, becoming everybody everywhere, in a pose that is at once a triumph of imaginative identification and a quick-change vaudeville act. But if Walt "leaks out into the universe," as D.H. Lawrence put it, it is not at the expense of his own memorable identity. He is comically egotistical (saying in "Song of Myself," with tongue firmly in cheek, "I dote on myself, there is that lot of me and all so luscious"), hungry to incorporate all experience, humble or exalted, male or female, minute or cosmic, spiritual or carnal. He is at once the act and the observer of the act: "My hurts turn livid upon me as I lean on a cane and observe." He can observe the particular and at the same time maintain the distance to see the "form, union, plan" of life.

Whitman's prosody strikes a similar balance between fluidity and form. He abandons the traditional meters of English verse in favor of a rhythmical "free verse," in which the rhetorical phrase, rather than the foot, becomes the basic unit, and the verse is given shape by such rhetorical devices as parallelism and repetition. The result is a highly oral style, reminiscent not only of the King James version of the Bible, but also of the high rhetoric of the nineteenth-century stage and the operatic arias Whitman admired so much.

"I Saw in Louisiana a Live-Oak Growing" is one of the group of forty-five poems that Whitman introduced into *Leaves of Grass* in the 1860 edition under the heading of "Calamus." ("Calamus," also called "sweet flag," is a tall, coarse grass that grows in marshy areas around ponds.) Whitman wrote that the Calamus poems celebrated "comradeship": "the adhesive love, at least rivaling the amative love hitherto possessing imaginative literature, if not going beyond it."

"Out of the Cradle Endlessly Rocking" was first published in the New York *Saturday Press* in 1859 and was added to *Leaves of Grass* in the 1860 edition. Originally entitled "A Child's Reminiscence," the poem belongs to

the tradition of such Romantic poems as Wordsworth's "Lines Composed a Few Miles above Tintern Abbey," in which the mature poet revisits a scene important in youth and meditates on its significance. "When I Heard the Learn'd Astronomer" was written in 1865 and included in the section called "Drum Taps" in the edition of *Leaves of Grass* of that year.

"When Lilacs Last in the Dooryard Bloom'd," Whitman's meditation on the death of Lincoln, for all its apparently free-associational spontaneity, is a carefully structured development of the triple images of lilac, star, and bird. Like such great predecessors in the poetic elegy as Milton's "Lycidas" and Shelley's "Adonais," the poem focuses not so much upon the person mourned as upon the sensibility of the mourner as he struggles to find meaning in the painful death and to come to terms with his grief.

FURTHER READING (*prepared by J.H.*): The standard biography is Gay Wilson Allen's *The Solitary Singer: A Critical Biography*, 1955, rev. 1967, repr. with a new preface, 1985, which has been supplemented but not superseded by biographies by Justin Kaplan, 1980, and Paul Zweig, 1984. James E. Miller Jr.'s *Walt Whitman*, updated ed. 1990, is a good general introduction. Allen's *The New Walt Whitman Handbook*, 1975, updated 1986, is a valuable guide through the poetry and the criticism. *Critical Essays on Walt Whitman*, ed. James Woodress, 1983, is a generous collection of previously published essays. George Hutchinson's *The Ecstatic Whitman: Literary Shamanism and the Crisis of the Union*, 1986, locates Whitman within his time, while James Perrin Warren's *Walt Whitman's Language Experiment*, 1990, deals authoritatively with Whitman's use of language.

I SAW IN LOUISIANA A LIVE-OAK[1] GROWING

I saw in Louisiana a live-oak growing,
All alone stood it and the moss hung down from the branches,
Without any companion it grew there uttering joyous leaves of dark
 green,
And its look, rude, unbending, lusty, made me think of myself,
But I wonder'd how it could utter joyous leaves standing alone there
 without its friend near, for I knew I could not, 5
And I broke off a twig with a certain number of leaves upon it,
 and twined around it a little moss,
And brought it away, and I have placed it in sight in my room,
It is not needed to remind me as of my own dear friends,
(For I believe lately I think of little else than of them,)
Yet it remains to me a curious token, it makes me think of manly
 love; 10
For all that, and though the live-oak glistens there in Louisiana
 solitary in a wide flat space,
Uttering joyous leaves all its life without a friend or lover near,
I know very well I could not.

[1] A live-oak is an evergreen oak that grows in the American South. Whitman pictures it as hung with Spanish moss.

OUT OF THE CRADLE ENDLESSLY ROCKING

Out of the cradle endlessly rocking,
Out of the mocking-bird's throat, the musical shuttle,
Out of the Ninth-month[1] midnight,
Over the sterile sands and the fields beyond, where the child leaving
 his bed wander'd alone, bareheaded, barefoot, 5
Down from the shower'd halo,
Up from the mystic play of shadows twining and twisting as if they
 were alive,
Out from the patches of briers and blackberries,
From the memories of the bird that chanted to me,
From your memories sad brother, from the fitful risings and fall-
 ings I heard,
From under that yellow half-moon late-risen and swollen as if with
 tears, 10
From those beginning notes of yearning and love there in the
 mist,
From the thousand responses of my heart never to cease,
From the myriad thence-arous'd words,
From the word stronger and more delicious than any,
From such as now they start the scene revisiting, 15
As a flock, twittering, rising, or overhead passing,
Borne hither, ere all eludes me, hurriedly,
A man, yet by these tears a little boy again,
Throwing myself on the sand, confronting the waves,
I, chanter of pains and joys, uniter of here and hereafter, 20
Taking all hints to use them, but swiftly leaping beyond them,
A reminiscence sing.

Once Paumanok,[2]
When the lilac-scent was in the air and Fifth-month grass was
 growing,
Up this seashore in some briers, 25
Two feather'd guests from Alabama, two together,
And their nest, and four light-green eggs spotted with brown,
And every day the he-bird to and fro near at hand,
And every day the she-bird crouch'd on her nest, silent, with
 bright eyes,
And every day I, a curious boy, never too close, never disturbing
 them, 30
Cautiously peering, absorbing, translating.

Shine! shine! shine!
Pour down your warmth, great sun!
While we bask, we two together.

[1] The Quaker term for September. Whitman uses the Quaker terms for the months
throughout his work.
[2] The Indian name for Long Island.

Two together!
Winds blow south, or winds blow north, 35
Day come white, or night come black,
Home, or rivers and mountains from home,
Singing all time, minding no time,
While we two keep together. 40

Till of a sudden,
May-be kill'd, unknown to her mate,
One forenoon the she-bird crouch'd not on the nest,
Nor return'd that afternoon, nor the next,
Nor ever appear'd again. 45

And thenceforward all summer in the sound of the sea,
And at night under the full of the moon in calmer weather,
Over the hoarse surging of the sea,
Or flitting from brier to brier by day,
I saw, I heard at intervals the remaining one, the he-bird, 50
The solitary guest from Alabama.

Blow! blow! blow!
Blow up sea-winds along Paumanok's shore;
I wait and I wait till you blow my mate to me.

Yes, when the stars glisten'd,
All night long on the prong of a moss-scallop'd stake, 55
Down almost amid the slapping waves,
Sat the lone singer wonderful causing tears.

He call'd on his mate,
He pour'd forth the meanings which I of all men know. 60

Yes my brother I know,
The rest might not, but I have treasur'd every note,
For more than once dimly down to the beach gliding,
Silent, avoiding the moonbeams, blending myself with the
 shadows,
Recalling now the obscure shapes, the echoes, the sounds and
 sights after their sorts, 65
The white arms out in the breakers tirelessly tossing,
I, with bare feet, a child, the wind wafting my hair,
Listen'd long and long.

Listen'd to keep, to sing, now translating the notes,
Following you my brother. 70

Soothe! soothe! soothe!
Close on its wave soothes the wave behind,
And again another behind embracing and lapping, every one close,
But my love soothes not me, not me.

Low hangs the moon, it rose late, 75
It is lagging—O I think it is heavy with love, with love.

O madly the sea pushes upon the land,
With love, with love.

O night! do I not see my love fluttering out among the breakers?
What is that little black thing I see there in the white? 80

Loud! loud! loud!
Loud I call to you, my love!
High and clear I shoot my voice over the waves,
Surely you must know who is here, is here,
You must know who I am, my love. 85

Low-hanging moon!
What is that dusky spot in your brown yellow?
O it is the shape, the shape of my mate!
O moon do not keep her from me any longer.

Land! land! O land! 90
Whichever way I turn, O I think you could give me my mate back again if
 you only would,
For I am almost sure I see her dimly whichever way I look.

O rising stars!
Perhaps the one I want so much will rise, will rise with some of you.

O throat! O trembling throat!
Sound clearer through the atmosphere! 95
Pierce the woods, the earth,
Somewhere listening to catch you must be the one I want.

Shake out carols!
Solitary here, the night's carols!
Carols of lonesome love! death's carols! 100
Carols under that lagging, yellow, waning moon!
O under that moon where she droops almost down into the sea!
O reckless despairing carols.

But soft! sink low!
Soft! let me just murmur, 105
And do you wait a moment you husky-nois'd sea,
For somewhere I believe I heard my mate responding to me,
So faint, I must be still, be still to listen,
But not altogether still, for then she might not come immediately to me. 110

Hither my love!
Here I am! here!
With this just-sustain'd note I announce myself to you,
This gentle call is for you my love, for you.

Do not be decoy'd elsewhere, 115
That is the whistle of the wind, it is not my voice,
That is the fluttering, the fluttering of the spray,
Those are the shadows of leaves.

O darkness! O in vain!
O I am very sick and sorrowful. 120

O brown halo in the sky near the moon, drooping upon the sea!
O troubled reflection in the sea!
O throat! O throbbing heart!
And I singing uselessly, uselessly all the night.

O past! O happy life! O songs of joy! 125
In the air, in the woods, over fields,
Loved! loved! loved! loved! loved!
But my mate no more, no more with me!
We two together no more.

The aria sinking, 130
All else continuing, the stars shining,
The winds blowing, the notes of the bird continuous echoing,
With angry moans the fierce old mother incessantly moaning,
On the sands of Paumanok's shore gray and rustling,
The yellow half-moon enlarged, sagging down, drooping, the face
 of the sea almost touching, 135
The boy ecstatic, with his bare feet the waves, with his hair the
 atmosphere dallying,
The love in the heart long pent, now loose, now at last tumultu-
 ously bursting,
The aria's meaning, the ears, the soul, swiftly depositing,
The strange tears down the cheeks coursing,
The colloquy there, the trio, each uttering, 140
The undertone, the savage old mother incessantly crying,
To the boy's soul's questions sullenly timing, some drown'd secret
 hissing,
To the outsetting bard.

Demon or bird! (said the boy's soul,)
Is it indeed toward your mate you sing? or is it really to me? 145
For I, that was a child, my tongue's use sleeping, now I have
 heard you,
Now in a moment I know what I am for, I awake,
And already a thousand singers, a thousand songs, clearer, louder
 and more sorrowful than yours,
A thousand warbling echoes have started to life within me, never
 to die.

O you singer solitary, singing by yourself, projecting me, 150
O solitary me listening, never more shall I cease perpetuating you,

Never more shall I escape, never more the reverberations,
Never more the cries of unsatisfied love be absent from me,
Never again leave me to be the peaceful child I was before what
 there in the night,
By the sea under the yellow and sagging moon, 155
The messenger there arous'd, the fire, the sweet hell within,
The unknown want, the destiny of me.

O give me the clew! (it lurks in the night here somewhere,)
O if I am to have so much, let me have more!

A word then, (for I will conquer it,) 160
The word final, superior to all,
Subtle, sent up—what is it?—I listen;
Are you whispering it, and have been all the time, you sea-waves?
Is that it from your liquid rims and wet sands?

Whereto answering, the sea, 165
Delaying not, hurrying not,
Whisper'd me through the night, and very plainly before day-
 break,
Lisp'd to me the low and delicious word death,
And again death, death, death, death,
Hissing melodious, neither like the bird nor like my arous'd child's
 heart,
But edging near as privately for me rustling at my feet, 170
Creeping thence steadily up to my ears and laving[3] me softly all
 over,
Death, death, death, death, death.

Which I do not forget,
But fuse the song of my dusky demon and brother, 175
That he sang to me in the moonlight on Paumanok's gray beach,
With the thousand responsive songs at random,
My own songs awaked from that hour,
And with them the key, the word up from the waves,
The word of the sweetest song and all songs, 180
That strong and delicious word which, creeping to my feet,
(Or like some old crone rocking the cradle, swathed in sweet gar-
 ments, bending aside,)
The sea whisper'd me.

WHEN I HEARD THE LEARN'D ASTRONOMER

When I heard the learn'd astronomer,
When the proofs, the figures, were ranged in columns before me,

[3] Bathing.

When I was shown the charts and diagrams, to add, divide, and mea-
 sure them,
When I sitting heard the astronomer where he lectured with much
 applause in the lecture-room,
How soon unaccountable I became tired and sick, 5
Till rising and gliding out I wander'd off by myself,
In the mystical moist night-air, and from time to time,
Look'd up in perfect silence at the stars.

WHEN LILACS LAST IN THE DOORYARD BLOOM'D.

1

When lilacs last in the dooryard bloom'd,
And the great star[1] early droop'd in the western sky in the night,
I mourn'd, and yet shall mourn with ever-returning spring.

Ever-returning spring, trinity sure to me you bring,
Lilac blooming perennial and drooping star in the west, 5
And thought of him I love.

2

O powerful western fallen star!
O shades of night—O moody, tearful night!
O great star disappear'd—O the black murk that hides the star!
O cruel hands that hold me powerless—O helpless soul of me! 10
O harsh surrounding cloud that will not free my soul.

3

In the dooryard fronting an old farm-house near the white-wash'd
 palings,
Stands the lilac-bush tall-growing with heart-shaped leaves of rich
 green,
With many a pointed blossom rising delicate, with the perfume strong
 I love,
With every leaf a miracle—and from this bush in the dooryard, 15
With delicate-color'd blossoms and heart-shaped leaves of rich
 green,
A sprig with its flower I break.

4

In the swamp in secluded recesses,
A shy and hidden bird is warbling a song.

Solitary the thrush, 20
The hermit withdrawn to himself, avoiding the settlements,
Sings by himself a song.

[1] Venus, the evening star.

Song of the bleeding throat,
Death's outlet song of life, (for well dear brother I know,
If thou wast not granted to sing thou would'st surely die.) 25

5

Over the breast of the spring, the land, amid cities,
Amid lanes and through old woods, where lately the violets peep'd
 from the ground, spotting the gray debris,
Amid the grass in the fields each side of the lanes, passing the endless
 grass,
Passing the yellow-spear'd wheat, every grain from its shroud in the
 dark-brown fields uprisen,
Passing the apple-tree blows of white and pink in the orchards, 30
Carrying a corpse to where it shall rest in the grave,
Night and day journeys a coffin.[2]

6

Coffin that passes through lanes and streets,
Through day and night with the great cloud darkening the land,
With the pomp of the inloop'd flags with the cities draped in black, 35
With the show of the States themselves as of crape-veil'd women
 standing,
With processions long and winding and the flambeaus[3] of the night,
With the countless torches lit, with the silent sea of faces and the
 unbared heads,
With the waiting depot, the arriving coffin, and the sombre faces,
With dirges through the night, with the thousand voices rising
 strong and solemn, 40
With all the mournful voices of the dirges pour'd around the
 coffin,
The dim-lit churches and the shuddering organs—where amid
 these you journey,
With the tolling tolling bells' perpetual clang,
Here, coffin that slowly passes,
I give you my sprig of lilac. 45

7

(Nor for you, for one alone,
Blossoms and branches green to coffins all I bring,
For fresh as the morning, thus would I chant a song for you O sane
 and sacred death.

All over bouquets of roses,
O death, I cover you over with roses and early lilies, 50
But mostly and now the lilac that blooms the first,

[2] Lincoln was assassinated on Good Friday, April 14, 1865. After a funeral service in Washington, his body was taken by train to Springfield, Illinois, for burial. The journey, at twenty miles an hour, took two weeks, through scenes of grief like those Whitman describes.
[3] Torches.

Copious I break, I break the sprigs from the bushes,
With loaded arms I come, pouring for you,
For you and the coffins all of you O death.)

8

O western orb sailing the heaven, 55
Now I know what you must have meant as a month since I walk'd,
As I walk'd in silence the transparent shadowy night,
As I saw you had something to tell as you bent to me night after
 night,
As you droop'd from the sky low down as if to my side, (while the
 other stars all look'd on,)
As we wander'd together the solemn night, (for something I know not
 what kept me from sleep,) 60
As the night advanced, and I saw on the rim of the west how full you
 were of woe,
As I stood on the rising ground in the breeze in the cool transparent
 night,
As I watch'd where you pass'd and was lost in the netherward black
 of the night,
As my soul in its trouble dissatisfied sank, as where you sad orb,
Concluded, dropt in the night, and was gone. 65

9

Sing on there in the swamp,
O singer bashful and tender, I hear your notes, I hear your call,
I hear, I come presently, I understand you,
But a moment I linger, for the lustrous star has detain'd me,
The star my departing comrade holds and detains me. 70

10

O how shall I warble myself for the dead one there I loved?
And how shall I deck my song for the large sweet soul that has gone?
And what shall my perfume be for the grave of him I love?

Sea-winds blown from east and west,
Blown from the Eastern sea and blown from the Western sea, till
 there on the prairies meeting, 75
These and with these and the breath of my chant,
I'll perfume the grave of him I love.

11

O what shall I hang on the chamber walls?
And what shall the pictures be that I hang on the walls,
To adorn the burial-house of him I love? 80

Pictures of growing spring and farms and homes,
With the Fourth-month[4] eve at sundown, and the gray smoke
 lucid and bright,

[4] The Quaker term for April.

With floods of the yellow gold of the gorgeous, indolent, sinking sun,
 burning, expanding the air,
With the fresh sweet herbage under foot, and the pale green leaves
 of the trees prolific,
In the distance the flowing glaze, the breast of the river, with a wind-
 dapple here and there, 85
With ranging hills on the banks, with many a line against the
 sky, and shadows,
And the city at hand with dwellings so dense, and stacks of
 chimneys,
And all the scenes of life and the workshops, and the workmen
 homeward returning.

<div align="center">12</div>

Lo, body and soul—this land,
My own Manhattan with spires, and the sparkling and hurrying tides,
 and the ships,
The varied and ample land, the South and the North in the light, 90
 Ohio's shores and flashing Missouri,
And ever the far-spreading prairies cover'd with grass and corn.

Lo, the most excellent sun so calm and haughty,
The violet and purple morn with just-felt breezes,
The gentle soft-born measureless light,
The miracle spreading bathing all, the fulfill'd noon, 95
The coming eve delicious, the welcome night and the stars,
Over my cities shining all, enveloping man and land.

<div align="center">13</div>

Sing on, sing on you gray-brown bird,
Sing from the swamps, the recesses, pour your chant from the bushes, 100
Limitless out of the dusk, out of the cedars and pines.

Sing on dearest brother, warble your reedy song,
Loud human song, with voice of uttermost woe.

O liquid and free and tender!
O wild and loose to my soul—O wondrous singer, 105
You only I hear—yet the star holds me, (but will soon depart,)
Yet the lilac with mastering odor holds me.

<div align="center">14</div>

Now while I sat in the day and look'd forth,
In the close of the day with its light and the fields of spring, and the
 farmers preparing their crops,
In the large unconscious scenery of my land with its lakes and forests, 110
In the heavenly aerial beauty, (after the perturb'd winds and the
 storms,)
Under the arching heavens of the afternoon swift passing, and the
 voices of children and women,

The many-moving sea-tides, and I saw the ships how they sail'd,
And the summer approaching with richness, and the fields all
　　busy with labor,
And the infinite separate houses, how they all went on, each with its
　　meals and minutia of daily usages, 115
And the streets how their throbbings throbb'd, and the cities
　　pent—lo, then and there,
Falling upon them all and among them all, enveloping me with
　　the rest,
Appear'd the cloud, appear'd the long black trail,
And I knew death, its thought, and the sacred knowledge of
　　death.

Then with the knowledge of death as walking one side of me, 120
And the thought of death close-walking the other side of me,
And I in the middle as with companions, and as holding the
　　hands of companions,
I fled forth to the hiding receiving night that talks not,
Down to the shores of the water, the path by the swamp in the
　　dimness,
To the solemn shadowy cedars and ghostly pines so still. 125

And the singer so shy to the rest receiv'd me,
The gray-brown bird I know receiv'd us comrades three,
And he sang the carol of death, and a verse for him I love.

From deep secluded recesses,
From the fragrant cedars and the ghostly pines so still, 130
Came the carol of the bird.

And the charm of the carol rapt me,
As I held as if by their hands my comrades in the night,
And the voice of my spirit tallied the song of the bird.

Come lovely and soothing death, 135
Undulate round the world, serenely arriving, arriving,
In the day, in the night, to all, to each,
Sooner or later delicate death.

Prais'd be the fathomless universe,
For life and joy, and for objects and knowledge curious, 140
And for love, sweet love—but praise! praise! praise!
For the sure-enwinding arms of cool-enfolding death.

Dark mother always gliding near with soft feet,
Have none chanted for thee a chant of fullest welcome?
Then I chant it for thee, I glorify thee above all, 145
I bring thee a song that when thou must indeed come, come unfalteringly.

Approach strong deliveress,
When it is so, when thou hast taken them I joyously sing the dead,

Lost in the loving floating ocean of thee,
Laved[5] in the flood of thy bliss O death. 150

From me to thee glad serenades,
Dances for thee I propose saluting thee, adornments and feastings for thee,
And the sights of the open landscape and the high-spread sky are fitting,
And life and the fields, and the huge and thoughtful night.

The night in silence under many a star, 155
The ocean shore and the husky whispering wave whose voice I know,
And the soul turning to thee O vast and well-veil'd death,
And the body gratefully nestling close to thee.

Over the tree-tops I float thee a song,
Over the rising and singing waves, over the myriad fields and the prairies
 wide,
 160
Over the dense-pack'd cities all and the teeming wharves and ways,
I float this carol with joy, with joy to thee O death.

15

To the tally of my soul,
Loud and strong kept up the gray-brown bird,
With pure deliberate notes spreading filling the night. 165

Loud in the pines and cedars dim,
Clear in the freshness moist and the swamp-perfume,
And I with my comrades there in the night.

While my sight that was bound in my eyes unclosed,
As to long panoramas of visions. 170

And I saw askant[6] the armies,
I saw as in noiseless dreams hundreds of battle-flags,
Borne through the smoke of the battles and pierc'd with missiles
 I saw them,
And carried hither and yon through the smoke, and torn and
 bloody,
And at last but a few shreds left on the staffs, (and all in silence,) 175
And the staffs all splinter'd and broken.

I saw battle-corpses, myriads of them,
And the white skeletons of young men, I saw them,
I saw the debris and debris of all the slain soldiers of the war,
But I saw they were not as was thought, 180
They themselves were fully at rest, they suffer'd not,
The living remain'd and suffer'd, the mother suffer'd,
And the wife and the child and the musing comrade suffer'd,
And the armies that remain'd suffer'd.

[5] Bathed. [6] With suspicion or mistrust.

16

Passing the visions, passing the night, 185
Passing, unloosing the hold of my comrades' hands,
Passing the song of the hermit bird and the tallying song of my
 soul,
Victorious song, death's outlet song, yet varying ever-altering song,
As low and wailing, yet clear the notes, rising and falling,
 flooding the night,
Sadly sinking and fainting, as warning and warning, and yet again
 bursting with joy, 190
Covering the earth and filling the spread of the heaven,
As that powerful psalm in the night I heard from recesses,
Passing, I leave thee lilac with heart-shaped leaves,
I leave thee there in the door-yard, blooming, returning with
 spring.

I cease from my song for thee, 195
From my gaze on thee in the west, fronting the west, communing with
 thee,
O comrade lustrous with silver face in the night.

Yet each to keep and all, retrievements out of the night,
The song, the wondrous chant of the gray-brown bird,
And the tallying chant, the echo arous'd in my soul, 200
With the lustrous and drooping star with the countenance full of
 woe,
With the holders holding my hand nearing the call of the bird,
Comrades mine and I in the midst, and their memory ever to keep,
 for the dead I loved so well,
For the sweetest, wisest soul of all my days and lands—and this for his
 dear sake,
Lilac and star and bird twined with the chant of my soul, 205
There in the fragrant pines and the cedars dusk and dim.

A NOISELESS PATIENT SPIDER

A noiseless patient spider,
I mark'd where on a little promontory it stood isolated,
Mark'd how to explore the vacant vast surrounding,
It launch'd forth filament, filament, filament, out of itself,
Ever unreeling them, ever tirelessly speeding them. 5

And you O my soul where you stand,
Surrounded, detached, in measureless oceans of space,
Ceaselessly musing, venturing, throwing, seeking the spheres to
 connect them,

Till the bridge you will need be form'd, till the ductile[1] anchor
 hold,
Till the gossamer thread you fling catch somewhere, O my soul. 10

Herman Melville
(1819–1891)

Masterpieces came close upon one another's heels in America in the 1850's.
Ralph Waldo Emerson's *Representative Men* and Nathaniel Hawthorne's *The
Scarlet Letter* were both published in 1850; Herman Melville's *Moby-Dick*
followed in 1851; Henry David Thoreau's *Walden* in 1854; and Walt Whit-
man's *Leaves of Grass* in 1855. All these books have had a major impact
upon modern world literature, but they are also intensely American; all
touch universal concerns through the local and the topical. Together, they
constitute a sort of five-voiced discussion of the question of the prospects of
the American Adam in an Edenic continent rapidly being filled up through
Yankee hustle. The five voices, it is generally held, are on two sides: on one,
Emerson, Thoreau, and Whitman, from their own particular points of
view, argue optimistically for the almost unlimited development of demo-
cratic man; on the other, Hawthorne and Melville point to the serpent in
the shrubbery, the blackness in the human situation that persists despite
changes in social organization.

Herman Melville, born in New York City in 1819, learned the lessons of
blackness early. When he was eleven, his father, a well-to-do merchant,
went bankrupt; two years later he died, driven insane through worry and
overwork. The widow moved with her children to Albany. By the time
Melville was twenty, he had worked as a bank clerk, a salesman, a farm-
hand, and a schoolteacher. In 1839, he signed on as a cabinboy for a voyage
to Liverpool and back, a shocking experience of brutality and vice. In 1841,
he sailed, this time as a seaman, on the whaler *Acushnet,* bound for the
South Seas. After eighteen months, he jumped ship in the Marquesas Is-
lands, encountered a tribe of cannibals, and left the islands on an Austra-
lian whaler, whose crew mutinied. Melville was briefly imprisoned in Tahiti
for his share in the mutiny. After a period of beachcombing in Tahiti and
clerking in Hawaii, he signed on as part of the crew of the American frigate
United States; during the fourteen-month voyage home, Melville witnessed
firsthand the injustice and brutality of navy life. The ship arrived in Boston
in October, 1844, and Melville was discharged along with the rest of the
crew. The experiences of this three-year adventure were to furnish him
with the materials of his books and to shape his attitudes for the rest of his
life.

Typee, a barely fictionalized account of his experiences in the Marquesas,
appeared in 1846, and *Omoo,* which continues the story of the voyage

[1] Capable of being drawn out in thin filaments.

through the mutiny and Tahiti, followed in 1847. Both books were success-
ful, but Melville's next book, *Mardi*, was greeted with bafflement. Again the
book dealt with a young American deserter in the South Seas, but the
narrative burst the bonds of the romantic adventure genre to become a
dense political and religious allegory. The protagonist Taji, in quest of the
beautiful Yillah, sails through the allegorical islands of the Mardi archipel-
ago, discussing metaphysical questions with the philosopher Babbalanja.
Stung by the failure of this strange, experimental book, Melville returned
to more conventional sea stories with *Redburn* (1849), the story of his first
voyage to Liverpool, and *White Jacket* (1850), based on his voyage home
from Hawaii aboard the *United States*.

 Melville had married in 1847, and in 1850, he moved with his wife to
the village of Pittsfield, Massachusetts, where he began a new sea novel,
Moby-Dick. Nathaniel Hawthorne lived only seven miles away, in the village
of Lenox, and the two writers developed a close friendship that was to leave
a lasting mark on Melville's work. Melville, as *Mardi* demonstrates, had
already begun to experiment with ways to enrich literal narrative, making it
suggest deeper levels of experience, and the personal influence of Haw-
thorne, as well as that of his cryptic, suggestive tales, led him to develop the
allusive and symbolic dimensions of his story. The first draft of *Moby-Dick*
seems to have been a fairly literal, documentary whaling narrative; the
second draft, completed under Hawthorne's influence, became a richly
symbolic quest story, "broiled in hell fire." It is narrated by a young man
named Ishmael, superficially at least much like the narrator of *Typee*, but it
deals with the obsessed, demonic Captain Ahab, perhaps Ishmael's double,
who, like many of Hawthorne's protagonists, has arrogantly isolated him-
self from life in a quest not only for the white whale but for more than
human knowledge.

 The commercial failure of *Moby-Dick*, which he knew was his master-
piece, embittered Melville, who became increasingly alienated from his
family and friends. He continued to write. *Pierre* (1852), a bitter, dreamlike
allegory, mystified readers even more than *Moby-Dick*. *Israel Potter*, a histor-
ical novel, appeared in 1855, and *Piazza Tales*, a collection of short stories
which included "Bartleby the Scrivener," appeared in 1856. *The Confidence
Man* (1857) explores, aboard a Mississippi riverboat, the theme of truth
and illusion.

 In 1866, Melville obtained the post of deputy customs inspector in New
York, a job that provided the financial security his books had never pro-
vided but which left him little time for writing. *Clarel*, a book-length sym-
bolic poem about a trip to Palestine, was published in 1876; three collec-
tions of shorter poems also appeared during Melville's lifetime. He
resigned the customs job in 1885 and died six years later, virtually forgot-
ten as a writer but leaving one of his finest stories, the novella *Billy Budd*, in
manuscript among his effects. It was not until the 1930's that Melville's
works were rediscovered and republished and he began the rapid rise to
fame that has now placed him with Hawthorne, Thoreau, and Whitman
among the giants of American literature.

 Melville's contemporaries (or those who had heard of him at all)
thought of him as a writer of adventure stories who had lapsed into writing
jumbled, possibly crazed, allegories. From our perspective, we can see his

work as perhaps complex and sometimes tortured but remarkably unified around a handful of rich and profoundly explored themes. The most important of these is evil and the individual's recognition and response to it, both in the outside world and in himself. Even the comparatively simple sea stories explore sardonically the intrusion of Western, "Christian" culture, with its burden of vice, disease, and guilt, into the Edenic societies of the South Seas. Captain Ahab, the Promethean Romantic individualist, thinks he is pursuing Evil itself in the form of the white whale. But is Moby-Dick "Evil" (or even "evil"?) As whiteness contains all colors, so the whiteness of the whale contains all possibilities; it is infinite in its possibilities and in its mysteriousness. And as Ahab pursues the monster upon which he has projected aspects of his own nature that he has denied, he ironically comes more and more to resemble his hated antagonist; at the end, he goes to his death bound by the harpoon lines to the whale. Captain Vere, in *Billy Budd*, for all his apparent humaneness and moral sensitivity, is Captain Ahab's brother in one respect; like him, he is blind to his own evil. He rationalizes his own actions by conservative appeals to law and institutions, but Billy hangs just the same.

Melville was at his best within the roominess of the novel, but he wrote a number of short stories and novellas as well, and in at least two, "Benito Cereno" and "Bartleby the Scrivener," he was able to achieve effective expressions of his sardonic vision. Bartleby is one of those isolates, dropouts from ordinary life, whom both Melville and his friend Hawthorne liked to dissect. But Bartleby is no Ahab, or even a Young Goodman Brown; he is just a crank, and his story is told as black comedy. Why does Bartleby decide that he "would prefer not to," and what does his polite but firm disengagement from life and drift toward death mean? Critics have varied widely in their answers. For one, the story is an economic allegory and Bartleby is a working-class hero who refuses to compete within the capitalist system. Another finds in the story a fable of Melville's attempts to write commercial magazine fiction in the 1850's (he would have preferred not to). But is Bartleby even the main character? A case could equally well be made that the real center of interest is the genial, liberal narrator, who prides himself on his connection with John Jacob Astor and who is "filled with a profound conviction that the easiest way of life is the best." The rest of his staff—the grotesque Turkey, Nippers, and Ginger Nut—seem to suggest some aspects of himself that he has repressed, and perhaps the sepulchral Bartleby, to whom he feels bound in so intimate and sympathetic a relationship, may represent the emergence of a hidden blackness in himself.

FURTHER READING *(prepared by W. J. R.):* A superior introduction to Melville is Newton Arvin's *Herman Melville*, 1950, rpt. 1957, which received a National Book Award. Tyrus Hillway's *Herman Melville*, 1963, rev. 1979, contains a fine critical survey of Melville, with chapters on his life and individual treatments of the major works. Further direction for the new reader can be found in James E. Miller, Jr.'s *A Reader's Guide to Herman Melville*, 1973, and in John Bryant's *A Companion to Melville Studies*, 1986. Critical reactions to a number of Melville works are offered in *Melville: A Collection of Critical Essays*, ed. Richard Chase, 1962, and *Herman Melville: Reassessments*, ed. by A. Robert Lee, 1984. The major criticism is collected in *Melville: The Critical Heritage*, ed. by Watson G. Branch, 1985.

BARTLEBY THE SCRIVENER

A STORY OF WALL STREET

I am a rather elderly man. The nature of my avocations, for the last thirty years, has brought me into more than ordinary contact with what would seem an interesting and somewhat singular set of men, of whom, as yet, nothing, that I know of, has ever been written—I mean, the law-copyists, or scriveners. I have known very many of them, professionally and privately, and, if I pleased, could relate divers histories, at which good-natured gentlemen might smile, and sentimental souls might weep. But I waive the biographies of all other scriveners, for a few passages in the life of Bartleby, who was a scrivener, the strangest I ever saw, or heard of. While, of other law-copyists, I might write the complete life, of Bartleby nothing of that sort can be done. I believe that no materials exist, for a full and satisfactory biography of this man. It is an irreparable loss to literature. Bartleby was one of those beings of whom nothing is ascertainable, except from the original sources, and, in his case, those are very small. What my own astonished eyes saw of Bartleby, *that* is all I know of him, except, indeed, one vague report, which will appear in the sequel.

Ere introducing the scrivener, as he first appeared to me, it is fit I make some mention of myself, my *employés*, my business, my chambers, and general surroundings; because some such description is indispensable to an adequate understanding of the chief character about to be presented. Imprimis:[1] I am a man who, from his youth upwards, has been filled with a profound conviction that the easiest way of life is the best. Hence, though I belong to a profession proverbially energetic and nervous, even to turbulence, at times, yet nothing of that sort have I ever suffered to invade my peace. I am one of those unambitious lawyers who never address a jury, or in any way draw down public applause; but, in the cool tranquillity of a snug retreat, do a snug business among rich men's bonds, and mortgages, and title-deeds. All who know me, consider me an eminently *safe* man. The late John Jacob Astor,[2] a personage little given to poetic enthusiasm, had no hesitation in pronouncing my first grand point to be prudence; my next, method. I do not speak it in vanity, but simply record the fact, that I was not unemployed in my profession by the late John Jacob Astor; a name which, I admit, I love to repeat; for it hath a rounded and orbicular sound to it, and rings like unto bullion. I will freely add, that I was not insensible to the late John Jacob Astor's good opinion.

Some time prior to the period at which this little history begins, my avocations had been largely increased. The good old office, now extinct in the State of New York, of a Master of Chancery,[3] had been conferred upon me. It was not a very arduous office, but very pleasantly remunerative. I seldom lose my temper; much more seldom indulge in dangerous indignation at wrongs and outrages; but I must be permitted to be rash here and

[1] In the first place.
[2] American merchant (1763–1848); at his death, the richest man in the United States.
[3] A Master of Chancery presided over equity cases, without a jury.

declare, that I consider the sudden and violent abrogation of the office of Master in Chancery, by the new Constitution, as a —— premature act; inasmuch as I had counted upon a life-lease of the profits, whereas I only received those of a few short years. But this is by the way.

My chambers were up stairs, at No. —— Wall Street. At one end, they looked upon the white wall of the interior of a spacious skylight shaft, penetrating the building from top to bottom.

This view might have been considered rather tame than otherwise, deficient in what landscape painters call "life." But, if so, the view from the other end of my chambers offered, at least, a contrast, if nothing more. In that direction, my windows commanded an unobstructed view of a lofty brick wall, black by age and everlasting shade; which wall required no spyglass to bring out its lurking beauties, but, for the benefit of all near-sighted spectators, was pushed up to within ten feet of my window-panes. Owing to the great height of the surrounding buildings, and my chambers being on the second floor, the interval between this wall and mine not a little resembled a huge square cistern.

At the period just preceding the advent of Bartleby, I had two persons as copyists in my employment, and a promising lad as an office-boy. First, Turkey; second, Nippers; third, Ginger Nut. These may seem names, the like of which are not usually found in the Directory. In truth, they were nicknames, mutually conferred upon each other by my three clerks, and were deemed expressive of their respective persons or characters. Turkey was a short, pursy Englishman, of about my own age—that is, somewhere not far from sixty. In the morning, one might say, his face was of a fine florid hue, but after twelve o'clock, meridian—his dinner hour—it blazed like a grate full of Christmas coals; and continued blazing—but, as it were, with a gradual wane—till six o'clock, P.M., or thereabouts; after which, I saw no more of the proprietor of the face, which, gaining its meridian with the sun, seemed to set with it, to rise, culminate, and decline the following day, with the like regularity and undiminished glory. There are many singular coincidences I have known in the course of my life, not the least among which was the fact, that, exactly when Turkey displayed his fullest beams from his red and radiant countenance, just then, too, at that critical moment, began the daily period when I considered his business capacities as seriously disturbed for the remainder of the twenty-four hours. Not that he was absolutely idle, or averse to business then; far from it. The difficulty was, he was apt to be altogether too energetic. There was a strange, inflamed, flurried, flighty recklessness of activity about him. He would be incautious in dipping his pen into his inkstand. All his blots upon my documents were dropped there after twelve o'clock, meridian. Indeed, not only would he be reckless, and sadly given to making blots in the afternoon, but, some days, he went further, and was rather noisy. At such times, too, his face flamed with augmented blazonry, as if cannel coal had been heaped on anthracite. He made an unpleasant racket with his chair; spilled his sandbox; in mending his pens, impatiently split them all to pieces, and threw them on the floor in a sudden passion; stood up, and leaned over his table, boxing his papers about in a most indecorous manner, very sad to behold in an elderly man like him. Nevertheless, as he was in many ways a most valuable person to me, and all the time before twelve o'clock, meridian, was

the quickest, steadiest creature, too, accomplishing a great deal of work in a style not easily to be matched—for these reasons, I was willing to overlook his eccentricities, though, indeed, occasionally, I remonstrated with him. I did this very gently, however, because, though the civilest, nay, the blandest and most reverential of men in the morning, yet, in the afternoon, he was disposed, upon provocation, to be slightly rash with his tongue—in fact, insolent. Now, valuing his morning services as I did, and resolved not to lose them—yet, at the same time, made uncomfortable by his inflamed ways after twelve o'clock—and being a man of peace, unwilling by my admonitions to call forth unseemly retorts from him, I took upon me, one Saturday noon (he was always worse on Saturdays) to hint to him, very kindly, that, perhaps, now that he was growing old, it might be well to abridge his labors; in short, he need not come to my chambers after twelve o'clock, but, dinner over, had best go home to his lodgings, and rest himself till tea-time. But no; he insisted upon his afternoon devotions. His countenance became intolerably fervid, as he oratorically assured me—gesticulating with a long ruler at the other end of the room—that if his services in the morning were useful, how indispensable, then, in the afternoon?

"With submission, sir" said Turkey, on this occasion, "I consider myself your right-hand man. In the morning I but marshall and deploy my columns; but in the afternoon I put myself at their head, and gallantly charge the foe, thus"—and he made a violent thrust with the ruler.

"But the blots, Turkey," intimated I.

"True; but, with submission, sir, behold these hairs! I am getting old. Surely, sir, a blot or two of a warm afternoon is not to be severely urged against gray hairs. Old age—even if it blot the page—is honorable. With submission, sir, we *both* are getting old."

This appeal to my fellow-feeling was hardly to be resisted. At all events, I saw that go he would not. So, I made up my mind to let him stay, resolving, nevertheless, to see to it that, during the afternoon, he had to do with my less important papers.

Nippers, the second on my list, was a whiskered, sallow, and, upon the whole, rather piratical-looking young man, of about five-and-twenty. I alway deemed him the victim of two evil powers—ambition and indigestion. The ambition was evinced by a certain impatience of the duties of a mere copyist, an unwarrantable usurpation of strictly professional affairs such as the original drawing up of legal documents. The indigestion seemed betokened in an occasional nervous testiness and grinning irritability, causing the teeth to audibly grind together over mistakes committed in copying; unnecessary maledictions, hissed, rather than spoken, in the heat of business; and especially by a continual discontent with the height of the table where he worked. Though of a very ingenious mechanical turn, Nippers could never get this table to suit him. He put chips under it, blocks of various sorts, bits of pasteboard, and at last went so far as to attempt an exquisite adjustment, by final pieces of folded blotting-paper. But no invention would answer. If, for the sake of easing his back, he brought the table-lid at a sharp angle well up towards his chin, and wrote there like a man using the steep roof of a Dutch house for his desk, then he declared that it stopped the circulation in his arms. If now he lowered the table to his waistbands, and stooped over it in writing, then there was a sore aching in

his back. In short, the truth of the matter was, Nippers knew not what he wanted. Or, if he wanted anything, it was to be rid of a scrivener's table altogether. Among the manifestations of his diseased ambition was a fondness he had for receiving visits from certain ambiguous-looking fellows in seedy coats, whom he called his clients. Indeed, I was aware that not only was he, at times, considerable of a ward-politician, but he occasionally did a little business at the justices' courts, and was not unknown on the steps of the Tombs.[4] I have good reason to believe, however, that one individual who called upon him at my chambers, and who, with a grand air, he insisted was his client, was no other than a dun, and the alleged title-deed, a bill. But, with all his failings, and the annoyances he caused me, Nippers, like his compatriot Turkey, was a very useful man to me; wrote a neat, swift hand; and, when he chose, was not deficient in a gentlemanly sort of deportment. Added to this, he always dressed in a gentlemanly sort of way; and so, incidentally, reflected credit upon my chambers. Whereas, with respect to Turkey, I had much ado to keep him from being a reproach to me. His clothes were apt to look oily, and smell of eating-houses. He wore his pantaloons very loose and baggy in summer. His coats were execrable; his hat not to be handled. But while the hat was a thing of indifference to me, inasmuch as his natural civility and deference, as a dependent Englishman, always led him to doff it the moment he entered the room, yet his coat was another matter. Concerning his coats, I reasoned with him; but with no effect. The truth was, I suppose, that a man with so small an income could not afford to sport such a lustrous face and a lustrous coat at one and the same time. As Nippers once observed, Turkey's money went chiefly for red ink. One winter day, I presented Turkey with a highly respectable-looking coat of my own—a padded gray coat, of a most comfortable warmth, and which buttoned straight up from the knee to the neck. I thought Turkey would appreciate the favor, and abate his rashness and obstreperousness of afternoons. But no; I verily believe that buttoning himself up in so downy and blanket-like a coat had a pernicious effect upon him—upon the same principle that too much oats are bad for horses. In fact, precisely as a rash, restive horse is said to feel his oats, so Turkey felt his coat. It made him insolent. He was a man whom prosperity harmed.

Though, concerning the self-indulgent habits of Turkey, I had my own private surmises, yet, touching Nippers, I was well persuaded that, whatever might be his faults in other respects, he was, at least, a temperate young man. But, indeed, nature herself seemed to have been his vintner, and, at his birth, charged him so thoroughly with an irritable, brandy-like disposition, that all subsequent potations were needless. When I consider how, amid the stillness of my chambers, Nippers would sometimes impatiently rise from his seat, and stooping over his table, spread his arms wide apart, seize the whole desk, and move it, and jerk it, with a grim, grinding motion on the floor, as if the table were a perverse voluntary agent, intent on thwarting and vexing him, I plainly perceive that, for Nippers, brandy-and-water were altogether superfluous.

[4] The New York Halls of Justice and House of Detention, familiarly called the "Tombs" because its architecture is reminiscent of Egyptian temples and tombs.

It was fortunate for me that, owing to its peculiar cause—indigestion—the irritability and consequent nervousness of Nippers were mainly observable in the morning, while in the afternoon he was comparatively mild. So that, Turkey's paroxysms only coming on about twelve o'clock, I never had to do with their eccentricities at one time. Their fits relieved each other, like guards. When Nippers' was on, Turkey's was off; and *vice versa*. This was a good natural arrangement, under the circumstances.

Ginger Nut, the third on my list, was a lad, some twelve years old. His father was a carman, ambitious of seeing his son on the bench instead of a cart, before he died. So he sent him to my office, as student at law, errand-boy, cleaner and sweeper, at the rate of one dollar a week. He had a little desk to himself, but he did not use it much. Upon inspection, the drawer exhibited a great array of the shells of various sorts of nuts. Indeed, to this quick-witted youth, the whole noble science of the law was contained in a nutshell. Not the least among the employments of Ginger Nut, as well as one which he discharged with the most alacrity, was his duty as cake and apple purveyor for Turkey and Nippers. Copying law-papers being proverbially a dry, husky sort of business, my two scriveners were fain to moisten their mouths very often with Spitzenbergs,[5] to be had at the numerous stalls nigh the Custom House and Post office. Also, they sent Ginger Nut very frequently for that peculiar cake—small, flat, round, and very spicy—after which he had been named by them. Of a cold morning, when business was but dull, Turkey would gobble up scores of these cakes, as if they were mere wafers—indeed, they sell them at the rate of six or eight for a penny—the scrape of his pen blending with the crunching of the crisp particles in his mouth. Rashest of all the fiery afternoon blunders and flurried rashnesses of Turkey, was his once moistening a ginger-cake between his lips, and clapping it on to a mortgage, for a seal. I came within an ace of dismissing him then. But he mollified me by making an oriental bow, and saying—

"With submission, sir, it was generous of me to find you in stationery on my own account."

Now my original business—that of a conveyancer and title hunter, and drawer-up of recondite documents of all sorts—was considerably increased by receiving the Master's office. There was now great work for scriveners. Not only must I push the clerks already with me, but I must have additional help.

In answer to my advertisement, a motionless young man one morning stood upon my office threshold, the door being open, for it was summer. I can see that figure now—pallidly neat, pitiably respectable, incurably forlorn! It was Bartleby.

After a few words touching his qualifications, I engaged him, glad to have among my corps of copyists a man of so singularly sedate an aspect, which I thought might operate beneficially upon the flighty temper of Turkey, and the fiery one of Nippers.

I should have stated before that ground-glass folding-doors divided my premises into two parts, one of which was occupied by my scriveners, the

[5] A kind of apple.

other by myself. According to my humor, I threw open these doors, or closed them. I resolved to assign Bartleby a corner by the folding-doors, but on my side of them, so as to have this quiet man within easy call, in case any trifling thing was to be done. I placed his desk close up to a small side-window in that part of the room, a window which originally had afforded a lateral view of certain grimy brickyards and bricks, but which, owing to subsequent erections, commanded at present no view at all, though it gave some light. Within three feet of the panes was a wall, and the light came down from far above, between two lofty buildings, as from a very small opening in a dome. Still further to a satisfactory arrangement, I procured a high green folding screen, which might entirely isolate Bartleby from my sight, though not remove him from my voice. And thus, in a manner, privacy and society were conjoined.

At first, Bartleby did an extraordinary quantity of writing. As if long famishing for something to copy, he seemed to gorge himself on my documents. There was no pause for digestion. He ran a day and night line, copying by sunlight and by candle-light. I should have been quite delighted with his application, had he been cheerfully industrious. But he wrote on silently, palely, mechanically.

It is, of course, an indispensable part of a scrivener's business to verify the accuracy of his copy, word by word. Where there are two or more scriveners in an office, they assist each other in this examination, one reading from the copy, the other holding the original. It is a very dull, wearisome, and lethargic affair. I can readily imagine that, to some sanguine temperaments, it would be altogether intolerable. For example, I cannot credit that the mettlesome poet, Byron, would have contentedly sat down with Bartleby to examine a law document of, say five hundred pages, closely written in a crimpy hand.

Now and then, in the haste of business, it had been my habit to assist in comparing some brief document myself, calling Turkey or Nippers for this purpose. One object I had, in placing Bartleby so handy to me behind the screen, was, to avail myself of his services on such trivial occasions. It was on the third day, I think, of his being with me, and before any necessity had arisen for having his own writing examined, that, being much hurried to complete a small affair I had in hand, I abruptly called to Bartleby. In my haste and natural expectancy of instant compliance, I sat with my head bent over the original on my desk, and my right hand sideways, and somewhat nervously extended with the copy, so that, immediately upon emerging from his retreat, Bartleby might snatch it and proceed to business without the least delay.

In this very attitude did I sit when I called to him, rapidly stating what it was I wanted him to do—namely, to examine a small paper with me. Imagine my surprise, nay, my consternation, when, without moving from his privacy, Bartleby, in a singularly mild, firm voice, replied, "I would prefer not to."

I sat awhile in perfect silence, rallying my stunned faculties. Immediately it occurred to me that my ears had deceived me, or Bartleby had entirely misunderstood my meaning. I repeated my request in the clearest tone I could assume; but in quite as clear a one came the previous reply, "I would prefer not to."

"Prefer not to," echoed I, rising in high excitement, and crossing the room with a stride. "What do you mean? Are you moonstruck? I want you to help me compare this sheet here—take it," and I thrust it towards him.

"I would prefer not to," said he.

I looked at him steadfastly. His face was leanly composed; his gray eye dimly calm. Not a wrinkle of agitation rippled him. Had there been the least uneasiness, anger, impatience or impertinence in his manner; in other words, had there been anything ordinarily human about him, doubtless I should have violently dismissed him from the premises. But as it was, I should have as soon thought of turning my pale plaster-of-paris bust of Cicero out of doors. I stood gazing at him awhile, as he went on with his own writing, and then reseated myself at my desk. This is very strange, thought I. What had one best do? But my business hurried me. I concluded to forget the matter for the present, reserving it for my future leisure. So, calling Nippers from the other room, the paper was speedily examined.

A few days after this, Bartleby concluded four lengthy documents, being quadruplicates of a week's testimony taken before me in my High Court of Chancery. It became necessary to examine them. It was an important suit, and great accuracy was imperative. Having all things arranged, I called Turkey, Nippers, and Ginger Nut, from the next room, meaning to place the four copies in the hands of my four clerks, while I should read from the original. Accordingly, Turkey, Nippers, and Ginger Nut had taken their seats in a row, each with his document in his hand, when I called to Bartleby to join this interesting group.

"Bartleby! quick, I am waiting."

I heard a slow scrape of his chair legs on the uncarpeted floor, and soon he appeared standing at the entrance of his hermitage.

"What is wanted?" said he, mildly.

"The copies, the copies," said I, hurriedly. "We are going to examine them. There"—and I held towards him the fourth quadruplicate.

"I would prefer not to," he said, and gently disappeared behind the screen.

For a few moments I was turned into a pillar of salt,[6] standing at the head of my seated column of clerks. Recovering myself, I advanced towards the screen, and demanded the reason for such extraordinary conduct.

"*Why* do you refuse?"

"I would prefer not to."

With any other man I should have flown outright into a dreadful passion, scorned all further words, and thrust him ignominiously from my presence. But there was something about Bartleby that not only strangely disarmed me, but, in a wonderful manner, touched and disconcerted me. I began to reason with him.

"These are your own copies we are about to examine. It is labor saving to you, because one examination will answer for your four papers. It is

[6]Lot's wife was turned into a pillar of salt when she disobeyed the Lord's command and looked back on Sodom. See Genesis 19:26.

common usage. Every copyist is bound to help examine his copy. Is it not
so? Will you not speak? Answer!"

"I prefer not to," he replied in a flute-like tone. It seemed to me that,
while I had been addressing him, he carefully revolved every statement
that I made; fully comprehended the meaning; could not gainsay the irre-
sistible conclusion; but, at the same time, some paramount consideration
prevailed with him to reply as he did.

"You are decided, then, not to comply with my request—a request
made according to common usage and common sense?"

He briefly gave me to understand, that on that point my judgment was
sound. Yes: his decision was irreversible.

It is not seldom the case that, when a man is browbeaten in some un-
precedented and violently unreasonable way, he begins to stagger in his
own plainest faith. He begins, as it were, vaguely to surmise that, wonderful
as it may be, all the justice and all the reason is on the other side. Accord-
ingly, if any disinterested persons are present, he turns to them for some
reinforcement for his own faltering mind.

"Turkey," said I, "what do you think of this? Am I not right?"

"With submission, sir," said Turkey, in his blandest tone, "I think that
you are."

"Nippers," said I, "what do *you* think of it?"

"I think I should kick him out of the office."

(The reader of nice perceptions will here perceive that, it being morn-
ing, Turkey's answer is couched in polite and tranquil terms, but Nippers
replies in ill-tempered ones. Or, to repeat a previous sentence, Nippers'
ugly mood was on duty, and Turkey's off.)

"Ginger Nut," said I, willing to enlist the smallest suffrage in my behalf,
"what do *you* think of it?"

"I think, sir, he's a little *luny*," replied Ginger Nut, with a grin.

"You hear what they say," said I, turning towards the screen, "come
forth and do your duty."

But he vouchsafed no reply. I pondered a moment in sore perplexity.
But once more business hurried me. I determined again to postpone the
consideration of this dilemma to my future leisure. With a little trouble we
made out to examine the papers without Bartleby, though at every page or
two Turkey deferentially dropped his opinion, that this proceeding was
quite out of the common; while Nippers, twitching in his chair with a
dyspeptic nervousness, ground out, between his set teeth, occasional hiss-
ing maledictions against the stubborn oaf behind the screen. And for his
(Nippers') part, this was the first and the last time he would do another
man's business without pay.

Meanwhile Bartleby sat in his hermitage, oblivious to everything but his
own peculiar business there.

Some days passed, the scrivener being employed upon another lengthy
work. His late remarkable conduct led me to regard his ways narrowly. I
observed that he never went to dinner; indeed, that he never went any-
where. As yet I had never, of my personal knowledge, known him to be
outside of my office. He was a perpetual sentry in the corner. At about
eleven o'clock though, in the morning, I noticed that Ginger Nut would
advance toward the opening in Bartleby's screen, as if silently beckoned

thither by a gesture invisible to me where I sat. The boy would then leave the office, jingling a few pence, and reappear with a handful of ginger-nuts, which he delivered in the hermitage, receiving two of the cakes for his trouble.

He lives, then, on ginger-nuts, thought I; never eats a dinner, properly speaking; he must be a vegetarian, then, but no; he never eats even vegeta-bles, he eats nothing but ginger-nuts. My mind then ran on in reveries concerning the probable effects upon the human constitution of living en-tirely on ginger-nuts. Ginger-nuts are so called, because they contain gin-ger as one of their peculiar constituents, and the final flavoring one. Now, what was ginger? A hot, spicy thing. Was Bartleby hot and spicy? Not at all. Ginger, then, had no effect upon Bartleby. Probably he preferred it should have none.

Nothing so aggravates an earnest person as a passive resistance. If the individual so resisted be of a not inhumane temper, and the resisting one perfectly harmless in his passivity, then, in the better moods of the former, he will endeavor charitably to construe to his imagination what proves im-possible to be solved by his judgment. Even so, for the most part, I re-garded Bartleby and his ways. Poor fellow! thought I, he means no mis-chief; it is plain he intends no insolence; his aspect sufficiently evinces that his eccentricities are involuntary. He is useful to me. I can get along with him. If I turn him away, the chances are he will fall in with some less indulgent employer, and then he will be rudely treated, and perhaps driven forth miserably to starve. Yes. Here I can cheaply purchase a deli-cious self-approval. To befriend Bartleby; to humor him in his strange wilfulness, will cost me little or nothing, while I lay up in my soul what will eventually prove a sweet morsel for my conscience. But this mood was not invariable with me. The passiveness of Bartleby sometimes irritated me. I felt strangely goaded on to encounter him in new opposition—to elicit some angry spark from him answerable to my own. But, indeed, I might as well have essayed to strike fire with my knuckles against a bit of Windsor soap. But one afternoon the evil impulse in me mastered me, and the following little scene ensued:

"Bartleby," said I, "when those papers are all copied, I will compare them with you."

"I would prefer not to."

"How? Surely you do not mean to persist in that mulish vagary?"

No answer.

I threw open the folding-doors nearby, and turning upon Turkey and Nippers, exclaimed:

"Bartleby a second time says, he won't examine his papers. What do you think of it, Turkey?"

It was afternoon, be it remembered. Turkey sat glowing like a brass boiler; his bald head steaming; his hands reeling among his blotted papers.

"Think of it?" roared Turkey. "I think I'll just step behind his screen, and black his eyes for him!"

So saying, Turkey rose to his feet and threw his arms into a pugilistic position. He was hurrying away to make good his promise, when I detained him, alarmed at the effect of incautiously rousing Turkey's combativeness after dinner.

"Sit down, Turkey," said I, "and hear what Nippers has to say. What do you think of it, Nippers? Would I not be justified in immediately dismissing Bartleby?"

"Excuse me, that is for you to decide, sir. I think his conduct quite unusual, and, indeed, unjust, as regards Turkey and myself. But it may only be a passing whim."

"Ah," exclaimed I, "you have strangely changed your mind, then—you speak very gently of him now."

"All beer," cried Turkey; "gentleness is effects of beer—Nippers and I dined together today. You see how gentle *I* am, sir. Shall I go and black his eyes?"

"You refer to Bartleby, I suppose. No, not today, Turkey," I replied; "pray, put up your fists."

I closed the doors, and again advanced towards Bartleby. I felt additional incentives tempting me to my fate. I burned to be rebelled against again. I remembered that Bartleby never left the office.

"Bartleby," said I, "Ginger Nut is away; just step around to the Post Office, won't you?" (it was but a three minutes' walk) "and see if there is anything for me."

"I would prefer not to."

"You *will* not?"

"I *prefer* not."

I staggered to my desk, and sat there in a deep study. My blind inveteracy returned. Was there any other thing in which I could procure myself to be ignominiously repulsed by this lean, penniless wight?—my hired clerk? What added thing is there, perfectly reasonable, that he will be sure to refuse to do?

"Bartleby!"

No answer.

"Bartleby," in a louder tone.

No answer.

"Bartleby," I roared.

Like a very ghost, agreeably to the laws of magical invocation, at the third summons, he appeared at the entrance of his hermitage.

"Go to the next room, and tell Nippers to come to me."

"I prefer not to," he respectfully and slowly said, and mildly disappeared.

"Very good, Bartleby," said I, in a quiet sort of serenely-severe self-possessed tone, intimating the unalterable purpose of some terrible retribution very close at hand. At the moment I half intended something of the kind. But upon the whole, as it was drawing towards my dinner-hour, I thought it best to put on my hat and walk home for the day, suffering much from perplexity and distress of mind.

Shall I acknowledge it? The conclusion of this whole business was, that it soon became a fixed fact of my chambers, that a pale young scrivener, by the name of Bartleby, had a desk there; that he copied for me at the usual rate of four cents a folio (one hundred words); but he was permanently exempt from examining the work done by him, that duty being transferred to Turkey and Nippers, out of compliment, doubtless, to their superior acuteness; moreover, said Bartleby was never, on any account, to be dis-

patched on the most trivial errand of any sort; and that even if entreated to take upon him such a matter, it was generally understood that he would "prefer not to"—in other words, that he would refuse point-blank.

As days passed on, I became considerably reconciled to Bartleby. His steadiness, his freedom from all dissipation, his incessant industry (except when he chose to throw himself into a standing revery behind his screen), his great stillness, his unalterableness of demeanor under all circumstances, made him a valuable acquisition. One prime thing was this—*he was always there*—first in the morning, continually through the day, and the last at night. I had a singular confidence in his honesty. I felt my most precious papers perfectly safe in his hands. Sometimes, to be sure, I could not, for the very soul of me, avoid falling into sudden spasmodic passions with him. For it was exceeding difficult to bear in mind all the time those strange peculiarities, privileges, and unheard-of exemptions, forming the tacit stipulations on Bartleby's part under which he remained in my office. Now and then, in the eagerness of dispatching pressing business, I would inadvertently summon Bartleby, in a short, rapid tone, to put his finger, say, on the incipient tie of a bit of red tape with which I was about compressing some papers. Of course, from behind the screen the usual answer, "I prefer not to," was sure to come; and then, how could a human creature, with the common infirmities of our nature, refrain from bitterly exclaiming upon such perverseness—such unreasonableness? However, every added repulse of this sort which I received only tended to lessen the probability of my repeating the inadvertence.

Here it must be said, that, according to the custom of most legal gentlemen occupying chambers in densely-populated law buildings, there were several keys to my door. One was kept by a woman residing in the attic, which person weekly scrubbed and daily swept and dusted my apartments. Another was kept by Turkey for convenience sake. The third I sometimes carried in my own pocket. The fourth I knew not who had.

Now, one Sunday morning I happened to go to Trinity Church,[7] to hear a celebrated preacher, and finding myself rather early on the ground I thought I would walk round to my chambers for a while. Luckily I had my key with me; but upon applying it to the lock, I found it resisted by something inserted from the inside. Quite surprised, I called out; when to my consternation a key was turned from within; and thrusting his lean visage at me, and holding the door ajar, the apparition of Bartleby appeared, in his shirt-sleeves, and otherwise in a strangely tattered deshabille, saying quietly that he was sorry, but he was deeply engaged just then, and—preferred not admitting me at present. In a brief word or two, he moreover added, that perhaps I had better walk round the block two or three times, and by that time he would probably have concluded his affairs.

Now, the utterly unsurmised appearance of Bartleby, tenanting my law-chambers of a Sunday morning, with his cadaverously gentlemanly *nonchalance*, yet withal firm and self-possessed, had such a strange effect upon me, that incontinently I slunk away from my own door, and did as desired. But not without sundry twinges of impotent rebellion against the mild effrontery of this unaccountable scrivener. Indeed, it was his wonder-

[7] A large and elaborate Episcopal church in the Wall Street area of New York.

ful mildness chiefly, which not only disarmed me, but unmanned me, as it were. For I consider that one, for the time, is sort of unmanned when he tranquilly permits his hired clerk to dictate to him, and order him away from his own premises. Furthermore, I was full of uneasiness as to what Bartleby could possibly be doing in my office in his shirt-sleeves, and in an otherwise dismantled condition of a Sunday morning. Was anything amiss going on? Nay, that was out of the question. It was not to be thought of for a moment that Bartleby was an immoral person. But what could he be doing there?—copying? Nay again, whatever might be his eccentricities, Bartleby was an eminently decorous person. He would be the last man to sit down to his desk in any state approaching to nudity. Besides, it was Sunday; and there was something about Bartleby that forbade the supposition that he would by any secular occupation violate the proprieties of the day.

Nevertheless, my mind was not pacified; and full of a restless curiosity, at last I returned to the door. Without hindrance I inserted my key, opened it, and entered. Bartleby was not to be seen. I looked round anxiously, peeped behind his screen; but it was very plain that he was gone. Upon more closely examining the place, I surmised that for an indefinite period Bartleby must have ate, dressed, and slept in my office, and that too without plate, mirror, or bed. The cushioned seat of a rickety old sofa in one corner bore the faint impress of a lean, reclining form. Rolled away under his desk, I found a blanket; under the empty grate, a blacking box and brush; on the chair, a tin basin, with soap and a ragged towel; in a newspaper a few crumbs of ginger-nuts and a morsel of cheese. Yes, thought I, it is evident enough that Bartleby has been making his home here, keeping bachelor's hall all by himself. Immediately then the thought came sweeping across me, what miserable friendlessness and loneliness are here revealed! His poverty is great; but his solitude, how horrible! Think of it. Of a Sunday, Wall Street is deserted as Petra;[8] and every night of every day it is an emptiness. This building, too, which of week-days hums with industry and life, at nightfall echoes with sheer vacancy, and all through Sunday is forlorn. And here Bartleby makes his home; sole spectator of a solitude which he has seen all populous—a sort of innocent and transformed Marius brooding among the ruins of Carthage![9]

For the first time in my life a feeling of overpowering stinging melancholy seized me. Before, I had never experienced aught but a not unpleasing sadness. The bond of a common humanity now drew me irresistibly to gloom. A fraternal melancholy! For both I and Bartleby were sons of Adam. I remembered the bright silks and sparkling faces I had seen that day, in gala trim, swan-like sailing down the Mississippi of Broadway; and I contrasted them with the pallid copyist, and thought to myself, Ah, happiness courts the light, so we deem the world is gay; but misery hides aloof, so we deem that misery there is none. These sad fancyings—chimeras, doubtless, of a sick and silly brain—led on to other and more special thoughts, concerning the eccentricities of Bartleby. Presentiments of strange discov-

[8] An ancient city of Jordan, it was forgotten until J. L. Burckhardt discovered its ruins in 1812.

[9] Caius Marius (c. 155–86 B.C.) was a Roman general who won a number of victories in Africa but was exiled by his enemy Sulla. He was a favorite subject of nineteenth-century painting.

eries hovered round me. The scrivener's pale form appeared to me laid out, among uncaring strangers, in its shivering winding-sheet.

Suddenly I was attracted by Bartleby's closed desk, the key in open sight left in the lock.

I mean no mischief, seek the gratification of no heartless curiosity, thought I; besides, the desk is mine, and its contents, too, so I will make bold to look within. Everything was methodically arranged, the papers smoothly placed. The pigeon-holes were deep, and removing the files of documents, I groped into their recesses. Presently I felt something there, and dragged it out. It was an old bandanna handkerchief, heavy and knotted. I opened it, and saw it was a saving's bank.

I now recalled all the quiet mysteries which I had noted in the man. I remembered that he never spoke but to answer; that, though at intervals he had considerable time to himself, yet I had never seen him reading—no, not even a newspaper; that for long periods he would stand looking out, at his pale window behind the screen, upon the dead brick wall; I was quite sure he never visited any refectory or eating-house; while his pale face clearly indicated that he never drank beer like Turkey, or tea and coffee even, like other men; that he never went anywhere in particular that I could learn; never went out for a walk, unless, indeed, that was the case at present; that he had declined telling who he was, or whence he came, or whether he had any relatives in the world; that though so thin and pale, he never complained of ill-health. And more than all, I remembered a certain unconscious air of pallid—how shall I call it?—of pallid haughtiness, say, or rather an austere reserve about him, which had positively awed me into my tame compliance with his eccentricities, when I had feared to ask him to do the slightest incidental thing for me, even though I might know, from his long-continued motionlessness, that behind his screen he must be standing in one of those dead-wall reveries of his.

Revolving all these things, and coupling them with the recently discovered fact, that he made my office his constant abiding place and home, and not forgetful of his morbid moodiness; revolving all these things, a prudential feeling began to steal over me. My first emotions had been those of pure melancholy and sincerest pity; but just in proportion as the forlornness of Bartleby grew and grew to my imagination, did that same melancholy merge into fear, that pity into repulsion. So true it is, and so terrible, too, that up to a certain point the thought or sight of misery enlists our best affections; but, in certain special cases, beyond that point it does not. They err who would assert that invariably this is owing to the inherent selfishness of the human heart. It rather proceeds from a certain hopelessness of remedying excessive and organic ill. To a sensitive being, pity is not seldom pain. And when at last it is perceived that such pity cannot lead to effectual succor, common sense bids the soul be rid of it. What I saw that morning persuaded me that the scrivener was the victim of innate and incurable disorder. I might give alms to his body; but his body did not pain him; it was his soul that suffered, and his soul I could not reach.

I did not accomplish the purpose of going to Trinity Church that morning. Somehow, the things I had seen disqualified me for the time from church-going. I walked homeward, thinking what I would do with Bartleby. Finally, I resolved upon this—I would put certain calm questions

to him the next morning, touching his history, etc., and if he declined to answer them openly and unreservedly (and I supposed he would prefer not), then to give him a twenty dollar bill over and above whatever I might owe him, and tell him his services were no longer required; but that if in any other way I could assist him, I would be happy to do so, especially if he desired to return to his native place, wherever that might be, I would willingly help to defray the expenses. Moreover, if, after reaching home, he found himself at any time in want of aid, a letter from him would be sure of a reply.

The next morning came.

"Bartleby," said I, gently calling to him behind his screen.

No reply.

"Bartleby," said I, in a still gentler tone, "come here; I am not going to ask you to do anything you would prefer not to do—I simply wish to speak to you."

Upon this he noiselessly slid into view.

"Will you tell me, Bartleby, where you were born?"

"I would prefer not to."

"Will you tell me *anything* about yourself?"

"I would prefer not to."

"But what reasonable objection can you have to speak to me? I feel friendly towards you."

He did not look at me while I spoke, but kept his glance fixed upon my bust of Cicero, which, as I then sat, was directly behind me, some six inches above my head.

"What is your answer, Bartleby?" said I, after waiting a considerable time for a reply, during which his countenance remained immovable, only there was the faintest conceivable tremor of the white attenuated mouth.

"At present I prefer to give no answer," he said, and retired into his hermitage.

It was rather weak in me I confess, but his manner, on this occasion, nettled me. Not only did there seem to lurk in it a certain calm disdain, but his perverseness seemed ungrateful, considering the undeniable good usage and indulgence he had received from me.

Again I sat ruminating what I should do. Mortified as I was at his behavior, and resolved as I had been to dismiss him when I entered my office, nevertheless I strangely felt something superstitious knocking at my heart, and forbidding me to carry out my purpose, and denouncing me for a villain if I dared to breathe one bitter word against this forlornest of mankind. At last, familiarly drawing my chair behind his screen, I sat down and said: "Bartleby, never mind, then, about revealing your history; but let me entreat you, as a friend, to comply as far as may be with the usages of this office. Say now, you will help to examine papers tomorrow or next day: in short, say now, that in a day or two you will begin to be a little reasonable:—say so, Bartleby."

"At present I would prefer not to be a little reasonable," was his mildly cadaverous reply.

Just then the folding-doors opened, and Nippers approached. He seemed suffering from an unusually bad night's rest, induced by severer indigestion than common. He overheard those final words of Bartleby.

"*Prefer not,* eh?" gritted Nippers—"I'd *prefer* him, if I were you, sir," addressing me—"I'd *prefer* him; I'd give him preferences, the stubborn mule! What is it, sir, pray, that he *prefers* not to do now?"

Bartleby moved not a limb.

"Mr. Nippers," said I, "I'd prefer that you would withdraw for the present."

Somehow, of late, I had got into the way of involuntarily using this word "prefer" upon all sorts of not exactly suitable occasions. And I trembled to think that my contact with the scrivener had already and seriously affected me in a mental way. And what further and deeper aberration might it not yet produce? This apprehension had not been without efficacy in determining me to summary measures.

As Nippers, looking very sour and sulky, was departing, Turkey blandly and deferentially approached.

"With submission, sir," said he, "yesterday I was thinking about Bartleby here, and I think that if he would but prefer to take a quart of good ale every day, it would do much towards mending him, and enabling him to assist in examining his papers."

"So you have got the word, too," said I, slightly excited.

"With submission, what word, sir?" asked Turkey, respectfully crowding himself into the contracted space behind the screen, and by so doing, making me jostle the scrivener. "What word, sir?"

"I would prefer to be left alone here," said Bartleby, as if offended at being mobbed in his privacy.

"*That's* the word, Turkey," said I—"*that's* it."

"Oh, *prefer?* Oh yes—queer word. I never use it myself. But, sir, as I was saying, if he would but prefer—"

"Turkey," interrupted I, "you will please withdraw."

"Oh certainly, sir, if you prefer that I should."

As he opened the folding-door to retire, Nippers at his desk caught a glimpse of me, and asked whether I would prefer to have a certain paper copied on blue paper or white. He did not in the least roguishly accent the word "prefer." It was plain that it involuntarily rolled from his tongue. I thought to myself, surely I must get rid of a demented man, who already has in some degree turned the tongues, if not the heads of myself and clerks. But I thought it prudent not to break the dismission at once.

The next day I noticed that Bartleby did nothing but stand at his window in his dead-wall revery. Upon asking him why he did not write, he said that he had decided upon doing no more writing.

"Why, how now? what next?" exclaimed I, "do no more writing?"

"No more."

"And what is the reason?"

"Do you not see the reason for yourself?" he indifferently replied.

I looked steadfastly at him, and perceived that his eyes looked dull and glazed. Instantly it occurred to me, that his unexampled diligence in copying by his dim window for the first few weeks of his stay with me might have temporarily impaired his vision.

I was touched. I said something in condolence with him. I hinted that of course he did wisely in abstaining from writing for a while; and urged him to embrace that opportunity of taking wholesome exercise in the open

air. This, however, he did not do. A few days after this, my other clerks being absent, and being in a great hurry to dispatch certain letters by the mail, I thought that, having nothing else earthly to do, Bartleby would surely be less inflexible than usual, and carry these letters to the post-office. But he blankly declined. So, much to my inconvenience, I went myself.

Still added days went by. Whether Bartleby's eyes improved or not, I could not say. To all appearance, I thought they did. But when I asked him if they did, he vouchsafed no answer. At all events, he would do no copying. At last, in reply to my urgings, he informed me that he had permanently given up copying.

"What!" exclaimed I; "suppose your eyes should get entirely well—better than ever before—would you not copy then?"

"I have given up copying," he answered, and slid aside.

He remained as ever, a fixture in my chamber. Nay—if that were possible—he became still more of a fixture than before. What was to be done? He would do nothing in the office; why should he stay there? In plain fact, he had now become a millstone to me, not only useless as a necklace, but afflictive to bear. Yet I was sorry for him. I speak less than truth when I say that, on his own account, he occasioned me uneasiness. If he would but have named a single relative or friend, I would instantly have written, and urged their taking the poor fellow away to some convenient retreat. But he seemed alone, absolutely alone in the universe. A bit of wreck in the mid-Atlantic. At length, necessities connected with my business tyrannized over all other considerations. Decently as I could, I told Bartleby that in six days' time he must unconditionally leave the office. I warned him to take measures, in the interval, for procuring some other abode. I offered to assist him in this endeavor, if he himself would but take the first step towards a removal. "And when you finally quit me, Bartleby," added I, "I shall see that you go not away entirely unprovided. Six days from this hour, remember."

At the expiration of that period, I peeped behind the screen, and lo! Bartleby was there.

I buttoned up my coat, balanced myself; advanced slowly towards him, touched his shoulder, and said, "The time has come; you must quit this place; I am sorry for you; here is money; but you must go."

"I would prefer not," he replied, with his back still towards me.

"You *must*."

He remained silent.

Now I had an unbounded confidence in this man's common honesty. He had frequently restored to me sixpences and shillings carelessly dropped upon the floor, for I am apt to be very reckless in such shirt-button affairs. The proceeding, then, which followed will not be deemed extraordinary.

"Bartleby," said I, "I owe you twelve dollars on account; here are thirty-two; the odd twenty are yours—Will you take it?" and I handed the bills towards him.

But he made no motion.

"I will leave them here, then," putting them under a weight on the table. Then taking my hat and cane and going to the door, I tranquilly turned

and added—"After you have removed your things from these offices, Bartleby, you will of course lock the door—since every one is now gone for the day but you—and if you please, slip your key underneath the mat, so that I may have it in the morning. I shall not see you again; so good-bye to you. If, hereafter, in your new place of abode, I can be of any service to you, do not fail to advise me by letter. Good-bye, Bartleby, and fare you well."

But he answered not a word; like the last column of some ruined temple, he remained standing mute and solitary in the middle of the otherwise deserted room.

As I walked home in a pensive mood, my vanity got the better of my pity. I could not but highly plume myself on my masterly management in getting rid of Bartleby. Masterly I call it, and such it must appear to any dispassionate thinker. The beauty of my procedure seemed to consist in its perfect quietness. There was no vulgar bullying, no bravado of any sort, no choleric hectoring, and striding to and fro across the apartment, jerking out vehement commands for Bartleby to bundle himself off with his beggarly traps. Nothing of the kind. Without loudly bidding Bartleby depart—as an inferior genius might have done—I *assumed* the ground that depart he must; and upon that assumption built all I had to say. The more I thought over my procedure, the more I was charmed with it. Nevertheless, next morning, upon awakening, I had my doubts—I had somehow slept off the fumes of vanity. One of the coolest and wisest hours a man has, is just after he awakes in the morning. My procedure seemed as sagacious as ever—but only in theory. How it would prove in practice—there was the rub. It was truly a beautiful thought to have assumed Bartleby's departure; but, after all, that assumption was simply my own, and none of Bartleby's. The great point was, not whether I had assumed that he would quit me, but whether he would prefer to do so. He was more a man of preferences than assumptions.

After breakfast, I walked down town, arguing the probabilities *pro* and *con.* One moment I thought it would prove a miserable failure, and Bartleby would be found all alive at my office as usual; the next moment it seemed certain that I should find his chair empty. And so I kept veering about. At the corner of Broadway and Canal Street, I saw quite an excited group of people standing in earnest conversation.

"I'll take odds he doesn't," said a voice as I passed.

"Doesn't go?—done!" said I, "put up your money."

I was instinctively putting my hand in my pocket to produce my own, when I remember that this was an election day. The words I had overheard bore no reference to Bartleby, but to the success or non-success of some candidate for the mayoralty. In my intent frame of mind, I had, as it were, imagined that all Broadway shared in my excitement, and were debating the same question with me. I passed on, very thankful that the uproar of the street screened my momentary absent-mindedness.

As I had intended, I was earlier than usual at my office door. I stood listening for a moment. All was still. He must be gone. I tried the knob. The door was locked. Yes, my procedure had worked to a charm; he indeed must be vanished. Yet a certain melancholy mixed with this: I was almost

sorry for my brilliant success. I was fumbling under the door mat for the key which Bartleby was to have left there for me, when accidentally my knee knocked against a panel, producing a summoning sound, and in response a voice came to me from within—"Not yet; I am occupied."

It was Bartleby.

I was thunderstruck. For an instant I stood like the man who, pipe in mouth, was killed one cloudless afternoon long ago in Virginia, by summer lightning; at his own warm open window he was killed, and remained leaning out there upon the dreamy afternoon, till some one touched him, when he fell.

"Not gone!" I murmured at last. But again obeying that wondrous ascendancy which the inscrutable scrivener had over me, and from which ascendancy, for all my chafing, I could not completely escape, I slowly went down stairs and out into the street, and while walking round the block, considered what I should next do in this unheard-of perplexity. Turn the man out by an actual thrusting I could not; to drive him away by calling him hard names would not do; calling in the police was an unpleasant idea; and yet, permit him to enjoy his cadaverous triumph over me—this, too, I could not think of. What was to be done? or, if nothing could be done, was there anything further that I could *assume* in the matter? Yes, as before I had prospectively assumed that Bartleby would depart, so now I might retrospectively assume that departed he was. In the legitimate carrying out of this assumption, I might enter my office in a great hurry, and pretending not to see Bartleby at all, walk straight against him as if he were air. Such a proceeding would in a singular degree have the appearance of a home-thrust. It was hardly possible that Bartleby could withstand such an application of the doctrine of assumption. But upon second thoughts the success of the plan seemed rather dubious. I resolved to argue the matter over with him again.

"Bartleby," said I, entering the office, with a quietly severe expression, "I am seriously displeased. I am pained, Bartleby. I had thought better of you. I had imagined you of such a gentlemanly organization, that in any delicate dilemma a slight hint would suffice—in short, an assumption. But it appears I am deceived. Why," I added, unaffectedly starting, "you have not even touched that money yet," pointing to it, just where I had left it the evening previous.

He answered nothing.

"Will you, or will you not, quit me?" I now demanded in a sudden passion, advancing close to him.

"I would prefer *not* to quit you," he replied, gently emphasizing the *not*.

"What earthly right have you to stay here? Do you pay any rent? Do you pay any taxes? Or is this property yours?"

He answered nothing.

"Are you ready to go on and write now? Are your eyes recovered? Could you copy a small paper for me this morning? or help examine a few lines? or step round to the post-office? In a word, will you do anything at all, to give a coloring to your refusal to depart the premises?"

He silently retired into his hermitage.

I was now in such a state of nervous resentment that I thought it but prudent to check myself at present from further demonstrations. Bartleby

and I were alone. I remembered the tragedy of the unfortunate Adams[10] and the still more unfortunate Colt in the solitary office of the latter; and how poor Colt, being dreadfully incensed by Adams, and imprudently permitting himself to get wildly excited, was at unawares hurried into his fatal act—an act which certainly no man could possibly deplore more than the actor himself. Often it had occurred to me in my ponderings upon the subject that had that altercation taken place in the public street, or at a private residence, it would not have terminated as it did. It was the circumstance of being alone in a solitary office, up stairs, of a building entirely unhallowed by humanizing domestic associations—an uncarpeted office, doubtless, of a dusty, haggard sort of appearance—this it must have been, which greatly helped to enhance the irritable desperation of the hapless Colt.

But when this old Adam of resentment rose in me and tempted me concerning Bartleby, I grappled him and threw him. How? Why, simply by recalling the divine injunction: "A new commandment give I unto you, that ye love one another."[11] Yes, this it was that saved me. Aside from higher considerations, charity often operates as a vastly wise and prudent principle—a great safeguard to its possessor. Men have committed murder for jealousy's sake, and anger's sake, and hatred's sake, and selfishness' sake, and spiritual pride's sake; but no man, that ever I heard of, ever committed a diabolical murder for sweet charity's sake. Mere self-interest, then, if no better motive can be enlisted, should, especially with high-tempered men, prompt all beings to charity and philanthropy. At any rate, upon the occasion in question, I strove to drown my exasperated feelings towards the scrivener by benevolently construing his conduct. Poor fellow, poor fellow! thought I, he don't mean anything; and besides, he has seen hard times, and ought to be indulged.

I endeavored, also, immediately to occupy myself, and at the same time to comfort my despondency. I tried to fancy, that in the course of the morning, at such time as might prove agreeable to him, Bartleby, of his own free accord, would emerge from his hermitage and take up some decided line of march in the direction of the door. But no. Half-past twelve o'clock came; Turkey began to glow in the face, overturn his inkstand, and become generally obstreperous; Nippers abated down into quietude and courtesy; Ginger Nut munched his noon apple; and Bartleby remained standing at his window in one of his profoundest dead-wall reveries. Will it be credited? Ought I to acknowledge it? That afternoon I left the office without saying one further word to him.

Some days now passed, during which, at leisure intervals I looked a little into "Edwards on the Will," and "Priestley on Necessity."[12] Under the circumstances, those books induced a salutary feeling. Gradually I slid into the persuasion that these troubles of mine, touching the scrivener, had

[10] Melville is alluding to a sensational murder case of 1842. John C. Colt killed Samuel Adams and was sentenced to be hanged but committed suicide just before the execution.

[11] These are Christ's words to his disciples, John 13:34.

[12] Jonathan Edwards (1703–1758), the American theologian, presented the Calvinist argument for predestination, especially in *The Freedom of the Will* (1754). Joseph Priestley (1773–1804), English scientist and Unitarian, also argued for determinism, though on scientific grounds.

been all predestinated from eternity, and Bartleby was billeted upon me for some mysterious purpose of an all-wise Providence, which it was not for a mere mortal like me to fathom. Yes, Bartleby, stay there behind your screen, thought I; I shall persecute you no more; you are harmless and noiseless as any of these old chairs; in short, I never feel so private as when I know you are here. At last I see it, I feel it; I penetrate to the predestinated purpose of my life. I am content. Others may have loftier parts to enact; but my mission in this world, Bartleby, is to furnish you with office-room for such period as you may see fit to remain.

I believe that this wise and blessed frame of mind would have continued with me, had it not been for the unsolicited and uncharitable remarks obtruded upon me by my professional friends who visited the rooms. But thus it often is, that the constant friction of illiberal minds wears out at last the best resolves of the more generous. Though to be sure, when I reflected upon it, it was not strange that people entering my office should be struck by the peculiar aspect of the unaccountable Bartleby, and so be tempted to throw out some sinister observations concerning him. Sometimes an attorney, having business with me, and calling at my office, and finding no one but the scrivener there, would undertake to obtain some sort of precise information from him touching my whereabouts; but without heeding his idle talk, Bartleby would remain standing immovable in the middle of the room. So after contemplating him in that position for a time, the attorney would depart, no wiser than he came.

Also, when a reference[13] was going on, and the room full of lawyers and witnesses, and business driving fast, some deeply-occupied legal gentleman present, seeing Bartleby wholly unemployed, would request him to run round to his (the legal gentleman's) office and fetch some papers for him. Thereupon, Bartleby would tranquilly decline, and yet remain idle as before. Then the lawyer would give a great stare, and turn to me. And what could I say? At last I was made aware that all through the circle of my professional acquaintance, a whisper of wonder was running round, having reference to the strange creature I kept at my office. This worried me very much. And as the idea came upon me of his possibly turning out a long-lived man, and keeping occupying my chambers, and denying my authority; and perplexing my visitors; and scandalizing my professional reputation; and casting a general gloom over the premises; keeping soul and body together to the last upon his savings (for doubtless he spent but half a dime a day), and in the end perhaps outlive me, and claim possession of my office by right of his perpetual occupancy: as all these dark anticipations crowded upon me more and more, and my friends continually intruded their relentless remarks upon the apparition in my room; a great change was wrought in me. I resolved to gather all my faculties together, and forever rid me of this intolerable incubus.[14]

Ere revolving any complicated project, however, adapted to this end, I first simply suggested to Bartleby the propriety of his permanent departure. In a calm and serious tone, I commended the idea to his careful and mature consideration. But, having taken three days to meditate upon it, he

[13] A conference with a legal referee.
[14] Something that weighs upon one like a nightmare.

apprised me, that his original determination remained the same; in short, that he still preferred to abide with me.

What shall I do? I now said to myself, buttoning up my coat to the last button. What shall I do? what ought I to do? what does conscience say I *should* do with this man, or, rather, ghost. Rid myself of him, I must; go, he shall. But how? You will not thrust him, the poor, pale, passive mortal—you will not thrust such a helpless creature out of your door? you will not dishonor yourself by such cruelty? No, I will not, I cannot do that. Rather would I let him live and die here, and then mason up his remains in the wall. What, then, will you do? For all your coaxing, he will not budge. Bribes he leaves under your own paper-weight on your table; in short, it is quite plain that he prefers to cling to you.

Then something severe, something unusual must be done. What! surely you will not have him collared by a constable, and commit his innocent pallor to the common jail? And upon what ground could you procure such a thing to be done?—a vagrant, is he? What! he a vagrant, a wanderer, who refuses to budge? It is because he will *not* be a vagrant, then, that you seek to count him *as* a vagrant. That is too absurd. No visible means of support: there I have him. Wrong again: for indubitably he *does* support himself, and that is the only unanswerable proof that any man can show of his possessing the means so to do. No more, then. Since he will not quit me, I must quit him. I will change my offices; I will move elsewhere, and give him fair notice, that if I find him on my new premises I will then proceed against him as a common trespasser.

Acting accordingly, next day I thus addressed him: "I find these chambers too far from the City Hall; the air is unwholesome. In a word, I propose to remove my offices next week, and shall no longer require your services. I tell you this now, in order that you may seek another place."

He made no reply, and nothing more was said.

On the appointed day I engaged carts and men, proceeded to my chambers, and, having but little furniture, everything was removed in a few hours. Throughout, the scrivener remained standing behind the screen, which I directed to be removed the last thing. It was withdrawn; and, being folded up like a huge folio, left him the motionless occupant of a naked room. I stood in the entry watching him a moment, while something from within me upbraided me.

I re-entered, with my hand in my pocket—and—and my heart in my mouth.

"Good-bye, Bartleby; I am going—good-bye, and God some way bless you; and take that," slipping something in his hand. But it dropped upon the floor, and then—strange to say—I tore myself from him whom I had so longed to be rid of.

Established in my new quarters, for a day or two I kept the door locked, and started at every footfall in the passages. When I returned to my rooms, after any little absence, I would pause at the threshold for an instant, and attentively listen, ere applying my key. But these fears were needless. Bartleby never came nigh me.

I thought all was going well, when a perturbed-looking stranger visited me, inquiring whether I was the person who had recently occupied rooms at No.—Wall Street.

Full of forebodings, I replied that I was.

"Then, sir," said the stranger, who proved a lawyer, "you are responsi-ble for the man you left there. He refuses to do any copying; he refuses to do anything; he says he prefers not to; and he refuses to quit the premises."

"I am very sorry, sir," said I, with assumed tranquillity, but an inward tremor, "but, really, the man you allude to is nothing to me—he is no relation or apprentice of mine, that you should hold me responsible for him."

"In mercy's name, who is he?"

"I certainly cannot inform you. I know nothing about him. Formerly I employed him as a copyist; but he has done nothing for me now for some time past."

"I shall settle him, then—good morning, sir."

Several days passed, and I heard nothing more; and, though I often felt a charitable prompting to call at the place and see poor Bartleby, yet a certain squeamishness, of I know not what, withheld me.

All is over with him, by this time, thought I, as last, when, through another week, no further intelligence reached me. But, coming to my room the day after, I found several persons waiting at my door in a high state of nervous excitement.

"That's the man—here he comes," cried the foremost one, whom I recognized as the lawyer who had previously called upon me alone.

"You must take him away, sir, at once," cried a portly person among them, advancing upon me, and whom I knew to be the landlord of No.— Wall Street. "These gentlemen, my tenants, cannot stand it any longer; Mr. B———," pointing to the lawyer, "has turned him out of his room, and he now persists in haunting the building generally, sitting upon the banisters of the stairs by day, and sleeping in the entry by night. Everybody is con-cerned; clients are leaving the offices; some fears are entertained of a mob; something you must do, and that without delay."

Aghast at this torrent, I fell back before it, and would fain have locked myself in my new quarters. In vain I persisted that Bartleby was nothing to me—no more than to any one else. In vain—I was the last person known to have anything to do with him, and they held me to the terrible account. Fearful, then, of being exposed in the papers (as one person present ob-scurely threatened), I considered the matter, and, at length, said, that if the lawyer would give me a confidential interview with the scrivener, in his (the lawyer's) own room, I would, that afternoon, strive my best to rid them of the nuisance they complained of.

Going up stairs to my old haunt, there was Bartleby silently sitting upon the banister at the landing.

"What are you doing here, Bartleby?" said I.

"Sitting upon the banister," he mildly replied.

I motioned him into the lawyer's room, who then left us.

"Bartleby," said I, "are you aware that you are the cause of great tribula-tion to me, by persisting in occupying the entry after being dismissed from the office?"

No answer.

"Now one of two things must take place. Either you must do something,

or something must be done to you. Now what sort of business would you like to engage in? Would you like to re-engage in copying for some one?"

"No; I would prefer not to make any change."

"Would you like a clerkship in a dry-goods store?"

"There is too much confinement about that. No, I would not like a clerkship; but I am not particular."

"Too much confinement," I cried, "why, you keep yourself confined all the time!"

"I would prefer not to take a clerkship," he rejoined, as if to settle that little item at once.

"How would a bar-tender's business suit you? There is no trying of the eye-sight in that."

"I would not like it at all; though, as I said before, I am not particular."

His unwonted wordiness inspirited me. I returned to the charge.

"Well, then, would you like to travel through the country collecting bills for the merchants? That would improve your health."

"No, I would prefer to be doing something else."

"How, then, would going as a companion to Europe, to entertain some young gentleman with your conversation—how would that suit you?"

"Not at all. It does not strike me that there is anything definite about that. I like to be stationary. But I am not particular."

"Stationary you shall be, then," I cried, now losing all patience, and, for the first time in all my exasperating connection with him, fairly flying into a passion. "If you do not go away from these premises before night, I shall feel bound—indeed, I *am* bound—to—to—to quit the premises myself!" I rather absurdly concluded, knowing not with what possible threat to try to frighten his immobility into compliance. Despairing of all further efforts, I was precipitately leaving him, when a final thought occurred to me—one which had not been wholly unindulged before.

"Bartleby," said I, in the kindest tone I could assume under such exciting circumstances, "will you go home with me now—not to my office, but my dwelling—and remain there till we can conclude upon some convenient arrangement for you at our leisure? Come, let us start now, right away."

"No: at present I would prefer not to make any change at all."

I answered nothing; but, effectually dodging every one by the suddenness and rapidity of my flight, rushed from the building, ran up Wall Street towards Broadway, and, jumping into the first omnibus, was soon removed from pursuit. As soon as tranquillity returned, I distinctly perceived that I had now done all that I possibly could, both in respect to the demands of the landlord and his tenants, and with regard to my own desire and sense of duty, to benefit Bartleby, and shield him from rude persecution. I now strove to be entirely care-free and quiescent; and my conscience justified me in the attempt; though, indeed, it was not so successful as I could have wished. So fearful was I of being again hunted out by the incensed landlord and his exasperated tenants, that, surrendering my business to Nippers, for a few days, I drove about the upper part of the town and through the suburbs, in my rockaway;[15] crossed over to Jersey City and Hoboken, and

[15] A light, four-wheeled carriage.

paid fugitive visits to Manhattanville and Astoria. In fact, I almost lived in my rockaway for the time.

When again I entered my office, lo, a note from the landlord lay upon the desk. I opened it with trembling hands. It informed me that the writer had sent to the police, and had Bartleby removed to the Tombs as a vagrant. Moreover, since I knew more about him than any one else, he wished me to appear at that place, and make a suitable statement of the facts. These tidings had a conflicting effect upon me. At first I was indignant; but, at last, almost approved. The landlord's energetic, summary disposition, had led him to adopt a procedure which I do not think I would have decided upon myself; and yet, as a last resort, under such peculiar circumstances, it seemed the only plan.

As I afterwards learned, the poor scrivener, when told that he must be conducted to the Tombs, offered not the slightest obstacle, but, in his pale, unmoving way, silently acquiesced.

Some of the compassionate and curious by-standers joined the party; and headed by one of the constables arm-in-arm with Bartleby, the silent procession filed its way through all the noise, and heat, and joy of the roaring thoroughfares at noon.

The same day I received the note, I went to the Tombs, or, to speak more properly, the Halls of Justice. Seeking the right officer, I stated the purpose of my call, and was informed that the individual I described was, indeed, within. I then assured the functionary that Bartleby was a perfectly honest man, and greatly to be compassionated, however unaccountably eccentric. I narrated all I knew, and closed by suggesting the idea of letting him remain in as indulgent confinement as possible, till something less harsh might be done—though, indeed, I hardly knew what. At all events, if nothing else could be decided upon, the alms-house must receive him. I then begged to have an interview.

Being under no disgraceful charge, and quite serene and harmless in all his ways, they had permitted him freely to wander about the prison, and, especially, in the inclosed grass-platted yards thereof. And so I found him there, standing all alone in the quietest of the yards, his face towards a high wall, while all around, from the narrow slits of the jail windows, I thought I saw peering out upon him the eyes of murderers and thieves.

"Bartleby!"

"I know you," he said, without looking round—"and I want nothing to say to you."

"It was not I that brought you here, Bartleby," said I, keenly pained at his implied suspicion. "And to you, this should not be so vile a place. Nothing reproachful attaches to you by being here. And see, it is not so sad a place as one might think. Look, there is the sky, and here is the grass."

"I know where I am," he replied, but would say nothing more, and so I left him.

As I entered the corridor again, a broad meat-like man, in an apron, accosted me, and, jerking his thumb over his shoulder, said—"Is that your friend?"

"Yes."

"Does he want to starve? If he does, let him live on the prison fare, that's all."

"Who are you?" asked I, not knowing what to make of such an unofficially speaking person in such a place.

"I am the grub-man. Such gentlemen as have friends here, hire me to provide them with something good to eat."

"Is this so?" said I, turning to the turnkey.

He said it was.

"Well, then," said I, slipping some silver into the grub-man's hands (for so they called him), "I want you to give particular attention to my friend there; let him have the best dinner you can get. And you must be as polite to him as possible."

"Introduce me, will you?" said the grub-man, looking at me with an expression which seemed to say he was all impatience for an opportunity to give a specimen of his breeding.

Thinking it would prove of benefit to the scrivener, I acquiesced; and, asking the grub-man his name, went up with him to Bartleby.

"Bartleby, this is a friend; you will find him very useful to you."

"Your sarvant, sir, your sarvant," said the grub-man, making a low salutation behind his apron. "Hope you find it pleasant here, sir; nice grounds—cool apartments—hope you'll stay with us some time—try to make it agreeable. What will you have for dinner today?"

"I prefer not to dine today," said Bartleby, turning away. "It would disagree with me; I am unused to dinners." So saying, he slowly moved to the other side of the inclosure, and took up a position fronting the dead-wall.

"How's this?" said the grub-man, addressing me with a stare of astonishment. "He's odd, ain't he?"

"I think he is a little deranged," said I, sadly.

"Deranged? deranged is it? Well, now, upon my word, I thought that friend of yourn was a gentleman forger; they are always pale and genteel-like, them forgers. I can't help pity 'em—can't help it, sir. Did you know Monroe Edwards?" he added, touchingly, and paused. Then, laying his hand piteously on my shoulder, sighed, "he died of consumption at Sing-Sing.[16] So you weren't acquainted with Monroe?"

"No, I was never socially acquainted with any forgers. But I cannot stop longer. Look to my friend yonder. You will not lose by it. I will see you again."

Some few days after this, I again obtained admission to the Tombs, and went through the corridors in quest of Bartleby; but without finding him.

"I saw him coming from his cell not long ago," said a turnkey, "may be he's gone to loiter in the yards."

So I went in that direction.

"Are you looking for the silent man?" said another turnkey, passing me. "Yonder he lies—sleeping in the yard there. 'Tis not twenty minutes since I saw him lie down."

The yard was entirely quiet. It was not accessible to the common prisoners. The surrounding walls, of amazing thickness, kept off all sounds behind them. The Egyptian character of the masonry weighed upon me with its gloom. But a soft imprisoned turf grew under foot. The heart of the

[16] New York state prison at Ossining.

eternal pyramids, it seemed, wherein, by some strange magic, through the clefts, grass-seed, dropped by birds, had sprung.

Strangely huddled at the base of the wall, his knees drawn up, and lying on his side, his head touching the cold stones, I saw the wasted Bartleby. But nothing stirred. I paused; then went close up to him; stooped over, and saw that his dim eyes were open; otherwise he seemed profoundly sleeping. Something prompted me to touch him. I felt his hand, when a tingling shiver ran up my arm and down my spine to my feet.

The round face of the grub-man peered upon me now. "His dinner is ready. Won't he dine today, either? Or does he live without dining?"

"Lives without dining," said I, and closed the eyes.

"Eh!—He's asleep, ain't he?"

"With kings and counselors,"[17] murmured I.

There would seem little need for proceeding further in this history. Imagination will readily supply the meager recital of poor Bartleby's interment. But, ere parting with the reader, let me say, that if this little narrative has sufficiently interested him, to awaken curiosity as to who Bartleby was, and what manner of life he led prior to the present narrator's making his acquaintance, I can only reply, that in such curiosity I fully share, but am wholly unable to gratify it. Yet here I hardly know whether I should divulge one little item of rumor, which came to my ear a few months after the scrivener's decease. Upon what basis it rested, I could never ascertain; and hence, how true it is I cannot now tell. But, inasmuch as this vague report has not been without a certain suggestive interest to me, however sad, it may prove the same with some others; and so I will briefly mention it. The report was this: that Bartleby had been a subordinate clerk in the Dead Letter Office at Washington, from which he had been suddenly removed by a change in the administration. When I think over this rumor, hardly can I express the emotions which seize me. Dead letters! does it not sound like dead men? Conceive a man by nature and misfortune prone to a pallid hopelessness, can any business seem more fitted to heighten it than that of continually handling these dead letters, and assorting them for the flames? For by the cart-load they are annually burned. Sometimes from out the folded paper the pale clerk takes a ring—the finger it was meant for, perhaps, moulders in the grave; a bank-note sent in swiftest charity—he whom it would relieve, nor eats nor hungers any more; pardon for those who died despairing; hope for those who died unhoping; good tidings for those who died stifled by unrelieved calamities. On errands of life, these letters speed to death.

Ah, Bartleby! Ah, humanity!

[17]Job wishes he were dead and "at rest, with kings and counselors of the earth." Job 3:13–14.

Emily Dickinson

(1830–1886)

The two greatest poets of nineteenth-century America are, arguably, Walt Whitman and Emily Dickinson. Their contemporaries would have been Lowell, Oliver Wendell Holmes, and a handful of lesser names seemed the best bets for time's palm. Whitman, until late in his life, was known as a faintly obscene bohemian with a barbaric yawp, and nobody had heard of Emily Dickinson at all. Two poets could not, at least superficially, be less similar. Whitman is a poet of expansiveness, Dickinson of compression; Whitman's poetic persona is that of a boisterous outdoorsman, Dickinson's that of a painfully self-conscious recluse; Whitman is an aggressively male rooster, Dickinson a little white hen. But they were parallel in one respect, which perhaps put the steel in their poetry: they were both outside the paralyzing genteelism of the public culture, Whitman through his defiance of dominant codes of taste and restraint, Dickinson through her withdrawal into an intensely private world.

Dickinson was born in 1830 in Amherst, Massachusetts. The family constellation is crucial, since family and home constituted almost her entire poetic world. There was her strong, upright father, a prominent lawyer and the treasurer of Amherst College; Dickinson adored and feared him, and his image lies just beneath the surface of many of her poems, including ones about God. Her fragile mother was a chronic invalid who required long periods of nursing by her daughters. Dickinson was very close both to her sister Lavinia, a competent, loving friend, and to her brother Austin, a lawyer like his father. Dickinson seems to have been normally lively and outgoing as a young girl, but during her teens, despite a brief period away from home at Mount Holyoke Female Seminary, she began a gradual withdrawal from the outside world back into the family home. By the time she was twenty-three, she could write, "I do not go from home," and she did not, except for brief, rare trips to Boston or Philadelphia in the early years of her seclusion, for the rest of her life. Her fellow villagers in Amherst came to think of her as a village eccentric, who always dressed in white and was seldom seen, even when they came to call, when she sometimes listened to music or conversation from behind a door left ajar. They called her "the myth."

Within the house, Dickinson carried on a regular domestic routine, supervising the gardening, tending the greenhouse, and, especially, baking bread, which her father regarded as her special talent. She also carried on an extensive correspondence with a small circle of friends, read voluminously, and wrote her poetry. Although she showed her poems occasionally to others throughout her life, apparently not even her family suspected the extent and the quality of her writing.

A personal crisis of some sort occurred between the ages of twenty-nine and thirty-four, peaking in 1862, when Dickinson was thirty-two. Early romantic biographers attributed this crisis, quite evident in her poems, to a love affair, and it is true that her emotional turbulence of 1862 was appar-

ently triggered by the departure, for California, of Charles Wadsworth, a Philadelphia minister with whom she seems to have been in love, although probably concealing the fact from him and everyone else. She had similarly ambiguous relationships with Benjamin Newton, a student in her father's law office, and with the distinguished critic Thomas Wentworth Higginson, both of whom she regarded, overtly at least, as mentors or "preceptors." But the 1862 breakdown, if it was that, now seems to have had much more complex causes than a disappointment in love, and certainly the poems which probably allude to this crisis, such as "I felt a Funeral, in my Brain," suggest a very serious and deep-seated mental disturbance.

The crisis passed, however, and Dickinson resumed the even tenor of her quiet life. Her father died suddenly in 1873, and her mother was paralyzed by a stroke a year later; Emily and Lavinia nursed her for seven years, until her death. Dickinson survived her for only four years, dying in 1886.

After her death, a box was found containing about nine hundred poems. Higginson assisted the family in editing a selection of them, published as *Poems by Emily Dickinson* in 1890; two more collections appeared in 1891 and 1896. Her reputation spread and more editions of her work appeared beginning in 1914 and culminating in Thomas Johnson's definitive edition of her complete poems—totaling 1775—in 1955. Dickinson did not title her poems or, of course, prepare them for publication by providing conventional capitalization and punctuation. The numbers given in this selection are those assigned by Johnson, and the capitalization and punctuation follow the manuscripts. The dates on the left are the approximate dates of composition, as determined by Johnson; those on the right are the original publication dates. (Only seven poems of her total production were published during her lifetime.)

Dickinson's poetry, as her life seems to have done, sets up a passionate tension between constraint and freedom. She works within the narrow limits of the rhymed quatrains of Protestant hymn-books, but she stretches the form as far as it will go with rhythmic variations and "slant rhymes" (*hand/ end, star/door*, etc.). For the most part, she assumes a persona of almost childlike naiveté, who "tells all the truth but tells it slant," but on occasion, she adopts a dramatic character (as she does in "I'm 'wife'—I've finished that," for example) or adopts a grave, mature tone very far from childlike whimsy (as in "I felt a Funeral, in my Brain," and "My life closed twice before its close—"). Her themes burst the limits of her characteristically small, domestic subjects to range out into cosmic speculations, especially on God, death, love, and nature. A description of a bird on her walk can become an unpretentious but powerful meditation upon both the cruelty and the grandeur of nature, and a complex and ambivalent attitude toward death can be expressed as an afternoon carriage-ride with a gentleman caller.

Some critics have insisted upon Dickinson's close, though eccentric, relation to her own time and have denied that she is, in any sense, a "modern" poet. It is true that, as her poetic form is an extension of traditional psalmody, so her themes show a post-Calvinist preoccupation with the relationships among man, God, and nature. It is nevertheless hard not to see, in her sense of the centrality and complexity of her own inner life and the frankness with which she deals with it and in her characteristic delight in

ambiguity, paradox, and "slantness," qualities which speak very directly to modern readers.

FURTHER READING *(prepared by J. H)*: The standard biography is Richard B. Sewell's *The Life of Emily Dickinson,* 1974, repr. in one volume, 1980. The monumental task of establishing the texts and chronology of Dickinson's work was accomplished in *The Poems of Emily Dickinson,* ed. by Thomas H. Johnson, 3 vols., 1955. One could do worse in beginning the study of Dickinson than read Adrienne Rich's brilliant essay "Vesuvius at Home: The Power of Emily Dickinson" [1976], repr. in *Critical Essays on Emily Dickinson,* ed. by Paul J. Ferlazzo, 1984. Ferlazzo is also the author of *Emily Dickinson,* 1976, in the Twayne United States Authors series. Another brief introduction is Donna Dickenson, *Emily Dickinson,* 1985, in the Berg Women's series. Among more advanced studies, Charles R. Anderson's *Emily Dickinson's Poetry: Stairway of Surprise,* 1960, despite its age, has not been superseded. John Cody's *After Great Pain: The Inner Life of Emily Dickinson,* 1971, is a sensitive and thorough account by a professional psychoanalyst of Dickinson's personality and its expression in her poetry. Karl Miller's *The Only Kangaroo among the Beauty: Emily Dickinson and America,* 1979, places Dickinson in her time. Vivian R. Pollak's *Dickinson: The Anxiety of Gender,* 1984, is a strong feminist reading. Paula Bennett, in *My Life a Loaded Gun: Female Creativity and Feminist Poetics,* 1986, considers the psychology of creativity, dealing with Sylvia Plath and Adrienne Rich as well as Dickinson. See also Wendy Barker, *Lunacy of Light: Emily Dickinson and the Experience of Metaphor,* 1987.

67

Success is counted sweetest
By those who ne'er succeed.
To comprehend a nectar
Requires sorest need.

Not one of all the purple Host 5
Who took the Flag today
Can tell the definition
So clear of Victory

As he defeated—dying—
On whose forbidden ear 10
The distant strains of triumph
Burst agonized and clear!

c. 1859 *1878*

199

I'm "wife"—I've finished that—
That other state—

I'm Czar—I'm "Woman" now—
It's safer so—

How odd the Girl's life looks 5
Behind this soft Eclipse—
I think that Earth feels so
To folks in Heaven—now—

This being comfort—then
That other kind—was pain— 10
But why compare?
I'm "Wife"! Stop there!

c. 1860 *1890*

214

I taste a liquor never brewed—
From Tankards scooped in Pearl—
Not all the Vats upon the Rhine
Yield such an Alcohol!

Inebriate of Air—am I— 5
And Debauchee of Dew—
Reeling—thro endless summer days—
From inns of Molten Blue—

When "Landlords" turn the drunken Bee
Out of the Foxglove's[1] door— 10
When Butterflies—renounce their "drams"[2]—
I shall but drink the more!

Till Seraphs swing their snowy Hats—
And Saints—to windows run—
To see the little Tippler 15
Leaning against the—Sun—

c. 1860 *1861*

258

There's a certain Slant of light,
Winter Afternoons—

[1] *Foxglove* is a flower with dotted white or purple tubular blossoms.
[2] Shots of liquor.

That oppresses, like the Heft[1]
Of Cathedral Tunes—

Heavenly Hurt, it gives us— 5
We can find no scar,
But internal difference,
Where the Meanings, are—

None may teach it—Any—
'Tis the Seal Despair— 10
An imperial affliction
Sent us of the Air—

When it comes, the Landscape listens—
Shadows—hold their breath—
When it goes, 'tis like the Distance 15
On the look of Death—

c. 1861 *1890*

280

I felt a Funeral, in my Brain,
And Mourners to and fro
Kept treading—treading—till it seemed
That Sense was breaking through—

And when they all were seated, 5
A Service, like a Drum—
Kept beating—beating—till I thought
My Mind was going numb—

And then I heard them lift a Box
And creak across my Soul 10
With those same Boots of Lead, again,
Then Space—began to toll,

As all the Heavens were a Bell,
And Being, but an Ear,
And I, and Silence, some strange Race 15
Wrecked, solitary, here—

And then a Plank in Reason, broke,
And I dropped down, and down—
And hit a World, at every plunge,
And Finished knowing—then— 20

c. 1861 *1896*

[1] A colloquial term for "weight," as in the "heft" of an ax.

<center>303</center>

The Soul selects her own Society—
Then—shuts the Door—
To her divine Majority—
Present no more—

Unmoved—she notes the Chariots—pausing— 5
At her low Gate—
Unmoved—an Emperor be kneeling
Upon her Mat—

I've known her—from an ample nation—
Choose One— 10
Then—close the Valves of her attention—
Like Stone—

c. 1862 *1890*

<center>327</center>

Before I got my eye put out
I liked as well to see—
As other Creatures, that have Eyes
And know no other way—

But were it told to me—Today— 5
That I might have the sky
For mine—I tell you that my Heart
Would split, for size of me—

The Meadows—mine—
The Mountains—mine— 10
All Forests—Stintless Stars—
As much of Noon as I could take
Between my finite eyes—

The Motions of the Dipping Birds—
The Morning's Amber Road— 15
For mine—to look at when I liked—
The News would strike me dead—

So safer—guess—with just my soul
Upon the Window pane—
Where other Creatures put their eyes— 20
Incautious—of the Sun—

c. 1862 *1891*

328

A Bird came down the Walk—
He did not know I saw—
He bit an Angleworm in halves
And ate the fellow, raw,

And then he drank a Dew 5
From a convenient Grass—
And then hopped sidewise to the Wall
To let a Beetle pass—

He glanced with rapid eyes
That hurried all around— 10
They looked like frightened Beads, I thought—
He stirred his Velvet Head

Like one in danger, Cautious,
I offered him a Crumb
And he unrolled his feathers 15
And rowed him softer home—

Than Oars divide the Ocean,
Too silver for a seam—
Or Butterflies, off Banks of Noon
Leap, plashless[1] as they swim. 20

c. 1862 *1891*

341

After great pain, a formal feeling comes—
The Nerves sit ceremonious, like Tombs—
The stiff Heart questions was it He, that bore,
And Yesterday, or Centuries before?

The Feet, mechanical, go round— 5
Of Ground, or Air, or Ought—
A Wooden way
Regardless grown,
A Quartz contentment, like a stone—

This is the Hour of Lead— 10
Remembered, if outlived,
As Freezing persons, recollect the Snow—
First—Chill—then Stupor—then the letting go—

c. 1862 *1929*

[1] Splashless.

401

What Soft—Cherubic Creatures—
These Gentlewomen are—
One would as soon assault a Plush[1]—
Or violate a Star—

Such Dimity[2] Convictions— 5
A Horror so refined
Of freckled Human Nature—
Of Deity—ashamed—

It's such a common—Glory—
A Fisherman's—Degree— 10
Redemption—Brittle Lady—
Be so—ashamed of Thee—

c. 1862 *1896*

435

Much Madness is divinest Sense—
To a discerning Eye—
Much Sense—the starkest Madness—
'Tis the Majority
In this, as All, prevail— 5
Assent—and you are sane—
Demur—you're straightway dangerous—
And handled with a Chain—

c. 1862 *1890*

465

I heard a Fly buzz—when I died—
The Stillness in the Room
Was like the Stillness in the Air—
Between the Heaves of Storm—

The Eyes around—had wrung them dry— 5
And Breaths were gathering firm
For that last Onset—when the King
Be witnessed—in the Room—

[1] A soft, piled fabric; perhaps, by extension, a cushion made of such a fabric.
[2] A sheer cotton fabric in checks or stripes often used in nineteenth-century ladies' clothing.

I willed my Keepsakes—Signed away
What portion of me be 10
Assignable—and then it was
There interposed a Fly—

With Blue—uncertain stumbling Buzz—
Between the light—and me—
And then the Windows failed—and then 15
I could not see to see—

c. 1862 *1896*

470

I am alive—I guess—
The Branches on my Hand
Are full of Morning Glory—
And at my finger's end—

The Carmine[1]—tingles warm— 5
And if I hold a Glass
Across my Mouth—it blurs it—
Physician's—proof of Breath—

I am alive—because
I am not in a Room— 10
The Parlor—Commonly—it is—
So Visitors may come—

And lean—and view it sidewise—
And add "How cold—it grew"—
And "Was it conscious—when it stepped 15
In Immortality?"

I am alive—because
I do not own a House—
Entitled to myself—precise—
And fitting no one else— 20

And marked my Girlhood's name—
So Visitors may know
Which Door is mine—and not mistake—
And try another Key—

How good—to be alive! 25
How infinite—to be

[1] Crimson (blood).

Alive—two-fold—The Birth I had—
And this—besides, in—Thee!

c. 1862 *1945*

585

I like to see it lap the Miles—
And lick the Valleys up—
And stop to feed itself at Tanks—
And then—prodigious step

Around a Pile of Mountains— 5
And supercilious peer
In Shanties—by the sides of Roads—
And then a Quarry pare

To fit its Ribs
And crawl between 10
Complaining all the while
In horrid—hooting stanza—
Then chase itself down Hill—

And neigh like Boanerges[1]—
Then—punctual as a Star 15
Stop—docile and omnipotent
At its own stable door—

c. 1862 *1891*

712

Because I could not stop for Death—
He kindly stopped for me—
The Carriage held but just Ourselves—
And Immortality.

We slowly drove—He knew no haste 5
And I had put away
My labor and my leisure too,
For His Civility—

We passed the School, where Children strove
At Recess—in the Ring— 10

[1] Name given by Christ to James and John, meaning "sons of thunder." See Mark 3:17. In Dickinson's day, it was a humorous term for any loud, ranting preacher or orator.

We passed the Fields of Gazing Grain—
We passed the Setting Sun—

Or rather—He passed Us—
The Dews drew quivering and chill—
For only Gossamer, my Gown— 15
My Tippet[1]—only Tulle[2]—

We paused before a House that seemed
A Swelling of the Ground—
The Roof was scarcely visible—
The Cornice—in the Ground— 20

Since then—'tis Centuries—and yet
Feels shorter than the Day
I first surmised the Horses' Heads
Were toward Eternity—

c. 1863 *1890*

764

Presentiment—is that long Shadow—on the Lawn—
Indicative that Suns go down—

The Notice to the startled Grass
That Darkness—is about to pass—

c. 1863 *1890*

829

Ample make this Bed—
Make this Bed with Awe—
In it wait till Judgment break
Excellent and Fair.

Be its Mattress straight— 5
Be its Pillow round—
Let no Sunrise' yellow noise
Interrupt this Ground—

c. 1864 *1891*

[1] Scarf. [2] A thin, fine, silk netting.

1129

Tell all the Truth but tell it slant—
Success in Circuit lies
Too bright for our infirm Delight
The Truth's superb surprise

As Lightning to the Children eased 5
With explanation kind
The Truth must dazzle gradually
Or every man be blind—

c. 1868 *1945*

1732

My life closed twice before its close—
It yet remains to see
If Immortality unveil
A third event to me

So huge, so hopeless to conceive 5
As these that twice befell.
Parting is all we know of heaven,
And all we need of hell.

(date uncertain) *1896*

Realism and Naturalism

T HERE is now only one consuming interest left in our life, the passion for the study of living reality," the Goncourt brothers, Jules and Edmond, wrote in 1865 in their great joint diary of the French literary life. "We are like a man accustomed to drawing from a wax dummy who has suddenly been presented with a living model, or rather life itself with its entrails warm and active, its guts palpitating." The Goncourts rather slyly and disingenuously reflect the baiting of the middle class inherent in the realist movement; a large portion of the reading public preferred its literature without the palpitating guts. But the Goncourts also express the heady exhilaration the realists felt when they took off (as they thought) the rosy glasses of romanticism and gazed unspectacled at "life itself." From a later, more disillusioned perspective, it may appear that they merely exchanged one pair of spectacles for another, darker pair. But if nineteenth-century realism sometimes seems somber and humorless, we would do well to remember how brave the new world of reality seemed to the realists, how deeply their assumptions about art have become embedded in the modern mind, and how vital the impulse toward "the study of living reality" has been in literature since their time.

The most straightforward definition of realism is probably the one given by the American realist William Dean Howells: it is "the truthful treatment of material." But what material? And what is truthful treatment? The realists tended to be highly selective in their choice of material, focusing upon what seemed real to their largely middle-class readers. The subjects of realistic fiction thus tended to be contemporary, ordinary, and middle-class. "Truthful" treatment of such subjects usually consisted of a faithful imitation of surface details with the goal of creating the illusion of reality. Henrik Ibsen spoke for most of his fellow realists when he said that the effect of his plays depended upon "making the spectator feel as if he were actually sitting, listening, and looking on events happening in real life."

Creating such an illusion required certain artistic choices. Characters had to be ordinary, average, contemporary people rather than the exceptional extremists—the Agamemnons, the King Lears, and the Werthers—who had formed the central subjects of much earlier literature. Plots had to be unobtrusive, made up of the trivial incidents of everyday life, as "natural" as possible in their development, capturing the wandering, indeterminate nature of ordinary experience rather than contriving the tensions and climaxes of traditional plots. And the language had to be equally natural or at least give the impression of being so; not only were characters made to speak in the intonations of everyday life but the authors themselves strove

to make their language as invisible as possible, a neutral reflector of impersonal reality.

Why this sudden interest, in the middle of the nineteenth century, in the direct imitation of ordinary life? Realism was to some extent an extension of romanticism, which included ordinary, "natural" life among its concerns. It was Wordsworth, after all, who proposed in *Lyrical Ballads* to "choose incidents and situations from common life, and to relate or describe them, throughout, as far as was possible in a selection of language really used by men." But the realists' concern with ordinary life represented a considerable shift in basic assumptions. Wordsworth proposed to throw over ordinary life " a certain colouring of imagination" and to trace through simple incidents "the primary laws of our nature," especially the ways "the passions of men are incorporated with the beautiful and permanent forms of nature." The realists' vision of ordinary life was a darker one. The "ordinary man" of the realists was not a rural laborer, in harmony with the cycles of nature, but an urban bourgeois, alienated from both nature and himself by the pressures of a scrambling, competitive, materialistic society.

Discontent with the optimistic premises of romanticism became evident in European literature as early as the 1840's, especially in France. Balzac's flood of novels during the 1830's and 1840's were basically antiromantic in their subordination of the individual will to external circumstance. His famous Preface to *The Human Comedy* (1842) sets forth some of the basic tenets of realism, including a materialistic determinism ("Tell me what you possess and I will tell you what you think"), and outlines a quasi-scientific project of producing a comprehensive classification of human types. His divisions resemble zoological categories: "By drawing up an inventory of vices and virtues, by collecting the chief facts of the passions, by depicting characters, by choosing the principal incidents of social life, by composing types out of a combination of homogeneous characteristics, I might perhaps succeed in writing the history which so many historians have neglected: that of Manners."

To see the reasons for the shift in emphasis between romanticism and realism, we must look outside literature to society and politics and especially to the triumph of the commercial middle class after the mid-century. The collapse of the 1848 revolutions that swept France, Germany, Austria, and Italy marked a major turning point in European life. Artists and intellectuals had taken an active part in these revolutions; the idealistic poet and novelist Alphonse de Lamartine had actually headed the French provisional government after the 1848 February Revolution, and the poet-patriot Giuseppe Mazzini was a leading figure in the 1848 Milan Revolution and in the 1849 Roman republic. The backlash of conservative reaction after 1848 drove artists all over Europe from the political arena and back into a kind of art that provided a refuge from a society they more and more perceived as crude, brutal, and unredeemable. In France, the decisive defeat of liberalism came with the 1851 *coup d'état* by which Napoleon III transformed the short-lived Second Republic into the Second Empire. Jules Goncourt spoke for many French intellectuals when he called the Second Empire "decadence in its vilest form, a new invasion of the barbarians." English intellectuals reacted similarly to the Crystal Palace exhibition

of the same year, a celebration which, from one point of view, magnified England's material progress and industrial dominance and, from another, more jaundiced one, her crassness, vulgarity, and social injustice.

The bourgeois triumph of the 1850's was far from the unqualified disaster that aesthetes considered it. The French Bonapartist government built broad boulevards and laid water lines and sewer pipes in Paris; the diplomacy of Cavour in Italy and Bismarck in Germany unified those countries at last; and all over Europe the wealth created by industrialization brought about a new prosperity, at least some of which trickled down to the working class. Growth was so rapid that the ordinary person came to believe in inevitable, limitless progress. But it was a kind of growth to which most artists felt irreconcilably hostile. The gap between the artist and society, already wide during the age of romanticism, became a yawning gulf even now not wholly bridged.

Middle-class expansionism found its ideology in Positivism and an exaggerated faith in science or "scientism." Positivism was the creation of the French philosopher Auguste Comte, who set forth the system in his *Course of Positive Philosophy* (1830–42). For Comte, the greatest of the sciences was sociology (a term he coined), and the goal of science was to reform society so that all people could live together in comfort and harmony. Metaphysics he rejected as superstition; trustworthy knowledge was derivable from sense experience and the "positive" sciences only. Comte's brisk, commonsense optimism and his faith in progress perfectly suited the temper of his age, and by the 1850's, Positivism was the ruling ideology of many European intellectuals. In England, the Utilitarianism preached by John Stuart Mill and others was thoroughly Positivistic in its insistence upon empiricism as the basis of all knowledge and its demystification of morality as "the greatest good for the greatest number." Karl Marx, whose *Communist Manifesto* (written with Friedrich Engels) appeared in 1848, was also Positivistic in his "scientific" theory of social change, a theory developed in full in *Capital,* the influential first volume of which appeared in 1867. Mill's Utilitarianism was paralleled in Germany by the philosophy of Ludwig Feuerbach, who defined religion as nothing more than a symbolic dream and philosophy as the study of man as defined by experience. Marx's attempt at scientific history was similarly pursued by the English historian Henry Thomas Buckle, whose *History of Civilization in England* (1857–61), with its broad sweep and its supposedly scientific method, created a sensation. Even Charles Darwin's evolutionary bombshell *The Origin of Species* (1859) was essentially Positivistic in its application of the methods of science to areas that had traditionally been the province of religion: humanity's origins, nature, and relation to the rest of the natural world.

The realist writers felt an uneasy ambivalence toward this world of explosive prosperity, dizzying progress, and scientific Positivism. On the one hand, they maintained their stance of disapproval and estrangement; on the other, they shaped an art based upon the methods if not the values of the larger society. None of the great realist writers was in any sense an apologist for his or her society; all were more or less in open revolt against it. And yet all to some degree brought to art the habits of mind pervasive in that society: a sceptical secularism, a concern for the here and now, and a loosely scientific objectivity. It is almost as if the realists were saying to their

1131

contemporaries: "We will use your own methods to reveal to you the meanness, the cruelty, and the vulgarity of the society you take such pride in." The result was a paradoxically avant-garde art in which the bourgeoisie was taunted in its own common-sense terms. This ambivalence is especially powerful in the work of the great French realist Gustave Flaubert, who had to drive himself to write about a contemporary reality he found nauseating and who periodically escaped into lush, neoromantic fantasies. "Do you really believe that this mean reality, whose reproduction disgusts you, does not make my gorge rise as much as yours?" he wrote to a friend who had taken exception to *Madame Bovary* (1857). "If you knew me better, you would know that I hold the everyday life in detestation. Personally I have always kept myself as far away from it as I could. But aesthetically I wanted this time, and only this time, to exhaust it thoroughly. So I took the thing in an heroic fashion, I mean a minute one, accepting everything, saying everything, depicting everything—an ambitious statement!"

The desire to shock the middle class became even more pointed when realism darkened still further into naturalism, the movement that dominated the 1870's and 1880's as realism had dominated the 1850's and 1860's. Naturalism is not merely an extreme form of realism; it is informed by a very different philosophical view, a post-Darwinian form of scientific determinism in which people are the prisoners of their biological inheritance and social environment. The naturalists abandoned the middle-class drawing rooms of the realists for the "lower depths," working-class settings where the impact of environment was especially clear, and for violent, animalistic characters whose inherited drives, especially hunger and sex, are particularly vivid. Naturalism, for all its claims to a scientific objectivity, was an even better stick with which to beat the middle class than realism had been. The Goncourt brothers, at the same time fastidious aesthetes and the first architects of the naturalistic novel, wrote in their preface to what has been called the first naturalistic novel, *Germinie Lacerteux* (1864), "The public loves to read pleasant, soothing stories, adventures that end happily, imaginative works that disturb neither its digestion nor its peace of mind: this book furnishes entertainment of a melancholy, violent sort calculated to disarrange the habits and injure the health of the public."

The Goncourts denied that their work, for all its disturbing qualities, was pessimistic or despairing; their aim, they said, was to make the novel a "serious, impassioned, living form of literary study and social investigation" and to bring about social reform. Their friend, Émile Zola, theoretician and practitioner of the "experimental novel"—the novel designed like a medical experiment—similarly denied that he was a fatalist: "We are not fatalists, we are determinists, which is not at all the same thing. . . . The moment that we can act, and that we do act, on the determining cause of phenomena—by modifying their surroundings, for example—we cease to be fatalists." Such explanations cut little ice with middle-class readers, however; Zola's works were frequently banned and Tennyson, speaking for the bourgeoisie, rejected modern literature as "wallowing in the troughs of Zolaism."

Realism and naturalism transcended national boundaries. France took the lead, but the realist impulse quickly spread throughout Europe. Scandinavia, long a backwater of European culture, became the center of a new

drama, vitalized by realism, when Henrik Ibsen, an obscure, failed Norwegian playwright living in exile in Germany, read the Danish critic Georg Brandes' lecture on "Main Currents in Nineteenth-Century Literature." Brandes had applied for the chair of aesthetics at the University of Copenhagen and, to demonstrate his qualifications for the post, had been asked to deliver a series of lectures. His opening lecture, delivered on November 3, 1871, was a scathing attack on Danish literature, which he said was forty years behind the times and lost in a haze of dreamy, abstract idealism. The only living literature, he said, pointing to the French writers as examples, was realistic literature, literature that "submitted contemporary social problems to debate." When Ibsen read the lecture in Dresden in 1872, he wrote to his friend Brandes: "No more dangerous book could fall into the hands of a pregnant writer. It is one of those works that place a yawning gulf between yesterday and today." Ibsen's *Pillars of Society* followed in 1877, the first in the series of twelve realistic dramas that debated contemporary social problems. The progression in the French novel from realism to naturalism was echoed in the Scandinavian drama when Ibsen's realistic plays were followed by August Strindberg's naturalistic ones, such as *The Father* (1887) and *Miss Julie* (1888). These display the quasi-Darwinian spectacle of brutal, primitive characters triumphing in the struggle for survival over more sensitive and highly developed types.

In England, George Eliot cultivated, in *Adam Bede* (1859), *Middlemarch* (1871–72), and other works, a gentle realism which she compared to Dutch genre paintings. "Let us always have men," she wrote, "ready to give the loving pains of a life to the faithful representation of commonplace things—men who see beauty in these commonplace things, and delight in showing how kindly the light of heaven falls on them." The realistic impulse touched Charles Dickens, too, as he turned from the romantic optimism of his early novels to the more somber studies of society that began to appear in the 1850's, especially *Bleak House* (1853), *Hard Times* (1854), and *Great Expectations* (1860–61). George Meredith, Thomas Hardy, George Moore, and Joseph Conrad carried the realist-naturalist tradition down to the early years of the twentieth century.

In Russia, a realistic movement flourished that surpassed even its French inspiration. Nikolay Gogol, though a conservative upholder of autocracy and serfdom, established, especially in his comedy *The Inspector General* (1836) and his story "The Overcoat" (1842), a "natural" school of writing that was to foster the greatest achievements of Russian fiction. Ivan Turgenev added to Gogol's influence that of his friends Flaubert in France and George Eliot in England. His *A Sportsman's Sketches* (1852), a series of realistic stories of Russian peasant life, played a role in the emancipation of the serfs in 1861, and his *Fathers and Sons* (1862) is one of the great works of nineteenth-century realism. The most brilliant member of the "natural" school, however, was Fyodor Dostoevsky, whose four greatest novels, *Crime and Punishment* (1866), *The Idiot* (1868–69), *The Possessed* (1871–72), and *The Brothers Karamazov* (1879–80), all probe in their different ways the classic realist theme: the fate of the individual living in a problematical modern world stripped of faith. Leo Tolstoy's *War and Peace* (1865–69) and *Anna Karenina* (1875–76), a book often compared to *Madame Bovary*, are also in the main realistic tradition, as are his "post-conversion" master-

1133

pieces "The Death of Ivan Ilyitch" (1886) and "The Kreutzer Sonata" (1891). Anton Chekhov, besides writing magnificent realistic short stories, carried realistic drama beyond even Ibsen, to a point where photographic and phonographic literalism takes on a shimmering intensity on the borders of symbolism.

Realism crossed the Atlantic, too, to generate a vigorous movement in America. The chief theoretician of American realism was William Dean Howells, who in his column "The Editor's Study" in *Harper's Magazine* vigorously advocated an American realism somewhat milder than that of Flaubert, Zola, and Dostoevsky. America, he thought, was dominated, as France and Russia were not, by "the large, cheerful average of health and success and happy life." Therefore, American realists should concern themselves with "the more smiling aspects of life, which are the more American." Timid as this program sounds, Howells' proselytizing and his example, in such novels as *The Rise of Silas Lapham* (1885), opened the way for the great American realists, Mark Twain and Henry James, and for the later American naturalists: Frank Norris, Hamlin Garland, Theodore Dreiser, Upton Sinclair, and Jack London.

America was somewhat late in following the realist-naturalist flag; in Europe the movement had run its course by the late 1880's, when the artists' withdrawal from society that had been latent in realism was extended in the symbolist movement, which like realism originated in France and spread thoughout Europe to dominate the closing years of the century.

Realism, of course, did not disappear when it ceased to be the dominant style of serious art. It has survived as the style of most popular literature, drama, film, and television, where frequently a realistic manner is used to present the most unrealistic views of life. But it has also survived in serious art as one of the styles available to modern writers and has found special favor with socially committed writers, such as the proletarian authors of the 1930's and the "Angry Young Men" novelists of post-World War II Britain. It seems likely that as long as writers are drawn to "the study of living reality," they will continue to draw upon the models of the great nineteenth-century realists.

FURTHER READING *(prepared by J. H.)*: A number of basic documents in which the nineteenth-century realists and naturalists directly declared their goals are available in the "Realism" section of *The Modern Tradition: Backgrounds of Modern Literature*, ed. by Richard Ellmann and Charles Feidelson, Jr., 1965. Two other useful collections are *Documents of Modern Literary Realism*, ed. by George L. Becker, 1963, and *Realism, Naturalism, and Symbolism: Modes of Thought and Expression in Europe, 1848–1914*, ed. by Roland N. Stromberg, 1968. The critical issues implied by the terms *realism* and *naturalism* are well treated in René Wellek's "The Concept of Realism in Literary Scholarship," in *Concepts of Criticism*, 1963, and in Harry Levin's "What is Realism?" in *Contexts of Criticism*, 1957. Levin's *The Gates of Horn*, 1963, is a standard study of the French nineteenth-century realist novelists. On the development of the realistic novel elsewhere, see Ian Watt, *The Rise of the Novel*, 1957, and John Vernon, *Money and Fiction: Literary Realism in the Nineteenth and Early Twentieth Centuries*, 1985. Erich Auerbach's masterful *Mimesis: The Representation of Reality in Western Literature*, trans. by Willard R. Trask, 1953, furnishes for the nineteenth-century realists the context of the treatment of reality throughout literary history. *The European Realist Tradition*, ed. by Gabriel P. Weisberg, 1983, contains a number of important essays.

Ivan Turgenev
(1818–1883)

Ivan Turgenev (pronounced Tur-GAIN-yef), though recognized everywhere as one of Russia's greatest literary artists, had the misfortune to be a contemporary of Dostoevsky and Tolstoy, two authors of such elemental force and visionary power as to make almost anyone else seem somewhat pale by comparison. As a result, critics and historians of literature have tended, even while strongly praising Turgenev, to dwell unduly and gratuitously on his alleged narrowness of range. But Turgenev's aims were not those of Tolstoy or Dostoevsky; like his American counterpart and disciple, Henry James, Turgenev was more an artist and psychologist than a prophet or visionary. This is not at all to say that Turgenev's works lack emotional power, any more than that is true of James. On the contrary, few if any writers have ever conveyed more piercingly than Turgenev the emotional turbulence—the bliss and the pain—of romantic love. Neither is it true, moreover, that Turgenev limited his focus to the private life of the heart; he was also a sensitive and alert recorder of social and political change. Yet there too he was historically unfortunate: his committed but moderate political liberalism, combined with his devotion to the civilized values of western Europe, ultimately pleased no one in the feverishly polarized Russia of his day. He was too advanced to suit mossbacked Russian traditionalists and, on the other hand, too much a believer in gradual progress to suit the impatient radical ideologues who raised the political stakes ever higher as the nineteenth century ran its course.

Turgenev was born in 1818 in Orel, a city in central Russia two hundred miles south of Moscow. His father, a military officer who had distinguished himself fighting against Napoleon, had married for her money a very wealthy landowner some six years his senior, to whom he was habitually unfaithful; in this and certain other respects, their situation parallels the marital relationship Turgenev described later in *First Love*. Although his father took some pains to assure a good education for Ivan, the boy was reared mainly by his strong-willed mother, whose ruthless treatment of the serfs on her estate, Spasskoe, made a powerful and unfavorable impression on her son. It seems very likely that Turgenev's later tendency to create strong-minded or imperious heroines (his father died when the boy was sixteen) owed something to his mother's influence.

Ivan was educated by tutors, then at private schools, then at Moscow University, which he entered when he was fifteen, and then at the university at St. Petersburg, to which he transferred a year later. After taking his degree in 1837, he returned to Spasskoe for a year, during which he acquainted himself sympathetically with the life of peasants on the estate. In 1838 he began a three-year soujourn in western Europe, enrolling at the University of Berlin for a time, absorbing the ideas of German romantic thinkers, discovering the wonders of the world of art through a trip to Italy, and in general coming under the spell of things European, much as Henry James was to do a quarter-century later.

Turgenev went back to Russia after this foreign excursion, but his drift toward Europe was accelerated by two developments of his mid-twenties.

One was his falling in love with the internationally famous (and already married) operatic soprano Pauline Viardot while she was performing in Russia in 1843. (She was, incidentally, a close friend of George Sand and a model for the adventurous heroine of Sand's gothic novel *Consuelo*.) Thus began a lifelong connection between Mme Viardot and Turgenev, which subsisted in some indefinable region between the platonic and the fleshly; Turgenev was often, later in his life, to settle in one part of Europe or another mainly so that he could remain close to her. The other development was his discovery that Europe afforded precious freedom and stimulus to the creative imagination of a writer. In his teens he had tried his hand as a poet, in the then-obligatory Byronic manner, and in 1843, while back in Russia, he achieved a success with the verse narrative *Parasha*. Gradually he modulated into his true vehicle, prose fiction, by way of a series of stories about country life, later collected and published in 1852 as *A Sportsman's Sketches*. The realistic and sympathetic portraits of peasants in this collection came to constitute a political statement, unpopular at the time with the court of Czar Nicholas I but subsequently, it is sometimes argued, instrumental in helping persuade his successor, Alexander II, to emancipate the serfs, as he did in 1861. Turgenev's exposure to western Europe had been essential to the gestation of *A Sportsman's Sketches*, giving him the distance and perspective he needed to focus his sense of opposition to the existence of serfdom.

During the 1840s and early 1850s, at home in Russia and abroad, Turgenev continued to experiment with a number of literary forms. Besides poems, he wrote literary criticism and several plays, some of which went unproduced at the time because of the censor's ban. One of the banned plays, *A Month in the Country* (1855), would later be staged memorably in 1909 by the renowned director Konstantin Stanislavsky (the founder of "method" acting) and thenceforth would enjoy a permanent place in the dramatic repertory. In 1850, in the novella *The Diary of a Superfluous Man*, Turgenev also introduced into Russian literature a type of weak-willed social and intellectual misfit that was to become a staple of the Russian literary imagination over the next few decades.

Ironically, one of Turgenev's most momentous publications at this time was a mere obituary, marking the death in 1852 of one of the great Russian writers, Nikolai Gogol. Czar Nicholas I had preferred to treat Gogol as a nonperson because of his satirical works, notably the play *The Inspector General* (1836) and the novel *Dead Souls* (1842). Turgenev was imprisoned for a month and then exiled to the Spasskoe estate, which he and his brother had inherited after their mother's death in 1850. The purported offense was violation of the censorship laws, but Turgenev believed his real offense to have been his sympathetic portraits of the serfs in *A Sportsman's Sketches*. It was not until 1855, when Nicholas I died, that Turgenev was allowed to travel abroad once more. Much of his later life, though punctuated by trips back to his native land, was to be spent in France, Germany, Italy, and England.

In the mid-1850s Turgenev began to explore still another literary genre: the novel. For him, the novel did not mean the blockbuster epics that Dostoevsky and Tolstoy would create; most of Turgenev's novels are hardly longer than novellas, focusing intensely on a few key characters in

specific situations rather than panning over vast social and spiritual land-scapes peopled by dozens of varied and far-flung characters. It would be wrong to regard these novels as mere cameo miniatures, however, or mere studies of manners; though many of them are love stories or otherwise explore character in intimate psychological close-up, most of them rever-berate also with larger social or political implications. *Rudin* (1856), the protagonist of which is modeled on the famous anarchist Mikhail Bakunin, whom Turgenev had known well as a student in Berlin, satirically deflates Rudin as an ineffectual idealist, all talk and no action, but in the end this antihero dies at the Paris barricades during the revolution of 1848. *Home of the Gentry* (1859) is a delicately conceived love story, but it is also a study of the difficulty in defining and realizing what is potentially best in Russian society. *On the Eve* (1860)—which Henry James for one regarded as Tur-genev's greatest novel—is mainly a personal portrait of its high-minded and fearless heroine, but ultimately the novel launches her onto politically perilous seas, in the cause of Bulgarian independence. The love interest in *Fathers and Sons* (1862), Turgenev's most widely read work today, is at the heart of the plot, but even more significant is the novel's delineation of a radical new social and political philosophy that, largely because Turgenev so named it, came to be called nihilism. On its personal level of action, *Smoke* (1867) is notable mainly for its wrenching account of the hero's at-traction to a morally ambiguous, irresistible heroine, but the novel includes also some lively social commentary, championing the progressive and civil-ized "European" values at the expense both of vapid, outdated Russian aristocrats and of their mindless revolutionary adversaries.

Through the earlier part of his career as a writer, Turgenev was re-garded as a man in the vanguard of events, a realist in his portrayal of Russian society and culture but also a spokesman for the most promising of Russian aspirations. This image of him changed with the publication of *Fathers and Sons* in 1862; many radicals considered the picture of its nihilist hero as a vicious slur, while conservatives believed that Turgenev had made the hero too sympathetic. Suddenly Turgenev seemed to his critics to have lost touch with what was really happening in the political and spiritual life of Russia. Indeed, Turgenev's acidulous depiction in *Smoke* of political idi-ocy both old and new seems to have been a piqued reaction to this double-barreled criticism from both left and right. Predictably, *Smoke* did nothing to appease Turgenev's critics; the traditionalist Dostoevsky, for example, in his novel *The Possessed* (1871), severely lampooned Turgenev as effetely Westernized and outdated.

There had always been a deep vein of pessimism in Turgenev; it is reflected strongly, for example, in the unhappy outcomes of most of his love stories. The despondency and alienation from Russia that he felt as a result of his compatriots' severe judgments of him deepened this pessimism in his latter years. Moreover, money had become a problem, largely be-cause of agents' mismanagement of his Russian landed estate and the fi-nancial burdens thrown upon him by the failed marriage of an illegitimate daughter whom he had fathered in 1842. With an exception or two such as the novel *Virgin Soil* (1877), in his last works he tended to avoid social-politi-cal themes. He remained something of a political activist, but in the capac-ity of private citizen rather than writer; indeed, after 1877 he virtually

ceased to be a writer at all. The decline in his spirits was temporarily arrested by several events that occurred shortly after he turned sixty: an honorary doctorate from Oxford in 1879 and trips to Russia in 1879 and 1880 during which Turgenev was enthusiastically acclaimed by Russians, old and young, as one of their country's greatest authors. He was even reconciled with Dostoevsky, personally if not ideologically. Moreover, outside of Russia his stature as the most admired of Russian writers was unimpaired. Nevertheless, his last years were mainly unhappy ones, and his health, which had been bad for some time, rapidly deteriorated. He died of spinal cancer in 1883, in the Parisian suburb of Bougival; Pauline Viardot was with him at the end. His body was returned to Russia, where he was buried in St. Petersburg (the city later called Leningrad). Like Henry James—another expatriate, explorer of international and European themes, meticulous artist and psychologist, and creator of heroic young female protagonists—Turgenev died abroad but was interred in his native country.

First Love (1860), written when Turgenev was at the height of his literary powers and prestige, was the work of his own that, he once remarked, he reread with the greatest pleasure and the keenest sense of conviction. His preference for it doubtless had something to do with its quasi-autobiographical content, but there are better reasons for placing it among his masterpieces. Although it is one of the most intimate and personal of his works, with little or no commentary on the state of Russia or of society, the story typifies Turgenev's artistic methods and his view of life. The plot is simple, the interest is primarily inner and psychological, and Zinaida, the heroine, is a good representative of the author's commanding female protagonists, endowed with powers of attraction, command, and personal presence that dwarf most of the people around them. The utter subjectivity of the experience of love is conveyed through a literary technique rooted in Turgenev's characteristic emphasis on narrative point of view; we are given privileged glimpses into the heart of the young narrator, Volodya, but we know also, less directly, that from other points of view, such as Zinaida's, equally stirring events and emotional crises are at work.

Moreover, *First Love* implies some far-reaching things about human experience and human personality, most obviously as regards the dynamics of love and of people in love. Seldom has the euphoria of young love been captured with such power and lyricism as in the adolescent Volodya. Yet we are also given to understand, almost from the very beginning and more emphatically as the story unfolds, that love is more than euphoria, that it involves a dynamic of both power and powerlessness (the imperious Zinaida is herself one of love's subjects, we come to learn), and that the happiness of love is inseparable from the giving and receiving of acute pain.

First Love, it is often said, illustrates Turgenev's deep pessimism: love is wondrous, but it cannot last and can seldom if ever be repeated. The somber last paragraphs of the story can be taken to bear out that gloomy emphasis. Yet *pessimism* may not be the right word to describe the final effect of this story. As a mode of bringing people together in joy or contentment, love may have failed; but as a way of opening people up to the paradoxical sense of human community-in-isolation, love has done fruitful and pre-

cious work. It could be argued that the revelation experienced by the disillusioned Volodya in the last sentences of the story—like the similar revelation, or "epiphany," experienced by a saddened Gabriel Conroy at the end of Joyce's "The Dead"—is both a testimony to irremediable loss and a glimpse of the profound spiritual roots that, exactly because they do suffer, human beings share with one another.

A NOTE ON RUSSIAN NAMES

Russian names are often a source of confusion to non-Russian readers. For example, in the opening paragraph of *First Love*, Nikolaich and Piotrovich are not the surnames of the two guests but rather their middle names, or "patronymics" (based on their fathers' first names). Russian names work as follows: A person has three names: a given name (such as Sergei or Vladimir), followed by a middle "patronymic" name (the person's father's first name followed by a suffix ending in -*ich*, "son of," for males and -*vna*, "daughter of," for females), followed by the surname or family name. Thus the two guests are identified as Sergei son of Nikolai and Vladimir son of Piotr; the narrator does not mention their surnames. A few paragraphs below, the host's wife is identified as Anna Ivanovna, that is, Anna daughter of Ivan; her surname is, again, unmentioned.

There are two further complications: 1) A woman's surname adds the feminine suffix -*a*, so that the surname of the wife or daughter of a man named Zasioskin is Zasioskina; and 2) First names often appear as familiar or affectionate nicknames; thus the heroine of this story, whose first name is Zinaida, is called Zenia by her mother. Her full name is Zinaida (nickname Zenia) Alexandrovna (daughter of a man whose first name is Alexander) Zasioskina (the feminine form of the family name, Zasioskin). *[Editors' headnote.]*

FURTHER READING *(prepared by S. M.):* *The Borzoi Turgenev,* 1950, includes in one handy volume good translations by Harry Stevens of four of Turgenev's best novels—*Rudin, On the Eve, Fathers and Sons,* and *Smoke*—along with three novellas including *The Diary of a Superfluous Man.* An excellent medium-length introduction to Turgenev, beginning with a brief biographical sketch and including also perceptive interpretations of the major works, is A. V. Knowles's *Ivan Turgenev,* 1988, in the Twayne's World Authors series; another good general introduction is Charles Moser, *Ivan Turgenev,* 1972. The considerable scholarly literature devoted to Turgenev includes at least four excellent critical biographies, of which the most recent is Leonard Schapiro's *Turgenev: His Life and Times,* 1978. V. S. Pritchett's *The Gentle Barbarian: The Life and Work of Turgenev,* 1977, is written for general readers and does not include an index but is perhaps the most enjoyable of the biographies. David Magarshack's *Turgenev: A Life,* 1954, and Avrahm Yarmolinsky's pioneering *Turgenev: The Man, His Art, and His Age,* 1926, are also excellent. (None of the four biographies mentioned discusses *First Love* at any great length.) Isaiah Berlin's *Fathers and Children,* 1972, is good on Turgenev's relation to the intellectual history of his era. On Turgenev's development, see Richard Freeborn, *Turgenev: The Novelist's Novelist,* 1963. A good sampling of recent criticism is *Critical Essays on Ivan Turgenev,* ed. David A. Lowe, 1988. Victor Ripp's *Turgenev's Russia,* 1980, includes in Chapter 8 a discussion of *First Love* as part of an extended treatment of Turgenev's views of love, and the novella is also analyzed in Chapter 3 of J. A. T. Lloyd's *Ivan Turgenev,* 1942, rpt. 1972.

FIRST LOVE

Translated by Harry Stevens

1

The guests had long since departed. The clock struck half past twelve. Only the host, Sergei Nikolaich, and Vladimir Piotrovich were left in the room.

The host rang and ordered the servant to clear the supper table.

"Well, so it's agreed," he said, making himself more comfortable in his armchair and lighting a cigar. "Each of us undertakes to tell the story of his first love. You begin, Sergei Nikolaich."

Sergei Nikolaich, a portly man with a fair, puffy face, first looked at his host, then fixed his eyes on the ceiling. "I never had a first love," he said at last. "I started with my second."

"But how could you have done that?"

"Quite simply. I was eighteen when I first began to chase after a certain very attractive young lady; but I courted her exactly as if it were nothing new for me at all, exactly as—I paid court to others, later. To tell the truth, the first time I fell in love—and the last—was at the age of six, with my nurse; but that was very long ago, I have quite forgotten the details of our relations, and even if I could remember them, who would be interested?"

"Well, what am I to say?" the host began. "There isn't much of interest to tell about my first love either. I never fell in love with anyone until I met Anna Ivanovna, my present wife; and everything went like clockwork then: our fathers arranged our betrothal, we very quickly fell in love with each other, and we got married without delay. So my story can be told in very few words. I confess, gentlemen, that when I raised this question of first love I was relying on you,—I won't say old bachelors, and yet you're not exactly young. Surely you'll amend matters for us with some story, Vladimir Piotrovich?"

"It so happens that my first love was not exactly ordinary," Vladimir Piotrovich replied after some hesitation. He was about forty years old, and had black hair streaked with gray.

"Ah!" The host and Sergei Nikolaich exclaimed in one voice. "So much the better. . . . Tell us the story."

"With pleasure. . . . But no, I won't tell you the story; I am no good at telling stories, I make them either dry and short, or long-winded and untrue to life. But if you'll allow me I'll write down all I can remember and read it to you."

At first his two friends would not agree, but he insisted on having his way. Two weeks later they met again, and he kept his promise.

This is what he had written.

At that time I was sixteen; it happened in the summer of 1833.

I was living with my parents in Moscow. They had rented a house for the summer close to the Kaluga Gate, opposite the Nieskuchny Gardens.[1] I

[1] The principal public park of Moscow, often called *Sans Souci,* "Carefree."

was preparing to enter the university, but I worked very little and at my leisure.

No one put any restraints on my freedom. I did what I liked, especially after I had parted from my last tutor, a Frenchman who could never get used to the idea that he had fallen "like a bomb" (*comme une bombe*) into Russia, and who spent days on end lying in bed with a fierce expression on his face. My father treated me with negligent kindness; my mother paid hardly any attention to me, though I was her only child: she was preoccupied with other cares. My father, a man still young and very handsome, had married her for money; she was ten years older than he. She had a miserable life; she was always getting upset, always jealous, always angry—but never in my father's presence. She was terribly afraid of him, and he treated her sternly, coldly, distantly. I have never known any other man so artificially calm, self-assured, and autocratic.

I shall never forget the first few weeks I spent in that house by the Kaluga Gate. The weather was perfect; we moved out of town on May 9, St. Nicholas's Day. I went walking in our garden, or about the Nieskuchny Gardens, or out beyond the city gate, taking a book with me—Kaidanov's *Course,*[2] for instance—but rarely opening it. I spent much of my time reciting poems, for I knew very many by heart. My blood was coursing through my veins, and I was melancholy, so delightfully and absurdly; I was always expecting something, always afraid of something, and I was astonished at everything, and always at the ready. My imagination played and danced continually around the same ideas, like swifts round a belfry at dawn. I was lost in thought, I sorrowed and even wept. But through the tears and through the sorrow inspired by some melodious poem, or by the beauty of the evening, a joyous feeling of youthful and effervescent life sprang up like grass in spring.

I had a saddle-horse. I saddled her myself and rode alone to some distant spot, the farther the better; I shook out the reins in a gallop and imagined myself a knight at a tourney (how merrily the wind blew in my ears!). Or, turning my face to the sky, I took its radiant light and azure into my soul.

I remember that in those days my mind hardly ever visualized the image of a woman, the apparition of woman's love, in any definite shape; but in all my thoughts, in all my feelings, lurked a half-recognized, bashful presentiment of something new, something inexpressibly sweet—something feminine.

This presentiment, this expectation, suffused all my being: I drew it in with my breath, it flowed through my veins in every drop of my blood . . . it was fated to have speedy realization.

Our house consisted of a large timber dwelling with a columned portico and two low wings; in the left-hand wing was a tiny manufactury of cheap wallpapers; I sometimes went there to watch a dozen thin and shock-headed, hollow-cheeked boys in greasy gowns, who jumped from time to time on the wooden levers that worked the square blocks of the press and so, with the weight of their puny bodies, stamped the patterns on the wall-paper. The small wing on the right was empty, but was to be rented. One

[2] A book of lectures on history.

day, three weeks or so after May 9, the shutters of this wing were thrown open, and women's faces appeared at the windows: a family had come to live there. I remember that same day at dinner my mother asked our butler who our new neighbors were, and, when he mentioned the name of Princess Zasiokina, remarked not without a touch of respect: "Ah, a princess!" then added: "She cannot be very well off."

"They arrived in three droshkies,"[3] the butler observed as he respectfully presented the dish. "They haven't a carriage of their own, and the furniture they brought is hardly worth mentioning."

"Maybe," my mother replied, "but all the same a princess is better."

My father gave her a frigid look; she said no more.

Certainly the Princess Zasiokina could not have been wealthy: the small wing she had rented was so tumbledown and tiny that anyone at all well off would never have agreed to live in it. However, I paid no attention to any of this conversation. The Princess's title made little impression on me: I had recently been reading Schiller's *Robbers*.[4]

2

I had the habit of wandering about our garden every evening with a gun and taking pot shots at the rooks. I had long felt hatred for those prudent, rapacious, and cunning birds. On the day I have already spoken of I went off into the garden as usual and, after walking fruitlessly along all the avenues (the rooks recognized me and only cawed brokenly in the distance), I happened to approach the low fence separating our domain from the narrow strip of garden extending beyond and attached to the right-hand wing. I walked along with my head sunk on my breast. Suddenly I heard voices. I looked over the fence and was petrified: I saw a strange sight.

A few paces away, in a glade between bushes of green raspberry, was a tall, graceful girl in a striped, rose-colored dress and with a white kerchief on her head; four young men were pressing round her, and she was smacking each of them in turn on the forehead with those small gray flowers—I don't know their names, but they are well known to children: the flowers form small bags and burst with a pop when you strike them against anything hard. The young men thrust out their foreheads so readily, and there was something so charming, so imperative, so gracious, amusing, and pleasant in the girl's movements, that I all but cried out with amazement and delight, and I think I would have given everything else on earth for those enchanting fingers to strike me on the forehead too. My gun slipped to the grass, I forgot everything; my eyes were fixed on that graceful waist and neck and the beautiful hands, and the rather untidy, fair hair beneath the white kerchief, and that one half-closed, intelligent eye (I was watch-

[3] Low, open carriages in which the passengers sat on a bench, facing sideways.

[4] *The Robbers* (1782), by the famous German poet Friedrich Schiller, is about outlaws who rebel against outmoded social forms.

ing her from the side) and those eyelashes and the tender cheek below them. . . .

"Young man! Now, young man!" I suddenly heard a voice right beside me. "Is it permissible to stare like that at strange young ladies?"

I trembled all over, I was put to confusion. Beside me, but beyond the fence, a man with close-cut black hair was standing and gazing at me with an ironical expression. The girl turned toward me at that same moment. I saw her large gray eyes in her vivid, animated face, and all that face suddenly began to quiver, to smile; her white teeth gleamed, her eyebrows were raised amusingly. I crimsoned, snatched up my gun from the ground, and, pursued by a ringing but not ill-natured laugh, ran to my room, flung myself on my bed, and covered my face with my hands. My heart was dancing within me; I felt deeply abashed and gay; I felt an agitation I had never known before.

After a rest I combed my hair, made myself tidy, and went downstairs to tea. The image of the young girl went before me; my heart ceased to dance, but it felt a pleasant twinge.

"What is the matter with you?" my father suddenly asked me. "Have you killed a rook?"

I felt like telling him everything, but I refrained and only smiled to myself. When I went to bed, for some unknown reason I spun round three or four times on one leg, greased my hair, got into bed, and slept like a log all night. In the early morning I woke for a moment, raised my head, looked around me rapturously, and fell off to sleep again.

3

"How can I make their acquaintance?" was my first thought the moment I awoke in the morning. I went out into the garden before tea, but did not go close to the fence and did not see anyone. After we had had tea I walked up and down the road in front of the house several times and took glances at the windows from this distance. . . . I thought I saw her face behind a curtain, and in my alarm I hurriedly retreated. "All the same, we must make their acquaintance," I thought as I wandered aimlessly over the sandy waste that extends beyond the Nieskuchny Gardens. "But how? That's the problem." I recalled the tiniest details of the previous day's meeting; for some reason I remembered very clearly how she had laughed at me. But while I was working myself up and making all kinds of plans, fate was already taking care of me.

While I was out, my mother received a letter from her new neighbor; it was on gray paper and sealed with a brown seal such as is used only for postal notices and to seal the corks of cheap wine-bottles. This letter, which was written in illiterate terms and slovenly handwriting, asked my mother to extend her protection to the Princess: according to her, my mother was intimately acquainted with certain important people who had the fate of the Princess and her children in their hands, as she was involved in very serious judicial cases. "I adress myself to you," she wrote, "as one noble lady to another, and moreover it is a plesure for me to have this oportunity." In

conclusion she asked my mother's permission for her to call. I found my mother in an unpleasant frame of mind: my father was not at home, and she had no one with whom to discuss the letter. It was impossible not to reply to a "noble lady," and a Princess at that, but how to reply my mother could not imagine. She thought it would not be correct to write a note in French,[5] but she herself was not very good at Russian orthography,[6] she knew that; and she was anxious not to compromise herself. She was delighted at my arrival and at once ordered me to go to the Princess and tell her in person that my mother was always ready to do Her Excellency any service that lay in her power, and to ask her to call at one o'clock. The unexpectedly rapid fulfillment of my secret desires both delighted and frightened me. But I did not reveal the confusion into which I was plunged, and first went to my room to put on a new coat and cravat, for when at home I still went about in a jacket and turn-down collar, though I was deeply mortified at having to wear them.

4

All my body trembling uncontrollably, I entered the close and unpleasant lobby of the Zasiokins' wing and was met by an old, gray-headed servant with a dark, copper-colored face, moody little pig's eyes, and such deep furrows on the forehead and temples as I had never seen in all my life. He was carrying a pickled herring backbone on a tray; shutting the door leading to the other room with his foot, he asked abruptly: "What do you want?"

"Is the Princess Zasiokina at home?" I asked.

"Vonifaty?" a jarring feminine voice shouted from the other side of the door.

The servant silently turned his back on me, revealing that the back of his livery was badly worn and had a single rusty button stamped with an armorial bearing,[7] and went off, after setting the tray on the floor.

"Have you been to the policeman?" the same voice asked. The servant muttered something. "What? Someone come? Our neighbor's son? Well, ask him in."

The servant returned to me. "Please go into the reception room," he said as he picked up the tray from the floor. I tidied myself and went in.

I found myself in a small and not very neatly arranged room with poor furniture that looked as though it had been set out in a hurry. A woman aged about fifty, straight-haired and plain-looking, in an old green dress and with a varicolored triangular worsted neckerchief round her neck, was sitting by the window, in an armchair with a broken arm. Her small black eyes were fixed on me.

I went up to her and bowed.

[5] French was often used by nineteenth-century Russians who were (or wanted to be considered) sophisticated Western Europeans.

[6] Spelling. [7] Part of an aristocratic coat-of-arms.

"Have I the honor of speaking to Princess Zasiokina?"

"I am Princess Zasiokina. And are you Mr. V.'s son?"

"That is so. I have called with a message from my mother."

"Please sit down. Vonifaty! Where are my keys? Have you seen them?"

I told the Princess my mother's answer to her note. As she listened she tapped her fat red fingers on the windowsill, and when I had finished she fixed her eyes on me once more.

"Very good; I shall call without fail," she said. "But how young you still are! How old are you, if I may ask?"

"Sixteen," I replied with an involuntary stammer.

The Princess took some greasy, scribbled papers out of her pocket, raised them right to her nose, and began to sort them over.

"A fine age!" she said suddenly, turning and fidgeting in her chair. "But please don't stand on ceremony. I have simple ways."

"Too simple," I thought, with involuntary squeamishness running my eyes over all her unsightly figure.

At that moment another door of the reception room was swiftly flung open and the girl I had seen in the garden the previous evening entered. She raised her hand, and a derisive smile flitted over her face.

"And this is my daughter," the Princess said, pointing to the girl with her elbow. "Zenia, my dear, this is the son of our neighbor, Mr. V. What is your name, if I may ask?" She turned to me.

"Vladimir," I replied, rising, and stuttering in my agitation.

"And your patronymic?"[8]

"Piotrovich."

"Indeed. I knew a chief of police once whose name was Vladimir Piotrovich too. Vonifaty! Don't look for the keys. I have them in my pocket."

The young girl was still gazing at me with the same smile, her eyes half-closed and her head cocked a little on one side.

"I've already seen M'sieur Voldemar," she began. (The silvery sound of her voice ran over me like a pleasant chilliness.) "You will allow me to call you that, won't you?"

"Please!" I stammered.

"Where did you see him?" her mother asked.

The young Princess did not reply. "Are you busy now?" she said, not taking her eyes off me.

"Not at all."

"Would you like to help me ball some wool? Come with me to my room." She nodded to me and went out. I followed her.

In the room we entered the furniture was rather better and was arranged with greater taste. At that moment, however, I was not in a state to notice anything: I walked as though in a dream, and in all my being I felt an idiotically tense felicity.

The Princess sat down, picked up a skein of crimson wool, and, pointing me to a chair opposite her, carefully opened the skein and put it over my hands. All this she did without saying a word, with an amusing deliberation of movement and with the same bright and crafty smile on her slightly

[8] On Russian names, see the Headnote to *First Love*.

parted lips. She began to wind the wool into a card folded double, and suddenly transfixed me with such a clear and swift glance that I involuntarily cast down my eyes. When her eyes, which usually were half-closed, were opened to their full extent, her face changed completely; it was as though light had flooded over it.

"What did you think of me yesterday, M'sieur Voldemar?" she asked, after a moment. "I expect you condemned me?"

"I—Princess—I didn't think anything—how could I?" I answered in some embarrassment.

"Listen! she retorted. "You don't know me yet; I am exceedingly strange; I always like to be told the truth. I heard that you're sixteen, and I am twenty-one; you see I am much older than you, and so you should always tell me the truth—and do as I tell you," she added. "Look at me; why don't you look at me?"

I was still more embarrassed; none the less, I raised my eyes to her. She smiled, only not with her previous, but with a different, approving smile. "Look at me," she said, caressingly lowering her voice. "I don't dislike being looked at. I like your face; I have a feeling we shall be friends. And do you like me?" She added craftily.

"Princess—" I began.

"To begin with, call me Zinaida Alexandrovna; and secondly, what is this habit children" (she corrected herself)—"young people have of not saying frankly what they feel? That's all right for grown-ups. Now, you do like me, don't you?"

Though I found it very pleasant to have her talking to me so frankly, none the less I was a little annoyed. I wanted to show her that she was not dealing with a boy, and so, adopting as nonchalant and serious an air as possible, I said: "Of course I like you very much, Zinaida Alexandrovna; I have no intention of concealing that."

She shook her head deliberately. "Have you a tutor?" she suddenly asked.

"No. I haven't had a tutor for a long time."

I was lying; it was not a month since I had parted with my Frenchman.

"Oh; why, so I see; you're quite big, really."

She gently tapped my fingers. "Hold your hands straight." And she set to work diligently to wind the wool.

I took advantage of the circumstance that she did not raise her eyes and began to scrutinize her, at first surreptitiously, then more and more openly. Her face seemed even more charming than it had looked the previous evening, so fine, intelligent, and pleasant was everything about it. She was sitting with her back to the window, which was hung with a white blind; the sunlight, filtering through this blind, flooded her fluffy, golden hair, her innocent neck, her drooping shoulders and tender, untroubled breast with soft light. I looked at her, and how dear and close she grew to me! I felt that I had known her a very long time, that I had never known anything and had never even lived until I met her. . . . She was wearing a dark, rather shabby dress and an apron; I think I would willingly have caressed every fold in that dress and that apron. The toes of her shoes peered out from under her dress: I would have bowed myself down to those shoes in adoration. "And so I am sitting in front of her," I thought; "I have made

her acquaintance. . . . What happiness—really, what happiness!" I all but sprang off the chair in my rapture, but I only kicked my feet a little, like an infant enjoying some treat.

I felt as good as a fish in water, and I would have remained in that room forever; I would never have left that spot.

Her eyelids slowly rose, and again her shining eyes beamed before me, and again she smiled.

"How you are staring at me!" she said slowly, and threatened me with one finger.

I crimsoned. . . . "She understands everything, she sees everything," the thought flashed through my head. "And how can she help understanding and seeing everything?"

Suddenly there was a tapping sound in the next room, and a saber clattered.

"Zenia!" the Princess called from that room. "Belovzorov has brought you a kitten."

"A kitten!" Zinaida exclaimed, and, rising impetuously from the chair, she flung the ball of wool onto my knees and ran out.

I also rose and, laying the skein and ball of wool on the window-sill, went into the reception room and halted in astonishment: in the middle of the room a tabby kitten was lying with her paws spread out, and Zinaida was on her knees before it, carefully raising its tiny head. Close to the Princess was a flaxen and curly-haired young hussar[9] with crimson face and goggling eyes; he covered almost all the wall space between the two windows.

"How funny it is!" Zinaida declared. "And its eyes are not gray, but green; and what big ears it has! Thank you, Victor Yegorich! You are very kind!"

The hussar, whom I recognized as one of the young men I had seen the previous evening, smiled and bowed, clattering his spurs and jingling the chain of his saber.

"You were so kind yesterday as to say that you wanted a tabby kitten with large ears—and here it is! Your word is law!" He bowed again.

The kitten squealed faintly and began to sniff the floor.

"Oh, it's hungry!" Zinaida exclaimed. "Vonifaty! Sonia! Bring some milk."

A maid in an old yellow dress, with a faded kerchief round her neck, brought in a saucer of milk and set it before the kitten. The kitten trembled, screwed up its eyes, and began to lap.

"What a rosy little tongue it has!" Zinaida observed, bending her head down almost to the floor and gazing at the animal from one side, with her eyes right by its nose.

The kitten drank till it had had enough and then began to purr, finically lifting its paws. Zinaida got up and, turning to the maid, said in an indifferent tone: "Take it out!"

"In exchange for the kitten, your little hand!" the hussar said, grinning and drawing up all his powerful body, which was tightly constricted in his new uniform.

[9] Cavalry soldier.

"Both hands!" Zinaida retorted, and held out her hands to him. While he was kissing them she looked at me across her shoulder.

I stood rooted to the spot and did not know whether I ought to smile, to say something, or keep silent. Suddenly through the wide-open door leading to the lobby I caught sight of our servant Fyodor. He made signs to me. I mechanically went out to him.

"What do you want?" I asked.

"Your mother has sent for you," he said in a whisper. "She is angry because you haven't come back with a reply."

"But have I been here so long, then?"

"An hour and more."

"An hour and more!" I involuntarily repeated. Going back to the reception room, I began to take my leave and scrape my feet.

"Where are you going?" the young Princess asked me, looking round the hussar's body.

"I must go home. So I am to say"—I turned to her mother—"that you will call on my mother at one o'clock."

"Yes, you tell her that, my boy."

She hurriedly picked up a snuffbox and took a pinch so noisily that I shuddered. "Yes, tell her that," she repeated, blinking tearfully and wheezing.

I bowed once more, turned, and left the room with the feeling of awkwardness in the back that a very young man always feels when he knows people are staring after him.

"But don't forget to come and see us, M'sieur Voldemar," Zinaida called, and she again burst into a laugh.

"What is she always laughing for?" I thought as I returned home with Fyodor, who said not one word to me, but followed me with a disapproving air. My mother scolded me and wondered what I could have been doing so long in that Princess's place. I did not tell her and went off to my room. I suddenly felt very sad. . . . I tried not to cry. . . . I was jealous of that hussar!

5

The Princess kept her promise and called on my mother, who did not take any liking to her. I was not present at their meeting, but at table my mother told my father that she thought Princess Zasiokina *une femme très vulgaire*,[10] that she had grown very tired of the Princess's requests that she should intercede with Princess Sergei on her behalf, that she was always involved in lawsuits and affairs, *des vilaines affaires d'argent*,[11] and that she must be a terrible intriguer. My mother added, however, that she had invited the Princess and her daughter to dine with us next day (when I heard the words "and her daughter," I bent my head over my plate), because, after all, she was our neighbor, and a Princess. To which my father said he

[10] French: "a very vulgar woman." [11] French: "sordid money matters."

remembered now what sort of lady she was: in his youth he had known the late Prince Zasiokin, who had been very well brought up, but had been an empty and quarrelsome fellow. In society he had been known as *"le Parisien,"* because he had lived many years in Paris; at one time he had been very wealthy, but he had gambled away all his fortune. And for some unknown reason, possibly for money—though in any case he could have made a better choice, my father added with a frigid smile—he married the daughter of some lawyer's clerk and then began to indulge in speculation and ruined himself completely.

"So long as she doesn't ask us to lend her money," my mother observed.

"That is extremely possible," my father said calmly. "Does she speak French?"

"Very badly."

"Hm! But that doesn't matter. I think you said you had invited her daughter too; someone has assured me that she is a very pleasant and well-educated girl."

"Ah! In that case she doesn't take after her mother."

"Nor her father!" my father retorted. "He was educated too, but stupid!"

Mother sighed and was lost in thought. My father said no more. During this conversation I felt very awkward.

After dinner I went into the garden, but without my gun. I had pledged myself not to go near the Zasiokin garden, but an irresistible force drew me that way—and not for nothing. When still some distance from the fence, I saw Zinaida. This time she was alone. She was holding a small book in one hand and was walking slowly along the path. She did not notice me.

I all but let her pass, but suddenly I stopped short and coughed.

She turned, but did not stop; with one hand she threw back the broad blue ribbon of her round straw hat, then she looked at me, quietly smiled, and fixed her eyes on her book again.

I took off my cap and hesitated for a moment, then turned away with a heavy heart. *"Que suis-je pour elle?"*[12] I thought (God knows why) in French.

I heard familiar steps behind me. I looked round: my father was coming toward me with his swift and easy stride.

"Is that the young Princess?" he asked me.

"Yes."

"Do you know her, then?"

"I saw her this morning when I called on her mother."

My father halted and, turning sharply on his heels, walked back. As he drew level with Zinaida he bowed to her politely. She bowed in reply, not without a look of astonishment, and let her book fall. I saw her following him with her eyes. My father always dressed exquisitely, in his own original and simple manner; but never had his figure seemed more finely proportioned, never had he worn his gray hat more beautifully on his still quite thick, curly hair.

I thought of going to Zinaida, but she did not even glance at me. She picked up her book and walked away.

[12] French: "What am I to her?"

6

I spent all that evening and the following morning in a despondent torpor. I remember I tried to work, and picked up Kaidanov, but the scrawling lines and pages of that famous primer flickered before me in vain. Ten times in succession I read the sentence: "Julius Caesar was distinguished by his martial courage"; I understood not one word and threw the book down. Before dinner I again greased my hair and put on my coat and cravat.

"What are you wearing them for?" my mother asked. "You're not a student yet, and goodness knows whether you'll pass the entrance examination. And it isn't so long since you had the jacket made for you. You mustn't stop wearing it altogether."

"We're having guests," I whispered almost in despair.

"What rubbish! What sort of guests do you call them?"

I had to submit. I exchanged my coat for the jacket, but I did not take off the cravat. The Princess and her daughter arrived half an hour or so before dinner; the older woman was wearing the green dress I had already seen, had thrown a yellow shawl round her shoulders, and had put on an old-fashioned bonnet with flame-colored ribbons. She at once began to talk about her promissory notes, complained of her poverty, and was "importunate," but did not stand on ceremony in the least: she took snuff just as noisily, and shifted and fidgeted on her chair just as freely. Apparently it did not even occur to her that she was a Princess. On the other hand, Zinaida behaved very correctly, almost haughtily, like a real princess. Her face wore a look of cold immobility and importance, and I did not recognize her, did not recognize her looks or her smiles, though in this new guise also she seemed beautiful to me. She was wearing a light *barège*[13] dress with pale blue figurework; her hair fell in long curls at the side of her cheeks, in the English fashion; this coiffure suited the cold expression of her face. My father sat next to her at dinnertime and entertained her with his own distinctive, elegant, and imperturbable courtesy. Occasionally he glanced at her, and occasionally she glanced at him, but so queerly, almost inimically.[14] They carried on conversation in French; I remember I was astonished by the purity of her pronunciation. At table the older Princess was just as unconstrained as before; she ate a great deal and praised the cooking. My mother was obviously depressed by her and replied with a mournful disdain; from time to time my father knitted his brows a little. My mother did not take to Zinaida either. "She's so haughty," she said next day. "And what has she got to be haughty about, *avec sa mine de grisette?*"[15]

"Evidently you've never seen grisettes," my father remarked.

"And thank goodness for that!"

"Of course, thank goodness—only, how can you pass judgment on them?"

Zinaida did not pay any attention to me whatever. Soon after dinner the Princess took her leave.

[13] A light, gauzy fabric, blended from silk or cotton. [14] With hostility.
[15] French: "with her lowbrow shopgirl's look."

"I shall hope to have your protection, Maria Nikolaevna and Piotr Vasilievich," she said in a drawling voice to my father and mother. "What can I do? There were days—but they have passed. And here am I, an Excellency," she added with an unpleasant laugh; "but what's the good of honor if you haven't any food for dinner?" My father bowed to her respectfully and accompanied her to the door of the lobby. I stood beside him in my tailless jacket and stared at the floor, as though condemned to death. Zinaida's treatment of me had completely overcome me. But imagine my surprise when, as she walked past me, with the old gracious expression in her eyes she hurriedly whispered: "Come along at eight o'clock, do you hear, without fail. . . . " I was astonished, but she was already departing, throwing a white scarf over her head as she went.

7

At eight o'clock exactly, wearing my coat and with my hair combed up at the front, I entered the lobby of the small wing that the Princess occupied. The old servant stared at me glumly and rose reluctantly from the bench. Merry voices could be heard coming from the reception room. I opened the door and started back in amazement. The young Princess was standing on a chair in the middle of the room, holding out a man's hat in front of her; five men were crowded round the chair. They were trying to put their hands into the hat, but she raised it and shook it vigorously. When she saw me she cried: "Wait, wait! We have a fresh guest; he must be given a ticket too." Lightly jumping down from the chair, she took me by the lapel of my coat. "Come on," she said, "what are you waiting for? Messieurs, let me introduce you. This is M'sieur Voldemar, our neighbor's son. And these," she added, turning to me and pointing to the guests one after another, "are Count Malevsky, Dr. Lushin, the poet Maidanov, retired Captain Nirmatsky, and Belovzorov, the hussar you have seen before. Please be friends, and good friends."

I was so embarrassed that I did not even bow to anyone. Dr. Lushin I recognized as the same swarthy gentleman who had so ruthlessly put me to shame in the garden. I did not know the others at all.

"Count!" Zinaida continued, "write a ticket for M'sieur Voldemar."

"That is unfair," the Count objected in a slightly Polish accent. He was a very handsome and fashionably dressed man with black hair, expressive hazel eyes, a thin white nose, and a scanty mustache above a very small mouth. "He hasn't played forfeits[16] with us."

"It's unfair," Belovzorov and the gentleman described as a retired captain both repeated. The captain was a man about forty years of age, hideously pockmarked, with hair as frizzy as a Negro's, rather stocky, bowleg-

[16] A parlor game in which articles are forfeited if one makes a mistake and bought back by paying a penalty.

ged, and wearing a military jacket without epaulets,[17] flung round his shoulders.

"Write a ticket, I tell you," the Princess repeated. "What do you call this, mutiny? M'sieur Voldemar is with us for the first time, and today the law does not apply to him. Stop grumbling and write a ticket; that is my wish."

The Count shrugged his shoulders but, humbly bowing his head, took the pen in his white, beringed hand, tore off a piece of paper, and began to write on it.

"At any rate, do let us explain to Mr. Voldemar what it is all about," Lushin said in a scoffing tone, "for he looks completely bewildered. You see, young man, we're playing forfeits. The Princess has had to pay a forfeit, and the one who draws the lucky ticket will have the right to kiss her hand. Did you understand what I said?"

I only glanced at him and continued standing as before. But the Princess jumped onto the chair again and shook the hat. All the men drew round her, and I with the others.

"Maidanov," she said to the tall young man with emaciated face, small, shortsighted eyes, and extraordinarily long black hair; "you, as a poet, should be magnanimous and surrender your ticket to M'sieur Voldemar, so that he has two chances instead of one."

But Maidanov shook his head and whirled his hair. I was the last to thrust my hand into the hat. I drew out a ticket and unfolded it. Lord, what did I feel like when I read the words: "A kiss!"

"A kiss!" I involuntarily exclaimed.

"Bravo! He's won!" Zinaida cried. "I am glad!" She got down from the chair and looked into my eyes so lucidly and sweetly that my heart beat violently. "But are you glad?" she asked me.

"I?" I stammered.

"Sell me your ticket," Belovzorov suddenly said ineptly right in my ear. "I'll give you a hundred rubles for it."

I gave him such an indignant look that Zinaida clapped her hands, while Lushin exclaimed: "Good lad!"

"But," Lushin went on, "I, as the master of ceremonies, am bound to see that all the rules are observed. M'sieur Voldemar, go down on one knee. That is our custom."

Zinaida stood in front of me with her head bent a little to one side, as though to examine me the better, and dignifiedly stretched out her hand. My eyes went misty; I tried to go down on one knee, but fell down on both my knees; and so clumsily did I press my lips against her fingers that I scratched the tip of my nose with her nail.

"Enough!" Lushin cried, and helped me to rise.

We went on playing at forfeits. Zinaida seated me beside her. The forfeits she thought of! In one case she had to represent a "statue," and she chose the ugly poet Maidanov as her pedestal; she ordered him to lie facedownward, and even to tuck his head into his chest. The merriment did not cease for one moment. I was a privately and soberly educated lad, brought up in a genteel, sedate home, and all this noise and racket, this unceremo-

[17] A shoulder decoration on a military uniform.

nious, almost violent gaiety, these unprecedented relations with strangers, went to my head. I was just as intoxicated as if I had drunk too much wine. I began to laugh and talk even louder than the others, so that even the old Princess, who was closeted in the next room with some lawyer's clerk summoned into conference with her, came out to stare at me. But I felt so happy that, as we say, I did not care a fig and took no notice of anyone's sneers and wry looks. Zinaida continued to show preference for me and did not let me leave her side. In one forfeit I had to sit beside her, our heads covered with the one silk kerchief: I was supposed to tell her my greatest secret. I still remember how close together our heads were in that stifling, translucent, scented veil, how in that twilight her eyes shone very mildly and very close to me, and her parted lips breathed on me hotly, and I saw her teeth, and her hair tickled and scorched me. I was silent; she smiled mysteriously and roguishly and whispered at last: "Well, and now what?" But I only went red and laughed and turned away, and could hardly get my breath. We grew tired of forfeits, so we began to play a game in which we all had to stand in a circle holding a string, while she was in the middle. And my goodness! What rapture I felt when I forgot what I was doing and she gave me a strong, sharp smack on my extended fingers! And how I tried after that to pretend that I was forgetting again! But she only teased me and would not smack my fingers, though I left them extended.

What else did we do in the course of that evening! We played the piano and we sang and we danced and we acted a gypsy encampment. Nirmatsky was dressed as a bear and given salt water to drink. Count Malevsky showed us card tricks and ended by shuffling the cards and dealing himself a hand that held all the trumps, at which Lushin "ventured to congratulate him." Maidanov recited parts of his poem "The Murderer" (this was at the height of the romantic period in our literature), which he proposed to publish in a black jacket with the title in blood red. We stole the hat off the knees of the lawyer's clerk and made him do the Cossack[18] dance as ransom; we dressed old Vonifaty in a bonnet, while Zinaida put on a man's hat. I could not tell you all we did. Only Belovzorov withdrew more and more into one corner, morose and angry. At times his eyes were suffused with blood, he flushed and looked as though at any moment he would charge down on us and scatter us in all directions, like splinters. But the Princess looked at him and threatened him with her finger, and once more he skulked in his corner.

At last we were worn out. Zinaida's mother was now ready for anything, as she herself expressed it, and no amount of shouting disturbed her; but even she felt tired and wanted to rest. Supper was served at midnight, and consisted of a piece of old, dry cheese and some cold patties of chopped ham, which I thought more tasty than any meat pie; there was only one bottle of wine, and that bottle was queer: dark, with a swollen neck, and the wine inside it was a rose color; however, no one drank any of it. When I left I was weary and happy to the point of exhaustion; at parting Zinaida squeezed my hand firmly and again smiled enigmatically.

The night breathed heavily and humidly into my flaming face; a storm appeared to be gathering; black clouds were growing and crawling over the

[18] South-Russian horseman.

sky, visibly changing their smoky outlines. A breeze trembled restlessly in the dark trees, and somewhere beyond the horizon thunder seemed to be grumbling to itself angrily and hollowly.

I made my way to my room through the back entrance. My servant was sleeping on the floor, and I had to step across him. He awoke, saw me, and reported that my mother had been annoyed with me again and had wanted to send for me to come home, but my father had restrained her. (I never went to bed without saying good-night to my mother and asking her blessing.) But there was nothing to be done about it now!

I told my man that I would undress and get myself to bed and put out the candle. . . . But I did not undress and I did not lie down.

I sat down on a chair, and sat there for a long time as though enchanted. What I felt was so new and so sweet: I sat looking about me and not stirring, breathing slowly, and only silently laughing at my memories from time to time, then going cold at the thought that I was in love, that this was it, this was love. Zinaida's face silently floated before me in the darkness—it floated up, and did not float past—her lips still enigmatically smiling, her eyes looking at me a little sidelong, interrogatively, thoughtfully, and tenderly, as they had at our parting. At last I rose, tiptoed over to my bed, and cautiously laid my head on the pillow without undressing, as though afraid that by some abrupt movement I would disturb the feeling with which I was overflowing. . . .

I lay down, but I did not even close my eyes. I quickly noticed that pallid gleams of light were continually flickering across the room toward me. I half raised myself and glanced at the window. Its transom showed up distinctly against the mysteriously and mournfully glimmering panes. A thunderstorm, I thought; and I was right, it was a thunderstorm. But it was a very long way off, and no thunder was to be heard; only dull, long, sheet lightning lit up the sky incessantly; it did not flash so much as flutter and quiver like the wings of a dying bird. I got up, went across to the window, and remained standing there till dawn came. . . . The lightning did not cease for a moment; it was what the common people call a "sparrows' night." I gazed at the silent sandy plain, at the dark mass of the Nieskuchny Gardens, at the yellowish façades of distant buildings, which seemed to be quivering with every feeble flash. I gazed and could not tear myself away; that mute lightning, those temperate flashes, seemed to be in accord with the mute and secret emotions that were flaming up inside me. The dawn began to break; the sunrise drew on in crimson patches. As the sun approached, the lightning grew paler and less frequent; it flickered more and more intermittently, and finally ceased, overborne by the sobering and indubitable light of the oncoming day . . .

Within me, too, my own lightnings faded. I felt a great weariness and stillness. . . . But Zinaida's image continued to hover triumphantly over my soul. Only, that very image seemed to grow composed: like a swan flying up from the reeds of a marsh, it separated from the other, unpleasant shapes surrounding it and, as I dropped off to sleep, I fell once more at its feet in a valedictory and trustful adoration.

O gentle feelings, tender sounds, the benignity and assuagement of the deeply moved soul, the melting joy of love's first emotions—where are you now, where are you now?

8

When I went down to tea next morning, my mother scolded me, but not so much as I had expected, and made me tell her how I had spent the previous evening. I replied in few words, omitting many of the details and trying to make it all appear as innocent as possible.

"All the same, they are not people *comme il faut*,"[19] Mother remarked, "and there is no reason why you should go chasing after them, instead of preparing for your examination and keeping yourself occupied."

As I knew that my mother's anxiety about my occupations was confined to these few words, I did not think it necessary to protest. But after tea my father took me by the arm and, leading me into the garden, made me tell him all I had seen at the Zasiokins' the previous evening.

My father had a strange influence over me, and our relations, too, were strange. He took hardly any interest in my education and upbringing, but he never upset me, he respected my freedom, and, if I may put it so, he was even polite to me . . . only he never let me draw close to him. I loved him, I admired him, he seemed to me the perfect pattern of a man, and, upon my word, how passionately I would have become attached to him if I had not continually felt that he was thrusting me off! On the other hand, if he wished, with just one word, one gesture, he could suddenly win my unbounded confidence in him. My soul would lay itself bare, I would talk to him as if he were an understanding friend, or an indulgent tutor . . . and then, just as abruptly, he would abandon me, and he again thrust me off, kindly and gently, but none the less he thrust me off.

Sometimes a spirit of gaiety came over him, and then he was ready to sport and romp with me like a boy (he was fond of all vigorous physical movement). Once—only once—he caressed me so tenderly that I all but burst into tears. But his gaiety and his tenderness vanished without trace, and the intimacy that had sprung up between us afforded me no hope whatever for the future—I might have dreamed it. There were times when I would study his intelligent, handsome, lucid face . . . my heart would begin to quiver, and all my being would be vehemently drawn toward him. . . . He seemed to feel what was going on inside me, he would pat me casually on the cheek, and either would go off or would occupy himself with something, or would go quite set and cold, as he alone could, and at once I would shrink and go cold too. His rare outbursts of feeling for me were never to be evoked by my mute but intelligible entreaties; they always came unexpectedly. In later days, when I pondered on my father's character, I came to the conclusion that he had no time for me, or for family life; he was fond of something else, and thoroughly enjoyed that something else. "You yourself take all you can, but never put yourself in someone else's hand; belong to yourself: that is the whole art of life," he once said to me. On another occasion I, as a young democrat, ventured to reflect on freedom in his presence (that day he was "good," as I used to say, and at such times I could talk with him about anything). "Freedom," he repeated. "But do you know what it is that can give man freedom?"

[19] French: "proper"; the "right kind" of people.

"No, what?"

"Will; his own will; and it gives him power too, which is better than freedom. Know how to desire, and then you will be free, and you will command."

First and foremost my father wanted to live . . . and he did live. Perhaps he had a presentiment that he would not be able to enjoy the "art" of life for long: he died at the age of forty-two.

I told my father all about my visit to the Zasiokins. He listened to me half-attentively, half-abstractedly, sitting on a bench and drawing in the sand with the butt of his whip. Very occasionally he smiled, and looked at me brightly and amusingly, and encouraged me to go on by asking brief questions and making interjections. At first I could not bring myself even to mention Zinaida's name, but I could not restrain myself, and I began to refer to her. My father went on smiling. Then he was lost in thought; he yawned and rose to his feet.

I remembered that on leaving the house he had ordered his horse to be saddled. He was an excellent horseman and could control the very wildest of horses.

"Shall I ride with you, Papa?" I asked him.

"No," he replied, and his face adopted its usual indifferent and kindly expression. "Go for a ride by yourself if you like; and tell the coachman I'm not going."

He turned his back on me and walked away swiftly. I followed him with my eyes; he vanished through the gate. I saw his hat moving along above the fence; he turned in at the Zasiokins' gate.

He remained there over an hour, but then went off at once to town and did not return home till the evening.

After dinner I myself went to call on the Zasiokins! I found only the old Princess in the reception room. When she saw me she scratched her head under her cap with the end of a knitting-needle and suddenly asked me if I would write out a soliciting letter for her.

"With pleasure," I replied, and sat down on the edge of a chair.

"Only write in large letters," she said and handed me a dirty sheet of paper. "But could you do it today, my dear?"

"I'll write it out this very day."

The door leading to the next room was opened very slightly and Zinaida's face appeared in the opening; it was pale, thoughtful, and the hair was thrown back negligently. She stared at me with great, cold eyes and quietly closed the door again.

"Zenia, Zenia!" her mother called. But Zinaida did not answer. I took away the Princess's letter and sat over it all the evening.

9

My "passion" began from that day. I remember I felt rather as a man must feel who has just entered the Czar's[20] service: I had ceased to be a boy; I

[20] The Russian emperor's.

was in love. I have said that my passion began from that day; I could add
that my torments also dated from that day. In Zinaida's absence I lan-
guished; my mind was a blank, everything dropped out of my hands, and
for days on end I thought tensely only about her. . . . I languished. . . . But
I felt no better in her presence. I was jealous, I realized my insignificance, I
stupidly sulked and stupidly fawned; and even so an irresistible power
drew me to her, and every time I crossed the threshold of her room I felt
an involuntary throb of happiness. She guessed at once that I was in love
with her, nor did I think to conceal the fact; she made fun of my passion,
played with me, petted and tormented me. It is sweet to be the sole source,
the autocratic and irresponsible cause, of another being's greatest joys and
deepest sorrows—and in Zinaida's hands I was as the softest wax. For that
matter, I was not the only one in love with her: all the men who visited her
home went crazy over her, and she kept them all in leading strings,[21] at her
feet. She found amusement in arousing their hopes, or their fears, in twist-
ing them round her finger at her whim (she called this knocking people
against one another), and they did not even think of resisting and readily
submitted to her. In all her being, so vital and beautiful, was a peculiarly
enchanting blend of cunning and unconcern, artificiality and simplicity,
stillness and high spirits; everything she did, or said, her every movement,
was invested with a light, subtle charm, a playful strength. Her face, too,
was incessantly changing, and it played too; almost in the same instant it
would express derision, thoughtfulness, and passion. The most varied of
feelings, light and swift, sped momentarily over her eyes and lips, like the
shadows of clouds on a sunny, windy day.

She had need of every one of her devotees. Belovzorov, whom she
sometimes called "my animal" and sometimes simply "mine," would readily
have thrown himself into the fire for her; though he could put no hope in
his mental capacity or any other qualities, he was continually proposing to
her, hinting that others only talked. Maidanov answered to the poetic ele-
ments in her soul: though he was rather cold, like almost all authors, he
tensely assured her, and possibly himself too, that he worshipped her, he
lauded her in innumerable poems and read them to her with an unnatural
yet sincere rapture. She felt sympathy for him, and at the same time she
rather made fun of him; she did not really believe him and, after listening
to his effusions, made him read Pushkin,[22] in order to clear the air, as she
said. Dr. Lushin, mocking and cynical of speech, knew her better than did
any of the others, and loved her more than any of the others, though he
ran her down behind her back and to her face. She respected him, but she
did not release him and sometimes took a particular, malignant pleasure in
making him feel that he, too, was in her hands. "I am a coquette, I am
heartless, I have an actress's nature," she said to him once in my presence.
"Well, all right! Give me your hand; I'll stick a pin in it; you will feel shame
in front of this young man, it will hurt you; but all the same, Mr. Self-right-
eous, you've got to laugh!" Lushin flushed, turned away and bit his lips, but
finished by putting out his hand. She pricked him, and he did begin to

[21] Restraint (literally, strings used to guide a child learning to walk).
[22] Alexander Pushkin (1799–1837), the great Russian poet.

laugh . . . and she laughed too as she pushed the pin in quite deep and looked into his eyes, which vainly tried to avoid her gaze.

Least of all could I understand the relations between Zinaida and Count Malevsky. He was good-looking, adroit, and intelligent, but even I, a six-teen-year-old lad, found something dubious, something false in him, and I was amazed that Zinaida did not notice it. But perhaps she did notice this falsity and was not repelled by it. Her unsatisfactory upbringing, her strange acquaintances and habits, her mother's constant presence, the pov-erty and disorder of the home—everything, beginning with the very liberty that this young woman enjoyed, and her consciousness of superiority to everybody around her, developed a half-contemptuous negligence and lack of squeamishness in her. There were times when it did not matter what happened—Vonifaty might come to report that there was no sugar in the house, some petty calumny would come out, or the guests would quarrel with one another—she only shook her curls, said: "It's all nothing," and was not worried in the least.

On the other hand, there were times when all my blood boiled as I saw Malevsky go up to her, his body swaying craftily, like a fox, and then ele-gantly lean on the back of her chair and whisper into her ear with a self-satisfied and ingratiating little smile, while she folded her arms on her breast, looked at him attentively, and she too smiled and gently swayed her head.

"What pleasure do you get out of seeing Monsieur Malevsky?" I asked her one day.

"But he has such handsome little mustaches!" she replied. "In any case, it's nothing to do with you."

"You mustn't think I'm in love with him," she said to me on another occasion. "No, I'm not. I cannot love a man like him, a man I have to look down at. I need someone who will break me. . . . But I shall never meet such a man, thank God! I shall never be caught by anyone; no, never!"

"So you will never fall in love?"

"But how about you? Don't I love you, then?" she said, and struck me on my nose with the end of her glove.

Yes, Zinaida was always making fun of me. For three weeks I saw her every day, and there was little that she did not do with me! She rarely called on us, and I did not regret this; in our house she was transformed into a young lady, into a young princess, and I shunned her. I was afraid of betraying myself in front of my mother, who was very unfriendly to Zinaida and watched us inimically. I was not so afraid of Father; he did not appear to notice me, and he talked only little with Zinaida, though when he did he talked with particular intelligence and meaning in his words. I stopped working, reading, I even stopped wandering about the district and riding. Like a beetle tied by one leg, I continually hovered about the home of my beloved; I think I would have remained there forever . . . but that was impossible: my mother grumbled at me, and sometimes Zinaida herself drove me away. Then I locked myself in my room or went off to the very end of the garden, climbed onto the ruins of a lofty stone conservatory, and, dangling my feet from the wall overlooking the road, sat there for hours and gazed and gazed, seeing nothing. Around me white butterflies lazily fluttered over the dusty nettles, a saucy sparrow settled not far away

on a broken red brick and irritatingly chirruped, incessantly twisting and
turning all its body and spreading wide its tail; the rooks, still distrustful of
me, occasionally cawed as they sat high up on the bare crown of a birch
tree, the sun and the wind played gently among the tree's supple branches,
from time to time the sounds of the bells of the Donskoi Monastery floated
calmly and despondently to my ears; but I sat, gazed, listened, and was
entirely filled with a nameless feeling that included all feelings: sadness,
and joy, and presentiment of the future, and desire, and fear of life. But at
that time I understood nothing of all this, and I could not have given a
name to any of the feelings that possessed me, or else I would have given all
of it just one name, the name of Zinaida.

But Zinaida went on playing with me, like a cat with a mouse. At one
moment she would flirt with me, and I grew excited and melted like wax;
the next instant she drove me away, and I did not dare to go near her, did
not dare to glance at her.

I remember she was very cold to me for several days in succession; I
grew quite diffident, and when I timidly went to call on them I tried to
keep near the old Princess, even though just then she was scolding and
shouting a great deal: she was in a bad way with her promissory notes, and
she had already had to see the police twice.

One day I was passing the well-known fence in the garden when I hap-
pened to see Zinaida: she was sitting very still on the grass, resting her head
on both hands. I tried quietly to retreat, but she suddenly raised her head
and beckoned to me imperatively. I was petrified: at first I did not under-
stand her gesture. She repeated it. I at once jumped over the fence and ran
up to her joyfully; but she halted me with a look and pointed to the path
two steps away from her. In my confusion, not knowing what to do, I went
down on my knees at the edge of the path. She was so pale, and such a
bitter sorrow, such profound weariness, was expressed in all her features
that my heart sank and I muttered involuntarily: "What is the matter?"

She stretched out her hand, pulled up some weed, bit it, and threw it
away, as far as she could throw it.

"Do you love me very much?" she said at last. "Do you?"

I made no answer; and besides, why should I answer?

"Yes," she said, looking at me as before. "That is true. Just the same
eyes," she added, then was lost in thought and covered her face with her
hands. "Everything has grown repulsive to me," she whispered. "I would
go off to the end of the world; I cannot bear this, I cannot cope with it. . . .
And what awaits me in the future? . . . Ah, it is hard for me. . . . My God,
how hard!"

"Why is it?" I asked timidly.

She did not answer and only shrugged her shoulders. I remained on my
knees, looking at her with deep despondency. Every word she uttered was a
stab in my heart. I think that at that moment I would willingly have given
my life if only she had ceased to grieve. I looked at her and, still not under-
standing why she was so depressed, I vividly pictured her coming suddenly,
in an outburst of uncontrollable sorrow, into the garden and falling to the
ground as though mown down. It was bright and green all around us; the
wind was rustling among the leaves of the trees and occasionally swaying
the long cane of a raspberry above Zinaida's head. Somewhere doves were

cooing, and the bees were humming as they flew low over the scanty grass. Above us the sky was a gracious azure—but I felt so sad. . . .

"Say some poetry to me," she said in an undertone, and leaned on her elbows. "I like you to say poems. You sing them, but that's nothing, that's the way of youth, Say 'On the Hills of Georgia'[23] to me. Only sit down first."

I sat down and recited "On the Hills of Georgia."

"'That my heart simply cannot help loving'"—Zinaida repeated the line. "That is where poetry is so good: it tells of something that is not, something that not only is better than the reality, but is even more like the truth. . . . 'That my heart simply cannot cease loving.' It would like to, but it cannot." She was silent again and suddenly started and rose. "Let's go. Maidanov is with Mamma; he brought me his poem, but I left him. And now he is upset too—but it cannot be helped. You will find out some day— only don't be angry with me!"

She hurriedly squeezed my hand and ran off in front. We returned to the house. Maidanov began to read us his "Murderer," which had just been printed; but I did not listen to it. He shouted out his four-foot iambics[24] in a singsong voice; the rhythms alternated and jingled like sleighbells, empty and loud; but I gazed continually at Zinaida and continually tried to fathom the meaning of her last words.

> "Or is it that a secret rival
> Suddenly has conquered thee?"

Maidanov exclaimed in a nasal tone, and my eyes met Zinaida's eyes. She let them drop and faintly blushed. I saw her blush, and I went cold with alarm. I had already felt jealous, but only at that moment did the thought that she was in love flash through my head. "My God! She's fallen in love!"

10

Now I was really tormented. I racked my brains, I thought, and thought again, and watched her persistently, though as far as possible secretly. A change had occurred in her, that was evident. Now she went off for walks by herself, and long walks too. Sometimes she did not come out of her room when there were visitors, but sat there for hours. This had not formerly been her habit. I suddenly became—or thought I became— extremely observant. "Isn't it he? Or perhaps it is he?" I asked myself, anxiously considering one devotee after another. Secretly I thought Count Malevsky more dangerous than the others, though for Zinaida's sake I felt ashamed of admitting this possibility.

My powers of observation did not extend beyond my own nose, and my secrecy probably did not deceive anybody; at least, Dr. Lushin soon saw through me. By the way, he, too, had changed of late: he had grown thin-

[23] A short poem (1829) by Pushkin.
[24] Poetic lines of four measures, each measure consisting of an iamb (a light syllable followed by an accented one).

ner, and though he laughed just as much, his laugh was more hollow, evil, and curt; his previous light irony and exaggerated cynicism were replaced by an involuntary nervous irritability.

"What are you always dragging along here for, young man?" he asked me one day when he was alone with me in the Zasiokins' reception room. (The young Princess had not yet returned from a walk, and her mother could be heard on the mezzanine floor loudly scolding her maid.) "You ought to be studying and working while you are young; but you—what are you doing?"

"You don't know whether I work or not at home," I retorted, not without a touch of hauteur,[25] but also in some embarrassment.

"What work is there to be done here? That's not what is worrying you. But I won't argue with you—at your age this is to be expected. Only your choice is far from commendable. Don't you see the kind of house this is?"

"I don't understand you," I remarked.

"You don't understand? So much the worse for you. I consider it my duty to warn you. People like me, old bachelors, may call here with safety, what can happen to us? We have been well steeled, nothing whatever can make any holes in us. But you've still got a delicate skin; and the air here is injurious to you, believe me. You may catch the infection."

"What do you mean?"

"What I say. Tell me, are you really well, even now? Are you in any normal state? Is what you are feeling of any value to you, any good to you?"

"Well, and what am I feeling?" I said, though in my heart of hearts I had to admit that he was right.

"Ah, young man, young man!" he went on in a tone of voice that suggested there was something very insulting to me in those two words. "What are you trying to be clever for? After all, thank God you still reveal in your face what is going on in your soul. But there, why talk? I myself would not come here if—" (he clenched his teeth)—"if I were not just as big a fool as you are. Only this is the thing that amazes me: how it is that you, with your intelligence, don't perceive what is happening all around you?"

"But what is happening, then?" I retorted, and I went tense with expectation.

The doctor looked at me with derisive commiseration.

"And I'm a fine one too," he said, apparently to himself. "Much need I have to say all this to him! In a word," he added, raising his voice, "I repeat: this atmosphere is not good for you. You like being here; but then, why shouldn't you? It is pleasant to smell the scents of a conservatory, only you cannot go and live in it. Now take my advice and go back to Kaidanov."

The Princess entered and began to complain to him of the toothache. A little later Zinaida returned.

"Now do scold her, doctor," her mother said. "All the day she is drinking nothing but ice water, and is it really good for her, with her weak chest?"

"Why do you do that?" Lushin asked Zinaida.

"What harm is there in it?"

"What harm is there in it? You may catch a chill and die."

[25] Haughtiness.

"Really? Surely not? And in any case, what of it? If that is the way I am to go."

"You don't say!" the doctor snorted. Zinaida's mother went out.

"You don't say!" Zinaida repeated. "Is life so cheerful, after all? Look around you. . . . Well, are you satisfied? Or do you think that I don't realize it all, don't feel it all? I enjoy drinking ice water, and can you seriously assure me that such a life is so worth while that it is not to be risked for a moment of enjoyment . . . I won't speak of happiness."

"That's just it," Lushin remarked. "Caprice and independence: those two words sum up all your being, they express the whole of your character."

She laughed a nervous laugh.

"You've missed the post, doctor. You are not very good at observation, you're left behind. Put your spectacles on. I am not interested in caprices now; making a fool of you, making a fool of myself—how very cheerful! And as for independence—M'sieur Voldemar," she suddenly cried, stamping her little foot, "don't pull that melancholy face. I cannot stand it when people show me commiseration." She swiftly left the room.

"This atmosphere is bad for you, young man; very bad," Lushin said to me once more.

11

That evening all the usual guests were gathered in the Zasiokins' reception room; I was among them.

The conversation turned to Maidanov's poem. Zinaida praised it, and quite sincerely. "But do you know what?" she said to him. "If I were a poet I would choose other subjects. Perhaps it is all nonsense, but sometimes strange thoughts come into my head, especially when I am lying awake, before dawn, when the sky begins to turn rosy and gray. For instance, I would—You won't laugh at me?"

"No! No!" we all exclaimed with one accord.

"I would picture a whole company of young girls in a large boat on a quiet river at night," she went on, folding her hands over her chest and gazing to one side. "The moon is shining, and they are all in white and wearing garlands of white flowers, and they're singing something, a kind of hymn, you know."

"I understand, I understand; go on," Maidanov said in a meaningful and dreamy tone.

"Suddenly there is noise, and laughter, torches, tambourines on the bank. . . . It is a crowd of bacchantes[26] running with singing and clamor. And here you have to describe the scene, Mr. Poet. . . . Only I would like the torches to be crimson and smoking a great deal, and the bacchantes' eyes must be glittering beneath their garlands, and the garlands should be

[26] Wild, orgiastic female devotees of the god Bacchus, or Dionysus.

of a dark color. And don't forget the tigerskins and the goblets . . . and gold, lots of gold."

"But where is the gold to be?" Maidanov asked, throwing back his straight hair and dilating his nostrils.

"Where? On their shoulders, on their arms, on their legs, everywhere. They say that in ancient times the women wore gold bangles round their ankles. The bacchantes call to the girls in the boat to join them. The girls have stopped singing their hymn—they cannot go on with it—but they do not stir. The river carries them to the bank. And now, suddenly, one of them quietly rises. . . . This must be described very well: how she quietly stands up in the moonlight, and how her friends are afraid. . . . She has stepped over the edge of the boat, the bacchantes surround her, they dash off into the night, into the darkness. . . . Here you must describe the smoke as floating in great billows, and everything is confused. Only their shrieks are to be heard, and her garland is left lying on the bank."

She was silent. ("Oh, she has fallen in love indeed!" I thought again.)

"And is that all?" Maidanov asked.

"Yes," she replied.

"That cannot be the subject for a whole poem," he said seriously. "But I shall make use of your idea in a lyric."

"In the romantic genre?" Malevsky added.

"Of course, in the romantic genre, the Byronic."

"But in my view Hugo is better than Byron," the young Count said with a negligent air. "He is more interesting."[27]

"Hugo is a first-class writer," Maidanov retorted, "and my friend Tonkosheev, in his Spanish novel *El Trovador*—"

"Ah, that is the book with the question marks round the wrong way, isn't it?" Zinaida interrupted him.

"Yes, that's the way the Spaniards write it. I was about to say that Tonkosheev—"

"Now you'll start arguing about classicism and romanticism again," Zinaida once more interrupted him. "I'd rather have a game—"

"Of forfeits?" Lushin broke in.

"No, forfeits are boring; we'll play comparisons." (This was a game she herself had invented; some object was named, and each player tried to compare it with something else, and the prize went to the one who made the best comparison.) She went across to the window. The sun had only just set; long, crimson clouds were floating high in the heavens.

"What are those clouds like?" she asked, and went on without waiting for us to answer: "I think they are like those purple sails on Cleopatra's golden vessel when she sailed to meet Antony.[28] Do you remember, Maidanov? You told me all about it recently."

[27] George Gordon, Lord Byron (1788–1824), creator of the gloomy, world-weary type known as the "Byronic hero," was the English Romantic poet most admired and influential on the Continent. Victor Hugo (1802–85), poet, novelist, and dramatist, was the greatest of the French Romantics.

[28] The gorgeous river-pageant by which Cleopatra, the voluptuous Egyptian queen, woos the Roman leader Marc Antony is described in Shakespeare's *Antony and Cleopatra*, II.ii.196–231.

Like Polonius in *Hamlet,* we all decided that the clouds did remind us of those very sails, and that not one of us could ever think of a better comparison.[29]

"But how old was Antony then?" she asked.

"I'm sure he was a young man," Malevsky remarked.

"Yes, he was young," Maidanov confirmed in a tone of conviction.

"Pardon me!" Lushin exclaimed; "he was over forty."[30]

"Over forty," Zinaida repeated, giving him a swift glance.

I went home soon after. "She's in love," my lips involuntarily whispered. "But with whom?"

12

The days passed. Zinaida grew more and more strange, more and more incomprehensible. One day I went to see her and found her sitting on a rush chair with her head pressed against the sharp edge of the table. She straightened up. . . . All her face was wet with tears.

"Ah! So it's you!" she said with a harsh, sneering smile. "Come here."

I went to her; she laid her hand on my head, suddenly seized my hair, and began to twist it.

"That hurts," I said at last.

"Ah! So it hurts, does it? But doesn't it hurt me? Doesn't it?" she repeated.

"Oh!" she cried out suddenly as she saw that she had torn out a thin strand of hair. "What have I done? Poor M'sieur Voldemar!"

She carefully straightened out the strand of hair, wound it round her finger, and twisted it in a little ring.

"I shall put your hair in a medallion, and I shall wear it," she said, while her eyes glittered with tears. "Perhaps that will comfort you a little. . . . But now good-by."

I returned home, to find an unpleasant situation awaiting me. My mother was having a scene with my father. She was reproaching him with something or other, but he, as usual, was coldly and courteously silent, and not long after, he drove off. I could not catch what my mother was saying, nor was I particularly interested. I remember only that afterward she sent for me to go to her room and talked in a very dissatisfied tone about my visits to the Princess, who, in her words, was *une femme capable de tout.*[31] I kissed her hand (I always did that when I wanted to cut short the conversation) and went to my room. Zinaida's tears had baffled me completely. I simply did not know what to make of it all, and I, too, was ready to cry: after all, I was a child, despite my sixteen years. Now I no longer thought of Malevsky, though Belovzorov grew more and more threatening every day and looked at the shifty Count like a wolf at a sheep. Indeed, I did not

[29] In Shakespeare's *Hamlet,* III.ii.391–99, Hamlet toys with the pompous councillor Polonius by getting him to agree that a cloud looks like a camel, then a weasel, then a whale.

[30] Lushin is right; Antony was about forty-two when he first met Cleopatra.

[31] French: "a woman capable of anything."

think of anything or anybody. I was lost in conjecture, and was always going off to lonely spots. I grew especially fond of the conservatory. I would climb up to the top of the high wall, would sit down, and go on sitting there, such an unhappy, lonely, and mournful lad that I began to feel sorry for myself. And how comforting did I find those mournful feelings, how I reveled in them!

Well, one day, as I was sitting on the wall, gazing into the distance and listening to the church bells, suddenly something passed over me . . . like a little breeze; not a shiver, but literally a waft, literally a sensation that someone was in the vicinity. . . . I looked down. Below me Zinaida was hurriedly walking along the road; she was in a gray dress and had a rose-colored parasol over her shoulder. She saw me, halted, and, throwing back the brim of her straw hat, raised her velvety eyes to me.

"What are you doing up there, so high?" she asked me with a strange smile. "Listen! You're always declaring that you love me; jump down here to me, if you really do love me."

She hardly had time to say the words before I flew down just as though someone had pushed me in the back. The wall was about fourteen feet high. I reached the ground on my feet, but the drop was so great that I could not keep my balance: I fell and lost consciousness for a moment. When I came to, without opening my eyes I felt that Zinaida was kneeling beside me. "My dear boy," she said as she bent over me, and an anxious tenderness sounded in her voice; "what made you do that, what made you do as I told you? . . . You see, I love you. . . . Get up."

Her breast rose and fell beside me, her hands touched my head, and suddenly—ah, what happened to me then!—her soft, fresh lips began to cover all my face with kisses . . . they touched my lips. . . . But then she must have guessed by the expression of my face that I had come round, though I had not opened my eyes, for, swiftly rising, she said: "Now get up, you madcap, you stupid! What are you lying in the dust for?" I got up. "Hand me my parasol," she said; "I dropped it somewhere. And don't stare at me like that. . . . What a stupid thing to do! You haven't hurt yourself, have you? I expect you've stung yourself in the nettles. Don't stare at me, I tell you. Oh, he doesn't understand a thing, he doesn't say a word," she added, as though to herself. "Go home, M'sieur Voldemar, and brush yourself off, and don't dare to follow me or I'll be angry, and then never again—"

She did not finish the sentence and briskly walked away, while I sat up in the road. My legs would not support me. The nettles had stung my hands, my back ached, and my head was swimming, but the feeling of bliss that I experienced at that moment has never visited me again. It was like a pleasant pain in all my limbs, and it was resolved at last in rapturous jumps and exclamations of joy. Truly, I was still a child.

13

I was so gay and proud all that day, I retained the feeling of Zinaida's kisses so vividly on my face, I remembered her every word with such shuddering

rapture, I cherished my unexpected happiness so deeply that I began to feel frightened, I did not even wish to see her, the cause of these new sensations. I felt that now I could demand nothing more of fate, that now I ought to "sigh deeply for the last time, and die." On the other hand, when I went to call on the Zasiokins next day, I felt great embarrassment, which I vainly tried to conceal beneath a modest jauntiness, proper to a man who wishes to indicate that he can keep a secret. Zinaida received me very simply, without any sign of agitation; she only threatened me with her finger and asked whether I had any bruises. All my modest jauntiness and mysterious secrecy vanished in a moment, and with it my embarrassment. Of course, I had not expected anything in particular, but Zinaida's calm was like a douche of cold water. I realized that in her eyes I was a child, and I felt very miserable. She walked backward and forward, smiling swiftly whenever she glanced at me; but her thoughts were far away, I saw that clearly. . . . "Shall I be the first to refer to yesterday?" I thought. "Shall I ask where she was off to in such a hurry, so that I can find out definitely? . . . " But I only dismissed the idea and sat down in a corner.

Belovzorov came in; I was glad to see him.

"I haven't found you a riding-horse, not a quiet one, yet," he began in a harsh tone. "Freitag says he has one, but I'm not sure about it. I'm afraid."

"What are you afraid of?" Zinaida inquired. "May I ask?"

"What am I afraid of? Why, you cannot ride yet. God preserve us from anything happening! And what is this mad idea that has suddenly come into your head?"

"Well, that's my business, M'sieur my animal. In that case I shall ask Piotr Vasilich." (My father's name was Piotr Vasilich, and I was surprised to hear her mention his name so lightly and easily, as though she was quite sure of his readiness to serve her.)

"So that's it?" Belovzorov retorted. "So it's with him that you want to go riding?"

"Either with him or with someone else, it makes no difference to you. In any case it won't be with you."

"Won't be with me?" Belovzorov repeated. "As you wish. What of it? I'll get you a horse."

"Only, listen, I don't want any old nag. I warn you that I want to gallop."

"Gallop by all means. But whom are you going to ride with? Malevsky, by any chance?"

"And why not, warrior knight? Now calm down," she added, "and don't flash your eyes. I'll take you with me too. You know what I think about Malevsky now—pooh!" She shook her head.

"You say that just to console me," he snorted.

Zinaida half closed her eyes. "Does it console you, then? Oh, oh, oh, you warrior!" she said at last, as though she could not think of anything else to call him. "And what about you, M'sieur Voldemar? Would you go riding with us?"

"I'm not fond of riding—with lots of other people," I muttered without raising my eyes.

"So you prefer it to be tête-à-tête?³² Well, the free has his choice, the

³² A party of two.

saved has—paradise," she said, sighing. "Go and see what you can do, Belovzorov. I need a horse for tomorrow."

"All very well, but where are we to get the money?" her mother intervened.

Zinaida knitted her brows.

"I shan't ask you for it. Belovzorov will give me credit."

"He will, he certainly will," the Princess replied, and suddenly shouted at the top of her voice: "Dunia!"

"*Maman,* I have given you a bell to ring," Zinaida observed.

"Dunia!" the old woman called again.

Belovzorov took his leave; I went with him. Zinaida did not detain me.

14

Next morning I rose early, cut myself a stick, and went for a walk out beyond the city turnpike. I thought I would walk off my misery. The day was beautiful, bright, and not too hot; a cheerful, fresh breeze was roving over the earth, and it blew and played gently, stirring everything and disturbing nothing. I wandered a long time over the hills, through the forest; I did not feel happy—I had left home with the intention of giving myself over to dejection; but my youth, the fine weather, the fresh air, the pleasure of the swift walk, the delight of lying alone on the thick grass, all had their way: the memory of those unforgettable words, of those kisses, again forced itself upon my soul. It was pleasant to think that at all events Zinaida would have to admit my resolution, my heroism. . . . "She may find others better than I," I thought, "and let her! On the other hand, others only say they'll do a thing, but I do it. And what else couldn't I do for her!" My imagination began to run riot. I imagined how I would save her from the hands of enemies, how, all streaming with blood, I would wrest her from a dungeon, how I would die at her feet. I remembered a picture that hung in our reception room; it depicted Maleque Adèle carrying off Mathilde[33] . . . and at that very moment my attention was distracted by the sight of a great spotted woodpecker, which fussily climbed the slender trunk of a birch and peered anxiously out from behind it, first to the right, then to the left, like a musician from behind the neck of his double-bass.

Then I began to sing: "Not white are the snows," and went on to a ballad well known at that time, "I wait for thee, whenas the playful zephyr";[34] then I began to declaim Yermak's apostrophe to the stars, from Khomyakov's tragedy of the same name;[35] I would have tried my hand at writing something in a sentimental style, I even thought of the line that was to end the poem: "O Zinaida, Zinaida!" But nothing came of it. Meanwhile the dinner hour was approaching. I dropped down into a valley; a narrow,

[33] The principal characters in *Mathilde* (1805), by the French novelist Sophie Cottin (1770–1807).

[34] The first of the songs is a Russian folk song; the second is a setting of a poem by P. A. Vyazemsky (1792–1878).

[35] The dramatist A. S. Khomyakov lived 1804–60.

sandy path wound along it in the direction of the city. I followed this path. . . . The hollow drumming of horse-hoofs sounded behind me. I looked round, involuntarily halted, and removed my cap: my father and Zinaida were riding toward me, side by side. My father was saying something to her, leaning all his body across and resting his hand on her horse's neck. He was smiling. Zinaida was listening to him without speaking, her eyes strictly cast down and her lips compressed. At first I saw no one else, but some moments later Belovzorov appeared round a bend in the valley; he was in his hussar uniform, with a pelisse,[36] and was riding a foaming black horse. The good horse shook its head, snorted, and fretted; the rider was continually reining it in and spurring it on. I stepped aside. My father gathered up his reins and drew away from Zinaida; she slowly raised her eyes to him, and they both set off at a gallop. . . . Belovzorov tore after them, his saber clattering. "He's as crimson as a lobster," I thought. "And she—why is she so pale? They've been riding all the morning, and yet she's pale."

I hastened my steps and arrived home just before dinnertime. My father, who had washed and changed his clothes, was already sitting by my mother's chair and reading a *feuilleton* from the *Journal des débats*[37] to her in his even, musical voice. But my mother was only half listening; when she saw me, she asked me where I had been all day, and added that she did not like people going off God knows where and God knows with whom. I felt like replying: "I have been for a walk by myself"; but I looked at my father, and for some reason I kept silent.

15

During the next five or six days I hardly saw Zinaida at all; she pleaded that she was unwell, which, however, did not prevent the usual visitors from reporting for duty, as they themselves put it—all except Maidanov, who grew depressed and bored as soon as he had no chance to rhapsodize. Belovzorov sat moodily in a corner, red of face, his coat tightly buttoned up. An unpleasant smile roved continually over Count Malevsky's thin features. The Count certainly had fallen out of favor with Zinaida and now waited diligently on the old Princess, even driving with her in a hired carriage to see the Governor General. This journey proved a failure, however, and even led to some unpleasantness for Malevsky; they reminded him of some incident or other in which he had been involved with road engineers, and he had to plead in his justification that at that time he was lacking in experience. Lushin called a couple of times every day, but did not remain long. I was a little afraid of him after our last talk, but at the same time I was genuinely drawn toward him. One day he went for a walk with me in the Nieskuchny Gardens; he was very good-natured and amiable, told me the names and properties of various herbs and flowers, and suddenly went off at a tangent and exclaimed, striking himself on the forehead: "But I,

[36] A fur-trimmed coat. [37] An article from the *Journal of Debates*.

fool that I am, thought she was a flirt! Evidently it is pleasant to sacrifice oneself for others!"

"What are you trying to convey?" I asked him.

"I'm not trying to convey anything to *you*," he retorted vehemently.

Zinaida avoided me: my arrival always made an unpleasant impression on her, as I could not help noticing. She involuntarily turned away from me—involuntarily, that was what made it so bitter, what upset me most of all. But there was nothing I could do about it, and I tried to keep out of her sight and watched over her only from a distance, which was not always possible. As before, something incomprehensible was happening to her: her features changed, she changed altogether. One warm, still evening I was particularly struck by the change that had occurred in her. I was sitting on a low bench under a spreading elder bush; I was fond of this spot, for from it I could see the window of Zinaida's room. I was sitting there, and above my head amid the darkened foliage a little bird was fidgeting; a gray kitten, arching its back, cautiously stole into the garden, and the first May bugs were buzzing noisily in the air, which was still translucent, though the day was fading. I sat and gazed at the window and waited to see whether it would open. Yes, it did open, and Zinaida appeared at it. She was wearing a white dress, and she herself, her face, her shoulders, her arms, were all as white as a sheet. She stood a long time without stirring and gazed a long time fixedly from under her wrinkled brows. I had not realized that she could look like that. Then she clenched her fists, strongly, very strongly, shook her curls, and, nodding with an air of decision, slammed the window shut again.

Three days later I met her in the garden. I tried to slip away, but she herself stopped me.

"Give me your hand," she said with all her former kindness. "You and I haven't had a talk for a long time."

I glanced at her. Her eyes were beaming mildly, and her face was smiling, as though through a mist.

"Are you still unwell?" I asked her.

"No, it's all past now," she replied as she picked a small red rose. "I'm a little tired, but that will pass too."

"And will you be again as you were before?" I asked.

She raised the rose to her face, and I had the impression that the brilliant color of the petals was reflected in her cheeks. "Have I changed, then?" she asked.

"Yes, you have changed," I replied in a low voice.

"I have been cold to you, I know, " she began. "But you shouldn't have taken any notice of it. . . . I could not be otherwise. But why talk about it?"

"You don't want me to love you, that's what it is, " I exclaimed moodily in an involuntary outburst.

"You're wrong; do go on loving me, but not as before."

"How, then?"

"We shall be friends, that's how." She held out the rose for me to smell. "Listen; after all, I am much older than you. I could quite well be your aunt, really I could; or if not your aunt, then your elder sister. But you—"

"You regard me as a child," I interrupted her.

"Why, yes. You are a child, but a dear, good, intelligent child whom I

love very much. Do you know what? From today I appoint you my page; and you must not forget that pages should never leave their mistresses' side. Here is the token of your new dignity," she added, putting the rose in my buttonhole. "A token of my favor."

"I have had other favors from you in the past," I muttered.

"Ah!" she said, and looked sidelong at me. "What a memory he has! Well, what if I did? I'm just as ready now."

And, bending toward me, she printed a pure, tranquil kiss on my forehead.

I only gazed at her; but she turned away and went toward the house, saying: "Follow me, my page." I followed her, continually in a muse. "Is this gentle and sober-minded girl the same Zinaida whom once I knew?" I thought. "Surely not?" Even her walk seemed more staid, and all her figure more majestic and harmonious.

But my goodness! With what new strength did my love flame up within me!

16

After dinner guests again gathered in the Zasiokins' reception room, and Zinaida came out to join them. All the company was present that had assembled on that first unforgettable evening. Even Nirmatsky dragged himself along. This time Maidanov was the first to arrive; he brought some new verse. We played forfeits again, but now they were lacking in the previous ingenuity, and there was not the former foolery and hubbub; the gypsy element had vanished. Zinaida set a new mood for our gathering. I sat beside her, as was my right as a page. Among other things she suggested that the one who drew a forfeit should tell a dream he had had. But this was not a success. The dreams proved either uninteresting (Belovzorov had dreamed that he fed his horse on carp, and that his mount had a wooden head) or unnatural, invented. . . . Maidanov treated us to a whole novel: it included graveyard vaults, and angels with lyres, and flowers that talked . . . and sounds coming from afar. Zinaida would not let him finish. "Now we have begun to make up stories," she said, "let each of us tell some story, only it must be really made up." It fell to Belovzorov to begin.

The young hussar was disconcerted. "I can't think of anything," he exclaimed.

"What nonsense!" Zinaida rebuked him. "Imagine, for instance, that you are married, and tell us how you would spend the time with your wife. Would you keep her locked in?"

"I would keep her locked in."

"And would you sit with her yourself?"

"Of course I would."

"Excellent. But supposing she got bored with all this and was false to you?"

"I would kill her."

"But supposing she ran away?"

"I would go after her, and I would kill her just the same."

"Yes, but supposing I were your wife, what would you do then?"

He was silent for a moment, then replied: "I would kill myself."

Zinaida laughed. "I see your song isn't a long one."

She herself drew the second forfeit. She gazed up at the ceiling and was lost in thought. "Now listen to what I have made up," she said at last, "Imagine a magnificent palace, a summer night, and a marvelous ball. The ball is being given by the young Queen. Everywhere there is gold, marble, crystal, silk, lights, amber, flowers, incense, all the whims of luxury."

"You're fond of luxury, aren't you?" Lushin interrupted.

"Luxury is beautiful," she retorted. "I am fond of all beautiful things."

"More than fine things?" he asked.

"That is too subtle, and I don't understand it. Don't interrupt me. And so, it is a magnificent ball. There are a large number of guests, they are all young, fine, and brave, they are all madly in love with the Queen."

"But aren't there any women among the guests?" Malevsky asked.

"No—but wait, yes, there are."

"And they're all ugly?"

"They're all charming, but all the men are in love with the Queen. She is tall and graceful . . . she has a small gold diadem on her black hair."

I gazed at Zinaida, and at that moment she seemed so much taller than the rest of us, and such lucid intelligence and such authority beamed from her white forehead, from her knitted brows, that I thought: "You yourself are this Queen."

"They all crowd round her," she continued, "they all make her highly flattering speeches."

"But is she fond of flattery?" Lushin asked.

"How unbearable you are! You're always interrupting. . . . Who doesn't like flattery?"

"Just one last question," Malevsky interposed. "Has the Queen a husband?"

"I hadn't thought about that. No, why should she have a husband?"

"Of course," Malevsky caught her up; "why should she have a husband?"

"*Silence!*" Maidanov, who spoke French badly, exclaimed in French.

"Merci," Zinaida said to him. "And so the Queen listens to these speeches, she listens to the music, but her eyes are not on any of her guests. Six windows are open from top to bottom, from ceiling to floor, and beyond them is the dark sky with great stars, and the dark garden with great trees. The Queen is gazing into the garden. There, by the tree, is a fountain; in the dusk it shows up white and long, very long, like an apparition. Through the talk and the music the Queen hears the quiet splashing of the water; she gazes and thinks: 'All you gentlemen are of noble birth, you are all intelligent, and wealthy, you crowd round me, you treasure my every word, every one of you is ready to die at my feet, I rule over you. . . . But there, by the fountain, by that splashing water, the one I love, the one who rules over me, is standing and waiting for me. He is wearing neither sumptuous attire nor precious gems; no one knows him, but he is waiting for me and is sure that I shall come. And I shall go to him, and there is no power that could halt me when I desire to go to him and remain with him, and to be lost with him there in the darkness of the garden, beneath the rustling of the trees, beneath the splashing of the fountain.' "

She was silent.

"Is this—all made up?" Malevsky asked craftily.

Zinaida did not even look at him.

"But, gentlemen, what would we do," Lushin suddenly asked, "if we were among those guests and knew about that fortunate one by the fountain?"

"Wait, wait!" Zinaida interrupted him. "I myself will tell you what each of you would do. You, Belovzorov, would challenge him to a duel; you, Maidanov, would write an epigram on him. But no, you don't know how to write epigrams; you would write long iambic verse about him, in the manner of Barbier, and you would publish your poem in the *Telegraph*.[38] You, Nirmatsky, would borrow from him. . . . No, you would lend him money at interest. You, Doctor—" She paused. "As for you, I don't know what you would do."

"In my capacity as court physician," he said, "I would advise the Queen not to give balls if she hadn't time for her guests."

"Perhaps you'd be right. But you, Count—"

"And I?" Malevsky asked, with his unpleasant smile.

"You would offer him a poisoned sweet."

Malevsky's face twisted a little in a grimace and looked Jewish for a moment, but he immediately burst into a roar of laughter.

"And as for you, Voldemar—" Zinaida continued. "But no more of this; let us play some other game."

"M'sieur Voldemar, in his capacity as the Queen's page, would hold her train as she ran into the garden," Malevsky observed venomously.

I flared up; but Zinaida swiftly laid her hand on my shoulder, rose a little in her seat, and declared in a voice that shook a little: "I have never given Your Excellency any right to be insolent, and so I must ask you to withdraw." She pointed to the door.

"Forgive me, Princess!" Malevsky muttered, turning pale.

"The Princess is right!" Belovzorov exclaimed, and he, too, rose.

"By God, I never expected you to take it like that," Malevsky added. "I don't think there was anything of that nature in what I said. . . . It never occurred to me to insult you even in thought. . . . Do pardon me."

Zinaida gave him a cold look and coldly laughed. "If you wish you can remain," she declared with a negligent gesture. "I and M'sieur Voldemar were angry over nothing. You find it pleasant to wound! May you enjoy it!"

"Forgive me!" Malevsky repeated yet again; and I, remembering Zinaida's gesture, thought again that even a real queen could not have pointed an audacious man to the door with greater dignity.

The game of forfeits did not continue for long after this little incident; everybody felt rather awkward, not so much because of what had happened as because of another, not altogether defined, yet oppressive feeling. No one referred to it, but each of us was conscious of it, both in himself and in his neighbor. Maidanov read his poems to us, and Malevsky praised them with exaggerated enthusiasm. "Isn't he anxious to show how kind he

[38] Henri Auguste Barbier (1805–82) was a French author of verse satires. The *Telegraph* was a journal published in Moscow in the earlier nineteenth century, at the time when the story takes place.

is!" Lushin whispered to me. We soon broke up. Suddenly Zinaida went into a reverie; the Princess sent in to say that she had a headache; Nirmatsky began to complain of his rheumatism.

I was a long time getting to sleep; I had been impressed by Zinaida's story. "Was she hinting at something, perhaps?" I asked myself. "And at whom, at what was she hinting? And if there really is something to hint at, how is one to decide? . . . No, no, it cannot be that," I whispered, turning over from one hot cheek to the other. But I remembered Zinaida's face as she told her story. I remembered the exclamation that had burst from Lushin in the Nieskuchny Gardens, the sudden changes in her behavior toward me, and I was lost in conjecture. "Who is he?" Those three words seemed to rise before my eyes, outlined in the darkness. I felt as though a low, sinister cloud were hanging over me, and I could feel its pressure and was waiting for it to burst any moment. Of recent times I had grown accustomed to a great deal, I had seen a great deal at the Zasiokins'. Their untidiness, the greasy candle-ends, the broken knives and forks, the glum old Vonifaty, the ragged maidservants, the manners of the old Princess herself—all this terrible existence no longer disturbed me. But I could not get accustomed to what I vaguely surmised was occurring in Zinaida now. "She's an adventuress," my mother had once said of her in my presence. An adventuress: my idol, my divinity! That term burned me, I tried to get away from it by burying myself in the pillow; I was indignant. . . . And at the same time what would I not have agreed to, what would I not have given, if I could have been that fortunate one at the fountain!

The blood began to burn and course through my veins. "The garden . . . the fountain," I thought. "I'll go into the garden." I briskly dressed and slipped out of the house. The night was dark; the trees were only faintly whispering; a gentle cool fell from the sky, the smell of parsley came from the garden. I walked along all the paths; the quiet sound of my footsteps both disconcerted and encouraged me. I halted, waited, and listened to the heavy and rapid beating of my heart. At last I approached the fence and leaned on the thin rail. Suddenly—or did I imagine it?—a woman's figure flitted past a few paces away. I strained my eyes into the darkness, I held my breath. What was that? Did I hear footsteps, or was it again my heart beating? "Who is there?" I stammered almost inaudibly. And what was that? A suppressed laugh? Or the leaves rustling, or a sigh close to my ear? I began to feel afraid. "Who is there?" I repeated still more softly.

The air streamed past me for a moment; a fiery streak glittered over the sky; a star fell: "Zinaida?" I wanted to ask; but the words died on my lips. And suddenly everything grew profoundly still all around me, as often happens in the middle of the night. Even the crickets ceased to chirrup among the trees; only a window was noisily shut somewhere. I went on standing and standing for a moment or two longer, then returned to my room, to my cold bed. I felt a strange agitation, as though I had been to keep an assignation[39] and had been left waiting alone and had passed by another's happiness.

[39] Prearranged meeting of lovers.

17

Next day I saw Zinaida only for a second: she drove off somewhere in a droshky with her mother. On the other hand I saw Lushin, who, by the way, hardly deigned to speak to me, and Malevsky. The young Count smirked and began to talk to me quite pleasantly. Of all the visitors to the Zasiokins' he alone had been able to insinuate himself into our house and to find favor with my mother. My father did not like him and treated him with insulting courtesy.

"Ah, *monsieur le page!*" Malevsky began. "Very glad to meet you. What is your excellent queen doing?"

His fresh, handsome face was so repellent to me at that moment, and he looked at me so contemptuously and playfully, that I made no answer whatever.

"Are you still angry?" he went on. "How absurd! After all, it was not I who called you a page, and pages are usually found in attendance on queens. But allow me to observe that you perform your duties badly."

"Why do I?"

"Pages should be inseparable from their sovereigns; pages should always know what their sovereigns are doing, they should even watch over them"; and he added, lowering his voice: "Day—and night."

"What do you mean?"

"What do I mean? I think I am expressing myself clearly enough. Day—and night. In the daytime it is easy enough; one can see in the daytime and there are people about. But at night—that is the time to expect trouble. I advise you not to sleep at night, but to watch, to watch with all your powers. Remember, in the garden, by the fountain at night—that is where one should be on guard. You'll be grateful to me."

He laughed and turned his back on me. Probably he did not attach any special importance to what he had said: he had the reputation of being fond of mystifying people, and boasted of his ability to take people in at the masquerades—a gift that depended a great deal on the almost unconscious hypocrisy that marked his character. He was only trying to tease me, but every word he said flowed like poison through my veins. The blood rushed to my head. "Ah, so that's it!" I said to myself. "Good! So I did not go into the garden for nothing. But it shall not be!" I exclaimed aloud and beat my breast with my fist, though to tell the truth I had no idea what it was that must not be. "Whether it is Malevsky himself that visits the garden," I thought (possibly he had said too much, and he was capable of such insolence), "or anyone else" (our garden wall was very low, and it was quite easy to climb over it), "it will be a bad lookout for anyone I come across. I don't advise anyone to fall in with me! I shall show all the world and her, the traitress" (so after all I did call her a traitress) "that I can take my revenge!"

I returned to my room, went to my writing-desk and took out a pen-knife I had recently bought, felt the sharp blades, and, with furrowed brows, with cold and concentrated resolution I thrust it into my pocket, as though such deeds were nothing surprising and my actions nothing new to me. My heart swelled angrily and went numb. I did not relax my displea-

sure or my compressed lips all that day, and I walked backward and forward with one hand in my pocket, clutching the heated knife and preparing myself for something terrible. These new and unprecedented feelings so greatly occupied and diverted me that, to tell the truth, I thought very little about Zinaida. I was continually thinking of Aleko, the young gypsy: "Whither, my handsome youth?" "Lie down!" And then: "Thou art all spattered with blood; oh, what hast thou done?" . . . "Nothing!"[40] With what a harsh smile did I repeat that word "nothing"! My father was not at home, but my mother, who for some time past had been in a state of almost speechless irritation, noticed my air of doom, and at supper she said to me: "What are you sulking for like a mouse in the groats?"[41] In reply I only smiled at her condescendingly and thought: "If she only knew!" Eleven o'clock struck; I went to my room, but I did not undress. I waited for midnight; at last it, too, struck. "Time!" I whispered between my teeth and, buttoning my coat right up and even rolling up my sleeves, I went out into the garden.

I had already chosen the spot where I would keep guard. At the end of the garden, where the fence separating our domain from that of the Zasiokins' ended in the common wall, grew a single fir; standing beneath its low, thick branches, I could have a good view of all that happened around me, so far as the nocturnal darkness would permit. Here, too, was a little path, which always seemed rather mysterious to me: it crawled like a snake up to the fence, which at this spot showed signs that someone had climbed over it, and led to a circular arbor of dense acacias. I reached the fir, leaned against its trunk, and began to watch.

That night was as still as the night before; but there were fewer clouds in the sky, and I could see the outlines of the bushes, and even the taller flowers, more clearly. Those first few moments of expectation were exhausting, almost frightening. I had not resolved on any step; I only pondered what action I should take. Should I thunder out: "Where are you going? Stop! Confess or die"? Or should I simply strike? Every sound, every rustle and whisper, seemed significant, extraordinary. . . . I made ready. . . . I leaned forward. . . . But half an hour passed; an hour passed; my blood grew still and cold; I began to realize that I was doing all this for nothing, that I was even rather ridiculous, that Malevsky had been making fun of me. I abandoned my ambush and walked right through the garden. As though of intent, not the least sound was to be heard anywhere; everything was at peace; even our dog was asleep, rolled into a ball by the wicket gate. I climbed onto the ruins of the conservatory, and before me I saw the far-stretching plain. I recalled my meeting with Zinaida and was lost in thought.

I started. . . . I thought I heard the creak of a door being opened, then the light crack of a twig snapping. In two bounds I was down from the ruins, and froze still. Swift, light, and cautious steps were clearly to be heard in the garden. They drew near to where I was standing. "Here he

[40] The reference is to Pushkin's poem "The Gipsies" (1824), in which Aleko kills his wife and her lover.
[41] Bin of grain.

comes—here he comes at last!" rushed through my mind. I convulsively drew the knife out of my pocket, convulsively opened it; crimson sparks danced before my eyes, in my fear and anger the hair stirred on my head. The footsteps came straight toward me; I bent down, I strained to meet them. A man appeared. . . . My God! It was my father!

I recognized him at once, though he was wrapped from head to foot in a dark cloak, and his hat was drawn down over his face. He went past me on tiptoe. He did not notice me, though nothing concealed me; but I crouched and cowered so low that I think I must have been level with the ground. The jealous Othello ready to commit murder was suddenly transformed into a schoolboy.[42] I was so frightened by my father's unexpected appearance that at first I did not even notice whence he had come or where he went. Only when everything was again still all around me did I straighten up and wonder: "What is father walking in the garden at night for?" In my fright I had dropped my pocketknife in the grass, but I did not even trouble to look for it: I felt deeply ashamed. I cooled down in a moment. But as I returned home, I went to my bench under the elder bush and glanced at the window of Zinaida's bedroom. The small, slightly convex panes showed as dim blue patches in the feeble light coming from the nocturnal sky. Suddenly their color began to change. Behind them—I saw it, I saw it clearly—the white blind was let down cautiously and quietly, was let down to the windowsill, and remained down, motionless.

"What is all this?" I said aloud, almost involuntarily, when I was back in my room once more. "A dream, chance, or—?" The suppositions that suddenly came to my mind were so new and strange that I did not even dare to give myself over to them.

18

Next morning I woke with a headache. The agitation of the night before had gone. It was replaced by a dull bewilderment and grief that I had never known before, as though something within me had died.

"What are you looking like a rabbit with half its brain extracted for?" Lushin asked me when we met. At breakfast time I took surreptitious glances first at my father, then at my mother. He was calm, as usual, and she, as usual, was secretly irritable. I waited for him to talk to me in his amiable way, as sometimes he did. But he did not even caress me with his everyday, cold caress. "Shall I tell Zinaida everything?" I thought. " . . . After all, it doesn't matter now, it's all over between us." I went to see her, but not only did I not say anything to her about it, I did not even succeed in saying more than a word to her, much as I wished to. Her brother, a twelve-year-old student in a military school, had arrived from Petersburg for a

[42] The reference is to Shakespeare's *Othello*, in which the hero, maddened by false suspicion of his wife's infidelity, murders her.

holiday. Zinaida at once placed him in my charge. "Here you are, my dear Volodya" (it was the first time she had used this diminutive), "here is a companion for you. His name is Volodya too. Please be nice to him; he's still shy, but he has a kind heart. Show him the Nieskuchny Gardens, take him for walks, and take him under your protection. You will do that, won't you? You're kind, too." She graciously laid both hands on my shoulders, and I was completely overcome. This boy's arrival turned me also into a boy. I gazed silently at the lad, who stared at me just as speechlessly. Zinaida burst into laughter and pushed us toward each other. "Now give each other a hug, children." We gave each other a hug.

"Would you like me to take you into the garden?" I asked him.

"If you please," he replied in a hoarse, genuinely cadet voice. Zinaida laughed again. I did manage to observe that never before had she had such a charming color in her cheeks. I went off with the cadet.

In our garden was an old swing. I seated him on the thin board and began to give him a swing. He sat very still in his new little uniform of stout cloth, with broad gold lace galloons,[43] and clung tightly to the rope. "But you should unbutton your collar," I said to him. "It's all right, we're used to it," he said, and cleared his throat. He was like his sister; his eyes especially reminded me of her. I enjoyed doing him a kindness, but meanwhile that same corrosive sorrow was gnawing at my heart. "Now indeed I am a child," I thought; "but yesterday—" I remembered where I had dropped my penknife the night before and went and found it. The boy asked me for it, broke off a stout stem of angelica, carved a pipe from it, and began to pipe. Othello whistled a little, too.

But then how he wept, that very same Othello, in Zinaida's arms, when, seeking him out in a corner of the garden that evening, she asked him why he was so sad. My tears poured down so torrentially that she was alarmed. "What's the matter with you, what's the matter, Volodya?" she asked, and as I did not answer and did not stop crying, she made to kiss my wet cheek. But I turned away from her and whispered through my sobs: "I know everything; why did you play with me? . . . What did you need my love for?"

"I have done you wrong, Volodya," she said. "Ah, I have done you great wrong," she said, and clenched her fists. "How much there is in me that is stupid, dark, sinful! . . . But I am not playing with you now; I love you— you don't even suspect why, or how. . . . But all the same—what do you know?"

What could I say to her? She stood before me and looked at me, and I belonged to her wholly, from my head to my feet, the moment she looked at me. . . . Fifteen minutes later I was running races with her and her brother; I was no longer weeping, I was laughing, though my swollen eyelids dropped tears with my laughter; round my neck Zinaida's ribbon was tied instead of a cravat, and I cried out with joy when I succeeded in catching her by the waist. She did just as she liked with me.

[43] Braid; trimming.

I should find it difficult if I were made to tell in detail all that happened to me during the week after my unfortunate nocturnal expedition. It was a strange, feverish time, a kind of chaos in which the most contradictory feelings, thoughts, suspicions, hopes, joys, and sufferings eddied like a whirlwind. I grew afraid to look into myself, if a sixteen-year-old boy can look into himself at all; I grew afraid to take stock of anything; I simply hastened to get through the day till the evening. On the other hand, I slept at night—the child's mental levity helped me there. I did not wish to know whether anyone loved me, and did not wish to confess to myself that no one loved me; I avoided my father, but Zinaida I could not avoid. I burned as though on fire in her presence; but what use was there in my knowing the sort of fire in which I burned and melted?—it was bliss for me to melt and burn so pleasantly. I gave myself over entirely to my sensations, and was cunning with myself, turning my back on my memories, and closing my eyes to what I anticipated ahead of me. . . . Without doubt this drain on me would not have continued for long in any case—a thunderclap ended it all with one stroke and flung me into a new path.

Returning toward dinnertime after a long walk one day, I was amazed to learn that I would be dining alone: my father had driven somewhere, and my mother was not well, did not want anything to eat, and had locked herself in her bedroom. By the servants' faces I guessed that something unusual had occurred. I did not dare to question them, but I had one friend, the young butler, Philip, a passionate lover of verse and an artist on the guitar, and I spoke to him. He told me there had been a terrible scene between my father and mother (and every word was heard in the maids' room; much of the quarrel was in French, but the maid Masha had lived five years with a sempstress from Paris, and she understood everything). My mother had charged my father with infidelity, with intimacy with the young lady next door; at first my father had denied everything, but then he had flared up and in his turn had said something very harsh, "apparently about their ages," at which my mother had burst into tears. My mother had also made mention of a promissory note of the Princess's that had been accepted, and she had spoken very unpleasantly about her and the young lady too. And then my father had used threats to her. "And all the trouble arose," Philip added, "over an anonymous letter; and no one knows who wrote it. Otherwise there would have been no reason for all this affair to come out at all."

"But really was there anything in it?" I said with difficulty, while my hands and feet turned cold and something began to quiver in the very depths of my breast.

Philip winked meaningly. "There was. You can't keep these things quiet, no matter how careful your father was this time. After all, you have to hire a carriage or something . . . and then you can't manage without the servants."

I sent Philip away and collapsed on my bed. I did not sob, or give way to despair; I did not ask myself when and how all this had happened; I was

not astonished that I had not already guessed, long since. I did not even rail against my father. What I had learned was beyond my power to bear: this sudden revelation shattered me. It was all over. All my flowers were torn up in one handful and lay around me, scattered and trampled.

20

Next day Mother announced that she was going back to town. In the morning my father had gone to her bedroom and had sat alone with her for a long time. No one heard what he said to her, but she did not cry any more; she grew calm, and asked for food—but she did not come downstairs and did not change her decision. I remember I wandered about all day; but I did not go into the garden, and did not look once at the Zasiokins' wing. But that evening I was witness of an astonishing incident: my father led Count Malevsky by the arm from the reception room to the lobby and, in our footman's presence, coldly told him: "Several days ago in a certain house Your Excellency was shown the door. I shall not give you any explanation now, but I have the honor to inform you that if you call on me again I shall throw you through the window. I do not like your handwriting." The Count bowed, clenched his teeth, bristled up, and disappeared.

Preparations were put in hand for our return to town, to our house in Arbat Square. In all probability my father himself no longer wished to remain in the country. But evidently he had persuaded Mother not to make a scene; everything was done quietly, unhurriedly; my mother even sent a servant to convey her respects and to express her regret that, as she was not at all well, she would not be seeing the Princess again before our departure. I roamed about as though crazy and only wanted it all to end as soon as possible. One thought never left my head: how could she, a young girl, and a Princess after all, resolve on such conduct, knowing that my father was not free, and when she could have married Belovzorov, for instance? What did she hope for? Why was she not afraid of ruining all her own future? "Yes," I thought, "this is love, this is passion, this is devotion"; and I recalled Lushin's words: to sacrifice oneself for others is sweet. I happened to see a white patch at one of the windows of the wing. "Surely that isn't Zinaida's face?" I thought. . . . Yes, it was her face. I could endure no more. I could not part from her without saying a last good-by to her. I seized a convenient moment and went to her home.

In the reception room the old Princess welcomed me with her usual unpleasant and negligent greeting.

"Why have your people taken flight so soon?" she said, thrusting snuff into both her nostrils. I looked at her and felt relieved. Philip's reference to a "promissory note" had been tormenting me. But she suspected nothing; at least, so it seemed to me then. Zinaida came in from the next room, in a black dress, her face pale, her hair unbound; she silently took me by the hand and led me out of the room.

"I heard your voice and came out at once," she began. "And was it so easy for you to desert us, you wicked boy?"

"I've come to say good-by to you, Princess," I replied, "and probably forever. You have heard that we are going away?"

She gazed at me fixedly.

"Yes, I have heard. Thank you for coming. I had begun to think I would not be seeing you. Don't think badly of me. I tormented you sometimes, but all the same I am not what you imagine me to be."

She turned away and leaned against the window.

"Really I am not. I know you have a bad opinion of me."

"I have?"

"Yes, you have—you have. . . . "

"I have?" I repeated sorrowfully, and my heart began to quiver as of old under the influence of her irresistible, inexpressible enchantment. "I? Believe me, Zinaida Alexandrovna, no matter what you did, no matter how much you tortured me, I would love you and adore you to the end of my days."

She turned swiftly to me and, opening her arms wide, took my head in her hands and impetuously and hotly kissed me. God knows whom that long, farewell kiss was seeking, but I greedily tasted of its sweetness, I knew that it would never be repeated. "Good-by, good-by . . . " I said again.

She tore herself away and went out. And I left the house. I am unable to convey the feeling with which I left. I would never wish it to be repeated, but I would regard myself as unfortunate if I had never known it.

We drove back to town. It took me a long time to cut myself off from the past, it took me a long time to settle down to work. My wound slowly healed; but really there was no bad feeling between my father and me. On the contrary, he seemed to grow even more in my eyes; let psychologists explain this contradiction as they wish. One day as I was walking along the boulevard, to my indescribable joy I ran into Lushin. I liked him for his direct and unhypocritical nature, and, besides, he was dear to me because of the memories he awoke within me. I rushed over to him. "Aha!" he said. "So it's you, young man! Let me have a look at you! You're still rather yellow, but I must say there isn't the former nasty look in your eyes. Now you look like a man, not a lapdog. Well, and what are you doing? Working hard?"

I sighed. I did not want to lie, but I was ashamed to tell the truth.

"Now, don't be afraid," Lushin went on, "don't be shy. The main thing is to live a normal life and not to give yourself over to distractions. For what good will they ever do you? No matter where the wave carries you, it is always bad; but a man may stand on stone so long as he stands on his own feet. I've got a bit of a cough, and Belovzorov—have you heard?"

"No, I haven't. What's happened?"

"Vanished without a trace; they say he's gone off to the Caucasus.[44] There's a lesson for you, young man. And all because they're not capable of getting out in time, of breaking the net. But you appear to have escaped without damage. Now see that you don't get caught again. Good-by."

"I shan't be caught again," I thought. "I shall never see her again." But I was fated to see Zinaida once more.

[44] A mountain range in the south, between the Black and Caspian Seas.

21

My father went riding every day; he had a magnificent roan and sorrel[45] English thoroughbred, untiring and wicked, with a long, slender neck and long legs; he was called Electric. No one but my father could ride him. One day Father came in to me in a good humor—a mood I had not known him to be in for a long time. He was intending to go for a ride and was already wearing spurs. I asked him to take me with him.

"We'd do better at a game of leapfrog," he replied. "On your hack you'll never keep up with me."

"Yes I shall; I'll wear spurs too."

"Come on, then."

We set off. I had a little shaggy raven horse, strong in the legs and quite skittish; true, he had to gallop at full speed when Electric was put into a fast trot, but even so I was not left behind. I have never seen another horseman like my father; he sat his horse so beautifully and with such careless ease that it seemed as though the horse beneath him were conscious of it and proud of him. We rode along all the boulevards, and through the Dvichye Fields, jumped several fences (at first I was afraid to jump, but my father felt contempt for timid people, and I ceased to be afraid), rode twice across the River Moskva, and I was just thinking that now we would be returning home, especially as my father himself had noticed that my horse was tired, when suddenly he turned away in the direction of the Crimean Ford and galloped along the bank. I set off after him. Drawing up to a lofty pile of old beams, he swung himself nimbly out of the saddle, ordered me to dismount, and, giving me his horse's reins, said I was to wait for him here by the beams. Then he turned into a narrow lane and was lost to sight. I began to walk up and down along the bank, leading the horses and swearing at Electric, who would keep throwing up or shaking his head, snorting and neighing. And when I halted he dug his hoofs into the earth one after another, squealed, and bit my mount on the neck; in a word, he behaved like a spoiled thoroughbred. My father did not return. An unpleasant dampness rose from the river; a fine rain fell softly and sprinkled tiny dark spots over the idiotic gray beams, which I now found thoroughly boring as I wandered about in their vicinity. I began to feel anxious, but still my father did not return. Some policeman, a Finn, who was all gray too, and had an enormous shako,[46] like a pot, on his head, and was armed with a halberd[47] (what was a policeman doing on the bank of the River Moskva, I wondered), came along and, turning his elderly, furrowed face in my direction, asked me:

"What are you doing here with those horses, young sir? Give them to me, I'll hold them."

I did not reply; he asked me for some tobacco. In order to get away from him (moreover, I was on tenterhooks with impatience), I went several paces in the direction my father had taken, then walked along the little lane

[45] Grayish-tan and pale red-brown.
[46] A cylindrical military hat, with a visor and an ornamental plume.
[47] A weapon with an ax-like blade mounted on a spear or shaft.

to its end, turned a corner, and stopped short. In a street some forty paces away, outside the open window of a small wooden house, I saw my father. He was standing with his back to me and leaning with his chest against the windowsill. Inside the house, half hidden by the curtain, a woman in a dark dress was sitting, talking to him. The woman was Zinaida.

I was petrified. I confess that I had had not the least expectation of what I saw. My first reaction was to turn and flee. "He will look round," I thought, "and I shall be done for." But a strange feeling, a feeling stronger than curiosity, stronger even than jealousy, stronger than fear, restrained me. I began to watch, I tried to overhear what they were saying. Apparently my father was insisting on something. Zinaida would not agree. I can see her face even now, mournful, serious, beautiful, and with an indescribable impress of devotion, sorrow, love, and a kind of despair—I cannot find another word for it. She spoke in monosyllables, did not raise her eyes, and only smiled, humbly and obstinately. In that smile alone did I recognize my former Zinaida. My father shrugged his shoulders and adjusted the hat on his head: a movement that was always a sign that he was getting impatient. Then I caught the words: *"Vous devez vous separer de cette . . ."*[48] Zinaida drew herself up and stretched out her hand. . . . Suddenly before my eyes, something unbelievable occurred; my father impetuously raised his whip, with which he had been beating the dust out of the edge of his coat, and I heard a sharp blow on that arm bared to the elbow. I could hardly refrain from crying out. But Zinaida shuddered, gazed silently at my father, and slowly raised her arm to her mouth, then kissed the weal[49] that showed livid across it. He threw his whip away and, running hurriedly up the steps of the veranda, burst into the house. Zinaida turned and, stretching out her arms, throwing back her head, also left the window.

My heart sinking with fear, possessed with a bewildered horror, I flung myself back and, running along the lane, all but letting go of Electric, returned to the riverbank. I could make nothing of what I had seen. I knew that my cold and restrained father sometimes had outbreaks of frenzy, yet I could not realize that I had just witnessed such an attack. But I felt at once that no matter how long I lived, it would never be possible for me to forget that movement, that look, that smile of Zinaida's; I felt that her image, this new image that had suddenly been revealed to me, was imprinted forever in my memory. I stared senselessly at the river and did not notice that tears were running from my eyes. "They beat her," I thought; "they beat her . . . beat her. . . ."

"Now what's the matter with you? Give me my horse!" I heard my father's voice behind me.

I mechanically gave him the rein. He sprang into the saddle. The animal was chilled, and he rose on his hind legs and took one bound of a good ten feet. But Father quickly had him under control; he drove the spurs into his flanks and struck him on the neck with his fist. "Pity I haven't got my whip!" he muttered.

I remembered how that same whip had whistled and the blow it had struck, and shuddered.

"What have you done with it?" I asked after a moment.

[48] French: "You must separate from that. . ." [49] Ridge raised on the skin.

He did not reply, but galloped on ahead. I overtook him. I simply had to see his face.

"Have you been bored while I was gone?" he asked through set teeth.

"A little. But where have you dropped your whip?" I asked him again.

He gave me a swift look. "I haven't dropped it," he said; "I threw it away." He was lost in thought and his head sank on his breast. And then, for the first and probably for the last time, I saw how much tenderness and regret could be expressed in his stern features.

He galloped on once more, and this time I could not overtake him: I arrived home fifteen minutes after him.

"Now, that is love," I said to myself again as I sat that evening before my writing-desk, which was now beginning to be littered with exercise books and primers. "That is passion. How could one help revolting, how could one endure a blow from anyone, least of all from the dearest of all hands! But evidently you can, if you really love. . . . Yet I—I imagined . . ."

The past month had aged me considerably, and even to me my love, with all its agitations and sufferings, seemed something petty, and childish, and miserable by comparison with this other, this unknown something, at which I could hardly surmise and which frightened me, like a strange, handsome, but threatening face that one vainly tries to discern in the dusk.

I dreamed a strange and terrible dream that night. I thought I was entering a low, dark room. . . . My father was standing with a whip in his hand and stamping his feet; Zinaida was huddled in one corner, and there was a crimson line, not on her hand, but on her forehead. . . . And behind them both Belovzorov rose covered with blood, grinning with his white teeth and angrily threatening him.

Two months later I entered the university, and six months afterward my father died of a stroke, in Petersburg, to which city we had recently moved. A few days before his death a letter arrived from Moscow that greatly agitated him. . . . He went to ask my mother for something, and they say he even wept—he, my father! On the very morning of the day he had the stroke he began to write a letter to me in French. "My son," he wrote, "fear woman's love; fear that happiness, that poison. . . ." After his death my mother sent quite a large sum of money to Moscow.

22

Four years passed. I had just left the university and still had no real idea what I intended to do with myself, at what door to knock; for the time being, I was loafing about in idleness. One fine evening I met Maidanov at the theater. He had married and gone into the civil service; but I did not notice any change in him. He still went into raptures just as unnecessarily, and grew depressed just as suddenly.

"Do you know," he said to me, in passing, "Madame Dolskaya is here?"

"Which Madame Dolskaya?"

"Why, have you forgotten? The former Princess Zasiokina, whom we were all in love with, including yourself. Do you remember, in the house you had for the summer near the Nieskuchny Gardens?"

"Has she married Dolsky, then?"

"Yes."

"And she is here, in the theater?"

"No, I mean she's in Petersburg. She arrived a day or two ago. She is planning to go abroad."

"What sort of man is her husband?" I asked.

"A splendid fellow, and wealthy. He was a colleague of mine in Moscow. You understand that after that affair—you must know all about it" (he smiled significantly)—"it was not easy for her to make a match; there were consequences. . . . But with her intelligence everything is possible. Go and call on her; she'll be very glad to see you. She has grown even more beautiful."

He gave me Zinaida's address. She was staying in the Hôtel Demuth. Old memories began to quicken within me. . . . I promised myself that I would call on my former "passion" the very next day. But something else came along; a week passed, then another; and when I did at last go to the Hôtel Demuth and ask for Mme Dolskaya, I learned that she had died four days previously, quite suddenly, in childbirth.

Something seemed to strike at my heart. The thought that I could have seen her and did not see her, and now never would see her—that bitter thought pierced me with all the strength of irresistible reproach. "She's dead!" I repeated, staring stupidly at the porter. I slowly made my way into the street and went, not knowing whither. All the past came back and rose before me in a moment. And so that was how it had been resolved, that was what that young, burning, brilliant life, hurrying and agitated, had striven to achieve! As I thought this, I imagined those dear features, those eyes, those curls, in a narrow box, in the damp underground gloom, here, not far from me, who was still alive, and perhaps only a few paces from my father. . . . I thought all this, I strained my imagination; but meanwhile:

> *"From indifferent lips I heard news of her death,*
> *And indifferently listened I to it . . ."*[50]

the words echoed in my soul. O youth! Youth! There seems to be nothing you cannot do, you would seem to have mastery over all the treasures of the universe, even sorrow is a comfort to you, even grief confers added beauty on your face, you are self-confident and audacious; you say: "I alone am alive, look at me." But with you, too, the days speed past and disappear without trace and without number, and everything within you vanishes, like wax in the sun, like snow. . . . And, maybe, all the secret of your charm consists not in the possibility that you can do anything, but in the possibility of thinking that you can do anything, consists just in the circumstance that you cast to the winds strength that you would not know how to use on anything else, in the circumstance that every one of us seriously regards himself as a spendthrift, seriously assumes that he has every right to say: "Oh, what would I have done if I had not wasted my time in vain!"

So too I. . . . How much I hoped for, how much I expected, what a rich future did I anticipate, even when I had only just carried out the momen-

[50] From Pushkin's poem "Beneath the blue sky of my native land" (1825).

tarily returning apparition of my first love, accompanying it with a single sigh, a single pang of mourning.

But of all that I hoped, what has come to pass? And now that the evening shadows are already beginning to speed over my life, what is left to me more fresh, more precious than the memory of that swiftly passed, vernal thunder of my morn?

But in vain do I upbraid myself. Even then, in that thoughtless, youthful time, I did not remain deaf to the mournful voice that called to me, the solemn sound that reached me from beyond the grave. I remember, a few days after I had learned of Zinaida's death, I was drawn by my own invincible attraction to be present at the deathbed of a poor old woman who lived in our house. Covered with rags, lying on hard boards, with a sack beneath her head, she died painfully and wretchedly. All her life had been passed in one bitter struggle with everyday need; she had never known joy, she had never tasted the honey of happiness; one would have thought that she could not but rejoice at death, at its freedom, its peace. And yet so long as her decrepit body still resisted, so long as her breast still heaved beneath the icy hand that lay on it, so long as her last strength had not departed from her, that old woman went on crossing herself and whispering: "Lord, forgive me my trespasses. . . ." And only with the last spark of consciousness did the expression of fear and terror of her end fade from her eyes. . . . And I remember that there, beside that poor old woman's deathbed, I suddenly felt afraid for Zinaida; and I wanted to pray for her, for my father . . . and for myself.

Gustave Flaubert
(1821–1880)

"The author, in his work," the great French novelist Gustave Flaubert wrote, "must be like God in the Universe, present everywhere and visible nowhere." The metaphor is significant. Flaubert conceived of the artist as a sort of God, bringing his own world into being in an act of creation analogous to God's, exercising so scrupulous a fidelity to the reality of that world that his own personality is totally subsumed in it. This rigorous conception of the novelist's work and Flaubert's realization of it in his fiction played a crucial role in the making of the modern novel, no longer a slightly tawdry medium of bourgeois diversion but as lofty a form as tragedy or the epic. With Flaubert, however, the ideal of perfect objectivity was a reaction to powerful contrary impulses in his own character. He possessed a lush romantic strain and a continual temptation to retreat into his own imagination which he subdued only by herculean effort and which constantly threatened to reassert itself. Flaubert's realism was born of a heroic struggle not to be romantic.

Flaubert was born in Rouen in 1821 into the sort of prosperous middle-class background he was to treat with profound ambivalence in his greatest fiction. His father was chief surgeon at the Hôtel-Dieu hospital in Rouen, while his mother, daughter of a doctor in the small town of Pont-l'Évêque, came from a family of distinguished magistrates. His father's profession and his contact with operating rooms and anatomy classes had a permanent influence upon Flaubert, who was later to hold that he observed his subjects with "a doctor's eye." While still at school, he formed a close friendship with a young philosopher named Alfred Le Poittevin. The two young men adopted pessimistic views and cultivated an anti-bourgeois stance, compiling lists of banal *idées reçues* ("received ideas") to be ridiculed. By the age of sixteen, Flaubert was writing stories, mostly in a fervent romantic style, which remained unpublished. He also wrote, when he was sixteen, a long manuscript he called *Memoirs of a Fool,* an impassioned account of his secret love for a much older married woman, Elisa Schlesinger.

Flaubert's family determined upon a law career for him, and he was enrolled at the age of twenty in the Faculty of Law at the University of Paris. Two years later, after failing his examinations, he suffered a severe nervous collapse, diagnosed at the time as epilepsy, and was forced to withdraw from his studies and return home. After the death of his father in 1846, he moved, with his mother and his orphaned infant niece, to the family estate of Croisset, near Rouen, and remained there for most of the rest of his life, devoting his full energies to literature.

The history of the composition of Flaubert's books is complex, because of his meticulous working habits and his protracted revisions. His first major book was *Madame Bovary,* published in 1856 but composed during an extended interlude of five years between work on other, very different books. One of the stories Flaubert had written when he was sixteen was "Passion and Virtue," which dealt with a woman much like Emma Bovary. Twelve years later, when he read the manuscript of his *Temptation of St. Anthony* to his friends Louis Bouilhet and Maxime du Camp, they condemned its romantic excesses, advised him to burn it, and recommended that he discipline his imagination by writing a "down-to-earth" novel of ordinary life; they suggested as a topic the true story of Delphine Delamare, wife of a country doctor in Normandy who had died of grief after she deceived and ruined him. Flaubert accepted the challenge and, drawing upon the story of Delphine Delamare as well as the similar one of an acquaintance named Louise Pradier, began the five-year composition of *Madame Bovary.* Flaubert's own letters and journals record the psychological as well as artistic struggle the novel required. Contemptuous of his commonplace characters and his sordid story of provincial adultery, he nevertheless forced himself to identify sympathetically with them and to re-create meticulously their constricted world. At the same time, he strove to find beauty even in the ordinary. Through an exacting search for *le seul mot juste* ("the only right word") he aimed to achieve a style that was "as rhythmical as verse and as precise as the language of science." Emma Bovary's conflict between romantic escapism and hard reality was Flaubert's own, so that he could justly say, when questioned about the model for Emma, "Madame Bovary is myself." *Madame Bovary* was pub-

lished in magazine installments in 1856, and Flaubert was almost immediately brought to trial on charges of "outraging public morals and religion"; he was acquitted only narrowly. The novel made Flaubert famous and has since come to be regarded as the cornerstone of the modern art novel.

After the long submission to reality that *Madame Bovary* required, Flaubert's next novel swung to the other extreme of his divided artistic personality. *Salammbô* (1862) is a lush historical novel set in ancient Carthage; to write it, Flaubert made a trip to Tunisia to inspect the ruins of the city and to gather material on the third-century B.C. revolt of mercenaries against Carthage which forms the background of the novel.

Publication of *The Sentimental Education* (1869) brought to an end a process of composition even more protracted than that of *Madame Bovary*. The story of the passion of the young Frederic Moreau for the older wife of a businessman, the novel had its roots in Flaubert's youthful *Memoirs of a Fool*. Flaubert had completely rewritten this manuscript twice before the final version, once in 1842 and again between 1843 and 1845. In the process, the novel became a large-scale social panorama in which the love story is set against the background of French society under the "July Monarchy" of King Louis Philippe.

The writing of *The Temptation of St. Anthony* (1874) was spread out over a period of thirty-five years. Again, it had its start in a youthful manuscript, *Smarh*, which Flaubert wrote when he was eighteen. He radically revised the plot in 1846–49, 1856, and 1870. The successive versions of the book reflect Flaubert's developing view of religion, from the anti-religious nihilism of the early versions to a final view that religion and science are complementary, a position influenced by his reading of the English evolutionary philosopher Herbert Spencer.

"A Simple Heart" appeared in 1877 as part of *Three Tales*, which also included the stories "The Legend of St. Julian the Hospitaller" and "Herodias." These three stories, sharply contrasted in content and style, are linked by the fact that all three deal with various kinds of saints. *Three Tales* challenges *Madame Bovary* as Flaubert's masterpiece, exhibiting the same consummate craftsmanship as the earlier novel but exercised upon a wider range of material.

When Flaubert died suddenly of an apoplectic stroke in 1880, at the age of fifty-eight, he left an unfinished novel named *Bouvard and Pecuchet*, a wry satirical work about two clerks who take advantage of an unexpected legacy to retire to the country and dabble with various utopian schemes. A satire on the naive bourgeois faith in half-understood science, the novel can also be seen as Flaubert's whimsical account of his own journey to understanding.

Flaubert's books tend to oscillate between the poles of romanticism and realism which he himself was quick to describe as the basic dichotomy in his art as in his life. But the opposition appears in individual works as well. "A Simple Heart" belongs with *Madame Bovary* among the works in which Flaubert develops with painstaking realism a story of ordinary, contemporary life. Flaubert seems, like the God of creation, to be "visible nowhere" in this simple tale of a humble life. Félicité's life is built up, detail by detail, from concrete reality, with the barest minimum of authorial commentary

or explicit interpretation. The servant's painful, lonely life is a deeply moving account of "the wretched of the earth," all the more touching because of the restraint and objectivity with which it is told.

And yet Flaubert's realism is very far from a merely photographic record of life in which reality is left to determine form and facts are presumed to "speak for themselves." Again like God, if Flaubert is "nowhere visible," he is "present everywhere," shaping Félicité's story artistically and providing a subtle, ironic commentary upon it by the most indirect of means. Félicité (even her name—"happiness"—is delicately ironic) is a secular saint; her story is a series of trials—including the losses of her lover, her nephew, her parrot—from which she emerges ambiguously triumphant. She defeats monsters (the bull in the field), is scourged like Christ by the angry coachman, and is finally vouchsafed a vision of God (and her parrot). And what are we to think of that parrot? When Félicité's simple heart stops beating as the vulgar but sumptuous festival procession pauses outside her window and the beatific vision of Loulou appears, are we to laugh or cry? Is Flaubert ironically satirizing the absurdity of a constrained life or asserting the holiness of the most ordinary details of a simple life? He is doing both, and the achievement exemplifies the richness and resonance of Flaubert's complex art.

FURTHER READING (*prepared by W. J. R.*): Good biographies include Stratton Buck's *Gustave Flaubert*, 1966, and Philip Spencer's *Flaubert: A Biography*, 1952. Victor Brombert's *The Novels of Flaubert*, 1966, devotes a chapter to "A Simple Heart," discussing the tenderness and irony of the piece. *Madame Bovary, Salammbô*, and several other major works are also discussed at length. Introductory discussions of *Madame Bovary, Three Tales*, and *The Sentimental Education*, as well as a survey of Flaubert criticism, are offered in Peter Cortland's *A Reader's Guide to Flaubert*, 1968. *Flaubert: A Collection of Critical Essays,* ed. Raymond Giraud, 1964, includes essays by Jean-Paul Sartre, Erich Auerbach, and others. A general appreciation of Flaubert's artistry is provided in Margaret G. Tillett's *On Reading Flaubert*, 1961. Tillett discusses six major works, among them "A Simple Heart." Michael Peled Ginsberg's *Flaubert Writing: A Study in Narrative Strategies*, 1986, is accurately described by its title. Julian Barnes' *Flaubert's Parrot*, 1984, is a witty, inventive novel built around themes from *A Simple Heart* that almost incidentally has a lot to say about Flaubert and his story.

A SIMPLE HEART

Translated by Arthur McDowall

I

Madame Aubain's servant Félicité was the envy of the ladies of Pont-l'Évêque[1] for half a century.

She received a hundred francs a year. For that she was cook and general

[1] A village in Normandy, home of Flaubert's mother.

servant, and did the sewing, washing, and ironing; she could bridle a horse, fatten poultry, and churn butter—and she remained faithful to her mistress, unamiable as the latter was.

Mme. Aubain had married a gay bachelor without money who died at the beginning of 1809, leaving her with two small children and a quantity of debts. She then sold all her property except the farms of Toucques and Geffosses, which brought in five thousand francs a year at most, and left her house in Saint-Melaine for a less expensive one that had belonged to her family and was situated behind the market.

This house had a slate roof and stood between an alley and a lane that went down to the river. There was an unevenness in the levels of the rooms which made you stumble. A narrow hall divided the kitchen from the "parlor" where Mme. Aubain spent her day, sitting in a wicker easy chair by the window. Against the panels, which were painted white, was a row of eight mahogany chairs. On an old piano under the barometer a heap of wooden and cardboard boxes rose like a pyramid. A stuffed armchair stood on either side of the Louis-Quinze chimney-piece, which was in yellow marble with a clock in the middle of it modelled like a temple of Vesta.[2] The whole room was a little musty, as the floor was lower than the garden.

The first floor began with "Madame's" room: very large, with a pale-flowered wallpaper and a portrait of "Monsieur" as a dandy of the period. It led to a smaller room, where there were two children's cots without mattresses. Next came the drawing-room, which was always shut up and full of furniture covered with sheets. Then there was a corridor leading to a study. The shelves of a large bookcase were respectably lined with books and papers, and its three wings surrounded a broad writing-table in darkwood. The two panels at the end of the room were covered with pen-drawings, water-color landscapes, and engravings by Audran,[3] all relics of better days and vanished splendor. Félicité's room on the top floor got its light from a dormer-window, which looked over the meadows.

She rose at daybreak to be in time for Mass, and worked till evening without stopping. Then, when dinner was over, the plates and dishes in order, and the door shut fast, she thrust the log under the ashes and went to sleep in front of the hearth with her rosary in her hand. Félicité was the stubbornest of all bargainers; and as for cleanness, the polish on her saucepans was the despair of other servants. Thrifty in all things, she ate slowly, gathering off the table in her fingers the crumbs of her loaf—a twelve-pound loaf expressly baked for her, which lasted for three weeks.

At all times of year she wore a print handkerchief fastened with a pin behind, a bonnet that covered her hair, gray stockings, a red skirt, and a bibbed apron—such as hospital nurses wear—over her jacket.

Her face was thin and her voice sharp. At twenty-five she looked like forty. From fifty onwards she seemed of no particular age; and with her silence, straight figure, and precise movements she was like a woman made of wood, and going by clockwork.

[2] Vesta was the Roman goddess of the hearth. *Louis-Quinze* is the fussy, rococo decorative style which prevailed in France in the first half of the eighteenth century.

[3] Gérard Audran was a seventeenth-century French engraver whose copies of famous paintings were popular household decorations.

II

She had had her love-story like another.

Her father, a mason, had been killed by falling off some scaffolding. Then her mother died, her sisters scattered, and a farmer took her in and employed her, while she was still quite little, to herd the cows at pasture. She shivered in rags and would lie flat on the ground to drink water from the ponds; she was beaten for nothing, and finally turned out for the theft of thirty sous[4] which she did not steal. She went to another farm, where she became dairy-maid; and as she was liked by her employers her companions were jealous of her.

One evening in August (she was then eighteen) they took her to the assembly at Colleville. She was dazed and stupefied in an instant by the noise of the fiddlers, the lights in the trees, the gay medley of dresses, the lace, the gold crosses, and the throng of people jigging all together. While she kept shyly apart a young man with a well-to-do air, who was leaning on the shaft of a cart and smoking his pipe, came up to ask her to dance. He treated her to cider, coffee, and cake, and bought her a silk handkerchief; and then, imagining she had guessed his meaning, offered to see her home. At the edge of a field of oats he pushed her roughly down. She was frightened and began to cry out; and he went off.

One evening later she was on the Beaumont road. A big hay-wagon was moving slowly along; she wanted to get in front of it, and as she brushed past the wheels she recognized Theodore. He greeted her quite calmly, saying she must excuse it all because it was "the fault of the drink." She could not think of any answer and wanted to run away.

He began at once to talk about the harvest and the worthies of the commune, for his father had left Colleville for the farm at Les Écots, so that now he and she were neighbors. "Ah!" she said. He added that they thought of settling him in life. Well, he was in no hurry; he was waiting for a wife to his fancy. She dropped her head; and then he asked her if she thought of marrying. She answered with a smile that it was mean to make fun of her.

"But I am not, I swear!"—and he passed his left hand round her waist. She walked in the support of his embrace; their steps grew slower. The wind was soft, the stars glittered, the huge wagon-load of hay swayed in front of them, and dust rose from the dragging steps of the four horses. Then, without a word of command, they turned to the right. He clasped her once more in his arms, and she disappeared into the shadow.

The week after Theodore secured some assignations with her.

They met at the end of farmyards, behind a wall, or under a solitary tree. She was not innocent as young ladies are—she had learned knowledge from the animals—but her reason and the instinct of her honor would not let her fall. Her resistance exasperated Theodore's passion; so much so that to satisfy it—or perhaps quite artlessly—he made her an offer of marriage. She was in doubt whether to trust him, but he swore great oaths of fidelity.

Soon he confessed to something troublesome; the year before his par-

[4] A very small sum of money. (A *sou* is worth five *centimes* or one twentieth of a *franc*.)

ents had bought him a substitute for the army, but any day he might be taken again, and the idea of serving was a terror to him. Félicité took this cowardice of his as a sign of affection, and it redoubled hers. She stole away at night to see him, and when she reached their meeting-place Theodore racked her with his anxieties and urgings.

At last he declared that he would go himself to the prefecture[5] for information, and would tell her the result on the following Sunday, between eleven and midnight.

When the moment came she sped towards her lover. Instead of him she found one of his friends.

He told her that she would not see Theodore any more. To ensure himself against conscription he had married an old woman, Madame Lehoussais, of Toucques, who was very rich.

There was an uncontrollable burst of grief. She threw herself on the ground, screamed, called to the God of mercy, and moaned by herself in the fields till daylight came. Then she came back to the farm and announced that she was going to leave; and at the end of the month she received her wages, tied all her small belongings with a handkerchief, and went to Pont-l'Évêque.

In front of the inn there she made inquiries of a woman in a widow's cap, who, as it happened, was just looking for a cook. The girl did not know much, but her willingness seemed so great and her demands so small that Mme. Aubain ended by saying:

"Very well, then, I will take you."

A quarter of an hour afterwards Félicité was installed in her house.

She lived there at first in a tremble, as it were, at "the style of the house" and the memory of "Monsieur" floating over it all. Paul and Virginie, the first aged seven and the other hardly four, seemed to her beings of a precious substance; she carried them on her back like a horse; it was a sorrow to her that Mme. Aubain would not let her kiss them every minute. And yet she was happy there. Her grief had melted in the pleasantness of things all round.

Every Thursday regular visitors came in for a game of boston,[6] and Félicité got the cards and foot-warmers ready beforehand. They arrived punctually at eight and left before the stroke of eleven.

On Monday mornings the dealer who lodged in the covered passage spread out all his old iron on the ground. Then a hum of voices began to fill the town, mingled with the neighing of horses, bleating of lambs, grunting of pigs, and the sharp rattle of carts along the street. About noon, when the market was at its height, you might see a tall, hook-nosed old countryman with his cap pushed back making his appearance at the door. It was Robelin, the farmer of Geffosses. A little later came Liébard, the farmer from Toucques—short, red, and corpulent—in a gray jacket and gaiters[7] shod with spurs.

Both had poultry or cheese to offer their landlord. Félicité was invariably a match for their cunning, and they went away filled with respect for her.

[5] Office of the prefect, or magistrate.
[6] Card game, played by four people with two decks of cards.
[7] Boots with fabric uppers.

At vague intervals Mme. Aubain had a visit from the Marquis de Gremanville, one of her uncles, who had ruined himself by debauchery and now lived at Falaise on his last remaining morsel of land. He invariably came at the luncheon hour, with a dreadful poodle whose paws left all the furniture in a mess. In spite of efforts to show his breeding, which he carried to the point of raising his hat every time he mentioned "my late father," habit was too strong for him; he poured himself out glass after glass and fired off improper remarks. Félicité edged him politely out of the house—"You have had enough, Monsieur de Gremanville! Another time!"—and she shut the door on him.

She opened it with pleasure to M. Bourais, who had been a lawyer. His baldness, his white stock, frilled shirt, and roomy brown coat, his way of rounding the arm as he took snuff—his whole person, in fact, created that disturbance of mind which overtakes us at the sight of extraordinary men.

As he looked after the property of "Madame" he remained shut up with her for hours in "Monsieur's" study, though all the time he was afraid of compromising himself. He respected the magistracy immensely, and had some pretensions to Latin.

To combine instruction and amusement he gave the children a geography book made up of a series of prints. They represented scenes in different parts of the world: cannibals with feathers on their heads, a monkey carrying off a young lady, Bedouins in the desert, the harpooning of a whale, and so on. Paul explained these engravings to Félicité; and that, in fact, was the whole of her literary education. The children's education was undertaken by Guyot, a poor creature employed at the town hall, who was famous for his beautiful hand and sharpened his penknife on his boots.

When the weather was bright the household set off early for a day at Geffosses Farm.

Its courtyard is on a slope, with the farmhouse in the middle, and the sea looks like a gray streak in the distance.

Félicité brought slices of cold meat out of her basket, and they breakfasted in a room adjoining the dairy. It was the only surviving fragment of a country house which was now no more. The wallpaper hung in tatters, and quivered in the draughts. Mme. Aubain sat with bowed head, overcome by her memories; the children became afraid to speak. "Why don't you play, then?" she would say, and off they went.

Paul climbed into the barn, caught birds, played at ducks and drakes over the pond, or hammered with his stick on the big casks which boomed like drums. Virginie fed the rabbits or dashed off to pick cornflowers, her quick legs showing their embroidered little drawers.

One autumn evening they went home by the fields. The moon was in its first quarter, lighting part of the sky; and mist floated like a scarf over the windings of the Toucques. Cattle, lying out in the middle of the grass, looked quietly at the four people as they passed. In the third meadow some of them got up and made a half-circle in front of the walkers. "There's nothing to be afraid of," said Félicité, as she stroked the nearest on the back with a kind of crooning song; he wheeled round and the others did the same. But when they crossed the next pasture there was a formidable bellow. It was a bull, hidden by the mist. Mme. Aubain was about to run. "No! no! don't go so fast!" They mended their pace, however, and heard a loud

breathing behind them which came nearer. His hoofs thudded on the meadow grass like hammers; why, he was galloping now! Félicité turned round, and tore up clods of earth with both hands and threw them in his eyes. He lowered his muzzle, waved his horns, and quivered with fury, bellowing terribly. Mme. Aubain, now at the end of the pasture with her two little ones, was looking wildly for a place to get over the high bank. Félicité was retreating, still with her face to the bull, keeping up a shower of clods which blinded him, and crying all the time, "Be quick! be quick!"

Mme. Aubain went down into the ditch, pushed Virginie first and then Paul, fell several times as she tried to climb the bank, and managed it at last by dint of courage.

The bull had driven Félicité to bay against a rail-fence; his slaver[8] was streaming into her face; another second, and he would have gored her. She had just time to slip between two of the rails, and the big animal stopped short in amazement.

This adventure was talked of at Pont-l'Évêque for many a year. Félicité did not pride herself on it in the least, not having the barest suspicion that she had done anything heroic.

Virginie was the sole object of her thoughts, for the child developed a nervous complaint as a result of her fright, and M. Poupart, the doctor, advised sea-bathing at Trouville. It was not a frequented place then. Mme. Aubain collected information, consulted Bourais, and made preparations as though for a long journey.

Her luggage started a day in advance, in Liébard's cart. The next day he brought round two horses, one of which had a lady's saddle with a velvet back to it, while a cloak was rolled up to make a kind of seat on the crupper of the other. Mme. Aubain rode on that, behind the farmer. Félicité took charge of Virginie, and Paul mounted M. Lechaptois' donkey, lent on condition that great care was taken of it.

The road was so bad that its five miles took two hours. The horses sank in the mud up to their pasterns, and their haunches jerked abruptly in the effort to get out; or else they stumbled in the ruts, and at other moments had to jump. In some places Liébard's mare came suddenly to a halt. He waited patiently until she went on again, talking about the people who had properties along the road, and adding moral reflections to their history. So it was that as they were in the middle of Toucques, and passed under some windows bowered with nasturtiums, he shrugged his shoulders and said: "There's a Mme. Lehoussais lives there; instead of taking a young man she. . ." Félicité did not hear the rest; the horses were trotting and the donkey galloping. They all turned down a bypath; a gate swung open and two boys appeared; and the party dismounted in front of a manure-heap at the very threshold of the farmhouse door.

When Mme. Liébard saw her mistress she gave lavish signs of joy. She served her a luncheon with a sirloin of beef, tripe, black-pudding, a fricassee of chicken, sparkling cider, a fruit tart, and brandied plums; seasoning it all with compliments to Madame, who seemed in better health; Mademoiselle, who was "splendid" now; and Monsieur Paul, who had "filled out" wonderfully. Nor did she forget their deceased grandparents, whom the

[8] Saliva.

Liébards had known, as they had been in the service of the family for several generations. The farm, like them, had the stamp of antiquity. The beams on the ceiling were worm-eaten, the walls blackened with smoke, and the window-panes gray with dust. There was an oak dresser laden with every sort of useful article—jugs, plates, pewter bowls, wolf-traps, and sheep-shears; and a huge syringe made the children laugh. There was not a tree in the three courtyards without mushrooms growing at the bottom of it or a tuft of mistletoe on its boughs. Several of them had been thrown down by the wind. They had taken root again at the middle; and all were bending under their wealth of apples. The thatched roofs, like brown velvet and of varying thickness, withstood the heaviest squalls. The cart-shed, however, was falling into ruin. Mme. Aubain said she would see about it, and ordered the animals to be saddled again.

It was another half-hour before they reached Trouville. The little caravan dismounted to pass Écores—it was an overhanging cliff with boats below it—and three minutes later they were at the end of the quay and entered the courtyard of the Golden Lamb, kept by good Mme. David.

From the first days of their stay Virginie began to feel less weak, thanks to the change of air and the effect of the sea-baths. These, for want of a bathing-dress, she took in her chemise; and her nurse dressed her afterwards in a coastguard's cabin which was used by the bathers.

In the afternoons they took the donkey and went off beyond the Black Rocks, in the direction of Hennequeville. The path climbed at first through ground with dells in it like the green sward of a park, and then reached a plateau where grass fields and arable lay side by side. Hollies rose stiffly out of the briary tangle at the edge of the road; and here and there a great withered tree made zigzags in the blue air with its branches.

They nearly always rested in a meadow, with Deauville on their left, Havre on their right, and the open sea in front. It glittered in the sunshine, smooth as a mirror and so quiet that its murmur was scarcely to be heard; sparrows chirped in hiding and the immense sky arched over it all. Mme. Aubain sat doing her needlework; Virginie plaited rushes by her side; Félicité pulled up lavender, and Paul was bored and anxious to start home.

Other days they crossed the Toucques in a boat and looked for shells. When the tide went out sea-urchins, starfish, and jelly-fish were left exposed; and the children ran in pursuit of the foam-flakes which scudded in the wind. The sleepy waves broke on the sand and unrolled all along the beach; it stretched away out of sight, bounded on the land-side by the dunes which parted it from the Marsh, a wide meadow shaped like an arena. As they came home that way, Trouville, on the hill-slope in the background, grew bigger at every step, and its miscellaneous throng of houses seemed to break into a gay disorder.

On days when it was too hot they did not leave their room. From the dazzling brilliance outside light fell in streaks between the laths of the blinds. There were no sounds in the village; and on the pavement below not a soul. This silence round them deepened the quietness of things. In the distance, where men were caulking,[9] there was a tap of hammers as they plugged the hulls, and a sluggish breeze wafted up the smell of tar.

[9] Filling the seams of ships with oakum or other material.

The chief amusement was the return of the fishing-boats. They began to tack[10] as soon as they had passed the buoys. The sails came down on two of the three masts; and they drew on with the foresail swelling like a balloon, glided through the splash of the waves, and when they had reached the middle of the harbor suddenly dropped anchor. Then the boats drew up against the quay. The sailors threw quivering fish over the side; a row of carts was waiting, and women in cotton bonnets darted out to take the baskets and give their men a kiss.

One of them came up to Félicité one day, and she entered the lodgings a little later in a state of delight. She had found a sister again—and then Nastasie Barette, "wife of Leroux," appeared, holding an infant at her breast and another child with her right hand, while on her left was a little cabin boy with his hands on his hips and a cap over his ear.

After a quarter of an hour Mme. Aubain sent them off; but they were always to be found hanging about the kitchen, or encountered in the course of a walk. The husband never appeared.

Félicité was seized with affection for them. She bought them a blanket, some shirts, and a stove; it was clear that they were making a good thing out of her. Mme. Aubain was annoyed by this weakness of hers, and she did not like the liberties taken by the nephew, who said "thee" and "thou" to Paul.[11] So as Virginie was coughing and the fine weather gone, she returned to Pont-l'Évêque.

There M. Bourais enlightened her on the choice of a boys' school. The one at Caen was reputed to be the best, and Paul was sent to it. He said his good-byes bravely, content enough at going to live in a house where he would have companions.

Mme. Aubain resigned herself to her son's absence as a thing that had to be. Virginie thought about it less and less. Félicité missed the noise he made. But she found an occupation to distract her; from Christmas onward she took the little girl to catechism every day.

III

After making a genuflexion at the door she walked up between the double rows of chairs under the lofty nave, opened Mme. Aubain's pew, sat down, and began to look about her. The choir stalls were filled with the boys on the right and the girls on the left, and the curé[12] stood by the lectern. On a painted window in the apse the Holy Ghost looked down upon the Virgin. Another window showed her on her knees before the child Jesus, and a group carved in wood behind the altar-shrine represented St. Michael overthrowing the dragon.

The priest began with a sketch of sacred history. The Garden, the Flood, the Tower of Babel, cities in flames, dying nations, and overturned idols passed like a dream before her eyes; and the dizzying vision left her with reverence for the Most High and fear of His wrath. Then she wept at

[10] Sail in a zigzag pattern against the wind.
[11] That is, the nephew used the familiar forms of the French second-person pronoun.
[12] Parish priest.

the story of the Passion. Why had they crucified Him, when He loved the children, fed the multitudes, healed the blind, and had willed, in His meekness, to be born among the poor, on the dung-heap of a stable? The sowings, harvests, wine-presses, all the familiar things that the Gospel speaks of, were a part of her life. They had been made holy by God's passing; and she loved the lambs more tenderly for her love of the Lamb, and the doves because of the Holy Ghost.

She found it hard to imagine Him in person, for He was not merely a bird, but a flame as well, and a breath at other times. It may be His light, she thought, which flits at night about the edge of the marshes, His breathing which drives on the clouds, His voice which gives harmony to the bells; and she would sit rapt in adoration, enjoying the cool walls and the quiet of the church.

Of doctrines she understood nothing—did not even try to understand. The curé discoursed, the children repeated their lesson, and finally she went to sleep, waking up with a start when their wooden shoes clattered on the flagstones as they went away.

It was thus that Félicité, whose religious education had been neglected in her youth, learned the catechism by dint of hearing it; and from that time she copied all Virginie's observances, fasting as she did and confessing with her. On Corpus Christi Day they made a festal altar together.

The first communion loomed distractingly ahead. She fussed over the shoes, the rosary, the book and gloves; and how she trembled as she helped Virginie's mother to dress her!

All through the mass she was racked with anxiety. She could not see one side of the choir because of M. Bourais but straight in front of her was the flock of maidens, with white crowns above their hanging veils, making the impression of a field of snow; and she knew her dear child at a distance by her dainty neck and thoughtful air. The bell tinkled. The heads bowed, and there was silence. As the organ pealed, singers and congregation took up the "Agnus Dei";[13] then the procession of the boys began, and after them the girls rose. Step by step, with their hands joined in prayer, they went towards the lighted altar, knelt on the first step, received the sacrament in turn, and came back in the same order to their places. When Virginie's turn came Félicité leaned forward to see her; and with the imaginativeness of deep and tender feeling it seemed to her that she actually was the child; Virginie's face became hers, she was dressed in her clothes, it was her heart beating in her breast. As the moment came to open her mouth she closed her eyes and nearly fainted.

She appeared early in the sacristy[14] next morning for Monsieur the curé to give her the communion. She took it with devotion, but it did not give her the same exquisite delight.

Mme. Aubain wanted to make her daughter into an accomplished person; and as Guyot could not teach her music or English she decided to place her in the Ursuline Convent at Honfleur as a boarder. The child made no objection. Félicité sighed and thought that Madame lacked feel-

[13] A liturgical prayer to Christ (from its opening words: "Lamb of God").
[14] Vestry, the room in a church where the sacred vestments and utensils are kept.

ing. Then she reflected that her mistress might be right; matters of this kind were beyond her.

So one day an old spring-van drew up at the door, and out of it stepped a nun to fetch the young lady. Félicité hoisted the luggage on to the top, admonished the driver, and put six pots of preserves, a dozen pears, and a bunch of violets under the seat.

At the last moment Virginie broke into a fit of sobbing; she threw her arms round her mother, who kissed her on the forehead, saying over and over "Come, be brave! be brave!" The step was raised, and the carriage drove off.

Then Mme. Aubain's strength gave way; and in the evening all her friends—the Lormeau family, Mme. Lechaptois, the Rochefeuille ladies, M. de Houppeville, and Bourais—came in to console her.

To be without her daughter was very painful for her at first. But she heard from Virginie three times a week, wrote to her on the other days, walked in the garden, and so filled up the empty hours.

From sheer habit Félicité went into Virginie's room in the mornings and gazed at the walls. It was boredom to her not to have to comb the child's hair now, lace up her boots, tuck her into bed—and not to see her charming face perpetually and hold her hand when they went out together. In this idle condition she tried making lace. But her fingers were too heavy and broke the threads; she could not attend to anything, she had lost her sleep, and was, in her own words, "destroyed."

To "divert herself" she asked leave to have visits from her nephew Victor.

He arrived on Sundays after mass, rosy-cheeked, bare-chested, with the scent of the country he had walked through still about him. She laid her table promptly and they had lunch, sitting opposite each other. She ate as little as possible herself to save expense, but stuffed him with food so generous that at last he went to sleep. At the first stroke of vespers she woke him up, brushed his trousers, fastened his tie, and went to church, leaning on his arm with maternal pride.

Victor was always instructed by his parents to get something out of her—a packet of moist sugar, it might be, a cake of soap, spirits, or even money at times. He brought his things for her to mend and she took over the task, only too glad to have a reason for making him come back.

In August his father took him off on a coasting voyage. It was holiday time, and she was consoled by the arrival of the children. Paul, however, was getting selfish, and Virginie was too old to be called "thou" any longer; this put a constraint and barrier between them.

Victor went to Morlaix, Dunkirk, and Brighton in succession and made Félicité a present on his return from each voyage. It was a box made of shells the first time, a coffee cup the next, and on the third occasion a large gingerbread man. Victor was growing handsome. He was well made, had a hint of a moustache, good honest eyes, and a small leather hat pushed backwards like a pilot's. He entertained her by telling stories embroidered with nautical terms.

On a Monday, July 14, 1819 (she never forgot the date), he told her that he had signed on for the big voyage and next night but one he would take

the Honfleur boat and join his schooner, which was to weigh anchor from Havre before long. Perhaps he would be gone two years.

The prospect of this long absence threw Félicité into deep distress; one more good-bye she must have, and on the Wednesday evening, when Madame's dinner was finished, she put on her clogs and made short work of the twelve miles between Pont-l'Évêque and Honfleur.

When she arrived in front of the Calvary she took the turn to the right instead of the left, got lost in the timber-yards, and retraced her steps; some people to whom she spoke advised her to be quick. She went all round the harbor basin, full of ships, and knocked against hawsers;[15] then the ground fell away, lights flashed across each other, and she thought her wits had left her, for she saw horses up in the sky.

Others were neighing by the quay-side, frightened at the sea. They were lifted by a tackle and deposited in a boat, where passengers jostled each other among cider casks, cheese baskets, and sacks of grain; fowls could be heard clucking, the captain swore; and a cabin-boy stood leaning over the bows, indifferent to it all. Félicité, who had not recognized him, called "Victor!" and he raised his head; all at once, as she was darting forwards, the gangway was drawn back.

The Honfleur packet, women singing as they hauled it, passed out of harbor. Its framework creaked and the heavy waves whipped its bows. The canvas had swung round, no one could be seen on board now; and on the moon-silvered sea the boat made a black speck which paled gradually, dipped, and vanished.

As Félicité passed by the Calvary she had a wish to commend to God what she cherished most, and she stood there praying a long time with her face bathed in tears and her eyes towards the clouds. The town was asleep, coastguards were walking to and fro; and water poured without cessation through the holes in the sluice, with the noise of a torrent. The clocks struck two.

The convent parlor would not be open before day. If Félicité were late Madame would most certainly be annoyed; and in spite of her desire to kiss the other child she turned home. The maids at the inn were waking up as she came in to Pont-l'Évêque.

So the poor slip of a boy was going to toss for months and months at sea! She had not been frightened by his previous voyages. From England or Brittany you came back safe enough; but America, the colonies, the islands—these were lost in a dim region at the other end of the world.

Félicité's thoughts from that moment ran entirely on her nephew. On sunny days she was harassed by the idea of thirst; when there was a storm she was afraid of the lightning on his account. As she listened to the wind growling in the chimney or carrying off the slates she pictured him lashed by that same tempest, at the top of a shattered mast, with his body thrown backwards under a sheet of foam; or else (with a reminiscence of the illustrated geography) he was being eaten by savages, captured in a wood by monkeys, or dying on a desert shore. And never did she mention her anxieties.

[15] Heavy ropes for mooring ships.

Mme. Aubain had anxieties of her own, about her daughter. The good sisters found her an affectionate but delicate child. The slightest emotion unnerved her. She had to give up the piano.

Her mother stipulated for regular letters from the convent. She lost patience one morning when the postman did not come, and walked to and fro in the parlor from her armchair to the window. It was really amazing; not a word for four days!

To console Mme. Aubain by her own example Félicité remarked:

"As for me, Madame, it's six months since I heard. . ."

"From whom, pray?"

"Why . . . from my nephew," the servant answered gently.

"Oh! your nephew!" And Mme. Aubain resumed her walk with a shrug of the shoulders, as much as to say: "I was not thinking of him! And what is more, it's absurd! A scamp of a cabin-boy—what does he matter? . . . whereas my daughter . . . why, just think!"

Félicité, though she had been brought up on harshness, felt indignant with Madame—and then forgot. It seemed the simplest thing in the world to her to lose one's head over the little girl. For her the two children were equally important; a bond in her heart made them one, and their destinies must be the same.

She heard from the chemist that Victor's ship had arrived at Havana. He had read this piece of news in a gazette.

Cigars—they made her imagine Havana as a place where no one does anything but smoke, and there was Victor moving among the negroes in a cloud of tobacco. Could you, she wondered, "in case you needed," return by land? What was the distance from Pont-l'Évêque? She questioned M. Bourais to find out.

He reached for his atlas and began explaining the longitudes; Félicité's consternation provoked a fine pedantic smile. Finally he marked with his pencil a black, imperceptible point in the indentations of an oval spot, and said as he did so, "Here it is." She bent over the map; the maze of colored lines wearied her eyes without conveying anything; and on an invitation from Bourais to tell him her difficulty she begged him to show her the house where Victor was living. Bourais threw up his arms, sneezed, and laughed immensely: a simplicity like hers was a positive joy. And Félicité did not understand the reason; how could she when she expected, very likely, to see the actual image of her nephew—so stunted was her mind!

A fortnight afterwards Liébard came into the kitchen at market-time as usual and handed her a letter from her brother-in-law. As neither of them could read she took it to her mistress.

Mme. Aubain, who was counting the stitches in her knitting, put the work down by her side, broke the seal of the letter, started, and said in a low voice, with a look of meaning:

"It is bad news . . . that they have to tell you. Your nephew. . ."

He was dead. The letter said no more.

Félicité fell on to a chair, leaning her head against the wainscot; and she closed her eyelids, which suddenly flushed pink. Then with bent forehead, hands hanging, and fixed eyes, she said at intervals:

"Poor little lad! poor little lad!"

Liébard watched her and heaved sighs. Mme. Aubain trembled a little.

She suggested that Félicité should go to see her sister at Trouville. Félicité answered by a gesture that she had no need.

There was a silence. The worthy Liébard thought it was time for them to withdraw.

Then Félicité said:

"They don't care, not they!"

Her head dropped again; and she took up mechanically, from time to time, the long needles on her work-table.

Women passed in the yard with a barrow of dripping linen.

As she saw them through the window-panes she remembered her washing; she had put it to soak the day before, to-day she must wring it out; and she left the room.

Her plank and tub were at the edge of the Touques. She threw a pile of linen on the bank, rolled up her sleeves, and taking her wooden beater dealt lusty blows whose sound carried to the neighboring gardens. The meadows were empty, the river stirred in the wind; and down below long grasses wavered, like the hair of corpses floating in the water. She kept her grief down and was very brave until the evening; but once in her room she surrendered to it utterly, lying stretched on the mattress with her face in the pillow and her hands clenched against her temples.

Much later she heard, from the captain himself, the circumstances of Victor's end. They had bled him too much at the hospital for yellow fever. Four doctors held him at once. He had died instantly, and the chief had said:

"Bah! there goes another!"

His parents had always been brutal to him. She preferred not to see them again; and they made no advances, either because they forgot her or from the callousness of the wretchedly poor.

Virginie began to grow weaker.

Tightness in her chest, coughing, continual fever, and veinings on her cheek-bones betrayed some deep-seated complaint. M. Poupart had advised a stay in Provence. Mme. Aubain determined on it, would have brought her daughter home at once but for the climate of Pont-l'Évêque.

She made an arrangement with a job-master, and he drove her to the convent every Tuesday. There is a terrace in the garden, with a view over the Seine. Virginie took walks there over the fallen vine-leaves, on her mother's arm. A shaft of sunlight through the clouds made her blink sometimes, as she gazed at the sails in the distance and the whole horizon from the castle of Tancarville to the lighthouses at Havre. Afterwards they rested in the arbor. Her mother had secured a little cask of excellent Malaga; and Virginie, laughing at the idea of getting tipsy, drank a thimble-full of it, no more.

Her strength came back visibly. The autumn glided gently away. Félicité reassured Mme. Aubain. But one evening, when she had been out on a commission in the neighborhood, she found M. Poupart's gig[16] at the door. He was in the hall, and Mme. Aubain was tying her bonnet.

"Give me my foot-warmer, purse, gloves! Quicker, come!"

Virginie had inflammation of the lungs; perhaps it was hopeless.

[16] A light two-wheeled carriage.

"Not yet!" said the doctor, and they both got into the carriage under whirling flakes of snow. Night was coming on and it was very cold.

Félicité rushed into the church to light a taper. Then she ran after the gig, came up with it in an hour, and jumped lightly in behind. As she hung on by the fringes a thought came into her mind: "The courtyard has not been shut up; supposing burglars got in!" And she jumped down.

At dawn next day she presented herself at the doctor's. He had come in and started for the country again. Then she waited in the inn, thinking that a letter would come by some hand or other. Finally, when it was twilight, she took the Lisieux coach.

The convent was at the end of a steep lane. When she was about half-way up it she heard strange sounds—a death-bell tolling. "It is for someone else," thought Félicité, and she pulled the knocker violently.

After some minutes there was a sound of trailing slippers, the door opened ajar, and a nun appeared.

The good sister, with an air of compunction, said that "she had just passed away." On the instant the bell of St. Leonard's tolled twice as fast.

Félicité went up to the second floor.

From the doorway she saw Virginie stretched on her back, with her hands joined, her mouth open, and head thrown back under a black cruci-fix that leaned towards her, between curtains that hung stiffly, less pale than was her face. Mme. Aubain, at the foot of the bed which she clasped with her arms, was choking with sobs of agony. The mother superior stood on the right. Three candlesticks on the chest of drawers made spots of red, and the mist came whitely through the windows. Nuns came and took Mme. Aubain away.

For two nights Félicité never left the dead child. She repeated the same prayers, sprinkled holy water over the sheets, came and sat down again, and watched her. At the end of the first vigil she noticed that the face had grown yellow, the lips turned blue, the nose was sharper, and the eyes sunk in. She kissed them several times, and would not have been immensely surprised if Virginie had opened them again; to minds like hers the super-natural is quite simple. She made the girl's toilette, wrapped her in her shroud, lifted her down into her bier, put a garland on her head, and spread out her hair. It was fair, and extraordinarily long for her age. Félicité cut off a big lock and slipped half of it into her bosom, determined that she should never part with it.

The body was brought back to Pont-l'Évêque, as Mme. Aubain intended; she followed the hearse in a closed carriage.

It took another three-quarters of an hour after the mass to reach the cemetery. Paul walked in front, sobbing. M. Bourais was behind, and then came the chief residents, the women shrouded in black mantles, and Félicité. She thought of her nephew; and because she had not been able to pay these honors to him her grief was doubled, as though the one were being buried with the other.

Mme. Aubain's despair was boundless. It was against God that she first rebelled, thinking it unjust of Him to have taken her daughter from her— she had never done evil and her conscience was so clear! Ah, no!—she ought to have taken Virginie off to the south. Other doctors would have saved her. She accused herself now, wanted to join her child, and broke

into cries of distress in the middle of her dreams. One dream haunted her above all. Her husband, dressed as a sailor, was returning from a long voyage, and shedding tears he told her that he had been ordered to take Virginie away. Then they consulted how to hide her somewhere.

She came in once from the garden quite upset. A moment ago—and she pointed out the place—the father and daughter had appeared to her, standing side by side, and they did nothing, but they looked at her.

For several months after this she stayed inertly in her room. Félicité lectured her gently; she must live for her son's sake, and for the other, in remembrance of "her."

"Her?" answered Mme. Aubain, as though she were just waking up. "Ah, yes! . . . yes! . . . You do not forget her!" This was an allusion to the cemetery, where she was strictly forbidden to go.

Félicité went there every day.

Precisely at four she skirted the houses, climbed the hill, opened the gate, and came to Virginie's grave. It was a little column of pink marble with a stone underneath and a garden plot enclosed by chains. The beds were hidden under a coverlet of flowers. She watered their leaves, freshened the gravel, and knelt down to break up the earth better. When Mme. Aubain was able to come there she felt a relief and a sort of consolation.

Then years slipped away, one like another, and their only episodes were the great festivals as they recurred—Easter, the Assumption, All Saints' Day. Household occurrences marked dates that were referred to afterwards. In 1825, for instance, two glaziers white-washed the hall; in 1827 a piece of the roof fell into the courtyard and nearly killed a man. In the summer of 1828 it was Madame's turn to offer the consecrated bread; Bourais, about this time, mysteriously absented himself; and one by one the old acquaintances passed away: Guyot, Liébard, Mme. Lechaptois, Robelin, and Uncle Gremanville, who had been paralyzed for a long time.

One night the driver of the mail-coach announced the Revolution of July[17] in Pont-l'Évêque. A new sub-prefect was appointed a few days later—Baron de Larsonnière, who had been consul in America, and brought with him, besides his wife, a sister-in-law and three young ladies, already growing up. They were to be seen about on their lawn, in loose blouses, and they had a negro and a parrot. They paid a call on Mme. Aubain which she did not fail to return. The moment they were seen in the distance Félicité ran to let her mistress know. But only one thing could really move her feelings—the letters from her son.

He was swallowed up in a tavern life and could follow no career. She paid his debts, he made new ones; and the sighs that Mme. Aubain uttered as she sat knitting by the window reached Félicité at her spinning-wheel in the kitchen.

They took walks together along the espaliered[18] wall, always talking of Virginie and wondering if such and such a thing would have pleased her and what, on some occasion, she would have been likely to say.

All her small belongings filled a cupboard in the two-bedded room.

[17] In 1830, when the Bourbons were expelled and Louis-Philippe was placed on the throne.
[18] Covered with fruit trees or shrubs trained to grow flat against the wall.

Mme. Aubain inspected them as seldom as she could. One summer day she made up her mind to it—and some moths flew out of the wardrobe.

Virginie's dresses were in a row underneath a shelf, on which there were three dolls, some hoops, a set of toy pots and pans, and the basin that she used. They took out her petticoats as well, and the stockings and handkerchiefs, and laid them out on the two beds before folding them up again. The sunshine lit up these poor things, bringing out their stains and the creases made by the body's movements. The air was warm and blue, a blackbird warbled, life seemed bathed in a deep sweetness. They found a little plush hat with thick, chestnut-colored pile; but it was eaten all over by moths. Félicité begged it for her own. Their eyes met fixedly and filled with tears; at last the mistress opened her arms, the servant threw herself into them, and they embraced each other, satisfying their grief in a kiss that made them equal.

It was the first time in their lives, Mme. Aubain's nature not being expansive. Félicité was as grateful as though she had received a favor, and cherished her mistress from that moment with the devotion of an animal and a religious worship.

The kindness of her heart unfolded.

When she heard the drums of a marching regiment in the street she posted herself at the door with a pitcher of cider and asked the soldiers to drink. She nursed cholera patients and protected the Polish refugees;[19] one of these even declared that he wished to marry her. They quarreled, however; for when she came back from the Angelus[20] one morning she found that he had got into her kitchen and made himself a vinegar salad which he was quietly eating.

After the Poles came father Colmiche, an old man who was supposed to have committed atrocities in '93.[21] He lived by the side of the river in the ruins of a pigsty. The little boys watched him through the cracks in the wall, and threw pebbles at him which fell on the pallet where he lay constantly shaken by a catarrh; his hair was very long, his eyes inflamed, and there was a tumor on his arm bigger than his head. She got him some linen and tried to clean up his miserable hole; her dream was to establish him in the bake-house, without letting him annoy Madame. When the tumor burst she dressed it every day; sometimes she brought him cake, and would put him in the sunshine on a truss of straw. The poor old man, slobbering and trembling, thanked her in his worn-out voice, was terrified that he might lose her, and stretched out his hands when he saw her go away. He died; and she had a mass said for the repose of his soul.

That very day a great happiness befell her; just at dinner-time appeared Mme. de Larsonnière's negro, carrying the parrot in its cage, with perch, chain, and padlock. A note from the baroness informed Mme. Aubain that her husband had been raised to a prefecture and they were starting that evening; she begged her to accept the bird as a memento and mark of her regard.

For a long time he had absorbed Félicité's imagination, because he came from America; and that name reminded her of Victor, so much so that she

[19] From the Polish uprisings against Russia in 1831. [20] Morning devotion.
[21] The Reign of Terror began in France in 1793.

made inquiries of the negro. She had once gone so far as to say "How Madame would enjoy having him!"

The negro repeated the remark to his mistress; and as she could not take the bird away with her she chose this way of getting rid of him.

IV

His name was Loulou. His body was green and the tips of his wings rose-pink; his forehead was blue and his throat golden.

But he had the tiresome habits of biting his perch, tearing out his feathers, sprinkling his dirt about, and spattering the water of his tub. He annoyed Mme. Aubain, and she gave him to Félicité for good.

She endeavored to train him; soon he could repeat "Nice boy! Your servant, sir! Good morning, Marie!" He was placed by the side of the door, and astonished several people by not answering to the name Jacquot, for all parrots are called Jacquot. People compared him to a turkey and a log of wood, and stabbed Félicité to the heart each time. Strange obstinacy on Loulou's part!—directly you looked at him he refused to speak.

None the less he was eager for society; for on Sundays, while the Rochefeuille ladies, M. de Houppeville, and new familiars—Onfroy the apothecary, Monsieur Varin, and Captain Mathieu—were playing their game of cards, he beat the windows with his wings and threw himself about so frantically that they could not hear each other speak.

Bourais' face, undoubtedly, struck him as extremely droll. Directly he saw it he began to laugh—and laugh with all his might. His peals rang through the courtyard and were repeated by the echo; the neighbors came to their windows and laughed too; while M. Bourais, gliding along under the wall to escape the parrot's eye, and hiding his profile with his hat, got to the river and then entered by the garden gate. There was a lack of tenderness in the looks which he darted at the bird.

Loulou had been slapped by the butcher-boy for making so free as to plunge his head into his basket; and since then he was always trying to nip him through his shirt. Fabu threatened to wring his neck, although he was not cruel, for all his tattooed arms and large whiskers. Far from it; he really rather liked the parrot, and in a jovial humor even wanted to teach him to swear. Félicité, who was alarmed by such proceedings, put the bird in the kitchen. His little chain was taken off and he roamed about the house.

His way of going downstairs was to lean on each step with the curve of his beak, raise the right foot, and then the left; and Félicité was afraid that these gymnastics brought on fits of giddiness. He fell ill and could not talk or eat any longer. There was a growth under his tongue, such as fowls have sometimes. She cured him by tearing the pellicle off with her finger-nails. Mr. Paul was thoughtless enough one day to blow some cigar smoke into his nostrils, and another time when Mme. Lormeau was teasing him with the end of her umbrella he snapped at the ferrule. Finally he got lost.

Félicité had put him on the grass to refresh him, and gone away for a minute, and when she came back—no sign of the parrot! She began by looking for him in the shrubs, by the waterside, and over the roofs, without listening to her mistress's cries of "Take care, do! You are out of your wits!"

Then she investigated all the gardens in Pont-l'Évêque, and stopped the passers-by. "You don't ever happen to have seen my parrot, by any chance, do you?" And she gave a description of the parrot to those who did not know him. Suddenly, behind the mills at the foot of the hill she thought she could make out something green that fluttered. But on the top of the hill there was nothing. A hawker assured her that he had come across the parrot just before, at Saint-Melaine, in Mère Simon's shop. She rushed there; they had no idea of what she meant. At last she came home exhausted, with her slippers in shreds and despair in her soul; and as she was sitting in the middle of the garden-seat at Madame's side, telling the whole story of her efforts, a light weight dropped on to her shoulder—it was Loulou! What on earth had he been doing? Taking a walk in the neighborhood, perhaps!

She had some trouble in recovering from this, or rather never did recover. As the result of a chill she had an attack of quinsy,[22] and soon afterwards an earache. Three years later she was deaf; and she spoke very loud, even in church. Though Félicité's sins might have been published in every corner of the diocese without dishonor to her or scandal to anybody, his Reverence the priest thought it right now to hear her confession in the sacristy only.

Imaginary noises in the head completed her upset. Her mistress often said to her, "Heavens! how stupid you are!" "Yes, Madame," she replied, and looked about for something.

Her little circle of ideas grew still narrower; the peal of church bells and the lowing of cattle ceased to exist for her. All living beings moved as silently as ghosts. One sound only reached her ears now—the parrot's voice.

Loulou, as though to amuse her, reproduced the click-clack of the turn-spit,[23] the shrill call of a man selling fish, and the noise of the saw in the joiner's house opposite; when the bell rang he imitated Mme. Aubain's "Félicité! the door! the door!"

They carried on conversations, he endlessly reciting the three phrases in his repertory, to which she replied with words that were just as disconnected but uttered what was in her heart. Loulou was almost a son and a lover to her in her isolated state. He climbed up her fingers, nibbled at her lips, and clung to her kerchief; and when she bent her forehead and shook her head gently to and fro, as nurses do, the great wings of her bonnet and the bird's wings quivered together.

When the clouds massed and the thunder rumbled Loulou broke into cries, perhaps remembering the downpours in his native forests. The streaming rain made him absolutely mad; he fluttered wildly about, dashed up to the ceiling, upset everything, and went out through the window to dabble in the garden; but he was back quickly to perch on one of the fire-dogs and hopped about to dry himself, exhibiting his tail and his beak in turn.

One morning in the terrible winter of 1837 she had put him in front of the fireplace because of the cold. She found him dead, in the middle of his cage: head downwards, with his claws in the wires. He had died from con-

[22] Tonsillitis. [23] Device to turn meat over a fire.

gestion, no doubt. But Félicité thought he had been poisoned with parsley, and though there was no proof of any kind her suspicions inclined to Fabu.

She wept so piteously that her mistress said to her, "Well, then, have him stuffed!"

She asked advice from the chemist, who had always been kind to the parrot. He wrote to Havre, and a person called Fellacher undertook the business. But as parcels sometimes got lost in the coach she decided to take the parrot as far as Honfleur herself.

Along the sides of the road were leafless apple-trees, one after the other. Ice covered the ditches. Dogs barked about the farms; and Félicité, with her hands under her cloak, her little black sabots[24] and her basket, walked briskly in the middle of the road.

She crossed the forest, passed High Oak, and reached St. Gatien.

A cloud of dust rose behind her, and in it a mail-coach, carried away by the steep hill, rushed down at full gallop like a hurricane. Seeing this woman who would not get out of the way, the driver stood up in front and the postilion shouted too. He could not hold in his four horses, which increased their pace, and the two leaders were grazing her when he threw them to one side with a jerk of the reins. But he was wild with rage, and lifting his arm as he passed at full speed, gave her such a lash from waist to neck with his big whip that she fell on her back.

Her first act, when she recovered consciousness, was to open her basket. Loulou was happily none the worse. She felt a burn in her right cheek, and when she put her hands against it they were red; the blood was flowing.

She sat down on a heap of stones and bound up her face with her handkerchief. Then she ate a crust of bread which she had put in the basket as a precaution, and found a consolation for her wound in gazing at the bird.

When she reached the crest of Ecquemauville she saw the Honfleur lights sparkling in the night sky like a company of stars; beyond, the sea stretched dimly. Then a faintness overtook her and she stopped; her wretched childhood, the disillusion of her first love, her nephew's going away, and Virginie's death all came back to her at once like the waves of an oncoming tide, rose to her throat, and choked her.

Afterwards, at the boat, she made a point of speaking to the captain, begging him to take care of the parcel, though she did not tell him what was in it.

Fellacher kept the parrot a long time. He was always promising it for the following week. After six months he announced that a packing-case had started, and then nothing more was heard of it. It really seemed as though Loulou was never coming back. "Ah, they have stolen him!" she thought.

He arrived at last, and looked superb. There he was, erect upon a branch which screwed into a mahogany socket, with a foot in the air and his head on one side, biting a nut which the bird-stuffer—with a taste for impressiveness—had gilded.

Félicité shut him up in her room. It was a place to which few people

[24] Wooden shoes.

were admitted, and held so many religious objects and miscellaneous things that it looked like a chapel and bazaar in one.

A big cupboard impeded you as you opened the door. Opposite the window commanding the garden a little round one looked into the court; there was a table by the folding-bed with a water-jug, two combs, and a cube of blue soap in a chipped plate. On the walls hung rosaries, medals, several benign Virgins, and a holy water vessel made out of coconut; on the chest of drawers, which was covered with a cloth like an altar, was the shell box that Victor had given her, and after that a watering-can, a toy-balloon, exercise-books, the illustrated geography, and a pair of young lady's boots; and, fastened by its ribbons to the nail of the looking-glass, hung the little plush hat! Félicité carried observances of this kind so far as to keep one of Monsieur's frock-coats. All the old rubbish which Mme. Aubain did not want any longer she laid hands on for her room. That was why there were artificial flowers along the edge of the chest of drawers and a portrait of the Comte d'Artois[25] in the little window recess.

With the aid of a bracket Loulou was established over the chimney, which jutted into the room. Every morning when she woke up she saw him there in the dawning light, and recalled old days and the smallest details of insignificant acts in a deep quietness which knew no pain.

Holding, as she did, no communication with anyone, Félicité lived as insensibly as if she were walking in her sleep. The Corpus Christi processions roused her to life again. Then she went round begging mats and candlesticks from the neighbors to decorate the altar they put up in the street.

In church she was always gazing at the Holy Ghost in the window, and observed that there was something of the parrot in him. The likeness was still clearer, she thought, on a crude color-print representing the baptism of Our Lord. With his purple wings and emerald body he was the very image of Loulou.

She bought him, and hung him up instead of the Comte d'Artois, so that she could see them both together in one glance. They were linked in her thoughts; and the parrot was consecrated by his association with the Holy Ghost, which became more vivid to her eye and more intelligible. The Father could not have chosen to express Himself through a dove, for such creatures cannot speak; it must have been one of Loulou's ancestors, surely. And though Félicité looked at the picture while she said her prayers she swerved a little from time to time towards the parrot.

She wanted to join the Ladies of the Virgin,[26] but Mme. Aubain dissuaded her.

And then a great event loomed up before them—Paul's marriage.

He had been a solicitor's clerk to begin with, and then tried business, the Customs, the Inland Revenue, and made efforts, even, to get into the Rivers and Forests. By an inspiration from heaven he had suddenly, at thirty-six, discovered his real line—the Registrar's Office. And there he showed such marked capacity that an inspector had offered him his daughter's hand and promised him his influence.

[25] Title of Charles X, last of the Bourbon kings, who ruled between 1824 and 1830.
[26] A lay religious organization.

So Paul, grown serious, brought the lady to see his mother.

She sniffed at the ways of Pont-l'Évêque, gave herself great airs, and wounded Félicité's feelings. Mme. Aubain was relieved at her departure.

The week after came news of M. Bourais' death in an inn in Lower Brittany. The rumor of suicide was confirmed, and doubts arose as to his honesty. Mme. Aubain studied his accounts, and soon found out the whole tale of his misdoings—embezzled arrears, secret sales of wood, forged receipts, etc. Besides that he had an illegitimate child, and "relations with a person at Dozulé."

These shameful facts distressed her greatly. In March 1853 she was seized with a pain in the chest; her tongue seemed to be covered with film, and leeches did not ease the difficult breathing. On the ninth evening of her illness she died, just at seventy-two.

She passed as being younger, owing to the bands of brown hair which framed her pale, pock-marked face. There were few friends to regret her, for she had a stiffness of manner which kept people at a distance.

But Félicité mourned for her as one seldom mourns for a master. It upset her ideas and seemed contrary to the order of things, impossible and monstrous, that Madame should die before her.

Ten days afterwards, which was the time it took to hurry there from Besançon, the heirs arrived. The daughter-in-law ransacked the drawers, chose some furniture, and sold the rest; and then they went back to their registering.

Madame's armchair, her small round table, her foot-warmer, and the eight chairs were gone! Yellow patches in the middle of the panels showed where the engravings had hung. They had carried off the two little beds and the mattresses, and all Virginie's belongings had disappeared from the cupboard. Félicité went from floor to floor dazed with sorrow.

The next day there was a notice on the door, and the apothecary shouted in her ear that the house was for sale.

She tottered, and was obliged to sit down. What distressed her most of all was to give up her room, so suitable as it was for poor Loulou. She enveloped him with a look of anguish when she was imploring the Holy Ghost, and formed the idolatrous habit of kneeling in front of the parrot to say her prayers. Sometimes the sun shone in at the attic window and caught his glass eye, and a great luminous ray shot out of it and put her in an ecstasy.

She had a pension of three hundred and eighty francs a year which her mistress had left her. The garden gave her a supply of vegetables. As for clothes, she had enough to last her to the end of her days, and she economized in candles by going to bed at dusk.

She hardly ever went out, as she did not like passing the dealer's shop, where some of the old furniture was exposed for sale. Since her fit of giddiness she dragged one leg; and as her strength was failing Mère Simon, whose grocery business had collapsed, came every morning to split the wood and pump water for her.

Her eyes grew feeble. The shutters ceased to be thrown open. Years and years passed, and the house was neither let nor sold.

Félicité never asked for repairs because she was afraid of being sent

away. The boards on the roof rotted; her bolster was wet for a whole winter. After Easter she spat blood.

Then Mère Simon called in a doctor. Félicité wanted to know what was the matter with her. But she was too deaf to hear, and the only word which reached her was "pneumonia." It was a word she knew, and she answered softly "Ah! like Madame," thinking it natural that she should follow her mistress.

The time for the festal shrines was coming near. The first one was always at the bottom of the hill, the second in front of the post office, and the third towards the middle of the street. There was some rivalry in the matter of this one, and the women of the parish ended by choosing Mme. Aubain's courtyard.

The hard breathing and fever increased. Félicité was vexed at doing nothing for the altar. If only she could at least have put something there! Then she thought of the parrot. The neighbors objected that it would not be decent. But the priest gave her permission, which so intensely delighted her that she begged him to accept Loulou, her sole possession, when she died.

From Tuesday to Saturday, the eve of the festival, she coughed more often. By the evening her face had shrivelled, her lips stuck to her gums, and she had vomitings; and at twilight next morning, feeling herself very low, she sent for a priest.

Three kindly women were round her during the extreme unction. Then she announced that she must speak to Fabu. He arrived in his Sunday clothes, by no means at his ease in the funereal atmosphere.

"Forgive me," she said, with an effort to stretch out her arm; "I thought it was you who had killed him."

What did she mean by such stories? She suspected him of murder—a man like him! He waxed indignant, and was on the point of making a row. "There," said the women, "she is no longer in her senses, you can see it well enough!"

Félicité spoke to shadows of her own from time to time. The women went away, and Mère Simon had breakfast. A little later she took Loulou and brought him close to Félicité with the words:

"Come, now, say good-bye to him!"

Loulou was not a corpse, but the worms devoured him; one of his wings was broken, and the tow was coming out of his stomach. But she was blind now; she kissed him on the forehead and kept him close against her cheek. Mère Simon took him back from her to put him on the altar.

V

Summer scents came up from the meadows; flies buzzed; the sun made the river glitter and heated the slates. Mère Simon came back into the room and fell softly asleep.

She woke at the noise of bells; the people were coming out from vespers. Félicité's delirium subsided. She thought of the procession and saw it as if she had been there.

All the school children, the church-singers, and the firemen walked on the pavement, while in the middle of the road the verger armed with his hallebard and the beadle with a large cross[27] advanced in front. Then came the schoolmaster, with an eye on the boys, and the sister, anxious about her little girls; three of the daintiest, with angelic curls, scattered rose-petals in the air; the deacon controlled the band with outstretched arms; and two censer-bearers turned back at every step towards the Holy Sacrament, which was borne by Monsieur the curé, wearing his beautiful chasuble,[28] under a canopy of dark-red velvet held up by four churchwardens. A crowd of people pressed behind, between the white cloths covering the house walls, and they reached the bottom of the hill.

A cold sweat moistened Félicité's temples. Mère Simon sponged her with a piece of linen, saying to herself that one day she would have to go that way.

The hum of the crowd increased, was very loud for an instant, and then went further away.

A fusillade shook the window-panes. It was the postilions saluting the monstrance.[29] Félicité rolled her eyes and said as audibly as she could: "Does he look well?" The parrot was weighing on her mind.

Her agony began. A death-rattle that grew more and more convulsed made her sides heave. Bubbles of froth came at the corners of her mouth and her whole body trembled.

Soon the booming of the ophicleides,[30] the high voices of the children, and the deep voices of the men were distinguishable. At intervals all was silent, and the tread of feet, deadened by the flowers they walked on, sounded like a flock pattering on grass.

The clergy appeared in the courtyard. Mère Simon clambered on to a chair to reach the attic window, and so looked down straight upon the shrine. Green garlands hung over the altar, which was decked with a flounce of English lace. In the middle was a small frame with relics in it; there were two orange-trees at the corners, and all along stood silver candlesticks and china vases, with sunflowers, lilies, peonies, foxgloves, and tufts of hortensia. This heap of blazing color slanted from the level of the altar to the carpet which went on over the pavement; and some rare objects caught the eye. There was a silver-gilt sugar-basin with a crown of violets; pendants of Alençon stone[31] glittered on the moss, and two Chinese screens displayed their landscapes. Loulou was hidden under roses, and showed nothing but his blue forehead, like a plaque of lapis lazuli.

The churchwardens, singers, and children took their places round the three sides of the court. The priest went slowly up the steps, and placed his great, radiant golden sun[32] upon the lace. Everyone knelt down. There was a deep silence; and the censers glided to and fro on the full swing of their chains.

[27] A verger is the official who carries the symbol of office (the hallebard) before a church dignitary. A beadle is a minor parish officer with such duties as keeping order during services.
[28] Outer vestment.
[29] Container in which the consecrated host is exposed for adoration.
[30] Old-fashioned bass horns.
[31] A semi-precious stone from the region around the town of Alençon in northern France.
[32] The monstrance.

An azure vapor rose up into Félicité's room. Her nostrils met it; she inhaled it sensuously, mystically; and then closed her eyes. Her lips smiled. The beats of her heart lessened one by one, vaguer each time and softer, as a fountain sinks, an echo disappears; and when she sighed her last breath she thought she saw an opening in the heavens, and a gigantic parrot hovering above her head.

Fyodor Dostoevsky
(1821–1881)

"It would be possible," the Russian philosopher Nikolai Berdyaev wrote, "to determine two patterns, two types among men's souls, the one inclined toward the spirit of Tolstoy, the other toward that of Dostoevsky." Even their contemporaries noted the contrasting, if complementary, qualities of the two men's works, and in our own time, the critic George Steiner has elaborated at book length the contrast between Tolstoy's "epic" vision and Dostoevsky's "tragic" one. The differences can be overstated—the two men had much in common—but it is true that it is as if a shadow had passed over the sun when we move from the outward-looking, rationalistic, social world of Tolstoy to the inward-looking, visionary, existential world of Dostoevsky.

Tolstoy's fervent, questing life is like the plot of a Tolstoy novel; Dostoevsky's painful life is like the outline of one by Dostoevsky. Born in Moscow in 1821, Dostoevsky had early experiences very different from those of the wealthy, privileged Tolstoy. One biographer comments that his family "could have provided a case-study of morbid pathology." His father, a former army surgeon and at the time of Dostoevsky's birth resident physician in a hospital for the poor, was a violent, domineering alcoholic, his mother a weak, defeated woman who died when Dostoevsky was sixteen. He entered the military engineering school in St. Petersburg; while he was in school, his father was murdered by serfs on his small estate, whom he had viciously mistreated. Dostoevsky brooded over this tragedy for forty years, finally exorcizing its horror in his last novel, *The Brothers Karamazov*. Dostoevsky was graduated from the engineering school in 1843 and was commissioned a lieutenant, almost immediately resigning his commission, however, to try to make his way as a writer. Two novels appeared in 1846: *Poor People* and *The Double*. *Poor People*, as the title suggests, is a realistic, proletarian novel; its originality lay, however, in Dostoevsky's sensitive psychological analysis of its clerk-protagonist's love for an orphan girl. The novel's public success was not matched by *The Double*, the story of a paranoid civil servant who meets a man who looks just like himself and who is conspiring against him. The novel inaugurated a long line of Dostoevskian studies of divided personalities. Over the next three years, Dostoevsky published a number of short stories and portions of a new novel.

In 1849, however, the most shattering event of Dostoevsky's life occurred. For some time he had been a member of the "Petrashevsky Circle," a socialist discussion group, and now the Czar's government arrested the group and sentenced twenty-one of them, including Dostoevsky, to be shot. The police staged a grisly mock-execution, actually leading the prisoners to the execution wall, before announcing that the sentences had been commuted. Dostoevsky's sentence was changed to four years in a Siberian labor camp, to be followed by four years as a soldier in the ranks. He later described his experiences in prison in *The House of the Dead* (1862): "A period of burial alive. I was put in a coffin. The torture was unutterable and unbearable." After four years, he was released from the camp and sent to the Siberian frontier post of Semipalatinsk as a soldier. In 1859, he was permitted to resign from the army and return to St. Petersburg.

The impact of these ten years upon Dostoevsky's life and work was incalculable. His sufferings aggravated a mild epilepsy he had had for several years; this condition was to plague him the rest of his life. Prolonged association with criminals was to influence his writings; each of his major novels turns around a serious crime. In prison, he also gained a deep respect for the Russian peasantry that was to shape his thinking, and repeated readings of the Bible, the only book permitted in the prison, deepened and confirmed his previous faith. But perhaps most crucially, and certainly most paradoxically, Dostoevsky, who had gone into prison a mild socialist, emerged a profound political conservative, believing that his punishment had been deserved and that the Czar was kind and merciful. His life is perhaps a classic case of "identifying with the oppressor."

Back in Petersburg, Dostoevsky struggled to reestablish his long-interrupted literary career. With his brother Mikhail he founded a journal, *Time,* in which he published *The House of the Dead* and *The Insulted and Injured* (both in 1861) and a travel book, *Winter Notes on Summer Impressions* (1863). He had taken the journey described in the latter book, through Germany, France, Italy, Switzerland, and England, in 1862 in the company of Appolinaria Suslova, a woman with whom he had a passionate and tempestuous love affair which ended in 1865. He had married in 1857, while still at Semipalatinsk, a high-tempered widow named Maria Isaeva, who suffered from tuberculosis. The marriage was a desperately unhappy one, and the two were frequently separated before her death from tuberculosis in 1864.

In 1865, plagued by debts in St. Petersburg, Dostoevsky fled to Germany to work on a new novel, *Crime and Punishment,* which he hoped would pay off his debts. He further exacerbated his financial difficulties, however, by obsessive and self-destructive gambling, for which he retained a passion all his life. Returning to Russia with the unfinished manuscript of *Crime and Punishment,* he interrupted work on it to write, in twenty-six days, *The Gambler,* in order to satisfy a publisher who threatened to seize the rights to all his works to satisfy claims against him. Dostoevsky fell in love with Anna Grigorevna Snitkina, the stenographer he hired to take his dictation of *The Gambler.* They were married in 1867, and for the rest of his life, she was to provide a quiet, stabilizing influence upon him.

Again pursued by creditors, Dostoevsky left St. Petersburg with his new wife in 1867, not to return until 1871. *Crime and Punishment,* a great critical

success but not a financial one, was published just before they left; *The Idiot* appeared serially in 1868.

The last decade of Dostoevsky's life was his most peaceful and fruitful period. He continued to be at the center of political and ideological quarrels—for a time he edited a reactionary magazine named *The Citizen*—but his wife's quiet efficiency brought a stable domestic routine and some relief from debt. *The Possessed* appeared in 1873, *A Raw Youth* in 1876, and his masterpiece, *The Brothers Karamazov*, in 1880. The climax of his public career came the same year, when he delivered a stirring speech in commemoration of the great poet Aleksandr Pushkin in Moscow, praising such "Russian" qualities in Pushkin as spirituality and faith and calling for contemporaries to draw upon those same qualities to lead the world toward peace and brotherhood. The crowd responded with chants of "Prophet! Prophet!" and he was lionized as a national hero. He died of complications of emphysema, from which he had suffered for years, only a few months after this triumph, in January, 1881.

Much of Dostoevsky's massive and complex achievement can be understood in terms of his central figure of "the underground man." The convicts in *The House of the Dead*, despised, thrust out of society, veering between self-hate and self-justification, anticipate this figure, but he takes center stage with the first words of *Notes from Underground* (1864): "I am a sick man. . . . I am a spiteful man. I am an unattractive man. I believe my liver is diseased." The speaker, like Raskolnikov, the main character in *Crime and Punishment*, lurks in his scruffy room, peering out at society, but spending most of his time spinning out great verbal webs rationalizing his own inner division. All Dostoevsky's subsequent protagonists are variations of the type, in their psychological positions if not in their living conditions: Natasha in *The Insulted and Injured*, Prince Myshkin in *The Idiot*, and all three of the Karamazov brothers—Dmitri, Ivan, and Alyosha. For Dostoevsky, to be Russian is, almost by definition, to be "underground"; Russians have been enslaved, impoverished, and degraded for centuries and have developed characteristic responses to their subjection: a permanent stance of resentment, wild swings between brutality and self-sacrificing altruism, a bewildering blend of sadism and masochism.

The "underground" position, however, is not confined to Russia; the Russian underground man is representative of the response of modern people everywhere to the conditions of society. Three centuries of scientific rationalism, capitalism, and industrialism have produced mass humanity, faceless, hopeless, deprived of their freedom by being regarded only as cogs in the economic machine. The person who would preserve his or her freedom in such a world must drop out of it, go "underground" in a refusal to be dehumanized and stripped of the right to choose. The underground man, for all his perverse absurdity, thus is humanity at its most real and most human; being "underground," in its broadest sense, becomes Dostoevsky's metaphor for the human condition itself. People, even when they are not oppressed by political despotism or by a soulless social philosophy, are thwarted in their fundamental drive toward freedom by their own reason and by their physical needs. The Dostoevskian underground man is not only divided from society but divided within himself, his drive toward freedom inevitably generating, in its act of revolt, cruel and aggressive impulses. The psychological results of this division appear in the studies of

extreme mental states—sadomasochism, schizophrenia, paranoia—that fill Dostoevsky's novels.

The underground man as modern man is almost inevitably a city man, and Dostoevsky's St. Petersburg is, along with Balzac's Paris and Dickens's London, one of the most powerful urban nightmares. The agrarian Tolstoy generally stayed out of Petersburg, artistically as well as personally, but Dostoevsky found in the city the perfect symbol for his view of the modern world. The impression we get of the city from his novels is of a labyrinth of winding passageways and narrow streets and of tiny, rathole-like rooms from which lonely strangers scurry out from time to time. The sun may shine on the fashionable crowd passing along Nevsky Prospect, but we see it, from the perspective of the underground, as a procession of vaguely threatening automatons, a polite battlefield of egotism and self-interest.

Dostoevsky is a wonderfully dramatic writer; George Steiner argues that he possessed "the most comprehensive and natural dramatic temper since Shakespeare's." *Notes from Underground* is, first of all, a great one-character play, a sustained dramatic monologue by a vivid, monstrous, tragicomic character. It began as a satirical attack on the popular utopian novel *What Is To Be Done?* (1863) by the Russian socialist Nikolai Chernyshevsky, and whole sections of the *Notes*—the attempt to bump into the officer on the Nevsky Prospect and the climactic encounter with the prostitute Liza—parody specific incidents in *What Is To Be Done?* Chernyshevsky's novel, an optimistic picture of a perfectly rational society, infuriated Dostoevsky, and he has his underground man reply at length, predicting that perverse, unregenerate, irrational man will do anything, even against his self-interest, to maintain the freedom that makes him human, to keep from being a mere "organ-stop" or "piano-key" in Chernyshevsky's Crystal Palace. The complexity and the comic irony of the story, and what raises it above the level of a satire on a long-forgotten novel, is that the underground man is not just a mouthpiece for Dostoevsky's ideas but an unforgettable character, crankily haranguing his imagined Chernyshevskian listeners on behalf of human freedom while at the same time demonstrating his own bondage, paralysis, and cruelty.

The dirty, spiteful, human "louse" of *Notes from Underground* seems very far from the Ivan Karamazov of "The Grand Inquisitor," but they are spiritual brothers. The Karamazov brothers—long separated but brought together by circumstances leading up to and including the murder of their drunken, profligate father—are all underground men, acutely self-conscious, deeply divided within themselves, torn between violent extremes. Each has made an existential, "underground" choice of self-definition, Dmitri of evil and Alyosha of saintliness, while the haunted Ivan has chosen rationalistic nihilism. (Criminal, saint, and rationalist are recurring figures throughout Dostoevsky's fiction.)

In "The Grand Inquisitor," Ivan Karamazov unfolds for his shocked brother Alyosha a sardonic view of human nature and of human history. The Grand Inquisitor speaks for Catholicism, but he might as well speak for socialism or "nihilism," any system which would deprive humans of their moral freedom in return for the comforting security of "miracle, mystery, and authority." The Inquisitor thinks of himself as the benefactor of mankind; he and his Church know that the mass of humanity cannot

bear the terrible burden of freedom which Christ laid upon them by refusing Satan's comforting escapes of bread, miracles, and authority, and so they have supplied these means of escape. The Inquisitor is satanically persuasive, but his counsel of moral slavery is refuted by Christ's silent kiss at the end, an act implying what the saintly Father Zossima makes explicit in the following section, that harmony is not attained through the reason but through freedom and love.

FURTHER READING (*prepared by W. J. R.*): Joseph Frank's four-volume critical biography of Dostoevsky, of which three volumes have appeared (1976, 1986, and 1986), is the fullest and most reliable account of Dostoevsky's life and works. Victor Terras's *F. M. Dostoevsky: Life, Work, and Criticism*, 1984, is a fine brief treatment. Ronald Hingley's well-illustrated *Dostoevsky, His Life and Work*, 1978, discusses the major works and some of the minor ones. William J. Leatherbarrow's *Fedor Dostoevsky*, 1981, contains good introductory discussions of *Crime and Punishment*, *The Idiot*, and several other works. John Jones' *Dostoevsky*, 1983; Robert L. Jackson's *Dostoevsky*, 1984; and Roger B. Anderson's *Dostoevsky: Myths of Duality*, 1986, are all valuable introductions. Collections of critical essays include *Dostoevsky: A Collection of Critical Essays*, ed. by René Wellek, 1962; *New Essays on Dostoevsky*, ed. by Malcolm V. Jones and Garth M. Terry, 1983; and *Dostoevsky and the Human Condition After a Century*, ed. by Alexej Ugrinsky, Frank S. Lambaska, and Valija K. Ozolino, 1986.

NOTES FROM UNDERGROUND[1]

Translated by Constance Garnett

PART I

UNDERGROUND

I

I am a sick man. . . . I am a spiteful man. I am an unattractive man. I believe my liver is diseased. However, I know nothing at all about my disease, and do not know for certain what ails me. I don't consult a doctor for it, and never have, though I have a respect for medicine and doctors. Besides, I am extremely superstitious, sufficiently so to respect medicine, anyway (I am well-educated enough not to be superstitious, but I am superstitious). No, I refuse to consult a doctor from spite. That you probably will not understand. Well, I understand it, though. Of course I can't explain

[1] The author of the diary and the diary itself are, of course, imaginary. Nevertheless, it is clear that such persons as the writer of these notes not only may, but positively must, exist in our society, when we consider the circumstances in the midst of which our society is formed. I have tried to expose to the view of the public, more distinctly than is commonly done, one of the characters of the recent past. He is one of the representatives of a generation still living. In this fragment, entitled "Underground," this person introduces himself and his views, and, as it were, tries to explain the causes owing to which he has made his appearance and was bound to make his appearance in our midst. In the second fragment there are added the actual notes of this person concerning certain events in his life. (Dostoevsky's note.)

who it is precisely that I am mortifying in this case by my spite: I am perfectly well aware that I cannot "pay out" the doctors by not consulting them; I know better than any one that by all this I am only injuring myself and no one else. But still, if I don't consult a doctor it is from spite. My liver is bad, well—let it get worse!

I have been going on like that for a long time—twenty years. Now I am forty. I used to be in the government service, but am no longer. I was a spiteful official. I was rude and took pleasure in being so. I did not take bribes, you see, so I was bound to find a recompense in that, at least. (A poor jest, but I will not scratch it out. I wrote it thinking it would sound very witty; but now that I have seen myself that I only wanted to show off in a despicable way, I will not scratch it out on purpose!)

When petitioners used to come for information to the table at which I sat, I used to grind my teeth at them, and felt intense enjoyment when I succeeded in making anybody unhappy. I almost always did succeed. For the most part they were all timid people—of course, they were petitioners. But of the uppish ones there was one officer in particular I could not endure. He simply would not be humble, and clanked his sword in a disgusting way. I carried on a feud with him for eighteen months over that sword. At last I got the better of him. He left off clanking it. That happened in my youth, though.

But do you know, gentlemen, what was the chief point about my spite? Why, the whole point, the real sting of it lay in the fact that continually, even in the moment of the acutest spleen, I was inwardly conscious with shame that I was not only not a spiteful but not even an embittered man, that I was simply scaring sparrows at random and amusing myself by it. I might foam at the mouth, but bring me a doll to play with, give me a cup of tea with sugar in it, and maybe I should be appeased. I might even be genuinely touched, though probably I should grind my teeth at myself afterwards and lie awake at night with shame for months after. That was my way.

I was lying when I said just now that I was a spiteful official. I was lying from spite. I was simply amusing myself with the petitioners and with the officer, and in reality I never could become spiteful. I was conscious every moment in myself of many, very many elements absolutely opposite to that. I felt them positively swarming in me, these opposite elements. I knew that they had been swarming in me all my life and craving some outlet from me, but I would not let them, would not let them, purposely would not let them come out. They tormented me till I was ashamed: they drove me to convulsions and—sickened me, at last, how they sickened me! Now, are not you fancying, gentlemen, that I am expressing remorse for something now, that I am asking your forgiveness for something? I am sure you are fancying that . . . However, I assure you I do not care if you are. . . .[2]

It was not only that I could not become spiteful, I did not know how to become anything: neither spiteful nor kind, neither a rascal nor an honest man, neither a hero nor an insect. Now, I am living out my life in my corner, taunting myself with the spiteful and useless consolation that an

[2] Here, as elsewhere in the text, repeated periods do not indicate an omission but are punctuation marks.

intelligent man cannot become anything seriously, and it is only the fool who becomes anything. Yes, a man in the nineteenth century must and morally ought to be pre-eminently a characterless creature; a man of character, an active man is preeminently a limited creature. That is my conviction of forty years. I am forty years old now, and you know forty years is a whole lifetime; you know it is extreme old age. To live longer than forty years is bad manners, is vulgar, immoral. Who lives beyond forty? Answer that, sincerely and honestly. I will tell you who do: fools and worthless fellows. I tell all old men that to their face, all these venerable old men, all these silver-haired and reverend seniors! I tell the whole world that to its face! I have a right to say so, for I shall go on living to sixty myself. To seventy! To eighty! . . . Stay, let me take breath. . . .

You imagine no doubt, gentlemen, that I want to amuse you. You are mistaken in that, too. I am by no means such a mirthful person as you imagine, or as you may imagine; however, irritated by all this babble (and I feel that you are irritated) you think fit to ask me who am I—then my answer is, I am a collegiate assessor.[3] I was in the service that I might have something to eat (and solely for that reason), and when last year a distant relation left me six thousand roubles in his will I immediately retired from the service and settled down in my corner. I used to live in this corner before, but now I have settled down in it. My room is a wretched, horrid one in the outskirts of the town. My servant is an old country-woman, ill-natured from stupidity, and, moreover, there is always a nasty smell about her. I am told that the Petersburg climate is bad for me, and that with my small means it is very expensive to live in Petersburg. I know all that better than all these sage and experienced counsellors and monitors. . . . But I am remaining in Petersburg; . . . I am not going away from Petersburg! I am not going away because . . . ech! Why, it is absolutely no matter whether I am going away or not going away.

But what can a decent man speak of with most pleasure?

Answer: Of himself.

Well, so I will talk about myself.

II

I want now to tell you, gentlemen, whether you care to hear it or not, why I could not even become an insect. I tell you solemnly, that I have many times tried to become an insect. But I was not equal even to that. I swear, gentlemen, that to be too conscious is an illness—a real thoroughgoing illness. For man's everyday needs, it would have been quite enough to have the ordinary human consciousness, that is, half or a quarter of the amount which falls to the lot of a cultivated man of our unhappy nineteenth century, especially one who has the fatal ill-luck to inhabit Petersburg, the most theoretical and intentional town on the whole terrestrial globe. (There are intentional and unintentional towns.) It would have been quite enough, for instance, to have the consciousness by which all so-called direct persons and men of action live. I bet you think I am writing all this from affectation, to

[3] A minor civil servant.

be witty at the expense of men of action; and what is more, that from ill-bred affectation, I am clanking a sword like my officer. But, gentlemen, whoever can pride himself on his diseases and even swagger over them?

Though, after all, every one does do that; people do pride themselves on their diseases, and I do, may be, more than any one else. We will not dispute it; my contention was absurd. But yet I am firmly persuaded that a great deal of consciousness, every sort of consciousness, in fact, is a disease. I stick to that. Let us leave that, too, for a minute. Tell me this: why does it happen that at the very, yes, at the very moments when I am most capable of feeling every refinement of all that is "good and beautiful," as they used to say at one time, it would, as though of design, happen to me not only to feel but to do such ugly things, such that . . . Well, in short, actions that all, perhaps, commit; but which, as though purposely, occurred to me at the very time when I was most conscious that they ought not to be committed. The more conscious I was of goodness and of all that was "good and beautiful," the more deeply I sank into my mire and the more ready I was to sink in it altogether. But the chief point was that all this was, as it were, not accidental in me, but as though it were bound to be so. It was as though it were my most normal condition, and not in the least disease or depravity, so that at last all desire in me to struggle against this depravity passed. It ended by my almost believing (perhaps actually believing) that this was perhaps my normal condition. But at first, in the beginning, what agonies I endured in that struggle! I did not believe it was the same with other people, and all my life I hid this fact about myself as a secret. I was ashamed (even now, perhaps, I am ashamed): I got to the point of feeling a sort of secret abnormal, despicable enjoyment in returning home to my corner on some disgusting Petersburg night, acutely conscious that that day I had committed a loathsome action again, that what was done could never be undone, and secretly, inwardly gnawing, gnawing at myself for it, tearing and consuming myself till at last the bitterness turned into a sort of shameful accursed sweetness, and at last—into positive real enjoyment! Yes into enjoyment, into enjoyment! I insist upon that. I have spoken of this because I keep wanting to know for a fact whether other people feel such enjoyment? I will explain; the enjoyment was just from the too intense consciousness of one's own degradation; it was from feeling oneself that one had reached the last barrier, that it was horrible, but that it could not be otherwise; that there was no escape for you; that you never could become a different man; that even if time and faith were still left you to change into something different you would most likely not wish to change; or if you did wish to, even then you would do nothing; because perhaps in reality there was nothing for you to change into.

And the worst of it was, and the root of it all, that it was all in accord with the normal fundamental laws of over-acute consciousness, and with the inertia that was the direct result of those laws, and that consequently one was not only unable to change but could do absolutely nothing. Thus it would follow, as the result of acute consciousness, that one is not to blame in being a scoundrel; as though that were any consolation to the scoundrel once he has come to realize that he actually is a scoundrel. But enough. . . . Ech, I have talked a lot of nonsense, but what have I explained? How

is enjoyment in this to be explained? But I will explain it. I will get to the bottom of it! That is why I have taken up my pen. . . .

I, for instance, have a great deal of *amour propre*.[4] I am as suspicious and prone to take offense as a hunchback or a dwarf. But upon my word I sometimes have had moments when if I had happened to be slapped in the face I should, perhaps, have been positively glad of it. I say, in earnest, that I should probably have been able to discover even in that a peculiar sort of enjoyment—the enjoyment, of course, of despair; but in despair there are the most intense enjoyments, especially when one is very acutely conscious of the hopelessness of one's position. And when one is slapped in the face—why then the consciousness of being rubbed into a pulp would positively overwhelm one. The worst of it is, look at it which way one will, it still turns out that I was always the most to blame in everything. And what is most humiliating of all, to blame for no fault of my own but, so to say, through the laws of nature. In the first place, to blame because I am cleverer than any of the people surrounding me. (I have always considered myself cleverer than any of the people surrounding me, and sometimes, would you believe it, have been positively ashamed of it. At any rate, I have all my life, as it were, turned my eyes away and never could look people straight in the face.) To blame, finally, because even if I had had magnanimity, I should only have had more suffering from the sense of its uselessness. I should certainly have never been able to do anything from being magnanimous—neither to forgive, for my assailant would perhaps have slapped me from the laws of nature, and one cannot forgive the laws of nature; nor to forget, for even if it were owing to the laws of nature, it is insulting all the same. Finally, even if I had wanted to be anything but magnanimous, had desired on the contrary to revenge myself on my assailant, I could not have revenged myself on any one for anything because I should certainly never have made up my mind to do anything, even if I had been able to. Why should I not have made up my mind? About that in particular I want to say a few words.

III

With people who know how to revenge themselves and to stand up for themselves in general, how is it done? Why, when they are possessed, let us suppose, by the feeling of revenge, then for the time there is nothing else but that feeling left in their whole being. Such a gentleman simply dashes straight for his object like an infuriated bull with its horns down, and nothing but a wall will stop him. (By the way: facing the wall, such gentlemen— that is, the "direct" persons and men of action—are genuinely nonplussed. For them a wall is not an evasion, as for us people who think and consequently do nothing; it is not an excuse for turning aside, an excuse for which we are always very glad, though we scarcely believe in it ourselves, as a rule. No, they are nonplussed in all sincerity. The wall has for them something tranquillizing, morally soothing, final—maybe even something mysterious . . . but of the wall later.)

Well, such a direct person I regard as the real normal man, as his tender mother nature wished to see him when she graciously brought him into

[4] Self-esteem.

being on the earth. I envy such a man till I am green in the face. He is
stupid. I am not disputing that, but perhaps the normal man should be
stupid, how do you know? Perhaps it is very beautiful, in fact. And I am the
more persuaded of that suspicion, if one can call it so, by the fact that if you
take, for instance, the antithesis of the normal man, that is, the man of
acute consciousness, who has come, of course, not out of the lap of nature
but out of a retort (this is almost mysticism, gentlemen, but I suspect this,
too), this retort-made man is sometimes so nonplussed in the presence of
his antithesis that with all his exaggerated consciousness he genuinely
thinks of himself as a mouse and not a man. It may be an acutely conscious
mouse, yet it is a mouse, while the other is a man, and therefore, et cetera,
et cetera. And the worst of it is, he himself, his very own self, looks on
himself as a mouse; no one asks him to do so; and that is an important
point. Now let us look at this mouse in action. Let us suppose, for instance,
that it feels insulted, too (and it almost always does feel insulted), and wants
to revenge itself, too. There may even be a greater accumulation of spite
in it than in *l'homme de la nature et de la vérité*.[5] The base and nasty desire to
vent that spite on its assailant rankles perhaps even more nastily in it than
in *l'homme de la nature et de la vérité*. For through his innate stupidity the
latter looks upon his revenge as justice pure and simple; while in conse-
quence of his acute consciousness the mouse does not believe in the justice
of it. To come at last to the deed itself, to the very act of revenge. Apart
from the one fundamental nastiness the luckless mouse succeeds in creat-
ing around it so many other nastinesses in the form of doubts and ques-
tions, adds to the one question so many unsettled questions that there inevi-
tably works up around it a sort of fatal brew, a stinking mess, made up of its
doubts, emotions, and of the contempt spat upon it by the direct men of
action who stand solemnly about it as judges and arbitrators, laughing at it
till their healthy sides ache. Of course the only thing left for it is to dismiss
all that with a wave of its paw, and, with a smile of assumed contempt in
which it does not even itself believe, creep ignominiously into its mouse-
hole. There in its nasty, stinking, underground home our insulted, crushed
and ridiculed mouse promptly becomes absorbed in cold, malignant and,
above all, everlasting spite. For forty years together it will remember its
injury down to the smallest, most ignominious details, and every time will
add, of itself, details still more ignominious, spitefully teasing and torment-
ing itself with its own imagination. It will itself be ashamed of its imagin-
ings, but yet it will recall it all, it will go over and over every detail, it will
invent unheard of things against itself, pretending that those things might
happen, and will forgive nothing. Maybe it will begin to revenge itself, too,
but, as it were, piecemeal, in trivial ways, from behind the stove, incognito,
without believing either in its own right to vengeance, or in the success of
its revenge, knowing that from all its efforts at revenge it will suffer a hun-
dred times more than he on whom it revenges itself, while he, I daresay,
will not even scratch himself. On its deathbed it will recall it all over again,
with interest accumulated over all the years and. . . .

But it is just in that cold, abominable half despair, half belief, in that

[5] "The man of nature and of truth." This is the phrase Rousseau uses to describe himself in
his *Confessions* (1781–88), somewhat disingenuously, the speaker suggests.

conscious burying oneself alive for grief in the underworld for forty years, in that acutely recognized and yet partly doubtful hopelessness of one's position, in that hell of unsatisfied desires turned inward, in that fever of oscillations, or resolutions determined for ever and repented of again a minute later—that the savor of that strange enjoyment of which I have spoken lies. It is so subtle, so difficult of analysis, that persons who are a little limited, or even simply persons of strong nerves, will not understand a single atom of it. "Possibly," you will add on your own account with a grin, "people will not understand it either who have never received a slap in the face," and in that way you will politely hint to me that I, too, perhaps, have had the experience of a slap in the face in my life, and so I speak as one who knows. I bet that you are thinking that. But set your minds at rest, gentlemen, I have not received a slap in the face, though it is absolutely a matter of indifference to me what you may think about it. Possibly, I even regret, myself, that I have given so few slaps in the face during my life. But enough . . . not another word on that subject of such extreme interest to you.

I will continue calmly concerning persons with strong nerves who do not understand a certain refinement of enjoyment. Though in certain circumstances these gentlemen bellow their loudest like bulls, though this, let us suppose, does them the greatest credit, yet, as I have said already, confronted with the impossible they subside at once. The impossible means the stone wall! What stone wall? Why, of course, the laws of nature, the deductions of natural science, mathematics. As soon as they prove to you, for instance, that you are descended from a monkey, then it is no use scowling, accept it for a fact. When they prove to you that in reality one drop of your own fat must be dearer to you than a hundred thousand of your fellow-creatures, and that this conclusion is the final solution of all so-called virtues and duties and all such prejudices and fancies, then you have just to accept it, there is no help for it, for twice two is a law of mathematics. Just try refuting it.

"Upon my word," they will shout at you, "it is no use protesting: it is a case of twice two makes four! Nature does not ask your permission, she has nothing to do with your wishes, and whether you like her laws or dislike them, you are bound to accept her as she is, and consequently all her conclusions. A wall, you see, is a wall . . ." and so on, and so on.

Merciful Heavens! but what do I care for the laws of nature and arithmetic, when, for some reason I dislike those laws and the fact that twice two makes four? Of course I cannot break through the wall by battering my head against it if I really have not the strength to knock it down, but I am not going to be reconciled to it simply because it is a stone wall and I have not the strength.

As though such a stone wall really were a consolation, and really did contain some word of conciliation, simply because it is as true as twice two makes four. Oh, absurdity of absurdities! How much better it is to understand it all, to recognize it all, all the impossibilities and the stone wall; not to be reconciled to one of those impossibilities and stone walls if it disgusts you to be reconciled to it; by the way of the most inevitable, logical combinations to reach the most revolting conclusions on the everlasting theme, that even for the stone wall you are yourself somehow to blame, though

again it is as clear as day you are not to blame in the least, and therefore grinding your teeth in silent impotence to sink into luxurious inertia, brooding on the fact that there is no one even for you to feel vindictive against, that you have not, and perhaps never will have, an object for your spite, that it is a sleight of hand, a bit of juggling, a card-sharper's trick, that it is simply a mess, no knowing what and no knowing who, but in spite of all these uncertainties and jugglings, still there is an ache in you, and the more you do not know, the worse the ache.

<div align="center">IV</div>

"Ha, ha, ha! You will be finding enjoyment in toothache next," you cry, with a laugh.

"Well? Even in toothache there is enjoyment," I answer. I had toothache for a whole month and I know there is. In that case, of course, people are not spiteful in silence, but moan; but they are not candid moans, they are malignant moans, and the malignancy is the whole point. The enjoyment of the sufferer finds expression in those moans; if he did not feel enjoyment in them he would not moan. It is a good example, gentlemen, and I will develop it. Those moans express in the first place all the aimlessness of your pain, which is so humiliating to your consciousness; the whole legal system of nature on which you spit disdainfully, of course, but from which you suffer all the same while she does not. They express the consciousness that you have no enemy to punish, but that you have pain; the consciousness that in spite of all possible Wagenheims[6] you are in complete slavery to your teeth; that if some one wishes it, your teeth will leave off aching, and if he does not, they will go on aching another three months; and that finally if you are still contumacious and still protest, all that is left you for your own gratification is to thrash yourself or beat your wall with your fist as hard as you can, and absolutely nothing more. Well, these mortal insults, these jeers on the part of some one unknown, end at last in an enjoyment which sometimes reaches the highest degree of voluptuousness. I ask you, gentlemen, listen sometimes to the moans of an educated man of the nineteenth century suffering from toothache, on the second or third day of the attack, when he is beginning to moan, not as he moaned on the first day, that is, not simply because he has toothache, not just as any coarse peasant, but as a man affected by progress and European civilization, a man who is "divorced from the soil and the national elements," as they express it nowadays. His moans become nasty, disgustingly malignant, and go on for whole days and nights. And of course he knows himself that he is doing himself no sort of good with his moans; he knows better than any one that he is only lacerating and harassing himself and others for nothing; he knows that even the audience before whom he is making his efforts, and his whole family, listen to him with loathing, do not put the least faith in him, and inwardly understand that he might moan differently, more simply, without trills and flourishes, and that he is only amusing himself like that from ill-humor, from malignancy. Well, in all these recognitions and disgraces it is that there lies a voluptuous pleasure. As though he would

[6]Two dentists, both named Wagenheim, advertised "painless dentistry" in the Petersburg newspaper in 1864.

say: "I am worrying you, I am lacerating your hearts, I am keeping every one in the house awake. Well, stay awake then, you, too, feel every minute that I have toothache. I am not a hero to you now, as I tried to seem before, but simply a nasty person, an impostor. Well, so be it, then! I am very glad that you see through me. It is nasty for you to hear my despicable moans: well, let it be nasty; here I will let you have a nastier flourish in a minute" You do not understand even now, gentlemen? No, it seems our development and our consciousness must go further to understand all the intricacies of this pleasure. You laugh? Delighted. My jests, gentlemen, are of course in bad taste, jerky, involved, lacking self-confidence. But of course that is because I do not respect myself. Can a man of perception respect himself at all?

<div align="center">V</div>

Come, can a man who attempts to find enjoyment in the very feeling of his own degradation possibly have a spark of respect for himself? I am not saying this now from any mawkish kind of remorse. And, indeed, I could never endure saying, "Forgive me, Papa, I won't do it again," not because I am incapable of saying that—on the contrary, perhaps just because I have been too capable of it, and in what a way, too! As though of design I used to get into trouble in cases when I was not to blame in any way. That was the nastiest part of it. At the same time I was genuinely touched and penitent, I used to shed tears and, of course, deceived myself, though I was not acting in the least and there was a sick feeling in my heart at the time. . . . For that one could not blame even the laws of nature, though the laws of nature have continually all my life offended me more than anything. It is loathsome to remember it all, but it was loathsome even then. Of course, a minute or so later I would realize wrathfully that it was all a lie, a revolting lie, an affected lie, that is, all this penitence, this emotion, these vows of reform. You will ask why did I worry myself with such antics: answer, because it was very dull to sit with one's hands folded, and so one began cutting capers. That is really it. Observe yourselves more carefully, gentlemen, then you will understand that it is so. I invented adventures for myself and made up a life, so as at least to live in some way. How many times it has happened to me—well, for instance, to take offense simply on purpose, for nothing; and one knows oneself, of course, that one is offended at nothing, that one is putting it on, but yet one brings oneself, at last, to the point of being really offended. All my life I have had an impulse to play such pranks, so that in the end I could not control it in myself. Another time, twice, in fact, I tried hard to be in love. I suffered, too, gentlemen, I assure you. In the depth of my heart there was no faith in my suffering, only a faint stir of mockery, but yet I did suffer, and in the real, orthodox way; I was jealous, beside myself . . . and it was all from *ennui*,[7] gentlemen, all from *ennui;* inertia overcame me. You know the direct, legitimate fruit of consciousness is inertia, that is, conscious sitting-with-the-hands-folded. I have referred to this already. I repeat, I repeat with emphasis: all "direct" persons and men of action are active just because they are stupid and limited. How explain that? I will tell you: in consequence of their limitation

[7] A feeling of weariness or dissatisfaction.

they take immediate and secondary causes for primary ones, and in that way persuade themselves more quickly and easily than other people do that they have found an infallible foundation for their activity, and their minds are at ease and you know that is the chief thing. To begin to act, you know, you must first have your mind completely at ease and no trace of doubt left in it. Why, how am I, for example, to set my mind at rest? Where are the primary causes on which I am to build? Where are my foundations? Where am I to get them from? I exercise myself in reflection, and consequently with me every primary cause at once draws after itself another still more primary, and so on to infinity. That is just the essence of every sort of consciousness and reflection. It must be a case of the laws of nature again. What is the result of it in the end? Why, just the same. Remember I spoke just now of vengeance. (I am sure you did not take it in.) I said that a man revenges himself because he sees justice in it. Therefore he has found a primary cause, that is, justice. And so he is at rest on all sides, and consequently he carries out his revenge calmly and successfully, being persuaded that he is doing a just and honest thing. But I see no justice in it, I find no sort of virtue in it either, and consequently if I attempt to revenge myself, it is only out of spite. Spite, of course, might overcome everything, all my doubts, and so might serve quite successfully in place of a primary cause, precisely because it is not a cause. But what is to be done if I have not even spite (I began with that just now, you know)? In consequence again of those accursed laws of consciousness, anger in me is subject to chemical disintegration. You look into it, the object flies off into air, your reasons evaporate, the criminal is not to be found, the wrong becomes not a wrong but a phantom, something like the toothache, for which no one is to blame, and consequently there is only the same outlet left again—that is, to beat the wall as hard as you can. So you give it up with a wave of the hand because you have not found a fundamental cause. And try letting yourself be carried away by your feelings, blindly, without reflection, without a primary cause, repelling consciousness at least for a time; hate or love, if only not to sit with your hands folded. The day after tomorrow, at the latest, you will begin despising yourself for having knowingly deceived yourself. Result: a soap-bubble and inertia. Oh, gentlemen, do you know, perhaps I consider myself an intelligent man, only because all my life I have been able neither to begin nor to finish anything. Granted I am a babbler,[8] a harmless vexatious babbler, like all of us. But what is to be done if the direct and sole vocation of every intelligent man is babble, that is, the intentional pouring of water through a sieve?

VI

Oh, if I had done nothing simply from laziness! Heavens, how I should have respected myself, then. I should have respected myself because I should at least have been capable of being lazy; there would at least have been one quality, as it were, positive in me, in which I could have believed myself. Question: What is he? Answer: A sluggard; how very pleasant it would have been to hear that of oneself! It would mean that I was positively defined, it would mean that there was something to say about me. "Slug-

[8] One who chatters or talks excessively.

gard"—why, it is a calling and vocation, it is a career. Do not jest, it is so. I should then be a member of the best club by right, and should find my occupation in continually respecting myself. I knew a gentlemen who prided himself all his life on being a connoisseur of Lafitte.[9] He considered this as his positive virtue, and never doubted himself. He died, not simply with a tranquil, but with a triumphant, conscience, and he was quite right, too. Then I should have chosen a career for myself, I should have been a sluggard and a glutton, not a simple one, but, for instance, one with sympathies for everything good and beautiful. How do you like that? I have long had visions of it. That "good and beautiful" weighs heavily on my mind at forty. But that is at forty; then—oh, then it would have been different! I should have found for myself a form of activity in keeping with it, to be precise, drinking to the health of everything "good and beautiful." I should have snatched at every opportunity to drop a tear into my glass and then to drain it to all that is "good and beautiful." I should then have turned everything into the good and the beautiful; in the nastiest, unquestionable trash, I should have sought out the good and the beautiful. I should have exuded tears like a wet sponge. An artist, for instance, paints a picture worthy of Gay.[10] At once I drink to the health of the artist who painted the picture worthy of Gay, because I love all that is "good and beautiful." An author has written *What you will:*[11] at once I drink to the health of "what you will" because I love all that is "good and beautiful."

I should claim respect for doing so. I should persecute any one who would not show me respect. I should live at ease, I should die with dignity, why, it is charming, perfectly charming! And what a good round belly I should have grown, what a triple chin I should have established, what a ruby nose I should have colored for myself, so that every one would have said, looking at me: "Here is an asset! Here is something real and solid!" And, say what you like, it is very agreeable to hear such remarks about oneself in this negative age.

VII

But these are all golden dreams. Oh, tell me, who was it first announced, who was it first proclaimed, that man only does nasty things because he does not know his own interests; and that if he were enlightened, if his eyes were opened to his real normal interests, man would at once cease to do nasty things, would at once become good and noble because, being enlightened and understanding his real advantage, he would see his own advantage in the good and nothing else, and we all know that not one man can, consciously, act against his own interests, consequently, so to say, through necessity, he would begin doing good? Oh, the babe! Oh, the pure, innocent child! Why, in the first place, when in all these thousands of years has there been a time when man has acted only from his own interest? What is to be done with the millions of facts that bear witness that men, *consciously*, that is fully understanding their real interests, have left them in the background and have rushed headlong on another path, to meet peril and danger, compelled to this course by nobody and by nothing, but, as it were,

[9] A kind of wine.　　[10] Nikolay Nikolaevich Gay, a popular painter of historical subjects.
[11] The subtitle of Shakespeare's *Twelfth Night*.

simply disliking the beaten track, and have obstinately, willfully, struck out
another difficult, absurd way, seeking it almost in the darkness. So, I sup-
pose, this obstinacy and perversity were pleasanter to them than any advan-
tage. . . . Advantage! What is advantage? And will you take it upon yourself
to define with perfect accuracy in what the advantage of man consists? And
what if it so happens that a man's advantage, *sometimes*, not only may, but
even must, consist in his desiring in certain cases what is harmful to himself
and not advantageous. And if so, if there can be such a case, the whole
principle falls into dust. What do you think—are there such cases? You
laugh; laugh away, gentlemen, but only answer me: have man's advantages
been reckoned up with perfect certainty? Are there not some which not
only have not been included but cannot possibly be included under any
classification? You see, you gentlemen have, to the best of my knowledge,
taken your whole register of human advantages from the averages of statis-
tical figures and politico-economical formulas. Your advantages are pros-
perity, wealth, freedom, peace—and so on, and so on. So that the man who
should, for instance, go openly and knowingly in opposition to all that list
would, to your thinking, and indeed mine, too, of course, be an obscurant-
ist[12] or an absolute madman: would not he? But, you know, this is what is
surprising: why does it so happen that all these statisticians, sages and lov-
ers of humanity, when they reckon up human advantages invariably leave
out one? They don't even take it into their reckoning in the form in which it
should be taken, and the whole reckoning depends upon that. It would be
no great matter, they would simply have to take it, this advantage, and add
it to the list. But the trouble is, that this strange advantage does not fall
under any classification and is not in place in any list. I have a friend for
instance . . . Ech! gentlemen, but of course he is your friend, too; and
indeed there is no one, no one, to whom he is not a friend! When he
prepares for any undertaking this gentleman immediately explains to you,
elegantly and clearly, exactly how he must act in accordance with the laws
of reason and truth. What is more, he will talk to you with excitement and
passion of the true normal interests of man; with irony he will upbraid the
shortsighted fools who do not understand their own interests, nor the true
significance of virtue; and, within a quarter of an hour, without any sudden
outside provocation, but simply through something inside him which is
stronger than all his interests, he will go off on quite a different tack—that
is, act in direct opposition to what he has just been saying about himself, in
opposition to the laws of reason, in opposition to his own advantage, in fact
in opposition to everything . . . I warn you that my friend is a compound
personality, and therefore it is difficult to blame him as an individual. The
fact is, gentlemen, it seems there must really exist something that is dearer
to almost every man than his greatest advantages, or (not to be illogical)
there is a most advantageous advantage (the very one omitted of which we
spoke just now) which is more important and more advantageous than all
other advantages, for the sake of which a man if necessary is ready to act in
opposition to all laws; that is, in opposition to reason, honor, peace, pros-
perity—in fact, in opposition to all those excellent and useful things if only
he can attain that fundamental, most advantageous advantage which is

[12]One who deliberately tries to make things obscure or vague.

dearer to him than all. "Yes, but it's advantage all the same," you will retort. But excuse me, I'll make the point clear, and it is not a case of playing upon words. What matters is, that this advantage is remarkable from the very fact that it breaks down all our classifications, and continually shatters every system constructed by lovers of mankind for the benefit of mankind. In fact, it upsets everything. But before I mention this advantage to you, I want to compromise myself personally, and therefore I boldly declare that all these fine systems, all these theories for explaining to mankind their real normal interests, in order that inevitably striving to pursue these interests they may at once become good and noble—are, in my opinion, so far, mere logical exercises! Yes, logical exercises. Why, to maintain this theory of the regeneration of mankind by means of the pursuit of his own advantage is to my mind almost the same thing as . . . as to affirm, for instance, following Buckle,[13] that through civilization mankind becomes softer, and consequently less bloodthirsty and less fitted for warfare. Logically it does seem to follow from his arguments. But man has such a predilection for systems and abstract deductions that he is ready to distort the truth intentionally, he is ready to deny the evidence of his senses only to justify his logic. I take this example because it is the most glaring instance of it. Only look about you: blood is being spilt in streams, and in the merriest way, as though it were champagne. Take the whole of the nineteenth century in which Buckle lived. Take Napoleon—the Great and also the present one. Take North America—the eternal union. Take the farce of Schleswig-Holstein.[14] . . . And what is it that civilization softens in us? The only gain of civilization for mankind is the greater capacity for variety of sensations—and absolutely nothing more. And through the development of this many-sidedness man may come to finding enjoyment in bloodshed. In fact, this has already happened to him. Have you noticed that it is the most civilized gentlemen who have been the subtlest slaughterers, to whom the Attilas[15] and Stenka Razins[16] could not hold a candle, and if they are not so conspicuous as the Attilas and Stenka Razins it is simply because they are so often met with, are so ordinary and have become so familiar to us. In any case civilization has made mankind if not more bloodthirsty, at least more vilely, more loathsomely bloodthirsty. In old days he saw justice in bloodshed and with his conscience at peace exterminated those he thought proper. Now we do think bloodshed abominable and yet we engage in this abomination, and with more energy than ever. Which is worse? Decide that for yourselves. They say that Cleopatra (excuse an instance from Roman history) was fond of sticking gold pins into her slave-girls' breasts and derived gratification from their screams and writhings. You will say that that was in the comparatively barbarous times; that these are barbarous times too, because also, comparatively speaking, pins are stuck in even now; that though man has

[13] Henry Thomas Buckle, in his popular *History of Civilization in England* (1857–61), maintained the thesis the speaker summarizes.

[14] An area disputed by Germany and Denmark and the subject of the Dano-Prussian War (1864). The English Lord Palmerston once said that of the three men who had ever understood the Schleswig-Holstein dispute, one was dead (Prince Albert), one was insane (a professor), and the third (Palmerston himself) had forgotten it.

[15] Attila was a notorious fifth-century A.D. King of the Huns.

[16] Stenka Razin was a seventeenth-century Cossack leader, noted for his fierce conquests.

now learned to see more clearly than in barbarous ages, he is still far from having learned to act as reason and science would dictate. But yet you are fully convinced that he will be sure to learn when he gets rid of certain old bad habits, and when common sense and science have completely re-educated human nature and turned it in a normal direction. You are confident that then man will cease from *intentional* error and will, so to say, be compelled not to want to set his will against his normal interests. That is not all; then, you say, science itself will teach man (though to my mind it's a superfluous luxury) that he never has really had any caprice or will of his own, and that he himself is something of the nature of a piano-key or the stop of an organ, and that there are, besides, things called the laws of nature; so that everything he does is not done by his willing it, but is done of itself, by the laws of nature. Consequently we have only to discover these laws of nature, and man will no longer have to answer for his actions and life will become exceedingly easy for him. All human actions will then, of course, be tabulated according to these laws, mathematically, like tables of logarithms up to 108,000, and entered in an index; or, better still, there would be published certain edifying works of the nature of encyclopedic lexicons, in which everything will be so clearly calculated and explained that there will be no more incidents or adventures in the world.

Then—this is all what you say—new economic relations will be established, all ready-made and worked out with mathematical exactitude, so that every possible question will vanish in the twinkling of an eye, simply because every possible answer to it will be provided. Then the "Crystal Palace"[17] will be built. Then In fact, those will be halcyon days. Of course there is no guaranteeing (this is my comment) that it will not be, for instance, frightfully dull then (for what will one have to do when everything will be calculated and tabulated), but on the other hand everything will be extraordinarily rational. Of course boredom may lead you to anything. It is boredom sets one sticking golden pins into people, but all that would not matter. What is bad (this is my comment again) is that I dare say people will be thankful for the gold pins then. Man is stupid, you know, phenomenally stupid; or rather he is not at all stupid, but he is so ungrateful that you could not find another like him in all creation. I, for instance, would not be in the least surprised if all of a sudden, *à propos* of nothing, in the midst of general prosperity a gentleman with an ignoble, or rather with a reactionary and ironical, countenance were to arise and, putting his arms akimbo, say to us all: "I say, gentlemen, hadn't we better kick over the whole show and scatter rationalism to the winds, simply to send these logarithms to the devil, and to enable us to live once more at our own sweet foolish will!" That again would not matter, but what is annoying is that he would be sure to find followers—such is the nature of man. And all that for

[17] The speaker is alluding to the utopian society, organized on wholly rational principles, in Nikolai Chernyshevsky's didactic novel *What Is To Be Done?* (1863). Chernyshevsky's "Crystal Palace" is closely based on the utopian "phalansteries" projected by the French social philosopher Charles Fourier (1772–1837), hypothetical communities so meticulously planned that one critic remarked that they were "the Arcadias of a bureaucrat." Chernyshevsky, for the name and architecture of his utopia (a great dome of iron and glass), drew upon London's Crystal Palace, built for the Great Exhibition of 1851 and widely regarded as a marvel of progressive architecture.

the most foolish reason, which, one would think, was hardly worth mentioning: that is, that man everywhere and at all times, whoever he may be, has preferred to act as he chose and not in the least as his reason and advantage dictated. And one may choose what is contrary to one's own interests, and sometimes one *positively ought* (that is my idea). One's own free unfettered choice, one's own caprice, however wild it may be, one's own fancy worked up at times to frenzy—is that very "most advantageous advantage" which we have overlooked, which comes under no classification and against which all systems and theories are continually being shattered to atoms. And how do these wiseacres know that man wants a normal, a virtuous choice? What has made them conceive that man must want a rationally advantageous choice? What man wants is simply *independent* choice, whatever that independence may cost and wherever it may lead. And choice, of course, the devil only knows what choice. . . .

VIII

"Ha! ha! ha! But you know there is no such thing as choice in reality, say what you like," you will interpose with a chuckle. "Science has succeeded in so far analyzing man that we know already that choice and what is called freedom of will is nothing else than——"

Stay, gentlemen, I meant to begin with that myself. I confess, I was rather frightened. I was just going to say that the devil only knows what choice depends on, and that perhaps that was a very good thing, but I remembered the teaching of science . . . and pulled myself up. And here you have begun upon it. Indeed, if there really is some day discovered a formula for all our desires and caprices—that is, an explanation of what they depend upon, by what laws they arise, how they develop, what they are aiming at in one case and in another and so on, that is, a real mathematical formula—then, most likely, man will at once cease to feel desire, indeed, he will be certain to. For who would want to choose by rule? Besides, he will at once be transformed from a human being into an organ-stop or something of the sort; for what is a man without desires, without freewill and without choice, if not a stop in an organ? What do you think? Let us reckon the chances—can such a thing happen or not?

"H'm!" you decide. "Our choice is usually mistaken from a false view of our advantage. We sometimes choose absolute nonsense because in our foolishness we see in that nonsense the easiest means for attaining a supposed advantage. But when all that is explained and worked out on paper (which is perfectly possible, for it is contemptible and senseless to suppose that some laws of nature man will never understand), then certainly so-called desires will no longer exist. For if a desire should come into conflict with reason we shall then reason and not desire, because it will be impossible retaining our reason to be *senseless* in our desires, and in that way knowingly act against reason and desire to injure ourselves. And as all choice and reasoning can be really calculated—because there will some day be discovered the laws of our so-called freewill—so, joking apart, there may one day be something like a table constructed of them, so that we really shall choose in accordance with it. If, for instance, some day they calculate and prove to me that I make a long nose at some one because I could not help making a long nose at him and that I had to do it in that particular way, what *freedom*

is left me, especially if I am a learned man and have taken my degree somewhere? Then I should be able to calculate my whole life for thirty years beforehand. In short, if this could be arranged there would be nothing left for us to do; anyway, we should have to understand that. And, in fact, we ought unweariedly to repeat to ourselves that at such and such a time and in such and such circumstances nature does not ask our leave; that we have got to take her as she is and not fashion her to suit our fancy, and if we really aspire to formulas and tables of rules, and well, even . . . to the chemical retort, there's no help for it, we must accept the retort too, or else it will be accepted without our consent. . . ."

Yes, but here I come to a stop! Gentlemen, you must excuse me for being over-philosophical; it's the result of forty years underground! Allow me to indulge my fancy. You see, gentlemen, reason is an excellent thing, there's no disputing that, but reason is nothing but reason and satisfies only the rational side of man's nature, while will is a manifestation of the whole life, that is, of the whole human life including reason and all the impulses. And although our life, in this manifestation of it, is often worthless, yet it is life and not simply extracting square roots. Here I, for instance, quite naturally want to live, in order to satisfy all my capacities for life, and not simply my capacity for reasoning, that is, not simply one twentieth of my capacity for life. What does reason know? Reason only knows what it has succeeded in learning (some things, perhaps, it will never learn; this is a poor comfort, but why not say so frankly?) and human nature acts as a whole, with everything that is in it, consciously or unconsciously, and, even if it goes wrong, it lives. I suspect, gentlemen, that you are looking at me with compassion; you tell me again that an enlightened and developed man, such, in short, as the future man will be, cannot consciously desire anything disadvantageous to himself, that that can be proved mathematically. I thoroughly agree, it can—by mathematics. But I repeat for the hundredth time, there is one case, one only, when man may consciously, purposely, desire what is injurious to himself, what is stupid, very stupid—simply in order to have the right to desire for himself even what is very stupid and not to be bound by an obligation to desire only what is sensible. Of course, this very stupid thing, this caprice of ours, may be in reality, gentlemen, more advantageous for us than anything else on earth, especially in certain cases. And in particular it may be more advantageous than any advantage even when it does us obvious harm, and contradicts the soundest conclusions of our reason concerning our advantage—for in any circumstances it preserves for us what is most precious and most important—that is, our personality, our individuality. Some, you see, maintain that this really is the most precious thing for mankind; choice can, of course, if it chooses, be in agreement with reason; and especially if this be not abused but kept within bounds. It is profitable and sometimes even praiseworthy. But very often, and even most often, choice is utterly and stubbornly opposed to reason . . . and . . . and . . . do you know that that, too, is profitable, sometimes even praiseworthy? Gentlemen, let us suppose that man is not stupid. (Indeed one cannot refuse to suppose that, if only from the one consideration, that, if man is stupid, then who is wise?) But if he is not stupid, he is monstrously ungrateful! Phenomenally ungrateful. In fact, I believe that the best definition of man is the ungrateful biped. But that is not all, that is

not his worst defect; his worst defect is his perpetual moral obliquity, perpetual—from the days of the Flood to the Schleswig-Holstein period. Moral obliquity and consequently lack of good sense; for it has long been accepted that lack of good sense is due to no other cause than moral obliquity. Put it to the test and cast your eyes upon the history of mankind. What will you see? Is it a grand spectacle? Grand, if you like. Take the Colossus of Rhodes,[18] for instance, that's worth something. With good reason Mr. Anaevsky[19] testifies of it that some say that it is the work of man's hands, while others maintain that it has been created by nature herself. Is it many-colored? May be it is many-colored, too: if one takes the dress uniforms, military and civilian, of all peoples in all ages—that alone is worth something, and if you take the undress uniforms you will never get to the end of it; no historian would be equal to the job. Is it monotonous? May be it's monotonous too: it's fighting and fighting; they are fighting now, they fought first and they fought last—you will admit, that it is almost too monotonous. In short, one may say anything about the history of the world—anything that might enter the most disordered imagination. The only thing one can't say is that it's rational. The very word sticks in one's throat. And, indeed, this is the odd thing that is continually happening: there are continually turning up in life moral and rational persons, sages and lovers of humanity who make it their object to live all their lives as morally and rationally as possible, to be, so to speak, a light to their neighbors simply in order to show them that it is possible to live morally and rationally in this world. And yet we all know that those very people sooner or later have been false to themselves, playing some queer trick, often a most unseemly one. Now I ask you: what can be expected of man since he is a being endowed with such strange qualities? Shower upon him every earthly blessing, drown him in a sea of happiness, so that nothing but bubbles of bliss can be seen on the surface; give him economic prosperity, such that he should have nothing else to do but sleep, eat cakes and busy himself with the continuation of his species, and even then out of sheer ingratitude, sheer spite, man would play you some nasty trick. He would even risk his cakes and would deliberately desire the most fatal rubbish, the most uneconomical absurdity, simply to introduce into all this positive good sense his fatal fantastic element. It is just his fantastic dreams, his vulgar folly that he will desire to retain, simply in order to prove to himself—as though that were so necessary—that men still are men and not the keys of a piano, which the laws of nature threaten to control so completely that soon one will be able to desire nothing but by the calendar. And that is not all: even if man were nothing but a piano-key, even if this were proved to him by natural science and mathematics, even then he would not become reasonable, but would purposely do something perverse out of simple ingratitude, simply to gain his point. And if he does not find means he will contrive destruction and chaos, will contrive sufferings of all sorts, only to gain his point! He will launch a curse upon the world, and as only man can curse (it

[18] Large bronze statue of the sun god Helios in Rhodes harbor. One of the ancient Seven Wonders of the World.
[19] A. E. Anaevsky (1788–1886) wrote a number of potboiler "reference" books in the 1850's and 1860's.

is his privilege, the primary distinction between him and other animals), may be by his curse alone he will attain his object—that is, convince himself that he is a man and not a piano-key! If you say that all this, too, can be calculated and tabulated—chaos and darkness and curses, so that the mere possibility of calculating it all beforehand would stop it all, and reason would reassert itself, then man would purposely go mad in order to be rid of reason and gain his point! I believe in it, I answer for it, for the whole work of man really seems to consist in nothing but proving to himself every minute that he is a man and not a piano-key! It may be at the cost of his skin, it may be by cannibalism! And this being so, can one help being tempted to rejoice that it has not yet come off, and that desire still depends on something we don't know?

You will scream at me (that is, if you condescend to do so) that no one is touching my free will, that all they are concerned with is that my will should of itself, of its own free will, coincide with my own normal interests, with the laws of nature and arithmetic.

Good Heavens, gentlemen, what sort of free will is left when we come to tabulation and arithmetic, when it will all be a case of twice two makes four? Twice two makes four without my will. As if free will meant that!

IX

Gentlemen, I am joking, and I know myself that my jokes are not brilliant, but you know one can't take everything as a joke. I am, perhaps, jesting against the grain. Gentlemen, I am tormented by questions; answer them for me. You, for instance, want to cure men of their old habits and reform their will in accordance with science and good sense. But how do you know, not only that it is possible, but also that it is *desirable*, to reform man in that way? And what leads you to the conclusion that man's inclinations *need* reforming? In short, how do you know that such a reformation will be a benefit to man? And to go to the root of the matter, why are you so positively convinced that not to act against his real normal interests guaranteed by the conclusions of reason and arithmetic is certainly always advantageous for man and must always be a law for mankind? So far, you know, this is only your supposition. It may be the law of logic, but not the law of humanity. You think, gentlemen, perhaps that I am mad? Allow me to defend myself. I agree that man is pre-eminently a creative animal, predestined to strive consciously for an object and to engage in engineering—that is, incessantly and eternally to make new roads, *wherever they may lead.* But the reason why he wants sometimes to go off at a tangent may just be that he is *predestined* to make the road, and perhaps, too, that however stupid the "direct" practical man may be, the thought sometimes will occur to him that the road almost always does lead *somewhere*, and that the destination it leads to is less important than the process of making it, and that the chief thing is to save the well-conducted child from despising engineering, and so giving way to the fatal idleness, which, as we all know, is the mother of all the vices. Man likes to make roads and to create, that is a fact beyond dispute. But why has he such a passionate love for destruction and chaos also? Tell me that! But on that point I want to say a couple of words myself. May it not be that he loves chaos and destruction (there can be no disputing

that he does sometimes love it) because he is instinctively afraid of attaining his object and completing the edifice he is constructing? Who knows, perhaps he only loves that edifice from a distance, and is by no means in love with it at close quarters; perhaps he only loves building it and does not want to live in it, but will leave it, when completed, for the use of *les animaux domestiques*[20]—such as the ants, the sheep, and so on. Now the ants have quite a different taste. They have a marvelous edifice of that pattern which endures for ever—the ant heap.

With the ant-heap the respectable race of ants began and with the ant-heap they will probably end, which does the greatest credit to their perseverance and good sense. But man is a frivolous and incongruous creature, and perhaps, like a chess player, loves the process of the game, not the end of it. And who knows (there is no saying with certainty), perhaps the only goal on earth to which mankind is striving lies in this incessant process of attaining, in other words, in life itself, and not in the thing to be attained, which must always be expressed as a formula, as positive as twice two makes four, and such positiveness is not life, gentlemen, but is the beginning of death. Anyway, man has always been afraid of this mathematical certainty, and I am afraid of it now. Granted that man does nothing but seek that mathematical certainty, he traverses oceans, sacrifices his life in the quest, but to succeed, really to find it, he dreads, I assure you. He feels that when he has found it there will be nothing for him to look for. When workmen have finished their work they do at least receive their pay, they go to the tavern, then they are taken to the police-station—and there is occupation for a week. But where can man go? Anyway, one can observe a certain awkwardness about him when he has attained such objects. He loves the process of attaining, but does not quite like to have attained, and that, of course, is very absurd. In fact, man is a comical creature; there seems to be a kind of jest in it all. But yet mathematical certainty is, after all, something insufferable. Twice two makes four seems to me simply a piece of insolence. Twice two makes four is a pert coxcomb[21] who stands with arms akimbo barring your path and spitting. I admit that twice two makes four is an excellent thing, but if we are to give everything its due, twice two makes five is sometimes a very charming thing too.

And why are you so firmly, so triumphantly, convinced that only the normal and the positive—in other words, only what is conducive to welfare—is for the advantage of man? Is not reason in error as regards advantage? Does not man, perhaps, love something besides well-being? Perhaps he is just as fond of suffering? Perhaps suffering is just as great a benefit to him as well-being? Man is sometimes extraordinarily, passionately, in love with suffering, and that is a fact. There is no need to appeal to universal history to prove that; only ask yourself, if you are a man and have lived at all. As far as my personal opinion is concerned, to care only for well-being seems to me positively ill-bred. Whether it's good or bad, it is sometimes very pleasant, too, to smash things. I hold no brief for suffering nor for well-being either. I am standing for . . . my caprice, and for its being guaranteed to me when necessary. Suffering would be out of place in vaudevilles, for instance; I know that. In the "Crystal Palace" it is unthinka-

[20] The domestic animals (French) [21] A conceited, foolish person.

ble; suffering means doubt, negation, and what would be the good of a crystal palace if there could be any doubt about it? And yet I think man will never renounce real suffering, that is, destruction and chaos. Why, suffering is the sole origin of consciousness. Though I did lay it down at the beginning that consciousness is the greatest misfortune for man, yet I know man prizes it and would not give it up for any satisfaction. Consciousness, for instance, is infinitely superior to twice two makes four. Once you have mathematical certainty there is nothing left to do or to understand. There will be nothing left but to bottle up your five senses and plunge into contemplation. While if you stick to consciousness, even though the same result is attained, you can at least flog yourself at times, and that will, at any rate, liven you up. Reactionary as it is, corporal punishment is better than nothing.

<div align="center">x</div>

You believe in a crystal palace that can never be destroyed—a palace at which one will not be able to put out one's tongue or make a long nose on the sly. And perhaps that is just why I am afraid of this edifice, that it is of crystal and can never be destroyed and that one cannot put one's tongue out at it even on the sly.

You see, if it were not a palace, but a hen-house, I might creep into it to avoid getting wet, and yet I would not call the hen-house a palace out of gratitude to it for keeping me dry. You laugh and say that in such circumstances a hen-house is as good as a mansion. Yes, I answer, if one had to live simply to keep out of the rain.

But what is to be done if I have taken it into my head that that is not the only object in life, and that if one must live one had better live in a mansion. That is my choice, my desire. You will only eradicate it when you have changed my preference. Well, do change it, allure me with something else, give me another ideal. But meanwhile I will not take a hen-house for a mansion. The crystal palace may be an idle dream, it may be that it is inconsistent with the laws of nature and that I have invented it only through my own stupidity, through the old-fashioned irrational habits of my generation. But what does it matter to me that it is inconsistent? That makes no difference since it exists in my desires, or rather exists as long as my desires exist. Perhaps you are laughing again? Laugh away; I will put up with any mockery rather than pretend that I am satisfied when I am hungry. I know, anyway, that I will not be put off with a compromise, with a recurring zero, simply because it is consistent with the laws of nature and actually exists. I will not accept as the crown of my desires a block of slum tenements on a lease of a thousand years, and perhaps with a sign-board of Wagenheim the dentist hanging out. Destroy my desires, eradicate my ideals, show me something better, and I will follow you. You will say, perhaps, that it is not worth your trouble; but in that case I can give you the same answer. We are discussing things seriously; but if you won't deign to give me your attention, I will drop your acquaintance. I can retreat into my underground hole.

But while I am alive and have desires I would rather my hand were withered off than bring one brick to such a building! Don't remind me that I have just rejected the crystal palace for the sole reason that one cannot

put out one's tongue at it. I did not say that because I am so fond of putting my tongue out. Perhaps the thing I resented was, that of all your edifices there has not been one at which one could not put out one's tongue. On the contrary, I would let my tongue be cut off out of gratitude if things could be so arranged that I should lose all desire to put it out. It is not my fault that things cannot be so arranged, and that one must be satisfied with model flats. Then why am I made with such desires? Can I have been constructed simply in order to come to the conclusion that all my construction is a cheat? Can this be my whole purpose? I do not believe it.

But do you know what: I am convinced that we underground folk ought to be kept on a curb. Though we may sit forty years underground without speaking, when we do come out into the light of day and break out we talk and talk and talk. . . .

XI

The long and the short of it is, gentlemen, that it is better to do nothing! Better conscious inertia! And so hurrah for underground! Though I have said that I envy the normal man to the last drop of my bile, yet I should not care to be in his place such as he is now (though I shall not cease envying him). No, no; anyway the underground life is more advantageous. There, at any rate, one can. . . . Oh, but even now I am lying! I am lying because I know myself that it is not underground that is better, but something different, quite different, for which I am thirsting, but which I cannot find! Damn underground!

I will tell you another thing that would be better, and that is, if I myself believed in anything of what I have just written. I swear to you, gentlemen, there is not one thing, not one word of what I have written that I really believe. That is, I believe it, perhaps, but at the same time I feel and suspect that I am lying like a cobbler.

"Then why have you written all this?" you will say to me. "I ought to put you underground for forty years without anything to do and then come to you in your cellar, to find out what stage you have reached! How can a man be left with nothing to do for forty years?"

"Isn't that shameful, isn't that humiliating?" you will say, perhaps, wagging your heads contemptuously. "You thirst for life and try to settle the problems of life by a logical tangle. And how persistent, how insolent are your sallies, and at the same time what a scare you are in! You talk nonsense and are pleased with it; you say impudent things and are in continual alarm and apologizing for them. You declare that you are afraid of nothing and at the same time try to ingratiate yourself in our good opinion. You declare that you are gnashing your teeth and at the same time you try to be witty so as to amuse us. You know that your witticisms are not witty, but you are evidently well satisfied with their literary value. You may, perhaps, have really suffered, but you have no respect for your own suffering. You may have sincerity, but you have no modesty; out of the pettiest vanity you expose your sincerity to publicity and ignominy. You doubtlessly mean to say something, but hide your last word through fear, because you have not the resolution to utter it, and only have a cowardly impudence. You boast of consciousness, but you are not sure of your ground, for though your mind works, yet your heart is darkened and corrupt, and you cannot have a

full, genuine consciousness without a pure heart. And how intrusive you are, how you insist and grimace! Lies, lies, lies!"

Of course I have myself made up all the things you say. That, too, is from underground. I have been for forty years listening to you through a crack under the floor. I have invented them myself, there was nothing else I could invent. It is no wonder that I have learned it by heart and it has taken a literary form. . .

But can you really be so credulous as to think that I will print all this and give it to you to read too? And another problem: why do I call you "gentlemen," why do I address you as though you really were my readers? Such confessions as I intend to make are never printed nor given to other people to read. Anyway, I am not strong-minded enough for that, and I don't see why I should be. But you see a fancy has occurred to me and I want to realize it at all costs. Let me explain.

Every man has reminiscences which he would not tell to every one, but only to his friends. He has other matters in his mind which he would not reveal even to his friends, but only to himself, and that in secret. But there are other things which a man is afraid to tell even to himself, and every decent man has a number of such things stored away in his mind. The more decent he is, the greater the number of such things in his mind. Anyway, I have only lately determined to remember some of my early adventures. Till now I have always avoided them, even with a certain uneasiness. Now, when I am not only recalling them, but have actually decided to write an account of them, I want to try the experiment whether one can, even with oneself, be perfectly open and not take fright at the whole truth. I will observe, in parenthesis, that Heine[22] says that a true autobiography is almost an impossibility, and that man is bound to lie about himself. He considers that Rousseau certainly told lies about himself in his *Confessions,* and even intentionally lied, out of vanity. I am convinced that Heine is right; I quite understand how sometimes one may, out of sheer vanity, attribute regular crimes to oneself, and indeed I can very well conceive that kind of vanity. But Heine judged of people who made their confessions to the public. I write only for myself, and I wish to declare once and for all that if I write as though I were addressing readers, that is simply because it is easier for me to write in that form. It is a form, an empty form—I shall never have readers. I have made this plain already. . .

I don't wish to be hampered by any restrictions in the compilation of my notes. I shall not attempt any system or method. I will jot things down as I remember them.

But here, perhaps, some one will catch at the word and ask me: if you really don't reckon on readers, why do you make such compacts with yourself—and on paper too—that is, that you won't attempt any system or method, that you jot things down as you remember them, and so on, and so on? Why are you explaining? Why do you apologize?

Well, there it is, I answer.

There is a whole psychology in all this, though. Perhaps it is simply that I am a coward. And perhaps that I purposely imagine an audience before

[22] Heinrich Heine, German poet, who, in his *Confessions* (1854), made these comments about autobiography and about Rousseau.

me in order that I may be more dignified while I write. There are perhaps thousands of reasons. Again, what is my object precisely in writing? If it is not for the benefit of the public why should I not simply recall these incidents in my own mind without putting them on paper?

Quite so; but yet it is more imposing on paper. There is something more impressive in it; I shall be better able to criticize myself and improve my style. Besides, I shall perhaps obtain actual relief from writing. Today, for instance, I am particularly oppressed by one memory of a distant past. It came back vividly to my mind a few days ago, and has remained haunting me like an annoying tune that one cannot get rid of. And yet I must get rid of it somehow. I have hundreds of such reminiscences; but at times some one stands out from the hundreds and oppresses me. For some reason I believe that if I write it down I should get rid of it. Why not try?

Besides, I am bored, and I never have anything to do. Writing will be a sort of work. They say work makes man kind-hearted and honest. Well, here is a chance for me, anyway.

Snow is falling today, yellow and dingy. It fell yesterday, too, and a few days ago. I fancy it is the wet snow that has reminded me of that incident which I cannot shake off now. And so let it be a story *à propos* of the falling snow.

PART II

À PROPOS OF THE WET SNOW

> When from dark error's subjugation
> My words of passionate exhortation
> Had wrenched thy fainting spirit free;
> And writhing prone in thine affliction
> Thou didst recall with malediction
> The vice that had encompassed thee:
> And when thy slumbering conscience, fretting
> By recollection's torturing flame,
> Thou didst reveal the hideous setting
> Of thy life's current ere I came:
> When suddenly I saw thee sicken,
> And weeping, hide thine anguished face,
> Revolted, maddened, horror-stricken,
> At memories of foul disgrace, etc., etc., etc.
> —Nekrasov[23] (*translated by Juliet Soskice*)

[23] Nikolay A. Nekrasov, Russian poet and radical. The poem deals with the favorite romantic theme of the redemption of a prostitute by love, the theme Dostoevsky in Part II is to present from a devastating, "underground" point of view. The speaker breaks off the poem with an impatient "etc., etc., etc." The omitted last lines—"Into my house come bold and free, / Its rightful mistress there to be"—appear ironically later in Part II.

I

At that time I was only twenty-four. My life was even then gloomy, ill-regulated, and as solitary as that of a savage. I made friends with no one and positively avoided talking, and buried myself more and more in my hole. At work in the office I never looked at any one, and I was perfectly well aware that my companions looked upon me, not only as a queer fellow, but even looked upon me—I always fancied this—with a sort of loathing. I sometimes wondered why it was that nobody except me fancied that he was looked upon with aversion? One of the clerks had a most repulsive, pock-marked face, which looked positively villainous. I believe I should not have dared to look at any one with such an unsightly countenance. Another had such a very dirty old uniform that there was an unpleasant odor in his proximity. Yet not one of these gentlemen showed the slightest self-consciousness—either about their clothes or their countenance or their character in any way. Neither of them ever imagined that they were looked at with repulsion; if they had imagined it they would not have minded—so long as their superiors did not look at them in that way. It is clear to me now that, owing to my unbounded vanity and to the high standard I set for myself, I often looked at myself with furious discontent, which verged on loathing, and so I inwardly attributed the same feeling to every one. I hated my face, for instance: I thought it disgusting, and even suspected that there was something base in my expression, and so every day when I turned up at the office I tried to behave as independently as possible, and to assume a lofty expression, so that I might not be suspected of being abject. "My face may be ugly," I thought, "but let it be lofty, expressive, and, above all, *extremely* intelligent." But I was positively and painfully certain that it was impossible for my countenance ever to express those qualities. And what was worst of all, I thought it actually stupid looking, and I would have been quite satisfied if I could have looked intelligent. In fact, I would even have put up with looking base if, at the same time, my face could have been thought strikingly intelligent.

Of course, I hated my fellow clerks one and all, and I despised them all, yet at the same time I was, as it were, afraid of them. In fact, it happened at times that I thought more highly of them than of myself. It somehow happened quite suddenly that I alternated between despising them and thinking them superior to myself. A cultivated and decent man cannot be vain without setting a fearfully high standard for himself, and without despising and almost hating himself at certain moments. But whether I despised them or thought them superior I dropped my eyes almost every time I met any one. I even made experiments whether I could face so and so's looking at me, and I was always the first to drop my eyes. This worried me to distraction. I had a sickly dread, too, of being ridiculous, and so had a slavish passion for the conventional in everything external. I loved to fall into the common rut, and had a whole-hearted terror of any kind of eccentricity in myself. But how could I live up to it? I was morbidly sensitive, as a man of our age should be. They were all stupid, and as like one another as so many sheep. Perhaps I was the only one in the office who fancied that I was a coward and a slave, and I fancied it just because I was more highly developed. But it was not only that I fancied it, it really was so. I was a coward and a slave. I say this without the slightest embarrassment. Every

decent man of our age must be a coward and a slave. That is his normal condition. Of that I am firmly persuaded. He is made and constructed to that very end. And not only at the present time owing to some casual circumstances, but always, at all times, a decent man is bound to be a coward and a slave. It is the law of nature for all decent people all over the earth. If any one of them happens to be valiant about something, he need not be comforted nor carried away by that; he would show the white feather just the same before something else. That is how it invariably and inevitably ends. Only donkeys and mules are valiant, and they only till they are pushed up to the wall. It is not worth while to pay attention to them for they really are of no consequence.

Another circumstance, too, worried me in those days: that there was no one like me and I was unlike any one else. "I am unique and they are all alike," I thought—and pondered.

From that it is evident that I was still a youngster.

The very opposite sometimes happened. It was loathsome sometimes to go to the office; things reached such a point that I often came home ill. But all at once à *propos* of nothing, there would come a phase of skepticism and indifference (everything happened in phases to me), and I would laugh myself at my intolerance and fastidiousness, I would reproach myself with being *romantic*. At one time I was unwilling to speak to any one, while at other times I would not only talk, but go to the length of contemplating making friends with them. All my fastidiousness would suddenly, for no rhyme or reason, vanish. Who knows, perhaps I never had really had it, and it had simply been affected, and got out of books. I have not decided that question even now. Once I quite made friends with them, visited their homes, played preference, drank vodka, talked of promotions. . . . But here let me make a digression.

We Russians, speaking generally, have never had those foolish transcendental "romantics"—German, and still more French—on whom nothing produces any effect; if there were an earthquake, if all France perished at the barricades, they would still be the same, they would not even have the decency to affect a change, but would still go on singing their transcendental songs to the hour of their death, because they are fools. We, in Russia, have no fools; that is well known. That is what distinguishes us from foreign lands. Consequently these transcendental natures are not found amongst us in their pure form. The idea that they are is due to our "realistic" journalists and critics of that day, always on the look out for Kostanzhoglos[24] and Uncle Pyotr Ivanichs[25] and foolishly accepting them as our ideal; they have slandered our romantics, taking them for the same transcendental sort as in Germany or France. On the contrary, the characteristics of our "romantics" are absolutely and directly opposed to the transcendental European type, and no European standard can be applied to them. (Allow me to make use of this word "romantic"—an old-fashioned and much respected word which has done good service and is familiar to all.) The characteristics of our romantic are to understand everything, *to see everything and to see it often incomparably more clearly than our most realistic minds*

[24] An idealized landowner in Nikolai Gogol's *Dead Souls*, Part II (1851).
[25] A sympathetic character in Ivan Goncharov's *A Common Story* (1847).

see it; to refuse to accept anyone or anything, but at the same time not to despise anything; to give way, to yield, from policy; never to lose sight of a useful practical object (such as rent-free quarters at the government expense, pensions, decorations), to keep their eye on that object through all the enthusiasms and volumes of lyrical poems, and at the same time to preserve "the good and the beautiful" inviolate within them to the hour of their death, and to preserve themselves also, incidentally, like some precious jewel wrapped in cotton wool if only for the benefit of "the good and the beautiful." Our "romantic" is a man of great breadth and the greatest rogue of all our rogues, I assure you. . . . I can assure you from experience, indeed. Of course, that is, if he is intelligent. But what am I saying! The romantic is always intelligent, and I only meant to observe that although we have had foolish romantics they don't count, and they were only so because in the flower of their youth they degenerated into Germans, and to preserve their precious jewel more comfortably, settled somewhere out there—by preference in Weimar or the Black Forest.[26]

I, for instance, genuinely despised my official work and did not openly abuse it simply because I was in it myself and got a salary for it. Anyway, take note, I did not openly abuse it. Our romantic would rather go out of his mind—a thing, however, which very rarely happens—than take to open abuse, unless he had some other career in view; and he is never kicked out. At most, they would take him to the lunatic asylum as "the King of Spain"[27] if he should go very mad. But it is only the thin, fair people who go out of their minds in Russia. Innumerable "romantics" attain later in life to considerable rank in the service. Their many-sidedness is remarkable! And what a faculty they have for the most contradictory sensations! I was comforted by this thought even in those days, and I am of the same opinion now. That is why there are so many "broad natures" among us who never lose their ideal even in the depths of degradation; and though they never stir a finger for their ideal, though they are arrant thieves and knaves, yet they tearfully cherish their first ideal and are extraordinarily honest at heart. Yes, it is only among us that the most incorrigible rogue can be absolutely and loftily honest at heart without in the least ceasing to be a rogue. I repeat, our romantics, frequently, become such accomplished rascals (I use the term "rascals" affectionately), suddenly display such a sense of reality and practical knowledge that their bewildered superiors and the public generally can only ejaculate in amazement.

Their many-sidedness is really amazing, and goodness knows what it may develop into later on, and what the future has in store for us. It is not a poor material! I do not say this from any foolish or boastful patriotism. But I feel sure that you are again imagining that I am joking. Or perhaps it's just the contrary and you are convinced that I really think so. Anyway, gentlemen, I shall welcome both views as an honor and a special favor. And do forgive my digression.

[26] The town of Weimar, in east Germany, was the home of Johann Wolfgang von Goethe and of such other Romantics as Johann Gottfried von Herder, Friedrich von Schiller, and Franz Liszt. The Black Forest, a mountainous area in southwest Germany, was also a favorite Romantic locale because of its natural beauty.

[27] The main character in Nikolai Gogol's story "Memoirs of a Madman" (1835) believes that he is the King of Spain and ends up in a lunatic asylum.

I did not, of course, maintain friendly relations with my comrades and soon was at loggerheads with them, and in my youth and inexperience I even gave up bowing to them, as though I had cut off all relations. That, however, only happened to me once. As a rule, I was always alone.

In the first place I spent most of my time at home, reading. I tried to stifle all that was continually seething within me by means of external impressions. And the only external means I had was reading. Reading, of course, was a great help—exciting me, giving me pleasure and pain. But at times it bored me fearfully. One longed for movement in spite of everything, and I plunged all at once into dark, underground, loathsome vice of the pettiest kind. My wretched passions were acute, smarting, from my continual, sickly irritability. I had hysterical impulses, with tears and convulsions. I had no resource except reading, that is, there was nothing in my surroundings which I could respect and which attracted me. I was overwhelmed with depression, too; I had a hysterical craving for incongruity and for contrast, and so I took to vice. I have not said all this to justify myself. . . . But, no! I am lying. I did want to justify myself. I make that little observation for my own benefit, gentlemen. I don't want to lie. I vowed to myself I would not.

And so, furtively, timidly, in solitude, at night, I indulged in filthy vice, with a feeling of shame which never deserted me, even at the most loathsome moments, and which at such moments nearly made me curse. Already even then I had my underground world in my soul. I was fearfully afraid of being seen, of being met, of being recognized. I visited various obscure haunts.

One night as I was passing a tavern I saw through a lighted window some gentlemen fighting with billiard cues, and saw one of them thrown out of a window. At other times I should have felt very much disgusted, but I was in such a mood at the time, that I actually envied the gentleman thrown out of a window—and I envied him so much that I even went into the tavern and into the billiard-room. "Perhaps," I thought, "I'll have a fight, too, and they'll throw me out of the window."

I was not drunk—but what is one to do—depression will drive a man to such a pitch of hysteria? But nothing happened. It seemed that I was not even equal to being thrown out of the window and I went away without having my fight.

An officer put me in my place from the first moment.

I was standing by the billiard-table and in my ignorance blocking up the way, and he wanted to pass; he took me by the shoulders and without a word—without a warning or explanation—moved me from where I was standing to another spot and passed by as though he had not noticed me. I could have forgiven blows, but I could not forgive his having moved me without noticing me.

Devil knows what I would have given for a real regular quarrel—a more decent, a more *literary* one, so to speak. I had been treated like a fly. This officer was over six foot, while I was a spindly little fellow. But the quarrel was in my hands. I had only to protest and I certainly would have been thrown out of the window. But I changed my mind and preferred to beat a resentful retreat.

I went out of the tavern straight home, confused and troubled, and the

next night I went out again with the same lewd intentions, still more fur-
tively, abjectly and miserably than before, as it were, with tears in my
eyes—but still I did go out again. Don't imagine, though, it was cowardice
made me slink away from the officer: I never have been a coward at heart,
though I have always been a coward in action. Don't be in a hurry to
laugh—I assure you I can explain it all.

Oh, if only that officer had been one of the sort who would consent to
fight a duel! But no, he was one of those gentlemen (alas, long extinct!)
who preferred fighting with cues or, like Gogol's Lieutenant Pirogov,[28]
appealing to the police. They did not fight duels and would have thought a
duel with a civilian like me an utterly unseemly procedure in any case—and
they looked upon the duel altogether as something impossible, something
free-thinking and French. But they were quite ready to bully, especially
when they were over six foot.

I did not slink away through cowardice, but through an unbounded
vanity. I was afraid not of his six foot, not of getting a sound thrashing and
being thrown out of the window; I should have had physical courage
enough, I assure you; but I had not the moral courage. What I was afraid
of was that every one present, from the insolent marker down to the lowest
little stinking, pimply clerk in a greasy collar, would jeer at me and fail to
understand when I began to protest and to address them in literary lan-
guage. For of the point of honor—not of honor, but of the point of honor
(*point d'honneur*)—one cannot speak among us except in literary language.
You can't allude to the "point of honor" in ordinary language. I was fully
convinced (the sense of reality, in spite of all my romanticism!) that they
would all simply split their sides with laughter, and that the officer would
not simply beat me, that is, without insulting me, but would certainly prod
me in the back with his knee, kick me round the billiard-table, and only
then perhaps have pity and drop me out of the window.

Of course, this trivial incident could not with me end in that. I often met
that officer afterwards in the street and noticed him very carefully. I am
not quite sure whether he recognized me, I imagine not; I judge from
certain signs. But I—I stared at him with spite and hatred and so it went
on . . . for several years! My resentment grew even deeper with years. At
first I began making stealthy inquiries about this officer. It was difficult for
me to do so, for I knew no one. But one day I heard some one shout his
surname in the street as I was following him at a distance, as though I were
tied to him—and so I learnt his surname. Another time I followed him to
his flat, and for ten kopecks learned from the porter where he lived, on
which story, whether he lived alone or with others, and so on—in fact,
everything one could learn from a porter. One morning, though I had
never tried my hand with the pen, it suddenly occurred to me to write a
satire on this officer in the form of a novel which would unmask his vil-
lainy. I wrote the novel with relish. I did unmask his villainy, I even exag-
gerated it; at first I so altered his surname that it could easily be recognized,
but on second thoughts I changed it, and sent the story to the *Otechestvenniye*

[28] This incident occurs in Nikolai Gogol's story "The Nevsky Prospect" (1835).

Zapiski.[29] But at that time such attacks were not the fashion and my story was not printed. That was a great vexation to me.

Sometimes I was positively choked with resentment. At last I determined to challenge my enemy to a duel. I composed a splendid, charming letter to him, imploring him to apologize to me, and hinting rather plainly at a duel in case of refusal. The letter was so composed that if the officer had had the least understanding of the good and the beautiful he would certainly have flung himself on my neck and have offered me his friendship. And how fine that would have been! How we should have got on together! "He could have shielded me with his higher rank, while I could have improved his mind with my culture, and, well . . . my ideas, and all sorts of things might have happened." Only fancy, this was two years after his insult to me, and my challenge would have been a ridiculous anachronism, in spite of all the ingenuity of my letter in disguising and explaining away the anachronism. But, thank God (to this day I thank the Almighty with tears in my eyes) I did not send the letter to him. Cold shivers run down my back when I think of what might have happened if I had sent it.

And all at once I revenged myself in the simplest way, by a stroke of genius! A brilliant thought suddenly dawned upon me. Sometimes on holidays I used to stroll along the sunny side of the Nevsky[30] about four o'clock in the afternoon. Though it was hardly a stroll so much as a series of innumerable miseries, humiliations and resentments; but no doubt that was just what I wanted. I used to wriggle along in a most unseemly fashion, like an eel, continually moving aside to make way for generals, for officers of the guards and the hussars, or for ladies. At such minutes there used to be a convulsive twinge at my heart, and I used to feel hot all down my back at the mere thought of the wretchedness of my attire, of the wretchedness and abjectness of my little scurrying figure. This was a regular martyrdom, a continual, intolerable humiliation at the thought, which passed into an incessant and direct sensation, that I was a mere fly in the eyes of all this world, a nasty, disgusting fly—more intelligent, more highly developed, more refined in feeling than any of them, of course—but a fly that was continually making way for every one, insulted and injured by every one. Why I inflicted this torture upon myself, why I went to the Nevsky, I don't know. I felt simply drawn there at every possible opportunity.

Already then I began to experience a rush of the enjoyment of which I spoke in the first chapter. After my affair with the officer I felt even more drawn there than before: it was on the Nevsky that I met him most frequently, there I could admire him. He, too, went there chiefly on holidays. He, too, turned out of his path for generals and persons of high rank, and he, too, wriggled between them like an eel; but people, like me, or even better dressed than me, he simply walked over; he made straight for them as though there was nothing but empty space before him, and never, under any circumstances, turned aside. I gloated over my resentment watching him and . . . always resentfully made way for him. It exasperated me that even in the street I could not be on an even footing with him.

[29] A well-known radical Russian journal. The title means *Notes of the Fatherland.*
[30] Nevsky Prospect, the fashionable main street of St. Petersburg.

"Why must you invariably be the first to move aside?" I kept asking myself in hysterical rage, waking up sometimes at three o'clock in the morning. "Why is it you and not he? There's no regulation about it; there's no written law. Let the making way be equal as it usually is when refined people meet: he moves half-way and you move half-way; you pass with mutual respect."

But that never happened, and I always moved aside, while he did not even notice my making way for him. And lo and behold a bright idea dawned upon me! "What," I thought, "if I meet him and don't move on one side? What if I don't move aside on purpose, even if I knock up against him? How would that be?" This audacious idea took such a hold on me that it gave me no peace. I was dreaming of it continually, horribly, and I purposely went more frequently to the Nevsky in order to picture more vividly how I should do it when I did do it. I was delighted. This intention seemed to me more and more practical and possible.

"Of course I shall not really push him," I thought, already more good-natured in my joy. "I will simply not turn aside, will run up against him, not very violently, but just shouldering each other—just as much as decency permits. I will push against him just as much as he pushes against me." At last I made up my mind completely. But my preparations took a great deal of time. To begin with, when I carried out my plan I should need to be looking rather more decent, and so I had to think of my get-up. "In case of emergency, if, for instance, there were any sort of public scandal (and the public there is of the most *recherché*:[31] the Countess walks there; Prince D. walks there; all the literary world is there), I must be well dressed; that inspires respect and of itself puts us on an equal footing in the eyes of society."

With this object I asked for some of my salary in advance, and bought at Churkin's a pair of black gloves and a decent hat. Black gloves seemed to me both more dignified and *bon ton*[32] than the lemon-colored ones which I had contemplated at first. "The color is too gaudy, it looks as though one were trying to be conspicuous," and I did not take the lemon-colored ones. I had got ready long beforehand a good shirt, with white bone studs; my overcoat was the only thing that held me back. The coat in itself was a very good one, it kept me warm; but it was wadded and it had a raccoon collar which was the height of vulgarity. I had to change the collar at any sacrifice, and to have a beaver one like an officer's. For this purpose I began visiting the Gostiny Dvor[33] and after several attempts I pitched upon a piece of cheap German beaver. Though these German beavers soon grow shabby and look wretched, yet at first they look exceedingly well, and I only needed it for one occasion. I asked the price; even so, it was too expensive. After thinking it over thoroughly I decided to sell my raccoon collar. The rest of the money—a considerable sum for me, I decided to borrow from Anton Antonich Syetochkin, my immediate superior, an unassuming person, though grave and judicious. He never lent money to any one, but I had, on entering the service, been specially recommended to him by an

[31] Exquisite, exceedingly refined (French).
[32] Literally, "good tone" (French); tasteful, fashionable. [33] Market for foreign goods.

important personage who had got me my berth. I was horribly worried. To
borrow from Anton Antonich seemed to me monstrous and shameful. I
did not sleep for two or three nights. Indeed, I did not sleep well at that
time, I was in a fever; I had a vague sinking at my heart or else a sudden
throbbing, throbbing, throbbing! Anton Antonich was surprised at first,
then he frowned, then he reflected, and did after all lend me the money,
receiving from me a written authorization to take from my salary a fort-
night later the sum that he had lent me.

In this way everything was at last ready. The handsome beaver replaced
the mean-looking raccoon, and I began by degrees to get to work. It would
never have done to act off-hand, at random; the plan had to be carried out
skillfully, by degrees. But I must confess that after many efforts I began to
despair: we simply could not run into each other. I made every prepara-
tion, I was quite determined—it seemed as though we should run into one
another directly—and before I knew what I was doing I had stepped aside
for him again and he had passed without noticing me. I even prayed as I
approached him that God would grant me determination. One time I had
made up my mind thoroughly, but it ended in my stumbling and falling at
his feet because at the very last instant when I was six inches from him my
courage failed me. He very calmly stepped over me, while I flew on one
side like a ball. That night I was ill again, feverish and delirious.

And suddenly it ended most happily. The night before I had made up
my mind not to carry out my fatal plan and to abandon it all, and with that
object I went to the Nevsky for the last time, just to see how I would aban-
don it all. Suddenly, three paces from my enemy, I unexpectedly made up
my mind—I closed my eyes, and we ran full tilt, shoulder to shoulder,
against one another! I did not budge an inch and passed him on a perfectly
equal footing! He did not even look round and pretended not to notice it;
but he was only pretending, I am convinced of that. I am convinced of that
to this day! Of course, I got the worst of it—he was stronger, but that was
not the point. The point was that I had attained my object, I had kept up
my dignity, I had not yielded a step, and had put myself publicly on an
equal social footing with him. I returned home feeling that I was fully
avenged for everything. I was delighted. I was triumphant and sang Italian
arias. Of course, I will not describe to you what happened to me three days
later; if you have read my first chapter you can guess that for yourself. The
officer was afterwards transferred; I have not seen him now for fourteen
years. What is the dear fellow doing now? Whom is he walking over?

II

But the period of my dissipation would end and I always felt very sick
afterwards. It was followed by remorse—I tried to drive it away: I felt too
sick. By degrees, however, I grew used to that too. I grew used to every-
thing, or rather I voluntarily resigned myself to enduring it. But I had a
means of escape that reconciled everything—that was to find refuge in "the
good and the beautiful," in dreams, of course. I was a terrible dreamer, I
would dream for three months on end, tucked away in my corner, and you
may believe me that at those moments I had no resemblance to the gentle-
man who, in the perturbation of his chicken heart, put a collar of German
beaver on his great coat. I suddenly became a hero. I would not have

admitted my six-foot lieutenant even if he had called on me. I could not even picture him before me then. What were my dreams and how I could satisfy myself with them—it is hard to say now, but at the time I was satisfied with them. Though, indeed, even now, I am to some extent satisfied with them. Dreams were particularly sweet and vivid after a spell of dissipation; they came with remorse and with tears, with curses and transports. There were moments of such positive intoxication, of such happiness, that there was not the faintest trace of irony within me, on my honor. I had faith, hope, love. I believed blindly at such times that by some miracle, by some external circumstance, all this would suddenly open out, expand; that suddenly a vista of suitable activity—beneficent, good, and, above all, *ready made* (what sort of activity I had no idea, but the great thing was that it should be all ready for me)—would rise up before me—and I should come out into the light of day, almost riding a white horse and crowned with laurel. Anything but the foremost place I could not conceive for myself, and for that very reason I quite contentedly occupied the lowest in reality. Either to be a hero or to grovel in the mud—there was nothing between. That was my ruin, for when I was in the mud I comforted myself with the thought that at other times I was a hero, and the hero was a cloak for the mud: for an ordinary man it was shameful to defile himself, but a hero was too lofty to be utterly defiled, and so he might defile himself. It is worth noting that these attacks of the "good and the beautiful" visited me even during the period of dissipation and just at the times when I was touching bottom. They came in separate spurts, as though reminding me of themselves, but did not banish the dissipation by their appearance. On the contrary, they seemed to add a zest to it by contrast, and were only sufficiently present to serve as an appetizing sauce. That sauce was made up of contradictions and sufferings, of agonizing inward analysis, and all these pangs and pinpricks gave a certain piquancy, even a significance to my dissipation—in fact, completely answered the purpose of an appetizing sauce. There was a certain depth of meaning in it. And I could hardly have resigned myself to the simple, vulgar, direct debauchery of a clerk and have endured all the filthiness of it. What could have allured me about it then and have drawn me at night into the street? No, I had a lofty way of getting out of it all.

And what loving-kindness, oh Lord, what loving-kindness I felt at times in those dreams of mine! in those "flights into the good and the beautiful"; though it was fantastic love, though it was never applied to anything human in reality, yet there was so much of this love that one did not feel afterwards even the impulse to apply it in reality; that would have been superfluous. Everything, however, passed satisfactorily by a lazy and fascinating transition into the sphere of art, that is, into the beautiful forms of life, lying ready, largely stolen from the poets and novelists and adapted to all sorts of needs and uses. I, for instance, was triumphant over every one; every one, of course, was in dust and ashes, and was forced spontaneously to recognize my superiority, and I forgave them all. I was a poet and a grand gentleman, I fell in love; I came in for countless millions and immediately devoted them to humanity, and at the same time I confessed before all the people my shameful deeds, which, of course, were not merely shameful, but had in them much that was "good and beautiful" something

in the Manfred style.[34] Every one would kiss me and weep (what idiots they would be if they did not), while I should go barefoot and hungry preaching new ideas and fighting a victorious Austerlitz[35] against the obscurantists. Then the band would play a march, an amnesty would be declared, the Pope would agree to retire from Rome to Brazil; then there would be a ball for the whole of Italy at the Villa Borghese[36] on the shores of the Lake of Como,[37] the Lake of Como being for that purpose transferred to the neighborhood of Rome; then would come a scene in the bushes, and so on, and so on—as though you did not know all about it? You will say that it is vulgar and contemptible to drag all this into public after all the tears and transports which I have myself confessed. But why is it contemptible? Can you imagine that I am ashamed of it all, and that it was stupider than anything in your life, gentlemen? And I can assure you that some of these fancies were by no means badly composed. . . . It did not all happen on the shores of Lake Como. And yet you are right—it really is vulgar and contemptible. And most contemptible of all it is that now I am attempting to justify myself to you. And even more contemptible than that is my making this remark now. But that's enough, or there will be no end to it: each step will be more contemptible than the last. . . .

I could never stand more than three months of dreaming at a time without feeling an irresistible desire to plunge into society. To plunge into society meant to visit my superior at the office, Anton Antonich Syetoch-kin. He was the only permanent acquaintance I have had in my life, and wonder at the fact myself now. But I only went to see him when that phase came over me, and when my dreams had reached such a point of bliss that it became essential at once to embrace my fellows and all mankind; and for that purpose I needed, at least, one human being, actually existing. I had to call on Anton Antonich, however, on Tuesday—his at-home day; so I had always to time my passionate desire to embrace humanity so that it might fall on a Tuesday.

This Anton Antonich lived on the fourth story in a house in Five Corners, in four low-pitched rooms, one smaller than the other, of a particularly frugal and sallow appearance. He had two daughters and their aunt, who used to pour out the tea. Of the daughters one was thirteen and another fourteen, they both had snub noses, and I was awfully shy of them because they were always whispering and giggling together. The master of the house usually sat in his study on a leather couch in front of the table with some gray-headed gentleman, usually a colleague from our office or some other department. I never saw more than two or three visitors there, always the same. They talked about the excise duty; about business in the Senate,[38] about salaries, about promotions, about His Excellency, and the best means of pleasing him, and so on. I had the patience to sit like a fool beside these people for four hours at a stretch, listening to them without knowing what to say to them or venturing to say a word. I became stupe-

[34] Manfred, the title hero of Byron's play (1817), has committed unspecified sins which serve to make him even more romantic and attractive.
[35] Battle in which Napoleon defeated the combined Austrian and Russian armies in 1805.
[36] In Rome. [37] Between Italy and Switzerland. [38] A high court.

fied, several times I felt myself perspiring, I was overcome by a sort of paralysis; but this was pleasant and good for me. On returning home I deferred for a time my desire to embrace all mankind.

I had however one other acquaintance of a sort, Simonov, who was an old schoolfellow. I had a number of schoolfellows, indeed, in Petersburg, but I did not associate with them and had even given up nodding to them in the street. I believe I had transferred into the department I was in simply to avoid their company and to cut off all connection with my hateful childhood. Curses on that school and all those terrible years of penal servitude! In short, I parted from my schoolfellows as soon as I got out into the world. There were two or three left to whom I nodded in the street. One of them was Simonov, who had been in no way distinguished at school, was of a quiet and equable disposition; but I discovered in him a certain independence of character and even honesty. I don't even suppose that he was particularly stupid. I had at one time spent some rather soulful moments with him, but these had not lasted long and had somehow been suddenly clouded over. He was evidently uncomfortable at these reminiscences, and was, I fancy, always afraid that I might take up the same tone again. I suspected that he had an aversion for me, but still I went on going to see him, not being quite certain of it.

And so on one occasion, unable to endure my solitude and knowing that as it was Thursday Anton Antonich's door would be closed, I thought of Simonov. Climbing up to his fourth story I was thinking that the man disliked me and that it was a mistake to go and see him. But as it always happened that such reflections impelled me, as though purposely, to put myself into a false position, I went in. It was almost a year since I had last seen Simonov.

III

I found two of my old schoolfellows with him. They seemed to be discussing an important matter. All of them took scarcely any notice of my entrance, which was strange, for I had not met them for years. Evidently they looked upon me as something on the level of a common fly. I had not been treated like that even at school, though they all hated me. I knew, of course, that they must despise me now for my lack of success in the service, and for my having let myself sink so low, going about badly dressed and so on—which seemed to them a sign of my incapacity and insignificance. But I had not expected such contempt. Simonov was positively surprised at my turning up. Even in old days he had always seemed surprised at my coming. All this disconcerted me: I sat down, feeling rather miserable, and began listening to what they were saying.

They were engaged in warm and earnest conversation about a farewell dinner which they wanted to arrange for the next day to a comrade of theirs called Zverkov, an officer in the army, who was going away to a distant province. This Zverkov had been all the time at school with me too. I had begun to hate him particularly in the upper grades. In the lower grades he had simply been a pretty, playful boy whom everybody liked. I had hated him, however, even in the lower grades, just because he was a pretty and playful boy. He was always bad at his lessons and got worse and worse as he went on; however, he left with a good certificate, as he had

powerful interest. During his last year at school he came in for an estate of two hundred serfs, and as almost all of us were poor he took up a swaggering tone among us. He was vulgar in the extreme, but at the same time he was a good-natured fellow, even in his swaggering. In spite of superficial, fantastic and sham notions of honor and dignity, all but very few of us positively grovelled before Zverkov, and the more so the more he swaggered. And it was not from any interested motive that they grovelled, but simply because he had been favored by the gifts of nature. Moreover, it was, as it were, an accepted idea among us that Zverkov was a specialist in regard to tact and the social graces. This last fact particularly infuriated me. I hated the abrupt self-confident tone of his voice, his admiration of his own witticisms, which were often frightfully stupid, though he was bold in his language; I hated his handsome, but stupid face (for which I would, however, have gladly exchanged my intelligent one), and the free-and-easy military manners in fashion in the 'forties. I hated the way in which he used to talk of his future conquests of women (he did not venture to begin his attack upon women until he had the epaulettes of an officer, and was looking forward to them with impatience), and boasted of the duels he would constantly be fighting. I remember how I, invariably so taciturn, suddenly fastened upon Zverkov, when one day talking at a leisure moment with his schoolfellows of his future relations with the fair sex, and growing as sportive as a puppy in the sun, he all at once declared that he would not leave a single village girl on his estate unnoticed, that that was his *droit de seigneur*,[39] and that if the peasants dared to protest he would have them all flogged and double the tax on them, the bearded rascals. Our servile rabble applauded, but I attacked him, not from compassion for the girls and their fathers, but simply because they were applauding such an insect. I got the better of him on that occasion, but though Zverkov was stupid he was lively and impudent, and so laughed it off, and in such a way that my victory was not really complete: the laugh was on his side. He got the better of me on several occasions afterwards, but without malice, jestingly, casually. I remained angrily and contemptuously silent and would not answer him. When we left school he made advances to me; I did not rebuff them, for I was flattered, but we soon parted and quite naturally. Afterwards I heard of his barrack-room success as a lieutenant, and of the fast life he was leading. Then there came other rumors—of his successes in the service. By then he had taken to cutting me in the street, and I suspected that he was afraid of compromising himself by greeting a personage as insignificant as me. I saw him once in the theater, in the third tier of boxes. By then he was wearing shoulder-straps. He was twisting and twirling about, ingratiating himself with the daughters of an ancient General. In three years he had gone off considerably, though he was still rather handsome and adroit. One could see that by the time he was thirty he would be corpulent. So it was to this Zverkov that my school-fellows were going to give a dinner on his departure. They had kept up with him for those three years, though privately they did not consider themselves on an equal footing with him, I am convinced of that.

Of Simonov's two visitors, one was Ferfichkin, a Russianized German—

[39] "The right of the master," that is, to all the peasant women (French).

a little fellow with the face of a monkey, a blockhead who was always deriding every one, a very bitter enemy of mine from our days in the lower grades—a vulgar, impudent, swaggering fellow, who affected a most sensitive feeling of personal honor, though, of course, he was a wretched little coward at heart. He was one of those worshippers of Zverkov who made up to the latter from interested motives, and often borrowed money from him. Simonov's other visitor, Trudolyubov, was a person in no way remarkable—a tall young fellow, in the army, with a cold face, fairly honest, though he worshipped success of every sort, and was only capable of thinking of promotion. He was some sort of distant relation of Zverkov's, and this, foolish as it seems, gave him a certain importance among us. He always thought me of no consequence whatever; his behavior to me, though not quite courteous, was tolerable.

"Well, with seven roubles each," said Trudolyubov, "twenty-one roubles between the three of us, we ought to be able to get a good dinner. Zverkov, of course, won't pay."

"Of course not, since we are inviting him," Simonov decided.

"Can you imagine," Ferfichkin interrupted hotly and conceitedly, like some insolent flunky boasting of his master the General's decorations, "can you imagine that Zverkov will let us pay alone? He will accept from delicacy, but he will order half a dozen bottles of champagne."

"Do we want half a dozen for the four of us?" observed Trudolyubov, taking notice only of the half dozen.

"So the three of us, with Zverkov for the fourth, twenty-one roubles, at the Hôtel de Paris at five o'clock tomorrow," Simonov, who had been asked to make the arrangements, concluded finally.

"How twenty-one roubles?" I asked in some agitation, with a show of being offended; "if you count me it will not be twenty-one, but twenty-eight roubles."

It seemed to me that to invite myself so suddenly and unexpectedly would be positively graceful, and that they would all be conquered at once and would look at me with respect.

"Do you want to join, too?" Simonov observed, with no appearance of pleasure, seeming to avoid looking at me. He knew me through and through.

It infuriated me that he knew me so thoroughly.

"Why not? I am an old schoolfellow of his, too, I believe, and I must own I feel hurt that you have left me out," I said, boiling over again.

"And where were we to find you?" Ferfichkin put in roughly.

"You never were on good terms with Zverkov," Trudolyubov added, frowning.

But I had already clutched at the idea and would not give it up.

"It seems to me that no one has a right to form an opinion upon that," I retorted in a shaking voice, as though something tremendous had happened. "Perhaps that is just my reason for wishing it now, that I have not always been on good terms with him."

"Oh, there's no making you out . . . with these refinements," Trudolyubov jeered.

"We'll put your name down," Simonov decided, addressing me. "Tomorrow at five o'clock at the Hôtel de Paris."

"What about the money?" Ferfichkin began in an undertone, indicating me to Simonov, but he broke off, for even Simonov was embarrassed.

"That will do," said Trudolyubov, getting up. "If he wants to come so much, let him."

"But it's a private thing, between us friends," Ferfichkin said crossly, as he, too, picked up his hat. "It's not an official gathering."

"We do not want at all, perhaps . . ."

They went away. Ferfichkin did not greet me in any way as he went out, Trudolyubov barely nodded. Simonov, with whom I was left *tête-à-tête*, was in a state of vexation and perplexity, and looked at me queerly. He did not sit down and did not ask me to.

"H'm . . . yes . . . tomorrow, then. Will you pay your subscription now? I just ask so as to know," he muttered in embarrassment.

I flushed crimson, and as I did so I remembered that I had owed Simonov fifteen roubles for ages—which I had, indeed, never forgotten, though I had not paid it.

"You will understand, Simonov, that I could have no idea when I came here. . . . I am very much vexed that I have forgotten. . . ."

"All right, all right, that doesn't matter. You can pay tomorrow after the dinner. I simply wanted to know. . . . Please don't . . ."

He broke off and began pacing the room still more vexed. As he walked he began to stamp with his heels.

"Am I keeping you?" I asked, after two minutes of silence.

"Oh!" he said, starting, "that is—to be truthful—yes. I have to go and see some one . . . not far from here," he added in an apologetic voice, somewhat abashed.

"My goodness, why didn't you say so?" I cried, seizing my cap, with an astonishingly free-and-easy air, which was the last thing I should have expected of myself.

"It's close by . . . not two paces away," Simonov repeated, accompanying me to the front door with a fussy air which did not suit him at all. "So five o'clock, punctually, tomorrow," he called down the stairs after me. He was very glad to get rid of me. I was in a fury.

"What possessed me, what possessed me to force myself upon them?" I wondered, grinding my teeth as I strode along the street, "for a scoundrel, a pig like that Zverkov! Of course, I had better not go; of course, I must just snap my fingers at them. I am not bound in any way. I'll send Simonov a note by tomorrow's post. . . ."

But what made me furious was that I knew for certain that I should go, that I should make a point of going; and the more tactless, the more unseemly my going would be, the more certainly I would go.

And there was a positive obstacle to my going: I had no money. All I had was nine roubles, I had to give seven of that to my servant, Apollon, for his monthly wages. That was all I paid him—he had to keep himself.

Not to pay him was impossible, considering his character. But I will talk about that fellow, about that plague of mine, another time.

However, I knew I should go and should not pay him his wages.

That night I had the most hideous dreams. No wonder; all the evening I had been oppressed by memories of my miserable days at school, and I could not shake them off. I was sent to the school by distant relations, upon

whom I was dependent and of whom I have heard nothing since—they sent me there a forlorn, silent boy, already crushed by their reproaches, already troubled by doubt, and looking with savage distrust at every one. My schoolfellows met me with spiteful and merciless jibes because I was not like any of them. But I could not endure their taunts; I could not give in to them with the ignoble readiness with which they gave in to one another. I hated them from the first, and shut myself away from every one in timid, wounded and disproportionate pride. Their coarseness revolted me. They laughed cynically at my face, at my clumsy figure; and yet what stupid faces they had themselves. In our school the boys' faces seemed in a special way to degenerate and grow stupider. How many fine-looking boys came to us! In a few years they became repulsive. Even at sixteen I wondered at them morosely; even then I was struck by the pettiness of their thoughts, the stupidity of their pursuits, their games, their conversations. They had no understanding of such essential things, they took no interest in such striking, impressive subjects, that I could not help considering them inferior to myself. It was not wounded vanity that drove me to it, and for God's sake do not thrust upon me your hackneyed remarks, repeated to nausea, that "I was only a dreamer," while they even then had an understanding of life. They understood nothing, they had no idea of real life, and I swear that that was what made me most indignant with them. On the contrary, the most obvious, striking reality they accepted with fantastic stupidity and even at that time were accustomed to respect success. Everything that was just, but oppressed and looked down upon, they laughed at heartlessly and shamefully. They took rank for intelligence; even at sixteen they were already talking about a snug berth. Of course, a great deal of it was due to their stupidity, to the bad examples with which they had always been surrounded in their childhood and boyhood. They were monstrously depraved. Of course a great deal of that, too, was superficial and an assumption of cynicism; of course there were glimpses of youth and freshness even in their depravity; but even that freshness was not attractive, and showed itself in a certain rakishness. I hated them horribly, though perhaps I was worse than any of them. They repaid me in the same way, and did not conceal their aversion for me. But by then I did not desire their affection: on the contrary I continually longed for their humiliation. To escape from their derision I purposely began to make all the progress I could with my studies and forced my way to the very top. This impressed them. Moreover, they all began by degrees to grasp that I had already read books none of them could read, and understood things (not forming part of our school curriculum) of which they had not even heard. They took a savage and sarcastic view of it, but were morally impressed, especially as the teachers began to notice me on those grounds. The mockery ceased, but the hostility remained, and cold and strained relations became permanent between us. In the end I could not put up with it: with years a craving for society, for friends, developed in me. I attempted to get on friendly terms with some of my schoolfellows; but somehow or other my intimacy with them was always strained and soon ended of itself. Once, indeed, I did have a friend. But I was already a tyrant at heart; I wanted to exercise unbounded sway over him; I tried to instill into him a contempt for his surroundings; I required of him a disdainful and complete break with those surroundings. I fright-

ened him with my passionate affection; I reduced him to tears, to hysterics. He was a simple and devoted soul; but when he devoted himself to me entirely I began to hate him immediately and repulsed him—as though all I needed him for was to win a victory over him, to subjugate him and nothing else. But I could not subjugate all of them; my friend was not at all like them either, he was, in fact, a rare exception. The first thing I did on leaving school was to give up the special job for which I had been destined so as to break all ties, to curse my past and shake the dust from off my feet. . . . And goodness knows why, after all that, I should go trudging off to Simonov's!

Early next morning I roused myself and jumped out of bed with excitement, as though it were all about to happen at once. But I believed that some radical change in my life was coming, and would inevitably come that day. Owing to its rarity, perhaps, any external event, however trivial, always made me feel as though some radical change in my life were at hand. I went to the office, however, as usual, but sneaked away home two hours earlier to get ready. The great thing, I thought, is not to be the first to arrive, or they will think I am overjoyed at coming. But there were thousands of such great points to consider, and they all agitated and overwhelmed me. I polished my boots a second time with my own hands; nothing in the world would have induced Apollon to clean them twice a day, as he considered that it was more than his duties required of him. I stole the brushes to clean them from the passage, being careful he should not detect it, for fear of his contempt. Then I minutely examined my clothes and thought that everything looked old, worn and threadbare. I had let myself get too slovenly. My uniform, perhaps, was tidy, but I could not go out to dinner in my uniform. The worst of it was that on the knee of my trousers was a big yellow stain. I had a foreboding that that stain would deprive me of nine-tenths of my personal dignity. I knew, too, that it was very bad to think so. "But this is no time for thinking: now I am in for the real thing," I thought, and my heart sank. I knew, too, perfectly well even then, that I was monstrously exaggerating the facts. But how could I help it? I could not control myself and was already shaking with fever. With despair I pictured to myself how coldly and disdainfully that "scoundrel" Zverkov would meet me; with what dull-witted, invincible contempt the blockhead Trudolyubov would look at me; with what impudent rudeness the insect Ferfichkin would snigger at me in order to curry favor with Zverkov; how completely Simonov would take it all in, and how he would despise me for the abjectness of my vanity and lack of spirit—and, worst of all, how paltry, *unliterary,* commonplace it would all be. Of course, the best thing would be not to go at all. But that was most impossible of all: if I feel impelled to do anything, I seem to be pitchforked into it. I should have jeered at myself ever afterwards: "So you funked it, you funked it, you funked the *real thing!*" On the contrary, I passionately longed to show all that "rabble" that I was by no means such a spiritless creature as I seemed to myself. What is more, even in the acutest paroxysm of this cowardly fever, I dreamed of getting the upper hand, of dominating them, carrying them away, making them like me—if only for my "elevation of thought and unmistakable wit." They would abandon Zverkov, he would sit on one side, silent and ashamed, while I should crush him. Then, perhaps, we would be recon-

ciled and drink to our everlasting friendship; but what was most bitter and most humiliating for me was that I knew even then, knew fully and for certain, that I needed nothing of all this really, that I did not really want to crush, to subdue, to attract them, and that I did not care a straw really for the result, even if I did achieve it. Oh, how I prayed for the day to pass quickly! In unutterable anguish I went to the window, opened the movable pane and looked out into the troubled darkness of the thickly falling wet snow. At last my wretched little clock hissed out five. I seized my hat and trying not to look at Apollon, who had been all day expecting his month's wages, but in his foolishness was unwilling to be the first to speak about it, I slipped between him and the door and jumping into a high-class sledge, on which I spent my last half rouble, I drove up in grand style to the Hôtel de Paris.

<p style="text-align:center">IV</p>

I had been certain the day before that I should be the first to arrive. But it was not a question of being the first to arrive. Not only were they not there, but I had difficulty in finding our room. The table was not laid even. What did it mean? After a good many questions I elicited from the waiters that the dinner had been ordered not for five, but for six o'clock. This was confirmed at the buffet too. I felt really ashamed to go on questioning them. It was only twenty-five minutes past five. If they changed the dinner hour they ought at least to have let me know—that is what the post is for, and not to have put me in an absurd position in my own eyes and . . . and even before the waiters. I sat down; the servant began laying the table; I felt even more humiliated when he was present. Towards six o'clock they brought in candles, though there were lamps burning in the room. It had not occurred to the waiter, however, to bring them in at once when I arrived. In the next room two gloomy, angry-looking persons were eating their dinners in silence at two different tables. There was a great deal of noise, even shouting, in a room further away; one could hear the laughter of a crowd of people, and nasty little shrieks in French: there were ladies at the dinner. It was sickening, in fact. I rarely passed more unpleasant moments, so much so that when they did arrive all together punctually at six I was overjoyed to see them, as though they were my deliverers, and even forgot that it was incumbent upon me to show resentment.

Zverkov walked in at the head of them; evidently he was the leading spirit. He and all of them were laughing; but, seeing me, Zverkov drew himself up a little, walked up to me deliberately with a slight, rather jaunty bend from the waist. He shook hands with me in a friendly, but not over-friendly, fashion, with a sort of circumspect courtesy like that of a General, as though in giving me his hand he were warding off something. I had imagined, on the contrary, that on coming in he would at once break into his habitual thin, shrill laugh and fall to making his insipid jokes and witticisms. I had been preparing for them ever since the previous day, but I had not expected such condescension, such high-official courtesy. So, then, he felt himself ineffably superior to me in every respect! If he only meant to insult me by that high-official tone, it would not matter, I thought—I could pay him back for it one way or another. But what if, in

reality, without the least desire to be offensive, that sheepshead had a notion in earnest that he was superior to me and could only look at me in a patronizing way? The very supposition made me gasp.

"I was surprised to hear of your desire to join us," he began, lisping and drawling, which was something new. "You and I seem to have seen nothing of one another. You fight shy of us. You shouldn't. We are not such terrible people as you think, Well, anyway, I am glad to renew our acquaintance."

And he turned carelessly to put down his hat on the window.

"Have you been waiting long?" Trudolyubov inquired.

"I arrived at five o'clock as you told me yesterday," I answered aloud, with an irritability that threatened an explosion.

"Didn't you let him know that we had changed the hour?" said Trudolyubov to Simonov.

"No, I didn't. I forgot," the latter replied, with no sign of regret, and without even apologizing to me he went off to order the *hors d'oeuvres.*

"So you've been here a whole hour? Oh, poor fellow!" Zverkov cried ironically, for to his notions this was bound to be extremely funny. That rascal Ferfichkin followed with his nasty little snigger like a puppy yapping. My position struck him, too, as exquisitely ludicrous and embarrassing.

"It isn't funny at all!" I cried to Ferfichkin, more and more irritated. "It wasn't my fault, but other people's. They neglected to let me know. It was . . . it was . . . it was simply absurd."

"It's not only absurd, but something else as well," muttered Trudolyubov, naïvely taking my part. "You are not hard enough upon it. It was simply rudeness—unintentional, of course. And how could Simonov . . . h'm!"

"If a trick like that had been played on me," observed Ferfichkin, "I should . . ."

"But you should have ordered something for yourself," Zverkov interrupted, "or simply asked for dinner without waiting for us."

"You will allow that I might have done that without your permission," I rapped out. "If I waited, it was. . ."

"Let us sit down, gentlemen," cried Simonov, coming in. "Everything is ready; I can answer for the champagne; it is capitally frozen. . . . You see, I did not know your address, where was I to look for you?" he suddenly turned to me, but again he seemed to avoid looking at me. Evidently he had something against me. It must have been what happened yesterday.

All sat down; I did the same. It was a round table. Trudolyubov was on my left, Simonov on my right. Zverkov was sitting opposite, Ferfichkin next to him, between him and Trudolyubov.

"Tell me, are you . . . in a government office?" Zverkov went on attending to me. Seeing that I was embarrassed, he seriously thought that he ought to be friendly to me, and, so to speak, cheer me up.

"Does he want me to throw a bottle at his head?" I thought, in a fury. In my novel surroundings I was unnaturally ready to be irritated.

"In the N—— office," I answered jerkily, with my eyes on my plate.

"And ha-ave you a go-od berth? I say, what ma-a-de you leave your original job?"

"What ma-a-de me was that I wanted to leave my original job," I

drawled more than he, hardly able to control myself. Ferfichkin went off
into a guffaw. Simonov looked at me ironically. Trudolyubov left off eating
and began looking at me with curiosity.

Zverkov winced, but he tried not to notice it.

"And the remuneration?"

"What remuneration?"

"I mean, your sa-a-lary?"

"Why are you cross-examining me?" However, I told him at once what
my salary was. I turned horribly red.

"It is not very handsome," Zverkov observed majestically.

"Yes, you can't afford to dine at cafés on that," Ferfichkin added
insolently.

"To my thinking it's very poor," Trudolyubov observed gravely.

"And how thin you have grown! How you have changed!" added
Zverkov, with a shade of venom in his voice, scanning me and my attire
with a sort of insolent compassion.

"Oh, spare his blushes," cried Ferfichkin, sniggering.

"My dear sir, allow me to tell you I am not blushing," I broke out at last;
"do you hear? I am dining here, at this café, at my own expense, not at
other people's—note that, Mr. Ferfichkin."

"Wha-at? Isn't every one here dining at his own expense? You would
seem to be . . ." Ferfichkin flew out at me, turning as red as a lobster, and
looking me in the face with fury.

"Tha-at," I answered, feeling I had gone too far, "and I imagine it
would be better to talk of something more intelligent."

"You intend to show off your intelligence, I suppose?"

"Don't disturb yourself, that would be quite out of place here."

"Why are you clacking away like that, my good sir, eh? Have you gone
out of your wits in your office?"

"Enough, gentlemen, enough!" Zverkov cried, authoritatively.

"How stupid it is!" muttered Simonov.

"It really is stupid. We have met here, a company of friends, for a
farewell dinner to a comrade and you carry on an altercation," said
Trudolyubov, rudely addressing himself to me alone. "You invited yourself
to join us, so don't disturb the general harmony."

"Enough, enough!" cried Zverkov. "Give over, gentlemen, it's out of
place. Better let me tell you how I nearly got married the day before yes-
terday. . . ."

And then followed a burlesque narrative of how this gentleman had
almost been married two days before. There was not a word about the
marriage, however, but the story was adorned with generals, colonels and
gentlemen-in-waiting, while Zverkov almost took the lead among them. It
was greeted with approving laughter; Ferfichkin positively squealed.

No one paid any attention to me, and I sat crushed and humiliated.

"Good Heavens, these are not the people for me!" I thought. "And what
a fool I have made of myself before them! I let Ferfichkin go too far,
though. The brutes imagine they are doing me an honor in letting me sit
down with them. They don't understand that it's an honor to them and not
to me! I've grown thinner! My clothes! Oh, damn my trousers! Zver-
kov noticed the yellow stain on the knee as soon as he came in. . . . But

what's the use! I must get up at once, this very minute, take my hat and simply go without a word . . . with contempt! And tomorrow I can send a challenge. The scoundrels! As though I cared about the seven roubles. They may think. . . . Damn it! I don't care about the seven roubles. I'll go this minute!"

Of course I remained. I drank sherry and Lafitte[40] by the glassful in my discomfiture. Being unaccustomed to it, I was quickly affected. My annoyance increased as the wine went to my head. I longed all at once to insult them all in a most flagrant manner and then go away. To seize the moment and show what I could do, so that they would say, "He's clever, though he is absurd," and . . . and . . . in fact, damn them all!

I scanned them all insolently with my drowsy eyes. But they seemed to have forgotten me altogether. They were noisy, vociferous, cheerful. Zverkov was talking all the time. I began listening. Zverkov was talking of some exuberant lady whom he had at last led on to declaring her love (of course, he was lying like a horse), and how he had been helped in this affair by an intimate friend of his, a Prince Kolya, an officer in the hussars, who had three thousand serfs.

"And yet this Kolya, who has three thousand serfs, has not put in an appearance here tonight to see you off," I cut in suddenly.

For a minute every one was silent. "You are drunk already." Trudolyubov deigned to notice me at last, glancing contemptuously in my direction. Zverkov, without a word, examined me as though I were an insect. I dropped my eyes. Simonov made haste to fill up the glasses with champagne.

Trudolyubov raised his glass, as did every one else but me.

"Your health and good luck on the journey!" he cried to Zverkov. "To old times, to our future, hurrah!"

They all tossed off their glasses, and crowded round Zverkov to kiss him. I did not move; my full glass stood untouched before me.

"Why, aren't you going to drink it?" roared Trudolyubov, losing patience and turning menacingly to me.

"I want to make a speech separately, on my own account . . . and then I'll drink it, Mr. Trudolyubov."

"Spiteful brute!" muttered Simonov. I drew myself up in my chair and feverishly seized my glass, prepared for something extraordinary, though I did not know myself precisely what I was going to say.

"*Silence!*" cried Ferfichkin. "Now for a display of wit!"

Zverkov waited very gravely, knowing what was coming.

"Mr. Lieutenant Zverkov," I began, "let me tell you that I hate phrases, phrasemongers and men in corsets . . . that's the first point, and there is a second one to follow it."

There was a general stir.

"The second point is: I hate ribaldry and ribald talkers. Especially ribald talkers! The third point: I love justice, truth and honesty." I went on almost mechanically, for I was beginning to shiver with horror myself and had no idea how I came to be talking like this. "I love thought, Monsieur Zverkov; I love true comradeship, on an equal footing and not . . . H'm . . . I

[40] A kind of wine.

love. . . . But, however, why not? I will drink your health, too, Mr. Zverkov. Seduce the Circassian[41] girls, shoot the enemies of the fatherland and . . . and . . . to your health, Monsieur Zverkov!"

Zverkov got up from his seat, bowed to me and said:

"I am very much obliged to you." He was frightfully offended and turned pale.

"Damn the fellow!" roared Trudolyubov, bringing his fist down on the table.

"Well, he wants a punch in the face for that," squealed Ferfichkin.

"We ought to turn him out," muttered Simonov.

"Not a word, gentlemen, not a movement!" cried Zverkov solemnly, checking the general indignation. "I thank you all, but I can show him for myself how much value I attach to his words."

"Mr. Ferfichkin, you will give me satisfaction tomorrow for your words just now!" I said aloud, turning with dignity to Ferfichkin.

"A duel, you mean? Certainly," he answered. But probably I was so ridiculous as I challenged him and it was so out of keeping with my appearance that everyone, including Ferfichkin, was prostrate with laughter.

"Yes, let him alone, of course! He is quite drunk," Trudolyubov said with disgust.

"I shall never forgive myself for letting him join us," Simonov muttered again.

"Now is the time to throw a bottle at their heads," I thought to myself. I picked up the bottle . . . and filled my glass. . . . "No, I'd better sit on to the end," I went on thinking; "you would be pleased, my friends, if I went away. Nothing will induce me to go. I'll go on sitting here and drinking to the end, on purpose, as a sign that I don't think you of the slightest consequence. I will go on sitting and drinking, because this is a public-house and I paid my entrance money. I'll sit here and drink, for I look upon you as so many pawns, as inanimate pawns. I'll sit here and drink . . . and sing if I want to, yes, sing, for I have the right to . . . to sing . . . H'm!"

But I did not sing. I simply tried not to look at any of them. I assumed most unconcerned attitudes and waited with impatience for them to speak *first*. But alas, they did not address me! And oh, how I wished, how I wished at that moment to be reconciled to them! It struck eight, at last nine. They moved from the table to the sofa. Zverkov stretched himself on a lounge and put one foot on a round table. Wine was brought there. He did, as a fact, order three bottles on his own account. I, of course, was not invited to join them. They all sat round him on the sofa. They listened to him, almost with reverence. It was evident that they were fond of him. "What for? What for?" I wondered. From time to time they were moved to drunken enthusiasm and kissed each other. They talked of the Caucasus, of the nature of true passion, of snug berths in the service, of the income of an hussar[42] called Podkharzhevsky, whom none of them knew personally, and rejoiced in the largeness of it, of the extraordinary grace and beauty of a Princess

[41] The Circassians were an Islamic people in the rebellious Caucasus area near the Black Sea, where Zverkov is to be stationed. See Lermontov's *A Hero of Our Time*.
[42] Cavalryman.

D., whom none of them had ever seen; then it came to Shakespeare's being immortal.

I smiled contemptuously and walked up and down the other side of the room, opposite the sofa, from the table to the stove and back again. I tried my very utmost to show them that I could do without them, and yet I purposely made a noise with my boots, thumping with my heels. But it was all in vain. They paid no attention. I had the patience to walk up and down in front of them from eight o'clock till eleven, in the same place, from the table to the stove and back again. "I walk up and down to please myself and no one can prevent me." The waiter who came into the room stopped, from time to time, to look at me. I was somewhat giddy from turning round so often; at moments it seemed to me that I was in delirium. During those three hours I was three times soaked with sweat and dry again. At times, with an intense, acute pang I was stabbed to the heart by the thought that ten years, twenty years, forty years would pass, and that even in forty years I would remember with loathing and humiliation those filthiest, most ludicrous, and most awful moments of my life. No one could have gone out of his way to degrade himself more shamelessly, and I fully realized it, fully, and yet I went on pacing up and down from the table to the stove. "Oh, if you only knew what thought and feelings I am capable of, how cultured I am!" I thought at moments, mentally addressing the sofa on which my enemies were sitting. But my enemies behaved as though I were not in the room. Once—only once—they turned towards me, just when Zverkov was talking about Shakespeare, and I suddenly gave a contemptuous laugh. I laughed in such an affected and disgusting way that they all at once broke off their conversation, and silently and gravely for two minutes watched me walking up and down from the table to the stove, *taking no notice of them.* But nothing came of it: they said nothing, and two minutes later they ceased to notice me again. It struck eleven.

"Friends," cried Zverkov getting up from the sofa, "let us all be off now, *there!*"

"Of course, of course," the others assented. I turned sharply to Zverkov. I was so harassed, so exhausted, that I would have cut my throat to put an end to it. I was in a fever; my hair, soaked with perspiration, stuck to my forehead and temples.

"Zverkov, I beg your pardon," I said abruptly and resolutely. "Ferfichkin, yours too, and every one's, every one's: I have insulted you all!"

"Aha! A duel is not in your line, old man," Ferfichkin hissed venomously.

It sent a sharp pang to my heart.

"No, it's not the duel I am afraid of, Ferfichkin! I am ready to fight you tomorrow, after we are reconciled. I insist upon it, in fact, and you cannot refuse. I want to show you that I am not afraid of a duel. You shall fire first and I shall fire into the air."

"He is comforting himself," said Simonov.

"He's simply raving," said Trudolyubov.

"But let us pass. Why are you barring our way? What do you want?" Zverkov answered disdainfully.

They were all flushed, their eyes were bright: they had been drinking heavily.

"I ask for your friendship, Zverkov; I insulted you, but . . ."

"Insulted? *You* insulted *me*? Understand, sir, that you never, under any circumstances, could possibly insult *me*."

"And that's enough for you. Out of the way!" concluded Trudolyubov.

"Olympia is mine, friends, that's agreed!" cried Zverkov.

"We won't dispute your right, we won't dispute your right," the others answered, laughing.

I stood as though spat upon. The party went noisily out of the room. Trudolyubov struck up some stupid song. Simonov remained behind for a moment to tip the waiters. I suddenly went up to him.

"Simonov! give me six roubles!" I said, with desperate resolution.

He looked at me in extreme amazement, with vacant eyes. He, too, was drunk.

"You don't mean you are coming with us?"

"Yes."

"I've no money," he snapped out, and with a scornful laugh he went out of the room.

I clutched at his overcoat. It was a nightmare.

"Simonov, I saw you had money. Why do you refuse me? Am I a scoundrel? Beware of refusing me: if you knew, if you knew why I am asking! My whole future, my whole plans depend upon it!"

Simonov pulled out the money and almost flung it at me.

"Take it, if you have no sense of shame!" he pronounced pitilessly, and ran to overtake them.

I was left for a moment alone. Disorder, the remains of dinner, a broken wine-glass on the floor, spilt wine, cigarette ends, fumes of drink and delirium in my brain, an agonizing misery in my heart and finally the waiter, who had seen and heard all and was looking inquisitively into my face.

"I am going there!" I cried. "Either they shall all go down on their knees to beg for my friendship, or I will give Zverkov a slap in the face!"

v

"So this is it, this is it at last—contact with real life," I muttered as I ran headlong downstairs. "This is very different from the Pope's leaving Rome and going to Brazil, very different from the ball on Lake Como!"

"You are a scoundrel," a thought flashed through my mind, "if you laugh at this now."

"No matter!" I cried, answering myself. "Now everything is lost!"

There was no trace to be seen of them, but that made no difference—I knew where they had gone.

At the steps was standing a solitary night sledge-driver in a rough peasant coat, powdered over with the still falling, wet, and as it were warm, snow. It was hot and steamy. The little shaggy piebald horse was also covered with snow and coughing, I remember that very well. I made a rush for the roughly made sledge; but as soon as I raised my foot to get into it, the recollection of how Simonov had just given me six roubles seemed to double me up and I tumbled into the sledge like a sack.

"No, I must do a great deal to make up for all that," I cried. "But I will make up for it or perish on the spot this very night. Start!"

We set off. There was a perfect whirl in my head.

"They won't go down on their knees to beg for my friendship. That is a mirage, cheap mirage, revolting, romantic and fantastical—that's another ball on Lake Como. And so I am bound to slap Zverkov's face! It is my duty to. And so it is settled; I am flying to give him a slap in the face. Hurry up!"

The driver tugged at the reins.

"As soon as I go in I'll give it him. Ought I before giving him the slap to say a few words by way of preface? No. I'll simply go in and give it him. They will all be sitting in the drawing-room, and he with Olympia on the sofa. That damned Olympia! She laughed at my looks on one occasion and refused me. I'll pull Olympia's hair, pull Zverkov's ears! No, better one ear, and pull him by it round the room. Maybe they will all begin beating me and will kick me out. That's most likely, indeed. No matter! Anyway, I shall first slap him; the initiative will be mine; and by the laws of honor that is everything: he will be branded and cannot wipe off the slap by any blows, by nothing but a duel. He will be forced to fight. And let them beat me now. Let them, the ungrateful wretches! Trudolyubov will beat me hardest, he is so strong; Ferfichkin will be sure to catch hold sideways and tug at my hair. But no matter, no matter! That's what I am going for. The blockheads will be forced at last to see the tragedy of it all! When they drag me to the door I shall call out to them that in reality they are not worth my little finger. Get on, driver, get on!" I cried to the driver. He started and flicked his whip, I shouted so savagely.

"We shall fight at daybreak, that's a settled thing. I've done with the office. Ferfichkin made a joke about it just now. But where can I get pistols? Nonsense! I'll get my salary in advance and buy them. And powder, and bullets? That the second's business. And how can it all be done by daybreak? And where am I to get a second? I have no friends. Nonsense!" I cried, lashing myself up more and more. "It's of no consequence! the first person I meet in the street is bound to be my second, just as he would be bound to pull a drowning man out of water. The most eccentric things may happen. Even if I were to ask the director himself to be my second tomorrow, he would be bound to consent, if only from a feeling of chivalry, and to keep the secret! Anton Antonich. . . ."

The fact is, that at that very minute the disgusting absurdity of my plan and the other side of the question was clearer and more vivid to my imagination than it could be to any one on earth. But. . . .

"Get on, driver, get on, you rascal, get on!"

"Ugh, sir!" said the son of toil.

Cold shivers suddenly ran down me.

Wouldn't it be better . . . to go straight home? My God, my God! Why did I invite myself to this dinner yesterday? But no, it's impossible. And my walking up and down for three hours from the table to the stove? No, they, they and no one else must pay for my walking up and down! They must wipe out this dishonor! Drive on!

And what if they give me into custody? They won't dare! They'll be afraid of the scandal. And what if Zverkov is so contemptuous that he refuses to fight a duel? He is sure to; but in that case I'll show them . . . I will turn up at the posting station when he is setting off tomorrow, I'll catch him by the leg, I'll pull off his coat when he gets into the carriage. I'll get

my teeth into his hand, I'll bite him. "See what lengths you can drive a desperate man to!" He may hit me on the head and they may belabor me from behind. I will shout to the assembled multitude: "Look at this young puppy who is driving off to captivate the Circassian girls after letting me spit in his face!"

Of course, after that everything will be over! The office will have vanished off the face of the earth. I shall be arrested, I shall be tried, I shall be dismissed from the service, thrown in prison, sent to Siberia. Never mind! In fifteen years when they let me out of prison I will trudge off to him, a beggar, in rags. I shall find him in some provincial town. He will be married and happy. He will have a grown-up daughter. . . . I shall say to him: "Look, monster, at my hollow cheeks and my rags! I've lost everything— my career, my happiness, art, science, *the woman I loved,* and all through you. Here are pistols. I have come to discharge my pistol and . . . and I . . . forgive you. Then I shall fire into the air and he will hear nothing more of me. . . ."

I was actually on the point of tears, though I knew perfectly well at that moment that all this was out of Pushkin's *Silvio*[43] and Lermontov's *Masquerade.*[44] And all at once I felt horribly ashamed, so ashamed that I stopped the horse, got out of the sledge, and stood still in the snow in the middle of the street. The driver gazed at me, sighing and astonished.

What was I to do? I could not go on there—it was evidently stupid, and I could not leave things as they were, because that would seem as though . . . Heavens, how could I leave things! And after such insults! "No!" I cried, throwing myself into the sledge again. "It is ordained! It is fate! Drive on, drive on!"

And in my impatience I punched the sledge-driver on the back of the neck.

"What are you up to? What are you hitting me for?" the peasant shouted, but he whipped up his nag so that it began kicking.

The wet snow was falling in big flakes; I unbuttoned myself, regardless of it. I forgot everything else, for I had finally decided on the slap, and felt with horror that it was going to happen *now, at once,* and that *no force could stop it.* The deserted street lamps gleamed sullenly in the snowy darkness like torches at a funeral. The snow drifted under my great-coat, under my coat, under my cravat, and melted there. I did not wrap myself up—all was lost, anyway.

At last we arrived. I jumped out, almost unconscious, ran up the steps and began knocking and kicking at the door. I felt fearfully weak, particularly in my legs and my knees. The door was opened quickly as though they knew I was coming. As a fact, Simonov had warned them that perhaps another gentleman would arrive, and this was a place in which one had to give notice and to observe certain precautions. It was one of those "millinery establishments" which were abolished by the police a good time ago. By day it really was a shop; but at night, if one had an introduction, one might visit it for other purposes.

[43] The speaker is thinking of Alexander Pushkin's story "The Shot" (1830), in which the main character is named Silvio and which turns around attempted revenge.

[44] A romantic verse play (1835) by Mikhail Lermontov.

I walked rapidly through the dark shop into the familiar drawing-room, where there was only one candle burning, and stood still in amazement: there was no one there. "Where are they?" I asked somebody. But by now, of course, they had separated. Before me was standing a person with a stupid smile, the "madam" herself, who had seen me before. A minute later a door opened and another person came in.

Taking no notice of anything I strode about the room, and, I believe, I talked to myself. I felt as though I had been saved from death and was conscious of this, joyfully, all over: I should have given that slap, I should certainly, certainly have given it! But now they were not here and . . . everything had vanished and changed! I looked round. I could not realize my condition yet. I looked mechanically at the girl who had come in: and had a glimpse of a fresh, young, rather pale face, with straight, dark eyebrows, and with grave, as it were wondering, eyes that attracted me at once; I should have hated her if she had been smiling. I began looking at her more intently and, as it were, with effort. I had not fully collected my thoughts. There was something simple and good-natured in her face, but something strangely grave. I am sure that this stood in her way here, and no one of those fools had noticed her. She could not, however, have been called a beauty, though she was tall, strong-looking, and well built. She was very simply dressed. Something loathsome stirred within me. I went straight up to her.

I chanced to look into the glass. My harassed face struck me as revolting in the extreme, pale, angry, abject, with dishevelled hair. "No matter, I am glad of it," I thought; "I am glad that I shall seem repulsive to her; I like that."

VI

. . . Somewhere behind a screen a clock began wheezing, as though oppressed by something, as though some one were strangling it. After an unnaturally prolonged wheezing there followed a shrill, nasty, and as it were unexpectedly rapid, chime—as though some one were suddenly jumping forward. It struck two. I woke up, though I had indeed not been asleep but lying half conscious.

It was almost completely dark in the narrow, cramped, low-pitched room, cumbered up with an enormous wardrobe and piles of cardboard boxes and all sorts of frippery and litter. The candle end that had been burning on the table was going out and gave a faint flicker from time to time. In a few minutes there would be complete darkness.

I was not long in coming to myself; everything came back to my mind at once, without an effort, as though it had been in ambush to pounce upon me again. And, indeed, even while I was unconscious a point seemed continually to remain in my memory unforgotten, and round it my dreams moved drearily. But strange to say, everything that had happened to me in that day seemed to me now, on waking, to be in the far, far away past, as though I had long, long ago lived all that down.

My head was full of fumes. Something seemed to be hovering over me, rousing me, exciting me, and making me restless. Misery and spite seemed surging up in me again and seeking an outlet. Suddenly I saw beside me two wide open eyes scrutinizing me curiously and persistently. The look in

those eyes was coldly detached, sullen, as it were utterly remote; it weighed upon me.

A grim idea came into my brain and passed all over my body, as a horrible sensation, such as one feels when one goes into a damp and moldy cellar. There was something unnatural in those two eyes, beginning to look at me only now. I recalled, too, that during those two hours I had not said a single word to this creature, and had, in fact, considered it utterly superfluous; in fact, the silence had for some reason gratified me. Now I suddenly realized vividly the hideous idea—revolting as a spider—of vice, which, without love, grossly and shamelessly begins with that in which true love finds its consummation. For a long time we gazed at each other like that, but she did not drop her eyes before mine and her expression did not change, so that at last I felt uncomfortable.

"What is your name?" I asked abruptly, to put an end to it.

"Liza," she answered almost in a whisper, but somehow far from graciously, and she turned her eyes away.

I was silent.

"What weather! The snow . . . it's disgusting!" I said, almost to myself, putting my arm under my head despondently, and gazing at the ceiling.

She made no answer. This was horrible.

"Have you always lived in Petersburg?" I asked a minute later, almost angrily, turning my head slightly towards her.

"No."

"Where do you come from?"

"From Riga," she answered reluctantly.

"Are you a German?"

"No, Russian."

"Have you been here long?"

"Where?"

"In this house?"

"A fortnight."

She spoke more and more jerkily. The candle went out; I could no longer distinguish her face.

"Have you a father and mother?"

"Yes . . . no . . . I have."

"Where are they?"

"There . . . in Riga."

"What are they?"

"Oh, nothing."

"Nothing? Why, what class are they?"

"Tradespeople."

"Have you always lived with them?"

"Yes."

"How old are you?"

"Twenty."

"Why did you leave them?"

"Oh, for no reason."

That answer meant "Let me alone; I feel sick, sad."

We were silent.

God knows why I did not go away. I felt myself more and more sick and

dreary. The images of the previous day began of themselves, apart from my will, flitting through my memory in confusion. I suddenly recalled something I had seen that morning when, full of anxious thoughts, I was hurrying to the office.

"I saw them carrying a coffin out yesterday and they nearly dropped it," I suddenly said aloud, not that I desired to open the conversation, but as it were by accident.

"A coffin?"

"Yes, in the Haymarket; they were bringing it up out of a cellar."

"From a cellar?"

"Not from a cellar, but from a basement. Oh, you know . . . down below . . . from a house of ill-fame. It was filthy all round . . . Egg-shells, litter . . . stench. It was loathsome."

Silence.

"A nasty day to be buried," I began, simply to avoid being silent.

"Nasty, in what way?"

"The snow, the wet." (I yawned.)

"It makes no difference," she said suddenly, after a brief silence.

"No, it's horrid." (I yawned again.) "The gravediggers must have sworn at getting drenched by the snow. And there must have been water in the grave."

"Why water in the grave?" she asked, with a sort of curiosity, but speaking even more harshly and abruptly than before.

I suddenly began to feel provoked.

"Why, there must have been water at the bottom a foot deep. You can't dig a dry grave in Volkovo Cemetery."

"Why?"

"Why? Why, the place is waterlogged. It's a regular marsh. So they bury them in water. I've seen it myself . . . many times."

(I had never seen it once, indeed I had never been in Volkovo, and had only heard stories of it.)

"Do you mean to say, you don't mind how you die?"

"But why should I die?" she answered, as though defending herself.

"Why, some day you will die, and you will die just the same as that dead woman. She was . . . a girl like you. She died of consumption."

"A wench would have died in a hospital . . ." (She knows all about it already: she said "wench," not "girl.")

"She was in debt to her madam," I retorted, more and more provoked by the discussion; "and went on earning money for her up to the end, though she was in consumption. Some sledge-drivers standing by were talking about her to some soldiers and telling them so. No doubt they knew her. They were laughing. They were going to meet in a pot-house to drink to her memory."

A great deal of this was my invention. Silence followed, profound silence. She did not stir.

"And is it better to die in a hospital?"

"Isn't it just the same? Besides, why should I die?" she added irritably.

"If not now, a little later."

"Why a little later?"

"Why, indeed? Now you are young, pretty, fresh, you fetch a high price.

But after another year of this life you will be very different—you will go off."

"In a year?"

"Anyway, in a year you will be worth less," I continued malignantly. "You will go from here to something lower, another house; a year later—to a third, lower and lower, and in seven years you will come to a basement in the Haymarket. That will be if you were lucky. But it would be much worse if you got some disease, consumption, say . . . and caught a chill, or something or other. It's not easy to get over an illness in your way of life. If you catch anything you may not get rid of it. And so you would die."

"Oh, well, then I shall die," she answered, quite vindictively, and she made a quick movement.

"But one is sorry."

"Sorry for whom?"

"Sorry for life."

Silence.

"Have you been engaged to be married? Eh?"

"What's that to you?"

"Oh, I am not cross-examining you. It's nothing to me. Why are you so cross? Of course you may have had your own troubles. What is it to me? It's simply that I felt sorry."

"Sorry for whom?"

"Sorry for you."

"No need," she whispered hardly audibly, and again made a faint movement.

That incensed me at once. What! I was so gentle with her, and she. . . .

"Why, do you think that you are on the right path?"

"I don't think anything."

"That's what's wrong, that you don't think. Realize it while there is still time. There still is time. You are still young, good-looking; you might love, be married, be happy. . . ."

"Not all married women are happy," she snapped out in the rude abrupt tone she used at first.

"Not all, of course, but anyway it is much better than the life here. Infinitely better. Besides, with love one can live even without happiness. Even in sorrow life is sweet; life is sweet, however one lives. But here what is there but . . . filth? Phew!"

I turned away with disgust; I was no longer reasoning coldly. I began to feel myself what I was saying and warmed to the subject. I was already longing to expound the cherished ideas I had brooded over in my corner. Something suddenly flared up in me. An object had appeared before me.

"Never mind my being here, I am not an example for you. I am, perhaps, worse than you are. I was drunk when I came here, though," I hastened, however, to say in self-defense. "Besides, a man is no example for a woman. It's a different thing. I may degrade and defile myself, but I am not any one's slave. I come and go, and that's an end of it. I shake it off, and I am a different man. But you are a slave from the start. Yes, a slave! You give up everything, your whole freedom. If you want to break your chains afterwards, you won't be able to: you will be more and more fast in the snares. It is an accursed bondage. I know it. I won't speak of anything else,

maybe you won't understand, but tell me: no doubt you are in debt to your madam? There, you see," I added, though she made no answer, but only listened in silence, entirely absorbed, "that's a bondage for you! You will never buy your freedom. They will see to that. It's like selling your soul to the devil. . . . And besides . . . perhaps I, too, am just as unlucky—how do you know—and wallow in the mud on purpose, out of misery? You know, men take to drink from grief; well, maybe I am here from grief. Come, tell me, what is there good here? Here you and I . . . came together . . . just now and did not say one word to one another all the time, and it was only afterwards you began staring at me like a wild creature, and I at you. Is that loving? Is that how one human being should meet another? It's hideous, that's what it is!"

"Yes!" she assented sharply and hurriedly.

I was positively astounded by the promptitude of this "Yes." So the same thought may have been straying through her mind when she was staring at me just before. So she, too, was capable of certain thoughts? "Damn it all, this was interesting, this was a point of likeness!" I thought, almost rubbing my hands. And indeed it's easy to turn a young soul like that!

It was the exercise of my power that attracted me most.

She turned her head nearer to me, and it seemed to me in the darkness that she propped herself on her arm. Perhaps she was scrutinizing me. How I regretted that I could not see her eyes. I heard her deep breathing.

"Why have you come here?" I asked her, with a note of authority already in my voice.

"Oh, I don't know."

"But how nice it would be to be living in your father's house! It's warm and free; and you have a home of your own."

"But what if it's worse than this?"

"I must take the right tone," flashed through my mind. "I may not get far with sentimentality." But it was only a momentary thought. I swear she really did interest me. Besides, I was exhausted and moody. And cunning so easily goes hand-in-hand with feeling.

"Who denies it!" I hastened to answer. "Anything may happen. I am convinced that some one has wronged you, and that you are more sinned against than sinning. Of course, I know nothing of your story, but it's not likely a girl like you has come here of her own inclination. . . ."

"A girl like me?" she whispered, hardly audibly; but I heard it.

Damn it all, I was flattering her. That was horrid. But perhaps it was a good thing. . . . She was silent.

"See, Liza, I will tell you about myself. If I had had a home from childhood, I shouldn't be what I am now. I often think that. However bad it may be at home, anyway they are your father and mother, and not enemies, strangers. Once a year at least, they'll show their love of you. Anyway, you know you are at home. I grew up without a home; and perhaps that's why I've turned so . . . unfeeling."

I waited again. "Perhaps she doesn't understand," I thought, "and, indeed, it is absurd—it's moralizing."

"If I were a father and had a daughter, I believe I should love my daughter more than my sons, really," I began indirectly, as though talking of something else, to distract her attention. I must confess I blushed.

"Why so?" she asked.

Ah! so she was listening!

"I don't know, Liza. I knew a father who was a stern, austere man, but used to go down on his knees to his daughter, used to kiss her hands, her feet, he couldn't make enough of her, really. When she danced at parties he used to stand for five hours at a stretch, gazing at her. He was mad over her: I understand that! She would fall asleep tired at night, and he would wake to kiss her in her sleep and make the sign of the cross over her. He would go about in a dirty old coat, he was stingy to every one else, but would spend his last penny for her, giving her expensive presents, and it was his greatest delight when she was pleased with what he gave her. Fathers always love their daughters more than the mothers do. Some girls live happily at home! And I believe I should never let my daughters marry."

"What next?" she said, with a faint smile.

"I should be jealous, I really should. To think that she should kiss any one else! That she should love a stranger more than her father! It's painful to imagine it. Of course, that's all nonsense, of course every father would be reasonable at last. But I believe before I should let her marry, I should worry myself to death; I should find fault with all her suitors. But I should end by letting her marry whom she herself loved. The one whom the daughter loves always seems the worst to the father, you know. That is always so. So many family troubles come from that."

"Some are glad to sell their daughters, rather than marrying them honorably."

Ah, so that was it!

"Such a thing, Liza, happens in those accursed families in which there is neither love nor God," I retorted warmly, "and where there is no love, there is no sense either. There are such families, it's true, but I am not speaking of them. You must have seen wickedness in your own family, if you talk like that. Truly, you must have been unlucky. H'm! . . . that sort of thing mostly comes about through poverty."

"And is it any better with the gentry? Even among the poor, honest people live happily."

"H'm . . . yes. Perhaps. Another thing, Liza, man is fond of reckoning up his troubles, but does not count his joys. If he counted them up as he ought, he would see that every lot has enough happiness provided for it. And what if all goes well with the family, if the blessing of God is upon it, if the husband is a good one, loves you, cherishes you, never leaves you! There is happiness in such a family! Even sometimes there is happiness in the midst of sorrow; and indeed sorrow is everywhere. If you marry *you will find out for yourself.* But think of the first years of married life with one you love: what happiness, what happiness there sometimes is in it! And indeed it's the ordinary thing. In those early days even quarrels with one's husband end happily. Some women get up quarrels with their husbands just because they love them. Indeed, I knew a woman like that: she seemed to say that because she loved him, she would torment him and make him feel it. You know that you may torment a man on purpose through love. Women are particularly given to that, thinking to themselves 'I will love him so, I will make so much of him afterwards, that it's no sin to torment him a little now.' And all in the house rejoice in the sight of you, and you are happy

and gay and peaceful and honorable. . . . Then there are some women who are jealous. If he went off anywhere—I knew one such woman, she couldn't restrain herself, but would jump up at night and run off on the sly to find out where he was, whether he was with some other woman. That's a pity. And the woman knows herself it's wrong, and her heart fails her and she suffers, but she loves—it's all through love. And how sweet it is to make it up after quarrels, to own herself in the wrong or to forgive him! And they are both so happy all at once—as though they had met anew, been married over again; as though their love had begun afresh. And no one, no one should know what passes between husband and wife if they love one another. And whatever quarrels there may be between them they ought not to call in their own mother to judge between them and tell tales of one another. They are their own judges. Love is a holy mystery and ought to be hidden from all other eyes, whatever happens. That makes it holier and better. They respect one another more, and much is built on respect. And if once there has been love, if they have been married for love, why should love pass away? Surely one can keep it! It is rare that one cannot keep it. And if the husband is kind and straightforward, why should not love last? The first phase of married love will pass, it is true, but then there will come a love that is better still. Then there will be the union of souls, they will have everything in common, there will be no secrets between them. And once they have children, the most difficult times will seem to them happy, so long as there is love and courage. Even toil will be a joy, you may deny yourself bread for your children and even that will be a joy. They will love you for it afterwards; so you are laying by for your future. As the children grow up you feel that you are an example, a support for them; that even after you die your children will always keep your thoughts and feelings, because they have received them from you, they will take on your semblance and likeness. So you see this is a great duty. How can it fail to draw the father and mother nearer? People say it's a trial to have children. Who says that? It is heavenly happiness! Are you fond of little children, Liza? I am awfully fond of them. You know—a little rosy baby boy at your bosom, and what husband's heart is not touched, seeing his wife nursing his child! A plump little rosy baby, sprawling and snuggling, chubby little hands and feet, clean tiny little nails, so tiny that it makes one laugh to look at them; eyes that look as if they understand everything. And while it sucks it clutches at your bosom with its little hand, plays. When its father comes up, the child tears itself away from the bosom, flings itself back, looks at its father, laughs, as though it were fearfully funny and falls to sucking again. Or it will bite its mother's breast when its little teeth are coming, while it looks sideways at her with its little eyes as though to say, 'Look, I am biting!' Is not all that happiness when they are the three together, husband, wife and child? One can forgive a great deal for the sake of such moments. Yes, Liza, one must first learn to live oneself before one blames others!"

"It's by pictures, pictures like that one must get at you," I thought to myself, though I did speak with real feeling, and all at once I flushed crimson. "What if she were suddenly to burst out laughing, what should I do then?" That idea drove me to fury. Towards the end of my speech I really was excited, and now my vanity was somehow wounded. The silence continued. I almost nudged her.

"Why are you——" she began and stopped. But I understood: there was a quiver of something different in her voice, not abrupt, harsh and unyielding as before, but something soft and shamefaced, so shamefaced that I suddenly felt ashamed and guilty.

"What?" I asked, with tender curiosity.

"Why, you . . ."

"What?"

"Why, you . . . speak somehow like a book," she said, and again there was a note of irony in her voice.

That remark sent a pang to my heart. It was not what I was expecting.

I did not understand that she was hiding her feelings under irony, that this is usually the last refuge of modest and chaste-souled people when the privacy of their soul is coarsely and intrusively invaded, and that their pride makes them refuse to surrender till the last moment and shrink from giving expression to their feelings before you. I ought to have guessed the truth from the timidity with which she had repeatedly approached her sarcasm, only bringing herself to utter it at last with an effort. But I did not guess, and an evil feeling took possession of me.

"Wait a bit!" I thought.

VII

"Oh, hush, Liza! How can you talk about being like a book, when it makes even me, an outsider, feel sick? Though I don't look at it as an outsider, for, indeed, it touches me to the heart. . . . Is it possible, is it possible that you do not feel sick at being here yourself? Evidently habit does wonders! God knows what habit can do with any one. Can you seriously think that you will never grow old, that you will always be good-looking, and that they will keep you here for ever and ever? I say nothing of the loathsomeness of the life here. . . . Though let me tell you this about it—about your present life, I mean; here though you are young now, attractive, nice, with soul and feeling, yet you know as soon as I came to myself just now I felt at once sick at being here with you! One can only come here when one is drunk. But if you were anywhere else, living as good people live, I should perhaps be more than attracted by you, should fall in love with you, should be glad of a look from you, let alone a word; I should hang about your door, should go down on my knees to you, should look upon you as my betrothed and think it an honor to be allowed to. I should not dare to have an impure thought about you. But here, you see, I know that I have only to whistle and you have to come with me whether you like it or not. I don't consult your wishes, but you mine. The lowest laborer hires himself as a workman, but he doesn't make a slave of himself altogether; besides, he knows that he will be free again presently. But when are you free? Only think what you are giving up here? What is it you are making a slave of? It is your soul, together with your body; you are selling your soul which you have no right to dispose of! You give your love to be outraged by every drunkard! Love! But that's everything, you know, it's a priceless diamond, it's a maiden's treasure, love—why, a man would be ready to give his soul, to face death to gain that love. But how much is your love worth now? You are sold, all of you, body and soul, and there is no need to strive for love when you can have everything without love. And you know there is no greater insult to a

girl than that, do you understand? To be sure, I have heard that they comfort you, poor fools, they let you have lovers of your own here. But you know that's simply a farce, that's simply a sham, it's just laughing at you, and you are taken in by it! Why, do you suppose he really loves you, that lover of yours? I don't believe it. How can he love you when he knows you may be called away from him any minute? He would be a low fellow if he did! Will he have a grain of respect for you? What have you in common with him? He laughs at you and robs you—that is all his love amounts to! You are lucky if he does not beat you. Very likely he does beat you, too. Ask him, if you have got one, whether he will marry you. He will laugh in your face, if he doesn't spit in it or give you a blow—though maybe he is not worth a bad halfpenny himself. And for what have you ruined your life, if you come to think of it? For the coffee they give you to drink and the plentiful meals? But with what object are they feeding you up? An honest girl couldn't swallow the food, for she would know what she was being fed for. You are in debt here, and, of course, you will always be in debt, and you will go on in debt to the end, till the visitors here begin to scorn you. And that will soon happen, don't rely upon your youth—all that flies by express train here, you know. You will be kicked out. And not simply kicked out; long before that she'll begin nagging at you, scolding you, abusing you, as though you had not sacrificed your health for her, had not thrown away your youth and your soul for her benefit, but as though you had ruined her, beggared her, robbed her. And don't expect any one to take your part: the others, your companions, will attack you, too, to win her favor, for all are in slavery here, and have lost all conscience and pity here long ago. They have become utterly vile, and nothing on earth is viler, more loathsome, and more insulting than their abuse. And you are laying down everything here, unconditionally, youth and health and beauty and hope, and at twenty-two you will look like a woman of five-and-thirty, and you will be lucky if you are not diseased, pray to God for that! No doubt you are thinking now that you have a gay time and no work to do! Yet there is no work harder or more dreadful in the world or ever has been. One would think that the heart alone would be worn out with tears. And you won't dare to say a word, not half a word when they drive you away from here; you will go away as though you were to blame. You will change to another house, then to a third, then somewhere else, till you come down at last to the Haymarket. There you will be beaten at every turn; that is good manners there, the visitors don't know how to be friendly without beating you. You don't believe that it is so hateful there? Go and look for yourself some time, you can see with your own eyes. Once, one New Year's Day, I saw a woman at a door. They had turned her out as a joke, to give her a taste of the frost because she had been crying so much, and they shut the door behind her. At nine o'clock in the morning she was already quite drunk, dishevelled, half-naked, covered with bruises, her face was powdered, but she had a black-eye, blood was trickling from her nose and her teeth; some cabman had just given her a drubbing. She was sitting on the stone steps, a salt fish of some sort was in her hand; she was crying, wailing something about her luck and beating with the fish on the steps, and cabmen and drunken soldiers were crowding in the doorway taunting her. You don't believe that you will ever be like that? I should be sorry to believe

it, too, but how do you know; maybe ten years, eight years ago that very woman with the salt fish came here fresh as a cherub, innocent, pure, knowing no evil, blushing at every word. Perhaps she was like you, proud, ready to take offense, not like the others; perhaps she looked like a queen, and knew what happiness was in store for the man who should love her and whom she should love. Do you see how it ended? And what if at that very minute when she was beating on the filthy steps with that fish, drunken and dishevelled—what if at that very minute she recalled the pure early days in her father's house, when she used to go to school and the neighbor's son watched for her on the way, declaring that he would love her as long as he lived, that he would devote his life to her, and when they vowed to love one another for ever and be married as soon as they were grown up! No, Liza, it would be happy for you if you were to die soon of consumption in some corner, in some cellar like that woman just now. In the hospital, do you say? You will be lucky if they take you, but what if you are still of use to the madam here? Consumption is a queer disease, it is not like fever. The patient goes on hoping till the last minute and says he is all right. He deludes himself. And that just suits your madam. Don't doubt it, that's how it is; you have sold your soul, and what is more you owe money, so you daren't say a word. But when you are dying, all will abandon you, all will turn away from you, for then there will be nothing to get from you. What's more, they will reproach you for cumbering the place, for being so long over dying. However you beg you won't get a drink of water without abuse: 'Whenever are you going off, you nasty hussy, you won't let us sleep with your moaning, you make the gentlemen sick.' That's true, I have heard such things said myself. They will thrust you dying into the filthiest corner in the cellar—in the damp and darkness; what will your thoughts be, lying there alone? When you die, strange hands will lay you out, with grumbling and impatience; no one will bless you, no one will sigh for you, they only want to get rid of you as soon as may be; they will buy a coffin, take you to the grave as they did that poor woman today, and celebrate your memory at the tavern. In the gravest sleet, filth, wet snow—no need to put themselves out for you—'Let her down, Vanyukha; it's just like her luck—even here, she is head-foremost,[45] the hussy. Shorten the cord, you rascal.' 'It's all right as it is.' 'All right, is it? Why, she's on her side! She was a fellow-creature, after all! But, never mind, throw the earth on her.' And they won't care to waste much time quarrelling over you. They will scatter the wet blue clay as quick as they can and go off to the tavern . . . and there your memory on earth will end; other women have children to go to their graves, fathers, husbands. While for you neither tear, nor sigh, nor remembrance; no one in the whole world will ever come to you, your name will vanish from the face of the earth—as though you had never existed, never been born at all! Nothing but filth and mud, however you knock at your coffin lid at night, when the dead arise, however you cry: 'Let me out, kind people, to live in the light of day! My life was no life at all; my life has been thrown away like a dish-clout;[46] it was drunk away in the tavern at the Haymarket; let me out, kind people, to live in the world again.'"

And I worked myself up to such a pitch that I began to have a lump in

[45] Both "head first" and "buffeted by fate." [46] Dishcloth.

my throat myself, and . . . and all at once I stopped, sat up in dismay, and bending over apprehensively, began to listen with a beating heart. I had reason to be troubled.

I had felt for some time that I was turning her soul upside down and rending her heart, and—and the more I was convinced of it, the more eagerly I desired to gain my object as quickly and as effectually as possible. It was the exercise of my skill that carried me away; yet it was not merely sport. . . .

I knew I was speaking stiffly, artificially, even bookishly, in fact, I could not speak except "like a book." But that did not trouble me: I knew, I felt that I should be understood and that this very bookishness might be an assistance. But now, having attained my effect, I was suddenly panic-stricken. Never before had I witnessed such despair! She was lying on her face, thrusting her face into the pillow and clutching it in both hands. Her heart was being torn. Her youthful body was shuddering all over as though in convulsions. Suppressed sobs rent her bosom and suddenly burst out in weeping and wailing, then she pressed closer into the pillow: she did not want any one here, not a living soul, to know of her anguish and her tears. She bit the pillow, bit her hand till it bled (I saw that afterwards), or, thrusting her fingers into her dishevelled hair, seemed rigid with the effort of restraint, holding her breath and clenching her teeth. I began saying something, begging her to calm herself, but felt that I did not dare; and all at once, in a sort of cold shiver, almost in terror, began fumbling in the dark, trying hurriedly to get dressed to go. It was dark: though I tried my best I could not finish dressing quickly. Suddenly I felt a box of matches and a candlestick with a whole candle in it. As soon as the room was lighted up, Liza sprang up, sat up in bed, and with a contorted face, with a half insane smile, looked at me almost senselessly. I sat down beside her and took her hands; she came to herself, made an impulsive movement towards me, would have caught hold of me, but did not dare, and slowly bowed her head before me.

"Liza, my dear, I was wrong . . . forgive me, my dear," I began, but she squeezed my hand in her fingers so tightly that I felt I was saying the wrong thing and stopped.

"This is my address, Liza, come to me."

"I will come," she answered resolutely, her head still bowed.

"But now I am going, good-bye . . . till we meet again."

I got up; she, too, stood up and suddenly flushed all over, gave a shudder, snatched up a shawl that was lying on a chair and muffled herself in it to her chin. As she did this she gave another sickly smile, blushed and looked at me strangely. I felt wretched; I was in haste to get away—to disappear.

"Wait a minute," she said suddenly, in the passage just at the doorway, stopping me with her hand on my overcoat. She put down the candle in hot haste and ran off; evidently she had thought of something or wanted to show me something. As she ran away she flushed, her eyes shone, and there was a smile on her lips—what was the meaning of it? Against my will I waited: she came back a minute later with an expression that seemed to ask forgiveness for something. In fact, it was not the same face, not the same look as the evening before: sullen, mistrustful and obstinate. Her eyes now

were imploring, soft, and at the same time trustful, caressing, timid. The expression with which children look at people they are very fond of, of whom they are asking a favor. Her eyes were a light hazel, they were lovely eyes, full of life, and capable of expressing love as well as sullen hatred.

Making no explanation, as though I, as a sort of higher being, must understand everything without explanations, she held out a piece of paper to me. Her whole face was positively beaming at that instant with naïve, almost childish, triumph. I unfolded it. It was a letter to her from a medical student or some one of that sort—a very high-flown and flowery, but extremely respectful, love-letter. I don't recall the words now, but I remember well that through the high-flown phrases there was apparent a genuine feeling, which cannot be feigned. When I had finished reading it I met her glowing, questioning, and childishly impatient eyes fixed upon me. She fastened her eyes upon my face and waited impatiently for what I should say. In a few words, hurriedly, but with a sort of joy and pride, she explained to me that she had been to a dance somewhere in a private house, a family of "very nice people *who knew nothing,* absolutely nothing, for she had only come here so lately and it had all happened . . . and she hadn't made up her mind to stay and was certainly going away as soon as she had paid her debt . . ." and at that party there had been the student who had danced with her all the evening. He had talked to her, and it turned out that he had known her in old days at Riga when he was a child, they had played together, but a very long time ago—and he knew her parents, but *about this* he knew nothing, nothing whatever, and had no suspicion! And the day after the dance (three days ago) he had sent her that letter through the friend with whom she had gone to the party . . . and . . . well, that was all."

She dropped her shining eyes with a sort of bashfulness as she finished.

The poor girl was keeping that student's letter as a precious treasure, and had run to fetch it, her only treasure, because she did not want me to go away without knowing that she, too, was honestly and genuinely loved; that she, too, was addressed respectfully. No doubt that letter was destined to lie in her box and lead to nothing. But none the less, I am certain that she would keep it all her life as a precious treasure, as her pride and justification, and now at such a minute she had thought of that letter and brought it with naïve pride to raise herself in my eyes that I might see, that I, too, might think well of her. I said nothing, pressed her hand and went out. I so longed to get away. . . . I walked all the way home, in spite of the fact that the melting snow was still falling in heavy flakes. I was exhausted, shattered, in bewilderment. But behind the bewilderment the truth was already gleaming. The loathsome truth.

VIII

It was some time, however, before I consented to recognize that truth. Waking up in the morning after some hours of heavy, leaden sleep, and immediately realizing all that had happened on the previous day, I was positively amazed at my last night's *sentimentality* with Liza, at all those "outcries of horror and pity." "To think of having such an attack of womanish hysteria, pah!" I concluded. And what did I thrust my address upon her for? What if she comes? Let her come, though; it doesn't matter. . . . But

obviously, that was not now the chief and the most important matter: I had to make haste and at all costs save my reputation in the eyes of Zverkov and Simonov as quickly as possible; that was the chief business. And I was so taken up that morning that I actually forgot all about Liza.

First of all I had at once to repay what I had borrowed the day before from Simonov. I resolved on a desperate measure: to borrow fifteen roubles straight off from Anton Antonich. As luck would have it he was in the best of humors that morning, and gave it to me at once, on the first asking. I was so delighted at this that, as I signed the I O U with a swaggering air, I told him casually that the night before "I had been keeping it up with some friends at the Hôtel de Paris; we were giving a farewell party to a comrade, in fact, I might say a friend of my childhood, and you know—a desperate rake, fearfully spoiled—of course, he belongs to a good family, and has considerable means, a brilliant career; he is witty, charming, a regular Lovelace,[47] you understand; we drank an extra 'half-dozen' and . . ."

And it went off all right; all this was uttered very easily, unconstrainedly and complacently.

On reaching home I promptly wrote to Simonov.

To this hour I am lost in admiration when I recall the truly gentlemanly, good-humored, candid tone of my letter. With tact and good-breeding, and, above all, entirely without superfluous words, I blamed myself for all that had happened. I defended myself, "if I really may be allowed to defend myself," by alleging that, being utterly unaccustomed to wine, I had been intoxicated with the first glass, which I said I had drunk before they arrived, while I was waiting for them at the Hôtel de Paris between five and six o'clock. I begged Simonov's pardon especially; I asked him to convey my explanations to all the others, especially to Zverkov, whom "I seemed to remember as though in a dream" I had insulted. I added that I would have called upon all of them myself, but my head ached, and besides I had not the face to. I was particularly pleased with a certain lightness, almost carelessness (strictly within the bounds of politeness, however), which was apparent in my style, and better than any possible arguments, gave them at once to understand that I took rather an independent view of "all that unpleasantness last night"; that I was by no means so utterly crushed as you, my friends, probably imagine; but on the contrary, looked upon it as a gentleman serenely respecting himself should look upon it. "On a young hero's past no censure is cast!"

"There is actually an aristocratic playfulness about it!" I thought admiringly, as I read over the letter. And it's all because I am an intellectual and cultivated man! Another man in my place would not have known how to extricate himself, but here I have got out of it and am as jolly as ever again, and all because I am "a cultivated and educated man of our day." And, indeed, perhaps, everything was due to the wine yesterday. H'm! . . . no, it was not the wine. I did not drink anything at all between five and six when I was waiting for them. I had lied to Simonov; I had lied shamelessly; and indeed I wasn't ashamed now. . . . Hang it all though, the great thing was that I was rid of it.

[47] A seducer, from a major character in Samuel Richardson's *Clarissa Harlowe* (1747–48).

I put six roubles in the letter, sealed it up, and asked Apollon to take it to Simonov. When he learned that there was money in the letter, Apollon became more respectful and agreed to take it. Towards evening I went out for a walk. My head was still aching and giddy after yesterday. But as evening came on and the twilight grew denser, my impressions and, following them, my thoughts, grew more and more different and confused. Something was not dead within me, in the depths of my heart and conscience it would not die, and it showed itself in acute depression. For the most part I jostled my way through the most crowded business streets, along Myeshchansky Street, along Sadovy Street and in Yusupov Garden. I always liked particularly sauntering along these streets in the dusk, just when there were crowds of working people of all sorts going home from their daily work, with faces looking cross with anxiety. What I liked was just that cheap bustle, that bare prose. On this occasion the jostling of the streets irritated me more than ever. I could not make out what was wrong with me, I could not find the clue, something seemed rising up continually in my soul, painfully, and refusing to be appeased. I returned home completely upset, it was just as though some crime were lying on my conscience.

The thought that Liza was coming worried me continually. It seemed queer to me that of all my recollections of yesterday this tormented me, as it were, especially, as it were, quite separately. Everything else I had quite succeeded in forgetting by the evening; I dismissed it all and was still perfectly satisfied with my letter to Simonov. But on this point I was not satisfied at all. It was as though I were worried only by Liza. "What if she comes," I thought incessantly, "well, it doesn't matter, let her come! H'm! it's horrid that she should see, for instance, how I live. Yesterday I seemed such a hero to her, while now, h'm! It's horrid, though, that I have let myself go so, the room looks like a beggar's. And I brought myself to go out to dinner in such a suit! And my American leather[48] sofa with the stuffing sticking out. And my dressing-gown, which will not cover me, such tatters, and she will see all this and she will see Apollon. That beast is certain to insult her. He will fasten upon her in order to be rude to me. And I, of course, shall be panic-stricken as usual, I shall begin bowing and scraping before her and pulling my dressing-gown round me, I shall begin smiling, telling lies. Oh, the beastliness! And it isn't the beastliness of it that matters most! There is something more important, more loathsome, viler! Yes, viler! And to put on that dishonest lying mask again!" . . .

When I reached that thought I fired up all at once.

"Why dishonest? How dishonest? I was speaking sincerely last night. I remember there was real feeling in me, too. What I wanted was to excite an honorable feeling in her. . . . Her crying was a good thing, it will have a good effect."

Yet I could not feel at ease. All that evening, even when I had come back home, even after nine o'clock, when I calculated that Liza could not possibly come, she still haunted me, and what was worse, she came back to my mind always in the same position. One moment out of all that had happened last night stood vividly before my imagination; the moment when I struck a match and saw her pale, distorted face, with its look of torture.

[48] A cheap kind of artificial leather.

And what a pitiful, what an unnatural, what a distorted smile she had at that moment! But I did not know then, that fifteen years later I should still in my imagination see Liza, always with the pitiful, distorted, inappropriate smile which was on her face at that minute.

Next day I was ready again to look upon it all as nonsense, due to over-excited nerves, and, above all, as *exaggerated*. I was always conscious of that weak point of mine, and sometimes very much afraid of it. "I exaggerate everything, that is where I go wrong," I repeated to myself every hour. But, however, "Liza will very likely come all the same," was the refrain with which all my reflections ended. I was so uneasy that I sometimes flew into a fury: "She'll come, she is certain to come!" I cried, running about the room, "if not today, she will come tomorrow; she'll find me out! The damnable romanticism of these pure hearts! Oh, the vileness—oh, the silliness—oh, the stupidity of these 'wretched sentimental souls!' Why, how fail to understand? How could one fail to understand?"

But at this point I stopped short, and in great confusion, indeed.

And how few, how few words, I thought, in passing, were needed; how little of the idyllic (and affectedly, bookishly, artificially idyllic too) had sufficed to turn a whole human life at once according to my will. That's virginity, to be sure! Freshness of soil!

At times a thought occurred to me, to go to her, "to tell her all," and beg her not to come to me. But this thought stirred such wrath in me that I believed I should have crushed that "damned" Liza if she had chanced to be near me at the time. I should have insulted her, have spat at her, have turned her out, have struck her!

One day passed, however, another and another; she did not come and I began to grow calmer. I felt particularly bold and cheerful after nine o'clock, I even sometimes began dreaming, and rather sweetly: I, for instance, became the salvation of Liza, simply through her coming to me and my talking to her. . . . I develop her, educate her. Finally, I notice that she loves me, loves me passionately. I pretend not to understand (I don't know, however, why I pretend, just for effect, perhaps). At last all confusion, transfigured, trembling and sobbing, she flings herself at my feet and says that I am her savior, and that she loves me better than anything in the world. I am amazed, but. . . . "Liza," I say, "can you imagine that I have not noticed your love, I saw it all, I divined it, but I did not dare to approach you first, because I had an influence over you and was afraid that you would force yourself, from gratitude, to respond to my love, would try to rouse in your heart a feeling which was perhaps absent, and I did not wish that . . . because it would be tyranny . . . it would be indelicate (in short, I launch off at that point into European, inexplicably lofty subtleties à la George Sand[49]), but now, now you are mine, you are my creation, you are pure, you are good, you are my noble wife.

> 'Into my house come bold and free,
> Its rightful mistress there to be.'"[50]

[49] Pseudonym of the French novelist and feminist Aurore Dupin (1804–76). Her novels are marked by a high moral idealism.

[50] These are the last lines of the poem by Nekrasov quoted at the beginning of Part II.

Then we begin living together, go abroad and so on, and so on. In fact, in the end it seemed vulgar to me myself, and I began putting out my tongue at myself.

Besides, they won't let her out, "the hussy!" I thought. They don't let them go out very readily, especially in the evening (for some reason I fancied she would come in the evening, and at seven o'clock precisely). Though she did say she was not altogether a slave there yet, and had certain rights; so, h'm! Damn it all, she will come, she is sure to come!

It was a good thing, in fact, that Apollon distracted my attention at that time by his rudeness. He drove me beyond all patience! He was the bane of my life, the curse laid upon me by Providence. We had been squabbling continually for years, and I hated him. My God, how I hated him! I believe I had never hated any one in my life as I hated him, especially at some moments. He was an elderly, dignified man, who worked part of his time as a tailor. But for some unknown reason he despised me beyond all measure, and looked down upon me insufferably. Though, indeed, he looked down upon every one. Simply to glance at that flaxen, smoothly brushed head, at the tuft of hair he combed up on his forehead and oiled with sunflower oil, at that dignified mouth, compressed into the shape of the letter V, made one feel one was confronting a man who never doubted of himself. He was a pedant, to the most extreme point, the greatest pedant I had met on earth, and with that had a vanity only befitting Alexander of Macedon.[51] He was in love with every button on his coat, every nail on his fingers—absolutely in love with them, and he looked it! In his behavior to me he was a perfect tyrant, he spoke very little to me, and if he chanced to glance at me he gave me a firm, majestically self-confident and invariably ironical look that drove me sometimes to fury. He did his work with the air of doing me the greatest favor. Though he did scarcely anything for me, and did not, indeed, consider himself bound to do anything. There could be no doubt that he looked upon me as the greatest fool on earth, and that if he did not "get rid of me" it was simply because he could get wages from me every month. He consented to do nothing for me for seven roubles a month. Many sins should be forgiven me for what I suffered from him. My hatred reached such a point that sometimes his very step almost threw me into convulsions. What I loathed particularly was his lisp. His tongue must have been a little too long or something of that sort, for he continually lisped, and seemed to be very proud of it, imagining that it greatly added to his dignity. He spoke in a slow, measured tone, with his hands behind his back and his eyes fixed on the ground. He maddened me particularly when he read aloud the psalms to himself behind his partition. Many a battle I waged over that reading! But he was awfully fond of reading aloud in the evenings, in a slow, even, sing-song voice, as though over the dead. It is interesting that that is how he has ended: he hires himself out to read the psalms over the dead, and at the same time he kills rats and makes blacking.[52] But at that time I could not get rid of him, it was as though he were chemically combined with my existence. Besides, nothing would have in-

[51] Alexander the Great (356–323 b.c.).
[52] Compound to make things black, either shoes or stoves.

duced him to consent to leave me. I could not live in furnished lodgings: my lodging was my private solitude, my shell, my cave, in which I concealed myself from all mankind, and Apollon seemed to me, for some reason, an integral part of that flat, and for seven years I could not turn him away.

To be two or three days behind with his wages, for instance, was impossible. He would have made such a fuss, I should not have known where to hide my head. But I was so exasperated with every one during those days, that I made up my mind for some reason and with some object to *punish* Apollon and not to pay him for a fortnight the wages that were owing him. I had for a long time—for the last two years—been intending to do this, simply in order to teach him not to give himself airs with me, and to show him that if I liked I could withhold his wages. I purposed to say nothing to him about it, and was purposely silent indeed, in order to score off his pride and force him to be the first to speak of his wages. Then I would take the seven roubles out of a drawer, show him I have the money put aside on purpose, but that I won't, I won't, I simply won't pay him his wages, I won't just because that is "what I wish," because "I am master, and it is for me to decide," because he has been disrespectful, because he has been rude; but if he were to ask respectfully I might be softened and give it to him, otherwise he might wait another fortnight, another three weeks, a whole month. . . .

But angry as I was, yet he got the better of me. I could not hold out for four days. He began as he always did begin in such cases, for there had been such cases already, there had been attempts (and it may be observed I knew all this beforehand, I knew his nasty tactics by heart). He would begin by fixing upon me an exceedingly severe stare, keeping it up for several minutes at a time, particularly on meeting me or seeing me out of the house. If I held out and pretended not to notice these stares, he would, still in silence, proceed to further tortures. All at once, *à propos* of nothing, he would walk softly and smoothly into my room, when I was pacing up and down or reading, stand at the door, one hand behind his back and one foot behind the other, and fix upon me a stare more than severe, utterly contemptuous. If I suddenly asked him what he wanted, he would make me no answer, but continue staring at me persistently for some seconds, then, with a peculiar compression of his lips and a most significant air, deliberately turn round and deliberately go back to his room. Two hours later he would come out again and again present himself before me in the same way. It had happened that in my fury I did not even ask him what he wanted, but simply raised my head sharply and imperiously and began staring back at him. So we stared at one another for two minutes; at last he turned with deliberation and dignity and went back again for two hours.

If I were still not brought to reason by all this, but persisted in my revolt, he would suddenly begin sighing while he looked at me, long, deep sighs as though measuring by them the depths of my moral degradation, and, of course, it ended at last by his triumphing completely: I raged and shouted, but still was forced to do what he wanted.

This time the usual staring maneuvers had scarcely begun when I lost my temper and flew at him in a fury. I was irritated beyond endurance apart from him.

"Stay," I cried, in a frenzy, as he was slowly and silently turning, with

one hand behind his back, to go to his room, "stay! Come back, come back, I tell you!" and I must have bawled so unnaturally, that he turned round and even looked at me with some wonder. However, he persisted in saying nothing, and that infuriated me.

"How dare you come and look at me like that without being sent for? Answer!"

After looking at me calmly for half a minute, he began turning round again.

"Stay!" I roared, running up to him, "don't stir! There. Answer, now: what did you come in to look at?"

"If you have any order to give me it's my duty to carry it out," he answered, after another silent pause, with a slow, measured lisp, raising his eyebrows and calmly twisting his head from one side to another, all this with exasperating composure.

"That's not what I am asking you about, you torturer!" I shouted, turning crimson with anger. "I'll tell you why you came here myself: you see, I don't give you your wages, you are so proud you don't want to bow down and ask for it, and so you come to punish me with your stupid stares, to worry me and you have no sus . . . pic . . . ion how stupid it is—stupid, stupid, stupid, stupid!" . . .

He would have turned round again without a word, but I seized him.

"Listen," I shouted to him. "Here's the money, do you see, here it is" (I took it out of the table drawer); "here's the seven roubles complete, but you are not going to have it, you . . . are . . . not . . . going . . . to . . . have it until you come respectfully with bowed head to beg my pardon. Do you hear?"

"That cannot be," he answered, with the most unnatural self-confidence.

"It shall be so," I said, "I give you my word of honor, it shall be!"

"And there's nothing for me to beg your pardon for," he went on, as though he had not noticed my exclamations at all. "Why, besides, you called me a 'torturer,' for which I can summon you at the police-station at any time for insulting behavior."

"Go, summon me," I roared, "go at once, this very minute, this very second! You are a torturer all the same! a torturer!"

But he merely looked at me, then turned, and regardless of my loud calls to him, he walked to his room with an even step and without looking round.

"If it had not been for Liza nothing of this would have happened," I decided inwardly. Then, after waiting a minute, I went myself behind his screen with a dignified and solemn air, though my heart was beating slowly and violently.

"Apollon," I said quietly and emphatically, though I was breathless, "go at once without a minute's delay and fetch the police-officer."

He had meanwhile settled himself at his table, put on his spectacles and taken up some sewing. But, hearing my order, he burst into a guffaw.

"At once, go this minute! Go on, or else you can't imagine what will happen."

"You are certainly out of your mind," he observed, without even raising his head, lisping as deliberately as ever and threading his needle. "Whoever

heard of a man sending for the police against himself? And as for being frightened—you are upsetting yourself about nothing, for nothing will come of it."

"Go!" I shrieked, clutching him by the shoulder. I felt I should strike him in a minute.

But I did not notice the door from the passage softly and slowly open at that instant and a figure come in, stop short, and begin staring at us in perplexity. I glanced, nearly swooned with shame, and rushed back to my room. There, clutching at my hair with both hands, I leaned my head against the wall and stood motionless in that position.

Two minutes later I heard Apollon's deliberate footsteps. "There is some woman asking for you," he said, looking at me with peculiar severity. Then he stood aside and let in Liza. He would not go away, but stared at us sarcastically.

"Go away, go away," I commanded in desperation. At that moment my clock began whirring and wheezing and struck seven.

IX

"Into my house come bold and free,
Its rightful mistress there to be."
(From the same poem)

I stood before her crushed, crestfallen, revoltingly confused, and I believe I smiled as I did my utmost to wrap myself in the skirts of my ragged wadded dressing-gown—exactly as I had imagined the scene not long before in a fit of depression. After standing over us for a couple of minutes Apollon went away, but that did not make me more at ease. What made it worse was that she, too, was overwhelmed with confusion, more so, in fact, than I should have expected. At the sight of me, of course.

"Sit down," I said mechanically, moving a chair up to the table, and I sat down on the sofa. She obediently sat down at once and gazed at me open-eyed, evidently expecting something from me at once. This naïveté of expectation drove me to fury, but I restrained myself.

She ought to have tried not to notice, as though everything had been as usual, while instead of that, she . . . and I dimly felt that I should make her pay dearly for *all this.*

"You have found me in a strange position, Liza," I began, stammering and knowing that this was the wrong way to begin. "No, no, don't imagine anything," I cried, seeing that she had suddenly flushed. "I am not ashamed of my poverty. . . . On the contrary I look with pride on my poverty. I am poor but honorable. . . . One can be poor and honorable," I muttered. "However . . . would you like tea?". . .

"No," she was beginning.

"Wait a minute."

I leaped up and ran to Apollon. I had to get out of the room somehow.

"Apollon," I whispered in feverish haste, flinging down before him the seven roubles which had remained all the time in my clenched fist, "here are your wages, you see I give them to you; but for that you must come to my rescue: bring me tea and a dozen rusks from the restaurant. If you

won't go, you'll make me a miserable man! You don't know what this woman is. . . . This is—everything! You may be imagining something. . . . But you don't know what that woman is!" . . .

Apollon, who had already sat down to his work and put on his spectacles again, at first glanced askance at the money without speaking or putting down his needle; then, without paying the slightest attention to me or making any answer he went on busying himself with his needle, which he had not yet threaded. I waited before him for three minutes with my arms crossed *à la Napoléon.* My temples were moist with sweat. I was pale, I felt it. But, thank God, he must have been moved to pity, looking at me. Having threaded his needle he deliberately got up from his seat, deliberately moved back his chair, deliberately took off his spectacles, deliberately counted the money, and finally asking me over his shoulder: "Shall I get a whole portion?" deliberately walked out of the room. As I was going back to Liza, the thought occurred to me on the way: shouldn't I run away just as I was in my dressing-gown, no matter where, and then let happen what would.

I sat down again. She looked at me uneasily. For some minutes we were silent.

"I will kill him," I shouted suddenly, striking the table with my fist so that the ink spurted out of the inkstand.

"What are you saying!" she cried, starting.

"I will kill him! kill him!" I shrieked, suddenly striking the table in absolute frenzy, and at the same time fully understanding how stupid it was to be in such a frenzy. "You don't know, Liza, what that torturer is to me. He is my torturer. . . . He has gone now to fetch some rusks; he . . ."

And suddenly I burst into tears. It was an hysterical attack. How ashamed I felt in the midst of my sobs; but still I could not restrain them.

She was frightened.

"What is the matter? What is wrong?" she cried, fussing about me.

"Water, give me water, over there!" I muttered in a faint voice, though I was inwardly conscious that I could have got on very well without water and without muttering in a faint voice. But I was, what is called, *putting it on,* to save appearances, though the attack was a genuine one.

She gave me water, looking at me in bewilderment. At that moment Apollon brought in the tea. It suddenly seemed to me that this commonplace, prosaic tea was horribly undignified and paltry after all that had happened, and I blushed crimson. Liza looked at Apollon with positive alarm. He went out without a glance at either of us.

"Liza, do you despise me?" I asked, looking at her fixedly, trembling with impatience to know what she was thinking.

She was confused, and did not know what to answer.

"Drink your tea," I said to her angrily. I was angry with myself, but, of course, it was she who would have to pay for it. A horrible spite against her suddenly surged up in my heart; I believe I could have killed her. To revenge myself on her I swore inwardly not to say a word to her all the time. "She is the cause of it all," I thought.

Our silence lasted for five minutes. The tea stood on the table; we did not touch it. I had got to the point of purposely refraining from beginning in order to embarrass her further; it was awkward for her to begin alone.

Several times she glanced at me with mournful perplexity. I was obstinately silent. I was, of course, myself the chief sufferer, because I was fully conscious of the disgusting meanness of my spiteful stupidity, and yet at the same time I could not restrain myself.

"I want to . . . get away . . . from there altogether," she began, to break the silence in some way, but, poor girl, that was just what she ought not to have spoken about at such a stupid moment to a man so stupid as I was. My heart positively ached with pity for her tactless and unnecessary straightforwardness. But something hideous at once stifled all compassion in me; it even provoked me to greater venom. I did not care what happened. Another five minutes passed.

"Perhaps I am in your way," she began timidly, hardly audibly, and was getting up.

But as soon as I saw this first impulse of wounded dignity I positively trembled with spite, and at once burst out.

"Why have you come to me, tell me that, please?" I began, gasping for breath and regardless of logical connection in my words. I longed to have it all out at once, at one burst; I did not even trouble how to begin. "Why have you come? Answer, answer," I cried, hardly knowing what I was doing. "I'll tell you, my good girl, why you have come. You've come because I talked sentimental stuff to you then. So now you are soft as butter and longing for fine sentiments again. So you may as well know that I was laughing at you then. And I am laughing at you now. Why are you shuddering? Yes, I was laughing at you! I had been insulted just before, at dinner, by the fellows who came that evening before me. I came to you, meaning to thrash one of them, an officer; but I didn't succeed, I didn't find him; I had to avenge the insult on some one to get back my own again; you turned up, I vented my spleen on you and laughed at you. I had been humiliated, so I wanted to humiliate; I had been treated like a rag, so I wanted to show my power. . . . That's what it was, and you imagined I had come there on purpose to save you. Yes? You imagined that? You imagined that?"

I knew that she would perhaps be muddled and not take it all in exactly, but I knew, too, that she would grasp the gist of it, very well indeed. And so, indeed, she did. She turned white as a handkerchief, tried to say something, and her lips worked painfully; but she sank on a chair as though she had been felled by an axe. And all the time afterwards she listened to me with her lips parted and her eyes wide open, shuddering with awful terror. The cynicism, the cynicism of my words overwhelmed her. . . .

"Save you!" I went on, jumping up from my chair and running up and down the room before her. "Save you from what? But perhaps I am worse than you myself. Why didn't you throw it in my teeth when I was giving you that sermon: 'But what did you come here yourself for? was it to read us a sermon?' Power, power was what I wanted then, sport was what I wanted, I wanted to wring out your tears, your humiliation, your hysteria—that was what I wanted then! Of course, I couldn't keep it up then, because I am a wretched creature, I was frightened, and, the devil knows why, gave you my address in my folly. Afterwards, before I got home, I was cursing and swearing at you because of that address, I hated you already because of the lies I had told you. Because I only like playing with words, only dreaming, but, do you know, what I really want is that you should all go to hell. That is

what I want. I want peace; yes, I'd sell the whole world for a farthing, straight off, so long as I was left in peace. Is the world to go to pot, or am I to go without my tea? I say that the world may go to pot for me so long as I always get my tea. Did you know that, or not? Well, anyway, I know that I am a blackguard, a scoundrel, an egoist, a sluggard. Here I have been shuddering for the last three days at the thought of your coming. And do you know what has worried me particularly for these three days? That I posed as such a hero to you, and now you would see me in a wretched torn dressing-gown, beggarly, loathsome. I told you just now that I was not ashamed of my poverty; so you may as well know that I am ashamed of it; I am more ashamed of it than of anything, more afraid of it than of being found out if I were a thief, because I am as vain as though I had been skinned and the very air blowing on me hurts. Surely by now you must realize that I shall never forgive you for having found me in this wretched dressing-gown, just as I was flying at Apollon like a spiteful cur. The savior, the former hero, was flying like a mangy, unkempt sheep-dog at his lackey, and the lackey was jeering at him! And I shall never forgive you for the tears I could not help shedding before you just now, like some silly woman put to shame! And for what I am confessing to you now, I shall never forgive *you* either! Yes—you must answer for it all because you turned up like this, because I am a blackguard, because I am the nastiest, stupidest, absurdest and most envious of all the worms on earth, who are not a bit better than I am, but, the devil knows why, are never put to confusion; while I shall always be insulted by every louse, that is my doom! And what is it to me that you don't understand a word of this! And what do I care, what do I care about you, and whether you go to ruin there or not? Do you understand? How I shall hate you now after saying this, for having been here and listening. Why, it's not once in a lifetime a man speaks out like this, and then it is in hysterics! . . . What more do you want? Why do you still stand confronting me, after all this? Why are you worrying me? Why don't you go?"

But at this point a strange thing happened. I was so accustomed to think and imagine everything from books, and to picture everything in the world to myself just as I had made it up in my dreams beforehand, that I could not all at once take in this strange circumstance. What happened was this: Liza, insulted and crushed by me, understood a great deal more than I imagined. She understood from all this what a woman understands first of all, if she feels genuine love, that is, that I was myself unhappy.

The frightened and wounded expression on her face was followed first by a look of sorrowful perplexity. When I began calling myself a scoundrel and a blackguard and my tears flowed (the tirade was accompanied throughout by tears) her whole face worked convulsively. She was on the point of getting up and stopping me; when I finished she took no notice of my shouting: "Why are you here, why don't you go away?" but realized only that it must have been very bitter to me to say all this. Besides, she was so crushed, poor girl; she considered herself infinitely beneath me; how could she feel anger or resentment? She suddenly leaped up from her chair with an irresistible impulse and held out her hands, yearning towards me, though still timid and not daring to stir. . . . At this point there was a revulsion in my heart, too. Then she suddenly rushed to me, threw her

arms round me and burst into tears. I, too, could not restrain myself, and sobbed as I never had before.

"They won't let me . . . I can't be good!" I managed to articulate; then I went to the sofa, fell on it face downwards, and sobbed on it for a quarter of an hour in genuine hysterics. She came close to me, put her arms round me and stayed motionless in that position. But the trouble was that the hysterics could not go on for ever, and (I am writing the loathsome truth) lyingface downwards on the sofa with my face thrust into my nasty leather pillow, I began by degrees to be aware of a far-away, involuntary but irresistible feeling that it would be awkward now for me to raise my head and look Liza straight in the face. Why was I ashamed? I don't know, but I was ashamed. The thought, too, came into my overwrought brain that our parts now were completely changed, that she was now the heroine, while I was just such a crushed and humiliated creature as she had been before me that night—four days before. . . . And all this came into my mind during the minutes I was lying on my face on the sofa.

My God! surely I was not envious of her then.

I don't know, to this day I cannot decide, and at the time, of course, I was still less able to understand what I was feeling than now. I cannot get on without domineering and tyrannizing over some one, but . . . there is no explaining anything by reasoning and so it is useless to reason.

I conquered myself, however, and raised my head; I had to do so sooner or later . . . and I am convinced to this day that it was just because I was ashamed to look at her that another feeling was suddenly kindled and flamed up in my heart . . . a feeling of mastery and possession. My eyes gleamed with passion, and I gripped her hands tightly. How I hated her and how I was drawn to her at that minute! The one feeling intensified the other. It was almost like an act of vengeance. At first there was a look of amazement, even of terror on her face, but only for one instant. She warmly and rapturously embraced me.

x

A quarter of an hour later I was rushing up and down the room in frenzied impatience, from minute to minute I went up to the screen and peeped through the crack at Liza. She was sitting on the ground with her head leaning against the bed, and must have been crying. But she did not go away, and that irritated me. This time she understood it all. I had insulted her finally, but . . . there's no need to describe it. She realized that my outburst of passion had been simply revenge, a fresh humiliation, and that to my earlier, almost causeless hatred was added a *personal hatred,* born of envy. . . . Though I do not maintain positively that she understood all this distinctly; but she certainly did fully understand that I was a despicable man, and what was worse, incapable of loving her.

I know I shall be told that this is incredible—but it is incredible to be as spiteful and stupid as I was; it may be added that it was strange I should not love her, or at any rate, appreciate her love. Why is it strange? In the first place, by then I was incapable of love, for I repeat, with me loving meant tyrannizing and showing my moral superiority. I have never in my life been able to imagine any other sort of love, and have nowadays come to the

point of sometimes thinking that love really consists in the right—freely given by the beloved object—to tyrannize over her.

Even in my underground dreams I did not imagine love except as a struggle. I began it always with hatred and ended it with moral subjugation, and afterwards I never knew what to do with the subjugated object. And what is there to wonder at in that, since I had succeeded in so corrupting myself, since I was so out of touch with "real life," as to have actually thought of reproaching her, and putting her to shame for having come to me to hear "fine sentiments"; and did not even guess that she had come not to hear fine sentiments, but to love me, because to a woman all reformation, all salvation from any sort of ruin, and all moral renewal is included in love and can only show itself in that form.

I did not hate her so much, however, when I was running about the room and peeping through the crack in the screen. I was only insufferably oppressed by her being here. I wanted her to disappear. I wanted "peace," to be left alone in my underground world. Real life oppressed me with its novelty so much that I could hardly breathe.

But several minutes passed and she still remained, without stirring, as though she were unconscious. I had the shamelessness to tap softly at the screen as though to remind her. . . . She started, sprang up, and flew to seek her kerchief, her hat, her coat, as though making her escape from me. . . . Two minutes later she came from behind the screen and looked with heavy eyes at me. I gave a spiteful grin, which was forced, however, to *keep up appearances,* and I turned away from her eyes.

"Good-bye," she said, going towards the door.

I ran up to her, seized her hand, opened it, thrust something in it and closed it again. Then I turned at once and dashed away in haste to the other corner of the room to avoid seeing her, anyway. . . .

I did not mean a moment since to tell a lie—to write that I did this accidentally, not knowing what I was doing through foolishness, through losing my head. But I don't want to lie, and so I will say straight out that I opened her hand and put the money in it . . . from spite. It came into my head to do this while I was running up and down the room and she was sitting behind the screen. But this I can say for certain: though I did that cruel thing purposely, it was not an impulse from the heart, but came from my evil brain. This cruelty was so affected, so purposely made up, so completely a product of the brain, of books, that I could not even keep it up a minute—first I dashed away to avoid seeing her, and then in shame and despair rushed after Liza. I opened the door in the passage and began listening.

"Liza! Liza!" I cried on the stairs, but in a low voice, not boldly.

There was no answer, but I fancied I heard her footsteps, lower down on the stairs.

"Liza!" I cried, more loudly.

No answer. But at that minute I heard the stiff outer glass door open heavily with a creak and slam violently, the sound echoed up the stairs.

She had gone. I went back to my room in hesitation. I felt horribly oppressed.

I stood still at the table, beside the chair on which she had sat and looked aimlessly before me. A minute passed, suddenly I started; straight

before me on the table I saw. . . . In short, I saw a crumpled blue five-rouble note, the one I had thrust into her hand a minute before. It was the same note; it could be no other, there was no other in the flat. So she had managed to fling it from her hand on the table at the moment when I had dashed into the further corner.

Well! I might have expected that she would do that. Might I have expected it? No, I was such an egoist, I was so lacking in respect for my fellow-creatures that I could not even imagine she would do so. I could not endure it. A minute later I flew like a madman to dress, flinging on what I could at random and ran headlong after her. She could not have got two hundred paces away when I ran out into the street.

It was a still night and the snow was coming down in masses and falling almost perpendicularly, covering the pavement and the empty street as though with a pillow. There was no one in the street, no sound was to be heard. The street lamps gave a disconsolate and useless glimmer. I ran two hundred paces to the cross-roads and stopped short.

Where had she gone? And why was I running after her?

Why? To fall down before her, to sob with remorse, to kiss her feet, to entreat her forgiveness! I longed for that, my whole breast was being rent to pieces, and never, never shall I recall that minute with indifference. But—what for? I thought. Should I not begin to hate her, perhaps, even tomorrow, just because I had kissed her feet today? Should I give her happiness? Had I not recognized that day, for the hundredth time, what I was worth? Should I not torture her?

I stood in the snow, gazing into the troubled darkness, and pondered this.

"And will it not be better?" I mused fantastically, afterwards at home, stifling the living pang of my heart with fantastic dreams. "Will it not be better that she should keep the resentment of the insult for ever? Resentment—why, it is purification; it is a most stinging and painful consciousness! Tomorrow I should have defiled her soul and have exhausted her heart, while now the feeling of insult will never die in her heart, and however loathsome the filth awaiting her—the feeling of insult will elevate and purify her . . . by hatred . . . h'm! . . . perhaps, too, by forgiveness. . . . Will all that make things easier for her though? . . ."

And, indeed, I will ask on my own account here, an idle question: which is better—cheap happiness or exalted sufferings? Well, which is better?

So I dreamed as I sat at home that evening, almost dead with the pain in my soul. Never had I endured such suffering and remorse, yet could there have been the faintest doubt when I ran out from my lodging that I should turn back half-way? I never met Liza again and I have heard nothing of her. I will add, too, that I remained for a long time afterwards pleased with the phrase about the benefit from resentment and hatred in spite of the fact that I almost fell ill from misery.

Even now, so many years later, all this is somehow a very evil memory. I have many evil memories now, but . . . hadn't I better end my "Notes" here? I believe I made a mistake in beginning to write them, anyway I have felt ashamed all the time I've been writing this story; so it's hardly literature so much as a corrective punishment. Why, to tell long stories, showing how

I have spoiled my life through morally rotting in my corner, through lack of fitting environment, through divorce from real life, and rankling spite in my underground world, would certainly not be interesting; a novel needs a hero, and all the traits for an anti-hero are *expressly* gathered together here, and what matters most, it all produces an unpleasant impression, for we are all divorced from life, we are all cripples, every one of us, more or less. We are so divorced from it that we feel at once a sort of loathing for real life, and so cannot bear to be reminded of it. Why, we have come almost to looking upon real life as an effort, almost as hard labor, and we are all privately agreed that it is better in books. And why do we fuss and fume sometimes? Why are we perverse and ask for something else? We don't know what ourselves. It would be the worse for us if our petulant prayers were answered. Come, try, give any one of us, for instance, a little more independence, untie our hands, widen the spheres of our activity, relax the control and we . . . yes, I assure you . . . we should be begging to be under control again at once. I know that you will very likely be angry with me for that, and will begin shouting and stamping. Speak for yourself, you will say, and for your miseries in your underground holes, and don't dare to say "all of us"—excuse me, gentlemen, I am not justifying myself with that "all of us." As for what concerns me in particular I have only in my life carried to an extreme what you have not dared to carry half-way, and what's more, you have taken your cowardice for good sense, and have found comfort in deceiving yourselves. So that perhaps, after all, there is more life in me than in you. Look into it more carefully! Why, we don't even know what living means now, what it is, and what it is called! Leave us alone without books and we shall be lost and in confusion at once. We shall not know what to join on to, what to cling to, what to love and what to hate, what to respect and what to despise. We are oppressed at being men—men with a real individual flesh and blood, we are ashamed of it, we think it a disgrace and try to contrive to be some sort of impossible generalized man. We are stillborn, and for generations past have been begotten, not by living fathers, and that suits us better and better. We are developing a taste for it. Soon we shall contrive to be born somehow from an idea. But enough; I don't want to write more from "Underground."

(The notes of this paradoxalist do not end here, however. He could not refrain from going on with them, but it seems to us that we may stop here.)

from *THE BROTHERS KARAMAZOV*

Translated by Constance Garnett

THE GRAND INQUISITOR

"You wrote a poem?"

"Oh, no, I didn't write it," laughed Ivan, "and I've never written two lines of poetry in my life. But I made up this poem in prose and I remembered it. I was carried away when I made it up. You will be my first

reader—that is, listener. Why should an author forego even one listener?" smiled Ivan. "Shall I tell it to you?"

"I am all attention," said Alyosha.

"My poem is called 'The Grand Inquisitor'; it's a ridiculous thing, but I want to tell it to you. . . ."

"Fifteen centuries have passed since He promised to come in His glory, fifteen centuries since His prophet wrote, 'Behold, I come quickly';[1] 'Of that day and that hour knoweth no man, neither the Son, but the Father,'[2] as He Himself predicted on earth. But humanity awaits Him with the same faith and with the same love. Oh, with greater faith, for it is fifteen centuries since man has ceased to see signs from heaven.

> No signs from heaven come today
> To add to what the heart doth say.

There was nothing left but faith in what the heart doth say. It is true there were many miracles in those days. There were saints who performed miraculous cures; some holy people, according to their biographies, were visited by the Queen of Heaven herself. But the devil did not slumber, and doubts were already arising among men of the truth of these miracles. And just then there appeared in the north of Germany a terrible new heresy. 'A huge star like to a torch' (that is, to a church) 'fell on the sources of the waters and they became bitter.' These heretics began blasphemously denying miracles. But those who remained faithful were all the more ardent in their faith. The tears of humanity rose up to Him as before, awaited His coming, loved Him, hoped for Him, yearned to suffer and die for Him as before. And so many ages mankind had prayed with faith and fervor, 'O Lord our God, hasten Thy coming,' so many ages called upon Him, that in His infinite mercy He deigned to come down to His servants. Before that day He had come down, He had visited some holy men, martyrs and hermits, as is written in their lives. Among us, Tyutchev,[3] with absolute faith in the truth of his words, bore witness that

> Bearing the Cross, in slavish dress,
> Weary and worn, the Heavenly King
> Our mother, Russia, came to bless,
> And through our land went wandering.

And that certainly was so, I assure you.

"And behold, He deigned to appear for a moment to the people, to the tortured, suffering people, sunk in iniquity, but loving Him like children. My story is laid in Spain, in Seville, in the most terrible time of the Inquisition, when fires were lighted every day to the glory of God, and 'in the splendid *auto da fé*[4] the wicked heretics were burnt.' Oh, of course, this was not the coming in which He will appear according to His promise at the end of time in all His heavenly glory, and which will be sudden 'as lightning

[1] Revelation 22:7. [2] Mark 13:32. [3] Fëdor Tyutchev, Russian poet (1803–73).
[4] Literally, "act of the faith" (Portuguese); the burning of a heretic.

flashing from east to west.'[5] No, He visited His children only for a moment, and there where the flames were crackling around the heretics. In His infinite mercy He came once more among men in that human shape in which He walked among men for three years fifteen centuries ago. He came down to the 'hot pavements' of the southern town in which on the day before almost a hundred heretics had, *ad majorem gloriam Dei*,[6] been burnt by the cardinal, the Grand Inquisitor, in a magnificent *auto da fé*, in the presence of the king, the court, the knights, the cardinals, the most charming ladies of the court, and the whole population of Seville.

"He came softly, unobserved, and yet, strange to say, every one recognized Him. That might be one of the best passages in the poem. I mean, why they recognized Him. The people are irresistibly drawn to Him, they surround Him, they flock about Him, follow Him. He moves silently in their midst with a gentle smile of infinite compassion. The sun of love burns in His heart, light and power shine from His eyes, and their radiance, shed on the people, stirs their hearts with responsive love. He holds out His hands to them, blesses them, and a healing virtue comes from contact with Him, even with His garments. An old man in the crowd, blind from childhood, cries out, 'O Lord, heal me and I shall see Thee!' and, as it were, scales fall from his eyes and the blind man sees Him. The crowd weeps and kisses the earth under His feet. Children throw flowers before Him, sing, and cry hosannah. 'It is He—it is He!' all repeat. 'It must be He, it can be no one but Him!' He stops at the steps of the Seville cathedral at the moment when the weeping mourners are bringing in a little open white coffin. In it lies a child of seven, the only daughter of a prominent citizen. The dead child lies hidden in flowers. 'He will raise your child,' the crowd shouts to the weeping mother. The priest, coming to meet the coffin, looks perplexed, and frowns, but the mother of the dead child throws herself at His feet with a wail. 'If it is Thou, raise my child!' she cries, holding out her hands to Him. The procession halts, the coffin is laid on the steps at His feet. He looks with compassion, and His lips once more softly pronounce, 'Maiden, arise!'[7] and the maiden arises. The little girl sits up in the coffin and looks round, smiling with wide-open wondering eyes, holding a bunch of white roses they had put in her hand.

"There are cries, sobs, confusion among the people, and at that moment the cardinal himself, the Grand Inquisitor, passes by the cathedral. He is an old man, almost ninety, tall and erect, with a withered face and sunken eyes, in which there is still a gleam of light. He is not dressed in his gorgeous cardinal's robes, as he was the day before, when he was burning the enemies of the Roman Church—at this moment he is wearing his coarse, old, monk's cassock. At a distance behind him come his gloomy assistants and slaves and the 'holy guard.' He stops at the sight of the crowd and watches it from a distance. He sees everything; he sees them set the coffin down at His feet, sees the child rise up, and his face darkens. He knits his thick gray brows and his eyes gleam with a sinister fire. He holds out his finger and bids the guards take Him. And such is his power, so completely are the people cowed into submission and trembling obedience

[5]Matthew 24:27. [6]"For the greater glory of God," the motto of the Jesuits.
[7]Mark 5:41.

to him, that the crowd immediately makes way for the guards, and in the midst of deathlike silence they lay hands on Him and lead Him away. The crowd instantly bows down to the earth, like one man, before the old Inquisitor. He blesses the people in silence and passes on. The guards lead their prisoner to the close, gloomy vaulted prison in the ancient palace of the Holy Inquisition and shut Him in it. The day passes and is followed by the dark, burning, 'breathless' night of Seville. The air is 'fragrant with laurel and lemon.' In the pitch darkness the iron door of the prison is suddenly opened and the Grand Inquisitor himself comes in with a light in his hand. He is alone; the door is closed at once behind him. He stands in the doorway and for a minute or two gazes into His face. At last he goes up slowly, sets the light on the table and speaks.

"'Is it Thou? Thou?' but receiving no answer, he adds at once, 'Don't answer, be silent. What canst Thou say, indeed? I know too well what Thou wouldst say. And Thou hast no right to add anything to what Thou hadst said of old. Why, then, art Thou come to hinder us? For Thou hast come to hinder us, and Thou knowest that. But dost Thou know what will be tomorrow? I know not who Thou art and care not to know whether it is Thou or only a semblance of Him, but tomorrow I shall condemn Thee and burn Thee at the stake as the worst of heretics. And the very people who have today kissed Thy feet, tomorrow at the faintest sign from me will rush to heap up the embers of Thy fire. Knowest Thou that? Yes, maybe Thou knowest it,' he added with thoughtful penetration, never for a moment taking his eyes off the Prisoner."

"I don't quite understand, Ivan. What does it mean?" Alyosha, who had been listening in silence, said with a smile. "Is it simply a wild fantasy, or a mistake on the part of the old man—some impossible *quiproquo*?"[8]

"Take it as the last," said Ivan, laughing, "if you are so corrupted by modern realism and can't stand anything fantastic. If you like it to be a case of mistaken identity, let it be so. It is true," he went on, laughing, "the old man was ninety, and he might well be crazy over his set idea. He might have been struck by the appearance of the Prisoner. It might, in fact, be simply his ravings, the delusion of an old man of ninety, over-excited by the *auto da fé* of a hundred heretics the day before. But does it matter to us after all whether it was a mistake of identity or a wild fantasy? All that matters is that the old man should speak out, should speak openly of what he has thought in silence for ninety years."

"And the Prisoner too is silent? Does He look at him and not say a word?"

"That's inevitable in any case," Ivan laughed again. "The old man has told Him He hasn't the right to add anything to what He has said of old. One may say it is the most fundamental feature of Roman Catholicism, in my opinion at least. 'All has been given by Thee to the Pope,' they say, 'and all, therefore, is still in the Pope's hands, and there is no need for Thee to come now at all. Thou must not meddle for the time, at least.' That's how they speak and write too—the Jesuits, at any rate. I have read it myself in the works of their theologians. 'Hast Thou the right to reveal to us one of the mysteries of that world from which Thou hast come?' my old man asks

[8] Misunderstanding.

Him, and answers the question for Him. 'No, Thou hast not; that Thou mayest not add to what has been said of old, and mayest not take from men the freedom which Thou didst exalt when Thou wast on earth. Whatsoever Thou revealest anew will encroach on men's freedom of faith; for it will be manifest as a miracle, and the freedom of their faith was dearer to Thee than anything in those days fifteen hundred years ago. Didst Thou not often say then, "I will make you free"?[9] But now Thou hast seen these "free" men,' the old man adds suddenly, with a pensive smile. 'Yes, we've paid dearly for it,' he goes on, looking sternly at Him, 'but at last we have completed that work in Thy name. For fifteen centuries we have been wrestling with Thy freedom, but now it is ended and over for good. Dost Thou not believe that it's over for good? Thou lookest meekly at me and deignest not even to be wroth with me. But let me tell Thee that now, today, people are more persuaded than ever that they have perfect freedom, yet they have brought their freedom to us and laid it humbly at our feet. But that has been our doing. Was this what Thou didst? Was this Thy freedom?'"

"I don't understand again," Alyosha broke in. "Is he ironical, is he jesting?"

"Not a bit of it! He claims it as a merit for himself and his Church that at last they have vanquished freedom and have done so to make men happy. 'For now' (he is speaking of the Inquisition, of course) 'for the first time it has become possible to think of the happiness of men. Man was created a rebel; and how can rebels be happy? Thou wast warned,' he says to Him. 'Thou hast had no lack of admonitions and warnings, but Thou didst not listen to those warnings; Thou didst reject the only way by which men might be made happy. But, fortunately, departing Thou didst hand on the work to us. Thou hast promised, Thou hast established by Thy word, Thou hast given to us the right to bind and to unbind, and now, of course, Thou canst not think of taking it away. Why, then, hast Thou come to hinder us?'"

"And what's the meaning of 'no lack of admonitions and warnings'?" asked Alyosha.

"Why, that's the chief part of what the old man must say.

"'The wise and dread spirit, the spirit of self-destruction and non-existence,' the old man goes on, 'the great spirit talked with Thee in the wilderness, and we are told in the books that he "tempted" Thee.[10] Is that so? And could anything truer be said than what he revealed to Thee in three questions and what Thou didst reject, and what in the books is called "the temptation"? And yet if there has ever been on earth a real stupendous miracle, it took place on that day, on the day of the three temptations. The statement of those three questions was itself the miracle. If it were possible to imagine simply for the sake of argument that those three questions of the dread spirit had perished utterly from the books, and that we had to restore them to invent them anew, and to do so had gathered to-

[9] See John 8:36.
[10] The story of Satan's temptation of Christ in the Wilderness appears in Matthew 4:1–11, Mark 1:12–13, and Luke 4:1–13. Satan first tempts him to turn stones into bread, then tempts him to test God by flinging himself off a pinnacle, and finally offers him all the kingdoms of the world.

gether all the wise men of the earth—rulers, chief priests, learned men, philosophers, poets—and had set them the task to invent three questions, such as would not only fit the occasion, but express in three words, three human phrases, the whole future history of the world and of humanity— dost Thou believe that all the wisdom of the earth united could have invented anything in depth and force equal to the three questions which were actually put to Thee then by the wise and mighty spirit in the wilderness? From those questions alone, from the miracle of their statement, we can see that we have here to do not with the fleeting human intelligence, but with the absolute and eternal. For in those three questions the whole subsequent history of mankind is, as it were, brought together into one whole, and foretold, and in them are united all the unsolved historical contradictions of human nature. At the time it could not be so clear, since the future was unknown; but now that fifteen hundred years have passed, we see that everything in those three questions was so justly divined and foretold, and has been so truly fulfilled, that nothing can be added to them or taken from them.

"'Judge Thyself who was right—Thou or he who questioned Thee then? Remember the first question; its meaning, in other words, was this: "Thou wouldst go into the world, and art going with empty hands, with some promise of freedom which men in their simplicity and their natural unruliness cannot even understand, which they fear and dread—for nothing has ever been more insupportable for a man and a human society than freedom. But seest Thou these stones in this parched and barren wilderness? Turn them into bread, and mankind will run after Thee like a flock of sheep, grateful and obedient, though for ever trembling, lest Thou withdraw Thy hand and deny them Thy bread." But Thou wouldst not deprive man of freedom and didst reject the offer, thinking, what is that freedom worth, if obedience is bought with bread? Thou didst reply that man lives not by bread alone. But dost Thou know that for the sake of that earthly bread the spirit of the earth will rise up against Thee and will strive with Thee and overcome Thee, and all will follow him, crying, "Who can compare with this beast? He has given us fire from heaven!"[11] Dost Thou know that the ages will pass, and humanity will proclaim by the lips of their sages that there is no crime, and therefore no sin; there is only hunger?' "Feed men, and then ask of them virtue!" that's what they'll write on the banner, which they will raise against Thee, and with which they will destroy Thy temple. Where Thy temple stood will rise a new building; the terrible tower of Babel[12] will be built again, and though, like the one of old, it will not be finished, yet Thou mightest have prevented that new tower and have cut short the sufferings of men for a thousand years; for they will come back to us after a thousand years of agony with their tower. They will seek us again, hidden underground in the catacombs,[13] for we shall be again persecuted and tortured. They will find us and cry to us, "Feed us, for those who have promised us fire from heaven haven't given it!" And then we shall finish

[11] Revelation 13:4, 13.
[12] The building of the Tower of Babel, an act of pride against God, is described in Genesis 11.
[13] Underground tombs, where early Christians met to avoid Roman persecution.

building their tower, for he finishes the building who feeds them. And we alone shall feed them in Thy name, declaring falsely that it is in Thy name. Oh, never, never can they feed themselves without us! No science will give them bread so long as they remain free. In the end they will lay their freedom at our feet, and say to us, "Make us your slaves, but feed us." They will understand themselves, at last, that freedom and bread enough for all are inconceivable together, for never, never will they be able to share between them! They will be convinced, too, that they can never be free, for they are weak, vicious, worthless and rebellious. Thou didst promise them the bread of Heaven, but, I repeat again, can it compare with earthly bread in the eyes of the weak, ever sinful and ignoble race of man? And if for the sake of the bread of Heaven thousands shall follow Thee, what is to become of the millions and tens of thousands of millions of creatures who will not have the strength to forego the earthly bread for the sake of the heavenly? Or dost Thou care only for the tens of thousands of the great and strong, while the millions, numerous as the sands of the sea, who are weak but love Thee, must exist only for the sake of the great and strong? No, we care for the weak too. They are sinful and rebellious, but in the end they too will become obedient. They will marvel at us and look on us as gods, because we are ready to endure the freedom which they have found so dreadful and to rule over them—so awful it will seem to them to be free. But we shall tell them that we are Thy servants and rule them in Thy name. We shall deceive them again, for we will not let Thee come to us again. That deception will be our suffering, for we shall be forced to lie.

"'This is the significance of the first question in the wilderness, and this is what Thou hast rejected for the sake of that freedom which Thou hast exalted above everything. Yet in this question lies hid the great secret of this world. Choosing "bread," Thou wouldst have satisfied the universal and everlasting craving of humanity—to find some one to worship. So long as man remains free he strives for nothing so incessantly and so painfully as to find some one to worship. But man seeks to worship what is established beyond dispute, so that all men would agree at once to worship it. For these pitiful creatures are concerned not only to find what one or the other can worship, but to find something that all would believe in and worship; what is essential is that all may be *together* in it. This craving for *community* of worship is the chief misery of every man individually and of all humanity from the beginning of time. For the sake of common worship they've slain each other with the sword. They have set up gods and challenged one another, "Put away your gods and come and worship ours, or we will kill you and your gods!" And so it will be to the end of the world, even when gods disappear from the earth; they will fall down before idols just the same. Thou didst know, Thou couldst not but have known, this fundamental secret of human nature, but Thou didst reject the one infallible banner which was offered Thee to make all men bow down to Thee alone—the banner of earthly bread; and Thou hast rejected it for the sake of freedom and the bread of Heaven. Behold what Thou didst further. And all again in the name of freedom! I tell Thee that man is tormented by no greater anxiety than to find some one quickly to whom he can hand over that gift of freedom with which the ill-fated creature is born. But only one who can appease their conscience can take over their freedom. In bread there was

offered Thee an invincible banner; give bread, and man will worship thee, for nothing is more certain than bread. But if some one else gains possession of his conscience—oh! then he will cast away Thy bread and follow after him who has ensnared his conscience. In that Thou wast right. For the secret of man's being is not only to live but to have something to live for. Without a stable conception of the object of life, man would not consent to go on living, and would rather destroy himself than remain on earth, though he had bread in abundance. That is true. But what happened? Instead of taking men's freedom from them, Thou didst make it greater than ever! Didst Thou forget that man prefers peace, and even death, to freedom of choice in the knowledge of good and evil? Nothing is more seductive for man than his freedom of conscience, but nothing is a greater cause of suffering. And behold, instead of giving a firm foundation for setting the conscience of man at rest for ever, Thou didst choose all that is exceptional, vague and enigmatic; Thou didst choose what was utterly beyond the strength of men, acting as though Thou didst not love them at all—Thou who didst come to give Thy life for them! Instead of taking possession of men's freedom, Thou didst increase it, and burdened the spiritual kingdom of mankind with its sufferings for ever. Thou didst desire man's free love, that he should follow Thee freely, enticed and taken captive by Thee. In place of the rigid ancient law, man must hereafter with free heart decide for himself what is good and what is evil, having only Thy image before him as his guide. But didst Thou not know that he would at last reject even Thy image and Thy truth, if he is weighed down with the fearful burden of free choice? They will cry aloud at last that the truth is not in Thee, for they could not have been left in greater confusion and suffering than Thou hast caused, laying upon them so many cares and unanswerable problems.

"'So that, in truth, Thou didst Thyself lay the foundation for the destruction of Thy kingdom, and no one is more to blame for it. Yet what was offered Thee? There are three powers, three powers alone, able to conquer and to hold captive for ever the conscience of these impotent rebels for their happiness—those forces are miracle, mystery and authority. Thou hast rejected all three and hast set the example for doing so. When the wise and dread spirit set Thee on the pinnacle of the temple and said to Thee, "If Thou wouldst know whether Thou art the Son of God then cast Thyself down, for it is written: the angels shall hold him up lest he fall and bruise himself, and Thou shalt know then whether Thou art the Son of God and shalt prove then how great is Thy faith in Thy Father." But Thou didst refuse and wouldst not cast Thyself down. Oh, of course, Thou didst proudly and well, like God; but the weak, unruly race of men, are they gods? Oh, Thou didst know then that in taking one step, in making one movement to cast Thyself down, Thou wouldst be tempting God and have lost all Thy faith in Him, and wouldst have been dashed to pieces against that earth which Thou didst come to save. And the wise spirit that tempted Thee would have rejoiced. But I ask again, are there many like Thee? And couldst Thou believe for one moment that men, too, could face such a temptation? Is the nature of men such, that they can reject miracle, and at the great moments of their life, the moments of their deepest, most agonizing spiritual difficulties, cling only to the free verdict of the heart? Oh,

Thou didst know that Thy deed would be recorded in books, would be handed down to remote times and the utmost ends of the earth, and Thou didst hope that man, following Thee, would cling to God and not ask for a miracle. But Thou didst not know that when man rejects miracle he rejects God too; for man seeks not so much God as the miraculous. And as man cannot bear to be without the miraculous, he will create new miracles of his own for himself, and will worship deeds of sorcery and witchcraft, though he might be a hundred times over a rebel, heretic and infidel. Thou didst not come down from the Cross when they shouted to Thee, mocking and reviling Thee, "Come down from the cross and we will believe that Thou art He." [14] Thou didst not come down, for again Thou wouldst not enslave man by a miracle, and didst crave faith given freely, not based on miracle. Thou didst crave for free love and not the base raptures of the slave before the might that has overawed him for ever. But Thou didst think too highly of men therein, for they are slaves, of course, though rebellious by nature. Look round and judge; fifteen centuries have passed, look upon them. Whom hast Thou raised up to Thyself? I swear, man is weaker and baser by nature than Thou hast believed him! Can he, can he do what Thou didst? By showing him so much respect, Thou didst, as it were, cease to feel for him, for Thou didst ask far too much from him—Thou who hast loved him more than Thyself! Respecting him less, Thou wouldst have asked less of him. That would have been more like love, for his burden would have been lighter. He is weak and vile. What though he is everywhere now rebelling against our power, and proud of his rebellion? It is the pride of a child and a schoolboy. They are little children rioting and barring out the teacher at school. But their childish delight will end; it will cost them dear. They will cast down temples and drench the earth with blood. But they will see at last, the foolish children, that, though they are rebels, they are impotent rebels, unable to keep up their own rebellion. Bathed in their foolish tears, they will recognize at last that He who created them rebels must have meant to mock at them. They will say this in despair, and their utterance will be a blasphemy which will make them more unhappy still, for man's nature cannot bear blasphemy, and in the end always avenges it on itself. And so unrest, confusion and unhappiness—that is the present lot of man after Thou didst bear so much for their freedom! The great prophet tells in vision and in image, that he saw all those who took part in the first resurrection and that there were of each tribe twelve thousand. But if there were so many of them, they must have been not men but gods. They had borne Thy cross, they had endured scores of years in the barren, hungry wilderness, living upon locusts and roots—and Thou mayest indeed point with pride at those children of freedom, of free love, of free and splendid sacrifice for Thy name. But remember that they were only some thousands; and what of the rest? And how are the other weak ones to blame, because they could not endure what the strong have endured? How is the weak soul to blame that it is unable to receive such terrible gifts? Canst Thou have simply come to the elect and for the elect? But if so, it is a mystery and we cannot understand it. And if it is a mystery, we too have a right to preach a mystery, and to teach them that it's not the free judgment

[14] Mark 15:32.

of their hearts, not love that matters, but a mystery which they must follow blindly, even against their conscience. So we have done. We have corrected Thy work and have founded it upon *miracle, mystery* and *authority*. And men rejoiced that they were again led like sheep, and that the terrible gift that had brought them such suffering was, at last, lifted from their hearts. Were we right teaching them this? Speak! Did we not love mankind, so meekly acknowledging their feebleness, lovingly lightening their burden, and permitting their weak nature even sin with our sanction? Why hast Thou come now to hinder us? And why dost Thou look silently and searchingly at me with Thy mild eyes? Be angry. I don't want Thy love, for I love Thee not. And what use is it for me to hide anything from Thee? Don't I know to Whom I am speaking? All that I can say is known to Thee already. And is it for me to conceal from Thee our mystery? Perhaps it is Thy will to hear it from my lips. Listen, then. We are not working with Thee, but with *him*—that is our mystery. It's long—eight centuries—since we have been on *his* side and not on Thine. Just eight centuries ago, we took from him what Thou didst reject with scorn, that last gift he offered Thee, showing Thee all the kingdoms of the earth.[15] We took from him Rome and the sword of Caesar, and proclaimed ourselves sole rulers of the earth, though hitherto we have not been able to complete our work. But whose fault is that? Oh, the work is only beginning, but it has begun. It has long to await completion and the earth has yet much to suffer, but we shall triumph and shall be Caesars, and then we shall plan the universal happiness of man. But Thou mightest have taken even then the sword of Caesar. Why didst Thou reject that last gift? Hadst Thou accepted that last counsel of the mighty spirit, Thou wouldst have accomplished all that man seeks on earth—that is, some one to worship, some one to keep his conscience, and some means of uniting all in one unanimous and harmonious ant-heap, for the craving for universal unity is the third and last anguish of men. Mankind as a whole has always striven to organize a universal state. There have been many great nations with great histories, but the more highly they were developed the more unhappy they were, for they felt more acutely than other people the craving for world-wide union. The great conquerors, Timours and Ghenghis-Khans,[16] whirled like hurricanes over the face of the earth striving to subdue its people, and they too were but the unconscious expression of the same craving for universal unity. Hadst Thou taken the world and Caesar's purple, Thou wouldst have founded the universal state and have given universal peace. For who can rule men if not he who holds their conscience and their bread in his hands? We have taken the sword of Caesar, and in taking it, of course, have rejected Thee and followed *him*. Oh, ages are yet to come of the confusion of free thought, of their science and cannibalism. For having begun to build their tower of Babel without us, they will end, of course, with cannibalism. But then the beast will crawl to us and lick our feet and spatter them with tears of blood. And we shall sit upon the beast and raise the cup, and on it will be written, "Mystery." But

[15] In 401, Pope Innocent I claimed jurisdiction over the entire Roman Church, thus replacing the Roman Empire as the only "universal" authority.

[16] Timour, or Tamerlane (c. 1336–1405), was the famous Mongol conqueror; Ghenghis-Khan (1167?–1227), also a Mongol, conquered most of China and penetrated into southeast Europe.

then, and only then, the reign of peace and happiness will come for men. Thou art proud of Thine elect, but Thou hast only the elect, while we give rest to all. And besides, how many of those elect, those mighty ones who could become elect, have grown weary waiting for Thee, and have transferred and will transfer the powers of their spirit and the warmth of their heart to the other camp, and end by raising their *free* banner against Thee. Thou didst Thyself lift up that banner. But with us all will be happy and will no more rebel nor destroy one another as under Thy freedom. Oh, we shall persuade them that they will only become free when they renounce their freedom to us and submit to us. And shall we be right or shall we be lying? They will be convinced that we are right, for they will remember the horrors of slavery and confusion to which Thy freedom brought them. Freedom, free thought and science, will lead them into such straits and will bring them face to face with such marvels and insoluble mysteries, that some of them, the fierce and rebellious, will destroy themselves, others, rebellious but weak, will destroy one another, while the rest, weak and unhappy, will crawl fawning to our feet and whine to us: "Yes, you were right, you alone possess His mystery, and we come back to you, save us from ourselves!"

"'Receiving bread from us, they will see clearly that we take the bread made by their hands from them, to give it to them, without any miracle. They will see that we do not change the stones to bread, but in truth they will be more thankful for taking it from our hands than for the bread itself! For they will remember only too well that in old days, without help, even the bread they made turned to stones in their hands, while since they have come back to us, the very stones have turned to bread in their hands. Too, too well will they know the value of complete submission! And until men know that, they will be unhappy. Who is most to blame for their not knowing it?—speak! Who scattered the flock and sent it astray on unknown paths? But the flock will come together again and will submit once more, and then it will be once for all. Then we shall give them the quiet humble happiness of weak creatures such as they are by nature. Oh, we shall persuade them at last not to be proud, for Thou didst lift them up and thereby taught them to be proud. We shall show them that they are weak, that they are only pitiful children, but that childlike happiness is the sweetest of all. They will become timid and will look to us and huddle close to us in fear, as chicks to the hen. They will marvel at us and will be awe-stricken before us,[17] and will be proud at our being so powerful and clever, that we have been able to subdue such a turbulent flock of thousands of millions. They will tremble impotently before our wrath, their minds will grow fearful, they will be quick to shed tears like women and children, but they will be just as ready at a sign from us to pass to laughter and rejoicing, to happy mirth and childish song. Yes, we shall set them to work, but in their leisure hours we shall make their life like a child's game, with children's songs and innocent dance. Oh, we shall allow them even sin, they are weak and helpless, and they will love us like children because we allow them to sin. We shall tell them that every sin will be expiated, if it is done with our permission, that we allow them to sin because we love them, and the punishment

[17] See Revelation 17:6.

for these sins we take upon ourselves. And we shall take it upon ourselves, and they will adore us as their saviors who have taken on themselves their sins before God. And they will have no secrets from us. We shall allow or forbid them to live with their wives and mistresses, to have or not to have children—according to whether they have been obedient or disobedient—and they will submit to us gladly and cheerfully. The most painful secrets of their conscience, all, all they will bring to us, and we shall have an answer for all. And they will be glad to believe our answer, for it will save them from the great anxiety and terrible agony they endure at present in making a free decision for themselves. And all will be happy, all the millions of creatures except the hundred thousand who rule over them. For only we, we who guard the mystery, shall be unhappy. There will be thousands of millions of happy babes, and a hundred thousand sufferers who have taken upon themselves the curse of the knowledge of good and evil. Peacefully they will die, peacefully they will expire in Thy name, and beyond the grave they will find nothing but death. But we shall keep the secret, and for their happiness we shall allure them with the reward of heaven and eternity. Though if there were anything in the other world, it certainly would not be for such as they. It is prophesied that Thou wilt come again in victory, Thou wilt come with Thy chosen, the proud and strong, but we will say that they have only saved themselves, but we have saved all. We are told that the harlot who sits upon the beast, and holds in her hands the *mystery*, shall be put to shame, that the weak will rise up again, and will rend her royal purple and will strip naked her loathsome body.[18] But then I will stand up and point out to Thee the thousand millions of happy children who have known no sin. And we who have taken their sins upon us for their happiness will stand up before Thee and say: "Judge us if Thou canst and darest." Know that I fear Thee not. Know that I too have been in the wilderness, I too have lived on roots and locusts, I too prized the freedom with which Thou hast blessed men, and I too was striving to stand among Thy elect, among the strong and powerful, thirsting "to make up the number." But I awakened and would not serve madness. I turned back and joined the ranks of those *who have corrected Thy work*. I left the proud and went back to the humble, for the happiness of the humble. What I say to Thee will come to pass, and our dominion will be built up. I repeat, tomorrow Thou shalt see that obedient flock who at a sign from me will hasten to heap up the hot cinders about the pile on which I shall burn Thee for coming to hinder us. For if any one has ever deserved our fires, it is Thou. Tomorrow I shall burn Thee. *Dixi*.'"[19]

Ivan stopped. He was carried away as he talked, and spoke with excitement; when he had finished, he suddenly smiled.

Alyosha had listened in silence; towards the end he was greatly moved and seemed several times on the point of interrupting, but restrained himself. Now his words came with a rush.

"But . . . that's absurd!" he cried, flushing. "Your poem is in praise of Jesus, not in blame of Him—as you meant it to be. And who will believe you about freedom? Is that the way to understand it? That's not the idea of

[18] The vision of the Whore of Babylon is described in Revelation 17.

[19] Literally, "I have spoken" (Latin), closing formula for an ecclesiastical pronouncement.

it in the Orthodox Church. . . . That's Rome, and not even the whole of Rome, it's false—those are the worst of the Catholics, the Inquisitors, the Jesuits! . . . And there could not be such a fantastic creature as your Inquisitor. What are these sins of mankind they take on themselves? Who are these keepers of the mystery who have taken some curse upon themselves for the happiness of mankind? When have they been seen? We know the Jesuits, they are spoken ill of, but surely they are not what you describe? They are not that at all, not at all. . . . They are simply the Romish army for the earthly sovereignty of the world in the future, with the Pontiff of Rome for Emperor . . . that's their ideal, but there's no sort of mystery or lofty melancholy about it. . . . It's simple lust of power, of filthy earthly gain, of domination—something like a universal serfdom with them as masters—that's all they stand for. They don't even believe in God perhaps. Your suffering Inquisitor is a mere fantasy."

"Stay, stay," laughed Ivan, "how hot you are! A fantasy you say, let it be so! Of course it's a fantasy. But allow me to say: do you really think that the Roman Catholic movement of the last centuries is actually nothing but the lust of power, of filthy earthly gain? Is that Father Païssy's teaching?"

"No, no, on the contrary, Father Païssy did once say something rather the same as you . . . but of course it's not the same, not a bit the same," Alyosha hastily corrected himself.

"A precious admission, in spite of your 'not a bit the same.' I ask you why your Jesuits and Inquisitors have united simply for vile material gain? Why can there not be among them one martyr oppressed by great sorrow and loving humanity? You see, only suppose that there was one such man among all those who desire nothing but filthy material gain—if there's only one like my old Inquisitor, who had himself eaten roots in the desert and made frenzied efforts to subdue his flesh to make himself free and perfect. But yet all his life he loved humanity, and suddenly his eyes were opened, and he saw that it is no great moral blessedness to attain perfection and freedom, if at the same time one gains the conviction that millions of God's creatures have been created as a mockery, that they will never be capable of using their freedom, that these poor rebels can never turn into giants to complete the tower, that it was not for such geese that the great idealist dreamt his dream of harmony. Seeing all that he turned back and joined—the clever people. Surely that could have happened?"

"Joined whom, what clever people?" cried Alyosha, completely carried away. "They have no such great cleverness and no mysteries and secrets. . . . Perhaps nothing but Atheism, that's all their secret. Your Inquisitor does not believe in God, that's his secret!"

"What if it is so! At last you have guessed it. It's perfectly true, it's true that that's the whole secret, but isn't that suffering, at least for a man like that, who has wasted his whole life in the desert and yet could not shake off his incurable love of humanity? In his old age he reached the clear conviction that nothing but the advice of the great dread spirit could build up any tolerable sort of life for the feeble, unruly, 'incomplete, empirical creatures created in jest.' And so, convinced of this, he sees that he must follow the counsel of the wise spirit, the dread spirit of death and destruction, and therefore accept lying and deception, and lead men consciously to death and destruction, and yet deceive them all the way so that they may not

notice where they are being led, that the poor blind creatures may at least on the way think themselves happy. And note, the deception is in the name of Him in Whose ideal the old man had so fervently believed all his life long. Is not that tragic? And if only one such stood at the head of the whole army 'filled with the lust of power only for the sake of filthy gain'—would not one such be enough to make a tragedy? More than that, one such standing at the head is enough to create the actual leading idea of the Roman Church with all its armies and Jesuits, its highest idea. I tell you frankly that I firmly believe that there has always been such a man among those who stood at the head of the movement. Who knows, there may have been some such even among the Roman Popes. Who knows, perhaps the spirit of that accursed old man who loves mankind so obstinately in his own way, is to be found even now in a whole multitude of such old men, existing not by chance but by agreement, as a secret league formed long ago for the guarding of the mystery, to guard it from the weak and the unhappy, so as to make them happy. No doubt it is so, and so it must be indeed. I fancy that even among the Masons there's something of the same mystery at the bottom, and that that's why the Catholics so detest the Masons as their rivals breaking up the unity of the idea, while it is so essential that there should be one flock and one shepherd. . . .[20] But from the way I defend my idea I might be an author impatient of your criticism. Enough of it."

"You are perhaps a Mason yourself!" broke suddenly from Alyosha. "You don't believe in God," he added, speaking this time very sorrowfully. He fancied besides that his brother was looking at him ironically. "How does your poem end?" he asked, suddenly looking down. "Or was it the end?"

"I meant to end it like this. When the Inquisitor ceased speaking he waited some time for his Prisoner to answer him. His silence weighed down upon him. He saw that the Prisoner had listened intently all the time, looking gently in his face and evidently not wishing to reply. The old man longed for Him to say something, however bitter and terrible. But He suddenly approached the old man in silence and softly kissed him on his bloodless aged lips. That was all His answer. The old man shuddered. His lips moved. He went to the door, opened it, and said to Him: 'Go, and come no more . . . come not at all, never, never!' And he let Him out into the dark alleys of the town. The Prisoner went away."

"And the old man?"

"The kiss glows in his heart, but the old man adheres to his idea."

"And you with him, you too?" cried Alyosha, mournfully.

Ivan laughed.

"Why, it's all nonsense, Alyosha. It's only a senseless poem of a senseless student, who could never write two lines of verse. Why do you take it so seriously? Surely you don't suppose I am going straight off to the Jesuits, to join the men who are correcting His work? Good Lord, it's no business of mine. I told you, all I want is to live on to thirty, and then . . . dash the cup to the ground!" . . .

[20] John 10:16. The Masons, or the order of Free and Accepted Masons, is a secret fraternal order originating in the medieval stoneworkers' guild. Its secrecy has inspired strong opposition from many sources, including the Roman Catholic Church.

Alyosha looked at him in silence.

"I thought that going away from here I have you at least," Ivan said suddenly, with unexpected feeling; "but now I see that there is no place for me even in your heart, my dear hermit. The formula, 'all is lawful,' I won't renounce—will you renounce me for that, yes?"

Alyosha got up, went to him and softly kissed him on the lips.

"That's plagiarism," cried Ivan, highly delighted. "You stole that from my poem. Thank you though. Get up, Alyosha, it's time we were going, both of us." . . .

Leo Tolstoy
(1828–1910)

The figure of Count Leo Tolstoy, both as writer and as man, towers over the remarkable flowering of Russian fiction in the nineteenth century. The titanic *War and Peace* and *Anna Karenina* are the greatest products of that flowering, and the conflicts and tensions in human life, which Tolstoy examined with such unflinching honesty in those works, were acted out in his own extraordinary life. They were the tensions and conflicts arising from Romantic liberalism—between the individual and society, between self-realization and self-abnegation in the service of others, between an inability to accept orthodox religion and a deep need to believe—but Tolstoy's agonized probings of them reach depths beyond those of his own intellectual milieu to reach a sort of bedrock of existential concerns.

Tolstoy was born in 1828 into a wealthy, aristocratic Russian family at Yasnaya Polyana, about a hundred miles south of Moscow, and he grew up on the family estate. His parents died when he was still a child, and he was reared by relatives and educated by private tutors. He studied at Kazan University, but returned home after three years to manage the family estate and lead a rather shallow, dissolute life in the upper social circles of Moscow and St. Petersburg. When he was twenty-three, he rejected this idle life and joined his soldier brother Nikolay in the Caucasus; he was a soldier for five years, distinguishing himself in engagements against the Caucasian hill tribes and taking part in the defense of Sevastopol in the Crimean War. While in the army, he began to write sketches and stories of his childhood and of military life; these tales were published in various Russian magazines. When he left the army, Tolstoy lived briefly in St. Petersburg, where he had already developed a literary reputation, but soon left to return to his estate and then to travel in Europe, continuing to write short stories and to pursue a growing interest in the education of the Russian peasantry.

In 1862, Tolstoy married Sonya Bers, a lively, intelligent young woman from a middle-class family, and returned to manage his estate and rear a

family which came to number thirteen children. He also wrote, between 1863 and 1877, his two great masterpieces, *War and Peace* (1869) and *Anna Karenina* (1877). *War and Peace,* an immense panorama of Russian life in the early nineteenth century, including Napoleon's 1812 invasion of Russia, centers upon the lives of five aristocratic Russian families and especially upon two major characters, Andrey and Pierre. These two men exemplify the major moral conflict of the book: between Romantic self-realization and service to others. Tolstoy also develops in the novel, sometimes directly and didactically, a theory of history which minimizes the influence of "great men" on historical events in favor of historical processes and natural laws which transcend individuals. *Anna Karenina,* set in the upper-class Russian society of the 1860's, while still large in scale, does not attempt the epic sweep of *War and Peace* but focuses more narrowly upon a private action, the adulterous love of Anna and Count Vronsky. The tone is darker and more pessimistic; the epigraph of the novel is "Vengeance is mine, I will repay," but the vengeance exacted from Anna is not the Lord's, but society's, not for her moral transgression but for her refusal to comply with society's hypocritical proprieties.

The inner tensions Tolstoy dramatized so powerfully in *War and Peace* and *Anna Karenina* began to overwhelm him personally. He underwent a shattering spiritual and perhaps psychological crisis which culminated in 1879 and was recorded in *A Confession* (written at the time, but not published until 1882). Tolstoy emerged from his agonized quest for the purpose of life with the simple answer that it was "to do good," an insight that he elaborated into a system of Christian anarchy. He renounced organized religion, government, and private property in favor of a faith in the individual's divinely given power to discern the good, a conviction derived from his perception of the simple faith of the peasants and from his study of Christ's words.

Most of Tolstoy's writing during the last thirty years of his life was devoted to advancing these ideas, most fully stated in *What Then Must We Do?* (1886). Didactic books, pamphlets, and articles poured from his pen; he transferred control of his estate to his family; and he attempted to bring his own daily life into conformity with his philosophical views. He gave up smoking and drinking, became a vegetarian, dressed in peasant clothes, and engaged in manual labor, attempting to avoid in every way dependence upon the labor of others. He also renounced sexual relations with his wife, in conformity with the commandment "Do not lust," one of five basic commandments he had derived from the words of Christ. Both Tolstoy's writings and the reports of his exemplary life began to attract disciples all over the world, many of whom made the pilgrimage to Yasnaya Polyana to talk with him.

Tolstoy developed the artistic implications of his new philosophy in *What is Art?* (1897). In this work, he rejected all art that does not achieve the moral purpose of communicating to the reader, through sympathetic identification, the state of the writer's soul. On these grounds, he developed his notorious rejection of Shakespeare's plays as "bad art," along with a number of other established masterpieces, including his own earlier works. Tolstoy tried to exemplify his new theory of art in a number of fictional and dramatic works, many of them marred by explicit moralizing but many

among his finest achievements, including "The Death of Ivan Ilyitch" (1886), "The Kreutzer Sonata" (1891), *Resurrection* (1899), the drama *The Power of Darkness* (1888), and the unfinished drama *The Light Shines in Darkness* (1910).

Tolstoy's commitment to his prophetic role increasingly alienated his wife and his older sons, who refused to join him in his ascetic life and who eventually obtained control of copyrights to all his works printed before 1880, in order to maintain an income satisfactory to them. The tensions of his domestic situation finally led Tolstoy, in 1910, at the age of eighty-two, to leave the estate secretly one night, in the company of his doctor and his youngest daughter Aleksandra, in order to seek a place where he could lead the kind of simple, hermit's life he sought. He caught a severe cold on the journey, however, and died a few days later of pneumonia in the house of a stationmaster on the railway.

Tolstoy's acute, conscience-stricken perception of the injustice of the Russian class system, his glorification of the people, and his vision of a stateless, classless society superficially seem to anticipate the revolutionary upheaval that was to transform Russia within a decade after his death. But in reality, Tolstoy's philosophy came out of a tradition of Romantic individualism and mysticism that was anathema to the makers of the Revolution; it derived not from Marx but from Rousseau, in its glorification of "natural man," its attempt to reconstruct a primitive Christianity, and its rejection of all received political or religious doctrine. For Tolstoy, the earthly paradise would not come through the inexorable unfolding of impersonal historical process or through violent class struggle; it would begin in the heart of each individual and would be achieved through the rule of love and nonviolence.

The post-conversion "Death of Ivan Ilyitch" is one of Tolstoy's finest works, profoundly moral in the sense that he defined in *What is Art?* and yet never (or seldom) marred by explicit, inorganic moralizing. Inevitably, it suggests comparison with the medieval *Everyman*, in which a journey to death similarly becomes a journey toward illumination. (The persistence of the theme is demonstrated by such recent works as Ingmar Bergman's *Wild Strawberries* and Iris Murdoch's *Bruno's Dream*.) The point of Ivan Ilyitch's life is its ordinariness; it is "the simplest, the most ordinary, and the most awful." Ivan Ilyitch's very name is ordinary, a Russian equivalent of "John Smith." The protagonist has not been a great sinner, any more than Everyman has; he has led a perfectly respectable life, always doing what was expected of him as best he could. But in the face of death, a terrible question pushes itself forward: "What if in reality all my life, my conscious life, has been not the right thing?" In his crisis, as in Everyman's, "Fellowship," "Kindred and Cousin," and "Goods" fall away from him. But—and here Tolstoy parts company with the conventionally Christian vision of *Everyman*—it is not the priesthood, the "sacraments seven," and "Good Deeds" that accompany Ivan Ilyitch to the grave; he receives the last rites but they are a speciously comforting deception, like the other conventions whose hollowness he now sees. The qualities that do bring about Ivan's final illumination are those that form the core of Tolstoy's deeply moving faith.

FURTHER READING *(prepared by J. H.):* Ernest J. Simmons's *Leo Tolstoy,* 1947, is still the standard English critical biography. Simmons has also written a briefer account in *Tolstoy,* 1974. Henry Gifford's *Tolstoy,* 1982, in the Past Masters series, is a good introductory overview. A more advanced overview is Richard F. Gustafson, *Leo Tolstoy: Resident and Stranger,* 1986. Ruth C. Benson's *Women in Tolstoy: The Ideal and the Erotic,* 1973, is excellent on its subject. Collections of critical essays include *Tolstoy: A Collection of Critical Essays,* ed. by Ralph E. Matlaw, 1967; *New Essays on Tolstoy,* ed. by Malcolm Jones, 1978; and *Tolstoy: The Critical Heritage,* ed. by A. V. Knowles, 1978. A useful guide to criticism in English up to its date is *Leo Tolstoy: An Annotated Bibliography of English-Language Sources to 1978,* comp. by David R. Egan and Melinda A. Egan, 1979.

THE DEATH OF IVAN ILYITCH

Translated by Constance Garnett

I

Inside the great building of the Law Courts, during the interval in the hearing of the Melvinsky case, the members of the judicial council and the public prosecutor were gathered together in the private room of Ivan Yegorovitch Shebek, and the conversation turned upon the celebrated Krasovsky case. Fyodor Vassilievitch hotly maintained that the case was not in the jurisdiction of the court. Yegor Ivanovitch stood up for his own view; but from the first Pyotr Ivanovitch, who had not entered into the discussion, took no interest in it, but was looking through the newspapers which had just been brought in.

"Gentlemen!" he said, "Ivan Ilyitch is dead!"

"You don't say so!"

"Here, read it," he said to Fyodor Vassilievitch, handing him the fresh still damp-smelling paper.

Within a black margin was printed: "Praskovya Fyodorovna Golovin with heartfelt affliction informs friends and relatives of the decease of her beloved husband, member of the Court of Justice, Ivan Ilyitch Golovin, who passed away on the 4th of February. The funeral will take place on Thursday at one o'clock."

Ivan Ilyitch was a colleague of the gentlemen present, and all liked him. It was some weeks now since he had been taken ill; his illness had been said to be incurable. His post had been kept open for him, but it had been thought that in case of his death Alexyeev might receive his appointment, and either Vinnikov or Shtabel would succeed to Alexyeev's. So that on hearing of Ivan Ilyitch's death, the first thought of each of the gentlemen in the room was of the effect this death might have on the transfer or promotion of themselves or their friends.

"Now I am sure of getting Shtabel's place or Vinnikov's," thought Fyodor Vassilievitch. "It was promised me long ago, and the promotion means eight hundred rubles additional income, besides the grants for office expenses."

"Now I shall have to petition for my brother-in-law to be transferred from Kaluga," thought Pyotr Ivanovitch. "My wife will be very glad. She won't be able to say now that I've never done anything for her family."

"I thought somehow that he'd never get up from his bed again," Pyotr Ivanovitch said aloud. "I'm sorry!"

"But what was it exactly was wrong with him?"

"The doctors could not decide. That's to say, they did decide, but differently. When I saw him last, I thought he would get over it."

"Well, I positively haven't called there ever since the holidays. I've kept meaning to go."

"Had he any property?"

"I think there's something, very small, of his wife's. But something quite trifling."

"Yes, one will have to go and call. They live such a terribly long way off."

"A long way from you, you mean. Everything's a long way from your place."

"There, he can never forgive me for living the other side of the river," said Pyotr Ivanovitch, smiling at Shebek. And they began to talk of the great distances between different parts of the town, and went back into the court.

Besides the reflections upon the changes and promotions in the service likely to ensue from this death, the very fact of the death of an intimate acquaintance excited in every one who heard of it, as such a fact always does, a feeling of relief that "it is he that is dead, and not I."

"Only think! he is dead, but here am I all right," each one thought or felt. The more intimate acquaintances, the so-called friends of Ivan Ilyitch, could not help thinking too that now they had the exceedingly tiresome social duties to perform of going to the funeral service and paying the widow a visit of condolence.

The most intimately acquainted with their late colleague were Fyodor Vassilievitch and Pyotr Ivanovitch.

Pyotr Ivanovitch had been a comrade of his at the school of jurisprudence, and considered himself under obligations to Ivan Ilyitch.

Telling his wife at dinner of the news of Ivan Ilyitch's death and his reflections as to the possibility of getting her brother transferred into their circuit, Pyotr Ivanovitch, without lying down for his usual nap, put on his frockcoat and drove to Ivan Ilyitch's.

At the entrance before Ivan Ilyitch's flat stood a carriage and two hired flies.[1] Downstairs in the entry near the hat-stand there was leaning against the wall a coffin-lid with tassels and braiding freshly rubbed up with pipeclay. Two ladies were taking off their cloaks. One of them he knew, the sister of Ivan Ilyitch; the other was a lady he did not know. Pyotr Ivanovitch's colleague, Shvarts, was coming down; and from the top stair, seeing who it was coming in, he stopped and winked at him, as though to say: "Ivan Ilyitch has made a mess of it; it's a very different matter with you and me."

Shvarts's face, with his English whiskers[2] and all his thin figure in his frockcoat, had, as it always had, an air of elegant solemnity; and this solem-

[1] Light, covered, horse-drawn cabs. [2] Long, flowing side whiskers.

nity, always such a contrast to Shvarts's playful character, had a special piquancy here. So thought Pyotr Ivanovitch.

Pyotr Ivanovitch let the ladies pass on in front of him, and walked slowly up the stairs after them. Shvarts had not come down, but was waiting at the top. Pyotr Ivanovitch knew what for; he wanted obviously to settle with him where their game of *vint*[3] was to be that evening. The ladies went up to the widow's room; while Shvarts, with his lips tightly and gravely shut and amusement in his eyes, with a twitch of his eyebrows motioned Pyotr Ivanovitch to the right, to the room where the dead man was.

Pyotr Ivanovitch went in, as people always do on such occasions, in uncertainty as to what he would have to do there. One thing he felt sure of—that crossing oneself never comes amiss on such occasions. As to whether it was necessary to bow down while doing so, he did not feel quite sure, and so chose a middle course. On entering the room he began crossing himself, and made a slight sort of bow. So far as the movements of his hands and head permitted him, he glanced while doing so about the room. Two young men, one a high school boy, nephews probably, were going out of the room, crossing themselves. An old lady was standing motionless; and a lady, with her eyebrows queerly lifted, was saying something to her in a whisper. A deacon in a frockcoat, resolute and hearty, was reading something aloud with an expression that precluded all possibility of contradiction. A young peasant who used to wait at table, Gerasim, walking with light footsteps in front of Pyotr Ivanovitch, was sprinkling something on the floor. Seeing this, Pyotr Ivanovitch was at once aware of the faint odor of the decomposing corpse. On his last visit to Ivan Ilyitch Pyotr Ivanovitch had seen this peasant in his room; he was performing the duties of a sicknurse, and Ivan Ilyitch liked him particularly. Pyotr Ivanovitch continued crossing himself and bowing in a direction intermediate between the coffin, the deacon, and the holy pictures on the table in the corner. Then when this action of making the sign of the cross with his hand seemed to him to have been unduly prolonged, he stood still and began to scrutinize the dead man.

The dead man lay, as dead men always do lie, in a peculiarly heavy dead way, his stiffened limbs sunk in the cushions of the coffin, and his head bent back forever on the pillow, and thrust up, as dead men always do, his yellow waxen forehead with bald spots on the sunken temples, and his nose that stood out sharply and, as it were, squeezed on the upper lip. He was much changed, even thinner since Pyotr Ivanovitch had seen him, but his face—as always with the dead—was more handsome, and, above all, more impressive than it had been when he was alive. On the face was an expression of what had to be done having been done, and rightly done. Besides this, there was too in that expression a reproach or a reminder for the living. This reminder seemed to Pyotr Ivanovitch uncalled for, or, at least, to have nothing to do with him. He felt something unpleasant; and so Pyotr Ivanovitch once more crossed himself hurriedly, and, as it struck him, too hurriedly, not quite in accordance with the proprieties, turned and went to the door. Shvarts was waiting for him in the adjoining room, standing with his legs apart and both hands behind his back playing with his top hat. A

[3] A game similar to auction bridge.

single glance at the playful, sleek, and elegant figure of Shvarts revived Pyotr Ivanovitch. He felt that he, Shvarts, was above it, and would not give way to depressing impressions. The mere sight of him said plainly: the incident of the service over the body of Ivan Ilyitch cannot possibly consti- tute a sufficient ground for recognizing the business of the session sus- pended,—in other words, in no way can it hinder us from shuffling and cutting a pack of cards this evening, while the footman sets four unsanctified candles on the table for us; in fact, there is no ground for supposing that this incident could prevent us from spending the evening agreeably. He said as much indeed to Pyotr Ivanovitch as he came out, proposing that the party should meet at Fyodor Vassilievitch's. But apparently it was Pyotr Ivanovitch's destiny not to play *vint* that evening. Praskovya Fyodorovna, a short, fat woman who, in spite of all efforts in a contrary direction, was steadily broader from her shoulders downwards, all in black, with lace on her head and her eyebrows as queerly arched as those of the lady standing beside the coffin, came out of her own apartments with some other ladies, and conducting them to the dead man's room, said: "The service will take place immediately; come in."

Shvarts, making an indefinite bow, stood still, obviously neither accept- ing nor declining this invitation. Praskovya Fyodorovna, recognizing Pyotr Ivanovitch, sighed, went right up to him, took his hand, and said, "I know that you were a true friend of Ivan Ilyitch's . . ." and looked at him, expect- ing from him the suitable action in response to these words. Pyotr Ivanovitch knew that, just as before he had to cross himself, now what he had to do was to press her hand, to sigh and to say, "Ah, I was indeed!" And he did so. And as he did so, he felt that the desired result had been attained; that he was touched, and she was touched.

"Come, since it's not begun yet, I have something I want to say to you," said the widow. "Give me your arm."

Pyotr Ivanovitch gave her his arm, and they moved towards the inner rooms, passing Shvarts, who winked gloomily at Pyotr Ivanovitch.

"So much for our *vint*! Don't complain if we find another partner. You can make a fifth when you do get away," said his humorous glance.

Pyotr Ivanovitch sighed still more deeply and despondently, and Praskovya Fyodorovna pressed his hand gratefully. Going into her draw- ing-room, which was upholstered with pink cretonne and lighted by a dis- mal-looking lamp, they sat down at the table, she on a sofa and Pyotr Ivanovitch on a low ottoman with deranged springs which yielded spas- modically under his weight. Praskovya Fyodorovna was about to warn him to sit on another seat, but felt such a recommendation out of keeping with her position, and changed her mind. Sitting down on the ottoman, Pyotr Ivanovitch remembered how Ivan Ilyitch had arranged this drawing-room, and had consulted him about this very pink cretonne with green leaves. Seating herself on the sofa, and pushing by the table (the whole drawing- room was crowded with furniture and things), the widow caught the lace of her black fichu[4] in the carving of the table. Pyotr Ivanovitch got up to disentangle it for her; and the ottoman, freed from his weight, began bob- bing up spasmodically under him. The widow began unhooking her lace

[4] Shawl or scarf draped over the shoulders and fastened in front to hide a low neckline.

herself, and Pyotr Ivanovitch again sat down, suppressing the mutinous ottoman springs under him. But the widow could not quite free herself, and Pyotr Ivanovitch rose again, and again the ottoman became mutinous and popped up with a positive snap. When this was all over, she took out a clean cambric handkerchief and began weeping. Pyotr Ivanovitch had been chilled off by the incident with the lace and the struggle with the ottoman springs, and he sat looking sullen. This awkward position was cut short by the entrance of Sokolov, Ivan Ilyitch's butler, who came in to announce that the place in the cemetery fixed on by Praskovya Fyodorovna would cost two hundred rubles. She left off weeping, and with the air of a victim glancing at Pyotr Ivanovitch, said in French that it was very terrible for her. Pyotr Ivanovitch made a silent gesture signifying his unhesitating conviction that it must indeed be so.

"Please, smoke," she said in a magnanimous, and at the same time, crushed voice, and she began discussing with Sokolov the question of the price of the site for the grave.

Pyotr Ivanovitch, lighting a cigarette, listened to her very circumstantial inquiries as to the various prices of sites and her decision as to the one to be selected. Having settled on the site for the grave, she made arrangements also about the choristers. Sokolov went away.

"I see to everything myself," she said to Pyotr Ivanovitch, moving on one side the albums that lay on the table; and noticing that the table was in danger from the cigarette-ash, she promptly passed an ash-tray to Pyotr Ivanovitch, and said: "I consider it affectation to pretend that my grief prevents me from looking after practical matters. On the contrary, if anything could—not console me . . . but distract me, it is seeing after everything for him." She took out her handkerchief again, as though preparing to weep again; and suddenly, as though struggling with herself, she shook herself, and began speaking calmly: "But I've business to talk about with you."

Pyotr Ivanovitch bowed, carefully keeping in check the springs of the ottoman, which had at once begun quivering under him.

"The last few days his sufferings were awful."

"Did he suffer very much?" asked Pyotr Ivanovitch.

"Oh, awfully! For the last moments, hours indeed, he never left off screaming. For three days and nights in succession he screamed incessantly. It was insufferable. I can't understand how I bore it; one could hear it through three closed doors. Ah, what I suffered!"

"And was he really conscious?" asked Pyotr Ivanovitch.

"Yes," she whispered, "up to the last minute. He said good-bye to us a quarter of an hour before his death, and asked Volodya to be taken away too."

The thought of the sufferings of a man he had known so intimately, at first as a light-hearted boy, a schoolboy, then grown up as a partner at whist, in spite of the unpleasant consciousness of his own and this woman's hypocrisy, suddenly horrified Pyotr Ivanovitch. He saw again that forehead, the nose that seemed squeezing the lip, and he felt frightened for himself. "Three days and nights of awful suffering and death. Why, that may at once, any minute, come upon me too," he thought, and he felt for an instant terrified. But immediately, he could not himself have said how, there came to his support the customary reflection that this had happened

to Ivan Ilyitch and not to him, and that to him this must not and could not happen; that in thinking thus he was giving way to depression, which was not the right thing to do, as was evident from Shvarts's expression of face. And making these reflections, Pyotr Ivanovitch felt reassured, and began with interest inquiring details about Ivan Ilyitch's end, as though death were a mischance peculiar to Ivan Ilyitch, but not at all incidental to himself.

After various observations about the details of the truly awful physical sufferings endured by Ivan Ilyitch (these details Pyotr Ivanovitch learned only through the effect Ivan Ilyitch's agonies had had on the nerves of Praskovya Fyodorovna), the widow apparently thought it time to get to business.

"Ah, Pyotr Ivanovitch, how hard it is, how awfully, awfully hard!" and she began to cry again.

Pyotr Ivanovitch sighed, and waited for her to blow her nose. When she had done so, he said, "Indeed it is," and again she began to talk, and brought out what was evidently the business she wished to discuss with him; that business consisted in the inquiry as to how on the occasion of her husband's death she was to obtain a grant from the government. She made a show of asking Pyotr Ivanovitch's advice about a pension. But he perceived that she knew already to the minutest details, what he did not know himself indeed, everything that could be got out of the government on the ground of this death; but that what she wanted to find out was, whether there were not any means of obtaining a little more? Pyotr Ivanovitch tried to imagine such means; but after pondering a little, and out of politeness abusing the government for its stinginess, he said that he believed that it was impossible to obtain more. Then she sighed and began unmistakably looking about for an excuse for getting rid of her visitor. He perceived this, put out his cigarette, got up, pressed her hand, and went out into the passage.

In the dining-room, where was the bric-à-brac clock that Ivan Ilyitch had been so delighted at buying, Pyotr Ivanovitch met the priest and several people he knew who had come to the service for the dead, and saw too Ivan Ilyitch's daughter, a handsome young lady. She was all in black. Her very slender figure looked even slenderer than usual. She had a gloomy, determined, almost wrathful expression. She bowed to Pyotr Ivanovitch as though he were to blame in some way. Behind the daughter, with the same offended air on his face, stood a rich young man, whom Pyotr Ivanovitch knew, too, an examining magistrate, the young lady's *fiancé*, as he had heard. He bowed dejectedly to him, and would have gone on into the dead man's room, when from the staircase there appeared the figure of the son, the high school boy, extraordinarily like Ivan Ilyitch. He was the little Ivan Ilyitch over again as Pyotr Ivanovitch remembered him at school. His eyes were red with crying, and had that look often seen in unclean boys of thirteen or fourteen.[5] The boy, seeing Pyotr Ivanovitch, scowled morosely and bashfully. Pyotr Ivanovitch nodded to him and went into the dead man's room. The service for the dead began—candles, groans, incense, tears, sobs. Pyotr Ivanovitch stood frowning, staring at his feet in front of

[5] Tolstoy apparently means the boy engages in masturbation.

him. He did not once glance at the dead man, and right through to the end did not once give way to depressing influences, and was one of the first to walk out. In the hall there was no one. Gerasim, the young peasant, darted out of the dead man's room, tossed over with his strong hand all the fur cloaks to find Pyotr Ivanovitch's, and gave it him.

"Well, Gerasim, my boy?" said Pyotr Ivanovitch, so as to say something. "A sad business, isn't it?"

"It's God's will. We shall come to the same," said Gerasim, showing his white, even, peasant teeth in a smile, and, like a man in a rush of extra work, he briskly opened the door, called up the coachman, saw Pyotr Ivanovitch into the carriage, and darted back to the steps as though bethinking himself of what he had to do next.

Pyotr Ivanovitch had a special pleasure in the fresh air after the smell of incense, of the corpse, and of carbolic acid.

"Where to?" asked the coachman.

"It's not too late, I'll still go round to Fyodor Vassilievitch's."

And Pyotr Ivanovitch drove there. And he did, in fact, find them just finishing the first rubber, so that he came just at the right time to take a hand.

II

The previous history of Ivan Ilyitch was the simplest, the most ordinary, and the most awful.

Ivan Ilyitch died at the age of forty-five, a member of the Judicial Council. He was the son of an official, whose career in Petersburg through various ministries and departments had been such as leads people into that position in which, though it is distinctly obvious that they are unfit to perform any kind of real duty, they yet cannot, owing to their long past service and their official rank, be dismissed; and they therefore receive a specially created fictitious post, and by no means fictitious thousands—from six to ten—on which they go on living till extreme old age. Such was the privy councilor, the superfluous member of various superfluous institutions, Ilya Efimovitch Golovin.

He had three sons. Ivan Ilyitch was the second son. The eldest son's career was exactly like his father's, only in a different department, and he was by now close upon that stage in the service in which the same sinecure would be reached. The third son was the unsuccessful one. He had in various positions always made a mess of things, and was now employed in the railway department. And his father and his brothers, and still more their wives, did not merely dislike meeting him, but avoided, except in extreme necessity, recollecting his existence. His sister had married Baron Greff, a Petersburg official of the same stamp as his father-in-law. Ivan Ilyitch was *le phénix de la famille*,[6] as people said. He was not so frigid and precise as the eldest son, nor so wild as the youngest. He was the happy mean between them—a shrewd, lively, pleasant, and well-bred man. He had been educated with his younger brother at the school of jurisprudence.

[6] *Le phénix de la famille.* "The phoenix of the family," a paragon (French).

The younger brother had not finished the school course, but was expelled when in the fifth class. Ivan Ilyitch completed the course successfully. At school he was just the same as he was later on all his life—an intelligent fellow, highly good-humored and sociable, but strict in doing what he considered to be his duty. His duty he considered whatever was so considered by those persons who were set in authority over him. He was not a toady as a boy, nor later on as a grown-up person; but from his earliest years he was attracted, as a fly to the light, to persons of good standing in the world, assimilated their manners and their views of life, and established friendly relations with them. All the enthusiasms of childhood and youth passed, leaving no great traces in him; he gave way to sensuality and to vanity, and latterly when in the higher classes at school to liberalism, but always keeping within certain limits which were unfailingly marked out for him by his instincts.

At school he had committed actions which had struck him beforehand as great vileness, and gave him a feeling of loathing for himself at the very time he was committing them. But later on, perceiving that such actions were committed also by men of good position, and were not regarded by them as base, he was able, not to regard them as good, but to forget about them completely, and was never mortified by recollections of them.

Leaving the school of jurisprudence in the tenth class, and receiving from his father a sum of money for his outfit, Ivan Ilyitch ordered his clothes at Sharmer's, hung on his watchchain a medallion inscribed *respice finem*,[7] said good-bye to the prince who was the principal of his school, had a farewell dinner with his comrades at Donon's, and with all his new fashionable belongings—traveling trunk, linen, suits of clothes, shaving and toilet appurtenances, and traveling rug, all ordered and purchased at the very best shops—set off to take the post of secretary on special commissions for the governor of a province, a post which had been obtained for him by his father.

In the province Ivan Ilyitch without loss of time made himself a position as easy and agreeable as his position had been in the school of jurisprudence. He did his work, made his career, and at the same time led a life of well-bred social gaiety. Occasionally he visited various districts on official duty, behaved with dignity both with his superiors and his inferiors; and with exactitude and an incorruptible honesty of which he could not help feeling proud, performed the duties with which he was entrusted, principally having to do with the dissenters.[8] When engaged in official work he was, in spite of his youth and taste for frivolous amusement, exceedingly reserved, official, and even severe. But in social life he was often amusing and witty, and always good-natured, well-bred, and *bon enfant*,[9] as was said of him by his chief and his chief's wife, with whom he was like one of the family.

In the province there was, too, a connection with one of the ladies who obtruded their charms on the stylish young lawyer. There was a dressmaker, too, and there were drinking bouts with smart officers visiting the

[7]"Look to the end" (Latin).
[8]The Old Believers, members of a sect broken off from the Russian Orthodox Church in the seventeenth century and subjects of a number of legal restrictions.
[9]Literally, "good child"; congenial (French).

neighborhood, and visits to a certain outlying street after supper; there was a rather cringing obsequiousness in his behavior, too, with his chief, and even his chief's wife. But all this was accompanied with such a tone of the highest breeding, that it could not be called by harsh names; it all came under the rubric of the French saying, *Il faut que la jeunesse se passe.*[10] Everything was done with clean hands, in clean shirts, with French phrases, and, what was of most importance, in the highest society, and consequently with the approval of people of rank.

Such was Ivan Ilyitch's career for five years, and then came a change in his official life. New methods of judicial procedure were established; new men were wanted to carry them out. And Ivan Ilyitch became such a new man. Ivan Ilyitch was offered the post of examining magistrate, and he accepted it in spite of the fact that this post was in another province, and he would have to break off all the ties he had formed and form new ones. Ivan Ilyitch's friends met together to see him off, had their photographs taken in a group, presented him with a silver cigarette-case, and he set off to his new post.

As an examining magistrate, Ivan Ilyitch was as *comme il faut,*[11] as well-bred, as adroit in keeping official duties apart from private life, and as successful in gaining universal respect, as he had been as secretary of private commissions. The duties of his new office were in themselves of far greater interest and attractiveness for Ivan Ilyitch. In his former post it had been pleasant to pass in his smart uniform from Sharmer's through the crowd of petitioners and officials waiting timorously and envying him, and to march with his easy swagger straight into the governor's private room, there to sit down with him to tea and cigarettes. But the persons directly subject to his authority were few. The only such persons were the district police superintendents and the dissenters, when he was serving on special commissions. And he liked treating such persons affably, almost like comrades; liked to make them feel that he, able to annihilate them, was behaving in this simple, friendly way with them. But such people were then few in number. Now as an examining magistrate Ivan Ilyitch felt that every one—every one without exception—the most dignified, the most self-satisfied people, all were in his hands, and that he had but to write certain words on a sheet of paper with a printed heading, and this dignified self-satisfied person would be brought before him in the capacity of a defendant or a witness; and if he did not care to make him sit down, he would have to stand up before him and answer his questions. Ivan Ilyitch never abused this authority of his; on the contrary, he tried to soften the expression of it. But the consciousness of this power and the possibility of softening its effect constituted for him the chief interest and attractiveness of his new position. In the work itself, in the preliminary inquiries, that is, Ivan Ilyitch very rapidly acquired the art of setting aside every consideration irrelevant to the official aspect of the case, and of reducing every case, however complex, to that form in which it could in a purely external fashion be put on paper, completely excluding his personal view of the matter, and what was of paramount importance, observing all the necessary formalities. All this

[10] French for "Youth must pass" (That's the way young people are).
[11] "As it should be"; proper (French).

work was new. And he was one of the first men who put into practical working the reforms in judicial procedure enacted in 1864.[12]

On settling in a new town in his position as examining magistrate, Ivan Ilyitch made new acquaintances, formed new ties, took up a new line, and adopted a rather different attitude. He took up an attitude of somewhat dignified aloofness towards the provincial authorities, while he picked out the best circle among the legal gentlemen and wealthy gentry living in the town, and adopted a tone of slight dissatisfaction with the government, moderate liberalism, and lofty civic virtue. With this, while making no change in the elegance of his get-up, Ivan Ilyitch in his new office gave up shaving, and left his beard free to grow as it liked. Ivan Ilyitch's existence in the new town proved to be very agreeable; the society which took the line of opposition to the governor was friendly and good; his income was larger, and he found a source of increased enjoyment in whist, at which he began to play at this time; and having a faculty for playing cards good-humoredly, and being rapid and exact in his calculations, he was as a rule on the winning side.

After living two years in the new town, Ivan Ilyitch met his future wife. Praskovya Fyodorovna Mihel was the most attractive, clever, and brilliant girl in the set in which Ivan Ilyitch moved. Among other amusements and recreations after his labors as a magistrate, Ivan Ilyitch started a light, playful flirtation with Praskovya Fyodorovna.

Ivan Ilyitch when he was an assistant secretary had danced as a rule; as an examining magistrate he danced only as an exception. He danced now as it were under protest, as though to show "that though I am serving on the new reformed legal code, and am of the fifth class in official rank, still if it comes to a question of dancing, in that line, too, I can do better than others." In this spirit he danced now and then towards the end of the evening with Praskovya Fyodorovna, and it was principally during these dances that he won the heart of Praskovya Fyodorovna. She fell in love with him. Ivan Ilyitch had no clearly defined intention of marrying; but when the girl fell in love with him, he put the question to himself: "After all, why not get married?"

The young lady, Praskovya Fyodorovna, was of good family, nice-looking. There was a little bit of property. Ivan Ilyitch might have reckoned on a more brilliant match, but this was a good match. Ivan Ilyitch had his salary; she, he hoped, would have as much of her own. It was a good family; she was a sweet, pretty, and perfectly *comme il faut* young woman. To say that Ivan Ilyitch got married because he fell in love with his wife and found in her sympathy with his views of life, would be as untrue as to say that he got married because the people of his world approved of the match. Ivan Ilyitch was influenced by both considerations; he was doing what was agreeable to himself in securing such a wife, and at the same time doing what persons of higher standing looked upon as the correct thing.

And Ivan Ilyitch got married.

The process itself of getting married and the early period of married life, with the conjugal caresses, the new furniture, the new crockery, the new house linen, all up to the time of his wife's pregnancy, went off very

[12] Russian law was reformed in 1864, following the emancipation of the serfs in 1861.

well; so that Ivan Ilyitch had already begun to think that so far from marriage breaking up that kind of frivolous, agreeable, lighthearted life, always decorous and always approved by society, which he regarded as the normal life, it would even increase its agreeableness. But at that point, in the early months of his wife's pregnancy, there came in a new element, unexpected, unpleasant, tiresome and unseemly, which could never have been anticipated, and from which there was no escape.

His wife, without any kind of reason, it seemed to Ivan Ilyitch, *de gaieté de coeur*,[13] as he expressed it, began to disturb the agreeableness and decorum of their life. She began without any sort of justification to be jealous, exacting in her demands on his attention, squabbled over everything, and treated him to the coarsest and most unpleasant scenes.

At first Ivan Ilyitch hoped to escape from the unpleasantness of this position by taking up the same frivolous and well-bred line that had served him well on other occasions of difficulty. He endeavored to ignore his wife's ill-humor, went on living lightheartedly and agreeably as before, invited friends to play cards, tried to get away himself to the club or to his friends. But his wife began on one occasion with such energy, abusing him in such coarse language, and so obstinately persisted in her abuse of him every time he failed in carrying out her demands, obviously having made up her mind firmly to persist till he gave way, that is, stayed at home and was as dull as she was, that Ivan Ilyitch took alarm. He perceived that matrimony, at least with his wife, was not invariably conducive to the pleasures and proprieties of life; but, on the contrary, often destructive of them, and that it was therefore essential to erect some barrier to protect himself from these disturbances. And Ivan Ilyitch began to look about for such means of protecting himself. His official duties were the only thing that impressed Praskovya Fyodorovna, and Ivan Ilyitch began to use his official position and the duties arising from it in his struggle with his wife to fence off his own independent world apart.

With the birth of the baby, the attempts at nursing it, and the various unsuccessful experiments with foods, with the illnesses, real and imaginary, of the infant and its mother, in which Ivan Ilyitch was expected to sympathize, though he never had the slightest idea about them, the need for him to fence off a world apart for himself outside his family life became still more imperative. As his wife grew more irritable and exacting, so did Ivan Ilyitch more and more transfer the center of gravity of his life to his official work. He became fonder and fonder of official life, and more ambitious than he had been.

Very quickly, not more than a year after his wedding, Ivan Ilyitch had become aware that conjugal life, though providing certain comforts, was in reality a very intricate and difficult business towards which one must, if one is to do one's duty, that is, lead the decorous life approved by society, work out for oneself a definite line, just as in the government service.

And such a line Ivan Ilyitch did work out for himself in his married life. He expected from his home life only those comforts—of dinner at home, of housekeeper and bed—which it could give him, and, above all, that perfect propriety in external observances required by public opinion. For the rest,

[13] "Out of gaiety of heart"; willfully or arbitrarily (French).

he looked for good-humored pleasantness, and if he found it he was very thankful. If he met with antagonism and querulousness, he promptly retreated into the separate world he had shut off for himself in his official life, and there he found solace.

Ivan Ilyitch was prized as a good official, and three years later he was made assistant public prosecutor. The new duties of this position, their dignity, the possibility of bringing any one to trial and putting any one in prison, the publicity of the speeches and the success Ivan Ilyitch had in that part of his work,—all this made his official work still more attractive to him.

Children were born to him. His wife became steadily more querulous and ill-tempered, but the line Ivan Ilyitch had taken up for himself in home life put him almost out of reach of her grumbling.

After seven years of service in the same town, Ivan Ilyitch was transferred to another province with the post of public prosecutor. They moved, money was short, and his wife did not like the place they had moved to. The salary was indeed a little higher than before, but their expenses were larger. Besides, a couple of children died, and home life consequently became even less agreeable for Ivan Ilyitch.

For every mischance that occurred in their new place of residence, Praskovya Fyodorovna blamed her husband. The greater number of subjects of conversation between husband and wife, especially the education of the children, led to questions which were associated with previous quarrels, and quarrels were ready to break out at every instant. There remained only those rare periods of being in love which did indeed come upon them, but never lasted long. These were the islands at which they put in for a time, but they soon set off again upon the ocean of concealed hostility, that was made manifest in their aloofness from one another. This aloofness might have distressed Ivan Ilyitch if he had believed that this ought not to be so, but by now he regarded this position as perfectly normal, and it was indeed the goal towards which he worked in his home life. His aim was to make himself more and more free from the unpleasant aspects of domestic life and to render them harmless and decorous. And he attained this aim by spending less and less time with his family; and when he was forced to be at home, he endeavored to secure his tranquillity by the presence of outsiders. The great thing for Ivan Ilyitch was having his office. In the official world all the interest of life was concentrated for him. And this interest absorbed him. The sense of his own power, the consciousness of being able to ruin any one he wanted to ruin, even the external dignity of his office, when he made his entry into the court or met subordinate officials, his success in the eyes of his superiors and his subordinates, and, above all, his masterly handling of cases, of which he was conscious,—all this delighted him and, together with chats with his colleagues, dining out, and whist, filled his life. So that, on the whole, Ivan's life still went on in the way he thought it should go—agreeably, decorously.

So he lived for another seven years. His eldest daughter was already sixteen, another child had died, and there was left only one other, a boy at the high school, a subject of dissension. Ivan Ilyitch wanted to send him to the school of jurisprudence, while Praskovya Fyodorovna to spite him sent him to the high school. The daughter had been educated at home, and had turned out well; the boy too did fairly well at his lessons.

III

Such was Ivan Ilyitch's life for seventeen years after his marriage. He had been prosecutor a long while by now, and had refused several appointments offered him, looking out for a more desirable post, when there occurred an unexpected incident which utterly destroyed his peace of mind. Ivan Ilyitch had been expecting to be appointed presiding judge in a university town, but a certain Goppe somehow stole a march on him and secured the appointment. Ivan Ilyitch took offense, began upbraiding him, and quarrelled with him and with his own superiors. A coolness was felt towards him, and on the next appointment that was made he was again passed over.

This was in the year 1880. That year was the most painful one in Ivan Ilyitch's life. During that year it became evident on the one hand that his pay was insufficient for his expenses; on the other hand, that he had been forgotten by every one, and that what seemed to him the most monstrous, the cruelest injustice, appeared to other people as a quite commonplace fact. Even his father felt no obligation to assist him. He felt that every one had deserted him, and that every one regarded his position with an income of three thousand five hundred rubles as a quite normal and even fortunate one. He alone, with a sense of the injustice done him, and the everlasting nagging of his wife and the debts he had begun to accumulate, living beyond his means, knew that his position was far from being normal.

The summer of that year, to cut down his expenses, he took a holiday and went with his wife to spend the summer in the country at her brother's.

In the country, with no official duties to occupy him, Ivan Ilyitch was for the first time a prey not to simple boredom, but to intolerable depression; and he made up his mind that things could not go on like that, and that it was absolutely necessary to take some decisive steps.

After a sleepless night spent by Ivan Ilyitch walking up and down the terrace, he determined to go to Petersburg to take active steps and to get transferred to some other department, so as to revenge himself on *them*, the people, that is, who had not known how to appreciate him.

Next day, in spite of all the efforts of his wife and his mother-in-law to dissuade him, he set off to Petersburg.

He went with a single object before him—to obtain a post with an income of five thousand. He was ready now to be satisfied with a post in any department, of any tendency, with any kind of work. He must only have a post—a post with five thousand, in the executive department, the banks, the railways, the Empress Marya's institutions,[14] even in the customs duties—what was essential was five thousand, and essential it was, too, to get out of the department in which they had failed to appreciate his value.

And, behold, this quest of Ivan Ilyitch's was crowned with wonderful, unexpected success. At Kursk there got into the same first-class carriage F. S. Ilyin, an acquaintance, who told him of a telegram just received by the governor of Kursk, announcing a change about to take place in the ministry—Pyotr Ivanovitch was to be superseded by Ivan Semyonovitch.

The proposed change, apart from its significance for Russia, had spe-

[14]The Empress Marya, wife of Paul I, founded a number of charitable institutions.

cial significance for Ivan Ilyitch from the fact that by bringing to the front a new person, Pyotr Petrovitch, and obviously, therefore, his friend Zahar Ivanovitch, it was in the highest degree propitious to Ivan Ilyitch's own plans. Zahar Ivanovitch was a friend and school-fellow of Ivan Ilyitch's.

At Moscow the news was confirmed. On arriving at Petersburg, Ivan Ilyitch looked up Zahar Ivanovitch, and received a positive promise of an appointment in his former department—that of justice.

A week later he telegraphed to his wife: *"Zahar Miller's place. At first report I receive appointment."*

Thanks to these changes, Ivan Ilyitch unexpectedly obtained, in the same department as before, an appointment which placed him two stages higher than his former colleagues, and gave him an income of five thousand, together with the official allowance of three thousand five hundred for traveling expenses. All his ill-humor with his former enemies and the whole department was forgotten, and Ivan Ilyitch was completely happy.

Ivan Ilyitch went back to the country more lighthearted and good-tempered than he had been for a very long while. Praskovya Fyodorovna was in better spirits, too, and peace was patched up between them. Ivan Ilyitch described what respect every one had shown him in Petersburg; how all those who had been his enemies had been put to shame, and were cringing now before him; how envious they were of his appointment, and still more of the high favor in which he stood at Petersburg.

Praskovya Fyodorovna listened to this, and pretended to believe it, and did not contradict him in anything, but confined herself to making plans for her new arrangements in the town to which they would be moving. And Ivan Ilyitch saw with delight that these plans were his plans; that they were agreed; and that his life after this disturbing hitch in its progress was about to regain its true, normal character of lighthearted agreeableness and propriety.

Ivan Ilyitch had come back to the country for a short stay only. He had to enter upon the duties of his new office on the 10th of September; and besides, he needed some time to settle in a new place, to move all his belongings from the other province, to purchase and order many things in addition; in short, to arrange things as settled in his own mind, and almost exactly as settled in the heart too of Praskovya Fyodorovna.

And now when everything was so successfully arranged, and when he and his wife were agreed in their aim, and were, besides, so little together, they got on with one another as they had not got on together since the early years of their married life. Ivan Ilyitch had thought of taking his family away with him at once; but his sister and his brother-in-law, who had suddenly become extremely cordial and intimate with him and his family, were so pressing in urging them to stay that he set off alone.

Ivan Ilyitch started off; and the lighthearted temper produced by his success, and his good understanding with his wife, one thing backing up another, did not desert him all the time. He found a charming set of apartments, the very thing both husband and wife had dreamed of. Spacious, lofty reception-rooms in the old style, a comfortable, dignified-looking study for him, rooms for his wife and daughter, a schoolroom for his son, everything as though planned on purpose for them. Ivan Ilyitch himself looked after the furnishing of them, chose the wallpapers, bought furni-

ture, by preference antique furniture, which had a peculiar *comme-il-faut* style to his mind, and it all grew up and grew up, and really attained the ideal he had set before himself. When he had half finished arranging the house, his arrangement surpassed his own expectations. He saw the *comme-il-faut* character, elegant and free from vulgarity, that the whole would have when it was all ready. As he fell asleep he pictured to himself the reception-room as it would be. Looking at the drawing-room, not yet finished, he could see the hearth, the screen, the *étagère*,[15] and the little chairs dotted here and there, the plates and dishes on the wall, and the bronzes as they would be when they were all put in their places. He was delighted with the thought of how he would impress Praskovya and Lizanka, who had taste too in this line. They would never expect anything like it. He was particularly successful in coming across and buying cheap old pieces of furniture, which gave a peculiarly aristocratic air to the whole. In his letters he purposely disparaged everything so as to surprise them. All this so absorbed him that the duties of his new office, though he was so fond of his official work, interested him less than he had expected. During sittings of the court he had moments of inattention; he pondered the question which sort of cornices to have on the window-blinds, straight or fluted. He was so interested in this business that he often set to work with his own hands, moved a piece of furniture, or hung up curtains himself. One day he went up a ladder to show a workman, who did not understand, how he wanted some hangings draped, made a false step and slipped; but, like a strong and nimble person, he clung on, and only knocked his side against the corner of a frame. The bruised place ached, but it soon passed off. Ivan Ilyich felt all this time particularly good-humored and well. He wrote: "I feel fifteen years younger." He thought his house-furnishing would be finished in September, but it dragged on to the middle of October. But then the effect was charming; not he only said so, but every one who saw it told him so too.

In reality, it was all just what is commonly seen in the houses of people who are not exactly wealthy but want to look like wealthy people, and so succeed only in being like one another—hangings, dark wood, flowers, rugs and bronzes, everything dark and highly polished, everything that all people of a certain class have so as to be like all people of a certain class. And in his case it was all so like that it made no impression at all; but it all seemed to him somehow special. When he met his family at the railway station and brought them to his newly furnished rooms, all lighted up in readiness, and a footman in a white tie opened the door into an entry decorated with flowers, and then they walked into the drawing-room and the study, uttering cries of delight, he was very happy, conducted them everywhere, eagerly drinking in their praises, and beaming with satisfaction. The same evening, while they talked about various things at tea, Praskovya Fyodorovna inquired about his fall, and he laughed and showed them how he had gone flying, and how he had frightened the upholsterer.

"It's as well I'm something of an athlete. Another man might have been killed, and I got nothing worse than a blow here; when it's touched it hurts, but it's going off already; just a bruise."

[15] Cabinet with a tier of open shelves; bookcase (French).

And they began to live in their new abode, which, as is always the case, when they had got thoroughly settled in they found to be short of just one room, and with their new income, which, as always, was only a little—some five hundred rubles—too little, and everything went very well. Things went particularly well at first, before everything was quite finally arranged, and there was still something to do to the place—something to buy, something to order, something to move, something to make to fit. Though there were indeed several disputes between husband and wife, both were so well satisfied, and there was so much to do, that it all went off without serious quarrels. When there was nothing left to arrange, it became a little dull, and something seemed to be lacking, but by then they were making acquaintances and forming habits, and life was filled up again.

Ivan Ilyitch, after spending the morning in the court, returned home to dinner, and at first he was generally in a good humor, although this was apt to be upset a little, and precisely on account of the new abode. Every spot on the table-cloth, on the hangings, the string of a window blind broken, irritated him. He had devoted so much trouble to the arrangement of the rooms that any disturbance of their order distressed him. But, on the whole, the life of Ivan Ilyitch ran its course as, according to his conviction, life ought to do—easily, agreeably, and decorously. He got up at nine, drank his coffee, read the newspaper, then put on his official uniform, and went to the court. There the routine of the daily work was ready mapped out for him, and he stepped into it at once. People with petitions, inquiries in the office, the office itself, the sittings—public and preliminary. In all this the great thing necessary was to exclude everything with the sap of life in it, which always disturbs the regular course of official business, not to admit any sort of relations with people except the official relations; the motive of all intercourse had to be simply the official motive, and the intercourse itself to be only official. A man would come, for instance, anxious for certain information. Ivan Ilyitch, not being the functionary on duty, would have nothing whatever to do with such a man. But if this man's relation to him as a member of the court is such as can be formulated on official stamped paper—within the limits of such a relation Ivan Ilyitch would do everything, positively everything he could, and in doing so would observe the semblance of human friendly relations, that is, the courtesies of social life. But where the official relation ended, there everything else stopped too. This art of keeping the official aspect of things apart from his real life, Ivan Ilyitch possessed in the highest degree; and through long practice and natural aptitude, he had brought it to such a pitch of perfection that he even permitted himself at times, like a skilled specialist as it were in jest, to let the human and official relations mingle. He allowed himself this liberty just because he felt he had the power at any moment if he wished it to take up the purely official line again and to drop the human relation. This thing was not simply easy, agreeable, and decorous; in Ivan Ilyitch's hands it attained a positively artistic character. In the intervals of business he smoked, drank tea, chatted a little about politics, a little about public affairs, a little about cards, but most of all about appointments in the service. And tired, but feeling like some artist who has skillfully played his part in the performance, one of the first violins in the orchestra, he returned home. At home his daughter and her mother had been paying calls

somewhere, or else some one had been calling on them; the son had been at school, had been preparing his lessons with his teachers, and duly learning correctly what was taught at the high school. Everything was as it should be. After dinner, if there were no visitors, Ivan Ilyitch sometimes read some book of which people were talking, and in the evening sat down to work, that is, read official papers, compared them with the laws, sorted depositions, and put them under the laws. This he found neither tiresome nor entertaining. It was tiresome when he might have been playing *vint;* but if there were no *vint* going on, it was better anyway than sitting alone or with his wife. Ivan Ilyitch's pleasures were little dinners, to which he invited ladies and gentlemen of good social position, and such methods of passing the time with them as were usual with such persons, so that his drawing-room might be like all other drawing-rooms.

Once they even gave a party—a dance. And Ivan Ilyitch enjoyed it, and everything was very successful, except that it led to a violent quarrel with his wife over the tarts and sweetmeats. Praskovya Fyodorovna had her own plan; while Ivan Ilyitch insisted on getting everything from an expensive pastry-cook, and ordered a great many tarts, and the quarrel was because these tarts were left over and the pastry-cook's bill came to forty-five rubles. The quarrel was a violent and unpleasant one, so much so that Praskovya Fyodorovna called him "Fool, imbecile." And he clutched at his head, and in his anger made some allusion to a divorce. But the party itself was enjoyable. There were all the best people, and Ivan Ilyitch danced with Princess Trufanov, the sister of the one so well known in connection with the charitable association called "Bear my Burden." His official pleasures lay in the gratification of his pride; his social pleasures lay in the gratification of his vanity. But Ivan Ilyitch's most real pleasure was the pleasure of playing *vint.* He admitted to himself that, after all, after whatever unpleasant incidents there had been in his life, the pleasure which burned like a candle before all others was sitting with good players, and not noisy partners, at *vint;* and, of course, a four-hand game (playing with five was never a success, though one pretends to like it particularly), and with good cards, to play a shrewd, serious game, then supper and a glass of wine. And after *vint,* especially after winning some small stakes (winning large sums was unpleasant), Ivan Ilyitch went to bed in a particularly happy frame of mind.

So they lived. They moved in the very best circle, and were visited by people of consequence and young people.

In their views of their circle of acquaintances, the husband, the wife, and the daughter were in complete accord; and without any expressed agreement on the subject, they all acted alike in dropping and shaking off various friends and relations, shabby persons who swooped down upon them in their drawing-room with Japanese plates on the walls, and pressed their civilities on them. Soon these shabby persons ceased fluttering about them, and none but the very best society was seen at the Golovins. Young men began to pay attention to Lizanka; and Petrishtchev, the son of Dmitry Ivanovitch Petrishtchev, and the sole heir of his fortune, an examining magistrate, began to be so attentive to Lizanka, that Ivan Ilyitch had raised the question with his wife whether it would not be as well to arrange a sledge drive for them, or to get up some theatricals. So they lived. And

everything went on in this way without change, and everything was very nice.

<div align="center">

IV

</div>

All were in good health. One could not use the word ill-health in connection with the symptoms Ivan Ilyitch sometimes complained of, namely, a queer taste in his mouth and a sort of uncomfortable feeling on the left side of the stomach.

But it came to pass that this uncomfortable feeling kept increasing, and became not exactly a pain, but a continual sense of weight in his side and the cause of an irritable temper. This irritable temper, continually growing, began at last to mar the agreeable easiness and decorum that had reigned in the Golovin household. Quarrels between the husband and wife became more and more frequent, and soon all the easiness and amenity of life had fallen away, and mere propriety was maintained with difficulty. Scenes became again more frequent. Again there were only islands in the sea of contention—and but few of these—at which the husband and wife could meet without an outbreak. And Praskovya Fyodorovna said now, not without grounds, that her husband had a trying temper. With her characteristic exaggeration, she said he had always had this awful temper, and she had needed all her sweetness to put up with it for twenty years. It was true that it was he now who began the quarrels. His gusts of temper always broke out just before dinner, and often just as he was beginning to eat, at the soup. He would notice that some piece of the crockery had been chipped, or that the food was not nice, or that his son put his elbow on the table, or his daughter's hair was not arranged as he liked it. And whatever it was, he laid the blame of it on Praskovya Fyodorovna. Praskovya Fyodorovna had at first retorted in the same strain, and said all sorts of horrid things to him; but on two occasions, just at the beginning of dinner, he had flown into such a frenzy that she perceived that it was due to physical derangement, and was brought on by taking food, and she controlled herself; she did not reply, but simply made haste to get dinner over. Praskovya Fyodorovna took great credit to herself for this exercise of self-control. Making up her mind that her husband had a fearful temper, and made her life miserable, she began to feel sorry for herself. And the more she felt for herself, the more she hated her husband. She began to wish he were dead; yet could not wish it, because then there would be no income. And this exasperated her against him even more. She considered herself dreadfully unfortunate, precisely because even his death could not save her, and she felt irritated and concealed it, and this hidden irritation on her side increased his irritability.

After one violent scene, in which Ivan Ilyitch had been particularly unjust, and after which he had said in explanation that he certainly was irritable, but that it was due to illness, she said that if he were ill he ought to take steps, and insisted on his going to see a celebrated doctor.

He went. Everything was as he had expected; everything was as it always is. The waiting and the assumption of dignity, that professional dignity he knew so well, exactly as he assumed it himself in court, and the sounding

and listening and questions that called for answers that were foregone con-
clusions and obviously superfluous, and the significant air that seemed to
insinuate—you only leave it all to us, and we will arrange everything, for us
it is certain and incontestable how to arrange everything, everything in one
way for every man of every sort. It was all exactly as in his court of justice.
Exactly the same air as he put on in dealing with a man brought up for
judgment, the doctor put on for him.

The doctor said: This and that proves that you have such-and-such a
thing wrong inside you; but if that is not confirmed by analysis of this and
that, then we must assume this and that. If we assume this and that, then—
and so on. To Ivan Ilyitch there was only one question of consequence, Was
his condition dangerous or not? But the doctor ignored that irrelevant
inquiry. From the doctor's point of view this was a side issue, not the subject
under consideration; the only real question was the balance of probabilities
between a loose kidney, chronic catarrh, and appendicitis. It was not a
question of the life of Ivan Ilyitch, but the question between the loose
kidney and the intestinal appendix. And this question, as it seemed to Ivan
Ilyitch, the doctor solved in a brilliant manner in favor of the appendix,
with the reservation that analysis of the water[16] might give a fresh clue, and
that then the aspect of the case would be altered. All this was point for
point identical with what Ivan Ilyitch had himself done in brilliant fashion a
thousand times over in dealing with some man on his trial. Just as brilliantly
the doctor made his summing-up, and triumphantly, gaily even, glanced
over his spectacles at the prisoner in the dock. From the doctor's sum-
ming-up Ivan Ilyitch deduced the conclusion—that things looked bad, and
that he, the doctor, and most likely every one else, did not care, but that
things looked bad for him. And this conclusion impressed Ivan Ilyitch mor-
bidly, arousing in him a great feeling of pity for himself, of great anger
against this doctor who could be unconcerned about a matter of such im-
portance.

But he said nothing of that. He got up, and, laying the fee on the table,
he said, with a sigh, "We sick people probably often ask inconvenient ques-
tions. Tell me, is this generally a dangerous illness or not?"

The doctor glanced severely at him with one eye through his spectacles,
as though to say: "Prisoner at the bar, if you will not keep within the limits
of the questions allowed you, I shall be compelled to take measures for
your removal from the precincts of the court." "I have told you what I
thought necessary and suitable already," said the doctor; "the analysis will
show anything further." And the doctor bowed him out.

Ivan Ilyitch went out slowly and dejectedly, got into his sledge, and
drove home. All the way home he was incessantly going over all the doctor
had said, trying to translate all these complicated, obscure, scientific
phrases into simple language, and to read in them an answer to the ques-
tion, Is it bad—is it very bad, or nothing much as yet? And it seemed to him
that the upshot of all the doctor had said was that it was very bad. Every-
thing seemed dismal to Ivan Ilyitch in the streets. The sledge-drivers were
dismal, the houses were dismal, the people passing, and the shops were
dismal. This ache, this dull gnawing ache, that never ceased for a second,

[16] Urine.

seemed, when connected with the doctor's obscure utterances, to have gained a new, more serious significance. With a new sense of misery Ivan Ilyitch kept watch on it now.

He reached home and began to tell his wife about it. His wife listened; but in the middle of his account his daughter came in with her hat on, ready to go out with her mother. Reluctantly she half sat down to listen to these tedious details, but she could not stand it for long, and her mother did not hear his story to the end.

"Well, I'm very glad," said his wife; "now you must be sure and take the medicine regularly. Give me the prescription; I'll send Gerasim to the chemist's!" And she went to get ready to go out.

He had not taken a breath while she was in the room, and he heaved a deep sigh when she was gone.

"Well," he said, "may be it really is nothing as yet."

He began to take the medicine, to carry out the doctor's directions, which were changed after the analysis of the water. But it was just at this point that some confusion arose, either in the analysis or in what ought to have followed from it. The doctor himself, of course, could not be blamed for it, but it turned out that things had not gone as the doctor had told him. Either he had forgotten or told a lie, or was hiding something from him.

But Ivan Ilyitch still went on just as exactly carrying out the doctor's direction, and in doing so he found comfort at first.

From the time of his visit to the doctor Ivan Ilyitch's principal occupation became the exact observance of the doctor's prescriptions as regards hygiene and medicine and the careful observation of his ailment in all the functions of his organism. Ivan Ilyitch's principal interest came to be people's ailments and people's health. When anything was said in his presence about sick people, about deaths and recoveries, especially in the case of an illness resembling his own, he listened, trying to conceal his excitement, asked questions, and applied what he heard to his own trouble.

The ache did not grow less; but Ivan Ilyitch made great efforts to force himself to believe that he was better. And he succeeded in deceiving himself so long as nothing happened to disturb him. But as soon as he had a mischance, some unpleasant words with his wife, a failure in his official work, an unlucky hand at *vint,* he was at once acutely sensible of his illness. In former days he had borne with such mishaps, hoping soon to retrieve the mistake, to make a struggle, to reach success later, to have a lucky hand. But now he was cast down by every mischance and reduced to despair. He would say to himself: "Here I'm only just beginning to get better, and the medicine has begun to take effect, and now this mischance or disappointment." And he was furious against the mischance or the people who were causing him the disappointment and killing him, and he felt that this fury was killing him, but could not check it. One would have thought that it should have been clear to him that this exasperation against circumstances and people was aggravating his disease, and that therefore he ought not to pay attention to the unpleasant incidents. But his reasoning took quite the opposite direction. He said that he needed peace, and was on the watch for everything that disturbed his peace, and at the slightest disturbance of it he flew into a rage. What made his position worse was that he read medical books and consulted doctors. He got worse so gradually that

he might have deceived himself, comparing one day with another, the difference was so slight. But when he consulted the doctors, then it seemed to him that he was getting worse, and very rapidly so indeed. And in spite of this, he was continually consulting the doctors.

That month he called on another celebrated doctor. The second celebrity said almost the same as the first, but put his questions differently; and the interview with this celebrity only redoubled the doubts and terrors of Ivan Ilyitch. A friend of a friend of his, a very good doctor, diagnosed the disease quite differently; and in spite of the fact that he guaranteed recovery, by his questions and his suppositions he confused Ivan Ilyitch even more and strengthened his suspicions. A homeopath[17] gave yet another diagnosis of the complaint, and prescribed medicine, which Ivan Ilyitch took secretly for a week; but after a week of the homeopathic medicine he felt no relief, and losing faith both in the other doctor's treatment and in this, he fell into even deeper depression. One day a lady of his acquaintance talked to him of the healing wrought by the holy pictures. Ivan Ilyitch caught himself listening attentively and believing in the reality of the facts alleged. This incident alarmed him. "Can I have degenerated to such a point of intellectual feebleness?" he said to himself. "Nonsense! it's all rubbish. I must not give way to nervous fears, but fixing on one doctor, adhere strictly to his treatment. That's what I will do. Now it's settled. I won't think about it, but till next summer I will stick to the treatment, and then I shall see. Now I'll put a stop to this wavering!" It was easy to say this, but impossible to carry it out. The pain in his side was always dragging at him, seeming to grow more acute and ever more incessant; it seemed to him that the taste in his mouth was queerer, and there was a loathsome smell even from his breath, and his appetite and strength kept dwindling. There was no deceiving himself; something terrible, new, and so important that nothing more important had ever been in Ivan Ilyitch's life, was taking place in him, and he alone knew of it. All about him did not or would not understand, and believed that everything in the world was going on as before. This was what tortured Ivan Ilyitch more than anything. Those of his own household, most of all his wife and daughter, who were absorbed in a perfect whirl of visits, did not, he saw, comprehend it at all, and were annoyed that he was so depressed and exacting, as though he were to blame for it. Though they tried indeed to disguise it, he saw he was a nuisance to them; but that his wife had taken up a definite line of her own in regard to his illness, and stuck to it regardless of what he might say and do. This line was expressed thus: "You know," she would say to acquaintances, "Ivan Ilyitch cannot, like all other simple-hearted folks, keep to the treatment prescribed him. One day he'll take his drops and eat what he's ordered, and go to bed in good time; the next day, if I don't see to it, he'll suddenly forget to take his medicine, eat sturgeon (which is forbidden by the doctors), yes, and sit up at *vint* till past midnight."

"Why, when did I do that?" Ivan Ilyitch asked in vexation one day at Pyotr Ivanovitch's.

[17] Practitioner of homeopathy, a system of medicine that treats illnesses by administering minute doses of substances that, in healthy persons, would produce symptoms of the disease treated.

"Why, yesterday, with Shebek."

"It makes no difference. I couldn't sleep for pain."

"Well, it doesn't matter what you do it for, only you'll never get well like that, and you make us wretched."

Praskovya Fyodorovna's external attitude to her husband's illness, openly expressed to others and to himself, was that Ivan Ilyitch was to blame in the matter of his illness, and that the whole illness was another injury he was doing to his wife. Ivan Ilyitch felt that the expression of this dropped from her unconsciously, but that made it no easier for him.

In his official life, too, Ivan Ilyitch noticed, or fancied he noticed, a strange attitude to him. At one time it seemed to him that people were looking inquisitively at him, as a man who would shortly have to vacate his position; at another time his friends would suddenly begin chaffing him in a friendly way over his nervous fears, as though that awful and horrible, unheard-of thing that was going on within him, incessantly gnawing at him, and irresistibly dragging him away somewhere, were the most agreeable subject for joking. Shvarts especially, with his jocoseness, his liveliness, and his *comme-il-faut* tone, exasperated Ivan Ilyitch by reminding him of himself ten years ago.

Friends came sometimes to play cards. They sat down to the card-table; they shuffled and dealt the new cards. Diamonds were led and followed by diamonds, the seven. His partner said, "Can't trump," and played the two of diamonds. What then? Why, delightful, capital, it should have been—he had a trump hand. And suddenly Ivan Ilyitch feels that gnawing ache, that taste in his mouth, and it strikes him as something grotesque that with that he could be glad of a trump hand.

He looks at Mihail Mihailovitch, his partner, how he taps on the table with his red hand, and affably and indulgently abstains from snatching up the trick, and pushes the cards towards Ivan Ilyitch so as to give him the pleasure of taking them up, without any trouble, without even stretching out his hand. "What, does he suppose that I'm so weak that I can't stretch out my hand?" thinks Ivan Ilyitch, and he forgets the trumps, and trumps his partner's cards, and plays his trump hand without making three tricks; and what's the most awful thing of all is that he sees how upset Mihail Mihailovitch is about it, while he doesn't care a bit, and it's awful for him to think why he doesn't care.

They all see that he's in pain, and say to him, "We can stop if you're tired. You go and lie down." Lie down? No, he's not in the least tired; they will play the rubber. All are gloomy and silent. Ivan Ilyitch feels that it is he who has brought this gloom upon them, and he cannot disperse it. They have supper, and the party breaks up, and Ivan Ilyitch is left alone with the consciousness that his life is poisoned for him and poisons the life of others, and that this poison is not losing its force, but is continually penetrating more and more deeply into his whole existence.

And with the consciousness of this, and with the physical pain in addition, and the terror in addition to that, he must lie in his bed, often not able to sleep for pain the greater part of the night; and in the morning he must get up again, dress, go to the law-court, speak, write, or, if he does not go out, stay at home for all the four-and-twenty hours of the day and night, of

which each one is a torture. And he had to live thus on the edge of the precipice alone, without one man who would understand and feel for him.

V

In this way one month, then a second, passed by. Just before the New Year his brother-in-law arrived in the town on a visit to them. Ivan Ilyitch was at the court when he arrived. Praskovya Fyodorovna had gone out shopping. Coming home and going into his study, he found there his brother-in-law, a healthy, florid man, engaged in unpacking his trunk. He raised his head, hearing Ivan Ilyitch's step, and for a second stared at him without a word. That stare told Ivan Ilyitch everything. His brother-in-law opened his mouth to utter an "Oh!" of surprise, but checked himself. That confirmed it all.

"What! have I changed?"

"Yes, there is a change."

And all Ivan Ilyitch's efforts to draw him into talking of his appearance his brother-in-law met with obstinate silence. Praskovya Fyodorovna came in; the brother-in-law went to see her. Ivan Ilyitch locked his door and began gazing at himself in the looking-glass, first full face, then in profile. He took up his photograph, taken with his wife, and compared the portrait with what he saw in the looking-glass. The change was immense. Then he bared his arm to the elbow, looked at it, pulled the sleeve down again, sat down on an ottoman and felt blacker than night.

"I mustn't, I mustn't," he said to himself, jumped up, went to the table, opened some official paper, tried to read it, but could not. He opened the door, went into the drawing-room. The door into the drawing-room was closed. He went up to it on tiptoe and listened.

"No, you're exaggerating," Praskovya Fyodorovna was saying.

"Exaggerating? You can't see it. Why, he's a dead man. Look at his eyes—there's no light in them. But what's wrong with him?"

"No one can tell. Nikolaev" (that was another doctor) "said something, but I don't know, Leshtchetitsky" (this was the celebrated doctor) "said the opposite."

Ivan Ilyitch walked away, went to his own room, lay down, and fell to musing. "A kidney—a loose kidney." He remembered all the doctors had told him, how it had been detached, and how it was loose; and by an effort of imagination he tried to catch that kidney and to stop it, to strengthen it. So little was needed, he fancied. "No, I'll go again to Pyotr Ivanovitch" (this was the friend who had a friend a doctor). He rang, ordered the horse to be put in, and got ready to go out.

"Where are you off too, Jean?"[18] asked his wife with a peculiarly melancholy and exceptionally kind expression.

This exceptionally kind expression exasperated him. He looked darkly at her.

"I want to see Pyotr Ivanovitch."

[18] French form of "Ivan."

He went to the friend who had a friend a doctor. And with him to the doctor's. He found him in, and had a long conversation with him.

Reviewing the anatomical and physiological details of what, according to the doctor's view, was taking place within him, he understood it all. It was just one thing—a little thing wrong with the intestinal appendix. It might all come right. Only strengthen one sluggish organ, and decrease the undue activity of another, and absorption would take place, and all would be set right. He was a little late for dinner. He ate his dinner, talked cheerfully, but it was a long while before he could go to his own room to work. At last he went to his study, and at once sat down to work. He read his legal documents and did his work, but the consciousness never left him of having a matter of importance very near to his heart which he had put off, but would look into later. When he had finished his work, he remembered that the matter near his heart was thinking about the intestinal appendix. But he did not give himself up to it; he went into the drawing-room to tea. There were visitors; and there was talking, playing on the piano, and singing; there was the young examining magistrate, the desirable match for the daughter. Ivan Ilyitch spent the evening, as Praskovya Fyodorovna observed, in better spirits than any of them; but he never forgot for an instant that he had the important matter of the intestinal appendix put off for consideration later. At eleven o'clock he said good night and went to his own room. He had slept alone since his illness in a little room adjoining his study. He went in, undressed, and took up a novel of Zola,[19] but did not read it; he fell to thinking. And in his imagination the desired recovery of the intestinal appendix had taken place. There had been absorption, rejection, re-establishment of the regular action.

"Why, it's all simply that," he said to himself. "One only wants to assist nature." He remembered the medicine, got up, took it, lay down on his back, watching for the medicine to act beneficially and overcome the pain. "It's only to take it regularly and avoid injurious influences; why, already I feel rather better, much better." He began to feel his side; it was not painful to the touch. "Yes, I don't feel it—really, much better already." He put out the candle and lay on his side. "The appendix is getting better, absorption." Suddenly he felt the familiar, old, dull, gnawing ache, persistent, quiet, in earnest. In his mouth the same familiar loathsome taste. His heart sank, and his brain felt dim, misty. "My God, my God!" he said, "again, again, and it will never cease." And suddenly the whole thing rose before him in quite a different aspect. "Intestinal appendix! kidney!" he said to himself. "It's not a question of the appendix, not a question of the kidney, but of life and . . . death. Yes, life has been and now it's going, going away, and I cannot stop it. Yes. Why deceive myself? Isn't it obvious to every one, except me, that I'm dying, and it's only a question of weeks, of days—at once perhaps. There was light, and now there is darkness. I was here, and now I am going! Where?" A cold chill ran over him, his breath stopped. He heard nothing but the throbbing of his heart.

"I shall be no more, then what will there be? There'll be nothing. Where

[19] Émile Zola, contemporary French naturalist writer. Tolstoy disliked Zola's work and regarded it as indecent and demoralizing.

then shall I be when I'm no more? Can this be dying? No; I don't want to!" He jumped up, tried to light the candle; and fumbling with trembling hands, he dropped the candle and the candlestick on the floor and fell back again on the pillow. "Why trouble? it doesn't matter," he said to himself, staring with open eyes into the darkness. "Death. Yes, death. And they—all of them—don't understand, and don't want to understand, and feel no pity. They are playing." (He caught through the closed doors the far-away cadence of a voice and the accompaniment.) "They don't care, but they will die too. Fools! Me sooner and them later; but it will be the same for them. And they are merry. The beasts!" Anger stifled him. And he was agonizingly, insufferably miserable. "It cannot be that all men always have been doomed to this awful horror!" He raised himself.

"There is something wrong in it; I must be calm. I must think it all over from the beginning." And then he began to consider. "Yes, the beginning of my illness. I knocked my side, and I was just the same, that day and the days after; it ached a little, then more, then doctors, then depression, misery, and again doctors; and I've gone on getting closer and closer to the abyss. Strength growing less. Nearer and nearer. And here I am, wasting away, no light in my eyes. I think of how to cure the appendix, but this is death. Can it be death?" Again a horror came over him; gasping for breath, he bent over, began feeling for the matches, and knocked his elbow against the bedside table. It was in his way and hurt him; he felt furious with it, in his anger knocked against it more violently, and upset it. And in despair, breathless, he fell back on his spine waiting for death to come that instant.

The visitors were leaving at that time. Praskovya Fyodorovna was seeing them out. She heard something fall, and came in.

"What is it?"

"Nothing. I dropped something by accident."

She went out, brought a candle. He was lying, breathing hard and fast, like a man who has run a mile, and staring with fixed eyes at her.

"What is it, Jean?"

"No—othing, I say. I dropped something."—"Why speak? She won't understand," he thought.

She certainly did not understand. She picked up the candle, lighted it for him, and went out hastily. She had to say good-bye to a departing guest. When she came back, he was lying in the same position on his back, looking upwards.

"How are you—worse?"

"Yes."

She shook her head, sat down.

"Do you know what, Jean? I wonder if we hadn't better send for Leshtchetitsky to see you here?"

This meant calling in the celebrated doctor, regardless of expense. He smiled malignantly, and said no. She sat a moment longer, went up to him, and kissed him on the forehead.

He hated her with all the force of his soul when she was kissing him, and had to make an effort not to push her away.

"Good night. Please God, you'll sleep."

"Yes."

VI

Ivan Ilyitch saw that he was dying, and was in continual despair.

At the bottom of his heart Ivan Ilyitch knew that he was dying; but so far from growing used to this idea, he simply did not grasp it—he was utterly unable to grasp it.

The example of the syllogism that he had learned in Kiseveter's logic[20]—Caius is a man, men are mortal, therefore Caius is mortal—had seemed to him all his life correct only as regards Caius, but not at all as regards himself. In that case it was a question of Caius, a man, an abstract man, and it was perfectly true, but he was not Caius, and was not an abstract man; he had always been a creature quite, quite different from all others; he had been little Vanya with a mamma and papa, and Mitya and Volodya, with playthings and a coachman and a nurse; afterwards with Katenka, with all the joys and griefs and ecstasies of childhood, boyhood, and youth. What did Caius know of the smell of the leathern ball Vanya had been so fond of? Had Caius kissed his mother's hand like that? Caius had not heard the silk rustle of his mother's skirts. He had not made a riot at school over the pudding. Had Caius been in love like that? Could Caius preside over the sittings of the court?

And Caius certainly was mortal, and it was right for him to die; but for me, little Vanya, Ivan Ilyitch, with all my feelings and ideas—for me it's a different matter. And it cannot be that I ought to die. That would be too awful.

That was his feeling.

"If I had to die like Caius, I should have known it was so, some inner voice would have told me so. But there was nothing of the sort in me. And I and all my friends, we felt that it was not at all the same as with Caius. And now here it is!" he said to himself. "It can't be! It can't be, but it is! How is it? How's one to understand it?" And he could not conceive it, and tried to drive away this idea as false, incorrect, and morbid, and to supplant it by other, correct, healthy ideas. But this idea, not as an idea merely, but as it were an actual fact, came back again and stood confronting him.

And to replace this thought he called up other thoughts, one after another, in the hope of finding support in them. He tried to get back into former trains of thought, which in old days had screened off the thought of death. But, strange to say, all that had in old days covered up, obliterated the sense of death, could not now produce the same effect. Latterly, Ivan Ilyitch spent the greater part of his time in these efforts to restore his old trains of thought which had shut off death. At one time he would say to himself, "I'll put myself into my official work; why, I used to live in it." And he would go to the law-courts, banishing every doubt. He would enter into conversation with his colleagues, and would sit carelessly, as his old habit was, scanning the crowd below dreamily, and with both his wasted hands he would lean on the arms of the oak arm-chair just as he always did; and bending over to a colleague, pass the papers to him and whisper to him, then suddenly dropping his eyes and sitting up straight, he would pro-

[20] Ivan is remembering a school textbook, *Outline of Logic* (1796), by the German Karl Kiesewetter.

nounce the familiar words that opened the proceedings. But suddenly in the middle, the pain in his side, utterly regardless of the stage he had reached in his conduct of the case, began its work. It riveted Ivan Ilyitch's attention. He drove away the thought of it, but it still did its work, and then *It* came and stood confronting him and looked at him, and he felt turned to stone, and the light died away in his eyes, and he began to ask himself again, "Can it be that It is the only truth?" And his colleagues and his subordinates saw with surprise and distress that he, the brilliant, subtle judge, was losing the thread of his speech, was making blunders. He shook himself, tried to regain his self-control, and got somehow to the end of the sitting, and went home with the painful sense that his judicial labors could not as of old hide from him what he wanted to hide; that he could not by means of his official work escape from *It*. And the worst of it was that It drew him to itself not for him to do anything in particular, but simply for him to look at It straight in the face, to look at It and, doing nothing, suffer unspeakably.

And to save himself from this, Ivan Ilyitch sought amusements, other screens, and these screens he found, and for a little while they did seem to save him; but soon again they were not so much broken down as let the light through, as though It pierced through everything, and there was nothing that could shut It off.

Sometimes during those days he would go into the drawing-room he had furnished, that drawing-room where he had fallen, for which—how bitterly ludicrous it was for him to think of it!—for the decoration of which he had sacrificed his life, for he knew that it was that bruise that had started his illness. He went in and saw that the polished table had been scratched by something. He looked for the cause, and found it in the bronze clasps of the album, which had been twisted on one side. He took up the album, a costly one, which he had himself arranged with loving care, and was vexed at the carelessness of his daughter and her friends. Here a page was torn, here the photographs had been shifted out of their places. He carefully put it to rights again and bent the clasp back.

Then the idea occurred to him to move all this setting up of the albums to another corner where the flowers stood. He called the footman; or his daughter or his wife came to help him. They did not agree with him, contradicted him; he argued, got angry. But all that was very well, since he did not think of It; It was not in sight.

But then his wife would say, as he moved something himself, "Do let the servants do it, you'll hurt yourself again," and all at once It peeped through the screen; he caught a glimpse of It. He caught a glimpse of It, but still he hoped It would hide itself. Involuntarily, though, he kept watch on his side; there it is just the same still, aching still, and now he cannot forget it, and *It* is staring openly at him from behind the flowers. What's the use of it all?

"And it's the fact that here, at that curtain, as if it had been storming a fort, I lost my life. Is it possible? How awful and how silly! It cannot be! It cannot be, and it is."

He went into his own room, lay down, and was again alone with It. Face to face with It, and nothing to be done with It. Nothing but to look at It and shiver.

VII

How it came to pass during the third month of Ivan Ilyitch's illness, it would be impossible to say, for it happened little by little, imperceptibly, but it had come to pass that his wife and his daughter and his son and their servants and their acquaintances, and the doctors, and, most of all, he himself—all were aware that all interest in him for other people consisted now in the question how soon he would leave his place empty, free the living from the constraint of his presence, and be set free himself from his sufferings.

He slept less and less; they gave him opium, and began to inject morphine. But this did not relieve him. The dull pain he experienced in the half-asleep condition at first only relieved him as a change, but then it became as bad, or even more agonizing, than the open pain. He had special things to eat prepared for him according to the doctors' prescriptions; but these dishes became more and more distasteful, more and more revolting to him.

Special arrangements, too, had to be made for his other physical needs, and this was a continual misery to him. Misery from the uncleanliness, the unseemliness, and the stench, from the feeling of another person having to assist in it.

But just from this most unpleasant side of his illness there came comfort to Ivan Ilyitch. There always came into his room on these occasions to clear up for him the peasant who waited on table, Gerasim.

Gerasim was a clean, fresh, young peasant, who had grown stout and hearty on the good fare in town. Always cheerful and bright. At first the sight of this lad, always cleanly dressed in the Russian style, engaged in this revolting task, embarrassed Ivan Ilyitch.

One day, getting up from the night-stool,[21] too weak to replace his clothes, he dropped on to a soft low chair and looked with horror at his bare, powerless thighs, with the muscles so sharply standing out on them.

Then there came in with light, strong steps Gerasim, in his thick boots, diffusing a pleasant smell of tar from his boots, and bringing in the freshness of the winter air. Wearing a clean hempen apron, and a clean cotton shirt, with his sleeves tucked up on his strong, bare young arms, without looking at Ivan Ilyitch, obviously trying to check the radiant happiness in his face so as not to hurt the sick man, he went up to the night-stool.

"Gerasim," said Ivan Ilyitch faintly.

Gerasim started, clearly afraid that he had done something amiss, and with a rapid movement turned towards the sick man his fresh, good-natured, simple young face, just beginning to be downy with the first growth of beard.

"Yes, your honor."

"I'm afraid this is very disagreeable for you. You must excuse me. I can't help it."

"Why, upon my word, sir!" And Gerasim's eyes beamed, and he showed his white young teeth in a smile. "What's a little trouble? It's a case of illness with you, sir."

[21] Commode; seat over a chamber pot.

And with his deft, strong arms he performed his habitual task, and went out, stepping lightly. And five minutes later, treading just as lightly, he came back.

Ivan Ilyitch was still sitting in the same way in the arm-chair.

"Gerasim," he said, when the latter had replaced the night-stool all sweet and clean, "please help me; come here." Gerasim went up to him. "Lift me up. It's difficult for me alone, and I've sent Dmitry away."

Gerasim went up to him; as lightly as he stepped he put his strong arms round him, deftly and gently lifted and supported him, with the other hand pulled up his trousers, and would have set him down again. But Ivan Ilyitch asked him to carry him to the sofa. Gerasim, without effort, carefully not squeezing him, led him, almost carrying him, to the sofa, and settled him there.

"Thank you; how neatly and well . . . you do everything."

Gerasim smiled again, and would have gone away. But Ivan Ilyitch felt his presence such a comfort that he was reluctant to let him go.

"Oh, move that chair near me, please. No, that one, under my legs. I feel easier when my legs are higher."

Gerasim picked up the chair, and without letting it knock, set it gently down on the ground just at the right place, and lifted Ivan Ilyitch's legs on to it. It seemed to Ivan Ilyitch that he was easier just at the moment when Gerasim lifted his legs higher.

"I'm better when my legs are higher," said Ivan Ilyitch. "Put that cushion under me."

Gerasim did so. Again he lifted his legs to put the cushion under them. Again it seemed to Ivan Ilyitch that he was easier at that moment when Gerasim held his legs raised. When he laid them down again, he felt worse.

"Gerasim," he said to him, "are you busy just now?"

"Not at all, sir," said Gerasim, who had learned among the town-bred servants how to speak to gentlefolks.

"What have you left to do?"

"Why, what have I to do? I've done everything, there's only the wood to chop for to-morrow."

"Then hold my legs up like that—can you?"

"To be sure, I can." Gerasim lifted the legs up. And it seemed to Ivan Ilyitch that in that position he did not feel the pain at all.

"But how about the wood?"

"Don't you trouble about that, sir. We shall have time enough."

Ivan Ilyitch made Gerasim sit and hold his legs, and began to talk to him. And, strange to say, he fancied he felt better while Gerasim had hold of his legs.

From that time forward Ivan Ilyitch would sometimes call Gerasim, and get him to hold his legs on his shoulders, and he liked talking with him. Gerasim did this easily, readily, simply, and with a good-nature that touched Ivan Ilyitch. Health, strength, and heartiness in all other people were offensive to Ivan Ilyitch; but the strength and heartiness of Gerasim did not mortify him, but soothed him.

Ivan Ilyitch's great misery was due to the deception that for some reason or other every one kept up with him—that he was simply ill, and not dying, and that he need only keep quiet and follow the doctor's orders, and

then some great change for the better would be the result. He knew that whatever they might do, there would be no result except more agonizing sufferings and death. And he was made miserable by this lie, made miserable at their refusing to acknowledge what they all knew and he knew, by their persisting in lying to him about his awful position, and in forcing him too to take part in this lie. Lying, lying, this lying carried on over him on the eve of his death, and destined to bring that terrible, solemn act of his death down to the level of all their visits, curtains, sturgeons for dinner . . . was a horrible agony for Ivan Ilyitch. And, strange to say, many times when they had been going through the regular performance over him, he had been within a hair's-breadth of screaming at them: "Cease your lying! You know, and I know, that I'm dying; so do, at least, give over lying!" But he had never had the spirit to do this. The terrible, awful act of his dying was, he saw, by all those about him, brought down to the level of a casual, unpleasant, and to some extent indecorous, incident (somewhat as they would behave with a person who should enter a drawing-room smelling unpleasant). It was brought down to this level by that very decorum to which he had been enslaved all his life. He saw that no one felt for him, because no one would even grasp his position. Gerasim was the only person who recognized the position, and felt sorry for him. And that was why Ivan Ilyitch was only at ease with Gerasim. He felt comforted when Gerasim sometimes supported his legs for whole nights at a stretch, and would not go away to bed, saying, "Don't you worry yourself, Ivan Ilyitch, I'll get sleep enough yet," or when suddenly dropping into the familiar peasant forms of speech, he added: "If thou weren't sick, but as 'tis, 'twould be strange if I didn't wait on thee." Gerasim alone did not lie; everything showed clearly that he alone understood what it meant, and saw no necessity to disguise it, and simply felt sorry for his sick, wasting master. He even said this once straight out, when Ivan Ilyitch was sending him away.

"We shall all die. So what's a little trouble?" he said, meaning by this to express that he did not complain of the trouble just because he was taking this trouble for a dying man, and he hoped that for him too some one would be willing to take the same trouble when his time came.

Apart from this deception, or in consequence of it, what made the greatest misery for Ivan Ilyitch was that no one felt for him as he would have liked them to feel for him. At certain moments, after prolonged suffering, Ivan Ilyitch, ashamed as he would have been to own it, longed more than anything for some one to feel sorry for him, as for a sick child. He longed to be petted, kissed, and wept over, as children are petted and comforted. He knew that he was an important member of the law-courts, that he had a beard turning grey, and that therefore it was impossible. But still he longed for it. And in his relations with Gerasim there was something approaching to that. And that was why being with Gerasim was a comfort to him. Ivan Ilyitch longs to weep, longs to be petted and wept over, and then there comes in a colleague, Shebek; and instead of weeping and being petted, Ivan Ilyitch puts on his serious, severe, earnest face, and from mere inertia gives his views on the effect of the last decision in the Court of Appeal, and obstinately insists upon them. This falsity around him and within him did more than anything to poison Ivan Ilyitch's last days.

VIII

It was morning. All that made it morning for Ivan Ilyitch was that Gerasim had gone away, and Pyotr the footman had come in; he had put out the candles, opened one of the curtains, and begun surreptitiously setting the room to rights. Whether it were morning or evening, Friday or Sunday, it all made no difference; it was always just the same thing. Gnawing, agonizing pain never ceasing for an instant; the hopeless sense of life always ebbing away, but still not yet gone; always swooping down on him that fearful, hated death, which was the only reality, and always the same falsity. What were days, or weeks, or hours of the day to him?

"Will you have tea, sir?"

"He wants things done in their regular order. In the morning the family should have tea," he thought, and only said—

"No."

"Would you care to move on to the sofa?"

"He wants to make the room tidy, and I'm in his way. I'm uncleanness, disorder," he thought, and only said—

"No, leave me alone."

The servant still moved busily about his work. Ivan Ilyitch stretched out his hand. Pyotr went up to offer his services.

"What can I get you?"

"My watch."

Pyotr got out the watch, which lay just under his hand, and gave it to him.

"Half-past eight. Are they up?"

"Not yet, sir. Vladimir Ivanovitch" (that was his son) "has gone to the high school, and Praskovya Fyodorovna gave orders that she was to be waked if you asked for her. Shall I send word?"

"No, no need." Should I try some tea? he thought. "Yes, tea . . . bring it."

Pyotr was on his way out. Ivan Ilyitch felt frightened of being left alone. "How keep him? Oh, the medicine. Pyotr, give me my medicine. Oh well, may be, medicine may still be some good." He took the spoon, drank it. "No, it does no good. It's all rubbish, deception," he decided, as soon as he tasted the familiar, mawkish, hopeless taste. "No, I can't believe it now. But the pain, why this pain? If it would only cease for a minute." And he groaned. Pyotr turned round. "No, go on. Bring the tea."

Pyotr went away. Ivan Ilyitch, left alone, moaned, not so much from the pain, awful as it was, as from misery. Always the same thing again and again, all these endless days and nights. If it would only be quicker. Quicker to what? Death, darkness. No, no. Anything better than death!

When Pyotr came in with the tea on a tray, Ivan Ilyitch stared for some time absent-mindedly at him, not grasping who he was and what he wanted. Pyotr was disconcerted by this stare. And when he showed he was disconcerted, Ivan Ilyitch came to himself.

"Oh yes," he said, "tea, good, set it down. Only help me to wash and put on a clean shirt."

And Ivan Ilyitch began his washing. He washed his hands slowly, and

then his face, cleaned his teeth, combed his hair, and looked in the looking-glass. He felt frightened at what he saw, especially at the way his hair clung limply to his pale forehead. When his shirt was being changed, he knew he would be still more terrified if he glanced at his body, and he avoided looking at himself. But at last it was all over. He put on his dressing-gown, covered himself with a rug, and sat in the armchair to drink his tea. For one moment he felt refreshed; but as soon as he began to drink the tea, again there was the same taste, the same pain. He forced himself to finish it, and lay down, stretched out his legs. He lay down and dismissed Pyotr.

Always the same. A gleam of hope flashes for a moment, then again the sea of despair roars about him again, and always pain, always pain, always heartache, and always the same thing. Alone it is awfully dreary; he longs to call some one, but he knows beforehand that with others present it will be worse. "Morphine again—only to forget again. I'll tell him, the doctor, that he must think of something else. It can't go on; it can't go on like this."

One hour, two hours pass like this. Then there is a ring at the front door. The doctor, perhaps. Yes, it is the doctor, fresh, hearty, fat, and cheerful, wearing that expression that seems to say, "You there are in a panic about something, but we'll soon set things right for you." The doctor is aware that this expression is hardly fitting here, but he has put it on once and for all, and can't take it off, like a man who has put on a frockcoat to pay a round of calls.

In a hearty, reassuring manner the doctor rubs his hands.

"I'm cold. It's a sharp frost. Just let me warm myself," he says with an expression, as though it's only a matter of waiting a little till he's warm, and as soon as he's warm he'll set everything to rights.

"Well, now, how are you?"

Ivan Ilyitch feels that the doctor would like to say, "How's the little trouble?" but that he feels that he can't talk like that, and says, "How did you pass the night?"

Ivan Ilyitch looks at the doctor with an expression that asks—

"Is it possible you're never ashamed of lying?"

But the doctor does not care to understand this look.

And Ivan Ilyitch says—

"It's always just as awful. The pain never leaves me, never ceases. If only there were something!"

"Ah, you're all like that, all sick people say that. Come, now, I do believe I'm thawed; even Praskovya Fyodorovna, who's so particular, could find no fault with my temperature. Well, now I can say good morning." And the doctor shakes hands.

And dropping his former levity, the doctor, with a serious face, proceeds to examine the patient, feeling his pulse, to take his temperature, and then the tappings and soundings begin.

Ivan Ilyitch knows positively and indubitably that it's all nonsense and empty deception; but when the doctor, kneeling down, stretches over him, putting his ear first higher, then lower, and goes through various gymnastic evolutions over him with a serious face, Ivan Ilyitch is affected by this, as he used sometimes to be affected by the speeches of the lawyers in court,

though he was perfectly well aware that they were telling lies all the while and why they were telling lies.

The doctor, kneeling on the sofa, was still sounding him, when there was the rustle of Praskovya Fyodorovna's silk dress in the doorway, and she was heard scolding Pyotr for not having let her know that the doctor had come.

She comes in, kisses her husband, and at once begins to explain that she has been up a long while, and that it was only through a misunderstanding that she was not there when the doctor came.

Ivan Ilyitch looks at her, scans her all over, and sets down against her her whiteness and plumpness, and the cleanness of her hands and neck, and the glossiness of her hair, and the gleam full of life in her eyes. With all the force of his soul he hates her. And when she touches him it makes him suffer from the thrill of hatred he feels for her.

Her attitude to him and his illness is still the same. Just as the doctor had taken up a certain line with the patient which he was not now able to drop, so she too had taken up a line with him—that he was not doing something he ought to do, and was himself to blame, and she was lovingly reproaching him for his neglect, and she could not now get out of this attitude.

"Why, you know, he won't listen to me; he doesn't take his medicine at the right times. And what's worse still, he insists on lying in a position that surely must be bad for him—with his legs in the air."

She described how he made Gerasim hold his legs up.

The doctor smiled with kindly condescension that said, "Oh well, it can't be helped, these sick people do take up such foolish fancies; but we must forgive them."

When the examination was over, the doctor looked at his watch, and then Praskovya Fyodorovna informed Ivan Ilyitch that it must, of course, be as he liked, but she had sent to-day for a celebrated doctor, and that he would examine him, and have a consultation with Mihail Danilovitch (that was the name of their regular doctor).

"Don't oppose it now, please. This I'm doing entirely for my own sake," she said ironically, meaning it to be understood that she was doing it all for his sake, and was only saying this to give him no right to refuse her request. He lay silent, knitting his brows. He felt that he was hemmed in by such a tangle of falsity that it was hard to disentangle anything from it.

Everything she did for him was entirely for her own sake, and she told him she was doing for her own sake what she actually was doing for her own sake as something so incredible that he would take it as meaning the opposite.

At half-past eleven the celebrated doctor came. Again came the sounding, and then grave conversation in his presence and in the other room about the kidney and the appendix, and questions and answers, with such an air of significance, that again, instead of the real question of life and death, which was now the only one that confronted him, the question that came uppermost was of the kidney and the appendix, which were doing something not as they ought to do, and were for that reason being attacked by Mihail Danilovitch and the celebrated doctor, and forced to mend their ways.

The celebrated doctor took leave of him with a serious, but not a hopeless face. And to the timid question that Ivan Ilyitch addressed to him while he lifted his eyes, shining with terror and hope, up towards him, Was there a chance of recovery? he answered that he could not answer for it, but that there was a chance. The look of hope with which Ivan Ilyitch watched the doctor out was so piteous that, seeing it, Praskovya Fyodorovna positively burst into tears, as she went out of the door to hand the celebrated doctor his fee in the next room.

The gleam of hope kindled by the doctor's assurance did not last long. Again the same room, the same pictures, the curtains, the wallpaper, the medicine-bottles, and ever the same, his aching suffering body. And Ivan Ilyitch began to moan; they gave him injections, and he sank into oblivion. When he waked up it was getting dark; they brought him his dinner. He forced himself to eat some broth; and again everything the same, and again the coming night.

After dinner at seven o'clock, Praskovya Fyodorovna came into his room, dressed as though to go to a *soirée*,[22] with her full bosom laced in tight, and traces of powder on her face. She had in the morning mentioned to him that they were going to the theatre. Sarah Bernhardt[23] was visiting the town, and they had a box, which he had insisted on their taking. By now he had forgotten about it, and her smart attire was an offense to him. But he concealed this feeling when he recollected that he had himself insisted on their taking a box and going, because it was an aesthetic pleasure, beneficial and instructive for the children.

Praskovya Fyodorovna came in satisfied with herself, but yet with something of a guilty air. She sat down, asked how he was, as he saw, simply for the sake of asking, and not for the sake of learning anything, knowing indeed that there was nothing to learn, and began telling him how absolutely necessary it was; how she would not have gone for anything, but the box had been taken, and Liza, their daughter, and Petrishtchev (the examining lawyer, the daughter's suitor) were going, and that it was out of the question to let them go alone. But that she would have liked much better to stay with him. If only he would be sure to follow the doctor's prescription while she was away.

"Oh, and Fyodor Dmitryevitch" (the suitor) "would like to come in. May he? And Liza?"

"Yes, let them come in."

The daughter came in, in evening clothes, her fresh young body showing, while his body made him suffer so. But she made a show of it; she was strong, healthy, obviously in love, and impatient of the illness, suffering, and death that hindered her happiness.

Fyodor Dmitryevitch came in too in evening dress, his hair curled *à la Capoul*,[24] with his long sinewy neck tightly fenced round by a white collar, with his vast expanse of white chest and strong thighs displayed in narrow black trousers, with one white glove in his hand and a crush opera hat.

[22] Evening affair.

[23] Immensely popular French actress (1844–1923), who toured widely in Europe, the United States, and Russia.

[24] In the fashionable Capoul style (French).

Behind him crept in unnoticed the little high school boy in his new uniform, poor fellow, in gloves, and with those awful blue rings under his eyes that Ivan Ilyitch knew the meaning of.

He always felt sorry for his son. And pitiable indeed was his scared face of sympathetic suffering. Except Gerasim, Ivan Ilyitch fancied that Volodya was the only one that understood and was sorry.

They all sat down; again they asked how he was. A silence followed. Liza asked her mother about the opera-glass. An altercation ensued between the mother and daughter as to who had taken it, and where it had been put. It turned into an unpleasant squabble.

Fyodor Dmitryevitch asked Ivan Ilyitch whether he had seen Sarah Bernhardt? Ivan Ilyitch could not at first catch the question that was asked him, but then he said, "No, have you seen her before?"

"Yes, in *Adrienne Lecouvreur.*"[25]

Praskovya Fyodorovna observed that she was particularly good in that part. The daughter made some reply. A conversation sprang up about the art and naturalness of her acting, that conversation that is continually repeated and always the same.

In the middle of the conversation Fyodor Dmitryevitch glanced at Ivan Ilyitch and relapsed into silence. The others looked at him and became mute, too. Ivan Ilyitch was staring with glittering eyes straight before him, obviously furious with them. This had to be set right, but it could not anyhow be set right. This silence had somehow to be broken. No one would venture on breaking it, and all began to feel alarmed that the decorous deception was somehow breaking down, and the facts would be exposed to all. Liza was the first to pluck up courage. She broke the silence. She tried to cover up what they were all feeling, but inadvertently she gave it utterance.

"*If we are going,* though, it's time to start," she said, glancing at her watch, a gift from her father; and with a scarcely perceptible meaning smile to the young man, referring to something only known to themselves, she got up with a rustle of her skirts.

They all got up, said good-bye, and went away. When they were gone, Ivan Ilyitch fancied he was easier; there was no falsity—that had gone away with them, but the pain remained. That continual pain, that continual terror, made nothing harder, nothing easier. It was always worse.

Again came minute after minute, hour after hour, still the same and still no end, and ever more terrible the inevitable end.

"Yes, send Gerasim," he said in answer to Pyotr's question.

IX

Late at night his wife came back. She came in on tiptoe, but he heard her, opened his eyes, and made haste to close them again. She wanted to send away Gerasim and sit up with him herself instead. He opened his eyes and said, "No, go away."

[25] A light, commercial play by the immensely prolific French playwright Eugène Scribe. Tolstoy disliked his work.

"Are you in great pain?"

"Always the same."

"Take some opium."

He agreed, and drank it. She went away.

Till three o'clock he slept a miserable sleep. It seemed to him that he and his pain were being thrust somewhere into a narrow, deep, black sack, and they kept pushing him further and further in, and still could not thrust him to the bottom. And this operation was awful to him, and was accompanied with agony. And he was afraid, and yet wanted to fall into it, and struggled and yet tried to get into it. And all of a sudden he slipped and fell and woke up. Gerasim, still the same, is sitting at the foot of the bed half-dozing peacefully, patient. And he is lying with his wasted legs clad in stockings, raised on Gerasim's shoulders, the same candle burning in the alcove, and the same interminable pain.

"Go away, Gerasim," he whispered.

"It's all right, sir. I'll stay a bit longer."

"No, go away."

He took his legs down, lay sideways on his arm, and he felt very sorry for himself. He only waited till Gerasim had gone away into the next room; he could restrain himself no longer, and cried like a child. He cried at his own helplessness, at his awful loneliness, at the cruelty of people, at the cruelty of God, at the absence of God.

"Why hast Thou done all this? What brought me to this? Why, why torture me so horribly?"

He did not expect an answer, and wept indeed that there was and could be no answer. The pain grew more acute again, but he did not stir, did not call.

He said to himself, "Come, more then; come, strike me! But what for? What have I done to Thee? what for?"

Then he was still, ceased weeping, held his breath, and was all attention; he listened, as it were, not to a voice uttering sounds, but to the voice of his soul, to the current of thoughts that rose up within him.

"What is it you want?" was the first clear idea capable of putting into words that he grasped.

"What? Not to suffer, to live," he answered.

And again he was utterly plunged into attention so intense that even the pain did not distract him.

"To live? Live how?" the voice of his soul was asking.

"Why, live as I used to live before—happily and pleasantly."

"As you used to live before—happily and pleasantly?" queried the voice. And he began going over in his imagination the best moments of his pleasant life. But strange to say, all these best moments of his pleasant life seemed now not at all what they had seemed then. All—except the first memories of childhood—there, in his childhood there had been something really pleasant in which one could have lived if it had come back. But the creature who had this pleasant experience was no more; it was like a memory of some one else.

As soon as he reached the beginning of what had resulted in him as he was now, Ivan Ilyitch, all that had seemed joys to him then now melted

away before his eyes and were transformed into something trivial, and often disgusting.

And the further he went from childhood, the nearer to the actual present, the more worthless and uncertain were the joys. It began with life at the school of jurisprudence. Then there had still been something genuinely good; then there had been gaiety; then there had been friendship; then there had been hopes. But in the higher classes these good moments were already becoming rarer. Later on, during the first period of his official life, at the governor's, good moments appeared; but it was all mixed, and less and less of it was good. And further on even less was good, and the further he went the less good there was.

His marriage . . . as gratuitous as the disillusion of it and the smell of his wife's breath and the sensuality, the hypocrisy! And that deadly official life, and anxiety about money, and so for one year, and two, and ten, and twenty, and always the same thing. And the further he went, the more deadly it became. "As though I had been going steadily downhill, imagining that I was going uphill. So it was in fact. In public opinion I was going uphill, and steadily as I got up it, life was ebbing away from me. . . . And now the work's done, there's nothing left but to die.

"But what is this? What for? It cannot be! It cannot be that life has been so senseless, so loathsome? And if it really was so loathsome and senseless, then why die, and die in agony? There's something wrong.

"Can it be I have not lived as one ought?" suddenly came into his head. "But how not so, when I've done everything as it should be done?" he said, and at once dismissed this only solution of all the enigma of life and death as something utterly out of the question.

"What do you want now? To live? Live how? Live as you live at the courts when the usher booms out: 'The Judge is coming!' . . . The judge is coming, the judge is coming," he repeated to himself. "Here he is, the judge! But I'm not to blame!" he shrieked in fury. "What's it for?" And he left off crying, and turning with his face to the wall, fell to pondering always on the same question, "What for, why all this horror?"

But however much he pondered, he could not find an answer. And whenever the idea struck him, as it often did, that it all came of his never having lived as he ought, he thought of all the correctness of his life and dismissed the strange idea.

X

Another fortnight had passed. Ivan Ilyitch could not now get up from the sofa. He did not like lying in bed, and lay on the sofa. And lying almost all the time facing the wall, in loneliness he suffered all the inexplicable agonies, and in loneliness pondered always that inexplicable question, "What is it? Can it be true that it's death?" And an inner voice answered, "Yes, it is true." "Why these agonies?" and a voice answered, "For no reason." Beyond and besides this there was nothing.

From the very beginning of his illness, ever since Ivan Ilyitch first went to the doctor's, his life had been split up into two contradictory moods,

which were continually alternating—one was despair and the anticipation of an uncomprehended and awful death; the other was hope and an absorbed watching over the actual condition of his body. First there was nothing confronting him but a kidney or intestine which had temporarily declined to perform its duties, then there was nothing but unknown awful death, which there was no escaping.

These two moods had alternated from the very beginning of the illness; but the further the illness progressed, the more doubtful and fantastic became the conception of the kidney, and the more real the sense of approaching death.

He had but to reflect on what he had been three months before and what he was now, to reflect how steadily he had been going downhill, for every possibility of hope to be shattered.

Of late, in the loneliness in which he found himself, lying with his face to the back of the sofa, a loneliness in the middle of a populous town and of his numerous acquaintances and his family, a loneliness than which none more complete could be found anywhere—not at the bottom of the sea, not deep down in the earth;—of late in this fearful loneliness Ivan Ilyitch had lived only in imagination in the past. One by one the pictures of his past rose up before him. It always began from what was nearest in time and went back to the most remote, to childhood, and rested there. If Ivan Ilyitch thought of the stewed prunes that had been offered him for dinner that day, his mind went back to the damp, wrinkled French plum of his childhood, of its peculiar taste and the flow of saliva when the stone was sucked; and along with this memory of a taste there rose up a whole series of memories of that period—his nurse, his brother, his playthings. "I mustn't . . . it's too painful," Ivan Ilyitch said to himself, and he brought himself back to the present. The button on the back of the sofa and the creases in the morocco.[26] "Morocco's dear, and doesn't wear well; there was a quarrel over it. But the morocco was different, and different too the quarrel when we tore father's portfolio and were punished, and mamma bought us the tarts." And again his mind rested on his childhood, and again it was painful, and he tried to drive it away and think of something else.

And again at that point, together with that chain of associations, quite another chain of memories came into his heart, of how his illness had grown up and become more acute. It was the same there, the further back the more 'ife there had been. There had been both more that was good in life and more of life itself. And the two began to melt into one. "Just as the pain goes on getting worse and worse, so has my whole life gone on getting worse and worse," he thought. One light spot was there at the back, at the beginning of life, and then it kept getting blacker and blacker, and going faster and faster. "In inverse ratio to the square of the distance from death," thought Ivan Ilyitch. And the image of a stone falling downwards with increasing velocity sank into his soul. Life, a series of increasing sufferings, falls more and more swiftly to the end, the most fearful sufferings. "I am falling." He shuddered, shifted himself, would have resisted, but he

[26] A fine leather made from goatskin, often used as a furniture-covering in the nineteenth century.

knew beforehand that he could not resist; and again, with eyes weary with gazing at it, but unable not to gaze at what was before him, he stared at the back of the sofa and waited, waited expecting that fearful fall and shock and dissolution. "Resistance is impossible," he said to himself. "But if one could at least comprehend what it's for? Even that's impossible. It could be explained if one were to say that I hadn't lived as I ought. But that can't be alleged," he said to himself, thinking of all the regularity, correctness, and propriety of his life. "That really can't be admitted," he said to himself, his lips smiling ironically as though some one could see his smile and be deceived by it. "No explanation! Agony, death. . . . What for?"

XI

So passed a fortnight. During that fortnight an event occurred that had been desired by Ivan Ilyitch and his wife. Petrishtchev made a formal proposal. This took place in the evening. Next day Praskovya Fyodorovna went in to her husband, resolving in her mind how to inform him of Fyodor Dmitryevitch's proposal, but that night there had been a change for the worse in Ivan Ilyitch. Praskovya Fyodorovna found him on the same sofa, but in a different position. He was lying on his face, groaning, and staring straight before him with a fixed gaze.

She began talking of remedies. He turned his stare on her. She did not finish what she had begun saying; such hatred of her in particular was expressed in that stare.

"For Christ's sake, let me die in peace," he said.

She would have gone away, but at that moment the daughter came in and went up to say good morning to him. He looked at his daughter just as at his wife, and to her inquiries how he was, he told her drily that they would soon all be rid of him. Both were silent, sat a little while, and went out.

"How are we to blame?" said Liza to her mother. "As though we had done it! I'm sorry for papa, but why punish us?"

At the usual hour the doctor came. Ivan Ilyitch answered, "Yes, no," never taking his exasperated stare from him, and towards the end he said, "Why, you know that you can do nothing, so let me be."

"We can relieve your suffering," said the doctor.

"Even that you can't do; let me be."

The doctor went into the drawing-room and told Praskovya Fyodorovna that it was very serious, and that the only resource left them was opium to relieve his sufferings, which must be terrible. The doctor said his physical sufferings were terrible, and that was true; but even more terrible than his physical sufferings were his mental sufferings, and in that lay his chief misery.

His moral sufferings were due to the fact that during that night, as he looked at the sleepy, good-natured, broad-cheeked face of Gerasim, the thought had suddenly come into his head, "What if in reality all my life, my conscious life, has been not the right thing?" The thought struck him that what he had regarded before as an utter impossibility, that he had spent his life not as he ought, might be the truth. It struck him that those scarcely

detected impulses of struggle within him against what was considered good by persons of higher position, scarcely detected impulses which he had dismissed, that they might be the real thing, and everything else might be not the right thing. And his official work, and his ordering of his daily life and of his family, and these social and official interests,—all that might be not the right thing. He tried to defend it all to himself. And suddenly he felt all the weakness of what he was defending. And it was useless to defend it.

"But if it's so," he said to himself, "and I am leaving life with the consciousness that I have lost all that was given me, and there's no correcting it, then what?" He lay on his back and began going over his whole life entirely anew. When he saw the footman in the morning, then his wife, then his daughter, then the doctor, every movement they made, every word they uttered, confirmed for him the terrible truth that had been revealed to him in the night. In them he saw himself, saw all in which he had lived, and saw distinctly that it was all not the right thing; it was a horrible, vast deception that concealed both life and death. This consciousness intensified his physical agonies, multiplied them tenfold. He groaned and tossed from side to side and pulled at the covering over him. It seemed to him that it was stifling him and weighing him down. And for that he hated them.

They gave him a big dose of opium; he sank into unconsciousness; but at dinner-time the same thing began again. He drove them all away, and tossed from side to side.

His wife came to him and said, "Jean, darling, do this for my sake" (for my sake?). "It can't do harm, and it often does good. Why, it's nothing. And often in health people——"

He opened his eyes wide.

"What? Take the sacrament? What for? No. Besides . . ."

She began to cry.

"Yes, my dear. I'll send for our priest, he's so nice."

"All right, very well," he said.

When the priest came and confessed him he was softened, felt as it were a relief from his doubts, and consequently from his sufferings, and there came a moment of hope. He began once more thinking of the intestinal appendix and the possibility of curing it. He took the sacrament with tears in his eyes.

When they laid him down again after the sacrament for a minute, he felt comfortable, and again the hope of life sprang up. He began to think about the operation which had been suggested to him. "To live, I want to live," he said to himself. His wife came in to congratulate him; she uttered the customary words and added—

"It's quite true, isn't it, that you're better?"

Without looking at her, he said, "Yes."

Her dress, her figure, the expression of her face, the tone of her voice,—all told him the same: "Not the right thing. All that in which you lived and are living is lying, deceit, hiding life and death away from you." And as soon as he had formed that thought, hatred sprang up in him, and with that hatred agonizing physical sufferings, and with these sufferings the sense of inevitable, approaching ruin. Something new was happening; there were screwing and shooting pains, and a tightness in his breathing.

The expression of his face as he uttered that "Yes" was terrible. After

uttering that "Yes," looking her straight in the face, he turned on to his face, with a rapidity extraordinary in his weakness, and shrieked—

"Go away, go away, let me be!"

XII

From that moment there began the scream that never ceased for three days, and was so awful that through two closed doors one could not hear it without horror. At the moment when he answered his wife he grasped that he had fallen, that there was no return, that the end had come, quite the end, while doubt was still as unsolved, still remained doubt.

"Oo! Oo—o! Oo!" he screamed in varying intonations. He had begun screaming, "I don't want to!" and so had gone on screaming on the same vowel sound—oo!

All those three days, during which time did not exist for him, he was struggling in that black sack into which he was being thrust by an unseen resistless force. He struggled as the man condemned to death struggles in the hands of the executioner, knowing that he cannot save himself. And every moment he felt that in spite of all his efforts to struggle against it, he was getting nearer and nearer to what terrified him. He felt that his agony was due both to his being thrust into this black hole and still more to his not being able to get right into it. What hindered him from getting into it was the claim that his life had been good. That justification of his life held him fast and would not let him get forward, and it caused him more agony than all.

All at once some force struck him in the chest, in the side, and stifled his breathing more than ever; he rolled forward into the hole, and there at the end there was some sort of light. It had happened with him, as it had sometimes happened to him in a railway carriage, when he had thought he was going forward while he was going back, and all of a sudden recognized his real direction.

"Yes, it has all been not the right thing," he said to himself, "but that's no matter." He could, he could do the right thing. "What is the right thing?" he asked himself, and suddenly he became quiet.

This was at the end of the third day, two hours before his death. At that very moment the schoolboy had stealthily crept into his father's room and gone up to his bedside. The dying man was screaming and waving his arms. His hand fell on the schoolboy's head. The boy snatched it, pressed it to his lips, and burst into tears.

At that very moment Ivan Ilyitch had rolled into the hole, and caught sight of the light, and it was revealed to him that his life had not been what it ought to have been, but that that could still be set right. He asked himself, "What is the right thing?"—and became quiet, listening. Then he felt some one was kissing his hand. He opened his eyes and glanced at his son. He felt sorry for him. His wife went up to him. He glanced at her. She was gazing at him with open mouth, the tears unwiped streaming over her nose and cheeks, a look of despair on her face. He felt sorry for her.

"Yes, I'm making them miserable," he thought. "They're sorry, but it will be better for them when I die." He would have said this, but had not

the strength to utter it. "Besides, why speak, I must act," he thought. With a glance to his wife he pointed to his son and said—

"Take away . . . sorry for him. . . . And you too . . ." He tried to say "forgive," but said "forgo" . . . and too weak to correct himself, shook his hand, knowing that He would understand Whose understanding mattered.

And all at once it became clear to him that what had tortured him and would not leave him was suddenly dropping away all at once on both sides and on ten sides and on all sides. He was sorry for them, must act so that they might not suffer. Set them free and be free himself of those agonies. "How right and how simple!" he thought. "And the pain?" he asked himself. "Where's it gone? Eh, where are you, pain?"

He began to watch for it.

"Yes, here it is. Well, what of it, let the pain be.

"And death. Where is it?"

He looked for his old accustomed terror of death, and did not find it. "Where is it? What death?" There was no terror, because death was not either.

In the place of death there was light.

"So this is it!" he suddenly exclaimed aloud.

"What joy!"

To him all this passed in a single instant, and the meaning of that instant suffered no change after. For those present his agony lasted another two hours. There was a rattle in his throat, a twitching in his wasted body. Then the rattle and the gasping came at longer and longer intervals.

"It is over!" some one said over him.

He caught those words and repeated them in his soul.

"Death is over," he said to himself. "It's no more."

He drew in a breath, stopped midway in the breath, stretched and died.

Henrik Ibsen
(1828–1906)

Henrik Ibsen, the schoolbook cliché has it, is the Father of Modern Drama. The label is an oversimplification; modern drama had a number of fathers (an artistic, if not a biological, possibility). And Father Ibsen has had more than his share of trouble with his children, whose attitudes have ranged from dutiful imitation to outright rebellion. But the label does suggest Ibsen's achievement, not only a dozen or so luminous, timeless plays, but the articulation of a viable "idea of a theater" for the modern age. In the longest view, the idea of a theater has appeared only three times in Western literature—in Periclean Athens in the fifth century B.C., in Renaissance Europe between about 1580 and 1700, and in the modern period since about 1880. At each of these points, playwrights have achieved the supremely difficult task of creating a theater and a dramatic form capable of

expressing their ages' views of human life richly and complexly. Ibsen took the debased and mechanical theater in which he served a long, wearying apprenticeship and forged from its elements a dramatic form rooted deeply enough in the popular theater to be stageworthy and accessible and at the same time rich and subtle enough to express a comprehensive view of modern life and to probe multiple levels of existence. His themes are not only the ills of society but also the most private problems of the inner life of the individual, problems of what Ibsen called "spiritual emancipation and purification." His artistic children, even the most rebellious, have not outgrown his influence.

The modern theater may be said to date from December 4, 1879, the publication date of *A Doll House*. It took Ibsen fifty-one years of grueling apprenticeship to reach that date. He was born in 1828 in Skien, Norway, a tiny logging town about a hundred miles southwest of what is now Oslo (then called Christiania). His childhood was lonely and poverty-stricken, especially after the bankruptcy of his businessman father when Ibsen was eight. When he was fifteen, he was sent as an apothecary's apprentice to Grimstad, another tiny town farther down the Oslo Fjord, where he remained for six years, feeling, as he recalled later, "on a war footing with the little community where I felt I was being suppressed by my situation and by circumstances in general." He fathered an illegitimate child upon a housemaid ten years his senior and contributed to the child's support for fifteen years—a "buried secret" like those which appear so frequently in his mature plays—and he wrote his first play, *Catiline* (1849). *Catiline* was a stiff, amateurish play which turned the first-century B.C. Roman revolutionary into a haunted, brooding, Byronic figure; it nevertheless announced, as Ibsen himself observed twenty-five years later, some of his major themes, including "the conflict between one's aims and one's abilities, between what man proposes and what is actually possible."

Ibsen left Grimstad when he was twenty-one, determined to be a writer rather than a druggist. Despite a rigorous program of self-education, he failed a portion of his entrance examinations for the University of Christiania and instead used *Catiline,* which had been privately printed in a tiny edition, as his entrée into the Norwegian theater, such as it was. In 1851, he was engaged as a resident playwright in Bergen. He worked in the theater for the next thirteen years, first in Bergen for six and then in Christiania for seven more. He did everything from sweeping the stage to stage-managing, and he wrote eight plays, mostly in verse and mostly on Norwegian legendary and historical subjects, which were produced, in several instances with modest success. Ibsen came to despise the workaday theater—he called it "a daily abortion"—but his consummate sense of the stage can be traced to this prolonged experience in actual production.

In 1864, Ibsen, depressed, defeated, and deeply in debt, obtained a small government travel grant and went to Italy, where he was soon joined by his wife Suzannah, whom he had married in 1858, and their young son Sigurd. They were not to return to Norway, except for short visits, for twenty-seven years. Ibsen felt, he later wrote, that he had "escaped from the darkness into the light, from the mists through a tunnel out into the sunlight," and in a sudden burst of joyful energy, he wrote the work that catapulted him into fame, *Brand* (1866). This was a "dramatic poem" not

intended for the stage about a Norwegian priest whose defiant creed of "All or Nothing" plunges him into a tragic inner conflict between love and will. The play was an enormous success, going through fourteen editions in two years, and was followed quickly by *Peer Gynt* (1867), a complementary "dramatic poem" about a folklore hero who becomes the prototype of what Ibsen saw as contemporary spiritual vacillation and compromise. Following the publication of *Peer Gynt,* the Ibsens moved to Germany; they were to divide their residence between Germany and Italy for the next twenty-three years. Several years were consumed in work on what Ibsen thought would be his masterpiece, *Emperor and Galilean* (1873), a mammoth "world-historical" closet drama about the Roman Emperor who attempted to restore paganism after the triumph of Christianity. *Emperor and Galilean* was followed by a transitional work, *Pillars of Society* (1877), in which Ibsen experimented with ways of constructing a prose play of modern life. *Pillars of Society* inaugurated the series of twelve plays to which Ibsen was to devote the rest of his life and which constitute his chief contribution to the modern theater.

In these plays, Ibsen renounced the romantic expansiveness of his earlier plays and adopted a radically different technique. All are set in contemporary Norway within middle-class homes, all are in prose, and all are thoroughly realistic, intended to make the spectator feel, as Ibsen said, "as if he were actually sitting, listening, and looking at events happening in real life." Style, in this case, is a direct expression of a philosophy of art. In these plays, Ibsen decisively renounced the idealist theory of art, in which its function is to inspire and uplift by presenting images of life as it should be, and adopted instead a realistic theory, in which art presents an interpretation of life as it is, thereby opening the way toward reform and improvement.

Ibsen's twelve realistic plays, which he suggested on at least one occasion formed an interrelated cycle, fall into four rather unequal groups. *Pillars of Society* presents a narrow, hypocritical village society in which the revelation of a guilty secret from the past becomes the instrument of purgation for the main character. *A Doll House* (1879) and *Ghosts* (1881) further explore this metaphor within the context of marriage. *A Doll House* provoked a major scandal, intensified by *Ghosts,* in which Ibsen advanced even more forcefully the theme of the individual's responsibility to himself as supreme over even the most hallowed of social institutions. The response to these plays perhaps contributed to the themes of a second group—*An Enemy of the People* (1886), *The Wild Duck* (1884), and *Rosmersholm* (1886)—in which Ibsen explored the ambiguities of truth-telling and its consequences. Already in *Rosmersholm* social criticism began to be subordinated to the exploration of individual personalities, especially extreme, neurotic ones, and realistic technique began to be modified by an extensive use of symbolism. These tendencies continued in *The Lady from the Sea* (1888) and *Hedda Gabler* (1890), both complex studies in the psychological consequences of female subordination. Ibsen himself explicitly linked his last four plays as an interrelated subgroup: *The Master Builder* (1892), *Little Eyolf* (1894), *John Gabriel Borkman* (1896), and *When We Dead Awaken* (1899). These plays have a rich, autumnal quality in their explorations of regret over failures and missed opportunities in the lives of strong-willed, titanic men; the style is

symbolist rather than realistic, as the literal narratives are invaded by dream- and fantasy-material.

The last few years of Ibsen's life were marked by a series of ambiguous but apparently platonic love affairs with much younger women: Helene Raff and Emilie Bardach ("the May sun in a September life") and a young pianist named Hildur Andersen. These relationships left their mark on the final plays, especially in the ambiguous figure of Hilde Wangel in *The Master Builder*.

Ibsen and his wife took up permanent residence back in Norway in 1891. He suffered a severe stroke in 1900, followed by a second the following year, which left him unable to write. He remained an invalid for five more years, dying in 1906. His last word was *"Tvertimod!"* ("On the contrary!").

Intellectually, Ibsen was a romantic liberal. Despite his reputation as a social critic, he never dealt in his plays with specific topical events. Even the more general targets of his criticism were matters hardly reformable by legislative measures: the pettiness and narrowness of small-town life, the excessive influence of the clergy, the power of commercial interests. Rather, he insisted throughout his life that reform must begin in the self-liberation of the individual.

Ibsen's craftsmanship has been much praised but frequently for the wrong reasons. His dramaturgy in the narrowest sense is very much of the nineteenth century, and modern audiences must adopt a historical perspective if they are to accept comfortably his use of coincidence, his sometimes melodramatic, "cliff-hanger" act curtains, his characters' powers of total recall, and the almost frightening explicitness with which characters announce the themes of the plays they are in ("The spirit of truth and the spirit of freedom—*those* are the pillars of society," "I've been your doll-wife here, just as at home I was Papa's doll-child," etc.). Ibsen's formal mastery is not in his manipulation of such dated conventions but in the larger matter of shaping an entire story dramatically. At the center of each Ibsen play is an individual human life, glimpsed at a climactic moment of decision but gradually unfolded in its entirety in the course of the play. The contours of the lives of all these protagonists have certain similarities: a critical, self-limiting choice of a "mission" early in life, the gradual unfolding of the consequences of that choice, and an ecstatic moment of self-understanding leading sometimes to liberation, sometimes to death. It is this recurring myth of the self and its resonating implications through the levels of the family, the society, and the cosmos that link Ibsen's plays and give the reader the sense of titanic conflicts being worked out below the sometimes trivial events of the plays, the sense that the young James Joyce perhaps had in mind when he found the power of Ibsen's plays in "the naked drama—either the perception of a great truth, or the opening up of a great question, or a great conflict which is almost independent of the conflicting actors."

All these generalizations apply to *A Doll House*. (The play is usually known in English as *A Doll's House*, but the present translator, Rolf Fjelde, sensibly uses the English idiom that corresponds to the Norwegian title, *Et dukkehjem*.) The action of the play covers only a little over a day, but in its course Nora's entire life unfolds before us; her childhood as a "doll-child,"

her transition into a "doll-wife," her adoption of the misguided "mission" to win Helmer's lasting love through her great "secret," the collapse of this project, and the resurgence of her long-suppressed individuality. Past and present are thus constantly juxtaposed in the tight, "revelatory" structure, in which the revelation of past events becomes a major part of present action.

A Doll House aroused a storm of controversy when it was first published. Conservative readers and audiences indignantly rejected the depiction of what was after all a fairly conventional marriage as the systematic enslavement of the wife. But what they found most outrageous was the proposition that a woman's "most sacred duties" were not to her husband and children but to herself. The actress who first played Nora in Germany flatly refused to play the final scene as written, exclaiming, "*I* would never leave *my* children," and she presented Nora as viewing her sleeping children and sinking to the floor, unable to leave them. That final scene (in its authentic version) still retains its power, even in an age when the "angel of the house" has been partially demythologized.

A Doll House is a strong, polemical plea for women's liberation, but this particular kind of liberation is placed in a more general context of human liberation. Nora's father and husband and her society have enslaved her, but more basically, she has enslaved herself years ago by choosing, however unconsciously, something less than full selfhood. And now her greatest challenge is not to free herself from Helmer but to overcome her own instincts toward self-enslavement. The play is thus not only an exposure of marital enslavement but also a searching study of the psychology of the enslaved. Nineteen years after he wrote *A Doll House*, Ibsen was honored by the leading Norwegian feminist society for his services to women's rights. In responding to their tribute, he said, "I thank you for the toast, but must disclaim the honor of having consciously worked for the women's rights movement. I am not even quite clear as to just what this women's rights movement really is. To me it has seemed a problem of mankind in general." Ibsen was undoubtedly indulging his love of placing himself "on the contrary" here, but his words suggest a profound truth about *A Doll House*. Nora is correct when she tells Helmer, "It's a great sin what you and Papa did to me. You're to blame that nothing's become of me." But she moves beyond this view of herself as passive victim, which merely perpetuates her status as object, and accepts her own responsibility to bring about "the greatest miracle" of self-transformation. And for Ibsen, this is the greatest liberation of all.

FURTHER READING *(prepared by J. H.):* Michael Meyer's massive *Ibsen: A Biography*, 1971, is the standard life, detailed and readable and with a great deal of information about the real-life sources of Ibsen's plays. A good short introduction is David Thomas's *Henrik Ibsen*, 1983. Of historical interest but transcending that level are George Brandes, *Henrik Ibsen: A Critical Study*, 1898 (translated by Jessie Muir, 1964), by the Danish critic who was one of Ibsen's closest friends; and Bernard Shaw's *The Quintessence of Ibsenism*, 1891, by Ibsen's most famous disciple in England. More recent critical overviews are provided by Maurice Valency, *The Flower and the Castle*, 1963; and G. Wilson Knight, *Ibsen*, 1962. M. C. Bradbrook's *Ibsen the Norwegian: A Revaluation*, 1966; Brian W. Downs' *Ibsen: The Intellectual Background*, 1948, and *A Study of Six Plays by Ibsen*, 1950; and P. F. D. Tennant's *Ibsen's Dramatic*

Technique, 1948, well represent Ibsen studies in England. James Hurt's *Catiline's Dream: An Essay on Ibsen's Plays*, 1972; and Charles R. Lyons' *Henrik Ibsen: The Divided Consciousness*, 1972, both attempt to relate the form of Ibsen's drama to his vision of life. On *A Doll House*, Austin Quigley's "*A Doll's House* Revisited," *Modern Drama*, Dec. 1984, is an interesting review of the critical issues. Good collections of essays on Ibsen, with introductory bibliographies, are *Ibsen: A Collection of Critical Essays*, ed. Rolf Fjelde, 1965; and *Henrik Ibsen: A Critical Anthology*, ed. James McFarlane, 1970. The important subject of Ibsen's women characters is well treated in Elizabeth Hardwick, "Ibsen's Women," in *Seduction and Betrayal*, 1974.

A DOLL HOUSE

Translated by Rolf Fjelde

THE CHARACTERS

TORVALD HELMER, *a lawyer*
NORA, *his wife*
DR. RANK
MRS. LINDE
NILS KROGSTAD, *a bank clerk*
THE HELMERS' THREE SMALL
 CHILDREN

ANNE-MARIE, *their nurse*
HELENE, *a maid*
A DELIVERY BOY

The action takes place in
 HELMER'*s residence.*

ACT ONE

A comfortable room, tastefully but not expensively furnished. A door to the right in the back wall leads to the entryway; another to the left leads to HELMER'*s study. Between these doors, a piano. Midway in the left-hand wall a door, and further back a window. Near the window a round table with an armchair and a small sofa. In the right-hand wall, toward the rear, a door, and nearer the foreground a porcelain stove with two armchairs and a rocking chair beside it. Between the stove and the side door, a small table. Engravings on the walls. An* etagère[1] *with china figures and other small art objects; a small bookcase with richly bound books; the floor carpeted; a fire burning in the stove. It is a winter day.*

[*A bell rings in the entryway; shortly after we hear the door being unlocked.* NORA *comes into the room, humming happily to herself; she is wearing street clothes and carries an armload of packages, which she puts down on the table to the right. She has left the hall door open; and through it a* DELIVERY BOY *is seen, holding a Christmas tree and a basket, which he gives to the* MAID *who let them in.*]

NORA. Hide the tree well, Helene. The children mustn't get a glimpse of it till this evening, after it's trimmed. [*To the* DELIVERY BOY, *taking out her purse.*] How much?
DELIVERY BOY. Fifty, ma'am.

[1] A piece of furniture with open shelves; a bookcase.

NORA. There's a crown. No, keep the change. [*The* BOY *thanks her and leaves.* NORA *shuts the door. She laughs softly to herself while taking off her street things. Drawing a bag of macaroons from her pocket, she eats a couple, then steals over and listens at her husband's study door.*] Yes, he's home. [*Hums again as she moves to the table right.*]

HELMER [*from the study*]. Is that my little lark twittering out there?

NORA [*busy opening some packages*]. Yes, it is.

HELMER. Is that my squirrel rummaging around?

NORA. Yes!

HELMER. When did my squirrel get in?

NORA. Just now. [*Putting the macaroon bag in her pocket and wiping her mouth.*] Do come in, Torvald, and see what I've bought.

HELMER. Can't be disturbed. [*After a moment he opens the door and peers in, pen in hand.*] Bought, you say? All that there? Has the little spendthrift been out throwing money around again?

NORA. Oh, but Torvald, this year we really should let ourselves go a bit. It's the first Christmas we haven't had to economize.

HELMER. But you know we can't go squandering.

NORA. Oh yes, Torvald, we can squander a little now. Can't we? Just a tiny, wee bit. Now that you've got a big salary and are going to make piles and piles of money.

HELMER. Yes—starting New Year's. But then it's a full three months till the raise comes through.

NORA. Pooh! We can borrow that long.

HELMER. Nora! [*Goes over and playfully takes her by the ear.*] Are your scatterbrains off again? What if today I borrowed a thousand crowns, and you squandered them over Christmas week, and then on New Year's Eve a roof tile fell on my head, and I lay there—

NORA [*putting her hand on his mouth*]. Oh! Don't say such things!

HELMER. Yes, but what if it happened—then what?

NORA. If anything so awful happened, then it just wouldn't matter if I had debts or not.

HELMER. Well, but the people I'd borrowed from?

NORA. Them? Who cares about them! They're strangers.

HELMER. Nora, Nora, how like a woman! No, but seriously, Nora, you know what I think about that. No debts! Never borrow! Something of freedom's lost—and something of beauty, too—from a home that's founded on borrowing and debt. We've made a brave stand up to now, the two of us; and we'll go right on like that the little while we have to.

NORA [*going toward the stove*]. Yes, whatever you say, Torvald.

HELMER [*following her*]. Now, now, the little lark's wings mustn't droop. Come on, don't be a sulky squirrel. [*Taking out his wallet.*] Nora, guess what I have here.

NORA [*turning quickly*]. Money!

HELMER. There, see. [*Hands her some notes.*] Good grief, I know how costs go up in a house at Christmastime.

NORA. Ten—twenty—thirty—forty. Oh, thank you, Torvald; I can manage no end on this.

HELMER. You really will have to.

NORA. Oh yes, I promise I will! But come here so I can show you every-

thing I bought. And so cheap! Look, new clothes for Ivar here—and a sword. Here a horse and a trumpet for Bob. And a doll and a doll's bed here for Emmy; they're nothing much, but she'll tear them to bits in no time anyway. And here I have dress material and handkerchiefs for the maids. Old Anne-Marie really deserves something more.

HELMER. And what's in that package there?

NORA [*with a cry*]. Torvald, no! You can't see that till tonight!

HELMER. I see. But tell me now, you little prodigal, what have you thought of for yourself?

NORA. For myself? Oh, I don't want anything at all.

HELMER. Of course you do. Tell me just what—within reason—you'd most like to have.

NORA. I honestly don't know. Oh, listen, Torvald—

HELMER. Well?

NORA [*fumbling at his coat buttons, without looking at him*]. If you want to give me something, then maybe you could—you could—

HELMER. Come on, out with it.

NORA [*hurriedly*]. You could give me money, Torvald. No more than you think you can spare; then one of these days I'll buy something with it.

HELMER. But Nora—

NORA. Oh, please, Torvald darling, do that! I beg you, please. Then I could hang the bills in pretty gilt paper on the Christmas tree. Wouldn't that be fun?

HELMER. What are those little birds called that always fly through their fortunes?

NORA. Oh yes, spendthrifts; I know all that. But let's do as I say, Torvald; then I'll have time to decide what I really need most. That's very sensible, isn't it?

HELMER [*smiling*]. Yes, very—that is, if you actually hung onto the money I give you, and you actually used it to buy yourself something. But it goes for the house and for all sorts of foolish things, and then I only have to lay out some more.

NORA. Oh, but Torvald—

HELMER. Don't deny it, my dear little Nora. [*Putting his arm around her waist.*] Spendthrifts are sweet, but they use up a frightful amount of money. It's incredible what it costs a man to feed such birds.

NORA. Oh, how can you say that! Really, I save everything I can.

HELMER [*laughing*]. Yes, that's the truth. Everything you can. But that's nothing at all.

NORA [*humming, with a smile of quiet satisfaction*]. Hm, if you only knew what expenses we larks and squirrels have, Torvald.

HELMER. You're an odd little one. Exactly the way your father was. You're never at a loss for scaring up money; but the moment you have it, it runs right out through your fingers; you never know what you've done with it. Well, one takes you as you are. It's deep in your blood. Yes, these things are hereditary, Nora.

NORA. Ah, I could wish I'd inherited many of Papa's qualities.

HELMER. And I couldn't wish you anything but just what you are, my sweet little lark. But wait; it seems to me you have a very—what should I call it?—a very suspicious look today—

NORA. I do?

HELMER. You certainly do. Look me straight in the eye.

NORA [*looking at him*]. Well?

HELMER [*shaking an admonitory finger*]. Surely my sweet tooth hasn't been running riot in town today, has she?

NORA. No. Why do you imagine that?

HELMER. My sweet tooth really didn't make a little detour through the confectioner's?

NORA. No, I assure you, Torvald—

HELMER. Hasn't nibbled some pastry?

NORA. No, not at all.

HELMER. Not even munched a macaroon or two?

NORA. No, Torvald, I assure you, really—

HELMER. There, there now. Of course I'm only joking.

NORA [*going to the table, right*]. You know I could never think of going against you.

HELMER. No, I understand that; and you *have* given me your word. [*Going over to her.*] Well, you keep your little Christmas secrets to yourself, Nora darling. I expect they'll come to light this evening, when the tree is lit.

NORA. Did you remember to ask Dr. Rank?

HELMER. No. But there's no need for that; it's assumed he'll be dining with us. All the same, I'll ask him when he stops by here this morning. I've ordered some fine wine. Nora, you can't imagine how I'm looking forward to this evening.

NORA. So am I. And what fun for the children, Torvald!

HELMER. Ah, it's so gratifying to know that one's gotten a safe, secure job, and with a comfortable salary. It's a great satisfaction, isn't it?

NORA. Oh, it's wonderful!

HELMER. Remember last Christmas? Three whole weeks before, you shut yourself in every evening till long after midnight, making flowers for the Christmas tree, and all the other decorations to surprise us. Ugh, that was the dullest time I've ever lived through.

NORA. It wasn't at all dull for me.

HELMER [*smiling*]. But the outcome *was* pretty sorry, Nora.

NORA. Oh, don't tease me with that again. How could I help it that the cat came in and tore everything to shreds.

HELMER. No, poor thing, you certainly couldn't. You wanted so much to please us all, and that's what counts. But it's just as well that the hard times are past.

NORA. Yes, it's really wonderful.

HELMER. Now I don't have to sit here alone, boring myself, and you don't have to tire your precious eyes and your fair little delicate hands—

NORA [*clapping her hands*]. No, is it really true, Torvald, I don't have to? Oh, how wonderfully lovely to hear! [*Taking his arm.*] Now I'll tell you just how I've thought we should plan things. Right after Christmas— [*The doorbell rings.*] Oh, the bell. [*Straightening the room up a bit.*] Somebody would have to come. What a bore!

HELMER. I'm not at home to visitors, don't forget.

MAID [*from the hall doorway*]. Ma'am, a lady to see you—

NORA. All right, let her come in.

MAID [*to* HELMER]. And the doctor's just come too.
HELMER. Did he go right to my study?
MAID. Yes, he did.

> [HELMER *goes into his room. The* MAID
> *shows in* MRS. LINDE, *dressed in travel-*
> *ing clothes, and shuts the door after her.*]

MRS. LINDE [*in a dispirited and somewhat hesitant voice*]. Hello, Nora.
NORA [*uncertain*]. Hello—
MRS. LINDE. You don't recognize me.
NORA. No, I don't know—but wait, I think—[*Exclaiming.*] What! Kristine!
Is it really you?
MRS. LINDE. Yes, it's me.
NORA. Kristine! To think I didn't recognize you. But then, how could I?
[*More quietly.*] How you've changed, Kristine!
MRS. LINDE. Yes, no doubt I have. In nine—ten long years.
NORA. Is it so long since we met! Yes, it's all of that. Oh, these last eight
years have been a happy time, believe me. And so now you've come in to
town, too. Made the long trip in the winter. That took courage.
MRS. LINDE. I just got here by ship this morning.
NORA. To enjoy yourself over Christmas, of course. Oh, how lovely! Yes,
enjoy ourselves, we'll do that. But take your coat off. You're not still
cold? [*Helping her.*] There now, let's get cozy here by the stove. No, the
easy chair there! I'll take the rocker here. [*Seizing her hands.*] Yes, now
you have your old look again; it was only in that first moment. You're a
bit more pale, Kristine—and maybe a bit thinner.
MRS. LINDE. And much, much older, Nora.
NORA. Yes, perhaps a bit older; a tiny, tiny bit; not much at all. [*Stopping
short; suddenly serious.*] Oh, but thoughtless me, to sit here, chattering
away. Sweet, good Kristine, can you forgive me?
MRS. LINDE. What do you mean, Nora?
NORA [*softly*]. Poor Kristine, you've become a widow.
MRS. LINDE. Yes, three years ago.
NORA. Oh, I knew it, of course; I read it in the papers. Oh, Kristine, you
must believe me; I often thought of writing you then, but I kept post-
poning it, and something always interfered.
MRS. LINDE. Nora dear, I understand completely.
NORA. No, it was awful of me, Kristine. You poor thing, how much you
must have gone through. And he left you nothing?
MRS. LINDE. No.
NORA. And no children?
MRS. LINDE. No.
NORA. Nothing at all, then?
MRS. LINDE. Not even a sense of loss to feed on.
NORA [*looking incredulously at her*]. But Kristine, how could that be?
MRS. LINDE [*smiling wearily and smoothing her hair*]. Oh, sometimes it hap-
pens, Nora.
NORA. So completely alone. How terribly hard that must be for you. I have
three lovely children. You can't see them now; they're out with the
maid. But now you must tell me everything—
MRS. LINDE. No, no, no, tell me about yourself.

NORA. No, you begin. Today I don't want to be selfish. I want to think only of you today. But there *is* something I must tell you. Did you hear of the wonderful luck we had recently?

MRS. LINDE. No, what's that?

NORA. My husband's been made manager in the bank, just think!

MRS. LINDE. Your husband? How marvelous!

NORA. Isn't it? Being a lawyer is such an uncertain living, you know, especially if one won't touch any cases that aren't clean and decent. And of course Torvald would never do that, and I'm with him completely there. Oh, we're simply delighted, believe me! He'll join the bank right after New Year's and start getting a huge salary and lots of commissions. From now on we can live quite differently—just as we want. Oh, Kristine, I feel so light and happy! Won't it be lovely to have stacks of money and not a care in the world?

MRS. LINDE. Well, anyway, it would be lovely to have enough for necessities.

NORA. No, not just for necessities, but stacks and stacks of money!

MRS. LINDE [*smiling*]. Nora, Nora, aren't you sensible yet? Back in school you were such a free spender.

NORA [*with a quiet laugh*]. Yes, that's what Torvald still says. [*Shaking her finger.*] But "Nora, Nora" isn't as silly as you all think. Really, we've been in no position for me to go squandering. We've had to work, both of us.

MRS. LINDE. You too?

NORA. Yes, at odd jobs—needlework, crocheting, embroidery, and such— [*Casually.*] and other things too. You remember that Torvald left the department when we were married? There was no chance of promotion in his office, and of course he needed to earn more money. But that first year he drove himself terribly. He took on all kinds of extra work that kept him going morning and night. It wore him down, and then he fell deathly ill. The doctors said it was essential for him to travel south.

MRS. LINDE. Yes, didn't you spend a whole year in Italy?

NORA. That's right. It wasn't easy to get away, you know. Ivar had just been born. But of course we had to go. Oh, that was a beautiful trip, and it saved Torvald's life. But it cost a frightful sum, Kristine.

MRS. LINDE. I can well imagine.

NORA. Four thousand, eight hundred crowns it cost. That's really a lot of money.

MRS. LINDE. But it's lucky you had it when you needed it.

NORA. Well, as it was, we got it from Papa.

MRS. LINDE. I see. It was just about the time your father died.

NORA. Yes, just about then. And, you know, I couldn't make that trip out to nurse him. I had to stay here, expecting Ivar any moment, and with my poor sick Torvald to care for. Dearest Papa, I never saw him again, Kristine. Oh, that was the worst time I've known in all my marriage.

MRS. LINDE. I know how you loved him. And then you went off to Italy?

NORA. Yes. We had the means now, and the doctors urged us. So we left a month after.

MRS. LINDE. And your husband came back completely cured?

NORA. Sound as a drum!

MRS. LINDE. But—the doctor?

NORA. Who?

MRS. LINDE. I thought the maid said he was a doctor, the man who came in with me.

NORA. Yes, that was Dr. Rank—but he's not making a sick call. He's our closest friend, and he stops by at least once a day. No, Torvald hasn't had a sick moment since, and the children are fit and strong, and I am, too. [*Jumping up and clapping her hands.*] Oh, dear God, Kristine, what a lovely thing to live and be happy! But how disgusting of me—I'm talking of nothing but my own affairs. [*Sits on a stool close by* KRISTINE, *arms resting across her knees.*] Oh, don't be angry with me! Tell me, is it really true that you weren't in love with your husband? Why did you marry him, then?

MRS. LINDE. My mother was still alive, but bedridden and helpless—and I had my two younger brothers to look after. In all conscience, I didn't think I could turn him down.

NORA. No, you were right there. But was he rich at the time?

MRS. LINDE. He was very well off, I'd say. But the business was shaky, Nora. When he died, it all fell apart, and nothing was left.

NORA. And then—?

MRS. LINDE. Yes, so I had to scrape up a living with a little shop and a little teaching and whatever else I could find. The last three years have been like one endless workday without a rest for me. Now it's over, Nora. My poor mother doesn't need me, for she's passed on. Nor the boys either; they're working now and can take care of themselves.

NORA. How free you must feel—

MRS. LINDE. No—only unspeakably empty. Nothing to live for now. [*Standing up anxiously.*] That's why I couldn't take it any longer out in that desolate hole. Maybe here it'll be easier to find something to do and keep my mind occupied. If I could only be lucky enough to get a steady job, some office work—

NORA. Oh, but Kristine, that's so dreadfully tiring, and you already look so tired. It would be much better for you if you could go off to a bathing resort.

MRS. LINDE [*going toward the window*]. I have no father to give me travel money, Nora.

NORA [*rising*]. Oh, don't be angry with me.

MRS. LINDE [*going to her*]. Nora dear, don't you be angry with me. The worst of my kind of situation is all the bitterness that's stored away. No one to work for, and yet you're always having to snap up your opportunities. You have to live; and so you grow selfish. When you told me the happy change in your lot, do you know I was delighted less for your sakes than for mine?

NORA. How so? Oh, I see. You think maybe Torvald could do something for you.

MRS. LINDE. Yes, that's what I thought.

NORA. And he will, Kristine! Just leave it to me; I'll bring it up so delicately—find something attractive to humor him with. Oh, I'm so eager to help you.

MRS. LINDE. How very kind of you, Nora, to be so concerned over me—doubly kind, considering you really know so little of life's burdens yourself.

NORA. I—? I know so little—?

MRS. LINDE [*smiling*]. Well, my heavens—a little needlework and such—Nora, you're just a child.

NORA [*tossing her head and pacing the floor*]. You don't have to act so superior.

MRS. LINDE. Oh?

NORA. You're just like the others. You all think I'm incapable of anything serious—

MRS. LINDE. Come now—

NORA. That I've never had to face the raw world.

MRS. LINDE. Nora dear, you've just been telling me all your troubles.

NORA. Hm! Trivia! [*Quietly.*] I haven't told you the big thing.

MRS. LINDE. Big thing? What do you mean?

NORA. You look down on me so, Kristine, but you shouldn't. You're proud that you worked so long and hard for your mother.

MRS. LINDE. I don't look down on a soul. But it *is* true: I'm proud—and happy, too—to think it was given to me to make my mother's last days almost free of care.

NORA. And you're also proud thinking of what you've done for your brothers.

MRS. LINDE. I feel I've a right to be.

NORA. I agree. But listen to this, Kristine—I've also got something to be proud and happy for.

MRS. LINDE. I don't doubt it. But whatever do you mean?

NORA. Not so loud. What if Torvald heard! He mustn't, not for anything in the world. Nobody must know, Kristine. No one but you.

MRS. LINDE. But what is it, then?

NORA. Come here. [*Drawing her down beside her on the sofa.*] It's true—I've also got something to be proud and happy for. I'm the one who saved Torvald's life.

MRS. LINDE. Saved—? Saved how?

NORA. I told you about the trip to Italy. Torvald never would have lived if he hadn't gone south—

MRS. LINDE. Of course; your father gave you the means—

NORA [*smiling*]. That's what Torvald and all the rest think, but—

MRS. LINDE. But—?

NORA. Papa didn't give us a pin. I was the one who raised the money.

MRS. LINDE. You? That whole amount?

NORA. Four thousand, eight hundred crowns. What do you say to that?

MRS. LINDE. But Nora, how was it possible? Did you win the lottery?

NORA [*disdainfully*]. The lottery? Pooh! No art to that.

MRS. LINDE. But where did you get it from then?

NORA [*humming, with a mysterious smile*]. Hmm, tra-la-la-la.

MRS. LINDE. Because you couldn't have borrowed it.

NORA. No? Why not?

MRS. LINDE. A wife can't borrow without her husband's consent.

NORA [*tossing her head*]. Oh, but a wife with a little business sense, a wife who knows how to manage—

MRS. LINDE. Nora, I simply don't understand—

NORA. You don't have to. Whoever said I *borrowed* the money? I could have gotten it other ways. [*Throwing herself back on the sofa.*] I could have gotten it from some admirer or other. After all, a girl with my ravishing appeal—

MRS. LINDE. You lunatic.

NORA. I'll bet you're eaten up with curiosity, Kristine.

MRS. LINDE. Now listen here, Nora—you haven't done something indiscreet?

NORA [*sitting up again*]. Is it indiscreet to save your husband's life?

MRS. LINDE. I think it's indiscreet that without his knowledge you—

NORA. But that's the point: he mustn't know! My Lord, can't you understand? He mustn't ever know the close call he had. It was to *me* the doctors came to say his life was in danger—that nothing could save him but a stay in the south. Didn't I try strategy then! I began talking about how lovely it would be for me to travel abroad like other young wives; I begged and I cried; I told him please to remember my condition, to be kind and indulge me; and then I dropped a hint that he could easily take out a loan. But at that, Kristine, he nearly exploded. He said I was frivolous, and it was his duty as man of the house not to indulge me in whims and fancies—as I think he called them. Aha, I thought, now you'll just have to be saved—and that's when I saw my chance.

MRS. LINDE. And your father never told Torvald the money wasn't from him?

NORA. No, never. Papa died right about then. I'd considered bringing him into my secret and begging him never to tell. But he was too sick at the time—and then, sadly, it didn't matter.

MRS. LINDE. And you've never confided in your husband since?

NORA. For heaven's sake, no! Are you serious? He's so strict on that subject. Besides—Torvald, with all his masculine pride—how painfully humiliating for him if he ever found out he was in debt to me. That would just ruin our relationship. Our beautiful, happy home would never be the same.

MRS. LINDE. Won't you ever tell him?

NORA [*thoughtfully, half smiling*]. Yes—maybe sometime, years from now, when I'm no longer so attractive. Don't laugh! I only mean when Torvald loves me less than now, when he stops enjoying my dancing and dressing up and reciting for him. Then it might be wise to have something in reserve—[*Breaking off.*] How ridiculous! That'll never happen— Well, Kristine, what do you think of my big secret? I'm capable of something too, hm? You can imagine, of course, how this thing hangs over me. It really hasn't been easy meeting the payments on time. In the business world there's what they call quarterly interest and what they call amortization, and these are always so terribly hard to manage. I've had to skimp a little here and there, wherever I could, you know. I could hardly spare anything from my house allowance, because Torvald has to live well. I couldn't let the children go poorly dressed; whatever I got for them, I felt I had to use up completely—the darlings!

MRS. LINDE. Poor Nora, so it had to come out of your own budget, then?

NORA. Yes, of course. But I was the one most responsible, too. Every time Torvald gave me money for new clothes and such, I never used more than half; always bought the simplest, cheapest outfits. It was a godsend that everything looks so well on me that Torvald never noticed. But it did weigh me down at times, Kristine. It *is* such a joy to wear fine things. You understand.

MRS. LINDE. Oh, of course.

NORA. And then I found other ways of making money. Last winter I was lucky enough to get a lot of copying to do. I locked myself in and sat writing every evening till late in the night. Ah, I was tired so often, dead tired. But still it was wonderful fun, sitting and working like that, earning money. It was almost like being a man.

MRS. LINDE. But how much have you paid off this way so far?

NORA. That's hard to say, exactly. These accounts, you know, aren't easy to figure. I only know that I've paid out all I could scrape together. Time and again I haven't known where to turn. [*Smiling.*] Then I'd sit here dreaming of a rich old gentleman who had fallen in love with me—

MRS. LINDE. What! Who is he?

NORA. Oh, really! And that he'd died, and when his will was opened, there in big letters it said, "All my fortune shall be paid over in cash, immediately, to that enchanting Mrs. Nora Helmer."

MRS. LINDE. But Nora dear—who *was* this gentleman?

NORA. Good grief, can't you understand? The old man never existed; that was only something I'd dream up time and again whenever I was at my wits' end for money. But it makes no difference now; the old fossil can go where he pleases for all I care; I don't need him or his will—because now I'm free. [*Jumping up.*] Oh, how lovely to think of that, Kristine! Carefree! To know you're carefree, utterly carefree; to be able to romp and play with the children, and to keep up a beautiful, charming home—everything just the way Torvald likes it! And think, spring is coming, with big blue skies. Maybe we can travel a little then. Maybe I'll see the ocean again. Oh yes, it *is* so marvelous to live and be happy!

[*The front doorbell rings.*]

MRS. LINDE [*rising*]. There's the bell. It's probably best that I go.

NORA. No, stay. No one's expected. It must be for Torvald.

MAID [*from the hall doorway*]. Excuse me, ma'am—there's a gentleman here to see Mr. Helmer, but I didn't know—since the doctor's with him—

NORA. Who is the gentleman?

KROGSTAD [*from the doorway*]. It's me, Mrs. Helmer.

[MRS. LINDE *starts and turns away toward the window.*]

NORA [*stepping toward him, tense, her voice a whisper*]. You? What is it? Why do you want to speak to my husband?

KROGSTAD. Bank business—after a fashion. I have a small job in the investment bank, and I hear now your husband is going to be our chief—

NORA. In other words, it's—

KROGSTAD. Just dry business, Mrs. Helmer. Nothing but that.

NORA. Yes, then please be good enough to step into the study. [*She nods*

indifferently as she sees him out by the hall door, then returns and begins stirring up the stove.]

MRS. LINDE. Nora—who was that man?

NORA. That was a Mr. Krogstad—a lawyer.

MRS. LINDE. Then it really was him.

NORA. Do you know that person?

MRS. LINDE. I did once—many years ago. For a time he was a law clerk in our town.

NORA. Yes, he's been that.

MRS. LINDE. How he's changed.

NORA. I understand he had a very unhappy marriage.

MRS. LINDE. He's a widower now.

NORA. With a number of children. There now, it's burning. [*She closes the stove door and moves the rocker a bit to one side.*]

MRS. LINDE. They say he has a hand in all kinds of business.

NORA. Oh? That may be true; I wouldn't know. But let's not think about business. It's so dull.

[DR. RANK *enters from* HELMER'S *study.*]

RANK [*still in the doorway*]. No, no, really—I don't want to intrude, I'd just as soon talk a little while with your wife. [*Shuts the door, then notices* MRS. LINDE.] Oh, beg pardon. I'm intruding here too.

NORA. No, not at all. [*Introducing him.*] Dr. Rank, Mrs. Linde.

RANK. Well now, that's a name much heard in this house. I believe I passed the lady on the stairs as I came.

MRS. LINDE. Yes, I take the stairs very slowly. They're rather hard on me.

RANK. Uh-hm, some touch of internal weakness?

MRS. LINDE. More overexertion, I'd say.

RANK. Nothing else? Then you're probably here in town to rest up in a round of parties?

MRS. LINDE. I'm here to look for work.

RANK. Is that the best cure for overexertion?

MRS. LINDE. One has to live, Doctor.

RANK. Yes, there's a common prejudice to that effect.

NORA. Oh, come on, Dr. Rank—you really do want to live yourself.

RANK. Yes, I really do. Wretched as I am, I'll gladly prolong my torment indefinitely. All my patients feel like that. And it's quite the same, too, with the morally sick. Right at this moment there's one of those moral invalids in there with Helmer—

MRS. LINDE [*softly*]. Ah!

NORA. Who do you mean?

RANK. Oh, it's a lawyer, Krogstad, a type you wouldn't know. His character is rotten to the root—but even he began chattering all-importantly about how he had to *live.*

NORA. Oh? What did he want to talk to Torvald about?

RANK. I really don't know. I only heard something about the bank.

NORA. I didn't know that Krog—that this man Krogstad had anything to do with the bank.

RANK. Yes, he's gotten some kind of berth down there. [*To* MRS. LINDE.] I don't know if you also have, in your neck of the woods, a type of person

who scuttles about breathlessly, sniffing out hints of moral corruption, and then maneuvers his victim into some sort of key position where he can keep an eye on him. It's the healthy these days that are out in the cold.

MRS. LINDE. All the same, it's the sick who most need to be taken in.

RANK [*with a shrug*]. Yes, there we have it. That's the concept that's turning society into a sanatorium.

> [NORA, *lost in her thoughts, breaks out into quiet laughter and claps her hands.*]

RANK. Why do you laugh at that? Do you have any real idea of what society is?

NORA. What do I care about dreary old society? I was laughing at something quite different—something terribly funny. Tell me, Doctor—is everyone who works in the bank dependent now on Torvald?

RANK. Is that what you find so terribly funny?

NORA [*smiling and humming*]. Never mind, never mind! [*Pacing the floor.*] Yes, that's really immensely amusing: that we—that Torvald has so much power now over all those people. [*Taking the bag out of her pocket.*] Dr. Rank, a little macaroon on that?

RANK. See here, macaroons! I thought they were contraband here.

NORA. Yes, but these are some that Kristine gave me.

MRS. LINDE. What? I—?

NORA. Now, now, don't be afraid. You couldn't possibly know that Torvald had forbidden them. You see, he's worried they'll ruin my teeth. But hmp! Just this once! Isn't that so, Dr. Rank? Help yourself! [*Puts a macaroon in his mouth.*] And you too, Kristine. And I'll also have one, only a little one—or two, at the most. [*Walking about again.*] Now I'm really tremendously happy. Now there's just one last thing in the world that I have an enormous desire to do.

RANK. Well! And what's that?

NORA. It's something I have such a consuming desire to say so Torvald could hear.

RANK. And why can't you say it?

NORA. I don't dare. It's quite shocking.

MRS. LINDE. Shocking?

RANK. Well, then it isn't advisable. But in front of us you certainly can. What do you have such a desire to say so Torvald could hear?

NORA. I have such a huge desire to say—to hell and be damned!

RANK. Are you crazy?

MRS. LINDE. My goodness, Nora!

RANK. Go on, say it. Here he is.

NORA [*hiding the macaroon bag*]. Shh, shh, shh!

> [HELMER *comes in from his study, hat in hand, overcoat over his arm.*]

NORA [*going toward him*]. Well, Torvald dear, are you through with him?

HELMER. Yes, he just left.

NORA. Let me introduce you—this is Kristine, who's arrived here in town.

HELMER. Kristine—? I'm sorry, but I don't know—

NORA. Mrs. Linde, Torvald dear. Mrs. Kristine Linde.

HELMER. Of course. A childhood friend of my wife's, no doubt?

MRS. LINDE. Yes, we knew each other in those days.

NORA. And just think, she made the long trip down here in order to talk with you.

HELMER. What's this?

MRS. LINDE. Well, not exactly—

NORA. You see, Kristine is remarkably clever in office work, and so she's terribly eager to come under a capable man's supervision and add more to what she already knows—

HELMER. Very wise, Mrs. Linde.

NORA. And then when she heard that you'd become a bank manager—the story was wired out to the papers—then she came in as fast as she could and—Really, Torvald, for my sake you can do a little something for Kristine, can't you?

HELMER. Yes, it's not at all impossible. Mrs. Linde, I suppose you're a widow?

MRS. LINDE. Yes.

HELMER. Any experience in office work?

MRS. LINDE. Yes, a good deal.

HELMER. Well, it's quite likely that I can make an opening for you—

NORA [*clapping her hands*]. You see, you see!

HELMER. You've come at a lucky moment, Mrs. Linde.

MRS. LINDE. Oh, how can I thank you?

HELMER. Not necessary. [*Putting his overcoat on.*] But today you'll have to excuse me—

RANK. Wait, I'll go with you. [*He fetches his coat from the hall and warms it at the stove.*]

NORA. Don't stay out long, dear.

HELMER. An hour; no more.

NORA. Are you going too, Kristine?

MRS. LINDE [*putting on her winter garments*]. Yes, I have to see about a room now.

HELMER. Then perhaps we can all walk together.

NORA [*helping her*]. What a shame we're so cramped here, but it's quite impossible for us to—

MRS. LINDE. Oh, don't even think of it! Good-bye, Nora dear, and thanks for everything.

NORA. Good-bye for now. Of course you'll be back this evening. And you too, Dr. Rank. What? If you're well enough? Oh, you've got to be! Wrap up tight now.

> [*In a ripple of small talk the company moves out into the hall; children's voices are heard outside on the steps.*]

NORA. There they are! There they are! [*She runs to open the door. The children come in with their nurse,* ANNE-MARIE.] Come in, come in! [*Bends down and kisses them.*] Oh, you darlings—! Look at them, Kristine. Aren't they lovely!

RANK. No loitering in the draft here.

HELMER. Come, Mrs. Linde—this place is unbearable now for anyone but
mothers.

> [DR. RANK, HELMER, *and* MRS. LINDE
> *go down the stairs.* ANNE-MARIE *goes
> into the living room with the children.*
> NORA *follows, after closing the hall door.*]

NORA. How fresh and strong you look. Oh, such red cheeks you have! Like
apples and roses. [*The children interrupt her throughout the following.*] And
it was so much fun? That's wonderful. Really? You pulled both Emmy
and Bob on the sled? Imagine, all together! Yes, you're a clever boy,
Ivar. Oh, let me hold her a bit, Anne-Marie. My sweet little doll baby!
[*Takes the smallest from the nurse and dances with her.*] Yes, yes, Mama will
dance with Bob as well. What? Did you throw snowballs? Oh, if I'd only
been there! No, don't bother, Anne-Marie—I'll undress them myself.
Oh yes, let me. It's such fun. Go in and rest; you look half frozen.
There's hot coffee waiting for you on the stove. [*The nurse goes into the
room to the left.* NORA *takes the children's winter things off, throwing them
about, while the children talk to her all at once.*] Is that so? A big dog chased
you? But it didn't bite? No, dogs never bite little, lovely doll babies.
Don't peek in the packages, Ivar! What is it? Yes, wouldn't you like to
know. No, no, it's an ugly something. Well? Shall we play? What shall we
play? Hide-and-seek? Yes, let's play hide-and-seek. Bob must hide first.
I must? Yes, let me hide first. [*Laughing and shouting, she and the children
play in and out of the living room and the adjoining room to the right. At last*
NORA *hides under the table. The children come storming in, search, but cannot
find her, then hear her muffled laughter, dash over to the table, lift the cloth up
and find her. Wild shouting. She creeps forward as if to scare them. More shouts.
Meanwhile, a knock at the hall door; no one has noticed it. Now the door half
opens, and* KROGSTAD *appears. He waits a moment; the game goes on.*]

KROGSTAD. Beg pardon. Mrs. Helmer—

NORA [*with a strangled cry, turning and scrambling to her knees*]. Oh! What do
you want?

KROGSTAD. Excuse me. The outer door was ajar; it must be someone for-
got to shut it—

NORA [*rising*]. My husband isn't home, Mr. Krogstad.

KROGSTAD. I know that.

NORA. Yes—then what do you want here?

KROGSTAD. A word with you.

NORA. With—? [*To the children, quietly.*] Go in to Anne-Marie. What? No,
the strange man won't hurt Mama. When he's gone, we'll play some
more. [*She leads the children into the room to the left and shuts the door after
them. Then, tense and nervous:*] You want to speak to me?

KROGSTAD. Yes, I want to.

NORA. Today? But it's not yet the first of the month—

KROGSTAD. No, it's Christmas Eve. It's going to be up to you how merry a
Christmas you have.

NORA. What is it you want? Today I absolutely can't—

KROGSTAD. We won't talk about that till later. This is something else. You
do have a moment to spare, I suppose?

NORA. Oh yes, of course—I do, except—

KROGSTAD. Good. I was sitting over at Olsen's Restaurant when I saw your husband go down the street—

NORA. Yes?

KROGSTAD. With a lady.

NORA. Yes. So?

KROGSTAD. If you'll pardon my asking: wasn't that lady a Mrs. Linde?

NORA. Yes.

KROGSTAD. Just now come into town?

NORA. Yes, today.

KROGSTAD. She's a good friend of yours?

NORA. Yes, she is. But I don't see—

KROGSTAD. I also knew her once.

NORA. I'm aware of that.

KROGSTAD. Oh? You know all about it. I thought so. Well, then let me ask you short and sweet: is Mrs. Linde getting a job in the bank?

NORA. What makes you think you can cross-examine me, Mr. Krogstad— you, one of my husband's employees? But since you ask, you might as well know—yes, Mrs. Linde's going to be taken on at the bank. And I'm the one who spoke for her, Mr. Krogstad. Now you know.

KROGSTAD. So I guessed right.

NORA [*pacing up and down*]. Oh, one does have a tiny bit of influence, I should hope. Just because I am a woman, don't think it means that— When one has a subordinate position, Mr. Krogstad, one really ought to be careful about pushing somebody who—hm—

KROGSTAD. Who has influence?

NORA. That's right.

KROGSTAD [*in a different tone*]. Mrs. Helmer, would you be good enough to use your influence on my behalf?

NORA. What? What do you mean?

KROGSTAD. Would you please make sure that I keep my subordinate position in the bank?

NORA. What does that mean? Who's thinking of taking away your position?

KROGSTAD. Oh, don't play the innocent with me. I'm quite aware that your friend would hardly relish the chance of running into me again; and I'm also aware now whom I can thank for being turned out.

NORA. But I promise you—

KROGSTAD. Yes, yes, yes, to the point: there's still time, and I'm advising you to use your influence to prevent it.

NORA. But Mr. Krogstad, I have absolutely no influence.

KROGSTAD. You haven't? I thought you were just saying—

NORA. You shouldn't take me so literally. I! How can you believe that I have any such influence over my husband?

KROGSTAD. Oh, I've known your husband from our student days. I don't think the great bank manager's more steadfast than any other married man.

NORA. You speak insolently about my husband, and I'll show you the door.

KROGSTAD. The lady has spirit.

NORA. I'm not afraid of you any longer. After New Year's, I'll soon be done with the whole business.

KROGSTAD [*restraining himself*]. Now listen to me, Mrs. Helmer. If necessary, I'll fight for my little job in the bank as if it were life itself.

NORA. Yes, so it seems.

KROGSTAD. It's not just a matter of income; that's the least of it. It's something else— All right, out with it! Look, this is the thing. You know, just like all the others, of course, that once, a good many years ago, I did something rather rash.

NORA. I've heard rumors to that effect.

KROGSTAD. The case never got into court; but all the same, every door was closed in my face from then on. So I took up those various activities you know about. I had to grab hold somewhere; and I dare say I haven't been among the worst. But now I want to drop all that. My boys are growing up. For their sakes, I'll have to win back as much respect as possible here in town. That job in the bank was like the first rung in my ladder. And now your husband wants to kick me right back down in the mud again.

NORA. But for heaven's sake, Mr. Krogstad, it's simply not in my power to help you.

KROGSTAD. That's because you haven't the will to—but I have the means to make you.

NORA. You certainly won't tell my husband that I owe you money?

KROGSTAD. Hm—what if I told him that?

NORA. That would be shameful of you. [*Nearly in tears.*] This secret—my joy and my pride—that he should learn it in such a crude and disgusting way—learn it from you. You'd expose me to the most horrible unpleasantness—

KROGSTAD. Only unpleasantness?

NORA [*vehemently*]. But go on and try. It'll turn out the worse for you, because then my husband will really see what a crook you are, and then you'll *never* be able to hold your job.

KROGSTAD. I asked if it was just domestic unpleasantness you were afraid of?

NORA. If my husband finds out, then of course he'll pay what I owe at once, and then we'd be through with you for good.

KROGSTAD [*a step closer*]. Listen, Mrs. Helmer—you've either got a very bad memory, or else no head at all for business. I'd better put you a little more in touch with the facts.

NORA. What do you mean?

KROGSTAD. When your husband was sick, you came to me for a loan of four thousand, eight hundred crowns.

NORA. Where else could I go?

KROGSTAD. I promised to get you that sum—

NORA. And you got it.

KROGSTAD. I promised to get you that sum, on certain conditions. You were so involved in your husband's illness, and so eager to finance your trip, that I guess you didn't think out all the details. It might just be a good idea to remind you. I promised you the money on the strength of a note I drew up.

NORA. Yes, and that I signed.

KROGSTAD. Right. But at the bottom I added some lines for your father to guarantee the loan. He was supposed to sign down there.

NORA. Supposed to? He did sign.

KROGSTAD. I left the date blank. In other words, your father would have dated his signature himself. Do you remember that?

NORA. Yes, I think—

KROGSTAD. Then I gave you the note for you to mail to your father. Isn't that so?

NORA. Yes.

KROGSTAD. And naturally you sent it at once—because only some five, six days later you brought me the note, properly signed. And with that, the money was yours.

NORA. Well, then; I've made my payments regularly, haven't I?

KROGSTAD. More or less. But—getting back to the point—those were hard times for you then, Mrs. Helmer.

NORA. Yes, they were.

KROGSTAD. Your father was very ill, I believe.

NORA. He was near the end.

KROGSTAD. He died soon after?

NORA. Yes.

KROGSTAD. Tell me, Mrs. Helmer, do you happen to recall the date of your father's death? The day of the month, I mean.

NORA. Papa died the twenty-ninth of September.

KROGSTAD. That's quite correct; I've already looked into that. And now we come to a curious thing—[*Taking out a paper.*] which I simply cannot comprehend.

NORA. Curious thing? I don't know—

KROGSTAD. This is the curious thing; that your father co-signed the note for your loan three days after his death.

NORA. How—? I don't understand.

KROGSTAD. Your father died the twenty-ninth of September. But look. Here your father dated his signature October second. Isn't that curious, Mrs. Helmer? [NORA *is silent.*] Can you explain it to me? [NORA *remains silent.*] It's also remarkable that the words "October second" and the year aren't written in your father's hand, but rather in one that I think I know. Well, it's easy to understand. Your father forgot perhaps to date his signature, and then someone or other added it, a bit sloppily, before anyone knew of his death. There's nothing wrong in that. It all comes down to the signature. And there's no question about *that,* Mrs. Helmer. It really *was* your father who signed his own name here, wasn't it?

NORA [*after a short silence, throwing her head back and looking squarely at him*]. No, it wasn't. *I* signed Papa's name.

KROGSTAD. Wait, now—are you fully aware that this is a dangerous confession?

NORA. Why? You'll soon get your money.

KROGSTAD. Let me ask you a question—why didn't you send the paper to your father?

NORA. That was impossible. Papa was so sick. If I'd asked him for his signature, I also would have had to tell him what the money was for. But I couldn't tell him, sick as he was, that my husband's life was in danger. That was just impossible.

KROGSTAD. Then it would have been better if you'd given up the trip abroad.

NORA. I couldn't possibly. The trip was to save my husband's life. I couldn't give that up.

KROGSTAD. But didn't you ever consider that this was a fraud against me?

NORA. I couldn't let myself be bothered by that. You weren't any concern of mine. I couldn't stand you, with all those cold complications you made, even though you knew how badly off my husband was.

KROGSTAD. Mrs. Helmer, obviously you haven't the vaguest idea of what you've involved yourself in. But I can tell you this: it was nothing more and nothing worse that I once did—and it wrecked my whole reputation.

NORA. You? Do you expect me to believe that you ever acted bravely to save your wife's life?

KROGSTAD. Laws don't inquire into motives.

NORA. Then they must be very poor laws.

KROGSTAD. Poor or not—if I introduce this paper in court, you'll be judged according to law.

NORA. This I refuse to believe. A daughter hasn't a right to protect her dying father from anxiety and care? A wife hasn't a right to save her husband's life? I don't know much about laws, but I'm sure that somewhere in the books these things are allowed. And you don't know anything about it—you who practice the law? You must be an awful lawyer, Mr. Krogstad.

KROGSTAD. Could be. But business—the kind of business we two are mixed up in—don't you think I know about that? All right. Do what you want now. But I'm telling you *this:* if I get shoved down a second time, you're going to keep me company. [*He bows and goes out through the hall.*]

NORA [*pensive for a moment, then tossing her head*]. Oh, really! Trying to frighten me! I'm not so silly as all that. [*Begins gathering up the children's clothes, but soon stops.*] But—? No, but that's impossible! I did it out of love.

THE CHILDREN [*in the doorway, left*]. Mama, that strange man's gone out the door.

NORA. Yes, yes, I know it. But don't tell anyone about the strange man. Do you hear? Not even Papa!

THE CHILDREN. No, Mama. But now will you play again?

NORA. No, not now.

THE CHILDREN. Oh, but Mama, you promised.

NORA. Yes, but I can't now. Go inside; I have too much to do. Go in, go in, my sweet darlings. [*She herds them gently back in the room and shuts the door after them. Settling on the sofa, she takes up a piece of embroidery and makes some stitches, but soon stops abruptly.*] No! [*Throws the work aside, rises, goes to the hall door and calls out.*] Helene! Let me have the tree in here. [*Goes to the table, left, opens the table drawer, and stops again.*] No, but that's utterly impossible!

MAID [*with the Christmas tree*]. Where should I put it, ma'am?

NORA. There. The middle of the floor.

MAID. Should I bring anything else?

NORA. No, thanks. I have what I need.

> [*The* MAID, *who has set the tree down,*
> *goes out.*]

NORA [*absorbed in trimming the tree*]. Candles here—and flowers here. That
terrible creature! Talk, talk, talk! There's nothing to it at all. The tree's
going to be lovely. I'll do anything to please you, Torvald. I'll sing for
you, dance for you—

> [HELMER *comes in from the hall, with a*
> *sheaf of papers under his arm.*]

NORA. Oh! You're back so soon?

HELMER. Yes. Has anyone been here?

NORA. Here? No.

HELMER. That's odd. I saw Krogstad leaving the front door.

NORA. So? Oh yes, that's true. Krogstad was here a moment.

HELMER. Nora, I can see by your face that he's been here, begging you to
put in a good word for him.

NORA. Yes.

HELMER. And it was supposed to seem like your own idea? You were to
hide it from me that he'd been here. He asked you that, too, didn't he?

NORA. Yes, Torvald, but—

HELMER. Nora, Nora, and you could fall for that? Talk with that sort of
person and promise him anything? And then in the bargain, tell me an
untruth.

NORA. An untruth—?

HELMER. Didn't you say that no one had been here? [*Wagging his finger.*]
My little songbird must never do that again. A songbird needs a clean
beak to warble with. No false notes. [*Putting his arm about her waist.*]
That's the way it should be, isn't it? Yes, I'm sure of it. [*Releasing her.*]
And so, enough of that. [*Sitting by the stove.*] Ah, how snug and cozy it is
here. [*Leafing among his papers.*]

NORA [*busy with the tree, after a short pause*]. Torvald!

HELMER. Yes.

NORA. I'm so much looking forward to the Stenborgs' costume party, day
after tomorrow.

HELMER. And I can't wait to see what you'll surprise me with.

NORA. Oh, that stupid business!

HELMER. What?

NORA. I can't find anything that's right. Everything seems so ridiculous, so
inane.

HELMER. So my little Nora's come to *that* recognition?

NORA [*going behind his chair, her arms resting on its back*]. Are you very busy,
Torvald?

HELMER. Oh—

NORA. What papers are those?

HELMER. Bank matters.

NORA. Already?

HELMER. I've gotten full authority from the retiring management to make
all necessary changes in personnel and procedure. I'll need Christmas
week for that. I want to have everything in order by New Year's.

NORA. So that was the reason this poor Krogstad—

HELMER. Hm.

NORA [*still leaning on the chair and slowly stroking the nape of his neck*]. If you weren't so very busy, I would have asked you an enormous favor, Torvald.

HELMER. Let's hear. What is it?

NORA. You know, there isn't anyone who has your good taste—and I want so much to look well at the costume party. Torvald, couldn't you take over and decide what I should be and plan my costume?

HELMER. Ah, is my stubborn little creature calling for a lifeguard?

NORA. Yes, Torvald, I can't get anywhere without your help.

HELMER. All right—I'll think it over. We'll hit on something.

NORA. Oh, how sweet of you. [*Goes to the tree again. Pauses.*] Aren't the red flowers pretty—? But tell me, was it really such a crime that this Krogstad committed?

HELMER. Forgery. Do you have any idea what that means?

NORA. Couldn't he have done it out of need?

HELMER. Yes, or thoughtlessness, like so many others. I'm not so heartless that I'd condemn a man categorically for just one mistake.

NORA. No, of course not, Torvald!

HELMER. Plenty of men have redeemed themselves by openly confessing their crimes and taking their punishment.

NORA. Punishment—?

HELMER. But now Krogstad didn't go that way. He got himself out by sharp practices, and that's the real cause of his moral breakdown.

NORA. Do you really think that would—?

HELMER. Just imagine how a man with that sort of guilt in him has to lie and cheat and deceive on all sides, has to wear a mask even with the nearest and dearest he has, even with his own wife and children. And with the children, Nora—that's where it's most horrible.

NORA. Why?

HELMER. Because that kind of atmosphere of lies infects the whole life of a home. Every breath the children take in is filled with the germs of something degenerate.

NORA [*coming closer behind him*]. Are you sure of that?

HELMER. Oh, I've seen it often enough as a lawyer. Almost everyone who goes bad early in life has a mother who's a chronic liar.

NORA. Why just—the mother?

HELMER. It's usually the mother's influence that's dominant, but the father's works in the same way, of course. Every lawyer is quite familiar with it. And still this Krogstad's been going home year in, year out, poisoning his own children with lies and pretense; that's why I call him morally lost. [*Reaching his hands out toward her.*] So my sweet little Nora must promise me never to plead his cause. Your hand on it. Come, come, what's this? Give me your hand. There, now. All settled. I can tell you it'd be impossible for me to work alongside of him. I literally feel physically revolted when I'm anywhere near such a person.

NORA [*withdraws her hand and goes to the other side of the Christmas tree*]. How hot it is here! And I've got so much to do.

HELMER [*getting up and gathering his papers*]. Yes, and I have to think about

getting some of these read through before dinner. I'll think about your costume, too. And something to hang on the tree in gilt paper, I may even see about that. [*Putting his hand on her head.*] Oh you, my darling little songbird. [*He goes into his study and closes the door after him.*]

NORA [*softly, after a silence*]. Oh, really! it isn't so. It's impossible. It must be impossible.

ANNE-MARIE [*in the doorway, left*]. The children are begging so hard to come in to Mama.

NORA. No, no, no, don't let them in to me! You stay with them, Anne-Marie.

ANNE-MARIE. Of course, ma'am. [*Closes the door.*]

NORA [*pale with terror*]. Hurt my children—! Poison my home? [*A moment's pause; then she tosses her head.*] That's not true. Never. Never in all the world.

ACT TWO

Same room. Beside the piano the Christmas tree now stands stripped of ornament, burned-down candle stubs on its ragged branches. NORA's street clothes lie on the sofa. NORA, alone in the room, moves restlessly about; at last she stops at the sofa and picks up her coat.

NORA [*dropping the coat again*]. Someone's coming! [*Goes toward the door, listens.*] No—there's no one. Of course—nobody's coming today, Christmas Day—or tomorrow, either. But maybe—[*Opens the door and looks out.*] No, nothing in the mailbox. Quite empty. [*Coming forward.*] What nonsense! He won't do anything serious. Nothing terrible could happen. It's impossible. Why, I have three small children.

> [ANNE-MARIE, *with a large carton,*
> *comes in from the room to the left.*]

ANNE-MARIE. Well, at last I found the box with the masquerade clothes.

NORA. Thanks. Put it on the table.

ANNE-MARIE [*does so*]. But they're all pretty much of a mess.

NORA. Ahh! I'd love to rip them in a million pieces!

ANNE-MARIE. Oh, mercy, they can be fixed right up. Just a little patience.

NORA. Yes, I'll go get Mrs. Linde to help me.

ANNE-MARIE. Out again now? In this nasty weather? Miss Nora will catch cold—get sick.

NORA. Oh, worse things could happen— How are the children?

ANNE-MARIE. The poor mites are playing with their Christmas presents, but—

NORA. Do they ask for me much?

ANNE-MARIE. They're so used to having Mama around, you know.

NORA. Yes, but Anne-Marie, I *can't* be together with them as much as I was.

ANNE-MARIE. Well, small children get used to anything.

NORA. You think so? Do you think they'd forget their mother if she was gone for good?

ANNE-MARIE. Oh, mercy—gone for good!

NORA. Wait, tell me, Anne-Marie—I've wondered so often—how could you ever have the heart to give your child over to strangers?

ANNE-MARIE. But I had to, you know, to become little Nora's nurse.

NORA. Yes, but how could you *do* it?

ANNE-MARIE. When I could get such a good place? A girl who's poor and who's gotten in trouble is glad enough for that. Because that slippery fish, he didn't do a thing for me, you know.

NORA. But your daughter's surely forgotten you.

ANNE-MARIE. Oh, she certainly has not. She's written to me, both when she was confirmed and when she was married.

NORA [*clasping her about the neck*]. You old Anne-Marie, you were a good mother for me when I was little.

ANNE-MARIE. Poor little Nora, with no other mother but me.

NORA. And if the babies didn't have one, then I know that you'd— What silly talk! [*Opening the carton.*] Go in to them. Now I'll have to— Tomorrow you can see how lovely I'll look.

ANNE-MARIE. Oh, there won't be anyone at the party as lovely as Miss Nora. [*She goes off into the room, left.*]

NORA [*begins unpacking the box, but soon throws it aside*]. Oh, if I dared to go out. If only nobody would come. If only nothing would happen here while I'm out. What craziness—nobody's coming. Just don't think. This muff—needs a brushing. Beautiful gloves, beautiful gloves. Let it go. Let it go! One, two, three, four, five, six— [*With a cry.*] Oh, there they are! [*Poises to move toward the door, but remains irresolutely standing.* MRS. LINDE *enters from the hall, where she has removed her street clothes.*]

NORA. Oh, it's you, Kristine. There's no one else out there? How good that you've come.

MRS. LINDE. I hear you were up asking for me.

NORA. Yes, I just stopped by. There's something you really can help me with. Let's get settled on the sofa. Look, there's going to be a costume party tomorrow evening at the Stenborgs' right above us, and now Torvald wants me to go as a Neapolitan peasant girl and dance the tarantella[2] that I learned in Capri.

MRS. LINDE. Really, are you giving a whole performance?

NORA. Torvald says yes, I should. See, here's the dress. Torvald had it made for me down there; but now it's all so tattered that I just don't know—

MRS. LINDE. Oh, we'll fix that up in no time. It's nothing more than the trimmings—they're a bit loose here and there. Needle and thread? Good, now we have what we need.

NORA. Oh, how sweet of you!

MRS. LINDE [*sewing*]. So you'll be in disguise tomorrow, Nora. You know what? I'll stop by then for a moment and have a look at you all dressed up. But listen, I've absolutely forgotten to thank you for that pleasant evening yesterday.

NORA [*getting up and walking about*]. I don't think it was as pleasant as usual

[2] A rapid, whirling southern Italian dance. Its name comes from the fact that it is popularly supposed to represent the death throes of someone bitten by a tarantula.

yesterday. You should have come to town a bit sooner, Kristine—Yes, Torvald really knows how to give a home elegance and charm.

MRS. LINDE. And you do, too, if you ask me. You're not your father's daughter for nothing. But tell me, is Dr. Rank always so down in the mouth as yesterday?

NORA. No, that was quite an exception. But he goes around critically ill all the time—tuberculosis of the spine, poor man. You know, his father was a disgusting thing who kept mistresses and so on—and that's why the son's been sickly from birth.

MRS. LINDE [*lets her sewing fall to her lap*]. But my dearest Nora, how do you know about such things?

NORA [*walking more jauntily*]. Hmp! When you've had three children, then you've had a few visits from—from women who know something of medicine, and they tell you this and that.

MRS. LINDE [*resumes sewing; a short pause*]. Does Dr. Rank come here every day?

NORA. Every blessed day. He's Torvald's best friend from childhood, and *my* good friend, too. Dr. Rank almost belongs to this house.

MRS. LINDE. But tell me—is he quite sincere? I mean, doesn't he rather enjoy flattering people?

NORA. Just the opposite. Why do you think that?

MRS. LINDE. When you introduced us yesterday, he was proclaiming that he'd often heard my name in this house; but later I noticed that your husband hadn't the slightest idea who I really was. So how could Dr. Rank—?

NORA. But it's all true, Kristine. You see, Torvald loves me beyond words, and, as he puts it, he'd like to keep me all to himself. For a long time he'd almost be jealous if I even mentioned any of my old friends back home. So of course I dropped that. But with Dr. Rank I talk a lot about such things, because he likes hearing about them.

MRS. LINDE. Now listen, Nora; in many ways you're still like a child. I'm a good deal older than you, with a little more experience. I'll tell you something: you ought to put an end to all this with Dr. Rank.

NORA. What should I put an end to?

MRS. LINDE. Both parts of it, I think. Yesterday you said something about a rich admirer who'd provide you with money—

NORA. Yes, one who doesn't exist—worse luck. So?

MRS. LINDE. Is Dr. Rank well off?

NORA. Yes, he is.

MRS. LINDE. With no dependents?

NORA. No, no one. But—

MRS. LINDE. And he's over here every day?

NORA. Yes, I told you that.

MRS. LINDE. How can a man of such refinement be so grasping?

NORA. I don't follow you at all.

MRS. LINDE. Now don't try to hide it, Nora. You think I can't guess who loaned you the forty-eight hundred crowns?

NORA. Are you out of your mind? How could you think such a thing! A friend of ours, who comes here every single day. What an intolerable situation that would have been!

MRS. LINDE. Then it really wasn't him.

NORA. No, absolutely not. It never even crossed my mind for a moment—
 And he had nothing to lend in those days; his inheritance came later.

MRS. LINDE. Well, I think that was a stroke of luck for you, Nora dear.

NORA. No, it never would have occurred to me to ask Dr. Rank— Still, I'm
 quite sure that if I had asked him—

MRS. LINDE. Which you won't, of course.

NORA. No, of course not. I can't see that I'd ever need to. But I'm quite
 positive that if I talked to Dr. Rank—

MRS. LINDE. Behind your husband's back?

NORA. I've got to clear up this other thing; *that's* also behind his back. I've
 got to clear it all up.

MRS. LINDE. Yes, I was saying that yesterday, but—

NORA [*pacing up and down*]. A man handles these problems so much better
 than a woman—

MRS. LINDE. One's husband does, yes.

NORA. Nonsense. [*Stopping.*] When you pay everything you owe, then you
 get your note back, right?

MRS. LINDE. Yes, naturally.

NORA. And can rip it into a million pieces and burn it up—that filthy scrap
 of paper!

MRS. LINDE [*looking hard at her, laying her sewing aside, and rising slowly*]. Nora,
 you're hiding something from me.

NORA. You can see it in my face?

MRS. LINDE. Something's happened to you since yesterday morning. Nora,
 what is it?

NORA [*hurrying toward her*]. Kristine! [*Listening.*] Shh! Torvald's home.
 Look, go in with the children a while. Torvald can't bear all this snip-
 ping and stitching. Let Anne-Marie help you.

MRS. LINDE [*gathering up some of the things*]. All right, but I'm not leaving
 here until we've talked this out. [*She disappears into the room, left, as*
 TORVALD *enters from the hall.*]

NORA. Oh, how I've been waiting for you, Torvald dear.

HELMER. Was that the dressmaker?

NORA. No, that was Kristine. She's helping me fix up my costume. You
 know, it's going to be quite attractive.

HELMER. Yes, wasn't that a bright idea I had?

NORA. Brilliant! But then wasn't I good as well to give in to you?

HELMER. Good—because you give in to your husband's judgment? All
 right, you little goose, I know you didn't mean it like that. But I won't
 disturb you. You'll want to have a fitting, I suppose.

NORA. And you'll be working?

HELMER. Yes. [*Indicating a bundle of papers.*] See. I've been down to the
 bank. [*Starts toward his study.*]

NORA. Torvald.

HELMER [*stops*]. Yes.

NORA. If your little squirrel begged you, with all her heart and soul, for
 something—?

HELMER. What's that?

NORA. Then would you do it?

HELMER. First, naturally, I'd have to know what it was.

NORA. Your squirrel would scamper about and do tricks, if you'd only be sweet and give in.

HELMER. Out with it.

NORA. Your lark would be singing high and low in every room—

HELMER. Come on, she does that anyway.

NORA. I'd be a wood nymph and dance for you in the moonlight.

HELMER. Nora—don't tell me it's that same business from this morning?

NORA [*coming closer*]. Yes, Torvald, I beg you, please!

HELMER. And you actually have the nerve to drag that up again?

NORA. Yes, yes, you've got to give in to me; you *have* to let Krogstad keep his job in the bank.

HELMER. My dear Nora, I've slated his job for Mrs. Linde.

NORA. That's awfully kind of you. But you could just fire another clerk instead of Krogstad.

HELMER. This is the most incredible stubbornness! Because you go and give an impulsive promise to speak up for him, I'm expected to—

NORA. That's not the reason, Torvald. It's for your own sake. That man does writing for the worst papers; you said it yourself. He could do you any amount of harm. I'm scared to death of him—

HELMER. Ah, I understand. It's the old memories haunting you.

NORA. What do you mean by that?

HELMER. Of course, you're thinking about your father.

NORA. Yes, all right. Just remember how those nasty gossips wrote in the papers about Papa and slandered him so cruelly. I think they'd have had him dismissed if the department hadn't sent you up to investigate, and if you hadn't been so kind and open-minded toward him.

HELMER. My dear Nora, there's a notable difference between your father and me. Your father's official career was hardly above reproach. But mine is; and I hope it'll stay that way as long as I hold my position.

NORA. Oh, who can ever tell what vicious minds can invent? We could be so snug and happy now in our quiet, carefree home—you and I and the children, Torvald! That's why I'm pleading with you so—

HELMER. And just by pleading for him you make it impossible for me to keep him on. It's already known at the bank that I'm firing Krogstad. What if it's rumored around now that the new bank manager was vetoed by his wife—

NORA. Yes, what then—?

HELMER. Oh yes—as long as our little bundle of stubbornness gets her way—! I should go and make myself ridiculous in front of the whole office—give people the idea I can be swayed by all kinds of outside pressure. Oh, you can bet I'd feel the effects of that soon enough! Besides—there's something that rules Krogstad right out at the bank as long as I'm the manager.

NORA. What's that?

HELMER. His moral failings I could maybe overlook if I had to—

NORA. Yes, Torvald, why not?

HELMER. And I hear he's quite efficient on the job. But he was a crony of mine back in my teens—one of those rash friendships that crop up again and again to embarrass you later in life. Well, I might as well say it

straight out: we're on a first-name basis. And that tactless fool makes no effort at all to hide it in front of others. Quite the contrary—he thinks that entitles him to take a familiar air around me, and so every other second he comes booming out with his "Yes, Torvald!" and "Sure thing, Torvald!" I tell you, it's been excruciating for me. He's out to make my place in the bank unbearable.

NORA. Torvald, you can't be serious about all this.

HELMER. Oh no? Why not?

NORA. Because these are such petty considerations.

HELMER. What are you saying? Petty? You think I'm petty!

NORA. No, just the opposite, Torvald dear. That's exactly why—

HELMER. Never mind. You call my motives petty; then I might as well be just that. Petty! All right! We'll put a stop to this for good. [*Goes to the hall door and calls.*] Helene!

NORA. What do you want?

HELMER [*searching among his papers*]. A decision. [*The* MAID *comes in.*] Look here; take this letter; go out with it at once. Get hold of a messenger and have him deliver it. Quick now. It's already addressed. Wait, here's some money.

MAID. Yes, sir. [*She leaves with the letter.*]

HELMER [*straightening his papers*]. There, now, little Miss Willful.

NORA [*breathlessly*]. Torvald, what was that letter?

HELMER. Krogstad's notice.

NORA. Call it back, Torvald! There's still time. Oh, Torvald, call it back! Do it for my sake—for your sake, for the children's sake! Do you hear, Torvald; do it? You don't know how this can harm us.

HELMER. Too late.

NORA. Yes, too late.

HELMER. Nora dear, I can forgive you this panic, even though basically you're insulting me. Yes, you are! Or isn't it an insult to think that *I* should be afraid of a courtroom hack's revenge? But I forgive you anyway, because this shows so beautifully how much you love me. [*Takes her in his arms.*] This is the way it should be, my darling Nora. Whatever comes, you'll see: when it really counts, I have strength and courage enough as a man to take on the whole weight myself.

NORA [*terrified*]. What do you mean by that?

HELMER. The whole weight, I said.

NORA [*resolutely*]. No, never in all the world.

HELMER. Good. So we'll share it, Nora, as man and wife. That's as it should be. [*Fondling her.*] Are you happy now? There, there, there—not these frightened dove's eyes. It's nothing at all but empty fantasies— Now you should run through your tarantella and practice your tambourine. I'll go to the inner office and shut both doors, so I won't hear a thing; you can make all the noise you like. [*Turning in the doorway.*] And when Rank comes, just tell him where he can find me. [*He nods to her and goes with his papers into the study, closing the door.*]

NORA [*standing as though rooted, dazed with fright, in a whisper*]. He really could do it. He will do it. He'll do it in spite of everything. No, not that, never, never! Anything but that! Escape! A way out— [*The doorbell rings.*] Dr. Rank! Anything but that! *Anything,* whatever it is! [*Her hands*

pass over her face, smoothing it; she pulls herself together, goes over and opens the hall door. DR. RANK *stands outside, hanging his fur coat up. During the following scene, it begins getting dark.*]

NORA. Hello, Dr. Rank. I recognized your ring. But you mustn't go in to Torvald yet; I believe he's working.

RANK. And you?

NORA. For you, I always have an hour to spare—you know that. [*He has entered, and she shuts the door after him.*]

RANK. Many thanks. I'll make use of these hours while I can.

NORA. What do you mean by that? While you can?

RANK. Does that disturb you?

NORA. Well, it's such an odd phrase. Is anything going to happen?

RANK. What's going to happen is what I've been expecting so long—but I honestly didn't think it would come so soon.

NORA [*gripping his arm*]. What is it you've found out? Dr. Rank, you have to tell me!

RANK [*sitting by the stove*]. It's all over with me. There's nothing to be done about it.

NORA [*breathing easier*]. Is it you—then—?

RANK. Who else? There's no point in lying to one's self. I'm the most miserable of all my patients, Mrs. Helmer. These past few days I've been auditing my internal accounts. Bankrupt! Within a month I'll probably be laid out and rotting in the churchyard.

NORA. Oh, what a horrible thing to say.

RANK. The thing itself is horrible. But the worst of it is all the other horror before it's over. There's only one final examination left; when I'm finished with that, I'll know about when my disintegration will begin. There's something I want to say. Helmer with his sensitivity has such a sharp distaste for anything ugly. I don't want him near my sickroom.

NORA. Oh, but Dr. Rank—

RANK. I won't have him in there. Under no condition. I'll lock my door to him—As soon as I'm completely sure of the worst, I'll send you my calling card marked with a black cross, and you'll know then the wreck has started to come apart.

NORA. No, today you're completely unreasonable. And I wanted you so much to be in a really good humor.

RANK. With death up my sleeve? And then to suffer this way for somebody else's sins. Is there any justice in that? And in every single family, in some way or another, this inevitable retribution of nature goes on—

NORA [*her hands pressed over her ears*]. Oh, stuff! Cheer up! Please—be gay!

RANK. Yes, I'd just as soon laugh at it all. My poor, innocent spine, serving time for my father's gay army days.

NORA [*by the table, left*]. He was so infatuated with asparagus tips and *pâté de foie gras,* wasn't that it?

RANK. Yes—and with truffles.

NORA. Truffles, yes. And then with oysters, I suppose?

RANK. Yes, tons of oysters, naturally.

NORA. And then the port and champagne to go with it. It's so sad that all these delectable things have to strike at our bones.

RANK. Especially when they strike at the unhappy bones that never shared in the fun.

NORA. Ah, that's the saddest of all.

RANK [*looks searchingly at her*]. Hm.

NORA [*after a moment*]. Why did you smile?

RANK. No, it was you who laughed.

NORA. No, it was you who smiled, Dr. Rank!

RANK [*getting up*]. You're even a bigger tease than I'd thought.

NORA. I'm full of wild ideas today.

RANK. That's obvious.

NORA [*putting both hands on his shoulders*]. Dear, dear Dr. Rank, you'll never die for Torvald and me.

RANK. Oh, that loss you'll easily get over. Those who go away are soon forgotten.

NORA [*looks fearfully at him*]. You believe that?

RANK. One makes new connections, and then—

NORA. Who makes new connections?

RANK. Both you and Torvald will when I'm gone. I'd say you're well under way already. What was that Mrs. Linde doing here last evening?

NORA. Oh, come—you can't be jealous of poor Kristine?

RANK. Oh yes, I am. She'll be my successor here in the house. When I'm down under, that woman will probably—

NORA. Shh! Not so loud. She's right in there.

RANK. Today as well. So you see.

NORA. Only to sew on my dress. Good gracious, how unreasonable you are. [*Sitting on the sofa.*] Be nice now, Dr. Rank. Tomorrow you'll see how beautifully I'll dance; and you can imagine then that I'm dancing only for you—yes, and of course for Torvald, too—that's understood. [*Takes various items out of the carton.*] Dr. Rank, sit over here and I'll show you something.

RANK [*sitting*]. What's that?

NORA. Look here. Look.

RANK. Silk stockings.

NORA. Flesh-colored. Aren't they lovely? Now it's so dark here, but tomorrow— No, no, no, just look at the feet. Oh well, you might as well look at the rest.

RANK. Hm—

NORA. Why do you look so critical? Don't you believe they'll fit?

RANK. I've never had any chance to form an opinion on that.

NORA [*glancing at him a moment*]. Shame on you. [*Hits him lightly on the ear with the stockings.*] That's for you. [*Puts them away again.*]

RANK. And what other splendors am I going to see now?

NORA. Not the least bit more, because you've been naughty. [*She hums a little and rummages among her things.*]

RANK [*after a short silence*]. When I sit here together with you like this, completely easy and open, then I don't know—I simply can't imagine—whatever would have become of me if I'd never come into this house.

NORA [*smiling*]. Yes, I really think you feel completely at ease with us.

RANK [*more quietly, staring straight ahead*]. And then to have to go away from
 it all—

NORA. Nonsense, you're not going away.

RANK [*his voice unchanged*]. —and not even be able to leave some poor show
 of gratitude behind, scarcely a fleeting regret—no more than a vacant
 place that anyone can fill.

NORA. And if I asked you now for—? No—

RANK. For what?

NORA. For a great proof of your friendship—

RANK. Yes, yes?

NORA. No, I mean—for an exceptionally big favor—

RANK. Would you really, for once, make me so happy?

NORA. Oh, you haven't the vaguest idea what it is.

RANK. All right, then tell me.

NORA. No, but I can't, Dr. Rank—it's all out of reason. It's advice and help,
 too—and a favor—

RANK. So much the better. I can't fathom what you're hinting at. Just speak
 out. Don't you trust me?

NORA. Of course. More than anyone else. You're my best and truest friend,
 I'm sure. That's why I want to talk to you. All right, then, Dr. Rank:
 there's something you can help me prevent. You know how deeply, how
 inexpressibly dearly Torvald loves me; he'd never hesitate a second to
 give up his life for me.

RANK [*leaning close to her*]. Nora—do you think he's the only one—

NORA [*with a slight start*]. Who—?

RANK. Who'd gladly give up his life for you.

NORA [*heavily*]. I see.

RANK. I swore to myself you should know this before I'm gone. I'll never
 find a better chance. Yes, Nora, now you know. And also you know now
 that you can trust me beyond anyone else.

NORA [*rising, natural and calm*]. Let me by.

RANK [*making room for her, but still sitting*]. Nora—

NORA [*in the hall doorway*]. Helene, bring the lamp in. [*Goes over to the stove.*]
 Ah, dear Dr. Rank, that was really mean of you.

RANK [*getting up*]. That I've loved you just as deeply as somebody else? Was
 that mean?

NORA. No, but that you came out and told me. That was quite unneces-
 sary—

RANK. What do you mean? Have you known—?

> [*The* MAID *comes in with the lamp, sets it
> on the table, and goes out again.*]

RANK. Nora—Mrs. Helmer—I'm asking you: have you known about it?

NORA. Oh, how can I tell what I know or don't know? Really, I don't know
 what to say— Why did you have to be so clumsy, Dr. Rank! Everything
 was so good.

RANK. Well, in any case, you now have the knowledge that my body and
 soul are at your command. So won't you speak out?

NORA [*looking at him*]. After that?

RANK. Please, just let me know what it is.

NORA. You can't know anything now.

RANK. I have to. You mustn't punish me like this. Give me the chance to do whatever is humanly possible for you.

NORA. Now there's nothing you can do for me. Besides, actually, I don't need any help. You'll see—it's only my fantasies. That's what it is. Of course! [*Sits in the rocker, looks at him, and smiles.*] What a nice one you are, Dr. Rank. Aren't you a little bit ashamed, now that the lamp is here?

RANK. No, not exactly. But perhaps I'd better go—for good?

NORA. No, you certainly can't do that. You must come here just as you always have. You know Torvald can't do without you.

RANK. Yes, but *you*?

NORA. You know how much I enjoy it when you're here.

RANK. That's precisely what threw me off. You're a mystery to me. So many times I've felt you'd almost rather be with me than with Helmer.

NORA. Yes—you see, there are some people that one loves most and other people that one would almost prefer being with.

RANK. Yes, there's something to that.

NORA. When I was back home, of course I loved Papa most. But I always thought it was so much fun when I could sneak down to the maids' quarters, because they never tried to improve me, and it was always so amusing, the way they talked to each other.

RANK. Aha, so it's *their* place that I've filled.

NORA [*jumping up and going to him*]. Oh, dear, sweet Dr. Rank, that's not what I meant at all. But you can understand that with Torvald it's just the same as with Papa—

[*The* MAID *enters from the hall.*]

MAID. Ma'am—please! [*She whispers to* NORA *and hands her a calling card.*]

NORA [*glancing at the card*]. Ah! [*Slips it into her pocket.*]

RANK. Anything wrong?

NORA. No, no, not at all. It's only some—it's my new dress—

RANK. Really? But—there's your dress.

NORA. Oh, that. But this is another one—I ordered it—Torvald mustn't know—

RANK. Ah, now we have the big secret.

NORA. That's right. Just go in with him—he's back in the inner study. Keep him there as long as—

RANK. Don't worry. He won't get away. [*Goes into the study.*]

NORA [*to the* MAID]. And he's standing waiting in the kitchen?

MAID. Yes, he came up by the back stairs.

NORA. But didn't you tell him somebody was here?

MAID. Yes, but that didn't do any good.

NORA. He won't leave?

MAID. No, he won't go till he's talked with you, ma'am.

NORA. Let him come in, then—but quietly. Helene, don't breathe a word about this. It's a surprise for my husband.

MAID. Yes, yes, I understand—[*Goes out.*]

NORA. This horror—it's going to happen. No, no, no, it can't happen, it mustn't. [*She goes and bolts* HELMER's *door. The* MAID *opens the hall door for* KROGSTAD *and shuts it behind him. He is dressed for travel in a fur coat, boots, and a fur cap.*]

NORA [*going toward him*]. Talk softly. My husband's home.

KROGSTAD. Well, good for him.

NORA. What do you want?

KROGSTAD. Some information.

NORA. Hurry up, then. What is it?

KROGSTAD. You know, of course, that I got my notice.

NORA. I couldn't prevent it, Mr. Krogstad. I fought for you to the bitter end, but nothing worked.

KROGSTAD. Does your husband's love for you run so thin? He knows everything I can expose you to, and all the same he dares to—

NORA. How can you imagine he knows anything about this?

KROGSTAD. Ah, no—I can't imagine it either, now. It's not at all like my fine Torvald Helmer to have so much guts—

NORA. Mr. Krogstad, I demand respect for my husband!

KROGSTAD. Why, of course—all due respect. But since the lady's keeping it so carefully hidden, may I presume to ask if you're also a bit better informed than yesterday about what you've actually done?

NORA. More than you ever could teach me.

KROGSTAD. Yes, I *am* such an awful lawyer.

NORA. What is it you want from me?

KROGSTAD. Just a glimpse of how you are, Mrs. Helmer. I've been thinking about you all day long. A cashier, a night-court scribbler, a—well, a type like me also has a little of what they call a heart, you know.

NORA. Then show it. Think of my children.

KROGSTAD. Did you or your husband ever think of mine? But never mind. I simply wanted to tell you that you don't need to take this thing too seriously. For the present, I'm not proceeding with any action.

NORA. Oh no, really! Well—I knew that.

KROGSTAD. Everything can be settled in a friendly spirit. It doesn't have to get around town at all; it can stay just among us three.

NORA. My husband must never know anything of this.

KROGSTAD. How can you manage that? Perhaps you can pay me the balance?

NORA. No, not right now.

KROGSTAD. Or you know some way of raising the money in a day or two?

NORA. No way that I'm willing to use.

KROGSTAD. Well, it wouldn't have done you any good, anyway. If you stood in front of me with a fistful of bills, you still couldn't buy your signature back.

NORA. Then tell me what you're going to do with it.

KROGSTAD. I'll just hold onto it—keep it on file. There's no outsider who'll even get wind of it. So if you've been thinking of taking some desperate step—

NORA. I have.

KROGSTAD. Been thinking of running away from home—

NORA. I have!

KROGSTAD. Or even of something worse—

NORA. How could you guess that?

KROGSTAD. You can drop those thoughts.

NORA. How could you guess I was thinking of *that*?

KROGSTAD. Most of us think about *that* at first. I thought about it too, but I
 discovered I hadn't the courage—
NORA [*lifelessly*]. I don't either.
KROGSTAD [*relieved*]. That's true, you haven't the courage? You too?
NORA. I don't have it—I don't have it.
KROGSTAD. It would be terribly stupid, anyway. After that first storm at
 home blows out, why, then— I have here in my pocket a letter for your
 husband—
NORA. Telling everything?
KROGSTAD. As charitably as possible.
NORA [*quickly*]. He mustn't ever get that letter. Tear it up. I'll find some
 way to get money.
KROGSTAD. Beg pardon, Mrs. Helmer, but I think I just told you—
NORA. Oh, I don't mean the money I owe you. Let me know how much you
 want from my husband, and I'll manage it.
KROGSTAD. I don't want any money from your husband.
NORA. What do you want, then?
KROGSTAD. I'll tell you what. I want to recoup, Mrs. Helmer; I want to get
 on in the world—and there's where your husband can help me. For a
 year and a half I've kept myself clean of anything disreputable—all that
 time struggling with the worst conditions; but I was satisfied, working
 my way up step by step. Now I've been written right off, and I'm just not
 in the mood to come crawling back. I tell you, I want to move on. I want
 to get back in the bank—in a better position. Your husband can set up a
 job for me—
NORA. He'll never do that!
KROGSTAD. He'll do it. I know him. He won't dare breathe a word of pro-
 test. And once I'm in there together with him, you just wait and see!
 Inside of a year, I'll be the manager's right-hand man. It'll be Nils Krog-
 stad, not Torvald Helmer, who runs the bank.
NORA. You'll never see the day!
KROGSTAD. Maybe you think you can—
NORA. I have the courage now—for *that*.
KROGSTAD. Oh, you don't scare me. A smart, spoiled lady like you—
NORA. You'll see; you'll see!
KROGSTAD. Under the ice, maybe? Down in the freezing, coal-black water?
 There, till you float up in the spring, ugly, unrecognizable, with your
 hair falling out—
NORA. You don't frighten me.
KROGSTAD. Nor do you frighten me. One doesn't do these things, Mrs.
 Helmer. Besides, what good would it be? I'd still have him safe in my
 pocket.
NORA. Afterwards? When I'm no longer—?
KROGSTAD. Are you forgetting that *I'll* be in control then over your final
 reputation? [NORA *stands speechless, staring at him.*] Good; now I've
 warned you. Don't do anything stupid. When Helmer's read my letter,
 I'll be waiting for his reply. And bear in mind that it's your husband
 himself who's forced me back to my old ways. I'll never forgive him for
 that. Good-bye, Mrs. Helmer. [*He goes out through the hall.*]

NORA [*goes to the hall door, opens it a crack, and listens*]. He's gone. Didn't leave the letter. Oh no, no, that's impossible too! [*Opening the door more and more.*] What's that? He's standing outside—not going downstairs. He's thinking it over? Maybe he'll—? [*A letter falls in the mailbox; then* KROGSTAD's *footsteps are heard, dying away down a flight of stairs.* NORA *gives a muffled cry and runs over toward the sofa table. A short pause.*] In the mailbox. [*Slips warily over to the hall door.*] It's lying there. Torvald, Torvald—now we're lost!

MRS. LINDE [*entering with the costume from the room, left*]. There now, I can't see anything else to mend. Perhaps you'd like to try—

NORA [*in a hoarse whisper*]. Kristine, come here.

MRS. LINDE [*tossing the dress on the sofa*]. What's wrong? You look upset.

NORA. Come here. See that letter? *There!* Look—through the glass in the mailbox.

MRS. LINDE. Yes, yes, I see it.

NORA. That letter's from Krogstad—

MRS. LINDE. Nora—it's Krogstad who loaned you the money!

NORA. Yes, and now Torvald will find out everything.

MRS. LINDE. Believe me, Nora, it's best for both of you.

NORA. There's more you don't know. I forged a name.

MRS. LINDE. But for heaven's sake—?

NORA. I only want to tell you that, Kristine, so that you can be my witness.

MRS. LINDE. Witness? Why should I—?

NORA. If I should go out of my mind—it could easily happen—

MRS. LINDE. Nora!

NORA. Or anything else occurred—so I couldn't be present here—

MRS. LINDE. Nora, Nora, you aren't yourself at all!

NORA. And someone should try to take on the whole weight, all of the guilt, you follow me—

MRS. LINDE. Yes, of course, but why do you think—?

NORA. Then you're the witness that it isn't true, Kristine. I'm very much myself; my mind right now is perfectly clear; and I'm telling you: nobody else has known about this; I alone did everything. Remember that.

MRS. LINDE. I will. But I don't understand all this.

NORA. Oh, how could you ever understand it? It's the miracle now that's going to take place.

MRS. LINDE. The miracle?

NORA. Yes, the miracle. But it's so awful, Kristine. It mustn't take place, not for anything in the world.

MRS. LINDE. I'm going right over and talk with Krogstad.

NORA. Don't go near him; he'll do you some terrible harm!

MRS. LINDE. There was a time once when he'd gladly have done anything for me.

NORA. He?

MRS. LINDE. Where does he live?

NORA. Oh, how do I know? Yes. [*Searches in her pocket.*] Here's his card. But the letter, the letter—!

HELMER [*from the study, knocking on the door*]. Nora!

NORA [*with a cry of fear*]. Oh! What is it? What do you want?

HELMER. Now, now, don't be so frightened. We're not coming in. You locked the door—are you trying on the dress?

NORA. Yes, I'm trying it. I'll look just beautiful, Torvald.

MRS. LINDE [*who has read the card*]. He's living right around the corner.

NORA. Yes, but what's the use? We're lost. The letter's in the box.

MRS. LINDE. And your husband has the key?

NORA. Yes, always.

MRS. LINDE. Krogstad can ask for his letter back unread; he can find some excuse—

NORA. But it's just this time that Torvald usually—

MRS. LINDE. Stall him. Keep him in there. I'll be back as quick as I can. [*She hurries out through the hall entrance.*]

NORA [*goes to* HELMER'S *door, opens it, and peers in*]. Torvald!

HELMER [*from the inner study*]. Well—does one dare set foot in one's own living room at last? Come on, Rank, now we'll get a look— [*In the doorway.*] But what's this?

NORA. What, Torvald dear?

HELMER. Rank had me expecting some grand masquerade.

RANK [*in the doorway*]. That was my impression, but I must have been wrong.

NORA. No one can admire me in my splendor—not till tomorrow.

HELMER. But Nora dear, you look so exhausted. Have you practiced too hard?

NORA. No, I haven't practiced at all yet.

HELMER. You know, it's necessary—

NORA. Oh, it's absolutely necessary, Torvald. But I can't get anywhere without your help. I've forgotten the whole thing completely.

HELMER. Ah, we'll soon take care of that.

NORA. Yes, take care of me, Torvald, please! Promise me that? Oh, I'm so nervous. That big party— You must give up everything this evening for me. No business—don't even touch your pen. Yes? Dear Torvald, promise?

HELMER. It's a promise. Tonight I'm totally at your service—you little helpless thing. Hm—but first there's one thing I want to— [*Goes toward the hall door.*]

NORA. What are you looking for?

HELMER. Just to see if there's any mail.

NORA. No, no, don't do that, Torvald!

HELMER. Now what?

NORA. Torvald, please. There isn't any.

HELMER. Let me look, though. [*Starts out.* NORA, *at the piano, strikes the first notes of the tarantella.* HELMER, *at the door, stops.*] Aha!

NORA. I can't dance tomorrow if I don't practice with you.

HELMER [*going over to her*]. Nora dear, are you really so frightened?

NORA. Yes, so terribly frightened. Let me practice right now; there's still time before dinner. Oh, sit down and play for me, Torvald. Direct me. Teach me, the way you always have.

HELMER. Gladly, if it's what you want. [*Sits at the piano.*]

NORA [*snatches the tambourine up from the box, then a long varicolored shawl,*

which she throws around herself, whereupon she springs forward and cries out:]
Play for me now! Now I'll dance!

[HELMER *plays and* NORA *dances.* RANK *stands behind* HELMER *at the piano and looks on.*]

HELMER [*as he plays*]. Slower. Slow down.

NORA. Can't change it.

HELMER. Not so violent, Nora!

NORA. Has to be just like this.

HELMER [*stopping*]. No, no, that won't do at all.

NORA [*laughing and swinging her tambourine*]. Isn't that what I told you?

RANK. Let me play for her.

HELMER [*getting up*]. Yes, go on. I can teach her more easily then.

[RANK *sits at the piano and plays;* NORA *dances more and more wildly.* HELMER *has stationed himself by the stove and repeatedly gives her directions; she seems not to hear them; her hair loosens and falls over her shoulders; she does not notice, but goes on dancing.* MRS. LINDE *enters.*]

MRS. LINDE [*standing dumbfounded at the door*]. Ah—!

NORA [*still dancing*]. See what fun, Kristine!

HELMER. But Nora darling, you dance as if your life were at stake.

NORA. And it is.

HELMER. Rank, stop! This is pure madness. Stop it, I say!

[RANK *breaks off playing, and* NORA *halts abruptly.*]

HELMER [*going over to her*]. I never would have believed it. You've forgotten everything I taught you.

NORA [*throwing away the tambourine*]. You see for yourself.

HELMER. Well, there's certainly room for instruction here.

NORA. Yes, you see how important it is. You've got to teach me to the very last minute. Promise me that, Torvald?

HELMER. You can bet on it.

NORA. You mustn't, either today or tomorrow, think about anything else but me; you mustn't open any letters—or the mailbox—

HELMER. Ah, it's still the fear of that man—

NORA. Oh yes, yes, that too.

HELMER. Nora, it's written all over you—there's already a letter from him out there.

NORA. I don't know. I guess so. But you mustn't read such things now; there mustn't be anything ugly between us before it's all over.

RANK [*quietly to* HELMER]. You shouldn't deny her.

HELMER [*putting his arm around her*]. The child can have her way. But tomorrow night, after you've danced—

NORA. Then you'll be free.

MAID [*in the doorway, right*]. Ma'am, dinner is served.

NORA. We'll be wanting champagne, Helene.

MAID. Very good, ma'am. [*Goes out.*]

HELMER. So—a regular banquet, hm?

NORA. Yes, a banquet—champagne till daybreak! [*Calling out.*] And some macaroons, Helene. Heaps of them—just this once.

HELMER [*taking her hands*]. Now, now, now—no hysterics. Be my own little lark again.

NORA. Oh, I will soon enough. But go on in—and you, Dr. Rank. Kristine, help me put up my hair.

RANK [*whispering, as they go*]. There's nothing wrong—really wrong, is there?

HELMER. Oh, of course not. It's nothing more than this childish anxiety I was telling you about. [*They go out, right.*]

NORA. Well?

MRS. LINDE. Left town.

NORA. I could see by your face.

MRS. LINDE. He'll be home tomorrow evening. I wrote him a note.

NORA. You shouldn't have. Don't try to stop anything now. After all, it's a wonderful joy, this waiting here for the miracle.

MRS. LINDE. What is it you're waiting for?

NORA. Oh, you can't understand that. Go in to them; I'll be along in a moment.

> [MRS. LINDE *goes into the dining room.* NORA *stands a short while as if composing herself; then she looks at her watch.*]

NORA. Five. Seven hours to midnight. Twenty-four hours to the midnight after, and then the tarantella's done. Seven and twenty-four? Thirty-one hours to live.

HELMER [*in the doorway, right*]. What's become of the little lark?

NORA [*going toward him with open arms*]. Here's your lark!

ACT THREE

Same scene. The table, with chairs around it, has been moved to the center of the room. A lamp on the table is lit. The hall door stands open. Dance music drifts down from the floor above. MRS. LINDE sits at the table, absently paging through a book, trying to read, but apparently unable to focus her thoughts. Once or twice she pauses, tensely listening for a sound at the outer entrance.

MRS. LINDE [*glancing at her watch*]. Not yet—and there's hardly any time left. If only he's not—[*Listening again.*] Ah, there he is. [*She goes out in the hall and cautiously opens the outer door. Quiet footsteps are heard on the stairs. She whispers:*] Come in. Nobody's here.

KROGSTAD [*in the doorway*]. I found a note from you at home. What's back of all this?

MRS. LINDE. I just *had* to talk to you.

KROGSTAD. Oh? And it just *had* to be here in this house?

MRS. LINDE. At my place it was impossible; my room hasn't a private entrance. Come in; we're all alone. The maid's asleep, and the Helmers are at the dance upstairs.

KROGSTAD [*entering the room*]. Well, well, the Helmers are dancing tonight? Really?

MRS. LINDE. Yes, why not?

KROGSTAD. How true—why not?

MRS. LINDE. All right, Krogstad, let's talk.

KROGSTAD. Do we two have anything more to talk about?

MRS. LINDE. We have a great deal to talk about.

KROGSTAD. I wouldn't have thought so.

MRS. LINDE. No, because you've never understood me, really.

KROGSTAD. Was there anything more to understand—except what's all too common in life? A calculating woman throws over a man the moment a better catch comes by.

MRS. LINDE. You think I'm so thoroughly calculating? You think I broke it off lightly?

KROGSTAD. Didn't you?

MRS. LINDE. Nils—is that what you really thought?

KROGSTAD. If you cared, then why did you write me the way you did?

MRS. LINDE. What else could I do? If I had to break off with you, then it was my job as well to root out everything you felt for me.

KROGSTAD [*wringing his hands*]. So that was it. And this—all this, simply for money!

MRS. LINDE. Don't forget I had a helpless mother and two small brothers. We couldn't wait for you, Nils; you had such a long road ahead of you then.

KROGSTAD. That may be; but you still hadn't the right to abandon me for somebody else's sake.

MRS. LINDE. Yes—I don't know. So many, many times I've asked myself if I did have that right.

KROGSTAD [*more softly*]. When I lost you, it was as if all the solid ground dissolved from under my feet. Look at me; I'm a half-drowned man now, hanging onto a wreck.

MRS. LINDE. Help may be near.

KROGSTAD. It was near—but then you came and blocked it off.

MRS. LINDE. Without my knowing it, Nils. Today for the first time I learned that it's you I'm replacing at the bank.

KROGSTAD. All right—I believe you. But now that you know, will you step aside?

MRS. LINDE. No, because that wouldn't benefit you in the slightest.

KROGSTAD. Not "benefit" me, hm! I'd step aside anyway.

MRS. LINDE. I've learned to be realistic. Life and hard, bitter necessity have taught me that.

KROGSTAD. And life's taught me never to trust fine phrases.

MRS. LINDE. Then life's taught you a very sound thing. But you do have to trust in actions, don't you?

KROGSTAD. What does that mean?

MRS. LINDE. You said you were hanging on like a half-drowned man to a wreck.

KROGSTAD. I've good reason to say that.

MRS. LINDE. I'm also like a half-drowned woman on a wreck. No one to suffer with; no one to care for.

KROGSTAD. You made your choice.

MRS. LINDE. There wasn't any choice then.

KROGSTAD. So—what of it?

MRS. LINDE. Nils, if only we two shipwrecked people could reach across to each other.

KROGSTAD. What are you saying?

MRS. LINDE. Two on one wreck are at least better off than each on his own.

KROGSTAD. Kristine!

MRS. LINDE. Why do you think I came into town?

KROGSTAD. Did you really have some thought of me?

MRS. LINDE. I have to work to go on living. All my born days, as long as I can remember, I've worked, and it's been my best and my only joy. But now I'm completely alone in the world; it frightens me to be so empty and lost. To work for yourself—there's no joy in that. Nils, give me something—someone to work for.

KROGSTAD. I don't believe all this. It's just some hysterical feminine urge to go out and make a noble sacrifice.

MRS. LINDE. Have you ever found me to be hysterical?

KROGSTAD. Can you honestly mean this? Tell me—do you know everything about my past?

MRS. LINDE. Yes.

KROGSTAD. And you know what they think I'm worth around here.

MRS. LINDE. From what you were saying before, it would seem that with me you could have been another person.

KROGSTAD. I'm positive of that.

MRS. LINDE. Couldn't it happen still?

KROGSTAD. Kristine—you're saying this in all seriousness? Yes, you are! I can see it in you. And do you really have the courage, then—?

MRS. LINDE. I need to have someone to care for; and your children need a mother. We both need each other. Nils, I have faith that you're good at heart—I'll risk everything together with you.

KROGSTAD [*gripping her hands*]. Kristine, thank you, thank you— Now I know I can win back a place in their eyes. Yes—but I forgot—

MRS. LINDE [*listening*]. Shh! The tarantella. Go now! Go on!

KROGSTAD. Why? What is it?

MRS. LINDE. Hear the dance up there? When that's over, they'll be coming down.

KROGSTAD. Oh, then I'll go. But—it's all pointless. Of course, you don't know the move I made against the Helmers.

MRS. LINDE. Yes, Nils, I know.

KROGSTAD. And all the same, you have the courage to—?

MRS. LINDE. I know how far despair can drive a man like you.

KROGSTAD. Oh, if I only could take it all back.

MRS. LINDE. You easily could—your letter's still lying in the mailbox.

KROGSTAD. Are you sure of that?

MRS. LINDE. Positive. But—

KROGSTAD [*looks at her searchingly*]. Is that the meaning of it, then? You'll save your friend at any price. Tell me straight out. Is that it?

MRS. LINDE. Nils—anyone who's sold herself for somebody else once isn't going to do it again.

KROGSTAD. I'll demand my letter back.

MRS. LINDE. No, no.

KROGSTAD. Yes, of course. I'll stay here till Helmer comes down; I'll tell him to give me my letter again—that it only involves my dismissal—that he shouldn't read it—

MRS. LINDE. No, Nils, don't call the letter back.

KROGSTAD. But wasn't that exactly why you wrote me to come here?

MRS. LINDE. Yes, in that first panic. But it's been a whole day and night since then, and in that time I've seen such incredible things in this house. Helmer's got to learn everything; this dreadful secret has to be aired; those two have to come to a full understanding; all these lies and evasions can't go on.

KROGSTAD. Well, then, if you want to chance it. But at least there's one thing I can do, and do right away—

MRS. LINDE [*listening*]. Go now, go quick! The dance is over. We're not safe another second.

KROGSTAD. I'll wait for you downstairs.

MRS. LINDE. Yes, please do; take me home.

KROGSTAD. I can't believe it; I've never been so happy. [*He leaves by way of the outer door; the door between the room and the hall stays open.*]

MRS. LINDE [*straightening up a bit and getting together her street clothes*]. How different now! How different! Someone to work for, to live for—a home to build. Well, it is worth the try! Oh, if they'd only come! [*Listening.*] Ah, there they are. Bundle up. [*She picks up her hat and coat.* NORA*'s and* HELMER*'s voices can be heard outside; a key turns in the lock, and* HELMER *brings* NORA *into the hall almost by force. She is wearing the Italian costume with a large black shawl about her; he has on evening dress, with a black domino[3] open over it.*]

NORA [*struggling in the doorway*]. No, no, no, not inside! I'm going up again. I don't want to leave so soon.

HELMER. But Nora dear—

NORA. Oh, I beg you, please, Torvald. From the bottom of my heart, *please*—only an hour more!

HELMER. Not a single minute, Nora darling. You know our agreement. Come on, in we go; you'll catch cold out here. [*In spite of her resistance, he gently draws her into the room.*]

MRS. LINDE. Good evening.

NORA. Kristine!

HELMER. Why, Mrs. Linde—are you here so late?

MRS. LINDE. Yes, I'm sorry, but I did want to see Nora in costume.

NORA. Have you been sitting here, waiting for me?

MRS. LINDE. Yes. I didn't come early enough; you were all upstairs; and then I thought I really couldn't leave without seeing you.

HELMER [*removing* NORA*'s shawl*]. Yes, take a good look. She's worth looking at, I can tell you that, Mrs. Linde. Isn't she lovely?

MRS. LINDE. Yes, I should say—

HELMER. A dream of loveliness, isn't she? That's what everyone thought at the party, too. But she's horribly stubborn—this sweet little thing. What's to be done with her? Can you imagine, I almost had to use force to pry her away.

[3] A large, loose, hooded cloak, designed to be worn with a mask for masquerades.

NORA. Oh, Torvald, you're going to regret you didn't indulge me, even for just a half hour more.

HELMER. There, you see. She danced her tarantella and got a tumultuous hand—which was well earned, although the performance may have been a bit too naturalistic—I mean it rather overstepped the proprieties of art. But never mind—what's important is, she made a success, an overwhelming success. You think I could let her stay on after that and spoil the effect? Oh no; I took my lovely little Capri girl—my capricious little Capri girl, I should say—took her under my arm; one quick tour of the ballroom, a curtsy to every side, and then—as they say in novels—the beautiful vision disappeared. An exit should always be effective, Mrs. Linde, but that's what I can't get Nora to grasp. Phew, it's hot in here. [*Flings the domino on a chair and opens the door to his room.*] Why's it dark in here? Oh yes, of course. Excuse me. [*He goes in and lights a couple of candles.*]

NORA [*in a sharp, breathless whisper*]. So?

MRS. LINDE [*quietly*]. I talked with him.

NORA. And—?

MRS. LINDE. Nora—you must tell your husband everything.

NORA [*dully*]. I knew it.

MRS. LINDE. You've got nothing to fear from Krogstad, but you have to speak out.

NORA. I won't tell.

MRS. LINDE. Then the letter will.

NORA. Thanks, Kristine. I know now what's to be done. Shh!

HELMER [*reentering*]. Well, then, Mrs. Linde—have you admired her?

MRS. LINDE. Yes, and now I'll say good night.

HELMER. Oh, come, so soon? Is this yours, this knitting?

MRS. LINDE. Yes, thanks. I nearly forgot it.

HELMER. Do you knit, then?

MRS. LINDE. Oh yes.

HELMER. You know what? You should embroider instead.

MRS. LINDE. Really? Why?

HELMER. Yes, because it's a lot prettier. See here, one holds the embroidery so, in the left hand, and then one guides the needle with the right— so—in an easy, sweeping curve—right?

MRS. LINDE. Yes, I guess that's—

HELMER. But, on the other hand, knitting—it can never be anything but ugly. Look, see here, the arms tucked in, the knitting needles going up and down—there's something Chinese about it. Ah, that was really a glorious champagne they served.

MRS. LINDE. Yes, good night, Nora, and don't be stubborn anymore.

HELMER. Well put, Mrs. Linde!

MRS. LINDE. Good night, Mr. Helmer.

HELMER [*accompanying her to the door*]. Good night, good night. I hope you get home all right. I'd be very happy to—but you don't have far to go. Good night, good night. [*She leaves. He shuts the door after her and returns.*] There, now, at last we got her out the door. She's a deadly bore, that creature.

NORA. Aren't you pretty tired, Torvald?

HELMER. No, not a bit.

NORA. You're not sleepy?

HELMER. Not at all. On the contrary, I'm feeling quite exhilarated. But you? Yes, you really look tired and sleepy.

NORA. Yes, I'm very tired. Soon now I'll sleep.

HELMER. See! You see! I was right all along that we shouldn't stay longer.

NORA. Whatever you do is always right.

HELMER [*kissing her brow*]. Now my little lark talks sense. Say, did you notice what a time Rank was having tonight?

NORA. Oh, was he? I didn't get to speak with him.

HELMER. I scarcely did either, but it's a long time since I've seen him in such high spirits. [*Gazes at her a moment, then comes nearer her.*] Hm—it's marvelous, though, to be back home again—to be completely alone with you. Oh, you bewitchingly lovely young woman!

NORA. Torvald, don't look at me like that!

HELMER. Can't I look at my richest treasure? At all that beauty that's mine, mine alone—completely and utterly.

NORA [*moving around to the other side of the table*]. You mustn't talk to me that way tonight.

HELMER [*following her*]. The tarantella is still in your blood, I can see—and it makes you even more enticing. Listen. The guests are beginning to go. [*Dropping his voice.*] Nora—it'll soon be quiet through this whole house.

NORA. Yes, I hope so.

HELMER. You do, don't you, my love? Do you realize—when I'm out at a party like this with you—do you know why I talk to you so little, and keep such a distance away; just send you a stolen look now and then— you know why I do it? It's because I'm imagining then that you're my secret darling, my secret young bride-to-be, and that no one suspects there's anything between us.

NORA. Yes, yes; oh, yes, I know you're always thinking of me.

HELMER. And then when we leave and I place the shawl over those fine young rounded shoulders—over that wonderful curving neck—then I pretend that you're my young bride, that we're just coming from the wedding, that for the first time I'm bringing you into my house—that for the first time I'm alone with you—completely alone with you, your trembling young beauty! All this evening I've longed for nothing but you. When I saw you turn and sway in the tarantella—my blood was pounding till I couldn't stand it—that's why I brought you down here so early—

NORA. Go away, Torvald! Leave me alone. I don't want all this.

HELMER. What do you mean? Nora, you're teasing me. You will, won't you? Aren't I your husband—?

[*A knock at the outside door.*]

NORA [*startled*]. What's that?

HELMER [*going toward the hall*]. Who is it?

RANK [*outside*]. It's me. May I come in a moment?

HELMER [*with quiet irritation*]. Oh, what does he want now? [*Aloud.*] Hold on. [*Goes and opens the door.*] Oh, how nice that you didn't just pass us by!

RANK. I thought I heard your voice, and then I wanted so badly to have a

look in. [*Lightly glancing about.*] Ah, me, these old familiar haunts. You
have it snug and cozy in here, you two.

HELMER. You seemed to be having it pretty cozy upstairs, too.

RANK. Absolutely. Why shouldn't I? Why not take in everything in life? As
much as you can, anyway, and as long as you can. The wine was su-
perb—

HELMER. The champagne especially.

RANK. You noticed that too? It's amazing how much I could guzzle down.

NORA. Torvald also drank a lot of champagne this evening.

RANK. Oh?

NORA. Yes, and that always makes him so entertaining.

RANK. Well, why shouldn't one have a pleasant evening after a well-spent
day?

HELMER. Well spent? I'm afraid I can't claim that.

RANK [*slapping him on the back*]. But I can, you see!

NORA. Dr. Rank, you must have done some scientific research today.

RANK. Quite so.

HELMER. Come now—little Nora talking about scientific research!

NORA. And can I congratulate you on the results?

RANK. Indeed you may.

NORA. Then they were good?

RANK. The best possible for both doctor and patient—certainty.

NORA [*quickly and searchingly*]. Certainty?

RANK. Complete certainty. So don't I owe myself a gay evening afterwards?

NORA. Yes, you're right, Dr. Rank.

HELMER. I'm with you—just so long as you don't have to suffer for it in the
morning.

RANK. Well, one never gets something for nothing in life.

NORA. Dr. Rank—are you very fond of masquerade parties?

RANK. Yes, if there's a good array of odd disguises—

NORA. Tell me, what should we two go as at the next masquerade?

HELMER. You little featherhead—already thinking of the next!

RANK. We two? I'll tell you what: you must go as Charmed Life—

HELMER. Yes, but find a costume for *that!*

RANK. Your wife can appear just as she looks every day.

HELMER. That was nicely put. But don't you know what you're going to be?

RANK. Yes, Helmer, I've made up my mind.

HELMER. Well?

RANK. At the next masquerade I'm going to be invisible.

HELMER. That's a funny idea.

RANK. They say there's a hat—black, huge—have you never heard of the
hat that makes you invisible? You put it on, and then no one on earth
can see you.

HELMER [*suppressing a smile*]. Ah, of course.

RANK. But I'm quite forgetting what I came for. Helmer, give me a cigar,
one of the dark Havanas.

HELMER. With the greatest pleasure. [*Holds out his case.*]

RANK. Thanks. [*Takes one and cuts off the tip.*]

NORA [*striking a match*]. Let me give you a light.

RANK. Thank you. [*She holds the match for him; he lights the cigar.*] And now good-bye.

HELMER. Good-bye, good-bye, old friend.

NORA. Sleep well, Doctor.

RANK. Thanks for that wish.

NORA. Wish me the same.

RANK. You? All right, if you like— Sleep well. And thanks for the light. [*He nods to them both and leaves.*]

HELMER [*his voice subdued*]. He's been drinking heavily.

NORA [*absently*]. Could be. [HELMER *takes his keys from his pocket and goes out in the hall.*] Torvald—what are you after?

HELMER. Got to empty the mailbox; it's nearly full. There won't be room for the morning papers.

NORA. Are you working tonight?

HELMER. You know I'm not. Why—what's this? Someone's been at the lock.

NORA. At the lock—?

HELMER. Yes, I'm positive. What do you suppose—? I can't imagine one of the maids—? Here's a broken hairpin. Nora, it's yours—

NORA [*quickly*]. Then it must be the children—

HELMER. You'd better break them of that. Hm, hm—well, opened it after all. [*Takes the contents out and calls into the kitchen.*] Helene! Helene, would you put out the lamp in the hall. [*He returns to the room, shutting the hall door, then displays the handful of mail.*] Look how it's piled up. [*Sorting through them.*] Now what's this?

NORA [*at the window*]. The letter! Oh, Torvald, no!

HELMER. Two calling cards—from Rank.

NORA. From Dr. Rank?

HELMER [*examining them*]. "Dr. Rank, Consulting Physician." They were on top. He must have dropped them in as he left.

NORA. Is there anything on them?

HELMER. There's a black cross over the name. See? That's a gruesome notion. He could almost be announcing his own death.

NORA. That's just what he's doing.

HELMER. What! You've heard something? Something he's told you?

NORA. Yes. That when those cards came, he'd be taking his leave of us. He'll shut himself in now and die.

HELMER. Ah, my poor friend! Of course I knew he wouldn't be here much longer. But so soon— And then to hide himself away like a wounded animal.

NORA. If it has to happen, then it's best it happens in silence—don't you think so, Torvald?

HELMER [*pacing up and down*]. He'd grown right into our lives. I simply can't imagine him gone. He with his suffering and loneliness—like a dark cloud setting off our sunlit happiness. Well, maybe it's best this way. For him, at least. [*Standing still.*] And maybe for us too, Nora. Now we're thrown back on each other, completely. [*Embracing her.*] Oh you, my darling wife, how can I hold you close enough? You know what, Nora—time and again I've wished you were in some terrible danger, just so I could stake my life and soul and everything, for your sake.

NORA [*tearing herself away, her voice firm and decisive*]. Now you must read your mail, Torvald.

HELMER. No, no, not tonight. I want to stay with you, dearest.

NORA. With a dying friend on your mind?

HELMER. You're right. We've both had a shock. There's ugliness between us—these thoughts of death and corruption. We'll have to get free of them first. Until then—we'll stay apart.

NORA [*clinging about his neck*]. Torvald—good night! Good night!

HELMER [*kissing her on the cheek*]. Good night, little songbird. Sleep well, Nora. I'll be reading my mail now. [*He takes the letters into his room and shuts the door after him.*]

NORA [*with bewildered glances, groping about, seizing* HELMER's *domino, throwing it around her, and speaking in short, hoarse, broken whispers*]. Never see him again. Never, never. [*Putting her shawl over her head.*] Never see the children either—them, too. Never, never. Oh, the freezing black water! The depths—down— Oh, I wish it were over— He has it now; he's reading it—now. Oh no, no, not yet. Torvald, good-bye, you and the children— [*She starts for the hall; as she does,* HELMER *throws open his door and stands with an open letter in his hand.*]

HELMER. Nora!

NORA [*screams*]. Oh—!

HELMER. What is this? You know what's in this letter?

NORA. Yes, I know. Let me go! Let me out!

HELMER [*holding her back*]. Where are you going?

NORA [*struggling to break loose*]. You can't save me, Torvald!

HELMER [*slumping back*]. True! Then it's true what he writes? How horrible! No, no, it's impossible—it can't be true.

NORA. It *is* true. I've loved you more than all this world.

HELMER. Ah, none of your slippery tricks.

NORA [*taking one step toward him*]. Torvald—!

HELMER. What *is* this you've blundered into!

NORA. Just let me loose. You're not going to suffer for my sake. You're not going to take on my guilt.

HELMER. No more playacting. [*Locks the hall door.*] You stay right here and give me a reckoning. You understand what you've done? Answer! You understand?

NORA [*looking squarely at him, her face hardening*]. Yes. I'm beginning to understand everything now.

HELMER [*striding about*]. Oh, what an awful awakening! In all these eight years—she who was my pride and joy—a hypocrite, a liar—worse, worse—a criminal! How infinitely disgusting it all is! The shame! [NORA *says nothing and goes on looking straight at him. He stops in front of her.*] I should have suspected something of the kind. I should have known. All your father's flimsy values— Be still! All your father's flimsy values have come out in you. No religion, no morals, no sense of duty— Oh, how I'm punished for letting him off! I did it for your sake, and you repay me like this.

NORA. Yes, like this.

HELMER. Now you've wrecked all my happiness—ruined my whole future.

Oh, it's awful to think of. I'm in a cheap little grafter's hands; he can do anything he wants with me, ask for anything, play with me like a puppet—and I can't breathe a word. I'll be swept down miserably into the depths on account of a featherbrained woman.

NORA. When I'm gone from this world, you'll be free.

HELMER. Oh, quit posing. Your father had a mess of those speeches too. What good would that ever do me if you were gone from this world, as you say? Not the slightest. He can still make the whole thing known; and if he does, I could be falsely suspected as your accomplice. They might even think that I was behind it—that I put you up to it. And all that I can thank you for—you that I've coddled the whole of our marriage. Can you see now what you've done to me?

NORA [*icily calm*]. Yes.

HELMER. It's so incredible, I just can't grasp it. But we'll have to patch up whatever we can. Take off the shawl. I said, take it off! I've got to appease him somehow or other. The thing has to be hushed up at any cost. And as for you and me, it's got to seem like everything between us is just as it was—to the outside world, that is. You'll go right on living in this house, of course. But you can't be allowed to bring up the children; I don't dare trust you with them—Oh, to have to say this to someone I've loved so much! Well, that's done with. From now on happiness doesn't matter; all that matters is saving the bits and pieces, the appearance—[*The doorbell rings.* HELMER *starts.*] What's that? And so late. Maybe the worst—? You think he'd—? Hide, Nora! Say you're sick. [NORA *remains standing motionless.* HELMER *goes and opens the door.*]

MAID [*half dressed, in the hall*]. A letter for Mrs. Helmer.

HELMER. I'll take it. [*Snatches the letter and shuts the door.*] Yes, it's from him. You don't get it; I'm reading it myself.

NORA. Then read it.

HELMER [*by the lamp*]. I hardly dare. We may be ruined, you and I. But— I've got to know. [*Rips open the letter, skims through a few lines, glances at an enclosure, then cries out joyfully.*] Nora! [NORA *looks inquiringly at him.*] Nora! Wait—better check it again— Yes, yes, it's true. I'm saved. Nora, I'm saved!

NORA. And I?

HELMER. You too, of course. We're both saved, both of us. Look. He's sent back your note. He says he's sorry and ashamed—that a happy development in his life—oh, who cares what he says! Nora, we're saved! No one can hurt you. Oh, Nora, Nora—but first, this ugliness all has to go. Let me see— [*Takes a look at the note.*] No, I don't want to see it; I want the whole thing to fade like a dream. [*Tears the note and both letters to pieces, throws them into the stove and watches them burn.*] There—now there's nothing left— He wrote that since Christmas Eve you—Oh, they must have been three terrible days for you, Nora.

NORA. I fought a hard fight.

HELMER. And suffered pain and saw no escape but—No, we're not going to dwell on anything unpleasant. We'll just be grateful and keep on repeating: it's over now, it's over! You hear me, Nora? You don't seem to realize—it's over. What's it mean—that frozen look? Oh, poor little

Nora, I understand. You can't believe I've forgiven you. But I have,
Nora; I swear I have. I know that what you did, you did out of love
for me.

NORA. That's true.

HELMER. You loved me the way a wife ought to love her husband. It's
simply the means that you couldn't judge. But you think I love you any
the less for not knowing how to handle your affairs? No, no—just lean
on me; I'll guide you and teach you. I wouldn't be a man if this feminine
helplessness didn't make you twice as attractive to me. You mustn't
mind those sharp words I said—that was all in the first confusion of
thinking my world had collapsed. I've forgiven you, Nora; I swear I've
forgiven you.

NORA. My thanks for your forgiveness. [*She goes out through the door, right.*]

HELMER. No, wait— [*Peers in.*] What are you doing in there?

NORA [*inside*]. Getting out of my costume.

HELMER [*by the open door*]. Yes, do that. Try to calm yourself and collect
your thoughts again, my frightened little songbird. You can rest easy
now; I've got wide wings to shelter you with. [*Walking about close by the
door.*] How snug and nice our home is, Nora. You're safe here; I'll keep
you like a hunted dove I've rescued out of a hawk's claws. I'll bring
peace to your poor, shuddering heart. Gradually it'll happen, Nora;
you'll see. Tomorrow all this will look different to you; then everything
will be as it was. I won't have to go on repeating I forgive you; you'll feel
it for yourself. How can you imagine I'd ever conceivably want to
disown you—or even blame you in any way? Ah, you don't know a
man's heart, Nora. For a man there's something indescribably sweet and
satisfying in knowing he's forgiven his wife—and forgiven her out of a
full and open heart. It's as if she belongs to him in two ways now: in a
sense he's given her fresh into the world again, and she's become his
wife and his child as well. From now on that's what you'll be to me—you
little, bewildered, helpless thing. Don't be afraid of anything, Nora; just
open your heart to me, and I'll be conscience and will to you both—
[NORA *enters in her regular clothes.*] What's this? Not in bed? You've
changed your dress?

NORA. Yes, Torvald, I've changed my dress.

HELMER. But why now, so late?

NORA. Tonight I'm not sleeping.

HELMER. But Nora dear—

NORA [*looking at her watch*]. It's still not so very late. Sit down, Torvald; we
have a lot to talk over. [*She sits at one side of the table.*]

HELMER. Nora—what is this? That hard expression—

NORA. Sit down, This'll take some time. I have a lot to say.

HELMER [*sitting at the table directly opposite her*]. You worry me, Nora. And I
don't understand you.

NORA. No, that's exactly it. You don't understand me. And I've never un-
derstood you either—until tonight. No, don't interrupt. You can just
listen to what I say. We're closing out accounts, Torvald.

HELMER. How do you mean that?

NORA [*after a short pause*]. Doesn't anything strike you about our sitting
here like this?

HELMER. What's that?

NORA. We've been married now eight years. Doesn't it occur to you that this is the first time we two, you and I, man and wife, have ever talked seriously together?

HELMER. What do you mean—seriously?

NORA. In eight whole years—longer even—right from our first acquaintance, we've never exchanged a serious word on any serious thing.

HELMER. You mean I should constantly go and involve you in problems you couldn't possibly help me with?

NORA. I'm not talking of problems. I'm saying that we've never sat down seriously together and tried to get to the bottom of anything.

HELMER. But dearest, what good would that ever do you?

NORA. That's the point right there: you've never understood me. I've been wronged greatly, Torvald—first by Papa, and then by you.

HELMER. What! By us—the two people who've loved you more than anyone else?

NORA [*shaking her head*]. You never loved me. You've thought it fun to be in love with me, that's all.

HELMER. Nora, what a thing to say!

NORA. Yes, it's true now, Torvald. When I lived at home with Papa, he told me all his opinions, so I had the same ones too; or if they were different I hid them, since he wouldn't have cared for that. He used to call me his doll-child, and he played with me the way I played with my dolls. Then I came into your house—

HELMER. How can you speak of our marriage like that?

NORA [*unperturbed*]. I mean, then I went from Papa's hands into yours. You arranged everything to your own taste, and so I got the same taste as you—or I pretended to; I can't remember. I guess a little of both, first one, then the other. Now when I look back, it seems as if I'd lived here like a beggar—just from hand to mouth. I've lived by doing tricks for you, Torvald. But that's the way you wanted it. It's a great sin what you and Papa did to me. You're to blame that nothing's become of me.

HELMER. Nora, how unfair and ungrateful you are! Haven't you been happy here?

NORA. No, never. I thought so—but I never have.

HELMER. Not—not happy!

NORA. No, only lighthearted. And you've always been so kind to me. But our home's been nothing but a playpen. I've been your doll-wife here, just as at home I was Papa's doll-child. And in turn the children have been my dolls. I thought it was fun when you played with me, just as they thought it fun when I played with them. That's been our marriage, Torvald.

HELMER. There's some truth in what you're saying—under all the raving exaggeration. But it'll all be different after this. Playtime's over; now for the schooling.

NORA. Whose schooling—mine or the children's?

HELMER. Both yours and the children's, dearest.

NORA. Oh, Torvald, you're not the man to teach me to be a good wife to you.

HELMER. And you can say that?

NORA. And I—how am I equipped to bring up children?

HELMER. Nora!

NORA. Didn't you say a moment ago that that was no job to trust me with?

HELMER. In a flare of temper! Why fasten on that?

NORA. Yes, but you were so very right. I'm not up to the job. There's another job I have to do first. I have to try to educate myself. You can't help me with that. I've got to do it alone. And that's why I'm leaving you now.

HELMER [*jumping up*]. What's that?

NORA. I have to stand completely alone, if I'm ever going to discover myself and the world out there. So I can't go on living with you.

HELMER. Nora, Nora!

NORA. I want to leave right away. Kristine should put me up for the night—

HELMER. You're insane! You've no right! I forbid you!

NORA. From here on, there's no use forbidding me anything. I'll take with me whatever is mine. I don't want a thing from you, either now or later.

HELMER. What kind of madness is this!

NORA. Tomorrow I'm going home—I mean, home where I came from. It'll be easier up there to find something to do.

HELMER. Oh, you blind, incompetent child!

NORA. I must learn to be competent, Torvald.

HELMER. Abandon your home, your husband, your children! And you're not even thinking what people will say.

NORA. I can't be concerned about that. I only know how essential this is.

HELMER. Oh, it's outrageous. So you'll run out like this on your most sacred vows.

NORA. What do you think are my most sacred vows?

HELMER. And I have to tell you that! Aren't they your duties to your husband and children?

NORA. I have other duties equally sacred.

HELMER. That isn't true. What duties are they?

NORA. Duties to myself.

HELMER. Before all else, you're a wife and a mother.

NORA. I don't believe in that anymore. I believe that, before all else, I'm a human being, no less than you—or anyway, I ought to try to become one. I know the majority thinks you're right, Torvald, and plenty of books agree with you, too. But I can't go on believing what the majority says, or what's written in books. I have to think over these things myself and try to understand them.

HELMER. Why can't you understand your place in your own home? On a point like that, isn't there one everlasting guide you can turn to? Where's your religion?

NORA. Oh, Torvald, I'm really not sure what religion is.

HELMER. What—?

NORA. I only know what the minister said when I was confirmed. He told me religion was this thing and that. When I get clear and away by myself, I'll go into that problem too. I'll see if what the minister said was right, or, in any case, if it's right for me.

HELMER. A young woman your age shouldn't talk like that. If religion can't move you, I can try to rouse your conscience. You do have some moral feeling? Or, tell me—has that gone too?

NORA. It's not easy to answer that, Torvald. I simply don't know. I'm all confused about these things. I just know I see them so differently from you. I find out, for one thing, that the law's not at all what I'd thought—but I can't get it through my head that the law is fair. A woman hasn't a right to protect her dying father or save her husband's life! I can't believe that.

HELMER. You talk like a child. You don't know anything of the world you live in.

NORA. No, I don't. But now I'll begin to learn for myself. I'll try to discover who's right, the world or I.

HELMER. Nora, you're sick; you've got a fever. I almost think you're out of your head.

NORA. I've never felt more clearheaded and sure in my life.

HELMER. And—clearheaded and sure—you're leaving your husband and children?

NORA. Yes.

HELMER. Then there's only one possible reason.

NORA. What?

HELMER. You no longer love me.

NORA. No. That's exactly it.

HELMER. Nora! You can't be serious!

NORA. Oh, this is so hard, Torvald—you've been so kind to me always. But I can't help it. I don't love you anymore.

HELMER [*struggling for composure*]. Are you also clearheaded and sure about that?

NORA. Yes, completely. That's why I can't go on staying here.

HELMER. Can you tell me what I did to lose your love?

NORA. Yes, I can tell you. It was this evening when the miraculous thing didn't come—then I knew you weren't the man I'd imagined.

HELMER. Be more explicit; I don't follow you.

NORA. I've waited now so patiently eight long years—for, my Lord, I know miracles don't come every day. Then this crisis broke over me, and such a certainty filled me: *now* the miraculous event would occur. While Krogstad's letter was lying out there, I never for an instant dreamed that you could give in to his terms. I was so utterly sure you'd say to him: go on, tell your tale to the whole wide world. And when he'd done that—

HELMER. Yes, what then? When I'd delivered my own wife into shame and disgrace—!

NORA. When he'd done that, I was so utterly sure that you'd step forward, take the blame on yourself and say: I am the guilty one.

HELMER. Nora—!

NORA. You're thinking I'd never accept such a sacrifice from you? No, of course not. But what good would my protests be against you? That was the miracle I was waiting for, in terror and hope. And to stave that off, I would have taken my life.

HELMER. I'd gladly work for you day and night, Nora—and take on pain and deprivation. But there's no one who gives up honor for love.

NORA. Millions of women have done just that.

HELMER. Oh, you think and talk like a silly child.

NORA. Perhaps. But you neither think nor talk like the man I could join myself to. When your big fright was over—and it wasn't from any threat against me, only for what might damage you—when all the danger was past, for you it was just as if nothing had happened. I was exactly the same, your little lark, your doll, that you'd have to handle with double care now that I'd turned out so brittle and frail. [*Gets up.*] Torvald—in that instant it dawned on me that for eight years I've been living here with a stranger, and that I'd even conceived three children—oh, I can't stand the thought of it! I could tear myself to bits.

HELMER [*heavily*]. I see. There's a gulf that's opened between us—that's clear. Oh, but Nora, can't we bridge it somehow?

NORA. The way I am now, I'm no wife for you.

HELMER. I have the strength to make myself over.

NORA. Maybe—if your doll gets taken away.

HELMER. But to part! To part from you! No, Nora, no—I can't imagine it.

NORA [*going out, right*]. All the more reason why it has to be. [*She reenters with her coat and a small overnight bag, which she puts on a chair by the table.*]

HELMER. Nora, Nora, not now! Wait till tomorrow.

NORA. I can't spend the night in a strange man's room.

HELMER. But couldn't we live here like brother and sister—

NORA. You know very well how long that would last. [*Throws her shawl about her.*] Good-bye, Torvald. I won't look in on the children. I know they're in better hands than mine. The way I am now, I'm no use to them.

HELMER. But someday, Nora—someday—?

NORA. How can I tell? I haven't the least idea what'll become of me.

HELMER. But you're my wife, now and wherever you go.

NORA. Listen, Torvald—I've heard that when a wife deserts her husband's house just as I'm doing, then the law frees him from all responsibility. In any case, I'm freeing you from being responsible. Don't feel yourself bound, any more than I will. There has to be absolute freedom for us both. Here, take your ring back. Give me mine.

HELMER. That too?

NORA. That too.

HELMER. There it is.

NORA. Good. Well, now it's all over. I'm putting the keys here. The maids know all about keeping up the house—better than I do. Tomorrow, after I've left town, Kristine will stop by to pack up everything that's mine from home. I'd like those things shipped up to me.

HELMER. Over! All over! Nora, won't you ever think about me?

NORA. I'm sure I'll think of you often, and about the children and the house here.

HELMER. May I write you?

NORA. No—never. You're not to do that.

HELMER. Oh, but let me send you—

NORA. Nothing. Nothing.

HELMER. Or help you if you need it.

NORA. No. I accept nothing from strangers.

HELMER. Nora—can I never be more than a stranger to you?

NORA [*picking up the overnight bag*]. Ah, Torvald—it would take the greatest miracle of all—

HELMER. Tell me the greatest miracle!

NORA. You and I both would have to transform ourselves to the point that—Oh, Torvald, I've stopped believing in miracles.

HELMER. But I'll believe. Tell me! Transform ourselves to the point that—?

NORA. That our living together could be a true marriage. [*She goes out down the hall.*]

HELMER [*sinks down on a chair by the door, face buried in his hands*]. Nora! Nora! [*Looking about and rising.*] Empty. She's gone. [*A sudden hope leaps in him.*] The greatest miracle—?

[*From below, the sound of a door slamming shut.*]

Joaquim Maria Machado de Assis
(*1839–1908*)

For most North American readers, Joaquim Maria Machado de Assis, Brazil's greatest writer, had, in effect, two careers. One was his productive and innovative writing life in the second half of the nineteenth century, which remained for decades almost totally unknown outside Brazil. The other was his gradual climb into international fame over the past thirty years, beginning with the publication in 1952 of an English translation of his *Posthumous Memoirs of Brás Cubas* (English title: *Epitaph for a Small Winner*) and continuing with the translation of four other major novels (and several minor ones) and two collections of short stories. Many American critics now rank him with Flaubert and James (to cite two of the most frequently made comparisons) as a master of the early modern novel. One does not have to look far to see the reasons for both the prolonged obscurity and the sudden fame, on the international scene. Machado wrote in Portuguese, which continues, much more than Spanish, to be an "exotic" language in the United States and Western Europe. Furthermore, his achievement was not very well understood, even in Brazil, during his own lifetime and for years after. The qualities in his work which seem so startlingly and attractively modern today—his dislocations of narrative structure, his experiments with narrative voice, his cool irony—tended to be regarded as flaws by his contemporaries. Machado's fame spread when there was an audience ready for him, one that had become accustomed to modernist fiction. It was an audience, too, that had learned to expect innovation and excitement in South American fiction and that was startled to find that one of the most exciting of the

"new" South American writers had done his major work almost a century before.

Machado was born in Rio de Janeiro in 1839. His father, a housepainter, was a mulatto Brazilian, the son of former slaves; his mother was a white Portuguese immigrant from the Azores. Machado attended only five years of elementary school; otherwise he educated himself. He did a good job; he became fluent in several languages, including French, Spanish, and English, and his writing shows an encyclopedic knowledge of world literature. He began supporting himself when he was fifteen, working at a variety of jobs, mostly connected with publishing: typesetting, proofreading, and editing. In 1874, he entered the civil service in the Ministry of Agriculture. For the last thirty-four years of his life, he led the quiet life of a happily married but childless government bureaucrat.

Machado used the financial security of his civil service position to carry on an astonishingly prolific career as a writer. This career began also when he was fifteen, when he published his first poem in a Rio magazine. His early love was the theater, and by the time he was thirty he had written nineteen plays and opera librettos, most of them produced by theater companies in the city. (The influence of dramatic form can be seen in some of his later fiction, in its skillful dialogue and clear-cut scenic structure.) He was also a facile poet and a regular newspaper columnist. After 1870, however, he turned his attention primarily to short stories and novels and between 1870 and 1880 wrote four rather conventional romantic novels: *Resurrection* (1872), *Hand and Glove* (1874), *Helena* (1876), and *Yaya García* (1878).

The year 1880 marked the turning point in Machado's literary career. If his reputation rested upon his work up to that point, he would be remembered merely as a gently satirical chronicler of middle-class manners during the years of Brazil's Second Empire (1840–90). In 1879, however, Machado fell ill and had to take a leave of absence from his job and spend several months in a health resort. During his convalescence, he wrote a novel, partially dictated to his wife, which was published in 1881. *Epitaph of a Small Winner* was a sharp departure from his early work (although in retrospect we can see its roots in that earlier work). The book had a startlingly original point of view, for one thing; the narrator, Brás Cubas, was dead. His "posthumous memoirs" were posthumous not just in the sense of being published after his death; they were *written* after his death. And he told the story of his life not in a continuous narration but in 160 short, abrupt, numbered sections, with a self-conscious bookishness modelled, according to a tongue-in-cheek preface, on the works of Laurence Sterne, the eighteenth-century English author of *Tristram Shandy*, and Xavier de Maistre, the eighteenth-century French author of the eccentric *Journey Round My Room*.

Machado continued to explore the fictional vein he had opened up in *Epitaph of a Small Winner* in four more novels: a sequel to *Small Winner* named *Quincas Borba* (1891; English title: *Philosopher or Dog?*), his masterpiece *Dom Casmurro* (1900), and two linked late novels, *Esau and Jacob* (1904) and *Memorial of Aires* (1908).

In Machado's day, the two dominant literary movements were romanticism (to which he somewhat inclined in his early work) and naturalism

(which he regularly denounced as superficial and photographic). The great achievement of *Small Winner* was that it swept away such distinctions and forged a completely original form of fiction that transcended them. Paradoxically, by going back to such eighteenth-century models as Sterne and Xavier de Maistre, Machado anticipated many of the features of the twentieth-century novel: a style of understatement and irony, a subjective and unreliable narrator, and a self-consciousness about how to tell the story that produces a text that talks about itself.

Despite the brilliance of Machado's achievement in the novel form, many Brazilian critics believe that his mastery of the short story was even greater. Machado once remarked that he liked to write "vertically," meaning presumably that he was less interested in the "horizontal" elaboration of plot than in exploring the depths of a situation, an ideal well suited to the short story form. Machado wrote short stories all his life, producing about a hundred, collected in five volumes beginning in 1882. "Dona Paula" was written in 1884. With its close attention to its protagonist's stream of consciousness, its coolly ironic narrator, and its structural juxtapositions of times, characters, and value systems, it is a small-scale but representative example of Machado's mature art.

FURTHER READING *(prepared by J. H.):* There is no authoritative critical biography of Machado in English (or in Portuguese either, for that matter). José Bettencourt Machado's *Machado of Brazil: The Life and Times of Machado de Assis, Brazil's Greatest Novelist*, 1962, is a popular, fictionalized work designed to acquaint American readers with the author. The basic critical introduction in English is Helen Caldwell's *Machado de Assis: The Brazilian Master and His Novels*, 1970. Samuel Putnam's chapter, "Machado de Assis and the End-of-the-Century Realists," in his *Marvelous Journey: A Survey of Four Centuries of Brazilian Writing*, 1948, is a pioneering effort that is still of some interest, especially for its discerning comparison of Machado with Henry James. Maria Luisa Nunes's *The Craft of An Absolute Winner: Characterization and Narratology in the Novels of Machado de Assis*, 1983, is a demanding but rewarding study. Among critics writing in English, less attention has been directed to Machado's short stories than to his novels; an exception is John Nist in his "The Short Stories of Machado de Assis," *Arizona Quarterly* 24 (1968), 5–22.

DONA PAULA

Translated by Jack Schmitt and Lorie Ishimatsu

She couldn't possibly have arrived at a more opportune time. Dona Paula entered the parlor precisely as her niece was drying her tear-swollen eyes. She was surprised, as was her niece Venancinha, who knew that her aunt rarely descended from the Tijuca district,[1] where she lived. It was May 1882, and Venancinha hadn't seen her aunt since Christmas. Dona Paula had come down the previous day to spend the night with her sister on Lavradio Street. Today, she had dressed and run off to visit her niece right after lunch. A slave who saw her wanted to announce her arrival, but Dona

[1] A fashionable suburb a little west of Rio de Janeiro, now part of the city.

Paula told her not to—to avoid rustling her skirts, she tiptoed ever so slowly to the parlor door, opened it, and went in.

"What's this all about?" she exclaimed.

Flinging herself into Dona Paula's arms, Venancinha burst into tears. Her aunt kissed, embraced, and comforted her and insisted that she tell her what the matter was. Was she sick, or . . .

"I wish to God I were sick! Death would be better!" interrupted the girl.

"Don't talk nonsense! What happened? Come now, tell me."

Venancinha dried her eyes and tried to talk. After five or six words, the tears flowed again, in such abundance and with such force that Dona Paula thought she'd best wait until they subsided. Meanwhile, she took off her black lace mantelet[2] and her gloves. She was a striking, elegant woman with large attractive eyes that must have been irresistible when she was younger. While her niece wept, she moved quietly to close the parlor door, then returned to the settee. After a few minutes, Venancinha stopped crying and told her aunt what had happened.

It was nothing less than a quarrel with her husband, so violent they had even spoken of separating. Jealousy had caused it. For some time her husband had been suspicious of a certain gentleman, but the evening before, after seeing his wife dance with the man twice and talk to him for a few minutes, he concluded they were in love. When they returned home he was sullen. The next morning after breakfast, he exploded and said cruel harsh things, which she answered in kind.

"Where's your husband now?" inquired her aunt.

"He's gone. I think he went to the office."

Dona Paula asked her if his office were still in the same building and told her not to worry; it wasn't a serious matter. Within two hours everything would be settled. She quickly put on her gloves.

"Are you going there, Auntie?"

"Going there? Of course I'm going! Your husband's a good man—it was just a lover's quarrel. Number 104? I'm on my way, and don't let the slaves see you looking like this!"

Dona Paula spoke with volubility, self-assurance, and kindness. She put on her gloves, and Venancinha, as she helped her aunt with her mantelet, swore she adored Conrad despite their quarrel. Conrad, her husband, had been practicing law since 1874. As Dona Paula left, her niece showered her with kisses of gratitude. In all truth, she couldn't possibly have arrived at a more opportune time. On her way to see Conrad, Dona Paula reflected upon the incident with curiosity, if not suspicion, a little uneasy as to what the whole truth of the matter might be. In any case, she was determined to restore domestic peace.

When she reached her nephew's office, he was not yet in, but shortly thereafter he arrived. After his initial surprise at seeing her there, he guessed the object of her visit. He confessed that he had overreacted with his wife and said he was not accusing her of loose morals or perverse intentions. But she was behaving like a scatterbrain: she was too friendly with other men and was given to coquettish glances and honeyed words in their

[2] A short mantle or cape.

presence. And indiscretion was one of the gateways to misconduct. Furthermore, he had no doubt that his wife and the man in question were in love with one another. Venancinha had only told her about the evening before—she had not mentioned four or five other incidents, one of which had occurred at the theater and had developed into a scandal of sorts. He wasn't about to accept the responsibility for his wife's reckless and indiscreet behavior. If she wanted to go around falling in love, she'd have to pay the price for it.

Dona Paula heard him out. Then it was her turn to speak. She agreed that her niece was flighty but attributed this to her youth. A pretty girl could not help attracting attention, and it was natural for Venancinha to be flattered by the admiring glances of other men. It was also understandable that her response to such flattery was interpreted as a sign of love, by other men as well as her husband—their infatuation and his jealousy were the cause of the quarrel. She, for her part, had just seen her niece crying in earnest. When she left, Venancinha was disconsolate and brokenhearted and had even talked of wanting to die because of what he had said to her. So if he really only attributed her actions to foolishness, why not proceed with discretion and understanding? He should use counsel and common sense—he could help her avoid similar situations in the future and show her how even the appearance of friendship and good will toward other men could be misinterpreted and harm her reputation.

The good lady spoke no less than twenty minutes, and she expressed herself so eloquently and diplomatically that her nephew felt his heart softening. He resisted, of course—two or three times, to avoid appearing overly lenient, he declared that everything between them was finished. In self-justification, he mentally evoked his arguments against a reconciliation. But Dona Paula looked down until his wave of indignation had passed and then looked up at him with her large, sagacious, imploring eyes.

Seeing that Conrad wasn't going to give in easily, Dona Paula proposed a compromise: "Forgive her, and make your peace together, then I'll take her to Tijuca to spend a month or two with me. It will be a kind of temporary exile for her. Meanwhile, I'll take it upon myself to straighten her out. Agreed?"

Conrad accepted. As soon as Dona Paula had his word, she prepared to leave to tell her niece the encouraging news. Conrad accompanied her to the stairs, where they shook hands. Dona Paula didn't release his hand until she had repeated her recommendation that he proceed with tenderness and discretion. Then, as though it were an afterthought, she added: "And you're going to see that the man in question isn't worth even a minute of the time we've spent worrying over him."

"His name is Vasco Maria Portela."

Dona Paula turned pale. What Vasco Maria Portela? An elderly gentleman, a former diplomat who . . . no, he was retired, had been in Europe for a few years, and had just received the title of baron. It was his son, a worthless rascal who had returned to Rio from Europe a short time before. Dona Paula squeezed Conrad's hand and hurried downstairs. Confused and excited, she spent several minutes at the landing going through the motions of adjusting her mantelet. She stared at the floor, pondering the

situation. Then she set out to meet her niece, carrying with her the pro-
posal for a reconciliation with Conrad and the conditions under which it
was to be achieved. Venancinha accepted everything.

Two days later, they went to Dona Paula's home in the Tijuca district. If
Venancinha seemed to have lost some of her earlier enthusiasm for the
trip, the loss was probably due to the idea of exile or to longing for what she
had left behind. In any event, Vasco's name went up to Tijuca. If it wasn't
in both heads, it was at least in Dona Paula's, where it was a kind of echo, a
remote and pleasant sound, something that seemed to hearken from the
time of the opera singer Stoltz and the Marquis of Paraná.[3] Those distant
echoes were just as fragile as youth itself, and where were those three
eternities now? They were scattered among the distant ruins of the past
thirty years. Dona Paula, having nothing else to look forward to, lived with
those memories of the past.

The elder Vasco had also been young once and had loved. Unbeknown
to their marriage partners, he and Dona Paula had filled their cups to the
brim and for several years had slaked their thirst for one another. Since the
passing winds are unable to record men's speeches, there is no way to
reveal here what was said at the time about their adventure, which eventu-
ally came to an end. It had been a series of sweet and bitter hours mixed
with pleasures and tears, ecstasy and anger, and various other intoxicants
the lady had used when she filled her loving cup to overflowing. She
drained the cup dry and never touched it again. Satiety was followed by
abstinence, and public opinion was formed by this final phase. Her hus-
band died and the years flowed by. Dona Paula was now an austere and
pious lady, prestigious and respected by all.

Dona Paula's thought had been carried to the past by her niece. The two
similar situations, mingled with the same name and blood, awakened some
old memories. They were going to be living together in Tijuca for a few
weeks, and Venancinha would be following her aunt's instructions. Dona
Paula would attempt to challenge her own memory—to what extent could
she reexperience those sensations from the past?

"Aren't we going to the city at all? Not even for a little visit?" asked
Venancinha the next morning, laughing.

"Are you bored already?"

"No, I'd never be bored here, I was just asking if . . ."

Dona Paula, also laughing, shook her finger negatively. Then she asked
her niece if she missed the city. Venancinha said no and gave more weight
to her answer by allowing the corners of her mouth to droop, in order to
reflect her disdain or indifference. It was as though she had written a letter
saying more than she had intended to say. Avoiding the reckless abandon
of someone rushing off to save his father from the hangman's noose, Dona
Paula had the good habit of reading slowly. She fixed her attention on the
spaces between the letters and the lines, took in everything, and found her
niece's response excessive.

"They're in love with one another," she thought.

[3] That is, the time of her youth. Rosine Stoltz (1815–1903) was a French operatic soprano
who toured Brazil and made a hit in the 1850's. The Marquis of Paraná (1801–56) was a
Brazilian politician under Dom Pedro II.

This discovery awakened her dormant memories of the past. Dona Paula struggled to shake off those persistent memories, but they returned like a group of chorus girls: some slowly and suggestively, others with quick and sprightly movements—they sang, laughed, and raised the very devil. Dona Paula's mind returned to the dances of yesteryear. She remembered the eternal waltzes that made everyone stare at her in wonder and boasted to her niece about the mazurkas, the most graceful dance in the world, the theater, cardgames, and, obliquely, the kisses. But everything—and this was the curious thing about her recollections—everything was described with the cold and faded ink of an old chronicle, an empty skeleton of history that lacked a living soul. Everything occurred in her head. Dona Paula tried synchronizing her heart and her head to see if she could feel something beyond a mere mental reproduction of her past, but despite all efforts to evoke the old feelings, none returned. Time had swallowed them.

If she could only peek into her niece's heart, she might be able to see her own image reflected there, and then . . . After Dona Paula was possessed by this idea, it became harder for her to concentrate on her niece's rehabilitation, even though she was sincerely preoccupied with her welfare and wanted to see her reunited with Conrad. In order to assure themselves of company in purgatory, habitual sinners may secretly desire to see others committing sins too, but sinning wasn't the issue here. Dona Paula stressed Conrad's virtues and superiority and also told her niece that uncontrolled passions could destroy her marriage and, even more tragic, cause her husband to disown her.

Conrad confirmed the validity of Dona Paula's warnings when he paid his first visit nine days later: he was cold when he entered and when he left. Venancinha was terrified. She had hoped that their nine-day separation would soften her husband, and, really, it had. But in order to avoid the appearance of an easy capitulation, he masked his true feelings and held back his emotions. And this had a greater effect than anything else. Venancinha's terrible fear of losing her husband was the principal factor in her rehabilitation. Exile alone could not have accomplished so much.

Just two days after Conrad's visit, when both ladies had approached the villa gate to set out on their daily stroll, they saw a gentleman on horseback coming in their direction. Venancinha fixed her eyes on him, let out a little cry, and ran to hide behind the wall. Dona Paula understood and waited. She wanted to see the man close-up. After two or three minutes he approached. Seated upright in his saddle, he was a handsome, proud-looking, elegant youth with fine polished boots. He looked just like the other Vasco—the same large deep-set eyes, the same tilt of the head, the same broad shoulders.

After Dona Paula had pried the first word out of her niece, Venancinha told her everything that very night. They had first seen one another at the horse races, right after his return from Europe. Two weeks later, she was introduced to him at a dance. He seemed so interesting and Parisian that she spoke to her husband about him the next morning. Conrad frowned in displeasure, and this reaction gave her an idea she had never before entertained. She began to see him with pleasure, and then she longed to see him. He spoke to her respectfully and told her nice things: that she was the loveliest and most elegant young woman in Rio, that in Paris he had re-

cently heard some ladies from the Alvarenga family praising her fine quali-
ties. He was witty when he criticized other people and expressed himself
more sensitively than anyone she had ever met. He didn't talk about love,
but he pursued her with his eyes—no matter how hard she tried to look
away from him, she couldn't help noticing. She began to think about him,
frequently and with interest, and her heart fluttered whenever they met. It
was probably easy for him to detect in her face the impression he made.

Leaning forward, Dona Paula listened to Venancinha's story with her
whole past concentrated in her eyes. With mouth agape, she seemed anx-
ious to drink in her niece's words, as if they were a cordial. And she asked
for more, telling Venancinha to omit nothing whatsoever. Dona Paula
looked so youthful and her request was so gentle and full of potential
forgiveness that she seemed like a confidant and friend, despite a few
harsh words interspersed among the pleasant remarks through a sort of
unconscious hypocrisy. It wasn't intentional, however: Dona Paula even
deceived herself. She was like an invalid general who struggles to recover
some of his old ardor by listening to the stories of another's campaigns.

"You can see your husband was right," she said. "You were foolish, very
foolish."

Venancinha agreed with her aunt and swore it was completely finished.

"I'm afraid it isn't. Did you really come to love him?"

"Auntie . . ."

"You still love him!"

"I swear I don't love him anymore, but I . . . yes, I confess I did. Forgive
me, and please don't say anything to Conrad! I wish none of this had ever
happened. Yes, I'll admit I was smitten at first . . . But what did you ex-
pect?"

"Did he reveal his feelings to you?"

"Yes, he did. It happened at the Lyric Theater one evening, as we were
about to leave. He usually came by my theater box to accompany me to the
carriage, and on our way out he uttered . . . three words."

Out of consideration, Dona Paula didn't ask for the gentleman's words,
but she imagined the circumstances: the galleries, the couples leaving, the
lights, the crowds, the sound of voices, and the scene she visualized allowed
her to piece together some of the sensations her niece had experienced.
With great interest and diplomacy, she asked her to describe her feelings in
greater detail.

"I don't know exactly what I felt," replied Venancinha, her tongue
gradually loosened by her growing emotion. "I don't remember the first
five minutes. I think I maintained my dignity—in any event, I didn't an-
swer him. I felt that everyone was staring at us, that they might have over-
heard him, and when people greeted me with a smile it seemed that they
were mocking me. Somehow I managed to go down the stairs and without
really knowing what I was doing, got into the carriage. I allowed my fingers
to go limp when we shook hands good-by. I can assure you that I wish I
hadn't heard anything he said. When we were inside the carriage, Conrad
told me he was tired and leaned back against the far side of the seat. It was
for the best, because I don't know what I would have said if we had talked
on the way home. I leaned back too, but not for long—I wasn't able to sit
still. I looked out the glass windows, and from time to time I could see only

the glare of streetlamps, and then not even that. Instead I saw the theater galleries, the stairs, the crowds of people, and him next to me whispering those words, just three words, and I'm not able to say what I thought then—my ideas were jumbled and confused, and I felt a churning inside me."

"But after you were back home?"

"At home, as I undressed, I was at last able to reflect a little, but very little. I slept poorly and late. The next morning I was bewildered. I cannot say I was happy or sad. I remember I thought about him a lot, and to get him out of my mind, I promised myself I would reveal everything to Conrad, but the thoughts returned again. From time to time I shuddered, imagining I heard his voice. Then I remembered that when I gave him my hand my fingers were limp, and I felt—I don't know exactly how to say it—a kind of regret, a fear of having offended him. Then I wanted to see him again . . . Forgive me, Auntie, but you asked me to tell everything."

Dona Paula's answer was a tight squeeze of the hand and an understanding nod. Through these ingenuously narrated sensations, she had at last found something from her own past. Sometimes, in a dreamy trance of reminiscence, her eyelids were half-closed; at other times her eyes were sparkling with warmth and curiosity. She heard everything: day by day and encounter by encounter, including the details of the scene in the theater, which her niece had initially hidden from her. And the rest followed: the hours of anxiety, longing, fear, hope, depression, and dissimulation, all the deeply felt emotions of a young girl in this situation. To satisfy her insatiable curiosity, Dona Paula insisted on knowing every detail of her niece's story, which was neither a book nor even a chapter of adultery, but a prologue, interesting and violent.

Venancinha finished. Her aunt, in a state of rapture, said nothing. Then she came to, took her niece by the hand, and drew her closer. She didn't talk right away. First she stared intently at her niece's deep-set eyes, fresh mouth, and restless, palpitating youthfulness. She wasn't drawn entirely out of her trance until Venancinha once again begged her forgiveness. Dona Paula said everything with a mother's tenderness and austerity. She spoke so eloquently of chastity, public opinion, and loving one's husband that Venancinha wept, unable to contain herself.

Tea was served, but it wasn't really an appropriate time for tea. Venancinha retired immediately—as it was still quite light, she left the room with her eyes lowered so the servant wouldn't see her in such a state of emotion. Dona Paula remained seated at the table, in the presence of the servant. She spent about twenty minutes drinking her tea and munching on a biscuit. As soon as she was alone, she went to lean against the window which looked out from the back of the villa.

The wind blew gently and the leaves rustled with a whispering sound. Although they weren't the leaves of her youth, they nevertheless questioned her: "Paula, do you remember the leaves of yesteryear?"[4] For that is the peculiar thing about leaves: the generations that pass on tell the newcomers what they saw, and that is why all leaves know and ask questions about everything. "Do you remember the leaves of yesteryear?"

[4] An echo from "But where are the snows of yesteryear?"—a line from a poem by the fifteenth-century French poet François Villon, as translated by D. G. Rossetti.

She did remember, of course, but that sensation she had felt a short time before, which was scarcely a reverberation, had ceased. In vain she repeated her niece's words as she breathed in the pungent evening air, but instead of recapturing sensations from the past, she was only able to evoke the scattered lifeless reminiscences in her head. Her heart slowed down, and her blood ran at its normal speed again. When her niece was absent she felt nothing. Nonetheless, she stayed there, staring out at the night, which had nothing in common with the nights of Stoltz and the Marquis of Paraná. But she stared out anyway, and in the kitchen the slave women fought off their drowsiness by telling stories. Now and then they commented impatiently, "Seems like the old missus ain't never going to bed tonight!"

Henry James
(1843–1916)

On each flank of Western Europe in the nineteenth century there emerged a civilization that increasingly regarded its relation to Western Europe as a symbolic test of national character. To the Russians in the east, the West symbolized futurist liberalism and secular enlightenment, things to be desired or abhorred depending on whether one considered Russia as embarrassingly backward or as holy soil, Mother Russia, endangered by corrupt modernity. Westward, across the Atlantic, Americans felt as ambivalent toward Western Europe as the Russians did—not, however, because it pointed toward the future but rather because it embodied the past. In America the future had already happened, as it were, but culturally the New World was still a gawky adolescent. Americans were resolved to throw off European "corruption" but were also fascinated with an Old-World culture that, however corrupt, incorporated a mature beauty and a civilized urbanity that had barely begun to emerge in America. Early- and mid-nineteenth-century American authors such as Washington Irving and Nathaniel Hawthorne had already begun to explore the European theme, not to mention later authors such as Mark Twain, but it remained for Henry James to make that theme the very center of his creative consciousness. It is probably no coincidence that one of James's most admired literary models was Ivan Turgenev, an expatriate from Russia and its most Westernized realist author.

James's internationalism proved, like many other aspects of his work, to be a herald of things to come in American literature. In the next generation or two such diverse authors as Edith Wharton, Gertrude Stein, F. Scott Fitzgerald, and Ernest Hemingway would all, through their work or lifestyle or both, explore European values and settings, often to help define what was most American in their own roots and values. James's long career, which bridges the transition from literary realism to modernism, is also

illuminating because through it flow the most powerful currents of turn-of-the-century literature—feminism, naturalism, aestheticism, and formalism. Except for the formalism, such currents generally flow a little beneath the surface of James's work, however, or cross it at an angle. Even his realism is more psychological than circumstantial. He was contrarian and independent artist enough not to become a committed devotee of the -isms that came thick and fast during his lifetime.

Henry James was born in 1843, in New York City. Although some of his formative years were to be spent in New England, the New York perspective afforded him a more cosmopolitan view of America than was typical of the pure New Englanders who had dominated much of earlier American literature. Nevertheless, James's life story—like the stories of the characters in the works he was to write—is mainly a chronicle of his imaginative life and of the perceptions that nourished it. Henry was the second of five children; his brother William James, one year older, was also to become famous, as one of the most distinguished American philosophers and psychologists. (It was William who coined the now-indispensable phrase "stream of consciousness.") Their wealthy father was a man of vivacious mind and spirit, whose aim was give his children—along with the money they would inherit—large views, freedom, cosmopolitanism, and a sense of purpose in whatever vocation they might follow. Largely in pursuance of these goals, he took the family abroad for several extensive stays while the children were growing up; Henry was educated as much by travel as by his tutors and the assortment of schools he attended. In 1860, when he was seventeen, the family settled down in Newport, Rhode Island, where Henry took up painting (he was later to write many stories about artists) but soon developed an even deeper passion for literature, especially for Balzac and other French authors. Ineligible for military service in the Civil War because of a mysterious disability, apparently the result of a back injury incurred while fighting a fire in Newport, he enrolled briefly at Harvard Law School, but once again literature claimed priority. Among American authors he had a special devotion to Hawthorne, another great anatomist of human psychology. When the family moved again in 1864, to Boston, and soon thereafter to Cambridge, Massachusetts, James met a number of important men of letters, including the young William Dean Howells, the writer whose name would become synonymous with the American school of realism. Howells helped James embark on a career as a magazine writer, at first mainly of reviews and essays but also of a few stories.

In 1869, at the age of twenty-six, James embarked on his first solo trip to Europe, which included also his first experience of Italy, a country that permanently impressed his imagination. Other trips to Europe followed, including an extended stay in Paris that brought James into contact with some of the mightiest writers of the time, including Turgenev and the foremost French realists and naturalists: Gustave Flaubert, Emile Zola, Guy de Maupassant, and others. James came to realize, however, that he would never be wholly accepted by the Parisians as one of their own, and so in 1876 he made the key decision to settle in England, permanently.

Except for trips to the continent and a very few trips back to the United States, James spent the rest of his life in England, first in bachelor's quarters in London and later in Rye, an English-Channel town in the southeast,

where he bought a house in 1897. His social schedule, especially while he lived in London, was impressively upscale and incredibly busy, with frequent dinner invitations that allowed James to hobnob with many eminent Victorians. He was also a frequent guest at English country houses. Later in his life he became a kind of cult figure to several important new writers such as Joseph Conrad, gradually moving into the role of their admired "master."

Despite being so sociable, James remained in many ways a private figure, intensely committed to the essentially inner world of his creative work. By the end of his life he had written twenty full-length novels and more than a hundred novellas and stories, besides plays, travel books, biographical works, and literary criticism. The spark of inspiration for most of his novels and stories came from casual sources such as conversation, not from his own direct experience, but the distinctive personal qualities of his characters (a matter James regarded as far more important than the outer events of their lives) came from his imagination, which fleshed out the characters and their circumstances from the slimmest of hints. He never married or even, apparently, ever had a love affair; his closest approach seems to have been a deep but tentative friendship with the American writer Constance Fenimore Woolson when they were in their forties. Her later death, apparently by suicide, came as a great shock to him. Questions about his emotional life are especially intriguing in light of his many stories and novels about people in love and people who miss out on their chances for love.

In 1904–1905 James returned to tour the United States extensively— not just the Northeast but the deepest reaches of the South and West. The journey revealed to James just how much his native country had grown and changed and, in his eyes, how much innocence it had lost. He recorded his impressions in a thoughtful travel book, *The American Scene* (1907). In his last years, in addition to two novels he left unfinished, he wrote about half of a projected five-volume autobiography and also undertook the major task of heavily revising many of his works for the "New York Edition" that appeared in the decade following 1907. This edition is notable not only for the new versions James produced of older works but also for a series of invaluable prefaces in which James commented on his own fiction and on the theory of fiction in general. He continues today to be regarded as one of the foremost theorists of literature.

Several bits of international symbolism came together in James's very last days. Despite his acclimatization to England and Europe, he had remained an American citizen for over seventy years. But in 1915, pained by American neutrality in the First World War, he became a British subject and soon thereafter was awarded the Order of Merit by King George V— one of many honors he received late in life. In February of 1916 James died, after a stroke and an attack of pneumonia, a little short of his seventy-third birthday. Appropriately, although he was cremated in England, his ashes were returned to the United States and interred in Cambridge.

The first phase of James's long career as a writer has an essential consistency, and so does his last phase, the two being separated by a period when experiments, not always successful, took him in various directions. In the first phase, through the early 1880's, he explored in a number of stories

and novels the international theme that so strongly preoccupied him. *Roderick Hudson* (1875), for example, narrates the ill-fated love and deterioration of an American sculptor in Rome, and *The American* (1877) examines an unsuccessful attempt by a naïve but high-minded American businessman to cope with the caste prejudice of an aristocratic French family. *The Europeans* (1878) reverses directions across the Atlantic, concentrating on an American expatriate who returns to her country in an unsuccessful attempt to fortune-hunt in Boston.

James's most impressive studies of this period, however, are of American womanhood. Sometimes, as in the exquisite and moving short novel *Washington Square* (1881), the setting is America, but James is most characteristic when he blends the international theme with the "American girl" theme in works narrating the social and psychological ordeals of young American women in an unfamiliar European setting. The most memorable of these works are the novella *Daisy Miller* (1878) and the novel *Portrait of a Lady* (1881), the two greatest popular successes among James's works. The latter narrates, in English and Italian settings, the disillusioning marriage of the independent-spirited and beautiful Isabel Archer to a morally shallow, mercenary American expatriate. At least among the novels James wrote before the century turned, *The Portrait of a Lady* is generally regarded as his masterpiece. In many of these novels, what America means is freshness or crudeness or innocence and what Europe means is ripeness or cultivation or corruption. But those distinctions are continually modified and complicated by James's subtle handling of values. For example, in both *Daisy Miller* and *The Portrait of a Lady* it is Europeanized Americans rather than Europeans as such who pose the most sinister obstacles to American innocence and idealism. Moreover, *innocent* is far too passive a term to apply to James's young American heroines, who, even when victimized by chicanery or by "Europe," tend to remain unbroken in character, however spiritually battered.

Between the early 1880s and about 1900, James's imagination began to take new turns. Having already heralded the end-of-the-century feminist revival, he now explored in his own offbeat way the other two main literary currents of the period: naturalism, by way of its hallmark, the social novel; and aestheticism. The social novels included *The Bostonians* (1886), a disturbing study of the struggle for the heroine's soul fought between her resolutely antifeminist southern lover and a militant female crusader for women's rights; and *The Princess Casamassima* (1886), a seemingly un-Jamesian melodrama about revolutionaries and the London underclass. A number of works began to explore intensively the subject of artists and art, including *The Tragic Muse* (1890), which brings alive convincingly the atmosphere of the painter's studio and of the theater, and a number of short stories including "The Real Thing" (1890), about a painter who finds that his low-life models are better subjects to work with in illustrating a book on high society than a couple of impoverished models who are authentic members of the upper class. To this mixed middle period belong also several studies James wrote of the consciousness of childhood as it confronts an adult or evil world. These include *What Maisie Knew* (1897), in which a young daughter of divorced, morally sleazy parents learns to cope with their world and values; and *The Turn of the Screw* (1898), one of the great

ghost stories. In this novella, two young children and their governess are confronted by sinister revenants who may or may not be projections of the governess's sex-starved and hysterical imagination. (Interpreters have endlessly disputed the matter.) James had by no means abandoned his theme of innocence corrupted.

Although attempts by James to write for the stage in the early 1890's were a humiliating failure, he may have profited from the experience, for through the decade he moved ever closer, experimentally, to a kind of fiction in which the "truth" is withheld and events are presented dramatically, unmediated by an authoritative, explanatory narrator, or else impressionistically, as they reveal themselves to the imperfect awareness of a point-of-view character. (The hazy indistinct light effects of late nineteenth-century Impressionist painting suggest a parallel.) In making this shift, James was in fact helping to usher in the mode of fiction that would dominate the entire first half of the twentieth century. His new approach came to a head in the three monumental novels of his last ("major") phase, which resume James's early theme of upright Americans really or supposedly ensnared in European intrigues: *The Wings of the Dove* (1902), *The Ambassadors* (1903), and *The Golden Bowl* (1904). These novels, the culmination of James's work, were written after the author had ceased to expect appreciation by a wide public, and they have had to wage an uphill fight for recognition even among sophisticated readers; indeed, they still provoke controversy. The problem for readers has been the superrefined subtlety with which perceptions and fleeting events are hinted at, so that it is sometimes hard to determine what is going on and why it is significant. This general problem is reflected specifically in the elaborate style James adopted, full of qualifications and half-retractions, so that the narrator seems to take away in any one phrase what he has given us in the preceding one. For some readers the sense of overfastidiousness is compounded by James's frequent resort to apologetic quotation marks that seem to retreat squeamishly from the most ordinary and natural of English idioms.

Though difficult, James's late novels and stories no longer seem quite so intimidating, partly because a number of great authors in James's wake have acclimated readers to psychological complexity and involuted sentences—notably Joseph Conrad, Marcel Proust, and William Faulkner. We can also now recognize as misleading the old notion that James came to value the cerebral, for its own sake, over the passionate; indeed, the whole point of such works as *The Ambassadors* and the late short-story masterpiece "The Beast in the Jungle" (1903) is the tragic waste that results when people cravenly avoid a commitment to passion and the fullest life. It can be argued that the genius of James's late work, including his prose style, lies in its implication of readers themselves in the groping uncertainties and evasions experienced by the characters in their faltering approaches to understanding and emotional commitment.

A great distance may seem to separate the obscurities of such late work by James from the apparently direct, uncomplicated novella *Daisy Miller*, which he wrote near the outset of his career. The plot itself is uncomplicated, and so, it might seem, is Daisy herself, who seems always to say just what she means and to do just what she wants to do. But the impression of simplicity one gets when first reading the story vanishes as soon as one

begins to think hard about it and ask just what James is up to. What, after all, is Daisy really like? Is she a naïve innocent or a young woman with a program? If we are drawn to her, is it because she is harmlessness persecuted or because she is an authentically subversive force? Winterbourne comes to classify her as a "flirt"; is that the truth? If so, what does that label mean and explain? What does Daisy feel toward Giovanelli? Is she flirting with him in a conventional sense or experimenting with a new mode of male-female relations? Or is she really looking past him toward Winterbourne? What, in fact, does she feel toward Winterbourne? Why, when leaving the Colosseum, does she tell him that she is indifferent to the danger of Roman fever?

These questions about Daisy are just the beginning; we may also ponder whether or not she is the true focal center of the story. Is it more concerned with Winterbourne's mind, values, and emotional resources than with Daisy herself? Is he on Daisy's side or does he only think he is? Why is it so essential to him to find the right formula for placing and understanding her? Does he make Daisy harder to understand than she really is, or does he give her too little credit for complexity? What is it that prevents his expressing and acting on the attraction he apparently feels toward her?

Or is *Daisy Miller* not really about either Daisy or Winterbourne but rather about society (a term Daisy, in her own way, likes to use), or about the contrast between America and Europe? Are Daisy and Winterbourne tokens used by James in order to explore the mentalities of people such as Mrs. Costello and Mrs. Walker and the social structures they insist on? If the America–Europe contrast is essential, and if Europe corrupts American innocence, why are most of Daisy's persecutors themselves Americans? What does it mean for Winterbourne to state that he has lived too long in foreign parts? Are the social rules the Costellos and Walkers insist on in Rome and Vevey really different from the rules they insist on in New York? What could Winterbourne have understood about Daisy in America that he cannot understand in Europe?

That so many questions can be asked about *Daisy Miller* reminds us that the late work of Henry James, with all its uncertainties, subtleties, and merely hinted-at recognitions, is not so different after all from his earliest work. His brother William was not the only psychologist in the family.

A NOTE ON THE TEXT

The version of *Daisy Miller* printed in this anthology is the original one, not the stylistically complex version James later wrote and published in 1909 in the New York Edition. The earlier version is the more familiar one, seems more appropriate for new readers of James, and is considered by many readers and authorities to be inherently superior.

FURTHER READING *(prepared by S. M.):* The definitive biography of James is Leon Edel's monumental but readable *Henry James,* which addresses in five volumes both James's life and his works: *The Untried Years: 1843–1870,* 1953; *The Conquest of London: 1870–1881,* 1962; *The Middle Years: 1882–1895,* 1962; *The Treacherous Years: 1895–1901,* 1969; and *The Master: 1901–1916,* 1973. There is also a good

one-volume condensation: *Henry James: A Life*, 1985. *The Conquest of London* discusses *Daisy Miller* in some detail—its background, reception, and place in the Jamesian scheme. Edel's introduction to his edition of *The Complete Tales of Henry James*, 1963, is good on James's international theme. Lyall Powers's *Henry James: An Introduction and Interpretation*, 1970, combining biography and criticism, is an excellent book for new readers of James. Harry T. Moore's *Henry James*, 1974, is a compact, well-illustrated biography. John Randall, in "The Genteel Reader and *Daisy Miller*," *American Quarterly*, vol. 17 (1965), outlines James's implied criticism of the genteel tradition. Paul Lukacs's "Unambiguous Ambiguity: The International Theme of *Daisy Miller*," *Studies in American Fiction*, vol. 16 (1988), is good on the subject it addresses. The essays collected in *James's "Daisy Miller": The Story, the Play, the Critics*, ed. William Stafford, 1963, are an accessible introduction to the novella; they include an informative introduction by Stafford as well as pieces by such well-known critics as Leslie Fiedler ("Daisy Miller: The Good Bad Girl") and Wayne Booth ("The Tragedy and the Comedy and the Irony").

DAISY MILLER

PART I

At the little town of Vevey,[1] in Switzerland, there is a particularly comfortable hotel. There are, indeed, many hotels; for the entertainment of tourists is the business of the place, which, as many travellers will remember, is seated upon the edge of a remarkably blue lake—a lake that it behoves every tourist to visit. The shore of the lake presents an unbroken array of establishments of this order, of every category, from the "grand hotel" of the newest fashion, with a chalk-white front, a hundred balconies, and a dozen flags flying from its roof, to the little Swiss *pension*[2] of an elder day, with its name inscribed in German-looking lettering upon a pink or yellow wall, and an awkward summer-house in the angle of the garden. One of the hotels at Vevey, however, is famous, even classical, being distinguished from many of its upstart neighbours by an air both of luxury and of maturity. In this region, in the month of June, American travellers are extremely numerous; it may be said, indeed, that Vevey assumes at this period some of the characteristics of an American watering-place. There are sights and sounds which evoke a vision, an echo, of Newport and Saratoga.[3] There is a flitting hither and thither of "stylish" young girls, a rustling of muslin flounces, a rattle of dance-music in the morning hours, a sound of high-pitched voices at all times. You receive an impression of these things at the excellent inn of the "Trois Couronnes," and are transported in fancy

[1] Vevey is near the eastern end of Lake Geneva, a sizable lake in the northwest part of the Swiss Alps. The city of Geneva lies at the western end of the lake, some thirty miles from Vevey.

[2] A boardinghouse, especially for tourists.

[3] Newport, on the Rhode Island coast, and Saratoga Springs, in upstate New York, were the two most fashionable resort towns in the United States in the late nineteenth century.

to the Ocean House or to Congress Hall.[4] But at the "Trois Couronnes," it must be added, there are other features that are much at variance with these suggestions: neat German waiters, who look like secretaries of legation; Russian princesses sitting in the garden; little Polish boys walking about, held by the hand, with their governors; a view of the snowy crest of the Dent du Midi and the picturesque towers of the Castle of Chillon.[5]

I hardly know whether it was the analogies or the differences that were uppermost in the mind of a young American, who, two or three years ago, sat in the garden of the "Trois Couronnes," looking about him, rather idly, at some of the graceful objects I have mentioned. It was a beautiful summer morning, and in whatever fashion the young American looked at things, they must have seemed to him charming. He had come from Geneva the day before, by the little steamer, to see his aunt, who was staying at the hotel—Geneva having been for a long time his place of residence. But his aunt had a headache—his aunt had almost always a headache—and now she was shut up in her room, smelling camphor, so that he was at liberty to wander about. He was some seven-and-twenty years of age; when his friends spoke of him, they usually said that he was at Geneva, "studying." When his enemies spoke of him they said—but, after all, he had no enemies; he was an extremely amiable fellow, and universally liked. What I should say is, simply, that when certain persons spoke of him they affirmed that the reason of his spending so much time at Geneva was that he was extremely devoted to a lady who lived there—a foreign lady—a person older than himself. Very few Americans—indeed I think none—had ever seen this lady, about whom there were some singular stories. But Winterbourne had an old attachment for the little metropolis of Calvinism;[6] he had been put to school there as a boy, and he had afterwards gone to college there—circumstances which had led to his forming a great many youthful friendships. Many of these he had kept, and they were a source of great satisfaction to him.

After knocking at his aunt's door and learning that she was indisposed, he had taken a walk about the town, and then he had come in to his breakfast. He had now finished his breakfast; but he was drinking a small cup of coffee, which had been served to him on a little table in the garden by one of the waiters who looked like an *attaché*.[7] At last he finished his coffee and lit a cigarette. Presently a small boy came walking along the path—an urchin of nine or ten. The child, who was diminutive for his years, had an aged expression of countenance, a pale complexion, and sharp little features. He was dressed in knickerbockers, with red stockings, which displayed his poor little spindleshanks; he also wore a brilliant red cravat. He

[4] *Trois Couronnes* (French): "Three Crowns." The Ocean House and Congress Hall were resort hotels in, respectively, Newport and Saratoga.

[5] *Dent du Midi* (French): "Tooth of the South," a mountain peak. The ancient Castle of Chillon, on Lake Geneva, was enhanced as a tourist attraction after Lord Byron wrote *The Prisoner of Chillon* (1816), a poem about the rigors endured by Bonivard, a sixteenth-century patriot imprisoned there.

[6] John Calvin (1509–64), one of the preeminent theologians of the Reformation era, turned Geneva into a bastion of Protestantism.

[7] Official at an embassy or legation.

carried in his hand a long alpenstock,[8] the sharp point of which he thrust into everything that he approached—the flower-beds, the garden-benches, the trains of the ladies' dresses. In front of Winterbourne he paused, looking at him with a pair of bright, penetrating little eyes.

"Will you give me a lump of sugar?" he asked, in a sharp, hard little voice—a voice immature, and yet, somehow, not young.

Winterbourne glanced at the small table near him, on which his coffee-service rested, and saw that several morsels of sugar remained. "Yes, you may take one," he answered; "but I don't think sugar is good for little boys."

This little boy stepped forward and carefully selected three of the coveted fragments, two of which he buried in the pocket of his knickerbockers, depositing the other as promptly in another place. He poked his alpenstock, lance-fashion, into Winterbourne's bench, and tried to crack the lump of sugar with his teeth.

"Oh, blazes; it's har-r-d!" he exclaimed, pronouncing the adjective in a peculiar manner.

Winterbourne had immediately perceived that he might have the honour of claiming him as a fellow-countryman. "Take care you don't hurt your teeth," he said, paternally.

"I haven't got any teeth to hurt. They have all come out. I have only got seven teeth. My mother counted them last night, and one came out right afterwards. She said she'd slap me if any more came out. I can't help it. It's this old Europe. It's the climate that makes them come out. In America they didn't come out. It's these hotels."

Winterbourne was much amused. "If you eat three lumps of sugar, your mother will certainly slap you," he said.

"She's got to give me some candy, then," rejoined his young interlocutor. "I can't get any candy here—any American candy. American candy's the best candy."

"And are American little boys the best little boys?" asked Winterbourne.

"I don't know. I'm an American boy," said the child.

"I see you are one of the best!" laughed Winterbourne.

"Are you an American man?" pursued this vivacious infant. And then, on Winterbourne's affirmative reply—"American men are the best," he declared.

His companion thanked him for the compliment; and the child, who had now got astride of his alpenstock, stood looking about him, while he attacked a second lump of sugar. Winterbourne wondered if he himself had been like this in his infancy, for he had been brought to Europe at about this age.

"Here comes my sister!" cried the child, in a moment. "She's an American girl."

Winterbourne looked along the path and saw a beautiful young lady advancing. "American girls are the best girls," he said, cheerfully, to his young companion.

"My sister ain't the best!" the child declared. "She's always blowing at me."

[8] A mountain-climber's staff, with a metal tip.

"I imagine that is your fault, not hers," said Winterbourne. The young lady meanwhile had drawn near. She was dressed in white muslin, with a hundred frills and flounces, and knots of pale-coloured ribbon. She was bare-headed; but she balanced in her hand a large parasol, with a deep border of embroidery; and she was strikingly, admirably pretty. "How pretty they are!" thought Winterbourne, straightening himself in his seat, as if he were prepared to rise.

The young lady paused in front of his bench, near the parapet of the garden, which overlooked the lake. The little boy had now converted his alpenstock into a vaulting-pole, by the aid of which he was springing about in the gravel, and kicking it up not a little.

"Randolph," said the young lady, "what *are* you doing?"

"I'm going up the Alps," replied Randolph. "This is the way!" And he gave another little jump, scattering the pebbles about Winterbourne's ears.

"That's the way they come down," said Winterbourne.

"He's an American man!" cried Randolph, in his little hard voice.

The young lady gave no heed to this announcement, but looked straight at her brother. "Well, I guess you had better be quiet," she simply observed.

It seemed to Winterbourne that he had been in a manner presented. He got up and stepped slowly towards the young girl, throwing away his cigarette. "This little boy and I have made acquaintance," he said, with great civility. In Geneva, as he had been perfectly aware, a young man was not at liberty to speak to a young unmarried lady except under certain rarely occurring conditions; but here at Vevey, what conditions could be better than these?—a pretty American girl coming and standing in front of you in a garden. This pretty American girl, however, on hearing Winterbourne's observation, simply glanced at him; she then turned her head and looked over the parapet, at the lake and the opposite mountains. He wondered whether he had gone too far; but he decided that he must advance farther, rather than retreat. While he was thinking of something else to say, the young lady turned to the little boy again.

"I should like to know where you got that pole," she said.

"I bought it!" responded Randolph.

"You don't mean to say you're going to take it to Italy."

"Yes, I am going to take it to Italy!" the child declared.

The young girl glanced over the front of her dress, and smoothed out a knot or two of ribbon. Then she rested her eyes upon the prospect again. "Well, I guess you had better leave it somewhere," she said, after a moment.

"Are you going to Italy?" Winterbourne inquired, in a tone of great respect.

The young lady glanced at him again. "Yes, sir," she replied. And she said nothing more.

"Are you—a—going over the Simplon?"[9] Winterbourne pursued, a little embarrassed.

"I don't know," she said. "I suppose it's some mountain. Randolph, what mountain are we going over?"

[9] A scenically spectacular mountain pass through the Alps, near the Italian border; like Chillon, it had been popularized in descriptions by early nineteenth-century English Romantic poets such as Wordsworth and Shelley.

"Going where?" the child demanded.

"To Italy," Winterbourne explained.

"I don't know," said Randolph. "I don't want to go to Italy. I want to go to America."

"Oh, Italy is a beautiful place!" rejoined the young man.

"Can you get candy there?" Randolph loudly inquired.

"I hope not," said his sister. "I guess you have had enough candy, and mother thinks so too."

"I haven't had any for ever so long—for a hundred weeks!" cried the boy, still jumping about.

The young lady inspected her flounces and smoothed her ribbons again; and Winterbourne presently risked an observation upon the beauty of the view. He was ceasing to be embarrassed, for he had begun to perceive that she was not in the least embarrassed herself. There had not been the slightest alteration in her charming complexion; she was evidently neither offended nor fluttered. If she looked another way when he spoke to her, and seemed not particularly to hear him, this was simply her habit, her manner. Yet, as he talked a little more, and pointed out some of the objects of interest in the view, with which she appeared quite unacquainted, she gradually gave him more of the benefit of her glance; and then he saw that this glance was perfectly direct and unshrinking. It was not, however, what would have been called an immodest glance, for the young girl's eyes were singularly honest and fresh. They were wonderfully pretty eyes; and, indeed, Winterbourne had not seen for a long time anything prettier than his fair countrywoman's various features—her complexion, her nose, her ears, her teeth. He had a great relish for feminine beauty; he was addicted to observing and analysing it; and as regards this young lady's face he made several observations. It was not at all insipid, but it was not exactly expressive; and though it was eminently delicate Winterbourne mentally accused it—very forgivingly—of a want of finish. He thought it very possible that Master Randolph's sister was a coquette; he was sure she had a spirit of her own; but in her bright, sweet, superficial little visage there was no mockery, no irony. Before long it became obvious that she was much disposed towards conversation. She told him that they were going to Rome for the winter—she and her mother and Randolph. She asked him if he was a "real American"; she wouldn't have taken him for one; he seemed more like a German—this was said after a little hesitation, especially when he spoke. Winterbourne, laughing, answered that he had met Germans who spoke like Americans; but that he had not, so far as he remembered, met an American who spoke like a German. Then he asked her if she would not be more comfortable in sitting upon the bench which he had just quitted. She answered that she liked standing up and walking about; but she presently sat down. She told him she was from New York State—"if you know where that is." Winterbourne learned more about her by catching hold of her small, slippery brother and making him stand a few minutes by his side.

"Tell me your name, my boy," he said.

"Randolph C. Miller," said the boy, sharply. "And I'll tell you her name," and he levelled his alpenstock at his sister.

"You had better wait till you are asked!" said this young lady, calmly.

"I should like very much to know your name," said Winterbourne.

"Her name is Daisy Miller!" cried the child. "But that isn't her real name; that isn't her name on her cards."

"It's a pity you haven't got one of my cards!" said Miss Miller.

"Her real name is Annie P. Miller," the boy went on.

"Ask him *his* name," said his sister, indicating Winterbourne.

But on this point Randolph seemed perfectly indifferent; he continued to supply information with regard to his own family. "My father's name is Ezra B. Miller," he announced. "My father ain't in Europe; my father's in a better place than Europe."

Winterbourne imagined for a moment that this was the manner in which the child had been taught to intimate that Mr Miller had been removed to the sphere of celestial rewards. But Randolph immediately added, "My father's in Schenectady. He's got a big business. My father's rich, you bet."

"Well!" ejaculated Miss Miller, lowering her parasol and looking at the embroidered border. Winterbourne presently released the child, who departed, dragging his alpenstock along the path. "He doesn't like Europe," said the young girl. "He wants to go back."

"To Schenectady, you mean?"

"Yes; he wants to go right home. He hasn't got any boys here. There is one boy here, but he always goes round with a teacher; they won't let him play."

"And your brother hasn't any teacher?" Winterbourne inquired.

"Mother thought of getting him one, to travel round with us. There was a lady told her of a very good teacher; an American lady—perhaps you know her—Mrs Sanders. I think she came from Boston. She told her of this teacher, and we thought of getting him to travel round with us. But Randolph said he didn't want a teacher travelling round with us. He said he wouldn't have lessons when he was in the cars.[10] And we *are* in the cars about half the time. There was an English lady we met in the cars—I think her name was Miss Featherstone; perhaps you know her. She wanted to know why I didn't give Randolph lessons—give him 'instruction,' she called it. I guess he could give me more instruction than I could give him. He's very smart."

"Yes," said Winterbourne; "he seems very smart."

"Mother's going to get a teacher for him as soon as we get to Italy. Can you get good teachers in Italy?"

"Very good, I should think," said Winterbourne.

"Or else she's going to find some school. He ought to learn some more. He's only nine. He's going to college." And in this way Miss Miller continued to converse upon the affairs of her family, and upon other topics. She sat there with her extremely pretty hands, ornamented with very brilliant rings, folded in her lap, and with her pretty eyes now resting upon those of Winterbourne, now wandering over the garden, the people who passed by, and the beautiful view. She talked to Winterbourne as if she had known him a long time. He found it very pleasant. It was many years since he had heard a young girl talk so much. It might have been said of this unknown young lady, who had come and sat down beside him upon a bench, that she

[10] Railway cars.

chattered. She was very quiet, she sat in a charming tranquil attitude; but her lips and her eyes were constantly moving. She had a soft, slender, agreeable voice, and her tone was decidedly sociable. She gave Winterbourne a history of her movements and intentions, and those of her mother and brother, in Europe, and enumerated, in particular, the various hotels at which they had stopped. "That English lady in the cars," she said—"Miss Featherstone—asked me if we didn't all live in hotels in America. I told her I had never been in so many hotels in my life as since I came to Europe. I have never seen so many—it's nothing but hotels." But Miss Miller did not make this remark with a querulous accent; she appeared to be in the best humour with everything. She declared that the hotels were very good, when once you got used to their ways, and that Europe was perfectly sweet. She was not disappointed—not a bit. Perhaps it was because she had heard so much about it before. She had ever so many intimate friends that had been there ever so many times. And then she had had ever so many dresses and things from Paris. Whenever she put on a Paris dress she felt as if she were in Europe.

"It was a kind of a wishing-cap,"[11] said Winterbourne.

"Yes," said Miss Miller, without examining this analogy; "it always made me wish I was here. But I needn't have done that for dresses. I am sure they send all the pretty ones to America; you see the most frightful things here. The only thing I don't like," she proceeded, "is the society. There isn't any society; or, if there is, I don't know where it keeps itself. Do you? I suppose there is some society somewhere, but I haven't seen anything of it. I'm very fond of society, and I have always had a great deal of it. I don't mean only in Schenectady, but in New York. I used to go to New York every winter. In New York I had lots of society. Last winter I had seventeen dinners given me; and three of them were by gentlemen," added Daisy Miller. "I have more friends in New York than in Schenectady—more gentlemen friends; and more young lady friends too," she resumed in a moment. She paused again for an instant; she was looking at Winterbourne with all her prettiness in her lively eyes and in her light, slightly monotonous smile. "I have always had," she said, "a great deal of gentlemen's society."

Poor Winterbourne was amused, perplexed, and decidedly charmed. He had never yet heard a young girl express herself in just this fashion; never, at least, save in cases where to say such things seemed a kind of demonstrative evidence of a certain laxity of deportment. And yet was he to accuse Miss Daisy Miller of actual or potential *inconduite*,[12] as they said at Geneva? He felt that he had lived at Geneva so long that he had lost a good deal; he had become dishabituated to the American tone. Never, indeed, since he had grown old enough to appreciate things, had he encountered a young American girl of so pronounced a type as this. Certainly she was very charming; but how deucedly sociable! Was she simply a pretty girl from New York State—were they all like that, the pretty girls who had a good deal of gentlemen's society? Or was she also a designing, an audacious, an unscrupulous young person? Winterbourne had lost his instinct

[11] A cap magically empowered to make one's wishes come true.
[12] French: Misconduct.

in this matter, and his reason could not help him. Miss Daisy Miller looked extremely innocent. Some people had told him that, after all, American girls were exceedingly innocent; and others had told him that, after all, they were not. He was inclined to think Miss Daisy Miller was a flirt—a pretty American flirt. He had never, as yet, had any relations with young ladies of this category. He had known, here in Europe, two or three women—persons older than Miss Daisy Miller, and provided, for respectability's sake, with husbands—who were great coquettes— dangerous, terrible women, with whom one's relations were liable to take a serious turn. But this young girl was not a coquette in that sense; she was very unsophisticated; she was only a pretty American flirt. Winterbourne was almost grateful for having found the formula that applied to Miss Daisy Miller. He leaned back in his seat; he remarked to himself that she had the most charming nose he had ever seen; he wondered what were the regular conditions and limitations of one's intercourse with a pretty American flirt. It presently became apparent that he was on the way to learn.

"Have you been to that old castle?" asked the young girl, pointing with her parasol to the far-gleaming walls of the Château de Chillon.

"Yes, formerly, more than once," said Winterbourne. "You too, I suppose, have seen it?"

"No; we haven't been there. I want to go there dreadfully. Of course I mean to go there. I wouldn't go away from here without having seen that old castle."

"It's a very pretty excursion," said Winterbourne, "and very easy to make. You can drive, you know, or you can go by the little steamer."

"You can go in the cars," said Miss Miller.

"Yes; you can go in the cars," Winterbourne assented.

"Our courier[13] says they take you right up to the castle," the young girl continued. "We were going last week; but my mother gave out. She suffers dreadfully from dyspepsia. She said she couldn't go. Randolph wouldn't go either; he says he doesn't think much of old castles. But I guess we'll go this week, if we can get Randolph."

"Your brother is not interested in ancient monuments?" Winterbourne inquired, smiling.

"He says he don't care much about old castles. He's only nine. He wants to stay at the hotel. Mother's afraid to leave him alone, and the courier won't stay with him; so we haven't been to many places. But it will be too bad if we don't go up there." And Miss Miller pointed again at the Château de Chillon.

"I should think it might be arranged," said Winterbourne. "Couldn't you get some one to stay—for the afternoon—with Randolph?"

Miss Miller looked at him a moment; and then, very placidly—"I wish *you* would stay with him!" she said.

Winterbourne hesitated a moment. "I would much rather go to Chillon with you."

"With me?" asked the young girl, with the same placidity.

She didn't rise, blushing, as a young girl at Geneva would have done; and yet Winterbourne, conscious that he had been very bold, thought it

[13] An assistant and guide to tourists.

possible she was offended. "With your mother," he answered very respect-
fully.

But it seemed that both his audacity and his respect were lost upon Miss
Daisy Miller."I guess my mother won't go, after all," she said. "She don't
like to ride round in the afternoon. But did you really mean what you said
just now; that you would like to go up there?"

"Most earnestly," Winterbourne declared.

"Then we may arrange it. If mother will stay with Randolph, I guess
Eugenio will."

"Eugenio?" the young man inquired.

"Eugenio's our courier. He doesn't like to stay with Randolph; he's the
most fastidious man I ever saw. But he's a splendid courier. I guess he'll
stay at home with Randolph if mother does, and then we can go to the
castle."

Winterbourne reflected for an instant as lucidly as possible—"we" could
only mean Miss Daisy Miller and himself. This programme seemed almost
too agreeable for credence; he felt as if he ought to kiss the young lady's
hand. Possibly he would have done so—and quite spoiled the project; but
at this moment another person—presumably Eugenio—appeared. A tall,
handsome man, with superb whiskers, wearing a velvet morning-coat and a
brilliant watch-chain, approached Miss Miller, looking sharply at her com-
panion. "Oh, Eugenio!" said Miss Miller, with the friendliest accent.

Eugenio had looked at Winterbourne from head to foot; he now bowed
gravely to the young lady. "I have the honour to inform mademoiselle that
luncheon is upon the table."

Miss Miller slowly rose. "See here, Eugenio," she said. "I'm going to that
old castle, any way."

"To the Château de Chillon, mademoiselle?" the courier inquired. "Ma-
demoiselle has made arrangements?" he added, in a tone which struck
Winterbourne as very impertinent.

Eugenio's tone apparently threw, even to Miss Miller's own apprehen-
sion, a slightly ironical light upon the young girl's situation. She turned to
Winterbourne, blushing a little—a very little. "You won't back out?" she
said.

"I shall not be happy till we go!" he protested.

"And you are staying in this hotel?" she went on. "And you are really an
American?"

The courier stood looking at Winterbourne, offensively. The young
man, at least, thought his manner of looking an offence to Miss Miller; it
conveyed an imputation that she "picked up" acquaintances. "I shall have
the honour of presenting to you a person who will tell you all about me," he
said smiling, and referring to his aunt.

"Oh, well, we'll go some day," said Miss Miller. And she gave him a smile
and turned away. She put up her parasol and walked back to the inn beside
Eugenio. Winterbourne stood looking after her; and as she moved away,
drawing her muslin furbelows[14] over the gravel, said to himself that she
had the *tournure*[15] of a princess.

He had, however, engaged to do more than proved feasible, in promis-

[14] Fancy, pleated trimmings at the hemline. [15] French: figure; lines.

ing to present his aunt, Mrs Costello, to Miss Daisy Miller. As soon as the former lady had got better of her headache he waited upon her in her apartment; and, after the proper inquiries in regard to her health, he asked her if she had observed, in the hotel, an American family—a mamma, a daughter, and a little boy.

"And a courier?" said Mrs Costello. "Oh, yes, I have observed them. Seen them—heard them—and kept out of their way." Mrs Costello was a widow with a fortune; a person of much distinction, who frequently intimated that, if she were not so dreadfully liable to sick-headaches, she would probably have left a deeper impress upon her time. She had a long pale face, a high nose, and a great deal of very striking white hair, which she wore in large puffs and *rouleaux*[16] over the top of her head. She had two sons married in New York, and another who was now in Europe. This young man was amusing himself at Hamburg, and, though he was on his travels, was rarely perceived to visit any particular city at the moment selected by his mother for her own appearance there. Her nephew, who had come up to Vevey expressly to see her, was therefore more attentive than those who, as she said, were nearer to her. He had imbibed at Geneva the idea that one must always be attentive to one's aunt. Mrs Costello had not seen him for many years, and she was greatly pleased with him, manifesting her approbation by initiating him into many of the secrets of that social sway which, as she gave him to understand, she exerted in the American capital.[17] She admitted that she was very exclusive; but, if he were acquainted with New York, he would see that one had to be. And her picture of the minutely hierarchical constitution of the society of that city, which she presented to him in many different lights, was, to Winterbourne's imagination, almost oppressively striking.

He immediately perceived, from her tone, that Miss Daisy Miller's place in the social scale was low. "I am afraid you don't approve of them," he said.

"They are very common," Mrs Costello declared. "They are the sort of Americans that one does one's duty by not—not accepting."

"Ah, you don't accept them?" said the young man.

"I can't, my dear Frederick. I would if I could, but I can't."

"The young girl is very pretty," said Winterbourne, in a moment.

"Of course she's pretty. But she is very common."

"I see what you mean, of course," said Winterbourne, after another pause.

"She has that charming look that they all have," his aunt resumed. "I can't think where they pick it up; and she dresses in perfection—no, you don't know how well she dresses. I can't think where they get their taste."

"But, my dear aunt, she is not, after all, a Comanche savage."

"She is a young lady," said Mrs Costello, "who has an intimacy with her mamma's courier."

"An intimacy with the courier?" the young man demanded.

"Oh, the mother is just as bad! They treat the courier like a familiar friend—like a gentleman. I shouldn't wonder if he dines with them. Very likely they have never seen a man with such good manners, such fine clothes, so like a gentleman. He probably corresponds to the young lady's

[16] French: coils. [17] Principal city—i.e., New York.

idea of a Count. He sits with them in the garden, in the evening. I think he smokes."

Winterbourne listened with interest to these disclosures; they helped him to make up his mind about Miss Daisy. Evidently she was rather wild. "Well," he said, "I am not a courier, and yet she was very charming to me."

"You had better have said at first," said Mrs Costello, with dignity, "that you had made her acquaintance."

"We simply met in the garden, and we talked a bit."

"*Tout bonnement!*[18] And pray what did you say?"

"I said I should take the liberty of introducing her to my admirable aunt."

"I am much obliged to you."

"It was to guarantee my respectability," said Winterbourne.

"And pray who is to guarantee hers?"

"Ah, you are cruel!" said the young man. "She's a very nice girl."

"You don't say that as if you believed it," Mrs Costello observed.

"She is completely uncultivated," Winterbourne went on. "But she is wonderfully pretty, and, in short, she is very nice. To prove that I believe it, I am going to take her to the Château de Chillon."

"You two are going off there together? I should say it proved just the contrary. How long had you known her, may I ask, when this interesting project was formed? You haven't been twenty-four hours in the house."

"I had known her half-an-hour!" said Winterbourne, smiling.

"Dear me!" cried Mrs Costello. "What a dreadful girl!"

Her nephew was silent for some moments. "You really think, then," he began, earnestly, and with a desire for trust-worthy information—"you really think that——" But he paused again.

"Think what, sir?" said his aunt.

"That she is the sort of young lady who expects a man—sooner or later—to carry her off?"

"I haven't the least idea what such young ladies expect a man to do. But I really think that you had better not meddle with little American girls that are uncultivated, as you call them. You have lived too long out of the country. You will be sure to make some great mistake. You are too innocent."

"My dear aunt, I am not so innocent," said Winterbourne, smiling and curling his moustache.

"You are too guilty, then!"

Winterbourne continued to curl his moustache, meditatively. "You won't let the poor girl know you then?" he asked at last.

"Is it literally true that she is going to the Château de Chillon with you?"

"I think that she fully intends it."

"Then, my dear Frederick," said Mrs Costello, "I must decline the honour of her acquaintance. I am an old woman, but I am not too old—thank Heaven—to be shocked!"

"But don't they all do these things—the young girls in America?" Winterbourne inquired.

Mrs Costello stared a moment. "I should like to see my granddaughters do them!" she declared, grimly.

[18] French: "Simply!" "Quite frankly!"

This seemed to throw some light upon the matter, for Winterbourne remembered to have heard that his pretty cousins in New York were "tremendous flirts." If, therefore, Miss Daisy Miller exceeded the liberal license allowed to these young ladies, it was probable that anything might be expected of her. Winterbourne was impatient to see her again, and he was vexed with himself that, by instinct, he should not appreciate her justly.

Though he was impatient to see her, he hardly knew what he should say to her about his aunt's refusal to become acquainted with her; but he discovered, promptly enough, that with Miss Daisy Miller there was no great need of walking on tiptoe. He found her that evening in the garden, wandering about in the warm starlight, like an indolent sylph,[19] and swinging to and fro the largest fan he had ever beheld. It was ten o'clock. He had dined with his aunt, had been sitting with her since dinner, and had just taken leave of her till the morrow. Miss Daisy Miller seemed very glad to see him; she declared it was the longest evening she had ever passed.

"Have you been all alone?" he asked.

"I have been walking round with mother. But mother gets tired walking round," she answered.

"Has she gone to bed?"

"No; she doesn't like to go to bed," said the young girl. "She doesn't sleep—not three hours. She says she doesn't know how she lives. She's dreadfully nervous. I guess she sleeps more than she thinks. She's gone somewhere after Randolph; she wants to try to get him to go to bed. He doesn't like to go to bed."

"Let us hope she will persuade him," observed Winterbourne.

"She will talk to him all she can; but he doesn't like her to talk to him," said Miss Daisy, opening her fan. "She's going to try to get Eugenio to talk to him. But he isn't afraid of Eugenio. Eugenio's a splendid courier, but he can't make much impression on Randolph! I don't believe he'll go to bed before eleven." It appeared that Randolph's vigil was in fact triumphantly prolonged, for Winterbourne strolled about with the young girl for some time without meeting her mother. "I have been looking round for that lady you want to introduce me to," his companion resumed. "She's your aunt." Then, on Winterbourne's admitting the fact, and expressing some curiosity as to how she had learned it, she said she had heard all about Mrs Costello from the chambermaid. She was very quiet and very *comme il faut;*[20] she wore white puffs; she spoke to no one, and she never dined at the *table d'hôte.*[21] Every two days she had a headache. "I think that's a lovely description, headache and all!" said Miss Daisy, chattering along in her thin, gay voice. "I want to know her ever so much. I know just what *your* aunt would be; I know I should like her. She would be very exclusive. I like a lady to be exclusive; I'm dying to be exclusive myself. Well, we *are* exclusive, mother and I. We don't speak to every one—or they don't speak to us. I suppose it's about the same thing. Any way, I shall be ever so glad to know your aunt."

Winterbourne was embarrassed. "She would be most happy," he said; "but I am afraid those headaches will interfere."

[19] Dainty inhabitant of the air. [20] French: proper; correct.
[21] French: "host's table," serving standard or prescribed dishes.

The young girl looked at him through the dusk. "But I suppose she doesn't have a headache every day," she said, sympathetically.

Winterbourne was silent a moment. "She tells me she does," he answered at last—not knowing what to say.

Miss Daisy Miller stopped and stood looking at him. Her prettiness was still visible in the darkness; she was opening and closing her enormous fan. "She doesn't want to know me!" she said, suddenly. "Why don't you say so? You needn't be afraid. I'm not afraid!" And she gave a little laugh.

Winterbourne fancied there was a tremor in her voice; he was touched, shocked, mortified by it. "My dear young lady," he protested, "she knows no one. It's her wretched health."

The young girl walked on a few steps, laughing still. "You needn't be afraid," she repeated. "Why should she want to know me?" Then she paused again; she was close to the parapet of the garden, and in front of her was the starlit lake. There was a vague sheen upon its surface, and in the distance were dimly seen mountain forms. Daisy Miller looked out upon the mysterious prospect, and then she gave another little laugh. "Gracious! she *is* exclusive!" she said. Winterbourne wondered whether she was seriously wounded, and for a moment almost wished that her sense of injury might be such as to make it becoming in him to attempt to reassure and comfort her. He had a pleasant sense that she would be very approachable for consolatory purposes. He felt then, for the instant, quite ready to sacrifice his aunt, conversationally; to admit that she was a proud, rude woman, and to declare that they needn't mind her. But before he had time to commit himself to this perilous mixture of gallantry and impiety, the young lady, resuming her walk, gave an exclamation in quite another tone. "Well; here's mother! I guess she hasn't got Randolph to go to bed." The figure of a lady appeared, at a distance, very indistinct in the darkness, and advancing with a slow and wavering movement. Suddenly it seemed to pause.

"Are you sure it is your mother? Can you distinguish her in this thick dusk?" Winterbourne asked.

"Well!" cried Miss Daisy Miller, with a laugh, "I guess I know my own mother. And when she has got on my shawl, too! She is always wearing my things."

The lady in question, ceasing to advance, hovered vaguely about the spot at which she had checked her steps.

"I am afraid your mother doesn't see you," said Winterbourne. "Or perhaps," he added—thinking, with Miss Miller, the joke permissible—"perhaps she feels guilty about your shawl."

"Oh, it's a fearful old thing!" the young girl replied, serenely. "I told her she could wear it. She won't come here, because she sees you."

"Ah, then," said Winterbourne, "I had better leave you."

"Oh no; come on!" urged Miss Daisy Miller.

"I'm afraid your mother doesn't approve of my walking with you."

Miss Miller gave him a serious glance. "It isn't for me; it's for you—that is, it's for *her*. Well; I don't know who it's for! But mother doesn't like any of my gentlemen friends. She's right down timid. She always makes a fuss if I introduce a gentleman. But I *do* introduce them—almost always. If I didn't

introduce my gentlemen friends to mother," the young girl added, in her little soft, flat monotone, "I shouldn't think I was natural."

"To introduce me," said Winterbourne, "you must know my name." And he proceeded to pronounce it.

"Oh, dear; I can't say all that!" said his companion, with a laugh. But by this time they had come up to Mrs Miller, who, as they drew near, walked to the parapet of the garden and leaned upon it, looking intently at the lake and turning her back upon them. "Mother!" said the young girl, in a tone of decision. Upon this the elder lady turned round. "Mr Winterbourne," said Miss Daisy Miller, introducing the young man very frankly and prettily. "Common," she was, as Mrs Costello had pronounced her; yet it was a wonder to Winterbourne that, with her commonness, she had a singularly delicate grace.

Her mother was a small, spare, light person, with a wandering eye, a very exiguous[22] nose, and a large forehead, decorated with a certain amount of thin, much-frizzled hair. Like her daughter, Mrs Miller was dressed with extreme elegance; she had enormous diamonds in her ears. So far as Winterbourne could observe, she gave him no greeting—she certainly was not looking at him. Daisy was near her, pulling her shawl straight. "What are you doing, poking round here?" this young lady inquired; but by no means with that harshness of accent which her choice of words may imply.

"I don't know," said her mother, turning towards the lake again.

"I shouldn't think you'd want that shawl!" Daisy exclaimed.

"Well—I do!" her mother answered, with a little laugh.

"Did you get Randolph to go to bed?" asked the young girl.

"No; I couldn't induce him," said Mrs Miller, very gently. "He wants to talk to the waiter. He likes to talk to that waiter."

"I was telling Mr Winterbourne," the young girl went on; and to the young man's ear her tone might have indicated that she had been uttering his name all her life.

"Oh, yes!" said Winterbourne; "I have the pleasure of knowing your son."

Randolph's mamma was silent; she turned her attention to the lake. But at last she spoke. "Well, I don't see how he lives!"

"Anyhow, it isn't so bad as it was at Dover,"[23] said Daisy Miller.

"And what occurred at Dover?" Winterbourne asked.

"He wouldn't go to bed at all. I guess he sat up all night—in the public parlour. He wasn't in bed at twelve o'clock: I know that."

"It was half-past twelve," declared Mrs Miller, with mild emphasis.

"Does he sleep much during the day?" Winterbourne demanded.

"I guess he doesn't sleep much," Daisy rejoined.

"I wish he would!" said her mother. "It seems as if he couldn't."

"I think he's real tiresome," Daisy pursued.

Then, for some moments, there was silence. "Well, Daisy Miller," said

[22] Small; meager.
[23] The city, on the English Channel, from which travelers generally embarked for France.

the elder lady, presently, "I shouldn't think you'd want to talk against your own brother!"

"Well, he *is* tiresome, mother," said Daisy, quite without the asperity of a retort.

"He's only nine," urged Mrs Miller.

"Well, he wouldn't go to that castle," said the young girl. "I'm going there with Mr Winterbourne."

To this announcement, very placidly made, Daisy's mamma offered no response. Winterbourne took for granted that she deeply disapproved of the projected excursion; but he said to himself that she was a simple, easily managed person, and that a few deferential protestations would take the edge from her displeasure. "Yes," he began; "your daughter has kindly allowed me the honour of being her guide."

Mrs Miller's wandering eyes attached themselves, with a sort of appealing air, to Daisy, who, however, strolled a few steps farther, gently humming to herself. "I presume you will go in the cars," said her mother.

"Yes; or in the boat," said Winterbourne.

"Well, of course, I don't know," Mrs Miller rejoined. "I have never been to that castle."

"It is a pity you shouldn't go," said Winterbourne, beginning to feel reassured as to her opposition. And yet he was quite prepared to find that, as a matter of course, she meant to accompany her daughter.

"We've been thinking ever so much about going," she pursued; "but it seems as if we couldn't. Of course Daisy—she wants to go round. But there's a lady here—I don't know her name—she says she shouldn't think we'd want to go to see castles *here;* she should think we'd want to wait till we got to Italy. It seems as if there would be so many there," continued Mrs Miller, with an air of increasing confidence. "Of course, we only want to see the principal ones. We visited several in England," she presently added.

"Ah, yes! in England there are beautiful castles," said Winterbourne. "But Chillon, here, is very well worth seeing."

"Well, if Daisy feels up to it——," said Mrs Miller, in a tone impregnated with a sense of the magnitude of the enterprise. "It seems as if there was nothing she wouldn't undertake."

"Oh, I think she'll enjoy it!" Winterbourne declared. And he desired more and more to make it a certainty that he was to have the privilege of a *tête-à-tête*[24] with the young lady, who was still strolling along in front of them, softly vocalising. "You are not disposed, madam," he inquired, "to undertake it yourself?"

Daisy's mother looked at him, an instant, askance, and then walked forward in silence. Then—"I guess she had better go alone," she said, simply.

Winterbourne observed to himself that this was a very different type of maternity from that of the vigilant matrons who massed themselves in the forefront of social intercourse in the dark old city at the other end of the lake. But his meditations were interrupted by hearing his name very distinctly pronounced by Mrs Miller's unprotected daughter.

"Mr Winterbourne!" murmured Daisy.

[24] A party of two.

"Mademoiselle!" said the young man.

"Don't you want to take me out in a boat?"

"At present?" he asked.

"Of course!" said Daisy.

"Well, Annie Miller!" exclaimed her mother.

"I beg you, madam, to let her go," said Winterbourne, ardently; for he had never yet enjoyed the sensation of guiding through the summer starlight a skiff freighted with a fresh and beautiful young girl.

"I shouldn't think she'd want to," said her mother. "I should think she'd rather go indoors."

"I'm sure Mr Winterbourne wants to take me," Daisy declared. "He's so awfully devoted!"

"I will row you over to Chillon, in the starlight."

"I don't believe it!" said Daisy.

"Well!" ejaculated the elder lady again.

"You haven't spoken to me for half-an-hour," her daughter went on.

"I have been having some very pleasant conversation with your mother," said Winterbourne.

"Well; I want you to take me out in a boat!" Daisy repeated. They had all stopped, and she had turned round and was looking at Winterbourne. Her face wore a charming smile, her pretty eyes were gleaming, she was swinging her great fan about. No; it's impossible to be prettier than that, thought Winterbourne.

"There are half-a-dozen boats moored at that landing-place," he said, pointing to certain steps which descended from the garden to the lake. "If you will do me the honour to accept my arm, we will go and select one of them."

Daisy stood there smiling; she threw back her head and gave a little light laugh. "I like a gentleman to be formal!" she declared.

"I assure you it's a formal offer."

"I was bound I would make you say something," Daisy went on.

"You see it's not very difficult," said Winterbourne. "But I am afraid you are chaffing[25] me."

"I think not, sir," remarked Mrs Miller, very gently.

"Do, then, let me give you a row," he said to the young girl.

"It's quite lovely, the way you say that!" cried Daisy.

"It will be still more lovely to do it."

"Yes, it would be lovely!" said Daisy. But she made no movement to accompany him; she only stood there laughing.

"I should think you had better find out what time it is," interposed her mother.

"It is eleven o'clock, madam," said a voice, with a foreign accent, out of the neighbouring darkness; and Winterbourne, turning, perceived the florid personage who was in attendance upon the two ladies. He had apparently just approached.

"Oh, Eugenio," said Daisy, "I am going out in a boat!"

Eugenio bowed. "At eleven o'clock, mademoiselle?"

"I am going with Mr Winterbourne. This very minute."

[25] Making fun of.

"Do tell her she can't," said Mrs Miller to the courier.

"I think you had better not go out in a boat, mademoiselle," Eugenio declared.

Winterbourne wished to Heaven this pretty girl were not so familiar with her courier; but he said nothing.

"I suppose you don't think it's proper!" Daisy exclaimed. "Eugenio doesn't think anything's proper."

"I am at your service," said Winterbourne.

"Does mademoiselle propose to go alone?" asked Eugenio of Mrs Miller.

"Oh, no; with this gentleman!" answered Daisy's mamma.

The courier looked for a moment at Winterbourne—the latter thought he was smiling—and then, solemnly, with a bow, "As mademoiselle pleases!" he said.

"Oh, I hoped you would make a fuss!" said Daisy. "I don't care to go now."

"I myself shall make a fuss if you don't go," said Winterbourne.

"That's all I want—a little fuss!" And the young girl began to laugh again.

"Mr Randolph has gone to bed!" the courier announced, frigidly.

"Oh, Daisy; now we can go!" said Mrs Miller.

Daisy turned away from Winterbourne, looking at him, smiling and fanning herself. "Good night," she said; "I hope you are disappointed, or disgusted, or something!"

He looked at her, taking the hand she offered him. "I am puzzled," he answered.

"Well; I hope it won't keep you awake!" she said, very smartly; and, under the escort of the privileged Eugenio, the two ladies passed towards the house.

Winterbourne stood looking after them; he was indeed puzzled. He lingered beside the lake for a quarter of an hour, turning over the mystery of the young girl's sudden familiarities and caprices. But the only very definite conclusion he came to was that he should enjoy deucedly "going off" with her somewhere.

Two days afterwards he went off with her to the Castle of Chillon. He waited for her in the large hall of the hotel, where the couriers, the servants, the foreign tourists were lounging about and staring. It was not the place he would have chosen, but she had appointed it. She came tripping downstairs, buttoning her long gloves, squeezing her folded parasol against her pretty figure, dressed in the perfection of a soberly elegant travelling-costume. Winterbourne was a man of imagination and, as our ancestors used to say, of sensibility; as he looked at her dress and, on the great stair-case, her little rapid, confiding step, he felt as if there were something romantic going forward. He could have believed he was going to elope with her. He passed out with her among all the idle people that were assembled there; they were all looking at her very hard; she had begun to chatter as soon as she joined him. Winterbourne's preference had been that they should be conveyed to Chillon in a carriage; but she expressed a lively wish to go in the little steamer; she declared that she had a passion for steam-

boats. There was always such a lovely breeze upon the water, and you saw such lots of people. The sail was not long, but Winterbourne's companion found time to say a great many things. To the young man himself their little excursion was so much of an escapade—an adventure—that, even allowing for her habitual sense of freedom, he had some expectation of seeing her regard it in the same way. But it must be confessed that, in this particular, he was disappointed. Daisy Miller was extremely animated, she was in charming spirits; but she was apparently not at all excited; she was not fluttered; she avoided neither his eyes nor those of any one else; she blushed neither when she looked at him nor when she saw that people were looking at her. People continued to look at her a great deal, and Winterbourne took much satisfaction in his pretty companion's distinguished air. He had been a little afraid that she would talk loud, laugh overmuch, and even, perhaps, desire to move about the boat a good deal. But he quite forgot his fears; he sat smiling, with his eyes upon her face, while, without moving from her place, she delivered herself of a great number of original reflections. It was the most charming garrulity he had ever heard. He had assented to the idea that she was "common," but was she so, after all, or was he simply getting used to her commonness? Her conversation was chiefly of what metaphysicians term the objective cast; but every now and then it took a subjective turn.

"What on *earth* are you so grave about?" she suddenly demanded, fixing her agreeable eyes upon Winterbourne's.

"Am I grave?" he asked. "I had an idea I was grinning from ear to ear."

"You look as if you were taking me to a funeral. If that's a grin, your ears are very near together."

"Should you like me to dance a hornpipe on the deck?"

"Pray do, and I'll carry round your hat. It will pay the expenses of our journey."

"I never was better pleased in my life," murmured Winterbourne.

She looked at him a moment, and then burst into a little laugh. "I like to make you say those things! You're a queer mixture!"

In the castle, after they had landed, the subjective element decidedly prevailed. Daisy tripped about the vaulted chambers, rustled her skirts in the corkscrew staircases, flirted back with a pretty little cry and a shudder from the edge of the *oubliettes*,[26] and turned a singularly well-shaped ear to everything that Winterbourne told her about the place. But he saw that she cared very little for feudal antiquities, and that the dusky traditions of Chillon made but a slight impression upon her. They had the good fortune to have been able to walk about without other companionship than that of the custodian; and Winterbourne arranged with this functionary that they should not be hurried—that they should linger and pause wherever they chose. The custodian interpreted the bargain generously—Winterbourne, on his side, had been generous—and ended by leaving them quite to themselves. Miss Miller's observations were not remarkable for logical consistency; for anything she wanted to say she was sure to find a pretext. She

[26] French: "Forget-places"; dungeons doorless except at the top, where prisoners could be left to die, "forgotten."

found a great many pretexts in the rugged embrasures[27] of Chillon for asking Winterbourne sudden questions about himself—his family, his previous history, his tastes, his habits, his intentions—and for supplying information upon corresponding points in her own personality. Of her own tastes, habits and intentions Miss Miller was prepared to give the most definite, and indeed the most favourable, account.

"Well; I hope you know enough!" she said to her companion, after he had told her the history of the unhappy Bonivard. "I never saw a man that knew so much!" The history of Bonivard had evidently, as they say, gone into one ear and out of the other. But Daisy went on to say that she wished Winterbourne would travel with them and "go round" with them; they might know something, in that case. "Don't you want to come and teach Randolph?" she asked. Winterbourne said that nothing could possibly please him so much; but that he had unfortunately other occupations. "Other occupations? I don't believe it!" said Miss Daisy. "What do you mean? You are not in business." The young man admitted that he was not in business; but he had engagements which, even within a day or two, would force him to go back to Geneva. "Oh, bother!" she said, "I don't believe it!" and she began to talk about something else. But a few moments later, when he was pointing out to her the pretty design of an antique fireplace, she broke out irrelevantly, "You don't mean to say you are going back to Geneva?"

"It is a melancholy fact that I shall have to return to Geneva tomorrow."

"Well, Mr Winterbourne," said Daisy; "I think you're horrid!"

"Oh, don't say such dreadful things!" said Winterbourne—"just at the last."

"The last!" cried the young girl; "I call it the first. I have half a mind to leave you here and go straight back to the hotel alone." And for the next ten minutes she did nothing but call him horrid. Poor Winterbourne was fairly bewildered; no young lady had as yet done him the honour to be so agitated by the announcement of his movements. His companion, after this, ceased to pay any attention to the curiosities of Chillon or the beauties of the lake; she opened fire upon the mysterious charmer in Geneva, whom she appeared to have instantly taken it for granted that he was hurrying back to see. How did Miss Daisy Miller know that there was a charmer in Geneva? Winterbourne, who denied the existence of such a person, was quite unable to discover; and he was divided between amazement at the rapidity of her induction and amusement at the frankness of her *persiflage*.[28] She seemed to him, in all this, an extraordinary mixture of innocence and crudity. "Does she never allow you more than three days at a time?" asked Daisy, ironically. "Doesn't she give you a vacation in summer? There's no one so hard worked but they can get leave to go off somewhere at this season. I suppose, if you stay another day, she'll come after you in the boat. Do wait over till Friday, and I will go down to the landing to see her arrive!" Winterbourne began to think he had been wrong to feel disappointed in the temper in which the young lady had embarked. If he had missed the personal accent, the personal accent was now making its appear-

[27] Tapered openings in the stone walls. [28] Playful, teasing talk.

ance. It sounded very distinctly, at last, in her telling him she would stop "teasing" him if he would promise her solemnly to come down to Rome in the winter.

"That's not a difficult promise to make," said Winterbourne. "My aunt has taken an apartment in Rome for the winter, and has already asked me to come and see her."

"I don't want you to come for your aunt," said Daisy; "I want you to come for me." And this was the only allusion that the young man was ever to hear her make to his invidious[29] kinswoman. He declared that, at any rate, he would certainly come. After this Daisy stopped teasing. Winterbourne took a carriage, and they drove back to Vevey in the dusk; the young girl was very quiet.

In the evening Winterbourne mentioned to Mrs Costello that he had spent the afternoon at Chillon, with Miss Daisy Miller.

"The Americans—of the courier?" asked this lady.

"Ah, happily," said Winterbourne, "the courier stayed at home."

"She went with you all alone?"

"All alone."

Mrs Costello sniffed a little at her smelling-bottle. "And that," she exclaimed, "is the young person you wanted me to know!"

PART II: ROME

Winterbourne, who had returned to Geneva the day after his excursion to Chillon, went to Rome towards the end of January. His aunt had been established there for several weeks, and he had received a couple of letters from her. "Those people you were so devoted to last summer at Vevey have turned up here, courier and all," she wrote. "They seem to have made several acquaintances, but the courier continues to be the most *intime*. The young lady, however, is also very intimate with some third-rate Italians, with whom she rackets about in a way that makes much talk. Bring me that pretty novel of Cherbuliez's—'Paule Méré'—and don't come later than the 23rd."

In the natural course of events, Winterbourne, on arriving in Rome, would presently have ascertained Mrs Miller's address at the American banker's and have gone to pay his compliments to Miss Daisy. "After what happened at Vevey I certainly think I may call upon them," he said to Mrs Costello.

"If, after what happens—at Vevey and everywhere—you desire to keep up the acquaintance, you are very welcome. Of course a man may know everyone. Men are welcome to the privilege!"

"Pray what is it that happens—here, for instance?" Winterbourne demanded.

"The girl goes about alone with her foreigners. As to what happens farther, you must apply elsewhere for information. She has picked up half-a-dozen of the regular Roman fortune-hunters, and she takes them about

[29] Offensive; hateful.

to people's houses. When she comes to a party she brings with her a gentle-man with a good deal of manner and a wonderful moustache."

"And where is the mother?"

"I haven't the least idea. They are very dreadful people."

Winterbourne meditated a moment. "They are very ignorant—very innocent only. Depend upon it they are not bad."

"They are hopelessly vulgar," said Mrs Costello. "Whether or no being hopelessly vulgar is being 'bad' is a question for the metaphysicians. They are bad enough to dislike, at any rate; and for this short life that is quite enough."

The news that Daisy Miller was surrounded by half-a-dozen wonderful moustaches checked Winterbourne's impulse to go straightway to see her. He had perhaps not definitely flattered himself that he had made an ineffaceable impression upon her heart, but he was annoyed at hearing of a state of affairs so little in harmony with an image that had lately flitted in and out of his own meditations; the image of a very pretty girl looking out of an old Roman window and asking herself urgently when Mr Winterbourne would arrive. If, however, he determined to wait a little before reminding Miss Miller of his claims to her consideration, he went very soon to call upon two or three other friends. One of these friends was an American lady who had spent several winters at Geneva, where she had placed her children at school. She was a very accomplished woman and she lived in the Via Gregoriana. Winterbourne found her in a little crimson drawing-room, on a third floor; the room was filled with southern sunshine. He had not been there ten minutes when the servant came in, announcing "Madame Mila!" This announcement was presently followed by the entrance of little Randolph Miller, who stopped in the middle of the room and stood staring at Winterbourne. An instant later his pretty sister crossed the threshold; and then, after a considerable interval, Mrs Miller slowly advanced.

"I know you!" said Randolph.

"I'm sure you know a great many things," exclaimed Winterbourne, taking him by the hand. "How is your education coming on?"

Daisy was exchanging greetings very prettily with her hostess; but when she heard Winterbourne's voice she quickly turned her head. "Well, I declare!" she said.

"I told you I should come, you know," Winterbourne rejoined, smiling.

"Well—I didn't believe it," said Miss Daisy.

"I am much obliged to you," laughed the young man.

"You might have come to see me!" said Daisy.

"I arrived only yesterday."

"I don't believe that!" the young girl declared.

Winterbourne turned with a protesting smile to her mother; but this lady evaded his glance, and seating herself, fixed her eyes upon her son. "We've got a bigger place than this," said Randolph. "It's all gold on the walls."

Mrs Miller turned uneasily in her chair. "I told you if I were to bring you, you would say something!" she murmured.

"I told *you!*" Randolph exclaimed. "I tell *you,* sir!" he added jocosely, giving Winterbourne a thump on the knee. "It *is* bigger, too!"

Daisy had entered upon a lively conversation with her hostess; Winterbourne judged it becoming to address a few words to her mother. "I hope you have been well since we parted at Vevey," he said.

Mrs Miller now certainly looked at him—at his chin. "Not very well, sir," she answered.

"She's got the dyspepsia," said Randolph. "I've got it too. Father's got it. I've got it worst!"

This announcement, instead of embarrassing Mrs Miller, seemed to relieve her. "I suffer from the liver," she said. "I think it's this climate; it's less bracing than Schenectady, especially in the winter season. I don't know whether you know we reside at Schenectady. I was saying to Daisy that I certainly hadn't found any one like Dr Davis, and I didn't believe I should. Oh, at Schenectady, he stands first; they think everything of him. He has so much to do, and yet there was nothing he wouldn't do for me. He said he never saw anything like my dyspepsia, but he was bound to cure it. I'm sure there was nothing he wouldn't try. He was just going to try something new when we came off. Mr Miller wanted Daisy to see Europe for herself. But I wrote to Mr Miller that it seems as if I couldn't get on without Dr Davis. At Schenectady he stands at the very top; and there's a great deal of sickness there, too. It affects my sleep."

Winterbourne had a good deal of pathological gossip with Dr Davis's patient, during which Daisy chattered unremittingly to her own companion. The young man asked Mrs Miller how she was pleased with Rome. "Well, I must say I am disappointed," she answered. "We had heard so much about it; I suppose we had heard too much. But we couldn't help that. We had been led to expect something different."

"Ah, wait a little, and you will become very fond of it," said Winterbourne.

"I hate it worse and worse every day!"cried Randolph.

"You are like the infant Hannibal,"[30] said Winterbourne.

"No, I ain't!" Randolph declared, at a venture.

"You are not much like an infant," said his mother. "But we have seen places," she resumed, "that I should put a long way before Rome." And in reply to Winterbourne's interrogation, "There's Zurich," she observed; "I think Zurich is lovely; and we hadn't heard half so much about it."

"The best place we've seen is the City of Richmond!" said Randolph.

"He means the ship," his mother explained. "We crossed in that ship. Randolph had a good time on the City of Richmond."

"It's the best place I've seen," the child repeated. "Only it was turned the wrong way."

"Well, we've got to turn the right way some time," said Mrs Miller, with a little laugh. Winterbourne expressed the hope that her daughter at least found some gratification in Rome, and she declared that Daisy was quite carried away. "It's on account of the society—the society's splendid. She goes round everywhere; she has made a great number of acquaintances. Of course she goes round more than I do. I must say they have been very

[30]Carthaginian general who in 218 B.C. led an invading army over the Alps into Italy, after which he severely defeated the Romans in a number of battles and threatened Rome itself. The Romans finally defeated him in north Africa.

sociable; they have taken her right in. And then she knows a great many gentlemen. Oh, she thinks there's nothing like Rome. Of course, it's a great deal pleasanter for a young lady if she knows plenty of gentlemen."

By this time Daisy had turned her attention again to Winterbourne. "I've been telling Mrs Walker how mean you were!" the young girl announced.

"And what is the evidence you have offered?" asked Winterbourne, rather annoyed at Miss Miller's want of appreciation of the zeal of an admirer who on his way down to Rome had stopped neither at Bologna nor at Florence, simply because of a certain sentimental impatience. He remembered that a cynical compatriot had once told him that American women—the pretty ones, and this gave a largeness to the axiom—were at once the most exacting in the world and the least endowed with a sense of indebtedness.

"Why, you were awfully mean at Vevey," said Daisy. "You wouldn't do anything. You wouldn't stay there when I asked you."

"My dearest young lady," cried Winterbourne, with eloquence, "have I come all the way to Rome to encounter your reproaches?"

"Just hear him say that!" said Daisy to her hostess, giving a twist to a bow on this lady's dress. "Did you ever hear anything so quaint?"

"So quaint, my dear?" murmured Mrs Walker, in the tone of a partisan of Winterbourne.

"Well, I don't know," said Daisy, fingering Mrs Walker's ribbons. "Mrs Walker, I want to tell you something."

"Mother," interposed Randolph, with his rough ends to his words, "I tell you you've got to go. Eugenio'll raise something!"

"I'm not afraid of Eugenio," said Daisy, with a toss of her head. "Look here, Mrs Walker," she went on, "you know I'm coming to your party."

"I am delighted to hear it."

"I've got a lovely dress."

"I am very sure of that."

"But I want to ask a favour—permission to bring a friend."

"I shall be happy to see any of your friends," said Mrs Walker, turning with a smile to Mrs Miller.

"Oh, they are not my friends," answered Daisy's mamma, smiling shyly, in her own fashion. "I never spoke to them!"

"It's an intimate friend of mine—Mr Giovanelli," said Daisy, without a tremor in her clear little voice or a shadow on her brilliant little face.

Mrs Walker was silent a moment, she gave a rapid glance at Winterbourne. "I shall be glad to see Mr Giovanelli," she then said.

"He's an Italian," Daisy pursued, with the prettiest serenity. "He's a great friend of mine—he's the handsomest man in the world—except Mr Winterbourne! He knows plenty of Italians, but he wants to know some Americans. He thinks ever so much of Americans. He's tremendously clever. He's perfectly lovely!"

It was settled that this brilliant personage should be brought to Mrs Walker's party, and then Mrs Miller prepared to take her leave. "I guess we'll go back to the hotel," she said.

"You may go back to the hotel, mother, but I'm going to take a walk," said Daisy.

"She's going to walk with Mr Giovanelli," Randolph proclaimed.

"I am going to the Pincio,"[31] said Daisy, smiling.

"Alone, my dear—at this hour?" Mrs Walker asked. The afternoon was drawing to a close—it was the hour for the throng of carriages and of contemplative pedestrians. "I don't think it's safe, my dear," said Mrs Walker.

"Neither do I," subjoined Mrs Miller. "You'll get the fever as sure as you live. Remember what Dr Davis told you!"

"Give her some medicine before she goes," said Randolph.

The company had risen to its feet; Daisy, still showing her pretty teeth, bent over and kissed her hostess. "Mrs Walker, you are too perfect," she said. "I'm not going alone; I am going to meet a friend."

"Your friend won't keep you from getting the fever," Mrs Miller observed.

"Is it Mr Giovanelli?" asked the hostess.

Winterbourne was watching the young girl; at this question his attention quickened. She stood there smiling and smoothing her bonnet-ribbons; she glanced at Winterbourne. Then, while she glanced and smiled, she answered without a shade of hesitation, "Mr Giovanelli—the beautiful Giovanelli."

"My dear young friend," said Mrs Walker, taking her hand, pleadingly, "don't walk off to the Pincio at this hour to meet a beautiful Italian."

"Well, he speaks English," said Mrs Miller.

"Gracious me!" Daisy exclaimed, "I don't want to do anything improper. There's an easy way to settle it." She continued to glance at Winterbourne. "The Pincio is only a hundred yards distant, and if Mr Winterbourne were as polite as he pretends he would offer to walk with me!"

Winterbourne's politeness hastened to affirm itself, and the young girl gave him gracious leave to accompany her. They passed down-stairs before her mother, and at the door Winterbourne perceived Mrs Miller's carriage drawn up, with the ornamental courier whose acquaintance he had made at Vevey seated within. "Good-bye, Eugenio!" cried Daisy, "I'm going to take a walk." The distance from the Via Gregoriana to the beautiful garden at the other end of the Pincian Hill is, in fact, rapidly traversed. As the day was splendid, however, and the concourse of vehicles, walkers, and loungers numerous, the young Americans found their progress much delayed. This fact was highly agreeable to Winterbourne, in spite of his consciousness of his singular situation. The slow-moving, idly-gazing Roman crowd bestowed much attention upon the extremely pretty young foreign lady who was passing through it upon his arm; and he wondered what on earth had been in Daisy's mind when she proposed to expose herself, unattended, to its appreciation. His own mission, to her sense, apparently, was to consign her to the hands of Mr Giovanelli; but Winterbourne, at once annoyed and gratified, resolved that he would do no such thing.

"Why haven't you been to see me?" asked Daisy. "You can't get out of that."

[31] A park in Rome, noted for its splendid view of the city and of the sunset; popular with both Romans and tourists.

"I have had the honour of telling you that I have only just stepped out of the train."

"You must have stayed in the train a good while after it stopped!" cried the young girl, with her little laugh. "I suppose you were asleep. You have had time to go to see Mrs Walker."

"I knew Mrs Walker—" Winterbourne began to explain.

"I knew where you knew her. You knew her at Geneva. She told me so. Well, you knew me at Vevey. That's just as good. So you ought to have come." She asked him no other question than this; she began to prattle about her own affairs. "We've got splendid rooms at the hotel; Eugenio says they're the best rooms in Rome. We are going to stay all winter—if we don't die of the fever; and I guess we'll stay then. It's a great deal nicer than I thought; I thought it would be fearfully quiet; I was sure it would be awfully poky. I was sure we should be going round all the time with one of those dreadful old men that explain about the pictures and things. But we only had about a week of that, and now I'm enjoying myself. I know ever so many people, and they are all so charming. The society's extremely select. There are all kinds—English, and Germans, and Italians. I think I like the English best. I like their style of conversation. But there are some lovely Americans. I never saw anything so hospitable. There's something or other every day. There's not much dancing; but I must say I never thought dancing was everything. I was always fond of conversation. I guess I shall have plenty at Mrs Walker's—her rooms are so small." When they had passed the gate of the Pincian Gardens, Miss Miller began to wonder where Mr Giovanelli might be. "We had better go straight to that place in front," she said, "where you look at the view."

"I certainly shall not help you to find him," Winterbourne declared.

"Then I shall find him without you," said Miss Daisy.

"You certainly won't leave me!" cried Winterbourne.

She burst into her little laugh. "Are you afraid you'll get lost—or run over? But there's Giovanelli, leaning against that tree. He's staring at the women in the carriages: did you ever see anything so cool?"

Winterbourne perceived at some distance a little man standing with folded arms, nursing his cane. He had a handsome face, an artfully poised hat, a glass in one eye and a nosegay in his button-hole. Winterbourne looked at him a moment and then said, "Do you mean to speak to that man?"

"Do I mean to speak to him? Why, you don't suppose I mean to communicate by signs?"

"Pray understand, then," said Winterbourne, "that I intend to remain with you."

Daisy stopped and looked at him, without a sign of troubled consciousness in her face; with nothing but the presence of her charming eyes and her happy dimples. "Well, she's a cool one!" thought the young man.

"I don't like the way you say that," said Daisy. "It's too imperious."

"I beg your pardon if I say it wrong. The main point is to give you an idea of my meaning."

The young girl looked at him more gravely, but with eyes that were prettier than ever. "I have never allowed a gentleman to dictate to me, or to interfere with anything I do."

"I think you have made a mistake," said Winterbourne. "You should sometimes listen to a gentleman—the right one."

Daisy began to laugh again. "I do nothing but listen to gentlemen!" she exclaimed. "Tell me if Mr Giovanelli is the right one."

The gentleman with the nosegay in his bosom had now perceived our two friends, and was approaching the young girl with obsequious rapidity. He bowed to Winterbourne as well as to the latter's companion; he had a brilliant smile, an intelligent eye; Winterbourne thought him not a bad-looking fellow. But he nevertheless said to Daisy—"No, he's not the right one."

Daisy evidently had a natural talent for performing introductions; she mentioned the name of each of her companions to the other. She strolled along with one of them on each side of her; Mr Giovanelli, who spoke English very cleverly—Winterbourne afterwards learned that he had practised the idiom upon a great many American heiresses—addressed her a great deal of very polite nonsense; he was extremely urbane, and the young American, who said nothing, reflected upon that profundity of Italian cleverness which enables people to appear more gracious in proportion as they are more acutely disappointed. Giovanelli, of course, had counted upon something more intimate; he had not bargained for a party of three. But he kept his temper in a manner which suggested far-stretching intentions. Winterbourne flattered himself that he had taken his measure. "He is not a gentleman," said the young American; "he is only a clever imitation of one. He is a music-master, or a penny-a-liner,[32] or a third-rate artist. Damn his good looks!" Mr Giovanelli had certainly a very pretty face; but Winterbourne felt a superior indignation at his own lovely fellow-countrywoman's not knowing the difference between a spurious gentleman and a real one. Giovanelli chattered and jested and made himself wonderfully agreeable. It was true that if he was an imitation the imitation was very skillful. "Nevertheless," Winterbourne said to himself, "a nice girl ought to know!" And then he came back to the question whether this was in fact a nice girl. Would a nice girl—even allowing for her being a little American flirt—make a rendezvous with a presumably low-lived foreigner? The rendezvous in this case, indeed, had been in broad daylight, and in the most crowded corner of Rome; but was it not possible to regard the choice of these circumstances as a proof of extreme cynicism? Singular though it may seem, Winterbourne was vexed that the young girl, in joining her *amoroso*,[33] should not appear more impatient of his own company, and he was vexed because of his inclination. It was impossible to regard her as a perfectly well-conducted young lady; she was wanting in a certain indispensable delicacy. It would therefore simplify matters greatly to be able to treat her as the object of one of those sentiments which are called by romancers "lawless passions." That she should seem to wish to get rid of him would help him to think more lightly of her, and to be able to think more lightly of her would make her much less perplexing. But Daisy, on this occasion, continued to present herself as an inscrutable combination of audacity and innocence.

[32] A hack writer. [33] Lover; beau.

She had been walking some quarter of an hour, attended by her two cavaliers, and responding in a tone of very childish gaiety, as it seemed to Winterbourne, to the pretty speeches of Mr Giovanelli, when a carriage that had detached itself from the revolving train drew up beside the path. At the same moment Winterbourne perceived that his friend Mrs Walker—the lady whose house he had lately left—was seated in the vehicle and was beckoning to him. Leaving Miss Miller's side, he hastened to obey her summons. Mrs Walker was flushed; she wore an excited air. "It is really too dreadful," she said. "That girl must not do this sort of thing. She must not walk here with you two men. Fifty people have noticed her."

Winterbourne raised his eyebrows. "I think it's a pity to make too much fuss about it."

"It's a pity to let the girl ruin herself!"

"She is very innocent," said Winterbourne.

"She's very crazy!" cried Mrs Walker. "Did you ever see anything so imbecile as her mother? After you had all left me, just now, I could not sit still for thinking of it. It seemed too pitiful, not even to attempt to save her. I ordered the carriage and put on my bonnet, and came here as quickly as possible. Thank heaven I have found you!"

"What do you propose to do with us?" asked Winterbourne, smiling.

"To ask her to get in, to drive her about here for half-an-hour, so that the world may see she is not running absolutely wild, and then to take her safely home."

"I don't think it's a very happy thought," said Winterbourne; "but you can try."

Mrs Walker tried. The young man went in pursuit of Miss Miller, who had simply nodded and smiled at his interlocutrix[34] in the carriage and had gone her way with her own companion. Daisy, on learning that Mrs Walker wished to speak to her, retraced her steps with a perfect good grace and with Mr Giovanelli at her side. She declared that she was delighted to have a chance to present this gentleman to Mrs Walker. She immediately achieved the introduction, and declared that she had never in her life seen anything so lovely as Mrs Walker's carriage-rug.

"I am glad you admire it," said this lady, smiling sweetly. "Will you get in and let me put it over you?"

"Oh, no, thank you," said Daisy. "I shall admire it much more as I see you driving round with it."

"Do get in and drive with me," said Mrs Walker.

"That would be charming, but it's so enchanting just as I am!" and Daisy gave a brilliant glance at the gentlemen on either side of her.

"It may be enchanting, dear child, but it is not the custom here," urged Mrs Walker, leaning forward in her victoria[35] with her hands devoutly clasped.

"Well, it ought to be, then!" said Daisy. "If I didn't walk I should expire."

"You should walk with your mother, dear," cried the lady from Geneva, losing patience.

[34] Woman he has been speaking with.
[35] A low-slung, light carriage, seating two, with a collapsible top.

"With my mother dear!" exclaimed the young girl. Winterbourne saw that she scented interference. "My mother never walked ten steps in her life. And then, you know," she added with a laugh, "I am more than five years old."

"You are old enough to be more reasonable. You are old enough, dear Miss Miller, to be talked about."

Daisy looked at Mrs Walker, smiling intensely. "Talked about? What do you mean?"

"Come into my carriage and I will tell you."

Daisy turned her quickened glance again from one of the gentlemen beside her to the other. Mr Giovanelli was bowing to and fro, rubbing down his gloves and laughing very agreeably; Winterbourne thought it a most unpleasant scene. "I don't think I want to know what you mean," said Daisy presently. "I don't think I should like it."

Winterbourne wished that Mrs Walker would tuck in her carriage-rug and drive away; but this lady did not enjoy being defied, as she afterwards told him.

"Should you prefer being thought a very reckless girl?" she demanded.

"Gracious me!" exclaimed Daisy. She looked again at Mr Giovanelli, then she turned to Winterbourne. There was a little pink flush in her cheek; she was tremendously pretty. "Does Mr Winterbourne think," she asked slowly, smiling, throwing back her head and glancing at him from head to foot, "that—to save my reputation—I ought to get into the carriage?"

Winterbourne coloured; for an instant he hesitated greatly. It seemed so strange to hear her speak that way of her "reputation." But he himself, in fact, must speak in accordance with gallantry. The finest gallantry, here, was simply to tell her the truth; and the truth, for Winterbourne, as the few indications I have been able to give have made him known to the reader, was that Daisy Miller should take Mrs Walker's advice. He looked at her exquisite prettiness; and then he said very gently, "I think you should get into the carriage."

Daisy gave a violent laugh. "I never heard anything so stiff! If this is improper, Mrs Walker," she pursued, "then I am all improper, and you must give me up. Good-bye; I hope you'll have a lovely ride!" and, with Mr Giovanelli, who made a triumphantly obsequious salute, she turned away.

Mrs Walker sat looking after her, and there were tears in Mrs Walker's eyes. "Get in here, sir," she said to Winterbourne, indicating the place beside her. The young man answered that he felt bound to accompany Miss Miller; whereupon Mrs Walker declared that if he refused her this favour she would never speak to him again. She was evidently in earnest. Winterbourne overtook Daisy and her companion, and, offering the young girl his hand, told her that Mrs Walker had made an imperious claim upon his society. He expected that in answer she would say something rather free, something to commit herself still farther to that "recklessness" from which Mrs Walker had so charitably endeavored to dissuade her. But she only shook his hand, hardly looking at him, while Mr Giovanelli bade him farewell with a too emphatic flourish of the hat.

Winterbourne was not in the best possible humour as he took his seat in

Mrs Walker's victoria. "That was not clever of you," he said candidly, while the vehicle mingled again with the throng of carriages.

"In such a case," his companion answered, "I don't wish to be clever, I wish to be *earnest!*"

"Well, your earnestness has only offended her and put her off."

"It has happened very well," said Mrs Walker. "If she is so perfectly determined to compromise herself, the sooner one knows it the better; one can act accordingly."

"I suspect she meant no harm," Winterbourne rejoined.

"So I thought a month ago. But she has been going too far."

"What has she been doing?"

"Everything that is not done here. Flirting with any man she could pick up; sitting in corners with mysterious Italians; dancing all the evening with the same partners; receiving visits at eleven o'clock at night. Her mother goes away when visitors come."

"But her brother, " said Winterbourne, laughing, "sits up till midnight."

"He must be edified by what he sees. I'm told that at their hotel every one is talking about her, and that a smile goes round among the servants when a gentleman comes and asks for Miss Miller."

"The servants be hanged!" said Winterbourne angrily. "The poor girl's only fault," he presently added, "is that she is very uncultivated."

"She is naturally indelicate," Mrs Walker declared. "Take that example this morning. How long had you known her at Vevey?"

"A couple of days."

"Fancy, then, her making it a personal matter that you should have left the place!"

Winterbourne was silent for some moments; then he said, "I suspect, Mrs Walker, that you and I have lived too long at Geneva!" And he added a request that she should inform him with what particular design she had made him enter her carriage.

"I wished to beg you to cease your relations with Miss Miller—not to flirt with her—to give her no farther opportunity to expose herself—to let her alone, in short."

"I'm afraid I can't do that," said Winterbourne. "I like her extremely."

"All the more reason that you shouldn't help her to make a scandal."

"There shall be nothing scandalous in my attentions to her."

"There certainly will be in the way she takes them. But I have said what I had on my conscience," Mrs Walker pursued. "If you wish to rejoin the young lady I will put you down. Here, by-the-way, you have a chance."

The carriage was traversing that part of the Pincian Garden which over-hangs the wall of Rome and overlooks the beautiful Villa Borghese.[36] It is bordered by a large parapet, near which there are several seats. One of the seats, at a distance, was occupied by a gentleman and a lady, towards whom Mrs Walker gave a toss of her head. At the same moment these persons rose and walked towards the parapet. Winterbourne had asked the coach-man to stop; he now descended from the carriage. His companion looked at him a moment in silence; then, while he raised his hat, she drove majes-tically away. Winterbourne stood there; he had turned his eyes towards

[36] A seventeenth-century estate; now a major public park.

Daisy and her cavalier. They evidently saw no one; they were too deeply occupied with each other. When they reached the low garden-wall they stood a moment looking off at the great flat-topped pine-clusters of the Villa Borghese; then Giovanelli seated himself familiarly upon the broad ledge of the wall. The western sun in the opposite sky sent out a brilliant shaft through a couple of cloud-bars; whereupon Daisy's companion took her parasol out of her hands and opened it. She came a little nearer and he held the parasol over her; then, still holding it, he let it rest upon her shoulder, so that both of their heads were hidden from Winterbourne. This young man lingered a moment, then he began to walk. But he walked— not towards the couple with the parasol; towards the residence of his aunt, Mrs Costello.

He flattered himself on the following day that there was no smiling among the servants when he, at least, asked for Mrs Miller at her hotel. This lady and her daughter, however, were not at home; and on the next day after, repeating his visit, Winterbourne again had the misfortune not to find them. Mrs Walker's party took place on the evening of the third day, and in spite of the frigidity of his last interview with the hostess Winterbourne was among the guests. Mrs Walker was one of those American ladies who, while residing abroad, make a point, in their own phrase, of studying European society; and she had on this occasion collected several specimens of her diversely born fellow-mortals to serve, as it were, as textbooks. When Winterbourne arrived Daisy Miller was not there; but in a few moments he saw her mother come in alone, very shyly and ruefully. Mrs Miller's hair, above her exposed-looking temples, was more frizzled than ever. As she approached Mrs Walker, Winterbourne also drew near.

"You see I've come all alone," said poor Mrs Miller. "I'm so frightened; I don't know what to do; it's the first time I've ever been to a party alone— especially in this country. I wanted to bring Randolph or Eugenio or some one, but Daisy just pushed me off by myself. I ain't used to going round alone."

"And does not your daughter intend to favour us with her society?" demanded Mrs Walker, impressively.

"Well, Daisy's all dressed," said Mrs Miller, with that accent of the dispassionate, if not of the philosophic, historian with which she always recorded the current incidents of her daughter's career. "She got dressed on purpose before dinner. But she's got a friend of hers there; that gentleman—the Italian—that she wanted to bring. They've got going at the piano; it seems as if they couldn't leave off. Mr Giovanelli sings splendidly. But I guess they'll come before very long," concluded Mrs Miller hopefully.

"I'm sorry she should come—in that way," said Mrs Walker.

"Well, I told her that there was no use in her getting dressed before dinner if she was going to wait three hours," responded Daisy's mamma. "I didn't see the use of her putting on such a dress as that to sit round with Mr Giovanelli."

"This is most horrible!" said Mrs Walker, turning away and addressing herself to Winterbourne. "*Elle s'affiche.*[37] It's her revenge for my having

[37] French: "She is making herself notorious."

ventured to remonstrate with her. When she comes I shall not speak to her."

Daisy came after eleven o'clock, but she was not, on such an occasion, a young lady to wait to be spoken to. She rustled forward in radiant loveliness, smiling and chattering, carrying a large bouquet and attended by Mr Giovanelli. Every one stopped talking, and turned and looked at her. She came straight to Mrs Walker. "I'm afraid you thought I never was coming, so I sent mother off to tell you. I wanted to make Mr Giovanelli practise some things before he came; you know he sings beautifully, and I want you to ask him to sing. This is Mr Giovanelli; you know I introduced him to you; he's got the most lovely voice and he knows the most charming set of songs. I made him go over them this evening, on purpose; we had the greatest time at the hotel." Of all this Daisy delivered herself with the sweetest, brightest audibleness, looking now at her hostess and now round the room, while she gave a series of little pats, round her shoulders, to the edges of her dress. "Is there any one I know?" she asked.

"I think every one knows you!" said Mrs Walker pregnantly, and she gave a very cursory greeting to Mr Giovanelli. This gentleman bore himself gallantly. He smiled and bowed and showed his white teeth, he curled his moustaches and rolled his eyes, and performed all the proper functions of a handsome Italian at an evening party. He sang, very prettily, half-a-dozen songs, though Mrs Walker afterwards declared that she had been quite unable to find out who asked him. It was apparently not Daisy who had given him his orders. Daisy sat at a distance from the piano, and though she had publicly, as it were, professed a high admiration for his singing, talked, not inaudibly, while it was going on.

"It's a pity these rooms are so small; we can't dance," she said to Winterbourne, as if she had seen him five minutes before.

"I am not sorry we can't dance," Winterbourne answered; "I don't dance."

"Of course you don't dance; you're too stiff," said Miss Daisy. "I hope you enjoyed your drive with Mrs Walker."

"No, I didn't enjoy it; I preferred walking with you."

"We paired off, that was much better," said Daisy. "But did you ever hear anything so cool as Mrs Walker's wanting me to get into her carriage and drop poor Mr Giovanelli; and under the pretext that it was proper? People have different ideas! It would have been most unkind; he had been talking about that walk for ten days."

"He should not have talked about it at all," said Winterbourne; "he would never have proposed to a young lady of this country to walk about the streets with him."

"About the streets?" cried Daisy, with her pretty stare. "Where then would he have proposed to her to walk? The Pincio is not the streets, either; and I, thank goodness, am not a young lady of this country. The young ladies of this country have a dreadfully poky time of it, so far as I can learn; I don't see why I should change my habits for *them*."

"I am afraid your habits are those of a flirt," said Winterbourne gravely.

"Of course they are," she cried, giving him her little smiling stare again. "I'm a fearful, frightful flirt! Did you ever hear of a nice girl that was not? But I suppose you will tell me now that I am not a nice girl."

"You're a very nice girl, but I wish you would flirt with me, and me only," said Winterbourne.

"Ah! thank you, thank you very much; you are the last man I should think of flirting with. As I have had the pleasure of informing you, you are too stiff."

"You say that too often," said Winterbourne.

Daisy gave a delighted laugh. "If I could have the sweet hope of making you angry, I would say it again."

"Don't do that; when I am angry I'm stiffer than ever. But if you won't flirt with me, do cease at least to flirt with your friend at the piano; they don't understand that sort of thing here."

"I thought they understood nothing else!" exclaimed Daisy.

"Not in young unmarried women."

"It seems to me much more proper in young unmarried women than in old married ones," Daisy declared.

"Well," said Winterbourne, "when you deal with natives you must go by the custom of the place. Flirting is a purely American custom; it doesn't exist here. So when you show yourself in public with Mr Giovanelli and without your mother——"

"Gracious! poor mother!" interposed Daisy.

"Though you may be flirting, Mr Giovanelli is not; he means something else."

"He isn't preaching, at any rate," said Daisy with vivacity. "And if you want very much to know, we are neither of us flirting; we are too good friends for that; we are very intimate friends."

"Ah!" rejoined Winterbourne, "if you are in love with each other it is another affair."

She had allowed him up to this point to talk so frankly that he had no expectation of shocking her by this ejaculation; but she immediately got up, blushing visibly, and leaving him to exclaim mentally that little American flirts were the queerest creatures in the world. "Mr Giovanelli, at least," she said, giving her interlocutor a single glance, "never says such very disagreeable things to me."

Winterbourne was bewildered; he stood staring. Mr Giovanelli had finished singing; he left the piano and came over to Daisy. "Won't you come into the other room and have some tea?" he asked, bending before her with his decorative smile.

Daisy turned to Winterbourne, beginning to smile again. He was still more perplexed, for this inconsequent smile made nothing clear, though it seemed to prove, indeed, that she had a sweetness and softness that reverted instinctively to the pardon of offences. "It has never occurred to Mr Winterbourne to offer me any tea," she said, with her little tormenting manner.

"I have offered you advice," Winterbourne rejoined.

"I prefer weak tea!" cried Daisy, and she went off with the brilliant Giovanelli. She sat with him in the adjoining room, in the embrasure of the window, for the rest of the evening. There was an interesting performance at the piano, but neither of these young people gave heed to it. When Daisy came to take leave of Mrs Walker, this lady conscientiously repaired the weakness of which she had been guilty at the moment of the young girl's

arrival. She turned her back straight upon Miss Miller and left her to depart with what grace she might. Winterbourne was standing near the door; he saw it all. Daisy turned very pale and looked at her mother, but Mrs Miller was humbly unconscious of any violation of the usual social forms. She appeared, indeed, to have felt an incongruous impulse to draw attention to her own striking observance of them. "Good night, Mrs Walker," she said; "we've had a beautiful evening. You see if I let Daisy come to parties without me, I don't want her to go away without me." Daisy turned away, looking with a pale, grave face at the circle near the door; Winterbourne saw that, for the first moment, she was too much shocked and puzzled even for indignation. He on his side was greatly touched.

"That was very cruel," he said to Mrs Walker.

"She never enters my drawing-room again," replied his hostess.

Since Winterbourne was not to meet her in Mrs Walker's drawing-room, he went as often as possible to Mrs Miller's hotel. The ladies were rarely at home, but when he found them the devoted Giovanelli was always present. Very often the polished little Roman was in the drawing-room with Daisy alone, Mrs Miller being apparently constantly of the opinion that discretion is the better part of surveillance. Winterbourne noted, at first with surprise, that Daisy on these occasions was never embarrassed or annoyed by his own entrance; but he very presently began to feel that she had no more surprises for him; the unexpected in her behaviour was the only thing to expect. She showed no displeasure at her *tête-à-tête* with Giovanelli being interrupted; she could chatter as freshly and freely with two gentlemen as with one; there was always, in her conversation, the same odd mixture of audacity and puerility. Winterbourne remarked to himself that if she was seriously interested in Giovanelli it was very singular that she should not take more trouble to preserve the sanctity of their interviews, and he liked her the more for her innocent-looking indifference and her apparently inexhaustible good humour. He could hardly have said why, but she seemed to him a girl who would never be jealous. At the risk of exciting a somewhat derisive smile on the reader's part, I may affirm that with regard to the women who had hitherto interested him it very often seemed to Winterbourne among the possibilities that, given certain contingencies, he should be afraid—literally afraid—of these ladies. He had a pleasant sense that he should never be afraid of Daisy Miller. It must be added that this sentiment was not altogether flattering to Daisy; it was part of his conviction, or rather of his apprehension, that she would prove a very light young person.

But she was evidently very much interested in Giovanelli. She looked at him whenever he spoke; she was perpetually telling him to do this and to do that; she was constantly "chaffing" and abusing him. She appeared completely to have forgotten that Winterbourne had said anything to displease her at Mrs Walker's little party. One Sunday afternoon, having gone to St Peter's[38] with his aunt, Winterbourne perceived Daisy strolling about the great church in company with the inevitable Giovanelli. Presently he

[38] The vast basilica, full of great works of art, adjoining the Pope's residence; the central church of Roman Catholicism.

pointed out the young girl and her cavalier to Mrs Costello. This lady looked at them a moment through her eyeglass, and then she said:

"That's what makes you so pensive in these days, eh?"

"I had not the least idea I was pensive," said the young man.

"You are very much pre-occupied, you are thinking of something."

"And what is it," he asked, "that you accuse me of thinking of?"

"Of that young lady's—Miss Baker's, Miss Chandler's—what's her name?—Miss Miller's intrigue with that little barber's block."[39]

"Do you call it an intrigue," Winterbourne asked—"an affair that goes on with such peculiar publicity?"

"That's their folly," said Mrs Costello, "it's not their merit."

"No," rejoined Winterbourne, with something of that pensiveness to which his aunt had alluded. "I don't believe that there is anything to be called an intrigue."

"I have heard a dozen people speak of it; they say she is quite carried away by him."

"They are certainly very intimate," said Winterbourne.

Mrs Costello inspected the young couple again with her optical instrument. "He is very handsome. One easily sees how it is. She thinks him the most elegant man in the world, the finest gentleman. She has never seen anything like him; he is better even than the courier. It was the courier probably who introduced him, and if he succeeds in marrying the young lady, the courier will come in for a magnificent commission."

"I don't believe she thinks of marrying him," said Winterbourne, "and I don't believe he hopes to marry her."

"You may be very sure she thinks of nothing. She goes on from day to day, from hour to hour, as they did in the Golden Age.[40] I can imagine nothing more vulgar. And at the same time," added Mrs Costello, "depend upon it that she may tell you any moment that she is 'engaged.'"

"I think that is more than Giovanelli expects," said Winterbourne.

"Who is Giovanelli?"

"The little Italian. I have asked questions about him and learned something. He is apparently a perfectly respectable little man. I believe he is in a small way a *cavaliere avvocato*.[41] But he doesn't move in what are called the first circles. I think it is really not absolutely impossible that the courier introduced him. He is evidently immensely charmed with Miss Miller. If she thinks him the finest gentleman in the world, he, on his side, has never found himself in personal contact with such splendour, such opulence, such expensiveness, as this young lady's. And then she must seem to him wonderfully pretty and interesting. I rather doubt whether he dreams of marrying her. That must appear to him too impossible a piece of luck. He has nothing but his handsome face to offer, and there is a substantial Mr Miller in that mysterious land of dollars. Giovanelli knows that he hasn't a title to offer. If he were only a count or a *marchese!*[42] He must wonder at his luck at the way they have taken him up."

[39] An artificial head for displaying wigs.

[40] The mythical period when the world was simple, natural, and without social organization.

[41] Italian: lawyer. [42] Marquis; a rank just above that of count.

"He accounts for it by his handsome face, and thinks Miss Miller a young lady *qui se passe ses fantaisies!*"[43] said Mrs Costello.

"It is very true," Winterbourne pursued, "that Daisy and her mamma have not yet risen to that stage of—what shall I call it?—of culture, at which the idea of catching a count or a *marchese* begins. I believe that they are intellectually incapable of that conception."

"Ah! but the *cavaliere* can't believe it," said Mrs Costello.

Of the observation excited by Daisy's "intrigue," Winterbourne gathered that day at St Peter's sufficient evidence. A dozen of the American colonists in Rome came to talk with Mrs Costello, who sat on a little portable stool at the base of one of the great pilasters.[44] The vesper-service[45] was going forward in splendid chants and organ-tones in the adjacent choir,[46] and meanwhile, between Mrs Costello and her friends, there was a great deal said about poor little Miss Miller's going really "too far." Winterbourne was not pleased with what he heard; but when, coming out upon the great steps of the church, he saw Daisy, who had emerged before him, get into an open cab with her accomplice and roll away through the cynical streets of Rome, he could not deny to himself that she was going very far indeed. He felt very sorry for her—not exactly that he believed that she had completely lost her head, but because it was painful to hear so much that was pretty and undefended and natural assigned to a vulgar place among the categories of disorder. He made an attempt after this to give a hint to Mrs Miller. He met one day in the Corso[47] a friend—a tourist like himself—who had just come out of the Doria Palace,[48] where he had been walking through the beautiful gallery. His friend talked for a moment about the superb portrait of Innocent X by Velasquez, which hangs in one of the cabinets[49] of the palace, and then said, "And in the same cabinet, by-the-way, I had the pleasure of contemplating a picture of a different kind—that pretty American girl whom you pointed out to me last week." In answer to Winterbourne's inquiries, his friend narrated that the pretty American girl—prettier than ever—was seated with a companion in the secluded nook in which the great papal portrait is enshrined.

"Who was her companion?" asked Winterbourne.

"A little Italian with a bouquet in his button-hole. The girl is delightfully pretty, but I thought I understood from you the other day that she was a young lady *du meilleur monde.*"[50]

"So she is!" answered Winterbourne; and having assured himself that his informant had seen Daisy and her companion but five minutes before, he jumped into a cab and went to call on Mrs Miller. She was at home; but she apologised to him for receiving him in Daisy's absence.

"She's gone out somewhere with Mr Giovanelli," said Mrs Miller. "She's always going round with Mr Giovanelli."

"I have noticed that they are very intimate," Winterbourne observed.

"Oh! it seems as if they couldn't live without each other!" said Mrs

[43] French: "who indulges her whims." [44] Imitation columns built into a wall.
[45] A late-afternoon or evening service. [46] Wing of the church.
[47] A principal street running through the center of Rome.
[48] A Renaissance-era palace. Its art gallery includes a famous portrait (1650) of Pope Innocent X by the Spanish painter Velasquez.
[49] Rooms. [50] French: "of the best society."

Miller. "Well, he's a real gentleman, anyhow. I keep telling Daisy she's engaged!"

"And what does Daisy say?"

"Oh, she says she isn't engaged. But she might as well be!" this impartial parent resumed. "She goes on as if she was. But I've made Mr Giovanelli promise to tell me, if *she* doesn't. I should want to write to Mr Miller about it—shouldn't you?"

Winterbourne replied that he certainly should; and the state of mind of Daisy's mamma struck him as so unprecedented in the annals of parental vigilance that he gave up as utterly irrelevant the attempt to place her upon her guard.

After this Daisy was never at home, and Winterbourne ceased to meet her at the houses of their common acquaintance, because, as he perceived, these shrewd people had quite made up their minds that she was going too far. They ceased to invite her, and they intimated that they desired to express to observant Europeans the great truth that, though Miss Daisy Miller was a young American lady, her behaviour was not representative— was regarded by her compatriots as abnormal. Winterbourne wondered how she felt about all the cold shoulders that were turned towards her, and sometimes it annoyed him to suspect that she did not feel at all. He said to himself that she was too light and childish, too uncultivated and unreasoning, too provincial, to have reflected upon her ostracism or even to have perceived it. Then at other moments he believed that she carried about in her elegant and irresponsible little organism a defiant, passionate, perfectly observant consciousness of the impression she produced. He asked himself whether Daisy's defiance came from the consciousness of innocence or from her being, essentially, a young person of the reckless class. It must be admitted that holding oneself to a belief in Daisy's "innocence" came to seem to Winterbourne more and more a matter of fine-spun gallantry. As I have already had occasion to relate, he was angry at finding himself re- duced to chopping logic about this young lady; he was vexed at his want of instinctive certitude as to how far her eccentricities were generic, national, and how far they were personal. From either view of them he had some- how missed her, and now it was too late. She was "carried away" by Mr Giovanelli.

A few days after his brief interview with her mother, he encountered her in that beautiful abode of flowering desolation known as the Palace of the Caesars. The early Roman spring had filled the air with bloom and perfume, and the rugged surface of the Palatine[51] was muffled with tender verdure. Daisy was strolling along the top of one of those great mounds of ruin that are embanked with mossy marble and paved with monumental inscriptions. It seemed to him that Rome had never been so lovely as just then. He stood looking off at the enchanting harmony of line and colour that remotely encircles the city, inhaling the softly humid odours and feel- ing the freshness of the year and the antiquity of the place reaffirm them- selves in mysterious interfusion. It seemed to him also that Daisy had never looked so pretty; but this had been an observation of his whenever he met

[51] On the Palatine, one of the seven hills of ancient Rome, are located the ruins of the emperors' palaces.

her. Giovanelli was at her side, and Giovanelli, too, wore an aspect of even unwonted brilliancy.

"Well," said Daisy, "I should think you would be lonesome!"

"Lonesome?" asked Winterbourne.

"You are always going round by yourself. Can't you get any one to walk with you?"

"I am not so fortunate," said Winterbourne, "as your companion."

Giovanelli, from the first, had treated Winterbourne with distinguished politeness; he listened with a deferential air to his remarks; he laughed, punctiliously, at his pleasantries, he seemed disposed to testify to his belief that Winterbourne was a superior young man. He carried himself in no degree like a jealous wooer; he had obviously a great deal of tact; he had no objection to your expecting a little humility of him. It even seemed to Winterbourne at times that Giovanelli would find a certain mental relief in being able to have a private understanding with him—to say to him, as an intelligent man, that, bless you, *he* knew how extraordinary was this young lady, and didn't flatter himself with delusive—or at least *too* delusive—hopes of matrimony and dollars. On this occasion he strolled away from his companion to pluck a sprig of almond blossom, which he carefully arranged in his button-hole.

"I know why you say that," said Daisy, watching Giovanelli. "Because you think I go round too much with *him*!" And she nodded at her attendant.

"Every one thinks so—if you care to know," said Winterbourne.

"Of course I care to know!" Daisy exclaimed seriously. "But I don't believe it. They are only pretending to be shocked. They don't really care a straw what I do. Besides, I don't go round so much."

"I think you will find they do care. They will show it—disagreeably."

Daisy looked at him a moment. "How—disagreeably?"

"Haven't you noticed anything?" Winterbourne asked.

"I have noticed you. But I noticed you were as stiff as an umbrella the first time I saw you."

"You will find I am not so stiff as several others," said Winterbourne, smiling.

"How shall I find it?"

"By going to see the others."

"What will they do to me?"

"They will give you the cold shoulder. Do you know what that means?"

Daisy was looking at him intently; she began to colour. "Do you mean as Mrs Walker did the other night?"

"Exactly!" said Winterbourne.

She looked away at Giovanelli, who was decorating himself with his almond-blossom. Then looking back at Winterbourne—"I shouldn't think you would let people be so unkind!" she said.

"How can I help it?" he asked.

"I should think you would say something."

"I do say something"; and he paused a moment. "I say that your mother tells me that she believes you are engaged."

"Well, she does," said Daisy very simply.

Winterbourne began to laugh. "And does Randolph believe it?" he asked.

"I guess Randolph doesn't believe anything," said Daisy. Randolph's scepticism excited Winterbourne to farther hilarity, and he observed that Giovanelli was coming back to them. Daisy, observing it too, addressed herself again to her countryman. "Since you have mentioned it," she said, "*I am* engaged." . . . Winterbourne looked at her; he had stopped laughing. "You don't believe it!" she added.

He was silent a moment; and then, "Yes, I believe it!" he said.

"Oh, no, you don't," she answered. "Well, then—I am not!"

The young girl and her cicerone[52] were on their way to the gate of the enclosure, so that Winterbourne, who had but lately entered, presently took leave of them. A week afterwards he went to dine at a beautiful villa on the Cælian Hill,[53] and, on arriving, dismissed his hired vehicle. The evening was charming, and he promised himself the satisfaction of walking home beneath the Arch of Constantine[54] and past the vaguely lighted monuments of the Forum.[55] There was a waning moon in the sky, and her radiance was not brilliant, but she was veiled in a thin cloud-curtain which seemed to diffuse and equalise it. When, on his return from the villa (it was eleven o'clock), Winterbourne approached the dusky circle of the Colosseum,[56] it occurred to him, as a lover of the picturesque, that the interior, in the pale moonshine, would be well worth a glance. He turned aside and walked to one of the empty arches, near which, as he observed, an open carriage—one of the little Roman street-cabs—was stationed. Then he passed in among the cavernous shadows of the great structure, and emerged upon the clear and silent arena. The place had never seemed to him more impressive. One-half of the gigantic circus[57] was in deep shade; the other was sleeping in the luminous dusk. As he stood there he began to murmur Byron's famous lines, out of "Manfred";[58] but before he had finished his quotation he remembered that if nocturnal meditations in the Colosseum are recommended by the poets, they are deprecated by the doctors. The historic atmosphere was there, certainly; but the historic atmosphere, scientifically considered, was no better than a villainous miasma.[59] Winterbourne walked to the middle of the arena, to take a more general glance, intending thereafter to make a hasty retreat. The great cross in the centre was covered with shadow; it was only as he drew near it

[52] Guide who conducts sightseers.

[53] Another of the hills of ancient Rome, adjacent to the Palatine hill and just south of the Colosseum.

[54] A well-preserved triumphal arch commemorating a victory (A.D. 312) of Constantine the Great, the emperor who later shifted the imperial capital to Byzantium (renamed Constantinople) and became a Christian.

[55] The civic center of ancient Rome, still crowded with the ruins of important buildings.

[56] The gigantic amphitheater, dating from the first century A.D., famous for gladiatorial combats and traditionally considered the site of Christian martyrdoms. Inside, a large cross had been erected (and still stands) on one side of the ground-level tier.

[57] Arena.

[58] In Byron's verse drama *Manfred* (1817), III.iv.1–41, the protagonist recalls fervently the awesomeness and beauty of the Colosseum and other Roman ruins seen by moonlight.

[59] Poisonous mist associated with decay.

that he made it out distinctly. Then he saw that two persons were stationed upon the low steps which formed its base. One of these was a woman, seated; her companion was standing in front of her.

Presently the sound of the woman's voice came to him distinctly in the warm night-air. "Well, he looks at us as one of the old lions or tigers may have looked at the Christian martyrs!" These were the words he heard, in the familiar accent of Miss Daisy Miller.

"Let us hope he is not very hungry," responded the ingenious Giovanelli. "He will have to take me first; you will serve for dessert!"

Winterbourne stopped, with a sort of horror; and, it must be added, with a sort of relief. It was as if a sudden illumination had been flashed upon the ambiguity of Daisy's behaviour and the riddle had become easy to read. She was a young lady whom a gentleman need no longer be at pains to respect. He stood there looking at her—looking at her companion, and not reflecting that though he saw them vaguely, he himself must have been more brightly visible. He felt angry with himself that he had bothered so much about the right way of regarding Miss Daisy Miller. Then, as he was going to advance again, he checked himself; not from the fear that he was doing her injustice, but from a sense of the danger of appearing unbecomingly exhilarated by this sudden revulsion from cautious criticism. He turned away towards the entrance of the place; but as he did so he heard Daisy speak again.

"Why, it was Mr Winterbourne! He saw me—and he cuts me!"

What a clever little reprobate she was, and how smartly she played an injured innocence! But he wouldn't cut her. Winterbourne came forward again, and went towards the great cross. Daisy had got up; Giovanelli lifted his hat. Winterbourne had now begun to think simply of the craziness, from a sanitary point of view, of a delicate young girl lounging away the evening in this nest of malaria. What if she *were* a clever little reprobate? That was no reason for her dying of the *perniciosa*.[60] "How long have you been here?" he asked, almost brutally.

Daisy, lovely in the flattering moonlight, looked at him a moment. Then—"All the evening," she answered gently. . . . "I never saw anything so pretty."

"I am afraid," said Winterbourne, "that you will not think Roman fever very pretty. This is the way people catch it. I wonder," he added, turning to Giovanelli, "that you, a native Roman, should countenance such a terrible indiscretion."

"Ah," said the handsome native, "for myself, I am not afraid."

"Neither am I—for you! I am speaking for this young lady."

Giovanelli lifted his well-shaped eyebrows and showed his brilliant teeth. But he took Winterbourne's rebuke with docility. "I told the Signorina it was a grave indiscretion; but when was the Signorina ever prudent?"

"I never was sick, and I don't mean to be!" the Signorina declared. "I don't look like much, but I'm healthy! I was bound to see the Colosseum by moonlight; I shouldn't have wanted to go home without that; and we have

[60] Italian: "malignant [fever]."

had the most beautiful time, haven't we, Mr Giovanelli? If there has been any danger, Eugenio can give me some pills. He has got some splendid pills."

"I should advise you," said Winterbourne, "to drive home as fast as possible and take one!"

"What you say is very wise," Giovanelli rejoined. "I will go and make sure the carriage is at hand." And he went forward rapidly.

Daisy followed with Winterbourne. He kept looking at her; she seemed not in the least embarrassed. Winterbourne said nothing; Daisy chattered about the beauty of the place. "Well, I *have* seen the Colosseum by moonlight!" she exclaimed. "That's one good thing." Then, noticing Winterbourne's silence, she asked him why he didn't speak. He made no answer; he only began to laugh. They passed under one of the dark archways; Giovanelli was in front with the carriage. Here Daisy stopped a moment, looking at the young American. "*Did* you believe I was engaged the other day?" she asked.

"It doesn't matter what I believed the other day," said Winterbourne, still laughing.

"Well, what do you believe now?"

"I believe that it makes very little difference whether you are engaged or not!"

He felt the young girl's pretty eyes fixed upon him through the thick gloom of the archway; she was apparently going to answer. But Giovanelli hurried her forward. "Quick, quick," he said; "if we get in by midnight we are quite safe."

Daisy took her seat in the carriage, and the fortunate Italian placed himself beside her. "Don't forget Eugenio's pills!" said Winterbourne, as he lifted his hat.

"I don't care," said Daisy, in a little strange tone, "whether I have Roman fever or not!" Upon this the cab-driver cracked his whip, and they rolled away over the desultory patches of the antique pavement.

Winterbourne—to do him justice, as it were—mentioned to no one that he had encountered Miss Miller, at midnight, in the Colosseum with a gentleman; but nevertheless, a couple of days later, the fact of her having been there under these circumstances was known to every member of the little American circle, and commented accordingly. Winterbourne reflected that they had of course known it at the hotel, and that, after Daisy's return, there had been an exchange of jokes between the porter and the cab-driver. But the young man was conscious at the same moment that it had ceased to be a matter of serious regret to him that the little American flirt should be "talked about" by low-minded menials. These people, a day or two later, had serious information to give: the little American flirt was alarmingly ill. Winterbourne, when the rumour came to him, immediately went to the hotel for more news. He found that two or three charitable friends had preceded him, and that they were being entertained in Mrs Miller's salon by Randolph.

"It's going round at night," said Randolph—"that's what made her sick. She's always going round at night. I shouldn't think she'd want to—it's so plaguey dark. You can't see anything here at night, except when there's a

moon. In America there's always a moon!" Mrs Miller was invisible; she was now, at least, giving her daughter the advantage of her society. It was evident that Daisy was dangerously ill.

Winterbourne went often to ask for news of her, and once he saw Mrs Miller, who, though deeply alarmed, was—rather to his surprise—perfectly composed, and, as it appeared, a most efficient and judicious nurse. She talked a good deal about Dr Davis, but Winterbourne paid her the compliment of saying to himself that she was not, after all, such a monstrous goose. "Daisy spoke of you the other day," she said to him. "Half the time she doesn't know what she's saying, but that time I think she did. She gave me a message; she told me to tell you. She told me to tell you that she never was engaged to that handsome Italian. I am sure I am very glad; Mr Giovanelli hasn't been near us since she was taken ill. I thought he was so much of a gentleman; but I don't call that very polite! A lady told me that he was afraid I was angry with him for taking Daisy round at night. Well, so I am; but I suppose he knows I'm a lady. I would scorn to scold him. Any way, she says she's not engaged. I don't know why she wanted you to know; but she said to me three times—'Mind you tell Mr Winterbourne.' And then she told me to ask if you remembered the time you went to that castle, in Switzerland. But I said I wouldn't give any such messages as that. Only, if she is not engaged, I'm sure I'm glad to know it."

But, as Winterbourne had said, it mattered very little. A week after this the poor girl died; it had been a terrible case of the fever. Daisy's grave was in the little Protestant cemetery,[61] in an angle of the wall of imperial Rome, beneath the cypresses and the thick spring-flowers. Winterbourne stood there beside it, with a number of other mourners; a number larger than the scandal excited by the young lady's career would have led you to expect. Near him stood Giovanelli, who came nearer still before Winterbourne turned away. Giovanelli was very pale; on this occasion he had no flower in his button-hole; he seemed to wish to say something. At last he said, "She was the most beautiful young lady I ever saw, and the most amiable." And then he added in a moment, "And she was the most innocent."

Winterbourne looked at him and presently repeated his words, "And the most innocent?"

"The most innocent!"

Winterbourne felt sore and angry. "Why the devil," he asked, "did you take her to that fatal place?"

Mr Giovanelli's urbanity was apparently imperturbable. He looked on the ground a moment, and then he said, "For myself, I had no fear; and she wanted to go."

"That was no reason!" Winterbourne declared.

The subtle Roman again dropped his eyes. "If she had lived, I should have got nothing. She would never have married me, I am sure."

"She would never have married you?"

"For a moment I hoped so. But no. I am sure."

[61] The Protestant Cemetery in Rome had become a shrine for English-speaking tourists; it was associated with memorable figures of the Romantic era, especially the English poet John Keats, who died in Rome in 1821 at the age of twenty-five and is buried in the cemetery.

Winterbourne listened to him; he stood staring at the raw protuberance among the April daisies. When he turned away again Mr Giovanelli, with his light slow step, had retired.

Winterbourne almost immediately left Rome; but the following summer he again met his aunt, Mrs Costello, at Vevey. Mrs Costello was fond of Vevey. In the interval Winterbourne had often thought of Daisy Miller and her mystifying manners. One day he spoke of her to his aunt—said it was on his conscience that he had done her injustice.

"I am sure I don't know," said Mrs Costello. "How did your injustice affect her?"

"She sent me a message before her death which I didn't understand at the time. But I have understood it since. She would have appreciated one's esteem."

"Is that a modest way," asked Mrs Costello, "of saying that she would have reciprocated one's affection?"

Winterbourne offered no answer to this question; but he presently said, "You were right in that remark that you made last summer. I was booked to make a mistake. I have lived too long in foreign parts."

Nevertheless, he went back to live at Geneva, whence there continue to come the most contradictory accounts of his motives of sojourn: a report that he is "studying" hard—an intimation that he is much interested in a very clever foreign lady.

Kate Chopin
(1851–1904)

One of the most striking events in the study of American literature in the last few decades has been the rediscovery of the late nineteenth-century novelist and short-story writer Kate Chopin. Beginning in the mid-1950s, a few scholars and critics began calling attention to Chopin's work, which had been out of print for over fifty years and which was remembered, if at all, only as minor local-color fiction. Within a dozen years, her complete works were republished and her masterpiece, *The Awakening*, established itself as one of the classic American novels. The story is paralleled in American literary history only by Herman Melville's forty-year critical eclipse after his death and by William Faulkner's long neglect during his own lifetime until he was rediscovered by Malcolm Cowley in 1946. Chopin, like Melville and Faulkner, was ahead of her time; it was not until the resurgence of American feminism that the quality of her work could be adequately recognized by an appreciable number of readers.

Kate Chopin was born Katherine O'Flaherty in St. Louis in 1851; her mother was a cultured French Creole and her father an Irish immigrant and a well-to-do merchant who died when Chopin was four years old. She attended private Catholic schools and was a fashionable nineteen-year-old

debutante when she met and married Oscar Chopin, a twenty-five-year-old cotton merchant of French ancestry from New Orleans. The couple settled there and moved in the social circles of the Creole aristocracy for nine years, until Oscar Chopin's business failed and they moved with their children to Natchitoches Parish in rural Louisiana, where he managed part of the family plantation.

Oscar Chopin died suddenly in 1883, and the young widow, still only thirty-two years old, moved with her six children to her mother's home in St. Louis. Her mother died in 1885, however, and left Chopin without any close family. The following five years were a period of intellectual growth and transformation for Chopin. Her closest friend was her family doctor, Frederick Kolbenheyer (partial model for Dr. Mandelet in *The Awakening*), a cultivated, well-read man who discussed books with her and encouraged her to try writing herself. She later said that she had "made her own acquaintance" during this period.

Chopin's first published work, two short stories, appeared in periodicals in 1889; a novel, *At Fault,* published in St. Louis at her own expense, followed in 1890. *At Fault* is a weak, didactic, anti-reform novel about a woman who makes the man she loves remarry the wife he divorced because of her alcoholism; the woman continues drinking and all three lives are ruined. A second novel was written almost immediately, but Chopin was unable to find a publisher for it. She eventually destroyed the manuscript. Meanwhile, she was having increasing success in publishing her stories and sketches in national magazines, and she achieved national recognition with *Bayou Folk* (1894), a selection of her Louisiana "local color" stories.

The critical success of *Bayou Folk* seems to have given Chopin more confidence in her own powers and perceptions and set her on a course that was eventually to alienate her from her popular audience. She began increasingly to write about passionate, freedom-loving women in stories which were increasingly rejected by editors on moral grounds. Her second collection of stories, *A Night in Acadie,* appeared in 1897; genteel reviewers were less affirmative than they had been with *Bayou Folk,* finding an unpleasant note of "sensuality" in the stories.

When *A Night in Acadie* appeared, Chopin was already completing *The Awakening*. It was accepted by a publisher and appeared in 1899, arousing a storm of shocked protest. A St. Louis reviewer pronounced it "not a healthy book," a Chicago one placed it in "the overworked field of sex fiction," while one in Los Angeles found it "unhealthily introspective and morbid." One of the most interesting reviews was by twenty-six-year-old Willa Cather, who disliked the book but shrewdly compared Edna Pontellier to Flaubert's Madame Bovary and interpreted the book as an examination of the kind of woman who with an "unbalanced idealism" expects "the passion of love to fill and gratify every need of life." "Next time," Cather concluded, "I hope that Miss Chopin will devote that flexible iridescent style of hers to a better cause."

There was to be no next time. Chopin's third collection of short stories was rejected a few months after the scandal of *The Awakening*. Depressed and discouraged, she gave up writing altogether. She died five years later, at the age of fifty-three.

In the context of the social and literary history of her time, Chopin was

only mildly liberal. She lived in the South through the racial conflict of Reconstruction and the ruthless expansionism of the Gilded Age, but issues of race or class appear obliquely if at all in her work. In her period of self-examination following the deaths of her husband and mother, she stopped being a practicing Catholic. She read Darwin and was profoundly influenced by him, insisting thereafter that no serious writer could ignore his account of human nature. She disliked reform and was basically pessimistic about the ability of men and women to escape their "biological fates."

At the same time, she was not a Naturalist. She disliked Zola's novels, finding them too grim, and had the same objection to Hardy. She seems either not to have known or to have been indifferent to the work of the American Naturalists who were writing at the same time: Dreiser, Norris, Crane, and Garland, though she rejected with some impatience Garland's "sociological" subjects. The major influences upon her seem to have been French: Flaubert and, especially, Guy de Maupassant, whose mild realism she greatly admired. She belongs among the realists who dealt, as William Dean Howells recommended, with "the smiling aspects" of life; she was a lover, she wrote, of "brightness and gaiety and life and sunshine."

Chopin's recurring subject, in her mature short stories, is a woman's "awakening" to her true nature, the theme she develops at length in her final novel. Edna Pontellier's awakening is primarily into sensuality, but this awakening comes to involve, for her, large existential issues. She begins to "realize her position in the universe as a human being, and to recognize her relations as an individual to the world within and about her." Sexual freedom becomes the chief expression of a sense of an independent self: "I give myself where I choose," she tells Robert, when he inquires whether Pontellier would free her.

Edna's growth into sensuality and selfhood would be a simpler and a less interesting action if it were not accompanied by a contrary movement in the novel—a "going to sleep" in tension with the "awakening." She has been "self-contained" as a child and has spent most of her girlhood lost in daydreams and fantasies. She drops off to sleep at crucial points throughout the novel, sleeping through most of the day she first openly spends with Robert and experiencing "the old ennui" at the dinner party at which she celebrates her break with her husband. The ending of the novel is anticipated by a number of escapes into unconsciousness throughout and by the ambiguous symbolism of the sea, promising both sensuality and danger.

Despite these foreshadowings, the logic of the ending is elusive. Edna's explicit motivations for her final decision are revulsion at promiscuity— "Today it is Arobin; tomorrow it will be some one else"—and fear for her children—"but Raoul and Etienne!" But her children have not figured in her motivations before—through most of the novel they are visiting their grandmother—and we may wonder why a succession of lovers would be unwelcome, or at any rate worse than what she chooses. Perhaps more crucial than conscious motivation is Chopin's Darwinian pessimism about the possibility of changing one's nature. The ending also raises the general problem of the limits of Romantic individualism. Swimming "far out, where no woman had swum before," carries with it, for man or woman, the danger of not being able to swim back.

FURTHER READING *(prepared by N. K. B.):* For other fiction by Chopin, see *The Complete Works of Kate Chopin,* 2 vols., 1969, ed. by Per Seyersted. Seyersted has also written the most extensive biography, *Kate Chopin: A Critical Biography,* 1969, which includes a thorough examination of her stylistic methods and critical reception. A good brief treatment is Barbara C. Ewell's *Kate Chopin,* 1986. Daniel Rankin's early biography, *Kate Chopin and Her Creole Stories,* 1932, is valuable for the personal reminiscences included, and his antagonistic reaction to *The Awakening* is an interesting contrast to later studies. Nina Baym's introductory essay to *The Awakening and Selected Stories,* 1981, provides an illuminating survey of Chopin's life and writing career, viewed in the context of nineteenth-century fiction and women's writings. Margaret Culley, ed., *The Awakening: An Authoritative Text, Contexts, Criticism,* 1977, offers a shorter introduction; this edition also includes a wide sampling of contemporary reviews. Warner Berthoff, *The Ferment of Realism: American Literature 1894– 1919,* 1965, acclaims Chopin for her rebellion against nineteenth-century social conventions. In "Local Color in *The Awakening,*" *Southern Review,* 6 (1970), 1031– 1040, John R. May discusses the importance of setting in the novel. Donald A. Ringe, "Romantic Imagery in Kate Chopin's *The Awakening,*" *American Literature,* 43 (1972), 580–588, articulates the Romantic themes of the novel. In a detailed and provocative analysis, "Thanatos and Eros: Kate Chopin's *The Awakening,*" *American Quarterly,* 25 (1973), 449–471, Cynthia Griffin Wolff uses a psychoanalytic model to explain Edna's character and action. Among many treatments of the novel's feminist themes, Gina M. Burchard's "Kate Chopin's Problematical Womanliness: The Frontier of American Feminism," in the *Journal of the American Studies Association of Texas,* 1984, provides a succinct overview.

THE AWAKENING

I

A green and yellow parrot, which hung in a cage outside the door, kept repeating over and over:

"*Allez vous-en! Allez vous-en! Sapristi!*[1] That's all right!"

He could speak a little Spanish, and also a language which nobody understood, unless it was the mocking-bird that hung on the other side of the door, whistling his fluty notes out upon the breeze with maddening persistence.

Mr. Pontellier, unable to read his newspaper with any degree of comfort, arose with an expression and an exclamation of disgust. He walked down the gallery and across the narrow "bridges" which connected the Lebrun cottages one with the other. He had been seated before the door of the main house. The parrot and the mocking-bird were the property of Madame Lebrun, and they had the right to make all the noise they wished. Mr. Pontellier had the privilege of quitting their society when they ceased to be entertaining.

He stopped before the door of his own cottage, which was the fourth one from the main building and next to the last. Seating himself in a wicker rocker which was there, he once more applied himself to the task of read-

[1] "Go away! Go away! Good lord!"

ing the newspaper. The day was Sunday; the paper was a day old. The Sunday papers had not yet reached Grand Isle.[2] He was already acquainted with the market reports, and he glanced restlessly over the editorials and bits of news which he had not had time to read before quitting New Orleans the day before.

Mr. Pontellier wore eye-glasses. He was a man of forty, of medium height and rather slender build; he stooped a little. His hair was brown and straight, parted on one side. His beard was neatly and closely trimmed.

Once in a while he withdrew his glance from the newspaper and looked about him. There was more noise than ever over at the house. The main building was called "the house," to distinguish it from the cottages. The chattering and whistling birds were still at it. Two young girls, the Farival twins, were playing a duet from "Zampa"[3] upon the piano. Madame Lebrun was bustling in and out, giving orders in a high key to a yard-boy whenever she got inside the house, and directions in an equally high voice to a dining-room servant whenever she got outside. She was a fresh, pretty woman, clad always in white with elbow sleeves. Her starched skirts crinkled as she came and went. Farther down, before one of the cottages, a lady in black was walking demurely up and down, telling her beads. A good many persons of the *pension* had gone over to the *Chênière Caminada*[4] in Beaudelet's lugger[5] to hear mass. Some young people were out under the water-oaks playing croquet. Mr. Pontellier's two children were there— sturdy little fellows of four and five. A quadroon[6] nurse followed them about with a far-away, meditative air.

Mr. Pontellier finally lit a cigar and began to smoke, letting the paper drag idly from his hand. He fixed his gaze upon a white sunshade that was advancing at snail's pace from the beach. He could see it plainly between the gaunt trunks of the water-oaks and across the stretch of yellow camomile. The gulf looked far away, melting hazily into the blue of the horizon. The sunshade continued to approach slowly. Beneath its pink-lined shelter were his wife, Mrs. Pontellier, and young Robert Lebrun. When they reached the cottage, the two seated themselves with some appearance of fatigue upon the upper step of the porch, facing each other, each leaning against a supporting post.

"What folly! to bathe at such an hour in such heat!" exclaimed Mr. Pontellier. He himself had taken a plunge at daylight. That was why the morning seemed long to him.

"You are burnt beyond recognition," he added, looking at his wife as one looks at a valuable piece of personal property which has suffered some damage. She held up her hands, strong, shapely hands, and surveyed them critically, drawing up her lawn sleeves above the wrists. Looking at them reminded her of her rings, which she had given to her husband before leaving for the beach. She silently reached out to him, and he, understanding, took the rings from his vest pocket and dropped them into her open palm. She slipped them upon her fingers; then clasping her knees, she

[2] An island fifty miles south of New Orleans in the Gulf of Mexico, popular as a summer resort among New Orleans Creoles.

[3] A once-popular opera by Louis Hérold. [4] Another island near Grand Isle.

[5] A small boat with "lugsails" (square sails on a slanting yard).

[6] A person who is one-fourth Negro.

looked across at Robert and began to laugh. The rings sparkled upon her fingers. He sent back an answering smile.

"What is it?" asked Pontellier, looking lazily and amused from one to the other. It was some utter nonsense; some adventure out there in the water, and they both tried to relate it at once. It did not seem half so amusing when told. They realized this, and so did Mr. Pontellier. He yawned and stretched himself. Then he got up, saying he had half a mind to go over to Klein's hotel and play a game of billiards.

"Come go along, Lebrun," he proposed to Robert. But Robert admitted quite frankly that he preferred to stay where he was and talk to Mrs. Pontellier.

"Well, send him about his business when he bores you, Edna," instructed her husband as he prepared to leave.

"Here, take the umbrella," she exclaimed, holding it out to him. He accepted the sunshade, and lifting it over his head descended the steps and walked away.

"Coming back to dinner?" his wife called after him. He halted a moment and shrugged his shoulders. He felt in his vest pocket; there was a ten-dollar bill there. He did not know; perhaps he would return for the early dinner and perhaps he would not. It all depended upon the company which he found over at Klein's and the size of "the game." He did not say this, but she understood it, and laughed, nodding good-by to him.

Both children wanted to follow their father when they saw him starting out. He kissed them and promised to bring them back bonbons and peanuts.

II

Mrs. Pontellier's eyes were quick and bright; they were a yellowish brown, about the color of her hair. She had a way of turning them swiftly upon an object and holding them there as if lost in some inward maze of contemplation or thought.

Her eyebrows were a shade darker than her hair. They were thick and almost horizontal, emphasizing the depth of her eyes. She was rather handsome than beautiful. Her face was captivating by reason of a certain frankness of expression and a contradictory subtle play of features. Her manner was engaging.

Robert rolled a cigarette. He smoked cigarettes because he could not afford cigars, he said. He had a cigar in his pocket which Mr. Pontellier had presented him with, and he was saving it for his after-dinner smoke.

This seemed quite proper and natural on his part. In coloring he was not unlike his companion. A clean-shaved face made the resemblance more pronounced than it would otherwise have been. There rested no shadow of care upon his open countenance. His eyes gathered in and reflected the light and languor of the summer day.

Mrs. Pontellier reached over for a palm-leaf fan that lay on the porch and began to fan herself, while Robert sent between his lips light puffs from his cigarette. They chatted incessantly: about the things around

them; their amusing adventure out in the water—it had again assumed its entertaining aspect; about the wind, the trees, the people who had gone to the *Chênière;* about the children playing croquet under the oaks, and the Farival twins, who were now performing the overture to "The Poet and the Peasant."[7]

Robert talked a good deal about himself. He was very young, and did not know any better. Mrs. Pontellier talked a little about herself for the same reason. Each was interested in what the other said. Robert spoke of his intention to go to Mexico in the autumn, where fortune awaited him. He was always intending to go to Mexico, but some way never got there. Meanwhile he held on to his modest position in a mercantile house in New Orleans, where an equal familiarity with English, French and Spanish gave him no small value as a clerk and correspondent.

He was spending his summer vacation, as he always did, with his mother at Grand Isle. In former times, before Robert could remember, "the house" had been a summer luxury of the Lebruns. Now, flanked by its dozen or more cottages, which were always filled with exclusive visitors from the *"Quartier Français,"*[8] it enabled Madame Lebrun to maintain the easy and comfortable existence which appeared to be her birthright.

Mrs. Pontellier talked about her father's Mississippi plantation and her girlhood home in the old Kentucky blue-grass country. She was an American woman, with a small infusion of French which seemed to have been lost in dilution. She read a letter from her sister, who was away in the East, and who had engaged herself to be married. Robert was interested, and wanted to know what manner of girls the sisters were, what the father was like, and how long the mother had been dead.

When Mrs. Pontellier folded the letter it was time for her to dress for the early dinner.

"I see Léonce isn't coming back," she said, with a glance in the direction whence her husband had disappeared. Robert supposed he was not, as there were a good many New Orleans club men over at Klein's.

When Mrs. Pontellier left him to enter her room, the young man descended the steps and strolled over toward the croquet players, where, during the half-hour before dinner, he amused himself with the little Pontellier children, who were very fond of him.

III

It was eleven o'clock that night when Mr. Pontellier returned from Klein's hotel. He was in an excellent humor, in high spirits, and very talkative. His entrance awoke his wife, who was in bed and fast asleep when he came in. He talked to her while he undressed, telling her anecdotes and bits of news and gossip that he had gathered during the day. From his trousers pockets he took a fistful of crumpled bank notes and a good deal of silver coin,

[7] This overture was another hackneyed parlor piece. *Poet and Peasant* is a light opera by Franz von Suppé.

[8] The French Quarter of New Orleans, home of the bulk of the Creole population.

which he piled on the bureau indiscriminately with keys, knife, handkerchief, and whatever else happened to be in his pockets. She was overcome with sleep, and answered him with little half utterances.

He thought it very discouraging that his wife, who was the sole object of his existence, evinced so little interest in things which concerned him, and valued so little his conversation.

Mr. Pontellier had forgotten the bonbons and peanuts for the boys. Notwithstanding he loved them very much, and went into the adjoining room where they slept to take a look at them and make sure that they were resting comfortably. The result of his investigation was far from satisfactory. He turned and shifted the youngsters about in bed. One of them began to kick and talk about a basket full of crabs.

Mr. Pontellier returned to his wife with the information that Raoul had a high fever and needed looking after. Then he lit a cigar and went and sat near the open door to smoke it.

Mrs. Pontellier was quite sure Raoul had no fever. He had gone to bed perfectly well, she said, and nothing had ailed him all day. Mr. Pontellier was too well acquainted with fever symptoms to be mistaken. He assured her the child was consuming at that moment in the next room.

He reproached his wife with her inattention, her habitual neglect of the children. If it was not a mother's place to look after children, whose on earth was it? He himself had his hands full with his brokerage business. He could not be in two places at once; making a living for his family on the street, and staying at home to see that no harm befell them. He talked in a monotonous, insistent way.

Mrs. Pontellier sprang out of bed and went into the next room. She soon came back and sat on the edge of the bed, leaning her head down on the pillow. She said nothing, and refused to answer her husband when he questioned her. When his cigar was smoked out he went to bed, and in half a minute he was fast asleep.

Mrs. Pontellier was by that time thoroughly awake. She began to cry a little, and wiped her eyes on the sleeve of her *peignoir*. Blowing out the candle, which her husband had left burning, she slipped her bare feet into a pair of satin *mules* at the foot of the bed and went out on the porch, where she sat down in the wicker chair and began to rock gently to and fro.

It was then past midnight. The cottages were all dark. A single faint light gleamed out from the hallway of the house. There was no sound abroad except the hooting of an old owl in the top of a water-oak, and the everlasting voice of the sea, that was not uplifted at that soft hour. It broke like a mournful lullaby upon the night.

The tears came so fast to Mrs. Pontellier's eyes that the damp sleeve of her *peignoir* no longer served to dry them. She was holding the back of her chair with one hand; her loose sleeve had slipped almost to the shoulder of her uplifted arm. Turning, she thrust her face, steaming and wet, into the bend of her arm, and she went on crying there, not caring any longer to dry her face, her eyes, her arms. She could not have told why she was crying. Such experiences as the foregoing were not uncommon in her married life. They seemed never before to have weighed much against the abundance of her husband's kindness and a uniform devotion which had come to be tacit and self-understood.

An indescribable oppression, which seemed to generate in some unfamiliar part of her consciousness, filled her whole being with a vague anguish. It was like a shadow, like a mist passing across her soul's summer day. It was strange and unfamiliar; it was a mood. She did not sit there inwardly upbraiding her husband, lamenting at Fate, which had directed her footsteps to the path which they had taken. She was just having a good cry all to herself. The mosquitoes made merry over her, biting her firm, round arms and nipping at her bare insteps.

The little stinging, buzzing imps succeeded in dispelling a mood which might have held her there in the darkness half a night longer.

The following morning Mr. Pontellier was up in good time to take the rockaway[9] which was to convey him to the steamer at the wharf. He was returning to the city to his business, and they would not see him again at the Island till the coming Saturday. He had regained his composure, which seemed to have been somewhat impaired the night before. He was eager to be gone, as he looked forward to a lively week in Carondelet Street.[10]

Mr. Pontellier gave his wife half of the money which he had brought away from Klein's hotel the evening before. She liked money as well as most women, and accepted it with no little satisfaction.

"It will buy a handsome wedding present for Sister Janet!" she exclaimed, smoothing out the bills as she counted them one by one.

"Oh! we'll treat Sister Janet better than that, my dear," he laughed, as he prepared to kiss her good-by.

The boys were tumbling about, clinging to his legs, imploring that numerous things be brought back to them. Mr. Pontellier was a great favorite, and ladies, men, children, even nurses, were always on hand to say good-by to him. His wife stood smiling and waving, the boys shouting, as he disappeared in the old rockaway down the sandy road.

A few days later a box arrived for Mrs. Pontellier from New Orleans. It was from her husband. It was filled with *friandises*, with luscious and toothsome bits—the finest of fruits, *patés*, a rare bottle or two, delicious syrups, and bonbons in abundance.

Mrs. Pontellier was always very generous with the contents of such a box; she was quite used to receiving them when away from home. The *patés* and fruit were brought to the dining-room; the bonbons were passed around. And the ladies, selecting with dainty and discriminating fingers and a little greedily, all declared that Mr. Pontellier was the best husband in the world. Mrs. Pontellier was forced to admit that she knew of none better.

IV

It would have been a difficult matter for Mr. Pontellier to define to his own satisfaction or any one else's wherein his wife failed in her duty toward their children. It was something which he felt rather than perceived, and

[9] A light four-wheeled carriage (named after Rockaway, New Jersey, where it was manufactured).
[10] Chief financial street in New Orleans and location of the Cotton Exchange.

he never voiced the feeling without subsequent regret and ample atone-
ment.

If one of the little Pontellier boys took a tumble whilst at play, he was
not apt to rush crying to his mother's arms for comfort; he would more
likely pick himself up, wipe the water out of his eyes and the sand out of his
mouth, and go on playing. Tots as they were, they pulled together and
stood their ground in childish battles with doubled fists and uplifted voices,
which usually prevailed against the other mother-tots. The quadroon nurse
was looked upon as a huge encumbrance, only good to button up waists
and panties and to brush and part hair; since it seemed to be a law of
society that hair must be parted and brushed.

In short, Mrs. Pontellier was not a mother-woman. The mother-women
seemed to prevail that summer at Grand Isle. It was easy to know them,
fluttering about with extended, protecting wings when any harm, real or
imaginary, threatened their precious brood. They were women who idol-
ized their children, worshiped their husbands, and esteemed it a holy privi-
lege to efface themselves as individuals and grow wings as ministering an-
gels.

Many of them were delicious in the rôle; one of them was the embodi-
ment of every womanly grace and charm. If her husband did not adore
her, he was a brute, deserving of death by slow torture. Her name was
Adèle Ratignolle. There are no words to describe her save the old ones that
have served so often to picture the bygone heroine of romance and the fair
lady of our dreams. There was nothing subtle or hidden about her charms;
her beauty was all there, flaming and apparent: the spun-gold hair that
comb nor confining pin could restrain; the blue eyes that were like nothing
but sapphires; two lips that pouted, that were so red one could only think
of cherries or some other delicious crimson fruit in looking at them. She
was growing a little stout, but it did not seem to detract an iota from the
grace of every step, pose, gesture. One would not have wanted her white
neck a mite less full or her beautiful arms more slender. Never were hands
more exquisite than hers, and it was a joy to look at them when she
threaded her needle or adjusted her gold thimble to her taper middle
finger as she sewed away on the little night-drawers or fashioned a bodice
or a bib.

Madame Ratignolle was very fond of Mrs. Pontellier, and often she took
her sewing and went over to sit with her in the afternoons. She was sitting
there the afternoon of the day the box arrived from New Orleans. She had
possession of the rocker, and she was busily engaged in sewing upon a
diminutive pair of night-drawers.

She had brought the pattern of the drawers for Mrs. Pontellier to cut
out—a marvel of construction, fashioned to enclose a baby's body so effect-
ually that only two small eyes might look out from the garment, like an
Eskimo's. They were designed for winter wear, when treacherous drafts
came down chimneys and insidious currents of deadly cold found their way
through key-holes.

Mrs. Pontellier's mind was quite at rest concerning the present material
needs of her children, and she could not see the use of anticipating and
making winter night garments the subject of her summer meditations. But
she did not want to appear unamiable and uninterested, so she had

brought forth newspapers, which she spread upon the floor of the gallery, and under Madame Ratignolle's directions she had cut a pattern of the impervious garment.

Robert was there, seated as he had been the Sunday before, and Mrs. Pontellier also occupied her former position on the upper step, leaning listlessly against the post. Beside her was a box of bonbons, which she held out at intervals to Madame Ratignolle.

That lady seemed at a loss to make a selection, but finally settled upon a stick of nougat, wondering if it were not too rich; whether it could possibly hurt her. Madame Ratignolle had been married seven years. About every two years she had a baby. At that time she had three babies, and was beginning to think of a fourth one. She was always talking about her "condition." Her "condition" was in no way apparent, and no one would have known a thing about it but for her persistence in making it the subject of conversation.

Robert started to reassure her, asserting that he had known a lady who had subsisted upon nougat during the entire—but seeing the color mount into Mrs. Pontellier's face he checked himself and changed the subject.

Mrs. Pontellier, though she had married a Creole,[11] was not thoroughly at home in the society of Creoles; never before had she been thrown so intimately among them. There were only Creoles that summer at Lebrun's. They all knew each other, and felt like one large family, among whom existed the most amicable relations. A characteristic which distinguished them and which impressed Mrs. Pontellier most forcibly was their entire absence of prudery. Their freedom of expression was at first incomprehensible to her, though she had no difficulty in reconciling it with a lofty chastity which in the Creole woman seems to be inborn and unmistakable.

Never would Edna Pontellier forget the shock with which she heard Madame Ratignolle relating to old Monsieur Farival the harrowing story of one of her *accouchements*,[12] withholding no intimate detail. She was growing accustomed to like shocks, but she could not keep the mounting color back from her cheeks. Oftener than once her coming had interrupted the droll story with which Robert was entertaining some amused group of married women.

A book had gone the rounds of the *pension*. When it came her turn to read it, she did so with profound astonishment. She felt moved to read the book in secret and solitude, though none of the others had done so—to hide it from view at the sound of approaching footsteps. It was openly criticized and freely discussed at table. Mrs. Pontellier gave over being astonished, and concluded that wonders would never cease.

V

They formed a congenial group sitting there that summer afternoon—Madame Ratignolle sewing away, often stopping to relate a story or incident with much expressive gesture of her perfect hands; Robert and Mrs.

[11] A Louisianan of French ancestry. Specifically, here, a member of the small circle of wealthy Creole "old families."
[12] "Periods of confinement in childbirth."

Pontellier sitting idle, exchanging occasional words, glances or smiles which indicated a certain advanced stage of intimacy and *camaraderie.*

He had lived in her shadow during the past month. No one thought anything of it. Many had predicted that Robert would devote himself to Mrs. Pontellier when he arrived. Since the age of fifteen, which was eleven years before, Robert each summer at Grand Isle had constituted himself the devoted attendant of some fair dame or damsel. Sometimes it was a young girl, again a widow; but as often as not it was some interesting married woman.

For two consecutive seasons he lived in the sunlight of Mademoiselle Duvigné's presence. But she died between summers; then Robert posed as an inconsolable, prostrating himself at the feet of Madame Ratignolle for whatever crumbs of sympathy and comfort she might be pleased to vouchsafe.

Mrs. Pontellier liked to sit and gaze at her fair companion as she might look upon a faultless Madonna.

"Could any one fathom the cruelty beneath that fair exterior?" murmured Robert. "She knew that I adored her once, and she let me adore her. It was 'Robert, come; go; stand up; sit down; do this; do that; see if the baby sleeps; my thimble, please, that I left God knows where. Come and read Daudet[13] to me while I sew.'"

"*Par example!*[14] I never had to ask. You were always there under my feet, like a troublesome cat."

"You mean like an adoring dog. And just as soon as Ratignolle appeared on the scene, then it *was* like a dog. '*Passez! Adieu! Allez vous-en!*'"[15]

"Perhaps I feared to make Alphonse jealous," she interjoined, with excessive naïveté. That made them all laugh. The right hand jealous of the left! The heart jealous of the soul! But for that matter, the Creole husband is never jealous; with him the gangrene passion is one which has become dwarfed by disuse.

Meanwhile Robert, addressing Mrs. Pontellier, continued to tell of his one time hopeless passion for Madame Ratignolle; of sleepless nights, of consuming flames till the very sea sizzled when he took his daily plunge. While the lady at the needle kept up a little running, contemptuous comment:

"*Blagueur—farceur—gros bête, va!*"[16]

He never assumed this serio-comic tone when alone with Mrs. Pontellier. She never knew precisely what to make of it; at that moment it was impossible for her to guess how much of it was jest and what proportion was earnest. It was understood that he had often spoken words of love to Madame Ratignolle, without any thought of being taken seriously. Mrs. Pontellier was glad he had not assumed a similar rôle toward herself. It would have been unacceptable and annoying.

Mrs. Pontellier had brought her sketching materials, which she some-

[13] Alphonse Daudet (1840–97) wrote lightly satirical, "local color" books about his native Provence.
[14] "For goodness sake!" [15] "Go on! Good bye! Go away!"
[16] "Humbug—joker—big blockhead, go on!"

times dabbled with in an unprofessional way. She liked the dabbling. She felt in it satisfaction of a kind which no other employment afforded her.

She had long wished to try herself on Madame Ratignolle. Never had that lady seemed a more tempting subject than at that moment, seated there like some sensuous Madonna, with the gleam of the fading day enriching her splendid color.

Robert crossed over and seated himself upon the step below Mrs. Pontellier, that he might watch her work. She handled her brushes with a certain ease and freedom which came, not from long and close acquaintance with them, but from a natural aptitude. Robert followed her work with close attention, giving forth little ejaculatory expressions of appreciation in French, which he addressed to Madame Ratignolle.

"*Mais ce n'est pas mal! Elle s'y connait, elle a de la force, oui.*"[17]

During his oblivious attention he once quietly rested his head against Mrs. Pontellier's arm. As gently she repulsed him. Once again he repeated the offense. She could not but believe it to be thoughtlessness on his part; yet that was no reason she should submit to it. She did not remonstrate, except again to repulse him quietly but firmly. He offered no apology.

The picture completed bore no resemblance to Madame Ratignolle. She was greatly disappointed to find that it did not look like her. But it was a fair enough piece of work, and in many respects satisfying.

Mrs. Pontellier evidently did not think so. After surveying the sketch critically she drew a broad smudge of paint across its surface, and crumpled the paper between her hands.

The youngsters came tumbling up the steps, the quadroon following at the respectful distance which they required her to observe. Mrs. Pontellier made them carry her paints and things into the house. She sought to detain them for a little talk and some pleasantry. But they were greatly in earnest. They had only come to investigate the contents of the bonbon box. They accepted without murmuring what she chose to give them, each holding out two chubby hands scoop-like, in the vain hope that they might be filled; and then away they went.

The sun was low in the west, and the breeze soft and languorous that came up from the south, charged with the seductive odor of the sea. Children, freshly befurbeloved,[18] were gathering for their games under the oaks. Their voices were high and penetrating.

Madame Ratignolle folded her sewing, placing thimble, scissors and thread all neatly together in the roll, which she pinned securely. She complained of faintness. Mrs. Pontellier flew for the cologne water and a fan. She bathed Madame Ratignolle's face with cologne, while Robert plied the fan with unnecessary vigor.

The spell was soon over, and Mrs. Pontellier could not help wondering if there were not a little imagination responsible for its origin, for the rose tint had never faded from her friend's face.

She stood watching the fair woman walk down the long line of galleries with the grace and majesty which queens are sometimes supposed to pos-

[17] "That's not bad! She knows what she's doing, she has talent!"
[18] Dressed up with ruffles and flounces.

sess. Her little ones ran to meet her. Two of them clung about her white skirts, the third she took from its nurse and with a thousand endearments bore it along in her own fond, encircling arms. Though, as everybody well knew, the doctor had forbidden her to lift so much as a pin!

"Are you going bathing?" asked Robert of Mrs. Pontellier. It was not so much a question as a reminder.

"Oh, no," she answered, with a tone of indecision. "I'm tired; I think not." Her glance wandered from his face away toward the Gulf, whose sonorous murmur reached her like a loving but imperative entreaty.

"Oh, come!" he insisted. "You mustn't miss your bath. Come on. The water must be delicious; it will not hurt you. Come."

He reached up for her big, rough straw hat that hung on a peg outside the door, and put it on her head. They descended the steps, and walked away together toward the beach. The sun was low in the west and the breeze was soft and warm.

VI

Edna Pontellier could not have told why, wishing to go to the beach with Robert, she should in the first place have declined, and in the second place have followed in obedience to one of the two contradictory impulses which impelled her.

A certain light was beginning to dawn dimly within her,—the light which, showing the way, forbids it.

At that early period it served but to bewilder her. It moved her to dreams, to thoughtfulness, to the shadowy anguish which had overcome her the midnight when she had abandoned herself to tears.

In short, Mrs. Pontellier was beginning to realize her position in the universe as a human being, and to recognize her relations as an individual to the world within and about her. This may seem like a ponderous weight of wisdom to descend upon the soul of a young woman of twenty-eight— perhaps more wisdom than the Holy Ghost is usually pleased to vouchsafe to any woman.

But the beginning of things, of a world especially, is necessarily vague, tangled, chaotic, and exceedingly disturbing. How few of us ever emerge from such beginning! How many souls perish in its tumult!

The voice of the sea is seductive; never ceasing, whispering, clamoring, murmuring, inviting the soul to wander for a spell in abysses of solitude; to lose itself in mazes of inward contemplation.

The voice of the sea speaks to the soul. The touch of the sea is sensuous, enfolding the body in its soft, close embrace.

VII

Mrs. Pontellier was not a woman given to confidences, a characteristic hitherto contrary to her nature. Even as a child she had lived her own small life all within herself. At a very early period she had apprehended instinctively

the dual life—that outward existence which conforms, the inward life which questions.

That summer at Grand Isle she began to loosen a little the mantle of reserve that had always enveloped her. There may have been—there must have been—influences, both subtle and apparent, working in their several ways to induce her to do this; but the most obvious was the influence of Adèle Ratignolle. The excessive physical charm of the Creole had first attracted her, for Edna had a sensuous susceptibility to beauty. Then the candor of the woman's whole existence, which every one might read, and which formed so striking a contrast to her own habitual reserve—this might have furnished a link. Who can tell what metals the gods use in forging the subtle bond which we call sympathy, which we might as well call love.

The two women went away one morning to the beach together, arm in arm, under the huge white sunshade. Edna had prevailed upon Madame Ratignolle to leave the children behind, though she could not induce her to relinquish a diminutive roll of needlework, which Adèle begged to be allowed to slip into the depths of her pocket. In some unaccountable way they had escaped from Robert.

The walk to the beach was no inconsiderable one, consisting as it did of a long, sandy path, upon which a sporadic and tangled growth that bordered it on either side made frequent and unexpected inroads. There were acres of yellow camomile reaching out on either hand. Further away still, vegetable gardens abounded, with frequent small plantations of orange or lemon trees intervening. The dark green clusters glistened from afar in the sun.

The women were both of goodly height, Madame Ratignolle possessing the more feminine and matronly figure. The charm of Edna Pontellier's physique stole insensibly upon you. The lines of her body were long, clean and symmetrical; it was a body which occasionally fell into splendid poses; there was no suggestion of the trim, stereotyped fashion-plate about it. A casual and indiscriminating observer, in passing, might not cast a second glance upon the figure. But with more feeling and discernment he would have recognized the noble beauty of its modeling, and the graceful severity of poise and movement, which made Edna Pontellier different from the crowd.

She wore a cool muslin that morning—white, with a waving vertical line of brown running through it; also a white linen collar and the big straw hat which she had taken from the peg outside the door. The hat rested any way on her yellow-brown hair, that waved a little, was heavy, and clung close to her head.

Madame Ratignolle, more careful of her complexion, had twined a gauze veil about her head. She wore dogskin gloves, with gauntlets that protected her wrists. She was dressed in pure white, with a fluffiness of ruffles that became her. The draperies and fluttering things which she wore suited her rich, luxuriant beauty as a greater severity of line could not have done.

There were a number of bath-houses along the beach, of rough but solid construction, built with small, protecting galleries facing the water. Each house consisted of two compartments, and each family at Lebrun's

possessed a compartment for itself, fitted out with all the essential para-
phernalia of the bath and whatever other conveniences the owners might
desire. The two women had no intention of bathing; they had just strolled
down to the beach for a walk and to be alone and near the water. The
Pontellier and Ratignolle compartments adjoined one another under the
same roof.

Mrs. Pontellier had brought down her key through force of habit. Un-
locking the door of her bath-room she went inside, and soon emerged,
bringing a rug, which she spread upon the floor of the gallery, and two
huge hair pillows covered with crash,[19] which she placed against the front
of the building.

The two seated themselves there in the shade of the porch, side by side,
with their backs against the pillows and their feet extended. Madame
Ratignolle removed her veil, wiped her face with a rather delicate handker-
chief, and fanned herself with the fan which she always carried suspended
somewhere about her person by a long, narrow ribbon. Edna removed her
collar and opened her dress at the throat. She took the fan from Madame
Ratignolle and began to fan both herself and her companion. It was very
warm, and for a while they did nothing but exchange remarks about the
heat, the sun, the glare. But there was a breeze blowing, a choppy, stiff
wind that whipped the water into froth. It fluttered the skirts of the two
women and kept them for a while engaged in adjusting, readjusting, tuck-
ing in, securing hair-pins and hat-pins. A few persons were sporting some
distance away in the water. The beach was very still of human sound at that
hour. The lady in black was reading her morning devotions on the porch of
a neighboring bath-house. Two young lovers were exchanging their hearts'
yearnings beneath the children's tent, which they had found unoccupied.

Edna Pontellier, casting her eyes about, had finally kept them at rest
upon the sea. The day was clear and carried the gaze out as far as the blue
sky went; there were a few white clouds suspended idly over the horizon. A
lateen sail[20] was visible in the direction of Cat Island, and others to the
south seemed almost motionless in the far distance.

"Of whom—of what are you thinking?" asked Adèle of her companion,
whose countenance she had been watching with a little amused attention,
arrested by the absorbed expression which seemed to have seized and fixed
every feature into a statuesque repose.

"Nothing," returned Mrs. Pontellier, with a start, adding at once: "How
stupid! But it seems to me it is the reply we make instinctively to such a
question. Let me see," she went on, throwing back her head and narrowing
her fine eyes till they shone like two vivid points of light. "Let me see. I was
really not conscious of thinking of anything; but perhaps I can retrace my
thoughts."

"Oh! never mind!" laughed Madame Ratignolle. "I am not quite so
exacting. I will let you off this time. It is really too hot to think, especially to
think about thinking."

"But for the fun of it," persisted Edna. "First of all, the sight of the
water stretching so far away, those motionless sails against the blue sky,

[19] A heavy cotton or linen fabric, with a rough, nubby surface.
[20] A long triangular sail.

made a delicious picture that I just wanted to sit and look at. The hot wind beating in my face made me think—without any connection that I can trace—of a summer day in Kentucky, of a meadow that seemed as big as the ocean to the very little girl walking through the grass, which was higher than her waist. She threw out her arms as if swimming when she walked, beating the tall grass as one strikes out in the water. Oh, I see the connection now!"

"Where were you going that day in Kentucky, walking through the grass?"

"I don't remember now. I was just walking diagonally across a big field. My sun-bonnet obstructed the view. I could see only the stretch of green before me, and I felt as if I must walk on forever, without coming to the end of it. I don't remember whether I was frightened or pleased. I must have been entertained.

"Likely as not it was Sunday," she laughed; "and I was running away from prayers, from the Presbyterian service, read in a spirit of gloom by my father that chills me yet to think of."

"And have you been running away from prayers ever since, *ma chère?*"[21] asked Madame Ratignolle, amused.

"No! oh, no!" Edna hastened to say. "I was a little unthinking child in those days, just following a misleading impulse without question. On the contrary, during one period of my life religion took a firm hold upon me; after I was twelve and until—until—why, I suppose until now, though I never thought much about it—just driven along by habit. But do you know," she broke off, turning her quick eyes upon Madame Ratignolle and leaning forward a little so as to bring her face quite close to that of her companion, "sometimes I feel this summer as if I were walking through the green meadow again; idly, aimlessly, unthinking and unguided."

Madame Ratignolle laid her hand over that of Mrs. Pontellier, which was near her. Seeing that the hand was not withdrawn, she clasped it firmly and warmly. She even stroked it a little, fondly, with the other hand, murmuring in an undertone, *"Pauvre chérie."*[22]

The action was at first a little confusing to Edna, but she soon lent herself readily to the Creole's gentle caress. She was not accustomed to an outward and spoken expression of affection, either in herself or in others. She and her younger sister, Janet, had quarreled a good deal through force of unfortunate habit. Her older sister, Margaret, was matronly and dignified, probably from having assumed matronly and housewifely responsibilities too early in life, their mother having died when they were quite young. Margaret was not effusive; she was practical. Edna had had an occasional girl friend, but whether accidentally or not, they seemed to have been all of one type—the self-contained. She never realized that the reserve of her own character had much, perhaps everything, to do with this. Her most intimate friend at school had been one of rather exceptional intellectual gifts, who wrote fine-sounding essays, which Edna admired and strove to imitate; and with her she talked and glowed over the English classics, and sometimes held religious and political controversies.

Edna often wondered at one propensity which sometimes had inwardly disturbed her without causing any outward show or manifestation on her

[21] "My dear." [22] "Poor dear."

part. At a very early age—perhaps it was when she traversed the ocean of waving grass—she remembered that she had been passionately enamored of a dignified and sad-eyed cavalry officer who visited her father in Kentucky. She could not leave his presence when he was there, nor remove her eyes from his face, which was something like Napoleon's, with a lock of black hair falling across the forehead. But the cavalry officer melted imperceptibly out of her existence.

At another time her affections were deeply engaged by a young gentleman who visited a lady on a neighboring plantation. It was after they went to Mississippi to live. The young man was engaged to be married to the young lady, and they sometimes called upon Margaret, driving over of afternoons in a buggy. Edna was a little miss, just merging into her teens; and the realization that she herself was nothing, nothing, nothing to the engaged young man was a bitter affliction to her. But he, too, went the way of dreams.

She was a grown young woman when she was overtaken by what she supposed to be the climax of her fate. It was when the face and figure of a great tragedian[23] began to haunt her imagination and stir her senses. The persistence of the infatuation lent it an aspect of genuineness. The hopelessness of it colored it with the lofty tones of a great passion.

The picture of the tragedian stood enframed upon her desk. Any one may possess the portrait of a tragedian without exciting suspicion or comment. (This was a sinister reflection which she cherished.) In the presence of others she expressed admiration for his exalted gifts, as she handed the photograph around and dwelt upon the fidelity of the likeness. When alone she sometimes picked it up and kissed the cold glass passionately.

Her marriage to Léonce Pontellier was purely an accident, in this respect resembling many other marriages which masquerade as the decrees of Fate. It was in the midst of her secret great passion that she met him. He fell in love, as men are in the habit of doing, and pressed his suit with an earnestness and an ardor which left nothing to be desired. He pleased her; his absolute devotion flattered her. She fancied there was a sympathy of thought and taste between them, in which fancy she was mistaken. Add to this the violent opposition of her father and her sister Margaret to her marriage with a Catholic, and we need seek no further for the motives which led her to accept Monsieur Pontellier for her husband.

The acme of bliss, which would have been a marriage with the tragedian, was not for her in this world. As the devoted wife of a man who worshiped her, she felt she would take her place with a certain dignity in the world of reality, closing the portals forever behind her upon the realm of romance and dreams.

But it was not long before the tragedian had gone to join the cavalry officer and the engaged young man and a few others; and Edna found herself face to face with the realities. She grew fond of her husband, realizing with some unaccountable satisfaction that no trace of passion or excessive and fictitious warmth colored her affection, thereby threatening its dissolution.

[23] Chopin probably had in mind the famous American Shakespearian actor Edwin Booth (1833–93).

She was fond of her children in an uneven, impulsive way. She would sometimes gather them passionately to her heart; she would sometimes forget them. The year before they had spent part of the summer with their grandmother Pontellier in Iberville. Feeling secure regarding their happiness and welfare, she did not miss them except with an occasional intense longing. Their absence was a sort of relief, though she did not admit this, even to herself. It seemed to free her of a responsibility which she had blindly assumed and for which Fate had not fitted her.

Edna did not reveal so much as all this to Madame Ratignolle that summer day when they sat with faces turned to the sea. But a good part of it escaped her. She had put her head down on Madame Ratignolle's shoulder. She was flushed and felt intoxicated with the sound of her own voice and the unaccustomed taste of candor. It muddled her like wine, or like a first breath of freedom.

There was the sound of approaching voices. It was Robert, surrounded by a troop of children, searching for them. The two little Pontelliers were with him, and he carried Madame Ratignolle's little girl in his arms. There were other children beside, and two nurse-maids followed, looking disagreeable and resigned.

The women at once rose and began to shake out their draperies and relax their muscles. Mrs. Pontellier threw the cushions and rug into the bath-house. The children all scampered off to the awning, and they stood there in a line, gazing upon the intruding lovers, still exchanging their vows and sighs. The lovers got up, with only a silent protest, and walked slowly away somewhere else.

The children possessed themselves of the tent, and Mrs. Pontellier went over to join them.

Madame Ratignolle begged Robert to accompany her to the house; she complained of cramp in her limbs and stiffness of the joints. She leaned draggingly upon his arm as they walked.

VIII

"Do me a favor, Robert," spoke the pretty woman at his side, almost as soon as she and Robert had started on their slow, homeward way. She looked up in his face, leaning on his arm beneath the encircling shadow of the umbrella which he had lifted.

"Granted; as many as you like," he returned, glancing down into her eyes that were full of thoughtfulness and some speculation.

"I only ask for one; let Mrs. Pontellier alone."

"*Tiens!*" he exclaimed, with a sudden, boyish laugh. "*Voilà que Madame Ratignolle est jalouse!*"[24]

"Nonsense! I'm in earnest; I mean what I say. Let Mrs. Pontellier alone."

"Why?" he asked; himself growing serious at his companion's solicitation.

[24] "So! Madame Ratignolle is jealous!"

"She is not one of us; she is not like us. She might make the unfortunate blunder of taking you seriously."

His face flushed with annoyance, and taking off his soft hat he began to beat it impatiently against his leg as he walked. "Why shouldn't she take me seriously?" he demanded sharply. "Am I a comedian, a clown, a jack-in-the-box? Why shouldn't she? You Creoles! I have no patience with you! Am I always to be regarded as a feature of an amusing programme? I hope Mrs. Pontellier does take me seriously. I hope she has discernment enough to find in me something besides the *blagueur*.[25] If I thought there was any doubt—"

"Oh, enough, Robert!" she broke into his heated outburst. "You are not thinking of what you are saying. You speak with about as little reflection as we might expect from one of those children down there playing in the sand. If your attentions to any married women here were ever offered with any intention of being convincing, you would not be the gentleman we all know you to be, and you would be unfit to associate with the wives and daughters of the people who trust you."

Madame Ratignolle had spoken what she believed to be the law and the gospel. The young man shrugged his shoulders impatiently.

"Oh! well! That isn't it," slamming his hat down vehemently upon his head. "You ought to feel that such things are not flattering to say to a fellow."

"Should our whole intercourse consist of an exchange of compliments? *Ma foi!*"[26]

"It isn't pleasant to have a woman tell you—" he went on, unheedingly, but breaking off suddenly: "Now if I were like Arobin—you remember Alcée Arobin and that story of the consul's wife at Biloxi?" And he related the story of Alcée Arobin and the consul's wife; and another about the tenor of the French Opera,[27] who received letters which should never have been written; and still other stories, grave and gay, till Mrs. Pontellier and her possible propensity for taking young men seriously was apparently forgotten.

Madame Ratignolle, when they had regained her cottage, went in to take the hour's rest which she considered helpful. Before leaving her, Robert begged her pardon for the impatience—he called it rudeness—with which he had received her well-meant caution.

"You made one mistake, Adèle," he said, with a light smile; "there is no earthly possibility of Mrs. Pontellier ever taking me seriously. You should have warned me against taking myself seriously. Your advice might then have carried some weight and given me subject for some reflection. *Au revoir.* But you look tired," he added, solicitously. "Would you like a cup of bouillon? Shall I stir you a toddy? Let me mix you a toddy with a drop of Angostura."

She acceded to the suggestion of bouillon, which was grateful and acceptable. He went himself to the kitchen, which was a building apart from the cottages and lying to the rear of the house. And he himself brought her

[25] "Humbug," "fool." [26] "My word!" (literally, "My faith!").

[27] The New Orleans French Opera was one of the finest early opera companies in America.

the golden-brown bouillon, in a dainty Sèvres cup, with a flaky cracker or two on the saucer.

She thrust a bare, white arm from the curtain which shielded her open door, and received the cup from his hands. She told him he was a *bon garçon*,[28] and she meant it. Robert thanked her and turned away toward "the house."

The lovers were just entering the grounds of the *pension*. They were leaning toward each other as the water-oaks bent from the sea. There was not a particle of earth beneath their feet. Their heads might have been turned upside-down, so absolutely did they tread upon blue ether. The lady in black, creeping behind them, looked a trifle paler and more jaded than usual. There was no sign of Mrs. Pontellier and the children. Robert scanned the distance for any such apparition. They would doubtless remain away till the dinner hour. The young man ascended to his mother's room. It was situated at the top of the house, made up of odd angles and a queer, sloping ceiling. Two broad dormer windows looked out toward the Gulf, and as far across it as a man's eye might reach. The furnishings of the room were light, cool, and practical.

Madame Lebrun was busily engaged at the sewing-machine. A little black girl sat on the floor, and with her hands worked the treadle of the machine. The Creole woman does not take any chances which may be avoided of imperiling her health.

Robert went over and seated himself on the broad sill of one of the dormer windows. He took a book from his pocket and began energetically to read it, judging by the precision and frequency with which he turned the leaves. The sewing-machine made a resounding clatter in the room; it was of a ponderous, by-gone make. In the lulls, Robert and his mother exchanged bits of desultory conversation.

"Where is Mrs. Pontellier?"

"Down at the beach with the children."

"I promised to lend her the Goncourt.[29] Don't forget to take it down when you go; it's there on the bookshelf over the small table." Clatter, clatter, clatter, bang! for the next five or eight minutes.

"Where is Victor going with the rockaway?"

"The rockaway? Victor?"

"Yes; down there in front. He seems to be getting ready to drive away somewhere."

"Call him." Clatter, clatter!

Robert uttered a shrill, piercing whistle which might have been heard back at the wharf.

"He won't look up."

Madame Lebrun flew to the window. She called "Victor!" She waved a handkerchief and called again. The young fellow below got into the vehicle and started the horse off at a gallop.

Madame Lebrun went back to the machine, crimson with annoyance.

[28] "Good waiter" or "good boy."
[29] The Goncourt brothers, Edmond (1822–96) and Jules (1830–70), were famous for their realistic novels of Parisian life.

Victor was the younger son and brother—a *tête montée*,[30] with a temper which invited violence and a will which no ax could break.

"Whenever you say the word I'm ready to thrash any amount of reason into him that he's able to hold."

"If your father had only lived!" Clatter, clatter, clatter, clatter, bang! It was a fixed belief with Madame Lebrun that the conduct of the universe and all things pertaining thereto would have been manifestly of a more intelligent and higher order had not Monsieur Lebrun been removed to other spheres during the early years of their married life.

"What do you hear from Montel?" Montel was a middle-aged gentleman whose vain ambition and desire for the past twenty years had been to fill the void which Monsieur Lebrun's taking off had left in the Lebrun household. Clatter, clatter, bang, clatter!

"I have a letter somewhere," looking in the machine drawer and finding the letter in the bottom of the work-basket. "He says to tell you he will be in Vera Cruz the beginning of next month"—clatter, clatter!—"and if you still have the intention of joining him"—bang! clatter, clatter, bang!

"Why didn't you tell me so before, mother? You know I wanted—" Clatter, clatter, clatter!

"Do you see Mrs. Pontellier starting back with the children? She will be in late to luncheon again. She never starts to get ready for luncheon till the last minute." Clatter, clatter! "Where are you going?"

"Where did you say the Goncourt was?"

IX

Every light in the hall was ablaze; every lamp turned as high as it could be without smoking the chimney or threatening explosion. The lamps were fixed at intervals against the wall, encircling the whole room. Some one had gathered orange and lemon branches, and with these fashioned graceful festoons between. The dark green of the branches stood out and glistened against the white muslin curtains which draped the windows, and which puffed, floated, and flapped at the capricious will of a stiff breeze that swept up from the Gulf.

It was Saturday night a few weeks after the intimate conversation held between Robert and Madame Ratignolle on their way from the beach. An unusual number of husbands, fathers, and friends had come down to stay over Sunday; and they were being suitably entertained by their families, with the material help of Madame Lebrun. The dining tables had all been removed to one end of the hall, and the chairs ranged about in rows and in clusters. Each little family group had had its say and exchanged its domestic gossip earlier in the evening. There was now an apparent disposition to relax; to widen the circle of confidences and give a more general tone to the conversation.

Many of the children had been permitted to sit up beyond their usual bedtime. A small band of them were lying on their stomachs on the floor looking at the colored sheets of the comic papers which Mr. Pontellier had

[30] "Hothead."

brought down. The little Pontellier boys were permitting them to do so, and making their authority felt.

Music, dancing, and a recitation or two were the entertainments furnished, or rather, offered. But there was nothing systematic about the programme, no appearance of prearrangement nor even premeditation.

At an early hour in the evening the Farival twins were prevailed upon to play the piano. They were girls of fourteen, always clad in the Virgin's colors, blue and white, having been dedicated to the Blessed Virgin at their baptism. They played a duet from "Zampa," and at the earnest solicitation of every one present followed it with the overture to "The Poet and the Peasant."

"*Allez vous-en! Sapristi!*" shrieked the parrot outside the door. He was the only being present who possessed sufficient candor to admit that he was not listening to these gracious performances for the first time that summer. Old Monsieur Farival, grandfather of the twins, grew indignant over the interruption, and insisted upon having the bird removed and consigned to regions of darkness. Victor Lebrun objected; and his decrees were as immutable as those of Fate. The parrot fortunately offered no further interruption to the entertainment, the whole venom of his nature apparently having been cherished up and hurled against the twins in that one impetuous outburst.

Later a young brother and sister gave recitations, which every one present had heard many times at winter evening entertainments in the city.

A little girl performed a skirt dance in the center of the floor. The mother played her accompaniments and at the same time watched her daughter with greedy admiration and nervous apprehension. She need have had no apprehension. The child was mistress of the situation. She had been properly dressed for the occasion in black tulle and black silk tights. Her little neck and arms were bare, and her hair, artificially crimped, stood out like fluffy black plumes over her head. Her poses were full of grace, and her little black-shod toes twinkled as they shot out and upward with a rapidity and suddenness which were bewildering.

But there was no reason why every one should not dance. Madame Ratignolle could not, so it was she who gaily consented to play for the others. She played very well, keeping excellent waltz time and infusing an expression into the strains which was indeed inspiring. She was keeping up her music on account of the children, she said; because she and her husband both considered it a means of brightening the home and making it attractive.

Almost every one danced but the twins, who could not be induced to separate during the brief period when one or the other should be whirling around the room in the arms of a man. They might have danced together, but they did not think of it.

The children were sent to bed. Some went submissively; others with shrieks and protests as they were dragged away. They had been permitted to sit up till after the ice-cream, which naturally marked the limit of human indulgence.

The ice-cream was passed around with cake—gold and silver cake arranged on platters in alternate slices; it had been made and frozen during the afternoon back of the kitchen by two black women, under the supervi-

sion of Victor. It was pronounced a great success—excellent if it had only contained a little less vanilla or a little more sugar, if it had been frozen a degree harder, and if the salt might have been kept out of portions of it. Victor was proud of his achievement, and went about recommending it and urging every one to partake of it to excess.

After Mrs. Pontellier had danced twice with her husband, once with Robert, and once with Monsieur Ratignolle, who was thin and tall and swayed like a reed in the wind when he danced, she went out on the gallery and seated herself on the low window-sill, where she commanded a view of all that went on in the hall and could look out toward the Gulf. There was a soft effulgence in the east. The moon was coming up, and its mystic shimmer was casting a million lights across the distant, restless water.

"Would you like to hear Mademoiselle Reisz play?" asked Robert, coming out on the porch where she was. Of course Edna would like to hear Mademoiselle Reisz play; but she feared it would be useless to entreat her.

"I'll ask her," he said. "I'll tell her that you want to hear her. She likes you. She will come." He turned and hurried away to one of the far cottages, where Mademoiselle Reisz was shuffling away. She was dragging a chair in and out of her room, and at intervals objecting to the crying of a baby, which a nurse in the adjoining cottage was endeavoring to put to sleep. She was a disagreeable little woman, no longer young, who had quarreled with almost every one, owing to a temper which was self-assertive and a disposition to trample upon the rights of others. Robert prevailed upon her without any too great difficulty.

She entered the hall with him during a lull in the dance. She made an awkward, imperious little bow as she went in. She was a homely woman, with a small weazened face and body and eyes that glowed. She had absolutely no taste in dress, and wore a batch of rusty black lace with a bunch of artificial violets pinned to the side of her hair.

"Ask Mrs. Pontellier what she would like to hear me play," she requested of Robert. She sat perfectly still before the piano, not touching the keys, while Robert carried her message to Edna at the window. A general air of surprise and genuine satisfaction fell upon every one as they saw the pianist enter. There was a settling down, and a prevailing air of expectancy everywhere. Edna was a trifle embarrassed at being thus signaled out for the imperious little woman's favor. She would not dare to choose, and begged that Mademoiselle Reisz would please herself in her selections.

Edna was what she herself called very fond of music. Musical strains, well rendered, had a way of evoking pictures in her mind. She sometimes liked to sit in the room of mornings when Madame Ratignolle played or practiced. One piece which that lady played Edna had entitled "Solitude." It was a short, plaintive, minor strain. The name of the piece was something else, but she called it "Solitude." When she heard it there came before her imagination the figure of a man standing beside a desolate rock on the seashore. He was naked. His attitude was one of hopeless resignation as he looked toward a distant bird winging its flight away from him.

Another piece called to her mind a dainty young woman clad in an Empire gown, taking mincing dancing steps as she came down a long avenue between tall hedges. Again, another reminded her of children at play, and still another of nothing on earth but a demure lady stroking a cat.

The very first chords which Mademoiselle Reisz struck upon the piano sent a keen tremor down Mrs. Pontellier's spinal column. It was not the first time she had heard an artist at the piano. Perhaps it was the first time she was ready, perhaps the first time her being was tempered to take an impress of the abiding truth.

She waited for the material pictures which she thought would gather and blaze before her imagination. She waited in vain. She saw no pictures of solitude, of hope, of longing, or of despair. But the very passions themselves were aroused within her soul, swaying it, lashing it, as the waves daily beat upon her splendid body. She trembled, she was choking, and the tears blinded her.

Mademoiselle had finished. She arose, and bowing her stiff, lofty bow, she went away, stopping for neither thanks nor applause. As she passed along the gallery she patted Edna upon the shoulder.

"Well, how did you like my music?" she asked. The young woman was unable to answer; she pressed the hand of the pianist convulsively. Mademoiselle Reisz perceived her agitation and even her tears. She patted her again upon the shoulder as she said:

"You are the only one worth playing for. Those others? Bah!" and she went shuffling and sidling on down the gallery toward her room.

But she was mistaken about "those others." Her playing had aroused a fever of enthusiasm. "What passion!" "What an artist!" "I have always said no one could play Chopin like Mademoiselle Reisz!" "That last prelude! *Bon Dieu!* It shakes a man!"

It was growing late, and there was a general disposition to disband. But some one, perhaps it was Robert, thought of a bath at that mystic hour and under that mystic moon.

X

At all events Robert proposed it, and there was not a dissenting voice. There was not one but was ready to follow when he led the way. He did not lead the way, however, he directed the way; and he himself loitered behind with the lovers, who had betrayed a disposition to linger and hold themselves apart. He walked between them, whether with malicious or mischievous intent was not wholly clear, even to himself.

The Pontelliers and Ratignolles walked ahead; the women leaning upon the arms of their husbands. Edna could hear Robert's voice behind them, and could sometimes hear what he said. She wondered why he did not join them. It was unlike him not to. Of late he had sometimes held away from her for an entire day, redoubling his devotion upon the next and the next, as though to make up for hours that had been lost. She missed him the days when some pretext served to take him away from her, just as one misses the sun on a cloudy day without having thought much about the sun when it was shining.

The people walked in little groups toward the beach. They talked and laughed; some of them sang. There was a band playing down at Klein's hotel, and the strains reached them faintly, tempered by the distance. There were strange, rare odors abroad—a tangle of the sea smell and of

weeds and damp, new-plowed earth, mingled with the heavy perfume of a field of white blossoms somewhere near. But the night sat lightly upon the sea and the land. There was no weight of darkness; there were no shadows. The white light of the moon had fallen upon the world like the mystery and the softness of sleep.

Most of them walked into the water as though into a native element. The sea was quiet now, and swelled lazily in broad billows that melted into one another and did not break except upon the beach in little foamy crests that coiled back like slow, white serpents.

Edna had attempted all summer to learn to swim. She had received instructions from both the men and women; in some instances from the children. Robert had pursued a system of lessons almost daily; and he was nearly at the point of discouragement in realizing the futility of his efforts. A certain ungovernable dread hung about her when in the water, unless there was a hand near by that might reach out and reassure her.

But that night she was like the little tottering, stumbling, clutching child, who of a sudden realizes its powers, and walks for the first time alone, boldly and with over-confidence. She could have shouted for joy. She did shout for joy, as with a sweeping stroke or two she lifted her body to the surface of the water.

A feeling of exultation overtook her, as if some power of significant import had been given her to control the working of her body and her soul. She grew daring and reckless, overestimating her strength. She wanted to swim far out, where no woman had swum before.

Her unlooked-for achievement was the subject of wonder, applause, and admiration. Each one congratulated himself that his special teachings had accomplished this desired end.

"How easy it is!" she thought. "It is nothing," she said aloud; "why did I not discover before that it was nothing. Think of the time I have lost splashing about like a baby!" She would not join the groups in their sports and bouts, but intoxicated with her newly conquered power, she swam out alone.

She turned her face seaward to gather in an impression of space and solitude, which the vast expanse of water, meeting and melting with the moonlit sky, conveyed to her excited fancy. As she swam she seemed to be reaching out for the unlimited in which to lose herself.

Once she turned and looked toward the shore, toward the people she had left there. She had not gone any great distance—that is, what would have been a great distance for an experienced swimmer. But to her unaccustomed vision the stretch of water behind her assumed the aspect of a barrier which her unaided strength would never be able to overcome.

A quick vision of death smote her soul, and for a second of time appalled and enfeebled her senses. But by an effort she rallied her staggering faculties and managed to regain the land.

She made no mention of her encounter with death and her flash of terror, except to say to her husband, "I thought I should have perished out there alone."

"You were not so very far, my dear; I was watching you," he told her.

Edna went at once to the bath-house, and she had put on her dry clothes and was ready to return home before the others had left the water.

She started to walk away alone. They all called to her and shouted to her. She waved a dissenting hand, and went on, paying no further heed to their renewed cries which sought to detain her.

"Sometimes I am tempted to think that Mrs. Pontellier is capricious," said Madame Lebrun, who was amusing herself immensely and feared that Edna's abrupt departure might put an end to the pleasure.

"I know she is," assented Mr. Pontellier; "sometimes, not often."

Edna had not traversed a quarter of the distance on her way home before she was overtaken by Robert.

"Did you think I was afraid?" she asked him, without a shade of annoyance.

"No; I knew you weren't afraid."

"Then why did you come? Why didn't you stay out there with the others?"

"I never thought of it."

"Thought of what?"

"Of anything. What difference does it make?"

"I'm very tired," she uttered, complainingly.

"I know you are."

"You don't know anything about it. Why should you know? I never was so exhausted in my life. But it isn't unpleasant. A thousand emotions have swept through me tonight. I don't comprehend half of them. Don't mind what I'm saying; I am just thinking aloud. I wonder if I shall ever be stirred again as Mademoiselle Reisz's playing moved me tonight. I wonder if any night on earth will ever again be like this one. It is like a night in a dream. The people about me are like some uncanny, half-human beings. There must be spirits abroad tonight."

"There are," whispered Robert. "Didn't you know this was the twenty-eighth of August?"

"The twenty-eighth of August?"

"Yes. On the twenty-eighth of August, at the hour of midnight, and if the moon is shining—the moon must be shining—a spirit that has haunted these shores for ages rises up from the Gulf. With its own penetrating vision the spirit seeks some one mortal worthy to hold him company, worthy of being exalted for a few hours into realms of the semi-celestials. His search has always hitherto been fruitless, and he has sunk back, disheartened, into the sea. But tonight he found Mrs. Pontellier. Perhaps he will never wholly release her from the spell. Perhaps she will never again suffer a poor, unworthy earthling to walk in the shadow of her divine presence."

"Don't banter me," she said, wounded at what appeared to be his flippancy. He did not mind the entreaty, but the tone with its delicate note of pathos was like a reproach. He could not explain; he could not tell her that he had penetrated her mood and understood. He said nothing except to offer her his arm, for, by her own admission, she was exhausted. She had been walking alone with her arms hanging limp, letting her white skirts trail along the dewy path. She took his arm, but she did not lean upon it. She let her hand lie listlessly, as though her thoughts were elsewhere—somewhere in advance of her body, and she was striving to overtake them.

Robert assisted her into the hammock which swung from the post be-
fore her door out to the trunk of a tree.

"Will you stay out here and wait for Mr. Pontellier?" he asked.

"I'll stay out here. Good-night."

"Shall I get you a pillow?"

"There's one here," she said, feeling about, for they were in the shadow.

"It must be soiled; the children have been tumbling it about."

"No matter." And having discovered the pillow, she adjusted it beneath
her head. She extended herself in the hammock with a deep breath of
relief. She was not a supercilious or an over-dainty woman. She was not
much given to reclining in the hammock, and when she did so it was with
no cat-like suggestion of voluptuous ease, but with a beneficent repose
which seemed to invade her whole body.

"Shall I stay with you till Mr. Pontellier comes?" asked Robert, seating
himself on the outer edge of one of the steps and taking hold of the ham-
mock rope which was fastened to the post.

"If you wish. Don't swing the hammock. Will you get my white shawl
which I left on the window-sill over at the house?"

"Are you chilly?"

"No; but I shall be presently."

"Presently?" he laughed. "Do you know what time it is? How long are
you going to stay out here?"

"I don't know. Will you get the shawl?"

"Of course I will," he said, rising. He went over to the house, walking
along the grass. She watched his figure pass in and out of the strips of
moonlight. It was past midnight. It was very quiet.

When he returned with the shawl she took it and kept it in her hand.
She did not put it around her.

"Did you say I should stay till Mr. Pontellier came back?"

"I said you might if you wished to."

He seated himself again and rolled a cigarette, which he smoked in
silence. Neither did Mrs. Pontellier speak. No multitude of words could
have been more significant than those moments of silence, or more preg-
nant with the first-felt throbbings of desire.

When the voices of the bathers were heard approaching, Robert said
good-night. She did not answer him. He thought she was asleep. Again she
watched his figure pass in and out of the strips of moonlight as he walked
away.

XI

"What are you doing out here, Edna? I thought I should find you in bed,"
said her husband, when he discovered her lying there. He had walked up
with Madame Lebrun and left her at the house. His wife did not reply.

"Are you asleep?" he asked, bending down close to look at her.

"No." Her eyes gleamed bright and intense, with no sleepy shadows, as
they looked into his.

"Do you know it is past one o'clock? Come on," and he mounted the
steps and went into their room.

"Edna!" called Mr. Pontellier from within, after a few moments had gone by.

"Don't wait for me," she answered. He thrust his head through the door.

"You will take cold out there," he said, irritably. "What folly is this? Why don't you come in?"

"It isn't cold; I have my shawl."

"The mosquitoes will devour you."

"There are no mosquitoes."

She heard him moving about the room; every sound indicating impatience and irritation. Another time she would have gone in at his request. She would, through habit, have yielded to his desire; not with any sense of submission or obedience to his compelling wishes, but unthinkingly, as we walk, move, sit, stand, go through the daily treadmill of the life which has been portioned out to us.

"Edna, dear, are you not coming in soon?" he asked again, this time fondly, with a note of entreaty.

"No; I am going to stay out here."

"This is more than folly," he blurted out. "I can't permit you to stay out there all night. You must come in the house instantly."

With a writhing motion she settled herself more securely in the hammock. She perceived that her will had blazed up, stubborn and resistant. She could not at that moment have done other than denied and resisted. She wondered if her husband had ever spoken to her like that before, and if she had submitted to his command. Of course she had; she remembered that she had. But she could not realize why or how she should have yielded, feeling as she then did.

"Léonce, go to bed," she said. "I mean to stay out here. I don't wish to go in, and I don't intend to. Don't speak to me like that again; I shall not answer you."

Mr. Pontellier had prepared for bed, but he slipped on an extra garment. He opened a bottle of wine, of which he kept a small and select supply in a buffet of his own. He drank a glass of the wine and went out on the gallery and offered a glass to his wife. She did not wish any. He drew up the rocker, hoisted his slippered feet on the rail, and proceeded to smoke a cigar. He smoked two cigars; then he went inside and drank another glass of wine. Mrs. Pontellier again declined to accept a glass when it was offered to her. Mr. Pontellier once more seated himself with elevated feet, and after a reasonable interval of time smoked some more cigars.

Edna began to feel like one who awakens gradually out of a dream, a delicious, grotesque, impossible dream, to feel again the realities pressing into her soul. The physical need for sleep began to overtake her; the exuberance which had sustained and exalted her spirit left her helpless and yielding to the conditions which crowded her in.

The stillest hour of the night had come, the hour before dawn, when the world seems to hold its breath. The moon hung low, and had turned from silver to copper in the sleeping sky. The old owl no longer hooted, and the water-oaks had ceased to moan as they bent their heads.

Edna arose, cramped from lying so long and still in the hammock. She

tottered up the steps, clutching feebly at the post before passing into the house.

"Are you coming in, Léonce?" she asked, turning her face toward her husband.

"Yes, dear," he answered, with a glance following a misty puff of smoke. "Just as soon as I have finished my cigar."

XII

She slept but a few hours. They were troubled and feverish hours, disturbed with dreams that were intangible, that eluded her, leaving only an impression upon her half-awakened senses of something unattainable. She was up and dressed in the cool of the early morning. The air was invigorating and steadied somewhat her faculties. However, she was not seeking refreshment or help from any source, either external or from within. She was blindly following whatever impulse moved her, as if she had placed herself in alien hands for direction, and freed her soul of responsibility.

Most of the people at that early hour were still in bed and asleep. A few, who intended to go over to the *Chênière* for mass, were moving about. The lovers, who had laid their plans the night before, were already strolling toward the wharf. The lady in black, with her Sunday prayer-book, velvet and gold-clasped, and her Sunday silver beads, was following them at no great distance. Old Monsieur Farival was up, and was more than half inclined to do anything that suggested itself. He put on his big straw hat, and taking his umbrella from the stand in the hall, followed the lady in black, never overtaking her.

The little negro girl who worked Madame Lebrun's sewing-machine was sweeping the galleries with long, absent-minded strokes of the broom. Edna sent her up into the house to awaken Robert.

"Tell him I am going to the *Chênière*. The boat is ready; tell him to hurry."

He had soon joined her. She had never sent for him before. She had never asked for him. She had never seemed to want him before. She did not appear conscious that she had done anything unusual in commanding his presence. He was apparently equally unconscious of anything extraordinary in the situation. But his face was suffused with a quiet glow when he met her.

They went together back to the kitchen to drink coffee. There was no time to wait for any nicety of service. They stood outside the window and the cook passed them their coffee and a roll, which they drank and ate from the window-sill. Edna said it tasted good. She had not thought of coffee nor of anything. He told her he had often noticed that she lacked forethought.

"Wasn't it enough to think of going to the *Chênière* and waking you up?" she laughed. "Do I have to think of everything?—as Léonce says when he's in a bad humor. I don't blame him; he'd never be in a bad humor if it weren't for me."

They took a short cut across the sands. At a distance they could see the

curious procession moving toward the wharf—the lovers, shoulder to shoulder, creeping; the lady in black, gaining steadily upon them; old Monsieur Farival, losing ground inch by inch, and a young barefooted Spanish girl, with a red kerchief on her head and a basket on her arm, bringing up the rear.

Robert knew the girl, and he talked to her a little in the boat. No one present understood what they said. Her name was Mariequita. She had a round, sly, piquant face and pretty black eyes. Her hands were small, and she kept them folded over the handle of her basket. Her feet were broad and coarse. She did not strive to hide them. Edna looked at her feet, and noticed the sand and slime between her brown toes.

Beaudelet grumbled because Mariequita was there, taking up so much room. In reality he was annoyed at having old Monsieur Farival, who considered himself the better sailor of the two. But he would not quarrel with so old a man as Monsieur Farival, so he quarreled with Mariequita. The girl was deprecatory at one moment, appealing to Robert. She was saucy the next, moving her head up and down, making "eyes" at Robert and making "mouths" at Beaudelet.

The lovers were all alone. They saw nothing, they heard nothing. The lady in black was counting her beads for the third time. Old Monsieur Farival talked incessantly of what he knew about handling a boat, and of what Beaudelet did not know on the same subject.

Edna liked it all. She looked Mariequita up and down, from her ugly brown toes to her pretty black eyes, and back again.

"Why does she look at me like that?" inquired the girl of Robert.

"Maybe she thinks you are pretty. Shall I ask her?"

"No. Is she your sweetheart?"

"She's a married lady, and has two children."

"Oh! well! Francisco ran away with Sylvano's wife, who had four children. They took all his money and one of the children and stole his boat."

"Shut up!"

"Does she understand?"

"Oh, hush!"

"Are those two married over there—leaning on each other?"

"Of course not," laughed Robert.

"Of course not," echoed Mariequita, with a serious, confirmatory bob of the head.

The sun was high up and beginning to bite. The swift breeze seemed to Edna to bury the sting of it into the pores of her face and hands. Robert held his umbrella over her.

As they went cutting sidewise through the water, the sails bellied taut, with the wind filling and overflowing them. Old Monsieur Farival laughed sardonically at something as he looked at the sails, and Beaudelet swore at the old man under his breath.

Sailing across the bay to the *Chênière Caminada*, Edna felt as if she were being borne away from some anchorage which had held her fast, whose chains had been loosening—had snapped the night before when the mystic spirit was abroad, leaving her free to drift whithersoever she chose to set her sails. Robert spoke to her incessantly; he no longer noticed Mariequita.

The girl had shrimps in her bamboo basket. They were covered with Spanish moss. She beat the moss down impatiently, and muttered to herself sullenly.

"Let us go to Grande Terre[31] tomorrow," said Robert in a low voice.

"What shall we do there?"

"Climb up the hill to the old fort and look at the little wriggling gold snakes, and watch the lizards sun themselves."

She gazed away toward Grande Terre and thought she would like to be alone there with Robert, in the sun, listening to the ocean's roar and watching the slimy lizards writhe in and out among the ruins of the old fort.

"And the next day or the next we can sail to the Bayou Brulow,"[32] he went on.

"What shall we do there?"

"Anything—cast bait for fish."

"No; we'll go back to Grande Terre. Let the fish alone."

"We'll go wherever you like," he said. "I'll have Tonie come over and help me patch and trim my boat. We shall not need Beaudelet nor any one. Are you afraid of the pirogue?"[33]

"Oh, no."

"Then I'll take you some night in the pirogue when the moon shines. Maybe your Gulf spirit will whisper to you in which of these islands the treasures are hidden—direct you to the very spot, perhaps."

"And in a day we should be rich!" she laughed. "I'd give it all to you, the pirate gold and every bit of treasure we could dig up. I think you would know how to spend it. Pirate gold isn't a thing to be hoarded or utilized. It is something to squander and throw to the four winds, for the fun of seeing the golden specks fly."

"We'd share it, and scatter it together," he said. His face flushed.

They all went together up to the quaint little Gothic church of Our Lady of Lourdes, gleaming all brown and yellow with paint in the sun's glare.

Only Beaudelet remained behind, tinkering at his boat, and Mariequita walked away with her basket of shrimps, casting a look of childish ill-humor and reproach at Robert from the corner of her eye.

XIII

A feeling of oppression and drowsiness overcame Edna during the service. Her head began to ache, and the lights on the altar swayed before her eyes. Another time she might have made an effort to regain her composure; but her one thought was to quit the stifling atmosphere of the church and reach the open air. She arose, climbing over Robert's feet with a muttered apology. Old Monsieur Farival, flurried, curious, stood up, but upon seeing that Robert had followed Mrs. Pontellier, he sank back into his seat. He whispered an anxious inquiry of the lady in black, who did not notice him

[31] An island near Grand Isle. [32] A village on the mainland near Grand Isle.
[33] Canoe.

or reply, but kept her eyes fastened upon the pages of her velvet prayer-book.

"I felt giddy and almost overcome," Edna said, lifting her hands instinctively to her head and pushing her straw hat up from her forehead. "I couldn't have stayed through the service." They were outside in the shadow of the church. Robert was full of solicitude.

"It was folly to have thought of going in the first place, let alone staying. Come over to Madame Antoine's; you can rest there." He took her arm and led her away, looking anxiously and continuously down into her face.

How still it was, with only the voice of the sea whispering through the reeds that grew in the salt-water pools! The long line of little gray, weather-beaten houses nestled peacefully among the orange trees. It must always have been God's day on that low, drowsy island, Edna thought. They stopped, leaning over a jagged fence made of sea-drift, to ask for water. A youth, a mild-faced Acadian,[34] was drawing water from the cistern, which was nothing more than a rusty buoy, with an opening on one side, sunk in the ground. The water which the youth handed to them in a tin pail was not cold to taste, but it was cool to her heated face, and it greatly revived and refreshed her.

Madame Antoine's cot[35] was at the far end of the village. She welcomed them with all the native hospitality, as she would have opened her door to let the sunlight in. She was fat, and walked heavily and clumsily across the floor. She could speak no English, but when Robert made her understand that the lady who accompanied him was ill and desired to rest, she was all eagerness to make Edna feel at home and to dispose of her comfortably.

The whole place was immaculately clean, and the big, four-posted bed, snow-white, invited one to repose. It stood in a small side room which looked out across a narrow grass plot toward the shed, where there was a disabled boat lying keel upward.

Madame Antoine had not gone to mass. Her son Tonie had, but she supposed he would soon be back, and she invited Robert to be seated and wait for him. But he went and sat outside the door and smoked. Madame Antoine busied herself in the large front room preparing dinner. She was boiling mullets over a few red coals in the huge fireplace.

Edna, left alone in the little side room, loosened her clothes, removing the greater part of them. She bathed her face, her neck and arms in the basin that stood between the windows. She took off her shoes and stockings and stretched herself in the very center of the high, white bed. How luxurious it felt to rest thus in a strange, quaint bed, with its sweet country odor of laurel lingering about the sheets and mattress! She stretched her strong limbs that ached a little. She ran her fingers through her loosened hair for a while. She looked at her round arms as she held them straight up and rubbed them one after the other, observing closely, as if it were something she saw for the first time, the fine, firm quality and texture of her flesh. She clasped her hands easily above her head, and it was thus she fell asleep.

[34] Descendant of the French Canadians expelled from Acadia (Nova Scotia) in the eighteenth century who settled in Louisiana. "Cajun" is a corruption of "Acadian."

[35] Cottage.

She slept lightly at first, half awake and drowsily attentive to the things about her. She could hear Madame Antoine's heavy, scraping tread as she walked back and forth on the sanded floor. Some chickens were clucking outside the windows, scratching for bits of gravel in the grass. Later she half heard the voices of Robert and Tonie talking under the shed. She did not stir. Even her eyelids rested numb and heavily over her sleepy eyes. The voices went on—Tonie's slow, Acadian drawl, Robert's quick, soft, smooth French. She understood French imperfectly unless directly addressed, and the voices were only part of the other drowsy, muffled sounds lulling her senses.

When Edna awoke it was with the conviction that she had slept long and soundly. The voices were hushed under the shed. Madame Antoine's step was no longer to be heard in the adjoining room. Even the chickens had gone elsewhere to scratch and cluck. The mosquito bar was drawn over her; the old woman had come in while she slept and let down the bar. Edna arose quietly from the bed, and looking between the curtains of the window, she saw by the slanting rays of the sun that the afternoon was far advanced. Robert was out there under the shed, reclining in the shade against the sloping keel of the overturned boat. He was reading from a book. Tonie was no longer with him. She wondered what had become of the rest of the party. She peeped out at him two or three times as she stood washing herself in the little basin between the windows.

Madame Antoine had laid some coarse, clean towels upon a chair, and had placed a box of *poudre de riz*[36] within easy reach. Edna dabbed the powder upon her nose and cheeks as she looked at herself closely in the little distorted mirror which hung on the wall above the basin. Her eyes were bright and wide awake and her face glowed.

When she had completed her toilet she walked into the adjoining room. She was very hungry. No one was there. But there was a cloth spread upon the table that stood against the wall, and a cover was laid for one, with a crusty brown loaf and a bottle of wine beside the plate. Edna bit a piece from the brown loaf, tearing it with her strong, white teeth. She poured some of the wine into the glass and drank it down. Then she went softly out of doors, and plucking an orange from the low-hanging bough of a tree, threw it at Robert, who did not know she was awake and up.

An illumination broke over his whole face when he saw her and joined her under the orange tree.

"How many years have I slept?" she inquired. "The whole island seems changed. A new race of beings must have sprung up, leaving only you and me as past relics. How many ages ago did Madame Antoine and Tonie die? and when did our people from Grand Isle disappear from the earth?"

He familiarly adjusted a ruffle upon her shoulder.

"You have slept precisely one hundred years. I was left here to guard your slumbers; and for one hundred years I have been out under the shed reading a book. The only evil I couldn't prevent was to keep a broiled fowl from drying up."

"If it has turned to stone, still will I eat it," said Edna, moving with him

[36] "Rice powder."

into the house. "But really, what has become of Monsieur Farival and the others?"

"Gone hours ago. When they found that you were sleeping they thought it best not to awake you. Any way, I wouldn't have let them. What was I here for?"

"I wonder if Léonce will be uneasy!" she speculated, as she seated herself at table.

"Of course not; he knows you are with me," Robert replied, as he busied himself among sundry pans and covered dishes which had been left standing on the hearth.

"Where are Madame Antoine and her son?" asked Edna.

"Gone to Vespers,[37] and to visit some friends, I believe. I am to take you back in Tonie's boat whenever you are ready to go."

He stirred the smoldering ashes till the broiled fowl began to sizzle afresh. He served her with no mean repast, dripping the coffee anew and sharing it with her. Madame Antoine had cooked little else than the mullets, but while Edna slept Robert had foraged the island. He was childishly gratified to discover her appetite, and to see the relish with which she ate the food which he had procured for her.

"Shall we go right away?" she asked, after draining her glass and brushing together the crumbs of the crusty loaf.

"The sun isn't as low as it will be in two hours," he answered.

"The sun will be gone in two hours."

"Well, let it go; who cares!"

They waited a good while under the orange trees, till Madame Antoine came back, panting, waddling, with a thousand apologies to explain her absence. Tonie did not dare to return. He was shy, and would not willingly face any woman except his mother.

It was very pleasant to stay there under the orange trees, while the sun dipped lower and lower, turning the western sky to flaming copper and gold. The shadows lengthened and crept out like stealthy, grotesque monsters across the grass.

Edna and Robert both sat upon the ground—that is, he lay upon the ground beside her, occasionally picking at the hem of her muslin gown.

Madame Antoine seated her fat body, broad and squat, upon a bench beside the door. She had been talking all the afternoon, and had wound herself up to the story-telling pitch.

And what stories she told them! But twice in her life she had left the *Chênière Caminada,* and then for the briefest span. All her years she had squatted and waddled there upon the island, gathering legends of the Baratarians[38] and the sea. The night came on, with the moon to lighten it. Edna could hear the whispering voices of dead men and the click of muffled gold.

When she and Robert stepped into Tonie's boat, with the red lateen sail, misty spirit forms were prowling in the shadows and among the reeds, and upon the water were phantom ships, speeding to cover.

[37] An evening church service.
[38] Pirates who operated in the area of Barataria Bay. The most famous was Jean Lafitte.

XIV

The youngest boy, Etienne, had been very naughty, Madame Ratignolle said, as she delivered him into the hands of his mother. He had been unwilling to go to bed and had made a scene; whereupon she had taken charge of him and pacified him as well as she could. Raoul had been in bed and asleep for two hours.

The youngster was in his long white nightgown, that kept tripping him up as Madame Ratignolle led him along by the hand. With the other chubby fist he rubbed his eyes, which were heavy with sleep and ill humor. Edna took him in her arms, and seating herself in the rocker, began to coddle and caress him, calling him all manner of tender names, soothing him to sleep.

It was not more than nine o'clock. No one had yet gone to bed but the children.

Léonce had been very uneasy at first, Madame Ratignolle said, and had wanted to start at once for the *Chênière*. But Monsieur Farival had assured him that his wife was only overcome with sleep and fatigue, that Tonie would bring her safely back later in the day; and he had thus been dissuaded from crossing the bay. He had gone over to Klein's, looking up some cotton broker whom he wished to see in regard to securities, exchanges, stocks, bonds, or something of the sort, Madame Ratignolle did not remember what. He said he would not remain away late. She herself was suffering from heat and oppression, she said. She carried a bottle of salts and a large fan. She would not consent to remain with Edna, for Monsieur Ratignolle was alone, and he detested above all things to be left alone.

When Etienne had fallen asleep Edna bore him into the back room, and Robert went and lifted the mosquito bar that she might lay the child comfortably in his bed. The quadroon had vanished. When they emerged from the cottage Robert bade Edna good-night.

"Do you know we have been together the whole livelong day, Robert— since early this morning?" she said at parting.

"All but the hundred years when you were sleeping. Good-night."

He pressed her hand and went away in the direction of the beach. He did not join any of the others, but walked alone toward the Gulf.

Edna stayed outside, awaiting her husband's return. She had no desire to sleep or to retire; nor did she feel like going over to sit with the Ratignolles, or to join Madame Lebrun and a group whose animated voices reached her as they sat in conversation before the house. She let her mind wander back over her stay at Grand Isle; and she tried to discover wherein this summer had been different from any and every other summer of her life. She could only realize that she herself—her present self—was in some way different from the other self. That she was seeing with different eyes and making the acquaintance of new conditions in herself that colored and changed her environment, she did not yet suspect.

She wondered why Robert had gone away and left her. It did not occur to her to think he might have grown tired of being with her the livelong day. She was not tired, and she felt that he was not. She regretted that he

had gone. It was so much more natural to have him stay when he was not absolutely required to leave her.

As Edna waited for her husband she sang low a little song that Robert had sung as they crossed the bay. It began with "Ah! *Si tu savais*," and every verse ended with "*si tu savais*."[39]

Robert's voice was not pretentious. It was musical and true. The voice, the notes, the whole refrain haunted her memory.

XV

When Edna entered the dining-room one evening a little late, as was her habit, an unusually animated conversation seemed to be going on. Several persons were talking at once, and Victor's voice was predominating, even over that of his mother. Edna had returned late from her bath, had dressed in some haste, and her face was flushed. Her head, set off by her dainty white gown, suggested a rich, rare blossom. She took her seat at table between old Monsieur Farival and Madame Ratignolle.

As she seated herself and was about to begin to eat her soup, which had been served when she entered the room, several persons informed her simultaneously that Robert was going to Mexico. She laid her spoon down and looked about her bewildered. He had been with her, reading to her all the morning, and had never even mentioned such a place as Mexico. She had not seen him during the afternoon; she had heard some one say he was at the house, upstairs with his mother. This she had thought nothing of, though she was surprised when he did not join her later in the afternoon, when she went down to the beach.

She looked across at him, where he sat beside Madame Lebrun, who presided. Edna's face was a blank picture of bewilderment, which she never thought of disguising. He lifted his eyebrows with the pretext of a smile as he returned her glance. He looked embarrassed and uneasy.

"When is he going?" she asked of everybody in general, as if Robert were not there to answer for himself.

"Tonight!" "This very evening!" "Did you ever!" "What possesses him!" were some of the replies she gathered, uttered simultaneously in French and English.

"Impossible!" she exclaimed. "How can a person start off from Grand Isle to Mexico at a moment's notice, as if he were going over to Klein's or to the wharf or down to the beach?"

"I said all along I was going to Mexico; I've been saying so for years!" cried Robert, in an excited and irritable tone, with the air of a man defending himself against a swarm of stinging insects.

Madame Lebrun knocked on the table with her knife handle.

"Please let Robert explain why he is going, and why he is going tonight," she called out. "Really, this table is getting to be more and more like Bedlam every day, with everybody talking at once. Sometimes—I hope God will

[39] "If you could know." Margaret Culley has identified this important song as a ballad, "Si Tu Savais," by Michael Balfe (1808–70), composer of *The Bohemian Girl.*

forgive me—but positively, sometimes I wish Victor would lose the power of speech."

Victor laughed sardonically as he thanked his mother for her holy wish, of which he failed to see the benefit to anybody, except that it might afford her a more ample opportunity and license to talk herself.

Monsieur Farival thought that Victor should have been taken out in mid-ocean in his earliest youth and drowned. Victor thought there would be more logic in thus disposing of old people with an established claim for making themselves universally obnoxious. Madame Lebrun grew a trifle hysterical; Robert called his brother some sharp, hard names.

"There's nothing much to explain, mother," he said; though he explained, nevertheless—looking chiefly at Edna—that he could only meet the gentleman whom he intended to join at Vera Cruz by taking such and such a steamer, which left New Orleans on such a day; that Beaudelet was going out with his lugger-load of vegetables that night, which gave him an opportunity of reaching the city and making his vessel in time.

"But when did you make up your mind to all this?" demanded Monsieur Farival.

"This afternoon," returned Robert, with a shade of annoyance.

"At what time this afternoon?" persisted the old gentleman, with nagging determination, as if he were cross-questioning a criminal in a court of justice.

"At four o'clock this afternoon, Monsieur Farival," Robert replied, in a high voice and with a lofty air, which reminded Edna of some gentleman on the stage.

She had forced herself to eat most of her soup, and now she was picking the flaky bits of a *court bouillon*[40] with her fork.

The lovers were profiting by the general conversation on Mexico to speak in whispers of matters which they rightly considered were interesting to no one but themselves. The lady in black had once received a pair of prayer-beads of curious workmanship from Mexico, with very special indulgence attached to them, but she had never been able to ascertain whether the indulgence extended outside the Mexican border. Father Fochel of the Cathedral had attempted to explain it; but he had not done so to her satisfaction. And she begged that Robert would interest himself, and discover, if possible, whether she was entitled to the indulgence accompanying the remarkably curious Mexican prayer-beads.

Madame Ratignolle hoped that Robert would exercise extreme caution in dealing with the Mexicans, who, she considered, were a treacherous people, unscrupulous and revengeful. She trusted she did them no injustice in thus condemning them as a race. She had known personally but one Mexican, who made and sold excellent tamales, and whom she would have trusted implicitly, so soft-spoken was he. One day he was arrested for stabbing his wife. She never knew whether he had been hanged or not.

Victor had grown hilarious, and was attempting to tell an anecdote about a Mexican girl who served chocolate one winter in a restaurant in Dauphine Street.[41] No one would listen to him but old Monsieur Farival, who went into convulsions over the droll story.

[40] Fish in wine sauce. [41] A street in the French Quarter.

Edna wondered if they had all gone mad, to be talking and clamoring at that rate. She herself could think of nothing to say about Mexico or the Mexicans.

"At what time do you leave?" she asked Robert.

"At ten," he told her. "Beaudelet wants to wait for the moon."

"Are you all ready to go?"

"Quite ready. I shall only take a hand-bag, and shall pack my trunk in the city."

He turned to answer some question put to him by his mother, and Edna, having finished her black coffee, left the table.

She went directly to her room. The little cottage was close and stuffy after leaving the outer air. But she did not mind; there appeared to be a hundred different things demanding her attention indoors. She began to set the toilet-stand to rights, grumbling at the negligence of the quadroon, who was in the adjoining room putting the children to bed. She gathered together stray garments that were hanging on the backs of chairs, and put each where it belonged in closet or bureau drawer. She changed her gown for a more comfortable and commodious wrapper. She rearranged her hair, combing and brushing it with unusual energy. Then she went in and assisted the quadroon in getting the boys to bed.

They were very playful and inclined to talk—to do anything but lie quiet and go to sleep. Edna sent the quadroon away to her supper and told her she need not return. Then she sat and told the children a story. Instead of soothing it excited them, and added to their wakefulness. She left them in heated argument, speculating about the conclusion of the tale which their mother promised to finish the following night.

The little black girl came in to say that Madame Lebrun would like to have Mrs. Pontellier go and sit with them over at the house till Mr. Robert went away. Edna returned answer that she had already undressed, that she did not feel quite well, but perhaps she would go over to the house later. She started to dress again, and got as far advanced as to remove her *peignoir.* But changing her mind once more she resumed the *peignoir,* and went outside and sat down before her door. She was overheated and irritable, and fanned herself energetically for a while. Madame Ratignolle came down to discover what was the matter.

"All that noise and confusion at the table must have upset me," replied Edna, "and moreover, I hate shocks and surprises. The idea of Robert starting off in such a ridiculously sudden and dramatic way! As if it were a matter of life and death! Never saying a word about it all morning when he was with me."

"Yes," agreed Madame Ratignolle. "I think it was showing us all—you especially—very little consideration. It wouldn't have surprised me in any of the others; those Lebruns are all given to heroics. But I must say I should never have expected such a thing from Robert. Are you not coming down? Come on, dear; it doesn't look friendly."

"No," said Edna, a little sullenly. "I can't go to the trouble of dressing again; I don't feel like it."

"You needn't dress; you look all right; fasten a belt around your waist. Just look at me!"

"No," persisted Edna; "but you go on. Madame Lebrun might be offended if we both stayed away."

Madame Ratignolle kissed Edna good-night, and went away, being in truth rather desirous of joining in the general and animated conversation which was still in progress concerning Mexico and the Mexicans.

Somewhat later Robert came up, carrying his hand-bag.

"Aren't you feeling well?" he asked.

"Oh, well enough. Are you going right away?"

He lit a match and looked at his watch. "In twenty minutes," he said. The sudden and brief flare of the match emphasized the darkness for a while. He sat down upon a stool which the children had left out on the porch.

"Get a chair," said Edna.

"This will do," he replied. He put on his soft hat and nervously took it off again, and wiping his face with his handkerchief, complained of the heat.

"Take the fan," said Edna, offering it to him.

"Oh, no! Thank you. It does no good; you have to stop fanning some time, and feel all the more uncomfortable afterward."

"That's one of the ridiculous things which men always say. I have never known one to speak otherwise of fanning. How long will you be gone?"

"Forever, perhaps. I don't know. It depends upon a good many things."

"Well, in case it shouldn't be forever, how long will it be?"

"I don't know."

"This seems to me perfectly preposterous and uncalled for. I don't like it. I don't understand your motive for silence and mystery, never saying a word to me about it this morning." He remained silent, not offering to defend himself. He only said, after a moment:

"Don't part from me in an ill-humor. I never knew you to be out of patience with me before."

"I don't want to part in any ill-humor," she said. "But can't you understand? I've grown used to seeing you, to having you with me all the time, and your action seems unfriendly, even unkind. You don't even offer an excuse for it. Why, I was planning to be together, thinking of how pleasant it would be to see you in the city next winter."

"So was I," he blurted. "Perhaps that's the—" He stood up suddenly and held out his hand. "Good-by, my dear Mrs. Pontellier; good-by. You won't—I hope you won't completely forget me." She clung to his hand, striving to detain him.

"Write to me when you get there, won't you, Robert?" she entreated.

"I will, thank you. Good-by."

How unlike Robert! The merest acquaintance would have said something more emphatic than "I will, thank you; good-by," to such a request.

He had evidently already taken leave of the people over at the house, for he descended the steps and went to join Beaudelet, who was out there with an oar across his shoulder waiting for Robert. They walked away in the darkness. She could only hear Beaudelet's voice; Robert had apparently not even spoken a word of greeting to his companion.

Edna bit her handkerchief convulsively, striving to hold back and to hide, even from herself as she would have hidden from another, the emo-

tion which was troubling—tearing—her. Her eyes were brimming with tears.

For the first time she recognized anew the symptoms of infatuation which she had felt incipiently as a child, as a girl in her earliest teens, and later as a young woman. The recognition did not lessen the reality, the poignancy of the revelation by any suggestion or promise of instability. The past was nothing to her; offered no lesson which she was willing to heed. The future was a mystery which she never attempted to penetrate. The present alone was significant; was hers, to torture her as it was doing then with the biting conviction that she had lost that which she had held, that she had been denied that which her impassioned, newly awakened being demanded.

XVI

"Do you miss your friend greatly?" asked Mademoiselle Reisz one morning as she came creeping up behind Edna, who had just left her cottage on her way to the beach. She spent much of her time in the water since she had acquired finally the art of swimming. As their stay at Grand Isle drew near its close, she felt that she could not give too much time to a diversion which afforded her the only real pleasurable moments that she knew. When Mademoiselle Reisz came and touched her upon the shoulder and spoke to her, the woman seemed to echo the thought which was ever in Edna's mind; or, better, the feeling which constantly possessed her.

Robert's going had some way taken the brightness, the color, the meaning out of everything. The conditions of her life were in no way changed, but her whole existence was dulled, like a faded garment which seems to be no longer worth wearing. She sought him everywhere—in others whom she induced to talk about him. She went up in the mornings to Madame Lebrun's room, braving the clatter of the old sewing-machine. She sat there and chatted at intervals as Robert had done. She gazed around the room at the pictures and photographs hanging upon the wall, and discovered in some corner an old family album, which she examined with the keenest interest, appealing to Madame Lebrun for enlightenment concerning the many figures and faces which she discovered between its pages.

There was a picture of Madame Lebrun with Robert as a baby, seated in her lap, a round-faced infant with a fist in his mouth. The eyes alone in the baby suggested the man. And that was he also in kilts, at the age of five, wearing long curls and holding a whip in his hand. It made Edna laugh, and she laughed, too, at the portrait in his first long trousers; while another interested her, taken when he left for college, looking thin, long-faced, with eyes full of fire, ambition and great intentions. But there was no recent picture, none which suggested the Robert who had gone away five days ago, leaving a void and wilderness behind him.

"Oh, Robert stopped having his pictures taken when he had to pay for them himself! He found wiser use for his money, he says," explained Madame Lebrun. She had a letter from him, written before he left New Orleans. Edna wished to see the letter, and Madame Lebrun told her to look

for it either on the table or the dresser, or perhaps it was on the mantel-piece.

The letter was on the bookshelf. It possessed the greatest interest and attraction for Edna; the envelope, its size and shape, the post-mark, the handwriting. She examined every detail of the outside before opening it. There were only a few lines, setting forth that he would leave the city that afternoon, that he had packed his trunk in good shape, that he was well, and sent her his love and begged to be affectionately remembered to all. There was no special message to Edna except a postscript saying that if Mrs. Pontellier desired to finish the book which he had been reading to her, his mother would find it in his room, among other books there on the table. Edna experienced a pang of jealousy because he had written to his mother rather than to her.

Every one seemed to take for granted that she missed him. Even her husband, when he came down the Saturday following Robert's departure, expressed regret that he had gone.

"How do you get on without him, Edna?" he asked.

"It's very dull without him," she admitted. Mr. Pontellier had seen Robert in the city, and Edna asked him a dozen questions or more. Where had they met? On Carondelet Street, in the morning. They had gone "in" and had a drink and cigar together. What had they talked about? Chiefly about his prospects in Mexico, which Mr. Pontellier thought were promising. How did he look? How did he seem—grave, or gay, or how? Quite cheerful, and wholly taken up with the idea of his trip, which Mr. Pontellier found altogether natural in a young fellow about to seek fortune and adventure in a strange, queer country.

Edna tapped her foot impatiently, and wondered why the children persisted in playing in the sun when they might be under the trees. She went down and led them out of the sun, scolding the quadroon for not being more attentive.

It did not strike her as in the least grotesque that she should be making of Robert the object of conversation and leading her husband to speak of him. The sentiment which she entertained for Robert in no way resembled that which she felt for her husband, or had ever felt, or ever expected to feel. She had all her life long been accustomed to harbor thoughts and emotions which never voiced themselves. They had never taken the form of struggles. They belonged to her and were her own, and she entertained the conviction that she had a right to them and that they concerned no one but herself. Edna had once told Madame Ratignolle that she would never sacrifice herself for her children, or for any one. Then had followed a rather heated argument; the two women did not appear to understand each other or to be talking the same language. Edna tried to appease her friend, to explain.

"I would give up the unessential; I would give my money, I would give my life for my children; but I wouldn't give myself. I can't make it more clear; it's only something which I am beginning to comprehend, which is revealing itself to me."

"I don't know what you would call the essential, or what you mean by the unessential," said Madame Ratignolle, cheerfully; "but a woman who

would give her life for her children could do no more than that—your Bible tells you so. I'm sure I couldn't do more than that."

"Oh, yes you could!" laughed Edna.

She was not surprised at Mademoiselle Reisz's question the morning that lady, following her to the beach, tapped her on the shoulder and asked if she did not greatly miss her young friend.

"Oh, good morning, Mademoiselle; is it you? Why, of course I miss Robert. Are you going down to bathe?"

"Why should I go down to bathe at the very end of the season when I haven't been in the surf all summer," replied the woman, disagreeably.

"I beg your pardon," offered Edna, in some embarrassment, for she should have remembered that Mademoiselle Reisz's avoidance of the water had furnished a theme for much pleasantry. Some among them thought it was on account of her false hair, or the dread of getting the violets wet, while others attributed it to the natural aversion for water sometimes believed to accompany the artistic temperament. Mademoiselle offered Edna some chocolates in a paper bag, which she took from her pocket, by way of showing that she bore no ill feeling. She habitually ate chocolates for their sustaining quality; they contained much nutriment in small compass, she said. They saved her from starvation, as Madame Lebrun's table was utterly impossible; and no one save so impertinent a woman as Madame Lebrun could think of offering such food to people and requiring them to pay for it.

"She must feel very lonely without her son," said Edna, desiring to change the subject. "Her favorite son, too. It must have been quite hard to let him go."

Mademoiselle laughed maliciously.

"Her favorite son! Oh, dear! Who could have been imposing such a tale upon you? Aline Lebrun lives for Victor, and for Victor alone. She has spoiled him into the worthless creature he is. She worships him and the ground he walks on. Robert is very well in a way, to give up all the money he can earn to the family, and keep the barest pittance for himself. Favorite son, indeed! I miss the poor fellow myself, my dear. I liked to see him and to hear him about the place—the only Lebrun who is worth a pinch of salt. He comes to see me often in the city. I like to play to him. That Victor! hanging would be too good for him. It's a wonder Robert hasn't beaten him to death long ago."

"I thought he had great patience with his brother," offered Edna, glad to be talking about Robert, no matter what was said.

"Oh! he thrashed him well enough a year or two ago," said Mademoiselle. "It was about a Spanish girl, whom Victor considered that he had some sort of claim upon. He met Robert one day talking to the girl, or walking with her, or bathing with her, or carrying her basket—I don't remember what;—and he became so insulting and abusive that Robert gave him a thrashing on the spot that has kept him comparatively in order for a good while. It's about time he was getting another."

"Was her name Mariequita?" asked Edna.

"Mariequita—yes, that was it; Mariequita. I had forgotten. Oh, she's a sly one, and a bad one, that Mariequita!"

Edna looked down at Mademoiselle Reisz and wondered how she could have listened to her venom so long. For some reason she felt depressed, almost unhappy. She had not intended to go into the water; but she donned her bathing suit, and left Mademoiselle alone, seated under the shade of the children's tent. The water was growing cooler as the season advanced. Edna plunged and swam about with an abandon that thrilled and invigorated her. She remained a long time in the water, half hoping that Mademoiselle Reisz would not wait for her.

But Mademoiselle waited. She was very amiable during the walk back, and raved much over Edna's appearance in her bathing suit. She talked about music. She hoped that Edna would go to see her in the city, and wrote her address with the stub of a pencil on a piece of card which she found in her pocket.

"When do you leave?" asked Edna.

"Next Monday; and you?"

"The following week," answered Edna, adding, "It has been a pleasant summer, hasn't it, Mademoiselle?"

"Well," agreed Mademoiselle Reisz, with a shrug, "rather pleasant, if it hadn't been for the mosquitoes and the Farival twins."

XVII

The Pontelliers possessed a very charming home on Esplanade Street[42] in New Orleans. It was a large, double cottage, with a broad front veranda, whose round, fluted columns supported the sloping roof. The house was painted a dazzling white; the outside shutters, or jalousies, were green. In the yard, which was kept scrupulously neat, were flowers and plants of every description which flourishes in South Louisiana. Within doors the appointments were perfect after the conventional type. The softest carpets and rugs covered the floors; rich and tasteful draperies hung at doors and windows. There were paintings, selected with judgment and discrimination, upon the walls. The cut glass, the silver, the heavy damask which daily appeared upon the table were the envy of many women whose husbands were less generous than Mr. Pontellier.

Mr. Pontellier was very fond of walking about his house examining its various appointments and details, to see that nothing was amiss. He greatly valued his possessions, chiefly because they were his, and derived genuine pleasure from contemplating a painting, a statuette, a rare lace curtain—no matter what—after he had bought it and placed it among his household gods.

On Tuesday afternoons—Tuesday being Mrs. Pontellier's reception day[43]—there was a constant stream of callers—women who came in carriages or in the street cars, or walked when the air was soft and distance permitted. A light-colored mulatto boy, in dress coat and bearing a diminutive silver tray for the reception of cards, admitted them. A maid, in white fluted cap, offered the callers liqueur, coffee, or chocolate, as they might

[42] One of the wealthiest and most fashionable streets in the French Quarter.
[43] The day set aside each week to receive callers.

desire. Mrs. Pontellier, attired in a handsome reception gown, remained in the drawing-room the entire afternoon receiving her visitors. Men sometimes called in the evening with their wives.

This had been the programme which Mrs. Pontellier had religiously followed since her marriage, six years before. Certain evenings during the week she and her husband attended the opera or sometimes the play.

Mr. Pontellier left his home in the mornings between nine and ten o'clock, and rarely returned before half-past six or seven in the evening—dinner being served at half-past seven.

He and his wife seated themselves at table one Tuesday evening, a few weeks after their return from Grand Isle. They were alone together. The boys were being put to bed; the patter of their bare, escaping feet could be heard occasionally, as well as the pursuing voice of the quadroon, lifted in mild protest and entreaty. Mrs. Pontellier did not wear her usual Tuesday reception gown; she was in ordinary house dress. Mr. Pontellier, who was observant about such things, noticed it, as he served the soup and handed it to the boy in waiting.

"Tired out, Edna? Whom did you have? Many callers?" he asked. He tasted his soup and began to season it with pepper, salt, vinegar, mustard—everything within reach.

"There were a good many," replied Edna, who was eating her soup with evident satisfaction. "I found their cards when I got home; I was out."

"Out!" exclaimed her husband, with something like genuine consternation in his voice as he laid down the vinegar cruet and looked at her through his glasses. "Why, what could have taken you out on Tuesday? What did you have to do?"

"Nothing. I simply felt like going out, and I went out."

"Well, I hope you left some suitable excuse," said her husband, somewhat appeased, as he added a dash of cayenne pepper to the soup.

"No, I left no excuse. I told Joe to say I was out, that was all."

"Why, my dear, I should think you'd understand by this time that people don't do such things; we've got to observe *les convenances*[44] if we ever expect to get on and keep up with the procession. If you felt that you had to leave home this afternoon, you should have left some suitable explanation for your absence.

"This soup is really impossible; it's strange that woman hasn't learned yet to make a decent soup. Any free-lunch stand in town serves a better one. Was Mrs. Belthrop here?"

"Bring the tray with the cards, Joe. I don't remember who was here."

The boy retired and returned after a moment, bringing the tiny silver tray, which was covered with ladies' visiting cards. He handed it to Mrs. Pontellier.

"Give it to Mr. Pontellier," she said.

Joe offered the tray to Mr. Pontellier, and removed the soup.

Mr. Pontellier scanned the names of his wife's callers, reading some of them aloud, with comments as he read.

"'The Misses Delasidas.' I worked a big deal in futures for their father this morning; nice girls; it's time they were getting married. 'Mrs. Belthrop.'

[44] The conventions or proprieties.

I tell you what it is, Edna; you can't afford to snub Mrs. Belthrop. Why, Belthrop could buy and sell us ten times over. His business is worth a good, round sum to me. You'd better write her a note. 'Mrs. James Highcamp.' Hugh! the less you have to do with Mrs. Highcamp, the better. 'Madame Laforcé.' Came all the way from Carrolton, too, poor old soul. 'Miss Wiggs,' 'Mrs. Eleanor Boltons.'" He pushed the cards aside.

"Mercy!" exclaimed Edna, who had been fuming. "Why are you taking the thing so seriously and making such a fuss over it?"

"I'm not making any fuss over it. But it's just such seeming trifles that we've got to take seriously; such things count."

The fish was scorched. Mr. Pontellier would not touch it. Edna said she did not mind a little scorched taste. The roast was in some way not to his fancy, and he did not like the manner in which the vegetables were served.

"It seems to me," he said, "we spend money enough in this house to procure at least one meal a day which a man could eat and retain his self-respect."

"You used to think the cook was a treasure," returned Edna, indifferently.

"Perhaps she was when she first came; but cooks are only human. They need looking after, like any other class of persons that you employ. Suppose I didn't look after the clerks in my office, just let them run things their own way; they'd soon make a nice mess of me and my business."

"Where are you going?" asked Edna, seeing that her husband arose from table without having eaten a morsel except a taste of the highly-seasoned soup.

"I'm going to get my dinner at the club. Good night." He went into the hall, took his hat and stick from the stand, and left the house.

She was somewhat familiar with such scenes. They had often made her very unhappy. On a few previous occcasions she had been completely deprived of any desire to finish her dinner. Sometimes she had gone into the kitchen to administer a tardy rebuke to the cook. Once she went to her room and studied the cookbook during an entire evening, finally writing out a menu for the week, which left her harassed with a feeling that, after all, she had accomplished no good that was worth the name.

But that evening Edna finished her dinner alone, with forced deliberation. Her face was flushed and her eyes flamed with some inward fire that lighted them. After finishing her dinner she went to her room, having instructed the boy to tell any other callers that she was indisposed.

It was a large, beautiful room, rich and picturesque in the soft, dim light which the maid had turned low. She went and stood at an open window and looked out upon the deep tangle of the garden below. All the mystery and witchery of the night seemed to have gathered there amid the perfumes and the dusky and tortuous outlines of flowers and foliage. She was seeking herself and finding herself in just such sweet half-darkness which met her moods. But the voices were not soothing that came to her from the darkness and the sky above and the stars. They jeered and sounded mournful notes without promise, devoid even of hope. She turned back into the room and began to walk to and fro down its whole length, without stopping, without resting. She carried in her hands a thin handkerchief, which she tore into ribbons, rolled into a ball, and flung from her. Once she

stopped, and taking off her wedding ring, flung it upon the carpet. When she saw it lying there, she stamped her heel upon it, striving to crush it. But her small boot heel did not make an indenture, not a mark upon the little glittering circlet.

In a sweeping passion she seized a glass vase from the table and flung it upon the tiles of the hearth. She wanted to destroy something. The crash and clatter were what she wanted to hear.

A maid, alarmed at the din of breaking glass, entered the room to discover what was the matter.

"A vase fell upon the hearth," said Edna. "Never mind; leave it till morning."

"Oh! you might get some of the glass in your feet, ma'am," insisted the young woman, picking up bits of the broken vase that were scattered upon the carpet. "And here's your ring, ma'am, under the chair."

Edna held out her hand, and taking the ring, slipped it upon her finger.

XVIII

The following morning Mr. Pontellier, upon leaving for his office, asked Edna if she would not meet him in town in order to look at some new fixtures for the library.

"I hardly think we need new fixtures, Léonce. Don't let us get anything new; you are too extravagant. I don't believe you ever think of saving or putting by."

"The way to become rich is to make money, my dear Edna, not to save it," he said. He regretted that she did not feel inclined to go with him and select new fixtures. He kissed her good-by, and told her she was not looking well and must take care of herself. She was unusually pale and very quiet.

She stood on the front veranda as he quitted the house, and absently picked a few sprays of jessamine that grew upon a trellis near by. She inhaled the odor of the blossoms and thrust them into the bosom of her white morning gown. The boys were dragging along the banquette[45] a small "express wagon," which they had filled with blocks and sticks. The quadroon was following them with little quick steps, having assumed a fictitious animation and alacrity for the occasion. A fruit vender was crying his wares in the street.

Edna looked straight before her with a self-absorbed expression upon her face. She felt no interest in anything about her. The street, the children, the fruit vender, the flowers growing there under her eyes, were all part and parcel of an alien world which had suddenly become antagonistic.

She went back into the house. She had thought of speaking to the cook concerning her blunders of the previous night; but Mr. Pontellier had saved her that disagreeable mission, for which she was so poorly fitted. Mr. Pontellier's arguments were usually convincing with those whom he employed. He left home feeling quite sure that he and Edna would sit down

[45] Sidewalk.

that evening, and possibly a few subsequent evenings, to a dinner deserving of the name.

Edna spent an hour or two in looking over some of her old sketches. She could see their shortcomings and defects, which were glaring in her eyes. She tried to work a little, but found she was not in the humor. Finally she gathered together a few of the sketches—those which she considered the least discreditable; and she carried them with her when, a little later, she dressed and left the house. She looked handsome and distinguished in her street gown. The tan of the seashore had left her face, and her forehead was smooth, white, and polished beneath her heavy yellow-brown hair. There were a few freckles on her face, and a small, dark mole near the under lip and one on the temple, half-hidden in her hair.

As Edna walked along the street she was thinking of Robert. She was still under the spell of her infatuation. She had tried to forget him, realizing the inutility of remembering. But the thought of him was like an obsession, ever pressing itself upon her. It was not that she dwelt upon details of their acquaintance, or recalled in any special or peculiar way his personality; it was his being, his existence, which dominated her thought, fading sometimes as if it would melt into the mist of the forgotten, reviving again with an intensity which filled her with an incomprehensible longing.

Edna was on her way to Madame Ratignolle's. Their intimacy, begun at Grand Isle, had not declined, and they had seen each other with some frequency since their return to the city. The Ratignolles lived at no great distance from Edna's home, on the corner of a side street, where Monsieur Ratignolle owned and conducted a drug store which enjoyed a steady and prosperous trade. His father had been in the business before him, and Monsieur Ratignolle stood well in the community and bore an enviable reputation for integrity and clear-headedness. His family lived in commodious apartments over the store, having an entrance on the side within the *porte cochère*.[46] There was something which Edna thought very French, very foreign, about their whole manner of living. In the large and pleasant salon which extended across the width of the house, the Ratignolles entertained their friends once a fortnight with a *soirée musicale*, sometimes diversified by card-playing. There was a friend who played upon the 'cello. One brought his flute and another his violin, while there were some who sang and a number who performed upon the piano with various degrees of taste and agility. The Ratignolles' *soirées musicales* were widely known, and it was considered a privilege to be invited to them.

Edna found her friend engaged in assorting the clothes which had returned that morning from the laundry. She at once abandoned her occupation upon seeing Edna, who had been ushered without ceremony into her presence.

"'Cité can do it as well as I; it is really her business," she explained to Edna, who apologized for interrupting her. And she summoned a young black woman, whom she instructed, in French, to be very careful in checking off the list which she handed her. She told her to notice particularly if a fine linen handkerchief of Monsieur Ratignolle's, which was missing last

[46] A porch at the door of a building for sheltering persons entering or leaving carriages.

week, had been returned; and to be sure to set to one side such pieces as required mending and darning.

Then placing an arm around Edna's waist, she led her to the front of the house, to the salon, where it was cool and sweet with the odor of great roses that stood upon the hearth in jars.

Madame Ratignolle looked more beautiful than ever there at home, in a negligé which left her arms almost wholly bare and exposed the rich, melting curves of her white throat.

"Perhaps I shall be able to paint your picture some day," said Edna with a smile when they were seated. She produced the roll of sketches and started to unfold them. "I believe I ought to work again. I feel as if I wanted to be doing something. What do you think of them? Do you think it worth while to take it up again and study some more? I might study for a while with Laidpore."

She knew that Madame Ratignolle's opinion in such a matter would be next to valueless, that she herself had not alone decided, but determined; but she sought the words of praise and encouragement that would help her to put heart into her venture.

"Your talent is immense, dear!"

"Nonsense!" protested Edna, well pleased.

"Immense, I tell you," persisted Madame Ratignolle, surveying the sketches one by one, at close range, then holding them at arm's length, narrowing her eyes, and dropping her head on one side. "Surely, this Bavarian peasant is worthy of framing; and this basket of apples! never have I seen anything more lifelike. One might almost be tempted to reach out a hand and take one."

Edna could not control a feeling which bordered upon complacency at her friend's praise, even realizing, as she did, its true worth. She retained a few of the sketches, and gave all the rest to Madame Ratignolle, who appreciated the gift far beyond its value and proudly exhibited the pictures to her husband when he came up from the store a little later for his midday dinner.

Mr. Ratignolle was one of those men who are called the salt of the earth. His cheerfulness was unbounded, and it was matched by his goodness of heart, his broad charity, and common sense. He and his wife spoke English with an accent which was only discernible through its un-English emphasis and a certain carefulness and deliberation. Edna's husband spoke English with no accent whatever. The Ratignolles understood each other perfectly. If ever the fusion of two human beings into one has been accomplished on this sphere it was surely in their union.

As Edna seated herself at table with them she thought, "Better a dinner of herbs," though it did not take her long to discover that it was no dinner of herbs, but a delicious repast, simple, choice, and in every way satisfying.

Monsieur Ratignolle was delighted to see her, though he found her looking not so well as at Grand Isle, and he advised a tonic. He talked a good deal on various topics, a little politics, some city news and neighborhood gossip. He spoke with an animation and earnestness that gave an exaggerated importance to every syllable he uttered. His wife was keenly

interested in everything he said, laying down her fork the better to listen, chiming in, taking the words out of his mouth.

Edna felt depressed rather than soothed after leaving them. The little glimpse of domestic harmony which had been offered her gave her no regret, no longing. It was not a condition of life which fitted her, and she could see in it but an appalling and hopeless ennui. She was moved by a kind of commiseration for Madame Ratignolle,—a pity for that colorless existence which never uplifted its possessor beyond the region of blind contentment, in which no moment of anguish ever visited her soul, in which she would never have the taste of life's delirium. Edna vaguely wondered what she meant by "life's delirium." It had crossed her thought like some unsought, extraneous impression.

XIX

Edna could not help but think that it was very foolish, very childish, to have stamped upon her wedding ring and smashed the crystal vase upon the tiles. She was visited by no more outbursts, moving her to such futile expedients. She began to do as she liked and to feel as she liked. She completely abandoned her Tuesdays at home, and did not return the visits of those who had called upon her. She made no ineffectual efforts to conduct her household *en bonne ménagère*,[47] going and coming as it suited her fancy, and, so far as she was able, lending herself to any passing caprice.

Mr. Pontellier had been a rather courteous husband so long as he met a certain tacit submissiveness in his wife. But her new and unexpected line of conduct completely bewildered him. It shocked him. Then her absolute disregard for her duties as a wife angered him. When Mr. Pontellier became rude, Edna grew insolent. She had resolved never to take another step backward.

"It seems to me the utmost folly for a woman at the head of a household, and the mother of children, to spend in an atelier[48] days which would be better employed contriving for the comfort of her family."

"I feel like painting," answered Edna. "Perhaps I shan't always feel like it."

"Then in God's name paint! but don't let the family go to the devil. There's Madame Ratignolle; because she keeps up her music, she doesn't let everything else go to chaos. And she's more of a musician than you are a painter."

"She isn't a musician, and I'm not a painter. It isn't on account of painting that I let things go."

"On account of what, then?"

"Oh! I don't know. Let me alone; you bother me."

It sometimes entered Mr. Pontellier's mind to wonder if his wife were not growing a little unbalanced mentally. He could see plainly that she was not herself. That is, he could not see that she was becoming herself and daily casting aside that fictitious self which we assume like a garment with which to appear before the world.

[47] "As a good housekeeper." [48] Studio.

Her husband let her alone as she requested, and went away to his office. Edna went up to her atelier—a bright room in the top of the house. She was working with great energy and interest, without accomplishing anything, however, which satisfied her even in the smallest degree. For a time she had the whole household enrolled in the service of art. The boys posed for her. They thought it amusing at first, but the occupation soon lost its attractiveness when they discovered that it was not a game arranged especially for their entertainment. The quadroon sat for hours before Edna's palette, patient as a savage, while the house-maid took charge of the children, and the drawing-room went undusted. But the house-maid, too, served her term as model when Edna perceived that the young woman's back and shoulders were molded on classic lines, and that her hair, loosened from its confining cap, became an inspiration. While Edna worked she sometimes sang low the little air, *"Ah! si tu savais!"*

It moved her with recollections. She could hear again the ripple of the water, the flapping sail. She could see the glint of the moon upon the bay, and could feel the soft, gusty beating of the hot south wind. A subtle current of desire passed through her body, weakening her hold upon the brushes and making her eyes burn.

There were days when she was very happy without knowing why. She was happy to be alive and breathing, when her whole being seemed to be one with the sunlight, the color, the odors, the luxuriant warmth of some perfect Southern day. She liked then to wander alone into strange and unfamiliar places. She discovered many a sunny, sleepy corner, fashioned to dream in. And she found it good to dream and to be alone and unmolested.

There were days when she was unhappy, she did not know why,—when it did not seem worth while to be glad or sorry, to be alive or dead; when life appeared to her like a grotesque pandemonium and humanity like worms struggling blindly toward inevitable annihilation. She could not work on such a day, nor weave fancies to stir her pulses and warm her blood.

XX

It was during such a mood that Edna hunted up Mademoiselle Reisz. She had not forgotten the rather disagreeable impression left upon her by their last interview; but she nevertheless felt a desire to see her—above all, to listen while she played upon the piano. Quite early in the afternoon she started upon her quest for the pianist. Unfortunately she had mislaid or lost Mademoiselle Reisz's card, and looking up her address in the city directory, she found that the woman lived on Bienville Street, some distance away. The directory which fell into her hands was a year or more old, however, and upon reaching the number indicated, Edna discovered that the house was occupied by a respectable family of mulattoes who had *chambres garnies*[49] to let. They had been living there for six months, and knew absolutely nothing of a Mademoiselle Reisz. In fact, they knew noth-

[49]"Furnished rooms."

ing of any of their neighbors; their lodgers were all people of the highest distinction, they assured Edna. She did not linger to discuss class distinctions with Madame Pouponne, but hastened to a neighboring grocery store, feeling sure that Mademoiselle would have left her address with the proprietor.

He knew Mademoiselle Reisz a good deal better than he wanted to know her, he informed his questioner. In truth, he did not want to know her at all, or anything concerning her—the most disagreeable and unpopular woman who ever lived in Bienville Street. He thanked heaven she had left the neighborhood, and was equally thankful that he did not know where she had gone.

Edna's desire to see Mademoiselle Reisz had increased tenfold since these unlooked-for obstacles had arisen to thwart it. She was wondering who could give her the information she sought, when it suddenly occurred to her that Madame Lebrun would be the one most likely to do so. She knew it was useless to ask Madame Ratignolle, who was on the most distant terms with the musician, and preferred to know nothing concerning her. She had once been almost as emphatic in expressing herself upon the subject as the corner grocer.

Edna knew that Madame Lebrun had returned to the city, for it was the middle of November. And she also knew where the Lebruns lived, on Chartres Street.

Their home from the outside looked like a prison, with iron bars before the door and lower windows. The iron bars were a relic of the old *régime*,[50] and no one had ever thought of dislodging them. At the side was a high fence enclosing the garden. A gate or door opening upon the street was locked. Edna rang the bell at this side garden gate, and stood upon the banquette, waiting to be admitted.

It was Victor who opened the gate for her. A black woman, wiping her hands upon her apron, was close at his heels. Before she saw them Edna could hear them in altercation, the woman—plainly an anomaly—claiming the right to be allowed to perform her duties, one of which was to answer the bell.

Victor was surprised and delighted to see Mrs. Pontellier, and he made no attempt to conceal either his astonishment or his delight. He was a dark-browed, good-looking youngster of nineteen, greatly resembling his mother, but with ten times her impetuosity. He instructed the black woman to go at once and inform Madame Lebrun that Mrs. Pontellier desired to see her. The woman grumbled a refusal to do part of her duty when she had not been permitted to do it all, and started back to her interrupted task of weeding the garden. Whereupon Victor administered a rebuke in the form of a volley of abuse, which, owing to its rapidity and incoherence, was all but incomprehensible to Edna. Whatever it was, the rebuke was convincing, for the woman dropped her hoe and went mumbling into the house.

Edna did not wish to enter. It was very pleasant there on the side porch, where there were chairs, a wicker lounge, and a small table. She seated herself, for she was tired from her long tramp; and she began to rock gently and smooth out the folds of her silk parasol. Victor drew up his chair

[50] That is, the period of Spanish rule (1762–1800).

beside her. He at once explained that the black woman's offensive conduct was all due to imperfect training, as he was not there to take her in hand. He had only come up from the island the morning before, and expected to return next day. He stayed all winter at the island; he lived there, and kept the place in order and got things ready for the summer visitors.

But a man needed occasional relaxation, he informed Mrs. Pontellier, and every now and again he drummed up a pretext to bring him to the city. My! but he had had a time of it the evening before! He wouldn't want his mother to know, and he began to talk in a whisper. He was scintillant with recollections. Of course, he couldn't think of telling Mrs. Pontellier all about it, she being a woman and not comprehending such things. But it all began with a girl peeping and smiling at him through the shutters as he passed by. Oh! but she was a beauty! Certainly he smiled back, and went up and talked to her. Mrs. Pontellier did not know him if she supposed he was one to let an opportunity like that escape him. Despite herself, the youngster amused her. She must have betrayed in her look some degree of interest or entertainment. The boy grew more daring, and Mrs. Pontellier might have found herself, in a little while, listening to a highly colored story but for the timely appearance of Madame Lebrun.

That lady was still clad in white, according to her custom of the summer. Her eyes beamed an effusive welcome. Would not Mrs. Pontellier go inside? Would she partake of some refreshment? Why had she not been there before? How was that dear Mr. Pontellier and how were those sweet children? Had Mrs. Pontellier ever known such a warm November?

Victor went and reclined on the wicker lounge behind his mother's chair, where he commanded a view of Edna's face. He had taken her parasol from her hands while he spoke to her, and he now lifted it and twirled it above him as he lay on his back. When Madame Lebrun complained that it was *so* dull coming back to the city; that she saw *so* few people now; that even Victor, when he came up from the island for a day or two, had *so* much to occupy him and engage his time; then it was that the youth went into contortions on the lounge and winked mischievously at Edna. She somehow felt like a confederate in crime, and tried to look severe and disapproving.

There had been but two letters from Robert, with little in them, they told her. Victor said it was really not worth while to go inside for the letters, when his mother entreated him to go in search of them. He remembered the contents, which in truth he rattled off very glibly when put to the test.

One letter was written from Vera Cruz and the other from the City of Mexico. He had met Montel, who was doing everything toward his advancement. So far, the financial situation was no improvement over the one he had left in New Orleans, but of course the prospects were vastly better. He wrote of the City of Mexico, the buildings, the people and their habits, the conditions of life which he found there. He sent his love to the family. He inclosed a check to his mother, and hoped she would affectionately remember him to all his friends. That was about the substance of the two letters. Edna felt that if there had been a message for her, she would have received it. The despondent frame of mind in which she had left home began again to overtake her, and she remembered that she wished to find Mademoiselle Reisz.

Madame Lebrun knew where Mademoiselle Reisz lived. She gave Edna the address, regretting that she would not consent to stay and spend the remainder of the afternoon, and pay a visit to Mademoiselle Reisz some other day. The afternoon was already well advanced.

Victor escorted her out upon the banquette, lifted her parasol, and held it over her while he walked to the car with her. He entreated her to bear in mind that the disclosures of the afternoon were strictly confidential. She laughed and bantered him a little, remembering too late that she should have been dignified and reserved.

"How handsome Mrs. Pontellier looked!" said Madame Lebrun to her son.

"Ravishing!" he admitted. "The city atmosphere has improved her. Some way she doesn't seem like the same woman."

XXI

Some people contended that the reason Mademoiselle Reisz always chose apartments up under the roof was to discourage the approach of beggars, peddlars and callers. There were plenty of windows in her little front room. They were for the most part dingy, but as they were nearly always open it did not make so much difference. They often admitted into the room a good deal of smoke and soot; but at the same time all the light and air that there was came through them. From her windows could be seen the crescent of the river, the masts of ships and the big chimneys of the Mississippi steamers. A magnificent piano crowded the apartment. In the next room she slept, and in the third and last she harbored a gasoline stove on which she cooked her meals when disinclined to descend to the neighboring restaurant. It was there also that she ate, keeping her belongings in a rare old buffet, dingy and battered from a hundred years of use.

When Edna knocked at Mademoiselle Reisz's front room door and entered, she discovered that person standing beside the window, engaged in mending or patching an old prunella gaiter.[51] The little musician laughed all over when she saw Edna. Her laugh consisted of a contortion of the face and all the muscles of the body. She seemed strikingly homely, standing there in the afternoon light. She still wore the shabby lace and the artificial bunch of violets on the side of her head.

"So you remembered me at last," said Mademoiselle. "I had said to myself, 'Ah, bah! she will never come.'"

"Did you want me to come?" asked Edna with a smile.

"I had not thought much about it," answered Mademoiselle. The two had seated themselves on a little bumpy sofa which stood against the wall. "I am glad, however, that you came. I have the water boiling back there, and was just about to make some coffee. You will drink a cup with me. And how is *la belle dame*?[52] Always handsome! always healthy! always contented!" She took Edna's hand between her strong wiry fingers, holding it

[51] A kind of shoe with a cloth upper. [52] "The beautiful lady."

loosely without warmth, and executing a sort of double theme upon the
back and palm.

"Yes," she went on; "I sometimes thought: 'She will never come. She
promised as those women in society always do, without meaning it. She will
not come.' For I really don't believe you like me, Mrs. Pontellier."

"I don't know whether I like you or not," replied Edna, gazing down at
the little woman with a quizzical look.

The candor of Mrs. Pontellier's admission greatly pleased Mademoiselle
Reisz. She expressed her gratification by repairing forthwith to the region
of the gasoline stove and rewarding her guest with the promised cup of
coffee. The coffee and the biscuit accompanying it proved very acceptable
to Edna, who had declined refreshment at Madame Lebrun's and was now
beginning to feel hungry. Mademoiselle set the tray which she brought in
upon a small table near at hand, and seated herself once again on the
lumpy sofa.

"I have had a letter from your friend," she remarked, as she poured a
little cream into Edna's cup and handed it to her.

"My friend?"

"Yes, your friend Robert. He wrote to me from the City of Mexico."

"Wrote to *you*?" repeated Edna in amazement, stirring her coffee
absently.

"Yes, to me. Why not? Don't stir all the warmth out of your coffee;
drink it. Though the letter might as well have been sent to you; it was
nothing but Mrs. Pontellier from beginning to end."

"Let me see it," requested the young woman, entreatingly.

"No; a letter concerns no one but the person who writes it and the one
to whom it is written."

"Haven't you just said it concerned me from beginning to end?"

"It was written about you, not to you. 'Have you seen Mrs. Pontellier?
How is she looking?' he asks. 'As Mrs. Pontellier says,' or 'as Mrs. Pontellier
once said.' 'If Mrs. Pontellier should call upon you, play for her that Im-
promptu of Chopin's, my favorite. I heard it here a day or two ago, but not
as you play it. I should like to know how it affects her,' and so on, as if he
supposed we were constantly in each other's society."

"Let me see the letter."

"Oh, no."

"Have you answered it?"

"No."

"Let me see the letter."

"No, and again, no."

"Then play the Impromptu for me."

"It is growing late; what time do you have to be home?"

"Time doesn't concern me. Your question seems a little rude. Play the
Impromptu."

"But you have told me nothing of yourself. What are you doing?"

"Painting!" laughed Edna. "I am becoming an artist. Think of it!"

"Ah! an artist! You have pretensions, Madame."

"Why pretensions? Do you think I could not become an artist?"

"I do not know you well enough to say. I do not know your talent or
your temperament. To be an artist includes much; one must possess

many gifts—absolute gifts—which have not been acquired by one's own effort. And, moreover, to succeed, the artist must possess the courageous soul."

"What do you mean by the courageous soul?"

"Courageous, *ma foi!* The brave soul. The soul that dares and defies."

"Show me the letter and play for me the Impromptu. You see that I have persistence. Does that quality count for anything in art?"

"It counts with a foolish old woman whom you have captivated," replied Mademoiselle, with her wriggling laugh.

The letter was right there at hand in the drawer of the little table upon which Edna had just placed her coffee cup. Mademoiselle opened the drawer and drew forth the letter, the topmost one. She placed it in Edna's hands, and without further comment arose and went to the piano.

Mademoiselle played a soft interlude. It was an improvisation. She sat low at the instrument, and the lines of her body settled into ungraceful curves and angles that gave it an appearance of deformity. Gradually and imperceptibly the interlude melted into the soft opening minor chords of the Chopin Impromptu.

Edna did not know when the Impromptu began or ended. She sat in the sofa corner reading Robert's letter by the fading light. Mademoiselle had glided from the Chopin into the quivering love-notes of Isolde's song,[53] and back again to the Impromptu with its soulful and poignant longing.

The shadows deepened in the little room. The music grew strange and fantastic—turbulent, insistent, plaintive and soft with entreaty. The shadows grew deeper. The music filled the room. It floated out upon the night, over the housetops, the crescent of the river, losing itself in the silence of the upper air.

Edna was sobbing, just as she had wept one midnight at Grand Isle when strange, new voices awoke in her. She arose in some agitation to take her departure. "May I come again, Mademoiselle?" she asked at the threshold.

"Come whenever you feel like it. Be careful; the stairs and landings are dark; don't stumble."

Mademoiselle reentered and lit a candle. Robert's letter was on the floor. She stooped and picked it up. It was crumpled and damp with tears. Mademoiselle smoothed the letter out, restored it to the envelope, and replaced it in the table drawer.

XXII

One morning on his way into town Mr. Pontellier stopped at the house of his old friend and family physician, Doctor Mandelet. The Doctor was a semi-retired physician, resting, as the saying is, upon his laurels. He bore a reputation for wisdom rather than skill—leaving the active practice of

[53] The *Liebestod* ("Love-death" in German) from Richard Wagner's *Tristan and Isolde* (1857–59). In this passionate aria, Isolde bids the dead Tristan farewell and falls dead herself.

medicine to his assistants and younger contemporaries—and was much sought for in matters of consultation. A few families, united to him by bonds of friendship, he still attended when they required the services of a physician. The Pontelliers were among these.

Mr. Pontellier found the Doctor reading at the open window of his study. His house stood rather far back from the street, in the center of a delightful garden, so that it was quiet and peaceful at the old gentleman's study window. He was a great reader. He stared up disapprovingly over his eye-glasses as Mr. Pontellier entered, wondering who had the temerity to disturb him at that hour of the morning.

"Ah, Pontellier! Not sick, I hope. Come and have a seat. What news do you bring this morning?" He was quite portly, with a profusion of gray hair, and small blue eyes which age had robbed of much of their brightness but none of their penetration.

"Oh! I'm never sick, Doctor. You know that I come of tough fiber—of that old Creole race of Pontelliers that dry up and finally blow away. I came to consult—no, not precisely to consult—to talk to you about Edna. I don't know what ails her."

"Madame Pontellier not well?" marveled the Doctor. "Why, I saw her—I think it was a week ago—walking along Canal Street, the picture of health, it seemed to me."

"Yes, yes; she seems quite well," said Mr. Pontellier, leaning forward and whirling his stick between his two hands; "but she doesn't act well. She's odd, she's not like herself. I can't make her out, and I thought perhaps you'd help me."

"How does she act?" inquired the doctor.

"Well, it isn't easy to explain," said Mr. Pontellier, throwing himself back in his chair. "She lets the housekeeping go to the dickens."

"Well, well; women are not all alike, my dear Pontellier. We've got to consider—"

"I know that; I told you I couldn't explain. Her whole attitude—toward me and everybody and everything—has changed. You know I have a quick temper, but I don't want to quarrel or be rude to a woman, especially my wife; yet I'm driven to it, and feel like ten thousand devils after I've made a fool of myself. She's making it devilishly uncomfortable for me," he went on nervously. "She's got some sort of notion in her head concerning the eternal rights of women; and—you understand—we meet in the morning at the breakfast table."

The old gentleman lifted his shaggy eyebrows, protruded his thick nether lip, and tapped the arms of his chair with his cushioned fingertips.

"What have you been doing to her, Pontellier?"

"Doing! *Parbleu!*"

"Has she," asked the Doctor, with a smile, "has she been associating of late with a circle of pseudo-intellectual women—super-spiritual superior beings? My wife has been telling me about them."

"That's the trouble," broke in Mr. Pontellier, "she hasn't been associating with any one. She has abandoned her Tuesdays at home, has thrown over all her acquaintances, and goes tramping about by herself, moping in the street-cars, getting in after dark. I tell you she's peculiar. I don't like it; I feel a little worried over it."

This was a new aspect for the Doctor. "Nothing hereditary?" he asked, seriously. "Nothing peculiar about her family antecedents, is there?"

"Oh, no, indeed! She comes of sound old Presbyterian Kentucky stock. The old gentleman, her father, I have heard, used to atone for his weekday sins with his Sunday devotions. I know for a fact, that his race horses literally ran away with the prettiest bit of Kentucky farming land I ever laid eyes upon. Margaret—you know Margaret—she has all the Presbyterianism undiluted. And the youngest is something of a vixen. By the way, she gets married in a couple of weeks from now."

"Send your wife up to the wedding," exclaimed the Doctor, foreseeing a happy solution. "Let her stay among her own people for a while; it will do her good."

"That's what I want her to do. She won't go to the marriage. She says a wedding is one of the most lamentable spectacles on earth. Nice thing for a woman to say to her husband!" exclaimed Mr. Pontellier, fuming anew at the recollection.

"Pontellier," said the Doctor, after a moment's reflection, "let your wife alone for a while. Don't bother her, and don't let her bother you. Woman, my dear friend, is a very peculiar and delicate organism—a sensitive and highly organized woman, such as I know Mrs. Pontellier to be, is especially peculiar. It would require an inspired psychologist to deal successfully with them. And when ordinary fellows like you and me attempt to cope with their idiosyncrasies the result is bungling. Most women are moody and whimsical. This is some passing whim of your wife, due to some cause or causes which you and I needn't try to fathom. But it will pass happily over, especially if you let her alone. Send her around to see me."

"Oh! I couldn't do that; there'd be no reason for it," objected Mr. Pontellier.

"Then I'll go around and see her," said the Doctor. "I'll drop in to dinner some evening *en bon ami*."[54]

"Do! by all means," urged Mr. Pontellier. "What evening will you come? Say Thursday. Will you come Thursday?" he asked, rising to take his leave.

"Very well; Thursday. My wife may possibly have some engagement for me Thursday. In case she has, I shall let you know. Otherwise, you may expect me."

Mr. Pontellier turned before leaving to say:

"I am going to New York on business very soon. I have a big scheme on hand, and want to be on the field proper to pull the ropes and handle the ribbons. We'll let you in on the inside if you say so, Doctor," he laughed.

"No, I thank you, my dear sir," returned the Doctor. "I leave such ventures to you younger men with the fever of life still in your blood."

"What I wanted to say," continued Mr. Pontellier, with his hand on the knob; "I may have to be absent a good while. Would you advise me to take Edna along?"

"By all means, if she wishes to go. If not, leave her here. Don't contradict her. The mood will pass, I assure you. It may take a month, two, three months—possibly longer, but it will pass; have patience."

"Well, good-by, *à jeudi*,"[55] said Mr. Pontellier, as he let himself out.

[54]"As a good friend." [55]"Until Thursday."

The Doctor would have liked during the course of conversation to ask, "Is there any man in the case?" but he knew his Creole too well to make such a blunder as that.

He did not resume his book immediately, but sat for a while meditatively looking out into the garden.

XXIII

Edna's father was in the city, and had been with them several days. She was not very warmly or deeply attached to him, but they had certain tastes in common, and when together they were companionable. His coming was in the nature of a welcome disturbance; it seemed to furnish a new direction for her emotions.

He had come to purchase a wedding gift for his daughter, Janet, and an outfit for himself in which he might make a creditable appearance at her marriage. Mr. Pontellier had selected the bridal gift, as every one immediately connected with him always deferred to his taste in such matters. And his suggestions on the question of dress—which too often assumes the nature of a problem—were of inestimable value to his father-in-law. But for the past few days the old gentleman had been upon Edna's hands, and in his society she was becoming acquainted with a new set of sensations. He had been a colonel in the Confederate army, and still maintained, with the title, the military bearing which had always accompanied it. His hair and mustache were white and silky, emphasizing the rugged bronze of his face. He was tall and thin, and wore his coats padded, which gave a fictitious breadth and depth to his shoulders and chest. Edna and her father looked very distinguished together, and excited a good deal of notice during their perambulations. Upon his arrival she began by introducing him to her atelier and making a sketch of him. He took the whole matter very seriously. If her talent had been ten-fold greater than it was, it would not have surprised him, convinced as he was that he had bequeathed to all of his daughters the germs of a masterful capability, which only depended upon their own efforts to be directed toward successful achievement.

Before her pencil he sat rigid and unflinching, as he had faced the cannon's mouth in days gone by. He resented the intrusion of the children, who gaped with wondering eyes at him, sitting so stiff up there in their mother's bright atelier. When they drew near he motioned them away with an expressive action of the foot, loath to disturb the fixed lines of his countenance, his arms, or his rigid shoulders.

Edna, anxious to entertain him, invited Mademoiselle Reisz to meet him, having promised him a treat in her piano playing; but Mademoiselle declined the invitation. So together they attended a *soirée musicale* at the Ratignolles'. Monsieur and Madame Ratignolle made much of the Colonel, installing him as the guest of honor and engaging him at once to dine with them the following Sunday, or any day which he might select. Madame coquetted with him in the most captivating and naïve manner, with eyes, gestures, and a profusion of compliments, till the Colonel's old head felt thirty years younger on his padded shoulders. Edna marveled, not comprehending. She herself was almost devoid of coquetry.

There were one or two men whom she observed at the *soirée musicale;* but she would never have felt moved to any kittenish display to attract their notice—to any feline or feminine wiles to express herself toward them. Their personality attracted her in an agreeable way. Her fancy selected them, and she was glad when a lull in the music gave them an opportunity to meet her and talk with her. Often on the street the glance of strange eyes had lingered in her memory, and sometimes had disturbed her.

Mr. Pontellier did not attend these *soirées musicales.* He considered them *bourgeois,* and found more diversion at the club. To Madame Ratignolle he said the music dispensed at her *soirées* was too "heavy," too far beyond his untrained comprehension. His excuse flattered her. But she disapproved of Mr. Pontellier's club, and she was frank enough to tell Edna so.

"It's a pity Mr. Pontellier doesn't stay home more in the evenings. I think you would be more—well, if you don't mind my saying it—more united, if he did."

"Oh! dear no!" said Edna, with a blank look in her eyes. "What should I do if he stayed home? We wouldn't have anything to say to each other."

She had not much of anything to say to her father, for that matter; but he did not antagonize her. She discovered that he interested her, though she realized that he might not interest her long; and for the first time in her life she felt as if she were thoroughly acquainted with him. He kept her busy serving him and ministering to his wants. It amused her to do so. She would not permit a servant or one of the children to do anything for him which she might do herself. Her husband noticed, and thought it was the expression of a deep filial attachment which he had never suspected.

The Colonel drank numerous "toddies" during the course of the day, which left him, however, imperturbed. He was an expert at concocting strong drinks. He had even invented some, to which he had given fantastic names, and for whose manufacture he required diverse ingredients that it devolved upon Edna to procure for him.

When Doctor Mandelet dined with the Pontelliers on Thursday he could discern in Mrs. Pontellier no trace of that morbid condition which her husband had reported to him. She was excited and in a manner radiant. She and her father had been to the race course, and their thoughts when they seated themselves at table were still occupied with the events of the afternoon, and their talk was still of the track. The Doctor had not kept pace with turf affairs. He had certain recollections of racing in what he called "the good old times" when the Lecompte stables flourished,[56] and he drew upon this fund of memories so that he might not be left out and seem wholly devoid of the modern spirit. But he failed to impose upon the Colonel, and was even far from impressing him with this trumped-up knowledge of bygone days. Edna had staked her father on his last venture, with the most gratifying results to both of them. Besides, they had met some very charming people, according to the Colonel's impressions. Mrs. Mortimer Merriman and Mrs. James Highcamp, who were there with Alcée Arobin, had joined them and had enlivened the hours in a fashion that warmed him to think of.

[56] Like most of Chopin's references to places in New Orleans, this is an actual institution.

Mr. Pontellier himself had no particular leaning toward horse-racing, and was even rather inclined to discourage it as a pastime, especially when he considered the fate of that blue-grass farm in Kentucky. He endeavored, in a general way, to express a particular disapproval, and only succeeded in arousing the ire and opposition of his father-in-law. A pretty dispute followed, in which Edna warmly espoused her father's cause and the Doctor remained neutral.

He observed his hostess attentively from under his shaggy brows, and noted a subtle change which had transformed her from the listless woman he had known into a being who, for the moment, seemed palpitant with the forces of life. Her speech was warm and energetic. There was no repression in her glance or gesture. She reminded him of some beautiful, sleek animal waking up in the sun.

The dinner was excellent. The claret was warm and the champagne was cold, and under their beneficent influence the threatened unpleasantness melted and vanished with the fumes of the wine.

Mr. Pontellier warmed up and grew reminiscent. He told some amusing plantation experiences, recollections of old Iberville and his youth, when he hunted 'possum in company with some friendly darky; thrashed the pecan trees, shot the grosbec,[57] and roamed the woods and fields in mischievous idleness.

The Colonel, with little sense of humor and of the fitness of things, related a somber episode of those dark and bitter days, in which he had acted a conspicuous part and always formed a central figure. Nor was the Doctor happier in his selection, when he told the old, ever new and curious story of the waning of a woman's love, seeking strange, new channels, only to return to its legitimate source after days of fierce unrest. It was one of the many little human documents which had been unfolded to him during his long career as a physician. The story did not seem especially to impress Edna. She had one of her own to tell, of a woman who paddled away with her lover one night in a pirogue and never came back. They were lost amid the Baratarian Islands, and no one ever heard of them or found trace of them from that day to this. It was a pure invention. She said that Madame Antoine had related it to her. That, also, was an invention. Perhaps it was a dream she had had. But every glowing word seemed real to those who listened. They could feel the hot breath of the Southern night; they could hear the long sweep of the pirogue through the glistening moonlit water, the beating of birds' wings, rising startled from among the reeds in the salt-water pools; they could see the faces of the lovers, pale, close together, rapt in oblivious forgetfulness, drifting into the unknown.

The champagne was cold, and its subtle fumes played fantastic tricks with Edna's memory that night.

Outside, away from the glow of the fire and the soft lamplight, the night was chill and murky. The Doctor doubled his old-fashioned cloak across his breast as he strode home through the darkness. He knew his fellow-creatures better than most men; knew that inner life which so seldom unfolds itself to unanointed eyes. He was sorry he had accepted Pontellier's invita-

[57] A kind of finch, hunted as a gamebird in the South.

tion. He was growing old, and beginning to need rest and an imperturbed spirit. He did not want the secrets of other lives thrust upon him.

"I hope it isn't Arobin," he muttered to himself as he walked. "I hope to heaven it isn't Alcée Arobin."

XXIV

Edna and her father had a warm, and almost violent dispute upon the subject of her refusal to attend her sister's wedding. Mr. Pontellier declined to interfere, to interpose either his influence or his authority. He was following Doctor Mandelet's advice, and letting her do as she liked. The Colonel reproached his daughter for her lack of filial kindness and respect, her want of sisterly affection and womanly consideration. His arguments were labored and unconvincing. He doubted if Janet would accept any excuse—forgetting that Edna had offered none. He doubted if Janet would ever speak to her again, and he was sure Margaret would not.

Edna was glad to be rid of her father when he finally took himself off with his wedding garments and his bridal gifts, with his padded shoulders, his Bible reading, his "toddies" and ponderous oaths.

Mr. Pontellier followed him closely. He meant to stop at the wedding on his way to New York and endeavor by every means which money and love could devise to atone somewhat for Edna's incomprehensible action.

"You are too lenient, too lenient by far, Léonce," asserted the Colonel. "Authority, coercion are what is needed. Put your foot down good and hard; the only way to manage a wife. Take my word for it."

The Colonel was perhaps unaware that he had coerced his own wife into her grave. Mr. Pontellier had a vague suspicion of it which he thought it needless to mention at that late day.

Edna was not so consciously gratified at her husband's leaving home as she had been over the departure of her father. As the day approached when he was to leave her for a comparatively long stay, she grew melting and affectionate, remembering his many acts of consideration and his repeated expressions of an ardent attachment. She was solicitous about his health and his welfare. She bustled around, looking after his clothing, thinking about heavy underwear, quite as Madame Ratignolle would have done under similar circumstances. She cried when he went away, calling him her dear, good friend, and she was quite certain she would grow lonely before very long and go to join him in New York.

But after all, a radiant peace settled upon her when she at last found herself alone. Even the children were gone. Old Madame Pontellier had come herself and carried them off to Iberville with their quadroon. The old madame did not venture to say she was afraid they would be neglected during Léonce's absence; she hardly ventured to think so. She was hungry for them—even a little fierce in her attachment. She did not want them to be wholly "children of the pavement," she always said when begging to have them for a space. She wished them to know the country, with its streams, its fields, its woods, its freedom, so delicious to the young. She wished them to taste something of the life their father had lived and known and loved when he, too, was a little child.

When Edna was at last alone, she breathed a big, genuine sigh of relief. A feeling that was unfamiliar but very delicious came over her. She walked all through the house, from one room to another, as if inspecting it for the first time. She tried the various chairs and lounges, as if she had never sat and reclined upon them before. And she perambulated around the outside of the house, investigating, looking to see if windows and shutters were secure and in order. The flowers were like new acquaintances; she approached them in a familiar spirit, and made herself at home among them. The garden walks were damp, and Edna called to the maid to bring out her rubber sandals. And there she stayed, and stooped, digging around the plants, trimming, picking dead, dry leaves. The children's little dog came out, interfering, getting in her way. She scolded him, laughed at him, played with him. The garden smelled so good and looked so pretty in the afternoon sunlight. Edna plucked all the bright flowers she could find, and went into the house with them, she and the little dog.

Even the kitchen assumed a sudden interesting character which she had never before perceived. She went in to give directions to the cook, to say that the butcher would have to bring much less meat, that they would require only half their usual quantity of bread, of milk and groceries. She told the cook that she herself would be greatly occupied during Mr. Pontellier's absence, and she begged her to take all thought and responsibility of the larder upon her own shoulders.

That night Edna dined alone. The candelabra, with a few candles in the center of the table, gave all the light she needed. Outside the circle of light in which she sat, the large dining-room looked solemn and shadowy. The cook, placed upon her mettle, served a delicious repast—a luscious tenderloin broiled *à point*. The wine tasted good; the *marron glacé*[58] seemed to be just what she wanted. It was so pleasant, too, to dine in a comfortable *peignoir*.

She thought a little sentimentally about Léonce and the children, and wondered what they were doing. As she gave a dainty scrap or two to the doggie, she talked intimately to him about Etienne and Raoul. He was beside himself with astonishment and delight over these companionable advances, and showed his appreciation by his little quick, snappy barks and a lively agitation.

Then Edna sat in the library after dinner and read Emerson until she grew sleepy. She realized that she had neglected her reading, and determined to start anew upon a course of improving studies, now that her time was completely her own to do with as she liked.

After a refreshing bath, Edna went to bed. And as she snuggled comfortably beneath the eiderdown a sense of restfulness invaded her, such as she had not known before.

XXV

When the weather was dark and cloudy Edna could not work. She needed the sun to mellow and temper her mood to the sticking point. She had reached a stage when she seemed to be no longer feeling her way, working,

[58] *à point.* "Perfectly." *marron glacé.* "Candied chestnut."

when in the humor, with sureness and ease. And being devoid of ambition, and striving not toward accomplishment, she drew satisfaction from the work in itself.

On rainy or melancholy days Edna went out and sought the society of the friends she had made at Grand Isle. Or else she stayed indoors and nursed a mood with which she was becoming too familiar for her own comfort and peace of mind. It was not despair; but it seemed to her as if life were passing by, leaving its promise broken and unfulfilled. Yet there were other days when she listened, was led on and deceived by fresh promises which her youth held out to her.

She went again to the races, and again. Alcée Arobin and Mrs. Highcamp called for her one bright afternoon in Arobin's drag.[59] Mrs. Highcamp was a worldly but unaffected, intelligent, slim, tall blonde woman in the forties, with an indifferent manner and blue eyes that stared. She had a daughter who served her as a pretext for cultivating the society of young men of fashion. Alcée Arobin was one of them. He was a familiar figure at the race course, the opera, the fashionable clubs. There was a perpetual smile in his eyes, which seldom failed to awaken a corresponding cheerfulness in any one who looked into them and listened to his good-humored voice. His manner was quiet, and at times a little insolent. He possessed a good figure, a pleasing face, not overburdened with depth of thought or feeling; and his dress was that of the conventional man of fashion.

He admired Edna extravagantly, after meeting her at the races with her father. He had met her before on other occasions, but she had seemed to him unapproachable until that day. It was at his instigation that Mrs. Highcamp called to ask her to go with them to the Jockey Club to witness the turf event of the season.

There were possibly a few track men out there who knew the race horse as well as Edna, but there was certainly none who knew it better. She sat between her two companions as one having authority to speak. She laughed at Arobin's pretensions, and deplored Mrs. Highcamp's ignorance. The race horse was a friend and intimate associate of her childhood. The atmosphere of the stables and the breath of the blue grass paddock revived in her memory and lingered in her nostrils. She did not perceive that she was talking like her father as the sleek geldings ambled in review before them. She played for very high stakes, and fortune favored her. The fever of the game flamed in her cheeks and eyes, and it got into her blood and into her brain like an intoxicant. People turned their heads to look at her, and more than one lent an attentive ear to her utterances, hoping thereby to secure the elusive but ever-desired "tip." Arobin caught the contagion of excitement which drew him to Edna like a magnet. Mrs. Highcamp remained, as usual, unmoved, with her indifferent stare and uplifted eyebrows.

Edna stayed and dined with Mrs. Highcamp upon being urged to do so. Arobin also remained and sent away his drag.

The dinner was quiet and uninteresting, save for the cheerful efforts of Arobin to enliven things. Mrs. Highcamp deplored the absence of her

[59] A large four-horse coach.

daughter from the races, and tried to convey to her what she had missed by going to the "Dante reading" instead of joining them. The girl held a geranium leaf up to her nose and said nothing, but looked knowing and non-committal. Mr. Highcamp was a plain, bald-headed man, who only talked under compulsion. He was unresponsive. Mrs. Highcamp was full of delicate courtesy and consideration toward her husband. She addressed most of her conversation to him at table. They sat in the library after dinner and read the evening papers together under the droplight;[60] while the younger people went into the drawing-room near by and talked. Miss Highcamp played some selections from Grieg upon the piano. She seemed to have apprehended all of the composer's coldness and none of his poetry. While Edna listened she could not help wondering if she had lost her taste for music.

When the time came for her to go home, Mr. Highcamp grunted a lame offer to escort her, looking down at his slippered feet with tactless concern. It was Arobin who took her home. The car ride was long, and it was late when they reached Esplanade Street. Arobin asked permission to enter for a second to light his cigarette—his match safe[61] was empty. He filled his match safe, but did not light his cigarette until he left her, after she had expressed her willingness to go to the races with him again.

Edna was neither tired nor sleepy. She was hungry again, for the Highcamp dinner, though of excellent quality, had lacked abundance. She rummaged in the larder and brought forth a slice of Gruyère and some crackers. She opened a bottle of beer which she found in the icebox. Edna felt extremely restless and excited. She vacantly hummed a fantastic tune as she poked at the wood embers on the hearth and munched a cracker.

She wanted something to happen—something, anything; she did not know what. She regretted that she had not made Arobin stay a half hour to talk over the horses with her. She counted the money she had won. But there was nothing else to do, so she went to bed, and tossed there for hours in a sort of monotonous agitation.

In the middle of the night she remembered that she had forgotten to write her regular letter to her husband; and she decided to do so next day and tell him about her afternoon at the Jockey Club. She lay wide awake composing a letter which was nothing like the one which she wrote next day. When the maid awoke her in the morning Edna was dreaming of Mr. Highcamp playing the piano at the entrance of a music store on Canal Street, while his wife was saying to Alcée Arobin, as they boarded an Esplanade Street car:

"What a pity that so much talent has been neglected! but I must go."

When, a few days later, Alcée Arobin again called for Edna in his drag, Mrs. Highcamp was not with him. He said they would pick her up. But as that lady had not been apprised of his intention of picking her up, she was not at home. The daughter was just leaving the house to attend the meeting of a branch Folk Lore Society, and regretted that she could not accompany them. Arobin appeared nonplused, and asked Edna if there were any one else she cared to ask.

She did not deem it worth while to go in search of any of the fashionable

[60] Suspended gas lamp. [61] Noncombustible container for matches.

acquaintances from whom she had withdrawn herself. She thought of
Madame Ratignolle, but knew that her fair friend did not leave the house,
except to take a languid walk around the block with her husband after
nightfall. Mademoiselle Reisz would have laughed at such a request from
Edna. Madame Lebrun might have enjoyed the outing, but for some rea-
son Edna did not want her. So they went alone, she and Arobin.

The afternoon was intensely interesting to her. The excitement came
back upon her like a remittent fever. Her talk grew familiar and confiden-
tial. It was no labor to become intimate with Arobin. His manner invited
easy confidence. The preliminary stage of becoming acquainted was one
which he always endeavored to ignore when a pretty and engaging woman
was concerned.

He stayed and dined with Edna. He stayed and sat beside the wood fire.
They laughed and talked; and before it was time to go he was telling her
how different life might have been if he had known her years before. With
ingenuous frankness he spoke of what a wicked, ill-disciplined boy he had
been, and impulsively drew up his cuff to exhibit upon his wrist the scar
from a saber cut which he had received in a duel outside of Paris when he
was nineteen. She touched his hand as she scanned the red cicatrice[62] on
the inside of his white wrist. A quick impulse that was somewhat spasmodic
impelled her fingers to close in a sort of clutch upon his hand. He felt the
pressure of her pointed nails in the flesh of his palm.

She arose hastily and walked toward the mantel.

"The sight of a wound or scar always agitates and sickens me," she said.
"I shouldn't have looked at it."

"I beg your pardon," he entreated, following her; "it never occurred to
me that it might be repulsive."

He stood close to her, and the effrontery in his eyes repelled the old,
vanishing self in her, yet drew all her awakening sensuousness. He saw
enough in her face to impel him to take her hand and hold it while he said
his lingering good night.

"Will you go to the races again?" he asked.

"No," she said. "I've had enough of the races. I don't want to lose all the
money I've won, and I've got to work when the weather is bright,
instead of—"

"Yes; work; to be sure. You promised to show me your work. What
morning may I come up to your atelier? Tomorrow?"

"No!"

"Day after?"

"No, no."

"Oh, please don't refuse me! I know something of such things. I might
help you with a stray suggestion or two."

"No. Good night. Why don't you go after you have said good night? I
don't like you," she went on in a high, excited pitch, attempting to draw
away her hand. She felt that her words lacked dignity and sincerity, and she
knew that he felt it.

"I'm sorry you don't like me. I'm sorry I offended you. How have I
offended you? What have I done? Can't you forgive me?" And he bent and

[62] Scar.

pressed his lips upon her hand as if he wished never more to withdraw them.

"Mr. Arobin," she complained, "I'm greatly upset by the excitement of the afternoon; I'm not myself. My manner must have misled you in some way. I wish you to go, please." She spoke in a monotonous, dull tone. He took his hat from the table, and stood with eyes turned from her, looking into the dying fire. For a moment or two he kept an impressive silence.

"Your manner has not misled me, Mrs. Pontellier," he said finally. "My own emotions have done that. I couldn't help it. When I'm near you, how could I help it? Don't think anything of it, don't bother, please. You see, I go when you command me. If you wish me to stay away, I shall do so. If you let me come back, I—oh! you will let me come back?"

He cast one appealing glance at her, to which she made no response. Alcée Arobin's manner was so genuine that it often deceived even himself.

Edna did not care or think whether it were genuine or not. When she was alone she looked mechanically at the back of her hand which he had kissed so warmly. Then she leaned her head down on the mantelpiece. She felt somewhat like a woman who in a moment of passion is betrayed into an act of infidelity, and realizes the significance of the act without being wholly awakened from its glamour. The thought was passing vaguely through her mind, "What would he think?"

She did not mean her husband; she was thinking of Robert Lebrun. Her husband seemed to her now like a person whom she had married without love as an excuse.

She lit a candle and went up to her room. Alcée Arobin was absolutely nothing to her. Yet his presence, his manners, the warmth of his glances, and above all the touch of his lips upon her hand had acted like a narcotic upon her.

She slept a languorous sleep, interwoven with vanishing dreams.

XXVI

Alcée Arobin wrote Edna an elaborate note of apology, palpitant with sincerity. It embarrassed her; for in a cooler, quieter moment it appeared to her absurd that she should have taken his action so seriously, so dramatically. She felt sure that the significance of the whole occurrence had lain in her own self-consciousness. If she ignored his note it would give undue importance to a trivial affair. If she replied to it in a serious spirit it would still leave in his mind the impression that she had in a susceptible moment yielded to his influence. After all, it was no great matter to have one's hand kissed. She was provoked at his having written the apology. She answered in as light and bantering a spirit as she fancied it deserved, and said she would be glad to have him look in upon her at work whenever he felt the inclination and his business gave him the opportunity.

He responded at once by presenting himself at her home with all his disarming naïveté. And then there was scarcely a day which followed that she did not see him or was not reminded of him. He was prolific in pretexts. His attitude became one of good-humored subservience and tacit

adoration. He was ready at all times to submit to her moods, which were as often kind as they were cold. She grew accustomed to him. They became intimate and friendly by imperceptible degrees, and then by leaps. He sometimes talked in a way that astonished her at first and brought the crimson into her face; in a way that pleased her at last, appealing to the animalism that stirred impatiently within her.

There was nothing which so quieted the turmoil of Edna's senses as a visit to Mademoiselle Reisz. It was then, in the presence of that personality which was offensive to her, that the woman, by her divine art, seemed to reach Edna's spirit and set it free.

It was misty, with heavy, lowering atmosphere, one afternoon, when Edna climbed the stairs to the pianist's apartments under the roof. Her clothes were dripping with moisture. She felt chilled and pinched as she entered the room. Mademoiselle was poking at a rusty stove that smoked a little and warmed the room indifferently. She was endeavoring to heat a pot of chocolate on the stove. The room looked cheerless and dingy to Edna as she entered. A bust of Beethoven, covered with a hood of dust, scowled at her from the mantelpiece.

"Ah! here comes the sunlight!" exclaimed Mademoiselle, rising from her knees before the stove. "Now it will be warm and bright enough; I can let the fire alone."

She closed the stove door with a bang, and approaching, assisted in removing Edna's dripping mackintosh.

"You are cold; you look miserable. The chocolate will soon be hot. But would you rather have a taste of brandy? I have scarcely touched the bottle which you brought me for my cold." A piece of red flannel was wrapped around Mademoiselle's throat; a stiff neck compelled her to hold her head on one side.

"I will take some brandy," said Edna, shivering as she removed her gloves and overshoes. She drank the liquor from the glass as a man would have done. Then flinging herself upon the uncomfortable sofa she said, "Mademoiselle, I am going to move away from my house on Esplanade Street."

"Ah!" ejaculated the musician, neither surprised nor especially interested. Nothing ever seemed to astonish her very much. She was endeavoring to adjust the bunch of violets which had become loose from its fastening in her hair. Edna drew her down upon the sofa, and taking a pin from her own hair, secured the shabby artificial flowers in their accustomed place.

"Aren't you astonished?"

"Passably. Where are you going? to New York? to Iberville? to your father in Mississippi? where?"

"Just two steps away," laughed Edna, "in a little four-room house around the corner. It looks so cozy, so inviting and restful, whenever I pass by; and it's for rent. I'm tired looking after that big house. It never seemed like mine, anyway—like home. It's too much trouble. I have to keep too many servants. I am tired bothering with them."

"That is not your true reason, *ma belle*. There is no use in telling me lies. I don't know your reason, but you have not told me the truth." Edna did not protest or endeavor to justify herself.

"The house, the money that provides for it, are not mine. Isn't that enough reason?"

"They are your husband's," returned Mademoiselle, with a shrug and a malicious elevation of the eyebrows.

"Oh! I see there is no deceiving you. Then let me tell you: It is a caprice. I have a little money of my own from my mother's estate, which my father sends me by driblets. I won a large sum this winter on the races, and I am beginning to sell my sketches. Laidpore is more and more pleased with my work; he says it grows in force and individuality. I cannot judge of that myself, but I feel that I have gained in ease and confidence. However, as I said, I have sold a good many through Laidpore. I can live in the tiny house for little or nothing, with one servant. Old Celestine, who works occasionally for me, says she will come stay with me and do my work. I know I shall like it, like the feeling of freedom and independence."

"What does your husband say?"

"I have not told him yet. I only thought of it this morning. He will think I am demented, no doubt. Perhaps you think so."

Mademoiselle shook her head slowly. "Your reason is not yet clear to me," she said.

Neither was it quite clear to Edna herself; but it unfolded itself as she sat for a while in silence. Instinct had prompted her to put away her husband's bounty in casting off her allegiance. She did not know how it would be when he returned. There would have to be an understanding, an explanation. Conditions would some way adjust themselves, she felt; but whatever came, she had resolved never again to belong to another than herself.

"I shall give a grand dinner before I leave the old house!" Edna exclaimed. "You will have to come to it, Mademoiselle. I will give you everything that you like to eat and to drink. We shall sing and laugh and be merry for once." And she uttered a sigh that came from the very depths of her being.

If Mademoiselle happened to have received a letter from Robert during the interval of Edna's visits, she would give her the letter unsolicited. And she would seat herself at the piano and play as her humor prompted her while the young woman read the letter.

The little stove was roaring; it was red-hot, and the chocolate in the tin sizzled and sputtered. Edna went forward and opened the stove door, and Mademoiselle rising, took a letter from under the bust of Beethoven and handed it to Edna.

"Another! so soon!" she exclaimed, her eyes filled with delight. "Tell me, Mademoiselle, does he know that I see his letters?"

"Never in the world! He would be angry and would never write to me again if he thought so. Does he write to you? Never a line. Does he send you a message? Never a word. It is because he loves you, poor fool, and is trying to forget you, since you are not free to listen to him or to belong to him."

"Why do you show me his letters, then?"

"Haven't you begged for them? Can I refuse you anything? Oh! you cannot deceive me," and Mademoiselle approached her beloved instrument and began to play. Edna did not at once read the letter. She sat

holding it in her hand, while the music penetrated her whole being like an effulgence, warming and brightening the dark places of her soul. It prepared her for joy and exultation.

"Oh!" she exclaimed, letting the letter fall to the floor. "Why did you not tell me?" She went and grasped Mademoiselle's hands up from the keys. "Oh! unkind! malicious! Why did you not tell me?"

"That he was coming back? No great news, *ma foi*. I wonder he did not come long ago."

"But when, when?" cried Edna, impatiently. "He does not say when."

"He says 'very soon.' You know as much about it as I do; it is all in the letter."

"But why? Why is he coming? Oh, if I thought—" and she snatched the letter from the floor and turned the pages this way and that way, looking for the reason, which was left untold.

"If I were young and in love with a man," said Mademoiselle, turning on the stool and pressing her wiry hands between her knees as she looked down at Edna, who sat on the floor holding the letter, "it seems to me he would have to be some *grand esprit*;[63] a man with lofty aims and ability to reach them; one who stood high enough to attract the notice of his fellow-men. It seems to me if I were young and in love I should never deem a man of ordinary caliber worthy of my devotion."

"Now it is you who are telling lies and seeking to deceive me, Mademoiselle; or else you have never been in love, and know nothing about it. Why," went on Edna, clasping her knees and looking up into Mademoiselle's twisted face, "do you suppose a woman knows why she loves? Does she select? Does she say to herself: 'Go to! Here is a distinguished statesman with presidential possibilities; I shall proceed to fall in love with him.' Or, 'I shall set my heart upon this musician, whose fame is on every tongue?' Or, 'This financier, who controls the world's money markets?'"

"You are purposely misunderstanding me, *ma reine*.[64] Are you in love with Robert?"

"Yes," said Edna. It was the first time she had admitted it, and a glow overspread her face, blotching it with red spots.

"Why?" asked her companion. "Why do you love him when you ought not to?"

Edna, with a motion or two, dragged herself on her knees before Mademoiselle Reisz, who took the glowing face between her two hands.

"Why? Because his hair is brown and grows away from his temples; because he opens and shuts his eyes, and his nose is a little out of drawing; because he has two lips and a square chin, and a little finger which he can't straighten from having played baseball too energetically in his youth. Because—"

"Because you do, in short," laughed Mademoiselle. "What will you do when he comes back?" she asked.

"Do? Nothing, except feel glad and happy to be alive."

She was already glad and happy to be alive at the mere thought of his return. The murky, lowering sky, which had depressed her a few hours

[63] "Great-spirited person." [64] "My dear" (literally, "my queen").

before, seemed bracing and invigorating as she splashed through the streets on her way home.

She stopped at a confectioner's and ordered a huge box of bonbons for the children in Iberville. She slipped a card in the box, on which she scribbled a tender message and sent an abundance of kisses.

Before dinner in the evening Edna wrote a charming letter to her husband, telling him of her intention to move for a while into the little house around the block, and to give a farewell dinner before leaving, regretting that he was not there to share it, to help her out with the menu and assist her in entertaining the guests. Her letter was brilliant and brimming with cheerfulness.

XXVII

"What is the matter with you?" asked Arobin that evening. "I never found you in such a happy mood." Edna was tired by that time, and was reclining on the lounge before the fire.

"Don't you know the weather prophet has told us we shall see the sun pretty soon?"

"Well, that ought to be reason enough," he acquiesced. "You wouldn't give me another if I sat here all night imploring you." He sat close to her on a low tabouret[65] and as he spoke his fingers lightly touched the hair that fell a little over her forehead. She liked the touch of his fingers through her hair, and closed her eyes sensitively.

"One of these days," she said, "I'm going to pull myself together for a while and think—try to determine what character of a woman I am; for, candidly, I don't know. By all the codes which I am acquainted with, I am a devilishly wicked specimen of the sex. But some way I can't convince myself that I am. I must think about it."

"Don't. What's the use? Why should you bother thinking about it when I can tell you what manner of woman you are." His fingers strayed occasionally down to her warm, smooth cheeks and firm chin, which was growing a little full and double.

"Oh, yes! You will tell me that I am adorable; everything that is captivating. Spare yourself the effort."

"No; I shan't tell you anything of the sort, though I shouldn't be lying if I did."

"Do you know Mademoiselle Reisz?" she asked irrelevantly.

"The pianist? I know her by sight. I've heard her play."

"She says queer things sometimes in a bantering way that you don't notice at the time and you find yourself thinking about afterward."

"For instance?"

"Well, for instance, when I left her today, she put her arms around me and felt my shoulder blades, to see if my wings were strong, she said. 'The bird that would soar above the level plain of tradition and prejudice must

[65] A padded stool.

have strong wings. It is a sad spectacle to see the weaklings bruised, exhausted, fluttering back to earth.'"

"Whither would you soar?"

"I'm not thinking of any extraordinary flights. I only half comprehend her."

"I've heard she's partially demented," said Arobin.

"She seems to me wonderfully sane," Edna replied.

"I'm told she's extremely disagreeable and unpleasant. Why have you introduced her at a moment when I desired to talk of you?"

"Oh! talk of me if you like," cried Edna, clasping her hands beneath her head; "but let me think of something else while you do."

"I'm jealous of your thoughts tonight. They're making you a little kinder than usual; but some way I feel as if they were wandering, as if they were not here with me." She only looked at him and smiled. His eyes were very near. He leaned upon the lounge with an arm extended across her, while the other hand still rested upon her hair. They continued silently to look into each other's eyes. When he leaned forward and kissed her, she clasped his head, holding his lips to hers.

It was the first kiss of her life to which her nature had really responded. It was a flaming torch that kindled desire.

XXVIII

Edna cried a little that night after Arobin left her. It was only one phase of the multitudinous emotions which had assailed her. There was with her an overwhelming feeling of irresponsibility. There was the shock of the unexpected and the unaccustomed. There was her husband's reproach looking at her from the external things around her which he had provided for her external existence. There was Robert's reproach making itself felt by a quicker, fiercer, more overpowering love, which had awakened within her toward him. Above all, there was understanding. She felt as if a mist had been lifted from her eyes, enabling her to look upon and comprehend the significance of life, that monster made up of beauty and brutality. But among the conflicting sensations which assailed her, there was neither shame nor remorse. There was a dull pang of regret because it was not the kiss of love which had inflamed her, because it was not love which had held this cup of life to her lips.

XXIX

Without even waiting for an answer from her husband regarding his opinion or wishes in the matter, Edna hastened her preparations for quitting her home on Esplanade Street and moving into the little house around the block. A feverish anxiety attended her every action in that direction. There was no moment of deliberation, no interval of repose between the thought and its fulfillment. Early upon the morning following those hours passed in Arobin's society, Edna set about securing her new abode and hurrying her

arrangements for occupying it. Within the precincts of her home she felt like one who has entered and lingered within the portals of some forbidden temple in which a thousand muffled voices bade her begone.

Whatever was her own in the house, everything which she had acquired aside from her husband's bounty, she caused to be transported to the other house, supplying simple and meager deficiencies from her own resources.

Arobin found her with rolled sleeves, working in company with the house-maid, when he looked in during the afternoon. She was splendid and robust, and had never appeared handsomer than in the old blue gown, with a red silk handkerchief knotted at random around her head to protect her hair from the dust. She was mounted upon a high step-ladder, unhooking a picture from the wall when he entered. He had found the front door open, and had followed his ring by walking in unceremoniously.

"Come down!" he said. "Do you want to kill yourself?" She greeted him with affected carelessness, and appeared absorbed in her occupation.

If he had expected to find her languishing, reproachful, or indulging in sentimental tears, he must have been greatly surprised.

He was no doubt prepared for any emergency, ready for any one of the foregoing attitudes, just as he bent himself easily and naturally to the situation which confronted him.

"Please come down," he insisted, holding the ladder and looking up at her.

"No," she answered; "Ellen is afraid to mount the ladder. Joe is working over at the 'pigeon house'—that's the name Ellen gives it, because it's so small and looks like a pigeon house—and some one has to do this."

Arobin pulled off his coat, and expressed himself ready and willing to tempt fate in her place. Ellen brought him one of her dust-caps, and went into contortions of mirth, which she found it impossible to control, when she saw him put it on before the mirror as grotesquely as he could. Edna herself could not refrain from smiling when she fastened it at his request. So it was he who in turn mounted the ladder, unhooking pictures and curtains, and dislodging ornaments as Edna directed. When he had finished he took off his dust-cap and went out to wash his hands.

Edna was sitting on the tabouret, idly brushing the tips of a feather duster along the carpet when he came in again.

"Is there anything more you will let me do?" he asked.

"That is all," she answered. "Ellen can manage the rest." She kept the young woman occupied in the drawing-room, unwilling to be left alone with Arobin.

"What about the dinner?" he asked; "the grand event, the *coup d'état*?"[66]

"It will be day after tomorrow. Why do you call it the '*coup d'état*'? Oh! it will be very fine; all my best of everything—crystal, silver and gold, Sèvres, flowers, music, and champagne to swim in. I'll let Léonce pay the bills. I wonder what he'll say when he sees the bills."

"And you ask me why I call it a *coup d'état*?" Arobin had put on his coat, and he stood before her and asked if his cravat was plumb. She told him it was, looking no higher than the tip of his collar.

[66] A sudden seizure of political power (literally, "stroke of state"). Arobin, in applying the term facetiously to the dinner party, is implying that Edna is deposing Pontellier.

"When do you go to the 'pigeon house?'—with all due acknowledgement to Ellen."

"Day after tomorrow, after the dinner. I shall sleep there."

"Ellen, will you very kindly get me a glass of water?" asked Arobin. "The dust in the curtains, if you will pardon me for hinting such a thing, has parched my throat to a crisp."

"While Ellen gets the water," said Edna, rising, "I will say good-by and let you go. I must get rid of this grime, and I have a million things to do and think of."

"When shall I see you?" asked Arobin, seeking to detain her, the maid having left the room.

"At the dinner, of course. You are invited."

"Not before?—not tonight or tomorrow morning or tomorrow noon or night? or the day after morning or noon? Can't you see yourself, without my telling you, what an eternity it is?"

He had followed her into the hall and to the foot of the stairway, looking up at her as she mounted with her face half turned to him.

"Not an instant sooner," she said. But she laughed and looked at him with eyes that at once gave him courage to wait and made it torture to wait.

XXX

Though Edna had spoken of the dinner as a very grand affair, it was in truth a very small affair and very select, in so much as the guests invited were few and were selected with discrimination. She had counted upon an even dozen seating themselves at her round mahogany board, forgetting for the moment that Madame Ratignolle was to the last degree *souffrante*[67] and unpresentable, and not foreseeing that Madame Lebrun would send a thousand regrets at the last moment. So there were only ten, after all, which made a cozy, comfortable number.

There were Mr. and Mrs. Merriman, a pretty, vivacious little woman in the thirties; her husband, a jovial fellow, something of a shallow-pate, who laughed a good deal at other people's witticisms, and had thereby made himself extremely popular. Mrs. Highcamp had accompanied them. Of course, there was Alcée Arobin; and Mademoiselle Reisz had consented to come. Edna had sent her a fresh bunch of violets with black lace trimmings for her hair. Monsieur Ratignolle brought himself and his wife's excuses. Victor Lebrun, who happened to be in the city, bent upon relaxation, had accepted with alacrity. There was a Miss Mayblunt, no longer in her teens, who looked at the world through lorgnettes and with the keenest interest. It was thought and said that she was intellectual; it was suspected of her that she wrote under a *nom de guerre*.[68] She had come with a gentleman by the name of Gouvernail, connected with one of the daily papers, of whom nothing special could be said, except that he was observant and seemed quiet and inoffensive. Edna herself made the tenth, and at half-past eight they seated themselves at table, Arobin and Monsieur Ratignolle on either side of their hostess.

[67] "Suffering"; "ill." [68] Pseudonym.

Mrs. Highcamp sat between Arobin and Victor Lebrun. Then came Mrs. Merriman, Mr. Gouvernail, Miss Mayblunt, Mr. Merriman, and Mademoiselle Reisz next to Monsieur Ratignolle.

There was something extremely gorgeous about the appearance of the table, an effect of splendor conveyed by a cover of pale yellow satin under strips of lace-work. There were wax candles in massive brass candelabra, burning softly under yellow silk shades; full, fragrant roses, yellow and red, abounded. There were silver and gold, as she had said there would be, and crystal which glittered like the gems which the women wore.

The ordinary stiff dining chairs had been discarded for the occasion and replaced by the most commodious and luxurious which could be collected throughout the house. Mademoiselle Reisz, being exceedingly diminutive, was elevated upon cushions, as small children are sometimes hoisted at table upon bulky volumes.

"Something new, Edna?" exclaimed Miss Mayblunt, with lorgnette directed toward a magnificent cluster of diamonds that sparkled, that almost sputtered, in Edna's hair, just over the center of her forehead.

"Quite new; 'brand' new, in fact; a present from my husband. It arrived this morning from New York. I may as well admit that this is my birthday, and that I am twenty-nine. In good time I expect you to drink my health. Meanwhile, I shall ask you to begin with this cocktail, composed—would you say 'composed?'" with an appeal to Miss Mayblunt—"composed by my father in honor of Sister Janet's wedding."

Before each guest stood a tiny glass that looked and sparkled like a garnet gem.

"Then, all things considered," spoke Arobin, "it might not be amiss to start out by drinking the Colonel's health in the cocktail which he composed, on the birthday of the most charming of women—the daughter whom he invented."

Mr. Merriman's laugh at this sally was such a genuine outburst and so contagious that it started the dinner with an agreeable swing that never slackened.

Miss Mayblunt begged to be allowed to keep her cocktail untouched before her, just to look at. The color was marvelous! She could compare it to nothing she had ever seen, and the garnet lights which it emitted were unspeakably rare. She pronounced the Colonel an artist, and stuck to it.

Monsieur Ratignolle was prepared to take things seriously: the *mets,* the *entre-mets,*[69] the service, the decorations, even the people. He looked up from his pompono[70] and inquired of Arobin if he were related to the gentleman of that name who formed one of the firm of Laitner and Arobin, lawyers. The young man admitted that Laitner was a warm personal friend, who permitted Arobin's name to decorate the firm's letterheads and to appear upon a shingle that graced Perdido Street.

"There are so many inquisitive people and institutions abounding," said Arobin, "that one is really forced as a matter of convenience these days to assume the virtue of an occupation if he has it not."[71]

[69] The main courses and the side dishes. [70] A fish, prized as a delicacy.
[71] Hamlet asks his mother Gertrude to "assume a virtue, if you have it not" (*Hamlet* III.iv.161).

Monsieur Ratignolle stared a little, and turned to ask Mademoiselle Reisz if she considered the symphony concerts up to the standard which had been set the previous winter. Mademoiselle Reisz answered Monsieur Ratignolle in French, which Edna thought a little rude, under the circumstances, but characteristic. Mademoiselle had only disagreeable things to say of the symphony concerts, and insulting remarks to make of all the musicians of New Orleans, singly and collectively. All her interest seemed to be centered upon the delicacies placed before her.

Mr. Merriman said that Mr. Arobin's remark about inquisitive people reminded him of a man from Waco the other day at the St. Charles Hotel—but as Mr. Merriman's stories were always lame and lacking point, his wife seldom permitted him to complete them. She interrupted him to ask if he remembered the name of the author whose book she had bought the week before to send to a friend in Geneva. She was talking "books" with Mr. Gouvernail and trying to draw from him his opinion upon current literary topics. Her husband told the story of the Waco man privately to Miss Mayblunt, who pretended to be greatly amused and to think it extremely clever.

Mrs. Highcamp hung with languid but unaffected interest upon the warm and impetuous volubility of her left-hand neighbor, Victor Lebrun. Her attention was never for a moment withdrawn from him after seating herself at table; and when he turned to Mrs. Merriman, who was prettier and more vivacious than Mrs. Highcamp, she waited with easy indifference for an opportunity to reclaim his attention. There was the occasional sound of music, of mandolins, sufficiently removed to be an agreeable accompaniment rather than an interruption to the conversation. Outside the soft, monotonous splash of a fountain could be heard; the sound penetrated into the room with the heavy odor of jessamine that came through the open windows.

The golden shimmer of Edna's satin gown spread in rich folds on either side of her. There was a soft fall of lace encircling her shoulders. It was the color of her skin, without the glow, the myriad living tints that one may sometimes discover in vibrant flesh. There was something in her attitude, in her whole appearance when she leaned her head against the high-backed chair and spread her arms, which suggested the regal woman, the one who rules, who looks on, who stands alone.

But as she sat there amid her guests, she felt the old ennui overtaking her; the hopelessness which so often assailed her, which came upon her like an obsession, like something extraneous, independent of volition. It was something which announced itself; a chill breath that seemed to issue from some vast cavern wherein discords wailed. There came over her the acute longing which always summoned into her spiritual vision the presence of the beloved one, overpowering her at once with a sense of the unattainable.

The moments glided on, while a feeling of good fellowship passed around the circle like a mystic cord, holding and binding these people together with jest and laughter. Monsieur Ratignolle was the first to break the pleasant charm. At ten o'clock he excused himself. Madame Ratignolle was waiting for him at home. She was *bien souffrante*,[72] and she was filled with vague dread, which only her husband's presence could allay.

[72] "Very ill."

Mademoiselle Reisz arose with Monsieur Ratignolle, who offered to escort her to the car. She had eaten well; she had tasted the good, rich wines, and they must have turned her head, for she bowed pleasantly to all as she withdrew from table. She kissed Edna upon the shoulder, and whispered: *"Bonne nuit, ma reine; soyez sage."*[73] She had been a little bewildered upon rising, or rather, descending from her cushions, and Monsieur Ratignolle gallantly took her arm and led her away.

Mrs. Highcamp was weaving a garland of roses, yellow and red. When she had finished the garland, she laid it lightly upon Victor's black curls. He was reclining far back in the luxurious chair, holding a glass of champagne to the light.

As if a magician's wand had touched him, the garland of roses transformed him into a vision of Oriental beauty. His cheeks were the color of crushed grapes, and his dusky eyes glowed with a languishing fire.

"Sapristi!" exclaimed Arobin.

But Mrs. Highcamp had one more touch to add to the picture. She took from the back of her chair a white silken scarf, with which she had covered her shoulders in the early part of the evening. She draped it across the boy in graceful folds, and in a way to conceal his black, conventional evening dress. He did not seem to mind what she did to him, only smiled, showing a faint gleam of white teeth, while he continued to gaze with narrowing eyes at the light through his glass of champagne.

"Oh! to be able to paint in color rather than in words!" exclaimed Miss Mayblunt, losing herself in a rhapsodic dream as she looked at him.

> "'There was a graven image of Desire
> Painted with red blood on a ground of gold.'"[74]

murmured Gouvernail, under his breath.

The effect of the wine upon Victor was to change his accustomed volubility into silence. He seemed to have abandoned himself to a reverie, and to be seeing pleasing visions in the amber bead.

"Sing," entreated Mrs. Highcamp. "Won't you sing to us?"

"Let him alone," said Arobin.

"He's posing," offered Mr. Merriman; "let him have it out."

"I believe he's paralyzed," laughed Mrs. Merriman. And leaning over the youth's chair, she took the glass from his hand and held it to his lips. He sipped the wine slowly, and when he had drained the glass she laid it upon the table and wiped his lips with her little filmy handkerchief.

"Yes, I'll sing for you," he said, turning in his chair toward Mrs. Highcamp. He clasped his hands behind his head, and looking up at the ceiling began to hum a little, trying his voice like a musician tuning an instrument. Then, looking at Edna, he began to sing:

> "Ah! si tu savais!"

"Stop!" she cried, "don't sing that. I don't want you to sing it," and she laid her glass so impetuously and blindly upon the table as to shatter it

[73] "Good night, my dear; be good."

[74] From "A Cameo," by A. C. Swinburne (1837–1909).

against a caraffe. The wine spilled over Arobin's legs and some of it trickled down upon Mrs. Highcamp's black gauze gown. Victor had lost all idea of courtesy, or else he thought his hostess was not in earnest, for he laughed and went on:

> "Ah! si tu savais
> Ce que tes yeux me disent"—[75]

"Oh! you mustn't! you mustn't," exclaimed Edna, and pushing back her chair she got up, and going behind him placed her hand over his mouth. He kissed the soft palm that pressed upon his lips.

"No, no, I won't, Mrs. Pontellier. I didn't know you meant it," looking up at her with caressing eyes. The touch of his lips was like a pleasing sting to her hand. She lifted the garland of roses from his head and flung it across the room.

"Come, Victor; you've posed long enough. Give Mrs. Highcamp her scarf."

Mrs. Highcamp undraped the scarf from about him with her own hands. Miss Mayblunt and Mr. Gouvernail suddenly conceived the notion that it was time to say good night. And Mr. and Mrs. Merriman wondered how it could be so late.

Before parting from Victor, Mrs. Highcamp invited him to call upon her daughter, who she knew would be charmed to meet him and talk French and sing French songs with him. Victor expressed his desire and intention to call upon Miss Highcamp at the first opportunity which presented itself. He asked if Arobin were going his way. Arobin was not.

The mandolin players had long since stolen away. A profound stillness had fallen upon the broad, beautiful street. The voices of Edna's disbanding guests jarred like a discordant note upon the quiet harmony of the night.

XXXI

"Well?" questioned Arobin, who had remained with Edna after the others had departed.

"Well," she reiterated, and stood up, stretching her arms, and feeling the need to relax her muscles after having been so long seated.

"What next?" he asked.

"The servants are all gone. They left when the musicians did. I have dismissed them. The house has to be closed and locked, and I shall trot around to the pigeon house, and shall send Celestine over in the morning to straighten things up."

He looked around, and began to turn out some of the lights.

"What about upstairs?" he inquired.

"I think it is all right; but there may be a window or two unlatched. We had better look; you might take a candle and see. And bring me my wrap and hat on the foot of the bed in the middle room."

[75]"Ah! couldst thou but know what thine eyes tell me," from the Balfe song Robert sang earlier.

He went up with the light, and Edna began closing doors and windows. She hated to shut in the smoke and the fumes of the wine. Arobin found her cape and hat, which he brought down and helped her to put on.

When everything was secured and the lights put out, they left through the front door, Arobin locking it and taking the key, which he carried for Edna. He helped her down the steps.

"Will you have a spray of jessamine?" he asked, breaking off a few blossoms as he passed.

"No; I don't want anything."

She seemed disheartened, and had nothing to say. She took his arm, which he offered her, holding up the weight of her satin train with the other hand. She looked down, noticing the black line of his leg moving in and out so close to her against the yellow shimmer of her gown. There was the whistle of a railway train somewhere in the distance, and the midnight bells were ringing. They met no one in their short walk.

The "pigeon-house" stood behind a locked gate, and a shallow *parterre*[76] that had been somewhat neglected. There was a small front porch, upon which a long window and the front door opened. The door opened directly into the parlor; there was no side entry. Back in the yard was a room for servants, in which old Celestine had been ensconced.

Edna had left a lamp burning low upon the table. She had succeeded in making the room look habitable and homelike. There were some books on the table and a lounge near at hand. On the floor was a fresh matting, covered with a rug or two; and on the walls hung a few tasteful pictures. But the room was filled with flowers. These were a surprise to her. Arobin had sent them, and had had Celestine distribute them during Edna's absence. Her bedroom was adjoining, and across a small passage were the dining-room and kitchen.

Edna seated herself with every appearance of discomfort.

"Are you tired?" he asked.

"Yes, and chilled, and miserable. I feel as if I had been wound up to a certain pitch—too tight—and something inside of me had snapped." She rested her head against the table upon her bare arm.

"You want to rest," he said, "and to be quiet. I'll go; I'll leave you and let you rest."

"Yes," she replied.

He stood up beside her and smoothed her hair with his soft, magnetic hand. His touch conveyed to her a certain physical comfort. She could have fallen quietly asleep there if he had continued to pass his hand over her hair. He brushed the hair upward from the nape of her neck.

"I hope you will feel better and happier in the morning," he said. "You have tried to do too much in the past few days. The dinner was the last straw; you might have dispensed with it."

"Yes," she admitted; "it was stupid."

"No, it was delightful; but it has worn you out." His hand had strayed to her beautiful shoulders, and he could feel the response of her flesh to his touch. He seated himself beside her and kissed her lightly upon the shoulder.

[76] "Garden with flower beds."

"I thought you were going away," she said, in an uneven voice.

"I am, after I have said good night."

"Good night," she murmured.

He did not answer, except to continue to caress her. He did not say good night until she had become supple to his gentle, seductive entreaties.

XXXII

When Mr. Pontellier learned of his wife's intention to abandon her home and take up her residence elsewhere, he immediately wrote her a letter of unqualified disapproval and remonstrance. She had given reasons which he was unwilling to acknowledge as adequate. He hoped she had not acted upon her rash impulse; and begged her to consider first, foremost, and above all else, what people would say. He was not dreaming of scandal when he uttered this warning; that was a thing which would never have entered into his mind to consider in connection with his wife's name or his own. He was simply thinking of his financial integrity. It might get noised about that the Pontelliers had met with reverses, and were forced to conduct their *ménage*[77] on a humbler scale than heretofore. It might do incalculable mischief to his business prospects.

But remembering Edna's whimsical turn of mind of late, and foreseeing that she had immediately acted upon her impetuous determination, he grasped the situation with his usual promptness and handled it with his well-known business tact and cleverness.

The same mail which brought to Edna his letter of disapproval carried instructions—the most minute instructions—to a well-known architect concerning the remodeling of his home, changes which he had long contemplated, and which he desired carried forward during his temporary absence.

Expert and reliable packers and movers were engaged to convey the furniture, carpets, pictures—everything movable, in short—to places of security. And in an incredibly short time the Pontellier house was turned over to the artisans. There was to be an addition—a small snuggery;[78] there was to be frescoing, and hardwood flooring was to be put into such rooms as had not yet been subjected to this improvement.

Furthermore, in one of the daily papers appeared a brief notice to the effect that Mr. and Mrs. Pontellier were contemplating a summer sojourn abroad, and that their handsome residence on Esplanade Street was undergoing sumptuous alterations, and would not be ready for occupancy until their return. Mr. Pontellier had saved appearances!

Edna admired the skill of his maneuver, and avoided any occasion to balk his intentions. When the situation as set forth by Mr. Pontellier was accepted and taken for granted, she was apparently satisfied that it should be so.

The pigeon-house pleased her. It at once assumed the intimate character of a home, while she herself invested it with a charm which it reflected like a warm glow. There was with her a feeling of having descended in the

[77]"Household." [78]A cozy room; a "den."

social scale, with a corresponding sense of having risen in the spiritual. Every step which she took toward relieving herself from obligations added to her strength and expansion as an individual. She began to look with her own eyes; to see and to apprehend the deeper undercurrents of life. No longer was she content to "feed upon opinion" when her own soul had invited her.

After a little while, a few days, in fact, Edna went up and spent a week with her children in Iberville. They were delicious February days, with all the summer's promise hovering in the air.

How glad she was to see the children! She wept for very pleasure when she felt their little arms clasping her; their hard, ruddy cheeks pressed against her own glowing cheeks. She looked into their faces with hungry eyes that could not be satisfied with looking. And what stories they had to tell their mother! About the pigs, the cows, the mules! About riding to the mill behind Gluglu; fishing back in the lake with their Uncle Jasper; picking pecans with Lidie's little black brood, and hauling chips in their express wagon. It was a thousand times more fun to haul real chips for old lame Susie's real fire than to drag painted blocks along the banquette on Esplanade Street!

She went with them herself to see the pigs and the cows, to look at the darkies laying the cane, to thrash the pecan trees, and catch fish in the back lake. She lived with them a whole week long, giving them all of herself, and gathering and filling herself with their young existence. They listened, breathless, when she told them the house in Esplanade Street was crowded with workmen, hammering, nailing, sawing, and filling the place with clatter. They wanted to know where their bed was; what had been done with their rocking-horse; and where did Joe sleep, and where had Ellen gone, and the cook? But, above all, they were fired with a desire to see the little house around the block. Was there any place to play? Were there any boys next door? Raoul, with pessimistic foreboding, was convinced that there were only girls next door. Where would they sleep, and where would papa sleep? She told them the fairies would fix it all right.

The old Madame was charmed with Edna's visit, and showered all manner of delicate attentions upon her. She was delighted to know that the Esplanade Street house was in a dismantled condition. It gave her the promise and pretext to keep the children indefinitely.

It was with a wrench and a pang that Edna left her children. She carried away with her the sound of their voices and the touch of their cheeks. All along the journey homeward their presence lingered with her like the memory of a delicious song. But by the time she had regained the city the song no longer echoed in her soul. She was again alone.

XXXIII

It happened sometimes when Edna went to see Mademoiselle Reisz that the little musician was absent, giving a lesson or making some small necessary household purchase. The key was always left in a secret hiding-place in the entry, which Edna knew. If Mademoiselle happened to be away, Edna would usually enter and wait for her return.

When she knocked at Mademoiselle Reisz's door one afternoon there was no response; so unlocking the door, as usual, she entered and found the apartment deserted, as she had expected. Her day had been quite filled up, and it was for a rest, for a refuge, and to talk about Robert, that she sought out her friend.

She had worked at her canvas—a young Italian character study—all the morning, completing the work without the model; but there had been many interruptions, some incident to her modest housekeeping, and others of a social nature.

Madame Ratignolle had dragged herself over, avoiding the too public thoroughfares, she said. She complained that Edna had neglected her much of late. Besides, she was consumed with curiosity to see the little house and the manner in which it was conducted. She wanted to hear all about the dinner party; Monsieur Ratignolle had left *so* early. What had happened after he left? The champagne and grapes which Edna sent over were *too* delicious. She had so little appetite; they had refreshed and toned her stomach. Where on earth was she going to put Mr. Pontellier in that little house, and the boys? And then she made Edna promise to go to her when her hour of trial overtook her.

"At any time—any time of the day or night, dear," Edna assured her.

Before leaving Madame Ratignolle said:

"In some way you seem to me like a child, Edna. You seem to act without a certain amount of reflection which is necessary in this life. That is the reason I want to say you mustn't mind if I advise you to be a little careful while you are living here alone. Why don't you have some one come and stay with you? Wouldn't Mademoiselle Reisz come?"

"No; she wouldn't wish to come, and I shouldn't want her always with me."

"Well, the reason—you know how evil-minded the world is—some one was talking of Alcée Arobin visiting you. Of course, it wouldn't matter if Mr. Arobin had not such a dreadful reputation. Monsieur Ratignolle was telling me that his attentions alone are considered enough to ruin a woman's name."

"Does he boast of his successes?" asked Edna, indifferently, squinting at her picture.

"No, I think not. I believe he is a decent fellow as far as that goes. But his character is so well known among the men. I shan't be able to come back and see you; it was very, very imprudent today."

"Mind the step!" cried Edna.

"Don't neglect me," entreated Madame Ratignolle; "and don't mind what I said about Arobin, or having some one to stay with you."

"Of course not," Edna laughed. "You may say anything you like to me." They kissed good-by. Madame Ratignolle had not far to go, and Edna stood on the porch a while watching her walk down the street.

Then in the afternoon Mrs. Merriman and Mrs. Highcamp had made their "party call." Edna felt that they might have dispensed with the formality. They had also come to invite her to play *vingt-et-un*[79] one evening at Mrs. Merriman's. She was asked to go early, to dinner, and Mr. Merriman

[79] "Twenty-one," a card game.

or Mr. Arobin would take her home. Edna accepted in a half-hearted way. She sometimes felt very tired of Mrs. Highcamp and Mrs. Merriman.

Late in the afternoon she sought refuge with Mademoiselle Reisz, and stayed there alone, waiting for her, feeling a kind of repose invade her with the very atmosphere of the shabby, unpretentious little room.

Edna sat at the window, which looked out over the house-tops and across the river. The window frame was filled with pots of flowers, and she sat and picked the dry leaves from a rose geranium. The day was warm, and the breeze which blew from the river was very pleasant. She removed her hat and laid it on the piano. She went on picking the leaves and digging around the plants with her hat pin. Once she thought she heard Mademoiselle Reisz approaching. But it was a young black girl, who came in, bringing a small bundle of laundry, which she deposited in the adjoining room, and went away.

Edna seated herself at the piano, and softly picked out with one hand the bars of a piece of music which lay open before her. A half-hour went by. There was the occasional sound of people going and coming in the lower hall. She was growing interested in her occupation of picking out the aria, when there was a second rap at the door. She vaguely wondered what these people did when they found Mademoiselle's door locked.

"Come in," she called, turning her face toward the door. And this time it was Robert Lebrun who presented himself. She attempted to rise; she could not have done so without betraying the agitation which mastered her at sight of him, so she fell back upon the stool, only exclaiming, "Why, Robert!"

He came and clasped her hand, seemingly without knowing what he was saying or doing.

"Mrs. Pontellier! How do you happen—oh! how well you look! Is Mademoiselle Reisz not here? I never expected to see you."

"When did you come back?" asked Edna in an unsteady voice, wiping her face with her handkerchief. She seemed ill at ease on the piano stool, and he begged her to take the chair by the window. She did so, mechanically, while he seated himself on the stool.

"I returned day before yesterday," he answered, while he leaned his arm on the keys, bringing forth a crash of discordant sound.

"Day before yesterday!" she repeated, aloud; and went on thinking to herself, "day before yesterday," in a sort of an uncomprehending way. She had pictured him seeking her at the very first hour, and he had lived under the same sky since day before yesterday; while only by accident had he stumbled upon her. Mademoiselle must have lied when she said, "Poor fool, he loves you."

"Day before yesterday," she repeated, breaking off a spray of Mademoiselle's geranium; "then if you had not met me here today you wouldn't—when—that is, didn't you mean to come and see me?"

"Of course, I should have gone to see you. There have been so many things—" he turned the leaves of Mademoiselle's music nervously. "I started in at once yesterday with the old firm. After all there is as much chance for me here as there was there—that is, I might find it profitable some day. The Mexicans were not very congenial."

So he had come back because the Mexicans were not congenial; because business was as profitable here as there; because of any reason, and not because he cared to be near her. She remembered the day she sat on the floor, turning the pages of his letter, seeking the reason which was left untold.

She had not noticed how he looked—only feeling his presence; but she turned deliberately and observed him. After all, he had been absent but a few months, and was not changed. His hair—the color of hers—waved back from his temples in the same way as before. His skin was not more burned than it had been at Grand Isle. She found in his eyes, when he looked at her for one silent moment, the same tender caress, with an added warmth and entreaty which had not been there before—the same glance which had penetrated to the sleeping places of her soul and awakened them.

A hundred times Edna had pictured Robert's return, and imagined their first meeting. It was usually at her home, whither he had sought her out at once. She always fancied him expressing or betraying in some way his love for her. And here, the reality was that they sat ten feet apart, she at the window, crushing geranium leaves in her hand and smelling them, he twirling around on the piano stool, saying:

"I was very much surprised to hear of Mr. Pontellier's absence; it's a wonder Mademoiselle Reisz did not tell me; and your moving—mother told me yesterday. I should think you would have gone to New York with him, or to Iberville with the children, rather than be bothered here with housekeeping. And you are going abroad, too, I hear. We shan't have you at Grand Isle next summer; it won't seem—do you see much of Mademoiselle Reisz? She often spoke of you in the few letters she wrote."

"Do you remember that you promised to write to me when you went away?" A flush overspread his whole face.

"I couldn't believe that my letters would be of any interest to you."

"That is an excuse; it isn't the truth." Edna reached for her hat on the piano. She adjusted it, sticking the hat pin through the heavy coil of hair with some deliberation.

"Are you not going to wait for Mademoiselle Reisz?" asked Robert.

"No; I have found when she is absent this long, she is liable not to come back till late." She drew on her gloves, and Robert picked up his hat.

"Won't you wait for her?" asked Edna.

"Not if you think she will not be back till late," adding, as if suddenly aware of some discourtesy in his speech, "and I should miss the pleasure of walking home with you." Edna locked the door and put the key back in its hiding-place.

They went together, picking their way across muddy streets and sidewalks encumbered with the cheap display of small tradesmen. Part of the distance they rode in the car, and after disembarking, passed the Pontellier mansion, which looked broken and half torn asunder. Robert had never known the house, and looked at it with interest.

"I never knew you in your home," he remarked.

"I am glad you did not."

"Why?" She did not answer. They went on around the corner, and it

seemed as if her dreams were coming true after all, when he followed her into the little house.

"You must stay and dine with me, Robert. You see I am all alone, and it is so long since I have seen you. There is so much I want to ask you." She took off her hat and gloves. He stood irresolute, making some excuse about his mother who expected him; he even muttered something about an engagement. She struck a match and lit the lamp on the table; it was growing dusk. When he saw her face in the lamp-light, looking pained, with all the soft lines gone out of it, he threw his hat aside and seated himself.

"Oh! you know I want to stay if you will let me!" he exclaimed. All the softness came back. She laughed, and went and put her hand on his shoulder.

"This is the first moment you have seemed like the old Robert. I'll go tell Celestine." She hurried away to tell Celestine to set an extra place. She even sent her off in search of some added delicacy which she had not thought of for herself. And she recommended great care in dripping the coffee and having the omelet done to a proper turn.

When she reëntered, Robert was turning over magazines, sketches, and things that lay upon the table in great disorder. He picked up a photograph, and exclaimed:

"Alcée Arobin! What on earth is his picture doing here?"

"I tried to make a sketch of his head one day," answered Edna, "and he thought the photograph might help me. It was at the other house. I thought it had been left there. I must have packed it up with my drawing materials."

"I should think you would give it back to him if you have finished with it."

"Oh! I have a great many such photographs. I never think of returning them. They don't amount to anything." Robert kept on looking at the picture.

"It seems to me—do you think his head worth drawing? Is he a friend of Mr. Pontellier's? You never said you knew him."

"He isn't a friend of Mr. Pontellier's; he's a friend of mine. I always knew him—that is, it is only of late that I know him pretty well. But I'd rather talk about you, and know what you have been seeing and doing and feeling out there in Mexico." Robert threw aside the picture.

"I've been seeing the waves and the white beach of Grand Isle; the quiet, grassy street of the *Chênière;* the old fort at Grande Terre. I've been working like a machine, and feeling like a lost soul. There was nothing interesting."

She leaned her head upon her hand to shade her eyes from the light.

"And what have you been seeing and doing and feeling all these days?" he asked.

"I've been seeing the waves and the white beach of Grand Isle; the quiet, grassy street of the *Chênière Caminada;* the old sunny fort at Grande Terre. I've been working with a little more comprehension than a machine, and still feeling like a lost soul. There was nothing interesting."

"Mrs. Pontellier, you are cruel," he said, with feeling, closing his eyes and resting his head back in his chair. They remained in silence till old Celestine announced dinner.

XXXIV

The dining-room was very small. Edna's round mahogany would have almost filled it. As it was there was but a step or two from the little table to the kitchen, to the mantel, the small buffet, and the side door that opened out on the narrow brick-paved yard.

A certain degree of ceremony settled upon them with the announcement of dinner. There was no return to personalities. Robert related incidents of his sojourn in Mexico, and Edna talked of events likely to interest him, which had occurred during his absence. The dinner was of ordinary quality, except for the few delicacies which she had sent out to purchase. Old Celestine, with a bandana *tignon*[80] twisted about her head, hobbled in and out, taking a personal interest in everything; and she lingered occasionally to talk *patois*[81] with Robert, whom she had known as a boy.

He went out to a neighboring cigar stand to purchase cigarette papers, and when he came back he found that Celestine had served the black coffee in the parlor.

"Perhaps I shouldn't have come back," he said. "When you are tired of me, tell me to go."

"You never tire me. You must have forgotten the hours and hours at Grand Isle in which we grew accustomed to each other and used to being together."

"I have forgotten nothing at Grand Isle," he said, not looking at her, but rolling a cigarette. His tobacco pouch, which he laid upon the table, was a fantastic embroidered silk affair, evidently the handiwork of a woman.

"You used to carry your tobacco in a rubber pouch," said Edna, picking up the pouch and examining the needlework.

"Yes; it was lost."

"Where did you buy this one? In Mexico?"

"It was given to me by a Vera Cruz girl; they are very generous," he replied, striking a match and lighting his cigarette.

"They are very handsome, I suppose, those Mexican women; very picturesque, with their black eyes and their lace scarfs."

"Some are; others are hideous. Just as you find women everywhere."

"What was she like—the one who gave you the pouch? You must have known her very well."

"She was very ordinary. She wasn't of the slightest importance. I knew her well enough."

"Did you visit at her house? Was it interesting? I should like to know and hear about the people you met, and the impressions they made on you."

"There are some people who leave impressions not so lasting as the imprint of an oar upon the water."

"Was she such a one?"

"It would be ungenerous for me to admit that she was of that order and kind." He thrust the pouch back in his pocket, as if to put away the subject with the trifle which had brought it up.

[80] "Chignon," head scarf.

[81] Cajun speech, a dialect of French with many borrowings from English, Spanish, and American Indian languages.

Arobin dropped in with a message from Mrs. Merriman, to say that the card party was postponed on account of the illness of one of her children.

"How do you do, Arobin?" said Robert, rising from the obscurity.

"Oh! Lebrun. To be sure! I heard yesterday you were back. How did they treat you down in Mexique?"

"Fairly well."

"But not well enough to keep you there. Stunning girls, though, in Mexico. I thought I should never get away from Vera Cruz when I was down there a couple of years ago."

"Did they embroider slippers and tobacco pouches and hat-bands and things for you?" asked Edna.

"Oh! my! no! I didn't get so deep in their regard. I fear they made more impression on me than I made on them."

"You were less fortunate than Robert, then."

"I am always less fortunate than Robert. Has he been imparting tender confidences?"

"I've been imposing myself long enough," said Robert, rising, and shaking hands with Edna. "Please convey my regards to Mr. Pontellier when you write."

He shook hands with Arobin and went away.

"Fine fellow, that Lebrun," said Arobin when Robert had gone. "I never heard you speak of him."

"I knew him last summer at Grand Isle," she replied. "Here is that photograph of yours. Don't you want it?"

"What do I want with it? Throw it away." She threw it back on the table.

"I'm not going to Mrs. Merriman's," she said. "If you see her, tell her so. But perhaps I had better write. I think I shall write now, and say that I am sorry her child is sick, and tell her not to count on me."

"It would be a good scheme," acquiesced Arobin. "I don't blame you; stupid lot!"

Edna opened the blotter, and having procured paper and pen, began to write the note. Arobin lit a cigar and read the evening paper, which he had in his pocket.

"What is the date?" she asked. He told her.

"Will you mail this for me when you go out?"

"Certainly." He read to her little bits out of the newspaper, while she straightened things on the table.

"What do you want to do?" he asked, throwing aside the paper. "Do you want to go out for a walk or a drive or anything? It would be a fine night to drive."

"No; I don't want to do anything but just be quiet. You go away and amuse yourself. Don't stay."

"I'll go away if I must; but I shan't amuse myself. You know that I only live when I am near you."

He stood up to bid her good night.

"Is that one of the things you always say to women?"

"I have said it before, but I don't think I ever came so near meaning it," he answered with a smile. There were no warm lights in her eyes; only a dreamy, absent look.

"Good night. I adore you. Sleep well," he said, and he kissed her hand and went away.

She stayed alone in a kind of reverie—a sort of stupor. Step by step she lived over every instant of the time she had been with Robert after he had entered Mademoiselle Reisz's door. She recalled his words, his looks. How few and meager they had been for her hungry heart! A vision—a transcendently seductive vision of a Mexican girl arose before her. She writhed with a jealous pang. She wondered when he would come back. He had not said he would come back. She had been with him, had heard his voice and touched his hand. But some way he had seemed nearer to her off there in Mexico.

XXXV

The morning was full of sunlight and hope. Edna could see before her no denial—only the promise of excessive joy. She lay in bed awake, with bright eyes full of speculation. "He loves you, poor fool." If she could but get that conviction firmly fixed in her mind, what mattered about the rest? She felt she had been childish and unwise the night before in giving herself over to despondency. She recapitulated the motives which no doubt explained Robert's reserve. They were not insurmountable; they would not hold if he really loved her; they could not hold against her own passion, which he must come to realize in time. She pictured him going to his business that morning. She even saw how he was dressed; how he walked down one street, and turned the corner of another; saw him bending over his desk, talking to people who entered the office, going to his lunch, and perhaps watching for her on the street. He would come to her in the afternoon or evening, sit and roll his cigarette, talk a little, and go away as he had done the night before. But how delicious it would be to have him there with her! She would have no regrets, nor seek to penetrate his reserve if he still chose to wear it.

Edna ate her breakfast only half dressed. The maid brought her a delicious printed scrawl from Raoul, expressing his love, asking her to send him some bonbons, and telling her they had found that morning ten tiny white pigs all lying in a row beside Lidie's big white pig.

A letter also came from her husband, saying he hoped to be back early in March, and then they would get ready for that journey abroad which he had promised her so long, which he felt now fully able to afford; he felt able to travel as people should, without any thought of small economies— thanks to his recent speculations in Wall Street.

Much to her surprise she received a note from Arobin, written at midnight from the club. It was to say good morning to her, to hope she had slept well, to assure her of his devotion, which he trusted she in some faintest manner returned.

All these letters were pleasing to her. She answered the children in a cheerful frame of mind, promising them bonbons, and congratulating them upon their happy find of the little pigs.

She answered her husband with friendly evasiveness,—not with any fixed design to mislead him, only because all sense of reality had gone out

of her life; she had abandoned herself to Fate, and awaited the conse-
quences with indifference.

To Arobin's note she made no reply. She put it under Celestine's stove-lid.

Edna worked several hours with much spirit. She saw no one but a
picture dealer, who asked her if it were true that she was going abroad to
study in Paris.

She said possibly she might, and he negotiated with her for some Pari-
sian studies to reach him in time for the holiday trade in December.

Robert did not come that day. She was keenly disappointed. He did not
come the following day, nor the next. Each morning she awoke with hope,
and each night she was a prey to despondency. She was tempted to seek
him out. But far from yielding to the impulse, she avoided any occasion
which might throw her in his way. She did not go to Mademoiselle Reisz's
nor pass by Madame Lebrun's, as she might have done if he had still been
in Mexico.

When Arobin, one night, urged her to drive with him, she went—out to
the lake, on the Shell Road.[82] His horses were full of mettle, and even a
little unmanageable. She liked the rapid gait at which they spun along, and
the quick, sharp sound of the horses' hoofs on the hard road. They did not
stop anywhere to eat or to drink. Arobin was not needlessly imprudent. But
they ate and they drank when they regained Edna's little dining-room—
which was comparatively early in the evening.

It was late when he left her. It was getting to be more than a passing
whim with Arobin to see her and be with her. He had detected the latent
sensuality, which unfolded under his delicate sense of her nature's require-
ments like a torpid, torrid, sensitive blossom.

There was no despondency when she fell asleep that night; nor was
there hope when she awoke in the morning.

XXXVI

There was a garden out in the suburbs; a small, leafy corner, with a few
green tables under the orange trees. An old cat slept all day on the stone
step in the sun, and an old *mulatresse*[83] slept her idle hours away in her chair
at the open window, till some one happened to knock on one of the green
tables. She had milk and cream cheese to sell, and bread and butter. There
was no one who could make such excellent coffee or fry a chicken so golden
brown as she.

The place was too modest to attract the attention of people of fashion,
and so quiet as to have escaped the notice of those in search of pleasure and
dissipation. Edna had discovered it accidentally one day when the high-
board gate stood ajar. She caught sight of a little green table, blotched with
the checkered sunlight that filtered through the quivering leaves overhead.
Within she had found the slumbering *mulatresse*, the drowsy cat, and a glass
of milk which reminded her of the milk she had tasted in Iberville.

She often stopped there during her perambulations; sometimes taking

[82] A wide, well-paved road around Lake Pontchartrain, popular for carriage rides.
[83] Mulatto woman, of mixed white and Negro descent.

a book with her, and sitting an hour or two under the trees when she found the place deserted. Once or twice she took a quiet dinner there alone, having instructed Celestine beforehand to prepare no dinner at home. It was the last place in the city where she would have expected to meet any one she knew.

Still she was not astonished when, as she was partaking of a modest dinner late in the afternoon, looking into an open book, stroking the cat, which had made friends with her—she was not greatly astonished to see Robert come in at the tall garden gate.

"I am destined to see you only by accident," she said, shoving the cat off the chair beside her. He was surprised, ill at ease, almost embarrassed at meeting her thus so unexpectedly.

"Do you come here often?" he asked.

"I almost live here," she said.

"I used to drop in very often for a cup of Catiche's good coffee. This is the first time since I came back."

"She'll bring you a plate, and you will share my dinner. There's always enough for two—even three." Edna had intended to be indifferent and as reserved as he when she met him; she had reached the determination by a laborious train of reasoning, incident to one of her despondent moods. But her resolve melted when she saw him before her, seated there beside her in the little garden, as if a designing Providence had led him into her path.

"Why have you kept away from me, Robert?" she asked, closing the book that lay open upon the table.

"Why are you so personal, Mrs. Pontellier? Why do you force me to idiotic subterfuges?" he exclaimed with sudden warmth. "I suppose there's no use telling you I've been very busy, or that I've been sick, or that I've been to see you and not found you at home. Please let me off with any one of these excuses."

"You are the embodiment of selfishness," she said. "You save yourself something—I don't know what—but there is some selfish motive, and in sparing yourself you never consider for a moment what I think, or how I feel your neglect and indifference. I suppose this is what you would call unwomanly; but I have got into a habit of expressing myself. It doesn't matter to me, and you may think me unwomanly if you like."

"No; I only think you cruel, as I said the other day. Maybe not intentionally cruel; but you seem to be forcing me into disclosures which can result in nothing; as if you would have me bare a wound for the pleasure of looking at it, without the intention or power of healing it."

"I'm spoiling your dinner, Robert; never mind what I say. You haven't eaten a morsel."

"I only came in for a cup of coffee." His sensitive face was all disfigured with excitement.

"Isn't this a delightful place?" she remarked. "I am so glad it has never actually been discovered. It is so quiet, so sweet, here. Do you notice there is scarcely a sound to be heard? It's so out of the way; and a good walk from the car. However, I don't mind walking. I always feel so sorry for women who don't like to walk; they miss so much—so many rare little glimpses of life; and we women learn so little of life on the whole.

"Catiche's coffee is always hot. I don't know how she manages it, here in the open air. Celestine's coffee gets cold bringing it from the kitchen to the dining-room. Three lumps! How can you drink it so sweet? Take some of the cress with your chop; it's so biting and crisp. Then there's the advantage of being able to smoke with your coffee out here. Now, in the city— aren't you going to smoke?"

"After a while," he said, laying a cigar on the table.

"Who gave it to you?" she laughed.

"I bought it. I suppose I'm getting reckless; I bought a whole box." She was determined not to be personal again and make him uncomfortable.

The cat made friends with him, and climbed into his lap when he smoked his cigar. He stroked her silky fur, and talked a little about her. He looked at Edna's book, which he had read; and he told her the end, to save her the trouble of wading through it, he said.

Again he accompanied her back to her home; and it was after dusk when they reached the little "pigeon-house." She did not ask him to remain, which he was grateful for, as it permitted him to stay without the discomfort of blundering through an excuse which he had no intention of considering. He helped her to light the lamp; then she went into her room to take off her hat and to bathe her face and hands.

When she came back Robert was not examining the pictures and magazines as before; he sat off in the shadow, leaning his head back on the chair as if in a reverie. Edna lingered a moment beside the table, arranging the books there. Then she went across the room to where he sat. She bent over the arm of his chair and called his name.

"Robert," she said, "are you asleep?"

"No," he answered, looking up at her.

She leaned over and kissed him—a soft, cool, delicate kiss, whose voluptuous sting penetrated his whole being—then she moved away from him. He followed, and took her in his arms, just holding her close to him. She put her hand up to his face and pressed his cheek against her own. The action was full of love and tenderness. He sought her lips again. Then he drew her down upon the sofa beside him and held her hand in both of his.

"Now you know," he said, "now you know what I have been fighting against since last summer at Grand Isle; what drove me away and drove me back again."

"Why have you been fighting against it?" she asked. Her face glowed with soft lights.

"Why? Because you were not free; you were Léonce Pontellier's wife. I couldn't help loving you if you were ten times his wife; but so long as I went away from you and kept away I could help telling you so." She put her free hand up to his shoulder, and then against his cheek, rubbing it softly. He kissed her again. His face was warm and flushed.

"There in Mexico I was thinking of you all the time, and longing for you."

"But not writing to me," she interrupted.

"Something put into my head that you cared for me; and I lost my

senses. I forgot everything but a wild dream of your some way becoming my wife."

"Your wife!"

"Religion, loyalty, everything would give way if only you cared."

"Then you must have forgotten that I was Léonce Pontellier's wife."

"Oh! I was demented, dreaming of wild, impossible things, recalling men who had set their wives free, we have heard of such things."

"Yes, we have heard of such things."

"I came back full of vague, mad intentions. And when I got here—"

"When you got here you never came near me!" She was still caressing his cheek.

"I realized what a cur I was to dream of such a thing, even if you had been willing."

She took his face between her hands and looked into it as if she would never withdraw her eyes more. She kissed him on the forehead, the eyes, the cheeks, and the lips.

"You have been a very, very foolish boy, wasting your time dreaming of impossible things when you speak of Mr. Pontellier setting me free! I am no longer one of Mr. Pontellier's possessions to dispose of or not. I give myself where I choose. If he were to say, 'Here, Robert, take her and be happy; she is yours,' I should laugh at you both."

His face grew a little white. "What do you mean?" he asked.

There was a knock at the door. Old Celestine came in to say that Madame Ratignolle's servant had come around the back way with a message that Madame had been taken sick and begged Mrs. Pontellier to go to her immediately.

"Yes, yes," said Edna, rising; "I promised. Tell her yes—to wait for me. I'll go back with her."

"Let me walk over with you," offered Robert.

"No," she said; "I will go with the servant." She went into her room to put on her hat, and when she came in again she sat once more upon the sofa beside him. He had not stirred. She put her arms about his neck.

"Good-by, my sweet Robert. Tell me good-by." He kissed her with a degree of passion which had not before entered into his caress, and strained her to him.

"I love you," she whispered, "only you; no one but you. It was you who awoke me last summer out of a life-long, stupid dream. Oh! you have made me so unhappy with your indifference. Oh! I have suffered, suffered! Now you are here we shall love each other, my Robert. We shall be everything to each other. Nothing else in the world is of any consequence. I must go to my friend; but you will wait for me? No matter how late; you will wait for me, Robert?"

"Don't go; don't go! Oh! Edna, stay with me," he pleaded. "Why should you go? Stay with me, stay with me."

"I shall come back as soon as I can; I shall find you here." She buried her face in his neck, and said good-by again. Her seductive voice, together with his great love for her, had enthralled his senses, had deprived him of every impulse but the longing to hold her and keep her.

XXXVII

Edna looked in at the drug store. Monsieur Ratignolle was putting up a mixture himself, very carefully, dropping a red liquid into a tiny glass. He was grateful to Edna for having come; her presence would be a comfort to his wife. Madame Ratignolle's sister, who had always been with her at such trying times, had not been able to come up from the plantation, and Adèle had been inconsolable until Mrs. Pontellier so kindly promised to come to her. The nurse had been with them at night for the past week, as she lived a great distance away. And Dr. Mandelet had been coming and going all the afternoon. They were then looking for him any moment.

Edna hastened upstairs by a private stairway that led from the rear of the store to the apartments above. The children were all sleeping in a back room. Madame Ratignolle was in the salon, whither she had strayed in her suffering impatience. She sat on the sofa, clad in an ample white *peignoir*, holding a handkerchief tight in her hand with a nervous clutch. Her face was drawn and pinched, her sweet blue eyes haggard and unnatural. All her beautiful hair had been drawn back and plaited. It lay in a long braid on the sofa pillow, coiled like a golden serpent. The nurse, a comfortable looking *Griffe* woman[84] in white apron and cap, was urging her to return to her bedroom.

"There is no use, there is no use," she said at once to Edna. "We must get rid of Mandelet; he is getting too old and careless. He said he would be here at half-past seven; now it must be eight. See what time it is, Joséphine."

The woman was possessed of a cheerful nature, and refused to take any situation too seriously, especially a situation with which she was so familiar. She urged Madame to have courage and patience. But Madame only set her teeth hard into her under lip, and Edna saw the sweat gather in beads on her white forehead. After a moment or two she uttered a profound sigh and wiped her face with the handkerchief rolled in a ball. She appeared exhausted. The nurse gave her a fresh handkerchief, sprinkled with cologne water.

"This is too much!" she cried. "Mandelet ought to be killed! Where is Alphonse? Is it possible I am to be abandoned like this—neglected by every one?"

"Neglected, indeed!" exclaimed the nurse. Wasn't she there? And here was Mrs. Pontellier leaving, no doubt, a pleasant evening at home to devote to her? And wasn't Monsieur Ratignolle coming that very instant through the hall? And Joséphine was quite sure she had heard Doctor Mandelet's *coupé*.[85] Yes, there it was, down at the door.

Adèle consented to go back to her room. She sat on the edge of a little low couch next to her bed.

Doctor Mandelet paid no attention to Madame Ratignolle's upbraidings. He was accustomed to them at such times, and was too well convinced of her loyalty to doubt it.

He was glad to see Edna, and wanted her to go with him into the salon

[84] A mulatto. [85] A short carriage for two people.

and entertain him. But Madame Ratignolle would not consent that Edna should leave her for an instant. Between agonizing moments, she chatted a little, and said it took her mind off her sufferings.

Edna began to feel uneasy. She was seized with a vague dread. Her own like experiences seemed far away, unreal, and only half remembered. She recalled faintly an ecstasy of pain, the heavy odor of chloroform, a stupor which had deadened sensation, and an awakening to find a little new life to which she had given being, added to the great unnumbered multitude of souls that come and go.

She began to wish she had not come; her presence was not necessary. She might have invented a pretext for staying away; she might even invent a pretext now for going. But Edna did not go. With an inward agony, with a flaming, outspoken revolt against the ways of Nature, she witnessed the scene of torture.

She was still stunned and speechless with emotion when later she leaned over her friend to kiss her and softly say good-by. Adèle, pressing her cheek, whispered in an exhausted voice: "Think of the children, Edna. Oh think of the children! Remember them!"

XXXVIII

Edna still felt dazed when she got outside in the open air. The Doctor's *coupé* had returned for him and stood before the *porte cochère*. She did not wish to enter the *coupé*, and told Doctor Mandelet she would walk; she was not afraid, and would go alone. He directed his carriage to meet him at Mrs. Pontellier's, and he started to walk home with her.

Up—away up, over the narrow street between the tall houses, the stars were blazing. The air was mild and caressing, but cool with the breath of spring and the night. They walked slowly, the Doctor with a heavy, measured tread and his hands behind him; Edna, in an absent-minded way, as she had walked one night at Grand Isle, as if her thoughts had gone ahead of her and she was striving to overtake them.

"You shouldn't have been there, Mrs. Pontellier," he said. "That was no place for you. Adèle is full of whims at such times. There were a dozen women she might have had with her, unimpressionable women. I felt that it was cruel, cruel. You shouldn't have gone."

"Oh, well!" she answered, indifferently. "I don't know that it matters after all. One has to think of the children some time or other; the sooner the better."

"When is Léonce coming back?"

"Quite soon. Some time in March."

"And you are going abroad?"

"Perhaps—no, I am not going. I'm not going to be forced into doing things. I don't want to go abroad. I want to be let alone. Nobody has any right—except children, perhaps—and even then, it seems to me—or it did seem—" She felt that her speech was voicing the incoherency of her thoughts, and stopped abruptly.

"The trouble is," sighed the Doctor, grasping her meaning intuitively, "that youth is given up to illusions. It seems to be a provision of Nature; a decoy to secure mothers for the race. And Nature takes no account of moral consequences, of arbitrary conditions which we create, and which we feel obliged to maintain at any cost."

"Yes," she said. "The years that are gone seem like dreams—if one might go on sleeping and dreaming—but to wake up and find—oh! well! perhaps it is better to wake up after all, even to suffer, rather than to remain a dupe to illusions all one's life."

"It seems to me, my dear child," said the Doctor at parting, holding her hand, "you seem to me to be in trouble. I am not going to ask for your confidence. I will only say that if ever you feel moved to give it to me, perhaps I might help you. I know I would understand, and I tell you there are not many who would—not many, my dear."

"Some way I don't feel moved to speak of things that trouble me. Don't think I am ungrateful or that I don't appreciate your sympathy. There are periods of despondency and suffering which take possession of me. But I don't want anything but my own way. That is wanting a good deal, of course, when you have to trample upon the lives, the hearts, the prejudices of others—but no matter—still, I shouldn't want to trample upon the little lives. Oh! I don't know what I'm saying, Doctor. Good night. Don't blame me for anything."

"Yes, I will blame you if you don't come and see me soon. We will talk of things you never have dreamt of talking about before. It will do us both good. I don't want you to blame yourself, whatever comes. Good night, my child."

She let herself in at the gate, but instead of entering she sat upon the step of the porch. The night was quiet and soothing. All the tearing emotion of the last few hours seemed to fall away from her like a somber, uncomfortable garment, which she had but to loosen to be rid of. She went back to that hour before Adèle had sent for her; and her senses kindled afresh in thinking of Robert's words, the pressure of his arms, and the feeling of his lips upon her own. She could picture at that moment no greater bliss on earth than possession of the beloved one. His expression of love had already given him to her in part. When she thought that he was there at hand, waiting for her, she grew numb with the intoxication of expectancy. It was so late; he would be asleep perhaps. She would awaken him with a kiss. She hoped he would be asleep that she might arouse him with her caresses.

Still, she remembered Adèle's voice whispering, "Think of the children; think of them." She meant to think of them; that determination had driven into her soul like a death wound—but not tonight. Tomorrow would be time to think of everything.

Robert was not waiting for her in the little parlor. He was nowhere at hand. The house was empty. But he had scrawled on a piece of paper that lay in the lamplight:

"I love you. Good-by—because I love you."

Edna grew faint when she read the words. She went and sat on the sofa. Then she stretched herself out there, never uttering a sound. She did not

sleep. She did not go to bed. The lamp sputtered and went out. She was still awake in the morning, when Celestine unlocked the kitchen door and came in to light the fire.

XXXIX

Victor, with hammer and nails and scraps of scantling,[86] was patching a corner of one of the galleries. Mariequita sat near by, dangling her legs, watching him work, and handing him nails from the tool-box. The sun was beating down upon them. The girl had covered her head with her apron folded into a square pad. They had been talking for an hour or more. She was never tired of hearing Victor describe the dinner at Mrs. Pontellier's. He exaggerated every detail, making it appear a veritable Lucullean[87] feast. The flowers were in tubs, he said. The champagne was quaffed from huge golden goblets. Venus rising from the foam[88] could have presented no more entrancing a spectacle than Mrs. Pontellier, blazing with beauty and diamonds at the head of the board, while the other women were all of them youthful houris,[89] possessed of incomparable charms.

She got it into her head that Victor was in love with Mrs. Pontellier, and he gave her evasive answers, framed so as to confirm her belief. She grew sullen and cried a little, threatening to go off and leave him to his fine ladies. There were a dozen men crazy about her at the *Chénière;* and since it was the fashion to be in love with married people, why, she could run away any time she liked to New Orleans with Célina's husband.

Célina's husband was a fool, a coward, and a pig, and to prove it to her, Victor intended to hammer his head into a jelly the next time he encountered him. This assurance was very consoling to Mariequita. She dried her eyes, and grew cheerful at the prospect.

They were still talking of the dinner and the allurements of city life when Mrs. Pontellier herself slipped around the corner of the house. The two youngsters stayed dumb with amazement before what they considered to be an apparition. But it was really she in flesh and blood, looking tired and a little travel-stained.

"I walked up from the wharf," she said, "and heard the hammering. I supposed it was you, mending the porch. It's a good thing. I was always tripping over those loose planks last summer. How dreary and deserted everything looks!"

It took Victor some little time to comprehend that she had come in Beaudelet's lugger, that she had come alone, and for no purpose but to rest.

"There's nothing fixed up yet, you see. I'll give you my room; it's the only place."

"Any corner will do," she assured him.

"And if you can stand Philomel's cooking," he went on, "though I might

[86] Small boards.

[87] Extravagant. Lucullus was a first-century B.C. Roman consul famous for his wealth and luxury.

[88] Venus, the Roman goddess of love, was born from the ocean foam.

[89] Nymphs; the beautiful virgins provided in Paradise to faithful Moslems.

try to get her mother while you are here. Do you think she would come?" turning to Mariequita.

Mariequita thought that perhaps Philomel's mother might come for a few days, and money enough.

Beholding Mrs. Pontellier make her appearance, the girl had at once suspected a lovers' rendezvous. But Victor's astonishment was so genuine, and Mrs. Pontellier's indifference so apparent, that the disturbing notion did not lodge long in her brain. She contemplated with the greatest interest this woman who gave the most sumptuous dinners in America, and who had all the men in New Orleans at her feet.

"What time will you have dinner?" asked Edna. "I'm very hungry; but don't get anything extra."

"I'll have it ready in little or no time," he said, bustling and packing away his tools. "You may go to my room to brush up and rest yourself. Mariequita will show you."

"Thank you," said Edna. "But, do you know, I have a notion to go down to the beach and take a good wash and even a little swim, before dinner?"

"The water is too cold!" they both exclaimed. "Don't think of it."

"Well, I might go down and try—dip my toes in. Why, it seems to me the sun is hot enough to have warmed the very depths of the ocean. Could you get me a couple of towels? I'd better go right away, so as to be back in time. It would be a little too chilly if I waited till this afternoon."

Mariequita ran over to Victor's room, and returned with some towels, which she gave to Edna.

"I hope you have fish for dinner," said Edna, as she started to walk away; "but don't do anything extra if you haven't."

"Run and find Philomel's mother," Victor instructed the girl. "I'll go to the kitchen and see what I can do. By Gimminy! Women have no consideration! She might have sent me word."

Edna walked on down to the beach rather mechanically, not noticing anything special except that the sun was hot. She was not dwelling upon any particular train of thought. She had done all the thinking which was necessary after Robert went away, when she lay awake upon the sofa till morning.

She had said over and over to herself: "Today it is Arobin; tomorrow it will be some one else. It makes no difference to me, it doesn't matter about Léonce Pontellier—but Raoul and Etienne!" She understood now clearly what she had meant long ago when she said to Adèle Ratignolle that she would give up the unessential, but she would never sacrifice herself for her children.

Despondency had come upon her there in the wakeful night, and had never lifted. There was no one thing in the world that she desired. There was no human being whom she wanted near her except Robert; and she even realized that the day would come when he, too, and the thought of him would melt out of her existence, leaving her alone. The children appeared before her like antagonists who had overcome her; who had overpowered her and sought to drag her into the soul's slavery for the rest of her days. But she knew a way to elude them. She was not thinking of these things when she walked down to the beach.

The water of the Gulf stretched out before her, gleaming with the mil-

lion lights of the sun. The voice of the sea is seductive, never ceasing, whispering, clamoring, murmuring, inviting the soul to wander in abysses of solitude. All along the white beach, up and down, there was no living thing in sight. A bird with a broken wing was beating the air above, reeling, fluttering, circling disabled down, down to the water.

Edna had found her old bathing suit still hanging, faded, upon its accustomed peg.

She put it on, leaving her clothing in the bath-house. But when she was there beside the sea, absolutely alone, she cast the unpleasant, pricking garments from her, and for the first time in her life she stood naked in the open air, at the mercy of the sun, the breeze that beat upon her, and the waves that invited her.

How strange and awful it seemed to stand naked under the sky! how delicious! She felt like some new-born creature, opening its eyes in a familiar world that it had never known.

The foamy wavelets curled up to her white feet, and coiled like serpents about her ankles. She walked out. The water was chill, but she walked on. The water was deep, but she lifted her white body and reached out with a long, sweeping stroke. The touch of the sea is sensuous, enfolding the body in its soft, close embrace.

She went on and on. She remembered the night she swam far out, and recalled the terror that seized her at the fear of being unable to regain the shore. She did not look back now, but went on and on, thinking of the blue-grass meadow that she had traversed when a little child, believing that it had no beginning and no end.

Her arms and legs were growing tired.

She thought of Léonce and the children. They were a part of her life. But they need not have thought that they could possess her, body and soul. How Mademoiselle Reisz would have laughed, perhaps sneered, if she knew! "And you call yourself an artist! What pretensions, Madame! The artist must possess the courageous soul that dares and defies."

Exhaustion was pressing upon and overpowering her.

"Good-by—because I love you." He did not know; he did not understand. He would never understand. Perhaps Doctor Mandelet would have understood if she had seen him—but it was too late; the shore was far behind her, and her strength was gone.

She looked into the distance, and the old terror flamed up for an instant, then sank again. Edna heard her father's voice and her sister Margaret's. She heard the barking of an old dog that was chained to the sycamore tree. The spurs of the cavalry officer clanged as he walked across the porch. There was the hum of bees, and the musky odor of pinks filled the air.

Anton Chekhov
(1860–1904)

Several streams flowed into the river that became the modern theater—the biting social realism of Ibsen, the hallucinatory dream visions of Strindberg, the defiant absurdism of Alfred Jarry—but none more important than that of the four major plays of the Russian dramatist Anton Chekhov. *Uncle Vanya, The Seagull, The Three Sisters,* and *The Cherry Orchard* are plays that altered dramatic form to make it expressive of a distinctly "modern" view of human personality—multilayered, governed at least as much by unconscious forces as by conscious ones, full of tensions and contradictions between desire and action, expressed in language which, oftener than not, is designed to conceal or relieve half-understood feelings rather than to communicate. The dramatist Chekhov, inimitable, has nevertheless been imitated in some ways by most of the major dramatists of the twentieth century. His impact has been just as great upon the modern short story, which he created in the same sense that he created modern drama, altering the traditional form of short fiction to express the same sort of modern perception of human reality that his dramas express.

Chekhov was born in 1860 in the southern Russian seaport town of Taganrog, where his father, a former serf and a rigid taskmaster to his family, ran a gradually failing grocery. Chekhov helped in the family business and attended the local schools, entering when he was nine the local *gymnasium* or high school, where he remained for ten years. When he was sixteen, his father went bankrupt and escaped creditors by moving the family to Moscow. Chekhov remained behind, supporting himself for the last three years of his schooling by tutoring younger students. When he graduated at the age of nineteen, he followed the family to Moscow, where his father was slipping into bankruptcy again. Chekhov took over financial support of the family as well as entering the five-year medical program at Moscow University; he paid his own expenses and those of his family by free-lance writing of comic sketches for humorous magazines. He continued writing even after he became a doctor in 1884; the humorous, popular writing of the years between 1879 and 1888 forms an enormous body of work largely unknown today but crucial in the forming of his technical skill.

The publication of a long story named "The Steppe" in a leading Russian literary journal in 1888 marked the beginning of a new phase in Chekhov's career. Already he had begun to experiment with stories and sketches in a more serious vein, and "The Steppe," an account of a journey through the Ukraine as seen through the eyes of a child, established the mode of his fiction for the last sixteen years of his life. A few of his earlier stories have been resurrected from the ephemeral journals in which they were published, but for the most part Chekhov's reputation in fiction rests upon about fifty stories written after 1888.

At the same time that Chekhov was moving in the direction of greater seriousness and complexity in his stories, he was experimenting with deepening and enriching his dramatic work. His *Ivanov* (1887), a comparatively traditional work, had been successful both in Moscow and Petersburg, and

he had written skillful short popular farces, or "vaudevilles"—"The Bear," "The Marriage Proposal," "The Wedding"—which are still frequently produced. But in 1888–89, he also wrote a long, rather verbose play named *The Wood Demon,* which, despite its failure in a Moscow production, represented a new experimental direction in Chekhov's playwriting. "The play is awfully strange," he confided to a friend, "and I wonder that such strange things should come from my pen." *The Wood Demon* was later to be transformed into *Uncle Vanya* (1897).

Between 1890 and 1892, Chekhov was also deeply involved in medical and scientific work. In 1890, he made an extended trip to a Russian penal settlement on the remote island of Sakhalin, off the east coast of Siberia; he published the results of his investigation in *The Island of Sakhalin* (1893–94). He also worked diligently in relief programs during the disastrous peasant famines of 1891 and 1892.

From 1892 until 1898, Chekhov lived on a small estate he bought in the village of Melikhova, about fifty miles south of Moscow. He moved his elderly parents to the estate and cared for them, with the help of his unmarried sister Mariya, who became the housekeeper. The Melikhova years were among the most productive of Chekhov's life; he wrote many of his greatest short stories here, as well as a second full-length play, *The Seagull,* disastrously produced in St. Petersburg in 1896 in one of the most humiliating experiences of Chekhov's life.

During the later Melikhova years, Chekhov began to develop troubling symptoms of tuberculosis, the disease which had killed his irresponsible but lovable brother Nikolay in 1889. In 1897, he experienced a serious lung hemorrhage and was forced to sell the Melikhova estate and move to a villa in the more temperate climate of Yalta, a resort on the Crimean coast. The remaining seven years of his life were largely devoted to drama, although several of his greatest short stories, including "The Lady with a Dog," date from the Yalta years. In 1898, the failed *Seagull* was revived as one of the first productions of the newly established Moscow Art Theater, under the direction of Konstantine Stanislavsky. It was an enormous success; the emblem of the Moscow Art Theater, one of the great theaters of the world, is still a stylized seagull. Chekhov, to provide Stanislavsky with a new play, offered *Uncle Vanya,* already radically revised from *The Wood Demon* and successfully produced in the provinces. It was produced at the Moscow Art Theater in 1899 and was also a success, though a more modest one than *The Seagull,* baffling many members of the audience.

Chekhov's physical condition was worsening rapidly and he was unable to attend the Moscow performances of either *The Seagull* or *Uncle Vanya.* He had, however, been able to attend one of the rehearsals of *The Seagull* and had fallen in love with Olga Knipper, the actress who played Nina; they were married in 1901, and the marriage was a very happy one, though Chekhov was confined to Yalta by his illness and Knipper, deeply committed to her work, remained in Moscow for the theater season each year. The Art Theater had toured the Crimea in 1900 and had performed both *The Seagull* and *Uncle Vanya* for Chekhov at Sevastapol and Yalta. His third play, *The Three Sisters,* was modestly successful in its first performance at the Moscow Art Theater in January, 1901; Chekhov, defying the advice of his doctors, had gone to Moscow and taken an active part in rehearsals.

Chekhov began his masterpiece, *The Cherry Orchard*, about the time of his marriage. The culmination of his rich, ironic technique, it took shape over a period of three years, reaching production on January 17, 1904, Chekhov's birthday and the occasion of an elaborate and moving series of tributes to him by his theatrical colleagues. He lived only six months more, dying in the German resort town of Badenweiler on July 14, 1904.

Sigmund Freud once replied, when asked for a definition of a healthy life, that it consisted of being able to love and being able to work. He might have been describing Chekhov's view of life. Chekhov's world is an uncertain, indeterminate one which seems to be slowly falling apart. Social change, economic pressure, and philosophical doubt have left his characters uncertain of who they are and what goals they should adopt. All his plays and most of his stories take place not in the great centers of social and intellectual life but in the country in little provincial towns, and the sense of being out of touch with things, of being somehow in the backwaters, becomes symbolic of his characters' psychological positions as well. Chekhov's stories and plays meticulously etch the discouragement and disillusionment Russian intellectuals felt in the years following the failed reforms of Czar Alexander II in the 1860's and '70's and, at the same time, anticipate the modern Wasteland.

But Chekhov's work is never depressing or despairing. His characters may be confused or defeated, but their successes and failures are consistently placed against a background of a deep faith in the redemptive power of love and work, love even when it is refused or unreciprocated, work even when its long-range effects cannot be seen. In every Chekhov play and in many of the stories, someone eventually expresses Chekhov's faith in work, as Trofimov does, for example, in *The Cherry Orchard:* "It is clear that to begin to live in the present we must first expiate our past, we must break with it; and we can expiate it only by suffering, by extraordinary unceasing labor." (The fact that, of all the characters in *The Cherry Orchard,* Trofimov is one of those least capable of either love or work is a Chekhovian irony that does not invalidate his point.)

Chekhov never developed his simple faith into a systematic philosophy, and he seems to have been completely indifferent to the many pre-Revolutionary political movements fermenting in Russia during his lifetime. On one issue, however, he seems to have taken something of a stand, though a characteristically mild and indirect one. In the late 1880's, he had been much influenced by Tolstoy's doctrines of the holiness of the simple life and of nonresistance to violence and evil. Tolstoy's passivity and quietism were fundamentally alien to Chekhov's character, however, and in a number of stories of the nineties and in at least one play, *The Three Sisters,* he deals tellingly with the necessity to resist evil actively and with the illusions involved in fantasies of simple, earthy life. In the great story "Ward Number Six" (1892), for example, he tells the story of a doctor who does nothing to improve conditions in the wretched mental ward in his charge and ends up committed there himself. In *The Three Sisters,* the voracious Natalya gradually takes over the entire house of her sisters-in-law, who are unwilling ever to take a firm stand against her. And in the trio of 1898 stories, "The Man in a Shell," "Gooseberries," and "About Love," Chekhov deals with various sorts of self-deluded retreats from life and reality.

"Gooseberries" is one of Chekhov's greatest and most characteristic stories. On the surface, it seems curiously actionless and unresolved, a comic but shallow anecdote about a petty civil servant who acts out a sort of pop-cult Tolstoyan fantasy. But on second reading, the foolish Nikolay recedes in importance; we realize that the protagonist of the story is the frame-narrator Ivan Ivanovitch and that the climax of the story is his own spiritual crisis which his visit to his brother has triggered, his own vision of "general hypnotism." It seems a valid and moving vision, but we wonder. It has brought Ivan Ivanovitch to the point that "there is no spectacle more painful" than the sight of "a happy family sitting around the table drinking tea." Perhaps it is true that "the fact that lovely Pelagea was moving noiselessly about was better than any story."

Chekhov usually expressed his aims in drama in terms of a quiet, literal realism: "A play should be written in which people arrive, go away, have dinner, talk about the weather, and play cards. Life must be exactly as it is, and people as they are—not on stilts. . . . Let everything on the stage be just as complicated, and at the same time just as simple as it is in life." This will do as a loose description of *The Cherry Orchard*, but it does not suggest the play's meticulous artistry, in which each detail is as carefully controlled as in a lyric poem. Chekhov's plays are sometimes said to be "plotless," perhaps because people have trouble recognizing familiar plot elements when they are presented in unfamiliar ways. *The Cherry Orchard* has buried in it the rigid structure of a nineteenth-century "dispossession" melodrama, complete with foreclosing villain, grieving old mother, and paired young lovers. But Chekhov shifts the emphasis from melodramatic action to human reaction; the climactic auction, like most of the rest of the story, takes place offstage. And the stock characters are humanized and given contradictory motives. Lopahin loves the Ranevskys and is desperate to help them save their estate (though the ex-serf in him is also capable of gloating, understandably, over owning it himself). Lyubov, passionate, sentimental, charming, and self-destructive, is poles away from the white-haired old mother of theatrical cliché. And Trofimov and Anya are a most unexpected set of young lovers, being "above love" (at least according to Trofimov).

For the mechanical tricks of melodramatic plotting, Chekhov substitutes a simple pattern of arrival and departure ("people arrive and go away"); for stock theatrical characters, he substitutes real people, lovingly and meticulously observed ("not on stilts"); and for theatrical rhetoric, he substitutes the shifting, treacherous currents of real speech, full of abrupt changes, apparent irrelevancies, and unconscious revelations of an emotional "subtext" under the "text" of rational intention. The result is one of the greatest of modern plays: a study of the decline and fall of a charming but doomed culture, a guarded but optimistic expression of hope for the future, and a timeless exploration of confused and groping but infinitely precious humanity.

FURTHER READING (*prepared by W. J. R.*): Ronald Hingley's *A New Life of Anton Chekhov*, 1976, is a thorough biography based on much new Chekhov material. Other substantial biographies are David Magarshack's *Chekhov: A Life*, 1953, and Ernest J. Simmons's *Chekhov, A Biography*, 1962. *Anton Chekhov's Life and Thought:*

Selected Letters and Commentary, ed. by Simon Karlinsky and trans. by Michael-Henry Heim and Simon Karlinsky, 1976, supplements a generous selection of Chekhov's letters with such extensive commentary that it amounts to a Chekhovian autobiography. Irina Kirk's *Anton Chekhov,* 1981, an introductory study, discusses Chekhov's artistic development, the short stories, and (more briefly) the major plays. David Magarshack's *Chekhov the Dramatist,* 1950, examines Chekhov's development as a playwright in terms of a distinction between plays of direct and of indirect action. Major plays are also discussed in Maurice Valency's *The Breaking String,* 1966, and J. L. Styan's *Chekhov in Performance,* 1971. Chekhov's artistry, his theater, and his personality are examined in *Chekhov: A Collection of Critical Essays,* ed. by Robert Louis Jackson, 1967. *Chekhov's Great Plays: A Critical Anthology,* ed. by Jean-Pierre Barricelli, 1981, is limited to drama and includes excellent essays by most of the leading recent Chekhov critics. Another good collection is *Chekhov: New Perspectives,* ed. by René Wellek and Nonna D. Wellek, 1984.

GOOSEBERRIES

Translated by Constance Garnett

The whole sky had been overcast with rain-clouds from early morning; it was a still day, not hot, but heavy, as it is in gray dull weather when the clouds have been hanging over the country for a long while, when one expects rain and it does not come. Ivan Ivanovitch, the veterinary surgeon, and Burkin, the high-school teacher, were already tired from walking, and the fields seemed to them endless. Far ahead of them they could just see the windmills of the village of Mironositskoe; on the right stretched a row of hillocks which disappeared in the distance behind the village, and they both knew that this was the bank of the river, that there were meadows, green willows, homesteads there, and that if one stood on one of the hillocks one could see from it the same vast plain, telegraph-wires, and a train which in the distance looked like a crawling caterpillar, and that in clear weather one could even see the town. Now, in still weather, when all nature seemed mild and dreamy, Ivan Ivanovitch and Burkin were filled with love of that countryside, and both thought how great, how beautiful a land it was.

"Last time we were in Prokofy's barn," said Burkin, "you were about to tell me a story."

"Yes; I meant to tell you about my brother."

Ivan Ivanovitch heaved a deep sigh and lighted a pipe to begin to tell his story, but just at that moment the rain began. And five minutes later heavy rain came down, covering the sky, and it was hard to tell when it would be over. Ivan Ivanovitch and Burkin stopped in hesitation; the dogs, already drenched, stood with their tails between their legs gazing at them feelingly.

"We must take shelter somewhere," said Burkin. "Let us go to Alehin's; it's close by."

"Come along."

They turned aside and walked through mown fields, sometimes going straight forward, sometimes turning to the right, till they came out on the road. Soon they saw poplars, a garden, then the red roofs of barns; there

was a gleam of the river, and the view opened on to a broad expanse of water with a windmill and a white bath-house: this was Sofino, where Alehin lived.

The watermill was at work, drowning the sound of the rain; the dam was shaking. Here wet horses with drooping heads were standing near their carts, and men were walking about covered with sacks. It was damp, muddy, and desolate; the water looked cold and malignant. Ivan Ivanovitch and Burkin were already conscious of a feeling of wetness, messiness, and discomfort all over; their feet were heavy with mud, and when, crossing the dam, they went up to the barns, they were silent, as though they were angry with one another.

In one of the barns there was the sound of a winnowing machine,[1] the door was open, and clouds of dust were coming from it. In the doorway was standing Alehin himself, a man of forty, tall and stout, with long hair, more like a professor or an artist than a landowner. He had on a white shirt that badly needed washing, a rope for a belt, drawers instead of trousers, and his boots, too, were plastered up with mud and straw. His eyes and nose were black with dust. He recognized Ivan Ivanovitch and Burkin, and was apparently much delighted to see them.

"Go into the house, gentlemen," he said, smiling; "I'll come directly, this minute."

It was a big two-storied house. Alehin lived in the lower story, with arched ceilings and little windows, where the bailiffs had once lived; here everything was plain, and there was a smell of rye bread, cheap vodka, and harness. He went upstairs into the best rooms only on rare occasions, when visitors came. Ivan Ivanovitch and Burkin were met in the house by a maid-servant, a young woman so beautiful that they both stood still and looked at one another.

"You can't imagine how delighted I am to see you, my friends," said Alehin, going into the hall with them. "It is a surprise! Pelagea," he said, addressing the girl, "give our visitors something to change into. Only I must first go and wash, for I almost think I have not washed since spring. Wouldn't you like to come into the bath-house? and meanwhile they will get things ready here."

Beautiful Pelagea, looking so refined and soft, brought them towels and soap, and Alehin went to the bath-house with his guests.

"It's a long time since I had a wash," he said, undressing. "I have got a nice bath-house, as you see—my father built it—but I somehow never have time to wash."

He sat down on the steps and soaped his long hair and his neck, and the water round him turned brown.

"Yes, I must say," said Ivan Ivanovitch meaningly, looking at his head.

"It's a long time since I washed . . ." said Alehin with embarrassment, giving himself a second soaping, and the water near him turned dark blue, like ink.

Ivan Ivanovitch went outside, plunged into the water with a loud splash, and swam in the rain, flinging his arms out wide. He stirred the water into waves which set the white lilies bobbing up and down; he swam to the very

[1] Threshing machine, to separate grain from chaff.

middle of the millpond and dived, and came up a minute later in another place, and swam on, and kept on diving, trying to touch the bottom.

"Oh, my goodness!" he repeated continually, enjoying himself thoroughly. "Oh, my goodness!" He swam to the mill, talked to the peasants there, then returned and lay on his back in the middle of the pond, turning his face to the rain. Burkin and Alehin were dressed and ready to go, but he still went on swimming and diving. "Oh, my goodness! . . ." he said. "Oh, Lord, have mercy on me! . . ."

"That's enough!" Burkin shouted to him.

They went back to the house. And only when the lamp was lighted in the big drawing-room upstairs, and Burkin and Ivan Ivanovitch, attired in silk dressing-gowns and warm slippers, were sitting in arm-chairs; and Alehin, washed and combed, in a new coat, was walking about the drawing-room, evidently enjoying the feeling of warmth, cleanliness, dry clothes, and light shoes; and when lovely Pelagea, stepping noiselessly on the carpet and smiling softly, handed tea and jam on a tray—only then Ivan Ivanovitch began on his story, and it seemed as though not only Burkin and Alehin were listening, but also the ladies, young and old, and the officers who looked down upon them sternly and calmly from their gold frames.

"There are two of us brothers," he began—"I, Ivan Ivanovitch, and my brother, Nikolay Ivanovitch, two years younger. I went in for a learned profession and became a veterinary surgeon, while Nikolay sat in a government office from the time he was nineteen. Our father, Tchimsha-Himalaisky, was a kantonist;[2] but he rose to be an officer and left us a little estate and the rank of nobility. After his death the little estate went in debts and legal expenses; but, anyway, we had spent our childhood running wild in the country. Like peasant children, we passed our days and nights in the fields and the woods, looked after horses, stripped the bark off the trees, fished, and so on. . . . And, you know, whoever has once in his life caught perch or has seen the migrating of the thrushes in autumn, watched how they float in flocks over the village on bright, cool days, he will never be a real townsman, and will have a yearning for freedom to the day of his death. My brother was miserable in the government office. Years passed by, and he went on sitting in the same place, went on writing the same papers and thinking of one and the same thing—how to get into the country. And this yearning by degrees passed into a definite desire, into a dream of buying himself a little farm somewhere on the banks of a river or a lake.

"He was a gentle, good-natured fellow, and I was fond of him, but I never sympathized with this desire to shut himself up for the rest of his life in a little farm of his own. It's the correct thing to say that a man needs no more than six feet of earth. But six feet is what a corpse needs, not a man. And they say, too, now, that if our intellectual classes are attracted to the land and yearn for a farm, it's a good thing. But these farms are just the same as six feet of earth. To retreat from town, from the struggle, from the bustle of life, to retreat and bury oneself in one's farm—it's not life, it's egoism, laziness, it's monasticism of a sort, but monasticism without good

[2] Son of a common soldier, registered at birth in the army.

works. A man does not need six feet of earth or a farm, but the whole globe, all nature, where he can have room to display all the qualities and peculiarities of his free spirit.

"My brother Nikolay, sitting in his government office, dreamed of how he would eat his own cabbages, which would fill the whole yard with such a savory smell, take his meals on the green grass, sleep in the sun, sit for whole hours on the seat by the gate gazing at the fields and the forest. Gardening books and the agricultural hints in calendars were his delight, his favorite spiritual sustenance; he enjoyed reading newspapers, too, but the only thing he read in them were the advertisements of so many acres of arable land and a grass meadow with farm-houses and buildings, a river, a garden, a mill and millponds, for sale. And his imagination pictured the garden-paths, flowers and fruit, starling cotes, the carp in the pond, and all that sort of thing, you know. These imaginary pictures were of different kinds according to the advertisements which he came across, but for some reason in every one of them he had always to have gooseberries. He could not imagine a homestead, he could not picture an idyllic nook, without gooseberries.

"'Country life has its conveniences,' he would sometimes say. 'You sit on the verandah and you drink tea, while your ducks swim on the pond, there is a delicious smell everywhere, and . . . and the gooseberries are growing.'

"He used to draw a map of his property, and in every map there were the same things—(*a*) house for the family, (*b*) servants' quarters, (*c*) kitchen garden, (*d*) gooseberry-bushes. He lived parsimoniously, was frugal in food and drink, his clothes were beyond description; he looked like a beggar, but kept on saving and putting money in the bank. He grew fearfully avaricious. I did not like to look at him, and I used to give him something and send him presents for Christmas and Easter, but he used to save that too. Once a man is absorbed by an idea there is no doing anything with him.

"Years passed: he was transferred to another province. He was over forty, and he was still reading the advertisements in the papers and saving up. Then I heard he was married. Still with the same object of buying a farm and having gooseberries, he married an elderly and ugly widow without a trace of feeling for her, simply because she had filthy lucre. He went on living frugally after marrying her, and kept her short of food, while he put her money in the bank in his name.

"Her first husband had been a postmaster, and with him she was accustomed to pies and home-made wines, while with her second husband she did not get enough black bread; she began to pine away with this sort of life, and three years later she gave up her soul to God. And I need hardly say that my brother never for one moment imagined that he was responsible for her death. Money, like vodka, makes a man queer. In our town there was a merchant who, before he died, ordered a plateful of honey and ate up all his money and lottery tickets with the honey, so that no one might get the benefit of it. While I was inspecting cattle at a railway-station, a cattle-dealer fell under an engine and had his leg cut off. We carried him into the waiting-room, the blood was flowing—it was a horrible thing—and he kept asking them to look for his leg and was very much worried about it; there were twenty roubles in the boot on the leg that had been cut off, and he was afraid they would be lost."

"That's a story from a different opera," said Burkin.

"After his wife's death," Ivan Ivanovitch went on, after thinking for half a minute, "my brother began looking out for an estate for himself. Of course, you may look about for five years and yet end by making a mistake, and buying something quite different from what you have dreamed of. My brother Nikolay bought through an agent a mortgaged estate of three hundred and thirty acres, with a house for the family, with servants' quarters, with a park, but with no orchard, no gooseberry-bushes, and no duck-pond; there was a river, but the water in it was the color of coffee, because on one side of the estate there was a brickyard and on the other a factory for burning bones. But Nikolay Ivanovitch did not grieve much, he ordered twenty gooseberry-bushes, planted them, and began living as a country gentleman.

"Last year I went to pay him a visit. I thought I would go and see what it was like. In his letters my brother called his estate 'Tchumbaroklov Waste, alias Himalaiskoe.' I reached 'alias Himalaiskoe' in the afternoon. It was hot. Everywhere there were ditches, fences, hedges, fir-trees planted in rows, and there was no knowing how to get to the yard, where to put one's horse. I went up to the house, and was met by a fat red dog that looked like a pig. It wanted to bark, but it was too lazy. The cook, a fat, barefooted woman, came out of the kitchen, and she, too, looked like a pig, and said that her master was resting after dinner. I went in to see my brother. He was sitting up in bed with a quilt over his legs; he had grown older, fatter, wrinkled; his cheeks, his nose, and his mouth all stuck out—he looked as though he might begin grunting into the quilt at any moment.

"We embraced each other, and shed tears of joy and of sadness at the thought that we had once been young and now were both gray-headed and near the grave. He dressed, and led me out to show me the estate.

"'Well, how are you getting on here?' I asked.

"'Oh, all right, thank God; I am getting on very well.'

"He was no more a poor timid clerk, but a real landowner, a gentleman. He was already accustomed to it, had grown used to it, and liked it. He ate a great deal, went to the bath-house, was growing stout, was already at law with the village commune and both factories, and was very much offended when the peasants did not call him 'Your Honor.' And he concerned himself with the salvation of his soul in a substantial, gentlemanly manner, and performed deeds of charity, not simply, but with an air of consequence. And what deeds of charity! He treated the peasants for every sort of disease with soda and castor oil, and on his name-day had a thanksgiving service in the middle of the village, and then treated the peasants to a gallon of vodka—he thought that was the thing to do. Oh, those horrible gallons of vodka! One day the fat landowner hauls the peasants up before the district captain for trespass, and next day, in honor of a holiday, treats them to a gallon of vodka, and they drink and shout 'Hurrah!' and when they are drunk bow down to his feet. A change of life for the better, and being well-fed and idle develop in a Russian the most insolent self-conceit. Nikolay Ivanovitch, who at one time in the government office was afraid to have any views of his own, now could say nothing that was not gospel truth, and uttered such truths in the tone of a prime minister. 'Education is essential, but for the peasants it is premature.' 'Corporal punishment is harmful

as a rule, but in some cases it is necessary and there is nothing to take its place.'

"'I know the peasants and understand how to treat them,' he would say. 'The peasants like me. I need only to hold up my little finger and the peasants will do anything I like.'

"And all this, observe, was uttered with a wise, benevolent smile. He repeated twenty times over 'We noblemen,' 'I as a noble'; obviously he did not remember that our grandfather was a peasant, and our father a soldier. Even our surname Tchimsha-Himalaisky, in reality so incongruous, seemed to him now melodious, distinguished, and very agreeable.

"But the point just now is not he, but myself. I want to tell you about the change that took place in me during the brief hours I spent at his country place. In the evening, when we were drinking tea, the cook put on the table a plateful of gooseberries. They were not bought, but his own gooseberries, gathered for the first time since the bushes were planted. Nikolay Ivanovitch laughed and looked for a minute in silence at the gooseberries, with tears in his eyes; he could not speak for excitement. Then he put one gooseberry in his mouth, looked at me with the triumph of a child who has at last received his favorite toy, and said:

"'How delicious!'

"And he ate them greedily, continually repeating, 'Ah, how delicious! Do taste them!'

"They were sour and unripe, but, as Pushkin says:

> "'Dearer to us the falsehood that exalts
> Than hosts of baser truths.'

"I saw a happy man whose cherished dream was so obviously fulfilled, who had attained his object in life, who had gained what he wanted, who was satisfied with his fate and himself. There is always, for some reason, an element of sadness mingled with my thoughts of human happiness, and, on this occasion, at the sight of a happy man I was overcome by an oppressive feeling that was close upon despair. It was particularly oppressive at night. A bed was made up for me in the room next to my brother's bedroom, and I could hear that he was awake, and that he kept getting up and going to the plate of gooseberries and taking one. I reflected how many satisfied, happy people there really are! What a suffocating force it is! You look at life: the insolence and idleness of the strong, the ignorance and brutishness of the weak, incredible poverty all about us, overcrowding, degeneration, drunkenness, hypocrisy, lying. . . . Yet all is calm and stillness in the houses and in the streets; of the fifty thousand living in a town, there is not one who would cry out, who would give vent to his indignation aloud. We see the people going to market for provisions, eating by day, sleeping by night, talking their silly nonsense, getting married, growing old, serenely escorting their dead to the cemetery; but we do not see and we do not hear those who suffer, and what is terrible in life goes on somewhere behind the scenes. . . . Everything is quiet and peaceful, and nothing protests but mute statistics: so many people gone out of their minds, so many gallons of vodka drunk, so many children dead from malnutrition. . . . And this order of things is evidently necessary; evidently the happy man only feels at

ease because the unhappy bear their burdens in silence, and without that silence happiness would be impossible. It's a case of general hypnotism. There ought to be behind the door of every happy, contented man some one standing with a hammer continually reminding him with a tap that there are unhappy people; that however happy he may be, life will show him her laws sooner or later, trouble will come for him—disease, poverty, losses—and no one will see or hear, just as now he neither sees nor hears others. But there is no man with a hammer; the happy man lives at his ease, and trivial daily cares faintly agitate him like the wind in the aspen-tree—and all goes well.

"That night I realized that I, too, was happy and contented," Ivan Ivanovitch went on, getting up. "I, too, at dinner and at the hunt liked to lay down the law on life and religion, and the way to manage the peasantry. I, too, used to say that science was light, that culture was essential, but for the simple people reading and writing was enough for the time. Freedom is a blessing, I used to say; we can no more do without it than without air, but we must wait a little. Yes, I used to talk like that, and now I ask, 'For what reason are we to wait?'" asked Ivan Ivanovitch, looking angrily at Burkin. "Why wait, I ask you? What grounds have we for waiting? I shall be told, it can't be done all at once; every idea takes shape in life gradually, in its due time. But who is it says that? Where is the proof that it's right? You will fall back upon the natural order of things, the uniformity of phenomena; but is there order and uniformity in the fact that I, a living, thinking man, stand over a chasm and wait for it to close of itself, or to fill up with mud at the very time when perhaps I might leap over it or build a bridge across it? And again, wait for the sake of what? Wait till there's no strength to live? And meanwhile one must live, and one wants to live!

"I went away from my brother's early in the morning, and ever since then it has been unbearable for me to be in town. I am oppressed by its peace and quiet; I am afraid to look at the windows, for there is no spectacle more painful to me now than the sight of a happy family sitting around the table drinking tea. I am old and am not fit for the struggle; I am not even capable of hatred; I can only grieve inwardly, feel irritated and vexed; but at night my head is hot from the rush of ideas, and I cannot sleep. . . . Ah, if I were young!"

Ivan Ivanovitch walked backwards and forwards in excitement, and repeated: "If I were young!"

He suddenly went up to Alehin and began pressing first one of his hands and then the other.

"Pavel Konstantinovitch," he said in an imploring voice, "don't be calm and contented, don't let yourself be put to sleep! While you are young, strong, confident, be not weary in well-doing! There is no happiness, and there ought not to be; but if there is a meaning and an object in life, that meaning and object is not our happiness, but something greater and more rational. Do good!"

And all this Ivan Ivanovitch said with a pitiful, imploring smile, as though he were asking him a personal favor.

Then all three sat in arm-chairs at different ends of the drawing-room and were silent. Ivan Ivanovitch's story had not satisfied either Burkin or Alehin. When the generals and ladies gazed down from their gilt frames,

looking in the dusk as though they were alive, it was dreary to listen to the story of the poor clerk who ate gooseberries. They felt inclined, for some reason, to talk about elegant people, about women. And their sitting in the drawing-room where everything—the chandeliers in their covers, the arm-chairs, and the carpet under their feet—reminded them that those very people who were now looking down from their frames had once moved about, sat, drunk tea in this room, and the fact that lovely Pelagea was moving noiselessly about was better than any story.

Alehin was fearfully sleepy; he had got up early, before three o'clock in the morning, to look after his work, and now his eyes were closing; but he was afraid his visitors might tell some interesting story after he had gone, and he lingered on. He did not go into the question whether what Ivan Ivanovitch had just said was right and true. His visitors did not talk of groats, nor of hay, nor of tar, but of something that had no direct bearing on his life, and he was glad and wanted them to go on.

"It's bed-time, though," said Burkin, getting up. "Allow me to wish you good-night."

Alehin said good-night and went downstairs to his own domain, while the visitors remained upstairs. They were both taken for the night to a big room where there stood two old wooden beds decorated with carvings, and in the corner was an ivory crucifix. The big cool beds, which had been made by the lovely Pelagea, smelt agreeably of clean linen.

Ivan Ivanovitch undressed in silence and got into bed.

"Lord forgive us sinners!" he said, and put his head under the quilt.

His pipe lying on the table smelt strongly of stale tobacco, and Burkin could not sleep for a long while, and kept wondering where the oppressive smell came from.

The rain was pattering on the window-panes all night.

THE CHERRY ORCHARD

Translated by Constance Garnett

CHARACTERS[1]

MADAME RANEVSKY (LYUBOV ANDREYEVNA), *the owner of the cherry orchard*	EPIHODOV, SEMYON PANTALEYEVITCH, *a clerk*
ANYA, *her daughter, aged seventeen*	DUNYASHA, *a maid*
	FIRS, *an old valet, aged eighty-seven*

[1] The variety of names for the same person in nineteenth-century Russian literature is sometimes a source of confusion. Russians have three names: a given name (Lyubov or Leonid), a patronymic (Andreyevna, or "daughter of Andrey"; Andreyevitch, or "son of Andrey"), and a surname. A person may be addressed in a number of ways: by title and surname, as in "Madame Ranevsky" (formal), by given name and patronymic, as in "Lyubov Andreyevna" (respectful, but less formal), by given name alone, as in "Lyubov" or "Pyotr" (familiar), or by a diminutive of the given name: "Lyuba" or "Petya" (intimate or affectionate).

VARYA, *her adopted daughter,*
 aged twenty-four
GAEV, LEONID ANDREYEVITCH,
 brother of Madame Ranevsky
LOPAHIN, YERMOLAY ALEXEYE-
VITCH, *a merchant*
TROFIMOV, PYOTR SERGEYE-
VITCH, *a student*
SEMYONOV-PISHTCHIK,
 a landowner
CHARLOTTA IVANOVNA,
 a governess

YASHA, *a young valet*
A VAGRANT
THE STATIONMASTER
A POST-OFFICE CLERK
VISITORS
SERVANTS

*The action takes place on the
estate of* MADAME RANEVSKY

ACT ONE

SCENE

A room, which has always been called the nursery. One of the doors leads into
ANYA'S *room. Dawn, sun rises during the scene. May, the cherry trees in flower, but
it is cold in the garden with the frost of early morning. Windows closed.*

[*Enter* DUNYASHA *with a candle and* LOPAHIN *with a book in his hand.*]
LOPAHIN. The train's in, thank God. What time is it?
DUNYASHA. Nearly two o'clock. [*Puts out the candle.*] It's daylight already.
LOPAHIN. The train's late! Two hours, at least. [*Yawns and stretches.*] I'm a
 pretty one; what a fool I've been. Came here on purpose to meet them
 at the station and dropped asleep. . . . Dozed off as I sat in the chair.
 It's annoying. . . . You might have waked me.
DUNYASHA. I thought you had gone. [*Listens.*] There, I do believe they're
 coming!
LOPAHIN. [*Listens.*] No, what with the luggage and one thing and another.
 [*A pause.*] Lyubov Andreyevna has been abroad five years; I don't know
 what she is like now. . . . She's a splendid woman. A good-natured,
 kind-hearted woman. I remember when I was a lad of fifteen, my poor
 father—he used to keep a little shop here in the village in those days—
 gave me a punch in the face with his fist and made my nose bleed. We
 were in the yard here, I forget what we'd come about—he had had a
 drop. Lyubov Andreyevna—I can see her now—she was a slim young
 girl then—took me to wash my face, and then brought me into this very
 room, into the nursery. "Don't cry, little peasant," says she, "it will be
 well in time for your wedding day." . . . [*A pause.*] Little peasant. . . . My
 father was a peasant, it's true, but here am I in a white waistcoat and
 brown shoes, like a pig in a bun shop. Yes, I'm a rich man, but for all my
 money, come to think, a peasant I was, and a peasant I am. [*Turns over
 the pages of the book.*] I've been reading this book and I can't make head
 or tail of it. I fell asleep over it. [*A pause.*]
DUNYASHA. The dogs have been awake all night, they feel that the mistress
 is coming.
LOPAHIN. Why, what's the matter with you, Dunyasha?
DUNYASHA. My hands are all of a tremble. I feel as though I should faint.

LOPAHIN. You're a spoilt soft creature, Dunyasha. And dressed like a lady too, and your hair done up. That's not the thing. One must know one's place.

[*Enter* EPIHODOV *with a nosegay; he wears a pea jacket and highly polished creaking topboots; he drops the nosegay as he comes in.*]

EPIHODOV [*picking up the nosegay*]. Here! the gardener's sent this, says you're to put it in the dining room. [*Gives* DUNYASHA *the nosegay.*]

LOPAHIN. And bring me some kvass.[2]

DUNYASHA. I will. [*Goes out.*]

EPIHODOV. It's chilly this morning, three degrees of frost, though the cherries are all in flower. I can't say much for our climate. [*Sighs.*] I can't. Our climate is not often propitious to the occasion. Yermolay Alexeyevitch, permit me to call your attention to the fact that I purchased myself a pair of boots the day before yesterday, and they creak, I venture to assure you, so that there's no tolerating them. What ought I to grease them with?

LOPAHIN. Oh, shut up! Don't bother me.

EPIHODOV. Every day some misfortune befalls me. I don't complain. I'm used to it, and I wear a smiling face. [DUNYASHA *comes in, hands* LOPAHIN *the kvass.*] I am going. [*Stumbles against a chair, which falls over.*] There! [*As though triumphant*] There you see now, excuse the expression, an accident like that among others. . . . It's positively remarkable. [*Goes out.*]

DUNYASHA. Do you know, Yermolay Alexeyevitch, I must confess, Epihodov has made me a proposal.

LOPAHIN. Ah!

DUNYASHA. I'm sure I don't know. . . . He's a harmless fellow, but sometimes when he begins talking, there's no making anything of it. It's all very fine and expressive, only there's no understanding it. I've a sort of liking for him too. He loves me to distraction. He's an unfortunate man; every day there's something. They tease him about it—two and twenty misfortunes they call him.

LOPAHIN [*listening*]. There! I do believe they're coming.

DUNYASHA. They are coming! What's the matter with me? . . . I'm cold all over.

LOPAHIN. They really are coming. Let's go and meet them. Will she know me? It's five years since I saw her.

DUNYASHA [*in a flutter*]. I shall drop this very minute. . . . Ah, I shall drop.

[*There is a sound of two carriages driving up to the house.* LOPAHIN *and* DUNYASHA *go out quickly. The stage is left empty. A noise is heard in the adjoining rooms.* FIRS, *who has driven to meet* MADAME RANEVSKY, *crosses the stage hurriedly leaning on a stick. He is wearing old-fashioned livery and a high hat. He says*]

[2]Russian beer made from barley, malt, and rye.

*something to himself, but not a word can
be distinguished. The noise behind the
scenes goes on increasing. A voice: "Come,
let's go in here." Enter* LYUBOV AN-
DREYEVNA, ANYA, *and* CHARLOTTA
IVANOVNA *with a pet dog on a chain, all
in travelling dresses.* VARYA *in an out-
door coat with a kerchief over her head,*
GAEV, SEMYONOV-PISHTCHIK, LOPA-
HIN, DUNYASHA *with bag and parasol,
servants with other articles. All walk
across the room.*]

ANYA. Let's come in here. Do you remember what room this is, mamma?

LYUBOV [*joyfully, through her tears*]. The nursery!

VARYA. How cold it is, my hands are numb. [*To* LYUBOV ANDREYEVNA]
Your rooms, the white room and the lavender one, are just the same as
ever, mamma.

LYUBOV. My nursery, dear delightful room. . . . I used to sleep here when
I was little. . . . [*Cries.*] And here I am, like a little child. . . . [*Kisses her
brother and* VARYA, *and then her brother again.*] Varya's just the same as
ever, like a nun. And I knew Dunyasha. [*Kisses* DUNYASHA.]

GAEV. The train was two hours late. What do you think of that? Is that the
way to do things?

CHARLOTTA [*to* PISHTCHIK]. My dog eats nuts, too.

PISHTCHIK [*wonderingly*]. Fancy that!

[*They all go out except* ANYA *and* DUN-
YASHA.]

DUNYASHA. We've been expecting you so long. [*Takes* ANYA'S *hat and coat.*]

ANYA. I haven't slept for four nights on the journey. I feel dreadfully cold.

DUNYASHA. You set out in Lent, there was snow and frost, and now? My
darling! [*Laughs and kisses her.*] I *have* missed you, my precious, my joy. I
must tell you . . . I can't put it off a minute. . . .

ANYA [*wearily*]. What now?

DUNYASHA. Epihodov, the clerk, made me a proposal just after Easter.

ANYA. It's always the same thing with you. . . . [*Straightening her hair*] I've
lost all my hairpins. . . . [*She is staggering from exhaustion.*]

DUNYASHA. I don't know what to think, really. He does love me, he does
love me so!

ANYA [*looking towards her door, tenderly*]. My own room, my windows just as
though I had never gone away. I'm home! Tomorrow morning I shall
get up and run into the garden. . . . Oh, if I could get to sleep! I haven't
slept all the journey, I was so anxious and worried.

DUNYASHA. Pyotr Sergeyevitch came the day before yesterday.

ANYA [*joyfully*]. Petya!

DUNYASHA. He's asleep in the bathhouse, he has settled in there. I'm afraid
of being in their way, says he. [*Glancing at her watch*] I was to have waked
him, but Varvara Mihalovna told me not to. Don't you wake him, says
she.

[*Enter* VARYA *with a bunch of keys at her
waist.*]

VARYA. Dunyasha, coffee and make haste. . . . Mamma's asking for coffee.
DUNYASHA. This very minute. [*Goes out.*]
VARYA. Well, thank God, you've come. You're home again [*petting her*]. My
 little darling has come back! My precious beauty has come back again!
ANYA. I have had a time of it!
VARYA. I can fancy.
ANYA. We set off in Holy Week—it was so cold then, and all the way Char-
 lotta would talk and show off her tricks. What did you want to burden
 me with Charlotta for?
VARYA. You couldn't have travelled all alone, darling. At seventeen!
ANYA. We got to Paris at last, it was cold there—snow. I speak French
 shockingly. Mamma lives on the fifth floor, I went up to her and there
 were a lot of French people, ladies, an old priest with a book. The place
 smelt of tobacco and so comfortless. I felt sorry, oh! so sorry for
 mamma all at once, I put my arms round her neck, and hugged her and
 wouldn't let her go. Mamma was as kind as she could be, and she
 cried. . . .
VARYA [*through her tears*]. Don't speak of it, don't speak of it!
ANYA. She had sold her villa at Mentone, she had nothing left, nothing. I
 hadn't a farthing left either, we only just had enough to get here. And
 mamma doesn't understand! When we had dinner at the stations, she
 always ordered the most expensive things and gave the waiters a whole
 rouble. Charlotta's just the same. Yasha too must have the same as we
 do; it's simply awful. You know Yasha is mamma's valet now, we
 brought him here with us.
VARYA. Yes, I've seen the young rascal.
ANYA. Well, tell me—have you paid the arrears on the mortgage?
VARYA. How could we get the money?
ANYA. Oh, dear! Oh, dear!
VARYA. In August the place will be sold.
ANYA. My goodness!
LOPAHIN. [*Peeps in at the door and moos like a cow.*] Moo! [*Disappears.*]
VARYA [*weeping*]. There, that's what I could do to him [*shakes her fist*].
ANYA [*embracing* VARYA, *softly*]. Varya, has he made you an offer? [VARYA
 shakes her head.] Why, but he loves you. Why is it you don't come to an
 understanding? What are you waiting for?
VARYA. I believe that there never will be anything between us. He has a lot
 to do, he has no time for me . . . and takes no notice of me. Bless the
 man, it makes me miserable to see him. . . . Everyone's talking of our
 being married, everyone's congratulating me, and all the while there's
 really nothing in it; it's all like a dream. [*In another tone*] You have a new
 brooch like a bee.
ANYA [*mournfully*]. Mamma bought it. [*Goes into her own room and in a light-
 hearted childish tone*] And you know, in Paris I went up in a balloon!
VARYA. My darling's home again! My pretty is home again!
 [DUNYASHA *returns with the coffee pot
 and is making the coffee.*]
VARYA [*standing at the door*]. All day long, darling, as I go about looking
 after the house, I keep dreaming all the time. If only we could marry
 you to a rich man, then I should feel more at rest. Then I would go off

by myself on a pilgrimage to Kiev, to Moscow . . . and so I would spend my life going from one holy place to another. . . . I would go on and on. . . . What bliss!

ANYA. The birds are singing in the garden. What time is it?

VARYA. It must be nearly three. It's time you were asleep, darling. [*Going into* ANYA'S *room*] What bliss!

> [YASHA *enters with a rug and a travelling bag.*]

YASHA. [*Crosses the stage, mincingly.*] May one come in here, pray?

DUNYASHA. I shouldn't have known you, Yasha. How you have changed abroad.

YASHA. H'm! . . . And who are you?

DUNYASHA. When you went away, I was that high. [*Shows distance from floor.*] Dunyasha, Fyodor's daughter. . . . You don't remember me!

YASHA. H'm! . . . You're a peach! [*Looks round and embraces her: she shrieks and drops a saucer.* YASHA *goes out hastily.*]

VARYA [*in the doorway, in a tone of vexation*]. What now?

DUNYASHA [*through her tears*]. I have broken a saucer.

VARYA. Well, that brings good luck.

ANYA [*coming out of her room*]. We ought to prepare mamma: Petya is here.

VARYA. I told them not to wake him.

ANYA [*dreamily*]. It's six years since father died. Then only a month later little brother Grisha was drowned in the river, such a pretty boy he was, only seven. It was more than mamma could bear, so she went away, went away without looking back [*shuddering*]. . . . How well I understand her, if only she knew! [*A pause.*] And Petya Trofimov was Grisha's tutor, he may remind her.

> [*Enter* FIRS: *he is wearing a pea jacket and a white waistcoat.*]

FIRS. [*Goes up to the coffee pot, anxiously.*] The mistress will be served here. [*Puts on white gloves.*] Is the coffee ready? [*Sternly to* DUNYASHA] Girl! Where's the cream?

DUNYASHA. Ah, mercy on us! [*Goes out quickly.*]

FIRS [*fussing round the coffee pot*]. Ech! you good-for-nothing! [*Muttering to himself*] Come back from Paris. And the old master used to go to Paris too . . . horses all the way. [*Laughs.*]

VARYA. What is it, Firs?

FIRS. What is your pleasure? [*Gleefully*] My lady has come home! I have lived to see her again! Now I can die. [*Weeps with joy.*]

> [*Enter* LYUBOV ANDREYEVNA, GAEV *and* SEMYONOV-PISHTCHIK; *the latter is in a short-waisted full coat of fine cloth, and full trousers.* GAEV, *as he comes in, makes a gesture with his arms and his whole body, as though he were playing billiards.*]

LYUBOV. How does it go? Let me remember. Cannon off the red!

GAEV. That's it—in off the white! Why, once, sister, we used to sleep together in this very room, and now I'm fifty-one, strange as it seems.

LOPAHIN. Yes, time flies.

GAEV. What do you say?

LOPAHIN. Time, I say, flies.

GAEV. What a smell of patchouli!³

ANYA. I'm going to bed. Good night, mamma. [*Kisses her mother.*]

LYUBOV. My precious darling. [*Kisses her hands.*] Are you glad to be home? I can't believe it.

ANYA. Good night, uncle.

GAEV [*kissing her face and hands*]. God bless you! How like you are to your mother! [*To his sister*] At her age you were just the same, Lyuba.

> [ANYA *shakes hands with* LOPAHIN *and* PISHTCHIK, *then goes out, shutting the door after her.*]

LYUBOV. She's quite worn out.

PISHTCHIK. Aye, it's a long journey, to be sure.

VARYA [*to* LOPAHIN *and* PISHTCHIK]. Well, gentlemen? It's three o'clock and time to say good-by.

LYUBOV. [*Laughs.*] You're just the same as ever, Varya. [*Draws her to her and kisses her.*] I'll just drink my coffee and then we will all go and rest. [FIRS *puts a cushion under her feet.*] Thanks, friend. I am so fond of coffee, I drink it day and night. Thanks, dear old man. [*Kisses* FIRS.]

VARYA. I'll just see whether all the things have been brought in. [*Goes out.*]

LYUBOV. Can it really be me sitting here? [*Laughs.*] I want to dance about and clap my hands. [*Covers her face with her hands.*] And I could drop asleep in a moment! God knows I love my country, I love it tenderly; I couldn't look out of the window in the train, I kept crying so. [*Through her tears*] But I must drink my coffee, though. Thank you, Firs, thanks, dear old man. I'm so glad to find you still alive.

FIRS. The day before yesterday.

GAEV. He's rather deaf.

LOPAHIN. I have to set off for Harkov directly, at five o'clock. . . . It is annoying! I wanted to have a look at you, and a little talk. . . . You are just as splendid as ever.

PISHTCHIK [*breathing heavily*]. Handsomer, indeed. . . . Dressed in Parisian style . . . completely bowled me over.

LOPAHIN. Your brother, Leonid Andreyevitch here, is always saying that I'm a low-born knave, that I'm a money grubber, but I don't care one straw for that. Let him talk. Only I do want you to believe in me as you used to. I do want your wonderful tender eyes to look at me as they used to in the old days. Merciful God! My father was a serf of your father and of your grandfather, but you—you—did so much for me once, that I've forgotten all that; I love you as though you were my kin . . . more than my kin.

LYUBOV. I can't sit still, I simply can't. . . . [*Jumps up and walks about in violent agitation.*] This happiness is too much for me. . . . You may laugh at me, I know I'm silly. . . . My own bookcase. [*Kisses the bookcase.*] My little table.

GAEV. Nurse died while you were away.

³A penetrating East Indian perfume.

LYUBOV. [*Sits down and drinks coffee.*] Yes, the Kingdom of Heaven be hers! You wrote me of her death.

GAEV. And Anastasy is dead. Squinting Petruchka has left me and is in service now with the police captain in the town. [*Takes a box of caramels out of his pocket and sucks one.*]

PISHTCHIK. My daughter, Dashenka, wishes to be remembered to you.

LOPAHIN. I want to tell you something very pleasant and cheering [*glancing at his watch*]. I'm going directly . . . there's no time to say much . . . well, I can say it in a couple of words. I needn't tell you your cherry orchard is to be sold to pay your debts; the 22nd of August is the date fixed for the sale; but don't you worry, dearest lady, you may sleep in peace, there is a way of saving it. . . . This is what I propose. I beg your attention! Your estate is not twenty miles from the town, the railway runs close by it, and if the cherry orchard and the land along the river bank were cut up into building plots and then let on lease for summer villas, you would make an income of at least 25,000 roubles a year out of it.

GAEV. That's all rot, if you'll excuse me.

LYUBOV. I don't quite understand you, Yermolay Alexeyevitch.

LOPAHIN. You will get a rent of at least 25 roubles a year for a three-acre plot from summer visitors, and if you say the word now, I'll bet you what you like there won't be one square foot of ground vacant by the autumn, all the plots will be taken up. I congratulate you; in fact, you are saved. It's a perfect situation with that deep river. Only, of course, it must be cleared—all the old buildings, for example, must be removed, this house too, which is really good for nothing and the old cherry orchard must be cut down.

LYUBOV. Cut down? My dear fellow, forgive me, but you don't know what you are talking about. If there is one thing interesting—remarkable indeed—in the whole province, it's just our cherry orchard.

LOPAHIN. The only thing remarkable about the orchard is that it's a very large one. There's a crop of cherries every alternate year, and then there's nothing to be done with them, no one buys them.

GAEV. This orchard is mentioned in the "Encyclopaedia."

LOPAHIN [*glancing at his watch*]. If we don't decide on something and don't take some steps, on the 22nd of August the cherry orchard and the whole estate too will be sold by auction. Make up your minds! There is no other way of saving it, I'll take my oath on that. No, no!

FIRS. In old days, forty or fifty years ago, they used to dry the cherries, soak them, pickle them, make jam too, and they used——

GAEV. Be quiet, Firs.

FIRS. And they used to send the preserved cherries to Moscow and to Harkov by the wagon-load. That brought the money in! And the preserved cherries in those days were soft and juicy, sweet and fragrant. . . . They knew the way to do them then. . . .

LYUBOV. And where is the recipe now?

FIRS. It's forgotten. Nobody remembers it.

PISHTCHIK [*to* LYUBOV ANDREYEVNA]. What's it like in Paris? Did you eat frogs there?

LYUBOV. Oh, I ate crocodiles.

PISHTCHIK. Fancy that now!

LOPAHIN. There used to be only the gentlefolks and the peasants in the country, but now there are these summer visitors. All the towns, even the small ones, are surrounded nowadays by these summer villas. And one may say for sure, that in another twenty years there'll be many more of these people and that they'll be everywhere. At present the summer visitor only drinks tea in his verandah, but maybe he'll take to working his bit of land too, and then your cherry orchard would become happy, rich and prosperous. . . .

GAEV [*indignant*]. What rot!

[*Enter* VARYA AND YASHA.]

VARYA. There are two telegrams for you, mamma. [*Takes out keys and opens an old-fashioned bookcase with a loud crack.*] Here they are.

LYUBOV. From Paris. [*Tears the telegrams, without reading them.*] I have done with Paris.

GAEV. Do you know, Lyuba, how old that bookcase is? Last week I pulled out the bottom drawer and there I found the date branded on it. The bookcase was made just a hundred years ago. What do you say to that? We might have celebrated its jubilee. Though it's an inanimate object, still it is a *book* case.

PISHTCHIK [*amazed*]. A hundred years! Fancy that now.

GAEV. Yes. . . . It is a thing . . . [*feeling the bookcase*]. Dear, honored, bookcase! Hail to thee who for more than a hundred years hast served the pure ideals of good and justice; thy silent call to fruitful labor has never flagged in those hundred years, maintaining [*in tears*] in the generations of man, courage and faith in a brighter future and fostering in us ideals of good and social consciousness. [*A pause.*]

LOPAHIN. Yes. . . .

LYUBOV. You are just the same as ever, Leonid.

GAEV [*a little embarrassed*]. Cannon off the right into the pocket!

LOPAHIN [*looking at his watch*]. Well, it's time I was off.

YASHA [*handing* LYUBOV ANDREYEVNA *medicine*]. Perhaps you will take your pills now.

PISHTCHIK. You shouldn't take medicines, my dear madam . . . they do no harm and no good. Give them here . . . honored lady. [*Takes the pillbox, pours the pills into the hollow of his hand, blows on them, puts them in his mouth and drinks off some kvass.*] There!

LYUBOV [*in alarm*]. Why, you must be out of your mind!

PISHTCHIK. I have taken all the pills.

LOPAHIN. What a glutton! [*All laugh.*]

FIRS. His honor stayed with us in Easter week, ate a gallon and a half of cucumbers. . . . [*Mutters.*]

LYUBOV. What is he saying?

VARYA. He has taken to muttering like that for the last three years. We are used to it.

YASHA. His declining years!

[CHARLOTTA IVANOVNA, *a very thin, lanky figure in a white dress with a lorgnette in her belt, walks across the stage.*]

LOPAHIN. I beg your pardon, Charlotta Ivanovna, I have not had time to greet you. [*Tries to kiss her hand.*]

CHARLOTTA [*pulling away her hand*]. If I let you kiss my hand, you'll be wanting to kiss my elbow, and then my shoulder.

LOPAHIN. I've no luck today! [*All laugh.*] Charlotta Ivanovna, show us some tricks!

LYUBOV. Charlotta, do show us some tricks!

CHARLOTTA. I don't want to. I'm sleepy. [*Goes out.*]

LOPAHIN. In three weeks' time we shall meet again. [*Kisses* LYUBOV ANDREYEVNA'S *hand.*] Good-by till then—I must go. [*To* GAEV] Good-by. [*Kisses* PISHTCHIK.] Good-by. [*Gives his hand to* VARYA, *then to* FIRS *and* YASHA.] I don't want to go. [*To* LYUBOV ANDREYEVNA] If you think over my plan for the villas and make up your mind, then let me know; I will lend you 50,000 roubles. Think of it seriously.

VARYA [*angrily*]. Well, do go, for goodness sake.

LOPAHIN. I'm going, I'm going. [*Goes out.*]

GAEV. Low-born knave! I beg pardon, though . . . Varya is going to marry him, he's Varya's fiancé.

VARYA. Don't talk nonsense, uncle.

LYUBOV. Well, Varya, I shall be delighted. He's a good man.

PISHTCHIK. He is, one must acknowledge, a most worthy man. And my Dashenka . . . says too that . . . she says . . . various things. [*Snores, but at once wakes up.*] But all the same, honored lady, could you oblige me . . . with a loan of 240 roubles . . . to pay the interest on my mortgage tomorrow?

VARYA [*dismayed*]. No, no.

LYUBOV. I really haven't any money.

PISHTCHIK. It will turn up. [*Laughs.*] I never lose hope. I thought everything was over, I was a ruined man, and lo and behold—the railway passed through my land and . . . they paid me for it. And something else will turn up again, if not today, then tomorrow . . . Dashenka'll win two hundred thousand . . . she's got a lottery ticket.

LYUBOV. Well, we've finished our coffee, we can go to bed.

FIRS. [*Brushes* GAEV, *reprovingly.*] You have got on the wrong trousers again! What am I to do with you?

VARYA [*softly*]. Anya's asleep. [*Softly opens the window.*] Now the sun's risen, it's not a bit cold. Look, mamma, what exquisite trees! My goodness! And the air! The starlings are singing!

GAEV. [*Opens another window.*] The orchard is all white. You've not forgotten it, Lyuba? That long avenue that runs straight, straight as an arrow, how it shines on a moonlight night. You remember? You've not forgotten?

LYUBOV [*looking out of the window into the garden*]. Oh, my childhood, my innocence! It was in this nursery I used to sleep, from here I looked out into the orchard, happiness waked with me every morning and in those days the orchard was just the same, nothing has changed. [*Laughs with delight.*] All, all white! Oh, my orchard! After the dark gloomy autumn, and the cold winter; you are young again, and full of happiness, the heavenly angels have never left you. . . . If I could cast off the burden that weighs on my heart, if I could forget the past!

GAEV. H'm! and the orchard will be sold to pay our debts; it seems strange. . . .

LYUBOV. See, our mother walking . . . all in white, down the avenue! [*Laughs with delight.*] It is she!

GAEV. Where?

VARYA. Oh, don't, mamma!

LYUBOV. There is no one. It was my fancy. On the right there, by the path to the arbor, there is a white tree bending like a woman. . . .

> [*Enter* TROFIMOV *wearing a shabby student's uniform and spectacles.*]

LYUBOV. What a ravishing orchard! White masses of blossom, blue sky. . . .

TROFIMOV. Lyubov Andreyevna! [*She looks round at him.*] I will just pay my respects to you and then leave you at once. [*Kisses her hand warmly.*] I was told to wait until morning, but I hadn't the patience to wait any longer. . . .

> [LYUBOV ANDREYEVNA *looks at him in perplexity.*]

VARYA [*through her tears*]. This is Petya Trofimov.

TROFIMOV. Petya Trofimov, who was your Grisha's tutor. . . . Can I have changed so much?

> [LYUBOV ANDREYEVNA *embraces him and weeps quietly.*]

GAEV [*in confusion*]. There, there, Lyuba.

VARYA [*crying*]. I told you, Petya, to wait till tomorrow.

LYUBOV. My Grisha . . . my boy . . . Grisha . . . my son!

VARYA. We can't help it, mamma, it is God's will.

TROFIMOV [*softly through his tears*]. There . . . there.

LYUBOV [*weeping quietly*]. My boy was lost . . . drowned. Why? Oh, why, dear Petya? [*More quietly*] Anya is asleep in there, and I'm talking loudly . . . making this noise. . . . But, Petya? Why have you grown so ugly? Why do you look so old?

TROFIMOV. A peasant woman in the train called me a mangy-looking gentleman.

LYUBOV. You were quite a boy then, a pretty little student, and now your hair's thin—and spectacles. Are you really a student still?

> [*Goes towards the door.*]

TROFIMOV. I seem likely to be a perpetual student.

LYUBOV. [*Kisses her brother, then* VARYA.] Well, go to bed. . . . You are older too, Leonid.

PISHTCHIK. [*Follows her.*] I suppose it's time we were asleep. . . . Ugh! my gout. I'm staying the night! Lyubov Andreyevna, my dear soul, if you could . . . tomorrow morning . . . 240 roubles.

GAEV. That's always his story.

PISHTCHIK. 240 roubles . . . to pay the interest on my mortgage.

LYUBOV. My dear man, I have no money.

PISHTCHIK. I'll pay it back, my dear . . . a trifling sum.

LYUBOV. Oh, well. Leonid will give it you. . . You give him the money, Leonid.

GAEV. Me give it him! Let him wait till he gets it!

LYUBOV. It can't be helped, give it him. He needs it. He'll pay it back. [LYUBOV ANDREYEVNA, TROFIMOV, PISHTCHIK *and* FIRS *go out.* GAEV, VARYA *and* YASHA *remain.*]

GAEV. Sister hasn't got out of the habit of flinging away her money. [*To* YASHA] Get away, my good fellow, you smell of the hen house.

YASHA [*with a grin*]. And you, Leonid Andreyevitch, are just the same as ever.

GAEV. What's that? [*To* VARYA] What did he say?

VARYA [*to* YASHA]. Your mother has come from the village; she has been sitting in the servants' room since yesterday, waiting to see you.

YASHA. Oh, bother her!

VARYA. For shame!

YASHA. What's the hurry? She might just as well have come tomorrow. [*Goes out.*]

VARYA. Mamma's just the same as ever, she hasn't changed a bit. If she had her own way, she'd give away everything.

GAEV. Yes. [*A pause.*] If a great many remedies are suggested for some disease, it means that the disease is incurable. I keep thinking and racking my brains; I have many schemes, a great many, and that really means none. If we could only come in for a legacy from somebody, or marry our Anya to a very rich man, or we might go to Yaroslavl and try our luck with our old aunt, the Countess. She's very, very rich, you know.

VARYA. [*Weeps.*] If God would help us.

GAEV. Don't blubber. Aunt's very rich, but she doesn't like us. First, sister married a lawyer instead of a nobleman. . . . [ANYA *appears in the doorway.*] And then her conduct, one can't call it virtuous. She is good, and kind, and nice, and I love her, but, however one allows for extenuating circumstances, there's no denying that she's an immoral woman. One feels it in her slightest gesture.

VARYA [*in a whisper*]. Anya's in the doorway.

GAEV. What do you say? [*A pause.*] It's queer, there seems to be something wrong with my right eye. I don't see as well as I did. And on Thursday when I was in the district Court . . . [*Enter* ANYA.]

VARYA. Why aren't you asleep, Anya?

ANYA. I can't get to sleep.

GAEV. My pet. [*Kisses* ANYA's *face and hands.*] My child. [*Weeps.*] You are not my niece, you are my angel, you are everything to me. Believe me, believe . . .

ANYA. I believe you, uncle. Everyone loves you and respects you . . . but, uncle dear, you must be silent . . . simply be silent. What were you saying just now about my mother, about your own sister? What made you say that?

GAEV. Yes, yes . . . [*Puts his hand over his face.*] Really, that was awful! My God, save me! And today I made a speech to the bookcase . . . so stupid! And only when I had finished, I saw how stupid it was.

VARYA. It's true, uncle, you ought to keep quiet. Don't talk, that's all.

ANYA. If you could keep from talking, it would make things easier for you, too.

GAEV. I won't speak. [*Kisses* ANYA *and* VARYA's *hands.*] I'll be silent. Only this is about business. On Thursday I was in the district Court; well, there was a large party of us there and we began talking of one thing and another, and this and that, and do you know, I believe that it will be possible to raise a loan on an I.O.U. to pay the arrears on the mortgage.

VARYA. If the Lord would help us!

GAEV. I'm going on Tuesday; I'll talk of it again. [*To* VARYA] Don't blubber. [*To* ANYA] Your mamma will talk to Lopahin; of course, he won't refuse her. And as soon as you're rested you shall go to Yaroslavl to the Countess, your great-aunt. So we shall all set to work in three directions at once, and the business is done. We shall pay off arrears, I'm convinced of it. [*Puts a caramel in his mouth.*] I swear on my honor, I swear by anything you like, the estate shan't be sold [*excitedly*]. By my own happiness, I swear it! Here's my hand on it, call me the basest, vilest of men, if I let it come to an auction! Upon my soul I swear it!

ANYA. [*Her equanimity has returned, she is quite happy.*] How good you are, uncle, and how clever! [*Embraces her uncle.*] I'm at peace now! Quite at peace! I'm happy!

[*Enter* FIRS.]

FIRS [*reproachfully*]. Leonid Andreyevitch, have you no fear of God? when are you going to bed?

GAEV. Directly, directly. You can go, Firs. I'll . . . yes, I will undress myself. Come, children, by-by. We'll go into details tomorrow, but now go to bed. [*Kisses* ANYA *and* VARYA] I'm a man of the eighties.[4] They run down that period, but still I can say I have had to suffer not a little for my convictions in my life. It's not for nothing that the peasant loves me. One must know the peasant! One must know how . . .

ANYA. At it again, uncle!

VARYA. Uncle dear, you'd better be quiet!

FIRS [*angrily*]. Leonid Andreyevitch!

GAEV. I'm coming. I'm coming. Go to bed. Potted the shot—there's a shot for you! A beauty! [*Goes out,* FIRS *hobbling after him.*]

ANYA. My mind's at rest now. I don't want to go to Yaroslavl, I don't like my great-aunt, but still my mind's at rest. Thanks to uncle.

[*Sits down.*]

VARYA. We must go to bed. I'm going. Something unpleasant happened while you were away. In the old servants' quarters there are only the old servants, as you know—Efimyushka, Polya and Yevstigney—and Karp too. They began letting stray people in to spend the night—I said nothing. But all at once I heard they had been spreading a report that I gave them nothing but pease pudding to eat. Out of stinginess, you know. . . . And it was all Yevstigney's doing. . . . Very well, I said to myself. . . . If that's how it is, I thought, wait a bit. I sent for Yevstigney. . . . [*Yawns.*] He comes. . . . "How's this, Yevstigney," I said,

[4] The 1880's (twenty years before the time of the play) were a period of repressive reaction in Russia. Gaev idealizes the political attitudes of his class.

"you could be such a fool as to? . . ." [*Looking at* ANYA] Anitchka! [*A pause.*] She's asleep. [*Puts her arm round* ANYA.] Come to bed . . . come along! [*Leads her.*] My darling has fallen asleep! Come . . . [*They go.*]

> [*Far away beyond the orchard a shepherd plays on a pipe.* TROFIMOV *crosses the stage and, seeing* VARYA *and* ANYA, *stands still.*]

VARYA. 'Sh! asleep, asleep. Come, my own.

ANYA [*softly, half asleep*]. I'm so tired. Still those bells. Uncle . . . dear . . . mamma and uncle. . . .

VARYA. Come, my own, come along.

> [*They go into* ANYA'S *room.*]

TROFIMOV [*tenderly*]. My sunshine! My spring.

ACT TWO

SCENE

The open country. An old shrine, long abandoned and fallen out of the perpendicular; near it a well, large stones that have apparently once been tombstones, and an old garden seat. The road to GAEV'S *house is seen. On one side rise dark poplars; and there the cherry orchard begins. In the distance a row of telegraph poles and far, far away on the horizon there is faintly outlined a great town, only visible in very fine clear weather. It is near sunset.* CHARLOTTA, YASHA *and* DUNYASHA *are sitting on the seat.* EPIHODOV *is standing near, playing something mournful on a guitar. All sit plunged in thought.* CHARLOTTA *wears an old forage cap; she has taken a gun from her shoulder and is tightening the buckle on the strap.*

CHARLOTTA [*musingly*]. I haven't a real passport of my own, and I don't know how old I am, and I always feel that I'm a young thing. When I was a little girl, my father and mother used to travel about to fairs and give performances—very good ones. And I used to dance *salto-mortale*[5] and all sorts of things. And when papa and mamma died, a German lady took me and had me educated. And so I grew up and became a governess. But where I came from, and who I am, I don't know. . . . Who my parents were, very likely they weren't married . . . I don't know. [*Takes a cucumber out of her pocket and eats.*] I know nothing at all. [*A pause.*] One wants to talk and has no one to talk to . . . I have nobody.

EPIHODOV. [*Plays on the guitar and sings.*] "What care I for the noisy world! What care I for friends or foes!" How agreeable it is to play on the mandolin!

DUNYASHA. That's a guitar, not a mandolin. [*Looks in a hand mirror and powders herself.*]

EPIHODOV. To a man mad with love, it's a mandolin. [*Sings.*] "Were her heart but aglow with love's mutual flame." [YASHA *joins in.*]

CHARLOTTA. How shockingly these people sing! Foo! Like jackals!

DUNYASHA [*to* YASHA]. What happiness, though, to visit foreign lands.

YASHA. Ah, yes! I rather agree with you there. [*Yawns, then lights a cigar.*]

[5] The "leap of death" (Italian), a standing somersault.

EPIHODOV. That's comprehensible. In foreign lands everything has long since reached full complexion.

YASHA. That's so, of course.

EPIHODOV. I'm a cultivated man, I read remarkable books of all sorts, but I can never make out the tendency I am myself precisely inclined for, whether to live or to shoot myself, speaking precisely, but nevertheless I always carry a revolver. Here it is . . . [*Shows revolver.*]

CHARLOTTA. I've had enough, and now I'm going. [*Puts on the gun.*] Epihodov, you're a very clever fellow, and a very terrible one too, all the women must be wild about you. Br-r-r! [*Goes.*] These clever fellows are all so stupid; there's not a creature for me to speak to. . . . Always alone, alone, nobody belonging to me . . . and who I am, and why I'm on earth, I don't know. [*Walks away slowly.*]

EPIHODOV. Speaking precisely, not touching upon other subjects, I'm bound to admit about myself, that destiny behaves mercilessly to me, as a storm to a little boat. If, let us suppose, I am mistaken, then why did I wake up this morning, to quote an example, and look round, and there on my chest was a spider of fearful magnitude . . . like this. [*Shows with both hands.*] And then I take up a jug of kvass, to quench my thirst, and in it there is something in the highest degree unseemly of the nature of a cockroach. [*A pause.*] Have you read Buckle?[6] [*A pause.*] I am desirous of troubling you, Dunyasha, with a couple of words.

DUNYASHA. Well, speak.

EPIHODOV. I should be desirous to speak with you alone. [*Sighs.*]

DUNYASHA [*embarrassed*]. Well—only bring me my mantle first. It's by the cupboard. It's rather damp here.

EPIHODOV. Certainly. I will fetch it. Now I know what I must do with my revolver. [*Takes the guitar and goes off playing on it.*]

YASHA. Two and twenty misfortunes! Between ourselves, he's a fool. [*Yawns.*]

DUNYASHA. God grant he doesn't shoot himself! [*A pause.*] I am so nervous, I'm always in a flutter. I was a little girl when I was taken into our lady's house, and now I have quite grown out of peasant ways, and my hands are white, as white as a lady's. I'm such a delicate, sensitive creature, I'm afraid of everything. I'm so frightened. And if you deceive me, Yasha, I don't know what will become of my nerves.

YASHA. [*Kisses her.*] You're a peach! Of course a girl must never forget herself; what I dislike more than anything is a girl being flighty in her behavior.

DUNYASHA. I'm passionately in love with you, Yasha; you are a man of culture—you can give your opinion about anything. [*A pause.*]

YASHA. [*Yawns.*] Yes, that's so. My opinion is this: if a girl loves anyone, that means that she has no principles. [*A pause.*] It's pleasant smoking a cigar in the open air. [*Listens.*] Someone's coming this way . . . it's the gentlefolk. [DUNYASHA *embraces him impulsively.*] Go home, as though

[6] Henry Thomas Buckle's *History of Civilization in England* (1857–61), popular in Russia for its presumably enlightened, rationalistic view of history. Epihodov's "ideas" are a jumble of half-understood "advanced thought."

you had been to the river to bathe; go by that path, or else they'll meet you and suppose I have made an appointment with you here. That I can't endure.

DUNYASHA [*coughing softly*]. The cigar has made my head ache. . . .

[*Goes off.* YASHA *remains sitting near the shrine. Enter* LYUBOV ANDREYEVNA, GAEV *and* LOPAHIN.]

LOPAHIN. You must make up your mind once for all—there's no time to lose. It's quite a simple question, you know. Will you consent to letting the land for building or not? One word in answer: Yes or no? Only one word!

LYUBOV. Who is smoking such horrible cigars here? [*Sits down.*]

GAEV. Now the railway line has been brought near, it's made things very convenient. [*Sits down.*] Here we have been over and lunched in town. Cannon off the white! I should like to go home and have a game.

LYUBOV. You have plenty of time.

LOPAHIN. Only one word! [*Beseechingly*] Give me an answer!

GAEV [*yawning*]. What do you say?

LYUBOV. [*Looks in her purse.*] I had quite a lot of money here yesterday, and there's scarcely any left today. My poor Varya feeds us all on milk soup for the sake of economy; the old folks in the kitchen get nothing but pease pudding, while I waste my money in a senseless way. [*Drops purse, scattering gold pieces.*] There, they have all fallen out [*annoyed*]!

YASHA. Allow me, I'll soon pick them up. [*Collects the coins.*]

LYUBOV. Pray do, Yasha. And what did I go off to the town to lunch for? Your restaurant's a wretched place with its music and the tablecloth smelling of soap. . . . Why drink so much, Leonid? And eat so much? And talk so much? Today you talked a great deal again in the restaurant, and all so inappropriately. About the era of the 'seventies, about the decadents. And to whom? Talking to waiters about decadents![7]

LOPAHIN. Yes.

GAEV [*waving his hand*]. I'm incorrigible; that's evident. [*Irritably to* YASHA] Why is it you keep fidgeting about in front of us!

YASHA. [*Laughs.*] I can't help laughing when I hear your voice.

GAEV [*to his sister*]. Either I or he . . .

LYUBOV. Get along! Go away, Yasha.

YASHA. [*Gives* LYUBOV ANDREYEVNA *her purse.*] Directly [*hardly able to suppress his laughter*]. This minute. . . . [*Goes off.*]

LOPAHIN. Deriganov, the millionaire, means to buy your estate. They say he is coming to the sale himself.

LYUBOV. Where did you hear that?

LOPAHIN. That's what they say in town.

GAEV. Our aunt in Yaroslavl has promised to send help; but when, and how much she will send, we don't know.

LOPAHIN. How much will she send? A hundred thousand? Two hundred?

LYUBOV. Oh, well! . . . Ten or fifteen thousand, and we must be thankful to get that.

[7] Members of an anti-bourgeois movement in the arts in the 1890s.

LOPAHIN. Forgive me, but such reckless people as you are—such queer, un-businesslike people—I never met in my life. One tells you in plain Russian your estate is going to be sold, and you seem not to understand it.

LYUBOV. What are we to do? Tell us what to do.

LOPAHIN. I do tell you every day. Every day I say the same thing. You absolutely must let the cherry orchard and the land on building leases; and do it at once, as quick as may be—the auction's close upon us! Do understand! Once make up your mind to build villas, and you can raise as much money as you like, and then you are saved.

LYUBOV. Villas and summer visitors—forgive me saying so—it's so vulgar.

GAEV. There I perfectly agree with you.

LOPAHIN. I shall sob, or scream, or fall into a fit. I can't stand it! You drive me mad! [*To* GAEV] You're an old woman!

GAEV. What do you say?

LOPAHIN. An old woman! [*Gets up to go.*]

LYUBOV [*in dismay*]. No, don't go! Do stay, my dear friend! Perhaps we shall think of something.

LOPAHIN. What is there to think of?

LYUBOV. Don't go, I entreat you! With you here it's more cheerful, anyway. [*A pause.*] I keep expecting something, as though the house were going to fall about our ears.

GAEV [*in profound dejection*]. Potted the white! It fails—a kiss.

LYUBOV. We have been great sinners. . . .

LOPAHIN. You have no sins to repent of.

GAEV. [*Puts a caramel in his mouth.*] They say I've eaten up my property in caramels. [*Laughs.*]

LYUBOV. Oh, my sins! I've always thrown my money away recklessly like a lunatic. I married a man who made nothing but debts. My husband died of champagne—he drank dreadfully. To my misery I loved another man, and immediately—it was my first punishment—the blow fell upon me, here, in the river . . . my boy was drowned and I went abroad—went away for ever, never to return, not to see that river again . . . I shut my eyes, and fled, distracted, and *he* after me . . . pitilessly, brutally. I bought a villa at Mentone,[8] for *he* fell ill there, and for three years I had no rest day or night. His illness wore me out, my soul was dried up. And last year, when my villa was sold to pay my debts, I went to Paris and there he robbed me of everything and abandoned me for another woman; and I tried to poison myself. . . . So stupid, so shameful! . . . And suddenly I felt a yearning for Russia, for my country, for my little girl. . . . [*Dries her tears.*] Lord, Lord, be merciful! Forgive my sins! Do not chastise me more! [*Takes a telegram out of her pocket.*] I got this today from Paris. He implores forgiveness, entreats me to return. [*Tears up the telegram.*] I fancy there is music somewhere. [*Listens.*]

GAEV. That's our famous Jewish orchestra. You remember, four violins, a flute and a double bass.

LYUBOV. That still in existence? We ought to send for them one evening, and give a dance.

[8] A resort on the Riviera.

LOPAHIN. [*Listens.*] I can't hear. . . . [*Hums softly.*] "For money the Germans will turn a Russian into a Frenchman." [*Laughs.*] I did see such a piece at the theater yesterday! It was funny!

LYUBOV. And most likely there was nothing funny in it. You shouldn't look at plays, you should look at yourself a little oftener. How gray your lives are! How much nonsense you talk.

LOPAHIN. That's true. One may say honestly, we live a fool's life. [*Pause.*] My father was a peasant, an idiot; he knew nothing and taught me nothing, only beat me when he was drunk, and always with his stick. In reality I am just such another blockhead and idiot. I've learnt nothing properly. I write a wretched hand. I write so that I feel ashamed before folks, like a pig.

LYUBOV. You ought to get married, my dear fellow.

LOPAHIN. Yes . . . that's true.

LYUBOV. You should marry our Varya, she's a good girl.

LOPAHIN. Yes.

LYUBOV. She's a good-natured girl, she's busy all day long, and what's more, she loves you. And you have liked her for ever so long.

LOPAHIN. Well? I'm not against it. . . . She's a good girl. [*Pause.*]

GAEV. I've been offered a place in the bank: 6,000 roubles a year. Did you know?

LYUBOV. You would never do for that! You must stay as you are.

[*Enter* FIRS *with overcoat.*]

FIRS. Put it on, sir, it's damp.

GAEV [*putting it on*]. You bother me, old fellow.

FIRS. You can't go on like this. You went away in the morning without leaving word. [*Looks him over.*]

LYUBOV. You look older, Firs!

FIRS. What is your pleasure?

LOPAHIN. You look older, she said.

FIRS. I've had a long life. They were arranging my wedding before your papa was born. . . . [*Laughs.*] I was the head footman before the emancipation came.[9] I wouldn't consent to be set free then; I stayed on with the old master. . . . [*A pause.*] I remember what rejoicings they made and didn't know themselves what they were rejoicing over.

LOPAHIN. Those were fine old times. There was flogging anyway.

FIRS [*not hearing*]. To be sure! The peasants knew their place, and the masters knew theirs; but now they're all at sixes and sevens, there's no making it out.

GAEV. Hold your tongue, Firs. I must go to town tomorrow. I have been promised an introduction to a general, who might let us have a loan.

LOPAHIN. You won't bring that off. And you won't pay your arrears, you may rest assured of that.

LYUBOV. That's all his nonsense. There is no such general.

[*Enter* TROFIMOV, ANYA, *and* VARYA.]

GAEV. Here come our girls.

ANYA. There's mamma on the seat.

[9]The serfs were emancipated in Russia in 1861.

LYUBOV [*tenderly*]. Come here, come along. My darlings! [*Embraces* ANYA *and* VARYA.] If you only knew how I love you both. Sit beside me, there, like that.

[*All sit down.*]

LOPAHIN. Our perpetual student is always with the young ladies.

TROFIMOV. That's not your business.

LOPAHIN. He'll soon be fifty, and he's still a student.

TROFIMOV. Drop your idiotic jokes.

LOPAHIN. Why are you so cross, you queer fish?

TROFIMOV. Oh, don't persist!

LOPAHIN. [*Laughs.*] Allow me to ask you what's your idea of me?

TROFIMOV. I'll tell you my idea of you, Yermolay Alexeyevitch: you are a rich man, you'll soon be a millionaire. Well, just as in the economy of nature a wild beast is of use, who devours everything that comes in his way, so you too have your use.

[*All laugh.*]

VARYA. Better tell us something about the planets, Petya.

LYUBOV. No, let us go on with the conversation we had yesterday.

TROFIMOV. What was it about?

GAEV. About pride.

TROFIMOV. We had a long conversation yesterday, but we came to no con-clusion. In pride, in your sense of it, there is something mystical. Per-haps you are right from your point of view; but if one looks at it simply, without subtlety, what sort of pride can there be, what sense is there in it, if a man in his physiological formation is very imperfect, if in the immense majority of cases he is coarse, dull-witted, profoundly un-happy? One must give up glorification of self. One should work, and nothing else.

GAEV. One must die in any case.

TROFIMOV. Who knows? And what does it mean—dying? Perhaps man has a hundred senses, and only the five we know are lost at death, while the other ninety-five remain alive.

LYUBOV. How clever you are, Petya!

LOPAHIN [*ironically*]. Fearfully clever!

TROFIMOV. Humanity progresses, perfecting its powers. Everything that is beyond its ken now will one day become familiar and comprehensible; only we must work, we must with all our powers aid the seeker after truth. Here among us in Russia the workers are few in number as yet. The vast majority of the intellectual people I know, seek nothing, do nothing, are not fit as yet for work of any kind. They call themselves intellectual, but they treat their servants as inferiors, behave to the peas-ants as though they were animals, learn little, read nothing seriously, do practically nothing, only talk about science and know very little about art. They are all serious people, they all have severe faces, they all talk of weighty matters and air their theories, and yet the vast majority of us—ninety-nine per cent—live like savages, at the least thing fly to blows and abuse, eat piggishly, sleep in filth and stuffiness, bugs every-where, stench and damp and moral impurity. And it's clear all our fine talk is only to divert our attention and other people's. Show me where to

find the crèches[10] there's so much talk about, and the reading rooms? They only exist in novels: in real life there are none of them. There is nothing but filth and vulgarity and Asiatic apathy. I fear and dislike very serious faces. I'm afraid of serious conversations. We should do better to be silent.

LOPAHIN. You know, I get up at five o'clock in the morning, and I work from morning to night; and I've money, my own and other people's, always passing through my hands, and I see what people are made of all round me. One has only to begin to do anything to see how few honest, decent people there are. Sometimes when I lie awake at night, I think: "Oh! Lord, thou hast given us immense forests, boundless plains, the widest horizons, and living here we ourselves ought really to be giants."

LYUBOV. You ask for giants! They are no good except in storybooks; in real life they frighten us.

[EPIHODOV *advances in the background, playing on the guitar.*]

LYUBOV [*dreamily*]. There goes Epihodov.

ANYA [*dreamily*]. There goes Epihodov.

GAEV. The sun has set, my friends.

TROFIMOV. Yes.

GAEV [*not loudly, but, as it were, declaiming*]. O nature, divine nature, thou art bright with eternal luster, beautiful and indifferent! Thou, whom we call mother, thou dost unite within thee life and death! Thou dost give life and dost destroy!

VARYA [*in a tone of supplication*]. Uncle!

ANYA. Uncle, you are at it again!

TROFIMOV. You'd much better be cannoning off the red!

GAEV. I'll hold my tongue, I will.

[*All sit plunged in thought. Perfect stillness. The only thing audible is the muttering of* FIRS. *Suddenly there is a sound in the distance, as it were from the sky—the sound of a breaking harp string, mournfully dying away.*]

LYUBOV. What is that?

LOPAHIN. I don't know. Somewhere far away a bucket fallen and broken in the pits. But somewhere very far away.

GAEV. It might be a bird of some sort—such as a heron.

TROFIMOV. Or an owl.

LYUBOV. [*Shudders.*] I don't know why, but it's horrid. [*A pause.*]

FIRS. It was the same before the calamity—the owl hooted and the samovar hissed all the time.

GAEV. Before what calamity?

FIRS. Before the emancipation. [*A pause.*]

LYUBOV. Come, my friends, let us be going; evening is falling. [*To* ANYA] There are tears in your eyes. What is it, darling? [*Embraces her.*]

ANYA. Nothing, mamma; it's nothing.

[10] Day nurseries or child-care centers.

TROFIMOV. There is somebody coming.

[*The* WAYFARER *appears in a shabby white forage cap and an overcoat; he is slightly drunk.*]

WAYFARER. Allow me to inquire, can I get to the station this way?

GAEV. Yes. Go along that road.

WAYFARER. I thank you most feelingly [*coughing*]. The weather is superb. [*Declaims*] My brother, my suffering brother! . . . Come out to the Volga! Whose groan do you hear? . . . [*To* VARYA] Mademoiselle, vouchsafe a hungry Russian thirty kopeks.

[VARYA *utters a shriek of alarm.*]

LOPAHIN [*angrily*]. There's a right and a wrong way of doing everything!

LYUBOV [*hurriedly*]. Here, take this. [*Looks in her purse.*] I've no silver. No matter—here's gold for you.

WAYFARER. I thank you most feelingly! [*Goes off.*]

[*Laughter.*]

VARYA [*frightened*]. I'm going home—I'm going . . . Oh, mamma, the servants have nothing to eat, and you gave him gold!

LYUBOV. There's no doing anything with me. I'm so silly! When we get home, I'll give you all I possess. Yermolay Alexeyevitch, you will lend me some more . . . !

LOPAHIN. I will.

LYUBOV. Come, friends, it's time to be going. And Varya, we have made a match of it for you. I congratulate you.

VARYA [*through her tears*]. Mamma, that's not a joking matter.

LOPAHIN. "Ophelia, get thee to a nunnery!" [11]

GAEV. My hands are trembling; it's a long while since I had a game of billiards.

LOPAHIN. "Ophelia! Nymph, in thy orisons be all my sins remember'd."

LYUBOV. Come, it will soon be suppertime.

VARYA. How he frightened me! My heart's simply throbbing.

LOPAHIN. Let me remind you, ladies and gentlemen: on the 22nd of August the cherry orchard will be sold. Think about that! Think about it!

[*All go off, except* TROFIMOV *and* ANYA.]

ANYA [*laughing*]. I'm grateful to the wayfarer! He frightened Varya and we are left alone.

TROFIMOV. Varya's afraid we shall fall in love with each other, and for days together she won't leave us. With her narrow brain she can't grasp that we are above love. To eliminate the petty and transitory which hinders us from being free and happy—that is the aim and meaning of our life. Forward! We go forward irresistibly towards the bright star that shines yonder in the distance. Forward! Do not lag behind, friends.

ANYA. [*Claps her hands.*] How well you speak! [*A pause.*] It is divine here today.

TROFIMOV. Yes, it's glorious weather.

[11] Lopahin is quoting in a garbled version *Hamlet* III.i.139–42, from a scene in which Hamlet alternately woos and abuses Ophelia. Lopahin seems merely to be trying to be "elegant," and fails to realize the horrible inappropriateness of the line.

ANYA. Somehow, Petya, you've made me so that I don't love the cherry orchard as I used to. I used to love it so dearly. I used to think that there was no spot on earth like our garden.

TROFIMOV. All Russia is our garden. The earth is great and beautiful—there are many beautiful places in it. [*A pause.*] Think only, Anya, your grandfather, and great-grandfather, and all your ancestors were slave owners—the owners of living souls—and from every cherry in the orchard, from every leaf, from every trunk there are human creatures looking at you. Cannot you hear their voices? Oh, it is awful! Your orchard is a fearful thing, and when in the evening or at night one walks about the orchard, the old bark on the trees glimmers dimly in the dusk, and the old cherry trees seem to be dreaming of centuries gone by and tortured by fearful visions. Yes! We are at least two hundred years behind, we have really gained nothing yet, we have no definite attitude to the past, we do nothing but theorize or complain of depression or drink vodka. It is clear that to begin to live in the present we must first expiate our past, we must break with it; and we can expiate it only by suffering, by extraordinary unceasing labor. Understand that, Anya.

ANYA. The house we live in has long ceased to be our own, and I shall leave it, I give you my word.

TROFIMOV. If you have the house keys, fling them into the well and go away. Be free as the wind.

ANYA [*in ecstasy*]. How beautifully you said that!

TROFIMOV. Believe me, Anya, believe me! I am not thirty yet, I am young, I am still a student, but I have gone through so much already! As soon as winter comes I am hungry, sick, careworn, poor as a beggar, and what ups and downs of fortune have I not known! And my soul was always, every minute, day and night, full of inexplicable forebodings. I have a foreboding of happiness, Anya. I see glimpses of it already.

ANYA [*pensively*]. The moon is rising.

> [EPIHODOV *is heard playing still the same mournful song on the guitar. The moon rises. Somewhere near the poplars* VARYA *is looking for* ANYA *and calling "Anya! where are you?"*]

TROFIMOV. Yes, the moon is rising. [*A pause.*] Here is happiness—here it comes! It is coming nearer and nearer; already I can hear its footsteps. And if we never see it—if we may never know it—what does it matter? Others will see it after us.

VARYA'S VOICE. Anya! Where are you?

TROFIMOV. That Varya again! [*Angrily*] It's revolting!

ANYA. Well, let's go down to the river. It's lovely there.

TROFIMOV. Yes, let's go.

> [*They go.*]

VARYA'S VOICE. Anya! Anya!

ACT THREE

SCENE

A drawing room divided by an arch from a larger drawing room. A chandelier burning. The Jewish orchestra, the same that was mentioned in Act II, is heard

playing in the anteroom. It is evening. In the larger drawing room they are dancing the grand chain.[12] *The voice of* SEMYONOV-PISHTCHIK: "Promenade à une paire!" *Then enter the drawing room in couples first* PISHTCHIK *and* CHARLOTTA IVANOVNA, *then* TROFIMOV *and* LYUBOV ANDREYEVNA, *thirdly* ANYA *with the* POST OFFICE CLERK, *fourthly* VARYA *with the* STATION MASTER, *and other guests.* VARYA *is quietly weeping and wiping away her tears as she dances. In the last couple is* DUNYASHA. *They move across the drawing room.* PISHTCHIK *shouts:* "Grand rond, balancez!" *and* "Les Cavaliers à genou et remerciez vos dames."

[FIRS *in a swallow-tail coat brings in seltzer water on a tray.* PISHTCHIK *and* TROFIMOV *enter the drawing room.*]

PISHTCHIK. I am a full-blooded man; I have already had two strokes. Dancing's hard work for me, but as they say, if you're in the pack, you must bark with the rest. I'm as strong, I may say, as a horse. My parent, who would have his joke—may the Kingdom of Heaven be his!—used to say about our origin that the ancient stock of the Semyonov-Pishtchiks was derived from the very horse that Caligula made a member of the senate. [*Sits down.*] But I've no money, that's where the mischief is. A hungry dog believes in nothing but meat. . . . [*Snores, but at once wakes up.*] That's like me . . . I can think of nothing but money.

TROFIMOV. There really is something horsy about your appearance.

PISHTCHIK. Well . . . a horse is a fine beast . . . a horse can be sold.

> [*There is the sound of billiards being played in an adjoining room.* VARYA *appears in the arch leading to the larger drawing room.*]

TROFIMOV [*teasing*]. Madame Lopahin! Madame Lopahin!

VARYA [*angrily*]. Mangy-looking gentleman!

TROFIMOV. Yes, I am a mangy-looking gentleman, and I'm proud of it!

VARYA [*pondering bitterly*]. Here we have hired musicians and nothing to pay them! [*Goes out.*]

TROFIMOV [*to* PISHTCHIK]. If the energy you have wasted during your lifetime in trying to find the money to pay your interest, had gone to something else, you might in the end have turned the world upside down.

PISHTCHIK. Nietzsche, the philosopher, a very great and celebrated man . . . of enormous intellect . . . says in his works, that one can make forged bank notes.[13]

TROFIMOV. Why, have you read Nietzsche?

PISHTCHIK. What next . . . Dashenka told me. . . . And now I am in such a position, I might just as well forge bank notes. The day after tomorrow

[12] A popular ballroom dance. In the following lines, *"Promenade à une paire"* (Promenade by couples), *"Grand rond, balancez"* (Grand round and swing), and *"Les Cavaliers à genou et remerciez vos dames"* (Gentlemen, kneel and thank your partners) are calls in the dance. Even in their reduced circumstances, the Ranevskys dance fashionable French dances rather than Russian ones.

[13] As usual, Pishtchik has everything garbled. The German philosopher Friedrich Nietzsche (1844–1900) argued that the Superman (the natural aristocrat) was "beyond good and evil," but Nietzsche did not issue a general warrant for forgery.

I must pay 310 roubles—130 I have procured. [*Feels in his pockets, in alarm.*] The money's gone! I have lost my money! [*Through his tears*] Where's the money? [*Gleefully*] Why, here it is behind the lining. . . . It has made me hot all over.

[*Enter* LYUBOV ANDREYEVNA *and* CHARLOTTA IVANOVNA.]

LYUBOV. [*Hums the Lezginka.*] Why is Leonid so long? What can he be doing in town? [*To* DUNYASHA] Offer the musicians some tea.

TROFIMOV. The sale hasn't taken place, most likely.

LYUBOV. It's the wrong time to have the orchestra, and the wrong time to give a dance. Well, never mind. [*Sits down and hums softly.*]

CHARLOTTA. [*Gives* PISHTCHIK *a pack of cards.*] Here's a pack of cards. Think of any card you like.

PISHTCHIK. I've thought of one.

CHARLOTTA. Shuffle the pack now. That's right. Give it here, my dear Mr. Pishtchik. *Ein, zwei, drei*[14]—now look, it's in your breast pocket.

PISHTCHIK [*taking a card out of his breast pocket*]. The eight of spades! Perfectly right! [*Wonderingly*] Fancy that now!

CHARLOTTA [*holding pack of cards in her hands, to* TROFIMOV]. Tell me quickly which is the top card.

TROFIMOV. Well, the queen of spades.

CHARLOTTA. It is! [*To* PISHTCHIK] Well, which card is uppermost?

PISHTCHIK. The ace of hearts.

CHARLOTTA. It is! [*Claps her hands, pack of cards disappears.*] Ah! what lovely weather it is today!

[*A mysterious feminine voice which seems coming out of the floor answers her. "Oh, yes, it's magnificent weather, madam."*]

CHARLOTTA. You are my perfect ideal.

VOICE. And I greatly admire you too, madam.

STATION MASTER [*applauding*]. The lady ventriloquist—bravo!

PISHTCHIK [*wonderingly*]. Fancy that now! Most enchanting Charlotta Ivanovna. I'm simply in love with you.

CHARLOTTA. In love? [*Shrugging shoulders*] What do you know of love, *guter Mensch, aber schlechter Musikant.*[15]

TROFIMOV. [*Pats* PISHTCHIK *on the shoulder.*] You dear old horse. . . .

CHARLOTTA. Attention, please! Another trick! [*Takes a travelling rug from a chair.*] Here's a very good rug; I want to sell it [*shaking it out*]. Doesn't anyone want to buy it?

PISHTCHIK [*wonderingly*]. Fancy that!

CHARLOTTA. *Ein, zwei, drei!* [*Quickly picks up rug she has dropped; behind the rug stands* ANYA; *she makes a curtsey, runs to her mother, embraces her and runs back into the larger drawing room amidst general enthusiasm.*]

LYUBOV. [*Applauds.*] Bravo! Bravo!

CHARLOTTA. Now again! *Ein, zwei, drei!* [*Lifts up the rug; behind the rug stands* VARYA, *bowing.*]

PISHTCHIK [*wonderingly*]. Fancy that now!

[14]"One, two, three" (German). [15]"A good man but a bad musician" (German).

CHARLOTTA. That's the end. [*Throws the rug at* PISHTCHIK, *makes a curtsey, runs into the larger drawing room.*]

PISHTCHIK. [*Hurries after her.*] Mischievous creature! Fancy! [*Goes out.*]

LYUBOV. And still Leonid doesn't come. I can't understand what he's doing in the town so long! Why, everything must be over by now. The estate is sold, or the sale has not taken place. Why keep us so long in suspense?

VARYA [*trying to console her*]. Uncle's bought it. I feel sure of that.

TROFIMOV [*ironically*]. Oh, yes!

VARYA. Great-aunt sent him an authorization to buy it in her name, and transfer the debt. She's doing it for Anya's sake, and I'm sure God will be merciful. Uncle will buy it.

LYUBOV. My aunt in Yaroslavl sent fifteen thousand to buy the estate in her name, she doesn't trust us—but that's not enough even to pay the arrears. [*Hides her face in her hands.*] My fate is being sealed today, my fate . . .

TROFIMOV [*teasing* VARYA]. Madame Lopahin.

VARYA [*angrily*]. Perpetual student! Twice already you've been sent down from the University.

LYUBOV. Why are you angry, Varya? He's teasing you about Lopahin. Well, what of that? Marry Lopahin if you like, he's a good man, and interesting; if you don't want to, don't! Nobody compels you, darling.

VARYA. I must tell you plainly, mamma, I look at the matter seriously; he's a good man, I like him.

LYUBOV. Well, marry him. I can't see what you're waiting for.

VARYA. Mamma. I can't make him an offer myself. For the last two years, everyone's been talking to me about him. Everyone talks; but he says nothing or else makes a joke. I see what it means. He's growing rich, he's absorbed in business, he has no thoughts for me. If I had money, were it ever so little, if I had only a hundred roubles, I'd throw everything up and go far away. I would go into a nunnery.

TROFIMOV. What bliss!

VARYA [*to* TROFIMOV]. A student ought to have sense! [*In a soft tone with tears*] How ugly you've grown, Petya! How old you look! [*To* LYUBOV ANDREYEVNA, *no longer crying*] But I can't do without work, mamma; I must have something to do every minute.

[*Enter* YASHA.]

YASHA [*hardly restraining his laughter*]. Epihodov has broken a billiard cue! [*Goes out.*]

VARYA. What is Epihodov doing here? Who gave him leave to play billiards? I can't make these people out. [*Goes out.*]

LYUBOV. Don't tease her, Petya. You see she has grief enough without that.

TROFIMOV. She is so very officious, meddling in what's not her business. All the summer she's given Anya and me no peace. She's afraid of a love affair between us. What's it to do with her? Besides, I have given no grounds for it. Such triviality is not in my line. We are above love!

LYUBOV. And I suppose I am beneath love. [*Very uneasily*] Why is it Leonid's not here? If only I could know whether the estate is sold or not! It seems such an incredible calamity that I really don't know what to think. I am distracted . . . I shall scream in a minute . . . I shall do something stupid. Save me, Petya, tell me something, talk to me!

TROFIMOV. What does it matter whether the estate is sold today or not? That's all done with long ago. There's no turning back, the path is overgrown. Don't worry yourself, dear Lyubov Andreyevna. You mustn't deceive yourself; for once in your life you must face the truth!

LYUBOV. What truth? You see where the truth lies, but I seem to have lost my sight, I see nothing. You settle every great problem so boldly, but tell me, my dear boy, isn't it because you're young—because you haven't yet understood one of your problems through suffering? You look forward boldly, and isn't it that you don't see and don't expect anything dreadful because life is still hidden from your young eyes? You're bolder, more honest, deeper than we are, but think, be just a little magnanimous, have pity on me. I was born here, you know, my father and mother lived here, my grandfather lived here, I love this house. I can't conceive of life without the cherry orchard, and if it really must be sold, then sell me with the orchard. [*Embraces* TROFIMOV, *kisses him on the forehead.*] My boy was drowned here. [*Weeps.*] Pity me, my dear kind fellow.

TROFIMOV. You know I feel for you with all my heart.

LYUBOV. But that should have been said differently, so differently. [*Takes out her handkerchief, telegram falls on the floor.*] My heart is so heavy today. It's so noisy here my soul is quivering at every sound, I'm shuddering all over, but I can't go away; I'm afraid to be quiet and alone. Don't be hard on me, Petya . . . I love you as though you were one of ourselves. I would gladly let you marry Anya—I swear I would—only, my dear boy, you must take your degree, you do nothing—you're simply tossed by fate from place to place. That's so strange. It is, isn't it? And you must do something with your beard to make it grow somehow. [*Laughs.*] You look so funny!

TROFIMOV. [*Picks up the telegram.*] I've no wish to be a beauty.

LYUBOV. That's a telegram from Paris. I get one every day. One yesterday and one today. That savage creature is ill again, he's in trouble again. He begs forgiveness, beseeches me to go, and really I ought to go to Paris to see him. You look shocked, Petya. What am I to do, my dear boy, what am I to do? He is ill, he is alone and unhappy, and who'll look after him, who'll keep him from doing the wrong thing, who'll give him his medicine at the right time? And why hide it or be silent? I love him, that's clear. I love him! I love him! He's a millstone about my neck, I'm going to the bottom with him, but I love that stone and can't live without it. [*Presses* TROFIMOV's *hand.*] Don't think ill of me, Petya, don't tell me anything, don't tell me . . .

TROFIMOV [*through his tears*]. For God's sake forgive my frankness: why, he robbed you!

LYUBOV. No! No! No! You mustn't speak like that. [*Covers her ears.*]

TROFIMOV. He is a wretch! You're the only person that doesn't know it! He's a worthless creature! A despicable wretch!

LYUBOV [*getting angry, but speaking with restraint*]. You're twenty-six or twenty-seven years old, but you're still a schoolboy.

TROFIMOV. Possibly.

LYUBOV. You should be a man at your age! You should understand what love means! And you ought to be in love yourself. You ought to fall in

love! [*Angrily*] Yes, yes, and it's not purity in you, you're simply a prude, a comic fool, a freak.

TROFIMOV [*in horror*]. The things she's saying!

LYUBOV. I am above love! You're not above love, but simply as our Firs here says, "You are a good-for-nothing." At your age not to have a mistress!

TROFIMOV [*in horror*]. This is awful! The things she is saying! [*Goes rapidly into the larger drawing room clutching his head.*] This is awful! I can't stand it! I'm going. [*Goes off, but at once returns.*] All is over between us! [*Goes off into the anteroom.*]

LYUBOV. [*Shouts after him.*] Petya! Wait a minute! You funny creature! I was joking! Petya!

[*There is a sound of somebody running quickly downstairs and suddenly falling with a crash. ANYA and VARYA scream, but there is a sound of laughter at once.*]

LYUBOV. What has happened?

[*ANYA runs in.*]

ANYA [*laughing*]. Petya's fallen downstairs! [*Runs out.*]

LYUBOV. What a queer fellow that Petya is!

[*The STATION MASTER stands in the middle of the larger room and reads "The Magdalene," by Alexey Tolstoy.[16] They listen to him, but before he has recited many lines strains of a waltz are heard from the anteroom and the reading is broken off. All dance. TROFIMOV, ANYA, VARYA and LYUBOV ANDREYEVNA come in from the anteroom.*]

LYUBOV. Come, Petya—come, pure heart! I beg your pardon. Let's have a dance! [*Dances with PETYA.*]

[*ANYA and VARYA dance. FIRS comes in, puts his stick down near the side door. YASHA also comes into the drawing room and looks on at the dancing.*]

YASHA. What is it, old man?

FIRS. I don't feel well. In the old days we used to have generals, barons and admirals dancing at our balls, and now we send for the post office clerk and the station master and even they're not overanxious to come. I am getting feeble. The old master, the grandfather, used to give sealing wax for all complaints. I have been taking sealing wax for twenty years or more. Perhaps that's what's kept me alive.

YASHA. You bore me, old man! [*Yawns.*] It's time you were done with.

FIRS. Ach, you're a good-for-nothing! [*Mutters.*]

[*TROFIMOV and LYUBOV ANDREYEVNA dance in the larger room and then on to the stage.*]

LYUBOV. *Merci.* I'll sit down a little. [*Sits down.*] I'm tired.

[16] A sentimental "parlor piece" in which Christ appears at a fashionable banquet.

[*Enter* ANYA.]

ANYA [*excitedly*]. There's a man in the kitchen has been saying that the cherry orchard's been sold today.

LYUBOV. Sold to whom?

ANYA. He didn't say to whom. He's gone away.

[*She dances with* TROFIMOV, *and they go off into the larger room.*]

YASHA. There was an old man gossiping there, a stranger.

FIRS. Leonid Andreyevitch isn't here yet, he hasn't come back. He has his light overcoat on, *demi-saison*,[17] he'll catch cold for sure. Ach! Foolish young things!

LYUBOV. I feel as though I should die. Go, Yasha, find out to whom it has been sold.

YASHA. But he went away long ago, the old chap. [*Laughs.*]

LYUBOV [*with slight vexation*]. What are you laughing at? What are you pleased at?

YASHA. Epihodov is so funny. He's a silly fellow, two and twenty misfortunes.

LYUBOV. Firs, if the estate is sold, where will you go?

FIRS. Where you bid me, there I'll go.

LYUBOV. Why do you look like that? Are you ill? You ought to be in bed.

FIRS. Yes [*ironically*]. Me go to bed and who's to wait here? Who's to see to things without me? I'm the only one in all the house.

YASHA [*to* LYUBOV ANDREYEVNA]. Lyubov Andreyevna, permit me to make a request of you; if you go back to Paris again, be so kind as to take me with you. It's positively impossible for me to stay here [*looking about him; in an undertone*]. There's no need to say it, you see for yourself—an uncivilized country, the people have no morals, and then the dullness! The food in the kitchen's abominable, and then Firs runs after one muttering all sorts of unsuitable words. Take me with you, please do!

[*Enter* PISHTCHIK.]

PISHTCHIK. Allow me to ask you for a waltz, my dear lady. [LYUBOV ANDREYEVNA *goes with him.*] Enchanting lady, I really must borrow of you just 180 roubles [*dances*], only 180 roubles. [*They pass into the larger room.*]

YASHA. [*Hums softly.*] "Knowest thou my soul's emotion."

[*In the larger drawing room, a figure in a gray top hat and in check trousers is gesticulating and jumping about. Shouts of "Bravo, Charlotta Ivanovna."*]

DUNYASHA. [*She has stopped to powder herself.*] My young lady tells me to dance. There are plenty of gentlemen, and too few ladies, but dancing makes me giddy and makes my heart beat. Firs, the post office clerk said something to me just now that quite took my breath away.

[*Music becomes more subdued.*]

FIRS. What did he say to you?

DUNYASHA. He said I was like a flower.

YASHA. [*Yawns.*] What ignorance! [*Goes out.*]

[17] "Between seasons"; light, "all-weather" clothing (French).

DUNYASHA. Like a flower. I am a girl of such delicate feelings, I am awfully fond of soft speeches.

FIRS. Your head's being turned.

[*Enter* EPIHODOV.]

EPIHODOV. You have no desire to see me, Dunyasha. I might be an insect. [*Sighs.*] Ah! life!

DUNYASHA. What is it you want?

EPIHODOV. Undoubtedly you may be right. [*Sighs.*] But of course, if one looks at it from that point of view, if I may so express myself, you have, excuse my plain speaking, reduced me to a complete state of mind. I know my destiny. Every day some misfortune befalls me and I have long ago grown accustomed to it, so that I look upon my fate with a smile. You gave me your word, and though I——

DUNYASHA. Let us have a talk later, I entreat you, but now leave me in peace, for I am lost in reverie. [*Plays with her fan.*]

EPIHODOV. I have a misfortune every day, and if I may venture to express myself, I merely smile at it, I even laugh.

[VARYA *enters from the larger drawing room.*]

VARYA. You still have not gone, Epihodov. What a disrespectful creature you are, really! [*To* DUNYASHA] Go along, Dunyasha! [*To* EPIHODOV] First you play billiards and break the cue, then you go wandering about the drawing room like a visitor!

EPIHODOV. You really cannot, if I may so express myself, call me to account like this.

VARYA. I'm not calling you to account, I'm speaking to you. You do nothing but wander from place to place and don't do your work. We keep you as a counting-house clerk, but what use you are I can't say.

EPIHODOV [*offended*]. Whether I work or whether I walk, whether I eat or whether I play billiards, is a matter to be judged by persons of understanding and my elders.

VARYA. You dare to tell me that! [*Firing up*] You dare! You mean to say I've no understanding. Begone from here! This minute!

EPIHODOV [*intimidated*]. I beg you to express yourself with delicacy.

VARYA [*beside herself with anger*]. This moment! get out! away! [*He goes towards the door, she following him.*] Two and twenty misfortunes! Take yourself off! Don't let me set eyes on you! [EPIHODOV *has gone out, behind the door his voice,* "I shall lodge a complaint against you."] What! You're coming back? [*Snatches up the stick* FIRS *has put down near the door.*] Come! Come! Come! I'll show you! What! You're coming? Then take that! [*She swings the stick, at the very moment that* LOPAHIN *comes in.*]

LOPAHIN. Very much obliged to you!

VARYA [*angrily and ironically*]. I beg your pardon!

LOPAHIN. Not at all! I humbly thank you for your kind reception!

VARYA. No need of thanks for it. [*Moves away, then looks round and asks softly*] I haven't hurt you?

LOPAHIN. Oh, no! Not at all! There's an immense bump coming up, though!

VOICES FROM LARGER ROOM. Lopahin has come! Yermolay Alexeyevitch!

PISHTCHIK. What do I see and hear? [*Kisses* LOPAHIN.] There's a whiff of cognac about you, my dear soul, and we're making merry here too!

[*Enter* LYUBOV ANDREYEVNA.]

LYUBOV. Is it you, Yermolay Alexeyevitch? Why have you been so long? Where's Leonid?

LOPAHIN. Leonid Andreyevitch arrived with me. He is coming.

LYUBOV [*in agitation*]. Well! Well! Was there a sale? Speak!

LOPAHIN [*embarrassed, afraid of betraying his joy*]. The sale was over at four o'clock. We missed our train—had to wait till half-past nine. [*Sighing heavily*] Ugh! I feel a little giddy.

[*Enter* GAEV. *In his right hand he has purchases, with his left hand is wiping away his tears.*]

LYUBOV. Well, Leonid? What news? [*Impatiently, with tears*] Make haste, for God's sake!

GAEV. [*Makes her no answer, simply waves his hand. To* FIRS, *weeping*] Here, take them; there's anchovies, Kertch herrings. I have eaten nothing all day. What I have been through! [*Door into the billiard room is open. There is heard a knocking of balls and the voice of* YASHA *saying "Eighty-seven."* GAEV'S *expression changes, he leaves off weeping.*] I am fearfully tired. Firs, come and help me change my things. [*Goes to his own room across the larger drawing room.*]

PISHTCHIK. How about the sale? Tell us, do!

LYUBOV. Is the cherry orchard sold?

LOPAHIN. It is sold.

LYUBOV. Who has bought it?

LOPAHIN. I have bought it.

[*A pause.* LYUBOV *is crushed; she would fall down if she were not standing near a chair and table.* VARYA *takes keys from her waistband, flings them on the floor in middle of drawing room and goes out.*]

LOPAHIN. I have bought it! Wait a bit, ladies and gentlemen, pray. My head's a bit muddled, I can't speak. [*Laughs.*] We came to the auction. Deriganov was there already. Leonid Andreyevitch only had 15,000 and Deriganov bid 30,000, besides the arrears, straight off. I saw how the land lay. I bid against him. I bid 40,000, he bid 45,000, I said 55, and so he went on, adding 5 thousands and I adding 10. Well . . . So it ended. I bid 90, and it was knocked down to me. Now the cherry orchard's mine! Mine! [*Chuckles.*] My God, the cherry orchard's mine! Tell me that I'm drunk, that I'm out of my mind, that it's all a dream. [*Stamps with his feet.*] Don't laugh at me! If my father and my grandfather could rise from their graves and see all that has happened! How their Yermolay, ignorant, beaten Yermolay, who used to run about barefoot in winter, how that very Yermolay has bought the finest estate in the world! I have bought the estate where my father and grandfather were slaves, where they weren't even admitted into the kitchen. I am asleep, I am dreaming! It is all fancy, it is the work of your imagination plunged in the darkness of ignorance. [*Picks up keys, smiling fondly.*] She threw

away the keys; she means to show she's not the housewife now. [*Jingles the keys.*] Well, no matter. [*The orchestra is heard tuning up.*] Hey, musicians! Play! I want to hear you. Come, all of you, and look how Yermolay Lopahin will take the axe to the cherry orchard, how the trees will fall to the ground! We will build houses on it and our grandsons and great-grandsons will see a new life springing up there. Music! Play up!

> [*Music begins to play.* LYUBOV ANDRE-
> YEVNA *has sunk into a chair and is weep-
> ing bitterly.*]

LOPAHIN [*reproachfully*]. Why, why didn't you listen to me? My poor friend! Dear lady, there's no turning back now. [*With tears*] Oh, if all this could be over, oh, if our miserable disjointed life could somehow soon be changed!

PISHTCHIK. [*Takes him by the arm, in an undertone.*] She's weeping, let us go and leave her alone. Come. [*Takes him by the arm and leads him into the larger drawing room.*]

LOPAHIN. What's that? Musicians, play up! All must be as I wish it. [*With irony*] Here comes the new master, the owner of the cherry orchard! [*Accidentally tips over a little table, almost upsetting the candelabra.*] I can pay for everything!

> [*Goes out with* PISHTCHIK. *No one re-
> mains on the stage or in the larger draw-
> ing room except* LYUBOV, *who sits hud-
> dled up, weeping bitterly. The music plays
> softly.* ANYA *and* TROFIMOV *come in
> quickly.* ANYA *goes up to her mother and
> falls on her knees before her.* TROFIMOV
> *stands at the entrance to the larger draw-
> ing room.*]

ANYA. Mamma! Mamma, you're crying, dear, kind, good mamma! My precious! I love you! I bless you! The cherry orchard is sold, it is gone, that's true, that's true! But don't weep, mamma! Life is still before you, you have still your good, pure heart! Let us go, let us go, darling, away from here! We will make a new garden, more splendid than this one; you will see it, you will understand. And joy, quiet, deep joy, will sink into your soul like the sun at evening! And you will smile, mamma! Come, darling, let us go!

ACT FOUR

SCENE

Same as in First Act. There are neither curtains on the windows nor pictures on the walls: only a little furniture remains piled up in a corner as if for sale. There is a sense of desolation; near the outer door and in the background of the scene are packed trunks, travelling bags, etc. On the left the door is open, and from here the voices of VARYA *and* ANYA *are audible.* LOPAHIN *is standing waiting.* YASHA *is holding a tray with glasses full of champagne. In front of the stage* EPIHODOV *is tying up a box. In the background behind the scene a hum of talk from the peasants who have come to say good-by. The voice of* GAEV: "Thanks, brothers, thanks!"*

YASHA. The peasants have come to say good-by. In my opinion, Yermolay Alexeyevitch, the peasants are good-natured, but they don't know much about things.

> [*The hum of talk dies away. Enter across front of stage* LYUBOV ANDREYEVNA *and* GAEV. *She is not weeping, but is pale; her face is quivering—she cannot speak.*]

GAEV. You gave them your purse, Lyuba. That won't do—that won't do!

LYUBOV. I couldn't help it! I couldn't help it!

> [*Both go out.*]

LOPAHIN [*in the doorway, calls after them*]. You will take a glass at parting? Please do. I didn't think to bring any from the town, and at the station I could only get one bottle. Please take a glass. [*A pause.*] What? You don't care for any? [*Comes away from the door.*] If I'd known, I wouldn't have bought it. Well, and I'm not going to drink it. [YASHA *carefully sets the tray down on a chair.*] You have a glass, Yasha, anyway.

YASHA. Good luck to the travellers, and luck to those that stay behind! [*Drinks.*] This champagne isn't the real thing, I can assure you.

LOPAHIN. It cost eight roubles the bottle. [*A pause.*] It's devilish cold here.

YASHA. They haven't heated the stove today—it's all the same since we're going. [*Laughs.*]

LOPAHIN. What are you laughing for?

YASHA. For pleasure.

LOPAHIN. Though it's October, it's as still and sunny as though it were summer. It's just right for building! [*Looks at his watch; says in doorway*] Take note, ladies and gentlemen, the train goes in forty-seven minutes; so you ought to start for the station in twenty minutes. You must hurry up!

> [TROFIMOV *comes in from out of doors wearing a greatcoat.*]

TROFIMOV. I think it must be time to start, the horses are ready. The devil only knows what's become of my galoshes; they're lost. [*In the doorway.*] Anya! My galoshes aren't here. I can't find them.

LOPAHIN. And I'm getting off to Harkov. I am going in the same train with you. I'm spending all the winter at Harkov. I've been wasting all my time gossiping with you and fretting with no work to do. I can't get on without work. I don't know what to do with my hands, they flap about so queerly, as if they didn't belong to me.

TROFIMOV. Well, we're just going away, and you will take up your profitable labors again.

LOPAHIN. Do take a glass.

TROFIMOV. No, thanks.

LOPAHIN. Then you're going to Moscow now?

TROFIMOV. Yes. I shall see them as far as the town, and tomorrow I shall go on to Moscow.

LOPAHIN. Yes, I daresay, the professors aren't giving any lectures, they're waiting for your arrival.

TROFIMOV. That's not your business.

LOPAHIN. How many years have you been at the University?

TROFIMOV. Do think of something newer than that—that's stale and flat.

[*Hunts for galoshes.*] You know we shall most likely never see each other again, so let me give you one piece of advice at parting: don't wave your arms about—get out of the habit. And another thing, building villas, reckoning up that the summer visitors will in time become independent farmers—reckoning like that, that's not the thing to do either. After all, I am fond of you: you have fine delicate fingers like an artist, you've a fine delicate soul.

LOPAHIN. [*Embraces him.*] Good-by, my dear fellow. Thanks for everything. Let me give you money for the journey, if you need it.

TROFIMOV. What for? I don't need it.

LOPAHIN. Why, you haven't got a halfpenny.

TROFIMOV. Yes, I have, thank you. I got some money for a translation. Here it is in my pocket, [*anxiously*] but where can my galoshes be!

VARYA [*from the next room*]. Take the nasty things! [*Flings a pair of galoshes onto the stage.*]

TROFIMOV. Why are you so cross, Varya? h'm! . . . but those aren't my galoshes.

LOPAHIN. I sowed three thousand acres with poppies in the spring, and now I have cleared forty thousand profit. And when my poppies were in flower, wasn't it a picture! So here, as I say, I made forty thousand, and I'm offering you a loan because I can afford to. Why turn up your nose? I am a peasant—I speak bluntly.

TROFIMOV. Your father was a peasant, mine was a chemist—and that proves absolutely nothing whatever. [LOPAHIN *takes out his pocketbook.*] Stop that—stop that. If you were to offer me two hundred thousand I wouldn't take it. I am an independent man, and everything that all of you, rich and poor alike, prize so highly and hold so dear, hasn't the slightest power over me—it's like so much fluff fluttering in the air. I can get on without you. I can pass by you. I am strong and proud. Humanity is advancing towards the highest truth, the highest happiness, which is possible on earth, and I am in the front ranks.

LOPAHIN. Will you get there?

TROFIMOV. I shall get there. [*A pause.*] I shall get there, or I shall show others the way to get there.

[*In the distance is heard the stroke of an axe on a tree.*]

LOPAHIN. Good-by, my dear fellow; it's time to be off. We turn up our noses at one another, but life is passing all the while. When I am working hard without resting, then my mind is more at ease, and it seems to me as though I too know what I exist for; but how many people there are in Russia, my dear boy, who exist, one doesn't know what for. Well, it doesn't matter. That's not what keeps things spinning. They tell me Leonid Andreyevitch has taken a situation. He is going to be a clerk at the bank—6,000 roubles a year. Only, of course, he won't stick to it—he's too lazy.

ANYA [*in the doorway*]. Mamma begs you not to let them chop down the orchard until she's gone.

TROFIMOV. Yes, really, you might have the tact. [*Walks out across the front of the stage.*]

LOPAHIN. I'll see to it! I'll see to it! Stupid fellows! [*Goes out after him.*]

ANYA. Has Firs been taken to the hospital?

YASHA. I told them this morning. No doubt they have taken him.

ANYA [*to* EPIHODOV, *who passes across the drawing room*]. Semyon Pantaleye-vitch, inquire, please, if Firs has been taken to the hospital.

YASHA [*in a tone of offense*]. I told Yegor this morning—why ask a dozen times?

EPIHODOV. Firs is advanced in years. It's my conclusive opinion no treatment would do him good; it's time he was gathered to his fathers. And I can only envy him. [*Puts a trunk down on a cardboard hatbox and crushes it.*] There, now, of course—I knew it would be so.

YASHA [*jeeringly*]. Two and twenty misfortunes!

VARYA [*through the door*]. Has Firs been taken to the hospital?

ANYA. Yes.

VARYA. Why wasn't the note for the doctor taken too?

ANYA [*from the adjoining room*]. Where's Yasha? Tell him his mother's come to say good-by to him.

YASHA. [*Waves his hand.*] They put me out of all patience! [DUNYASHA *has all this time been busy about the luggage. Now, when* YASHA *is left alone, she goes up to him.*]

DUNYASHA. You might just give me one look, Yasha. You're going away. You're leaving me. [*Weeps and throws herself on his neck.*]

YASHA. What are you crying for? [*Drinks the champagne.*] In six days I shall be in Paris again. Tomorrow we shall get into the express train and roll away in a flash. I can scarcely believe it! *Vive la France!* It doesn't suit me here—it's not the life for me; there's no doing anything. I have seen enough of the ignorance here. I have had enough of it. [*Drinks champagne.*] What are you crying for? Behave yourself properly, and then you won't cry.

DUNYASHA. [*Powders her face, looking in a pocket mirror.*] Do send me a letter from Paris. You know how I loved you, Yasha—how I loved you! I am a tender creature, Yasha.

YASHA. Here they are coming!

[*Busies himself about the trunks, humming softly. Enter* LYUBOV ANDRE-YEVNA, GAEV, ANYA *and* CHARLOTTA IVANOVNA.]

GAEV. We ought to be off. There's not much time now [*looking at* YASHA]. What a smell of herrings!

LYUBOV. In ten minutes we must get into the carriage. [*Casts a look about the room.*] Farewell, dear house, dear old home of our fathers! Winter will pass and spring will come, and then you will be no more; they will tear you down! How much those walls have seen! [*Kisses her daughter passionately.*] My treasure, how bright you look! Your eyes are sparkling like diamonds! Are you glad? Very glad?

ANYA. Very glad! A new life is beginning, mamma.

GAEV. Yes, really, everything is all right now. Before the cherry orchard was sold, we were all worried and wretched, but afterwards, when once the question was settled conclusively, irrevocably, we all felt calm and

even cheerful. I am a bank clerk now—I am a financier—cannon off
the red. And you, Lyuba, after all, you are looking better; there's no
question of that.

LYUBOV. Yes. My nerves are better, that's true. [*Her hat and coat are handed
to her.*] I'm sleeping well. Carry out my things, Yasha. It's time. [*To
ANYA*] My darling, we shall soon see each other again. I am going to
Paris. I can live there on the money your Yaroslavl auntie sent us to buy
the estate with—hurrah for auntie!—but that money won't last long.

ANYA. You'll come back soon, mamma, won't you? I'll be working up for
my examination in the high school, and when I have passed that, I shall
set to work and be a help to you. We will read all sorts of things to-
gether, mamma, won't we? [*Kisses her mother's hands.*] We will read in the
autumn evenings. We'll read lots of books, and a new wonderful world
will open out before us [*dreamily*]. Mamma, come soon.

LYUBOV. I shall come, my precious treasure. [*Embraces her.*]

[*Enter* LOPAHIN. CHARLOTTA *softly
hums a song.*]

GAEV. Charlotta's happy; she's singing!

CHARLOTTA. [*Picks up a bundle like a swaddled baby.*] By, by, my baby. [*A baby
is heard crying: "Ooah! ooah!"*] Hush, hush, my pretty boy! [*Ooah! ooah!*]
Poor little thing! [*Throws the bundle back.*] You must please find me a
situation. I can't go on like this.

LOPAHIN. We'll find you one, Charlotta Ivanovna. Don't you worry your-
self.

GAEV. Everyone's leaving us. Varya's going away. We have become of no
use all at once.

CHARLOTTA. There's nowhere for me to be in the town. I must go away.
[*Hums.*] What care I . . .

[*Enter* PISHTCHIK.]

LOPAHIN. The freak of nature!

PISHTCHIK [*gasping*]. Oh! . . . let me get my breath. . . . I'm worn out . . .
my most honored . . . Give me some water.

GAEV. Want some money, I suppose? Your humble servant! I'll go out of
the way of temptation. [*Goes out.*]

PISHTCHIK. It's a long while since I have been to see you . . . dearest lady.
[*To LOPAHIN*] You are here . . . glad to see you . . . a man of immense
intellect . . . take . . . here [*gives LOPAHIN*] . . . 400 roubles. That leaves
me owing 840.

LOPAHIN [*shrugging his shoulders in amazement*]. It's like a dream. Where did
you get it?

PISHTCHIK. Wait a bit . . . I'm hot . . . a most extraordinary occurrence!
Some Englishmen came along and found in my land some sort of white
clay. [*To LYUBOV ANDREYEVNA*] And 400 for you . . . most lovely . . .
wonderful. [*Gives money.*] The rest later. [*Sips water.*] A young man in
the train was telling me just now that a great philosopher advises jump-
ing off a housetop. "Jump!" says he; "the whole gist of the problem lies
in that." [*Wonderingly*] Fancy that, now! Water, please!

LOPAHIN. What Englishmen?

PISHTCHIK. I have made over to them the rights to dig the clay for
twenty-four years . . . and now, excuse me . . . I can't stay . . . I must

be trotting on. I'm going to Znoikovo . . . to Kardamanovo. . . . I'm in debt all round. [*Sips.*] . . . To your very good health! . . . I'll come in on Thursday.

LYUBOV. We are just off to the town, and tomorrow I start for abroad.

PISHTCHIK. What! [*In agitation*] Why to the town? Oh, I see the furniture . . . the boxes. No matter . . . [*through his tears*] . . . no matter . . . men of enormous intellect . . . these Englishmen. . . . Never mind . . . be happy. God will succor you . . . no matter . . . everything in this world must have an end. [*Kisses* LYUBOV ANDREYEVNA'S *hand.*] If the rumor reaches you that my end has come, think of this . . . old horse, and say: "There once was such a man in the world . . . Semyonov Pishtchik . . . the Kingdom of Heaven be his!" . . . most extraordinary weather . . . yes. [*Goes out in violent agitation, but at once returns and says in the doorway*] Dashenka wishes to be remembered to you. [*Goes out.*]

LYUBOV. Now we can start. I leave with two cares in my heart. The first is leaving Firs ill. [*Looking at her watch*] We have still five minutes.

ANYA. Mamma, Firs has been taken to the hospital. Yasha sent him off this morning.

LYUBOV. My other anxiety is Varya. She is used to getting up early and working; and now, without work, she's like a fish out of water. She is thin and pale, and she's crying, poor dear! [*A pause.*] You are well aware, Yermolay Alexeyevitch, I dream of marrying her to you, and everything seemed to show that you would get married. [*Whispers to* ANYA *and motions to* CHARLOTTA *and both go out.*] She loves you—she suits you. And I don't know—I don't know why it is you seem, as it were, to avoid each other. I can't understand it!

LOPAHIN. I don't understand it myself, I confess. It's queer somehow, altogether. If there's still time, I'm ready now at once. Let's settle it straight off, and go ahead; but without you, I feel I shan't make her an offer.

LYUBOV. That's excellent. Why, a single moment's all that's necessary. I'll call her at once.

LOPAHIN. And there's champagne all ready too [*looking into the glasses*]. Empty! Someone's emptied them already. [YASHA *coughs.*] I call that greedy.

LYUBOV [*eagerly*]. Capital! We will go out. Yasha, *allez!*[18] I'll call her in. [*At the door*] Varya, leave all that; come here. Come along! [*Goes out with* YASHA.]

LOPAHIN [*looking at his watch*]. Yes.

> [*A pause. Behind the door, smothered laughter and whispering, and, at last, enter* VARYA.]

VARYA [*looking a long while over the things*]. It is strange, I can't find it anywhere.

LOPAHIN. What are you looking for?

VARYA. I packed it myself, and I can't remember. [*A pause.*]

LOPAHIN. Where are you going now, Varvara Mihailova?

VARYA. I? To the Ragulins. I have arranged to go to them to look after the house—as a housekeeper.

[18] "Go!"

LOPAHIN. That's in Yashnovo? It'll be seventy miles away. [*A pause.*] So this is the end of life in this house!

VARYA [*looking among the things*]. Where is it? Perhaps I put it in the trunk. Yes, life in this house is over—there will be no more of it.

LOPAHIN. And I'm just off to Harkov—by this next train. I've a lot of business there. I'm leaving Epihodov here, and I've taken him on.

VARYA. Really!

LOPAHIN. This time last year we had snow already, if you remember; but now it's so fine and sunny. Though it's cold, to be sure—three degrees of frost.

VARYA. I haven't looked. [*A pause.*] And besides, our thermometer's broken.

> [*A pause. Voice at the door from the yard:* "Yermolay Alexeyevitch!"]

LOPAHIN [*as though he had long been expecting this summons*]. This minute!

> [LOPAHIN *goes out quickly.* VARYA *sitting on the floor and laying her head on a bag full of clothes, sobs quietly. The door opens.* LYUBOV ANDREYEVNA *comes in cautiously.*]

LYUBOV. Well? [*A pause.*] We must be going.

VARYA. [*Has wiped her eyes and is no longer crying.*] Yes, mamma, it's time to start. I shall have time to get to the Ragulins today, if only you're not late for the train.

LYUBOV [*in the doorway*]. Anya, put your things on.

> [*Enter* ANYA, *then* GAEV *and* CHARlotta Ivanovna. Gaev *has on a warm coat with a hood. Servants and cabmen come in.* EPIHODOV *bustles about the luggage.*]

LYUBOV. Now we can start on our travels.

ANYA [*joyfully*]. On our travels!

GAEV. My friends—my dear, my precious friends! Leaving this house forever, can I be silent? Can I refrain from giving utterance at leave-taking to those emotions which now flood all my being?

ANYA [*supplicatingly*]. Uncle!

VARYA. Uncle, you mustn't!

GAEV [*dejectedly*]. Cannon and into the pocket . . . I'll be quiet. . . .

> [*Enter* TROFIMOV *and afterwards* LOPAHIN.]

TROFIMOV. Well, ladies and gentlemen, we must start.

LOPAHIN. Epihodov, my coat!

LYUBOV. I'll stay just one minute. It seems as though I have never seen before what the walls, what the ceilings in this house were like, and now I look at them with greediness, with such tender love.

GAEV. I remember when I was six years old sitting in that window on Trinity Day watching my father going to church.

LYUBOV. Have all the things been taken?

LOPAHIN. I think all. [*Putting on overcoat, to* EPIHODOV] You, Epihodov, mind you see everything is right.

EPIHODOV [*in a husky voice*]. Don't you trouble, Yermolay Alexeyevitch.

LOPAHIN. Why, what's wrong with your voice?

EPIHODOV. I've just had a drink of water, and I choked over something.

YASHA [*contemptuously*]. The ignorance!

LYUBOV. We are going—and not a soul will be left here.

LOPAHIN. Not till the spring.

VARYA. [*Pulls a parasol out of a bundle, as though about to hit someone with it.* LOPAHIN *makes a gesture as though alarmed.*] What is it? I didn't mean anything.

TROFIMOV. Ladies and gentlemen, let us get into the carriage. It's time. The train will be in directly.

VARYA. Petya, here they are, your galoshes, by that box. [*With tears*] And what dirty old things they are!

TROFIMOV [*putting on his galoshes*]. Let us go, friends!

GAEV [*greatly agitated, afraid of weeping*]. The train—the station! Double balk, ah!

LYUBOV. Let us go!

LOPAHIN. Are we all here? [*Locks the side door on left.*] The things are all here. We must lock up. Let us go!

ANYA. Good-by, home! Good-by to the old life!

TROFIMOV. Welcome to the new life!

> [TROFIMOV *goes out with* ANYA. VARYA *looks round the room and goes out slowly.* YASHA *and* CHARLOTTA IVANOVNA, *with her dog, go out.*]

LOPAHIN. Till the spring, then! Come, friends, till we meet!

> [*Goes out.* LYUBOV ANDREYEVNA *and* GAEV *remain alone. As though they had been waiting for this, they throw themselves on each other's necks, and break into subdued smothered sobbing, afraid of being overheard.*]

GAEV [*in despair*]. Sister, my sister!

LYUBOV. Oh, my orchard!—my sweet, beautiful orchard! My life, my youth, my happiness, good-by! good-by!

VOICE OF ANYA [*calling gaily*]. Mamma!

VOICE OF TROFIMOV [*gaily, excitedly*]. Aa—oo!

LYUBOV. One last look at the walls, at the windows. My dear mother loved to walk about this room.

GAEV. Sister, sister!

VOICE OF ANYA. Mamma!

VOICE OF TROFIMOV. Aa—oo!

LYUBOV. We are coming.

> [*They go out. The stage is empty. There is the sound of the doors being locked up, then of the carriages driving away. There is silence. In the stillness there is the dull stroke of an axe on a tree, clanging with a mournful lonely sound. Footsteps are heard.* FIRS *appears in the doorway on the*

*right. He is dressed as always—in a pea
jacket and white waistcoat with slippers on
his feet. He is ill.*]

FIRS. [*Goes up to the doors, and tries the handles.*] Locked! They have
gone. . . . [*Sits down on sofa.*] They have forgotten me. . . . Never mind
. . . I'll sit here a bit. . . . I'll be bound Leonid Andreyevitch hasn't put
his fur coat on and has gone off in his thin overcoat. [*Sighs anxiously.*] I
didn't see after him. . . . These young people . . . [*Mutters something that
can't be distinguished.*] Life has slipped by as though I hadn't lived. [*Lies
down.*] I'll lie down a bit. . . . There's no strength in you, nothing left
you—all gone! Ech! I'm good for nothing.

> [*Lies motionless. A sound is heard that
> seems to come from the sky, like a breaking
> harp string, dying away mournfully. All is
> still again, and there is heard nothing but
> the strokes of the axe far away in the
> orchard.*]

Moderns and Contemporaries

I T is hard to get a clear perspective on the literature of our own century. For one thing, we are too close to it; for another, it is still writing itself. Like Menelaus seizing Proteus, we can take a grip on it for a moment, but the minute we let go, it changes shape again. Or, to change the metaphor, looking at recent literature sometimes seems less like looking through a lens than like peering into a kaleidoscope (or perhaps the "collideorscape" through which James Joyce peered at history in *Finnegans Wake*). One moment we get a fix upon a pattern, the next moment another takes its place. Nevertheless, as we approach the end of the century, literary historians have arrived at some tentative, working generalizations about twentieth-century literature. It seems useful, to begin with, to divide this literature into two phases, Modern and Contemporary. The Modern period seems to have come to an end about the time of the Second World War, when new currents began to emerge that we call Contemporary and that we are still experiencing.

Moderns

"Modern," in general usage, just means "up-to-date" or "pertaining to the present time," and so as time passes the period referred to is continually changing. Therefore, there may appear to be something paradoxical about saying that the Modern period ended about the time of the Second World War. But the fact is that historians of art and culture use the term "Modern" in a special way to refer to the period roughly coinciding with the first half of this century. The term, awkward as it is, was used by the artists themselves; and it may be significant that early twentieth-century artists settled upon such a slippery, ever-changing word to describe their work, which itself demonstrated a pattern of rapid and accelerating change. But change itself can be a principle of continuity; there can be, paradoxically, a "tradition of the new," as the art critic Harold Rosenberg has pointed out. Throughout the history of Western literature, writers have rejected the models of their predecessors, but never has the rejection been so total and the search for continually new forms been so determined as it was in the Modern period.

Behind the quest for new forms lay the conviction that modern experience was unique, qualitatively different from that of any time in the past. "In or about December, 1910," Virginia Woolf wrote, "human character

1605

changed." D. H. Lawrence had the same feeling, though he dated the change five years later: "It was in 1915 the old world ended," he wrote in *Kangaroo*. One is tempted to ask the exact time of day and if Woolf and Lawrence were sure that their watches were accurate. But of course their comparative precision was a rhetorical flourish as well as an allusion to certain symbolic events: the death of England's King Edward VII and the opening of the first Post-Impressionist exhibition in London (both 1910) and the first full year of World War I (1915).

More important than getting an exact fix on precise dates is understanding what this presumed change in "human character" amounted to. At its most fundamental level, the change was a massive disillusionment, an erosion of faith not only in religion but in a number of secular principles as well, principles that at least seemed to form the basis of all of Western civilization. The disillusionment was to some degree intellectual, the result of a wide range of late nineteenth-century theories and discoveries that collectively implied a radical revision of traditional Western ideas. Karl Marx's *Capital* (1867–94) shook the imperialist ideology of Western Europe by finding in history not the pattern of progress toward domination of the world by the "enlightened" bourgeoisie of Europe but an inevitable movement, to be hurried along by revolution, toward a struggle between the capitalist middle class and the nonpropertied proletariat that would end in the triumph of the workers. Charles Darwin's *Origin of Species* (1859) and *The Descent of Man* (1871) similarly seemed to remove mind from human history, on an even broader scale, by placing human beings in the animal world in the grip of determinative forces not of reason but of brute survival. Sir James G. Frazer, in *The Golden Bough* (1890), struck another blow against the popular theory of progress by showing the continuities and similarities between "primitive" and "civilized" cultures. The German philosopher Friedrich Nietzsche's *Birth of Tragedy* (1872), which glorified the Dionysian forces in life, has an enormous impact on late nineteenth-century Europe; in Nietzsche's reconsideration of Greek history, Apollo and Socrates became the villains rather than the heroic light-bringers that they had seemed to the nineteenth-century imagination. Faith in ordinary, cause-and-effect reasoning was further eroded from a very different source by Max Planck's proposal in 1900 of the quantum theory of atomic and subatomic particles; its model of discrete bits (*quanta*) of energy behaving in apparently discontinuous and unpredictable ways seized the imaginations of people who took the theory far beyond the limits of physics. And Sigmund Freud's *Interpretation of Dreams* (1899) created a new model of human personality itself as complex, multilayered, and governed, in large part, by irrational and unconscious survivals of infantile fantasy.

In a sense, these ideas were not new; class struggle, the animal side of humanity, primitivism, the power of the irrational, and the unconscious had been central to much nineteenth-century thought. But these ideas had never succeeded, in the nineteenth century, in destroying the generally prevailing faith in religion, progress, and materialism. That faith weakened in the face of contrary evidence late in the century and died in the apocalyptic experience of the First World War.

Modern artists just after World War I (and some in the years just before it) found themselves in a world deprived of a number of traditional ways of

ordering experience. They could no longer accept the premises of the existence of a God, of the human race's right to a certain dignity by virtue of its special place in creation, of the supremacy of reason in human affairs, or even of life as being self-evidently worth living. The heavens were, for the first time in history, empty. Of course, not all people rejected these premises any more than all people reject them now. (A perennial piece of graffiti reads: "God is dead—Nietzsche." "Nietzsche is dead—God.") But the main tendency of Modern culture was to deny or question them.

Much of Modern literature was born from this new spiritual confrontation with emptiness. But the exploration of the void was not always despairing or nihilistic. Just as frequently, it was joyful and affirmative. The search for new ways of ordering experience meaningfully ended as often in hope as in despair, whether the ground for affirmation was personal relationships, social idealism, rediscovery of our roots in nature, or a kind of indefinable animal vitality. As often as not, "gaiety," in William Butler Yeats's words, "transfigures all that dread."

Disillusioned and contemplating a cosmos and a society either without order or so complexly ordered as to defy understanding, most Modern writers looked within themselves for a principle of order. The most striking feature of Modern literature, therefore, was its overwhelming preoccupation with the self, the nature of consciousness, and the processes of perception. In its subjectivity, Modern literature paralleled the development of other arts, such as painting, which moved in the late nineteenth century from the Impressionistic concern with the viewer's coloring of the external world in the act of perception, through a gradual withdrawal from the outside world into the viewer's consciousness, to the complete immersion in the mind typical of Modern abstract painting.

Crucial to early modern literary explorations of individual perception were the theory and practice of the French Symbolist poets. Charles Baudelaire (1821–67), Arthur Rimbaud (1854–91), Paul Verlaine (1844–96), and Stéphane Mallarmé (1842–98) reacted against both the materialism of their society and the crudity of naturalism by withdrawing into an ideal world of art. The Symbolists aimed to capture the most evanescent of personal experiences in shimmering, open-ended, essentially private symbols. Their quixotic goal was to express the inexpressible, or rather to evoke it subtly. "Poetry," Mallarmé wrote, "should not inform but suggest and evoke, not name things but create their atmosphere." Echoes of Symbolist doctrine linger not only in the pervasive symbolic method of the early Modern novelists, poets, and dramatists but also in a number of explicit statements about narrative form and meaning, such as Conrad's description of Marlow's narrative method in *Heart of Darkness:* "To him the meaning of an episode was not inside like a kernel but outside, enveloping the tale which brought it out only as a glow brings out a haze, in the likeness of one of those misty halos that sometimes are made visible by the spectral illumination of moonshine." They linger also in Virginia Woolf's description of life as the novelist should seek to represent it—"not a series of gig lamps symmetrically arranged; but a luminous halo, a semi-transparent envelope surrounding us from the beginning of consciousness to the end"—and in the young James Joyce's quest for epiphanic moments of enlightenment through bits of concrete experience.

The Symbolists' concentration upon single moments of individual perception anticipated the Moderns' pervasive concern with fragmentation. As general laws and large systems lost their persuasiveness, they left behind small fragments of irreducible experience to be manipulated and reordered in new ways. As the Cubist painters shattered the features of a human face and reassembled them, perhaps with both eyes on one side of a profile, so Modern writers shattered and reassembled the elements of their art. Conrad's literary impressionism approaches a kind of literary cubism in a novel such as *Lord Jim,* a series of nonchronological fragments glimpsed, to use Marlow's own metaphor, through brief rifts in an enveloping fog. Character, too, is disassembled into its fragmentary components, not held together by an overarching theory of human types or any other simple psychology. The Swedish dramatist August Strindberg's "characterless" dramatic characters are of this complex sort. "I have depicted my characters as modern characters," he pointed out in his preface to *Miss Julie* (1888), "vacillating, disjointed: a blending of the old and the new. . . . My characters are conglomerates of a past stage of civilization and our present one, scraps from books and newspapers, pieces of humanity, torn-off tatters of holiday clothes that have disintegrated and become rags—exactly as the soul is patched together." The "heap of broken images" that is T. S. Eliot's *The Waste Land,* the disjointed fragments of a story the six characters bring to the theater in Luigi Pirandello's *Six Characters in Search of an Author* (1921), and the brief, snapshot scenes of Bertolt Brecht's Epic Theater are all expressions of the Modern writer's sense that fragments were all that one could honestly treat. Fragments alone were freed from suspect traditional systems of order.

The disintegration of experience into fragments suggests the negative side of Modernism; the Symbolists' attempt to divine the significance of each luminous bit and the search for new forms of organizing the fragments suggest the positive side. The simplest organizational method was juxtaposition, as in collage. Early Modern painters experimented with this method, and Ezra Pound used it when he edited the first version of Eliot's *The Waste Land* to remove the transitions between the separate sections. Even more far-reaching was stream-of-consciousness, a technique associated ordinarily with fiction but implicit also in poetry or even drama that takes its form from the fluid, associational, often illogical, moment-to-moment sequence of ideas, feelings, and impressions of a single mind. Inevitably, traditional literary forms melt before such subjectivity and are replaced by unique, make-it-up-as-you-go-along ones in which each work seems tailored to its own content. Genres overlap and merge, so that poetry can incorporate sections of flat prose and novels can employ the lyricism, the rhythmic qualities, and the symbolism traditionally associated with poetry. The forms of the past are shamelessly raided and employed, but mainly for ironic effect, as when *The Waste Land* briefly shapes itself into a series of sonnets, *Heart of Darkness* reminds us for a moment of a boys' adventure story, or the Producer of *Six Characters* tries to force the characters' inchoate tale into the iron form of melodrama.

An equally important shaping principle in Modern literature was what might be called the "stream-of-*un*consciousness," the use of the irrational logic of dreams and fantasies. The Moderns' search for an alternative logic

to what they perceived as a sterile, exhausted rationality led them repeatedly to the shadowy structures of the dream. Strindberg, in his preface to *A Dream Play* (1902), described his idea of these structures: "The author has sought to reproduce the disconnected, yet apparently logical, form of the dream. Anything is possible and plausible. Time and space do not exist; the imagination, grounding itself only slightly in reality, spins and weaves new patterns, mixing memory, experience, free invention, absurdity, and improvisation. Characters divide, double, redouble, evaporate, condense, float out of each other, converge. But there is a consciousness transcending all—the consciousness of the dreamer." Like Strindberg, the French Surrealists of the 1920's sought to capture the dream for literature, through hypnosis, drugs, revery, and automatic writing; for them, the "surreality" of dreams held a truth more profound than the logic of waking reality. But even for other writers who did not attempt to recreate dreams directly, the workings of the unconscious held a fascination so great that Freud's explanations in *The Interpretation of Dreams* of the principles of dream-logic—its symbolizings, compressions and divisions of characters and ideas, and its mysterious redistributions of emotional associations—are almost as useful for interpreting modern literature as they are for interpreting dreams.

Myth, as a kind of collective dream, was mined also for its power to give shape to experience, but myth in Modernism was stripped, for the most part, of its religious and magical associations. When James Joyce built *Ulysses*, the story of a day in Dublin, June 16, 1904, on the foundation of the *Odyssey*, T. S. Eliot found the idea promising for Modern literature: "In using the myth, in manipulating the continuous parallel between contemporaneity and antiquity, Mr. Joyce is pursuing a method which others must pursue after him. . . . It is simply a way of controlling, of ordering, of giving a shape and a significance to the immense panorama of futility and anarchy which is contemporary history. . . . It is, I seriously believe, a step toward making the modern world possible for art." Eliot himself employed the "mythic method" in 1922, the same year *Ulysses* was published, when he built *The Waste Land* upon the structure of the ancient fertility myth of the dying and reviving king. Eliot was right in predicting that many later writers would find in allusion and myth a way of structuring modern experience: Yeats with both Greek and Celtic hero-tales, Mann with the Faust legend and the biblical story of Joseph and his brothers, Faulkner with his vision of southern history as reenacting the Fall of Man, and dozens of other writers with dozens of other myths.

The Modern writer's quest for order created by individual consciousness led inevitably to a preoccupation with the artist himself and with the artistic process. The early twentieth century was the great age of the *Bildungsroman* (the growing-up story) and the *Kunstlerroman* (the artist-story), along with their equivalents in poetry and drama. One of the great Modern masterpieces, Marcel Proust's *Remembrance of Things Past* (1913–27), is a seven-volume narrative about the writer himself and his quest for an artistic subject. D. H. Lawrence's *Sons and Lovers* (1913), Thomas Mann's *Death in Venice* (1913) and *Doctor Faustus* (1947), James Joyce's *A Portrait of the Artist as a Young Man* (1916), Virginia Woolf's *To the Lighthouse* (1927), and a host of other works explore either the writer's own development as an artist or that of a thinly veiled surrogate. The themes of these works were seldom

narrowly esthetic; art became an exemplary activity, representing the pattern-making which the openness and indeterminacy of modern life forced everyone to engage in. Thus the artist became the Modernist hero, the prototype of the modern person thinking and feeling.

The same pattern-making impulse may account for the formalism and the reflexivity of much Modern art. It is as if the artist were saying, "If I cannot see an order in the world around me, I can at least explore the order within the microcosm of my work. And perhaps that order will help me perceive order in the larger world as well." Modern literature is full of metafiction, metapoetry, and metatheater, self-reflexive literature about literature, in which literary forms come to stand for the forms of life. Much Modern drama carries to its logical conclusion Jaques' observation in *As You Like It* that "all the world's a stage, and all the men and women merely players." In Pirandello's *Six Characters in Search of an Author*, the six characters invade a play rehearsal and launch an attack upon the actors' definitions of "theater" and "life," leaving them at least half-convinced that life consists only in wearing a series of "naked masks." Or perhaps all the world's a novel, as it seems to be in the work of writers from Joseph Conrad on through Proust and Joyce. Or perhaps it's a poem, as it is in *The Waste Land* and in William Butler Yeats's "Sailing to Byzantium." Art folds back upon itself in "the act of finding," as Wallace Stevens wrote, "what will suffice."

It hardly needs saying that this description of a subjective, self-conscious Modern literature of fragments, dreams, and myths hardly applies to much of the literature of the first half of the twentieth century. Not all modern writers were Modernists, and a characteristic feature of the Modern period was the coexistence of a proliferation of styles, ranging from survivals of nineteenth-century realism to an astonishing variety of experimental styles.

Contemporaries

If several of the major Modern movements in the arts were a direct response to the shock of the First World War, some important threads in Contemporary literature can be traced back to the impact of the Second World War. Virginia Woolf said human character changed in December, 1910; it probably changed again in August, 1945, when a mushroom cloud rose over Hiroshima, Japan, ending a war of unprecedented horror with the additional horror of the destruction of 130,000 civilians. After the First World War, the idea of Western civilization had to be reconciled with the fact of the million dead at Verdun; after the Second, it had to allow for the systematic, bureaucratized slaughter of six million Jews, the division of the planet between superpowers in a seemingly permanent stance of confrontation, and weapons in the hands of these superpowers that made the annihilation of the human race a genuine possibility. To these new facts of life were to be added over the next four decades constantly accelerating innovations in technology that were to place humans in space and on the moon,

to alter transportation so radically as to bend our perceptions of time and space, and to bombard us constantly with electronically processed information.

If art, as Hamlet said, shows "the very age and body of the time his form and pressure," it is not surprising that the extraordinary forms and pressures of the recent past should have demanded new forms of literary expression. What is surprising is that these new forms should have been comparatively slow in developing and even slower in winning critical recognition and understanding. The wholesale rejection of traditional forms and the aggressive experimentation that followed the disillusionment of the First World War were not duplicated after the even deeper disillusionment of the Second World War. The transition from Modern to Contemporary literature was less obvious, and only very recently have critics begun to define the changes involved.

Even more than in the Modern period, the hallmark of the Contemporary period has been pluralism, and no brief survey can pretend even to mention all the important trends in Contemporary literature. But some of those trends can be suggested by referring to the dozen works that represent that literature (hardly adequately) in this anthology.

First, as Samuel Beckett's *Krapp's Last Tape* suggests, the energies of Modernism are far from exhausted in Contemporary literature. The world has shrunk, for Krapp, to the pool of white light that represents his own consciousness. He seems to spend his time obsessively going over his own life, exploded into achronological fragments through the medium of the tape recorder, and reassembling it along lines that have more meaning for him. Here are the preoccupation with perception, the fragmentation, the loss of stable belief in anything outside the self, the pervasive irony that we identify with Modernism. Beckett, friend and contemporary of Joyce, has been called the "last Modernist." But he has also been called the "first postmodernist," in an attempt to suggest the commanding position he holds in the literature of the present rather than only the past.

The notion of "postmodernism" is the subject of a great deal of controversy and disagreement. But one reasonable view holds that postmodernism represents an extension of Modernist experimentation; perhaps "neo-Modernism" would be a less confusing way to express this view. Postmodernism's principal extension of Modernism is in the direction of a preoccupation—sometimes it seems an exclusive one—with the text itself. The American experimental novelist Ronald Sukenick has put the matter dramatically (and significantly not in his own voice but in that of one of his characters): "The contemporary writer is forced to start from scratch: reality doesn't exist, time doesn't exist, personality doesn't exist. In view of these annihilations it should be no surprise that literature also does not exist—how could it? There is only reading and writing."

"Only reading and writing": not a bad description of Krapp, if we extend it to include listening and recording. Krapp's world is a text, the boxes of tapes he has recorded over the years, analogues of his progressive consciousness of self. In a sense, Beckett's text about Krapp's text is Modernist reflexivity; Beckett is commenting upon his own art by implicitly equating it with Krapp's futile tape. (And what is "Krapp's last tape"? Is it the tape

Krapp tries to record and impatiently throws away, or is the play itself "Krapp's last tape"?) But Beckett's denial of the external world goes beyond Modernist limits. Here the world is not merely chaotic; as Sukenick says, it does not exist at all. Its ties to reality cut, the play can incorporate various modalities freely and without incongruity; Krapp is both a real old man and a timeless clown existing only "on stage."

A world in which "reality" does not exist, only verbal constructs, sounds impossibly sterile and claustrophobic. But oddly enough postmodernist principles lead writers as often toward the real world as away from it. Jorge Luis Borges's brief, haunting "fictions" and Gabriel García Márquez's "magical and realistic" stories, among the works in the anthology, perhaps have most claim to be read along with *Krapp's Last Tape* as postmodern writing. Borges's and García Márquez's stories create alternative worlds of possibility and wonder, but they have meaning only as they point back to aspects of the world we know, aspects not ordinarily accessible to realistic fiction.

The postmodern self-consciousness about narrative texts probably derives not only from philosophical premises but also, to some extent impossible to assess, from the electronic media, especially television. The American writer Norman Mailer has described the contemporary reading public as having "had their minds jabbed and poked and twitched and probed and finally galvanized into surrealistic modes of response by commercials cutting into dramatic narratives, and parents flipping from network to network." It is hard to make the suspension of disbelief required of traditional fiction when a narrative on television has its main scenes anticipated in a "teaser" introduction and then is periodically interrupted by commercials and station breaks, when one sees the events of the day regularly reduced and packaged in neat chunks on the evening news, or when, by means of communications satellites, *The Muppets* or *Kojak* is ripped out of its original context and becomes the most popular show in, say, Hong Kong. We suffer from a surfeit of narrative and, out of self-defense if nothing else, are forced to become conscious of its workings.

At the same time that some Contemporary writers have extended Modernism into postmodernism, others have brought about a strong resurgence of realistic writing, in which the text is treated as a transparent window onto reality, rather than the object of contemplation in itself. Realism remains the main form of popular fiction and drama, but it is also favored by a number of serious writers with strong political convictions. Many such writers seem to regard postmodern experimentation as too close to estheticism and are drawn instead to realism's traditional power to make a faithful report of social conditions. Thus Richard Wright, driven by the urgency of his opposition to American racism, writes a story like the blunt, brutally literal "Big Boy Leaves Home." In this anthology, James Baldwin's "Sonny's Blues," Alice Walker's "To Hell With Dying," and, in a very different way, Joyce Carol Oates's "Did You Ever Slip on Red Blood?" also illustrate contemporary realism at its most artful. Athol Fugard's "Master Harold" . . . and the boys" is an example of a similar Contemporary realism in drama.

Contemporary "literature of the Western world" has also been vastly enriched by voices long silent or suppressed. From classical times through the modern period, what has been traditionally regarded as Western litera-

ture has been overwhelmingly Western European and American, white, and male. The international women's movement of the past quarter of a century has been reflected in the emergence of a great many gifted women writers who have given the distinctive life experience of women a greater prominence in literature than ever before. They are represented here by Adrienne Rich, Joyce Carol Oates, and Alice Walker, three fine writers who must stand for many more. To turn from gender to geography, Jorge Luis Borges and Gabriel García Márquez represent in the anthology the extraordinary emergence in the 1960's of Latin American literature into international prominence. Athol Fugard similarly represents the strength and power of recent South African writing, while the gifted Milan Kundera represents a sizable body of fine Contemporary Eastern European literature.

It used to be fashionable, in the first fine flush of the electronic revolution, to speak of the "death of the book." Books—clumsy, old-fashioned, and wasteful of time and space—were to be superseded by various sorts of instant-access data banks. Things have not worked out that way. Contemporary literature has not only survived, it has flourished. It is hard to see its shape from our close perspective, and future generations may read it very differently, but it seems likely that the writers who to us are Contemporary will have a high place in the history of world literature.

FURTHER READING (*prepared by J. H.*): A good starting point for the study of Modern literature is *Modernism*, ed. Malcolm Bradbury and James McFarlane, 1974, in the Pelican Guides to European Literature series. This volume includes thirty-four essays by a number of critics on important topics in Modernism, including its history in different countries and its expression in various genres. *The Modern Tradition: Backgrounds of Modern Literature*, ed. Richard Ellmann and Charles Feidelson, Jr., 1965, constitutes a small library in itself of key documents in the intellectual history of Modernism. Of the many collections of essays on Modernism, one of the best is *Literary Modernism*, ed. Irving Howe, 1967. Howe's introduction, "The Idea of the Modern," is a good short treatment of the subject. A classic essay not included in the Howe collection is Harry Levin's "What Was Modernism?" in *Refractions*, 1966. Maurice Beebe's "What Modernism Was," his introduction to a special issue on Modernism in the *Journal of Modern Literature*, 3 (1973–74), 1065–84, is also excellent; he includes a bibliography of the subject. Alistair Davies has produced a book-length *Annotated Critical Bibliography of Modernism*, 1982.

On the relation of Modernism to Symbolism, see Edmund Wilson's *Axel's Castle: A Study in the Imaginative Literature of 1870–1930*, 1945. On the relation of Modernism to Romanticism, see Robert Langbaum, *The Modern Spirit: Essays on the Continuity of Nineteenth- and Twentieth-Century Literature*, 1970; Gabriel Josipovici, "Modernism and Romanticism," in *The World and the Book*, 1971; and John Lucas, *Romantic to Modern Literature*, 1982.

On Contemporary literature, see Ihab Hassan's *The Dismemberment of Orpheus: Toward a Postmodern Literature*, 2nd ed., 1982, and *The Postmodern Turn: Essays on Postmodern Theory and Culture*, 1986. David Lodge's "Modernism, Antimodernism, and Postmodernism," in *Working with Structuralism*, 1981, is clear and provocative. Charles Russell's *Poets, Prophets, and Revolutionaries: The Literary Avant-Garde from Rimbaud through Postmodernism*, 1985, is detailed and discriminating; his final chapter on postmodernism is especially good. Ivar Ivask's *World Literature Since 1945: Critical Surveys of the Contemporary Literatures of Europe and the Americas*, 1973, is notable for its breadth, including not only experimental work but more traditional work as well. A reference guide to contemporary fiction is *Postmodern Fiction: A Bio-Bibliographical Guide*, ed. by Larry McCaffrey, 1986.

French Symbolist and Modernist Poetry
(c.1840—c.1920)

The mapping of literary history can be an arbitrary thing. It would be reasonable, from one point of view, to define the French poetry produced between the mid-nineteenth and the early twentieth centuries as a magnificent achievement for which Romanticism had been a preparatory dawn and which faded into the twilight of modernism. For our present purposes, we are examining the period differently, as a transition between the Romantics and the modernists. This perspective is, more or less, the one adopted by the modernists themselves, who, despite their tendency at times to disavow the past in one large gesture, admitted a special kind of fraternal debt to the symbolists. To outline this transition we present eight poets, all of whom can, at least in certain respects, be called symbolists: Charles Baudelaire (1821–67), Tristan Corbière (1845–75), Paul Verlaine (1844–96), Arthur Rimbaud (1854–91), Stéphane Mallarmé (1842–98), Jules Laforgue (1860–87), Guillaume Apollinaire (1880–1918), and Paul Valéry (1871–1945). As these dates indicate, our arrangement is not strictly chronological; rather, it reflects, roughly, the order of the poets' most important or typical work. Some of them died very young; others entered the stream of literary history very early or very late in their lives (in the case of Corbière, posthumously).

The label *symbolist* must be elasticized somewhat if it is to comprehend all eight of these poets; strictly speaking, the label was consciously adopted by only some of them or for only part of their creative careers. Moreover, the term meant something significantly different from what it means today in ordinary usage, even literary usage. For the French symbolists, generally speaking, the symbol did not mean a specific figure of speech akin to a simile; nor did it mean a clear, concrete object that represents some identifiable entity (as, say, whiteness in Conrad's *Heart of Darkness* symbolizes the veneer of hypocritical civilization). Rather, symbolism meant the interconnectedness of an image with a whole range of things (as in Rimbaud's sonnet "Vowels") or even the more cosmic interconnectedness of everything with everything else (as in Baudelaire's sonnet "Correspondences"). The function of symbolism was not to clarify but rather almost the opposite: to evoke mysterious overtones, along with the overtones of mystery. Indeed, the word *tones* here is crucial, for one of the symbolists' main goals was to approach the condition of music, a condition of pure feeling, pure esthetic experience divorced from statement (especially didactic statement), narrative, or even sharply-etched description. The analogues with French impressionism in the other arts are strong, and indeed impressionist composers such as Debussy were often inspired by the symbolist poets.

Perhaps the best realizations of symbolist poetry in the sense just described are the poems of Verlaine, with their pastel colors, their gentle pianissimo harmonies, their power to suggest, their quiet but intense lyricism. (Not that he couldn't also be acerb or a little naughty, as in "Sentimental Conversation" and "Song of the Ingenues.") His "Art of Poetry" outlines perfectly several planks in the symbolist program. The fact that in this

highly polished, eloquent, and epigrammatic poem he recommends to poets a fine carelessness, urges them to wring the neck of eloquence, and calls epigram a murderer, produces some amusing ironies, but his points get made.

All this sounds invertebrate and misty, closer to the nostalgic escapism of pre-Raphaelite painting than to modernism, and indeed what appealed to the modernists were certain other faces of the symbolist practice and esthetic. (Some modern poets, however, started out sounding a little like Verlaine—Yeats, for example.) To appreciate these other faces, one must go back a little earlier to the poet whose work and vision underlie all the others we are discussing: Charles Baudelaire, the greatest of the group. There is plenty of exotic sound and perfume in Baudelaire's poetry, and an even deeper commitment than Verlaine's to the primacy of esthetic experience, but there is also harshness, horror, and stench. These, for him, are an inescapable part of the anguished reality of human existence; a woman's hair can be redolent of tropical balms ("The Head of Hair"), but her body will decay like that of the rotting animal in "Carrion." Few poets have celebrated sexual pleasure more ardently, but probably none has confronted the other face of sex more uncompromisingly than Baudelaire does in his picture of the hanged voluptuary, his body devoured by animals, in "A Voyage to Cythera." It is not a long step from these visions to Yeats's description of his condition in "Sailing to Byzantium": "sick with desire / And fastened to a dying animal." For that matter, Yeats's image, in the same poem, of his soul divorced from living flesh has something in common with the vision of an inorganic (though surrealistic and somewhat nightmarish) world in "Parisian Dream." The concreteness of such poems, and their un-Romantic, unflinching explorations of the brute facts about human life, exerted a stronger fascination for twentieth-century poets than did the more delicate musicality of Verlaine.

The dilemma of spirit mired or trapped in matter can hardly be regarded as a discovery of the nineteenth and twentieth centuries; the dilemma is at the heart of Plato's philosophy, and it has been explored by Christian and other ascetics for many ages. The new twist given to this dualism in Baudelaire and his successors comes largely from the new esthetic context in which they place the old problem. The question is not only what poetry should *say* about the conflict between "higher" and "lower" aspects of existence; more urgent, for the poets we are considering, is the question how this dualism affects the very role and nature of art. That the dualism is an urgent moral problem for Baudelaire is unquestionable; he, for one, strongly believed in the reality of sin. For Mallarmé, the moral aspect becomes more equivocal; poems such as "Windows" and "The Azure" seem to express a genuinely moral revulsion toward the fallen human condition, but the moral revulsion blends into an esthetic one, disgusted less with sin than with the vulgarity and banality of mundane life. Indeed, as Mallarmé grew older, he became the mentor of a dedicated group of younger symbolists who, along with him, had come to be less concerned with the purity of the soul than with the purity of art. (Paul Valéry was for a time one of these disciples.) Indeed, some esthetes deliberately and proudly called themselves "decadents." With Mallarmé showing the way, his followers came to believe that poetry should achieve a calcu-

lated obscurity, not only as a means necessary to expressing certain things but also, to some extent, as a protective coating insulating poetry from the vulgar throng of philistines.

One form cerebral poetry could take in later literature can be seen in poems like Valéry's "Song of the Columns," which is a kind of hymn to the mind by way of its enshrinement in the aloof, abstract principles of architecture. The other modernist side of all this, the side that, in the name of "the new," wants to lovingly embrace all of humanity and the cosmos, to extend and publicize art rather than protect it against trespassers, appears in the gregarious Guillaume Apollinaire, pioneer of cubist, dadaist, and surrealist movements. Indeed, this paradox, of wanting at the same time to erect elitist walls and to break down the old conventional barriers, is the distinctive mark of almost all the avant-garde movements that have appeared in the arts in the twentieth century. Arthur Rimbaud, the demonic *enfant terrible* of nineteenth-century French poetry (all his poetry was written by the time he was twenty), had helped prepare the way for such avant-gardism. His notorious poem "The Drunken Boat" is on the one hand a bacchic bath, a phantasmagoria of sense impressions and exotic images, a welcoming of all experience, and on the other hand an exercise in poetic obscurity fully accessible to, at most, a small circle of diligent explicators.

The most inclusive term for these paradoxes and dualisms, discerned by the symbolists or apparent in their work, is irony. Sometimes, as we have suggested, the ironies are large matters of morality, metaphysics, and esthetics, and twentieth-century artists, living in an even more fragmented world, have been especially receptive to such tensions of attitude. But the symbolists were also ironists in another, more ordinary sense. In bitter or in comic veins, they were especially aware of the disparity between pretensions and commonplace reality—an awareness that typifies their revolt against Romanticism. In "The Pretty Redhead," Apollinaire, addressing the Establishment, ironically takes "ardent Reason" as his emblem of the spirit of adventure he has been describing, and then takes as his emblem of ardent reason "an adorable redhead." In this characteristically jaunty vein he had had a number of forerunners. One of them was Corbière, who, in "The End," had taken the eminent Romantic poet Victor Hugo down a peg by showing him how sailors really talk and look at things, and who in "Paris by Day" had imaged Divine Providence as God's great casserole dish. Another forerunner was Laforgue, who in "The Approach of Winter" takes as his ironic target the typical Romantic theme and imagery of the changing seasons, but with a difference: the sun, for example, is "white as spittle on a barroom floor" and "like a gland torn out of a neck." It is hard not to think of T. S. Eliot's "Prufrock": "the evening is spread out against the sky / Like a patient etherised upon a table." Other resemblances also suggest themselves: Laforgue was one of the inventors of "free verse," in which lines have no set pattern of meter or rhyme. Such stylistic unbuttonedness is in parallel with the free-and-easy tone achieved in some of the symbolist poems, which in turn is in parallel with the highly unconventional lives certain of them led—most notably Arthur Rimbaud and Paul Verlaine (who went to jail for a while for shooting Rimbaud). The symbolists contributed, in their lives or works or both, a good deal to what the word

bohemianism has come to mean, whether we are thinking of the Left Bank in Paris or the Beat Poets of the 1950's.

FURTHER READING *(prepared by B. W.):* For students who wish to read other works by the poets collected here, the following bilingual collections are recommended: Angel Flores, ed., *An Anthology of French Poetry from Nerval to Valéry in English Translation,* 1958; C. F. MacIntyre, trans., *French Symbolist Poetry,* 1958; and *The Penguin Book of French Verse* (with plain prose translations), parts 3 and 4, ed. Anthony Hartley, 1959. Excellent translations of Baudelaire, by various hands, appear in Charles Baudelaire, *Flowers of Evil,* ed. Marthiel and Jackson Mathews, rev, ed. 1962. The translations, in the present anthology, of Baudelaire by Richard Howard and of Verlaine and Corbière by C. F. MacIntyre are drawn from excellent book-length translations of the respective poets. For brief general introductions to the individual poets, one place to start is with the histories of French literature; *A Literary History of France,* of which the pertinent volumes, 4 and 5 (1967), are by P. E. Charvet, is especially good. Lengthier discussions of the most important of the eight poets appear in Wallace Fowlie, *Climate of Violence: The French Literary Tradition from Baudelaire to the Present,* 1967. On Baudelaire's life, see Enid Starkie, *Baudelaire,* rev. ed., 1957; a good critical study is Martin Turnell, *Baudelaire: A Study of His Poetry,* 1954. See also *Baudelaire: A Collection of Critical Essays,* ed. Henri Peyre, 1962. On the other poets, the following books are recommended: Antoine Adam, *The Art of Paul Verlaine,* trans. Carl Morse, 1963 (biography and criticism); Wallace Fowlie, *Mallarmé,* 1953 (biography and criticism); Robert Greer Cohn, *Toward the Poems of Mallarmé,* 1965 (criticism); Frederic C. St. Aubyn, *Arthur Rimbaud,* updated ed., 1990; Enid Starkie, *Arthur Rimbaud,* rev. ed. 1968 (biography); Wallace Fowlie, *Rimbaud: A Critical Study,* 1966 (includes a brief biography); Warren Ramsey, *Jules Laforgue and the Ironic Inheritance,* 1953 (criticism); Francis Steegmuller, *Apollinaire: Poet Among the Painters,* 1963 (biography); Scott Bates, *Apollinaire,* 1967 (criticism); Henry A. Grubbs, *Paul Valéry,* 1968 (biography and criticism). Two recent general studies are Carol de Dobay Rifelj's *Word and Figure: The Language of Nineteenth-Century French Poetry,* 1986; and David Michael Hertz's *The Tuning of the Word: The Musico-literary Poetics of the Symbolist Movement,* 1987.

Charles Baudelaire
(1821–1867)

TO THE READER[1]

Ignorance, error, cupidity, and sin
Possess our souls and exercise our flesh;
Habitually we cultivate remorse
As beggars entertain and nurse their lice.

[1] French title: *Au lecteur;* translated by Stanley Kunitz.

Our sins are stubborn. Cowards when contrite
We overpay confession with our pains,
And when we're back again in human mire
Vile tears, we think, will wash away our stains.

Thrice-potent Satan in our cursèd bed
Lulls us to sleep, our spirit overkissed,
Until the precious metal of our will 10
Is vaporized—that cunning alchemist!²

Who but the Devil pulls our waking-strings!
Abominations lure us to their side;
Each day we take another step to hell,
Descending through the stench, unhorrified.

Like an exhausted rake³ who mouths and chews
The martyrized breast of an old withered whore
We steal, in passing, whatever joys we can,
Squeezing the driest orange all the more. 20

Packed in our brains incestuous as worms
Our demons celebrate in drunken gangs,
And when we breathe, that hollow rasp is Death
Sliding invisibly down into our lungs.

If the dull canvas of our wretched life
Is unembellished with such pretty ware
As knives or poison, pyromania,⁴ rape,
It is because our soul's too weak to dare!

But in this den of jackals, monkeys, curs,
Scorpions, buzzards, snakes . . . this paradise 30
Of filthy beasts that screech, howl, grovel, grunt—
In this menagerie of mankind's vice

There's one supremely hideous and impure!
Soft-spoken, not the type to cause a scene,
He'd willingly make rubble of the earth
And swallow up creation in a yawn.

I mean *Ennui!*⁵ who in his hookah-dreams⁶
Produces hangmen and real tears together.
How well you know this fastidious monster, reader,
—Hypocrite reader, you!—my double! my brother! 40

²The alchemists of the middle ages performed experiments designed to transform matter, especially by turning base metals into precious ones.
³A man addicted to vice. ⁴A compulsion to commit arson.
⁵Boredom; to Baudelaire and the French Symbolists, *ennui* (pronounced on-wee) was a diseased cosmic weariness of soul.
⁶Opium dreams; a hookah is a pipe for drawing smoke through water.

THE ALBATROSS[1]

Often, to pass the time on board, the crew
will catch an albatross, one of those big birds
which nonchalantly chaperone a ship
across the bitter fathoms of the sea.

Tied to the deck, this sovereign of space,
as if embarrassed by its clumsiness,
pitiably lets its great white wings
drag at its sides like a pair of unshipped oars.[2]

How weak and awkward, even comical
this traveller but lately so adroit— 10
one deckhand sticks a pipestem in its beak,
another mocks the cripple that once flew!

The Poet is like this monarch of the clouds
riding the storm above the marksman's range;
exiled on the ground, hooted and jeered,
he cannot walk because of his great wings.

CORRESPONDENCES[1]

Nature is a temple from whose living columns
Commingling voices emerge at times;
Here man wanders through forests of symbols
Which seem to observe him with familiar eyes.

Like long-drawn echoes afar converging
In harmonies darksome and profound,
Vast as the night and vast as light,
Colors, scents and sounds correspond.

There are fragrances fresh as the flesh of children,
Sweet as the oboe, green as the prairie,
—And others overpowering, rich and corrupt, 10

Possessing the pervasiveness of everlasting things,
Like benjamin,[2] frankincense, amber, myrrh,
Which the raptures of the senses and the spirit sing.

[1] *L'Albatros;* translated by Richard Howard.
[2] Oars removed from their rowing position.
[1] *Correspondances;* translated by Kate Flores. [2] An Indonesian gum used in perfumes.

THE HEAD OF HAIR[1]

Ecstatic fleece that ripples to your nape
and reeks of negligence in every curl!
To people my dim cubicle tonight
with memories shrouded in that head of hair,
I'd have it flutter like a handkerchief!

For torpid Asia, torrid Africa
—the wilderness I thought a world away—
survive at the heart of this dark continent. . . .
As other souls set sail to music, mine,
O my love! embarks on your redolent[2] hair. 10

Take me, tousled current, to where men
as mighty as the trees they live among
submit like them to the sun's long tyranny;
ebony sea, you bear a brilliant dream
of sails and pennants, mariners and masts,

a harbor where my soul can slake its thirst
for color, sound and smell—where ships that glide
among the seas of golden silk throw wide
their yardarms to embrace a glorious sky
palpitating in eternal heat. 20

Drunk, and in love with drunkenness, I'll dive
into this ocean where the other lurks,
and solaced by these waves, my restlessness
will find a fruitful lethargy at last,
rocking forever at aromatic ease.

Blue hair, vault of shadows, be for me
the canopy of overarching sky;
here at the downy roots of every strand
I stupefy myself on the mingled scent
of musk and tar and coconut oil for hours. . . 30

For hours? Forever! Into that splendid mane
let me braid rubies, ropes of pearls to bind
you indissolubly to my desire—
you the oasis where I dream, the gourd
from which I gulp the wine of memory.

CARRION[1]

Remember, my soul, the thing we saw
that lovely summer day?

[1]*La Chevelure;* translated by Richard Howard. [2]Suggestively fragrant.
[1]*Une Charogne;* translated by Richard Howard.

On a pile of stones where the path turned off,
　　the hideous carrion—

legs in the air, like a whore—displayed,
　　indifferent to the last,
a belly slick with lethal sweat
　　and swollen with foul gas.

the sun lit up that rottenness
　　as though to roast it through,
restoring to Nature a hundredfold 10
　　what she had here made one.

And heaven watched the splendid corpse
　　like a flower open wide—
you nearly fainted dead away
　　at the perfume it gave off.

Flies kept humming over the guts
　　from which a gleaming clot
of maggots poured to finish off
　　what scraps of flesh remained. 20

The tide of trembling vermin sank,
　　then bubbled up afresh
as if the carcass, drawing breath,
　　by *their* lives lived again

and made a curious music there—
　　like running water, or wind,
or the rattle of chaff the winnower
　　loosens in his fan.[2]

Shapeless—nothing was left but a dream
　　the artist had sketched in, 30
forgotten, and only later on
　　finished from memory.

Behind the rocks an anxious bitch
　　eyed us reproachfully,
waiting for the chance to resume
　　her interrupted feast.

—Yet you will come to this offence,
　　this horrible decay,
you, the light of my life, the sun
　　and moon and stars of my love! 40

[2] Air currents from the winnowing-fan separated grain from inedible chaff.

Yes, you will come to this, my queen,
 after the sacraments,[3]
when you rot underground among
 the bones already there.

But as their kisses eat you up,
 my Beauty, tell the worms
I've kept the sacred essence, saved
 the form of my rotted loves!

MUSIC[1]

On music drawn away, a sea-borne mariner
 Star over bowsprit[2] pale,
Beneath a roof of mist or depths of lucid air
 I put out under sail;

Breastbone my steady bow and lungs full, running free
 Before a following gale,
I ride the rolling back and mass of every sea
 By Night wrapt in her veil;

All passions and all joys that vessels undergo
 Tremble alike in me;
Fair wind or waves in havoc when the tempests blow 10

 On the enormous sea
Rock me, and level calms come silvering sea and air,
 A glass[3] for my despair.

THE CRACKED BELL[1]

It is bitter and sweet, during the Winter nights,
To listen, by the quivering and smoking hearth-log,
To the memories withdrawn that ascend in slow flights
On the carillons whose music sings out through the fog.

Thrice fortunate the bell with a vigorous throat
That, in spite of old age, alert and still robust,
Flings faithfully the challenge of its religious note,
Like a veteran campaigner keeping watch at his post.

[3] Extreme Unction, the Roman Catholic sacramental rite for the dying.
[1] *La Musique;* translated by Robert Fitzgerald.
[2] The tapered pole projecting forward from the bow of a ship. [3] Mirror.
[1] *La Cloche fêlée;* translated by Vernon Watkins.

As for me, my soul's cracked, and when in gloom it longs
To people the chill air of the night with its songs, 10
It often befalls me that its enfeebled call

Seems a wounded man's rattle, forgotten by all
By a lake of blood under a vast heap of dead,
And who dies, without moving, in immense throes of dread!

SPLEEN (IV)[1]

When skies are low and heavy as a lid
over the mind tormented by disgust,
and hidden in the gloom the sun pours down
on us a daylight dingier than the dark;

when earth becomes a trickling dungeon where
Trust like a bat keeps lunging through the air,
beating tentative wings along the walls
and bumping its head against the rotten beams;

when rain falls straight from unrelenting clouds,
forging the bars of some enormous jail, 10
and silent hordes of obscene spiders spin
their webs across the basements of our brains;

then all at once the raging bells break loose,
hurling to heaven their awful caterwaul,[2]
like homeless ghosts with no one left to haunt
whimpering their endless grievances.

—And giant hearses, without dirge or drums,
parade at half-step in my soul, where Hope,
defeated, weeps, and the oppressor Dread
plants his black flag on my assenting skull. 20

HEAUTON TIMOROUMENOS[1]

No rage, no rancor: I shall beat you
 as butchers fell an ox,

[1] *Spleen (IV);* translated by Richard Howard. Baudelaire wrote several poems with this title.
Like *ennui, spleen* (moroseness) was a favorite term with Baudelaire and the Symbolists. The
word suggests a disease of the spirit.
[2] Discordant screeching and howling.
[1] *L'Héautontimorouménos;* translated by Richard Howard. The title, Greek for "the self-
tormentor," is the name of a play by the Roman dramatist Terence (second century B.C.).

as Moses smote the rock in Horeb[2]—
 I shall make you weep,

and by waters of affliction
 my desert will be slaked.
My desire, that hope has made monstrous,
 will frolic in your tears

as a ship tosses on the ocean—
 in my besotted heart
your adorable sobs will echo
 like an ecstatic drum.

 10

For I—am I not dissonance
 in the divine accord,
because of the greedy Irony
 which infiltrates my soul?

I hear it in my voice—that shrillness,
 that poison in my blood!
I am the sinister glass in which
 the Fury[3] sees herself!

 20

I am the knife and the wound it deals,
 I am the slap and the cheek,
I am the wheel and the broken limbs,
 hangman and victim both!

I am the vampire at my own veins,
 one of the great lost horde
doomed for the rest of time, and beyond,
 'to laugh—but smile no more.'[4]

PARISIAN DREAM[1]

1

It is a terrible terrain
 no mortal eye has seen
whose image still seduces me
 this morning as it fades . . .

[2] Another name for Mt. Sinai. During the Israelites' ordeal in the desert after their exodus from Egypt, their leader Moses drew water from a rock by striking it with his rod. The Lord then named the spring Meribah, "contention" or "affliction." See Numbers 20:1–13.

[3] In classical mythology, the Furies were infernal agents of retribution for evil.

[4] The translator identifies the last line as derived from "The Haunted Palace," by the American author Edgar Allan Poe (1809–49).

[1] *Rêve parisien;* translated by Richard Howard.

Sleep is full of miracles!
 Some impulse in my dream
had rid the region I devised
 of every growing thing,

and proud of the resulting scene
 I savored in my art 10
the rapturous monotony
 of metal, water, stone . . .

A maze of stairs and arches formed
 an endless palace filled
with basins where the bright cascades
 fell into tarnished gold;

Like crystal curtains, cataracts
 streamed down metal walls,
shimmering where the ripples made
 perpetual descent; 20

colonnades instead of trees
 shaded sleeping pools
where, vain as women, huge naiads[2]
 marveled at themselves;

pale-blue sheets of water spread
 between the marble quays[3]—
their rims of rose and green converged
 a universe away;

unimaginable gems
 glowed in magic streams; 30
mirrors dizzily exchanged
 the dazzling world they showed!

Sacred rivers crossed the sky
 in silent unconcern,
pouring the treasure of their urns
 into diamond gulfs.

Architect of such conceits,
 I sent submissive seas
into the jewelled conduits[4]
 my will erected there; 40

and every color, even black,
 became a lustrous prism;

[2] In mythology, nymphs inhabiting streams and pools. [3] Piers; docks.
[4] Channels.

liquid turned to glowing glass
 and what was crystal flowed;

yet neither sun nor moon appeared,
 and no horizon paled
to light such wonders—from *within*
 each thing was luminous!

And on these marvels as they moved
 there weighed (without a sound— 50
the eye alone was master here)
 the silence of the Void.

 2

Waking, dazzled, I was back
 in my familiar slum
and felt returning to my soul
 the curse of all my cares;

with unrelenting strokes the clock
 insisted it was noon,
and shadows poured out of the sky
 upon a sluggish world. 60

A VOYAGE TO CYTHERA[1]

My heart flew up like a bird before the mast,
circled the shrouds and mounted free and clear;
the ship rolled on beneath a cloudless sky
like an angel drunk on the glory of the sun.

What is that dreary island—the black one there?
Cythera, someone says, the one in the song
insipid Eldorado[2] of good old boys:
it isn't much of a place, as you can see.

Island of feasting hearts and secret joys!
Like a fragrance, the voluptuary ghost 10
of Aphrodite floats above your shores,
inflaming minds with languor and with love.

Island green with myrtle,[3] rich with bloom,
revered forever by all mortal men
from whose adoring hearts wells up a sigh
soft as the fallen petals of a rose

[1] *Un Voyage à Cythère;* translated by Richard Howard. The Greek island of Cythera, near the place where Aphrodite, goddess of sex and love, was born of the sea foam, was a principal center of her sensual rites.
[2] The legendary Realm of Gold. [3] The flower of love, sacred to Aphrodite.

or the relentless moan of doves[4] . . . Cythera now
was nothing more than a thistled promontory
vexed by the wheeling gulls' unruly cries.
Yet there was something . . . I could see it now; 20

no temple sheltered by its sacred grove,
no priestess gathering blossoms, her loose robe
half-opened to the breezes as they passed,
her flesh ignited by a secret fire;

but as we cleared the coastline—close enough
to scare the shorebirds with our flapping sails—
we saw what it was: black against the sky,
no cypress but a branching gallows-tree.

Perched on their provender,[5] ferocious birds
were ravaging the ripe corpse hanging there, 30
driving their filthy beaks like cruel drills
into each cranny of its rotten flesh;

the eyes were holes, and from the ruined groin
a coil of heavy guts had tumbled out—
the greedy creatures, gorged on hideous sweets,
had peck by vicious peck castrated him.

Below his feet, among a whining pack
that waited, muzzles lifted for their share,
some bigger beast was prowling back and forth
like a hangman huge among his underlings. 40

Inhabitant of Cythera, rapture's child,
how silently you suffered these affronts
in expiation of your shameful rites
and sins that have proscribed[6] your burial.

Ludicrous carcass! I hung there with you,
and at the sight of your insulted limbs
I tasted, like a vomit in my mouth,
the bitter tide of age-old sufferings.

Knowing what you were and what you are,
I felt each saber-tooth and jabbing beak 50
of jet-black panthers and of carrion-crows
that once so loved to lacerate my flesh.

. . . The sky was suave, the sea serene; for me
from now on everything was bloody and black

[4] The birds associated with Aphrodite. [5] Feed for animals.
[6] Outlawed; forbidden.

—the worse for me—and as if in a shroud
my heart lay buried in this allegory.

On Aphrodite's island all I found
was a token gallows where my image hung. . .
Lord give me strength and courage to behold
my body and my heart without disgust! 60

TRAVELERS[1]

to Maxime Du Camp

1

The child enthralled by lithographs and maps
can satisfy his hunger for the world:
how limitless it is beneath the lamp,
and how it shrinks in the eyes of memory!

One morning we set out. Our heart is full,
our mind ablaze with rancor and disgust—
we yield it all to the rhythm of the waves,
our infinite self awash on the finite sea:

some are escaping from their country's shame,
some from the horror of life at home, and some 10
—astrologers blinded by a woman's stare—
are fugitives from Circe's tyranny;

rather than be turned to swine they drug
themselves on wind and sea and glowing skies;[2]
rain and snow and incinerating suns
gradually erase her kisses' scars.

But only those who leave for leaving's sake
are *travelers;* hearts tugging like balloons,
they never balk at what they call their fate
and, not knowing why, keep muttering "away!" . . . 20

those whose longings have the shape of clouds,
who dream—as conscripts dream of guns—of huge
and fluctuating and obscure delights,
none of which has ever had a name.

2

As if we wanted to be a ball or a top!
bouncing and twirling—even in our sleep

[1] *Le Voyage;* translated by Richard Howard.
[2] Circe was the very beautiful witch who, in Homer's *Odyssey*, Book X, lures Odysseus' men
with her charms and then transforms them into swine.

we look for something, driven round and round
like a sun some cruel Angel spins in space.

Preposterous quest! whose goal cannot be known
but, being nowhere, can be anywhere; 30
only our hope is inexhaustible,
and Man pursues repose until he drops!

Our soul is a schooner seeking a free port,
and when the question rises from the deck,
a voice from the topmast eagerly replies:
"Happiness! . . . Glory! . . . Love! . . . " Another reef.

The lookout hails each island, after dark,
as El Dorado[3] and the Promised Land;
imagination readies for its feast—
and sights a sandbar by the morning light. 40

Irons or overboard with the drunken tar,[4]
pathetic lover of chimerical[5] coasts
who dreams Atlantis[6] and then finds the sea
emptier for one more fond mirage!

One more old sailor in the muddy slums
who meditates, half blind, on Happy Isles
and thinks he sees the beacons of Dakar[7]
each time a candle gutters in the dark.

3
Awesome travelers! What noble chronicles
we read in your unfathomable eyes! 50
Open the sea-chests of your memories
and show us jewels made of storms and stars.

We long to journey without steam or sail!
Help us forget the prison of our days
and on the canvas of our minds unfurl
your visions framed by the horizon's gold.

Tell us what you've seen!

4
 "We've seen the stars,
the waves, and shoals we failed to see—we saw;
and though destruction came in many forms,
we were too often bored, the same as here. 60

[3] The legendary Realm of Gold, eagerly sought by explorers. [4] Sailor.
[5] Fanciful, like the Chimera, a fabled beast.
[6] The legendary lost continent beneath the Atlantic Ocean.
[7] The city on the farthest-western coast of Africa. The mythical Fortunate Isles were imagined to exist in that vicinity.

The glory of the sun on Tyrian seas,[8]
the glow of cities when the sun goes down,
awakened in our hearts a restless urge
to plunge into a still more distant sky.

None of the famous landscapes that we saw
equalled the mysterious allure
of those that Chance arranges in the clouds . . .
And our desire would let us have no peace!

Enjoyment breeds desire tenfold . . . Desire!
Old tree manured by pleasure, all the while 70
your bark will coarsen, growing thick and hard,
your branches seek the sun at closer range!

Great tree, will you grow forever, hardier
than the cypress? All the same, we've brought
these images for your albums, stay-at-homes
who prize whatever comes from far away:

idols we saw, hideous gods whose thrones
were set with emeralds the size of plums;
and palaces of marble lace whose cost
would ruin your most reckless millionaires; 80

robes embroidered by a thousand slaves;
women who filed their lacquered teeth to points;
jugglers sinous as the snakes they charmed . . ."

 5
Yes, and what else?

 6
 "You talk just like a child!

Chief among all the wonders that we glimpsed
in every hole and corner, forced on our sight
at every turn of Fortune's fatal wheel—
the boring pageant of immortal sin:

Woman a slave and yet vainglorious,
stupid and unashamed in her self-love; 90
Man a greedy tyrant, slave of his slaves,
swelling the sewer to a stinking flood;

victims in tears, the hangman glorified;
the banquet seasoned and festooned with blood:

[8] Tyre was a great city of ancient Phoenicia, in what is now Lebanon.

the poison of power clogs the despot's veins,
and the people kiss the knout[9] that scourges them;

several religions similar to ours,
besieging heaven—the holy everywhere
like sybarites[10] on rose-beds (only on
beds of nails) in hot pursuit of bliss; 100

Humanity enslaved by rhetoric
and mad today as it has ever been,
screaming to God in a tantrum of despair:
'I curse You in my Image—Father, be damned!'

And the least stupid, Ecstasy's elect,
fleeing the herd where Fate has penned them fast,
take refuge in the wards of Opium!
—So much for what is news around the world!"

7

It is a bitter truth our travels teach!
Tiny and monotonous, the world 110
has shown—will always show us—what we are:
oases of fear in the wasteland of ennui![11]

Choose your desolation—stay if you can,
stir if you must. One man chooses sloth
to cheat a tireless adversary, Time,
out of his triumph in the funeral games.

Another journeys, like the Wandering Jew,[12]
forever, but no roving can evade
the merciless net; still others seem to know
how to kill Time before they're even weaned! 120

Yet we are his in the end. One hope remains:
to venture forth, with "Onward!" as our cry . . .
Just as once we set sail for Cathay,[13]
wind in our hair, eyes on the open sea,

we shall embark upon the Sea of Shades
with all the elation of a boy's first cruise . . .
Do you hear those lovely voices? They have death
in their appeal: "Come with us, come and eat

[9] A leather whip. [10] Devotees of voluptuous pleasure. [11] Bored weariness.
[12] In medieval legend, one of the mockers during the Passion of Christ, condemned to wander endlessly without the hope of death.
[13] The old poetical name for China.

the fragrant Lotus![14] Here is where we reap
the magic harvest that you hunger for! 130
Come and revel in the sweet delight
of days where it is always afternoon!"

Pylades is there, his arms held out;
we know the sound by heart, we guess the ghost!
It is her voice—we used to kiss her knees—
"Orestes, come—Electra waits for you . . ."[15]

<center>8</center>

Death, old admiral, up anchor now,
this country wearies us. Put out to sea!
What if the waves and winds are black as ink,
our hearts are filled with light. You know our hearts! 140

Pour us your poison, let us be comforted!
Once we have burned our brains out, we can plunge
to Hell or Heaven—any abyss will do—
deep in the Unknown to find the *new!*

SCRUTINY AT MIDNIGHT[1]

The clock ironically summons us
to account for what we did with this day past,
Friday the thirteenth, ominous date! and yet,
knowing the risks, we have defiled our life—

blasphemed the most incontestable of Gods
and (worthy slave of Hell) like a parasite
at Croesus'[2] feast, to please our monstrous host,
mocked what we love and what we loathe acclaimed!

oppressed the weak we wrongfully despise
and (servile bully) cringed to stupid Power, 10
genuflected[3] before the throne of Things
and blessed the phosphorescence of decay!

Last, to cheat our moods with madness, we
whose Muse's priesthood serves a world of death
have drunk without thirst and eaten without hunger!
—Let darkness hide us: quick, blow out the lamp!

[14] In Homer's *Odyssey*, Book IX, Odysseus and his crew find a land where eaters of the lotus-fruit are sapped of all their memory, energy, and will.

[15] In Greek myth, Pylades was the supportive friend and Electra the supportive older sister of Orestes, who killed his mother in revenge for her murder of his father.

[1] *L'Examen de minuit;* translated by Richard Howard.

[2] An enormously rich king of Lydia, in Asia Minor, sixth century B.C.

[3] Bent the knee, in adoration.

Tristan Corbière
(1845–1875)

OH! THAT?[1]

What? . . .
(Shakespeare)

Essays?—Nonsense, I have not essayed!
A study?—I'm lazy, I've never pilfered around.
A volume?—Too brochure-like to be bound . . .
Copy?—For that, alas, you don't get paid!

A poem?—Thanks, but I have hocked my lyre.
A book?— . . . A book, that's something to be read! . . .
Loose sheets?—No, thank God, it's tight-sewn and entire!
Album!—Not blank, but it lacks a coherent thread.

Rhymed ends?—By which end? . . . And it's little use!
An opus?—It's not polished and polished again. 10
Songs?—I'd just love that, my little Muse! . . .
Pastime?—You think it's mere amusement, then?

Verses? . . . a flux of verse? . . . —No, it's jerky, see.
—Ah, you've been chasing Originality? . . .
—No . . . she's an odd hussy,—*from the streets*—it's
odd, when you proposition her, she beats it.

Is it pure *chic*?—And who'd teach me that game?
—Does it soar? Or sink convulsed?—Neither flight nor fall!
—A thing for the ashcan?— . . . Or for a house of ill fame.
—The reformatory, even?—Not at all! 20

—Good, it's not classic?—It is barely French!
—Amateur?—Do I suggest success?
—Old-fashioned?—Well, not forty years off the bench . . .
—New style?—With years, one remedies that vice.

. . . *THAT* is naïvely just an impudent *pose;*
it is or it isn't *that:* all or nothing, say.
—A masterpiece?—Maybe; I've never made one of those.
—Is it in the style of the Hurons, of Gagne, or Musset?[2]

[1] *Ça?;* translated by C. F. MacIntyre. *Ça* (French for "that") is also the title of the opening
section of the volume that contains this poem, which is a kind of manifesto.
[2] *Hurons:* primitives. Paulin Gagne was an eccentric French poet of the century, Alfred de
Musset a distinguished Romantic poet.

—It's like . . . I've signed my humble *nom d'auteur*,[3]
and my child has no title that's a lie. 30
It may be right, or wrong; a hit-or-miss try . . .
Art has never met me. And I don't know Her.

Central police station,[4] May 20, 1873.

PARIS BY NIGHT[1]

It's not a city, it's a world.

It's the sea,—dead calm.—And the spring's great tide,[2]
snarling distantly now, has retreated wide . . .
Rumbling, it will roll in from the ebb.
Do you hear the scratching of nocturnal crabs?

It's the dried Styx:[3] here comes Diogenes,[4]
ragpicker, with lantern, wandering at his ease.
The perverse poets by the somber river,
with their hollow skulls for bait-cans, fish forever.

It's the fields: in wheeling flight the hideous hags,
harpies,[5] swoop to glean the dirty rags; 10
the gutter-rabbit, alert for rats, takes flight
from Bondy's boys,[6] the vintagers of night.

It's death: the cop's laid out.—In an upper room
at rest, love sucks the flesh of a heavy arm
where the slaked kisses leave their rouge in smudges.
The hour's alone. Listen: not a dream budges.

It's life: listen, the living waters shed
the eternal song upon the slimy head
of a sea-god with green naked limbs who lies
on a bed in the Morgue . . . with great wide-open eyes.[7] 20

[3] Author's name. [4] The identification of the locale is whimsical.
[1] *Paris nocturne;* translated by C. F. MacIntyre.
[2] The "spring tide" is the half-monthly tide that rises highest and retreats lowest, at the periods of new and full moon.
[3] In classical mythology, the river bordering the realm of the dead.
[4] A Greek philosopher, fourth century B.C., who lived in a tub and carried a lantern while searching for an honest man.
[5] In classical myth, foul monsters, part woman and part bird.
[6] Robbers (named for a forest near Paris).
[7] The translator notes that, before modern refrigeration, running water was used on corpses in the Morgue.

PARIS BY DAY[1]

Look at the great red copper disk above,
glowing where God heats up in his casserole
manna, scraps, the eternal daily dole:
it's simmering in sweat and peppered with love.

In the vague sizzle of rancid meat that burns,
the scullions[2] squat in a circle round the oven.
The drunks are there, too, holding out their flagons;
a poor wretch has the shakes as he waits his turn.

You think it's for all and sundry the sun fries
those seething gobs of fat in golden grease?
No, on us drips dog-soup from the skies.

Some have sunshine; we live under the eaves.
For us the kettle that's black, no longer hot.
Bah! I'd as lief have that as the honey-pot!

10

THE END[1]

Oh! how many mariners, how many captains
Who set off lighthearted for faraway journeys
Are vanished in this mournful horizon! . . .

. .

How many skippers dead with their crews!
The Ocean took all the pages of their lives
And with one puff scattered them over the waves.
None will know their end sunk in the deep . . .

. .

None will know their names, not even the humble stone
In the narrow cemetery where echoes answer us,
Not even the green weeping willow shedding its leaves in the fall,
Not even the plaintive monotonous song
Of the blindman singing in the corner of an old bridge.

VICTOR HUGO: *Oceano nox*[2]

Well now, these mariners—sailors, captains,
All in their great Ocean swallowed forever . . .
Who left nonchalant for their faraway journeys,
Are dead—as true as they left.

[1] *Paris diurne;* translated by C. F. MacIntyre. [2] Kitchen drudges; wretches.
[1] *La Fin;* translated by Kate Flores.
[2] Victor Hugo (1802–85), poet and novelist, was the most eminent French writer of the time. *Oceano Nox* (Latin) means "Night on the Ocean."

What then! It's their trade; they died with their boots on!
Their snifters to their hearts, all alive inside their capotes . . .
—Dead . . . No thanks: Lady Death has no sea legs;
Let her sleep with you: She's your good wife . . .
—As for them, none of it: Complete! washed away by the wave!
 Or lost in a squall . . . 10

A squall . . . that's death, you think? The lower sail
Pounding across the water!—That's *floundering* . . .
A blast of the leaden sea, then the high mast
Whipping at wave level—and that's *foundering*.

—Foundering.—Fathom this word. Your *death* is mighty pale
And nothing much on board, in a raging gale . . .
Nothing much against the great bitter smile
Of the sailor struggling.—Come now, make way!—
Death the windy old phantom changes face:
 The Sea! . . . 20

Drowned?—Aw, go on! You drown in *fresh* water!
—Sunk! Crew and cargo! And, down to the little ship's-boy,
Defiance in their eyes, in their teeth curses!
Spitting a death-rattle quid to the spume,
And downing without puking *the big salty cup* . . .
 —The way they downed their snifters—
. .
—No six-foot-under for them, or cemetery rats:
Them, they head for the sharks! The soul of a sailor,
Instead of oozing in your potatoes,
 Breathes with every wave! 30

—See there on the horizon the billow heaving;
 The amorous belly, you'd say,
Of a whore in heat, half-soused . . .
 They're there!—The billow has a cave—

—Listen, listen to the storm bellow! . . .
Their anniversary.—It returns quite often—
O poet, keep your blindman's songs to yourself;
—For them: the *De Profundis*[3] the wind trumpets!

. . . Let them roll eternally in the virgin spaces! . . .
 Let them roll green and bare, 40
Without pine and without nails, without lid, without candles . . .
—O let them roll, parvenu[4] landlubbers!

[3] Latin for "Out of the depths," the first words of Psalm 130.
[4] Recently arrived; amateurish.

Paul Verlaine
(1844–1896)

MY FAMILIAR DREAM[1]

I often have this strange and piercing dream
of a nameless woman—that we love each other;
she loves and understands me; never the same
woman, nor yet at any time another.

She understands me, and my heart grows clear
for her alone—no problem; she knows how
to wipe away the sweat from my pale brow,
and only she can cool it with her tears.

Blonde, auburn, or brunette?—I do not know.
Her name? I remember it is sonorous 10
and sweet as the names of those loved long ago,

exiled by Life. And like a statue's wide
gaze is hers. Serene and grave, her voice
has the tone of those dear voices that have died.

SONG OF THE INGENUES[1]

Ingenues, not quite grown,
blue-eyed, braids round the head,
we live almost unknown
in novels not much read.

With our arms intertwined,
we walk; pure as sunbeams
is our subconscious mind,
and we have azure dreams;

laughing, we race through the meadows,
prattling, from sunrise 10
to the fall of evening shadows,
chasing the butterflies;

[1] *Mon rêve familier;* translated by C. F. MacIntyre.
[1] *La Chanson des ingénues;* translated by C. F. MacIntyre. Ingenues are simple, unsophisticated girls.

shepherdess bonnets quite
preserve our young fresh skin,
and our frocks—so thin—
are of immaculate white;

the Richelieus[2] and rakes make passes,
the cavaliers sheep's eyes,
all prodigal of sighs
and greetings and 'alases!' 20

in vain—they have no luck;
they get their noses hurt
on the ironic tucks
of the evasive skirt.

Ingenuously we rail
at the imaginations
of these climbers of the wall,
although the perturbations,

wild thumpings of our hearts,
inform our secret dreams 30
that we're the future tarts
of these same libertines.

SENTIMENTAL CONVERSATION[1]

In the old solitary frozen park
two forms just passed and vanished in the dark.

Their lips were soft and slack, their eyes were dead,
and one could scarcely hear the words they said.

In the old lonely park nipped by the frost,
two specters have called back the past they lost.

—Do you remember our old ecstasies?
—Why would you have me waken those memories?

—When you hear my name does your heart always glow?
Do you always see my soul in dreams?—No. 10

—Ah, the good days of joy unspeakable
when our lips mingled!—That is possible.

[2] Lecherous noblemen. [1] *Colloque sentimental;* translated by C. F. MacIntyre.

—How blue the sky was then, and hope beat high!
—But hope fled, vanquished, down the gloomy sky.

Even so they walked through the wild oats, these dead,
and only the night heard the words they said.

THE WHITE MOON[1]

The white moon
Gleams in the wood;
From every branch
There comes a voice
Beneath the bower . . .

O my love.

The pond reflects,
Shimmering mirror,
The silhouette
Of the dim willow 10
Where the wind laments . . .

Let us dream, it is the hour.

Vast and tender
An appeasement
Seems to lower
From the firmament
Star-bedecked . . .

Exquisite hour.

SONGS WITHOUT WORDS, VIII[1]

In the ennui[2] unending
of the flat land
the vague snow descending
shines like sand.

With no gleam of light
in the copper sky,
one imagines he might
see the moon live and die.

[1] *La Lune blanche;* translated by Kate Flores.
[1] *Romances sans paroles, VIII;* translated by C. F. MacIntyre. [2] Monotony; tedium.

In the near-by woods
among the mist 10
gray oaks twist
like floating clouds.

With no gleam of light
in the copper sky,
one imagines he might
see the moon live and die.

Wind-broken crow,
and starving wolves too,
when sharp winds blow
what happens to you? 20

In the ennui unending
of the flat land
the vague snow descending
shines like sand.

WISDOM, BOOK III: V[1]

Black and heavy sleep
Falls upon my life;
Sleep, my every hope,
Sleep, desire and strife.

Now my eyes are blind;
Recollections fail,
Bitter ones and kind—
Melancholy tale!

Cradled in a deep
Pit beneath the ground, 10
I am rocked asleep.
Silence! Not a sound!

THE ART OF POETRY[1]

You must have music first of all,
and for that a rhythm uneven[2] is best,
vague in the air and soluble,
with nothing heavy and nothing at rest.

[1] *Sagesse, III: V;* translated by Brandon Witherspoon.
[1] *Art poétique;* translated by C. F. MacIntyre.
[2] Having lines of uneven length or having an odd rather than even number of syllables in
the line.

You must not scorn to do some wrong
in choosing the words to fill your lines:
nothing more dear than the tipsy song
where the Undefined and Exact combine.

It is the veiled and lovely eye,
the full noon quivering with light; 10
it is, in the cool of an autumn sky,
the blue confusion of stars at night!

Never the Color, always the Shade,
always the nuance is supreme!
Only by shade is the trothal³ made
between flute and horn, of dream with dream!

Epigram's an assassin! Keep
away from him, fierce Wit, and vicious
laughter that makes the Azure weep,
and from all that garlic of vulgar dishes! 20

Take Eloquence and wring his neck!
You would do well, by force and care,
wisely to hold Rhyme in check,
or she's off—if you don't watch—God knows where!

Oh, who will tell the wrongs of Rhyme?
What crazy negro or deaf child
made this trinket for a dime,
sounding hollow and false when filed?

Let there be music, again and forever!
Let your verse be a quick-wing'd thing and light— 30
such as one feels when a new love's fervor
to other skies wings the soul in flight.

Happy-go-lucky, let your lines
disheveled run where the dawn winds lure,
smelling of wild mint, smelling of thyme . . .
and all the rest is literature.

³ Betrothal; pledge of marriage.

Arthur Rimbaud
(1854–1891)

MY BOHEMIA[1]

Fists in torn pockets I departed.
My overcoat grew ideal too.
I walked, your knight, O Muse,
And dreamed, O my! what glorious loves.

My only trousers had a hole.
Little Tom Thumb, I dropped my dreaming rhymes.
My lodging was the Great Bear Inn,
And in the sky my stars were rustling.

I listened, seated by the road—
In soft September—where the dew 10
Was wine of vigor on my face;

And in weird shadows rhyming, plucked like lyres,
The laces of my martyred shoes,
One foot against my heart.

THE DRUNKEN BOAT[1]

As I descended black, impassive Rivers,
I sensed that haulers[2] were no longer guiding me:
Screaming Redskins took them for their targets,
Nailed nude to colored stakes: barbaric trees.

I was indifferent to all my crews;
I carried English cottons, Flemish[3] wheat.
When the disturbing din of haulers ceased,
The Rivers let me ramble where I willed.

Through the furious ripping of the sea's mad tides,
Last winter, deafer than an infant's mind, 10
I ran! And drifting, green Peninsulas
Did not know roar more gleefully unkind.

[1] *Ma Bohème;* translated by Louise Varèse. Here "Bohemia" means both the "gipsy" life of wandering and the unconventional, "bohemian" life.
[1] *Le Bateau ivre;* translated by Stephen Stepanchev. [2] Men with tow ropes.
[3] From Flanders (approximately, modern Belgium).

A tempest blessed my vigils on the sea.
Lighter than a cork I danced on the waves,
Those endless rollers, as they say, of graves:
Ten nights beyond a lantern's silly eye!

Sweeter than sourest apple-flesh to children,
Green water seeped into my pine-wood hull
And washed away blue wine stains, vomitings,
Scattering rudder, anchor, man's lost rule. 20

And then I, trembling, plunged into the Poem
Of the Sea, infused with stars, milk-white,
Devouring azure greens; where remnants, pale
And gnawed, of pensive corpses fell from light;

Where, staining suddenly the blueness, delirium,
The slow rhythms of the pulsing glow of day,
Stronger than alcohol and vaster than our lyres,
The bitter reds of love ferment the way!

I know skies splitting into light, whirled spouts
Of water, surfs, and currents: I know the night, 30
The dawn exalted like a flock of doves, pure wing,
And I have seen what men imagine they have seen.

I saw the low sun stained with mystic horrors,
Lighting long, curdled clouds of violet,
Like actors in a very ancient play,
Waves rolling distant thrills like lattice light!

I dreamed of green night, stirred by dazzling snows,
Of kisses rising to the sea's eyes, slowly,
The sap-like coursing of surprising currents,
And singing phosphors, flaring blue and gold! 40

I followed, for whole months, a surge like herds
Of insane cattle in assault on the reefs,
Unhopeful that three Marys, come on luminous feet,
Could force a muzzle on the panting seas!

Yes, I struck incredible Floridas
That mingled flowers and the eyes of panthers
In skins of men! And rainbows bridled green
Herds beneath the horizon of the seas.

I saw the ferment of enormous marshes, weirs[4]
Where a whole Leviathan[5] lies rotting in the weeds! 50
Collapse of waters within calms at sea,
And distances in cataract toward chasms!

[4] Artificial enclosures in rivers or the sea. [5] Sea monster.

Glaciers, silver suns, pearl waves, and skies like coals,
Hideous wrecks at the bottom of brown gulfs
Where giant serpents eaten by red bugs
Drop from twisted trees and shed a black perfume!

I should have liked to show the young those dolphins
In blue waves, those golden fish, those fish that sing.
—Foam like flowers rocked my sleepy drifting,
And, now and then, fine winds supplied me wings. 60

When, feeling like a martyr, I tired of poles and zones,
The sea, whose sobbing made my tossing sweet,
Raised me its dark flowers, deep and yellow whirled,
And, like a woman, I fell on my knees . . .

Peninsula, I tossed upon my shores
The quarrels and droppings of clamorous, blond-eyed birds.
I sailed until, across my rotting cords,
Drowned men, spinning backwards, fell asleep! . . .

Now I, a lost boat in the hair of coves,
Hurled by tempest into a birdless air, 70
I, whose drunken carcass neither Monitors
Nor Hansa[6] ships would fish back for men's care;

Free, smoking, rigged with violet fogs,
I, who pierced the red sky like a wall
That carries exquisite mixtures for good poets,
Lichens of sun and azure mucus veils;

Who, spotted with electric crescents, ran
Like a mad plank, escorted by seahorses,
When cudgel blows of hot Julys struck down
The sea-blue skies upon wild water spouts; 80

I, who trembled, feeling the moan at fifty leagues
Of rutting Behemoths and thick Maelstroms,[7] I,
Eternal weaver of blue immobilities,
I long for Europe with its ancient quays![8]

I saw sidereal[9] archipelagoes! and isles
Whose delirious skies are open to the voyager:
—Is it in depthless nights you sleep your exile,
A million golden birds, O future Vigor?—

But, truly, I have wept too much! The dawns disturb.
All moons are painful, and all suns break bitterly: 90

[6] A medieval league of north-German commercial cities.
[7] *Behemoths:* huge animals. *Maelstroms:* whirlpools. [8] Wharves; docks. [9] Starry.

Love has swollen me with drunken torpors.
Oh, that my keel might break and spend me in the sea!

Of European waters I desire
Only the black, cold puddle in a scented twilight
Where a child of sorrows squats and sets the sails
Of a boat as frail as a butterfly in May.

I can no longer, bathed in languors, O waves,
Cross the wake of cotton-bearers on long trips,
Nor ramble in a pride of flags and flares,
Nor swim beneath the horrible eyes of prison ships. 100

VOWELS[1]

A black, E white, I red, U green, O blue;
Someday I'll tell your latent birth O vowels:
A, a black corset hairy with gaudy flies
That bumble round all stinking putrefactions,

Gulfs of darkness; E, candors of steam and tents,
Icicles' proud spears, white kings, and flutter of parasols;
I, purple blood coughed up, laughter of lovely lips
In anger or ecstatic penitence;

U, cycles, divine vibrations of virescent[2] seas,
Peace of the pastures sown with animals, peace 10
Of the wrinkles that alchemy[3] stamps on studious brows;

O, Clarion supreme, full of strange stridences,[4]
Silences crossed by Angels and Worlds:
—Omega, the violet ray of His Eyes!

LIVES[1]

I

Oh the enormous avenues of the holy land, the terraces of the temple!
What has become of the Brahmin[2] who once taught me Proverbs? Now,
further down, I can still see even old women! I recall the silver hours, and
sun by the rivers, and my girl's hand on my shoulders, and our caresses as
we stood in the peppered heath. A flight of scarlet pigeons thundered in

[1] *Voyelles:* translated by Louise Varèse. It is interesting to compare this poem with
Baudelaire's "Correspondences."
[2] Becoming green. [3] The medieval pseudo-science of chemical transformations.
[4] Loud, harsh sounds. [1] *Vies;* translated by Angel Flores.
[2] A member of the highest Hindu caste; a learned aristocrat.

my brain. —Exiled here, I had a stage on which I performed the master-
pieces of literatures the world over. I might point out to you incredible
riches. I have been following up the history of treasures you might find—
and I know what is next! My wisdom is rejected as chaos. What is my void
when compared to the surprise awaiting you?

II

I am an inventor far more deserving of attention than all those who
have preceded me; a musician who has moreover discovered something
like the key of love. Now a country squire from a lean land with a tranquil
sky, I endeavor to throw off lethargy by remembering my mendicant[3]
childhood, my years of apprenticeship or my arrival in wooden shoes, my
polemics, my five or six widowings, and a few carousals when my level head
kept me from emulating my comrades' folly. I do not miss my former share
of divine gaiety. The quietude of this harsh countryside feeds my dreadful
skepticism rather bountifully. But since this skepticism can no longer be
put to use, and since, furthermore, I have devoted myself to a new anxiety,
I believe I shall end up as a very dangerous madman.

III

In an attic where I was locked up when I was twelve I got to know the
world—I illustrated the human comedy. In a gin mill I learned history. At
some night revel, in a northern city, I met all the women of the Old Mas-
ters. In an old Paris arcade I was taught the classical sciences. In a magnifi-
cent mansion, reeking with oriental luxury, I completed my exhaustive
tasks and spent my luxurious retreat. I have burned up my blood. My duty
has been remitted to me. But that need no longer even concern us. I am
really from beyond the grave, and accept no new commitments.

Stéphane Mallarmé
(*1842–1898*)

WINDOWS[1]

Disgusted with the dreary hospital, and the rank fumes
Rising with the banal whiteness of the curtains
Toward the great crucifix tired of the bare wall,
The man destined for death slyly straightens his old spine,

Shuffles, less to warm his rotting body
Than to watch the sun on the stones, to press
His ashen gaunt and skeletal face
To the panes which a clear beautiful ray attempts to tinge,

[3] Beggar-like. [1] *Les Fenêtres;* translated by Daisy Aldan.

And his mouth, feverish and greedy for the azure,
As when young, he breathed his prize, 10
A virginal cheek! soils
With a long bitter kiss the warm golden panes.

Drunk, forgetting the horror of the holy oil,
The herb teas, the clock and the inflicted bed,
The cough, he lives again; and when twilight bleeds on the tiles,[2]
His eye on the horizon gorged with light,

Sees golden ships, fine as swans,
On a scented river of purple, sleepily
Rocking the rich faun flash of their lines
In a great calm charged with memory! 20

In this way, disgusted with the blunt-souled man
Who wallows in contentment, where only his appetites
Devour him, and who insists on fetching this filth
To present to his wife nursing her children,

I flee and I cling to all those windows
From where one turns one's back on life, and hallowed,
In their glass, washed by eternal dews,
Gilded by the chaste morning of the Infinite

I see myself and I brag I am an angel! and I die, and I long
—Let the glass be art, let it be mysticism— 30
To be reborn, wearing my dream as a crown,
In a past heaven where Beauty flourished!

But, alas! Here-below is master; its curse
Sickens me at times even in this safe shelter,
And the foul vomit of Stupidity
Makes me stop up my nose in face of the azure.[3]

Is there a way for Me who knows bitterness,
To shatter the crystal insulted by the monster
And to escape with my two featherless wings
—Even at the risk of falling in eternity? 40

SIGH[1]

Towards your brow where an autumn dreams
freckled with russet scatterings,
calm sister, and towards the sky,

[2] Tile roofs. [3] The (blue) sky; the heavens.
[1] *Soupir;* translated by Frederick Morgan.

wandering, of your angelic eye
my soul ascends: thus, white and true,
within some melancholy garden
a fountain sighs towards the Blue!
—Towards October's softened Blue
that pure and pale in the great pools
mirrors its endless lassitude 10
and, on dead water where the leaves
wind-strayed in tawny anguish cleave
cold furrows, lets the yellow sun
in one long lingering ray crawl on.

THE AZURE[1]

In serene irony the infinite azure,
Languidly lovely as the flowers, smites
The impotent poet cursing his genius
Across a barren wilderness of Sorrows.

Fleeing with eyes closed, I feel it probe
Deep as a racking remorse
My empty soul. Where escape? And what eerie night
To hurl, O remains, against this heart-mangling scorn?

O fogs, come forth! Pour your monotonous ashes
In long shreds of haze across the skies, 10
Drowning the livid quagmire of the autumns
And rearing a vast ceiling of silence!

And you, from the lethal morasses emerge and gather
As you come the slime and the vapid reeds,
Dear Ennui,[2] to stuff with untiring hands
The great blue holes the birds maliciously make.

More! Let the sad chimneys unceasingly
Smoke, and a wandering prison of soot
Blot out in the horror of their murky trails
The sun dying yellowish on the horizon! 20

—The Sky is dead.—Toward you I run! O matter, give
Oblivion of the cruel Ideal and of Sin
To this martyr who comes to share the straw
Where men's contented cattle lie,

For here I wish, since at the last my brain, empty
As the pot of paint lying at the foot of a wall,

[1] *L'Azur;* translated by Kate Flores. The Azure is the blue sky, the heavens.
[2] Bored weariness.

The art to adorn the woeful Idea possesses no more,
To yawn disconsolately to a desolate death . . .

In vain! The Azure triumphs, and in the bells
I hear it sing. My soul, it becomes a voice　　　　　　　　　　　　30
Instilling us with fear anew of its awful victory,
And from the living metal comes in bluenesses the Angelus![3]

It whirls through the mist as of old and cleaves
Like a resolute sword your intrinsic agony;
In the helpless and hopeless revolt what escape?
I am obsessed. The Azure! The Azure! The Azure! The Azure!

Jules Laforgue
(1860–1887)

LAMENT OF THE ORGANIST
OF NOTRE-DAME DE NICE[1]

Hark, already the winter crows
Have said their psalm among our bells;
The autumn showers are near, like knells;
Farewell the woods of the casinos.

Last night her cheek had a paler dye
And her body shivered, numbed quite through;
This church of ours is icy, too.
Ah, none loves her down here but I.

I! I shall cut my heart out, tooled
For the sake of a smile so sad from her,　　　　　　　　　　　　10
And remain true to her image there
Forever, in this victorious world.

The day that she leaves this world
A *Miserere*[2] I mean to play
So cosmic in its despairing way
That God will have to return me word.

[3] A prayer in honor of the Virgin Mary, announced by church bells.
[1] *Complainte de l'Organiste de Notre-Dame de Nice;* translated by Vernon Watkins. Nice is a French resort city on the Riviera.
[2] Latin, "Have mercy"; a musical setting of the 51st Psalm.

No, I shall stay down here, all dark,
Loyal to my dear phthisic[3] dead,
Rocking my heart too deeply fed
With the eternal fugues of Bach.[4] 20

And every year, at the new year's birth,
On our anniversary, constant then,
I shall unroll this *Requiem*[5]
I have made for the death of the Earth.

FOR THE BOOK OF LOVE[1]

I can die tomorrow and I have not loved.
My lips never touched a woman's while I lived.
None has given me her soul in a look; none in heat
Has held me, exhausted with love, to her heart.

I have but suffered for all nature, each moment,
For the beings, the wind, the flowers, the firmament,
Suffered through all my nerves minutely, like a knife,
Suffered to have a soul still not yet pure enough.

I spat upon love, and I have killed the flesh.
Mad with pride on this Earth enslaved by Instinct's leash, 10
I alone stood and stiffened myself against life.
I challenged the Instinct with a bitter laugh.

Everywhere, in the salons, at the theater, in church,
Before these cold great men, these men of finest touch,
And these women with gentle, or jealous, or proud eyes
Whose tender, ravished soul one might virginally rechase,[2]

I thought: all these are come to it. I heard in their rites
The roarings of the unclean coupling of brutes.
So much mire with an access of three minutes in mind!
Men, be correct! O women, keep your smiles refined! 20

[3] Suffering from consumption (tuberculosis).
[4] Johann Sebastian Bach (1685–1750), the great German composer, is especially famous for church music, much of it contrapuntal.
[5] A musical setting of the church service for the dead.
[1] *Pour le Livre d'amour;* translated by Vernon Watkins.
[2] Restore the elegant surface of; readorn.

THE APPROACH OF WINTER[1]

Blockade of the senses! Mail steamers from the Levant![2] . . .
O downpour of rain! O downpour of night,
O! the wind! . . .
All Hallow's Eve, Christmas, and the New Year,
Oh, in the drizzling, all my chimneys! . . .
Of factories . . .

It is impossible to sit down any more, all the benches are wet;
Believe me, everything is over until next year,
All the benches are wet, the woods are so rusted,
And the horns[3] have so many times sounded your note, your
 sound of *ton* and *taine!* . . . 10

Ah! storm clouds flocking here from the shores of the Channel,
You have spoiled us our last Sunday.

It drizzles;
In the wet forest, spider webs
Bend under the drops of water, and it is their ruin.
Plenipotentiary[4] suns from the washing of golden riversands,
From country fairs,
Where are you buried?
This evening a squandered sun lies helpless at the top of the slope,
Lies on the hillside, in the broom, on his cloak. 20
A sun white as spittle on a barroom floor
Lies in a litter of yellow broom,
The yellow broom-flowers of autumn.
And the horns call him!
May he come back . . .
May he come to himself again!
Tallyho! Tallyho![5] and the hunting horn at the kill!
O sad anthem, have you ended! . . . And they play the fool! . . .
And he lies there, the sun, like a gland torn out of a neck,
And he shivers, without a friend! . . . 30

Forward, forward, and the horn at the kill!
It is well-known Winter blowing in;
Oh! the turnings, the bends of the highroads,
And without Little Red Ridinghood making her way! . . .
Oh! their ruts from the wagons of another month,
Ascending like quixotic[6] rails
Towards the patrols of fleeing storm clouds

[1] *L'Hiver qui vient;* translated by Joseph Bennett. [2] The eastern Mediterranean.
[3] The horns sounded in the fox-hunt. [4] Invested with total authority.
[5] The hunters' cry when the fox is sighted.
[6] Romantic, visionary, impractical (like Don Quixote).

Which the wind knocks towards the transatlantic sheep-folds! . . .
Let us hasten, hasten, it is the well-known season, this time,
And the wind, this night, he has made beautiful clouds! 40
O havoc, O nests, O modest little gardens!
My heart and my drowsiness: O echoes of hatchets! . . .

All these branches still have their green leaves,
The underbrush is now nothing but a dung heap of dead leaves;
Leaves, leaflets, may a fair wind carry you away
In swarms toward the ponds,
Or for the gamekeeper's fire,
Or for the mattresses of ambulances
For soldiers far from France.

It is the season, it is the season, rust overruns the masses, 50
Rust gnaws in their kilometric spleens
The telegraphic wires on the highroads where no one passes.

The horns, the horns, the horns—melancholic! . . .
Melancholic! . . .
They depart, changing their tone,
Changing their tone and their music,
Your note, your sound of *ton* and *taine* and *ton!* . . .
The horns, the horns, the horns! . . .
Have departed with the north wind.

I cannot leave this tone: such echoes! . . . 60
It is the season, it is the season, the grape harvest is over! . . .
Here come the rains with their angel's patience,
The business is over and done with, adieu grape harvests and all
 the baskets,
All the Watteau[7] baskets of the peasant dances under the chestnut
 trees,
It is the coughing in high-school dormitories which returns,
It is herb tea without a hearth, far from home,
Pulmonary consumption[8] saddening the neighborhood,
And all the misery concentrated in great cities.

But, woolens, rubber overshoes, pharmacy, dream,
Parted curtains on balconies high up above the riverbanks 70
Facing the sea of roofs of the quarters of the city,
Lamps, engravings, tea, *petits fours*,[9]
Will you not be my only amours! . . .
(Oh! and then, are you versed in, besides the pianos,
The sober and vespertine[10] weekly mystery

[7]Jean-Antoine Watteau (1684–1721), a French painter who created elegant garden-scenes.
[8]When he wrote the poem Laforgue was himself dying of this disease. He was twenty-seven when he died.
[9]Cupcakes. [10]Appearing in the evening.

Of the sanitation statistics
In the newspapers?)

No, no! it is the season and the planet is curiously quaint!
May the south wind, may the south wind
Ravel out the old shoes which time runs off with!　　　　　80
It is the season, oh rending! it is the season!
Every year, every year,
In chorus I will try to give it its note.

Guillaume Apollinaire
(*1880–1918*)

THE MIRABEAU BRIDGE[1]

Under the Mirabeau Bridge the Seine
　　　Flows and our love
　　Must I be reminded again
How joy came always after pain

　　　Night comes the hour is rung
　　　The days go I remain

Hands within hands we stand face to face
　　　While underneath
　　The bridge of our arms passes
The loose wave of our gazing which is endless　　　　10

　　　Night comes the hour is rung
　　　The days go I remain

Love slips away like this water flowing
　　　Love slips away
　　How slow life is in its going
And hope is so violent a thing

　　　Night comes the hour is rung
　　　The days go I remain

The days pass the weeks pass and are gone
　　　Neither time that is gone　　　　20

[1] *Le Pont Mirabeau;* translated by W. S. Merwin.

Nor love ever returns again
Under the Mirabeau Bridge flows the Seine

Night comes the hour is rung
The days go I remain

ANNIE[1]

On the Texas coast
Between Mobile and Galveston there's
A large garden full of roses
And the villa there
Is one great rose

Time and again a woman walks
In that garden all alone
And when I pass by on the lime-shaded road
Our eyes lock

As this woman is a Mennonite[2] 10
Her rosebushes and her frocks are buttonless
There are two missing from my coat
The lady and I profess almost the same rite

WHITE SNOW[1]

Angels angels in the sky
One's dressed as an officer
One as a cook
And the others are singing

Smart officer color of the sky
Long after Christmas soft spring will bring
A shining sun to medal you
A shining sun

And now the cook is plucking geese
Ah! fall of snow 10
Falling and no
Darling girl in my arms' embrace

[1] *Annie;* translated by Dudley Fitts.
[2] Mennonites are evangelical Christians opposed to military service, the holding of public office, and adornments in dress.
[1] *La Blanche neige;* translated by Dudley Fitts.

HILLS[1]

Overhead in the Paris sky
Two airplanes fought it out one day
And one was red and one was black
And all the while in the zenith flamed
The everlasting sun-airplane

And one of them was my whole youth
The other was my days to come
The fury of their fight was like
The Archangel's[2] with radiant wings
The day he fought with Lucifer 10

Set the sum against the problem thus
And the night thus against the day
Thus what I love makes its attack
Upon my love thus a great storm
Tears up the roots of a crying tree

There is such sweetness everywhere
Paris like a waking girl
Rises languid from her sleep
Shakes out the long coils of her hair
Singing and what she sings is fair 20

My youth has fallen where is it now
See all my future is in flames
Let the whole world hear me today
When I pronounce that now at last
Prophecy is an art newborn

You will find men who stand like hills
Towering from the run of men
Seeing the distant future's shape
Better than what surrounds them now
Clearer than what is past and gone 30

Adornment of roadways and of times
Passing and lasting without stay
Let us give the serpents leave to hiss
Vainly against the southern wind
The Psylli and the wave are gone[3]

[1] *Les Collines;* translated by Dudley Fitts.
[2] The archangel Michael, who opposed the rebellious Lucifer (Satan) in the war in Heaven.
[3] The Psylli were mythological prophets and magicians of ancient Cyrenaica, in North Africa, who derived their powers from the primitive art of snake-charming. They were drowned in a feud with the god of the hot South Wind, who had ruined their crops.

Schedule of days if our machines
Should set themselves to think at last
Waves of gold would comb and break
On stretches of a jeweled shore
The foam would be a womb once more 40

An eagle's pitch is less than man's
Man's is the joy that the sea knows
He frees himself in that upper air
From shadows and the muzzying blues[4]
And so the spirit regains the dream

This is the time of sorcery
It's ours again prepare to see
A thousand million prodigies
Beyond the scope of myth itself
Since none has yet imagined them 50

The inner depths of consciousness
Tomorrow they will be explored
Who knows what living entities
Will be drawn up from that abyss
What new and whole cosmologies

Prophets rising up to speak
On the blue line of the distant hills
Will know the certitude of things
That learned men pretend to know
And they will carry us where they will 60

Desire is the greatest force
Come let me kiss you on the brow
Ah you are light as a tongue of flame
All of whose suffering you know
All of whose fervor burning bright

The time will come when we shall know
All that's to know of suffering
An age neither of taking heart
Nor of letting what we cherish go
Nor of doing all that we can do 70

In man himself we shall seek out
More than was ever sought before
And we shall weigh with no machines
Or instruments the will of man
And the drive engendered by that will

[4] Befuddling depression.

And even those who most would help
Are wrong in their ministering to us
Since the times that made us one
Nothing is ended nothing's begun
Look on your finger there's a ring 80

Time of deserts and crossroads
Time of hills and of city squares
I am here for a stroll or two
Where a talisman[5] enacts his role
Dead and more subtile than life itself

At last I've set myself apart
From every natural concern
Die I may but I cannot sin
And whatever any man has touched
My hands have touched my hands have felt 90

I have investigated un-
imagined things and many times
I have taken the very weight
Of life unweighable and now
I can perish with a smile

How often I have soared so high
So high that everything disappeared
Good-bye bizarreries ghosts good-bye
Then how shall I be imposed upon
By a small boy's pantomime of fear 100

Farewell my youth jasmine of time
I have breathed that fresh perfume
At Rome upon the floral floats
Gay with masks and tinkling bells
And the bright wreaths of carnival

Pure Christmas farewell now my youth
When all life was a single star
And I could see it mirrored in
The Mediterranean water far
Pearlier than a meteor 110

Downy as an archangelical
Nest with a garland made of clouds
Brighter than haloes are and all
Splendors and emanating fires
Single sweetness Harmonies

[5] An instrument of magic power.

But now I make a halt to watch
Upon the incandescent grass
A straying snake and it is I
I am the flute I play upon
I am the whip I am the lash 120

There is a time for suffering
There is a time for goodness too
My youth farewell the time has come
To know what it is the future holds
To know and not to die of it

This is the time of burning grace
When only a man's will can act
Seven years of tests beyond belief
Will bring him back to his true self
More pure more wise and more alive 130

He will discover worlds beyond
Now his mind shrivels like those flowers
That bring to birth delicious fruits
And we shall see them ripening
Upon the hill in the thick sun

I sing of very life and I
Alone am fit to sing this song
My music falls like scattered seed
You other singers be still You shall
Not mingle your tares[6] with my wheat 140

A vessel came into the port
A great ship fine with all her flags
On her we found no one at all
But a woman she was rosy fair
And she lay murdered at our feet

I was begging another time
And all they gave me was a flame
That burnt me to the lips I could
Not say a single word of thanks
Torch that nothing can put out 150

And where are you dear friend of mine
Withdrawn so deep into yourself
That only a pit was left behind
For me to hurl myself into
Down to the neutral shades below

[6] Biblical term for harmful weeds.

I hear my footsteps coming back
Along those pathways that no foot
Has ever taken I hear my steps
Always passing there below
Slow or swift as they come and go 160

Winter you with your whiskered chin
It's snowing I am out of sorts
I have traversed a glory of skies
Where human life is music and
The sun is too white for my eyes

Become familiar as I have
With the wonders that I proclaim
The goodness that is to prevail
The suffering that I endure
Then you will know what is to come 170

From suffering with goodness joined
A purer beauty shall be born
Than any beauty found before
In balanced counterweight of forms
Snow falls I shudder and I burn

Here at my table I write down
Whatever it may be I have felt
Whatever I have sung up there
A thrusting tree that sways against
The wind and its light streaming hair 180

A silk hat on the tablecloth
In a jumble of fruit the gloves lie dead
Beside an apple a lady cranes
Her neck to see the gentleman
Stands next her and engulfs himself

The dance whirls on at the back of time
I have killed the handsome band leader
And for the pleasure of my friends
I peel an orange now whose taste
Is a marvel of fireworks in the sky 190

They are all dead the headwaiter comes
And pours them an unreal champagne
That bubbles as though it were a snail
Or as though it were a poet's brain
A rose was singing all the while

The slave raises a naked sword
Like rivers and their springing wells

And every time he lowers it
The guts of a universe are drawn
And new worlds issue forth from it 200

The chauffeur hangs on to the wheel
And every time along the road
He honks at a corner there beyond
Just at the edge of his eye's reach
A virgin universe recedes

Third on the program's the lady who
Takes the elevator up
Up she goes forever up
And light streams round about her and
She stands transfigured in that light 210

But these are minor secrets There
Are others you'll find more profound
To be disclosed in a little while
And they will cut you through and through
With a thought forever unparalleled

Weep then and weep and weep again
What though the moon is full tonight
Or only crescent in the sky
Ah weep and weep and weep again
We have laughed so long in the sunlight 220

Arms of gold support this life
The golden secret must be pierced
There's nothing but a rapid flame
Touched by a rose adorably
And all the fragrance of the rose

COMPANY COMMANDER[1]

My mouth will flame the sulphurs of the Pit
You will find my mouth a hell of sweetness and seduction
My mouth's angels will hold sway in your heart
My mouth's soldiers will take you by storm
The priests of my mouth will cense[2] your beauty
Your soul will shake like a terrain in an earthquake
Your eyes will be charged with all the love that humanity has stored
 up in its eyes since the beginning
My mouth will be an army against you a stumbling awkward army
Tricky as a magician with his sleight of changing shapes

[1] *Chef de section;* translated by Dudley Fitts. [2] Worship with incense.

The choirs and orchestra of my mouth will tell you my love 10
It murmurs to you now from far away
While I stand here eyes fastened to my watch waiting for the exact
　　moment to go over the top[3]

THE PRETTY REDHEAD[1]

Here I am before all a man of sense
Knowing life and of death as much as a human being can know
Having experienced the pangs and the joys of love
Having known at times how to impose his ideas
Acquainted with several languages
Having traveled not a little
Having seen war in the Artillery and the Infantry
Wounded in the head trepanned[2] under chloroform
Having lost his best friends in the frightful struggle
I know of the old and the new as much as one man can know of
　　the two 10
And without being disturbed today by this war
Between us and for us my friends
I judge this long quarrel about tradition and invention
　　　　About Order and Adventure

You whose mouth is made in the image of God's
Mouth which is order itself
Be indulgent when you compare us
With those who were the perfection of order
We who seek adventure everywhere

We are not your enemies 20
We strive to give you vast and strange domains
Where mystery flowers for all who would gather it
There are new fires of colors there never seen before
A thousand imponderable phantasms
To which reality must be given
We strive to explore kindness enormous country where all is still
There is also time which can be banished or recaptured
Pity us who struggle ever on the frontiers
Of the limitless and the future
Pity us our errors pity us our sins 30

Here now comes summer the violent season
And my youth as well as the spring is dead
O Sun this is the time of ardent Reason
　　　　And I expect

[3] Move out of the trenches into battle.　　[1] *La Jolie rousse;* translated by Kate Flores.
[2] Having had a disk cut out of the skull. Though he lived until 1918, the year the First
World War ended, Apollinaire died of wounds received early in the war.

To follow ever the sweet and noble form
Which she takes that I may love only her
She comes and draws me as a magnet iron
 She has the charming aspect
 Of an adorable redhead

Her hair is of gold one might say 40
A lovely flash of lightning that endures
Or those flames which flaunt
In tea roses that wither

But laugh laugh at me
Men everywhere especially people here
For there are so many things that I do not dare tell you
So many things that you would not permit me to say
Have pity on me

Paul Valéry
(1871–1945)

HELEN[1]

Azure![2] behold me . . . I come from the caverns of death
To hear once more the measured sounding of waves,
And once more I see long galleys in the dawn
Revive from darkness in a file of golden oars.

My solitary hands call forth those monarchs
Whose beards of salt entwined my simple fingers.
I wept. They sang of their obscure triumphs
And of buried seas in the wake of their barques.[3]

I hear deep hollow shells and the compelling
Clarions of war, pacing the flight of the oars— 10
The clear song of the oarsmen chains this tumult.

[1] *Hélène;* translated by Andrew Chiappe. Helen of Troy recalls events of the Trojan War, fought three thousand years ago. After she ran away from her husband Menelaus with the Trojan prince Paris, Menelaus and the other Greek kings launched an armada of a thousand ships to reclaim her. The ensuing war lasted ten years, ending with Greek victory and Helen's return.
[2] The blue (sky). [3] Sailing ships.

And gods raised high on the heroic prow,
Their ancient smile insulted by the spray,
Hold forth toward me forgiving sculptured arms.

THE BEE[1]

So deadly delicate your sting!
Yet, O golden bee, I place
Over this soft curve, saddening,
Nothing but a dream of lace.

Prick the breast's fine gourd and press
Home where love dies, where sleeps his spell!
Thus may some of my rosiness
Rise to the round and stubborn flesh!

I need a hurt that's keen and swift.
A torment prompt and soon done with 10
Is better than one that sleeping lies.

O may my body be made warm
By this tiny gold alarm
Without which love sleeps or dies!

SONG OF THE COLUMNS[1]

Sweet columns, with
Chaplets[2] adorned with day,
Crowned with true birds, no myth,
That walk the stone-fledged way,

Sweet columns, O
The bobbins'[3] orchestra!
Each one confides its own
Hush to the unison.

—What do you bear so high
Equal in radiance? 10
—For desire's faultless eye
Our studious elegance.

We sing by mutual choice
That we bear up the skies.

[1] *L'Abeille;* translated by Lionel Abel.
[1] *Cantique des colonnes;* translated by Vernon Watkins.
[2] Headdresses; also, moldings resembling strings of beads. [3] Spindles'.

O sage and single voice
Singing for the eyes!

See what clear hymns!
What sonority
Our light-enamoured limbs
Draw from limpidity![4] 20

So chill, chased[5] with dawn,
We from our beds early
By the chisel were drawn
To become these lilies!

From our beds of cold crystal
We were awakened,
Talons of metal
Gripped us and slackened.

To face the moon,
The moon and sun-glow, 30
We were polished each one
Like a nail of the toe!

Servant-maids inflexuous,[6]
Smiles with no viewer,
The girl before us
Feels her legs pure.

Piously matched peers,
The nose beneath the string-course[7]
And our rich ears
Deaf to the white load's force, 40

A temple on our eyes,
Dark for eternity,
Without the gods we rise
To that divinity!

Our antique youths,
Dull flesh, fair shades of mirth,
Are bright with subtle truths
Which numbers bring to birth.

[4] Clarity; transparency. [5] Gold-coated.
[6] Unbending; or, perhaps, bent inward. (Translates the French *sans genoux*, "without knees.")
[7] In architecture, a decorative horizontal molding.

Girls of the golden numbers,[8]
Strong with heaven's laws and rod, 50
On us there falls and slumbers
A honey-colored god.

He sleeps at ease, the Day,
Whom every day with vows
We on love's table lay,
Slack-tided[9] on our brows.

Incorruptible sisters,
Half fire, half cool as eves,
We took for dancers
Breezes and dry leaves, 60

And the centuries, by ten,
And the past peoples' tide,
It is a deep-found Then,
Then never satisfied!

Beneath our loves that raise
A weight than Earth more grave
Silent we cross the days
Like a stone the wave!

We walk in time, and these
Our dazzling bodies 70
Have steps ineffable
That mark in fable . . .

ASIDES[1]

What do you do? Why, everything.
What are you worth? Worth, well,
The worth of mastery and disgust,
Presentiment and trial . . .
What are you worth? Worth, well . . .
What do you want? Nothing, all.

What do you know? Boredom.
What can you do? Dream.
And with the power of the mind
Can turn the morning into night. 10

[8] The "golden numbers," derived from a lunar calendar, are used in calculating the date of Easter. There may also be a reference to the "golden section," a mathematically elegant ratio (approximately 3 to 5) honored in the arts since antiquity.
[9] Slack tide is the moment when the tide is neither rising nor ebbing.
[1] *Chanson à part;* translated by William Jay Smith.

What can you do? Dream,
And so drive boredom from the mind.

What do you want? My own good.
What must you do? Learn.
Learn and master and foresee,
All, of course, to no good.
What do you fear? The will.
Who are you? Nothing, nothing at all.

Where are you going? To death.
What will you do there? Die; 20
Nor ever return to this rotten game,
Forever and ever and ever the same.
Where are you going? To die.
What will you do there? Be dead.

Sigmund Freud
(1856–1939)

The question of whether the work of Sigmund Freud is science or art has
never been settled, least of all by Freud himself, who recognized and de-
lighted in the ambiguity. Through his early work, especially, he held him-
self to the precision of a scientific method and vocabulary, while at the
same time drawing freely for examples and language upon a wide range of
literature and art; his pages are studded with references to his favorite
literary works: Greek tragedy, Shakespeare's plays, Milton's *Paradise Lost*,
and the works of German Romanticism. He insisted throughout his life
that not he but the poets had discovered the unconscious and that his
contribution had consisted of systematizing their insights through "a few
psychological formulas." He was a magnificent writer himself; *The Interpre-
tation of Dreams* and the great case studies are monuments of Austrian liter-
ature. It is not a denigration of psychoanalysis to say it is a great imagina-
tive creation, the flowering of the literary tradition which was rooted in
Rousseau and which flourished throughout the nineteenth century in the
Romantics' abiding interest in the individual self and how it emerges from
childhood experience. It is no wonder that a recent student of psychoanaly-
sis has concluded that it is faltering as a science and that "Freud's future
place will be in that realm of art, not science."

Freud was born in 1856 in Freiberg, Moravia (now Příbor, Czechoslo-
vakia), the son of a prosperous Jewish wool merchant. The family moved to
Vienna when Freud was four and he was educated there at the excellent
Sperl Gymnasium and the University of Vienna, where he received his

medical degree in 1881. Plans for a research career were changed in 1882, when he met and fell in love with Martha Bernays and decided that, if he was to support a wife, he would have to go into private practice. Over the four years of their engagement, he was on the staff first of the Vienna General Hospital and then of a private psychiatric clinic. He treated patients, continued research on the physiology of the brain which he had begun as a medical student, became a lecturer in neuropathology at the University, and attended a crucial four-month series of lectures in Paris by the famous neurologist Jean Charcot, who had begun to experiment with the treatment of hysteria by hypnotism. In 1886, Freud married Martha Bernays and set up a private psychiatric practice in Vienna, which was to continue for the next fifty-one years.

The story of the rest of Freud's life is essentially the story of the development of psychoanalysis, a rigorous and deeply personal exploration against heavy odds into unknown territories of the human mind. The beginnings of psychoanalysis were in a series of hysteric patients Freud treated, along with another Viennese physician, Josef Breuer, beginning in 1882. ("Hysteria" is a neurotic condition characterized by violent emotional outbursts, depression, and various impairments of sensory and motor functions.) Breuer, like Charcot, was experimenting with hypnosis in the treatment of these patients and had discovered that if a patient could be induced to remember and describe the circumstances of the onset of his illness, the symptoms tended to disappear, at least temporarily. The most famous of these patients was "Anna O.," a twenty-one-year-old girl who had suffered a partial paralysis and impairments of speech and sight after the death of her father; Breuer broke off her treatment abruptly when he discovered that she was sexually attracted to him. The success of "the talking cure" suggested a psychological rather than a physiological basis for hysteria, and this insight became the subject of *Studies on Hysteria* (1895), upon which Breuer and Freud collaborated. By the time the book was published, Breuer and Freud had already gone their separate ways, because of Breuer's inability to accept Freud's growing conviction that sexual experiences were invariably at the basis of hysterical conditions. Between 1892 and 1897, Freud gradually abandoned hypnosis in favor of "free association," a process of encouraging the patient to talk freely about his or her memories, withholding and censoring nothing, while the therapist quietly listened. He also developed his theory of "childhood seduction"; on the evidence of a detailed study of thirteen cases, he concluded that "the cause of hysteria is a passive sexual experience before puberty: i.e., a traumatic seduction."

Perhaps the most important creative period in Freud's life was the three years between 1897 and 1900. His father, Jakob Freud, died in 1896, triggering powerful conflicts in Freud which amounted to a serious psychoneurosis. He embarked upon a rigorous, systematic psychoanalysis (he began to use the word first in 1896) of himself, to which he devoted an hour at the end of each working day and which he reported, sometimes cryptically, in letters to his intimate friend Wilhelm Fliess. The product of this self-analysis was the abandonment of the seduction theory, the formulation of the theory of the Oedipus complex, and the writing of *The Interpretation of Dreams*. Freud abandoned the seduction theory when he real-

ized that sexual molestation of children, though doubtless more common than generally acknowledged, could not be as universal as it appeared to be among his patients (and at the same time discovered that his own father was not free from "incestuous incrimination"). He concluded that effects like those of actual molestation could be produced by fantasies representing the wishes of children to sleep with parents of the opposite sex, the basis of the theory of the Oedipus complex. The extent to which *The Interpretation of Dreams* grew out of his own self-analysis Freud himself acknowledged in his preface to the second edition in 1908: "For this book has a further subjective significance for me personally—a significance which I only grasped after I completed it. It was, I found, a portion of my own self-analysis, my reaction to my father's death—that is to say, to the most important event, the most poignant loss, of a man's life." On the foundation of his own self-examination, Freud established the main outlines of psychoanalysis in *The Interpretation of Dreams:* the theory of the unconscious, the ways in which dreams represent reality, and the development of infantile sexuality, including the Oedipus complex.

For the rest of his life Freud elaborated and modified the model of psychoanalysis presented in *The Interpretation of Dreams. The Psychopathology of Everyday Life* (1901) and *Jokes and their Relation to the Unconscious* (1905) explained how everyday "slips" and jokes, respectively, reveal the workings of unconscious wishes. Also appearing in 1905 were the important *Three Essays on the Theory of Sexuality* ("The Sexual Aberrations," "Infantile Sexuality," and "The Transformations of Puberty") and the first of the great case studies: "Dora." "Little Hans" and "The Rat Man" appeared in 1909, "Dr. Schreber" and "The Wolf Man" in 1911 and 1918. *Beyond the Pleasure Principle* (1920) introduced, in connection with a study of the "repetition compulsion" (the drive to repeat patterns of behavior), the important, and controversial, theory of a "death instinct." *The Ego and the Id* (1923) elaborated Freud's spatial metaphor of the mind as divided into ego, superego, and id. *The Future of an Illusion* (1927), *Civilization and Its Discontents* (1930), and *Moses and Monotheism* (1939) turned from individual psychology to apply psychoanalytical insights to broad questions of human culture.

Much of Freud's energy during the latter part of his life was also devoted to defending and disseminating the principles of psychoanalysis personally. A small group of interested friends which met on Wednesday evenings at Freud's house beginning in 1902 grew into the Vienna Psychoanalytical Society in 1908 and the International Psychoanalytical Association in 1910. Freud's relationships with his disciples and associates were often difficult; one after another broke away, often with much bitterness; first Alfred Adler, then Wilhelm Stekel, and finally Carl Jung.

In 1917, Freud, a heavy cigar-smoker, first noticed a painful swelling in the roof of his mouth, eventually diagnosed as cancer in 1923. Over the next sixteen years, he underwent thirty-three painful operations; in his last years, he had to wear a bulky prosthetic device to separate his mouth from his nasal cavity. In 1938, the Nazis marched into Vienna, with Freud and his "Jewish" psychology high on their blacklists; his books had been publicly burned in Berlin in 1933. The Nazis, under international pressure, agreed to allow him to leave Austria, and Freud reluctantly yielded to his friends' urgings and left Vienna for London. He died there in 1939.

Freud's masterpiece is undoubtedly *The Interpretation of Dreams,* but among his shorter works the case studies stand very high. Freud himself noted that the case studies read like carefully constructed fiction: "It strikes me myself as strange that the case histories I write should read like short stories and that, as one might say, they lack the serious stamp of science." *Fragment of an Analysis of a Case of Hysteria* (or *Dora,* as it is usually referred to) is perhaps the most fascinating of the case histories. Dora's story, as it unfolds under Freud's probing, has the quality of fiction; it is like, as Peter Gay has pointed out, one of Arthur Schnitzler's ironic, disillusioned dissections of sexual mores in contemporary Vienna. Eighteen-year-old Dora is caught between two families: her own, with a handsome, self-indulgent father and a dull, withdrawn mother; and that of Frau K., engaged in a long-term affair with Dora's father, and Herr K., in hot pursuit of Dora herself. Small wonder that Dora is showing signs of stress: breathlessness, laryngitis, and erratic swings of mood. But the chief interest of *Dora* is not medical or therapeutic but narrative. As the critic Steven Marcus has pointed out, *Dora* is a creative narrative that includes its own analysis and interpretation. The world of *Dora* is the world of modern fiction, in which narrative is not the presentation of finished conclusions about reality but a series of probing, often inconclusive investigations into a problematical world inhabited by complex, multilayered human beings who do not yield up their secrets easily. One of these complex people is Freud himself, who in the course of the case study is forced to acknowledge his own failure; Dora abruptly broke off the analysis after less than three months and it remained a "fragment" of an analysis. Part of the failure, Freud acknowledges, was his inadequate attention to the "transference" (Dora's attitude toward him, including her tendency to make him a stand-in for significant figures in her life) and the "counter-transference" (his own attitude toward his "intelligent and engaging" but immensely irritating patient). The question in *"Dora"* is how Dora's story can be told, by Dora to herself and to Freud and by Freud to himself and to the reader. The answer, never quite satisfactory, is in the narrative fragments that make up the story, the pervasive self-conscious analysis and interpretation, and the tentative voice of Freud himself as problematic narrator, never sure of what has happened, always reaching for truths that elude his grasp. Conrad did not have to read Freud before he created his Marlow, brooding out the secrets of a Lord Jim or a Kurtz, nor did Joyce have to read him before he stripped away Gabriel Conroy's layers of defenses to bring him to self-confrontation. But both they and the other great fictionalists of the twentieth century reflect the view of human beings in the world that Freud first mapped.

FURTHER READING *(prepared by J. H.):* Peter Gay's biography, *Freud: A Life for Our Time,* 1988, offers not only an authoritative account of Freud's life but also a lucid and accurate account of Freud's thought and its implications for modern culture. The best brief account of Freud's thought is Richard Wollheim's *Freud,* 1971. Also excellent is Philip Rieff's *Freud: The Mind of the Moralist,* 3rd ed., 1979. A pioneering study of Freud as a writer is Stanley Edgar Hyman's *The Tangled Bank,* 1962, which also includes studies of Darwin, Marx, and Frazer as literary figures. More contemporary in critical approach is Patrick J. Mahony's *Freud as a Writer,* 1982. *Freud: A Collection of Critical Essays,* ed. Perry Meisel, 1981, in the Twentieth Century Views series, has a long, excellent introduction by the editor on "Freud as Literature" and

assembles a number of major essays on Freud's significance to literature, including Steven Marcus's important 1974 essay, "Freud and Dora: Story, History, Case History." This essay is also reprinted in *In Dora's Case: Freud—Hysteria—Feminism*, ed. Charles Bernheimer and Claire Kahane, 1985, along with eleven other critical essays on "*Dora*." Phillip McCaffrey's *Freud and Dora: The Artful Dream*, 1984, brings the methods of literary analysis to Dora's second dream to supplement and critique Freud's analysis. On the related topic of the psychoanalytic interpretation of literature, the novice might well start with Norman Holland's *The Dynamics of Literary Response*, 1968; Holland's later turn toward "identity theory" as a tool of literary analysis is well represented in *Poems in Persons*, 1973. Ernst Kris's *Psychoanalytic Explorations in Art*, 1952, and Simon O. Lesser's *Fiction and the Unconscious*, 1957, can also be recommended. There are a number of useful collections of psychoanalytical essays on literature; among them are *Psychoanalysis and Literature*, ed. Hendrik M. Ruitenbeek, 1964, and *The Practice of Psychoanalytic Criticism*, ed. Leonard Tennenhouse, 1976. Current issues are well covered in *The Talking Cure: Essays in Psychoanalysis and Language*, ed. Colin MacCabe, 1986.

DORA: FRAGMENT OF AN ANALYSIS OF A CASE OF HYSTERIA

Translated by Alix and James Strachey

[1.] THE CLINICAL PICTURE

* * * *

The family circle of the eighteen-year-old girl who is the subject of this paper included, besides herself, her two parents and a brother who was one and a half years her senior. Her father was the dominating figure in this circle, owing to his intelligence and his character as much as to the circumstances of his life. It was those circumstances which provided the framework for the history of the patient's childhood and illness. At the time at which I began the girl's treatment her father was in the late forties, a man of rather unusual activity and talents, a large manufacturer in very comfortable circumstances. His daughter was most tenderly attached to him, and for that reason her critical powers, which developed early, took all the more offense at many of his actions and peculiarities.

Her affection for him was still further increased by the many severe illnesses which he had been through since her sixth year. At that time he had fallen ill with tuberculosis and the family had consequently moved to a small town in a good climate, situated in one of our southern provinces. There his lung trouble rapidly improved; but, on account of the precautions which were still considered necessary, both parents and children continued for the next ten years or so to reside chiefly in this spot, which I shall call B——. When her father's health was good, he used at times to be away, on visits to his factories. During the hottest part of the summer the family used to move to a health-resort in the hills.

When the girl was about ten years old, her father had to go through a course of treatment in a darkened room on account of a detached retina. As a result of this misfortune his vision was permanently impaired. His gravest illness occurred some two years later. It took the form of a confusional attack, followed by symptoms of paralysis and slight mental disturbances. A friend of his (who plays a part in the story with which we shall be concerned later on) persuaded him, while his condition had scarcely improved, to travel to Vienna with his physician and come to me for advice. I hesitated for some time as to whether I ought not to regard the case as one of tabo-paralysis, but I finally decided upon a diagnosis of a diffuse vascular affection; and since the patient admitted having had a specific infection before his marriage, I prescribed an energetic course of anti-luetic treatment, as a result of which all the remaining disturbances passed off.[1] It is no doubt owing to this fortunate intervention of mine that four years later he brought his daughter, who had meanwhile grown unmistakably neurotic, and introduced her to me, and that after another two years he handed her over to me for psychotherapeutic treatment.

I had in the meantime also made the acquaintance in Vienna of a sister of his, who was a little older than himself. She gave clear evidence of a severe form of psychoneurosis without any characteristically hysterical symptoms. After a life which had been weighed down by an unhappy marriage, she died of a marasmus[2] which made rapid advances and the symptoms of which were, as a matter of fact, never fully cleared up. An elder brother of the girl's father, whom I once happened to meet, was a hypochondriacal bachelor.

The sympathies of the girl herself, who, as I have said, became my patient at the age of eighteen, had always been with the father's side of the family, and ever since she had fallen ill she had taken as her model the aunt who has just been mentioned. There could be no doubt, too, that it was from her father's family that she had derived not only her natural gifts and her intellectual precocity but also the predisposition to her illness. I never made her mother's acquaintance. From the accounts given me by the girl and her father I was led to imagine her as an uncultivated woman and above all as a foolish one, who had concentrated all her interests upon domestic affairs, especially since her husband's illness and the estrangement to which it led. She presented the picture, in fact, of what might be called the "housewife's psychosis." She had no understanding for her children's more active interests, and was occupied all day long in cleaning the house with its furniture and utensils and in keeping them clean—to such an extent as to make it almost impossible to use or enjoy them. This condition, traces of which are to be found often enough in normal housewives, inevitably reminds one of forms of obsessional washing and other kinds of obsessional cleanliness. But such women (and this applied to the patient's mother) are entirely without insight into their illness, so that one essential characteristic of an "obsessional neurosis" is lacking. The relations between the girl and her mother had been unfriendly for years. The daughter

[1] *Tabo-paralysis:* syphilitic paralysis. *Diffuse vascular affection:* generalized circulatory disorder. *Anti-luetic treatment:* treatment for syphilis (lues).
[2] A generalized degeneration, wasting away.

looked down on her mother and used to criticize her mercilessly, and she had withdrawn completely from her influence.

During the girl's earlier years, her only brother (her elder brother by a year and a half) had been the model which her ambitions had striven to follow. But in the last few years the relations between the brother and sister had grown more distant. The young man used to try so far as he could to keep out of the family disputes; but when he was obliged to take sides he would support his mother. So that the usual sexual attraction had drawn together the father and daughter on the one side and the mother and son on the other.

The patient, to whom I shall in future give the name of Dora,[3] had even at the age of eight begun to develop neurotic symptoms. She became subject at that time to chronic dyspnoea[4] with occasional accesses during which the symptom was very much aggravated. The first onset occurred after a short expedition in the mountains and was accordingly put down to over-exertion. In the course of six months, during which she was made to rest and was carefully looked after, this condition gradually passed off. The family doctor seems to have had not a moment's hesitation in diagnosing the disorder as purely nervous and in excluding any organic cause for the dyspnoea; but he evidently considered this diagnosis compatible with the aetiology of over-exertion.

The little girl went through the usual infectious diseases of childhood without suffering any permanent damage. As she herself told me—and her words were intended to convey a deeper meaning—her brother was as a rule the first to start the illness and used to have it very slightly, and she would then follow suit with a severe form of it. When she was about twelve she began to suffer from hemicranial headaches in the nature of a migraine, and from attacks of nervous coughing. At first these two symptoms always appeared together, but they became separated later on and ran different courses. The migraine grew rarer, and by the time she was sixteen she had quite got over it. But attacks of *tussis nervosa*,[5] which had no doubt been started by a common catarrh, continued to occur over the whole period. When, at the age of eighteen, she came to me for treatment, she was again coughing in a characteristic manner. The number of these attacks could not be determined; but they lasted from three to five weeks, and on one occasion for several months. The most troublesome symptom during the first half of an attack of this kind, at all events in the last few years, used to be a complete loss of voice. The diagnosis that this was once more a nervous complaint had been established long since; but the various methods of treatment which are usual, including hydrotherapy and the local application of electricity, had produced no result. It was in such circumstances as these that the child had developed into a mature young

[3] Freud analyzed the unconscious reasons for his choosing the pseudonym Dora for his patient (whose real name was Ida Bauer) in *The Psychopathology of Everyday Life* (1901). The nurse of his sister Rosa's children was supposedly named Dora, but Freud had discovered that her name was really Rosa and that she had changed it in order to avoid confusion with her employer. On learning this, he had remarked, "Poor people! They cannot even retain their own names!" "Thus," Freud wrote, "when I sought a name for a person *who could not retain her own name* no other except 'Dora' occurred to me."

[4] Difficult or labored breathing. [5] Nervous coughing.

woman of very independent judgment, who had grown accustomed to laugh at the efforts of doctors, and in the end to renounce their help entirely. Moreover, she had always been against calling in medical advice, though she had no personal objection to her family doctor. Every proposal to consult a new physician aroused her resistance, and it was only her father's authority which induced her to come to me at all.

I first saw her when she was sixteen, in the early summer. She was suffering from a cough and from hoarseness, and even at that time I proposed giving her psychological treatment. My proposal was not adopted, since the attack in question, like the others, passed off spontaneously, though it had lasted unusually long. During the winter of the next year she came and stayed in Vienna with her uncle and his daughters after the death of the aunt of whom she had been so fond. There she fell ill of a feverish disorder which was diagnosed at the time as appendicitis. In the following autumn, since her father's health seemed to justify the step, the family left the health-resort of B—— for good and all. They first moved to the town where her father's factory was situated, and then, scarcely a year later, settled permanently in Vienna.

Dora was by that time in the first bloom of youth—a girl of intelligent and engaging looks. But she was a source of heavy trials for her parents. Low spirits and an alteration in her character had now become the main features of her illness. She was clearly satisfied neither with herself nor with her family; her attitude towards her father was unfriendly, and she was on very bad terms with her mother, who was bent upon drawing her into taking a share in the work of the house. She tried to avoid social intercourse, and employed herself—so far as she was allowed to by the fatigue and lack of concentration of which she complained—with attending lectures for women and with carrying on more or less serious studies. One day her parents were thrown into a state of great alarm by finding upon the girl's writing-desk, or inside it, a letter in which she took leave of them because, as she said, she could not longer endure her life. Her father, indeed, being a man of some perspicacity, guessed that the girl had no serious suicidal intentions. But he was none the less very much shaken; and when one day, after a slight passage of words between him and his daughter, she had a first attack of loss of consciousness—an event which was subsequently covered by an amnesia—it was determined, in spite of her reluctance, that she should come to me for treatment.

No doubt this case history, as I have so far outlined it, does not upon the whole seem worth recording. It is merely a case of *"petite hystérie"* with the commonest of all somatic and mental symptoms: dyspnoea, *tussis nervosa*, aphonia, and possibly migraines, together with depression, hysterical unsociability, and a *taedium vitae* which was probably not entirely genuine.[6] More interesting cases of hysteria have no doubt been published, and they have very often been more carefully described; for nothing will be found in the following pages on the subject of stigmata of cutaneous sensibility, limitation of the visual field, or similar matters. I may venture to remark, however, that all such collections of the strange and wonderful phenomena of

[6] *Petite hystérie:* minor hysteria. *Aphonia:* loss of voice. *Taedium vitae:* an overwhelming feeling that life is tedious.

hysteria have but slightly advanced our knowledge of a disease which still remains as great a puzzle as ever. What is wanted is precisely an elucidation of the commonest cases and of their most frequent and typical symptoms. I should have been very well satisfied if the circumstances had allowed me to give a complete elucidation of this case of *petite hystérie*. And my experiences with other patients leave me no doubt that my analytic method would have enabled me to do so.

In 1896, shortly after the appearance of my *Studies on Hysteria* (written in conjunction with Dr. J. Breuer), I asked an eminent fellow-specialist for his opinion upon the psychological theory of hysteria put forward in that work. He bluntly replied that he considered it an unjustifiable generalization of conclusions which might hold good for a few cases. Since then I have seen an abundance of cases of hysteria, and I have been occupied with each case for a number of days, weeks, or years. In not a single one of them have I failed to discover the psychological determinants which were postulated in the *Studies*, namely, a psychic trauma, a conflict of affects, and—an additional factor which I brought forward in later publications—a disturbance in the sphere of sexuality. It is of course not to be expected that the patient will come to meet the physician half-way with material which has become pathogenic for the very reason of its efforts to lie concealed; nor must the inquirer rest content with the first "No" that crosses his path.

In Dora's case, thanks to her father's shrewdness, which I have remarked upon more than once already, there was no need for me to look about for the points of contact between the circumstances of the patient's life and her illness, at all events in its most recent form. Her father told me that he and his family while they were at B—— had formed an intimate friendship with a married couple who had been settled there for several years. Frau K. had nursed him during his long illness, and had in that way, he said, earned a title to his undying gratitude. Herr K. had always been most kind to Dora. He had gone on walks with her when he was there, and had made her small presents; but no one had thought any harm of that. Dora had taken the greatest care of the K.'s two little children, and been almost a mother to them. When Dora and her father had come to see me two years before in the summer, they had been just on their way to stop with Herr and Frau K., who were spending the summer on one of our lakes in the Alps. Dora was to have spent several weeks at the K.'s, while her father had intended to return after a few days. During that time Herr K. had been living there as well. As her father was preparing for his departure the girl had suddenly declared with the greatest determination that she was going with him, and she had in fact put her decision into effect. It was not until some days later that she had thrown any light upon her strange behavior. She had then told her mother—intending that what she said should be passed on to her father—that Herr K. had had the audacity to make her a proposal while they were on a walk after a trip upon the lake. Herr K. had been called to account by her father and uncle on the next occasion of their meeting, but he had denied in the most emphatic terms having on his side made any advances which could have been open to such a construction. He had then proceeded to throw suspicion upon the girl, saying that he had heard from Frau K. that she took no interest in anything but sexual mat-

ters, and that she used to read Mantegazza's *Physiology of Love*[7] and books of that sort in their house on the lake. It was most likely, he had added, that she had been over-excited by such reading and had merely "fancied" the whole scene she had described.

"I have no doubt," continued her father, "that this incident is responsible for Dora's depression and irritability and suicidal ideas. She keeps pressing me to break off relations with Herr K. and more particularly with Frau K., whom she used positively to worship formerly. But that I cannot do. For, to begin with, I myself believe that Dora's tale of the man's immoral suggestions is a phantasy that has forced its way into her mind; and besides, I am bound to Frau K. by ties of honorable friendship and I do not wish to cause her pain. The poor woman is most unhappy with her husband, of whom, by the by, I have no very high opinion. She herself has suffered a great deal with her nerves, and I am her only support. With my state of health I need scarcely assure you that there is nothing wrong in our relations. We are just two poor wretches who give one another what comfort we can by an exchange of friendly sympathy. You know already that I get nothing out of my own wife. But Dora, who inherits my obstinacy, cannot be moved from her hatred of the K.'s. She had her last attack after a conversation in which she had again pressed me to break with them. Please try and bring her to reason."

Her father's words did not always quite tally with this pronouncement; for on other occasions he tried to put the chief blame for Dora's impossible behavior upon her mother—whose peculiarities made the house unbearable for every one. But I had resolved from the first to suspend my judgment of the true state of affairs till I had heard the other side as well.

The experience with Herr K.—his making love to her and the insult to her honor which was involved—seems to provide in Dora's case the psychic trauma which Breuer and I declared long ago to be the indispensable prerequisite for the production of a hysterical disorder. But this new case also presents all the difficulties which have since led me to go beyond that theory, besides an additional difficulty of a special kind. For, as so often happens in histories of cases of hysteria, the trauma that we know of as having occurred in the patient's past life is insufficient to explain or to determine the particular character of the symptoms; we should understand just as much or just as little of the whole business if the result of the trauma had been symptoms quite other than *tussis nervosa*, aphonia, depression, and *taedium vitae*. But there is the further consideration that some of these symptoms (the cough and the loss of voice) had been produced by the patient years before the time of the trauma, and that their earliest appearances belong to her childhood, since they occurred in her eighth year. If, therefore, the trauma theory is not to be abandoned, we must go back to her childhood and look about there for any influences or impressions which might have had an effect analogous to that of a trauma. Moreover, it deserves to be remarked that in the investigation even of cases in which the

[7] Paolo Mantegazza's *Physiology of Love* (1873) was an explicitly illustrated textbook on the sexual organs.

first symptoms had not already set in in childhood I have been driven to trace back the patients' life history to their earliest years.

When the first difficulties of the treatment had been overcome, Dora told me of an earlier episode with Herr K., which was even better calculated to act as a sexual trauma. She was fourteen years old at the time. Herr K. had made an arrangement with her and his wife that they should meet him one afternoon at his place of business in the principal square of B—— so as to have a view of a church festival. He persuaded his wife, however, to stay at home, and sent away his clerks, so that he was alone when the girl arrived. When the time for the procession approached, he asked the girl to wait for him at the door which opened upon the staircase leading to the upper story, while he pulled down the outside shutters. He then came back, and, instead of going out by the open door, suddenly clasped the girl to him and pressed a kiss upon her lips. This was surely just the situation to call up a distinct feeling of sexual excitement in a girl of fourteen who had never before been approached. But Dora had at that moment a violent feeling of disgust, tore herself free from the man, and hurried past him to the staircase and from there to the street door. She nevertheless continued to meet Herr K. Neither of them ever mentioned the little scene; and according to her account Dora kept it a secret till her confession during the treatment. For some time afterwards, however, she avoided being alone with Herr K. The K.'s had just made plans for an expedition which was to last for some days and on which Dora was to have accompanied them. After the scene of the kiss she refused to join the party, without giving any reason.

In this scene—second in order of mention, but first in order of time— the behavior of this child of fourteen was already entirely and completely hysterical. I should without question consider a person hysterical in whom an occasion for sexual excitement elicited feelings that were preponderantly or exclusively unpleasurable; and I should do so whether or no the person were capable of producing somatic symptoms. The elucidation of the mechanism of this *reversal of affect* is one of the most important and at the same time one of the most difficult problems in the psychology of the neuroses. In my own judgment I am still some way from having achieved this end; and I may add that within the limits of the present paper I shall be able to bring forward only a part of such knowledge as I do possess. . . .

I did not find it easy to direct the patient's attention to her relations with Herr K. She declared that she had done with him. The uppermost layer of all her associations during the sittings, and everything of which she was easily conscious and of which she remembered having been conscious the day before was always connected with her father. It was quite true that she could not forgive her father for continuing his relations with Herr K. and more particularly with Frau K. But she viewed those relations in a very different light from that in which her father wished them to appear. In her mind there was no doubt that what bound her father to this young and beautiful woman was a common love-affair. Nothing that could help to confirm this view had escaped her perception, which in this connection was pitilessly sharp; *here there were no gaps to be found in her memory.* Their acquaintance with the K.'s had begun before her father's serious illness; but it had not become intimate until the young woman had officially taken on the

position of nurse during that illness, while Dora's mother had kept away from the sick-room. During the first summer holidays after his recovery things had happened which must have opened every one's eyes to the true character of this "friendship." The two families had taken a suite of rooms in common at the hotel. One day Frau K. had announced that she could not keep the bedroom which she had up till then shared with one of her children. A few days later Dora's father had given up his bedroom, and they had both moved into new rooms—the end rooms, which were only separated by the passage, while the rooms they had given up had not offered any such security against interruption. Later on, whenever she had reproached her father about Frau K., he had been in the habit of saying that he could not understand her hostility and that, on the contrary, his children had every reason for being grateful to Frau K. Her mother, whom she had asked for an explanation of this mysterious remark, had told her that her father had been so unhappy at that time that he had made up his mind to go into the wood and kill himself, and that Frau K., suspecting as much, had gone after him and had persuaded him by her entreaties to preserve his life for the sake of his family. Of course, Dora went on, she herself did not believe this story; no doubt the two of them had been seen together in the wood, and her father had thereupon invented this fairy tale of his suicide so as to account for their rendezvous.

When they had returned to B——, her father had visited Frau K. every day at definite hours, while her husband was at his business. Everybody had talked about it and had questioned her about it pointedly. Herr K. himself had often complained bitterly to her mother, though he had spared her herself any allusions to the subject—which she seemed to attribute to the delicacy of his feelings. When they had all gone for walks together, her father and Frau K. had always known how to manage things so as to be alone with each other. There could be no doubt that she had taken money from him, for she spent more than she could possibly have afforded out of her own purse or her husband's. Dora added that her father had begun to make handsome presents to Frau K., and in order to make these less conspicuous had at the same time become especially liberal towards her mother and herself. And, while previously Frau K. had been an invalid and had even been obliged to spend months in a sanatorium for nervous disorders because she had been unable to walk, she had now become a healthy and lively woman.

Even after they had left B—— for the manufacturing town, these relations, already of many years' standing, had been continued. From time to time her father used to declare that he could not endure the rawness of the climate, and that he must do something for himself; he would begin to cough and complain, until suddenly he would start off to B——, and from there write the most cheerful letters home. All these illnesses had only been pretexts for seeing his friend again. Then one day it had been decided that they were to move to Vienna, and Dora began to suspect a hidden connection. And sure enough, they had scarcely been three weeks in Vienna when she heard that the K.'s had moved there as well. They were in Vienna, so she told me, at that very moment, and she frequently met her father with Frau K. in the street. She also met Herr K. very often, and he always used to turn round and look after her; and once when he had met her out by

herself he had followed her for a long way, so as to make sure where she was going and whether she might not have a rendezvous.

On one occasion during the course of the treatment her father again felt worse, and went off to B—— for several weeks; and the sharp-sighted Dora had soon unearthed the fact that Frau K. had started off to the same place on a visit to her relatives there. It was at this time that Dora's criticisms of her father were the most frequent: he was insincere, he had a strain of falseness in his character, he only thought of his own enjoyment, and he had a gift for seeing things in the light which suited him best.

I could not in general dispute Dora's characterization of her father; and there was one particular respect in which it was easy to see that her reproaches were justified.When she was feeling embittered she used to be overcome by the idea that she had been handed over to Herr K. as the price of his tolerating the relations between her father and his wife; and her rage at her father's making such a use of her was visible behind her affection for him. At other times she was quite well aware that she had been guilty of exaggeration in talking like this. The two men had of course never made a formal agreement in which she was treated as an object for barter; her father in particular would have been horrified at any such suggestion. But he was one of those men who know how to evade a dilemma by falsifying their judgment upon one of the conflicting alternatives. If it had been pointed out to him that there might be danger for a growing girl in the constant and uncontrolled companionship of a man who had no satisfaction from his own wife, he would have been certain to answer that he could rely upon his daughter, that a man like K. could never be dangerous to her, and that his friend was himself incapable of such intentions, or that Dora was still a child and was treated as a child by K. But as a matter of fact things were in a position in which each of the two men avoided drawing any conclusions from the other's behavior which would have been awkward for his own plans. It was possible for Herr K. to send Dora flowers every day for a whole year while he was in the neighborhood, to take every opportunity of giving her valuable presents, and to spend all his spare time in her company, without her parents noticing anything in his behavior that was characteristic of love-making.

When the patient brings forward a sound and incontestable train of argument during psychoanalytic treatment, the physician is liable to feel a moment's embarrassment, and the patient may take advantage of it by asking: "This is all perfectly correct and true, isn't it? What do you want to change in it now that I've told it you?" But it soon becomes evident that the patient uses thoughts of this kind, which the analysis cannot attack, for the purpose of cloaking others which are anxious to escape from criticism and from consciousness. A string of reproaches against other people leads one to suspect the existence of a string of self-reproaches with the same content. All that need be done is to turn back each single reproach on to the speaker himself. There is something undeniably automatic about this method of defending oneself against a self-reproach by making the same reproach against some one else. A model of it is to be found in the *tu quoque* arguments of children; if one of them is accused of being a liar, he will reply without an instant's hesitation: "You're another." A grown-up person who wanted to throw back abuse would look for some really exposed spot

in his antagonist and would not lay the chief stress upon the same content being repeated. In paranoia the projection of a reproach on to another person without any alteration in its content and therefore without any consideration for reality becomes manifest as the process of delusion-formation.

Dora's reproaches against her father also had a "lining" or "backing" of self-reproaches with a corresponding content in every case, as I shall show in detail. She was right in thinking that her father did not wish to look too closely into Herr K.'s behavior to his daughter, for fear of being disturbed in his own love-affair with Frau K. But Dora herself had done precisely the same thing. She had made herself an accomplice in the affair, and had dismissed from her mind every sign which tended to show its true character. It was not until after her adventure by the lake that her eyes were opened and that she began to apply such a severe standard to her father. During all the previous years she had given every possible assistance to her father's relations with Frau K. She would never go to see her if she thought her father was there; but, knowing that in that case the children would have been sent out, she would turn her steps in a direction where she would be sure to meet them, and would go for a walk with them. There had been some one in the house who had been anxious at an early stage to open her eyes to the nature of her father's relations with Frau K., and to induce her to take sides against her. This was her last governess, an unmarried woman, no longer young, who was well-read and of advanced views. The teacher and her pupil were for a while upon excellent terms, until suddenly Dora became hostile to her and insisted upon her dismissal. So long as the governess had any influence she used it for stirring up feeling against Frau K. She explained to Dora's mother that it was incompatible with her dignity to tolerate such an intimacy between her husband and another woman; and she drew Dora's attention to all the striking features of their relations. But her efforts were vain. Dora remained devoted to Frau K. and would hear of nothing that might make her think ill of her relations with her father. On the other hand she very easily fathomed the motives by which her governess was actuated. She might be blind in one direction, but she was sharp-sighted enough in the other. She saw that the governess was in love with her father. When he was there, she seemed to be quite another person: at such times she could be amusing and obliging. While the family were living in the manufacturing town and Frau K. was not on the horizon, her hostility was directed against Dora's mother, who was then her more immediate rival. Up to this point Dora bore her no ill-will. She did not become angry until she observed that she herself was a subject of complete indifference to the governess, whose pretended affection for her was really meant for her father. While her father was away from the manufacturing town the governess had no time to spare for her, would not go for walks with her, and took no interest in her studies. No sooner had her father returned from B—— than she was once more ready with every sort of service and assistance. Thereupon Dora dropped her.

The poor woman had thrown a most unwelcome light upon a part of Dora's own behavior. What the governess had from time to time been to Dora, Dora had been to Herr K.'s children. She had been a mother to them, she had taught them, she had gone for walks with them, she had

offered them a complete substitute for the slight interest which their own mother showed in them. Herr K. and his wife had often talked of getting a divorce; but it never took place, because Herr K., who was an affectionate father, would not give up either of the two children. A common interest in the children had from the first been a bond between Herr K. and Dora. Her preoccupation with his children was evidently a cloak for something else that Dora was anxious to hide from herself and from other people.

The same inference was to be drawn both from her behavior towards the children, regarded in the light of the governess's behavior towards herself, and from her silent acquiescence in her father's relations with Frau K.—namely, that she had all these years been in love with Herr K. When I informed her of this conclusion she did not assent to it. It is true that she once told me that other people besides (one of her cousins, for instance—a girl who had stopped with them for some time at B——) had said to her: "Why, you're simply wild about that man!" But she herself could not be got to recollect any feelings of the kind. Later on, when the quantity of material that had come up had made it difficult for her to persist in her denial, she admitted that she might have been in love with Herr K. at B——, but declared that since the scene by the lake it had all been over. In any case it was quite certain that the reproaches which she made against her father of having been deaf to the most imperative calls of duty and of having seen things in the light which was most convenient from the point of view of his own passions—these reproaches recoiled upon her own head.[8] Her other reproach against her father was that his ill-health was only a pretext and that he exploited it for his own purposes. This reproach, too, concealed a whole section of her own secret history. One day she complained of a professedly new symptom, which consisted of piercing gastric pains. "Whom are you copying now?" I asked her, and I found I had hit the mark. The day before she had visited her cousins, the daughters of the aunt who had died. The younger one had become engaged, and this had given occasion to the elder one for falling ill with gastric pains, and she was to be sent off to Semmering.[9] Dora thought it was all just envy on the part of the elder sister; she always got ill when she wanted something, and what she wanted now was to be away from home so as not to have to look on her sister's happiness. But Dora's own gastric pains proclaimed the fact that she identified herself with her cousin, who, according to her, was a malingerer. Her grounds for this identification were either that she too envied the luckier girl her love, or that she saw her own story reflected in that of the elder sister, who had recently had a love-affair which had ended unhappily. But she had also learned from observing Frau K. what useful things illnesses could become. Herr K. spent part of the year in travelling. Whenever he came back, he used to find his wife in bad health, although, as Dora knew, she had been quite well only the day before. Dora realized that the presence of the husband had the effect of making his wife ill, and that she was glad to be ill so as to be able to escape the conjugal duties which she so

[8]"The question then arises: If Dora loved Herr K., what was the reason for her refusing him in the scene by the lake? Or at any rate, why did her refusal take such a brutal form, as though she were embittered against him? And how could a girl who was in love feel insulted by a proposal which was made in a manner neither tactless nor offensive?" [Freud].

[9]A fashionable health resort about fifty miles south of Vienna.

much detested. At this point in the discussion Dora suddenly brought in an allusion to her own alterations between good and bad health during the first years of her girlhood at B——; and I was thus driven to suspect that her states of health were to be regarded as depending upon something else, in the same way as Frau K.'s. (It is a rule of psychoanalytic technique that an internal connection which is still undisclosed will announce its presence by means of a contiguity—a temporal proximity—of associations; just as in writing, if "a" and "b" are put side by side, it means that the syllable "ab" is to be formed out of them.) Dora had had a very large number of attacks of coughing accompanied by loss of voice. Could it be that the presence or absence of the man she loved had had an influence upon the appearance and disappearance of the symptoms of her illness? If this were so, it must be possible to discover some coincidence or other which would betray the fact. I asked her what the average length of these attacks had been. "From three to six weeks, perhaps." How long had Herr K.'s absences lasted? "Three to six weeks, too," she was obliged to admit. Her illness was therefore a demonstration of her love for K., just as his wife's was a demonstration of her dislike. It was only necessary to suppose that she had behaved in the opposite way from Frau K., and had been ill when he was absent and well when he had come back. And this really seemed to have been so, at least during the first period of the attacks. Later on it no doubt became necessary to obscure the coincidence between her attacks of illness and the absence of the man she secretly loved, lest its regularity should betray her secret. The length of the attacks would then remain as a trace of their original significance.

I remembered that long before, while I was working at Charcot's clinic, I had seen and heard how in cases of hysterical mutism writing operated vicariously in the place of speech. Such patients were able to write more fluently, quicker, and better than others did or than they themselves had done previously. The same thing had happened with Dora. In the first days of her attacks of aphonia "writing had always come specially easy to her." No psychological elucidation was really required for this peculiarity, which was the expression of a physiological substitutive function enforced by necessity; it was noticeable, however, that such an elucidation was easily to be found. Herr K. used to write to her at length while he was travelling and to send her picture post-cards. It used to happen that she alone was informed as to the date of his return, and that his arrival took his wife by surprise. Moreover, that a person will correspond with an absent friend whom he cannot talk to is scarcely less obvious than that if he has lost his voice he will try to make himself understood in writing. Dora's aphonia, then, allowed of the following symbolic interpretation. When the person she loved was away she gave up speaking; speech had lost its value since she could not speak to *him*. On the other hand, writing gained in importance, as being the only means of communication with the absent person. . . .

None of her father's actions seemed to have embittered her so much as his readiness to consider the scene by the lake as a product of her imagination. She was almost beside herself at the idea of its being supposed that she had merely fancied something on that occasion. For a long time I was in perplexity as to what the self-reproach could be which lay behind her passionate repudiation of this explanation of the episode. It was justifiable to

suspect that there was something concealed, for a reproach which misses the mark gives no lasting offense. On the other hand, I came to the conclusion that Dora's story must correspond to the facts in every respect. No sooner had she grasped Herr K.'s intention than, without letting him finish what he had to say, she had given him a slap in the face and hurried away. Her behavior must have seemed as incomprehensible to the man after she had left him as to us, for he must long before have gathered from innumerable small signs that he was secure of the girl's affections. In our discussion of Dora's second dream we shall come upon the solution of this riddle as well as upon the self-reproach which we have hitherto failed to discover.

As she kept on repeating her complaints against her father with a wearisome monotony, and as at the same time her cough continued, I was led to think that this symptom might have some meaning in connection with her father. And apart from this, the explanation of the symptom which I had hitherto obtained was far from fulfilling the requirements which I am accustomed to make of such explanations. According to a rule which I had found confirmed over and over again by experience, though I had not yet ventured to erect it into a general principle, a symptom signifies the representation—the realization— of a phantasy with a sexual content, that is to say, it signifies a sexual situation. It would be better to say that at least *one* of the meanings of a symptom is the representation of a sexual phantasy, but that no such limitation is imposed upon the content of its other meanings. Any one who takes up psychoanalytic work will quickly discover that a symptom has more than one meaning and serves to represent several unconscious mental processes simultaneously. And I should like to add that in my estimation a single unconscious mental process or phantasy will scarcely ever suffice for the production of a symptom.

An opportunity very soon occurred for interpreting Dora's nervous cough in this way by means of an imagined sexual situation. She had once again been insisting that Frau K. only loved her father because he was *"ein vermögender Mann"* ["a man of means"]. Certain details of the way in which she expressed herself (which I pass over here, like most other purely technical parts of the analysis) led me to see that behind this phrase its opposite lay concealed, namely, that her father was *"ein unvermögender Mann"* ["a man without means"].[10] This could only be meant in a sexual sense—that her father, as a man, was without means, was impotent. Dora confirmed this interpretation from her conscious knowledge; whereupon I pointed out the contradiction she was involved in if on the one hand she continued to insist that her father's relation with Frau K. was a common love-affair, and on the other hand maintained that her father was impotent, or in other words incapable of carrying on an affair of such a kind. Her answer showed that she had no need to admit the contradiction. She knew very well, she said, that there was more than one way of obtaining sexual gratification. (The source of this piece of knowledge, however, was once more untraceable.) I questioned her further, whether she referred to the use of organs other than the genitals for the purpose of sexual intercourse, and she replied in the affirmative. I could then go on to say that in that case she must be thinking of precisely those parts of the body which in her case were

[10] *Unvermögend* ("unable") is used in the senses of both "not rich" and "impotent."

in a state of irritation,—the throat and the oral cavity. To be sure, she would not hear of going so far as this in recognizing her own thoughts; and indeed, if the occurrence of the symptom was to be made possible at all, it was essential that she should not be completely clear on the subject. But the conclusion was inevitable that with her spasmodic cough, which, as is usual, was referred for its exciting cause to a tickling in her throat, she pictured to herself a scene of sexual gratification *per os*[11] between the two people whose love-affair occupied her mind so incessantly. A very short time after she had tacitly accepted this explanation her cough vanished—which fitted in very well with my view; but I do not wish to lay too much stress upon this development, since her cough had so often before spontaneously disappeared. . . .

Dora's incessant repetition of the same thoughts about her father's relations with Frau K. made it possible to derive still further important material from the analysis.

A train of thought such as this may be described as exaggerated, or better *reinforced*, or "supervalent," in Wernicke's sense of the word.[12] It shows its pathological character, in spite of its apparently reasonable content, by the single peculiarity that no amount of conscious and voluntary effort of thought on the patient's part is able to dissipate or remove it. A normal train of thought, however intense it may be, can eventually be disposed of. Dora felt quite rightly that her thoughts about her father required to be judged in a special way. "I can think of nothing else," she complained again and again. "I know my brother says we children have no right to criticize this behavior of father's. He declares that we ought not to trouble ourselves about it, and ought even to be glad, perhaps, that he has found a woman he can love, since mother understands him so little. I can quite see that, and I should like to think the same as my brother, but I can't. I can't forgive him for it."

Now what is one to do in the face of a supervalent thought like this, after one has heard what its conscious grounds are and listened to the ineffectual protests made against it? Reflection will suggest that *this exaggerated train of thought must owe its reinforcement to the unconscious.* It cannot be resolved by any effort of thought, either because it itself reaches with its root down into unconscious, repressed material, or because another unconscious thought lies concealed behind it. In the latter case, the concealed thought is usually the direct contrary of the supervalent one. Contrary thoughts are always closely connected with each other and are often paired off in such a way that *the one thought is exaggeratedly conscious while its counterpart is repressed and unconscious.* This relation between the two thoughts is an effect of the process of repression. For repression is often achieved by means of an excessive reinforcement of the thought contrary to the one which is to be repressed. This process I call *reactive reinforcement,* and the thought which asserts itself exaggeratedly in consciousness and (in the same way as a prejudice) cannot be removed I call a *reactive thought.* The two thoughts then act towards each other much like the two needles of an astatic galvanometer. The reactive thought keeps the objectionable one under repression by means of a certain surplusage of intensity; but for that

[11] "By mouth." [12] C. Wernicke was the author of *Outline of Psychiatry* (1900).

reason it itself is "damped" and proof against conscious efforts of thought. So that the way to deprive the exaggerated thought of its reinforcement is by bringing its repressed contrary into consciousness.

We must also be prepared to meet with instances in which the supervalency of a thought is due not to the presence of one only of these two causes but to a concurrence of both of them. Other complications, too, may arise, but they can easily be fitted into the general scheme.

Let us now apply our theory to the instance provided by Dora's case. We will begin with the first hypothesis, namely, that her preoccupation with her father's relations to Frau K. owed its obsessive character to the fact that its root was unknown to her and lay in the unconscious. It is not difficult to divine the nature of that root from her circumstances and her conduct. Her behavior obviously went far beyond what would have been appropriate to filial concern. She felt and acted more like a jealous wife—in a way which would have been comprehensible in her mother. By her ultimatum to her father ("either her or me"), by the scenes she used to make, by the suicidal intentions she allowed to transpire,—by all this she was clearly putting herself in her mother's place. If we have rightly guessed the nature of the imaginary sexual situation which underlay her cough, in that phantasy she must have been putting herself in Frau K.'s place. She was therefore identifying herself with the woman her father had once loved and with the woman he loved now. The inference is obvious that her affection for her father was a much stronger one than she knew or than she would have cared to admit: in fact, that she was in love with him.

I have learned to look upon unconscious love relations like this (which may be recognized by their abnormal consequences)—between a father and a daughter, or between a mother and a son—as a revival of germs of feeling in infancy. I have shown at length elsewhere at what an early age sexual attraction makes itself felt between parents and children, and I have explained that the myth of Oedipus is probably to be regarded as a poetical rendering of what is typical in these relations. Distinct traces are probably to be found in most people of an early partiality of this kind—on the part of a daughter for her father, or on the part of a son for his mother; but it must be assumed to be more intense from the very first in the case of those children whose constitution marks them down for a neurosis, who develop prematurely and have a craving for love. At this point certain other influences, which need not be discussed here, come into play, and lead to a fixation of this rudimentary feeling of love or to a reinforcement of it; so that it turns into something (either while the child is still young or not until it has reached the age of puberty) which must be put on a par with a sexual inclination and which, like the latter, has the forces of the libido at its command. The external circumstances of our patient were by no means unfavorable to such an assumption. The nature of her disposition had always drawn her towards her father, and his numerous illnesses were bound to have increased her affection for him. In many of these illnesses he would allow no one but her to discharge the lighter duties of nursing. He had been so proud of the early growth of her intelligence that he had made her his confidante while she was still a child. It was really she and not her mother whom Frau K.'s appearance had driven out of more than one position.

When I told Dora that I could not avoid supposing that her affection for her father must at a very early moment have amounted to her being completely in love with him, she of course gave me her usual reply: "I don't remember that." But she immediately went on to tell me something analogous about a seven-year-old girl who was her cousin (on her mother's side) and in whom she often thought she saw a kind of reflection of her own childhood. This little girl had (not for the first time) been the witness of a heated dispute between her parents, and, when Dora happened to come in on a visit soon afterwards, whispered in her ear: "You can't think how I hate that person!" (pointing to her mother), "and when she's dead I shall marry papa." I am in the habit of regarding associations such as this, which bring forward something that agrees with the content of an assertion of mine, as a confirmation from the unconscious of what I have said. No other kind of "Yes" can be extracted from the unconscious; there is no such thing at all as an unconscious "No."

For years on end she had given no expression to this passion for her father. On the contrary, she had for a long time been on the closest terms with the woman who had supplanted her with her father, and she had actually, as we know from her self-reproaches, facilitated this woman's relations with her father. Her own love for her father had therefore been recently revived; and, if so, the question arises to what end this had happened. Clearly as a reactive symptom, so as to suppress something else— something, that is, that still exercised power in the unconscious. Considering how things stood, I could not help supposing in the first instance that what was suppressed was her love of Herr K. I could not avoid the assumption that she was still in love with him but that, for unknown reasons, since the scene by the lake her love had aroused in her violent feelings of opposition, and that the girl had brought forward and reinforced her old affection for her father in order to avoid any further necessity for paying conscious attention to the love which she had felt in the first years of her girlhood and which had now become painful to her. In this way I gained an insight into a conflict which was well calculated to unhinge the girl's mind. On the one hand she was filled with regret at having rejected the man's proposal, and with longing for his company and all the little signs of his affection; while on the other hand these feelings of tenderness and longing were combated by powerful forces, amongst which her pride was one of the most obvious. Thus she had succeeded in persuading herself that she had done with Herr K.—that was the advantage she derived from this typical process of repression; and yet she was obliged to summon up her infantile affection for her father and to exaggerate it, in order to protect herself against the feelings of love which were constantly pressing forward into consciousness. The further fact that she was almost incessantly a prey to the most embittered jealousy seemed to admit of still another determination.

My expectations were by no means disappointed when this explanation of mine was met by Dora with a most emphatic negative. The "No" uttered by a patient after a repressed thought has been presented to his conscious perception for the first time does no more than register the existence of a repression and its severity; it acts, as it were, as a gauge of the repression's strength. If this "No," instead of being regarded as the expression of an impartial judgment (of which, indeed, the patient is incapable), is ignored,

and if work is continued, the first evidence soon begins to appear that in such a case "No" signifies the desired "Yes." Dora admitted that she found it impossible to be as angry with Herr K. as he had deserved. She told me that one day she had met Herr K. in the street while she was walking with a cousin of hers who did not know him. The other girl had exclaimed all at once: "Why, Dora, what's wrong with you? You've gone as white as a sheet!" She herself had felt nothing of this change of color; but I explained to her that the expression of emotion and the play of features obey the unconscious rather than the conscious, and are a means of betraying the former. Another time Dora came to me in the worst of tempers after having been uniformly cheerful for several days. She could give no explanation of this. She felt so contrary to-day, she said; it was her uncle's birthday, and she could not bring herself to congratulate him, and she did not know why. My powers of interpretation had run dry that day; I let her go on talking, and she suddenly recollected that it was Herr K.'s birthday too—a fact which I did not neglect to use against her. And it was then no longer hard to explain why the handsome presents she had had on her own birthday a few days before had given her no pleasure. One gift was missing, and that was Herr K.'s, the gift which had plainly once been the most prized of all.

Nevertheless Dora persisted in denying my contention for some time longer, until, towards the end of the analysis, the conclusive proof of its correctness came to light.

I must now turn to consider a further complication, to which I should certainly give no space if I were a man of letters engaged upon the creation of a mental state like this for a short story, instead of being a medical man engaged upon its dissection. The element to which I must now allude can only serve to obscure and efface the outlines of the fine poetic conflict which we have been able to ascribe to Dora. This element would rightly fall a sacrifice to the censorship of a writer, for he, after all, simplifies and abstracts when he appears in the character of a psychologist. But in the world of reality, which I am trying to depict here, a complication of motives, an accumulation and conjunction of mental activities—in a word, overdetermination—is the rule. For behind Dora's supervalent train of thought which was concerned with her father's relations with Frau K. there lay concealed a feeling of jealousy which had that lady as its *object*—a feeling, that is, which could only be based upon an affection on Dora's part for one of her own sex. It has long been known and often been pointed out that at the age of puberty boys and girls show clear signs, even in normal cases, of the existence of an affection for people of their own sex. A romantic and sentimental friendship with one of her school-friends, accompanied by vows, kisses, promises of eternal correspondence, and all the sensibility of jealousy, is a common precursor of a girl's first serious passion for a man. Thenceforward, in favorable circumstances, the homosexual current of feeling often runs completely dry. But if a girl is not happy in her love for a man, the current is often set flowing again by the libido in later years and is increased up to a greater or lesser degree of intensity. If this much can be established without difficulty of healthy persons, and if we take into account what has already been said upon the fuller development in neurotics of the normal germs of perversion, we shall expect to find in these latter too a fairly strong homosexual predisposition. It must, indeed, be so; for I

have never yet come through a single psychoanalysis of a man or woman without having to take into account a very considerable current of homosexuality. When, in a hysterical woman or girl, the sexual libido which is directed towards men has been energetically suppressed, it will regularly be found that the libido which is directed towards women has become vicariously reinforced and even to some extent conscious.

I shall not in this place go any further into this important subject, which is especially indispensable to an understanding of hysteria in men, because Dora's analysis came to an end before it could throw any light upon this side of her mental life. But I should like to recall the governess, whom I have already mentioned, and with whom Dora had at first enjoyed the closest interchange of thought, until she discovered that she was being admired and fondly treated not for her own sake but for her father's; whereupon she had obliged the governess to leave. She used also to dwell with noticeable frequency and a peculiar emphasis upon the story of another estrangement which appeared inexplicable even to herself. She had always been on particularly good terms with the younger of her two cousins—the girl who had later on become engaged—and had shared all sorts of secrets with her. When, for the first time after Dora had broken off her stay by the lake, her father was going back to B——, she had naturally refused to go with him. This cousin had then been asked to travel with him instead, and she had accepted the invitation. From that time forward Dora had felt a coldness towards her, and she herself was surprised to find how indifferent she had become, although, as she admitted, she had very little ground for complaint against her. These instances of sensitiveness led me to inquire what her relations with Frau K. had been up till the time of the breach. I then found that the young woman and the scarcely grown girl had lived for years on a footing of the closest intimacy. When Dora stayed with the K.'s she used to share a bedroom with Frau K., and the husband used to be quartered elsewhere. She had been the wife's confidante and adviser in all the difficulties of her married life. There was nothing they had not talked about. Medea had been quite content that Creusa should make friends with her two children;[13] and she certainly did nothing to interfere with the relations between the girl and the children's father. How Dora managed to fall in love with the man about whom her beloved friend had so many bad things to say is an interesting psychological problem. We shall not be far from solving it when we realize that thoughts in the unconscious live very comfortably side by side, and even contraries get on together without disputes—a state of things which persists often enough even in the conscious.

When Dora talked about Frau K., she used to praise her "adorable white body" in accents more appropriate to a lover than to a defeated rival. Another time she told me, more in sorrow than in anger, that she was convinced the presents her father had brought her had been chosen by Frau K., for she recognized her taste. Another time, again, she pointed out that, evidently through the agency of Frau K., she had been given a present of some jewellery which was exactly like some that she had seen in Frau K.'s

[13] Medea, in Euripides's play, is cast off by her husband Jason in favor of the princess Creusa.

possession and had wished for aloud at the time. Indeed, I can say in general that I never heard her speak a harsh or angry word against the lady, although from the point of view of her supervalent thought she should have regarded her as the prime author of her misfortunes. She seemed to behave inconsequently; but her apparent inconsequence was precisely the manifestation of a complicating current of feeling. For how had this woman to whom Dora was so enthusiastically devoted behaved to her? After Dora had brought forward her accusation against Herr K., and her father had written to him demanding an explanation, Herr K. had replied in the first instance by protesting sentiments of the highest esteem for her and by proposing that he should come to the manufacturing town to clear up every misunderstanding. A few weeks later, when her father spoke to him at B——, there was no longer any question of esteem. On the contrary, Herr K. spoke of her with disparagement, and produced as his trump card the reflection that no girl who read such books and was interested in such things could have any title to a man's respect. Frau K., therefore, had betrayed her and had calumniated her; for it had only been with her that she had read Mantegazza and discussed forbidden topics. It was a repetition of what had happened with the governess: Frau K. had not loved her for her own sake but on account of her father. Frau K. had sacrificed her without a moment's hesitation so that her relations with her father might not be disturbed. This mortification touched her, perhaps, more nearly and had a greater pathogenic effect than the other one, which she tried to use as a screen for it,—the fact that she had been sacrificed by her father. Did not the obstinacy with which she retained the particular amnesia concerning the sources of her forbidden knowledge point directly to the great emotional importance for her of the accusation against her upon that score, and consequently to her betrayal by her friend?

I believe, therefore, that I am not mistaken in supposing that Dora's supervalent train of thought, which was concerned with her father's relations with Frau K., was designed not only for the purpose of suppressing her love for Herr K., which had once been conscious, but also to conceal her love for Frau K., which was in a deeper sense unconscious. The train of thought was directly contrary to the latter current of feeling. She told herself incessantly that her father had sacrificed her to this woman, and made noisy demonstrations to show that she grudged her the possession of her father; and in this way she concealed from herself the contrary fact, which was that she grudged her father Frau K.'s love, and had not forgiven the woman she loved for the disillusionment she had been caused by her betrayal. The jealous emotions of a woman were linked in the unconscious with a jealousy such as might have been felt by a man. These masculine or, more properly speaking, *gynaecophilic* currents of feeling are to be regarded as typical of the unconscious erotic life of hysterical girls.

[2.] THE FIRST DREAM

Just at a moment when there was a prospect that the material that was coming up for analysis would throw light upon an obscure point in Dora's

childhood, she reported that a few nights earlier she had once again had a dream which she had already dreamed in exactly the same way on many previous occasions. A periodically recurrent dream was by its very nature particularly well calculated to arouse my curiosity; and in any case it was justifiable in the interests of the treatment to consider the way in which the dream worked into the analysis as a whole. I therefore determined to make an especially careful investigation of it.

Here is the dream as related by Dora: "*A house was on fire.*[14] *My father was standing beside my bed and woke me up. I dressed myself quickly. Mother wanted to stop and save her jewel-case; but Father said: 'I refuse to let myself and my two children be burned for the sake of your jewel-case.' We hurried downstairs, and as soon as I was outside I woke up.*"

As the dream was a recurrent one, I naturally asked her when she had first dreamed it. She told me she did not know. But she remembered having had the dream three nights in succession at L—— (the place on the lake where the scene with Herr K. had taken place), and it had now come back again a few nights earlier, here in Vienna.[15] My expectations from the clearing-up of the dream were naturally heightened when I heard of its connection with the events at L——. But I wanted to discover first what had been the exciting cause of its recent recurrence, and I therefore asked Dora to take the dream bit by bit and tell me what occurred to her in connection with it. She had already had some training in dream interpretation from having previously analyzed a few minor specimens.

"Something occurs to me," she said, "but it cannot belong to the dream, for it is quite recent, whereas I have certainly had the dream before."

"That makes no difference," I replied. "Start away! It will simply turn out to be the most recent thing that fits in with the dream."

"Very well, then. Father has been having a dispute with Mother in the last few days, because she locks the dining-room door at night. My brother's room, you see, has no separate entrance, but can only be reached through the dining-room. Father does not want my brother to be locked in like that at night. He says it will not do: something might happen in the night so that it might be necessary to leave the room."

"And that made you think of the risk of fire?"

"Yes."

"Now, I should like you to pay close attention to the exact words you used. We may have to make use of them. You said that '*something might happen in the night so that it might be necessary to leave the room.*'"[16]

But Dora had now discovered the connecting link between the recent exciting cause of the dream and the original one, for she continued:

[14] "In answer to an inquiry Dora told me that there had never really been a fire at their house" [Freud].

[15] "The content of the dream makes it possible to establish that it in fact occurred *for the first time* at L——" [Freud].

[16] "I laid stress on these words because they took me aback. They seemed to have an ambiguous ring about them. Are not certain physical needs referred to in the same words? Now, in a line of associations ambiguous words (or, as we may call them, 'switch-words') act like points at a junction. If the points are switched across from the position in which they appear to lie in the dream, then we find ourselves on another set of rails; and along this second track run the thoughts which we are in search of but which still lie concealed behind the dream" [Freud].

"When we arrived at L—— that time, Father and I, he openly said he was afraid of fire. We arrived in a violent thunderstorm, and saw the small wooden house without any lightning-conductor. So his anxiety was quite natural."

What I now had to do was to establish the relation between the events at L—— and the recurrent dreams which she had had there. I therefore said: "Did you have the dream during your first nights at L—— or during your last ones? in other words, before or after the scene in the wood by the lake of which we have heard so much?" (I must explain that I knew that scene had not occurred on the very first day, and that she had remained at L—— for a few days after it without giving any hint of the incident.)

Her first reply was that she did not know, but after a while she added: "Yes. I think it was after the scene."

So now I knew that the dream was a reaction to that experience. But why had it recurred there three times? I continued my questions: "How long did you stop on at L—— after the scene?"

"Four days more. On the fifth I went away with Father."

"Now I am certain that the dream was an immediate effect of your experience with Herr K. It was at L—— that you dreamed it for the first time, and not before. You have only introduced this uncertainty in your memory so as to obliterate the connection in your mind. But the figures do not quite fit in to my satisfaction yet. If you stayed at L—— for four nights longer, the dream might have occurred four times over. Perhaps this was so?"

She no longer disputed my contention; but instead of answering my question she proceeded: "In the afternoon after our trip on the lake, from which we (Herr K. and I) returned at midday, I had gone to lie down as usual on the sofa in the bedroom to have a short sleep. I suddenly awoke and saw Herr K. standing beside me. . . . "

"In fact, just as you saw your father standing beside your bed in the dream?"

"Yes. I asked him sharply what it was he wanted there. By way of reply he said he was not going to be prevented from coming into his own bedroom when he wanted; besides, there was something he wanted to fetch. This episode put me on my guard, and I asked Frau K. whether there was not a key to the bedroom door. The next morning (on the second day) I locked myself in while I was dressing. In the afternoon, when I wanted to lock myself in so as to lie down again on the sofa, the key was gone. I am convinced that Herr K. had removed it."

"Then here we have the theme of locking or not locking a room which appeared in the first association to the dream and also happened to occur in the exciting cause of the recent recurrence of the dream.[17] I wonder whether the phrase '*I dressed myself quickly*' may not also belong to this context?"

[17]"I suspected, though I did not as yet say so to Dora, that she had seized upon this element on account of a symbolic meaning which it possessed. *Zimmer* ['room'] in dreams stands very frequently for *Frauenzimmer* [literally, 'women's apartments,' but often used as a slightly derogatory term for 'woman']. The question whether a woman is 'open' or 'shut' can naturally not be a matter of indifference. It is well known, too, what sort of 'key' effects the opening in such a case" [Freud].

"It was then that I made up my mind not to stay with Herr K. without Father. On the subsequent mornings I could not help feeling afraid that Herr K. would surprise me while I was dressing: *so I always dressed myself very quickly.* You see, Father lived at the hotel, and Frau K. used always to go out early so as to go on expeditions with him. But Herr K. did not annoy me again."

"I understand. On the afternoon of the second day after the scene in the wood you resolved to escape from his persecution, and during the second, third, and fourth nights you had time to repeat that resolution in your sleep. (You already knew on the second afternoon—before the dream, therefore—that you would not have the key on the following—the third—morning to lock yourself in with while you were dressing; and you could then form the design of dressing as quickly as possible.) But your dream recurred each night, for the very reason that it corresponded to a resolution. A resolution remains in existence until it has been carried out. You said to yourself, as it were: 'I shall have no rest and I can get no quiet sleep until I am out of this house.' In your account of the dream you turned it the other way and said: *'As soon as I was outside I woke up.'*"

At this point I shall interrupt my report of the analysis in order to compare this small piece of dream interpretation with the general statements I have made upon the mechanism of the formation of dreams. I argued in my book [*The Interpretation of Dreams*] that every dream is a wish which is represented as fulfilled, that the representation acts as a disguise if the wish is a repressed one, belonging to the unconscious, and that except in the case of children's dreams only an unconscious wish or one which reaches down into the unconscious has the force necessary for the formation of a dream. I fancy my theory would have been more certain of general acceptance if I had contented myself with maintaining that every dream had a meaning, which could be discovered by means of a certain process of interpretation; and that when the interpretation had been completed the dream could be replaced by thoughts which would fall into place at an easily recognizable point in the waking mental life of the dreamer. I might then have gone on to say that the meaning of a dream turned out to be of as many different sorts as the processes of waking thought; that in one case it would be a fulfilled wish, in another a realized fear, or again a reflection persisting on into sleep, or a resolution (as in the instance of Dora's dream), or a piece of creative thought during sleep, and so on. Such a theory would no doubt have proved attractive from its very simplicity, and it might have been supported by a great many examples of dreams that had been satisfactorily interpreted, as for instance by the one which has been analyzed in these pages.

But instead of this I formulated a generalization according to which the meaning of dreams is limited to a single form, to the representation of wishes, and by so doing I aroused a universal inclination to dissent. I must, however, observe that I did not consider it either my right or my duty to simplify a psychological process so as to make it more acceptable to my readers, when my researches had shown me that it presented a complication which could not be reduced to uniformity until the inquiry had been carried into another field. It is therefore of special importance to me to

show that apparent exceptions—such as this dream of Dora's, which has shown itself in the first instance to be the continuation into sleep of a resolution formed during the day—nevertheless lend fresh support to the rule which is in dispute.

Much of the dream, however, still remained to be interpreted, and I proceeded with my questions: "What is this about the jewel-case that your mother wanted to save?"

"Mother is very fond of jewelery and had had a lot given her by Father."

"And you?"

"I used to be very fond of jewelery too, once; but I have not worn any since my illness.—Once, four years ago" (a year before the dream), "Father and Mother had a great dispute about a piece of jewelery. Mother wanted to be given a particular thing—pearl drops to wear in her ears. But Father does not like that kind of thing, and he bought her a bracelet instead of the drops. She was furious, and told him that as he had spent so much money on a present she did not like he had better just give it to some one else."

"I dare say you thought to yourself you would accept it with pleasure."

"I don't know.[18] I don't in the least know how Mother comes into the dream; she was not with us at L—— at the time."[19]

"I will explain that to you later. Does nothing else occur to you in connection with the jewel-case? So far you have only talked about jewellery and have said nothing about a case."

"Yes, Herr K. had made me a present of an expensive jewel-case a little time before."

"Then a return-present would have been very appropriate. Perhaps you do not know that 'jewel-case' ['*Schmuckkästchen*'] is a favorite expression for the same thing that you alluded to not long ago by means of the reticule you were wearing—for the female genitals, I mean."

"I knew you would say that."

"That is to say, you knew that it *was* so.—The meaning of the dream is now becoming even clearer. You said to yourself: 'This man is persecuting me; he wants to force his way into my room. My "jewel-case" is in danger, and if anything happens it will be Father's fault.' For that reason in the dream you chose a situation which expresses the opposite—a danger from which your father is saving you. In this part of the dream everything is turned into its opposite; you will soon discover why. As you say, the mystery turns upon your mother. You ask how she comes into the dream? She is, as you know, your former rival in your father's affections. In the incident of the bracelet, you would have been glad to accept what your mother had rejected. Now let us put 'give' instead of 'accept' and 'withhold' instead of 'reject.' Then it means that you were ready to give your father what your mother withheld from him; and the thing in question was connected with

18 "The regular formula with which she confessed to anything that had been repressed" [Freud].

19 "This remark gave evidence of a complete misunderstanding of the rules of dream-interpretation, though on other occasions Dora was perfectly familiar with them. This fact, coupled with the hesitancy and meagerness of her associations with the jewel-case, showed me that we were here dealing with material which had been very intensely repressed" [Freud].

jewellry. Now bring your mind back to the jewel-case which Herr K. gave you. You have there the starting-point for a parallel line of thoughts, in which Herr K. is to be put in the place of your father just as he was in the matter of standing beside your bed. He gave you a jewel-case; so you are to give him your jewel-case. That was why I spoke just now of a 'return-present.' In this line of thoughts your mother must be replaced by Frau K. (You will not deny that she, at any rate, was present at the time.) So you are ready to give Herr K. what his wife withholds from him. That is the thought which has had to be repressed with so much energy, and which has made it necessary for every one of its elements to be turned into its opposite. The dream confirms once more what I had already told you before you dreamed it—that you are summoning up your old love for your father in order to protect yourself against your love for Herr K. But what do all these efforts show? Not only that you are afraid of Herr K., but that you are still more afraid of yourself, and of the temptation you feel to yield to him. In short, these efforts prove once more how deeply you loved him."

Naturally Dora would not follow me in this part of the interpretation. I myself, however, had been able to arrive at a further step in the interpretation, which seemed to me indispensable both for the anamnesis[20] of the case and for the theory of dreams. I promised to communicate this to Dora at the next sitting.

The fact was that I could not forget the hint which seemed to be conveyed by the ambiguous words already noticed—*that it might be necessary to leave the room; that an accident might happen in the night.* Added to this was the fact that the elucidation of the dream seemed to me incomplete so long as a particular requirement remained unsatisfied; for, though I do not wish to insist that this requirement is a universal one, I have a predilection for discovering a means of satisfying it. A regularly formed dream stands, as it were, upon two legs, one of which is in contact with the main and current exciting cause, and the other with some momentous occurrence in the years of childhood. The dream sets up a connection between those two factors—the event during childhood and the event of the present day—and it endeavors to re-shape the present upon the model of the remote past. For the wish which creates the dream always springs from the period of childhood; and it is continually trying to summon childhood back into reality and to correct the present day by the measure of childhood. I believed that I could already clearly detect the elements of Dora's dream, which could be pieced together into an allusion to an event in childhood.

I opened the discussion of the subject with a little experiment, which was, as usual, successful. There happened to be a large match-stand on the table. I asked Dora to look round and see whether she noticed anything special on the table, something that was not there as a rule. She noticed nothing. I then asked her if she knew why children were forbidden to play with matches.

"Yes; on account of the risk of fire. My uncle's children are very fond of playing with matches."

"Not only on that account. They are warned not to 'play with fire,' and a particular belief is associated with the warning."

[20] History; recollection.

She knew nothing about it. —"Very well, then; the fear is that if they do they will wet their bed. The antithesis of 'water' and 'fire' must be at the bottom of this. Perhaps it is believed that they will dream of fire and then try and put it out with water. I cannot say exactly. But I notice that the antithesis of water and fire has been extremely useful to you in the dream. Your mother wanted to save the jewel-case so that it should not be *burned;* while in the dream-thoughts it is a question of the 'jewel-case' not being *wetted.* But fire is not only used as the contrary of water, it also serves directly to represent love (as in the phrase 'to be *consumed* with love'). So that from 'fire' one set of rails runs by this symbolic meaning to thoughts of love; while the other set runs by way of the contrary 'water,' and, after sending off a branch line which provides another connection with 'love' (for love also makes things wet), leads in a different direction. And what direction can that be? Think of the expressions you used: that *an accident might happen in the night,* and that *it might be necessary to leave the room.* Surely the allusion must be to a physical exigency? And if you transpose the accident into childhood what can it be but bed-wetting? But what is usually done to prevent children from wetting their bed? Are they not woken up in the night out of their sleep, *exactly as your father woke you up in the dream?* This, then, must be the actual occurrence which enabled you to substitute your father for Herr K., who really woke you up out of your sleep. I am accordingly driven to conclude that you were addicted to bed-wetting up to a later age than is usual with children. The same must also have been true of your brother; for your father said: '*I refuse to let my two children go to destruction. . . . '* Your brother has no other sort of connection with the real situation at the K.'s; he had not gone with you to L——. And now, what have your recollections to say to this?"

"I know nothing about myself," was her reply, "but my brother used to wet his bed up till his sixth or seventh year; and it used sometimes to happen to him in the daytime too."

I was on the point of remarking to her how much easier it is to remember things of that kind about one's brother than about oneself, when she continued the train of recollections which had been revived: "Yes. I used to do it too, for some time, but not until my seventh or eighth year. It must have been serious, because I remember now that the doctor was called in. It lasted till a short time before my nervous asthma."

"And what did the doctor say to it?"

"He explained it as a nervous weakness; it would soon pass off, he thought; and he prescribed a tonic."

The interpretation of the dream now seemed to me to be complete. But Dora brought me an addendum to the dream on the very next day. She had forgotten to relate, she said, that each time after waking up she had smelled smoke. Smoke, of course, fitted in well with fire, but it also showed that the dream had a special relation to myself; for when she used to assert that there was nothing concealed behind this or that, I would often say by way of rejoinder:"There can be no smoke without fire!" Dora objected, however, to such a purely personal interpretation, saying that Herr K. and her father were passionate smokers—as I am too, for the matter of that. She herself had smoked during her stay by the lake, and Herr K. had rolled a cigarette for her before he began his unlucky proposal. She thought, too,

that she clearly remembered noticing the smell of smoke on the three occasions of the dream's occurrence at L——, and not for the first time at its recent reappearance. As she would give me no further information, it was left to me to determine how this addendum was to be introduced into the texture of the dream-thoughts. One thing which I had to go upon was the fact that the smell of smoke had only come up as an addendum to the dream, and must therefore have had to overcome a particularly strong effort on the part of repression. Accordingly it was probably related to the thoughts which were the most obscurely presented and the most successfully repressed in the dream, to the thoughts, that is, concerned with the temptation to show herself willing to yield to the man. If that were so, the addendum to the dream could scarcely mean anything else than the longing for a kiss, which, with a smoker, would necessarily smell of smoke. But a kiss had passed between Herr K. and Dora some two years earlier, and it would certainly have been repeated more than once if she had given way to him. So the thoughts of temptation seemed in this way to have harked back to the earlier scene, and to have revived the memory of the kiss against whose seductive influence the little "suck-a-thumbs" had defended herself at the time by the feeling of disgust. Taking into consideration, finally, the indications which seemed to point to there having been a transference on to me—since I am a smoker too—I came to the conclusion that the idea had probably occurred to her one day during a sitting that she would like to have a kiss from me. This would have been the exciting cause which led her to repeat the warning dream and to form her resolution of stopping the treatment. Everything fits together very satisfactorily upon this view; but owing to the characteristics of "transference" its validity is not susceptible of definite proof.

I might at this point hesitate whether I should first consider the light thrown by this dream upon the history of the case, or whether I should rather begin by dealing with the objection to my theory of dreams which may be based upon it. I shall take the former course.

The significance of bed-wetting in the early history of neurotics is worth going into thoroughly. For the sake of clearness I will confine myself to remarking that Dora's case of bed-wetting was not the usual one. The disorder was not simply that the habit had persisted beyond what is considered the normal period, but, according to her explicit account, it had begun by disappearing and had then returned at a relatively late age—after her sixth year. Bed-wetting of this kind has, to the best of my knowledge, no more likely cause than masturbation, a habit whose importance in the aetiology of bed-wetting in general is still insufficiently appreciated. In my experience, the children concerned have themselves at one time been very well aware of this connection, and all its psychological consequences follow from it as though they had never forgotten it. Now, at the time when Dora reported the dream, we were engaged upon a line of inquiry which led straight towards an admission that she had masturbated in childhood. A short while before, she had raised the question of why it was precisely *she* that had fallen ill, and, before I could answer, had put the blame on her father. The justification for this was forthcoming not out of her unconscious thoughts but from her conscious knowledge. It turned out, to my astonishment, that the girl knew what the nature of her father's illness had

been. After his return from consulting me she had overheard a conversation in which the name of the disease had been mentioned. At a still earlier period—at the time of the detached retina—an oculist who was called in must have hinted at a luetic aetiology; for the inquisitive and anxious girl overheard an old aunt of hers saying to her mother: "He was ill before his marriage, you know," and adding something which she could not understand, but which she subsequently connected in her mind with improper subjects.

Her father, then, had fallen ill through leading a loose life, and she assumed that he handed on his bad health to her by heredity. I was careful not to tell her that, as I have already mentioned, I was of opinion, too, that the offspring of luetics were very specially predisposed to severe neuropsychoses. The line of thought in which she brought this accusation against her father was continued in her unconscious material. For several days on end she identified herself with her mother by means of slight symptoms and peculiarities of manner, which gave her an opportunity for some really remarkable achievements in the direction of intolerable behavior. She then allowed it to transpire that she was thinking of a stay she had made at Franzensbad,[21] which she had visited with her mother—I forget in what year. Her mother was suffering from abdominal pains and from a discharge (a catarrh) which necessitated a cure at Franzensbad. It was Dora's view—and here again she was probably right—that this illness was due to her father, who had thus handed on his venereal disease to her mother. It was quite natural that in drawing this conclusion she should, like the majority of laymen, have confused gonorrhoea and syphilis—what is contagious and what is hereditary. The persistence with which she held to this identification with her mother forced me almost to ask her whether she too was suffering from a venereal disease; and I then learned that she was afflicted with a catarrh (leucorrhoea)[22] whose beginning, she said, she could not remember.

I then understood that behind the train of thought in which she brought these open accusations against her father there lay concealed as usual a self-accusation. I met her half-way by assuring her that in my view the occurrence of leucorrhoea in young girls pointed primarily to masturbation, and I considered that all the other causes which were commonly assigned to that complaint were put in the background by masturbation.[23] I added that she was now on the way to finding an answer to her own question of why it was precisely *she* that had fallen ill—by confessing that she had masturbated, probably in childhood. Dora denied flatly that she could remember any such thing. But a few days later she did something which I could not help regarding as a further step towards the confession. For on that day she wore at her waist—a thing she never did on any other occasion before or after—a small reticule of a shape which had just come into fashion; and, as she lay on the sofa and talked, she kept playing with it—opening it, putting a finger into it, shutting it again, and so on. I looked on for some time, and then explained to her the nature of a *symptomatic act.* . . .

There is a great deal of symbolism of this kind in life, but as a rule we

[21] A spa in west Bohemia, now Czechoslovakia. [22] A vaginal discharge.
[23] "This is an extreme view which I should no longer maintain today" [Freud, 1923].

pass it by without heeding it. When I set myself the task of bringing to light what human beings keep hidden within them, not by the compelling power of hypnosis, but by observing what they say and what they show, I thought the task was a harder one than it really is. He that has eyes to see and ears to hear may convince himself that no mortal can keep a secret. If his lips are silent, he chatters with his finger-tips; betrayal oozes out of him at every pore. And thus the task of making conscious the most hidden recesses of the mind is one which it is quite possible to accomplish.

Dora's symptomatic act with the reticule did not immediately precede the dream. She started the sitting which brought us the narrative of the dream with another symptomatic act. As I came into the room in which she was waiting she hurriedly concealed a letter which she was reading. I naturally asked her whom the letter was from, and at first she refused to tell me. Something then came out which was a matter of complete indifference and had no relation to the treatment. It was a letter from her grandmother, in which she begged Dora to write to her more often. I believe that Dora only wanted to play "secrets" with me, and to hint that she was on the point of allowing her secret to be torn from her by the physician. I was then in a position to explain her antipathy to every new physician. She was afraid lest he might arrive at the foundation of her illness, either by examining her and discovering her catarrh, or by questioning her and eliciting the fact of her addiction to bed-wetting—lest he might guess, in short, that she had masturbated. And afterwards she would speak very contemptuously of the physicians whose perspicacity she had evidently over-estimated beforehand.

The reproaches against her father for having made her ill, together with the self-reproach underlying them, the leucorrhoea, the playing with the reticule, the bed-wetting after her sixth year, the secret which she would not allow the physicians to tear from her—the circumstantial evidence of her having masturbated in childhood seems to me complete and without a flaw. In the present case I had begun to suspect the masturbation when she had told me of her cousin's gastric pains, and had then identified herself with her by complaining for days together of similar painful sensations. It is well known that gastric pains occur especially often in those who masturbate. According to a personal communication made to me by W. Fliess,[24] it is precisely gastralgias of this character which can be interpreted by an application of cocaine to the "gastric spot" discovered by him in the nose, and which can be cured by the cauterization of the same spot. In confirmation of my suspicion Dora gave me two facts from her conscious knowledge: she herself had frequently suffered from gastric pains, and she had good reasons for believing that her cousin was a masturbator. It is a very common thing for patients to recognize in other people a connection which, on account of their emotional resistances, they cannot perceive in themselves. And, indeed, Dora no longer denied my supposition, although she still remembered nothing. Even the date which she assigned to the bed-wetting, when she said that it lasted "till a short time before the appearance of the nervous asthma," appears to me to be of clinical significance.

[24] Wilhelm Fliess, a Berlin ear-nose-and-throat specialist who was Freud's closest friend and confidant during the 1890's.

Hysterical symptoms hardly ever appear so long as children are masturbating, but only afterwards, when a period of abstinence has set in; they form a substitute for masturbatory satisfaction, the desire for which continues to persist in the unconscious until another and more normal kind of satisfaction appears—where that is still attainable. For upon whether it is still attainable or not depends the possibility of a hysteria being cured by marriage and normal sexual intercourse. But if the satisfaction afforded in marriage is again removed—as it may be owing to *coitus interruptus*,[25] psychological estrangement, or other causes—then the libido flows back again into its old channel and manifests itself once more in hysterical symptoms. . . .

We will now attempt to put together the various determinants that we have found for Dora's attacks of coughing and hoarseness. In the lowest stratum we must assume the presence of a real and organically determined irritation of the throat—which acted like the grain of sand around which an oyster forms its pearl. This irritation was susceptible to fixation, because it concerned a part of the body which in Dora had to a high degree retained its significance as an erotogenic zone. And the irritation was consequently well fitted to give expression to excited states of the libido. It was brought to fixation by what was probably its first psychological wrapping—her sympathetic imitation of her father—and by her subsequent self-reproaches on account of her "catarrh." The same group of symptoms, moreover, showed itself capable of representing her relations with Herr K.; it could express her regret at his absence and her wish to make him a better wife. After a part of her libido had once more turned towards her father, the symptom obtained what was perhaps its last meaning; it came to represent sexual intercourse with her father by means of Dora's identifying herself with Frau K. I can guarantee that this series is by no means complete. Unfortunately, an incomplete analysis cannot enable us to follow the temporal sequence of the changes in a symptom's meaning, or to display clearly the succession and coexistence of its various meanings. It may legitimately be expected of a complete analysis that it should fulfill these demands.

I must now proceed to touch upon some further relations existing between Dora's genital catarrh and her hysterical symptoms. At a time when any psychological elucidation of hysteria was still very remote, I used to hear experienced fellow-doctors who were my seniors maintain that in the case of hysterical patients suffering from leucorrhoea any increase in the catarrh was regularly followed by an intensification of the hysterical troubles, and especially of anorexia and vomiting. No one was very clear about the nature of the connection, but I fancy the general inclination was towards the opinion held by gynaecologists. According to their hypothesis, as is well known, disorders of the genitals exercise upon the nervous functions a direct and far-reaching influence in the nature of an organic disturbance—though a therapeutic test of this theory is apt to leave one in the lurch. In the light of our present knowledge we cannot exclude the possibility of the existence of a direct organic influence of this sort; but it is at all events easier to determine its psychological wrappings. The pride taken by women in the appearance of their genitals is quite a special feature of their vanity;

[25] Sexual intercourse which is deliberately interrupted (for contraceptive purposes).

and disorders of the genitals which they think calculated to inspire feelings of repugnance or even disgust have an incredible power of humiliating them, of lowering their self-esteem, and of making them irritable, sensitive, and distrustful. An abnormal secretion of the mucous membrane of the vagina is looked upon as a source of disgust.

It will be remembered that Dora had a lively feeling of disgust after being kissed by Herr K. We now learn further that the same governess whom Dora cast off on account of her faithlessness had, from her own experience of life, propounded to Dora the view that all men were frivolous and untrustworthy. To Dora that must mean that all men were like her father. But she thought her father suffered from venereal disease—for had he not handed it on to her and her mother? She might therefore have imagined to herself that all men suffered from venereal disease, and naturally her conception of venereal disease was modelled upon her one experience of it—a personal one at that. To suffer from venereal disease, therefore, meant for her to be afflicted with a disgusting discharge. So may we not have here a further motive for the disgust she felt at the moment of the embrace? Thus the disgust which was transferred on to the contact of the man would be a feeling which had been projected according to the primitive mechanism I have already mentioned, and would be related ultimately to her own leucorrhoea.

I suspect that we are here concerned with unconscious processes of thought which are twined around a pre-existing structure of organic connections, much as festoons of flowers are twined around a wire; so that on another occasion one might find other lines of thought inserted between the same points of departure and termination. Yet a knowledge of the thought-connections which have been effective in the individual case is of a value which cannot be exaggerated for clearing up the symptoms. It is only because the analysis was prematurely broken off that we have been obliged in Dora's case to resort to framing conjectures and filling in deficiencies. What I have brought forward for filling up the gaps is invariably supported by other cases which have been more thoroughly analyzed.

The dream from the analysis of which we have derived this information corresponded, as we have seen, to a resolution which Dora carried with her into her sleep. It was therefore repeated each night until the resolution had been carried out; and it reappeared years later when an occasion arose for forming an analogous resolution. The resolution might have been consciously expressed in some such words as these: "I must fly from this house, for I see that my virginity is threatened here; I shall go away with my father, and I shall take precautions not to be surprised while I am dressing in the morning." These thoughts are clearly expressed in the dream; they form part of a mental current which has achieved consciousness and a dominating position in waking life. Behind them can be discerned obscure traces of a train of thought which forms part of a contrary current and has consequently been suppressed. This other train of thought culminated in the temptation to yield to the man, out of gratitude for the love and tenderness he had shown her during the last few years, and it may perhaps have revived the memory of the only kiss she had so far had from him. But according to the theory which I developed in my *Interpretation of Dreams*

such elements as these are not enough for the formation of a dream. On that theory a dream is not a resolution represented as having been carried out, but a wish represented as having been fulfilled, and, moreover, in most cases a wish dating from childhood. It is our business now to discover whether this principle may not be contradicted by the present dream.

The dream does in fact contain infantile material, though it is impossible at a first glance to discover any connection between that material and Dora's resolution to fly from Herr K.'s house and the temptation of his presence. Why should a recollection have emerged of her bed-wetting when she was a child and of the trouble her father used to take to teach the child clean habits? We may answer this by saying that it was only by the help of this train of thought that it was possible to suppress the other thoughts which were so intensely occupied with the temptation to yield, or that it was possible to secure the domination of the resolution which had been formed to combat those other thoughts. The child decided to fly *with* her father; in reality she fled *to* her father because she was afraid of the man who was pursuing her; she summoned up an infantile affection for her father so that it might protect her against her present affection for a stranger. Her father was himself partly responsible for her present danger, for he had handed her over to this strange man in the interests of his own love-affair. And how much better it had been when that same father of hers had loved no one more than her, and had exerted all his strength to save her from the dangers that had then threatened her. The infantile, and now unconscious, wish to put her father in the strange man's place had the potency necessary for the formation of a dream. If there had been a past situation similar to a present one, and differing from it only in being concerned with one instead of with the other of the two persons mentioned in the wish, that situation would become the main one in the dream. But there *had* been such a situation. Her father had once stood beside her bed, just as Herr K. had the day before, and had woken her up, with a kiss perhaps, as Herr K. may have intended to do. Thus her resolution to fly from the house was not in itself capable of producing a dream; but it became so by being associated with another resolution which was founded upon infantile wishes. The wish to replace Herr K. by her father provided the necessary motive power for the dream. Let me recall the interpretation I was led to adopt of Dora's intensified train of thought about her father's relations with Frau K. My interpretation was that she had at that point summoned up an infantile affection for her father so as to be able to keep her repressed love for Herr K. in its state of repression. This same sudden revulsion in the patient's mental life was reflected in the dream. . . .

Any one who has learned to appreciate the delicacy of the fabric of structures such as dreams will not be surprised to find that Dora's wish that her father might take the place of the man who was her tempter called up in her memory not merely a casual collection of material from her childhood, but precisely such material as was most intimately bound up with the suppression of her temptation. For if Dora felt unable to yield to her love for the man, if in the end she repressed that love instead of surrendering to it, there was no factor upon which her decision depended more directly than upon her premature sexual enjoyment and its consequences—her bed-wetting, her catarrh, and her disgust. An early history of this kind can

afford a basis for two kinds of behavior in response to the demands of love in maturity—which of the two will depend upon the summation of constitutional determinants in the individual. He will either exhibit an abandonment to sexuality which is entirely without resistances and borders upon perversity; or there will be a reaction—he will repudiate sexuality, and will at the same time fall ill of a neurosis. In the case of our present patient, her constitution and the high level of her intellectual and moral education decided in favor of the latter course.

I should like, further, to draw special attention to the fact that the analysis of this dream has given us access to certain details of the pathogenically operative events which had otherwise been inaccessible to memory, or at all events to reproduction. The recollection of the bed-wetting in childhood had, as we have seen, already been repressed. And Dora had never mentioned the details of her persecution by Herr K.; they had never occurred to her mind. . . .

[3.] THE SECOND DREAM

A few weeks after the first dream the second occurred, and when it had been dealt with the analysis was broken off. It cannot be made as completely intelligible as the first, but it afforded a desirable confirmation of an assumption which had become necessary about the patient's mental state, it filled up a gap in her memory, and it made it possible to obtain a deep insight into the origin of another of her symptoms.

Dora described the dream as follows: "*I was walking about in a town which I did not know. I saw streets and squares which were strange to me.*[26] *Then I came into a house where I lived, went to my room, and found a letter from Mother lying there. She wrote saying that as I had left home without my parents' knowledge she had not wished to write to me to say that Father was ill. 'Now he is dead, and if you like*[27] *you can come.' I then went to the station ['Bahnhof'] and asked about a hundred times: 'Where is the station?' I always got the answer: 'Five minutes.' I then saw a thick wood before me which I went into, and there I asked a man whom I met. He said to me: 'Two and a half hours more.'*[28] *He offered to accompany me. But I refused and went alone. I saw the station in front of me and could not reach it. At the same time I had the usual feeling of anxiety that one has in dreams when one cannot move forward. Then I was at home. I must have been travelling in the meantime, but I know nothing about that. I walked into the porter's lodge, and inquired for our flat. The maidservant opened the door to me and replied that Mother and the others were already at the cemetery ['Friedhof'].*"[29]

It was not without some difficulty that the interpretation of this dream

[26] "To this she subsequently made an important addendum: '*I saw a monument in one of the squares*'" [Freud].

[27] "To this came the addendum: '*There was a question-mark after this word, thus: 'like?''*" [Freud].

[28] "In repeating the dream she said: '*Two hours*'" [Freud].

[29] "In the next session Dora brought me two addenda to this: '*I saw myself particularly distinctly going up the stairs,*' and '*After she had answered I went to my room, but not the least sadly, and began reading a big book that lay on my writing-table.*'" [Freud].

proceeded. In consequence of the peculiar circumstances in which the analysis was broken off—circumstances connected with the content of the dream—the whole of it was not cleared up. And for this reason, too, I am not equally certain at every point of the order in which my conclusions were reached. I will begin by mentioning the subject-matter with which the current analysis was dealing at the time when the dream intervened. For some time Dora herself had been raising a number of questions about the connection between some of her actions and the motives which presumably underlay them. One of these questions was: "Why did I say nothing about the scene by the lake for some days after it had happened?" Her second question was: "Why did I then suddenly tell my parents about it?" Moreover, her having felt so deeply injured by Herr K.'s proposal seemed to me in general to need explanation, especially as I was beginning to realize that Herr K. himself had not regarded his proposal to Dora as a mere frivolous attempt at seduction. I looked upon her having told her parents of the episode as an action which she had taken when she was already under the influence of a morbid craving for revenge. A normal girl, I am inclined to think, will deal with a situation of this kind by herself. I shall thus present the material produced during the analysis of this dream in the somewhat haphazard order in which it recurs to my mind.

She was wandering about alone in a strange town, and saw streets and squares. Dora assured me that it was certainly not B——, which I had first hit upon, but a town in which she had never been. It was natural to suggest that she might have seen some pictures or photographs and have taken the dream-pictures from them. After this remark of mine came the addendum about the monument in one of the squares and immediately afterwards her recognition of its source. At Christmas[30] she had been sent an album from a German health-resort, containing views of the town; and the very day before the dream she had looked this up to show it to some relatives who were stopping with them. It had been put in a box for keeping pictures in, and she could not lay her hands on it at once. She had therefore said to her mother: "Where is the box?" One of the pictures was of a square with a monument in it. The present had been sent to her by a young engineer, with whom she had once had a passing acquaintance in the manufacturing town. The young man had accepted a post in Germany, so as to become sooner self-supporting; and he took every opportunity of reminding Dora of his existence. It was easy to guess that he intended to come forward as a suitor one day, when his position had improved. But that would take time, and it meant waiting.

The wandering about in a strange town was overdetermined. It led back to one of the exciting causes from the day before. A young cousin of Dora's had come to stay with them for the holidays, and Dora had had to show him round Vienna. This cause was, it is true, a matter of complete indifference to her. But her cousin's visit reminded her of her own first brief visit to Dresden. On that occasion she had been a stranger and had wandered about, not failing, of course, to visit the famous picture gallery. Another cousin of hers, who was with them and knew Dresden, had wanted to act as

[30] This session, we later learn, occurred during the week between Christmas and New Year's.

a guide and take her round the gallery. *But she declined, and went alone,* and stopped in front of the pictures that appealed to her. She remained *two hours* in front of the Sistine Madonna, rapt in silent admiration. When I asked her what had pleased her so much about the picture she could find no clear answer to make. At last she said: "The Madonna."

There could be no doubt that these associations really belonged to the material concerned in forming the dream. They contained portions which reappeared in the dream unchanged ("she declined, and went alone" and "two hours"). I may remark at once that "pictures" was a point of junction in the network of her dream-thoughts (the pictures in the album, the pictures at Dresden). I should also like to single out, with a view to subsequent investigation, the theme of the "Madonna," of the virgin mother. But what was most evident was that in this first part of the dream she was identifying herself with a young man. This young man was wandering about in a strange place, he was striving to reach a goal, but he was being kept back, he needed patience and must wait. If in all this she had been thinking of the engineer, it would have been appropriate for the goal to have been the possession of a woman, of herself. But instead of this it was—a station. Nevertheless, the relation of the question in the dream to the question which had actually been put allows us to substitute *"box"* for "station."[31] A box and a woman: the notions begin to agree better.

She asked quite a hundred times. . . . This led to another exciting cause of the dream, and this time to one that was less indifferent. On the previous evening they had had company, and afterwards her father had asked her to fetch him the brandy: he could not get to sleep unless he had taken some brandy. She had asked her mother for the key of the sideboard; but the latter had been deep in conversation, and had not answered her, until Dora had exclaimed with the exaggeration of impatience: "I've asked you *a hundred times* already where the key is." As a matter of fact, she had of course only repeated the question about *five times.*[32]

"Where is the *key?*" seems to me to be the masculine counterpart to the question "Where is the *box?*" They are therefore questions referring to— the genitals.

Dora went on to say that during this same family gathering some one had toasted her father and had expressed the hope that he might continue to enjoy the best of health for many years to come, etc. At this a strange quiver had passed over her father's tired face, and she had understood what thoughts he was having to keep down. Poor sick man! Who could tell what span of life was still to be his?

This brings us to the *contents of the letter* in the dream. Her father was dead, and she had left home by her own choice. In connection with this letter I at once reminded Dora of the farewell letter which she had written to her parents or had at least composed for their benefit. This letter had been intended to give her father a fright, so that he should give up Frau K.; or at any rate to take revenge on him if he could not be induced to do that.

[31] The German *Schachtel,* like its English equivalent "box," is a vulgarism for "woman."

[32] "In the dream the number five occurs in the mention of the period of 'five minutes.' In my book on the interpretation of dreams I have given several examples of the way in which numbers occurring in the dream-thoughts are treated by dreams. We frequently find them torn out of their true context and inserted in a new one" [Freud].

We are here concerned with the subject of her death and of her father's death. (Cf. "cemetery" later on in the dream.) Shall we be going astray if we suppose that the situation which formed the façade of the dream was a phantasy of revenge directed against her father? The feelings of pity for him which she remembered from the day before would be quite in keeping with this. According to the phantasy she had left home and gone among strangers, and her father's heart had broken with grief and with longing for her. Then she would be revenged. She understood very clearly what it was that her father needed when he could not get to sleep without a drink of brandy.[33] We will make a note of Dora's *craving for revenge* as a new element to be taken into account in any subsequent synthesis of her dream-thoughts.

But the contents of the letter must be capable of further determination. What was the source of the words "if you like"? It was at this point that the addendum of there having been a question-mark after the word "like" occurred to Dora, and she then recognized these words as a quotation out of the letter from Frau K. which had contained the invitation to L——, the place by the lake. In that letter there had been a question-mark placed, in a most unusual fashion, in the very middle of a sentence, after the intercalated words "if you would like to come."

So here we were back again at the scene by the lake and at the problems connected with it. I asked Dora to describe the scene to me in detail. At first she produced little that was new. Herr K.'s exordium had been somewhat serious; but she had not let him finish what he had to say. No sooner had she grasped the purport of his words than she had slapped him in the face and hurried away. I inquired what his actual words had been. Dora could only remember one of his pleas: "You know I get nothing out of my wife." In order to avoid meeting him again she had wanted to get back to L—— on foot, by walking round the lake, and *she had asked a man whom she met how far it was.* On his replying that it was *"Two and a half hours,"* she had given up her intention and had after all gone back to the ship, which left soon afterwards. Herr K. had been there too, and had come up to her and begged her to forgive him and not to mention the incident. But she had made no reply.—Yes. The *wood* in the dream had been just like the wood by the shore of the lake, the wood in which the scene she had just described once more had taken place. But she had seen precisely the same thick wood the day before, in a picture at the Secessionist exhibition. In the background of the picture there were *nymphs.*[34]

At this point a certain suspicion of mine became a certainty. The use of *"Bahnhof"* ["station"; literally, "railway-court"][35] and *"Friedhof"* ["ceme-

[33] "There can be no doubt that sexual satisfaction is the best soporific, just as sleeplessness is almost always the consequence of lack of satisfaction. Her father could not sleep because he was debarred from sexual intercourse with the woman he loved. (Compare in this connection the phrase discussed just below: 'I get nothing out of my wife.')" [Freud].

[34] "Here for the third time we come upon 'picture' (views of towns, the Dresden gallery), but in a much more significant connection. Because of what appears in the picture (the wood, the nymphs), the *Bild* ['picture'] is turned into a *Weibsbild* [literally, 'picture of a woman': another vulgarism for 'woman']" [Freud].

[35] "Moreover, a 'station' is used for purposes of *Verkehr* ['traffic,' 'intercourse,' 'sexual intercourse']: this fact determines the psychical coating in a number of cases of railway phobia" [Freud].

tery"; literally, "peace-court"] to represent the female genitals was striking enough in itself, but it also served to direct my awakened curiosity to the similarly formed *"Vorhof"* ["vestibulum"; literally, "fore-court"]—an anatomical term for a particular region of the female genitals. This might have been no more than a misleading joke. But now, with the addition of "nymphs" visible in the background of a "thick wood," no further doubts could be entertained. Here was a symbolic geography of sex! "Nymphae," as is known to physicians though not to laymen (and even by the former the term is not very commonly used), is the name given to the labia minora, which lie in the background of the "thick wood" of the pubic hair. But any one who employed such technical names as "vestibulum" and "nymphae" must have derived his knowledge from books, and not from popular ones either, but the anatomical text-books or from an encyclopaedia—the common refuge of youth when it is devoured by sexual curiosity. If this interpretation were correct, therefore, there lay concealed behind the first situation in the dream a phantasy of defloration, the phantasy of a man seeking to force an entrance into the female genitals.[36]

I informed Dora of the conclusions I had reached. The impression made upon her must have been forcible, for there immediately appeared a piece of the dream which had been forgotten: *"she went calmly to her room, and began reading a big book that lay on her writing-table."* The emphasis here was upon the two details "calmly" and "big" in connection with "book." I asked whether the book was in encyclopaedia *format,* and she said it was. Now children never read about forbidden subjects in an encyclopaedia *calmly.* They do it in fear and trembling, with an uneasy look over their shoulder to see if some one may not be coming. Parents are very much in the way while reading of this kind is going on. But this uncomfortable situation had been radically improved, thanks to the dream's power of fulfilling wishes. Dora's father was dead, and the others had already gone to the cemetery. She might calmly read whatever she chose. Did not this mean that one of her motives for revenge was a revolt against her parents' constraint? If her father was dead she could read or love as she pleased.

At first she would not remember ever having read anything in an encyclopaedia; but she then admitted that a recollection of an occasion of the kind did occur to her, though it was of an innocent enough nature. At the time when the aunt she was so fond of had been so seriously ill and it had already been settled that Dora was to go to Vienna, a *letter* had come from another uncle, to say that they could not go to Vienna, as a boy of his, a cousin of Dora's therefore, had fallen dangerously ill with appendicitis. Dora had thereupon looked up in the encyclopaedia to see what the symp-

[36] "The phantasy of defloration formed the second component of the situation. The emphasis upon the difficulty of getting forward and the anxiety felt in the dream indicated the stress which the dreamer was so ready to lay upon her virginity—a point alluded to in another place by means of the Sistine Madonna. These sexual thoughts gave an unconscious ground-coloring to the wishes (which were perhaps merely kept secret) concerned with the suitor who was waiting for her in Germany. We have already recognized the phantasy of revenge as the first component of the same situation in the dream. The two components do not coincide completely, but only in part. We shall subsequently come upon the traces of a third and still more important train of thought" [Freud].

toms of appendicitis were. From what she had then read she still recollected the characteristic localization of the abdominal pain.

I then remembered that shortly after her aunt's death Dora had had an attack of what had been alleged to be appendicitis. Up till then I had not ventured to count that illness among her hysterical productions. She told me that during the first few days she had had high fever and had felt the pain in her abdomen that she had read about in the encyclopaedia. She had been given cold fomentations but had not been able to bear them. On the second day her period had set in, accompanied by violent pains. (Since her health had been bad, the periods had been very irregular.) At that time she used to suffer continually from constipation.

It was not really possible to regard this state as a purely hysterical one. Although hysterical fever does undoubtedly occur, yet it seemed too arbitrary to put down the fever accompanying this questionable illness to hysteria instead of to some organic cause operative at the time. I was on the point of abandoning the track, when she herself helped me along it by producing her last addendum to the dream: *"she saw herself particularly distinctly going up the stairs."*

I naturally required a special determinant for this. Dora objected that she would anyhow have had to go upstairs if she had wanted to get to her flat, which was on an upper floor. It was easy to brush aside this objection (which was probably not very seriously intended) by pointing out that if she had been able to travel in her dream from the unknown town to Vienna without making a railway journey she ought also to have been able to leave out a flight of stairs. She then proceeded to relate that after the appendicitis she had not been able to walk properly and had dragged her right foot. This state of things had continued for a long time, and on that account she had been particularly glad to avoid stairs. Even now her foot sometimes dragged. The doctors whom she had consulted at her father's desire had been very much astonished at this most unusual after-effect of an appendicitis, especially as the abdominal pains had not recurred and did not in any way accompany the dragging of the foot.

Here, then, we have a true hysterical symptom. The fever may have been organically determined—perhaps by one of those very frequent attacks of influenza that are not localized in any particular part of the body. Nevertheless it was now established that the neurosis had seized upon this chance event and made use of it for an utterance of its own. Dora had therefore given herself an illness which she had read up about in the encyclopaedia, and she had punished herself for dipping into its pages. But she was forced to recognize that the punishment could not possibly apply to her reading the innocent article in question. It must have been inflicted as the result of a process of displacement, after another occasion of more guilty reading had become associated with this one; and the guilty occasion must lie concealed in her memory behind the contemporaneous innocent one. It might still be possible, perhaps, to discover the nature of the subjects she had read about on that other occasion.

What, then, was the meaning of this condition, of this attempted simulation of a perityphlitis?[37] The remainder of the disorder, the dragging of

[37] Intestinal inflammation.

one leg, was entirely out of keeping with perityphlitis. It must, no doubt, fit in better with the secret and possibly sexual meaning of the clinical picture; and if it were elucidated might in its turn throw light upon the meaning which we were in search of. I looked about for a means of approaching the puzzle. Periods of time had been mentioned in the dream; and time is assuredly never a matter of indifference in any biological event. I therefore asked Dora when this attack of appendicitis had taken place; whether it had been before or after the scene by the lake. Every difficulty was resolved at a single blow by her prompt reply: "Nine months later." The period of time is sufficiently characteristic. Her supposed attack of appendicitis had thus enabled the patient with the modest means at her disposal (the pains and the menstrual flow) to realize a phantasy of *childbirth*. Dora was naturally aware of the significance of this period of time, and could not dispute the probability of her having, on the occasion under discussion, read up in the encyclopaedia about pregnancy and childbirth. But what was all this about her dragging her leg? I could now hazard a guess. That is how people walk when they have twisted a foot. So she had made a "false step": which was true indeed if she could give birth to a child nine months after the scene by the lake. But there was still another requirement upon the fulfillment of which I had to insist. I am convinced that a symptom of this kind can only arise where it has an *infantile* prototype. All my experience hitherto has led me to hold firmly to the view that recollections derived from the impressions of later years do not possess sufficient force to enable them to establish themselves as symptoms. I scarcely dared hope that Dora would provide me with the material that I wanted from her childhood, for the fact is that I am not yet in a position to assert the general validity of this rule, much as I should like to be able to do so. But in this case there came an immediate confirmation of it. Yes, said Dora, once when she was a child she had twisted the same foot; she had slipped on one of the steps as she was going *downstairs*. The foot—and it was actually the same one that she afterwards dragged—had swelled up and had to be bandaged and she had had to lie up for some weeks. This had been a short time before the attack of nervous asthma in her eighth year.

The next thing to do was to turn to account our knowledge of the existence of this phantasy: "If it is true that you were delivered of a child nine months after the scene by the lake, and that you are going about to this very day carrying the consequences of your false step with you, then it follows that in your unconscious you must have regretted the upshot of the scene. In your unconscious thoughts, that is to say, you have made an emendation in it. The assumption that underlies your phantasy of childbirth is that on that occasion something took place,[38] that on that occasion you experienced and went through everything that you were in fact obliged to pick up later on from the encyclopaedia. So you see that your love for Herr K. did not come to an end with the scene, but that (as I

[38] "The phantasy of defloration is thus found to have an application to Herr K., and we begin to see why this part of the dream contained material taken from the scene by the lake—the refusal, two and a half hours, the wood, the invitation to L——" [Freud].

maintained) it has persisted down to the present day—though it is true that you are unconscious of it."—And Dora disputed the fact no longer.[39]

The labor of elucidating the second dream had so far occupied two hours. At the end of the second sitting, when I expressed my satisfaction at the result, Dora replied in a depreciatory tone: "Why, has anything so very remarkable come out?" These words prepared me for the advent of fresh revelations.

She opened the third sitting with these words: "Do you know that I am here for the last time to-day?"—"How can I know, as you have said nothing to me about it?"—"Yes. I made up my mind to put up with it till the New Year.[40] But I shall wait no longer than that to be cured."—"You know that you are free to stop the treatment at any time. But for to-day we will go on with our work. When did you come to this decision?"—"A fortnight ago, I think."—"That sounds just like a maidservant or a governess—a fortnight's warning."—"There was a governess who gave warning with the K.'s, when I was on my visit to them that time at L——, by the lake."—"Really? You have never told me about her. Tell me."

"Well, there was a young girl in the house, who was the children's governess; and she behaved in the most extraordinary way to Herr K. She never said good morning to him, never answered his remarks, never

[39] "I may here add a few supplementary interpretations to those that have already been given. The 'Madonna' was obviously Dora herself; in the first place because of the 'adorer' who had sent her the pictures, in the second place because she had won Herr K.'s love chiefly by the motherliness she had shown towards his children, and lastly because she had had a child though she was still a girl (this being a direct allusion to the phantasy of childbirth). Moreover, the notion of the 'Madonna' is a favorite counter-idea in the minds of girls who feel themselves oppressed by imputations of sexual guilt,—which was the case with Dora. A first suspicion of this connection came to me while I was working as a physician at the Psychiatric Clinic of the University. I there came across a case of confusional insanity with hallucinations, in which the attack, which ran a rapid course, turned out to be a reaction to a reproach made against the patient by her *fiancé*. If the analysis had been continued, Dora's maternal longing for a child would probably have been revealed as an obscure though powerful motive in her behavior. The numerous questions which she had been raising latterly seem to have been belated derivatives of questions inspired by the sexual curiosity which she had tried to gratify with the encyclopaedia. The subjects which she read up in it were presumably pregnancy, childbirth, virginity, and so on. —In reproducing the dream Dora had forgotten one of the questions which need to be inserted into the course of the second situation in the dream. This question could only be: 'Does Herr —— live here?' or 'Where does Herr —— live?' There must have been some reason for her having forgotten this apparently innocent question, especially as she need not have brought it into the dream at all. This reason, it seems to me, lay in her surname itself, which also denoted an object and in fact more than one kind of object, and which could therefore be regarded as an 'ambiguous' word. Unluckily I cannot give the name and show how well designed it was to indicate something 'ambiguous' and 'improper.' [*Bauer*, Dora's real surname, means 'bird-cage' in German but is used vulgarly to refer to the female genitals.] This interpretation was supported by the discovery of a similar play upon words in another part of the dream, where the material was derived from Dora's recollections of her aunt's death ('they have already gone to the cemetery') and where there was similarly a play upon her aunt's name. These improper words seemed to point to a second and *oral* source of information, since the encyclopaedia would not cover them. I should not have been surprised to hear that this source had been Frau K. herself, Dora's calumniator. In that case she would have been the one person whom Dora generously spared, while she pursued the others with an almost malignant vindictiveness. Behind the almost limitless series of displacements which were thus brought to light, it was possible to divine the operation of a single simple factor— Dora's deep-rooted homosexual love for Frau K." [Freud].

[40] This session took place on December 31, 1900.

handed him anything at table when he asked for it, and in short treated him like thin air. For that matter he was hardly any politer to her. A day or two before the scene by the lake, the girl took me aside and said she had something to tell me. She then told me that Herr K. had made advances to her at a time when his wife was away for several weeks; he had made violent love to her and had implored her to yield to his entreaties, saying that he got nothing from his wife, and so on."—"Why, those are the very words he used afterwards, when he made his proposal to you and you gave him the slap in his face."—"Yes. She had given way to him, but after a little while he had ceased to care for her, and since then she hated him."—"And this governess had given warning?"—"No. She meant to give warning. She told me that as soon as she felt she was thrown over she had told her parents what had happened. They were respectable people living in Germany somewhere. Her parents said that she must leave the house instantly; and, as she failed to do so, they wrote to her saying that they would have nothing more to do with her, and that she was never to come home again."—"And why had she not gone away?"—"She said she meant to wait a little longer, to see if there might not be some change in Herr K. She could not bear living like that any more, she said, and if she saw no change she should give warning and go away."—"And what became of the girl?"—"I only know that she went away."—"And she did not have a child as a result of the adventure?"—"No."

Here, therefore (and quite in accordance with the rules), was a piece of material information coming to light in the middle of the analysis and helping to solve problems which had previously been raised. I was able to say to Dora: "Now I know your motive for the slap in the face with which you answered Herr K.'s proposal. It was not that you were offended at his suggestions; you were actuated by jealousy and revenge. At the time when the governess was telling you her story you were still able to make use of your gift for putting on one side everything that is not agreeable to your feelings. But at the moment when Herr K. used the words 'I get nothing out of my wife'—which were the same words he had used to the governess—fresh emotions were aroused in you and tipped the balance. 'Does he dare,' you said to yourself, 'to treat me like a governess, like a servant?' Wounded pride added to jealousy and to the conscious motives of common sense—it was too much.[41] To prove to you how deeply impressed you were by the governess's story, let me draw your attention to the repeated occasions upon which you have identified yourself with her both in your dream and in your conduct. You told your parents what happened—a fact which we have hitherto been unable to account for—just as the governess wrote and told *her* parents. You give me a fortnight's warning, just like a governess. The letter in the dream which gave you leave to go home is the counterpart of the governess's letter from her parents forbidding her to do so."

"Then why did I not tell my parents at once?"

"How much time did you allow to elapse?"

[41] "It is not a matter of indifference, perhaps, that Dora may have heard her father make the same complaint about his wife, just as I myself did from his own lips. She was perfectly well aware of its meaning" [Freud].

"The scene took place on the last day of June; I told my mother about it on July 14th."

"Again a fortnight, then—the time characteristic for a person in service. Now I can answer your question. You understood the poor girl very well. She did not want to go away at once, because she still had hopes, because she expected that Herr K.'s affections would return to her again. So that must have been your motive too. You waited for that length of time so as to see whether he would repeat his proposals; if he had, you would have concluded that he was in earnest, and did not mean to play with you as he had done with the governess."

"A few days after I had left he sent me a picture postcard."[42]

"Yes, but when after that nothing more came, you gave free rein to your feelings of revenge. I can even imagine that at that time you were still able to find room for a subsidiary intention, and thought that your accusation might be a means of inducing him to travel to the place where you were living."—"As he actually offered to do at first," Dora threw in.—"In that way your longing for him would have been appeased"—here she nodded assent, a thing which I had not expected—"and he might have made you the amends you desired."

"What amends?"

"The fact is, I am beginning to suspect that you took the affair with Herr K. much more seriously than you have been willing to admit so far. Had not the K.'s often talked of getting a divorce?"

"Yes, certainly. At first she did not want to, on account of the children. And now she wants to, but he no longer does."

"May you not have thought that he wanted to get divorced from his wife so as to marry you? And that now he no longer wants to because he has no one to replace her? It is true that two years ago you were very young. But you told me yourself that your mother was engaged at seventeen and then waited two years for her husband. A daughter usually takes her mother's love-story as her model. So you too wanted to wait for him, and you took it that he was only waiting till you were grown up enough to be his wife. I imagine that this was a perfectly serious plan for the future in your eyes. You have not even got the right to assert that it was out of the question for Herr K. to have had any such intention; you have told me enough about him that points directly towards his having such an intention. Nor does his behavior at L—— contradict this view. After all, you did not let him finish his speech and do not know what he meant to say to you. Incidentally, the scheme would by no means have been so impracticable. Your father's relations with Frau K.—and it was probably only for this reason that you lent them your support for so long—made it certain that her consent to a divorce could be obtained; and you can get anything you like out of your father. Indeed, if your temptation at L—— had had a different upshot, this would have been the only possible solution for all the parties concerned. And I think that is why you regretted the actual event so deeply and emended it in the phantasy which made its appearance in the shape of the appendicitis. So it must have been a bitter piece of disillusionment for you

[42] "Here is the point of contact with the engineer, who was concealed behind the figure of Dora herself in the first situation in the dream" [Freud].

when the effect of your charges against Herr K. was not that he renewed his proposals but that he replied instead with denials and slanders. You will agree that nothing makes you so angry as having it thought that you merely fancied the scene by the lake. I know now—and this is what you do not want to be reminded of—that you *did* fancy that Herr K.'s proposals were serious, and that he would not leave off until you had married him."

Dora had listened to me without any of her usual contradictions. She seemed to be moved; she said good-bye to me very warmly, with the heartiest wishes for the New Year, and—came no more. Her father, who called on me two or three times afterwards, assured me that she would come back again, and said it was easy to see that she was eager for the treatment to continue. But it must be confessed that Dora's father was never entirely straightforward. He had given his support to the treatment so long as he could hope that I should "talk" Dora out of her belief that there was something more than a friendship between him and Frau K. His interest faded when he observed that it was not my intention to bring about that result. I knew Dora would not come back again. Her breaking off so unexpectedly, just when my hopes of a successful termination of the treatment were at their highest, and her thus bringing those hopes to nothing—this was an unmistakable act of vengeance on her part. Her purpose of self-injury also profited by this action. No one who, like me, conjures up the most evil of those half-tamed demons that inhabit the human breast, and seeks to wrestle with them, can expect to come through the struggle unscathed. Might I perhaps have kept the girl under my treatment if I myself had acted a part, if I had exaggerated the importance to me of her staying on, and had shown a warm personal interest in her—a course which, even after allowing for my position as her physician, would have been tantamount to providing her with a substitute for the affection she longed for? I do not know. Since in every case a part of the factors that are encountered under the form of resistance remains unknown, I have always avoided acting a part, and have contented myself with practicing the humbler arts of psychology. In spite of every theoretical interest and of every endeavor to be of assistance as a physician, I keep the fact in mind that there must be some limits set to the extent to which psychological influence may be used, and I respect as one of these limits the patient's own will and understanding.

Nor do I know whether Herr K. would have done any better if it had been revealed to him that the slap Dora gave him by no means signified a final "No" on her part, but that it expressed the jealousy which had lately been roused in her, while her strongest feelings were still on his side. If he had disregarded that first "No," and had continued to press his suit with a passion which left room for no doubts, the result might very well have been a triumph of the girl's affection for him over all her internal difficulties. But I think she might just as well have been merely provoked into satisfying her craving for revenge upon him all the more thoroughly. It is never possible to calculate towards which side the decision will incline in such a conflict of motives: whether towards the removal of the repression or towards its reinforcement. Incapacity for meeting a *real* erotic demand is one of the most essential features of a neurosis. Neurotics are dominated by the opposition between reality and phantasy. If what they long for the most intensely in their phantasies is presented to them in reality, they none the

less flee from it; and they abandon themselves to their phantasies the most readily where they need no longer fear to see them realized. Nevertheless, the barrier erected by repression can fall before the onslaught of a violent emotional excitement produced by a real cause; it is possible for a neurosis to be overcome by reality. But we have no general means of calculating through what person or what event such a cure can be effected.[43]

[4.] POSTSCRIPT

*** * * ***

In publishing this paper, incomplete though it is, I had two objects in view. In the first place, I wished to supplement my book on the interpretation of dreams by showing how an art, which would otherwise be useless, can be turned to account for the discovery of the hidden and repressed parts of mental life. (Incidentally, in the process of analyzing the two dreams dealt with in the paper, the technique of dream interpretation, which is similar to that of psychoanalysis, has come under consideration.) In the second place, I wished to stimulate interest in a whole group of phenomena of which science is still in complete ignorance to-day because they can only be brought to light by the use of this particular method. No one, I believe, can have had any true conception of the complexity of the psychological events in a case of hysteria—the juxtaposition of the most dissimilar tendencies, the mutual dependence of contrary ideas, the repressions and displacements, and so on. The emphasis laid by Janet upon the *"idée fixe"*[44] which becomes transformed into a symptom amounts to no

[43] "I will add a few remarks on the structure of this dream, though it is not possible to understand it thoroughly enough to allow of a synthesis being attempted. A prominent piece of the dream is to be seen in the phantasy of revenge against her father, which stands out like a façade in front of the rest. (She had gone away from home by her own choice; her father was ill, and then dead. . . . Then she went home; all the others were already at the cemetery. She went to her room, not the least sadly, and calmly began reading the encyclopaedia.) This part of the material also contained two allusions to her other act of revenge, which she had actually carried out, when she let her parents discover a farewell letter from her. (The letter—from her mother, in the dream—and the mention of the funeral of the aunt who had always been her model.) —Behind this phantasy lie concealed her thoughts of revenge against Herr K., for which she found an outlet in her behavior to me. (The maidservant, the invitation, the wood, the two and a half hours—all these came from material connected with the events at L——.) Her recollection of the governess, and of the latter's exchange of letters with her parents, is related, no less than her farewell letter, to the letter in the dream allowing her to come home. Her refusal to let herself be accompanied and her decision to go alone may perhaps be translated into these words: 'Since you have treated me like a servant, I shall take no more notice of you, I shall go my own way by myself, and not marry.' —Screened by these thoughts of revenge, glimpses can be caught in other places of material derived from tender phantasies based upon the love for Herr K. which still persisted unconsciously in Dora. ('I would have waited for you till I could be your wife'—defloration—childbirth.) —Finally, we can see the action of the fourth and most deeply buried group of thoughts—those relating to her love for Frau K.—in the fact that the phantasy of defloration is represented from the man's point of view (her identification of herself with her admirer who lived abroad) and in the fact that in two places there are the clearest allusions to ambiguous speeches ('Does Herr —— live here?') and to that source of her sexual knowledge which had not been oral (the encyclopedia). Cruel and sadistic tendencies find satisfaction in this dream" [Freud].

[44] Pierre Janet, the French neurologist, attributed hysteria to obsessively held "fixed ideas."

more than an extremely meager attempt at schematization. Moreover, it is impossible to avoid the suspicion that, when the ideas attaching to certain excitations are incapable of becoming conscious, those excitations must act upon one another differently, run a different course, and manifest themselves differently from those other excitations which we describe as "normal" and which have ideas attaching to them of which we become conscious. When once things have been made clear up to this point, no obstacle can remain in the way of an understanding of a therapeutic method which removes neurotic symptoms by transforming ideas of the former kind into normal ones.

I was further anxious to show that sexuality does not simply intervene, like a *deus ex machina,* on one single occasion, at some point in the working of the processes which characterize hysteria, but that it provides the motive power for every single symptom, and for every single manifestation of a symptom. The symptoms of the disease are nothing else than *the patient's sexual activity.* A single case can never be capable of proving a theorem so general as this one; but I can only repeat over and over again—for I never find it otherwise—that sexuality is the key to the problem of the psychoneuroses and of the neuroses in general. No one who disdains the key will ever be able to unlock the door. I still await news of the investigations which are to make it possible to contradict this theorem or to limit its scope. What I have hitherto heard against it have been expressions of personal dislike or disbelief. To these it is enough to reply in the words of Charcot: *"Ça n'empêche pas d'exister."*[45]

Nor is the case of whose history and treatment I have published a fragment in these pages well calculated to put the value of psychoanalytic therapy in its true light. Not only the briefness of the treatment (which hardly lasted three months), but another factor inherent in the nature of the case, prevented an improvement from being effected such as is attainable in other instances, where the improvement will be admitted by the patient and his relatives and will approximate more or less closely to a complete recovery. Satisfactory results of this kind are reached when the symptoms are maintained solely by the internal conflict between the tendencies concerned with sexuality. In such cases the patient's condition will be seen improving in proportion as he is helped towards a solution of his mental problems by the translation of pathogenic into normal material. The course of events is very different when the symptoms have become enlisted in the service of external motives, as had happened with Dora during the last two years. It is surprising, and might easily be misleading, to find that the patient's condition shows no noticeable alteration even though considerable progress has been made with the work of analysis. But in reality things are not as bad as they seem. It is true that the symptoms do not disappear while the work is proceeding; but they disappear a little while later, when the relations between patient and physician have been dissolved. The postponement of recovery or improvement is really only caused by the physician's own person.

I must go back a little, in order to make the matter intelligible. It may be safely said that during psychoanalytic treatment the formation of new

[45] "That does not prevent it from being true."

symptoms is invariably stopped. But the productive powers of the neurosis are by no means extinguished; they are occupied in the creation of a special class of mental structures, for the most part unconscious, to which the name of *"transferences"* may be given.

What are transferences? They are new editions or facsimiles of the tendencies and phantasies which are aroused and made conscious during the progress of the analysis; but they have this peculiarity, which is characteristic for their species, that they replace some earlier person by the person of the physician. To put it another way: a whole series of psychological experiences are revived, not as belonging to the past, but as applying to the person of the physician at the present moment. Some of these transferences have a content which differs from that of their model in no respect whatever except for the substitution. These, then—to keep to the same metaphor—are merely new impressions or reprints. Others are more ingeniously constructed; their content has been subjected to a moderating influence—to *sublimation*, as I call it—and they may even become conscious, by cleverly taking advantage of some real peculiarity in the physician's person or circumstances and attaching themselves to that. These, then, will no longer be new impressions, but revised editions.

If the theory of analytic technique is gone into, it becomes evident that transference is an inevitable necessity. Practical experience, at all events, shows conclusively that there is no means of avoiding it, and that this latest creation of the disease must be combated like all the earlier ones. This happens, however, to be by far the hardest part of the whole task. It is easy to learn how to interpret dreams, to extract from the patient's associations his unconscious thoughts and memories, and to practice similar explanatory arts: for these the patient himself will always provide the text. Transference is the one thing the presence of which has to be detected almost without assistance and with only the slightest clues to go upon, while at the same time the risk of making arbitrary inferences has to be avoided. Nevertheless, transference cannot be evaded, since use is made of it in setting up all the obstacles that make the material inaccessible to treatment, and since it is only after the transference has been resolved that a patient arrives at a sense of conviction of the validity of the connections which have been constructed during the analysis.

Some people may feel inclined to look upon it as a serious objection to a method which is in any case troublesome enough that it itself should multiply the labors of the physician by creating a new species of pathological mental products. They may even be tempted to infer from the existence of transferences that the patient will be injured by analytic treatment. Both these suppositions would be mistaken. The physician's labors are not multiplied by transference; it need make no difference to him whether he has to overcome any particular tendency of the patient's in connection with himself or with some one else. Nor does the treatment force upon the patient, in the shape of transference, any new task which he would not otherwise have performed. It is true that neuroses may be cured in institutions from which psychoanalytic treatment is excluded, that hysteria may be said to be cured not by the method but by the physician, and that there is usually a sort of blind dependence and a permanent bond between a patient and the

physician who has removed his symptoms by hypnotic suggestion; but the scientific explanation of all these facts is to be found in the existence of "transferences" such as are regularly directed by patients on to their physicians. Psychoanalytic treatment does not create transferences, it merely brings them to light, like so many other hidden psychical factors. The only difference is this—that spontaneously a patient will only call up affectionate and friendly transferences to help towards his recovery; if they cannot be called up, he feels the physician is "antipathetic" to him, and breaks away from him as fast as possible and without having been influenced by him. In psychoanalysis, on the other hand, since the play of motives is different, all the patient's tendencies, including hostile ones, are aroused; they are then turned to account for the purposes of the analysis by being made conscious, and in this way the transference is constantly being destroyed. Transference, which seems ordained to be the greatest obstacle to psychoanalysis, becomes its most powerful ally, if its presence can be detected each time and explained to the patient.

I have been obliged to speak of transference, for it is only by means of this factor that I can elucidate the peculiarities of Dora's analysis. Its great merit, namely, the unusual clarity which makes it seem so suitable as a first introductory publication, is closely bound up with its great defect, which led to its being broken off prematurely. I did not succeed in mastering the transference in good time. Owing to the readiness with which Dora put one part of the pathogenic material at my disposal during the treatment, I neglected the precaution of looking out for the first signs of transference, which was being prepared in connection with another part of the same material—a part of which I was in ignorance. At the beginning it was clear that I was replacing her father in her imagination, which was not unlikely, in view of the difference between our ages. She was even constantly comparing me with him consciously, and kept anxiously trying to make sure whether I was being quite straightforward with her, for her father "always preferred secrecy and roundabout ways." But when the first dream came, in which she gave herself the warning that she had better leave my treatment just as she had formerly left Herr K.'s house, I ought to have listened to the warning myself. "Now," I ought to have said to her, "it is from Herr K. that you have made a transference on to me. Have you noticed anything that leads you to suspect me of evil intentions similar (whether openly or in some sublimated form) to Herr K.'s? Or have you been struck by anything about me or got to know anything about me which has caught your fancy, as happened previously with Herr K.?" Her attention would then have been turned to some detail in our relations, or in my person or circumstances, behind which there lay concealed something analogous but immeasurably more important concerning Herr K. And when this transference had been cleared up, the analysis would have obtained access to new memories, dealing, probably, with actual events. But I was deaf to this first note of warning, thinking I had ample time before me, since no further stages of transference developed and the material for the analysis had not yet run dry. In this way the transference took me unawares, and, because of the unknown quantity in me which reminded Dora of Herr K., she took her revenge on me as she wanted to take her revenge on him, and deserted

me as she believed herself to have been deceived and deserted by him. Thus she *acted* an essential part of her recollections and phantasies instead of reproducing it in the treatment. What this unknown quantity was I naturally cannot tell. I suspect that it had to do with money, or with jealousy of another patient who had kept up relations with my family after her recovery. When it is possible to work transferences into the analysis at an early stage, the course of the analysis is retarded and obscured, but its existence is better guaranteed against sudden and overwhelming resistances.

In Dora's second dream there are several clear allusions to transference. At the time she was telling me the dream I was still unaware (and did not learn until two days later) that we had only *two hours* more work before us. This was the same length of time which she had spent in front of the Sistine Madonna, and which (by making a correction and putting "two hours" instead of "two and a half hours") she had taken as the length of the walk which she had not made around the lake. The striving and waiting in the dream, which related to the young man in Germany, and had their origin in her waiting till Herr K. could marry her, had been expressed in the transference a few days before. The treatment, she had thought, was too long for her; she would never have the patience to wait so long. And yet in the first few weeks she had had discernment enough to listen without making any such objections when I informed her that her complete recovery would require perhaps a year. Her refusing in the dream to be accompanied, and preferring to go alone, also originated from her visit to the gallery at Dresden, and I was myself to experience them on the appointed day. What they meant was, no doubt: "Men are all so detestable that I would rather not marry. This is my revenge."

If cruel impulses and revengeful motives, which have already been used in the patient's ordinary life for maintaining her symptoms, become transferred on to the physician during treatment, before he has had time to detach them from himself by tracing them back to their sources, then it is not to be wondered at if the patient's condition is unaffected by his therapeutic efforts. For how could the patient take a more effective revenge than by demonstrating upon her own person the helplessness and incapacity of the physician? Nevertheless, I am not inclined to put too low a value upon the therapeutic results even of such a fragmentary treatment as Dora's.

It was not until fifteen months after the case was over and this paper drafted that I had news of my patient's condition and the effects of my treatment. On a date which is not a matter of complete indifference, on the first of April (times and dates, as we know, were never without significance for her), Dora came to see me again: to finish her story and to ask for help once more. One glance at her face, however, was enough to tell me that she was not in earnest over her request. For four or five weeks after stopping the treatment she had been "all in a muddle," as she said. A great improvement had then set in; her attacks had become less frequent and her spirits had risen. In the May of that year one of the K.'s two children (it had always been delicate) had died. She took the opportunity of their loss to pay them a visit of condolence, and they received her as though nothing had happened in the last three years. She made it up with them, she took her

revenge on them, and she brought her own business to a satisfactory conclusion. To the wife she said: "I know you have an affair with my father"; and the other did not deny it. From the husband she drew an admission of the scene by the lake which he had disputed, and brought the news of her vindication home to her father. Since then she had not resumed her relations with the family.

After this she had gone on quite well till the middle of October, when she had had another attack of aphonia which had lasted for six weeks. I was surprised at this news, and, on my asking her whether there had been any exciting cause, she told me that the attack had followed upon a violent fright. She had seen some one run over by a cart. Finally she came out with the fact that the accident had occurred to no less a person than Herr K. himself. She had come across him in the street one day; they had met in a place where there was a great deal of traffic; he had stopped in front of her as though in bewilderment, and in his abstraction he had allowed himself to be knocked down by a cart. She had been able to convince herself, however, that he escaped without serious injury. She still felt some slight emotion if she heard any one speak of her father's affair with Frau K., but otherwise she had no further concern with the matter. She was absorbed in her work, and had no thoughts of marrying.

She went on to tell me that she had come for help on account of a right-sided facial neuralgia, from which she was now suffering day and night. "How long has it been going on?" "Exactly a fortnight." I could not help smiling; for I was able to show her that exactly a fortnight earlier she had read a piece of news that concerned me in the newspaper.[46] (This was in 1902.) And this she confirmed.

Her alleged facial neuralgia was thus a self-punishment—remorse at having once given Herr K. a box on the ear, and at having transferred her feelings of revenge on to me. I do not know what kind of help she wanted from me, but I promised to forgive her for having deprived me of the satisfaction of affording her a far more radical cure for her troubles.

Years have again gone by since her visit. In the meantime the girl has married, and indeed—unless all the signs mislead me—she has married the young man who came into her associations at the beginning of the analysis of the second dream.[47] Just as the first dream represented her turning away from the man she loved to her father—that is to say, her flight from life into disease—so the second dream announced that she was about to tear herself free from her father and had been reclaimed once more by the realities of life.

[46] The news was probably that Freud had been appointed to a Professorship (March 1902).
[47] "This, as I afterwards learned, was a mistaken notion" [Freud, 1909].

Joseph Conrad
(1857–1924)

To take up a new language at the age of twenty, as Joseph Conrad did, is to accept a challenge. To make a career as a professional, indeed a creative, writer in the new language is an act of hardihood, and Conrad did that too. *More* (as William Faulkner would say): he became one of the masters of English prose style, in a highly adjectival vein disastrous to imitate (unless one is Faulkner, who did so) but eminently right for Conrad himself in his heavily atmospheric tales. Even this linguistic miracle, however, is only the beginning of Conrad's achievement. Author of some of the best adventure fiction in any language, he also—and more fundamentally—explored troubled minds and souls. Starting from the realist tradition of the nineteenth-century novels, and retaining much of their rich texture and verisimilitude, he went on to pioneer modernist methods, especially in the handling of narrative time and multiple or less-than-reliable points of view. He was one of the great symbolists. In short, he was close to being the complete literary artist. And even if, some centuries hence, the world should lose all interest in art, Conrad will remain indispensable to cultural history, for his vivid anatomies of colonialism, imperialism, the Third World as it appears to the Westerner, and—still more broadly—his critique of the Western *mythos* of Enlightened Progress. Indeed, those two words come startlingly alive in *Heart of Darkness,* with its complex symbolic title and its ironically labeled "pilgrims" whose heavenly city is made not of ethereal alabaster but of material ivory.

Conrad's life divides into two halves: an adventurous far-flung career as a seaman and a second career as a writer, spent almost entirely in a small corner of England. He was born in 1857, as Józef Teodor Konrad Nalecz Korzeniowski, in Berdyczew, a Polish town that had been absorbed into Russia (and today again is part of the Soviet Union). His parents, Apollo and Evelina Korzeniowski, were descended from landed gentry. When his son was four, Apollo—poet, translator, and fervent Polish nationalist—was consigned for political reasons to exile in northern Russia; mother and son joined him there. Climatic hardships took their toll, Evelina dying when the boy was seven. The despondent Apollo died four years later, in Krakow. (Conrad's fiction is haunted by the image of a selfless yet egotistic believer willing to risk disaster for his ideals.) The orphan Józef came under the care of his benevolent uncle Tadeusz Bobrowski, who saw to his ward's schooling in that city. The restless and romantic teenager, like the Marlow he created in his later fiction, aspired to explore the great world, and, after having eroded his uncle's opposition, he took a social step down by entering the French merchant marine at the age of sixteen as an apprentice seaman. For four years he sailed in French ships (steamers he despised as "locomotives"), to the West Indies and South America. During this period Conrad seems to have had some covert escapades, in Latin America and in Spain, where he smuggled guns in the service of Don Carlos, the claimant of the Spanish throne. In Marseilles he also incurred a mysterious chest-wound, possibly from a duel over a woman (as he wanted people to be-

lieve), possibly from an attempted suicide (which would be consistent with his chronic tendency to depression).

When he was twenty, Conrad took a decisive step by shifting from the French to the English merchant service, partly in order to evade the Russian draft, from which British ships claimed exemption for their men. In the next sixteen years, under the British flag, Conrad continued to see the world—chiefly in voyages to Australia, India, and the Indonesian islands—while also getting to know England and, more important, English. He worked and studied his way up, qualifying as mate, then captain, and becoming a British citizen along the way. In 1890, between sea assignments, he commanded a river boat on the Congo. The million square miles of the Belgian Congo region, only recently opened up by the famous explorer Henry Morton Stanley, were at the time the personal property of King Leopold II, a rapacious man whose philanthropic rhetoric was a screen for one of the most infamous chapters in the history of European imperialism. Conrad, whose moral sensibilities had not been nurtured in a hothouse, later called the episode "the vilest scramble for loot that ever disfigured the history of human conscience and geographical exploration." Some of the atrocities committed in the Congo are evoked by Marlow's account in *Heart of Darkness,* which in other ways too follows closely the author's real-life experiences. Conrad's health was permanently impaired, and the inner man was likewise transformed, according to his own testimony. Before that time, he said, he had been "a mere animal"—a curious and intriguing metaphor in view of the discoveries Marlow makes about human nature in the story.

By 1894, when Conrad's seagoing career ended, he had been writing for several years, and in 1895, under his simplified and Englished name, he launched his prolific career as an author of fiction with *Almayer's Folly,* which like many of Conrad's novels still to come drew on his experiences and observations in places remote from Europe. In the following year he married Jessie George, an Englishwoman, and settled down in the county of Kent, in southeast England, his home for the rest of his life. Over the next seventeen years he produced in steady succession sixteen books, some of them ranking with the best fiction in English, including such masterpieces as *Heart of Darkness* (1899, included in *Youth,* 1902), *Lord Jim* (1900), *Nostromo* (1904), *The Secret Agent* (1907), and *Under Western Eyes* (1911). His friends and admirers were a kind of turn-of-the-century pantheon, including Stephen Crane, Henry James, H. G. Wells, Rudyard Kipling, W. H. Hudson, John Galsworthy, Arnold Bennett, Ford Madox Ford (who coauthored three books with Conrad), and several other eminent people. Yet despite this kind of backing, for novels of the highest excellence with the inherent popular appeal of exotic places and adventurous action, Conrad's works did not sell widely, and his life was a grinding struggle with low spirits, poor health, and poverty. Not until *Chance* (1912-14) and *Victory* (1915) were published did he score popular and financial success. Thereafter he was a celebrity, idolized during an American visit in 1923 and offered British knighthood (which he declined) in 1924. He died of a heart attack that same year and was buried in the Roman Catholic churchyard in Canterbury, the city at the spiritual center of his adopted country.

Although it lacks the epic scale of, say, *Nostromo, Heart of Darkness* is

Conrad at his best and near his most characteristic. The presence of Conrad's alter ego Marlow (who appears in several other works); the skillful dislocations of narrative sequence, which moves psychologically toward climactic insight rather than chronologically; the appropriately tropical luxuriance of the heightened language; the gropings toward understanding, by Marlow, implicitly by his shipboard listeners, and by the reader; the portentous mood infused into words, events, objects, and setting; perhaps above all the nearly unparalleled density of the relentless but somehow unobtrusive symbolic imagery—all these working together make up a novel that, for power disciplined by art, has few equals in fiction. At no point in *Heart of Darkness* can one sink a drill without discovering several of its many strata. It synthesizes historical epochs—from the Roman to the Elizabethan to the modern English and European. It penetrates anthropological time and space as well, tracing a deceptively long path from "civilization" to the "primitive" that, we come to see, is at most a single step. It makes a timely statement about Belgium and other colonial powers, its theme transcending the 1890s without blurring the journalistic details. It relates a particular man's growth—or attempt to grow—into knowledge of the world and of himself. It explores not only for the truth but for the meaning and usefulness of the very notion of truth. Its images are unforgettable, especially in their eerie juxtapositions and superimpositions: grass growing through the pavements of a white city, and, far away, through the rib cage of a human skeleton; a woman's arms extended in grief on a jungle riverbank and in a European drawing room; the popping of a gunboat's shells into an impassive continent and a fusillade directed as idly into riverside foliage; the "scientific" measurement of heads by a European doctor and the impaled heads around a jungle station; an accountant's immaculate starched collar and an adventurer's clownlike patchwork apparel; the preternatural stillness of the jungle and the voice of a fallen missionary, at once the symbol of his power and of his ineffectuality.

Heart of Darkness is an endlessly discussed, endlessly discussable work. Does Marlow find and face truth, or does he finally take refuge in still another saving form of illusion? If the "civilized" pilgrim-profiteers and the deluded emissaries of spiritual light are more contemptible than the "savages," why is "restraint," normally considered a civilized trait, so imperative when the wild is calling? What, exactly, does Marlow mean by the "inborn strength" and "deliberate belief" that he contrasts with mere "principles" as the only safeguard against the darkness without and within the human heart? And how is that bulwark related to the saving power of practical work? In what sense are Kurtz's appalling last words an "affirmation, a moral victory"? Why does Marlow lie to Kurtz's "Intended"? Does he, in fact, lie to her or does he ironically equivocate? In the dense thematic interweaving of *Heart of Darkness*, each of these and of many similar questions is the end of a string that, unlike Ariadne's in the ancient myth, leads into a labyrinth without guaranteeing that it has an exit. It is an interesting fact, and symptomatic of Conrad's power and insight, that readers continue to debate such issues even while wondering whether they are resolvable, either as critical problems within the novel itself or outside it, as questions about the real-life darkness of the human heart.

FURTHER READING (*prepared by W. J. R.*): The three finest biographies in order of usefulness for the student of Conrad's art are Jocelyn Baines's *Joseph Conrad: A Critical Biography*, 1960; Frederick R. Karl's *Joseph Conrad: The Three Lives*, 1979; and Bernard C. Meyer's *Joseph Conrad: A Psychoanalytic Biography*, 1967. Norman Page's *A Conrad Companion*, 1985, provides work-by-work commentary. For important studies of the real-life sources of Conrad's stories, see J. D. Gordan's *Joseph Conrad: The Making of a Novelist*, 1940, and Norman Sherry's *Conrad's Eastern World*, 1966, and *Conrad's Western World*, 1971. The ideology and politics of Conrad's fiction have been studied by Eloise Knapp Hay, *The Political Novels of Joseph Conrad*, 1963; Avrom Fleishman, *Conrad's Politics: Community and Anarchy in the Fiction of Joseph Conrad*, 1967; and R. F. Lee, *Conrad's Colonialism*, 1969. Ian Watt's *Conrad in the Nineteenth Century*, 1979, is probably the most significant study of the novelist since Albert Guerard's *Conrad the Novelist*, 1958. Benita Parry's *Conrad and Imperialism*, 1983, is authoritative on its topic. Other valuable studies of his fiction may be found in Thomas Moser's *Joseph Conrad: Achievement and Decline*, 1957; Leo Gurko's *Joseph Conrad: Giant in Exile*, 1962; Adam Gillon's *The Eternal Solitary*, 1960; Frederick R. Karl's *A Reader's Guide to Joseph Conrad*, 1960; and Suresh Raval's *The Art of Failure: Conrad's Fiction*, 1986. The Norton Critical Edition of *Heart of Darkness*, ed. Robert Kimbrough, 3rd ed., 1983, includes background material and critical essays, including Chinua Achebe's important "An Image of Africa: Racism in Conrad's *Heart of Darkness*."

HEART OF DARKNESS

I

The Nellie, a cruising yawl, swung to her anchor without a flutter of the sails, and was at rest. The flood had made, the wind was nearly calm, and being bound down the river, the only thing for it was to come to[1] and wait for the turn of the tide.

The sea-reach of the Thames stretched before us like the beginning of an interminable waterway. In the offing[2] the sea and the sky were welded together without a joint, and in the luminous space the tanned sails of the barges drifting up with the tide seemed to stand still in red clusters of canvas sharply peaked, with gleams of varnished sprits. A haze rested on the low shores that ran out to sea in vanishing flatness. The air was dark above Gravesend,[3] and farther back still seemed condensed into a mournful gloom, brooding motionless over the biggest, and the greatest, town on earth.

The Director of Companies was our captain and our host. We four affectionately watched his back as he stood in the bows looking to seaward. On the whole river there was nothing that looked half so nautical. He resembled a pilot, which to a seaman is trustworthiness personified. It was difficult to realize his work was not out there in the luminous estuary, but behind him, within the brooding gloom.

[1] Anchor. [2] Horizon.

[3] A town twenty-five miles east of London, where the Thames begins to widen toward the sea.

Between us there was, as I have already said somewhere, the bond of the sea. Besides holding our hearts together through long periods of separation, it had the effect of making us tolerant of each other's yarns—and even convictions. The Lawyer—the best of old fellows—had, because of his many years and many virtues, the only cushion on deck, and was lying on the only rug. The Accountant had brought out already a box of dominoes, and was toying architecturally with the bones. Marlow sat cross-legged right aft, leaning against the mizzen-mast. He had sunken cheeks, a yellow complexion, a straight back, an ascetic aspect, and, with his arms dropped, the palms of hands outwards, resembled an idol. The director, satisfied the anchor had good hold, made his way aft and sat down amongst us. We exchanged a few words lazily. Afterwards there was silence on board the yacht. For some reason or other we did not begin that game of dominoes. We felt meditative, and fit for nothing but placid staring. The day was ending in a serenity of still and exquisite brilliance. The water shone pacifically; the sky, without a speck, was a benign immensity of unstained light; the very mist on the Essex marshes was like a gauzy and radiant fabric, hung from the wooded rises inland, and draping the low shores in diaphanous folds. Only the gloom to the west, brooding over the upper reaches, became more sombre every minute, as if angered by the approach of the sun.

And at last, in its curved and imperceptible fall, the sun sank low, and from glowing white changed to a dull red without rays and without heat, as if about to go out suddenly, stricken to death by the touch of that gloom brooding over a crowd of men.

Forthwith a change came over the waters, and the serenity became less brilliant but more profound. The old river in its broad reach rested unruffled at the decline of day, after ages of good service done to the race that peopled its banks, spread out in the tranquil dignity of a waterway leading to the uttermost ends of the earth. We looked at the venerable stream not in the vivid flush of a short day that comes and departs for ever, but in the august light of abiding memories. And indeed nothing is easier for a man who has, as the phrase goes, "followed the sea" with reverence and affection, than to evoke the great spirit of the past upon the lower reaches of the Thames. The tidal current runs to and fro in its unceasing service, crowded with memories of men and ships it has borne to the rest of home or to the battles of the sea. It had known and served all the men of whom the nation is proud, from Sir Francis Drake to Sir John Franklin,[4] knights all, titled and untitled—the great knights-errant of the sea. It had borne all the ships whose names are like jewels flashing in the night of time, from the *Golden Hind* returning with her round flanks full of treasure, to be visited by the Queen's Highness and thus pass out of the gigantic tale, to the *Erebus* and *Terror*, bound on other conquests—and that never returned. It had known the ships and the men. They had sailed from Deptford, from Greenwich, from Erith[5]—the adventurers and the settlers; kings' ships and the ships of men on 'Change;[6] captains, admirals, the dark "interlopers" of the Eastern

[4] Drake was the Elizabethan admiral who sailed around the globe in the *Golden Hind* (Deer) in 1577–1580. Franklin was a seeker of the Northwest Passage, in the ships *Erebus* and *Terror*, in 1845–1847.

[5] *Deptford . . . Erith.* Ports downstream from London. [6] The financial market.

trade, and the commissioned "generals" of East India[7] fleets. Hunters for gold or pursuers of fame, they all had gone out on that stream, bearing the sword, and often the torch, messengers of the might within the land, bearers of a spark from the sacred fire. What greatness had not floated on the ebb of that river into the mystery of an unknown earth! . . . The dreams of men, the seed of commonwealths, the germs of empires.

The sun set; the dusk fell on the stream, and lights began to appear along the shore. The Chapman lighthouse, a three-legged thing erect on a mud-flat, shone strongly. Lights of ships moved in the fairway[8]—a great stir of lights going up and going down. And farther west on the upper reaches the place of the monstrous town was still marked ominously on the sky, a brooding gloom in sunshine, a lurid glare under the stars.

"And this also," said Marlow suddenly, "has been one of the dark places of the earth."

He was the only man of us who still "followed the sea." The worst that could be said of him was that he did not represent his class. He was a seaman, but he was a wanderer, too, while most seamen lead, if one may so express it, a sedentary life. Their minds are of the stay-at-home order, and their home is always with them—the ship; and so is their country—the sea. One ship is very much like another, and the sea is always the same. In the immutability of their surroundings the foreign shores, the foreign faces, the changing immensity of life, glide past, veiled not by a sense of mystery but by a slightly disdainful ignorance; for there is nothing mysterious to a seaman unless it be the sea itself, which is the mistress of his existence and as inscrutable as Destiny. For the rest, after his hours of work, a casual stroll or a casual spree on shore suffices to unfold for him the secret of a whole continent, and generally he finds the secret not worth knowing. The yarns of seamen have a direct simplicity, the whole meaning of which lies within the shell of a cracked nut. But Marlow was not typical (if his propensity to spin yarns be excepted), and to him the meaning of an episode was not inside like a kernel but outside, enveloping the tale which brought it out only as a glow brings out a haze, in the likeness of one of those misty halos that sometimes are made visible by the spectral illumination of moonshine.

His remark did not seem at all surprising. It was just like Marlow. It was accepted in silence. No one took the trouble to grunt even; and presently he said, very slow—

"I was thinking of very old times, when the Romans[9] first came here, nineteen hundred years ago—the other day. . . . Light came out of this river since—you say Knights? Yes; but it is like a running blaze on a plain, like a flash of lightning in the clouds. We live in the flicker—may it last as long as the old earth keeps rolling! But darkness was here yesterday. Imagine the feelings of a commander of a fine—what d'ye call 'em?—trireme[10] in the Mediterranean, ordered suddenly to the north; run overland

[7] The East India Company was officially chartered; "interlopers" were unauthorized traders.

[8] Main channel.

[9] Beginning with Julius Caesar, the Romans conquered and then occupied much of Britain between 54 B.C. and 442 A.D.

[10] Galley with three levels of oars.

across the Gauls[11] in a hurry; put in charge of one of these craft the legionaries—a wonderful lot of handy men they must have been, too—used to build, apparently by the hundred, in a month or two, if we may believe what we read. Imagine him here—the very end of the world, a sea the colour of lead, a sky the colour of smoke, a kind of ship about as rigid as a concertina—and going up this river with stores, or orders, or what you like. Sand-banks, marshes, forests, savages,—precious little to eat fit for a civilized man, nothing but Thames water to drink. No Falernian[12] wine here, no going ashore. Here and there a military camp lost in a wilderness, like a needle in a bundle of hay—cold, fog, tempests, disease, exile, and death,—death skulking in the air, in the water, in the bush. They must have been dying like flies here. Oh, yes—he did it. Did it very well, too, no doubt, and without thinking much about it either, except afterwards to brag of what he had gone through in his time, perhaps. They were men enough to face the darkness. And perhaps he was cheered by keeping his eye on a chance of promotion to the fleet at Ravenna[13] by and by, if he had good friends in Rome and survived the awful climate. Or think of a decent young citizen in a toga—perhaps too much dice, you know—coming out here in the train of some prefect,[14] or tax-gatherer, or trader even, to mend his fortunes. Land in a swamp, march through the woods, and in some inland post feel the savagery, the utter savagery, had closed round him,—all that mysterious life of the wilderness that stirs in the forest, in the jungles, in the hearts of wild men. There's no initiation either into such mysteries. He has to live in the midst of the incomprehensible, which is also detestable. And it has a fascination, too, that goes to work upon him. The fascination of the abomination—you know, imagine the growing regrets, the longing to escape, the powerless disgust, the surrender, the hate."

He paused.

"Mind," he began again, lifting one arm from the elbow, the palm of the hand outwards, so that, with his legs folded before him, he had the pose of a Buddha[15] preaching in European clothes and without a lotus-flower— "Mind, none of us would feel exactly like this. What saves us is efficiency— the devotion to efficiency. But these chaps were not much account, really. They were no colonists; their administration was merely a squeeze, and nothing more, I suspect. They were conquerors, and for that you want only brute force—nothing to boast of, when you have it, since your strength is just an accident arising from the weakness of others. They grabbed what they could get for the sake of what was to be got. It was just robbery with violence, aggravated murder on a great scale, and men going at it blind—as is very proper for those who tackle a darkness. The conquest of the earth, which mostly means the taking it away from those who have a different complexion or slightly flatter noses than ourselves, is not a pretty thing when you look into it too much. What redeems it is the idea only. An idea at the back of it; not a sentimental pretence but an idea; and an unselfish

[11] Inhabitants of what is now France and Belgium. [12] A gourmet wine.
[13] An important base of the Roman fleet, on the Adriatic Sea.
[14] High Roman administrator.
[15] Statue of the Indian founder of Buddhism, often represented atop a lotus flower; also, a Buddhist wise man.

belief in the idea—something you can set up, and bow down before, and offer a sacrifice to. . . ."

He broke off. Flames glided in the river, small green flames, red flames, white flames, pursuing, overtaking, joining, crossing each other—then separating slowly or hastily. The traffic of the great city went on in the deepening night upon the sleepless river. We looked on, waiting patiently—there was nothing else to do till the end of the flood; but it was only after a long silence, when he said, in a hesitating voice, "I suppose you fellows remember I did once turn fresh-water sailor for a bit," that we knew we were fated, before the ebb began to run, to hear about one of Marlow's inconclusive experiences.

"I don't want to bother you much with what happened to me personally," he began, showing in this remark the weakness of many tellers of tales who seem so often unaware of what their audience would best like to hear; "yet to understand the effect of it on me you ought to know how I got out there, what I saw, how I went up that river to the place were I first met the poor chap. It was the farthest point of navigation and the culminating point of my experience. It seemed somehow to throw a kind of light on everything about me—and into my thoughts. It was sombre enough, too— and pitiful—not extraordinary in any way–not very clear either. No, not very clear. And yet it seemed to throw a kind of light.

"I had then, as you remember, just returned to London after a lot of Indian Ocean, Pacific, China Seas—a regular dose of the East—six years or so, and I was loafing about, hindering you fellows in your work and invading your homes, just as though I had got a heavenly mission to civilize you. It was very fine for a time, but after a bit I did get tired of resting. Then I began to look for a ship—I should think the hardest work on earth. But the ships wouldn't even look at me. And I got tired of that game, too.

"Now when I was a little chap I had a passion for maps. I would look for hours at South America, or Africa, or Australia, and lose myself in all the glories of exploration. At that time there were many blank spaces on the earth, and when I saw one that looked particularly inviting on a map (but they all look that) I would put my finger on it and say, When I grow up I will go there. The North Pole was one of these places, I remember. Well, I haven't been there yet, and shall not try now. The glamour's off. Other places were scattered about the Equator, and in every sort of latitude all over the two hemispheres. I have been in some of them, and . . . well, we won't talk about that. But there was one yet—the biggest, the most blank, so to speak—that I had a hankering after.

"True, by this time it was not a blank space any more. It had got filled since my boyhood with rivers and lakes and names. It had ceased to be a blank space of delightful mystery—a white patch for a boy to dream gloriously over. It had become a place of darkness. But there was in it one river[16] especially, a mighty big river, that you could see on the map, resembling an immense snake uncoiled, with its head in the sea, its body at rest curving afar over a vast country, and its tail lost in the depths of the land. And as I looked at the map of it in a shop-window, it fascinated me as a snake would a bird—a silly little bird. Then I remembered there was a big

[16] The Congo, flowing through central Africa into the South Atlantic.

concern, a Company for trade on that river. Dash it all! I thought to myself, they can't trade without using some kind of craft on that lot of fresh water—steamboats! Why shouldn't I try to get charge of one? I went on along Fleet Street,[17] but could not shake off the idea. The snake had charmed me.

"You understand it was a Continental concern, that Trading society; but I have a lot of relations living on the Continent, because it's cheap and not so nasty as it looks, they say.

"I am sorry to own I began to worry them. This was already a fresh departure for me. I was not used to get things that way, you know. I always went my own road and on my own legs where I had a mind to go. I wouldn't have believed it of myself; but, then—you see—I felt somehow I must get there by hook or by crook. So I worried them. The men said 'My dear fellow,' and did nothing. Then—would you believe it?—I tried the women. I, Charlie Marlow, set the women to work—to get a job. Heavens! Well, you see, the notion drove me. I had an aunt, a dear enthusiastic soul. She wrote: 'It will be delightful. I am ready to do anything, anything for you. It is a glorious idea. I know the wife of a very high personage in the Administration, and also a man who has lots of influence with,' etc., etc. She was determined to make no end of fuss to get me appointed skipper of a river steamboat, if such was my fancy.

"I got my appointment—of course; and I got it very quick. It appears the Company had received news that one of their captains had been killed in a scuffle with the natives. This was my chance, and it made me the more anxious to go. It was only months and months afterwards, when I made the attempt to recover what was left of the body, that I heard the original quarrel arose from a misunderstanding about some hens. Yes, two black hens. Fresleven—that was the fellow's name, a Dane—thought himself wronged somehow in the bargain, so he went ashore and started to hammer the chief of the village with a stick. Oh, it didn't surprise me in the least to hear this, and at the same time to be told that Fresleven was the gentlest, quietest creature that ever walked on two legs. No doubt he was; but he had been a couple of years already out there engaged in the noble cause, you know, and he probably felt the need at last of asserting his self-respect in some way. Therefore he whacked the old nigger mercilessly, while a big crowd of his people watched him, thunderstruck, till some man—I was told the chief's son—in desperation at hearing the old chap yell, made a tentative jab with a spear at the white man—and of course it went quite easy between the shoulder-blades. Then the whole population cleared into the forest, expecting all kinds of calamities to happen, while, on the other hand, the steamer Fresleven commanded left also in a bad panic, in charge of the engineer, I believe. Afterwards nobody seemed to trouble much about Fresleven's remains, till I got out and stepped into his shoes. I couldn't let it rest, though; but when an opportunity offered at last to meet my predecessor, the grass growing through his ribs was tall enough to hide his bones. They were all there. The supernatural being had not been touched after he fell. And the village was deserted, the huts gaped black, rotting, all askew within the fallen enclosures. A calamity had come to it,

[17] Busy commercial street in London.

sure enough. The people had vanished. Mad terror had scattered them, men, women, and children, through the bush, and they had never returned. What became of the hens I don't know either. I should think the cause of progress got them, anyhow. However, through this glorious affair I got my appointment, before I had fairly begun to hope for it.

"I flew around like mad to get ready, and before forty-eight hours I was crossing the Channel to show myself to my employers, and sign the contract. In a very few hours I arrived in a city[18] that always makes me think of a whited sepulchre.[19] Prejudice no doubt. I had no difficulty in finding the Company's offices. It was the biggest thing in the town, and everybody I met was full of it. They were going to run an over-sea empire, and make no end of coin by trade.

"A narrow and deserted street in deep shadow, high houses, innumerable windows with venetian blinds, a dead silence, grass sprouting between the stones, imposing carriage archways right and left, immense double doors standing ponderously ajar. I slipped through one of these cracks, went up a swept and ungarnished staircase, as arid as a desert, and opened the first door I came to. Two women, one fat and the other slim, sat on straw-bottomed chairs, knitting black wool. The slim one got up and walked straight at me—still knitting with down-cast eyes—and only just as I began to think of getting out of her way, as you would for a somnambulist,[20] stood still, and looked up. Her dress was as plain as an umbrella-cover, and she turned round without a word and preceded me into a waiting-room. I gave my name, and looked about. Deal[21] table in the middle, plain chairs all round the walls, on one end a large shining map, marked with all the colours of a rainbow. There was a vast amount of red—good to see at any time, because one knows that some real work is done in there, a deuce of a lot of blue, a little green, smears of orange, and, on the East Coast, a purple patch, to show where the jolly pioneers of progress drink the jolly lager-beer. However, I wasn't going into any of these. I was going into the yellow.[22] Dead in the centre. And the river was there—fascinating—deadly—like a snake. Ough! A door opened, a whitehaired secretarial head, but wearing a compassionate expression, appeared, and a skinny forefinger beckoned me into the sanctuary. Its light was dim, and a heavy writing-desk squatted in the middle. From behind that structure came out an impression of pale plumpness in a frock-coat. The great man himself. He was five feet six, I should judge, and had his grip on the handle-end of ever so many millions. He shook hands, I fancy, murmured vaguely, was satisfied with my French. *Bon voyage.*

"In about forty-five seconds I found myself again in the waiting-room with the compassionate secretary, who, full of desolation and sympathy, made me sign some document. I believe I undertook amongst other things not to disclose any trade secrets. Well, I am not going to.

[18] Brussels, capital of Belgium, whose king, Leopold II, owned the vast Congo region in 1890, the approximate time of this story.

[19] Jesus, in accusing the Pharisees of hypocrisy, likened them to whited sepulchers (tombs), gleaming without but corrupt within. See Matthew 23:27.

[20] Sleepwalker. [21] Plain fir or pine.

[22] The colors distinguish lands controlled by the various European colonial powers; for example, red is British, purple German or perhaps Dutch, yellow the Belgian Congo.

"I began to feel slightly uneasy. You know I am not used to such ceremonies, and there was something ominous in the atmosphere. It was just as though I had been let into some conspiracy—I don't know—something not quite right; and I was glad to get out. In the outer room the two women knitted black wool feverishly. People were arriving, and the younger one was walking back and forth introducing them. The old one sat on her chair. Her flat cloth slippers were propped up on a foot-warmer, and a cat reposed on her lap. She wore a starched white affair on her head, had a wart on one cheek, and silver-rimmed spectacles hung on the tip of her nose. She glanced at me above the glasses. The swift and indifferent placidity of that look troubled me. Two youths with foolish and cheery countenances were being piloted over, and she threw at them the same quick glance of unconcerned wisdom. She seemed to know all about them and about me, too. An eerie feeling came over me. She seemed uncanny and fateful. Often far away there I thought of these two, guarding the door of Darkness, knitting black wool as for a warm pall,[23] one introducing, introducing continuously to the unknown, the other scrutinizing the cheery and foolish faces with unconcerned old eyes. *Ave!* Old knitter of black wool. *Morituri te salutant.*[24] Not many of those she looked at ever saw her again— not half, by a long way.

"There was yet a visit to the doctor. 'A simple formality,' assured me the secretary, with an air of taking an immense part in all my sorrows. Accordingly a young chap wearing his hat over the left eyebrow, some clerk I suppose,—there must have been clerks in the business, though the house was as still as a house in a city of the dead—came from somewhere up-stairs, and led me forth. He was shabby and careless, with inkstains on the sleeves of his jacket, and his cravat was large and billowy, under a chin shaped like the toe of an old boot. It was a little too early for the doctor, so I proposed a drink, and thereupon he developed a vein of joviality. As we sat over our vermouths he glorified the Company's business, and by and by I expressed casually my surprise at him not going out there. He became very cool and collected all at once. 'I am not such a fool as I look, quoth Plato to his disciples,' he said sententiously, emptied his glass with great resolution, and we rose.

"The old doctor felt my pulse, evidently thinking of something else the while. 'Good, good for there,' he mumbled, and then with a certain eagerness asked me whether I would let him measure my head. Rather surprised, I said Yes, when he produced a thing like calipers and got the dimensions back and front and every way, taking notes carefully. He was an unshaven little man in a threadbare coat like a gaberdine, with his feet in slippers, and I thought him a harmless fool. 'I always ask leave, in the interests of science, to measure the crania of those going out there,' he said. 'And when they come back, too?' I asked. 'Oh, I never see them,' he remarked; 'and, moreover, the changes take place inside, you know.' He smiled, as if at some quiet joke. 'So you are going out there. Famous.[25]

[23] Cloth spread over a coffin.

[24] *Ave . . . salutant.* The salute to the Emperor by the Roman gladiators in the arena: "Hail! Those who are about to die salute you."

[25] Splendid.

Interesting, too.' He gave me a searching glance, and made another note. 'Ever any madness in your family?' he asked, in a matter-of-fact tone. I felt very annoyed. 'Is that question in the interests of science, too?' 'It would be,' he said, without taking notice of my irritation, 'interesting for science to watch the mental changes of individuals, on the spot, but . . .' 'Are you an alienist?'[26] I interrupted. 'Every doctor should be— a little,' answered that original, imperturbably. 'I have a little theory which you Messieurs who go out there must help me to prove. This is my share in the advantages my country shall reap from the possession of such a magnificent dependency. The mere wealth I leave to others. Pardon my questions, but you are the first Englishman coming under my observation . . .' I hastened to assure him I was not in the least typical. 'If I were,' said I, 'I wouldn't be talking like this with you.' 'What you say is rather profound, and probably erroneous,' he said, with a laugh. 'Avoid irritation more than exposure to the sun. Adieu. How do you English say, eh? Good-bye. Ah! Good-bye. Adieu. In the tropics one must before everything keep calm.' . . . He lifted a warning forefinger. . . . *'Du calme, du calme. Adieu.'*

"One thing more remained to do—say good-bye to my excellent aunt. I found her triumphant. I had a cup of tea—the last decent cup of tea for many days—and in a room that most soothingly looked just as you would expect a lady's drawing-room to look, we had a long quiet chat by the fireside. In the course of these confidences it became quite plain to me I had been represented to the wife of the high dignitary, and goodness knows to how many more people besides, as an exceptional and gifted creature—a piece of good fortune for the Company—a man you don't get hold of every day. Good heavens! and I was going to take charge of a two-penny-half-penny river-steamboat with a penny whistle[27] attached! It appeared, however, I was also one of the Workers, with a capital—you know. Something like an emissary of light, something like a lower sort of apostle. There had been a lot of such rot let loose in print and talk just about that time, and the excellent woman, living right in the rush of all that humbug, got carried off her feet. She talked about 'weaning those ignorant millions from their horrid ways,' till, upon my word, she made me quite uncomfortable. I ventured to hint that the Company was run for profit.

" 'You forget, dear Charlie, that the labourer is worthy of his hire,'[28] she said, brightly. It's queer how out of touch with truth women are. They live in a world of their own, and there has never been anything like it, and never can be. It is too beautiful altogether, and if they were to set it up it would go to pieces before the first sunset. Some confounded fact we men have been living contentedly with ever since the day of creation would start up and knock the whole thing over.

"After this I got embraced, told to wear flannel, be sure to write often, and so on—and I left. In the street—I don't known why—a queer feeling came to me that I was an impostor. Odd thing that I, who used to clear out for any part of the world at twenty-four hours' notice, with less thought than most men give to the crossing of a street, had a moment—I won't say

[26] Psychiatrist. [27] A small, inexpensive musical pipe.
[28] *labourer . . . hire.* Jesus' words to his disciples in sending them forth as missionaries; Luke 10:7.

of hesitation, but of startled pause, before this commonplace affair. The best way I can explain it to you is by saying that, for a second or two, I felt as though, instead of going to the centre of a continent, I were about to set off for the centre of the earth.

"I left in a French steamer, and she called in every blamed port they have out there, for, as far as I could see, the sole purpose of landing soldiers and custom-house officers. I watched the coast. Watching a coast as it slips by the ship is like thinking about an enigma. There it is before you—smiling, frowning, inviting, grand, mean, insipid, or savage, and always mute with an air of whispering, Come and find out. This one was almost featureless, as if still in the making, with an aspect of monotonous grimness. The edge of a colossal jungle, so dark-green as to be almost black, fringed with white surf, ran straight, like a ruled line, far, far away along a blue sea whose glitter was blurred by a creeping mist. The sun was fierce, the land seemed to glisten and drip with steam. Here and there grayish-whitish specks showed up clustered inside the white surf, with a flag flying above them perhaps. Settlements some centuries old, and still no bigger than pinheads on the untouched expanse of their background. We pounded along, stopped, landed soldiers; went on, landed custom-house clerks to levy toll in what looked like a God-forsaken wilderness, with a tin shed and a flagpole lost in it; landed more soldiers—to take care of the custom-house clerks, presumably. Some, I heard, got drowned in the surf; but whether they did or not, nobody seemed particularly to care. They were just flung out there, and on we went. Every day the coast looked the same, as though we had not moved; but we passed various places—trading places—with names like Gran' Bassam, Little Popo; names that seemed to belong to some sordid farce acted in front of a sinister back-cloth. The idleness of a passenger, my isolation amongst all these men with whom I had no point of contact, the oily and languid sea, the uniform sombreness of the coast, seemed to keep me away from the truth of things, within the toil[29] of a mournful and senseless delusion. The voice of the surf heard now and then was a positive pleasure, like the speech of a brother. It was something natural, that had its reason, that had a meaning. Now and then a boat from the shore gave one a momentary contact with reality. It was paddled by black fellows. You could see from afar the white of their eyeballs glistening. They shouted, sang; their bodies streamed with perspiration; they had faces like grotesque masks—these chaps; but they had bone, muscle, a wild vitality, an intense energy of movement, that was as natural and true as the surf along their coast. They wanted no excuse for being there. They were a great comfort to look at. For a time I would feel I belonged still to a world of straightforward facts; but the feeling would not last long. Something would turn up to scare it away. Once, I remember, we came upon a man-of-war anchored off the coast. There wasn't even a shed there, and she was shelling the bush. It appears the French had one of their wars going on thereabouts. Her ensign[30] dropped limp like a rag; the muzzles of the long six-inch guns stuck out all over the low hull; the greasy, slimy swell swung her up lazily and let her down, swaying her thin masts. In the empty immensity of earth, sky, and water, there she was, incomprehen-

[29] Net; trap. [30] Flag.

sible, firing into a continent. Pop, would go one of the six-inch guns; a small flame would dart and vanish, a little white smoke would disappear, a tiny projectile would give a feeble screech—and nothing happened. Nothing could happen. There was a touch of insanity in the proceeding, a sense of lugubrious drollery in the sight; and it was not dissipated by somebody on board assuring me earnestly there was a camp of natives—he called them enemies!—hidden out of sight somewhere.

"We gave her her letters (I heard the men in that lonely ship were dying of fever at the rate of three a day) and went on. We called at some more places with farcical names, where the merry dance of death and trade goes on in a still and earthy atmosphere as of an overheated catacomb;[31] all along the formless coast bordered by dangerous surf, as if Nature herself had tried to ward off intruders; in and out of rivers, streams of death in life, whose banks were rotting into mud, whose waters, thickened into slime, invaded the contorted mangroves,[32] that seemed to writhe at us in the extremity of an impotent despair. Nowhere did we stop long enough to get a particularized impression, but the general sense of vague and oppressive wonder grew upon me. It was like a weary pilgrimage amongst hints for nightmares.

"It was upward of thirty days before I saw the mouth of the big river. We anchored off the seat of the government. But my work would not begin till some two hundred miles farther on. So as soon as I could I made a start for a place thirty miles higher up.

"I had my passage on a little sea-going steamer. Her captain was a Swede, and knowing me for a seaman, invited me on the bridge. He was a young man, lean, fair, and morose, with lanky hair and a shuffling gait. As we left the miserable little wharf, he tossed his head contemptuously at the shore. 'Been living there?' he asked. I said, 'Yes.' 'Fine lot these government chaps—are they not?' he went on, speaking English with great precision and considerable bitterness. 'It is funny what some people will do for a few francs a month. I wonder what becomes of that kind when it goes up country?' I said to him I expected to see that soon. 'So-o-o!' he exclaimed. He shuffled athwart,[33] keeping one eye ahead vigilantly. 'Don't be too sure,' he continued. 'The other day I took up a man who hanged himself on the road. He was a Swede, too.' 'Hanged himself! Why, in God's name?' I cried. He kept on looking out watchfully. 'Who knows? The sun too much for him, or the country perhaps.'

"At last we opened a reach.[34] A rocky cliff appeared, mounds of turned-up earth by the shore, houses on a hill, others with iron roofs, amongst a waste of excavations, or hanging to the declivity. A continuous noise of the rapids above hovered over this scene of inhabited devastation. A lot of people, mostly black and naked, moved about like ants. A jetty projected into the river. A blinding sunlight drowned all this at times in a sudden recrudescence of glare. 'There's your Company's station,' said the Swede, pointing to three wooden barrack-like structures on the rocky slope. 'I will send your things up. Four boxes did you say? So. Farewell.'

"I came upon a boiler wallowing in the grass, then found a path leading

[31] Underground tunnel containing graves. [32] Tropical evergreens. [33] Sideways.
[34] Straight stretch between curves of the river.

up the hill. It turned aside for the boulders, and also for an undersized railway-truck lying there on its back with its wheels in the air. One was off. The thing looked as dead as the carcass of some animal. I came upon more pieces of decaying machinery, a stack of rusty rails. To the left a clump of trees made a shady spot, where dark things seemed to stir feebly. I blinked, the path was steep. A horn tooted to the right, and I saw the black people run. A heavy and dull detonation shook the ground, a puff of smoke came out of the cliff, and that was all. No change appeared on the face of the rock. They were building a railway. The cliff was not in the way or anything; but this objectless blasting was all the work going on.

"A slight clinking behind me made me turn my head. Six black men advanced in a file, toiling up the path. They walked erect and slow, balancing small baskets full of earth on their heads, and the clink kept time with their footsteps. Black rags were wound round their loins, and the short ends behind waggled to and fro like tails. I could see every rib, the joints of their limbs were like knots in a rope; each had an iron collar on his neck, and all were connected together with a chain whose bights[35] swung between them, rhythmically clinking. Another report from the cliff made me think suddenly of that ship of war I had seen firing into a continent. It was the same kind of ominous voice; but these men could by no stretch of imagination be called enemies. They were called criminals, and the outraged law, like the bursting shells, had come to them, an insoluble mystery from the sea. All their meagre breasts panted together, the violently dilated nostrils quivered, the eyes stared stonily up-hill. They passed me within six inches, without a glance, with that complete, deathlike indifference of unhappy savages. Behind this raw matter one of the reclaimed, the product of the new forces at work, strolled despondently, carrying a rifle by its middle. He had a uniform jacket with one button off, and seeing a white man on the path, hoisted his weapon to his shoulder with alacrity. This was simple prudence, white men being so much alike at a distance that he could not tell who I might be. He was speedily reassured, and with a large, white, rascally grin, and a glance at his charge,[36] seemed to take me into partnership in his exalted trust. After all, I also was a part of the great cause of these high and just proceedings.

"Instead of going up, I turned and descended to the left. My idea was to let that chain-gang get out of sight before I climbed the hill. You know I am not particularly tender; I've had to strike and to fend off. I've had to resist and to attack sometimes—that's only one way of resisting—without counting the exact cost, according to the demands of such sort of life as I had blundered into. I've seen the devil of violence, and the devil of greed, and the devil of hot desire; but, by all the stars! these were strong, lusty, red-eyed devils, that swayed and drove men—men, I tell you. But as I stood on this hillside, I foresaw that in the blinding sunshine of that land I would become acquainted with a flabby, pretending, weak-eyed devil of a rapacious and pitiless folly. How insidious he could be, too, I was only to find out several months later and a thousand miles farther. For a moment I stood appalled, as though by a warning. Finally I descended the hill, obliquely, towards the trees I had seen.

[35] Slack lengths. [36] Those in his custody.

"I avoided a vast artificial hole somebody had been digging on the slope, the purpose of which I found it impossible to divine. It wasn't a quarry or a sandpit, anyhow. It was just a hole. It might have been connected with the philanthropic desire of giving the criminals something to do. I don't know. Then I nearly fell into a very narrow ravine, almost no more than a scar in the hillside. I discovered that a lot of imported drainage-pipes for the settlement had been tumbled in there. There wasn't one that was not broken. It was a wanton smash-up. At last I got under the trees. My purpose was to stroll into the shade for a moment; but no sooner within than it seemed to me I had stepped into the gloomy circle of some Inferno. The rapids were near, and an uninterrupted, uniform, headlong, rushing noise filled the mournful stillness of the grove, where not a breath stirred, not a leaf moved, with a mysterious sound—as though the tearing pace of the launched earth had suddenly become audible.

"Black shapes crouched, lay, sat between the trees leaning against the trunks, clinging to the earth, half coming out, half effaced within the dim light, in all the attitudes of pain, abandonment, and despair. Another mine[37] on the cliff went off, followed by a slight shudder of the soil under my feet. The work was going on. The work! And this was the place where some of the helpers had withdrawn to die.

"They were dying slowly—it was very clear. They were not enemies, they were not criminals, they were nothing earthly now,—nothing but black shadows of disease and starvation, lying confusedly in the greenish gloom. Brought from all the recesses of the coast in all the legality of time contracts, lost in uncongenial surroundings, fed on unfamiliar food, they sickened, became inefficient, and were then allowed to crawl away and rest. These moribund shapes were free as air—and nearly as thin. I began to distinguish the gleam of the eyes under the trees. Then, glancing down, I saw a face near my hand. The black bones reclined at full length with one shoulder against the tree, and slowly the eyelids rose and the sunken eyes looked up at me, enormous and vacant, a kind of blind, white flicker in the depths of the orbs, which died out slowly. The man seemed young—almost a boy—but you know with them it's hard to tell. I found nothing else to do but to offer him one of my good Swede's ship's biscuits I had in my pocket. The fingers closed slowly on it and held—there was no other movement and no other glance. He had tied a bit of white worsted round his neck—Why? Where did he get it? Was it a badge—an ornament—a charm—a propitiatory act? Was there any idea at all connected with it? It looked startling round his black neck, this bit of white thread from beyond the seas.

"Near the same tree two more bundles of acute angles sat with their legs drawn up. One, with his chin propped on his knees, stared at nothing, in an intolerable and appalling manner: his brother phantom rested its forehead, as if overcome with a great weariness; and all about others were scattered in every pose of contorted collapse, as in some picture of a massacre or a pestilence. While I stood horror-struck, one of these creatures rose to his hands and knees, and went off on all-fours towards the river to drink. He lapped out of his hand, then sat up in the sunlight, crossing his

[37] Explosive device.

shins in front of him, and after a time let his woolly head fall on his breast-bone.

"I didn't want any more loitering in the shade, and I made haste towards the station. When near the buildings I met a white man, in such an unexpected elegance of get-up that in the first moment I took him for a sort of vision. I saw a high starched collar, white cuffs, a light alpaca jacket, snowy trousers, a clean necktie, and varnished boots. No hat. Hair parted, brushed, oiled, under a green-lined parasol held in a big white hand. He was amazing, and had a pen-holder behind his ear.

"I shook hands with this miracle, and I learned he was the Company's chief accountant, and that all the book-keeping was done at this station. He had come out for a moment, he said, 'to get a breath of fresh air.' The expression sounded wonderfully odd, with its suggestion of sedentary desk-life. I wouldn't have mentioned the fellow to you at all, only it was from his lips that I first heard the name of the man who is so indissolubly connected with the memories of that time. Moreover, I respected the fellow. Yes; I respected his collars, his vast cuffs, his brushed hair. His appearance was certainly that of a hairdresser's dummy; but in the great demoralization of the land he kept up his appearance. That's backbone. His starched collars and got-up shirt-fronts were achievements of character. He had been out nearly three years; and, later, I could not help asking him how he managed to sport such linen. He had just the faintest blush, and said modestly, 'I've been teaching one of the native women about the station. It was difficult. She had a distaste for the work.' Thus this man had verily accomplished something. And he was devoted to his books, which were in apple-pie order.

"Everything else in the station was in a muddle,—heads, things, buildings. Strings of dusty niggers with splay feet arrived and departed; a stream of manufactured goods, rubbishy cottons, beads, and brass-wire sent into the depths of darkness, and in return came a precious trickle of ivory.

"I had to wait in the station for ten days—an eternity. I lived in a hut in the yard, but to be out of the chaos I would sometimes get into the accountant's office. It was built of horizontal planks, and so badly put together that, as he bent over his high desk, he was barred from neck to heels with narrow strips of sunlight. There was no need to open the big shutter to see. It was hot there, too; big flies buzzed fiendishly, and did not sting, but stabbed. I sat generally on the floor, while, of faultless appearance (and even slightly scented), perching on a high stool, he wrote, he wrote. Sometimes he stood up for exercise. When a truckle-bed with a sick man (some invalid agent from up-country) was put in there, he exhibited a gentle annoyance. 'The groans of this sick person,' he said, 'distract my attention. And without that it is extremely difficult to guard against clerical errors in this climate.'

"One day he remarked, without lifting his head, 'In the interior you will no doubt meet Mr. Kurtz.' On my asking who Mr. Kurtz was, he said he was a first-class agent; and seeing my disappointment at this information, he added slowly, laying down his pen, 'He is a very remarkable person.' Further questions elicited from him that Mr. Kurtz was at present in charge of a trading post, a very important one, in the true ivory-country, at 'the very bottom of there. Sends in as much ivory as all the others put

together. . . .' He began to write again. The sick man was too ill to groan. The flies buzzed in a great peace.

"Suddenly there was a growing murmur of voices and a great tramping of feet. A caravan had come in. A violent babble of uncouth sounds burst out on the other side of the planks. All the carriers were speaking together, and in the midst of the uproar the lamentable voice of the chief agent was heard 'giving it up' tearfully for the twentieth time that day. . . . He rose slowly. 'What a frightful row,' he said. He crossed the room gently to look at the sick man, and returning, said to me, 'He does not hear.' 'What! Dead?' I asked, startled. 'No, not yet,' he answered, with great composure. Then, alluding with a toss of the head to the tumult in the station-yard, 'When one has got to make correct entries, one comes to hate those savages—hate them to the death.' He remained thoughtful for a moment. 'When you see Mr. Kurtz,' he went on, 'tell him from me that everything here'—he glanced at the desk—'is very satisfactory. I don't like to write to him—with those messengers of ours you never know who may get hold of your letter—at that Central Station.' He stared at me for a moment with his mild, bulging eyes. 'Oh, he will go far, very far,' he began again. 'He will be a somebody in the Administration before long. They, above—the Council in Europe, you know—mean him to be.'

"He turned to his work. The noise outside had ceased, and presently in going out I stopped at the door. In the steady buzz of flies the homeward-bound agent was lying flushed and insensible; the other, bent over his books, was making correct entries of perfectly correct transactions; and fifty feet below the doorstep I could see the still treetops of the grove of death.

"Next day I left that station at last, with a caravan of sixty men, for a two-hundred-mile tramp.

"No use telling you much about that. Paths, paths, everywhere; a stamped-in network of paths spreading over the empty land, through long grass, through burnt grass, through thickets, down and up chilly ravines, up and down stony hills ablaze with heat; and a solitude, a solitude, nobody, not a hut. The population had cleared out a long time ago. Well, if a lot of mysterious niggers armed with all kinds of fearful weapons suddenly took to traveling on the road between Deal[38] and Gravesend, catching the yokels right and left to carry heavy loads for them, I fancy every farm and cottage thereabouts would get empty very soon. Only here the dwellings were gone, too. Still I passed through several abandoned villages. There's something pathetically childish in the ruins of grass walls. Day after day, with the stamp and shuffle of sixty pair of bare feet behind me, each pair under a 60-lb. load. Camp, cook, sleep, strike camp, march. Now and then a carrier dead in harness, at rest in the long grass near the path, with an empty water-gourd and his long staff lying by his side. A great silence around and above. Perhaps on some quiet night the tremor of far-off drums, sinking, swelling, a tremor vast, faint; a sound weird, appealing, suggestive, and wild—and perhaps with as profound a meaning as the sound of bells in a Christian country. Once a white man in an unbuttoned

[38] A port on the English Channel.

uniform, camping on the path with an armed escort of lank Zanzibaris,[39] very hospitable and festive—not to say drunk. Was looking after the upkeep of the road, he declared. Can't say I saw any road or any upkeep, unless the body of a middle-aged negro, with a bullet-hole in the forehead, upon which I absolutely stumbled three miles farther on, may be considered as a permanent improvement. I had a white companion, too, not a bad chap, but rather too fleshy and with the exasperating habit of fainting on the hot hillsides, miles away from the least bit of shade and water. Annoying, you know, to hold your own coat like a parasol over a man's head while he is coming-to. I couldn't help asking him once what he meant by coming there at all. 'To make money, of course. What do you think?' he said, scornfully. Then he got fever, and had to be carried in a hammock slung under a pole. As he weighed sixteen stone[40] I had no end of rows with the carriers. They jibbed,[41] ran away, sneaked off with their loads in the night—quite a mutiny. So, one evening, I made a speech in English with gestures, not one of which was lost to the sixty pairs of eyes before me, and the next morning I started the hammock off in front all right. An hour afterwards I came upon the whole concern wrecked in a bush—man, hammock, groans, blankets, horrors. The heavy pole had skinned his poor nose. He was very anxious for me to kill somebody, but there wasn't the shadow of a carrier near. I remembered the old doctor—'It would be interesting for science to watch the mental changes of individuals, on the spot.' I felt I was becoming scientifically interesting. However, all that is to no purpose. On the fifteenth day I came in sight of the big river again, and hobbled into the Central Station. It was on a back water surrounded by scrub and forest, with a pretty border of smelly mud on one side, and on the three others enclosed by a crazy fence of rushes. A neglected gap was all the gate it had, and the first glance at the place was enough to let you see the flabby devil was running that show. White men with long staves in their hands appeared languidly from amongst the buildings, strolling up to take a look at me, and then retired out of sight somewhere. One of them, a stout, excitable chap with black moustaches, informed me with great volubility and many digressions, as soon as I told him who I was, that my steamer was at the bottom of the river. I was thunderstruck. What, how, why? Oh, it was 'all right.' The 'manager himself' was there. All quite correct. 'Everybody had behaved splendidly! splendidly!'—'you must,' he said in agitation, 'go and see the general manager at once. He is waiting!'

"I did not see the real significance of that wreck at once. I fancy I see it now, but I am not sure—not at all. Certainly the affair was too stupid—when I think of it—to be altogether natural. Still . . . But at the moment it presented itself simply as a confounded nuisance. The steamer was sunk. They had started two days before in a sudden hurry up the river with the manager on board, in charge of some volunteer skipper, and before they had been out three hours they tore the bottom out of her on stones, and she sank near the south bank. I asked myself what I was to do there, now my boat was lost. As a matter of fact, I had plenty to do in fishing my

[39] Hired men from Zanzibar, a large island off the east coast of Africa.
[40] Fourteen-pound British unit of weight; thus, 224 pounds. [41] Balked.

command out of the river. I had to set about it the very next day. That, and the repairs when I brought the pieces to the station, took some months.

"My first interview with the manager was curious. He did not ask me to sit down after my twenty-mile walk that morning. He was commonplace in complexion, in feature, in manners, and in voice. He was of middle size and of ordinary build. His eyes, of the usual blue, were perhaps remarkably cold, and he certainly could make his glance fall on one as trenchant and heavy as an axe. But even at these times the rest of his person seemed to disclaim the intention. Otherwise there was only an indefinable, faint expression of his lips, something stealthy—a smile—not a smile—I remember it, but I can't explain. It was unconscious, this smile was, though just after he had said something it got intensified for an instant. It came at the end of his speeches like a seal applied on the words to make the meaning of the commonest phrase appear absolutely inscrutable. He was a common trader, from his youth up employed in these parts—nothing more. He was obeyed, yet he inspired neither love nor fear, nor even respect. He inspired uneasiness. That was it! Uneasiness. Not a definite mistrust—just uneasiness—nothing more. You have no idea how effective such a . . . a . . . faculty can be. He had no genius for organizing, for initiative, or for order even. That was evident in such things as the deplorable state of the station. He had no learning, and no intelligence. His position had come to him—why? Perhaps because he was never ill . . . He had served three terms of three years out there . . . Because triumphant health in the general rout of constitutions is a kind of power in itself. When he went home on leave he rioted on a large scale—pompously. Jack[42] ashore—with a difference—in externals only. This one could gather from his casual talk. He originated nothing, he could keep the routine going—that's all. But he was great. He was great by this little thing that it was impossible to tell what could control such a man. He never gave that secret away. Perhaps there was nothing within him. Such a suspicion made one pause—for out there there were no external checks. Once when various tropical diseases had laid low almost every 'agent' in the station, he was heard to say, 'Men who come out here should have no entrails.' He sealed the utterance with that smile of his, as though it had been a door opening into a darkness he had in his keeping. You fancied you had seen things—but the seal was on. When annoyed at mealtimes by the constant quarrels of the white men about precedence, he ordered an immense round table to be made, for which a special house had to be built. This was the station's mess-room. Where he sat was the first place—the rest were nowhere. One felt this to be his unalterable conviction. He was neither civil nor uncivil. He was quiet. He allowed his 'boy'—an overfed young negro from the coast—to treat the white men, under his very eyes, with provoking insolence.

"He began to speak as soon as he saw me. I had been very long on the road. He could not wait. Had to start without me. The up-river stations had to be relieved. There had been so many delays already that he did not know who was dead and who was alive, and how they got on—and so on, and so on. He paid no attention to my explanations, and, playing with a stick of

[42] Jack-tar; sailor.

sealing-wax, repeated several times that the situation was 'very grave, very grave.' There were rumours that a very important station was in jeopardy, and its chief, Mr. Kurtz, was ill. Hoped it was not true. Mr. Kurtz was . . . I felt weary and irritable. Hang Kurtz, I thought. I interrupted him by saying I had heard of Mr. Kurtz on the coast. 'Ah! So they talk of him down there,' he murmured to himself. Then he began again, assuring me Mr. Kurtz was the best agent he had, an exceptional man, of the greatest importance to the Company; therefore I could understand his anxiety. He was, he said, 'very, very uneasy.' Certainly he fidgeted on his chair a good deal, exclaimed, 'Ah, Mr. Kurtz!' broke the stick of sealing-wax and seemed dumfounded by the accident. Next thing he wanted to know 'how long it would take to' . . . I interrupted him again. Being hungry, you know, and kept on my feet too, I was getting savage. 'How can I tell?' I said. 'I haven't even seen the wreck yet—some months, no doubt.' All this talk seemed to me so futile. 'Some months,' he said. 'Well, let us say three months before we can make a start. Yes. That ought to do the affair.' I flung out of his hut (he lived all alone in a clay hut with a sort of verandah) muttering to myself my opinion of him. He was a chattering idiot. Afterwards I took it back when it was borne in upon me startlingly with what extreme nicety he had estimated the time requisite for the 'affair.'

"I went to work the next day, turning, so to speak, my back on that station. In that way only it seemed to me I could keep my hold on the redeeming facts of life. Still, one must look about sometimes; and then I saw this station, these men strolling aimlessly about in the sunshine of the yard. I asked myself sometimes what it all meant. They wandered here and there with their absurd long staves in their hands, like a lot of faithless pilgrims bewitched inside a rotten fence. The word 'ivory' rang in the air, was whispered, was sighed. You would think they were praying to it. A taint of imbecile rapacity blew through it all, like a whiff from some corpse. By Jove! I've never seen anything so unreal in my life. And outside, the silent wilderness surrounding this cleared speck on the earth struck me as something great and invincible, like evil or truth, waiting patiently for the passing away of this fantastic invasion.

"Oh, those months! Well, never mind. Various things happened. One evening a grass shed full of calico, cotton prints, beads, and I don't know what else, burst into a blaze so suddenly that you would have thought the earth had opened to let an avenging fire consume all that trash. I was smoking my pipe quietly by my dismantled steamer, and saw them all cutting capers in the light, with their arms lifted high, when the stout man with moustaches came tearing down to the river, a tin pail in his hand, assured me that everybody was 'behaving splendidly, splendidly,' dipped about a quart of water and tore back again. I noticed there was a hole in the bottom of his pail.

"I strolled up. There was no hurry. You see the thing had gone off like a box of matches. It had been hopeless from the very first. The flame had leaped high, driven everybody back, lighted up everything—and collapsed. The shed was already a heap of embers glowing fiercely. A nigger was being beaten near by. They said he had caused the fire in some way; be that as it may, he was screeching most horribly. I saw him, later, for several days, sitting in a bit of shade looking very sick and trying to recover him-

self: afterwards he arose and went out—and the wilderness without a sound took him into its bosom again. As I approached the glow from the dark I found myself at the back of two men, talking. I heard the name of Kurtz pronounced, then the words, 'take advantage of this unfortunate accident.' One of the men was the manager. I wished him a good evening. 'Did you ever see anything like it—eh? it is incredible,' he said, and walked off. The other man remained. He was a first-class agent, young, gentlemanly, a bit reserved, with a forked little beard and a hooked nose. He was stand-offish with the other agents, and they on their side said he was the manager's spy upon them. As to me, I had hardly ever spoken to him before. We got into talk, and by and by we strolled away from the hissing ruins. Then he asked me to his room, which was in the main building of the station. He struck a match, and I perceived that this young aristocrat had not only a silver-mounted dressing-case but also a whole candle all to himself. Just at that time the manager was the only man supposed to have any right to candles. Native mats covered the clay walls; a collection of spears, assegais,[43] shields, knives was hung up in trophies. The business intrusted to this fellow was the making of bricks—so I had been informed; but there wasn't a fragment of a brick anywhere in the station, and he had been there more than a year—waiting. It seems he could not make bricks without something, I don't know what—straw[44] maybe. Anyways, it could not be found there, and as it was not likely to be sent from Europe, it did not appear clear to me what he was waiting for. An act of special creation[45] perhaps. However, they were all waiting—all the sixteen or twenty pilgrims of them—for something; and upon my word it did not seem an uncongenial occupation, from the way they took it, though the only thing that ever came to them was disease—as far as I could see. They beguiled the time by backbiting and intriguing against each other in a foolish kind of way. There was an air of plotting about that station, but nothing came of it, of course. It was as unreal as everything else—as the philanthropic pretence of the whole concern, as their talk, as their government, as their show of work. The only real feeling was a desire to get appointed to a trading-post where ivory was to be had, so that they could earn percentages. They intrigued and slandered and hated each other only on that account,—but as to effectually lifting a little finger—oh, no. By heavens! there is something after all in the world allowing one man to steal a horse while another must not look at a halter. Steal a horse straight out. Very well. He has done it. Perhaps he can ride. But there is a way of looking at a halter that would provoke the most charitable of saints into a kick.

"I had no idea why he wanted to be sociable, but as we chatted in there it suddenly occurred to me the fellow was trying to get at something—in fact, pumping me. He alluded constantly to Europe, to the people I was supposed to know there—putting leading questions as to my acquaintances in the sepulchral city, and so on. His little eyes glittered like mica discs—with curiosity—though he tried to keep up a bit of superciliousness. At first I

[43] Javelins used by south-African tribes.

[44] The ancient Hebrews, enslaved in Egypt, were required to deliver their usual quota of bricks though deprived of the straw needed to make them, an instance of senseless tyranny. See Exodus 5.

[45] The belief, rejected by evolutionists, that God created each species separately.

was astonished, but very soon I became awfully curious to see what he would find out from me. I couldn't possibly imagine what I had in me to make it worth his while. It was very pretty to see how he baffled himself, for in truth my body was full only of chills, and my head had nothing in it but that wretched steamboat business. It was evident he took me for a perfectly shameless prevaricator. At last he got angry, and, to conceal a movement of furious annoyance, he yawned. I rose. Then I noticed a small sketch in oils, on a panel, representing a woman, draped and blindfolded, carrying a lighted torch. The background was sombre—almost black. The movement of the woman was stately, and the effect of the torch-light on the face was sinister.

"It arrested me, and he stood by civilly, holding an empty half-pint champagne bottle (medical comforts) with the candle stuck in it. To my question he said Mr. Kurtz had painted this—in this very station more than a year ago—while waiting for means to go to his trading-post. "Tell me, pray,' said I, 'who is this Mr. Kurtz?'

"'The chief of the Inner Station,' he answered in a short tone, looking away. 'Much obliged,' I said, laughing. 'And you are the brickmaker of the Central Station. Everyone knows that.' He was silent for a while. 'He is a prodigy,' he said at last. 'He is an emissary of pity, and science, and progress, and devil knows what else. We want,' he began to declaim suddenly, 'for the guidance of the cause intrusted to us by Europe, so to speak, higher intelligence, wide sympathies, a singleness of purpose.' 'Who says that?' I asked. 'Lots of them,' he replied. 'Some even write that; and so *he* comes here, a special being, as you ought to know.' 'Why ought I to know?' I interrupted, really surprised. He paid no attention. 'Yes. To-day he is chief of the best station, next year he will be assistant-manager, two years more and . . . but I daresay you know what he will be in two years' time. You are of the new gang—the gang of virtue. The same people who sent him specially also recommended you. Oh, don't say no. I've my own eyes to trust.' Light dawned upon me. My dear aunt's influential acquaintances were producing an unexpected effect upon that young man. I nearly burst into a laugh. 'Do you read the Company's confidential correspondence?' I asked. He hadn't a word to say. It was great fun. 'When Mr. Kurtz,' I continued, severely, 'is General Manager, you won't have the opportunity.'

"He blew the candle out suddenly, and we went outside. The moon had risen. Black figures strolled about listlessly, pouring water on the glow, whence proceeded a sound of hissing; steam ascended in the moonlight, the beaten nigger groaned somewhere. 'What a row the brute makes!' said the indefatigable man with the moustaches, appearing near us. 'Serve him right. Transgression—punishment—bang! Pitiless, pitiless. That's the only way. This will prevent all conflagrations for the future. I was just telling the manager . . .' He noticed my companion, and became crestfallen all at once. 'Not in bed yet,' he said, with a kind of servile heartiness; 'it's so natural. Ha! Danger—agitation.' He vanished. I went on to the river-side, and the other followed me. I heard a scathing murmur at my ear. 'Heap of muffs—go to.' The pilgrims could be seen in knots gesticulating, discussing. Several had still their staves in their hands. I verily believe they took these sticks to bed with them. Beyond the fence the forest stood up spectrally in the moonlight, and through the dim stir, through the faint

sounds of that lamentable courtyard, the silence of the land went home to one's very heart—its mystery, its greatness, the amazing reality of its concealed life. The hurt nigger moaned feebly somewhere near by, and then fetched a deep sigh that made me mend my pace away from there. I felt a hand introducing itself under my arm. 'My dear sir,' said the fellow, 'I don't want to be misunderstood, and especially by you, who will see Mr. Kurtz long before I can have that pleasure. I wouldn't like him to get a false idea of my disposition. . . .'

"I let him run on, this papier-maché Mephistopheles,[46] and it seemed to me that if I tried I could poke my forefinger through him, and would find nothing inside but a little loose dirt, maybe. He, don't you see, had been planning to be assistant-manager by and by under the present man, and I could see that the coming of that Kurtz had upset them both not a little. He talked precipitately, and I did not try to stop him. I had my shoulders against the wreck of my steamer, hauled up on the slope like a carcass of some big river animal. The smell of mud, of primeval mud, by Jove! was in my nostrils, the high stillness of primeval forest was before my eyes; there were shiny patches on the black creek. The moon had spread over everything a thin layer of silver—over the rank grass, over the mud, upon the wall of matted vegetation standing higher than the wall of a temple, over the great river I could see through a sombre gap glittering, glittering, as it flowed broadly by without a murmur. All this was great, expectant, mute, while the man jabbered about himself. I wondered whether the stillness on the face of the immensity looking at us two were meant as an appeal or as a menace. What were we who had strayed in here? Could we handle that dumb thing, or would it handle us? I felt how big, how confoundedly big, was that thing that couldn't talk, and perhaps was deaf as well. What was in there? I could see a little ivory coming out from there, and I had heard Mr. Kurtz was in there. I had heard enough about it, too—God knows! Yet somehow it didn't bring any image with it—no more than if I had been told an angel or a fiend was in there. I believed it in the same way one of you might believe there are inhabitants in the planet Mars. I knew once a Scotch sailmaker who was certain, dead sure, there were people in Mars. If you asked him for some idea how they looked and behaved, he would get shy and mutter something about 'walking on all-fours.' If you as much as smiled, he would—though a man of sixty—offer to fight you. I would not have gone so far as to fight for Kurtz, but I went for him near enough to a lie. You know I hate, detest, and can't bear a lie, not because I am straighter than the rest of us, but simply because it appalls me. There is a taint of death, a flavour of mortality in lies—which is exactly what I hate and detest in the world—what I want to forget. It makes me miserable and sick, like biting something rotten would do. Temperament, I suppose. Well, I went near enough to it by letting the young fool there believe anything he liked to imagine as to my influence in Europe. I became in an instant as much of a pretence as the rest of the bewitched pilgrims. This simply because I had a notion it somehow would be of help to that Kurtz whom at the time I did not see—you understand. He was just a word for me. I did not see the man in the name any more than you do. Do you see him? Do you see the story?

[46] The devil who bargains for the legendary Faust's soul.

Do you see anything? It seems to me I am trying to tell you a dream—making a vain attempt, because no relation of a dream can convey the dream-sensation, that commingling of absurdity, surprise, and bewilderment in a tremor of struggling revolt, that notion of being captured by the incredible which is of the very essence of dreams . . .”

He was silent for a while.

“. . . No, it is impossible; it is impossible to convey the life-sensation of any given epoch of one’s existence—that which makes its truth, its meaning—its subtle and penetrating essence. It is impossible. We live, as we dream—alone. . . .”

He paused again as if reflecting, then added—

“Of course in this you fellows see more than I could then. You see me, whom you know. . . .”

It had become so pitch dark that we listeners could hardly see one another. For a long time already he, sitting apart, had been no more to us than a voice. There was not a word from anybody. The others might have been asleep, but I was awake. I listened, I listened on the watch for the sentence, for the word, that would give me the clue to the faint uneasiness inspired by this narrative that seemed to shape itself without human lips in the heavy night-air of the river.

“. . . Yes—I let him run on,” Marlow began again, “and think what he pleased about the powers that were behind me. I did! And there was nothing behind me! There was nothing but that wretched, old, mangled steamboat I was leaning against, while he talked fluently about ‘the necessity for every man to get on.’ ‘And when one comes out here, you conceive, it is not to gaze at the moon.’ Mr. Kurtz was a ‘universal genius,’ but even a genius would find it easier to work with ‘adequate tools—intelligent men.’ He did not make bricks—why, there was a physical impossibility in the way—as I was well aware; and if he did secretarial work for the manager, it was because ‘no sensible man rejects wantonly the confidence of his superiors.’ Did I see it? I saw it. What more did I want? What I really wanted was rivets, by heaven! Rivets. To get on with the work—to stop the hole. Rivets I wanted. There were cases of them down at the coast—cases—piled up—burst—split! You kicked a loose rivet at every second step in that station yard on the hillside. Rivets had rolled into the grove of death. You could fill your pockets with rivets for the trouble of stooping down—and there wasn’t one rivet to be found where it was wanted. We had plates that would do, but nothing to fasten them with. And every week the messenger, a lone negro, letter-bag on shoulder and staff in hand, left our station for the coast. And several times a week a coast caravan came in with trade goods—ghastly glazed calico that made you shudder only to look at it, glass beads value about a penny a quart, confounded spotted cotton handkerchiefs. And no rivets. Three carriers could have brought all that was wanted to set that steamboat afloat.

“He was becoming confidential now, but I fancy my unresponsive attitude must have exasperated him at last, for he judged it necessary to inform me he feared neither God nor devil, let alone any mere man. I said I could see that very well, but what I wanted was a certain quantity of rivets—and rivets were what really Mr. Kurtz wanted, if he had only known it. Now letters went to the coast every week. . . . ‘My dear sir,’ he cried, ‘I

write from dictation.' I demanded rivets. There was a way—for an intelligent man. He changed his manner; became very cold, and suddenly began to talk about a hippopotamus; wondered whether sleeping on board the steamer (I stuck to my salvage night and day) I wasn't disturbed. There was an old hippo that had the bad habit of getting out on the bank and roaming at night over the station grounds. The pilgrims used to turn out in a body and empty every rifle they could lay hands on at him. Some even had sat up o' nights for him. All this energy was wasted, though. 'That animal has a charmed life,' he said; 'but you can say this only of brutes in this country. No man—you apprehend me?—no man here bears a charmed life.' He stood there for a moment in the moonlight with his delicate hooked nose set a little askew, and his mica eyes glittering without a wink, then, with a curt Good-night, he strode off. I could see he was disturbed and considerably puzzled, which made me feel more hopeful than I had been for days. It was a great comfort to turn from that chap to my influential friend, the battered, twisted, ruined, tin-pot steamboat. I clambered on board. She rang under my feet like an empty Huntley & Palmer biscuit-tin kicked along a gutter; she was nothing so solid in make, and rather less pretty in shape, but I had expended enough hard work on her to make me love her. No influential friend would have served me better. She had given me a chance to come out a bit—to find out what I could do. No, I don't like work. I had rather laze about and think of all the fine things that can be done. I don't like work—no man does—but I like what is in the work,—the chance to find yourself. Your own reality—for yourself, not for others— what no other man can ever know. They can only see the mere show, and never can tell what it really means.

"I was not surprised to see somebody sitting aft, on the deck, with his legs dangling over the mud. You see I rather chummed with the few mechanics there were in that station, whom the other pilgrims naturally despised—on account of their imperfect manners, I suppose. This was the foreman—a boiler-maker by trade—a good worker. He was a lank, bony, yellow-faced man, with big intense eyes. His aspect was worried, and his head was as bald as the palm of my hand; but his hair in falling seemed to have stuck to his chin, and had prospered in the new locality, for his beard hung down to his waist. He was a widower with six young children (he had left them in charge of a sister of his to come out there), and the passion of his life was pigeon-flying. He was an enthusiast and a connoisseur. He would rave about pigeons. After work hours he used sometimes to come over from his hut for a talk about his children and his pigeons; at work, when he had to crawl in the mud under the bottom of the steamboat, he would tie up that beard of his in a kind of white serviette[47] he brought for the purpose. It had loops to go over his ears. In the evening he could be seen squatted on the bank rinsing that wrapper in the creek with great care, then spreading it solemnly on a bush to dry.

"I slapped him on the back and shouted, 'We shall have rivets!' He scrambled to his feet exclaiming, 'No! Rivets!' as though he couldn't believe his ears. Then in a low voice, 'You . . . eh?' I don't know why we behaved like lunatics. I put my finger to the side of my nose and nodded mysteri-

[47] Napkin.

ously. 'Good for you!' he cried, snapped his fingers above his head, lifting
one foot. I tried a jig. We capered on the iron deck. A frightful clatter came
out of that hulk, and the virgin forest on the other bank of the creek sent it
back in a thundering roll upon the sleeping station. It must have made
some of the pilgrims sit up in their hovels. A dark figure obscured the
lighted doorway of the manager's hut, vanished, then, a second or so after,
the doorway itself vanished, too. We stopped, and the silence driven away
by the stamping of our feet flowed back again from the recesses of the land.
The great wall of vegetation, an exuberant and entangled mass of trunks,
branches, leaves, boughs, festoons, motionless in the moonlight, was like a
rioting invasion of soundless life, a rolling wave of plants, piled up, crested,
ready to topple over the creek, to sweep every little man of us out of his
little existence. And it moved not. A deadened burst of mighty splashes
and snorts reached us from afar, as though an ichthyosaurus[48] had been
taking a bath of glitter in the great river. 'After all,' said the boiler-maker in
a reasonable tone, 'why shouldn't we get the rivets?' Why not, indeed! I did
not know of any reason why we shouldn't. 'They'll come in three weeks,' I
said, confidently.

"But they didn't. Instead of rivets there came an invasion, an infliction,
a visitation. It came in sections during the next three weeks, each section
headed by a donkey carrying a white man in new clothes and tan shoes,
bowing from that elevation right and left to the impressed pilgrims. A
quarrelsome band of footsore sulky niggers trod on the heels of the don-
key; a lot of tents, camp-stools, tin boxes, white cases, brown bales would be
shot down in the courtyard, and the air of mystery would deepen a little
over the muddle of the station. Five such instalments came, with their ab-
surd air of disorderly flight with the loot of innumerable outfit shops and
provision stores, that, one would think, they were lugging, after a raid, into
the wilderness for equitable division. It was an inextricable mess of things
decent in themselves but that human folly made look like the spoils of
thieving.

"This devoted band called itself the Eldorado[49] Exploring Expedition,
and I believe they were sworn to secrecy. Their talk, however, was the talk
of sordid buccaneers: it was reckless without hardihood, greedy without
audacity, and cruel without courage; there was not an atom of foresight or
of serious intention in the whole batch of them, and they did not seem
aware these things are wanted for the work of the world. To tear treasure
out of the bowels of the land was their desire, with no more moral purpose
at the back of it than there is in burglars breaking into a safe. Who paid the
expenses of the noble enterprise I don't know; but the uncle of our man-
ager was leader of that lot.

"In exterior he resembled a butcher in a poor neighbourhood, and his
eyes had a look of sleepy cunning. He carried his fat paunch with ostenta-
tion on his short legs, and during the time his gang infested the station
spoke to no one but his nephew. You could see these two roaming about all
day long with their heads close together in an everlasting confab.[50]

[48] Primeval marine reptile.
[49] The name of a legendary Latin American kingdom supposed to be rich in gold and
gems.
[50] Talk.

"I had given up worrying myself about the rivets. One's capacity for that kind of folly is more limited than you would suppose. I said Hang!—and let things slide. I had plenty of time for meditation, and now and then I would give some thought to Kurtz. I wasn't very interested in him. No. Still, I was curious to see whether this man, who had come out equipped with moral ideas of some sort, would climb to the top after all and how he would set about his work when there."

II

"One evening as I was lying flat on the deck of my steamboat, I heard voices approaching—and there were the nephew and the uncle strolling along the bank. I laid my head on my arm again, and had nearly lost myself in a doze, when somebody said in my ear, as it were: 'I am as harmless as a little child, but I don't like to be dictated to. Am I the manager—or am I not? I was ordered to send him there. It's incredible.' . . . I became aware that the two were standing on the shore alongside the forepart of the steamboat, just below my head. I did not move; it did not occur to me to move: I was sleepy. 'It *is* unpleasant,' grunted the uncle. 'He has asked the Administration to be sent there,' said the other, 'with the idea of showing what he could do; and I was instructed accordingly. Look at the influence that man must have. Is it not frightful?' They both agreed it was frightful, then made several bizarre remarks: 'Make rain and fine weather—one man—the Council—by the nose'—bits of absurd sentences that got the better of my drowsiness, so that I had pretty near the whole of my wits about me when the uncle said, 'The climate may do away with this difficulty for you. Is he alone there?' 'Yes,' answered the manager; 'he sent his assistant down the river with a note to me in these terms: "Clear this poor devil out of the country, and don't bother sending more of that sort. I had rather be alone than have the kind of men you can dispose of with me." It was more than a year ago. Can you imagine such impudence!' 'Anything since then?' asked the other, hoarsely. 'Ivory,' jerked the nephew; 'lots of it— prime sort—lots—most annoying, from him.' 'And with that?' questioned the heavy rumble. 'Invoice,' was the reply fired out, so to speak. Then silence. They had been talking about Kurtz.

"I was broad awake by this time, but, lying perfectly at ease, remained still, having no inducement to change my position. 'How did that ivory come all this way?' growled the elder man, who seemed very vexed. The other explained that it had come with a fleet of canoes in charge of an English half-caste clerk Kurtz had with him; that Kurtz had apparently intended to return himself, the station being by that time bare of goods and stores, but after coming three hundred miles, had suddenly decided to go back, which he started to do alone in a small dugout with four paddlers, leaving the half-caste to continue down the river with the ivory. The two fellows there seemed astounded at anybody attempting such a thing. They were at a loss for an adequate motive. As to me, I seemed to see Kurtz for the first time. It was a distinct glimpse: the dugout, four paddling savages, and the lone white man turning his back suddenly on the headquarters, on relief, on thoughts of home—perhaps; setting his face towards the depths

of the wilderness, towards his empty and desolate station. I did not know the motive. Perhaps he was just simply a fine fellow who stuck to his work for its own sake. His name, you understand, had not been pronounced once. He was 'that man.' The half-caste, who, as far as I could see, had conducted a difficult trip with great prudence and pluck, was invariably alluded to as 'that scoundrel.' The 'scoundrel' had reported that the 'man' had been very ill—had recovered imperfectly. . . . The two below me moved away then a few paces, and strolled back and forth at some little distance. I heard: 'Military post—doctor—two hundred miles—quite alone now—unavoidable delays—nine months—no news—strange rumours.' They approached again, just as the manager was saying, 'No one, as far as I know, unless a species of wandering trader—a pestilential fellow, snapping ivory from the natives.' Who was it they were talking about now? I gathered in snatches that this was some man supposed to be in Kurtz's district, and of whom the manager did not approve. 'We will not be free from unfair competition till one of these fellows is hanged for an example,' he said. 'Certainly,' grunted the other; 'get him hanged! Why not? Anything—anything can be done in this country. That's what I say; nobody here, you understand, *here*, can endanger your position. And why? You stand the climate—you outlast them all. The danger is in Europe; but there before I left I took care to——' They moved off and whispered, then their voices rose again. 'The extraordinary series of delays is not my fault. I did my best.' The fat man sighed. 'Very sad.' 'And the pestiferous absurdity of his talk,' continued the other; 'he bothered me enough when he was here. "Each station should be like a beacon on the road towards better things, a centre for trade of course, but also for humanizing, improving, instructing." Conceive you—that ass! And he wants to be manager! No, it's——' Here he got choked by excessive indignation, and I lifted my head the least bit. I was surprised to see how near they were—right under me. I could have spat upon their hats. They were looking on the ground, absorbed in thought. The manager was switching his leg with a slender twig: his sagacious relative lifted his head. 'You have been well since you came out this time?' he asked. The other gave a start. 'Who? I? Oh! Like a charm—like a charm. But the rest—oh, my goodness! All sick. They die so quick, too, that I haven't the time to send them out of the country—it's incredible!' 'H'm. Just so,' grunted the uncle. 'Ah! my boy, trust to this—I say, trust to this.' I saw him extend his short flipper of an arm for a gesture that took in the forest, the creek, the mud, the river,—seemed to beckon with a dishonouring flourish before the sunlit face of the land a treacherous appeal to the lurking death, to the hidden evil, to the profound darkness of its heart. It was so startling that I leaped to my feet and looked back at the edge of the forest, as though I had expected an answer of some sort to that black display of confidence. You know the foolish notions that come to one sometimes. The high stillness confronted these two figures with its ominous patience, waiting for the passing away of a fantastic invasion.

"They swore aloud together—out of sheer fright, I believe—then pretending not to know anything of my existence, turned back to the station. The sun was low; and leaning forward side by side, they seemed to be tugging painfully uphill their two ridiculous shadows of unequal length,

that trailed behind them slowly over the tall grass without bending a single blade.

"In a few days the Eldorado Expedition went into the patient wilderness, that closed upon it as the sea closes over a diver. Long afterwards the news came that all the donkeys were dead. I know nothing as to the fate of the less valuable animals. They, no doubt, like the rest of us, found what they deserved. I did not inquire. I was then rather excited at the prospect of meeting Kurtz very soon. When I say very soon I mean it comparatively. It was just two months from the day we left the creek when we came to the bank below Kurtz's station.

"Going up that river was like travelling back to the earliest beginnings of the world, when vegetation rioted on the earth and the big trees were kings. An empty stream, a great silence, an impenetrable forest. The air was warm, thick, heavy, sluggish. There was no joy in the brilliance of sunshine. The long stretches of the waterway ran on, deserted, into the gloom of overshadowed distances. On silvery sandbanks hippos and alligators sunned themselves side by side. The broadening waters flowed through a mob of wooded islands; you lost your way on that river as you would in a desert, and butted all day long against shoals, trying to find the channel, till you thought yourself bewitched and cut off for ever from everything you had known once—somewhere—far away—in another existence perhaps. There were moments when one's past came back to one, as it will sometimes when you have not a moment to spare to yourself; but it came in the shape of an unrestful and noisy dream, remembered with wonder amongst the overwhelming realities of this strange world of plants, and water, and silence. And this stillness of life did not in the least resemble a peace. It was the stillness of an implacable force brooding over an inscrutable intention. It looked at you with a vengeful aspect. I got used to it afterwards; I did not see it any more; I had no time. I had to keep guessing at the channel; I had to discern, mostly by inspiration, the signs of hidden banks; I watched for sunken stones; I was learning to clap my teeth smartly before my heart flew out, when I shaved by a fluke some infernal sly old snag that would have ripped the life out of the tin-pot steamboat and drowned all the pilgrims; I had to keep a look-out for the signs of dead wood we could cut up in the night for next day's steaming. When you have to attend to things of that sort, to the mere incidents of the surface, the reality—the reality, I tell you—fades. The inner truth is hidden—luckily, luckily. But I felt it all the same; I felt often its mysterious stillness watching me at my monkey tricks, just as it watches you fellows performing on your respective tight-ropes for—what is it? half-a-crown a tumble——"

"Try to be civil, Marlow," growled a voice, and I knew there was at least one listener awake besides myself.

"I beg your pardon. I forgot the heartache which makes up the rest of the price. And indeed what does the price matter, if the trick be well done? You do your tricks very well. And I didn't do badly either, since I managed not to sink that steamboat on my first trip. It's a wonder to me yet. Imagine a blindfolded man set to drive a van over a bad road. I sweated and shivered over that business considerably, I can tell you. After all, for a seaman, to scrape the bottom of the thing that's supposed to float all the time under

his care is the unpardonable sin. No one may know of it, but you never forget the thump—eh? A blow on the very heart. You remember it, you dream of it, you wake up at night and think of it—years after—and go hot and cold all over. I don't pretend to say that steamboat floated all the time. More than once she had to wade for a bit, with twenty cannibals splashing around and pushing. We had enlisted some of these chaps on the way for a crew. Fine fellows—cannibals—in their place. They were men one could work with, and I am grateful to them. And, after all, they did not eat each other before my face: they had brought along a provision of hippo-meat which went rotten, and made the mystery of the wilderness stink in my nostrils. Phoo! I can sniff it now. I had the manager on board and three or four pilgrims with their staves—all complete. Sometimes we came upon a station close by the bank, clinging to the skirts of the unknown, and the white men rushing out of a tumble-down hovel, with great gestures of joy and surprise and welcome, seemed very strange—had the appearance of being held there captive by a spell. The word ivory would ring in the air for a while—and on we went again into the silence, along empty reaches, round the still bends, between the high walls of our winding way, reverberating in hollow claps the ponderous beat of the stern-wheel. Trees, trees, millions of trees, massive, immense, running up high; and at their foot, hugging the bank against the stream, crept the little begrimed steamboat, like a sluggish beetle crawling on the floor of a lofty portico.[51] It made you feel very small, very lost, and yet it was not altogether depressing, that feeling. After all, if you were small, the grimy beetle crawled on—which was just what you wanted it to do. Where the pilgrims imagined it crawled to I don't know. To some place where they expected to get something. I bet! For me it crawled towards Kurtz—exclusively; but when the steam-pipes started leaking we crawled very slow. The reaches opened before us and closed behind, as if the forest had stepped leisurely across the water to bar the way for our return. We penetrated deeper and deeper into the heart of darkness. It was very quiet there. At night sometimes the roll of drums behind the curtain of trees would run up the river and remain sustained faintly, as if hovering in the air high over our heads, till the first break of day. Whether it meant war, peace, or prayer we could not tell. The dawns were heralded by the descent of a chill stillness; the wood-cutters slept, their fires burned low; the snapping of a twig would make you start. We were wanderers on a prehistoric earth, on an earth that wore the aspect of an unknown planet. We could have fancied ourselves the first of men taking possession of an accursed inheritance, to be subdued at the cost of profound anguish and of excessive toil. But suddenly, as we struggled round a bend, there would be a glimpse of rush walls, of peaked grass-roofs, a burst of yells, a whirl of black limbs, a mass of hands clapping, of feet stamping, of bodies swaying, of eyes rolling, under the droop of heavy and motionless foliage. The steamer toiled along slowly on the edge of a black and incomprehensible frenzy. The prehistoric man was cursing us, praying to us, welcoming us—who could tell? We were cut off from the comprehension of our surroundings; we glided past like phantoms, wondering and secretly appalled, as sane men would be before an enthusiastic

[51] Porch with tall columns.

outbreak in a madhouse. We could not understand because we were too far and could not remember, because we were travelling in the night of first ages, of those ages that are gone, leaving hardly a sign—and no memories.

"The earth seemed unearthly. We are accustomed to look upon the shackled form of a conquered monster, but there—there you could look at a thing monstrous and free. It was unearthly, and the men were—— No, they were not inhuman. Well, you know, that was the worst of it—this suspicion of their not being inhuman. It would come slowly to one. They howled and leaped, and spun, and made horrid faces; but what thrilled you was just the thought of their humanity—like yours—the thought of your remote kinship with this wild and passionate uproar. Ugly. Yes, it was ugly enough; but if you were man enough you would admit to yourself that there was in you just the faintest trace of a response to the terrible frankness of that noise, a dim suspicion of there being a meaning in it which you—you so remote from the night of first ages—could comprehend. And why not? The mind of man is capable of anything—because everything is in it, all the past as well as all the future. What was there after all? Joy, fear, sorrow, devotion, valour, rage—who can tell?—but truth—truth stripped of its cloak of time. Let the fool gape and shudder—the man knows, and can look on without a wink. But he must at least be as much of a man as these on the shore. He must meet that truth with his own true stuff—with his own inborn strength. Principles won't do. Acquisitions, clothes, pretty rags—rags that would fly off at the first good shake. No; you want a deliberate belief. An appeal to me in this fiendish row—is there? Very well; I hear; I admit, but I have a voice, too, and for good or evil mine is the speech that cannot be silenced. Of course, a fool, what with sheer fright and fine sentiments, is always safe. Who's that grunting? You wonder I didn't go ashore for a howl and a dance? Well, no—I didn't. Fine sentiments, you say? Fine sentiments, be hanged! I had no time. I had to mess about with white-lead and strips of woollen blanket helping to put bandages on those leaky steampipes—I tell you. I had to watch the steering, and circumvent those snags, and get the tin-pot along by hook or by crook. There was surface-truth enough in these things to save a wiser man. And between whiles I had to look after the savage who was fireman. He was an improved specimen; he could fire up a vertical boiler. He was there below me, and, upon my word, to look at him was as edifying as seeing a dog in a parody of breeches and a feather hat, walking on his hind-legs. A few months of training had done for that really fine chap. He squinted at the steam-gauge and at the water-gauge with an evident effort of intrepidity— and he had filed teeth, too, the poor devil, and the wool of his pate shaved into queer patterns, and three ornamental scars on each of his cheeks. He ought to have been clapping his hands and stamping his feet on the bank, instead of which he was hard at work, a thrall to strange witchcraft, full of improving knowledge. He was useful because he had been instructed; and what he knew was this—that should the water in that transparent thing disappear, the evil spirit inside the boiler would get angry through the greatness of his thirst, and take a terrible vengeance. So he sweated and fired up and watched the glass fearfully (with an impromptu charm, made of rags, tied to his arm, and a piece of polished bone, as big as a watch, stuck flatways through his lower lip), while the wooded banks slipped past

us slowly, the short noise was left behind, the interminable miles of silence—and we crept on, towards Kurtz. But the snags were thick, the water was treacherous and shallow, the boiler seemed indeed to have a sulky devil in it, and thus neither that fireman nor I had any time to peer into our creepy thoughts.

"Some fifty miles below the Inner Station we came upon a hut of reeds, an inclined and melancholy pole, with the unrecognizable tatters of what had been a flag of some sort flying from it, and a neatly stacked wood-pile. This was unexpected. We came to the bank, and on the stack of firewood found a flat piece of board with some faded pencil-writing on it. When deciphered it said: 'Wood for you. Hurry up. Approach cautiously.' There was a signature, but it was illegible—not Kurtz— a much longer word. 'Hurry up.' Where? Up the river? 'Approach cautiously.' We had not done so. But the warning could not have been meant for the place where it could be only found after approach. Something was wrong above. But what— and how much? That was the question. We commented adversely upon the imbecility of that telegraphic style. The bush around said nothing, and would not let us look very far, either. A torn curtain of red twill hung in the doorway of the hut, and flapped sadly in our faces. The dwelling was dismantled; but we could see a white man had lived there not very long ago. There remained a rude table—a plank on two posts; a heap of rubbish reposed in a dark corner, and by the door I picked up a book. It had lost its covers, and the pages had been thumbed into a state of extremely dirty softness; but the back had been lovingly stitched afresh with white cotton thread, which looked clean yet. It was an extraordinary find. Its title was, *An Inquiry into some Points of Seamanship,* by a man Towser, Towson—some such name—Master in his Majesty's Navy. The matter looked dreary reading enough, with illustrative diagrams and repulsive tables of figures, and the copy was sixty years old. I handled this amazing antiquity with the greatest possible tenderness, lest it should dissolve in my hands. Within, Towson or Towser was inquiring earnestly into the breaking strain of ships' chains and tackle, and other such matters. Not a very enthralling book; but at the first glance you could see there a singleness of intention, an honest concern for the right way of going to work, which made these humble pages, thought out so many years ago, luminous with another than a professional light. The simple old sailor, with his talk of chains and purchases,[52] made me forget the jungle and the pilgrims in a delicious sensation of having come upon something unmistakably real. Such a book being there was wonderful enough; but still more astounding were the notes penciled in the margin, and plainly referring to the text. I couldn't believe my eyes! They were in cipher! Yes, it looked like cipher. Fancy a man lugging with him a book of that description into this nowhere and studying it—and making notes—in cipher at that! It was an extravagant mystery.

"I had been dimly aware for some time of a worrying noise, and when I lifted my eyes I saw the wood-pile was gone, and the manager, aided by all the pilgrims, was shouting at me from the river-side. I slipped the book into my pocket. I assure you to leave off reading was like tearing myself away from the shelter of an old and solid friendship.

[52] Instruments such as blocks-and-tackle used to move objects.

"I started the lame engine ahead. 'It must be this miserable trader—this intruder,' exclaimed the manager, looking back malevolently at the place we had left. 'He must be English,' I said. 'It will not save him from getting into trouble if he is not careful,' muttered the manager darkly. I observed with assumed innocence that no man was safe from trouble in this world.

"The current was more rapid now, the steamer seemed at her last gasp, the stern-wheel flopped languidly, and I caught myself listening on tiptoe for the next beat of the boat, for in sober truth I expected the wretched thing to give up every moment. It was like watching the last flickers of a life. But still we crawled. Sometimes I would pick out a tree a little way ahead to measure our progress towards Kurtz by, but I lost it invariably before we got abreast. To keep the eyes so long on one thing was too much for human patience. The manager displayed a beautiful resignation. I fretted and fumed and took to arguing with myself whether or no I would talk openly with Kurtz; but before I could come to any conclusion it occurred to me that my speech or my silence, indeed any action of mine, would be a mere futility. What did it matter what any one knew or ignored? What did it matter who was manager? One gets sometimes such a flash of insight. The essentials of this affair lay deep under the surface, beyond my reach, and beyond my power of meddling.

"Towards the evening of the second day we judged ourselves about eight miles from Kurtz's station. I wanted to push on; but the manager looked grave, and told me the navigation up there was so dangerous that it would be advisable, the sun being very low already, to wait where we were till next morning. Moreover, he pointed out that if the warning to approach cautiously were to be followed, we must approach in daylight—not at dusk, or in the dark. This was sensible enough. Eight miles meant nearly three hours' steaming for us, and I could also see suspicious ripples at the upper end of the reach. Nevertheless, I was annoyed beyond expression at the delay, and most unreasonably, too, since one night more could not matter much after so many months. As we had plenty of wood, and caution was the word, I brought up in the middle of the stream. The reach was narrow, straight, with high sides like a railway cutting. The dusk came gliding into it long before the sun had set. The current ran smooth and swift, but a dumb immobility sat on the banks. The living trees, lashed together by the creepers and every living bush of the undergrowth, might have been changed into stone, even to the slenderest twig, to the lightest leaf. It was not sleep—it seemed unnatural, like a state of trance. Not the faintest sound of any kind could be heard. You looked on amazed, and began to suspect yourself of being deaf—then the night came suddenly, and struck you blind as well. About three in the morning some large fish leaped, and the loud splash made me jump as though a gun had been fired. When the sun rose there was a white fog, very warm and clammy, and more blinding than the night. It did not shift or drive; it was just there, standing all round you like something solid. At eight or nine, perhaps, it lifted as a shutter lifts. We had a glimpse of the towering multitude of trees, of the immense matted jungle, with the blazing little ball of the sun hanging over it—all perfectly still—and then the white shutter came down again, smoothly, as if sliding in greased grooves. I ordered the chain, which we had begun to heave in, to be paid out again. Before it stopped running with

a muffled rattle, a cry, a very loud cry as of infinite desolation soared slowly in the opaque air. It ceased. A complaining clamour, modulated in savage discords, filled our ears. The sheer unexpectedness of it made my hair stir under my cap. I don't know how it struck the others: to me it seemed as though the mist itself had screamed, so suddenly, and apparently from all sides at once, did this tumultuous and mournful uproar arise. It culminated in a hurried outbreak of almost intolerably excessive shrieking, which stopped short, leaving us stiffened in a variety of silly attitudes, and obstinately listening to the nearly as appalling and excessive silence. 'Good God! What is the meaning——' stammered at my elbow one of the pilgrims, a little fat man, with sandy hair and red whiskers, who wore side-spring boots, and pink pyjamas tucked into his socks. Two others remained open-mouthed a whole minute, then dashed into the little cabin, to rush out incontinently and stand darting scared glances, with Winchesters[53] at 'ready' in their hands. What we could see was just the steamer we were on, her outlines blurred as though she had been on the point of dissolving, and a misty strip of water, perhaps two feet broad, around her—and that was all. The rest of the world was nowhere, as far as our eyes and ears were concerned. Just nowhere. Gone, disappeared; swept off without leaving a whisper or a shadow behind.

"I went forward, and ordered the chain to be hauled in short, so as to be ready to trip the anchor and move the steamboat at once if necessary. 'Will they attack?' whispered an awed voice. 'We will be all butchered in this fog,' murmured another. The faces twitched with the strain, the hands trembled slightly, the eyes forgot to wink. It was very curious to see the contrast of expressions of the white men and of the black fellows of our crew, who were as much strangers to that part of the river as we, though their homes were only eight hundred miles away. The whites, of course greatly discomposed, had besides a curious look of being painfully shocked by such an outrageous row. The others had an alert, naturally interested expression; but their faces were essentially quiet, even those of the one or two who grinned as they hauled at the chain. Several exchanged short, grunting phrases, which seemed to settle the matter to their satisfaction. Their headman, a young, broad-chested black, severely draped in dark-blue fringed cloths, with fierce nostrils and his hair all done up artfully in oily ringlets, stood near me. 'Aha!' I said, just for good fellowship's sake. 'Catch 'im,' he snapped, with a bloodshot widening of his eyes and a flash of sharp teeth—'catch 'im. Give 'im to us.' 'To you, eh?' I asked; 'what would you do with them?' 'Eat 'im!' he said, curtly, and, leaning his elbow on the rail, looked out into the fog in a dignified and profoundly pensive attitude. I would no doubt have been properly horrified, had it not occurred to me that he and his chaps must be very hungry; that they must have been growing increasingly hungry for at least this month past. They had been engaged for six months (I don't think a single one of them had any clear idea of time, as we at the end of countless ages have. They still belonged to the beginnings of time—had no inherited experience to teach them as it were), and of course, as long as there was a piece of paper written over in accordance with some farcical law or other made down the river, it didn't

[53] A brand of repeater rifle.

enter anybody's head to trouble how they would live. Certainly they had brought with them some rotten hippo-meat, which couldn't have lasted very long, anyway, even if the pilgrims hadn't, in the midst of a shocking hullabaloo, thrown a considerable quantity of it overboard. It looked like a high-handed proceeding; but it was really a case of legitimate self-defense. You can't breathe dead hippo waking, sleeping, and eating, and at the same time keep your precarious grip on existence. Besides that, they had given them every week three pieces of brass wire, each about nine inches long; and the theory was they were to buy their provisions with that currency in river-side villages. You can see how *that* worked. There were either no villages, or the people were hostile, or the director, who like the rest of us fed out of tins, with an occasional old he-goat thrown in, didn't want to stop the steamer for some more or less recondite reason. So, unless they swallowed the wire itself, or made loops of it to snare the fishes with, I don't see what good their extravagant salary could be to them. I must say it was paid with a regularity worthy of a large and honourable trading company. For the rest, the only thing to eat—though it didn't look eatable in the least—I saw in their possession was a few lumps of some stuff like half-cooked dough, of a dirty lavender colour, they kept wrapped in leaves, and now and then swallowed a piece of, but so small that it seemed done more for the looks of the thing than for any serious purpose of sustenance. Why in the name of all the gnawing devils of hunger they didn't go for us—they were thirty to five—and have a good tuck-in[54] for once, amazes me now when I think of it. They were big powerful men, with not much capacity to weigh the consequences, with courage, with strength, even yet, though their skins were no longer glossy and their muscles no longer hard. And I saw that something restraining, one of those human secrets that baffle probability, had come into play there. I looked at them with a swift quickening of interest—not because it occurred to me I might be eaten by them before very long, though I own to you that just then I perceived—in a new light, as it were—how unwholesome the pilgrims looked, and I hoped, yes I positively hoped, that my aspect was not so—what shall I say?—so—unappetizing: a touch of fantastic vanity which fitted well with the dream-sensation that pervaded all my days at that time. Perhaps I had a little fever, too. One can't live with one's finger everlastingly on one's pulse. I had often 'a little fever,' or a little touch of other things—the playful paw-strokes of the wilderness, the preliminary trifling before the more serious onslaught which came in due course. Yes; I looked at them as you would on any human being, with a curiosity of their impulses, motives, capacities, weaknesses, when brought to the test of an inexorable physical necessity. Restraint! What possible restraint? Was it superstition, disgust, patience, fear—or some kind of primitive honour? No fear can stand up to hunger, no patience can wear it out, disgust simply does not exist where hunger is; and as to superstition, beliefs, and what you may call principles, they are less than chaff in a breeze. Don't you know the devilry of lingering starvation, its exasperating torment, its black thoughts, its sombre and brooding ferocity? Well, I do. It takes a man all his inborn strength to fight hunger properly. It's really easier to face bereavement, dishonour, and the perdi-

[54] Dinner.

tion of one's soul—than this kind of prolonged hunger. Sad, but true. And these chaps, too, had no earthly reason for any kind of scruple. Restraint! I would just as soon have expected restraint from a hyena prowling amongst the corpses of a battlefield. But there was the fact facing me—the fact dazzling, to be seen, like the foam on the depths of the sea, like a ripple on an unfathomable enigma, a mystery greater—when I thought of it—than the curious, inexplicable note of desperate grief in this savage clamour that had swept by us on the river-bank, behind the blind whiteness of the fog.

"Two pilgrims were quarrelling in hurried whispers as to which bank. 'Left.' 'No, no; how can you? Right, right, of course.' 'It is very serious,' said the manager's voice behind me; 'I would be desolated if anything should happen to Mr. Kurtz before we came up.' I looked at him, and had not the slightest doubt he was sincere. He was just the kind of man who would wish to preserve appearances. That was his restraint. But when he muttered something about going on at once, I did not even take the trouble to answer him. I knew, and he knew, that it was impossible. Were we to let go our hold of the bottom, we would be absolutely in the air—in space. We wouldn't be able to tell where we were going to—whether up or down stream, or across—till we fetched against one bank or the other,—and then we wouldn't know at first which it was. Of course I made no move. I had no mind for a smash-up. You couldn't imagine a more deadly place for a shipwreck. Whether drowned at once or not, we were sure to perish speedily in one way or another. 'I authorize you to take all the risks,' he said, after a short silence. 'I refuse to take any,' I said, shortly; which was just the answer he expected, though its tone might have surprised him. 'Well, I must defer to your judgment. You are captain,' he said, with marked civility. I turned my shoulder to him in sign of my appreciation, and looked into the fog. How long would it last? It was the most hopeless look-out. The approach to this Kurtz grubbing for ivory in the wretched bush was beset by as many dangers as though he had been an enchanted princess sleeping in a fabulous castle. 'Will they attack, do you think?' asked the manager, in a confidential tone.

"I did not think they would attack, for several obvious reasons. The thick fog was one. If they left the bank in their canoes they would get lost in it, as we would be if we attempted to move. Still, I had also judged the jungle of both banks quite impenetrable—and yet eyes were in it, eyes that had seen us. The river-side bushes were certainly very thick; but the undergrowth behind was evidently penetrable. However, during the short lift I had seen no canoes anywhere in the reach—certainly not abreast of the steamer. But what made the idea of attack inconceivable to me was the nature of the noise—of the cries we had heard. They had not the fierce character boding immediate hostile intention. Unexpected, wild, and violent as they had been, they had given me an irresistible impression of sorrow. The glimpse of the steamboat had for some reason filled those savages with unrestrained grief. The danger, if any, I expounded, was from our proximity to a great human passion let loose. Even extreme grief may ultimately vent itself in violence—but more generally takes the form of apathy. . . .

"You should have seen the pilgrims stare! They had no heart to grin, or even to revile me: but I believe they thought me gone mad—with fright,

maybe. I delivered a regular lecture. My dear boys, it was no good bothering. Keep a lookout? Well, you may guess I watched the fog for the signs of lifting as a cat watches a mouse; but for anything else our eyes were of no more use to us than if we had been buried miles deep in a heap of cotton-wool. It felt like it, too—choking, warm, stifling. Besides, all I said, though it sounded extravagant, was absolutely true to fact. What we afterwards alluded to as an attack was really an attempt at repulse. The action was very far from being aggressive—it was not even defensive, in the usual sense: it was undertaken under the stress of desperation, and in its essence was purely protective.

"It developed itself, I should say, two hours after the fog lifted, and its commencement was at a spot, roughly speaking, about a mile and a half below Kurtz's station. We had just floundered and flopped round a bend, when I saw an islet, a mere grassy hummock of bright green, in the middle of the stream. It was the only thing of the kind; but as we opened the reach more, I perceived it was the head of a long sandbank, or rather of a chain of shallow patches stretching down the middle of the river. They were discoloured, just awash, and the whole lot was seen just under the water, exactly as a man's backbone is seen running down the middle of his back under the skin. Now, as far as I did see, I could go to the right or to the left of this. I didn't know either channel, of course. The banks looked pretty well alike, the depth appeared the same; but as I had been informed the station was on the west side, I naturally headed for the western passage.

"No sooner had we fairly entered it than I became aware it was much narrower than I had supposed. To the left of us there was the long uninterrupted shoal, and to the right a high, steep bank heavily overgrown with bushes. Above the bush the trees stood in serried[55] ranks. The twigs overhung the current thickly, and from distance to distance a large limb of some tree projected rigidly over the stream. It was then well on in the afternoon, the face of the forest was gloomy, and a broad strip of shadow had already fallen on the water. In this shadow we steamed up—very slowly, as you may imagine. I sheered her well inshore—the water being deepest near the bank, as the sounding-pole informed me.

"One of my hungry and forbearing friends was sounding in the bows just below me. This steamboat was exactly like a decked scow.[56] On the deck, there were two little teak-wood houses, with doors and windows. The boiler was in the fore-end, and the machinery right astern. Over the whole there was a light roof, supported on stanchions. The funnel projected through that roof, and in front of the funnel a small cabin built of light planks served for a pilot-house. It contained a couch, two camp-stools, a loaded Martini-Henry[57] leaning in one corner, a tiny table, and the steering-wheel. It had a wide door in front and a broad shutter at each side. All these were always thrown open, of course. I spent my days perched up there on the extreme fore-end of that roof, before the door. At night I slept, or tried to, on the couch. An athletic black belonging to some coast tribe, and educated by my poor predecessor, was the helmsman. He sported a pair of brass earrings, wore a blue cloth wrapper from the waist

[55] In dense rows. [56] Flat-bottomed rectangular-shaped boat. [57] A powerful rifle.

to the ankles, and thought all the world of himself. He was the most unstable kind of fool I had ever seen. He steered with no end of a swagger while you were by; but if he lost sight of you, he became instantly the prey of an abject funk,[58] and would let that cripple of a steamboat get the upper hand of him in a minute.

"I was looking down at the sounding-pole, and feeling much annoyed to see at each try a little more of it stick out of that river, when I saw my poleman give up the business suddenly, and stretch himself flat on the deck, without even taking the trouble to haul his pole in. He kept hold on it though, and it trailed in the water. At the same time the fireman, whom I could also see below me, sat down abruptly before his furnace and ducked his head. I was amazed. Then I had to look at the river mighty quick, because there was a snag in the fairway. Sticks, little sticks, were flying about—thick: they were whizzing before my nose, dropping below me, striking behind me against my pilot-house. All this time the river, the shore, the woods, were very quiet—perfectly quiet. I could only hear the heavy splashing thump of the stern-wheel and the patter of these things. We cleared the snag clumsily. Arrows, by Jove! We were being shot at! I stepped in quickly to close the shutter on the land-side. That fool-helmsman, his hands on the spokes, was lifting his knees high, stamping his feet, champing his mouth, like a reined-in horse. Confound him! And we were staggering within ten feet of the bank. I had to lean right out to swing the heavy shutter, and I saw a face amongst the leaves on the level with my own, looking at me very fierce and steady; and then suddenly, as though a veil had been removed from my eyes, I made out, deep in the tangled gloom, naked breasts, arms, legs, glaring eyes,—the bush was swarming with human limbs in movement, glistening, of bronze colour. The twigs shook, swayed, and rustled, the arrows flew out of them, and then the shutter came to. 'Steer her straight,' I said to the helmsman. He held his head rigid, face forward; but his eyes rolled, he kept on lifting and setting down his feet gently, his mouth foamed a little. 'Keep quiet!' I said in a fury. I might just as well have ordered a tree not to sway in the wind. I darted out. Below me there was a great scuffle of feet on the iron deck; confused exclamations; a voice screamed, 'Can you turn back?' I caught sight of a V-shaped ripple on the water ahead. What? Another snag! A fusillade burst out under my feet. The pilgrims had opened with their Winchesters, and were simply squirting lead into that bush. A deuce of a lot of smoke came up and drove slowly forward. I swore at it. Now I couldn't see the ripple of the snag either. I stood in the doorway, peering, and the arrows came in swarms. They might have been poisoned, but they looked as though they wouldn't kill a cat. The bush began to howl. Our woodcutters raised a warlike whoop; the report of a rifle just at my back deafened me. I glanced over my shoulder, and the pilot-house was yet full of noise and smoke when I made a dash at the wheel. The fool-nigger had dropped everything, to throw the shutter open and let off that Martini-Henry. He stood before the wide opening, glaring, and I yelled at him to come back, while I straightened the sudden twist out of that steamboat. There was no room to turn even if I had wanted to, the snag was some-

[58] Panic or depression.

where very near ahead in that confounded smoke, there was no time to lose, so I just crowded her into the bank—right into the bank, where I knew the water was deep.

"We tore slowly along the overhanging bushes in a whirl of broken twigs and flying leaves. The fusillade below stopped short, as I had foreseen it would when the squirts got empty. I threw my head back to a glinting whizz that traversed the pilot-house, in at one shutter hole and out at the other. Looking past that mad helmsman, who was shaking the empty rifle and yelling at the shore, I saw vague forms of men running bent double, leaping, gliding, distinct, incomplete, evanescent. Something big appeared in the air before the shutter, the rifle went overboard, and the man stepped back swiftly, looked at me over his shoulder in an extraordinary, profound, familiar manner, and fell upon my feet. The side of his head hit the wheel twice, and the end of what appeared a long cane clattered round and knocked over a little camp-stool. It looked as though after wrenching that thing from somebody ashore he had lost his balance in the effort. The thin smoke had blown away, we were clear of the snag, and looking ahead I could see that in another hundred yards or so I would be free to sheer off, away from the bank; but my feet felt so very warm and wet that I had to look down. The man had rolled on his back and stared straight up at me; both his hands clutched that cane. It was the shaft of a spear that, either thrown or lunged through the opening, had caught him in the side just below the ribs; the blade had gone in out of sight, after making a frightful gash; my shoes were full; a pool of blood lay very still, gleaming dark-red under the wheel; his eyes shone with an amazing lustre. The fusillade burst out again. He looked at me anxiously, gripping the spear like something precious, with an air of being afraid I would try to take it away from him. I had to make an effort to free my eyes from his gaze and attend to the steering. With one hand I felt above my head for the line of the steam whistle, and jerked out screech after screech hurriedly. The tumult of angry and warlike yells was checked instantly, and then from the depths of the woods went out such a tremulous and prolonged wail of mournful fear and utter despair as may be imagined to follow the flight of the last hope from the earth. There was a great commotion in the bush; the shower of arrows stopped, a few dropping shots rang out sharply—then silence, in which the languid beat of the stern-wheel came plainly to my ears. I put the helm hard a-starboard at the moment when the pilgrim in pink pyjamas, very hot and agitated, appeared in the doorway. 'The manager sends me ——' he began in an official tone, and stopped short. 'Good God!' he said, glaring at the wounded man.

"We two whites stood over him, and his lustrous and inquiring glance enveloped us both. I declare it looked as though he would presently put to us some question in an understandable language; but he died without uttering a sound, without moving a limb, without twitching a muscle. Only in the very last moment, as though in response to some sign we could not see, to some whisper we could not hear, he frowned heavily, and that frown gave to his black death-mask an inconceivably sombre, brooding, and menacing expression. The lustre of inquiring glance faded swiftly into vacant glassiness. 'Can you steer?' I asked the agent eagerly. He looked very dubious; but I made a grab at his arm, and he understood at once I meant him

to steer whether or no. To tell you the truth, I was morbidly anxious to change my shoes and socks. 'He is dead,' murmured the fellow, immensely impressed. 'No doubt about it,' said I, tugging like mad at the shoe-laces. 'And by the way, I suppose Mr. Kurtz is dead as well by this time.'

"For the moment that was the dominant thought. There was a sense of extreme disappointment, as though I had found out I had been striving after something altogether without a substance. I couldn't have been more disgusted if I had travelled all this way for the sole purpose of talking with Mr. Kurtz. Talking with . . . I flung one shoe overboard, and became aware that that was exactly what I had been looking forward to—a talk with Kurtz. I made the strange discovery that I had never imagined him as doing, you know, but as discoursing. I didn't say to myself, 'Now I will never see him,' or 'Now I will never shake him by the hand,' but, 'now I will never hear him.' The man presented himself as a voice. Not of course that I did not connect him with some sort of action. Hadn't I been told in all the tones of jealousy and admiration that he had collected, bartered, swindled, or stolen more ivory than all the other agents together? That was not the point. The point was in his being a gifted creature, and that of all his gifts the one that stood out preëminently, that carried with it a sense of real presence, was his ability to talk, his words—the gift of expression, the bewildering, the illuminating, the most exalted and the most contemptible, the pulsating stream of light, or the deceitful flow from the heart of an impenetrable darkness.

"The other shoe went flying unto the devil-god of that river. I thought, By Jove! it's all over. We are too late; he has vanished—the gift has vanished, by means of some spear, arrow, or club. I will never hear that chap speak after all,—and my sorrow had a startling extravagance of emotion, even such as I had noticed in the howling sorrow of these savages in the bush. I couldn't have felt more of lonely desolation somehow, had I been robbed of a belief or had missed my destiny in life. . . . Why do you sigh in this beastly way, somebody? Absurd? Well, absurd. Good Lord! mustn't a man ever—— Here, give me some tobacco." . . .

There was a pause of profound stillness, then a match flared, and Marlow's lean face appeared, worn, hollow, with downward folds and dropped eyelids, with an aspect of concentrated attention; and as he took vigorous draws at his pipe, it seemed to retreat and advance out of the night in the regular flicker of the tiny flame. The match went out.

"Absurd!" he cried. "This is the worst of trying to tell. . . . Here you all are, each moored with two good addresses, like a hulk with two anchors, a butcher round one corner, a policeman round another, excellent appetites, and temperature normal—you hear—normal from year's end to year's end. And you say, Absurd! Absurd be—exploded! Absurd! My dear boys, what can you expect from a man who out of sheer nervousness had just flung overboard a pair of new shoes! Now I think of it, it is amazing I did not shed tears. I am, upon the whole, proud of my fortitude. I was cut to the quick at the idea of having lost the inestimable privilege of listening to the gifted Kurtz. Of course I was wrong. The privilege was waiting for me. Oh, yes, I heard more than enough. And I was right, too. A voice. He was very little more than a voice. And I heard—him—it—this voice—other voices—all of them were so little more than voices—and the memory of

that time itself lingers around me, impalpable, like a dying vibration of one immense jabber, silly, atrocious, sordid, savage, or simply mean, without any kind of sense. Voices, voices—even the girl herself—now—"

He was silent for a long time.

"I laid[59] the ghost of his gifts at last with a lie," he began, suddenly. "Girl! What? Did I mention a girl? Oh, she is out of it—completely. They—the women I mean—are out of it—should be out of it. We must help them to stay in that beautiful world of their own, lest ours gets worse. Oh, she had to be out of it. You should have heard the disinterred body of Mr. Kurtz saying, 'My Intended.' You would have perceived directly then how completely she was out of it. And the lofty frontal bone of Mr. Kurtz! They say the hair goes on growing sometimes, but this—ah—specimen, was impressively bald. The wilderness had patted him on the head, and, behold, it was like a ball—an ivory ball; it had caressed him, and—lo!—he had withered; it had taken him, loved him, embraced him, got into his veins, consumed his flesh, and sealed his soul to its own by the inconceivable ceremonies of some devilish initiation. He was its spoiled and pampered favourite. Ivory? I should think so. Heaps of it, stacks of it. The old mud shanty was bursting with it. You would think there was not a single tusk left either above or below the ground in the whole country. 'Mostly fossil,' the manager had remarked, disparagingly. It was no more fossil than I am; but they call it fossil when it is dug up. It appears these niggers do bury the tusks sometimes—but evidently they couldn't bury this parcel deep enough to save the gifted Mr. Kurtz from his fate. We filled the steamboat with it, and had to pile a lot on the deck. Thus he could see and enjoy as long as he could see, because the appreciation of this favour had remained with him to the last. You should have heard him say, 'My ivory.' Oh yes, I heard him. 'My Intended, my ivory, my station, my river, my——' everything belonged to him. It made me hold my breath in expectation of hearing the wilderness burst into a prodigious peal of laughter that would shake the fixed stars in their places. Everything belonged to him—but that was a trifle. The thing was to know what he belonged to, how many powers of darkness claimed him for their own. That was the reflection that made you creepy all over. It was impossible—it was not good for one either—trying to imagine. He had taken a high seat amongst the devils of the land—I mean literally. You can't understand. How could you?—with solid pavement under your feet, surrounded by kind neighbours ready to cheer you or to fall on you, stepping delicately between the butcher and the policeman, in the holy terror of scandal and gallows and lunatic asylums—how can you imagine what particular region of the first ages a man's untrammelled feet may take him into by the way of solitude—utter solitude without a policeman—by the way of silence—utter silence, where no warning voice of a kind neighbour can be heard whispering of public opinion? These little things make all the great difference. When they are gone you must fall back upon your own innate strength, upon your own capacity for faithfulness. Of course you may be too much of a fool to go wrong—too dull even to know you are being assaulted by the powers of darkness. I take it, no fool ever made a bargain for his soul with the devil: the fool is too

[59] Put to rest.

much of a fool, or the devil too much of a devil—I don't know which. Or you may be such a thunderingly exalted creature as to be altogether deaf and blind to anything but heavenly sights and sounds. Then the earth for you is only a standing place—and whether to be like this is your loss or your gain I won't pretend to say. But most of us are neither one nor the other. The earth for us is a place to live in, where we must put up with sights, with sounds, with smells, too, by Jove!—breathe dead hippo, so to speak, and not be contaminated. And there, don't you see? your strength comes in, the faith in your ability for the digging of unostentatious holes to bury the stuff in—your power of devotion, not to yourself, but to an obscure, back-breaking business. And that's difficult enough. Mind, I am not trying to excuse or even explain—I am trying to account to myself for—for—Mr. Kurtz—for the shade of Mr. Kurtz. This initiated wraith from the back of Nowhere honoured me with its amazing confidence before it vanished altogether. This was because it could speak English to me. The orginal Kurtz had been educated partly in England, and—as he was good enough to say himself—his sympathies were in the right place. His mother was half-English, his father was half-French. All Europe contributed to the making of Kurtz; and by and by I learned that, most appropriately, the International Society for the Suppression of Savage Customs had intrusted him with the making of a report, for its future guidance. And he had written it, too. I've seen it. I've read it. It was eloquent, vibrating with eloquence, but too high-strung, I think. Seventeen pages of close writing he had found time for! But this must have been before his—let us say—nerves, went wrong, and caused him to preside at certain midnight dances ending with unspeakable rites, which—as far as I reluctantly gathered from what I heard at various times—were offered up to him—do you understand?—to Mr. Kurtz himself. But it was a beautiful piece of writing. The opening paragraph, however, in the light of later information, strikes me now as ominous. He began with the argument that we whites, from the point of development we had arrived at, 'must necessarily appear to them [savages] in the nature of supernatural beings—we approach them with the might as of a deity,' and so on, and so on. 'By the simple exercise of our will we can exert a power for good practically unbounded,' etc., etc. From that point he soared and took me with him. The peroration was magnificent, though difficult to remember, you know. It gave me the notion of an exotic Immensity ruled by an august Benevolence. It made me tingle with enthusiasm. This was the unbounded power of eloquence—of words—of burning noble words. There were no practical hints to interrupt the magic current of phrases, unless a kind of note at the foot of the last page, scrawled evidently much later, in an unsteady hand, may be regarded as the exposition of a method. It was very simple, and at the end of that moving appeal to every altruistic sentiment it blazed at you, luminous and terrifying, like a flash of lightning in a serene sky: 'Exterminate all the brutes!' The curious part was that he had apparently forgotten all about that valuable postscriptum, because, later on, when he in a sense came to himself, he repeatedly entreated me to take good care of 'my pamphlet' (he called it), as it was sure to have in the future a good influence upon his career. I had full information about all these things, and, besides, as it turned out, I was to have the care of his memory. I've done enough for it to give me the indisputable right to lay it, if I

choose, for an everlasting rest in the dust-bin[60] of progress amongst all the sweepings and, figuratively speaking, all the dead cats of civilization. But then, you see, I can't choose. He won't be forgotten. Whatever he was, he was not common. He had the power to charm or frighten rudimentary souls into an aggravated witch-dance in his honour; he could also fill the small souls of the pilgrims with bitter misgivings: he had one devoted friend at least, and he had conquered one soul in the world that was neither rudimentary nor tainted with self-seeking. No; I can't forget him, though I am not prepared to affirm the fellow was exactly worth the life we lost in getting to him. I missed my late helmsman awfully,—I missed him even while his body was still lying in the pilot-house. Perhaps you will think it passing strange this regret for a savage who was no more account than a grain of sand in a black Sahara. Well, don't you see, he had done something, he had steered; for months I had him at my back—a help—an instrument. It was a kind of partnership. He steered for me—I had to look after him, I worried about his deficiencies, and thus a subtle bond had been created, of which I only became aware when it was suddenly broken. And the intimate profundity of that look he gave me when he received his hurt remains to this day in my memory—like a claim of distant kinship affirmed in a supreme moment.

"Poor fool! If he had only left that shutter alone. He had no restraint, no restraint—just like Kurtz—a tree swayed by the wind. As soon as I had put on a dry pair of slippers, I dragged him out after first jerking the spear out of his side, which operation I confess I performed with my eyes shut tight. His heels leaped together over the little door-step; his shoulders were pressed to my breast; I hugged him from behind desperately. Oh! he was heavy, heavy; heavier than any man on earth, I should imagine. Then without more ado I tipped him overboard. The current snatched him as though he had been a wisp of grass, and I saw the body roll over twice before I lost sight of it for ever. All the pilgrims and the manager were then congregated on the awning-deck about the pilot-house, chattering at each other like a flock of excited magpies, and there was a scandalized murmur at my heartless promptitude. What they wanted to keep that body hanging about for I can't guess. Embalm it, maybe. But I had also heard another, and a very ominous, murmur on the deck below. My friends the woodcutters were likewise scandalized, and with a better show of reason—though I admit that the reason itself was quite inadmissible. Oh, quite! I had made up my mind that if my late helmsman was to be eaten, the fishes alone should have him. He had been a very second-rate helmsman while alive, but now he was dead he might have become a first-class temptation, and possibly cause some startling trouble. Besides, I was anxious to take the wheel, the man in pink pyjamas showing himself a hopeless duffer at the business.

"This I did directly the simple funeral was over. We were going half-speed, keeping right in the middle of the stream, and I listened to the talk about me. They had given up Kurtz, they had given up the station; Kurtz was dead, and the station had been burnt—and so on—and so on. The red-haired pilgrim was beside himself with the thought that at least this

[60] British term for garbage can.

poor Kurtz had been properly avenged. 'Say! We must have made a glori-
ous slaughter of them in the bush. Eh? What do you think? Say?' He posi-
tively danced, the bloodthirsty little gingery[61] beggar. And he had nearly
fainted when he saw the wounded man! I could not help saying, 'You made
a glorious lot of smoke, anyhow.' I had seen, from the way the tops of the
bushes rustled and flew, that almost all the shots had gone too high. You
can't hit anything unless you take aim and fire from the shoulder; but these
chaps fired from the hip with their eyes shut. The retreat, I maintained—
and I was right—was caused by the screeching of the steam-whistle. Upon
this they forgot Kurtz, and began to howl at me with indignant protests.

"The manager stood by the wheel murmuring confidentially about the
necessity of getting well away down the river before dark at all events, when
I saw in the distance a clearing on the river-side and the outlines of some
sort of building. 'What's this?' I asked. He clapped his hands in wonder.
'The station!' he cried. I edged in at once, still going half-speed.

"Through my glasses I saw the slope of a hill interspersed with rare
trees and perfectly free from undergrowth. A long decaying building on
the summit was half buried in the high grass; the large holes in the peaked
roof gaped black from afar; the jungle and the woods made a background.
There was no enclosure or fence of any kind; but there had been one
apparently, for near the house half-a-dozen slim posts remained in a row,
roughly trimmed, and with their upper ends ornamented with round
carved balls. The rails, or whatever there had been between, had disap-
peared. Of course the forest surrounded all that. The river-bank was clear,
and on the water-side I saw a white man under a hat like a cart-wheel
beckoning persistently with his whole arm. Examining the edge of the for-
est above and below, I was almost certain I could see movements—human
forms gliding here and there. I steamed past prudently, then stopped the
engines and let her drift down. The man on the shore began to shout,
urging us to land. 'We have been attacked,' screamed the manager. 'I
know—I know. It's all right,' yelled back the other, as cheerful as you
please. 'Come along. It's all right. I am glad.'

"His aspect reminded me of something I had seen—something funny I
had seen somewhere. As I manoeuvred to get alongside, I was asking my-
self, 'What does this fellow look like?' Suddenly I got it. He looked like a
harlequin.[62] His clothes had been made of some stuff that was brown hol-
land[63] probably, but it was covered with patches all over, with bright
patches, blue, red, and yellow,—patches on the back, patches on the front,
patches on elbows, on knees; coloured binding around his jacket, scarlet
edging at the bottom of his trousers; and the sunshine made him look
extremely gay and wonderfully neat withal, because you could see how
beautifully all this patching had been done. A beardless, boyish face, very
fair, no features to speak of, nose peeling, little blue eyes, smiles and
frowns chasing each other over that open countenance like sunshine and
shadow on a wind-swept plain. 'Look out, captain!' he cried; 'there's a snag

[61] Red-headed.
[62] The gaudily dressed clown in the style of Italian improvised comedy called *commedia
dell'arte.*
[63] Unbleached, often glazed, cotton or linen.

lodged in here last night.' What! Another snag? I confess I swore shame-fully. I had nearly holed my cripple, to finish off that charming trip. The harlequin on the bank turned his little pug-nose up to me. 'You English?' he asked, all smiles. 'Are you?' I shouted from the wheel. The smiles van-ished, and he shook his head as if sorry for my disappointment. Then he brightened up. 'Never mind!' he cried, encouragingly. 'Are we in time?' I asked. 'He is up there,' he replied, with a toss of the head up the hill, and becoming gloomy all of a sudden. His face was like the autumn sky, over-cast one moment and bright the next.

"When the manager, escorted by the pilgrims, all of them armed to the teeth, had gone to the house this chap came on board. 'I say, I don't like this. These natives are in the bush,' I said. He assured me earnestly it was all right. 'They are simple people,' he added; 'well, I am glad you came. It took me all my time to keep them off.' 'But you said it was all right,' I cried. 'Oh, they meant no harm,' he said; and as I stared he corrected himself, 'Not exactly.' Then vivaciously, 'My faith, your pilot-house wants a clean-up!' In the next breath he advised me to keep enough steam on the boiler to blow the whistle in case of any trouble. 'One good screech will do more for you than all your rifles. They are simple people,' he repeated. He rat-tled away at such a rate he quite overwhelmed me. He seemed to be trying to make up for lots of silence, and actually hinted, laughing, that such was the case. 'Don't you talk with Mr. Kurtz?' I said. 'You don't talk with that man—you listen to him,' he exclaimed with severe exaltation. 'But now ——' He waved his arm, and in the twinkling of an eye was in the uttermost depths of despondency. In a moment he came up again with a jump, pos-sessed himself of both my hands, shook them continuously, while he gabbled: 'Brother sailor . . . honour . . . pleasure . . . delight . . . introduce myself . . . Russian . . . son of an arch-priest . . . Government of Tambov[64] . . . What? Tobacco! English tobacco; the excellent English tobacco! Now, that's brotherly. Smoke? Where's a sailor that does not smoke?'

"The pipe soothed him, and gradually I made out he had run away from school, had gone to sea in a Russian ship; ran away again; served some time in English ships; was now reconciled with the arch-priest. He made a point of that. 'But when one is young one must see things, gather experience, ideas; enlarge the mind.' 'Here!' I interrupted. 'You can never tell! Here I met Mr. Kurtz,' he said, youthfully solemn and reproachful. I held my tongue after that. It appears he had persuaded a Dutch trading-house on the coast to fit him out with stores and goods, and had started for the interior with a light heart, and no more idea of what would happen to him than a baby. He had been wandering about that river for nearly two years alone, cut off from everybody and everything. 'I am not so young as I look. I am twenty-five,' he said. 'At first old Van Shuyten would tell me to go to the devil,' he narrated with keen enjoyment; 'but I stuck to him, and talked and talked, till at last he got afraid I would talk the hind-leg off his favourite dog, so he gave me some cheap things and a few guns, and told me he hoped he would never see my face again. Good old Dutchman, Van Shuyten. I've sent him one small lot of ivory a year ago, so that he can't call me a little thief when I get back. I hope he got it. And for the rest I don't

[64] Region in central Russia.

care. I had some wood stacked for you. That was my old house. Did you see?'

"I gave him Towson's book. He made as though he would kiss me, but restrained himself. 'The only book I had left, and I thought I had lost it,' he said, looking at it ecstatically. 'So many accidents happen to a man going about alone, you know. Canoes get upset sometimes—and sometimes you've got to clear out so quick when the people get angry.' He thumbed the pages. 'You made notes in Russian?' I asked. He nodded. 'I thought they were written in cipher,' I said. He laughed, then became serious. 'I had lots of trouble to keep these people off,' he said. 'Did they want to kill you?' I asked. 'Oh, no!' he cried, and checked himself. 'Why did they attack us?' I pursued. He hesitated, then said shamefacedly, 'They don't want him to go.' 'Don't they?' I said, curiously. He nodded a nod full of mystery and wisdom. 'I tell you,' he cried, 'this man has enlarged my mind.' He opened his arms wide, staring at me with his little blue eyes that were perfectly round."

III

"I looked at him, lost in astonishment. There he was before me, in motley,[65] as though he had absconded from a troupe of mimes, enthusiastic, fabulous.[66] His very existence was improbable, inexplicable, and altogether bewildering. He was an insoluble problem. It was inconceivable how he had existed, how he had succeeded in getting so far, how he had managed to remain—why he did not instantly disappear. 'I went a little farther,' he said, 'then still a little farther—till I had gone so far that I don't know how I'll ever get back. Never mind. Plenty time. I can manage. You take Kurtz away quick—quick—I tell you.' The glamour of youth enveloped his particoloured rags, his destitution, his loneliness, the essential desolation of his futile wanderings. For months—for years—his life hadn't been worth a day's purchase; and there he was gallantly, thoughtlessly alive, to all appearance indestructible solely by the virtue of his few years and of his unreflecting audacity. I was seduced into something like admiration—like envy. Glamour urged him on, glamour kept him unscathed. He surely wanted nothing from the wilderness but space to breathe in and to push on through. His need was to exist, and to move onwards at the greatest possible risk, and with a maximum of privation. If the absolutely pure, uncalculating, unpractical spirit of adventure had ever ruled a human being, it ruled this be-patched youth. I almost envied him the possession of this modest and clear flame. It seemed to have consumed all thought of self so completely, that even while he was talking to you, you forgot that it was he—the man before your eyes—who had gone through these things. I did not envy him his devotion to Kurtz, though. He had not meditated over it. It came to him, and he accepted it with a sort of eager fatalism. I must say that to me it appeared about the most dangerous thing in every way he had come upon so far.

"They had come together unavoidably, like two ships becalmed near

[65] Clown's many-colored apparel. [66] Like a creature of fable.

each other, and lay rubbing sides at last. I suppose Kurtz wanted an audience, because on a certain occasion, when encamped in the forest, they had talked all night, or more probably Kurtz had talked. 'We talked of everything,' he said, quite transported at the recollection. 'I forgot there was such a thing as sleep. The night did not seem to last an hour. Everything! Everything! . . . Of love, too.' 'Ah, he talked to you of love!' I said, much amused. 'It isn't what you think,' he cried, almost passionately. 'It was in general. He made me see things—things.'

"He threw his arms up. We were on deck at the time, and the headman of my wood-cutters, lounging near by, turned upon him his heavy and glittering eyes. I looked around, and I don't know why, but I assure you that never, never before, did this land, this river, this jungle, the very arch of this blazing sky, appear to me so hopeless and so dark, so impenetrable to human thought, so pitiless to human weakness. 'And, ever since, you have been with him, of course?' I said.

"On the contrary. It appears their intercourse had been very much broken by various causes. He had, as he informed me proudly, managed to nurse Kurtz through two illnesses (he alluded to it as you would to some risky feat), but as a rule Kurtz wandered alone, far in the depths of the forest. 'Very often coming to this station, I had to wait days and days before he would turn up,' he said. 'Ah, it was worth waiting for!—sometimes.' 'What was he doing? exploring or what?' I asked. 'Oh, yes, of course'; he had discovered lots of villages, a lake, too—he did not know exactly in what direction; it was dangerous to inquire too much—but mostly his expeditions had been for ivory. 'But he had no goods to trade with by that time,' I objected. 'There's a good lot of cartridges left even yet,' he answered, looking away. 'To speak plainly, he raided the country,' I said. He nodded. 'Not alone, surely!' He muttered something about the villages round that lake. 'Kurtz got the tribe to follow him, did he?' I suggested. He fidgeted a little. 'They adored him,' he said. The tone of these words was so extraordinary that I looked at him searchingly. It was curious to see his mingled eagerness and reluctance to speak of Kurtz. The man filled his life, occupied his thoughts, swayed his emotions. 'What can you expect?' he burst out; 'he came to them with thunder and lightning, you know—and they had never seen anything like it—and very terrible. He could be very terrible. You can't judge Mr. Kurtz as you would an ordinary man. No, no, no! Now—just to give you an idea—I don't mind telling you, he wanted to shoot me, too, one day—but I don't judge him.' 'Shoot you!' I cried. 'What for?' 'Well, I had a small lot of ivory the chief of that village near my house gave me. You see I used to shoot game for them. Well, he wanted it, and wouldn't hear reason. He declared he would shoot me unless I gave him the ivory and then cleared out of the country, because he could do so, and had a fancy for it, and there was nothing on earth to prevent him killing whom he jolly well pleased. And it was true, too. I gave him the ivory. What did I care! But I didn't clear out. No, no. I couldn't leave him. I had to be careful, of course, till we got friendly again for a time. He had his second illness then. Afterwards I had to keep out of the way; but I didn't mind. He was living for the most part in those villages on the lake. When he came down to the river, sometimes he would talk to me, and sometimes it was better for me to be careful. This man suffered too much. He hated all this,

and somehow he couldn't get away. When I had a chance I begged him to try and leave while there was time; I offered to go back with him. And he would say yes, and then he would remain; go off on another ivory hunt; disappear for weeks; forget himself amongst these people—forget himself—you know.' 'Why! he's mad,' I said. He protested indignantly. Mr. Kurtz couldn't be mad. If I had heard him talk, only two days ago, I wouldn't dare hint at such a thing. . . . I had taken up my binoculars while we talked, and was looking at the shore, sweeping the limit of the forest at each side and at the back of the house. The consciousness of there being people in that bush, so silent, so quiet—as silent and quiet as the ruined house on the hill—made me uneasy. There was no sign on the face of nature of this amazing tale that was not so much told as suggested to me in desolate exclamations, completed by shrugs, in interrupted phrases, in hints ending in deep sighs. The woods were unmoved, like a mask—heavy, like the closed door of a prison—they looked with their air of hidden knowledge, of patient expectation, of unapproachable silence. The Russian was explaining to me that it was only lately that Mr. Kurtz had come down to the river, bringing along with him all the fighting men of that lake tribe. He had been absent for several months—getting himself adored, I suppose—and had come down unexpectedly, with the intention to all appearance of making a raid either across the river or down stream. Evidently the appetite for more ivory had got the better of the—what shall I say?—less material aspirations. However he had got much worse suddenly. 'I heard he was lying helpless, and so I came up—took my chance,' said the Russian. 'Oh, he is bad, very bad.' I directed my glass to the house. There were no signs of life, but there was the ruined roof, the long mud wall peeping above the grass, with three little square window-holes, no two of the same size; all this brought within reach of my hand, as it were. And then I made a brusque movement, and one of the remaining posts of that vanished fence leaped up in the field of my glass. You remember I told you I had been struck at the distance by certain attempts at ornamentation, rather remarkable in the ruinous aspect of the place. Now I had suddenly a nearer view, and its first result was to make me throw my head back as if before a blow. Then I went carefully from post to post with my glass, and I saw my mistake. These round knobs were not ornamental but symbolic; they were expressive and puzzling, striking and disturbing—food for thought and also for vultures if there had been any looking down from the sky; but at all events for such ants as were industrious enough to ascend the pole. They would have been even more impressive, those heads on the stakes, if their faces had not been turned to the house. Only one, the first I had made out, was facing my way. I was not so shocked as you may think. The start back I had given was really nothing but a movement of surprise. I had expected to see a knob of wood there, you know. I returned deliberately to the first I had seen—and there it was, black, dried, sunken, with closed eyelids,—a head that seemed to sleep at the top of that pole, and, with the shrunken dry lips showing a narrow white line of the teeth, was smiling, too, smiling continuously at some endless and jocose dream of that eternal slumber.

"I am not disclosing any trade secrets. In fact, the manager said afterwards that Mr. Kurtz's methods had ruined the district. I have no opinion on that point, but I want you clearly to understand that there was nothing

exactly profitable in these heads being there. They only showed that Mr. Kurtz lacked restraint in the gratification of his various lusts, that there was something wanting in him—some small matter which, when the pressing need arose, could not be found under his magnificent eloquence. Whether he knew of this deficiency himself I can't say. I think the knowledge came to him at last—only at the very last. But the wilderness had found him out early, and had taken on him a terrible vengeance for the fantastic invasion. I think it had whispered to him things about himself which he did not know, things of which he had no conception till he took counsel with this great solitude—and the whisper had proved irresistibly fascinating. It echoed loudly within him because he was hollow at the core. . . . I put down the glass, and the head that had appeared near enough to be spoken to seemed at once to have leaped away from me into inaccessible distance.

"The admirer of Mr. Kurtz was a bit crestfallen. In a hurried, indistinct voice he began to assure me he had not dared to take these—say, symbols—down. He was not afraid of the natives; they would not stir till Mr. Kurtz gave the word. His ascendancy was extraordinary. The camps of these people surrounded the place, and the chiefs came every day to see him. They would crawl. . . . 'I don't want to know anything of the ceremonies used when approaching Mr. Kurtz,' I shouted. Curious, this feeling that came over me that such details would be more intolerable than those heads drying on the stakes under Mr. Kurtz's windows. After all, that was only a savage sight, while I seemed at one bound to have been transported into some lightless region of subtle horrors, where pure, uncomplicated savagery was a positive relief, being something that had a right to exist—obviously—in the sunshine. The young man looked at me with surprise. I suppose it did not occur to him that Mr. Kurtz was no idol of mine. He forgot I hadn't heard any of these splendid monologues on, what was it? on love, justice, conduct of life—or what not. If it had come to crawling before Mr. Kurtz, he crawled as much as the veriest savage of them all. I had no idea of the conditions, he said: these heads were the heads of rebels. I shocked him excessively by laughing. Rebels! What would be the next definition I was to hear? There had been enemies, criminals, workers—and these were rebels. Those rebellious heads looked very subdued to me on their sticks. 'You don't know how such a life tries a man like Kurtz,' cried Kurtz's last disciple. 'Well, and you?' I said. 'I! I! I am a simple man. I have no great thoughts. I want nothing from anybody. How can you compare me to . . . ?' His feelings were too much for speech, and suddenly he broke down. 'I don't understand,' he groaned. 'I've been doing my best to keep him alive, and that's enough. I had no hand in all this. I have no abilities. There hasn't been a drop of medicine or a mouthful of invalid food for months here. He was shamefully abandoned. A man like this, with such ideas. Shamefully! Shamefully! I—I—haven't slept for the last ten nights. . .'

"His voice lost itself in the calm of the evening. The long shadows of the forest had slipped down hill while we talked, had gone far beyond the ruined hovel, beyond the symbolic row of stakes. All this was in the gloom, while we down there were yet in the sunshine, and the stretch of the river abreast of the clearing glittered in a still and dazzling splendour, with a

murky and overshadowed bend above and below. Not a living soul was seen on the shore. The bushes did not rustle.

"Suddenly round the corner of the house a group of men appeared, as though they had come up from the ground. They waded waist-deep in the grass, in a compact body, bearing an improvised stretcher in their midst. Instantly, in the emptiness of the landscape, a cry arose whose shrillness pierced the still air like a sharp arrow flying straight to the very heart of the land; and, as if by enchantment, streams of human beings—of naked human beings—with spears in their hands, with bows, with shields, with wild glances and savage movements, were poured into the clearing by the dark-faced and pensive forest. The bushes shook, the grass swayed for a time, and then everything stood still in attentive immobility.

"'Now, if he does not say the right thing to them we are all done for,' said the Russian at my elbow. The knot of men with the stretcher had stopped, too, half-way to the steamer, as if petrified. I saw the man on the stretcher sit up, lank and with an uplifted arm, above the shoulders of the bearers. 'Let us hope that the man who can talk so well of love in general will find some particular reason to spare us this time,' I said. I resented bitterly the absurd danger of our situation, as if to be at the mercy of that atrocious phantom had been a dishonouring necessity. I could not hear a sound, but through my glasses I saw the thin arm extended commandingly, the lower jaw moving, the eyes of that apparition shining darkly far in its bony head that nodded with grotesque jerks. Kurtz—Kurtz—that means short in German—don't it? Well, the name was as true as everything else in his life—and death. He looked at least seven feet long. His covering had fallen off, and his body emerged from it pitiful and appalling as from a winding-sheet.[67] I could see the cage of his ribs all astir, the bones of his arm waving. It was as though an animated image of death carved out of old ivory had been shaking its hand with menaces at a motionless crowd of men made of dark and glittering bronze. I saw him open his mouth wide—it gave him a weirdly voracious aspect, as though he had wanted to swallow all the air, all the earth, all the men before him. A deep voice reached me faintly. He must have been shouting. He fell back suddenly. The stretcher shook as the bearers staggered forward again, and almost at the same time I noticed that the crowd of savages was vanishing without any perceptible movement of retreat, as if the forest that had ejected these beings so suddenly had drawn them in again as the breath is drawn in a long aspiration.

"Some of the pilgrims behind the stretcher carried his arms—two shot-guns, a heavy rifle, and a light revolver-carbine—the thunderbolts of that pitiful Jupiter.[68] The manager bent over him murmuring as he walked beside his head. They laid him down in one of the little cabins—just a room for a bedplace and a camp-stool or two, you know. We had brought his belated correspondence, and a lot of torn envelopes and open letters littered his bed. His hand roamed feebly amongst these pages. I was struck by the fire of his eyes and the composed languor of his expression. It was not so much the exhaustion of disease. He did not seem in pain. This shadow looked satiated and calm, as though for the moment it had had its fill of all the emotions.

[67] Wrapping for a corpse. [68] Ruler of the classical gods.

"He rustled one of the letters, and looking straight in my face said, 'I am glad.' Somebody had been writing to him about me. These special recommendations were turning up again. The volume of tone he emitted without effort, almost without the trouble of moving his lips, amazed me. A voice! a voice! It was grave, profound, vibrating, while the man did not seem capable of a whisper. However, he had enough strength in him—factitious no doubt—to very nearly make an end of us, as you shall hear directly.

"The manager appeared silently in the doorway; I stepped out at once and he drew the curtain after me. The Russian, eyed curiously by the pilgrims, was staring at the shore. I followed the direction of his glance.

"Dark human shapes could be made out in the distance, flitting indistinctly against the gloomy border of the forest, and near the river two bronze figures, leaning on tall spears, stood in the sunlight under fantastic head-dresses of spotted skins, warlike and still in statuesque repose. And from right to left along the lighted shore moved a wild and gorgeous apparition of a woman.

"She walked with measured steps, draped in striped and fringed cloths, treading the earth proudly, with a slight jingle and flash of barbarous ornaments. She carried her head high; her hair was done in the shape of a helmet; she had brass leggings to the knee, brass wire gauntlets to the elbow, a crimson spot on her tawny cheek, innumerable necklaces of glass beads on her neck; bizarre things, charms, gifts of witch-men, that hung about her, glittered and trembled at every step. She must have had the value of several elephant tusks upon her. She was savage and superb, wild-eyed and magnificent; there was something ominous and stately in her deliberate progress. And in the hush that had fallen suddenly upon the whole sorrowful land, the immense wilderness, the colossal body of the fecund and mysterious life seemed to look at her, pensive, as though it had been looking at the image of its own tenebrous[69] and passionate soul.

"She came abreast of the steamer, stood still, and faced us. Her long shadow fell to the water's edge. Her face had a tragic and fierce aspect of wild sorrow and of dumb pain mingled with the fear of some struggling, half-shaped resolve. She stood looking at us without a stir, and like the wilderness itself, with an air of brooding over an inscrutable purpose. A whole minute passed, and then she made a step forward. There was a low jingle, a glint of yellow metal, a sway of fringed draperies, and she stopped as if her heart had failed her. The young fellow by my side growled. The pilgrims murmured at my back. She looked at us all as if her life had depended upon the unswerving steadiness of her glance. Suddenly she opened her bared arms and threw them up rigid above her head, as though in an uncontrollable desire to touch the sky, and at the same time the swift shadows darted out on the earth, swept around on the river, gathering the steamer into a shadowy embrace. A formidable silence hung over the scene.

"She turned away slowly, walked on, following the bank, and passed into the bushes to the left. Once only her eyes gleamed back at us in the dusk of the thickets before she disappeared.

"'If she had offered to come aboard I really think I would have tried to

[69] Dark.

shoot her,' said the man of patches, nervously. 'I have been risking my life every day for the last fortnight to keep her out of the house. She got in one day and kicked up a row about those miserable rags I picked up in the storeroom to mend my clothes with. I wasn't decent. At least it must have been that, for she talked like a fury to Kurtz for an hour, pointing at me now and then. I don't understand the dialect of this tribe. Luckily for me, I fancy Kurtz felt too ill that day to care, or there would have been mischief. I don't understand. . . . No—it's too much for me. Ah, well, it's all over now.'

"At this moment I heard Kurtz's deep voice behind the curtain: 'Save me!—save the ivory, you mean. Don't tell me. Save *me!* Why, I've had to save you. You are interrupting my plans now. Sick! Sick! Not so sick as you would like to believe. Never mind. I'll carry my ideas out yet—I will return. I'll show you what can be done. You with your little peddling notions—you are interfering with me. I will return. I. . . .'

"The manager came out. He did me the honour to take me under the arm and lead me aside. 'He is very low, very low,' he said. He considered it necessary to sigh, but neglected to be consistently sorrowful. 'We have done all we could for him—haven't we? But there is no disguising the fact, Mr. Kurtz has done more harm than good to the Company. He did not see the time was not ripe for vigorous action. Cautiously, cautiously—that's my principle. We must be cautious yet. The district is closed to us for a time. Deplorable! Upon the whole, the trade will suffer. I don't deny there is a remarkable quantity of ivory—mostly fossil. We must save it, at all events—but look how precarious the position is—and why? Because the method is unsound.' 'Do you,' said I, looking at the shore, 'call it "unsound method?"' 'Without doubt,' he exclaimed, hotly. 'Don't you?' . . . 'No method at all,' I murmured after a while. 'Exactly,' he exulted. 'I anticipated this. Shows a complete want of judgment. It is my duty to point it out in the proper quarter.' 'Oh,' said I, 'that fellow—what's his name?—the brickmaker, will make a readable report for you.' He appeared confounded for a moment. It seemed to me I had never breathed an atmosphere so vile, and I turned mentally to Kurtz for relief—positively for relief. 'Nevertheless I think Mr. Kurtz is a remarkable man,' I said with emphasis. He started, dropped on me a cold heavy glance, said very quietly, 'he *was*,' and turned his back on me. My hour of favour was over; I found myself lumped along with Kurtz as a partisan of methods for which the time was not ripe: I was unsound! Ah! but it was something to have at least a choice of nightmares.

"I had turned to the wilderness really, not to Mr. Kurtz, who, I was ready to admit, was as good as buried. And for a moment it seemed to me as if I also were buried in a vast grave full of unspeakable secrets. I felt an intolerable weight oppressing my breast, the smell of the damp earth, the unseen presence of victorious corruption, the darkness of an impenetrable night. . . . The Russian tapped me on the shoulder. I heard him mumbling and stammering something about 'brother seaman—couldn't conceal—knowledge of matters that would affect Mr. Kurtz's reputation.' I waited. For him evidently Mr. Kurtz was not in his grave; I suspect that for him Mr. Kurtz was one of the immortals. 'Well!' said I at last, 'speak out. As it happens, I am Mr. Kurtz's friend—in a way.'

"He stated with a good deal of formality that had we not been 'of the

same profession,' he would have kept the matter to himself without regard to consequences. 'He suspected there was an active ill will towards him on the part of these white men that——' 'You are right,' I said, remembering a certain conversation I had overheard. 'The manager thinks you ought to be hanged.' He showed a concern at this intelligence which amused me at first. 'I had better get out of the way quietly,' he said, earnestly. 'I can do no more for Kurtz now, and they would soon find some excuse. What's to stop them? There's a military post three hundred miles from here.' 'Well, upon my word,' said I, 'perhaps you had better go if you have any friends amongst the savages near by.' 'Plenty,' he said, 'They are simple people— and I want nothing, you know.' He stood biting his lip, then: 'I don't want any harm to happen to these whites here, but of course I was thinking of Mr. Kurtz's reputation—but you are a brother seaman and——' 'All right,' said I, after a time. 'Mr. Kurtz's reputation is safe with me.' I did not know how truly I spoke.

"He informed me, lowering his voice, that it was Kurtz who had ordered the attack to be made on the steamer. 'He hated sometimes the idea of being taken away—and then again. . . . But I don't understand these matters. I am a simple man. He thought it would scare you away—that you would give it up, thinking him dead. I could not stop him. Oh, I had an awful time of it this last month.' 'Very well,' I said. 'He is all right now.' 'Ye-e-es,' he muttered, not very convinced apparently. 'Thanks,' said I; 'I shall keep my eyes open.' 'But quiet—eh?' he urged, anxiously. 'It would be awful for his reputation if anybody here——' I promised a complete discretion with great gravity. 'I have a canoe and three black fellows waiting not very far. I am off. Could you give me a few Martini-Henry cartridges?' I could, and did, with proper secrecy. He helped himself, with a wink at me, to a handful of my tobacco. 'Between sailors—you know—good English tobacco.' At the door of the pilot-house he turned round—'I say, haven't you a pair of shoes you could spare?' He raised one leg. 'Look.' The soles were tied with knotted strings sandal-wise under his bare feet. I rooted out an old pair, at which he looked with admiration before tucking it under his left arm. One of his pockets (bright red) was bulging with cartridges, from the other (dark blue) peeped 'Towson's Inquiry,' etc., etc. He seemed to think himself excellently well equipped for a renewed encounter with the wilderness. 'Ah! I'll never, never meet such a man again. You ought to have heard him recite poetry—his own, too, it was, he told me. Poetry!' He rolled his eyes at the recollection of these delights. 'Oh, he enlarged my mind!' 'Good-bye,' said I. He shook hands and vanished in the night. Sometimes I ask myself whether I had ever really seen him— whether it was possible to meet such a phenomenon! . . .

"When I woke up shortly after midnight his warning came to my mind with its hint of danger that seemed, in the starred darkness, real enough to make me get up for the purpose of having a look round. On the hill a big fire burned, illuminating fitfully a crooked corner of the station-house. One of the agents with a picket[70] of a few of our blacks, armed for the purpose, was keeping guard over the ivory; but deep within the forest, red gleams that wavered, that seemed to sink and rise from the ground

[70] Band of sentries.

amongst confused columnar shapes of intense blackness, showed the exact position of the camp where Mr. Kurtz's adorers were keeping their uneasy vigil. The monotonous beating of a big drum filled the air with muffled shocks and a lingering vibration. A steady droning sound of many men chanting each to himself some weird incantation came out from the black, flat wall of the woods as the humming of bees comes out of a hive, and had a strange narcotic effect upon my half-awake senses. I believe I dozed off leaning over the rail, till an abrupt burst of yells, an overwhelming outbreak of a pent-up and mysterious frenzy, woke me up in a bewildered wonder. It was cut short all at once, and the low droning went on with an effect of audible and soothing silence. I glanced casually into the little cabin. A light was burning within, but Mr. Kurtz was not there.

"I think I would have raised an outcry if I had believed my eyes. But I didn't believe them at first—the thing seemed so impossible. The fact is I was completely unnerved by a sheer blank fright, pure abstract terror, unconnected with any distinct shape of physical danger. What made this emotion so overpowering was—how shall I define it?—the moral shock I received, as if something altogether monstrous, intolerable to thought and odious to the soul, had been thrust upon me unexpectedly. This lasted of course the merest fraction of a second, and then the usual sense of commonplace, deadly danger, the possibility of a sudden onslaught and massacre, or something of the kind, which I saw impending, was positively welcome and composing. It pacified me, in fact, so much, that I did not raise an alarm.

"There was an agent buttoned up inside an ulster[71] and sleeping on a chair on deck within three feet of me. The yells had not awakened him; he snored very slightly; I left him to his slumbers and leaped ashore. I did not betray Mr. Kurtz—it was ordered I should never betray him—it was written I should be loyal to the nightmare of my choice. I was anxious to deal with this shadow by myself alone,—and to this day I don't know why I was so jealous of sharing with any one the peculiar blackness of that experience.

"As soon as I got on the bank I saw a trail—a broad trail through the grass. I remember the exultation with which I said to myself, 'He can't walk—he is crawling on all-fours—I've got him.' The grass was wet with dew. I strode rapidly with clenched fists. I fancy I had some vague notion of falling upon him and giving him a drubbing. I don't know. I had some imbecile thoughts. The knitting old woman with the cat obtruded herself upon my memory as a most improper person to be sitting at the other end of such an affair. I saw a row of pilgrims squirting lead in the air out of Winchesters held to the hip. I thought I would never get back to the steamer, and imagined myself living alone and unarmed in the woods to an advanced age. Such silly things—you know. And I remember I confounded the beat of the drum with the beating of my heart, and was pleased at its calm regularity.

"I kept to the track though—then stopped to listen. The night was very clear; a dark blue space, sparkling with dew and starlight, in which black things stood very still. I thought I could see a kind of motion ahead of me. I was strangely cocksure of everything that night. I actually left the track and

[71] Long, heavy overcoat.

ran in a wide semicircle (I verily believe chuckling to myself) so as to get in front of that stir, of that motion I had seen—if indeed I had seen anything. I was circumventing Kurtz as though it had been a boyish game.

"I came upon him, and, if he had not heard me coming, I would have fallen over him, too, but he got up in time. He rose, unsteady, long, pale, indistinct, like a vapour exhaled by the earth, and swayed slightly, misty and silent before me; while at my back the fires loomed between the trees, and the murmur of many voices issued from the forest. I had cut him off cleverly; but when actually confronting him I seemed to come to my senses, I saw the danger in its right proportion. It was by no means over yet. Suppose he began to shout? Though he could hardly stand, there was still plenty of vigour in his voice. 'Go away—hide yourself,' he said, in that profound tone. It was very awful. I glanced back. We were within thirty yards from the nearest fire. A black figure stood up, strode on long black legs, waving long black arms, across the glow. It had horns—antelope horns, I think—on its head. Some sorcerer, some witch-man, no doubt: it looked fiend-like enough. 'Do you know what you are doing?' I whispered. 'Perfectly,' he answered, raising his voice for that single word: it sounded to me far off and yet loud, like a hail through a speaking-trumpet. If he makes a row we are lost, I thought to myself. This clearly was not a case for fisticuffs, even apart from the very natural aversion I had to beat that Shadow—this wandering and tormented thing. 'You will be lost,' I said— 'utterly lost.' One gets sometimes such a flash of inspiration, you know. I did say the right thing, though indeed he could not have been more irretrievably lost than he was at this very moment, when the foundations of our intimacy were being laid—to endure—to endure—even to the end—even beyond.

"'I had immense plans,' he muttered irresolutely. 'Yes,' said I; 'but if you try to shout I'll smash your head with——' There was not a stick or a stone near. 'I will throttle you for good,' I corrected myself. 'I was on the threshold of great things,' he pleaded, in a voice of longing, with a wistfulness of tone that made my blood run cold. 'And now for this stupid scoundrel——' 'Your success in Europe is assured in any case,' I affirmed, steadily. I did not want to have the throttling of him, you understand—and indeed it would have been very little use for any practical purpose. I tried to break the spell—the heavy, mute spell of the wilderness—that seemed to draw him to its pitiless breast by the awakening of forgotten and brutal instincts, by the memory of gratified and monstrous passions. This alone, I was convinced, had driven him out to the edge of the forest, to the bush, towards the gleam of fires, the throb of drums, the drone of weird incantations; this alone had beguiled his unlawful soul beyond the bounds of permitted aspirations. And, don't you see, the terror of the position was not in being knocked on the head—though I had a very lively sense of that danger, too—but in this, that I had to deal with a being to whom I could not appeal in the name of anything high or low. I had, even like the niggers, to invoke him—himself—his own exalted and incredible degradation. There was nothing either above or below him, and I knew it. He had kicked himself loose of the earth. Confound the man! he had kicked the very earth to pieces. He was alone, and I before him did not know whether I stood on the ground or floated in the air. I've been telling you what we said—

repeating the phrases we pronounced—but what's the good? They were common everyday words—the familiar, vague sounds exchanged on every waking day of life. But what of that? They had behind them, to my mind, the terrific suggestiveness of words heard in dreams, of phrases spoken in nightmares. Soul! If anybody had ever struggled with a soul, I am the man. And I wasn't arguing with a lunatic either. Believe me or not, his intelligence was perfectly clear—concentrated, it is true, upon himself with horrible intensity, yet clear; and therein was my only chance—barring, of course, the killing him there and then, which wasn't so good, on account of unavoidable noise. But his soul was mad. Being alone in the wilderness, it had looked within itself, and, by heavens! I tell you, it had gone mad. I had—for my sins, I suppose—to go through the ordeal of looking into it myself. No eloquence could have been so withering to one's belief in mankind as his final burst of sincerity. He struggled with himself, too. I saw it,—I heard it. I saw the inconceivable mystery of a soul that knew no restraint, no faith, and no fear, yet struggling blindly with itself. I kept my head pretty well; but when I had him at last stretched on the couch, I wiped my forehead, while my legs shook under me as though I had carried half a ton on my back down that hill. And yet I had only supported him, his bony arm clasped round my neck—and he was not much heavier than a child.

"When next day we left at noon, the crowd, of whose presence behind the curtain of trees I had been acutely conscious all the time, flowed out of the woods again, filled the clearing, covered the slope with a mass of naked, breathing, quivering, bronze bodies. I steamed up a bit, then swung downstream, and two thousand eyes followed the evolutions of the splashing, thumping, fierce river-demon beating the water with its terrible tail and breathing black smoke into the air. In front of the first rank, along the river, three men, plastered with bright red earth from head to foot, strutted to and fro restlessly. When we came abreast again, they faced the river, stamped their feet, nodded their horned heads, swayed their scarlet bodies; they shook towards the fierce river-demon a bunch of black feathers, a mangy skin with a pendent tail—something that looked like a dried gourd; they shouted periodically together strings of amazing words that resembled no sounds of human language; and the deep murmurs of the crowd, interrupted suddenly, were like the responses of some satanic litany.

"We had carried Kurtz into the pilot-house: there was more air there. Lying on the couch, he stared through the open shutter. There was an eddy in the mass of human bodies, and the woman with helmeted head and tawny cheeks rushed out to the very brink of the stream. She put out her hands, shouted something, and all that wild mob took up the shout in a roaring chorus of articulated, rapid, breathless utterance.

"'Do you understand this?' I asked.

"He kept on looking out past me with fiery, longing eyes, with a mingled expression of wistfulness and hate. He made no answer, but I saw a smile, a smile of indefinable meaning, appear on his colourless lips that a moment after twitched convulsively. 'Do I not?' he said slowly, gasping, as if the words had been torn out of him by a supernatural power.

"I pulled the string of the whistle, and I did this because I saw the pilgrims on deck getting out their rifles with an air of anticipating a jolly

lark. At the sudden screech there was a movement of abject terror through that wedged mass of bodies. 'Don't! don't you frighten them away,' cried someone on deck disconsolately. I pulled the string time after time. They broke and ran, they leaped, they crouched, they swerved, they dodged the flying terror of the sound. The three red chaps had fallen flat, face down on the shore, as though they had been shot dead. Only the barbarous and superb woman did not so much as flinch, and stretched tragically her bare arms after us over the sombre and glittering river.

"And then that imbecile crowd down on the deck started their little fun, and I could see nothing more for smoke.

"The brown current ran swiftly out of the heart of darkness, bearing us down towards the sea with twice the speed of our upward progress; and Kurtz's life was running swiftly, too, ebbing, ebbing out of his heart into the sea of inexorable time. The manager was very placid, he had no vital anxieties now, he took us both in with a comprehensive and satisfied glance: the 'affair' had come off as well as could be wished. I saw the time approaching when I would be left alone of the party of 'unsound method.' The pilgrims looked upon me with disfavour. I was, so to speak, numbered with the dead. It is strange how I accepted this unforeseen partnership, this choice of nightmares forced upon me in the tenebrous land invaded by these mean and greedy phantoms.

"Kurtz discoursed. A voice! a voice! It rang deep to the very last. It survived his strength to hide in the magnificent folds of eloquence the barren darkness of his heart. Oh, he struggled! he struggled! The wastes of his weary brain were haunted by shadowy images now—images of wealth and fame revolving obsequiously round his unextinguishable gift of noble and lofty expression. My Intended, my station, my career, my ideas—these were the subjects for the occasional utterances of elevated sentiments. The shade of the original Kurtz frequented the bedside of the hollow sham, whose fate it was to be buried presently in the mould of primeval earth. But both the diabolic love and the unearthly hate of the mysteries it had penetrated fought for the possession of that soul satiated with primitive emotions, avid of lying fame, of sham distinction, of all the appearances of success and power.

"Sometimes he was contemptibly childish. He desired to have kings meet him at railway-stations on his return from some ghastly Nowhere, where he intended to accomplish great things. 'You show them you have in you something that is really profitable, and then there will be no limits to the recognition of your ability,' he would say. 'Of course you must take care of the motives—right motives—always.' The long reaches that were like one and the same reach, monotonous bends that were exactly alike, slipped past the steamer with their multitude of secular[72] trees looking patiently after this grimy fragment of another world, the forerunner of change, of conquest, of trade, of massacres, of blessings. I looked ahead—piloting. 'Close the shutter,' said Kurtz suddenly one day; 'I can't bear to look at this.' I did so. There was a silence. 'Oh, but I will wring your heart yet!' he cried at the invisible wilderness.

"We broke down—as I had expected—and had to lie up for repairs at

[72] Enduring for ages.

the head of an island. This delay was the first thing that shook Kurtz's confidence. One morning he gave me a packet of papers and a photograph—the lot tied together with a shoe-string. 'Keep this for me,' he said. 'This noxious fool' (meaning the manager) 'is capable of prying into my boxes when I am not looking.' In the afternoon I saw him. He was lying on his back with closed eyes, and I withdrew quietly, but I heard him mutter, 'Live rightly, die, die . . .' I listened. There was nothing more. Was he rehearsing some speech in his sleep, or was it a fragment of a phrase from some newspaper article? He had been writing for the papers and meant to do so again, 'for the furthering of my ideas. It's a duty.'

"His was an impenetrable darkness. I looked at him as you peer down at a man who is lying at the bottom of a precipice where the sun never shines. But I had not much time to give him, because I was helping the engine-driver to take to pieces the leaky cylinders, to straighten a bent connecting-rod, and in other such matters. I lived in an infernal mess of rust, filings, nuts, bolts, spanners, hammers, ratchet-drills—things I abominate, because I don't get on with them. I tended the little forge we fortunately had aboard; I toiled wearily in a wretched scrap-heap—unless I had the shakes too bad to stand.

"One evening coming in with a candle I was startled to hear him say a little tremulously, 'I am lying here in the dark waiting for death.' The light was within a foot of his eyes. I forced myself to murmur, 'Oh, nonsense!' and stood over him as if transfixed.

"Anything approaching the change that came over his features I have never seen before, and hope never to see again. Oh, I wasn't touched. I was fascinated. It was as though a veil had been rent. I saw on that ivory face the expression of sombre pride, of ruthless power, of craven terror—of an intense and hopeless despair. Did he live his life again in every detail of desire, temptation, and surrender during that supreme moment of complete knowledge? He cried in a whisper at some image, at some vision—he cried out twice, a cry that was no more than a breath—

"'The horror! The horror!'

"I blew the candle out and left the cabin. The pilgrims were dining in the mess-room, and I took my place opposite the manager, who lifted his eyes to give me a questioning glance, which I successfully ignored. He leaned back, serene, with that peculiar smile of his sealing the unexpressed depths of his meanness. A continuous shower of small flies streamed upon the lamp, upon the cloth, upon our hands and faces. Suddenly the manager's boy put his insolent black head in the doorway, and said in a tone of scathing contempt—

"'Mistah Kurtz—he dead.'

"All the pilgrims rushed out to see. I remained, and went on with my dinner. I believe I was considered brutally callous. However, I did not eat much. There was a lamp in there—light, don't you know—and outside it was so beastly, beastly dark. I went no more near the remarkable man who had pronounced a judgment upon the adventures of his soul on this earth. The voice was gone. What else had been there? But I am of course aware that next day the pilgrims buried something in a muddy hole.

"And then they very nearly buried me.

"However, as you see, I did not go to join Kurtz there and then. I did

not. I remained to dream the nightmare out to the end, and to show my loyalty to Kurtz once more. Destiny. My destiny! Droll thing life is—that mysterious arrangement of merciless logic for a futile purpose. The most you can hope from it is some knowledge of yourself—that comes too late—a crop of unextinguishable regrets. I have wrestled with death. It is the most unexciting contest you can imagine. It takes place in an impalpable grayness, with nothing under foot, with nothing around, without spectators, without clamour, without glory, without the great desire of victory, without the great fear of defeat, in a sickly atmosphere of tepid scepticism, without much belief in your own right, and still less in that of your adversary. If such is the form of ultimate wisdom, then life is a greater riddle than some of us think it to be. I was within a hair's breadth of the last opportunity for pronouncement, and I found with humiliation that probably I would have nothing to say. This is the reason why I affirm that Kurtz was a remarkable man. He had something to say. He said it. Since I had peeped over the edge myself, I understand better the meaning of his stare, that could not see the flame of the candle, but was wide enough to embrace the whole universe, piercing enough to penetrate all the hearts that beat in the darkness. He had summed up—he had judged. 'The horror!' He was a remarkable man. After all, this was the expression of some sort of belief; it had candour, it had conviction, it had a vibrating note of revolt in its whisper, it had the appalling face of a glimpsed truth—the strange commingling of desire and hate. And it is not my own extremity I remember best—a vision of grayness without form filled with physical pain, and a careless contempt for the evanescence of all things—even of this pain itself. No! It is his extremity that I seem to have lived through. True, he had made that last stride, he had stepped over the edge, while I had been permitted to draw back my hesitating foot. And perhaps in this is the whole difference; perhaps all the wisdom, and all truth, and all sincerity, are just compressed into that inappreciable moment of time in which we step over the threshold of the invisible. Perhaps! I like to think my summing-up would not have been a word of careless contempt. Better his cry—much better. It was an affirmation, a moral victory paid for by innumerable defeats, by abominable terrors, by abominable satisfactions. But it was a victory! That is why I have remained loyal to Kurtz to the last, and even beyond, when a long time after I heard once more, not his own voice, but the echo of his magnificent eloquence thrown to me from a soul as translucently pure as a cliff of crystal.

"No, they did not bury me, though there is a period of time which I remember mistily, with a shuddering wonder, like a passage through some inconceivable world that had no hope in it and no desire. I found myself back in the sepulchral city resenting the sight of people hurrying through the streets to filch a little money from each other, to devour their infamous cookery, to gulp their unwholesome beer, to dream their insignificant and silly dreams. They trespassed upon my thoughts. They were intruders whose knowledge of life was to me an irritating pretence, because I felt so sure they could not possibly know the things I knew. Their bearing, which was simply the bearing of commonplace individuals going about their business in the assurance of perfect safety, was offensive to me like the outrageous flauntings of folly in the face of a danger it is unable to comprehend.

I had no particular desire to enlighten them, but I had some difficulty in restraining myself from laughing in their faces, so full of stupid importance. I daresay I was not very well at that time. I tottered about the streets—there were various affairs to settle—grinning bitterly at perfectly respectable persons. I admit my behaviour was inexcusable, but then my temperature was seldom normal in these days. My dear aunt's endeavours to 'nurse up my strength' seemed altogether beside the mark. It was not my strength that wanted nursing, it was my imagination that wanted soothing. I kept the bundle of papers given me by Kurtz, not knowing exactly what to do with it. His mother had died lately, watched over, as I was told, by his Intended. A clean-shaved man, with an official manner and wearing gold-rimmed spectacles, called on me one day and made inquiries, at first circuitous, afterwards suavely pressing, about what he was pleased to denominate certain 'documents.' I was not surprised, because I had had two rows with the manager on the subject out there. I had refused to give up the smallest scrap out of that package, and I took the same attitude with the spectacled man. He became darkly menacing at last, and with much heat argued that the Company had the right to every bit of information about its 'territories.' And, said he, 'Mr. Kurtz's knowledge of unexplored regions must have been necessarily extensive and peculiar—owing to his great abilities and to the deplorable circumstances in which he had been placed: therefore——' I assured him Mr. Kurtz's knowledge, however extensive, did not bear upon the problems of commerce or administration. He invoked then the name of science. 'It would be an incalculable loss if,' etc., etc. I offered him the report on the 'Suppression of Savage Customs,' with the postscriptum torn off. He took it eagerly, but ended by sniffing at it with an air of contempt. 'This is not what we had a right to expect,' he remarked. 'Expect nothing else,' I said. 'There are only private letters.' He withdrew upon some threat of legal proceedings, and I saw him no more; but another fellow, calling himself Kurtz's cousin, appeared two days later, and was anxious to hear all the details about his dear relative's last moments. Incidentally he gave me to understand that Kurtz had been essentially a great musician. 'There was the making of an immense success,' said the man, who was an organist, I believe, with lank gray hair flowing over a greasy coat-collar. I had no reason to doubt his statement; and to this day I am unable to say what was Kurtz's profession, whether he ever had any—which was the greatest of his talents. I had taken him for a painter who wrote for the papers, or else for a journalist who could paint—but even the cousin (who took snuff during the interview) could not tell me what he had been—exactly. He was a universal genius—on that point I agreed with the old chap, who thereupon blew his nose noisily into a large cotton handkerchief and withdrew in senile agitation, bearing off some family letters and memoranda without importance. Ultimately a journalist anxious to know something of the fate of his 'dear colleague' turned up. This visitor informed me Kurtz's proper sphere ought to have been politics 'on the popular side.' He had furry straight eyebrows, bristly hair cropped short, an eye-glass on a broad ribbon, and becoming expansive, confessed his opinion that Kurtz really couldn't write a bit—'but heavens! how that man could talk. He electrified large meetings. He had faith—don't you see?—he had the faith. He could get himself to believe anything—anything. He would

have been a splendid leader of an extreme party.' 'What party?' I asked. 'Any party,' answered the other. 'He was an—an—extremist.' Did I not think so? I assented. Did I know, he asked, with a sudden flash of curiosity, 'what it was that had induced him to go out there?' 'Yes,' said I, and forthwith handed him the famous Report for publication, if he thought fit. He glanced through it hurriedly, mumbling all the time, judged 'it would do,' and took himself off with this plunder.

"Thus I was left at last with a slim packet of letters and the girl's portrait. She struck me as beautiful—I mean she had a beautiful expression. I know that the sunlight can be made to lie, too, yet one felt that no manipulation of light and pose could have conveyed the delicate shade of truthfulness upon those features. She seemed ready to listen without mental reservation, without suspicion, without a thought for herself. I concluded I would go and give her back her portrait and those letters myself. Curiosity? Yes; and also some other feeling perhaps. All that had been Kurtz's had passed out of my hands: his soul, his body, his station, his plans, his ivory, his career. There remained only his memory and his Intended—and I wanted to give that up, too, to the past, in a way—to surrender personally all that remained of him with me to that oblivion which is the last word of our common fate. I don't defend myself. I had no clear perception of what it was I really wanted. Perhaps it was an impulse of unconscious loyalty, or the fulfilment of one of those ironic necessities that lurk in the facts of human existence. I don't know. I can't tell. But I went.

"I thought his memory was like the other memories of the dead that accumulate in every man's life—a vague impress on the brain of shadows that had fallen on it in their swift and final passage; but before the high and ponderous door, between the tall houses of a street as still and decorous as a well-kept alley in a cemetery, I had a vision of him on the stretcher, opening his mouth voraciously, as if to devour all the earth with all its mankind. He lived then before me; he lived as much as he had ever lived—a shadow insatiable of splendid appearances, of frightful realities; a shadow darker than the shadow of the night, and draped nobly in the folds of a gorgeous eloquence. The vision seemed to enter the house with me—the stretcher, the phantom-bearers, the wild crowd of obedient worshippers, the gloom of the forests, the glitter of the reach between the murky bends, the beat of the drum, regular and muffled like the beating of a heart—the heart of a conquering darkness. It was a moment of triumph for the wilderness, an invading and vengeful rush which, it seemed to me, I would have to keep back alone for the salvation of another soul. And the memory of what I had heard him say afar there, with the horned shapes stirring at my back, in the glow of fires, within the patient woods, those broken phrases came back to me, were heard again in their ominous and terrifying simplicity. I remembered his abject pleading, his abject threats, the colossal scale of his vile desires, the meanness, the torment, the tempestuous anguish of his soul. And later on I seemed to see his collected languid manner, when he said one day, 'This lot of ivory now is really mine. The Company did not pay for it. I collected it myself at a very great personal risk. I am afraid they will try to claim it as theirs though. H'm. It is a difficult case. What do you think I ought to do—resist? Eh? I want no more than justice.' . . . He wanted no more than justice—no more than justice. I

rang the bell before a mahogany door on the first floor,[73] and while I waited he seemed to stare at me out of the glassy panel—stare with that wide and immense stare embracing, condemning, loathing all the universe. I seemed to hear the whispered cry, 'The horror! The horror!'

"The dusk was falling. I had to wait in a lofty drawing-room with three long windows from floor to ceiling that were like three luminous and bedraped columns. The bent gilt legs and backs of the furniture shone in indistinct curves. The tall marble fireplace had a cold and monumental whiteness. A grand piano stood massively in a corner; with dark gleams on the flat surfaces like a sombre and polished sarcophagus.[74] A high door opened—closed. I rose.

"She came forward, all in black, with a pale head, floating towards me in the dusk. She was in mourning. It was more than a year since his death, more than a year since the news came; she seemed as though she would remember and mourn forever. She took both my hands in hers and murmured, 'I had heard you were coming.' I noticed she was not very young— I mean not girlish. She had a mature capacity for fidelity, for belief, for suffering. The room seemed to have grown darker, as if all the sad light of the cloudy evening had taken refuge on her forehead. This fair hair, this pale visage, this pure brow, seemed surrounded by an ashy halo from which the dark eyes looked out at me. Their glance was guileless, profound, confident, and trustful. She carried her sorrowful head as though she were proud of that sorrow, as though she would say, I—I alone know how to mourn for him as he deserves. But while we were still shaking hands, such a look of awful desolation came upon her face that I perceived she was one of those creatures that are not the playthings of Time. For her he had died only yesterday. And, by Jove! the impression was so powerful that for me, too, he seemed to have died only yesterday—nay, this very minute. I saw her and him in the same instant of time—his death and her sorrow—I saw her sorrow in the very moment of his death. Do you understand? I saw them together—I heard them together. She had said, with a deep catch of the breath, 'I have survived'; while my strained ears seemed to hear distinctly, mingled with her tone of despairing regret, the summing-up whisper of his eternal condemnation. I asked myself what I was doing there, with a sensation of panic in my heart as though I had blundered into a place of cruel and absurd mysteries not fit for a human being to behold. She motioned me to a chair. We sat down. I laid the packet gently on the little table, and she put her hand over it. . . . 'You knew him well,' she murmured, after a moment of mourning silence.

"'Intimacy grows quickly out there,' I said. 'I knew him as well as it is possible for one man to know another.'

"'And you admired him,' she said. 'It was impossible to know him and not to admire him. Was it?'

"'He was a remarkable man,' I said, unsteadily. Then before the appealing fixity of her gaze, that seemed to watch for more words on my lips, I went on, 'It was impossible not to——'

"'Love him,' she finished eagerly, silencing me into an appalled

[73] What Americans call the second floor. [74] Stately stone coffin.

dumbness. 'How true! how true! But when you think that no one knew him so well as I! I had all his noble confidence. I knew him best.'

"'You knew him best,' I repeated. And perhaps she did. But with every word spoken the room was growing darker, and only her forehead, smooth and white, remained illumined by the unextinguishable light of belief and love.

"'You were his friend,' she went on. 'His friend,' she repeated, a little louder. 'You must have been, if he had given you this, and sent you to me. I feel I can speak to you—and oh! I must speak. I want you—you who have heard his last words—to know I have been worthy of him. . . . It is not pride. . . . Yes! I am proud to know I understood him better than any one on earth—he told me so himself. And since his mother died I have had no one—no one—to—to——'

"I listened. The darkness deepened. I was not even sure whether he had given me the right bundle. I rather suspect he wanted me to take care of another batch of his papers which, after his death, I saw the manager examining under the lamp. And the girl talked, easing her pain in the certitude of my sympathy; she talked as thirsty men drink. I had heard that her engagement with Kurtz had been disapproved by her people. He wasn't rich enough or something. And indeed I don't know whether he had not been a pauper all his life. He had given me some reason to infer that it was his impatience of comparative poverty that drove him out there.

"'. . . Who was not his friend who had heard him speak once?' she was saying. 'He drew men towards him by what was best in them.' She looked at me with intensity. 'It is the gift of the great,' she went on, and the sound of her low voice seemed to have the accompaniment of all the other sounds, full of mystery, desolation, and sorrow, I had ever heard—the ripple of the river, the soughing of the trees swayed by the wind, the murmurs of the crowds, the faint ring of incomprehensible words cried from afar, the whisper of a voice speaking from beyond the threshold of an eternal darkness. 'But you have heard him! You know!' she cried.

"'Yes, I know,' I said with something like despair in my heart, but bowing my head before the faith that was in her, before that great and saving illusion that shone with an unearthly glow in the darkness, in the triumphant darkness from which I could not have defended her—from which I could not even defend myself.

"'What a loss to me—to us!'—she corrected herself with beautiful generosity; then added in a murmur, 'To the world.' By the last gleams of twilight I could see the glitter of her eyes, full of tears—of tears that would not fall.

"'I have been very happy—very fortunate—very proud,' she went on. 'Too fortunate. Too happy for a little while. And now I am unhappy for—for life.'

"She stood up; her fair hair seemed to catch all the remaining light in a glimmer of gold. I rose, too.

"'And of all this,' she went on, mournfully, 'of all his promise, and of all his greatness, of his generous mind, of his noble heart, nothing remains—nothing but a memory. You and I——'

"'We shall always remember him,' I said, hastily.

"'No!' she cried. 'It is impossible that all this should be lost—that such a life should be sacrificed to leave nothing—but sorrow. You know what vast plans he had. I knew of them, too—I could not perhaps understand—but others knew of them. Something must remain. His words, at least, have not died.'

"'His words will remain,' I said.

"'And his example,' she whispered to herself. 'Men looked up to him—his goodness shone in every act. His example——

"'True,' I said; 'his example, too. Yes, his example. I forgot that.'

"'But I do not. I cannot—I cannot believe—not yet. I cannot believe that I shall never see him again, that nobody will see him again, never, never, never.'

"She put out her arms as if after a retreating figure, stretching them back and with clasped pale hands across the fading and narrow sheen of the window. Never see him! I saw him clearly enough then. I shall see this eloquent phantom as long as I live, and I shall see her, too, a tragic and familiar Shade, resembling in this gesture another one, tragic also, and bedecked with powerless charms, stretching bare brown arms over the glitter of the infernal stream, the stream of darkness. She said suddenly very low, 'He died as he lived.'

"'His end,' said I, with dull anger stirring in me, 'was in every way worthy of his life.'

"'And I was not with him,' she murmured. My anger subsided before a feeling of infinite pity.

"'Everything that could be done—— I mumbled.

"'Ah, but I believed in him more than any one on earth—more than his own mother, more than—himself. He needed me! Me! I would have treasured every sigh, every word, every sign, every glance.'

"I felt like a chill grip on my chest. 'Don't,' I said, in a muffled voice.

"'Forgive me. I—I—have mourned so long in silence—in silence. . . . You were with him—to the last? I think of his loneliness. Nobody near to understand him as I would have understood. Perhaps no one to hear. . . .'

"'To the very end,' I said, shakily. 'I heard his very last words. . . .' I stopped in a fright.

"'Repeat them,' she murmured in a heart-broken tone. 'I want—I want—something—something—to—live with.'

"I was on the point of crying at her, 'Don't you hear them?' The dusk was repeating them in a persistent whisper all around us, in a whisper that seemed to swell menacingly like the first whisper of a rising wind. 'The horror! the horror!'

"'His last word—to live with,' she insisted. 'Don't you understand I loved him—I loved him—I loved him!'

"I pulled myself together and spoke slowly.

"'The last word he pronounced was—your name.'

"I heard a light sigh and then my heart stood still, stopped dead short by an exulting and terrible cry, by the cry of inconceivable triumph and of unspeakable pain. 'I knew it—I was sure!' . . . She knew. She was sure. I heard her weeping; she had hidden her face in her hands. It seemed to me that the house would collapse before I could escape, that the heavens would fall upon my head. But nothing happened. The heavens do not fall

for such a trifle. Would they have fallen, I wonder, if I had rendered Kurtz that justice which was his due? Hadn't he said he wanted only justice? But I couldn't. I could not tell her. It would have been too dark—too dark altogether. . . ."

Marlow ceased, and sat apart, indistinct and silent, in the pose of a meditating Buddha. Nobody moved for a time. "We have lost the first of the ebb," said the Director, suddenly. I raised my head. The offing was barred by a black bank of clouds, and the tranquil waterway leading to the uttermost ends of the earth flowed sombre under an overcast sky—seemed to lead into the heart of an immense darkness.

William Butler Yeats
(1865–1939)

"The greatest poet of our time—certainly the greatest in this language, and so far as I am able to judge, in any language"—this was T. S. Eliot's judgment of William Butler Yeats soon after his death in 1939. Another fellow poet, W. H. Auden, paid, in verse, an equally strong, if more ambiguous, tribute: "You were silly like us: your gift survived it all; / The parish of rich women, physical decay, / Yourself; mad Ireland hurt you into poetry." The silliness is certainly there in Yeats; the greatness is in his power to pass his experiences through the Byzantine fire of his imagination and turn them into great poetry.

Yeats's life and personality were battlefields of ambivalence and contradiction. A shy, retiring man, he nevertheless was a vigorous crusader for Irish national literature, an efficient manager of the Abbey Theatre, and eventually an Irish senator ("a smiling public man"). One of the most local of poets, combing Irish folklore and history for his subjects and his imagery, he was at the same time profoundly modern in his intellectual cosmopolitanism, not only drawing upon the classics of Western literature and thought but also, often for the first time in the West, tapping the riches of Japan, China, and India. Rejecting the often acrimonious division between Catholic and Protestant in his native land, he nevertheless immersed himself in a sort of composite religious mysticism drawn from a wide range of world religions and partially devised by himself. It is no wonder that Yeats constructed an elaborate mythological system based upon "masks" and "anti-selves" and that his poems are full of rich, unresolved tensions between recurring opposites.

Yeats's life and career do not present an orderly progression through certain "periods," but rather a restless oscillation among his central preoccupations: a fierce devotion to "pure" art, an equally fierce commitment to an Irish national art, withdrawal into ecstatic mysticism, and involvement in the affairs of the world. Born in Dublin in 1865, Yeats was the first of four children of John Butler Yeats, who had thrown over the practice of the law

to become a portrait painter, and Susan Pollexfen Yeats, the quiet and devout daughter of a prominent family in County Sligo, in northwestern Ireland. Yeats's childhood and youth were divided among Dublin; London, where his father was studying art and seeking commissions; and Sligo, with his mother's family. After a brief flirtation with art school in Dublin, Yeats settled for a time in London, where his first book—*The Wanderings of Oisin*—appeared in 1889. Despite its Irish proper names, the book was a lengthy, ethereal, Shelleyan allegory.

The 1890's were a period of rapid development for Yeats. He had already become interested in the patriot John O'Leary's calls for an Irish national literature, and he was further galvanized by his first meeting, in 1889, with Maud Gonne, a famous Dublin beauty and a fervent nationalist, for whom he cherished a hopeless love the rest of his life. Yeats wrote a play, *The Countess Cathleen* (1892), for Maud Gonne, and in *The Celtic Twilight,* a collection of essays published in 1893, he renewed O'Leary's call for Irish art to express Irish nationalism. His meeting in 1896 with Lady Augusta Gregory, a wealthy Irish widow with an interest in writing, led to the founding of the Irish Literary Theatre in 1899 and of the Abbey Theatre in 1904. The Abbey became one of the greatest of twentieth-century theater companies, nurturing the dramatic talents not only of Yeats and Lady Gregory, who became a skilled writer of folk comedies, but also of John Millington Synge and, later, Sean O'Casey.

The other major thread of Yeats's development during the '90s was his evolving of an elaborate body of symbolism. His study of Shelley, Blake (whose works he edited during this decade), and the French Symbolists led him to a conviction that most major poets had drawn upon a fully developed system of complementary symbols, and he consciously set out to elaborate such a system for himself. He drew not only upon the symbols of Shelley and Blake but also upon the mystical systems of the Theosophists, the Rosicrucians, and the spiritualists. He had always been attracted to magic and in London had been a member of the Theosophical Society, a late-nineteenth-century cult which, under its charismatic leader Madame Helena Petrovna Blavatsky, sought to unite mankind by reviving ancient occult knowledge; he also belonged to the Order of the Golden Dawn, led by MacGregor Mathers, which shared many of the Theosophists' concerns but was more willing to attempt "phenomena," or feats of magic. From both literary and occult sources, Yeats built up a body of recurring symbols—the rose, the lily, the swan, the cross—and he added to them symbols of his own devising, many from Irish legend.

This body of symbolism first appeared fully in *The Wind Among the Reeds* (1899), a book whose impact upon the modern movement the Yeats critic Richard Ellmann has compared to that of Wordsworth's *Lyrical Ballads* (1798) upon the Romantic movement. Almost precisely a century before, Wordsworth had called for man to return to the "mighty presence" of nature for strength and renewal; Yeats called for man to turn back into himself to discover a second nature, a nature not "half created, half perceived" as for Wordsworth, but almost wholly created by the human mind, for whom seas, stars, and roses were merely emblems of inner reality.

After the achievement of *The Wind Among the Reeds,* and under the influence of his practical, public work with the Abbey Theatre and his study

of translations of Irish poetry, Yeats characteristically swung back from the symbolic pole of his work toward the realistic one. The poems in *In the Seven Woods* (1903), *The Green Helmet* (1910), and *Responsibilities* (1914), though they retained some Yeatsian symbolism, for the most part used more themes from ordinary life, a more concrete imagery, and a more direct, colloquial diction. This spirit is expressed in a short poem in *Responsibilities*, "A Coat," in which the poet rejects his coat "covered with embroideries / Out of old mythologies" and asserts that "there's more enterprise / In walking naked."

Ezra Pound, American expatriate and fervent crusader for the "modern," whom Yeats first met in 1909, helped interest Yeats, who was already disillusioned by the coarse literal-mindedness of Abbey audiences, in the Noh plays of Japan, and Yeats wrote the first of his many small chamber plays for dancers in 1916: *At the Hawk's Well*. In the same year, the Easter Rising, which was planned as a general rebellion against English rule but diminished to a gallant defense of the Dublin General Post Office, held by nationalists who proclaimed an Irish republic, was swiftly and brutally put down by the English. With a Yeatsian doubleness of vision, the arcane withdrawal of *At the Hawk's Well* was balanced by the guarded but genuine celebration, in a series of poems, of the "terrible beauty" of the Rising.

In 1917, Yeats proposed marriage to Iseult Gonne, daughter of the Maud Gonne who had refused his repeated proposals. Iseult, too, refused, and a few weeks later, Yeats proposed to Georgie Hyde-Lees and was accepted. On his honeymoon, Yeats suggested that his bride try automatic writing, by which the subject lets the hand move, ouija-board style, without conscious control. Yeats was delighted with the results, concluded that Mrs. Yeats had strong psychic powers, and used the texts produced as the basis of *A Vision* (1925), the exposition of his comprehensive mythology. The Yeatses paid £35 for a ruined Norman tower at Ballylee, in Galway, near Coole Park, Lady Gregory's home, where Yeats had spent many summers, and had it remodeled into a home. They divided their time between the tower and a house in Dublin. A daughter was born in 1919 and a son in 1921. In 1922 Yeats became a senator of the new Irish Free State, and in 1923 he received the Nobel Prize.

Whether because of his marriage, the satisfaction of recognition both in Ireland and internationally, or the achievement of a creatively balanced tension among the potentially conflicting elements of his art, Yeats's poetry of the 1920s represents his finest achievement. The volumes *The Tower* (1928) and *The Winding Stair* (1933), which contain such masterpieces as the two Byzantium poems, "Leda and the Swan," and "Among School Children," combine a direct, concrete diction and a rich and suggestive, though unobtrusive, symbolism to speak powerfully of many of Yeats's central concerns.

The last decade of Yeats's life was dominated by yet another conflict, that between mortality and the urge to live, and this conflict found its way into a surprising group of poems of his old age. In 1927, Yeats contracted a serious lung ailment from which he was never to recover fully. He had to give up residence in the Ballylee tower after 1929 and spent much of his time during these later years in Italy and the south of France. In 1934, he underwent a "Steinach operation," a procedure to retard aging by regulat-

ing the production of hormones; Yeats regarded it as a success. Much of his writing during the '30s was devoted to drama and to rewriting *A Vision*, a revised version of which appeared in 1937. But he also continued to write poetry voluminously, much of which was published posthumously, in *Last Poems and Plays* (1940). In many of these last poems, Yeats adopted the mask of a "wild old wicked man" raging against the dying of the light and returning, his "ladder" of speculation and mythologizing gone, to the "foul rag-and-bone shop of the heart." He died in southern France in 1939. His heirs had to wait until 1948, after World War II, to bring his body back to Sligo and reinter it in the churchyard at Drumcliffe, under the epitaph stipulated in "Under Ben Bulben": "Cast a cold eye on life, on death. Horseman, pass by!"

The serious reader of Yeats must sooner or later come to terms with the symbolism of the system outlined in *A Vision*, either reading all the poems after 1922 as fully understandable only in the light of the system, ignoring it completely and attending only to the poems' intrinsic meanings, or (most sensibly) consulting the system when it is needed and ignoring it otherwise. *A Vision* is very complex, but the elements of it needed for reading all but a few of the poems are fairly simple. Its basis is a cyclic system which, in good occult fashion, can show the "correspondences" among world history, national history, and the individual life. The cycle is the "Great Wheel," a circle divided into twenty-eight segments derived from the phases of the moon. Each of the twenty-eight phases is identified with certain characteristics and values; phases opposite each other on the circle are opposite in qualities as well. The Great Wheel thus yields twenty-eight phases through which world history and national histories pass, as well as twenty-eight personality types, each with its implicit opposite or "mask."

The other basic conceptual representation in *A Vision* consists of two "gyres." These gyres, or whirling cones, are represented as pointed in opposite directions and interpenetrating each other. Like the lunar phases of the Great Wheel, the gyres represent a balancing of opposites, one gyre representing external fate, the other standing for internal destiny (as well as a number of other opposites). A cross section of these two whirling, interlocked cones will produce a representation of the mingled qualities of an individual personality, with complex balancings of fate and free will, the physical and the spiritual, space and time, the moral and the esthetic, the "objective" and the "subjective," and other oppositions. The gyres, like the wheel, have historical and cosmic meanings as well as personal ones.

A Vision is also of interest in its own right, not just as a guide to the poems based on it. It can be read as an intensely subjective veiled self-analysis in which Yeats tries to come to terms with the divisions he feels in his own personality. But from another point of view, it is an essentially objective attempt to escape the divisions of a single self and attain a "unity" (a favorite Yeats word) in which all possible individual conflicts and antitheses can be contained. It is, in other words, Yeats's most elaborate poetic metaphor, if not his richest.

Yeats's attitude toward his system was ambiguous. At times, he seemed to imply a literal belief in it; at other times, he seemed to regard it merely as scaffolding to be kicked away after it had been used, mere "stylistic arrangements of experience." The ordinary reader of Yeats will be more

likely to adopt the latter attitude and be moved not by the system but by the poetry.

In imagining vividly the rape of Leda by the swan Zeus, Yeats wonders, "Did she put on his knowledge with his power / Before the indifferent beak could let her drop?" "Knowledge" and "power"—these are favorite words of Yeats's throughout his career. They suggest the choice (seldom clear-cut) the individual must make between cultivation of the self and involvement in the external world, with the danger that knowledge will make one "lack all conviction," while power will fill one with a misguided "passionate intensity." A few of Yeats's poems may be identified as "knowledge" poems or "power" poems, but in most of them knowledge and power are held in a dynamic balance, along with the other resonant oppositions that radiate out from this central one. It is this complex, essentially dramatic sense of the world, along with Yeats's miraculous mastery of language, that has made him the most memorable poet of the twentieth century.

An important, though paradoxical, part of Yeats's involvement in Irish public life was his work with the Abbey Theatre. The paradox is that, though Yeats was one of the founders of the theater and was for many years its manager, most of his own plays were written for a very different sort of theater. Yeats wrote over two dozen plays, most of them short, most of them in verse, and most of them intellectually demanding. While the Abbey strove to be a popular theater, producing more or less realistic plays of Irish life, Yeats's ideal "theater" seemed to be an aristocratic drawing-room with a handful of sophisticated spectators. And indeed many of his most characteristic plays were produced under such circumstances.

Deirdre, though, Yeats's dramatization of the most famous of Irish legends, was written for the Abbey and performed there in 1906 and many times subsequently. The story of Deirdre appears in the "Exile of the Sons of Uisliu," dating from the eighth or ninth century. (It is reprinted in the first volume of this anthology.) The tale begins with the birth of Derdriu (or Deirdre), of whom it is prophesied both that she will be wonderfully beautiful and that she will bring great harm to the kingdom of Ulster. King Conchobar orders that she be isolated and reared to be his bride. But when she is grown, she elopes with Noisiu (Naoise), one of the "sons of Uisliu." They flee to Alba (Britain), where they stay for some time, but are forced to flee again when the British king tries to kill Noisiu and kidnap Derdriu. Conchobar allows them to return to Ireland under pledges of safety, but he immediately kills Noisiu and takes Derdriu. Yeats, who begins his play with the return of the couple to Ireland, considerably compresses the action of the original story, in which Derdriu remains with Conchobar for a year, grieving for Noisiu, before committing suicide by dashing her head against a stone.

Yeats wrote of the story: "Deirdre was the Irish Helen, and Naisi her Paris, and Conchubar her Menelaus, and the events took place, according to the conventional chronology of the Bards, about the time of the birth of Christ." Yeats may have had a personal reason for his interest in the Deirdre story in 1904, when he began the play. Maud Gonne had married the dashing young Major John MacBride a year before. Thus Deirdre, Naoise, and Conchubar (Yeats's spelling) parallel not only the triangle of Helen, Paris, and Menelaus but also that of Maud Gonne, MacBride, and

Yeats. But Yeats is not only Conchubar, he is also Fergus, the ex-king who has given up power for knowledge. And so the conflict is not merely between Conchubar and Naoise but is also a very Yeatsian one between Conchubar and Fergus, power and knowledge, the crafty wielder of force and the easily deceived friend of the lovers. The modern theater has not taken the route implied by Yeats's compressed, poetic, and elliptical dramas, like *Deirdre*, but they remain a fascinating extension, at least, of his poetic achievement.

FURTHER READING (*prepared by J. H.*): There has been a recent flurry in the editing of Yeats's poems. The long-standard *Collected Poems* of 1951 has now been superseded by two new complete editions: *Yeats, The Poems: A New Edition*, ed. R. J. Finneran, 1983, and *W. B. Yeats: The Poems*, ed. Daniel Albright, 1990. Richard Ellmann's fine biography, *Yeats: The Man and the Masks*, rev. ed. 1979, has now been supplemented, though not replaced, by A. Norman Jeffares, *W. B. Yeats: A New Biography*, 1988. As short general introductions, Richard F. Peterson's *William Butler Yeats*, 1982, and Augustine Martin's *W. B. Yeats*, 1983, may both be recommended. For more extended overviews, see Ellmann's *The Identity of Yeats*, 2nd ed. 1964, and Harold Bloom's *Yeats*, 1970. Jeffares's *A New Commentary on the Poems of W. B. Yeats*, 1984, offers poem-by-poem commentaries and annotations. On Yeats's relation to Irish culture, see the chapter on Yeats in Seamus Deane, *Celtic Revivals*, 1985, and Conor Cruise O'Brien's classic essay, "Passion and Cunning: An Essay on the Politics of W. B. Yeats," in *In Excited Revery*, ed. A. Norman Jeffares and K. G. W. Cress, 1965, reprinted in O'Brien's *Passion and Cunning and Other Essays*, 1988. On the plays, A. Norman Jeffares and A. S. Knowland offer play-by-play commentaries in *A Commentary on the Collected Plays of W. B. Yeats*, 1975. Knowland has also written *W. B. Yeats: Dramatist of Vision*, 1983. Karen Dorn's *Players and Painted Stage: The Theatre of W. B. Yeats*, 1984, is not so much an interpretation of specific plays as an account of Yeats's theatrical practices in general.

THE LAKE ISLE OF INNISFREE[1]

I will arise and go now, and go to Innisfree,
And a small cabin build there, of clay and wattles[2] made:
Nine bean-rows will I have there, a hive for the honeybee,
And live alone in the bee-loud glade.

And I shall have some peace there, for peace comes dropping slow, 5
Dropping from the veils of the morning to where the cricket sings;
There midnight's all a glimmer, and noon a purple glow,
And evening full of the linnet's wings.

I will arise and go now, for always night and day
I hear lake water lapping with low sounds by the shore;
While I stand on the roadway, or on the pavements grey, 10
I hear it in the deep heart's core.

[1] An island in Lough Gill in County Sligo. This poem was suggested by Henry David Thoreau's *Walden* (1854).
[2] Interwoven poles and branches.

TO IRELAND IN THE COMING TIMES

Know, that I would accounted be
True brother of a company
That sang, to sweeten Ireland's wrong,
Ballad and story, rann[1] and song;
Nor be I any less of them, 5
Because the red-rose-bordered hem
Of her,[2] whose history began
Before God made the angelic clan,
Trails all about the written page.
When Time began to rant and rage 10
The measure of her flying feet
Made Ireland's heart begin to beat;
And Time bade all his candles flare
To light a measure here and there;
And may the thoughts of Ireland brood 15
Upon a measured quietude.

Nor may I less be counted one
With Davis, Mangan, Ferguson,[3]
Because, to him who ponders well,
My rhymes more than their rhyming tell 20
Of things discovered in the deep,
Where only body's laid asleep.
For the elemental creatures[4] go
About my table to and fro,
That hurry from unmeasured mind 25
To rant and rage in flood and wind;
Yet he who treads in measured ways
May surely barter gaze for gaze.
Man ever journeys on with them
After the red-rose-bordered hem. 30
Ah, faeries, dancing under the moon,
A Druid[5] land, a Druid tune!

While still I may, I write for you
The love I lived, the dream I knew.
From our birthday, until we die, 35
Is but the winking of an eye;
And we, our singing and our love,
What measurer Time has lit above,

[1] Verse or stanza (an Irish term).
[2] The rose. Yeats identified this as "the Eternal Rose of Beauty and of Peace," but it has many more complex meanings for him, including mystic rapture and divinity.
[3] Irish poets: Thomas Osborne Davis (1814–45), James Clarence Mangan (1803–49), and Samuel Ferguson (1810–86).
[4] Spirits associated with the four elements (earth, air, fire, and water).
[5] Having to do with an ancient Celtic priesthood.

And all benighted things that go
About my table to and fro, 40
Are passing on to where may be,
In truth's consuming ecstasy,
No place for love and dream at all;
For God goes by with white footfall.
I cast my heart into my rhymes, 45
That you, in the dim coming times,
May know how my heart went with them
After the red-rose-bordered hem.

HE REMEMBERS FORGOTTEN BEAUTY

When my arms wrap you round I press
My heart upon the loveliness
That has long faded from the world;
The jewelled crowns that kings have hurled
In shadowy pools, when armies fled; 5
The love-tales wrought with silken thread
By dreaming ladies upon cloth
That has made fat the murderous moth;
The roses that of old time were
Woven by ladies in their hair, 10
The dew-cold lilies ladies bore
Through many a sacred corridor
Where such grey clouds of incense rose
That only God's eyes did not close:
For that pale breast and lingering hand 15
Come from a more dream-heavy land,
A more dream-heavy hour than this;
And when you sigh from kiss to kiss
I hear white Beauty sighing, too,
For hours when all must fade like dew, 20
But flame on flame, and deep on deep,
Throne over throne where in half sleep,
Their swords upon their iron knees,
Brood her high lonely mysteries.

A COAT

I made my song a coat
Covered with embroideries
Out of old mythologies
From heel to throat;
But the fools caught it, 5
Wore it in the world's eyes

As though they'd wrought it.
Song, let them take it,
For there's more enterprise
In walking naked. 10

EASTER 1916[1]

I have met them at close of day
Coming with vivid faces
From counter or desk among grey
Eighteenth-century houses.
I have passed with a nod of the head 5
Or polite meaningless words,
Or have lingered awhile and said
Polite meaningless words,
And thought before I had done
Of a mocking tale or a gibe 10
To please a companion
Around the fire at the club,
Being certain that they and I
But lived where motley is worn:
All changed, changed utterly: 15
A terrible beauty is born.

That woman's[2] days were spent
In ignorant good-will,
Her nights in argument
Until her voice grew shrill. 20
What voice more sweet than hers
When, young and beautiful,
She rode to harriers?[3]
This man[4] had kept a school
And rode our wingèd horse;[5] 25
This other[6] his helper and friend
Was coming into his force;

[1] A general rebellion against British rule in Ireland was planned for Easter Sunday, 1916. When a German ship bringing arms was intercepted by the British, attempts were made to postpone the Rising, but they failed and the rebellion began on the Monday after Easter. The nationalists seized the Dublin General Post Office and proclaimed an Irish Republic. The British regained the Post Office, however, and executed sixteen of the nationalist leaders and imprisoned about two thousand of the participants. As Yeats indicates, he was personally acquainted with many of the leaders.

[2] Constance Gore-Booth, a fervent nationalist from the Sligo aristocracy. She was imprisoned for her role in the Rising.

[3] Hunting dogs that resemble small foxhounds.

[4] Padraic Pearse, headmaster of St. Enda's school and a poet. He was one of the seven signers of the proclamation of independence and was executed by the British.

[5] Pegasus, horse of the Muses (since Pearse was a poet).

[6] Thomas MacDonagh, executed for his part in the Rising, was a poet and playwright.

He might have won fame in the end,
So sensitive his nature seemed,
So daring and sweet his thought. 30
This other man[7] I had dreamed
A drunken, vainglorious lout.
He had done most bitter wrong
To some who are near my heart,
Yet I number him in the song; 35
He, too, has resigned his part
In the casual comedy;
He, too, has been changed in his turn,
Transformed utterly:
A terrible beauty is born. 40

Hearts with one purpose alone
Through summer and winter seem
Enchanted to a stone
To trouble the living stream.
The horse that comes from the road, 45
The rider, the birds that range
From cloud to tumbling cloud,
Minute by minute they change;
A shadow of cloud on the stream
Changes minute by minute; 50
A horse-hoof slides on the brim,
And a horse plashes within it;
The long-legged moor-hens dive,
And hens to moor-cocks call;
Minute by minute they live: 55
The stone's in the midst of all.

Too long a sacrifice
Can make a stone of the heart.
O when may it suffice?
That is Heaven's part, our part 60
To murmur name upon name,
As a mother names her child
When sleep at last has come
On limbs that had run wild.
What is it but nightfall? 65
No, no, not night but death;
Was it needless death after all?
For England may keep faith
For all that is done and said.[8]
We know their dream; enough 70

[7] Major John MacBride, who had married Maud Gonne, whom Yeats loved. They separated after two years.

[8] The English Parliament had voted Home Rule for Ireland, but it had not yet been implemented.

To know they dreamed and are dead;
And what if excess of love
Bewildered them till they died?
I write it out in a verse—
MacDonagh and MacBride 75
And Connolly⁹ and Pearse
Now and in time to be,
Wherever green is worn,
Are changed, changed utterly:
A terrible beauty is born. 80

THE SECOND COMING¹

Turning and turning in the widening gyre²
The falcon cannot hear the falconer;
Things fall apart; the centre cannot hold;
Mere anarchy is loosed upon the world,
The blood-dimmed tide is loosed, and everywhere 5
The ceremony of innocence is drowned;
The best lack all conviction, while the worst
Are full of passionate intensity.³

Surely some revelation is at hand;
Surely the Second Coming is at hand. 10
The Second Coming! Hardly are those words out
When a vast image out of *Spiritus Mundi*⁴
Troubles my sight: somewhere in sands of the desert
A shape with lion body and the head of a man,
A gaze blank and pitiless as the sun, 15
Is moving its slow thighs, while all about it
Reel shadows of the indignant desert birds.
The darkness drops again; but now I know
That twenty centuries of stony sleep
Were vexed to nightmare by a rocking cradle,⁵ 20
And what rough beast, its hour come round at last,
Slouches towards Bethlehem to be born?

⁹ James Connolly was commander in chief of the Easter Rising and was among those executed.

¹ An ironic allusion to Christ's promised return. Yeats saw history, as he explained in *A Vision* (1925, 1937), as a series of cycles ("gyres"). This poem suggests that the end of the Christian "gyre" is at hand and that it will be succeeded by an irrational, authoritarian cycle.

² A cone-shaped spiral. The reference here is to the falcon's literal flight, but the gyre-shape had a mystical meaning for Yeats and formed the basis of his diagram of history in *A Vision*.

³ *The blood-dimmed tide . . . passionate intensity.* A reference to the Russian Revolution (1917).

⁴ Latin for "Spirit of the World," a collective unconscious which Yeats held to be the storehouse of archetypal images such as that of the Sphinx.

⁵ The cradle of Christ.

SAILING TO BYZANTIUM[1]

I

That is no country for old men. The young
In one another's arms, birds in the trees
—Those dying generations—at their song,
The salmon-falls, the mackerel-crowded seas,
Fish, flesh, or fowl, commend all summer long 5
Whatever is begotten, born, and dies.
Caught in that sensual music all neglect
Monuments of unageing intellect.

II

An aged man is but a paltry thing,
A tattered coat upon a stick, unless 10
Soul clap its hands and sing, and louder sing
For every tatter in its mortal dress,
Nor is there singing school but studying
Monuments of its own magnificence;
And therefore I have sailed the seas and come 15
To the holy city of Byzantium.

III

O sages standing in God's holy fire
As in the gold mosaic of a wall,[2]
Come from the holy fire, perne in a gyre,[3]
And be the singing-masters of my soul. 20
Consume my heart away; sick with desire
And fastened to a dying animal
It knows not what it is; and gather me
Into the artifice of eternity.

IV

Once out of nature I shall never take 25
My bodily form from any natural thing,
But such a form as Grecian goldsmiths make
Of hammered gold and gold enamelling
To keep a drowsy Emperor awake;[4]
Or set upon a golden bough to sing 30
To lords and ladies of Byzantium
Of what is past, or passing, or to come.

[1] Byzantium (modern Istanbul) was the capital of the Byzantine Empire in the fifth and sixth centuries. Yeats makes it a symbol of the timeless world of art, but he was interested in the historical city as well, writing in *A Vision* of the integration of matter and spirit in Byzantine art. He regarded the highly stylized Byzantine art as "impersonal" and expressive of "the vision of a whole people."

[2] Yeats is referring to Byzantine mosaics like those on the walls of the famous Church of Hagia Sophia in Byzantium.

[3] Whirl in a spiral, a mystical movement for Yeats.

[4] *But such a form . . . Emperor awake.* Yeats said he had read of such singing artificial birds in the Byzantine Emperor's palace.

TWO SONGS FROM A PLAY[1]

I

I saw a staring virgin[2] stand
Where holy Dionysus died,
And tear the heart out of his side,
And lay the heart upon her hand
And bear that beating heart away; 5
And then did all the Muses[3] sing
Of Magnus Annus[4] at the spring,
As though God's death were but a play.

Another Troy must rise and set,
Another lineage feed the crow,[5] 10
Another Argo's painted prow
Drive to a flashier bauble yet.
The Roman Empire stood appalled:
It dropped the reigns of peace and war
When that fierce virgin and her Star[6] 15
Out of the fabulous darkness called.

II

In pity for man's darkening thought
He walked that room and issued thence
In Galilean turbulence;
The Babylonian starlight brought
A fabulous, formless darkness in; 5
Odour of blood when Christ was slain
Made all Platonic tolerance vain
And vain all Doric discipline.[7]

[1] The play was *The Resurrection* (1927). These two closely related songs refer to Yeats's cyclic theory of history. In the first, the death and rebirth of Dionysus are paralleled with those of Christ in the succeeding cycle. The second song develops the contrast between "Babylonian starlight" and Christ's "Galilean turbulence," but internalizes the contrast to man's own imagination ("resinous heart").

[2] Athene. Dionysus' heart was removed and swallowed by Zeus so that Dionysus might be reborn.

[3] The nine sister goddesses in Greek mythology who presided over the arts.

[4] Latin for the "Great Year," the 26,000 years in which a complete cycle of the precession of the equinoxes takes place. In Yeats's system, it represents one turning of the "Great Wheel" and is made up of twelve cycles of approximately two thousand years each.

[5] That is, the equivalent of the Trojan War must take place in another cycle. The crow is thought of as the scavenger of battlefields. Argo was the name of the ship in which Jason sailed to seek the Golden Fleece.

[6] Mary and Christ, paralleled with Athene and Dionysus.

[7] *Platonic tolerance . . . Doric discipline.* The teachings of Plato and other Greek philosophers.

Everything that man esteems
Endures a moment or a day. 10
Love's pleasure drives his love away,
The painter's brush consumes his dreams;
The herald's cry, the soldier's tread
Exhaust his glory and his might:
Whatever flames upon the night 15
Man's own resinous heart has fed.

LEDA AND THE SWAN[1]

A sudden blow: the great wings beating still
Above the staggering girl, her thighs caressed
By the dark webs, her nape caught in his bill,
He holds her helpless breast upon his breast.

How can those terrified vague fingers push 5
The feathered glory from her loosening thighs?
And how can body, laid in that white rush,
But feel the strange heart beating where it lies?

A shudder in the loins engenders there
The broken wall, the burning roof and tower 10
And Agamemnon dead.
 Being so caught up,
So mastered by the brute blood of the air,
Did she put on his knowledge with his power
Before the indifferent beak could let her drop?

AMONG SCHOOL CHILDREN

I

I walk through the long schoolroom questioning;
A kind old nun in a white hood replies;
The children learn to cipher and to sing,
To study reading-books and history,
To cut and sew, be neat in everything 5
In the best modern way—the children's eyes
In momentary wonder stare upon
A sixty-year-old smiling public man.[1]

[1] In Greek mythology, Zeus took the form of a swan to rape the mortal Leda. From the union, in Yeats's version of the myth, were born the twin sisters Clytemnestra (wife and slayer of Agamemnon) and Helen, cause of the Trojan War ("the burning roof and tower"). Yeats thinks of Zeus's act as an "annunciation" inaugurating Greek civilization.

[1] Yeats was not only a famous poet, but after 1922 an Irish Senator.

II

I dream of a Ledaean body,[2] bent
Above a sinking fire, a tale that she 10
Told of a harsh reproof, or trivial event
That changed some childish day to tragedy—
Told, and it seemed that our two natures blent
Into a sphere from youthful sympathy,
Or else, to alter Plato's parable,[3] 15
Into the yolk and white of the one shell.

III

And thinking of that fit of grief or rage
I look upon one child or t'other there
And wonder if she stood so at that age—
For even daughters of the swan can share 20
Something of every paddler's heritage—
And had that colour upon cheek or hair,
And thereupon my heart is driven wild:
She stands before me as a living child.

IV

Her present image floats into the mind— 25
Did Quattrocento finger[4] fashion it
Hollow of cheek as though it drank the wind
And took a mess of shadows for its meat?
And I though never of Ledaean kind
Had pretty plumage once—enough of that, 30
Better to smile on all that smile, and show
There is a comfortable kind of old scarecrow.

V

What youthful mother, a shape upon her lap
Honey of generation had betrayed,
And that must sleep, shriek, struggle to escape 35
As recollection or the drug decide,
Would think her son, did she but see that shape
With sixty or more winters on its head,
A compensation for the pang of his birth,
Or the uncertainty of his setting forth? 40

VI

Plato thought nature but a spume that plays
Upon a ghostly paradigm of things;[5]
Solider Aristotle played the taws

[2] A body like Leda's. (See "Leda and the Swan.") Yeats is referring to Maud Gonne.
[3] Aristophanes, in Plato's *Symposium*, says that the two sexes were originally one but were divided like an egg cut in two.
[4] The hand of a fifteenth-century Italian artist, such as Leonardo da Vinci.
[5] *Plato thought . . . of things.* An allusion to Plato's theory of forms, in which the visible world merely reflects ideal forms, which are the true reality.

Upon the bottom of a king of kings;[6]
World-famous golden-thighed Pythagoras 45
Fingered upon a fiddle-stick or strings
What a star sang and careless Muses heard:[7]
Old clothes upon old sticks to scare a bird.

VII

Both nuns and mothers worship images,
But those the candles light are not as those 50
That animate a mother's reveries,
But keep a marble or a bronze repose.
And yet they too break hearts—O Presences
That passion, piety or affection knows,
And that all heavenly glory symbolise— 55
O self-born mockers of man's enterprise;

VIII

Labour is blossoming or dancing where
The body is not bruised to pleasure soul,
Nor beauty born out of its own despair,
Nor blear-eyed wisdom out of midnight oil.
O chestnut-tree, great-rooted blossomer, 60
Are you the leaf, the blossom or the bole?[8]
O body swayed to music, O brightening glance,
How can we know the dancer from the dance?

CRAZY JANE TALKS WITH THE BISHOP[1]

I met the Bishop on the road
And much said he and I.
'Those breasts are flat and fallen now,
Those veins must soon be dry;
Live in a heavenly mansion, 5
Not in some foul sty.'

'Fair and foul are near of kin,
And fair needs foul,' I cried.
'My friends are gone, but that's a truth
Nor grave nor bed denied, 10

[6] *Solider Aristotle . . . king of kings.* Aristotle was tutor to the young Alexander the Great, whom he presumably whipped ("played the taws"). Aristotle was "solider" than Plato because he emphasized the close study of the visible world.

[7] The sixth-century B.C. Greek philosopher Pythagoras developed the theory of musical harmony. According to legend, he had a thighbone of gold.

[8] Trunk.

[1] This is one of a series of seven "Crazy Jane" poems, in which old, half-mad Jane speaks wisdom as King Lear's Fool does.

Learned in bodily lowliness
And in the heart's pride.

'A woman can be proud and stiff
When on love intent;
But Love has pitched his mansion in 15
The place of excrement;
For nothing can be sole or whole
That has not been rent.'

LAPIS LAZULI[1]

(FOR HARRY CLIFTON)

I have heard that hysterical women say
They are sick of the palette and fiddle-bow,
Of poets that are always gay,
For everybody knows or else should know
That if nothing drastic is done 5
Aeroplane and Zeppelin[2] will come out,
Pitch like King Billy[3] bomb-balls in
Until the town lie beaten flat.

All perform their tragic play,
There struts Hamlet, there is Lear, 10
That's Ophelia, that Cordelia;
Yet they, should the last scene be there,
The great stage curtain about to drop,
If worthy their prominent part in the play,
Do not break up their lines to weep. 15
They know that Hamlet and Lear are gay;
Gaiety transfiguring all that dread.
All men have aimed at, found and lost;
Black out; Heaven blazing into the head:
Tragedy wrought to its uttermost. 20
Though Hamlet rambles and Lear rages,
And all the drop-scenes drop at once
Upon a hundred thousand stages,
It cannot grow by an inch or an ounce.

On their own feet they came, or on shipboard, 25
Camel-back, horse-back, ass-back, mule-back,

[1] A deep-blue, semiprecious stone. Yeats actually had a piece carved in the manner he describes.

[2] A lighter-than-air dirigible used for military purposes by the Germans in World War I.

[3] King William III, who defeated the army of the deposed King James II at the Battle of the Boyne in 1690.

Old civilisations put to the sword.
Then they and their wisdom went to rack:
No handiwork of Callimachus,[4]
Who handled marble as if it were bronze, 30
Made draperies that seemed to rise
When sea-wind swept the corner, stands;
His long lamp-chimney shaped like the stem
Of a slender palm, stood but a day;
All things fall and are built again, 35
And those that build them again are gay.

Two Chinamen, behind them a third,
Are carved in lapis lazuli,
Over them flies a long-legged bird,
A symbol of longevity; 40
The third, doubtless a serving-man,
Carries a musical instrument.

Every discoloration of the stone,
Every accidental crack or dent,
Seems a water-course or an avalanche, 45
Or lofty slope where it still snows
Though doubtless plum or cherry-branch
Sweetens the little half-way house
Those Chinamen climb towards, and I
Delight to imagine them seated there; 50
There, on the mountain and the sky,
On all the tragic scene they stare.
One asks for mournful melodies;
Accomplished fingers begin to play.
Their eyes mid many wrinkles, their eyes, 55
Their ancient, glittering eyes, are gay.

THE CIRCUS ANIMALS' DESERTION

I

I sought a theme and sought for it in vain,
I sought it daily for six weeks or so.
Maybe at last, being but a broken man,
I must be satisfied with my heart, although
Winter and summer till old age began 5
My circus animals were all on show,

[4] Fifth-century B.C. Greek sculptor, famous for his carved draperies, produced with a running drill.

Those stilted boys, that burnished chariot,
Lion and woman and the Lord knows what.[1]

II

What can I but enumerate old themes?
First that sea-rider Oisin[2] led by the nose 10
Through three enchanted islands, allegorical dreams,
Vain gaiety, vain battle, vain repose,
Themes of the embittered heart, or so it seems,
That might adorn old songs or courtly shows;
But what cared I that set him on to ride, 15
I, starved for the bosom of his faery bride?

And then a counter-truth filled out its play,
The Countess Cathleen was the name I gave it;
She, pity-crazed, had given her soul away,
But masterful Heaven had intervened to save it.[3] 20
I thought my dear must her own soul destroy,
So did fanaticism and hate enslave it,[4]
And this brought forth a dream and soon enough
This dream itself had all my thought and love.

And when the Fool and Blind Man stole the bread 25
Cuchulain fought the ungovernable sea;[5]
Heart-mysteries there, and yet when all is said
It was the dream itself enchanted me:
Character isolated by a deed
To engross the present and dominate memory. 30
Players and painted stage took all my love,
And not those things that they were emblems of.

III

Those masterful images because complete
Grew in pure mind, but out of what began?
A mound of refuse or the sweepings of a street, 35
Old kettles, old bottles, and a broken can,
Old iron, old bones, old rags, that raving slut
Who keeps the till. Now that my ladder's gone,
I must lie down where all the ladders start,
In the foul rag-and-bone shop of the heart. 40

[1] *Those stilted boys . . . the Lord knows what.* The "stilted boys" are the tragic characters (wearing *cotherni*, or Greek thick-soled shoes) in Yeats's plays. The "burnished chariot" is Fergus's in such poems by Yeats as "Who Goes with Fergus?" The "lion and woman" are the sphinx in both "The Double Vision of Michael Robartes" and "The Second Coming."
[2] *that sea-rider Oisin.* In Yeats's 1889 poem *The Wanderings of Oisin* (pronounced "ush-een").
[3] *The Countess Cathleen . . . to save it.* *The Countess Cathleen* (1892) deals with an Irish countess who sells her soul to the devil to get food for her starving people, but whom God saves anyway, valuing the spirit above the deed.
[4] Maud Gonne, whose nationalist fervor Yeats disapproved of.
[5] *And when the Fool . . . ungovernable sea.* In the play *On Baile's Strand* (1904).

UNDER BEN BULBEN[1]

I

Swear by what the sages spoke
Round the Mareotic Lake
That the Witch of Atlas knew,
Spoke and set the cocks a-crow.[2]

Swear by those horsemen, by those women[3] 5
Complexion and form prove superhuman,
That pale, long-visaged company
That air in immortality
Completeness of their passions won;
Now they ride the wintry dawn 10
Where Ben Bulben sets the scene.

Here's the gist of what they mean.

II

Many times man lives and dies
Between his two eternities,
That of race and that of soul, 15
And ancient Ireland knew it all.
Whether man die in his bed
Or the rifle knocks him dead,
A brief parting from those dear
Is the worst man has to fear. 20
Though grave-diggers' toil is long,
Sharp their spades, their muscles strong,
They but thrust their buried men
Back in the human mind again.

III

You that Mitchel's prayer have heard, 25
'Send war in our time, O Lord!'[4]
Know that when all words are said
And a man is fighting mad,
Something drops from eyes long blind,

[1] One of Yeats's last poems, written September 4, 1938. Ben Bulben is a mountain in County Sligo, overlooking the village of Drumcliff, where Yeats left directions that he be buried.

[2] *Round the Mareotic Lake . . . cocks a-crow.* The Mareotic Lake is Lake Mareotis, near Alexandria, where both the Neo-Pythagorean philosophers (first century A.D.) and the Christian Neo-Platonists (third century A.D.) flourished. *The Witch of Atlas* is a poem by Percy Bysshe Shelley which mentions Lake Mareotis. Presumably what both the "sages" and the Witch of Atlas knew was the secret of timeless beauty.

[3] *those horsemen . . . those women.* The *sidhe* or Irish fairies who ride through the countryside around Ben Bulben.

[4] *'Send war . . . O Lord.'* John Mitchel (1815-75?), founder of the United Irishmen, wrote in his journal from prison, "Give us war in our time, O Lord!"

He completes his partial mind, 30
For an instant stands at ease,
Laughs aloud, his heart at peace.
Even the wisest man grows tense
With some sort of violence
Before he can accomplish fate, 35
Know his work or choose his mate.

IV

Poet and sculptor, do the work,
Nor let the modish painter shirk
What his great forefathers did,
Bring the soul of man to God. 40
Make him fill the cradles right.

Measurement began our might:[5]
Forms a stark Egyptian thought,
Forms that gentler Phidias wrought.
Michael Angelo left a proof 45
On the Sistine Chapel roof,
Where but half-awakened Adam
Can disturb globe-trotting Madam
Till her bowels are in heat,
Proof that there's a purpose set 50
Before the secret working mind:
Profane perfection of mankind.

Quattrocento[6] put in paint
On backgrounds for a God or Saint
Gardens where a soul's at ease; 55
Where everything that meets the eye,
Flowers and grass and cloudless sky,
Resemble forms that are or seem
When sleepers wake and yet still dream,
And when it's vanished still declare, 60
With only bed and bedstead there,
That heavens had opened.
 Gyres run on;
When that greater dream had gone
Calvert and Wilson, Blake and Claude,[7]
Prepared a rest for the people of God, 65

[5] Yeats is reviewing the development of art and thought according to his view of history. "Measurement" is Babylonian mathematics; Phidias was a fifth-century B.C. Greek sculptor; Michael Angelo (or Michelangelo) was the sixteenth-century Italian painter and sculptor who designed and painted the Sistine Chapel.

[6] The art of fifteenth-century Italy.

[7] *Calvert . . . Claude.* Edward Calvert, nineteenth-century wood-engraver; Richard Wilson, eighteenth-century landscape painter; William Blake, nineteenth-century poet and engraver; Claude Lorrain, seventeenth-century landscape painter. All these provided images for Yeats's poetry, as did Samuel Palmer (line 66), nineteenth-century landscape painter and etcher.

Palmer's phrase, but after that
Confusion fell upon our thought.

V

Irish poets, learn your trade,
Sing whatever is well made,
Scorn the sort now growing up 70
All out of shape from toe to top,
Their unremembering hearts and heads
Base-born products of base beds.
Sing the peasantry, and then
Hard-riding country gentlemen, 75
The holiness of monks, and after
Porter-drinkers' randy laughter;
Sing the lords and ladies gay
That were beaten into the clay
Through seven heroic centuries; 80
Cast your mind on other days
That we in coming days may be
Still the indomitable Irishry.

VI

Under bare Ben Bulben's head
In Drumcliff churchyard Yeats is laid. 85
An ancestor was rector there
Long years ago, a church stands near,
By the road an ancient cross.
No marble, no conventional phrase;
On limestone quarried near the spot 90
By his command these words are cut:
 Cast a cold eye
 On life, on death.
 Horseman, pass by![8]

DEIRDRE

PERSONS IN THE PLAY

MUSICIANS
FERGUS, *an old man*
NAOISE [*pronounced*
 Neesh-e], *a young king*
DEIRDRE, *his queen*

A DARK-FACED MESSENGER
CONCHUBAR [*pronounced*
 Conohar], *the old King of*
 Uladh,[1] *who is still strong*
 and vigorous
A DARK-FACED EXECUTIONER

[8] *Cast a cold eye . . . pass by!* The inscription on Yeats's tombstone. [1] Ulster.

*A Guest-house in a wood. It is a rough house of timber; through the doors and some
of the windows one can see the great spaces of the wood, the sky dimming, night
closing in. But a window to the left shows the thick leaves of a coppice; the landscape
suggests silence and loneliness. There is a door to right and left, and through the side
windows one can see anybody who approaches either door, a moment before he enters.
In the centre, a part of the house is curtained off; the curtains are drawn. There are
unlighted torches in brackets on the walls. There is, at one side, a small table with a
chessboard and chessmen upon it. At the other side of the room there is a brazier with
a fire; two women, with musical instruments beside them, crouch about the brazier:
they are comely women of about forty. Another woman, who carries a stringed instru-
ment, enters hurriedly; she speaks, at first standing in the doorway.*

FIRST MUSICIAN. I have a story right, my wanderers,
 That has so mixed with fable in our songs
 That all seemed fabulous. We are come, by chance,
 Into King Conchubar's country, and this house
 Is an old guest-house built for travellers
 From the seashore to Conchubar's royal house,
 And there are certain hills among these woods
 And there Queen Deirdre grew.
SECOND MUSICIAN. That famous queen
 Who has been wandering with her lover Naoise
 Somewhere beyond the edges of the world? 10
FIRST MUSICIAN [*going nearer to the brazier*]. Some dozen years ago,
 King Conchubar found
 A house upon a hillside in this wood,
 And there a child with an old witch to nurse her,
 And nobody to say if she were human,
 Or of the gods, or anything at all
 Of who she was or why she was hidden there,
 But that she'd too much beauty for good luck.
 He went up thither daily, till at last
 She put on womanhood, and he lost peace,
 And Deirdre's tale began. The King was old. 20
 A month or so before the marriage-day,
 A young man, in the laughing scorn of his youth,
 Naoise, the son of Usna, climbed up there,
 And having wooed, or, as some say, been wooed,
 Carried her off.
SECOND MUSICIAN. The tale were well enough
 Had it a finish.
FIRST MUSICIAN. Hush! I have more to tell;
 But gather close about that I may whisper
 The secrets of a king.
SECOND MUSICIAN. There's none to hear!
FIRST MUSICIAN. I have been to Conchubar's house and followed
 up
 A crowd of servants going out and in 30
 With loads upon their heads: embroideries
 To hang upon the walls, or new-mown rushes

To strew upon the floors, and came at length
To a great room.
SECOND MUSICIAN. Be silent; there are steps!

> *Enter* FERGUS, *an old man,*[2] *who*
> *moves about from door to window*
> *excitedly through what follows.*

FERGUS. I thought to find a message from the King.
You are musicians by these instruments,
And if as seems—for you are comely women—
You can praise love, you'll have the best of luck,
For there'll be two, before the night is in,
That bargained for their love, and paid for it 40
All that men value. You have but the time
To weigh a happy music with a sad,
To find what is most pleasing to a lover,
Before the son of Usna and his queen
Have passed this threshold.
FIRST MUSICIAN. Deirdre and her man!
FERGUS. I was to have found a message in this house,
And ran to meet it. Is there no messenger
From Conchubar to Fergus, son of Rogh?
FIRST MUSICIAN. Are Deirdre and her lover tired of life?
FERGUS. You are not of this country, or you'd know 50
That they are in my charge and all forgiven.
FIRST MUSICIAN. We have no country but the roads of the world.
FERGUS. Then you should know that all things change in the
 world,
And hatred turns to love and love to hate,
And even kings forgive.
FIRST MUSICIAN. An old man's love
Who casts no second line is hard to cure;
His jealousy is like his love.
FERGUS. And that's but true.
You have learned something in your wanderings.
He was so hard to cure that the whole court,
But I alone, thought it impossible; 60
Yet after I had urged it at all seasons,
I had my way, and all's forgiven now;
And you shall speak the welcome and the joy
That I lack tongue for.
FIRST MUSICIAN. Yet old men are jealous.
FERGUS [*going to door*]. I am Conchubar's near friend, and that
 weighed somewhat,
And it was policy to pardon them.
The need of some young, famous, popular man
To lead the troops, the murmur of the crowd,

[2] Fergus Mac Roigh. He was the former king of Ulster, having been tricked into giving up
the throne to Conchubar.

And his own natural impulse, urged him to it.
They have been wandering half a dozen years. 70
FIRST MUSICIAN. And yet old men are jealous.
FERGUS [*coming from door*]. Sing the more sweetly
　Because, though age is arid as a bone,
　This man has flowered. I've need of music, too;
　If this grey head would suffer no reproach,
　I'd dance and sing—

> [*Dark-faced men with strange, bar-
> baric dress and arms begin to pass by
> the doors and windows. They pass
> one by one and in silence.*]

　　　　　　　　and dance till the hour ran out,
　Because I have accomplished this good deed.
FIRST MUSICIAN. Look there—there at the window, those dark
　　men,
　With murderous and outlandish-looking arms—
　They've been about the house all day.
FERGUS [*looking after them*]. What are you?
　Where do you come from, who is it sent you here? 80
FIRST MUSICIAN. They will not answer you.
FERGUS. They do not hear.
FIRST MUSICIAN. Forgive my open speech, but to these eyes
　That have seen many lands they are such men
　As kings will gather for a murderous task
　That neither bribes, commands, nor promises
　Can bring their people to.
FERGUS. And that is why
　You harped upon an old man's jealousy.
　A trifle sets you quaking. Conchubar's fame
　Brings merchandise on every wind that blows.
　They may have brought him Libyan dragon-skin, 90
　Or the ivory of the fierce unicorn.
FIRST MUSICIAN. If these be merchants, I have seen the goods
　They have brought to Conchubar, and understood
　His murderous purpose.
FERGUS. Murderous, you say?
　Why, what new gossip of the roads is this?
　But I'll not hear.
FIRST MUSICIAN. It may be life or death.
　There is a room in Conchubar's house, and there—
FERGUS. Be silent, or I'll drive you from the door.
　There's many a one that would do more than that,
　And make it prison, or death, or banishment 100
　To slander the High King.

> [*Suddenly restraining himself and
> speaking gently.*]

　　　　　　　　　　　He is my friend;
　I have his oath, and I am well content.

I have known his mind as if it were my own
These many years, and there is none alive
Shall buzz against him, and I there to stop it.
I know myself, and him, and your wild thought
Fed on extravagant poetry, and lit
By such a dazzle of old fabulous tales
That common things are lost, and all that's strange
Is true because 'twere pity if it were not. 110

[*Going to the door again.*]

Quick! quick! your instruments! they are coming now.
I hear the hoofs a-clatter. Begin that song!
But what is it to be? I'd have them hear
A music foaming up out of the house
Like wine out of a cup. Come now, a verse
Of some old time not worth remembering,
And all the lovelier because a bubble.
Begin, begin, of some old king and queen,
Of Lugaidh Redstripe[3] or another; no, not him,
He and his lady perished wretchedly. 120

FIRST MUSICIAN [*singing*]
 "Why is it," Queen Edain[4] said,
 "If I do but climb the stair . . ."
FERGUS. Ah! that is better. . . . They are alighted now.
Shake all your cockscombs, children; these are lovers.

[FERGUS *goes out.*]

FIRST MUSICIAN
 "Why is it," Queen Edain said,
 "If I do but climb the stair
 To the tower overhead,
 When the winds are calling there,
 Or the gannets calling out
 In waste places of the sky, 130
 There's so much to think about
 That I cry, that I cry?"

SECOND MUSICIAN
 But her goodman answered her:
 "Love would be a thing of naught
 Had not all his limbs a stir
 Born out of immoderate thought;
 Were he anything by half,

[3] Lugaidh Redstripe is one of the heroes of the Cuchulain saga. The story of how he and
his wife, Dervorgil, played chess on the night they were killed is used throughout the play as
a foreshadowing of the deaths of Deirdre and Naoise.
[4] Edain is an Irish analogue of Persephone in Greek mythology. She was a mortal who was
wooed by Midhir, the king of the *Sidhe* (fairies), and taken to the Otherworld. Midhir's wife
changed her to a fly, and she was blown back to the world of mortals three times until Midhir,
in a game of chess, won her back to the Otherworld permanently.

Were his measure running dry.
　Lovers, if they may not laugh,
　　Have to cry, have to cry." 　　　　　　　　　　　140

> [DEIRDRE, NAOISE, *and* FERGUS
> *have been seen for a moment
> through the windows, but now they
> have entered.*]

THE THREE MUSICIANS [*together*]
But is Edain worth a song
　Now the hunt begins anew?
Praise the beautiful and strong;
　Praise the redness of the yew;
Praise the blossoming apple-stem.
　But our silence had been wise.
What is all our praise to them
　That have one another's eyes?

DEIRDRE. Silence your music, though I thank you for it;
　But the wind's blown upon my hair, and I 　　　　　150
　Must set the jewels on my neck and head
　For one that's coming.
NAOISE. 　　　　　　　Your colour has all gone
　As 'twere with fear, and there's no cause for that.
DEIRDRE. These women have the raddle[5] that they use
　To make them brave and confident, although
　Dread, toil, or cold may chill the blood o' their cheeks.
　You'll help me, women. It is my husband's will
　I show my trust in one that may be here
　Before the mind can call the colour up.
　My husband took these rubies from a king 　　　　160
　Of Surracha[6] that was so murderous
　He seemed all glittering dragon. Now wearing them
　Myself wars on myself, for I myself—
　That do my husband's will, yet fear to do it—
　Grow dragonish to myself.

> [*The women have gathered about
> her.* NAOISE *has stood looking at
> her, but* FERGUS *brings him to the
> chess-table.*]

NAOISE. 　　　　　　　No messenger!
　It's strange that there is none to welcome us.
FERGUS. King Conchubar has sent no messenger
　That he may come himself.
NAOISE. 　　　　　　　　And being himself,
　Being High King, he cannot break his faith.
　I have his word and I must take that word, 　　　　170

────────────

[5] Rouge.
[6] Yeats seems to mean Sorcha, the Irish Otherworld. If so, the rubies are supernatural.

Or prove myself unworthy of my nurture
Under a great man's roof.

FERGUS. We'll play at chess
Till the King comes. It is but natural
That she should doubt him, for her house has been
The hole of the badger and the den of the fox.

NAOISE. If I had not King Conchubar's word I'd think
That chess-board ominous.

FERGUS. How can a board
That has been lying there these many years
Be lucky or unlucky?

NAOISE. It is the board
Where Lugaidh Redstripe and that wife of his, 180
Who had a seamew's[7] body half the year,
Played at the chess upon the night they died.

FERGUS. I can remember now, a tale of treachery,
A broken promise and a journey's end—
But it were best forgot.

> [DEIRDRE *has been standing with
> the women about her. They have
> been helping her to put on her jewels
> and to put the pigment on her cheeks
> and arrange her hair. She has grad-
> ually grown attentive to what* FER-
> GUS *is saying.*]

NAOISE. If the tale's true,
When it was plain that they had been betrayed,
They moved the men and waited for the end
As it were bedtime, and had so quiet minds
They hardly winked their eyes when the sword flashed.

FERGUS. She never could have played so, being a woman, 190
If she had not the cold sea's blood in her.

DEIRDRE. The gods turn clouds and casual accidents
Into omens.

NAOISE. It would but ill become us,
Now that King Conchubar has pledged his word,
Should we be startled by a cloud or a shadow.

DEIRDRE. There's none to welcome us.

NAOISE. Being his guest,
Words that would wrong him can but wrong ourselves.

DEIRDRE. An empty house upon the journey's end!
Is that the way a king that means no mischief
Honours a guest?

FERGUS. He is but making ready 200
A welcome in his house, arranging where
The moorhen and the mallard go, and where
The speckled heathcock on a golden dish.

DEIRDRE. Had he no messenger?

[7] A seagull's.

NAOISE. Such words and fears
Wrong this old man who's pledged his word to us.
We must not speak or think as women do,
That when the house is all abed sit up
Marking among the ashes with a stick
Till they are terrified.—Being what we are
We must meet all things with an equal mind. 210
[*To* FERGUS.] Come, let us look if there's a messenger
From Conchubar. We cannot see from this
Because we are blinded by the leaves and twigs,
But it may be the wood will thin again.
It is but kind that when the lips we love
Speak words that are unfitting for kings' ears
Our ears be deaf.
FERGUS. But now I had to threaten
These wanderers because they would have weighed
Some crazy fantasy of their own brain
Or gossip of the road with Conchubar's word. 220
If I had thought so little of mankind
I never could have moved him to this pardon.
I have believed the best of every man,
And find that to believe it is enough
To make a bad man show him at his best,
Or even a good man swing his lantern higher.

> [NAOISE *and* FERGUS *go out. The
> last words are spoken as they go
> through the door. One can see them
> through part of what follows, either
> through door or window. They move
> about, talking or looking along
> the road towards* CONCHUBAR'*s
> house.*]

FIRST MUSICIAN. If anything lies heavy on your heart,
Speak freely of it, knowing it is certain
That you will never see my face again.
DEIRDRE. You've been in love?
FIRST MUSICIAN. If you would speak of love 230
Speak freely. There is nothing in the world
That has been friendly to us but the kisses
That were upon our lips, and when we are old
Their memory will be all the life we have.
DEIRDRE. There was a man that loved me. He was old;
I could not love him. Now I can but fear.
He has made promises, and brought me home;
But though I turn it over in my thoughts,
I cannot tell if they are sound and wholesome,
Or hackles on the hook.
FIRST MUSICIAN. I have heard he loved you 240
As some old miser loves the dragon-stone
He hides among the cobwebs near the roof.

DEIRDRE. You mean that when a man who has loved like that
 Is after crossed, love drowns in its own flood,
 And that love drowned and floating is but hate;
 And that a king who hates sleeps ill at night
 Till he has killed; and that, though the day laughs,
 We shall be dead at cock-crow.
FIRST MUSICIAN. You've not my thought.
 When I lost one I loved distractedly,
 I blamed my crafty rival and not him, 250
 And fancied, till my passion had run out,
 That could I carry him away with me,
 And tell him all my love, I'd keep him yet.
DEIRDRE. Ah! now I catch your meaning, that this king
 Will murder Naoise, and keep me alive.
FIRST MUSICIAN. 'Tis you that put that meaning upon words
 Spoken at random.
DEIRDRE. Wanderers like you,
 Who have their wit alone to keep their lives,
 Speak nothing that is bitter to the ear
 At random; if they hint at it at all 260
 Their eyes and ears have gathered it so lately
 That it is crying out in them for speech.
FIRST MUSICIAN. We have little that is certain.
DEIRDRE. Certain or not,
 Speak it out quickly, I beseech you to it;
 I never have met any of your kind
 But that I gave them money, food, and fire.
FIRST MUSICIAN. There are strange, miracle-working, wicked
 stones,
 Men tear out of the heart and the hot brain
 Of Libyan dragons.
DEIRDRE. The hot Istain stone,
 And the cold stone of Fanes,[8] that have power 270
 To stir even those at enmity to love.
FIRST MUSICIAN. They have so great an influence, if but sewn
 In the embroideries that curtain in
 The bridal bed.
DEIRDRE. O Mover of the stars
 That made this delicate house of ivory,[9]
 And made my soul its mistress, keep it safe!
FIRST MUSICIAN. I have seen a bridal bed, so curtained in,
 So decked for miracle in Conchubar's house,
 And learned that a bride's coming.
DEIRDRE. And I the bride?
 Here is worse treachery than the seamew suffered, 280

[8] Yeats seems to have taken the names of these magic stones from a medieval textbook
rather than from Irish mythology.
[9] Her skull or her body.

For she but died and mixed into the dust
Of her dear comrade, but I am to live
And lie in the one bed with him I hate.
Where is Naoise? I was not alone like this
When Conchubar first chose me for his wife;
I cried in sleeping or waking and he came,
But now there is worse need.

NAOISE [*entering with* FERGUS]. Why have you called?
I was but standing there, without the door.

DEIRDRE. I have heard terrible mysterious things,
Magical horrors and the spells of wizards. 290

FERGUS. Why, that's no wonder. You have been listening
To singers of the roads that gather up
The stories of the world.

DEIRDRE. But I have one
To make the stories of the world but nothing.

NAOISE. Be silent if it is against the King
Whose guest you are.

FERGUS. No, let her speak it out.
I know the High King's heart as it were my own,
And can refute a slander, but already
I have warned these women that it may be death.

NAOISE. I will not weigh the gossip of the roads 300
With the King's word. I ask your pardon for her:
She has the heart of the wild birds that fear
The net of the fowler or the wicker cage.

DEIRDRE. Am I to see the fowler and the cage
And speak no word at all?

NAOISE. You would have known,
Had they not bred you in that mountainous place,
That when we give a word and take a word
Sorrow is put away, past wrong forgotten.

DEIRDRE. Though death may come of it?

NAOISE. Though death may come.

DEIRDRE. When first we came into this empty house 310
You had foreknowledge of our death, and even
When speaking of the paleness of my cheek
Your own cheek blanched.

NAOISE. Listen to this old man.
He can remember all the promises
We trusted to.

DEIRDRE. You speak from the lips out,
And I am pleading for your life and mine.

NAOISE. Listen to this old man, for many think
He has a golden tongue.[10]

DEIRDRE. Then I will say
What it were best to carry to the grave.

[10] Fergus was sometimes given the epithet "Honey-mouth."

Look at my face where the leaf raddled it 320
And at these rubies on my hair and breast.
It was for him, to stir him to desire,
I put on beauty; yes, for Conchubar.

NAOISE. What frenzy put these words into your mouth?

DEIRDRE. No frenzy, for what need is there for frenzy
To change what shifts with every change of the wind,
Or else there is no truth in men's old sayings?
Was I not born a woman?

NAOISE. You're mocking me.

DEIRDRE. And is there mockery in this face and eyes,
Or in this body, in these limbs that brought 330
So many mischiefs? Look at me and say
If that that shakes my limbs be mockery.

NAOISE. What woman is there that a man can trust
But at the moment when he kisses her
At the first midnight?

DEIRDRE. Were it not most strange
That women should put evil in men's hearts
And lack it in themselves? And yet I think
That being half good I might change round again
Were we aboard our ship and on the sea.

NAOISE. We'll to the horses and take ship again. 340

FERGUS. Fool, she but seeks to rouse your jealousy
With crafty words.

DEIRDRE. Were we not born to wander?
These jewels have been reaped by the innocent sword
Upon a mountain, and a mountain bred me;
But who can tell what change can come to love
Among the valleys? I speak no falsehood now.
Away to windy summits, and there mock
The night-jar and the valley-keeping bird!

FERGUS. Men blamed you that you stirred a quarrel up
That has brought death to many. I have made peace, 350
Poured water on the fire, but if you fly
King Conchubar may think that he is mocked
And the house blaze again: and in what quarter,
If Conchubar were the treacherous man you think,
Would you find safety now that you have come
Into the very middle of his power,
Under his very eyes?

DEIRDRE. Under his eyes
And in the very middle of his power!
Then there is but one way to make all safe:
I'll spoil this beauty that brought misery
And houseless wandering on the man I loved. 360
These wanderers will show me how to do it;
To clip this hair to baldness, blacken my skin
With walnut juice, and tear my face with briars.

O that the creatures of the woods had torn
My body with their claws!
FERGUS. What, wilder yet!
DEIRDRE [*to* NAOISE]. Whatever were to happen to my face
I'd be myself, and there's not any way
But this to bring all trouble to an end.
NAOISE. Leave the gods' handiwork unblotched, and wait 370
For their decision, our decision is past.
 [*A Dark-faced* MESSENGER *comes
 to the threshold.*]
FERGUS. Peace, peace; the messenger is at the door;
He stands upon the threshold; he stands there;
He stands, King Conchubar's purpose on his lips.
MESSENGER. Supper is on the table. Conchubar
Is waiting for his guests.
FERGUS. All's well again!
All's well! All's well! You cried your doubts so loud
That I had almost doubted.
NAOISE. We doubted him,
And he the while but busy in his house
For the more welcome.
DEIRDRE. The message is not finished. 380
FERGUS. Come quickly. Conchubar will laugh, that I—
Although I held out boldly in my speech—
That I, even I—
DEIRDRE. Wait, wait! He is not done.
MESSENGER. Deirdre and Fergus, son of Rogh, are summoned;
But not the traitor that bore off the Queen.
It is enough that the King pardon her,
And call her to his table and his bed.
NAOISE. So, then, it's treachery.
FERGUS. I'll not believe it.
NAOISE. Lead on and I will follow at your heels
That I may challenge him before his court 390
To match me there, or match me in some place
Where none can come between us but our swords,
For I have found no truth on any tongue
That's not of iron.
MESSENGER. I am Conchubar's man,
I am content to serve an iron tongue:
That Tongue commands that Fergus, son of Rogh,
And Deirdre come this night into his house,
And none but they. [*He goes, followed by* NAOISE.]
FERGUS. Some rogue, some enemy,
Has bribed him to embroil us with the King;
I know that he has lied because I know 400
King Conchubar's mind as if it were my own,
But I'll find out the truth.

 [*He is about to follow* NAOISE, *but*
 DEIRDRE *stops him.*]
DEIRDRE. No, no, old man.
 You thought the best, and the worst came of it;
 We listened to the counsel of the wise,
 And so turned fools. But ride and bring your friends.
 Go, and go quickly. Conchubar has not seen me;
 It may be that his passion is asleep,
 And that we may escape.
FERGUS. But I'll go first,
 And follow up that Libyan heel, and send
 Such words to Conchubar that he may know 410
 At how great peril he lays hands upon you.
 [NAOISE *enters*]
NAOISE. The Libyan, knowing that a servant's life
 Is safe from hands like mine, but turned and mocked.
FERGUS. I'll call my friends, and call the reaping-hooks,[11]
 And carry you in safety to the ships.
 My name has still some power. I will protect,
 Or, if that is impossible, revenge.
 [*Goes out by other door.*]
NAOISE [*who is calm, like a man who has passed beyond life*].
 The crib has fallen and the birds are in it;
 There is not one of the great oaks about us
 But shades a hundred men.
DEIRDRE. Let's out and die, 420
 Or break away, if the chance favour us.
NAOISE. They would but drag you from me, stained with blood.
 Their barbarous weapons would but mar that beauty,
 And I would have you die as a queen should—
 In a death-chamber. You are in my charge.
 We will wait here, and when they come upon us,
 I'll hold them from the doors, and when that's over,
 Give you a cleanly death with this grey edge.
DEIRDRE. I will stay here; but you go out and fight.
 Our way of life has brought no friends to us, 430
 And if we do not buy them leaving it,
 We shall be ever friendless.
NAOISE. What do they say?
 That Lugaidh Redstripe and that wife of his
 Sat at this chess-board, waiting for their end.
 They knew that there was nothing that could save them,
 And so played chess as they had any night
 For years, and waited for the stroke of sword.
 I never heard a death so out of reach
 Of common hearts, a high and comely end.
 What need have I, that gave up all for love, 440

[11] The local farmers.

To die like an old king out of a fable,
Fighting and passionate? What need is there
For all that ostentation at my setting?
I have loved truly and betrayed no man.
I need no lightning at the end, no beating
In a vain fury at the cage's door.
[*To* MUSICIANS.] Had you been here when that man and his
 queen
Played at so high a game, could you have found
An ancient poem for the praise of it?
It should have set out plainly that those two, 450
Because no man and woman have loved better,
Might sit on there contentedly, and weigh
The joy comes after. I have heard the seamew
Sat there, with all the colour in her cheeks,
As though she'd say: "There's nothing happening
But that a king and queen are playing chess."
DEIRDRE. He's in the right, though I have not been born
Of the cold, haughty waves, my veins being hot,
And though I have loved better than that queen,
I'll have as quiet fingers on the board. 460
O, singing women, set it down in a book,
That love is all we need, even though it is
But the last drops we gather up like this;
And though the drops are all we have known of life,
For we have been most friendless—praise us for it,
And praise the double sunset, for naught's lacking
But a good end to the long, cloudy day.
NAOISE. Light torches there and drive the shadows out,
 For day's grey end comes up.
 [*A* MUSICIAN *lights a torch in the*
 fire and then crosses before the
 chess-players, and slowly lights the
 torches in the sconces. The light is
 almost gone from the wood, but there
 is a clear evening light in the sky,
 increasing the sense of solitude and
 loneliness.]
DEIRDRE. Make no sad music. 470
What is it but a king and queen at chess?
They need a music that can mix itself
Into imagination, but not break
The steady thinking that the hard game needs.
 [*During the chess, the* MUSICIANS
 sing this song]
 Love is an immoderate thing
 And can never be content
 Till it dip an ageing wing
 Where some laughing element

 Leaps and Time's old lanthorn dims.
 What's the merit in love-play, 480
 In the tumult of the limbs
 That dies out before 'tis day,
 Heart on heart, or mouth on mouth,
 All that mingling of our breath,
When love-longing is but drouth
 For the things come after death?

 [During the last verses DEIRDRE
 rises from the board and kneels at
 NAOISE'S *feet.]*

DEIRDRE. I cannot go on playing like that woman
 That had but the cold blood of the sea in her veins.
NAOISE. It is your move. Take up your man again.
DEIRDRE. Do you remember that first night in the woods 490
 We lay all night on leaves, and looking up,
 When the first grey of the dawn awoke the birds,
 Saw leaves above us? You thought that I still slept,
 And bending down to kiss me on the eyes,
 Found they were open. Bend and kiss me now,
 For it may be the last before our death.
 And when that's over, we'll be different;
 Imperishable things, a cloud or a fire.
 And I know nothing but this body, nothing
 But that old vehement, bewildering kiss. 500
 *[*CONCHUBAR *comes to the door.]*
FIRST MUSICIAN. Children, beware!
NAOISE [*laughing*]. He has taken up my challenge;
 Whether I am a ghost or living man
 When day has broken, I'll forget the rest,
 And say that there is kingly stuff in him.
 [Turns to fetch spear and shield,
 and then sees that CONCHUBAR *has*
 gone.]
FIRST MUSICIAN. He came to spy upon you, not to fight.
NAOISE. A prudent hunter, therefore, but no king.
 He'd find if what has fallen in the pit
 Were worth the hunting, but has come too near,
 And I turn hunter. You're not man, but beast.
 Go scurry in the bushes, now, beast, beast, 510
 For now it's topsy-turvy, I upon you.
 [He rushes out after CONCHUBAR.*]*
DEIRDRE. You have a knife there, thrust into your girdle.
 I'd have you give it me.
FIRST MUSICIAN. No, but I dare not.
DEIRDRE. No, but you must.
FIRST MUSICIAN. If harm should come to you,
 They'd know I gave it.
DEIRDRE [*snatching knife*]. There is no mark on this

To make it different from any other
Out of a common forge.

[*Goes to the door and looks out.*]

FIRST MUSICIAN. You have taken it,
 I did not give it you; but there are times
 When such a thing is all the friend one has.

DEIRDRE. The leaves hide all, and there's no way to find 520
 What path to follow. Why is there no sound?

[*She goes from door to window.*]

FIRST MUSICIAN. Where would you go?

DEIRDRE. To strike a blow for Naoise,
 If Conchubar call the Libyans to his aid.
 But why is there no clash? They have met by this!

FIRST MUSICIAN. Listen. I am called wise. If Conchubar win,
 You have a woman's wile that can do much,
 Even with men in pride of victory.
 He is in love and old. What were one knife
 Among a hundred?

DEIRDRE [*going towards them*]. Women, if I die,
 If Naoise die this night, how will you praise? 530
 What words seek out? for that will stand to you;
 For being but dead we shall have many friends.
 All through your wanderings, the doors of kings
 Shall be thrown wider open, the poor man's hearth
 Heaped with new turf, because you are wearing this

[*Gives* MUSICIAN *a bracelet.*]

 To show that you have Deirdre's story right.

FIRST MUSICIAN. Have you not been paid servants in love's house
 To sweep the ashes out and keep the doors?
 And though you have suffered all for mere love's sake
 You'd live your lives again.

DEIRDRE. Even this last hour. 540

[CONCHUBAR *enters with dark-faced men*]

CONCHUBAR. One woman and two men; that is the quarrel
 That knows no mending. Bring in the man she chose
 Because of his beauty and the strength of his youth.

[*The dark-faced men drag in* NAOISE *entangled in a net.*]

NAOISE. I have been taken like a bird or a fish.

CONCHUBAR. He cried "Beast, beast!" and in a blind-beast rage
 He ran at me and fell into the nets,
 But we were careful for your sake, and took him
 With all the comeliness that woke desire
 Unbroken in him. I being old and lenient,
 I would not hurt a hair upon his head. 550

DEIRDRE. What do you say? Have you forgiven him?

NAOISE. He is but mocking us. What's left to say
 Now that the seven years' hunt is at an end?

DEIRDRE. He never doubted you until I made him,
 And therefore all the blame for what he says
 Should fall on me.
CONCHUBAR. But his young blood is hot,
 And if we're of one mind, he shall go free,
 And I ask nothing for it, or, if something,
 Nothing I could not take. There is no king
 In the wide world that, being so greatly wronged, 560
 Could copy me, and give all vengeance up.
 Although her marriage-day had all but come,
 You carried her away; but I'll show mercy.
 Because you have the insolent strength of youth
 You carried her away; but I've had time
 To think it out through all these seven years.
 I will show mercy.
NAOISE. You have many words.
CONCHUBAR. I will not make a bargain; I but ask
 What is already mine.

 [DEIRDRE *moves slowly towards*
 CONCHUBAR *while he is speaking,*
 her eyes fixed upon him.]
 You may go free
 If Deirdre will but walk into my house 570
 Before the people's eyes, that they may know,
 When I have put the crown upon her head,
 I have not taken her by force and guile.
 The doors are open, and the floors are strewed
 And in the bridal chamber curtains sewn
 With all enchantments that give happiness
 By races that are germane to the sun,
 And nearest him, and have no blood in their veins—
 For when they're wounded the wound drips with wine—
 Nor speech but singing. At the bridal door 580
 Two fair king's daughters carry in their hands
 The crown and robe.
DEIRDRE. O no! Not that, not that!
 Ask any other thing but that one thing.
 Leave me with Naoise. We will go away
 Into some country at the ends of the earth.
 We'll trouble you no more; and there is no one
 That will not praise you if you pardon us.
 "He is good, he is good," they'll say to one another;
 "There's nobody like him, for he forgave
 Deirdre and Naoise."
CONCHUBAR. Do you think that I 590
 Shall let you go again, after seven years
 Of longing and of planning here and there,
 And trafficking with merchants for the stones

That make all sure,[12] and watching my own face
That none might read it?
DEIRDRE [*to* NAOISE]. It's better to go with him.
 Why should you die when one can bear it all?
 My life is over; it's better to obey.
 Why should you die? I will not live long, Naoise.
 I'd not have you believe I'd long stay living;
 O no, no, no! You will go far away. 600
 You will forget me. Speak, speak, Naoise, speak,
 And say that it is better that I go.
 I will not ask it. Do not speak a word,
 For I will take it all upon myself.
 Conchubar, I will go.
NAOISE. And do you think
 That, were I given life at such a price,
 I would not cast it from me? O my eagle!
 Why do you beat vain wings upon the rock
 When hollow night's above?
DEIRDRE. It's better, Naoise.
 It may be hard for you, but you'll forget. 610
 For what am I, to be remembered always?
 And there are other women. There was one,
 The daughter of the King of Leodas;[13]
 I could not sleep because of her. Speak to him;
 Tell it out plain, and make him understand.
 And if it be he thinks I shall stay living,
 Say that I will not.
NAOISE. Would I had lost life
 Among those Scottish kings that sought it of me
 Because you were my wife, or that the worst
 Had taken you before this bargaining! 620
 O eagle! If you were to do this thing,
 And buy my life of Conchubar with your body,
 Love's law being broken, I would stand alone
 Upon the eternal summits, and call out,
 And you could never come there, being banished.
DEIRDRE [*kneeling to* CONCHUBAR]. I would obey, but cannot. Par-
 don us.
 I know that you are good. I have heard you praised
 For giving gifts; and you will pardon us,
 Although I cannot go into your house.
 It was my fault. I only should be punished. 630
 [*Unseen by* DEIRDRE, NAOISE *is
 gagged.*]
 The very moment these eyes fell on him,
 I told him; I held out my hands to him;

[12] The stones referred to in ll. 269–70. [13] Yeats seems to have made up this name.

How could he refuse? At first he would not—
I am not lying—he remembered you.
What do I say? My hands?—No, no, my lips—
For I had pressed my lips upon his lips—
I swear it is not false—my breast to his;

> [CONCHUBAR motions; NAOISE,
> unseen by DEIRDRE, is taken behind
> the curtain.]

Until I woke the passion that's in all,
And how could he resist? I had my beauty.
You may have need of him, a brave, strong man, 640
Who is not foolish at the council-board,
Nor does he quarrel by the candle-light
And give hard blows to dogs. A cup of wine
Moves him to mirth, not madness.

> [She stands up.]
 What am I saying?
You may have need of him, for you have none
Who is so good a sword, or so well loved
Among the common people. You may need him,
And what king knows when the hour of need may come?
You dream that you have men enough. You laugh.
Yes; you are laughing to yourself. You say, 650
"I am Conchubar—I have no need of him."
You will cry out for him some day and say,
"If Naoise were but living"—[she misses NAOISE]. Where is he?
Where have you sent him? Where is the son of Usna?
Where is he, O, where is he?

> [She staggers over to the MUSI-
> CIANS. The EXECUTIONER has
> come out with a sword on which
> there is blood; CONCHUBAR points
> to it. The MUSICIANS give a wail.]

CONCHUBAR. The traitor who has carried off my wife
 No longer lives. Come to my house now, Deirdre,
 For he that called himself your husband's dead.
DEIRDRE. O, do not touch me. Let me go to him.

> [Pause.]

 King Conchubar is right. My husband's dead. 660
 A single woman is of no account,
 Lacking array of servants, linen cupboards,
 The bacon hanging—and King Conchubar's house
 All ready, too—I'll to King Conchubar's house.
 It is but wisdom to do willingly
 What has to be.
CONCHUBAR. But why are you so calm?
 I thought that you would curse me and cry out,
 And fall upon the ground and tear your hair.
DEIRDRE [laughing]. You know too much of women to think so;

Though, if I were less worthy of desire, 670
I would pretend as much; but, being myself,
It is enough that you were master here.
Although we are so delicately made,
There's something brutal in us, and we are won
By those who can shed blood. It was some woman
That taught you how to woo; but do not touch me:
I shall do all you bid me, but not yet,
Because I have to do what's customary.
We lay the dead out, folding up the hands,
Closing the eyes, and stretching out the feet, 680
And push a pillow underneath the head,
Till all's in order; and all this I'll do
For Naoise, son of Usna.

CONCHUBAR. It is not fitting.
You are not now a wanderer, but a queen,
And there are plenty that can do these things.

DEIRDRE [*motioning* CONCHUBAR *away*]. No, no. Not yet. I cannot be
 your queen
Till the past's finished, and its debts are paid.
When a man dies, and there are debts unpaid,
He wanders by the debtor's bed and cries,
"There's so much owing."

CONCHUBAR. You are deceiving me. 690
You long to look upon his face again.
Why should I give you now to a dead man
That took you from a living?

 [*He makes a step towards her.*]

DEIRDRE. In good time.
You'll stir me to more passion than he could,
And yet, if you are wise, you'll grant me this:
That I go look upon him that was once
So strong and comely and held his head so high
That women envied me. For I will see him
All blood-bedabbled and his beauty gone.
It's better, when you're beside me in your strength, 700
That the mind's eye should call up the soiled body,
And not the shape I loved. Look at him, women.
He heard me pleading to be given up,
Although my lover was still living, and yet
He doubts my purpose. I will have you tell him
How changeable all women are; how soon
Even the best of lovers is forgot
When his day's finished.

CONCHUBAR. No; but I will trust
The strength that you have praised, and not your purpose.

DEIRDRE [*almost with a caress*]. It is so small a gift and you will
 grant it 710
Because it is the first that I have asked.

He has refused. There is no sap in him;
Nothing but empty veins. I thought as much.
He has refused me the first thing I have asked—
Me, me, his wife. I understand him now;
I know the sort of life I'll have with him;
But he must drag me to his house by force.
If he refuses [*she laughs*], he shall be mocked of all.
They'll say to one another, "Look at him
That is so jealous that he lured a man 720
From over sea, and murdered him, and yet
He trembled at the thought of a dead face!"
 [*She has her hand upon the cur-
 tain.*]
CONCHUBAR. How do I know that you have not some knife,
 And go to die upon his body?
DEIRDRE. Have me searched,
 If you would make so little of your queen.
 It may be that I have a knife hid here
 Under my dress. Bid one of these dark slaves
 To search me for it. [*Pause.*]
CONCHUBAR. Go to your farewells, Queen.
DEIRDRE. Now strike the wire, and sing to it a while,
 Knowing that all is happy, and that you know 730
 Within what bride-bed I shall lie this night,
 And by what man, and lie close up to him,
 For the bed's narrow, and there outsleep the cockcrow.
 [*She goes behind the curtain.*]
FIRST MUSICIAN. They are gone, they are gone. The proud may lie
 by the proud.
SECOND MUSICIAN. Though we were bidden to sing, cry nothing
 loud.
FIRST MUSICIAN. They are gone, they are gone.
SECOND MUSICIAN. Whispering were enough.
FIRST MUSICIAN. Into the secret wilderness of their love.
SECOND MUSICIAN. A high, grey cairn. What more is to be said?
FIRST MUSICIAN. Eagles have gone into their cloudy bed.
 [*Shouting outside.* FERGUS *enters.
 Many men with scythes and sickles
 and torches gather about the doors.
 The house is lit with the glare of
 their torches.*]
FERGUS. Where's Naoise, son of Usna, and his queen? 740
 I and a thousand reaping-hooks and scythes
 Demand him of you.
CONCHUBAR. You have come too late.
 I have accomplished all. Deirdre is mine;
 She is my queen, and no man now can rob me.
 I had to climb the topmost bough, and pull
 This apple among the winds. Open the curtain
 That Fergus learn my triumph from her lips.

[*The curtain is drawn back. The*
MUSICIANS *begin to keen with low
voices.*]

No, no; I'll not believe it. She is not dead—
She cannot have escaped a second time!

FERGUS. King, she is dead; but lay no hand upon her. 750
What's this but empty cage and tangled wire,
Now the bird's gone? But I'll not have you touch it.

CONCHUBAR. You are all traitors, all against me—all.
And she has deceived me for a second time;
And every common man can keep his wife,
But not the King.

[*Loud shouting outside:* "Death
to Conchubar!" "Where is
Naoise?" *etc. The dark-faced men
gather round* CONCHUBAR *and
draw their swords; but he motions
them away.*]

I have no need of weapons,
There's not a traitor that dare stop my way.
Howl, if you will; but I, being King, did right
In choosing her most fitting to be Queen,
And letting no boy lover take the sway. 760

THE END

Luigi Pirandello
(*1867–1936*)

"Life," Luigi Pirandello wrote, "is a continuous flow which we continually
try to stop, to fix in concepts and ideals. But inside ourselves, in what we
call our soul, the flow continues indistinctly, under the wire, past the limits
that we set when we formed consciousness and built a personality. During
certain stormy moments, inundated by the flow, all our fictitious forms
collapse ignominiously."

Pirandello's perception of the tension between humanity's fragile, par-
tial, provisional conscious mind and the surging, vital, unknowable forces
of "life" is a distinctly and painfully modern one. (His "flood within our-
selves" is very close to Freud's Unconscious.) It was Pirandello's achieve-
ment as a dramatist to find a dramatic form that not only expressed this
perception but actually embodied it. The stage itself, in Pirandello's hands,
becomes a metaphor for a view of human personality as dizzyingly multiple

and of reality as essentially unknowable. *Six Characters in Search of an Author,* as his English translator Frederick May rightly suggests, is to the theater what Eliot's *Waste Land* is to poetry: a work which redefines the medium itself to express a radically modern sense of the world.

Pirandello was born in Sicily in 1867, the son of a prosperous family of sulfur-merchants. He resisted his father's desire for him to enter the family business and attended first the University of Rome and then the University of Bonn, where he received a doctorate in philology in 1891; his thesis was on the dialect of his hometown in Sicily. Three years later he entered into an arranged marriage with Antonietta Portulano, the daughter of another family of wealthy sulfur-dealers. The marriage gave Pirandello an independent income and allowed the couple to settle in Rome, where he led the life of a leisured man of letters, publishing an occasional volume of poetry and contributing short stories to literary magazines. The marriage produced three children.

In 1903, a catastrophic landslide destroyed the sulfur mines of both the Pirandellos and the Portulanos, plunging both families into poverty. Pirandello had to seek employment teaching Italian in a girls' school in Rome. His wife, already weakened by a difficult childbirth, reacted to the disaster first with a six-month hysterical paralysis and then with a progressive psychosis. Pirandello cared for her at home for sixteen years, the victim of her paranoia and irrational jealousy, until her increasing violence forced him to commit her to an institution in 1919. (Amazingly, she remained there for forty years, dying in 1959.) It is hard not to see in this tragedy the roots of Pirandello's later themes. The essential unknowability of other people, the fragility of surface forms and ideals, and the multiple selves within each personality were not merely theoretical issues for Pirandello.

Now driven by financial need, Pirandello began to write voluminously. His early career was devoted mainly to fiction; solid success came in 1904 with *The Late Mattia Pascal,* a novel which anticipated the conflict between being and seeming which dominated his later writing. Other successes followed: several collections of earthy, realistic short stories and several novels, including *The Old and Young* (1913), *The Notebooks of Serafino Gubbio, Cinematograph Operator* (1916), and *One, None, and a Hundred Thousand* (1925–26).

Pirandello wrote his first play, *The Vise,* in 1898, but discouraged by difficulties in getting it produced, he did not return to the theater until 1915. *Right You Are (If You Think So)* (1917), an ironic study of the relativity of truth, was a modest success and ignited an enormous burst of dramatic creativity that was to continue through the '20s. His first major theatrical success was *As Before, Better than Before* (1920); immediately after its production, he wrote, within a five-week period, both *Six Characters in Search of an Author* and *Henry IV,* his masterpieces. (Pirandello was always an extraordinarily fast writer; he wrote *Right You Are* in six days, *Six Characters* in three weeks, and *Henry IV* in two weeks.) The productions in Rome of *Six Characters* in 1921 and *Henry IV* in 1922 brought Pirandello international fame. Productions of the two plays followed in Paris, London, Berlin, and New York, and Pirandello's subsequent plays were eagerly competed for: *To Clothe the Naked* (1923), *The Life I Gave You* (1924), *Each in His Own Way* (1924), *Diana and Tuda* (1927), *The New Colony* (1928), *Lazarus* (1929), *To-*

night We Improvise (1930), *As You Desire Me* (1930), and *When Somebody is Somebody* (1933). He received the Nobel Prize in 1934.

World fame achieved, Pirandello in 1925 founded the Art Theater, an Italian national theater based in Rome but committed to touring the world with his plays; the company appeared all over Europe and even toured South America. Financial losses forced the theater to close, however, in 1928. When Mussolini assumed dictatorial powers in the same year, Pirandello committed himself enthusiastically to the new regime, accepting subsidies and honors from the Fascists and publicly supporting their policies, even contributing his Nobel medal to be melted down to support the Italian invasion of Abyssinia. Many attempts have been made to reconcile Pirandello's Fascism with the ironic skepticism toward all systems that characterizes his creative work. It is unnecessary to conclude that he was merely cynically opportunistic; if all systems are equally suspect, there is a temptation to accept one that at least promises order. The plays of the Fascist period—especially *The New Colony, Lazarus,* and *The Mountain Giants* (1936, unfinished)—have been read as withdrawals into myth in reaction to the rigors of the Fascist state. These later years were also marked by a deep, continuing love for the Italian actress Marta Abba. Pirandello died in 1936, leaving instructions for the most private and spartan of funerals: "Dead, let me not be clothed. Let me be placed, naked, in a sheet. No flowers on the bed, no lighted candle. . . . The cart, the horse, the driver, *e basta!*"

Italian critics have held that Pirandello's achievement is greater in fiction than in drama, but there is no doubt that his world stature rests primarily upon his plays, especially *Henry IV* and the plays that he called his trilogy of "the theater in the theater": *Six Characters in Search of An Author, Each in His Own Way,* and *Tonight We Improvise.* "Pirandellism," as it has influenced modern drama, is the self-conscious exposure of the theater itself as a metaphor for human life. This "metatheater" (to use the American critic Lionel Abel's term), the exploration of the proposition that "all the world's a stage," is perhaps as old as the theater itself, but it was Pirandello who revived it in peculiarly modern terms and placed it at the center of his art.

The basic premise of *Six Characters in Search of an Author*—six (ultimately seven) "characters" invade the rehearsal of a play—sets up a situation which generates a series of dazzling paradoxes about the relation of art to life and initiates a dramatic action designed to lead the commonsensical Producer and his actors to that vertiginous, Pirandellian moment when the "fictitious forms" of consciousness collapse under the surging "flood" of life, a moment reached at the very end of the play.

The spine of the play is the ongoing debate between the Father and the Producer over the comparative "reality" of ordinary human beings and "characters." Insofar as anyone wins the debate, it is probably the Father, who superficially seems to be Pirandello's spokesman. (In some productions, the Father has even been made up to look like Pirandello, pointed beard and all.) But it is a serious misreading of the play to miss the dramatic irony in the presentation of the Father. His arguments that the characters of art are more "real" than ordinary people because they are exempt from temporal change and because they can be seen from only one point of view are absurd (in several senses); his defense of the fixed and the unchanging

sounds suspiciously like not a defense of life but a wish for death. The unthinking animal vitality of the actors is much more attractive than the Father's tortured self-consciousness.

The crucial character in this play is perhaps not the Father but one who never appears, that mysteriously absent Author. Why did he abandon his characters and their shadowy, half-finished plot? The critic Eric Bentley has pointed out that the three incidents in the fragmentary "characters" plot are close to primitive fantasy: a father seducing his daughter, a son seeing his parents making love, and a child murdering a sibling. Perhaps our absent Author has abandoned his characters because they have led him onto psychologically dangerous ground. But behind even the Author, in a Pirandellian layering of reality, is Pirandello himself, who dramatizes, in the finished play, not merely the Father's specious philosophizing but all the paradoxes and conflicts of the parallel projects of playwriting and encountering the mysterious flood of life.

NOTE ON THE TEXT

The text of *Six Characters in Search of an Author* reprinted here differs considerably from the version generally known in America. Previous English translations of the play have been based upon Pirandello's original 1921 version. Frederick May's translation is the first English version based on Pirandello's final, definitive version of the play.

FURTHER READING (*prepared by N. K. B.*): *Naked Masks*, ed. Eric Bentley, 1952, contains other plays by Pirandello, an excellent introduction, a biographical note, and Pirandello's Preface to *Six Characters in Search of an Author*. Bentley's perceptive analyses of Pirandello have been collected in *The Pirandello Commentaries*, 1986. Gaspare Giudice, *Pirandello*, 1975, trans. by Alastair Hamilton, provides the fullest account of the writer's absorbing life; Renate Matthaei, *Luigi Pirandello*, 1973, also contains much biographical detail, in addition to analyzing the major plays. Anthony Caputi, *Pirandello and the Crisis of Modern Consciousness*, 1988, is a good exploration of the important subject of consciouness in the works. Anne Paolucci's *Pirandello's Theater*, 1974, focuses on the experimental quality of the later plays but argues for the unity of his entire work. Olga Ragusa, *Luigi Pirandello*, 1981, provides explications of selected plays in order to demonstrate Pirandello's early interest in psychology and the occult. Glauco Cambon, ed., *Pirandello: A Collection of Critical Essays*, 1967, is a valuable compendium of critical views, including Francis Fergusson's essay on theatricality in *Six Characters*. Oscar Büdel, *Pirandello*, 1966, rev. 1969, establishes the importance of Relativism in Pirandello's technique. Roger W. Oliver, *Dreams of Passion: The Theater of Luigi Pirandello*, 1979, interprets the drama according to the theory of perception articulated in Pirandello's essay "On Humor," with a lengthy analysis of *Six Characters*. A well-documented, thorough study, A. Richard Sogliuzzo's *Luigi Pirandello, Director: The Playwright in the Theatre*, 1982, demonstrates the role of Pirandello's theories in his own productions.

SIX CHARACTERS
IN SEARCH OF AN AUTHOR

A PLAY IN THE MAKING

Translated by Frederick May

THE CHARACTERS OF THE PLAY IN THE MAKING

THE FATHER	THE BOY *(non-speaking)*
THE MOTHER	THE LITTLE GIRL *(non-speaking)*
THE STEPDAUGHTER	MADAME PACE[1] *(who is called into being)*
THE SON	

THE ACTORS IN THE COMPANY

THE PRODUCER[2]	THE PROMPTER
THE LEADING LADY	THE PROPERTY MAN
THE LEADING MAN	THE FOREMAN OF THE STAGE CREW
THE SECOND FEMALE LEAD[3]	THE PRODUCER'S SECRETARY
THE INGENUE	THE COMMISSIONAIRE[4]
THE JUVENILE LEAD	STAGE HANDS AND OTHER THEATER
OTHER ACTORS AND ACTRESSES	PERSONNEL
THE STAGE MANAGER	

DAYTIME: THE STAGE OF A THEATER

N.B.—*The play has neither acts nor scenes. Its performance will be interrupted twice: once—though the curtain will not be lowered—when the* PRODUCER *and the principal* CHARACTERS *go away to write the script and the* ACTORS *leave the stage, and a second time when the Man on the Curtain lets it fall by mistake.*

When the audience enters the auditorium the curtain is up and the stage is just as it would be during the daytime. There is no set and there are no wings; it is empty and in almost total darkness. This is in order that right from the very beginning the audience shall receive the impression of being present, not at a performance of a carefully rehearsed play, but at a performance of a play that suddenly happens.

Two small flights of steps, one right and one left, give access to the stage from the auditorium.

On the stage itself, the prompter's dome has been removed, and is standing just to one side of the prompt box.[5]

[1] Pronounced "pah-chay" ("peace" in Italian).
[2] "Director" in American theater-terminology.
[3] Referred to as "The Second Actress" in the text. [4] Doorman, caretaker.
[5] Older theaters and opera houses had a pit in the stage down center for a prompter or chorus conductor. His head was concealed by a shield called the "prompter's dome."

Downstage, on the other side, a small table and an armchair with its back turned to the audience have been set for the PRODUCER.

Two more small tables, one rather larger than the other, together with several chairs, have been set downstage so that they are ready if needed for the rehearsal. There are other chairs scattered about to the left and to the right for the actors, and, in the background, to one side and almost hidden, there is a piano.

When the house lights go down the FOREMAN *comes on to the stage through the door back. He is dressed in blue dungarees and carries his tools in a bag slung at his belt. From a corner at the back of the stage he takes one or two slats of wood, brings them down front, kneels down and starts nailing them together. At the sound of his hammer the* STAGE-MANAGER *rushes in from the direction of the dressing rooms.*

STAGE-MANAGER. Hey! What are you doing?

FOREMAN. What am I doing? Hammering . . . nails.

STAGE-MANAGER. At this time of day? [*He looks at his watch.*] It's gone half-past ten! The Producer'll be here any minute now and he'll want to get on with his rehearsal.

FOREMAN. And let me tell *you* something . . . I've got to have time to do *my* work, too.

STAGE-MANAGER. You'll get it, you'll get it. . . . But you can't do that *now*.

FOREMAN. When can I do it then?

STAGE-MANAGER. After the rehearsal. Now, come on. . . . Clear up all this mess, and let me get on with setting the second act of *The Game As He Played It.*[6]

[*The* FOREMAN *gathers his pieces of wood together, muttering and grumbling all the while, and goes off. Meanwhile, the* ACtors of the Company *have begun to come on to the stage through the door back. First one comes in, then another, then two together . . . just as they please. There are nine or ten of them in all—as many as you would suppose you would need for the rehearsal of Pirandello's play,* The Game As He Played It, *which has been called for today. As they come in they greet one another and the* STAGE-MANAGER *with a cheery "Good morning." Some of them go off to their dressing-rooms; others, and among them the* PROMPTER, *who is carrying the prompt copy rolled up under his arm, remain on the stage, waiting for the* PRODUCER *to come and start the rehearsal. While they are waiting—some of them standing, some seated about in small groups—they exchange a few words among themselves. One lights a cigarette,*

[6] A (nonexistent) play by Pirandello.

another complains about the part that he's been given and a third reads out an item of news from a theatrical journal for the benefit of the other actors. It would be best if all the ACTORS AND ACTRESSES *could be dressed in rather bright and gay clothes. This first improvised scene should be played very naturally and with great vivacity. After a while, one of the comedy men can sit down at the piano and start playing a dance-tune. The younger* ACtors and Actresses *start dancing.*]

STAGE-MANAGER [*clapping his hands to restore order*]. Come on, now, come on! That's enough of that! Here's the producer!

> [*The music and dancing come to a sudden stop. The* ACTORS *turn and look out into the auditorium and see the* PRODUCER, *who is coming in through the door. He comes up the gangway between the stalls, bowler hat on head, stick under arm, and a large cigar in his mouth, to the accompaniment of a chorus of "Good-mornings" from the* ACTORS *and climbs up one of the flights of steps on to the stage. His* SECREtary *offers him his post—a newspaper or so, a script.*]

PRODUCER. Any letters?

SECRETARY. None at all. This is all the post there is.

PRODUCER [*handing him back the script*]. Put it in my office. [*Then, looking around and turning to the* STAGE-MANAGER.] Oh, you can't see a thing here! Ask them to give us a spot of light, please.

STAGE-MANAGER. Right you are!

> [*He goes off to give the order and a short while after the whole of the right side of the stage, where the* ACTORS *are standing, is lit up by a bright white light. In the meantime the* PROMPTER *has taken his place in his box, switched on his light and spread his script out in front of him.*]

PRODUCER [*clapping his hands*]. Come on, let's get started! [*To the* STAGE-MANAGER.] Anyone missing?

STAGE-MANAGER. The Leading Lady.

PRODUCER. As usual! [*Looks at his watch.*] We're ten minutes late already. Make a note, will you, please, to remind me to give her a good talking-to about being so late? It might teach her to get to rehearsals on time in the future.

> [*He has scarely finished his rebuke when the voice of the* LEADING LADY *is heard at the back of the auditorium.*]

LEADING LADY. No, please don't! Here I am! Here I am!

[*She is dressed completely in white, with a large and rather dashing and provocative hat, and is carrying a dainty little lap-dog. She runs down the aisle and hastily climbs up the steps on to the stage.*]

PRODUCER. You've set your heart on always keeping us waiting, haven't you?

LEADING LADY. Forgive me! I hunted everywhere for a taxi so that I should get here on time! But you haven't started yet, anyway. And I don't come on immediately. [*Then, calling the* STAGE-MANAGER *by name, she gives him the lap-dog.*] Please put him in my dressing-room . . . and mind you shut the door!

PRODUCER [*grumblingly*]. And she has to bring a dog along too! As if there weren't enough dogs around here! [*He claps his hands again and turns to the* PROMPTER.] Come on now, let's get on with Act II of *The Game As He Played It*. [*He sits down in the armchair.*] Now, ladies and gentlemen, who's on?

[*The* ACTORS AND ACTRESSES *clear away from the front of the stage and go and sit to one side, except for the three who start the scene, and the* LEADING LADY. *She had paid no attention to the* PRODUC-*er's question and has seated herself at one of the little tables.*]

PRODUCER [*to the* LEADING LADY]. Ah! So you're in this scene, are you?

LEADING LADY. Me? Oh, no!

PRODUCER [*annoyed*]. Then for God's sake get off!

[*And the* LEADING LADY *gets up and goes and sits with the others.*]

PRODUCER [*to the* PROMPTER]. Now, let's get started!

PROMPTER [*reading from his script*]. "The house of Leone Gala. A strange room, half dining-room, half study."

PRODUCER [*turning to the* STAGE-MANAGER]. We'll use the red set.

STAGE-MANAGER [*making a note on a sheet of paper*]. The red set. Right!

PROMPTER [*continuing to read from his script*]. "A table laid for a meal and a desk with books and papers. Bookshelves with books on them. Glass-fronted cupboards containing valuable china. A door back leading into Leone's bedroom. A side door left, leading into the kitchen. The main entrance is right."

PRODUCER [*getting up and pointing*]. Right! Now listen carefully—over there, the main entrance. And over here, the kitchen. [*Turning to the actor who is to play the part of Socrates.*] You'll make your entrances and exits this side. [*To the* STAGE-MANAGER.] We'll have that green-baize door at the back there . . . and some curtains. [*He goes and sits down again.*]

STAGE-MANAGER [*making a note*]. Right you are!

PROMPTER [*reading*]. "Scene I. Leone Gala, Guido Venanzi, Filippo, who is called Socrates." [*To the* PRODUCER.] Do I have to read the stage directions as well?

PRODUCER. Yes, yes, of course! I've told you that a hundred times!

PROMPTER [*reading*]. "When the curtain rises, Leone Gala, wearing a cook's hat and apron, is busy beating an egg in a basin with a wooden spoon. Filippo, also dressed as a cook, is beating another egg. Guido Venanzi is sitting listening to them."

LEADING MAN [*to the* PRODUCER]. Excuse me, but do I really have to wear a cook's hat?

PRODUCER [*irritated by this observation*]. So it seems! That's certainly what's written there! [*He points to the script.*]

LEADING MAN. Forgive me for saying so, but it's ridiculous.

PRODUCER [*bounding to his feet in fury*]. Ridiculous! Ridiculous! What do you expect me to do if the French haven't got any more good comedies to send us, and we're reduced to putting on plays by Pirandello? And if you can understand *his* plays . . . you're a better man than I am! He deliberately goes out of his way to annoy people, so that by the time the play's through everybody's fed up . . . actors, critics, audience, everybody!

> [*The* ACTORS *laugh. Then getting up and going over to the* LEADING MAN, *the* PRODUCER *cries*]:

Yes, my dear fellow, a cook's hat! And you beat eggs! And do you think that, having these eggs to beat, you then have nothing more on your hands? Oh, no, not a bit of it. . . . You have to represent the shell of the eggs that you're beating!

> [*The* ACTORS *start laughing again and begin to make ironical comments among themselves.*]

Shut up! And listen when I'm explaining things! [*Turning again to the* LEADING MAN.] Yes, my dear fellow, the shell . . . or, as you might say, the empty form of reason, without that content of instinct which is blind! You are reason and your wife is instinct, in a game where you play the parts which have been given you. And all the time you're playing your part, you are the self-willed puppet of yourself. Understand?

LEADING MAN [*spreading out his hands*]. Me? No!

PRODUCER [*returning to his seat*]. Neither do I! However, let's get on with it! It's going to be a wonderful flop, anyway! [*In a confidential tone.*] I suggest you turn to the audience a bit more . . . about three-quarters face. Otherwise, what with the abstruseness of the dialogue, and the audience's not being able to hear you, the whole thing'll go to hell. [*Clapping his hands again.*] Now, come along! *Come along!* Let's get started!

PROMPTER. Excuse me, sir, do you mind if I put the top back on my box? There's a bit of a draft.

PRODUCER. Of course! Go ahead! Go ahead!

> [*Meanwhile the* COMMISSIONAIRE *has entered the auditorium. He is wearing a braided cap and having covered the length of the aisle, he comes up to the edge of the stage to announce the arrival of the* SIX CHARACTERS *to the* PRODUCER. *They have followed the* COMMISSIONAIRE *into*

the auditorium and have walked behind
him as he has come up to the stage. They
look about them, a little perplexed and a
little dismayed.

In any production of this play it is
imperative that the producer should
use every means possible to avoid any
confusion between the SIX CHARACTERS
and the ACTORS. The placings of the two
groups, as they will be indicated in the
stage-directions once the CHARACTERS
are on the stage, will no doubt help. So,
too, will their being lit in different colors.
But the most effective and most suitable
method of distinguishing them that sug-
gests itself, is the use of special masks for
the CHARACTERS, masks specially made
from some material which will not grow
limp with perspiration and will at the
same time be light enough to be worn by
the actors playing these parts. They should
be cut so as to leave the eyes, the nose and
the mouth free. In this way the deep signif-
icance of the play can be brought out. The
CHARACTERS should not, in fact, appear
as phantasms, but as created realities,
unchangeable creations of the imagina-
tion and, therefore, more real and more
consistent than the ever-changing natu-
ralness of the ACTORS. The masks will
assist in giving the impression of figures
constructed by art, each one fixed immuta-
bly in the expression of that sentiment
which is fundamental to it. That is to say
in REMORSE for the FATHER, REVENGE
for the STEPDAUGHTER, CONTEMPT for
the SON and SORROW for the MOTHER.
Her mask should have wax tears fixed in
the corners of the eyes and coursing down
the cheeks, just like those which are carved
and painted in the representations of the
Mater Dolorosa[7] that are to be seen in
churches. Her dress, too, should be of a
special material and cut. It should be se-
verely plain, its folds stiff, giving in fact
the appearance of having been carved,
and not of being made of any material that

[7] Mary, mother of Christ, sorrowing for her son, a favorite subject of ecclesiastical art.

you can just go out and buy or have cut out and made up into a dress by any ordinary dressmaker.

The FATHER *is a man of about fifty. He is not bald but his reddish hair is thin at the temples. His moustache is thick and coils over his still rather youthful-looking mouth, which all too often falls open in a purposeless, uncertain smile. His complexion is pale and this is especially noticeable when one has occasion to look at his forehead, which is particularly broad. His blue, oval-shaped eyes are very clear and piercing. He is wearing a dark jacket and light-colored trousers. At times his manner is all sweetness and light, at others it is hard and harsh.*

The MOTHER *appears as a woman crushed and terrified by an intolerable weight of shame and abasement. She is dressed in a modest black and wears a thick crêpe widow's veil. When she lifts her veil she reveals a wax-like face; it is not, however, at all sickly-looking. She keeps her eyes downcast all the time. The* STEP-daughter, *who is eighteen, is defiant, bold, arrogant—almost shamelessly so. She is very beautiful. She, too, is dressed in mourning but carries it with a decided air of showy elegance. She shows contempt for the very timid, dejected, half-frightened manner of her younger brother, a rather grubby and unprepossessing* BOY *of fourteen, who is also dressed in black. On the other hand she displays a very lively tenderness for her small sister, a* LITTLE GIRL *of about four, who is wearing a white frock with a black silk sash round her waist.*

The SON *is a tall young man of twenty-two. He is wearing a mauve colored overcoat and has a long green scarf twisted round his neck. He appears as if he has stiffened into an attitude of contempt for the* FATHER *and of supercilious indifference towards the* MOTHER.]

COMMISSIONAIRE [*cap in hand*]. Excuse me, sir.
PRODUCER [*snapping at him rudely*]. Now what's the matter?
COMMISSIONAIRE. There are some people here, sir, asking for you.

[*The* PRODUCER *and the* ACTORS *turn
in astonishment and look out into the
auditorium.*]

PRODUCER [*furiously*]. But I've got a rehearsal on at the moment! And you
 know quite well that no one's allowed in here while a rehearsal's going
 on. [*Then addressing the* CHARACTERS.] Who are you? What do you want?

FATHER [*he steps forward, followed by the others, and comes to the foot of one of the
 flights of steps*]. We are here in search of an author.

PRODUCER [*caught between anger and utter astonishment*]. In search of an au-
 thor? Which author?

FATHER. Any author, sir.

PRODUCER. But there's no author here. . . . We're not rehearsing a new
 play.

STEPDAUGHTER [*vivaciously, as she rushes up the steps*]. So much the better!
 Then so much the better, sir! *We* can be your new play.

ONE OF THE ACTORS [*amidst the lively comments and laughter of the others*]. Oh,
 just listen to her! *Listen* to her!

FATHER [*following the* STEPDAUGHTER *on to the stage*]. Yes, but if there isn't
 any author. . . . [*To the* PRODUCER.] Unless *you'd* like to be the author. . . .

[*Holding the* LITTLE GIRL *by the hand,
the* MOTHER, *followed by the* BOY, *climbs
up the first few steps leading to the stage
and stands there expectantly. The* SON
remains morosely below.]

PRODUCER. Are you people trying to be funny?

FATHER. No. . . . How can you suggest such a thing? On the contrary, we
 are bringing you a terrible and grievous drama.

STEPDAUGHTER. And we might make your fortune for you.

PRODUCER. Perhaps you'll do me the kindness of getting out of this the-
 ater! We've got no time to waste on lunatics!

FATHER [*he is wounded by this, but replies in a gentle tone*]. Oh. . . . But you
 know very well, don't you, that life is full of things that are infinitely
 absurd, things that, for all their impudent absurdity, have no need to
 masquerade as truth, because they are true.

PRODUCER. What the devil are you talking about?

FATHER. What I'm saying is that reversing the usual order of things, forc-
 ing oneself to a contrary way of action, may well be construed as madness.
 As, for instance, when we create things which have all the appearance of
 reality in order that they shall look like the realities themselves.
 But allow me to observe that if this indeed be madness, it is, nonetheless,
 the sole *raison d'être* of your profession.

[*The* ACTORS *stir indignantly at this.*]

PRODUCER [*getting up and looking him up and down*]. Oh, yes? So you think
 ours is a profession of lunatics, do you?

FATHER. Yes, making what isn't true *seem* true . . . without having to . . .
 for fun. . . . Isn't it your function to give life on the stage to imaginary
 characters?

PRODUCER [*immediately, making himself spokesman for the growing anger of his
 actors*]. I should like you to know, my dear sir, that the actor's profes-
 sion is a most noble one. And although nowadays, with things in the

state they are, our playwrights give us stupid comedies to act, and pup-
pets to represent instead of men, I'd have you know that it is our boast
that we have given life, here on these very boards, to immortal works!

[*The* ACTORS *satisfiedly murmur their
approval and applaud the* PRODUCER.]

FATHER [*breaking in and following hard on his argument*]. There you are! Oh,
that's it exactly! To living beings . . . to beings who are more alive than
those who breathe and wear clothes! Less real, perhaps, but truer!
We're in complete agreement!

[*The* ACTORS *look at each other in utter
astonishment.*]

PRODUCER. But . . . What on earth! . . . But you said just now . . .

FATHER. No, I said that because of your . . . because you shouted at us that
you had no time to waste on lunatics . . . while nobody can know better
than you that nature makes use of the instrument of human fantasy to
pursue her work of creation on a higher level.

PRODUCER. True enough! True enough! But where does all this get us?

FATHER. Nowhere. I only wish to show you that one is born into life in so
many ways, in so many forms. . . . As a tree, or as a stone; as water or as
a butterfly. . . . Or as a woman. And that one can be born a character.

PRODUCER [*ironically, feigning amazement*]. And you, together with these
other people, were born a character?

FATHER. Exactly. And alive, as you see. [*The* PRODUCER *and the* ACTORS *burst
out laughing as if at some huge joke.*] [*Hurt.*] I'm sorry that you laugh like
that because, I repeat, we carry within ourselves a terrible and grievous
drama, as you can deduce for yourselves from this woman veiled in
black.

[*And so saying, he holds out his hand to
the* MOTHER *and helps her up the last few
steps and, continuing to hold her hand,
leads her with a certain tragic solemnity to
the other side of the stage, which immedi-
ately lights up with a fantastic kind of
light. The* LITTLE GIRL *and the* BOY *fol-
low their* MOTHER. *Next the* SON *comes
up and goes and stands to one side, in the
background. Then the* STEPDAUGHTER
*follows him on to the stage; she stands
downstage, leaning against the prosce-
nium arch. The* ACTORS *are at first com-
pletely taken aback and then, caught in
admiration at this development, they burst
into applause—just as if they had had a
show put on for their benefit.*]

PRODUCER [*at first utterly astonished and then indignant*]. Shut up! What
the . . .! [*Then turning to the* CHARACTERS.] And you get out of here!
Clear out of here! [*To the* STAGE-MANAGER.] For God's sake, clear
them out!

STAGE-MANAGER [*coming forward, but then stopping as if held back by some
strange dismay*]. Go away! Go away!

FATHER [*to the* PRODUCER]. No, no! Listen. . . . We. . . .

PRODUCER [*shouting*]. I tell you, we've got work to do!

LEADING MAN. You can't go about playing practical jokes like this. . . .

FATHER [*resolutely coming forward*]. I wonder at your incredulity. Is it perhaps that you're not accustomed to seeing the characters created by an
author leaping to life up here on the stage, when they come face to face
with each other? Or is it, perhaps, that there's no script there [*he points to
the prompt box*] that contains us?

STEPDAUGHTER [*smiling, she steps towards the* PRODUCER; *then, in a wheedling
voice*]. Believe me, sir, we really are six characters . . . and very, very
interesting! But we've been cut adrift.

FATHER [*brushing her aside*]. Yes, that's it, we've been cut adrift. [*And then
immediately to the* PRODUCER.] In the sense, you understand, that the author who created us as living beings, either couldn't or wouldn't put us
materially into the world of art. And it was truly a crime . . . because he
who has the good fortune to be born a living character may snap his
fingers at Death even. He will never die! Man . . . The writer . . . The
instrument of creation . . . Will die. . . . But what is created by him will
never die. And in order to live eternally he has not the slightest need of
extraordinary gifts or of accomplishing prodigies. Who was Sancho
Panza? Who was Don Abbondio?[8] And yet they live eternally because—
living seeds—they had the good fortune to find a fruitful womb—a
fantasy which knew how to raise and nourish them, and to make them
live through all eternity.

PRODUCER. All this is very, very fine indeed. . . . But what do you want
here?

FATHER. We wish to live, sir!

PRODUCER [*ironically*]. Through all eternity?

FATHER. No, sir; just for a moment . . . in you.

AN ACTOR. Listen to him! . . . listen to him!

LEADING LADY. They want to live in us!

JUVENILE LEAD [*pointing to the* STEPDAUGHTER]. I've no objection . . . so
long as I get her.

FATHER. Listen! Listen! The play is in the making. [*To the* PRODUCER.] But
if you and your actors are willing, we can settle it all between us without
further delay.

PRODUCER [*annoyed*]. But what do you want to settle? We don't go in for
that sort of concoction here! We put on comedies and dramas here.

FATHER. Exactly! That's the very reason why we came to you.

PRODUCER. And where's the script?

FATHER. It is in us, sir. [*The* ACTORS *laugh.*] The drama is in us. *We* are the
drama and we are impatient to act it—so fiercely does our inner passion
urge us on.

STEPDAUGHTER [*scornful, treacherous, alluring, with deliberate shamelessness*].
My passion. . . . If you only knew! My passion . . . for him!
[*She points to the* FATHER *and makes as if*

[8] *Sancho Panza . . . Don Abbondio.* Sancho Panza is the groom in Miguel de Cervantes' *Don
Quixote* (1605, 1616). Don Abbondio is the parish priest in Alessandro Manzoni's romantic
novel *I Promessi Sposi (The Betrothed,* 1825–26).

to embrace him, but then bursts into stri-
dent laughter.]
FATHER [*at once, angrily*]. You keep out of this for the moment! And please
don't laugh like that!
STEPDAUGHTER. Oh . . . mayn't I? Then perhaps *you'll* allow me, ladies and
gentlemen. . . . Although it's scarcely two months since my father died
. . . just you watch how I can dance and sing!
[*Mischievously she starts to sing Dave
Stamper's "Prends garde à Tchou-Tchin-
Tchou" in the fox-trot or slow one-step
version by François Salabert. She sings the
first verse, accompanying it with a dance.*]

Les chinois sont un peuple malin,
De Shangaï à Pékin,
Ils ont mis des écriteaux partout:
Prenez garde à Tchou-Tchin-Tchou![9]

[*While she is singing and dancing, the
ACTORS, and especially the younger ones,
as if attracted by some strange fascination,
move towards her and half raise their
hands as though to catch hold of her. She
runs away, and when the ACTORS burst
into applause, and the PRODUCER rebukes
her, she stands where she is, quietly,
abstractedly, and as if her thoughts were
far away.*]
ACTORS AND ACTRESSES [*laughing and clapping*]. Well done! Jolly good!
PRODUCER [*irately*]. Shut up! What do you think this is . . . a cabaret? [*Then
taking the FATHER a little to one side, he says with a certain amount of
consternation.*] Tell me something. . . . Is she mad?
FATHER. What do you mean, mad? It's worse than that!
STEPDAUGHTER [*immediately rushing up to the PRODUCER*]. Worse! Worse! Oh
it's something very much worse than that! Listen! Let's put this drama
on at once. . . . Please! Then you'll see that at a certain moment I . . .
when this little darling here. . . . [*Takes the LITTLE GIRL by the hand and
brings her over to the PRODUCER.*] . . . Isn't she a dear? [*Takes her in her arms
and kisses her.*] You little darling! . . . You dear little darling! [*Puts her
down again, adding in a moved tone, almost without wishing to.*] Well, when
God suddenly takes this child away from her poor mother, and that
little imbecile there [*roughly grabbing hold of the BOY by the sleeve and
thrusting him forward*] does the stupidest of all stupid things, like the idiot
he is [*pushing him back towards the MOTHER*] . . . Then you will see me run
away. Yes, I shall run away! And, oh, how I'm longing for that moment
to come! Because after all the very intimate things that have happened

[9]*Prends garde à Tchou-Tchin-Tchou.* French version of "Beware of Chu-Chin-Chow," a popu-
lar song of 1917. *Chou Chin Chow* was an enormously popular New York musical revue by
Frederic Norton and Oscar Asche, and this song, from the *Ziegfeld Follies of 1917*, alludes to its
success: "The Chinese are a cunning folk / From Shanghai to Peking, / They've put up posters
everywhere: / Beware of *Chu Chin Chow!*"

between him and me [*with a horrible wink in the direction of the* FATHER] I can't remain any longer with these people . . . having to witness my mother's anguish because of that queer fish there [*pointing to the* SON]. Look at him! Look at him! See how indifferent, how frigid he is . . . because he's the legitimate son . . . *he* is! He despises me, he despises him [*pointing to the* BOY], he despises that dear little creature. . . . Because we're bastards! Do you understand? . . . Because we're *bastards!* [*She goes up to the* MOTHER *and embraces her.*] And he doesn't want to recognize this poor woman as his mother. . . . This poor woman . . . who is the mother of us all! He looks down on her as if she were only the mother of us three bastards! The wretch! [*She says all this very quickly and very excitedly. She raises her voice at the word 'bastards' and the final 'wretch' is delivered in a low voice and almost spat out.*]

MOTHER [*to the* PRODUCER, *an infinity of anguish in her voice*]. Please, in the name of these two little children . . . I beg you. . . . [*She grows faint and sways on her feet.*] Oh, my God! [*Consternation and bewilderment among the* ACTORS.]

FATHER [*rushing over to support her, accompanied by most of the* ACTORS]. Quick . . . a chair. . . . A chair for this poor widow!

ACTORS [*rushing over*]. Has she fainted? Has she fainted?

PRODUCER. Quick, get a chair . . . get a chair!

> [*One of the* ACTORS *brings a chair, the others stand around, anxious to help in any way they can. The* MOTHER *sits on the chair; she attempts to prevent the* FA- *ther from lifting the veil which hides her face.*]

FATHER. Look at her. . . . Look at her. . . .

MOTHER. No, No! My God! Stop it, please!

FATHER. Let them see you. [*He lifts her veil.*]

MOTHER [*rising and covering her face with her hands in desperation*]. I beg you, sir, . . . Don't let this man carry out his plan! You must prevent him. . . . It's horrible!

PRODUCER [*utterly dumbfounded*]. I don't get this at all. . . . I haven't got the slightest idea what you're talking about. [*To the* FATHER.] Is this lady your wife?

FATHER [*immediately*]. Yes, sir, my wife.

PRODUCER. Then how does it come about that she's a widow if you're still alive?

> [*The* ACTORS *find relief for their bewilderment and astonishment in a noisy burst of laughter.*]

FATHER [*wounded, speaking with sharp resentment*]. Don't laugh! Don't laugh like that, for pity's sake! It is in this fact that her drama lies. She had another man. Another man who ought to be here.

MOTHER [*with a cry*]. No! No!

STEPDAUGHTER. He's got the good luck to be dead. . . . He died two months ago, as I just told you. We're still wearing mourning for him, as you can see.

FATHER. But it's not because he's dead that he's not here. No, he's not here

because . . . Look at her! Look at her, please, and you'll understand immediately! Her drama does not lie in the love of two men for whom she, being incapable of love, could feel nothing. . . . Unless, perhaps, it be a little gratitude . . . to him, not to me. She is not a woman. . . . She is a mother. And her drama. . . . And how powerful it is! How powerful it is! . . . Her drama lies entirely, in fact, in these four children. . . . The children of the two men that she had.

MOTHER. Did you say that I had them? Do you dare to say that I *had* these two men . . . to suggest that I wanted them? [*To the* PRODUCER.] It was his doing. He gave him to me! He forced him on me! He forced me. . . . He forced me to go away with that other man!

STEPDAUGHTER [*at once, indignantly*]. It's not true!

MOTHER [*startled*]. Not true?

STEPDAUGHTER. It's not true! It's not true, I say.

MOTHER. And what can you possibly know about it?

STEPDAUGHTER. It's not true! [*To the* PRODUCER.] Don't believe her! Do you know why she said that? Because of him. [*Pointing to the* SON.] That's why she said it! Because she tortures herself, wears herself out with anguish, because of the indifference of that son of hers. She wants him to believe that if she abandoned him when he was two years old it was because he [*pointing to the* FATHER] forced her to do it.

MOTHER [*forcefully*]. He forced me to do it! He forced me, as God is my witness! [*To the* PRODUCER.] Ask him [*pointing to her* HUSBAND] if it's not true! Make him tell my son! She [*pointing to her* DAUGHTER] knows nothing at all about the matter.

STEPDAUGHTER. I know that while my father lived you were always happy. . . . You had a peaceful and contented life together. Deny it if you can!

MOTHER. I don't deny it! No. . . .

STEPDAUGHTER. He was always most loving, always kindness itself towards you. [*To the* BOY, *angrily*.] Isn't it true? Go on. . . . Say it's true! Why don't you speak, you stupid little idiot?

MOTHER. Leave the poor boy alone! Why do you want to make me appear an ungrateful woman? I don't want to say anything against your father. . . . I only said that it wasn't my fault, and that it wasn't just to satisfy my own desires that I left his house and abandoned my son.

FATHER. What she says is true. It was my doing.

[*There is a pause.*]

LEADING MAN [*to the other* ACTORS]. My God! What a show!

LEADING LADY. And we're the audience this time!

JUVENILE LEAD. For once in a while.

PRODUCER [*who is beginning to show a lively interest*]. Let's listen to this! Let's hear what they've got to say!

[*And saying this he goes down the steps into the auditorium and stands in front of the stage, as if to get an impression of the scene from the audience's point of view.*]

SON [*without moving from where he is, speaking coldly, softly, ironically*]. Yes! Listen to the chunk of philosophy you're going to get now! He will tell you all about the Daemon of Experiment.

FATHER. You're a cynical idiot, as I've told you a hundred times. [*Down to the* PRODUCER.] He mocks me because of this expression that I've discovered in my own defense.

SON [*contemptuously*]. Words! Words!

FATHER. Yes! Words! Words! They can always bring consolation to us. . . . To everyone of us. . . . When we're confronted by something for which there's no explanation. . . . When we're face to face with an evil that consumes us. . . . The consolation of finding a word that tells us nothing, but that brings us peace.

STEPDAUGHTER. And dulls our sense of remorse, too. Yes! That above all!

FATHER. Dulls our sense of remorse? No, that's not true. It wasn't with words alone that I quietened remorse within me.

STEPDAUGHTER. No, you did it with a little money as well. Yes! Oh, yes! with a little money as well! With the hundred lire that he was going to offer me . . . as payment, ladies and gentlemen!

> [*A movement of horror on the part of the* ACTORS.]

SON [*contemptuously to his* STEPSISTER]. That was vile!

STEPDAUGHTER. Vile? There they were, in a pale blue envelope, on the little mahogany table in the room behind Madame Pace's shop. Madame Pace. . . . One of those *Madames* who pretend to sell *Robes et Manteaux*[10] so that they can attract us poor girls from decent families into their workrooms.

SON. And she's bought the right to tyrannize over the whole lot of us with those hundred lire that he was going to pay her. . . . But by good fortune. . . . And let me emphasize this. . . . He had no reason to pay her anything.

STEPDAUGHTER. Yes, but it was a very near thing! Oh, yes, it was, you know! [*She bursts out laughing.*]

MOTHER [*rising to protest*]. For shame! For shame!

STEPDAUGHTER [*immediately*]. Shame? No! This is my revenge! I'm trembling with desire. . . . Simply trembling with desire to live that scene! That room. . . . Over here is the shop-window with all the coats in it. . . . And over there the divan, the long mirror and a screen. . . . And in front of the window that little mahogany table. . . . And the pale blue envelope with the hundred lire inside. Yes, I can see it quite clearly! I'd only have to stretch out my hand and I could pick it up! But you gentlemen really ought to turn your backs now, because I'm almost naked. I no longer blush, because he's the one who does the blushing now [*pointing to the* FATHER]. But, let me tell you, he was very pale then. . . . Very pale indeed! [*To the* PRODUCER.] You can believe *me*!

PRODUCER. I haven't the vaguest idea what you're talking about!

FATHER. I can well believe it! When you get things hurled at you like that. Put your foot down. . . . And let me speak before you believe all these horrible slanders she's so viciously heaping upon me. . . . Without letting me get a word of explanation in.

STEPDAUGHTER. Ah, but this isn't the place for your long-winded fairy-stories, you know!

[10] Dresses and cloaks (French).

FATHER. But I'm not going to. . . . I want to explain things to him!

STEPDAUGHTER. Oh yes . . . I bet you do! You'll explain everything so that it suits you, won't you?

[*At this point the* PRODUCER *comes back on stage to restore order.*]

FATHER. But can't you see that here we have the cause of all the trouble! In the use of words! Each one of us has a whole world of things inside him. . . . And each one of us has his own particular world. How can we understand each other if into the words which I speak I put the sense and the value of things as I understand them within myself. . . . While at the same time whoever is listening to them inevitably assumes them to have the sense and value that they have for him. . . . The sense and value that they have in the world that he has within him? We think we understand one another. . . . But we never really do understand! Look at this situation, for example! All my pity, all the pity that I feel for this woman [*pointing to the* MOTHER] *she* sees as the most ferocious cruelty.

MOTHER. But you turned me out of the house!

FATHER. There! Do you hear? I turned her out! She really believed that I was turning her out!

MOTHER. You know how to talk . . . I don't. . . . But believe me [*turning to the* PRODUCER] after he had married me. . . . Goodness knows why! For I was a poor, humble woman. . . .

FATHER. But it was just because of that. . . . It was your humility that I loved in you. I married you for your humility, believing . . . [*He breaks off, for she is making gestures of contradiction. Then, seeing how utterly impossible it is to make her understand him, he opens his arms wide in a gesture of despair and turns to the* PRODUCER.] No! . . . You see? She says no! It's terrifying, believe me! It's really terrifying, this deafness [*he taps his forehead*]. . . . This mental deafness of hers! Affection. . . . Yes! . . . For her children! But deaf. . . . Mentally deaf. . . . Deaf to the point of desperation.

STEPDAUGHTER. True enough! But now you make him tell us what good all his cleverness has ever done us.

FATHER. If we could only foresee all the ill that can result from the good that we believe we are doing.

[*Meanwhile the* LEADING LADY, *with ever-increasing fury, has been watching the* LEADING MAN, *who is busy carrying on a flirtation with the* STEPDAUGHTER. *Unable to stand it any longer she now steps forward and says to the* PRODUCER.]

LEADING LADY. Excuse me, but are you going on with the rehearsal?

PRODUCER. Why, of course! Of course! But just at the moment I want to hear what these people have to say!

JUVENILE LEAD. This is really something quite new!

INGENUE. It's most interesting!

LEADING LADY. For those that are interested! [*And she looks meaningly in the direction of the* LEADING MAN.]

PRODUCER [*to the* FATHER]. But you'll have to explain everything clearly. [*He goes and sits down.*]

FATHER. Yes. . . . Well. . . . You see . . . I had a poor man working under me. . . . He was my secretary, and devoted to me. . . . Who understood *her* in every way. . . . In everything [*pointing to the* MOTHER]. Oh, there wasn't the slightest suspicion of anything wrong. He was a good man. A humble man. . . . Just like her. . . . They were incapable . . . both of them . . . not only of doing evil . . . but even of thinking it!

STEPDAUGHTER. So, instead, he thought about it for them! And then got on with it.

FATHER. It's not true! I thought that what I should be doing would be for their good. . . . And for mine, too. . . . I confess it! Yes, things had come to such a pass that I couldn't say a single word to either of them without their immediately exchanging an understanding look. . . . Without the one's immediately trying to catch the other's eye. . . . For advice as to how to take what I had said. . . . So that I shouldn't get into a bad temper. As you'll readily appreciate it was enough to keep me in a state of continual fury. . . . Of intolerable exasperation!

PRODUCER. But. . . . Forgive my asking. . . . Why didn't you give this secretary of yours the sack?

FATHER. That's exactly what I did do, as a matter of fact. But then I had to watch that poor woman wandering forlornly about the house like some poor lost creature. . . . Like one of those stray animals you take in out of charity.

MOTHER. But . . .

FATHER [*immediately turning on her, as if to forestall what she is about to say*]. Your son! You were going to tell him about your son, weren't you?

MOTHER. But first of all he tore my son away from me!

FATHER. Not out of any desire to be cruel though! I took him away so that, by living in the country, in contact with Nature, he might grow up strong and healthy.

STEPDAUGHTER [*pointing to him, ironically*]. And just look at him!

FATHER [*immediately*]. And is it my fault, too, that he's grown up the way he has? I sent him to a wet-nurse in the country . . . a peasant's wife . . . because my wife didn't seem strong enough to me. . . . Although she came of a humble family, and it was for that reason that I'd married her! Just a whim maybe. . . . But then . . . what was I to do? I've always had this cursed longing for a certain solid moral healthiness.

> [*At this the* STEPDAUGHTER *breaks out afresh into noisy laughter.*]

Make her stop that noise! I can't stand it!

PRODUCER. Be quiet! Let me hear what he has to say, for God's sake!

> [*At the* PRODUCER'S *rebuke she immediately returns to her former attitude. . . . Absorbed and distant, a half-smile on her lips. The* PRODUCER *comes down off the stage again to see how it looks from the auditorium.*]

FATHER. I could no longer stand the sight of that woman near me [*pointing to the* MOTHER]. Not so much because of the irritation she caused me . . . the nausea . . . the very real nausea with which she inspired me. . . .

But rather because of the pain . . . the pain and the anguish that I was suffering on her account.

MOTHER. And he sent me away!

FATHER. Well provided with everything. . . . To that other man. . . . So that she might be free of me.

MOTHER. And so that he might be free as well!

FATHER. Yes, I admit it. And a great deal of harm came as a result of it. . . . But I meant well. . . . And I did it more for her sake than for my own. I swear it! [*He folds his arms. Then immediately turning to the* MOTHER.] Did I ever lose sight of you? Tell me, did I ever lose sight of you until that fellow took you away suddenly to some other town . . . all unknown to me. . . . Just because he'd got some queer notion into his head about the interest I was showing in you. . . . An interest which was pure, I assure you, sir. . . . Without the slightest suspicion of any ulterior motive about it! I watched the new little family that grew up around her with incredible tenderness. She can testify to that [*he points to the* STEPDAUGHTER].

STEPDAUGHTER. Oh, I most certainly can! I was such a sweet little girl. . . . Such a sweet little girl, you see. . . . With plaits down to my shoulders . . . and my knickers a little bit longer than my frock. I used to see him standing there by the door of the school as I came out. He came to see how I was growing up. . . .

FATHER. Oh, this is vile! Treacherous! Infamous!

STEPDAUGHTER. Oh, no! What makes you say it's infamous?

FATHER. It's infamous! Infamous! [*Then turning excitedly to the* PRODUCER *he goes on in an explanatory tone.*] After she'd gone away [*pointing to the* MOTHER], my house suddenly seemed empty. She had been a burden on my spirit, but she had filled my house with her presence! Left alone I wandered through the rooms like some lost soul. This boy here [*pointing to the* SON], having been brought up away from home . . . I don't know . . . But . . . But when he returned home he no longer seemed to be my son. With no mother to link him to me, he grew up entirely on his own. . . . A creature apart . . . absorbed in himself . . . with no tie of intellect or affection to bind him to me. And then. . . . And, strange as it may seem, it's the simple truth . . . I became curious about her little family. . . . Gradually I was attracted to this family which had come into being as a result of what I had done. And the thought of it began to fill the emptiness that I felt all around me. I felt a real need . . . a very real need . . . to believe that she was happy, at peace, absorbed in the simple everyday duties of life. I wanted to look on her as being fortunate because she was far removed from the complicated torments of my spirit. And so, to have some proof of this, I used to go and watch that little girl come out of school.

STEPDAUGHTER. I should just say he did! He used to follow me along the street. He would smile at me and when I reached home he'd wave to me . . . like this. I would look at him rather provocatively, opening my eyes wide. I didn't know who he might be. I told my mother about him and she knew at once who it must be. [*The* MOTHER *nods agreement.*] At first she didn't want to let me go to school again. . . . And she kept me away

for several days. And when I did go back, I saw him waiting for me at the door again . . . looking so ridiculous . . . with a brown paper bag in his hand. He came up to me and patted me. . . . And then he took a lovely large straw hat out of the bag . . . with lots of lovely little roses on it. . . . And all for me.

PRODUCER. This is a bit off the point, you know.

SON [*contemptuously*]. Yes. . . . Literature! Literature!

FATHER. Literature indeed! This is life! Passion!

PRODUCER. It may be. But you certainly can't act this sort of stuff!

FATHER. I agree with you. Because all this is only leading up to the main action. I'm not suggesting that this part should be acted. And as a matter of fact, as you can quite well see, she [*pointing to the* STEPDAUGHTER] is no longer that little girl with plaits down to her shoulders. . . .

STEPDAUGHTER. . . . and her knickers a little bit longer than her frock!

FATHER. It is now that the drama comes! Something new, something complex. . . .

STEPDAUGHTER [*coming forward, her voice gloomy, fierce*]. As soon as my father died. . . .

FATHER [*at once, not giving her a chance to continue*]. . . . they fell into the most wretched poverty! They came back here. . . . And because of her stupidity [*pointing to the* MOTHER] I didn't know a thing about it. It's true enough that she can hardly write her own name. . . . But she might have got her daughter or that boy to write and tell me that they were in need!

MOTHER. Now tell me, sir, how was I to know that this was how he'd feel?

FATHER. That's exactly where you went wrong, in never having got to know how I felt about anything.

MOTHER. After so many years away from him. . . . And after all that had happened. . . .

FATHER. And is it my fault that that fellow took you away from here as he did? [*Turning to the* PRODUCER.] I tell you, they disappeared overnight. . . . He'd found some sort of a job away from here . . . I couldn't trace them at all. . . . So, of necessity, my interest in them dwindled. And this was how it was for quite a number of years. The drama broke out, unforeseen and violent in its intensity, when they returned. . . . When I was impelled by the demands of my miserable flesh, which is still alive with desire. . . . Oh, the wretchedness, the unutterable wretchedness of the man who's alone and who detests the vileness of casual affairs! When he's not old enough to do without a woman, and not really young enough to be able to go and look for one without feeling a sense of shame. Wretchedness, did I say? It's horrible! It's horrible! Because no woman is any longer capable of giving him love. And when he realizes this, he ought to do without. . . . Yes, yes, I know! . . . Each one of us, when he appears before his fellow men, is clothed with a certain dignity. But deep down inside himself he knows what unconfessable things go on in the secrecy of his own heart. We give way . . . we give way to temptation. . . . Only to rise up again immediately, filled with a great eagerness to re-establish our dignity in all its solid entirety. . . . Just as if it were a tombstone on some grave in which we had buried, in which we had hidden from our eyes, every sign, and the

very memory itself of our shame. And everyone is just like that! Only there are some of us who lack the courage to talk about certain things.

STEPDAUGHTER. They've got the courage to do them, though. . . . All of them!

FATHER. Yes, all of them! But only in secret! And that's why it needs so much more courage to talk about them! A man's only got to mention these things, and the words have hardly left his lips before he's been labelled a cynic. And all the time it's not true. He's just like everybody else. . . . In fact he's better than they are, because he's not afraid to reveal with the light of his intelligence that red blush of shame which is inherent in human bestiality. . . . That shame to which bestial man closes his eyes, in order not to see it. And woman. . . . Yes, woman. . . . What kind of a being is she? She looks at you, tantalizingly, invitingly. You take her in your arms! And no sooner is she clasped firmly in your arms than she shuts her eyes. It is the sign of her mission, the sign by which she says to man, "Blind yourself, for I am blind."

STEPDAUGHTER. And what about when she no longer shuts her eyes? When she no longer feels the need to hide her blushing shame from herself by closing her eyes? When she sees instead . . . dry-eyed and dispassionate . . . the blushing shame of man, who has blinded himself without love? Oh, what disgust, what unutterable disgust, does she feel then for all these intellectual complications, for all this philosophy which reveals the beast in man and then tries to save him, tries to excuse him . . . I just can't stand here and listen to him! Because when a man is obliged to "simplify" life bestially like that—when he throws overboard every vestige of "humanity," every chaste desire, every pure feeling. . . . All sense of idealism, of duty, of modesty and of shame. . . . Then nothing is more contemptible, infuriating and revoltingly nauseating than their maudlin remorse. . . . Those crocodile tears!

PRODUCER. Now let's get back to the point! Let's get to the point! This is just a lot of beating about the bush!

FATHER. Very well. But a fact is like a sack. . . . When it's empty it won't stand up. And in order to make it stand up you must first of all pour into it all the reasons and all the feelings which have caused it to exist. I couldn't possibly be expected to know that when that man died and they returned here in such utter poverty, she [*pointing to the* MOTHER] would go out to work as a dress-maker in order to support the children. . . . Nor that, of all people, she'd gone to work for that . . . for Madame Pace.

STEPDAUGHTER. Who's a high-class dress-maker, if you ladies and gentlemen would really like to know. On the surface she does work for only the best sort of people. But she arranges things so that these fine ladies act as a screen . . . without prejudice to the others . . . who are only so-so.

MOTHER. Believe me, it never entered my head for one moment that that old hag gave me work because she had her eye on my daughter. . . .

STEPDAUGHTER. Poor Mummy! Do you know what that woman used to do when I took her back the work that my mother had done? She would point out to me how the material had been ruined by giving it to my mother to sew. . . . Oh, she'd grumble about this! And she'd grumble

about that! And so, you understand, I had to pay for it. . . . And all the
time this poor creature thought she was sacrificing herself for me and
for those two children, as she sat up all night sewing away at work for
Madame Pace. [*Gestures and exclamations of indignation from the* ACTORS.]

PRODUCER [*immediately*]. And it was there, one day, that you met . . .

STEPDAUGHTER [*pointing to the* FATHER]. . . . him! Yes, him! An old client!
Now there's a scene for you to put on! Absolutely superb!

FATHER. With her . . . the Mother . . . arriving. . . .

STEPDAUGHTER [*immediately, treacherously*]. . . . almost in time!

FATHER [*a cry*]. No! In time! In time! Fortunately I recognized her in time!
And I took them all back home with me! Now you can imagine what the
situation is like for both of us. She, just as you see her. . . . And I, no
longer able to look her in the face.

STEPDAUGHTER. It's utterly ridiculous! How can I possibly be expected,
after all that, to be a modest young miss . . . well-bred and virtuous . . .
in accordance with his confounded aspirations for a "solid moral health-
iness"?

FATHER. My drama lies entirely in this one thing. . . . In my being con-
scious that each one of us believes himself to be a single person. But it's
not true. . . . Each one of us is many persons. . . . Many persons . . .
according to all the possibilities of being that there are within us. . . .
With some people we are one person. . . . With others we are somebody
quite different. . . . And all the time we are under the illusion of always
being one and the same person for everybody. . . . We believe that we
are always this one person in whatever it is we may be doing. But it's not
true! It's not true! And we see this very clearly when by some tragic
chance we are, as it were, caught up whilst in the middle of doing some-
thing and find ourselves suspended in mid-air. And then we perceive
that all of us was not in what we were doing, and that it would, there-
fore, be an atrocious injustice to us to judge us by that action alone. . . .
To keep us suspended like that. . . . To keep us in a pillory . . .
throughout all existence . . . as if our whole life were completely sum-
med up in that one deed. Now do you understand the treachery of this
girl? She surprised me somewhere where I shouldn't have been . . . and
doing something that I shouldn't have been doing with her. . . . She
surprised an aspect of me that should never have existed for her. And
now she is trying to attach to me a reality such as I could never have
expected I should have to assume for her. . . . The reality that lies in
one fleeting, shameful moment of my life. And this, this above all, is
what I feel most strongly about. And as you can see, the drama acquires
a tremendous value from this concept. Then there's the position of the
others. . . . His . . . [*pointing to the* SON].

SON [*shrugging his shoulders scornfully*]. Leave me alone! I've got nothing to
do with all this!

FATHER. What do you mean . . . you've got nothing to do with all this?

SON. I've got nothing to do with it. . . . And I don't want to have anything
to do with it, because, as you quite well know, I wasn't meant to be
mixed up in all this with the rest of you!

STEPDAUGHTER. Common, that's what we are! And he's a fine gentleman!
But, as you may have noticed, every now and again I fix him with a

contemptuous look, and he lowers his eyes. . . . Because he knows the harm he's done me!

SON [*scarcely looking at her*]. I?

STEPDAUGHTER. Yes, you! You! It's all your fault that I became a prostitute! [*A movement of horror from the* ACTORS.] Did you or did you not deny us, by the attitude you adopted—I won't say the intimacy of your home— but even that mere hospitality which makes guests feel at their ease? We were invaders who had come to disturb the kingdom of your legitimacy. I should just like you [*this to the* PRODUCER] to be present at certain little scenes that took place between him and me. He says that I tyrannized over everybody. . . . But it was just because of the way that he behaved that I took advantage of the thing that he calls "vile". . . . Why I exploited the reason for my coming into his house with my mother. . . . Who is his mother as well! And I went into that house as mistress of it!

SON [*slowly coming forward*]. It's all very easy for them. . . . It's fine sport. . . . All of them ganging-up against me. But just imagine the position of a son whose fate it is one fine day, while he's sitting quietly at home, to see arriving an impudent and brazen young woman who asks for his father—and heaven knows what her business is with him! Later he sees her come back, as brazen as ever, bringing that little girl with her. And finally he sees her treating his father—without knowing in the least why—in a very equivocal and very much to-the-point manner . . . asking him for money, in a tone of voice which leads you to suppose that he must give it to her. . . . Must give it to her, because he has every obligation to do so. . . .

FATHER. As indeed I have! It's an obligation I owe your mother!

SON. How should I know that? When had I ever seen or even heard of her? Then one day I see her arrive with *her* [*pointing to the* STEPDAUGHTER] together with that boy and the little girl. And they say to me, "This is *your* mother, too, you know." Little by little I begin to understand. . . . Largely as a result of the way she goes on [*pointing to the* STEPDAUGHTER *again*]. . . . Why it is that they've come to live with us. . . . So suddenly. . . . So unexpectedly. . . . What I feel, what I experience, I neither wish, nor am able, to express. I wouldn't even wish to confess it to myself. No action, therefore, can be hoped for from me in this affair. Believe me, I am a dramatically unrealized character . . . and I do not feel the least bit at ease in their company. So please leave me out of it!

FATHER. What! But it's just because you're like that. . . .

SON [*in violent exasperation*]. And what do you know about it? How do you know what I'm like? When have you ever bothered yourself about me?

FATHER. I admit it! I admit it! But isn't that a dramatic situation in itself? This aloofness of yours, which is so cruel to me and to your mother. . . . Your mother who returns home and sees you almost for the first time. . . . You're so grown up that she doesn't recognize you, but she knows that you're her son. [*Pointing to the* MOTHER *and addressing the* PRODUCER.] There, look! She's crying!

STEPDAUGHTER [*angrily, stamping her foot*]. Like the fool she is!

FATHER [*pointing to the* STEPDAUGHTER]. She can't stand him! [*Then returning to the subject of the* SON.] He says he's got nothing to do with all this, when, as a matter of fact, almost the whole action hinges on him. Look

at that little boy. . . . See how he clings to his mother all the time, fright-
ened and humiliated. . . . And it's *his* fault that he's like that! Perhaps
his position is the most painful of all. . . . More than any of them he
feels himself to be an outsider. And so the poor little chap feels morti-
fied, humiliated at being taken into my home . . . out of charity, as it
were. [*Confidentially.*] He's just like his father. Humble. . . . Doesn't say
a word. . . .

PRODUCER. I don't think it's a good idea to have him in. You've no idea
what a nuisance boys are on the stage.

FATHER. Oh, . . . but he won't be a nuisance for long. . . . He disappears
almost immediately. And the little girl, too. . . . In fact, she's the first
to go.

PRODUCER. This is excellent! I assure you I find this all very interest-
ing. . . . Very interesting indeed! I can see we've got the makings of a
pretty good play here.

STEPDAUGHTER [*trying to butt in*]. When you've got a character like me!

FATHER [*pushing her to one side in his anxiety to hear what decision the* PRODUCER
has come to]. You be quiet!

PRODUCER [*continuing, heedless of the interruption*]. And it's certainly some-
thing new. . . . Ye-es! . . .

FATHER. Absolutely brand new!

PRODUCER. You had a nerve, though, I must say. . . . Coming here and
chucking the idea at me like that. . . .

FATHER. Well, you understand, born as we are for the stage. . . .

PRODUCER. Are you amateur actors?

FATHER. No . . . I say that we're born for the stage because . . .

PRODUCER. Oh, don't try and come that one with me! You're an old hand at
this game.

FATHER. No. I only act as much as anyone acts the part that he sets himself
to perform, or the part that he is given in life. And in me it is passion
itself, as you can see, that always becomes a little theatrical of its own
accord . . . as it does in everyone . . . once it becomes exalted.

PRODUCER. Oh well, that as may be! That as may be! . . . But you do under-
stand, without an author . . . I could give you the address of somebody
who'd . . .

FATHER. No! . . . Look here. . . . You be the author!

PRODUCER. Me? What the devil are you talking about?

FATHER. Yes, you! You! Why not?

PRODUCER. Because I've never written anything in my life! That's why not!

FATHER. Then why not try your hand at it now? There's nothing to it.
Everybody's doing it! And your job's made all the easier for you because
we are here, all of us, alive before you. . . .

PRODUCER. That's not enough!

FATHER. Not enough? When you see us live our drama. . . .

PRODUCER. Yes! Yes! But we'll still need somebody to write the play.

FATHER. No. . . . Someone to take it down possibly, while we act it out,
scene by scene. It'll be quite sufficient if we make a rough sketch of it
first and then have a run through.

PRODUCER [*climbing back on to the stage, tempted by this*]. H'm! . . . You almost

succeed in tempting me. . . . H'm! It would be rather fun! We could certainly have a shot at it.

FATHER. Of course! Oh, you'll see what wonderful scenes 'll emerge! I can tell you what they are here and now.

PRODUCER. You tempt me. . . . You tempt me. . . . Let's have a go at it! . . . Come with me into my office. [*Turning to the* ACTORS.] You can have a few minutes' break. . . . But don't go too far away. I want you all back again in about a quarter of an hour or twenty minutes. [*To the* FATHER.] Well, let's see what we can make of it! We might get something really extraordinary out of it. . . .

FATHER. There's no *might* about it! They'd better come along too, don't you think? [*Pointing to the other* CHARACTERS.]

PRODUCER. Yes, bring 'em along! Bring 'em along! [*Starts going off and then turns back to the* ACTORS.] Now remember, don't be late back! You've got a quarter of an hour!

> [*The* PRODUCER *and the* SIX CHARAC-
> ters *cross the stage and disappear. The*
> ACTORS *remain looking at one another in*
> *astonishment.*]

LEADING MAN. Is he serious? What's he going to do?

JUVENILE LEAD. This is utter madness!

A THIRD ACTOR. Does he expect us to knock up a play in five minutes?

JUVENILE LEAD. Yes . . . like the actors in the old Commedia dell' Arte.[11]

LEADING LADY. Well, if he thinks that I'm going to have anything to do with fun and games of that sort. . . .

INGENUE. And you certainly don't catch me joining in!

A FOURTH ACTOR. I should like to know who those people are. [*He is allud-ing to the* CHARACTERS.]

THIRD ACTOR. Who do you think they're likely to be? They're probably escaped lunatics. . . . Or crooks!

JUVENILE LEAD. And does he really take what they say seriously?

INGENUE. Vanity! That's what it is. . . . The vanity of appearing as an author!

LEADING MAN. It's absolutely unheard of! If the stage has come to this. . . .

A FIFTH ACTOR. I'm rather enjoying it!

THIRD ACTOR. Oh, well! After all, we shall have the pleasure of seeing what comes of it all!

And talking among themselves in this way the ACTORS *leave the stage. Some go out through the door back, some go in the direction of the dressing-rooms. The curtain remains up.*

The performance is suspended for twenty minutes.

The call-bells ring, warning the audience that the performance is about to be re-sumed.

The ACTORS, *the* STAGE-MANAGER, *the* FOREMAN *of the stage crew, the* PROMPTER *and the* PROPERTY MAN *reassemble on stage. Some come from the dress-*

[11] Form of comic theater in sixteenth- to eighteenth-century Italy. It used improvised dia-logue and masked, stock characters such as Harlequin, Columbine, and Scaramouche.

ing-rooms, some through the door back, some even from the auditorium. The PRO-
ducer *enters from his office accompanied by the* SIX CHARACTERS.

The houselights are extinguished and the stage lighting is as before.

PRODUCER. Now come on, ladies and gentlemen! Are we all here? Let me
have your attention please! Now let's make a start! [*Then calls the*
FOREMAN.]
FOREMAN. Yes, sir?
PRODUCER. Set the stage for the parlor scene. A couple of flats and a door
will do. As quickly as you can!

> [*The* FOREMAN *runs off at once to carry
> out this order and is setting the stage as
> directed whilst the* PRODUCER *is making
> his arrangements with the* STAGE-MAN-
> ager, *the* PROPERTY MAN, *the* PROMP-
> ter *and the* ACTORS. *The flats he has set
> up are painted in pink and gold stripes.*]

PRODUCER [*to* PROPERTY MAN]. Just have a look, please, and see if we've got
some sort of sofa or divan in the props room.
PROPERTY MAN. There's the green one, sir.
STEPDAUGHTER. No, no, green won't do! It was yellow . . . yellow flowered
plush. . . . A huge thing . . . and most comfortable.
PROPERTY MAN. Well, we haven't got anything like that.
PRODUCER. It doesn't matter! Give me what there is!
STEPDAUGHTER. What do you mean, it doesn't matter? Madame Pace's
famous sofa!
PRODUCER. We only want it for this run-through. Please don't interfere. [*To
the* STAGE-MANAGER.] Oh, and see if we've got a shop-window . . . some-
thing rather long and narrowish is what we want.
STEPDAUGHTER. And a little table . . . the little mahogany table for the pale
blue envelope!
STAGE-MANAGER [*to* PRODUCER]. There's that little one. . . . You know, the
gold-painted one.
PRODUCER. That'll do fine! Shove it on!
FATHER. You need a long mirror.
STEPDAUGHTER. And the screen! I must have a screen, please. . . . Else
how can I manage?
STAGE-MANAGER. Don't you worry, Miss! We've got masses of them!
PRODUCER [*to the* STEPDAUGHTER]. And some clothes-hangers and so on,
h'm?
STEPDAUGHTER. Oh, yes, lots!
PRODUCER [*to the* STAGE-MANAGER]. See how many we've got and get some-
body to bring them up.
STAGE-MANAGER. Right you are, sir, I'll see to it!

> [*The* STAGE-MANAGER *goes off about his
> business and while the* PRODUCER *is talk-
> ing to the* PROMPTER *and later to the*
> CHARACTERS *and* ACTORS, *he gets the*

> *stage hands to bring up the furniture and properties and proceeds to arrange them in what he thinks is the best sort of order.*]

PRODUCER [*to the* PROMPTER]. Now if you'll get into position while they're setting the stage. . . . Look, here's an outline of the thing. . . . Act I . . . Act II . . . [*he holds out some sheets of paper to him*]. But you'll really have to excel yourself this time.

PROMPTER. You mean, take it down in shorthand?

PRODUCER [*pleasantly surprised*]. Oh, good man! Can you do shorthand?

PROMPTER. I mayn't know much about prompting, but shorthand. . . .

PRODUCER. Better and better. [*Turning to a* STAGE-HAND.] Go and get some paper out of my room. . . . A large stack. . . . As much as you can find!

> [*The* STAGE-HAND *hurries off and returns shortly with a thick stack of paper which he gives to the* PROMPTER.]

PRODUCER [*to the* PROMPTER]. Follow the scenes closely as we play them and try and fix the lines . . . or at least the most important ones. [*Then, turning to the* ACTORS.] Right, ladies and gentlemen, clear the stage, please! No, come over this side [*he waves them over to his left*] . . . and pay careful attention to what goes on.

LEADING LADY. Excuse me, but we . . .

PRODUCER [*forestalling what she is going to say*]. There won't be any improvising to do, don't you worry!

LEADING MAN. What *do* we have to do, then?

PRODUCER. Nothing. For the moment all you've got to do is to stay over there and watch what happens. You'll get your parts later. Just now we're going to have a rehearsal . . . or as much of one as we can in the circumstances! And *they'll* be doing the rehearsing [*he points to the* CHARACTERS].

FATHER [*in consternation, as if he had tumbled from the clouds into the midst of all the confusion on stage*]. We are? But, excuse me, in what way will it be a rehearsal?

PRODUCER. Well . . . a rehearsal . . . a rehearsal for *their* benefit. [*He points to the* ACTORS.]

FATHER. But if we're the characters . . .

PRODUCER. Just so, "the characters." But it's not characters that act here. It's actors who do the acting here. The characters remain there, in the script [*he points to the prompt box*]. . . . When there is a script!

FATHER. Precisely! And since there is no script and you have the good fortune to have the characters here alive before your very eyes. . . .

PRODUCER. Oh, this is wonderful! Do you want to do everything on your own? Act . . . present yourselves to the public?

FATHER. Yes, just as we are.

PRODUCER. And let me tell you you'd make a wonderful sight!

LEADING MAN. And what use should we be then?

PRODUCER. You're not going to pretend that you can act, are you? Why, it's enough to make a cat laugh. . . . [*And as a matter of fact, the* ACTORS *burst out laughing.*] There you are, you see, they're laughing at the idea! [*Then, remembering.*] But, to the point! I must tell you what your parts

are. That's not so very difficult. They pretty well cast themselves. [*To the* SECOND ACTRESS.] You, the Mother. [*To the* FATHER.] We'll have to find a name for her.

FATHER. Amalia.

PRODUCER. But that's your wife's name. We can hardly call her by her real name.

FATHER. And why not, when that's her name? But, perhaps, if it has to be that lady . . . [*a slight gesture to indicate the* SECOND ACTRESS] I see *her* [*pointing to the* MOTHER] as Amalia. But do as you like. . . . [*His confusion grows.*] I don't know what to say to you. . . . I'm already beginning. . . . I don't know how to express it . . . to hear my own words ringing false . . . as if they had another sound from the one I had meant to give them. . . .

PRODUCER. Now don't you worry about that! Don't you worry about it at all! We'll think about how to get the right tone of voice. And as for the name. . . . If you want it to be Amalia, Amalia it shall be. Or we'll find some other name. Just for the present we'll refer to the characters in this way. [*To the* JUVENILE LEAD.] You, the Son. . . [*To the* LEADING LADY.] And you'll play the Stepdaughter, of course. . . .

STEPDAUGHTER [*excitedly*]. What! What did you say? That woman there. . . . Me! [*She bursts out laughing.*]

PRODUCER [*angrily*]. And what's making you laugh?

LEADING LADY [*indignantly*]. Nobody has ever dared to laugh at me before! Either you treat me with respect or I'm walking out!

STEPDAUGHTER. Oh, no, forgive me! I wasn't laughing at you.

PRODUCER [*to* STEPDAUGHTER]. You should feel yourself honored to be played by . . .

LEADING LADY [*immediately, disdainfully*]. . . . "that woman there."

STEPDAUGHTER. But my remark wasn't meant as a criticism of you . . . I was thinking about myself. . . . Because I can't see myself in you at all. I don't know how to . . . you're not a bit like me!

FATHER. Yes, that's the point I wanted to make! Look . . . all that we express. . . .

PRODUCER. What do you mean . . . *all that you express*? Do you think that this whatever-it-is that you express is something you've got inside you? Not a bit of it.

FATHER. Why . . . aren't even the things we express our own?

PRODUCER. Of course they aren't! The things that you express become material here for the actors, who give it body and form, voice and gesture. And, let me tell you, my actors have given expression to much loftier material than this. This stuff of yours is so trivial that, believe me, if it comes off on the stage, the credit will all be due to my actors.

FATHER. I don't dare to contradict you! But please believe me when I tell you that we . . . who have these bodies . . . these features. . . . Who are as you see us now. . . . We are suffering horribly. . . .

PRODUCER [*cutting in impatiently*]. . . . But the make-up will remedy all that. . . . At least as far as your faces are concerned!

FATHER. Perhaps. . . . But what about our voices? . . . What about our gestures? . . .

PRODUCER. Now, look here! You, as yourself, just cannot exist here! Here
there's an actor who'll play you. And let that be an end to all this argu-
ment!

FATHER. I understand. . . . And now I think I see why our author didn't
wish to put us on the stage after all. . . . He saw us as we are. . . .
Alive. . . . He saw us as living beings. . . . I don't want to offend your
actors. . . . Heaven forbid that I should! . . . But I think that seeing
myself acted now . . . by I don't know whom . . .

LEADING MAN [*rising with some dignity and coming over, followed by a laughing
group of young actresses*]. By me, if you have no objection.

FATHER [*humbly, mellifluously*]. I am deeply honored, sir. [*He bows.*] But. . . .
Well. . . . I think that however much of his art this gentleman puts into
absorbing me into himself. . . . However much he wills it. . . . [*He be-
comes confused.*]

LEADING MAN. Go on! Go on! [*The* ACTRESSES *laugh.*]

FATHER. Well, I should say that the performance he'll give. . . . Even if he
makes himself up to look as much like me as he can. . . .I should say that
with his figure . . . [*All the* ACTORS *laugh*] . . . it will be difficult for it to
be a performance of me . . . of me as I really am. It will rather be . . .
leaving aside the question of his appearance. . . . It will be how he in-
terprets what I am . . . how he sees me. . . . If he sees me as anything at
all. . . . And not as I, deep down within myself, feel myself to be.
And it certainly seems to me that whoever is called upon to criticize us
will have to take this into account.

PRODUCER. So you're already thinking about what the critics will say, are
you? And here am I, still trying to get the play straight! The critics can
say what they like. We'd be much better occupied in thinking about
getting the play on. . . . If we can. [*Stepping out of the group and looking
around him.*] Now, come on, let's make a start! Is everything ready? [*To
the* ACTORS *and* CHARACTERS.] Come on, don't clutter up the place! Let
me see how it looks! [*He comes down from the stage.*] And now, don't let's
lose any more time! [*To the* STEPDAUGHTER.] Do you think the set looks
all right?

STEPDAUGHTER. To be perfectly honest, I just don't recognize it at all!

PRODUCER. Good Lord, you surely didn't hope that we were going to re-
construct that room behind Madame Pace's shop here on the stage, did
you? [*To the* FATHER.] You did tell me it had flowered wallpaper, didn't
you?

FATHER. Yes, white.

PRODUCER. Well, it's not white—and it's got stripes on it—but it'll have to
do! As for the furniture, I think we've more or less got everything we
need. Bring that little table down here a bit! [*The* STAGE HANDS *do so.
Then he says to the* PROPERTY MAN.] Now, will you go and get an enve-
lope. . . . A pale blue one if you can. . . . And give it to that gentle-
man. [*He points to the* FATHER.]

PROPERTY MAN. The kind you put letters in?

PRODUCER and FATHER. Yes, the kind you put letters in!

PROPERTY MAN. Yes, sir! At once, sir! [*Exit.*]

PRODUCER. Now, come on! First scene—the young lady. [*The* LEADING
LADY *comes forward.*] No! No! Wait a moment! I said the young lady!

[*Pointing to the* STEPDAUGHTER.] You stay there and watch. . . .

STEPDAUGHTER [*immediately adding*]. . . . how I make it live!

LEADING LADY [*resentfully*]. I'll know how to make it live, don't you worry, once I get started!

PRODUCER [*with his hands to his head*]. Ladies and gentlemen, don't let's have any arguing! Please! Right! Now . . . The first scene is between the young lady and Madame Pace. Oh! [*He looks around rather helplessly and then comes back on stage.*] What about this Madame Pace?

FATHER. She's not with us, sir.

PRODUCER. And what do we do about her?

FATHER. But she's alive! She's alive too!

PRODUCER. Yes, yes! But where is she?

FATHER. If you'll just allow me to have a word with your people. . . . [*Turning to the* ACTRESSES.] I wonder if you ladies would do me the kindness of lending me your hats for a moment.

THE ACTRESSES [*a chorus . . . half-laughing, half-surprised*]. What? Our hats?
What did he say?
Why?
Listen to the man!

PRODUCER. What are you going to do with the women's hats?
 [*The* ACTORS *laugh.*]

FATHER. Oh, nothing . . . I just want to put them on these pegs for a moment. And perhaps one of you ladies would be so kind as to take off your coat, too.

THE ACTORS [*laughter and surprise in their voices*]. Their coats as well? And after that?
The man must be mad!

ONE OR TWO OF THE ACTRESSES [*surprise and laughter in their voices*]. But why?
Only our coats?

FATHER. So that I can hang them here. . . . Just for a moment or so. . . . Please do me this favor. Will you?

THE ACTRESSES [*they take off their hats. One or two take off their coats as well, all laughing the while. They go over and hang the coats here and there on the pegs and hangers*].
And why not?
Here you are!
This really is funny!
Do we have to put them on show?

FATHER. Precisely. . . . You have to put them on show. . . . Like this!

PRODUCER. Is one allowed to know what you're up to?

FATHER. Why, yes. If we set the stage better, who knows whether she may not be attracted by the objects of her trade and perhaps appear among us. . . . [*He invites them to look towards the door at the back of the stage.*] Look! Look!

> [*The door opens and* MADAME PACE *comes in and takes a few steps forward. She is an enormously fat old harridan of a woman, wearing a pompous carrot-col-*

ored tow wig with a red rose stuck into one side of it, in the Spanish manner. She is heavily made up and dressed with clumsy elegance in a stylish red silk dress. In one hand she carries an ostrich feather fan; the other hand is raised and a lighted cigarette is poised between two fingers. Immediately they see this apparition, the Ac-tors and the Producer bound off the stage with howls of fear, hurling them-selves down the steps into the auditorium and making as if to dash up the aisle. The Stepdaughter, however, rushes humbly up to Madame Pace, as if greeting her mistress.]

Stepdaughter [*rushing up to her*]. Here she is! Here she is!

Father [*beaming*]. It's Madame Pace! What did I tell you? Here she is!

Producer [*his first surprise overcome, he is now indignant*]. What sort of a game do you call this?

Leading Man. ⎤
Juvenile Lead. ⎥ *Almost at the* Hang it all, what's going on?
Ingenue. ⎥ *same moment* Where did *she* spring from?
Leading Lady. ⎦ *and all* They were keeping her in
 speaking at reserve!
 once. So it's back to the music hall and conjuring tricks, is it?

Father [*dominating the protesting voices*]. One moment, please! Why should you wish to destroy this prodigy of reality, which was born, which was evoked, attracted and formed by this scene itself? . . . A reality which has more right to live here than you have. . . . Because it is so very much more alive than you are. . . . Why do you want to spoil it all, just because of some niggling, vulgar convention of truth? . . . Which of you actresses will be playing the part of Madame Pace? Well, *that* woman is Madame Pace! Grant me at least that the actress who plays her will be less true than she is. . . . For *she* is Madame Pace in person! Look! My daughter recognized her and went up to her at once. Now, watch this scene! Just watch it! [*Hesitantly the Producer and the Actors climb back on to the stage. But while the Actors have been protesting and the Father has been replying to them, the scene between the Stepdaughter and Madame Pace has begun. It is carried on in an undertone, very quietly—naturally in fact—in a manner that would be quite impossible on the stage. When the Actors obey the Father's demand that they shall watch what is happening, they see that Madame Pace has already put her hand under the Stepdaughter's chin to raise her head and is talking to her. Hearing her speak in a completely unintelligible manner they are held for a moment. But almost immediately their attention flags.*]

Producer. Well?

Leading Man. But what's she saying?

Leading Lady. We can't hear a thing!

Juvenile Lead. Speak up! Louder!

Stepdaughter [*she leaves Madame Pace and comes down to the group of Ac-*

tors. MADAME PACE *smiles—a priceless smile*]. Did you say, "Louder?" What do you mean, "Louder?" What we're talking about is scarcely the sort of thing to be shouted from the roof-tops. I was able to yell it out just now so that I could shame *him* [*pointing to the* FATHER]. . . . So that I could have my revenge! But it's quite another matter for Madame Pace. . . . It would mean prison for her.

PRODUCER. Indeed? So that's how it is, is it? But let me tell you something, my dear young lady. . . . Here in the theater you've got to make yourself heard! The way you're doing this bit at the moment even those of us who're on stage can't hear you! Just imagine what it'll be like with an audience out front. This scene's got to be got over. And anyway there's nothing to prevent you from speaking up when you're on together. . . . We shan't be here to listen to you. . . . We're only here now because it's a rehearsal. Pretend you're alone in the room behind the shop, where nobody can hear you.

> [*The* STEPDAUGHTER *elegantly, charmingly—and with a mischievous smile— wags her finger two or three times in disagreement.*]

PRODUCER. What do you mean, "No?"

STEPDAUGHTER [*in a mysterious whisper*]. There's someone who'll hear us if *she* [*pointing to* MADAME PACE] speaks up.

PRODUCER [*in utter consternation*]. Do you mean to say that there's somebody else who's going to burst in on us? [*The* ACTORS *make as if to dive off the stage again.*]

FATHER. No! No! They're alluding to me. I have to be there, waiting behind the door. . . . And Madame Pace knows it. So, if you'll excuse me, I'll go. . . . So that I'm all ready to make my entrance. [*He starts off towards the back of the stage.*]

PRODUCER [*stopping him*]. No! No! Wait a moment! When you're here you have to respect the conventions of the theater! Before you get ready to go on to that bit. . . .

STEPDAUGHTER. No! Let's get on with it at once! At once! I'm dying with desire, I tell you . . . to live this scene. . . . To live it! If he wants to get on with it right away, I'm more than ready!

PRODUCER [*shouting*]. But first of all, the scene between you and her [*pointing to* MADAME PACE] has got to be got over! Do you understand?

STEPDAUGHTER. Oh, my God! She's just been telling me what *you* already know. . . . That once again my mother's work has been badly done. . . . That the dress is spoiled. . . . And that I must be patient if she is to go on helping us in our misfortune.

MADAME PACE [*stepping forward, a grand air of importance about her*]. But, yes, señor, porque I not want to make profit . . . to take advantàge. . . .

PRODUCER [*more than a touch of terror in his voice*]. What? Does she speak like that?

> [*The* ACTORS *burst into noisy laughter.*]

STEPDAUGHTER [*laughing too*]. Yes, she speaks like that, half in English, half in Spanish. . . . It's most comical.

MADAME PACE. Ah, no, it does not to me seem good manners that you

laugh of me when I . . . force myself to . . . *hablar,* as I can, English, *señor*

PRODUCER. Indeed, no! It's very wrong of us! You speak like that! Yes, speak like that, Madame! It'll bring the house down! We couldn't ask for anything better. It'll bring a little comic relief into the crudity of the situation. Yes, you talk like that! It's absolutely wonderful!

STEPDAUGHTER. Wonderful! And why not? When you hear a certain sort of suggestion made to you in a lingo like that. . . . There's not much doubt about what your answer's going to be. . . . Because it almost seems like a joke. You feel inclined to laugh when you hear there's an "old *señor*" who wants to "amuse himself with me." An "old *señor,*" eh, Madame?

MADAME PACE. Not so very old. . . . Not quite so young, yes? And if he does not please to you. . . . Well, he has . . . *prudencia.*

MOTHER [*absorbed as they are in the scene the* ACTORS *have been paying no attention to her. Now, to their amazement and consternation, she leaps up and attacks* MADAME PACE. *At her cry they jump, then hasten smilingly to restrain her, for she, meanwhile, has snatched off* MADAME PACE'S *wig and has thrown it to the ground*]. You old devil! You old witch! You murderess! Oh, my daughter!

STEPDAUGHTER [*rushing over to restrain her* MOTHER]. No, Mummy, no! Please!

FATHER [*rushing over at the same time*]. Calm yourself, my dear! Just be calm! Now . . . come and sit down again!

MOTHER. Take that woman out of my sight, then!

> [*In the general excitement the* PRODUCER, *too, has rushed over and the* STEPDAUGHTER *now turns to him.*]

STEPDAUGHTER. It's impossible for my mother to remain here!

FATHER [*to the* PRODUCER]. They can't be here together. That's why, when we first came, that woman wasn't with us. If they're on at the same time the whole thing is inevitably given away in advance.

PRODUCER. It doesn't matter! It doesn't matter a bit! This is only a first run-through. . . . Just to give us a rough idea how it goes. Everything'll come in useful . . . I can sort out the bits and pieces later. . . . I'll make something out of it, even if it is all jumbled up. [*Turning to the* MOTHER *and leading her back to her chair.*] Now, please be calm, and sit down here, nice and quietly.

> [*Meanwhile the* STEPDAUGHTER *has gone down center stage again. She turns to* MADAME PACE.]

STEPDAUGHTER. Go on, Madame, go on!

MADAME PACE [*offended*]. Ah, no thank you! Here I do not do nothing more with your mother present!

STEPDAUGHTER. Now, come on! Show in the "old *señor*" who wants to "amuse himself with me." [*Turning imperiously on the rest.*] Yes, this scene has got to be played. So let's get on with it! [*To* MADAME PACE.] You can go!

MADAME PACE. Ah, I am going . . . I am going. . . . Most assuredly I

am going! [*Exit furiously, ramming her wig back on and glowering at the* ACTORS, *who mockingly applaud her.*]

STEPDAUGHTER [*to the* FATHER]. And now you make your entrance! There's no need for you to go out and come in again! Come over here! Pretend that you've already entered! Now, I'm standing here modestly, my eyes on the ground. Come on! Speak up! Say, "Good afternoon, Miss," in that special tone of voice . . . you know. . . . Like somebody who's just come in from the street.

PRODUCER [*by this time he is down off the stage*]. Listen to her! Are you running this rehearsal, or am I? [*To the* FATHER, *who is looking perplexed and undecided.*] Go on, do as she tells you! Go to the back of the stage. . . . Don't exit! . . . And then come forward again.

> [*The* FATHER *does as he is told. He is troubled and very pale. But as he approaches from the back of the stage he smiles, already absorbed in the reality of his created life. He smiles as if the drama which is about to break upon him is as yet unknown to him. The* AC- TORS *become intent on the scene which is beginning.*]

PRODUCER [*whispering quickly to the* PROMPTER, *who has taken up his position*]. Get ready to write now!

THE SCENE

FATHER [*coming forward, a new note in his voice*]. Good afternoon, Miss.

STEPDAUGHTER [*her head bowed, speaking with restrained disgust*]. Good afternoon!

FATHER [*studying her a little, looking up into her face from under the brim of her hat (which almost hides it), and perceiving that she is very young, exclaims, almost to himself, a little out of complacency, a little, too, from the fear of compromising himself in a risky adventure*]. H'm! But. . . . M'm. . . . This won't be the first time, will it? The first time that you've been here?

STEPDAUGHTER [*as before*]. No, sir.

FATHER. You've been here before? [*And since the* STEPDAUGHTER *nods in affirmation*] More than once? [*He waits a little while for her reply, resumes his study of her, again looking up into her face from under the brim of her hat, smiles and then says.*] Then . . . well . . . it shouldn't any longer be so. . . . May I take off your hat?

STEPDAUGHTER [*immediately forestalling him, unable to restrain her disgust*]. No, sir, I'll take it off myself! [*Convulsed, she hurriedly takes it off.*]

> [*The* MOTHER *is on tenterhooks throughout. The* TWO CHILDREN *cling to their* MOTHER *and they, she and the* SON *form a group on the side opposite the* ACTORS, *watching the scene. The* MOTHER *follows the words and the actions of the* STEPDAUGHTER *and the*

FATHER *with varying expressions of sorrow, of indignation, of anxiety and of horror; from time to time she hides her face in her hands and sobs.*]

MOTHER. Oh, my God! My God!

FATHER [*he remains for a moment as if turned to stone by this sob. Then he resumes in the same tone of voice as before*]. Here, let me take it. I'll hang it up for you. [*He takes the hat from her hands.*] But such a charming, such a dear little head really ought to have a much smarter hat than this! Would you like to come and help me choose one from among these hats of Madame's? Will you?

INGENUE [*breaking in*]. Oh, I say! Those are *our* hats!

PRODUCER [*at once, furiously*]. For God's sake, shut up! Don't try to be funny! We're doing our best to rehearse this scene, in case you weren't aware of the fact! [*Turning to* STEPDAUGHTER.] Go on from where you left off, please.

STEPDAUGHTER [*continuing*]. No thank you, sir.

FATHER. Come now, don't say no. Do say you'll accept it. . . . Just to please me. I shall be most upset if you won't. . . . Look, here are some rather nice ones. And then it would please Madame. She puts them out on show on purpose, you know.

STEPDAUGHTER. No . . . listen! I couldn't wear it.

FATHER. You're thinking perhaps about what they'll say when you come home wearing a new hat? Well now, shall I tell you what to do? Shall I tell you what to say when you get home?

STEPDAUGHTER [*quickly—she is at the end of her tether*]. No, it's not that! I couldn't wear it because I'm . . . As you see. . . . You should have noticed already . . . [*indicating her black dress*].

FATHER. That you're in mourning! Of course. . . . Oh, forgive me! Of course! Oh, I beg your pardon! Believe me. . . . I'm most profoundly sorry. . . .

STEPDAUGHTER [*summoning all her strength and forcing herself to conquer her contempt, her indignation and her nausea*]. Stop! Please don't say any more! I really ought to be thanking you. There's no need for you to feel so very sorry or upset! Please don't give another thought to what I said! I, too, you understand. . . . [*Tries hard to smile and adds.*] I really must forget that I'm dressed like this!

PRODUCER [*interrupting them; he climbs back on to the stage and turns to the* PROMPTER]. Hold it! Stop a minute! Don't write that down. Leave out that last bit. [*Turning to the* FATHER *and the* STEPDAUGHTER.] It's going very well! Very well indeed! [*Then to the* FATHER.] And then you go on as we arranged. [*To the* ACTORS.] Rather delightful, that bit where he offers her the hat, don't you think?

STEPDAUGHTER. Ah, but the best bit's coming now! Why aren't we going on?

PRODUCER. Now be patient, please! Just for a little while! [*Turning to the* ACTORS.] Of course it'll have to be treated rather lightly. . . .

LEADING MAN. . . . M'm . . . and put over slickly. . . .

LEADING LADY. Of course! There's nothing difficult about it at all. [*To the* LEADING MAN.] Shall we try it now?

LEADING MAN. As far as I'm . . . I'll go and get ready for my entrance. [*Exit to take up his position outside the door back.*]

PRODUCER [*to the* LEADING LADY]. Now, look. . . . The scene between you and Madame Pace is finished. I'll get down to writing it up properly afterwards. You're standing. . . . Where are you going?

LEADING LADY. Just a moment! I want to put my hat back on. . . . [*Goes over, takes her hat down and puts it on.*]

PRODUCER. Good! Now you stand here. With your head bowed down a bit.

STEPDAUGHTER [*amused*]. But she's not dressed in black!

LEADING LADY. I *shall* be dressed in black. . . . And much more becomingly than you are!

PRODUCER [*to the* STEPDAUGHTER]. Shut up . . . please! And watch! You'll learn something. [*Claps his hands.*] Now come on! Let's get going! Entrance! [*He goes down from the stage again to see how it looks from out front. The door back opens and the* LEADING MAN *steps forward. He has the lively, raffish, self-possessed air of an elderly gallant. The playing of this scene by the* ACTORS *will appear from the very first words as something completely different from what was played before, without its having, even in the slightest degree, the air of a parody. It should appear rather as if the scene has been touched up. Quite naturally the* FATHER *and the* STEPDAUGHTER, *not being able to recognize themselves at all in the* LEADING LADY *and* LEADING MAN, *yet hearing them deliver the very words they used, react in a variety of ways, now with a gesture, now with a smile, with open protest even, to the impression they receive. They are surprised, lost in wonder, in suffering . . . as we shall see. The* PROMPTER's *voice is clearly heard throughout the scene.*]

LEADING MAN. Good afternoon, Miss!

FATHER [*immediately, unable to restrain himself*]. No! No! [*And the* STEP-daughter, *seeing the* LEADING MAN *enter in this way, bursts out laughing.*]

PRODUCER [*infuriated*]. Shut up! And once and for all . . . Stop that laughing! We shan't get anywhere if we go on like this!

STEPDAUGHTER [*moving away from the proscenium*]. Forgive me . . . but I couldn't help laughing! This lady [*pointing to the* LEADING LADY] stands just where you put her, without budging an inch . . . But if she's meant to be me. . . . I can assure you that if I heard anybody saying "Good afternoon" to me in that way and in that tone of voice I'd burst out laughing. . . . So I had to, you see.

FATHER [*coming forward a little, too*]. Yes, that's it exactly. . . . His manner. . . . The tone of voice. . . .

PRODUCER. To hell with your manner and your tone of voice! Just stand to one side, if you don't mind, and let me get a look at this rehearsal.

LEADING MAN [*coming forward*]. Now if I've got to play an old fellow who's coming into a house of rather doubtful character. . . .

PRODUCER. Oh, don't take any notice of him! Now, *please!* Start again, please! It was going very nicely. [*There is a pause—he is clearly waiting for the* LEADING MAN *to begin again.*] Well?

LEADING MAN. Good afternoon, Miss.

LEADING LADY. Good afternoon!

LEADING MAN [*repeating the* FATHER's *move—that is, looking up into the* LEAD-ING LADY's *face from under the brim of her hat; but then expressing very clearly*

first his satisfaction and then his fear]. M'm . . . this won't be the first time, I hope. . . .

FATHER [*unable to resist the temptation to correct him*]. Not "hope"—"will it?", "will it?"

PRODUCER. You say "will it?" . . . It's a question.

LEADING MAN [*pointing to the* PROMPTER]. I'm sure he said "hope."

PRODUCER. Well, it's all one! "Hope" or whatever it was! Go on, please! Go on. . . . Oh, there was one thing . . . I think perhaps it ought not to be quite so heavy. . . . Hold on, I'll show you what I mean. Watch me. . . . [*Comes back on to the stage. Then, making his entrance, he proceeds to play the part.*] Good afternoon, Miss.

LEADING LADY. Good afternoon. . . .

PRODUCER. M'm. . . . [*Turning to the* LEADING MAN *to impress on him the way he has looked up at the* LEADING LADY *from under the brim of her hat.*] Surprise, fear and satisfaction. [*Then turning back to the* LEADING LADY.] It won't be the first time, will it, that you've been here? [*Turning again to the* LEADING MAN *inquiringly.*] Is that clear? [*To the* LEADING LADY.] And then you say, "No, sir." [*To the* LEADING MAN.] There you are. . . . It wants to be a little more . . . what shall I say? . . . A little more *flexible*. A little more *souple!* [*He goes down from the stage again.*]

LEADING LADY. No, sir. . . .

LEADING MAN. You've been here before? More than once?

PRODUCER. Wait a minute! You must let her [*pointing to the* LEADING LADY] get her nod in first. You've been here before? [*The* LEADING LADY *lifts her head a little, closing her eyes painfully as if in disgust and then when the* PRODUCER *says* Down, *nods twice.*]

STEPDAUGHTER [*unable to restrain herself*]. Oh, my God! [*And immediately she puts her hand over her mouth to stifle her laughter.*]

PRODUCER [*turning*]. What's the matter?

STEPDAUGHTER [*immediately*]. Nothing! Nothing!

PRODUCER [*to the* LEADING MAN]. It's your cue. . . . Carry straight on.

LEADING MAN. More than once? Well then . . . Come along. . . . May I take off your hat?

[*The* LEADING MAN *says this last line in such a tone of voice and accompanies it with such a gesture that the* STEPDAUGHTER, *who has remained with her hands over her mouth, can no longer restrain herself. She tries desperately to prevent herself from laughing but a noisy burst of laughter comes irresistibly through her fingers.*]

LEADING LADY [*turning indignantly*]. I'm not going to stand here and be made a fool of by that woman!

LEADING MAN. And neither am I. Let's pack the whole thing in.

PRODUCER [*shouting at the* STEPDAUGHTER]. Once and for all, will you shut up!

STEPDAUGHTER. Yes. . . . Forgive me, please! . . . Forgive me!

PRODUCER. The trouble with you is that you've got no manners! You go too far!

FATHER [*trying to intervene*]. Yes, sir, you're quite right! Quite right! But you must forgive her. . . .

PRODUCER [*climbing back on to the stage*]. What do you want me to forgive? It's absolutely disgusting the way she's behaving!

FATHER. Yes. . . . But . . . Oh, believe me . . . Believe me, it has such a strange effect. . . .

PRODUCER. Strange! How do you mean, "Strange"? What's so strange about it?

FATHER. You see, sir, I admire . . . I admire your actors. . . . That gentleman there [*pointing to the* LEADING MAN] and that lady [*pointing to the* LEADING LADY] . . . But . . . Well . . . The truth is . . . They're certainly not us!

PRODUCER. I should hope not! How do you expect them to be *you* if they're actors?

FATHER. Just so, actors. And they play our parts well, both of them. But when they act . . . To us they seem to be doing something quite different. They want to be the same . . . And all the time they just aren't.

PRODUCER. But how aren't they the same? What are they then?

FATHER. Something that becomes theirs . . . And no longer ours.

PRODUCER. But that's inevitable! I've told you that already.

FATHER. Yes, I understand . . . I understand that. . . .

PRODUCER. Well then, let's hear no more on the subject! [*Turning to the* ACTORS.] We'll run through it later by ourselves in the usual way. I've always had a strong aversion to holding rehearsals with the author present. He's never satisfied! [*Turning to the* FATHER *and the* STEPDAUGHTER.] Now, come on, let's get on with it! And let's see if we can have no more laughing! [*To the* STEPDAUGHTER.]

STEPDAUGHTER. Oh, I shan't laugh any more! I promise you! My big bit's coming now. . . . Just you wait and see!

PRODUCER. Well, then. . . . When you say, "Please don't give another thought to what I said! I, too, you understand. . . ." [*Turning to the* FATHER.] You come in at once with, "I understand! I understand!" and immediately ask . . .

STEPDAUGHTER [*interrupting him*]. What? What does he ask?

PRODUCER. . . . why you're in mourning.

STEPDAUGHTER. Oh, no! That's not it at all! Listen! When I told him that I mustn't think about my being in mourning, do you know what his answer was? "Well, then, let's take this little frock off at once, shall we?"

PRODUCER. That would be wonderful! Wonderful! That *would* bring the house down!

STEPDAUGHTER. But it's the truth!

PRODUCER. But what's the truth got to do with it? Acting's what *we're* here for! Truth's all very fine . . . But only up to a point.

STEPDAUGHTER. And what do you want then?

PRODUCER. You'll see! You'll see! Leave everything to me.

STEPDAUGHTER. No, I won't! What you'd like to do, no doubt, is to concoct a romantic, sentimental little affair out of my disgust, out of all the reasons, each more cruel, each viler than the other, why I am this sort of woman, why I am what I am! An affair with him! He asks me why I'm in

mourning and I reply with tears in my eyes that my father died only two months ago. No! No! He must say what he said then, "Well, then, let's take this little frock off at once, shall we?" And I . . . my heart still grieving for my father's death. . . . I went behind there . . . Do you understand? . . . There, behind that screen! And then, my fingers trembling with shame and disgust, I took off my frock, undid my brassière. . . .

PRODUCER [*running his hands through his hair*]. For God's sake! What on earth are you saying, girl?

STEPDAUGHTER [*crying out excitedly*]. The truth! The truth!

PRODUCER. Yes, it probably is the truth! I'm not denying it! And I understand . . . I fully appreciate all your horror. But you must realize that we simply can't put this kind of thing on the stage.

STEPDAUGHTER. Oh, you can't, can't you? If that's how things are, thanks very much! I'm going!

PRODUCER. No! No! Look here! . . .

STEPDAUGHTER. I'm going! I'm not stopping here! You worked it all out together, didn't you? . . . The pair of you. . . . You and him. . . . When you were in there. . . . You worked out what was going to be possible on the stage. Oh, thanks very much! I understand! He wants to jump to the bit where he presents his spiritual torments! [*This is said harshly.*] But I want to present my own drama! *Mine! Mine!*

PRODUCER [*his shoulders shaking with annoyance*]. Ah! There we have it! *Your* drama! Look here . . . you'll have to forgive me for telling you this . . . but there isn't only your part to be considered! Each of the others has his drama, too. [*He points to the* FATHER.] He has his and your Mother has hers. You can't have one character coming along like this, becoming too prominent, invading the stage in and out of season and overshadowing all the rest. All the characters must be contained within one harmonious picture, and presenting only what it is proper to present. I'm very well aware that everyone carries a complete life within himself and that he wants to put it before the whole world. But it's here that we run into difficulties: how are we to bring out only just so much as is absolutely necessary? . . . And at the same time, of course, to take into account all the other characters. . . . And yet in that small fragment we have to be able to hint at all the rest of the secret life of that character. Ah, it would be all very pleasant if each character could have a nice little monologue. . . . Or without making any bones about it, give a lecture, in which he could tell his audience what's bubbling and boiling away inside him. [*His tone is good-humored, conciliatory.*] You must restrain yourself. And believe me, it's in your own interest, too. Because all this fury . . . this exasperation and this disgust . . . They make a bad impression. Especially when . . . And pardon me for mentioning this. . . . You yourself have confessed that you'd had other men there at Madame Pace's before him. . . . And more than once!

STEPDAUGHTER [*bowing her head. She pauses a moment in recollection and then, a deeper note in her voice*]. That is true! But you must remember that those other men mean *him* for me, just as much as he himself does!

PRODUCER [*uncomprehending*]. What? The other men mean *him*? What do you mean?

STEPDAUGHTER. Isn't it true that in the case of someone who's gone wrong, the person who was responsible for the first fault is responsible for all the faults which follow? And in my case, he is responsible. . . . Has been ever since before I was born. Look at him, and see if it isn't true!

PRODUCER. Very well, then! And does this terrible weight of remorse that is resting on his spirit seem so slight a thing to you? Give him the chance of acting it!

STEPDAUGHTER. How? How can he act all his "noble" remorse, all his "moral" torments, if you want to spare him all the horror of one day finding in his arms. . . . After he had asked her to take off her frock . . . her grief still undulled by time. . . . The horror of finding in his arms that child. . . . A woman now, and a fallen woman already. . . . That child whom he used to go and watch as she came out of school? [*She says these last words in a voice trembling with emotion. The* MOTHER, *hearing her talk like this, is overcome by distress which expresses itself at first in stifled sobs. Finally she breaks out into a fit of bitter crying. Everyone is deeply moved. There is a long pause.*]

STEPDAUGHTER [*gravely and resolutely, as soon as the* MOTHER *shows signs of becoming a little quieter*]. At the moment we are here, unknown as yet by the public. Tomorrow you will present us as you wish. . . . Making up your play in your own way. But would you really like to see our drama? To see it flash into life as it did in reality?

PRODUCER. Why, of course! I couldn't ask for anything better, so that from now on I can use as much as possible of it.

STEPDAUGHTER. Well, then, ask my Mother to leave us.

MOTHER [*rising, her quiet weeping changed to a sharp cry*]. No! No! Don't you allow them to do it! Don't allow them to do it!

PRODUCER. But it's only so that I can see how it goes.

MOTHER. I can't bear it! I can't bear it!

PRODUCER. But since it's already happened, I don't understand!

MOTHER. No, it's happening now! It happens all the time! My torment is no pretense, sir. I am alive and I am present always. . . . At every moment of my torment. . . . A torment which is for ever renewing itself. Always alive and always present. But those two children there. . . . Have you heard them say a single word? They can no longer speak! They cling to me still. . . . In order to keep my torment living and present! But for themselves they no longer exist! They no longer exist! And she [*pointing to the* STEPDAUGHTER] . . . She has run away. . . . Run away from me and is lost. . . . Lost! . . . And if I see her here before me it is for this reason and for this reason alone. . . . To renew at all times. . . . Forever. . . . To bring before me again, present and living, the anguish that I have suffered on her account too.

FATHER [*solemnly*]. The eternal moment, as I told you, sir. She [*he points to the* STEPDAUGHTER] . . . She is here in order to fix me. . . . To hold me suspended throughout all eternity. . . . In the pillory of that one fleeting shameful moment in my life. She cannot renounce her rôle. . . . And you, sir, cannot really spare me my agony.

PRODUCER. Quite so, but I didn't say that I wouldn't present it. As a matter of fact it'll form the basis of the first act. . . . Up to the point where she surprises you [*pointing to the* MOTHER].

FATHER. That is right. Because it is my sentence. All our passion. . . . All our suffering. . . . Which must culminate in *her* cry [*pointing to the* MOTHER].

STEPDAUGHTER. I can still hear it ringing in my ears! That cry sent me mad! You can play me just as you like. . . . It doesn't matter. Dressed, if you like, provided that I can have my arms bare at least. . . . Just my arms bare. . . . Because, you see, standing there . . . [*She goes up to the* FATHER *and rests her head on his chest.*] With my head resting on his chest like this . . . and with my arms round his neck . . . I could see a vein throbbing away in my arm. And then . . . Just as if that pulsing vein alone gave me a sense of horror . . . I shut my eyes tight and buried my head in his chest. [*Turning towards the* MOTHER.] Scream, Mummy! Scream! [*She buries her head in the* FATHER'S *chest and, raising her shoulders as if in order not to hear the cry, adds in a voice stifled with torment.*] Scream, as you screamed then!

MOTHER [*rushing upon them to separate them*]. No! No! She's my daughter! [*And having torn her daughter away.*] You brute! You brute! She's my daughter! Can't you see that she's my daughter?

PRODUCER [*retreating at the cry right up to the footlights, amid the general dismay of the* ACTORS]. Excellent! Excellent! And then . . . Curtain! Curtain!

FATHER [*rushing over to him convulsively*]. Yes, because that's how it really happened!

PRODUCER [*quite convinced, admiration in his voice*]. Oh, yes, we must have the curtain there. . . . That cry and then . . . Curtain! Curtain!

> [*At the repeated shouts of the* PRODUCER *the* STAGE-HAND *on the curtain lets it down, leaving the* PRODUCER *and the* FAther *between it and the footlights.*]

PRODUCER [*looking up, his arms raised*]. Oh, the damned fool! I say, "Curtain" . . . Meaning that I want the act to end there. . . . And he really does go and bring the curtain down. [*To the* FATHER, *lifting up a corner of the curtain.*] Oh, yes! That's absolutely wonderful! Very good indeed! That'll get them! There's no *if or but* about it. . . . That line and then . . . *Curtain!* We've got something in that first act . . . or I'm a Dutchman! [*Disappears through the curtain with the* FATHER.]

When the curtain goes up again the audience sees that the STAGE-HANDS *have dismantled the previous set and put on in its place a small garden fountain. On one side of the stage the* ACTORS *are sitting in a row, and on the other side, the* CHARACters. *The* PRODUCER *is standing in a meditative attitude in the middle of the stage with his hand clenched over his mouth. There is a brief pause; then:*

PRODUCER [*with a shrug of his shoulders*]. Oh, well! . . . Let's get on with Act II! Now if you'll only leave it all to me, as we agreed, everything'll sort itself out.

STEPDAUGHTER. This is where we make our entry into his house . . . [*Pointing to the* FATHER.] In spite of him! [*Pointing to the* SON.]

PRODUCER [*out of patience*]. Yes, yes! But leave it to me, I tell you!

STEPDAUGHTER. Well. . . . So long as it's made quite clear that it was against his wishes.

MOTHER [*from the corner, shaking her head*]. For all the good that's come of it. . . .

STEPDAUGHTER [*turning to her quickly*]. That doesn't matter! The more harm that it's done us, the more remorse for him!

PRODUCER [*impatiently*]. I understand all that! I'll take it all into account! Don't you worry about it!

MOTHER [*a supplicant note in her voice*]. But I do beg you, sir . . . To set my conscience at rest. . . . To make it quite plain that I tried in every way I could to . . .

STEPDAUGHTER [*interrupting contemptuously and continuing her* MOTHER's *speech*]. . . . to pacify me, to persuade me not to get my own back. . . . [*To the* PRODUCER.] Go on . . . do what she asks you! Give her that satisfaction. . . . Because she's quite right, you know! I'm enjoying myself no end, because . . . Well, just look. . . . The meeker she is, the more she tries to wriggle her way into his heart, the more he holds himself aloof, the more distant he becomes. I can't think why she bothers!

PRODUCER. Are we going to get started on the second act or are we not?

STEPDAUGHTER. I won't say another word! But, you know, it won't be possible to play it all in the garden, as you suggested.

PRODUCER. Why not?

STEPDAUGHTER. Because he [*pointing to the* SON *again*] shuts himself up in his room all the time. . . . Holding himself aloof. . . . And, what's more, there's all the boy's part. . . . Poor bewildered little devil. . . . As I told you, all that takes place indoors.

PRODUCER. I know all about that! On the other hand you do understand that we can hardly stick up notices telling the audience what the scene is. . . . *Or* change the set three or four times in one act.

LEADING MAN. They used to in the good old days.

PRODUCER. Oh, yes. . . . When the intelligence of the audience was about up to the level of that little girl's there. . . .

LEADING LADY. And it does make it easier to get the sense of illusion.

FATHER [*immediately, rising*]. Illusion, did you say? For Heaven's sake, please don't use the word illusion! Please don't use that word. . . . It's a particularly cruel one for us!

PRODUCER [*astounded*]. And why's that?

FATHER. It's cruel! Cruel! You should have known that!

PRODUCER. What ought we to say then? We were referring to the illusion that we have to create on this stage . . . for the audience. . . .

LEADING MAN. . . . with our acting. . . .

PRODUCER. . . . the illusion of a reality!

FATHER. I understand, sir. But you . . . Perhaps you can't understand us. Forgive me! Because . . . you see . . . for you and for your actors, all this is only . . . and quite rightly so. . . . All this is only a game.

LEADING LADY [*indignantly interrupting him*]. What do you mean, a game? We're not children! We're serious actors!

FATHER. I don't deny it! And in fact, in using the term, I was referring to your art which must, as this gentleman has said, create a perfect illusion of reality.

PRODUCER. Precisely!

FATHER. Now just consider the fact that we [*pointing quickly to himself and to the other* FIVE CHARACTERS] as ourselves, have no other reality outside this illusion!

PRODUCER [*in utter astonishment, looking round at his actors who show the same bewildered amazement*]. And what does all that mean?

FATHER [*the ghost of a smile on his face. There is a brief pause while he looks at them all*]. As I said. . . . What other reality should we have? What for you is an illusion that you have to create, for us, on the other hand, is our sole reality. The only reality we know. [*There is a short pause. Then he takes a step or two towards the* PRODUCER *and adds*.] But it's not only true in our case, you know. Just think it over. [*He looks into his eyes.*] Can you tell me who you are? [*And he stands there pointing his index finger at him.*]

PRODUCER [*disturbed, a half-smile on his lips*]. What? Who am I? I'm myself!

FATHER. And suppose I were to tell you that that wasn't true? Suppose I told you that you were me? . . .

PRODUCER. I should say that you were mad! [*The* ACTORS *laugh.*]

FATHER. You're quite right to laugh, because here everything's a game. [*To the* PRODUCER.] And you can object, therefore, that it's only in fun that that gentleman [*pointing to the* LEADING MAN] who is *himself* must be *me* who, on the contrary, am myself. . . . That is, *the person you see here*. There, you see. I've caught you in a trap! [*The* ACTORS *laugh again.*]

PRODUCER [*annoyed*]. But you said all this not ten minutes ago! Do we have to go over all that again?

FATHER. No. As a matter of fact that wasn't what I intended. I should like to invite you to abandon this game. . . . [*Looking at the* LEADING LADY *as if to forestall what she will say.*] Your art! Your art! . . . The game that it is customary for you and your actors to play here in this theater. And once again I ask you in all seriousness. . . . Who are you?

PRODUCER [*turning to the* ACTORS *in utter amazement, an amazement not unmixed with irritation*]. What a cheek the fellow has! A man who calls himself a character comes here and asks me who I am!

FATHER [*with dignity, but in no way haughtily*]. A character, sir, may always ask a man who he is. Because a character has a life which is truly his, marked with his own special characteristics. . . . And as a result he is always somebody! Whilst a man. . . . And I'm not speaking of you personally at the moment. . . . Man in general . . . Can quite well be nobody.

PRODUCER. That as may be! But you're asking *me* these questions. Me, do you understand? The Producer! The boss!

FATHER [*softly, with gentle humility*]. But only in order to know if you, you as you really are now, are seeing yourself as, for instance, after all the time that has gone by, you see yourself as you were at some point in the past. . . . With all the illusions that you had then . . . with everything . . . all the things you had deep down inside you . . . everything that made up your external world . . . everything as it appeared to you then . . . and as it *was*, as it was in reality for you then! Well . . . thinking back on those illusions which you no longer have . . . on all those things that no longer *seem* to be what they *were* once upon a time . . . don't you feel that . . . I won't say these boards. . . . No! . . . That the very earth

itself is slipping away from under your feet, when you reflect that in the
same way this *you* that you now feel yourself to be . . . all your reality as
it is today . . . is destined to seem an illusion tomorrow?

PRODUCER [*not having understood much of all this, and somewhat taken aback by
this specious argument*]. Well? And where does all this get us, anyway?

FATHER. Nowhere. I only wanted to make you see that if we [*again pointing
to himself and to the other* CHARACTERS] have no reality outside the world
of illusion, it would be as well if you mistrusted your own reality. . . .
The reality that you breathe and touch today. . . . Because like the
reality of yesterday, it is fated to reveal itself as a mere illusion tomor-
row.

PRODUCER [*deciding to make fun of him*]. Oh, excellent! And so you'd say that
you and this play of yours that you've been putting on for my benefit
are more real than I am?

FATHER [*with the utmost seriousness*]. Oh, without a doubt.

PRODUCER. Really?

FATHER. I thought that you'd understood that right from the very begin-
ning.

PRODUCER. More real than I am?

FATHER. If your reality can change from one day to the next. . . .

PRODUCER. But everybody knows that it can change like that! It's always
changing. . . . Just like everybody else's!

FATHER [*with a cry*]. No, ours doesn't change! You see. . . . That's the dif-
ference between us! Our reality doesn't change. . . . It can't change. . . .
It can never be in any way different from what it is. . . . Because it is
already fixed. . . . Just as it is. . . . For ever! For ever it is *this* reality. . . .
It's terrible! . . . This immutable reality. . . . It should make you shud-
der to come near us!

PRODUCER [*quickly, suddenly struck by an idea. He moves over and stands squarely
in front of him*]. I should like to know, however, when anyone ever saw a
character step out of his part and begin a long dissertation on it like the
one you've just been making. . . . Expounding it. . . . Explaining it. . . .
Can you tell me? . . . I've never seen it happen before!

FATHER. You have never seen it happen before because authors usually
hide the details of their work of creation. Once the characters are
alive. . . . Once they are standing truly alive before their author. . . .
He does nothing but follow the words and gestures that they suggest to
him. . . . And he must want them to be what they themselves want to be.
For woe betide him if he doesn't do what they wish him to do! When a
character is born he immediately acquires such an independence. . . .
Even of his own author. . . . That everyone can imagine him in a whole
host of situations in which his author never thought of placing him. . . .
They can even imagine his acquiring, sometimes, a significance that the
author never dreamed of giving him.

PRODUCER. Yes. . . . I know all that!

FATHER. Well, then, why are you so astonished at seeing us? Just imagine
what a misfortune it is for a character to be born alive. . . . Created
by the imagination of an author who afterwards sought to deny him
life. . . . Now tell me whether a character who has been left unrealized
in this way. . . . Living, yet without a life. . . . Whether this character

hasn't the right to do what we are doing now. . . . Here and now. . . . For your benefit? . . . After we had spent . . . Oh, such ages, believe me! . . . Doing it for his benefit . . . Trying to persuade him, trying to urge him to realize us. . . . First of all I would present myself to him. . . . Then she would . . . [*pointing to the* STEPDAUGHTER]. . . . And then her poor Mother. . . .

STEPDAUGHTER [*coming forward as if in a trance*]. Yes, what he says is true. . . . I would go and tempt him. . . . There, in his gloomy study. . . . Just at twilight. . . . He would be sitting there, sunk in an armchair. . . . Not bothering to stir himself and switch on the light. . . . Content to let the room get darker and darker. . . . Until the whole room was filled with a darkness that was alive with our presence. . . . We were there to tempt him. . . . [*And then, as if she saw herself as still in that study and irritated by the presence of all those actors.*] Oh, go away. . . . All of you! Leave us alone! Mummy . . . and her son. . . . I and the little girl. . . . The boy by himself. . . . Always by himself. . . . Then he and I together [*a faint gesture in the direction of the* FATHER]. And then. . . . By myself. . . . By myself . . . alone in that darkness [*a sudden turn round as if she wished to seize and fix the vision that she has of herself, the living vision of herself that she sees shining in the darkness*]. Yes, my life! Ah, what scenes, what wonderful scenes we suggested to him! And I . . . I tempted him more than any of them. . . .

FATHER. Indeed you did! And it may well be that it's all your fault that he wouldn't give us the life we asked for. . . . You were too persistent. . . . Too impudent. . . . You exaggerated too much. . . .

STEPDAUGHTER. What? When it was he who wanted me to be what I am? [*She goes up to the* PRODUCER *and says confidentially.*] I think it's much more likely that he refused because he felt depressed . . . or because of his contempt for the theater. . . . Or at least, for the present-day theater with all its pandering to the box-office. . . .

PRODUCER. Let's get on! Let's get on, for God's sake! Let's have some action!

STEPDAUGHTER. It looks to me as if we've got too much action for you already. . . . Just staging our entry into his house [*pointing to the* FATHER]. You yourself said that you couldn't stick up notices or be changing the set every five minutes.

PRODUCER. And neither can we! Of course we can't! What we've got to do is to combine and group all the action into one continuous well-knit scene. . . . Not the sort of thing that you want. . . . With, first of all, your younger brother coming home from school and wandering about the house like some lost soul. . . . Hiding behind doors and brooding on a plan that . . . What did you say it does to him?

STEPDAUGHTER. Dries him up. . . . Shrivels him up completely.

PRODUCER. M'm! Well, as you said. . . . And all the time you can see it more and more clearly in his eyes. . . . Wasn't that what you said?

STEPDAUGHTER. Yes. . . . Just look at him! [*Pointing to where he is standing by his* MOTHER.]

PRODUCER. And then, at the same time, you want the child to be playing in the garden, blissfully unaware of everything. The boy in the house, the little girl in the garden. . . . I ask you!

STEPDAUGHTER. Yes . . . happily playing in the sun! That is the only plea-
sure that I have. . . . Her happiness. . . . All the joy that she gets from
playing in the garden. . . . After the wretchedness and the squalor of
that horrible room where we all four slept together. . . . And she had to
sleep with me. . . . Just think of it. . . . My vile contaminated body next
to hers! . . . With her holding me tight in her loving, innocent, little
arms! She only had to get a glimpse of me in the garden and she'd run
up to me and take me by the hand. She wasn't interested in the big
flowers . . . she'd run about looking for the . . . "weeny" ones. . . . So
that she could point them out to me. . . . And she'd be so happy. . . . So
excited. . . .

> [*As she says this she is torn by the memory
> of it all and gives a long, despairing cry,
> dropping her head on to her hands which
> are lying loosely on the little table in front
> of her. At the sight of her emotion everyone
> is deeply moved. The* PRODUCER *goes up
> to her almost paternally and says comfort-
> ingly.*]

PRODUCER. We'll have the garden in. . . . Don't you worry. . . . We'll have
the garden scene in. . . . Just you wait and see. . . . You'll be quite
satisfied with how I arrange it. . . . We'll play everything in the garden.
[*Calling a* STAGE-HAND.] Hey [*his name*]! Let me have something in the
shape of a tree or two. . . . A couple of not-too-large cypresses in front
of this fountain! [*Two small cypress trees descend from the flies. The* FOREMAN
dashes up and fixes them with struts and nails.]

PRODUCER [*to the* STEPDAUGHTER]. That'll do. . . . For the moment any-
way. . . . It'll give us a rough idea. [*Calls to the* STAGE-HAND *again.*] Oh
[*his name*], let me have something for a sky, will you?

STAGE-HAND [*up aloft*]. Eh?

PRODUCER. Something for a sky! A backcloth to go behind the fountain!
[*And a white backcloth descends from the flies.*]

PRODUCER. Not white! I said I wanted a sky! Oh, well, it doesn't mat-
ter. . . . Leave it! Leave it! . . . I'll fix it myself. . . . [*Calls.*] Hey! . . . You
there on the lights! . . . Everything off. . . . And let me have the moon-
light blues on! . . . Blues in the batten! . . . A couple of blue spots on the
backcloth! . . . Yes, that's it! That's just right!

> [*There is now a mysterious moonlit effect
> about the scene, and the* ACTORS *are
> prompted to move about and to speak as
> they would if they were indeed walking in
> a moonlit garden.*]

PRODUCER [*to the* STEPDAUGHTER]. There, do you see? Now the Boy, instead
of hiding behind doors inside the house, can move about the garden
and hide behind these trees. But, you know, it'll be rather difficult to
find a little girl to play that scene with you. . . . The one where she
shows you the flowers. [*Turning to the* BOY.] Now come down here a bit!
Let's see how it works out! [*Then, since the* BOY *doesn't move.*] Come on!
Come on! [*He drags him forward and tries to make him hold his head up. But
after every attempt down it falls again.*] Good God, here's a fine how d'ye

do. . . . There's something queer about this boy. . . . What's the matter with him? . . . My God, he'll have to say *something*. . . . [*He goes up to him, puts a hand on his shoulder and places him behind one of the trees.*] Now. . . . Forward a little! . . . Let me see you! . . . M'm! . . . Now hide yourself. . . . That's it! Now try popping your head out a bit . . . Take a look round. . . . [*He goes to one side to study the effect and the* BOY *does what he has been told to do. The* ACTORS *look on, deeply affected and quite dismayed.*] That's excellent! . . . Yes, excellent! [*Turning again to the* STEPDAUGHTER.] Suppose the little girl were to catch sight of him there as he was looking out, and run over to him. . . . Wouldn't that drag a word or two out of him?

STEPDAUGHTER [*rising*]. It's no use your hoping that he'll speak. . . . At least not so long as *he's* here [*pointing to the* SON]. If you want him to speak, you'll have to send *him* away first.

SON [*going resolutely towards the steps down into the auditorium*]. Willingly! I'm only too happy to oblige! Nothing could possibly suit me better!

PRODUCER [*immediately catching hold of him*]. Hey! Oh no you don't! Where are you going? You hang on a minute!

> [*The* MOTHER *rises in dismay, filled with anguish at the thought that he really is going away. She instinctively raises her arms to prevent him from going, without, however, moving from where she is standing.*]

SON [*he has reached the footlights*]. I tell you . . . There's absolutely nothing for me to do here! Let me go, please! Let me go! [*This to the* PRODUCER.]

PRODUCER. What do you mean . . . There's nothing for you to do?

STEPDAUGHTER [*placidly, ironically*]. Don't bother to hold him back! He won't go away!

FATHER. He has to play that terrible scene with his Mother in the garden.

SON [*immediately, fiercely, resolutely*]. I'm not playing anything! I've said that all along! [*To the* PRODUCER.] Let me go!

STEPDAUGHTER [*running over, then addressing the* PRODUCER]. Do you mind? [*She gets him to lower the hand with which he has been restraining the* SON.] Let him go! [*Then turning to the* SON, *as soon as the* PRODUCER *has dropped his arm.*] Well, go on. . . . Leave us!

> [*The* SON *stands where he is, still straining in the direction of the steps, but, as if held back by some mysterious force, he cannot go down them. Then, amidst the utter dismay and anxious bewilderment of the* ACTORS, *he wanders slowly along the length of the footlights in the direction of the other flight of steps. Once there, he again finds himself unable to descend, much as he would wish to. The* STEPDAUGHTER *has watched his progress intently, her eyes challenging, defiant. Now she bursts out laughing.*]

STEPDAUGHTER. He can't, you see! He can't leave us! He must remain

here. . . . He has no choice but to remain with us! He's chained to
us. . . . Irrevocably! But if I . . . Who really do run away when what is
inevitable happens. . . . And I run away because of my hatred for
him. . . . I run away just because I can no longer bear the sight of
him. . . . Well, if I can still stay here. . . . If I can still put up with his
company and with having to have him here before my eyes. . . . Do you
think it's likely that he can run away? Why, he has to stay here with that
precious father of his. . . . With his mother. . . . Because now she has
no other children but him. . . . [*Turning to her* MOTHER.] Come on,
Mummy! Come on. . . . [*Turning to the* PRODUCER *and pointing to the*
MOTHER.] There. . . . You see. . . . She'd got up to prevent him from
going. . . . [*To her* MOTHER, *as if willing her actions by some magic power.*]
Come on! Come on! [*Then to the* PRODUCER.] You can imagine just how
reluctant she is to give this proof of her affection in front of your actors.
But so great is her desire to be with him that . . . There! . . . You
see? . . . She's willing to live out again her scene with him! [*And as a
matter of fact the* MOTHER *has gone up to her* SON, *and scarcely has the* STEP-
DAUGHTER *finished speaking before she makes a gesture to indicate her
agreement.*]

SON [*immediately*]. No! No! You're not going to drag me into this! If I can't
get away, I shall stay here! But I repeat that I'm not going to do any
acting at all!

FATHER [*trembling with excitement, to the* PRODUCER]. You can force him to
act!

SON. Nobody can force me!

FATHER. I can and I will!

STEPDAUGHTER. Wait! Wait! First of all the little girl has to go to the foun-
tain. . . . [*Goes over to the* LITTLE GIRL. *She drops on to her knees in front of
her and takes her face in her hands.*] Poor little darling. . . . You're looking
so bewildered. . . . With those beautiful big eyes. . . . You must be won-
dering just where you are. We're on a stage, dear! What's a stage? Well
. . . It's a place where you play at being serious. They put on plays here.
And now *we're* putting a play on. Really and truly! Even you. . . .
[*Embracing her, clasping her to her breast and rocking her for a moment or so.*]
Oh, you little darling. . . . My dear little darling, what a terrible play for
you. . . . What a horrible end they've thought out for you! The garden,
the fountain. . . . Yes, it's a make-believe fountain. . . . The pity is, dar-
ling, that everything's make-believe here. . . . But perhaps you like a
make-believe fountain better than a real one. . . . So that you can play
in it. . . . M'm? No. . . . It'll be a game for the others. . . . Not for you
unfortunately . . . Because you're real. . . . And you really play by a real
fountain. . . . A lovely big green one, with masses of bamboo palms
casting shadows. . . . Looking at your reflection in the water. . . . And
lots and lots of little baby ducklings swimming about in it, breaking the
shadow into a thousand little ripples. You try to take hold of one of the
ducklings. . . . [*With a shriek which fills everybody with dismay.*] No, Rosetta,
no! Your Mummy's not looking after you. . . . And all because of that
swine there. . . . Her son! I feel as if all the devils in hell were loose
inside me. . . . And he . . . [*Leaves the* LITTLE GIRL *and turns with her
usual scorn to the* BOY.] What are you doing . . . drooping there like

that? . . . Always the little beggar-boy! It'll be your fault too if that baby drowns. . . . Because of the way you go on. . . . As if I didn't pay for everybody when I got you into his house. [*Seizing his arm to make him take his hand out of his pocket.*] What have you got there? What are you trying to hide? Out with it! Take that hand out of your pocket! [*She snatches his hand out of his pocket and to everybody's horror reveals that it is clenched round a revolver. She looks at him for a little while, as if satisfied. Then she says somberly.*] M'm! Where did you get that gun from? . . . And how did you manage to lay your hands on it? [*And since the* BOY, *in his utter dismay—his eyes are staring and vacant—does not reply.*] You idiot! If I'd been you I shouldn't have killed myself. . . . I'd have killed one of *them.* . . . Or the pair of them! Father and son together!

> [*She hides him behind the cypress tree where he was lurking before. Then she takes the* LITTLE GIRL *by the hand and leads her towards the fountain. She puts her into the basin of the fountain, and makes her lie down so that she is completely hidden. Finally she goes down on her knees and buries her head in her hands on the rim of the basin of the fountain.*]

PRODUCER. That's it! Good! [*Turning to the* SON.] And at the same time. . . .

SON [*angrily*]. What do you mean . . . "And at the same time"? Oh, no! . . . Nothing of the sort! There never was any scene between her and me! [*Pointing to the* MOTHER.] You make her tell you what really happened! [*Meanwhile the* SECOND ACTRESS *and the* JUVENILE LEAD *have detached themselves from the group of* ACTORS *and are standing gazing intently at the* MOTHER *and the* SON *so that later they can act these parts.*]

MOTHER. Yes, it's true, sir! I'd gone to his room at the time.

SON. There! Did you hear? To my room! Not into the garden!

PRODUCER. That doesn't matter at all! As I said we'll have to run all the action together into one composite scene!

SON [*becoming aware that the* JUVENILE LEAD *is studying him*]. What do *you* want?

JUVENILE LEAD. Nothing! I was just looking at you.

SON [*turning to the* SECOND ACTRESS]. Oh! . . . And *you're* here too, are you? All ready to play *her* part, I suppose? [*Pointing to the* MOTHER.]

PRODUCER. That's the idea! And if you want my opinion you ought to be damned grateful for all the attention they're paying you.

SON. Indeed? Thank you! But hasn't it dawned on you yet that you aren't going to be able to stage this play? Not even the tiniest vestige of us is to be found in you. . . . And all the time your actors are studying us from the outside. Do you think it's possible for us to live confronted by a mirror which, not merely content with freezing us in that particular picture which is the fixing of our expression, has to throw an image back at us which we can no longer recognize? . . . Our own features, yes. . . . But twisted into a horrible grimace.

FATHER. He's quite right! He's quite right, you know!

PRODUCER [*to the* JUVENILE LEAD *and* SECOND ACTRESS]. Right you are! Get back with the others!

SON. It's no use your bothering! I'm not having anything to do with this!

PRODUCER. You be quiet for the moment, and let me listen to what your mother has to say! [*To the* MOTHER.] You were saying? . . . You'd gone to his room? . . .

MOTHER. Yes, I'd gone to his room. . . . I couldn't bear the strain any longer! I wanted to pour out my heart to him. . . . I wanted to tell him of all the anguish that was tormenting me. . . . But as soon as he saw me come in . .

SON. There was no scene between us! I rushed out of the room. . . . I didn't want to get involved in any scenes! Because I never have been involved in any! Do you understand?

MOTHER. Yes! That *is* what happened! That is what happened.

PRODUCER. But for the purposes of this play we've simply *got* to have a scene between you and him! Why . . . it's absolutely *essential*!

MOTHER. I'm quite ready to take part in one! Oh, if you could only find some way to give me an opportunity of speaking to him . . . if only for a moment. . . . So that I can pour out my heart to him!

FATHER [*going up to the* SON, *in a great rage*]. You'll do what she asks, do you understand? You'll do what your Mother asks!

SON [*more stubbornly than ever*]. I'm doing nothing!

FATHER [*taking hold of him by the lapels of his coat and shaking him*]. My God, you'll do what I tell you! Or else . . . Can't you hear how she's pleading with you? Haven't you a spark of feeling in you for your Mother?

SON [*grappling with the* FATHER]. No, I haven't! For God's sake let's have done with all this. . . . Once and for all, let's have done with it!

> [*General agitation. The* MOTHER *is terrified and tries to get between them in order to separate them.*]

MOTHER. Please! *Please!*

FATHER [*without relinquishing his hold*]. You must obey me! You *must!*

SON [*struggling with him and finally hurling him to the ground. He falls near the steps amidst general horror*]. What's come over you? Why are you in this terrible state of frenzy? Haven't you any sense of decency? . . . Going about parading your shame. . . . And ours, too. I'm having nothing to do with this affair! Nothing, do you hear? And by making this stand I am interpreting the wishes of our author, who didn't wish to put us on the stage!

PRODUCER. Oh, God! You come along here and . . .

SON [*pointing to the* FATHER]. *He* did! I didn't!

PRODUCER. Aren't you here now?

SON. It was he who wanted to come. . . . And he dragged us all along with him. Then the pair of them went in there with you and agreed on what was to go into the play. But he didn't only stick to what really did occur. . . . No, as if that wasn't enough for any man, he had to put in things that never even happened.

PRODUCER. Well, then, you tell me what really happened! You can at least do that! You rushed out of your room without saying a word?

SON [*he hesitates for a moment*]. Without saying a word! I didn't want to get involved in a scene!

PRODUCER [*pressing him*]. And then? What did you do then?

SON [*everybody's attention is on him; amidst the anguished silence he takes a step or two across the front of the stage*]. Nothing. . . . As I was crossing the garden . . . [*he breaks off and becomes gloomy and absorbed*].

PRODUCER [*urging him to speak, very much moved by this extraordinary reserve*]. Well? As you were crossing the garden?

SON [*in exasperation, shielding his face with his arm*]. Why do you want to force me to tell you? It's horrible!

[*The* MOTHER *is trembling all over and stifled sobs come from her as she looks towards the fountain.*]

PRODUCER [*slowly, quietly . . . he has seen where the* MOTHER *is looking and he now turns to the* SON *with growing apprehension*]. The little girl?

SON [*staring straight in front of him, out into the auditorium*]. There . . . In the fountain. . . .

FATHER [*from where he is on the floor, pointing with tender pity to the* MOTHER]. She was following him. . . .

PRODUCER [*anxiously to the* SON]. And what did you do?

SON [*slowly, continuing to stare in front of him*]. I rushed up to the fountain. . . . I was about to dive in and fish her out. . . . Then all of a sudden I pulled up short. . . . Behind that tree I saw something that made my blood run cold. . . . The boy. . . . The boy was standing there. . . . Stock still. . . . With madness in his eyes. . . . Staring like some insane creature at his little sister, who was lying drowned in the fountain! [*The* STEPDAUGHTER, *who has all this while been bent over the fountain in order to hide the* LITTLE GIRL, *is sobbing desperately—her sobs coming like an echo from the background. There is a pause.*] I moved towards him. . . . And then . . . [*And from behind the trees where the* BOY *is hidden a revolver shot rings out.*]

MOTHER [*with a heartrending cry she rushes behind the trees accompanied by the* SON *and all the* ACTORS. *There is general confusion*]. Oh, my son! My son! [*And then amidst the general hubbub and shouting.*] Help! Oh, help!

PRODUCER [*amidst all the shouting, he tries to clear a space while the* BOY *is carried off behind the skycloth*]. Is he wounded? Is he badly hurt?

[*By now everybody, except for the* PRODUCER *and the* FATHER, *who is still on the ground by the steps, has disappeared behind the skycloth. They can be heard muttering and exclaiming in great consternation. Then first from one side, then from the other, the* ACTORS *re-enter.*]

LEADING LADY [*re-entering right, very much moved*]. He's dead, poor boy! He's dead! Oh what a terrible thing to happen!

LEADING MAN [*re-entering left, laughing*]. What do you mean, dead? It's all make-believe! It's all just a pretense! Don't get taken in by it!

OTHER ACTORS [*entering from the right*]. Make-believe? Pretense? Reality! Reality! He's dead!

OTHERS [*from the left*]. No! Make-believe! It's all a pretense!

FATHER [*rising and crying out to them*]. What do you mean, pretense? Reality, ladies and gentlemen, reality! Reality! [*And desperation in his face, he too disappears behind the backcloth*].

PRODUCER [*at the end of his tether*]. Pretense! Reality! Go to hell, the whole lot of you! Lights! Lights! Lights!

> [*The stage and the auditorium are suddenly flooded with very bright light. The* PRODUCER *breathes again as if freed from a tremendous burden. They all stand there looking into one another's eyes, in an agony of suspense and dismay.*]

PRODUCER. My God! Nothing like this has ever happened to me before! I've lost a whole day on their account! [*He looks at his watch.*] You can go home now. . . . All of you! There's nothing we can do now! It's too late to start rehearsing again! I'll see you all this evening. [*And as soon as the* ACTORS *have said "Goodbye!" and gone he calls out to the* ELECTRICIAN.] Hey [*his name*]! Everything off! [*He has hardly got the words out before the theater is plunged for a moment into utter darkness.*] Hell! You might at least leave me one light on, so that I can see where I'm going!

And immediately behind the backcloth, a green flood lights up. It projects the silhouettes of the CHARACTERS (*minus the* BOY *and the* LITTLE GIRL), *clear-cut and huge, on to the backcloth. The* PRODUCER *is terrified and leaps off the stage. As he does so the green flood is switched off—rather as if its having come on in the first instance had been due to the* ELECTRICIAN'S *having pulled the wrong switch—and the stage is again lit in blue. Slowly the* CHARACTERS *come in and advance to the front of the stage. The* SON *comes in first, from the right, followed by the* MOTHER, *who has her arms outstretched towards him. Then the* FATHER *comes in from the left. They stop half-way down the stage and stand there like people in a trance. Last of all the* STEPDAUGHTER *comes in from the left and runs towards the steps which lead down into the auditorium. With her foot on the top step she stops for a moment to look at the other three and bursts into strident laughter. Then she hurls herself down the steps and runs up the aisle. She stops at the back of the auditorium and turns to look at the three figures standing on the stage. She bursts out laughing again. And when she has disappeared from the auditorium you can still hear her terrible laughter coming from the foyer beyond. A short pause and then,*

CURTAIN

Thomas Mann
(*1875–1955*)

To be a German citizen in the first half of the twentieth century, to be deeply committed to German culture and to feel that one is in the tradition of Goethe, Schiller, and Wagner, and at the same time be forced to witness and participate in the debacle that is modern German history is a fearful challenge for an artist. Yet this was the position of Thomas Mann, the

greatest German novelist of his time, and the dilemma provided the underlying subject, at least indirectly, of much of his voluminous work. A profoundly philosophical novelist, Mann concerned himself even in his early stories with the contrary forces that lead to social growth or decay. Mann was forced to revise many of his views, but he remained throughout his career an eloquent spokesman for traditional, humane values and an acute analyst of the forces in modern life that threaten those values.

Mann was born in 1875 in the Baltic seaport town of Lübeck, in west Germany, into a family that had been prosperous merchants in the region since medieval times. After his father's death when Mann was sixteen, he moved with his family to Munich, where he attended the university (without, however, taking a degree), worked briefly in an insurance office, and wrote for a satirical magazine. In his early twenties, he decided to devote himself to writing, as his older brother Heinrich had already done. (Heinrich had a successful career as a novelist; he is now best remembered for the novel dramatized in Josef von Sternberg's 1930 film *The Blue Angel*.) Mann's early stories, of which a collection appeared in 1898, dealt recurringly with the ambiguities of the artist's role, as both interpreter and falsifier of life. They also showed the influence of the romantic irrationalism of Schopenhauer and Nietzsche and the composer Wagner.

Mann's first novel, *Buddenbrooks* (1900), was a massive family novel which continued the exploration of the tension between art and ordinary, middle-class life by showing, over three generations, how a preoccupation with art saps the vitality of the younger heirs of a vigorous family of businessmen. A nostalgia for the virtues of bourgeois culture also pervaded the novellas *Tonio Kröger* and *Tristan* (both 1903), and the great novella *Death in Venice* (1912) further explored the threat of decadence inherent in the artist's role.

The outbreak of World War I led Mann first to a polemical articulation of his social views and ultimately to a rethinking and modification of them. Reacting to his brother Heinrich's open criticism of the conservatism and nationalism of German culture, Mann in 1918 published a polemical treatise, *Reflections of an Unpolitical Man*, in which he hotly defended "creative" irrationalism, conservatism, and authoritarianism against the claims of rationalistic democracy. Germany's defeat in the war and the chaos and extremism of German life under the short-lived Weimar Republic of the 1920s led him gradually to revise his views, and in a series of essays, he began to espouse democratic principles. This intellectual development is reflected in *The Magic Mountain* (1924), in which a mountaintop tuberculosis sanitarium comes to serve as a model of the spiritual state of Europe. Much of this long novel of ideas is devoted to debates between the humanistic and democratic Settembrini and the cynical, totalitarian Naphta. At the end, the protagonist, Hans Castorp, who has come to spend three weeks but spends seven years in the death-haunted enchantment of the sanitarium, sides, somewhat skeptically but decisively, with Settembrini and leaves for a life of action and service to others. Some of the same tensions between traditional values and newer ones appear in *Disorder and Early Sorrow* (1926).

As the shadow of the coming of Nazism began to fall across Germany, Mann became even more outspoken in his defense of humane values. In

Mario and the Magician (1930), he caricatured the Nazis in the figure of a shabby, cynical illusionist; in the same year, he delivered a courageous address in Berlin, "An Appeal to Reason," calling for the middle and working classes to join together to oppose the rising barbarity of the Nazis. When Hitler took power in 1933, Mann and his wife were on vacation in Switzerland. Warned by friends, they did not return to Germany, but spent the following five years near Zurich. They came to America in 1938, settling first in Princeton, New Jersey, and then in southern California. The Nazis had stripped him of German citizenship in 1936; he became a U.S. citizen in 1944.

Mann spent much of the 1930's and 1940's working on his cycle of novels *Joseph and His Brothers,* in which he reinterpreted the biblical story as a fable of the issues of his own day. Israel, in his treatment, is the home of the mythic, the tribal, and the collective. Joseph is forced out of this traditional environment into Egypt, the home of change, history, and individualism, thus paralleling Mann's own spiritual history and that of his time, as he saw it. Some of these same themes appear in the witty, ironic *Lotte in Weimar* (1939), known in America as *The Beloved Returns;* here Lotte Kestner, the heroine of Goethe's semi-autobiographical *Werther,* comes as an old woman to renew her relationship with her old lover, now a world-famous writer. But Goethe refuses to return to the past and teaches Lotte that one must accept time and change. The novels of the war years also include *Doctor Faustus* (1947), begun in 1943; it traces, through the music of the German composer Adrian Leverkühn, the movement of Germany from humanism to Nazi primitivism. The novel has been called the greatest literary treatment of music as well as the most profound artistic treatment of Nazism.

Mann refused to live again in Germany after the war, although he visited both East and West Germany several times. He left the United States in 1952 to settle once more in Switzerland, where he died in 1955.

The conflict of citizen and artist is a basic theme in Mann's work (as it is in that of his great contemporary Joyce, who dramatized the conflict in the figures of Leopold Bloom and Stephen Dedalus in *Ulysses*). Professor Cornelius is one of Mann's most moving portraits of the bourgeois citizen. His story is consummately crafted; Mann, despite his skill in the large-scale novel, is perhaps at his best in his tightly constructed novellas. *Disorder and Early Sorrow* seems at first to be a fragile, almost eventless story of domestic life. But as it develops, the story becomes a complex layering of social values and generational conflict. The professor's traditional world is crumbling under the pressures of post-war economic and social disorder. He is far from unsympathetic with the values of the "big folks," his children, but he finds them disturbing and hard to understand, and he sits in his study upstairs, surrounded by his books and listening to the tumult of the party downstairs, in a rich image of social disjunction. The story moves from "disorder" to "early sorrow" in the culminating episode of Ellie's bedtime suffering. Her painful fall from innocence into experience is paralleled by her father's reaction. The small, domestic action of the story opens up into large perspectives as Cornelius meditates upon his own love of history, his "timeless" love for his daughter, and his own fear of falling from the death-

like, artlike stasis of finished history into the experience of the frightening but living present.

FURTHER READING (*prepared by N. K. B.*): Nigel Hamilton, *The Brothers Mann: The Lives of Heinrich and Thomas Mann, 1871–1950 and 1875–1955*, 1979, is a major study of the background and biographies of the two figures. For concise introductions to Mann's life and writing, see Joseph R. Stern, *Thomas Mann*, 1967; R. J. Hollingdale, *Thomas Mann: A Critical Study*, 1971; and Martin Swales, *Thomas Mann: A Study*, 1980. Henry Hatfield, *Thomas Mann*, 1951, rev. 1962, contains a biographical sketch and surveys Mann's artistic development. Ignace Feuerlicht, *Thomas Mann*, 1968, discusses *Disorder and Early Sorrow* in his introductory study, which stresses the autobiographical features of Mann's work. In *Thomas Mann: The Uses of Tradition*, 1974, T. J. Reed views Mann in the context of German and European literary traditions. Erich Heller's provocative study *Thomas Mann: The Ironic German*, 1958, rev. 1961, also examines Mann's debt to the cultural milieu. T. E. Apter's *Thomas Mann: The Devil's Advocate*, 1979, demonstrates the strong influence of German Romanticism on Mann's career. Inta M. Ezergailis, ed., *Critical Essays on Thomas Mann*, 1988, reprints many of the most important essays on Mann's work.

DISORDER AND EARLY SORROW

Translated by H. T. Lowe–Porter

The principal dish at dinner had been croquettes made of turnip greens. So there follows a trifle,[1] concocted out of those dessert powders we use nowadays,[2] that taste like almond soap. Xaver, the youthful manservant, in his outgrown striped jacket, white woolen gloves, and yellow sandals, hands it round, and the "big folk" take this opportunity to remind their father, tactfully, that company is coming today.

The "big folk" are two, Ingrid and Bert. Ingrid is brown-eyed, eighteen, and perfectly delightful. She is on the eve of her exams, and will probably pass them, if only because she knows how to wind masters, and even headmasters, round her finger. She does not, however, mean to use her certificate once she gets it; having leanings towards the stage, on the ground of her ingratiating smile, her equally ingratiating voice, and a marked and irresistible talent for burlesque. Bert is blond and seventeen. He intends to get done with school somehow, anyhow, and fling himself into the arms of life. He will be a dancer, or a cabaret actor, possibly even a waiter—but not a waiter anywhere else save at Cairo, the night-club, whither he has once already taken flight, at five in the morning, and been brought back crestfallen. Bert bears a strong resemblance to the youthful manservant, Xaver Kleinsgutl, of about the same age as himself; not because he looks common—in features he is strikingly like his father, Professor Cornelius—but by reason of an approximation of types, due in its turn to far-

[1] A dessert made of sponge cake spread with a jam or other filling and covered with custard.

[2] That is, during the difficult inflationary period that followed World War I. *Disorder and Early Sorrow* was written in 1925.

reaching compromises in matters of dress and bearing generally. Both lads wear their heavy hair very long on top, with a cursory parting in the middle, and give their heads the same characteristic toss to throw it off the forehead. When one of them leaves the house, by the garden gate, bareheaded in all weathers, in a blouse rakishly girded with a leather strap, and sheers off bent well over with his head on one side; or else mounts his push-bike—Xaver makes free with his employers', of both sexes, or even, in acutely irresponsible mood, with the Professor's own—Dr. Cornelius from his bedroom window cannot, for the life of him, tell whether he is looking at his son or his servant. Both, he thinks, look like young moujiks.[3] And both are impassioned cigarette-smokers, though Bert has not the means to compete with Xaver, who smokes as many as thirty a day, of a brand named after a popular cinema star. The big folk call their father and mother the "old folk"—not behind their backs, but as a form of address and in all affection: "Hullo, old folks," they will say; though Cornelius is only forty-seven years old and his wife eight years younger. And the Professor's parents, who lead in his household the humble and hesitant life of the really old, are on the big folk's lips the "ancients." As for the "little folk," Ellie and Snapper, who take their meals upstairs with blue-faced Ann—so-called because of her prevailing facial hue—Ellie and Snapper follow their mother's example and address their father by his first name, Abel. Unutterably comic it sounds, in its pert, confiding familiarity; particularly on the lips, in the sweet accents, of five-year-old Eleanor, who is the image of Frau Cornelius's baby pictures and whom the Professor loves above everything else in the world.

"Darling old thing," says Ingrid affably, laying her large but shapely hand on his, as he presides in proper middle-class style over the family table, with her on his left and the mother opposite: "Parent mine, may I ever so gently jog your memory, for you have probably forgotten: this is the afternoon we were to have our little jollification, our turkey-trot with eats to match. You haven't a thing to do but just bear up and not funk it; everything will be over by nine o'clock."

"Oh—ah!" says Cornelius, his face falling. "Good!" he goes on, and nods his head to show himself in harmony with the inevitable. "I only meant—is this really the day? Thursday, yes. How time flies! Well, what time are they coming?"

"Half past four they'll be dropping in, I should say," answers Ingrid, to whom her brother leaves the major rôle in all dealings with the father. Upstairs, while he is resting, he will hear scarcely anything, and from seven to eight he takes his walk. He can slip out by the terrace if he likes.

"Tut!" says Cornelius deprecatingly, as who should say: "You exaggerate." But Bert puts in: "It's the one evening in the week Wanja doesn't have to play. Any other night he'd have to leave by half past six, which would be painful for all concerned."

Wanja is Ivan Herzl, the celebrated young leading man at the Stadttheater.[4] Bert and Ingrid are on intimate terms with him, they often visit him in his dressing-room and have tea. He is an artist of the modern school, who stands on the stage in strange and, to the Professor's mind,

[3] Russian peasants. [4] Municipal theater.

utterly affected dancing attitudes, and shrieks lamentably. To a professor of history, all highly repugnant; but Bert has entirely succumbed to Herzl's influence, blackens the lower rim of his eyelids—despite painful but fruitless scenes with the father—and with youthful carelessness of the ancestral anguish declares that not only will he take Herzl for his model if he becomes a dancer, but in case he turns out to be a waiter at the Cairo he means to walk precisely thus.

Cornelius slightly raises his brows and makes his son a little bow—indicative of the unassumingness and self-abnegation that befits his age. You could not call it a mocking bow or suggestive in any special sense. Bert may refer it to himself or equally to his so talented friend.

"Who else is coming?" next inquires the master of the house. They mention various people, names all more or less familiar, from the city, from the suburban colony, from Ingrid's school. They still have some telephoning to do, they say. They have to phone Max. This is Max Hergesell, an engineering student; Ingrid utters his name in the nasal drawl which according to her is the traditional intonation of all the Hergesells. She goes on to parody it in the most abandonedly funny and lifelike way, and the parents laugh until they nearly choke over the wretched trifle. For even in these times when something funny happens people have to laugh.

From time to time the telephone bell rings in the Professor's study, and the big folk run across, knowing it is their affair. Many people had to give up their telephones the last time the price rose, but so far the Corneliuses have been able to keep theirs, just as they have kept their villa, which was built before the war, by dint of the salary Cornelius draws as professor of history—a million marks,[5] and more or less adequate to the chances and changes of postwar life. The house is comfortable, even elegant, though sadly in need of repairs that cannot be made for lack of materials, and at present disfigured by iron stoves with long pipes. Even so, it is still the proper setting of the upper middle class, though they themselves look odd enough in it, with their worn and turned clothing and altered way of life. The children, of course, know nothing else; to them it is normal and regular, they belong by birth to the "villa proletariat." The problem of clothing troubles them not at all. They and their like have evolved a costume to fit the time, by poverty out of taste for innovation: in summer it consists of scarcely more than a belted linen smock and sandals. The middle-class parents find things rather more difficult.

The big folk's table napkins hang over their chair-backs, they talk with their friends over the telephone. These friends are the invited guests who have rung up to accept or decline or arrange; and the conversation is carried on in the jargon of the clan, full of slang and high spirits, of which the old folk understand hardly a word. These consult together meantime about the hospitality to be offered to the impending guests. The Professor displays a middle-class ambitiousness: he wants to serve a sweet—or something that looks like a sweet—after the Italian salad and brownbread sandwiches. But Frau Cornelius says that would be going too far. The guests would not expect it, she is sure—and the big folk, returning once more to their trifle, agree with her.

[5] This high monthly salary reflects the runaway inflation in postwar Germany.

The mother of the family is of the same general type as Ingrid, though not so tall. She is languid; the fantastic difficulties of the housekeeping have broken and worn her. She really ought to go and take a cure,[6] but feels incapable; the floor is always swaying under her feet, and everything seems upside down. She speaks of what is uppermost in her mind: the eggs, they simply must be bought today. Six thousand marks apiece they are, and just so many are to be had on this one day of the week at one single shop fifteen minutes' journey away. Whatever else they do, the big folk must go and fetch them immediately after luncheon, with Danny, their neighbor's son, who will soon be calling for them; and Xaver Kleinsgutl will don civilian garb and attend his young master and mistress. For no single household is allowed more than five eggs a week; therefore the young people will enter the shop singly, one after another, under assumed names, and thus wring twenty eggs from the shopkeeper for the Cornelius family. This enterprise is the sporting event of the week for all participants, not excepting the moujik Kleinsgutl, and most of all for Ingrid and Bert, who delight in misleading and mystifying their fellowmen and would revel in the performance even if it did not achieve one single egg. They adore impersonating fictitious characters; they love to sit in a bus and carry on long lifelike conversations in a dialect which they otherwise never speak, the most commonplace dialogue about politics and people and the price of food, while the whole bus listens open-mouthed to this incredibly ordinary prattle, though with a dark suspicion all the while that something is wrong somewhere. The conversation waxes ever more shameless, it enters into revolting detail about these people who do not exist. Ingrid can make her voice sound ever so common and twittering and shrill as she impersonates a shopgirl with an illegitimate child, said child being a son with sadistic tendencies, who lately out in the country treated a cow with such unnatural cruelty that no Christian could have borne to see it. Bert nearly explodes at her twittering, but restrains himself and displays a grisly sympathy; he and the unhappy shopgirl entering into a long, stupid, depraved, and shuddery conversation over the particular morbid cruelty involved; until an old gentleman opposite, sitting with his ticket folded between his index finger and his seal ring, can bear it no more and makes public protest against the nature of the themes these young folk are discussing with such particularity. He uses the Greek plural: "themata." Whereat Ingrid pretends to be dissolving in tears, and Bert behaves as though his wrath against the old gentleman was with difficulty being held in check and would probably burst out before long. He clenches his fists, he gnashes his teeth, he shakes from head to foot; and the unhappy old gentleman, whose intentions had been of the best, hastily leaves the bus at the next stop.

Such are the diversions of the big folk. The telephone plays a prominent part in them: they ring up any and everybody—members of government, opera singers, dignitaries of the Church—in the character of shop assistants, or perhaps as Lord or Lady Doolittle. They are only with difficulty persuaded that they have the wrong number. Once they emptied their parents' card-tray[7] and distributed its contents among the neighbors' letter-boxes, wantonly, yet not without enough impish sense of the fitness

[6] Rest cure, at a spa. [7] Tray where visitors left their calling-cards.

of things to make it highly upsetting, God only knowing why certain people should have called where they did.

Xaver comes in to clear away, tossing the hair out of his eyes. Now that he has taken off his gloves you can see the yellow chain-ring[8] on his left hand. And as the Professor finishes his watery eight-thousand-mark beer and lights a cigarette, the little folk can be heard scrambling down the stair, coming, by established custom, for their after-dinner call on Father and Mother. They storm the dining-room, after a struggle with the latch, clutched by both pairs of little hands at once; their clumsy small feet twinkle over the carpet, in red felt slippers with the socks falling down on them. With prattle and shoutings each makes for his own place: Snapper to Mother, to climb on her lap, boast of all he has eaten, and thump his fat little tum; Ellie to her Abel, so much hers because she is so very much his; because she consciously luxuriates in the deep tenderness—like all deep feeling, concealing a melancholy strain—with which he holds her small form embraced; in the love in his eyes as he kisses her little fairy hand or the sweet brow with its delicate tracery of tiny blue veins.

The little folk look like each other, with the strong undefined likeness of brother and sister. In clothing and haircut they are twins. Yet they are sharply distinguished after all, and quite on sex lines. It is a little Adam and a little Eve. Not only is Snapper the sturdier and more compact, he appears consciously to emphasize his four-year-old masculinity in speech, manner, and carriage, lifting his shoulders and letting the little arms hang down quite like a young American athlete, drawing down his mouth when he talks and seeking to give his voice a gruff and forthright ring. But all this masculinity is the result of effort rather than natively his. Born and brought up in these desolate, distracted times, he has been endowed by them with an unstable and hypersensitive nervous system and suffers greatly under life's disharmonies. He is prone to sudden anger and outbursts of bitter tears, stamping his feet at every trifle; for this reason he is his mother's special nursling and care. His round, round eyes are chestnut brown and already inclined to squint, so that he will need glasses in the near future. His little nose is long, the mouth small—the father's nose and mouth they are, more plainly than ever since the Professor shaved his pointed beard and goes smooth-faced. The pointed beard had become impossible—even professors must make some concession to the changing times.

But the little daughter sits on her father's knee, his Eleonorchen,[9] his little Eve, so much more gracious a little being, so much sweeter-faced than her brother—and he holds his cigarette away from her while she fingers his glasses with her dainty wee hands. The lenses are divided for reading and distance, and each day they tease her curiosity afresh.

At bottom he suspects that his wife's partiality may have a firmer basis than his own: that Snapper's refractory masculinity perhaps is solider stuff than his own little girl's more explicit charm and grace. But the heart will not be commanded, that he knows; and once and for all his heart belongs to the little one, as it has since the day she came, since the first time he saw

[8] Wrist chain affected by young bohemians of the time.

[9] "Little Eleanor," an affectionate diminutive form of "Eleanor."

her. Almost always when he holds her in his arms he remembers that first time: remembers the sunny room in the Women's Hospital, where Ellie first saw the light, twelve years after Bert was born. He remembers how he drew near, the mother smiling the while, and cautiously put aside the canopy of the diminutive bed that stood beside the large one. There lay the little miracle among the pillows: so well formed, so encompassed, as it were, with the harmony of sweet proportions, with little hands that even then, though so much tinier, were beautiful as now; with wide-open eyes blue as the sky and brighter than the sunshine—and almost in that very second he felt himself captured and held fast. This was love at first sight, love everlasting: a feeling unknown, unhoped for, unexpected—in so far as it could be a matter of conscious awareness; it took entire possession of him, and he understood, with joyous amazement, that this was for life.

But he understood more. He knows, does Dr. Cornelius, that there is something not quite right about this feeling, so unaware, so undreamed of, so involuntary. He has a shrewd suspicion that it is not by accident it has so utterly mastered him and bound itself up with his existence; that he had— even subconsciously—been preparing for it, or, more precisely, been prepared for it. There is, in short, something in him which at a given moment was ready to issue in such a feeling; and this something, highly extraordinary to relate, is his essence and quality as a professor of history. Dr. Cornelius, however, does not actually say this, even to himself; he merely realizes it, at odd times, and smiles a private smile. He knows that history professors do not love history because it is something that comes to pass, but only because it is something that *has* come to pass; that they hate a revolution like the present one[10] because they feel it is lawless, incoherent, irrelevant—in a word, unhistoric; that their hearts belong to the coherent, disciplined, historic past. For the temper of timelessness, the temper of eternity—thus the scholar communes with himself when he takes his walk by the river before supper—that temper broods over the past; and it is a temper much better suited to the nervous system of a history professor than are the excesses of the present. The past is immortalized; that is to say, it is dead; and death is the root of all godliness and all abiding significance. Dr. Cornelius, walking alone in the dark, has a profound insight into this truth. It is this conservative instinct of his, his sense of the eternal, that has found in his love for his little daughter a way to save itself from the wounding inflicted by the times. For father love, and a little child on its mother's breast—are not these timeless, and thus very, very holy and beautiful? Yet Cornelius, pondering there in the dark, descries something not perfectly right and good in his love. Theoretically, in the interests of science, he admits it to himself. There is something ulterior about it, in the nature of it; that something is hostility, hostility against the history of today, which is still in the making and thus not history at all, in behalf of the genuine history that has already happened—that is to say, death. Yes, passing strange though all this is, yet it is true; true in a sense, that is. His devotion to this priceless little morsel of life and new growth has something to do with death, it clings to death as against life; and that is neither right nor beautiful—in a sense. Though only the most fanatical asceticism could be capa-

[10] That is, the revolution in society after the war.

ble, on no other ground than such casual scientific perception, of tearing this purest and most precious of feelings out of his heart.

He holds his darling on his lap and her slim rosy legs hang down. He raises his brows as he talks to her, tenderly, with a half-teasing note of respect, and listens enchanted to her high, sweet little voice calling him Abel. He exchanges a look with the mother, who is caressing her Snapper and reading him a gentle lecture. He must be more reasonable, he must learn self-control; today again, under the manifold exasperations of life, he has given way to rage and behaved like a howling dervish. Cornelius casts a mistrustful glance at the big folk now and then, too; he thinks it not unlikely they are not unaware of those scientific preoccupations of his evening walks. If such be the case they do not show it. They stand there leaning their arms on their chair-backs and with a benevolence not untinctured with irony look on at the parental happiness.

The children's frocks are of a heavy, brick-red stuff, embroidered in modern "arty" style. They once belonged to Ingrid and Bert and are precisely alike, save that little knickers come out beneath Snapper's smock. And both have their hair bobbed. Snapper's is a streaky blond, inclined to turn dark. It is bristly and sticky and looks for all the world like a droll, badly fitting wig. But Ellie's is chestnut brown, glossy and fine as silk, as pleasing as her whole little personality. It covers her ears—and these ears are not a pair, one of them being the right size, the other distinctly too large. Her father will sometimes uncover this little abnormality and exclaim over it as though he had never noticed it before, which both makes Ellie giggle and covers her with shame. Her eyes are now golden brown, set far apart and with sweet gleams in them—such a clear and lovely look! The brows above are blond; the nose still unformed, with thick nostrils and almost circular holes; the mouth large and expressive, with a beautifully arching and mobile upper lip. When she laughs, dimples come in her cheeks and she shows her teeth like loosely strung pearls. So far she has lost but one tooth, which her father gently twisted out with his handkerchief after it had grown very wobbling. During this small operation she had paled and trembled very much. Her cheeks have the softness proper to her years, but they are not chubby; indeed, they are rather concave, due to her facial structure, with its somewhat prominent jaw. On one, close to the soft fall of her hair, is a downy freckle.

Ellie is not too well pleased with her looks—a sign that already she troubles about such things. Sadly she thinks it is best to admit it once for all, her face is "homely"; though the rest of her, "on the other hand," is not bad at all. She loves expressions like "on the other hand"; they sound choice and grown-up to her, and she likes to string them together, one after the other: "very likely," "probably," "after all." Snapper is self-critical too, though more in the moral sphere: he suffers from remorse for his attacks of rage and considers himself a tremendous sinner. He is quite certain that heaven is not for such as he; he is sure to go to "the bad place" when he dies, and no persuasions will convince him to the contrary—as that God sees the heart and gladly makes allowances. Obstinately he shakes his head, with the comic, crooked little peruke,[11] and vows there is no place for him

[11] Wig. (Snapper's hair looks like a wig.)

in heaven. When he has a cold he is immediately quite choked with mucus; rattles and rumbles from top to toe if you even look at him; his temperature flies up at once and he simply puffs. Nursy is pessimistic on the score of his constitution: such fat-blooded children as he might get a stroke any minute. Once she even thought she saw the moment at hand: Snapper had been in one of his berserker rages, and in the ensuing fit of penitence stood himself in the corner with his back to the room. Suddenly Nursy noticed that his face had gone all blue, far bluer, even, than her own. She raised the alarm, crying out that the child's all too rich blood had at length brought him to his final hour; and Snapper, to his vast astonishment, found himself, so far from being rebuked for evil-doing, encompassed in tenderness and anxiety—until it turned out that his color was not caused by apoplexy but by the distempering[12] on the nursery wall, which had come off on his tear-wet face.

Nursy has come downstairs too, and stands by the door, sleek-haired, owl-eyed, with her hands folded over her white apron, and a severely dignified manner born of her limited intelligence. She is very proud of the care and training she gives her nurslings and declares that they are "enveloping wonderfully." She has had seventeen suppurated teeth lately removed from her jaws and been measured for a set of symmetrical yellow ones in dark rubber gums; these now embellish her peasant face. She is obsessed with the strange conviction that these teeth of hers are the subject of general conversation, that, as it were, the sparrows on the housetops chatter of them. "Everybody knows I've had a false set put in," she will say; "there has been a great deal of foolish talk about them." She is much given to dark hints and veiled innuendo: speaks, for instance, of a certain Dr. Bleifuss,[13] whom every child knows, and "there are even some in the house who pretend to be him." All one can do with talk like this is charitably to pass it over in silence. But she teaches the children nursery rhymes: gems like:

> "Puff, puff, here comes the train!
> Puff, puff, toot, toot,
> Away it goes again,"

Or that gastronomical jingle, so suited, in its sparseness, to the times, and yet seemingly with a blitheness of its own:

> "Monday we begin the week,
> Tuesday there's a bone to pick.
> Wednesday we're half way through,
> Thursday what a great to-do!
> Friday we eat what fish we're able,
> Saturday we dance round the table.
> Sunday brings us pork and greens—
> Here's a feast for kings and queens!"

[12] Water-soluble paint. [13] "Dr. Leadfoot."

Also a certain four-line stanza with a romantic appeal, unutterable and unuttered:

> "Open the gate, open the gate
> And let the carriage drive in.
> Who is it in the carriage sits?
> A lordly sir with golden hair."

Or, finally that ballad about golden-haired Marianne who sat on a, sat on a, sat on a stone, and combed out her, combed out her, combed out her hair; and about bloodthirsty Rudolph, who pulled out a, pulled out a, pulled out a knife—and his ensuing direful end. Ellie enunciates all these ballads charmingly, with her mobile little lips, and sings them in her sweet little voice—much better than Snapper. She does everything better than he does, and he pays her honest admiration and homage and obeys her in all things except when visited by one of his attacks. Sometimes she teaches him, instructs him upon the birds in the picture book and tells him their proper names: "This is a chaffinch, Buddy, this is a bullfinch, this is a cowfinch." He has to repeat them after her. She gives him medical instruction too, teaches him the names of diseases, such as infammation of the lungs, infammation of the blood, infammation of the air. If he does not pay attention and cannot say the words after her, she stands him in the corner. Once she even boxed his ears, but was so ashamed that she stood herself in the corner for a long time. Yes, they are fast friends, two souls with but a single thought, and have all their adventures in common. They come home from a walk and relate as with one voice that they have seen two moolies and a teenty-weenty baby calf. They are on familiar terms with the kitchen, which consists of Xaver and the ladies Hinterhofer, two sisters once of the lower middle class who, in these evil days, are reduced to living *"au pair"*[14] as the phrase goes and officiating as cook and housemaid for their board and keep. The little ones have a feeling that Xaver and the Hinterhofers are on much the same footing with their father and mother as they are themselves. At least sometimes, when they have been scolded, they go downstairs and announce that the master and mistress are cross. But playing with the servants lacks charm compared with the joys of playing upstairs. The kitchen could never rise to the height of the games their father can invent. For instance, there is "four gentlemen taking a walk." When they play it Abel will crook his knees until he is the same height with themselves and go walking with them, hand in hand. They never get enough of this sport; they could walk round and round the dining-room a whole day on end, five gentlemen in all, counting the diminished Abel.

Then there is the thrilling cushion game. One of the children, usually Ellie, seats herself, unbeknownst to Abel, in his seat at table. Still as a mouse she awaits his coming. He draws near with his head in the air, descanting in loud, clear tones upon the surpassing comfort of his chair; and sits down on top of Ellie. "What's this, what's this?" says he. And bounces about, deaf to the smothered giggles exploding behind him. "Why have they put a cushion in my chair? And what a queer, hard, awkward-shaped cushion it

[14] As unpaid servants who work for their room and board.

is!" he goes on. "Frightfully uncomfortable to sit on!" And keeps pushing and bouncing about more and more on the astonishing cushion and clutching behind him into the rapturous giggling and squeaking, until at last he turns round, and the game ends with a magnificent climax of discovery and recognition. They might go through all this a hundred times without diminishing by an iota its power to thrill.

Today is no time for such joys. The imminent festivity disturbs the atmosphere, and besides there is work to be done, and, above all, the eggs to be got. Ellie has just time to recite "Puff, puff," and Cornelius to discover that her ears are not mates, when they are interrupted by the arrival of Danny, come to fetch Bert and Ingrid. Xaver, meantime, has exchanged his striped livery for an ordinary coat, in which he looks rather rough-and-ready, though as brisk and attractive as ever. So then Nursy and the children ascend to the upper regions, the Professor withdraws to his study to read, as always after dinner, and his wife bends her energies upon the sandwiches and salad that must be prepared. And she has another errand as well. Before the young people arrive she has to take her shopping basket and dash into town on her bicycle, to turn into provisions a sum of money she has in hand, which she dares not keep lest it lose all value.

Cornelius reads, leaning back in his chair, with his cigar between his middle and index fingers. First he reads Macaulay[15] on the origin of the English public debt at the end of the seventeenth century; then an article in a French periodical on the rapid increase in the Spanish debt towards the end of the sixteenth. Both these for his lecture on the morrow. He intends to compare the astonishing prosperity which accompanied the phenomenon in England with its fatal effects a hundred years earlier in Spain, and to analyze the ethical and psychological grounds of the difference in results. For that will give him a chance to refer back from the England of William III, which is the actual subject in hand, to the time of Philip II and the Counter-Reformation, which is his own special field. He has already written a valuable work on this period; it is much cited and got him his professorship. While his cigar burns down and gets strong, he excogitates a few pensive sentences in a key of gentle melancholy, to be delivered before his class next day: about the practically hopeless struggle carried on by the belated Philip against the whole trend of history: against the new, the kingdom-disrupting power of the Germanic ideal of freedom and individual liberty. And about the persistent, futile struggle of the aristocracy, condemned by God and rejected of man, against the forces of progress and change. He savors his sentences; keeps on polishing them while he puts back the books he has been using; then goes upstairs for the usual pause in his day's work, the hour with drawn blinds and closed eyes, which he so imperatively needs. But today, he recalls, he will rest under disturbed conditions, amid the bustle of preparations for the feast. He smiles to find his

[15] Thomas Babington Macaulay, English historian (1800–1859). The lecture Cornelius is planning relates economic conditions to ethical and religious matters by comparing conditions in seventeenth-century England, the time of William III, to those in sixteenth-century Spain, the time of Philip II and the Counter-Reformation (a reform movement within the Roman Catholic Church in response to the sixteenth-century Reformation, led by Martin Luther). The topic obviously concerns him because of the implicit parallel with the Germany of his own day.

heart giving a mild flutter at the thought. Disjointed phrases on the theme
of black-clad Philip and his times mingle with a confused consciousness that
they will soon be dancing down below. For five minutes or so he falls
asleep.

As he lies and rests he can hear the sound of the garden gate and the
repeated ringing at the bell. Each time a little pang goes through him, of
excitement and suspense, at the thought that the young people have begun
to fill the floor below. And each time he smiles at himself again—though
even his smile is slightly nervous, is tinged with the pleasurable anticipa-
tions people always feel before a party. At half past four—it is already
dark—he gets up and washes at the wash-stand. The basin has been out of
repair for two years. It is supposed to tip, but has broken away from its
socket on one side and cannot be mended because there is nobody to mend
it; neither replaced because no shop can supply another. So it has to be
hung up above the vent and emptied by lifting in both hands and pouring
out the water. Cornelius shakes his head over this basin, as he does several
times a day—whenever, in fact, he has occasion to use it. He finishes his
toilet with care, standing under the ceiling light to polish his glasses till they
shine. Then he goes downstairs.

On his way to the dining-room he hears the gramophone already going,
and the sound of voices. He puts on a polite, society air; at his tongue's end
is the phrase he means to utter: "Pray don't let me disturb you," as he
passes directly into the dining-room for his tea. "Pray don't let me disturb
you"—it seems to him precisely the *mot juste*;[16] towards the guests cordial
and considerate, for himself a very bulwark.

The lower floor is lighted up, all the bulbs in the chandelier are burning
save one that has burned out. Cornelius pauses on a lower step and surveys
the entrance hall. It looks pleasant and cozy in the bright light, with its copy
of Marées[17] over the brick chimney-piece, its wainscoted walls—wainscoted
in soft wood—and red-carpeted floor, where the guests stand in groups,
chatting, each with his tea-cup and slice of bread-and-butter spread with
anchovy paste. There is a festal haze, faint scents of hair and clothing and
human breath come to him across the room, it is all characteristic and
familiar and highly evocative. The door into the dressing-room is open,
guests are still arriving.

A large group of people is rather bewildering at first sight. The Profes-
sor takes in only the general scene. He does not see Ingrid, who is standing
just at the foot of the steps, in a dark silk frock with a pleated collar falling
softly over the shoulders, and bare arms. She smiles up at him, nodding
and showing her lovely teeth.

"Rested?" she asks, for his private ear. With a quite unwarranted start
he recognizes her, and she presents some of her friends.

"May I introduce Herr Zuber?" she says. "And this is Fräulein
Plaichinger."

Herr Zuber is insignificant. But Fräulein Plaichinger is a perfect

[16] The exact word (French).
[17] The works of the German painter Hans von Marées (1837–1887) had been rediscovered
and become popular in the 1890s.

Germania,[18] blond and voluptuous, arrayed in floating draperies. She has a snub nose, and answers the Professor's salutation in the high, shrill pipe so many stout women have.

"Delighted to meet you," he says. "How nice of you to come! A class-mate of Ingrid's, I suppose?"

And Herr Zuber is a golfing partner of Ingrid's. He is in business; he works in his uncle's brewery. Cornelius makes a few jokes about the thin-ness of the beer and professes to believe that Herr Zuber could easily do something about the quality if he would. "But pray don't let me disturb you," he goes on, and turns towards the dining-room.

"There comes Max," says Ingrid. "Max, you sweep, what do you mean by rolling up at this time of day?" For such is the way they talk to each other, offensively to an older ear; of social forms, of hospitable warmth, there is no faintest trace. They all call each other by their first names.

A young man comes up to them out of the dressing-room and makes his bow; he has an expanse of white shirt-front and a little black string tie. He is as pretty as a picture, dark, with rosy cheeks, clean-shaven of course, but with just a sketch of side-whisker. Not a ridiculous or flashy beauty, not like a gypsy fiddler, but just charming to look at, in a winning, well-bred way, with kind dark eyes. He even wears his dinner-jacket a little awkwardly.

"Please don't scold me, Cornelia," he says; "it's the idiotic lectures." And Ingrid presents him to her father as Herr Hergesell.

Well, and so this is Herr Hergesell. He knows his manners, does Herr Hergesell, and thanks the master of the house quite ingratiatingly for his invitation as they shake hands. "I certainly seem to have missed the bus," says he jocosely. "Of course I have lectures today up to four o'clock; I would have; and after that I had to go home to change." Then he talks about his pumps, with which he has just been struggling in the dressing-room.

"I brought them with me in a bag," he goes on. "Mustn't tramp all over the carpet in our brogues—it's not done. Well, I was ass enough not to fetch along a shoe-horn, and I find I simply can't get in! What a sell! They are the tightest I've ever had, the numbers don't tell you a thing, and all the leather today is just cast iron. It's not leather at all. My poor finger"—he confidingly displays a reddened digit and once more characterizes the whole thing as a "sell," and a putrid sell into the bargain. He really does talk just as Ingrid said he did, with a peculiar nasal drawl, not affectedly in the least, but merely because that is the way of all the Hergesells.

Dr. Cornelius says it is very careless of them not to keep a shoe-horn in the cloak-room and displays proper sympathy with the mangled finger. "But now you *really* must not let me disturb you any longer," he goes on. "*Auf wiedersehen!*"[19] And he crosses the hall into the dining-room.

There are guests there too, drinking tea; the family table is pulled out. But the Professor goes at once to his own little upholstered corner with the electric light bulb above it—the nook where he usually drinks his tea. His wife is sitting there talking with Bert and two other young men, one of them Herzl, whom Cornelius knows and greets; the other a typical

[18] Female figure embodying Germany. [19]"Until we meet again!"; Goodbye.

"Wandervogel"[20] named Möller, a youth who obviously neither owns nor cares to own the correct evening dress of the middle classes (in fact, there is no such thing any more), nor to ape the manners of a gentleman (and, in fact, there is no such thing any more either). He has a wilderness of hair, horn spectacles, and a long neck, and wears golf stockings and a belted blouse. His regular occupation, the Professor learns, is banking, but he is by way of being an amateur folklorist and collects folksongs from all localities and in all languages. He sings them, too, and at Ingrid's command has brought his guitar; it is hanging in the dressing-room in an oilcloth case. Herzl, the actor, is small and slight, but he has a strong growth of black beard, as you can tell by the thick coat of powder on his cheeks. His eyes are larger than life, with a deep and melancholy glow. He has put on rouge besides the powder—those dull carmine high-lights on the cheeks can be nothing but a cosmetic. "Queer," thinks the Professor. "You would think a man would be one thing or the other—not melancholic and use face paint at the same time. It's a psychological contradiction. How can a melancholy man rouge? But here we have a perfect illustration of the abnormality of the artist soul-form. It can make possible a contradiction like this—perhaps it even consists in the contradiction. All very interesting— and no reason whatever for not being polite to him. Politeness is a primitive convention—and legitimate. . . . Do take some lemon, Herr Hofschauspieler!"[21]

Court actors and court theaters—there are no such things any more, really. But Herzl relishes the sound of the title, notwithstanding he is a revolutionary artist. This must be another contradiction inherent in his soul-form; so, at least, the Professor assumes, and he is probably right. The flattery he is guilty of is a sort of atonement for his previous hard thoughts about the rouge.

"Thank you so much—it's really too good of you, sir," says Herzl, quite embarrassed. He is so overcome that he almost stammers; only his perfect enunciation saves him. His whole bearing towards his hostess and the master of the house is exaggeratedly polite. It is almost as though he had a bad conscience in respect of his rouge; as though an inward compulsion had driven him to put it on, but now, seeing it through the Professor's eyes, he disapproves of it himself, and thinks, by an air of humility towards the whole of unrouged society, to mitigate its effect.

They drink their tea and chat: about Möller's folksongs, about Basque folksongs and Spanish folksongs; from which they pass to the new production of *Don Carlos*[22] at the Stadttheater, in which Herzl plays the title-rôle. He talks about his own rendering of the part and says he hopes his conception of the character has unity. They go on to criticize the rest of the cast, the setting, and the production as a whole; and Cornelius is struck, rather painfully, to find the conversation trending towards his own special province, back to Spain and the Counter-Reformation. He has done nothing at all to give it this turn, he is perfectly innocent, and hopes it does not look as though he had sought an occasion to play the professor. He won-

[20] A "bird of passage," a wanderer belonging to a German youth movement.
[21] "Mr. Court-Theater Actor!"
[22] A play by the German Romantic playwright Friedrich Schiller (1759–1805).

ders, and falls silent, feeling relieved when the little folk come up to the table. Ellie and Snapper have on their blue velvet Sunday frocks; they are permitted to partake in the festivities up to bed-time. They look shy and large-eyed as they say how-do-you-do to the strangers and, under pressure, repeat their names and ages. Herr Möller does nothing but gaze at them solemnly, but Herzl is simply ravished. He rolls his eyes up to heaven and puts his hands over his mouth; he positively blesses them. It all, no doubt, comes from his heart, but he is so addicted to theatrical methods of making an impression and getting an effect that both words and behavior ring frightfully false. And even his enthusiasm for the little folk looks too much like part of his general craving to make up for the rouge on his cheeks.

The tea-table has meanwhile emptied of guests, and dancing is going on in the hall. The children run off, the Professor prepares to retire. "Go and enjoy yourselves," he says to Möller and Herzl, who have sprung from their chairs as he rises from his. They shake hands and he withdraws into his study, his peaceful kingdom, where he lets down the blinds, turns on the desk lamp, and sits down to his work.

It is work which can be done, if necessary, under disturbed conditions: nothing but a few letters and a few notes. Of course, Cornelius's mind wanders. Vague impressions float through it: Herr Hergesell's refractory pumps, the high pipe in that plump body of the Plaichinger female. As he writes, or leans back in his chair and stares into space, his thoughts go back to Herr Möller's collection of Basque folksongs, to Herzl's posings and humility, to "his" Carlos and the court of Philip II. There is something strange, he thinks, about conversations. They are so ductile, they will flow of their own accord in the direction of one's dominating interest. Often and often he has seen this happen. And while he is thinking, he is listening to the sounds next door—rather subdued, he finds them. He hears only voices, no sound of footsteps. The dancers do not glide or circle round the room; they merely walk about over the carpet, which does not hamper their movements in the least. Their way of holding each other is quite different and strange, and they move to the strains of the gramophone, to the weird music of the new world. He concentrates on the music and makes out that it is a jazz-band record, with various percussion instruments and the clack and clatter of castanets, which, however, are not even faintly suggestive of Spain, but merely jazz like the rest. No, not Spain. . . . His thoughts are back at their old round.

Half an hour goes by. It occurs to him it would be no more than friendly to go and contribute a box of cigarettes to the festivities next door. Too bad to ask the young people to smoke their own—though they have probably never thought of it. He goes into the empty dining-room and takes a box from his supply in the cupboard: not the best ones, nor yet the brand he himself prefers, but a certain long, thin kind he is not averse to getting rid of—after all, they are nothing but youngsters. He takes the box into the hall, holds it up with a smile, and deposits it on the mantel-shelf. After which he gives a look round and returns to his own room.

There comes a lull in dance and music. The guests stand about the room in groups or round the table at the window or are seated in a circle by the fireplace. Even the built-in stairs, with their worn velvet carpet, are

crowded with young folk as in an amphitheater: Max Hergesell is there, leaning back with one elbow on the step above and gesticulating with his free hand as he talks to the shrill, voluptuous Plaichinger. The floor of the hall is nearly empty, save just in the center: there, directly beneath the chandelier, the two little ones in their blue velvet frocks clutch each other in an awkward embrace and twirl silently round and round, oblivious of all else. Cornelius, as he passes, strokes their hair, with a friendly word; it does not distract them from their small solemn preoccupation. But at his own door he turns to glance round and sees young Hergesell push himself off the stair by his elbow—probably because he noticed the Professor. He comes down into the arena, takes Ellie out of her brother's arms, and dances with her himself. It looks very comic, without the music, and he crouches down just as Cornelius does when he goes walking with the four gentlemen, holding the fluttered Ellie as though she were grown up and taking little "shimmying" steps. Everybody watches with huge enjoyment, the gramophone is put on again, dancing becomes general. The Professor stands and looks, with his hand on the door-knob. He nods and laughs; when he finally shuts himself into his study the mechanical smile still lingers on his lips.

Again he turns over pages by his desk lamp, takes notes, attends to a few simple matters. After a while he notices that the guests have forsaken the entrance hall for his wife's drawing-room, into which there is a door from his own study as well. He hears their voices and the sounds of a guitar being tuned. Herr Möller, it seems, is to sing—and does so. He twangs the strings of his instrument and sings in a powerful bass a ballad in a strange tongue, possibly Swedish. The Professor does not succeed in identifying it, though he listens attentively to the end, after which there is great applause. The sound is deadened by the portière that hangs over the dividing door. The young bank-clerk begins another song. Cornelius goes softly in.

It is half-dark in the drawing-room; the only light is from the shaded standard lamp, beneath which Möller sits, on the divan, with his legs crossed, picking his strings. His audience is grouped easily about; as there are not enough seats, some stand, and more, among them many young ladies, are simply sitting on the floor with their hands clasped round their knees or even with their legs stretched out before them. Hergesell sits thus, in his dinner-jacket, next the piano, with Fräulein Plaichinger beside him. Frau Cornelius is holding both children on her lap as she sits in her easy-chair opposite the singer. Snapper, the Boeotian,[23] begins to talk loud and clear in the middle of the song and has to be intimidated with hushings and finger-shakings. Never, never would Ellie allow herself to be guilty of such conduct. She sits there daintily erect and still on her mother's knee. The Professor tries to catch her eye and exchange a private signal with his little girl; but she does not see him. Neither does she seem to be looking at the singer. Her gaze is directed lower down.

Möller sings the "joli tambour":[24]

[23] A barbarian. (The ancient Athenians joked about the provinciality of the residents of Boeotia, a remote area of Greece.)
[24] The "pretty drum" (French), a kind of folksong.

"Sire, mon roi, donnez-moi votre fille—"[25]

They are all enchanted. "How good!" Hergesell is heard to say, in the odd, nasally condescending Hergesell tone. The next one is a beggar ballad, to a tune composed by young Möller himself; it elicits a storm of applause:

> "Gypsy lassie a-goin' to the fair,
> Huzza!
> Gypsy laddie a-goin' to be there—
> Huzza, diddlety umpty dido!"

Laughter and high spirits, sheer reckless hilarity, reigns after this jovial ballad. "Frightfully good!" Hergesell comments again, as before. Follows another popular song, this time a Hungarian one; Möller sings it in its own outlandish tongue, and most effectively. The Professor applauds with ostentation. It warms his heart and does him good, this outcropping of artistic, historic, and cultural elements all amongst the shimmying. He goes up to young Möller and congratulates him, talks about the songs and their sources, and Möller promises to lend him a certain annotated book of folksongs. Cornelius is the more cordial because all the time, as fathers do, he has been comparing the parts and achievements of this young stranger with those of his own son, and being gnawed by envy and chagrin. This young Möller, he is thinking, is a capable bank clerk (though about Möller's capacity he knows nothing whatever) and has this special gift besides, which must have taken talent and energy to cultivate. "And here is my poor Bert, who knows nothing and can do nothing and thinks of nothing except playing the clown, without even talent for that!" He tries to be just; he tells himself that, after all, Bert has innate refinement; that probably there is a good deal more to him than there is to the successful Möller; that perhaps he has even something of the poet in him, and his dancing and table-waiting are due to mere boyish folly and the distraught times. But paternal envy and pessimism win the upper hand; when Möller begins another song, Dr. Cornelius goes back to his room.

He works as before, with divided attention, at this and that, while it gets on for seven o'clock. Then he remembers a letter he may just as well write, a short letter and not very important, but letter-writing is wonderful for the way it takes up the time, and it is almost half past when he has finished. At half past eight the Italian salad will be served; so now is the prescribed moment for the Professor to go out into the wintry darkness to post his letters and take his daily quantum of fresh air and exercise. They are dancing again, and he will have to pass through the hall to get his hat and coat; but they are used to him now, he need not stop and beg them not to be disturbed. He lays away his papers, takes up the letters he has written, and goes out. But he sees his wife sitting near the door of his room and pauses a little by her easy-chair.

She is watching the dancing. Now and then the big folk or some of their guests stop to speak to her; the party is at its height, and there are more onlookers than these two: blue-faced Ann is standing at the bottom of the

[25]"Lord, my king, give me your daughter."

stairs, in all the dignity of her limitations. She is waiting for the children, who simply cannot get their fill of these unwonted festivities, and watching over Snapper, lest his all too rich blood be churned to the danger-point by too much twirling round. And not only the nursery but the kitchen takes an interest: Xaver and the two ladies Hinterhofer are standing by the pantry door looking on with relish. Fräulein Walburga, the elder of the two sunken sisters (the culinary section—she objects to being called a cook), is a whimsical, good-natured sort, brown-eyed, wearing glasses with thick circular lenses; the nose-piece is wound with a bit of rag to keep it from pressing on her nose. Fräulein Cecilia is younger, though not so precisely young either. Her bearing is as self-assertive as usual, this being her way of sustaining her dignity as a former member of the middle class. For Fräulein Cecilia feels acutely her descent into the ranks of domestic service. She positively declines to wear a cap or other badge of servitude, and her hardest trial is on the Wednesday evening when she has to serve the dinner while Xaver has his afternoon out. She hands the dishes with averted face and elevated nose—a fallen queen; and so distressing is it to behold her degradation that one evening when the little folk happened to be at table and saw her they both with one accord burst into tears. Such anguish is unknown to young Xaver. He enjoys serving and does it with an ease born of practice as well as talent, for he was once a "piccolo."[26] But otherwise he is a thorough-paced good-for-nothing and windbag—with quite distinct traits of character of his own, as his long-suffering employers are always ready to concede, but perfectly impossible and a bag of wind for all that. One must just take him as he is, they think, and not expect figs from thistles. He is the child and product of the disrupted times, a perfect specimen of his generation, follower of the revolution, Bolshevist sympathizer. The Professor's name for him is the "minute-man," because he is always to be counted on in any sudden crisis, if only it address his sense of humor or love of novelty, and will display therein amazing readiness and resource. But he utterly lacks a sense of duty and can as little be trained to the performance of the daily round and common task as some kinds of dog can be taught to jump over a stick. It goes so plainly against the grain that criticism is disarmed. One becomes resigned. On grounds that appealed to him as unusual and amusing he would be ready to turn out of his bed at any hour of the night. But he simply cannot get up before eight in the morning, he cannot do it, he will not jump over the stick. Yet all day long the evidence of this free and untrammelled existence, the sound of his mouth organ, his joyous whistle, or his raucous but expressive voice lifted in song, rises to the hearing of the world abovestairs; and the smoke of his cigarettes fills the pantry. While the Hinterhofer ladies work he stands and looks on. Of a morning while the Professor is breakfasting, he tears the leaf off the study calendar—but does not lift a finger to dust the room. Dr. Cornelius has often told him to leave the calendar alone, for he tends to tear off two leaves at a time and thus to add to the general confusion. But young Xaver appears to find joy in this activity, and will not be deprived of it.

Again, he is fond of children, a winning trait. He will throw himself into

[26] Apprentice waiter.

games with the little folk in the garden, make and mend their toys with great ingenuity, even read aloud from their books—and very droll it sounds in his thick-lipped pronunciation. With his whole soul he loves the cinema; after an evening spent there he inclines to melancholy and yearning and talking to himself. Vague hopes stir in him that some day he may make his fortune in that gay world and belong to it by rights—hopes based on his shock of hair and his physical agility and daring. He likes to climb the ash tree in the front garden, mounting branch by branch to the very top and frightening everybody to death who sees him. Once there he lights a cigarette and smokes it as he sways to and fro, keeping a lookout for a cinema director who might chance to come along and engage him.

If he changed his striped jacket for mufti,[27] he might easily dance with the others and no one would notice the difference. For the big folk's friends are rather anomalous in their clothing: evening dress is worn by a few, but it is by no means the rule. There is quite a sprinkling of guests, both male and female, in the same general style as Möller the ballad-singer. The Professor is familiar with the circumstances of most of this young generation he is watching as he stands beside his wife's chair; he has heard them spoken of by name. They are students at the high school or at the School of Applied Art; they lead, at least the masculine portion, that precarious and scrambling existence which is purely the product of the time. There is a tall, pale, spindling youth, the son of a dentist, who lives by speculation. From all the Professor hears, he is a perfect Aladdin.[28] He keeps a car, treats his friends to champagne suppers, and showers presents upon them on every occasion, costly little trifles in mother-of-pearl and gold. So today he has brought gifts to the young givers of the feast: for Bert a gold lead-pencil, and for Ingrid a pair of earrings of barbaric size, great gold circlets that fortunately do not have to go through the little ear lobe, but are fastened over it by means of a clip. The big folk come laughing to their parents to display these trophies; and the parents shake their heads even while they admire—Aladdin bowing over and over from afar.

The young people appear to be absorbed in their dancing—if the performance they are carrying out with so much still concentration can be called dancing. They stride across the carpet, slowly, according to some unfathomable prescript, strangely embraced; in the newest attitude, tummy advanced and shoulders high, waggling the hips. They do not get tired, because nobody could. There is no such thing as heightened color or heaving bosoms. Two girls may dance together or two young men—it is all the same. They move to the exotic strains of the gramophone, played with the loudest needles to procure the maximum of sound: shimmies, foxtrots, one-steps, double foxes, African shimmies, Java dances, and Creole polkas, the wild musky melodies follow one another, now furious, now languishing, a monotonous Negro program in unfamiliar rhythm, to a clacking, clashing, and strumming orchestral accompaniment.

"What is that record?" Cornelius inquires of Ingrid, as she passes him by in the arms of the pale young speculator, with reference to the piece

[27] Ordinary street clothing.
[28] Fabulously rich person (from a story in the *Arabian Nights:* "Aladdin and His Wonderful Lamp").

then playing, whose alternate languors and furies he finds comparatively pleasing and showing a certain resourcefulness in detail.

"*Prince of Pappenheim:* 'Console thee, dearest child,' " she answers, and smiles pleasantly back at him with her white teeth.

The cigarette smoke wreathes beneath the chandelier. The air is blue with a festal haze compact of sweet and thrilling ingredients that stir the blood with memories of green-sick pains and are particularly poignant to those whose youth—like the Professor's own—has been oversensitive. . . . The little folk are still on the floor. They are allowed to stay up until eight, so great is their delight in the party. The guests have got used to their presence; in their own way, they have their place in the doings of the evening. They have separated, anyhow: Snapper revolves all alone in the middle of the carpet, in his little blue velvet smock, while Ellie is running after one of the dancing couples, trying to hold the man fast by his coat. It is Max Hergesell and Fräulein Plaichinger. They dance well, it is a pleasure to watch them. One has to admit that these mad modern dances, when the right people dance them, are not so bad after all—they have something quite taking. Young Hergesell is a capital leader, dances according to rule, yet with individuality. So it looks. With what aplomb can he walk backwards—when space permits! And he knows how to be graceful standing still in a crowd. And his partner supports him well, being unsuspectedly lithe and buoyant, as fat people often are. They look at each other, they are talking, paying no heed to Ellie, though others are smiling to see the child's persistence. Dr. Cornelius tries to catch up his little sweetheart as she passes and draw her to him. But Ellie eludes him, almost peevishly; her dear Abel is nothing to her now. She braces her little arms against his chest and turns her face away with a persecuted look. Then escapes to follow her fancy once more.

The Professor feels an involuntary twinge. Uppermost in his heart is hatred for this party, with its power to intoxicate and estrange his darling child. His love for her—that not quite disinterested, not quite unexceptionable love of his—is easily wounded. He wears a mechanical smile, but his eyes have clouded, and he stares fixedly at a point in the carpet, between the dancers' feet.

"The children ought to go to bed," he tells his wife. But she pleads for another quarter of an hour; she has promised already, and they do love it so! He smiles again and shakes his head, stands so a moment and then goes across to the cloakroom, which is full of coats and hats and scarves and overshoes. He has trouble in rummaging out his own coat, and Max Hergesell comes out of the hall, wiping his brow.

"Going out, sir?" he asks, in Hergesellian accents, dutifully helping the older man on with his coat. "Silly business this, with my pumps," he says. "They pinch like hell. The brutes are simply too tight for me, quite apart from the bad leather. They press just here on the ball of my great toe"—he stands on one foot and holds the other in his hand—"it's simply unbearable. There's nothing for it but to take them off; my brogues will have to do the business. . . . Oh, let me help you, sir."

"Thanks," says Cornelius. "Don't trouble. Get rid of your own tormentors. . . . Oh, thanks very much!" For Hergesell has gone on one knee to snap the fasteners of his snowboots.

Once more the Professor expresses his gratitude; he is pleased and touched by so much sincere respect and youthful readiness to serve. "Go and enjoy yourself," he counsels. "Change your shoes and make up for what you have been suffering. Nobody can dance in shoes that pinch. Good-bye, I must be off to get a breath of fresh air."

"I'm going to dance with Ellie now," calls Hergesell after him. "She'll be a first-rate dancer when she grows up, and that I'll swear to."

"Think so?" Cornelius answers, already half out. "Well, you are a connoisseur, I'm sure. Don't get curvature of the spine with stooping."

He nods again and goes. 'Fine lad," he thinks as he shuts the door. "Student of engineering. Knows what he's bound for, got a good clear head, and so well set up and pleasant too." And again paternal envy rises as he compares his poor Bert's status with this young man's, which he puts in the rosiest light that his son's may look the darker. Thus he sets out on his evening walk.

He goes up the avenue, crosses the bridge, and walks along the bank on the other side as far as the next bridge but one. The air is wet and cold, with a little snow now and then. He turns up his coat collar and slips the crook of his cane over the arm behind his back. Now and then he ventilates his lungs with a long deep breath of the night air. As usual when he walks, his mind reverts to his professional preoccupations, he thinks about his lectures and the things he means to say tomorrow about Philip's struggle against the Germanic revolution, things steeped in melancholy and penetratingly just. Above all just, he thinks. For in one's dealings with the young it behooves one to display the scientific spirit, to exhibit the principles of enlightenment—not only for purposes of mental discipline, but on the human and individual side, in order not to wound them or indirectly offend their political sensibilities; particularly in these days, when there is so much tinder in the air, opinions are so frightfully split up and chaotic, and you may so easily incur attacks from one party or the other, or even give rise to scandal, by taking sides on a point of history. "And taking sides is unhistoric anyhow," so he muses. "Only justice, only impartiality is historic." And could not, properly considered, be otherwise. . . . For justice can have nothing of youthful fire and blithe, fresh, loyal conviction. It is by nature melancholy. And, being so, has secret affinity with the lost cause and the forlorn hope rather than with the fresh and blithe and loyal—perhaps this affinity is its very essence and without it it would not exist at all! . . . "And is there then no such thing as justice?" the Professor asks himself, and ponders the question so deeply that he absently posts his letters in the next box and turns round to go home. This thought of his is unsettling and disturbing to the scientific mind—but is it not after all itself scientific, psychological, conscientious, and therefore to be accepted without prejudice, no matter how upsetting? In the midst of which musings Dr. Cornelius finds himself back at his own door.

On the outer threshold stands Xaver, and seems to be looking for him.

"Herr Professor," says Xaver, tossing back his hair, "go upstairs to Ellie straight off. She's in a bad way."

"What's the matter?" asks Cornelius in alarm. "Is she ill?"

"No-o, not to say ill," answers Xaver. "She's just in a bad way and crying

fit to bust her little heart. It's along o' that chap with the shirtfront that danced with her—Herr Hergesell. She couldn't be got to go upstairs peaceably, not at no price at all, and she's b'en crying bucketfuls."

"Nonsense," says the Professor, who has entered and is tossing off his things in the cloakroom. He says no more; opens the glass door and without a glance at the guests turns swiftly to the stairs. Takes them two at a time, crosses the upper hall and the small room leading into the nursery. Xaver follows at his heels, but stops at the nursery door.

A bright light still burns within, showing the gay frieze that runs all round the room, the large row of shelves heaped with a confusion of toys, the rocking-horse on his swaying platform, with red-varnished nostrils and raised hoofs. On the linoleum lie other toys—building blocks, railway trains, a little trumpet. The two white cribs stand not far apart, Ellie's in the window corner, Snapper's out in the room.

Snapper is asleep. He has said his prayers in loud, ringing tones, prompted by Nurse, and gone off at once into vehement, profound, and rosy slumber—from which a cannonball fired at close range could not rouse him. He lies with both fists flung back on the pillows on either side of the tousled head with its funny crooked little slumber-tossed wig.

A circle of females surrounds Ellie's bed: not only blue-faced Ann is there, but the Hinterhofer ladies too, talking to each other and to her. They make way as the Professor comes up and reveal the child sitting all pale among her pillows, sobbing and weeping more bitterly than he has ever seen her sob and weep in her life. Her lovely little hands lie on the coverlet in front of her, the nightgown with its narrow lace border has slipped down from her shoulder—such a thin, birdlike little shoulder— and the sweet head Cornelius loves so well, set on the neck like a flower on its stalk, her head is on one side, with the eyes rolled up to the corner between wall and ceiling above her head. For there she seems to envisage the anguish of her heart and even to nod to it—either on purpose or because her head wobbles as her body is shaken with the violence of her sobs. Her eyes rain down tears. The bow-shaped lips are parted, like a little *mater dolorosa's,*[29] and from them issue long, low wails that in nothing resemble the unnecessary and exasperating shrieks of a naughty child, but rise from the deep extremity of her heart and wake in the Professor's own a sympathy that is well-nigh intolerable. He has never seen his darling so before. His feelings find immediate vent in an attack on the ladies Hinterhofer.

"What about the supper?" he asks sharply. "There must be a great deal to do. Is my wife being left to do it alone?"

For the acute sensibilities of the former middle class this is quite enough. The ladies withdraw in righteous indignation, and Xaver Kleingutl jeers at them as they pass out. Having been born to low life instead of achieving it, he never loses a chance to mock at their fallen state.

"Childie, childie," murmurs Cornelius, and sitting down by the crib enfolds the anguished Ellie in his arms. "What is the trouble with my darling?"

[29] A *mater dolorosa* is the conventional figure in art of Mary grieving for Christ.

She bedews his face with her tears.

"Abel . . . Abel . . ." she stammers between sobs. "Why—isn't Max—my brother? Max ought to be—my brother!"

Alas, alas! What mischance is this? Is this what the party has wrought, with its fatal atmosphere? Cornelius glances helplessly up at blue-faced Ann standing there in all the dignity of her limitations with her hands before her on her apron. She purses up her mouth and makes a long face. "It's pretty young," she says, "for the female instincts to be showing up."

"Hold your tongue," snaps Cornelius, in his agony. He has this much to be thankful for, that Ellie does not turn from him now; she does not push him away as she did downstairs, but clings to him in her need, while she reiterates her absurd, bewildered prayer that Max might be her brother, or with a fresh burst of desire demands to be taken downstairs so that he can dance with her again. But Max, of course, is dancing with Fräulein Plaichinger, that behemoth who is his rightful partner and has every claim upon him; whereas Ellie—never, thinks the Professor, his heart torn with the violence of his pity, never has she looked so tiny and birdlike as now, when she nestles to him shaken with sobs and all unaware of what is happening in her little soul. No, she does not know. She does not comprehend that her suffering is on account of Fraülein Plaichinger, fat, overgrown, and utterly within her rights in dancing with Max Hergesell, whereas Ellie may only do it once, by way of a joke, although she is incomparably the more charming of the two. Yet it would be quite mad to reproach young Hergesell with the state of affairs or to make fantastic demands upon him. No, Ellie's suffering is without help or healing and must be covered up. Yet just as it is without understanding, so it is also without restraint—and that is what makes it so horribly painful. Xaver and blue-faced Ann do not feel this pain, it does not affect them—either because of native callousness or because they accept it as the way of nature. But the Professor's fatherly heart is quite torn by it, and by a distressful horror of this passion, so hopeless and so absurd.

Of no avail to hold forth to poor Ellie on the subject of the perfectly good little brother she already has. She only casts a distraught and scornful glance over at the other crib, where Snapper lies vehemently slumbering, and with fresh tears calls again for Max. Of no avail either the promise of a long, long walk tomorrow, all five gentlemen, round and round the dining room table; or a dramatic description of the thrilling cushion games they will play. No, she will listen to none of all this, nor to lying down and going to sleep. She will not sleep, she will sit bolt upright and suffer. . . . But on a sudden they stop and listen, Abel and Ellie; listen to something miraculous that is coming to pass, that is approaching by strides, two strides, to the nursery door, that now overwhelmingly appears. . . .

It is Xaver's work, not a doubt of that. He has not remained by the door where he stood to gloat over the ejection of the Hinterhofers. No, he has bestirred himself, taken a notion; likewise steps to carry it out. Downstairs he has gone, twitched Herr Hergesell's sleeve, and made a thick-lipped request. So here they both are. Xaver, having done his part, remains by the door; but Max Hergesell comes up to Ellie's crib; in his dinner jacket, with his sketchy side-whiskers and charming black eyes; obviously quite pleased

with his rôle of swan knight[30] and fairy prince, as one who should say: "See, here am I, now all losses are restored and sorrows end!"[31]

Cornelius is almost as much overcome as Ellie herself.

"Just look," he says feebly, "look who's here. This is uncommonly good of you, Herr Hergesell."

"Not a bit of it," says Hergesell. "Why shouldn't I come to say good-night to my fair partner?"

And he approaches the bars of the crib, behind which Ellie sits struck mute. She smiles blissfully through her tears. A funny, high little note that is half a sigh of relief comes from her lips, then she looks dumbly up at her swan knight with her golden-brown eyes—tear-swollen though they are, so much more beautiful than the fat Plaichinger's. She does not put up her arms. Her joy, like her grief, is without understanding; but she does not do that. The lovely little hands lie quiet on the coverlet, and Max Hergesell stands with his arms leaning over the rail as on a balcony.

"And now," he says smartly, "she need not 'sit the livelong night and weep upon her bed'!"[32] He looks at the Professor to make sure he is receiving due credit for the quotation. "Ha ha!" he laughs, "she's beginning young. 'Console thee, dearest child!' Never mind, you're all right! Just as you are you'll be wonderful! You've only got to grow up. . . . And you'll lie down and go to sleep like a good girl, now I've come to say good-night? And not cry any more, little Lorelei?"[33]

Ellie looks up at him, transfigured. One birdlike shoulder is bare; the Professor draws the lace-trimmed nighty over it. There comes into his mind a sentimental story he once read about a dying child who longs to see a clown he had once, with unforgettable ecstasy, beheld in a circus. And they bring the clown to the bedside marvellously arrayed, embroidered before and behind with silver butterflies; and the child dies happy. Max Hergesell is not embroidered, and Ellie, thank God, is not going to die, she has only been "in a bad way." But, after all, the effect is the same. Young Hergesell leans over the bars of the crib and rattles on, more for the father's ear than the child's, but Ellie does not know that—and the father's feelings towards him are a most singular mixture of thankfulness, embarrassment, and hatred.

"Good night, little Lorelei," says Hergesell, and gives her his hand through the bars. Her pretty, soft, white little hand is swallowed up in the grasp of his big, strong, red one. "Sleep well," he says, "and sweet dreams! But don't dream about me—God forbid! Not at your age—ha ha!" And then the fairy clown's visit is at an end. Cornelius accompanies him to the door. "No, no, positively, no thanks called for, don't mention it," he large-heartedly protests; and Xaver goes downstairs with him, to help serve the Italian salad.

[30] Lohengrin, in Wagner's opera (1847) of that name, enters in one scene in a boat drawn by swans.

[31] Shakespeare's Sonnet 30: "But if the while I think on thee, dear friend, / All losses are restor'd and sorrows end."

[32] From a lyric in Johann Wolfgang von Goethe's *Wilhelm Meister's Apprenticeship* (1796), Chapter 13.

[33] A siren who, in German legend, lured sailors onto rocks along the Rhine with her singing.

But Dr. Cornelius returns to Ellie, who is now lying down, with her cheek pressed into her flat little pillow.

"Well, wasn't that lovely?" he says as he smooths the covers. She nods, with one last little sob. For a quarter of an hour he sits beside her and watches while she falls asleep in her turn, beside the little brother who found the right way so much earlier than she. Her silky brown hair takes the enchanting fall it always does when she sleeps; deep, deep lie the lashes over the eyes that late so abundantly poured forth their sorrow; the angelic mouth with its bowed upper lip is peacefully relaxed and a little open. Only now and then comes a belated catch in her slow breathing.

And her small hands, like pink and white flowers, lie so quietly, one on the coverlet, the other on the pillow by her face—Dr. Cornelius, gazing, feels his heart melt with tenderness as with strong wine.

"How good," he thinks, "that she breathes in oblivion with every breath she draws! That in childhood each night is a deep wide gulf between one day and the next. Tomorrow, beyond all doubt, young Hergesell will be a pale shadow, powerless to darken her little heart. Tomorrow, forgetful of all but present joy, she will walk with Abel and Snapper, all five gentlemen, round and round the table, will play the ever-thrilling cushion game."

Heaven be praised for that!

James Joyce
(*1882–1941*)

It is extraordinary that the greatest poet of the twentieth century, William Butler Yeats, and the greatest novelist, James Joyce, were both from the tiny island of Ireland. And both were not only from Ireland but quintessentially of Ireland; Irish life provided the materials of their art, cosmopolitan as that art came to be. Both wrote primarily of themselves, transforming their self-perceptions, their experiences, and their friends into symbols. But Yeats's art was essentially compressive; remaining in Ireland, he distilled his observations into brief, luminous lyrics. Joyce's was expansive; through his prolonged, self-imposed exile from Ireland, he wove his memories of Irish life into a series of ever longer and more inclusive books, climaxing his career with an extraordinary Dublin epic grounded in the story of a Dublin publican's family but reaching out to include all of human history. *Dubliners* (1914), *A Portrait of the Artist as a Young Man* (1916), *Ulysses* (1922), and *Finnegans Wake* (1939) remain stories of Dublin life at the turn of the century while at the same time they stand at the pinnacle of international modern fiction.

Joyce was born in Dublin in 1882. The members of his family were to cast their shadows over his major fictional characters. The father was John Stanislaus Joyce, the mother was Mary Jane ("May") Murray Joyce, and there were nine brothers and sisters who survived infancy; the one closest

to Joyce was Stanislaus, two years younger than he. Joyce described his father, under the guise of "Simon Dedalus" in *A Portrait of the Artist as a Young Man,* as "a medical student, an oarsman, a tenor, an amateur actor, a shouting politician, a small landlord, a small investor, a drinker, a good fellow, a storyteller, somebody's secretary, something in a distillery, a tax-gatherer, a bankrupt and at present a praiser of his own past." May Joyce was a gentle, devout woman with a good training in music. "Stannie" was a quiet, studious boy who remained unflinchingly loyal to his older brother and whom Joyce came to regard, with considerable ambivalence, as a sort of shadow self.

The story of Joyce's childhood and youth in Dublin is one of the gradual but steady decline of the family fortunes and of his own self-separation from them. John Joyce had begun his marriage with a good income from inherited property and from a political appointment as collector of taxes for the city of Dublin. When Joyce was six, he was sent to Clongowes Wood College, an expensive boarding school run by the Jesuits. John Joyce lost his job as tax collector, however, because of irregularities in his accounts, and drifted through a series of jobs toward bankruptcy. Joyce had to drop out of Clongowes Wood; after two years at home, he completed his elementary education at Belvedere College, where he and Stanislaus were admitted without fees. He remained there between the ages of eleven and sixteen, distinguishing himself academically, and then entered University College, Dublin, a Jesuit institution founded by Cardinal Newman as an alternative to the almost wholly Protestant Trinity College, Dublin. During his university years, Joyce read widely, often outside the curriculum, and began to write seriously, producing not only several published critical essays but also poems and notebooks of "epiphanies," the word Joyce borrowed from theology to refer to intense moments when the truth about a person or thing was revealed. He graduated in 1902, with a respectable second-class degree in Latin.

After graduating, Joyce considered studying medicine, attended a few lectures in Dublin, and then went to Paris, where he spent a few months, quickly giving up the idea of becoming a doctor. He returned to Dublin in April, 1903, after receiving the telegram, memorable from its use in *Ulysses,* "MOTHER DYING COME HOME FATHER." His mother died in August, and Joyce remained in Dublin for a little over a year more, teaching for a short time, beginning an autobiographical novel named *Stephen Hero,* writing some short stories for a farmers' magazine, *The Irish Homestead,* and sharing, for ten days, a rented Martello tower with a medical-student friend named Oliver St. John Gogarty, later to become the "Buck Mulligan" of *Ulysses.*

In June, 1904, Joyce met a girl from Galway named Nora Barnacle, then working as a chambermaid in Finn's Hotel in Dublin. Their first date was on June 16, 1904 (commemorated by Joyce's selection of that date for "Bloomsday," the day of the entire action of *Ulysses*). The two fell in love; since Joyce was opposed to marriage as an institution and could not live unmarried with Nora in Dublin, he persuaded her to go abroad with him. They left Dublin in October, 1904, and went to Pola, a small Adriatic seaport then controlled by Austria, now part of Yugoslavia. After a few months they moved to Trieste, where they remained, with a brief interlude

in Rome, until 1915, Joyce supporting them by teaching English in the local Berlitz school. Stanislaus joined them in Trieste in 1905; a son, Georgio, was born the same year, and a daughter, Lucia Anna, in 1907.

In 1905, too, Joyce submitted the first version of *Dubliners,* a collection of short stories, to a publisher; it was repeatedly rejected and even after acceptance was subjected to censorship by publishers and printers who objected to the stories' sexual frankness, their use of such obscenities as "bloody," and their use of real names of people and places. Joyce meanwhile had begun in 1907 to revise *Stephen Hero* into a tighter, more carefully controlled "work in five chapters." Both *Dubliners* and *A Portrait of the Artist as a Young Man* were published in 1914 (*A Portrait* in serial form in a literary review named *The Egoist,* with book publication following in 1916). Both works were favorably reviewed and began to bring Joyce a wide reputation.

When World War I broke out in 1915, the Joyces were allowed to leave Trieste for neutral Zurich. They remained there until 1919, with Joyce giving private English lessons and working on the early chapters of *Ulysses.* This book had started as another short story for *Dubliners* about a "Mr. Hunter" but quickly grew into a massive novel which recreates the action of the *Odyssey* in a single day in 1904 Dublin, with the Stephen Dedalus of *A Portrait* in the role of Telemachus and Leopold Bloom, an advertising solicitor, and his musical wife Molly as Odysseus and Penelope. After the war, the Joyces returned to Trieste briefly and then moved to Paris in 1920. By now Joyce had obtained some measure of relief from money worries, first through grants from the Royal Literary Society and Mrs. Edith Rockefeller McCormick and later through a continuing series of subsidies from Harriet Shaw Weaver, a well-to-do English feminist and patron of the arts. In 1917, however, he had begun to suffer from increasing difficulties with his eyesight; between that time and 1930, he underwent twenty-five painful operations for iritis, glaucoma, and cataracts which left his vision seriously impaired.

When *Ulysses* was published on Joyce's fortieth birthday, February 2, 1922, a storm of outrage broke around his head. Serial publication of the early chapters of the book in the American *Little Review* had already been banned in 1920, and now the postal authorities banned it in both England and America. For more than ten years, English and American readers could get the book only in smuggled, surreptitious copies from Paris. Finally in 1933, an American court ruled that it was not obscene. An American edition appeared the following year, and the English followed suit in 1936. (The book was never banned in Ireland, but it was not allowed for sale either until long after it was available elsewhere.)

Even before the completion of *Ulysses,* Joyce had been planning a "night" book to complement his "day" book, *Ulysses,* and he wrote the first pages of the new work in March, 1923. Its composition was to stretch out over sixteen years, with sections appearing periodically in magazines and in pamphlet form as parts of a "Work in Progress." Joyce's last years were saddened by the mental illness of his daughter; what began as mild eccentricity gradually became advanced schizophrenia, and it was necessary to place her in a mental hospital in 1932. "Work in Progress," completed and given the title *Finnegans Wake,* was published in 1939, its long-awaited ap-

pearance disappointingly neglected under the urgency of news of the im-
pending war. When France fell to the Nazis in 1940, the Joyces fled again
to Zurich, where Joyce died in January, 1941, of a perforated ulcer.

In Joyce's own day, his work was greeted with incomprehension and
hostility by the general public and by a sizable portion of the literary estab-
lishment. (And even by a number of his fellow modernist novelists: Vir-
ginia Woolf thought *Ulysses* was the work of "a queasy undergraduate
scratching his pimples," although she later relented, and D. H. Lawrence
told his wife that Molly's monologue was "the dirtiest, most indecent, ob-
scene thing ever written. Yes, it is, Frieda. . . . It is filthy.") His admirers
generally praised his work for its technical experimentation and stylistic
brilliance. T. S. Eliot praised Joyce for his use in *Ulysses* of the "mythical
method" and recognized the parallel (not really a very close one) with his
own treatment of the Fisher King myth in a modern setting in *The Waste
Land*, published the same year as *Ulysses*. A great deal of attention has been
paid to Joyce's "stream of consciousness" technique, by which the narrative
follows the flow of consciousness of one or more characters, a technique
Joyce experimented with in *Dubliners*, developed fully in *A Portrait* and
Ulysses, and transcended in the flowing, multilayered dream language of
Finnegans Wake.

Joyce was a daring experimentalist, and the difficulty of his books can
still intimidate. *A Portrait* is by no means easy reading; it takes a number of
deep breaths to get through *Ulysses* the first time; and *Finnegans Wake* re-
mains literally a closed book to all except a growing but still comparatively
small number of enthusiasts who have accepted the challenge, if not of
spending their entire lives on it, as Joyce suggested (only half facetiously),
of spending enough time on it to open up its flood of comic invention and
warm humanity.

It is the comedy and the humanity that are likely to strike contemporary
readers more than the obscenity and the obscurity, accustomed as we are to
sexual frankness greater than Molly's and puzzles more difficult than *Ulys-
ses*. Joyce is above all a great comic writer, not only in the Irish blarneying
that fills his pages but in his vision of life. Joyce's world, like that of the
other great modernists, was fragmented, the fragmentation defined for
him, as the critic Charles Peake has pointed out, as the split between the
extraordinariness of the romantic, self-absorbed Artist (Stephen Dedalus)
and the ordinariness of the earthy, life-accepting Citizen (Leopold Bloom).
This split, which Joyce found within himself as well as in his family and in
the modern world, he was able to resolve through the reconciling power of
the comic imagination, which can soar into the ethereal while carrying the
ordinary with it all the way.

Dubliners is a collection of fifteen stories of Dublin life. On the first page
of the first story, "The Sisters," the nameless young narrator whispers the
word "paralysis" to himself and says that he "longed to be nearer to it and
to look upon its deadly work." In a sense, all the stories in the collection
explore paralysis in Irish life, through successive sequences devoted to
childhood, adolescence, mature life, and public life (Joyce's own catego-
ries).

Joyce wrote "The Dead," the last and greatest story in *Dubliners*, in 1907,
two years after he had submitted the first version of *Dubliners* to a pub-

lisher. Part of the impulse for the story came from Joyce's feeling that he had not been quite fair to Dublin in the other stories of *Dubliners;* he had left out, he told his brother Stanislaus, "its ingenuous insularity and its hospitality." He also drew upon an experience of his wife Nora; in Galway in 1903, Michael ("Sonny") Bodkin had courted her and had died after standing in the rain under her window and singing to her. The model for Gabriel was partially Joyce himself; other partial models were his father and a friend named Constantine Curran. One critic has aptly suggested that Gabriel may be Joyce's portrait of himself if he had remained in the paralysis of Dublin.

The finished story, however, transforms whatever is autobiographical in the material into a polished and complex work of art. Every detail from the opening line ("Lily, the caretaker's daughter, was literally run off her feet") contributes to the title metaphor and leads Gabriel inexorably to his moving and epiphanic moment of self-realization in the last lines.

Ulysses is hard to sample. Its eighteen chapters, based loosely on the structure of the *Odyssey*, are so intricately woven together that touching one episode sends vibrations throughout the entire web. But "Calypso" gives a sense of at least some features of the book, even outside the rich matrix in which it is set in its original context. "Calypso" is the first chapter devoted to the main character, Leopold Bloom. It is preceded by three chapters devoted to Stephen Dedalus and followed by fourteen more devoted to Bloom's travelings around Dublin on June 16, 1904, and his eventual return home with Stephen.

The materials introduced in "Calypso" are to be endlessly developed and scrutinized from every angle in the rest of *Ulysses*: Bloom's relationship with Molly, who has a sexual assignation with the vulgar billsticker Blazes Boylan at four that afternoon; the death of Paddy Dignam, whose funeral Bloom is attending at eleven in the morning; his affection and concern for Milly, his fifteen-year-old daughter who is working as a photographer's assistant in Mullingar; his continuing grief over the death of his infant son Rudy, eleven years before; and, most pervasive of all, his nostalgia for happier days and his resilience in coping with the present. More important than external facts, which we pick up in bits and pieces, is the glimpse we get of how Bloom's mind works, the earthy, practical, often touching, frequently comic workings of the mind of, as one of the characters later calls him, a good "allroundman."

FURTHER READING (*prepared by J. H.*): One of the finest literary biographies ever written is Richard Ellmann's *James Joyce*, 2nd ed., 1982. There are a great many introductory books that briefly survey the major works. Perhaps the best of these is the *Cambridge Companion to James Joyce*, ed. Derek Attridge, 1990, which contains eleven essays on Joycean works and topics by major Joyce scholars. A similar compendium that is also useful is *A Companion to Joyce Studies*, ed. Zack Bowen and James F. Carens, 1984. Of the many "introductions" by single authors, Patrick Parrinder's *James Joyce*, 1984, and Bernard Benstock, *James Joyce*, 1985, may be recommended. In the same category, but more ambitious and correspondingly more lastingly useful, are Hugh Kenner's *Dublin's Joyce*, 1955, repr. 1987, and Charles H. Peake's *James Joyce: The Citizen and the Artist*, 1977. On *Dubliners*, *James Joyce's "Dubliners": Critical Essays*, ed. Clive Hart, 1969, provides essays on each of the stories, while Don Gifford, *Joyce Annotated: Notes for "Dubliners" and "A Portrait of the Artist as*

a Young Man," 2nd ed., 1982, identifies references and allusions. Gifford's *"Ulysses" Annotated*, rev. ed. 1989, does the same thing for *Ulysses*. The general books listed all provide introductions to *Ulysses*; a perceptive and more extended treatment is Hugh Kenner, *Ulysses*, rev. ed., 1987. Important essays on Joyce are collected in *James Joyce*, ed. Harold Bloom, 1986, in the Modern Critical Views series.

THE DEAD

Lily, the caretaker's daughter, was literally run off her feet. Hardly had she brought one gentleman into the little pantry behind the office on the ground floor and helped him off with his overcoat than the wheezy hall-door bell clanged again and she had to scamper along the bare hallway to let in another guest. It was well for her she had not to attend to the ladies also. But Miss Kate and Miss Julia had thought of that and had converted the bathroom upstairs into a ladies' dressing-room. Miss Kate and Miss Julia were there, gossiping and laughing and fussing, walking after each other to the head of the stairs, peering down over the banisters and calling down to Lily to ask her who had come.

It was always a great affair, the Misses Morkan's annual dance. Every-body who knew them came to it, members of the family, old friends of the family, the members of Julia's choir, any of Kate's pupils that were grown up enough, and even some of Mary Jane's pupils too. Never once had it fallen flat. For years and years it had gone off in splendid style as long as anyone could remember; ever since Kate and Julia, after the death of their brother Pat, had left the house in Stoney Batter and taken Mary Jane, their only niece, to live with them in the dark gaunt house on Usher's Island, the upper part of which they had rented from Mr Fulham, the corn-factor[1] on the ground floor. That was a good thirty years ago if it was a day. Mary Jane, who was then a little girl in short clothes, was now the main prop of the household, for she had the organ in Haddington Road.[2] She had been through the Academy and gave a pupils' concert every year in the upper room of the Antient Concert Rooms.[3] Many of her pupils belonged to the better-class families on the Kingstown and Dalkey line. Old as they were, her aunts also did their share. Julia, though she was quite grey, was still the leading soprano in Adam and Eve's,[4] and Kate, being too feeble to go about much, gave music lessons to beginners on the old square piano in the back room. Lily, the caretaker's daughter, did housemaid's work for them. Though their life was modest, they believed in eating well; the best of everything: diamond-bone sirloins, three-shilling tea and the best bottled stout. But Lily seldom made a mistake in the orders so that she got on well with her three mistresses. They were fussy, that was all. But the only thing they would not stand was back answers.

Of course they had good reason to be fussy on such a night. And then it was long after ten o'clock and yet there was no sign of Gabriel and his wife.

[1] Grain merchant.
[2] That is, had the organist's job in a church on Haddington Road.
[3] A Dublin concert hall. Joyce competed in a singing contest there in 1904.
[4] A large church on Merchant's Quay in central Dublin.

Besides they were dreadfully afraid that Freddy Malins might turn up screwed.[5] They would not wish for worlds that any of Mary Jane's pupils should see him under the influence; and when he was like that it was sometimes very hard to manage him. Freddy Malins always came late but they wondered what could be keeping Gabriel: and that was what brought them every two minutes to the banisters to ask Lily had Gabriel or Freddy come.

—O, Mr Conroy, said Lily to Gabriel when she opened the door for him, Miss Kate and Miss Julia thought you were never coming. Goodnight, Mrs Conroy.

—I'll engage they did, said Gabriel, but they forget that my wife here takes three mortal hours to dress herself.

He stood on the mat, scraping the snow from his goloshes, while Lily led his wife to the foot of the stairs and called out:

—Miss Kate, here's Mrs Conroy.

Kate and Julia came toddling down the dark stairs at once. Both of them kissed Gabriel's wife, said she must be perished alive and asked was Gabriel with her.

—Here I am as right as the mail, Aunt Kate! Go on up. I'll follow, called out Gabriel from the dark.

He continued scraping his feet vigorously while the three women went upstairs, laughing, to the ladies' dressing-room. A light fringe of snow lay like a cape on the shoulders of his overcoat and like toecaps on the toes of his goloshes; and, as the buttons of his overcoat slipped with a squeaking noise through the snow-stiffened frieze,[6] a cold fragrant air from out-of-doors escaped from crevices and folds.

—Is it snowing again, Mr Conroy? asked Lily.

She had preceded him into the pantry to help him off with his overcoat. Gabriel smiled at the three syllables she had given his surname and glanced at her. She was a slim, growing girl pale in complexion and with hay-coloured hair. The gas in the pantry made her look still paler. Gabriel had known her when she was a child and used to sit on the lowest step nursing a rag doll.

—Yes, Lily, he answered, and I think we're in for a night of it.

He looked up at the pantry ceiling, which was shaking with the stamping and shuffling of feet on the floor above, listened for a moment to the piano and then glanced at the girl, who was folding his overcoat carefully at the end of a shelf.

—Tell me, Lily, he said in a friendly tone, do you still go to school?

—O no, sir, she answered. I'm done schooling this year and more.

—O, then, said Gabriel gaily, I suppose we'll be going to your wedding one of these fine days with your young man, eh?

The girl glanced back at him over her shoulder and said with great bitterness:

—The men that is now is only all palaver and what they can get out of you.

Gabriel coloured as if he felt he had made a mistake and, without looking at her, kicked off his goloshes and flicked actively with his muffler at his patent-leather shoes.

[5] Drunk. [6] A heavy, woolen cloth.

He was a stout tallish young man. The high colour of his cheeks pushed upwards even to his forehead where it scattered itself in a few formless patches of pale red; and on his hairless face there scintillated restlessly the polished lenses and the bright gilt rims of the glasses which screened his delicate and restless eyes. His glossy black hair was parted in the middle and brushed in a long curve behind his ears where it curled slightly beneath the groove left by his hat.

When he had flicked lustre into his shoes he stood up and pulled his waistcoat down more tightly on his plump body. Then he took a coin rapidly from his pocket.

—O Lily, he said, thrusting it into her hands, it's Christmas-time, isn't it? Just . . . here's a little. . . .

He walked rapidly towards the door.

—O no, sir! cried the girl, following him. Really, sir, I wouldn't take it.

—Christmas-time! Christmas-time! said Gabriel, almost trotting to the stairs and waving his hand to her in deprecation.

The girl, seeing that he had gained the stairs, called out after him:

—Well, thank you, sir.

He waited outside the drawing-room door until the waltz should finish, listening to the skirts that swept against it and to the shuffling of feet. He was still discomposed by the girl's bitter and sudden retort. It had cast a gloom over him which he tried to dispel by arranging his cuffs and the bows of his tie. He then took from his waistcoat pocket a little paper and glanced at the headings he had made for his speech. He was undecided about the lines from Robert Browning for he feared they would be above the heads of his hearers. Some quotation that they would recognise from Shakespeare or from the Melodies[7] would be better. The indelicate clacking of the men's heels and the shuffling of their soles reminded him that their grade of culture differed from his. He would only make himself ridiculous by quoting poetry to them which they could not understand. They would think that he was airing his superior education. He would fail with them just as he had failed with the girl in the pantry. He had taken up a wrong tone. His whole speech was a mistake from first to last, an utter failure.

Just then his aunts and his wife came out of the ladies' dressing-room. His aunts were two small plainly dressed old women. Aunt Julia was an inch or so the taller. Her hair, drawn low over the tops of her ears, was grey; and grey also, with darker shadows, was her large flaccid face. Though she was stout in build and stood erect her slow eyes and parted lips gave her the appearance of a woman who did not know where she was or where she was going. Aunt Kate was more vivacious. Her face, healthier than her sister's, was all puckers and creases, like a shrivelled red apple, and her hair, braided in the same old-fashioned way, had not lost its ripe nut colour.

They both kissed Gabriel frankly. He was their favourite nephew, the son of their dead elder sister, Ellen, who had married T. J. Conroy of the Port and Docks.[8]

[7] Thomas Moore's *Irish Melodies* (1807–34), a popular collection in which Moore wrote new words to traditional Irish melodies.

[8] That is, of the government office regulating the harbor.

—Gretta tells me you're not going to take a cab back to Monkstown to-night, Gabriel, said Aunt Kate.

—No, said Gabriel, turning to his wife, we had quite enough of that last year, hadn't we? Don't you remember, Aunt Kate, what a cold Gretta got out of it? Cab windows rattling all the way, and the east wind blowing in after we passed Merrion. Very jolly it was. Gretta caught a dreadful cold.

Aunt Kate frowned severely and nodded her head at every word.

—Quite right, Gabriel, quite right, she said. You can't be too careful.

—But as for Gretta there, said Gabriel, she'd walk home in the snow if she were let.

Mrs Conroy laughed.

—Don't mind him, Aunt Kate, she said. He's really an awful bother, what with green shades for Tom's eyes at night and making him do the dumb-bells, and forcing Eva to eat the stirabout.[9] The poor child! And she simply hates the sight of it! . . . O, but you'll never guess what he makes me wear now!

She broke out into a peal of laughter and glanced at her husband, whose admiring and happy eyes had been wandering from her dress to her face and hair. The two aunts laughed heartily too, for Gabriel's solicitude was a standing joke with them.

—Goloshes! said Mrs Conroy. That's the latest. Whenever it's wet underfoot I must put on my goloshes. To-night even he wanted me to put them on, but I wouldn't. The next thing he'll buy me will be a diving suit.

Gabriel laughed nervously and patted his tie reassuringly while Aunt Kate nearly doubled herself, so heartily did she enjoy the joke. The smile soon faded from Aunt Julia's face and her mirthless eyes were directed towards her nephew's face. After a pause she asked:

—And what are goloshes, Gabriel?

—Goloshes, Julia! exclaimed her sister. Goodness me, don't you know what goloshes are? You wear them over your . . . over your boots, Gretta, isn't it?

—Yes, said Mrs Conroy. Guttapercha[10] things. We both have a pair now. Gabriel says everyone wears them on the continent.

—O, on the continent, murmured Aunt Julia, nodding her head slowly.

Gabriel knitted his brows and said, as if he were slightly angered:

—It's nothing very wonderful but Gretta thinks it very funny because she says the word reminds her of Christy Minstrels.[11]

—But tell me, Gabriel, said Aunt Kate, with brisk tact. Of course, you've seen about the room. Gretta was saying . . .

—O, the room is all right, replied Gabriel. I've taken one in the Gresham.[12]

—To be sure, said Aunt Kate, by far the best thing to do. And the children, Gretta, you're not anxious about them?

—O, for one night, said Mrs Conroy. Besides, Bessie will look after them.

—To be sure, said Aunt Kate again. What a comfort it is to have a girl

[9] Porridge, oatmeal. [10] A tough plastic substance resembling rubber.
[11] Famous minstrel company organized by E. P. Christy. American blackface minstrels were popular in nineteenth-century Dublin.
[12] A fashionable Dublin hotel.

like that, one you can depend on! There's that Lily, I'm sure I don't know what has come over her lately. She's not the girl she was at all.

Gabriel was about to ask his aunt some questions on this point but she broke off suddenly to gaze after her sister who had wandered down the stairs and was craning her neck over the banisters.

—Now, I ask you, she said, almost testily, where is Julia going? Julia! Julia! Where are you going?

Julia, who had gone halfway down one flight, came back and announced blandly:

—Here's Freddy.

At the same moment a clapping of hands and a final flourish of the pianist told that the waltz had ended. The drawing-room door was opened from within and some couples came out. Aunt Kate drew Gabriel aside hurriedly and whispered into his ear:

—Slip down, Gabriel, like a good fellow and see if he's all right, and don't let him up if he's screwed. I'm sure he's screwed. I'm sure he is.

Gabriel went to the stairs and listened over the banisters. He could hear two persons talking in the pantry. Then he recognised Freddy Malins' laugh. He went down the stairs noisily.

—It's such a relief, said Aunt Kate to Mrs Conroy, that Gabriel is here. I always feel easier in my mind when he's here. . . . Julia, there's Miss Daly and Miss Power will take some refreshment. Thanks for your beautiful waltz, Miss Daly. It made lovely time.

A tall wizen-faced man, with a stiff grizzled moustache and swarthy skin, who was passing out with his partner, said:

—And may we have some refreshment, too, Miss Morkan?

—Julia, said Aunt Kate summarily, and here's Mr Browne and Miss Furlong. Take them in, Julia, with Miss Daly and Miss Power.

—I'm the man for the ladies, said Mr Browne, pursing his lips until his moustache bristled and smiling in all his wrinkles. You know, Miss Morkan, the reason they are so fond of me is—

He did not finish his sentence, but, seeing that Aunt Kate was out of earshot, at once led the three young ladies into the back room. The middle of the room was occupied by two square tables placed end to end, and on these Aunt Julia and the caretaker were straightening and smoothing a large cloth. On the sideboard were arrayed dishes and plates, and glasses and bundles of knives and forks and spoons. The top of the closed square piano served also as a sideboard for viands and sweets. At a smaller sideboard in one corner two young men were standing, drinking hop-bitters.[13]

Mr Browne led his charges thither and invited them all, in jest, to some ladies' punch, hot, strong and sweet. As they said they never took anything strong he opened three bottles of lemonade for them. Then he asked one of the young men to move aside, and, taking hold of the decanter, filled out for himself a goodly measure of whisky. The young men eyed him respectfully while he took a trial sip.

—God help me, he said, smiling, it's the doctor's orders.

His wizened face broke into a broader smile, and the three young ladies

[13] A kind of malt liquor.

laughed in musical echo to his pleasantry, swaying their bodies to and fro, with nervous jerks of their shoulders. The boldest said:

—O, now, Mr Browne, I'm sure the doctor never ordered anything of the kind.

Mr Browne took another sip of his whisky and said, with sidling mimicry:

—Well, you see, I'm like the famous Mrs Cassidy, who is reported to have said: *Now, Mary Grimes, if I don't take it, make me take it, for I feel I want it.*

His hot face had leaned forward a little too confidentially and he had assumed a very low Dublin accent so that the young ladies, with one instinct, received his speech in silence. Miss Furlong, who was one of Mary Jane's pupils, asked Miss Daly what was the name of the pretty waltz she had played; and Mr Browne, seeing that he was ignored, turned promptly to the two young men who were more appreciative.

A red-faced young woman, dressed in pansy,[14] came into the room, excitedly clapping her hands and crying:

—Quadrilles! Quadrilles![15]

Close on her heels came Aunt Kate, crying:

—Two gentlemen and three ladies, Mary Jane!

—O, here's Mr Bergin and Mr Kerrigan, said Mary Jane. Mr Kerrigan, will you take Miss Power? Miss Furlong, may I get you a partner, Mr Bergin. O, that'll just do now.

—Three ladies, Mary Jane, said Aunt Kate.

The two young gentlemen asked the ladies if they might have the pleasure, and Mary Jane turned to Miss Daly.

—O, Miss Daly, you're really awfully good, after playing for the last two dances, but really we're so short of ladies to-night.

—I don't mind in the least, Miss Morkan.

—But I've a nice partner for you, Mr Bartell D'Arcy, the tenor. I'll get him to sing later on. All Dublin is raving about him.

—Lovely voice, lovely voice! said Aunt Kate.

As the piano had twice begun the prelude to the first figure Mary Jane led her recruits quickly from the room. They had hardly gone when Aunt Julia wandered slowly into the room, looking behind her at something.

—What is the matter, Julia? asked Aunt Kate anxiously. Who is it?

Julia, who was carrying in a column of table-napkins, turned to her sister and said, as if the question had surprised her:

—It's only Freddy, Kate, and Gabriel with him.

In fact right behind her Gabriel could be seen piloting Freddy Malins across the landing. The latter, a young man of about forty, was of Gabriel's size and build, with very round shoulders. His face was fleshy and pallid, touched with colour only at the thick hanging lobes of his ears and at the wide wings of his nose. He had coarse features, a blunt nose, a convex and receding brow, tumid and protruded lips. His heavy-lidded eyes and the disorder of his scanty hair made him look sleepy. He was laughing heartily in a high key at a story which he had been telling Gabriel on the stairs and at the same time rubbing the knuckles of his left fist backwards and forwards into his left eye.

—Good-evening, Freddy, said Aunt Julia.

[14] Violet. [15] A ballroom dance for four-couple "sets."

Freddy Malins bade the Misses Morkan good-evening in what seemed an offhand fashion by reason of the habitual catch in his voice and then, seeing that Mr Browne was grinning at him from the sideboard, crossed the room on rather shaky legs and began to repeat in an undertone the story he had just told to Gabriel.

—He's not so bad, is he? said Aunt Kate to Gabriel.

Gabriel's brows were dark but he raised them quickly and answered:

—O, no, hardly noticeable.

—Now, isn't he a terrible fellow! she said. And his poor mother made him take the pledge on New Year's Eve. But come on, Gabriel, into the drawing-room.

Before leaving the room with Gabriel she signalled to Mr Browne by frowning and shaking her forefinger in warning to and fro. Mr Browne nodded in answer and, when she had gone, said to Freddy Malins:

—Now, then, Teddy, I'm going to fill you out a good glass of lemonade just to buck you up.

Freddy Malins, who was nearing the climax of his story, waved the offer aside impatiently but Mr Browne, having first called Freddy Malins' attention to a disarray in his dress, filled out and handed him a full glass of lemonade. Freddy Malins' left hand accepted the glass mechanically, his right hand being engaged in the mechanical readjustment of his dress. Mr Browne, whose face was once more wrinkling with mirth, poured out for himself a glass of whisky while Freddy Malins exploded, before he had well reached the climax of his story, in a kink of high-pitched bronchitic laughter and, setting down his untasted and overflowing glass, began to rub the knuckles of his left fist backwards and forwards into his left eye, repeating words of his last phrase as well as his fit of laughter would allow him.

. .

Gabriel could not listen while Mary Jane was playing her Academy piece,[16] full of runs and difficult passages, to the hushed drawing-room. He liked music but the piece she was playing had no melody for him and he doubted whether it had any melody for the other listeners, though they had begged Mary Jane to play something. Four young men, who had come from the refreshment-room to stand in the doorway at the sound of the piano, had gone away quietly in couples after a few minutes. The only persons who seemed to follow the music were Mary Jane herself, her hands racing along the key-board or lifted from it at the pauses like those of a priestess in momentary imprecation, and Aunt Kate standing at her elbow to turn the page.

Gabriel's eyes, irritated by the floor, which glittered with beeswax under the heavy chandelier, wandered to the wall above the piano. A picture of the balcony scene in *Romeo and Juliet* hung there and beside it was a picture of the two murdered princes in the Tower[17] which Aunt Julia had worked

[16] Demonstration piece prepared as part of her study at the Dublin Royal Academy of Music.

[17] Richard III was said to have ordered the murders of his two nephews, sons of Edward IV, in the Tower of London, 1483.

in red, blue and brown wools when she was a girl. Probably in the school they had gone to as girls that kind of work had been taught, for one year his mother had worked for him as a birthday present a waistcoat of purple tabinet, with little foxes' heads upon it, lined with brown satin and having round mulberry buttons. It was strange that his mother had had no musical talent though Aunt Kate used to call her the brains carrier of the Morkan family. Both she and Julia had always seemed a little proud of their serious and matronly sister. Her photograph stood before the pierglass.[18] She held an open book on her knees and was pointing out something in it to Constantine who, dressed in a man-o'-war suit, lay at her feet. It was she who had chosen the names of her sons for she was very sensible of the dignity of family life. Thanks to her, Constantine was now senior curate in Balbriggan and, thanks to her, Gabriel himself had taken his degree in the Royal University. A shadow passed over his face as he remembered her sullen opposition to his marriage. Some slighting phrases she had used still rankled in his memory; she had once spoken of Gretta as being country cute and that was not true of Gretta at all. It was Gretta who had nursed her during all her last long illness in their house at Monkstown.

He knew that Mary Jane must be near the end of her piece for she was playing again the opening melody with runs of scales after every bar and while he waited for the end the resentment died down in his heart. The piece ended with a trill of octaves in the treble and a final deep octave in the bass. Great applause greeted Mary Jane as, blushing and rolling up her music nervously, she escaped from the room. The most vigorous clapping came from the four young men in the doorway who had gone away to the refreshment-room at the beginning of the piece but had come back when the piano had stopped.

Lancers[19] were arranged. Gabriel found himself partnered with Miss Ivors. She was a frank-mannered talkative young lady, with a freckled face and prominent brown eyes. She did not wear a low-cut bodice and the large brooch which was fixed in the front of her collar bore on it an Irish device.

When they had taken their places she said abruptly:

—I have a crow to pluck with you.

—With me? said Gabriel.

She nodded her head gravely.

—What is it? asked Gabriel, smiling at her solemn manner.

—Who is G. C.? answered Miss Ivors, turning her eyes upon him.

Gabriel coloured and was about to knit his brows, as if he did not understand, when she said bluntly:

—O, innocent Amy! I have found out that you write for *The Daily Express.* Now, aren't you ashamed of yourself?

—Why should I be ashamed of myself? asked Gabriel, blinking his eyes and trying to smile.

—Well, I'm ashamed of you, said Miss Ivors frankly. To say you'd write for a rag like that. I didn't think you were a West Briton.[20]

A look of perplexity appeared on Gabriel's face. It was true that he wrote a literary column every Wednesday in *The Daily Express,* for which he

[18] A large mirror filling the space between two windows.
[19] A kind of quadrille. [20] Pejorative term for an English-oriented Irishman.

was paid fifteen shillings. But that did not make him a West Briton surely. The books he received for review were almost more welcome than the paltry cheque. He loved to feel the covers and turn over the pages of newly printed books. Nearly every day when his teaching in the college was ended he used to wander down the quays to the second-hand booksellers, to Hickey's on Bachelor's Walk, to Web's or Massey's on Aston's Quay, or to O'Clohissey's in the by-street. He did not know how to meet her charge. He wanted to say that literature was above politics. But they were friends of many years' standing and their careers had been parallel, first at the University and then as teachers: he could not risk a grandiose phrase with her. He continued blinking his eyes and trying to smile and murmured lamely that he saw nothing political in writing reviews of books.

When their turn to cross[21] had come he was still perplexed and inattentive. Miss Ivors promptly took his hand in a warm grasp and said in a soft friendly tone:

—Of course, I was only joking. Come, we cross now.

When they were together again she spoke of the University question[22] and Gabriel felt more at ease. A friend of hers had shown her his review of Browning's poems. That was how she had found out the secret: but she liked the review immensely. Then she said suddenly:

—O, Mr Conroy, will you come for an excursion to the Aran Isles[23] this summer? We're going to stay there a whole month. It will be splendid out in the Atlantic. You ought to come. Mr Clancy is coming, and Mr Kilkelly and Kathleen Kearney. It would be splendid for Gretta too if she'd come. She's from Connacht,[24] isn't she?

—Her people are, said Gabriel shortly.

—But you will come, won't you? said Miss Ivors, laying her warm hand eagerly on his arm.

—That fact is, said Gabriel, I have already arranged to go—

—Go where? asked Miss Ivors.

—Well, you know, every year I go for a cycling tour with some fellows and so—

—But where? asked Miss Ivors.

—Well, we usually go to France or Belgium or perhaps Germany, said Gabriel awkwardly.

—And why do you go to France and Belgium, said Miss Ivors, instead of visiting your own land?

—Well, said Gabriel, it's partly to keep in touch with the languages and partly for a change.

—And haven't you your own language to keep in touch with—Irish? asked Miss Ivors.

—Well, said Gabriel, if it comes to that, you know, Irish is not my language.

Their neighbours had turned to listen to the cross-examination. Gabriel

[21] A step in the Lancers quadrille.

[22] The question of how to provide Roman Catholics with educational opportunities other than those offered by the heavily Protestant Trinity College, Dublin.

[23] Islands off the west coast of Ireland, valued by nationalists as a place where the Irish language and customs had been preserved.

[24] An area in western Ireland.

glanced right and left nervously and tried to keep his good humour under the ordeal which was making a blush invade his forehead.

—And haven't you your own land to visit, continued Miss Ivors, that you know nothing of, your own people, and your own country?

—O, to tell you the truth, retorted Gabriel suddenly, I'm sick of my own country, sick of it!

—Why? asked Miss Ivors.

Gabriel did not answer for his retort had heated him.

—Why? repeated Miss Ivors.

They had to go visiting together[25] and, as he had not answered her, Miss Ivors said warmly:

—Of course, you've no answer.

Gabriel tried to cover his agitation by taking part in the dance with great energy. He avoided her eyes for he had seen a sour expression on her face. But when they met in the long chain he was surprised to feel his hand firmly pressed. She looked at him from under her brows for a moment quizzically until he smiled. Then, just as the chain was about to start again, she stood on tiptoe and whispered into his ear:

—West Briton!

When the lancers were over Gabriel went away to a remote corner of the room where Freddy Malins' mother was sitting. She was a stout feeble old woman with white hair. Her voice had a catch in it like her son's and she stuttered slightly. She had been told that Freddy had come and that he was nearly all right. Gabriel asked her whether she had had a good crossing. She lived with her married daughter in Glasgow and came to Dublin on a visit once a year. She answered placidly that she had had a beautiful crossing and that the captain had been most attentive to her. She spoke also of the beautiful house her daughter kept in Glasgow, and of all the friends they had there. While her tongue rambled on Gabriel tried to banish from his mind all memory of the unpleasant incident with Miss Ivors. Of course the girl or woman, or whatever she was, was an enthusiast but there was a time for all things. Perhaps he ought not to have answered her like that. But she had no right to call him a West Briton before people, even in joke. She had tried to make him ridiculous before people, heckling him and staring at him with her rabbit's eyes.

He saw his wife making her way towards him through the waltzing couples. When she reached him she said into his ear:

—Gabriel, Aunt Kate wants to know won't you carve the goose as usual. Miss Daly will carve the ham and I'll do the pudding.

—All right, said Gabriel.

—She's sending in the younger ones first as soon as this waltz is over so that we'll have the table to ourselves.

—Were you dancing? asked Gabriel.

—Of course I was. Didn't you see me? What row had you with Molly Ivors?

—No row. Why? Did she say so?

—Something like that. I'm trying to get that Mr D'Arcy to sing. He's full of conceit, I think.

[25] Another step in the Lancers quadrille.

—There were no words, said Gabriel moodily, only she wanted me to go for a trip to the west of Ireland and I said I wouldn't.

His wife clasped her hands excitedly and gave a little jump.

—O, do go, Gabriel, she cried. I'd love to see Galway again.

—You can go if you like, said Gabriel coldly.

She looked at him for a moment, then turned to Mrs Malins and said:

—There's a nice husband for you, Mrs Malins.

While she was threading her way back across the room Mrs Malins, without adverting to the interruption, went on to tell Gabriel what beautiful places there were in Scotland and beautiful scenery. Her son-in-law brought them every year to the lakes and they used to go fishing. Her son-in-law was a splendid fisher. One day he caught a fish, a beautiful big fish, and the man in the hotel boiled it for their dinner.

Gabriel hardly heard what she said. Now that supper was coming near he began to think again about his speech and about the quotation. When he saw Freddy Malins coming across the room to visit his mother Gabriel left the chair free for him and retired into the embrasure of the window. The room had already cleared and from the back room came the clatter of plates and knives. Those who still remained in the drawing-room seemed tired of dancing and were conversing quietly in little groups. Gabriel's warm trembling fingers tapped the cold pane of the window. How cool it must be outside! How pleasant it would be to walk out alone, first along by the river and then through the park![26] The snow would be lying on the branches of the trees and forming a bright cap on the top of the Wellington Monument.[27] How much more pleasant it would be there than at the supper-table!

He ran over the headings of his speech: Irish hospitality, sad memories, the Three Graces, Paris, the quotation from Browning. He repeated to himself a phrase he had written in his review: *One feels that one is listening to a thought-tormented music.* Miss Ivors had praised the review. Was she sincere? Had she really any life of her own behind all her propagandism? There had never been any ill-feeling between them until that night. It unnerved him to think that she would be at the supper-table, looking up at him while he spoke with her critical quizzing eyes. Perhaps she would not be sorry to see him fail in his speech. An idea came into his mind and gave him courage. He would say, alluding to Aunt Kate and Aunt Julia: *Ladies and Gentlemen, the generation which is now on the wane among us may have had its faults but for my part I think it had certain qualities of hospitality, of humour, of humanity, which the new and very serious and hypereducated generation that is growing up around us seems to me to lack.* Very good: that was one for Miss Ivors. What did he care that his aunts were only two ignorant old women?

A murmur in the room attracted his attention. Mr Browne was advancing from the door, gallantly escorting Aunt Julia, who leaned upon his arm, smiling and hanging her head. An irregular musketry of applause escorted her also as far as the piano and then, as Mary Jane seated herself on the stool, and Aunt Julia, no longer smiling, half turned so as to pitch her voice fairly into the room, gradually ceased. Gabriel recognised the

[26] Phoenix Park, on the west side of Dublin.

[27] A large monument to the Duke of Wellington at the east end of Phoenix Park.

prelude. It was that of an old song of Aunt Julia's—*Arrayed for the Bridal*.[28]
Her voice, strong and clear in tone, attacked with great spirit the runs
which embellish the air and though she sang very rapidly she did not miss
even the smallest of the grace notes. To follow the voice, without looking at
the singer's face, was to feel and share the excitement of swift and secure
flight. Gabriel applauded loudly with all the others at the close of the song
and loud applause was borne in from the invisible supper-table. It sounded
so genuine that a little colour struggled into Aunt Julia's face as she bent to
replace in the music-stand the old leather-bound song-book that had her
initials on the cover. Freddy Malins, who had listened with his head
perched sideways to hear her better, was still applauding when everyone
else had ceased and talking animatedly to his mother who nodded her head
gravely and slowly in acquiescence. At last, when he could clap no more, he
stood up suddenly and hurried across the room to Aunt Julia whose hand
he seized and held in both his hands, shaking it when words failed him or
the catch in his voice proved too much for him.

—I was just telling my mother, he said, I never heard you sing so well,
never. No, I never heard your voice so good as it is to-night. Now! Would
you believe that now? That's the truth. Upon my word and honour that's
the truth. I never heard your voice sound so fresh and so . . . so clear and
fresh, never.

Aunt Julia smiled broadly and murmured something about compli-
ments as she released her hand from his grasp. Mr Browne extended his
open hand towards her and said to those who were near him in the manner
of a showman introducing a prodigy to an audience:

—Miss Julia Morkan, my latest discovery!

He was laughing very heartily at this himself when Freddy Malins
turned to him and said:

—Well, Browne, if you're serious you might make a worse discovery. All
I can say is I never heard her sing half so well as long as I am coming here.
And that's the honest truth.

—Neither did I, said Mr Browne. I think her voice has greatly im-
proved.

Aunt Julia shrugged her shoulders and said with meek pride:

—Thirty years ago I hadn't a bad voice as voices go.

—I often told Julia, said Aunt Kate emphatically, that she was simply
thrown away in that choir. But she never would be said by me.

She turned as if to appeal to the good sense of the others against a
refractory child while Aunt Julia gazed in front of her, a vague smile of
reminiscence playing on her face.

—No, continued Aunt Kate, she wouldn't be said or led by anyone,
slaving there in that choir night and day, night and day. Six o'clock on
Christmas morning! And all for what?

—Well, isn't it for the honour of God, Aunt Kate? asked Mary Jane,
twisting round on the piano-stool and smiling.

Aunt Kate turned fiercely on her niece and said:

[28] A "parlor" arrangement by George Linley of the aria *"Son vergin vezzosa"* from Bellini's
opera *I Puritani*. The song, an ecstatic description of a girl on her wedding day, contrasts
sharply with Aunt Julia's aged appearance.

—I know all about the honour of God, Mary Jane, but I think it's not at all honourable for the pope to turn out the women out of the choirs that have slaved there all their lives and put little whipper-snappers of boys over their heads.[29] I suppose it is for the good of the Church if the pope does it. But it's not just, Mary Jane, and it's not right.

She had worked herself into a passion and would have continued in defence of her sister for it was a sore subject with her but Mary Jane, seeing that all the dancers had come back, intervened pacifically:

—Now, Aunt Kate, you're giving scandal to Mr Browne who is of the other persuasion.[30]

Aunt Kate turned to Mr Browne, who was grinning at this allusion to his religion, and said hastily:

—O, I don't question the pope's being right. I'm only a stupid old woman and I wouldn't presume to do such a thing. But there's such a thing as common everyday politeness and gratitude. And if I were in Julia's place I'd tell that Father Healey straight up to his face . . .

—And besides, Aunt Kate, said Mary Jane, we really are all hungry and when we are hungry we are all very quarrelsome.

—And when we are thirsty we are also quarrelsome, added Mr Browne.

—So that we had better go to supper, said Mary Jane, and finish the discussion afterwards.

On the landing outside the drawing-room Gabriel found his wife and Mary Jane trying to persuade Miss Ivors to stay for supper. But Miss Ivors, who had put on her hat and was buttoning her cloak, would not stay. She did not feel in the least hungry and she had already overstayed her time.

—But only for ten minutes, Molly, said Mrs Conroy. That won't delay you.

—To take a pick itself, said Mary Jane, after all your dancing.

—I really couldn't, said Miss Ivors.

—I am afraid you didn't enjoy yourself at all, said Mary Jane hopelessly.

—Ever so much, I assure you, said Miss Ivors, but you really must let me run off now.

—But how can you get home? asked Mrs Conroy.

—O, it's only two steps up the quay.[31]

Gabriel hesitated a moment and said:

—If you will allow me, Miss Ivors, I'll see you home if you really are obliged to go.

But Miss Ivors broke away from them.

—I won't hear of it, she cried. For goodness sake go in to your suppers and don't mind me. I'm quite well able to take care of myself.

—Well, you're the comical girl, Molly, said Mrs Conroy frankly.

—*Beannacht libh*,[32] cried Miss Ivors, with a laugh, as she ran down the staircase.

Mary Jane gazed after her, a moody puzzled expression on her face, while Mrs Conroy leaned over the banisters to listen for the hall-door. Gabriel asked himself was he the cause of her abrupt departure. But she

[29] Pope Pius X, in 1903, forbade women to sing in choirs and ordered the use of boys' choirs instead.
[30] Protestant. [31] One of the docks along the Liffey River in Dublin.
[32] "Farewell" (Gaelic).

did not seem to be in ill humour: she had gone away laughing. He stared blankly down the staircase.

At that moment Aunt Kate came toddling out of the supper-room, almost wringing her hands in despair.

—Where is Gabriel? she cried. Where on earth is Gabriel? There's everyone waiting in there, stage to let,[33] and nobody to carve the goose!

—Here I am, Aunt Kate! cried Gabriel, with sudden animation, ready to carve a flock of geese, if necessary.

A fat brown goose lay at one end of the table and at the other end, on a bed of creased paper strewn with sprigs of parsley, lay a great ham, stripped of its outer skin and peppered over with crust crumbs, a neat paper frill round its shin and beside this was a round of spiced beef. Between these rival ends ran parallel lines of side-dishes: two little minsters of jelly, red and yellow; a shallow dish full of blocks of blancmange and red jam, a large green leaf-shaped dish with a stalk-shaped handle, on which lay bunches of purple raisins and peeled almonds, a companion dish on which lay a solid rectangle of Smyrna figs, a dish of custard topped with grated nutmeg, a small bowl full of chocolates and sweets wrapped in gold and silver papers and a glass vase in which stood some tall celery stalks. In the centre of the table there stood, as sentries to a fruit-stand which upheld a pyramid of oranges and American apples, two squat old-fashioned decanters of cut glass, one containing port and the other dark sherry. On the closed square piano a pudding in a huge yellow dish lay in waiting and behind it were three squads of bottles of stout and ale and minerals, drawn up according to the colours of their uniforms, the first two black, with brown and red labels, the third and smallest squad white, with transverse green sashes.

Gabriel took his seat boldly at the head of the table and, having looked to the edge of the carver, plunged his fork firmly into the goose. He felt quite at ease now for he was an expert carver and liked nothing better than to find himself at the head of a well-laden table.

—Miss Furlong, what shall I send you? he asked. A wing or a slice of the breast?

—Just a small slice of the breast.

—Miss Higgins, what for you?

—O, anything at all, Mr Conroy.

While Gabriel and Miss Daly exchanged plates of goose and plates of ham and spiced beef Lily went from guest to guest with a dish of hot floury potatoes wrapped in a white napkin. This was Mary Jane's idea and she had also suggested apple sauce for the goose but Aunt Kate had said that plain roast goose without any apple sauce had always been good enough for her and she hoped she might never eat worse. Mary Jane waited on her pupils and saw that they got the best slices and Aunt Kate and Aunt Julia opened and carried across from the piano bottles of stout and ale for the gentlemen and bottles of minerals for the ladies. There was a great deal of confusion and laughter and noise, the noise of orders and counter-orders, of knives and forks, of corks and glass-stoppers. Gabriel began to carve second helpings as soon as he had finished the first round without serving himself.

[33] *stage to let.* An expression meaning things are delayed.

Everyone protested loudly so that he compromised by taking a long draught of stout for he had found the carving hot work. Mary Jane settled down quietly to her supper but Aunt Kate and Aunt Julia were still toddling round the table, walking on each other's heels, getting in each other's way and giving each other unheeded orders. Mr Browne begged of them to sit down and eat their suppers and so did Gabriel but they said there was time enough, so that, at last, Freddy Malins stood up and, capturing Aunt Kate, plumped her down on her chair amid general laughter.

When everyone had been well served Gabriel said, smiling:

—Now, if anyone wants a little more of what vulgar people call stuffing let him or her speak.

A chorus of voices invited him to begin his own supper and Lily came forward with three potatoes which she had reserved for him.

—Very well, said Gabriel amiably, as he took another preparatory draught, kindly forget my existence, ladies and gentlemen, for a few minutes.

He set to his supper and took no part in the conversation with which the table covered Lily's removal of the plates. The subject of talk was the opera company which was then at the Theatre Royal. Mr Bartell D'Arcy, the tenor, a dark-complexioned young man with a smart moustache, praised very highly the leading contralto of the company but Miss Furlong thought she had a rather vulgar style of production. Freddy Malins said there was a negro chieftain singing in the second part of the Gaiety pantomime who had one of the finest tenor voices he had ever heard.

—Have you heard him? he asked Mr Bartell D'Arcy across the table.

—No, answered Mr Bartell D'Arcy carelessly.

—Because, Freddy Malins explained, now I'd be curious to hear your opinion of him. I think he has a grand voice.

—It takes Teddy to find out the really good things, said Mr Browne familiarly to the table.

—And why couldn't he have a voice too? asked Freddy Malins sharply. Is it because he's only a black?

Nobody answered this question and Mary Jane led the table back to the legitimate opera. One of her pupils had given her a pass for *Mignon*.[34] Of course it was very fine, she said, but it made her think of poor Georgina Burns. Mr Browne could go back farther still, to the old Italian companies that used to come to Dublin—Tietjens, Ilma de Murzka, Campanini, the great Trebelli, Giuglini, Ravelli, Aramburo.[35] Those were the days, he said, when there was something like singing to be heard in Dublin. He told too of how the top gallery of the old Royal[36] used to be packed night after night, of how one night an Italian tenor had sung five encores to *Let Me Like a Soldier Fall*,[37] introducing a high C every time, and of how the gallery boys would sometimes in their enthusiasm unyoke the horses from the carriage of some great *prima donna* and pull her themselves through the

[34] Opera by Ambroise Thomas (1866).

[35] These are all names of famous opera singers of the nineteenth century.

[36] A Dublin theater that burned down in 1880.

[37] A melodramatic tenor aria from the opera *Maritana* (1845), by William Vincent Wallace, words by Edward Fitzball.

streets to her hotel. Why did they never play the grand old operas now, he asked, *Dinorah, Lucrezia Borgia?*[38] Because they could not get the voices to sing them: that was why.

—Oh, well, said Mr Bartell D'Arcy, I presume there are as good singers to-day as there were then.

—Where are they? asked Mr Browne defiantly.

—In London, Paris, Milan, said Mr Bartell D'Arcy warmly. I suppose Caruso,[39] for example, is quite as good, if not better than any of the men you have mentioned.

—Maybe so, said Mr Browne. But I may tell you I doubt it strongly.

—O, I'd give anything to hear Caruso sing, said Mary Jane.

—For me, said Aunt Kate, who had been picking a bone, there was only one tenor. To please me, I mean. But I suppose none of you ever heard of him.

—Who was he, Miss Morkan? asked Mr Bartell D'Arcy politely.

—His name, said Aunt Kate, was Parkinson. I heard him when he was in his prime and I think he had then the purest tenor voice that was ever put into a man's throat.

—Strange, said Mr Bartell D'Arcy. I never even heard of him.

—Yes, yes, Miss Morkan is right, said Mr Browne. I remember hearing of old Parkinson but he's too far back for me.

—A beautiful pure sweet mellow English tenor, said Aunt Kate with enthusiasm.

Gabriel having finished, the huge pudding was transferred to the table. The clatter of forks and spoons began again. Gabriel's wife served out spoonfuls of the pudding and passed the plates down the table. Midway down they were held up by Mary Jane, who replenished them with raspberry or orange jelly or with blancmange and jam. The pudding was of Aunt Julia's making and she received praises for it from all quarters. She herself said that it was not quite brown enough.

—Well, I hope, Miss Morkan, said Mr Browne, that I'm brown enough for you because, you know, I'm all brown.

All the gentlemen, except Gabriel, ate some of the pudding out of compliment to Aunt Julia. As Gabriel never ate sweets the celery had been left for him. Freddy Malins also took a stalk of celery and ate it with his pudding. He had been told that celery was a capital thing for the blood and he was just then under doctor's care. Mrs Malins, who had been silent all through the supper, said that her son was going down to Mount Melleray[40] in a week or so. The table then spoke of Mount Melleray, how bracing the air was down there, how hospitable the monks were and how they never asked for a penny-piece from their guests.

—And do you mean to say, asked Mr Browne incredulously, that a chap can go down there and put up there as if it were a hotel and live on the fat of the land and then come away without paying a farthing?

[38] *Dinorah* (1859) is an opera by Giacomo Meyerbeer; *Lucrezia Borgia* (1833) is by Gaetano Donizetti.

[39] The great tenor Enrico Caruso (1874–1921) was at the height of his career in 1904, the time of the story.

[40] Trappist monastery in southern Ireland.

—O, most people give some donation to the monastery when they leave, said Mary Jane.

—I wish we had an institution like that in our Church, said Mr Browne candidly.

He was astonished to hear that the monks never spoke, got up at two in the morning and slept in their coffins. He asked what they did it for.

—That's the rule of the order, said Aunt Kate firmly.[41]

—Yes, but why? asked Mr Browne.

Aunt Kate repeated that it was the rule, that was all. Mr Browne still seemed not to understand. Freddy Malins explained to him, as best he could, that the monks were trying to make up for the sins committed by all the sinners in the outside world. The explanation was not very clear for Mr Browne grinned and said:

—I like that idea very much but wouldn't a comfortable spring bed do them as well as a coffin?

—The coffin, said Mary Jane, is to remind them of their last end.

As the subject had grown lugubrious it was buried in a silence of the table during which Mrs Malins could be heard saying to her neighbour in an indistinct undertone:

—They are very good men, the monks, very pious men.

The raisins and almonds and figs and apples and oranges and chocolates and sweets were now passed about the table and Aunt Julia invited all the guests to have either port or sherry. At first Mr Bartell D'Arcy refused to take either but one of his neighbours nudged him and whispered something to him upon which he allowed his glass to be filled. Gradually as the last glasses were being filled the conversation ceased. A pause followed, broken only by the noise of the wine and by unsettlings of chairs. The Misses Morkan, all three, looked down at the tablecloth. Someone coughed once or twice and then a few gentlemen patted the table gently as a signal for silence. The silence came and Gabriel pushed back his chair and stood up.

The patting at once grew louder in encouragement and then ceased altogether. Gabriel leaned his ten trembling fingers on the tablecloth and smiled nervously at the company. Meeting a row of upturned faces he raised his eyes to the chandelier. The piano was playing a waltz tune and he could hear the skirts sweeping against the drawing-room door. People, perhaps, were standing in the snow on the quay outside, gazing up at the lighted windows and listening to the waltz music. The air was pure there. In the distance lay the park where the trees were weighted with snow. The Wellington Monument wore a gleaming cap of snow that flashed westward over the white field of Fifteen Acres.[42]

He began:

—Ladies and Gentlemen.

—It has fallen to my lot this evening, as in years past, to perform a very pleasing task but a task for which I am afraid my poor powers as a speaker are all too inadequate.

—No, no! said Mr Browne.

[41] Aunt Kate is misinformed; the Trappists have no such rule.
[42] Part of Phoenix Park.

—But, however that may be, I can only ask you to-night to take the will for the deed and to lend me your attention for a few moments while I endeavour to express to you in words what my feelings are on this occasion.

—Ladies and Gentlemen. It is not the first time that we have gathered together under this hospitable roof, around this hospitable board. It is not the first time that we have been the recipients—or perhaps, I had better say, the victims—of the hospitality of certain good ladies.

He made a circle in the air with his arm and paused. Everyone laughed or smiled at Aunt Kate and Aunt Julia and Mary Jane who all turned crimson with pleasure. Gabriel went on more boldly:

—I feel more strongly with every recurring year that our country has no tradition which does it so much honour and which it should guard so jealously as that of its hospitality. It is a tradition that is unique as far as my experience goes (and I have visited not a few places abroad) among the modern nations. Some would say, perhaps, that with us it is rather a failing than anything to be boasted of. But granted even that, it is, to my mind, a princely failing, and one that I trust will long be cultivated among us. Of one thing, at least, I am sure. As long as this one roof shelters the good ladies aforesaid—and I wish from my heart it may do so for many and many a long year to come—the tradition of genuine warm-hearted courte- ous Irish hospitality, which our forefathers have handed down to us and which we in turn must hand down to our descendants, is still alive among us.

A hearty murmur of assent ran round the table. It shot through Gabriel's mind that Miss Ivors was not there and that she had gone away discourteously: and he said with confidence in himself:

—Ladies and Gentlemen.

—A new generation is growing up in our midst, a generation actuated by new ideas and new principles. It is serious and enthusiastic for these new ideas and its enthusiasm, even when it is misdirected, is, I believe, in the main sincere. But we are living in a sceptical and, if I may use the phrase, a thought-tormented age: and sometimes I fear that this new generation, educated or hypereducated as it is, will lack those qualities of humanity, of hospitality, of kindly humour which belonged to an older day. Listening to-night to the names of all those great singers of the past it seemed to me, I must confess, that we were living in a less spacious age. Those days might, without exaggeration, be called spacious days: and if they are gone beyond recall let us hope, at least, that in gatherings such as this we shall still speak of them with pride and affection, still cherish in our hearts the memory of those dead and gone great ones whose fame the world will not willingly let die.[43]

—Hear, hear! said Mr Browne loudly.

—But yet, continued Gabriel, his voice falling into a softer inflection, there are always in gatherings such as this sadder thoughts that will recur to our minds: thoughts of the past, of youth, of changes, of absent faces that we miss here to-night. Our path through life is strewn with many such sad memories: and were we to brood upon them always we could not find the

[43] *the world . . . die.* Gabriel is echoing a phrase of Milton's here, about his hopes as a poet (*The Reason of Church Government,* Preface to Book II).

heart to go on bravely with our work among the living. We have all of us living duties and living affections which claim, and rightly claim, our strenuous endeavours.

—Therefore, I will not linger on the past. I will not let any gloomy moralising intrude upon us here to-night. Here we are gathered together for a brief moment from the bustle and rush of our everyday routine. We are met here as friends, in the spirit of good-fellowship, as colleagues, also to a certain extent, in the true spirit of *camaraderie,* and as the guests of— what shall I call them?—the Three Graces[44] of the Dublin musical world.

The table burst into applause and laughter at this sally. Aunt Julia vainly asked each of her neighbours in turn to tell her what Gabriel had said.

—He says we are the Three Graces, Aunt Julia, said Mary Jane.

Aunt Julia did not understand but she looked up, smiling, at Gabriel, who continued in the same vein:

—Ladies and Gentlemen.

—I will not attempt to play to-night the part that Paris played on another occasion.[45] I will not attempt to choose between them. The task would be an invidious one and one beyond my poor powers. For when I view them in turn, whether it be our chief hostess herself, whose good heart, whose too good heart, has become a byword with all who know her, or her sister, who seems to be gifted with perennial youth and whose singing must have been a surprise and a revelation to us all to-night, or, last but not least, when I consider our youngest hostess, talented, cheerful, hardworking and the best of nieces, I confess, Ladies and Gentlemen, that I do not know to which of them I should award the prize.

Gabriel glanced down at his aunts and, seeing the large smile on Aunt Julia's face and the tears which had risen to Aunt Kate's eyes, hastened to his close. He raised his glass of port gallantly, while every member of the company fingered a glass expectantly, and said loudly:

—Let us toast them all three together. Let us drink to their health, wealth, long life, happiness and prosperity and may they long continue to hold the proud and self-won position which they hold in their profession and the position of honour and affection which they hold in our hearts.

All the guests stood up, glass in hand, and turning towards the three seated ladies, sang in unison, with Mr Browne as leader:

> *For they are jolly gay fellows,*
> *For they are jolly gay fellows,*
> *For they are jolly gay fellows,*
> *Which nobody can deny.*

Aunt Kate was making frank use of her handkerchief and even Aunt Julia seemed moved. Freddy Malins beat time with his pudding-fork and the singers turned towards one another, as if in melodious conference, while they sang with emphasis:

[44] In classical mythology, the three Graces, daughters of Zeus, were Aglaia (brilliance), Euphrosyne (joy), and Thalia (bloom). They presided over all beauty and charm.

[45] The shepherd Paris had to judge the beauty of Hera, Athena, and Aphrodite. His choice of Aphrodite began the Trojan War.

> *Unless he tells a lie,*
> *Unless he tells a lie,*

Then, turning once more towards their hostesses, they sang:

> *For they are jolly gay fellows,*
> *For they are jolly gay fellows,*
> *For they are jolly gay fellows,*
> *Which nobody can deny.*

The acclamation which followed was taken up beyond the door of the supper-room by many of the other guests and renewed time after time, Freddy Malins acting as officer with his fork on high.

. .

The piercing morning air came into the hall where they were standing so that Aunt Kate said:

—Close the door, somebody. Mrs Malins will get her death of cold.

—Browne is out there, Aunt Kate, said Mary Jane.

—Browne is everywhere, said Aunt Kate, lowering her voice.

Mary Jane laughed at her tone.

—Really, she said archly, he is very attentive.

—He has been laid on[46] here like the gas, said Aunt Kate in the same tone, all during the Christmas.

She laughed herself this time good-humouredly and then added quickly:

—But tell him to come in, Mary Jane, and close the door. I hope to goodness he didn't hear me.

At that moment the hall-door was opened and Mr Browne came in from the doorstep, laughing as if his heart would break. He was dressed in a long green overcoat with mock astrakhan cuffs and collar and wore on his head an oval fur cap. He pointed down the snow-covered quay from where the sound of shrill prolonged whistling was borne in.

—Teddy will have all the cabs in Dublin out, he said.

Gabriel advanced from the little pantry behind the office, struggling into his overcoat and, looking round the hall, said:

—Gretta not down yet?

—She's getting on her things, Gabriel, said Aunt Kate.

—Who's playing up there? asked Gabriel.

—Nobody. They're all gone.

—O no, Aunt Kate, said Mary Jane. Bartell D'Arcy and Miss O'Callaghan aren't gone yet.

—Someone is strumming at the piano, anyhow, said Gabriel.

Mary Jane glanced at Gabriel and Mr Browne and said with a shiver:

—It makes me feel cold to look at you two gentlemen muffled up like that. I wouldn't like to face your journey home at this hour.

—I'd like nothing better this minute, said Mr Browne stoutly, than a

[46] Provided like one of the utilities.

rattling fine walk in the country or a fast drive with a good spanking goer between the shafts.

—We used to have a very good horse and trap at home, said Aunt Julia sadly.

—The never-to-be-forgotten Johnny, said Mary Jane, laughing.

Aunt Kate and Gabriel laughed too.

—Why, what was wonderful about Johnny? asked Mr Browne.

—The late lamented Patrick Morkan, our grandfather, that is, explained Gabriel, commonly known in his later years as the old gentleman, was a glue-boiler.

—O, now, Gabriel, said Aunt Kate, laughing, he had a starch mill.

—Well, glue or starch, said Gabriel, the old gentleman had a horse by the name of Johnny. And Johnny used to work in the old gentleman's mill, walking round and round in order to drive the mill. That was all very well; but now comes the tragic part about Johnny. One fine day the old gentleman thought he'd like to drive out with the quality to a military review in the park.

—The Lord have mercy on his soul, said Aunt Kate compassionately.

—Amen, said Gabriel. So the old gentleman, as I said, harnessed Johnny and put on his very best tall hat and his very best stock collar and drove out in grand style from his ancestral mansion somewhere near Back Lane, I think.

Everyone laughed, even Mrs Malins, at Gabriel's manner and Aunt Kate said:

—O now, Gabriel, he didn't live in Back Lane, really. Only the mill was there.

—Out from the mansion of his forefathers, continued Gabriel, he drove with Johnny. And everything went on beautifully until Johnny came in sight of King Billy's statue:[47] and whether he fell in love with the horse King Billy sits on or whether he thought he was back again in the mill, anyhow he began to walk round the statue.

Gabriel paced in a circle round the hall in his goloshes amid the laughter of the others.

—Round and round he went, said Gabriel, and the old gentleman, who was a very pompous old gentleman, was highly indignant. *Go on, sir! What do you mean, sir? Johnny! Johnny! Most extraordinary conduct! Can't understand the horse!*

The peal of laughter which followed Gabriel's imitation of the incident was interrupted by a resounding knock at the hall-door. Mary Jane ran to open it and let in Freddy Malins. Freddy Malins, with his hat well back on his head and his shoulders humped with cold, was puffing and steaming after his exertions.

—I could only get one cab, he said.

—O, we'll find another along the quay, said Gabriel.

—Yes, said Aunt Kate. Better not keep Mrs Malins standing in the draught.

Mrs Malins was helped down the front steps by her son and Mr Browne

[47] Statue of King William III, who defeated the army of the deposed Catholic King James II at the Battle of the Boyne in 1690.

and, after many manoeuvres, hoisted into the cab. Freddy Malins clambered in after her and spent a long time settling her on the seat, Mr Browne helping him with advice. At last she was settled comfortably and Freddy Malins invited Mr Browne into the cab. There was a good deal of confused talk, and then Mr Browne got into the cab. The cabman settled his rug over his knees, and bent down for the address. The confusion grew greater and the cabman was directed differently by Freddy Malins and Mr Browne, each of whom had his head out through a window of the cab. The difficulty was to know where to drop Mr Browne along the route and Aunt Kate, Aunt Julia and Mary Jane helped the discussion from the doorstep with cross-directions and contradictions and abundance of laughter. As for Freddy Malins he was speechless with laughter. He popped his head in and out of the window every moment, to the great danger of his hat, and told his mother how the discussion was progressing till at last Mr Browne shouted to the bewildered cabman above the din of everybody's laughter:

—Do you know Trinity College?

—Yes, sir, said the cabman.

—Well, drive bang up against Trinity College gates, said Mr Browne, and then we'll tell you where to go. You understand now?

—Yes, sir, said the cabman.

—Make like a bird for Trinity College.

—Right, sir, cried the cabman.

The horse was whipped up and the cab rattled off along the quay amid a chorus of laughter and adieus.

Gabriel had not gone to the door with the others. He was in a dark part of the hall gazing up the staircase. A woman was standing near the top of the first flight, in the shadow also. He could not see her face but he could see the terracotta and salmonpink panels of her skirt which the shadow made appear black and white. It was his wife. She was leaning on the banisters, listening to something. Gabriel was surprised at her stillness and strained his ear to listen also. But he could hear little save the noise of laughter and dispute on the front steps, a few chords struck on the piano and a few notes of a man's voice singing.

He stood still in the gloom of the hall, trying to catch the air that the voice was singing and gazing up at his wife. There was grace and mystery in her attitude as if she were a symbol of something. He asked himself what is a woman standing on the stairs in the shadow, listening to distant music, a symbol of. If he were a painter he would paint her in that attitude. Her blue felt hat would show off the bronze of her hair against the darkness and the dark panels of her skirt would show off the light ones. *Distant Music* he would call the picture if he were a painter.

The hall-door was closed; and Aunt Kate, Aunt Julia and Mary Jane came down the hall, still laughing.

—Well, isn't Freddy terrible? said Mary Jane. He's really terrible.

Gabriel said nothing but pointed up the stairs towards where his wife was standing. Now that the hall-door was closed the voice and the piano could be heard more clearly. Gabriel held up his hand for them to be silent. The song seemed to be in the old Irish tonality and the singer seemed uncertain both of his words and of his voice. The voice, made plaintive by

distance and by the singer's hoarseness, faintly illuminated the cadence of the air with words expressing grief:

> *O, the rain falls on my heavy locks*
> *And the dew wets my skin,*
> *My babe lies cold . . .*[48]

—O, exclaimed Mary Jane. It's Bartell D'Arcy singing and he wouldn't sing all the night. O, I'll get him to sing a song before he goes.

—O, do, Mary Jane, said Aunt Kate.

Mary Jane brushed past the others and ran to the staircase but before she reached it the singing stopped and the piano was closed abruptly.

—O, what a pity! she cried. Is he coming down, Gretta?

Gabriel heard his wife answer yes and saw her come down towards them. A few steps behind her were Mr Bartell D'Arcy and Miss O'Callaghan.

—O, Mr D'Arcy, cried Mary Jane, it's downright mean of you to break off like that when we were all in raptures listening to you.

—I have been at him all the evening, said Miss O'Callaghan, and Mrs Conroy too and he told us he had a dreadful cold and couldn't sing.

—O, Mr D'Arcy, said Aunt Kate, now that was a great fib to tell.

—Can't you see that I'm as hoarse as a crow? said Mr D'Arcy roughly.

He went into the pantry hastily and put on his overcoat. The others, taken aback by his rude speech, could find nothing to say. Aunt Kate wrinkled her brows and made signs to the others to drop the subject. Mr D'Arcy stood swathing his neck carefully and frowning.

—It's the weather, said Aunt Julia, after a pause.

—Yes, everybody has colds, said Aunt Kate readily, everybody.

—They say, said Mary Jane, we haven't had snow like it for thirty years; and I read this morning in the newspapers that the snow is general all over Ireland.

—I love the look of snow, said Aunt Julia sadly.

—So do I, said Miss O'Callaghan. I think Christmas is never really Christmas unless we have the snow on the ground.

—But poor Mr D'Arcy doesn't like the snow, said Aunt Kate, smiling.

Mr D'Arcy came from the pantry, fully swathed and buttoned, and in a repentant tone told them the history of his cold. Everyone gave him advice and said it was a great pity and urged him to be very careful of his throat in the night air. Gabriel watched his wife who did not join in the conversation. She was standing right under the dusty fanlight and the flame of the gas lit up the rich bronze of her hair which he had seen her drying at the fire a few days before. She was in the same attitude and seemed unaware of the talk about her. At last she turned towards them and Gabriel saw that there was colour on her cheeks and that her eyes were shining. A sudden tide of joy went leaping out of his heart.

[48] The song is "The Lass of Aughrim," a version of a song also known as "Lord Gregory" (Child ballad number 76). The lass stands in the rain outside the castle of Lord Gregory, her child's father, begging to be taken in. Joyce learned this song from his Galway wife Nora.

—Mr D'Arcy, she said, what is the name of that song you were singing?

—It's called *The Lass of Aughrim,* said Mr D'Arcy, but I couldn't remember it properly. Why? Do you know it?

—*The Lass of Aughrim,* she repeated. I couldn't think of the name.

—It's a very nice air, said Mary Jane. I'm sorry you were not in voice tonight.

—Now, Mary Jane, said Aunt Kate, don't annoy Mr D'Arcy. I won't have him annoyed.

Seeing that all were ready to start she shepherded them to the door where good-night was said:

—Well, good-night, Aunt Kate, and thanks for the pleasant evening.

—Good-night, Gabriel. Good-night, Gretta!

—Good-night, Aunt Kate, and thanks ever so much. Good-night Aunt Julia.

—O, good-night, Gretta, I didn't see you.

—Good-night, Mr D'Arcy. Good-night, Miss O'Callaghan.

—Good-night, Miss Morkan.

—Good-night, again.

—Good-night, all. Safe home.

—Good-night. Good night.

The morning was still dark. A dull yellow light brooded over the houses and the river; and the sky seemed to be descending. It was slushy underfoot; and only streaks and patches of snow lay on the roofs, on the parapets of the quay and on the area railings. The lamps were still burning redly in the murky air and, across the river, the palace of the Four Courts[49] stood out menacingly against the heavy sky.

She was walking on before him with Mr Bartell D'Arcy, her shoes in a brown parcel tucked under one arm and her hands holding her skirt up from the slush. She had no longer any grace of attitude but Gabriel's eyes were still bright with happiness. The blood went bounding along his veins; and the thoughts went rioting through his brain, proud, joyful, tender, valorous.

She was walking on before him so lightly and so erect that he longed to run after her noiselessly, catch her by the shoulders and say something foolish and affectionate into her ear. She seemed to him so frail that he longed to defend her against something and then to be alone with her. Moments of their secret life together burst like stars upon his memory. A heliotrope envelope was lying beside his breakfast-cup and he was caressing it with his hand. Birds were twittering in the ivy and the sunny web of the curtain was shimmering along the floor: he could not eat for happiness. They were standing on the crowded platform and he was placing a ticket inside the warm palm of her glove. He was standing with her in the cold, looking in through a grated window at a man making bottles in a roaring furnace. It was very cold. Her face, fragrant in the cold air, was quite close to his; and suddenly he called out to the man at the furnace:

—Is the fire hot, sir?

But the man could not hear with the noise of the furnace. It was just as well. He might have answered rudely.

[49] The Irish law courts.

A wave of yet more tender joy escaped from his heart and went coursing in warm flood along his arteries. Like the tender fire of stars moments of their life together, that no one knew of or would ever know of, broke upon and illumined his memory. He longed to recall to her those moments, to make her forget the years of their dull existence together and remember only their moments of ecstasy. For the years, he felt, had not quenched his soul or hers. Their children, his writing, her household cares had not quenched all their souls' tender fire. In one letter that he had written to her then he had said: *Why is it that words like these seem to me so dull and cold? Is it because there is no word tender enough to be your name?*

Like distant music these words that he had written years before were borne towards him from the past. He longed to be alone with her. When the others had gone away, when he and she were in their room in the hotel, then they would be alone together. He would call her softly:

—Gretta!

Perhaps she would not hear at once: she would be undressing. Then something in his voice would strike her. She would turn and look at him. . . .

At the corner of Winetavern Street they met a cab. He was glad of its rattling noise as it saved him from conversation. She was looking out of the window and seemed tired. The others spoke only a few words, pointing out some building or street. The horse galloped along wearily under the murky morning sky, dragging his old rattling box after his heels, and Gabriel was again in a cab with her, galloping to catch the boat, galloping to their honeymoon.

As the cab drove across O'Connell Bridge Miss O'Callaghan said:

—They say you never cross O'Connell Bridge without seeing a white horse.

—I see a white man this time, said Gabriel.

—Where? asked Mr Bartell D'Arcy.

Gabriel pointed to the statue, on which lay patches of snow.[50] Then he nodded familiarly to it and waved his hand.

—Good-night, Dan, he said gaily.

When the cab drew up before the hotel Gabriel jumped out and, in spite of Mr Bartell D'Arcy's protest, paid the driver. He gave the man a shilling over his fare. The man saluted and said:

—A prosperous New Year to you, sir.

—The same to you, said Gabriel cordially.

She leaned for a moment on his arm in getting out of the cab and while standing at the curbstone, bidding the others good-night. She leaned lightly on his arm, as lightly as when she had danced with him a few hours before. He had felt proud and happy then, happy that she was his, proud of her grace and wifely carriage. But now, after the kindling again of so many memories, the first touch of her body, musical and strange and perfumed, sent through him a keen pang of lust. Under cover of her silence he pressed her arm closely to his side; and, as they stood at the hotel door, he felt that they had escaped from their lives and duties, escaped from home

[50] The statue is of Daniel O'Connell (1775–1847), the Irish nationalist after whom the bridge is named.

and friends and run away together with wild and radiant hearts to a new adventure.

An old man was dozing in a great hooded chair in the hall. He lit a candle in the office and went before them to the stairs. They followed him in silence, their feet falling in soft thuds on the thickly carpeted stairs. She mounted the stairs behind the porter, her head bowed in the ascent, her frail shoulders curved as with a burden, her skirt girt tightly about her. He could have flung his arms about her hips and held her still for his arms were trembling with desire to seize her and only the stress of his nails against the palms of his hands held the wild impulse of his body in check. The porter halted on the stairs to settle his guttering candle. They halted too on the steps below him. In the silence Gabriel could hear the falling of the molten wax into the tray and the thumping of his own heart against his ribs.

The porter led them along a corridor and opened a door. Then he set his unstable candle down on a toilet-table and asked at what hour they were to be called in the morning.

—Eight, said Gabriel.

The porter pointed to the tap of the electric-light and began a muttered apology but Gabriel cut him short.

—We don't want any light. We have light enough from the street. And I say, he added, pointing to the candle, you might remove that handsome article, like a good man.

The porter took up his candle again, but slowly for he was surprised by such a novel idea. Then he mumbled good-night and went out. Gabriel shot the lock to.

A ghostly light from the street lamp lay in a long shaft from one window to the door. Gabriel threw his overcoat and hat on a couch and crossed the room towards the window. He looked down into the street in order that his emotion might calm a little. Then he turned and leaned against a chest of drawers with his back to the light. She had taken off her hat and cloak and was standing before a large swinging mirror, unhooking her waist. Gabriel paused for a few moments, watching her, and then said:

—Gretta!

She turned away from the mirror slowly and walked along the shaft of light towards him. Her face looked so serious and weary that the words would not pass Gabriel's lips. No, it was not the moment yet.

—You looked tired, he said.

—I am a little, she answered.

—You don't feel ill or weak?

—No, tired: that's all.

She went on to the window and stood there, looking out. Gabriel waited again and then, fearing that diffidence was about to conquer him, he said abruptly:

—By the way, Gretta!

—What is it?

—You know that poor fellow Malins? he said quickly.

—Yes. What about him?

—Well, poor fellow, he's a decent sort of chap, after all, continued Gabriel in a false voice. He gave me back that sovereign I lent him and I didn't

expect it really. It's a pity he wouldn't keep away from that Browne, because he's not a bad fellow at heart.

He was trembling now with annoyance. Why did she seem so abstracted? He did not know how he could begin. Was she annoyed, too, about something? If she would only turn to him or come to him of her own accord! To take her as she was would be brutal. No, he must see some ardour in her eyes first. He longed to be master of her strange mood.

—When did you lend him the pound? she asked, after a pause.

Gabriel strove to restrain himself from breaking out in brutal language about the sottish Malins and his pound. He longed to cry to her from his soul, to crush her body against his, to overmaster her. But he said:

—O, at Christmas, when he opened that little Christmas-card shop in Henry Street.

He was in such a fever of rage and desire that he did not hear her come from the window. She stood before him for an instant, looking at him strangely. Then, suddenly raising herself on tiptoe and resting her hands lightly on his shoulders, she kissed him.

—You are a very generous person, Gabriel, she said.

Gabriel, trembling with delight at her sudden kiss and at the quaintness of her phrase, put his hands on her hair and began smoothing it back, scarcely touching it with his fingers. The washing had made it fine and brilliant. His heart was brimming over with happiness. Just when he was wishing for it she had come to him of her own accord. Perhaps her thoughts had been running with his. Perhaps she had felt the impetuous desire that was in him, and then the yielding mood had come upon her. Now that she had fallen to him so easily he wondered why he had been so diffident.

He stood, holding her head between his hands. Then, slipping one arm swiftly about her body and drawing her towards him, he said softly:

—Gretta dear, what are you thinking about?

She did not answer nor yield wholly to his arm. He said again, softly:

—Tell me what it is, Gretta. I think I know what is the matter. Do I know?

She did not answer at once. Then she said in an outburst of tears:

—O, I am thinking about that song, *The Lass of Aughrim.*

She broke loose from him and ran to the bed and, throwing her arms across the bed-rail, hid her face. Gabriel stood stock-still for a moment in astonishment and then followed her. As he passed in the way of the cheval-glass[51] he caught sight of himself in full length, his broad, well-filled shirt-front, the face whose expression always puzzled him when he saw it in a mirror and his glimmering gilt-rimmed eyeglasses. He halted a few paces from her and said:

—What about the song? Why does that make you cry?

She raised her head from her arms and dried her eyes with the back of her hand like a child. A kinder note than he had intended went into his voice.

—Why, Gretta? he asked.

—I am thinking about a person long ago who used to sing that song.

[51] A long mirror mounted to swing in a frame.

—And who was the person long ago? asked Gabriel, smiling.

—It was a person I used to know in Galway when I was living with my grandmother, she said.

The smile passed away from Gabriel's face. A dull anger began to gather again at the back of his mind and the dull fires of his lust began to glow angrily in his veins.

—Someone you were in love with? he asked ironically.

—It was a young boy I used to know, she answered, named Michael Furey. He used to sing that song, *The Lass of Aughrim*. He was very delicate.

Gabriel was silent. He did not wish her to think that he was interested in this delicate boy.

—I can see him so plainly, she said, after a moment. Such eyes as he had: big dark eyes! And such an expression in them—an expression!

—O then, you were in love with him? said Gabriel.

—I used to go out walking with him, she said, when I was in Galway.

A thought flew across Gabriel's mind.

—Perhaps that was why you wanted to go to Galway with that Ivors girl? he said coldly.

She looked at him and asked in surprise:

—What for?

Her eyes made Gabriel feel awkward. He shrugged his shoulders and said:

—How do I know? To see him perhaps.

She looked away from him along the shaft of light towards the window in silence.

—He is dead, she said at length. He died when he was only seventeen. Isn't it a terrible thing to die so young as that?

—What was he? asked Gabriel, still ironically.

—He was in the gasworks, she said.

Gabriel felt humiliated by the failure of his irony and by the evocation of this figure from the dead, a boy in the gasworks. While he had been full of memories of their secret life together, full of tenderness and joy and desire, she had been comparing him in her mind with another. A shameful consciousness of his own person assailed him. He saw himself as a ludicrous figure, acting as a pennyboy[52] for his aunts, a nervous well-meaning sentimentalist, orating to vulgarians and idealising his own clownish lusts, the pitiable fatuous fellow he had caught a glimpse of in the mirror. Instinctively he turned his back more to the light lest she might see the shame that burned upon his forehead.

He tried to keep up his tone of cold interrogation but his voice when he spoke was humble and indifferent.

—I suppose you were in love with this Michael Furey, Gretta, he said.

—I was great with him at that time, she said.

Her voice was veiled and sad. Gabriel, feeling now how vain it would be to try to lead her whither he had purposed, caressed one of her hands and said, also sadly:

—And what did he die of so young, Gretta? Consumption, was it?

—I think he died for me, she answered.

[52] Errand boy.

A vague terror seized Gabriel at this answer as if, at that hour when he had hoped to triumph, some impalpable and vindictive being was coming against him, gathering forces against him in its vague world. But he shook himself free of it with an effort of reason and continued to caress her hand. He did not question her again for he felt that she would tell him of herself. Her hand was warm and moist: it did not respond to his touch but he continued to caress it just as he had caressed her first letter to him that spring morning.

—It was in the winter, she said, about the beginning of the winter when I was going to leave my grandmother's and come up here to the convent. And he was ill at the time in his lodgings in Galway and wouldn't be let out and his people in Oughterard[53] were written to. He was in decline, they said, or something like that. I never knew rightly.

She paused for a moment and sighed.

—Poor fellow, she said. He was very fond of me and he was such a gentle boy. We used to go out together, walking, you know, Gabriel, like the way they do in the country. He was going to study singing only for his health. He had a very good voice, poor Michael Furey.

—Well; and then? asked Gabriel.

—And then when it came to the time for me to leave Galway and come up to the convent he was much worse and I wouldn't be let see him so I wrote a letter saying I was going up to Dublin and would be back in the summer and hoping he would be better then.

She paused for a moment to get her voice under control and then went on;

—Then the night before I left I was in my grandmother's house in Nuns' Island, packing up, and I heard gravel thrown up against the window. The window was so wet I couldn't see so I ran downstairs as I was and slipped out the back into the garden and there was the poor fellow at the end of the garden, shivering.

—And did you not tell him to go back? asked Gabriel.

—I implored of him to go home at once and told him he would get his death in the rain. But he said he did not want to live. I can see his eyes as well as well! He was standing at the end of the wall where there was a tree.

—And did he go home? asked Gabriel.

—Yes, he went home. And when I was only a week in the convent he died and he was buried in Oughterard where his people came from. O, the day I heard that, that he was dead!

She stopped, choking with sobs, and, overcome by emotion flung herself downward on the bed, sobbing in the quilt. Gabriel held her hand for a moment longer, irresolutely, and then, shy of intruding on her grief, let it fall gently and walked quietly to the window.

She was fast asleep.

Gabriel, leaning on his elbow, looked for a few moments unresentfully on her tangled hair and half-open mouth, listening to her deep-drawn breath. So she had had that romance in her life: a man had died for her sake. It hardly pained him now to think how poor a part he, her husband,

[53] A village near Galway, in western Ireland.

had played in her life. He watched her while she slept as though he and she had never lived together as man and wife. His curious eyes rested long upon her face and on her hair: and, as he thought of what she must have been then, in that time of her first girlish beauty, a strange, friendly pity for her entered his soul. He did not like to say even to himself that her face was no longer beautiful but he knew that it was no longer the face for which Michael Furey had braved death.

Perhaps she had not told him all the story. His eyes moved to the chair over which she had thrown some of her clothes. A petticoat string dangled to the floor. One boot stood upright, its limp upper fallen down: the fellow of it lay upon its side. He wondered at his riot of emotions of an hour before. From what had it proceeded? From his aunt's supper, from his own foolish speech, from the wine and dancing, the merry-making when saying good-night in the hall, the pleasure of the walk along the river in the snow. Poor Aunt Julia! She, too, would soon be a shade with the shade of Patrick Morkan and his horse. He had caught that haggard look upon her face for a moment when she was singing *Arrayed for the Bridal*. Soon, perhaps, he would be sitting in that same drawing-room, dressed in black, his silk hat on his knees. The blinds would be drawn down and Aunt Kate would be sitting beside him, crying and blowing her nose and telling him how Julia had died. He would cast about in his mind for some words that might console her, and would find only lame and useless ones. Yes, yes: that would happen very soon.

The air of the room chilled his shoulders. He stretched himself cautiously along under the sheets and lay down beside his wife. One by one they were all becoming shades. Better pass boldly into that other world, in the full glory of some passion, than fade and wither dismally with age. He thought of how she who lay beside him had locked in her heart for so many years that image of her lover's eyes when he had told her that he did not wish to live.

Generous tears filled Gabriel's eyes. He had never felt like that himself towards any woman but he knew that such a feeling must be love. The tears gathered more thickly in his eyes and in the partial darkness he imagined he saw the form of a young man standing under a dripping tree. Other forms were near. His soul had approached that region where dwell the vast hosts of the dead. He was conscious of, but could not apprehend, their wayward and flickering existence. His own identity was fading out into a grey impalpable world: the solid world itself which these dead had one time reared and lived in was dissolving and dwindling.

A few light taps upon the pane made him turn to the window. It had begun to snow again. He watched sleepily the flakes, silver and dark, falling obliquely against the lamplight. The time had come for him to set out on his journey westward. Yes, the newspapers were right: snow was general all over Ireland. It was falling on every part of the dark central plain, on the treeless hills, falling softly upon the Bog of Allen[54] and, farther westward, softly falling into the dark mutinous Shannon waves.[55] It was falling, too, upon every part of the lonely churchyard on the hill where Michael Furey

[54] The Bog of Allen is just southwest of Dublin.
[55] Waves on the Shannon river, near Limerick, in southwest Ireland.

lay buried. It lay thickly drifted on the crooked crosses and headstones, on the spears of the little gate, on the barren thorns. His soul swooned slowly as he heard the snow falling faintly through the universe and faintly falling, like the descent of their last end, upon all the living and the dead.

from *ULYSSES*

CALYPSO

Mr Leopold Bloom ate with relish the inner organs of beasts and fowls. He liked thick giblet soup, nutty gizzards, a stuffed roast heart, liverslices fried with crustcrumbs, fried hencods' roes. Most of all he liked grilled mutton kidneys which gave to his palate a fine tang of faintly scented urine.

Kidneys were in his mind as he moved about the kitchen softly, righting her breakfast things on the humpy tray. Gelid light and air were in the kitchen but out of doors gentle summer morning everywhere. Made him feel a bit peckish.

The coals were reddening.

Another slice of bread and butter: three, four: right. She didn't like her plate full. Right. He turned from the tray, lifted the kettle off the hob and set it sideways on the fire. It sat there, dull and squat, its spout stuck out. Cup of tea soon. Good. Mouth dry.

The cat walked stiffly round a leg of the table with tail on high.

—Mkgnao!

—O, there you are, Mr Bloom said, turning from the fire.

The cat mewed in answer and stalked again stiffly round a leg of the table, mewing. Just how she stalks over my writingtable. Prr. Scratch my head. Prr.

Mr Bloom watched curiously, kindly the lithe black form. Clean to see: the gloss of her sleek hide, the white button under the butt of her tail, the green flashing eyes. He bent down to her, his hands on his knees.

—Milk for the pussens, he said.

—Mrkgnao! the cat cried.

They call them stupid. They understand what we say better than we understand them. She understands all she wants to. Vindictive too. Cruel. Her nature. Curious mice never squeal. Seem to like it. Wonder what I look like to her. Height of a tower? No, she can jump me.

—Afraid of the chickens she is, he said mockingly. Afraid of the chook-chooks. I never saw such a stupid pussens as the pussens.

—Mrkrgnao! the cat said loudly.

She blinked up out of her avid shameclosing eyes, mewing plaintively and long, showing him her milkwhite teeth. He watched the dark eyeslits narrowing with greed till her eyes were green stones. Then he went to the dresser, took the jug Hanlon's milkman had just filled for him, poured warmbubbled milk on a saucer and set it slowly on the floor.

—Gurrhr! she cried, running to lap.

He watched the bristles shining wirily in the weak light as she tipped three times and licked lightly. Wonder is it true if you clip them they can't mouse after. Why? They shine in the dark, perhaps, the tips. Or kind of feelers in the dark, perhaps.

He listened to her licking lap. Ham and eggs, no. No good eggs with this drouth. Want pure fresh water. Thursday: not a good day either for a mutton kidney at Buckley's. Fried with butter, a shake of pepper. Better a pork kidney at Dlugacz's. While the kettle is boiling. She lapped slower, then licking the saucer clean. Why are their tongues so rough? To lap better, all porous holes. Nothing she can eat? He glanced round him. No.

On quietly creaky boots he went up the staircase to the hall, paused by the bedroom door. She might like something tasty. Thin bread and butter she likes in the morning. Still perhaps: once in a way.

He said softly in the bare hall:

—I'm going round the corner. Be back in a minute.

And when he had heard his voice say it he added:

—You don't want anything for breakfast?

A sleepy soft grunt answered:

—Mn.

No. She didn't want anything. He heard then a warm heavy sigh, softer, as she turned over and the loose brass quoits of the bedstead jingled. Must get those settled really. Pity. All the way from Gibraltar. Forgotten any little Spanish she knew. Wonder what her father gave for it. Old style. Ah yes! of course. Bought it at the governor's auction. Got a short knock. Hard as nails at a bargain, old Tweedy. Yes, sir. At Plevna that was. I rose from the ranks, sir, and I'm proud of it. Still he had brains enough to make that corner in stamps. Now that was farseeing.

His hand took his hat from the peg over his initialled heavy overcoat and his lost property office secondhand waterproof. Stamps: stickyback pictures. Daresay lots of officers are in the swim too. Course they do. The sweated legend in the crown of his hat told him mutely: Plasto's high grade ha. He peeped quickly inside the leather headband. White slip of paper. Quite safe.[1]

On the doorstep he felt in his hip pocket for the latchkey. Not there. In the trousers I left off. Must get it. Potato I have.[2] Creaky wardrobe. No use disturbing her. She turned over sleepily that time. He pulled the halldoor to after him very quietly, more, till the footleaf dropped gently over the threshold, a limp lid. Looked shut. All right till I come back anyhow.

He crossed to the bright side, avoiding the loose cellarflap of number seventyfive. The sun was nearing the steeple of George's church.[3] Be a warm day I fancy. Specially in these black clothes feel it more. Black conducts, reflects, (refracts is it?), the heat. But I couldn't go in that light suit. Make a picnic of it. His eyelids sank quietly often as he walked in happy warmth. Boland's breadvan delivering with trays our daily but she prefers

[1] Bloom has hidden in his hat the false name ("Henry Flower") and the post office address he uses to carry on a clandestine correspondence with a woman named Martha Clifford.

[2] Bloom, like many Irishmen of his day, carries a shrivelled potato in his pocket as a reminder of the Potato Famine of the 1840's. Bloom's was given to him by his mother.

[3] Bloom's house is at 7 Eccles Street, in northwest Dublin. St. George's Church is in Hardwicke Place, just east of Eccles Street.

yesterday's loaves turnovers crisp crowns hot. Makes you feel young. Somewhere in the east: early morning: set off at dawn. Travel round in front of the sun, steal a day's march on him. Keep it up for ever never grow a day older technically. Walk along a strand, strange land, come to a city gate, sentry there, old ranker too, old Tweedy's big moustaches, leaning on a long kind of a spear. Wander through awned streets. Turbaned faces going by. Dark caves of carpet shops, big man, Turko the terrible,[4] seated cross-legged, smoking a coiled pipe. Cries of sellers in the streets. Drink water scented with fennel, sherbet. Dander along all day. Might meet a robber or two. Well, meet him. Getting on to sundown. The shadows of the mosques among the pillars: priest with a scroll rolled up. A shiver of the trees, signal, the evening wind. I pass on. Fading gold sky. A mother watches me from her doorway. She calls her children home in their dark language. High wall: beyond strings twanged. Night sky, moon, violet, colour of Molly's new garters. Strings. Listen. A girl playing one of those instruments what do you call them: dulcimers. I pass.

Probably not a bit like it really. Kind of stuff you read: in the track of the sun.[5] Sunburst on the title page. He smiled, pleasing himself. What Arthur Griffith said about the headpiece over the *Freeman* leader: a homerule sun rising up in the northwest from the laneway behind the bank of Ireland.[6] He prolonged his pleased smile. Ikey touch that: homerule sun rising up in the northwest.

He approached Larry O'Rourke's. From the cellar grating floated up the flabby gush of porter. Through the open doorway the bar squirted out whiffs of ginger, teadust, biscuitmush. Good house, however: just the end of the city traffic. For instance M'Auley's down there: n. g.[7] as position. Of course if they ran a tramline along the North Circular from the cattlemarket to the quays value would go up like a shot.

Baldhead over the blind. Cute old codger. No use canvassing him for an ad. Still he knows his own business best. There he is, sure enough, my bold Larry, leaning against the sugarbin in his shirtsleeves watching the aproned curate swab up with mop and bucket. Simon Dedalus takes him off to a tee with his eyes screwed up. Do you know what I'm going to tell you? What's that, Mr O'Rourke? Do you know what? The Russians, they'd only be an eight o'clock breakfast for the Japanese.[8]

Stop and say a word: after the funeral perhaps. Sad thing about poor Dignam, Mr O'Rourke.

Turning into Dorset street he said freshly in greeting through the doorway:

—Good day, Mr O'Rourke.

—Good day to you.

[4] Turko the Terrible was the main character in a popular pantomime of that name by Edwin Hamilton.
[5] Bloom is thinking of a book: Frederick Diodati Thompson's *In the Track of the Sun: Diary of a Globe Trotter* (1893).
[6] *The Freeman's Journal and National Press* was a daily Dublin newspaper. The headpiece does show the sun rising over the Bank of Ireland (and thus in the northwest). Arthur Griffith was an Irish patriot and editor of the *United Irishman*.
[7] "No good."
[8] World attention in 1904 was focused on the Russo-Japanese War (February, 1904–September, 1905).

—Lovely weather, sir.

—'Tis all that.

Where do they get the money? Coming up redheaded curates from the county Leitrim, rinsing empties and old man in the cellar.[9] Then, lo and behold, they blossom out as Adam Findlaters or Dan Tallons.[10] Then think of the competition. General thirst. Good puzzle would be cross Dublin without passing a pub. Save it they can't. Off the drunks perhaps. Put down three and carry five. What is that, a bob here and there, dribs and drabs. On the wholesale orders perhaps. Doing a double shuffle with the town travellers. Square it you with the boss and we'll split the job, see?

How much would that tot to off the porter in the month? Say ten barrels of stuff. Say he got ten per cent off. O more. Fifteen. He passed Saint Joseph's National school. Brats' clamour. Windows open. Fresh air helps memory. Or a lilt. Ahbeesee defeegee kelomen opeecue rustyouvee doubleyou. Boys are they? Yes. Inishturk. Inishark. Inishboffin. At their joggerfry. Mine. Slieve Bloom.[11]

He halted before Dlugacz's window, staring at the hanks of sausages, polonies, black and white. Fifteen multiplied by. The figures whitened in his mind, unsolved: displeased, he let them fade. The shiny links, packed with forcemeat, fed his gaze and he breathed in tranquilly the lukewarm breath of cooked spicy pigs' blood.

A kidney oozed bloodgouts on the willowpatterned dish: the last. He stood by the nextdoor girl at the counter. Would she buy it too, calling the items from a slip in her hand? Chapped: washingsoda. And a pound and a half of Denny's sausages. His eyes rested on her vigorous hips. Woods his name is. Wonder what he does. Wife is oldish. New blood. No followers allowed. Strong pair of arms. Whacking a carpet on the clothesline. She does whack it, by George. The way her crooked skirt swings at each whack.

The ferreteyed porkbutcher folded the sausages he had snipped off with blotchy fingers, sausagepink. Sound meat there: like a stallfed heifer.

He took a page up from the pile of cut sheets: the model farm at Kinnereth on the lakeshore of Tiberias.[12] Can become ideal winter sanatorium. Moses Montefiore.[13] I thought he was. Farmhouse, wall round it, blurred cattle cropping. He held the page from him: interesting: read it nearer, the title, the blurred cropping cattle, the page rustling. A young white heifer. Those mornings in the cattlemarket,[14] the beasts lowing in their pens, branded sheep, flop and fall of dung, the breeders in hobnailed boots trudging through the litter, slapping a palm on a ripemeated hindquarter, there's a prime one, unpeeled switches in their hands. He held the page aslant patiently, bending his senses and his will, his soft subject gaze at rest. The crooked skirt swinging, whack by whack by whack.

The porkbutcher snapped two sheets from the pile, wrapped up her prime sausages and made a red grimace.

[9]*Curates:* slang for bartenders. *Old man:* the drink that customers leave in their glasses.
[10]Prosperous Dublin grocers and wine merchants.
[11]Slieve Bloom: a range of mountains in central Ireland.
[12]Tiberias is another name for the Sea of Galilee. A model farm was founded at Kinnereth (or Kinneret) in 1908 by the Palestine Land Development Company.
[13]A prominent Anglo-Jewish Zionist.
[14]Bloom worked in 1893–94 for Joseph Cuffe in the Dublin cattle market.

—Now, my miss, he said.

She tendered a coin, smiling boldly, holding her thick wrist out.

—Thank you, my miss. And one shilling threepence change. For you, please?

Mr Bloom pointed quickly. To catch up and walk behind her if she went slowly, behind her moving hams. Pleasant to see first thing in the morning. Hurry up, damn it. Make hay while the sun shines. She stood outside the shop in sunlight and sauntered lazily to the right. He sighed down his nose: they never understand. Sodachapped hands. Crusted toenails too. Brown scapulars in tatters, defending her both ways. The sting of disregard glowed to weak pleasure within his breast. For another: a constable off duty cuddling her in Eccles lane. They like them sizeable. Prime sausage. O please, Mr Policeman, I'm lost in the wood.[15]

—Threepence, please.

His hand accepted the moist tender gland and slid it into a sidepocket. Then it fetched up three coins from his trousers' pocket and laid them on the rubber prickles. They lay, were read quickly and quickly slid, disc by disc, into the till.

—Thank you, sir. Another time.

A speck of eager fire from foxeyes thanked him. He withdrew his gaze after an instant. No: better not: another time.

—Good morning, he said, moving away.

—Good morning, sir.

No sign. Gone. What matter?

He walked back along Dorset street, reading gravely. Agendath Netaim: planter's company.[16] To purchase waste sandy tracts from Turkish government and plant with eucalyptus trees. Excellent for shade, fuel and construction. Orangegroves and immense melonfields north of Jaffa. You pay eighty marks and they plant a dunam of land for you with olives, oranges, almonds or citrons. Olives cheaper: oranges need artificial irrigation. Every year you get a sending of the crop. Your name entered for life as owner in the book of the union. Can pay ten down and the balance in yearly instalments. Bleibtreustrasse 34, Berlin, W. 15.

Nothing doing. Still an idea behind it.

He looked at the cattle, blurred in silver heat. Silverpowdered olivetrees. Quiet long days: pruning, ripening. Olives are packed in jars, eh? I have a few left from Andrews. Molly spitting them out. Knows the taste of them now. Oranges in tissue paper packed in crates. Citrons too. Wonder is poor Citron still in Saint Kevin's parade. And Mastiansky with the old cither.[17] Pleasant evenings we had then. Molly in Citron's basketchair. Nice to hold, cool waxen fruit, hold in the hand, lift it to the nostrils and smell the perfume. Like that, heavy, sweet, wild perfume. Always the same, year after year. They fetched high prices too, Moisel told me. Arbutus place: Pleasants street: pleasant old times. Must be without a

[15] Bloom is thinking of a music hall song, "Oh Please, Mr. P'liceman, Oh! Oh! Oh!," popular in the 1890's.

[16] *Agendath Netaim*, as Bloom notes, is Hebrew for "planters' company." Bloom is reading an ad for a cooperative Zionist colony. (The actual Hebrew word would be *Agudath*.)

[17] Bloom is remembering his neighbors when he lived in Lombard Street, in south-central Dublin, 1892–93.

flaw, he said. Coming all that way: Spain, Gibraltar, Mediterranean, the Levant. Crates lined up on the quayside at Jaffa, chap ticking them off in a book, navvies handling them barefoot in soiled dungarees. There's what-doyoucallhim out of. How do you? Doesn't see. Chap you know just to salute bit of a bore. His back is like that Norwegian captain's.[18] Wonder if I'll meet him today. Watering cart. To provoke the rain. On earth as it is in heaven.

A cloud began to cover the sun slowly, wholly. Grey. Far.

No, not like that. A barren land, bare waste. Vulcanic lake, the dead sea: no fish, weedless, sunk deep in the earth. No wind could lift those waves, grey metal, poisonous foggy waters. Brimstone they called it raining down: the cities of the plain: Sodom, Gomorrah, Edom. All dead names. A dead sea in a dead land, grey and old. Old now. It bore the oldest, the first race. A bent hag crossed from Cassidy's, clutching a naggin bottle by the neck. The oldest people. Wandered far away over all the earth, captivity to captivity, multiplying, dying, being born everywhere. It lay there now. Now it could bear no more. Dead: an old woman's: the grey sunken cunt of the world.

Desolation.

Grey horror seared his flesh. Folding the page into his pocket he turned into Eccles street, hurrying homeward. Cold oils slid along his veins, chilling his blood: age crusting him with a salt cloak. Well, I am here now. Yes, I am here now. Morning mouth bad images. Got up wrong side of the bed. Must begin again those Sandow's exercises.[19] On the hands down. Blotchy brown brick houses. Number eighty still unlet. Why is that? Valuation is only twentyeight. Towers, Battersby, North, MacArthur: parlour windows plastered with bills. Plasters on a sore eye. To smell the gentle smoke of tea, fume of the pan, sizzling butter. Be near her ample bedwarmed flesh. Yes, yes.

Quick warm sunlight came running from Berkeley road, swiftly, in slim sandals, along the brightening footpath. Runs, she runs to meet me, a girl with gold hair on the wind.

Two letters and a card lay on the hallfloor. He stooped and gathered them. Mrs Marion Bloom. His quickened heart slowed at once. Bold hand. Mrs Marion.

—Poldy!

Entering the bedroom he halfclosed his eyes and walked through warm yellow twilight towards her tousled head.

—Who are the letters for?

He looked at them. Mullingar. Milly.[20]

—A letter for me from Milly, he said carefully, and a card to you. And a letter for you.

He laid her card and letter on the twill bedspread near the curve of her knees.

[18] That is, hunched. Joyce's father told a comic tale about a tailor and a hunchbacked Norwegian captain, later the basis for an episode in *Finnegans Wake.*

[19] Eugene Sandow wrote *Physical Strength and How to Obtain It* (1897), a book of exercises that, we later learn, Bloom owns.

[20] Fifteen-year-old Milly Bloom has recently taken a job as a photographer's assistant in Mullingar, about fifty miles west of Dublin.

—Do you want the blind up?

Letting the blind up by gentle tugs halfway his backward eye saw her glance at the letter and tuck it under her pillow.

—That do? he asked, turning.

She was reading the card, propped on her elbow.

—She got the things, she said.

He waited till she had laid the card aside and curled herself back slowly with a snug sigh.

—Hurry up with that tea, she said. I'm parched.

—The kettle is boiling, he said.

But he delayed to clear the chair: her striped petticoat, tossed soiled linen: and lifted all in an armful on to the foot of the bed.

As he went down the kitchen stairs she called:

—Poldy!

—What?

—Scald the teapot.

On the boil sure enough: a plume of steam from the spout. He scalded and rinsed out the teapot and put in four full spoons of tea, tilting the kettle then to let the water flow in. Having set it to draw he took off the kettle, crushed the pan flat on the live coals and watched the lump of butter slide and melt. While he unwrapped the kidney the cat mewed hungrily against him. Give her too much meat she won't mouse. Say they won't eat pork. Kosher. Here. He let the bloodsmeared paper fall to her and dropped the kidney amid the sizzling butter sauce. Pepper. He sprinkled it through his fingers ringwise from the chipped eggcup.

Then he slit open his letter, glancing down the page and over. Thanks: new tam: Mr Coghlan: lough Owel picnic: young student: Blazes Boylan's seaside girls.

The tea was drawn. He filled his own moustachecup, sham crown Derby, smiling. Silly Milly's birthday gift. Only five she was then. No, wait: four. I gave her the amberoid necklace she broke. Putting pieces of folded brown paper in the letterbox for her. He smiled, pouring.

> O, Milly Bloom, you are my darling.
> You are my lookingglass from night to morning.
> I'd rather have you without a farthing
> Than Katey Keogh with her ass and garden.[21]

Poor old professor Goodwin. Dreadful old case. Still he was a courteous old chap. Oldfashioned way he used to bow Molly off the platform. And the little mirror in his silk hat. The night Milly brought it into the parlour. O, look what I found in professor Goodwin's hat! All we laughed. Sex breaking out even then. Pert little piece she was.

He prodded a fork into the kidney and slapped it over: then fitted the teapot on the tray. Its hump bumped as he took it up. Everything on it? Bread and butter, four, sugar, spoon, her cream. Yes. He carried it upstairs, his thumb hooked in the teapot handle.

Nudging the door open with his knee he carried the tray in and set it on the chair by the bedhead.

[21] Bloom is thinking of a song by Samuel Lover, "O Thady Brady you are my darlin'."

—What a time you were! she said.

She set the brasses jingling as she raised herself briskly, an elbow on the pillow. He looked calmly down on her bulk and between her large soft bubs, sloping within her nightdress like a shegoat's udder. The warmth of her couched body rose on the air, mingling with the fragrance of the tea she poured.

A strip of torn envelope peeped from under the dimpled pillow. In the act of going he stayed to straighten the bedspread.

—Who was the letter from? he asked.

Bold hand. Marion.

—O, Boylan, she said. He's bringing the programme.[22]

—What are you singing?

—*Là ci darem* with J. C. Doyle, she said, and *Love's Old Sweet Song*.[23]

Her full lips, drinking, smiled. Rather stale smell that incense leaves next day. Like foul flowerwater.

—Would you like the window open a little?

She doubled a slice of bread into her mouth, asking:

—What time is the funeral?

—Eleven, I think, he answered. I didn't see the paper.

Following the pointing of her finger he took up a leg of her soiled drawers from the bed. No? Then, a twisted grey garter looped round a stocking: rumpled, shiny sole.

—No: that book.

Other stocking. Her petticoat.

—It must have fell down, she said.

He felt here and there. *Voglio e non vorrei*.[24] Wonder if she pronounces that right: *voglio*. Not in the bed. Must have slid down. He stooped and lifted the valance. The book, fallen, sprawled against the bulge of the orangekeyed chamberpot.

—Show here, she said. I put a mark in it. There's a word I wanted to ask you.

She swallowed a draught of tea from her cup held by nothandle and, having wiped her fingertips smartly on the blanket, began to search the text with the hairpin till she reached the word.

—Met him what? he asked.

—Here, she said. What does that mean?

He leaned downward and read near her polished thumbnail.

—Metempsychosis?

—Yes. Who's he when he's at home?

—Metempsychosis, he said, frowning. It's Greek: from the Greek. That means the transmigration of souls.

—O, rocks! she said. Tell us in plain words.

He smiled, glancing askance at her mocking eyes. The same young eyes. The first night after the charades. Dolphin's Barn. He turned over the

[22] Hugh "Blazes" Boylan, a Dublin billboard contractor and part-time concert manager, has arranged a concert tour to Belfast.

[23] *La ci darem la mano* ("Then we'll go hand in hand") is a duet from Mozart's *Don Giovanni*. "Love's Old Sweet Song" is a sentimental ballad (1884) by J. L. Molloy.

[24] The words (in *La ci darem la mano*) are actually *Vorrei e non vorrei*. Bloom changes *vorrei* ("I would like to") to the more positive *voglio* ("I want to").

smudged pages. *Ruby: the Pride of the Ring.* Hello. Illustration. Fierce Italian with carriagewhip. Must be Ruby pride of the on the floor naked. Sheet kindly lent. *The monster Maffei desisted and flung his victim from him with an oath.* Cruelty behind it all. Doped animals. Trapeze at Hengler's.[25] Had to look the other way. Mob gaping. Break your neck and we'll break our sides. Families of them. Bone them young so they metamspychosis. That we live after death. Our souls. That a man's soul after he dies, Dignam's soul. . . .

—Did you finish it? he asked.

—Yes, she said. There's nothing smutty in it. Is she in love with the first fellow all the time?

—Never read it. Do you want another?

—Yes. Get another of Paul de Kock's. Nice name he has.

She poured more tea into her cup, watching it flow sideways.

Must get that Capel street library book renewed or they'll write to Kearney, my guarantor. Reincarnation: that's the word.

—Some people believe, he said, that we go on living in another body after death, that we lived before. They call it reincarnation. That we all lived before on the earth thousands of years ago or some other planet. They say we have forgotten it. Some say they remember their past lives.

The sluggish cream wound curdling spirals through her tea. Better remind her of the word: metempsychosis. An example would be better. An example?

The Bath of the Nymph over the bed. Given away with the Easter number of *Photo Bits:* splendid masterpiece in art colours. Tea before you put milk in. Not unlike her with her hair down: slimmer. Three and six I gave for the frame. She said it would look nice over the bed. Naked nymphs: Greece: and for instance all the people that lived then.

He turned the pages back.

—Metempsychosis, he said, is what the ancient Greeks called it. They used to believe you could be changed into an animal or a tree, for instance. What they called nymphs, for example.

Her spoon ceased to stir up the sugar. She gazed straight before her, inhaling through her arched nostrils.

—There's a smell of burn, she said. Did you leave anything on the fire?

—The kidney! he cried suddenly.

He fitted the book roughly into his inner pocket and, stubbing his toes against the broken commode, hurried out towards the smell, stepping hastily down the stairs with a flurried stork's legs. Pungent smoke shot up in an angry jet from a side of the pan. By prodding a prong of the fork under the kidney he detached it and turned it turtle on its back. Only a little burnt. He tossed it off the pan on to a plate and let the scanty brown gravy trickle over it.

Cup of tea now. He sat down, cut and buttered a slice of the loaf. He shore away the burnt flesh and flung it to the cat. Then he put a forkful into his mouth, chewing with discernment the toothsome pliant meat. Done to a turn. A mouthful of tea. Then he cut away dies of bread, sopped one in the gravy and put it in his mouth. What was that about some young student

[25] The Hengler brothers, Charles and Albert, ran a "permanent circus" (as opposed to a traveling one) in Dublin.

and a picnic? He creased out the letter at his side, reading it slowly as he chewed, sopping another die of bread in the gravy and raising it to his mouth.

Dearest Papli

Thanks ever so much for the lovely birthday present. It suits me splendid. Everyone says I am quite the belle in my new tam. I got mummy's lovely box of creams and am writing. They are lovely. I am getting on swimming in the photo business now. Mr Coghlan took one of me and Mrs. Will send when developed. We did great biz yesterday. Fair day and all the beef to the heels were in. We are going to lough Owel on Monday with a few friends to make a scrap picnic. Give my love to mummy and to yourself a big kiss and thanks. I hear them at the piano downstairs. There is to be a concert in the Greville Arms on Saturday. There is a young student comes here some evenings named Bannon his cousins or something are big swells and he sings Boylan's (I was on the pop of writing Blazes Boylan's) song about those seaside girls. Tell him silly Milly sends my best respects. I must now close with fondest love

<div align="center">

Your fond daughter

Milly

</div>

P.S. Excuse bad writing am in hurry. Byby.

<div align="center">

M.

</div>

Fifteen yesterday. Curious, fifteenth of the month too. Her first birthday away from home. Separation. Remember the summer morning she was born, running to knock up Mrs Thornton in Denzille street. Jolly old woman. Lot of babies she must have helped into the world. She knew from the first poor little Rudy wouldn't live. Well, God is good, sir. She knew at once. He would be eleven now if he had lived.

His vacant face stared pityingly at the postscript. Excuse bad writing. Hurry. Piano downstairs. Coming out of her shell. Row with her in the XL Café about the bracelet. Wouldn't eat her cakes or speak or look. Saucebox. He sopped other dies of bread in the gravy and ate piece after piece of kidney. Twelve and six a week. Not much. Still, she might do worse. Musichall stage. Young student. He drank a draught of cooler tea to wash down his meal. Then he read the letter again: twice.

O, well: she knows how to mind herself. But if not? No, nothing has happened. Of course it might. Wait in any case till it does. A wild piece of goods. Her slim legs running up the staircase. Destiny. Ripening now. Vain: very.

He smiled with troubled affection at the kitchen window. Day I caught her in the street pinching her cheeks to make them red. Anemic a little. Was given milk too long. On the *Erin's King* that day round the Kish.[26] Damned old tub pitching about. Not a bit funky. Her pale blue scarf loose in the wind with her hair.

[26] The *Erin's King* was an excursion steamer in Dublin Bay that took passengers around the Kish, a lightship anchored at the south end of the bay.

All dimpled cheeks and curls,
Your head it simply swirls.[27]

Seaside girls. Torn envelope. Hands stuck in his trousers' pockets, jarvey off for the day, singing. Friend of the family. *Swurls,* he says. Pier with lamps, summer evening, band.

Those girls, those girls,
Those lovely seaside girls.

Milly too. Young kisses: the first. Far away now past. Mrs Marion. Reading, lying back now, counting the strands of her hair, smiling, braiding.

A soft qualm, regret, flowed down his backbone, increasing. Will happen, yes. Prevent. Useless; can't move. Girl's sweet light lips. Will happen too. He felt the flowing qualm spread over him. Useless to move now. Lips kissed, kissing, kissed. Full gluey woman's lips.

Better where she is down there: away. Occupy her. Wanted a dog to pass the time. Might take a trip down there. August bank holiday, only two and six return. Six weeks off, however. Might work a press pass. Or through M'Coy.

The cat, having cleaned all her fur, returned to the meatstained paper, nosed at it and stalked to the door. She looked back at him, mewing. Wants to go out. Wait before a door sometime it will open. Let her wait. Has the fidgets. Electric. Thunder in the air. Was washing at her ear with her back to the fire too.

He felt heavy, full: then a gentle loosening of his bowels. He stood up, undoing the waistband of his trousers. The cat mewed to him.

—Miaow! he said in answer. Wait till I'm ready.

Heaviness: hot day coming. Too much trouble to fag up the stairs to the landing.

A paper. He liked to read at stool. Hope no ape comes knocking just as I'm.

In the tabledrawer he found an old number of *Titbits.* He folded it under his armpit, went to the door and opened it. The cat went up in soft bounds. Ah, wanted to go upstairs, curl up in a ball on the bed.

Listening, he heard her voice:

—Come, come, pussy. Come.

He went out through the backdoor into the garden: stood to listen towards the next garden. No sound. Perhaps hanging clothes out to dry. The maid was in the garden. Fine morning.

He bent down to regard a lean file of spearmint growing by the wall. Make a summerhouse here. Scarlet runners. Virginia creepers. Want to manure the whole place over, scabby soil. A coat of liver of sulphur. All soil like that without dung. Household slops. Loam, what is this that is? The hens in the next garden: their droppings are very good top dressing. Best

[27] The song, referred to in Milly's letter, is "Seaside Girls" (1899), a music hall song by Harry B. Norris.

of all though are the cattle, especially when they are fed on those oilcakes. Mulch of dung. Best thing to clean ladies' kid gloves. Dirty cleans. Ashes too. Reclaim the whole place. Grow peas in that corner there. Lettuce. Always have fresh greens then. Still gardens have their drawbacks. That bee or bluebottle here Whitmonday.

He walked on. Where is my hat, by the way? Must have put it back on the peg. Or hanging up on the floor. Funny I don't remember that. Hallstand too full. Four umbrellas, her raincloak. Picking up the letters. Drago's shopbell ringing. Queer I was just thinking that moment. Brown brillantined hair over his collar. Just had a wash and brushup. Wonder have I time for a bath this morning. Tara street. Chap in the paybox there got away James Stephens, they say. O'Brien.[28]

Deep voice that fellow Dlugacz has. Agendath what is it? Now, my miss. Enthusiast.

He kicked open the crazy door of the jakes. Better be careful not to get these trousers dirty for the funeral. He went in, bowing his head under the low lintel. Leaving the door ajar, amid the stench of mouldy limewash and stale cobwebs he undid his braces. Before sitting down he peered through a chink up at the nextdoor windows. The king was in his countinghouse. Nobody.

Asquat on the cuckstool he folded out his paper, turning its pages over on his bared knees. Something new and easy. No great hurry. Keep it a bit. Our prize titbit: *Matcham's Masterstroke*. Written by Mr Philip Beaufoy, Playgoers' Club, London. Payment at the rate of one guinea a column has been made to the writer. Three and a half. Three pounds three. Three pounds, thirteen and six.

Quietly he read, restraining himself, the first column and, yielding but resisting, began the second. Midway, his last resistance yielding, he allowed his bowels to ease themselves quietly as he read, reading still patiently that slight constipation of yesterday quite gone. Hope it's not too big bring on piles again. No, just right. So. Ah! Costive. One tabloid of cascara sagrada. Life might be so. It did not move or touch him but it was something quick and neat. Print anything now. Silly season. He read on, seated calm above his own rising smell. Neat certainly. *Matcham often thinks of the masterstroke by which he won the laughing witch who now.* Begins and ends morally. *Hand in hand.* Smart. He glanced back through what he had read and, while feeling his water flow quietly, he envied kindly Mr Beaufoy who had written it and received payment of three pounds, thirteen and six.

Might manage a sketch. By Mr and Mrs L. M. Bloom. Invent a story for some proverb. Which? Time I used to try jotting down on my cuff what she said dressing. Dislike dressing together. Nicked myself shaving. Biting her nether lip, hooking the placket of her skirt. Timing her. 9.15. Did Roberts pay you yet? 9.20. What had Gretta Conroy on? 9.23. What possessed me to buy this comb? 9.24. I'm swelled after that cabbage. A speck of dust on the patent leather of her boot: rubbing smartly in turn each welt against her stockinged calf. Morning after the bazaar dance when May's band played

[28]James Stephens, a leading Fenian, escaped from Richmond Gaol in 1865. A certain J. P. O'Brien ran the Tara Street baths, but apparently he had nothing to do with Stephens' escape.

Ponchielli's dance of the hours.[29] Explain that: morning hours, noon, then evening coming on, then night hours. Washing her teeth. That was the first night. Her head dancing. Her fansticks clicking. Is that Boylan well off? He has money. Why? I noticed he had a good rich smell off his breath dancing. No use humming then. Allude to it. Strange kind of music that last night. The mirror was in shadow. She rubbed her handglass briskly on her woollen vest against her full wagging bub. Peering into it. Lines in her eyes. It wouldn't pan out somehow.

Evening hours, girls in grey gauze. Night hours then: black with daggers and eyemasks. Poetical idea: pink, then golden, then grey, then black. Still, true to life also. Day: then the night.

He tore away half the prize story sharply and wiped himself with it. Then he girded up his trousers, braced and buttoned himself. He pulled back the jerky shaky door of the jakes and came forth from the gloom into the air.

In the bright light, lightened and cooled in limb, he eyed carefully his black trousers: the ends, the knees, the houghs of the knees. What time is the funeral? Better find out in the paper.

A creak and a dark whirr in the air high up. The bells of George's church. They tolled the hour: loud dark iron.

Heigho! Heigho!
Heigho! Heigho!
Heigho! Heigho!

Quarter to. There again: the overtone following through the air. A third.

Poor Dignam!

[29]"The Dance of the Hours" is a ballet in Amilcare Ponchielli's opera *La Gioconda*. It represents, as Bloom remembers, the passing of the hours from dawn to dark.

Virginia Woolf
(1882–1941)

"Examine for a moment," Virginia Woolf wrote, "an ordinary mind on an ordinary day. The mind receives a myriad impressions—trivial, fantastic, evanescent, or engraved with the sharpness of steel. . . . Life is not a series of gig lamps symmetrically arranged; but a luminous halo, a semi-transparent envelope surrounding us from the beginning of consciousness to the end. Is it not the task of the novelist to convey this varying, this unknown and uncircumscribed spirit, whatever aberration or complexity it may display, with as little mixture of the alien and external as possible?" Woolf's

project of placing an individual consciousness at the center of fiction, as opposed to the "alien and external," is one she shares with many other major modern novelists. Her "luminous halo" reminds us of the famous description of Marlow's symbolist narrative style in Conrad's *Heart of Darkness:* "To him the meaning of an episode was not inside like a kernel but outside, enveloping the tale which brought it out only as a glow brings out a haze, in the likeness of one of these misty halos that sometimes are made visible by the spectral illumination of moonshine." And the project of exploring "an ordinary mind on an ordinary day" has been undertaken repeatedly by modern novelists from Conrad through Joyce, Proust, and Faulkner up to current writers. But the statement is also a very precise description of Woolf's own fluid and subtle fiction and its exploration of the flow of consciousness, "whatever aberration or complexity it may display."

Woolf was born in London in 1882. Her father was Sir Leslie Stephen, one of the leading men of letters of Victorian England, author of a *History of English Thought in the Eighteenth Century* and editor of the *Dictionary of National Biography;* her mother was Julia Pattle Stephen, a famous beauty and equally famous hostess to the literary figures who gathered at the Stephen home: George Meredith, Henry James, J. A. Symonds, and most of the other prominent writers of the day. Her father's learning and industry and her mother's social and domestic mastery were models Woolf struggled with all her life, until she exorcised them in her greatest novel, *To the Lighthouse* (1927).

Julia Stephen died when Woolf was thirteen. Leslie Stephen reacted by plunging into an exaggerated and melodramatic mourning that was to continue for the rest of his life, while Woolf had the first of a series of mental breakdowns that were to recur periodically the rest of her life. A second breakdown, including a suicide attempt, followed the death of her father in 1904, when she was twenty-two. When she recovered, she moved, with her sister Vanessa and her brothers Thoby and Adrian, from the family home in Kensington, London, to 46 Gordon Square in the less fashionable and more bohemian area of Bloomsbury. The Stephen sisters and brothers, in their new Bloomsbury home, formed the initial nucleus of what within a few years would be famous as the "Bloomsbury group," a circle of artists and intellectuals who would have a major impact upon the culture of England between the wars. The circle, many of whom knew the Stephen sons at Cambridge, eventually included the biographer Lytton Strachey, the economist J. M. Keynes, the art critic Roger Fry, the novelist E. M. Forster, and a number of lesser names.

Virginia Stephen married Leonard Woolf, a journalist and political writer, in 1912; the following year, her first novel, which she had worked on for six years, appeared: *The Voyage Out.* Publication of the book was followed by a third breakdown, which lasted, with brief respites, for four years.

In 1917, the Woolfs bought a hand press and founded the Hogarth Press in their home, partly as a therapeutic diversion for Virginia. It had a long and distinguished history, publishing not only some of Woolf's books but such other important works as T. S. Eliot's *Poems* (1919). A second novel, *Night and Day*, appeared in 1919 as well, followed by *Monday or Tues-*

day, a collection of stories, in 1920. Both *The Voyage Out* and *Night and Day* had been comparatively traditional in form, but in the stories of *Monday or Tuesday,* Woolf began to experiment with a more fluid, subjective style that deemphasized external action, capturing instead the moment-to-moment flow of consciousness of her characters. She pursued this style in her next novel, *Jacob's Room* (1922), and in *Mrs. Dalloway* (1925). Her finest novel, *To the Lighthouse,* appeared in 1927. Woolf used the language of psychoanalysis to describe the personal meaning of this novel, which explored through the character of Lily Briscoe her struggles to come to terms with the images of her parents, depicted in Mr. and Mrs. Ramsey. "I suppose that I did for myself what psychoanalysts do for their patients. I expressed some very long felt and deeply felt emotion. And in expressing it I explained it and then laid it to rest." The three-part structure of *To the Lighthouse*—a long, stream-of-consciousness account of a day in the life of the Ramseys and their guests, a shorter poetic account of the passing of ten years, and then another stream-of-consciousness description of another day—perfectly achieves the organic relation between fluid consciousness and form Woolf aspired to.

A love affair with Vita Sackville-West inspired the amusing but uncharacteristic *Orlando* (1928), a mock-biography that pursues a single character from Elizabethan times to the present, the protagonist changing sexes to fit each age. In *The Waves* (1931), Woolf returned to her more characteristic kind of experimentation, following the streams of consciousness of six characters at selected moments throughout their lives and juxtaposing them with a fragmented account of a single day on the seashore. The concern with the contrast between personal time and larger, more impersonal temporal units continued in *The Years* (1937), which traces, in a more traditional form than her immediately preceding novels, the history of the Pargiter family from 1880 to 1936, and in *Between the Acts* (1941), a short novel that balances a single day in the lives of a group of villagers against a village pageant embodying the whole range of English history.

Woolf's voluminous writing of the 1930's also included several volumes of her collected literary criticism, which had made her one of the most admired critics of her age; *Flush* (1933), a fanciful biography of the Brownings presented as the biography of Mrs. Browning's dog; and a long biography of her friend the art critic Roger Fry (1940). In *A Room of One's Own* (1929) and *Three Guineas* (1938), as well as many of her critical essays, she championed the cause of women writers and the more general emancipation of women.

In 1941, sensing the coming of another mental breakdown, Virginia Woolf, then living with her husband in a rural cottage near Rodmell, drowned herself in the nearby river Ouse.

To Woolf, her life as a writer was inseparable from her life as a woman. "A woman's writing is always feminine; it cannot help being feminine; at its best it is most feminine," she wrote (though characteristically complicating her position by adding, "the only difficulty lies in defining what we mean by feminine"). Feminine experience, she believed, had not received adequate expression in literature because of conventions that denied women education equal to men's and burdened them with social and domestic duties that stood in the way of writing. "Five hundred pounds and a room

of one's own" was the famous formula she proposed as the prerequisite for success as a writer. But Woolf's feminism was not confined to external social conditions; she explored feminine psychology in her greatest characters—Clarissa Dalloway, Mrs. Ramsey, Lily Briscoe—despite her awareness of the difficulty in "defining what we mean by feminine."

Woolf wrote "The Mark on the Wall" in 1917, as a diversion while working on *Night and Day.* "I shall never forget the day I wrote 'The Mark on the Wall,' " she wrote years later, "all in a flash, as if flying, after being kept stone-breaking for months." It was published in the summer of 1917 by the Hogarth Press, along with a short story by Leonard Woolf named "Three Jews," in a pamphlet called *Two Stories* and was subsequently collected in *Monday or Tuesday* (1921). The story contains its own self-referential description: "As we face each other in omnibuses and underground railways we are looking into the mirror; that accounts for the vagueness, the gleam of glassiness, in our eyes. And the novelists in future will realize more and more the importance of these reflections, for of course there is not one reflection but an almost infinite number; those are the depths they will explore, those the phantoms they will pursue, leaving the description of reality more and more out of their stories, taking a knowledge of it for granted, as the Greeks did and Shakespeare perhaps." "The Mark on the Wall" is nothing but such "reflections" (in both the senses of that punning word). Woolf never allowed herself such freedom from ordinary requirements of plot and characterization in her extended fictions. It is only in "The Mark on the Wall" and a few other short stories that she pared the "description of reality" down to such a minimum.

A Room of One's Own had its origin in two lectures given to the two women's colleges of Cambridge, Newnham and Girton, in 1928, and the short book she developed from the lectures retains their intimate, conversational tone—and not only conversational, but poetic as well. If "The Mark on the Wall" implies the provocative question, "Why is this fiction?" *A Room of One's Own* implies the question, "Why is this not fiction?" Woolf develops her feminist argument clearly and forcefully, raising and developing questions that still form many of the central issues in feminism. But she does so through narration, description, and imagery, culminating in one of those slight, resonant images that form the content of her fiction, in this case, the sight, glimpsed in London, of a young couple getting into a taxicab. "The sight was ordinary enough," she writes; "what was strange was the rhythmical order with which my imagination had invested it; and the fact that the ordinary sight of two people getting into a cab had the power to communicate something of their own seeming satisfaction." She uses the image to develop, over several pages, her final ideal of the androgynous personality. *A Room of One's Own* is the extraordinary combination of a keen, logical argument with the methods of stream-of-consciousness fiction. It is a classic of the modernist style to which Woolf made so single a contribution throughout her career.

FURTHER READING *(prepared by N. K. B.):* The standard biography is Quentin Bell's *Virginia Woolf,* 2 vols., 1972, a balanced, detailed account. Phyllis Rose's *Woman of Letters: A Life of Virginia Woolf,* 1978, is a feminist reading of Woolf's life, stressing her role as a professional writer and social critic. The best supplements to

these biographies are *The Diary of Virginia Woolf*, 5 vols., ed. Anne Oliver Bell, 1977ff., and *The Letters of Virginia Woolf*, 6 vols., ed. Nigel Nicolson and Joanne Trautmann, 1975ff. The hundredth anniversary of Woolf's birth inspired a number of collections of critical essays. See *Virginia Woolf: Centennial Essays*, ed. Elaine K. Ginsberg and Laura Moss Gottlieb, 1983; *Virginia Woolf: A Centenary Perspective*, ed. Eric Warner, 1984; and *Virginia Woolf and Bloomsbury: A Centenary Celebration*, ed. Jane Marcus, 1985. Jane Marcus has also written *Virginia Woolf: A Feminist Slant*, 1983; and *Virginia Woolf and the Languages of Patriarchy*, 1987, both provocative studies. Woolf's concern with various kinds of "reality" is well treated in Alex Zwerdling's *Virginia Woolf and the Real World*, 1987. The reception of Woolf's works during her own lifetime is well documented in *Virginia Woolf: The Critical Heritage*, ed. by Robin Majumdar and Allen McLaurin, 1975. Important recent essays are reprinted in *Critical Essays on Virginia Woolf*, ed. Morris Beja, 1985.

THE MARK ON THE WALL

Perhaps it was the middle of January in the present year that I first looked up and saw the mark on the wall. In order to fix a date it is necessary to remember what one saw. So now I think of the fire; the steady film of yellow light upon the page of my book; the three chrysanthemums in the round glass bowl on the mantelpiece. Yes, it must have been the winter time, and we had just finished our tea, for I remember that I was smoking a cigarette when I looked up and saw the mark on the wall for the first time. I looked up through the smoke of my cigarette and my eye lodged for a moment upon the burning coals, and that old fancy of the crimson flag flapping from the castle tower came into my mind, and I thought of the cavalcade of red knights riding up the side of the black rock. Rather to my relief the sight of the mark interrupted the fancy, for it is an old fancy, an automatic fancy, made as a child perhaps. The mark was a small round mark, black upon the white wall, about six or seven inches above the mantelpiece.

How readily our thoughts swarm upon a new object, lifting it a little way, as ants carry a blade of straw so feverishly, and then leave it. . . . If that mark was made by a nail, it can't have been for a picture, it must have been for a miniature—the miniature of a lady with white powdered curls, powder-dusted cheeks, and lips like red carnations. A fraud of course, for the people who had this house before us would have chosen pictures in that way—an old picture for an old room. That is the sort of people they were— very interesting people, and I think of them so often, in such queer places, because one will never see them again, never know what happened next. They wanted to leave this house because they wanted to change their style of furniture, so he said, and he was in process of saying that in his opinion art should have ideas behind it when we were torn asunder, as one is torn from the old lady about to pour out tea and the young man about to hit the tennis ball in the back garden of the suburban villa as one rushes past in the train.

But for that mark, I'm not sure about it; I don't believe it was made by a nail after all; it's too big, too round, for that. I might get up, but if I got up and looked at it, ten to one I shouldn't be able to say for certain; because

once a thing's done, no one ever knows how it happened. Oh! dear me, the mystery of life; the inaccuracy of thought! The ignorance of humanity! To show how very little control of our possessions we have—what an accidental affair this living is after all our civilization—let me just count over a few of the things lost in one lifetime, beginning, for that seems always the most mysterious of losses—what cat would gnaw, what rat would nibble—three pale blue canisters of book-binding tools? Then there were the bird cages, the iron hoops, the steel skates, the Queen Anne coal-scuttle, the bagatelle board,[1] the hand organ—all gone, and jewels, too. Opals and emeralds, they lie about the roots of turnips. What a scraping paring affair it is to be sure! The wonder is that I've any clothes on my back, that I sit surrounded by solid furniture at this moment. Why, if one wants to compare life to anything, one must liken it to being blown through the Tube[2] at fifty miles an hour—landing at the other end without a single hairpin in one's hair! Shot out at the feet of God entirely naked! Tumbling head over heels in the asphodel meadows[3] like brown paper parcels pitched down a shoot in the post office! With one's hair flying back like the tail of a race-horse. Yes, that seems to express the rapidity of life, the perpetual waste and repair; all so casual, all so haphazard. . . .

But after life. The slow pulling down of thick green stalks so that the cup of the flower, as it turns over, deluges one with purple and red light. Why, after all, should one not be born there as one is born here, helpless, speechless, unable to focus one's eyesight, groping at the roots of the grass, at the toes of the Giants? As for saying which are trees, and which are men and women, or whether there are such things, that one won't be in a condition to do for fifty years or so. There will be nothing but spaces of light and dark, intersected by thick stalks, and rather higher up perhaps, rose-shaped blots of an indistinct colour—dim pinks and blues—which will, as time goes on, become more definite, become—I don't know what. . . .

And yet that mark on the wall is not a hole at all. It may even be caused by some round black substance, such as a small rose leaf, left over from the summer, and I, not being a very vigilant housekeeper—look at the dust on the mantelpiece, for example, the dust which, so they say, buried Troy three times over, only fragments of pots utterly refusing annihilation, as one can believe.

The tree outside the window taps very gently on the pane. . . . I want to think quietly, calmly, spaciously, never to be interrupted, never to have to rise from my chair, to slip easily from one thing to another, without any sense of hostility, or obstacle. I want to sink deeper and deeper, away from the surface, with its hard separate facts. To steady myself, let me catch hold of the first idea that passes . . . Shakespeare. . . . Well, he will do as well as another. A man who sat himself solidly in an arm-chair, and looked into the fire, so— A shower of ideas fell perpetually from some very high Heaven down through his mind. He leant his forehead on his hand, and people, looking in through the open door—for this scene is supposed to take place

[1] Bagatelle is a game played on a board with holes in one end through which balls are driven with a cue.

[2] London subway.

[3] Heaven. (In Greek mythology, asphodel flowers grew in the Elysian fields, the happy otherworld reserved for heroes favored by the gods.)

on a summer's evening—But how dull this is, this historical fiction! It doesn't interest me at all. I wish I could hit upon a pleasant track of thought, a track indirectly reflecting credit upon myself, for those are the pleasantest thoughts, and very frequent even in the minds of modest mouse-coloured people, who believe genuinely that they dislike to hear their own praises. They are not thoughts directly praising oneself; that is the beauty of them; they are thoughts like this:

"And then I came into the room. They were discussing botany. I said how I'd seen a flower growing on a dust heap on the site of an old house in Kingsway.[4] The seed, I said, must have been sown in the reign of Charles the First. What flowers grew in the reign of Charles the First?" I asked— (But I don't remember the answer.) Tall flowers with purple tassels to them perhaps. And so it goes on. All the time I'm dressing up the figure of myself in my own mind, lovingly, stealthily, not openly adoring it, for if I did that, I should catch myself out, and stretch my hand at once for a book in self-protection. Indeed, it is curious how instinctively one protects the image of oneself from idolatry or any other handling that could make it ridiculous, or too unlike the original to be believed in any longer. Or is it not so very curious after all? It is a matter of great importance. Suppose the looking-glass smashes, the image disappears, and the romantic figure with the green of forest depths all about it is there no longer, but only that shell of a person which is seen by other people—what an airless, shallow, bald, prominent world it becomes! A world not to be lived in. As we face each other in omnibuses and underground railways we are looking into the mirror; that accounts for the vagueness, the gleam of glassiness, in our eyes. And the novelists in future will realize more and more the importance of these reflections, for of course there is not one reflection but an almost infinite number; those are the depths they will explore, those the phantoms they will pursue, leaving the description of reality more and more out of their stories, taking a knowledge of it for granted, as the Greeks did and Shakespeare perhaps—but these generalizations are very worthless. The military sound of the word is enough. It recalls leading articles, cabinet ministers—a whole class of things indeed which, as a child, one thought the thing itself, the standard thing, the real thing, from which one could not depart save at the risk of nameless damnation. Generalizations bring back somehow Sunday in London, Sunday afternoon walks, Sunday luncheons, and also ways of speaking of the dead, clothes, and habits—like the habit of sitting all together in one room until a certain hour, although nobody liked it. There was a rule for everything. The rule for tablecloths at that particular period was that they should be made of tapestry with little yellow compartments marked upon them, such as you may see in photographs of the carpets in the corridors of the royal palaces. Tablecloths of a different kind were not real tablecloths. How shocking, and yet how wonderful it was to discover that these real things, Sunday luncheons, Sunday walks, country houses, and tablecloths were not entirely real, were indeed half phantoms, and the damnation which visited the disbeliever in them was only a sense of illegitimate freedom. What now takes the place of those things I wonder, those real standard things? Men perhaps, should you be a woman; the

[4] Street in London.

masculine point of view which governs our lives, which sets the standard, which establishes Whitaker's Table of Precedency,[5] which has become, I suppose, since the war, half a phantom to many men and women, which soon, one may hope, will be laughed into the dustbin where the phantoms go, the mahogany sideboards and the Landseer prints,[6] Gods and Devils, Hell and so forth, leaving us all with an intoxicating sense of illegitimate freedom—if freedom exists. . . .

In certain lights that mark on the wall seems actually to project from the wall. Nor is it entirely circular. I cannot be sure, but it seems to cast a perceptible shadow, suggesting that if I ran my finger down that strip of the wall it would, at a certain point, mount and descend a small tumulus, a smooth tumulus[7] like those barrows on the South Downs which are, they say, either tombs or camps. Of the two I should prefer them to be tombs, desiring melancholy like most English people, and finding it natural at the end of a walk to think of the bones stretched beneath the turf. . . . There must be some book about it. Some antiquary must have dug up those bones and given them a name. . . . What sort of a man is an antiquary, I wonder? Retired Colonels for the most part, I daresay, leading parties of aged labourers to the top here, examining clods of earth and stone, and getting into correspondence with the neighbouring clergy, which, being opened at breakfast time, gives them a feeling of importance, and the comparison of arrow-heads necessitates cross-country journeys to the country towns, an agreeable necessity both to them and to their elderly wives, who wish to make plum jam or to clean out the study, and have every reason for keeping that great question of the camp or the tomb in perpetual suspension, while the Colonel himself feels agreeably philosophic in accumulating evidence on both sides of the question. It is true that he does finally incline to believe in the camp; and, being opposed, indites a pamphlet which he is about to read at the quarterly meeting of the local society when a stroke lays him low, and his last conscious thoughts are not of wife or child, but of the camp and that arrow-head there, which is now in the case at the local museum, together with the foot of a Chinese murderess, a handful of Elizabethan nails, a great many Tudor clay pipes, a piece of Roman pottery, and the wineglass that Nelson drank out of—proving I really don't know what.

No, no, nothing is proved, nothing is known. And if I were to get up at this very moment and ascertain that the mark on the wall is really—what shall we say?—the head of a gigantic old nail, driven in two hundred years ago, which has now, owing to the patient attrition of many generations of housemaids, revealed its head above the coat of paint, and is taking its first view of modern life in the sight of a white-walled fire-lit room, what should I gain?—Knowledge? Matter for further speculation? I can think sitting still as well as standing up. And what is knowledge? What are our learned men save the descendants of witches and hermits who crouched in caves and in woods brewing herbs, interrogating shrew-mice and writing down

[5] *Whitaker's Almanack,* an English reference work published annually, includes a "Table of Precedency" that shows the hierarchy of aristocratic and ecclesiastical ranks.

[6] Sir Edwin Henry Landseer was a Victorian painter famous for animal pictures. Reproductions of his work were popular in Victorian homes.

[7] A man-made mound of earth. The South Downs, hills in southern England, have a number of prehistoric burial mounds or barrows.

the language of the stars? And the less we honour them as our superstitions dwindle and our respect for beauty and health of mind increases. . . . Yes, one could imagine a very pleasant world. A quiet, spacious world, with the flowers so red and blue in the open fields. A world without professors or specialists or house-keepers with the profiles of policemen, a world which one could slice with one's thought as a fish slices the water with his fin, grazing the stems of the water-lilies, hanging suspended over nests of white sea eggs. . . . How peaceful it is down here, rooted in the centre of the world and gazing up through the grey waters, with their sudden gleams of light, and their reflections—if it were not for Whitaker's Almanack—if it were not for the Table of Precedency!

I must jump up and see for myself what that mark on the wall really is—a nail, a rose-leaf, a crack in the wood?

Here is nature once more at her old game of self-preservation. This train of thought, she perceives, is threatening mere waste of energy, even some collision with reality, for who will ever be able to lift a finger against Whitaker's Table of Precedency? The Archbishop of Canterbury is followed by the Lord High Chancellor; the Lord High Chancellor is followed by the Archbishop of York. Everybody follows somebody, such is the philosophy of Whitaker; and the great thing is to know who follows whom. Whitaker knows, and let that, so Nature counsels, comfort you, instead of enraging you; and if you can't be comforted, if you must shatter this hour of peace, think of the mark on the wall.

I understand Nature's game—her prompting to take action as a way of ending any thought that threatens to excite or to pain. Hence, I suppose, comes our slight contempt for men of action—men, we assume, who don't think. Still, there's no harm in putting a full stop to one's disagreeable thoughts by looking at a mark on the wall.

Indeed, now that I have fixed my eyes upon it, I feel that I have grasped a plank in the sea; I feel a satisfying sense of reality which at once turns the two Archbishops and the Lord High Chancellor to the shadows of shades. Here is something definite, something real. Thus, waking from a midnight dream of horror, one hastily turns on the light and lies quiescent, worshipping the chest of drawers, worshipping solidity, worshipping reality, worshipping the impersonal world which is a proof of some existence other than ours. That is what one wants to be sure of. . . . Wood is a pleasant thing to think about. It comes from a tree; and trees grow, and we don't know how they grow. For years and years they grow, without paying any attention to us, in meadows, in forests, and by the side of rivers—all things one likes to think about. The cows swish their tails beneath them on hot afternoons; they paint rivers so green that when a moorhen dives one expects to see its feathers all green when it comes up again. I like to think of the fish balanced against the stream like flags blown out; and of water-beetles slowly raising domes of mud upon the bed of the river. I like to think of the tree itself: first of the close dry sensation of being wood; then the grinding of the storm; then the slow, delicious ooze of sap; I like to think of it, too, on winter's nights standing in the empty field with all leaves close-furled, nothing tender exposed to the iron bullets of the moon, a naked mast upon an earth that goes tumbling, tumbling, all night long. The song of birds must sound very loud and strange in June; and how cold

the feet of insects must feel upon it, as they make laborious progresses up the creases of the bark, or sun themselves upon the thin green awning of the leaves, and look straight in front of them with diamond-cut red eyes. . . . One by one the fibres snap beneath the immense cold pressure of the earth, then the last storm comes and, falling, the highest branches drive deep into the ground again. Even so, life isn't done with; there are a million patient, watchful lives still for a tree, all over the world, in bedrooms, in ships, on the pavement, lining rooms, where men and women sit after tea, smoking cigarettes. It is full of peaceful thoughts, happy thoughts, this tree. I should like to take each one separately—but something is getting in the way. . . . Where was I? What has it all been about? A tree? A river? The Downs? Whitaker's Almanack? The fields of asphodel? I can't remember a thing. Everything's moving, falling, slipping, vanishing. . . . There is a vast upheaval of matter. Someone is standing over me and saying:

"I'm going out to buy a newspaper."

"Yes?"

"Though it's no good buying newspapers. . . . Nothing ever happens. Curse this war;[8] God damn this war! . . . All the same, I don't see why we should have a snail on our wall."

Ah, the mark on the wall! It was a snail.

from *A ROOM OF ONE'S OWN*

SHAKESPEARE'S SISTER[1]

It was disappointing not to have brought back in the evening some important statement, some authentic fact.[2] Women are poorer than men because— this or that. Perhaps now it would be better to give up seeking for the truth, and receiving on one's head an avalanche of opinion hot as lava, discoloured as dish-water. It would be better to draw the curtains; to shut out distractions; to light the lamp; to narrow the enquiry and to ask the historian, who records not opinions but facts, to describe under what conditions women lived, not throughout the ages, but in England, say in the time of Elizabeth.

For it is a perennial puzzle why no woman wrote a word of that extraordinary literature when every other man, it seemed, was capable of song or sonnet. What were the conditions in which women lived, I asked myself; for fiction, imaginative work that is, is not dropped like a pebble upon the ground, as science may be; fiction is like a spider's web, attached ever so lightly perhaps, but still attached to life at all four corners. Often the attachment is scarcely perceptible; Shakespeare's plays, for instance, seem to

[8] The First World War. ("The Mark on the Wall" was written in 1917.)

[1] Editorial title. This selection consists of Chapter 3 and the conclusion to the final chapter.

[2] In the preceding chapter, Woolf has described her visit to the British Museum, where she read about the status of women.

hang there complete by themselves. But when the web is pulled askew, hooked up at the edge, torn in the middle, one remembers that these webs are not spun in midair by incorporeal creatures, but are the work of suffering human beings, and are attached to grossly material things, like health and money and the houses we live in.

I went, therefore, to the shelf where the histories stand and took down one of the latest, Professor Trevelyan's *History of England*.[3] Once more I looked up Women, found "position of," and turned to the pages indicated. "Wife-beating," I read, "was a recognised right of man, and was practised without shame by high as well as low. . . . Similarly," the historian goes on, "the daughter who refused to marry the gentleman of her parents' choice was liable to be locked up, beaten and flung about the room, without any shock being inflicted on public opinion. Marriage was not an affair of personal affection, but of family avarice, particularly in the 'chivalrous' upper classes. . . . Betrothal often took place while one or both of the parties was in the cradle, and marriage when they were scarcely out of the nurses' charge." That was about 1470, soon after Chaucer's time. The next reference to the position of women is some two hundred years later, in the time of the Stuarts. "It was still the exception for women of the upper and middle class to choose their own husbands, and when the husband had been assigned, he was lord and master, so far at least as law and custom could make him. Yet even so," Professor Trevelyan concludes, "neither Shakespeare's women nor those of authentic seventeenth-century memoirs, like the Verneys and the Hutchinsons,[4] seem wanting in personality and character." Certainly, if we consider it, Cleopatra must have had a way with her; Lady Macbeth, one would suppose, had a will of her own; Rosalind, one might conclude, was an attractive girl.[5] Professor Trevelyan is speaking no more than the truth when he remarks that Shakespeare's women do not seem wanting in personality and character. Not being a historian, one might go even further and say that women have burnt like beacons in all the works of all the poets from the beginning of time— Clytemnestra, Antigone, Cleopatra, Lady Macbeth, Phèdre, Cressida, Rosalind, Desdemona, the Duchess of Malfi, among the dramatists; then among the prose writers: Millamant, Clarissa, Becky Sharp, Anna Karenina, Emma Bovary, Madame de Guermantes[6]—the names flock to mind, nor do they recall women "lacking in personality and character." Indeed, if woman had no existence save in the fiction written by men, one would imagine her a person of the utmost importance; very various; heroic and mean; splendid and sordid; infinitely beautiful and hideous in the ex-

[3] G. M. Trevelyan's *History of England* was published in 1926.
[4] *Memoirs of the Verney Family* (1892) and Lucy Hutchinson's *Memoirs of Colonel Hutchinson* (1806) were both written just after the English Civil War (1647-49), though not published until the nineteenth century.
[5] The Shakespeare plays in which these characters appear are *Antony and Cleopatra, Macbeth*, and *As You Like It*.
[6] The works in which these characters appear are, respectively, Aeschylus's *Oresteia*, Sophocles's *Antigone*, Shakespeare's *Antony and Cleopatra* and *Macbeth*, Racine's *Phèdre*, Shakespeare's *Troilus and Cressida, As You Like It*, and *Othello*, Webster's *The Duchess of Malfi*, Congreve's *The Way of the World*, Richardson's *Clarissa*, Thackeray's *Vanity Fair*, Tolstoy's *Anna Karenina*, Flaubert's *Madame Bovary*, and Proust's *Remembrance of Things Past*.

treme; as great as a man, some think even greater.[7] But this is woman in fiction. In fact, as Professor Trevelyan points out, she was locked up, beaten and flung about the room.

A very queer, composite being thus emerges. Imaginatively she is of the highest importance; practically she is completely insignificant. She pervades poetry from cover to cover; she is all but absent from history. She dominates the lives of kings and conquerors in fiction; in fact she was the slave of any boy whose parents forced a ring upon her finger. Some of the most inspired words, some of the most profound thoughts in literature fall from her lips; in real life she could hardly read, could scarcely spell, and was the property of her husband.

It was certainly an odd monster that one made up by reading the historians first and the poets afterwards—a worm winged like an eagle; the spirit of life and beauty in a kitchen chopping up suet. But these monsters, however amusing to the imagination, have no existence in fact. What one must do to bring her to life was to think poetically and prosaically at one and the same moment, thus keeping in touch with fact—that she is Mrs. Martin, aged thirty-six, dressed in blue, wearing a black hat and brown shoes; but not losing sight of fiction either—that she is a vessel in which all sorts of spirits and forces are coursing and flashing perpetually. The moment, however, that one tries this method with the Elizabethan woman, one branch of illumination fails; one is held up by the scarcity of facts. One knows nothing detailed, nothing perfectly true and substantial about her. History scarcely mentions her. And I turned to Professor Trevelyan again to see what history meant to him. I found by looking at his chapter headings that it meant—

"The Manor Court and the Methods of Open-field Agriculture . . . The Cistercians and Sheep-farming . . . The Crusades . . . The University . . . The House of Commons . . . The Hundred Years' War . . . The Wars of the Roses . . . The Renaissance Scholars . . . The Dissolution of the Monasteries . . . Agrarian and Religious Strife . . . The Origin of English Seapower . . . The Armada . . ." and so on. Occasionally an individual woman is mentioned, an Elizabeth, or a Mary; a queen or a great lady. But by no possible means could middle-class women with nothing but brains and character at their command have taken part in any one of the great movements which, brought together, constitute the historian's view of the past.

[7] "It remains a strange and almost inexplicable fact that in Athena's city, where women were kept in almost Oriental suppression as odalisques or drudges, the stage should yet have produced figures like Clytemnestra and Cassandra, Atossa and Antigone, Phèdre and Medea, and all the other heroines who dominate play after play of the 'misogynist' Euripides. But the paradox of this world where in real life a respectable woman could hardly show her face alone in the street, and yet on the stage woman equals or surpasses man, has never been satisfactorily explained. In modern tragedy the same predominance exists. At all events, a very cursory survey of Shakespeare's work (similarly with Webster, though not with Marlowe or Jonson) suffices to reveal how this dominance, this initiative of women, persists from Rosalind to Lady Macbeth. So too in Racine; six of his tragedies bear their heroines' names; and what male characters of his shall we set against Hermione and Andromaque, Bérénice and Roxane, Phèdre and Athalie? So again with Ibsen; what men shall we match with Solveig and Nora, Hedda and Hilda Wangel and Rebecca West?"—F. L. Lucas, *Tragedy*, pp. 114–15." [Woolf's note.]

Nor shall we find her in any collection of anecdotes. Aubrey[8] hardly mentions her. She never writes her own life and scarcely keeps a diary; there are only a handful of her letters in existence. She left no plays or poems by which we can judge her. What one wants, I thought—and why does not some brilliant student at Newnham or Girton[9] supply it?—is a mass of information; at what age did she marry; how many children had she as a rule; what was her house like; had she a room to herself; did she do the cooking; would she be likely to have a servant? All these facts lie somewhere, presumably, in parish registers and account books; the life of the average Elizabethan woman must be scattered about somewhere, could one collect it and make a book of it. It would be ambitious beyond my daring, I thought, looking about the shelves for books that were not there, to suggest to the students of those famous colleges that they should re-write history, though I own that it often seems a little queer as it is, unreal, lop-sided; but why should they not add a supplement to history? calling it, of course, by some inconspicuous name so that women might figure there without impropriety? For one often catches a glimpse of them in the lives of the great, whisking away into the background, concealing, I sometimes think, a wink, a laugh, perhaps a tear. And, after all, we have lives enough of Jane Austen; it scarcely seems necessary to consider again the influence of the tragedies of Joanna Baillie[10] upon the poetry of Edgar Allan Poe; as for myself, I should not mind if the homes and haunts of Mary Russell Mitford[11] were closed to the public for a century at least. But what I find deplorable, I continued, looking about the bookshelves again, is that nothing is known about women before the eighteenth century. I have no model in my mind to turn about this way and that. Here am I asking why women did not write poetry in the Elizabethan age, and I am not sure how they were educated; whether they were taught to write; whether they had sitting-rooms to themselves; how many women had children before they were twenty-one; what, in short, they did from eight in the morning till eight at night. They had no money evidently; according to Professor Trevelyan they were married whether they liked it or not before they were out of the nursery, at fifteen or sixteen very likely. It would have been extremely odd, even upon this showing, had one of them suddenly written the plays of Shakespeare, I concluded, and I thought of that old gentleman, who is dead now, but was a bishop, I think, who declared that it was impossible for any woman, past, present, or to come, to have the genius of Shakespeare. He wrote to the papers about it. He also told a lady who applied to him for information that cats do not as a matter of fact go to heaven, though they have, he added, souls of a sort. How much thinking those old gentlemen used to save one! How the borders of ignorance shrank back at their approach! Cats do not go to heaven. Women cannot write the plays of Shakespeare.

Be that as it may, I could not help thinking, as I looked at the works of

[8] John Aubrey (1626–97), author of *Brief Lives*.

[9] The two women's colleges of Cambridge. Woolf delivered an early version of parts of *A Room of One's Own* as lectures at both Newnham and Girton.

[10] Joanna Baillie (1762–1851) was a Romantic English dramatist who published four series of *Plays on the Passions* between 1798 and 1836.

[11] Mary Russell Mitford wrote *Our Village* (1819), sketches of rural life.

Shakespeare on the shelf, that the bishop was right at least in this; it would have been impossible, completely and entirely, for any woman to have written the plays of Shakespeare in the age of Shakespeare. Let me imagine, since facts are so hard to come by, what would have happened had Shakespeare had a wonderfully gifted sister, called Judith, let us say. Shakespeare himself went, very probably—his mother was an heiress—to the grammar school, where he may have learnt Latin—Ovid, Virgil and Horace—and the elements of grammar and logic. He was, it is well known, a wild boy who poached rabbits, perhaps shot a deer, and had, rather sooner than he should have done, to marry a woman in the neighbourhood, who bore him a child rather quicker than was right. That escapade sent him to seek his fortune in London. He had, it seemed, a taste for the theatre; he began by holding horses at the stage door. Very soon he got work in the theatre, became a successful actor, and lived at the hub of the universe, meeting everybody, knowing everybody, practising his art on the boards, exercising his wits in the streets, and even getting access to the palace of the queen. Meanwhile his extraordinarily gifted sister, let us suppose, remained at home. She was as adventurous, as imaginative, as agog to see the world as he was. But she was not sent to school. She had no chance of learning grammar and logic, let alone of reading Horace and Virgil. She picked up a book now and then, one of her brother's perhaps, and read a few pages. But then her parents came in and told her to mend the stockings or mind the stew and not moon about with books and papers. They would have spoken sharply but kindly, for they were substantial people who knew the conditions of life for a woman and loved their daughter—indeed, more likely than not she was the apple of her father's eye. Perhaps she scribbled some pages up in an apple loft on the sly, but was careful to hide them or set fire to them. Soon, however, before she was out of her teens, she was to be betrothed to the son of a neighbouring wool-stapler.[12] She cried out that marriage was hateful to her, and for that she was severely beaten by her father. Then he ceased to scold her. He begged her instead not to hurt him, not to shame him in this matter of her marriage. He would give her a chain of beads or a fine petticoat, he said; and there were tears in his eyes. How could she disobey him? How could she break his heart? The force of her own gift alone drove her to it. She made up a small parcel of her belongings, let herself down by a rope one summer's night and took the road to London. She was not seventeen. The birds that sang in the hedge were not more musical than she was. She had the quickest fancy, a gift like her brother's, for the tune of words. Like him, she had a taste for the theatre. She stood at the stage door; she wanted to act, she said. Men laughed in her face. The manager—a fat, loose-lipped man—guffawed. He bellowed something about poodles dancing and women acting[13]—no woman, he said, could possibly be an actress.[14] He hinted—you can imagine what. She could get no training in her craft. Could she even seek her

[12] Wool dealer. (A "stapler" is a dealer in "staple" goods.)

[13] An allusion to an anecdote in James Boswell's *Life of Johnson* (1791): "Next day, Sunday, July 31, I told him I had been that morning at a meeting of the people called Quakers, where I had heard a woman preach. JOHNSON. 'Sir, a woman's preaching is like a dog's walking on his hinder legs. It is not done well; but you are surprised to find it done at all.'"

[14] Women's roles were played by boys in the Elizabethan theater.

dinner in a tavern or roam the streets at midnight? Yet her genius was for fiction and lusted to feed abundantly upon the lives of men and women and the study of their ways. At last—for she was very young, oddly like Shakespeare the poet in her face, with the same grey eyes and rounded brows—at last Nick Greene the actor-manager took pity on her; she found herself with child by that gentleman and so—who shall measure the heat and violence of the poet's heart when caught and tangled in a woman's body?—killed herself one winter's night and lies buried at some cross-roads where the omnibuses now stop outside the Elephant and Castle.[15]

That, more or less, is how the story would run, I think, if a woman in Shakespeare's day had had Shakespeare's genius. But for my part, I agree with the deceased bishop, if such he was—it is unthinkable that any woman in Shakespeare's day should have had Shakespeare's genius. For genius like Shakespeare's is not born among labouring, uneducated, servile people. It was not born in England among the Saxons and the Britons. It is not born today among the working classes. How, then, could it have been born among women whose work began, according to Professor Trevelyan, almost before they were out of the nursery, who were forced to it by their parents and held to it by all the power of law and custom? Yet genius of a sort must have existed among women as it must have existed among the working classes. Now and again an Emily Brontë or a Robert Burns blazes out and proves its presence. But certainly it never got itself on to paper. When, however, one reads of a witch being ducked, of a woman possessed by devils, of a wise woman selling herbs, or even of a very remarkable man who had a mother, then I think we are on the track of a lost novelist, a suppressed poet, of some mute and inglorious[16] Jane Austen, some Emily Brontë who dashed her brains out on the moor or mopped and mowed[17] about the highways crazed with the torture that her gift had put her to. Indeed, I would venture to guess that Anon, who wrote so many poems without signing them, was often a woman. It was a woman, Edward Fitzgerald,[18] I think, suggested, who made the ballads and the folk-songs, crooning them to her children, beguiling her spinning with them, or the length of the winter's night.

This may be true or it may be false—who can say?—but what is true in it, so it seemed to me, reviewing the story of Shakespeare's sister as I had made it, is that any woman born with a great gift in the sixteenth century would certainly have gone crazed, shot herself, or ended her days in some lonely cottage outside the village, half witch, half wizard, feared and mocked at. For it needs little skill in psychology to be sure that a highly gifted girl who had tried to use her gift for poetry would have been so thwarted and hindered by other people, so tortured and pulled asunder by

[15]Elephant and Castle, now a station on the London Underground, was originally a pub south of the Thames where a number of roads joined; it was named for its pictorial sign showing an elephant with a castle-like *howdah*, or rider's seat, on its back. Suicides were buried at crossroads.

[16]Thomas Gray, in his *Elegy Written in a Country Churchyard* (1751), wrote that "some mute inglorious Milton" might rest there.

[17]To "mop and mow" is to make grotesque and perhaps insane faces.

[18]English poet (1809-83) famous for his translation and adaptation of the Persian *Rubáiyát* of Omar Khayyam.

her own contrary instincts, that she must have lost her health and sanity to a certainty. No girl could have walked to London and stood at a stage door and forced her way into the presence of actor-managers without doing herself a violence and suffering an anguish which may have been irrational—for chastity may be a fetish invented by certain societies for unknown reasons—but were none the less inevitable. Chastity had then, it has even now, a religious importance in a woman's life, and has so wrapped itself round with nerves and instincts that to cut it free and bring it to the light of day demands courage of the rarest. To have lived a free life in London in the sixteenth century would have meant for a woman who was poet and playwright a nervous stress and dilemma which might well have killed her. Had she survived, whatever she had written would have been twisted and deformed, issuing from a strained and morbid imagination. And undoubtedly, I thought, looking at the shelf where there are no plays by women, her work would have gone unsigned. That refuge she would have sought certainly. It was the relic of the sense of chastity that dictated anonymity to women even so late as the nineteenth century. Currer Bell, George Eliot, George Sand,[19] all the victims of inner strife as their writings prove, sought ineffectively to veil themselves by using the name of a man. Thus they did homage to the convention, which if not implanted by the other sex was liberally encouraged by them (the chief glory of a woman is not to be talked of, said Pericles,[20] himself a much-talked-of man), that publicity in women is detestable. Anonymity runs in their blood. The desire to be veiled still possesses them. They are not even now as concerned about the health of their fame as men are, and, speaking generally, will pass a tombstone or a signpost without feeling an irresistible desire to cut their names on it, as Alf, Bert or Chas. must do in obedience to their instinct, which murmurs if it sees a fine woman go by, or even a dog, *Ce chien est à moi.*[21] And, of course, it may not be a dog, I thought, remembering Parliament Square, the Sieges Allee and other avenues;[22] it may be a piece of land or a man with curly black hair. It is one of the great advantages of being a woman that one can pass even a very fine negress without wishing to make an Englishwoman of her.

That woman, then, who was born with a gift of poetry in the sixteenth century, was an unhappy woman, a woman at strife against herself. All the conditions of her life, all her own instincts, were hostile to the state of mind which is needed to set free whatever is in the brain. But what is the state of mind that is most propitious to the act of creation, I asked. Can one come by any notion of the state that furthers and makes possible that strange activity? Here I opened the volume containing the Tragedies of Shakespeare. What was Shakespeare's state of mind, for instance, when he wrote *Lear* and *Antony and Cleopatra?* It was certainly the state of mind most favourable to poetry that there has ever existed. But Shakespeare himself

[19] The male pseudonyms of, respectively, Charlotte Brontë, Mary Anne Evans, and Aurore Dupin.
[20] Athenian statesman (c. 495–429 B.C.) who presided over the zenith of Athens' wealth and power.
[21] "That dog is mine" (French).
[22] That is, centers of colonialist governments. Woolf is referring to the colonialism that she attributes to male acquisitiveness.

said nothing about it. We only know casually and by chance that he "never blotted a line."[23] Nothing indeed was ever said by the artist himself about his state of mind until the eighteenth century perhaps. Rousseau perhaps began it. At any rate, by the nineteenth century self-consciousness had developed so far that it was the habit for men of letters to describe their minds in confessions and autobiographies. Their lives also were written, and their letters were printed after their deaths. Thus, though we do not know what Shakespeare went through when he wrote *Lear,* we do know what Carlyle went through when he wrote the *French Revolution;* what Flaubert went through when he wrote *Madame Bovary;* what Keats was going through when he tried to write poetry against the coming of death and the indifference of the world.[24]

And one gathers from this enormous modern literature of confession and self-analysis that to write a work of genius is almost always a feat of prodigious difficulty. Everything is against the likelihood that it will come from the writer's mind whole and entire. Generally material circumstances are against it. Dogs will bark; people will interrupt; money must be made; health will break down. Further, accentuating all these difficulties and making them harder to bear is the world's notorious indifference. It does not ask people to write poems and novels and histories; it does not need them. It does not care whether Flaubert finds the right word[25] or whether Carlyle scrupulously verifies this or that fact. Naturally, it will not pay for what it does not want. And so the writer, Keats, Flaubert, Carlyle, suffers, especially in the creative years of youth, every form of distraction and discouragement. A curse, a cry of agony, rises from those books of analysis and confession. "Mightly poets in their misery dead"[26]—that is the burden of their song. If anything comes through in spite of all this, it is a miracle, and probably no book is born entire and uncrippled as it was conceived.

But for women, I thought, looking at the empty shelves, these difficulties were infinitely more formidable. In the first place, to have a room of her own, let alone a quiet room or a sound-proof room, was out of the question, unless her parents were exceptionally rich or very noble, even up to the beginning of the nineteenth century. Since her pin money, which depended on the good will of her father, was only enough to keep her clothed, she was debarred from such alleviations as came even to Keats or Tennyson or Carlyle, all poor men, from a walking tour, a little journey to France, from the separate lodging which, even if it were miserable enough, sheltered them from the claims and tyrannies of their families. Such material difficulties were formidable; but much worse were the immaterial. The indifference of the world which Keats and Flaubert and other men of ge-

[23] Ben Jonson said this in *Timber, or Discoveries* (1641).

[24] The works mentioned were all written against various obstacles. The manuscript of the first volume of Thomas Carlyle's *The French Revolution* (1837) was accidentally burned and had to be reconstructed. Gustave Flaubert struggled for five years to write *Madame Bovary* (1857), and he immediately had to defend it in court against charges of obscenity. During the last year of his life, Keats was aware of his imminent death from tuberculosis; he died in 1821 at the age of twenty-five. The personal letters of all three, describing their difficulties, have been published.

[25] A reference to Flaubert's ideal, in writing *Madame Bovary*, of finding *le seul mot juste* ("the only right word").

[26] A line from William Wordsworth's "Resolution and Independence," line 116.

nius have found so hard to bear was in her case not indifference but hostility. The world did not say to her as it said to them, Write if you choose; it makes no difference to me. The world said with a guffaw, Write? What's the good of your writing? Here the psychologists of Newnham and Girton might come to our help, I thought, looking again at the blank spaces on the shelves. For surely it is time that the effect of discouragement upon the mind of the artist should be measured, as I have seen a dairy company measure the effect of ordinary milk and Grade A milk upon the body of the rat. They set two rats in cages side by side, and of the two one was furtive, timid and small, and the other was glossy, bold and big. Now what food do we feed women as artists upon? I asked, remembering, I suppose, that dinner of prunes and custard.[27] To answer that question I had only to open the evening paper and to read that Lord Birkenhead is of opinion— but really I am not going to trouble to copy out Lord Birkenhead's opinion upon the writing of women.[28] What Dean Inge[29] says I will leave in peace. The Harley Street specialist[30] may be allowed to rouse the echoes of Harley Street with his vociferations without raising a hair on my head. I will quote, however, Mr. Oscar Browning,[31] because Mr. Oscar Browning was a great figure in Cambridge at one time, and used to examine the students at Girton and Newnham. Mr. Oscar Browning was wont to declare "that the impression left on his mind, after looking over any set of examination papers, was that, irrespective of the marks he might give, the best woman was intellectually the inferior of the worst man." After saying that Mr. Browning went back to his rooms—and it is this sequel that endears him and makes him a human figure of some bulk and majesty—he went back to his rooms and found a stable-boy lying on the sofa—"a mere skeleton, his cheeks were cavernous and sallow, his teeth were black, and he did not appear to have the full use of his limbs. . . . 'That's Arthur' [said Mr. Browning]. 'He's a dear boy really and most high-minded.'" The two pictures always seem to me to complete each other. And happily in this age of biography the two pictures often do complete each other, so that we are able to interpret the opinions of great men not only by what they say, but by what they do.

But though this is possible now, such opinions coming from the lips of important people must have been formidable enough even fifty years ago. Let us suppose that a father from the highest motives did not wish his daughter to leave home and become writer, painter or scholar. "See what

[27] In Chapter 1, Woolf had told of eating prunes and custard at "Fernham," a women's college, after eating a gourmet meal at "Oxbridge," a men's college.

[28] The Earl of Birkenhead was Lord Chancellor of England from 1919 to 1922. Woolf probably was referring to a recent biography, *Lord Birkenhead* (1926), by "Ephesian" (Carl E. B. Roberts), in which Birkenhead was quoted thus: "I venture to say that the sum total of human happiness, knowledge, and achievement would have been almost unaffected if Sappho had never sung, if Joan of Arc had never fought, if Siddons had never played, and if George Eliot had never written" (pp. 95–96).

[29] William Ralph Inge was Dean of St. Paul's Cathedral, London, from 1911 to 1934.

[30] Harley Street, London, is the location of fashionable doctors' offices. The "Harley Street specialist" referred to is unidentified.

[31] Oscar Browning (1837–1923) was Lecturer in History at King's College, Cambridge, from 1880 to 1908. Woolf got the quotation and the anecdote from H. E. Williams's *Oscar Browning* (1927).

Mr. Oscar Browning says," he would say; and there was not only Mr. Oscar Browning; there was the *Saturday Review;*[32] there was Mr. Greg[33]—the "essentials of a woman's being," said Mr. Greg emphatically, "are that *they are supported by, and they minister to, men*"—there was an enormous body of masculine opinion to the effect that nothing could be expected of women intellectually. Even if her father did not read out loud these opinions, any girl could read them for herself; and the reading, even in the nineteenth century, must have lowered her vitality, and told profoundly upon her work. There would always have been that assertion—you cannot do this, you are incapable of doing that—to protest against, to overcome. Probably for a novelist this germ is no longer of much effect; for there have been women novelists of merit. But for painters it must still have some sting in it; and for musicians, I imagine, is even now active and poisonous in the extreme. The woman composer stands where the actress stood in the time of Shakespeare. Nick Greene, I thought, remembering the story I had made about Shakespeare's sister, said that a woman acting put him in mind of a dog dancing. Johnson repeated the phrase two hundred years later of women preaching. And here, I said, opening a book about music, we have the very words used again in this year of grace, 1928, of women who try to write music. "Of Mlle. Germaine Tailleferre one can only repeat Dr. Johnson's dictum concerning a woman preacher, transposed into terms of music. 'Sir, a woman's composing is like a dog's walking on his hind legs. It is not done well, but you are surprised to find it done at all.'"[34] So accurately does history repeat itself.

Thus, I concluded, shutting Mr. Oscar Browning's life and pushing away the rest, it is fairly evident that even in the nineteenth century a woman was not encouraged to be an artist. On the contrary, she was snubbed, slapped, lectured and exhorted. Her mind must have been strained and her vitality lowered by the need of opposing this, of disproving that. For here again we come within range of that very interesting and obscure masculine complex which has had so much influence upon the woman's movement; that deep-seated desire, not so much that *she* shall be inferior as that *he* shall be superior, which plants him wherever one looks, not only in front of the arts, but barring the way to politics too, even when the risk to himself seems infinitesimal and the suppliant humble and devoted. Even Lady Bessborough,[35] I remembered, with all her passion for politics, must humbly bow herself and write to Lord Granville Leveson-Gower: ". . . notwithstanding all my violence in politics and talking so much on that subject, I perfectly agree with you that no woman has any business to meddle with that or any other serious business, farther than giving her opinion (if she is ask'd)." And so she goes on to spend her

[32] Influential London literary periodical.

[33] W. W. Greg (1875–1959) was an editor, bibliographer, reviewer, and, from 1907 to 1913, librarian of Trinity College, Cambridge.

[34] "*A Survey of Contemporary Music* [1924], Cecil Gray, p. 246." [Woolf's note.] Germaine Tailleferre (1892–1983) was a French composer, a member of the group known as *Les Six*, followers of Erik Satie.

[35] Henrietta Spencer, wife of the Earl of Bessborough, carried on a famous correspondence with Lord Granville Leveson-Gower (1815–91), British Foreign Secretary under William Gladstone. Woolf quotes from the published correspondence of Lord Granville.

enthusiasm where it meets with no obstacle whatsoever upon that immensely important subject, Lord Granville's maiden speech in the House of Commons. The spectacle is certainly a strange one, I thought. The history of men's opposition to women's emancipation is more interesting perhaps than the story of that emancipation itself. An amusing book might be made of it if some young student at Girton or Newnham would collect examples and deduce a theory—but she would need thick gloves on her hands, and bars to protect her of solid gold.

But what is amusing now, I recollected, shutting Lady Bessborough, had to be taken in desperate earnest once. Opinions that one now pastes in a book labelled cock-a-doodle-dum and keeps for reading to select audiences on summer nights once drew tears, I can assure you. Among your grandmothers and great-grandmothers there were many that wept their eyes out. Florence Nightingale shrieked aloud in her agony.[36] Moreover, it is all very well for you, who have got yourselves to college and enjoy sitting-rooms—or is it only bed-sitting-rooms?—of your own to say that genius should disregard such opinions; that genius should be above caring what is said of it. Unfortunately, it is precisely the men or women of genius who mind most what is said of them. Remember Keats. Remember the words he had cut on his tombstone.[37] Think of Tennyson; think—but I need hardly multiply instances of the undeniable, if very unfortunate, fact that it is the nature of the artist to mind excessively what is said about him. Literature is strewn with the wreckage of men who have minded beyond reason the opinions of others.

And this susceptibility of theirs is doubly unfortunate, I thought, returning again to my original enquiry into what state of mind is most propitious for creative work, because the mind of an artist, in order to achieve the prodigious effort of freeing whole and entire the work that is in him, must be incandescent, like Shakespeare's mind, I conjectured, looking at the book which lay open at *Antony and Cleopatra*. There must be no obstacle in it, no foreign matter unconsumed.

For though we say that we know nothing about Shakespeare's state of mind, even as we say that, we are saying something about Shakespeare's state of mind. The reason perhaps why we know so little of Shakespeare—compared with Donne or Ben Jonson or Milton—is that his grudges and spites and antipathies are hidden from us. We are not held up by some "revelation" which reminds us of the writer. All desire to protest, to preach, to proclaim an injury, to pay off a score, to make the world the witness of some hardship or grievance was fired out of him and consumed. Therefore his poetry flows from him free and unimpeded. If ever a human being got his work expressed completely, it was Shakespeare. If ever a mind was incandescent, unimpeded, I thought, turning again to the bookcase, it was Shakespeare's mind. . . .

I told you in the course of this paper that Shakespeare had a sister; but

[36]"See *Cassandra*, by Florence Nightingale, printed in *The Cause*, by R. Strachey." [Woolf's note.] Ray Strachey's *The Cause: A Short History of the Women's Movement in Great Britain* was published in 1928. Florence Nightingale's impassioned essay "Cassandra" (1852) was published as an appendix.

[37]"Here lies one whose name was writ in water."

do not look for her in Sir Sidney Lee's life of the poet.[38] She died young—
alas, she never wrote a word. She lies buried where the omnibuses now
stop, opposite the Elephant and Castle. Now my belief is that this poet who
never wrote a word and was buried at the crossroads still lives. She lives in
you and in me, and in many other women who are not here tonight, for
they are washing up the dishes and putting the children to bed. But she
lives; for great poets do not die; they are continuing presences; they need
only the opportunity to walk among us in the flesh. This opportunity, as I
think, it is now coming within your power to give her. For my belief is that
if we live another century or so—I am talking of the common life which is
the real life and not of the little separate lives which we live as individuals—
and have five hundred a year each of us and rooms of our own; if we have
the habit of freedom and the courage to write exactly what we think; if we
escape a little from the common sitting-room and see human beings not
always in their relation to each other but in relation to reality; and the sky,
too, and the trees or whatever it may be in themselves; if we look past
Milton's bogey,[39] for no human being should shut out the view; if we face
the fact, for it is a fact, that there is no arm to cling to, but that we go alone
and that our relation is to the world of reality and not only to the world of
men and women, then the opportunity will come and the dead poet who
was Shakespeare's sister will put on the body which she has so often laid
down. Drawing her life from the lives of the unknown who were her fore-
runners, as her brother did before her, she will be born. As for her coming
without that preparation, without that effort on our part, without that de-
termination that when she is born again she shall find it possible to live and
write her poetry, that we cannot expect, for that would be impossible. But I
maintain that she would come if we worked for her, and that so to work,
even in poverty and obscurity, is worth while.

[38] Sidney Lee was the author of a rather romantic *Life of William Shakespeare* (1898).
[39] That is, Milton's misogyny: Of Adam and Eve, "Not equal, as their sex not equal seemed;
/ For contemplation he and valor formed, / For softness she and sweet attractive grace; / He
for God only, she for God in him" (*Paradise Lost* IV. 296–99).

Franz Kafka
(1883–1924)

Dreams and nightmares have had an important place in literature since its
beginning, from Cassandra's visionary hallucinations in *Agamemnon*
through Dante's great dream-vision of the afterlife in *The Divine Comedy* to
Joyce's "funferall" dream-novel, *Finnegans Wake*. Some of the most power-
ful and characteristic modern literary dreams were those of a tall, lanky,
melancholy Jewish lawyer from Prague, who spent his days in a bureau-
cratic insurance office listening to workers' insurance claims and his nights

in writing stories that read like a series of nightmares. Dreams, as Freud pointed out, are among the most personal and idiosyncratic of phenomena, but paradoxically, Kafka's dream-stories, while profoundly rooted in his own lonely, neurotic personality, have struck deep chords in a wide range of readers. It is almost as if Kafka's nightmares of faceless, anonymous authority and of the individual's loneliness, alienation, and despair were collective dreams of the twentieth century.

Franz Kafka was born in 1883, in Prague, Czechoslovakia, a city whose twentieth-century history strangely echoes Kafka's fables of mindless tyranny and oppression. He was the oldest surviving child of six children; his father was a wealthy, self-made Jewish merchant whose struggles to succeed had made him an outspoken and domineering defender of traditional authority, while his mother was a simple, submissive woman with little sympathy for her son's artistic interests. He distinguished himself at a fine high school in Prague and then studied law at the University of Prague, receiving his doctorate when he was twenty-three. After a year of legal apprenticeship, he took a job with the accident claims division of the Workers' Accident Insurance Institute for the Kingdom of Bohemia. He stuck to that job steadily for nine years and then, after he developed tuberculosis, intermittently for another five, resigning only two years before his early death. Listening to stories of accidents and hardships and of dealing with governmental and business bureaucracy, tasks to which he devoted each day from eight to two, undoubtedly contributed to the themes of the stories he began writing after working hours.

Kafka's first published work appeared in a Prague magazine in 1909; he was to publish very little during his lifetime, most of his work appearing posthumously. He moved, however, in the circles of Prague Jewish intellectuals and artists, including the theologian Martin Buber, the novelist Franz Werfel, and especially Max Brod, his closest friend and, later, his editor and biographer. By 1913, Kafka had written enough short pieces to publish a collection, *Meditation;* the same year, he wrote "The Judgment," a story about his father, which he felt represented a great personal and artistic breakthrough, as well as "The Metamorphosis" and the first sections of the novel published after his death as *Amerika* (1927).

Also in 1913, Kafka met and fell in love with a German girl named Felice Bauer. Their odd courtship continued for five years, Kafka vacillating between the desire to marry and the desire to devote all his time to his art. During these years, he wrote the famous short story "The Penal Colony" and the novel *The Trial* (posthumously published in 1925). When World War I broke out, Kafka, as a civil servant, was exempt from military service, but the war's senselessness and brutality confirmed his own vision of the nightmarishness of history.

In 1917, Kafka discovered that he had tuberculosis. He took a medical leave from his job and began a series of treatments that were to continue the rest of his life. In 1920, he was in a sanitarium in the Tatra Mountains on the Polish border in northern Czechoslovakia. About this time he had an intense, tortured love affair with his Czech translator, Milena Jesenska, which again he broke off, ostensibly to devote all his time to writing. He was also working on his famous novel *The Castle* (1926), about a land surveyor

named K. and his attempts to enter the castle to which he has been summoned.

During the final years of his life, Kafka's health deteriorated rapidly. In 1923, he fell in love with Dora Dymant and settled with her in Berlin; he asked Dora's father for permission to marry her but was refused. In the winter of 1923–24 he moved into a series of clinics and sanitariums. He died, Dora at his side, on June 3, 1924, at a sanitarium in Kierling, near Vienna. His surviving family, including his sisters, all perished several years later in Nazi concentration camps.

Kafka left instructions that all his manuscripts were to be destroyed and that work already published was not to be republished. His friend Max Brod took the responsibility of disregarding these instructions, however, and published, over a period of several years, the bulk of Kafka's work. By the 1930's Kafka was well-known in France, England, and the United States; his fame in Germany had to wait until the fall of the Hitler regime in 1945, but since then he has become one of the most famous and influential of German-language authors there as well.

The American critic Philip Rahv has pointed out a "nuclear fable" that underlies Kafka's most characteristic works. In each of them, a unique, intelligent, unpredictable individual is thrust into a baffling, automatic, depersonalized world where he must struggle to maintain his individuality against a system that tries to force him into a dazed, acquiescent behavior which fits the externally imposed expectations of the system. The result is a painful, disorienting conflict between one's inner sense of self and the pressures of the identity imposed from without. The personal roots of this recurring fable were undoubtedly Kafka's relations with his domineering, intimidating father. This relationship, as Kafka saw it, is recorded in the painful, self-lacerating "Letter to His Father" (1919), a letter which never reached Hermann Kafka:

Dear Father:

You asked me recently why I maintain that I am afraid of you. As usual, I was unable to think of any answer to your question, partly for the very reason that I am afraid of you, and partly because an explanation of the grounds for this fear would mean going into far more details than I could even approximately keep in mind while talking.

The letter does not ultimately answer the question of why Hermann Kafka, overpowering as he was, remained so potent a force in his son's life. But he did remain so, not only in the stories of explicit paternal tyranny but in others in which the father's power is projected upon a frightening, depersonalizing universe.

It would be a mistake, however, to regard Kafka's stories as merely transcriptions of his neurotic fantasies, ripped raw from his unconscious. Kafka is one of the most artful of writers, and his oneiric tales are the products of careful craftsmanship and laborious revision. He was a close student not only of the German Romantic writers, including Goethe, Kleist,

Grillparzer, and Von Hofmannstal (a major influence), but also of Flaubert, Dostoevsky, Tolstoy, and Dickens, all of whom left some mark upon his work. He also took a lively interest in social and political affairs; from his adolescence he was a socialist, and in his later years he was a supporter of Zionism, under the influence of both Max Brod and Dora Dymant. Despite his atheism, he took an intense interest in Judaism and was especially influenced by the Jewish mystical movement known as Hasidism. Many of the most apparently private of Kafka's stories have social, philosophical, and religious dimensions that reflect these varied interests.

The first sentence of "The Metamorphosis"—"As Gregor Samsa awoke one morning from uneasy dreams he found himself transformed in his bed into a gigantic insect"—is one of the most famous in modern fiction, not only for its startling content but also for its calm, matter-of-fact style, which sets the tone for the rest of the story. The premise of the story is dreamlike; as Freud pointed out, one of the most important mechanisms of the "dream-work" is symbolization. Gregor Samsa feels himself to be an insect and has been treated like an insect; the story makes the dreamlike leap from "I feel like an insect" to "I am an insect." Gregor has been treated like an insect by his family and by his employer, and he is not blameless: he may feel like an insect for having displaced his father as breadwinner and head of the family. The causes are complex, but whatever they are, they have led Gregor to the ultimate alienation, loss of even his physical humanity. He is the ultimate "underground man," and his plight may even have been suggested by the incident in Dostoevsky's *Notes from Underground* in which the officer on the Nevsky Prospect takes the narrator by the shoulders and moves him to the side, as if he were nothing more than "a curious insect."

Once Gregor's metamorphosis has been accomplished, in that opening line, the story proceeds inexorably to his death, as it does for the protagonist in another story often linked to Kafka's: Tolstoy's *The Death of Ivan Ilyitch*, in which Ivan, like Gregor, feels that he is being punished but has committed no crime. But Ivan's story ends in illumination and joy at the last moment: " 'So this is it!' he suddenly exclaimed aloud, 'What joy!' " The only affirmative note in "The Metamorphosis" comes after Gregor's death, when his loved sister ambiguously and with an unconscious callousness reaffirms life by springing to her feet and stretching her young body.

FURTHER READING *(prepared by J. H.)*: There are several excellent biographies of Kafka. Max Brod, his close friend and literary executor, wrote *Franz Kafka: A Biography*, rev. Engl. trans. 1960. Ronald Hayman's massive *Kafka: A Biography*, 1982, emphasizes the links between Kafka's life and his writing, and Ernst Pawel's *The Nightmare of Reason: A Life of Franz Kafka*, 1984, is insightful on Kafka's personality. Klaus Wagenbach's *Franz Kafka: Pictures of a Life*, 1984, offers a brief biography accompanying a great many pictures of Kafka and his world. Introductory overviews of Kafka's writing are provided by Kurt J. Fickert's *Franz Kafka: Life, Works, and Criticism*, 1984, in the Authoritative Studies in World Literature series, and by Meno Spann's *Franz Kafka*, 1976, in the Twayne World Authors series. The section on Kafka in Margot Norris's *Beasts of the Modern Imagination: Darwin, Nietzsche, Kafka, and Lawrence*, 1985, is distinguished criticism. On *The Metamorphosis*, see *The Commentators' Despair: The Interpretations of Kafka's "Metamorphosis,"* ed. by Stanley Corngold, 1973. A more general collection of essays is the Kafka volume in the Twentieth Century Views series, ed. by Ronald Gray, 1962.

THE METAMORPHOSIS

Translated by Willa and Edwin Muir

I

As Gregor Samsa awoke one morning from uneasy dreams he found himself transformed in his bed into a gigantic insect. He was lying on his hard, as it were armor-plated, back and when he lifted his head a little he could see his dome-like brown belly divided into stiff arched segments on top of which the bed quilt could hardly keep in position and was about to slide off completely. His numerous legs, which were pitifully thin compared to the rest of his bulk, waved helplessly before his eyes.

What has happened to me? he thought. It was no dream. His room, a regular human bedroom, only rather too small, lay quiet between the four familiar walls. Above the table on which a collection of cloth samples was unpacked and spread out—Samsa was a commercial traveler—hung the picture which he had recently cut out of an illustrated magazine and put into a pretty gilt frame. It showed a lady, with a fur cap on and a fur stole, sitting upright and holding out to the spectator a huge fur muff into which the whole of her forearm had vanished!

Gregor's eyes turned next to the window, and the overcast sky—one could hear rain drops beating on the window gutter—made him quite melancholy. What about sleeping a little longer and forgetting all this nonsense, he thought, but it could not be done, for he was accustomed to sleep on his right side and in his present condition he could not turn himself over. However violently he forced himself towards his right side he always rolled on to his back again. He tried it at least a hundred times, shutting his eyes to keep from seeing his struggling legs, and only desisted when he began to feel in his side a faint dull ache he had never experienced before.

Oh God, he thought, what an exhausting job I've picked on! Traveling about day in, day out. It's much more irritating work than doing the actual business in the office, and on top of that there's the trouble of constant traveling, of worrying about train connections, the bed and irregular meals, casual acquaintances that are always new and never become intimate friends. The devil take it all! He felt a slight itching up on his belly; slowly pushed himself on his back nearer to the top of the bed so that he could lift his head more easily; identified the itching place which was surrounded by many small white spots the nature of which he could not understand and made to touch it with a leg, but drew the leg back immediately, for the contact made a cold shiver run through him.

He slid down again into his former position. This getting up early, he thought, makes one quite stupid. A man needs his sleep. Other commercials live like harem women. For instance, when I come back to the hotel of a morning to write up the orders I've got, these others are only sitting down to breakfast. Let me just try that with my chief; I'd be sacked on the spot. Anyhow, that might be quite a good thing for me, who can tell? If I didn't have to hold my hand because of my parents I'd have given notice long ago, I'd have gone to the chief and told him exactly what I think of him. That

would knock him endways from his desk! It's a queer way of doing, too, this sitting on high at a desk and talking down to employees, especially when they have to come quite near because the chief is hard of hearing. Well, there's still hope; once I've saved enough money to pay back my parents' debts to him—that should take another five or six years—I'll do it without fail. I'll cut myself completely loose then. For the moment, though, I'd better get up, since my train goes at five.

He looked at the alarm clock ticking on the chest. Heavenly Father! he thought. It was half-past six o'clock and the hands were quietly moving on, it was even past the half-hour, it was getting on toward a quarter to seven. Had the alarm clock not gone off? From the bed one could see that it had been properly set for four o'clock; of course it must have gone off. Yes, but was it possible to sleep quietly through that ear-splitting noise? Well, he had not slept quietly, yet apparently all the more soundly for that. But what was he to do now? The next train went at seven o'clock; to catch that he would need to hurry like mad and his samples weren't even packed up, and he himself wasn't feeling particularly fresh and active. And even if he did catch the train he wouldn't avoid a row with the chief, since the firm's porter would have been waiting for the five o'clock train and would have long since reported his failure to turn up. The porter was a creature of the chief's, spineless and stupid. Well, supposing he were to say he was sick? But that would be most unpleasant and would look suspicious, since during his five years' employment he had not been ill once. The chief himself would be sure to come with the sick-insurance doctor, would reproach his parents with their son's laziness and would cut all excuses short by referring to the insurance doctor, who of course regarded all mankind as perfectly healthy malingerers. And would he be so far wrong on this occasion? Gregor really felt quite well, apart from a drowsiness that was utterly superfluous after such a long sleep, and he was even unusually hungry.

As all this was running through his mind at top speed without his being able to decide to leave his bed—the alarm clock had just struck a quarter to seven—there came a cautious tap at the door behind the head of his bed. "Gregor," said a voice—it was his mother's—"it's a quarter to seven. Hadn't you a train to catch?" That gentle voice! Gregor had a shock as he heard his own voice answering hers, unmistakably his own voice, it was true, but with a persistent horrible twittering squeak behind it like an undertone, that left the words in their clear shape only for the first moment and then rose up reverberating round them to destroy their sense, so that one could not be sure one had heard them rightly. Gregor wanted to answer at length and explain everything, but in the circumstances he confined himself to saying: "Yes, yes, thank you, Mother, I'm getting up now." The wooden door between them must have kept the change in his voice from being noticeable outside, for his mother contented herself with this statement and shuffled away. Yet this brief exchange of words had made the other members of the family aware that Gregor was still in the house, as they had not expected, and at one of the side doors his father was already knocking, gently, yet with his fist. "Gregor, Gregor," he called, "what's the matter with you?" And after a little while he called again in a deeper voice: "Gregor! Gregor!" At the other side door his sister was saying in a low, plaintive tone: "Gregor? Aren't you well? Are you needing anything?" He answered them

both at once: "I'm just ready," and did his best to make his voice sound as normal as possible by enunciating the words very clearly and leaving long pauses between them. So his father went back to his breakfast, but his sister whispered: "Gregor, open the door, do." However, he was not thinking of opening the door, and felt thankful for the prudent habit he had acquired in traveling of locking all doors during the night, even at home.

His immediate intention was to get up quietly without being disturbed, to put on his clothes and above all eat his breakfast, and only then to consider what else was to be done, since in bed, he was well aware, his meditations would come to no sensible conclusion. He remembered that often enough in bed he had felt small aches and pains, probably caused by awkward postures, which had proved purely imaginary once he got up, and he looked forward eagerly to seeing this morning's delusions gradually fall away. That the change in his voice was nothing but the precursor of a severe chill, a standing ailment of commercial travelers, he had not the least possible doubt.

To get rid of the quilt was quite easy; he had only to inflate himself a little and it fell off by itself. But the next move was difficult, especially because he was so uncommonly broad. He would have needed arms and hands to hoist himself up; instead he had only the numerous little legs which never stopped waving in all directions and which he could not control in the least. When he tried to bend one of them it was the first to stretch itself straight; and did he succeed at last in making it do what he wanted, all the other legs meanwhile waved the more wildly in a high degree of unpleasant agitation. "But what's the use of lying idle in bed," said Gregor to himself.

He thought that he might get out of bed with the lower part of his body first, but this lower part, which he had not yet seen and of which he could form no clear conception, proved too difficult to move; it shifted so slowly; and when finally, almost wild with annoyance, he gathered his forces together and thrust out recklessly, he had miscalculated the direction and bumped heavily against the lower end of the bed, and the stinging pain he felt informed him that precisely this lower part of his body was at the moment probably the most sensitive.

So he tried to get the top part of himself out first, and cautiously moved his head towards the edge of the bed. That proved easy enough, and despite its breadth and mass the bulk of his body at last slowly followed the movement of his head. Still, when he finally got his head free over the edge of the bed he felt too scared to go on advancing, for after all if he let himself fall in this way it would take a miracle to keep his head from being injured. And at all costs he must not lose consciousness now, precisely now; he would rather stay in bed.

But when after a repetition of the same efforts he lay in his former position again, sighing, and watched his little legs struggling against each other more wildly than ever, if that were possible, and saw no way of bringing any order into this arbitrary confusion, he told himself again that it was impossible to stay in bed and that the most sensible course was to risk everything for the smallest hope of getting away from it. At the same time he did not forget meanwhile to remind himself that cool reflection, the coolest possible, was much better than desperate resolves. In such moments

he focused his eyes as sharply as possible on the window, but, unfortunately, the prospect of the morning fog, which muffled even the other side of the narrow street, brought him little encouragement and comfort. "Seven o'clock already," he said to himself when the alarm clock chimed again, "seven o'clock already and still such a thick fog." And for a little while he lay quiet, breathing lightly, as if perhaps expecting such complete repose to restore all things to their real and normal condition.

But then he said to himself: "Before it strikes a quarter past seven I must be quite out of this bed, without fail. Anyhow, by that time someone will have come from the office to ask for me, since it opens before seven." And he set himself to rocking his whole body at once in a regular rhythm, with the idea of swinging it out of the bed. If he tipped himself out in that way he could keep his head from injury by lifting it at an acute angle when he fell. His back seemed to be hard and was not likely to suffer from a fall on the carpet. His biggest worry was the loud crash he would not be able to help making, which would probably cause anxiety, if not terror, behind all the doors. Still, he must take the risk.

When he was already half out of the bed—the new method was more a game than an effort, for he needed only to hitch himself across by rocking to and fro—it struck him how simple it would be if he could get help. Two strong people—he thought of his father and the servant girl—would be amply sufficient; they would only have to thrust their arms under his convex back, lever him out of the bed, bend down with their burden and then be patient enough to let him turn himself right over on to the floor, where it was to be hoped his legs would then find their proper function. Well, ignoring the fact that the doors were all locked, ought he really to call for help? In spite of his misery he could not suppress a smile at the very idea of it.

He had got so far that he could barely keep his equilibrium when he rocked himself strongly, and he would have to nerve himself very soon for the final decision since in five minutes' time it would be a quarter past seven—when the front doorbell rang. "That's someone from the office," he said to himself, and grew almost rigid, while his little legs only jigged about all the faster. For a moment everything stayed quiet. "They're not going to open the door," said Gregor to himself, catching at some kind of irrational hope. But then of course the servant girl went as usual to the door with her heavy tread and opened it. Gregor needed only to hear the first good morning of the visitor to know immediately who it was—the chief clerk himself. What a fate, to be condemned to work for a firm where the smallest omission at once gave rise to the gravest suspicion! Were all employees in a body nothing but scoundrels, was there not among them one single loyal devoted man who, had he wasted only an hour or so of the firm's time in a morning, was so tormented by conscience as to be driven out of his mind and actually incapable of leaving his bed? Wouldn't it really have been sufficient to send an apprentice to inquire—if any inquiry were necessary at all—did the chief clerk himself have to come and thus indicate to the entire family, an innocent family, that this suspicious circumstance could be investigated by no one less versed in affairs than himself? And more through the agitation caused by these reflections than through any act of will Gregor swung himself out of bed with all his strength. There was

a loud thump, but it was not really a crash. His fall was broken to some extent by the carpet, his back, too, was less stiff than he thought, and so there was merely a dull thud, not so very startling. Only he had not lifted his head carefully enough and had hit it; he turned it and rubbed it on the carpet in pain and irritation.

"That was something falling down in there," said the chief clerk in the next room to the left. Gregor tried to suppose to himself that something like what had happened to him today might some day happen to the chief clerk; one really could not deny that it was possible. But as if in brusque reply to this supposition the chief clerk took a couple of firm steps in the next-door room and his patent-leather boots creaked. From the right-hand room his sister was whispering to inform him of the situation: "Gregor, the chief clerk's here." "I know," muttered Gregor to himself; but he didn't dare to make his voice loud enough for his sister to hear it.

"Gregor," said his father now from the left-hand room, "the chief clerk has come and wants to know why you didn't catch the early train. We don't know what to say to him. Besides, he wants to talk to you in person. So open the door, please. He will be good enough to excuse the untidiness of your room." "Good morning, Mr. Samsa," the chief clerk was calling amiably meanwhile. "He's not well," said his mother to the visitor, while his father was still speaking through the door, "he's not well, sir, believe me. What else would make him miss a train! The boy thinks about nothing but his work. It makes me almost cross the way he never goes out in the evenings; he's been here the last eight days and has stayed at home every single evening. He just sits there quietly at the table reading a newspaper or looking through railway timetables. The only amusement he gets is doing fretwork. For instance, he spent two or three evenings cutting out a little picture frame; you would be surprised to see how pretty it is; it's hanging in his room; you'll see it in a minute when Gregor opens the door. I must say I'm glad you've come, sir; we should never have got him to unlock the door by ourselves; he's so obstinate; and I'm sure he's unwell, though he wouldn't have it to be so this morning." "I'm just coming," said Gregor slowly and carefully, not moving an inch for fear of losing one word of the conversation. "I can't think of any other explanation, madam," said the chief clerk. "I hope it's nothing serious. Although on the other hand I must say that we men of business—fortunately or unfortunately—very often simply have to ignore any slight indisposition, since business must be attended to." "Well, can the chief clerk come in now?" asked Gregor's father impatiently, again knocking on the door. "No," said Gregor. In the left-hand room a painful silence followed this refusal; in the right-hand room his sister began to sob.

Why didn't his sister join the others? She was probably newly out of bed and hadn't even begun to put on her clothes yet. Well, why was she crying? Because he wouldn't get up and let the chief clerk in, because he was in danger of losing his job, and because the chief would begin dunning his parents again for the old debts? Surely these were things one didn't need to worry about for the present. Gregor was still at home and not in the least thinking of deserting the family. At the moment, true, he was lying on the carpet and no one who knew the condition he was in could seriously expect him to admit the chief clerk. But for such a small discourtesy, which could

plausibly be explained away somehow later on, Gregor could hardly be dismissed on the spot. And it seemed to Gregor that it would be much more sensible to leave him in peace for the present than to trouble him with tears and entreaties. Still, of course, their uncertainty bewildered them all and excused their behavior.

"Mr. Samsa," the chief clerk called now in a louder voice, "what's the matter with you? Here you are, barricading yourself in your room, giving only 'yes' and 'no' for answers, causing your parents a lot of unnecessary trouble and neglecting—I mention this only in passing—neglecting your business duties in an incredible fashion. I am speaking here in the name of your parents and of your chief, and I beg you quite seriously to give me an immediate and precise explanation. You amaze me, you amaze me. I thought you were a quiet, dependable person, and now all at once you seem bent on making a disgraceful exhibition of yourself. The chief did hint to me early this morning a possible explanation for your disappearance—with reference to the cash payments that were entrusted to you recently—but I almost pledged my solemn word of honor that this could not be so. But now that I see how incredibly obstinate you are, I no longer have the slightest desire to take your part at all. And your position in the firm is not so unassailable. I came with the intention of telling you all this in private, but since you are wasting my time so needlessly I don't see why your parents shouldn't hear it too. For some time past your work has been most unsatisfactory; this is not the season of the year for a business boom, of course, we admit that, but a season of the year for doing no business at all, that does not exist, Mr. Samsa, must not exist."

"But, sir," cried Gregor, beside himself and in his agitation forgetting everything else, "I'm just going to open the door this very minute. A slight illness, an attack of giddiness, has kept me from getting up. I'm still lying in bed. But I feel all right again. I'm getting out of bed now. Just give me a moment or two longer! I'm not quite so well as I thought. But I'm all right, really. How a thing like that can suddenly strike one down! Only last night I was quite well, my parents can tell you, or rather I did have a slight presentiment. I must have showed some sign of it. Why didn't I report it at the office! But one always thinks that an indisposition can be got over without staying in the house. Oh, sir, do spare my parents! All that you're reproaching me with now has no foundation; no one has ever said a word to me about it. Perhaps you haven't looked at the last orders I sent in. Anyhow, I can still catch the eight-o'clock train, I'm much the better for my few hours' rest. Don't let me detain you here, sir; I'll be attending to business very soon, and do be good enough to tell the chief so and to make my excuses to him!"

And while all this was tumbling out pell-mell and Gregor hardly knew what he was saying, he had reached the chest quite easily, perhaps because of the practice he had had in bed, and was now trying to lever himself upright by means of it. He meant actually to open the door, actually to show himself and speak to the chief clerk; he was eager to find out what the others, after all their insistence, would say at the sight of him. If they were horrified then the responsibility was no longer his and he could stay quiet. But if they took it calmly, then he had no reason either to be upset, and could really get to the station for the eight-o'clock train if he hurried. At

first he slipped down a few times from the polished surface of the chest, but at length with a last heave he stood upright; he paid no more attention to the pains in the lower part of his body, however they smarted. Then he let himself fall against the back of a near-by chair, and clung with his little legs to the edges of it. That brought him into control of himself again and he stopped speaking, for now he could listen to what the chief clerk was saying.

"Did you understand a word of it?" the chief clerk was asking; "surely he can't be trying to make fools of us?" "Oh dear," cried his mother, in tears, "perhaps he's terribly ill and we're tormenting him. Grete! Grete!" she called out then. "Yes, Mother?" called his sister from the other side. They were calling to each other across Gregor's room. "You must go this minute for the doctor. Gregor is ill. Go for the doctor, quick. Did you hear how he was speaking?" "That was no human voice," said the chief clerk in a voice noticeably low beside the shrillness of the mother's. "Anna! Anna!" his father was calling through the hall to the kitchen, clapping his hands, "get a locksmith at once!" And the two girls were already running through the hall with a swish of skirts—how could his sister have got dressed so quickly?—and were tearing the front door open. There was no sound of its closing again; they had evidently left it open, as one does in houses where some great misfortune has happened.

But Gregor was now much calmer. The words he uttered were no longer understandable, apparently, although they seemed clear enough to him, even clearer than before, perhaps because his ear had grown accustomed to the sound of them. Yet at any rate people now believed that something was wrong with him, and were ready to help him. The positive certainty with which these first measures had been taken comforted him. He felt himself drawn once more into the human circle and hoped for great and remarkable results from both the doctor and the locksmith, without really distinguishing precisely between them. To make his voice as clear as possible for the decisive conversation that was now imminent he coughed a little, as quietly as he could, of course, since this noise too might not sound like a human cough for all he was able to judge. In the next room meanwhile there was complete silence. Perhaps his parents were sitting at the table with the chief clerk, whispering, perhaps they were all leaning against the door and listening.

Slowly Gregor pushed the chair towards the door, then let go of it, caught hold of the door for support—the soles at the end of his little legs were somewhat sticky—and rested against it for a moment after his efforts. Then he set himself to turning the key in the lock with his mouth. It seemed, unhappily, that he hadn't really any teeth—what could he grip the key with?—but on the other hand his jaws were certainly very strong; with their help he did manage to set the key in motion, heedless of the fact that he was undoubtedly damaging them somewhere, since a brown fluid issued from his mouth, flowed over the key and dripped on the floor. "Just listen to that," said the chief clerk next door; "he's turning the key." That was a great encouragement to Gregor; but they should all have shouted encouragement to him, his father and mother too: "Go on, Gregor," they should have called out, "keep going, hold on to that key!" And in the belief that they were all following his efforts intently, he clenched his jaws recklessly

on the key with all the force at his command. As the turning of the key progressed he circled round the lock, holding on now only with his mouth, pushing on the key, as required, or pulling it down again with all the weight of his body. The louder click of the finally yielding lock literally quickened Gregor. With a deep breath of relief he said to himself: "So I didn't need the locksmith," and laid his head on the handle to open the door wide.

Since he had to pull the door towards him, he was still invisible when it was really wide open. He had to edge himself slowly round the near half of the double door, and to do it very carefully if he was not to fall plump upon his back just on the threshold. He was still carrying out this difficult manoeuvre, with no time to observe anything else, when he heard the chief clerk utter a loud "Oh!"—it sounded like a gust of wind—and now he could see the man, standing as he was nearest to the door, clapping one hand before his open mouth and slowly backing away as if driven by some invisible steady pressure. His mother—in spite of the chief clerk's being there her hair was still undone and sticking up in all directions—first clasped her hands and looked at his father, then took two steps towards Gregor and fell on the floor among her outspread skirts, her face quite hidden on her breast. His father knotted his fist with a fierce expression on his face as if he meant to knock Gregor back into his room, then looked uncertainly round the living room, covered his eyes with his hands and wept till his great chest heaved.

Gregor did not go now into the living room, but leaned against the inside of the firmly shut wing of the door, so that only half his body was visible and his head above it bending sideways to look at the others. The light had meanwhile strengthened; on the other side of the street one could see clearly a section of the endlessly long, dark-gray building opposite—it was a hospital—abruptly punctuated by its row of regular windows; the rain was still falling, but only in large singly discernible and literally singly splashing drops. The breakfast dishes were set out on the table lavishly, for breakfast was the most important meal of the day to Gregor's father, who lingered it out for hours over various newspapers. Right opposite Gregor on the wall hung a photograph of himself on military service, as a lieutenant, hand on sword, a carefree smile on his face, inviting one to respect his uniform and military bearing. The door leading to the hall was open, and one could see that the front door stood open too, showing the landing beyond and the beginning of the stairs going down.

"Well," said Gregor, knowing perfectly that he was the only one who had retained any composure, "I'll put my clothes on at once, pack up my samples and start off. Will you only let me go? You see, sir, I'm not obstinate, and I'm willing to work; traveling is a hard life, but I couldn't live without it. Where are you going, sir? To the office? Yes? Will you give a true account of all this? One can be temporarily incapacitated, but that's just the moment for remembering former services and bearing in mind that later on, when the incapacity has been got over, one will certainly work with all the more industry and concentration. I'm loyally bound to serve the chief, you know that very well. Besides, I have to provide for my parents and my sister. I'm in great difficulties, but I'll get out of them again. Don't make things any worse for me than they are. Stand up for me in the firm. Travelers are not popular there, I know. People think they earn sacks of

money and just have a good time. A prejudice there's no particular reason for revising. But you, sir, have a more comprehensive view of affairs than the rest of the staff, yes, let me tell you in confidence, a more comprehensive view than the chief himself, who, being the owner, lets his judgment easily be swayed against one of his employees. And you know very well that the traveler, who is never seen in the office almost the whole year round, can so easily fall a victim to gossip and ill luck and unfounded complaints, which he mostly knows nothing about, except when he comes back exhausted from his rounds, and only then suffers in person from their evil consequences, which he can no longer trace back to the original causes. Sir, sir, don't go away without a word to me to show that you think me in the right at least to some extent!"

But at Gregor's very first words the chief clerk had already backed away and only stared at him with parted lips over one twitching shoulder. And while Gregor was speaking he did not stand still one moment but stole away towards the door, without taking his eyes off Gregor, yet only an inch at a time, as if obeying some secret injunction to leave the room. He was already at the hall, and the suddenness with which he took his last step out of the living room would have made one believe he had burned the sole of his foot. Once in the hall he stretched his right arm before him towards the staircase, as if some supernatural power were waiting there to deliver him.

Gregor perceived that the chief clerk must on no account be allowed to go away in this frame of mind if his position in the firm were not to be endangered to the utmost. His parents did not understand this so well; they had convinced themselves in the course of years that Gregor was settled for life in this firm, and besides they were so preoccupied with their immediate troubles that all foresight had forsaken them. Yet Gregor had this foresight. The chief clerk must be detained, soothed, persuaded and finally won over; the whole future of Gregor and his family depended on it! If only his sister had been there! She was intelligent; she had begun to cry while Gregor was still lying quietly on his back. And no doubt the chief clerk, so partial to ladies, would have been guided by her; she would have shut the door of the flat and in the hall talked him out of his horror. But she was not there, and Gregor would have to handle the situation himself. And without remembering that he was still unaware what powers of movement he possessed, without even remembering that his words in all possibility, indeed in all likelihood, would again be unintelligible, he let go the wing of the door, pushed himself through the opening, started to walk towards the chief clerk, who was already ridiculously clinging with both hands to the railing on the landing; but immediately, as he was feeling for a support, he fell down with a little cry upon all his numerous legs. Hardly was he down when he experienced for the first time this morning a sense of physical comfort; his legs had firm ground under them; they were completely obedient, as he noted with joy; they even strove to carry him forward in whatever direction he chose; and he was inclined to believe that a final relief from all his sufferings was at hand. But in the same moment as he found himself on the floor, rocking with suppressed eagerness to move, not far from his mother, indeed just in front of her, she, who had seemed so completely crushed, sprang all at once to her feet, her arms and fingers outspread, cried: "Help, for God's sake, help!" bent her head down as if to

see Gregor better, yet on the contrary kept backing senselessly away; had quite forgotten that the laden table stood behind her; sat upon it hastily, as if in absence of mind, when she bumped into it; and seemed altogether unaware that the big coffee pot beside her was upset and pouring coffee in a flood over the carpet.

"Mother, Mother," said Gregor in a low voice, and looked up at her. The chief clerk, for the moment, had quite slipped from his mind; instead, he could not resist snapping his jaws together at the sight of the streaming coffee. That made his mother scream again. She fled from the table and fell into the arms of his father, who hastened to catch her. But Gregor had now no time to spare for his parents; the chief clerk was already on the stairs; with his chin on the banister he was taking one last backward look. Gregor made a spring, to be as sure as possible of overtaking him; the chief clerk must have divined his intention, for he leaped down several steps and vanished; he was still yelling "Ugh!" and it echoed through the whole staircase.

Unfortunately, the flight of the chief clerk seemed completely to upset Gregor's father, who had remained relatively calm until now, for instead of running after the man himself, or at least not hindering Gregor in his pursuit, he seized in his right hand the walking stick which the chief clerk had left behind on a chair, together with a hat and greatcoat, snatched in his left hand a large newspaper from the table and began stamping his feet and flourishing the stick and the newspaper to drive Gregor back into his room. No entreaty of Gregor's availed, indeed no entreaty was even understood; however humbly he bent his head his father only stamped on the floor the more loudly. Behind his father his mother had torn open a window, despite the cold weather, and was leaning far out of it with her face in her hands. A strong draught set in from the street to the staircase, the window curtains blew in, the newspapers on the table fluttered, stray pages whisked over the floor. Pitilessly Gregor's father drove him back, hissing and crying "Shoo!" like a savage. But Gregor was quite unpracticed in walking backwards, it really was a slow business. If he only had a chance to turn round he could get back to his room at once, but he was afraid of exasperating his father by the slowness of such a rotation and at any moment the stick in his father's hand might hit him a fatal blow on the back or on the head. In the end, however, nothing else was left for him to do since to his horror he observed that in moving backwards he could not even control the direction he took; and so, keeping an anxious eye on his father all the time over his shoulder, he began to turn round as quickly as he could, which was in reality very slowly. Perhaps his father noted his good intentions, for he did not interfere except every now and then to help him in the manoeuvre from a distance with the point of the stick. If only he would have stopped making that unbearable hissing noise! It made Gregor quite lose his head. He had turned almost completely round when the hissing noise so distracted him that he even turned a little the wrong way again. But when at last his head was fortunately right in front of the doorway, it appeared that his body was too broad simply to get through the opening. His father, of course, in his present mood was far from thinking of such a thing as opening the other half of the door, to let Gregor have enough space. He had merely the fixed idea of driving Gregor back into his

room as quickly as possible. He would never have suffered Gregor to make the circumstantial preparations for standing up on end and perhaps slipping his way through the door. Maybe he was now making more noise than ever to urge Gregor forward, as if no obstacle impeded him; to Gregor, anyhow, the noise in his rear sounded no longer like the voice of one single father; this was really no joke, and Gregor thrust himself—come what might—into the doorway. One side of his body rose up, he was tilted at an angle in the doorway, his flank was quite bruised, horrid blotches stained the white door, soon he was stuck fast and, left to himself, could not have moved at all, his legs on one side fluttered trembling in the air, those on the other were crushed painfully to the floor—when from behind his father gave him a strong push which was literally a deliverance and he flew far into the room, bleeding freely. The door was slammed behind with the stick, and then at last there was silence.

II

Not until it was twilight did Gregor awake out of a deep sleep, more like a swoon than a sleep. He would certainly have waked up of his own accord not much later, for he felt himself sufficiently rested and well-slept, but it seemed to him as if a fleeting step and a cautious shutting of the door leading into the hall had aroused him. The electric lights in the street cast a pale sheen here and there on the ceiling and the upper surfaces of the furniture, but down below, where he lay, it was dark. Slowly, awkwardly trying out his feelers, which he now first learned to appreciate, he pushed his way to the door to see what had been happening there. His left side felt like one single long, unpleasantly tense scar, and he had actually to limp on his two rows of legs. One little leg, moreover, had been severely damaged in the course of that morning's events—it was almost a miracle that only one had been damaged—and trailed uselessly behind him.

He had reached the door before he discovered what had really drawn him to it: the smell of food. For there stood a basin filled with fresh milk in which floated little sops of white bread. He could almost have laughed with joy, since he was now still hungrier than in the morning, and he dipped his head almost over the eyes straight into the milk. But soon in disappointment he withdrew it again; not only did he find it difficult to feed because of his tender left side—and he could only feed with the palpitating collaboration of his whole body—he did not like the milk either, although milk had been his favorite drink and that was certainly why his sister had set it there for him; indeed it was almost with repulsion that he turned away from the basin and crawled back to the middle of the room.

He could see through the crack of the door that the gas was turned on in the living room, but while usually at this time his father made a habit of reading the afternoon newspaper in a loud voice to his mother and occasionally to his sister as well, not a sound was now to be heard. Well, perhaps his father had recently given up this habit of reading aloud, which his sister had mentioned so often in conversation and in her letters. But there was the same silence all around, although the flat was certainly not empty of occupants. "What a quiet life our family has been leading," said Gregor to

himself, and as he sat there motionless staring into the darkness he felt great pride in the fact that he had been able to provide such a life for his parents and sister in such a fine flat. But what if all the quiet, the comfort, the contentment were now to end in horror? To keep himself from being lost in such thoughts Gregor took refuge in movement and crawled up and down the room.

Once during the long evening one of the side doors was opened a little and quickly shut again, later the other side door too; someone had apparently wanted to come in and then thought better of it. Gregor now stationed himself immediately before the living-room door, determined to persuade any hesitating visitor to come in or at least to discover who it might be; but the door was not opened again and he waited in vain. In the early morning, when the doors were locked, they had all wanted to come in; now that he had opened one door and the other had apparently been opened during the day, no one came in and even the keys were on the other side of the doors.

It was late at night before the gas went out in the living room, and Gregor could easily tell that his parents and his sister had all stayed awake until then, for he could clearly hear the three of them stealing away on tiptoe. No one was likely to visit him, not until the morning, that was certain; so he had plenty of time to meditate at his leisure on how he was to arrange his life afresh. But the lofty, empty room in which he had to lie flat on the floor filled him with an apprehension he could not account for, since it had been his very own room for the past five years—and with a half-unconscious action, not without a slight feeling of shame, he scuttled under the sofa, where he felt comfortable at once, although his back was a little cramped and he could not lift his head up, and his only regret was that his body was too broad to get the whole of it under the sofa.

He stayed there all night, spending the time partly in a light slumber, from which his hunger kept waking him up with a start, and partly in worrying and sketching vague hopes, which all led to the same conclusion, that he must lie low for the present and, by exercising patience and the utmost consideration, help the family to bear the inconvenience he was bound to cause them in his present condition.

Very early in the morning, it was still almost night, Gregor had the chance to test the strength of his new resolutions, for his sister, nearly fully dressed, opened the door from the hall and peered in. She did not see him at once, yet when she caught sight of him under the sofa—well, he had to be somewhere, he couldn't have flown away, could he?—she was so startled that without being able to help it she slammed the door shut again. But as if regretting her behavior she opened the door again immediately and came in on tiptoe, as if she were visiting an invalid or even a stranger. Gregor had pushed his head forward to the very edge of the sofa and watched her. Would she notice that he had left the milk standing, and not for lack of hunger, and would she bring in some other kind of food more to his taste? If she did not do it of her own accord, he would rather starve than draw her attention to the fact, although he felt a wild impulse to dart out from under the sofa, throw himself at her feet and beg her for something to eat. But his sister at once noticed, with surprise, that the basin was still full, except for a little milk that had been spilt all around it, she lifted it

immediately, not with her bare hands, true, but with a cloth and carried it away. Gregor was wildly curious to know what she would bring instead, and made various speculations about it. Yet what she actually did next, in the goodness of her heart, he could never have guessed at. To find out what he liked she brought him a whole selection of food, all set out on an old newspaper. There were old, half-decayed vegetables, bones from last night's supper covered with a white sauce that had thickened; some raisins and almonds; a piece of cheese that Gregor would have called uneatable two days ago; a dry roll of bread, a buttered roll, and a roll both buttered and salted. Besides all that, she set down again the same basin, into which she had poured some water, and which was apparently to be reserved for his exclusive use. And with fine tact, knowing that Gregor would not eat in her presence, she withdrew quickly and even turned the key, to let him understand that he could take his ease as much as he liked. Gregor's legs all whizzed towards the food. His wounds must have healed completely, moreover, for he felt no disability, which amazed him and made him reflect how more than a month ago he had cut one finger a little with a knife and had still suffered pain from the wound only the day before yesterday. Am I less sensitive now? he thought, and sucked greedily at the cheese, which above all the other edibles attracted him at once and strongly. One after another and with tears of satisfaction in his eyes he quickly devoured the cheese, the vegetables and the sauce; the fresh food, on the other hand, had no charms for him, he could not even stand the smell of it and actually dragged away to some little distance the things he could eat. He had long finished his meal and was only lying lazily on the same spot when his sister turned the key slowly as a sign for him to retreat. That roused him at once, although he was nearly asleep, and he hurried under the sofa again. But it took considerable self-control for him to stay under the sofa, even for the short time his sister was in the room, since the large meal had swollen his body somewhat and he was so cramped he could hardly breathe. Slight attacks of breathlessness afflicted him and his eyes were starting a little out of his head as he watched his unsuspecting sister sweeping together with a broom not only the remains of what he had eaten but even the things he had not touched, as if these were now of no use to anyone, and hastily shoveling it all into a bucket, which she covered with a wooden lid and carried away. Hardly had she turned her back when Gregor came from under the sofa and stretched and puffed himself out.

In this manner Gregor was fed, once in the early morning while his parents and the servant girl were still asleep, and a second time after they had all had their midday dinner, for then his parents took a short nap and the servant girl could be sent out on some errand or other by his sister. Not that they would have wanted him to starve, of course, but perhaps they could not have borne to know more about his feeding than from hearsay, perhaps too his sister wanted to spare them such little anxieties wherever possible, since they had quite enough to bear as it was.

Under what pretext the doctor and the locksmith had been got rid of on that first morning Gregor could not discover, for since what he said was not understood by the others, it never struck any of them, not even his sister, that he could understand what they said, and so whenever his sister came into his room he had to content himself with hearing her utter only a sigh

now and then and an occasional appeal to the saints. Later on, when she had got a little used to the situation—of course she could never get completely used to it—she sometimes threw out a remark which was kindly meant or could be so interpreted. "Well, he liked his dinner today," she would say when Gregor had made a good clearance of his food; and when he had not eaten, which gradually happened more and more often, she would say almost sadly: "Everything's been left standing again."

But although Gregor could get no news directly, he overheard a lot from the neighboring rooms, and as soon as voices were audible, he would run to the door of the room concerned and press his whole body against it. In the first few days especially there was no conversation that did not refer to him somehow, even if only indirectly. For two whole days there were family consultations at every mealtime about what should be done; but also between meals the same subject was discussed, for there were always at least two members of the family at home, since no one wanted to be alone in the flat and to leave it quite empty was unthinkable. And on the very first of these days the household cook—it was not quite clear what and how much she knew of the situation—went down on her knees to his mother and begged leave to go and when she departed, a quarter of an hour later, gave thanks for her dismissal with tears in her eyes as if for the greatest benefit that could have been conferred on her, and without any prompting swore a solemn oath that she would never say a single word to anyone about what had happened.

Now Gregor's sister had to cook too, helping her mother; true, the cooking did not amount to much, for they ate scarcely anything. Gregor was always hearing one of the family vainly urging another to eat and getting no answer but: "Thanks, I've had all I want," or something similar. Perhaps they drank nothing either. Time and again his sister kept asking his father if he wouldn't like some beer and offered kindly to go and fetch it herself, and when he made no answer suggested that she could ask the concierge to fetch it, so that he need feel no sense of obligation, but then a round "No" came from his father and no more was said about it.

In the course of that very first day Gregor's father explained the family's financial position and prospects to both his mother and his sister. Now and then he rose from the table to get some voucher or memorandum out of the small safe he had rescued from the collapse of his business five years earlier. One could hear him opening the complicated lock and rustling papers out and shutting it again. This statement made by his father was the first cheerful information Gregor had heard since his imprisonment. He had been of the opinion that nothing at all was left over from his father's business; at least his father had never said anything to the contrary, and of course he had not asked him directly. At that time Gregor's sole desire was to do his utmost to help the family to forget as soon as possible the catastrophe which had overwhelmed the business and thrown them all into a state of complete despair. And so he had set to work with unusual ardor and almost overnight had become a commercial traveler instead of a little clerk, with of course much greater chances of earning money, and his success was immediately translated into good round coin which he could lay on the table for his amazed and happy family. These had been fine times, and they had never recurred, at least not with the same sense of glory, although

later on Gregor had earned so much money that he was able to meet the expenses of the whole household and did so. They had simply got used to it, both the family and Gregor; the money was gratefully accepted and gladly given, but there was no special uprush of warm feeling. With his sister alone had he remained intimate, and it was a secret plan of his that she, who loved music, unlike himself, and could play movingly on the violin, should be sent next year to study at the Conservatorium, despite the great expense that would entail, which must be made up in some other way. During his brief visits home the Conservatorium was often mentioned in the talks he had with his sister, but always merely as a beautiful dream which could never come true, and his parents discouraged even these innocent references to it; yet Gregor had made up his mind firmly about it and meant to announce the fact with due solemnity on Christmas Day.

Such were the thoughts, completely futile in his present condition, that went through his head as he stood clinging upright to the door and listening. Sometimes out of sheer weariness he had to give up listening and let his head fall negligently against the door, but he always had to pull himself together again at once, for even the slight sound his head made was audible next door and brought all conversation to a stop. "What can he be doing now?" his father would say after a while, obviously turning towards the door, and only then would the interrupted conversation gradually be set going again.

Gregor was now informed as amply as he could wish—for his father tended to repeat himself in his explanations, partly because it was a long time since he had handled such matters and partly because his mother could not always grasp things at once—that a certain amount of investments, a very small amount it was true, had survived the wreck of their fortunes and had even increased a little because the dividends had not been touched meanwhile. And besides that, the money Gregor brought home every month—he had kept only a few dollars for himself—had never been quite used up and now amounted to a small capital sum. Behind the door Gregor nodded his head eagerly, rejoiced at this evidence of unexpected thrift and foresight. True, he could really have paid off some more of his father's debts to the chief with this extra money, and so brought much nearer the day on which he could quit his job, but doubtless it was better the way his father had arranged it.

Yet this capital was by no means sufficient to let the family live on the interest of it; for one year, perhaps, or at the most two, they could live on the principal, that was all. It was simply a sum that ought not to be touched and should be kept for a rainy day; money for living expenses would have to be earned. Now his father was still hale enough but an old man, and he had done no work for the past five years and could not be expected to do much; during these five years, the first years of leisure in his laborious though unsuccessful life, he had grown rather fat and become sluggish. And Gregor's old mother, how was she to earn a living with her asthma, which troubled her even when she walked through the flat and kept her lying on a sofa every other day panting for breath beside an open window? And was his sister to earn her bread, she who was still a child of seventeen and whose life hitherto had been so pleasant, consisting as it did in dressing herself nicely, sleeping long, helping in the housekeeping, going out to a

few modest entertainments and above all playing the violin? At first when-
ever the need for earning money was mentioned Gregor let go his hold on
the door and threw himself down on the cool leather sofa beside it, he felt
so hot with shame and grief.

Often he just lay there the long nights through without sleeping at all,
scrabbling for hours on the leather. Or he nerved himself to the great
effort of pushing an armchair to the window, then crawled up over the
window sill and, braced against the chair, leaned against the windowpanes,
obviously in some recollection of the sense of freedom that looking out of a
window always used to give him. For in reality day by day things that were
even a little way off were growing dimmer to his sight; the hospital across
the street, which he used to execrate for being all too often before his eyes,
was now quite beyond his range of vision, and if he had not known that he
lived in Charlotte Street, a quiet street but still a city street, he might have
believed that his window gave on a desert waste where gray sky and gray
land blended indistinguishably into each other. His quick-witted sister only
needed to observe twice that the armchair stood by the window; after that
whenever she had tidied the room she always pushed the chair back to the
same place at the window and even left the inner casements open.

If he could have spoken to her and thanked her for all she had to do for
him, he could have borne her ministrations better; as it was, they oppressed
him. She certainly tried to make as light as possible of whatever was disa-
greeable in her task, and as time went on she succeeded, of course, more
and more, but time brought more enlightenment to Gregor too. The very
way she came in distressed him. Hardly was she in the room when she
rushed to the window, without even taking time to shut the door, careful as
she was usually to shield the sight of Gregor's room from the others, and as
if she were almost suffocating tore the casements open with hasty fingers,
standing then in the open draught for a while even in the bitterest cold and
drawing deep breaths. This noisy scurry of hers upset Gregor twice a day;
he would crouch trembling under the sofa all the time, knowing quite well
that she would certainly have spared him such a disturbance had she found
it at all possible to stay in his presence without opening the window.

On one occasion, about a month after Gregor's metamorphosis, when
there was surely no reason for her to be still startled at his appearance, she
came a little earlier than usual and found him gazing out of the window,
quite motionless, and thus well placed to look like a bogey. Gregor would
not have been surprised had she not come in at all, for she could not
immediately open the window while he was there, but not only did she
retreat, she jumped back as if in alarm and banged the door shut; a stran-
ger might well have thought that he had been lying in wait for her there
meaning to bite her. Of course he hid himself under the sofa at once, but
he had to wait until midday before she came again, and she seemed more ill
at ease than usual. This made him realize how repulsive the sight of him
still was to her, and that it was bound to go on being repulsive, and what an
effort it must cost her not to run away even from the sight of the small
portion of his body that stuck out from under the sofa. In order to spare
her that, therefore, one day he carried a sheet on his back to the sofa—it
cost him four hours' labor—and arranged it there in such a way as to hide
him completely, so that even if she were to bend down she could not see

him. Had she considered the sheet unnecessary, she would certainly have stripped it off the sofa again, for it was clear enough that this curtaining and confining of himself was not likely to conduce to Gregor's comfort, but she left it where it was, and Gregor even fancied that he caught a thankful glance from her eye when he lifted the sheet carefully a very little with his head to see how she was taking the new arrangement.

For the first fortnight his parents could not bring themselves to the point of entering his room, and he often heard them expressing their appreciation of his sister's activities, whereas formerly they had frequently scolded her for being as they thought a somewhat useless daughter. But now, both of them often waited outside the door, his father and his mother, while his sister tidied his room, and as soon as she came out she had to tell them exactly how things were in the room, what Gregor had eaten, how he had conducted himself this time and whether there was not perhaps some slight improvement in his condition. His mother, moreover, began relatively soon to want to visit him, but his father and sister dissuaded her at first with arguments which Gregor listened to very attentively and altogether approved. Later, however, she had to be held back by main force, and when she cried out: "Do let me in to Gregor, he is my unfortunate son! Can't you understand that I must go to him?" Gregor thought that it might be well to have her come in, not every day, of course, but perhaps once a week; she understood things, after all, much better than his sister, who was only a child despite the efforts she was making and had perhaps taken on so difficult a task merely out of childish thoughtlessness.

Gregor's desire to see his mother was soon fulfilled. During the daytime he did not want to show himself at the window, out of consideration for his parents, but he could not crawl very far around the few square yards of floor space he had, nor could he bear lying quietly at rest all during the night, while he was fast losing any interest he had ever taken in food, so that for mere recreation he had formed the habit of crawling crisscross over the walls and ceiling. He especially enjoyed hanging suspended from the ceiling; it was much better than lying on the floor; one could breathe more freely; one's body swung and rocked lightly; and in the almost blissful absorption induced by this suspension it could happen to his own surprise that he let go and fell plump on the floor. Yet he now had his body much better under control than formerly, and even such a big fall did him no harm. His sister at once remarked the new distraction Gregor had found for himself—he left traces behind him of the sticky stuff on his soles wherever he crawled—and she got the idea in her head of giving him as wide a field as possible to crawl in and of removing the pieces of furniture that hindered him, above all the chest of drawers and the writing desk. But that was more than she could manage all by herself; she did not dare ask her father to help her; and as for the servant girl, a young creature of sixteen who had had the courage to stay on after the cook's departure, she could not be asked to help, for she had begged as an especial favor that she might keep the kitchen door locked and open it only on a definite summons; so there was nothing left but to apply to her mother at an hour when her father was out. And the old lady did come, with exclamations of joyful eagerness, which, however, died away at the door of Gregor's room. Gregor's sister, of course, went in first, to see that everything was in order

before letting his mother enter. In great haste Gregor pulled the sheet lower and rucked it more in folds so that it really looked as if it had been thrown accidentally over the sofa. And this time he did not peer out from under it; he renounced the pleasure of seeing his mother on this occasion and was only glad that she had come at all. "Come in, he's out of sight," said his sister, obviously leading her mother in by the hand. Gregor could now hear the two women struggling to shift the heavy old chest from its place, and his sister claiming the greater part of the labor for herself, without listening to the admonitions of her mother who feared she might overstrain herself. It took a long time. After at least a quarter of an hour's tugging his mother objected that the chest had better be left where it was, for in the first place it was too heavy and could never be got out before his father came home; standing in the middle of the room like that it would only hamper Gregor's movements, while in the second place it was not at all certain that removing the furniture would be doing a service to Gregor. She was inclined to think to the contrary; the sight of the naked walls made her own heart heavy, and why shouldn't Gregor have the same feeling, considering that he had been used to his furniture for so long and might feel forlorn without it. "And doesn't it look," she concluded in a low voice—in fact she had been almost whispering all the time as if to avoid letting Gregor, whose exact whereabouts she did not know, hear even the tones of her voice, for she was convinced that he could not understand her words—"doesn't it look as if we were showing him, by taking away his furniture, that we have given up hope of his ever getting better and are just leaving him coldly to himself? I think it would be best to keep his room exactly as it has always been, so that when he comes back to us he will find everything unchanged and be able all the more easily to forget what has happened in between."

On hearing these words from his mother Gregor realized that the lack of all direct human speech for the past two months together with the monotony of family life must have confused his mind, otherwise he could not account for the fact that he had quite earnestly looked forward to having his room emptied of furnishing. Did he really want his warm room, so comfortably fitted with old family furniture, to be turned into a naked den in which he would certainly be able to crawl unhampered in all directions but at the price of shedding simultaneously all recollection of his human background? He had indeed been so near the brink of forgetfulness that only the voice of his mother, which he had not heard for so long, had drawn him back from it. Nothing should be taken out of his room; everything must stay as it was; he could not dispense with the good influence of the furniture on his state of mind; and even if the furniture did hamper him in his senseless crawling round and round, that was no drawback but a great advantage.

Unfortunately his sister was of the contrary opinion; she had grown accustomed, and not without reason, to consider herself an expert in Gregor's affairs as against her parents, and so her mother's advice was now enough to make her determined on the removal not only of the chest and the writing desk, which had been her first intention, but of all the furniture except the indispensable sofa. This determination was not, of course, merely the outcome of childish recalcitrance and of the self-confidence she

had recently developed so unexpectedly and at such cost; she had in fact perceived that Gregor needed a lot of space to crawl about in, while on the other hand he never used the furniture at all, so far as could be seen. Another factor might have been also the enthusiastic temperament of an adolescent girl, which seeks to indulge itself on every opportunity and which now tempted Grete to exaggerate the horror of her brother's circumstances in order that she might do all the more for him. In a room where Gregor lorded it all alone over empty walls no one save herself was likely ever to set foot.

And so she was not to be moved from her resolve by her mother, who seemed moreover to be ill at ease in Gregor's room and therefore unsure of herself, was soon reduced to silence and helped her daughter as best she could to push the chest outside. Now, Gregor could do without the chest, if need be, but the writing desk he must retain. As soon as the two women had got the chest out of his room, groaning as they pushed it, Gregor stuck his head out from under the sofa to see how he might intervene as kindly and cautiously as possible. But as bad luck would have it, his mother was the first to return, leaving Grete clasping the chest in the room next door where she was trying to shift it all by herself, without of course moving it from the spot. His mother however was not accustomed to the sight of him; it might sicken her and so in alarm Gregor backed quickly to the other end of the sofa, yet could not prevent the sheet from swaying a little in front. That was enough to put her on the alert. She paused, stood still for a moment and then went back to Grete.

Although Gregor kept reassuring himself that nothing out of the way was happening, but only a few bits of furniture were being changed round, he soon had to admit that all this trotting to and fro of the two women, their little ejaculations and the scraping of furniture along the floor affected him like a vast disturbance coming from all sides at once, and however much he tucked in his head and legs and cowered to the very floor he was bound to confess that he would not be able to stand it for long. They were clearing his room out; taking away everything he loved; the chest in which he kept his fret saw and other tools was already dragged off; they were now loosening the writing desk which had almost sunk into the floor, the desk at which he had done all his homework when he was at the commercial academy, at the grammar school before that, and, yes, even at the primary school—he had no more time to waste in weighing the good intentions of the two women, whose existence he had by now almost forgotten, for they were so exhausted that they were laboring in silence and nothing could be heard but the heavy scuffling of their feet.

And so he rushed out—the women were just leaning against the writing desk in the next room to give themselves a breather—and four times changed his direction, since he really did not know what to rescue first; then on the wall opposite, which was already otherwise cleared, he was struck by the picture of the lady muffled in so much fur and quickly crawled up to it and pressed himself to the glass, which was a good surface to hold on to and comforted his hot belly. This picture at least, which was entirely hidden beneath him, was going to be removed by nobody. He turned his head towards the door of the living room so as to observe the women when they came back.

They had not allowed themselves much of a rest and were already coming; Grete had twined her arm round her mother and was almost supporting her. "Well, what shall we take now?" said Grete, looking round. Her eyes met Gregor's on the wall. She kept her composure, presumably because of her mother, bent her head down to her mother, to keep her from looking up, and said, although in a fluttering, unpremeditated voice: "Come, hadn't we better go back to the living room for a moment?" Her intentions were clear enough to Gregor; she wanted to bestow her mother in safety and then chase him down from the wall. Well, just let her try it! He clung to his picture and would not give it up. He would rather fly in Grete's face.

But Grete's words had succeeded in disquieting her mother, who took a step to one side, caught sight of the huge brown mass on the flowered wallpaper, and before she was really conscious that what she saw was Gregor screamed in a loud, hoarse voice: "Oh God, oh God!" fell with outspread arms over the sofa as if giving up and did not move. "Gregor!" cried his sister, shaking her fist and glaring at him. This was the first time she had directly addressed him since his metamorphosis. She ran into the next room for some aromatic essence with which to rouse her mother from her fainting fit. Gregor wanted to help too—there was still time to rescue the picture—but he was stuck fast to the glass and had to tear himself loose; he then ran after his sister into the next room as if he could advise her, as he used to do; but then had to stand helplessly behind her; she meanwhile searched among various small bottles and when she turned round started in alarm at the sight of him; one bottle fell on the floor and broke; a splinter of glass cut Gregor's face and some kind of corrosive medicine splashed him; without pausing a moment longer Grete gathered up all the bottles she could carry and ran to her mother with them; she banged the door shut with her foot. Gregor was now cut off from his mother, who was perhaps nearly dying because of him; he dared not open the door for fear of frightening away his sister, who had to stay with her mother; there was nothing he could do but wait; and harassed by self-reproach and worry he began now to crawl to and fro, over everything, walls, furniture and ceiling, and finally in his despair, when the whole room seemed to be reeling round him, fell down on to the middle of the big table.

A little while elapsed. Gregor was still lying there feebly and all around was quiet; perhaps that was a good omen. Then the doorbell rang. The servant girl was of course locked in her kitchen, and Grete would have to open the door. It was his father. "What's been happening?" were his first words; Grete's face must have told him everything. Grete answered in a muffled voice, apparently hiding her head on his breast: "Mother has been fainting, but she's better now. Gregor's broken loose." "Just what I expected," said his father, "just what I've been telling you, but you women would never listen." It was clear to Gregor that his father had taken the worst interpretation of Grete's all too brief statement and was assuming that Gregor had been guilty of some violent act. Therefore Gregor must now try to propitiate his father, since he had neither time nor means for an explanation. And so he fled to the door of his own room and crouched against it, to let his father see as soon as he came in from the hall that his son had the good intention of getting back into his room immediately and

that it was not necessary to drive him there, but that if only the door were opened he would disappear at once.

Yet his father was not in the mood to perceive such fine distinctions. "Ah!" he cried as soon as he appeared, in a tone which sounded at once angry and exultant. Gregor drew his head back from the door and lifted it to look at his father. Truly, this was not the father he had imagined to himself; admittedly he had been too absorbed of late in his new recreation of crawling over the ceiling to take the same interest as before in what was happening elsewhere in the flat, and he ought really to be prepared for some changes. And yet, and yet, could that be his father? The man who used to lie wearily sunk in bed whenever Gregor set out on a business journey; who welcomed him back of an evening lying in a long chair in a dressing gown; who could not really rise to his feet but only lifted his arms in greeting, and on the rare occasions when he did go out with his family, on one or two Sundays a year and on high holidays, walked between Gregor and his mother, who were slow walkers anyhow, even more slowly than they did, muffled in his old greatcoat, shuffling laboriously forward with the help of his crook-handled stick which he set down most cautiously at every step and, whenever he wanted to say anything, nearly always came to a full stop and gathered his escort around him? Now he was standing there in fine shape; dressed in a smart blue uniform with gold buttons, such as bank messengers wear; his strong double chin bulged over the stiff high collar of his jacket; from under his bushy eyebrows his black eyes darted fresh and penetrating glances; his onetime tangled white hair had been combed flat on either side of a shining and carefully exact parting. He pitched his cap, which bore a gold monogram, probably the badge of some bank, in a wide sweep across the whole room on to a sofa and with the tail-ends of his jacket thrown back, his hands in his trouser pockets, advanced with a grim visage towards Gregor. Likely enough he did not himself know what he meant to do; at any rate he lifted his feet uncommonly high, and Gregor was dumbfounded at the enormous size of his shoe soles. But Gregor could not risk standing up to him, aware as he had been from the very first day of his new life that his father believed only the severest measures suitable for dealing with him. And so he ran before his father, stopping when he stopped and scuttling forward again when his father made any kind of move. In this way they circled the room several times without anything decisive happening; indeed the whole operation did not even look like a pursuit because it was carried out so slowly. And so Gregor did not leave the floor, for he feared that his father might take as a piece of peculiar wickedness any excursion of his over the walls or the ceiling. All the same, he could not stay this course much longer, for while his father took one step he had to carry out a whole series of movements. He was already beginning to feel breathless, just as in his former life his lungs had not been very dependable. As he was staggering along, trying to concentrate his energy on running, hardly keeping his eyes open; in his dazed state never even thinking of any other escape than simply going forward; and having almost forgotten that the walls were free to him, which in this room were well provided with finely carved pieces of furniture full of knobs and crevices—suddenly something lightly flung landed close behind him and rolled before him. It was an apple; a second apple followed imme-

diately; Gregor came to a stop in alarm; there was no point in running on, for his father was determined to bombard him. He had filled his pockets with fruit from the dish on the sideboard and was now shying apple after apple, without taking particularly good aim for the moment. The small red apples rolled about the floor as if magnetized and cannoned into each other. An apple thrown without much force grazed Gregor's back and glanced off harmlessly. But another following immediately landed right on his back and sank in; Gregor wanted to drag himself forward, as if this startling, incredible pain could be left behind him; but he felt as if nailed to the spot and flattened himself out in a complete derangement of all his senses. With his last conscious look he saw the door of his room being torn open and his mother rushing out ahead of his screaming sister, in her underbodice, for her daughter had loosened her clothing to let her breathe more freely and recover from her swoon, he saw his mother rushing towards his father, leaving one after another behind her on the floor her loosened petticoats, stumbling over her petticoats straight to his father and embracing him, in complete union with him—but here Gregor's sight began to fail—with her hands clasped round his father's neck as she begged for her son's life.

III

The serious injury done to Gregor, which disabled him for more than a month—the apple went on sticking in his body as a visible reminder, since no one ventured to remove it—seemed to have made even his father recollect that Gregor was a member of the family, despite his present unfortunate and repulsive shape, and ought not to be treated as an enemy, that, on the contrary, family duty required the suppression of disgust and the exercise of patience, nothing but patience.

And although his injury had impaired, probably forever, his powers of movement, and for the time being it took him long, long minutes to creep across his room like an old invalid—there was no question now of crawling up the wall—yet in his own opinion he was sufficiently compensated for this worsening of his condition by the fact that towards evening the living-room door, which he used to watch intently for an hour or two beforehand, was always thrown open, so that lying in the darkness of his room, invisible to the family, he could see them all at the lamp-lit table and listen to their talk, by general consent as it were, very different from his earlier eaves-dropping.

True, their intercourse lacked the lively character of former times, which he had always called to mind with a certain wistfulness in the small hotel bedrooms where he had been wont to throw himself down, tired out, on damp bedding. They were now mostly very silent. Soon after supper his father would fall asleep in his armchair; his mother and sister would admonish each other to be silent; his mother, bending low over the lamp, stitched at fine sewing for an underwear firm; his sister, who had taken a job as a salesgirl, was learning shorthand and French in the evenings on the chance of bettering herself. Sometimes his father woke up, and as if quite unaware that he had been sleeping said to his mother: "What a lot of

sewing you're doing today!" and at once fell asleep again, while the two women exchanged a tired smile.

With a kind of mulishness his father persisted in keeping his uniform on even in the house; his dressing gown hung uselessly on its peg and he slept fully dressed where he sat, as if he were ready for service at any moment and even here only at the beck and call of his superior. As a result, his uniform, which was not brand-new to start with, began to look dirty, despite all the loving care of the mother and sister to keep it clean, and Gregor often spent whole evenings gazing at the many greasy spots on the garment, gleaming with gold buttons always in a high state of polish, in which the old man sat sleeping in extreme discomfort and yet quite peacefully.

As soon as the clock struck ten his mother tried to rouse his father with gentle words and to persuade him after that to get into bed, for sitting there he could not have a proper sleep and that was what he needed most, since he had to go on duty at six. But with the mulishness that had obsessed him since he became a bank messenger he always insisted on staying longer at the table, although he regularly fell asleep again and in the end only with the greatest trouble could be got out of his armchair and into his bed. However insistently Gregor's mother and sister kept urging him with gentle reminders, he would go on slowly shaking his head for a quarter of an hour, keeping his eyes shut, and refuse to get to his feet. The mother plucked at his sleeve, whispering endearments in his ear, the sister left her lessons to come to her mother's help, but Gregor's father was not to be caught. He would only sink down deeper in his chair. Not until the two women hoisted him up by the armpits did he open his eyes and look at them both, one after the other, usually with the remark: "This is a life. This is the peace and quiet of my old age." And leaning on the two of them he would heave himself up, with difficulty, as if he were a great burden to himself, suffer them to lead him as far as the door and then wave them off and go on alone, while the mother abandoned her needlework and the sister her pen in order to run after him and help him farther.

Who could find time, in this overworked and tired-out family, to bother about Gregor more than was absolutely needful? The household was reduced more and more; the servant girl was turned off; a gigantic bony charwoman with white hair flying round her head came in morning and evening to do the rough work; everything else was done by Gregor's mother, as well as great piles of sewing. Even various family ornaments, which his mother and sister used to wear with pride at parties and celebrations, had to be sold, as Gregor discovered of an evening from hearing them all discuss the prices obtained. But what they lamented most was the fact that they could not leave the flat which was much too big for their present circumstances, because they could not think of any way to shift Gregor. Yet Gregor saw well enough that consideration for him was not the main difficulty preventing the removal, for they could have easily shifted him in some suitable box with a few air holes in it; what really kept them from moving into another flat was rather their own complete hopelessness and the belief that they had been singled out for a misfortune such as had never happened to any of their relations or acquaintances. They fulfilled to the uttermost all that the world demands of poor people: the father

fetched breakfast for the small clerks in the bank, the mother devoted her energy to making underwear for strangers, the sister trotted to and fro behind the counter at the behest of customers, but more than this they had not the strength to do. And the wound in Gregor's back began to nag at him afresh when his mother and sister, after getting his father into bed, came back again, left their work lying, drew close to each other and sat cheek by cheek; when his mother, pointing towards his room, said: "Shut that door now, Grete," and he was left again in darkness, while next door the women mingled their tears or perhaps sat dry-eyed staring at the table.

Gregor hardly slept at all by night or by day. He was often haunted by the idea that next time the door opened he would take the family's affairs in hand again just as he used to do; once more, after this long interval, there appeared in his thoughts the figures of the chief and the chief clerk, the commercial travelers and the apprentices, the porter who was so dull-witted, two or three friends in other firms, a chambermaid in one of the rural hotels, a sweet and fleeting memory, a cashier in a milliner's shop, whom he had wooed earnestly but too slowly—they all appeared, together with strangers or people he had quite forgotten, but instead of helping him and his family they were one and all unapproachable and he was glad when they vanished. At other times he would not be in the mood to bother about his family, he was only filled with rage at the way they were neglecting him, and although he had no clear idea of what he might care to eat he would make plans for getting into the larder to take the food that was after all his due, even if he were not hungry. His sister no longer took thought to bring him what might especially please him, but in the morning and at noon before she went to business hurriedly pushed into his room with her foot any food that was available, and in the evening cleared it out again with one sweep of the broom, heedless of whether it had been merely tasted, or—as most frequently happened—left untouched. The cleaning of his room, which she now did always in the evenings, could not have been more hastily done. Streaks of dirt stretched along the walls, here and there lay balls of dust and filth. At first Gregor used to station himself in some particularly filthy corner when his sister arrived, in order to reproach her with it, so to speak. But he could have sat there for weeks without getting her to make any improvement; she could see the dirt as well as he did, but she had simply made up her mind to leave it alone. And yet, with a touchiness that was new to her, which seemed anyhow to have infected the whole family, she jealously guarded her claim to be the sole caretaker of Gregor's room. His mother once subjected his room to a thorough cleaning, which was achieved only by means of several buckets of water—all this dampness of course upset Gregor too and he lay widespread, sulky and motionless on the sofa—but she was well punished for it. Hardly had his sister noticed the changed aspect of his room that evening than she rushed in high dudgeon into the living room and, despite the imploringly raised hands of her mother, burst into a storm of weeping, while her parents—her father had of course been startled out of his chair—looked on at first in helpless amazement; then they too began to go into action; the father reproached the mother on his right for not having left the cleaning of Gregor's room to his sister; shrieked at the sister on his left that never again was she to be allowed to clean Gregor's room; while the mother tried to pull the father

into his bedroom, since he was beyond himself with agitation; the sister, shaken with sobs, then beat upon the table with her small fists; and Gregor hissed loudly with rage because not one of them thought of shutting the door to spare him such a spectacle and so much noise.

Still, even if the sister, exhausted by her daily work, had grown tired of looking after Gregor as she did formerly, there was no need for his mother's intervention or for Gregor's being neglected at all. The charwoman was there. This old widow, whose strong bony frame had enabled her to survive the worst a long life could offer, by no means recoiled from Gregor. Without being in the least curious she had once by chance opened the door of his room and at the sight of Gregor, who, taken by surprise, began to rush to and fro although no one was chasing him, merely stood there with her arms folded. From that time she never failed to open his door a little for a moment, morning and evening, to have a look at him. At first she even used to call him to her, with words which apparently she took to be friendly, such as: "Come along, then, you old dung beetle!" or "Look at the old dung beetle, then!" To such allocutions Gregor made no answer, but stayed motionless where he was, as if the door had never been opened. Instead of being allowed to disturb him so senselessly whenever the whim took her, she should rather have been ordered to clean out his room daily, that charwoman! Once, early in the morning—heavy rain was lashing on the windowpanes, perhaps a sign that spring was on the way—Gregor was so exasperated when she began addressing him again that he ran at her, as if to attack her, although slowly and feebly enough. But the charwoman instead of showing fright merely lifted high a chair that happened to be beside the door, and as she stood there with her mouth wide open it was clear that she meant to shut it only when she brought the chair down on Gregor's back. "So you're not coming any nearer?" she asked, as Gregor turned away again, and quietly put the chair back into the corner.

Gregor was now eating hardly anything. Only when he happened to pass the food laid out for him did he take a bit of something in his mouth as a pastime, kept it there for an hour at a time and usually spat it out again. At first he thought it was chagrin over the state of his room that prevented him from eating, yet he soon got used to the various changes in his room. It had become a habit in the family to push into his room things there was no room for elsewhere, and there were plenty of these now, since one of the rooms had been let to three lodgers. These serious gentlemen—all three of them with full beards, as Gregor once observed through a crack in the door—had a passion for order, not only in their own room but, since they were now members of the household, in all its arrangements, especially in the kitchen. Superfluous, not to say dirty, objects they could not bear. Besides, they had brought with them most of the furnishings they needed. For this reason many things could be dispensed with that it was no use trying to sell but that should not be thrown away either. All of them found their way into Gregor's room. The ash can likewise and the kitchen garbage can. Anything that was not needed for the moment was simply flung into Gregor's room by the charwoman, who did everything in a hurry; fortunately Gregor usually saw only the object, whatever it was, and the hand that held it. Perhaps she intended to take the things away again as time and opportunity offered, or to collect them until she could throw them all out

in a heap, but in fact they just lay wherever she happened to throw them, except when Gregor pushed his way through the junk heap and shifted it somewhat, at first out of necessity, because he had not room enough to crawl, but later with increasing enjoyment, although after such excursions, being sad and weary to death, he would lie motionless for hours. And since the lodgers often ate their supper at home in the common living room, the living-room door stayed shut many an evening, yet Gregor reconciled himself quite easily to the shutting of the door, for often enough on evenings when it was opened he had disregarded it entirely and lain in the darkest corner of his room, quite unnoticed by the family. But on one occasion the charwoman left the door open a little and it stayed ajar even when the lodgers came in for supper and the lamp was lit. They set themselves at the top end of the table where formerly Gregor and his father and mother had eaten their meals, unfolded their napkins and took knife and fork in hand. At once his mother appeared in the other doorway with a dish of meat and close behind her his sister with a dish of potatoes piled high. The food steamed with a thick vapor. The lodgers bent over the food set before them as if to scrutinize it before eating; in fact the man in the middle, who seemed to pass for an authority with the other two, cut a piece of meat as it lay on the dish, obviously to discover if it were tender or should be sent back to the kitchen. He showed satisfaction, and Gregor's mother and sister, who had been watching anxiously, breathed freely and began to smile.

The family itself took its meals in the kitchen. None the less, Gregor's father came into the living room before going into the kitchen and with one prolonged bow, cap in hand, made a round of the table. The lodgers all stood up and murmured something in their beards. When they were alone again they ate their food in almost complete silence. It seemed remarkable to Gregor that among the various noises coming from the table he could always distinguish the sound of their masticating teeth, as if this were a sign to Gregor that one needed teeth in order to eat, and that with toothless jaws even of the finest make one could do nothing. "I'm hungry enough," said Gregor sadly to himself, "but not for that kind of food. How these lodgers are stuffing themselves, and here am I dying of starvation!"

On that very evening—during the whole of his time there Gregor could not remember ever having heard the violin—the sound of violin-playing came from the kitchen. The lodgers had already finished their supper, the one in the middle had brought out a newspaper and given the other two a page apiece, and now they were leaning back at ease reading and smoking. When the violin began to play they pricked up their ears, got to their feet, and went on tiptoe to the hall door where they stood huddled together. Their movements must have been heard in the kitchen, for Gregor's father called out: "Is the violin-playing disturbing you, gentlemen? It can be stopped at once." "On the contrary," said the middle lodger, "could not Fräulein Samsa come and play in this room, beside us, where it is much more convenient and comfortable?" "Oh, certainly," cried Gregor's father, as if he were the violin-player. The lodgers came back into the living room and waited. Presently Gregor's father arrived with the music stand, his mother carrying the music and his sister with the violin. His sister quietly made everything ready to start playing; his parents, who had never let

rooms before and so had an exaggerated idea of the courtesy due to lodgers, did not venture to sit down on their own chairs; his father leaned against the door, the right hand thrust between two buttons of his livery coat, which was formally buttoned up; but his mother was offered a chair by one of the lodgers and, since she left the chair just where he had happened to put it, sat down in a corner to one side.

Gregor's sister began to play; the father and mother, from either side, intently watched the movements of her hands. Gregor, attracted by the playing, ventured to move forward a little until his head was actually inside the living room. He felt hardly any surprise at his growing lack of consideration for the others; there had been a time when he prided himself on being considerate. And yet just on this occasion he had more reason than ever to hide himself, since owing to the amount of dust which lay thick in his room and rose into the air at the slightest movement, he too was covered with dust; fluff and hair and remnants of food trailed with him, caught on his back and along his sides; his indifference to everything was much too great for him to turn on his back and scrape himself clean on the carpet, as once he had done several times a day. And in spite of his condition, no shame deterred him from advancing a little over the spotless floor of the living room.

To be sure, no one was aware of him. The family was entirely absorbed in the violin-playing; the lodgers, however, who first of all had stationed themselves, hands in pockets, much too close behind the music stand so that they could all have read the music, which must have bothered his sister, had soon retreated to the window, half-whispering with downbent heads, and stayed there while his father turned an anxious eye on them. Indeed, they were making it more than obvious that they had been disappointed in their expectation of hearing good or enjoyable violin-playing, that they had had more than enough of the performance and only out of courtesy suffered a continued disturbance of their peace. From the way they all kept blowing the smoke of their cigars high in the air through nose and mouth one could divine their irritation. And yet Gregor's sister was playing so beautifully. Her face leaned sideways, intently and sadly her eyes followed the notes of music. Gregor crawled a little farther forward and lowered his head to the ground so that it might be possible for his eyes to meet hers. Was he an animal, that music had such an effect upon him? He felt as if the way were opening before him to the unknown nourishment he craved. He was determined to push forward till he reached his sister, to pull at her skirt and so let her know that she was to come into his room with her violin, for no one here appreciated her playing as he would appreciate it. He would never let her out of his room, at least, not so long as he lived; his frightful appearance would become, for the first time, useful to him; he would watch all the doors of his room at once and spit at intruders; but his sister should need no constraint, she should stay with him of her own free will; she should sit beside him on the sofa, bend down her ear to him and hear him confide that he had had the firm intention of sending her to the Conservatorium, and that, but for his mishap, last Christmas—surely Christmas was long past?—he would have announced it to everybody without allowing a single objection. After this confession his sister would be so

touched that she would burst into tears, and Gregor would then raise himself to her shoulder and kiss her on the neck, which, now that she went to business, she kept free of any ribbon or collar.

"Mr. Samsa!" cried the middle lodger, to Gregor's father, and pointed, without wasting any more words, at Gregor, now working himself slowly forwards. The violin fell silent, the middle lodger first smiled to his friends with a shake of the head and then looked at Gregor again. Instead of driving Gregor out, his father seemed to think it more needful to begin by soothing down the lodgers, although they were not at all agitated and apparently found Gregor more entertaining than the violin-playing. He hurried towards them and, spreading out his arms, tried to urge them back into their own room and at the same time to block their view of Gregor. They now began to be really a little angry, one could not tell whether because of the old man's behavior or because it had just dawned on them that all unwittingly they had such a neighbor as Gregor next door. They demanded explanations of his father, they waved their arms like him, tugged uneasily at their beards, and only with reluctance backed towards their room. Meanwhile Gregor's sister, who stood there as if lost when her playing was so abruptly broken off, came to life again, pulled herself together all at once after standing for a while holding violin and bow in nervelessly hanging hands and staring at her music, pushed her violin into the lap of her mother, who was still sitting in her chair fighting asthmatically for breath, and ran into the lodgers' room to which they were now being shepherded by her father rather more quickly than before. One could see the pillows and blankets on the beds flying under her accustomed fingers and being laid in order. Before the lodgers had actually reached their room she had finished making the beds and slipped out.

The old man seemed once more to be so possessed by his mulish self-assertiveness that he was forgetting all the respect he should show to his lodgers. He kept driving them on and driving them on until in the very door of the bedroom the middle lodger stamped his foot loudly on the floor and so brought him to a halt. "I beg to announce," said the lodger, lifting one hand and looking also at Gregor's mother and sister, "that because of the disgusting conditions prevailing in this household and family"—here he spat on the floor with emphatic brevity—"I give you notice on the spot. Naturally I won't pay you a penny for the days I have lived here; on the contrary I shall consider bringing an action for damages against you, based on claims—believe me—that will be easily susceptible of proof." He ceased and stared straight in front of him, as if he expected something. In fact his two friends at once rushed into the breach with these words: "And we too give notice on the spot." On that he seized the door-handle and shut the door with a slam.

Gregor's father, groping with his hands, staggered forward and fell into his chair; it looked as if he were stretching himself there for his ordinary evening nap, but the marked jerkings of his head, which was as if uncontrollable, showed that he was far from asleep. Gregor had simply stayed quietly all the time on the spot where the lodgers had espied him. Disappointment at the failure of his plan, perhaps also the weakness arising from extreme hunger, made it impossible for him to move. He feared, with a fair degree of certainty, that at any moment the general tension would dis-

charge itself in a combined attack upon him, and he lay waiting. He did not react even to the noise made by the violin as it fell off his mother's lap from under her trembling fingers and gave out a resonant note.

"My dear parents," said his sister, slapping her hand on the table by way of introduction. "things can't go on like this. Perhaps you don't realize that, but I do. I won't utter my brother's name in the presence of this creature, and so all I say is: we must try to get rid of it. We've tried to look after it and to put up with it as far as is humanly possible, and I don't think anyone could reproach us in the slightest."

"She is more than right," said Gregor's father to himself. His mother, who was still choking for lack of breath, began to cough hollowly into her hand with a wild look in her eyes.

His sister rushed over to her and held her forehead. His father's thoughts seemed to have lost their vagueness at Grete's words; he sat more upright, fingering his service cap that lay among the plates still lying on the table from the lodgers' supper, and from time to time looked at the still form of Gregor.

"We must try to get rid of it," his sister now said explicitly to her father, since her mother was coughing too much to hear a word. "It will be the death of both of you, I can see that coming. When one has to work as hard as we do, all of us, one can't stand this continual torment at home on top of it. At least I can't stand it any longer." And she burst into such a passion of sobbing that her tears dropped on her mother's face, where she wiped them off mechanically.

"My dear," said the old man sympathetically, and with evident understanding, "but what can we do?"

Gregor's sister merely shrugged her shoulders to indicate the feeling of helplessness that had now overmastered her during her weeping fit, in contrast to her former confidence.

"If he could understand us," said her father, half questioningly; Grete, still sobbing, vehemently waved a hand to show how unthinkable that was.

"If he could understand us," repeated the old man, shutting his eyes to consider his daughter's conviction that understanding was impossible, "then perhaps we might come to some agreement with him. But as it is—"

"He must go," cried Gregor's sister, "that's the only solution, Father. You must just try to get rid of the idea that this is Gregor. The fact that we've believed it for so long is the root of all our trouble. But how can it be Gregor? If this were Gregor, he would have realized long ago that human beings can't live with such a creature, and he'd have gone away on his own accord. Then we wouldn't have any brother, but we'd be able to go on living and keep his memory in honor. As it is, this creature persecutes us, drives away our lodgers, obviously wants the whole apartment to himself and would have us all sleep in the gutter. Just look, Father," she shrieked all at once, "he's at it again!" And in an access of panic that was quite incomprehensible to Gregor she even quitted her mother, literally thrusting the chair from her as if she would rather sacrifice her mother than stay so near to Gregor, and rushed behind her father, who also rose up, being simply upset by her agitation, and half-spread his arms out as if to protect her.

Yet Gregor had not the slightest intention of frightening anyone, far less his sister. He had only begun to turn round in order to crawl back to his

room, but it was certainly a startling operation to watch, since because of his disabled condition he could not execute the difficult turning movements except by lifting his head and then bracing it against the floor over and over again. He paused and looked round. His good intentions seemed to have been recognized; the alarm had only been momentary. Now they were all watching him in melancholy silence. His mother lay in her chair, her legs stiffly outstretched and pressed together, her eyes almost closing for sheer weariness; his father and his sister were sitting beside each other, his sister's arm around the old man's neck.

Perhaps I can go on turning round now, thought Gregor, and began his labors again. He could not stop himself from panting with the effort, and had to pause now and then to take breath. Nor did anyone harass him; he was left entirely to himself. When he had completed the turn-round he began at once to crawl straight back. He was amazed at the distance separating him from his room and could not understand how in his weak state he had managed to accomplish the same journey so recently, almost without remarking it. Intent on crawling as fast as possible, he barely noticed that not a single word, not an ejaculation from his family, interfered with his progress. Only when he was already in the doorway did he turn his head round, not completely, for his neck muscles were getting stiff, but enough to see that nothing had changed behind him except that his sister had risen to her feet. His last glance fell on his mother, who was not quite overcome by sleep.

Hardly was he well inside his room when the door was hastily pushed shut, bolted and locked. The sudden noise in his rear startled him so much that his little legs gave beneath him. It was his sister who had shown such haste. She had been standing ready waiting and had made a light spring forward. Gregor had not even heard her coming, and she cried "At last!" to her parents as she turned the key in the lock.

"And what now?" said Gregor to himself, looking round in the darkness. Soon he made the discovery that he was now unable to stir a limb. This did not surprise him, rather it seemed unnatural that he should ever actually have been able to move on these feeble little legs. Otherwise he felt relatively comfortable. True, his whole body was aching, but it seemed that the pain was gradually growing less and would finally pass away. The rotting apple in his back and the inflamed area around it, all covered with soft dust, already hardly troubled him. He thought of his family with tenderness and love. The decision that he must disappear was one that he held to even more strongly than his sister, if that were possible. In this state of vacant and peaceful meditation he remained until the tower clock struck three in the morning. The first broadening of light in the world outside the window entered his consciousness once more. Then his head sank to the floor of its own accord and from his nostrils came the last faint flicker of his breath.

When the charwoman arrived early in the morning—what between her strength and her impatience she slammed all the doors so loudly, never mind how often she had been begged not to do so, that no one in the whole apartment could enjoy any quiet sleep after her arrival—she noticed nothing unusual as she took her customary peep into Gregor's room. She thought he was lying motionless on purpose, pretending to be in the sulks;

she credited him with every kind of intelligence. Since she happened to have the long-handled broom in her hand she tried to tickle him up with it from the doorway. When that too produced no reaction she felt provoked and poked at him a little harder, and only when she had pushed him along the floor without meeting any resistance was her attention aroused. It did not take her long to establish the truth of the matter, and her eyes widened, she let out a whistle, yet did not waste much time over it but tore open the door of the Samsas' bedroom and yelled into the darkness at the top of her voice: "Just look at this, it's dead; it's lying here dead and done for!"

Mr. and Mrs. Samsa started up in their double bed and before they realized the nature of the charwoman's announcement had some difficulty in overcoming the shock of it. But then they got out of bed quickly, one on either side, Mr. Samsa throwing a blanket over his shoulders, Mrs. Samsa in nothing but her nightgown; in this array they entered Gregor's room. Meanwhile the door of the living room opened, too, where Grete had been sleeping since the advent of the lodgers; she was completely dressed as if she had not been to bed, which seemed to be confirmed also by the paleness of her face. "Dead?" said Mrs. Samsa, looking questioningly at the charwoman, although she could have investigated for herself, and the fact was obvious enough without investigation. "I should say so," said the charwoman, proving her words by pushing Gregor's corpse a long way to one side with her broomstick. Mrs. Samsa made a movement as if to stop her, but checked it. "Well," said Mr. Samsa, "now thanks be to God." He crossed himself, and the three women followed his example. Grete, whose eyes never left the corpse, said: "Just see how thin he was. It's such a long time since he's eaten anything. The food came out again just as it went in." Indeed, Gregor's body was completely flat and dry, as could only now be seen when it was no longer supported by the legs and nothing prevented one from looking closely at it.

"Come in beside us, Grete, for a little while," said Mrs. Samsa with a tremulous smile, and Grete, not without looking back at the corpse, followed her parents into their bedroom. The charwoman shut the door and opened the window wide. Although it was so early in the morning a certain softness was perceptible in the fresh air. After all, it was already the end of March.

The three lodgers emerged from their room and were surprised to see no breakfast; they had been forgotten. "Where's our breakfast?" said the middle lodger peevishly to the charwoman. But she put her finger to her lips and hastily, without a word, indicated by gestures that they should go into Gregor's room. They did so and stood, their hands in the pockets of their somewhat shabby coats, around Gregor's corpse in the room where it was now fully light.

At that the door of the Samsas' bedroom opened and Mr. Samsa appeared in his uniform, his wife on one arm, his daughter on the other. They all looked a little as if they had been crying; from time to time Grete hid her face on her father's arm.

"Leave my house at once!" said Mr. Samsa, and pointed to the door without disengaging himself from the women. "What do you mean by that?" said the middle lodger, taken somewhat aback, with a feeble smile. The two others put their hands behind them and kept rubbing them to-

gether, as if in gleeful expectation of a fine set-to in which they were bound
to come off the winners. "I mean just what I say," answered Mr. Samsa, and
advanced in a straight line with his two companions towards the lodger. He
stood his ground at first quietly, looking at the floor as if his thoughts
were taking a new pattern in his head. "Then let us go, by all means," he
said, and looked up at Mr. Samsa as if in a sudden access of humility he
were expecting some renewed sanction for this decision. Mr. Samsa merely
nodded briefly once or twice with meaningful eyes. Upon that the lodger
really did go with long strides into the hall, his two friends had been listen-
ing and had quite stopped rubbing their hands for some moments and now
went scuttling after him as if afraid that Mr. Samsa might get into the hall
before them and cut them off from their leader. In the hall they all three
took their hats from the rack, their sticks from the umbrella stand, bowed
in silence and quitted the apartment. With a suspiciousness which proved
quite unfounded Mr. Samsa and the two women followed them out to the
landing; leaning over the banister they watched the three figures slowly but
surely going down the long stairs, vanishing from sight at a certain turn of
the staircase on every floor and coming into view again after a moment or
so; the more they dwindled, the more the Samsa family's interest in them
dwindled, and when a butcher's boy met them and passed them on the
stairs coming up proudly with a tray on his head, Mr. Samsa and the two
women soon left the landing and as if a burden had been lifted from them
went back into their apartment.

They decided to spend this day in resting and going for a stroll; they
had not only deserved such a respite from work, but absolutely needed
it. And so they sat down at the table and wrote three notes of excuse,
Mr. Samsa to his board of management, Mrs. Samsa to her employer and
Grete to the head of her firm. While they were writing, the charwoman
came in to say that she was going now, since her morning's work was fin-
ished. At first they only nodded without looking up, but as she kept hover-
ing there they eyed her irritably. "Well?" said Mr. Samsa. The charwoman
stood grinning in the doorway as if she had good news to impart to the
family but meant not to say a word unless properly questioned. The small
ostrich feather standing upright on her hat, which had annoyed Mr. Samsa
ever since she was engaged, was waving gaily in all directions. "Well, what is
it then?" asked Mrs. Samsa, who obtained more respect from the char-
woman than the others. "Oh," said the charwoman, giggling so amiably
that she could not at once continue, "just this, you don't need to bother
about how to get rid of the thing next door. It's been seen to already." Mrs.
Samsa and Grete bent over their letters again, as if preoccupied; Mr.
Samsa, who perceived that she was eager to begin describing it all in detail,
stopped her with a decisive hand. But since she was not allowed to tell her
story, she remembered the great hurry she was in, being obviously deeply
huffed: "Bye, everybody," she said, whirling off violently, and departed
with a frightful slamming of doors.

"She'll be given notice tonight," said Mr. Samsa, but neither from his
wife nor his daughter did he get any answer, for the charwoman seemed to
have shattered again the composure they had barely achieved. They rose,
went to the window and stayed there, clasping each other tight. Mr. Samsa
turned in his chair to look at them and quietly observed them for a little.

Then he called out: "Come along, now, do. Let bygones be bygones. And you might have some consideration for me." The two of them complied at once, hastened to him, caressed him and quickly finished their letters.

Then they all three left the apartment together, which was more than they had done for months, and went by tram into the open country outside the town. The tram, in which they were the only passengers, was filled with warm sunshine. Leaning comfortably back in their seats they canvassed their prospects for the future, and it appeared on closer inspection that these were not at all bad, for the jobs they had got, which so far they had never really discussed with each other, were all three admirable and likely to lead to better things later on. The greatest immediate improvement in their condition would of course arise from moving to another house; they wanted to take a smaller and cheaper but also better situated and more easily run apartment than the one they had, which Gregor had selected. While they were thus conversing, it struck both Mr. and Mrs. Samsa, almost at the same moment, as they became aware of their daughter's increasing vivacity, that in spite of all the sorrow of recent times, which had made her cheeks pale, she had bloomed into a pretty girl with a good figure. They grew quieter and half unconsciously exchanged glances of complete agreement, having come to the conclusion that it would soon be time to find a good husband for her. And it was like a confirmation of their new dreams and excellent intentions that at the end of their journey their daughter sprang to her feet first and stretched her young body.

D. H. Lawrence
(1885–1930)

D. H. Lawrence and James Joyce had a great deal in common: both spent most of their lives in exile from their native lands, England and Ireland, both labored to expand the boundaries of the novel, and both paid the price of having their major works banned because of their daring. But they greeted each other's work with hostility and incomprehension. Lawrence was repelled by Joyce's meticulous attention to detail: "'Did I feel a twinge in my little toe, or didn't I?' asks every character of Mr. Joyce," he wrote. Joyce, for his part, had this reaction to *Lady Chatterley's Lover* (which he called *"Lady Chatterbox's Lover"*): "I read the first 2 pages of the usual sloppy English, and S. G. [Stuart Gilbert] read me a lyrical bit about nudism in the wood and the end which is a piece of propaganda in favor of something which, outside D. H. L.'s country at any rate, makes all the propaganda for itself." The incomprehension is understandable. Joyce, for all his daring, was fundamentally a classicist who packed as much of the Western literary tradition as he could into his books and then sought to retire behind them, "paring his fingernails." Lawrence was the quintessential romantic, re-

nouncing tradition and placing himself squarely before the reader on every page of his books.

D. H. Lawrence (the initials stand for David Herbert) was born in 1885 at Eastwood, Nottinghamshire, in the middle of the coal-mining area of England. His father was a miner, his mother a cultivated ex-schoolteacher who felt that she had married beneath her; their conflicts are recorded in *Sons and Lovers*, Lawrence's first mature novel, and in many other works. Lawrence was able to attend Nottingham High School through a scholarship and, after a short period as a clerk and a pupil-teacher, went to University College, Nottingham. When he was twenty-three, he left college to become a teacher in Croydon and to write. His first novel, *The White Peacock*, appeared in 1911 and his second, *The Trespasser*, in 1912.

In 1912, the crucial event in Lawrence's personal life occurred: he met Frieda von Richthofen Weekley, the aristocratic German wife of one of his professors at Nottingham. A month later, they eloped to the continent and began a lifetime of wandering and intense, strained involvement with each other that was to form a major subject of Lawrence's writing. After two years in Germany and Italy, Lawrence and Frieda returned to England and were married there in 1914. *Sons and Lovers,* an autobiographical novel of his youth, was published in 1913; it was not a financial success but brought Lawrence's name to public attention. A collection of poems also appeared in 1913; *The Prussian Officer and Other Stories* appeared a year later.

While Lawrence was abroad, he had been working on a long novel which became *The Rainbow*, completed in 1915, and *Women in Love*, completed in 1916. *The Rainbow* was published in an expurgated edition in 1916 but was nevertheless officially condemned as obscene; *Women in Love* did not find a publisher for several years. Discouraged by this and other reverses, Lawrence spent the war years in restless movement. He became a friend of Lady Ottoline Morrell, a wealthy patroness of the arts, and hoped that she would help him set up a utopian community called "Rananim." Other friends included the critic John Middleton Murry, his writer-wife Katherine Mansfield, and the mathematician-philosopher Bertrand Russell, whom Lawrence met at Garsington Manor, Lady Ottoline's estate near Oxford. All of these friends appear in veiled form in *Women in Love*. In 1916, the Lawrences settled in a cottage in Cornwall, where they were persecuted by the police because of Lawrence's reputation as a critic of the war and because of Frieda's German background; they were finally forced to leave and settle in London for the duration of the war.

After it ended, the Lawrences resumed their wanderings, living for short times in Germany, Italy, and Sicily. In 1920, a London publisher finally agreed to reissue *The Rainbow* and to publish *Women in Love*, which appeared in 1921. *The Lost Girl* was published in 1920 and *Aaron's Rod* in 1922. The harsh attacks, especially upon *Women in Love*, in the English press hardened Lawrence's resolve to remain abroad; he and Frieda went to Ceylon in 1922 and then on to Australia, where he wrote *Kangaroo* (1923).

Late in 1922, the Lawrences accepted an invitation from a wealthy American woman, Mabel Dodge Luhan, to join her in Taos, New Mexico; it was the beginning of an infatuation with the American Southwest and Mexico that was profoundly to affect Lawrence's thinking and his late

works. In 1923, he left Taos for Mexico, where he studied Aztec civilization and began *The Plumed Serpent* (1926). He returned to London late the same year and tried to persuade his friends to return with him to Mexico and establish his long-delayed utopian society. Only one agreed, and the project collapsed when Lawrence became seriously ill in Mexico in the winter of 1924–25 with what was initially diagnosed as malaria but eventually was discovered to be an advanced case of tuberculosis.

Lawrence's last years were devoted to voluminous writing, carried out as he struggled against his illness. Settling in Florence, he wrote *Etruscan Places* (1932), the last of a number of fine travel books, and his last novel, *Lady Chatterley's Lover*, a passionate love story in which Lawrence also summed up his appeal for a new relationship between men and women, which would, he believed, imply a regeneration of society. The novel was published in limited editions in Florence (1928) and Paris (1929) and in an expurgated edition in 1932; it was not to be published in an authentic version until 1959, when it provoked a famous obscenity trial. He also wrote the major stories "The Woman Who Rode Away" (1928) and "The Man Who Died" (1931), a great deal of poetry, and *Apocalypse* (1931), a commentary on the Book of Revelation. He died in 1930 in a tuberculosis sanitarium in the south of France, and his ashes were taken to New Mexico for burial. He was only forty-four.

Lawrence was an intense, tormented man with a strong messianic streak. Underlying all his writing is a deep discontent with the modern world. He shared with many post-World War I writers the conviction that civilization was on the wrong track, that science, industrialization, and urbanization had produced a race of dehumanized robots, and that the solution lay in reawakening our irrational, emotional layers of being. "My great religion," he wrote, "is a belief in the blood, the flesh, as being wiser than the intellect." But more than most of his contemporaries, he was driven to translate his beliefs into ideologies and programs; a good part of his work is rather shrill polemic, calling for such projects as deindustrialization, the destruction of universal education, and compulsory training for boys in primitive combat.

At the heart of Lawrence's thinking, however, is his exploration of the marriage relationship. His thinking on this subject fluctuated considerably in the course of his career, but generally it tended toward an ambivalent emphasis both upon the violence and power struggles within the marriage bond and upon intimacy as a means of mystic knowledge. A key passage is Birkin's ideal of "star equilibrium" in *Women in Love*: "not meeting and mingling, but an equilibrium, a pure balance of two single beings:—as the stars balance each other." Such an ideal combines ecstatic intimacy and an awareness of the essential otherness of the partner, precluding both sterile hostility and parasitic dependency.

Lawrence was a fluent and prolific writer; he wrote more than sixty-five books, very uneven in quality. His finest achievements are his fourteen novels and his eight volumes of short stories. As a novelist, Lawrence did not share the "classical temper" of his contemporary Joyce; his novels are intense, lyrical, and visionary, with little attempt to create an objective world or autonomous characters. In his best novels—*The Rainbow* and *Women in Love*—the reader is swept along by the intensity of their vision,

the richness of their imagery, and the ecstatic rhythms of the prose. (Characteristically, Lawrence described even his prose style in sexual terms: the "continual, slightly modified repetition," he wrote, is a "pulsing, frictional to-and-fro which works up to culmination.")

Many critics, however, have identified Lawrence's best work as his short stories, which combine the lyric qualities of the novels with a tighter discipline and sense of craftsmanship and, frequently, an earthy realism. Recurringly, the major conflict in Lawrence's stories is between the forces of repression and those of the vital unconscious. The protagonist has often stifled his own desires out of a middle-class genteelism, a fear of his own impulses, or too great a vulnerability to the needs of others. In the course of the action, he (or, often, she) must confront the "return of the repressed" and choose the forces of life or the forces of death. Sometimes it is too late, as it is for Elizabeth Bates, standing over the body of her dead husband, whom she realizes she has "known falsely." And sometimes it is not, as it is not for Mabel Pervin and Jack Fergusson, as they move out of the death-pond into each other's arms, "amazed, bewildered, and afraid."

FURTHER READING *(prepared by J. H.):* An excellent critical biography of Lawrence is Harry T. Moore's *The Intelligent Heart,* 1954, revised as *The Priest of Love,* 1974. Keith Sagar's *D. H. Lawrence: Life into Art,* 1985, emphasizes, as the title suggests, Lawrence's transformations of his experiences into fiction. Sagar has also edited the useful *D. H. Lawrence Handbook,* 1982. Philip Hobsbaum's *Reader's Guide to D. H. Lawrence,* 1981, offers work-by-work commentaries. Janice H. Harris, in *The Short Fiction of D. H. Lawrence,* 1984, offers intelligent interpretations of Lawrence's short stories, including "Odour of Chrysanthemums" and "The Horse Dealer's Daughter." On Lawrence's ideas, Mark Spilka's *The Love Ethic of D. H. Lawrence,* 1963, is still valuable. See also Graham Holderness's *D. H. Lawrence: History, Ideology, and Fiction,* 1981, and Daniel J. Schneider's *The Consciousness of D. H. Lawrence: An Intellectual Biography,* 1986. The important topic of Lawrence's artistic treatment of women is well treated in Carol Dix's *D. H. Lawrence and Women,* 1980, and in Hilary Simpson's *D. H. Lawrence and Feminism,* 1982. Two good collections of essays are *D. H. Lawrence: A Centenary Consideration,* ed. by Peter Balbert and Phillip L. Marcus, 1985; and *D. H. Lawrence: New Studies,* ed. by Christopher Heywood, 1986. A thorough guide to Lawrence criticism is Thomas J. Rice's *D. H. Lawrence: A Guide to Research,* 1982.

ODOUR OF CHRYSANTHEMUMS

I

The small locomotive engine, Number 4, came clanking, stumbling down from Selston with seven full wagons. It appeared round the corner with loud threats of speed, but the colt that it startled from among the gorse,[1] which still flickered indistinctly in the raw afternoon, outdistanced it at a canter. A woman, walking up the railway line to Underwood, drew back into the hedge, held her basket aside, and watched the footplate of the

[1] A low, spiny shrub that grows on wastelands in Britain.

engine advancing. The trucks thumped heavily past, one by one, with slow inevitable movement, as she stood insignificantly trapped between the jolting black wagons and the hedge; then they curved away toward the coppice[2] where the withered oak leaves dropped noiselessly, while the birds, pulling at the scarlet hips[3] beside the track, made off into the dusk that had already crept into the spinney.[4] In the open, the smoke from the engine sank and cleaved to the rough grass. The fields were dreary and forsaken, and in the marshy strip that led to the whimsey,[5] a reedy pit-pond, the fowls had already abandoned their run among the alders, to roost in the tarred fowl-house. The pit-bank[6] loomed up beyond the pond, flames like red sores licking its ashy sides, in the afternoon's stagnant light. Just beyond rose the tapering chimneys and the clumsy black headstocks[7] of Brinsley Colliery. The two wheels were spinning fast up against the sky, and the winding-engine[8] rapped out its little spasms. The miners were being turned up.

The engine whistled as it came into the wide bay of railway lines beside the colliery, where rows of trucks stood in harbour.

Miners, single, trailing and in groups, passed like shadows diverging home. At the edge of the ribbed level of sidings squat[9] a low cottage, three steps down from the cinder track. A large bony vine clutched at the house, as if to claw down the tiled roof. Round the bricked yard grew a few wintry primroses. Beyond, the long garden sloped down to a bush-covered brook course. There were some twiggy apple trees, winter-crack trees, and ragged cabbages. Beside the path hung dishevelled pink chrysanthemums, like pink cloths hung on bushes. A woman came stooping out of the felt-covered fowl-house, halfway down the garden. She closed and padlocked the door, then drew herself erect, having brushed some bits from her white apron.

She was a tall woman of imperious mien, handsome, with definite black eyebrows. Her smooth black hair was parted exactly. For a few moments she stood steadily watching the miners as they passed along the railway: then she turned toward the brook course. Her face was calm and set, her mouth was closed with disillusionment. After a moment she called: "John!" There was no answer. She waited, and then said distinctly: "Where are you?"

"Here!" replied a child's sulky voice from among the bushes. The woman looked piercingly through the dusk.

"Are you at that brook?" she asked sternly.

For answer the child showed himself before the raspberry-canes that rose like whips. He was a small, sturdy boy of five. He stood quite still, defiantly.

"Oh!" said the mother, conciliated. "I thought you were down at that wet brook—and you remember what I told you—"

The boy did not move or answer.

[2]Thicket. [3]Seed pods of wild roses. [4]Grove of trees.
[5]A piece of mining equipment that raises water or ore out of the mine.
[6]Bank of slag or waste from the mine.
[7]Structure over a mine shaft that houses the surface part of the machinery. A colliery is a coal mine.
[8]Engine that raises and lowers men and materials in the mine. [9]Squatted.

"Come, come on in," she said more gently, "it's getting dark. There's your grandfather's engine coming down the line!"

The lad advanced slowly, with resentful, taciturn movement. He was dressed in trousers and waistcoat of cloth that was too thick and hard for the size of the garments. They were evidently cut down from a man's clothes.

As they went slowly toward the house he tore at the ragged wisps of chrysanthemums and dropped the petals in handfuls along the path.

"Don't do that—it does look nasty," said his mother. He refrained, and she, suddenly pitiful, broke off a twig with three or four wan flowers and held them against her face. When mother and son reached the yard her hand hesitated, and instead of laying the flower aside, she pushed it in her apron-band. The mother and son stood at the foot of the three steps looking across the bay of lines at the passing home of the miners. The trundle of the small train was imminent. Suddenly the engine loomed past the house and came to a stop opposite the gate.

The engine-driver, a short man with round grey beard, leaned out of the cab high above the woman.

"Have you got a cup of tea?" he said in a cheery, hearty fashion.

It was her father. She went in, saying she would mash.[10] Directly she returned.

"I didn't come to see you on Sunday," began the little grey-bearded man.

"I didn't expect you," said his daughter.

The engine-driver winced; then, reassuming his cheery, airy manner, he said:

"Oh, have you heard then? Well, and what do you think—?"

"I think it is soon enough," she replied.

At her brief censure the little man made an impatient gesture, and said coaxingly, yet with dangerous coldness:

"Well, what's a man to do? It's no sort of life for a man of my years, to sit at my own hearth like a stranger. And if I'm going to marry again it may as well be soon as late—what does it matter to anybody?"

The woman did not reply, but turned and went into the house. The man in the engine-cab stood assertive, till she returned with a cup of tea and a piece of bread and butter on a plate. She went up the steps and stood near the footplate of the hissing engine.

"You needn't 'a' brought me bread an' butter," said her father. "But a cup of tea"—he sipped appreciatively—"it's very nice." He sipped for a moment or two, then: "I hear as Walter's got another bout on," he said.

"When hasn't he?" said the woman bitterly.

"I heered tell of him in the 'Lord Nelson'[11] braggin' as he was going to spend that b— afore he went: half a sovereign that was."

"When?" asked the woman.

"A' Sat'day night—I know that's true."

"Very likely," she laughed bitterly. "He gives me twenty-three shillings."

"Aye, it's a nice thing, when a man can do nothing with his money but make a beast of himself!" said the grey-whiskered man. The woman turned

[10] Put the tea in to steep. [11] Name of a pub.

her head away. Her father swallowed the last of his tea and handed her the cup.

"Aye," he sighed, wiping his mouth. "It's a settler,[12] it is—"

He put his hand on the lever. The little engine strained and groaned, and the train rumbled toward the crossing. The woman again looked across the metals. Darkness was settling over the spaces of the railway and trucks: the miners, in grey sombre groups, were still passing home. The winding-engine pulsed hurriedly, with brief pauses. Elizabeth Bates looked at the dreary flow of men, then she went indoors. Her husband did not come.

The kitchen was small and full of firelight; red coals piled glowing up the chimney mouth. All the life of the room seemed in the white, warm hearth and the steel fender reflecting the red fire. The cloth was laid for tea; cups glinted in the shadows. At the back, where the lowest stairs protruded into the room, the boy sat struggling with a knife and a piece of whitewood. He was almost hidden in the shadow. It was half-past four. They had but to await the father's coming to begin tea. As the mother watched her son's sullen little struggle with the wood, she saw herself in his silence and pertinacity; she saw the father in her child's indifference to all but himself. She seemed to be occupied by her husband. He had probably gone past his home, slunk past his own door, to drink before he came in, while his dinner spoiled and wasted in waiting. She glanced at the clock, then took the potatoes to strain them in the yard. The garden and fields beyond the brook were closed in uncertain darkness. When she rose with the saucepan, leaving the drain steaming into the night behind her, she saw the yellow lamps were lit along the high road that went up the hill away beyond the space of the railway lines and the field.

Then again she watched the men trooping home, fewer now and fewer.

Indoors the fire was sinking and the room was dark red. The woman put her saucepan on the hob,[13] and set a batter pudding near the mouth of the oven. Then she stood unmoving. Directly, gratefully, came quick young steps to the door. Someone hung on the latch a moment, then a little girl entered and began pulling off her outdoor things, dragging a mass of curls, just ripening from gold to brown, over her eyes with her hat.

Her mother chid[14] her for coming late from school, and said she would have to keep her at home the dark winter days.

"Why, mother, it's hardly a bit dark yet. The lamp's not lighted, and my father's not home."

"No, he isn't. But it's a quarter to five! Did you see anything of him?"

The child became serious. She looked at her mother with large, wistful blue eyes.

"No, mother, I've never seen him. Why? Has he come up an' gone past, to Old Brinsley? He hasn't, mother, 'cos I never saw him."

"He'd watch that," said the mother bitterly, "he'd take care as you didn't see him. But you may depend upon it, he's seated in the 'Prince o' Wales.'[15] He wouldn't be this late."

The girl looked at her mother piteously.

[12] Final blow. [13] Shelf on the side of a fireplace. [14] Chided; scolded.
[15] Another pub.

"Let's have our teas, mother, should we?" said she.

The mother called John to table. She opened the door once more and looked out across the darkness of the lines. All was deserted: she could not hear the winding-engines.

"Perhaps," she said to herself, "he's stopped to get some ripping[16] done."

They sat down to tea. John, at the end of the table near the door, was almost lost in the darkness. Their faces were hidden from each other. The girl crouched against the fender slowly moving a thick piece of bread before the fire. The lad, his face a dusky mark on the shadow, sat watching her who was transfigured in the red glow.

"I do think it's beautiful to look in the fire," said the child.

"Do you?" said her mother. "Why?"

"It's so red, and full of little caves—and it feels so nice, and you can fair smell it."

"It'll want mending directly," replied the mother, "and then if your father comes he'll carry on and say there never is a fire when a man comes home sweating from the pit. A public-house is always warm enough."

There was silence till the boy said complainingly: "Make haste, our Annie."

"Well, I am doing! I can't make the fire do it no faster, can I?"

"She keeps wafflin'[17] it about so's to make 'er slow," grumbled the boy.

"Don't have such an evil imagination, child," replied the mother.

Soon the room was busy in the darkness with the crisp sound of crunching. The mother ate very little. She drank her tea determinedly, and sat thinking. When she rose her anger was evident in the stern unbending of her head. She looked at the pudding in the fender, and broke out:

"It is a scandalous thing as a man can't even come home to his dinner! If it's crozzled up[18] to a cinder I don't see why I should care. Past his very door he goes to get to a public-house, and here I sit with his dinner waiting for him—"

She went out. As she dropped piece after piece of coal on the red fire, the shadows fell on the walls, till the room was almost in total darkness.

"I canna see," grumbled the invisible John. In spite of herself, the mother laughed.

"You know the way to your mouth," she said. She set the dustpan outside the door. When she came again like a shadow on the hearth, the lad repeated, complaining sulkily:

"I canna see."

"Good gracious!" cried the mother irritably, "you're as bad as your father if it's a bit dusk!"

Nevertheless she took a paper spill[19] from a sheaf on the mantelpiece and proceeded to light the lamp that hung from the ceiling in the middle of the room. As she reached up, her figure displayed itself just rounding with maternity.

"Oh, mother—!" exclaimed the girl.

"What?" said the woman, suspended in the act of putting the lamp glass

[16] Cutting away coal. [17] Waving. [18] Shrivelled and burned.
[19] A long twist of paper.

over the flame. The copper reflector shone handsomely on her, as she stood with uplifted arm, turning to face her daughter.

"You've got a flower in your apron!" said the child, in a little rapture at this unusual event.

"Goodness me!" exclaimed the woman, relieved. "One would think the house was afire." She replaced the glass and waited a moment before turning up the wick. A pale shadow was seen floating vaguely on the floor.

"Let me smell!" said the child, still rapturously, coming forward and putting her face to her mother's waist.

"Go along, silly!" said the mother, turning up the lamp. The light revealed their suspense so that the woman felt it almost unbearable. Annie was still bending at her waist. Irritably, the mother took the flowers out from her apron-band.

"Oh, mother—don't take them out!" Annie cried, catching her hand and trying to replace the sprig.

"Such nonsense!" said the mother, turning away. The child put the pale chrysanthemums to her lips, murmuring:

"Don't they smell beautiful!"

Her mother gave a short laugh.

"No," she said, "not to me. It was chrysanthemums when I married him, and chrysanthemums when you were born, and the first time they ever brought him home drunk, he'd got brown chrysanthemums in his button-hole."

She looked at the children. Their eyes and their parted lips were wondering. The mother sat rocking in silence for some time. Then she looked at the clock.

"Twenty minutes to six!" In a tone of fine bitter carelessness she continued: "Eh, he'll not come now till they bring him. There he'll stick! But he needn't come rolling in here in his pit-dirt, for *I* won't wash him. He can lie on the floor—Eh, what a fool I've been, what a fool! And this is what I came here for, to this dirty hole, rats and all, for him to slink past his very door. Twice last week—he's begun now—"

She silenced herself, and rose to clear the table.

While for an hour or more the children played, subduedly intent, fertile of imagination, united in fear of the mother's wrath, and in dread of their father's home-coming, Mrs. Bates sat in her rocking-chair making a "singlet" of thick cream-coloured flannel, which gave a dull wounded sound as she tore off the grey edge. She worked at her sewing with energy, listening to the children, and her anger wearied itself, lay down to rest, opening its eyes from time to time and steadily watching, its ears raised to listen. Sometimes even her anger quailed and shrank, and the mother suspended her sewing, tracing the footsteps that thudded along the sleepers[20] outside; she would lift her head sharply to bid the children "hush," but she recovered herself in time, and the footsteps went past the gate, and the children were not flung out of their play-world.

But at last Annie sighed, and gave in. She glanced at her wagon of slippers, and loathed the game. She turned plaintively to her mother.

"Mother!"—but she was inarticulate.

[20]Cross ties of the railway track.

John crept out like a frog from under the sofa. His mother glanced up. "Yes," she said, "just look at those shirt-sleeves!"

The boy held them out to survey them, saying nothing. Then somebody called in a hoarse voice away down the line, and suspense bristled in the room, till two people had gone by outside, talking.

"It is time for bed," said the mother.

"My father hasn't come," wailed Annie plaintively. But her mother was primed with courage.

"Never mind. They'll bring him when he does come—like a log." She meant there would be no scene. "And he may sleep on the floor till he wakes himself. I know he'll not go to work tomorrow after this!"

The children had their hands and faces wiped with a flannel. They were very quiet. When they had put on their nightdresses, they said their prayers, the boy mumbling. The mother looked down at them, at the brown silken bush of intertwining curls in the nape of the girl's neck, at the little black head of the lad, and her heart burst with anger at their father who caused all three such distress. The children hid their faces in her skirts for comfort.

When Mrs. Bates came down, the room was strangely empty, with a tension of expectancy. She took up her sewing and stitched for some time without raising her head. Meantime her anger was tinged with fear.

II

The clock struck eight and she rose suddenly, dropping her sewing on her chair. She went to the stairfoot door, opened it, listening. Then she went out, locking the door behind her.

Something scuffled in the yard, and she started, though she knew it was only the rats with which the place was overrun. The night was very dark. In the great bay of railway lines, bulked with trucks, there was no trace of light, only away back she could see a few yellow lamps at the pit-top, and the red smear of the burning pit-bank on the night. She hurried along the edge of the track, then, crossing the converging lines, came to the stile by the white gates, whence she emerged on the road. Then the fear which had led her shrank. People were walking up to New Brinsley; she saw the lights in the houses; twenty yards further on were the broad windows of the "Prince of Wales," very warm and bright, and the loud voices of men could be heard distinctly. What a fool she had been to imagine that anything had happened to him! He was merely drinking over there at the "Prince of Wales." She faltered. She had never yet been to fetch him, and she never would go. So she continued her walk toward the long straggling line of houses, standing blank on the highway. She entered a passage between the dwellings.

"Mr. Rigley?—Yes! Did you want him? No, he's not in at this minute."

The raw-boned woman leaned forward from her dark scullery and peered at the other, upon whom fell a dim light through the blind of the kitchen window.

"Is it Mrs. Bates?" she asked in a tone tinged with respect.

"Yes. I wondered if your Master was at home. Mine hasn't come yet."

"'Asn't 'e! Oh, Jack's been 'ome an' 'ad 'is dinner an' gone out. 'E's just gone for 'alf an hour afore bedtime. Did you call at the 'Prince of Wales'?"

"No—"

"No, you didn't like—! It's not very nice." The other woman was indulgent. There was an awkward pause. "Jack never said nothink about—about your Mester," she said.

"No!—I expect he's stuck in there!"

Elizabeth Bates said this bitterly, and with recklessness. She knew that the woman across the yard was standing at her door listening, but she did not care. As she turned:

"Stop a minute! I'll just go an' ask Jack if 'e knows anythink," said Mrs. Rigley.

"Oh, no—I wouldn't like to put—!"

"Yes, I will, if you'll just step inside an' see as th' childer doesn't come downstairs and set theirselves afire."

Elizabeth Bates, murmuring a remonstrance, stepped inside. The other woman apologized for the state of the room.

The kitchen needed apology. There were little frocks and trousers and childish undergarments on the squab[21] and on the floor, and a litter of playthings everywhere. On the black American cloth[22] of the table were pieces of bread and cake, crusts, slops, and a teapot with cold tea.

"Eh, ours is just as bad," said Elizabeth Bates, looking at the woman, not at the house. Mrs. Rigley put a shawl over her head and hurried out, saying:

"I shanna be a minute."

The other sat, noting with faint disapproval the general untidiness of the room. Then she fell to counting the shoes of various sizes scattered over the floor. There were twelve. She sighed and said to herself, "No wonder!"—glancing at the litter. There came the scratching of two pairs of feet on the yard, and the Rigleys entered. Elizabeth Bates rose. Rigley was a big man, with very large bones. His head looked particularly bony. Across his temple was a blue scar, caused by a wound got in the pit, a wound in which the coal-dust remained blue like tattooing.

"'Asna 'e come whoam yit?" asked the man, without any form of greeting, but with deference and sympathy. "I couldna say wheer 'e is—'e's non ower theer!"—he jerked his head to signify the "Prince of Wales."

"'E's 'appen gone up to th' 'Yew,'"[23] said Mrs. Rigley.

There was another pause. Rigley had evidently something to get off his mind:

"Ah left 'im finishin' a stint," he began. "Loose-all[24] 'ad bin gone about ten minutes when we com'n away, an' I shouted, 'Are ter comin', Walt?' an' 'e said, 'Go on, Ah shanna be but a'ef a minnit,' so we com'n ter th' bottom, me an' Bowers, thinkin' as 'e wor just behint, an' 'ud come up i' th' next bantle[25]—"

He stood perplexed, as if answering a charge of deserting his mate. Elizabeth Bates, now again certain of disaster, hastened to reassure him:

[21] Couch. [22] Oilcloth.
[23] "Maybe he's gone up to the 'Yew'" (another pub, the Yew Tree).
[24] The signal to stop work. [25] Group.

"I expect 'e's gone up to th' 'Yew Tree,' as you say. It's not the first time. I've fretted myself into a fever before now. He'll come home when they carry him."

"Ay, isn't it too bad!" deplored the other woman.

"I'll just step up to Dick's an' see if 'e *is* theer," offered the man, afraid of appearing alarmed, afraid of taking liberties.

"Oh, I wouldn't think of bothering you that far," said Elizabeth Bates, with emphasis, but he knew she was glad of his offer.

As they stumbled up the entry, Elizabeth Bates heard Rigley's wife run across the yard and open her neighbour's door. At this, suddenly all the blood in her body seemed to switch away from her heart.

"Mind!" warned Rigley. "Ah've said many a time as Ah'd fill up them ruts in this entry, sumb'dy 'll be breakin' their legs yit."

She recovered herself and walked quickly along with the miner.

"I don't like leaving the children in bed, and nobody in the house," she said.

"No, you dunna!" he replied courteously. They were soon at the gate of the cottage.

"Well, I shanna be many minnits. Dunna you be frettin' now, 'e'll be all right," said the butty.[26]

"Thank you very much, Mr. Rigley," she replied.

"You're welcome!" he stammered, moving away. "I shanna be many minnits."

The house was quiet. Elizabeth Bates took off her hat and shawl, and rolled back the rug. When she had finished, she sat down. It was a few minutes past nine. She was startled by the rapid chuff of the winding-engine at the pit, and the sharp whirr of the brakes on the rope as it descended. Again she felt the painful sweep of her blood, and she put her hand to her side, saying aloud, "Good gracious!—it's only the nine o'clock deputy[27] going down," rebuking herself.

She sat still, listening. Half an hour of this, and she was wearied out.

"What am I working myself up like this for?" she said pitiably to herself, "I s'll only be doing myself some damage."

She took out her sewing again.

At a quarter to ten there were footsteps. One person! She watched for the door to open. It was an elderly woman, in a black bonnet and a black woollen shawl—his mother. She was about sixty years old, pale, with blue eyes, and her face all wrinkled and lamentable. She shut the door and turned to her daughter-in-law peevishly.

"Eh, Lizzie, whatever shall we do, whatever shall we do!" she cried.

Elizabeth drew back a little, sharply.

"What is it, mother?" she said.

The elder woman seated herself on the sofa.

"I don't know, child, I can't tell you!"—she shook her head slowly. Elizabeth sat watching her, anxious and vexed.

"I don't know," replied the grandmother, sighing very deeply. "There's

[26] Buddy or workmate, sometimes with the special meaning of "foreman."
[27] Minor official in the mine; inspector.

no end to my troubles, there isn't. The things I've gone through, I'm sure it's enough—" She wept without wiping her eyes, the tears running.

"But, mother," interrupted Elizabeth, "what do you mean? What is it?"

The grandmother slowly wiped her eyes. The fountains of her tears were stopped by Elizabeth's directness. She wiped her eyes slowly.

"Poor child! Eh, you poor thing!" she moaned. "I don't know what we're going to do, I don't—and you as you are—it's a thing, it is indeed!"

Elizabeth waited.

"Is he dead?" she asked, and at the words her heart swung violently, though she felt a slight flush of shame at the ultimate extravagance of the question. Her words sufficiently frightened the old lady, almost brought her to herself.

"Don't say so, Elizabeth! We'll hope it's not as bad as that; no, may the Lord spare us that, Elizabeth. Jack Rigley came just as I was sittin' down to a glass afore going to bed, an' 'e said, "'Appen[28] you'll go down th' line, Mrs. Bates. Walt's had an accident. 'Appen you'll go an' sit wi' 'er till we can get him home.' I hadn't time to ask him a word afore he was gone. An' I put my bonnet on an' come straight down, Lizzie. I thought to myself, 'Eh, that poor blessed child, if anybody should come an' tell her of a sudden, there's no knowin' what'll 'appen to 'er.' You mustn't let it upset you, Lizzie—or you know what to expect. How long is it, six months—or is it five, Lizzie? Ay!"—the old woman shook her head—"time slips on, it slips on! Ay!"

Elizabeth's thoughts were busy elsewhere. If he was killed—would she be able to manage on the little pension and what she could earn?—she counted up rapidly. If he was hurt—they wouldn't take him to the hospital—how tiresome he would be to nurse!—but perhaps she'd be able to get him away from the drink and his hateful ways. She would—while he was ill. The tears offered to come to her eyes at the picture. But what sentimental luxury was this she was beginning? She turned to consider the children. At any rate she was absolutely necessary for them. They were her business.

"Ay!" repeated the old woman, "it seems but a week or two since he brought me his first wages. Ay—he was a good lad, Elizabeth, he was, in his way. I don't know why he got to be such a trouble, I don't. He was a happy lad at home, only full of spirits. But there's no mistake he's been a handful of trouble, he has! I hope the Lord'll spare him to mend his ways. I hope so, I hope so. You've had a sight o' trouble with him, Elizabeth, you have indeed. But he was a jolly enough lad wi' me, he was, I can assure you. I don't know how it is. . . ."

The old woman continued to muse aloud, a monotonous irritating sound, while Elizabeth thought concentratedly, startled once, when she heard the winding-engine chuff quickly, and the brakes skirr with a shriek. Then she heard the engine more slowly, and the brakes made no sound. The old woman did not notice. Elizabeth waited in suspense. The mother-in-law talked, with lapses into silence.

"But he wasn't your son, Lizzie, an' it makes a difference. Whatever he was, I remember him when he was little, an' I learned to understand him and to make allowances. You've got to make allowances for them—"

[28]Maybe.

It was half-past ten, and the old woman was saying: "But it's trouble from beginning to end; you're never too old for trouble, never too old for that—" when the gate banged back, and there were heavy feet on the steps.

"I'll go, Lizzie, let me go," cried the old woman, rising. But Elizabeth was at the door. It was a man in pit-clothes.

"They're bringin' 'im, Missis," he said. Elizabeth's heart halted a moment. Then it surged on again, almost suffocating her.

"Is he—is it bad?" she asked.

The man turned away, looking at the darkness:

"The doctor says 'e'd been dead hours. 'E saw 'im i' th' lamp-cabin."

The old woman, who stood just behind Elizabeth, dropped into a chair, and folded her hands, crying: "Oh, my boy, my boy!"

"Hush!" said Elizabeth, with a sharp twitch of a frown. "Be still, mother, don't waken th' children: I wouldn't have them down for anything!"

The old woman moaned softly, rocking herself. The man was drawing away. Elizabeth took a step forward.

"How was it?" she asked.

"Well, I couldn't say for sure," the man replied, very ill at ease. "'E wor finishin' a stint an' th' butties 'ad gone, an' a lot o' stuff come down atop 'n 'im."

"And crushed him?" cried the widow, with a shudder.

"No," said the man, "it fell at th' back of 'im. 'E wor under th' face,[29] an' it niver touched 'im. It shut 'im in. It seems 'e wor smothered."

Elizabeth shrank back. She heard the old woman behind her cry:

"What?—what did 'e say it was?"

The man replied, more loudly: "'E wor smothered!"

Then the old woman wailed aloud, and this relieved Elizabeth.

"Oh, mother," she said, putting her hand on the old woman, "don't waken th' children, don't waken th' children."

She wept a little, unknowing, while the old mother rocked herself and moaned. Elizabeth remembered that they were bringing him home, and she must be ready. "They'll lay him in the parlour," she said to herself, standing a moment pale and perplexed.

Then she lighted a candle and went into the tiny room. The air was cold and damp, but she could not make a fire, there was no fireplace. She set down the candle and looked round. The candlelight glittered on the luster-glasses, on the two vases that held some of the pink chrysanthemums, and on the dark mahogany. There was a cold, deathly smell of chrysanthemums in the room. Elizabeth stood looking at the flowers. She turned away, and calculated whether there would be room to lay him on the floor, between the couch and the chiffonier. She pushed the chairs aside. There would be room to lay him down and to step round him. Then she fetched the old red tablecloth, and another old cloth, spreading them down to save her bit of carpet. She shivered on leaving the parlour; so, from the dresser-drawer she took a clean shirt and put it at the fire to air. All the time her mother-in-law was rocking herself in the chair and moaning.

"You'll have to move from there, mother," said Elizabeth. "They'll be bringing him in. Come in the rocker."

[29] The coal-face, exposed edge of the seam.

The old mother rose mechanically, and seated herself by the fire, continuing to lament. Elizabeth went into the pantry for another candle, and there, in the little penthouse under the naked tiles, she heard them coming. She stood still in the pantry doorway, listening. She heard them pass the end of the house, and come awkwardly down the three steps, a jumble of shuffling footsteps and muttering voices. The old woman was silent. The men were in the yard.

Then Elizabeth heard Matthews, the manager of the pit, say: "You go in first, Jim. Mind!"

The door came open, and the two women saw a collier backing into the room, holding one end of a stretcher, on which they could see the nailed pit-boots of the dead man. The two carriers halted, the man at the head stooping to the lintel of the door.

"Wheer will you have him?" asked the manager, a short, white-bearded man.

Elizabeth roused herself and came from the pantry carrying the unlighted candle.

"In the parlour," she said.

"In there, Jim!" pointed the manager, and the carriers backed round into the tiny room. The coat with which they had covered the body fell off as they awkwardly turned through the two doorways, and the women saw their man, naked to the waist, lying stripped for work. The old woman began to moan in a low voice of horror.

"Lay th' stretcher at th' side," snapped the manager, "an' put 'im on th' cloths. Mind now, mind! Look you now—!"

One of the men had knocked off a vase of chrysanthemums. He stared awkwardly, then they set down the stretcher. Elizabeth did not look at her husband. As soon as she could get in the room, she went and picked up the broken vase and the flowers.

"Wait a minute!" she said.

The three men waited in silence while she mopped up the water with a duster.

"Eh, what a job, what a job, to be sure!" the manager was saying, rubbing his brow with trouble and perplexity. "Never knew such a thing in my life, never! He'd no business to ha' been left. I never knew such a thing in my life! Fell over him clean as a whistle, an' shut him in. Not four foot of space, there wasn't—yet it scarce bruised him."

He looked down at the dead man, lying prone, half naked, all grimed with coal-dust.

"'Sphyxiated,' the doctor said. It *is* the most terrible job I've ever known. Seems as if it was done o' purpose. Clean over him, an' shut 'im in, like a mouse-trap"—he made a sharp, descending gesture with his hand.

The colliers standing by jerked aside their heads in hopeless comment.

The horror of the thing bristled upon them all.

Then they heard the girl's voice upstairs calling shrilly: "Mother, mother—who is it? Mother, who is it?"

Elizabeth hurried to the foot of the stairs and opened the door:

"Go to sleep!" she commanded sharply. "What are you shouting about? Go to sleep at once—there's nothing—"

Then she began to mount the stairs. They could hear her on the boards,

and on the plaster floor of the little bedroom. They could hear her distinctly:

"What's the matter now?—what's the matter with you, silly thing?"— her voice was much agitated, with an unreal gentleness.

"I thought it was some men come," said the plaintive voice of the child. "Has he come?"

"Yes, they've brought him. There's nothing to make a fuss about. Go to sleep now, like a good child."

They could hear her voice in the bedroom, they waited whilst she covered the children under the bedclothes.

"Is he drunk?" asked the girl, timidly, faintly.

"No! No—he's not! He—he's asleep."

"Is he asleep downstairs?"

"Yes—and don't make a noise."

There was silence for a moment, then the men heard the frightened child again:

"What's that noise?"

"It's nothing, I tell you, what are you bothering for?"

The noise was the grandmother moaning. She was oblivious of everything, sitting on her chair rocking and moaning. The manager put his hand on her arm and bade her "Sh—sh!!"

The old woman opened her eyes and looked at him. She was shocked by this interruption, and seemed to wonder.

"What time is it?"—the plaintive thin voice of the child, sinking back unhappily into sleep, asked this last question.

"Ten o'clock," answered the mother more softly. Then she must have bent down and kissed the children.

Matthews beckoned to the men to come away. They put on their caps and took up the stretcher. Stepping over the body, they tiptoed out of the house. None of them spoke till they were far from the wakeful children.

When Elizabeth came down she found his mother alone on the parlour floor, leaning over the dead man, the tears dropping on him.

"We must lay him out," the wife said. She put on the kettle, then returning knelt at the feet, and began to unfasten the knotted leather laces. The room was clammy and dim with only one candle, so that she had to bend her face almost to the floor. At last she got off the heavy boots and put them away.

"You must help me now," she whispered to the old woman. Together they stripped the man.

When they arose, saw him lying in the naïve dignity of death, the women stood arrested in fear and respect. For a few moments they remained still, looking down, the old mother whimpering. Elizabeth felt countermanded. She saw him, how utterly inviolable he lay in himself. She had nothing to do with him. She could not accept it. Stooping, she laid her hand on him, in claim. He was still warm, for the mine was hot where he had died. His mother had his face between her hands, and was murmuring incoherently. The old tears fell in succession as drops from wet leaves; the mother was not weeping, merely her tears flowed. Elizabeth embraced the body of her husband, with cheek and lips. She seemed to be listening,

inquiring, trying to get some connection. But she could not. She was driven away. He was impregnable.

She rose, went into the kitchen, where she poured warm water into a bowl, brought soap and flannel and a soft towel.

"I must wash him," she said.

Then the old mother rose stiffly, and watched Elizabeth as she carefully washed his face, carefully brushing the big blond moustache from his mouth with the flannel. She was afraid with a bottomless fear, so she ministered to him. The old woman, jealous, said:

"Let me wipe him!"—and she kneeled on the other side drying slowly as Elizabeth washed, her big black bonnet sometimes brushing the dark head of her daughter-in-law. They worked thus in silence for a long time. They never forgot it was death, and the touch of the man's dead body gave them strange emotions, different in each of the women; a great dread possessed them both, the mother felt the lie was given to her womb, she was denied; the wife felt the utter isolation of the human soul, the child within her was a weight apart from her.

At last it was finished. He was a man of handsome body, and his face showed no traces of drink. He was blond, full-fleshed, with fine limbs. But he was dead.

"Bless him," whispered his mother, looking always at his face, and speaking out of sheer terror. "Dear lad—bless him!" She spoke in a faint, sibilant ecstasy of fear and mother love.

Elizabeth sank down again to the floor, and put her face against his neck, and trembled and shuddered. But she had to draw away again. He was dead, and her living flesh had no place against his. A great dread and weariness held her: she was so unavailing. Her life was gone like this.

"White as milk he is, clear as a twelve-month baby, bless him, the darling!" the old mother murmured to herself. "Not a mark on him, clear and clean and white, beautiful as ever a child was made," she murmured with pride. Elizabeth kept her face hidden.

"He went peaceful, Lizzie—peaceful as sleep. Isn't he beautiful, the lamb? Ay—he must ha' made his peace, Lizzie. 'Appen he made it all right, Lizzie, shut in there. He'd have time. He wouldn't look like this if he hadn't made his peace. The lamb, the dear lamb. Eh, but he had a hearty laugh. I loved to hear it. He had the heartiest laugh, Lizzie, as a lad—"

Elizabeth looked up. The man's mouth was fallen back, slightly open under the cover of the moustache. The eyes, half shut, did not show glazed in the obscurity. Life with its smoky burning gone from him, had left him apart and utterly alien to her. And she knew what a stranger he was to her. In her womb was ice of fear, because of this separate stranger with whom she had been living as one flesh. Was this what it all meant—utter, intact separateness, obscured by heat of living? In dread she turned her face away. The fact was too deadly. There had been nothing between them, and yet they had come together, exchanging their nakedness repeatedly. Each time he had taken her, they had been two isolated beings, far apart as now. He was no more responsible than she. The child was like ice in her womb. For as she looked at the dead man, her mind, cold and detached, said clearly: "Who am I? What have I been doing? I have been fighting a hus-

band who did not exist. *He* existed all the time. What wrong have I done? What was that I have been living with? There lies the reality, this man." And her soul died in her for fear: she knew she had never seen him, he had never seen her, they had met in the dark and had fought in the dark, not knowing whom they met nor whom they fought. And now she saw, and turned silent in seeing. For she had been wrong. She had said he was something he was not; she had felt familiar with him. Whereas he was apart all the while, living as she never lived, feeling as she never felt.

In fear and shame she looked at his naked body, that she had known falsely. And he was the father of her children. Her soul was torn from her body and stood apart. She looked at his naked body and was ashamed, as if she had denied it. After all, it was itself. It seemed awful to her. She looked at his face, and she turned her own face to the wall. For his look was other than hers, his way was not her way. She had denied him what he was—she saw it now. She had refused him as himself. And this had been her life, and his life. She was grateful to death, which restored the truth. And she knew she was not dead.

And all the while her heart was bursting with grief and pity for him. What had he suffered? What stretch of horror for this helpless man! She was rigid with agony. She had not been able to help him. He had been cruelly injured, this naked man, this other being, and she could make no reparation. There were the children—but the children belonged to life. This dead man had nothing to do with them. He and she were only channels through which life had flowed to issue in the children. She was a mother—but how awful she knew it now to have been a wife. And he, dead now, how awful he must have felt it to be a husband. She felt that in the next world he would be a stranger to her. If they met there, in the beyond, they would only be ashamed of what had been before. The children had come, for some mysterious reason, out of both of them. But the children did not unite them. Now he was dead, she knew how eternally he was apart from her, how eternally he had nothing more to do with her. She saw this episode of her life closed. They had denied each other in life. Now he had withdrawn. An anguish came over her. It was finished then: it had become hopeless between them long before he died. Yet he had been her husband. But how little!

"Have you got his shirt, 'Lizabeth?"

Elizabeth turned without answering, though she strove to weep and behave as her mother-in-law expected. But she could not, she was silenced. She went into the kitchen and returned with the garment.

"It is aired," she said, grasping the cotton shirt here and there to try. She was almost ashamed to handle him; what right had she or any one to lay hands on him; but her touch was humble on his body. It was hard work to clothe him. He was so heavy and inert. A terrible dread gripped her all the while: that he could be so heavy and utterly inert, unresponsive, apart. The horror of the distance between them was almost too much for her—it was so infinite a gap she must look across.

At last it was finished. They covered him with a sheet and left him lying, with his face bound. And she fastened the door of the little parlour, lest the children should see what was lying there. Then, with peace sunk heavy on her heart, she went about making tidy the kitchen. She knew she submitted

to life, which was her immediate master. But from death, her ultimate master, she winced with fear and shame.

THE HORSE DEALER'S DAUGHTER

"Well, Mabel, and what are you going to do with yourself ?" asked Joe, with foolish flippancy. He felt quite safe himself. Without listening for an answer, he turned aside, worked a grain of tobacco to the tip of his tongue, and spat it out. He did not care about anything, since he felt safe himself.

The three brothers and the sister sat round the desolate breakfast table, attempting some sort of desultory consultation. The morning's post had given the final tap to the family fortune, and all was over. The dreary dining-room itself, with its heavy mahogany furniture, looked as if it were waiting to be done away with.

But the consultation amounted to nothing. There was a strange air of ineffectuality about the three men, as they sprawled at table, smoking and reflecting vaguely on their own condition. The girl was alone, a rather short, sullen-looking young woman of twenty-seven. She did not share the same life as her brothers. She would have been good-looking, save for the impassive fixity of her face, "bull-dog," as her brothers called it.

There was a confused tramping of horses' feet outside. The three men all sprawled round in their chairs to watch. Beyond the dark holly-bushes that separated the strip of lawn from the highroad, they could see a cavalcade of shire horses[1] swinging out of their own yard, being taken for exercise. This was the last time. These were the last horses that would go through their hands. The young men watched with critical, callous look. They were all frightened at the collapse of their lives, and the sense of disaster in which they were involved left them no inner freedom.

Yet they were three fine, well-set fellows enough. Joe, the eldest, was a man of thirty-three, broad and handsome in a hot, flushed way. His face was red, he twisted his black moustache over a thick finger, his eyes were shallow and restless. He had a sensual way of uncovering his teeth when he laughed, and his bearing was stupid. Now he watched the horses with a glazed look of helplessness in his eyes, a certain stupor of downfall.

The great draught-horses swung past. They were tied head to tail, four of them, and they heaved along to where a lane branched off from the highroad, planting their great hoofs floutingly in the fine black mud, swinging their great rounded haunches sumptuously, and trotting a few sudden steps as they were led into the lane, round the corner. Every movement showed a massive, slumbrous strength, and a stupidity which held them in subjection. The groom at the head looked back, jerking the leading rope. And the cavalcade moved out of sight up the lane, the tail of the last horse bobbed up tight and stiff, held out taut from the swinging great haunches as they rocked behind the hedges in a motion like sleep.

Joe watched with glazed hopeless eyes. The horses were almost like his own body to him. He felt he was done for now. Luckily he was engaged to

[1] A breed of draft horses, bred in the English Midlands.

a woman as old as himself, and therefore her father, who was steward of a neighbouring estate, would provide him with a job. He would marry and go into harness. His life was over, he would be a subject animal now.

He turned uneasily aside, the retreating steps of the horses echoing in his ears. Then, with foolish restlessness, he reached for the scraps of bacon-rind from the plates, and making a faint whistling sound, flung them to the terrier that lay against the fender. He watched the dog swallow them, and waited till the creature looked into his eyes. Then a faint grin came on his face, and in a high, foolish voice he said:

"You won't get much more bacon, shall you, you little bitch?"

The dog faintly and dismally wagged its tail, then lowered its haunches, circled round, and lay down again.

There was another helpless silence at the table. Joe sprawled uneasily in his seat, not willing to go till the family conclave was dissolved. Fred Henry, the second brother, was erect, clean-limbed, alert. He had watched the passing of the horses with more sang-froid.[2] If he was an animal, like Joe, he was an animal which controls, not one which is controlled. He was master of any horse, and he carried himself with a well-tempered air of mastery. But he was not master of the situations of life. He pushed his coarse brown moustache upwards, off his lip, and glanced irritably at his sister, who sat impassive and inscrutable.

"You'll go and stop with Lucy for a bit, shan't you?" he asked. The girl did not answer.

"I don't see what else you can do," persisted Fred Henry.

"Go as a skivvy,"[3] Joe interpolated laconically.

The girl did not move a muscle.

"If I was her, I should go in for training for a nurse," said Malcolm, the youngest of them all. He was the baby of the family, a young man of twenty-two, with a fresh, jaunty *museau*.[4]

But Mabel did not take any notice of him. They had talked at her and round her for so many years, that she hardly heard them at all.

The marble clock on the mantelpiece softly chimed the half-hour, the dog rose uneasily from the hearthrug and looked at the party at the breakfast table. But still they sat on in ineffectual conclave.

"Oh, all right," said Joe suddenly, apropos of nothing. "I'll get a move on."

He pushed back his chair, straddled his knees with a downward jerk, to get them free, in horsey fashion, and went to the fire. Still he did not go out of the room; he was curious to know what the others would do or say. He began to charge his pipe, looking down at the dog and saying, in a high, affected voice:

"Going wi' me? Going wi' me are ter? Tha'rt goin' further than tha counts on just now, dost hear?"

The dog faintly wagged its tail, the man stuck out his jaw and covered his pipe with his hands, and puffed intently, losing himself in the tobacco, looking down all the while at the dog with an absent brown eye. The dog

[2] Coolness, composure. [3] Servant.
[4] Face (French slang; literally "muzzle" or "snout").

looked up at him in mournful distrust. Joe stood with his knees stuck out, in real horsey fashion.

"Have you had a letter from Lucy?" Fred Henry asked of his sister.

"Last week," came the neutral reply.

"And what does she say?"

There was no answer.

"Does she *ask* you to go and stop there?" persisted Fred Henry.

"She says I can if I like."

"Well, then, you'd better. Tell her you'll come on Monday."

This was received in silence.

"That's what you'll do then, is it?" said Fred Henry, in some exasperation.

But she made no answer. There was a silence of futility and irritation in the room. Malcolm grinned fatuously.

"You'll have to make up your mind between now and next Wednesday," said Joe loudly, "or else find yourself lodgings on the kerbstone."

The face of the young woman darkened, but she sat on immutable.

"Here's Jack Fergusson!" exclaimed Malcolm, who was looking aimlessly out of the window.

"Where?" exclaimed Joe, loudly.

"Just gone past."

"Coming in?"

Malcolm craned his neck to see the gate.

"Yes," he said.

There was a silence. Mabel sat on like one condemned, at the head of the table. Then a whistle was heard from the kitchen. The dog got up and barked sharply. Joe opened the door and shouted:

"Come on."

After a moment a young man entered. He was muffled up in an overcoat and a purple woollen scarf, and his tweed cap, which he did not remove, was pulled down on his head. He was of medium height, his face was rather long and pale, his eyes looked tired.

"Hello, Jack, Well, Jack!" exclaimed Malcolm and Joe. Fred Henry merely said, "Jack."

"What's doing?" asked the newcomer, evidently addressing Fred Henry.

"Same. We've got to be out by Wednesday. Got a cold?"

"I have—got it bad, too."

"Why don't you stop in?"

"*Me* stop in? When I can't stand on my legs, perhaps I shall have a chance." The young man spoke huskily. He had a slight Scotch accent.

"It's a knock-out, isn't it," said Joe, boisterously, "if a doctor goes round croaking with a cold. Looks bad for the patients, doesn't it?"

The young doctor looked at him slowly.

"Anything the matter with *you*, then?" he asked sarcastically.

"Not as I know of. Damn your eyes, I hope not. Why?"

"I thought you were very concerned about the patients, wondered if you might be one yourself."

"Damn it, no, I've never been patient to no flaming doctor, and hope I never shall be," returned Joe.

At this point Mabel rose from the table, and they all seemed to become aware of her existence. She began putting the dishes together. The young doctor looked at her, but did not address her. He had not greeted her. She went out of the room with the tray, her face impassive and unchanged.

"When are you off then, all of you?" asked the doctor.

"I'm catching the eleven-forty," replied Malcolm. "Are you goin' down wi' th' trap, Joe?"

"Yes, I've told you I'm going down wi' th' trap, haven't I?"

"We'd better be getting her in then. So long, Jack, if I don't see you before I go," said Malcolm, shaking hands.

He went out, followed by Joe, who seemed to have his tail between his legs.

"Well, this is the devil's own," exclaimed the doctor, when he was left alone with Fred Henry. "Going before Wednesday, are you?"

"That's the orders," replied the other.

"Where, to Northampton?"

"That's it."

"The devil!" exclaimed Fergusson, with quiet chagrin.

And there was silence between the two.

"All settled up, are you?" asked Fergusson.

"About."

There was another pause.

"Well, I shall miss yer, Freddy, boy," said the young doctor.

"And I shall miss thee, Jack," returned the other.

"Miss you like hell," mused the doctor.

Fred Henry turned aside. There was nothing to say. Mabel came in again, to finish clearing the table.

"What are *you* going to do, then, Miss Pervin?" asked Fergusson. "Going to your sister's, are you?"

Mabel looked at him with her steady, dangerous eyes, that always made him uncomfortable, unsettling his superficial ease.

"No," she said.

"Well, what in the name of fortune *are* you going to do? Say what you mean to do," cried Fred Henry, with futile intensity.

But she only averted her head, and continued her work. She folded the white table-cloth, and put on the chenille cloth.

"The sulkiest bitch that ever trod!" muttered her brother.

But she finished her task with perfectly impassive face, the young doctor watching her interestedly all the while. Then she went out.

Fred Henry stared after her, clenching his lips, his blue eyes fixing in sharp antagonism, as he made a grimace of sour exasperation.

"You could bray[5] her into bits, and that's all you'd get out of her," he said in a small, narrowed tone.

The doctor smiled faintly.

"What's she *going* to do, then?" he asked.

"Strike me if *I* know!" returned the other.

There was a pause. Then the doctor stirred.

[5] Break.

"I'll be seeing you to-night, shall I?" he said to his friend.

"Ay—where's it to be? Are we going over to Jessdale?"

"I don't know. I've got such a cold on me. I'll come round to the Moon and Stars, anyway."

"Let Lizzie and May miss their night for once, eh?"

"That's it—if I feel as I do now."

"All's one—"

The two young men went through the passage and down to the back door together. The house was large, but it was servantless now, and desolate. At the back was a small bricked house-yard, and beyond that a big square, gravelled fine and red, and having stables on two sides. Sloping, dank, winter-dark fields stretched away on the open sides.

But the stables were empty. Joseph Pervin, the father of the family, had been a man of no education, who had become a fairly large horse dealer. The stables had been full of horses, there was a great turmoil and come-and-go of horses and of dealers and grooms. Then the kitchen was full of servants. But of late things had declined. The old man had married a second time, to retrieve his fortunes. Now he was dead and everything was gone to the dogs, there was nothing but debt and threatening.

For months, Mabel had been servantless in the big house, keeping the home together in penury for her ineffectual brothers. She had kept house for ten years. But previously it was with unstinted means. Then, however brutal and coarse everything was, the sense of money had kept her proud, confident. The men might be foul-mouthed, the women in the kitchen might have bad reputations, her brothers might have illegitimate children. But so long as there was money, the girl felt herself established, and brutally proud, reserved.

No company came to the house, save dealers and coarse men. Mabel had no associates of her own sex, after her sister went away. But she did not mind. She went regularly to church, she attended to her father. And she lived in the memory of her mother, who had died when she was fourteen, and whom she had loved. She had loved her father, too, in a different way, depending upon him, and feeling secure in him, until at the age of fifty-four he married again. And then she had set hard against him. Now he had died and left them all hopelessly in debt.

She had suffered badly during the period of poverty. Nothing, however, could shake the curious sullen, animal pride that dominated each member of the family. Now, for Mabel, the end had come. Still she would not cast about her. She would follow her own way just the same. She would always hold the keys of her own situation. Mindless and persistent, she endured from day to day. Why should she think? Why should she answer anybody? It was enough that this was the end, and there was no way out. She need not pass any more darkly along the main street of the small town, avoiding every eye. She need not demean herself any more, going into the shops and buying the cheapest food. This was at an end. She thought of nobody, not even of herself. Mindless and persistent, she seemed in a sort of ecstasy to be coming nearer to her fulfilment, her own glorification, approaching her dead mother, who was glorified.

In the afternoon she took a little bag, with shears and sponge and a

small scrubbing brush, and went out. It was a grey, wintry day, with saddened, dark green fields and an atmosphere blackened by the smoke of foundries not far off. She went quickly, darkly along the causeway, heeding nobody, through the town to the churchyard.

There she always felt secure, as if no one could see her, although as a matter of fact she was exposed to the stare of every one who passed along under the churchyard wall. Nevertheless, once under the shadow of the great looming church, among the graves, she felt immune from the world, reserved within the thick churchyard wall as in another country.

Carefully she clipped the grass from the grave, and arranged the pinky white, small chrysanthemums in the tin cross. When this was done, she took an empty jar from a neighbouring grave, brought water, and carefully, most scrupulously sponged the marble head-stone and the coping-stone.

It gave her sincere satisfaction to do this. She felt in immediate contact with the world of her mother. She took minute pains, went through the park in a state bordering on pure happiness, as if in performing this task she came into a subtle, intimate connection with her mother. For the life she followed here in the world was far less real than the world of death she inherited from her mother.

The doctor's house was just by the church. Fergusson, being a mere hired assistant, was slave to the country-side. As he hurried now to attend to the outpatients in the surgery, glancing across the graveyard with his quick eye, he saw the girl at her task at the grave. She seemed so intent and remote, it was like looking into another world. Some mystical element was touched in him. He slowed down as he walked, watching her as if spell-bound.

She lifted her eyes, feeling him looking. Their eyes met. And each looked away again at once, each feeling, in some way, found out by the other. He lifted his cap and passed on down the road. There remained distinct in his consciousness, like a vision, the memory of her face, lifted from the tombstone in the churchyard, and looking at him with slow, large, portentous eyes. It *was* portentous, her face. It seemed to mesmerize him. There was a heavy power in her eyes which laid hold of his whole being, as if he had drunk some powerful drug. He had been feeling weak and done before. Now the life came back into him, he felt delivered from his own fretted, daily self.

He finished his duties at the surgery as quickly as might be, hastily filling up the bottles of the waiting people with cheap drugs. Then, in perpetual haste, he set off again to visit several cases in another part of his round, before teatime. At all times he preferred to walk if he could, but particularly when he was not well. He fancied the motion restored him.

The afternoon was falling. It was grey, deadened, and wintry, with a slow, moist, heavy coldness sinking in and deadening all the faculties. But why should he think or notice? He hastily climbed the hill and turned across the dark green fields, following the black cinder-track. In the distance, across a shallow dip in the country, the small town was clustered like smouldering ash, a tower, a spire, a heap of low, raw, extinct houses. And on the nearest fringe of the town, sloping into the dip, was Oldmeadow, the Pervins' house. He could see the stables and the outbuildings distinctly, as they lay towards him on the slope. Well, he would not go there many more

times! Another resource would be lost to him, another place gone: the only company he cared for in the alien, ugly little town he was losing. Nothing but work, drudgery, constant hastening from dwelling to dwelling among the colliers and the ironworkers. It wore him out, but at the same time he had a craving for it. It was a stimulant to him to be in the homes of the working people, moving as it were through the innermost body of their life. His nerves were excited and gratified. He could come so near, into the very lives of the rough, inarticulate, powerfully emotional men and women. He grumbled, he said he hated the hellish hole. But as a matter of fact it excited him, the contact with the rough, strongly-feeling people was a stimulant applied direct to his nerves.

Below Oldmeadow, in the green, shallow, soddened hollow of fields, lay a square, deep pond. Roving across the landscape, the doctor's quick eye detected a figure in black passing through the gate of the field, down towards the pond. He looked again. It would be Mabel Pervin. His mind suddenly became alive and attentive.

Why was she going down there? He pulled up on the path on the slope above, and stood staring. He could just make sure of the small black figure moving in the hollow of the failing day. He seemed to see her in the midst of such obscurity, that he was like a clairvoyant, seeing rather with the mind's eye than with ordinary sight. Yet he could see her positively enough, whilst he kept his eye attentive. He felt, if he looked away from her, in the thick, ugly falling dusk, he would lose her altogether.

He followed her minutely as she moved, direct and intent, like something transmitted rather than stirring in voluntary activity, straight down the field towards the pond. There she stood on the bank for a moment. She never raised her head. Then she waded slowly into the water.

He stood motionless as the small black figure walked slowly and deliberately towards the centre of the pond, very slowly, gradually moving deeper into the motionless water, and still moving forward as the water got up to her breast. Then he could see her no more in the dusk of the dead afternoon.

"There!" he exclaimed. "Would you believe it?"

And he hastened straight down, running over the wet, soddened fields, pushing through the hedges, down into the depression of callous wintry obscurity. It took him several minutes to come to the pond. He stood on the bank, breathing heavily. He could see nothing. His eyes seemed to penetrate the dead water. Yes, perhaps that was the dark shadow of her black clothing beneath the surface of the water.

He slowly ventured into the pond. The bottom was deep, soft clay, he sank in, and the water clasped dead cold round his legs. As he stirred he could smell the cold, rotten clay that fouled up into the water. It was objectionable in his lungs. Still, repelled and yet not heeding, he moved deeper into the pond. The cold water rose over his thighs, over his loins, upon his abdomen. The lower part of his body was all sunk in the hideous cold element. And the bottom was so deeply soft and uncertain, he was afraid of pitching with his mouth underneath. He could not swim, and was afraid.

He crouched a little, spreading his hands under the water and moving them round, trying to feel for her. The dead cold pond swayed upon his chest. He moved again, a little deeper, and again, with his hands under-

neath, he felt all around under the water. And he touched her clothing. But it evaded his fingers. He made a desperate effort to grasp it.

And so doing he lost his balance and went under, horribly, suffocating in the foul earthy water, struggling madly for a few moments. At last, after what seemed an eternity, he got his footing, rose again into the air and looked around. He gasped, and knew he was in the world. Then he looked at the water. She had risen near him. He grasped her clothing, and drawing her nearer, turned to take his way to land again.

He went very slowly, carefully, absorbed in the slow progress. He rose higher, climbing out of the pond. The water was now only about his legs; he was thankful, full of relief to be out of the clutches of the pond. He lifted her and staggered on to the bank, out of the horror of wet, grey clay.

He laid her down on the bank. She was quite unconscious and running with water. He made the water come from her mouth, he worked to restore her. He did not have to work very long before he could feel the breathing begin again in her; she was breathing naturally. He worked a little longer. He could feel her live beneath his hands; she was coming back. He wiped her face, wrapped her in his overcoat, looked round into the dim, dark grey world, then lifted her and staggered down the bank and across the fields.

It seemed an unthinkably long way, and his burden so heavy he felt he would never get to the house. But at last he was in the stable-yard, and then in the house-yard. He opened the door and went into the house. In the kitchen he laid her down on the hearthrug, and called. The house was empty. But the fire was burning in the grate.

Then again he kneeled to attend to her. She was breathing regularly, her eyes were wide open and as if conscious, but there seemed something missing in her look. She was conscious in herself, but unconscious of her surroundings.

He ran upstairs, took blankets from a bed, and put them before the fire to warm. Then he removed her saturated, earthy-smelling clothing, rubbed her dry with a towel, and wrapped her naked in the blankets. Then he went into the dining-room, to look for spirits. There was a little whisky. He drank a gulp himself, and put some into her mouth.

The effect was instantaneous. She looked full into his face, as if she had been seeing him for some time, and yet had only just become conscious of him.

"Dr. Fergusson?" she said.

"What?" he answered.

He was divesting himself of his coat, intending to find some dry clothing upstairs. He could not bear the smell of the dead, clayey water, and he was mortally afraid for his own health.

"What did I do?" she asked.

"Walked into the pond," he replied. He had begun to shudder like one sick, and could hardly attend to her. Her eyes remained full on him, he seemed to be going dark in his mind, looking back at her helplessly. The shuddering became quieter in him, his life came back in him, dark and unknowing, but strong again.

"Was I out of my mind?" she asked, while her eyes were fixed on him all the time.

"Maybe, for the moment," he replied. He felt quiet, because his strength had come back. The strange fretful strain had left him.

"Am I out of my mind now?" she asked.

"Are you?" he reflected a moment. "No," he answered truthfully, "I don't see that you are." He turned his face aside. He was afraid now, because he felt dazed, and felt dimly that her power was stronger than his, in this issue. And she continued to look at him fixedly all the time. "Can you tell me where I shall find some dry things to put on?" he asked.

"Did you dive into the pond for me?" she asked.

"No," he answered. "I walked in. But I went in overhead as well."

There was silence for a moment. He hesitated. He very much wanted to go upstairs to get into dry clothing. But there was another desire in him. And she seemed to hold him. His will seemed to have gone to sleep, and left him, standing there slack before her. But he felt warm inside himself. He did not shudder at all, though his clothes were sodden on him.

"Why did you?" she asked.

"Because I didn't want you to do such a foolish thing," he said.

"It wasn't foolish," she said, still gazing at him as she lay on the floor, with a sofa cushion under her head. "It was the right thing to do. *I* knew best, then."

"I'll go and shift these wet things," he said. But still he had not the power to move out of her presence, until she sent him. It was as if she had the life of his body in her hands, and he could not extricate himself. Or perhaps he did not want to.

Suddenly she sat up. Then she became aware of her own immediate condition. She felt the blankets about her, she knew her own limbs. For a moment it seemed as if her reason were going. She looked round, with wild eye, as if seeking something. He stood still with fear. She saw her clothing lying scattered.

"Who undressed me?" she asked, her eyes resting full and inevitable on his face.

"I did," he replied, "to bring you round."

For some moments she sat and gazed at him awfully, her lips parted.

"Do you love me, then?" she asked.

He only stood and stared at her, fascinated. His soul seemed to melt.

She shuffled forward on her knees, and put her arms round him, round his legs, as he stood there, pressing her breasts against his knees and thighs, clutching him with strange, convulsive certainty, pressing his thighs against her, drawing him to her face, her throat, as she looked up at him with flaring, humble eyes of transfiguration, triumphant in first possession.

"You love me," she murmured, in strange transport, yearning and triumphant and confident. "You love me. I know you love me, I know."

And she was passionately kissing his knees, through the wet clothing, passionately and indiscriminately kissing his knees, his legs, as if unaware of everything.

He looked down at the tangled wet hair, the wild, bare, animal shoulders. He was amazed, bewildered, and afraid. He had never thought of loving her. He had never wanted to love her. When he rescued her and restored her, he was a doctor, and she was a patient. He had had no single personal thought of her. Nay, this introduction of the personal element

was very distasteful to him, a violation of his professional honour. It was horrible to have her there embracing his knees. It was horrible. He revolted from it, violently. And yet—and yet—he had not the power to break away.

She looked at him again, with the same supplication of powerful love, and that same transcendent, frightening light of triumph. In view of the delicate flame which seemed to come from her face like a light, he was powerless. And yet he had never intended to love her. He had never intended. And something stubborn in him could not give way.

"You love me," she repeated, in a murmur of deep rhapsodic assurance. "You love me."

Her hands were drawing him, drawing him down to her. He was afraid, even a little horrified. For he had, really, no intention of loving her. Yet her hands were drawing him towards her. He put out his hand quickly to steady himself, and grasped her bare shoulder. A flame seemed to burn the hand that grasped her soft shoulder. He had no intention of loving her: his whole will was against his yielding. It was horrible. And yet wonderful was the touch of her shoulders, beautiful the shining of her face. Was she perhaps mad? He had a horror of yielding to her. Yet something in him ached also.

He had been staring away at the door, away from her. But his hand remained on her shoulder. She had gone suddenly very still. He looked down at her. Her eyes were now wide with fear, with doubt, the light was dying from her face, a shadow of terrible greyness was returning. He could not bear the touch of her eyes' question upon him, and the look of death behind the question.

With an inward groan he gave way, and let his heart yield towards her. A sudden gentle smile came on his face. And her eyes, which never left his face, slowly, slowly filled with tears. He watched the strange water rise in her eyes, like some slow fountain coming up. And his heart seemed to burn and melt away in his breast.

He could not bear to look at her any more. He dropped on his knees, caught her head with his arms and pressed her face against his throat. She was very still. His heart, which seemed to have broken, was burning with a kind of agony in his breast. And he felt her slow, hot tears wetting his throat. But he could not move.

He felt the hot tears wet his neck and the hollows of his neck, and he remained motionless, suspended through one of man's eternities. Only now it had become indispensable to him to have her face pressed close to him; he could never let her go again. He could never let her head go away from the close clutch of his arm. He wanted to remain like that for ever, with his heart hurting him in a pain that was also life to him. Without knowing, he was looking down on her damp, soft brown hair.

Then, as it were suddenly, he smelt the horrid stagnant smell of that water. And at the same moment she drew away from him and looked at him. Her eyes were wistful and unfathomable. He was afraid of them, and he fell to kissing her, not knowing what he was doing. He wanted her eyes not to have that terrible, wistful, unfathomable look.

When she turned her face to him again, a faint delicate flush was glowing, and there was again dawning that terrible shining of joy in her eyes,

which really terrified him, and yet which he now wanted to see, because he feared the look of doubt still more.

"You love me?" she said, rather faltering.

"Yes." The word cost him a painful effort. Not because it wasn't true. But because it was too newly true, the *saying* seemed to tear open again his newly-torn heart. And he hardly wanted it to be true, even now.

She lifted her face to him, and he bent forward and kissed her on the mouth, gently, with the one kiss that is an eternal pledge. And as he kissed her his heart strained again in his breast. He never intended to love her. But now it was over. He had crossed over the gulf to her, and all that he had left behind had shrivelled and become void.

After the kiss, her eyes again slowly filled with tears. She sat still, away from him, with her face drooped aside, and her hands folded in her lap. The tears fell very slowly. There was complete silence. He too sat there motionless and silent on the hearthrug. The strange pain of his heart that was broken seemed to consume him. That he should love her? That this was love! That he should be ripped open in this way! Him, a doctor! How they would all jeer if they knew! It was agony to him to think they might know.

In the curious naked pain of the thought he looked again to her. She was sitting there drooped into a muse. He saw a tear fall, and his heart flared hot. He saw for the first time that one of her shoulders was quite uncovered, one arm bare, he could see one of her small breasts; dimly, because it had become almost dark in the room.

"Why are you crying?" he asked, in an altered voice.

She looked up at him, and behind her tears the consciousness of her situation for the first time brought a dark look of shame to her eyes.

"I'm not crying, really," she said, watching him half frightened.

He reached his hand, and softly closed it on her bare arm.

"I love you! I love you!" he said in a soft, low vibrating voice, unlike himself.

She shrank, and dropped her head. The soft, penetrating grip of his hand on her arm distressed her. She looked up at him.

"I want to go," she said. "I want to go and get you some dry things."

"Why?" he said. "I'm all right."

"But I want to go," she said. "And I want you to change your things."

He released her arm, and she wrapped herself in the blanket, looking at him rather frightened. And still she did not rise.

"Kiss me," she said wistfully.

He kissed her, but briefly, half in anger.

Then, after a second, she rose nervously, all mixed up in the blanket. He watched her in her confusion, as she tried to extricate herself and wrap herself up so that she could walk. He watched her relentlessly, as she knew. And as she went, the blanket trailing, and as he saw a glimpse of her feet and her white leg, he tried to remember her as she was when he had wrapped her in the blanket. But then he didn't want to remember, because she had been nothing to him then, and his nature revolted from remembering her as she was when she was nothing to him.

A tumbling, muffled noise from within the dark house startled him. Then he heard her voice:—"There are clothes." He rose and went to the

foot of the stairs, and gathered up the garments she had thrown down. Then he came back to the fire, to rub himself down and dress. He grinned at his own appearance when he had finished.

The fire was sinking, so he put on coal. The house was now quite dark, save for the light of a street-lamp that shone in faintly from beyond the holly trees. He lit the gas with matches he found on the mantelpiece. Then he emptied the pockets of his own clothes, and threw all his wet things in a heap into the scullery. After which he gathered up her sodden clothes, gently, and put them in a separate heap on the copper-top in the scullery.

It was six o'clock on the clock. His own watch had stopped. He ought to go back to the surgery. He waited, and still she did not come down. So he went to the foot of the stairs and called:

"I shall have to go."

Almost immediately he heard her coming down. She had on her best dress of black voile, and her hair was tidy, but still damp. She looked at him—and in spite of herself, smiled.

"I don't like you in those clothes," she said.

"Do I look a sight?" he answered.

They were shy of one another.

"I'll make you some tea," she said.

"No, I must go."

"Must you?" And she looked at him again with the wide, strained, doubtful eyes. And again, from the pain of his breast, he knew how he loved her. He went and bent to kiss her, gently, passionately, with his heart's painful kiss.

"And my hair smells so horrible," she murmured in distraction. "And I'm so awful, I'm so awful! Oh, no, I'm too awful." And she broke into bitter, heartbroken sobbing. "You can't want to love me, I'm horrible."

"Don't be silly, don't be silly," he said, trying to comfort her, kissing her, holding her in his arms. "I want you, I want to marry you, we're going to be married, quickly, quickly—tomorrow if I can."

But she only sobbed terribly, and cried:

"I feel awful. I feel awful. I feel I'm horrible to you."

"No, I want you, I want you," was all he answered, blindly, with that terrible intonation which frightened her almost more than her horror lest he should *not* want her.

T. S. Eliot
(1888–1965)

"Our civilization comprehends great variety and complexity, and this variety and complexity, playing upon a refined sensibility, must produce various and complex results. The poet must become more and more comprehensive, more allusive, more indirect, in order to force, to dislocate if

necessary, language into his meaning." These lines, from T. S. Eliot's 1921 essay on "The Metaphysical Poets," come as close to describing and justifying the sometimes frustrating difficulties of modern poetry as any short statement could. And the image of the modern poet that they present—a "refined sensibility" bombarded by "great variety and complexity" and shattering and distorting his language in order to express that complexity—is a precise description of the quintessential modern poet, Eliot himself. As poet, critic, editor, and playwright, Eliot exerted an enormous influence on literature between the two wars, not only in England but internationally; the critic Richard Ellmann has pointed out that "for a span of years the latest verses in Arabic, Swahili, or Japanese were far more likely to be written like Eliot than like earlier poets in those languages or like other poets in English." And if contemporary poets are not so directly overwhelmed by Eliot's magisterial presence, they still build upon the general foundations that he laid down early in the century.

Thomas Stearns Eliot was born in St. Louis, Missouri, in 1888, into a prosperous, prominent family that had moved to Missouri from Massachusetts two generations before. Eliot's grandfather, who had come to St. Louis just after graduation from Harvard Divinity School, founded the first Unitarian church in St. Louis and established Washington University there. His son, the poet's father, departed somewhat from family tradition by going into business; he became a prosperous brick manufacturer. Eliot's mother, Charlotte Champe Stearns, had literary interests; she wrote poetry, a biography of her father-in-law, and a verse drama about the fifteenth-century religious reformer Savonarola. Many of Eliot's mature beliefs—his respect for tradition, his religious leanings, his class biases—can be traced back to his displaced New England family.

Eliot was educated at private schools in St. Louis and Massachusetts and then at Harvard, where he enrolled in 1906 and received a degree in philosophy only three years later. Two of his Harvard teachers, George Santayana and Irving Babbitt, exercised a continuing influence upon him; from Babbitt, especially, he acquired a strong anti-Romantic attitude. The following five years were full of turbulence and indecision for Eliot. He enrolled in graduate school in philosophy at Harvard where he was a teaching assistant for a year and then went to Paris to attend lectures by the philosopher Henri Bergson. While in France he read widely in the French Symbolist poets. The Symbolist movement, which had as its goal the expression of unique, personal, emotional responses at given moments through symbols that were often indefinite, apparently illogical, and sometimes private in their meaning, was to be one of the major influences upon Eliot's poetry. Charles Baudelaire, Jules Laforgue, and Stéphane Mallarmé were especially impressive figures for him. After two years back at Harvard, during which he read widely in Sanskrit and Oriental philosophy, Eliot returned to Europe on a travel grant; when war broke out, he settled in London. By 1915, he had decided to give up philosophy to pursue a career as a writer, to remain in England permanently, and to marry. He supported himself first by teaching French and Latin in a grammar school, and then, for eight years, by working as a clerk in Lloyd's Bank. He married Vivien Haigh-Wood in 1915. His wife was subject to bouts of mental illness and the marriage was desperately unhappy, although they remained together for sev-

enteen years, before separating in 1932. Eliot completed his Ph.D. thesis on the philosophy of F. H. Bradley in 1916, but the war prevented his returning to Harvard for his final oral examination and he never received the degree. Bradley's philosophy, which emphasized the uniqueness of individual experience, was to have a continuing influence upon Eliot's thought and poetry.

Eliot had written "The Love Song of J. Alfred Prufrock" in 1910, but it was not published until 1915, after Eliot's friend Ezra Pound had sent it to Harriet Monroe, editor of the famous *Poetry* magazine in Chicago, and persuaded her to publish it, despite her initial judgment that it was "not poetry." Its publication in *Poetry* and as part of the collection *Prufrock and Other Observations* (1917) has been compared to the publication of William Wordsworth's and Samuel Taylor Coleridge's *Lyrical Ballads* in 1798; both inaugurated new ages in English poetry. The timid, anti-Romantic protagonist of "Prufrock," its dry, ironic tone, and its startlingly fresh imagery presented a model for modernist poetry that was to influence several generations of poets throughout the world.

The years from 1915 to 1921 were difficult for Eliot. Financial and marital problems and a punishing schedule of work at the bank, voluminous journalism, and intensive poetic composition led him to a severe mental breakdown in 1921. Friends were able to arrange a leave of absence from the bank and complete rest and psychiatric care in Switzerland. He took the manuscript of *The Waste Land* with him and with the editorial assistance of Ezra Pound gave the poem its final form. Its publication in 1922, first in Eliot's own review, the *Criterion*, then in the American *Dial*, and finally in book form, is generally regarded as the single most important event in the history of modern poetry. The promise of "The Love Song of J. Alfred Prufrock" was amply fulfilled in this frightening collage of fragments of memories, overheard conversations, and quotations, welded together only by the implied presence of a "refined sensibility" upon whom all this "variety and complexity" are being heaped and who staggers under their burden. Not even Eliot, apparently, was prepared either for the violent opposition to the poem ("a piece of tripe," was Amy Lowell's judgment) or for the fervency with which its admirers regarded it as the definitive description of their age. He regarded the claim that the poem expressed "the disillusionment of a generation" as "nonsense"; "I may have expressed for them," he wrote, "their own illusion of being disillusioned, but that did not form part of my intention." Nevertheless, the phrase *waste land* entered the language, along with *jazz age* and *lost generation*, as a definitive term for post-World War I disillusionment.

In 1925, Eliot was able to leave Lloyd's Bank and join the publishing firm of Faber and Faber as an editor, a position he retained for the rest of his life. His reputation as a critic had already begun to rival his stature as a poet, and in a series of volumes of essays, he developed a critical position second only to his own poetic practice in its influence upon modern poetry: *The Sacred Wood* (1920), *Homage to John Dryden* (1924), *For Lancelot Andrewes* (1928), and *Selected Essays* (1932).

Eliot's development after *The Waste Land* was steadily in the direction of literary, political, and religious conservatism and orthodoxy. In 1927, he became both an Anglo-Catholic and a British subject and was able to de-

scribe himself, apparently with a minimum of irony, as "classicist in litera-
ture, royalist in politics, and anglo-catholic in religion." The first major
poetic fruit of his conversion was "Ash-Wednesday" (1930), a poem based
on the Anglican service and the Christian ascetic disciplines. The *Four
Quartets*, long, interrelated poems that explored mystical experience, each
with a five-part "meditative" structure like that of *The Waste Land*, began to
appear in 1936 and were completed in 1943. Some critics have regarded
the *Four Quartets* as Eliot's masterpiece; others have found them garrulous,
mannered, and lacking in the intensity of the earlier poetry.

Much of Eliot's energy in his later years was devoted to an attempt to
create a modern poetic drama. His first completed play, *Murder in the Cathe-
dral* (1935), revived the style of Greek tragedy to tell the story of Thomas à
Becket's martyrdom. In his later plays—*The Family Reunion* (1939), *The
Cocktail Party* (1950), *The Confidential Clerk* (1954), and *The Elder Statesman*
(1959)—he turned instead to the form of modern high comedy, in the
manner of Noel Coward, a form which coexisted rather uneasily with the
plays' mythic and religious themes.

Vivien Eliot died in 1947; the couple had lived apart for the last fifteen
years of her life. In 1957, Eliot married Valerie Fletcher and seems to have
experienced a long-delayed personal happiness and peace. He died in
1965, at the age of seventy-seven.

Eliot's major poems are all essentially dramatic monologues of a start-
lingly innovative kind. Prufrock is a speaker so timid that, if we are to
believe the epigraph, he can persuade himself to talk only on the assurance
that what he says will never be heard. He seems to be speaking to himself.
Eliot denied that the "you and I" of the first line are merely two sides of
Prufrock and said that "you" was a male companion, but it hardly matters,
since Prufrock's self-preoccupation is so complete that any second party
functions only as a mirror for himself. His soliloquy is a "love song" only in
the most ironic sense; the whole poem is an elaborate rationalization for
not seeking love. Love remains, for Prufrock, beneath the layers of fear,
self-consciousness, and self-hate, only as a hopeless, fantasized yearning for
the vitality of "a pair of ragged claws" and of "the mermaids singing, each
to each."

The Waste Land is probably also best read as a dramatic monologue.
Eliot's original title, as we now know from the publication of the original
manuscript in 1971, was "He Do the Police in Different Voices." This line is
from Dickens's *Our Mutual Friend*, from a scene in which a widow praises her
adopted son, Sloppy: "I do love a newspaper," she says. "You mightn't think it,
but Sloppy is a beautiful reader of a newspaper. He do the Police in different
voices." *The Waste Land* retains something of this air of a bravura display of
mimicry. But who is the mimic? Eliot muddied the issue in his notes by identify-
ing Tiresias as "the most important personage in the poem, uniting all the rest."
But Tiresias cannot literally be the central consciousness, except perhaps as the
most comprehensive of the many avatars of the speaker in this poem in which
all the men are one man, all the women are one woman, and "the two sexes meet
in Tiresias." The speaker of *The Waste Land* is the "refined sensibility" of Eliot's
essay on the Metaphysical poets, upon whom the variety and complexity of the
modern world are impinging. His mind is packed with cultural tradition—an
anthropological account of the Grail legend, *The Divine Comedy*, the operas of

Wagner, the story of the Crucifixion, French Symbolist poetry, and Jacobean drama—as well as such scraps of popular culture as music hall songs, bits of slang, and contemporary fashions. These bits of "found material" are set into a matrix of the flowing stream of consciousness of a man at the end of his tether, desperately shoring fragments against his ruin. Paradoxically, this portrait of an age gains its power from being first a dramatic portrait of a single mind.

"Burnt Norton" (like the *Four Quartets* as a whole) deals with a single question: "Of what significance in our lives are ecstatic, intense moments when we seem to escape time and glimpse a supraordinary reality?" The two epigraphs from Heraclitus, at first affixed to "Burnt Norton" and later extended to all four Quartets, are important clues to the direction the answer will take. The first contrasts the general wisdom of the race with moments of private, individual insight. It also suggests the dualism of the individual's status both as part of the body of mankind, located in history and tradition, and as a unique person. The second epigraph—"The way up and the way down are one and the same"—suggests another duality, between two ways of apprehending the timeless truths that underlie the surface of life: an active embrace of ecstatic experience ("the way up") and a passive withdrawal from experience into the self ("the way down"). (At least that is what they suggest as Eliot develops them; they mean something rather different in their original Heraclitian contexts.)

The *Four Quartets*, including "Burnt Norton," have a reputation for great obscurity, a reputation reinforced by critics who have emphasized their philosophical content. But despite their philosophical richness, they are far from inaccessible. For one thing, they are built upon the materials of ordinary experience. "Burnt Norton," and eventually the Quartets as a whole, grow out of the experience in the rose-garden described in the first movement, a subtle and provocative incident but one that is eminently concrete and understandable. The third movement is similarly built from commonplace materials: a ride on a subway. The beautiful lyric that constitutes the fourth movement, however heavy its symbolic overlay, remains a remarkably simple description of nightfall, with a bird's wing catching the last rays of the sun.

For another thing, the Quartets, as their collective title suggests, are intensely musical. Eliot's model is the string quartet. Because of their complexity and because they were written late in the poet's life, the Quartets have often been loosely compared with the late quartets of Beethoven, but the specific model, according to Eliot, was the Quartets, nos. 2–6, of the Hungarian composer Béla Bartók. In an essay called "The Music of Poetry," written while he was at work on the *Four Quartets*, Eliot wrote: "I believe that the properties in which music concerns the poet most nearly are the sense of rhythm and the sense of structure. . . . The use of recurrent themes is as natural to poetry as to music. There are possibilities for verse which bear some analogy to the development of a theme by different groups of instruments; there are possibilities of transitions in a poem comparable to the different moments of a symphony or a quartet; there are possibilities of contrapuntal arrangement of subject matter." Eliot explores all these possibilities in "Burnt Norton," in the poem's division into five "movements," in the multivoiced texture analogous to the four instrumental voices in a string quartet, in the use of motifs that return like musi-

cal themes (birds, roses, light, and many others), and, most important, in the varied verbal music of the language, from the grave notes of the opening lines, to the fluent quick-tempo of the rose-garden scene and the magical incantations of the "Time and the bell" lyric.

FURTHER READING *(prepared by J. H.)*: The fullest biography of Eliot (who distrusted biographers and wanted to remain "invisible" behind his work) is that by Peter Ackroyd: *T. S. Eliot: A Life,* 1984. Good general treatments of Eliot's work are Hugh Kenner's *The Invisible Poet,* 1959; Northrop Frye's *T. S. Eliot,* rev. ed. 1968; and Bernard Bergonzi's *T. S. Eliot,* 1972. See also Louis Menaud's *Discovering Modernism: T. S. Eliot and His Context,* 1986. George Williamson's *Reader's Guide to T. S. Eliot,* 2nd ed. 1966, provides poem-by-poem analyses, as does Martin Scofield, *T.S. Eliot: The Poems,* 1988. Basic to the study of *The Waste Land* is *The Waste Land: A Facsimile and Transcript of the Original Drafts Including the Annotations of Ezra Pound,* ed. Valerie Eliot, 1971. A fascinating, if controversial, study of the autobiographical origins of *The Waste Land* is James E. Miller's *T. S. Eliot's Personal Waste Land: Exorcism of the Demons,* 1977. Grover Smith's *"The Waste Land,"* 1983, in the Unwin Critical Library series, is a book-length study of the poem. On "Burnt Norton," see Harry Blamires' *Word Unheard: A Guide Through Eliot's "Four Quartets,"* 1969; *"Four Quartets": A Casebook,* ed. by Bernard Bergonzi, 1969; and Julia M. Reibetanz's *A Reading of T. S. Eliot's "Four Quartets,"* 1983. Derek Traversi's *T. S. Eliot: The Longer Poems,* 1976, includes detailed, sensitive readings of both *The Waste Land* and *Four Quartets. T. S. Eliot: The Critical Heritage,* 2 vols., ed. by Michael Grant, 1982, is a generous collection of criticism, emphasizing initial reception. Another good collection is *T. S. Eliot,* ed. by Harold Bloom, 1985, in the Modern Critical Views series.

THE LOVE SONG
OF J. ALFRED PRUFROCK

> *S'io credesse che mia risposta fosse*
> *A persona che mai tornasse al mondo,*
> *Questa fiamma staria senza piu scosse.*
> *Ma perciocche giammai di questo fondo*
> *Non torno vivo alcun, s'i'odo il vero,*
> *Senza tema d'infamia ti rispondo.*[1]

Let us go then, you and I,
When the evening is spread out against the sky
Like a patient etherised upon a table;
Let us go, through certain half-deserted streets,
The muttering retreats

[1] These words are spoken to Dante by the spirit of Guido da Montefeltro, speaking from a flickering flame in the eighth circle of Hell.
> If I believed that my reply were to anyone
> who would ever return to the world,
> this flame would remain quiet,
> but since no one from this ditch
> has ever returned alive, if I hear the truth,
> I will answer without fear of infamy.
> —(DANTE, *Inferno* XXVII. 61–66)

Of restless nights in one-night cheap hotels
And sawdust restaurants with oyster-shells:
Streets that follow like a tedious argument
Of insidious intent
To lead you to an overwhelming question. . . 10
Oh, do not ask, "What is it?"
Let us go and make our visit.

In the room the women come and go
Talking of Michelangelo.

The yellow fog that rubs its back upon the window-panes,
The yellow smoke that rubs its muzzle on the window-panes
Licked its tongue into the corners of the evening,
Lingered upon the pools that stand in drains,
Let fall upon its back the soot that falls from chimneys,
Slipped by the terrace, made a sudden leap, 20
And seeing that it was a soft October night,
Curled once about the house, and fell asleep.

And indeed there will be time
For the yellow smoke that slides along the street,
Rubbing its back upon the window-panes;
There will be time, there will be time
To prepare a face to meet the faces that you meet;
There will be time to murder and create,
And time for all the works and days[2] of hands
That lift and drop a question on your plate; 30
Time for you and time for me,
And time yet for a hundred indecisions,
And for a hundred visions and revisions,
Before the taking of a toast and tea.

In the room the women come and go
Talking of Michelangelo.

And indeed there will be time
To wonder, "Do I dare?" and, "Do I dare?"
Time to turn back and descend the stair,
With a bald spot in the middle of my hair— 40
[They will say: "How his hair is growing thin!"]
My morning coat, my collar mounting firmly to the chin,
My necktie rich and modest, but asserted by a simple pin—
[They will say: "But how his arms and legs are thin!"]
Do I dare
Disturb the universe?

[2] *works and days.* An allusion to the *Works and Days* of the eighth-century B.C. Greek poet
Hesiod. The allusion is ironic, since the *Works and Days* deals with the real labors of peasants
rather than the idle chatter of this scene.

In a minute there is time
For decisions and revisions which a minute will reverse.

For I have known them all already, known them all:—
Have known the evenings, mornings, afternoons, 50
I have measured out my life with coffee spoons;
I know the voices dying with a dying fall
Beneath the music from a farther room.
 So how should I presume?

And I have known the eyes already, known them all—
The eyes that fix you in a formulated phrase,
And when I am formulated, sprawling on a pin,
When I am pinned and wriggling on the wall,
Then how should I begin
To spit out all the butt-ends of my days and ways? 60
 And how should I presume?

And I have known the arms already, known them all—
Arms that are braceleted and white and bare
[But in the lamplight, downed with light brown hair!]
Is it perfume from a dress
That makes me so digress?
Arms that lie along a table, or wrap about a shawl.
 And should I then presume?
 And how should I begin?

Shall I say, I have gone at dusk through narrow streets 70
And watched the smoke that rises from the pipes
Of lonely men in shirt-sleeves, leaning out of windows? . . .

 I should have been a pair of ragged claws
Scuttling across the floors of silent seas.

And the afternoon, the evening, sleeps so peacefully!
Smoothed by long fingers,
Asleep . . . tired . . . or it malingers,
Stretched on the floor, here beside you and me.
Should I, after tea and cakes and ices,
Have the strength to force the moment to its crisis? 80
But though I have wept and fasted, wept and prayed,
Though I have seen my head [grown slightly bald] brought in upon
 a platter,[3]
I am no prophet—and here's no great matter;
I have seen the moment of my greatness flicker,

[3] John the Baptist was beheaded and his head brought in upon a platter at the request of
Salome. See Matthew 14:1–12.

And I have seen the eternal Footman hold my coat, and snicker,
And in short, I was afraid.

 And would it have been worth it, after all,
After the cups, the marmalade, the tea,
Among the porcelain, among some talk of you and me,
Would it have been worth while, 90
To have bitten off the matter with a smile,
To have squeezed the universe into a ball
To roll it toward some overwhelming question,
To say: "I am Lazarus,[4] come from the dead,
Come back to tell you all, I shall tell you all"—
If one, settling a pillow by her head,
 Should say: "That is not what I meant at all.
 That is not it, at all."

 And would it have been worth it, after all,
Would it have been worth while, 100
After the sunsets and the dooryards and the sprinkled streets,
After the novels, after the teacups, after the skirts that trail along the
 floor—
And this, and so much more?—
It is impossible to say just what I mean!
But as if a magic lantern threw the nerves in patterns on a screen:
Would it have been worth while
If one, settling a pillow or throwing off a shawl,
And turning toward the window, should say:
 "That is not it at all,
 That is not what I meant, at all." 110

No! I am not Prince Hamlet, nor was meant to be;
Am an attendant lord, one that will do
To swell a progress,[5] start a scene or two,
Advise the prince; no doubt, an easy tool,
Deferential, glad to be of use,
Politic, cautious, and meticulous;
Full of high sentence,[6] but a bit obtuse;
At times, indeed, almost ridiculous—
Almost, at times, the Fool.

 I grow old . . . I grow old . . . 120
I shall wear the bottoms of my trousers rolled.

[4] Lazarus was raised from the dead by Jesus. See John 11:1–44.
[5] A ceremonial procession, often represented in Elizabethan plays.
[6] Sententiously expressed opinions.

Shall I part my hair behind? Do I dare to eat a peach?
I shall wear white flannel trousers, and walk upon the beach.
I have heard the mermaids singing, each to each.

I do not think that they will sing to me.

I have seen them riding seaward on the waves
Combing the white hair of the waves blown back
When the wind blows the water white and black.

We have lingered in the chambers of the sea
By sea-girls wreathed with seaweed red and brown 130
Till human voices wake us, and we drown.

THE WASTE LAND[1]

*"Nam Sibyllam quidem Cumis ego ipse oculis meis vidi in ampulla pendere, et
cum illi pueri dicerent:* Σίβυλλα τί θέλεις; *respondebat illa:* ἀποθανεῖν
θέλω.*"*[2]

FOR EZRA POUND
il miglior fabbro.[3]

I. THE BURIAL OF THE DEAD[4]

April is the cruellest month, breeding
Lilacs out of the dead land, mixing

[1] Eliot provided fifty-two notes for *The Waste Land* when it was first published in book form
in 1922 ("in order," according to his later statement, "to provide a few more pages of printed
matter"). The notes given here are by the editors, except for those identified as quoted or
abbreviated from Eliot's. Eliot's general note for the entire poem is as follows: "Not only the
title, but the plan and a good deal of the incidental symbolism of the poem were suggested by
Miss Jessie L. Weston's book on the Grail legend: *From Ritual to Romance* (Cambridge). Indeed,
so deeply am I indebted, Miss Weston's book will elucidate the difficulties of the poem much
better than my notes can do; and I recommend it (apart from the great interest of the book
itself) to any who think such elucidation of the poem worth the trouble. To another work of
anthropology I am indebted in general, one which has influenced our generation profoundly;
I mean *The Golden Bough;* I have used especially the two volumes *Adonis, Attis, Osiris.* Anyone
who is acquainted with these works will immediately recognise in the poem certain references
to vegetation ceremonies."
[2] "For I saw with my own eyes the Sibyl hanging in a jar at Cumae, and when the boys
asked, 'Sibyl, what do you want?' she answered, 'I want to die.'" This is from the *Satyricon* of
Petronius (first century A.D.). The Cumaean Sibyl was a famous prophetess whom Virgil has
guide Aeneas through Hades in the *Aeneid.* She had been granted eternal life by Apollo but
she forgot to ask for eternal youth and so shrivelled until she was so small that she was kept in
a jar.
[3] "The better maker" (Italian). Pound edited the original manuscript of *The Waste Land.*
The phrase is quoted from Dante's *Purgatory* XXVI.117, where Dante applies it to the
Provençal poet Arnaut Daniel.
[4] The title is from the Anglican burial service.

Memory and desire, stirring
Dull roots with spring rain.
Winter kept us warm, covering
Earth in forgetful snow, feeding
A little life with dried tubers.
Summer surprised us, coming over the Starnbergersee[5]
With a shower of rain; we stopped in the colonnade,
And went on in sunlight, into the Hofgarten,[6] 10
And drank coffee, and talked for an hour.
Bin gar keine Russin, stamm' aus Litauen, echt deutsch.[7]
And when we were children, staying at the archduke's,
My cousin's, he took me out on a sled,
And I was frightened. He said, Marie,
Marie, hold on tight. And down we went.
In the mountains, there you feel free.
I read, much of the night, and go south in the winter.

What are the roots that clutch, what branches grow
Out of this stony rubbish? Son of man,[8] 20
You cannot say, or guess, for you know only
A heap of broken images, where the sun beats,
And the dead tree gives no shelter, the cricket no relief,[9]
And the dry stone no sound of water. Only
There is shadow under this red rock,
(Come in under the shadow of this red rock),[10]
And I will show you something different from either
Your shadow at morning striding behind you
Or your shadow at evening rising to meet you;
I will show you fear in a handful of dust. 30
 Frisch weht der Wind
 Der Heimat zu
 Mein Irisch Kind,
 Wo weilest du?[11]
"You gave me hyacinths first a year ago;
"They called me the hyacinth girl."
—Yet when we came back, late, from the Hyacinth garden,

[5] A lake near Munich. The following lines echo a passage in *My Past*, the memoirs of the Austrian countess Marie Larisch, but according to Eliot's widow, Eliot derived them not from the book but from personal conversation with the countess.

[6] A public park in Munich.

[7] "I am no Russian, I'm from Lithuania, a true German" (German).

[8] Eliot cites Ezekiel 2:1 as the source of this passage. The Lord says to Ezekiel, "Son of man, stand upon thy feet, and I will speak unto thee."

[9] Eliot cites Ecclesiastes 12:5. The passage is describing the aged, who "are afraid also of what is high, and terrors are in the way; the almond tree blossoms, the grasshopper drags itself along and desire fails."

[10] Isaiah 32:2 describes a great king who will be "like the shade of a great rock in a weary land," thus, according to Christian interpretation, foreshadowing Christ.

[11] Eliot identifies this verse as the sailor's song in Richard Wagner's *Tristan and Isolde* (1857–59), Act I: "Fresh blows the wind to the homeland; my Irish child, where are you waiting?"

Your arms full, and your hair wet, I could not
Speak, and my eyes failed, I was neither
Living nor dead, and I knew nothing, 40
Looking into the heart of light, the silence.
Oed' und leer das Meer.[12]

Madame Sosostris,[13] famous clairvoyante,
Had a bad cold, nevertheless
Is known to be the wisest woman in Europe,
With a wicked pack of cards.[14] Here, said she,
Is your card, the drowned Phoenician Sailor,
(Those are pearls that were his eyes.[15] Look!)
Here is Belladonna,[16] the Lady of the Rocks,
The lady of situations. 50
Here is the man with three staves, and here the Wheel,[17]
And here is the one-eyed merchant, and this card,
Which is blank, is something he carries on his back,
Which I am forbidden to see. I do not find
The Hanged Man. Fear death by water.
I see crowds of people, walking round in a ring.
Thank you. If you see dear Mrs. Equitone,
Tell her I bring the horoscope myself:
One must be so careful these days.

[12] Eliot identifies this line also as from *Tristan and Isolde*, Act III: "Waste and empty is the sea." This is the report of a shepherd watching for the sail of a ship bringing Isolde from Cornwall to the dying Tristan.

[13] Eliot apparently derived the fortune-teller's fake Egyptian name from Aldous Huxley's novel *Chrome Yellow* (1921), in which a character uses the name "Sesostris, the Sorceress of Ecbatana" while telling fortunes at a fair.

[14] "I am not familiar with the exact constitution of the Tarot pack of cards, from which I have obviously departed to suit my own convenience. The Hanged Man, a member of the traditional pack, fits my purpose in two ways: because he is associated in my mind with the Hanged God of Frazer, and because I associate him with the hooded figure in the passage of the disciples to Emmaus in Part V. The Phoenician Sailor and the Merchant appear later; also the 'crowds of people,' and Death by Water. The Man with Three Staves (an authentic member of the Tarot pack) I associate, quite arbitrarily, with the Fisher King himself" (Eliot). The Tarot deck of cards, used widely for fortune-telling, is very old and uses as the names of suits the cup, lance, sword, and dish of the Grail legend. Jessie Weston discusses it in *From Ritual to Romance*. The figures on the cards, as Eliot notes, are identified with various characters in the poem. The Phoenician Sailor is both Mr. Eugenides (Part III) and Phlebas the Phoenician (Part IV). The Hanged Man is the "hooded figure" (Christ) of Part V. As Eliot also notes, the correspondences are not exact, and not every character has a corresponding card.

[15] *Those . . . his eyes.* A line from "Full Fathom Five Thy Father Lies," Ariel's song in Act I of Shakespeare's *The Tempest*. Ariel is alluding to the presumed drowning of Ferdinand's father King Alonso.

[16] Both "beautiful lady" (Italian) and the name of a poison, deadly nightshade. She anticipates the neurotic lady of Part II. She is the "Lady of the Rocks" in ironic reference to Leonardo da Vinci's "Lady of the Rocks," a painting of the Virgin Mary, and to sirens who lure sailors onto the rocks (a typically ambivalent pairing of opposites in the poem). She is a "lady of situations" because of her presumed gossiping and intrigues.

[17] The Wheel of Fortune in the Tarot deck.

Unreal City,[18] 60
Under the brown fog of a winter dawn,
A crowd flowed over London Bridge, so many,
I had not thought death had undone so many.[19]
Sighs, short and infrequent, were exhaled,[20]
And each man fixed his eyes before his feet.
Flowed up the hill and down King William Street,
To where Saint Mary Woolnoth kept the hours
With a dead sound on the final stroke of nine.[21]
There I saw one I knew, and stopped him, crying: "Stetson!
"You who were with me in the ships at Mylae![22] 70
"That corpse you planted last year in your garden,
"Has it begun to sprout? Will it bloom this year?
"Or has the sudden frost disturbed its bed?
"Oh keep the Dog far hence, that's friend to men,
"Or with his nails he'll dig it up again![23]
"You! hypocrite lecteur!—mon semblable,—mon frère!"[24]

II. A GAME OF CHESS[25]

The Chair she sat in, like a burnished throne,[26]
Glowed on the marble, where the glass
Held up by standards wrought with fruited vines
From which a golden Cupidon peeped out 80

[18] "Cf. Baudelaire: *'Fourmillante cité, cité pleine de rêves, / Ou le spectre en plein jour raccroche le passant'*" (Eliot). The poem Eliot refers to is "The Seven Old Men" in Charles Baudelaire's *The Flowers of Evil* (1857): "Swarming city, city fitted with dreams, / Where the spectre in broad daylight accosts the passerby."

[19] "Cf. *Inferno* III, 55–57" (Eliot). When Dante arrives in Hell, he sees a long train of people and exclaims, "I had not thought death had undone so many!"

[20] "Cf. *Inferno* IV, 25–27" (Eliot). Here Dante is describing the virtuous pagans in the first circle of Hell.

[21] "A phenomenon which I have often noticed" (Eliot). Saint Mary Woolnoth is a church in the "City," the financial district of London. King William Street is in the same area. The crowd is flowing over London Bridge to go to work.

[22] Naval battle in the First Punic War (260 B.C.), in which Rome defeated Carthage. The speaker merges this ancient war with the First World War, in which he and "Stetson" (a generalized figure, not a specific person) have recently fought.

[23] "Cf. the Dirge in Webster's *White Devil*" (Eliot). The lines Eliot refers to, in John Webster's play *The White Devil* (1612), are "But keep the wolf far thence, that's foe to men, / For with his nails he'll dig them up again" (V.iv.97–98). The switch from wolf to dog and the cliché of "man's best friend" domesticate the line but at the same time grotesquely juxtapose ancient fertility rites and modern suburban life.

[24] "V. Baudelaire, Preface to *Fleurs du Mal*" (Eliot). The line means, "Hypocrite reader!— my likeness—my brother!"

[25] The title of this section alludes to a play, *A Game at Chess*, by the Jacobean dramatist Thomas Middleton (c. 1570–1627). Closer to the action, though, is another Middleton play, *Women Beware Women*, in which an on-stage chess game parallels a cynical seduction in the next room. See note 36.

[26] "Cf. [Shakespeare's] *Antony and Cleopatra*, II.ii.190" (Eliot). The line is part of Enobarbus's description of Cleopatra: "The barge she sat in, like a burnished throne, / Burn'd on the water."

(Another hid his eyes behind his wing)
Doubled the flames of sevenbranched candelabra
Reflecting light upon the table as
The glitter of her jewels rose to meet it,
From satin cases poured in rich profusion;
In vials of ivory and coloured glass
Unstoppered, lurked her strange synthetic perfumes,
Unguent, powdered, or liquid—troubled, confused
And drowned the sense in odours; stirred by the air
That freshened from the window, these ascended 90
In fattening the prolonged candle-flames,
Flung their smoke into the laquearia,²⁷
Stirring the pattern on the coffered ceiling.
Huge sea-wood fed with copper
Burned green and orange, framed by the coloured stone,
In which sad light a carvèd dolphin swam.
Above the antique mantel was displayed
As though a window gave upon the sylvan scene²⁸
The change of Philomel,²⁹ by the barbarous king
So rudely forced;³⁰ yet there the nightingale 100
Filled all the desert with inviolable voice
And still she cried, and still the world pursues,
"Jug Jug"³¹ to dirty ears.
And other withered stumps of time
Were told upon the walls; staring forms
Leaned out, leaning, hushing the room enclosed.
Footsteps shuffled on the stair.
Under the firelight, under the brush, her hair
Spread out in fiery points
Glowed into words, then would be savagely still. 110

"My nerves are bad to-night. Yes, bad. Stay with me.
"Speak to me. Why do you never speak. Speak.
"What are you thinking of? What thinking? What?
"I never know what you are thinking. Think."

²⁷"V. *Aeneid*, I.726" (Eliot). A "laquearia" is a panelled ceiling; the passage in the *Aeneid* Eliot cites as his source for the word describes Dido's lavish banquet for her lover Aeneas.
²⁸*sylvan scene*. "V. Milton, *Paradise Lost*, IV. 140" (Eliot). The passage Eliot refers to is a description of Eden, as first seen by Satan.
²⁹"V. Ovid, *Metamorphoses*, VI, Philomela" (Eliot). In the *Metamorphoses*, Philomela is raped by her brother-in-law King Tereus, who cuts her tongue out so that she cannot denounce him. She is turned into a nightingale.
³⁰"Cf. Part III, l. 204" (Eliot). In the line Eliot refers to, he returns to Tereus and the nightingale's song. There may be an echo here, too, of Milton's lines in "Lycidas" (1637): "I come to pluck your berries harsh and crude, / And with forced fingers rude, / Shatter your leaves before the mellowing year" (ll. 3–5). An important sub-theme in both "Lycidas" and *The Waste Land* is the difficulty of writing the poems, Milton's because of his immaturity, Eliot's because of the fragmentation of his culture. ("Lycidas" also involves a "death by water.")
³¹A conventional representation of the nightingale's song in Elizabethan verse.

I think we are in rats' alley[32]
Where the dead men lost their bones.

"What is that noise?"
 The wind under the door.[33]
"What is that noise now? What is the wind doing?"
 Nothing again nothing.
 "Do 120
"You know nothing? Do you see nothing? Do you remember
"Nothing?"

 I remember
Those are pearls that were his eyes.[34]
"Are you alive, or not? Is there nothing in your head?"
 But
O O O O that Shakespeherian Rag—
It's so elegant
So intelligent
"What shall I do now? What shall I do?"[35] 130
"I shall rush out as I am, and walk the street
"With my hair down, so. What shall we do to-morrow?
"What shall we ever do?"
 The hot water at ten.
And if it rains, a closed car at four.
And we shall play a game of chess,[36]
Pressing lidless eyes and waiting for a knock upon the door.

 When Lil's husband got demobbed,[37] I said—
I didn't mince my words, I said to her myself,
HURRY UP PLEASE ITS TIME[38] 140
Now Albert's coming back, make yourself a bit smart.
He'll want to know what you done with that money he gave you
To get yourself some teeth. He did, I was there.
You have them all out, Lil, and get a nice set,
He said, I swear, I can't bear to look at you.
And no more can't I, I said, and think of poor Albert,
He's been in the army four years, he wants a good time,
And if you don't give it him, there's others will, I said.
Oh is there, she said. Something o' that, I said.
Then I'll know who to thank, she said, and give me a straight look. 150
HURRY UP PLEASE ITS TIME

[32]"Cf. Part III, l. 195" (Eliot): "bones cast in a little low dry garret, / Rattled by the rat's foot only, year to year."
[33]"Cf. Webster: 'Is the wind in that door still?'" (Eliot). The line is in John Webster's play *The Devil's Law Case* (1623), III.ii.162, where it is a question about whether a dying man is still breathing.
[34]"Cf. Part I, ll. 37, 48" (Eliot). The reference is again to Ariel's song in *The Tempest*.
[35]Lines 128–31 are quoted from a 1912 popular song, "That Shakespearian Rag."
[36]"Cf. the game of chess in Middleton's *Women Beware Women*" (Eliot). See note 25.
[37]British slang for *demobilized* or discharged from the army.
[38]Traditional bartender's call at closing time in an English pub.

If you don't like it you can get on with it, I said.
Others can pick and choose if you can't.
But if Albert makes off, it won't be for lack of telling.
You ought to be ashamed, I said, to look so antique.
(And her only thirty-one.)
I can't help it, she said, pulling a long face,
It's them pills I took, to bring it off, she said.
(She's had five already, and nearly died of young George.) 160
The chemist[39] said it would be all right, but I've never been the same.
You *are* a proper fool, I said.
Well, if Albert won't leave you alone, there it is, I said,
What you get married for if you don't want children?
HURRY UP PLEASE ITS TIME
Well, that Sunday Albert was home, they had a hot gammon,[40]
And they asked me in to dinner, to get the beauty of it hot—
HURRY UP PLEASE ITS TIME
HURRY UP PLEASE ITS TIME
Goonight Bill. Goonight Lou. Goonight May. Goonight. 170
Ta ta. Goonight. Goonight.
Good night, ladies, good night, sweet ladies, good night, good night.[41]

III. THE FIRE SERMON[42]

The river's tent is broken: the last fingers of leaf
Clutch and sink into the wet bank. The wind
Crosses the brown land, unheard. The nymphs are departed.
Sweet Thames, run softly, till I end my song.[43]
The river bears no empty bottles, sandwich papers,
Silk handkerchiefs, cardboard boxes, cigarette ends
Or other testimony of summer nights. The nymphs are departed.
And their friends, the loitering heirs of city directors; 180
Departed, have left no addresses.
By the waters of Leman I sat down and wept . . .[44]
Sweet Thames, run softly till I end my song,
Sweet Thames, run softly, for I speak not loud or long.
But at my back in a cold blast I hear[45]

[39] Druggist. [40] Ham.

[41] This line quotes Ophelia's last words in her mad scene before she drowns herself (*Hamlet*, IV.v. 72–73). The lines blend with their modern analogue, the drinking song "Good Night, Ladies."

[42] The title alludes to the "Fire Sermon" of Buddha, sixth-century B.C. founder of Buddhism. See note 74.

[43] "V. Spenser, *Prothalamion*" (Eliot). This line is the refrain of the *Prothalamion* (or "wedding song") by Edmund Spenser (c. 1552–1599), which also includes the river-nymphs, the "silver-streaming" Thames, and the description of London which this section parodies.

[44] See Psalm 137: "By the waters of Babylon, there we sat down and wept, when we remembered Zion." Eliot wrote *The Waste Land* in Switzerland, near Lake Leman (Lake Geneva). "Leman" is also the Middle English word for "mistress."

[45] "Cf. Marvell, *To His Coy Mistress*" (Eliot). Eliot is alluding to a line in the poem by Andrew Marvell (1627–78): "But at my back I always hear / Time's winged chariot hurrying near."

The rattle of the bones, and chuckle spread from ear to ear.
A rat crept softly through the vegetation
Dragging its slimy belly on the bank
While I was fishing in the dull canal
On a winter evening round behind the gashouse 190
Musing upon the king my brother's wreck
And on the king my father's death before him.[46]
White bodies naked on the low damp ground
And bones cast in a little low dry garret,
Rattled by the rat's foot only, year to year.
But at my back from time to time I hear[47]
The sound of horns and motors,[48] which shall bring
Sweeney to Mrs. Porter in the spring.
O the moon shone bright on Mrs. Porter
And on her daughter
They wash their feet in soda water[49] 200
Et O ces voix d'enfants, chantant dans la coupole![50]

　　Twit twit twit
Jug jug jug jug jug jug
So rudely forc'd.
Tereu[51]

　　　Unreal City[52]
Under the brown fog of a winter noon
Mr. Eugenides, the Smyrna merchant[53]
Unshaven, with a pocket full of currants 210

[46]"Cf. *The Tempest*, I,ii" (Eliot). The lines are Ferdinand's: "Sitting upon a bank, / Weeping again the King my father's wrack, / This music crept by me upon the waters."

[47]Another allusion to "To His Coy Mistress." See note 45.

[48]"Cf. Day, *Parliament of Bees:*
　　　　　　'When of a sudden, listening, you shall hear,
　　　　　　'A noise of horns and hunting, which shall bring
　　　　　　'Actaeon to Diana in the spring,
　　　　　　'Where all shall see her naked skin. . .'" (Eliot).
John Day (1547–c. 1640) was a minor Elizabethan poet. Actaeon, while hunting, accidentally came upon the goddess Diana bathing naked; as punishment, he was changed to a stag and torn apart by his own hounds.

[49]"I do not know the origins of the ballad from which these lines are taken: it was reported to me from Sydney, Australia" (Eliot). The song is an obscene parody of "Red Wing," sung in World War I: "O the moon shone bright on Mrs. Porter / And on the daughter / of Mrs. Porter. / They wash their feet in soda water, / And so they oughter, / To keep them clean."

[50]"V. Verlaine, *Parsifal*" (Eliot). The line is from a sonnet by Paul Verlaine (1844–1896). It means, "And O those voices of children, singing in the cupola!" The children are the children's choir at the end of Wagner's opera *Parsifal* (1877–82), singing as Parsifal's feet are ceremonially washed in preparation for his worship of the Grail. Here the children's voices ironically accompany, instead, the washing of Mrs. Porter's and her daughter's feet in soda water.

[51]See notes 30 and 31. "Tereu" is King Tereus; the line also echoes John Lyly's line in *Alexander and Campaspe* (1581): "'Tis the ravished nightingale; / Jug, jug, jug, jug, tereu, she cries."

[52]See note 18.

[53]Mr. Eugenides' name, ironically, means "well-born" in Greek. Smyrna is a Turkish seaport.

C.i.f. London: documents at sight,[54]
Asked me in demotic[55] French
To luncheon at the Cannon Street Hotel
Followed by a weekend at the Metropole.[56]

At the violet hour, when the eyes and back
Turn upward from the desk, when the human engine waits
Like a taxi throbbing waiting,
I Tiresias, though blind, throbbing between two lives,[57]
Old man with wrinkled female breasts, can see
At the violet hour, the evening hour that strives 220
Homeward, and brings the sailor home from the sea,[58]
The typist home at teatime, clears her breakfast, lights
Her stove, and lays out food in tins.
Out of the window perilously spread
Her drying combinations[59] touched by the sun's last rays,
On the divan are piled (at night her bed)
Stockings, slippers, camisoles, and stays.
I Tiresias, old man with wrinkled dugs
Perceived the scene, and foretold the rest—
I too awaited the expected guest. 230
He, the young man carbuncular,[60] arrives,
A small house agent's clerk, with one bold stare,
One of the low on whom assurance sits
As a silk hat on a Bradford millionaire.[61]
The time is now propitious, as he guesses,
The meal is ended, she is bored and tired,

[54] "The currants were quoted at a price 'carriage and insurance free to London'; and the Bill of Lading etc. were to be handed to the buyer upon payment of the sight draft" (Eliot).

[55] Colloquial, vulgar.

[56] The Cannon Street Hotel in London was a large hotel near the Cannon Street Station, where boat trains departed for and arrived from the Continent; it was thus frequented by foreign businessmen. The Metropole was a luxury resort hotel in Brighton. Both hotels were said to be favorite meeting places for homosexual and other irregular liaisons. Weston, in *From Ritual to Romance*, describes how the Grail cult was spread by Levantine merchants. This modern merchant spreads a somewhat different cult.

[57] "Tiresias, although a mere spectator and not indeed a 'character,' is yet the most important personage in the poem, uniting all the rest. Just as the one-eyed merchant, seller of currants, melts into the Phoenician Sailor, and the latter is not wholly distinct from Ferdinand Prince of Naples, so all the women are one woman, and the two sexes meet in Tiresias. What Tiresias *sees*, in fact, is the substance of the poem. The whole passage from Ovid is of great anthropological interest" (Eliot). Eliot then quotes a passage from Ovid's *Metamorphoses* (III.320–38) which tells how Tiresias spent seven years as a woman. Later, asked to settle a quarrel between Jove and Juno over whether men or women enjoyed sex more, Tiresias agreed with Jove that women did. Angered, Juno blinded him, but Jove compensated him by giving him prophetic powers.

[58] "This may not appear as exact as Sappho's lines, but I had in mind the 'longshore' or 'day' fisherman, who returns at nightfall" (Eliot). Eliot seems to have in mind Sappho's poem to Hesperus, the evening star, that brings home "all things bright morning scattered." The line also recalls Robert Louis Stevenson's line in "Requiem": "Home is the sailor, home from the sea."

[59] One-piece underwear. [60] With boils.

[61] From the industrial town of Bradford, which thrived on war contracts during World War I; hence, a *nouveau riche* and a war profiteer.

Endeavours to engage her in caresses
Which still are unreproved, if undesired.
Flushed and decided, he assaults at once;
Exploring hands encounter no defence; 240
His vanity requires no response,
And makes a welcome of indifference.
(And I Tiresias have foresuffered all
Enacted on this same divan or bed;
I who have sat by Thebes below the wall
And walked among the lowest of the dead.)[62]
Bestows one final patronising kiss,
And gropes his way, finding the stairs unlit . . .

She turns and looks a moment in the glass,
Hardly aware of her departed lover;
Her brain allows one half-formed thought to pass: 250
"Well now that's done: and I'm glad it's over."
When lovely woman stoops to folly[63] and
Paces about her room again, alone,
She smoothes her hair with automatic hand,
And puts a record on the gramophone.

"This music crept by me upon the waters"[64]
And along the Strand, up Queen Victoria Street.
O City city, I can sometimes hear
Beside a public bar in Lower Thames Street,
The pleasant whining of a mandoline 260
And a clatter and a chatter from within
Where fishmen lounge at noon: where the walls
Of Magnus Martyr[65] hold
Inexplicable splendour of Ionian white and gold.

[62] Tiresias lived in Thebes, where he foresaw the fates of Oedipus and Creon. After his death, he continued to prophesy in Hades.

[63] "V. Goldsmith, the song in *The Vicar of Wakefield*" (Eliot). The song, in Oliver Goldsmith's 1766 novel, runs:

> When lovely woman stoops to folly,
> And finds too late that men betray;
> What charm can soothe her melancholy,
> What art can wash her guilt away?
>
> The only art her guilt to cover,
> To hide her shame from every eye,
> To give repentance to her lover
> And wring his bosom—is to die.

[64] "V. *The Tempest*, as above" (Eliot). See note 46.

[65] "The interior of St. Magnus Martyr is to my mind one of the finest among Wren's interiors. See *The Proposed Demolition of Nineteen City Churches*: (P. S. King & Son, Ltd.)" (Eliot). The church of St. Magnus Martyr, designed by the seventeenth-century architect Christopher Wren, is located near London Bridge.

The river sweats[66]
Oil and tar
The barges drift
With the turning tide
Red sails
Wide 270
To leeward, swing on the heavy spar.
The barges wash
Drifting logs
Down Greenwich reach
Past the Isle of Dogs.[67]
 Weialala leia
 Wallala leialala[68]
Elizabeth and Leicester[69]
Beating oars 280
The stern was formed
A gilded shell
Red and gold
The brisk swell
Rippled both shores
Southwest wind
Carried down stream
The peal of bells
White towers
 Weialala leia 290
 Wallala leialala

"Trams and dusty trees.
Highbury bore me. Richmond and Kew
Undid me.[70] By Richmond I raised my knees
Supine on the floor of a narrow canoe."

[66]"The Song of the (three) Thames-daughters begins here. From line 292 to 306 inclusive they speak in turn. V. *Gotterdämmerung*, III.i: the Rhine-daughters" (Eliot). Eliot is referring to the Rhine Maidens in Richard Wagner's opera *The Twilight of the Gods* (1874). The modern women whose statements begin with line 292 ironically echo not only Wagner's Rhine Maidens but also Spenser's river nymphs.

[67]Greenwich reach is the stretch of the Thames near Greenwich; the Isle of Dogs is a peninsula extending into the Thames.

[68]This refrain is from the song of the Rhine Maidens in *The Twilight of the Gods*.

[69]"V. Froude, *Elizabeth*, Vol. I, ch. iv, letter of De Quadra to Philip of Spain: 'In the afternoon we were in a barge, watching the games on the river. (The queen) was alone with Lord Robert and myself on the poop, when they began to talk nonsense, and went so far that Lord Robert at last said, as I was on the spot there was no reason why they should not be married if the queen pleased'" (Eliot). Eliot quotes from *The Reign of Elizabeth*, by J. A. Froude (1818–1894). De Quadra was Spanish Ambassador to Elizabeth's court; Sir Robert was Robert Dudley, Earl of Leicester, a favorite of Elizabeth. Their sexual play on the Thames parallels the modern vignettes which follow.

[70]"Cf. *Purgatorio*, V, 133" (Eliot). The lines Eliot cites are translated, "Siena bore me; Maremma undid me," and are spoken by a woman named La Pia, who died in Maremma. Highbury is a suburb of London; Richmond and Kew are resort gardens near London.

"My feet are at Moorgate,[71] and my heart
Under my feet. After the event
He wept. He promised 'a new start.'
I made no comment. What should I resent?"

"On Margate Sands.[72] 300
I can connect
Nothing with nothing.
The broken fingernails of dirty hands.
My people humble people who expect
Nothing."
 la la

To Carthage then I came[73]

Burning burning burning burning[74]
O Lord Thou pluckest me out[75]
O Lord Thou pluckest 310

burning

IV. DEATH BY WATER[76]

Phlebas the Phoenician, a fortnight dead,
Forgot the cry of gulls, and the deep sea swell
And the profit and loss.
 A current under sea
Picked his bones in whispers. As he rose and fell
He passed the stages of his age and youth
Entering the whirlpool.
 Gentile or Jew
O you who turn the wheel and look to windward, 320
Consider Phlebas, who was once handsome and tall as you.

[71] A slum area of London. [72] Seaside resort on the Thames.

[73] "V. St. Augustine's *Confessions:* 'to Carthage then I came, where a cauldron of unholy loves sang all about mine ears' " (Eliot). St. Augustine (354–430) is describing his youthful debauchery.

[74] "The complete text of the Buddha's Fire Sermon (which corresponds in importance to the Sermon on the Mount, from which these words are taken, will be found translated in the late Henry Clarke Warren's *Buddhism in Translation* (Harvard Oriental Series). Mr. Warren was one of the great pioneers of Buddhist studies in the Occident" (Eliot).

[75] "From St. Augustine's *Confessions* again. The collocation of these two representatives of eastern and western asceticism, as the culmination of this part of the poem, is not an accident" (Eliot).

[76] This section is translated and adapted by Eliot from his poem in French "Dans le Restaurant."

V. WHAT THE THUNDER SAID[77]

After the torchlight red on sweaty faces
After the frosty silence in the gardens[78]
After the agony in stony places
The shouting and the crying
Prison and palace and reverberation
Of thunder of spring over distant mountains
He who was living is now dead
We who were living are now dying
With a little patience 330

 Here is no water but only rock
Rock and no water and the sandy road
The road winding above among the mountains
Which are mountains of rock without water
If there were water we should stop and drink
Amongst the rock one cannot stop or think
Sweat is dry and feet are in the sand
If there were only water amongst the rock
Dead mountain mouth of carious[79] teeth that cannot spit
Here one can neither stand nor lie nor sit 340
There is not even silence in the mountains
But dry sterile thunder without rain
There is not even solitude in the mountains
But red sullen faces sneer and snarl
From doors of mudcracked houses
 If there were water
 And no rock
 If there were rock
 And also water
 And water
 A spring 350
 A pool among the rock
 If there were the sound of water only
 Not the cicada
 And dry grass singing
 But sound of water over a rock

[77] "In the first part of Part V three themes are employed: the journey to Emmaus, the approach to the Chapel Perilous (see Miss Weston's book) and the present decay of eastern Europe" (Eliot). The "journey to Emmaus" is the journey upon which the resurrected Christ's disciples met him but did not recognize him. (See Luke 24:13–16.) The "approach to the Chapel Perilous" is the final stage of the Grail hero's quest. The "present decay of eastern Europe" alludes to the aftermath of World War I and the Russian Revolution.

[78] Gethsemane, where Christ prayed before his arrest, and Golgotha, where he was crucified. This section is from the point of view of Christ's disciples between his crucifixion and the resurrection.

[79] Decayed.

Where the hermit-thrush sings in the pine trees[80]
Drip drop drip drop drop drop drop
But there is no water
Who is the third who walks always beside you?[81] 360
When I count, there are only you and I together
But when I look ahead up the white road
There is always another one walking beside you
Gliding wrapt in a brown mantle, hooded
I do not know whether a man or a woman
—But who is that on the other side of you?

 What is that sound high in the air
Murmur of maternal lamentation
Who are those hooded hordes swarming
Over endless plains, stumbling in cracked earth 370
Ringed by the flat horizon only
What is the city over the mountains
Cracks and reforms and bursts in the violet air
Falling towers
Jerusalem Athens Alexandria
Vienna London
Unreal[82]

 A woman drew her long black hair out tight
And fiddled whisper music on those strings
And bats with baby faces in the violet light 380
Whistled, and beat their wings
And crawled head downward down a blackened wall
And upside down in air were towers
Tolling reminiscent bells, that kept the hours
And voices singing out of empty cisterns and exhausted wells.

 In this decayed hole among the mountains
In the faint moonlight, the grass is singing
Over the tumbled graves, about the chapel

[80]"This is *Turdus aonalaschkae pallasii*, the hermit-thrush which I have heard in Quebec Province. Chapman says (*Handbook of Birds of Eastern North America*) 'it is most at home in secluded woodland and thickety retreats. . . . Its notes are not remarkable for variety or volume, but in purity and sweetness of tone and exquisite modulation they are unequalled.' Its 'water-dripping song' is justly celebrated" (Eliot). (This faintly absurd Eliotic note may gently parody Eliot's own notes as well as those of literal-minded academic editors.)

[81]"The following lines were stimulated by the account of one of the Antarctic expeditions (I forget which, but I think one of Shackleton's): it was related that the party of explorers, at the extremity of their strength, had the constant delusion that there was *one more member* than could actually be counted" (Eliot). The "third" is, however, Christ on the road to Emmaus.

[82]"Cf. Hermann Hesse, *Blick ins Chaos*" (Eliot). The lines Eliot quotes from Hesse's *A Glimpse into Chaos* (1920) may be translated: "Already half of Europe, already at least half of Eastern Europe, is on the way to chaos, going drunkenly, in spiritual madness, along the edge of the abyss, singing drunkenly and rhapsodically, as Dimitri Karamazov [in Dostoevsky's *The Brothers Karamazov*] sang. The shocked bourgeoisie laughs at these songs; the saint and the seer hear them with tears."

There is the empty chapel,[83] only the wind's home.
It has no windows, and the door swings, 390
Dry bones can harm no one.
Only a cock stood on the rooftree
Co co rico co co rico[84]
In a flash of lightning. Then a damp gust
Bringing rain

Ganga[85] was sunken, and the limp leaves
Waited for rain, while the black clouds
Gathered far distant, over Himavant.[86]
The jungle crouched, humped in silence.
Then spoke the thunder 400
DA
Datta:[87] what have we given?
My friend, blood shaking my heart
The awful daring of a moment's surrender
Which an age of prudence can never retract
By this, and this only, we have existed
Which is not to be found in our obituaries
Or in memories draped by the beneficent spider[88]
Or under seals broken by the lean solicitor
In our empty rooms 410
DA
Dayadhvam: I have heard the key[89]
Turn in the door once and turn once only
We think of the key, each in his prison
Thinking of the key, each confirms a prison
Only at nightfall, aethereal rumours
Revive for a moment a broken Coriolanus[90]
DA

[83] The Chapel Perilous, where the Grail Knight prepares for the final quest.
[84] Cockadoodledoo. The cock's crow heralds rebirth, dispels evil spirits, and recalls Peter's denial of Christ (Matthew 26).
[85] The Ganges river. [86] The Himalaya mountains.
[87] "'Datta, dayadhvam, damyata' (Give, sympathise, control). The fable of the meaning of the Thunder is found in the *Brihadaranyaka—Upanishad*, 5, 1'" (Eliot). The fable Eliot refers to in the sacred Hindu text, the Upanishads, tells of how gods, men, and demons ask the god Prajápati what their duty is. He responds, in thunder, to each with the single syllable "Da." The men interpret this as *datta* (give alms), the demons as *dayadhvam* (sympathize with others), and the gods as *damyata* (control, practice self-restraint). All are correct, and the voice of the thunder ("da, da, da") continues to remind us of "the three great disciplines."
[88] "Cf. Webster, *The White Devil*, V,vi:
 '. . . they'll remarry
 Ere the worm pierce your winding-sheet, ere the spider
 Make a thick curtain for your epitaphs'" (Eliot).
[89] lines 412–415. Eliot gives as the source of this passage Dante's line (*Inferno* XXXIII.46): "and below I heard the door of the horrible tower nailed up." Count Ugolino is describing how he and his young sons were starved to death. Eliot also quotes from F. H. Bradley, the philosopher upon whose work he wrote his doctoral dissertation, on how each person is locked within his own self: "the whole world for each [soul] is peculiar and private to that soul."
[90] Title character in Shakespeare's play. Coriolanus's pride and scorn for the masses make him a good example of one who fails to "sympathize."

Damyata: The boat responded
Gaily, to the hand expert with sail and oar 420
The sea was calm, your heart would have responded
Gaily, when invited, beating obedient
To controlling hands

 I sat upon the shore
Fishing,[91] with the arid plain behind me
Shall I at least set my lands in order?
London Bridge is falling down falling down falling down
Poi s'ascose nel foco che gli affina[92]
Quando fiam uti chelidon[93]—O swallow swallow
Le Prince d'Aquitaine á la tour abolie[94] 430
These fragments I have shored against my ruins
Why then Ile fit you. Hieronymo's mad againe.[95]
Datta. Dayadhvam. Damyata.
 Shantih shantih shantih[96]

[91] "V. Weston: *From Ritual to Romance;* chapter on the Fisher King" (Eliot).
[92] "V. *Purgatorio,* XXVI, 148" (Eliot). In Dante's passage, the poet Arnaut Daniel describes how he is purging his earthly lusts in Purgatory. With additional lines which Eliot provides in the note, the passage reads, "'And so I pray you, by that Virtue which guides you to the top of the stair, be reminded in time of my pain.' Then he hid himself in the fire which purifies them." The last sentence translates the Italian of line 428.
[93] "V. *Pervigilium Veneris.* Cf. Philomela in Parts II and III" (Eliot). The line means "When shall I become as the swallow?" The *Pervigilium Veneris* (or "Vigil of Venus") is an anonymous late Latin poem which celebrates spring and Venus. It contains a reference to the Philomela myth used earlier in *The Waste Land;* Philomela longs to "become as the swallow" so that she "may cease to be silent."
[94] "V[]. Gerard de Nerval, Sonnet *El Desdichado*" (Eliot). The line (French), from "The Disinherited," by de Nerval (1808–1855), means, "The Prince of Aquitaine at the ruined tower." The line is a romantically melancholy self-description of the poet. The "ruined tower," a symbol of impotence, suggests the fall of civilizations and the "Tower Struck by Lightning" of the Tarot deck.
[95] "V. Kyd's *Spanish Tragedy*" (Eliot). In Thomas Kyd's Elizabethan revenge tragedy (c. 1587), subtitled "Hieronymo Is Mad Again," the main character, whose son has been murdered, is asked to write a court masque. Seeing a chance to take revenge through the play, he replies, "Why then Ile fit [or accommodate] you." Eliot seems to imply a comparison with himself and with *The Waste Land* as a poem to "fit" his audience.
[96] *Shantih.* "Repeated as here, a formal ending to an Upanishad. 'The Peace which passeth understanding' is our equivalent to this word" (Eliot).

from *FOUR QUARTETS*

BURNT NORTON[1]

τοῦ λόγου δ'ἐόντος ξυνοῦ ζώουσιν οἱ πολλοί
ὡς ἰδίαν ἔχοντες φρόνησιν.

I. p. 77. Fr. 2.

ὁδὸς ἄνω κάτω μία καὶ ὡυτή.

I. p. 89. Fr. 60

Diels: *Die Fragmente der Vorsokratiker* (Herakleitos).[2]

I

Time present and time past
Are both perhaps present in time future,
And time future contained in time past.
If all time is eternally present
All time is unredeemable.
What might have been is an abstraction
Remaining a perpetual possibility
Only in a world of speculation.
What might have been and what has been
Point to one end, which is always present. 10
Footfalls echo in the memory
Down the passage which we did not take
Towards the door we never opened
Into the rose-garden. My words echo
Thus, in your mind.
 But to what purpose
Disturbing the dust on a bowl of rose-leaves
I do not know.
 Other echoes
Inhabit the garden. Shall we follow?
Quick, said the bird, find them, find them,
Round the corner. Through the first gate, 20
Into our first world, shall we follow
The deception of the thrush? Into our first world.
There they were, dignified, invisible,
Moving without pressure, over the dead leaves,
In the autumn heat, through the vibrant air,

[1] A large, uninhabited country house near the village of Chipping Campden in Gloucestershire, England, erected on the site of an earlier mansion which burned in the seventeenth century (hence "burnt"). Eliot visited it in 1934.
[2] The Greek epigraphs are from the pre-Socratic philosopher Heraclitus (540–475 B.C.). The first reads: "Although the law of reason (the *Logos* or Word) is common to all, the majority of people live as though they had an understanding (or wisdom) of their own." The second: "The way up and the way down are one and the same."

And the bird called, in response to
The unheard music hidden in the shrubbery,
And the unseen eyebeam[3] crossed, for the roses
Had the look of flowers that are looked at.
There they were as our guests, accepted and accepting. 30
So we moved, and they, in a formal pattern,
Along the empty alley, into the box circle,[4]
To look down into the drained pool.
Dry the pool, dry concrete, brown edged,
And the pool was filled with water out of sunlight,
And the lotos[5] rose, quietly, quietly,
The surface glittered out of heart of light,[6]
And they were behind us, reflected in the pool.
Then a cloud passed, and the pool was empty.
Go, said the bird, for the leaves were full of children, 40
Hidden excitedly, containing laughter.
Go, go, go, said the bird: human kind
Cannot bear very much reality.
Time past and time future
What might have been and what has been
Point to one end, which is always present.

 II

Garlic and sapphires in the mud
Clot the bedded axle-tree.
The trilling wire in the blood
Sings below inveterate scars
Appeasing long forgotten wars. 50
The dance along the artery
The circulation of the lymph
Are figured in the drift of stars
Ascend to summer in the tree
We move above the moving tree
In light upon the figured leaf
And hear upon the sodden floor
Below, the boarhound and the boar
Pursue their pattern as before
But reconciled among the stars. 60

[3] A seventeenth-century metaphor for sight, conceived of as invisible rays of light going out from the eyes, making it possible to see things. See John Donne, "The Ecstasy," lines 6–7: "Our eye-beams twisted, and did thread / Our eyes upon one double string."
[4] A circular hedge of boxwood.
[5] The lotus is a water plant with large pink blossoms, sacred in several Eastern religions. In Buddhism, it symbolizes contemplation.
[6] An echo in reverse of Joseph Conrad's title *Heart of Darkness*. Eliot also used the phrase, in a similar context, in *The Waste Land*, line 41. Light, throughout the poem, has overtones of the divine light that floods Dante in God's presence at the end of the *Divine Comedy*.

 At the still point of the turning world.[7] Neither flesh nor
 fleshless;
Neither from nor towards; at the still point, there the dance is,
But neither arrest nor movement. And do not call it fixity,
Where past and future are gathered. Neither movement from nor
 towards,
Neither ascent nor decline. Except for the point, the still point,
There would be no dance, and there is only the dance.
I can only say, *there* we have been: but I cannot say where.
And I cannot say, how long, for that is to place it in time.
The inner freedom from the practical desire, 70
The release from action and suffering, release from the inner
And the outer compulsion, yet surrounded
By a grace of sense, a white light still and moving,
Erhebung[8] without motion, concentration
Without elimination, both a new world
And the old made explicit, understood
In the completion of its partial ecstasy,
The resolution of its partial horror.
Yet the enchainment of past and future
Woven in the weakness of the changing body, 80
Protects mankind from heaven and damnation
Which flesh cannot endure.
 Time past and time future
Allow but a little consciousness.
To be conscious is not to be in time
But only in time can the moment in the rose-garden,
The moment in the arbour where the rain beat,
The moment in the draughty church at smokefall
Be remembered; involved with past and future.
Only through time time is conquered.

 III

 Here[9] is a place of disaffection 90
 Time before and time after
 In a dim light: neither daylight
 Investing form with lucid stillness
 Turning shadow into transient beauty

[7] At the center of a turning wheel or globe, there is presumably a point which is still and around which everything else moves. This point is associated with God (the Unmoved Mover) or with divine experience.

[8] "Exaltation" (German).

[9] In the London Underground. Eliot said that he had a particular station in mind: the Gloucester Road Station, where he transferred from the Circle Line to the Piccadilly Line to go to Russell Square where his office was at Faber and Faber. To transfer, he had to go to a lower platform ("descend lower") by stairs ("one way") or by an elevator ("the other / Is the same, not in movement / But abstention from movement"). These details are, of course, only a private joke; Eliot builds from the materials an elaborate metaphor for the "disaffection" of ordinary life and the two modes of spiritual enlightenment.

With slow rotation suggesting permanence
Nor darkness to purify the soul
Emptying the sensual with deprivation
Cleansing affection from the temporal.
Neither plenitude nor vacancy. Only a flicker
Over the strained time-ridden faces 100
Distracted from distraction by distraction
Filled with fancies and empty of meaning
Tumid apathy with no concentration
Men and bits of paper, whirled by the cold wind
That blows before and after time,
Wind in and out of unwholesome lungs
Time before and time after.
Eructation of unhealthy souls
Into the faded air, the torpid
Driven on the wind that sweeps the gloomy hills of London, 110
Hampstead and Clerkenwell, Campden and Putney,
Highgate, Primrose and Ludgate.[10] Not here
Not here the darkness, in this twittering world.

 Descend lower, descend only
Into the world of perpetual solitude,
World not world, but that which is not world,
Internal darkness, deprivation
And destitution of all property,
Desiccation of the world of sense,
Evacuation of the world of fancy, 120
Inoperancy of the world of spirit;
This is the one way, and the other
Is the same, not in movement
But abstention from movement; while the world moves
In appetency, on its metalled ways
Of time past and time future.

 IV

Time and the bell have buried the day,
The black cloud carries the sun away.
Will the sunflower[11] turn to us, will the clematis[12]
Stray down, bend to us; tendril and spray 130
Clutch and cling?

 Chill
Fingers of yew[13] be curled

[10]Places in London.
[11]The sunflower, both because of its name and because it is heliotropic (growing toward the light), suggests light, as well as Christ ("son" as well as "sun").
[12]The clematis (also called "virgin's bower" in the United States) suggests the Virgin Mary.
[13]An evergreen tree, traditionally planted in graveyards, symbolic of both death and immortality.

Down on us? After the kingfisher's wing[14]
Has answered light to light, and is silent, the light is still
At the still point of the turning world.

V

Words move, music moves
Only in time; but that which is only living
Can only die. Words, after speech, reach
Into the silence. Only by the form, the pattern, 140
Can words or music reach
The stillness, as a Chinese jar still
Moves perpetually in its stillness.
Not the stillness of the violin, while the note lasts,
Not that only, but the co-existence,
Or say that the end precedes the beginning,
And the end and the beginning were always there
Before the beginning and after the end.
And all is always now. Words strain,
Crack and sometimes break, under the burden, 150
Under the tension, slip, slide, perish,
Decay with imprecision, will not stay in place,
Will not stay still. Shrieking voices
Scolding, mocking, or merely chattering,
Always assail them. The Word in the desert[15]
Is most attacked by voices of temptation,
The crying shadow in the funeral dance,
The loud lament of the disconsolate chimera.[16]

 The detail of the pattern is movement,
As in the figure of the ten stairs.[17] 160
Desire itself is movement
Not in itself desirable;
Love is itself unmoving,
Only the cause and end of movement,
Timeless, and undesiring
Except in the aspect of time
Caught in the form of limitation
Between un-being and being.
Sudden in a shaft of sunlight

[14]A small, fish-eating bird found near lakes and streams. One species has a crested head and a white bar on its wings. The name also suggests the Fisher King of *The Waste Land* and perhaps Christ's apostles ("fishers of men").

[15]A reference to Christ's temptation in the wilderness (Luke 4:1–4).

[16]A monster in Greek mythology with a lion's head, a goat's body, and a serpent's tail. Often interpreted as a symbol of the diseased imagination, it was killed by Bellerophon with the aid of Pegasus, a winged horse symbolic of poetic inspiration.

[17]Reference to the ten steps on the "mystic ladder" of the soul's ascent to God in the writings of St. John of the Cross (1542–91), a Spanish mystic.

Even while the dust moves
There rises the hidden laughter 170
Of children in the foliage
Quick now, here, now, always—
Ridiculous the waste sad time
Stretching before and after.

Isaac Babel
(1894–1941)

In 1920, Isaac Babel wrote to a friend from the Ukraine, where, as a member of the new Soviet Union's First Cavalry Division, he was fighting in the civil wars that sprang up in the wake of the Russian Revolution. In the letter, he defined his ambivalent stance toward the Revolution and his own artistic goals. "I went through two weeks of utter despair here," he wrote. "That was because of the ferocious cruelty that never lets up for a minute and because I clearly understood how unfit I am for the business of destruction, how difficult it is for me to break away from the past—from that which was bad, perhaps, but that which smelled of poetry for me as the hive smells of honey. I'm all right again now. So what—some will make the Revolution and I, I will sing that which is off to the side, that which goes deeper. I feel that I can do that and there will be a place and a time to do it." There was a time for Babel to sing "that which is off to the side, that which goes deeper," though a tragically short one. He produced only a handful of short stories—they would fit into a single volume—but they were enough to win him recognition as one of the masters of modern fiction.

Babel was born in 1894 in the flourishing Black Sea port of Odessa to a middle-class Jewish family. Both his Jewishness and his Odessa origins were of critical importance to Babel. Jews constituted as much as half of the population of Odessa at that time, although they faced constant discrimination and occasional violent repression. Babel's Jewishness gave him a solid background in Hebrew and Biblical studies as well as a lifelong sense of being an outsider, both of which marked his later writing. Odessa itself, with its sprawling, lively Jewish quarter, the Moldavanka, was to furnish the background for many of Babel's stories and to stand, in his mind, against Petersburg as the embodiment of the qualities he aspired to contribute to Russian literature. The Petersburg tradition of Gogol, Turgenev, and Dostoevsky, he wrote, was a literature that could not describe the sun; it was preoccupied with the gloomy and the morbid. Odessa, with its "sunny steppes washed by the sea," could be the setting for a new Russian literature, characterized by lightness, clarity, and joy.

Barred by his Jewishness from the University of Odessa, Babel enrolled at the age of seventeen in the Institute of Financial and Business Studies in

the Ukrainian capital of Kiev. Upon graduating in 1915, he moved immediately to Petersburg, the literary center of Russia, and launched himself upon a literary career. He landed a job on a newspaper, *The Journal of Journals,* and met the prominent writer and patron of young writers, Maxim Gorky, editor of a journal called *The Chronicle.* Gorky introduced him to other writers and published two of his first stories. In 1917, he enlisted in the army, possibly acting on Gorky's advice to "go to the people" in order to enrich his writing. He was soon discharged because of illness and returned to Petersburg. He rejoined the army two years later and in the summer of 1920 was assigned to the First Cavalry Division, then fighting in the Ukraine against Poland. Babel was not involved in actual combat— he was a staff writer for the Division newspaper, *The Red Cavalryman*—but his few months with the Cavalry Division were a turning point in his life, both personally and artistically. He returned to Odessa in 1921 and over the next few years, drawing upon his military diary and notebooks, wrote the thirty-four very short stories that make up *Red Cavalry* (1926). Even before book publication, the stories had created quite a stir, not least because they became the focus for debates over what a new Soviet literature should be. Most sensationally, General Semyon Budenny, commander of the First Cavalry, charged that Babel had slandered his soldiers, a charge against which Babel sharply defended himself. His position as one of Soviet Russia's most talented younger writers was consolidated by the appearance in book form of the four *Odessa Tales* (1927), which he had written and published in magazines in the early twenties.

In the 1930's, Babel lapsed into his famous "silence," a long period of unproductivity. In a witty, ironic speech to the first Soviet Writers' Congress in 1934, he described himself as practicing a "new literary genre—the genre of silence." The silence was certainly not absolute; Babel continued to publish, infrequently but regularly, throughout the decade, and some of his finest stories date from this period. But he did not fulfill his own or his readers' expectations of quantity. Part of the difficulty was domestic and financial. His wife (whom he married in 1919) had emigrated to France in 1925, and although he visited her there several times, she refused to return to Russia, and it was clear that his marriage was over. He began living with another woman in Moscow in 1935 and had a daughter by her in 1937. He was also plagued by financial worries; much of his time was taken up with hack editing and translating and with adapting his and other writers' work for films. (The great Russian film director Serge Eisenstein knew and admired Babel and in a well-known essay remarked on the cinematic quality of his stories.) But the silence also had political roots. The atmosphere for writers in Stalinist Russia was increasingly hostile and repressive, and beginning with *Red Cavalry,* Babel's works had attracted negative criticism. He made some efforts to accommodate his work to the rigid requirements of Social Realism; at one point he planned and partially completed a cycle of stories set on a collective farm. But basically his artistic vision could not be accommodated to the affirmative pieties demanded by the state. Finally he fell victim to Stalin's frightful purges. He was arrested in 1939 and sent to a prison camp, where he died in 1941. The date of his death was not divulged until years later, and no cause of death was given. A large number of unpublished manuscripts were seized when he was arrested; they have

never been recovered. In 1956, after Stalin's death, Babel was "rehabili-tated"; he was posthumously cleared of the charges against him, and re-publication of his work was permitted. He remains better known, however, in the West than in the Soviet Union, where his modernist ambiguities and his Jewish subjects are not popular.

The form to which Babel devoted his artistic life was the short story cycle. His individual stories are very short. Many are only two or three pages long; "The Story of My Dovecot," at about four thousand words, is one of his longest. But by arranging the stories in cycles, Babel achieved something of the scale and sweep of a novel, creating a large structure with small, discrete narrative units. Within each cycle, the stories are very care-fully arranged; he experimented for years with the best order for the *Red Cavalry* stories. Stories within a cycle are linked by common themes, a simi-lar narrative point of view, recurring characters, and, sometimes, a sequen-tial chronology. Babel wrote three such cycles: the Odessa stories, *Red Cav-alry,* and a cycle, which includes "The Story of My Dovecot," of stories about growing up and coming of age. He planned several other cycles, including one to be called "From a Petersburg Diary," but only a few stories survive from these.

The form of the cycle of very short stories was ideally suited to Babel's artistic practices, which were almost obsessively devoted to reduction and compression. Scholars who have examined Babel's surviving manuscripts report that they are full of deletions, of words, phrases, and entire sections, all in the interest of paring the stories down to an irreducible minimum. This art of the miniature is also to be seen in the way small details are used to build up the larger picture. In his use of narrative "fragments," as in his careful manipulation of point of view and in the movement in his stories toward an "epiphany," Babel reminds us of his affinity with his Modernist contemporaries in the West: Virginia Woolf, T. S. Eliot, and James Joyce.

Just as striking as the compression in Babel's work is its use of violence. A great many stories in *Red Cavalry* turn upon a brutal, shocking act of violence. One might expect violence in stories of war experience, but the violence is almost as pronounced in the *Odessa Stories* and the childhood cycle. The American critic Lionel Trilling has commented on two sides of Babel's character by analyzing a well-known photograph of him. The be-spectacled face is that of a Jewish intellectual: "long and thin, charged with emotion and internality; bitter, intense, very sensitive, touched with humor, full of consciousness and contradiction." But this intellectual face peers out at us from above a Cossack's uniform! The idea of a Jewish Cossack, Trilling points out, itself has the quality of a Jewish joke; the Cossack is traditionally the hated and feared enemy of the Jew. But Jew and Cossack meet in *Red Cavalry,* as they do in Babel's personality: in his sensitive irony and contemplativeness, combined with his shocked fascina-tion with the Cossack's primitive energy and violence.

The qualities of the Jew and the Cossack clash also in "The Story of My Dovecot" (1925), one of the earliest stories in the childhood cycle. This story of a bookish Jewish boy who is good at examinations unwinds with a deceptive casualness until violence explodes, shattering his sense of what is real. As he lies on the ground, surveying the "tiny," "awful" world before his eye, he protests, "This trampled earth in no way resembled real life,

waiting for exams in real life." But of course it is real life, with a
fearful Cossack reality, and by the end of the story we can see how artfully
Babel has arranged the small world of the story so as to engage the largest
of questions.

FURTHER READING *(prepared by J. H.):* The best book on Babel in English is Patri-
cia Carden's *The Art of Isaac Babel*, 1972. As a result of the long suppression of
Babel's work in the Soviet Union, a great deal of misinformation circulated about
him in the West for a number of years. Judith Stora-Sandor's 1968 biography (in
French) corrected most of these errors, and Carden presents Stora-Sandor's cor-
rected version of Babel's life in an introductory biographical chapter. Maurice
Friedberg's entry on Babel in *Handbook of Russian Literature*, ed. Victor Terras, 1985,
is brief but authoritative. Also useful are R. W. Hallett, *Isaac Babel*, 1972, in the
British series Russian Literary Profiles, and Milton Ehre, *Isaac Babel*, 1988. The
essay by Lionel Trilling quoted in the introduction appeared as the Introduction to
Babel's *Collected Stories*, trans. Walter Morison, 1955, and was reprinted in Trilling's
Beyond Culture: Essays on Literature and Learning, 1965. It contains many factual er-
rors (the result of the unavailability of facts about Babel's life at the time) but is a
provocative assessment of Babel's work. Also recommended are Renato Poggioli,
"Isaak Babel in Retrospect," in *The Phoenix and the Spider*, 1957; Stanley Edgar
Hyman, "Identities of Isaac Babel," in *The Promised End*, 1963; Marc Slonim, "Isaac
Babel: The Romantic Storyteller," in *Soviet Russian Literature: Writers and Problems*,
1964; Frank O'Connor, "The Romanticization of Violence," in *The Lonely Voice*,
1968; and Avrahm Yarmolinsky, "Isaac Babel (1894–1941)—An Odessa Maupas-
sant?" in *The Russian Literary Imagination*, 1969. *Isaac Babel*, ed. Harold Bloom, 1987,
in the Modern Critical Views series, reprints important critical essays.

THE STORY OF MY DOVECOT

Translated by Walter Morison

TO M. GORKY[1]

When I was a kid I longed for a dovecot.[2] Never in all my life have I
wanted a thing more. But not till I was nine did father promise the where-
withal to buy the wood to make one and three pairs of pigeons to stock it
with. It was then 1904, and I was studying for the entrance exam to the
preparatory class of the secondary school at Nikolayev in the Province of
Kherson, where my people were at that time living. This province of course
no longer exists, and our town has been incorporated in the Odessa Re-
gion.

I was only nine, and I was scared stiff of the exams. In both subjects,
Russian language and arithmetic, I couldn't afford to get less than top

[1] Maxim Gorky (1868–1936), great Russian novelist and playwright, was a lifelong friend
of Babel's. Gorky published Babel's first stories in 1916 in his St. Petersburg journal *The
Chronicle.*
[2] A dovecot, or dovecote, is a house for tame pigeons, usually mounted at a height above
the ground.

marks. At our secondary school the *numerus clausus*[3] was stiff: a mere five percent. So that out of forty boys only two that were Jews could get into the preparatory class. The teachers used to put cunning questions to Jewish boys; no one else was asked such devilish questions. So when father promised to buy the pigeons he demanded top marks with distinction in both subjects. He absolutely tortured me to death. I fell into a state of permanent daydream, into an endless, despairing, childish reverie. I went to the exam deep in this dream, and nevertheless did better than everybody else.

I had a knack for book-learning. Even though they asked cunning questions, the teachers could not rob me of my intelligence and my avid memory. I was good at learning, and got top marks in both subjects. But then everything went wrong. Khariton Efrussi, the corn-dealer who exported wheat to Marseille, slipped someone a 500-rouble bribe. My mark was changed from A to A – , and Efrussi Junior went to the secondary school instead of me. Father took it very badly. From the time I was six he had been cramming me with every scrap of learning he could, and that A – drove him to despair. He wanted to beat Efrussi up, or at least bribe two longshoremen to beat Efrussi up, but mother talked him out of the idea, and I started studying for the second exam the following year, the one for the lowest class. Behind my back my people got the teacher to take me in one year through the preparatory and first-year courses simultaneously, and conscious of the family's despair, I got three whole books by heart. These were Smirnovsky's *Russian Grammar,* Yevtushevsky's *Problems,* and Putsykovich's *Manual of Early Russian History.* Children no longer cram from these books, but I learned them by heart line upon line, and the following year in the Russian exam Karavayev gave me an unrivaled A + .

This Karavayev was a red-faced, irritable fellow, a graduate of Moscow University. He was hardly more than thirty. Crimson glowed in his manly cheeks as it does in the cheeks of peasant children. A wart sat perched on one cheek, and from it there sprouted a tuft of ash-colored cat's whiskers. At the exam, besides Karavayev, there was the Assistant Curator Pyatnitsky, who was reckoned a big noise in the school and throughout the province. When the Assistant Curator asked me about Peter the Great, a feeling of complete oblivion came over me, an awareness that the end was near: an abyss seemed to yawn before me, an arid abyss lined with exultation and despair.

About Peter the Great I knew things by heart from Putsykovich's book and Pushkin's verses.[4] Sobbing, I recited these verses, while the faces before me suddenly turned upside down, were shuffled as a pack of cards is shuffled. This card-shuffling went on, and meanwhile, shivering, jerking my back straight, galloping headlong, I was shouting Pushkin's stanzas at the top of my voice. On and on I yelled them, and no one broke into my crazy mouthings. Through a crimson blindness, through the sense of absolute freedom that had filled me, I was aware of nothing but Pyatnitsky's old face with its silver-touched beard bent toward me. He didn't interrupt me,

[3] Quota for Jewish students.

[4] Probably lines from Pushkin's *Poltava* (1828), a narrative poem celebrating Peter the Great's victory over Charles XII of Sweden at the Battle of Poltava (1709), marking the beginning of Russian supremacy in eastern Europe.

and merely said to Karavayev, who was rejoicing for my sake and Push-kin's:

"What a people," the old man whispered, "those little Jews of yours! There's a devil in them!"

And when at last I could shout no more, he said:

"Very well, run along, my little friend."

I went out from the classroom into the corridor, and there, leaning against a wall that needed a coat of white-wash, I began to awake from my trance. About me Russian boys were playing, the school bell hung not far away above the stairs, the caretaker was snoozing on a chair with a broken seat. I looked at the caretaker, and gradually woke up. Boys were creeping toward me from all sides. They wanted to give me a jab, or perhaps just have a game, but Pyatnitsky suddenly loomed up in the corridor. As he passed me he halted for a moment, the frock coat flowing down his back in a slow heavy wave. I discerned embarrassment in that large, fleshy, upper-class back, and got closer to the old man.

"Children," he said to the boys, "don't touch this lad." And he laid a fat hand tenderly on my shoulder.

"My little friend," he went on, turning me towards him, "tell your father that you are admitted to the first class."

On his chest a great star flashed, and decorations jingled in his lapel. His great black uniformed body started to move away on its stiff legs. Hemmed in by the shadowy walls, moving between them as a barge moves through a deep canal, it disappeared in the doorway of the head-master's study. The little servingman took in a tray of tea, clinking solemnly, and I ran home to the shop.

In the shop a peasant customer, tortured by doubt, sat scratching him-self. When he saw me my father stopped trying to help the peasant make up his mind, and without a moment's hesitation believed everything I had to say. Calling to the assistant to start shutting up shop, he dashed out into Cathedral Street to buy me a school cap with a badge on it. My poor mother had her work cut out getting me away from the crazy fellow. She was pale at that moment, she was experiencing destiny. She kept smoothing me, and pushing me away as though she hated me. She said there was always a notice in the paper about those who had been admitted to the school, and that God would punish us, and that folk would laugh at us if we bought a school cap too soon. My mother was pale; she was experiencing destiny through my eyes. She looked at me with bitter compassion as one might look at a little cripple boy, because she alone knew what a family ours was for misfortunes.

All the men in our family were trusting by nature, and quick to ill-considered actions. We were unlucky in everything we undertook. My grandfather had been a rabbi somewhere in the Belaya Tserkov region. He had been thrown out for blasphemy, and for another forty years he lived noisily and sparsely, teaching foreign languages. In his eightieth year he started going off his head. My Uncle Leo, my father's brother, had studied at the Talmudic Academy in Volozhin. In 1892 he ran away to avoid doing military service, eloping with the daughter of someone serving in the com-missariat in the Kiev military district. Uncle Leo took this woman to Cali-fornia, to Los Angeles, and there he abandoned her, and died in a house of

ill fame among Negroes and Malays. After his death the American police sent us a heritage from Los Angeles, a large trunk bound with brown iron hoops. In this trunk there were dumbbells, locks of women's hair, uncle's talith,[5] horsewhips with gilt handles, scented tea in boxes trimmed with imitation pearls. Of all the family there remained only crazy Uncle Simon-Wolf, who lived in Odessa, my father, and I. But my father had faith in people, and he used to put them off with the transports of first love. People could not forgive him for this, and used to play him false. So my father believed that his life was guided by an evil fate, an inexplicable being that pursued him, a being in every respect unlike him. And so I alone of all our family was left to my mother. Like all Jews I was short, weakly, and had headaches from studying. My mother saw all this. She had never been dazzled by her husband's pauper pride, by his incomprehensible belief that our family would one day be richer and more powerful than all others on earth. She desired no success for us, was scared of buying a school jacket too soon, and all she would consent to was that I should have my photo taken.

On September 20, 1905, a list of those admitted to the first class was hung up at the school. In the list my name figured too. All our kith and kin kept going to look at this paper, and even Shoyl, my granduncle, went along. I loved that boastful old man, for he sold fish at the market. His fat hands were moist, covered with fish-scales, and smelled of worlds chill and beautiful. Shoyl also differed from ordinary folk in the lying stories he used to tell about the Polish Rising of 1861.[6] Years ago Shoyl had been a tavern-keeper at Skvira. He had seen Nicholas I's soldiers shooting Count Godlevski and other Polish insurgents. But perhaps he hadn't. *Now* I know that Shoyl was just an old ignoramus and a simple-minded liar, but his cock-and-bull stories I have never forgotten: they were good stories. Well now, even silly old Shoyl went along to the school to read the list with my name on it, and that evening he danced and pranced at our pauper ball.

My father got up the ball to celebrate my success, and asked all his pals—grain-dealers, real-estate brokers, and the traveling salesmen who sold agricultural machinery in our parts. These salesmen would sell a machine to anyone. Peasants and landowners went in fear of them: you couldn't break loose without buying something or other. Of all Jews, salesmen are the widest-awake and the jolliest. At our party they sang Hasidic[7] songs consisting of three words only but which took an awful long time to sing, songs performed with endless comical intonations. The beauty of these intonations may only be recognized by those who have had the good fortune to spend Passover with the Hasidim or who have visited their noisy Volhynian synagogues. Besides the salesmen, old Lieberman who had taught me the Torah[8] and ancient Hebrew honored us with his presence.

[5] A Jewish prayer-mantle, with fringes at the four corners.
[6] The Congress of Vienna (1814–15) divided Poland between Germany and Russia. The Russian portion had its own constitution, which was, however, suspended after general insurrections in 1830–31. Further Polish risings against the Russians followed in the early 1860's.
[7] The Hasidim are a sect of Jews founded in Poland in the eighteenth century. They oppose the formalistic aspects of rabbinic Judaism and emphasize personal communion with God and emotional exaltation in prayer.
[8] Hebrew name for the first five books of the Bible, the Law of Moses.

In our circle he was known as Monsieur Lieberman. He drank more Bessa-rabian wine than he should have. The ends of the traditional silk tassels poked out from beneath his waistcoat, and in ancient Hebrew he proposed my health. In this toast the old man congratulated my parents and said that I had vanquished all my foes in single combat: I had vanquished the Rus-sian boys with their fat cheeks, and I had vanquished the sons of our own vulgar parvenus. So too in ancient times David King of Judah had over-come Goliath,[9] and just as I had triumphed over Goliath, so too would our people by the strength of their intellect conquer the foes who had encircled us and were thirsting for our blood. Monsieur Lieberman started to weep as he said this, drank more wine as he wept, and shouted *"Vivat!"*[10] The guests formed a circle and danced an old-fashioned quadrille with him in the middle, just as at a wedding in a little Jewish town. Everyone was happy at our ball. Even mother took a sip of vodka, though she neither liked the stuff nor understood how anyone else could—because of this she consid-ered all Russians cracked, and just couldn't imagine how women managed with Russian husbands.

But our happy days came later. For mother they came when of a morn-ing, before I set off for school, she would start making me sandwiches; when we went shopping to buy my school things—pencil box, money box, satchel, new books in cardboard bindings, and exercise books in shiny cov-ers. No one in the world has a keener feeling for new things than children have. Children shudder at the smell of newness as a dog does when it scents a hare, experiencing the madness which later, when we grow up, is called inspiration. And mother acquired this pure and childish sense of the own-ership of new things. It took us a whole month to get used to the pencil box, to the morning twilight as I drank my tea on the corner of the large, brightly-lit table and packed my books in my satchel. It took us a month to grow accustomed to our happiness, and it was only after the first half-term that I remembered about the pigeons.

I had everything ready for them: one rouble fifty and a dovecot made from a box by Grandfather Shoyl, as we called him. The dovecot was painted brown. It had nests for twelve pairs of pigeons, carved strips on the roof, and a special grating that I had devised to facilitate the capture of strange birds. All was in readiness. On Sunday, October 20, I set out for the bird market, but unexpected obstacles arose in my path.

The events I am relating, that is to say my admission to the first class at the secondary school, occurred in the autumn of 1905. The Emperor Nich-olas was then bestowing a constitution on the Russian people.[11] Orators in shabby overcoats were clambering onto tall curbstones and haranguing the people. At night shots had been heard in the streets, and so mother didn't want me to go to the bird market. From early morning on October 20 the boys next door were flying a kite right by the police station, and our water carrier, abandoning all his buckets, was walking about the streets with a red

[9] The story of the defeat of the giant Goliath by the shepherd-boy David is told in I Samuel 17.

[10] "Hurrah!" (French).

[11] In October 1905, Czar Nicholas II granted a parliamentary constitution to Russia. His manifesto granted certain civil rights to Jews; in response, anti-Semitic demonstrations and pogroms broke out across Russia.

face and brilliantined hair. Then we saw baker Kalistov's sons drag a
leather vaulting-horse out into the street and start doing gym in the middle
of the roadway. No one tried to stop them: Semernikov the policeman even
kept inciting them to jump higher. Semernikov was girt with a silk belt his
wife had made him, and his boots had been polished that day as they had
never been polished before. Out of his customary uniform, the policeman
frightened my mother more than anything else. Because of him she didn't
want me to go out, but I sneaked out by the back way and ran to the bird
market, which in our town was behind the station.

At the bird market Ivan Nikodimych, the pigeon-fancier, sat in his cus-
tomary place. Apart from pigeons, he had rabbits for sale too, and a pea-
cock. The peacock, spreading its tail, sat on a perch moving a passionless
head from side to side. To its paw was tied a twisted cord, and the other end
of the cord was caught beneath one leg of Ivan Nikodimych's wicker chair.
The moment I got there I bought from the old man a pair of cherry-
colored pigeons with luscious tousled tails, and a pair of crowned pigeons,
and put them away in a bag on my chest under my shirt. After these pur-
chases I had only forty copecks left, and for this price the old man was not
prepared to let me have a male and female pigeon of the Kryukov breed.
What I liked about Kryukov pigeons was their short, knobbly, good-
natured beaks. Forty copecks was the proper price, but the fancier insisted
on haggling, averting from me a yellow face scorched by the unsociable
passions of bird-snarers. At the end of our bargaining, seeing that there
were no other customers, Ivan Nikodimych beckoned me closer. All went
as I wished, and all went badly.

Toward twelve o'clock, or perhaps a bit later, a man in felt boots passed
across the square. He was stepping lightly on swollen feet, and in his worn-
out face lively eyes glittered.

"Ivan Nikodimych," he said as he walked past the bird-fancier, "pack up
your gear. In town the Jerusalem aristocrats are being granted a constitu-
tion. On Fish Street Grandfather Babel has been constituted to death."

He said this and walked lightly on between the cages like a barefoot
ploughman walking along the edge of a field.

"They shouldn't," murmured Ivan Nikodimych in his wake. "They
shouldn't!" he cried more sternly. He started collecting his rabbits and his
peacock, and shoved the Kryukov pigeons at me for forty copecks. I hid
them in my bosom and watched the people running away from the bird
market. The peacock on Ivan Nikodimych's shoulder was last of all to de-
part. It sat there like the sun in a raw autumnal sky; it sat as July sits on a
pink riverbank, a white-hot July in the long cool grass. No one was left in
the market, and not far off shots were rattling. Then I ran to the station,
cut across a square that had gone topsy-turvy, and flew down an empty lane
of trampled yellow earth. At the end of the lane, in a little wheeled arm-
chair, sat the legless Makarenko, who rode about town in his wheel-chair
selling cigarettes from a tray. The boys in our street used to buy smokes
from him, children loved him, I dashed toward him down the lane.

"Makarenko," I gasped, panting from my run, and I stroked the legless
one's shoulder, "have you seen Shoyl?"

The cripple did not reply. A light seemed to be shining through his
coarse face built up of red fat, clenched fists, chunks of iron. He was fidget-

ing on his chair in his excitement, while his wife Kate, presenting a wadded behind, was sorting out some things scattered on the ground.

"How far have you counted?" asked the legless man, and moved his whole bulk away from the woman, as though aware in advance that her answer would be unbearable.

"Fourteen pair of leggings," said Kate, still bending over, "six undersheets. Now I'm a-counting the bonnets."

"Bonnets!" cried Makarenko, with a choking sound like a sob, "it's clear, Catherine, that God has picked on me, that I must answer for all. People are carting off whole rolls of cloth, people have everything they should, and we're stuck with bonnets."

And indeed a woman with a beautiful burning face ran past us down the lane. She was clutching an armful of fezzes[12] in one arm and a piece of cloth in the other, and in a voice of joyful despair she was yelling for her children, who had strayed. A silk dress and a blue blouse fluttered after her as she flew, and she paid no attention to Makarenko who was rolling his chair in pursuit of her. The legless man couldn't catch up. His wheels clattered as he turned the handles for all he was worth.

"Little lady," he cried in a deafening voice, "where did you get that striped stuff?"

But the woman with the fluttering dress was gone. Round the corner to meet her leaped a rickety cart in which a peasant lad stood upright.

"Where've they all run to?" asked the lad, raising a red rein above the nags jerking in their collars.

"Everybody's on Cathedral Street," said Makarenko pleadingly, "everybody's there, sonny. Anything you happen to pick up, bring it along to me. I'll give you a good price."

The lad bent down over the front of the cart and whipped up his piebald nags. Tossing their filthy croups[13] like calves, the horses shot off at a gallop. The yellow lane was once more yellow and empty. Then the legless man turned his quenched eyes upon me.

"God's picked on me, I reckon," he said lifelessly, "I'm a son of man, I reckon."

And he stretched a hand spotted with leprosy toward me.

"What's that you've got in your sack?" he demanded, and took the bag that had been warming my heart.

With his fat hand the cripple fumbled among the tumbler pigeons and dragged to light a cherry-colored she-bird. Jerking back its feet, the bird lay still on his palm.

"Pigeons," said Makarenko, and squeaking his wheels he rode right up to me. "Damned pigeons," he repeated, and struck me on the cheek.

He dealt me a flying blow with the hand that was clutching the bird. Kate's wadded back seemed to turn upside down, and I fell to the ground in my new overcoat.

"Their spawn must be wiped out," said Kate, straightening up over the bonnets. "I can't a-bear their spawn, nor their stinking menfolk."

She said more things about our spawn, but I heard nothing of it. I lay on the ground, and the guts of the crushed bird trickled down from my

[12] Turkish felt caps, usually red. [13] Hindquarters.

temple. They flowed down my cheek, winding this way and that, splashing, blinding me. The tender pigeon-guts slid down over my forehead, and I closed by solitary unstopped-up eye so as not to see the world that spread out before me. This world was tiny, and it was awful. A stone lay just before my eyes, a little stone so chipped as to resemble the face of an old woman with a large jaw. A piece of string lay not far away, and a bunch of feathers that still breathed. My world was tiny, and it was awful. I closed by eyes so as not to see it, and pressed myself tight into the ground that lay beneath me in soothing dumbness. This trampled earth in no way resembled real life, waiting for exams in real life. Somewhere far away Woe rode across it on a great steed, but the noise of the hoofbeats grew weaker and died away, and silence, the bitter silence that sometimes overwhelms children in their sorrow, suddenly deleted the boundary between my body and the earth that was moving nowhither. The earth smelled of raw depths, of the tomb, of flowers. I smelled its smell and started crying, unafraid. I was walking along an unknown street set on either side with white boxes, walking in a getup of bloodstained feathers, alone between the pavements swept clean as on Sunday, weeping bitterly, fully and happily as I never wept again in all my life. Wires that had grown white hummed above my head, a watchdog trotted on in front, in the lane on one side a young peasant in a waistcoat was smashing a window frame in the house of Khariton Efrussi. He was smashing it with a wooden mallet, striking out with his whole body. Sighing, he smiled all around with the amiable grin of drunkenness, sweat, and spiritual power. The whole street was filled with a splitting, a snapping, the song of flying wood. The peasant's whole existence consisted in bending over, sweating, shouting queer words in some unknown, non-Russian language. He shouted the words and sang, shot out his blue eyes; till in the street there appeared a procession bearing the Cross and moving from the Municipal Building. Old men bore aloft the portrait of the neatly-combed Tsar, banners with graveyard saints swayed above their heads, inflamed old women flew on in front. Seeing the procession, the peasant pressed his mallet to his chest and dashed off in pursuit of the banners, while I, waiting till the tail-end of the procession had passed, made my furtive way home. The house was empty. Its white doors were open, the grass by the dovecot had been trampled down. Only Kuzma was still in the yard. Kuzma the yardman was sitting in the shed laying out the dead Shoyl.

"The wind bears you about like an evil wood-chip," said the old man when he saw me. "You've been away ages. And now look what they've done to granddad."

Kuzma wheezed, turned away from me, and started pulling a fish out of a rent in grandfather's trousers. Two pike perch had been stuck into grandfather: one into the rent in his trousers, the other into his mouth. And while grandfather was dead, one of the fish was still alive, and struggling.

"They've done grandfather in, but nobody else," said Kuzma, tossing the fish to the cat. "He cursed them all good and proper, a wonderful damning and blasting it was. You might fetch a couple of pennies to put on his eyes."

But then, at ten years of age, I didn't know what need the dead had of pennies.

"Kuzma," I whispered, "save us."

And I went over to the yardman, hugged his crooked old back with its one shoulder higher than the other, and over this back I saw grandfather. Shoyl lay in the sawdust, his chest squashed in, his beard twisted upwards, battered shoes on his bare feet. His feet, thrown wide apart, were dirty, lilac-colored, dead. Kuzma was fussing over him. He tied the dead man's jaws and kept glancing over the body to see what else he could do. He fussed as though over a newly-purchased garment, and only cooled down when he had given the dead man's beard a good combing.

"He cursed the lot of 'em right and left," he said, smiling, and cast a loving look over the corpse. "If Tartars had crossed his path he'd have sent them packing, but Russians came, and their women with them, Rooski women. Russians just can't bring themselves to forgive, I know what Rooskis are."

The yardman spread some more sawdust beneath the body, threw off his carpenter's apron, and took me by the hand.

"Let's go to father," he mumbled, squeezing my hand tighter and tighter. "Your father has been searching for you since morning, sure as fate you was dead."

And so with Kuzma I went to the house of the tax-inspector, where my parents, escaping the pogrom, had sought refuge.

William Faulkner
(1897–1962)

The South has been to modern American literature what Ireland has been to modern British literature—the source of a body of writing distinguished for its rich, poetic language and its power to evoke a particular culture, rooted in a specific time and place, and at the same time to escape parochialism and speak with a universality that can capture an international audience. There are many literary Souths—Thomas Wolfe's North Carolina, Katherine Anne Porter's Texas, Eudora Welty's Mississippi—but the most famous is an imaginary one, Yoknapatawpha County, "William Faulkner, sole owner and proprietor" (as Faulkner once wrote on a map of his fictional world). The history, geography, and demography of Yoknapatawpha County gradually evolved in a dozen novels and many more short stories over a period of thirty years. The course of its development was, to quote the title of one of the best books on Faulkner, "from Jefferson to the world." Rooted in the Southern yarning and tale-telling of his hometown of Jefferson, Mississippi, Faulkner's saga, as it unfolds, becomes a spiritual history of the South, a meditation on the course of American history, and ultimately a mythic chronicle of man's fall into experience.

Faulkner was born in 1897 in New Albany, Mississippi, but his parents moved while he was still young to Oxford, home of the University of Missis-

sippi, where his father first ran a livery stable and a hardware store and then became business manager of the university. Faulkner grew up among family tales of the South and of the Civil War; many centered around his great-grandfather, Colonel William C. Falkner (Faulkner added the "u" to the family name), who had fought for the Confederacy and after the war had built a railroad from Ripley into Tennessee and had even written a popular romantic novel, *The White Rose of Memphis.*

Always more interested in reading than in schooling, Faulkner dropped out of high school after two years and took a job in a bank, hoping to marry his sweetheart, Estelle Oldham. In 1918, when Estelle married another man and went to live with him in China, Faulkner joined the Canadian Royal Air Force. The war ended before he had finished his basic training, and he returned to Oxford, where he held a string of miscellaneous jobs, including a three-year stint as postmaster of the university post office. Meanwhile, he was learning to write; *The Marble Faun,* a collection of poems, appeared in 1924 in a private edition. Part of 1925 was spent in New Orleans, where he met a number of writers, including Sherwood Anderson, who helped him arrange for the publication of his first novel, *Soldiers' Pay* (1926). Back in Oxford, Faulkner continued to work at a series of odd jobs while he wrote in the evenings and on weekends. *Mosquitoes,* a novel about literary life in New Orleans, appeared in 1927, but his third novel, *Flags in the Dust,* was rejected. Faulkner immediately set to work revising *Flags in the Dust* and writing a new novel, *The Sound and the Fury.* The revised *Flags in the Dust* appeared early in 1929 as *Sartoris; The Sound and the Fury* appeared later the same year. These two novels marked the end of Faulkner's apprenticeship and inaugurated the Yoknapatawpha cycle.

Estelle Oldham returned to Oxford when her marriage ended in divorce, and she and Faulkner were married in 1929. They bought a run-down antebellum house just outside Oxford; Faulkner worked on it for years with his own hands. During the following twelve years, from 1930 to 1942, Faulkner produced the main body of his Yoknapatawpha series: *As I Lay Dying* (1930), *Sanctuary* (1931), *Light in August* (1932), *Absalom, Absalom!* (1936), *The Unvanquished* (1938), *The Wild Palms* (1939), *The Hamlet* (1940), and *Go Down, Moses* (1942). These books were highly admired by a small circle of his fellow writers and by foreign readers, especially in France, but popular success escaped him; the lurid *Sanctuary* was the only one of his novels of the 1930's to succeed commercially. By 1945, Faulkner's books were out of print, and he had largely given up fiction and was writing films in Hollywood.

The turning point in Faulkner's reputation came in 1945 with the publication of a collection of excerpts from his work, *The Portable Faulkner,* edited by the prominent critic Malcolm Cowley. Cowley, in his long introduction, made clear the essential unity of Faulkner's work and arranged the selections so as to demonstrate the interrelationships among the Yoknapatawpha books. *The Portable Faulkner* was widely and favorably reviewed, and Faulkner's publisher responded to public demand by putting his novels back in print. A new novel, *Intruder in the Dust,* was a popular success in 1948. The following year, Faulkner was awarded the Nobel

Prize. His *Collected Stories* appeared in 1950, *A Fable* in 1954, and *The Town* and *The Mansion,* the concluding volumes of the Snopes trilogy which he had begun with *The Hamlet,* in 1957 and 1959. His last novel, *The Reivers,* was published only a month before his death in Oxford in 1962.

Faulkner's technique, like his materials, was an unexpected combination of down-home earthiness and cosmopolitan sophistication. He had studied closely the great works of the early Modernists, the Symbolist poetry of Charles Baudelaire, Paul Verlaine, and Stéphane Mallarmé, the poetry of T. S. Eliot, and the fiction of James Joyce, and he learned much from their intense concentration upon the ebb and flow of a single consciousness and from their use of symbolism and stream-of-consciousness narrative styles. *The Sound and the Fury* broke new ground by making one of the four points of view from which the story is told that of a mentally retarded man; it is literally "a tale told by an idiot." Other novels are Conradian in their use of a ruminating, Marlow-like narrator whose spiralling meditations on the meaning of the action become the chief center of interest.

The imaginary Yoknapatawpha County was built up like a jigsaw puzzle, not in historic sequence but in bits and pieces. In its completed form, the history of the county spans more than a century, from the displacement of its Indian inhabitants by white settlers through the creation of a plantation society, the collapse of that society in the Civil War, and the aftermath, the coming of the Snopeses, a new breed of sterile, locust-like scramblers displacing the Sartorises and their ordered world. The meaning of the history of the county lies, above all, in the values its people live by. The Sartoris world is a genuine community, bound together by deep respect for the wilderness and the land and by living codes of honor and chivalry. It is doomed, though, by the tragic flaw of slavery, and the War opens the gates to new values from the North and from the embittered misfits within the South, codes based on sterility, voracious self-interest, and exploitation of the land and of other people. There is thus a Chekhovian quality in Faulkner's work, a plangent sense of a lost world which, however, never becomes sentimentally nostalgic; he defends not an idealized past but the enduring qualities which, as he asserted in his Nobel Prize address, will make man "prevail."

"An Odor of Verbena" was originally published as a short story and later became a section of *The Unvanquished;* the full novel traces the career of Colonel John Sartoris as seen through the eyes of his son Bayard. (Even Bayard's name contributes to the story's examination of codes of honor; he is named after a famous fifteenth-century French chivalric hero.) When *The Unvanquished* first appeared, many readers regarded it as a conventional Civil War romance, complete with dashing cavalrymen charging with plumes flying, sentimentalized Blacks defending their masters against the Yankees, and an idealized code of honor. "An Odor of Verbena" alone, the concluding section of the novel, is enough to refute this interpretation. Bayard, in the course of the story, is forced to confront the meaning of his father's code, now embodied in its "Greek amphora priestess," Drusilla Hawk. His choice of action places him among Faulkner's heroes, heroes not of flying plumes but of the human heart.

FURTHER READING *(prepared by J. H.):* Joseph Blotner's *Faulkner,* 1974, one-volume edition 1984, is the definitive biography. A good introductory survey of Faulkner's work is Roy K. Bird's *William Faulkner: Life, Works, and Criticism,* 1984, in the Authoritative Studies in World Literature series; another is Alan Warren Friedman's *William Faulkner,* 1984, in the Literature and Life series. Cleanth Brooks has been an important interpreter of Faulkner for many years. His *William Faulkner: The Yoknapatawpha Country,* 1963, and *William Faulkner: Toward Yoknapatawpha and Beyond,* 1978, are both still standard. *William Faulkner: First Encounters,* 1983, is a transcription of Brooks's lectures on Faulkner's short stories and six major novels. Robert D. Parker's *Faulkner and the Novelistic Imagination,* 1985, is a thoughtful and well-written study of Faulkner's story-telling. Specifically on the short stories, see James B. Carothers' *William Faulkner's Short Stories,* 1985; and Hans H. Skei's *William Faulkner: The Novelist as Short Story Writer,* 1985. *Faulkner: A Collection of Critical Essays,* ed. by Richard Brodhead, 1983, supplements an older volume edited by Robert Penn Warren in the Twentieth Century Views series.

AN ODOR OF VERBENA

1

It was just after supper. I had just opened my *Coke*[1] on the table beneath the lamp; I heard Professor Wilkins' feet in the hall and then the instant of silence as he put his hand to the door knob, and I should have known. People talk glibly of presentiment, but I had none. I heard his feet on the stairs and then in the hall approaching and there was nothing in the feet because although I had lived in this house for three college years now and although both he and Mrs. Wilkins called me Bayard in the house, he would no more have entered my room without knocking than I would have entered his—or hers. Then he flung the door violently inward against the doorstop with one of those gestures with or by which an almost painfully unflagging preceptory of youth ultimately aberrates,[2] and stood there saying, "Bayard. Bayard, my son, my dear son."

I should have known; I should have been prepared. Or maybe I was prepared because I remember how I closed the book carefully, even marking the place, before I rose. He (Professor Wilkins) was doing something, bustling at something; it was my hat and cloak which he handed me and which I took although I would not need the cloak, unless even then I was thinking (although it was October, the equinox had not occurred) that the rains and the cool weather would arrive before I should see this room again and so I would need the cloak anyway to return to it if I returned, thinking "God, if he had only done this last night, flung that door crashing and bouncing against the stop last night without knocking so I could have gotten there before it happened, been there when it did, beside him on whatever spot, wherever it was that he would have to fall and lie in the dust and dirt."

[1] A law book, *Coke on Littleton,* by Sir Edward Coke (1552–1634).
[2] *preceptory . . . aberrates.* A teacher of youth breaks his pattern.

"Your boy is downstairs in the kitchen," he said. It was not until years later that he told me (someone did; it must have been Judge Wilkins) how Ringo had apparently flung the cook aside and come on into the house and into the library where he and Mrs. Wilkins were sitting and said without preamble and already turning to withdraw: "They shot Colonel Sartoris this morning. Tell him I be waiting in the kitchen" and was gone before either of them could move. "He has ridden forty miles yet he refuses to eat anything." We were moving toward the door now—the door on my side of which I had lived for three years now with what I knew, what I knew now I must have believed and expected, yet beyond which I had heard the approaching feet yet heard nothing in the feet. "If there was just anything I could do."

"Yes, sir," I said. "A fresh horse for my boy. He will want to go back with me."

"By all means take mine—Mrs. Wilkins'," he cried. His tone was no different yet he did cry it and I suppose that at the same moment we both realised that was funny—a short-legged deep-barreled mare who looked exactly like a spinster music teacher, which Mrs. Wilkins drove to a basket phaeton[3]—which was good for me, like being doused with a pail of cold water would have been good for me.

"Thank you, sir," I said. "We won't need it. I will get a fresh horse for him at the livery stable when I get my mare." Good for me, because even before I finished speaking I knew that would not be necessary either, that Ringo would have stopped at the livery stable before he came out to the college and attended to that and that the fresh horse for him and my mare both would be saddled and waiting now at the side fence and we would not have to go through Oxford at all. Loosh would not have thought of that if he had come for me, he would have come straight to the college, to Professor Wilkins', and told his news and then sat down and let me take charge from then on. But not Ringo.

He followed me from the room. From now until Ringo and I rode away into the hot thick dusty darkness quick and strained for the overdue equinox like a laboring delayed woman, he would be somewhere either just beside me or just behind me and I never to know exactly nor care which. He was trying to find the words with which to offer me his pistol too. I could almost hear him: "Ah, this unhappy land, not ten years recovered from the fever yet still men must kill one another, still we must pay Cain's price in his own coin."[4] But he did not actually say it. He just followed me, somewhere beside or behind me as we descended the stairs toward where Mrs. Wilkins waited in the hall beneath the chandelier—a thin gray woman who reminded me of Granny, not that she looked like Granny probably but because she had known Granny—a lifted anxious still face which was thinking *Who lives by the sword shall die by it*[5] just as Granny would have thought, toward which I walked, had to walk not because I was Granny's grandson and had lived in her house for three college years and was about the age of

[3] A light, four-wheeled carriage.
[4] That is, through violence, as Cain killed Abel (Genesis 4).
[5] Jesus' words to a companion who cuts off the ear of a servant of the high priest (Matthew 26:52).

her son when he was killed in almost the last battle nine years ago, but because I was now The Sartoris. (The Sartoris: that had been one of the concomitant flashes, along with the *at last it has happened* when Professor Wilkins opened my door.) She didn't offer me a horse and pistol, not because she liked me any less than Professor Wilkins but because she was a woman and so wiser than any man, else the men would not have gone on with the War for two years after they knew they were whipped. She just put her hands (a small woman, no bigger than Granny had been) on my shoulders and said, "Give my love to Drusilla and your Aunt Jenny. And come back when you can."

"Only I don't know when that will be," I said. "I don't know how many things I will have to attend to." Yes, I lied even to her; it had not been but a minute yet since he had flung that door bouncing into the stop yet already I was beginning to realise, to become aware of that which I still had no yard-stick to measure save that one consisting of what, despite myself, despite my raising and background (or maybe because of them) I had for some time known I was becoming and had feared the test of it; I remember how I thought while her hands still rested on my shoulders: *At least this will be my chance to find out if I am what I think I am or if I just hope; if I am going to do what I have taught myself is right or if I am just going to wish I were.*

We went on to the kitchen, Professor Wilkins still somewhere beside or behind me and still offering me the pistol and horse in a dozen different ways. Ringo was waiting; I remember how I thought then that no matter what might happen to either of us, I would never be The Sartoris to him. He was twenty-four too, but in a way he had changed even less than I had since that day when we had nailed Grumby's body to the door of the old compress.[6] Maybe it was because he had outgrown me, had changed so much that summer while he and Granny traded mules with the Yankees that since then I had had to do most of the changing just to catch up with him. He was sitting quietly in a chair beside the cold stove, spent-looking too who had ridden forty miles (at one time, either in Jefferson or when he was alone at last on the road somewhere, he had cried; dust was now caked and dried in the tear-channels on his face) and would ride forty more yet would not eat, looking up at me a little red-eyed with weariness (or maybe it was more than just weariness and so I would never catch up with him) then rising without a word and going on toward the door and I following and Professor Wilkins still offering the horse and the pistol without speaking the words and still thinking (I could feel that too) *Dies by the sword. Dies by the sword.*

Ringo had the two horses saddled at the side gate, as I had known he would—the fresh one for himself and my mare father had given me three years ago, that could do a mile under two minutes any day and a mile every eight minutes all day long. He was already mounted when I realised that what Professor Wilkins wanted was to shake my hand. We shook hands; I know he believed he was touching flesh which might not be alive tomorrow night and I thought for a second how if I told him what I was going to do, since we had talked about it, about how if there was anything at all in the Book, anything of hope and peace for His blind and bewildered spawn

[6] A building where cotton is compressed into bales.

which He had chosen above all others to offer immortality, *Thou shalt not kill*[7] must be it, since maybe he even believed that he had taught it to me except that he had not, nobody had, not even myself since it went further than just having been learned. But I did not tell him. He was too old to be forced so, to condone even in principle such a decision; he was too old to have to stick to principle in the face of blood and raising and background, to be faced without warning and made to deliver like by a highwayman out of the dark: only the young could do that—one still young enough to have his youth supplied him gratis as a reason (not an excuse) for cowardice.

So I said nothing. I just shook his hand and mounted too, and Ringo and I rode on. We would not have to pass through Oxford now and so soon (there was a thin sickle of moon like the heel print of a boot in wet sand) the road to Jefferson lay before us, the road which I had travelled for the first time three years ago with Father and travelled twice at Christmas time and then in June and September and twice at Christmas time again and then June and September again each college term since alone on the mare, not even knowing that this was peace; and now this time and maybe last time who would not die (I knew that) but who maybe forever after could never again hold up his head. The horses took the gait which they would hold for forty miles. My mare knew the long road ahead and Ringo had a good beast too, had talked Hilliard at the livery stable out of a good horse too. Maybe it was the tears, the channels of dried mud across which his strain-reddened eyes had looked at me, but I rather think it was that same quality which used to enable him to replenish his and Granny's supply of United States Army letterheads[8] during that time—some outrageous assurance gained from too long and too close association with white people: the one whom he called Granny, the other with whom he had slept from the time we were born until Father rebuilt the house. We spoke one time, then no more:

"We could bushwhack him," he said. "Like we done Grumby that day. But I reckon that wouldn't suit that white skin you walks around in."

"No," I said. We rode on; it was October; there was plenty of time still for verbena although I would have to reach home before I would realise there was a need for it; plenty of time for verbena yet from the garden where Aunt Jenny puttered beside old Joby, in a pair of Father's old cavalry gauntlets, among the coaxed and ordered beds, the quaint and odorous old names, for though it was October no rain had come yet and hence no frost to bring (or leave behind) the first half-warm half-chill nights of Indian Summer—the drowsing air cool and empty for geese yet languid still with the old hot dusty smell of fox grape and sassafras—the nights when before I became a man and went to college to learn law Ringo and I, with lantern and axe and crokersack[9] and six dogs (one to follow the trail and five more just for the tonguing, the music) would hunt possum in the pasture where, hidden, we had seen our first Yankee that afternoon on the bright horse, where for the last year now you could hear the whistling of the trains which had no longer belonged to Mr. Redmond for a long while now and which at some instant, some second during the morning Father

[7] The sixth of the Ten Commandments (Exodus 20:13). [8] Official stationery.
[9] Burlap bag.

too had relinquished along with the pipe which Ringo said he was smoking, which slipped from his hand as he fell. We rode on, toward the house where he would be lying in the parlor now, in his regimentals[10] (sabre too) and where Drusilla would be waiting for me beneath all the festive glitter of the chandeliers, in the yellow ball gown and the sprig of verbena in her hair, holding the two loaded pistols (I could see that too, who had had no presentiment; I could see her, in the formal brilliant room arranged formally for obsequy, not tall, not slender as a woman is but as a youth, a boy, is motionless, in yellow, the face calm, almost bemused, the head simple and severe, the balancing sprig of verbena above each ear, the two arms bent at the elbows, the two hands shoulder high, the two identical duelling pistols lying upon, not clutched in, one to each: the Greek amphora priestess[11] of a succinct and formal violence).

2

Drusilla said that he had a dream. I was twenty then and she and I would walk in the garden in the summer twilight while we waited for Father to ride in from the railroad. I was just twenty then: that summer before I entered the University to take the law degree which Father decided I should have and four years after the one, the day, the evening when Father and Drusilla had kept old Cash Benbow from becoming United States Marshal and returned home still unmarried and Mrs. Habersham herded them into her carriage and drove them back to town and dug her husband out of his little dim hole in the new bank and made him sign Father's peace bond for killing the two carpet baggers,[12] and took Father and Drusilla to the minister herself and saw that they were married. And Father had rebuilt the house too, on the same blackened spot, over the same cellar, where the other had burned, only larger, much larger: Drusilla said that the house was the aura of Father's dream just as a bride's trousseau and veil is the aura of hers. And Aunt Jenny had come to live with us now so we had the garden (Drusilla would no more have bothered with flowers than Father himself would have, who even now, even four years after it was over, still seemed to exist, breathe, in that last year of it while she had ridden in man's clothes and with her hair cut short like any other member of Father's troop, across Georgia and both Carolinas in front of Sherman's army)[13] for her to gather sprigs of verbena from to wear in her hair because she said verbena was the only scent you could smell above the smell of the horses and courage and so it was the only one that was worth the wearing. The railroad was hardly begun then and Father and Mr. Redmond were not only still partners, they were still friends, which as George Wyatt said was easily a record for Father, and he would leave the house at daybreak on Jupiter, riding up

[10] Dress uniform. [11] Painting of a priestess on a Greek amphora, or vase.

[12] Northerners who went to the South after the Civil War to profit personally by the Reconstruction laws; so called because they were said to carry all their belongings in "carpet bags."

[13] In one of the decisive campaigns of the Civil War, the Northern general William Tecumseh Sherman took Atlanta in 1864 and then marched east across the South, devastating the countryside as he went.

and down the unfinished line with two saddlebags of gold coins borrowed on Friday to pay the men on Saturday, keeping just two cross-ties ahead of the sheriff as Aunt Jenny said. So we walked in the dusk, slowly between Aunt Jenny's flower beds while Drusilla (in a dress now, who still would have worn pants all the time if Father had let her) leaned lightly on my arm and I smelled the verbena in her hair as I had smelled the rain in it and in Father's beard that night four years ago when he and Drusilla and Uncle Buck McCaslin found Grumby and then came home and found Ringo and me more than just asleep: escaped into that oblivion which God or Nature or whoever it was had supplied us with for the time being, who had had to perform more than should be required of children because there should be some limit to the age, the youth at least below which one should not have to kill. This was just after the Saturday night when I returned and I watched him clean the derringer[14] and reload it and we learned that the dead man was almost a neighbor, a hill man who had been in the first infantry regiment when it voted Father out of command: and we never to know if the man actually intended to rob Father or not because Father had shot too quick, but only that he had a wife and several children in a dirt-floored cabin in the hills, to whom Father the next day sent some money and she (the wife) walked into the house two days later while we were sitting at the dinner table and flung the money at Father's face.

"But nobody could have more of a dream than Colonel Sutpen," I said. He had been Father's second-in-command in the first regiment and had been elected colonel when the regiment deposed Father after Second Manassas, and it was Sutpen and not the regiment whom Father never forgave. He was underbred, a cold ruthless man who had come into the country about thirty years before the War, nobody knew from where except Father said you could look at him and know he would not dare to tell. He had got some land and nobody knew how he did that either, and he got money from somewhere—Father said they all believed he robbed steamboats, either as a card sharper or as an out-and-out highwayman—and built a big house and married and set up as a gentleman. Then he lost everything in the War like everybody else, all hope of descendants too (his son killed his daughter's fiancé on the eve of the wedding and vanished) yet he came back home and set out singlehanded to rebuild his plantation. He had no friends to borrow from and he had nobody to leave it to and he was past sixty years old, yet he set out to rebuild his place like it used to be; they told how he was too busy to bother with politics or anything; how when Father and the other men organised the nightriders to keep the carpet baggers from organising the Negroes into an insurrection, he refused to have anything to do with it. Father stopped hating him long enough to ride out to see Sutpen himself and he (Sutpen) came to the door with a lamp and did not even invite them to come in and discuss it; Father said, "Are you with us or against us?" and he said, "I'm for my land. If every man of you would rehabilitate his own land, the country will take care of itself" and Father challenged him to bring the lamp out and set it on a stump where they could both see to shoot and Sutpen would not. "Nobody could have more of a dream than that."

[14] A short-barreled pocket pistol.

"Yes. But his dream is just Sutpen. John's is not. He is thinking of this whole country which he is trying to raise by its bootstraps, so that all the people in it, not just his kind nor his old regiment, but all the people, black and white, the women and children back in the hills who don't even own shoes—Don't you see?"

"But how can they get any good from what he wants to do for them if they are—after he has—"

"Killed some of them? I suppose you include those two carpet baggers he had to kill to hold that first election, don't you?"

"They were men. Human beings."

"They were Northerners, foreigners who had no business here. They were pirates." We walked on, her weight hardly discernible on my arm, her head just reaching my shoulder. I had always been a little taller than she, even on that night at Hawkhurst while we listened to the niggers passing in the road, and she had changed but little since—the same boy-hard body, the close implacable head with its savagely cropped hair which I had watched from the wagon above the tide of crazed singing niggers as we went down into the river—the body not slender as women are but as boys are slender. "A dream is not a very safe thing to be near, Bayard. I know; I had one once. It's like a loaded pistol with a hair trigger: if it stays alive long enough, somebody is going to be hurt. But if it's a good dream, it's worth it. There are not many dreams in the world, but there are a lot of human lives. And one human life or two dozen—"

"Are not worth anything?"

"No. Not anything.—Listen. I hear Jupiter. I'll beat you to the house." She was already running, the skirts she did not like to wear lifted almost to her knees, her legs beneath it running as boys run just as she rode like men ride.

I was twenty then. But the next time I was twenty-four; I had been three years at the University and in another two weeks I would ride back to Oxford for the final year and my degree. It was just last summer, last August, and Father had just beat Redmond for the State legislature. The railroad was finished now and the partnership between Father and Redmond had been dissolved so long ago that most people would have forgotten they were ever partners if it hadn't been for the enmity between them. There had been a third partner but nobody hardly remembered his name now; he and his name both had vanished in the fury of the conflict which set up between Father and Redmond almost before they began to lay the rails, between Father's violent and ruthless dictatorialness and will to dominate (the idea was his; he did think of the railroad first and then took Redmond in) and that quality in Redmond (as George Wyatt said, he was not a coward or Father would never have teamed with him) which permitted him to stand as much as he did from Father, to bear and bear and bear until something (not his will nor his courage) broke in him. During the War Redmond had not been a soldier, he had had something to do with cotton for the Government; he could have made money himself out of it but he had not and everybody knew he had not, Father knew it, yet Father would even taunt him with not having smelled powder. He was wrong; he knew he was when it was too late for him to stop just as a drunkard reaches a point where it is too late for him to stop, where he promises himself that he

will and maybe believes he will or can but it is too late. Finally they reached
the point (they had both put everything they could mortgage or borrow
into it for Father to ride up and down the line, paying the workmen and
the waybills[15] on the rails at the last possible instant) where even Father
realised that one of them would have to get out. So (they were not speaking
then; it was arranged by Judge Benbow) they met and agreed to buy or sell,
naming a price which, in reference to what they had put into it, was ridicu-
lously low but which each believed the other could not raise—at least Fa-
ther claimed that Redmond did not believe he could raise it. So Redmond
accepted the price, and found out that Father had the money. And accord-
ing to Father, that's what started it, although Uncle Buck McCaslin said
Father could not have owned a half interest in even one hog, let alone a
railroad, and not dissolve the business either sworn enemy or death-
pledged friend to his recent partner. So they parted and Father finished
the road. By that time, seeing that he was going to finish it, some Northern
people sold him a locomotive on credit which he named for Aunt Jenny,
with a silver oil can in the cab with her name engraved on it; and last
summer the first train ran into Jefferson, the engine decorated with flow-
ers and Father in the cab blowing blast after blast on the whistle when he
passed Redmond's house; and there were speeches at the station, with
more flowers and a Confederate flag and girls in white dresses and red
sashes and a band, and Father stood on the pilot of the engine and made a
direct and absolutely needless allusion to Mr. Redmond. That was it. He
wouldn't let him alone. George Wyatt came to me right afterward and told
me. "Right or wrong," he said, "us boys and most of the other folks in this
country know John's right. But he ought to let Redmond alone. I know
what's wrong: he's had to kill too many folks, and that's bad for a man. We
all know Colonel's brave as a lion, but Redmond ain't no coward either and
there ain't any use in making a brave man that made one mistake eat crow
all the time. Can't you talk to him?"

"I don't know," I said. "I'll try." But I had no chance. That is, I could
have talked to him and he would have listened, but he could not have heard
me because he had stepped straight from the pilot of that engine into the
race for the Legislature. Maybe he knew that Redmond would have to
oppose him to save his face even though he (Redmond) must have known
that, after that train ran into Jefferson, he had no chance against Father, or
maybe Redmond had already announced his candidacy and Father entered
the race just because of that, I don't remember. Anyway they ran, a bitter
contest in which Father continued to badger Redmond without reason or
need, since they both knew it would be a landslide for Father. And it was,
and we thought he was satisfied. Maybe he thought so himself, as the
drunkard believes that he is done with drink; and it was that afternoon and
Drusilla and I walked in the garden in the twilight and I said something
about what George Wyatt had told me and she released my arm and turned
me to face her and said, "This from you? You? Have you forgotten
Grumby?"

"No," I said. "I never will forget him."

"You never will. I wouldn't let you. There are worse things than killing

[15] Invoices; statements of charges due.

men, Bayard. There are worse things than being killed. Sometimes I think the finest thing that can happen to a man is to love something, a woman preferably, well, hard hard hard, then to die young because he believed what he could not help but believe and was what he could not (could not? would not) help but be." Now she was looking at me in a way she never had before. I did not know what it meant then and was not to know until to-night since neither of us knew then that two months later Father would be dead. I just knew that she was looking at me as she never had before and that the scent of the verbena in her hair seemed to have increased a hun-dred times, to have got a hundred times stronger, to be everywhere in the dusk in which something was about to happen which I had never dreamed of. Then she spoke. "Kiss me, Bayard."

"No. You are Father's wife."

"And eight years older than you are. And your fourth cousin too. And I have black hair. Kiss me, Bayard."

"No."

"Kiss me, Bayard." So I leaned my face down to her. But she didn't move, standing so, bent lightly back from me from the waist, looking at me; now it was she who said, "No." So I put my arms around her. Then she came to me, melted as women will and can, the arms with the wrist- and elbow-power to control horses about my shoulders, using the wrists to hold my face to hers until there was no longer need for the wrists; I thought then of the woman of thirty, the symbol of the ancient and eternal Snake[16] and of the men who have written of her, and I realised then the im-mitigable chasm between all life and all print—that those who can, do, those who cannot and suffer enough because they can't, write about it. Then I was free, I could see her again, I saw her still watching me with that dark inscrutable look, looking up at me now across her down-slanted face; I watched her arms rise with almost the exact gesture with which she had put them around me as if she were repeating the empty and formal gesture of all promise so that I should never forget it, the elbows angling outward as she put her hands to the sprig of verbena in her hair, I standing straight and rigid facing the slightly bent head, the short jagged hair, the rigid curiously formal angle of the bare arms gleaming faintly in the last of light as she removed the verbena sprig and put it into my lapel, and I thought how the War had tried to stamp all the women of her generation and class in the South into a type and how it had failed—the suffering, the identical experience (hers and Aunt Jenny's had been almost the same except that Aunt Jenny had spent a few nights with her husband before they brought him back home in an ammunition wagon while Gavin Breckbridge was just Drusilla's fiancé) was there in the eyes, yet beyond that was the incorrigibly individual woman: not like so many men who return from wars to live on Government reservations like so many steers, emasculate and empty of all save an identical experience which they cannot forget and dare not, else they would cease to live at that moment, almost interchangeable save for the old habit of answering to a given name.

"Now I must tell Father," I said.

"Yes," she said. "You must tell him. Kiss me." So again it was like it had

[16] That is, the Serpent of the Garden of Eden (Genesis 3).

been before. No. Twice, a thousand times and never like—the eternal and symbolical thirty to a young man, a youth, each time both cumulative and retroactive, immitigably unrepetitive, each wherein remembering excludes experience, each wherein experience antedates remembering; the skill without weariness, the knowledge virginal to surfeit, the cunning secret muscles to guide and control just as within the wrists and elbows lay slumbering the mastery of horses: she stood back, already turning, not looking at me when she spoke, never having looked at me, already moving swiftly on in the dusk: "Tell John. Tell him tonight."

I intended to. I went to the house and into the office at once; I went to the center of the rug before the cold hearth, I don't know why, and stood there rigid like soldiers stand, looking at eye level straight across the room and above his head and said, "Father" and then stopped. Because he did not even hear me. He said, "Yes, Bayard?" but he did not hear me although he was sitting behind the desk doing nothing, immobile, as still as I was rigid, one hand on the desk with a dead cigar in it, a bottle of brandy and a filled and untasted glass beside his hand, clothed quiet and bemused in whatever triumph it was he felt since the last overwhelming return of votes had come in late in the afternoon. So I waited until after supper. We went to the dining room and stood side by side until Aunt Jenny entered and then Drusilla, in the yellow ball gown, who walked straight to me and gave me one fierce inscrutable look then went to her place and waited for me to draw her chair while Father drew Aunt Jenny's. He had roused by then, not to talk himself but rather to sit at the head of the table and reply to Drusilla as she talked with a sort of feverish and glittering volubility—to reply now and then to her with that courteous intolerant pride which had lately become a little forensic, as if merely being in a political contest filled with fierce and empty oratory had retroactively made a lawyer of him who was anything and everything except a lawyer. Then Drusilla and Aunt Jenny rose and left us and he said, "Wait" to me who had made no move to follow and directed Joby to bring one of the bottles of wine which he had fetched back from New Orleans when he went there last to borrow money to liquidate his first private railroad bonds. Then I stood again like soldiers stand, gazing at eye level above his head while he sat half-turned from the table, a little paunchy now though not much, a little grizzled too in the hair though his beard was as strong as ever, with that spurious forensic air of lawyers and the intolerant eyes which in the last two years had acquired that transparent film which the eyes of carnivorous animals have and from behind which they look at a world which no ruminant ever sees, perhaps dares to see, which I have seen before on the eyes of men who have killed too much, who have killed so much that never again as long as they live will they ever be alone. I said again, "Father," then I told him.

"Hah?" he said. "Sit down." I sat down, I looked at him, watched him fill both glasses and this time I knew it was worse with him than not hearing: it didn't even matter. "You are doing well in the law, Judge Wilkins tells me. I am pleased to hear that. I have not needed you in my affairs so far, but from now on I shall. I have now accomplished the active portion of my aims in which you could not have helped me; I acted as the land and the time demanded and you were too young for that, I wished to shield you. But now the land and the time too are changing; what will follow will be a

matter of consolidation, of pettifogging and doubtless chicanery in which I would be a babe in arms but in which you, trained in the law, can hold your own—our own. Yes, I have accomplished my aim, and now I shall do a little moral house-cleaning. I am tired of killing men, no matter what the necessity nor the end. Tomorrow, when I go to town and meet Ben Redmond, I shall be unarmed."

3

We reached home just before midnight; we didn't have to pass through Jefferson either. Before we turned in the gates I could see the lights, the chandeliers—hall, parlor, and what Aunt Jenny (without any effort or perhaps even design on her part) had taught even Ringo to call the drawing room, the light falling outward across the portico, past the columns. Then I saw the horses, the faint shine of leather and buckle-glints on the black silhouettes and then the men too—Wyatt and others of Father's old troop— and I had forgot that they would be there. I had forgot that they would be there; I remember how I thought, since I was tired and spent with strain, *Now it will have to begin tonight. I won't even have until tomorrow in which to begin to resist.* They had a watchman, a picquet[17] out, I suppose, because they seemed to know at once that we were in the drive. Wyatt met me, I halted the mare, I could look down at him and at the others gathered a few yards behind him with that curious vulture-like formality which Southern men assume in such situations.

"Well, boy," George said.

"Was it—" I said. "Was he—"

"It was all right. It was in front. Redmond ain't no coward. John had the derringer inside his cuff like always, but he never touched it, never made a move toward it." I have seen him do it, he showed me once: the pistol (it was not four inches long) held flat inside his left wrist by a clip he made himself of wire and an old clock spring; he would raise both hands at the same time, cross them, fire the pistol from beneath his left hand almost as if he were hiding from his own vision what he was doing; when he killed one of the men he shot a hole through his own coat sleeve. "But you want to get on to the house," Wyatt said. He began to stand aside, then he spoke again: "We'll take this off your hands, any of us. Me." I hadn't moved the mare yet and I had made no move to speak, yet he continued quickly, as if he had already rehearsed all this, his speech and mine, and knew what I would say and only spoke himself as he would have removed his hat on entering a house or used "sir" in conversing with a stranger: "You're young, just a boy, you ain't had any experience in this kind of thing. Besides, you got them two ladies in the house to think about. He would understand, all right."

"I reckon I can attend to it," I said.

"Sure," he said; there was no surprise, nothing at all, in his voice because he had already rehearsed this: "I reckon we all knew that's what you would say." He stepped back then; almost it was as though he and not I

[17] Guard.

bade the mare to move on. But they all followed, still with that unctuous and voracious formality. Then I saw Drusilla standing at the top of the front steps, in the light from the open door and the windows like a theatre scene, in the yellow ball gown and even from here I believed that I could smell the verbena in her hair, standing there motionless yet emanating something louder than the two shots must have been—something voracious too and passionate. Then, although I had dismounted and someone had taken the mare, I seemed to be still in the saddle and to watch myself enter that scene which she had postulated like another actor while in the background for chorus Wyatt and the others stood with the unctuous formality which the Southern man shows in the presence of death—that Roman holiday engendered by mist-born Protestantism grafted onto this land of violent sun, of violent alteration from snow to heat-stroke which has produced a race impervious to both. I mounted the steps toward the figure straight and yellow and immobile as a candle which moved only to extend one hand; we stood together and looked down at them where they stood clumped, the horses too gathered in a tight group beyond them at the rim of light from the brilliant door and windows. One of them stamped and blew his breath and jangled his gear.

"Thank you, gentlemen," I said. "My aunt and my—Drusilla thank you. There's no need for you to stay. Goodnight." They murmured, turning. George Wyatt paused, looking back at me.

"Tomorrow?" he said.

"Tomorrow." Then they went on, carrying their hats and tiptoeing, even on the ground, the quiet and resilient earth, as though anyone in that house awake would try to sleep, anyone already asleep in it whom they could have wakened. Then they were gone and Drusilla and I turned and crossed the portico, her hand lying light on my wrist yet discharging into me with a shock like electricity that dark and passionate voracity, the face at my shoulder—the jagged hair with a verbena sprig above each ear, the eyes staring at me with that fierce exaltation. We entered the hall and crossed it, her hand guiding me without pressure, and entered the parlor. Then for the first time I realised it—the alteration which is death—not that he was now just clay but that he was lying down. But I didn't look at him yet because I knew that when I did I would begin to pant; I went to Aunt Jenny who had just risen from a chair behind which Louvinia stood. She was Father's sister, taller than Drusilla but no older, whose husband had been killed at the very beginning of the War, by a shell from a Federal frigate at Fort Moultrie, come to us from Carolina six years ago. Ringo and I went to Tennessee Junction in the wagon to meet her. It was January, cold and clear and with ice in the ruts; we returned just before dark with Aunt Jenny on the seat beside me holding a lace parasol and Ringo in the wagon bed nursing a hamper basket containing two bottles of old sherry and the two jasmine cuttings which were bushes in the garden now, and the panes of colored glass which she had salvaged from the Carolina house where she and Father and Uncle Bayard were born and which Father had set in a fanlight above one of the drawing room windows for her—who came up the drive and Father (home now from the railroad) went down the steps and lifted her from the wagon and said, "Well, Jenny," and she said, "Well, Johnny," and began to cry. She stood too, looking at me as I approached—

the same hair, the same high nose, the same eyes as Father's except that
they were intent and very wise instead of intolerant. She said nothing at all,
she just kissed me, her hands light on my shoulders. Then Drusilla spoke,
as if she had been waiting with a sort of dreadful patience for the empty
ceremony to be done, in a voice like a bell: clear, unsentient, on a single
pitch, silvery and triumphant: "Come, Bayard."

"Hadn't you better go to bed now?" Aunt Jenny said.

"Yes," Drusilla said in that silvery ecstatic voice, "Oh yes. There will be
plenty of time for sleep." I followed her, her hand again guiding me without
pressure; now I looked at him. It was just as I had imagined it—sabre,
plumes, and all—but with that alteration, that irrevocable difference which
I had known to expect yet had not realised, as you can put food into your
stomach which for a while the stomach declines to assimilate—the illimita-
ble grief and regret as I looked down at the face which I knew—the nose,
the hair, the eyelids closed over the intolerance—the face which I realised I
now saw in repose for the first time in my life; the empty hands still now
beneath the invisible stain of what had been (once, surely) needless blood,
the hands now appearing clumsy in their very inertness, too clumsy to have
performed the fatal actions which forever afterward he must have waked
and slept with and maybe was glad to lay down at last—those curious ap-
pendages clumsily conceived to begin with yet with which man has taught
himself to do so much, so much more than they were intended to do or
could be forgiven for doing, which had now surrendered that life to which
his intolerant heart had fiercely held; and then I knew that in a minute I
would begin to pant. So Drusilla must have spoken twice before I heard her
and turned and saw in the instant Aunt Jenny and Louvinia watching us,
hearing Drusilla now, the unsentient bell quality gone now, her voice whis-
pering into that quiet death-filled room with a passionate and dying fall:
"Bayard." She faced me, she was quite near; again the scent of the verbena
in her hair seemed to have increased a hundred times as she stood holding
out to me, one in either hand, the two duelling pistols. "Take them, Bay-
ard," she said, in the same tone in which she had said "Kiss me" last sum-
mer, already pressing them into my hands, watching me with that passion-
ate and voracious exaltation, speaking in a voice fainting and passionate
with promise: "Take them. I have kept them for you. I give them to you.
Oh you will thank me, you will remember me who put into your hands
what they say is an attribute only of God's, who took what belongs to
heaven and gave it to you. Do you feel them? the long true barrels true as
justice, the triggers (you have fired them) quick as retribution, the two of
them slender and invincible and fatal as the physical shape of love?" Again
I watched her arms angle out and upward as she removed the two verbena
sprigs from her hair in two motions faster than the eye could follow, al-
ready putting one of them into my lapel and crushing the other in her
other hand while she still spoke in that rapid passionate voice not much
louder than a whisper: "There. One I give to you to wear tomorrow (it will
not fade), the other I cast away, like this—" dropping the crushed bloom at
her feet. "I abjure it. I abjure verbena forever more; I have smelled it above
the odor of courage; that was all I wanted. Now let me look at you." She
stood back, staring at me—the face tearless and exalted, the feverish eyes
brilliant and voracious. "How beautiful you are: do you know it? How

beautiful: young, to be permitted to kill, to be permitted vengeance, to take into your bare hands the fire of heaven that cast down Lucifer.[18] No; I. I gave it to you; I put it into your hands; Oh you will thank me, you will remember me when I am dead and you are an old man saying to himself, 'I have tasted all things.'—It will be the right hand, won't it?" She moved; she had taken my right hand which still held one of the pistols before I knew what she was about to do; she had bent and kissed it before I comprehended why she took it. Then she stopped dead still, still stooping in that attitude of fierce exultant humility, her hot lips and her hot hands still touching my flesh, light on my flesh as dead leaves yet communicating to it that battery charge dark, passionate and damned forever of all peace. Because they are wise, women are—a touch, lips or fingers, and the knowledge, even clairvoyance, goes straight to the heart without bothering the laggard brain at all. She stood erect now, staring at me with intolerable and amazed incredulity which occupied her face alone for a whole minute while her eyes were completely empty; it seemed to me that I stood there for a full minute while Aunt Jenny and Louvinia watched us, waiting for her eyes to fill. There was no blood in her face at all, her mouth open a little and pale as one of those rubber rings women seal fruit jars with. Then her eyes filled with an expression of bitter and passionate betrayal. "Why, he's not—" she said. "He's not—And I kissed his hand," she said in an aghast whisper; "*I kissed his hand!*" beginning to laugh, the laughter, rising, becoming a scream yet still remaining laughter, screaming with laughter, trying herself to deaden the sound by putting her hand over her mouth, the laughter spilling between her fingers like vomit, the incredulous betrayed eyes still watching me across the hand.

"Louvinia!" Aunt Jenny said. They both came to her. Louvinia touched and held her and Drusilla turned her face to Louvinia.

"I kissed his hand, Louvinia!" she cried. "Did you see it? *I kissed his hand!*" the laughter rising again, becoming the scream again yet still remaining laughter, she still trying to hold it back with her hand like a small child who has filled its mouth too full.

"Take her upstairs," Aunt Jenny said. But they were already moving toward the door, Louvinia half-carrying Drusilla, the laughter diminishing as they neared the door as though it waited for the larger space of the empty and brilliant hall to rise again. Then it was gone; Aunt Jenny and I stood there and I knew soon that I would begin to pant. I could feel it beginning like you feel regurgitation beginning, as though there were not enough air in the room, the house, not enough air anywhere under the heavy hot low sky where the equinox couldn't seem to accomplish, nothing in the air for breathing, for the lungs. Now it was Aunt Jenny who said "Bayard" twice before I heard her. "You are not going to try to kill him. All right."

"All right?" I said.

"Yes. All right. Don't let it be Drusilla, a poor hysterical young woman. And don't let it be him, Bayard, because he's dead now. And don't let it be George Wyatt and those others who will be waiting for you tomorrow morning. I know you are not afraid."

[18] The rebel archangel whom God cast out of Heaven.

"But what good will that do?" I said. "What good will that do?" It almost began then; I stopped it just in time. "I must live with myself, you see."

"Then it's not just Drusilla? Not just him? Not just George Wyatt and Jefferson?"

"No," I said.

"Will you promise to let me see you before you go to town tomorrow?" I looked at her; we looked at one another for a moment. Then she put her hands on my shoulders and kissed me and released me, all in one motion. "Goodnight, son," she said. Then she was gone too and now it could begin. I knew that in a minute I would look at him and it would begin and I did look at him, feeling the long-held breath, the hiatus before it started, thinking how maybe I should have said, "Goodbye, Father" but did not. Instead I crossed to the piano and laid the pistols carefully on it, still keeping the panting from getting too loud too soon. Then I was outside on the porch and (I don't know how long it had been) I looked in the window and saw Simon squatting on a stool beside him. Simon had been his body servant during the War and when they came home Simon had a uniform too—a Confederate private's coat with a Yankee brigadier's star on it and he had put it on now too, like they had dressed Father, squatting on the stool beside him, not crying, not weeping the facile tears which are the white man's futile trait and which Negroes know nothing about but just sitting there, motionless, his lower lip slacked down a little; he raised his hand and touched the coffin, the black hand rigid and fragile-looking as a clutch of dead twigs, then dropped the hand; once he turned his head and I saw his eyes roll red and unwinking in his skull like those of a cornered fox. It had begun by that time; I panted, standing there, and this was it—the regret and grief, the despair out of which the tragic mute insensitive bones stand up that can bear anything, anything.

4

After a while the whippoorwills stopped and I heard the first day bird, a mockingbird. It had sung all night too but now it was the day song, no longer the drowsy moony fluting. Then they all began—the sparrows from the stable, the thrush that lived in Aunt Jenny's garden, and I heard a quail too from the pasture and now there was light in the room. But I didn't move at once. I still lay on the bed (I hadn't undressed) with my hands under my head and the scent of Drusilla's verbena faint from where my coat lay on a chair, watching the light grow, watching it turn rosy with the sun. After a while I heard Louvinia come up across the back yard and go into the kitchen; I heard the door and then the long crash of her armful of stovewood into the box. Soon they would begin to arrive—the carriages and buggies in the drive—but not for a while yet because they too would wait first to see what I was going to do. So the house was quiet when I went down to the diningroom, no sound in it except Simon snoring in the parlor, probably still sitting on the stool though I didn't look in to see. Instead I stood at the diningroom window and drank the coffee which Louvinia brought me, then I went to the stable; I saw Joby watching me from the kitchen door as I crossed the yard and in the stable Loosh looked up at me

across Betsy's head, a curry comb in his hand, though Ringo didn't look at me at all. We curried Jupiter then. I didn't know if we would be able to without trouble or not, since always Father would come in first and touch him and tell him to stand and he would stand like a marble horse (or pale bronze rather) while Loosh curried him. But he stood for me too, a little restive but he stood, then that was done and now it was almost nine o'clock and soon they would begin to arrive and I told Ringo to bring Betsy on to the house.

I went on to the house and into the hall. I had not had to pant in some time now but it was there, waiting, a part of the alteration, as though by being dead and no longer needing air he had taken all of it, all that he had compassed and claimed and postulated between the walls which he had built, along with him. Aunt Jenny must have been waiting; she came out of the diningroom at once, without a sound, dressed, the hair that was like Father's combed and smooth above the eyes that were different from Father's eyes because they were not intolerant but just intent and grave and (she was wise too) without pity. "Are you going now?" she said.

"Yes." I looked at her. Yes, thank God, without pity. "You see, I want to be thought well of."

"I do," she said. "Even if you spend the day hidden in the stable loft, I still do."

"Maybe if she knew that I was going. Was going to town anyway."

"No," she said. "No, Bayard." We looked at one another. Then she said quietly, "All right. She's awake." So I mounted the stairs. I mounted steadily, not fast because if I had gone fast the panting would have started again or I might have had to slow for a second at the turn or at the top and I would not have gone on. So I went slowly and steadily, across the hall to her door and knocked and opened it. She was sitting at the window, in something soft and loose for morning in her bedroom only she never did look like morning in a bedroom because here was no hair to fall about her shoulders. She looked up, she sat there looking at me with her feverish brilliant eyes and I remembered I still had the verbena sprig in my lapel and suddenly she began to laugh again. It seemed to come not from her mouth but to burst out all over her face like sweat does and with a dreadful and painful convulsion as when you have vomited until it hurts you yet still you must vomit again—burst out all over her face except her eyes, the brilliant incredulous eyes looking at me out of the laughter as if they belonged to somebody else, as if they were two inert fragments of tar or coal lying on the bottom of a receptacle filled with turmoil: "I kissed his hand! *I kissed his hand!*" Louvinia entered, Aunt Jenny must have sent her directly after me; again I walked slowly and steadily so it would not start yet, down the stairs where Aunt Jenny stood beneath the chandelier in the hall as Mrs. Wilkins had stood yesterday at the University. She had my hat in her hand. "Even if you hid all day in the stable, Bayard," she said. I took the hat; she said quietly, pleasantly, as if she were talking to a stranger, a guest: "I used to see a lot of blockade runners[19] in Charleston. They were heroes in a way, you see—not heroes because they were helping to prolong the

[19] During the Civil War, the North blockaded Southern ports. Blockade runners were sailors who slipped through the blockade.

Confederacy but heroes in the sense that David Crockett or John Sevier[20] would have been to small boys or fool young women. There was one of them, an Englishman. He had no business there; it was the money of course, as with all of them. But he was the Davy Crockett to us because by that time we had all forgot what money was, what you could do with it. He must have been a gentleman once or associated with gentlemen before he changed his name, and he had a vocabulary of seven words, though I must admit he got along quite well with them. The first four were, 'I'll have rum, thanks,' and then, when he had the rum, he would use the other three— across the champagne, to whatever ruffled bosom or low gown: 'No bloody moon.' No bloody moon, Bayard."

Ringo was waiting with Betsy at the front steps. Again he did not look at me, his face sullen, downcast even while he handed me the reins. But he said nothing, nor did I look back. And sure enough I was just in time; I passed the Compson carriage at the gates, General Compson lifted his hat as I did mine as we passed. It was four miles to town but I had not gone two of them when I heard the horse coming up behind me and I did not look back because I knew it was Ringo. I did not look back; he came up on one of the carriage horses, he rode up beside me and looked me full in the face for one moment, the sullen determined face, the eyes rolling at me defiant and momentary and red; we rode on. Now we were in town—the long shady street leading to the square, the new courthouse at the end of it; it was eleven o'clock now: long past breakfast and not yet noon so there were only women on the street, not to recognise me perhaps or at least not the walking stopped sudden and dead in midwalking as if the legs contained the sudden eyes, the caught breath, that not to begin until we reached the square and I thinking *If I could only be invisible until I reach the stairs to his office and begin to mount.* But I could not, I was not; we rode up to the Holston House and I saw the row of feet along the gallery rail come suddenly and quietly down and I did not look at them, I stopped Betsy and waited until Ringo was down then I dismounted and gave him the reins. "Wait for me here," I said.

"I'm going with you," he said, not loud; we stood there under the still circumspect eyes and spoke quietly to one another like two conspirators. Then I saw the pistol, the outline of it inside his shirt, probably the one we had taken from Grumby that day we killed him.

"No you ain't," I said.

"Yes I am."

"No you ain't." So I walked on, along the street in the hot sun. It was almost noon now and I could smell nothing except the verbena in my coat, as if it had gathered all the sun, all the suspended fierce heat in which the equinox could not seem to occur and were distilling it so that I moved in a cloud of verbena as I might have moved in a cloud of smoke from a cigar. Then George Wyatt was beside me (I don't know where he came from) and five or six others of Father's old troop a few yards behind, George's hand on my arm, drawing me into a doorway out of the avid eyes like caught breaths.

[20] Famous frontiersmen. Crockett (1786–1836) was U.S. Representative from Tennessee; he died at the Alamo. Sevier (1745–1815) became Governor of Tennessee.

"Have you got that derringer?" George said.

"No," I said.

"Good," George said. "They are tricky things to fool with. Couldn't nobody but Colonel ever handle one right; I never could. So you take this. I tried it this morning and I know it's right. Here." He was already fumbling the pistol into my pocket, then the same thing seemed to happen to him that happened to Drusilla last night when she kissed my hand—something communicated by touch straight to the simple code by which he lived, without going through the brain at all: so that he too stood suddenly back, the pistol in his hand, staring at me with his pale outraged eyes and speaking in a whisper thin with fury: "Who are you? Is your name Sartoris? By God, if you don't kill him, I'm going to." Now it was not panting, it was a terrible desire to laugh, to laugh as Drusilla had, and say, "That's what Drusilla said." But I didn't. I said,

"I'm tending to this. You stay out of it. I don't need any help." Then his fierce eyes faded gradually, exactly as you turn a lamp down.

"Well," he said, putting the pistol back into his pocket. "You'll have to excuse me, son. I should have knowed you wouldn't do anything that would keep John from laying quiet. We'll follow you and wait at the foot of the steps. And remember: he's a brave man, but he's been sitting in that office by himself since yesterday morning waiting for you and his nerves are on edge."

"I'll remember," I said. "I don't need any help." I had started on when suddenly I said it without having any warning that I was going to: "No bloody moon."

"What?" he said. I didn't answer. I went on across the square itself now, in the hot sun, they following though not close so that I never saw them again until afterward, surrounded by the remote still eyes not following me yet either, just stopped where they were before the stores and about the door to the courthouse, waiting. I walked steadily on enclosed in the now fierce odor of the verbena sprig. Then shadow fell upon me; I did not pause, I looked once at the small faded sign nailed to the brick *B. J. Redmond. Atty at Law* and began to mount the stairs, the wooden steps scuffed by the heavy bewildered boots of countrymen approaching litigation and stained by tobacco spit, on down the dim corridor to the door which bore the name again, *B. J. Redmond* and knocked once and opened it. He sat behind the desk, not much taller than Father but thicker as a man gets who spends most of his time sitting and listening to people, freshly shaven and with fresh linen; a lawyer yet it was not a lawyer's face—a face much thinner than the body would indicate, strained (and yes, tragic; I know that now) and exhausted beneath the neat recent steady strokes of the razor, holding a pistol flat on the desk before him, loose beneath his hand and aimed at nothing. There was no smell of drink, not even of tobacco in the neat clean dingy room although I knew he smoked. I didn't pause. I walked steadily toward him. It was not twenty feet from door to desk yet I seemed to walk in a dreamlike state in which there was neither time nor distance, as though the mere act of walking was no more intended to encompass space than was his sitting. We didn't speak. It was as if we both knew what the passage of words would be and the futility of it; how he might have said, "Go out, Bayard. Go away, boy" and then, "Draw then. I will allow you to

draw" and it would have been the same as if he had never said it. So we did not speak; I just walked steadily toward him as the pistol rose from the desk. I watched it, I could see the foreshortened slant of the barrel and I knew it would miss me though his hand did not tremble. I walked toward him, toward the pistol in the rocklike hand, I heard no bullet. Maybe I didn't even hear the explosion though I remember the sudden orange bloom and smoke as they appeared against his white shirt as they had appeared against Grumby's greasy Confederate coat; I still watched that foreshortened slant of barrel which I knew was not aimed at me and saw the second orange flash and smoke and heard no bullet that time either. Then I stopped; it was done then. I watched the pistol descend to the desk in short jerks; I saw him release it and sit back, both hands on the desk, I looked at his face and I knew too what it was to want air when there was nothing in the circumambience for the lungs. He rose, shoved the chair back with a convulsive motion and rose, with a queer ducking motion of his head; with his head still ducked aside and one arm extended as though he couldn't see and the other hand resting on the desk as if he couldn't stand alone, he turned and crossed to the wall and took his hat from the rack and with his head still ducked aside and one hand extended he blundered along the wall and passed me and reached the door and went through it. He was brave; no one denied that. He walked down those stairs and out onto the street where George Wyatt and the other six of Father's old troop waited and where the other men had begun to run now; he walked through the middle of them with his hat on and his head up (they told me how someone shouted at him: "Have you killed that boy too?"), saying no word, staring straight ahead and with his back to them, on to the station where the southbound train was just in and got on it with no baggage, nothing, and went away from Jefferson and from Mississippi and never came back.

I heard their feet on the stairs then in the corridor then in the room, but for a while yet (it wasn't that long, of course) I still sat behind the desk as he had sat, the flat of the pistol still warm under my hand, my hand growing slowly numb between the pistol and my forehead. Then I raised my head; the little room was full of men. "My God!" George Wyatt cried. "You took the pistol away from him and then missed him, missed him *twice*?" Then he answered himself—that same rapport for violence which Drusilla had and which in George's case was actual character judgment: "No; wait. You walked in here without even a pocket knife and let him miss you twice. My God in heaven." He turned, shouting: "Get to hell out of here! You, White, ride out to Sartoris and tell his folks it's all over and he's all right. Ride!" So they departed, went away; presently only George was left, watching me with that pale bleak stare which was speculative yet not at all ratiocinative. "Well by God," he said. "—Do you want a drink?"

"No," I said. "I'm hungry. I didn't eat any breakfast."

"I reckon not, if you got up this morning aiming to do what you did. Come on. We'll go to the Holston House."

"No," I said. "No. Not there."

"Why not? You ain't done anything to be ashamed of. I wouldn't have done it that way, myself. I'd a shot at him once, anyway. But that's your way or you wouldn't have done it."

"Yes," I said. "I would do it again."

"Be damned if I would.—You want to come home with me? We'll have time to eat and then ride out there in time for the——" But I couldn't do that either.

"No," I said. "I'm not hungry after all. I think I'll go home."

"Don't you want to wait and ride out with me?"

"No, I'll go on."

"You don't want to stay here, anyway." He looked around the room again, where the smell of powder smoke still lingered a little, still lay somewhere on the hot dead air though invisible now, blinking a little with his fierce pale unintroverted eyes. "Well by God," he said again. "Maybe you're right, maybe there has been enough killing in your family without—Come on." We left the office. I waited at the foot of the stairs and soon Ringo came up with the horses. We crossed the square again. There were no feet on the Holston House railing now (it was twelve o'clock) but a group of men stood before the door who raised their hats and I raised mine and Ringo and I rode on.

We did not go fast. Soon it was one, maybe after; the carriages and buggies would begin to leave the square soon, so I turned from the road at the end of the pasture and I sat the mare, trying to open the gate without dismounting, until Ringo dismounted and opened it. We crossed the pasture in the hard fierce sun; I could have seen the house now but I didn't look. Then we were in the shade, the close thick airless shade of the creek bottom; the old rails still lay in the undergrowth where we had built the pen to hide the Yankee mules. Presently I heard the water, then I could see the sunny glints. We dismounted. I lay on my back, I thought *Now it can begin again if it wants to.* But it did not. I went to sleep. I went to sleep almost before I had stopped thinking. I slept for almost five hours and I didn't dream anything at all yet I waked myself up crying, crying too hard to stop it. Ringo was squatting beside me and the sun was gone though there was a bird of some sort still singing somewhere and the whistle of the north-bound evening train sounded and the short broken puffs of starting where it had evidently stopped at our flag station. After a while I began to stop and Ringo brought his hat full of water from the creek but instead I went down to the water myself and bathed my face.

There was still a good deal of light in the pasture, though the whippoor-wills had begun, and when we reached the house there was a mockingbird singing in the magnolia, the night song now, the drowsy moony one, and again the moon like the rim print of a heel in wet sand. There was just one light in the hall now and so it was all over though I could still smell the flowers even above the verbena in my coat. I had not looked at him again. I had started to before I left the house but I did not, I did not see him again and all the pictures we had of him were bad ones because a picture could no more have held him dead than the house could have kept his body. But I didn't need to see him again because he was there, he would always be there; maybe what Drusilla meant by his dream was not something which he possessed but something which he had bequeathed us which we could never forget, which would even assume the corporeal shape of him whenever any of us, black or white, closed our eyes. I went into the house. There was no light in the drawing room except the last of the afterglow which came through the western window where Aunt Jenny's colored glass was; I

was about to go on upstairs when I saw her sitting there beside the window. She didn't call me and I didn't speak Drusilla's name, I just went to the door and stood there. "She's gone," Aunt Jenny said. "She took the evening train. She has gone to Montgomery, to Dennison." Denny had been married about a year now; he was living in Montgomery, reading law.

"I see," I said. "Then she didn't——" But there wasn't any use in that either; Jed White must have got there before one o'clock and told them. And besides, Aunt Jenny didn't answer. She could have lied to me but she didn't, she said,

"Come here." I went to her chair. "Kneel down. I can't see you."

"Don't you want the lamp?"

"No. Kneel down." So I knelt beside the chair. "So you had a perfectly splendid Saturday afternoon, didn't you? Tell me about it." Then she put her hands on my shoulders. I watched them come up as though she were trying to stop them; I felt them on my shoulders as if they had a separate life of their own and were trying to do something which for my sake she was trying to restrain, prevent. Then she gave up or she was not strong enough because they came up and took my face between them, hard, and suddenly the tears sprang and streamed down her face like Drusilla's laughing had. "Oh, damn you Sartorises!" she said. "Damn you! Damn you!"

As I passed down the hall the light came up in the diningroom and I could hear Louvinia laying the table for supper. So the stairs were lighted quite well. But the upper hall was dark. I saw her open door (that unmistakable way in which an open door stands open when nobody lives in the room any more) and I realised I had not believed that she was really gone. So I didn't look into the room. I went on to mine and entered. And then for a long moment I thought it was the verbena in my lapel which I still smelled. I thought that until I had crossed the room and looked down at the pillow on which it lay—the single sprig of it (without looking she would pinch off a half dozen of them and they would be all of a size, almost all of a shape, as if a machine had stamped them out) filling the room, the dusk, the evening with that odor which she said you could smell alone above the smell of horses.

Bertolt Brecht
(1898–1956)

Marxism, like Darwinism and Freudianism, has resonated through the culture of the twentieth century. Money, as a subject of literature, has had almost as long a history as love, but only with the publication of the first volume of Karl Marx's *Capital* in 1869 did anyone try to see all culture—art, philosophy, religion, human nature itself—as a logical extension of

economic conditions, a "superstructure" that sublimates the fundamental relationships of individuals and classes to the means of production. Marxist ideas have been expressed in literature in the productions of Socialist Realism, the style dictated by the Soviet Union and other Communist countries; in the plays of Bernard Shaw and Sean O'Casey; in the "proletarian" literature that appeared in the wake of the Great Depression of the 1930's; and in the post-World War II fiction of France, Germany, and England. The preeminent Marxist writer of the twentieth century, however, is the German dramatist Bertolt Brecht, who not only explored the implications of Marxist thought in a series of masterful plays and poems but also created a Marxist theory of drama that has had a wide influence upon the other arts as well.

Brecht was born in 1898 into a prosperous and pious middle-class family in Augsburg, Bavaria. His father, the manager of a paper mill, was a Roman Catholic, but Brecht was raised in his mother's Lutheran faith; Brecht later mentioned the vigorous earthiness of Luther's translation of the Bible as a major influence upon his own style.

When Brecht was nineteen, he enrolled as a medical student at the University of Munich. His studies were interrupted by a year of military service during which he was assigned to a military hospital in his hometown of Augsburg. After the war, he returned to Munich but gradually drifted away from his medical studies into Munich theatrical life. Brecht played the guitar and sang his own songs in cafes. He also began to experiment with playwriting; *Baal* (1918), a wildly romantic play about a violently self-destructive young poet, was heavily influenced by the French symbolist poets Paul Verlaine and Arthur Rimbaud and by the expressionist playwrights August Strindberg and Frank Wedekind. *Drums in the Night* (1918), an equally nihilistic and cynical play about a returned German soldier set against the background of the communist Spartakist uprising of 1918, was produced by the Munich Kammerspiele Theater, won the prestigious Kleist Prize, and brought Brecht immediate fame. *In the Jungle of Cities* (1923) and an adaptation of Christopher Marlowe's *Life of Edward II* (1924) were also produced successfully in Munich.

The first, Munich phase of Brecht's career ended in 1924 with a move to Berlin and a job as dramaturg (play reader and literary advisor) in the Deutsches Theater, run by the great director Max Reinhardt. The cynicism and anarchy of Brecht's early plays had struck a responsive chord in members of his generation, many of them embittered and disillusioned by the bourgeois culture that had produced, it seemed, the horrors of the First World War. Now he turned in reaction, as many of his young contemporaries did, to Marxism, which seemed to promise a positive alternative to capitalism. The first fruit of his intensive study of Marxism was *A Man's a Man* (1925), a sardonic comedy that examines, against a background of a Kiplingesque India, the power of external conditions over even such seemingly immutable facts as human identity. *The Threepenny Opera*, an updating of John Gay's eighteenth-century satire *The Beggar's Opera*, with music by Kurt Weill, gave Brecht his first major popular success in 1928. Also belonging to this period are a series of short didactic plays developing points of Marxist doctrine and intended to be produced by amateur groups: *The Flight of the Lindberghs* (1929), *The Didactic Play of Baden: On Consent* (1929),

The Exception and the Rule (1930), *The Measures Taken* (1930), and several others.

Brecht's outspoken Communist stance made it impossible for him to remain in Germany when Hitler came to power, and in 1933 he began a period of exile that was to last for fourteen years. He settled first in Denmark, moved to Sweden in 1939 and to Finland in 1940, and finally fled to the United States in 1941, settling in Santa Monica, California. Brecht wrote his greatest plays during this period of enforced exile when his native land was in the grip of the forces that Brecht hated most. During the Nazi regime, he wrote a series of rather ephemeral anti-Nazi propaganda plays, including *Fears and Miseries of the Third Reich* (1938) and *The Resistible Rise of Arturo Ui* (1941), which depicts Hitler as a Chicago gangster. But the major work of the war years was a series of powerful, poetic plays that combined the vitality of the first, nihilist period with the discipline of the second, didactic period: *Mother Courage and Her Children* (1939), *Galileo* (1939), *The Good Woman of Setzuan* (1940), and *The Caucasian Chalk Circle* (1945). In 1947, Brecht was called to testify before the House Committee on Un-American Activities; the Committee was poorly prepared, questioned Brecht ineptly, and dismissed him with thanks for his cooperation. He moved to Europe permanently the following day.

The nine years that remained to Brecht were devoted more to production of his plays and to creating the famous Berliner Ensemble than to writing new plays. Settling first in Switzerland, Brecht, in 1949, accepted an offer from the government of East Germany to direct his own company in East Berlin. The company, which eventually occupied the old Schiffbauerdamm theater, where *The Threepenny Opera* had played in 1928, became one of the finest theater companies of the world, rivalling the Moscow Art Theater and Dublin's Abbey Theatre in its influence upon world drama. Here Brecht directed the first German productions of many of his greatest plays and wrote a series of adaptations to furnish a repertoire for the new company: *The Private Tutor* (1950), based on an eighteenth-century play by Jacob Lenz; *Don Juan* (1952), based on the play by Molière; *Coriolanus* (1953), based on Shakespeare's play; and *Trumpets and Drums* (1956), based on George Farquhar's Restoration comedy *The Recruiting Officer*. The relationship between Brecht and the East German government was not always smooth; Brecht's practice did not follow the official government line of Socialist Realism, and in 1951, the government banned the production of his *Trial of Lucullus* on the grounds that it was too pacifist. Brecht died in Berlin in 1956.

Surprisingly, despite Brecht's vehement rejection of the German tradition of philosopher-artists from Goethe through Nietzsche and Wagner to Thomas Mann, he can best be seen as belonging in some ways to that tradition. He had a profoundly moral conception of his art, one that he elaborated into a theory of drama, most fully expressed in *A Little Organum for the Theater* (1948). This theory has come under fire from both Communist critics, who regard it as elitist and over-intellectualized, and Western capitalist critics, especially in America, who, when they want to praise Brecht, often insist that he "transcended" his theory to produce fundamentally traditional, "universal" plays. Basically, Brecht's theory of the "epic" (narrative) theater is a theory of the psychology of audience response. Tra-

ditional theater (what he called "Aristotelian" theater) encourages the spectator to identify uncritically with the main character and thereby to accept without question the values of the play's dramatic world. The playwright seeks to create the illusion that the play is happening in the present and to encourage the audience in a "willing suspension of disbelief" (to use Coleridge's phrase). Epic theater, in contrast, encourages the audience to maintain a skeptical detachment toward the characters and events of the play, not identifying uncritically with them but seeing them as examples of the relationship between "human nature" and social conditions. The epic playwright therefore organizes the action of his play into short, discrete segments and employs a number of "distancing devices" (*Verfremdungs-Effekts*) to discourage identification and to remind the spectators that they are watching a play, not real life: visible stage machinery, shifts in mode such as the introduction of verses, songs, and direct addresses to the audience, and stage settings that place realistic elements against nonrealistic backgrounds.

It is easy to disagree with the theory of the Epic Theater as a general theory of drama, but Brecht was obviously writing what Eliot called "programmatic criticism," intended to explain and justify his own practice. And Brecht's great plays, far from "transcending" his theories, brilliantly validate them.

The Good Woman of Setzuan, like all of Brecht's major plays, is set in a distant, largely imaginary society. Brecht cared little for historical realism; his India of *A Man's a Man*, his Chicago of *In the Jungle of Cities* and *St. Joan of the Stockyards* (1930), and his Yukon of *Mahagonny* (1929) are ludicrously inaccurate, and the Setzuan of *The Good Woman of Setzuan* has little to do with the real China. (When someone pointed out to Brecht that Setzuan, or Szechwan, was a province rather than a city, he merely laughed and declined to change his description.) Setzuan, like Brecht's India, Chicago, and Yukon, is modern capitalist society; its dreamlike unreality is a distancing device to throw into relief not historical or geographic fact but the theme of how a society based on competition can determine human nature. The Good Woman's enforced splitting into Shen Te and Shui Ta is a theatrical metaphor for the self-division inherent in a society that makes goodness and survival incompatible. The Good Woman becomes two people, as Kafka's Gregor Samsa in "The Metamorphosis" becomes an insect and Eliot's protagonist in *The Waste Land* becomes a schizophrenic when they are faced with similar modern threats to identity. And if Brecht, unlike Kafka or Eliot, believes that there is a political answer to these modern ills of alienation and self-division, he wisely withholds that answer. Shen Te's final desperate questions—"Could one change people? Can the world be changed?"—can be answered only by the audience.

FURTHER READING (*prepared by J. H.*): Ronald Hayman's *Brecht: A Biography*, 1983, is perhaps the best account in English. A companion volume by Hayman, *Brecht: The Plays*, 1984, offers good interpretations of the major plays. John Willett's *The Theatre of Bertolt Brecht*, 1959, rev. 1968, has long been a standard work. Willett's *Brecht in Context: Comparative Approaches*, 1983, explores Brecht's relation to other arts and sciences. Martin Esslin's *Brecht: A Choice of Evils*, 4th rev. ed. 1984, is a sensible, readable overview. So is Karl-Heinz Schoeps' *Bertolt Brecht*, 1977. Eric Bentley has been a long-time champion of Brecht's works in America. His edition of

Seven Plays by Bertolt Brecht, 1961, provides a good sampling of other plays, as well as a splendid introduction. Bentley's interpretations of Brecht's plays are collected in *The Brecht Commentaries*, 1981. His personal encounters with Brecht are recorded in *The Brecht Memoir*, 1985. Elizabeth Wright's *Postmodern Brecht*, 1989, is an interesting recent treatment.

THE GOOD WOMAN OF SETZUAN

Translated by Eric Bentley

CHARACTERS

WONG, *a water seller*
THREE GODS
SHEN TE, *a prostitute, later
a shopkeeper*
MRS. SHIN, *former owner of
Shen Te's shop*
A FAMILY OF EIGHT (*husband,
wife, brother, sister-in-
law, grandfather, nephew,
niece, boy*)
AN UNEMPLOYED MAN
A CARPENTER

MRS. MI TZU, *Shen Te's
landlady*
YANG SUN, *an unemployed pi-
lot, later a factory manager*
AN OLD WHORE
A POLICEMAN
AN OLD MAN
AN OLD WOMAN, *his wife*
MR. SHU FU, *a barber*
MRS. YANG, *mother of Yang Sun*
GENTLEMEN, VOICES, CHILDREN
(3), etc.

PROLOGUE

At the gates of the half-westernized city of Setzuan. Evening. WONG *the Water Seller
introduces himself to the audience.*

WONG. I sell water here in the city of Setzuan. It isn't easy. When water is scarce, I have long distances to go in search of it, and when it is plentiful, I have no income. But in our part of the world there is nothing unusual about poverty. Many people think only the gods can save the situation. And I hear from a cattle merchant—who travels a lot—that some of the highest gods are on their way here at this very moment. Informed sources have it that heaven is quite disturbed at all the complaining. I've been coming out here to the city gates for three days now to bid these gods welcome. I want to be the first to greet them. What about those fellows over there? No, no, they *work*. And that one there has ink on his fingers, he's no god, he must be a clerk from the cement factory. *Those* two are another story. They look as though they'd like to beat you. But gods don't need to beat you, do they? [*Enter* THREE Gods.] What about those three? Old-fashioned clothes—dust on their feet—they *must* be gods! [*He throws himself at their feet.*] Do with me what you will, illustrious ones!

FIRST GOD [*with an ear trumpet*]. Ah! [*He is pleased.*] So we were expected?

WONG [*giving them water*]. Oh, yes. And I *knew* you'd come.

FIRST GOD. We need somewhere to stay the night. You know of a place?

WONG. The whole town is at your service, illustrious ones! What sort of a place would you like?

[*The* GODS *eye each other.*]

FIRST GOD. Just try the first house you come to, my son.

WONG. That would be Mr. Fo's place.

FIRST GOD. Mr. Fo.

WONG. One moment! [*He knocks at the first house.*]

VOICE FROM MR. FO'S. No!

[WONG *returns a little nervously.*]

WONG. It's too bad. Mr. Fo isn't in. And his servants don't dare do a thing without his consent. He'll have a fit when he finds out who they turned away, won't he?

FIRST GOD [*smiling*]. He will, won't he?

WONG. One moment! The next house is Mr. Cheng's. Won't he be thrilled?

FIRST GOD. Mr. Cheng.

[WONG *knocks.*]

VOICE FROM MR. CHENG'S. Keep your gods. We have our own troubles!

WONG [*back with the* GODS]. Mr. Cheng is very sorry, but he has a houseful of relations. I think some of them are a bad lot, and naturally, he wouldn't like you to see them.

THIRD GOD. Are we so terrible?

WONG. Well, only with bad people, of course. Everyone knows the province of Kwan is always having floods.

SECOND GOD. Really? How's *that*?

WONG. Why, because they're so irreligious.

SECOND GOD. Rubbish. It's because they neglected the dam.

FIRST GOD [*to* SECOND]. Sh! [*To* WONG.] You're still in hopes, aren't you, my son?

WONG. Certainly. All Setzuan is competing for the honor! What happened up to now is pure coincidence. I'll be back. [*He walks away, but then stands undecided.*]

SECOND GOD. What did I tell you?

THIRD GOD. It *could* be pure coincidence.

SECOND GOD. The same coincidence in Shun, Kwan, and Setzuan? People just aren't religious any more, let's face the fact. Our mission has failed!

FIRST GOD. Oh come, we might run into a good person any minute.

THIRD GOD. How did the resolution read? [*Unrolling a scroll and reading from it.*] "The world can stay as it is if enough people are found living lives worthy of human beings." Good people, that is. Well, what about this Water Seller himself? *He's* good, or I'm very much mistaken.

SECOND GOD. You're very much mistaken. When he gave us a drink, I had the impression there was something odd about the cup. Well, look! [*He shows the cup to the* FIRST GOD.]

FIRST GOD. A false bottom!

SECOND GOD. The man is a swindler.

FIRST GOD. Very well, count *him* out. That's one man among millions. And as a matter of fact, we only need one on *our* side. These atheists are saying, "The world must be changed because no one can *be* good and

stay good." No one, eh? I say: let us find one—just one—and we have those fellows where we want them!

THIRD GOD [*to* WONG]. Water Seller, is it so hard to find a place to stay?

WONG. Nothing could be easier. It's just me. I don't go about it right.

THIRD GOD. Really? [*He returns to the others. A* GENTLEMAN *passes by.*]

WONG. Oh dear, they're catching on. [*He accosts the* GENTLEMAN.] Excuse the intrusion, dear sir, but three gods have just turned up. Three of the very highest. They need a place for the night. Seize this rare opportunity—to have real gods as your guests!

GENTLEMAN [*laughing*]. A new way of finding free rooms for a gang of crooks.

[*Exit* GENTLEMAN.]

WONG [*shouting at him*]. Godless rascal! Have you no religion, gentlemen of Setzuan? [*Pause.*] Patience, illustrious ones! [*Pause.*] There's only one person left. Shen Te, the prostitute. She *can't* say no. [*Calls up to a window.*] Shen Te!

[SHEN TE *opens the shutters and looks out.*]

WONG. *They're* here, and nobody wants them. Will you take them?

SHEN TE. Oh, no, Wong, I'm expecting a gentleman.

WONG. Can't you forget about him for tonight?

SHEN TE. The rent has to be paid tomorrow or I'll be out on the street.

WONG. This is no time for calculation, Shen Te.

SHEN TE. Stomachs rumble even on the Emperor's birthday, Wong.

WONG. Setzuan is one big dung hill!

SHEN TE. Oh, very well! I'll hide till my gentleman has come and gone. Then I'll take them. [*She disappears.*]

WONG. They mustn't see her gentleman or they'll know what she is.

FIRST GOD [*who hasn't heard any of this*]. I think it's hopeless.

[*They approach* WONG.]

WONG [*jumping, as he finds them behind him*]. A room has been found, illustrious ones! [*He wipes sweat off his brow.*]

SECOND GOD. Oh, good.

THIRD GOD. Let's see it.

WONG [*nervously*]. Just a minute. It has to be tidied up a bit.

THIRD GOD. Then we'll sit down here and wait.

WONG [*still more nervous*]. No, no! [*Holding himself back.*] Too much traffic, you know.

THIRD GOD [*with a smile*]. Of course, if you *want* us to move.

[*They retire a little. They sit on a doorstep.* WONG *sits on the ground.*]

WONG [*after a deep breath*]. You'll be staying with a single girl—the finest human being in Setzuan!

THIRD GOD. That's nice.

WONG [*to the audience*]. They gave me such a look when I picked up my cup just now.

THIRD GOD. You're worn out, Wong.

WONG. A little, maybe.

FIRST GOD. Do people here have a hard time of it?

WONG. The good ones do.

FIRST GOD. What about yourself?

WONG. You mean I'm not good. That's true. And I don't have an easy time either!

[*During this dialogue, a* GENTLEMAN *has turned up in front of* SHEN TE'S *house, and has whistled several times. Each time* WONG *has given a start.*]

THIRD GOD [*to* WONG, *softly*]. Psst! I think he's gone now.

WONG [*confused and surprised*]. Ye-e-es.

[*The* GENTLEMAN *has left now, and* SHEN TE *has come down to the street.*]

SHEN TE [*softly*]. Wong!

[*Getting no answer, she goes off down the street.* WONG *arrives just too late, forgetting his carrying pole.*]

WONG [*softly*]. Shen Te! Shen Te! [*To himself.*] So she's gone off to earn the rent. Oh dear, I can't go to the gods *again* with no room to offer them. Having failed in the service of the gods, I shall run to my den in the sewer pipe down by the river and hide from their sight!

[*He rushes off.* SHEN TE *returns, looking for him, but finding the gods. She stops in confusion.*]

SHEN TE. You are the illustrious ones? My name is Shen Te. It would please me very much if my simple room could be of use to you.

THIRD GOD. Where is the Water Seller, Miss . . . Shen Te?

SHEN TE. I missed him, somehow.

FIRST GOD. Oh, he probably thought you weren't coming, and was afraid of telling us.

THIRD GOD [*picking up the carrying pole*]. We'll leave this with you. He'll be needing it.

[*Led by* SHEN TE, *they go into the house. It grows dark, then light. Dawn. Again escorted by* SHEN TE, *who leads them through the half-light with a little lamp, the* GODS *take their leave.*]

FIRST GOD. Thank you, thank you, dear Shen Te, for your elegant hospitality! We shall not forget! And give our thanks to the Water Seller—he showed us a good human being.

SHEN TE. Oh, *I'm* not good. Let me tell you something: when Wong asked me to put you up, I hesitated.

FIRST GOD. It's all right to hesitate if you then go ahead! And in giving us that room you did much more than you knew. You proved that good people still exist, a point that has been disputed of late—even in heaven. Farewell!

SECOND GOD. Farewell!

THIRD GOD. Farewell!

SHEN TE. Stop, illustrious ones! I'm not sure you're right. I'd like to be good, it's true, but there's the rent to pay. And that's not all: I sell myself for a living. Even so I can't make ends meet, there's too much competition. I'd like to honor my father and mother and speak nothing but the

truth and not covet my neighbor's house. I should love to stay with one
man. But how? How is it done? Even breaking only a *few* of your com-
mandments, I can hardly manage.

FIRST GOD [*clearing his throat*]. These thoughts are but, um, the misgivings
of an unusually good woman!

THIRD GOD. Goodbye, Shen Te! Give our regards to the Water Seller!

SECOND GOD. And above all: be good! Farewell!

FIRST GOD. Farewell!

THIRD GOD. Farewell!

[*They start to wave goodbye.*]

SHEN TE. But everything is so expensive, I don't feel sure I can do it!

SECOND GOD. That's not in our sphere. We never meddle with economics.

THIRD GOD. One moment.

[*They stop.*]

Isn't it true she might do better if she had more money?

SECOND GOD. Come, come! How could we ever account for it Up Above?

FIRST GOD. Oh, there are ways. [*They put their heads together and confer in
dumb show. To* SHEN TE, *with embarrassment.*] As you say you can't pay
your rent, well, um, we're not paupers, so of course we *insist* on paying
for our room. [*Awkwardly thrusting money into her hands.*] There! [*Quickly.*]
But don't tell anyone! The incident is open to misinterpretation.

SECOND GOD. It certainly is!

FIRST GOD [*defensively*]. But there's no law against it! It was never decreed
that a god mustn't pay hotel bills!

[*The* GODS *leave.*]

SCENE I

*A small tobacco shop. The shop is not as yet completely furnished and hasn't started
doing business.*

SHEN TE [*to the audience*]. It's three days since the gods left. When they said
they wanted to pay for the room, I looked down at my hand, and there
was more than a thousand silver dollars! I bought a tobacco shop with
the money, and moved in yesterday. I don't own the building, of course,
but I can pay the rent, and I hope to do a lot of good here. Beginning
with Mrs. Shin, who's just coming across the square with her pot. She
had the shop before me, and yesterday she dropped in to ask for rice
for her children.

[*Enter* MRS. SHIN. *Both women bow.*]

How do you do, Mrs. Shin.

MRS. SHIN. How do you do, Miss Shen Te. You like your new home?

SHEN TE. Indeed, yes. Did your children have a good night?

MRS. SHIN. In that hovel? The youngest is coughing already.

SHEN TE. Oh, dear!

MRS. SHIN. You're going to learn a thing or two in these slums.

SHEN TE. Slums? That's not what you said when you sold me the shop!

MRS. SHIN. Now don't start nagging! Robbing me and my innocent chil-
dren of their home and then calling it a slum! That's the limit! [*She weeps.*]

SHEN TE [*tactfully*]. I'll get your rice.

MRS. SHIN. And a little cash while you're at it.

SHEN TE. I'm afraid I haven't sold anything yet.

MRS. SHIN [*screeching*]. I've got to have it. Strip the clothes from my back and then cut my throat, will you? I know what I'll do: I'll leave my children on your doorstep! [*She snatches the pot out of* SHEN TE'S *hands.*]

SHEN TE. Please don't be angry. You'll spill the rice.

[*Enter an elderly* HUSBAND *and* WIFE *with their shabbily-dressed* NEPHEW.]

WIFE. Shen Te, dear! You've come into money, they tell me. And we haven't a roof over our heads! A tobacco shop. We had one too. But it's gone. Could we spend the night here, do you think?

NEPHEW [*appraising the shop*]. Not bad!

WIFE. He's our nephew. We're inseparable!

MRS. SHIN. And who are these . . . ladies and gentlemen?

SHEN TE. They put me up when I first came in from the country. [*To the audience.*] Of course, when my small purse was empty, they put me out on the street, and they may be afraid I'll do the same to them. [*To the newcomers, kindly.*] Come in, and welcome, though I've only one little room for you—it's behind the shop.

HUSBAND. That'll do. Don't worry.

WIFE [*bringing* SHEN TE *some tea*]. We'll stay over here, so we won't be in your way. Did you make it a tobacco shop in memory of your first real home? We can certainly give you a hint or two! That's one reason we came.

MRS. SHIN [*to* SHEN TE]. Very nice! As long as you have a few customers too!

HUSBAND. Sh! A customer!

[*Enter an* UNEMPLOYED MAN, *in rags.*]

UNEMPLOYED MAN. Excuse me. I'm unemployed.

[MRS. SHIN *laughs.*]

SHEN TE. Can I help you?

UNEMPLOYED MAN. Have you any damaged cigarettes? I thought there might be some damage when you're unpacking.

WIFE. What nerve, begging for tobacco! [*Rhetorically.*] Why don't they ask for bread?

UNEMPLOYED MAN. Bread is expensive. One cigarette butt and I'll be a new man.

SHEN TE [*giving him cigarettes*]. That's very important—to be a new man. You'll be my first customer and bring me luck.

[*The* UNEMPLOYED MAN *quickly lights a cigarette, inhales, and goes off, coughing.*]

WIFE. Was that right, Shen Te, dear?

MRS. SHIN. If this is the opening of a shop, you can hold the closing at the end of the week.

HUSBAND. I bet he had money on him.

SHEN TE. Oh, no, he said he hadn't!

NEPHEW. How d'you know he wasn't lying?

SHEN TE [*angrily*]. How do you know he was?

WIFE [*wagging her head*]. You're too good, Shen Te, dear. If you're going to keep this shop, you'll have to learn to say No.

HUSBAND. Tell them the place isn't yours to dispose of. Belongs to . . . some relative who insists on all accounts being strictly in order . . .

MRS. SHIN. That's right! What do you think you are—a philanthropist?

SHEN TE [*laughing*]. Very well, suppose I ask you for my rice back, Mrs. Shin?

WIFE [*combatively, at* MRS. SHIN]. So that's *her* rice?

[*Enter the* CARPENTER, *a small man.*]

MRS. SHIN [*who, at the sight of him, starts to hurry away*]. See you tomorrow, Miss Shen Te! [*Exit* MRS. SHIN.]

CARPENTER. Mrs. Shin, it's you I want!

WIFE [*to* SHEN TE]. Has she some claim on you?

SHEN TE. She's hungry. That's a claim.

CARPENTER. Are you the new tenant? And filling up the shelves already? Well, they're not yours till they're paid for, ma'am. I'm the carpenter, so I should know.

SHEN TE. I took the shop "furnishings included."

CARPENTER. You're in league with that Mrs. Shin, of course. All right: I demand my hundred silver dollars.

SHEN TE. I'm afraid I haven't got a hundred silver dollars.

CARPENTER. Then you'll find it. Or I'll have you arrested.

WIFE [*whispering to* SHEN TE]. That relative: make it a cousin.

SHEN TE. Can't it wait till next month?

CARPENTER. No!

SHEN TE. Be a little patient, Mr. Carpenter, I can't settle all claims at once.

CARPENTER. Who's patient with me? [*He grabs a shelf from the wall.*] Pay up—or I take the shelves back!

WIFE. Shen Te! Dear! Why don't you let your . . . cousin settle this affair? [*To* CARPENTER.] Put your claim in writing. Shen Te's cousin will see you get paid.

CARPENTER [*derisively*]. Cousin, eh?

HUSBAND. Cousin, yes.

CARPENTER. I know these cousins!

NEPHEW. Don't be silly. He's a personal friend of mine.

HUSBAND. What a man! Sharp as a razor!

CARPENTER. All right. I'll put my claim in writing. [*Puts shelf on floor, sits on it, writes out bill.*]

WIFE [*to* SHEN TE]. He'd tear the dress off your back to get his shelves. Never recognize a claim! That's my motto.

SHEN TE. He's done a job, and wants something in return. It's shameful that I can't give it to him. What will the gods say?

HUSBAND. You did your bit when you took *us* in.

[*Enter the* BROTHER, *limping, and the* SISTER-IN-LAW, *pregnant.*]

BROTHER [*to* HUSBAND *and* WIFE]. So this is where you're hiding out! There's family feeling for you! Leaving us on the corner!

WIFE [*embarrassed, to* SHEN TE]. It's my brother and his wife. [*To them.*] Now stop grumbling, and sit quietly in that corner. [*To* SHEN TE.] It can't be helped. She's in her fifth month.

SHEN TE. Oh yes. Welcome!

WIFE [*to the couple*]. Say thank you.

[*They mutter something.*]
The cups are here. [*To* SHEN TE.] Lucky you bought this shop when you did!

SHEN TE [*laughing and bringing tea*]. Lucky indeed!
[*Enter* MRS. MI TZU, *the landlady.*]

MRS. MI TZU. Miss Shen Te? I am Mrs. Mi Tzu, your landlady. I hope our relationship will be a happy one. I like to think I give my tenants modern, personalized service. Here is your lease. [*To the others, as* SHEN TE *reads the lease.*] There's nothing like the opening of a little shop, is there? A moment of true beauty! [*She is looking around.*] Not very much on the shelves, of course. But everything in the gods' good time! Where are your references, Miss Shen Te?

SHEN TE. Do I *have* to have references?

MRS. MI TZU. After all, I haven't a notion who you are!

HUSBAND. Oh, *we'd* be glad to vouch for Miss Shen Te! We'd go through fire for her!

MRS. MI TZU. And who may *you* be?

HUSBAND [*stammering*]. Ma Fu, tobacco dealer.

MRS. MI TZU. Where is your shop, Mr. . . . Ma Fu?

HUSBAND. Well, um, I haven't a shop—I've just sold it.

MRS. MI TZU. I see. [*To* SHEN TE.] Is there no one else that knows you?

WIFE [*whispering to* SHEN TE]. Your cousin! Your cousin!

MRS. MI TZU. This is a respectable house, Miss Shen Te. I never sign a lease without certain assurances.

SHEN TE [*slowly, her eyes downcast*]. I have . . . a cousin.

MRS. MI TZU. On the square? Let's go over and see him. What does he do?

SHEN TE [*as before*]. He lives . . . in another city.

WIFE [*prompting*]. Didn't you say he was in Shung?

SHEN TE. That's right. Shung.

HUSBAND [*prompting*]. I had his name on the tip of my tongue. Mr. . . .

SHEN TE [*with an effort*]. Mr. . . . Shui . . . Ta.

HUSBAND. That's it! Tall, skinny fellow!

SHEN TE. Shui Ta!

NEPHEW [*to* CARPENTER]. *You* were in touch with him, weren't you? About the shelves?

CARPENTER [*surlily*]. Give him this bill. [*He hands it over.*] I'll be back in the morning.
[*Exit* CARPENTER.]

NEPHEW [*calling after him, but with his eyes on* MRS. MI TZU]. Don't worry! Mr. Shui Ta pays on the nail!

MRS. MI TZU [*looking closely at* SHEN TE]. I'll be happy to make his acquaintance, Miss Shen Te. [*Exit* MRS. MI TZU.]
[*Pause.*]

WIFE. By tomorrow morning she'll know more about you than you do yourself.

SISTER-IN-LAW [*to* NEPHEW]. This thing isn't built to last.
[*Enter* GRANDFATHER.]

WIFE. It's Grandfather! [*To* SHEN TE.] Such a good old soul!
[*The* BOY *enters.*]

BOY [*over his shoulder*]. Here they are!

WIFE. And the boy, how he's grown! But he always could eat enough for ten.

[*Enter the* NIECE.]

WIFE [*to* SHEN TE]. Our little niece from the country. There are more of us now than in your time. The less we had, the more there were of us; the more there were of us, the less we had. Give me the key. We must protect ourselves from unwanted guests. [*She takes the key and locks the door.*] Just make yourself at home. I'll light the little lamp.

NEPHEW [*a big joke*]. I hope her cousin doesn't drop in tonight! The strict Mr. Shui Ta!

[SISTER-IN-LAW *laughs.*]

BROTHER [*reaching for a cigarette*]. One cigarette more or less . . .

HUSBAND. One cigarette more or less.

[*They pile into the cigarettes. The* BROTHER *hands a jug of wine round.*]

NEPHEW. Mr. Shui Ta'll pay for it!

GRANDFATHER [*gravely, to* SHEN TE]. How do you do?

[SHEN TE, *a little taken aback by the belatedness of the greeting, bows. She has the* CARPENTER'S *bill in one hand, the landlady's lease in the other.*]

WIFE. How about a bit of a song? To keep Shen Te's spirits up?

NEPHEW. Good idea. Grandfather: you start!

SONG OF THE SMOKE

GRANDFATHER.

> I used to think (before old age beset me)
> That brains could fill the pantry of the poor.
> But where did all my cerebration get me?
> I'm just as hungry as I was before.
>> So what's the use?
>> See the smoke float free
>> Into ever colder coldness!
>> It's the same with me.

HUSBAND.

> The straight and narrow path leads to disaster
> And so the crooked path I tried to tread.
> That got me to disaster even faster.
> (They say we shall be happy when we're dead.)
>> So what's the use, etc.

NIECE.

> You older people, full of expectation,
> At any moment now you'll walk the plank!
> The future's for the younger generation!
> Yes, even if that future is a blank.
>> So what's the use, etc.

NEPHEW [*to the* BROTHER]. Where'd you get that wine?

SISTER-IN-LAW [*answering for the* BROTHER]. He pawned the sack of tobacco.

HUSBAND [*stepping in*]. What? That tobacco was all we had to fall back on! You pig!

BROTHER. *You'd* call a man a pig because your wife was frigid! Did you refuse to drink it?

[*They fight. The shelves fall over.*]

SHEN TE [*imploringly*]. Oh, don't! Don't break everything! Take it, take it all, but don't destroy a gift from the gods!

WIFE [*disparagingly*]. This shop isn't big enough. I should never have mentioned it to Uncle and the others. When *they* arrive, it's going to be disgustingly overcrowded.

SISTER-IN-LAW. And did you hear our gracious hostess? She cools off quick!

[*Voices outside. Knocking at the door.*]

UNCLE'S VOICE. Open the door!

WIFE. Uncle? Is that you, Uncle?

UNCLE'S VOICE. Certainly, it's me. Auntie says to tell you she'll have the children here in ten minutes.

WIFE [*to* SHEN TE]. I'll have to let him in.

SHEN TE [*who scarcely hears her*].

The little lifeboat is swiftly sent down
Too many men too greedily
Hold on to it as they drown.

SCENE IA
WONG'S *den in a sewer pipe.*

WONG [*crouching there*]. All quiet! It's four days now since I left the city. The gods passed this way on the second day. I heard their steps on the bridge over there. They must be a long way off by this time, so I'm safe.

[*Breathing a sigh of relief, he curls up and goes to sleep. In his dream the pipe becomes transparent, and the* GODS *appear.*]

[*Raising an arm, as if in self-defense.*] I know, I know, illustrious ones! I found no one to give you a room—not in all Setzuan! There, it's out. Please continue on your way!

FIRST GOD [*mildly*]. But you did find someone. Someone who took us in for the night, watched over us in our sleep, and in the early morning lighted us down to the street with a lamp.

WONG. It was . . . Shen Te, that took you in?

THIRD GOD. Who else?

WONG. And I ran away! "She isn't coming," I thought, "she just can't afford it."

GODS [*singing*].

O you feeble, well-intentioned, and yet feeble chap!
Where there's need the fellow thinks there is no goodness!
When there's danger he thinks courage starts to ebb away!
Some people only see the seamy side!
What hasty judgment! What premature desperation!

WONG. I'm *very* ashamed, illustrious ones.

FIRST GOD. Do us a favor, Water Seller. Go back to Setzuan. Find Shen Te,

and give us a report on her. We hear that she's come into a little money. Show interest in her goodness—for no one can be good for long if goodness is not in demand. Meanwhile we shall continue the search, and find other good people. After which, the idle chatter about the impossibility of goodness will stop!

[*The* GODS *vanish.*]

SCENE II

[*A knocking.*]

WIFE. Shen Te! Someone at the door. Where is she anyway?

NEPHEW. She must be getting the breakfast. Mr. Shui Ta will pay for it.

[*The* WIFE *laughs and shuffles to the door. Enter* MR. SHUI TA *and the* CARPENTER.]

WIFE. Who is it?

SHUI TA. I am Miss Shen Te's cousin.

WIFE. What?

SHUI TA. My name is Shui Ta.

WIFE. Her cousin?

NEPHEW. Her cousin?

NIECE. But that was a joke. She hasn't got a cousin.

HUSBAND. So early in the morning?

BROTHER. What's all the noise?

SISTER-IN-LAW. This fellow says he's her cousin.

BROTHER. Tell him to prove it.

NEPHEW. Right. If you're Shen Te's cousin, prove it by getting the breakfast.

SHUI TA [*whose regime begins as he puts out the lamp to save oil. Loudly, to all present, asleep or awake*]. Would you all please get dressed! Customers will be coming! I wish to open my shop!

HUSBAND. *Your* shop? Doesn't it belong to our good friend Shen Te?

[SHUI TA *shakes his head.*]

SISTER-IN-LAW. So we've been cheated. Where *is* the little liar?

SHUI TA. Miss Shen Te has been delayed. She wishes me to tell you there will be nothing she can do—now I am here.

WIFE [*bowled over*]. I thought she was *good!*

NEPHEW. Do you have to believe *him?*

HUSBAND. *I* don't.

NEPHEW. Then do something.

HUSBAND. Certainly! I'll send out a search party at once. You, you, you, and you, go out and look for Shen Te.

[*As the* GRANDFATHER *rises and makes for the door.*]

Not you, Grandfather, you and I will hold the fort.

SHUI TA. You won't find Miss Shen Te. She has suspended her hospitable activity for an unlimited period. There are too many of you. She asked me to say: this is a tobacco shop, not a gold mine.

HUSBAND. Shen Te never said a thing like that. Boy, food! There's a bakery on the corner. Stuff your shirt full when they're not looking!

SISTER-IN-LAW. Don't overlook the raspberry tarts.

HUSBAND. And don't let the policeman see you.

[*The* BOY *leaves.*]

SHUI TA. Don't you depend on this shop now? Then why give it a bad name, by stealing from the bakery?

NEPHEW. Don't listen to him. Let's find Shen Te. She'll give him a piece of her mind.

SISTER-IN-LAW. Don't forget to leave us some breakfast.

[BROTHER, SISTER-IN-LAW, *and* NEPHEW *leave.*]

SHUI TA [*to the* CARPENTER]. You see, Mr. Carpenter, nothing has changed since the poet, eleven hundred years ago, penned these lines:

A governor was asked what was needed
To save the freezing people in the city.
He replied:
"A blanket ten thousand feet long
To cover the city and all its suburbs."

[*He starts to tidy up the shop.*]

CARPENTER. Your cousin owes me money. I've got witnesses. For the shelves.

SHUI TA. Yes, I have your bill. [*He takes it out of his pocket.*] Isn't a hundred silver dollars rather a lot?

CARPENTER. No deductions! I have a wife and children.

SHUI TA. How many children?

CARPENTER. Three.

SHUI TA. I'll make you an offer. Twenty silver dollars.

[*The* HUSBAND *laughs.*]

CARPENTER. You're crazy. Those shelves are real walnut.

SHUI TA. Very well. Take them away.

CARPENTER. What?

SHUI TA. They cost too much. Please take them away.

WIFE. Not bad! [*And she, too, is laughing.*]

CARPENTER [*a little bewildered*]. Call Shen Te, someone! [*To* SHUI TA.] She's good!

SHUI TA. Certainly. She's ruined.

CARPENTER [*provoked into taking some of the shelves*]. All right, you can keep your tobacco on the floor.

SHUI TA [*to the* HUSBAND]. Help him with the shelves.

HUSBAND [*grins and carries one shelf over to the door where the* CARPENTER *now is*]. Goodbye, shelves!

CARPENTER [*to the* HUSBAND]. You dog! You want my family to starve?

SHUI TA. I repeat my offer. I have no desire to keep my tobacco on the floor. Twenty silver dollars.

CARPENTER [*with desperate aggressiveness*]. One hundred!

[SHUI TA *shows indifference, looks through the window. The* HUSBAND *picks up several shelves.*]

[*To* HUSBAND.] You needn't smash them against the doorpost, you idiot!

[*To* SHUI TA.] These shelves were made to measure. They're no use anywhere else!

SHUI TA. Precisely.

[*The* WIFE *squeals with pleasure.*]

CARPENTER [*giving up, sullenly*]. Take the shelves. Pay what you want to pay.

SHUI TA [*smoothly*]. Twenty silver dollars.

[*He places two large coins on the table. The* CARPENTER *picks them up.*]

HUSBAND [*brings the shelves back in*]. And quite enough too!

CARPENTER [*slinking off*]. Quite enough to get drunk on.

HUSBAND [*happily*]. Well, we got rid of him!

WIFE [*weeping with fun, gives a rendition of the dialogue just spoken*]. "Real walnut," says he. "Very well, take them away," says his lordship. "I have children," says he. "Twenty silver dollars," says his lordship. "They're no use anywhere else," says he. "Precisely," said his lordship! [*She dissolves into shrieks of merriment.*]

SHUI TA. And now: go!

HUSBAND. What's that?

SHUI TA. You're thieves, parasites. I'm giving you this chance. Go!

HUSBAND [*summoning all his ancestral dignity*]. That sort deserves no answer. Besides, one should never shout on an empty stomach.

WIFE. Where's that boy?

SHUI TA. Exactly. The boy. I want no stolen goods in this shop. [*Very loudly.*] I strongly advise you to leave! [*But they remain seated, noses in the air. Quietly.*] As you wish.

[SHUI TA *goes to the door. A* POLICEMAN *appears.* SHUI TA *bows.*]

I am addressing the officer in charge of this precinct?

POLICEMAN. That's right, Mr., um . . . what was the name, sir?

SHUI TA. Mr. Shui Ta.

POLICEMAN. Yes, of course, sir.

[*They exchange a smile.*]

SHUI TA. Nice weather we're having.

POLICEMAN. A little on the warm side, sir.

SHUI TA. Oh, a little on the warm side.

HUSBAND [*whispering to the* WIFE]. If he keeps it up till the boy's back, we're done for. [*Tries to signal* SHUI TA.]

SHUI TA [*ignoring the signal*]. Weather, of course, is one thing indoors, another out on the dusty street!

POLICEMAN. Oh, quite another, sir!

WIFE [*to the* HUSBAND]. It's all right as long as he's standing in the doorway—the boy will see him.

SHUI TA. Step inside for a moment! It's quite cool indoors. My cousin and I have just opened the place. And we attach the greatest importance to being on good terms with the, um, authorities.

POLICEMAN [*entering*]. Thank you, Mr. Shui Ta. It *is* cool!

HUSBAND [*whispering to the* WIFE]. And now the boy *won't* see him.

SHUI TA [*showing* HUSBAND *and* WIFE *to the* POLICEMAN]. Visitors, I think my cousin knows them. They were just leaving.

HUSBAND [*defeated*]. Ye-e-es, we were . . . just leaving.

SHUI TA. I'll tell my cousin you couldn't wait.

> [*Noise from the street. Shouts of "Stop, thief!"*]

POLICEMAN. What's that?

> [*The* BOY *is in the doorway with cakes and buns and rolls spilling out of his shirt. The* WIFE *signals desperately to him to leave. He gets the idea.*]

No, you don't! [*He grabs the* BOY *by the collar.*] Where's all this from?

BOY [*vaguely pointing*]. Down the street.

POLICEMAN [*grimly*]. So that's it. [*Prepares to arrest the* BOY.]

WIFE [*stepping in*]. And *we* knew nothing about it. [*To the* BOY.] Nasty little thief!

POLICEMAN [*dryly*]. Can you clarify the situation, Mr. Shui Ta?

> [SHUI TA *is silent.*]

POLICEMAN [*who understands silence*]. Aha. You're all coming with me—to the station.

SHUI TA. I can hardly say how sorry I am that *my* establishment . . .

WIFE. Oh, he saw the boy leave not ten minutes ago!

SHUI TA. And to conceal the theft asked a policeman in?

POLICEMAN. Don't listen to her, Mr. Shui Ta, I'll be happy to relieve you of their presence one and all! [*To all three.*] Out! [*He drives them before him.*]

GRANDFATHER [*leaving last. Gravely*]. Good morning!

POLICEMAN. Good morning!

> [SHUI TA, *left alone, continues to tidy up.* MRS. MI TZU *breezes in.*]

MRS. MI TZU. *You're* her cousin, are you? Then have the goodness to explain what all this means—police dragging people from a respectable house! By what right does your Miss Shen Te turn my property into a house of assignation?—Well, as you see, I know all!

SHUI TA. Yes. My cousin has the worst possible reputation: that of being poor.

MRS. MI TZU. No sentimental rubbish, Mr. Shui Ta. Your cousin was a common . . .

SHUI TA. Pauper. Let's use the uglier word.

MRS. MI TZU. I'm speaking of her conduct, not her earnings. But there must have *been* earnings, or how did she buy all this? Several elderly gentlemen took care of it, I suppose. I repeat: this is a respectable house! I have tenants who prefer not to live under the same roof with such a person.

SHUI TA [*quietly*]. How much do you want?

MRS. MI TZU [*he is ahead of her now*]. I beg your pardon?

SHUI TA. To reassure yourself. To reassure your tenants. How much will it cost?

MRS. MI TZU. You're a cool customer.

SHUI TA [*picking up the lease*]. The rent is high. [*He reads on.*] I assume it's payable by the month?

MRS. MI TZU. Not in her case.

SHUI TA [*looking up*]. What?

MRS. MI TZU. Six months' rent payable in advance. Two hundred silver dollars.

SHUI TA. Six . . . ! Sheer usury! And where am I to find it?

MRS. MI TZU. You should have thought of that before.

SHUI TA. Have you no heart, Mrs. Mi Tzu? It's true Shen Te acted fool-
ishly, being kind to all those people, but she'll improve with time. I'll see
to it she does. She'll work her fingers to the bone to pay her rent, and all
the time be as quiet as a mouse, as humble as a fly.

MRS. MI TZU. Her social background . . .

SHUI TA. Out of the depths! She came out of the depths! And before she'll
go back there, she'll work, sacrifice, shrink from nothing. . . . Such a
tenant is worth her weight in gold, Mrs. Mi Tzu.

MRS. MI TZU. It's silver we were talking about, Mr. Shui Ta. Two hundred
silver dollars or . . .

[*Enter the* POLICEMAN.]

POLICEMAN. Am I intruding, Mr. Shui Ta?

MRS. MI TZU. This tobacco shop is well-known to the police, I see.

POLICEMAN. Mr. Shui Ta has done us a service, Mrs. Mi Tzu. I am here to
present our official felicitations!

MRS. MI TZU. That means less than nothing to me, sir. Mr. Shui Ta, all I
can say is: I hope your cousin will find my terms acceptable. Good day,
gentlemen. [*Exit.*]

SHUI TA. Good day, ma'am.

[*Pause.*]

POLICEMAN. Mrs. Mi Tzu a bit of a stumbling block, sir?

SHUI TA. She wants six months' rent in advance.

POLICEMAN. And you haven't got it, eh?

[SHUI TA *is silent.*]

But surely you can get it, sir? A man like you?

SHUI TA. What about a woman like Shen Te?

POLICEMAN. You're not staying, sir?

SHUI TA. No, and I won't be back. Do you smoke?

POLICEMAN [*taking two cigars, and placing them both in his pocket*]. Thank you,
sir—I see your point. Miss Shen Te—let's mince no words—Miss Shen
Te lived by selling herself. "What else could she have done?" you ask.
"How else was she to pay the rent?" True. But the fact remains, Mr.
Shui Ta, it is not respectable. Why not? A very deep question. But, in
the first place, love—love isn't bought and sold like cigars, Mr. Shui Ta.
In the second place, it isn't respectable to go waltzing off with someone
that's paying his way, so to speak—it must be for love! Thirdly and
lastly, as the proverb has it: not for a handful of rice but for love! [*Pause.
He is thinking hard.*] "Well," you may say, "and what good is all this
wisdom if the milk's already spilt?" Miss Shen Te is what she is. Is *where*
she is. We have to face the fact that if she doesn't get hold of six months'
rent pronto, she'll be back on the streets. The question then as I see
it—everything in this world is a matter of opinion—the question as I see
it is: *how* is she to get hold of this rent? How? Mr. Shui Ta: I don't know.
[*Pause.*] I take that back, sir. It's just come to me. A husband. We must
find her a husband!

[*Enter a little* OLD WOMAN.]

OLD WOMAN. A good cheap cigar for my husband, we'll have been married
forty years tomorrow and we're having a little celebration.

SHUI TA. Forty years? And you still want to celebrate?

OLD WOMAN. As much as we can afford to. We have the carpet shop across the square. We'll be good neighbors, I hope?

SHUI TA. I hope so too.

POLICEMAN [*who keeps making discoveries*]. Mr. Shui Ta, you know what we need? We need capital. And how do we acquire capital? We get married.

SHUI TA [*to* OLD WOMAN]. I'm afraid I've been pestering this gentleman with my personal worries.

POLICEMAN [*lyrically*]. We can't pay six months' rent, so what do we do? We marry money.

SHUI TA. That might not be easy.

POLICEMAN. Oh, I don't know. She's a good match. Has a nice, growing business. [*To the* OLD WOMAN.] What do you think?

OLD WOMAN [*undecided*]. Well—

POLICEMAN. Should she put an ad in the paper?

OLD WOMAN [*not eager to commit herself*]. Well, if *she* agrees—

POLICEMAN. I'll write it for her. *You* lend us a hand, and *we* write an ad for you! [*He chuckles away to himself, takes out his notebook, wets the stump of a pencil between his lips, and writes away.*]

SHUI TA [*slowly*]. Not a bad idea.

POLICEMAN. "What . . . *respectable* . . . man . . . with small capital . . . widower . . . not excluded . . . desires . . . marriage . . . into flourishing . . . tobacco shop?" And now let's add: "am . . . pretty . . . " No! . . . "Prepossessing appearance."

SHUI TA. If you don't think that's an exaggeration?

OLD WOMAN. Oh, not a bit. I've seen her.

[*The* POLICEMAN *tears the page out of his notebook, and hands it over to* SHUI TA.]

SHUI TA [*with horror in his voice*]. How much luck we need to keep our heads above water! How many ideas! How many friends! [*To the* POLICEMAN.] Thank you, sir. I think I see my way clear.

SCENE III

Evening in the municipal park. Noise of a plane overhead. YANG SUN, *a young man in rags, is following the plane with his eyes: one can tell that the machine is describing a curve above the park.* YANG SUN *then takes a rope out of his pocket, looking anxiously about him as he does so. He moves toward a large willow. Enter* TWO PROSTITUTES, *one old, the other the* NIECE *whom we have already met.*

NIECE. Hello. Coming with me?

YANG SUN [*taken aback*]. If you'd like to buy me a dinner.

OLD WHORE. Buy you a dinner! [*To the* NIECE.] Oh, we know him—it's the unemployed pilot. Waste no time on him!

NIECE. But he's the only man left in the park. And it's going to rain.

OLD WHORE. Oh, how do you know?

[*And they pass by.* YANG SUN *again looks about him, again takes his rope, and this time throws it round a branch of the wil-*

> *low tree. Again he is interrupted. It is the*
> Two Prostitutes *returning—and in*
> *such a hurry they don't notice him.*]

Niece. It's going to pour!

[*Enter* Shen Te.]

Old Whore. There's that *gorgon* Shen Te! That *drove* your family out into the cold!

Niece. It wasn't her. It was that cousin of hers. She offered to *pay* for the cakes. I've nothing against her.

Old Whore. I have, though. [*So that* Shen Te *can hear.*] Now where could the little lady be off to? She may be rich now but that won't stop her snatching our young men, will it?

Shen Te. I'm going to the tearoom by the pond.

Niece. Is it true what they say? You're marrying a widower—with three children?

Shen Te. Yes. I'm just going to see him.

Yang Sun [*his patience at breaking point*]. Move on there! This is a park, not a whorehouse!

Old Whore. Shut your mouth!

[*But the* Two Prostitutes *leave.*]

Yang Sun. Even in the farthest corner of the park, even when it's raining, you can't get rid of them! [*He spits.*]

Shen Te [*overhearing this*]. And what right have you to scold them? [*But at this point she sees the rope.*] Oh!

Yang Sun. Well, what are you staring at?

Shen Te. That rope. What is it for?

Yang Sun. Think! Think! I haven't a penny. Even if I had, I wouldn't spend it on you. I'd buy a drink of water.

[*The rain starts.*]

Shen Te [*still looking at the rope*]. What is the rope for? You mustn't!

Yang Sun. What's it to you? Clear out!

Shen Te [*irrelevantly*]. It's raining.

Yang Sun. Well, don't try to come under this tree.

Shen Te. Oh, no. [*She stays in the rain.*]

Yang Sun. Now go away. [*Pause.*] For one thing, I don't like your looks, you're bowlegged.

Shen Te [*indignantly*]. That's not true!

Yang Sun. Well, don't show 'em to me. Look, it's raining. You better come under this tree.

[*Slowly, she takes shelter under the tree.*]

Shen Te. Why did you want to do it?

Yang Sun. You really want to know? [*Pause.*] To get rid of you! [*Pause.*] You know what a flyer is?

Shen Te. Oh yes, I've met a lot of pilots. At the tearoom.

Yang Sun. You call *them* flyers? Think they know what a machine *is*? Just 'cause they have leather helmets? They gave the airfield director a bribe, that's the way *those* fellows got up in the air! Try one of them out sometime. "Go up to two thousand feet," tell him, "then let it fall, then pick it up again with a flick of the wrist at the last moment." Know what he'll say to that? "It's not in my contract." Then again, there's the land-

ing problem. It's like landing on your own backside. It's no different, planes are human. Those fools don't understand. [*Pause.*] And I'm the biggest fool for reading the book on flying in the Peking school and skipping the page where it says: "we've got enough flyers and we don't need you." I'm a mail pilot and no mail. You understand that?

SHEN TE [*shyly*]. Yes. I do.

YANG SUN. No, you don't. You'd never understand that.

SHEN TE. When we were little we had a crane with a broken wing. He made friends with us and was very good-natured about our jokes. He would strut along behind us and call out to stop us going too fast for him. But every spring and autumn when the cranes flew over the villages in great swarms, he got quite restless. [*Pause.*] I understood that. [*She bursts out crying.*]

YANG SUN. Don't!

SHEN TE [*quieting down*]. No.

YANG SUN. It's bad for the complexion.

SHEN TE [*sniffling*]. I've stopped.

> [*She dries her tears on her big sleeve.
> Leaning against the tree, but not looking
> at her, he reaches for her face.*]

YANG SUN. You can't even wipe your own face. [*He is wiping it for her with his handkerchief. Pause.*]

SHEN TE [*still sobbing*]. I don't know *anything!*

YANG SUN. You interrupted me! What for?

SHEN TE. It's such a rainy day. You only wanted to do . . . *that* because it's such a rainy day.

> [*To the audience.*]

In our country
The evenings should never be somber
High bridges over rivers
The gray hour between night and morning
And the long, long winter:
Such things are dangerous
For, with all the misery,
A very little is enough
And men throw away an unbearable life.

> [*Pause.*]

YANG SUN. Talk about yourself for a change.

SHEN TE. What about me? I have a shop.

YANG SUN [*incredulous*]. You have a shop, do you? Never thought of walking the streets?

SHEN TE. I *did* walk the streets. Now I have a shop.

YANG SUN [*ironically*]. A gift of the gods, I suppose!

SHEN TE. How did you know?

YANG SUN [*even more ironical*]. One fine evening the gods turned up saying: here's some money!

SHEN TE [*quickly*]. One fine morning.

YANG SUN [*fed up*]. This isn't much of an entertainment.

> [*Pause.*]

SHEN TE. I can play the zither a little. [*Pause.*] And I can mimic men.

[*Pause.*] I got the shop, so the first thing I did was to give my zither away. I can be as stupid as a fish now, I said to myself, and it won't matter.

I'm rich now, I said
I walk alone, I sleep alone
For a whole year, I said
I'll have nothing to do with a man.

YANG SUN. And now you're marrying one! The one at the tearoom by the pond?

[SHEN TE *is silent.*]

YANG SUN. What do you know about love?

SHEN TE. Everything.

YANG SUN. Nothing. [*Pause.*] Or d'you just mean you enjoyed it?

SHEN TE. No.

YANG SUN [*again without turning to look at her, he strokes her cheek with his hand*]. You like that?

SHEN TE. Yes.

YANG SUN [*breaking off*]. You're easily satisfied, I must say. [*Pause.*] What a town!

SHEN TE. You have no friends?

YANG SUN [*defensively*]. Yes, I have! [*Change of tone.*] But they don't want to hear I'm still unemployed. "What?" they ask. "Is there still water in the sea?" You have friends?

SHEN TE [*hesitating*]. Just a . . . cousin.

YANG SUN. Watch him carefully.

SHEN TE. He only came once. Then he went away. He won't be back.

[YANG SUN *is looking away.*]

But to be without hope, they say, is to be without goodness!

[*Pause.*]

YANG SUN. Go on talking. A voice is a voice.

SHEN TE. Once, when I was a little girl, I fell, with a load of brushwood. An old man picked me up. He gave me a penny too. Isn't it funny how people who don't have very much like to give some of it away? They must like to show what they can do, and how could they show it better than by being kind? Being wicked is just like being clumsy. When we sing a song, or build a machine, or plant some rice, we're being kind. You're kind.

YANG SUN. You make it sound easy.

SHEN TE. Oh, no. [*Little pause.*] Oh! A drop of rain!

YANG SUN. Where'd you feel it?

SHEN TE. Between the eyes.

YANG SUN. Near the right eye? Or the left?

SHEN TE. Near the left eye.

YANG SUN. Oh, good. [*He is getting sleepy.*] So you're through with men, eh?

SHEN TE [*with a smile*]. But I'm not bowlegged.

YANG SUN. Perhaps not.

SHEN TE. Definitely not.

[*Pause.*]

YANG SUN [*leaning wearily against the willow*]. I haven't had a drop to

drink all day, I haven't eaten anything for *two* days. I couldn't love you if I tried.

[*Pause.*]

SHEN TE. I like it in the rain.

[*Enter* WONG *the Water Seller, singing.*]

THE SONG OF THE WATER SELLER IN THE RAIN

"Buy my water," I am yelling
And my fury restraining
For no water I'm selling
'Cause it's raining, 'cause it's raining!
 I keep yelling: "Buy my water!"
 But no one's buying
 Athirst and dying
 And drinking and paying!
 Buy water!
 Buy water, you dogs!

Nice to dream of lovely weather!
Think of all the consternation
Were there no precipitation
Half a dozen years together!
Can't you hear them shrieking: "Water!"
Pretending they adore me!
They all would go down on their knees before me!
 Down on your knees!
 Go down on your knees, you dogs!

What are lawns and hedges thinking?
What are fields and forests saying?
"At the cloud's breast we are drinking!
And we've no idea who's paying!"
 I keep yelling: "Buy my water!"
 But no one's buying
 Athirst and dying
 And drinking and paying!
 Buy water!
 Buy water, you dogs!

[*The rain has stopped now.* SHEN TE *sees* WONG *and runs toward him.*]

SHEN TE. Wong! You're back! Your carrying pole's at the shop.

WONG. Oh, thank you, Shen Te. And how is life treating *you?*

SHEN TE. I've just met a brave and clever man. And I want to buy him a cup of your water.

WONG [*bitterly*]. Throw back your head and open your mouth and you'll have all the water you need—

SHEN TE [*tenderly*].

I want *your* water, Wong
The water that has tired you so
The water that you carried all this way
The water that is hard to sell because it's been raining
I need it for the young man over there—he's a flyer!
A flyer is a bold man:
Braving the storms
In company with the clouds
He crosses the heavens
And brings to friends in far-away lands
The friendly mail!

> [*She pays* WONG, *and runs over to* YANG
> SUN *with the cup. But* YANG SUN *is fast
> asleep.*]

[*Calling to* WONG, *with a laugh.*] He's fallen asleep! Despair and rain and
I have worn him out!

SCENE IIIA

WONG's *den. The sewer pipe is transparent, and the* GODS *again appear to* WONG
in a dream.

WONG [*radiant*]. I've seen her, illustrious ones! And she hasn't changed!
FIRST GOD. That's good to hear.
WONG. She loves someone.
FIRST GOD. Let's hope the experience gives her the strength to stay good!
WONG. It does. She's doing good deeds all the time.
FIRST GOD. Ah? What sort? What sort of good deeds, Wong?
WONG. Well, she has a kind word for everybody.
FIRST GOD [*eagerly*]. And then?
WONG. Hardly anyone leaves her shop without tobacco in his pocket—
even if he can't pay for it.
FIRST GOD. Not bad at all. Next?
WONG. She's putting up a family of eight.
FIRST GOD [*gleefully, to the* SECOND GOD]. Eight! [*To* WONG.] And that's not
all, of course!
WONG. She bought a cup of water from me even though it was raining.
FIRST GOD. Yes, yes, yes, all these smaller good deeds!
WONG. Even they run into money. A little tobacco shop doesn't make
so much.
FIRST GOD [*sententiously*]. A prudent gardener works miracles on the
smallest plot.
WONG. She hands out rice every morning. That eats up half her earnings.
FIRST GOD [*a little disappointed*]. Well, as a beginning . . .
WONG. They call her the Angel of the Slums—whatever the Carpenter
may say!
FIRST GOD. What's this? A carpenter speaks ill of her?
WONG. Oh, he only says her shelves weren't paid for in full.
SECOND GOD [*who has a bad cold and can't pronounce his n's and m's*]. What's
this? Not paying a carpenter? Why was that?

WONG. I suppose she didn't have the money.

SECOND GOD [*severely*]. One pays what one owes, that's in our book of rules! First the letter of the law, then the spirit!

WONG. But it wasn't Shen Te, illustrious ones, it was her cousin. She called *him* in to help.

SECOND GOD. Then her cousin must never darken her threshold again!

WONG. Very well, illustrious ones! But in fairness to Shen Te, let me say that her cousin is a businessman.

FIRST GOD. Perhaps we should inquire what is customary? I find business quite unintelligible. But everybody's doing it. Business! Did the Seven Good Kings do business? Did Kung the Just sell fish?

SECOND GOD. In any case, such a thing must not occur again!

[*The GODS start to leave.*]

THIRD GOD. Forgive us for taking this tone with you. Wong, we haven't been getting enough sleep. The rich recommended us to the poor, and the poor tell us they haven't enough room.

SECOND GOD. Feeble, feeble, the best of them!

FIRST GOD. No great deeds! No heroic daring!

THIRD GOD. On such a *small* scale!

SECOND GOD. Sincere, yes, but what is actually *achieved*?

[*One can no longer hear them.*]

WONG [*calling after them*]. I've thought of something, illustrious ones: Perhaps you shouldn't ask—too—much—all—at—once!

SCENE IV

The square in front of SHEN TE's *tobacco shop. Beside* SHEN TE's *place, two other shops are seen: the carpet shop and a barber's. Morning. Outside* SHEN TE's *the* GRANDFATHER, *the* SISTER-IN-LAW, *the* UNEMPLOYED MAN, *and* MRS. SHIN *stand waiting.*

SISTER-IN-LAW. She's been out all night again.

MRS. SHIN. No sooner did we get rid of that crazy cousin of hers than Shen Te herself starts carrying on! Maybe she does give us an ounce of rice now and then, but can you depend on her? Can you depend on her?

[*Loud voices from the barber's.*]

VOICE OF SHU FU. What are you doing in my shop? Get out—at once!

VOICE OF WONG. But sir. They all let me sell . . .

[WONG *comes staggering out of the barber's shop pursued by* MR. SHU FU, *the barber, a fat man carrying a heavy curling iron.*]

SHU FU. Get out, I said! Pestering my customers with your slimy old water! Get out! Take your cup!

[*He holds out the cup.* WONG *reaches out for it.* MR. SHU FU *strikes his hand with the curling iron, which is hot.* WONG *howls.*]

You had it coming, my man!

[*Puffing, he returns to his shop. The* UNEMPLOYED MAN *picks up the cup and gives it to* WONG.]

UNEMPLOYED MAN. You can report that to the police.

WONG. My hand! It's smashed up!

UNEMPLOYED MAN. Any bones broken?

WONG. I can't move my fingers.

UNEMPLOYED MAN. Sit down. I'll put some water on it.

[WONG *sits.*]

MRS. SHIN. The water won't cost you anything.

SISTER-IN-LAW. You might have got a bandage from Miss Shen Te till she took to staying out all night. It's a scandal.

MRS. SHIN [*despondently*]. If you ask me, she's forgotten we ever existed!

[*Enter* SHEN TE *down the street, with a dish of rice.*]

SHEN TE [*to the audience*]. How wonderful to see Setzuan in the early morning! I always used to stay in bed with my dirty blanket over my head afraid to wake up. This morning I saw the newspapers being delivered by little boys, the streets being washed by strong men, and fresh vegetables coming in from the country on ox carts. It's a long walk from where Yang Sun lives, but I feel lighter at every step. They say you walk on air when you're in love, but it's even better walking on the rough earth, on the hard cement. In the early morning, the old city looks like a great rubbish heap. Nice, though—with all its little lights. And the sky, so pink, so transparent, before the dust comes and muddies it! What a lot you miss if you never see your city rising from its slumbers like an honest old craftsman pumping his lungs full of air and reaching for his tools, as the poet says! [*Cheerfully, to her waiting guests.*] Good morning, everyone, here's your rice! [*Distributing the rice, she comes upon* WONG.] Good morning, Wong, I'm quite lightheaded today. On my way over, I looked at myself in all the shop windows. I'd love to be beautiful.

[*She slips into the carpet shop.* MR. SHU FU *has just emerged from his shop.*]

SHU FU [*to the audience*]. It surprises me how beautiful Miss Shen Te is looking today! I never gave her a passing thought before. But now I've been gazing upon her comely form for exactly three minutes! I begin to suspect I am in love with her. She is overpoweringly attractive! [*Crossly, to* WONG.] Be off with you, rascal!

[*He returns to his shop.* SHEN TE *comes back out of the carpet shop with the* OLD MAN *its proprietor and his wife—whom we have already met—the* OLD WOMAN. SHEN TE *is wearing a shawl. The* OLD MAN *is holding up a looking glass for her.*]

OLD WOMAN. Isn't it lovely? We'll give you a reduction because there's a little hole in it.

SHEN TE [*looking at another shawl on the* OLD WOMAN'S *arm*]. The other one's nice too.

OLD WOMAN [*smiling*]. Too bad there's no hole in that!

SHEN TE. That's right. My shop doesn't make very much.

OLD WOMAN. And your good deeds eat it all up! Be more careful, my dear . . .

SHEN TE [*trying on the shawl with the hole*]. Just now, I'm light-headed! Does the color suit me?

OLD WOMAN. You'd better ask a man.

SHEN TE [*to the* OLD MAN]. Does the color suit me?

OLD MAN. You'd better ask your young friend.

SHEN TE. I'd like to have your opinion.

OLD MAN. It suits you, very well. But wear it this way: the dull side out.
[SHEN TE *pays up.*]

OLD WOMAN. If you decide you don't like it, you can exchange it. [*She pulls* SHEN TE *to one side.*] Has he got money?

SHEN TE [*with a laugh*]. Yang Sun? Oh, no.

OLD WOMAN. Then how're you going to pay your rent?

SHEN TE. I'd forgotten about that.

OLD WOMAN. And next Monday is the first of the month! Miss Shen Te, I've got something to say to you. After we [*indicating her husband*] got to know you, we had our doubts about that marriage ad. We thought it would be better if you'd let *us* help you. Out of our savings. We reckon we could lend you two hundred silver dollars. We don't need anything in writing—you could pledge us your tobacco stock.

SHEN TE. You're prepared to lend money to a person like me?

OLD WOMAN. It's folks like you that need it. We'd think twice about lending anything to your cousin.

OLD MAN [*coming up*]. All settled, my dear?

SHEN TE. I wish the gods could have heard what your wife was just saying, Mr. Ma. They're looking for good people who're happy—and helping me makes you happy because you know it was love that got me into difficulties!

[*The old couple smile knowingly at each other.*]

OLD MAN. And here's the money, Miss Shen Te.

[*He hands her an envelope.* SHEN TE *takes it. She bows. They bow back. They return to their shop.*]

SHEN TE [*holding up her envelope*]. Look, Wong, here's six month's rent! Don't you believe in miracles now? And how do you like my new shawl?

WONG. For the young fellow I saw you with in the park?

[SHEN TE *nods.*]

MRS. SHIN. Never mind all that. It's time you took a look at his hand!

SHEN TE. Have you hurt your hand?

MRS. SHIN. That barber smashed it with his hot curling iron. Right in front of our eyes.

SHEN TE [*shocked at herself*]. And I never noticed! We must get you to a doctor this minute or who knows what will happen?

UNEMPLOYED MAN. It's not a doctor he should see, it's a judge. He can ask for compensation. The barber's filthy rich.

WONG. You think I have a chance?

MRS. SHIN [*with relish*]. If it's really good and smashed. But is it?

WONG. I think so. It's very swollen. Could I get a pension?

MRS. SHIN. You'd need a witness.

WONG. Well, you all saw it. You could all testify.

> [*He looks round. The* UNEMPLOYED MAN, *the* GRANDFATHER, *and the* SIS-TER-IN-LAW *are all sitting against the wall of the shop eating rice. Their concentration on eating is complete.*]

SHEN TE [*to* MRS. SHIN]. You saw it yourself.

MRS. SHIN. I want nothin' to do with the police. It's against my principles.

SHEN TE [*to* SISTER-IN-LAW]. What about you?

SISTER-IN-LAW. Me? I wasn't looking.

SHEN TE [*to the* GRANDFATHER, *coaxingly*]. Grandfather, *you'll* testify, won't you?

SISTER-IN-LAW. And a lot of good that will do. He's simple-minded.

SHEN TE [*to the* UNEMPLOYED MAN]. You seem to be the only witness left.

UNEMPLOYED MAN. My testimony would only hurt him. I've been picked up twice for begging.

SHEN TE. Your brother is assaulted, and you shut your eyes?
> He is hit, cries out in pain, and you are silent?
> The beast prowls, chooses and seizes his victim, and you say:
> "Because we showed no displeasure, he has spared us."
> If no one present will be a witness, I will. I'll say I saw it.

MRS. SHIN [*solemnly*]. The name for that is perjury.

WONG. I don't know if I can accept that. Though maybe I'll have to. [*Looking at his hand.*] Is it swollen enough, do you think? The swelling's not going down?

UNEMPLOYED MAN. No, no, the swelling's holding up well.

WONG. Yes. It's *more* swollen if anything. Maybe my wrist is broken after all. I'd better see a judge at once.

> [*Holding his hand very carefully, and fixing his eyes on it, he runs off.* MRS. SHIN *goes quickly into the barber's shop.*]

UNEMPLOYED MAN [*seeing her*]. She is getting on the right side of Mr. Shu Fu.

SISTER-IN-LAW. You and I can't change the world, Shen Te.

SHEN TE. Go away! Go away all of you!

> [*The* UNEMPLOYED MAN, *the* SISTER-IN-LAW, *and the* GRANDFATHER *stalk off, eating and sulking.*]
> [*To the audience.*]

They've stopped answering
They stay put
They do as they're told
They don't care
Nothing can make them look up
But the smell of food.

[*Enter* MRS. YANG, YANG SUN'S *mother, out of breath.*]

MRS. YANG. Miss Shen Te. My son has told me everything. I am Mrs. Yang, Sun's mother. Just think. He's got an offer. Of a job as a pilot. A letter has just come. From the director of the airfield in Peking!

SHEN TE. So he can fly again? Isn't that wonderful!

MRS. YANG [*less breathlessly all the time*]. They won't give him the job for nothing. They want five hundred silver dollars.

SHEN TE. We can't let money stand in his way, Mrs. Yang!

MRS. YANG. If only you could help him out!

SHEN TE. I have the shop. I can try! [*She embraces* MRS. YANG.] I happen to have two hundred with me now. Take it. [*She gives her the old couple's money.*] It was a loan but they said I could repay it with my tobacco stock.

MRS. YANG. And they were calling Sun the Dead Pilot of Setzuan! A friend in need!

SHEN TE. We must find another three hundred.

MRS. YANG. How?

SHEN TE. Let me think. [*Slowly.*] I know someone who can help. I didn't want to call on his services again, he's hard and cunning. But a flyer must fly. And I'll make this the last time.

[*Distant sound of a plane.*]

MRS. YANG. If the man you mentioned can do it. . . . Oh, look, there's the morning mail plane, heading for Peking!

SHEN TE. The pilot can see us, let's wave!

[*They wave. The noise of the engine is louder.*]

MRS. YANG. You know that pilot up there?

SHEN TE. Wave, Mrs. Yang! I know the pilot who *will* be up there. He gave up hope. But he'll do it now. One man to raise himself above the misery, above us all.

[*To the audience.*]

Yang Sun, my lover:
Braving the storms
In company with the clouds
Crossing the heavens
And bringing to friends in far-away lands
The friendly mail!

SCENE IVA

In front of the inner curtain. Enter SHEN TE, *carrying* SHUI TA'S *mask. She sings.*

THE SONG OF DEFENSELESSNESS

In our country
A useful man needs luck
Only if he finds strong backers can he prove himself useful
The good can't defend themselves and
Even the gods are defenseless.

Oh, why don't the gods have their own ammunition
And launch against badness their own expedition
Enthroning the good and preventing sedition
And bringing the world to a peaceful condition?

Oh, why don't the gods do the buying and selling
Injustice forbidding, starvation dispelling
Give bread to each city and joy to each dwelling?
Oh, why don't the gods do the buying and selling?

> [*She puts on* SHUI TA's *mask and sings in
> his voice.*]

You can only help one of your luckless brothers
By trampling down a dozen others

Why is it the gods do not feel indignation
And come down in fury to end exploitation
Defeat all defeat and forbid desperation
Refusing to tolerate such toleration?

Why is it?

SCENE V

SHEN TE's *tobacco shop. Behind the counter,* MR. SHUI TA, *reading the paper.*
MRS. SHIN *is cleaning up. She talks and he takes no notice.*

MRS. SHIN. And when certain rumors get about, what *happens* to a little
place like this? It goes to pot. *I* know. So, if you want my advice, Mr.
Shui Ta, find out just what exactly has been going on between Miss
Shen Te and that Yang Sun from Yellow Street. And remember: a cer-
tain interest in Miss Shen Te has been expressed by the barber next
door, a man with twelve houses and only one wife, who, for that matter,
is likely to drop off at any time. A certain interest has been expressed.
[*She relishes the phrase.*] He was even inquiring about her means and, if
that doesn't prove a man is getting serious, what would? [*Still getting no
response, she leaves with her bucket.*]
YANG SUN'S VOICE. Is that Miss Shen Te's tobacco shop?
MRS. SHIN'S VOICE. Yes, it is, but it's Mr. Shui Ta who's here today.

> [SHUI TA *runs to the looking glass with
> the short, light steps of* SHEN TE, *and is
> just about to start primping, when he real-
> izes his mistake, and turns away, with a
> short laugh. Enter* YANG SUN. MRS.
> SHIN *enters behind him and slips into the
> back room to eavesdrop.*]

YANG SUN. I am Yang Sun.

> [SHUI TA *bows.*]

Is Miss Shen Te in?
SHUI TA. No.

YANG SUN. I guess you know our relationship? [*He is inspecting the stock.*] Quite a place! And I thought she was just talking big. I'll be flying again, all right. [*He takes a cigar, solicits and receives a light from* SHUI TA.] You think we can squeeze the other three hundred out of the tobacco stock?

SHUI TA. May I ask if it is your intention to sell at once?

YANG SUN. It was decent of her to come out with the two hundred but they aren't much use with the other three hundred still missing.

SHUI TA. Shen Te was overhasty promising so much. She might have to sell the shop itself to raise it. Haste, they say, is the wind that blows the house down.

YANG SUN. Oh, she isn't a girl to keep a man waiting. For one thing or the other, if you take my meaning.

SHUI TA. I take your meaning.

YANG SUN [*leering*]. Uh, huh.

SHUI TA. Would you explain what the five hundred silver dollars are for?

YANG SUN. Trying to sound me out? Very well. The director of the Peking airfield is a friend of mine from flying school. I give him five hundred: he gets me the job.

SHUI TA. The price is high.

YANG SUN. Not as these things go. He'll have to fire one of the present pilots—for negligence. Only the man he has in mind isn't negligent. Not easy, you understand. You needn't mention that part of it to Shen Te.

SHUI TA [*looking intently at* YANG SUN]. Mr. Yang Sun, you are asking my cousin to give up her possessions, leave her friends, and place her entire fate in your hands. I presume you intend to marry her?

YANG SUN. I'd be prepared to.

[*Slight pause.*]

SHUI TA. Those two hundred silver dollars would pay the rent here for six months. If you were Shen Te wouldn't you be tempted to continue business?

YANG SUN. What? Can you imagine Yang Sun the Flyer behind a counter? [*In an oily voice.*] "A strong cigar or a mild one, worthy sir?" Not in this century!

SHUI TA. My cousin wishes to follow the promptings of her heart, and, from her own point of view, she may even have what is called the right to love. Accordingly, she has commissioned me to help you to this post. There is nothing here that I am not empowered to turn immediately into cash. Mrs. Mi Tzu, the landlady, will advise me about the sale.

[*Enter* Mrs. Mi Tzu.]

MRS. MI TZU. Good morning, Mr. Shui Ta, you wish to see me about the rent? As you know it falls due the day after tomorrow.

SHUI TA. Circumstances have changed, Mrs. Mi Tzu: my cousin is getting married. Her future husband here, Mr. Yang Sun, will be taking her to Peking. I am interested in selling the tobacco stock.

MRS. MI TZU. How much are you asking, Mr. Shui Ta?

YANG SUN. Three hundred sil—

SHUI TA. Five hundred silver dollars.

MRS. MI TZU. How much did she pay for it, Mr. Shui Ta?

SHUI TA. A thousand. And very little has been sold.

MRS. MI TZU. She was robbed. But I'll make you a special offer if you'll promise to be out by the day after tomorrow. Three hundred silver dollars.

YANG SUN [*shrugging*]. Take it, man, take it.

SHUI TA. It is not enough.

YANG SUN. Why not? Why not? Certainly, it's enough.

SHUI TA [*to* MRS. MI TZU]. Excuse me. [*Takes* YANG SUN *on one side.*] The tobacco stock is pledged to the old couple who gave my cousin the two hundred.

YANG SUN. Is it in writing?

SHUI TA. No.

YANG SUN [*to* MRS. MI TZU]. Three hundred will do.

MRS. MI TZU. Of course, I need an assurance that Miss Shen Te is not in debt.

YANG SUN. Mr. Shui Ta?

SHUI TA. She is not in debt.

YANG SUN. When can you let us have the money?

MRS. MI TZU. The day after tomorrow. And remember: I'm doing this because I have a soft spot in my heart for young lovers! [*Exit.*]

YANG SUN [*calling after her*]. Boxes, jars and sacks—three hundred for the lot and the pain's over! [*To* SHUI TA.] Where else can we raise money by the day after tomorrow?

SHUI TA. Nowhere. Haven't you enough for the trip and the first few weeks?

YANG SUN. Oh, certainly.

SHUI TA. How much, exactly?

YANG SUN. Oh, I'll dig it up, if I have to steal it.

SHUI TA. I see.

YANG SUN. Well, don't fall off the roof. I'll get to Peking somehow.

SHUI TA. Two people can't travel for nothing.

YANG SUN [*not giving* SHUI TA *a chance to answer*]. I'm leaving *her* behind. No millstones around *my* neck!

SHUI TA. Oh.

YANG SUN. Don't look at me like that!

SHUI TA. How precisely is my cousin to live?

YANG SUN. Oh, you'll think of something.

SHUI TA. A small request, Mr. Yang Sun. Leave the two hundred silver dollars here until you can show me two tickets for Peking.

YANG SUN. You learn to mind your own business, Mr. Shui Ta.

SHUI TA. I'm afraid Miss Shen Te may not wish to sell the shop when she discovers that. . .

YANG SUN. You don't know women. She'll want to. Even then.

SHUI TA [*a slight outburst*]. She is a human being, sir! And not devoid of common sense!

YANG SUN. Shen Te is a woman: she *is* devoid of common sense. I only have to lay my hand on her shoulder, and church bells ring.

SHUI TA [*with difficulty*]. Mr. Yang Sun!

YANG SUN. Mr. Shui Whatever-it-is!

SHUI TA. My cousin is devoted to you . . . because. . .

YANG SUN. Because I have my hands on her breasts. Give me a cigar. [*He*

takes one for himself, stuffs a few more in his pocket, then changes his mind and takes the whole box.] Tell her I'll marry her, then bring me the three hundred. Or let her bring it. One or the other. [*Exit.*]

MRS. SHIN [*sticking her head out of the back room*]. Well, he has your cousin under his thumb, and doesn't care if all Yellow Street knows it!

SHUI TA [*crying out*]. I've lost my shop! And he doesn't love me! [*He runs berserk through the room, repeating these lines incoherently. Then stops suddenly and addresses* MRS. SHIN.] Mrs. Shin, you grew up in the gutter, like me. Are we lacking in hardness? I doubt it. If you steal a penny from me, I'll take you by the throat till you spit it out! You'd do the same to me. The times are bad, this city is hell, but we're like ants, we keep coming, up and up the walls, however smooth! Till bad luck comes. Being in love, for instance. *One* weakness is enough, and love is the deadliest.

MRS. SHIN [*emerging from the back room*]. You should have a little talk with Mr. Shu Fu the Barber. He's a real gentleman and just the thing for your cousin. [*She runs off.*]

SHUI TA.
A caress becomes a stranglehold
A sigh of love turns to a cry of fear
Why are there vultures circling in the air?
A girl is going to meet her lover.

[SHUI TA *sits down and* MR. SHU FU *enters with* MRS. SHIN.]

Mr. Shu Fu?

SHU FU. Mr. Shui Ta.

[*They both bow.*]

SHUI TA. I am told that you have expressed a certain interest in my cousin Shen Te. Let me set aside all propriety and confess: she is at this moment in grave danger.

SHU FU. Oh, dear!

SHUI TA. She has lost her shop, Mr. Shu Fu.

SHU FU. The charm of Miss Shen Te, Mr. Shui Ta, derives from the goodness, not of her shop, but of her heart. Men call her the Angel of the Slums.

SHUI TA. Yet her goodness has cost her two hundred silver dollars in a single day: we must put a stop to it.

SHU FU. Permit me to differ, Mr. Shui Ta. Let us rather open wide the gates to such goodness! Every morning, with pleasure tinged by affection, I watch her charitable ministrations. For they are hungry, and she giveth them to eat! Four of them, to be precise. Why only four? I ask. Why not four hundred? I hear she has been seeking shelter for the homeless. What about my humble cabins behind the cattle run? They are at her disposal. And so forth. And so on. Mr. Shui Ta, do you think Miss Shen Te could be persuaded to listen to certain ideas of mine? Ideas like these?

SHUI TA. Mr. Shu Fu, she would be honored.

[*Enter* WONG *and the* POLICEMAN. MR. SHU FU *turns abruptly away and studies the shelves.*]

WONG. Is Miss Shen Te here?

SHUI TA. No.

WONG. I am Wong the Water Seller. You are Mr. Shui Ta?

SHUI TA. I am.

WONG. I am a friend of Shen Te's.

SHUI TA. An intimate friend, I hear.

WONG [*to the* POLICEMAN]. You see? [*To* SHUI TA.] It's because of my hand.

POLICEMAN. He hurt his hand, sir, that's a fact.

SHUI TA [*quickly*]. You need a sling, I see. [*He takes a shawl from the back room, and throws it to* WONG.]

WONG. But that's her new shawl!

SHUI TA. She has no more use for it.

WONG. But she bought it to please someone!

SHUI TA. It happens to be no longer necessary.

WONG [*making the sling*]. She is my only witness.

POLICEMAN. Mr. Shui Ta, your cousin is supposed to have seen the Barber hit the Water Seller with a curling iron.

SHUI TA. I'm afraid my cousin was not present at the time.

WONG. But she was, sir! Just ask her! Isn't she in?

SHUI TA [*gravely*]. Mr. Wong, my cousin has her own troubles. You wouldn't wish her to add to them by committing perjury?

WONG. But it was she that told me to go to the judge!

SHUI TA. Was the judge supposed to heal your hand?

[MR. SHU FU *turns quickly around.* SHUI TA *bows to* SHU FU, *and vice versa.*]

WONG [*taking the sling off, and putting it back*]. I see how it is.

POLICEMAN. Well, I'll be on my way. [*To* WONG.] And you be careful. If Mr. Shu Fu wasn't a man who tempers justice with mercy, as the saying is, you'd be in jail for libel. Be off with you!

[*Exit* WONG, *followed by* POLICEMAN.]

SHUI TA. Profound apologies, Mr. Shu Fu.

SHU FU. Not at all, Mr. Shui Ta. [*Pointing to the shawl.*] The episode is over?

SHUI TA. It may take her time to recover. There are some fresh wounds.

SHU FU. We shall be discreet. Delicate. A short vacation could be arranged. . .

SHUI TA. First, of course, you and she would have to talk things over.

SHU FU. At a small supper in a small, but high-class, restaurant.

SHUI TA. I'll go and find her. [*Exit into back room.*]

MRS. SHIN [*sticking her head in again*]. Time for congratulations, Mr. Shu Fu?

SHU FU. Ah, Mrs. Shin! Please inform Miss Shen Te's guests they may take shelter in the cabins behind the cattle run!

[MRS. SHIN *nods, grinning.*]

[*To the audience.*] Well? What do you think of me, ladies and gentlemen? What could a man do more? Could he be less selfish? More farsighted? A small supper in a small but . . . Does that bring rather vulgar and clumsy thoughts into your mind? Ts, ts, ts. Nothing of the sort will occur. She won't even be touched. Not even accidentally while passing the salt. An exchange of ideas only. Over the flowers on the table— white chrysanthemums by the way [*he writes down a note of this*]— yes, over the white chrysanthemums, two young souls will . . . shall

I say "find each other"? We shall NOT exploit the misfortune of others. Understanding? Yes. An offer of assistance? Certainly. But quietly. Almost inaudibly. Perhaps with a single glance. A glance that could also—mean more.

MRS. SHIN [*coming forward*]. Everything under control, Mr. Shu Fu?

SHU FU. Oh, Mrs. Shin, what do you know about this worthless rascal Yang Sun?

MRS. SHIN. Why, he's the most worthless rascal. . .

SHU FU. Is he really? You're sure? [*As she opens her mouth.*] From now on, he doesn't exist! Can't be found anywhere!

[*Enter* YANG SUN.]

YANG SUN. What's been going on here?

MRS. SHIN. Shall I call Mr. Shui Ta, Mr. Shu Fu? He wouldn't want strangers in here!

SHU FU. Mr. Shui Ta is in conference with Miss Shen Te. Not to be disturbed!

YANG SUN. Shen Te here? I didn't see her come in. What kind of conference?

SHU FU [*not letting him enter the back room*]. Patience, dear sir! And if by chance I have an inkling who you are, pray take note that Miss Shen Te and I are about to announce our engagement.

YANG SUN. What?

MRS. SHIN. You didn't expect that, did you?

[YANG SUN *is trying to push past the barber into the back room when* SHEN TE *comes out.*]

SHU FU. My dear Shen Te, ten thousand apologies! Perhaps you. . .

YANG SUN. What is it, Shen Te? Have you gone crazy?

SHEN TE [*breathless*]. My cousin and Mr. Shu Fu have come to an understanding. They wish me to hear Mr. Shu Fu's plans for helping the poor.

YANG SUN. Your cousin wants to part us.

SHEN TE. Yes.

YANG SUN. And you've agreed to it?

SHEN TE. Yes.

YANG SUN. They told you I was bad.

[SHEN TE *is silent.*]

And suppose I am. Does that make me need you less? I'm low. Shen Te, I have no money, I don't do the right thing but at least I put up a fight! [*He is near her now, and speaks in an undertone.*] Have you no eyes? Look at him. Have you forgotten already?

SHEN TE. No.

YANG SUN. How it was raining?

SHEN TE. No.

YANG SUN. How you cut me down from the willow tree? Bought me water? Promised me money to fly with?

SHEN TE [*shakily*]. Yang Sun, what do you want?

YANG SUN. I want you to come with me.

SHEN TE [*in a small voice*]. Forgive me, Mr. Shu Fu, I want to go with Mr. Yang Sun.

YANG SUN. We're lovers you know. Give me the key to the shop.

[SHEN TE *takes the key from around her neck.* YANG SUN *puts it on the counter. To* MRS. SHIN.]

Leave it under the mat when you're through. Let's go, Shen Te.

SHU FU. But this is rape! Mr. Shui Ta!!

YANG SUN [*to* SHEN TE]. Tell him not to shout.

SHEN TE. Please don't shout for my cousin, Mr. Shu Fu. He doesn't agree with me, I know, but he's wrong. [*To the audience.*]

I want to go with the man I love
I don't want to count the cost
I don't want to consider if it's wise
I don't want to know if he loves me
I want to go with the man I love.

YANG SUN. That's the spirit.

[*And the couple leave.*]

SCENE VA

In front of the inner curtain. SHEN TE *in her wedding clothes, on the way to her wedding.*

SHEN TE. Something terrible has happened. As I left the shop with Yang Sun, I found the old carpet dealer's wife waiting in the street, trembling all over. She told me her husband has taken to his bed—sick with all the worry and excitement over the two hundred silver dollars they lent me. She said it would be best if I gave it back now. Of course, I had to say I would. She said she couldn't quite trust my cousin Shui Ta or even my fiancé Yang Sun. There were tears in her eyes. With my emotions in an uproar, I threw myself into Yang Sun's arms, I couldn't resist him. The things he'd said to Shui Ta had taught Shen Te nothing. Sinking into his arms, I said to myself:

To let no one perish, not even oneself
To fill everyone with happiness, even oneself
Is so good

How could I have forgotten those two old people? Yang Sun swept me away like a small hurricane. But he's not a bad man, and he loves me. He'd rather work in the cement factory than owe his flying to a crime. Though, of course, flying *is* a great passion with Sun. Now, on the way to my wedding, I waver between fear and joy.

SCENE VI

The "private dining room" on the upper floor of a cheap restaurant in a poor section of town. With SHEN TE: *the* GRANDFATHER, *the* SISTER-IN-LAW, *the* NIECE, MRS. SHIN, *the* UNEMPLOYED MAN. *In a corner, alone, a* PRIEST. *A* WAITER *pouring wine. Downstage,* YANG SUN *talking to his mother. He wears a dinner jacket.*

YANG SUN. Bad news, Mamma. She came right out and told me she can't sell the shop for me. Some idiot is bringing a claim because he lent her the two hundred she gave you.

MRS. YANG. What did *you* say? Of course, you can't marry her now.

YANG SUN. It's no use saying anything to *her*. I've sent for her cousin, Mr. Shui Ta. He said there was nothing in writing.

MRS. YANG. Good idea. I'll go out and look for him. Keep an eye on things. [*Exit* MRS. YANG. SHEN TE *has been pouring wine.*]

SHEN TE [*to the audience, pitcher in hand*]. I wasn't mistaken in him. He's bearing up well. Though it must have been an awful blow—giving up flying. I do love him so. [*Calling across the room to him.*] Sun, you haven't drunk a toast with the bride!

YANG SUN. What do we drink to?

SHEN TE. Why, to the future!

YANG SUN. When the bridegroom's dinner jacket won't be a hired one!

SHEN TE. But when the bride's dress will still get rained on sometimes!

YANG SUN. To everything we ever wished for!

SHEN TE. May all our dreams come true!

[*They drink.*]

YANG SUN [*with loud conviviality*]. And now, friends, before the wedding gets under way, I have to ask the bride a few questions. I've no idea what k'nd of a wife she'll make, and it worries me. [*Wheeling on* SHEN TE.] For example. Can you make five cups of tea with three tea leaves?

SHEN TE. No.

YANG SUN. So I won't be getting very much tea. Can you sleep on a straw mattress the size of that book? [*He points to the large volume the* PRIEST *is reading.*]

SHEN TE. The two of us?

YANG SUN. The one of you.

SHEN TE. In that case, no.

YANG SUN. What a wife! I'm shocked!

[*While the audience is laughing, his mother returns. With a shrug of her shoulders, she tells* YANG SUN *the expected guest hasn't arrived. The* PRIEST *shuts the book with a bang, and makes for the door.*]

MRS. YANG. Where are *you* off to? It's only a matter of minutes.

PRIEST [*watch in hand*]. Time goes on, Mrs. Yang, and I've another wedding to attend to. Also a funeral.

MRS. YANG [*irately*]. D'you think we planned it this way? I was hoping to manage with one pitcher of wine, and we've run through two already. [*Points to empty pitcher. Loudly.*] My dear Shen Te, I don't know where your cousin can be keeping himself!

SHEN TE. My cousin?

MRS. YANG. Certainly. I'm old fashioned enough to think such a close relative should attend the wedding.

SHEN TE. Oh, Sun, is it the three hundred silver dollars?

YANG SUN [*not looking her in the eye*]. Are you deaf? Mother says she's old

fashioned. And I say I'm considerate. We'll wait another fifteen minutes.

HUSBAND. Another fifteen minutes.

MRS. YANG [addressing the company]. Now you all know, don't you, that my son is getting a job as a mail pilot?

SISTER-IN-LAW. In Peking, too, isn't it?

MRS. YANG. In Peking, too! The two of us are moving to Peking!

SHEN TE. Sun, tell your mother Peking is out of the question now.

YANG SUN. Your cousin'll tell her. If he agrees. I don't agree.

SHEN TE [amazed, and dismayed]. Sun!

YANG SUN. I hate this godforsaken Setzuan. What people! Know what they look like when I half close my eyes? Horses! Whinnying, fretting, stamping, screwing their necks up! [Loudly.] And what is it the thunder says? They are su-per-flu-ous! [He hammers out the syllables.] They've run their last race! They can go trample themselves to death! [Pause.] I've got to get out of here.

SHEN TE. But I've promised the money to the old couple.

YANG SUN. And since you always do the wrong thing, it's lucky your cousin's coming. Have another drink.

SHEN TE [quietly]. My cousin can't be coming.

YANG SUN. How d'you mean?

SHEN TE. My cousin can't be where I am.

YANG SUN. Quite a conundrum!

SHEN TE [desperately]. Sun, I'm the one that loves you. Not my cousin. He was thinking of the job in Peking when he promised you the old couple's money—

YANG SUN. Right. And that's why he's bringing the three hundred silver dollars. Here—to my wedding.

SHEN TE. He is not bringing the three hundred silver dollars.

YANG SUN. Huh? What makes you think that?

SHEN TE [looking into his eyes]. He says you only bought one ticket to Peking.

[Short pause.]

YANG SUN. That was yesterday. [He pulls two tickets part way out of his inside pocket, making her look under his coat.] Two tickets. I don't want Mother to know. She'll get left behind. I sold her furniture to buy these tickets, so you see. . .

SHEN TE. But what's to become of the old couple?

YANG SUN. What's to become of me? Have another drink. Or do you believe in moderation? If I drink, I fly again. And if you drink, you may learn to understand me.

SHEN TE. You want to fly. But I can't help you.

YANG SUN. "Here's a plane, my darling—but it's only got one wing!"

[The WAITER enters.]

WAITER. Mrs. Yang! Mrs. Yang!

MRS. YANG. Yes?

WAITER. Another pitcher of wine, ma'am?

MRS. YANG. We have enough, thanks. Drinking makes me sweat.

WAITER. Would you mind paying, ma'am?

MRS. YANG [to everyone]. Just be patient a few moments longer, everyone, Mr. Shui Ta is on his way over! [To the WAITER.] Don't be a spoilsport.

WAITER. I can't let you leave till you've paid your bill, ma'am.

MRS. YANG. But they know me here.

WAITER. That's just it.

PRIEST [*ponderously getting up*]. I humbly take my leave. [*And he does.*]

MRS. YANG [*to the others, desperately*]. Stay where you are, everybody! The priest says he'll be back in two minutes!

YANG SUN. It's no good, Mamma. Ladies and gentlemen, Mr. Shui Ta still hasn't arrived and the priest has gone home. We won't detain you any longer.

[*They are leaving now.*]

GRANDFATHER [*in the doorway, having forgotten to put his glass down*]. To the bride! [*He drinks, puts down the glass, and follows the others.*]

[*Pause.*]

SHEN TE. Shall I go too?

YANG SUN. You? Aren't you the bride? Isn't this your wedding? [*He drags her across the room, tearing her wedding dress.*] If we can wait, you can wait. Mother calls me her falcon. She wants to see me in the clouds. But I think it may be St. Nevercome's Day before she'll go to the door and see my plane thunder by. [*Pause. He pretends the guests are still present.*] Why such a lull in the conversation, ladies and gentlemen? Don't you like it here? The ceremony is only slightly postponed—because an important guest is expected at any moment. Also because the bride doesn't know what love is. While we're waiting, the bridegroom will sing a little song. [*He does so.*]

THE SONG OF ST. NEVERCOME'S DAY

On a certain day, as is generally known,
 One and all will be shouting: Hooray, hooray!
For the beggar maid's son has a solid-gold throne
 And the day is St. Nevercome's Day
On St. Nevercome's, Nevercome's, Nevercome's Day
 He'll sit on his solid-gold throne

Oh, hooray, hooray! That day goodness will pay!
 That day badness will cost you your head!
And merit and money will smile and be funny
 While exchanging salt and bread
On St. Nevercome's, Nevercome's, Nevercome's Day
 While exchanging salt and bread

And the grass, oh, the grass will look down at the sky
 And the pebbles will roll up the stream
And all men will be good without batting an eye
 They will make of our earth a dream
On St. Nevercome's, Nevercome's, Nevercome's Day
 They will make of our earth a dream

And as for me, that's the day I shall be
 A flyer and one of the best

Unemployed man, you will have work to do
 Washerwoman, you'll get your rest
On St. Nevercome's, Nevercome's, Nevercome's Day
 Washerwoman, you'll get your rest

MRS. YANG. It looks like he's not coming.

[The three of them sit looking at the door.]

SCENE VIA

WONG's *den. The sewer pipe is again transparent and again the* GODS *appear to* WONG *in a dream.*

WONG. I'm so glad you've come, illustrious ones. It's Shen Te. She's in great trouble from following the rule about loving thy neighbor. Perhaps she's *too* good for this world!

FIRST GOD. Nonsense! You are eaten up by lice and doubts!

WONG. Forgive me, illustrious one, I only meant you might deign to intervene.

FIRST GOD. Out of the question! My colleague here intervened in some squabble or other only yesterday. *[He points to the* THIRD GOD *who has a black eye.]* The results are before us!

WONG. She had to call on her cousin again. But not even he could help. I'm afraid the shop is done for.

THIRD GOD *[a little concerned].* Perhaps we should help after all?

FIRST GOD. The gods help those that help themselves.

WONG. What if we *can't* help ourselves, illustrious ones?

[Slight pause.]

SECOND GOD. Try, anyway! Suffering ennobles!

FIRST GOD. Our faith in Shen Te is unshaken!

THIRD GOD. We certainly haven't found any *other* good people. You can see where we spend our nights from the straw on our clothes.

WONG. You might help her find her way by—

FIRST GOD. The good man finds his own way here below!

SECOND GOD. The good woman too.

FIRST GOD. The heavier the burden, the greater her strength!

THIRD GOD. We're only onlookers, you know.

FIRST GOD. And everything will be all right in the end, O ye of little faith!

[They are gradually disappearing through these last lines.]

SCENE VII

The yard behind SHEN TE's *shop. A few articles of furniture on a car.* SHEN TE *and* MRS. SHIN *are taking the washing off the line.*

MRS. SHIN. If you ask me, you should fight tooth and nail to keep the shop.

SHEN TE. How can I? I have to sell the tobacco to pay back the two hundred silver dollars today.

MRS. SHIN. No husband, no tobacco, no house and home! What are you going to live on?

SHEN TE. I can work. I can sort tobacco.

MRS. SHIN. Hey, look, Mr. Shui Ta's trousers! He must have left here stark naked!

SHEN TE. Oh, he may have another pair, Mrs. Shin.

MRS. SHIN. But if he's gone for good as you say, why has he left his pants behind?

SHEN TE. Maybe he's thrown them away.

MRS. SHIN. Can I take them?

SHEN TE. Oh, no.

[*Enter* MR. SHU FU, *running.*]

SHU FU. Not a word! Total silence! I know all. You have sacrificed your own love and happiness so as not to hurt a dear old couple who had put their trust in you! Not in vain does this district—for all its malevolent tongues!—call you the Angel of the Slums! That young man couldn't rise to your level, so you left him. And now, when I see you closing up the little shop, that veritable haven of rest for the multitude, well, I cannot, I cannot let it pass. Morning after morning I have stood watching in the doorway not unmoved—while you graciously handed out rice to the wretched. Is that never to happen again? Is the good woman of Setzuan to disappear? If only you would allow *me* to assist you! Now don't say anything! No assurances, no exclamations of gratitude! [*He has taken out his check book.*] Here! A blank check. [*He places it on the cart.*] Just my signature. Fill it out as you wish. Any sum in the world. I herewith retire from the scene, quietly, unobtrusively, making no claims, on tiptoe, full of veneration, absolutely selflessly . . . [*He has gone.*]

MRS. SHIN. Well! You're saved. There's always some idiot of a man . . . Now hurry! Put down a thousand silver dollars and let me fly to the bank before he comes to his senses.

SHEN TE. I can pay you for the washing without any check.

MRS. SHIN. What? You're not going to cash it just because you might have to marry him? Are you crazy? Men like him *want* to be led by the nose! Are you still thinking of that flyer? All Yellow Street knows how he treated you!

SHEN TE.

When I heard his cunning laugh, I was afraid

But when I saw the holes in his shoes, I loved him dearly.

MRS. SHIN. Defending that good for nothing after all that's happened!

SHEN TE [*staggering as she holds some of the washing*]. Oh!

MRS. SHIN [*taking the washing from her, dryly*]. So you feel dizzy when you stretch and bend? There couldn't be a little visitor on the way? If that's it, you can forget Mr. Shu Fu's blank check: it wasn't meant for a christening present!

[*She goes to the back with a basket.* SHEN TE's *eyes follow* MRS. SHIN *for a moment. Then she looks down at her own body, feels her stomach, and a great joy comes into her eyes.*]

SHEN TE. O joy! A new human being is on the way. The world awaits him.

In the cities the people say: he's got to be reckoned with, this new human being! [*She imagines a little boy to be present, and introduces him to the audience.*]

This is my son, the well-known flyer!

Say: Welcome

To the conqueror of unknown mountains and unreachable regions

Who brings us our mail across the impassable deserts!

[*She leads him up and down by the hand.*]

Take a look at the world, my son. That's a tree. Tree, yes. Say: "Hello, tree!" And bow. Like this. [*She bows.*] Now you know each other. And, look, here comes the Water Seller. He's a friend, give him your hand. A cup of fresh water for my little son, please. Yes, it *is* a warm day. [*Handing the cup.*] Oh dear, a policeman, we'll have to make a circle round *him*. Perhaps we can pick a few cherries over there in the rich Mr. Pung's garden. But we mustn't be seen. You want cherries? Just like children with fathers. No, no, you can't go straight at them like that. Don't pull. We must learn to be reasonable. Well, have it your own way. [*She has let him make for the cherries.*] Can you reach? Where to put them? Your mouth is the best place. [*She tries one herself.*] Mmm, they're good. But the policeman, we must run! [*They run.*] Yes, back to the street. Calm now, so no one will notice us. [*Walking the street with her child, she sings.*]

Once a plum—'twas in Japan—

Made a conquest of a man

But the man's turn soon did come

For he gobbled up the plum

[*Enter* WONG, *with a* CHILD *by the hand. He coughs.*]

SHEN TE. Wong!

WONG. It's about the Carpenter, Shen Te. He's lost his shop, and he's been drinking. His children are on the streets. This is one. Can you help?

SHEN TE [*to the child*]. Come here, little man. [*Takes him down to the footlights. To the audience.*]

You there! A man is asking you for shelter!

A man of tomorrow says: what about today?

His friend the conqueror, whom you know,

Is his advocate!

[*To* WONG.] He can live in Mr. Shu Fu's cabin. I may have to go there myself. I'm going to have a baby. That's a secret—don't tell Yang Sun—we'd only be in his way. Can you find the Carpenter for me?

WONG. I knew you'd think of something. [*To the* CHILD.] Goodbye, son, I'm going for your father.

SHEN TE. What about your hand, Wong? I wanted to help, but my cousin . . .

WONG. Oh, I can get along with one hand, don't worry. [*He shows how he can handle his pole with his left hand alone.*]

SHEN TE. But your right hand! Look, take this cart, sell everything that's on it, and go to the doctor with the money . . .

WONG. She's still good. But first I'll bring the Carpenter. I'll pick up the cart when I get back. [*Exit* WONG.]

SHEN TE [*to the* CHILD]. Sit down over here, son, till your father comes.

> [*The* CHILD *sits crosslegged on the ground. Enter the* HUSBAND *and* WIFE, *each dragging a large, full sack.*]

WIFE [*furtively*]. You're alone, Shen Te, dear?

> [*Shen Te nods. The* WIFE *beckons to the* NEPHEW *offstage. He comes on with another sack.*]

Your cousin's away?

> [SHEN TE *nods.*]

He's not coming back?

SHEN TE. No. I'm giving up the shop.

WIFE. That's why we're here. We want to know if we can leave these things in your new home. Will you do us this favor?

SHEN TE. Why, yes, I'd be glad to.

HUSBAND [*cryptically*]. And if anyone asks about them, say they're yours.

SHEN TE. Would anyone ask?

WIFE [*with a glance back at her* HUSBAND]. Oh, someone might. The police, for instance. They don't seem to like us. Where can we put it?

SHEN TE. Well, I'd rather not get in any more trouble . . .

WIFE. Listen to her! The good woman of Setzuan!

> [SHEN TE *is silent.*]

HUSBAND. There's enough tobacco in those sacks to give us a new start in life. We could have our own tobacco factory!

SHEN TE [*slowly*]. You'll have to put them in the back room.

> [*The sacks are taken offstage, while the* CHILD *is left alone. Shyly glancing about him, he goes to the garbage can, starts playing with the contents, and eating some of the scraps. The others return.*]

WIFE. We're counting on you, Shen Te!

SHEN TE. Yes. [*She sees the* CHILD *and is shocked.*]

HUSBAND. We'll see you in Mr. Shu Fu's cabins.

NEPHEW. The day after tomorrow.

SHEN TE. Yes. Now, go. Go! I'm not feeling well.

> [*Exeunt all three, virtually pushed off.*]

He is eating the refuse in the garbage can!
Only look at his little gray mouth!

> [*Pause. Music.*]

As this is the world *my* son will enter
I will study to defend him.
To be good to you, my son,
I shall be a tigress to all others
If I have to.
And I shall have to.
[*She starts to go.*] One more time, then. I hope really the last.

> [*Exit* SHEN TE, *taking* SHUI TA'S *trousers.* MRS. SHIN *enters and watches her with marked interest. Enter the* SISTER-IN-LAW *and the* GRANDFATHER.]

SISTER-IN-LAW. So it's true, the shop has closed down. And the furniture's in the back yard. It's the end of the road!

MRS. SHIN [*pompously*]. The fruit of high living, selfishness, and sensuality! Down the primrose path to Mr. Shu Fu's cabins—with you!

SISTER-IN-LAW. Cabins? Rat holes! He gave them to us because his soap supplies only went mouldy there!

[*Enter the* UNEMPLOYED MAN.]

UNEMPLOYED MAN. Shen Te is moving?

SISTER-IN-LAW. Yes. She was sneaking away.

MRS. SHIN. She's ashamed of herself, and no wonder!

UNEMPLOYED MAN. Tell her to call Mr. Shui Ta or she's done for this time!

SISTER-IN-LAW. Tell her to call Mr. Shui Ta or *we're* done for this time.

[*Enter* WONG *and* CARPENTER, *the latter with a* CHILD *on each hand.*]

CARPENTER. So we'll have a roof over our heads for a change!

MRS. SHIN. Roof? Whose roof?

CARPENTER. Mr. Shu Fu's cabins. And we have little Feng to thank for it. [FENG, *we find, is the name of the child already there; his* FATHER *now takes him. To the other two.*] Bow to your little brother, you two! [*The* CARPENTER *and the two new arrivals bow to* FENG.]

[*Enter* SHUI TA.]

UNEMPLOYED MAN. Sst! Mr. Shui Ta!

[*Pause.*]

SHUI TA. And what is this crowd here for, may I ask?

WONG. How do you do, Mr. Shui Ta? This is the Carpenter. Miss Shen Te promised him space in Mr. Shu Fu's cabins.

SHUI TA. That will not be possible.

CARPENTER. We can't go there after all?

SHUI TA. All the space is needed for other purposes.

SISTER-IN-LAW. You mean we have to get out? But we've got nowhere to go.

SHUI TA. Miss Shen Te finds it possible to provide employment. If the proposition interests you, you may stay in the cabins.

SISTER-IN-LAW [*with distaste*]. You mean *work*? Work for Miss Shen Te?

SHUI TA. Making tobacco, yes. There are three bales here already. Would you like to get them?

SISTER-IN-LAW [*trying to bluster*]. We have our own tobacco! We were in the tobacco business before you were born!

SHUI TA [*to the* CARPENTER *and the* UNEMPLOYED MAN]. You *don't* have your own tobacco. What about you?

[*The* CARPENTER *and the* UNEMPLOYED MAN *get the point, and go for the sacks. Enter* MRS. MI TZU.]

MRS. MI TZU. Mr. Shui Ta? I've brought you your three hundred silver dollars.

SHUI TA. I'll sign your lease instead. I've decided not to sell.

MRS. MI TZU. What? You don't need the money for that flyer?

SHUI TA. No.

MRS. MI TZU. And you can pay six months' rent?

SHUI TA [*takes the barber's blank check from the cart and fills it out*]. Here is a check for ten thousand silver dollars. On Mr. Shu Fu's account.

Look! [*He shows her the signature on the check.*] Your six months' rent will be in your hands by seven this evening. And now, if you'll excuse me.

MRS. MI TZU. So it's Mr. Shu Fu now. The flyer has been given his walking papers. These modern girls! In my day they'd have said she was flighty. That poor, deserted Mr. Yang Sun!

> [*Exit* MRS. MI TZU. *The* CARPENTER *and the* UNEMPLOYED MAN *drag the three sacks back on the stage.*]

CARPENTER [*to* SHUI TA]. I don't know why I'm doing this for you.

SHUI TA. Perhaps your children want to eat, Mr. Carpenter.

SISTER-IN-LAW [*catching sight of the sacks*]. Was my brother-in-law here?

MRS. SHIN. Yes, he was.

SISTER-IN-LAW. I thought as much. I know those sacks! That's our tobacco!

SHUI TA. Really? I thought it came from my back room! Shall we consult the police on the point?

SISTER-IN-LAW [*defeated*]. No.

SHUI TA. Perhaps you will show me the way to Mr. Shu Fu's cabins?

> [SHUI TA *goes off, followed by the* CAR-PENTER *and his two older children, the* SISTER-IN-LAW, *the* GRANDFATHER, *and the* UNEMPLOYED MAN. *Each of the last three drags a sack. Enter* OLD MAN *and* OLD WOMAN.]

MRS. SHIN. A pair of pants—missing from the clothes line one minute—and next minute on the honorable backside of Mr. Shui Ta!

OLD WOMAN. We thought Miss Shen Te was here.

MRS. SHIN [*preoccupied*]. Well, she's not.

OLD MAN. There was something she was going to give us.

WONG. She was going to help me too. [*Looking at his hand.*] It'll be too late soon. But she'll be back. This cousin has never stayed long.

MRS. SHIN [*approaching a conclusion*]. No, he hasn't, has he?

SCENE VIIA

The sewer pipe. WONG *asleep. In his dream, he tells the* GODS *his fears. The* GODS *seem tired from all their travels. They stop for a moment and look over their shoulders at the Water Seller.*

WONG. Illustrious ones, I've been having a bad dream. Our beloved Shen Te was in great distress in the rushes down by the river—the spot where the bodies of suicides are washed up. She kept staggering and holding her head down as if she was carrying something and it was dragging her down into the mud. When I called out to her, she said she had to take your Book of Rules to the other side, and not get it wet, or the ink would all come off. You had talked to her about the virtues, you know, the time she gave you shelter in Setzuan.

THIRD GOD. Well, but what do you suggest, my dear Wong?

WONG. Maybe a little relaxation of the rules, Benevolent One, in view of
the bad times.

THIRD GOD. As for instance?

WONG. Well, um, good-will, for instance, might do instead of love?

THIRD GOD. I'm afraid that would create new problems.

WONG. Or, instead of justice, good sportsmanship?

THIRD GOD. That would only mean more work.

WONG. Instead of honor, outward propriety?

THIRD GOD. Still more work! No, no! The rules will have to stand, my dear
Wong!

> [*Wearily shaking their heads, all three
> journey on.*]

SCENE VIII

SHUI TA'S *tobacco factory in* SHU FU'S *cabins. Huddled together behind bars, sev-
eral families, mostly women and children. Among these people the* SISTER-IN-LAW,
the GRANDFATHER, *the* CARPENTER, *and his three children. Enter* MRS. YANG
followed by YANG SUN.

MRS. YANG [*to the audience*]. There's something I just *have* to tell you:
strength and wisdom are wonderful things. The strong and wise
Mr. Shui Ta has transformed my son from a dissipated good-for-
nothing into a model citizen. As you may have heard, Mr. Shui Ta
opened a small tobacco factory near the cattle runs. It flourished.
Three months ago—I shall never forget it—I asked for an appoint-
ment, and Mr. Shui Ta agreed to see us—me and my son. I can see
him now as he came through the door to meet us . . .

> [*Enter* SHUI TA, *from a door.*]

SHUI TA. What can I do for you, Mrs. Yang?

MRS. YANG. This morning the police came to the house. We find you've
brought an action for breach of promise of marriage. In the name of
Shen Te. You also claim that Sun came by two hundred silver dollars by
improper means.

SHUI TA. That is correct.

MRS. YANG. Mr. Shui Ta, the money's all gone. When the Peking job didn't
materialize, he ran through it all in three days. I know he's a good-
for-nothing. He sold my furniture. He was moving to Peking without
me. Miss Shen Te thought highly of him at one time.

SHUI TA. What do *you* say, Mr. Yang Sun?

YANG SUN. The money's gone.

SHUI TA [*to* MRS. YANG]. Mrs. Yang, in consideration of my cousin's incom-
prehensible weakness for your son, I am prepared to give him another
chance. He can have a job—here. The two hundred silver dollars will be
taken out of his wages.

YANG SUN. So it's the factory or jail?

SHUI TA. Take your choice.

YANG SUN. May I speak with Shen Te?

SHUI TA. You may not.

> [*Pause.*]

YANG SUN [*sullenly*]. Show me where to go.

MRS. YANG. Mr. Shui Ta, you are kindness itself: the gods will reward you! [*To* YANG SUN.] And honest work will make a man of you, my boy.

> [YANG SUN *follows* SHUI TA *into the factory.* MRS. YANG *comes down again to the footlights.*]

Actually, honest work didn't agree with him—at first. And he got no opportunity to distinguish himself till—in the third week—when the wages were being paid. . . .

> [SHUI TA *has a bag of money. Standing next to his foreman—the former* UNEMPLOYED MAN—*he counts out the wages. It is* YANG SUN'S *turn.*]

UNEMPLOYED MAN [*reading*]. Carpenter, six silver dollars. Yang Sun, six silver dollars.

YANG SUN [*quietly*]. Excuse me, sir. I don't think it can be more than five. May I see? [*He takes the foreman's list.*] It says six working days. But that's a mistake, sir. I took a day off for court business. And I won't take what I haven't earned, however miserable the pay is!

UNEMPLOYED MAN. Yang Sun. Five silver dollars. [*To* SHUI TA.] A rare case, Mr. Shui Ta!

SHUI TA. How is it the book says six when it should say five?

UNEMPLOYED MAN. I must've made a mistake, Mr. Shui Ta. [*With a look at* YANG SUN.] It won't happen again.

SHUI TA [*taking* YANG SUN *aside*]. You don't hold back, do you? You give your all to the firm. You're even honest. Do the foreman's mistakes always favor the workers?

YANG SUN. He does have . . . friends.

SHUI TA. Thank you. May I offer you any little recompense?

YANG SUN. Give me a trial period of one week, and I'll prove my intelligence is worth more to you than my strength.

MRS. YANG SUN [*still down at the footlights*]. Fighting words, fighting words! That evening, I said to Sun: "If you're a flyer, then fly, my falcon! Rise in the world!" And he got to be foreman. Yes, in Mr. Shui Ta's tobacco factory, he worked real miracles.

> [*We see* YANG SUN *with his legs apart standing behind the workers who are handing along a basket of raw tobacco above their heads.*]

YANG SUN. Faster! Faster! You, there, d'you think you can just stand around now you're not foreman any more? It'll be your job to lead us in song. Sing!

> [UNEMPLOYED MAN *starts singing. The others join in the refrain.*]

SONG OF THE EIGHTH ELEPHANT

> Chang had seven elephants—all much the same—
>> But then there was Little Brother
> The seven, they were wild, Little Brother, he was tame

And to guard them Chang chose Little Brother
 Run faster!
Mr. Chang has a forest park
Which must be cleared before tonight
And already it's growing dark!

When the seven elephants cleared that forest park
 Mr. Chang rode high on Little Brother
While the seven toiled and moiled till dark
 On his big behind sat Little Brother
 Dig faster!
Mr. Chang has a forest park
Which must be cleared before tonight
And already it's growing dark!

And the seven elephants worked many an hour
 Till none of them could work another
Old Chang, he looked sour, on the seven, he did glower
 But gave a pound of rice to Little Brother
 What was that?
Mr. Chang has a forest park
Which must be cleared before tonight
And already it's growing dark!

And the seven elephants hadn't any tusks
 The one that had the tusks was Little Brother!
Seven are no match for one, if the one has a gun!
 How old Chang did laugh at Little Brother!
 Keep on digging!
Mr. Chang has a forest park
Which must be cleared before tonight
And already it's growing dark!

> [*Smoking a cigar,* SHUI TA *strolls by.*
> YANG SUN, *laughing, has joined in the
> refrain of the third stanza and speeded up
> the tempo of the last stanza by clapping his
> hands.*]

MRS. YANG. And that's why I say: strength and wisdom are wonderful
 things. It took the strong and wise Mr. Shui Ta to bring out the best in
 Yang Sun. A real superior man is like a bell. If you ring it, it rings, and if
 you don't, it don't, as the saying is.

SCENE IX

SHEN TE'S *shop, now an office with club chairs and fine carpets. It is raining.* SHUI
TA, *now fat, is just dismissing the* OLD MAN *and* OLD WOMAN. MRS. SHIN, *in
obviously new clothes, looks on, smirking.*

SHUI TA. No! I can NOT tell you when we expect her back.

OLD WOMAN. The two hundred silver dollars came today. In an envelope. There was no letter, but it must be from Shen Te. We want to write and thank her. May we have her address?

SHUI TA. I'm afraid I haven't got it.

OLD MAN [*pulling* OLD WOMAN's *sleeve*]. Let's be going.

OLD WOMAN. She's got to come back some time! [*They move off, uncertainly, worried.* SHUI TA *bows.*]

MRS. SHIN. They lost the carpet shop because they couldn't pay their taxes. The money arrived too late.

SHUI TA. They could have come to me.

MRS. SHIN. People don't like coming to you.

SHUI TA [*sits suddenly, one hand to his head*]. I'm dizzy.

MRS. SHIN. After all, you *are* in your seventh month. But old Mrs. Shin will be there in your hour of trial! [*She cackles feebly.*]

SHUI TA [*in a satisfied voice*]. Can I count on that?

MRS. SHIN. We all have our price, and mine won't be too high for the great Mr. Shui Ta! [*She opens* SHUI TA's *collar.*]

SHUI TA. It's for the child's sake. All of this.

MRS. SHIN. "All for the child," of course.

SHUI TA. I'm so fat. People must notice.

MRS. SHIN. Oh no, they think it's 'cause you're rich.

SHUI TA [*more feelingly*]. What will happen to the child?

MRS. SHIN. You ask that nine times a day. Why, it'll have the best that money can buy!

SHUI TA. He must never see Shui Ta.

MRS. SHIN. Oh, no. Always Shen Te.

SHUI TA. What about the neighbors? There are rumors, aren't there?

MRS. SHIN. As long as Mr. Shu Fu doesn't find out, there's nothing to worry about. Drink this.

[*Enter* YANG SUN *in a smart business suit, and carrying a businessman's brief case.* SHUI TA *is more or less in* MRS. SHIN's *arms.*]

YANG SUN [*surprised*]. I seem to be in the way.

SHUI TA [*ignoring this, rises with an effort*]. Till tomorrow, Mrs. Shin.

[MRS. SHIN *leaves with a smile, putting her new gloves on.*]

YANG SUN. Gloves now! She couldn't be fleecing you? And since when did *you* have a private life? [*Taking a paper from the brief case.*] You haven't been at your best lately, and things are getting out of hand. The police want to close us down. They say that at the most they can only permit twice the lawful number of workers.

SHUI TA [*evasively*]. The cabins are quite good enough.

YANG SUN. For the workers maybe, not for the tobacco. They're too damp. We must take over some of Mrs. Mi Tzu's buildings.

SHUI TA. Her price is double what I can pay.

YANG SUN. Not unconditionally. If she has me to stroke her knees she'll come down.

SHUI TA. I'll never agree to that.

YANG SUN. What's wrong? Is it the rain? You get so irritable whenever it rains.

SHUI TA. Never! I will never . . .

YANG SUN. Mrs. Mi Tzu'll be here in five minutes. *You* fix it. And Shu Fu will be with her. . . . What's all that noise?

> [*During the above dialogue,* WONG *is heard off stage calling:* "The good Shen Te, where is she? Which of you has seen Shen Te, good people? Where is Shen Te?" *A knock. Enter* WONG.]

WONG. Mr. Shui Ta, I've come to ask when Miss Shen Te will be back, it's six months now . . . There are rumors. People say something's happened to her.

SHUI TA. I'm busy. Come back next week.

WONG [*excited*]. In the morning there was always rice on her doorstep—for the needy. It's been there again lately!

SHUI TA. And what do people conclude from this?

WONG. That Shen Te is still in Setzuan! She's been . . . [*He breaks off.*]

SHUI TA. She's been what? Mr. Wong, if you're Shen Te's friend, talk a little less about her, that's my advice to you.

WONG. I don't want your advice! Before she disappeared, Miss Shen Te told me something very important—she's pregnant!

YANG SUN. What? What was that?

SHUI TA [*quickly*]. The man is lying.

WONG. A good woman isn't so easily forgotten, Mr. Shui Ta.

> [*He leaves.* SHUI TA *goes quickly into the back room.*]

YANG SUN [*to the audience*]. Shen Te pregnant? So that's why. Her cousin sent her away, so I wouldn't get wind of it. I have a son, a Yang appears on the scene, and what happens? Mother and child vanish into thin air! That scoundrel, that unspeakable . . . [*The sound of sobbing is heard from the back room.*] What was that? Someone sobbing? Who was it? Mr. Shui Ta the Tobacco King doesn't weep his heart out. And where does the rice come from that's on the doorstep in the morning?

> [SHUI TA *returns. He goes to the door and looks out into the rain.*]

Where is she?

SHUI TA. Sh! It's nine o'clock. But the rain's so heavy, you can't hear a thing.

YANG SUN. What do you want to hear?

SHUI TA. The mail plane.

YANG SUN. What?

SHUI TA. I've been told *you* wanted to fly at one time. Is that all forgotten?

YANG SUN. Flying mail is night work. I prefer the daytime. And the firm is very dear to me—after all it belongs to my ex-fiancée, even if she's not around. And she's not, is she?

SHUI TA. What do you mean by that?

YANG SUN. Oh, well, let's say I haven't altogether—lost interest.

SHUI TA. My cousin might like to know that.

YANG SUN. I might not be indifferent—if I found she was being kept under lock and key.

SHUI TA. By whom?

YANG SUN. By you.

SHUI TA. What could you do about it?

YANG SUN. I could submit for discussion—my position in the firm.

SHUI TA. You are now my Manager. In return for a more appropriate position, you might agree to drop the enquiry into your ex-fiancée's whereabouts?

YANG SUN. I might.

SHUI TA. What position *would* be more appropriate?

YANG SUN. The one at the top.

SHUI TA. My own? [*Silence.*] And if I preferred to throw you out on your neck?

YANG SUN. I'd come back on my feet. With suitable escort.

SHUI TA. The police?

YANG SUN. The police.

SHUI TA. And when the police found no one?

YANG SUN. I might ask them not to overlook the back room. [*Ending the pretense.*] In short, Mr. Shui Ta, my interest in this young woman has not been officially terminated. I should like to see more of her. [*Into* SHUI TA's *face.*] Besides, she's pregnant and needs a friend. [*He moves to the door.*] I shall talk about it with the Water Seller. [*Exit.*]

> [SHUI TA *is rigid for a moment, then he quickly goes into the back room. He returns with* SHEN TE's *belongings: underwear, etc. He takes a long look at the shawl of the previous scene. He then wraps the things in a bundle which, upon hearing a noise, he hides under the table. Enter* MRS. MI TZU *and* MR. SHU FU. *They put away their umbrellas and galoshes.*]

MRS. MI TZU. I thought your manager was here, Mr. Shui Ta. He combines charm with business in a way that can only be to the advantage of all of us.

SHU FU. You sent for us, Mr. Shui Ta?

SHUI TA. The factory is in trouble.

SHU FU. It always is.

SHUI TA. The police are threatening to close us down unless I can show that the extension of our facilities is imminent.

SHU FU. Mr. Shui Ta, I'm sick and tired of your constantly expanding projects. I place cabins at your cousin's disposal; you make a factory of them. I hand your cousin a check; you present it. Your cousin disappears and you find the cabins too small and talk of yet more . . .

SHUI TA. Mr. Shu Fu, I'm authorized to inform you that Miss Shen Te's return is now imminent.

SHU FU. Imminent? It's becoming his favorite word.

MRS. MI TZU. Yes, what does it mean?

SHUI TA. Mrs. Mi Tzu, I can pay you exactly half what you asked for your

buildings. Are you ready to inform the police that I am taking them over?

MRS. MI TZU. Certainly, if I can take over your manager.

SHU FU. What?

MRS. MI TZU. He's so efficient.

SHUI TA. I'm afraid I need Mr. Yang Sun.

MRS. MI TZU. So do I.

SHUI TA. He will call on you tomorrow.

SHU FU. So much the better. With Shen Te likely to turn up at any moment, the presence of that young man is hardly in good taste.

SHUI TA. So we have reached a settlement. In what was once the good Shen Te's little shop we are laying the foundations for the great Mr. Shui Ta's twelve magnificent super tobacco markets. You will bear in mind that though they call me the Tobacco King of Setzuan, it is my cousin's interests that have been served . . .

VOICES [off]. The police, the police! Going to the tobacco shop! Something must have happened! [Etc.]

[Enter YANG SUN, WONG, and the POLICEMAN.]

POLICEMAN. Quiet there, quiet, quiet! [They quiet down.] I'm sorry, Mr. Shui Ta, but there's a report that you've been depriving Miss Shen Te of her freedom. Not that I believe all I hear but the whole city's in an uproar.

SHUI TA. That's a lie.

POLICEMAN. Mr. Yang Sun has testified that he heard someone sobbing in the back room.

SHU FU. Mrs. Mi Tzu and myself will testify that no one here has been sobbing.

MRS. MI TZU. We have been quietly smoking our cigars.

POLICEMAN. Mr. Shui Ta, I'm afraid I shall have to take a look at that room. [He does so. The room is empty.] No one there, of course, sir.

YANG SUN. But I heard sobbing. What's that? [He finds the clothes.]

WONG. Those are Shen Te's things. [To crowd.] Shen Te's clothes are here!

VOICES [off. In sequence]. Shen Te's clothes! They've been found under the table! Body of murdered girl still missing! Tobacco King suspected!

POLICEMAN. Mr. Shui Ta, unless you can tell us where the girl is, I'll have to ask you to come along.

SHUI TA. I do not know.

POLICEMAN. I can't say how sorry I am, Mr. Shui Ta. [He shows him the door.]

SHUI TA. Everything will be cleared up in no time. There are still judges in Setzuan.

YANG SUN. I heard sobbing!

SCENE IXA

WONG's *den. For the last time, the* GODS *appear to the Water Seller in his dream. They have changed and show signs of a long journey, extreme fatigue, and plenty of mishaps. The* FIRST *no longer has a hat; the* THIRD *has lost a leg; all* THREE *are barefoot.*

WONG. Illustrious ones, at last you're here. Shen Te's been gone for months and today her cousin's been arrested. They think he murdered her to get the shop. But I had a dream and in this dream Shen Te said her cousin was keeping her prisoner. You must find her for us, illustrious ones!

FIRST GOD. We've found very few good people anywhere, and even they didn't keep it up. Shen Te is still the only one that stayed good.

SECOND GOD. If she *has* stayed good.

WONG. Certainly she has. But she's vanished.

FIRST GOD. That's the last straw. All is lost!

SECOND GOD. A little moderation, dear colleague!

FIRST GOD [*plaintively*]. What's the good of moderation now? If she can't be found, we'll have to resign! The world is a terrible place! Nothing but misery, vulgarity, and waste! Even the countryside isn't what it used to be. The trees are getting their heads chopped off by telephone wires, and there's such a noise from all the gunfire, and I can't stand those heavy clouds of smoke, and—

THIRD GOD. The place is absolutely unlivable! Good intentions bring people to the brink of the abyss, and good deeds push them over the edge. I'm afraid our book of rules is destined for the scrap heap—

SECOND GOD. It's people! They're a worthless lot!

THIRD GOD. The world is too cold!

SECOND GOD. It's people! They are too weak!

FIRST GOD. Dignity, dear colleagues, dignity! Never despair! As for this world, didn't we agree that we only have to find one human being who can stand the place? Well, we found her. True, we lost her again. We must find her again, that's all! And at once!

[*They disappear.*]

SCENE X

Courtroom. Groups: SHU FU and MRS. MI TZU; YANG SUN and MRS. YANG; WONG, the CARPENTER, the GRANDFATHER, the NIECE, the OLD MAN, the OLD WOMAN; MRS. SHIN, the POLICEMAN; the UNEMPLOYED MAN, the SISTER-IN-LAW.

OLD MAN. So much power isn't good for one man.

UNEMPLOYED MAN. And he's going to open twelve super tobacco markets!

WIFE. One of the judges is a friend of Mr. Shu Fu's.

SISTER-IN-LAW. Another one accepted a present from Mr. Shui Ta only last night. A great fat goose.

OLD WOMAN [*to* WONG]. And Shen Te is nowhere to be found.

WONG. Only the gods will ever know the truth.

POLICEMAN. Order in the court! My lords the judges!

[*Enter the* THREE GODS *in judges' robes. We overhear their conversation as they pass along the footlights to their bench.*]

THIRD GOD. We'll never get away with it, our certificates were so badly forged.

SECOND GOD. My predecessor's "sudden indigestion" will certainly cause comment.

FIRST GOD. But he *had* just eaten a whole goose.

UNEMPLOYED MAN. Look at that! *New* judges!

WONG. New judges. And what good ones!

> [*The* THIRD GOD *hears this, and turns to smile at* WONG. *The* GODS *sit. The* FIRST GOD *beats on the bench with his gavel. The* POLICEMAN *brings in* SHUI TA *who walks with lordly steps. He is whistled at.*]

POLICEMAN [*to* SHUI TA]. Be prepared for a surprise. The judges have been changed.

> [SHUI TA *turns quickly round, looks at them, and staggers.*]

NIECE. What's the matter now?

WIFE. The great Tobacco King nearly fainted.

HUSBAND. Yes, as soon as he saw the new judges.

WONG. Does *he* know who they are?

> [SHUI TA *picks himself up, and the proceedings open.*]

FIRST GOD. Defendant Shui Ta, you are accused of doing away with your cousin Shen Te in order to take possession of her business. Do you plead guilty or not guilty?

SHUI TA. Not guilty, my lord.

FIRST GOD [*thumbing through the documents of the case*]. The first witness is the Policeman. I shall ask him to tell us something of the respective reputations of Miss Shen Te and Mr. Shui Ta.

POLICEMAN. Miss Shen Te was a young lady who aimed to please, my lord. She liked to live and let live, as the saying goes. Mr. Shui Ta, on the other hand, is a man of principle. Though the generosity of Miss Shen Te forced him at times to abandon half measures, unlike the girl, he was always on the side of the law, my lord. One time, he even unmasked a gang of thieves to whom his too trustful cousin had given shelter. The evidence, in short, my lord, proves that Mr. Shui Ta was *incapable* of the crime of which he stands accused!

FIRST GOD. I see. And are there others who could testify along, shall we say, the same lines?

> [SHU FU *rises.*]

POLICEMAN [*whispering to* GODS]. Mr. Shu Fu—a very important person.

FIRST GOD [*inviting him to speak*]. Mr. Shu Fu!

SHU FU. Mr. Shui Ta is a businessman, my lord. Need I say more?

FIRST GOD. Yes.

SHU FU. Very well, I will. He is Vice President of the Council of Commerce and is about to be elected a Justice of the Peace. [*He returns to his seat.*]

WONG. Elected! *He* gave him the job!

> [*With a gesture the* FIRST GOD *asks who* MRS. MI TZU *is.*]

POLICEMAN. Another very important person. Mrs. Mi Tzu.

FIRST GOD [*inviting her to speak*]. Mrs. Mi Tzu!

MRS. MI TZU. My lord, as Chairman of the Committee on Social Work, I wish to call attention to just a couple of eloquent facts: Mr. Shui Ta not only has erected a model factory with model housing in our city, he is a regular contributor to our home for the disabled. [*She returns to her seat.*]

POLICEMAN [*whispering*]. And she's a great friend of the judge that ate the goose!

FIRST GOD [*to the* POLICEMAN]. Oh, thank you. What next? [*To the Court, genially.*] Oh, yes. We should find out if any of the evidence is less favorable to the Defendant.

> [WONG, *the* CARPENTER, *the* OLD MAN, *the* OLD WOMAN, *the* UNEMPLOYED MAN, *the* SISTER-IN-LAW, *and the* NIECE *come forward.*]

POLICEMAN [*whispering*]. Just the riff raff, my lord.

FIRST GOD [*addressing the "riff raff"*]. Well, um, riff raff—do you know anything of the Defendant, Mr. Shui Ta?

WONG. Too much, my lord.

UNEMPLOYED MAN. What don't we know, my lord?

CARPENTER. He ruined us.

SISTER-IN-LAW. He's a cheat.

NIECE. Liar.

WIFE. Thief.

BOY. Blackmailer.

BROTHER. Murderer.

FIRST GOD. Thank you. We should now let the Defendant state his point of view.

SHUI TA. I only came on the scene when Shen Te was in danger of losing what I had understood was a gift from the gods. Because I did the filthy jobs which someone had to do, they hate me. My activities were held down to the minimum, my lord.

SISTER-IN-LAW. He had us arrested]!

SHUI TA. Certainly. You stole from the bakery!

SISTER-IN-LAW. Such concern for the bakery! You didn't want the shop for yourself, I suppose!

SHUI TA. I didn't want the shop overrun with parasites.

SISTER-IN-LAW. We had nowhere else to go.

SHUI TA. There were too many of you.

WONG. What about this old couple. Were *they* parasites?

OLD MAN. We lost our shop because of you!

OLD WOMAN. And we gave your cousin money!

SHUI TA. My cousin's fiancé was a flyer. The money had to go to *him*.

WONG. Did you care whether he flew or not? Did you care whether she married him or not? You wanted her to marry someone else! [*He points at* SHU FU.]

SHUI TA. The flyer unexpectedly turned out to be a scoundrel.

YANG SUN [*jumping up*]. Which was the reason you made him your Manager?

SHUI TA. Later on he improved.

WONG. And when he improved, you sold him to her? [*He points out* MRS. MI TZU.]

SHUI TA. She wouldn't let me have her premises unless she had him to stroke her knees!

MRS. MI TZU. What? The man's a pathological liar. [*To him.*] Don't mention my property to me as long as you live! Murderer! [*She rustles off, in high dudgeon.*]

YANG SUN [*pushing in*]. My lord, I wish to speak for the Defendant.

SISTER-IN-LAW. Naturally. He's your employer.

UNEMPLOYED MAN. And the worst slave driver in the country.

MRS. YANG. That's a lie! My lord, Mr. Shui Ta is a great man. He . . .

YANG SUN. He's this and he's that, but he is not a murderer, my lord. Just fifteen minutes before his arrest I heard Shen Te's voice in his own back room.

FIRST GOD. Oh? Tell us more!

YANG SUN. I heard sobbing, my lord!

FIRST GOD. But lots of women sob, we've been finding.

YANG SUN. Could I fail to recognize her voice?

SHU FU. No, you made her sob so often yourself, young man!

YANG SUN. Yes. But I also made her happy. Till he [*pointing at* SHUI TA] decided to sell her to you!

SHUI TA. Because you didn't love her.

WONG. Oh, no: it was for the money, my lord!

SHUI TA. And what was the money for, my lord? For the poor! And for Shen Te so she could go on being good!

WONG. For the poor? That he sent to his sweatshops? And why didn't you let Shen Te be good when you signed the big check?

SHUI TA. For the child's sake, my lord.

CARPENTER. What about *my* children? What did he do about them?
 [SHUI TA *is silent.*]

WONG. The shop was to be a fountain of goodness. That was the gods' idea. You came and spoiled it!

SHUI TA. If I hadn't, it would have run dry!

MRS. SHIN. There's a lot in that, my lord.

WONG. What have you done with the good Shen Te, bad man? She *was* good, my lords, she was, I swear it! [*He raises his hand in an oath.*]

THIRD GOD. What's happened to your hand, Water Seller?

WONG [*pointing to* SHUI TA]. It's all his fault, my lord, *she* was going to send me to a doctor— [*To* SHUI TA.] You were her worst enemy!

SHUI TA. I was her only friend!

WONG. Where is she then? Tell us where your good friend is!
 [*The excitement of this exchange has run through the whole crowd.*]

ALL. Yes, where is she? Where is Shen Te? [*Etc.*]

SHUI TA. Shen Te had to go.

WONG. Where? Where to?

SHUI TA. I cannot tell you! I cannot tell you!

ALL. Why? Why did she have to go away? [*Etc.*]

WONG [*into the din with the first words, but talking on beyond the others*]. Why not, why not? Why did she have to go away?

SHUI TA [*shouting*]. Because you'd all have torn her to shreds, that's why! My lords, I have a request. Clear the court! When only the judges remain, I will make a confession.

ALL [*except* WONG, *who is silent, struck by the new turn of events*]. So he's guilty? He's confessing! [*Etc.*]

FIRST GOD [*using the gavel*]. Clear the court!

POLICEMAN. Clear the court!

WONG. Mr. Shui Ta has met his match this time.

MRS. SHIN [*with a gesture toward the judges*]. You're in for a little surprise.

> [*The court is cleared. Silence.*]

SHUI TA. Illustrious ones!

> [*The* GODS *look at each other, not quite believing their ears.*]

SHUI TA. Yes, I recognize you!

SECOND GOD [*taking matters in hand, sternly*]. What have you done with our good woman of Setzuan?

SHUI TA. I have a terrible confession to make: I am she! [*He takes off his mask, and tears away his clothes.* SHEN TE *stands there.*]

SECOND GOD. Shen Te!

SHEN TE. Shen Te, yes. Shui Ta *and* Shen Te. Both.

> Your injunction
> To be good and yet to live
> Was a thunderbolt:
> It has torn me in two
> I can't tell how it was
> But to be good to others
> And myself at the same time
> I could not do it
> Your world is not an easy one, illustrious ones!
> When we extend our hand to a beggar, he tears it off for us
> When we help the lost, we are lost ourselves.
> And so
> Since not to eat is to die
> Who can long refuse to be bad?
> As I lay prostrate beneath the weight of good intentions
> Ruin stared me in the face
> It was when I was unjust that I ate good meat
> And hobnobbed with the mighty
> Why?
> Why are bad deeds rewarded?
> Good ones punished?
> I enjoy giving
> I truly wished to be the Angel of the Slums
> But washed by a foster-mother in the water of the gutter
> I developed a sharp eye
> The time came when pity was a thorn in my side
> And, later, when kind words turned to ashes in my mouth

And anger took over
I became a wolf
Find me guilty, then, illustrious ones,
But know:
All that I have done I did
To help my neighbor
To love my lover
And to keep my little one from want
For your great, godly deeds, I was too poor, too small.

[*Pause.*]

FIRST GOD [*shocked*]. Don't go on making yourself miserable, Shen Te! We're overjoyed to have found you!

SHEN TE. I'm telling you I'm the bad man who committed all those crimes!

FIRST GOD [*using—or failing to use—his ear trumpet*]. The good woman who did all those good deeds?

SHEN TE. Yes, but the bad man too!

FIRST GOD [*as if something had dawned*]. Unfortunate coincidences! Heartless neighbors!

THIRD GOD [*shouting in his ear*]. But how is she to continue?

FIRST GOD. Continue? Well, she's a strong, healthy girl . . .

SECOND GOD. You didn't hear what she said!

FIRST GOD. I heard every word! She is confused, that's all! [*He begins to bluster.*] And what about this book of rules—we can't renounce our rules, can we? [*More quietly.*] Should the world be changed? How? By whom? The world should *not* be changed! [*At a sign from him, the lights turn pink, and music plays.*]

And now the hour of parting is at hand.
Dost thou behold, Shen Te, yon fleecy cloud?
It is our chariot. At a sign from me
'Twill come and take us back to whence we came
Above the azure vault and silver stars . . .

SHEN TE. No! Don't go, illustrious ones!

FIRST GOD.

Our cloud has landed now in yonder field
From whence it will transport us back to heaven.
Farewell, Shen Te, let not thy courage fail thee . . .

[*Exeunt* GODS.]

SHEN TE. What about the old couple? They've lost their shop! What about the Water Seller and his hand? And I've got to defend myself against the barber, because I don't love him! And against Sun, because I do love him! How? How?

[Shen Te's *eyes follow the* GODS *as they are imagined to step into a cloud which rises and moves forward over the orchestra and up beyond the balcony.*]

FIRST GOD [*from on high*]. We have faith in you, Shen Te!

SHEN TE. There'll be a child. And he'll have to be fed. I can't stay here. Where shall I go?

FIRST GOD. Continue to be good, good woman of Setzuan!

SHEN TE. I need my bad cousin!

FIRST GOD. But not very often!
SHEN TE. Once a week at least!
FIRST GOD. Once a month will be quite enough!
SHEN TE [*shrieking*]. No, no! Help!

> [*But the cloud continues to recede as the*
> GODS *sing.*]

VALEDICTORY HYMN

What rapture, oh, it is to know
 A good thing when you see it
And having seen a good thing, oh,
 What rapture 'tis to flee it

Be good, sweet maid of Setzuan
 Let Shui Ta be clever
Departing, we forget the man
 Remember your endeavor

Because through all the length of days
 Her goodness faileth never
Sing hallelujah! May Shen Te's
 Good name live on forever!

SHEN TE. Help!

EPILOGUE

You're thinking, aren't you, that this is no right
Conclusion to the play you've seen tonight?
After a tale, exotic, fabulous,
A nasty ending was slipped up on us.
We feel deflated too. We too are nettled
To see the curtain down and nothing settled.
How could a better ending be arranged?
Could one change people? Can the world be changed?
Would new gods do the trick? Will atheism?
Moral rearmament? Materialism?
It is for you to find a way, my friends,
To help good men arrive at happy ends.
You write the happy ending to the play!
There must, there must, there's got to be a way!

Jean-Paul Sartre

(1905–1980)

Jean-Paul Sartre came close to being for the mid-twentieth century what Voltaire was for the Enlightenment and Goethe was for the Romantic movement, an artist-philosopher who both shaped and reflected the spirit of his age and who expressed that spirit in a flood of writing in a variety of forms, theoretical and philosophical as well as imaginative. For many of his contemporaries, even those who knew his work only secondhand, existentialism was the only persuasive faith in a frightening age notably lacking in faith, and Sartre was existentialism's exemplary figure, both because of his writings and because of his active, "committed" life.

Sartre was born in 1905 in Paris. His father died when he was still a baby, and he was reared by his grandfather, an uncle of Albert Schweitzer, the famous philosopher, musician, and African missionary. In *The Words* (1964), an account of his early years, Sartre described himself as an ugly, lonely child who retreated into fantasy, which formed the basis of his mature concerns, metaphysics and fiction. He studied at the École Normale Supérieure in Paris, graduating in philosophy in 1929, and did further academic work in Egypt, Italy, Greece, and Germany, where he studied German philosophy under the famous existential phenomenologists Edmund Husserl and Martin Heidegger. In 1931, Sartre accepted a post as professor of philosophy in Le Havre. His early philosophical works showed the influence of Husserl and Heidegger: *Imagination* (1936), *Sketch for a Theory of the Emotions* (1939), and *The Psychology of Imagination* (1940).

When World War II broke out, Sartre joined the French army; he was captured and spent nine months as a prisoner of war (1940–41). When he returned to Paris, he became an active member of the French Resistance and wrote for the underground newspapers that the Resistance published in defiance of the Nazi occupation. He never returned to teaching and after 1944 devoted all his time to writing.

Sartre's major philosophical work, *Being and Nothingness*, appeared in 1943. In this book, Sartre presented a full existentialist theory of Being. The starting point for this philosophy is that God is dead and that therefore any ethical system must be based upon atheism. In the absence of God or any universal moral law, people are free to construct their own ethical system and their own meaning for their lives; indeed, "condemned to freedom," they are obliged to do so. The emphasis in Sartre's ethics is upon action; people are not what they *are* but rather what they *do*, the sum total of all their actions. They must therefore become "engaged" in active life and take sides upon the issues of their time.

Being and Nothingness brought Sartre world fame as a philosopher, but by the time it was published he was already well known as a writer of fiction. (Sartre always regarded his philosophy and his fiction as complementary; indeed, fiction could sometimes deal more sensitively with the problems of individual existence with which he was concerned than formal philosophy could.) His first novel, *Nausea*, and his first collection of short shories, *The*

Wall, both appeared in 1938. *Nausea* is the diary of a writer named Antoine Roquentin who finds himself nauseated by the variety and chaos of the external world and yearns for an orderly, controllable one, which he eventually finds in art. Sartre's only other novel was a massive, four-part work he never completed. Collectively entitled *Paths of Freedom*, it included *The Age of Reason* (1945), *The Reprieve* (1945), *Iron in the Soul* (1949), and an unfinished fourth part, two chapters of which were published in 1949 under the title "Strange Friendship."

During the war years, Sartre turned more to drama than to fiction. *No Exit* (1944) and *The Flies* (1946), a version of the Orestes legend, reveal indirectly a disillusionment with the saving power of art suggested by *Nausea*. Under the growing influence of Marxism, Sartre began to suggest in these plays an escape from "nausea" through action in the world. The title of his 1948 play *Dirty Hands* makes this theme explicit; a person must be willing to "dirty his hands" in the real world, a theme developed further in *The Devil and the Good Lord* (1951), *Nekrassov* (1956), and *The Condemned of Altona* (1960).

In a series of philosophical works written after the war, Sartre continued to develop his ideas, moving away from the pessimism of *Being and Nothingness* toward humanism. In *Existentialism and Humanism* (1946), *The Problem of Method* (1960), and *Critique of Dialectical Reasoning* (1960), he continued to emphasize human freedom, but argued that one's own freedom inevitably depends upon the freedom of others and that one must accept responsibility for all the values implied by one's own way of living.

In the 1950's, Sartre moved steadily closer to Communism, although he never became a party member. He traveled in the Soviet Union and in Cuba, where he supported Fidel Castro's regime. In 1967, he served as chairman of the Stockholm Vietnam War Crimes Tribunal, organized by Bertrand Russell to protest United States policy in Vietnam, and he urged Soviet intervention on behalf of the North in Vietnam. In 1964, he was awarded the Nobel Prize in literature, which he refused, explaining, "A writer must not accept official awards, because he would be adding the influence of the institution that crowned his work to the power of his pen. That is not fair to the reader."

Never married and firmly opposed to bourgeois marriage, Sartre formed a union in his student days with Simone de Beauvoir, who became as famous a writer as he; it was a stable relationship throughout his life. He died in 1980 at the age of seventy-four.

For a writer whose ideas are so complex and radical, Sartre's fiction is, at least on the surface, surprisingly traditional. It was influenced as strongly by detective stories, which he loved, as by philosophy. "The Wall," which first won him fame as a writer, is a suspense story with a melodramatic, O. Henry-like twist at the end. Nevertheless, it contains a cluster of Sartrian ideas, realized in a concrete, personal situation. Like many of his stories, "The Wall" reveals Sartre's interest in what he called "extreme cases"; it is under the pressure of desperate situations, he believed, that a person gains most in self-knowledge. Pablo Ibbieta's condemnation forces him into the crucial existential experience of confronting the reality of his own "absurd" mortality. In the space of a night, he undergoes a spiritual development

that might ordinarily consume years (or never take place at all). The end-
ing, contrived as it may seem, is an ironic, existentialist meditation upon the
relation between one's self and one's actions in the world.

FURTHER READING *(prepared by J. H.):* A good introduction to Sartre as a writer is
Catherine Savage Brosman's *Jean-Paul Sartre,* 1983, a volume in the Twayne World
Authors series. Another good introduction is Rhiannon Goldthorpe's *Sartre: Litera-
ture and Theory,* 1984, in the Cambridge Studies in French series. Philip Thody's
Sartre: A Biographical Introduction, 1971, is still valuable, especially in tracing com-
mon themes through the literary, philosophical, and political writings. Two collec-
tions of essays on Sartre are *Sartre: A Collection of Critical Essays,* ed. by Edith Kern,
1962, and *Sartre: A Collection of Critical Essays,* ed. by Mary Warnock, 1971. The
Warnock volume contains a useful introduction to Existentialism by Alisdair
MacIntyre. Robert Wilcocks, ed., *Critical Essays on Jean-Paul Sartre,* 1988, is a useful
collection.

THE WALL

Translated by Maria Jolas

They pushed us into a large white room and my eyes began to blink be-
cause the light hurt them. Then I saw a table and four fellows seated at the
table, civilians, looking at some papers. The other prisoners were herded
together at one end and we were obliged to cross the entire room to join
them. There were several I knew, and others who must have been foreign-
ers. The two in front of me were blond with round heads. They looked
alike. I imagine they were French. The smaller one kept pulling at his
trousers, out of nervousness.

This lasted about three hours. I was dog-tired and my head was empty.
But the room was well-heated, which struck me as rather agreeable; we had
not stopped shivering for twenty-four hours. The guards led the prisoners
in one after another in front of the table. Then the four fellows asked them
their names and what they did. Most of the time that was all—or perhaps
from time to time they would ask such questions as: "Did you help sabotage
the munitions?" or, "Where were you on the morning of the ninth and
what were you doing?" They didn't even listen to the replies, or at least
they didn't seem to. They just remained silent for a moment and looked
straight ahead, then they began to write. They asked Tom if it was true he
had served in the International Brigade.[1] Tom couldn't say he hadn't be-
cause of the papers they had found in his jacket. They didn't ask Juan
anything, but after he told them his name, they wrote for a long while.

"It's my brother José who's the anarchist," Juan said. "You know per-
fectly well he's not here now. I don't belong to any party. I never did take
part in politics." They didn't answer.

Then Juan said, "I didn't do anything. And I'm not going to pay for
what the others did."

[1] Units of international volunteers fighting on the Republican side in the Spanish Civil War
(1936–1939).

His lips were trembling. A guard told him to stop talking and led him away. It was my turn.

"Your name is Pablo Ibbieta?"

I said yes.

The fellow looked at his papers and said, "Where is Ramon Gris?"

"I don't know."

"You hid him in your house from the sixth to the nineteenth."

"I did not."

They continued to write for a moment and the guards led me away. In the hall, Tom and Juan were waiting between two guards. We started walking. Tom asked one of the guards, "What's the idea?" "How do you mean?" the guard asked. "Was that just the preliminary questioning, or was that the trial?" "That was the trial," the guard said. "So now what? What are they going to do with us?" The guard answered drily, "The verdict will be told you in your cell."

In reality, our cell was one of the cellars of the hospital. It was terribly cold there because it was very drafty. We had been shivering all night long and it had hardly been any better during the day. I had spent the preceding five days in a cellar in the archbishop's palace, a sort of dungeon that must have dated back to the Middle Ages. There were lots of prisoners and not much room, so they housed them just anywhere. But I was not homesick for my dungeon. I hadn't been cold there, but I had been alone, and that gets to be irritating. In the cellar I had company. Juan didn't say a word; he was afraid, and besides, he was too young to have anything to say. But Tom was a good talker and knew Spanish well.

In the cellar there were a bench and four straw mattresses. When they led us back we sat down and waited in silence. After a while Tom said, "Our goose is cooked."

"I think so too," I said. "But I don't believe they'll do anything to the kid."

Tom said, "They haven't got anything on him. He's the brother of a fellow who's fighting, and that's all."

I looked at Juan. He didn't seem to have heard.

Tom continued, "You know what they do in Saragossa?[2] They lay the guys across the road and then they drive over them with trucks. It was a Moroccan deserter who told us that. They say it's just to save ammunition."

I said, "Well, it doesn't save gasoline."

I was irritated with Tom; he shouldn't have said that.

He went on, "There are officers walking up and down the roads with their hands in their pockets, smoking, and they see that it's done right. Do you think they'd put 'em out of their misery? Like hell they do. They just let 'em holler. Sometimes as long as an hour. The Moroccan said the first time he almost puked."

"I don't believe they do that here," I said, "unless they really are short of ammunition."

The daylight came in through four air vents and a round opening that had been cut in the ceiling, to the left, and which opened directly onto the sky. It was through this hole, which was ordinarily closed by means of a

[2] Province in northeast Spain.

trapdoor, that they unloaded coal into the cellar. Directly under the hole, there was a big pile of coal dust; it had been intended for heating the hospital, but at the beginning of the war they had evacuated the patients and the coal had stayed there unused; it even got rained on from time to time, when they forgot to close the trapdoor.

Tom started to shiver. "God damn it," he said, "I'm shivering. There, it is starting again."

He rose and began to do gymnastic exercises. At each movement, his shirt opened and showed his white, hairy chest. He lay down on his back, lifted his legs in the air and began to do the scissors movement. I watched his big buttocks tremble. Tom was tough, but he had too much fat on him. I kept thinking that soon bullets and bayonet points would sink into that mass of tender flesh as though it were a pat of butter.

I wasn't exactly cold, but I couldn't feel my shoulders or my arms. From time to time, I had the impression that something was missing and I began to look around for my jacket. Then I would suddenly remember they hadn't given me a jacket. It was rather awkward. They had taken our clothes to give them to their own soldiers and had left us only our shirts and these cotton trousers the hospital patients wore in mid-summer. After a moment, Tom got up and sat down beside me, breathless.

"Did you get warmed up?"

"Damn it, no. But I'm all out of breath."

Around eight o'clock in the evening, a Major came in with two falangists.[3]

"What are the names of those three over there?" he asked the guard.

"Steinbock, Ibbieta and Mirbal," said the guard.

The Major put on his glasses and examined his list.

"Steinbock—Steinbock . . . Here it is. You are condemned to death. You'll be shot tomorrow morning."

He looked at his list again.

"The other two, also," he said.

"That's not possible," said Juan. "Not me."

The Major looked at him with surprise. "What's your name?"

"Juan Mirbal."

"Well, your name is here," said the Major, "and you're condemned to death."

"I didn't do anything," said Juan.

The Major shrugged his shoulders and turned toward Tom and me.

"You are both Basque?"

"No, nobody's Basque."

He appeared exasperated.

"I was told there were three Basques. I'm not going to waste my time running after them. I suppose you don't want a priest?"

We didn't even answer.

Then he said, "A Belgian doctor will be around in a little while. He has permission to stay with you all night."

[3] Fascists fighting against the Republic. The *Falange*, founded by José Antonio Primo de Rivera, son of the dictator, was a nationalist anti-Marxist youth group formed to oppose Socialist youth groups.

He gave a military salute and left.

"What did I tell you?" Tom said. "We're in for something swell."

"Yes," I said. "It's a damned shame for the kid."

I said that to be fair, but I really didn't like the kid. His face was too refined and it was disfigured by fear and suffering, which had twisted all his features. Three days ago, he was just a kid with a kind of affected manner some people like. But now he looked like an aging fairy, and I thought to myself he would never be young again, even if they let him go. It wouldn't have been a bad thing to show him a little pity, but pity makes me sick, and besides, I couldn't stand him. He hadn't said anything more, but he had turned gray. His face and hands were gray. He sat down again and stared, round-eyed, at the ground. Tom was goodhearted and tried to take him by the arm, but the kid drew himself away violently and made an ugly face. "Leave him alone," I said quietly. "Can't you see he's going to start to bawl?" Tom obeyed regretfully. He would have liked to console the kid; that would have kept him occupied and he wouldn't have been tempted to think about himself. But it got on my nerves. I had never thought about death, for the reason that the question had never come up. But now it had come up, and there was nothing else to do but think about it.

Tom started talking. "Say, did you ever bump anybody off?" he asked me. I didn't answer. He started to explain to me that he had bumped off six fellows since August. He hadn't yet realized what we were in for, and I saw clearly he didn't *want* to realize it. I myself hadn't quite taken it in. I wondered if it hurt very much. I thought about the bullets; I imagined their fiery hail going through my body. All that was beside the real question; but I was calm, we had all night in which to realize it. After a while Tom stopped talking and I looked at him out of the corner of my eye. I saw that he, too, had turned gray and that he looked pretty miserable. I said to myself, "It's starting." It was almost dark, a dull light filtered through the air vents across the coal pile and made a big spot under the sky. Through the hole in the ceiling I could already see a star. The night was going to be clear and cold.

The door opened and two guards entered. They were followed by a blond man in a tan uniform. He greeted us.

"I'm the doctor," he said. "I've been authorized to give you any assistance you may require in these painful circumstances."

He had an agreeable, cultivated voice.

I said to him, "What are you going to do here?"

"Whatever you want me to do. I shall do everything in my power to lighten these few hours."

"Why did you come to us? There are lots of others: the hospital's full of them."

"I was sent here," he answered vaguely. "You'd probably like to smoke, wouldn't you?" he added suddenly. "I've got some cigarettes and even some cigars."

He passed around some English cigarettes and some *puros*,[4] but we re-

[4] Small cigars.

fused them. I looked him straight in the eye and he appeared uncomfortable.

"You didn't come here out of compassion," I said to him. "In fact, I know who you are. I saw you with some fascists in the barracks yard the day I was arrested."

I was about to continue, when all at once something happened to me which surprised me: the presence of this doctor had suddenly ceased to interest me. Usually, when I've got hold of a man I don't let go. But somehow the desire to speak had left me. I shrugged my shoulders and turned away. A little later, I looked up and saw he was watching me with an air of curiosity. The guards had sat down on one of the mattresses. Pedro, the tall thin one, was twiddling his thumbs, while the other one shook his head occasionally to keep from falling asleep.

"Do you want some light?" Pedro suddenly asked the doctor. The other fellow nodded, "Yes." I think he was not over-intelligent, but doubtless he was not malicious. As I looked at his big, cold, blue eyes, it seemed to me the worst thing about him was his lack of imagination. Pedro went out and came back with an oil lamp which he set on the corner of the bench. It gave a poor light, but it was better than nothing; the night before we had been left in the dark. For a long while I stared at the circle of light the lamp threw on the ceiling. I was fascinated. Then, suddenly, I came to, the light circle paled, and I felt as if I were being crushed under an enormous weight. It wasn't the thought of death, and it wasn't fear; it was something anonymous. My cheeks were burning hot and my head ached.

I roused myself and looked at my two companions. Tom had his head in his hands and only the fat, white nape of his neck was visible. Juan was by far the worst off; his mouth was wide open and his nostrils were trembling. The doctor came over to him and touched him on the shoulder, as though to comfort him; but his eyes remained cold. Then I saw the Belgian slide his hand furtively down Juan's arm to his wrist. Indifferent, Juan let himself be handled. Then, as though absent-mindedly, the Belgian laid three fingers over his wrist; at the same time, he drew away somewhat and managed to turn his back to me. But I leaned over backward and saw him take out his watch and look at it a moment before relinquishing the boy's wrist. After a moment, he let the inert hand fall and went and leaned against the wall. Then, as if he had suddenly remembered something very important that had to be noted down immediately, he took a notebook from his pocket and wrote a few lines in it. "The son-of-a-bitch," I thought angrily. "He better not come and feel my pulse; I'll give him a punch in his dirty jaw."

He didn't come near me, but I felt he was looking at me. I raised my head and looked back at him. In an impersonal voice, he said, "Don't you think it's frightfully cold here?"

He looked purple with cold.

"I'm not cold," I answered him.

He kept looking at me with a hard expression. Suddenly I understood, and I lifted my hands to my face. I was covered with sweat. Here, in this cellar, in mid-winter, right in a draft, I was sweating. I ran my fingers through my hair, which was stiff with sweat; at the same time, I realized my shirt was damp and sticking to my skin. I had been streaming with perspi-

ration for an hour, at least, and had felt nothing. But this fact hadn't escaped that Belgian swine. He had seen the drops rolling down my face and had said to himself that it showed an almost pathological terror; and he himself had felt normal and proud of it because he was cold. I wanted to get up and go punch his face in, but I had hardly started to make a move before my shame and anger had disappeared. I dropped back onto the bench with indifference.

I was content to rub my neck with my handkerchief because now I felt the sweat dripping from my hair onto the nape of my neck and that was disagreeable. I soon gave up rubbing myself, however, for it didn't do any good; my handkerchief was already wringing wet and I was still sweating. My buttocks, too, were sweating, and my damp trousers stuck to the bench.

Suddenly, Juan said, "You're a doctor, aren't you?"

"Yes," said the Belgian.

"Do people suffer—very long?"

"Oh! When . . . ? No, no," said the Belgian, in a paternal voice, "it's quickly over."

His manner was as reassuring as if he had been answering a paying patient.

"But I . . . Somebody told me—they often have to fire two volleys."

"Sometimes," said the Belgian, raising his head, "it just happens that the first volley doesn't hit any of the vital organs."

"So then they have to reload their guns and aim all over again?" Juan thought for a moment, then added hoarsely, "But that takes time!"

He was terribly afraid of suffering. He couldn't think about anything else, but that went with his age. As for me, I hardly thought about it any more and it certainly was not fear of suffering that made me perspire.

I rose and walked toward the pile of coal dust. Tom gave a start and looked at me with a look of hate. I irritated him because my shoes squeaked. I wondered if my face was as putty-colored as his. Then I noticed that he, too, was sweating. The sky was magnificent; no light at all came into our dark corner and I had only to lift my head to see the Big Bear.[5] But it didn't look the way it had looked before. Two days ago, from my cell in the archbishop's palace, I could see a big patch of sky and each time of day brought back a different memory. In the morning, when the sky was a deep blue, and light, I thought of beaches along the Atlantic; at noon, I could see the sun, and I remembered a bar in Seville where I used to drink manzanilla[6] and eat anchovies and olives; in the afternoon, I was in the shade, and I thought of the deep shadow which covers half of the arena while the other half gleams in the sunlight: it really gave me a pang to see the whole earth reflected in the sky like that. Now, however, no matter how much I looked up in the air, the sky no longer recalled anything. I liked it better that way. I came back and sat down next to Tom. There was a long silence.

Then Tom began to talk in a low voice. He had to keep talking, otherwise he lost his way in his own thoughts. I believe he was talking to me, but he didn't look at me. No doubt he was afraid to look at me, because I was

[5] A constellation. [6] Apple brandy.

gray and sweating. We were both alike and worse than mirrors for each other. He looked at the Belgian, the only one who was alive.

"Say, do you understand? I don't."

Then I, too, began to talk in a low voice. I was watching the Belgian. "Understand what? What's the matter?"

"Something's going to happen to us that I don't understand."

There was a strange odor about Tom. It seemed to me that I was more sensitive to odors than ordinarily. With a sneer, I said, "You'll understand, later."

"That's not so sure," he said stubbornly. "I'm willing to be courageous, but at least I ought to know. . . . Listen, they're going to take us out into the courtyard. All right. The fellows will be standing in line in front of us. How many of them will there be?"

"Oh, I don't know. Five, or eight. Not more."

"That's enough. Let's say there'll be eight of them. Somebody will shout 'Shoulder arms!' and I'll see all eight rifles aimed at me. I'm sure I'm going to feel like going through the wall. I'll push against the wall as hard as I can with my back, and the wall won't give in. The way it is in a nightmare. . . . I can imagine all that. Ah, if you only knew how well I can imagine it!"

"Skip it!" I said. "I can imagine it too."

"It must hurt like the devil. You know they aim at your eyes and mouth so as to disfigure you," he added maliciously. "I can feel the wounds already. For the last hour I've been having pains in my head and neck. Not real pains—it's worse still. They're the pains I'll feel tomorrow morning. And after that, then what?"

I understood perfectly well what he meant, but I didn't want to seem to understand. As for the pains, I, too, felt them all through my body, like a lot of little gashes. I couldn't get used to them, but I was like him, I didn't think they were very important.

"After that," I said roughly, "you'll be eating daisies."

He started talking to himself, not taking his eyes off the Belgian, who didn't seem to be listening to him. I knew what he had come for, and that what we were thinking didn't interest him. He had come to look at our bodies, our bodies which were dying alive.

"It's like in a nightmare," said Tom. "You want to think of something, you keep having the impression you've got it, that you're going to understand, and then it slips away from you, it eludes you and it's gone again. I say to myself, afterwards, there won't be anything. But I don't really understand what that means. There are moments when I almost do—and then it's gone again. I start to think of the pains, the bullets, the noise of the shooting. I am a materialist, I swear it; and I'm not going crazy, either. But there's something wrong. I see my own corpse. That's not hard, but it's *I* who see it, with *my* eyes. I'll have to get to the point where I think—where I think I won't see anything more. I won't hear anything more, and the world will go on for the others. We're not made to think that way, Pablo. Believe me, I've already stayed awake all night waiting for something. But this is not the same thing. This will grab us from behind, Pablo, and we won't be ready for it."

"Shut up," I said. "Do you want me to call a father confessor?"

He didn't answer. I had already noticed that he had a tendency to

prophesy and call me "Pablo" in a kind of pale voice. I didn't like that very much, but it seems all the Irish are like that. I had a vague impression that he smelled of urine. Actually, I didn't like Tom very much, and I didn't see why, just because we were going to die together, I should like him any better. There are certain fellows with whom it would be different—with Ramon Gris, for instance. But between Tom and Juan, I felt alone. In fact, I liked it better that way. With Ramon I might have grown soft. But I felt terribly hard at that moment, and I wanted to stay hard.

Tom kept on muttering, in a kind of absent-minded way. He was certainly talking to keep from thinking. Naturally, I agreed with him, and I could have said everything he was saying. It's not *natural* to die. And since I was going to die, nothing seemed natural any more: neither the coal pile, nor the bench, nor Pedro's dirty old face. Only it was disagreeable for me to think the same things Tom thought. And I knew perfectly well that all night long, within five minutes of each other, we would keep on thinking things at the same time, sweating or shivering at the same time. I looked at him sideways and, for the first time, he seemed strange to me. He had death written on his face. My pride was wounded. For twenty-four hours I had lived side by side with Tom, I had listened to him, I had talked to him, and I knew we had nothing in common. And now we were as alike as twin brothers, simply because we were going to die together. Tom took my hand without looking at me.

"Pablo, I wonder . . . I wonder if it's true that we just cease to exist."

I drew my hand away.

"Look between your feet, you dirty dog."

There was a puddle between his feet and water was dripping from his trousers.

"What's the matter?" he said, frightened.

"You're wetting your pants," I said to him.

"It's not true," he said furiously. "I can't be . . . I don't feel anything."

The Belgian had come closer to him. With an air of false concern, he asked, "Aren't you feeling well?"

Tom didn't answer. The Belgian looked at the puddle without comment.

"I don't know what that is," Tom said savagely, "but I'm not afraid. I swear to you, I'm not afraid."

The Belgian made no answer. Tom rose and went to the corner. He came back, buttoning his fly, and sat down, without a word. The Belgian was taking notes.

We were watching the doctor. Juan was watching him too. All three of us were watching him because he was alive. He had the gestures of a living person, the interests of a living person; he was shivering in this cellar the way living people shiver; he had an obedient, well-fed body. We, on the other hand, didn't feel our bodies any more—not the same way, in any case. I felt like touching my trousers, but I didn't dare to. I looked at the Belgian, well-planted on his two legs, master of his muscles—and able to plan for tomorrow. We were like three shadows deprived of blood; we were watching him and sucking his life like vampires.

Finally he came over to Juan. Was he going to lay his hand on the nape of Juan's neck for some professional reason, or had he obeyed a charitable

impulse? If he had acted out of charity, it was the one and only time during
the whole night. He fondled Juan's head and the nape of his neck. The kid
let him do it, without taking his eyes off him. Then, suddenly, he took hold
of the doctor's hand and looked at it in a funny way. He held the Belgian's
hand between his own two hands and there was nothing pleasing about
them, those two gray paws squeezing that fat red hand. I sensed what was
going to happen and Tom sensed it, too. But all the Belgian saw was emo-
tion, and he smiled paternally. After a moment, the kid lifted the big red
paw to his mouth and started to bite it. The Belgian drew back quickly and
stumbled toward the wall. For a second, he looked at us with horror. He
must have suddenly understood that we were not men like himself. I began
to laugh, and one of the guards started up. The other had fallen asleep
with his eyes wide open, showing only the whites.

I felt tired and over-excited at the same time. I didn't want to think any
more about what was going to happen at dawn—about death. It didn't
make sense, and I never got beyond just words, or emptiness. But when-
ever I tried to think about something else I saw the barrels of rifles aimed at
me. I must have lived through my execution twenty times in succession; one
time I thought it was the real thing; I must have dozed off for a moment.
They were dragging me toward the wall and I was resisting; I was
imploring their pardon. I woke with a start and looked at the Belgian. I was
afraid I had cried out in my sleep. But he was smoothing his mustache; he
hadn't noticed anything. If I had wanted to, I believe I could have slept for
a while. I had been awake for the last forty-eight hours, and I was worn out.
But I didn't want to lose two hours of life. They would have had to come
and wake me at dawn. I would have followed them, drunk with sleep, and I
would have gone off without so much as "Gosh!" I didn't want it that way, I
didn't want to die like an animal. I wanted to understand. Besides, I was
afraid of having nightmares. I got up and began to walk up and down and,
so as to think about something else, I began to think about my past life.
Memories crowded in on me, helter-skelter. Some were good and some
were bad—at least that was how I had thought of them *before*. There were
faces and happenings. I saw the face of a little *novilero*[7] who had gotten
himself horned during the *Feria*, in Valencia. I saw the face of one of my
uncles, of Ramon Gris. I remembered all kinds of things that had hap-
pened: how I had been on strike for three months in 1926, and had almost
died of hunger. I recalled a night I had spent on a beach in Granada; I
hadn't eaten for three days, I was nearly wild, I didn't want to give up the
sponge. I had to smile. With what eagerness I had run after happiness, and
women, and liberty! And to what end? I had wanted to liberate Spain, I
admired Py Margall,[8] I had belonged to the anarchist movement, I had
spoken at public meetings. I took everything as seriously as if I had been
immortal.

At that time I had the impression that I had my whole life before me,
and I thought to myself, "It's all a god-damned lie." Now it wasn't worth
anything because it was finished. I wondered how I had ever been able to

[7] Boy assigned to tend cattle, in this case bulls for bullfights. The *Feria* is a bullfighting
festival.
[8] Revolutionary leader.

go out and have a good time with girls. I wouldn't have lifted my little finger if I had ever imagined that I would die like this. I saw my life before me finished, closed, like a bag, and yet what was inside was not finished. For a moment I tried to appraise it. I would have liked to say to myself, "It's been a good life." But it couldn't be appraised, it was only an outline. I had spent my time writing checks on eternity, and had understood nothing. Now, I didn't miss anything. There were a lot of things I might have missed: the taste of manzanilla, for instance, or the swims I used to take in summer in a little creek near Cadiz. But death had taken the charm out of everything.

Suddenly the Belgian had a wonderful idea.

"My friends," he said to us, "if you want me to—and providing the military authorities give their consent—I could undertake to deliver a word or some token from you to your loved ones. . . . "

Tom growled, "I haven't got anybody."

I didn't answer. Tom waited for a moment, then he looked at me with curiosity. "Aren't you going to send any message to Concha?"

"No."

I hated that sort of sentimental conspiracy. Of course, it was my fault, since I had mentioned Concha the night before, and I should have kept my mouth shut. I had been with her for a year. Even as late as last night, I would have cut my arm off with a hatchet just to see her again for five minutes. That was why I had mentioned her. I couldn't help it. Now I didn't care any more about seeing her. I hadn't anything more to say to her. I didn't even want to hold her in my arms. I loathed my body because it had turned gray and was sweating—and I wasn't even sure that I didn't loathe hers too. Concha would cry when she heard about my death; for months she would have no more interest in life. But still it was I who was going to die. When she looked at me something went from her to me. But I thought to myself that it was all over; if she looked at me *now* her gaze would not leave her eyes, it would not reach out to me. I was alone.

Tom, too, was alone, but not the same way. He was seated astride his chair and had begun to look at the bench with a sort of smile, with surprise, even. He reached out his hand and touched the wood cautiously, as though he were afraid of breaking something, then he drew his hand back hurriedly, and shivered. I wouldn't have amused myself touching that bench, if I had been Tom, that was just some more Irish play-acting. But somehow it seemed to me too that the different objects had something funny about them. They seemed to have grown paler, less massive than before. I had only to look at the bench, the lamp or the pile of coal dust to feel I was going to die. Naturally, I couldn't think clearly about my death, but I saw it everywhere, even on the different objects, the way they had withdrawn and kept their distance, tactfully, like people talking at the bedside of a dying person. It was *his own death* Tom had just touched on the bench.

In the state I was in, if they had come and told me I could go home quietly, that my life would be saved, it would have left me cold. A few hours, or a few years of waiting are all the same, when you've lost the illusion of being eternal. Nothing mattered to me any more. In a way, I was calm. But it was a horrible kind of calm—because of my body. My body—I saw with its eyes and I heard with its ears, but it was no longer I. It sweat

and trembled independently, and I didn't recognize it any longer. I was
obliged to touch it and look at it to know what was happening to it, just as
if it had been someone else's body. At times I still felt it, I felt a slipping, a
sort of headlong plunging, as in a falling airplane, or else I heard my heart
beating. But this didn't give me confidence. In fact, everything that came
from my body had something damned dubious about it. Most of the time it
was silent, it stayed put and I didn't feel anything other than a sort of
heaviness, a loathsome presence against me. I had the impression of being
bound to an enormous vermin.

The Belgian took out his watch and looked at it.

"It's half-past three," he said.

The son-of-a-bitch! He must have done it on purpose. Tom jumped up.
We hadn't yet realized the time was passing. The night surrounded us like a
formless, dark mass; I didn't even remember it had started.

Juan started to shout. Wringing his hands, he implored, "I don't want to
die! I don't want to die!"

He ran the whole length of the cellar with his arms in the air, then he
dropped down onto one of the mattresses, sobbing. Tom looked at him
with dismal eyes and didn't even try to console him any more. The fact was,
it was no use; the kid made more noise than we did, but he was less af-
fected, really. He was like a sick person who defends himself against his
malady with a high fever. When there's not even any fever left, it's much
more serious.

He was crying. I could tell he felt sorry for himself; he was thinking
about death. For one second, one single second, I too felt like crying, crying
out of pity for myself. But just the contrary happened. I took one look at
the kid, saw his thin, sobbing shoulders, and I felt I was inhuman. I
couldn't feel pity either for these others or for myself. I said to myself, "I
want to die decently."

Tom had gotten up and was standing just under the round opening
looking out for the first signs of daylight. I was determined, I wanted to die
decently, and I only thought about that. But underneath, ever since the
doctor had told us the time, I felt time slipping, flowing by, one drop at
a time.

It was still dark when I heard Tom's voice.

"Do you hear them?"

"Yes."

People were walking in the courtyard.

"What the hell are they doing? After all, they can't shoot in the dark."

After a moment, we didn't hear anything more. I said to Tom, "There's
the daylight."

Pedro got up yawning, and came and blew out the lamp. He turned to
the man beside him. "It's hellish cold."

The cellar had grown gray. We could hear shots at a distance.

"It's about to start," I said to Tom. "That must be in the back court-
yard."

Tom asked the doctor to give him a cigarette. I didn't want any; I didn't
want either cigarettes or alcohol. From that moment on, the shooting
didn't stop.

"Can you take it in?" Tom said.

He started to add something, then he stopped and began to watch the door. The door opened and a lieutenant came in with four soldiers. Tom dropped his cigarette.

"Steinbock?"

Tom didn't answer. Pedro pointed him out.

"Juan Mirbal?"

"He's the one on the mattress."

"Stand up," said the Lieutenant.

Juan didn't move. Two soldiers took hold of him by the armpits and stood him up on his feet. But as soon as they let go of him he fell down.

The soldiers hesitated a moment.

"He's not the first one to get sick," said the Lieutenant. "You'll have to carry him, the two of you. We'll arrange things when we get there." He turned to Tom. "All right, come along."

Tom left between two soldiers. Two other soldiers followed, carrying the kid by his arms and legs. He was not unconscious; his eyes were wide open and tears were rolling down his cheeks. When I started to go out, the Lieutenant stopped me.

"Are you Ibbieta?"

"Yes."

"You wait here. They'll come and get you later on."

They left. The Belgian and the two jailers left too, and I was alone. I didn't understand what had happened to me, but I would have liked it better if they had ended it all right away. I heard the volleys at almost regular intervals; at each one, I shuddered. I felt like howling and tearing my hair. But instead, I gritted my teeth and pushed my hands deep into my pockets, because I wanted to stay decent.

An hour later, they came to fetch me and took me up to the first floor in a little room which smelt of cigar smoke and was so hot it seemed to me suffocating. Here there were two officers sitting in comfortable chairs, smoking, with papers spread out on their knees.

"Your name is Ibbieta?"

"Yes."

"Where is Ramon Gris?"

"I don't know."

The man who questioned me was small and stocky. He had hard eyes behind his glasses.

"Come nearer," he said to me.

I went nearer. He rose and took me by the arms, looking at me in a way calculated to make me go through the floor. At the same time he pinched my arms with all his might. He didn't mean to hurt me; it was quite a game; he wanted to dominate me. He also seemed to think it was necessary to blow his fetid breath right into my face. We stood like that for a moment, only I felt more like laughing than anything else. It takes a lot more than that to intimidate a man who's about to die: it didn't work. He pushed me away violently and sat down again.

"It's your life or his," he said. "You'll be allowed to go free if you tell us where he is."

After all, these two bedizened fellows with their riding crops and boots were just men who were going to die one day. A little later than I, perhaps,

but not a great deal. And there they were, looking for names among their papers, running after other men in order to put them in prison or do away with them entirely. They had their opinions on the future of Spain and on other subjects. Their petty activities seemed to me to be offensive and ludicrous. I could no longer put myself in their place. I had the impression they were crazy.

The little fat fellow kept looking at me, tapping his boots with his riding crop. All his gestures were calculated to make him appear like a spirited, ferocious animal.

"Well? Do you understand?"

"I don't know where Gris is," I said. "I thought he was in Madrid."

The other officer lifted his pale hand indolently. This indolence was also calculated. I saw through all their little tricks, and I was dumbfounded that men should still exist who took pleasure in that kind of thing.

"You have fifteen minutes to think it over," he said slowly. "Take him to the linen-room, and bring him back here in fifteen minutes. If he continues to refuse, he'll be executed at once."

They knew what they were doing. I had spent the night waiting. After that, they had made me wait another hour in the cellar, while they shot Tom and Juan, and now they locked me in the linen-room. They must have arranged the whole thing the night before. They figured that sooner or later people's nerves wear out and they hoped to get me that way.

They made a big mistake. In the linen-room I sat down on a ladder because I felt very weak, and I began to think things over. Not their proposition, however. Naturally I knew where Gris was. He was hiding in his cousins' house, about two miles outside the city. I knew, too, that I would not reveal his hiding place, unless they tortured me (but they didn't seem to be considering that). All that was definitely settled and didn't interest me in the least. Only I would have liked to understand the reasons for my own conduct. I would rather die than betray Gris. Why? I no longer liked Ramon Gris. My friendship for him had died shortly before dawn along with my love for Concha, along with my own desire to live. Of course I still admired him—he was hard. But it was not for that reason that I was willing to die in his place; his life was no more valuable than mine. No life was of any value. A man was going to be stood up against a wall and fired at till he dropped dead. It didn't make any difference whether it was I or Gris or somebody else. I knew perfectly well he was more useful to the Spanish cause than I was, but I didn't give a god-damn about Spain or anarchy, either; nothing had any importance now. And yet, there I was. I could save my skin by betraying Gris and I refused to do it. It seemed more ludicrous to me than anything else; it was stubbornness.

I thought to myself, "Am I hard-headed!" And I was seized with a strange sort of cheerfulness.

They came to fetch me and took me back to the two officers. A rat darted out under our feet and that amused me. I turned to one of the falangists and said to him, "Did you see that rat?"

He made no reply. He was gloomy, and took himself very seriously. As for me, I felt like laughing, but I restrained myself because I was afraid that if I started, I wouldn't be able to stop. The falangist wore mustaches. I kept after him, "You ought to cut off those mustaches, you fool."

I was amused by the fact that he let hair grow all over his face while he was still alive. He gave me a kind of half-hearted kick, and I shut up.

"Well," said the fat officer, "have you thought things over?"

I looked at them with curiosity, like insects of a very rare species.

"I know where he is," I said. "He's hiding in the cemetery. Either in one of the vaults, or in the gravediggers' shack."

I said that just to make fools of them. I wanted to see them get up and fasten their belts and bustle about giving orders.

They jumped to their feet.

"Fine. Moles, go ask Lieutenant Lopez for fifteen men. And as for you," the little fat fellow said to me, "if you've told the truth, I don't go back on my word. But you'll pay for this, if you're pulling our leg."

They left noisily and I waited in peace, still guarded by the falangists. From time to time I smiled at the thought of the face they were going to make. I felt dull and malicious. I could see them lifting up the gravestones, or opening the doors of the vaults one by one. I saw the whole situation as though I were another person: the prisoner determined to play the hero, the solemn falangists with their mustaches and the men in uniform running around among the graves. It was irresistibly funny.

After half an hour, the little fat fellow came back alone. I thought he had come to give the order to execute me. The others must have stayed in the cemetery.

The officer looked at me. He didn't look at all foolish.

"Take him out in the big courtyard with the others," he said. "When military operations are over, a regular tribunal will decide his case."

I thought I must have misunderstood.

"So they're not—they're not going to shoot me?" I asked.

"Not now, in any case. Afterwards, that doesn't concern me."

I still didn't understand.

"But why?" I said to him.

He shrugged his shoulders without replying, and the soldiers led me away. In the big courtyard there were a hundred or so prisoners, women and children and a few old men. I started to walk around the grass plot in the middle. I felt absolutely idiotic. At noon we were fed in the dining hall. Two or three fellows spoke to me. I must have known them, but I didn't answer. I didn't even know where I was.

Toward evening about ten new prisoners were pushed into the courtyard. I recognized Garcia, the baker.

He said to me, "Lucky dog! I didn't expect to find you alive."

"They condemned me to death," I said, "and then they changed their minds. I don't know why."

"I was arrested at two o'clock," Garcia said.

"What for?"

Garcia took no part in politics.

"I don't know," he said. "They arrest everybody who doesn't think the way they do."

He lowered his voice.

"They got Gris."

I began to tremble.

"When?"

"This morning. He acted like a damned fool. He left his cousins' house Tuesday because of a disagreement. There were any number of fellows who would have hidden him, but he didn't want to be indebted to anybody any more. He said, 'I would have hidden at Ibbieta's, but since they've got him, I'll go hide in the cemetery.'"

"In the cemetery?"

"Yes. It was the god-damnedest thing. Naturally they passed by there this morning; that had to happen. They found him in the gravediggers' shack. They opened fire at him and they finished him off."

"In the cemetery!"

Everything went around in circles, and when I came to I was sitting on the ground. I laughed so hard the tears came to my eyes.

Albert Camus

(1913–1960)

Albert Camus' last published work was a collection of short stories entitled *Exile and the Kingdom,* a phrase that encapsulates the painful division in human life around which all his work spirals. "Exile" is the condition of modern human beings—stripped of God, alienated from nature, tyrannized by frightening political ideologies, isolated from their fellows, and divided even against themselves. "The Kingdom" is a kingdom of humanity people dream of, in which, acknowledging the emptiness of the heavens, people can nevertheless take joy in their own animal vitality and in that of nature, living justly and lovingly with their fellows and with themselves. Although he was identified with the post-World War II existentialists in France, Camus was less a formal philosopher than a novelist and meditative essayist whose intensely personal explorations of the human condition led him from a bleak vision of the absurdity of life to the guarded but moving humanism of his later works. A worldwide audience still finds this humanism timely and meaningful.

Camus was born in 1913 in the town of Mondovi in Algeria. His father died less than a year later, in the First Battle of the Marne in World War I; his mother, who worked as a cleaning woman, then moved with her two children, her mother, and a brother into a two-room apartment in the working-class section of Algiers. There Camus spent his childhood. After grade school, he won a scholarship to high school. At sixteen, he enrolled as a philosophy student at the University of Algiers, but his studies were interrupted when he suffered the first of the tuberculosis attacks that recurred all his life. He was forced to abandon his plans for a career in college teaching.

Through the 1930's, Camus supported himself with a series of miscellaneous jobs in Algiers. He also read widely in both classic and modern French authors and was active in the theater, founding a company, the

Workers' Theater, dedicated to performing for working-class audiences. For several years he acted, directed, and wrote plays for this company. He joined the Algerian Communist Party in 1934 but resigned a year later, disillusioned with its program. His first articles had been published while he was still at the university, and in 1937 he became a reporter, reviewer, and editorial writer for the *Alger-Républicain*. In the same year his first book was published: *Betwixt and Between*, a collection of childhood reminiscences and travel sketches. In these sketches and in *Nuptials*, published the following year, Camus dealt with a theme that was to recur throughout his work: the contrast between humanity's loneliness, suffering, and mortality and the joy in life, a joy represented especially by the sensuality of the North African landscape.

Camus left Algeria in 1942 for Paris to work in the French Resistance and to edit the underground Resistance newspaper *Combat*. *The Stranger* was published just before he left Algeria, and he took with him the completed manuscript of *The Myth of Sisyphus*; the two works were to bring him international fame. Both works explore Camus' conception of the "absurd," human beings' position confronted with a world without hope or meaning and faced with the painful contradiction between their longing for immortality and their knowledge of their inevitable death. Meursault, the protagonist of *The Stranger*, is condemned to death less for killing an Arab (actually an act of self-defense) than for being a "stranger" to society's rituals (he did not weep at his mother's funeral). As Sartre does in "The Wall," Camus explores the spiritual development of a person awaiting imminent death. In prison, Meursault, while still rejecting society's dead conventions, moves beyond his previous perception of life as merely a series of meaningless sensual experiences to a vision of life as infinitely precious, not in spite of its absurdity but because of it. Similarly, in the famous ending of *The Myth of Sisyphus*, the mythic hero, condemned forever to roll a boulder up a mountain in Hades, triumphs over his fate by accepting its inherent meaninglessness: "The struggle itself toward the heights is enough to fill a man's heart. One must imagine Sisyphus happy."

In Paris, Camus continued to write for the theater. *The Misunderstanding* was produced in Paris in 1944, and *Caligula* followed in 1945; both developed the absurdist themes of *The Stranger* and *The Myth of Sisyphus*. Camus' most disastrous theatrical failure, *The State of Siege* (1948), was followed by his most brilliant success, *The Just Assassins* (1950). These four plays constitute his major achievement in drama, although he also adapted the work of several other writers for the stage, including William Faulkner's *Requiem for a Nun* (1956) and Fyodor Dostoevsky's *The Possessed* (1959).

The Plague (1947), a novel (or "chronicle," as Camus called it) about an epidemic in Oran, signals a shift in his concerns from the plight of the individual absurdist hero to the problem of values available to social man in an absurd world. Camus finds the answer in the human dignity and cooperation with which the people of Oran confront the plague, an epidemic that symbolizes both the universal threat of an indifferent universe and specifically the political tyranny of Nazi-style totalitarianism. In *The Plague* and the works following it, Camus' emphasis shifts from absurdity to revolt, an option he explores fully and directly in the long philosophical essay *The Rebel* (1951). A person becomes a rebel at the point where he or she says no

to the oppressive patterns of society and accepts the challenge of forging personal and social values that affirm life. Camus' criticisms of collective, political "revolution," as opposed to individual, metaphysical "rebellion," alienated many of his politically committed contemporaries and led to an open break with Sartre.

The Fall (1956), a brilliantly ironic monologue, reveals yet another facet of Camus' thought, a new awareness of human duality. Evil is partially something we impose upon ourselves rather than something inflicted by a hostile universe. The complexity of the individual human being remains a central theme in the six stories, including "The Adulterous Woman," that make up *Exile and the Kingdom* (1957). In this same year, Camus was awarded the Nobel Prize at the unusually young age of forty-four. Less than three years later, in 1960, he was killed in an automobile accident.

One of the earliest reviewers of *Exile and the Kingdom*, Gaetan Picon, pointed to the fact that many of Camus' titles consist of a singular noun with a definite article: *The Stranger, The Plague, The Fall*. But in *Exile and the Kingdom*, he chose two opposing nouns as his title. Picon suggested that this change reflected a new note in Camus' writing, a willingness to give up the rather abstract unity of the earlier works in favor of the ambiguities and unresolved conflicts of reality. In *Exile and the Kingdom*, Picon wrote, "the answer is always given with the question, the right with the wrong side, the kingdom with the exile."

The idea for "The Adulterous Woman" came to Camus in 1952, when he was visiting the Saharan oasis town of Laghouat, 270 miles south of Algiers. "In Laghouat," he wrote in a preface to the first edition, "I met the characters of this story. I am not certain, of course, that their day ended as I have told it. Doubtless they did not go forth to the desert. But *I* went, some hours after that, and during all that time their image pursued me and challenged what I saw." The first edition was a pamphlet published by a small Algerian press run by a friend of Camus. When the publisher heard the title of the story, he objected that the public might think that the story was pornographic. Camus, with some dignity (and perhaps some irony), replied, "My dear friend, if it bears my name it will be a very proper title." And of course the ironies and ambiguities of the title form an important part of the meaning of this moving portrait of a complex and wholly credible woman.

FURTHER READING *(prepared by N. K. B.):* Patrick McCarthy's *Camus*, 1982, is an excellent critical biography that combines a detailed account of Camus' life with good critical analyses of his work. Camus' eventful life has also been detailed in Herbert R. Lottman's massive *Albert Camus: A Biography*, 1979. Germaine Brée's *Camus*, rev. ed. 1972, is a comprehensive and insightful critical study; it includes a short analysis of "The Adulterous Woman." Phillip H. Rhein's *Albert Camus*, rev. ed. 1989, in the Twayne World Authors series, is an informative introductory survey. In *Albert Camus and the Literature of Revolt*, 1960, John Cruickshank discusses Camus' persistent concern with political and existential freedom, focusing on the fictional and dramatic heroes and anti-heroes. Emmett Parker's *Albert Camus: The Artist in the Arena*, 1966, contains a detailed account of the political context for Camus' fiction and nonfiction. Donald Lazere's *The Unique Creation of Albert Camus*, 1973, is psychoanalytically oriented; it contains a detailed and persuasive account of the sexual imagery in "The Adulterous Woman." English Showalter Jr. devotes an excellent

chapter to "The Adulterous Woman" in *Exiles and Strangers: A Reading of Camus' "Exile and the Kingdom,"* 1984. See also Judith D. Suther's *Essays on Camus' "Exile and the Kingdom,"* 1982, and Susan Tarrow, *Exile from the Kingdom: A Political Rereading of Albert Camus,* 1985. Harold Bloom, ed., *Albert Camus,* 1989, reprints important critical essays.

THE ADULTEROUS WOMAN

Translated by Justin O'Brien

A housefly had been circling for the last few minutes in the bus, though the windows were closed. An odd sight here, it had been silently flying back and forth on tired wings. Janine lost track of it, then saw it light on her husband's motionless hand. The weather was cold. The fly shuddered with each gust of sandy wind that scratched against the windows. In the meager light of the winter morning, with a great fracas of sheet metal and axles, the vehicle was rolling, pitching, and making hardly any progress. Janine looked at her husband. With wisps of graying hair growing low on a narrow forehead, a broad nose, a flabby mouth, Marcel looked like a pouting faun. At each hollow in the pavement she felt him jostle against her. Then his heavy torso would slump back on his widespread legs and he would become inert again and absent, with vacant stare. Nothing about him seemed active but his thick hairless hands, made even shorter by the flannel underwear extending below his cuffs and covering his wrists. His hands were holding so tight to a little canvas suitcase set between his knees that they appeared not to feel the fly's halting progress.

Suddenly the wind was distinctly heard to howl and the gritty fog surrounding the bus became even thicker. The sand now struck the windows in packets as if hurled by invisible hands. The fly shook a chilled wing, flexed its legs, and took flight. The bus slowed and seemed on the point of stopping. But the wind apparently died down, the fog lifted slightly, and the vehicle resumed speed. Gaps of light opened up in the dust-drowned landscape. Two or three frail, whitened palm trees which seemed cut out of metal flashed into sight in the window only to disappear the next moment.

"What a country!" Marcel said.

The bus was full of Arabs pretending to sleep, shrouded in their burnooses.[1] Some had folded their legs on the seat and swayed more than the others in the car's motion. Their silence and impassivity began to weigh upon Janine; it seemed to her as if she had been traveling for days with that mute escort. Yet the bus had left only at dawn from the end of the rail line and for two hours in the cold morning it had been advancing on a stony, desolate plateau which, in the beginning at least, extended its straight lines all the way to reddish horizons. But the wind had risen and gradually swallowed up the vast expanse. From that moment on, the passengers had seen nothing more; one after another, they had ceased talking and were silently progressing in a sort of sleepless night, occasionally wiping their lips and eyes irritated by the sand that filtered into the car.

[1] Hooded cloaks, worn by Arabs.

"Janine!" She gave a start at her husband's call. Once again she thought how ridiculous that name was for someone tall and sturdy like her. Marcel wanted to know where his sample case was. With her foot she explored the empty space under the seat and encountered an object which she decided must be it. She could not stoop over without gasping somewhat. Yet in school she had won the first prize in gymnastics and hadn't known what it was to be winded. Was that so long ago? Twenty-five years. Twenty-five years were nothing, for it seemed to her only yesterday when she was hesitating between an independent life and marriage, just yesterday when she was thinking anxiously of the time she might be growing old alone. She was not alone and that law-student who always wanted to be with her was now at her side. She had eventually accepted him although he was a little shorter than she and she didn't like his eager, sharp laugh or his black protruding eyes. But she liked his courage in facing up to life, which he shared with all the French of this country.[2] She also liked his crestfallen look when events or men failed to live up to his expectations. Above all, she liked being loved, and he had showered her with attentions. By so often making her aware that she existed for him he made her exist in reality. No, she was not alone. . . .

The bus, with many loud honks, was plowing its way through invisible obstacles. Inside the car, however, no one stirred. Janine suddenly felt someone staring at her and turned toward the seat across the aisle. He was not an Arab, and she was surprised not to have noticed him from the beginning. He was wearing the uniform of the French regiments of the Sahara and an unbleached linen cap above his tanned face, long and pointed like a jackal's. His gray eyes were examining her with a sort of glum disapproval, in a fixed stare. She suddenly blushed and turned back to her husband, who was still looking straight ahead in the fog and wind. She snuggled down in her coat. But she could still see the French soldier, long and thin, so thin in his fitted tunic that he seemed constructed of a dry, friable material, a mixture of sand and bone. Then it was that she saw the thin hands and burned faces of the Arabs in front of her and noticed that they seemed to have plenty of room, despite their ample garments, on the seat where she and her husband felt wedged in. She pulled her coat around her knees. Yet she wasn't so fat—tall and well rounded rather, plump and still desirable, as she was well aware when men looked at her, with her rather childish face, her bright, naïve eyes contrasting with this big body she knew to be warm and inviting.

No, nothing had happened as she had expected. When Marcel had wanted to take her along on his trip she had protested. For some time he had been thinking of this trip—since the end of the war, to be precise, when business had returned to normal. Before the war the small dry-goods business he had taken over from his parents on giving up his study of law had provided a fairly good living. On the coast the years of youth can be happy ones. But he didn't much like physical effort and very soon had given up taking her to the beaches. The little car took them out of town solely for the Sunday afternoon ride. The rest of the time he preferred his shop full of multicolored piece-goods shaded by the arcades of this half-

[2] Algeria.

native, half-European quarter. Above the shop they lived in three rooms furnished with Arab hangings and furniture from the Galerie Barbès. They had not had children. The years had passed in the semi-darkness behind the half-closed shutters. Summer, the beaches, excursions, the mere sight of the sky were things of the past. Nothing seemed to interest Marcel but business. She felt she had discovered his true passion to be money, and, without really knowing why, she didn't like that. After all, it was to her advantage. Far from being miserly, he was generous, especially where she was concerned. "If something happened to me," he used to say, "you'd be provided for." And, in fact, it is essential to provide for one's needs. But for all the rest, for what is not the most elementary need, how to provide? This is what she felt vaguely, at infrequent intervals. Meanwhile she helped Marcel keep his books and occasionally substituted for him in the shop. Summer was always the hardest, when the heat stifled even the sweet sensation of boredom.

Suddenly, in summer as it happened, the war, Marcel called up then rejected on grounds of health, the scarcity of piece-goods, business at a standstill, the streets empty and hot. If something happened now, she would no longer be provided for. This is why, as soon as piece-goods came back on the market, Marcel had thought of covering the villages of the Upper Plateaus and of the South himself in order to do without a middle-man and sell directly to the Arab merchants. He had wanted to take her along. She knew that travel was difficult, she had trouble breathing, and she would have preferred staying at home. But he was obstinate and she had accepted because it would have taken too much energy to refuse. Here they were and, truly, nothing was like what she had imagined. She had feared the heat, the swarms of flies, the filthy hotels reeking of aniseed. She had not thought of the cold, of the biting wind, of these semi-polar plateaus cluttered with moraines.[3] She had dreamed too of palm trees and soft sand. Now she saw that the desert was not that at all, but merely stone, stone everywhere, in the sky full of nothing but stone-dust, rasping and cold, as on the ground, where nothing grew among the stones except dry grasses.

The bus stopped abruptly. The driver shouted a few words in that language she had heard all her life without ever understanding it. "What's the matter?" Marcel asked. The driver, in French this time, said that the sand must have clogged the carburetor, and again Marcel cursed this country. The driver laughed hilariously and asserted that it was nothing, that he would clean the carburetor and they'd be off again. He opened the door and the cold wind blew into the bus, lashing their faces with myriad grains of sand. All the Arabs silently plunged their noses into their burnooses and huddled up. "Shut the door," Marcel shouted. The driver laughed as he came back to the door. Without hurrying, he took some tools from under the dashboard, then, tiny in the fog, again disappeared ahead without closing the door. Marcel sighed. "You may be sure he's never seen a motor in his life." "Oh, be quiet!" said Janine. Suddenly she gave a start. On the shoulder of the road close to the bus, draped forms were standing still. Under the burnoose's hood and behind a rampart of veils, only their eyes

[3] Ridges of earth and rock left by glaciers.

were visible. Mute, come from nowhere, they were staring at the travelers. "Shepherds," Marcel said.

Inside the car there was total silence. All the passengers, heads lowered, seemed to be listening to the voice of the wind loosed across these endless plateaus. Janine was all of a sudden struck by the almost complete absence of luggage. At the end of the railroad line the driver had hoisted their trunk and a few bundles onto the roof. In the racks inside the bus could be seen nothing but gnarled sticks and shopping-baskets. All these people of the South apparently were traveling empty-handed.

But the driver was coming back, still brisk. His eyes alone were laughing above the veils with which he too had masked his face. He announced that they would soon be under way. He closed the door, the wind became silent, and the rain of sand on the windows could be heard better. The motor coughed and died. After having been urged at great length by the starter, it finally sparked and the driver raced it by pressing on the gas. With a big hiccough the bus started off. From the ragged clump of shepherds, still motionless, a hand rose and then faded into the fog behind them. Almost at once the vehicle began to bounce on the road, which had become worse. Shaken up, the Arabs constantly swayed. Nonetheless, Janine was feeling overcome with sleep when there suddenly appeared in front of her a little yellow box filled with lozenges. The jackal-soldier was smiling at her. She hesitated, took one, and thanked him. The jackal pocketed the box and simultaneously swallowed his smile. Now he was staring at the road, straight in front of him. Janine turned toward Marcel and saw only the solid back of his neck. Through the window he was watching the denser fog rising from the crumbly embankment.

They had been traveling for hours and fatigue had extinguished all life in the car when shouts burst forth outside. Children wearing burnooses, whirling like tops, leaping, clapping their hands, were running around the bus. It was now going down a long street lined with low houses; they were entering the oasis. The wind was still blowing, but the walls intercepted the grains of sand which had previously cut off the light. Yet the sky was still cloudy. Amidst shouts, in a great screeching of brakes, the bus stopped in front of the adobe arcades of a hotel with dirty windows. Janine got out and, once on the pavement, staggered. Above the houses she could see a slim minaret.[4] On her left rose the first palm trees of the oasis, and she would have liked to go toward them. But although it was close to noon, the cold was bitter; the wind made her shiver. She turned toward Marcel and saw the soldier coming toward her. She was expecting him to smile or salute. He passed without looking at her and disappeared. Marcel was busy getting down the trunk of piece-goods, a black foot-locker perched on the bus's roof. It would not be easy. The driver was the only one to take care of the luggage and he had already stopped, standing on the roof, to hold forth to the circle of burnooses gathered around the bus. Janine, surrounded with faces that seemed cut out of bone and leather, besieged by guttural shouts, suddenly became aware of her fatigue. "I'm going in," she said to Marcel, who was shouting impatiently to the driver.

[4] Slender tower attached to a Muslim mosque. From its balcony, the *muezzin*, or crier, calls the people to prayer.

She entered the hotel. The manager, a thin, laconic Frenchman, came to meet her. He led her to a second-floor balcony overlooking the street and into a room which seemed to have but an iron bed, a white-enameled chair, an uncurtained wardrobe, and, behind a rush screen, a washbasin covered with fine sand-dust. When the manager had closed the door, Janine felt the cold coming from the bare, white-washed walls. She didn't know where to put her bag, where to put herself. She had either to lie down or to remain standing, and to shiver in either case. She remained standing, holding her bag and staring at a sort of window-slit that opened onto the sky near the ceiling. She was waiting, but she didn't know for what. She was aware only of her solitude, and of the penetrating cold, and of a greater weight in the region of her heart. She was in fact dreaming, almost deaf to the sounds rising from the street along with Marcel's vocal outbursts, more aware on the other hand of that sound of a river coming from the window-slit and caused by the wind in the palm trees, so close now, it seemed to her. Then the wind seemed to increase and the gentle ripple of waters became a hissing of waves. She imagined, beyond the walls, a sea of erect, flexible palm trees unfurling in the storm. Nothing was like what she had expected, but those invisible waves refreshed her tired eyes. She was standing, heavy, with dangling arms, slightly stooped, as the cold climbed her thick legs. She was dreaming of the erect and flexible palm trees and of the girl she had once been.

After having washed, they went down to the dining-room. On the bare walls had been painted camels and palm trees drowned in a sticky background of pink and lavender. The arcaded windows let in a meager light. Marcel questioned the hotel manager about the merchants. Then an elderly Arab wearing a military decoration on his tunic served them. Marcel, preoccupied, tore his bread into little pieces. He kept his wife from drinking water. "It hasn't been boiled. Take wine." She didn't like that, for wine made her sleepy. Besides, there was pork on the menu. "They don't eat it because of the Koran.[5] But the Koran didn't know that well-done pork doesn't cause illness. We French know how to cook. What are you thinking about?" Janine was not thinking of anything, or perhaps of that victory of the cooks over the prophets. But she had to hurry. They were to leave the next morning for still farther south; that afternoon they had to see all the important merchants. Marcel urged the elderly Arab to hurry the coffee. He nodded without smiling and pattered out. "Slowly in the morning, not too fast in the afternoon," Marcel said, laughing. Yet eventually the coffee came. They barely took time to swallow it and went out into the dusty, cold street. Marcel called a young Arab to help him carry the trunk, but as a matter of principle quibbled about the payment. His opinion, which he once more expressed to Janine, was in fact based on the vague principle that they always asked for twice as much in the hope of settling for a quarter of the amount. Janine, ill at ease, followed the two trunk-bearers. She had put on a wool dress under her heavy coat and would have liked to take up less space. The pork, although well done, and the small quantity of wine she had drunk also bothered her somewhat.

[5] Sacred scripture of Islam. Muslims are forbidden to eat pork.

They walked along a diminutive public garden planted with dusty trees. They encountered Arabs who stepped out of their way without seeming to see them, wrapping themselves in their burnooses. Even when they were wearing rags, she felt they had a look of dignity unknown to the Arabs of her town. Janine followed the trunk, which made a way for her through the crowd. They went through the gate in an earthen rampart and emerged on a little square planted with the same mineral trees and bordered on the far side, where it was widest, with arcades and shops. But they stopped on the square itself in front of a small construction shaped like an artillery shell and painted a chalky blue. Inside, in the single room lighted solely by the entrance, an old Arab with white mustaches stood behind a shiny plank. He was serving tea, raising and lowering the teapot over three tiny multicolored glasses. Before they could make out anything else in the darkness, the cool scent of mint tea greeted Marcel and Janine at the door. Marcel had barely crossed the threshold and dodged the garlands of pewter teapots, cups and trays, and the postcard displays when he was up against the counter. Janine stayed at the door. She stepped a little aside so as not to cut off the light. At that moment she perceived in the darkness behind the old merchant two Arabs smiling at them, seated on the bulging sacks that filled the back of the shop. Red-and-black rugs and embroidered scarves hung on the walls; the floor was cluttered with sacks and little boxes filled with aromatic seeds. On the counter, beside a sparkling pair of brass scales and an old yardstick with figures effaced, stood a row of loaves of sugar. One of them had been unwrapped from its coarse blue paper and cut into on top. The smell of wool and spices in the room became apparent behind the scent of tea when the old merchant set down the teapot and said good-day.

Marcel talked rapidly in the low voice he assumed when talking business. Then he opened the trunk, exhibited the wools and silks, pushed back the scale and yardstick to spread out his merchandise in front of the old merchant. He got excited, raised his voice, laughed nervously, like a woman who wants to make an impression and is not sure of herself. Now, with hands spread wide, he was going through the gestures of selling and buying. The old man shook his head, passed the tea tray to the two Arabs behind him, and said just a few words that seemed to discourage Marcel. He picked up his goods, piled them back into the trunk, then wiped an imaginary sweat from his forehead. He called the little porter and they started off toward the arcades. In the first shop, although the merchant began by exhibiting the same Olympian manner, they were a little luckier. "They think they're God almighty," Marcel said, "but they're in business too! Life is hard for everyone."

Janine followed without answering. The wind had almost ceased. The sky was clearing in spots. A cold, harsh light came from the deep holes that opened up in the thickness of the clouds. They had now left the square. They were walking in narrow streets along earthen walls over which hung rotted December roses, or from time to time, a pomegranate, dried and wormy. An odor of dust and coffee, the smoke of a wood fire, the smell of stone and of sheep permeated this quarter. The shops, hollowed out of the walls, were far from one another; Janine felt her feet getting heavier. But her husband was gradually becoming more cheerful. He was beginning to sell and was feeling more kindly; he called Janine "Baby"; the trip would

not be wasted. "Of course," Janine said mechanically, "it's better to deal directly with them."

They came back by another street, toward the center. It was late in the afternoon; the sky was now almost completely clear. They stopped in the square. Marcel rubbed his hands and looked affectionately at the trunk in front of them. "Look," said Janine. From the other end of the square was coming a tall Arab, thin, vigorous, wearing a sky-blue burnoose, soft brown boots and gloves, and bearing his bronzed aquiline face loftily. Nothing but the *chèche*[6] that he was wearing swathed as a turban distinguished him from those French officers in charge of native affairs whom Janine had occasionally admired. He was advancing steadily toward them, but seemed to be looking beyond their group as he slowly removed the glove from one hand. "Well," said Marcel as he shrugged his shoulders, "there's one who thinks he's a general." Yes, all of them here had that look of pride; but this one, really, was going too far. Although they were surrounded by the empty space of the square, he was walking straight toward the trunk without seeing it, without seeing them. Then the distance separating them decreased rapidly and the Arab was upon them when Marcel suddenly seized the handle of the foot-locker and pulled it out of the way. The Arab passed without seeming to notice anything and headed with the same regular step toward the ramparts. Janine looked at her husband; he had his crestfallen look. "They think they can get away with anything now," he said. Janine did not reply. She loathed that Arab's stupid arrogance and suddenly felt unhappy. She wanted to leave and thought of her little apartment. The idea of going back to the hotel, to that icy room, discouraged her. It suddenly occurred to her that the manager had advised her to climb up to the terrace around the fort to see the desert. She said this to Marcel and that he could leave the trunk at the hotel. But he was tired and wanted to sleep a little before dinner. "Please," said Janine. He looked at her, suddenly attentive. "Of course, my dear," he said.

She waited for him in the street in front of the hotel. The white-robed crowd was becoming larger and larger. Not a single woman could be seen, and it seemed to Janine that she had never seen so many men. Yet none of them looked at her. Some of them, without appearing to see her, slowly turned toward her that thin, tanned face that made them all look alike to her, the face of the French soldier in the bus and that of the gloved Arab, a face both shrewd and proud. They turned that face toward the foreign woman, they didn't see her, and then, light and silent, they walked around her as she stood there with swelling ankles. And her discomfort, her need of getting away increased. "Why did I come?" But already Marcel was coming back.

When they climbed the stairs to the fort, it was five o'clock. The wind had died down altogether. The sky, completely clear, was now periwinkle blue. The cold, now drier, made their cheeks smart. Halfway up the stairs an old Arab, stretched out against the wall, asked them if they wanted a guide, but didn't budge, as if he had been sure of their refusal in advance. The stairs were long and steep despite several landings of packed earth. As they climbed, the space widened and they rose into an ever broader light,

[6]Cloth sun screen at the back of a military cap.

cold and dry, in which every sound from the oasis reached them pure and distinct. The bright air seemed to vibrate around them with a vibration increasing in length as they advanced, as if their progress struck from the crystal of light a sound wave that kept spreading out. And as soon as they reached the terrace and their gaze was lost in the vast horizon beyond the palm grove, it seemed to Janine that the whole sky rang with a single short and piercing note, whose echoes gradually filled the space above her, then suddenly died and left her silently facing the limitless expanse.

From east to west, in fact, her gaze swept slowly, without encountering a single obstacle, along a perfect curve. Beneath her, the blue-and-white terraces of the Arab town overlapped one another, splattered with the dark-red spots of peppers drying in the sun. Not a soul could be seen, but from the inner courts, together with the aroma of roasting coffee, there rose laughing voices or incomprehensible stamping of feet. Farther off, the palm grove, divided into uneven squares by clay walls, rustled its upper foliage in a wind that could not be felt upon the terrace. Still farther off and all the way to the horizon extended the ocher-and-gray realm of stones, in which no life was visible. At some distance from the oasis, however, near the wadi[7] that bordered the palm grove on the west could be seen broad black tents. All around them a flock of motionless dromedaries, tiny at that distance, formed against the gray ground the black signs of a strange handwriting, the meaning of which had to be deciphered. Above the desert, the silence was as vast as the space.

Janine, leaning her whole body against the parapet, was speechless, unable to tear herself away from the void opening before her. Beside her, Marcel was getting restless. He was cold; he wanted to go back down. What was there to see here, after all? But she could not take her gaze from the horizon. Over yonder, still farther south, at that point where sky and earth met in a pure line—over yonder it suddenly seemed there was awaiting her something of which, though it had always been lacking, she had never been aware until now. In the advancing afternoon the light relaxed and softened; it was passing from the crystalline to the liquid. Simultaneously, in the heart of a woman brought there by pure chance a knot tightened by the years, habit, and boredom was slowly loosening. She was looking at the nomads' encampment. She had not even seen the men living in it; nothing was stirring among the black tents, and yet she could think only of them whose existence she had barely known until this day. Homeless, cut off from the world, they were a handful wandering over the vast territory she could see, which however was but a paltry part of an even greater expanse whose dizzying course stopped only thousands of miles farther south, where the first river finally waters the forest. Since the beginning of time, on the dry earth of this limitless land scraped to the bone, a few men had been ceaselessly trudging, possessing nothing but serving no one, poverty-stricken but free lords of a strange kingdom. Janine did not know why this thought filled her with such a sweet, vast melancholy that it closed her eyes. She knew that this kingdom had been eternally promised her and yet that it would never be hers, never again, except in this fleeting moment perhaps when she opened her eyes again on the suddenly motionless sky and on its

[7]Bed of a stream, dry except during periods of rainfall.

waves of steady light, while the voices rising from the Arab town suddenly fell silent. It seemed to her that the world's course had just stopped and that, from that moment on, no one would ever age any more or die. Everywhere, henceforth, life was suspended—except in her heart, where, at the same moment, someone was weeping with affliction and wonder.

But the light began to move; the sun, clear and devoid of warmth, went down toward the west, which became slightly pink, while a gray wave took shape in the east ready to roll slowly over the vast expanse. A first dog barked and its distant bark rose in the now even colder air. Janine noticed that her teeth were chattering. "We are catching our death of cold," Marcel said. "You're a fool. Let's go back." But he took her hand awkwardly. Docile now, she turned away from the parapet and followed him. Without moving, the old Arab on the stairs watched them go down toward the town. She walked along without seeing anyone, bent under a tremendous and sudden fatigue, dragging her body, whose weight now seemed to her unbearable. Her exaltation had left her. Now she felt too tall, too thick, too white too, for this world she had just entered. A child, the girl, the dry man, the furtive jackal were the only creatures who could silently walk that earth. What would she do there henceforth except to drag herself toward sleep, toward death?

She dragged herself, in fact, toward the restaurant with a husband suddenly taciturn unless he was telling how tired he was, while she was struggling weakly against a cold, aware of a fever rising within her. Then she dragged herself toward her bed, where Marcel came to join her and put the light out at once without asking anything of her. The room was frigid. Janine felt the cold creeping up while the fever was increasing. She breathed with difficulty, her blood pumped without warming her; a sort of fear grew within her. She turned over and the old iron bedstead groaned under her weight. No, she didn't want to fall ill. Her husband was already asleep; she too had to sleep; it was essential. The muffled sounds of the town reached her through the window-slit. With a nasal twang old phonographs in the Moorish cafés ground out tunes she recognized vaguely; they reached her borne on the sound of a slow-moving crowd. She must sleep. But she was counting black tents; behind her eyelids motionless camels were grazing; immense solitudes were whirling within her. Yes, why had she come? She fell asleep on that question.

She awoke a little later. The silence around her was absolute. But, on the edges of town, hoarse dogs were howling in the soundless night. Janine shivered. She turned over, felt her husband's hard shoulder against hers, and suddenly, half asleep, huddled against him. She was drifting on the surface of sleep without sinking in and she clung to that shoulder with unconscious eagerness as her safest haven. She was talking, but no sound issued from her mouth. She was talking, but she herself hardly heard what she was saying. She could feel only Marcel's warmth. For more than twenty years every night thus, in his warmth, just the two of them, even when ill, even when traveling, as at present . . . Besides, what would she have done alone at home? No child! Wasn't that what she lacked? She didn't know. She simply followed Marcel, pleased to know that someone needed her. The only joy he gave her was the knowledge that she was necessary. Probably he didn't love her. Love, even when filled with hate, doesn't have that

sullen face. But what is his face like? They made love in the dark by feel, without seeing each other. Is there another love than that of darkness, a love that would cry aloud in daylight? She didn't know, but she did know that Marcel needed her and that she needed that need, that she lived on it night and day, at night especially—every night, when he didn't want to be alone, or to age or die, with that set expression he assumed which she occasionally recognized on other men's faces, the only common expression of those madmen hiding under an appearance of wisdom until the madness seizes them and hurls them desperately toward a woman's body to bury in it, without desire, everything terrifying that solitude and night reveals to them.

Marcel stirred as if to move away from her. No, he didn't love her; he was merely afraid of what was not she, and she and he should long ago have separated and slept alone until the end. But who can always sleep alone? Some men do, cut off from others by a vocation or misfortune, who go to bed every night in the same bed as death. Marcel never could do so—he above all, a weak and disarmed child always frightened by suffering, her own child indeed who needed her and who, just at that moment, let out a sort of whimper. She cuddled a little closer and put her hand on his chest. And to herself she called him with the little love-name she had once given him, which they still used from time to time without even thinking of what they were saying.

She called him with all her heart. After all, she too needed him, his strength, his little eccentricities, and she too was afraid of death. "If I could overcome that fear, I'd be happy. . . . " Immediately, a nameless anguish seized her. She drew back from Marcel. No, she was overcoming nothing, she was not happy, she was going to die, in truth, without having been liberated. Her heart pained her; she was stifling under a huge weight that she suddenly discovered she had been dragging around for twenty years. Now she was struggling under it with all her strength. She wanted to be liberated even if Marcel, even if the others, never were! Fully awake, she sat up in bed and listened to a call that seemed very close. But from the edges of night the exhausted and yet indefatigable voices of the dogs of the oasis were all that reached her ears. A slight wind had risen and she heard its light waters flow in the palm grove. It came from the south, where desert and night mingled now under the again unchanging sky, where life stopped, where no one would ever age or die any more. Then the waters of the wind dried up and she was not even sure of having heard anything except a mute call that she could, after all, silence or notice. But never again would she know its meaning unless she responded to it at once. At once—yes, that much was certain at least!

She got up gently and stood motionless beside the bed, listening to her husband's breathing. Marcel was asleep. The next moment, the bed's warmth left her and the cold gripped her. She dressed slowly, feeling for her clothes in the faint light coming through the blinds from the street-lamps. Her shoes in her hand, she reached the door. She waited a moment more in the darkness, then gently opened the door. The knob squeaked and she stood still. Her heart was beating madly. She listened with her body tense and, reassured by the silence, turned her hand a little more. The knob's turning seemed to her interminable. At last she opened the door,

slipped outside, and closed the door with the same stealth. Then, with her cheek against the wood, she waited. After a moment she made out, in the distance, Marcel's breathing. She faced about, felt the icy night air against her cheek, and ran the length of the balcony. The outer door was closed. While she was slipping the bolt, the night watchman appeared at the top of the stairs, his face blurred with sleep, and spoke to her in Arabic. "I'll be back," said Janine as she stepped out into the night.

Garlands of stars hung down from the black sky over the palm trees and houses. She ran along the short avenue, now empty, that led to the fort. The cold, no longer having to struggle against the sun, had invaded the night; the icy air burned her lungs. But she ran, half blind, in the darkness. At the top of the avenue, however, lights appeared, then descended toward her zigzagging. She stopped, caught the whir of turning sprockets and, behind the enlarging lights, soon saw vast burnooses surmounting fragile bicycle wheels. The burnooses flapped against her; then three red lights sprang out of the black behind her and disappeared at once. She continued running toward the fort. Halfway up the stairs, the air burned her lungs with such cutting effect that she wanted to stop. A final burst of energy hurled her despite herself onto the terrace, against the parapet, which was now pressing her belly. She was panting and everything was hazy before her eyes. Her running had not warmed her and she was still trembling all over. But the cold air she was gulping down soon flowed evenly inside her and a spark of warmth began to glow amidst her shivers. Her eyes opened at last on the expanse of night.

Not a breath, not a sound—except at intervals the muffled crackling of stones that the cold was reducing to sand—disturbed the solitude and silence surrounding Janine. After a moment, however, it seemed to her that the sky above her was moving in a sort of slow gyration. In the vast reaches of the dry, cold night, thousands of stars were constantly appearing, and their sparkling icicles, loosened at once, began to slip gradually toward the horizon. Janine could not tear herself away from contemplating those drifting flares. She was turning with them, and the apparently stationary progress little by little identified her with the core of her being, where cold and desire were now vying with each other. Before her the stars were falling one by one and being snuffed out among the stones of the desert, and each time Janine opened a little more to the night. Breathing deeply, she forgot the cold, the dead weight of others, the craziness or stuffiness of life, the long anguish of living and dying. After so many years of mad, aimless fleeing from fear, she had come to a stop at last. At the same time, she seemed to recover her roots and the sap again rose in her body, which had ceased trembling. Her whole belly pressed against the parapet as she strained toward the moving sky; she was merely waiting for her fluttering heart to calm down and establish silence within her. The last stars of the constellations dropped their clusters a little lower on the desert horizon and became still. Then, with unbearable gentleness, the water of night began to fill Janine, drowned the cold, rose gradually from the hidden core of her being and overflowed in wave after wave, rising up even to her mouth full of moans. The next moment, the whole sky stretched out over her, fallen on her back on the cold earth.

When Janine returned to the room, with the same precautions, Marcel

was not awake. But he whimpered as she got back in bed and a few seconds later sat up suddenly. He spoke and she didn't understand what he was saying. He got up, turned on the light, which blinded her. He staggered toward the washbasin and drank a long draught from the bottle of mineral water. He was about to slip between the sheets when, one knee on the bed, he looked at her without understanding. She was weeping copiously, unable to restrain herself. "It's nothing, dear," she said, "it's nothing."

Jorge Luis Borges
(1899–1986)

A group of remarkable writers, including Gabriel García Márquez, Jorge Amado, Julio Cortázar, and Mario Vargas Llosa, have transformed Latin American literature, in the last quarter of a century, from a placid backwater of world literature into an important current in the main stream. The most prominent of these writers was the Argentinian Jorge Luis Borges. Borges' reputation, although he wrote voluminously in a number of forms, rests almost exclusively upon about forty short prose tales, not quite sketches, not quite short stories—"fictions," he preferred to call them—which he wrote between about 1937 and 1955. Some of these fictions are brief, dreamlike fantasies, and others read, initially at least, like short autobiographical sketches that gradually open upon vistas of alternative realities. The effect is often vertiginous, as if the reader had rounded a corner or reached the top of a hill and suddenly glimpsed new worlds of the imagination.

Borges was born in Buenos Aires in 1899 into a family that had included a number of famous Argentine patriots. His father, a lawyer, teacher, and man of letters, was half English, and Borges learned English before he learned Spanish. In his father's well-stocked library, he read, as a child, many of the classics of storytelling—the *Arabian Nights, Don Quixote,* Greek mythology, and the novels of Charles Dickens, Mark Twain, and H. G. Wells—which were to leave their mark on his own later fiction-making. In 1914, the family was in Europe when World War I broke out. They spent the war in Switzerland, where Borges completed his education at the Collège de Genève, becoming proficient in Latin, French, and German. After the war, he lived for a year in Majorca and a year in Spain, where at the age of twenty-one he became friends with members of the avant-garde Ultraist movement, who, influenced by the French Symbolists, advocated free verse and the supremacy of metaphor over direct statement.

Borges returned to Buenos Aires in 1921, and over the next sixteen years, he led the life of an independent young man of letters in the artistic circles of the capital. He founded three literary magazines, which he used to promote Ultraist ideas in Argentina, published several volumes of po-

etry and essays, and wrote reviews and translations. *A Universal History of Infamy*, a collection of bizarre sketches of criminals, some imaginary, appeared in 1936, and *The History of Eternity*, a collection of essays on ideas of eternity throughout history, in 1937; both foreshadowed some of Borges' later preoccupations.

The turning point in Borges' career came in 1937–38, when he took a job in the Buenos Aires library, his father died, and he suffered a serious accident that left him with a severe head wound, blood poisoning, and a prolonged period of high fever. While convalescing from this close encounter with death, he began to write the fictions that were to make him famous, initially, he said, to see if he could still develop a lucid argument. The first collection of these pieces, *The Garden of Forking Paths*, appeared in 1941; an expanded version, *Fictions*, followed in 1944. The main body of Borges' most characteristic work was completed with *The Aleph* (1949).

Although Borges defined politics as "one of the forms of tedium," he strongly opposed Hitler in pro-German Argentina, and he was equally outspoken in his opposition to the dictatorship of Juan Perón, who came to power in 1946. Perón's government dismissed Borges from his library job and offered him a position as chicken inspector in the Buenos Aires city market. He was able to find a teaching post instead, but he remained under surveillance and his mother and sister were arrested. When Perón was overthrown in 1955, Borges became director of the National Library of Argentina, a member of the National Academy, and, a year later, Professor of English and North American Literature at the University of Buenos Aires.

Borges' eyesight began to deteriorate rapidly in the 1950's, as the result of the same hereditary eye disease that had blinded his father, and he eventually went almost totally blind. After 1955, he turned his attention more to poetry than to prose; his poetry, rather formal and classical, is radically different from his fictions. He did, however, publish a collection of stories which he regarded as experiments in "straightforward storytelling," *Doctor Brodie's Report*, in 1970. He traveled widely in his later years, especially in the United States, where he taught and delivered lectures on a number of university campuses. He died in 1986.

Borges' brief, unsettling fictions have often been compared to Kafka's dream stories. In certain obvious ways, the parallel is not very exact; Kafka writes of the unconscious and irrational, whereas the pleasures of Borges' stories seem to be those of the conscious, rational mind. He is one of the most bookish of writers, and his stories often seem like his own "Library of Babel," where the whole world is reduced to a collection of books that include "the faithful catalogue of the Library, thousands and thousands of false catalogues, a demonstration of the fallacy of the true catalogue," and "a version of each book in all languages, the interpolations of every book in all books." His stories are highly rational, artificial constructions, full of logical puzzles, perceptual tricks, and dazzling paradoxes. The title of *Labyrinths*, a collection of his stories in English, might be taken as descriptive of all his work. "Tlön, Uqbar, Orbis Tertius," for example, is among other things a progress through a labyrinth in which the reader, with the narrator, is repeatedly offered a choice between two "turnings": the real *Encyclopaedia Britannica* and its double, the plagiarized *Anglo-American Cyclopaedia*;

a copy of the *Anglo-American Cyclopaedia* that contains an article on Uqbar and one that does not; a faulty, half-remembered quotation from an Uqbar thinker and the true version; and a dozen other "forking paths."

Beneath the witty artificiality of Borges' fictions, however, there is a core of mystery that makes the comparison with Kafka just, despite their superficial differences. Borges' stories all play with systems of order, ways man has tried to make sense of the world, whether they be obscure heresies, philosophical systems, or artistic forms. But ultimately, all systems become equally provisional, and we are left with a sense of life as irreducibly enigmatic, all attempts to order it being merely fragments shored against our ruins. "Through the years," Borges has written, "a man peoples a space with images of provinces, kingdoms, mountains, bays, ships, islands, fishes, rooms, tools, stars, horses, and people. Shortly before his death he discovers that the patient labyrinth of lines traces the image of his own face."

FURTHER READING *(prepared by N. K. B.):* For an extensive collection of Borges' fiction, essays, and poetry, see Emir Rodriquez Monegal and Alastair Reid, eds., *Borges: A Reader,* 1981, which includes both little-known selections and major works spanning his entire career. *Borges at Eighty: Conversations,* ed. by Willis Barnstone, 1982, offers insights into Borges' view of his own work and that of others. Emir Rodriquez Monegal's *Jorge Luis Borges,* 1978, gives a detailed account of Borges' life, integrating critical commentary on the poetry and prose. For good introductions to Borges' major themes and artistry, see Martin Stabb's *Jorge Luis Borges,* 1970, a study of form that includes chapters on the poetry, fiction, and critical essays, including an analysis of "The Circular Ruins," and J. M. Cohen's *Jorge Luis Borges,* 1972, which analyzes the Argentinian context for Borges' early work. George McMurray's *Jorge Luis Borges,* 1980, emphasizes the philosophical concerns in the fiction. Gene H. Bell-Villada's *Borges and His Fictions: A Guide to His Mind and Art,* 1981, is very useful. Lowell Dunham and Ivar Ivask have edited a wide-ranging collection of essays on Borges, *The Cardinal Points of Borges,* 1971, which includes articles on his narrative style and critical reception. A guide to Borges criticism is David W. Foster's *Jorge Luis Borges: An Annotated Primary and Secondary Bibliography,* 1984.

TLÖN, UQBAR, ORBIS TERTIUS

Translated by James E. Irby

1

I owe the discovery of Uqbar to the conjunction of a mirror and an encyclopedia. The mirror troubled the depths of a corridor in a country house on Gaona Street in Ramos Mejía; the encyclopedia is fallaciously called *The Anglo-American Cyclopaedia* (New York, 1917) and is a literal but delinquent reprint of the *Encyclopaedia Britannica* of 1902. The event took place some five years ago. Bioy Casares[1] had had dinner with me that evening and we became lengthily engaged in a vast polemic concerning the composition of

[1] Adolfo Bioy Casares (b. 1914) is a well-known Argentine author and a friend and collaborator of Borges. Throughout the story, Borges mingles real and fictitious people.

a novel in the first person, whose narrator would omit or disfigure the facts and indulge in various contradictions which would permit a few readers— very few readers—to perceive an atrocious or banal reality. From the remote depths of the corridor, the mirror spied upon us. We discovered (such a discovery is inevitable in the late hours of the night) that mirrors have something monstrous about them. Then Bioy Casares recalled that one of the heresiarchs[2] of Uqbar had declared that mirrors and copulation are abominable, because they increase the number of men. I asked him the origin of this memorable observation and he answered that it was reproduced in *The Anglo-American Cyclopaedia*, in its article on Uqbar. The house (which we had rented furnished) had a set of this work. On the last pages of Volume XLVI we found an article on Upsala; on the first pages of Volume XLVII, one on Ural-Altaic Languages, but not a word about Uqbar. Bioy, a bit taken aback, consulted the volumes of the index. In vain he exhausted all of the imaginable spellings: Ukbar, Ucbar, Ooqbar, Ookbar, Ouk-bahr . . . Before leaving, he told me that it was a region of Iraq or of Asia Minor. I must confess that I agreed with some discomfort. I conjectured that this undocumented country and its anonymous heresiarch were a fiction devised by Bioy's modesty in order to justify a statement. The fruitless examination of one of Justus Perthes' atlases fortified my doubt.

The following day, Bioy called me from Buenos Aires. He told me he had before him the article on Uqbar, in Volume XLVI of the encyclopedia. The heresiarch's name was not forthcoming, but there was a note on his doctrine, formulated in words almost identical to those he had repeated, though perhaps literarily inferior. He had recalled: *Copulation and mirrors are abominable.* The text of the encyclopedia said: *For one of those gnostics, the visible universe was an illusion or (more precisely) a sophism. Mirrors and fatherhood are abominable because they multiply and disseminate that universe.* I told him, in all truthfulness, that I should like to see that article. A few days later he brought it. This surprised me, since the scrupulous cartographical indices of Ritter's *Erdkunde*[3] were plentifully ignorant of the name Uqbar.

The tome Bioy brought was, in fact, Volume XLVI of the *Anglo-American Cyclopaedia*. On the half-title page and the spine, the alphabetical marking (Tor-Ups) was that of our copy, but, instead of 917, it contained 921 pages. These four additional pages made up the article on Uqbar, which (as the reader will have noticed) was not indicated by the alphabetical marking. We later determined that there was no other difference between the volumes. Both of them (as I believe I have indicated) are reprints of the tenth *Encyclopaedia Britannica*. Bioy had acquired his copy at some sale or other.

We read the article with some care. The passage recalled by Bioy was perhaps the only surprising one. The rest of it seemed very plausible, quite in keeping with the general tone of the work and (as is natural) a bit boring. Reading it over again, we discovered beneath its rigorous prose a fundamental vagueness. Of the fourteen names which figured in the geographical part, we only recognized three—Khorasan, Armenia, Erzerum[4]—interpolated in the text in an ambiguous way. Of the historical names, only

[2]Those who advance heresies, or unorthodox opinions. [3]Geography.
[4]Actual places in the Middle East.

one: the impostor magician Smerdis,[5] invoked more as a metaphor. The note seemed to fix the boundaries of Uqbar, but its nebulous reference points were rivers and craters and mountain ranges of that same region. We read, for example, that the lowlands of Tsai Khaldun and the Axa Delta marked the southern frontier and that on the islands of the delta wild horses procreate. All this, on the first part of page 918. In the historical section (page 920) we learned that as a result of the religious persecutions of the thirteenth century, the orthodox believers sought refuge on these islands, where to this day their obelisks remain and where it is not uncommon to unearth their stone mirrors. The section on Language and Literature was brief. Only one trait is worthy of recollection: it noted that the literature of Uqbar was one of fantasy and that its epics and legends never referred to reality, but to the two imaginary regions of Mlejnas and Tlön . . . The bibliography enumerated four volumes which we have not yet found, though the third—Silas Haslam: *History of the Land Called Uqbar,* 1874—figures in the catalogues of Bernard Quaritch's book shop.[6] The first, *Lesbare und lesenswerthe Bemerkungen über das Land Ukkbar in Klein-Asien,* dates from 1641 and is the work of Johannes Valentinus Andreä.[7] This fact is significant; a few years later, I came upon that name in the unsuspected pages of De Quincey[8] (*Writings,* Volume XIII) and learned that it belonged to a German theologian who, in the early seventeenth century, described the imaginary community of Rosae Crucis[9]—a community that others founded later, in imitation of what he had prefigured.

That night we visited the National Library. In vain we exhausted atlases, catalogues, annuals of geographical societies, travelers' and historians' memoirs: no one had ever been in Uqbar. Neither did the general index of Bioy's encyclopedia register that name. The following day, Carlos Mastronardi (to whom I had related the matter) noticed the black and gold covers of the *Anglo-American Cyclopaedia* in a bookshop on Corrientes and Talcahuano . . . He entered and examined Volume XLVI. Of course, he did not find the slightest indication of Uqbar.

<div style="text-align:center">2</div>

Some limited and waning memory of Herbert Ashe, an engineer of the southern railways, persists in the hotel at Adrogué, amongst the effusive honeysuckles and in the illusory depths of the mirrors. In his lifetime, he suffered from unreality, as do so many Englishmen; once dead, he is not even the ghost he was then. He was tall and listless and his tired rectangular beard had once been red. I understand he was a widower, without children. Every few years he would go to England, to visit (I judge from some

[5] A usurper who seized the throne of Persia in the sixth century B.C.

[6] "Haslam has also published *A General History of Labyrinths*" (Borges' note). Bernard Quaritch ran a famous London bookshop in the nineteenth century.

[7] *Readable and Valuable Observations on the Land of Uqbar in Asia Minor.* Andreä (1586–1654) was an actual German theologian, although the book is fictitious.

[8] Thomas De Quincey (1785–1859), English essayist.

[9] The Brotherhood of the Rosy Cross, an occult group. The modern movement originated in the writings of Andreä, but it claims roots in ancient Egypt.

photographs he showed us) a sundial and a few oaks. He and my father had entered into one of those close (the adjective is excessive) English friendships that begin by excluding confidences and very soon dispense with dialogue. They used to carry out an exchange of books and newspapers and engage in taciturn chess games . . . I remember him in the hotel corridor, with a mathematics book in his hand, sometimes looking at the irrecoverable colors of the sky. One afternoon, we spoke of the duodecimal system of numbering (in which twelve is written as 10). Ashe said that he was converting some kind of tables from the duodecimal to the sexagesimal system (in which sixty is written as 10). He added that the task had been entrusted to him by a Norwegian, in Rio Grande do Sul. We had known him for eight years and he had never mentioned his sojourn in that region . . . We talked of country life, of the *capangas*,[10] of the Brazilian etymology of the word *gaucho*[11] (which some old Uruguayans still pronounce *gaúcho*) and nothing more was said—may God forgive me—of duodecimal functions. In September of 1937 (we were not at the hotel), Herbert Ashe died of a ruptured aneurysm. A few days before, he had received a sealed and certified package from Brazil. It was a book in large octavo. Ashe left it at the bar, where—months later—I found it. I began to leaf through it and experienced an astonished and airy feeling of vertigo which I shall not describe, for this is not the story of my emotions but of Uqbar and Tlön and Orbis Tertius. On one of the nights of Islam called the Night of Nights, the secret doors of heaven open wide and the water in the jars becomes sweeter; if those doors opened, I would not feel what I felt that afternoon. The book was written in English and contained 1001 pages. On the yellow leather back I read these curious words which were repeated on the title page: *A First Encyclopaedia of Tlön, Vol. XI. Hlaer to Jangn.* There was no indication of date or place. On the first page and on a leaf of silk paper that covered one of the color plates there was stamped a blue oval with this inscription: *Orbis Tertius.* Two years before I had discovered, in a volume of a certain pirated encyclopedia, a superficial description of a nonexistent country; now chance afforded me something more precious and arduous. Now I held in my hands a vast methodical fragment of an unknown planet's entire history, with its architecture and its playing cards, with the dread of its mythologies and the murmur of its languages, with its emperors and its seas, with its minerals and its birds and its fish, with its algebra and its fire, with its theological and metaphysical controversy. And all of it articulated, coherent, with no visible doctrinal intent or tone of parody.

In the "Eleventh Volume" which I have mentioned, there are allusions to preceding and succeeding volumes. In an article in the *N. R. F.* which is now classic, Néstor Ibarra has denied the existence of those companion volumes; Ezequiel Martínez Estrada[12] and Drieu La Rochelle have refuted that doubt, perhaps victoriously. The fact is that up to now the most diligent inquiries have been fruitless. In vain we have upended the libraries of the two Americas and of Europe. Alfonso Reyes,[13] tired of these subordinate sleuthing procedures, proposes that we should all undertake the task of reconstructing the many and weighty tomes that are lacking: *ex ungue*

[10] Thugs (Brazilian Portuguese). [11] Cowboy (Brazilian Portuguese).
[12] Actual Argentine essayist (1895–1964). [13] An actual Mexican writer (1889–1959).

leonem.[14] He calculates, half in earnest and half jokingly, that a generation of *tlönistas* should be sufficient. This venturesome computation brings us back to the fundamental problem: Who are the inventors of Tlön? The plural is inevitable, because the hypothesis of a lone inventor—an infinite Leibniz[15] laboring away darkly and modestly—has been unanimously discounted. It is conjectured that this brave new world is the work of a secret society of astronomers, biologists, engineers, metaphysicians, poets, chemists, algebraists, moralists, painters, geometers . . . directed by an obscure man of genius. Individuals mastering these diverse disciplines are abundant, but not so those capable of inventiveness and less so those capable of subordinating that inventiveness to a rigorous and systematic plan. This plan is so vast that each writer's contribution is infinitesimal. At first it was believed that Tlön was a mere chaos, an irresponsible license of the imagination; now it is known that it is a cosmos and that the intimate laws which govern it have been formulated, at least provisionally. Let it suffice for me to recall that the apparent contradictions of the Eleventh Volume are the fundamental basis for the proof that the other volumes exist, so lucid and exact is the order observed in it. The popular magazines, with pardonable excess, have spread news of the zoology and topography of Tlön; I think its transparent tigers and towers of blood perhaps do not merit the continued attention of *all* men. I shall venture to request a few minutes to expound its concept of the universe.

Hume noted for all time that Berkeley's arguments did not admit the slightest refutation nor did they cause the slightest conviction.[16] This dictum is entirely correct in its application to the earth, but entirely false in Tlön. The nations of this planet are congenitally idealist. Their language and the derivations of their language—religion, letters, metaphysics—all presuppose idealism. The world for them is not a concourse of objects in space; it is a heterogeneous series of independent acts. It is successive and temporal, not spatial. There are no nouns in Tlön's conjectural *Ursprache*,[17] from which the "present" languages and the dialects are derived: there are impersonal verbs, modified by monosyllabic suffixes (or prefixes) with an adverbial value. For example: there is no word corresponding to the word "moon," but there is a verb which in English would be "to moon" or "to moonate." "The moon rose above the river" is *hlör u fang axaxaxas mlö*, or literally: "upward behind the on-streaming it mooned."

The preceding applies to the languages of the southern hemisphere. In those of the northern hemisphere (on whose *Ursprache* there is very little data in the Eleventh Volume) the prime unit is not the verb, but the monosyllabic adjective. The noun is formed by an accumulation of adjectives.

[14] "By the claw of the lion" (Latin). The full saying is "By the claw of the lion we know him," that is, the part implies the whole.

[15] Gottfried Wilhelm Leibniz, seventeenth-century German mathematician and philosopher, invented the infinitesimal calculus. The English mathematician Sir Isaac Newton invented it independently at about the same time.

[16] The British idealist philosopher Bishop George Berkeley (1685–1753) argued that matter does not exist apart from its being perceived and that objects have a continuing existence only because they are continually observed by God. His theories were attacked by the Scottish skeptical philosopher David Hume (1711–1776).

[17] Original language (German).

They do not say "moon," but rather "round airy-light on dark" or "pale-orange-of-the-sky" or any other such combination. In the example selected the mass of adjectives refers to a real object, but this is purely fortuitous. The literature of this hemisphere (like Meinong's[18] subsistent world) abounds in ideal objects, which are convoked and dissolved in a moment, according to poetic needs. At times they are determined by mere simultaneity. There are objects composed of two terms, one of visual and another of auditory character: the color of the rising sun and the faraway cry of a bird. There are objects of many terms: the sun and the water on a swimmer's chest, the vague tremulous rose color we see with our eyes closed, the sensation of being carried along by a river and also by sleep. These second-degree objects can be combined with others; through the use of certain abbreviations, the process is practically infinite. There are famous poems made up of one enormous word. This word forms a *poetic object* created by the author. The fact that no one believes in the reality of nouns paradoxically causes their number to be unending. The languages of Tlön's northern hemisphere contain all the nouns of the Indo-European languages—and many others as well.

It is no exaggeration to state that the classic culture of Tlön comprises only one discipline: psychology. All others are subordinated to it. I have said that the men of this planet conceive the universe as a series of mental processes which do not develop in space but successively in time. Spinoza[19] ascribes to his inexhaustible divinity the attributes of extension and thought; no one in Tlön would understand the juxtaposition of the first (which is typical only of certain states) and the second—which is a perfect synonym of the cosmos. In other words, they do not conceive that the spatial persists in time. The perception of a cloud of smoke on the horizon and then of the burning field and then of the half-extinguished cigarette that produced the blaze is considered an example of association of ideas.

This monism or complete idealism invalidates all science. If we explain (or judge) a fact, we connect it with another; such linking, in Tlön, is a later state of the subject which cannot affect or illuminate the previous state. Every mental state is irreducible: the mere fact of naming it—i.e., of classifying it—implies a falsification. From which it can be deduced that there are no sciences on Tlön, not even reasoning. The paradoxical truth is that they do exist, and in almost uncountable number. The same thing happens with philosophies as happens with nouns in the northern hemisphere. The fact that every philosophy is by definition a dialectical game, a *Philosophie des Als Ob*,[20] has caused them to multiply. There is an abundance of incredible systems of pleasing design or sensational type. The metaphysicians of Tlön do not seek for the truth or even for verisimilitude, but rather for the astounding. They judge that metaphysics is a branch of fantastic literature. They know that a system is nothing more than the subordination of all aspects of the universe to any one such aspect. Even the phrase "all aspects"

[18] Alexius Meinong (1853–1920), Austrian philosopher and psychologist.
[19] The Dutch Jewish philosopher Baruch Spinoza (1632–1677) argued that all existence is embraced in one substance—God.
[20] A "philosophy of 'as if' " (German).

is rejectable, for it supposes the impossible addition of the present and of all past moments. Neither is it licit to use the plural "past moments," since it supposes another impossible operation . . . One of the schools of Tlön goes so far as to negate time: it reasons that the present is indefinite, that the future has no reality other than as a present hope, that the past has no reality other than as a present memory.[21] Another school declares that *all time* has already transpired and that our life is only the crepuscular and no doubt falsified and mutilated memory or reflection of an irrecoverable process. Another, that the history of the universe—and in it our lives and the most tenuous detail of our lives—is the scripture produced by a subordinate god in order to communicate with a demon.[22] Another, that the universe is comparable to those cryptographs in which not all the symbols are valid and that only what happens every three hundred nights is true. Another, that while we sleep here, we are awake elsewhere and that in this way every man is two men.

Amongst the doctrines of Tlön, none has merited the scandalous reception accorded to materialism. Some thinkers have formulated it with less clarity than fervor, as one might put forth a paradox. In order to facilitate the comprehension of this inconceivable thesis, a heresiarch of the eleventh century[23] devised the sophism of the nine copper coins, whose scandalous renown is in Tlön equivalent to that of the Eleatic paradoxes.[24] There are many versions of this "specious reasoning," which vary the number of coins and the number of discoveries; the following is the most common:

On Tuesday, X crosses a deserted road and loses nine copper coins. On Thursday, Y finds in the road four coins, somewhat rusted by Wednesday's rain. On Friday, Z discovers three coins in the road. On Friday morning, X finds two coins in the corridor of his house. The heresiarch would deduce from this story the reality—i.e., the continuity—of the nine coins which were recovered. *It is absurd* (he affirmed) *to imagine that four of the coins have not existed between Tuesday and Thursday, three between Tuesday and Friday afternoon, two between Tuesday and Friday morning. It is logical to think that they have existed—at least in some secret way, hidden from the comprehension of men—at every moment of those three periods.*

The language of Tlön resists the formulation of this paradox; most people did not even understand it. The defenders of common sense at first did no more than negate the veracity of the anecdote. They repeated that it was a verbal fallacy, based on the rash application of two neologisms not authorized by usage and alien to all rigorous thought: the verbs "find" and

[21] "Russell (*The Analysis of Mind*, 1921, page 159) supposes that the planet has been created a few minutes ago, furnished with a humanity that 'remembers' an illusory past" (Borges' note). The book is by the English mathematician and philosopher Bertrand Russell (1872–1970).

[22] Borges is alluding to Gnosticism, a second-century A.D. religious movement that stressed knowledge rather than faith as the key to salvation and postulated a number of gods, some of them evil. The early Christians declared it a heresy. Borges wrote extensively on Gnosticism, especially in his essay "A Vindication of the False Basílides" in *Other Inquisitions* (1952).

[23] "A century, according to the duodecimal system, signifies a period of a hundred and forty-four years" (Borges' note).

[24] A series of paradoxes proposed by the fifth-century B.C. Greek philosopher Zeno, of the Eleatic school.

"lose," which beg the question, because they presuppose the identity of the first and of the last nine coins. They recalled that all nouns (man, coin, Thursday, Wednesday, rain) have only a metaphorical value. They denounced the treacherous circumstance "somewhat rusted by Wednesday's rain," which presupposes what is trying to be demonstrated: the persistence of the four coins from Tuesday to Thursday. They explained that *equality* is one thing and *identity* another, and formulated a kind of *reductio ad absurdum*:[25] the hypothetical case of nine men who on nine successive nights suffer a severe pain. Would it not be ridiculous—they questioned—to pretend that this pain is one and the same?[26] They said that the heresiarch was prompted only by the blasphemous intention of attributing the divine category of *being* to some simple coins and that at times he negated plurality and at other times did not. They argued: if equality implies identity, one would also have to admit that the nine coins are one.

Unbelievably, these refutations were not definitive. A hundred years after the problem was stated, a thinker no less brilliant than the heresiarch but of orthodox tradition formulated a very daring hypothesis. This happy conjecture affirmed that there is only one subject, that this indivisible subject is every being in the universe and that these beings are the organs and masks of the divinity. X is Y and is Z. Z discovers three coins because he remembers that X lost them; X finds two in the corridor because he remembers that the others have been found . . . The Eleventh Volume suggests that three prime reasons determined the complete victory of this idealist pantheism. The first, its repudiation of solipsism;[27] the second, the possibility of preserving the psychological basis of the sciences; the third, the possibility of preserving the cult of the gods. Schopenhauer[28] (the passionate and lucid Schopenhauer) formulates a very similar doctrine in the first volume of *Parerga und Paralipomena*.

The geometry of Tlön comprises two somewhat different disciplines: the visual and the tactile. The latter corresponds to our own geometry and is subordinated to the first. The basis of visual geometry is the surface, not the point. This geometry disregards parallel lines and declares that man in his movement modifies the forms which surround him. The basis of its arithmetic is the notion of indefinite numbers. They emphasize the importance of the concepts of greater and lesser, which our mathematicians symbolize as * and †. They maintain that the operation of counting modifies quantities and converts them from indefinite into definite sums. The fact that several individuals who count the same quantity should obtain the same result is, for the psychologists, an example of association of ideas or of a good exercise of memory. We already know that in Tlön the subject of knowledge is one and eternal.

[25] "Reduction to absurdity" (Latin), a way of disproving a proposition by showing that an absurdity results if it is pushed to its logical conclusion.

[26] "Today, one of the churches of Tlön Platonically maintains that a certain pain, a certain greenish tint of yellow, a certain temperature, a certain sound, are the only reality. All men, in the vertiginous moment of coitus, are the same man. All men who repeat a line from Shakespeare *are* William Shakespeare" (Borges' note).

[27] The theory that the self is the only thing that exists and that it can know only itself.

[28] Arthur Schopenhauer (1788–1869), German philosopher. The work referred to is a collection of essays on various topics published in 1851.

In literary practices the idea of a single subject is also all-powerful. It is uncommon for books to be signed. The concept of plagiarism does not exist: it has been established that all works are the creation of one author, who is atemporal and anonymous. The critics often invent authors: they select two dissimilar works—the *Tao Te Ching* and the *1001 Nights*, say—attribute them to the same writer and then determine most scrupulously the psychology of this interesting *homme de lettres* . . .[29]

Their books are also different. Works of fiction contain a single plot, with all its imaginable permutations. Those of a philosophical nature invariably include both the thesis and the antithesis, the rigorous pro and con of a doctrine. A book which does not contain its counterbook is considered incomplete.

Centuries and centuries of idealism have not failed to influence reality. In the most ancient regions of Tlön, the duplication of lost objects is not infrequent. Two persons look for a pencil; the first finds it and says nothing; the second finds a second pencil, no less real, but closer to his expectations. These secondary objects are called *hrönir* and are, though awkward in form, somewhat longer. Until recently, the *hrönir* were the accidental products of distraction and forgetfulness. It seems unbelievable that their methodical production dates back scarcely a hundred years, but this is what the Eleventh Volume tells us. The first efforts were unsuccessful. However, the *modus operandi*[30] merits description. The director of one of the state prisons told his inmates that there were certain tombs in an ancient river bed and promised freedom to whoever might make an important discovery. During the months preceding the excavation the inmates were shown photographs of what they were to find. This first effort proved that expectation and anxiety can be inhibitory; a week's work with pick and shovel did not manage to unearth anything in the way of a *hrön* except a rusty wheel of a period posterior to the experiment. But this was kept in secret and the process was repeated later in four schools. In three of them the failure was almost complete; in the fourth (whose director died accidentally during the first excavations) the students unearthed—or produced—a gold mask, an archaic sword, two or three clay urns and the moldy and mutilated torso of a king whose chest bore an inscription which it has not yet been possible to decipher. Thus was discovered the unreliability of witnesses who knew of the experimental nature of the search . . . Mass investigations produce contradictory objects; now individual and almost improvised jobs are preferred. The methodical fabrication of *hrönir* (says the Eleventh Volume) has performed prodigious services for archaeologists. It has made possible the interrogation and even the modification of the past, which is now no less plastic and docile than the future. Curiously, the *hrönir* of second and third degree—the *hrönir* derived from another *hrön*, those derived from the *hrön* of a *hrön*—exaggerate the aberrations of the initial one; those of fifth degree are almost uniform; those of ninth degree become confused with those of the second; in those of the eleventh there is a purity of line not found in the original. The process is cyclical: the *hrön* of twelfth degree begins to fall off in quality. Stranger and more pure than any *hrön* is, at

[29] Man of letters (French). [30] "Mode of operating" (Latin); procedure.

times, the *ur:* the object produced through suggestion, educed by hope. The great golden mask I have mentioned is an illustrious example.

Things become duplicated in Tlön; they also tend to become effaced and lose their details when they are forgotten. A classic example is the doorway which survived so long as it was visited by a beggar and disappeared at his death. At times some birds, a horse, have saved the ruins of an amphitheater.

Postscript (1947). I reproduce the preceding article just as it appeared in the *Anthology of Fantastic Literature* (1940), with no omission other than that of a few metaphors and a kind of sarcastic summary which now seems frivolous. So many things have happened since then . . . I shall do no more than recall them here.

In March of 1941 a letter written by Gunnar Erfjord was discovered in a book by Hinton which had belonged to Herbert Ashe. The envelope bore a cancellation from Ouro Preto; the letter completely elucidated the mystery of Tlön. Its text corroborated the hypotheses of Martínez Estrada. One night in Lucerne or in London, in the early seventeenth century, the splendid history has its beginning. A secret and benevolent society (amongst whose members were Dalgarno and later George Berkeley)[31] arose to invent a country. Its vague initial program included "hermetic studies," philanthropy and the cabala.[32] From this first period dates the curious book by Andreä. After a few years of secret conclaves and premature syntheses it was understood that one generation was not sufficient to give articulate form to a country. They resolved that each of the masters should elect a disciple who would continue his work. This hereditary arrangement prevailed; after an interval of two centuries the persecuted fraternity sprang up again in America. In 1824, in Memphis (Tennessee), one of its affiliates conferred with the ascetic millionaire Ezra Buckley. The latter, somewhat disdainfully, let him speak—and laughed at the plan's modest scope. He told the agent that in America it was absurd to invent a country and proposed the invention of a planet. To this gigantic idea he added another, a product of his nihilism:[33] that of keeping the enormous enterprise secret. At that time the twenty volumes of the *Encyclopaedia Britannica* were circulating in the United States; Buckley suggested that a methodical encyclopedia of the imaginary planet be written. He was to leave them his mountains of gold, his navigable rivers, his pasture lands roamed by cattle and buffalo, his Negroes, his brothels and his dollars, on one condition: "The work will make no pact with the impostor Jesus Christ." Buckley did not believe in God, but he wanted to demonstrate to this nonexistent God that mortal man was capable of conceiving a world. Buckley was poisoned in Baton Rouge in 1828; in 1914 the society delivered to its collaborators, some three hundred in number, the last volume of the First

[31] George Dalgarno (1626?–1687) was a Scottish educator who developed a system of teaching the deaf and attempted to develop a universal writing system independent of particular languages. For Berkeley, see note 16.
[32] A Jewish mystical system that views creation as taking place through "emanation" or radiations from the Godhead and interprets the Scriptures through numerological ciphers.
[33] "Buckley was a freethinker, a fatalist and a defender of slavery" (Borges' note). Nihilism is a doctrine that denies any objective basis for truth.

Encyclopedia of Tlön. The edition was a secret one; its forty volumes (the vastest undertaking ever carried out by man) would be the basis for another more detailed edition, written not in English but in one of the languages of Tlön. This revision of an illusory world, was called, provisionally, *Orbis Tertius*[34] and one of its modest demiurgi[35] was Herbert Ashe, whether as an agent of Gunnar Erfjord or as an affiliate, I do not know. His having received a copy of the Eleventh Volume would seem to favor the latter assumption. But what about the others?

In 1942 events became more intense. I recall one of the first of these with particular clarity and it seems that I perceived then something of its premonitory character. It happened in an apartment on Laprida Street, facing a high and light balcony which looked out toward the sunset. Princess Faucigny Lucinge had received her silverware from Poitiers. From the vast depths of a box embellished with foreign stamps, delicate immobile objects emerged: silver from Utrecht and Paris covered with hard heraldic fauna, and a samovar. Amongst them—with the perceptible and tenuous tremor of a sleeping bird—a compass vibrated mysteriously. The Princess did not recognize it. Its blue needle longed for magnetic north; its metal case was concave in shape; the letters around its edge corresponded to one of the alphabets of Tlön. Such was the first intrusion of this fantastic world into the world of reality.

I am still troubled by a stroke of chance which made me the witness of the second intrusion as well. It happened some months later, at a country store owned by a Brazilian in Cuchilla Negra. Amorim[36] and I were returning from Sant' Anna. The River Tacuarembó had flooded and we were obliged to sample (and endure) the proprietor's rudimentary hospitality. He provided us with some creaking cots in a large room cluttered with barrels and hides. We went to bed, but were kept from sleeping until dawn by the drunken ravings of an unseen neighbor, who intermingled inexplicable insults with snatches of *milongas*[37]—or rather with snatches of the same *milonga*. As might be supposed, we attributed this insistent uproar to the store owner's fiery cane liquor. By daybreak, the man was dead in the hallway. The roughness of his voice had deceived us: he was only a youth. In his delirium a few coins had fallen from his belt, along with a cone of bright metal, the size of a die. In vain a boy tried to pick up this cone. A man was scarcely able to raise it from the ground. I held it in my hand for a few minutes; I remember that its weight was intolerable and that after it was removed, the feeling of oppressiveness remained. I also remember the exact circle it pressed into my palm. This sensation of a very small and at the same time extremely heavy object produced a disagreeable impression of repugnance and fear. One of the local men suggested we throw it into the swollen river; Amorim acquired it for a few pesos. No one knew anything about the dead man, except that "he came from the border." These small, very heavy cones (made from a metal which is not of this world) are images of the divinity in certain regions of Tlön.

[34]"Third World" (Latin).
[35]Minor gods who create the material world, in Gnostic thought.
[36]Enrique Amorim (1900–1960), Uruguayan novelist. [37]Dance tunes.

Here I bring the personal part of my narrative to a close. The rest is in the memory (if not in the hopes or fears) of all my readers. Let it suffice for me to recall or mention the following facts, with a mere brevity of words which the reflective recollection of all will enrich or amplify. Around 1944, a person doing research for the newspaper *The American* (of Nashville, Tennessee) brought to light in a Memphis library the forty volumes of the First Encyclopedia of Tlön. Even today there is a controversy over whether this discovery was accidental or whether it was permitted by the directors of the still nebulous *Orbis Tertius*. The latter is most likely. Some of the incredible aspects of the Eleventh Volume (for example, the multiplication of the *hrönir*) have been eliminated or attenuated in the Memphis copies; it is reasonable to imagine that these omissions follow the plan of exhibiting a world which is not too incompatible with the real world. The dissemination of objects from Tlön over different countries would complement this plan[38]. . . . The fact is that the international press infinitely proclaimed the "find." Manuals, anthologies, summaries, literal versions, authorized re-editions and pirated editions of the Greatest Work of Man flooded and still flood the earth. Almost immediately, reality yielded on more than one account. The truth is that it longed to yield. Ten years ago any symmetry with a semblance of order—dialectical materialism, anti-Semitism, Nazism—was sufficient to entrance the minds of men. How could one do other than submit to Tlön, to the minute and vast evidence of an orderly planet? It is useless to answer that reality is also orderly. Perhaps it is, but in accordance with divine laws—I translate: inhuman laws—which we never quite grasp. Tlön is surely a labyrinth, but it is a labyrinth devised by men, a labyrinth destined to be deciphered by men.

The contact and the habit of Tlön have disintegrated this world. Enchanted by its rigor, humanity forgets over and again that it is a rigor of chess masters, not of angels. Already the schools have been invaded by the (conjectural) "primitive language" of Tlön; already the teaching of its harmonious history (filled with moving episodes) has wiped out the one which governed in my childhood; already a fictitious past occupies in our memories the place of another, a past of which we know nothing with certainty—not even that it is false. Numismatology,[39] pharmacology and archaeology have been reformed. I understand that biology and mathematics also await their avatars[40] . . . A scattered dynasty of solitary men has changed the face of the world. Their task continues. If our forecasts are not in error, a hundred years from now someone will discover the hundred volumes of the Second Encyclopedia of Tlön.

Then English and French and mere Spanish will disappear from the globe. The world will be Tlön. I pay no attention to all this and go on revising, in the still days at the Adrogué hotel, an uncertain Quevedian translation (which I do not intend to publish) of Browne's *Urn Burial*.[41]

[38] "There remains, of course, the problem of the *material* of some objects" (Borges' note).
[39] The study of coins. [40] Variant versions.
[41] An eccentric meditative work by the English writer Sir Thomas Browne (1605–1682).

THE CIRCULAR RUINS

Translated by Norman Thomas di Giovanni
in collaboration with the author

And if he left off dreaming about you. . . .
—THROUGH THE LOOKING-GLASS, *IV*

Nobody saw him come ashore in the encompassing night, nobody saw the bamboo craft run aground in the sacred mud, but within a few days everyone knew that the quiet man had come from the south and that his home was among the numberless villages upstream on the steep slopes of the mountain, where the Zend[1] language is barely tainted by Greek and where lepers are rare. The fact is that the gray man pressed his lips to the mud, scrambled up the bank without parting (perhaps without feeling) the brushy thorns that tore his flesh, and dragged himself, faint and bleeding, to the circular opening watched over by a stone tiger, or horse, which once was the color of fire and is now the color of ash. This opening is a temple which was destroyed ages ago by flames, which the swampy wilderness later desecrated, and whose god no longer receives the reverence of men. The stranger laid himself down at the foot of the image.

Wakened by the sun high overhead, he noticed—somehow without amazement—that his wounds had healed. He shut his pale eyes and slept again, not because of weariness but because he willed it. He knew that this temple was the place he needed for his unswerving purpose; he knew that downstream the encroaching trees had also failed to choke the ruins of another auspicious temple with its own fire-ravaged, dead gods; he knew that his first duty was to sleep. Along about midnight, he was awakened by the forlorn call of a bird. Footprints, some figs, and a water jug told him that men who lived nearby had looked on his sleep with a kind of awe and either sought his protection or else were in dread of his witchcraft. He felt the chill of fear and searched the crumbling walls for a burial niche, where he covered himself over with leaves he had never seen before.

His guiding purpose, though it was supernatural, was not impossible. He wanted to dream a man; he wanted to dream him down to the last detail and project him into the world of reality. This mystical aim had taxed the whole range of his mind. Had anyone asked him his own name or anything about his life before then, he would not have known what to answer. This forsaken, broken temple suited him because it held few visible things, and also because the neighboring villagers would look after his frugal needs. The rice and fruit of their offerings were nourishment enough for his body, whose one task was to sleep and to dream.

At the outset, his dreams were chaotic; later on, they were of a dialectic nature. The stranger dreamed himself at the center of a circular amphitheater which in some way was also the burnt-out temple. Crowds of silent

[1]There is no such language, but the name suggests the *Zend Avesta*, the scripture of Zoroastrianism, a religion originating in Persia in the sixth century B.C. and predicating a dualistic world dominated by the struggle between gods of goodness and gods of evil.

disciples exhausted the tiers of seats; the faces of the farthest of them hung centuries away from him and at a height of the stars, but their features were clear and exact. The man lectured on anatomy, cosmography, and witchcraft. The faces listened, bright and eager, and did their best to answer sensibly, as if they felt the importance of his questions, which would raise one of them out of an existence as a shadow and place him in the real world. Whether asleep or awake, the man pondered the answers of his phantoms and, not letting himself be misled by impostors, divined in certain of their quandaries a growing intelligence. He was in search of a soul worthy of taking a place in the world.

After nine or ten nights he realized, feeling bitter over it, that nothing could be expected from those pupils who passively accepted his teaching but that he might, however, hold hopes for those who from time to time hazarded reasonable doubts about what he taught. The former, although they deserved love and affection, could never become real; the latter, in their dim way, were already real. One evening (now his evenings were also given over to sleeping, now he was only awake for an hour or two at dawn) he dismissed his vast dream-school forever and kept a single disciple. He was a quiet, sallow, and at times rebellious young man with sharp features akin to those of his dreamer. The sudden disappearance of his fellow pupils did not disturb him for very long, and his progress, at the end of a few private lessons, amazed his teacher. Nonetheless, a catastrophe intervened. One morning, the man emerged from his sleep as from a sticky wasteland, glanced up at the faint evening light, which at first he confused with the dawn, and realized that he had not been dreaming. All that night and the next day, the hideous lucidity of insomnia weighed down on him. To tire himself out he tried to explore the surrounding forest, but all he managed, there in a thicket of hemlocks, were some snatches of broken sleep, fleetingly tinged with visions of a crude and worthless nature. He tried to reassemble his school, and barely had he uttered a few brief words of counsel when the whole class went awry and vanished. In his almost endless wakefulness, tears of anger stung his old eyes.

He realized that, though he may penetrate all the riddles of the higher and lower orders, the task of shaping the senseless and dizzying stuff of dreams is the hardest that a man can attempt—much harder than weaving a rope of sand or of coining the faceless wind. He realized that an initial failure was to be expected. He then swore he would forget the populous vision which in the beginning had led him astray, and he sought another method. Before attempting it, he spent a month rebuilding the strength his fever had consumed. He gave up all thoughts of dreaming and almost at once managed to sleep a reasonable part of the day. The few times he dreamed during this period he did not dwell on his dreams. Before taking up his task again, he waited until the moon was a perfect circle. Then, in the evening, he cleansed himself in the waters of the river, worshiped the gods of the planets, uttered the prescribed syllables of an all-powerful name, and slept. Almost at once, he had a dream of a beating heart.

He dreamed it throbbing, warm, secret. It was the size of a closed fist, a darkish red in the dimness of a human body still without a face or sex. With anxious love he dreamed it for fourteen lucid nights. Each night he perceived it more clearly. He did not touch it, but limited himself to witnessing

it, to observing it, to correcting it now and then with a look. He felt it, he lived it from different distances and from many angles. On the fourteenth night he touched the pulmonary artery with a finger and then the whole heart, inside and out. The examination satisfied him. For one night he deliberately did not dream; after that he went back to the heart again, invoked the name of a planet, and set out to envision another of the principal organs. Before a year was over he came to the skeleton, the eyelids. The countless strands of hair were perhaps the hardest task of all. He dreamed a whole man, a young man, but the young man could not stand up or speak, nor could he open his eyes. Night after night, the man dreamed him asleep.

In the cosmogonies of the Gnostics,[2] the demiurges mold a red Adam who is unable to stand on his feet; as clumsy and crude and elementary as that Adam of dust was the Adam of dreams wrought by the nights of the magician. One evening the man was at the point of destroying all his handiwork (it would have been better for him had he done so), but in the end he restrained himself. Having exhausted his prayers to the gods of the earth and river, he threw himself down at the feet of the stone image that may have been a tiger or a stallion, and asked for its blind aid. That same evening he dreamed of the image. He dreamed it alive, quivering; it was no unnatural cross between tiger and stallion but at one and the same time both these violent creatures and also a bull, a rose, a thunderstorm. This manifold god revealed to him that its earthly name was Fire, that there in the circular temple (and in others like it) sacrifices had once been made to it, that it had been worshiped, and that through its magic the phantom of the man's dreams would be wakened to life in such a way that—except for Fire itself and the dreamer—every being in the world would accept him as a man of flesh and blood. The god ordered that, once instructed in the rites, the disciple should be sent downstream to the other ruined temple, whose pyramids still survived, so that in that abandoned place some human voice might exalt him. In the dreamer's dream, the dreamed one awoke.

The magician carried out these orders. He devoted a period of time (which finally spanned two years) to initiating his disciple into the riddles of the universe and the worship of Fire. Deep inside, it pained him to say goodbye to his creature. Under the pretext of teaching him more fully, each day he drew out the hours set aside for sleep. Also, he reshaped the somewhat faulty right shoulder. From time to time, he was troubled by the feeling that all this had already happened, but for the most part his days were happy. On closing his eyes he would think, "Now I will be with my son." Or, less frequently, "The son I have begotten awaits me and he will not exist if I do not go to him."

Little by little, he was training the young man for reality. On one occasion he commanded him to set up a flag on a distant peak. The next day, there on the peak, a fiery pennant shone. He tried other, similar exercises, each bolder than the one before. He realized with a certain bitterness that

[2] According to the doctrines of the second-century A.D. Gnostics, there was a hierarchy of 365 worlds, each identical with the one above it and each ruled by a "demiurge." The lowest world is our own, and its demiurge, our God, created man and the rest of the material world. See also "Tlön, Uqbar, Orbis Tertius," note 22.

his son was ready—and perhaps impatient—to be born. That night he kissed him for the first time and sent him down the river to the other temple, whose whitened ruins were still to be glimpsed over miles and miles of impenetrable forest and swamp. At the very end (so that the boy would never know he was a phantom, so that he would think himself a man like all men), the magician imbued with total oblivion his disciple's long years of apprenticeship.

His triumph and his peace were blemished by a touch of weariness. In the morning and evening dusk, he prostrated himself before the stone idol, perhaps imagining that his unreal son was performing the same rites farther down the river in other circular ruins. At night he no longer dreamed, or else he dreamed the way all men dream. He now perceived with a certain vagueness the sounds and shapes of the world, for his absent son was taking nourishment from the magician's decreasing consciousness. His life's purpose was fulfilled; the man lived on in a kind of ecstasy. After a length of time that certain tellers of the story count in years and others in half-decades, he was awakened one midnight by two rowers. He could not see their faces, but they spoke to him about a magic man in a temple up north who walked on fire without being burned. The magician suddenly remembered the god's words. He remembered that of all the creatures in the world, Fire was the only one who knew his son was a phantom. This recollection, comforting at first, ended by tormenting him. He feared that his son might wonder at this strange privilege and in some way discover his condition as a mere appearance. Not to be a man but to be the projection of another man's dreams—what an unparalleled humiliation, how bewildering! Every father cares for the child he has begotten—he has allowed—in some moment of confusion or happiness. It is understandable, then, that the magician should fear for the future of a son thought out organ by organ and feature by feature over the course of a thousand and one secret nights.

The end of these anxieties came suddenly, but certain signs foretold it. First (after a long drought), a far-off cloud on a hilltop, as light as a bird; next, toward the south, the sky, which took on the rosy hue of a leopard's gums; then, the pillars of smoke that turned the metal of the nights to rust; finally, the headlong panic of the forest animals. For what had happened many centuries ago was happening again. The ruins of the fire god's shrine were destroyed by fire. In a birdless dawn the magician saw the circling sheets of flame closing in on him. For a moment, he thought of taking refuge in the river, but then he realized that death was coming to crown his years and to release him from his labors. He walked into the leaping pennants of flame. They did not bite into his flesh, but caressed him and flooded him without heat or burning. In relief, in humiliation, in terror, he understood that he, too, was an appearance, that someone else was dreaming him.

Samuel Beckett
(1906–1989)

When the Nobel committee awarded its prize to Samuel Beckett in 1969, part of its citation read, "In the realm of annihilation, the writing of Samuel Beckett rises like a miserere from all mankind, its muffled minor key sounding liberation to the oppressed and comfort to those in need." "Liberation" and "comfort" are not words that occur to most first readers of Beckett's spare, bleak stories and plays, but the further one travels in Beckett's strange world, the more just the committee's emphasis seems. The liberation and comfort did not come easily for Beckett; much of his work was devoted to stripping away the superficial reassurances—material possessions, social status, ideologies—by which most of us arrive at a more or less uneasy accommodation with existence. But when, the stripping done, we arrive at Beckett's unblinking vision of the core human condition, there is comfort. Tragedy and comedy converge, as they do for Yeats, with "gaiety transfiguring all that dread."

Beckett was born in 1906 at Foxrock, just outside Dublin, of Protestant, Anglo-Irish parents. He attended a good private school, Portora Royal School, in what later became Northern Ireland and then earned a bachelor's degree in Romance languages at Trinity College, Dublin. Having settled, he thought, upon an academic career, he became a lecturer in English at the École Normale Supérieure in Paris when he was twenty-two. In Paris, he met a number of avant-garde artists, among them James Joyce, who became a close friend. After two years, he returned to Dublin and a post as lecturer in French at Trinity, but resigned after two more years and decided to become a writer. For the next five years, he traveled restlessly around Europe, finally settling in 1937 in Paris. A volume of short stories, *More Pricks than Kicks*, appeared in 1934 and his first novel, *Murphy*, in 1938.

When war broke out, Beckett remained in Paris and joined the French Underground. In 1942, learning that members of his group, "Gloria S.M.H.," had been arrested by the Nazis, he fled Paris for the unoccupied zone of France. He spent the rest of the war working as a farm laborer near Roussillon, in southeast France, and completing a second novel, *Watt*, not published until 1953.

When Beckett returned to Paris after the war, he plunged into an extraordinarily intensive four-year period of writing, between 1946 and 1950, during which he produced most of his major works. These included, in addition to a number of short stories, the trilogy of unconventional novels *Molloy, Malone Dies*, and *The Unnamable* and the play *Waiting for Godot*. All of these works were written in French, because, Beckett explained, "in French, it is easier to write without style"; he himself later translated them into English. None of them was published until Beckett's wife (a pianist and a member of his Resistance group) finally persuaded a publisher to issue *Molloy* and *Malone Dies* (both in 1951) and *The Unnamable* (1953). International fame, however, did not come until the famous production in 1953 of *Waiting for Godot* at the tiny Théâtre de Babylone in Paris. The play ran for

more than a year, to baffled but intrigued audiences, and soon found pro-
ducers in London and New York.

Beckett commented, "I wrote all my work very fast—between 1946 and
1950. Since then I haven't written anything. Or at least nothing that has
seemed to me valid." This seems to be a bit of Beckettian ironic self-depre-
cation, for he kept up a steady output of works which, whether "valid" or
not in whatever sense he had in mind, represented a logical development
of the implications of the great works of the 1940's. Some of the later pieces
reworked earlier ones, but many of them were fresh work that moved in
the direction of greater and greater compression and economy, perhaps in
the direction of the silence that seemed to be Beckett's ultimate ideal. Post-
1950 fiction includes *Stories and Texts for Nothing* (1955), which contains
stories written in the 1940's; *How It Is* (1960), regarded by some as Beckett's
finest fictional work; *The Lost Ones* (1966), an evocation of a purgatory-like
world reminiscent of both Dante and science fiction; *Lessness* (1969), a five-
page lyrical monologue; and *Company* (1980), a short, lyrical prose piece.
His plays after *Waiting for Godot* followed a similar course of reduction and
compression: *Endgame* (1956), perhaps Beckett's greatest play; *All That Fall*
(1956), one of a number of plays Beckett wrote for radio; *Krapp's Last Tape*
(1958); *Happy Days* (1961); *Play* (1962); *Film* (1963), a one-character
filmscript written for Buster Keaton; *Eh Joe* (1965), a play for television;
Not I (1972) and *That Time* (1975), both brief plays for one actor; *Rockaby*
(1981); *Disjecta, Ohio Impromptu, Catastrophe,* and *What Where* (all 1984).

The paradox of Beckett's work is its uniting of great philosophical so-
phistication and immediate, visceral appeal. Beckett dissociated himself
from the post-war French existentialists, but his work deals with the same
fundamental questions of individual Being, taken as antecedent to more
elaborate systems of meaning. What does it mean to say "I"? When I at-
tempt to define myself, how can I unite the "I" who defines with the "I"
being defined? How can I live my life meaningfully in the face of the
absurd fact of my mortality?

Such questions define the area Beckett seemed to refer to when he said,
"My little exploration is the whole zone of being that has always been set
aside by artists as something unusable—as something by definition incom-
patible with art." He carried out his exploration with a full consciousness of
the work of philosophers who have dealt with this "zone of being," preemi-
nently the seventeenth-century French philosopher René Descartes and his
little-known Dutch disciple Arnold Geulincx.

But Beckett was a writer rather than a philosopher, and a comic writer
at that. His triumph was not his contributions to ontology but his resonant,
heartbreaking metaphors for existence—an old man writing as he dies, two
tramps waiting by the side of the road, a woman sinking slowly into the
ground—and his mastery of dramatic monologue. The vision on the jetty
that the thirty-nine-year-old, tape-recorded Krapp reports echoes a similar
experience Beckett had at the same age on a pier in Dublin harbor when he
realized that dramatic monologue was the natural form for his work to
take. Beckett's greatest works, in both fiction and drama, are flowing,
stream-of-consciousness monologues in which particular characters and
events seem to swim up out of the stream briefly and then sink back in.
Even Didi and Gogo in *Waiting for Godot* or Hamm and Clov in *Endgame*

seem to be splittings of a single mind talking to itself. And the great *Trilogy* consists of a receding series of talkers who drop away until we arrive at the last monologist, the Unnamable, the voice of existence itself condemned to go on talking forever.

Krapp's Last Tape is a small masterpiece of Beckett's complex art. Krapp, like most of Beckett's protagonists, is basically a clown, and his routines with his keys, his bananas, and his bottle are broad music-hall gags. But the play is a metaphysical clown show: "Pascal's *Pensées* as played by the Fratel-lini clowns," in the words of the playwright Jean Anouilh about *Waiting for Godot.* The tape-recorder is used for all the slapstick comedy Beckett can get out of it, but it also becomes, with Krapp's bank of autobiographical tapes, a plangent metaphor for the time-cursed pathos of human existence.

FURTHER READING *(prepared by J. H.):* Deirdre Bair's massive biography *Samuel Beckett,* 1978, while perhaps premature, offers a wealth of information on Beckett's life and some rather dubious interpretations of its relevance to his work. Hugh Kenner has been a fine interpreter of Beckett over a long period; his *Samuel Beckett: A Critical Study,* 1962, rev. 1968; and *Reader's Guide to Samuel Beckett,* 1973, are still valuable, though they necessarily omit the later work. Ronald Hayman's *Samuel Beckett,* 3rd ed. 1980, is a good general introduction, as is Charles R. Lyons' *Samuel Beckett,* 1983, a volume in the Grove Press Modern Dramatists series. Beryl S. and John Fletcher's *A Student Guide to the Plays of Samuel Beckett,* rev. ed. 1985, is useful on a rather elementary level. Good collections of essays include *Samuel Beckett: Humanistic Perspectives,* ed. by Morris Beja, S. E. Gontarski, and Pierre Astier, 1983; *Beckett at 80 / Beckett in Context,* ed. by Enoch Brater, 1986; and *On Beckett: Essays and Criticism,* ed. by S. E. Gontarski, 1986. The Brater volume contains an excellent essay by Andrew Kenney on *Krapp's Last Tape.*

KRAPP'S LAST TAPE

A PLAY IN ONE ACT

A late evening in the future.

KRAPP'*s den.*

Front centre a small table, the two drawers of which open towards audience.

Sitting at the table, facing front, i.e. across from the drawers, a wearish[1] old man: KRAPP.

Rusty black narrow trousers too short for him. Rusty black sleeveless waistcoat, four capacious pockets. Heavy silver watch and chain. Grimy white shirt open at neck, no collar. Surprising pair of dirty white boots, size ten at least, very narrow and pointed.

White face. Purple nose. Disordered grey hair. Unshaven.

Very near-sighted (but unspectacled). Hard of hearing.

Cracked voice. Distinctive intonation.

[1] Lean, wizened.

Laborious walk.

On the table a tape-recorder with microphone and a number of cardboard boxes containing reels of recorded tapes.

Table and immediately adjacent area in strong white light. Rest of stage in darkness.

KRAPP *remains a moment motionless, heaves a great sigh, looks at his watch, fumbles in his pockets, takes out an envelope, puts it back, fumbles, takes out a small bunch of keys, raises it to his eyes, chooses a key, gets up and moves to front of table. He stoops, unlocks first drawer, peers into it, feels about inside it, takes out a reel of tape, peers at it, puts it back, locks drawer, unlocks second drawer, peers into it, feels about inside it, takes out a large banana, peers at it, locks drawer, puts keys back in his pocket. He turns, advances to edge of stage, halts, strokes banana, peels it, drops skin at his feet, puts end of banana in his mouth and remains motionless, staring vacuously before him. Finally he bites off the end, turns aside and begins pacing to and fro at edge of stage, in the light, i.e. not more than four or five paces either way, meditatively eating banana. He treads on skin, slips, nearly falls, recovers himself, stoops and peers at skin and finally pushes it, still stooping, with his foot over the edge of stage into pit. He resumes his pacing, finishes banana, returns to table, sits down, remains a moment motionless, heaves a great sigh, takes keys from his pockets, raises them to his eyes, chooses key, gets up and moves to front of table, unlocks second drawer, takes out a second large banana, peers at it, locks drawer, puts back keys in his pocket, turns, advances to edge of stage, halts, strokes banana, peels it, tosses skin into pit, puts end of banana in his mouth and remains motionless, staring vacuously before him. Finally he has an idea, puts banana in his waistcoat pocket, the end emerging, and goes with all the speed he can muster backstage into darkness. Ten seconds. Loud pop of cork. Fifteen seconds. He comes back into light carrying an old ledger and sits down at table. He lays ledger on table, wipes his mouth, wipes his hands on the front of his waistcoat, brings them smartly together and rubs them.*

KRAPP [*briskly*]. Ah! [*He bends over ledger, turns the pages, finds the entry he wants, reads.*] Box . . . thrree . . . spool . . . five. [*He raises his head and stares front. With relish.*] Spool! [*Pause.*] Spooool! [*Happy smile. Pause. He bends over table, starts peering and poking at the boxes.*] Box . . . thrree . . . thrree . . . four . . . two . . . [*with surprise*] nine! good God! . . . seven . . . ah! the little rascal! [*He takes up box, peers at it.*] Box thrree. [*He lays it on table, opens it and peers at spools inside.*] Spool . . . [*he peers at ledger*] . . . five . . . [*he peers at spools*] . . . five . . . five . . . ah! the little scoundrel! [*He takes out a spool, peers at it.*] Spool five. [*He lays it on table, closes box three, puts it back with the others, takes up the spool.*] Box thrree, spool five. [*He bends over the machine, looks up. With relish.*] Spooool! [*Happy smile. He bends, loads spool on machine, rubs his hands.*] Ah! [*He peers at ledger, reads entry at foot of page.*] Mother at rest at last . . . Hm . . . The black ball . . . [*He raises his head, stares blankly front. Puzzled.*] Black ball? . . . [*He peers again at ledger, reads.*] The dark nurse . . . [*He raises his head, broods, peers again at ledger, reads.*] Slight improvement in bowel condition . . . Hm . . . Memorable . . . what? [*He peers closer.*] Equinox, memorable equinox. [*He raises his head, stares blankly front. Puzzled.*] Memorable equinox? . . . [*Pause. He shrugs his shoulders, peers again at ledger, reads.*] Farewell to—[*he turns the page*]—love.

He raises his head, broods, bends over machine, switches on and assumes listening posture, i.e. leaning forward, elbows on table, hand cupping ear towards machine, face front.

TAPE [*strong voice, rather pompous, clearly* KRAPP's *at a much earlier time*].
 Thirty-nine today, sound as a—[*Settling himself more comfortably he knocks one of the boxes off the table, curses, switches off, sweeps boxes and ledger violently to the ground, winds tape back to beginning, switches on, resumes posture.*] Thirty-nine today, sound as a bell, apart from my old weakness, and intellectually I have now every reason to suspect at the . . . [*hesitates*] . . . crest of the wave—or thereabouts. Celebrated the awful occasion, as in recent years, quietly at the Winehouse. Not a soul. Sat before the fire with closed eyes, separating the grain from the husks. Jotted down a few notes, on the back of an envelope. Good to be back in my den, in my old rags. Have just eaten I regret to say three bananas and only with difficulty refrained from a fourth. Fatal things for a man with my condition. [*Vehemently.*] Cut 'em out! [*Pause.*] The new light above my table is a great improvement. With all this darkness round me I feel less alone. [*Pause.*] In a way. [*Pause.*] I love to get up and move about in it, then back here to . . . [*hesitates*] . . . me. [*Pause.*] Krapp.
 [*Pause.*]
The grain, now what I wonder do I mean by that, I mean . . . [*hesitates*] . . . I suppose I mean those things worth having when all the dust has—when all *my* dust has settled. I close my eyes and try and imagine them.
 [*Pause.* KRAPP *closes his eyes briefly.*]
Extraordinary silence this evening, I strain my ears and do not hear a sound. Old Miss McGlome always sings at this hour. But not tonight. Songs of her girlhood, she says. Hard to think of her as a girl. Wonderful woman though. Connaught,[2] I fancy. [*Pause.*] Shall I sing when I am her age, if I ever am? No. [*Pause.*] Did I sing as a boy? No. [*Pause.*] Did I ever sing? No.
 [*Pause.*]
Just been listening to an old year, passages at random. I did not check in the book, but it must be at least ten or twelve years ago. At that time I think I was still living on and off with Bianca in Kedar Street. Well out of that, Jesus yes! Hopeless business. [*Pause.*] Not much about her, apart from a tribute to her eyes. Very warm. I suddenly saw them again. [*Pause.*] Incomparable! [*Pause.*] Ah well . . . [*Pause.*] These old P.M.s[3] are gruesome, but I often find them—[KRAPP *switches off, broods, switches on*]—a help before embarking on a new . . . [*hesitates*] . . . retrospect. Hard to believe I was ever that young whelp. The voice! Jesus! And the aspirations! [*Brief laugh in which* KRAPP *joins.*] And the resolutions! [*Brief laugh in which* KRAPP *joins.*] To drink less, in particular. [*Brief laugh of* KRAPP *alone.*] Statistics. Seventeen hundred hours, out of the preceding eight thousand odd, consumed on licensed premises[4] alone. More than 20%, say 40% of his waking life. [*Pause.*] Plans for a less . . . [*hesitates*]

[2] Northwestern province of Ireland. [3] Post mortems.
[4] Shops licensed to sell liquor.

. . . engrossing sexual life. Last illness of his father. Flagging pursuit of happiness.

Unattainable laxation.[5] Sneers at what he calls his youth and thanks to God that it's over. [*Pause.*] False ring there. [*Pause.*] Shadows of the opus . . . magnum.[6] Closing with a—[*brief laugh*]—yelp to Providence. [*Prolonged laugh in which* KRAPP *joins.*] What remains of all that misery? A girl in a shabby green coat, on a railway-station platform? No?

[*Pause.*]

When I look—

KRAPP *switches off, broods, looks at his watch, gets up, goes backstage into darkness. Ten seconds. Pop of cork. Ten seconds. Second cork. Ten seconds. Third cork. Ten seconds. Brief burst of quavering song.*

KRAPP [*sings*]. Now the day is over,
　　　　　　Night is drawing nigh-igh,
　　　　　　Shadows—

Fit of coughing. He comes back into light, sits down, wipes his mouth, switches on, resumes his listening posture.

TAPE. —back on the year that is gone, with what I hope is perhaps a glint of the old eye to come, there is of course the house on the canal where mother lay a-dying, in the late autumn, after her long viduity [KRAPP *gives a start*], and the—[KRAPP *switches off, winds back tape a little, bends his ear closer to machine, switches on*]—a-dying, after her long viduity, and the—

KRAPP *switches off, raises his head, stares blankly before him. His lips move in the syllables of "viduity." No sound. He gets up, goes backstage into darkness, comes back with an enormous dictionary, lays it on table, sits down and looks up the word.*

KRAPP [*reading from dictionary*]. State—or condition of being—or remaining—a widow—or widower. [*Looks up. Puzzled.*] Being—or remaining? . . . [*Pause. He peers again at dictionary. Reading.*] "Deep weeds of viduity" . . . Also of an animal, especially a bird . . . the vidua or weaver-bird . . . Black plumage of male . . . [*He looks up. With relish.*] The vidua-bird!

[*Pause. He closes dictionary, switches on, resumes listening posture.*]

TAPE. —bench by the weir[7] from where I could see her window. There I sat, in the biting wind, wishing she were gone. [*Pause.*] Hardly a soul, just a few regulars, nursemaids, infants, old men, dogs. I got to know them quite well—oh by appearance of course I mean! One dark young beauty I recollect particularly, all white and starch, incomparable bosom, with a big black hooded perambulator, most funereal thing. Whenever I looked in her direction she had her eyes on me. And yet when I was bold enough to speak to her—not having been introduced—she threatened to call a policeman. As if I had designs on her virtue! [*Laugh. Pause.*] The face she had! The eyes! Like . . . [*hesi-

[5] Unwinding, relaxation.　　[6] Of the great work (especially of literature).
[7] Millpond.

tates] . . . chrysolite!⁸ [*Pause.*] Ah well . . . [*Pause.*] I was there when—
[Krapp *switches off, broods, switches on again*]—the blind went down, one
of those dirty brown roller affairs, throwing a ball for a little white
dog, as chance would have it. I happened to look up and there it was.
All over and done with, at last. I sat on for a few moments with the
ball in my hand and the dog yelping and pawing at me. [*Pause.*] Mo-
ments. Her moments, my moments. [*Pause.*] The dog's moments.
[*Pause.*] In the end I held it out to him and he took it in his mouth,
gently, gently. A small, old, black, hard, solid rubber ball. [*Pause.*] I
shall feel it, in my hand, until my dying day. [*Pause.*] I might have
kept it. [*Pause.*] But I gave it to the dog.

 [*Pause.*]
Ah well. . .

 [*Pause.*]
Spiritually a year of profound gloom and indigence until that memora-
ble night in March, at the end of the jetty,⁹ in the howling wind, never to
be forgotten, when suddenly I saw the whole thing. The vision, at last.
This I fancy is what I have chiefly to record this evening, against the day
when my work will be done and perhaps no place left in my memory,
warm or cold, for the miracle that . . . [*hesitates*] . . . for the fire that set
it alight. What I suddenly saw then was this, that the belief I had been
going on all my life, namely—[Krapp *switches off impatiently, winds tape
forward, switches on again*]—great granite rocks the foam flying up in the
light of the lighthouse and the wind-gauge spinning like a propellor,
clear to me at last that the dark I have always struggled to keep under is
in reality my most—[Krapp *curses, switches off, winds tape forward, switches
on again*]—unshatterable association until my dissolution of storm and
night with the light of the understanding and the fire—[Krapp *curses
louder, switches off, winds tape forward, switches on again*]—my face in her
breasts and my hand on her. We lay there without moving. But under
us all moved, and moved us, gently, up and down, and from side to side.

 [*Pause.*]
Past midnight. Never knew such silence. The earth might be uninhab-
ited.

 [*Pause.*]
Here I end—

 [Krapp *switches off, winds tape back,
 switches on again.*]
—upper lake, with the punt, bathed off the bank, then pushed out into
the stream and drifted. She lay stretched out on the floorboards with
her hands under her head and her eyes closed. Sun blazing down, bit of
a breeze, water nice and lively. I noticed a scratch on her thigh and
asked her how she came by it. Picking gooseberries, she said. I said
again I thought it was hopeless and no good going on, and she agreed,
without opening her eyes. [*Pause.*] I asked her to look at me and after a
few moments—[*pause*]—after a few moments she did, but the eyes just
slits, because of the glare. I bent over her to get them in the shadow and
they opened. [*Pause. Low.*] Let me in. [*Pause.*] We drifted in among the

⁸Olivine, a pale green precious stone. ⁹Wharf or pier.

flags and stuck. The way they went down, sighing, before the stem! [*Pause.*] I lay down across her with my face in her breasts and my hand on her. We lay there without moving. But under us all moved, and moved us, gently, up and down, and from side to side.

 [*Pause.*]
Past midnight. Never knew—

KRAPP *switches off, broods. Finally he fumbles in his pockets, encounters the banana, takes it out, peers at it, puts it back, fumbles, brings out the envelope, fumbles, puts back envelope, looks at his watch, gets up and goes backstage into darkness. Ten seconds. Sound of bottle against glass, then brief siphon. Ten seconds. Bottle against glass alone. Ten seconds. He comes back a little unsteadily into light, goes to front of table, takes out keys, raises them to his eyes, chooses key, unlocks first drawer, peers into it, feels about inside, takes out reel, peers at it, locks drawer, puts keys back in his pocket, goes and sits down, takes reel off machine, lays it on dictionary, loads virgin reel on machine, takes envelope from his pocket, consults back of it, lays it on table, switches on, clears his throat and begins to record.*

KRAPP. Just been listening to that stupid bastard I took myself for thirty years ago, hard to believe I was ever as bad as that. Thank God that's all done with anyway. [*Pause.*] The eyes she had! [*Broods, realizes he is recording silence, switches off, broods. Finally.*] Everything there, everything, all the—[*Realizes this is not being recorded, switches on.*] Everything there, everything on this old muckball, all the light and dark and famine and feasting of . . . [*hesitates*] . . . the ages! [*In a shout.*] Yes! [*Pause.*] Let that go! Jesus! Take his mind off his homework! Jesus! [*Pause. Weary.*] Ah well, maybe he was right. [*Pause.*] Maybe he was right. [*Broods. Realizes. Switches off. Consults envelope.*] Pah! [*Crumples it and throws it away. Broods. Switches on.*] Nothing to say, not a squeak. What's a year now? The sour cud and the iron stool. [*Pause.*] Revelled in the word spool. [*With relish.*] Spooool! Happiest moment of the past half million. [*Pause.*] Seventeen copies sold, of which eleven at trade price to free circulating libraries beyond the seas. Getting known. [*Pause.*] One pound six and something, eight I have little doubt. [*Pause.*] Crawled out once or twice, before the summer was cold. Sat shivering in the park, drowned in dreams and burning to be gone. Not a soul. [*Pause.*] Last fancies. [*Vehemently.*] Keep 'em under! [*Pause.*] Scalded the eyes out of me reading *Effie*[10] again, a page a day, with tears again. Effie . . . [*Pause.*] Could have been happy with her, up there on the Baltic, and the pines, and the dunes. [*Pause.*] Could I? [*Pause.*] And she? [*Pause.*] Pah! [*Pause.*] Fanny came in a couple of times. Bony old ghost of a whore. Couldn't do much, but I suppose better than a kick in the crutch. The last time wasn't so bad. How do you manage it, she said, at your age? I told her I'd been saving up for her all my life. [*Pause.*] Went to Vespers once, like when I was in short trousers. [*Pause. Sings.*]

 Now the day is over,
 Night is drawing nigh-igh,

[10] *Effi Briest* (1895), by the German novelist Theodor Fontane.

Shadows—[*coughing, then almost inaudible*]—of the evening
Steal across the sky.

[*Gasping.*] Went to sleep and fell off the pew. [*Pause.*] Sometimes won-
dered in the night if a last effort mightn't—][*Pause.*] Ah finish your
booze now and get to your bed. Go on with this drivel in the morning.
Or leave it at that. [*Pause.*] Leave it at that. [*Pause.*] Lie propped up in the
dark—and wander. Be again in the dingle[11] on a Christmas Eve, gath-
ering holly, the red-berried. [*Pause.*] Be again on Croghan on a Sunday
morning, in the haze, with the bitch, stop and listen to the bells. [*Pause.*]
And so on. [*Pause.*] Be again, be again. [*Pause.*] All that old misery.
[*Pause.*] Once wasn't enough for you. [*Pause.*] Lie down across her.

*Long pause. He suddenly bends over machine, switches off, wrenches off tape, throws
it away, puts on the other, winds it forward to the passage he wants, switches on,
listens staring front.*

TAPE.—gooseberries, she said. I said again I thought it was hopeless and no
good going on, and she agreed, without opening her eyes. [*Pause.*] I
asked her to look at me and after a few moments—[*pause*]—after a few
moments she did, but the eyes just slits, because of the glare. I bent over
her to get them in the shadow and they opened. [*Pause. Low.*] Let me in.
[*Pause.*] We drifted in among the flags and stuck. The way they went
down, sighing, before the stem! [*Pause.*] I lay down across her with my
face in her breasts and my hand on her. We lay there without moving.
But under us all moved, and moved us, gently, up and down, and from
side to side.

 [*Pause.* KRAPP'S *lips move. No sound.*]
Past midnight. Never knew such silence. The earth might be uninhab-
ited.

 [*Pause.*]
Here I end this reel. Box—[*pause*]—three, spool—[*pause*]—five. [*Pause.*]
Perhaps my best years are gone. When there was a chance of happi-
ness. But I wouldn't want them back. Not with the fire in me now. No, I
wouldn't want them back.

 [KRAPP *motionless staring before him.
 The tape runs on in silence.*]

 CURTAIN

[11] Wooded hollow.

Richard Wright
(*1908–1960*)

"The Negro is America's metaphor," Richard Wright once wrote, and else-where, "Negro life in the U.S. dramatically symbolizes the struggles of a people whose forefathers lived in a warm, simple culture and who are now trying to live the new way of life that dominates our time: machine-civiliza-tion and all the consequences flowing from it. It must be understood that when I talk of the American Negroes, I am talking about everybody." For Wright, universality, or "talking about everybody," was not a flight away from engagement with the very specific issue of American racism; *Native Son* (1940) tore the veil from the rage and frustration of urban American blacks and permanently changed the way both blacks and whites saw racial relations. But it was Wright's ability to see the Negro as metaphor as well as suffering individual that gave his work its psychological complexity and philosophical depth and made him a writer of international significance.

Wright was born in Natchez, Mississippi, in 1908, the son of a share-cropper father and a mother trained as a schoolteacher but employed as a domestic servant. The father deserted the family when Wright was five, and for several years the family led a wandering existence through Missis-sippi, Tennessee, and Arkansas as the mother searched for employment. After she was disabled by a stroke when Wright was seven, he and his five-year-old brother Leon were placed in an orphanage. Eventually the family was reunited in Mississippi in the home of Wright's maternal grand-mother, a stern Seventh Day Adventist with whom Wright was in constant conflict. When he graduated from high school in Jackson, Mississippi, he left home and found a job in Memphis, Tennessee.

After two years, the nineteen-year-old Wright determined to leave the South and made his way to Chicago, where he worked at a string of miscel-laneous manual jobs before landing a job as a postal clerk. He had already begun writing before he left Memphis, and in Chicago he continued to write and to read widely. He joined the leftist John Reed Club, a writers' group, in 1933 and shortly afterward joined the Communist Party. He moved to New York in 1937 to become an editor and writer for the *Daily Worker*. The following year his first book appeared: *Uncle Tom's Children*, a group of brutally naturalistic novellas about Southern racism.

The publication of *Native Son* in 1940 propelled Wright into interna-tional fame and was a landmark in black writing in America. The novel is a grim story of a black man named Bigger Thomas, who, after he uninten-tionally kills a white girl, comes to find in the role of murderer an alterna-tive identity preferable to that imposed upon him by white society as a projection of its own weakness and cruelty. Unlike much previous black writing, including Wright's own, *Native Son* does not portray passive vic-tims; it forces its readers to confront their own creation, a desperate, en-raged killer. The book is a psychologically keen analysis of the making of a "nigger" (a word with which Bigger's name is intended to chime). *Native Son* was a commercial as well as critical success, a best seller, a Book of the

Month Club selection, and the basis of a successful play directed on Broadway by Orson Welles the following year.

During the early 1940s, Wright became increasingly disillusioned with Communism, resenting the restrictions it placed upon his work and coming to believe that the issue of racism was of minor importance in its program; he left the Party in 1944. As his enthusiasm for Communism waned, he read more intensively in Dostoevsky, Nietzsche, and Freud and in such existentialist philosophers as Kierkegaard. The influence of existentialism can be seen already in *Native Son*, and it becomes prominent in "The Man Who Lived Underground," two sections of which were published in the literary magazine *Accent* in 1942 and which appeared complete in 1944. Wright's autobiography, *Black Boy* (1945), gave him another best-selling commercial success.

Gertrude Stein admired Wright's work, and in 1945 she used her influence to have the French government invite him to Paris. His cordial reception and the absence of race prejudice there encouraged him to settle permanently in France with his wife and daughter. He became friends with Jean-Paul Sartre and Albert Camus and, with a group of French writers, founded *Présence Africaine*, a journal of African culture. The fiction of the Paris years is generally regarded as representing a decline from the novels written in America. It includes *The Outsider* (1953), a Nietzschean study in identity; *Savage Holiday* (1954), a rather mechanical Freudian novel; and *The Long Dream* (1958), a maturation novel about a young Southern black who flees to Paris. *Black Power* (1954), *The Color Curtain* (1956), and *White Man, Listen* (1957) were all polemical books dealing with problems of the emerging nations of Africa.

Wright died unexpectedly in 1960 of amoebic dysentery, contracted during one of his African trips. Three more books were published posthumously: *Eight Men* (1961), a collection of stories; *Lawd Today* (1963), a novel written in the thirties but previously unpublished; and *American Hunger* (1977), an autobiographical continuation of *Black Boy*.

"Big Boy Leaves Home" is the first story in *Uncle Tom's Children*, and no one of Wright's works better illustrates his combination of focused anger and artistic control. On the first reading, one is likely to be overwhelmed by the brutality of the lynching, presented in graphic detail. (The brutality is not exaggerated, however; Wright based the account on several cases he had known in Mississippi.) On the second reading, the richness of the artistry of the story is likely to become apparent: the dreadful inexorability by which the action unfolds through the five numbered sections; the way the pastoral sweetness of the first section turns into the nightmare of the subsequent ones, as if the boys were playing on the edge of a volcano; and the precision by which Wright reveals the sexual anxieties, the violence, and the projective dehumanization that racism directs toward the racial Other. The title "Big Boy Leaves Home" has the hopeful note of youthful questing in it, but the circumstances of Big Boy's flight turn that hope into bitter irony. This is the world, Wright seems to be saying, that young black men enter in a violent, racist society.

FURTHER READING (*prepared by J. H.*): Michel Fabre's *The Unfinished Quest of Richard Wright*, 1973, remains the standard biography. Fabre has also published *The*

World of Richard Wright, 1985, twelve essays on aspects of Wright's work. Robert Felgar's *Richard Wright*, 1980; Russell Carl Brignano's *Richard Wright: An Introduction to the Man and His Works*, 1970; and C. James Trotman's *Richard Wright*, 1988, are all useful introductory overviews. Keneth Kinnamon's *The Emergence of Richard Wright*, 1972, is a perceptive study of Wright's early career. Kinnamon has also produced *A Richard Wright Bibliography*, 1988, a massive guide through Wright criticism and commentary. Important critical articles are collected in *Richard Wright*, ed. Harold Bloom, 1987, and in *Critical Essays on Richard Wright*, ed. Yoshinobu Hakutani, 1982.

BIG BOY LEAVES HOME

I

Yo mama don wear no drawers . . .

Clearly, the voice rose out of the woods, and died away. Like an echo another voice caught it up:

Ah seena when she pulled em off . . .

Another, shrill, cracking, adolescent:

N she washed 'em in alcohol . . .

Then a quartet of voices, blending in harmony, floated high above the tree tops:

N she hung 'em out in the hall . . .

Laughing easily, four black boys came out of the woods into cleared pasture. They walked lollingly in bare feet, beating tangled vines and bushes with long sticks.

"Ah wished Ah knowed some mo lines t tha song."

"Me too."

"Yeah, when yuh gits t where she hangs em out in the hall yuh has t stop."

"Shucks, whut goes wid *hall?*"

"*Call.*"

"*Fall.*"

"*Wall.*"

"*Quall.*"

They threw themselves on the grass, laughing.

"Big Boy?"

"Huh?"

"Yuh know one thing?"

"Whut?"

"Yuh sho is crazy!"

"Crazy?"

"Yeah, yuh crazys a bed-bug!"

"Crazy bout whut?"

"Man, whoever hearda *quall?*"

"Yuh said yuh wanted something to go wid *hall,* didn't yuh?"

"Yeah, but whuts a *quall?*"

"Nigger, a *qualls* a *quall*."

They laughed easily, catching and pulling long green blades of grass with their toes.

"Waal, ef a *qualls* a *quall*, whut IS a *quall*?"

"Oh, Ah know."

"Whut?"

"Tha ol song goes something like this:

> Yo mama don wear no drawers,
> > Ah seena when she pulled em off,
> N she washed em in alcohol,
> > N she hung em out in the hall,
> N then she put em back on her QUALL!"

They laughed again. Their shoulders were flat to the earth, their knees propped up, and their faces square to the sun.

"Big Boy, yuhs CRAZY!"

"Don ax me nothin else."

"Nigger, yuhs CRAZY!"

They fell silent, smiling, dropping the lids of their eyes softly against the sunlight.

"Man, don the groun feel warm?"

"Jus lika bed."

"Jeeesus, Ah could stay here ferever."

"Me too."

"Ah kin feel tha ol sun goin all thu me."

"Feels like mah bones is warm."

In the distance a train whistled mournfully.

"There goes number fo!"

"Hittin on all six!"

"Highballin it down the line!"

"Boun fer up Noth, Lawd, bound fer up Noth!"

They began to chant, pounding bare heels in the grass.

> Dis train bound fo Glory
> Dis train, Oh Hallelujah
> Dis train bound fo Glory
> Dis train, Oh Hallelujah
> Dis train bound fo Glory
> Ef yuh ride no need fer fret er worry
> Dis train, Oh Hallelujah
> Dis train . . .
> Dis train don carry no gambler
> Dis train, Oh Hallelujah
> Dis train don carry no gambler
> Dis train, Oh Hallelujah
> Dis train don carry no gambler
> No fo day creeper er midnight rambler
> Dis train, Oh Hallelujah
> Dis train . . .

When the song ended they burst out laughing, thinking of a train bound for Glory.

"Gee, thas a good ol song!"

"Huuuuummmmmmmmman . . ."

"Whut?"

"Geeee whiiiiiiz . . ."

"Whut?"

"Somebody done let win! Das whut!"

Buck, Bobo and Lester jumped up. Big Boy stayed on the ground, feigning sleep.

"Jeeesus, tha sho stinks!"

"Big Boy!"

Big Boy feigned to snore.

"Big Boy!"

Big Boy stirred as though in sleep.

"Big Boy!"

"Hunh?"

"Yuh rotten inside!"

"Rotten?"

"Lawd, cant yuh smell it?"

"Smell whut?"

"Nigger, yuh mus gotta bad col!"

"*Smell whut?*"

"NIGGER, YUH BROKE WIN!"

Big Boy laughed and fell back on the grass, closing his eyes.

"The hen whut cackles is the hen whut laid the egg."

"We ain no hens."

"Yuh cackled, didnt yuh?"

The three moved off with noses turned up.

"C mon!"

"Where yuh-all goin?"

"T the creek fer a swim."

"Yeah, les swim."

"Naw buddy naw!" said Big Boy, slapping the air with a scornful palm.

"Aa, c mon! Don be a heel!"

"N git *lynched?* Hell naw!"

"He ain gonna see us."

"How yuh know?"

"Cause he ain."

"Yuh-all go on. Ahma stay right here," said Big Boy.

"Hell, let im stay! C mon, les go," said Buck.

The three walked off, swishing at grass and bushes with sticks. Big Boy looked lazily at their backs.

"Hey!"

Walking on, they glanced over their shoulders.

"Hey, niggers!"

"C mon!"

Big Boy grunted, picked up his stick, pulled to his feet, and stumbled off.

"Wait!"

"C mon!"

He ran, caught up with them, leaped upon their backs, bearing them to the ground.

"Quit, Big Boy!"

"Gawddam, nigger!"

"Git t hell offa me!"

Big Boy sprawled in the grass beside them, laughing and pounding his heels in the ground.

"Nigger, whut yuh think we is, hosses?"

"How come yuh awways hoppin on us?"

"Lissen, wes gonna doubt-team on yuh one of these days n beat yo ol ass good."

Big Boy smiled.

"Sho nough?"

"Yeah, don yuh like it?"

"We gonna beat yuh sos yuh cant walk!"

"N dare yuh t do nothin erbout it!"

Big Boy bared his teeth.

"C mon! Try it now!"

The three circled around him.

"Say, Buck, yuh grab his feets!"

"N yuh git his head, Lester!"

"N Bobo, yuh get berhin n grab his arms!"

Keeping more than arm's length, they circled round and round Big Boy.

"C mon!" said Big Boy, feinting at one and then the other.

Round and round they circled, but could not seem to get any closer. Big Boy stopped and braced his hands on his hips.

"Is all three of yuh-all scareda me?"

"Les git im some other time," said Bobo, grinning.

"Yeah, we kin ketch yuh when yuh ain thinkin," said Lester.

"We kin trick yuh," said Buck.

They laughed and walked together.

Big Boy belched.

"Ahm hongry," he said.

"Me too."

"Ah wished Ah hada big hot pota belly-busters!"

"Cooked wid some good ol salty ribs . . ."

"N some good ol egg cornbread . . ."

"N some buttermilk . . ."

"N some hot peach cobbler swimmin in juice . . ."

"Nigger, hush!"

They began to chant, emphasizing the rhythm by cutting at grass with sticks.

> Bye n bye
> Ah wanna piece of pie
> Pies too sweet
> Ah wanna piece of meat
> Meats too red

> *Ah wanna piece of bread*
> *Breads too brown*
> *Ah wanna go t town*
> *Towns too far*
> *Ah wanna ketcha a car*
> *Cars too fas*
> *Ah fall n break mah ass*
> *Ahll understan it better bye n bye . . .*

They climbed over a barbed-wire fence and entered a stretch of thick woods. Big Boy was whistling softly, his eyes half-closed.

"LES GIT IM!"

Buck, Lester, and Bobo whirled, grabbed Big Boy about the neck, arms, and legs, bearing him to the ground. He grunted and kicked wildly as he went back into weeds.

"Hol im tight!"

"Git his arms! Git his arms!"

"Set on his legs so he cant kick!"

Big Boy puffed heavily, trying to get loose.

"WE GOT YUH NOW, GAWDDAMMIT, WE GOT YUH NOW!"

"Thas a Gawddam lie!" said Big Boy. He kicked, twisted, and clutched for a hold on one and then the other.

"Say, yuh-all hep me hol his arms!" said Bobo.

"Aw, we got this bastard now!" said Lester.

"Thas a Gawddam lie!" said Big Boy again.

"Say, yah-all hep me hol his arms!" called Bobo.

Big Boy managed to encircle the neck of Bobo with his left arm. He tightened his elbow scissors-like and hissed through his teeth:

"Yuh got me, ain yuh?"

"Hol im!"

"Les beat this bastard's ass!"

"Say, hep me hol his *arms!* Hes got aholda mah *neck!*" cried Bobo.

Big Boy squeezed Bobo's neck and twisted his head to the ground.

"Yuh got me, ain yuh?"

"Quit, Big Boy, yuh chokin me! Yuh hurtin mah neck!" cried Bobo.

"Turn me loose!" said Big Boy.

"Ah ain got yuh! Its the others whut got yuh!" pleaded Bobo.

"Tell them others t git t hell offa me or Ahma break yo neck," said Big Boy.

"Ssssay, yyyuh-al gggit ooooffa Bbig Boy. Hhhes got me," gurgled Bobo.

"Cant yuh hol im?"

"Nnaw, hhes ggot mmah nneck . . ."

Big Boy squeezed tighter.

"N Ahma break it too les yuh tell em t git t hell offa me!"

"Ttturn mmmeee llloose," panted Bobo, tears gushing.

"Cant yuh hol im, Bobo?" asked Buck.

"Nnaw, yuh-all tturn im lloose; hhhes got mah nnneck . . ."

"Grab his neck, Bobo . . ."

"Ah cant; yugurgur . . ."

To save Bobo, Lester and Buck got up and ran to a safe distance. Big Boy released Bobo, who staggered to his feet, slobbering and trying to stretch a crick out of his neck.

"Shucks, nigger, yuh almos broke mah neck," whimpered Bobo.

"Ahm gonna break yo ass nex time," said Big Boy.

"Ef Bobo coulda hel yuh we woulda had yuh," yelled Lester.

"Ah waznt gonna let im do that," said Big Boy.

They walked together again, swishing sticks.

"Yuh see," began Big Boy, "when a ganga guys jump on yuh, all yuh gotta do is put the heat on one of them n make im tell the others t let up, see?"

"Gee, thas a good idee!"

"Yeah, thas a good idee!"

"But yuh almos broke mah neck, man," said Bobo.

"Ahma smart nigger," said Big Boy, thrusting out his chest.

II

They came to the swimming hole.

"Ah ain goin in," said Bobo.

"Done got scared?" asked Big Boy.

"Naw, Ah ain scared . . ."

"How come yuh ain goin in?"

"Yuh know ol man Harvey don erllow no niggers t swim in this hole."

"N jus las year he took a shot at Bob fer swimming in here," said Lester.

"Shucks, ol man Harvey ain studyin bout us niggers," said Big Boy.

"Hes at home thinking about his jelly-roll," said Buck.

They laughed.

"Buck, yo mins lowern a snakes belly," said Lester.

"Ol man Harveys too doggone ol t think erbout jelly-roll," said Big Boy.

"Hes dried up; all the saps done lef im," said Bobo.

"C mon, les go!" said Big Boy.

Bobo pointed.

"See tha sign over yonder?"

"Yeah."

"Whut it say?"

"NO TRESPASSIN," read Lester.

"Know whut tha mean?"

"Mean ain no dogs n niggers erllowed," said Buck.

"Waal, wes here now," said Big Boy. "Ef he ketched us even like this thered be trouble, so we just as waal go on in . . ."

"Ahm wid the nex one!"

"Ahll go ef anybody else goes!"

Big Boy looked carefully in all directions. Seeing nobody, he began jerking off his overalls.

"LAS ONE INS A OL DEAD DOG!"

"THAS YO MA!"

"THAS YO PA!"

"THAS BOTH YO MA N YO PA!"

They jerked off their clothes and threw them in a pile under a tree. Thirty seconds later they stood, black and naked, on the edge of the hole under a sloping embankment. Gingerly Big Boy touched the water with his foot.

"Man, this waters col," he said.

"Ahm gonna put mah cloes back on," said Bobo, withdrawing his foot.

Big Boy grabbed him about the waist.

"Like hell yuh is!"

"Git outta the way, nigger!" Bobo yelled.

"Thow im in!" said Lester.

"Duck im!"

Bobo crouched, spread his legs, and braced himself against Big Boy's body. Locked in each other's arms, they tussled on the edge of the hole, neither able to throw the other.

"C mon, les me n yuh push em in."

"O.K."

Laughing, Lester and Buck gave the two locked bodies a running push. Big Boy and Bobo splashed, sending up silver spray in the sunlight. When Big Boy's head came up he yelled:

"Yuh bastard!"

"Tha wuz yo ma yuh pushed!" said Bobo, shaking his head to clear the water from his eyes.

They did a surface dive, came up and struck out across the creek. The muddy water foamed. They swam back, waded into shallow water, breathing heavily and blinking eyes.

"C mon in!"

"Man, the water's fine!"

Lester and Buck hesitated.

"Les wet em," Big Boy whispered to Bobo.

Before Lester and Buck could back away, they were dripping wet from handfuls of scooped water.

"Hey, quit!"

"Gawddam, nigger; tha waters col!"

"C mon in!" called Big Boy.

"We just as waal go on in now," said Buck.

"Look n see ef anybody's comin."

Kneeling, they squinted among the trees.

"Ain nobody."

"C mon, les go."

They waded in slowly, pausing each few steps to catch their breath. A desperate water battle began. Closing eyes and backing away, they shunted water into one another's faces with the flat palms of hands.

"Hey, cut it out!"

"Yeah, Ahm bout drownin!"

They came together in water up to their navels, blowing and blinking. Big Boy ducked, upsetting Bobo.

"Look out, nigger!"

"Don holler so loud!"

"Yeah, they kin hear yo ol big mouth a mile erway."

"This waters too col fer me."

"Thas cause it rained yistiddy."

They swam across and back again.

"Ah wish we hada bigger place t swim in."

"The white folks got plenty swimming pools n we ain got none."

"Ah useta swim in the ol Missippi when we lived in Vicksburg."

Big Boy put his head under the water and blew his breath. A sound came like that of a hippopotamus.

"C mon, les be hippos."

Each went to a corner of the creek and put his mouth just below the surface and blew like a hippopotamus. Tiring, they came and sat under the embankment.

"Look like Ah gotta chill."

"Me too."

"Les stay here n dry off."

"Jeeesus, Ahm col!"

They kept still in the sun, suppressing shivers. After some of the water had dried off their bodies they began to talk through clattering teeth.

"Whut would yuh do ef ol man Harveyd come erlong right now?"

"Run like hell!"

"Man, Ahd run so fas hed thinka black streaka lightnin shot pass im."

"But spose he hada gun?"

"Aw, nigger, shut up!"

They were silent. They ran their hands over wet, trembling legs, brushing water away. Then their eyes watched the sun sparkling on the restless creek.

Far away a train whistled.

"There goes number seven!"

"Headin fer up Noth!"

"Blazin it down the line!"

"Lawd, Ahm goin Noth some day."

"Me too, man."

"They say colored folks up Noth is got ekual rights."

They grew pensive. A black winged butterfly hovered at the water's edge. A bee droned. From somewhere came the sweet scent of honeysuckles. Dimly they could hear sparrows twittering in the woods. They rolled from side to side, letting sunshine dry their skins and warm their blood. They plucked blades of grass and chewed them.

"Oh!"

They looked up, their lips parting.

"Oh!"

A white woman, poised on the edge of the opposite embankment, stood directly in front of them, her hat in her hand and her hair lit by the sun.

"Its a woman!" whispered Big Boy in an underbreath. "A *white* woman!"

They stared, their hands instinctively covering their groins. Then they scrambled to their feet. The white woman backed slowly out of sight. They stood for a moment, looking at one another.

"Les git outta here!" Big Boy whispered.

"Wait till she goes erway."

"Les run, theyll ketch us here naked like this!"

"Mabbe theres a man wid her."

"C mon, les git our cloes," said Big Boy.

They waited a moment longer, listening.

"What t hell! Ahma git mah cloes," said Big Boy.

Grabbing at short tufts of grass, he climbed the embankment.

"Don run out there now!"

"C mon back, fool!"

Bobo hesitated. He looked at Big Boy, and then at Buck and Lester.

"Ahm goin wid Big Boy n git mah cloes," he said.

"Don run out there naked like tha, fool!" said Buck. "Yuh don know whos out there!"

Big Boy was climbing over the edge of the embankment.

"C mon," he whispered.

Bobo climbed after. Twenty-five feet away the woman stood. She had one hand over her mouth. Hanging by fingers, Buck and Lester peeped over the edge.

"C mon back; that womans scared," said Lester.

Big Boy stopped, puzzled. He looked at the woman. He looked at the bundle of clothes. Then he looked at Buck and Lester.

"C mon, les git our cloes!"

He made a step.

"Jim!" the woman screamed.

Big Boy stopped and looked around. His hands hung loosely at his side. The woman, her eyes wide, her hand over her mouth, backed away to the tree where their clothes lay in a heap.

"Big Boy, come back here n wait till shes gone!"

Bobo ran to Big Boy's side.

"Les go home! Theyll ketch us here," he urged.

Big Boy's throat felt tight.

"Lady, we wanna git our cloes," he said.

Buck and Lester climbed the embankment and stood indecisively. Big Boy ran toward the tree.

"Jim!" the woman screamed. "Jim! Jim!"

Black and naked, Big Boy stopped three feet from her.

"We wanna git our cloes," he said again, his words coming mechanically.

He made a motion.

"You go away! You go away! I tell you, you go away!"

Big Boy stopped again, afraid. Bobo ran and snatched the clothes. Buck and Lester tried to grab theirs out of his hands.

"You go away! You go away! You go away!" the woman screamed.

"Les go!" said Bobo, running toward the woods.

CRACK!

Lester grunted, stiffened, and pitched forward. His forehead struck a toe of the woman's shoes.

Bobo stopped, clutching the clothes. Buck whirled. Big Boy stared at Lester, his lips moving.

"Hes gotta gun; hes gotta gun!" yelled Buck, running wildly.

CRACK!

Buck stopped at the edge of the embankment, his head jerked backward, his body arched stiffly to one side; he toppled headlong, sending up a shower of bright spray to the sunlight. The creek bubbled.

Big Boy and Bobo backed away, their eyes fastened fearfully on a white man who was running toward them. He had a rifle and wore an army officer's uniform. He ran to the woman's side and grabbed her hand.

"You hurt, Bertha, you hurt?"

She stared at him and did not answer.

The man turned quickly. His face was red. He raised the rifle and pointed it at Bobo. Bobo ran back, holding the clothes in front of his chest.

"Don shoot me, Mistah, don shoot me . . ."

Big Boy lunged for the rifle, grabbing the barrel.

"You black sonofabitch!"

Big Boy clung desperately.

"Let go, you black bastard!"

The barrel pointed skyward.

CRACK!

The white man, taller and heavier, flung Big Boy to the ground. Bobo dropped the clothes, ran up, and jumped onto the white man's back.

"You black sonsofbitches!"

The white man released the rifle, jerked Bobo to the ground, and began to batter the naked boy with his fists. Then Big Boy swung, striking the man in the mouth with the barrel. His teeth caved in, and he fell, dazed. Bobo was on his feet.

"C mon, Big Boy, les go!"

Breathing hard, the white man got up and faced Big Boy. His lips were trembling, his neck and chin wet with blood. He spoke quietly.

"Give me that gun, boy!"

Big Boy leveled the rifle and backed away.

The white man advanced.

"Boy, I said give me that gun!"

Bobo had the clothes in his arms.

"Run, Big Boy, run!"

The man came at Big Boy.

"Ahll kill yuh; Ahll kill yuh!" said Big Boy.

His fingers fumbled for the trigger.

The man stopped, blinked, spat blood. His eyes were bewildered. His face whitened. Suddenly, he lunged for the rifle, his hands outstretched.

CRACK!

He fell forward on his face.

"Jim!"

Big Boy and Bobo turned in surprise to look at the woman.

"Jim!" she screamed again, and fell weakly at the foot of the tree.

Big Boy dropped the rifle, his eyes wide. He looked around. Bobo was crying and clutching the clothes.

"Big Boy, Big Boy . . ."

Big Boy looked at the rifle, started to pick it up, but didn't. He seemed at a loss. He looked at Lester, then at the white man; his eyes followed a thin stream of blood that seeped to the ground.

"Yuh done killed im," mumbled Bobo.

"Les go home!"

Naked, they turned and ran toward the wood. When they reached the barbed-wire fence they stopped.

"Les git our cloes on," said Big Boy.

They slipped quickly into overalls. Bobo held Lester's and Buck's clothes.

"Whut we gonna do wid these?"

Big Boy stared. His hands twitched.

"Leave em."

They climbed the fence and ran through the woods. Vines and leaves switched their faces. Once Bobo tripped and fell.

"C mon!" said Big Boy.

Bobo started crying, blood streaming from his scratches.

"Ahm scared!"

"C mon! Don cry! We wanna git home fo they ketches us!"

"Ahm scared!" said Bobo again, his eyes full of tears.

Big Boy grabbed his hand and dragged him along.

"C mon!"

III

They stopped when they got to the end of the woods. They could see the open road leading home, to ma and pa. But they hung back, afraid. The thick shadows cast from the trees were friendly and sheltering. But the wide glare of sun stretching out over the fields was pitiless. They crouched behind an old log.

"We gotta git home," said Big Boy.

"Theys gonna lynch us," said Bobo, half-questioningly.

Big Boy did not answer.

"Theys gonna lynch us," said Bobo again.

Big Boy shuddered.

"Hush!" he said. He did not want to think of it. He could not think of it; there was but one thought, and he clung to that one blindly. He had to get home, home to ma and pa.

Their heads jerked up. Their ears had caught the rhythmic jingle of a wagon. They fell to the ground and clung flat to the side of a log. Over the crest of the hill came the top of a hat. A white face. Then shoulders in a blue shirt. A wagon drawn by two horses pulled into full view.

Big Boy and Bobo held their breath, waiting. Their eyes followed the wagon till it was lost in dust around a bend of the road.

"We gotta git home," said Big Boy.

"Ahm scared," said Bobo.

"C mon! Les keep t the fields."

They ran till they came to the cornfields. Then they went slower, for last year's corn stubbles bruised their feet.

They came in sight of a brickyard.

"Wait a minute," gasped Big Boy.

They stopped.

"Ahm goin on t mah home n yuh better go on t yos."

Bobo's eyes grew round.

"Ahm scared!"

"Yuh better go on!"

"Lemme go wid yuh; theyll ketch me . . ."

"Ef yuh kin git home mabbe yo folks kin hep yuh t git erway."

Big Boy started off. Bobo grabbed him.

"Lemme go wid yuh!"

Big Boy shook free.

"Ef yuh stay here theys gonna lynch yuh!" he yelled, running.

After he had gone about twenty-five yards he turned and looked; Bobo was flying through the woods like the wind.

Big Boy slowed when he came to the railroad. He wondered if he ought to go through the streets or down the track. He decided on the tracks. He could dodge a train better than a mob.

He trotted along the ties, looking ahead and back. His cheek itched, and he felt it. His hand came away smeared with blood. He wiped it nervously on his overalls.

When he came to his back fence he heaved himself over. He landed among a flock of startled chickens. A bantam rooster tried to spur him. He slipped and fell in front of the kitchen steps, grunting heavily. The ground was slick with greasy dishwater.

Panting, he stumbled through the doorway.

"Lawd, Big Boy, whuts wrong wid yuh?"

His mother stood gaping in the middle of the floor. Big Boy flopped wordlessly onto a stool, almost toppling over. Pots simmered on the stove. The kitchen smelled of food cooking.

"Whuts the matter, Big Boy?"

Mutely, he looked at her. Then he burst into tears. She came and felt the scratches on his face.

"Whut happened t yuh, Big Boy? Somebody been botherin yuh?"

"They after me, Ma! They after me . . ."

"Who!"

"Ah . . . Ah . . . We . . ."

"Big Boy, whuts wrong wid yuh?"

"He killed Lester n Buck," he muttered simply.

"Killed!"

"Yessum."

"Lester n Buck!"

"Yessum, Ma!"

"How killed?"

"He shot em, Ma!"

"Lawd Gawd in Heaven, have mercy on us all! This is mo trouble, mo trouble," she moaned, wringing her hands.

"N Ah killed im, Ma . . ."

She stared, trying to understand.

"Whut happened, Big Boy?"

"We tried t git our cloes from the tree . . ."

"Whut tree?"

"We wuz swimmin, Ma. N the white woman . . ."

"*White* woman? . . ."

"Yessum. She wuz at the swimmin hole . . ."

"Lawd have mercy! Ah knowed yuh boys wuz gonna keep on till yuh got into somethin like this!"

She ran into the hall.

"Lucy!"

"Mam?"

"C mere!"

"Mam?"

"C mere, Ah say!"

"Whutcha wan, Ma? Ahm sewin."

"Chile, will yuh c mere like Ah ast yuh?"

Lucy came to the door holding an unfinished apron in her hands. When she saw Big Boy's face she looked wildly at her mother.

"Whuts the matter?"

"Wheres Pa?"

"He's out front, Ah reckon."

"Git im, quick!"

"Whuts the matter, Ma?"

"Go git yo Pa, Ah say!"

Lucy ran out. The mother sank into a chair, holding a dish rag. Suddenly, she sat up.

"Big Boy, Ah thought yuh wuz at school?"

Big Boy looked at the floor.

"How come yuh didn't go t school?"

"We went t the woods."

She sighed.

"Ah done done all Ah kin fer yuh, Big Boy. Only Gawd kin help yuh now."

"Ma, don let em git me; don let em git me . . ."

His father came into the doorway. He stared at Big Boy, then at his wife.

"Whuts Big Boy inter now?" he asked sternly.

"Saul, Big Boys done gone n got inter trouble wid the white folks."

The old man's mouth dropped, and he looked from one to the other.

"Saul, we gotta git im erway from here."

"Open yo mouth n talk! Whut yuh been doin?" The old man gripped Big Boy's shoulders and peered at the scratches on his face.

"Me n Lester n Buck n Bobo wuz out on ol man Harveys place swimmin . . ."

"Saul, its a *white* woman!"

Big Boy winced. The old man compressed his lips and stared at his wife. Lucy gaped at her brother as though she had never seen him before.

"Whut happened? Cant yuh all talk?" the old man thundered, with a certain helplessness in his voice.

"We wuz swimmin," Big Boy began, "n then a white woman comes up t the hole. We got up right erway to git our cloes sos we could git erway, n she started screamin. Our cloes wuz right by the tree where she wuz standin, n when we started t git em she just screamed. We told her we wanted our

cloes . . . Yuh see, Pa, she was standin' right *by* our cloes; n when we went t git em she jus screamed . . . Bobo got the cloes, n then he shot Lester . . ."

"*Who* shot Lester?"

"The white man."

"Whut white man?"

"Ah dunno, Pa. He wuz a soljer, n he had a rifle."

"A soljer?"

"Yessuh."

"A *soljer?*"

"Yessuh, Pa. A soljer."

The old man frowned.

"N then what yuh-all do?"

"Waal, Buck said, 'Hes gotta gun!' N we started runnin. N then he shot Buck, n he fell in the swimmin hole. We didn't see im no mo . . . He wuz close on us then. He looked at the white woman n then he started t shoot Bobo. Ah grabbed the gun, n we started fightin. Bobo jumped on his back. He started beatin Bobo. Then Ah hit im wid the gun. Then he started at me n Ah shot im. Then we run . . ."

"Who seen?"

"Nobody."

"Wheres Bobo?"

"He went home."

"Anybody run after yuh-all?"

"Nawsuh."

"Yuh see anybody?"

"Nawsuh. Nobody but a white man. But he didnt see us."

"How long fo yuh-all lef the swimmin hole?"

"Little while ergo."

The old man nervously brushed his hand across his eyes and walked to the door. His lips moved, but no words came.

"Saul, whut we gonna do?"

"Lucy," began the old man, "go t Brother Sanders n tell im Ah said c mere; n go t Brother Jenkins n tell im Ah said c mere; n go t Elder Peters n tell im Ah said c mere. N don say nothin t nobody but whut Ah tol yuh. N when yuh git thu come straight back. Now go!"

Lucy dropped her apron across the back of a chair and ran down the steps. The mother bent over, crying and praying. The old man walked slowly over to Big Boy.

"Big Boy?"

Big Boy swallowed.

"Ahm talkin t yuh!"

"Yessuh."

"How come yuh didnt go t school this mawnin?"

"We went t the woods."

"Didnt yo ma send yuh t school?"

"Yessuh."

"How come yuh didnt go?"

"We went t the woods."

"Don yuh know thas wrong?"

"Yessuh."

"How come yuh go?"

Big Boy looked at his fingers, knotted them, and squirmed in his seat.

"AHM TALKIN T YUH!"

His wife straightened up and said reprovingly:

"Saul!"

The old man desisted, yanking nervously at the shoulder straps of his overalls.

"How long wuz the woman there?"

"Not long."

"Wuz she young?"

"Yessuh. Lika gal."

"Did yuh-all say anythin t her?"

"Nawsuh. We jes said we wanted our cloes."

"N what she say?"

"Nothin, Pa. She jus backed erway t the tree n screamed."

The old man stared, his lips trying to form a question.

"Big Boy, did yuh-all bother her?"

"Nawsuh, Pa. We didnt *touch* her."

"How long fo the white man come up?"

"Right erway."

"Whut he say?"

"Nothin. He jus cussed us."

Abruptly the old man left the kitchen.

"Ma, cant Ah go fo they ketches me?"

"Sauls doin whut he kin."

"Ma, Ma, Ah don want em t ketch me . . ."

"Sauls doin what he kin. Nobody but the good Lawd kin hep us now."

The old man came back with a shotgun and leaned it in a corner. Fascinatedly, Big Boy looked at it.

There was a knock at the front door.

"Liza, see whos there."

She went. They were silent, listening. They could hear her talking.

"Whos there?"

"Me."

"Who?"

"Me, Brother Sanders."

"C mon in. Sauls waitin fer yuh."

Sanders paused in the doorway, smiling.

"Yuh sent fer me, Brother Morrison?"

"Brother Sanders, wes in deep trouble here."

Sanders came all the way into the kitchen.

"Yeah?"

"Big Boy done gone n killed a white man."

Sanders stopped short, then came forward, his face thrust out, his mouth open. His lips moved several times before he could speak.

"A *white* man?"

"They gonna kill me; they gonna kill me!" Big Boy cried, running to the old man.

"Saul, cant we git im erway somewhere?"

"Here now, take it easy; take it easy," said Sanders, holding Big Boy's wrists.

"They gonna kill me; they gonna lynch me!"

Big Boy slipped to the floor. They lifted him to a stool. His mother held him closely, pressing his head to her bosom.

"Whut we gonna do?" asked Sanders.

"Ah done sent fer Brother Jenkins n Elder Peters."

Sanders leaned his shoulders against the wall. Then, as the full meaning of it came to him, he exclaimed:

"Theys gonna git a mob! . . ." His voice broke off and his eyes fell on the shotgun.

Feet came pounding on the steps. They turned toward the door. Lucy ran in crying. Jenkins followed. The old man met him in the middle of the room, taking his hand.

"Wes in bad trouble here, Brother Jenkins. Big Boy's done gone n killed a white man. Yuh-alls gotta hep me . . ."

Jenkins looked hard at Big Boy.

"Elder Peters says hes comin," said Lucy.

"When all this happen?" asked Jenkins.

"Near bout a hour ergo, now," said the old man.

"Whut we gonna do?" asked Jenkins.

"Ah wanna wait till Elder Peters come," said the old man helplessly.

"But we gotta work fas ef we gonna do anythin," said Sanders. "We'll git in trouble jus standin here like this."

Big Boy pulled away from his mother.

"Pa, lemma go now! Lemma go now!"

"Be still, Big Boy!"

"Where kin yuh go?"

"Ah could ketch a freight!"

"Thas *sho* death!" said Jenkins. "They'll be watchin em all!"

"Kin yuh-all hep me wid some money?" the old man asked.

They shook their heads.

"Saul, whut kin we do? Big Boy cant stay here."

There was another knock at the door.

The old man backed stealthily to the shotgun.

"Lucy, go!"

Lucy looked at him, hesitating.

"Ah better go," said Jenkins.

It was Elder Peters. He came in hurriedly.

"Good evenin, everybody!"

"How yuh, Elder?"

"Good evenin."

"How yuh today?"

Peters looked around the crowded kitchen.

"Whuts the matter?"

"Elder, wes in deep trouble," began the old man. "Big Boy n some mo boys . . ."

". . . Lester n Buck n Bobo . . ."

". . . wuz over on ol man Harveys place swimmin . . ."

"N he don like us niggers *none*," said Peters emphatically. He widened his legs and put his thumbs in the armholes of his vest.

". . . n some white woman . . ."

"Yeah?" said Peters, coming closer.

". . . comes erlong n the boys tries t git their cloes where they done lef em under a tree. Waal, she started screamin n all, see? Reckon she thought the boys wuz after her. Then a white man in a soljers suit shoots two of em . . ."

". . . Lester n Buck . . ."

"Huummm," said Peters. "Tha wuz old man Harveys son."

"Harveys son?"

"Yuh mean the one that wuz in the Army?"

"Yuh mean Jim?"

"Yeah," said Peters. "The papers said he wuz here fer a vacation from his regiment. N tha woman the boys saw wuz jus erbout his wife . . ."

They stared at Peters. Now that they knew what white person had been killed, their fears became definite.

"N whut else happened?"

"Big Boy shot the man . . ."

"Harveys *son?*"

"He had t, Elder. He wuz gonna shoot im ef he didnt . . ."

"Lawd!" said Peters. He looked around and put his hat back on.

"How long ergo wuz this?"

"Mighty near an hour, now, Ah reckon."

"Do the white folks know yit?"

"Don know, Elder."

"Yuh-all better git this boy outta here right now," said Peters. "Cause ef yuh don theres gonna be a lynchin . . ."

"Where kin Ah go, Elder?" Big Boy ran up to him.

They crowded around Peters. He stood with his legs wide apart, looking up at the ceiling.

"Mabbe we kin hide im in the church till he kin git erway," said Jenkins. Peters' lips flexed.

"Naw, Brother, thall never do! Theyll git im there sho. N anyhow, ef they ketch im there itll ruin us all. We gotta git the boy outta town . . ."

Sanders went up to the old man.

"Lissen," he said in a whisper. "Mah son, Will, the one whut drives fer the Magnolia Express Comny, is takin a truck o goods t Chicawgo in the mawnin. If we kin hide Big Boy somewhere till then, we kin put him on the truck . . ."

"Pa, please, lemme go wid Will when he goes in the mawnin," Big Boy begged.

The old man stared at Sanders.

"Yuh reckon thas safe?"

"Its the only thing yuh *kin* do," said Peters.

"But where we gonna hide im till then?"

"Whut time yo boy leavin out in the mawnin?"

"At six."

They were quiet, thinking. The water kettle on the stove sang.

"Pa, Ah knows where Will passes erlong wid the truck out on Bullards Road. Ah kin hide in one of them ol kilns . . ."

"Where?"

"In one of them kilns we built . . ."

"But they'll git yuh there," wailed the mother.

"But there ain no place else fer im t go."

"Theres some holes big enough fer me t git in n stay till Will comes erlong," said Big Boy. "Please, Pa, lemme go fo they ketches me . . ."

"Let im go!"

"Please, Pa . . ."

The old man breathed heavily.

"Lucy, git his things!"

"Saul, theyll git im out there!" wailed the mother, grabbing Big Boy. Peters pulled her away.

"Sister Morrison, ef yuh don let im go n git erway from here hes gonna be caught shos theres a Gawd in Heaven!"

Lucy came running with Big Boy's shoes and pulled them on his feet. The old man thrust a battered hat on his head. The mother went to the stove and dumped the skillet of corn pone into her apron. She wrapped it, and unbuttoning Big Boy's overalls, pushed it into his bosom.

"Heres something fer yuh t eat; n pray, Big Boy, cause thas all anybody kin do now . . ."

Big Boy pulled to the door, his mother clinging to him.

"Let im go, Sister Morrison!"

"Run fas, Big Boy!"

Big Boy raced across the yard, scattering the chickens. He paused at the fence and hollered back:

"Tell Bobo where Ahm hidin n tell im t c mon!"

IV

He made for the railroad, running straight toward the sunset. He held his left hand tightly over his heart, holding the hot pone of corn bread there. At times he stumbled over the ties, for his shoes were tight and hurt his feet. His throat burned from thirst; he had had no water since noon.

He veered off the track and trotted over the crest of a hill, following Bullard's Road. His feet slipped and slid in the dust. He kept his eyes straight ahead, fearing every clump of shrubbery, every tree. He wished it were night. If he could only get to the kilns without meeting anyone. Suddenly a thought came to him like a blow. He recalled hearing the old folks tell tales of blood-hounds, and fear made him run slower. None of them had thought of that. Spose blood-houns wuz put on his trail? Lawd! Spose a whole pack of em, foamin n howlin, tore im t pieces? He went limp and his feet dragged. Yeah, thas whut they wuz gonna send after im, blood-houns! N then thered be no way fer im t dodge! Why hadnt Pa let im take tha shotgun? He stopped. He oughta go back n git tha shotgun. And then when the mob came he would take some with him.

In the distance he heard the approach of a train. It jarred him back to a sharp sense of danger. He ran again, his big shoes sopping up and down in the dust. He was tired and his lungs were bursting from running. He wet

his lips, wanting water. As he turned from the road across a plowed field he heard the train roaring at his heels. He ran faster, gripped in terror.

He was nearly there now. He could see the black clay on the sloping hillside. Once inside a kiln he would be safe. For a little while, at least. He thought of the shotgun again. If he only had something! Someone to talk to . . . Thas right! Bobo! Bobod be wid im. Hed almost fergot Bobo. Bobod bringa gun; he knowed he would. N tergether they could kill the whole mob. Then in the mawning theyd git inter Will's truck n go far erway, t Chicawgo . . .

He slowed to a walk, looking back and ahead. A light wind skipped over the grass. A beetle lit on his cheek and he brushed it off. Behind the dark pines hung a red sun. Two bats flapped against that sun. He shivered, for he was growing cold; the sweat on his body was drying.

He stopped at the foot of the hill, trying to choose between two patches of black kilns high above him. He went to the left, for there lay the ones he, Bobo, Lester, and Buck had dug only last week. He looked around again; the landscape was bare. He climbed the embankment and stood before a row of black pits sinking four and five feet deep into the earth. He went to the largest and peered in. He stiffened when his ears caught the sound of a whir. He ran back a few steps and poised on his toes. Six foot of snake slid out of the pit and went into a coil. Big Boy looked around wildly for a stick. He ran down the slope, peering into the grass. He stumbled over a tree limb. He picked it up and tested it by striking it against the ground.

Warily, he crept back up the slope, his stick poised. When about seven feet from the snake he stopped and waved the stick. The coil grew tighter, the whir sounded louder, and a flat head reared to strike. He went to the right, and the flat head followed him, the blue-black tongue darting forth; he went to the left, and the flat head followed him there too.

He stopped, teeth clenched. He had to kill this snake. Jus had t kill im! This wuz the safest pit on the hillside. He waved the stick again, looking at the snake before, thinking of a mob behind. The flat head reared higher. With stick over shoulder, he jumped in, swinging. The stick sang through the air, catching the snake on the side of the head, sweeping him out of coil. There was a brown writhing mass. Then Big Boy was upon him, pounding blows home, one on top of the other. He fought viciously, his eyes red, his teeth bared in a snarl. He beat till the snake lay still; then he stomped it with his heel, grinding its head into the dirt.

He stopped, limp, wet. The corners of his lips were white with spittle. He spat and shuddered.

Cautiously, he went to the hole and peered. He longed for a match. He imagined whole nests of them in there waiting. He put the stick into the hole and waved it around. Stooping, he peered again. It mus be awright. He looked over the hillside, his eyes coming back to the dead snake. Then he got to his knees and backed slowly into the hole.

When inside he felt there must be snakes about him, ready to strike. It seemed he could see and feel them there, waiting tensely in coil. In the dark he imagined long, white fangs ready to sink into his neck, his side, his legs. He wanted to come out, but kept still. Shucks, he told himself, ef there wuz any snakes in here they sho woulda done bit me by now. Some of his fear left, and he relaxed.

With elbows on ground and chin on palms, he settled. The clay was cold to his knees and thighs, but his bosom was kept warm by the hot pone of corn bread. His thirst returned and he longed for a drink. He was hungry, too. But he did not want to eat the corn pone. Naw, not now. Mabbe after erwhile, after Bobo came. Then theyd both eat the corn pone.

The view from his hole was fringed by the long tufts of grass. He could see all the way to Bullard's Road, and even beyond. The wind was blowing, and in the east the first touch of dusk was rising. Every now and then a bird floated past, a spot of wheeling black printed against the sky. Big Boy sighed, shifted his weight, and chewed at a blade of grass. A wasp droned. He heard number nine, far away and mournful.

The train made him remember how they had dug these kilns on long hot summer days, how they had made boilers out of big tin cans, filled them with water, fixed stoppers for steam, cemented them in holes with wet clay, and built fires under them. He recalled how they had danced and yelled when a stopper blew out of a boiler, letting out a big spout of steam and a shrill whistle. There were times when they had the whole hillside blazing and smoking. Yeah, yuh see, Big Boy wuz Casey Jones n wuz speedin it down the gleamin rails of the Southern Pacific. Bobo had number two on the Santa Fe. Buck wuz on the Illinoy Central. Lester the Nickel Plate. Lawd, how they sheveled the wood in! The boiling water would almost jar the cans loose from the clay. More and more pine-knots and dry leaves would be piled under the cans. Flames would grow so tall they would have to shield their eyes. Sweat would pour off their faces. Then, suddenly, a peg would shoot high into the air, and

Pssseeeezzzzzzzzzzzzzzzzzz . . .

Big Boy sighed and stretched out his arm, quenching the flames and scattering the smoke. Why didnt Bobo c mon? He looked over the fields; there was nothing but dying sunlight. His mind drifted back to the kilns. He remembered the day when Buck, jealous of his winning, had tried to smash his kiln. Yeah, that ol sonofabitch! Naw, Lawd! He didnt go t say tha! Whut wuz he thinkin erbout? Cussin the dead! Yeah, po ol Buck wuz dead now. N Lester too. Yeah, it wuz awright fer Buck t smash his kiln. Sho. N he wished he hadnt socked ol Buck so hard tha day. He wuz sorry fer Buck now. N he sho wished he hadnt cussed po ol Bucks ma, neither. Tha wuz sinful! Mabbe Gawd would git im fer that? But he didnt go t do it! Po Buck! Po Lester! Hed never treat anybody like tha ergin, never . . .

Dusk was slowly deepening. Somewhere, he could not tell exactly where, a cricket took up a fitful song. The air was growing soft and heavy. He looked over the fields, longing for Bobo . . .

He shifted his body to ease the cold damp of the ground, and thought back over the day. Yeah, hed been dam right erbout not wantin t go swimmin. N ef hed followed his right min hed neverve gone n got inter all this trouble. At first hed said naw. But shucks, somehow hed just went on wid the res. Yeah he shoulda went on t school tha mawnin, like Ma told im t do. But, hell, who wouldnt git tireda awways drivin a guy to school! Tha wuz the big trouble awways drivin a guy t school. He wouldnt be in all this trouble now if it wuznt fer that Gawddam school! Impatiently, he took the grass out of his mouth and threw it away, demolishing the little red school house . . .

Yeah, if they had all kept still n quiet when tha ol white woman showed-up, mabbe shedve went on off. But yuh never kin tell erbout these white folks. Mabbe she wouldntve went. Mabbe tha white man woulda killed all of em! All *fo* of em! Yeah, yuh never kin tell erbout white folks. Then, ergin, mabbe tha white woman woulda went on off n laffed. Yeah, mabbe tha white man woulda said: *Yuh nigger bastards git t hell outta here! Yuh know Gawddam well yuh don berlong here!* N then they woulda grabbed their cloes n run like all hell . . . He blinked the white man away. Where wuz Bobo? Why didnt he hurry up n c mon?

He jerked another blade and chewed. Yeah, ef Pa had only let im have tha shotgun! He could stan off a whole mob wid a shotgun. He looked at the ground as he turned a shotgun over in his hands. Then he leveled it at an advancing white man. *Boooom!* The man curled up. Another came. He reloaded quickly, and let him have what the other had got. He too curled up. Then another came. He got the same medicine. Then the whole mob swirled around him, and he blazed away, getting as many as he could. They closed in; but, by Gawd, he had done his part, hadnt he? N the newpapersd say: NIGGER KILLS DOZEN OF MOB BEFO LYNCHED! Er mabbe theyd say: TRAPPED NIGGER SLAYS TWENTY BEFO KILLED! He smiled a little. Tha wouldnt be so bad, would it? Blinking the newspaper away, he looked over the fields. Where wuz Bobo? Why didnt he hurry up n c mon?

He shifted, trying to get a crick out of his legs. Shucks, he wuz gettin tireda this. N it was almos dark now. Yeah, there wuz a little bittie star way over yonder in the eas. Mabbe tha white man wuznt dead? Mabbe they wuznt even lookin fer im? Mabbe he could go back home now? Naw, better wait erwhile. Thad be bes. But, Lawd, ef he only had some water! He could hardly swallow, his throat was so dry. Gawddam them white folks! Thas all they wuz good fer, t run a nigger down lika rabbit! Yeah, they git yuh in a corner n then they let yuh have it. A thousan of em! He shivered, for the cold of the clay was chilling his bones. Lawd, spose they found im here in this hole? N wid nobody t help im? . . . But ain no use in thinkin erbout tha; wait till trouble come fo yuh start fightin it. But if tha mob came one by one hed wipe em all out. Clean up the whole bunch. He caught one by the neck and choked him long and hard, choked him till his tongue and eyes popped out. Then he jumped upon his chest and stomped him like he had stomped that snake. When he had finished with one, another came. He choked him too. Choked till he sank slowly to the ground, gasping . . .

"Hoalo!"

Big Boy snatched his fingers from the white man's neck and looked over the fields. He saw nobody. Had someone spied him? He was sure that somebody had hollered. His heart pounded. But, shucks, nobody couldnt see im here in this hole . . . But mabbe theyd seen im when he wuz comin n had laid low n wuz now closin in on im! Praps they wuz signalin fer the others? Yeah, they wuz creepin up on im! Mabbe he oughta git up n run . . . Oh! Mabbe tha wuz Bobo! Yeah, Bobo! He oughta clim out n see if Bobo wuz lookin fer im . . . He stiffened.

"Hoalo!"

"Hoalo!"

"Wheres yuh?"

"Over here on Bullards Road!"

"C mon over!"

"Awright!"

He heard footsteps. Then voices came again, low and far away this time.

"Seen anybody?"

"Naw. Yuh?"

"Naw."

"Yuh reckon they got erway?"

"Ah dunno. Its hard t tell."

"Gawddam them sonofabitchin niggers!"

"We oughta kill ever black bastard in this country!"

"Waal, Jim got two of em, anyhow."

"But Bertha said there wuz *fo!*"

"Where in hell they hidin?"

"She said one of em wuz named Big Boy, or somethin like tha."

"We went t his shack lookin fer im."

"Yeah?"

"But we didnt fin im."

"These niggers stick tergether; they don never tell on each other."

"We looked all thu the shack n couldnt fin hide ner hair of im. Then we drove the ol woman n man out n set the shack on fire . . ."

"Jeesus! Ah wished Ah coulda been there!"

"Yuh shoulda heard the ol nigger woman howl . . ."

"Hoalo!"

"C mon over!"

Big Boy eased to the edge and peeped. He saw a white man with a gun slung over his shoulder running down the slope. Wuz they gonna search the hill? Lawd, there wuz no way fer im t git erway now; he wuz caught! He shoulda knowed theyd git im here. N he didn't hava thing, notta thing t fight wid. Yeah, soon as the blood-houns came theyd fin im. Lawd, have mercy! Theyd lynch im right here on the hill . . . Theyd git im n tie im t a stake n burn im erlive! Lawd! Nobody but the good Lawd could hep im now, nobody . . .

He heard more feet running. He nestled deeper. His chest ached. Nobody but the good Lawd could hep now. They wuz crowdn all round im n when they hada big crowd theyd close in on im. Then itd be over . . . The good Lawd would have t hep im, cause nobody could hep im now, nobody . . .

And then he went numb when he remembered Bobo. Spose Bobod come now? Hed be caught sho! Both of em would be caught! Theyd make Bobo tell where he wuz! Bobo oughta not try to come now. Somebody oughta tell im . . . But there wuz nobody; there wuz no way . . .

He eased slowly back to the opening. There was a large group of men. More were coming. Many had guns. Some had coils of rope slung over shoulders.

"Ah tell yuh they still here, somewhere . . ."

"But we looked all over!"

"What t hell! Wouldnt do t let em git erway!"

"Naw. Ef they git erway notta woman in this town would be safe."

"Say, whuts tha yuh got?"

"Er pillar."

"Fer whut?"

"Feathers, fool!"

"Chris! Thisll be hot if we kin ketch them niggers!"

"Ol Anderson said he wuz gonna bringa barrela tar!"

"Ah got some gasolin in mah car if yuh need it."

Big Boy had no feelings now. He was waiting. He did not wonder if they were coming after him. He just waited. He did not wonder about Bobo. He rested his cheek against the cold clay, waiting.

A dog barked. He stiffened. It barked again. He balled himself into a knot at the bottom of the hole, waiting. Then he heard the patter of dog feet.

"Look!"

"Whuts he got?"

"Its a snake!"

"Yeah, the dogs foun a snake!"

"Gee, its a big one!"

"Shucks, Ah wish he could fin one of them sonofabitchin niggers!"

The voices sank to low murmurs. Then he heard number twelve, its bell tolling and whistle crying as it slid along the rails. He flattened himself against the clay. Someone was singing:

We'll hang ever nigger t a sour apple tree . . .

When the song ended there was hard laughter. From the other side of the hill he heard the dog barking furiously. He listened. There was more than one dog now. There were many and they were barking their throats out.

"Hush. Ah hear them dogs!"

"When theys barkin like tha theys foun somethin!"

"Here they come over the hill!"

"WE GOT IM! WE GOT IM!"

There came a roar. Tha must be Bobo; tha mus be Bobo . . . In spite of his fear, Big Boy looked. The road, and half of the hillside across the road, were covered with men. A few were at the top of the hill, stenciled against the sky. He could see dark forms moving up the slopes. They were yelling.

"By Gawd, we got im!"

"C mon!"

"Where is he?"

"Theyre bringin im over the hill!"

"Ah got a rope fer im!"

"Say, somebody go n git the others!"

"Where is he? Cant we see im, Mister?"

"They say Berthas comin, too."

"Jack! Jack! Don leave me! Ah wanna see im!"

"Theyre bringin im over the hill, sweetheart!"

"AH WANNA BE THE FIRS T PUT A ROPE ON THA BLACK BAS-TARDS NECK!"

"Les start the fire!"

"Heat the tar!"

"Ah got some chains t chain im."

"Bring im over this way!"

"Chris, Ah wished Ah hada drink . . ."

Big Boy saw men moving over the hill. Among them was a long dark spot. Tha mus be Bobo; tha mus be Bobo theys carryin . . . Theyll git im here. He oughta git up n run. He clamped his teeth and ran his hand across his forehead, bringing it away wet. He tried to swallow, but could not; his throat was dry.

They had started the song again:

> *We'll hang ever nigger t a sour apple tree . . .*

There were women singing now. Their voices made the song round and full. Song waves rolled over the top of pine trees. The sky sagged low, heavy with clouds. Wind was rising. Sometimes cricket cries cut surprisingly across the mob song. A dog had gone to the utmost top of the hill. At each lull of the song his howl floated full into the night.

Big Boy shrank when he saw the first flame light the hillside. Would they see im here? Then he remembered you could not see into the dark if you were standing in the light. As flames leaped higher he saw two men rolling a barrel up the slope.

"Say, gimme a han here, will yuh?"

"Awright, heave!"

"C mon! Straight up! Git t the other end!"

"Ah got the feathers here in this pillar!"

"BRING SOME MO WOOD!"

Big Boy could see the barrel surrounded by flames. The mob fell back, forming a dark circle. Theyd fin im here! He had a wild impulse to climb out and fly across the hills. But his legs would not move. He stared hard, trying to find Bobo. His eyes played over a long, dark spot near the fire. Fanned by wind, flames leaped higher. He jumped. That dark spot had moved. Lawd, thas Bobo; thas Bobo . . .

He smelt the scent of tar, faint at first, then stronger. The wind brought it full into his face, then blew it away. His eyes burned and he rubbed them with his knuckles. He sneezed.

"LES GIT SOURVINEERS!"

He saw the mob close in around the fire. Their faces were hard and sharp in the light of the flames. More men and women were coming over the hill. The long, dark spot was smudged out.

"Everybody git back!"

"Look! Hes gotta finger!"

"C MON! GIT THE GALS BACK FROM THE FIRE!"

"He's got one of his ears, see?"

"Whuts the matter!"

"A woman fell out! Fainted, Ah reckon . . ."

The stench of tar permeated the hillside. The sky was black and the wind was blowing hard.

"HURRY UP N BURN THE NIGGER FO IT RAINS!"

Big Boy saw the mob fall back, leaving a small knot of men about the fire. Then, for the first time, he had a full glimpse of Bobo. A black body

flashed in the light. Bobo was struggling, twisting; they were binding his arms and legs.

When he saw them tilt the barrel he stiffened. A scream quivered. He knew the tar was on Bobo. The mob fell back. He saw a tar-drenched body glistening and turning.

"THE BASTARDS GOT IT!"

There was a sudden quiet. Then he shrank violently as the wind carried, like a flurry of snow, a widening spiral of white feathers into the night. The flames leaped tall as the trees. The scream came again. Big Boy trembled and looked. The mob was running down the slopes, leaving the fire clear. Then he saw a writhing white mass cradled in yellow flame, and heard screams, one on top of the other, each shriller and shorter than the last. The mob was quiet now, standing still, looking up the slopes at the writhing white mass gradually growing black, growing black in a cradle of yellow flame.

"PO ON MO GAS!"

"Gimme a lif, will yuh!"

Two men were struggling, carrying between them a heavy can. They set it down, tilted it, leaving it so that the gas would trickle down to the hollowed earth around the fire.

Big Boy slid back into the hole, his face buried in clay. He had no feelings now, no fears. He was numb, empty, as though all blood had been drawn from him. Then his muscles flexed taut when he heard a faint patter. A tiny stream of cold water seeped to his knees, making him push back to a drier spot. He looked up; rain was beating in the grass.

"It's rainin!"

"C mon, les git t town!"

". . . don worry, when the fire git thu wid im hell be gone . . ."

"Wait, Charles! Don leave me; its slippery here . . ."

"Ahll take some of yuh ladies back in mah car . . ."

Big Boy heard the dogs barking again, this time closer. Running feet pounded past. Cold water chilled his ankles. He could hear raindrops steadily hissing.

Now a dog was barking at the mouth of the hole, barking furiously, sensing a presence there. He balled himself into a knot and clung to the bottom, his knees and shins buried in water. The bark came louder. He heard paws scraping and felt the hot scent of dog breath on his face. Green eyes glowed and drew nearer as the barking, muffled by the closeness of the hole, beat upon his eardrums. Backing till his shoulders pressed against the clay, he held his breath. He pushed out his hands, his fingers stiff. The dog yawped louder, advancing, his bark rising sharp and thin. Big Boy rose to his knees, his hands before him. Then he flattened out still more against the bottom, breathing lungsful of hot dog scent, breathing it slowly, hard, but evenly. The dog came closer, bringing hotter dog scent. Big Boy could go back no more. His knees were slipping and slopping in the water. He braced himself, ready. Then, he never exactly knew how—he never knew whether he had lunged or the dog had lunged—they were together, rolling in the water. The green eyes were beneath him, between his legs. Dognails bit into his arms. His knees slipped backward and he landed full on the dog; the dog's breath left in a heavy gasp. Instinctively, he fumbled for the

throat as he felt the dog twisting between his knees. The dog snarled, long and low, as though gathering strength. Big Boy's hands traveled swiftly over the dog's back, groping for the throat. He felt dognails again and saw green eyes, but his fingers had found the throat. He choked, feeling his fingers sink; he choked, throwing back his head and stiffening his arms. He felt the dog's body heave, felt dognails digging into his loins. With strength flowing from fear, he closed his fingers, pushing his full weight on the dog's throat. The dog heaved again, and lay still . . . Big Boy heard the sound of his own breathing filling the hole, and heard shouts and footsteps above him going past.

For a long time he held the dog, held it long after the last footstep had died out, long after the rain had stopped.

V

Morning found him still on his knees in a puddle of rainwater, staring at the stiff body of a dog. As the air brightened he came to himself slowly. He held still for a long time, as though waking from a dream, as though trying to remember.

The chug of a truck came over the hill. He tried to crawl to the opening. His knees were stiff and a thousand needle-like pains shot from the bottom of his feet to the calves of his legs. Giddiness made his eyes blur. He pulled up and looked. Through brackish light he saw Will's truck standing some twenty-five yards away, the engine running. Will stood on the running board, looking over the slopes of the hill.

Big Boy scuffled out, falling weakly in the wet grass. He tried to call to Will, but his dry throat would make no sound. He tried again.

"Will!"

Will heard, answering:

"Big Boy, c mon!"

He tried to run, and fell. Will came, meeting him in the tall grass.

"C mon," Will said, catching his arm.

They struggled to the truck.

"Hurry up!" said Will, pushing him onto the running board.

Will pushed back a square trapdoor which swung above the back of the driver's seat. Big Boy pulled through, landing with a thud on the bottom. On hands and knees he looked around in the semi-darkness.

"Wheres Bobo?"

Big Boy stared.

"Wheres Bobo?"

"They got im."

"When?"

"Las night."

"The mob?"

Big Boy pointed in the direction of a charred sapling on the slope of the opposite hill. Will looked. The trapdoor fell. The engine purred, the gears whined, and the truck lurched forward over the muddy road, sending Big Boy on his side.

For a while he lay as he had fallen, on his side, too weak to move. As he felt the truck swing around a curve he straightened up and rested his back against a stack of wooden boxes. Slowly, he began to make out objects in the darkness. Through two long cracks fell thin blades of daylight. The floor was of smooth steel, and cold to his thighs. Splinters and bits of sawdust danced with the rumble of the truck. Each time they swung around a curve he was pulled over the floor; he grabbed at corners of boxes to steady himself. Once he heard the crow of a rooster. It made him think of home, of ma and pa. He thought he remembered hearing somewhere that the house had burned, but could not remember where . . . It all seemed unreal now.

He was tired. He dozed, swaying with the lurch. Then he jumped awake. The truck was running smoothly, on gravel. Far away he heard two short blasts from the Buckeye Lumber Mill. Unconsciously, the thought sang through his mind: Its six erclock . . .

The trapdoor swung in. Will spoke through a corner of his mouth.

"How yuh comin?"

"Awright."

"How they git Bobo?"

"He wuz comin over the hill."

"Whut they do?"

"They burnt im . . . Will, Ah wan some water; mah throats like fire . . ."

"Well git some when we pas a fillin station."

Big Boy leaned back and dozed. He jerked awake when the truck stopped. He heard Will get out. He wanted to peep through the trapdoor, but was afraid. For a moment, the wild fear he had known in the hole came back. Spose theyd search n fin im? He quieted when he heard Will's footsteps on the running board. The trapdoor pushed in. Will's hat came through, dripping.

"Take it, quick!"

Big Boy grabbed, spilling water into his face. The truck lurched. He drank. Hard cold lumps of brick rolled into his hot stomach. A dull pain made him bend over. His intestines seemed to be drawing into a tight knot. After a bit it eased, and he sat up, breathing softly.

The truck swerved. He blinked his eyes. The blades of daylight had turned brightly golden. The sun had risen.

The truck sped over the asphalt miles, sped northward, jolting him, shaking out of his bosom the crumbs of corn bread, making them dance with the splinters and sawdust in the golden blades of sunshine.

He turned on his side and slept.

James Baldwin
(1924–1987)

The urgency and violence of twentieth-century history have often forced writers into especially close relationships with current events. William Butler Yeats's poetry is colored by the "terrible beauty" of the 1916 Easter Rising in Ireland, much of Thomas Mann's fiction is a complex reaction to the German defeat in World War I, and the work of the French existentialists of the 1940's was shaped in major ways by the Nazi occupation of France. The American civil rights movement of the 1960's similarly found its major literary interpreter in James Baldwin, who explored its meaning in a series of powerfully written and widely read essays and, less directly, in a number of fine novels and short stories. The essays collected in *Notes of a Native Son* (1955), *Nobody Knows My Name* (1961), and *The Fire Next Time* (1963) brought Baldwin worldwide attention as one of the most accomplished essayists in American literary history, but they also placed him at the eye of a storm of controversy over his readings of racial issues. As the high passions of the 1960's receded with time, Baldwin came to be regarded less as the spokesman of a movement and more as an imaginative writer whose interpretations of racial issues were grounded in his own complex personality.

Baldwin was born in Harlem in 1924 to Berdis Jones, a domestic servant who three years later married David Baldwin, a brutal, paranoid laborer and storefront preacher by whom she had eight children. David Baldwin resented his wife's illegitimate son and subjected him to constant ridicule and abuse, from which Baldwin withdrew into a close relationship with his mother and into reading and schoolwork. While he was in De Witt Clinton High School, he also became a successful child preacher at the Fireside Pentecostal Church in Harlem, drawing large crowds for three years before losing his faith when he was sixteen.

Baldwin had already begun to write seriously while he was in high school, where he edited the school magazine, and he continued to write after graduation, while working in a defense plant in New Jersey. In 1943, Baldwin left home and settled in Greenwich Village, determined to become a writer. For the next five years, he supported himself by menial jobs and wrote at night, managing to sell a few magazine articles and beginning a novel. Richard Wright, whom he met in 1944, befriended him and helped him get a fellowship in 1945. A second award, the Rosenwald Fellowship, in 1948 enabled him to leave New York for Europe, where he remained for the next ten years, living in Paris, Switzerland, and the south of France.

The novel Baldwin had begun in Greenwich Village, *Go Tell It on the Mountain*, was completed in Europe and published in 1953. In this powerful and beautifully written novel, Baldwin drew upon his own early experiences for the story of a young Harlem boy named John Grimes with a gentle mother and a tyrannical stepfather and of Grimes's emotional conversion to fundamentalist religion. The critical praise with which *Go Tell It on the Mountain* was received was repeated in 1955, when *Notes of a Native Son* appeared. This collection of ten deeply personal essays on race had previously appeared in various magazines. In 1956, Baldwin's play *The*

Amen Corner was produced at Howard University in Washington, D.C., and his second novel, *Giovanni's Room*, appeared. *The Amen Corner* returned to Baldwin's early religious experiences, telling the story of a woman evangelist, who is modeled upon a preacher named Mother Horn he had known in Harlem; the play was subsequently produced on Broadway in 1965. *Giovanni's Room*, in which the characters are white, deals not with race but with Baldwin's other major subject, homosexuality, in a story of an American student in Paris torn between two loves, for an Italian bartender named Giovanni and for the student's American fiancée.

Baldwin's return to the United States in 1957 inaugurated a second major stage in his career, a period of intense involvement with the civil rights movement. He visited the South for the first time soon after his return, became a member of the national advisory board of the Congress on Racial Equality, for several years wrote voluminously on civil rights issues, and spoke frequently and eloquently for the cause in person and on television. The essays of this period were collected in *Nobody Knows My Name* and *The Fire Next Time*. *Nobody Knows My Name* reprinted fifteen magazine articles and lectures, including three essays sharply critical of Richard Wright. These essays brought down upon Baldwin's head the wrath of the black radical leader Eldridge Cleaver, who in *Soul on Ice* (1968) defended Wright for his "profound political, economic, and social reference" and found in Baldwin a hatred of blacks and "a racial death-wish." Most of *The Fire Next Time* consisted of a long essay, "Down at the Cross; Letter From a Region of My Mind," which had created a sensation when it was first published in *The New Yorker* in 1962; it is perhaps Baldwin's finest essay.

Baldwin's first novel after his return to the United States was *Another Country* (1962), an ambitious work in which Baldwin brought his themes of race and sexuality together in the story of the suicide of a gifted black jazz drummer named Rufus Scott and the quests for love of his survivors: his sister Ida, his white friend Vivaldo Moore, and his bisexual white Southern lover Eric. Critics found the novel flawed and uneven, but it is Baldwin's fullest development of his interpretation of racism as rooted in white sexual repression and projected self-hate. *Blues for Mr. Charlie*, a play loosely based upon the killing of Emmett Till, a young black man lynched in 1955, ran for four months on Broadway in 1964, and *Going to Meet the Man*, a collection of short stories, was published in 1965.

A third period in Baldwin's career began in 1965 when he left the United States again and settled in Paris and Istanbul. His publications after this move included the novels *Tell Me How Long the Train's Been Gone* (1968), *If Beale Street Could Talk* (1974), *Just Above My Head* (1979), and *The Evidence of Things Not Seen* (1985); a novella, *This Morning, This Evening, So Soon* (1967); three collections of essays; and miscellaneous other works, including screenplays, tape-recorded interviews, and a children's book. *Jimmy's Blues: Selected Poems* appeared in 1986. He died the following year.

"Sonny's Blues," originally published in 1957 and reprinted in 1965 in *Going to Meet the Man*, is one of Baldwin's most beautifully crafted stories and one of his richest explorations of the relationship between black culture and black identity. The story might equally well be called "Sonny's Brother's Blues," for as it unfolds, it becomes the story less of Sonny's life than of the narrator's rediscovery of his own family and racial ties, his

"brotherhood," in more than one sense. Sonny's arrest (which his brother, significantly, has to learn about from the newspaper) triggers a process of initiation for the narrator in which memories of the past become mingled with present encounters with Sonny and his world. In the final, climactic scene in the jazz club, when Sonny plays his triumphant "Am I Blue," his brother can join him in "leaving the shoreline and striking out for the deep water."

FURTHER READING (*prepared by J. H.*): A good starting point for the study of Baldwin is Carolyn Wedin Sylvander's *James Baldwin*, 1980, which includes a short biography, critical appraisals of the major works, and a survey of Baldwin criticism up to its date. Baldwin's own *The Price of the Ticket: Collected Nonfiction, 1948–1985* was published in 1985; it is valuable in connection with the fiction as well. Stanley Macebuh's *James Baldwin: A Critical Study*, 1973, is still valuable, especially in its treatment of Baldwin's place in the tradition of Afro-American writers. Trudier Harris considers an important topic in *Black Women in the Fiction of James Baldwin*, 1985. A good collection of criticism is *James Baldwin: A Collection of Critical Essays*, ed. by Keneth Kinnamon, 1974; it includes Eldridge Cleaver's famous attack on Baldwin from his 1968 *Soul on Ice*. A more recent collection is *Critical Essays on James Baldwin*, ed. Fred L. Standley and Nancy V. Burt, 1988. A guide to secondary material is Fred L. Standley, *James Baldwin: A Reference Guide*, 1980.

SONNY'S BLUES

I read about it in the paper, in the subway, on my way to work. I read it, and I couldn't believe it, and I read it again. Then perhaps I just stared at it, at the newsprint spelling out his name, spelling out the story. I stared at it in the swinging lights of the subway car, and in the faces and bodies of the people, and in my own face, trapped in the darkness which roared outside.

It was not to be believed and I kept telling myself that, as I walked from the subway station to the high school. And at the same time I couldn't doubt it. I was scared, scared for Sonny. He became real to me again. A great block of ice got settled in my belly and kept melting there slowly all day long, while I taught my classes algebra. It was a special kind of ice. It kept melting, sending trickles of ice water all up and down my veins, but it never got less. Sometimes it hardened and seemed to expand until I felt my guts were going to come spilling out or that I was going to choke or scream. This would always be at a moment when I was remembering some specific thing Sonny had once said or done.

When he was about as old as the boys in my classes his face had been bright and open, there was a lot of copper in it; and he'd had wonderfully direct brown eyes, and great gentleness and privacy. I wondered what he looked like now. He had been picked up, the evening before, in a raid on an apartment downtown, for peddling and using heroin.

I couldn't believe it: but what I mean by that is that I couldn't find any room for it anywhere inside me. I had kept it outside me for a long time. I hadn't wanted to know. I had had suspicions, but I didn't name them, I kept putting them away. I told myself that Sonny was wild, but he wasn't

crazy. And he'd always been a good boy, he hadn't ever turned hard or evil or disrespectful, the way kids can, so quick, so quick, especially in Harlem. I didn't want to believe that I'd ever see my brother going down, coming to nothing, all that light in his face gone out, in the condition I'd already seen so many others. Yet it had happened and here I was, talking about algebra to a lot of boys who might, every one of them for all I knew, be popping off needles every time they went to the head.[1] Maybe it did more for them than algebra could.

I was sure that the first time Sonny had ever had horse,[2] he couldn't have been much older than these boys were now. These boys, now, were living as we'd been living then, they were growing up with a rush and their heads bumped abruptly against the low ceiling of their actual possibilities. They were filled with rage. All they really knew were two darknesses, the darkness of their lives, which was now closing in on them, and the darkness of the movies, which had blinded them to that other darkness, and in which they now, vindictively, dreamed, at once more together than they were at any other time, and more alone.

When the last bell rang, the last class ended, I let out my breath. It seemed I'd been holding it for all that time. My clothes were wet—I may have looked as though I'd been sitting in a steam bath, all dressed up, all afternoon. I sat alone in the classroom a long time. I listened to the boys outside, downstairs, shouting and cursing and laughing. Their laughter struck me for perhaps the first time. It was not the joyous laughter which—God knows why—one associates with children. It was mocking and insular, its intent was to denigrate. It was disenchanted, and in this, also, lay the authority of their curses. Perhaps I was listening to them because I was thinking about my brother and in them I heard my brother. And myself.

One boy was whistling a tune, at once very complicated and very simple, it seemed to be pouring out of him as though he were a bird, and it sounded very cool and moving through all that harsh, bright air, only just holding its own through all those other sounds.

I stood up and walked over to the window and looked down into the courtyard. It was the beginning of the spring and the sap was rising in the boys. A teacher passed through them every now and again, quickly, as though he or she couldn't wait to get out of that courtyard, to get those boys out of their sight and off their minds. I started collecting my stuff. I thought I'd better get home and talk to Isabel.

The courtyard was almost deserted by the time I got downstairs. I saw this boy standing in the shadow of a doorway, looking just like Sonny. I almost called his name. Then I saw that it wasn't Sonny, but somebody we used to know, a boy from around our block. He'd been Sonny's friend. He'd never been mine, having been too young for me, and, anyway, I'd never liked him. And now, even though he was a grown-up man, he still hung around that block, still spent hours on the street corners, was always high and raggy. I used to run into him from time to time and he'd often work around to asking me for a quarter or fifty cents. He always had some real good excuse, too, and I always gave it to him. I don't know why.

But now, abruptly, I hated him. I couldn't stand the way he looked at

[1] Toilet. [2] Heroin.

me, partly like a dog, partly like a cunning child. I wanted to ask him what the hell he was doing in the school courtyard.

He sort of shuffled over to me, and he said, "I see you got the papers. So you already know about it."

"You mean about Sonny? Yes, I already know about it. How come they didn't get you?"

He grinned. It made him repulsive and it also brought to mind what he'd looked like as a kid. "I wasn't there. I stay away from them people."

"Good for you." I offered him a cigarette and I watched him through the smoke. "You come all the way down here just to tell me about Sonny?"

"That's right." He was sort of shaking his head and his eyes looked strange, as though they were about to cross. The bright sun deadened his damp dark brown skin and it made his eyes look yellow and showed up the dirt in his kinked hair. He smelled funky. I moved a little away from him and I said, "Well, thanks. But I already know about it and I got to get home."

"I'll walk you a little ways," he said. We started walking. There were a couple of kids still loitering in the courtyard and one of them said goodnight to me and looked strangely at the boy beside me.

"What're you going to do?" he asked me. "I mean, about Sonny?"

"Look. I haven't seen Sonny for over a year, I'm not sure I'm going to do anything. Anyway, what the hell *can* I do?"

"That's right," he said quickly, "ain't nothing you can do. Can't much help old Sonny no more, I guess."

It was what I was thinking and so it seemed to me he had no right to say it.

"I'm surprised at Sonny, though," he went on—he had a funny way of talking, he looked straight ahead as though he were talking to himself—"I thought Sonny was a smart boy, I thought he was too smart to get hung."

"I guess he thought so too," I said sharply, "and that's how he got hung. And how about you? You're pretty goddamn smart, I bet."

Then he looked directly at me, just for a minute. "I ain't smart," he said. "If I was smart, I'd have reached for a pistol a long time ago."

"Look. Don't tell *me* your sad story, if it was up to me, I'd give you one." Then I felt guilty—guilty, probably, for never having supposed that the poor bastard *had* a story of his own, much less a sad one, and I asked, quickly, "What's going to happen to him now?"

He didn't answer this. He was off by himself some place.

"Funny thing," he said, and from his tone we might have been discussing the quickest way to get to Brooklyn, "when I saw the papers this morning, the first thing I asked myself was if I had anything to do with it. I felt sort of responsible."

I began to listen more carefully. The subway station was on the corner, just before us, and I stopped. He stopped, too. We were in front of a bar and he ducked slightly, peering in, but whoever he was looking for didn't seem to be there. The juke box was blasting away with something black and bouncy and I half watched the barmaid as she danced her way from the juke box to her place behind the bar. And I watched her face as she laughingly responded to something someone said to her, still keeping time to the

music. When she smiled one saw the little girl, one sensed the doomed, still-struggling woman beneath the battered face of the semi-whore.

"I never *give* Sonny nothing," the boy said finally, "but a long time ago I come to school high and Sonny asked me how it felt." He paused, I couldn't bear to watch him, I watched the barmaid, and I listened to the music which seemed to be causing the pavement to shake. "I told him it felt great." The music stopped, the barmaid paused and watched the juke box until the music began again. "It did."

All this was carrying me some place I didn't want to go. I certainly didn't want to know how it felt. It filled everything, the people, the houses, the music, the dark, quicksilver barmaid, with menace; and this menace was their reality.

"What's going to happen to him now?" I asked again.

"They'll send him away some place and they'll try to cure him." He shook his head. "Maybe he'll even think he's kicked the habit. Then they'll let him loose"—he gestured, throwing his cigarette into the gutter. "That's all."

"What do you mean, that's *all*?"

But I knew what he meant.

"I *mean*, that's *all*." He turned his head and looked at me, pulling down the corners of his mouth. "Don't you know what I mean?" he asked, softly.

"How the hell *would* I know what you mean?" I almost whispered it, I don't know why.

"That's right," he said to the air, "how would *he* know what I mean?" He turned toward me again, patient and calm, and yet I somehow felt him shaking, shaking as though he were going to fall apart. I felt that ice in my guts again, the dread I'd felt all afternoon; and again I watched the barmaid, moving about the bar, washing glasses, and singing. "Listen. They'll let him out and then it'll just start all over again. That's what I mean."

"You mean—they'll let him out. And then he'll just start working his way back in again. You mean he'll never kick the habit. Is that what you mean?"

"That's right," he said, cheerfully. "*You* see what I mean."

"Tell me," I said at last, "why does he want to die? He must want to die, he's killing himself, why does he want to die?"

He looked at me in surprise. He licked his lips. "He don't want to die. He wants to live. Don't nobody want to die, ever."

Then I wanted to ask him—too many things. He could not have answered, or if he had, I could not have borne the answers. I started walking. "Well, I guess it's none of my business."

"It's going to be rough on old Sonny," he said. We reached the subway station. "This is your station?" he asked. I nodded. I took one step down. "Damn!" he said, suddenly. I looked up at him. He grinned again. "Damn it if I didn't leave all my money home. You ain't got a dollar on you, have you? Just for a couple of days, is all."

All at once something inside gave and threatened to come pouring out of me. I didn't hate him any more. I felt that in another moment I'd start crying like a child.

"Sure," I said. "Don't sweat." I looked in my wallet and didn't have a dollar, I only had a five. "Here," I said. "That hold you?"

He didn't look at it—he didn't want to look at it. A terrible, closed look came over his face, as though he were keeping the number on the bill a secret from him and me. "Thanks," he said, and now he was dying to see me go. "Don't worry about Sonny. Maybe I'll write him or something."

"Sure," I said. "You do that. So long."

"Be seeing you," he said. I went on down the steps.

And I didn't write Sonny or send him anything for a long time. When I finally did, it was just after my little girl died, and he wrote me back a letter which made me feel like a bastard.

Here's what he said:

Dear brother,

You don't know how much I needed to hear from you. I wanted to write you many a time but I dug how much I must have hurt you and so I didn't write. But now I feel like a man who's been trying to climb up out of some deep, real deep and funky hole and just saw the sun up there, outside. I got to get outside.

I can't tell you much about how I got here. I mean I don't know how to tell you. I guess I was afraid of something or I was trying to escape from something and you know I have never been very strong in the head (smile). I'm glad Mama and Daddy are dead and can't see what's happened to their son and I swear if I'd known what I was doing I would never have hurt you so, you and a lot of other fine people who were nice to me and who believed in me.

I don't want you to think it had anything to do with me being a musician. It's more than that. Or maybe less than that. I can't get anything straight in my head down here and I try not to think about what's going to happen to me when I get outside again. Sometime I think I'm going to flip and *never* get outside and sometime I think I'll come straight back. I tell you one thing, though, I'd rather blow my brains out than go through this again. But that's what they all say, so they tell me. If I tell you when I'm coming to New York and if you could meet me, I sure would appreciate it. Give my love to Isabel and the kids and I was sure sorry to hear about little Gracie. I wish I could be like Mama and say the Lord's will be done, but I don't know it seems to me that trouble is the one thing that never does get stopped and I don't know what good it does to blame it on the Lord. But maybe it does some good if you believe it.

Your brother,
Sonny

Then I kept in constant touch with him and I sent him whatever I could and I went to meet him when he came back to New York. When I saw him many things I thought I had forgotten came flooding back to me. This was because I had begun, finally, to wonder about Sonny, about the life that Sonny lived inside. This life, whatever it was, had made him older and thinner and it had deepened the distant stillness in which he had always moved. He looked very unlike my baby brother. Yet, when he smiled, when we shook hands, the baby brother I'd never known looked out from the depths of his private life, like an animal waiting to be coaxed into the light.

"How you been keeping?" he asked me.

"All right. And you?"

"Just fine." He was smiling all over his face. "It's good to see you again."

"It's good to see you."

The seven years' difference in our ages lay between us like a chasm: I wondered if these years would ever operate between us as a bridge. I was remembering, and it made it hard to catch my breath, that I had been there when he was born; and I had heard the first words he had ever spoken. When he started to walk, he walked from our mother straight to me. I caught him just before he fell when he took the first steps he ever took in this world.

"How's Isabel?"

"Just fine. She's dying to see you."

"And the boys?"

"They're fine, too. They're anxious to see their uncle."

"Oh, come on. You know they don't remember me."

"Are you kidding? Of course they remember you."

He grinned again. We got into a taxi. We had a lot to say to each other, far too much to know how to begin.

As the taxi began to move, I asked, "You still want to go to India?"

He laughed. "You still remember that. Hell, no. This place is Indian enough for me."

"It used to belong to them," I said.

And he laughed again. "They damn sure knew what they were doing when they got rid of it."

Years ago, when he was around fourteen, he'd been all hipped on the idea of going to India. He read books about people sitting on rocks, naked, in all kinds of weather, but mostly bad, naturally, and walking barefoot through hot coals and arriving at wisdom. I used to say that it sounded to me as though they were getting away from wisdom as fast as they could. I think he sort of looked down on me for that.

"Do you mind," he asked, "if we have the driver drive alongside the park?[3] On the west side—I haven't seen the city in so long."

"Of course not," I said. I was afraid that I might sound as though I were humoring him, but I hoped he wouldn't take it that way.

So we drove along, between the green of the park and the stony, lifeless elegance of hotels and apartment buildings, toward the vivid, killing streets of our childhood. These streets hadn't changed, though housing projects jutted up out of them now like rocks in the middle of a boiling sea. Most of the houses in which we had grown up had vanished, as had the stores from which we had stolen, the basements in which we had first tried sex, the rooftops from which we had hurled tin cans and bricks. But houses exactly like the houses of our past yet dominated the landscape, boys exactly like the boys we once had been found themselves smothering in these houses, came down into the streets for light and air and found themselves encircled by disaster. Some escaped the trap, most didn't. Those who got out always left something of themselves behind, as some animals amputate a leg and leave it in the trap. It might be said, perhaps, that I had escaped, after all, I was a school teacher; or that Sonny had, he hadn't lived in Harlem for

[3] Central Park in Manhattan.

years. Yet, as the cab moved uptown through streets which seemed, with a rush, to darken with dark people, and as I covertly studied Sonny's face, it came to me that what we both were seeking through our separate cab windows was that part of ourselves which had been left behind. It's always at the hour of trouble and confrontation that the missing member aches.

We hit 110th Street and started rolling up Lenox Avenue.[4] And I'd known this avenue all my life, but it seemed to me again, as it had seemed on the day I'd first heard about Sonny's trouble, filled with a hidden menace which was its very breath of life.

"We almost there," said Sonny.

"Almost." We were both too nervous to say anything more.

We live in a housing project. It hasn't been up long. A few days after it was up it seemed uninhabitably new, now, of course, it's already rundown. It looks like a parody of the good, clean, faceless life—God knows the people who live in it do their best to make it a parody. The beat-looking grass lying around isn't enough to make their lives green, the hedges will never hold out the streets, and they know it. The big windows fool no one, they aren't big enough to make space out of no space. They don't bother with the windows, they watch the TV screen instead. The playground is most popular with the children who don't play at jacks, or skip rope, or roller skate, or swing, and they can be found in it after dark. We moved in partly because it's not too far from where I teach, and partly for the kids; but it's really just like the houses in which Sonny and I grew up. The same things happen, they'll have the same things to remember. The moment Sonny and I started into the house I had the feeling that I was simply bringing him back into the danger he had almost died trying to escape.

Sonny has never been talkative. So I don't know why I was sure he'd be dying to talk to me when supper was over the first night. Everything went fine, the oldest boy remembered him, and the youngest boy liked him, and Sonny had remembered to bring something for each of them; and Isabel, who is really much nicer than I am, more open and giving, had gone to a lot of trouble about dinner and was genuinely glad to see him. And she's always been able to tease Sonny in a way that I haven't. It was nice to see her face so vivid again and to hear her laugh and watch her make Sonny laugh. She wasn't, or, anyway, she didn't seem to be, at all uneasy or embarrassed. She chatted as though there were no subject which had to be avoided and she got Sonny past his first, faint stiffness. And thank God she was there, for I was filled with that icy dread again. Everything I did seemed awkward to me, and everything I said sounded freighted with hidden meaning. I was trying to remember everything I'd heard about dope addiction and I couldn't help watching Sonny for signs. I wasn't doing it out of malice. I was trying to find out something about my brother. I was dying to hear him tell me he was safe.

"Safe!" my father grunted, whenever Mama suggested trying to move to a neighborhood which might be safer for children. "Safe, hell! Ain't no place safe for kids, nor nobody."

He always went on like this, but he wasn't, ever, really as bad as he

[4] Major street in Harlem, in north Manhattan; 110th Street is usually regarded as the southern boundary of Harlem.

sounded, not even on weekends, when he got drunk. As a matter of fact, he was always on the lookout for "something a little better," but he died before he found it. He died suddenly, during a drunken weekend in the middle of the war, when Sonny was fifteen. He and Sonny hadn't ever got on too well. And this was partly because Sonny was the apple of his father's eye. It was because he loved Sonny so much and was frightened for him, that he was always fighting with him. It doesn't do any good to fight with Sonny. Sonny just moves back, inside himself, where he can't be reached. But the principal reason that they never hit it off is that they were so much alike. Daddy was big and rough and loud-talking, just the opposite of Sonny, but they both had—that same privacy.

Mama tried to tell me something about this, just after Daddy died. I was home on leave from the army.

This was the last time I ever saw my mother alive. Just the same, this picture gets all mixed up in my mind with pictures I had of her when she was younger. The way I always see her is the way she used to be on a Sunday afternoon, say, when the old folks were talking after the big Sunday dinner. I always see her wearing pale blue. She'd be sitting on the sofa. And my father would be sitting in the easy chair, not far from her. And the living room would be full of church folks and relatives. There they sit, in chairs all around the living room, and the night is creeping up outside, but nobody knows it yet. You can see the darkness growing against the windowpanes and you hear the street noises every now and again, or maybe the jangling beat of a tambourine from one of the churches close by, but it's real quiet in the room. For a moment nobody's talking, but every face looks darkening, like the sky outside. And my mother rocks a little from the waist, and my father's eyes are closed. Everyone is looking at something a child can't see. For a minute they've forgotten the children. Maybe a kid is lying on the rug, half asleep. Maybe somebody's got a kid in his lap and is absent-mindedly stroking the kid's head. Maybe there's a kid, quiet and big-eyed, curled up in a big chair in the corner. The silence, the darkness coming, and the darkness in the faces frighten the child obscurely. He hopes that the hand which strokes his forehead will never stop—will never die. He hopes that there will never come a time when the old folks won't be sitting around the living room, talking about where they've come from, and what they've seen, and what's happened to them and their kinfolk.

But something deep and watchful in the child knows that this is bound to end, is already ending. In a moment someone will get up and turn on the light. Then the old folks will remember the children and they won't talk any more that day. And when light fills the room, the child is filled with darkness. He knows that every time this happens he's moved just a little closer to that darkness outside. The darkness outside is what the old folks have been talking about. It's what they've come from. It's what they endure. The child knows that they won't talk any more because if he knows too much about what's happened to *them*, he'll know too much too soon, about what's going to happen to *him*.

The last time I talked to my mother, I remember I was restless. I wanted to get out and see Isabel. We weren't married then and we had a lot to straighten out between us.

There Mama sat, in black, by the window. She was humming an old

church song, *Lord, you brought me from a long ways off*. Sonny was out some-
where. Mama kept watching the streets.

"I don't know," she said, "if I'll ever see you again, after you go off from
here. But I hope you'll remember the things I tried to teach you."

"Don't talk like that," I said, and smiled. "You'll be here a long time yet."

She smiled, too, but she said nothing. She was quiet for a long time. And
I said, "Mama, don't you worry about nothing. I'll be writing all the time,
and you be getting the checks. . . ."

"I want to talk to you about your brother," she said, suddenly. "If any-
thing happens to me he ain't going to have nobody to look out for him."

"Mama," I said, "ain't nothing going to happen to you *or* Sonny. Sonny's
all right. He's a good boy and he's got good sense."

"It ain't a question of his being a good boy," Mama said, "nor of his
having good sense. It ain't only the bad ones, nor yet the dumb ones that
gets sucked under." She stopped, looking at me. "Your Daddy once had a
brother," she said, and she smiled in a way that made me feel she was in
pain. "You didn't never know that, did you?"

"No," I said, "I never knew that," and I watched her face.

"Oh, yes," she said, "your Daddy had a brother." She looked out of the
window again. "I know you never saw your Daddy cry. But *I* did—many a
time, through all these years."

I asked her, "What happened to his brother? How come nobody's ever
talked about him?"

This was the first time I ever saw my mother look old.

"His brother got killed," she said, "when he was just a little younger
than you are now. I knew him. He was a fine boy. He was maybe a little full
of the devil, but he didn't mean nobody no harm."

Then she stopped and the room was silent, exactly as it had sometimes
been on those Sunday afternoons. Mama kept looking out into the streets.

"He used to have a job in the mill," she said, "and, like all young folks,
he just liked to perform on Saturday nights. Saturday nights, him and your
father would drift around to different places, go to dances and things like
that, or just sit around with people they knew, and your father's brother
would sing, he had a fine voice, and play along with himself on his guitar.
Well, this particular Saturday night, him and your father was coming home
from some place, and they were both a little drunk and there was a moon
that night, it was bright like day. Your father's brother was feeling kind of
good, and he was whistling to himself, and he had his guitar slung over his
shoulder. They was coming down a hill and beneath them was a road that
turned off from the highway. Well, your father's brother, being always
kind of frisky, decided to run down this hill, and he did, with that guitar
banging and clanging behind him, and he ran across the road, and he was
making water behind a tree. And your father was sort of amused at him
and he was still coming down the hill, kind of slow. Then he heard a car
motor and that same minute his brother stepped from behind the tree, into
the road, in the moonlight. And he started to cross the road. And your
father started to run down the hill, he says he don't know why. This car was
full of white men. They was all drunk, and when they seen your father's
brother they let out a great whoop and holler and they aimed the car
straight at him. They was having fun, they just wanted to scare him, the way

they do sometimes, you know. But they was drunk. And I guess the boy, being drunk, too, and scared, kind of lost his head. By the time he jumped it was too late. Your father says he heard his brother scream when the car rolled over him, and he heard the wood of that guitar when it give, and he heard them strings go flying, and he heard them white men shouting, and the car kept on a-going and it ain't stopped till this day. And, time your father got down the hill, his brother weren't nothing but blood and pulp."

Tears were gleaming on my mother's face. There wasn't anything I could say.

"He never mentioned it," she said, "because I never let him mention it before you children. Your Daddy was like a crazy man that night and for many a night thereafter. He says he never in his life seen anything as dark as that road after the lights of that car had gone away. Weren't nothing, weren't nobody on that road, just your Daddy and his brother and that busted guitar. Oh, yes. Your Daddy never did really get right again. Till the day he died he weren't sure but that every white man he saw was the man that killed his brother."

She stopped and took out her handkerchief and dried her eyes and looked at me.

"I ain't telling you all this," she said, "to make you scared or bitter or to make you hate nobody. I'm telling you this because you got a brother. And the world ain't changed."

I guess I didn't want to believe this. I guess she saw this in my face. She turned away from me, toward the window again, searching those streets.

"But I praise my Redeemer," she said at last, "that He called your Daddy home before me. I ain't saying it to throw no flowers at myself, but, I declare, it keeps me from feeling too cast down to know I helped your father get safely through this world. Your father always acted like he was the roughest, strongest man on earth. And everybody took him to be like that. But if he hadn't had me there—to see his tears!"

She was crying again. Still, I couldn't move. I said, "Lord, Lord, Mama, I didn't know it was like that."

"Oh, honey," she said, "there's a lot that you don't know. But you are going to find out." She stood up from the window and came over to me. "You got to hold on to your brother," she said, "and don't let him fall, no matter what it looks like is happening to him and no matter how evil you gets with him. You going to be evil with him many a time. But don't you forget what I told you, you hear?"

"I won't forget," I said. "Don't you worry, I won't forget. I won't let nothing happen to Sonny."

My mother smiled as though she were amused at something she saw in my face. Then, "You may not be able to stop nothing from happening. But you got to let him know you's *there*."

Two days later I was married, and then I was gone. And I had a lot of things on my mind and I pretty well forgot my promise to Mama until I got shipped home on a special furlough for her funeral.

And, after the funeral, with just Sonny and me alone in the empty kitchen, I tried to find out something about him.

"What do you want to do?" I asked him.

"I'm going to be a musician," he said.

For he had graduated, in the time I had been away, from dancing to the juke box to finding out who was playing what, and what they were doing with it, and he had bought himself a set of drums.

"You mean, you want to be a drummer?" I somehow had the feeling that being a drummer might be all right for other people but not for my brother Sonny.

"I don't think," he said, looking at me very gravely, "that I'll ever be a good drummer. But I think I can play a piano."

I frowned. I'd never played the role of the older brother quite so seriously before, had scarcely ever, in fact, *asked* Sonny a damn thing. I sensed myself in the presence of something I didn't really know how to handle, didn't understand. So I made my frown a little deeper as I asked: "What kind of musician do you want to be?"

He grinned. "How many kinds do you think there are?"

"Be *serious*," I said.

He laughed, throwing his head back, and then looked at me. "I *am* serious."

"Well, then, for Christ's sake, stop kidding around and answer a serious question. I mean, do you want to be a concert pianist, you want to play classical music and all that, or—or what?" Long before I finished he was laughing again. "For Christ's *sake*, Sonny!"

He sobered, but with difficulty. "I'm sorry. But you sound so—*scared*!" and he was off again.

"Well, you may think it's funny now, baby, but it's not going to be so funny when you have to make your living at it, let me tell you *that*." I was furious because I knew he was laughing at me and I didn't know why.

"No," he said, very sober now, and afraid, perhaps, that he'd hurt me, "I don't want to be a classical pianist. That isn't what interests me. I mean"—he paused, looking hard at me, as though his eyes would help me to understand, and then gestured helplessly, as though perhaps his hand would help—"I mean, I'll have a lot of studying to do, and I'll have to study *everything*, but, I mean, I want to play *with*—jazz musicians." He stopped. "I want to play jazz," he said.

Well the word had never before sounded as heavy, as real, as it sounded that afternoon in Sonny's mouth. I just looked at him and I was probably frowning a real frown by this time. I simply couldn't see why on earth he'd want to spend his time hanging around nightclubs, clowning around on bandstands, while people pushed each other around a dance floor. It seemed—beneath him, somehow. I had never thought about it before, had never been forced to, but I suppose I had always put jazz musicians in a class with what Daddy called "good-time people."

"Are you *serious*?"

"Hell, *yes*, I'm serious."

He looked more helpless than ever, and annoyed, and deeply hurt.

I suggested, helpfully: "You mean—like Louis Armstrong?"[5]

[5] Louis Armstrong (1900–1971), perhaps the greatest trumpet player in jazz history. He remained rooted in the "down home" Dixieland style, while also popularizing jazz for a white, middle-class audience.

His face closed as though I'd struck him. "No. I'm not talking about none of that old-time, down home crap."

"Well, look, Sonny, I'm sorry, don't get mad. I just don't altogether get it, that's all. Name somebody—you know, a jazz musician you admire."

"Bird."

"Who?"

"Bird! Charlie Parker![6] Don't they teach you nothing in the goddamn army?"

I lit a cigarette. I was surprised and then a little amused to discover that I was trembling. "I've been out of touch," I said. "You'll have to be patient with me. Now. Who's this Parker character?"

"He's just one of the greatest jazz musicians alive," said Sonny, sullenly, his hands in his pockets, his back to me. "Maybe *the* greatest," he added, bitterly, "that's probably why *you* never heard of him."

"All right," I said, "I'm ignorant. I'm sorry. I'll go out and buy all the cat's records right away, all right?"

"It don't," said Sonny, with dignity, "make any difference to me. I don't care what you listen to. Don't do me any favors."

I was beginning to realize that I'd never seen him so upset before. With another part of my mind I was thinking that this would probably turn out to be one of those things kids go through and that I shouldn't make it seem important by pushing it too hard. Still, I didn't think it would do any harm to ask: "Doesn't all this take a lot of time? Can you make a living at it?"

He turned back to me and half leaned, half sat, on the kitchen table. "Everything takes time," he said, "and—well, yes, sure, I can make a living at it. But what I don't seem to be able to make you understand is that it's the only thing I want to do."

"Well, Sonny," I said, gently, "you know people can't always do exactly what they *want* to do—"

"*No*, I don't know that," said Sonny, surprising me. "I think people *ought* to do what they want to do, what else are they alive for?"

"You getting to be a big boy," I said desperately, "it's time you started thinking about your future."

"I'm thinking about my future," said Sonny, grimly. "I think about it all the time."

I gave up. I decided, if he didn't change his mind, that we could always talk about it later. "In the meantime," I said, "you got to finish school." We had already decided that he'd have to move in with Isabel and her folks. I knew this wasn't the ideal arrangement because Isabel's folks are inclined to be dicty[7] and they hadn't especially wanted Isabel to marry me. But I didn't know what else to do. "And we have to get you fixed up at Isabel's."

There was a long silence. He moved from the kitchen table to the window. "That's a terrible idea. You know it yourself."

"Do you have a *better* idea?"

He just walked up and down the kitchen for a minute. He was as tall as

[6] Charlie "Bird" Parker (1920–1955), alto saxophonist and one of the finest improvisers in the history of jazz. The central figure in the "bop" movement of the 1940's, he was also addicted to heroin.

[7] Dictatorial, bossy.

I was. He had started to shave. I suddenly had the feeling that I didn't know him at all.

He stopped at the kitchen table and picked up my cigarettes. Looking at me with a kind of mocking, amused defiance, he put one between his lips. "You mind?"

"You smoking already?"

He lit the cigarette and nodded, watching me through the smoke. "I just wanted to see if I'd have the courage to smoke in front of you." He grinned and blew a great cloud of smoke to the ceiling. "It was easy." He looked at my face. "Come on, now. I bet you was smoking at my age, tell the truth."

I didn't say anything but the truth was on my face, and he laughed. But now there was something very strained in his laugh. "Sure. And I bet that ain't all you was doing."

He was frightening me a little. "Cut the crap," I said. "We already decided that you was going to go and live at Isabel's. Now what's got into you all of a sudden?"

"*You* decided it," he pointed out. "*I* didn't decide nothing." He stopped in front of me, leaning against the stove, arms loosely folded. "Look, brother. I don't want to stay in Harlem no more, I really don't." He was very earnest. He looked at me, then over toward the kitchen window. There was something in his eyes I'd never seen before, some thoughtfulness, some worry all his own. He rubbed the muscle of one arm. "It's time I was getting out of here."

"Where do you want to *go*, Sonny?"

"I want to join the army. Or the navy, I don't care. If I say I'm old enough, they'll believe me."

Then I got mad. It was because I was so scared. "You must be crazy. You goddamn fool, what the hell do you want to go and join the *army* for?"

"I just told you. To get out of Harlem."

"Sonny, you haven't even finished *school*. And if you really want to be a musician, how do you expect to study if you're in the *army*?"

He looked at me, trapped, and in anguish. "There's ways. I might be able to work out some kind of deal. Anyway, I'll have the G.I. Bill when I come out."

"*If* you come out." We stared at each other. "Sonny, please. Be reasonable. I know the setup is far from perfect. But we got to do the best we can."

"I ain't learning nothing in school," he said. "Even when I go." He turned away from me and opened the window and threw his cigarette out into the narrow alley. I watched his back. "At least, I ain't learning nothing you'd want me to learn." He slammed the window so hard I thought the glass would fly out, and turned back to me. "And I'm sick of the stink of these garbage cans!"

"Sonny," I said, "I know how you feel. But if you don't finish school now, you're going to be sorry later that you didn't." I grabbed him by the shoulders. "And you only got another year. It ain't so bad. And I'll come back and I swear I'll help you do *whatever* you want to do. Just try to put up with it till I come back. Will you please do that? For me?"

He didn't answer and he wouldn't look at me.

"Sonny. You hear me?"

He pulled away. "I hear you. But you never hear anything *I* say."

I didn't know what to say to that. He looked out of the window and then back at me. "OK," he said, and sighed. "I'll try."

Then I said, trying to cheer him up a little, "They got a piano at Isabel's. You can practice on it."

And as a matter of fact, it did cheer him up for a minute. "That's right," he said to himself. "I forgot that." His face relaxed a little. But the worry, the thoughtfulness, played on it still, the way shadows play on a face which is staring into the fire.

But I thought I'd never hear the end of that piano. At first, Isabel would write me, saying how nice it was that Sonny was so serious about his music and how, as soon as he came in from school, or wherever he had been when he was supposed to be at school, he went straight to that piano and stayed there until suppertime. And, after supper, he went back to that piano and stayed there until everybody went to bed. He was at the piano all day Saturday and all day Sunday. Then he bought a record player and started playing records. He'd play one record over and over again, all day long sometimes, and he'd improvise along with it on the piano. Or he'd play one section of the record, one chord, one change, one progression, then he'd do it on the piano. Then back to the record. Then back to the piano.

Well, I really don't know how they stood it. Isabel finally confessed that it wasn't like living with a person at all, it was like living with sound. And the sound didn't make any sense to her, didn't make any sense to any of them—naturally. They began, in a way, to be afflicted by this presence that was living in their home. It was as though Sonny were some sort of god, or monster. He moved in an atmosphere which wasn't like theirs at all. They fed him and he ate, he washed himself, he walked in and out of their door; he certainly wasn't nasty or unpleasant or rude, Sonny isn't any of those things; but it was as though he were all wrapped up in some cloud, some fire, some vision all his own; and there wasn't any way to reach him.

At the same time, he wasn't really a man yet, he was still a child, and they had to watch out for him in all kinds of ways. They certainly couldn't throw him out. Neither did they dare to make a great scene about that piano because even they dimly sensed, as I sensed, from so many thousands of miles away, that Sonny was at that piano playing for his life.

But he hadn't been going to school. One day a letter came from the school board and Isabel's mother got it—there had, apparently, been other letters but Sonny had torn them up. This day, when Sonny came in, Isabel's mother showed him the letter and asked where he'd been spending his time. And she finally got it out of him that he'd been down in Greenwich Village, with musicians and other characters, in a white girl's apartment. And this scared her and she started to scream at him and what came up, once she began—though she denies it to this day—was what sacrifices they were making to give Sonny a decent home and how little he appreciated it.

Sonny didn't play the piano that day. By evening, Isabel's mother had calmed down but then there was the old man to deal with, and Isabel herself. Isabel says she did her best to be calm but she broke down and started crying. She says she just watched Sonny's face. She could tell, by watching him, what was happening with him. And what was happening was

that they penetrated his cloud, they had reached him. Even if their fingers had been a thousand times more gentle than human fingers ever are, he could hardly help feeling that they had stripped him naked and were spitting on that nakedness. For he also had to see that his presence, that music, which was life or death to him, had been torture for them and that they had endured it, not at all for his sake, but only for mine. And Sonny couldn't take that. He can take it a little better today than he could then but he's still not very good at it and, frankly, I don't know anybody who is.

The silence of the next few days must have been louder than the sound of all the music ever played since time began. One morning, before she went to work, Isabel was in his room for something and she suddenly realized that all of his records were gone. And she knew for certain that he was gone. And he was. He went as far as the navy would carry him. He finally sent me a postcard from some place in Greece and that was the first I knew that Sonny was still alive. I didn't see him any more until we were both back in New York and the war had long been over.

He was a man by then, of course, but I wasn't willing to see it. He came by the house from time to time, but we fought almost every time we met. I didn't like the way he carried himself, loose and dreamlike all the time, and I didn't like his friends, and his music seemed to be merely an excuse for the life he led. It sounded just that weird and disordered.

Then we had a fight, a pretty awful fight, and I didn't see him for months. By and by I looked him up, where he was living, in a furnished room in the Village, and I tried to make it up. But there were lots of other people in the room and Sonny just lay on his bed, and he wouldn't come downstairs with me, and he treated these other people as though they were his family and I weren't. So I got mad and then he got mad, and then I told him that he might just as well be dead as live the way he was living. Then he stood up and he told me not to worry about him any more in life, that he *was* dead as far as I was concerned. Then he pushed me to the door and the other people looked on as though nothing were happening, and he slammed the door behind me. I stood in the hallway, staring at the door. I heard somebody laugh in the room and then the tears came to my eyes. I started down the steps, whistling to keep from crying, I kept whistling to myself, *You going to need me, baby, one of these cold, rainy days.*

I read about Sonny's trouble in the spring. Little Grace died in the fall. She was a beautiful little girl. But she only lived a little over two years. She died of polio and she suffered. She had a slight fever for a couple of days, but it didn't seem like anything and we just kept her in bed. And we would certainly have called the doctor, but the fever dropped, she seemed to be all right. So we thought it had just been a cold. Then, one day, she was up, playing, Isabel was in the kitchen fixing lunch for the two boys when they'd come in from school, and she heard Grace fall down in the living room. When you have a lot of children you don't always start running when one of them falls, unless they start screaming or something. And, this time, Gracie was quiet. Yet, Isabel says that when she heard that *thump* and then that silence, something happened to her to make her afraid. And she ran to the living room and there was little Grace on the floor, all twisted up, and the reason she hadn't screamed was that she couldn't get her breath. And when she did scream, it was the worst sound, Isabel says, that she'd ever

heard in all her life, and she still hears it sometimes in her dreams. Isabel will sometimes wake me up with a low, moaning, strangling sound and I have to be quick to awaken her and hold her to me and where Isabel is weeping against me seems a mortal wound.

I think I may have written Sonny the very day that little Grace was buried. I was sitting in the living room in the dark, by myself, and I suddenly thought of Sonny. My trouble made his real.

One Saturday afternoon, when Sonny had been living with us, or anyway, been in our house, for nearly two weeks, I found myself wandering aimlessly about the living room, drinking from a can of beer, and trying to work up courage to search Sonny's room. He was out, he was usually out whenever I was home, and Isabel had taken the children to see their grandparents. Suddenly I was standing still in front of the living room window, watching Seventh Avenue. The idea of searching Sonny's room made me still. I scarcely dared to admit to myself what I'd be searching for. I didn't know what I'd do if I found it. Or if I didn't.

On the sidewalk across from me, near the entrance to a barbecue joint, some people were holding an old-fashioned revival meeting. The barbecue cook, wearing a dirty white apron, his conked[8] hair reddish and metallic in the pale sun, and a cigarette between his lips, stood in the doorway, watching them. Kids and older people paused in their errands and stood there, along with some older men and a couple of very tough-looking women who watched everything that happened on the avenue, as though they owned it, or were maybe owned by it. Well, they were watching this, too. The revival was being carried on by three sisters in black, and a brother. All they had were their voices and their Bibles and a tambourine. The brother was testifying[9] and while he testified two of the sisters stood together, seeming to say, amen, and the third sister walked around with the tambourine outstretched and a couple of people dropped coins into it. Then the brother's testimony ended and the sister who had been taking up the collection dumped the coins into her palm and transferred them to the pocket of her long black robe. Then she raised both hands, striking the tambourine against the air, and then against one hand, and she started to sing. And the two other sisters and the brother joined in.

It was strange, suddenly, to watch, though I had been seeing these meetings all my life. So, of course, had everybody else down there. Yet, they paused and watched and listened and I stood still at the window. "*'Tis the old ship of Zion*," they sang, and the sister with the tambourine kept a steady, jangling beat, "*it has rescued many a thousand!*" Not a soul under the sound of their voices was hearing this song for the first time, not one of them had been rescued. Nor had they seen much in the way of rescue work being done around them. Neither did they especially believe in the holiness of the three sisters and the brother, they knew too much about them, knew where they lived, and how. The woman with the tambourine, whose voice dominated the air, whose face was bright with joy, was divided by very little from the woman who stood watching her, a cigarette between her heavy, chapped lips, her hair a cuckoo's nest, her face scarred and swollen from

[8] Chemically straightened.
[9] Making emotional declarations of religious beliefs and experiences.

many beatings, and her black eyes glittering like coal. Perhaps they both knew this, which was why, when, as rarely, they addressed each other, they addressed each other as Sister. As the singing filled the air the watching, listening faces underwent a change, the eyes focusing on something within; the music seemed to soothe a poison out of them; and time seemed, nearly, to fall away from the sullen, belligerent, battered faces, as though they were fleeing back to their first condition, while dreaming of their last. The barbecue cook half shook his head and smiled, and dropped his cigarette and disappeared into his joint. A man fumbled in his pockets for change and stood holding it in his hand impatiently, as though he had just remembered a pressing appointment further up the avenue. He looked furious. Then I saw Sonny, standing on the edge of the crowd. He was carrying a wide, flat notebook with a green cover, and it made him look, from where I was standing, almost like a schoolboy. The coppery sun brought out the copper in his skin, he was very faintly smiling, standing very still. Then the singing stopped, the tambourine turned into a collection plate again. The furious man dropped in his coins and vanished, so did a couple of the women, and Sonny dropped some change in the plate, looking directly at the woman with a little smile. He started across the avenue, toward the house. He has a slow, loping walk, something like the way Harlem hipsters walk, only he's imposed on this his own half-beat. I had never really noticed it before.

I stayed at the window, both relieved and apprehensive. As Sonny disappeared from my sight, they began singing again. And they were still singing when his key turned in the lock.

"Hey," he said.

"Hey, yourself. You want some beer?"

"No. Well, maybe." But he came up to the window and stood beside me, looking out. "What a warm voice," he said.

They were singing *If I could only hear my mother pray again!*

"Yes," I said, "and she can sure beat that tambourine."

"But what a terrible song," he said, and laughed. He dropped his notebook on the sofa and disappeared into the kitchen. "Where's Isabel and the kids?"

"I think they went to see their grandparents. You hungry?"

"No." He came back into the living room with his can of beer. "You want to come some place with me tonight?"

I sensed, I don't know how, that I couldn't possibly say no. "Sure. Where?"

He sat down on the sofa and picked up his notebook and started leafing through it. "I'm going to sit in with some fellows in a joint in the Village."

"You mean, you're going to play, tonight?"

"That's right." He took a swallow of his beer and moved back to the window. He gave me a sidelong look. "If you can stand it."

"I'll try," I said.

He smiled to himself and we both watched as the meeting across the way broke up. The three sisters and the brother, heads bowed, were singing *God be with you till we meet again.* The faces around them were very quiet. Then the song ended. The small crowd dispersed. We watched the three women and the lone man walk slowly up the avenue.

"When she was singing before," said Sonny, abruptly, "her voice reminded me for a minute of what heroin feels like sometimes—when it's in your veins. It makes you feel sort of warm and cool at the same time. And distant. And—and sure." He sipped his beer, very deliberately not looking at me. I watched his face. "It makes you feel—in control. Sometimes you've got to have that feeling."

"Do you?" I sat down slowly in the easy chair.

"Sometimes." He went to the sofa and picked up his notebook again. "Some people do."

"In order," I asked, "to play?" And my voice was very ugly, full of contempt and anger.

"Well"—he looked at me with great, troubled eyes, as though, in fact, he hoped his eyes would tell me things he could never otherwise say—"they *think* so. And *if* they think so—!"

"And what do *you* think?" I asked.

He sat on the sofa and put his can of beer on the floor. "I don't know," he said, and I couldn't be sure if he were answering my question or pursuing his thoughts. His face didn't tell me. "It's not so much to *play*. It's to *stand* it, to be able to make it at all. On any level." He frowned and smiled: "In order to keep from shaking to pieces."

"But these friends of yours," I said, "they seem to shake themselves to pieces pretty goddamn fast."

"Maybe." He played with the notebook. And something told me that I should curb my tongue, that Sonny was doing his best to talk, that I should listen. "But of course you only know the ones that've gone to pieces. Some don't—or at least they haven't *yet* and that's just about all *any* of us can say." He paused. "And then there are some who just live, really, in hell, and they know it and they see what's happening and they go right on. I don't know." He sighed, dropped the notebook, folded his arms. "Some guys, you can tell from the way they play, they on something *all* the time. And you can see that, well, it makes something real for them. But of course," he picked up his beer from the floor and sipped it and put the can down again, "they *want* to, too, you've got to see that. Even some of them that say they don't—*some*, not all."

"And what about you?" I asked—I couldn't help it. "What about you? Do *you* want to?"

He stood up and walked to the window and I remained silent for a long time. Then he sighed. "Me," he said. Then: "While I was downstairs before, on my way here, listening to that woman sing, it struck me all of a sudden how much suffering she must have had to go through—to sing like that. It's *repulsive* to think you have to suffer that much."

I said: "But there's no way not to suffer—is there, Sonny?"

"I believe not," he said and smiled, "but that's never stopped anyone from trying." He looked at me. "Has it?" I realized, with this mocking look, that there stood between us, forever, beyond the power of time or forgiveness, the fact that I had held silence—so long!—when he had needed human speech to help him. He turned back to the window. "No, there's no way not to suffer. But you try all kinds of ways to keep from drowning in it, to keep on top of it, and to make it seem—well, like *you*. Like you did

something, all right, and now you're suffering for it. You know?" I said nothing. "Well you know," he said, impatiently, "why *do* people suffer? Maybe it's better to do something to give it a reason, *any* reason."

"But we just agreed," I said, "that there's no way not to suffer. Isn't it better, then, just to—take it?"

"But nobody just takes it," Sonny cried, "that's what I'm telling you! *Everybody* tries not to. You're just hung up on the *way* some people try—it's not *your* way!"

The hair on my face began to itch, my face felt wet. "That's not true," I said, "that's not true. I don't give a damn what other people do, I don't even care how they suffer. I just care how *you* suffer." And he looked at me. "Please believe me," I said, "I don't want to see you—die—trying not to suffer."

"I won't," he said flatly, "die trying not to suffer. At least, not any faster than anybody else."

"But there's no need," I said, trying to laugh, "is there? in killing yourself."

I wanted to say more, but I couldn't. I wanted to talk about will power and how life could be—well, beautiful. I wanted to say that it was all within; but was it? or, rather, wasn't that exactly the trouble? And I wanted to promise that I would never fail him again. But it would all have sounded—empty words and lies.

So I made the promise to myself and prayed that I would keep it.

"It's terrible sometimes, inside," he said, "that's what's the trouble. You walk these streets, black and funky and cold, and there's not really a living ass to talk to, and there's nothing shaking, and there's no way of getting it out—that storm inside. You can't talk it and you can't make love with it, and when you finally try to get with it and play it, you realize *nobody's* listening. So *you've* got to listen. You got to find a way to listen."

And then he walked away from the window and sat on the sofa again, as though all the wind had suddenly been knocked out of him. "Sometimes you'll do *anything* to play, even cut your mother's throat." He laughed and looked at me. "Or your brother's." Then he sobered. "Or your own." Then: "Don't worry. I'm all right now and I think I'll *be* all right. But I can't forget—where I've been. I don't mean just the physical place I've been, I mean where I've *been*. And *what* I've been."

"What have you been, Sonny?" I asked.

He smiled—but sat sideways on the sofa, his elbow resting on the back, his fingers playing with his mouth and chin, not looking at me. "I've been something I didn't recognize, didn't know I could be. Didn't know anybody could be." He stopped, looking inward, looking helplessly young, looking old. "I'm not talking about it now because I feel *guilty* or anything like that—maybe it would be better if I did, I don't know. Anyway, I can't really talk about it. Not to you, not to anybody," and now he turned and faced me. "Sometimes, you know, and it was actually when I was most *out* of the world, I felt that I was in it, that I was *with* it, really, and I could play or I didn't really have to *play*, it just came out of me, it was there. And I don't know how I played, thinking about it now, but I know I did awful things, those times, sometimes, to people. Or it wasn't that I *did* anything to them—it was that they weren't real." He picked up the beer can; it was

empty; he rolled it between his palms: "And other times—well, I needed a fix, I needed to find a place to lean, I needed to clear a space to *listen*—and I couldn't find it, and I—went crazy, I did terrible things to *me*, I was terrible *for* me." He began pressing the beer can between his hands, I watched the metal begin to give. It glittered, as he played with it like a knife, and I was afraid he would cut himself, but I said nothing. "Oh well. I can never tell you. I was all by myself at the bottom of something, stinking and sweating and crying and shaking, and I smelled it, you know? *my* stink, and I thought I'd die if I couldn't get away from it and yet, all the same, I knew that everything I was doing was just locking me in with it. And I didn't know," he paused, still flattening the beer can, "I didn't know, I still *don't* know, something kept telling me that maybe it was good to smell your own stink, but I didn't think that *that* was what I'd been trying to do—and—who can stand it?" and he abruptly dropped the ruined beer can, looking at me with a small, still smile, and then rose, walking to the window as though it were the lodestone rock. I watched his face, he watched the avenue. "I couldn't tell you when Mama died—but the reason I wanted to leave Harlem so bad was to get away from drugs. And then, when I ran away, that's what I was running from—really. When I came back, nothing had changed, *I* hadn't changed, I was just—older." And he stopped, drumming with his fingers on the windowpane. The sun had vanished, soon darkness would fall. I watched his face. "It can come again," he said, almost as though speaking to himself. Then he turned to me. "It can come again," he repeated. "I just want you to know that."

"All right," I said, at last. "So it can come again. All right."

He smiled, but the smile was sorrowful. "I had to try to tell you," he said.

"Yes," I said. "I understand that."

"You're my brother," he said, looking straight at me, and not smiling at all.

"Yes," I repeated, "yes. I understand that."

He turned back to the window, looking out. "All that hatred down there," he said, "all that hatred and misery and love. It's a wonder it doesn't blow the avenue apart."

We went to the only nightclub on a short, dark street, downtown. We squeezed through the narrow, chattering, jampacked bar to the entrance of the big room, where the bandstand was. And we stood there for a moment, for the lights were very dim in this room and we couldn't see. Then, "Hello, boy," said the voice and an enormous black man, much older than Sonny or myself, erupted out of all that atmospheric lighting and put an arm around Sonny's shoulder. "I been sitting right here," he said, "waiting for you."

He had a big voice, too, and heads in the darkness turned toward us.

Sonny grinned and pulled a little away, and said, "Creole, this is my brother. I told you about him."

Creole shook my hand. "I'm glad to meet you, son," he said, and it was clear that he was glad to meet me *there*, for Sonny's sake. And he smiled, "You got a real musician in *your* family," and he took his arm from Sonny's shoulder and slapped him, lightly, affectionately, with the back of his hand.

"Well. Now I've heard it all," said a voice behind us. This was another

musician, and a friend of Sonny's, a coal-black, cheerful-looking man, built close to the ground. He immediately began confiding to me, at the top of his lungs, the most terrible things about Sonny, his teeth gleaming like a lighthouse and his laugh coming up out of him like the beginning of an earthquake. And it turned out that everyone at the bar knew Sonny, or almost everyone; some were musicians, working there, or nearby, or not working, some were simply hangers-on, and some were there to hear Sonny play. I was introduced to all of them and they were all very polite to me. Yet, it was clear that, for them, I was only Sonny's brother. Here, I was in Sonny's world. Or, rather: his kingdom. Here, it was not even a question that his veins bore royal blood.

They were going to play soon and Creole installed me, by myself, at a table in a dark corner. Then I watched them, Creole, and the little black man, and Sonny, and the others, while they horsed around, standing just below the bandstand. The light from the bandstand spilled just a little short of them and, watching them laughing and gesturing and moving about, I had the feeling that they, nevertheless, were being most careful not to step into that circle of light too suddenly: that if they moved into the light too suddenly, without thinking, they would perish in flame. Then, while I watched, one of them, the small black man, moved into the light and crossed the bandstand and started fooling around with his drums. Then— being funny and being, also, extremely ceremonious—Creole took Sonny by the arm and led him to the piano. A woman's voice called Sonny's name and a few hands started clapping. And Sonny, also being funny and being ceremonious, and so touched, I think, that he could have cried, but neither hiding it nor showing it, riding it like a man, grinned, and put both hands to his heart and bowed from the waist.

Creole then went to the bass fiddle and a lean, very bright-skinned brown man jumped up on the bandstand and picked up his horn. So there they were, and the atmosphere on the bandstand and in the room began to change and tighten. Someone stepped up to the microphone and announced them. Then there were all kinds of murmurs. Some people at the bar shushed others. The waitress ran around, frantically getting in the last orders, guys and chicks got closer to each other, and the lights on the bandstand, on the quartet, turned to a kind of indigo. Then they all looked different there. Creole looked about him for the last time, as though he were making certain that all his chickens were in the coop, and then he— jumped and struck the fiddle. And there they were.

All I know about music is that not many people ever really hear it. And even then, on the rare occasions when something opens within, and the music enters, what we mainly hear, or hear corroborated, are personal, private, vanishing evocations. But the man who creates the music is hearing something else, is dealing with the roar rising from the void and imposing order on it as it hits the air. What is evoked in him, then, is of another order, more terrible because it has no words, and triumphant, too, for that same reason. And his triumph, when he triumphs, is ours. I just watched Sonny's face. His face was troubled, he was working hard, but he wasn't with it. And I had the feeling that, in a way, everyone on the bandstand was waiting for him, both waiting for him and pushing him along. But as I began to watch Creole, I realized that it was Creole who held them all back.

He had them on a short rein. Up there, keeping the beat with his whole body, wailing on the fiddle, with his eyes half closed, he was listening to everything, but he was listening to Sonny. He was having a dialogue with Sonny. He wanted Sonny to leave the shoreline and strike out for the deep water. He was Sonny's witness that deep water and drowning were not the same thing—he had been there, and he knew. And he wanted Sonny to know. He was waiting for Sonny to do the things on the keys which would let Creole know that Sonny was in the water.

And, while Creole listened, Sonny moved, deep within, exactly like someone in torment. I had never before thought of how awful the relationship must be between the musician and his instrument. He has to fill it, this instrument, with the breath of life, his own. He has to make it do what he wants it to do. And a piano is just a piano. It's made out of so much wood and wires and little hammers and big ones, and ivory. While there's only so much you can do with it, the only way to find this out is to try; to try and make it do everything.

And Sonny hadn't been near a piano for over a year. And he wasn't on much better terms with his life, not the life that stretched before him now. He and the piano stammered, started one way, got scared, stopped; started another way, panicked, marked time, started again; then seemed to have found a direction, panicked again, got stuck. And the face I saw on Sonny I'd never seen before. Everything had been burned out of it, and, at the same time, things usually hidden were being burned in, by the fire and fury of the battle which was occurring in him up there.

Yet, watching Creole's face as they neared the end of the first set, I had the feeling that something had happened, something I hadn't heard. Then they finished, there was scattered applause, and then, without an instant's warning, Creole started into something else, it was almost sardonic, it was *Am I Blue*. And, as though he commanded, Sonny began to play. Something began to happen. And Creole let out the reins. The dry, low, black man said something awful on the drums, Creole answered, and the drums talked back. Then the horn insisted, sweet and high, slightly detached perhaps, and Creole listened, commenting now and then, dry, and driving, beautiful and calm and old. Then they all came together again, and Sonny was part of the family again. I could tell this from his face. He seemed to have found, right there beneath his fingers, a damn brand-new piano. It seemed that he couldn't get over it. Then, for a while, just being happy with Sonny, they seemed to be agreeing with him that brand-new pianos certainly were a gas.

Then Creole stepped forward to remind them that what they were playing was the blues. He hit something in all of them, he hit something in me, myself, and the music tightened and deepened, apprehension began to beat the air. Creole began to tell us what the blues were all about. They were not about anything very new. He and his boys up there were keeping it new, at the risk of ruin, destruction, madness, and death, in order to find new ways to make us listen. For, while the tale of how we suffer, and how we are delighted, and how we may triumph is never new, it always must be heard. There isn't any other tale to tell, it's the only light we've got in all this darkness.

And this tale, according to that face, that body, those strong hands on

those strings, has another aspect in every country, and a new depth in every generation. Listen, Creole seemed to be saying, listen. Now these are Sonny's blues. He made the little black man on the drums know it, and the bright, brown man on the horn. Creole wasn't trying any longer to get Sonny in the water. He was wishing him Godspeed. Then he stepped back, very slowly, filling the air with the immense suggestion that Sonny speak for himself.

Then they all gathered around Sonny and Sonny played. Every now and again one of them seemed to say, amen. Sonny's fingers filled the air with life, his life. But that life contained so many others. And Sonny went all the way back, he really began with the spare, flat statement of the opening phrase of the song. Then he began to make it his. It was very beautiful because it wasn't hurried and it was no longer a lament. I seemed to hear with what burning he had made it his, with what burning we had yet to make it ours, how we could cease lamenting. Freedom lurked around us and I understood, at last, that he could help us to be free if we would listen, that he would never be free until we did. Yet, there was no battle in his face now, I heard what he had gone through, and would continue to go through until he came to rest in earth. He had made it his: that long line, of which we knew only Mama and Daddy. And he was giving it back, as everything must be given back, so that, passing through death, it can live forever. I saw my mother's face again, and felt, for the first time, how the stones of the road she had walked on must have bruised her feet. I saw the moonlit road where my father's brother died. And it brought something else back to me, and carried me past it, I saw my little girl again and felt Isabel's tears again, and I felt my own tears begin to rise. And I was yet aware that this was only a moment, that the world waited outside, as hungry as a tiger, and that trouble stretched above us, longer than the sky.

Then it was over. Creole and Sonny let out their breath, both soaking wet, and grinning. There was a lot of applause and some of it was real. In the dark, the girl came by and I asked her to take drinks to the bandstand. There was a long pause, while they talked up there in the indigo light and after awhile I saw the girl put a Scotch and milk on top of the piano for Sonny. He didn't seem to notice it, but just before they started playing again, he sipped from it and looked toward me, and nodded. Then he put it back on top of the piano. For me, then, as they began to play again, it glowed and shook above my brother's head like the very cup of trembling.[10]

[10] "Behold, I have taken out of thine hand the cup of trembling, even the dregs of the cup of my fury; thou shalt no more drink it again" (Isaiah 51:22).

Gabriel García Márquez
(1928–)

In 1965, Gabriel García Márquez, a Columbian journalist who wrote fiction on the side, had published four books: three short, experimental novels and a collection of short stories. He had never received any royalties; his work had been well received critically and had won several literary prizes in Colombia, but none had sold enough copies to pay the publishing expenses. He had been suffering for several years from writer's block and could not make progress on a novel about several generations of a family in his small hometown in Colombia. One day while driving through the Mexican countryside, he suddenly had a vision about his book. The first chapter was as clear to him, he later said, as if it were already written. He returned to his home in Mexico City, where he had been working on film scripts and advertising copy, refused any more assignments, and holed up in his study. Eighteen months later he came out with the completed manuscript of the novel; he handed it to his wife, and, according to family legend, she handed him household bills for $10,000. The novel was *One Hundred Years of Solitude*. It was published in 1967, and immediately became an immense international critical and commercial success. A bestseller throughout Latin America, it was over the next few years translated into more than twenty-five languages. In France, it was named Best Foreign Book of 1969 by the Académie Française; in Italy, it received the prestigious Chianchiano Prize; and in the United States, it was named one of the twelve best books of 1970. In 1982, García Márquez was awarded the Nobel Prize for Literature.

This story, which sounds like every struggling unknown writer's fantasy, is actually less surprising when one considers not only García Márquez's long, inquiring apprenticeship as a writer but also the fertile ground into which he cast his artistic seed. By 1967, a generation of Latin-American writers had already caught the attention of the world: the Argentinian Jorge Luis Borges, with his brief, haunting, fictional "labyrinths"; the Guatemalan Miguel Angel Asturias, who won the Nobel Prize in 1967 for novels blending Mayan myths with hard political realities; the experimental Cuban novelist Alejo Carpentier; and the Chilean political poet Pablo Neruda, recipient of the 1971 Nobel Prize. The extraordinary success of *One Hundred Years of Solitude* called the world's attention to the fact that a second generation of Latin-American writers had arrived: not only García Márquez but also Julio Cortazar of Argentina, Guillermo Cabrera Infante of Cuba, Carlos Fuentes of Mexico, and Mario Vargas Llosa of Peru, to mention only a few of the best-known names. *One Hundred Years of Solitude* encouraged readers all over the world to read other Latin American novels and made it easier for new ones to be published and translated. The Boom (as the flowering of Latin American literature, beginning in the sixties, came to be called) was continuing.

García Márquez was born in 1928 in Aracataca, a small town on the Caribbean coast of Colombia in the area called the "banana zone." His parents left him in the care of his maternal grandparents for the first eight years of his life. Both Aracataca and the grandparents were to become primary sources of García Márquez's fiction. Aracataca served as the model

for the mythic "Macondo" of *One Hundred Years of Solitude* and other works, and the grandfather, an old soldier who had served in the civil wars in Colombia in the 1890's, provided a probable model for many of the old men, some battered, some heroic, who appear in his grandson's works. As for the grandmother, García Márquez later said that the revelation in the car in Mexico about how to write *One Hundred Years of Solitude* was the realization that he should write it as his grandmother talked. "She told things that sounded supernatural and fantastic, but she told them with complete naturalness," he said. "In previous attempts to tell the story without believing in it, I discovered that what I had to do was believe in them myself and write them with the same expressionless face with which my grandmother told them."

García Márquez enrolled at the age of nineteen in the law school of the National University in Bogotá but dropped out three years later to work as a writer. From 1950 to 1965, he worked as a newspaperman in Colombia and in Europe on a series of papers and as a correspondent for the Cuban news agency Prensa Latina. On his own time, he wrote fiction, at first a series of short, eerie stories, heavily influenced by Franz Kafka ("a disaster of Kafkaesque experimentation," the critic Regina Janes has called them), and then three novels: *Leaf Storm* (1955), *No One Writes to the Colonel* (1961), and *In Evil Hour* (1962). In these novels, the outlines of García Márquez's fictional world gradually took shape. William Faulkner probably inspired him to create a rural microcosm (Yoknapatawpha County in Faulkner, Macondo in García Márquez) and to employ, in *Leaf Storm,* a spiraling, meditative style, assigned to four subjective narrators, a style also probably indebted to Virginia Woolf. Later, in *No One Writes to the Colonel* and *In Evil Hour,* he borrowed from Ernest Hemingway his detached, objective third-person narrator and his spare, economical style. In *Big Mama's Funeral* (1962), a collection of eight short stories, these various influences had been thoroughly absorbed and García Márquez's distinctive fictional voice began to emerge, especially in the title story, which concluded the volume. The ground had been laid for *One Hundred Years of Solitude.*

The miracle of *One Hundred Years of Solitude* is the way it combines enormous complexity and sophistication with utter simplicity and accessibility. Like its classic Spanish predecessor *Don Quixote,* it is a favorite of critics and has engendered a hefty body of commentary, while at the same time it has charmed and delighted a mass audience who read for fun. Basically it is a mock-history of the imaginary town of Macondo and of its leading family, the Buendías, through six generations. But in its course, like a snowball rolling downhill, it picks up other stories: the history of Colombia, the history of South America, the biblical history of mankind, the histories of the families of Greek tragedy, the history of science, the history of literature, and several other narratives. All this encyclopedic material is held together by the narrative voice, a voice, we are told, like that of García Márquez's grandmother, telling the most incredible and marvelous things "with complete naturalness." At the end of the book, we learn that we have been reading a manuscript by one of the characters, the old gypsy Melquíades. The novel ends by folding back upon itself, leaving us with the vertiginous feeling that we have witnessed a complete world sprung from the imagination—as of course we have.

The five years of silence that preceded *One Hundred Years of Solitude* were matched by five years of silence following publication of the book, as García Márquez explored the direction his work should take. A second collection of short stories, *The Incredible and Sad Tale of Innocent Eréndira and Her Heartless Grandmother*, appeared in 1972. *The Autumn of the Patriarch* (1975) was the "dictator novel" which every Latin American writer seems compelled to write, a dream-like evocation of all dictators everywhere. *Chronicle of a Death Foretold* (1981) was a fictional treatment of an actual 1951 murder case in Colombia, in which a twenty-two-year-old student was hacked to death by two brothers who believed that he had seduced their sister, rejected by her husband on their wedding night. *Love in the Time of Cholera* appeared in 1985. It is a long novel, written at the pace of such nineteenth-century masters as Flaubert and Tolstoy. Most of the novel is about the obsession of a man for a woman he first met when he was eighteen. She repudiates him much of the time; indeed, in old age, just after her husband dies, she repudiates him again when he approaches her. He is persistent, however, and finally during a long paddle-boat ride on the Magdalena river, they give vent to their passions. (For part of the trip they have the boat to themselves because they have persuaded the captain to display the "cholera flag" and no one, therefore, will come near them.) In their eighties, they make love over and over, and, as the ending suggests, forever. *The General in His Labyrinth* (1989) is a novel about the great South American liberator Simón Bolívar.

A fundamental issue implied by all of García Márquez's work, and that of most other contemporary Latin American writers, is the relationship between literature and social change. García Márquez is a committed socialist who regards the Cuban Revolution as a model, however ambiguous, for the future of Latin America. He has consistently opposed right-wing dictatorships in Latin America and United States intervention in left-wing revolutionary activity, and through the years of his literary fame, he has continued to write political and social commentary. On the other hand, he is known to his readers as a writer who deals less with political realities than with a marvelous realm of the imagination. García Márquez has addressed this apparent contradiction. "After having written *Leaf Storm*," he has said, "I decided that writing about the village and my childhood was really an escape from having to face and write about the political reality of the country." *No One Writes to the Colonel, In Evil Hour,* and *Big Mama's Funeral* were attempts to deal directly with society and politics. "But when I finished *In Evil Hour*," he said, "I saw that all my views were wrong again. I came to see that in fact my writings about my childhood were *more* political and had more to do with the reality of my country than I had thought." He now believes that a revolutionary literature may operate not by a realistic depiction of suffering and injustice but by freeing the imagination to envision a better world. He strongly resists the label of "fantasy" for his work. "However fantastic may be the notion of a man who wakes to find himself transformed into a giant insect," he has written, "no one would argue that fantasy is the creative virtue of Franz Kafka; on the other hand, there is no doubt that it is the genius of Walt Disney. I believe that imagination is the particular faculty artists possess that enables them to create a new reality from the one they live in. That is the only artistic creation that seems valid

to me. Let us talk, then, about imagination in Latin America's artistic crea-
tion, and let us leave fantasy to the exclusive use of evil governments."

"Big Mama's Funeral" occupies a pivotal place in García Márquez's
work in that here many of the major elements of his mature style came
together. Big Mama is one of the earliest of his grotesque embodiments of
corrupt power; the story might equally well be called "The Autumn of the
Matriarch." A voice like García Márquez's grandmother's tells the most
extravagant stories in the most matter-of-fact way. And as the Pope floats
in his canoe down the Tiber and across the boundary between "the Roman
Empire and the ranches of Big Mama," we realize that we have entered a
magic kingdom, full of the magic, however, of neither Walt Disney nor
Franz Kafka but of the inimitable García Márquez.

FURTHER READING *(prepared by J.H.):* Regina Janes's *Gabriel García Márquez: Rev-
olutions in Wonderland,* 1981, is an elegant and insightful survey of the writer's work.
Other book-length introductions include George R. McMurray, *Gabriel García Már-
quez,* 1977, and Raymond Williams, *Gabriel García Márquez,* 1984. John S. Brush-
wood's chapter on García Márquez in *The Spanish-American Novel: A Twentieth Cen-
tury Survey,* 1975, offers good readings of his work in the context of other
Spanish-American writers. Michael Palencia-Roth's *Myth and the Modern Novel: Gar-
cía Márquez, Mann, and Joyce,* 1987, has a long chapter on García Márquez that
focuses on *One Hundred Years of Solitude,* placing it in the apocalyptic tradition. Many
interviews with García Márquez are available, including an important one with
Peter H. Stone, *Paris Review,* Winter, 1981. *The Fragrance of the Guava: Plinio Apuleyo
Mendoza in Conversation with Gabriel García Márquez,* 1983, is very important. On "Big
Mama's Funeral," see the relevant section in Regina Janes's book, as well as R. M.
Peel, "The Short Stories of Gabriel García Márquez," *Studies in Short Fiction,* Vol. 8,
1971; and David William Foster, "The Double Inscription of the *Narrataire* in 'Los
funerales de la Mamá Grande,' " in *Studies in the Contemporary Spanish American Short
Story,* 1979. *Gabriel García Márquez,* ed. Harold Bloom, 1989, is a collection of critical
essays.

BIG MAMA'S FUNERAL

Translated by J. S. Bernstein

This is, for all the world's unbelievers, the true account of Big Mama,
absolute sovereign of the Kingdom of Macondo, who lived for ninety-two
years, and died in the odor of sanctity one Tuesday last September, and
whose funeral was attended by the Pope.

Now that the nation, which was shaken to its vitals, has recovered its
balance; now that the bagpipers of San Jacinto, the smugglers of Guajira,
the rice planters of Sinú, the prostitutes of Caucamayal, the wizards of
Sierpe, and the banana workers of Aracataca have folded up their tents to
recover from the exhausting vigil and have regained their serenity, and the
President of the Republic and his Ministers and all those who represented
the public and supernatural powers on the most magnificent funeral occa-

sion recorded in the annals of history have regained control of their estates; now that the Holy Pontiff has risen up to Heaven in body and soul; and now that it is impossible to walk around in Macondo because of the empty bottles, the cigarette butts, the gnawed bones, the cans and rags and excrement that the crowd which came to the burial left behind; now is the time to lean a stool against the front door and relate from the beginning the details of this national commotion, before the historians have a chance to get at it.

Fourteen weeks ago, after endless nights of poultices, mustard plasters, and leeches, and weak with the delirium of her death agony, Big Mama ordered them to seat her in her old rattan rocker so she could express her last wishes. It was the only thing she needed to do before she died. That morning, with the intervention of Father Anthony Isabel, she had put the affairs of her soul in order, and now she needed only to put her worldly affairs in order with her nine nieces and nephews, her sole heirs, who were standing around her bed. The priest, talking to himself and on the verge of his hundredth birthday, stayed in the room. Ten men had been needed to take him up to Big Mama's bedroom, and it was decided that he should stay there so they should not have to take him down and then take him up again at the last minute.

Nicanor, the eldest nephew, gigantic and savage, dressed in khaki and spurred boots, with a .38-caliber long-barreled revolver holstered under his shirt, went to look for the notary. The enormous two-story mansion, fragrant from molasses and oregano, with its dark apartments crammed with chests and the odds and ends of four generations turned to dust, had become paralyzed since the week before, in expectation of that moment. In the long central hall, with hooks on the walls where in another time butchered pigs had been hung and deer were slaughtered on sleepy August Sundays, the peons were sleeping on farm equipment and bags of salt, awaiting the order to saddle the mules to spread the bad news to the four corners of the huge hacienda. The rest of the family was in the living room. The women were limp, exhausted by the inheritance proceedings and lack of sleep; they kept a strict mourning which was the culmination of countless accumulated mournings. Big Mama's matriarchal rigidity had surrounded her fortune and her name with a sacramental fence, within which uncles married the daughters of their nieces, and the cousins married their aunts, and brothers their sisters-in-law, until an intricate mesh of consanguinity was formed, which turned procreation into a vicious circle. Only Magdalena, the youngest of the nieces, managed to escape it. Terrified by hallucinations, she made Father Anthony Isabel exorcise her, shaved her head, and renounced the glories and vanities of the world in the novitiate of the Mission District.

On the margin of the official family, and in exercise of the *jus primae noctis*,[1] the males had fertilized ranches, byways, and settlements with an entire bastard line, which circulated among the servants without surnames, as godchildren, employees, favorites, and protégés of Big Mama.

[1] "Right of the first night"; right of a lord to spend the first night with the bride of a dependent.

The imminence of her death stirred the exhausting expectation. The dying woman's voice, accustomed to homage and obedience, was no louder than a bass organ pipe in the closed room, but it echoed in the most far-flung corners of the hacienda. No one was indifferent to this death. During this century, Big Mama had been Macondo's center of gravity, as had her brothers, her parents, and the parents of her parents in the past, in a dominance which covered two centuries. The town was founded on her surname. No one knew the origin, or the limits or the real value of her estate, but everyone was used to believing that Big Mama was the owner of the waters, running and still, of rain and drought, and of the district's roads, telegraph poles, leap years, and heat waves, and that she had furthermore a hereditary right over life and property. When she sat on her balcony in the cool afternoon air, with all the weight of her belly and authority squeezed into her old rattan rocker, she seemed, in truth, infinitely rich and powerful, the richest and most powerful matron in the world.

It had not occurred to anyone to think that Big Mama was mortal, except the members of her tribe, and Big Mama herself, prodded by the senile premonitions of Father Anthony Isabel. But she believed that she would live more than a hundred years, as did her maternal grandmother, who in the War of 1885 confronted a patrol of Colonel Aureliano Buendía's, barricaded in the kitchen of the hacienda. Only in April of this year did Big Mama realize that God would not grant her the privilege of personally liquidating, in an open skirmish, a horde of Federalist Masons.

During the first week of pain, the family doctor maintained her with mustard plasters and woolen stockings. He was a hereditary doctor, a graduate of Montpellier,[2] hostile by philosophical conviction to the progress of his science, whom Big Mama had accorded the lifetime privilege of preventing the establishment in Macondo of any other doctors. At one time he covered the town on horseback, visiting the doleful, sick people at dusk, and Nature had accorded him the privilege of being the father of many another's children. But arthritis kept him stiff-jointed in bed, and he ended up attending to his patients without calling on them, by means of suppositions, messengers, and errands. Summoned by Big Mama, he crossed the plaza in his pajamas, leaning on two canes, and he installed himself in the sick woman's bedroom. Only when he realized that Big Mama was dying did he order a chest with porcelain jars labeled in Latin brought, and for three weeks he besmeared the dying woman inside and out with all sorts of academic salves, magnificent stimulants, and masterful suppositories. Then he applied bloated toads to the site of her pain, and leeches to her kidneys, until the early morning of that day when he had to face the dilemma of either having her bled by the barber or exorcised by Father Anthony Isabel.

Nicanor sent for the priest. His ten best men carried him from the parish house to Big Mama's bedroom, seated on a creaking willow rocker, under the mildewed canopy reserved for great occasions. The little bell of the Viaticum[3] in the warm September dawn was the first notification to the inhabitants of Macondo. When the sun rose, the little plaza in front of Big Mama's house looked like a country fair.

[2] Famous medical school in France. [3] Communion given to the dying.

It was like a memory of another era. Until she was seventy, Big Mama used to celebrate her birthday with the most prolonged and tumultuous carnivals within memory. Demijohns of rum were placed at the townspeople's disposal, cattle were sacrificed in the public plaza, and a band installed on top of a table played for three days without stopping. Under the dusty almond trees, where, in the first week of the century, Colonel Aureliano Buendía's troops had camped, stalls were set up which sold banana liquor, rolls, blood puddings, chopped fried meat, meat pies, sausage, yucca breads, crullers, buns, corn breads, puff paste, *longanizas*,[4] tripes, coconut nougats, rum toddies, along with all sorts of trifles, gewgaws, trinkets, and knicknacks, and cockfights and lottery tickets. In the midst of the confusion of the agitated mob, prints and scapularies[5] with Big Mama's likeness were sold.

The festivities used to begin two days before and end on the day of her birthday, with the thunder of fireworks and a family dance at Big Mama's house. The carefully chosen guests and the legitimate members of the family, generously attended by the bastard line, danced to the beat of the old pianola which was equipped with the rolls most in style. Big Mama presided over the party from the rear of the hall in an easy chair with linen pillows, imparting discreet instructions with her right hand, adorned with rings on all her fingers. On that night the coming year's marriages were arranged, at times in complicity with the lovers, but almost always counseled by her own inspiration. To finish off the jubilation, Big Mama went out to the balcony, which was decorated with diadems and Japanese lanterns, and threw coins to the crowd.

That tradition had been interrupted, in part because of the successive mournings of the family and in part because of the political instability of the last few years. The new generations only heard stories of those splendid celebrations. They never managed to see Big Mama at High Mass, fanned by some functionary of the Civil Authority, enjoying the privilege of not kneeling, even at the moment of the elevation,[6] so as not to ruin her Dutch-flounced skirt and her starched cambric petticoats. The old people remembered, like a hallucination out of their youth, the two hundred yards of matting which were laid down from the manorial house to the main altar the afternoon on which Maria del Rosario Castañeda y Montero attended her father's funeral and returned along the matted street endowed with a new and radiant dignity, turned into Big Mama at the age of twenty-two. That medieval vision belonged then not only to the family's past but also to the nation's past. Ever more indistinct and remote, hardly visible on her balcony, stifled by the geraniums on hot afternoons, Big Mama was melting into her own legend. Her authority was exercised through Nicanor. The tacit promise existed, formulated by tradition, that the day Big Mama sealed her will the heirs would declare three nights of public merrymaking. But at the same time it was known that she had decided not to express her last wishes until a few hours before dying, and no one thought seriously about the possibility that Big Mama was mortal. Only this morning, awakened by the tinkling of the Viaticum, did the inhabitants of Macondo be-

[4] Pork sausages. [5] Vests with religious symbols worn under ordinary clothing.
[6] The elevation of the Host, in the mass.

come convinced not only that Big Mama was mortal but also that she was dying.

Her hour had come. Seeing her in her linen bed, bedaubed with aloes up to her ears, under the dust-laden canopy of Oriental crêpe, one could hardly make out any life in the thin respiration of her matriarchal breasts. Big Mama, who until she was fifty rejected the most passionate suitors, and who was well enough endowed by Nature to suckle her whole issue all by herself, was dying a virgin and childless. At the moment of extreme unction, Father Anthony Isabel had to ask for help in order to apply the oils to the palms of her hands, for since the beginning of her death throes Big Mama had had her fists closed. The attendance of the nieces was useless. In the struggle, for the first time in a week, the dying woman pressed against her chest the hand bejeweled with precious stones and fixed her colorless look on the nieces, saying, "Highway robbers." Then she saw Father Anthony Isabel in his liturgical habit and the acolyte with the sacramental implements, and with calm conviction she murmured, "I am dying." Then she took off the ring with the great diamond and gave it to Magdalena, the novice, to whom it belonged since she was the youngest heir. That was the end of a tradition: Magdalena had renounced her inheritance in favor of the Church.

At dawn Big Mama asked to be left alone with Nicanor to impart her last instructions. For half an hour, in perfect command of her faculties, she asked about the conduct of her affairs. She gave special instructions about the disposition of her body, and finally concerned herself with the wake. "You have to keep your eyes open," she said. "Keep everything of value under lock and key, because many people come to wakes only to steal." A moment later, alone with the priest, she made an extravagant confession, sincere and detailed, and later on took Communion in the presence of her nieces and nephews. It was then that she asked them to seat her in her rattan rocker so that she could express her last wishes.

Nicanor had prepared, on twenty-four folios written in a very clear hand, a scrupulous account of her possessions. Breathing calmly, with the doctor and Father Anthony Isabel as witnesses, Big Mama dictated to the notary the list of her property, the supreme and unique source of her grandeur and authority. Reduced to its true proportions, the real estate was limited to three districts, awarded by Royal Decree at the founding of the Colony; with the passage of time, by dint of intricate marriages of convenience, they had accumulated under the control of Big Mama. In that unworked territory, without definite borders, which comprised five townships and in which not one single grain had ever been sown at the expense of the proprietors, three hundred and fifty-two families lived as tenant farmers. Every year, on the eve of her name day,[7] Big Mama exercised the only act of control which prevented the lands from reverting to the state: the collection of rent. Seated on the back porch of her house, she personally received the payment for the right to live on her lands, as for more than a century her ancestors had received it from the ancestors of the tenants. When the three-day collection was over, the patio was crammed

[7] The day of the saint for whom she was named.

with pigs, turkeys, and chickens, and with the tithes and first fruits[8] of the land which were deposited there as gifts. In reality, that was the only harvest the family ever collected from a territory which had been dead since its beginnings, and which was calculated on first examination at a hundred thousand hectares.[9] But historical circumstances had brought it about that within those boundaries the six towns of Macondo district should grow and prosper, even the county seat, so that no person who lived in a house had any property rights other than those which pertained to the house itself, since the land belonged to Big Mama, and the rent was paid to her, just as the government had to pay her for the use the citizens made of the streets.

On the outskirts of the settlements, a number of animals, never counted and even less looked after, roamed, branded on the hindquarters with the shape of a padlock. This hereditary brand, which more out of disorder than out of quantity had become familiar in distant districts where the scattered cattle, dying of thirst, strayed in summer, was one of the most solid supports of the legend. For reasons which no one had bothered to explain, the extensive stables of the house had progressively emptied since the last civil war, and lately sugarcane presses, milking parlors, and a rice mill had been installed in them.

Aside from the items enumerated, she mentioned in her will the existence of three containers of gold coins buried somewhere in the house during the War of Independence, which had not been found after periodic and laborious excavations. Along with the right to continue the exploitation of the rented land, and to receive the tithes and first fruits and all sorts of extraordinary donations, the heirs received a chart kept up from generation to generation, and perfected by each generation, which facilitated the finding of the buried treasure.

Big Mama needed three hours to enumerate her earthly possessions. In the stifling bedroom, the voice of the dying woman seemed to dignify in its place each thing named. When she affixed her trembling signature, and the witnesses affixed theirs below, a secret tremor shook the hearts of the crowds which were beginning to gather in front of the house, in the shade of the dusty almond trees of the plaza.

The only thing lacking then was the detailed listing of her immaterial possessions. Making a supreme effort—the same kind that her forebears made before they died to assure the dominance of their line—Big Mama raised herself up on her monumental buttocks, and in a domineering and sincere voice, lost in her memories, dictated to the notary this list of her invisible estate:

The wealth of the subsoil, the territorial waters, the colors of the flag, national sovereignty, the traditional parties, the rights of man, civil rights, the nation's leadership, the right of appeal, Congressional hearings, letters of recommendation, historical records, free elections, beauty queens, transcendental speeches, huge demonstrations, distinguished young ladies, proper gentlemen, punctilious military men, His Illustrious Eminence, the

[8] Tithes (tenth parts) and first fruits (the earliest part of the harvest) are both religious contributions.

[9] An hectare is a metric unit of area, equivalent to 2.47 acres.

Supreme Court, goods whose importation was forbidden, liberal ladies, the meat problem, the purity of the language, setting a good example, the free but responsible press, the Athens of South America, public opinion, the lessons of democracy, Christian morality, the shortage of foreign exchange, the right of asylum, the Communist menace, the ship of state, the high cost of living, republican traditions, the underprivileged classes, statements of political support.

She didn't manage to finish. The laborious enumeration cut off her last breath. Drowning in the pandemonium of abstract formulas which for two centuries had constituted the moral justification of the family's power, Big Mama emitted a loud belch and expired.

That afternoon the inhabitants of the distant and somber capital saw the picture of a twenty-year-old woman on the first page of the extra editions, and thought that it was a new beauty queen. Big Mama lived again the momentary youth of her photograph, enlarged to four columns and with needed retouching, her abundant hair caught up atop her skull with an ivory comb and a diadem on her lace collar. That image, captured by a street photographer who passed through Macondo at the beginning of the century, and kept in the newspaper's morgue for many years in the section of unidentified persons, was destined to endure in the memory of future generations. In the dilapidated buses, in the elevators at the Ministries, and in the dismal tearooms hung with pale decorations, people whispered with veneration and respect about the dead personage in her sultry, malarial region, whose name was unknown in the rest of the country a few hours before—before it had been sanctified by the printed word. A fine drizzle covered the passers-by with misgiving and mist. All the church bells tolled for the dead. The President of the Republic, taken by surprise by the news when on his way to the commencement exercises for the new cadets, suggested to the War Minister, in a note in his own hand on the back of the telegram, that he conclude his speech with a minute of silent homage to Big Mama.

The social order had been brushed by death. The President of the Republic himself, who was affected by urban feelings as if they reached him through a purifying filter, managed to perceive from his car in a momentary but to a certain extent brutal vision the silent consternation of the city. Only a few low cafés remained open; the Metropolitan Cathedral was readied for nine days of funeral rites. At the National Capitol, where the beggars wrapped in newspapers slept in the shelter of the Doric columns and the silent statues of dead Presidents, the lights of Congress were lit. When the President entered his office, moved by the vision of the capital in mourning, his Ministers were waiting for him dressed in funereal garb, standing, paler and more solemn than usual.

The events of that night and the following ones would later be identified as a historic lesson. Not only because of the Christian spirit which inspired the most lofty personages of public power, but also because of the abnegation with which dissimilar interests and conflicting judgments were conciliated in the common goal of burying the illustrious body. For many years Big Mama had guaranteed the social peace and political harmony of her empire, by virtue of the three trunks full of forged electoral certificates which formed part of her secret estate. The men in her service, her

protégés and tenants, elder and younger, exercised not only their own rights of suffrage but also those of electors dead for a century. She exercised the priority of traditional power over transitory authority, the predominance of class over the common people, the transcendence of divine wisdom over human improvisation. In times of peace, her dominant will approved and disapproved canonries, benefices, and sinecures, and watched over the welfare of her associates, even if she had to resort to clandestine maneuvers or election fraud in order to obtain it. In troubled times, Big Mama contributed secretly for weapons for her partisans, but came to the aid of her victims in public. That patriotic zeal guaranteed the highest honors for her.

The President of the Republic had not needed to consult with his advisers in order to weigh the gravity of his responsibility. Between the Palace reception hall and the little paved patio which had served the viceroys as a *cochère*,[10] there was an interior garden of dark cypresses where a Portuguese monk had hanged himself out of love in the last days of the Colony. Despite his noisy coterie of bemedaled officials, the President could not suppress a slight tremor of uncertainty when he passed that spot after dusk. But that night his trembling had the strength of a premonition. Then the full awareness of his historical destiny dawned on him, and he decreed nine days of national mourning, and posthumous honors for Big Mama at the rank befitting a heroine who had died for the fatherland on the field of battle. As he expressed it in the dramatic address which he delivered that morning to his compatriots over the national radio and television network, the Nation's Leader trusted that the funeral rites for Big Mama would set a new example for the world.

Such a noble aim was to collide nevertheless with certain grave inconveniences. The judicial structure of the country, built by remote ancestors of Big Mama, was not prepared for events such as those which began to occur. Wise Doctors of Law, certified alchemists of the statutes, plunged into hermeneutics and syllogisms in search of the formula which would permit the President of the Republic to attend the funeral. The upper strata of politics, the clergy, the financiers lived through entire days of alarm. In the vast semicircle of Congress, rarefied by a century of abstract legislation, amid oil paintings of National Heroes and busts of Greek thinkers, the vocation of Big Mama reached unheard-of proportions, while her body filled with bubbles in the harsh Macondo September. For the first time, people spoke of her and conceived of her without her rattan rocker, her afternoon stupors, and her mustard plasters, and they saw her ageless and pure, distilled by legend.

Interminable hours were filled with words, words, words, which resounded throughout the Republic, made prestigious by the spokesmen of the printed word. Until, endowed with a sense of reality in that assembly of aseptic lawgivers, the historic blahblahblah was interrupted by the reminder that Big Mama's corpse awaited their decision at 104° in the shade. No one batted an eye in the face of that eruption of common sense in the pure atmosphere of the written law. Orders were issued to embalm the cadaver, while formulas were adduced, viewpoints were reconciled, or con-

[10] Porte cochere; covered area for vehicles to load and unload passengers.

stitutional amendments were made to permit the President to attend the burial.

So much had been said that the discussions crossed the borders, traversed the ocean, and blew like an omen through the pontifical apartments at Castel Gandolfo.[11] Recovered from the drowsiness of the torpid days of August, the Supreme Pontiff was at the window watching the lake where the divers were searching for the head of a decapitated young girl. For the last few weeks, the evening newspapers had been concerned with nothing else, and the Supreme Pontiff could not be indifferent to an enigma located such a short distance from his summer residence. But that evening, in an unforeseen substitution, the newspapers changed the photographs of the possible victims for that of one single twenty-year-old woman, marked off with black margins. "Big Mama," exclaimed the Supreme Pontiff, recognizing instantly the hazy daguerreotype which many years before had been offered to him on the occasion of his ascent to the Throne of Saint Peter. "Big Mama," exclaimed in chorus the members of the College of Cardinals in their private apartments, and for the third time in twenty centuries there was an hour of confusion, chagrin, and bustle in the limitless empire of Christendom, until the Supreme Pontiff was installed in his long black limousine en route to Big Mama's fantastic and far-off funeral.

The shining peach orchards were left behind, the Via Appia Antica with warm movie stars tanning on terraces without as yet having heard any news of the commotion, and then the somber promontory of Castel Sant' Angelo on the edge of the Tiber. At dusk the resonant pealing of St. Peter's Basilica mingled with the cracked tinklings of Macondo. Inside his stifling tent across the tangled reeds and the silent bogs which marked the boundary between the Roman Empire and the ranches of Big Mama, the Supreme Pontiff heard the uproar of the monkeys agitated all night long by the passing of the crowds. On his nocturnal itinerary, the canoe had been filled with bags of yucca, stalks of green bananas, and crates of chickens, and with men and women who abandoned their customary pursuits to try their luck at selling things at Big Mama's funeral. His Holiness suffered that night, for the first time in the history of the Church, from the fever of insomnia and the torment of mosquitoes. But the marvelous dawn over the Great Old Woman's domains, the primeval vision of the balsam apple and the iguana, erased from his memory the suffering of his trip and compensated him for his sacrifice.

Nicanor had been awakened by three knocks at the door which announced the imminent arrival of His Holiness. Death had taken possession of the house. Inspired by successive and urgent Presidential addresses, by the feverish controversies which had been silenced but continued to be heard by means of conventional symbols, men and congregations the world over dropped everything and with their presence filled the dark hallways, the jammed passageways, the stifling attics; and those who arrived later climbed up on the low walls around the church, the palisades, vantage points, timberwork, and parapets, where they accommodated themselves as best they could. In the central hall, Big Mama's cadaver lay mummifying while it waited for the momentous decisions contained in a quivering

[11] Village near Rome; summer residence of the Pope.

mound of telegrams. Weakened by their weeping, the nine nephews sat the wake beside the body in an ecstasy of reciprocal surveillance.

And still the universe was to prolong the waiting for many more days. In the city-council hall, fitted out with four leather stools, a jug of purified water, and a burdock hammock, the Supreme Pontiff suffered from a perspiring insomnia, diverting himself by reading memorials and administrative orders in the lengthy, stifling nights. During the day, he distributed Italian candy to the children who approached to see him through the window, and lunched beneath the hibiscus arbor with Father Anthony Isabel, and occasionally with Nicanor. Thus he lived for interminable weeks and months which were protracted by the waiting and the heat, until the day Father Pastrana appeared with his drummer in the middle of the plaza and read the proclamation of the decision. It was declared that Public Order was disturbed, ratatatat, and that the President of the Republic, ratatatat, had in his power the extraordinary prerogatives, ratatatat, which permitted him to attend Big Mama's funeral, ratatatat, tatatat, tatat, tatat.

The great day had arrived. In the streets crowded with carts, hawkers of fried foods, and lottery stalls, and men with snakes wrapped around their necks who peddled a balm which would definitively cure erysipelas and guarantee eternal life; in the mottled little plaza where the crowds had set up their tents and unrolled their sleeping mats, dapper archers cleared the Authorities' way. There they were, awaiting the supreme moment: the washerwomen of San Jorge, the pearl fishers from Cabo de la Vela, the fishermen from Ciénaga, the shrimp fishermen from Tasajera, the sorcerers from Mojajana, the salt miners from Manaure, the accordionists from Valledupar, the fine horsemen of Ayapel, the ragtag musicians from San Pelayo, the cock breeders from La Cueva, the improvisers from Sábanas de Bolívar, the dandies from Rebolo, the oarsmen of the Magdalena, the shysters from Monpox, in addition to those enumerated at the beginning of this chronicle, and many others. Even the veterans of Colonel Aureliano Buendía's camp—the Duke of Marlborough at their head, with the pomp of his furs and tiger's claws and teeth—overcame their centenarian hatred of Big Mama and those of her line and came to the funeral to ask the President of the Republic for the payment of their veterans' pensions which they had been waiting for for sixty years.

A little before eleven the delirious crowd which was sweltering in the sun, held back by an imperturbable élite force of warriors decked out in embellished jackets and filigreed morions,[12] emitted a powerful roar of jubilation. Dignified, solemn in their cutaways and top hats, the President of the Republic and his Ministers, the delegations from parliament, the Supreme Court, the Council of State, the traditional parties and the clergy, and representatives of Banking, Commerce, and Industry made their appearance around the corner of the telegraph office. Bald and chubby, the old and ailing President of the Republic paraded before the astonished eyes of the crowds who had seen him inaugurated without knowing who he was and who only now could give a true account of his existence. Among the archbishops enfeebled by the gravity of their ministry, and the military

[12] High-crested, visorless helmets.

men with robust chests armored with medals, the Leader of the Nation exuded the unmistakable air of power.

In the second rank, in a serene array of mourning crêpe, paraded the national queens of all things that have been or ever will be. Stripped of their earthly splendor for the first time, they marched by, preceded by the universal queen: the soybean queen, the green-squash queen, the banana queen, the meal yucca queen, the guava queen, the coconut queen, the kidney-bean queen, the 255-mile-long-string-of-iguana-eggs queen, and all the others who are omitted so as not to make this account interminable.

In her coffin draped in purple, separated from reality by eight copper turnbuckles, Big Mama was at that moment too absorbed in her formaldehyde eternity to realize the magnitude of her grandeur. All the splendor which she had dreamed of on the balcony of her house during her heat-induced insomnia was fulfilled by those forty-eight glorious hours during which all the symbols of the age paid homage to her memory. The Supreme Pontiff himself, whom she in her delirium imagined floating above the gardens of the Vatican in a resplendent carriage, conquered the heat with a plaited palm fan, and honored with his Supreme Dignity the greatest funeral in the world.

Dazzled by the show of power, the common people did not discern the covetous bustling which occurred on the rooftree of the house when agreement was imposed on the town grandees' wrangling and the catafalque was taken into the street on the shoulders of the grandest of them all. No one saw the vigilant shadow of the buzzards which followed the cortege through the sweltering little streets of Macondo, nor did they notice that as the grandees passed they left a pestilential train of garbage in the street. No one noticed that the nephews, godchildren, servants, and protégés of Big Mama closed the doors as soon as the body was taken out, and dismantled the doors, pulled the nails out of the planks, and dug up the foundations to divide up the house. The only thing which was not missed by anyone amid the noise of that funeral was the thunderous sigh of relief which the crowd let loose when fourteen days of supplications, exaltations, and dithyrambs were over, and the tomb was sealed with a lead plinth. Some of those present were sufficiently aware as to understand that they were witnessing the birth of a new era. Now the Supreme Pontiff could ascend to Heaven in body and soul, his mission on earth fulfilled, and the President of the Republic could sit down and govern according to his good judgment, and the queens of all things that have been or ever will be could marry and be happy and conceive and give birth to many sons, and the common people could set up their tents where they damn well pleased in the limitless domains of Big Mama, because the only one who could oppose them and had sufficient power to do so had begun to rot beneath a lead plinth. The only thing left then was for someone to lean a stool against the doorway to tell this story, lesson and example for future generations, so that not one of the world's disbelievers would be left who did not know the story of Big Mama, because tomorrow, Wednesday, the garbage men will come and will sweep up the garbage from her funeral, forever and ever.

Adrienne Rich
(1929–)

When Adrienne Rich published her collected poems in 1984, she titled the volume *The Fact of a Doorframe* and headed the collection with a 1974 poem by that name. The doorframe in the poem is a metaphor for poetry: "violent, arcane, common, / hewn of the commonest living substance / into archway, portal, frame." If the reader reads straight through the volume, though, and then returns to the epigraphic poem, it takes on a greater resonance. Doors stud the volume as a recurring metaphor for change and transformation. In "Snapshots of a Daughter-in-Law" (1958–60), the daughter-in-law stands "Poised, trembling and unsatisfied, before / an unlocked door, that cage of cages." "Prospective Immigrants Please Note" (1962) is completely devoted to a development of the image: "Either you will / go through this door / or you will not go through." If the "prospective immigrant" goes through the door, she may remember her name; if not, she may "live worthily," but "much will evade" her. These Richian doors probably carry a buried allusion to the famous door that Nora slams when she leaves her husband at the end of Ibsen's *A Doll House*; in "Juvenilia" (1960), a young Rich tries to write poetry under the stern eye of her father while the title of that play comically peers down at her from her father's bookshelf. There is also an implicit reference, in Rich's many rooms and doors, to Virginia Woolf's *A Room of One's Own*. But whereas for Woolf the room (along with five hundred pounds a year) represents security and autonomy, for Rich, as for Nora, it is something to get out of; hence the shift of emphasis from the room to the door.

To pass through a door is to change, and Rich has passed through many such doors in her life and her career. She grew up in Baltimore, Maryland, and was educated in private schools and at Radcliffe College, where she graduated in 1951. The same year she won the Yale Series of Younger Poets award for her first book, *A Change of World*. Her style in these early poems is controlled and rather formal; her chief models seemed to be William Butler Yeats and W. H. Auden. Auden wrote a foreword for the book; not surprisingly, he liked Rich's style, praised the poems' neatness and control, and compared them, rather quaintly in retrospect, to obedient little girls ("neatly and modestly dressed"). Other readers, however, looked behind the technique and found a powerful and truthful expression of female experience. In 1973, the critic Helen Vendler remembered reading *A Change of World* "in almost disbelieving wonder: someone my age was writing down my life."

Rich published three more volumes over the next decade. Meanwhile, in 1953, she married Alfred Conrad, a professor of economics at Harvard, and had three sons between 1955 and 1959. The important collection *Snapshots of a Daughter-in-Law* appeared in 1963. The fleeting, rather wistful references to female renunciation in *A Change of World* have now grown to recurring images of entrapment. Rich has said of the title poem that it "was jotted in fragments during children's naps, brief hours in a library, or at 3 A.M. after rising with a wakeful child. I despaired of doing any continuous

work at this time. Yet I began to feel that my fragments and scraps had a common consciousness and a common theme, one which I would have been very unwilling to put on paper at an earlier time because I had been taught that poetry should be 'universal,' which meant, of course, non-female." The forms of the poems have changed too. A few of the poems are in the regular patterns of the earlier volume, but several, again notably the title poem, employ lines of widely varying length and irregular rhythms and begin to incorporate prose quotations, a technique that Rich was to employ frequently in her later poems.

In 1966, Rich and her family moved to New York, where she took the first of a series of academic appointments; she taught at City College from 1968 to 1976. During the late sixties, she was preoccupied with her active participation in the resistance to the Vietnam War and with her disintegrating marriage, both major themes in the four volumes she published between 1966 and 1969. In 1970, she moved out of the household. Shockingly, Conrad killed himself a few months later.

The Will to Change appeared in 1971, and *Diving into the Wreck* in 1973; the latter won the 1974 National Book Award. These books represent yet another shift in Rich's work, turning from the nightmare images of entrapment, destruction, and death in both marriage poems and Vietnam poems to new images of strength and survival, manifesting "the will to change." Paradoxically, a number of poems that look toward the future in these volumes do so by mining the past, as Rich evolves her project of reconstructing women's history and culture, a collective undertaking that she has called "the most complex, subtle, and drastic revaluation ever attempted of the condition of the species." A number of these poems, then, are a "Study of History" (to quote the title of one of them). She returns to historical figures such as Caroline Herschel ("Planetarium") to unearth women's contributions to culture, or less literally she dives into the wreck of human culture "to see the damage that was done / and the treasures that prevail." Her technique continues to evolve in the direction of freedom and flexibility. Significantly, the still pictures of *Snapshots of a Daughter-in-Law* are here replaced by the dynamic and fluid qualities of film. A number of the poems experiment with cinematic structures and one is even named "Shooting Script."

Beginning in the early seventies, Rich began to identify herself increasingly with a lesbian-feminist position, a position she elaborated in a 1976 talk called " 'It Is the Lesbian in Us. . . .' " In 1976, too, she published both *Twenty-One Love Poems* and *Of Woman Born: Motherhood as Experience and Institution,* a lengthy study of motherhood not merely as a biological function but as an "institution" that has been shaped by male myths and expectations. *On Lies, Secrets, and Silence: Selected Prose, 1966–1978* appeared in 1979; *Blood, Bread, and Poetry: Selected Prose, 1979–1985,* was published in 1986. From 1976 to 1978 Rich taught at Douglass College in New Jersey. In 1978, she left academic life and moved to western Massachusetts where she coedited *Sinister Wisdom,* a lesbian-feminist journal. She now lives in California.

The themes of reclaiming female culture and the female past continue through *The Dream of a Common Language* (1978), *A Wild Patience Has Taken Me This Far* (1981), and the recent poems in the retrospective *The Fact of a*

Doorframe. Your Native Land, Your Life (1986) represents yet another door through which Rich seems to be passing. The title of the collection is rather ironic, since Rich's relationship, as a woman, a lesbian, and a Jew, to her native land is necessarily ambivalent. Much of the book, especially "Sources," a sequence of twenty-three linked poems, explores Rich's personal past and seeks spiritual reconciliation with her dead father and husband. "Contradictions: Tracking Poems" is a sequence of twenty-nine unconventional sonnets which turn from the past to the present to construct a portrait of the artist, considering and questioning both her life and the words by which she has lived. Rich's most recent collection is *Time's Power,* 1989.

There is something of the prophet in Adrienne Rich. She belongs among twentieth-century writers like D. H. Lawrence and Doris Lessing who have surveyed Western culture, found it out of joint, and attempted to set it right. She can speak without irony of her mission as a "revaluation of the condition of the species." Significantly, too, like Lawrence and Lessing, she locates the fatal flaw in civilization in the relations between the sexes. Rich's feminism has given her work direction, power, and energy. As the poet Hayden Carruth wrote, in reference to *The Dream of a Common Language,* "If the actual state of the world has driven her to devote part of her energy to polemic, she remains a poet primarily. And I do not imply by this that the ideology is unimportant to the poetry. On the contrary, the ideology is what has permitted her to combine traditional poetic resources with continual personal experiment, exactly the combination that has always produced the strongest literature."

However the strength of Rich's work is explained, it is undeniable. Over a period of thirty-five years, she has produced a distinguished body of poetry that has attracted a wide audience and has done much to restore poetry to a significant place in American life.

FURTHER READING *(prepared by J. H.):* A basic resource for the study of Rich is *Reading Adrienne Rich: Reviews and Re-Visions, 1951–81,* ed. Jane Roberta Cooper, 1984. This volume includes nine original essays on Rich's work, a substantial selection of reviews of individual volumes of her poetry, a section on Rich's prose, and a thirty-five-page bibliography of primary and secondary material. The Norton Critical Edition, *Adrienne Rich's Poetry,* ed. Barbara Charlesworth Gelpi and Albert Gelpi, 1975, is useful up to its date; it includes a good selection of poems through *Poems: Selected and New,* 1975; a section of Rich's own commentary on her work; and eight good critical essays. The illuminating interview with Rich in the Gelpi volume should be supplemented by more recent interviews, listed in the Cooper book. Rich's essay "When We Dead Awaken: Writing as Re-vision" (1971) is very important; it is reprinted in the Gelpi volume and in Rich's *On Lies, Secrets, and Silence: Selected Prose, 1966–1978,* 1979. Equally illuminating is the title essay in *Blood, Bread, and Poetry: Selected Prose, 1979–1985,* 1986. See, too, Claire Keyes' *The Aesthetics of Power: The Poetry of Adrienne Rich,* 1986. Otherwise, the most useful commentary is to be found in chapters of books. See David Kalstone, *Five Temperaments,* 1977; Rachel Blau DuPlessis, "The Critique of Consciousness and Myth in Levertov, Rich, and Rukeyser," in *Shakespeare's Sisters: Feminist Essays on Women Poets,* ed. Sandra M. Gilbert and Susan Gubar, 1979; and Cary Nelson, *Our Last First Poets: Vision and History in Contemporary American Poetry,* 1981.

AUNT JENNIFER'S TIGERS

Aunt Jennifer's tigers prance across a screen,
Bright topaz denizens of a world of green.
They do not fear the men beneath the tree;
They pace in sleek chivalric certainty.

Aunt Jennifer's fingers fluttering through her wool
Find even the ivory needle hard to pull.
The massive weight of Uncle's wedding band
Sits heavily upon Aunt Jennifer's hand.

When Aunt is dead, her terrified hands will lie
Still ringed with ordeals she was mastered by. 10
The tigers in the panel that she made
Will go on prancing, proud and unafraid.

1951

SNAPSHOTS OF A DAUGHTER-IN-LAW

1.
You, once a belle in Shreveport,
with henna-colored hair, skin like a peachbud,
still have your dresses copied from that time,
and play a Chopin prelude
called by Cortot: *"Delicious recollections
float like perfume through the memory."*[1]

Your mind now, moldering like wedding-cake,
heavy with useless experience, rich
with suspicion, rumor, fantasy,
crumbling to pieces under the knife-edge 10
of mere fact. In the prime of your life.

Nervy, glowering, your daughter
wipes the teaspoons, grows another way.

2.
Banging the coffee-pot into the sink
she hears the angels chiding, and looks out
past the raked gardens to the sloppy sky.
Only a week since They said: *Have no patience.*

[1] The French pianist and music critic Alfred Cortot used this phrase to describe Frédéric
Chopin's Seventh Prelude in his book *Chopin: 24 Preludes* (1930).

The next time it was: *Be insatiable.*
Then: *Save yourself; others you cannot save.*
Sometimes she's let the tapstream scald her arm, 20
a match burn to her thumbnail,

or held her hand above the kettle's snout
right in the woolly steam. They are probably angels,
since nothing hurts her anymore, except
each morning's grit blowing into her eyes.

3.
A thinking woman sleeps with monsters.
The beak that grips her, she becomes. And Nature,
that sprung-lidded, still commodious
steamer-trunk of *tempora* and *mores*[2]
gets stuffed with it all: the mildewed orange-flowers, 30
the female pills, the terrible breasts
of Boadicea[3] beneath flat foxes' heads and orchids.

Two handsome women, gripped in argument,
each proud, acute, subtle, I hear scream
across the cut glass and majolica
like Furies[4] cornered from their prey:
The argument *ad feminam,*[5] all the old knives
that have rusted in my back, I drive in yours,
ma semblable, ma soeur![6]

4.
Knowing themselves too well in one another: 40
their gifts no pure fruition, but a thorn,
the prick filed sharp against a hint of scorn . . .
Reading while waiting
for the iron to heat,
writing, *My Life had stood—a Loaded Gun—*[7]
in that Amherst pantry while the jellies boil and scum,
or, more often,
iron-eyed and beaked and purposed as a bird,
dusting everything on the whatnot every day of life.

[2] "Times" and "customs" (Latin), from the Roman orator Cicero's phrase "O tempora! O mores!" lamenting the presumed degeneracy of his age.

[3] British queen (first century A.D.) who led a revolt against the Roman occupiers of Britain.

[4] Goddesses of vengeance in Greek mythology.

[5] Argument "to the woman," a play upon the phrase *ad hominem* ("to the man"). An argument *ad hominem* is directed against an opponent personally rather than against his or her reasoning.

[6] "My likeness, my sister" (French). Charles Baudelaire ended his poem "To the Reader" with the line *"Hypocrite lecteur!"—mon semblable—mon frère!"* ("Hypocrite reader, my likeness, my brother!"). Eliot also uses this line in *The Waste Land* (l. 76).

[7] "Emily Dickinson, *Complete Poems,* ed. T. H. Johnson, 1960, p. 369." (Rich's note.) The following lines refer to Dickinson, who lived in Amherst, Massachusetts.

5.
Dulce ridens, dulce loquens,[8] 50
she shaves her legs until they gleam
like petrified mammoth-tusk.

6.
When to her lute Corinna sings[9]
neither words nor music are her own;
only the long hair dipping
over her cheek, only the song
of silk against her knees
and these
adjusted in reflections of an eye.

Poised, trembling and unsatisfied, before 60
an unlocked door, that cage of cages,
tell us, you bird, you tragical machine—
is this *fertilisante douleur?*[10] Pinned down
by love, for you the only natural action,
are you edged more keen
to prise the secrets of the vault? has Nature shown
her household books to you, daughter-in-law,
that her sons never saw?

7.
"To have in this uncertain world some stay
which cannot be undermined, is 70
of the utmost consequence."[11]
 Thus wrote
a woman, partly brave and partly good,
who fought with what she partly understood.
Few men about her would or could do more,
hence she was labeled harpy, shrew and whore.

8.
"You all die at fifteen," said Diderot,[12]
and turn part legend, part convention.
Still, eyes inaccurately dream
behind closed windows blankening with steam.
Deliciously, all that we might have been, 80

[8] "Sweetly laughing, sweetly speaking" (Latin), from Horace's Ode I.22: "Integer Vitae." In the original, the lines refer to the poet's lover, Lalage.

[9] First line of a poem by the Elizabethan poet Thomas Campion.

[10] "Fertilizing (or fruitful) sorrow" (French).

[11] "From Mary Wollstonecraft, *Thoughts on the Education of Daughters*, London, 1787." (Rich's note.)

[12] " 'You all die at fifteen': *'Vous mourez toutes à quinze ans,'* from the *Lettres à Sophie Volland*, quoted by Simone de Beauvoir in *Le Deuxième Sexe*, Vol. II, pp. 123–24." (Rich's note.) Denis Diderot (1713–84) was a French philosopher and encyclopedist. *Le Deuxième Sexe [The Second Sex]* (1949) by the French novelist and essayist Simone de Beauvoir was an important document in the early stage of contemporary feminism.

all that we were—fire, tears,
wit, taste, martyred ambition—
stirs like the memory of refused adultery
the drained and flagging bosom of our middle years.

9.
Not that it is done well, but
that it is done at all?[13] Yes, think
of the odds! or shrug them off forever.
This luxury of the precocious child,
Time's precious chronic invalid,—
would we, darlings, resign it if we could? 90
Our blight has been our sinecure:
mere talent was enough for us—
glitter in fragments and rough drafts.

Sigh no more, ladies.[14]
 Time is male
and in his cups drinks to the fair.
Bemused by gallantry, we hear
our mediocrities over-praised,
indolence read as abnegation,
slattern thought styled intuition,
every lapse forgiven, our crime 100
only to cast too bold a shadow
or smash the mold straight off.
For that, solitary confinement,
tear gas, attrition shelling.
Few applicants for that honor.

10.
 Well,
she's long about her coming, who must be
more merciless to herself than history.
Her mind full to the wind, I see her plunge
breasted and glancing through the currents,
taking the light upon her 110
at least as beautiful as any boy
or helicopter,[15]
 poised, still coming,
her fine blades making the air wince

[13] An allusion to an anecdote in James Boswell's *Life of Johnson* (1791): "Next day, Sunday, July 31, I told him I had been that morning at a meeting of the people called Quakers, where I had heard a woman preach. JOHNSON. 'Sir, a woman's preaching is like a dog's walking on his hinder legs. It is not done well; but you are surprised to find it done at all.' "

[14] From a song sung by Balthasar in Shakespeare's *Much Ado About Nothing*. The first two lines: "Sigh no more, ladies, sigh no more! / Men were deceivers ever."

[15] In a note, Rich cites in French a passage from *The Second Sex* which reads in English, "She comes down from the remoteness of ages, from Thebes, from Crete, from Chichén-Itzá; and she is also the totem set deep in the African jungle; she is a helicopter and she is a bird; and there is this, the greatest wonder of all: under her tinted hair the forest murmur becomes a thought, and words issue from her breasts." (Translated H. M. Parshley.)

but her cargo
no promise then:
delivered
palpable
ours.

1958–1960

THE BURNING OF PAPER INSTEAD OF CHILDREN

I was in danger of
verbalizing my moral
impulses out of existence.
—Daniel Berrigan,[1]
on trial in Baltimore.

1. My neighbor, a scientist and art-collector, telephones me in a state of
violent emotion. He tells me that my son and his, aged eleven and twelve,
have on the last day of school burned a mathematics textbook in the back-
yard. He has forbidden my son to come to his house for a week, and has
forbidden his own son to leave the house during that time. "The burning of
a book," he says, "arouses terrible sensations in me, memories of Hitler;
there are few things that upset me so much as the idea of burning a book."

 Back there: the library, walled
 with green Britannicas
 Looking again
 in Dürer's *Complete Works* 10
 for MELANCOLIA, the baffled woman[2]

 the crocodiles in Herodotus[3]
 the Book of the Dead[4]
 the *Trial of Jeanne d'Arc,*[5] so blue
 I think, It is her color

 and they take the book away
 because I dream of her too often

 love and fear in a house
 knowledge of the oppressor 20
 I know it hurts to burn

[1] Berrigan, a Catholic priest, was convicted with eight other defendants in 1968 of burning
draft records in Catonsville, Maryland, in protest against the Vietnam war.

[2] Melancholy is personified as a woman in an engraving by the German artist Albrecht
Dürer (1471–1528).

[3] In his *History* of the Persian Wars, the Greek historian Herodotus (fifth century B.C.)
describes the crocodiles of Egypt.

[4] Ancient Egyptian religious text.

[5] Transcript of the trial of Joan of Arc, who led the French forces against the English in the
Hundred Years War and was burned at the stake as a witch in 1431.

2. To imagine a time of silence
or few words
a time of chemistry and music

the hollows above your buttocks
traced by my hand
or, *hair is like flesh,* you said

an age of long silence

relief

from this tongue this slab of limestone 30
or reinforced concrete
fanatics and traders
dumped on this coast wildgreen clayred
that breathed once
in signals of smoke
sweep of the wind

knowledge of the oppressor
this is the oppressor's language

yet I need it to talk to you

3. *People suffer highly in poverty and it takes dignity and intelligence to* 40
overcome this suffering. Some of the suffering are: a child did not had dinner
last night: a child steal because he did not have money to buy it: to hear a
mother say she do not have money to buy food for her children and to see a child
without cloth it will make tears in your eyes.[6]

(the fracture of order
the repair of speech
to overcome this suffering)

4. We lie under the sheet
after making love, speaking
of loneliness 50
relieved in a book
relived in a book
so on that page
the clot and fissure
of it appears
words of a man
in pain
a naked word
entering the clot

[6] This paragraph is quoted from a paper Rich received from a student in the open admissions program of the City College of New York.

a hand grasping 60
through bars:

deliverance

What happens between us
has happened for centuries
we know it from literature

still it happens

sexual jealousy
outflung hand
beating bed

dryness of mouth 70
after panting

there are books that describe all this
and they are useless

You walk into the woods behind a house
there in that country
you find a temple
built eighteen hundred years ago
you enter without knowing
what it is you enter

so it is with us 80

no one knows what may happen
though the books tell everything

burn the texts said Artaud[7]

5. I am composing on the typewriter late at night, thinking of today.
How well we all spoke. A language is a map of our failures. Frederick
Douglass wrote an English purer than Milton's.[8] People suffer highly in
poverty. There are methods but we do not use them. Joan, who could not
read, spoke some peasant form of French. Some of the suffering are: it is
hard to tell the truth; this is America; I cannot touch you now. In America
we have only the present tense. I am in danger. You are in danger. The
burning of a book arouses no sensation in me. I know it hurts to burn.

[7] Antonin Artaud (1895–1948), French playwright, director, and theorist of the "Theater
of Cruelty." In *The Theater and Its Double* (1938), he called for the abandonment of dramatic
texts in favor of a nonverbal theater of intense feeling. Artaud appeared as an actor in Carl
Dreyer's film *The Passion of Joan of Arc* (1928); in his theater, he said, actors would be "like
victims burnt at the stake, signaling through the flames."

[8] Frederick Douglass, an escaped slave, wrote a famous autobiography, *Narrative of the Life
of Frederick Douglass* (1845). John Milton wrote *Paradise Lost* (1667).

There are flames of napalm in Catonsville, Maryland. I know it hurts to burn. The typewriter is overheated, my mouth is burning, I cannot touch you and this is the oppressor's language.

1968

DIVING INTO THE WRECK

First having read the book of myths,
and loaded the camera,
and checked the edge of the knife-blade,
I put on
the body-armor of black rubber
the absurd flippers
the grave and awkward mask.
I am having to do this
not like Cousteau[1] with his
assiduous team 10
aboard the sun-flooded schooner
but here alone.

There is a ladder.
The ladder is always there
hanging innocently
close to the side of the schooner.
We know what it is for,
we who have used it.
Otherwise
it's a piece of maritime floss 20
some sundry equipment.

I go down.
Rung after rung and still
the oxygen immerses me
the blue light
the clear atoms
of our human air.
I go down.
My flippers cripple me,
I crawl like an insect down the ladder 30
and there is no one
to tell me when the ocean
will begin.

First the air is blue and then
it is bluer and then green and then

[1] Jacques Cousteau founded the French navy's undersea research group in 1945 and, for years, had a popular program on American television.

black I am blacking out and yet
my mask is powerful
it pumps my blood with power
the sea is another story
the sea is not a question of power 40
I have to learn alone
to turn my body without force
in the deep element.

And now: it is easy to forget
what I came for
among so many who have always
lived here
swaying their crenellated fans
between the reefs
and besides 50
you breathe differently down here.

I came to explore the wreck.
The words are purposes.
The words are maps.
I came to see the damage that was done
and the treasures that prevail.
I stroke the beam of my lamp
slowly along the flank
of something more permanent
than fish or weed 60

the thing I came for:
the wreck and not the story of the wreck
the thing itself and not the myth
the drowned face always staring
toward the sun
the evidence of damage
worn by salt and sway into this threadbare beauty
the ribs of the disaster
curving their assertion
among the tentative haunters. 70

This is the place.
And I am here, the mermaid whose dark hair
streams black, the merman in his armored body
We circle silently
about the wreck
we dive into the hold.
I am she: I am he

whose drowned face sleeps with open eyes
whose breasts still bear the stress
whose silver, copper, vermeil cargo lies 80

obscurely inside barrels
half-wedged and left to rot
we are the half-destroyed instruments
that once held to a course
the water-eaten log
the fouled compass

We are, I am, you are
by cowardice or courage
the one who find our way
back to this scene 90
carrying a knife, a camera
a book of myths
in which
our names do not appear.

1972

PAULA BECKER TO CLARA WESTHOFF[1]

PAULA BECKER 1876–1907
CLARA WESTHOFF 1878–1954

*became friends at Worpswede, an artists' colony near Bremen, Germany, summer
1899. In January 1900, spent a half-year together in Paris, where Paula
painted and Clara studied sculpture with Rodin. In August they returned to
Worpswede, and spent the next winter together in Berlin. In 1901, Clara mar-
ried the poet Rainer Maria Rilke; soon after, Paula married the painter Otto
Modersohn. She died in a hemorrhage after childbirth, murmuring,* What a
shame!

The autumn feels slowed down,
summer still holds on here, even the light
seems to last longer than it should
or maybe I'm using it to the thin edge.
The moon rolls in the air. I didn't want this child.
You're the only one I've told.
I want a child maybe, someday, but not now.
Otto has a calm, complacent way
of following me with his eyes, as if to say
Soon you'll have your hands full! 10
And yes, I will; this child will be mine
not his, the failures, if I fail
will be all mine. We're not good, Clara,

[1] "Some phrases in this poem are quoted from actual diaries and letters of Paula Moder-
sohn-Becker, which were shown me in unpublished translations by Liselotte Glozer. Since
then, an annotated translation of the manuscripts has been published by Diane Radycki: *The
Letters and Journals of Paula Modersohn-Becker* (Metuchen, N. J.: Scarecrow Press, 1980)." (Rich's
note.)

at learning to prevent these things,
and once we have a child, it *is* ours.
But lately, I feel beyond Otto or anyone.
I know now the kind of work I have to do.
It takes such energy! I have the feeling I'm
moving somewhere, patiently, impatiently,
in my loneliness. I'm looking everywhere in nature 20
for new forms, old forms in new places,
the planes of an antique mouth, let's say, among the leaves.
I know and do not know
what I am searching for.
Remember those months in the studio together,
you up to your strong forearms in wet clay,
I trying to make something of the strange impressions
assailing me—the Japanese
flowers and birds on silk, the drunks
sheltering in the Louvre,[2] that river-light, 30
those faces. . . . Did we know exactly
why we were there? Paris unnerved you,
you found it too much, yet you went on
with your work . . . and later we met there again,
both married then, and I thought you and Rilke
both seemed unnerved. I felt a kind of joylessness
between you. Of course he and I
have had our difficulties. Maybe I was jealous
of him, to begin with, taking you from me,
maybe I married Otto to fill up 40
my loneliness for you.
Rainer, of course, *knows* more than Otto knows,
he believes in women. But he feeds on us,
like all of them. His whole life, his art
is protected by women. Which of us could say that?
Which of us, Clara, hasn't had to take that leap
out beyond our being women
to save our work? or is it to save ourselves?
Marriage is lonelier than solitude.
Do you know: I was dreaming I had died 50
giving birth to the child.
I couldn't paint or speak or even move.
My child—I think—survived me. But what was funny
in the dream was, Rainer had written my requiem—
a long, beautiful poem, and calling me his friend.
I was *your* friend
but in the dream you didn't say a word.
In the dream his poem was like a letter
to someone who has no right
to be there but must be treated gently, like a guest 60
who comes on the wrong day. Clara, why don't I dream of you?

[2] Famous Paris art museum, formerly a royal palace.

That photo of the two of us—I have it still,
you and I looking hard into each other
and my painting behind us. How we used to work
side by side! And how I've worked since then
trying to create according to our plan
that we'd bring, against all odds, our full power
to every subject. Hold back nothing
because we were women. Clara, our strength still lies
in the things we used to talk about: 70
how life and death take one another's hands,
the struggle for truth, our old pledge against guilt.
And now I feel dawn and the coming day.
I love waking in my studio, seeing my pictures
come alive in the light. Sometimes I feel
it is myself that kicks inside me,
myself I must give suck to, love . . .
I wish we could have done this for each other
all our lives, but we can't . . .
They say a pregnant woman 80
dreams of her own death. But life and death
take one another's hands. Clara, I feel so full
of work, the life I see ahead, and love
for you, who of all people
however badly I say this
will hear all I say and cannot say.

1975–1976

FOR JULIA IN NEBRASKA

*Here on the divide between the Republican and the Little Blue lived some of the
most courageous people of the frontier. Their fortunes and their loves live again
in the writings of Willa Cather, daughter of the plains and interpreter of man's
growth in these fields and in the valleys beyond.*

*On this beautiful, ever-changing land, man fought to establish a home. In her
vision of the plow against the sun, symbol of the beauty and importance of work,
Willa Cather caught the eternal blending of earth and sky. . . .*[1]

In the Midwest of Willa Cather
the railroad looks like a braid of hair
a grandmother's strong hands plaited
straight down a grand-daughter's back.
Out there last autumn the streets

[1] "Epigraph quoted from the Willa Cather Educational Foundation, Historical Landmark
Council, marker at the intersection of Highways 281 and 4, fourteen miles north of Red
Cloud, Nebraska." (Rich's note.)

dreamed copper-lustre, the fields
of winter wheat whispered long snows yet to fall
we were talking of matrices

and now it's spring again already.
This stormy Sunday lashed with rain 10
I call you in Nebraska
hear you're planting your garden
sanding and oiling a burl of wood
hear in your voice the intention to
survive the long war between mind and body
and we make a promise to talk
this year, about growing older

and I think: we're making a pledge.
Though not much in books of ritual
is useful between women 20
we still can make vows together
long distance, in electrical code:
Today you were promising me
to live, and I took your word,
Julia, as if it were my own:
we'll live to grow old and talk about it too.

I've listened to your words
seen you stand by the caldron's glare
rendering grammar by the heat
of your womanly wrath. 30
Brave linguist, bearing your double axe and shield
painfully honed and polished,
no word lies cool on your tongue
bent on restoring meaning to
our lesbian names, in quiet fury
weaving the chronicle so violently torn.

On this beautiful, ever-changing land
—the historical marker says—
man fought to establish a home
(fought whom? the marker is mute.) 40
They named this Catherland, for Willa Cather,
lesbian—the marker is mute,
the marker white men set on a soil
of broken treaties, Indian blood,
women wiped out in childbirths, massacres—
for Willa Cather, lesbian,
whose letters were burnt in shame.

Dear Julia, Willa knew at her death
that the very air was changing

that her Archbishop's skies 50
would hardly survive his life[2]
she knew as well that history
is neither your script nor mine
it is the pictograph
from which the young must learn
like Tom Outland,[3] from people
discredited or dead
that it needs a telling as plain
as the prairie, as the tale
of a young girl or an old woman 60
told by tongues that loved them

And Willa who could not tell
her own story as it was
left us her stern and delicate
respect for the lives she loved—
How are we going to do better?
for that's the question that lies
beyond our excavations,
the question I ask of you
and myself, when our maps diverge, 70
when we miss signals, fail—

And if I've written in passion,
Live, Julia! what was I writing
but my own pledge to myself
where the love of women is rooted?
And what was I invoking
but the matrices we weave
web upon web, delicate rafters
flung in audacity to the prairie skies
nets of telepathy contrived 80
to outlast the iron road
laid out in blood across the land they called virgin—
nets, strands, a braid of hair
a grandmother's strong hands plaited
straight down a grand-daughter's back.

1978, 1981

[2] An allusion to Cather's novel *Death Comes for the Archbishop* (1921).
[3] In Cather's *The Professor's House* (1925), Tom Outland discovers the stone city of an extinct tribe of cliff-dwellers.

from *CONTRADICTIONS: TRACKING POEMS*

1.

Look: this is January the worst onslaught
is ahead of us Don't be lured
by these soft grey afternoons these sunsets cut
from pink and violet tissue-paper by the thought
the days are lengthening
Don't let the solstice fool you:
our lives will always be
a stew of contradictions
the worst moment of winter can come in April
when the peepers are stubbornly still and our bodies 10
plod on without conviction
and our thoughts cramp down before the sheer
arsenal of everything that tries us:
this battering, blunt-edged life

9.

Tearing but not yet torn: this page
The long late-winter rage
wild rain on the windshield
clenched stems unyielding sticks
of maple, birch bleached grass the range
of things resisting change
And this is how I am
and this is how you are
when we resist the charmer's open sesame
the thief's light-fingered touch
staying closed because we will 10
not give ourselves away
until the agent the manipulator the false toucher
has left and it is May

10.

Night over the great and the little worlds
of Brooklyn the shredded communities
in Chicago Argentina Poland
in Holyoke Massachusetts Amsterdam Manchester England

Night falls⠀⠀the day of atonement[1] begins
in how many divided hearts⠀⠀how many defiant lives
Toronto⠀⠀Managua⠀⠀St. Johnsbury
and the great and little worlds of the women
Something ancient passes across the earth
lifting the dust of the blasted ghettos⠀⠀⠀⠀⠀⠀⠀⠀⠀⠀10
You ask if I will eat and I say, Yes,
I have never fasted
but something crosses my life
not a shadow⠀⠀⠀the reflection of a fire

14.

Lately in my dreams I hear long sentences
meaningless in ordinary American
like, *Your mother, too, was a missionary of poets*
and in another dream one of my old teachers
shows me a letter of reference
he has written for me, in a language
I know to be English but cannot understand,
telling me it's in "transformational grammar"
and that the student who typed the letter
does not understand this grammar either.⠀⠀⠀⠀⠀⠀10
Lately I dreamed about my father,
how I found him, alive, seated on an old chair.
I think what he said to me was,
You don't know how lonely I am.

17.

I have backroads I take⠀⠀⠀to places
like the hospital where night pain
is never tended enough but I can drive
under the overlacing boughs
of wineglass elm, oak, maple
from Mosquitoville to Wells River[2]
along the double track with the greened hump
the slope with the great sugar-grove
New Age talk calls it "visualizing"[3]⠀⠀⠀but I know
under torture I would travel⠀⠀⠀⠀⠀⠀⠀⠀⠀⠀⠀⠀10

[1] The Jewish holiday of Yom Kippur (late September or early October), a day of penitence, fasting, and meditation.
[2] Place names, like West Barnet, in central Vermont.
[3] *New Age* is a glossy, "consciousness-raising" magazine published in Brighton, Massachusetts. Rich is probably referring to an article on dreams published in the issue of October, 1983.

from the West Barnet burying-ground
to Joe's Brook by heart I know
all of those roads by heart
by heart I know what, and all, I have left behind

27.

The Tolstoyans[4] the Afro-American slaves
knew this: you could be killed
for teaching people to read and write
I used to think the worst affliction
was to be forbidden pencil and paper
well, Ding Ling[5] recited poems to prison walls
for years of the Cultural Revolution
and truly, the magic of written characters
looms and dwindles shrinks small grows swollen
depending on where you stand 10
and what is in your hand
and who can read and why
I think now the worst affliction
is not to know who you are or have been
I have learned this in part
from writers Reading and writing
aren't sacred yet people have been killed
as if they were

28.

This high summer we love will pour its light
the fields grown rich and ragged in one strong moment
then before we're ready will crash into autumn
with a violence we can't accept
a bounty we can't forgive
Night frost will strike when the noons are warm
the pumpkins wildly glowing the green tomatoes
straining huge on the vines
queen anne and blackeyed susan will straggle rusty
as the milkweed stakes her claim 10
she who will stand at last dark sticks barely rising
up through the snow her testament of continuation
We'll dream of a longer summer

[4] Followers of Leo Tolstoy (1828–1910), Russian novelist and religious philosopher, whose social program of service to others included teaching peasants to read.
[5] One of China's most popular twentieth-century authors. She was imprisoned for five years during the Cultural Revolution (1966–76) for her outspoken criticism of the Communist Party, especially on the issue of women's rights.

but this is the one we have:
I lay my sunburnt hand
on your table: this is the time we have

29.

You who think I find words for everything
this is enough for now
cut it short cut loose from my words

You for whom I write this
in the night hours when the wrecked cartilage
sifts round the mystical jointure of the bones
when the insect of detritus crawls
from shoulder to elbow to wristbone
remember: the body's pain and the pain on the streets
are not the same but you can learn 10
from the edges that blur O you who love clear edges
more than anything watch the edges that blur

1983–1985

Milan Kundera
(1929–)

Milan Kundera's novel *The Joke* was one of many victims of the Russian
takeover of Czechoslovakia in 1968. Denied publication by state censors for
two years, it had been published in 1967 and had quickly become a best-
seller in the "Prague Spring" of 1968, when it appeared that Czechoslo-
vakia might achieve independence from Soviet Russian domination. Soon
after Russian tanks rolled into the streets of Prague, however, *The Joke* was
proscribed and copies were removed from all bookstores and libraries.
Kundera himself was expelled from the Communist Party, fired from his
job at the Prague Film Institute, and after 1969 forbidden to publish any-
thing in his native country. He moved to France in 1975; four years later,
the Czech government stripped him of his citizenship. Yet in 1980, when a
television panelist called *The Joke* "a major indictment of Stalinism," Kun-
dera objected; "Spare me your Stalinism, please. *The Joke* is a love story."

The fear and suspicion with which the Soviet bloc and the Western
nations regarded each other during the Cold War was echoed in the way
they regarded one another's literature. The Russians and Eastern Europe-
ans saw American literature as dominated by such naturalistic critics of

American society as Jack London and Upton Sinclair, while Americans focused the same sort of distorting lens on Russian and Eastern European literature, focusing on only "dissident" writers like Boris Pasternak and Alexander Solzhenitsyn. Kundera has protested against distortion of this kind. "People write about the literature of the so-called East European countries as if it were indeed nothing more than a propaganda instrument, be it pro- or anti-Communist. I must confess I don't like the word 'dissident,' particularly when applied to art. It is part and parcel of that same politicizing, ideological distortion which cripples a work of art." Over the past decade, Western readers have come to recognize Kundera not just as an exotic "dissident" writer but as one of the great masters of contemporary fiction.

Kundera, born in 1929 in Brno, Czechoslovakia, at first studied music and worked as a jazz musician for some years. (His father was the famous Czech pianist Ludvik Kundera.) He joined the Communist Party in Czechoslovakia when he was seventeen, a year before the Communist takeover of the country in 1947. Two years later he was expelled for saying, as he puts it, "something I would better have left unsaid." His first publications were poetry: *Man: A Broad Garden* (1953), *The Last May* (1955), and *Monologues* (1957). The poems attracted unfavorable attention from the authorities for their political unorthodoxy and their eroticism; Kundera, however, was admitted back into the Communist Party in 1957. He enrolled as a student in the Prague Film Institute in 1956 and two years later became an assistant professor there. He briefly experimented with playwriting: *The Owners of the Keys* was produced by the National Theater in Prague in 1962 with great success. He has periodically returned to the dramatic form, perhaps most notably in *Jacques and His Master* (1968), based on Diderot's *Jacques the Fatalist*. Three volumes of short stories, *Laughable Loves*, Volumes I, II, and III, appeared in 1963, 1965, and 1968. Most of these stories deal with erotic adventures, often carried out between an incorrigible Don Juan and strong, sensual, believable women, against a background of institutional bureaucracy. Kundera's literary interest in jokes and games appears frequently in these stories as well. Many of them are told in short, discrete episodes, often numbered or subtitled; the tone is lightly ironic and humorous. In short, they have most of the characteristics of Kundera's later fiction.

The Joke is a complexly organized, darkly comic novel about a student at the University of Prague who is expelled and sent to work in the coal mines because he jokingly wrote on a postcard to a girl he was pursuing: "Optimism is the opium of the people! A healthy atmosphere stinks of stupidity! Long live Trotsky!" The novel takes place years later when the ex-student decides to revenge himself on the Communist official who expelled him by seducing the man's wife. Not only was the novel an enormous success, Kundera was allowed to make it into a film, which he wrote and directed himself; the film was equally successful, both in Czechoslovakia and abroad.

The third volume of *Laughable Loves* was the last book by Kundera permitted to be published in Czechoslovakia. *Life is Elsewhere*, written in 1970, was published in French in 1973 and in English in 1974; the original Czech text was published in 1979 by an emigré press. A similar pattern was fol-

lowed in the publication of *The Farewell Party* (1976). *Life Is Elsewhere* is a satirical novel about a young man who, urged on by his doting mother, becomes a bad poet and a posturing romantic revolutionary. *The Farewell Party* again mingles sexual farce with political satire in a story set in a government health spa for infertile women.

Kundera's masterpiece is probably either *The Book of Laughter and Forgetting* (1979) or *The Unbearable Lightness of Being* (1984). The title of the former identifies it as a "book" rather than a "novel," and its structure and style test the limits of the novel's form. The book is made up of seven sections, and the narrator, who identifies himself as "Milan Kundera," tells us that they are true stories about his own life. Impossible to summarize, *The Book of Laughter and Forgetting* verges on a short-story collection, an ironic essay, a fragmentary autobiography, and a fanciful history. At one point, the narrator calls it " a novel in the form of variations." In an interview, the American novelist Philip Roth asked Kundera if it was a novel, and Kundera replied: "As far as my own personal esthetic judgment goes, it really is a novel, but I have no wish to force this opinion on anyone. There is enormous freedom latent within the novelistic form. It is a mistake to regard a certain stereotyped structure as the inviolable essence of the novel."

The Unbearable Lightness of Being also takes full advantage of "the enormous freedom" of the novel form, although superficially it seems more traditional. It tells a more or less continuous story, following the progress of two sets of lovers: one, a young woman and a man who returns her love and yet cannot give up his pursuit of other women, and the other, one of the man's mistresses and her adoring lover. It, too, is structured in seven discrete parts, each further divided into short, numbered sections, which move dazzlingly through incidents in the plot, interspersed with short, ironic essays, historical anecdotes, and a wealth of other material. This variety is held together by the witty, meditative voice of the third-person narrator. The book won a number of awards in Europe and America and was greeted with great critical enthusiasm. The reviewer for *The Washington Times* wrote, for example: "Let me say it simply: *The Unbearable Lightness of Being* is one of the greatest novels of the twentieth century, and with its publication Kundera has firmly established himself as the world's greatest living writer."

Extravagant as such praise sounds, many readers would find themselves in agreement with it. Kundera, while completely original, has an affinity with a number of contemporary novelists—Gabriel García Márquez of Colombia and Margaret Atwood of Canada come to mind—who have found a way of writing about the harsh political realities of the contemporary world without lapsing into a hopeless recital of atrocities. In his own, idiosyncratic way, he is a "magic realist" who can encompass an astonishing range of experience within a single narrative, from the gray boredom of life under an authoritarian, bureaucratic regime to the sometimes ambiguous ecstasies of the private erotic life.

"Nobody Will Laugh," one of the best stories in *Laughable Loves*, characteristically combines politics and eroticism. Like a number of Kundera protagonists, Klima is both too intelligent and too highly sexed, perhaps, for his own good. Like several other stories in *Laughable Loves*, the story ex-

plores some of the same terrain as *The Joke* in tracing out the consequences of a piece of lighthearted folly in a society that is anything but lighthearted. But ultimately Klíma is not the victim of the bureaucracy but of himself, and the story, like *The Joke*, is less about Stalinism than about love.

FURTHER READING *(prepared by J. H.):* The American novelist and critic Philip Roth played an early, important role in introducing Kundera's work to an American audience. He included *Laughable Loves* and *The Book of Laughter and Forgetting* in a paperback series called "Writers from the Other Europe." Roth's introduction to *Laughable Loves* is excellent. An interesting interview by Roth is printed as an "Afterword" to *The Book of Laughter and Forgetting*. A lengthy, more recent interview by Lois Oppenheimer is "Clarifications, Elucidations: An Interview with Milan Kundera," in *Review of Contemporary Fiction*, Summer, 1989. David Lodge's "Milan Kundera and the Idea of the Author in Modern Criticism," *Critical Quarterly*, Spring/Summer, 1984, is good on Kundera's characteristic fictional structures. Kundera's roots in Czech literature are traced in Antonín J. Liehm's "Milan Kundera: Czech Writer," in *Czech Literature Since 1956*, ed. William E. Harkins and Paul I. Trensky, 1980. A guide to the criticism is Glen Brand, *Milan Kundera: An Annotated Bibliography*, 1988. Kundera's own *The Art of the Novel*, 1988, casts light on his own fiction.

NOBODY WILL LAUGH

Translated by Suzanne Rappaport

1

"Pour me some more slivovits,"[1] said Klara, and I wasn't against it. It was by no means unusual for us to open a bottle and this time there was a genuine excuse for it. That day I had received a considerable sum for the last part of a study, which was being published in installments by a professional visual arts magazine.

Publishing the study hadn't been so easy—what I'd written was polemical and controversial. That's why my studies had previously been rejected by *Visual Arts Journal,* where the editors were old and cautious, and had then been published only in a minor rival periodical, where the editors were younger and not so conservative.

The mailman brought the payment to the university along with another letter; an unimportant letter; in the morning in the first flush of beatitude I had hardly read the letter. But now at home, when it was approaching midnight and the wine was nearly gone, I took it off the table to amuse us.

"Esteemed comrade and if you will permit the expression—my colleague!" I read aloud to Klara. "Please excuse me, a man whom you have never met, for writing to you. I am turning to you with a request that you should read the enclosed article. True, I do not know you, but I respect you as a man whose judgments, reflections, and conclusions astonish me by their agreement with the results of my own research; I am completely amazed by it. Thus, for example, even though I bow before your conclu-

[1] Plum brandy.

sions and your excellent comparative analysis, I wish to call attention emphatically to the thought that Czech art has always been close to the people. I voiced this opinion before reading your treatise. I could prove this quite easily, for among other things, I even have witnesses. However, this is only marginal, for your treatise . . ." There followed further praise of my excellence and then a request. Would I kindly write a review of his article, that is, a specialist's evaluation for *Visual Arts Journal,* where they had been underestimating and rejecting his article for more than six months. They had told him that my opinion would be decisive, so now I had become the writer's only hope, a single light in an otherwise total darkness.

We made fun of Mr. Zaturetsky, whose aristocratic name fascinated us. But it was just fun; fun that meant no harm, for the praise which he had lavished on me, along with the excellent slivovits, softened me. It softened me so that in those unforgettable moments I loved the whole world. However, out of the whole world, especially Klara, because she was sitting opposite me, while the rest of the world was hidden from me by the walls of my Vrshovits[2] attic. And because at that moment I didn't have anything to reward the world with, I rewarded Klara; at least with promises.

Klara was a twenty-year-old girl from a good family. What am I saying, from a good family? From an excellent family! Her father had been a bank manager, and some time in the fifties, as a representative of the upper bourgeoisie, had been exiled to the village of Chelakovits, which was some distance from Prague. As a result, his daughter had a bad party record and worked as a seamstress in a large Prague dress factory. I can't bear prejudice. I don't believe that the extent of a father's property can leave its mark on his child's genes. I ask you, who today is really a plebeian and who is a patrician? Everything has been mixed up and has changed places so completely, that it's sometimes difficult to understand anything in terms of sociological concepts. I was far from feeling that I was sitting opposite a class enemy; on the contrary, I was sitting opposite a beautiful seamstress and trying to make her like me more by telling her lightheartedly about the advantages of a job I'd promised to get her through connections. I assured her that it was absurd for such a pretty girl to lose her beauty over a sewing machine, and I decided that she should become a model.

Klara didn't offer any resistance and we spent the night in happy understanding.

2

Man passes through the present with his eyes blindfolded. He is permitted merely to sense and guess at what he is actually experiencing. Only later when the cloth is untied can he glance at the past and find out *what* he has experienced and what meaning it has had.

That evening I thought I was drinking to my successes and didn't in the least suspect that it was the prelude to my undoing.

And because I didn't suspect anything I woke up the next day in a good mood, and while Klara was still breathing contentedly by my side, I took

[2] Area of southeastern Prague.

the article, which was attached to the letter, and skimmed through it with amused indifference.

It was called "Mikolash Alesh, Master of Czech Drawing," and it really wasn't worth even the half hour of inattention that I devoted to it. It was a collection of platitudes heaped together with no sense of continuity and without the least intention of advancing through them some original thought.

Quite clearly it was pure nonsense. The very same day Dr. Kalousek, the editor of *Visual Arts Journal* (in other respects an unusually hostile man), confirmed my opinion over the telephone; he called me at the university: "Say, did you get that treatise from the Zaturetsky guy? . . . Then take care of it. Five lecturers have already cut him to pieces, but he keeps on bugging us; he's got it into his head that you're the only genuine authority. Tell him in two sentences that it's crap, you know how to do that, you know how to be really venomous; and then we'll all have some peace."

But something inside me protested: why should I have to be Mr. Zaturetsky's executioner? Was *I* the one receiving an editor's salary for this? Besides, I remembered very well that they had refused my article at *Visual Arts Journal* out of overcautiousness; what's more, Mr. Zaturetsky's name was firmly connected in my mind with Klara, slivovits, and a beautiful evening. And finally, I shan't deny it, it's human—I could have counted on one finger the people who think me "a genuine authority": why should I lose this only one?

I closed the conversation with some clever vaguery, which Kalousek considered a promise and I, an excuse. I put down the receiver firmly convinced that I would never write the review for Mr. Zaturetsky.

Instead I took some writing paper out of the drawer and wrote a letter to Mr. Zaturetsky, in which I avoided any kind of judgment of his work, excusing myself by saying that my opinions on nineteenth century art were commonly considered devious and eccentric, and therefore my intercession—especially with the editors of *Visual Arts Journal*—would harm rather than benefit his cause. At the same time, I overwhelmed Mr. Zaturetsky with friendly loquacity, from which it was impossible not to detect approval on my part.

As soon as I had put the letter in the mailbox I forgot Mr. Zaturetsky. But Mr. Zaturetsky did not forget me.

<div align="center">3</div>

One day when I was about to end my lecture—I lecture at college in the history of art—there was a knock at the door; it was our secretary, Mary, a kind elderly lady, who occasionally prepares coffee for me, and says that I'm out when there are undesirable female voices on the telephone. She put her head in the doorway and said that some gentleman was looking for me.

I'm not afraid of gentlemen and so I took leave of the students and went good-humoredly out into the corridor. A smallish man in a shabby black suit and a white shirt bowed to me. He very respectfully informed me that he was Zaturetsky.

I invited the visitor into an empty room, offered him an armchair, and

began pleasantly discussing everything possible with him, for instance what a bad summer it was and what exhibitions were on in Prague. Mr. Zaturetsky politely agreed with all of my chatter, but he soon tried to apply every remark of mine to his article, which lay invisibly between us like an irresistible magnet.

"Nothing would make me happier than to write a review of your work," I said finally, "but as I explained to you in the letter, I am not considered an expert on the Czech nineteenth century, and, in addition, I'm on bad terms with the editors of *Visual Arts Journal*, who take me for a hardened modernist, so that a positive review from me could only harm you."

"Oh, you're too modest," said Mr. Zaturetsky, "how can you, who are such an expert, judge your own standing so blackly! In the editors' office they told me that everything depends on your review. If you support my article they'll publish it. You are my only recourse. It's the work of three years of study and three years of toil. Everything is now in your hands."

How carelessly and from what bad masonry does a man build his excuses! I didn't know how to reply to Mr. Zaturetsky. I involuntarily looked at his face and noticed there not only small, ancient, and innocent spectacles staring at me, but also a powerful, deep vertical wrinkle on his forehead. In a brief moment of clairvoyance a shiver shot down my spine. This wrinkle, concentrated and stubborn, betrayed not only the intellectual torment which its owner had gone through over Mikolash Alesh's drawings, but also unusually strong willpower. I lost my presence of mind and failed to find any clever excuse. I knew that I wouldn't write the review, but I also knew that I didn't have the strength to say so to this pathetic little man's face.

And then I began to smile and promise something vague. Mr. Zaturetsky thanked me and said that he would come again soon. We parted smiling.

In a couple of days he did come. I cleverly avoided him, but the next day I was told that he was searching for me again at the university. I realized that bad times were on the way; I went quickly to Mary so as to take appropriate steps.

"Mary dear, I beg you, if that man should come looking for me again, say that I've gone to do some research in Germany and I'll be back in a month. And you should know about this: I have, as you know, all my lectures on Tuesday and Wednesday. I'll shift them secretly to Thursday and Friday. Only the students will know about this, don't tell anyone, and leave the schedule uncorrected. I'll have to disobey the rules."

4

Indeed Mr. Zaturetsky did soon come back to look me up and was miserable when the secretary informed him that I'd suddenly gone off to Germany. "But this is not possible. Mr. Klima has to write a review about me. How could he go away like this?" "I don't know," said Mary. "However, he'll be back in a month." "Another month . . . ," moaned Mr. Zaturetsky: "And you don't know his address in Germany?" "I don't," said Mary.

And then I had a month of peace, but the month passed more quickly

than I expected and Mr. Zaturetsky stood once again in the office. "No, he still hasn't returned," said Mary, and when she met me later about something she asked me imploringly: "Your little man was here again, what in heaven's name should I tell him?" "Tell him, Mary, that I got jaundice and am in the hospital in Jena."[3] "In the hospital!" cried Mr. Zaturetsky, when Mary told him the story a few days later. "It's not possible! Don't you know that Mr. Klima has to write a review about me!" "Mr. Zaturetsky," said the secretary reproachfully, "Mr. Klima is lying in a hospital somewhere abroad seriously ill, and you think only about your review." Mr. Zaturetsky backed down and went away, but two weeks later was once again in the office: "I sent a registered letter to Mr. Klima in Jena. It is a small town, there can only be one hospital there, and the letter came back to me!" "Your little man is driving me crazy," said Mary to me the next day. "You mustn't get angry with me, what could I say to him? I told him that you've come back. You must deal with him by yourself now."

I didn't get angry with Mary. She had done what she could. Besides, I was far from considering myself beaten. I knew that I was not to be caught. I lived under cover all the time. I lectured secretly on Thursday and Friday; and every Tuesday and Wednesday, crouching in the doorway of a house opposite the school, I would rejoice at the sight of Mr. Zaturetsky, who kept watch in front of the school waiting for me to come out. I longed to put on a bowler hat and stick on a beard. I felt like Sherlock Holmes or the Invisible Man,[4] who strides stealthily; I felt like a little boy.

One day, however, Mr. Zaturetsky finally got tired of keeping watch and jumped on Mary. "Where exactly does Comrade Klima lecture?" "There's the schedule," said Mary, pointing to the wall, where the times of all the lectures were laid out in exemplary fashion on a large, checkered board.

"I see that," said Mr. Zaturetsky, refusing to be put off. "Only Comrade Klima never lectures here on either Tuesday or Wednesday. Is he reported sick?"

"No," said Mary hesitantly. And then the little man turned again on Mary. He reproached her for the confusion in the schedule. He inquired ironically how it was that she didn't know where every teacher was at a given time. He told her that he was going to complain about her. He shouted. He said that he was also going to complain about Comrade Assistant Klima, who wasn't lecturing, although he was supposed to be. He asked if the dean was in.

Unfortunately, the dean was in. Mr. Zaturetsky knocked on his door and went in. Ten minutes later he returned to Mary's office and demanded the address of my apartment.

"Twenty Skalnik Street in Litomyshl," said Mary. "In Prague, Mr. Klima only has a temporary address and he doesn't want it disclosed . . . " "I'm asking you to give me the address of Assistant Klima's Prague apartment," cried the little man in a trembling voice.

[3] In East Germany
[4] Sherlock Holmes in the detective stories of Arthur Conan Doyle (1859–1930); the Invisible Man in the novel by that name (1897) by H. G. Wells.

Somehow Mary lost her presence of mind. She gave him the address of my attic, my poor little refuge, my sweet den, in which I would be caught.

5

Yes, my permanent address is in Litomyshl; there I have my mother, my friends, and memories of my father; I flee from Prague, as often as I can, and write at home in my mother's small apartment. So it happened that I kept my mother's apartment as my permanent residence and in Prague I didn't manage to get myself a proper bachelor's apartment, as you're supposed to do, but lived in Vrshovits in lodgings, in a small, completely private attic, whose existence I concealed as much as possible. I didn't register[5] anywhere so as to prevent unnecessary meetings between undesirable guests and my various transient female roommates or visitors, whose comings and goings, I confess, were sometimes most disorganized. For precisely these reasons I didn't enjoy the best reputation in the house. Also, during my stays in Litomyshl I had several times lent my cozy little room to friends, who amused themselves only too well there, and didn't allow anyone in the house to get a wink of sleep. All this scandalized some of the occupants, who conducted a quiet war against me. Sometimes they had the local committee express unfavorable opinions of me and they even handed in a complaint to the apartment office.

At that time it was inconvenient for Klara to get to work from such a distance as Chelakovits, and so she began to stay overnight at my place. At first she stayed timidly and as an exception, then she left one dress, then several dresses, and within a short time my two suits were stuffed into a corner of the wardrobe, and my little room was transformed into a woman's boudoir.

I really liked Klara; she was beautiful; it pleased me that people turned their heads when we went out together; she was at least thirteen years younger than me, which increased the students' respect for me; I had a thousand reasons for taking good care of her. But I didn't want it to be known that she was living with me. I was afraid of rumors and gossip about us in the house; I was afraid that someone would start attacking my good old landlord, who lived for the greater part of the year outside Prague, was discreet, and didn't concern himself about me; I was afraid that one day he would come to me, unhappy and with a heavy heart, and ask me to send the young lady away for the sake of his good name.

Klara had been strictly ordered not to open the door to anyone.

One day she was alone in the house. It was a sunny day and rather stuffy in the attic. She was lounging almost naked on my couch, occupying herself with an examination of the ceiling, when suddenly there was a pounding on the door.

There was nothing alarming in this. I didn't have a bell, so anyone who

[5] Under the Communist regime, Czechoslovakians are required to register their addresses with the police.

came had to knock. So Klara wasn't going to let herself be disturbed by the noise and didn't stop examining the ceiling. But the pounding didn't cease; on the contrary, it went on with imperturbable persistence. Klara was getting nervous. She began to imagine a man standing behind the door, a man who slowly and significantly turns up the lapels of his jacket, and who will later pounce on her demanding why she hadn't opened the door, what she was concealing, and whether she was registered. A feeling of guilt seized her; she lowered her eyes from the ceiling and tried to think where she had left her dress lying. But the pounding continued so stubbornly, that in the confusion she found nothing but my raincoat hanging in the hall. She put it on and opened the door.

Instead of an evil, querying face, she only saw a little man, who bowed: "Is Mr. Klima at home?" "No, he isn't." "That's a pity," said the little man and apologized for having disturbed her. "The thing is that Mr. Klima has to write a review about me. He promised me and it's very urgent. If you would permit it, I could at least leave him a message."

Klara gave him paper and pencil, and in the evening I read that the fate of the article about Mikolash Alesh was in my hands alone, and that Mr. Zaturetsky was waiting most respectfully for my review and would try to look me up again at the university.

6

The next day, Mary told me how Mr. Zaturetsky had threatened her, and how he had gone to complain about her; her voice trembled and she was on the verge of tears; I flew into a rage. I realized that the secretary, who until now had been laughing at my game of hide-and-seek (though I would bet anything that she did what she did out of kindness toward me, rather than simply from a sense of fun), was now feeling hurt and conceivably saw me as the cause of her troubles. When I also included the exposure of my attic, the ten-minute pounding on the door, and Klara's fright—my anger grew to a frenzy.

As I was walking back and forth in Mary's office, biting my lips, boiling with rage and thinking about revenge, the door opened and Mr. Zaturetsky appeared.

When he saw me a glimmer of happiness flashed over his face. He bowed and greeted me. He had come a little prematurely, he had come before I had managed to consider my revenge.

He asked if I had received his message yesterday.

I was silent. He repeated his question. "I received it," I replied.

"And will you, please, write the review?"

I saw him in front of me: sickly, obstinate, beseeching; I saw the vertical wrinkle—etched on his forehead, the line of a single passion—I examined this line and grasped that it was a straight line determined by two points, my review and his article; that beyond the vice of this maniacal straight line nothing existed in his life but saintly asceticism; and then a spiteful trick occurred to me.

"I hope that you understand that after yesterday I can't speak to you," I said.

"I don't understand you."

"Don't pretend. She told me everything. It's unnecessary for you to deny it."

"I don't understand you," repeated the little man once again; but this time more decidedly.

I assumed a genial, almost friendly tone. "Look here, Mr. Zaturetsky, I don't blame you. I chase women as well and I understand you. In your position I would have tried to seduce a beautiful girl like that, if I'd found myself alone in an apartment with her and she'd been naked beneath a man's raincoat."

"This is an outrage!" The little man turned pale.

"No, it's the truth, Mr. Zaturetsky."

"Did the lady tell you this?"

"She has no secrets from me."

"Comrade Assistant, this is an outrage! I'm a married man. I have a wife! I have children!" The little man took a step forward, so that I had to step back.

"So much the worse for you, Mr. Zaturetsky."

"What do you mean, so much the worse?"

"I think being married must be a drawback to chasing women."

"Take it back!" said Mr. Zaturetsky menacingly.

"Well, all right," I conceded, "the matrimonial state need not always be an obstacle. Sometimes it can, on the contrary, excuse all sorts of things. But it makes no difference. I've already told you that I'm not angry with you and I understand you quite well. There's only one thing I don't understand. How can you still want a review from a man whose woman you've been trying to make?"

"Comrade Assistant! Dr. Kalousek, the editor of the magazine of the Academy of Sciences, *Visual Arts Journal,* is asking you for this review. And you must write the review!"

"The review or the woman. You can't ask for both."

"What kind of behavior is this, comrade!" screamed Mr. Zaturetsky in desperate anger.

The odd thing is that I suddenly felt that Mr. Zaturetsky had really wanted to seduce Klara. Seething with rage, I shouted, "You have the audacity to tell me off? You who should humbly apologize to me in front of my secretary."

I turned my back on Mr. Zaturetsky, and, confused, he staggered out.

"Well then," I sighed with relief like a general after the victorious conclusion of a hard campaign, and I said to Mary, "Perhaps he won't want a review by me any more."

Mary smiled and after a moment timidly asked, "Just why is it you don't want to write this review?"

"Because, Mary my dear, what he's written is the most awful crap."

"Then why don't you write in your review that it's crap?"

"Why should I write it? Why do I have to antagonize people?"—but hardly had I said this when I realized that Mr. Zaturetsky was my enemy all the same and that my struggle not to write the review was an aimless and

absurd struggle—unfortunately, there was nothing I could do either to stop it or to back down.

Mary was looking at me with an indulgent smile, as women look upon the foolishness of children; then the door opened and there stood Mr. Zaturetsky with his arm raised. "It's not me! It's you who will have to apologize," he shouted in a trembling voice and disappeared again.

7

I don't remember exactly when, perhaps that same day or perhaps a few days later, we found an envelope in my mailbox without an address.

Inside there was a letter in a clumsy, almost primitive handwriting:

Dear Madame:
Present yourself at my house on Sunday regarding the insult to my husband. I shall be at home all day. If you don't present yourself, I shall be forced to take measures.
Anna Zaturetsky, 14 Dalimilova Street, Prague 3.

Klara was scared and began saying something about my guilt. I waved my hand, declaring that the purpose of life is to give amusement, and if life is too lazy for this, there is nothing left but to help it along a little. Man must constantly saddle events, those swift mares without which he would be dragging his feet in the dust like a weary foot-slogger. When Klara said that she didn't want to saddle any events, I assured her that she would never meet Mr. or Mrs. Zaturetsky, and that the event into whose saddle I had jumped, I'd take care of with one hand tied behind my back.

In the morning when we were leaving the house, the porter stopped us. The porter wasn't an enemy. Prudently, I had once bribed him with a fifty-crown bill, and I had lived until this time in the agreeable conviction that he'd learned not to know anything about me, and didn't add fuel to the fire, which my enemies in the house kept alight.

"Some couple was here looking for you yesterday," he said.

"What sort of couple?"

"A little guy with a woman."

"What did the woman look like?"

"Two heads taller. Terribly energetic. A stern woman. She was asking about all sorts of things." He turned to Klara. "Chiefly about you. Who you are and what your name is."

"Good heavens, what did you say to her?" exclaimed Klara.

"What could I say? How do I know who comes to see Mr. Klíma? I told her that a different person comes every evening."

"Great!" I laughed and drew ten crowns from my pocket. "Just go on talking like that."

"Don't be afraid," I then said to Klara, "you won't go anywhere on Sunday and nobody will find you."

And Sunday came, and after Sunday, Monday, Tuesday, Wednesday; nothing happened. "You see," I said to Klara. But then came Thursday. I was lecturing to my students at the customary secret lecture about how

feverishly and in what an atmosphere of unselfish camaraderie the young Fauvists[6] had liberated color from its former impressionistic character, when Mary opened the door and whispered to me, "The wife of that Zaturetsky is here." "But I'm not here," I said, "just show her the schedule!" But Mary shook her head. "I showed her, but she peeped into your office and saw your raincoat on the stand. Just then Assistant Professor Zeleny came by and assured her that it was yours. So now she's sitting in the corridor waiting."

Had fate been able to pursue me more systematically, it is quite possible that I would have been a success. A blind alley is the place for my best inspirations. I said to my favorite student:

"Be so kind as to do me a small favor. Run to my office, put on my raincoat, and go out of the building in it. Some woman will try to prove that you are me, and your task will be not to admit it at any price."

The student went off and returned in about a quarter of an hour. He told me that the mission had been completed, the coast was clear, and the woman was out of the building.

This time I had won. But then came Friday, and in the afternoon Klara returned from work trembling almost like a leaf.

The polite gentleman who received customers in the tidy office of the dress factory had suddenly opened the door leading to the workroom, where my Klara and fifteen other seamstresses were sitting over their sewing machines, and cried:

"Does any one of you live at 5 Pushkin Street?"

Klara knew that it concerned her, because 5 Pushkin Street was my address. However, well-advised caution kept her quiet, for she knew that her living with me was a secret and that nobody knew anything about it.

"You see, that's what I've been telling her," said the polished gentleman when none of the seamstresses spoke up, and he went out again. Klara learned later that a strict female voice on the telephone had made him search through the directory of employees, and had talked for a quarter of an hour trying to convince him there must be a woman employee from 5 Pushkin Street in the factory.

The shadow of Mrs. Zaturetsky was cast over our idyllic room.

"But how could she have found out where you work? After all, here in the house nobody knows about you!" I yelled.

Yes, I was really convinced that nobody knew about us. I lived like an eccentric who thinks that he lives unobserved behind a high wall, while all the time one detail escapes him: the wall is made of transparent glass.

I had bribed the porter not to reveal that Klara lived with me, I had forced Klara into the most troublesome inconspicuousness and concealment and, meanwhile, the whole house knew about her. It was enough that once she had entered into an ill-advised conversation with a woman on the second floor—and they got to know where Klara was working.

Without suspecting it we had been living exposed for quite some time.

[6] School of French painters at the turn of the century, including most prominently Henri Matisse; they used pure, brilliant, unmixed color and a strongly expressive approach to their subjects.

2318

segmentnavigation>

What remained concealed from our persecutors was merely Klara's name and then one small detail: that she lived with me unregistered. These two were the final and only secrets behind which, for the time being, we eluded Mrs. Zaturetsky, who launched her attack so consistently and methodically that I was horror-struck.

I understood that it was going to be tough. The horse of my story was damnably saddled.

<div style="text-align:center">

8

</div>

This was on Friday. And when Klara came back from work on Saturday, she was trembling again. Here is what had happened:

Mrs. Zaturetsky had set out with her husband for the factory. She had called beforehand and asked the manager to allow her and her husband to visit the workshop, to examine the faces of the seamstresses. It's true that this request astonished the comrade manager, but Mrs. Zaturetsky put on such an air that it was impossible to refuse. She said something vague about an insult, about a ruined existence, and about court. Mr. Zaturetsky stood beside her, frowned, and was silent.

They were shown into the workroom. The seamstresses raised their heads indifferently, and Klara recognized the little man; she turned pale and with conspicuous inconspicuousness quickly went on with her needlework.

"Here you are," exclaimed the manager with ironic politeness to the stiff-looking pair. Mrs. Zaturetsky realized that she must take the initiative and she urged her husband: "Well look!" Mr. Zaturetsky assumed a scowl and looked around. "Is it one of them?" whispered Mrs. Zaturetsky.

Even with his glasses Mr. Zaturetsky couldn't see clearly enough to examine the large room, which in any case wasn't easy to survey, full as it was of piled-up junk and dresses hanging from long horizontal bars, with fidgety seamstresses, who didn't sit neatly with their faces toward the door, but in various positions; they were turning round, getting up and down, and involuntarily averting their faces. Therefore, Mr. Zaturetsky had to step forward and try not to skip anyone.

When the women understood that they were being examined by someone, and in addition by someone so unsightly and unattractive, they felt vaguely insulted, and sneers and grumbling began to be heard. One of them, a robust young girl, impertinently burst out:

"He's searching all over Prague for the shrew who made him pregnant!"

The noisy, ribald mockery of the women overwhelmed the couple; they stood downcast, and then became resolute with a peculiar sort of dignity.

"Ma'am," the impertinent girl yelled again at Mrs. Zaturetsky, "you look after your little son badly! I would never have let such a nice little boy out of the house."

"Look some more," she whispered to her husband, and sullenly and timidly he went forward step by step as if he were running the gauntlet, but firmly all the same—and he didn't miss a face.

All the time the manager was smiling noncommittally; he knew his

women and he knew that you couldn't do anything with them; and so he pretended not to hear their clamor, and he asked Mr. Zaturetsky, "Now please tell me, what is this woman supposed to look like?"

Mr. Zaturetsky turned to the manager and spoke slowly and seriously: "She was beautiful . . . She was very beautiful . . . "

Meanwhile Klara crouched in a corner, setting herself off from all the playful women by her agitation, her bent head, and her dogged activity. Oh, how badly she feigned her inconspicuousness and insignificance! And Mr. Zaturetsky was only a little way away from her; in the next minute he must look into her face.

"That isn't much, when you only remember that she was beautiful," said the police comrade manager to Mr. Zaturetsky. "There are many beautiful women. Was she short or tall?"

"Tall," said Mr. Zaturetsky.

"Was she brunette or blond?" Mr. Zaturetsky thought a moment and said, "She was blond."

This part of the story could serve as a parable on the power of beauty. When Mr. Zaturetsky had seen Klara for the first time at my place, he was so dazzled that he actually hadn't seen her. Beauty created before her some opaque screen. A screen of light, behind which she was hidden as if beneath a veil.

For Klara is neither tall nor blonde. Only the inner greatness of beauty lent her in Mr. Zaturetsky's eyes a semblance of great physical size. And the glow, which emanates from beauty, lent her hair the appearance of gold.

And so when the little man finally approached the corner where Klara, in a brown work smock, was huddled over a shirt, he didn't recognize her, because he had never seen her.

9

When Klara had finished an incoherent and barely intelligible account of this event I said, "You see, we're lucky."

But amid sobs Klara said to me, "What kind of luck? If they didn't find me today, they'll find me tomorrow."

"I should like to know how."

"They'll come here for me, to your place."

"I won't let anyone in."

"And what when they send the police?"

"Come now, I'll make a joke of it. After all, it was just a joke and fun."

"Today there's no time for jokes, today everything gets serious. They'll say that I wanted to blacken his reputation. When they take a look at him, how could they ever believe that he was capable of trying to seduce a woman?"

"You're right, Klara," I said, "they'll probably lock you up. But look, Karel Havlichek Borovsky[7] was also in jail and think how far he got; you must have learned about him in school."

[7] Czech author and political journalist (1821–56). In 1851, he was imprisoned and later exiled for his political views.

"Stop chattering," said Klara. "You know it looks bad for me. I'll have to go before the disciplinary committee and I'll have it on my record, and I'll never get out of the workshop. Anyway, I'd like to know what's happening about the modeling job you promised me. I can't sleep at your place any longer. I'll always be afraid that they're coming for me. Today I'm going back to Chelakovits." This was one conversation.

And that afternoon after a departmental meeting I had a second.

The chairman of the department, a gray-haired art historian and a wise man, invited me into his office.

"I hope you know that you haven't helped yourself with that study that has just come out," he said to me.

"Yes, I know," I replied.

"Many of our professors think that it applies to them and the dean thinks that it was an attack on his views."

"What can be done about it?" I said.

"Nothing," replied the professor, "but your three-year period as a lecturer has expired and candidates will compete to fill the position. It is customary for the committee to give the position to someone who has already taught in the school, but are you so sure that this custom will be upheld in your case? But this is not what I wanted to speak about. So far it has spoken in your favor that you lectured regularly, that you were popular with the students, and that you taught them something. But now you can't even rely on this. The dean has informed me that for the last three months you haven't lectured at all. And quite without excuse. Well, this in itself would be enough for immediate dismissal."

I explained to the professor that I hadn't missed a single lecture, that it had all been a joke, and I told him the whole story about Mr. Zaturetsky and Klara.

"Fine, I believe you," said the professor, "but what does it matter if I believe you? Today the whole school says that you don't lecture and don't do anything. It has already been discussed at the union meeting and yesterday they took the matter to the board of regents."

"But why didn't they speak to me about it first?"

"What should they speak to you about? Everything is clear to them. Now they are only looking back over your whole performance trying to find connections between your past and your present."

"What can they find bad in my past? You know yourself how much I like my work! I've never shirked! My conscience is clear."

"Every human life has many aspects," said the professor. "The past of each one of us can be just as easily arranged into the biography of a beloved statesman as into that of a criminal. Only look thoroughly at yourself. Nobody is denying that you like your work. But what if it served you above all as an opportunity for escape? You weren't often seen at meetings and when you did come, for the most part, you were silent. Nobody really knew what you thought. I myself remember that several times when a serious matter was being discussed you suddenly made a joke, which caused embarrassment. This embarrassment was of course immediately forgotten, but today, when it is retrieved from the past, it acquires a particular significance. Or remember how various women came looking for you at the university and how you refused to see them. Or else your last article, about which anyone

who wishes can allege that it was written from suspicious premises. All these, of course, are isolated facts; but just look at them in the light of today's offense, and they suddenly unite into a totality of significant testimony about your character and attitude."

"But what sort of offense! Everything can be explained so easily! The facts are quite simple and clear!"

"Facts mean little compared to attitudes. To contradict rumor or sentiment is as futile as arguing against a believer's faith in the Immaculate Conception. You have simply become a victim of faith, Comrade Assistant."

"There's a lot of truth in what you say," I said, "but if a sentiment has arisen against me like an act of faith, I shall fight faith with reason. I shall explain before everyone the things that took place. If people are human they will have to laugh at it."

"As you like. But you'll learn either that people aren't human or that you don't know what humans are like. They will not laugh. If you place before them everything as it happened, it will then appear that not only did you fail to fulfill your obligations as they were indicated on the schedule— that you did not do what you should have done—but on top of this, you lectured secretly, that is, you did what you shouldn't have done. It will appear that you insulted a man who was asking for your help. It will appear that your private life is not in order, that you have some unregistered girl living with you, which will make a very unfavorable impression on the female chairman of the union. The issue will become confused and God knows what further rumors will arise. Whatever they are they will certainly be useful to those who have been provoked by your views, but were ashamed to be against you on account of them."

I knew that the professor wasn't trying to alarm or deceive me. In this matter, however, I considered him a crank and didn't want to give myself up to his skepticism. The scandal with Mr. Zaturetsky made me go cold all over, but it hadn't tired me out yet. For I had saddled this horse myself, so I couldn't let it tear the reins from my hands and carry me off wherever it wished. I was prepared to engage in a contest with it. And the horse did not avoid the contest. When I reached home, there in the mailbox was a summons to a meeting of the local committee, and I had no doubt as to what it was about.

10

I was not mistaken. The local committee, which was in session in what had been a store, was seated around a long table. The members assumed a gloomy expression when I came in. A grizzled man with glasses and a receding chin pointed to a chair. I said thank you, sat down, and this man took the floor. He informed me that the local committee had been watching me for some time, that it knew very well that I led an irregular private life; that this did not produce a good impression in my neighborhood; that the tenants from my apartment house had already complained about me once, when they couldn't sleep because of the uproar in my apartment; that all this was enough for the local committee to have formed a proper conception of me. And now, on top of all this, Comrade Madame Zaturetsky,

the wife of a scientific worker, had turned to them for help. Six months ago I should have written a review about her husband's scientific work, and I hadn't done so, even though I well knew that the fate of the said work depended on my review.

"What the devil d'you mean by scientific work!" I interrupted the man with the little chin: "It's a patchwork of plagiarized thoughts."

"That is interesting, comrade." A fashionably dressed blonde of about thirty now joined in the discussion; on her face was permanently glued a beaming smile. "Permit me a question; what is your field?"

"I am an art theoretician."

"And Comrade Zaturetsky?"

"I don't know. Perhaps he's trying at something similar."

"You see," the blonde turned enthusiastically to the remaining members, "Comrade Klima sees a worker in the same field as a competitor and not as a comrade. This is the way that almost all our intellectuals think today."

"I shall continue," said the man with the receding chin. "Comrade Madame Zaturetsky told us that her husband visited your apartment and met some woman there. It is said that this woman accused Mr. Zaturetsky of wanting to molest her sexually. Comrade Madame Zaturetsky has in her hand documents which prove that her husband is not capable of such a thing. She wants to know the name of this woman who accused her husband, and to transfer the matter to the disciplinary section of the people's committee, because she claims this false accusation has damaged her husband's good name."

I tried again to cut this ridiculous affair short. "Look here, comrades," I said, "it isn't worth all the trouble. It's not a question of damaged reputation. The work is so weak that no one else could recommend it either. And if some misunderstanding occurred between this woman and Mr. Zaturetsky, it shouldn't really be necessary to summon a meeting."

"Fortunately, it is not you who will decide about our meetings, comrade," replied the man with the receding chin. "And when you now assert that Comrade Zaturetsky's work is bad, then we must look upon this as revenge. Comrade Madame Zaturetsky gave us a letter to read, which you wrote, after reading her husband's work."

"Yes. Only in that letter I didn't say a word about what the work was like."

"That is true. But you did write that you would be glad to help him; in this letter it is clearly implied that you respect Comrade Zaturetsky's work. And now you declare that it's a patchwork. Why didn't you say it to his face?"

"Comrade Klima has two faces," said the blonde.

At this moment an elderly woman with a permanent wave joined the discussion (she had an expression of self-sacrificing goodwill in examining the lives of others); she passed at once to the heart of the matter. "We would need to know, comrade, who this woman was whom Mr. Zaturetsky met at your home."

I understood unmistakably that it wasn't within my power to remove the senseless gravity from the whole affair, and that I could dispose of it in only

one way: to confuse the traces, to lure them away from Klara, to lead them away from her as the partridge leads the hound away from its nest, offering its own body for the sake of its young.

"It's a bad business, I don't remember her name," I said.

"How is it that you don't remember the name of the woman you live with?" questioned the woman with the permanent wave.

"At one time, I used to write all this down, but then it occurred to me that it was stupid and I dropped it. It's hard for a man to rely on his memory."

"Perhaps, Comrade Klima, you have an exemplary relationship with women," said the blonde.

"Perhaps I could remember, but I should have to think about it. Do you know when it was that Mr. Zaturetsky visited me?"

"That was . . . wait a moment," the man with the receding chin looked at his papers, "the fourteenth, on Wednesday afternoon."

"On Wednesday . . . the fourteenth . . . wait . . . " I held my head in my hand and did some thinking. "Oh I remember. That was Helena." I saw that they were all hanging expectantly on my words.

"Helena what?"

"What? I'm sorry, I don't know. I didn't want to ask her that. As a matter of fact, speaking frankly, I'm not even sure that her name was Helena. I only called her that because her husband seemed to me to be like red-haired Menelaus.[8] But anyway she very much liked being called that. On Tuesday evening I met her in a wineshop and managed to talk to her for a while, when her Menelaus went to the bar to drink a cognac. The next day she came to my place and was there the whole afternoon. Only I had to leave her in the evening for a couple of hours, I had a meeting at the university. When I returned she was disgusted because some little man had molested her and she thought that I had put him up to it; she took offense and didn't want to know me any more. And so, you see, I didn't even manage to learn her correct name."

"Comrade Klima, whether you are telling the truth or not," went on the blonde, "it seems to me to be absolutely incomprehensible that you can educate our youth. Does our life really inspire in you nothing but the desire to carouse and abuse women? Be assured, we shall give our opinion about this in the proper places."

"The porter didn't speak about any Helena," broke in the elderly lady with the permanent wave, "but he did inform us that some unregistered girl from the dress factory has been living with you for a month. Don't forget, comrade, that you are in lodgings. How can you imagine that someone can live with you like this? Do you think that your house is a brothel?"

There flashed before my eyes the ten crowns which I'd given to the porter a couple of days ago, and I understood that the encirclement was complete. And the woman from the local committee continued: "If you don't want to tell us her name, the police will find it out."

[8] In Homer's *Iliad* and *Odyssey*, Menelaus, husband of Helen of Troy, is said to have red hair.

11

The ground was slipping away beneath my feet. At the university I began to sense the malicious atmosphere which the professor had told me about. For the time being, I wasn't summoned to any interviews, but here and there I caught an allusion, and now and then Mary let something out, for the teachers drank coffee in her office and didn't watch their tongues. In a couple of days the selection committee, which was collecting evidence on all sides, was to meet. I imagined that its members had read the report of the local committee, a report about which I knew only that it was secret and that I couldn't refer to it.

There are moments in life when a man retreats defensively, when he must give ground, when he must surrender less important positions in order to protect the more important ones. But should it come to the very last, the most important one, at this point a man must halt and stand firm if he doesn't want to begin life all over again with idle hands and a feeling of being shipwrecked.

It seemed to me that this single, most important position was my love. Yes, in those troubled days I suddenly began to realize that I loved my fragile and unfortunate seamstress, who had been both beaten and pampered by life, and that I clung to her.

That day I met Klara at the museum. No, not at home. Do you think that home was still home? Is home a room with glass walls? A room observed through binoculars? A room where you must keep your beloved more carefully hidden than contraband?

Home was not home. There we felt like housebreakers who might be caught at any minute. Footsteps in the corridor made us nervous; we kept expecting someone to start pounding on the door. Klara was commuting from Chelakovits and we didn't feel like meeting in our alienated home for even a short while. So I had asked an artist friend to lend me his studio at night. That day I had got the key for the first time.

And so we found ourselves beneath a high roof in Vinohrady,[9] in an enormous room with one small couch and a huge, slanting window, from which we could see all the lights of Prague. Amid the many paintings propped against the walls, the untidiness, and the carefree artist's squalor, a blessed feeling of freedom returned to me. I sprawled on the couch, pushed in the corkscrew and opened a bottle of wine. I chattered gaily and freely, and was looking forward to a beautiful evening and night.

However, the pressure, which I no longer felt, had fallen with its full weight on Klara.

I have already mentioned how Klara without any scruples and with the greatest naturalness had lived at one time in my attic. But now, when we found ourselves for a short time in someone else's studio, she felt put out. More than put out: "It's humiliating," she said.

"What's humiliating?" I asked her.

"That we have to borrow an apartment."

"Why is it humiliating that we have to borrow an apartment?"

"Because there's something humiliating about it," she replied.

[9] Area on the eastern side of Prague.

"But we couldn't do anything else."

"I guess," she replied, "but in a borrowed apartment I feel like a whore."

"Good God, why should you feel like a whore in a *borrowed* apartment. Whores mostly operate in their own apartments, not in borrowed ones—"

It was futile to attack with reason the stout wall of irrational feelings that, as is known, is the stuff of which the female mind is made. From the beginning our conversation was ill-omened.

I told Klara what the professor had said, I told her what had happened at the local committee, and I was trying to convince her that in the end we would win if we loved each other and were together.

Klara was silent for a while and then said that I myself was guilty.

"Will you at least help me to get away from those seamstresses?"

I told her that this would have to be, at least temporarily, a time of forbearance.

"You see," said Klara, "you promised and in the end you do nothing. I won't be able to get out, even if somebody else wanted to help me, because I shall have my reputation ruined on your account."

I gave Klara my word that the incident with Mr. Zaturetsky couldn't harm her.

"I also don't understand," said Klara, "why you won't write the review. If you'd write it, then there'd be peace at once."

"It's too late, Klara," I said. "If I write this review they'll say that I'm condemning the work out of revenge and they'll be still more furious."

"And why must you condemn it? Write a favorable review!"

"I can't, Klara. This work is thoroughly absurd."

"So what? Why are you being truthful all of a sudden? Wasn't it a lie when you told the little man that they don't think much of you at *Visual Arts Journal*? And wasn't it a lie when you told the little man that he had tried to seduce me? And wasn't it a lie when you invented Helena? When you've told so many lies, what does it matter if you tell one more and praise him in the review? That's the only way you can smooth things out."

"You see, Klara," I said, "you think that a lie is a lie and it would seem that you're right. But you aren't. I can invent anything, make a fool of someone, carry out hoaxes and practical jokes—and I don't feel like a liar and I don't have a bad conscience. These lies, if you want to call them that, represent myself as I really am. With such lies I'm not simulating anything, with such lies I am in fact speaking the truth. But there are things which I can't lie about, things I've penetrated, whose meaning I've grasped, which I love and take seriously. It's impossible, don't ask me to do it, I can't."

We didn't understand each other.

But I really loved Klara and decided to do everything so that she would have nothing to reproach me for. The following day I wrote a letter to Mrs. Zaturetsky, saying that I would expect her the day after tomorrow at two o'clock in my office.

<div align="center">12</div>

True to her terrifying methodicalness, Mrs. Zaturetsky knocked precisely at the appointed time. I opened the door and asked her in.

Then I finally saw her. She was a tall woman, very tall with a thin peasant's face and pale blue eyes. "Take off your things," I said, and with awkward movements she took off a long, dark coat, narrow at the waist and oddly styled, a coat which God knows why evoked the image of an ancient greatcoat.

I didn't want to attack at once; I wanted my adversary to show me her cards first. After Mrs. Zaturetsky sat down, I got her to speak by making a remark or two.

"Mr. Klima," she said in a serious voice, but without any aggressiveness, "you know why I was looking for you. My husband has always respected you very much as a specialist and as a man of character. Everything depended on your review and you didn't want to do it for him. It took my husband three years to write this study. His life was harder than yours. He was a teacher, he commuted daily twenty miles outside Prague. Last year I forced him to stop that and devote himself to research."

"Mr. Zaturetsky isn't employed?" I asked.

"No . . . "

"What does he live on?"

"For the time being I have to work hard myself. This research, Mr. Klima, is my husband's passion. If you knew how he studied everything. If you knew how many pages he rewrote. He always says that a real scholar must write three hundred pages so as to keep thirty. And on top of it, this woman. Believe me, Mr. Klima, I know him, I'm sure he didn't do it, so why did this woman accuse him? I don't believe it. Let her say it before me and before him. I know women, perhaps she likes you very much and you don't care for her. Perhaps she wanted to make you jealous. But you can believe me, Mr. Klima, my husband would never have dared!"

I was listening to Mrs. Zaturetsky, and all at once something strange happened to me: I ceased being aware that this was the woman for whose sake I should have to leave the university, and that this was the woman who caused the tension between myself and Klara, and for whose sake I'd wasted so many days in anger and unpleasantness. The connection between her and the incident, in which we'd both played a sad role, suddenly seemed vague, arbitrary, accidental, and not our fault. All at once I understood that it had only been my illusion that we ourselves saddle events and control their course. The truth is that they aren't *our* stories at all, that they are foisted upon us from somewhere *outside;* that in no way do they represent us; that we are not to blame for the queer path that they follow. They carry us away, since they are controlled by some *other* forces; no, I don't mean by supernatural forces, but by human forces, by the forces of those people who, when they unite, unfortunately still remain mutually *alien.*

When I looked at Mrs. Zaturetsky's eyes it seemed to me that these eyes couldn't see the consequences of my actions, that these eyes weren't seeing at all, that they were merely swimming in her face; that they were only stuck on.

"Perhaps you're right, Mrs. Zaturetsky," I said in a conciliatory tone: "Perhaps my girl didn't speak the truth, but you know how it is when a man's jealous . . . I believed her and was carried away. This can happen to anyone."

"Yes, certainly," said Mrs. Zaturetsky and it was evident that a weight

had been lifted from her heart. "When you yourself see it, it's good. We were afraid that you believed her. This woman could have ruined my husband's whole life. I'm not speaking of the moral light it casts upon him. But my husband swears by your opinion. The editors assured him that it depended on you. My husband is convinced that if his article were published, he would finally be recognized as a scientific worker. I ask you, now that everything has been cleared up, will you write this review for him? And can you do it quickly?"

Now came the moment to avenge myself on everything and appease my rage, only at this moment I didn't feel any rage, and when I spoke it was only because there was no escaping it: "Mrs. Zaturetsky, there is some difficulty regarding the review. I shall confess to you how it all happened. I don't like to say unpleasant things to people's faces. This is my weakness. I avoided Mr. Zaturetsky, and I thought that he would figure out why I was avoiding him. His paper is weak. It has no scientific value. Do you believe me?"

"I find it hard to believe. I can't believe you," said Mrs. Zaturetsky.

"Above all, this work is not original. Please understand, a scholar must always arrive at something new; a scholar can't copy what we already know, what others have written."

"My husband definitely didn't copy."

"Mrs. Zaturetsky, you've surely read this study . . . " I wanted to continue, but Mrs. Zaturetsky interrupted me: "No, I haven't." I was surprised. "You will read it then for yourself."

"I can't see," said Mrs. Zaturetsky. "I see only light and shadow, my eyes are bad. I haven't read a single line for five years, but I don't need to read to know if my husband's honest or not. This can be recognized in other ways. I know my husband, as a mother her children, I know everything about him. And I know that what he does is always honest."

I had to undergo worse. I read aloud to Mrs. Zaturetsky paragraphs from Mateychek, Pechirka, and Michek, whose thoughts and formulations Mr. Zaturetsky had taken over. It wasn't a question of willful plagiarism, but rather an unconscious submission to those authorities who inspired in Mr. Zaturetsky a feeling of sincere and inordinate respect. But anyone who had seen these passages compared must have understood that no serious scholarly magazine could publish Mr. Zaturetsky's work.

I don't know how much Mrs. Zaturetsky concentrated on my exposition, how much of it she followed and understood; she sat humbly in the armchair, humbly and obediently like a soldier, who knows that he may not leave his post. It took about half an hour for us to finish. Mrs. Zaturetsky got up from the armchair, fixed her transparent eyes upon me, and in a dull voice begged my pardon; but I knew that she hadn't lost faith in her husband and she didn't reproach anyone except herself for not knowing how to resist my arguments, which seemed obscure and unintelligible to her. She put on her military raincoat and I understood that this woman was a soldier in body and spirit, a sad and loyal soldier, a soldier tired from long marches, a soldier who doesn't understand the sense of an order and yet carries it out without objections, a soldier who goes away defeated but without dishonor.

After she'd gone, something remained in my office of her weariness,

her loyalty, and her sadness. I suddenly forgot myself and my sorrows. The sorrow which seized me at that moment was purer, because it didn't issue from within me, but flowed from without, from afar.

13

"So now you don't have to be afraid of anything," I said to Klara, when later in the Dalmatian wineshop I repeated to her my conversation with Mrs. Zaturetsky.

"I didn't have anything to fear anyhow," replied Klara with a self-assurance that astonished me.

"How's that, you didn't? If it wasn't for you I wouldn't have met Mrs. Zaturetsky at all!"

"It's good that you did meet her, because what you did to them was cruel. Dr. Kalousek said that it's hard for an intelligent man to understand this."

"When did you meet Kalousek?"

"I've met him," said Klara.

"And did you tell him everything?"

"What? Is it a secret perhaps? Now I know exactly what you are."

"H'm."

"May I tell you what you are?"

"Please."

"A stereotyped cynic."

"You got that from Kalousek."

"Why from Kalousek? Do you think that I can't figure it out for myself? You actually think that I'm not capable of forming an opinion about you. You like to lead people by the nose. You promised Mr. Zaturetsky a review."

"I didn't promise him a review."

"That's one thing. And you promised me a job. You used me as an excuse to Mr. Zaturetsky, and you used Mr. Zaturetsky as an excuse to me. But you may be sure that I'll get that job."

"Through Kalousek?" I tried to be scornful.

"Not from you. You've gambled so much away and you don't even know yourself how much."

"And do you know?"

"Yes. Your contract won't be renewed and you'll be glad if they'll let you in some gallery as a clerk. But you must realize that all this was only your own mistake. If I can give you some advice: another time be honest and don't lie, because a man who lies can't be respected by any woman."

She got up, gave me (clearly for the last time) her hand, turned, and left.

Only after a while did it occur to me (in spite of the chilly silence which surrounded me) that my story was not of the tragic sort, but rather of the comic variety.

At any rate that afforded me some comfort.

Athol Fugard

(1932–)

When the South African playwright Athol Fugard was asked recently about the autobiographical element in his work, he replied by paraphrasing Adrienne Rich's comment on Emily Dickinson: "What is under most pressure to be concealed explodes into poetry." Fugard went on to say, "A play gets written when the external specifics of a story run parallel to a very private need to make a personal statement. If you've got a secret, you can create. It's almost like building the labyrinth at Knossos. Your Minotaur is at the center." Such statements may seem surprising to readers and theatergoers who think of Fugard primarily as a political playwright who over thirty years has written a series of powerful plays about the pain of life under apartheid, South Africa's harsh, bureaucratic system of racial segregation. But what gives Fugard's work its power is his ability to combine the political and the personal, to make "external specifics" and his "very private need" coincide. He writes from within the South African labyrinth not only geographically—he continues to live there—but emotionally as well. Apartheid is his personal tragedy as well as his country's, and he has traced out this tragedy in a series of searing dramas that have made him one of the world's two or three greatest living dramatists.

Fugard was born in Middelburg, South Africa, in 1932, and moved with his family when he was three to Port Elizabeth, which he still regards as his home. His father, who lost a leg in an accident as a child, was a jazz pianist who gradually sank into idleness and alcoholism. His strong-willed mother ran first a boarding house and then a small cafe named St. George's Park Tearoom. Fugard went to the Port Elizabeth schools, then to an automechanics course at the Port Elizabeth Technical College, and finally on a scholarship to the University of Cape Town, where he majored in sociology and anthropology. A few months short of a degree, he dropped out of the university and set out with a friend to hitchhike from Cape Town to Cairo, the length of Africa. At the end of the trip, out of money and at loose ends, he was offered a job as a seaman on a ship bound for Singapore, Yokohama, and eventually Great Britain. Fugard later traced his liberation from racism back to his two years as a sailor and the friendships he made with his fellow crewmen of all races.

Fugard returned to South Africa in 1956 and started work as a freelance writer and newswriter for the South African Broadcasting Company, first in Port Elizabeth and later in Cape Town. His serious involvement with the theater began in 1957, when he met and married an actress named Sheila Meiring. (She has since become a prominent novelist and poet.) Together, they began an experimental theater group in Cape Town, performing plays they wrote as well as plays by other South African writers. After a year, they moved to Johannesburg, where Fugard found work as a clerk in a Native Commissioner's court, which tried cases of passbook violations. (Under the system of apartheid, blacks have to carry identification; if they are found without it or in violation of the terms of their passbook, they can be arrested.) Though Fugard remained in the job for only three months,

the exposure to the inhuman realities of the racial system left a permanent mark on him. He left the court for a job as a stage manager with South Africa's National Theater and began to spend time in Sophiatown, a black township on the outskirts of Johannesburg. Here he helped form an amateur theater group for which he wrote his first two full-length plays: *No-Good Friday* (1958) and *Nongogo* (1959). In 1959, the Fugards went to England, where they spent an unsuccessful year trying to find theater work.

The turning point in Fugard's career came in 1961, when, back in South Africa, he wrote *The Blood Knot,* a play about two brothers of mixed race, one light enough to pass for white, the other very dark. It was first performed in an abandoned factory by Fugard himself and Zakes Mokae, a brilliant black actor whom Fugard had met in the Sophiatown theater and who became his closest friend. The play created a sensation, and a commercial production was arranged at the Intimate Theatre in Johannesburg. Fugard and Mokae toured through all South Africa with the play, which was subsequently produced in London, where it had limited success, and in New York, where, with James Earl Jones and J. D. Cannon, it was received enthusiastically and was voted Best Play of the Year by the *New York Times* critics.

The Blood Knot established the pattern of Fugard's future work: plays with minimal plots dealing with the intensely emotional relationships of only two or three people, linked by ties of blood, marriage, or friendship, produced first in small private theaters in South Africa, directed by Fugard and often acted by him, and subsequently given full professional productions abroad.

While *The Blood Knot* was winning applause in New York, Fugard continued to work with a small amateur theater group in Port Elizabeth named the Serpent Players, under conditions of steadily increasing harassment from the security police. In a crackdown on dissent in 1964, two of Fugard's actors were arrested and sent to Robben Island, the South African prison for political prisoners; there they performed *Antigone,* an incident Fugard was later to use in *The Island.* Meanwhile he wrote *People Are Living There* (1963), a tragicomedy set in a boarding house like the one his mother had run; *Hello and Goodbye* (1965), about an emotional encounter between a brother and sister; and *Boesman and Lena* (1969), about a homeless "Coloured" married couple encamped for the night in the middle of a long tramp. In retrospect, Fugard came to regard *The Blood Knot, Hello and Goodbye,* and *Boesman and Lena* as a trilogy of linked plays about "the nexus of family relationships."

After *Boesman and Lena,* Fugard moved into a new phase of his career, in which he experimented with collaborative development of plays. In 1972, he began working with a company of actors at The Space, an interracial experimental theater in Cape Town. Under the influence of the writings of the Polish avant-garde director Jerzy Grotowski, he collaboratively developed two plays with the actors John Kani and Winston Ntshona: *Sizwe Banzi Is Dead* (1972) and *The Island* (1973). *Sizwe Banzi Is Dead* deals with a black factory worker's quest for an identity card, *The Island* with the production of *Antigone* in Robben Island. Both were great international successes. To this period also belongs a play Fugard wrote alone: *Statements After an Arrest Under the Immorality Act* (1972), inspired by a newspaper pho-

tograph of a white librarian and a "Colored" schoolteacher who had a love affair, in violation of South African law. *Dimetos* (1975), an obscure, mythic play inspired by a quotation from Albert Camus, was Fugard's only play not specifically set in South Africa and his only notable failure.

Fugard has always kept detailed, meticulous notebooks of ideas for plays; they were published in 1983 as *Athol Fugard: Notebooks 1960–1977*. The germ of his next major play appears in the notebooks in a 1961 incident in which police raided a party Fugard was attending and arrested a young "Coloured" man who was there in violation of a police order forbidding him to meet with more than one person at a time. It was suspected that an informer had notified the police. Fugard repeatedly tried to write a play about this episode over the next several years. Finally in 1977 he combined the story of the young man with that of a white bus driver and his mentally disturbed wife and produced *A Lesson from Aloes*. Produced in New York in 1980, it won the New York Critics Award as the best play of the year.

Fugard reached even deeper into his past for *"Master Harold"* . . . *and the boys* (1982), to his childhood in the St. George's Park Tearoom in Port Elizabeth and an incident when, grieved and angered by his alcoholic father, he spit in the face of his own best friend, a black waiter named Sam Semela. The incident happened when Fugard was ten years old; he makes Hally seventeen in the play. Otherwise, he leaves even the names unchanged; his own full name is Harold Athol Lannigan Fugard, and he was known as Hally as a boy. In the first production, at the Yale Repertory Theater, and later in New York, Fugard's old friend Zakes Mokae played the role of Sam. Fugard called Sam Semela in South Africa on the night of the New York opening of the play. Semela was going to see the play in South Africa when it opened there in 1983, but when John Kani, who played the role there, went to pick up the old man, he found that he had just died.

Fugard has created a number of memorable roles for women, from Lena in *Boesman and Lena* to Gladys Bezuidenhout in *A Lesson from Aloes,* but in the early eighties, an actress friend pointed out to him that he had never written scenes between two women. The result of this and other factors led to *The Road to Mecca,* about the life of an eccentric woman who had committed suicide near Fugard's home. It was first performed in London, under Fugard's direction, in 1985. *A Place with the Pigs* was first produced in 1988, *My Children! My Africa!* in 1989.

In the tense political and racial situation of South Africa, Fugard and his drama have not escaped criticism. There is now a vigorous black theater movement in South Africa, and black playwrights, actors, and directors have questioned Fugard's right to speak for their people. Duma Ndlovu, a black director, for example, was quoted in 1986 as saying, "Athol Fugard has taken all the credit for black theater in South Africa. The West looks on him as the representative of black aspirations in South Africa through theater, a role that was not bestowed on him by black people, a role that black people say is not true." White Western critics have also had reservations. Dennis Walder, who has written a perceptive book on Fugard, says, "It is his greatest strength as a dramatist to move us deeply by his account of the South African experience; it is his greatest weakness that he is unable to

analyze that experience, or be clear about its social and historical implications."

Such criticisms have some validity but perhaps demand from Fugard what he has never pretended to offer. It is doubtful that Fugard would ever claim to be "the representative of black aspirations in South Africa through theater" or to offer a political analysis of "the social and historical implications" of his plays. It is true that he writes principally about the white experience in South Africa for primarily white audiences. And his position is essentially that of a liberal humanist; he is more likely to put his faith in understanding and forgiveness like that which Sam Semela shows than in revolution. But within these terms, he has placed South African concerns before an international theater audience and has created powerful, honest plays that explore the personal responsibilities that lie behind political and institutional injustice.

FURTHER READING (*prepared by J. H.*): The best book on Athol Fugard is Russell Vandenbroucke's *Truths the Hand Can Touch: The Theatre of Athol Fugard*, 1985. Vandenbroucke offers a wealth of biographical information, based on many conversations with Fugard, and detailed, perceptive readings of the plays. Dennis Walder's *Athol Fugard*, 1984, is a balanced, judicious interpretation of the major plays. Robert J. Green's "The Drama of Athol Fugard," in *Aspects of South African Literature,* ed. Christopher Heywood, 1976, is a good brief overview, up to its date. Stephen Gray has edited an important collection of essays, *Athol Fugard*, 1982. Mel Gussow's "Profile: Witness [Athol Fugard]," *New Yorker*, December 20, 1982, is a lively, thoughtful portrait with many quotations from Fugard. On *"Master Harold" . . . and the boys,* see Rob Amato, "Fugard's Confessional Analysis: '*Master Harold*' . . . *and the boys*," in *Momentum: On Recent South African Writing*, ed. M. J. Daymond, J. U. Jacobs, and Margaret Lenta, 1984.

"MASTER HAROLD"
. . . AND THE BOYS

The St. George's Park Tea Room on a wet and windy Port Elizabeth afternoon.

Tables and chairs have been cleared and are stacked on one side except for one which stands apart with a single chair. On this table a knife, fork, spoon and side plate in anticipation of a simple meal, together with a pile of comic books.

Other elements: a serving counter with a few stale cakes under glass and a not very impressive display of sweets, cigarettes and cool drinks, etc.; a few cardboard advertising handouts—Cadbury's Chocolate, Coca-Cola—and a blackboard on which an untrained hand has chalked up the prices of Tea, Coffee, Scones, Milkshakes—all flavors—and Cool Drinks; a few sad ferns in pots; a telephone; an old-style jukebox.

There is an entrance on one side and an exit into a kitchen on the other.

Leaning on the solitary table, his head cupped in one hand as he pages through one of the comic books, is SAM. *A black man in his mid-forties. He wears the white coat of a waiter. Behind him on his knees, mopping down the floor with a bucket of water*

and a rag, is WILLIE. *Also black and about the same age as Sam. He has his sleeves and trousers rolled up.*

The year: 1950

WILLIE [*singing as he works*].
 "She was scandalizin' my name,
 She took my money
 She called me honey
 But she was scandalizin' my name.
 Called it love but was playin' a game . . . "

> [*He gets up and moves the bucket. Stands thinking for a moment, then, raising his arms to hold an imaginary partner, he launches into an intricate ballroom dance step. Although a mildly comic figure, he reveals a reasonable degree of accomplishment.*]

Hey, Sam.

> [SAM, *absorbed in the comic book, does not respond.*]

Hey, Boet[1] Sam!

> [SAM *looks up.*]

I'm getting it. The quickstep. Look now and tell me. [*He repeats the step.*] Well?

SAM [*encouragingly*]. Show me again.
WILLIE. Okay, count for me.
SAM. Ready?
WILLIE. Ready.
SAM. Five, six, seven, eight . . . [WILLIE *starts to dance.*] A-n-d one two three four . . . and one two three four. . . . [*Ad libbing as* WILLIE *dances*] Your shoulders, Willie . . . your shoulders! Don't look down! Look happy, Willie! Relax, Willie!
WILLIE [*desperate but still dancing*]. I am relax.
SAM. No, you're not.
WILLIE. [*He falters.*] Ag no man, Sam! Mustn't talk. You make me make mistakes.
SAM. But you're too stiff.
WILLIE. Yesterday I'm not straight . . . today I'm too stiff!
SAM. Well, you are. You asked me and I'm telling you.
WILLIE. Where?
SAM. Everywhere. Try to glide through it.
WILLIE. Glide?
SAM. Ja, make it smooth. And give it more style. It must look like you're enjoying yourself.
WILLIE [*emphatically*]. I wasn't.
SAM. Exactly.
WILLIE. How can I enjoy myself? Not straight, too stiff and now it's also

[1] "Brother" (affectionate form of address).

glide, give it more style, make it smooth . . . Haai! Is hard to remember
all those things, Boet Sam.

SAM. That's your trouble. You're trying too hard.

WILLIE. I try hard because it *is* hard.

SAM. But don't let me see it. The secret is to make it look easy. Ballroom
must look happy, Willie, not like hard work. It must . . . Ja! . . . it must
look like romance.

WILLIE. Now another one! What's romance?

SAM. Love story with happy ending. A handsome man in tails, and in his
arms, smiling at him, a beautiful lady in evening dress!

WILLIE. Fred Astaire, Ginger Rogers.

SAM. You got it. Tapdance or ballroom, it's the same. Romance. In two
weeks' time when the judges look at you and Hilda, they must see a man
and a woman who are dancing their way to a happy ending. What I saw
was you holding her like you were frightened she was going to run
away.

WILLIE. Ja! Because that is what she wants to do! I got no romance left for
Hilda anymore, Boet Sam.

SAM. Then pretend. When you put your arms around Hilda, imagine she
is Ginger Rogers.

WILLIE. With no teeth? You try.

SAM. Well, just remember, there's only two weeks left.

WILLIE. I know, I know! [*to the jukebox*] I do it better with music. You got
sixpence for Sarah Vaughan?

SAM. That's a slow foxtrot. You're practicing the quick-step.

WILLIE. I'll practice slow foxtrot.

SAM [*shaking his head*]. It's your turn to put money in the jukebox.

WILLIE. I only got bus fare to go home. [*He returns disconsolately to his work.*]
Love story and happy ending! She's doing it all right, Boet Sam, but
is not me she's giving happy endings. Fuckin' whore! Three nights
now she doesn't come practice. I wind up gramophone, I get record
ready and I sit and wait. What happens? Nothing. Ten o'clock I start
dancing with my pillow. You try and practice romance by yourself,
Boet Sam. Struesgod, she doesn't come tonight I take back my dress
and ballroom shoes and I find me new partner. Size twenty-six. Shoes
size seven. And now she's also making trouble for me with the baby
again. Reports me to Child Wellfed, that I'm not giving her money.
She lies! Every week I am giving her money for milk. And how do
I know is my baby? Only his hair looks like me. She's fucking around
all the time I turn my back. Hilda Samuels is a bitch! [*Pause*] Hey,
Sam!

SAM. Ja.

WILLIE. You listening?

SAM. Ja.

WILLIE. So what you say?

SAM. About Hilda?

WILLIE. Ja.

SAM. When did you last give her a hiding?

WILLIE [*reluctantly*]. Sunday night.

SAM. And today is Thursday.

WILLIE. [*He knows what's coming.*] Okay.

SAM. Hiding on Sunday night, then Monday, Tuesday and Wednesday she doesn't come to practice . . . and you are asking me why?

WILLIE. I said okay, Boet Sam!

SAM. You hit her too much. One day she's going to leave you for good.

WILLIE. So? She makes me the hell-in too much.

SAM [*emphasizing his point*]. *Too* much and *too* hard. You had the same trouble with Eunice.

WILLIE. Because she also make the hell-in, Boet Sam. She never got the steps right. Even the waltz.

SAM. Beating her up every time she makes a mistake in the waltz? [*Shaking his head*] No, Willie! That takes the pleasure out of ballroom dancing.

WILLIE. Hilda is not too bad with the waltz, Boet Sam. Is the quickstep where the trouble starts.

SAM [*teasing him gently*]. How's your pillow with the quickstep?

WILLIE [*ignoring the tease*]. Good! And why? Because it got no legs. That's her trouble. She can't move them quick enough. Boet Sam, I start the record and before halfway Count Basie is already winning. Only time we catch up with him is when gramophone runs down.

[SAM *laughs.*]

Haaikona,[2] Boet Sam, is not funny.

SAM [*snapping his fingers*]. I got it! Give her a handicap.

WILLIE. What's that?

SAM. Give her a ten-second start and then let Count Basie go. Then I put my money on her. Hot favorite in the Ballroom Stakes: Hilda Samuels ridden by Willie Malopo.

WILLIE [*turning away*]. I'm not talking to you no more.

SAM [*relenting*]. Sorry, Willie . . .

WILLIE. It's finish between us.

SAM. Okay, okay . . . I'll stop.

WILLIE. You can also fuck off.

SAM. Willie, listen! I want to help you!

WILLIE. No more jokes?

SAM. I promise.

WILLIE. Okay. Help me.

SAM [*his turn to hold an imaginary partner*]. Look and learn. Feet together. Back straight. Body relaxed. Right hand placed gently in the small of her back and wait for the music. Don't start worrying about making mistakes or the judges or the other competitors. It's just you, Hilda and the music, and you're going to have a good time. What Count Basie do you play?

WILLIE. "You the cream in my coffee, you the salt in my stew."

SAM. Right. Give it to me in strict tempo.

WILLIE. Ready?

SAM. Ready.

WILLIE. A-n-d . . . [*singing*]
"You the cream in my coffee.
You the salt in my stew.

2"Not on your life!"

You will always be my necessity.
I'd be lost without you . . . " *(etc.)*

> [SAM *launches into the quickstep. He is obviously a much more accomplished dancer than* WILLIE. HALLY *enters. A seventeen-year-old white boy. Wet raincoat and school case. He stops and watches* SAM. *The demonstration comes to an end with a flourish. Applause from* HALLY *and* WILLIE]

HALLY. Bravo! No question about it. First place goes to Mr. Sam Semela.

WILLIE [*in total agreement*]. You was gliding with style, Boet Sam.

HALLY [*cheerfully*]. How's it, chaps?

SAM. Okay, Hally.

WILLIE [*springing to attention like a soldier and saluting*]. At your service, Master Harold!

HALLY. Not long to the big event, hey!

SAM. Two weeks.

HALLY. You nervous?

SAM. No.

HALLY. Think you stand a chance?

SAM. Let's just say I'm ready to go out there and dance.

HALLY. It looked like it. What about you, Willie?

> [WILLIE *groans*]

What's the matter?

SAM. He's got leg trouble.

HALLY. [*innocently*]. Oh, sorry to hear that, Willie.

WILLIE. Boet Sam! You promised. [WILLIE *returns to his work.*]

> [HALLY *deposits his school case and takes off his raincoat. His clothes are a little neglected and untidy: black blazer with school badge, gray flannel trousers in need of an ironing, khaki shirt and tie, black shoes.* SAM *has fetched a towel for* HALLY *to dry his hair.*]

HALLY. God, what a lousy bloody day. It's coming down cats and dogs out there. Bad for business, chaps . . . [*conspiratorial whisper*] . . . but it also means we're in for a nice quiet afternoon.

SAM. You can speak loud. Your Mom's not here.

HALLY. Out shopping?

SAM. No. The hospital.

HALLY. But it's Thursday. There's no visiting on Thursday afternoons. Is my Dad okay?

SAM. Sounds like it. In fact, I think he's going home.

HALLY [*stopped short by* SAM's *remark*]. What do you mean?

SAM. The hospital phoned.

HALLY. To say what?

SAM. I don't know. I just heard your Mom talking.

HALLY. So what makes you say he's going home?

SAM. It sounded as if they were telling her to come and fetch him.

> [HALLY *thinks about what* SAM *has said for a few seconds.*]

HALLY. When did she leave?

SAM. About an hour ago. She said she would phone you. Want to eat?

> [HALLY *doesn't respond.*]

Hally, want your lunch?

HALLY. I suppose so. [*His mood has changed.*] What's on the menu? . . . as if I don't know.

SAM. Soup, followed by meat pie and gravy.

HALLY. Today's?

SAM. No.

HALLY. And the soup?

SAM. Nourishing pea soup.

HALLY. Just the soup. [*the pile of comic books on the table*] And these?

SAM. For your Dad. Mr. Kempston brought them.

HALLY. You haven't been reading them, have you?

SAM. Just looking.

HALLY [*examining the comics*]. Jungle Jim . . . Batman and Robin . . . Tarzan . . . God, what rubbish! Mental pollution. Take them away.

> [SAM *exits waltzing into the kitchen.*
> HALLY *turns to* WILLIE.]

HALLY. Did you hear my Mom talking on the telephone, Willie?

WILLIE. No, Master Hally. I was at the back.

HALLY. And she didn't say anything to you before she left?

WILLIE. She said I must clean the floors.

HALLY. I mean about my Dad.

WILLIE. She didn't say nothing to me about him, Master Hally.

HALLY [*with conviction*]. No! It can't be. They said he needed at least another three weeks of treatment. Sam's definitely made a mistake. [*Rummages through his school case, finds a book and settles down at the table to read*] So, Willie!

WILLIE. Yes, Master Hally! Schooling okay today?

HALLY. Yes, okay. . . . [*He thinks about it.*] . . . No, not really. Ag, what's the difference? I don't care. And Sam says you've got problems.

WILLIE. Big problems.

HALLY. Which leg is sore?

> [WILLIE *groans.*]

Both legs.

WILLIE. There is nothing wrong with my legs. Sam is just making jokes.

HALLY. So then you *will* be in the competition.

WILLIE. Only if I can find me a partner.

HALLY. But what about Hilda?

SAM [*returning with a bowl of soup*]. She's the one who's got trouble with her legs.

HALLY. What sort of trouble, Willie?

SAM. From the way he describes it, I think the lady has gone a bit lame.

HALLY. Good God! Have you taken her to see a doctor?

SAM. I think a vet would be better.

HALLY. What do you mean?

SAM. What do you call it again when a racehorse goes very fast?

HALLY. Gallop?

SAM. That's it!

WILLIE. Boet Sam!

HALLY. "A gallop down the homestretch to the winning post." But what's that got to do with Hilda?

SAM. Count Basie always gets there first.

> [WILLIE *lets fly with his slop rag. It misses* SAM *and hits* HALLY.]

HALLY [*furious*]. For Christ's sake, Willie! What the hell do you think you're doing!

WILLIE. Sorry, Master Hally, but it's him. . . .

HALLY. Act your bloody age! [*Hurls the rag back at* WILLIE] Cut out the nonsense now and get on with your work. And you too, Sam. Stop fooling around.

> [SAM *moves away.*]

No. Hang on. I haven't finished! Tell me exactly what my Mom said.

SAM. I have. "When Hally comes, tell him I've gone to the hospital and I'll phone him."

HALLY. She didn't say anything about taking my Dad home?

SAM. No. It's just that when she was talking on the phone . . .

HALLY [*interrupting him*]. No, Sam. They can't be discharging him. She would have said so if they were. In any case, we saw him last night and he wasn't in good shape at all. Staff nurse even said there was talk about taking more X-rays. And now suddenly today he's better? If anything, it sounds more like a bad turn to me . . . which I sincerely hope it isn't. Hang on . . . how long ago did you say she left?

SAM. Just before two . . . [*his wrist watch*] . . . hour and a half.

HALLY. I know how to settle it. [*Behind the counter to the telephone. Talking as he dials*] Let's give her ten minutes to get to the hospital, ten minutes to load him up, another ten, at the most, to get home and another ten to get him inside. Forty minutes. They should have been home for at least half an hour already. [*Pause—he waits with the receiver to his ear.*] No reply, chaps. And you know why? Because she's at his bedside in hospital helping him pull through a bad turn. You definitely heard wrong.

SAM. Okay.

> [As far as HALLY *is concerned, the matter is settled. He returns to his table, sits down and divides his attention between the book and his soup.* SAM *is at his school case and picks up a textbook.*]

Modern Graded Mathematics for Standards Nine and Ten.

> [Opens it at random and laughs at something he sees]

Who is this supposed to be?

HALLY. Old fart-face Prentice.

SAM. Teacher?

HALLY. Thinks he is. And believe me, that is not a bad likeness.

SAM. Has he seen it?

HALLY. Yes.

SAM. What did he say?

HALLY. Tried to be clever, as usual. Said I was no Leonardo da Vinci and that bad art had to be punished. So, six of the best, and his are bloody good.

SAM. On your bum?

HALLY. Where else? The days when I got them on my hands are gone forever, Sam.

SAM. With your trousers down!

HALLY. No. He's not quite that barbaric.

SAM. That's the way they do it in jail.

HALLY [*flicker of morbid interest*]. Really?

SAM. Ja. When the magistrate sentences you to "strokes with a light cane."

HALLY. Go on.

SAM. They make you lie down on a bench. One policeman pulls down your trousers and holds your ankles, another one pulls your shirt over your head and holds your arms . . .

HALLY. Thank you! That's enough.

SAM. . . . and the one that gives you the strokes talks to you gently and for a long time between each one.

[*He laughs.*]

HALLY. I've heard enough, Sam! Jesus! It's a bloody awful world when you come to think of it. People can be real bastards.

SAM. That's the way it is, Hally.

HALLY. It doesn't *have* to be that way. There is something called progress, you know. We don't exactly burn people at the stake anymore.

SAM. Like Joan of Arc.

HALLY. Correct. If she was captured today, she'd be given a fair trial.

SAM. And then the death sentence.

HALLY [*a world-weary sigh*]. I know, I know! I oscillate between hope and despair for this world as well, Sam. But things will change, you wait and see. One day somebody is going to get up and give history a kick up the backside and get it going again.

SAM. Like who?

HALLY [*after thought*]. They're called social reformers. Every age, Sam, has got its social reformer. My history book is full of them.

SAM. So where's ours?

HALLY. Good question. And I hate to say it, but the answer is: I don't know. Maybe he hasn't even been born yet. Or is still only a babe in arms at his mother's breast. God, what a thought.

SAM. So we just go on waiting.

HALLY. Ja, looks like it. [*back to his soup and the book*]

SAM [*reading from the textbook*]. "Introduction: In some mathematical problems only the magnitude . . . " [*He mispronounces the word "magnitude"*]

HALLY [*correcting him without looking up*]. Magnitude.

SAM. What's it mean?

HALLY. How big it is. The size of the thing.

SAM [*reading*]. " . . . magnitude of the quantities is of importance. In other problems we need to know whether these quantities are negative or positive. For example, whether there is a debit or credit bank balance . . . "

HALLY. Whether you're broke or not.

SAM. " . . . whether the temperature is above or below Zero . . . "

HALLY. Naught degrees. Cheerful state of affairs! No cash and you're freezing to death. Mathematics won't get you out of that one.

SAM. "All these quantities are called . . ." [*Spelling the word*] . . . s-c-a-l . . .

HALLY. Scalars.

SAM. Scalars! [*shaking his head with a laugh*] You understand all that?

HALLY [*turning a page*]. No. And I don't intend to try.

SAM. So what happens when the exams come?

HALLY. Failing a math exam isn't the end of the world, Sam. How many times have I told you that examination results don't measure intelligence?

SAM. I would say about as many times as you've failed one of them.

HALLY [*mirthlessly*]. Ha, ha, ha.

SAM [*simultaneously*]. Ha, ha, ha.

HALLY. Just remember Winston Churchill didn't do particularly well at school.

SAM. You've also told me that one many times.

HALLY. Well, it just so happens to be the truth.

SAM [*enjoying the word*]. Magnitude! Magnitude! Show me how to use it.

HALLY [*after thought*]. An intrepid social reformer will not be daunted by the magnitude of the task he has undertaken.

SAM [*impressed*]. Couple of jaw-breakers in there!

HALLY. I gave you three for the price of one. Intrepid, daunted and magnitude. I did that once in an exam. Put five of the words I had to explain in one sentence. It was half a page long.

SAM. Well, I'll put my money on you in the English exam.

HALLY. Piece of cake. Eighty percent without even trying.

SAM [*another textbook from* HALLY'S *case*]. And history?

HALLY. So-so. I'll scrape through. In the fifties if I'm lucky.

SAM. You didn't do too badly last year.

HALLY. Because we had World War One. That at least had some action. You try to find that in the South African Parliamentary system.

SAM [*reading from the history textbook*]. "Napoleon and the principle of equality." Hey! This sounds interesting. "After concluding peace with Britain in 1802, Napoleon used a brief period of calm to in-sti-tute . . . "

HALLY. Introduce.

SAM. " . . . many reforms. Napoleon regarded all people as equal before the law and wanted them to have equal opportunities for advancement. All ves-ti-ges of the feu-dal system with its oppression of the poor were abolished." Vestiges, feudal system and abolished. I'm all right on oppression.

HALLY. I'm thinking. He swept away . . . abolished . . . the last remains . . . vestiges . . . of the bad old days . . . feudal system.

SAM. Ha! There's the social reformer we're waiting for. He sounds like a man of some magnitude.

HALLY. I'm not so sure about that. It's a damn good title for a book, though. A man of magnitude!

SAM. He sounds pretty big to me, Hally.

HALLY. Don't confuse historical significance with greatness. But maybe I'm

being a bit prejudiced. Have a look in there and you'll see he's two chapters long. And hell! . . . has he only got dates, Sam, all of which you've got to remember! This campaign and that campaign, and then, because of all the fighting, the next thing is we get Peace Treaties all over the place. And what's the end of the story? Battle of Waterloo, which he loses. Wasn't worth it. No, I don't know about him as a man of magnitude.

SAM. Then who would you say was?

HALLY. To answer that, we need a definition of greatness, and I suppose that would be somebody who . . . somebody who benefited all mankind.

SAM. Right. But like who?

HALLY. [*He speaks with total conviction.*] Charles Darwin. Remember him? That big book from the library. *The Origin of the Species.*

SAM. Him?

HALLY. Yes. For his Theory of Evolution.

SAM. You didn't finish it.

HALLY. I ran out of time. I didn't finish it because my two weeks was up. But I'm going to take it out again after I've digested what I read. It's safe. I've hidden it away in the Theology section. Nobody ever goes in there. And anyway who are you to talk? You hardly even looked at it.

SAM. I tried. I looked at the chapters in the beginning and I saw one called "The Struggle for an Existence." Ah ha, I thought. At last! But what did I get? Something called the mistiltoe which needs the apple tree and there's too many seeds and all are going to die except one . . . ! No, Hally.

HALLY [*intellectually outraged*]. What do you mean, No! The poor man had to start somewhere. For God's sake, Sam, he revolutionized science. Now we know.

SAM. What?

HALLY. Where we come from and what it all means.

SAM. And that's a benefit to mankind? Anyway, I still don't believe it.

HALLY. God, you're impossible. I showed it to you in black and white.

SAM. Doesn't mean I got to believe it.

HALLY. It's the likes of you that kept the Inquisition in business. It's called bigotry. Anyway, that's my man of magnitude. Charles Darwin! Who's yours?

SAM [*without hesitation*]. Abraham Lincoln.

HALLY. I might have guessed as much. Don't get sentimental, Sam. You've never been a slave, you know. And anyway we freed your ancestors here in South Africa long before the Americans. But if you want to thank somebody on their behalf, do it to Mr. William Wilberforce.[3] Come on. Try again. I want a real genius.

> [*Now enjoying himself, and so is* SAM.
> HALLY *goes behind the counter and helps
> himself to a chocolate.*]

SAM. William Shakespeare.

[3] William Wilberforce (1759–1833) was an English abolitionist, a Member of Parliament who waged a successful campaign for the abolition of slavery throughout the British Empire.

HALLY [*no enthusiasm*]. Oh. So you're also one of them, are you? You're
 basing that opinion on only one play, you know. You've only read my
 Julius Caesar and even I don't understand half of what they're talking
 about. They should do what they did with the old Bible: bring the lan-
 guage up to date.

SAM. That's all you've got. It's also the only one *you've* read.

HALLY. I know. I admit it. That's why I suggest we reserve our judgment
 until we've checked up on a few others. I've got a feeling, though, that
 by the end of this year one is going to be enough for me, and I can give
 you the names of twenty-nine other chaps in the Standard Nine class of
 the Port Elizabeth Technical College who feel the same. But if you want
 him, you can have him. My turn now. [*pacing*] This is a damned good
 exercise, you know! It started off looking like a simple question and
 here it's got us really probing into the intellectual heritage of our civili-
 zation.

SAM. So who is it going to be?

HALLY. My next man . . . and he gets the title on two scores: social reform
 and literary genius . . . is Leo Nikolaevich Tolstoy.

SAM. That Russian.

HALLY. Correct. Remember the picture of him I showed you?

SAM. With the long beard.

HALLY [*trying to look like Tolstoy*]. And those burning, visionary eyes. My
 God, the face of a social prophet if ever I saw one! And remember my
 words when I showed it to you? Here's a *man*, Sam!

SAM. Those were words, Hally.

HALLY. Not many intellectuals are prepared to shovel manure with the
 peasants and then go home and write a "little book" called *War and
 Peace*. Incidentally, Sam, he was somebody else who, to quote, " . . . did
 not distinguish himself scholastically."

SAM. Meaning?

HALLY. He was also no good at school.

SAM. Like you and Winston Churchill.

HALLY [*mirthlessly*]. Ha, ha, ha.

SAM [*simultaneously*]. Ha, ha, ha.

HALLY. Don't get clever, Sam. That man freed his serfs of his own free will.

SAM. No argument. He was a somebody, all right. I accept him.

HALLY. I'm sure Count Tolstoy will be very pleased to hear that. Your
 turn. Shoot. [*another chocolate from behind the counter*] I'm waiting, Sam.

SAM. I've got him.

HALLY. Good. Submit your candidate for examination.

SAM. Jesus.

HALLY [*stopped dead in his tracks*]. Who?

SAM. Jesus Christ.

HALLY. Oh, come on, Sam!

SAM. The Messiah.

HALLY. Ja, but still . . . No, Sam. Don't let's get started on religion. We'll
 just spend the whole afternoon arguing again. Suppose I turn around
 and say Mohammed?

SAM. All right.

HALLY. You can't have them both on the same list!

SAM. Why not? You like Mohammed, I like Jesus.

HALLY. I *don't* like Mohammed. I never have. I was merely being hypothetical. As far as I'm concerned, the Koran is as bad as the Bible. No. Religion is out! I'm not going to waste my time again arguing with you about the existence of God. You know perfectly well I'm an atheist . . . and I've got homework to do.

SAM. Okay, I take him back.

HALLY. You've got time for one more name.

SAM [*after thought*]. I've got one I know we'll agree on. A simple straightforward great Man of Magnitude . . . and no arguments. And *he* really *did* benefit all mankind.

HALLY. I wonder. After your last contribution I'm beginning to doubt whether anything in the way of an intellectual agreement is possible between the two of us. Who is he?

SAM. Guess.

HALLY. Socrates? Alexandre Dumas? Karl Marx? Dostoevsky? Nietzsche?

[SAM *shakes his head after each name.*]

Give me a clue.

SAM. The letter P is important . . .

HALLY. Plato!

SAM. . . . and his name begins with an F.

HALLY. I've got it. Freud and Psychology.

SAM. No. I didn't understand him.

HALLY. That makes two of us.

SAM. Think of mouldy apricot jam.

HALLY [*after a delighted laugh*]. Penicillin and Sir Alexander Fleming! And the title of the book: *The Microbe Hunters.* [*delighted*] Splendid, Sam! Splendid. For once we are in total agreement. The major breakthrough in medical science in the Twentieth Century. If it wasn't for him, we might have lost the Second World War. It's deeply gratifying, Sam, to know that I haven't been wasting my time in talking to you. [*Strutting around proudly*] Tolstoy may have educated his peasants, but I've educated you.

SAM. Standard Four to Standard Nine.

HALLY. Have we been at it as long as that?

SAM. Yep. And my first lesson was geography.

HALLY [*intrigued*]. Really? I don't remember.

SAM. My room there at the back of the old Jubilee Boarding House. I had just started working for your Mom. Little boy in short trousers walks in one afternoon and asks me seriously: "Sam, do you want to see South Africa?" Hey man! Sure I wanted to see South Africa!

HALLY. Was that me?

SAM. . . . So the next thing I'm looking at a map you had just done for homework. It was your first one and you were very proud of yourself.

HALLY. Go on.

SAM. Then came my first lesson. "Repeat after me, Sam: Gold in the Transvaal, mealies[4] in the Free State, sugar in Natal and grapes in the Cape." I still know it!

[4] Corn.

HALLY. Well, I'll be buggered. So that's how it all started.

SAM. And your next map was one with all the rivers and the mountains they came from. The Orange, the Vaal, the Limpopo, the Zambezi . . .

HALLY. You've got a phenomenal memory!

SAM. You should be grateful. That is why you started passing your exams. You tried to be better than me.

[*They laugh together.* WILLIE *is attracted by the laughter and joins them.*]

HALLY. The old Jubilee Boarding House. Sixteen rooms with board and lodging, rent in advance and one week's notice. I haven't thought about it for donkey's years . . . and I don't think that's an accident. God, was I glad when we sold it and moved out. Those years are not remembered as the happiest ones of an unhappy childhood.

WILLIE [*knocking on the table and trying to imitate a woman's voice*]. "Hally, are you there?"

HALLY. Who's that supposed to be?

WILLIE. "What you doing in there, Hally? Come out at once!"

HALLY [*to* SAM]. What's he talking about?

SAM. Don't you remember?

WILLIE. "Sam, Willie . . . is he in there with you boys?"

SAM. Hiding away in our room when your mother was looking for you.

HALLY [*another good laugh*]. Of course! I used to crawl and hide under your bed! But finish the story, Willie. Then what used to happen? You chaps would give the game away by telling her I was in there with you. So much for friendship.

SAM. We couldn't lie to her. She knew.

HALLY. Which meant I got another rowing for hanging around the "servants' quarters." I think I spent more time in there with you chaps than anywhere else in that dump. And do you blame me? Nothing but bloody misery wherever you went. Somebody was always complaining about the food, or my mother was having a fight with Micky Nash because she'd caught her with a petty officer in her room. Maud Meiring was another one. Remember those two? They were prostitutes, you know. Soldiers and sailors from the troopships. Bottom fell out of the business when the war ended. God, the flotsam and jetsam that life washed up on our shores! No joking, if it wasn't for your room, I would have been the first certified ten-year-old in medical history. Ja, the memories are coming back now. Walking home from school and thinking: "What can I do this afternoon?" Try out a few ideas, but sooner or later I'd end up in there with you fellows. I bet you I could still find my way to your room with my eyes closed. [*He does exactly that.*] Down the corridor . . . telephone on the right, which my Mom keeps locked because somebody is using it on the sly and not paying . . . past the kitchen and unappetizing cooking smells . . . around the corner into the backyard, hold my breath again because there are more smells coming when I pass your lavatory, then into that little passageway, first door on the right and into your room. How's that?

SAM. Good. But, as usual, you forgot to knock.

HALLY. Like that time I barged in and caught you and Cynthia . . . at it.

Remember? God, was I embarrassed! I didn't know what was going on at first.

SAM. Ja, that taught you a lesson.

HALLY. And about a lot more than knocking on doors, I'll have you know, and I don't mean geography either. Hell, Sam, couldn't you have waited until it was dark?

SAM. No.

HALLY. Was it that urgent?

SAM. Yes, and if you don't believe me, wait until your time comes.

HALLY. No, thank you. I am not interested in girls. [*Back to his memories . . . Using a few chairs he recreates the room as he lists the items*] A gray little room with a cold cement floor. Your bed against that wall . . . and I now know why the mattress sags so much! . . . Willie's bed . . . it's propped up on bricks because one leg is broken . . . that wobbly little table with the washbasin and jug of water . . . Yes! . . . stuck to the wall above it are some pin-up pictures from magazines. Joe Louis . . .

WILLIE. Brown Bomber. World Title. [*boxing pose*] Three rounds and knockout.

HALLY. Against who?

SAM. Max Schmeling.

HALLY. Correct. I can also remember Fred Astaire and Ginger Rogers, and Rita Hayworth in a bathing costume which always made me hot and bothered when I looked at it. Under Willie's bed is an old suitcase with all his clothes in a mess, which is why I never hide there. Your things are neat and tidy in a trunk next to your bed, and on it there is a picture of you and Cynthia in your ballroom clothes, your first silver cup for third place in a competition and an old radio which doesn't work anymore. Have I left out anything?

SAM. No.

HALLY. Right, so much for the stage directions. Now the characters. [SAM *and* WILLIE *move to their appropriate positions in the bedroom.*] Willie is in bed, under his blankets with his clothes on, complaining nonstop about something, but we can't make out a word of what he's saying because he's got his head under the blankets as well. You're on your bed trimming your toenails with a knife—not a very edifying sight—and as for me . . . What am I doing?

SAM. You're sitting on the floor giving Willie a lecture about being a good loser while you get the checker board and pieces ready for a game. Then you go to Willie's bed, pull off the blankets and make him play with you first because you know you're going to win, and that gives you the second game with me.

HALLY. And you certainly were a bad loser, Willie!

WILLIE. Haai!

HALLY. Wasn't he, Sam? And so slow! A game with you almost took the whole afternoon. Thank God I gave up trying to teach you how to play chess.

WILLIE. You and Sam cheated.

HALLY. I never saw Sam cheat, and mine were mostly the mistakes of youth.

WILLIE. Then how is it you two was always winning?

HALLY. Have you ever considered the possibility, Willie, that it was because we were better than you?

WILLIE. Every time better?

HALLY. Not every time. There were occasions when we deliberately let you win a game so that you would stop sulking and go on playing with us. Sam used to wink at me when you weren't looking to show me it was time to let you win.

WILLIE. So then you two didn't play fair.

HALLY. It was for your benefit, Mr. Malopo, which is more than being fair. It was an act of self-sacrifice. [*to* SAM] But you know what my best memory is, don't you?

SAM. No.

HALLY. Come on, guess. If your memory is so good, you must remember it as well.

SAM. We got up to a lot of tricks in there, Hally.

HALLY. This one was special, Sam.

SAM. I'm listening.

HALLY. It started off looking like another of those useless nothing-to-do afternoons. I'd already been down to Main Street looking for adventure, but nothing had happened. I didn't feel like climbing trees in the Donkin Park or pretending I was a private eye and following a stranger . . . so as usual: See what's cooking in Sam's room. This time it was you on the floor. You had two thin pieces of wood and you were smoothing them down with a knife. It didn't look particularly interesting, but when I asked you what you were doing, you just said, "Wait and see, Hally. Wait . . . and see" . . . in that secret sort of way of yours, so I knew there was a surprise coming. You teased me, you bugger, by being deliberately slow and not answering my questions!

[SAM *laughs*]

And whistling while you worked away! God, it was infuriating! I could have brained you! It was only when you tied them together in a cross and put that down on the brown paper that I realized what you were doing. "Sam is making a kite?" And when I asked you and you said "Yes" . . . [*Shaking his head with disbelief*] The sheer audacity of it took my breath away. I mean, seriously, what the hell does a black man know about flying a kite? I'll be honest with you, Sam, I had no hopes for it. If you think I was excited and happy, you got another guess coming. In fact, I was shit-scared that we were going to make fools of ourselves. When we left the boarding house to go up onto the hill, I was praying quietly that there wouldn't be any other kids around to laugh at us.

SAM [*enjoying the memory as much as* HALLY]. Ja, I could see that.

HALLY. I made it obvious, did I?

SAM. Ja. You refused to carry it.

HALLY. Do you blame me? Can you remember what the poor thing looked like? Tomato-box wood and brown paper! Flour and water for glue! Two of my mother's old stockings for a tail, and then all those bits and pieces of string you made me tie together so that we could fly it! Hell, no, that was now only asking for a miracle to happen.

SAM. Then the big argument when I told you to hold the string and run with it when I let go.

HALLY. I was prepared to run, all right, but straight back to the boarding house.

SAM [*knowing what's coming*]. So what happened?

HALLY. Come on, Sam, you remember as well as I do.

SAM. I want to hear it from you.

> [HALLY *pauses. He wants to be as accurate as possible.*]

HALLY. You went a little distance from me down the hill, you held it up ready to let it go. . . . "This is it," I thought. "Like everything else in my life, here comes another fiasco." Then you shouted, "Go, Hally!" and I started to run. [*another pause*] I don't know how to describe it, Sam, Ja! The miracle happened! I was running, waiting for it to crash to the ground, but instead suddenly there was something alive behind me at the end of the string, tugging at it as if it wanted to be free. I looked back . . . [*Shakes his head*] . . . I still can't believe my eyes. It was flying! Looping around and trying to climb even higher into the sky. You shouted to me to let it have more string. I did, until there was none left and I was just holding that piece of wood we had tied it to. You came up and joined me. You were laughing.

SAM. So were you. And shouting, "It works, Sam! We've done it!"

HALLY. And we had! I was so proud of us! It was the most splendid thing I had ever seen. I wished there were hundreds of kids around to watch us. The part that scared me, though, was when you showed me how to make it dive down to the ground and then just when it was on the point of crashing, swoop up again!

SAM. You didn't want to try yourself.

HALLY. Of course not! I would have been suicidal if anything had happened to it. Watching you do it made me nervous enough. I was quite happy just to see it up there with its tail fluttering behind it. You left me after that, didn't you? You explained how to get it down, we tied it to the bench so that I could sit and watch it, and you went away. I wanted you to stay, you know. I was a little scared of having to look after it by myself.

SAM [*quietly*]. I had work to do, Hally.

HALLY. It was sort of sad bringing it down, Sam. And it looked sad again when it was lying there on the ground. Like something that had lost its soul. Just tomato-box wood, brown paper and two of my mother's old stockings! But, hell, I'll never forget that first moment when I saw it up there. I had a stiff neck the next day from looking up so much.

> [SAM *laughs.* HALLY *turns to him with a question he never thought of asking before.*]

Why did you make that kite, Sam?

SAM [*evenly*]. I can't remember.

HALLY. Truly?

SAM. Too long ago, Hally.

HALLY. Ja, I suppose it was. It's time for another one, you know.

SAM. Why do you say that?

HALLY. Because it feels like that. Wouldn't be a good day to fly it, though.

SAM. No. You can't fly kites on rainy days.

HALLY. [*He studies* SAM. *Their memories have made him conscious of the man's presence in his life.*] How old are you, Sam?

SAM. Two score and five.

HALLY. Strange, isn't it?

SAM. What?

HALLY. Me and you.

SAM. What's strange about it?

HALLY. Little white boy in short trousers and a black man old enough to be his father flying a kite. It's not every day you see that.

SAM. But why strange? Because the one is white and the other black?

HALLY. I don't know. Would have been just as strange, I suppose, if it had been me and my Dad . . . cripple man and a little boy! Nope! There's no chance of me flying a kite without it being strange. [*simple statement of fact—no self-pity*] There's a nice little short story there. "The Kite-Flyers." But we'd have to find a twist in the ending.

SAM. Twist?

HALLY. Yes. Something unexpected. The way it ended with us was too straightforward . . . me on the bench and you going back to work. There's no drama in that.

WILLIE. And me?

HALLY. You?

WILLIE. Yes me.

HALLY. You want to get into the story as well, do you? I got it! Change the title: "Afternoons in Sam's Room" . . . expand it and tell all the stories. It's on its way to being a novel. Our days in the old Jubilee. Sad in a way that they're over. I almost wish we were still in that little room.

SAM. We're still together.

HALLY. That's true. It's just that life felt the right size in there . . . not too big and not too small. Wasn't so hard to work up a bit of courage. It's got so bloody complicated since then.

[*The telephone rings.* SAM *answers it.*]

SAM. St. George's Park Tea Room . . . Hello, Madam . . . Yes, Madam, he's here. . . . Hally, it's your mother.

HALLY. Where is she phoning from?

SAM. Sounds like the hospital. It's a public telephone.

HALLY [*relieved*]. You see! I told you. [*the telephone*] Hello, Mom . . . Yes . . . Yes no fine. Everything's under control here. How's things with poor old Dad? . . .Has he had a bad turn? . . . What? . . . Oh, God! . . . Yes, Sam told me, but I was sure he'd made a mistake. But what's this all about, Mom? He didn't look at all good last night. How can he get better so quickly? . . . Then very obviously you must say no. Be firm with him. You're the boss. . . . You know what it's going to be like if he comes home. . . . Well then, don't blame me when I fail my exams at the end of the year. . . . Yes! How am I expected to be fresh for school when I spend half the night massaging his gammy[5] leg? . . . So am I! . . . So

[5] Lame.

tell him a white lie. Say Dr. Colley wants more X-rays of his stump. Or bribe him. We'll sneak in double tots of brandy in future. . . . What? . . . Order him to get back into bed at once! If he's going to behave like a child, treat him like one. . . . All right, Mom! I was just trying to . . . I'm sorry. . . . I said I'm sorry. . . . Quick, give me your number. I'll phone you back. [*He hangs up and waits a few seconds.*] Here we go again! [*He dials.*] I'm sorry, Mom. . . . Okay . . . But now listen to me carefully. All it needs is for you to put your foot down. Don't take no for an answer. . . . Did you hear me? And whatever you do, don't discuss it with him. . . . Because I'm frightened you'll give in to him. . . . Yes, Sam gave me lunch. . . . I ate all of it! . . . No, Mom not a soul. It's still raining here. . . . Right, I'll tell them. I'll just do some homework and then lock up. . . . But remember now, Mom. Don't listen to anything he says. And phone me back and let me know what happens. . . . Okay. Bye, Mom. [*He hangs up. The men are staring at him.*] My Mom says that when you're finished with the floors you must do the windows. [*Pause*] Don't misunderstand me, chaps. All I want is for him to get better. And if he was, I'd be the first person to say: "Bring him home." But he's not, and we can't give him the medical care and attention he needs at home. That's what hospitals are there for. [*brusquely*] So don't just stand there! Get on with it!

[SAM *clears* HALLY's *table.*]

You heard right. My Dad wants to go home.

SAM. Is he better?

HALLY [*sharply*]. No! How the hell can he be better when last night he was groaning with pain? This is not an age of miracles!

SAM. Then he should stay in hospital.

HALLY [*seething with irritation and frustration*]. Tell me something I don't know, Sam. What the hell do you think I was saying to my Mom? All I can say is fuck-it-all.

SAM. I'm sure he'll listen to your Mom.

HALLY. You don't know what she's up against. He's already packed his shaving kit and pajamas and is sitting on his bed with his crutches, dressed and ready to go. I know him when he gets in that mood. If she tries to reason with him, we've had it. She's no match for him when it comes to a battle of words. He'll tie her up in knots. [*Trying to hide his true feelings*]

SAM. I suppose it gets lonely for him in there.

HALLY. With all the patients and nurses around? Regular visits from the Salvation Army? Balls! It's ten times worse for him at home. I'm at school and my mother is here in the business all day.

SAM. He's at least got you at night.

HALLY [*before he can stop himself*]. And we've got him! Please! I don't want to talk about it anymore. [*Unpacks his school case, slamming down books on the table*] Life is just a plain bloody mess, that's all. And people are fools.

SAM. Come on, Hally.

HALLY. Yes, they are! They bloody well deserve what they get.

SAM. Then don't complain.

HALLY. Don't try to be clever, Sam. It doesn't suit you. Anybody who thinks there's nothing wrong with this world needs to have his head

examined. Just when things are going along all right, without fail some-
one or something will come along and spoil everything. Somebody
should write that down as a fundamental law of the Universe. The prin-
ciple of perpetual disappointment. If there is a God who created this
world, he should scrap it and try again.

SAM. All right, Hally, all right. What you got for homework?

HALLY. Bullshit, as usual. [*Opens an exercise book and reads*] "Write five hun-
dred words describing an annual event of cultural or historical signifi-
cance."

SAM. That should be easy enough for you.

HALLY. And also plain bloody boring. You know what he wants, don't you?
One of their useless old ceremonies. The commemoration of the land-
ing of the 1820 Settlers,[6] or if it's going to be culture, Carols by Candle-
light every Christmas.

SAM. It's an impressive sight. Make a good description, Hally. All those
candles glowing in the dark and the people singing hymns.

HALLY. And it's called religious hysteria. [*intense irritation*] Please, Sam! Just
leave me alone and let me get on with it. I'm not in the mood for games
this afternoon. And remember my Mom's orders . . . you're to help
Willie with the windows. Come on now, I don't want any more nonsense
in here.

SAM. Okay, Hally, okay.

> [HALLY *settles down to his homework; de-
> termined preparations . . . pen, ruler,
> exercise book, dictionary, another
> cake . . . all of which will lead to nothing.
> SAM waltzes over to WILLIE and starts to
> replace tables and chairs. He practices a
> ballroom step while doing so. WILLIE
> watches. When SAM is finished, WILLIE
> tries*]

Good! But just a little bit quicker on the turn and only move in to her
after she's crossed over. What about this one?

> [*Another step. When* SAM *is finished,*
> WILLIE *again has a go.*]

Much better. See what happens when you just relax and enjoy yourself?
Remember that in two weeks' time and you'll be all right.

WILLIE. But I haven't got partner, Boet Sam.

SAM. Maybe Hilda will turn up tonight.

WILLIE. No, Boet Sam. [*reluctantly*] I gave her a good hiding.

SAM. You mean a bad one.

WILLIE. Good bad one.

SAM. Then you mustn't complain either. Now you pay the price for losing
your temper.

WILLIE. I also pay two pounds ten shilling entrance fee.

SAM. They'll refund you if you withdraw now.

WILLIE. [*appalled*]. You mean, don't dance?

[6] First Dutch (Afrikaner) immigrants into South Africa.

SAM. Yes.

WILLIE. No! I wait too long and I practice too hard. If I find me new partner, you think I can be ready in two weeks? I ask Madam for my leave now and we practice every day.

SAM. Quickstep non-stop for two weeks. World record, Willie, but you'll be mad at the end.

WILLIE. No jokes, Boet Sam.

SAM. I'm not joking.

WILLIE. So then what?

SAM. Find Hilda. Say you're sorry and promise you won't beat her again.

WILLIE. No.

SAM. Then withdraw. Try again next year.

WILLIE. No.

SAM. Then I give up.

WILLIE. Haaikona, Boet Sam, you can't.

SAM. What do you mean, I can't? I'm telling you: I give up.

WILLIE. [*adamant*]. No! [*accusingly*] It was you who start me ballroom dancing.

SAM. So?

WILLIE. Before that I use to be happy. And is you and Miriam who bring me to Hilda and say here's partner for you.

SAM. What are you saying, Willie?

WILLIE. You!

SAM. But me what? To blame?

WILLIE. Yes.

SAM. Willie . . . ? [*Bursts into laughter*]

WILLIE. And now all you do is make jokes at me. You wait. When Miriam leaves you is my turn to laugh. Ha! Ha! Ha!

SAM. [*He can't take* WILLIE *seriously any longer.*] She can leave me tonight! I know what to do. [*Bowing before an imaginary partner*] May I have the pleasure? [*He dances and sings.*]
"Just a fellow with his pillow . . .
Dancin' like a willow . . .
In an autumn breeze . . ."

WILLIE. There you go again!

[SAM *goes on dancing and singing.*]

Boet Sam!

SAM. There's the answer to your problem! Judges' announcement in two weeks' time: "Ladies and gentlemen, the winner in the open section . . . Mr. Willie Malopo and his pillow!"

[*This is too much for a now really angry* WILLIE. *He goes for* SAM, *but the latter is too quick for him and puts* HALLY'S *table between the two of them.*]

HALLY [*exploding*]. For Christ's sake, you two!

WILLIE [*still trying to get at* SAM]. I donner[7] you, Sam! Struesgod!

SAM [*still laughing*]. Sorry, Willie . . . Sorry . . .

[7] "Beat up; thrash."

HALLY. Sam! Willie! [*Grabs his ruler and gives* WILLIE *a vicious whack on the bum*] How the hell am I supposed to concentrate with the two of you behaving like bloody children!

WILLIE. Hit him too!

HALLY. Shut up, Willie.

WILLIE. He started jokes again.

HALLY. Get back to your work. You too, Sam. [*his ruler*] Do you want another one, Willie?

> [SAM *and* WILLIE *return to their work.* HALLY *uses the opportunity to escape from his unsuccessful attempt at homework. He struts around like a little despot, ruler in hand, giving vent to his anger and frustration.*]

Suppose a customer had walked in then? Or the Park Superintendent. And seen the two of you behaving like a pair of hooligans. That would have been the end of my mother's license, you know. And your jobs! Well, this is the end of it. From now on there will be no more of your ballroom nonsense in here. This is a business establishment, not a bloody New Brighton dancing school. I've been far too lenient with the two of you. [*Behind the counter for a green cool drink and a dollop of ice cream. He keeps up his tirade as he prepares it.*] But what really makes me bitter is that I allow you chaps a little freedom in here when business is bad and what do you do with it? The foxtrot! Specially you, Sam. There's more to life than trotting around a dance floor and I thought at least you knew it.

SAM. It's a harmless pleasure, Hally. It doesn't hurt anybody.

HALLY. It's also a rather simple one, you know.

SAM. You reckon so? Have you ever tried?

HALLY. Of course not.

SAM. Why don't you? Now.

HALLY. What do you mean? Me dance?

SAM. Yes. I'll show you a simple step—the waltz—then you try it.

HALLY. What will that prove?

SAM. That it might not be as easy as you think.

HALLY. I didn't say it was easy. I said it was simple—like in simple-minded, meaning mentally retarded. You can't exactly say it challenges the intellect.

SAM. It does other things.

HALLY. Such as?

SAM. Make people happy.

HALLY [*the glass in his hand*]. So do American cream sodas with ice cream. For God's sake, Sam, you're not asking me to take ballroom dancing seriously, are you?

SAM. Yes.

HALLY [*sigh of defeat*]. Oh, well, so much for trying to give you a decent education. I've obviously achieved nothing.

SAM. You still haven't told me what's wrong with admiring something that's beautiful and then trying to do it yourself.

HALLY. Nothing. But we happen to be talking about a foxtrot, not a thing of beauty.

SAM. But that is just what I'm saying. If you were to see two champions doing, two masters of the art . . . !

HALLY. Oh, God, I give up. So now it's also art!

SAM. Ja.

HALLY. There's a limit, Sam. Don't confuse art and entertainment.

SAM. So then what is art?

HALLY. You want a definition?

SAM. Ja.

HALLY. [*He realizes he has got to be careful. He gives the matter a lot of thought before answering.*] Philosophers have been trying to do that for centuries. What is Art? What is Life? But basically I suppose it's . . . the giving of meaning to matter.

SAM. Nothing to do with beautiful?

HALLY. It goes beyond that. It's the giving of form to the formless.

SAM. Ja, well, maybe it's not art, then. But I still say it's beautiful.

HALLY. I'm sure the word you mean to use is entertaining.

SAM. [*adamant*]. No. Beautiful. And if you want proof, come along to the Centenary Hall in New Brighton in two weeks' time.

[*The mention of the Centenary Hall draws* WILLIE *over to them.*]

HALLY. What for? I've seen the two of you prancing around in here often enough.

SAM. [*He laughs.*] This isn't the real thing, Hally. We're just playing around in here.

HALLY. So? I can use my imagination.

SAM. And what do you get?

HALLY. A lot of people dancing around and having a so-called good time.

SAM. That all?

HALLY. Well, basically it is that, surely.

SAM. No, it isn't. Your imagination hasn't helped you at all. There's a lot more to it than that. We're getting ready for the championships, Hally, not just another dance. There's going to be a lot of people, all right, and they're going to have a good time, but they'll only be spectators, sitting around and watching. It's just the competitors out there on the dance floor. Party decorations and fancy lights all around the walls! The ladies in beautiful evening dresses!

HALLY. My mother's got one of those, Sam, and, quite frankly, it's an embarrassment every time she wears it.

SAM. [*undeterred*]. Your imagination left out the excitement.

[HALLY *scoffs.*]

Oh, yes. The finalists are not going to be out there just to have a good time. One of those couples will be the 1950 Eastern Province Champions. And your imagination left out the music.

WILLIE. Mr. Elijah Gladman Guzana and his Orchestral Jazzonions.

SAM. The sound of the big band, Hally. Trombone, trumpet, tenor and alto sax. And then, finally, your imagination also left out the climax of the evening when the dancing is finished, the judges have stopped whis-

pering among themselves and the Master of Ceremonies collects their
scorecards and goes up onto the stage to announce the winners.

HALLY. All right. So you make it sound like a bit of a do. It's an occasion.
Satisfied?

SAM. [*victory*]. So you admit that!

HALLY. Emotionally yes, intellectually no.

SAM. Well, I don't know what you mean by that, all I'm telling you is that it
is going to be *the* event of the year in New Brighton. It's been sold out
for two weeks already. There's only standing room left. We've got com-
petitors coming from Kingwilliamstown, East London, Port Alfred.

[HALLY *starts pacing thoughtfully.*]

HALLY. Tell me a bit more.

SAM. I thought you weren't interested . . . intellectually.

HALLY [*mysteriously*]. I've got my reasons.

SAM. What do you want to know?

HALLY. It takes place every year?

SAM. Yes. But only every third year in New Brighton. It's East London's
turn to have the championships next year.

HALLY. Which, I suppose, makes it an even more significant event.

SAM. Ah ha! We're getting somewhere. Our "occasion" is now a "significant
event."

HALLY. I wonder.

SAM. What?

HALLY. I wonder if I would get away with it.

SAM. But what?

HALLY [*to the table and his exercise book*]. "Write five hundred words describ-
ing an annual event of cultural or historical significance." Would I be
stretching poetic license a little too far if I called your ballroom champi-
onships a cultural event?

SAM. You mean . . . ?

HALLY. You think we could get five hundred words out of it, Sam?

SAM. Victor Sylvester has written a whole book on ballroom dancing.

WILLIE. You going to write about it, Master Hally?

HALLY. Yes, gentlemen, that is precisely what I am considering doing. Old
Doc Bromely—he's my English teacher—is going to argue with me, of
course. He doesn't like natives. But I'll point out to him that in strict
anthropological terms the culture of a primitive black society includes
its dancing and singing. To put my thesis in a nutshell: The war-dance
has been replaced by the waltz. But it still amounts to the same thing:
the release of primitive emotions through movement. Shall we give it
a go?

SAM. I'm ready.

WILLIE. Me also.

HALLY. Ha! This will teach the old bugger a lesson. [*decision taken*] Right.
Let's get ourselves organized. [*This means another cake on the table. He sits.*]
I think you've given me enough general atmosphere, Sam, but to build
the tension and suspense I need facts. [*pencil poised*]

WILLIE. Give him facts, Boet Sam.

HALLY. What you called the climax . . . how many finalists?

SAM. Six couples.

HALLY [*making notes*]. Go on. Give me the picture.

SAM. Spectators seated right around the hall. [WILLIE *becomes a spectator.*]

HALLY. . . . and it's a full house.

SAM. At one end, on the stage, Gladman and his Orchestral Jazzonions. At the other end is a long table with the three judges. The six finalists go onto the dance floor and take up their positions. When they are ready and the spectators have settled down, the Master of Ceremonies goes to the microphone. To start with, he makes some jokes to get the people laughing . . .

HALLY. Good touch! [*As he writes*] " . . . creating a relaxed atmosphere which will change to one of tension and drama as the climax is approached."

SAM [*onto a chair to act out the M.C.*]. "Ladies and gentlemen, we come now to the great moment you have all been waiting for this evening. . . . The finals of the 1950 Eastern Province Open Ballroom Dancing Championships. But first let me introduce the finalists! Mr. and Mrs. Welcome Tchabalala from Kingwilliamstown . . ."

WILLIE [*He applauds after every name.*] Is when the people clap their hands and whistle and make a lot of noise, Master Hally.

SAM. "Mr. Mulligan Njikelane and Miss Nomhle Nkonyeni of Grahamstown; Mr. and Mrs. Norman Nchinga from Port Alfred; Mr. Fats Bokolane and Miss Dina Plaatjies from East London; Mr. Sipho Dugu and Mrs. Mable Magada from Peddie; and from New Brighton our very own Mr. Willie Malopo and Miss Hilda Samuels."

> [WILLIE *can't believe his ears. He abandons his role as spectator and scrambles into position as a finalist.*]

WILLIE. Relaxed and ready to romance!

SAM. The applause dies down. When everybody is silent, Gladman lifts up his sax, nods at the Orchestral Jazzonions . . .

WILLIE. Play the jukebox please, Boet Sam!

SAM. I also only got bus fare, Willie.

HALLY. Hold it, everybody. [*Heads for the cash register behind the counter*] How much is in the till, Sam?

SAM. Three shillings. Hally . . . your Mom counted it before she left.

> [HALLY *hesitates.*]

HALLY. Sorry, Willie. You know how she carried on the last time I did it. We'll just have to pool our combined imaginations and hope for the best. [*Returns to the table*] Back to work. How are the points scored, Sam?

SAM. Maximum of ten points each for individual style, deportment, rhythm and general appearance.

WILLIE. Must I start?

HALLY. Hold it for a second, Willie. And penalties?

SAM. For what?

HALLY. For doing something wrong. Say you stumble or bump into somebody . . . do they take off any points?

SAM. [*aghast*]. Hally . . . !

HALLY. When you're dancing. If you and your partner collide into another couple.

[HALLY *can get no further.* SAM *has col-*
lapsed with laughter. He explains to
WILLIE.]

SAM. If me and Miriam bump into you and Hilda . . . [WILLIE *joins him in*
another good laugh.] Hally, Hally . . . !

HALLY [*perplexed*]. Why? What did I say?

SAM. There's no collisions out there, Hally. Nobody trips or stumbles or
bumps into anybody else. That's what that moment is all about. To be
one of those finalists on that dance floor is like . . . like being in a dream
about a world in which accidents don't happen.

HALLY [*genuinely moved by* SAM'S *image*]. Jesus, Sam! That's beautiful!

WILLIE [*can endure waiting no longer*]. I'm starting!

[WILLIE *dances while* SAM *talks.*]

SAM. Of course it is. That's what I've been trying to say to you all after-
noon. And it's beautiful because that is what we want life to be like. But
instead, like you said, Hally, we're bumping into each other all the time.
Look at the three of us this afternoon: I've bumped into Willie, the two
of us have bumped into you, you've bumped into your mother, she
bumping into your Dad. . . . None of us knows the steps and there's no
music playing. And it doesn't stop with us. The whole world is doing it
all the time. Open a newspaper and what do you read? America has
bumped into Russia, England is bumping into India, rich man bumps
into poor man. Those are big collisions, Hally. They make for a lot of
bruises. People get hurt in all that bumping, and we're sick and tired of
it now. It's been going on for too long. Are we never going to get it
right? . . . Learn to dance life like champions instead of always being
just a bunch of beginners at it?

HALLY [*deep and sincere admiration of the man*]. You've got a vision, Sam!

SAM. Not just me. What I'm saying to you is that everybody's got it. That's
why there's only standing room left for the Centenary Hall in two
weeks' time. For as long as the music lasts, we are going to see six cou-
ples get it right, the way we want life to be.

HALLY. But is that the best we can do, Sam . . . watch six finalists dreaming
about the way it should be?

SAM. I don't know. But it starts with that. Without the dream we won't
know what we're going for. And anyway I reckon there are a few people
who have got past just dreaming about it and are trying for something
real. Remember that thing we read once in the paper about the Ma-
hatma Gandhi? Going without food to stop those riots in India?

HALLY. You're right. He certainly was trying to teach people to get the
steps right.

SAM. And the Pope.

HALLY. Yes, he's another one. Our old General Smuts[8] as well, you know.
He's also out there dancing. You know, Sam, when you come to think of
it, that's what the United Nations boils down to . . . a dancing school for
politicians!

SAM. And let's hope they learn.

[8]Jan Christian Smuts was Premier and Minister of Native Affairs in South Africa from
1919 to 1924.

HALLY [*a little surge of hope*]. You're right. We mustn't despair. Maybe there's some hope for mankind after all. Keep it up, Willie. [*Back to his table with determination*] This is a lot bigger than I thought. So what have we got? Yes, our title: "A World Without Collisions."

SAM. That sounds good! "A World Without Collisions."

HALLY. Subtitle: "Global Politics on the Dance Floor." No. A bit too heavy, hey? What about "Ballroom Dancing as a Political Vision"?

[*The telephone rings. SAM answers it.*]

SAM. St. George's Park Tea Room . . . Yes, Madam . . . Hally, it's your Mom.

HALLY [*back to reality*]. Oh, God, yes! I'd forgotten all about that. Shit! Remember my words, Sam? Just when you're enjoying yourself, someone or something will come along and wreck everything.

SAM. You haven't heard what she's got to say yet.

HALLY. Public telephone?

SAM. No.

HALLY. Does she sound happy or unhappy?

SAM. I couldn't tell. [*pause*] She's waiting, Hally.

HALLY [*to the telephone*] Hello, Mom . . . No, everything is okay here. Just doing my homework. . . . What's your news? . . . You've what? . . . [*Pause. He takes the receiver away from his ear for a few seconds. In the course of HALLY's telephone conversation, SAM and WILLIE discreetly position the stacked tables and chairs. HALLY places the receiver back to his ear.*] Yes, I'm still here. Oh, well, I give up now. Why did you do it, Mom? . . . Well, I just hope you know what you've let us in for. . . . [*loudly*] I said I hope you know what you've let us in for! It's the end of the peace and quiet we've been having. [*softly*] Where is he? [*normal voice*] He can't hear us from in there. But for God's sake, Mom, what happened? I told you to be firm with him. . . . Then you and the nurses should have held him down, taken his crutches away. . . . I know only too well he's my father! . . . I'm not being disrespectful, but I'm sick and tired of emptying stinking chamberpots full of phlegm and piss. . . . Yes, I do! When you're not there, he asks *me* to do it. . . . If you really want to know the truth, that's why I've got no appetite for my food. . . . Yes! There's a lot of things you don't know about. For your information, I still haven't got that science textbook I need. And you know why? He borrowed the money you gave me for it. . . . Because I didn't want to start another fight between you two. . . . He says that every time. . . . All right, Mom! [*viciously*] Then just remember to start hiding your bag away again, because he'll be at your purse before long for money for booze. And when he's well enough to come down here, you better keep an eye on the till as well, because that is also going to develop a leak. . . . Then don't complain to me when he starts his old tricks. . . . Yes, you do. I get it from you on one side and from him on the other, and it makes life hell for me. I'm not going to be the peacemaker anymore. I'm warning you now: when the two of you start fighting again, I'm leaving home. . . . Mom, if you start crying, I'm going to put down the receiver. . . . Okay . . . [*Lowering his voice to a vicious whisper*] Okay, Mom, I heard you. [*desperate*] No. . . . Because I don't want to. I'll see him when I get home! Mom! . . . [*Pause. When he speaks again, his tone changes completely.*

It is not simply pretense. We sense a genuine emotional conflict.] Welcome
home, chum! . . . What's that? . . . Don't be silly, Dad. You being home
is just about the best news in the world. . . . I bet you are. Bloody de-
pressing there with everybody going on about their ailments, hey! . . .
How you feeling? . . .Good . . . Here as well, pal. Coming down cats
and dogs. . . .That's right. Just the day for a kip and a toss in your old
Uncle Ned.[9] . . . Everything's just hunky-dory on my side, Dad. . . .
Well, to start with, there's a nice pile of comics for you on the
counter. . . . Yes, old Kemple brought them in. *Batman and Robin, Sub-
mariner* . . . just your cup of tea . . . I will. . . . Yes, we'll spin a few
yarns tonight. . . . Okay, chum, see you in a little while. . . . No, I
promise. I'll come straight home. . . . [*Pause—his mother comes back on the
phone.*] Mom? Okay. I'll lock up now. . . . What? . . . Oh, the brandy . . .
Yes, I'll remember! . . . I'll put it in my suitcase now, for God's sake. I
know well enough what will happen if he doesn't get it. . . . [*Places a
bottle of brandy on the counter*] I *was* kind to him, Mom, I didn't say any-
thing nasty! . . . All right. Bye. [*End of telephone conversation. A desolate
HALLY doesn't move. A strained silence*]

SAM. [*quietly*]. That sounded like a bad bump, Hally.
HALLY. [*having a hard time controlling his emotions. He speaks carefully.*] Mind
your own business, Sam.
SAM. Sorry. I wasn't trying to interfere. Shall we carry on? Hally? [*He indi-
cates the exercise book. No response from* HALLY]
WILLIE. [*also trying*]. Tell him about when they give out the cups, Boet Sam.
SAM. Ja! That's another big moment. The presentation of the cups after
the winners have been announced. You've got to put that in.
 [*Still no response from* HALLY]
WILLIE. A big silver one, Master Hally, called floating trophy for the cham-
pions.
SAM. We always invite some big-shot personality to hand them over. Guest
of honor this year is going to be His Holiness Bishop Jabulani of the All
African Free Zionist Church.
 [HALLY *gets up abruptly, goes to his table
 and tears up the page he was writing on.*]
HALLY. So much for a bloody world without collisions.
SAM. Too bad. It was on its way to being a good composition.
HALLY. Let's stop bullshitting ourselves, Sam.
SAM. Have we been doing that?
HALLY. Yes! That's what all our talk about a decent world has been . . .just
so much bullshit.
SAM. We did say it was still only a dream.
HALLY. And a bloody useless one at that. Life's a fuck-up and it's never
going to change.
SAM. Ja, maybe that's true.
HALLY. There's no maybe about it. It's a blunt and brutal fact. All we've
done this afternoon is waste our time.
SAM. Not if we'd got your homework done.
HALLY. I don't give a shit about my homework, so, for Christ's sake, just

[9] Kip: nap. Toss: sleep. Uncle Ned: rhyming slang for "bed."

shut up about it. [*Slamming books viciously into his school case*] Hurry up now and finish your work. I want to lock up and get out of here. [*pause*] And then go where? Home-sweet-fucking-home. Jesus, I hate that word.

> [HALLY *goes to the counter to put the brandy bottle and comics in his school case. After a moment's hesitation, he smashes the bottle of brandy. He abandons all further attempts to hide his feelings.* SAM *and* WILLIE *work away as unobtrusively as possible.*]

Do you want to know what is really wrong with your lovely little dream, Sam? It's not just that we are all bad dancers. That does happen to be perfectly true, but there's more to it than just that. You left out the cripples.

SAM. Hally!

HALLY. [*now totally reckless*]. Ja! Can't leave them out, Sam. That's why we always end up on our backsides on the dance floor. They're also out there dancing . . . like a bunch of broken spiders trying to do the quickstep! [*An ugly attempt at laughter*] When you come to think of it, it's a bloody comical sight. I mean, it's bad enough on two legs . . . but one and a pair of crutches! Hell, no, Sam. That's guaranteed to turn that dance floor into a shambles. Why you shaking your head? Picture it, man. For once this afternoon let's use our imaginations sensibly.

SAM. Be careful, Hally.

HALLY. Of what? The truth? I seem to be the only one around here who is prepared to face it. We've had the pretty dream, it's time now to wake up and have a good long look at the way things really are. Nobody knows the steps, there's no music, the cripples are also out there tripping up everybody and trying to get into the act, and it's all called the All-Comers-How-to-Make-a-Fuckup-of-Life Championships. [*another ugly laugh*] Hang on, Sam! The best bit is still coming. Do you know what the winner's trophy is? A beautiful big chamber-pot with roses on the side, and it's full to the brim with piss. And guess who I think is going to be this year's winner.

SAM [*almost shouting*]. Stop now!

HALLY [*suddenly appalled by how far he has gone*]. Why?

SAM. Hally? It's your father you're talking about.

HALLY. So?

SAM. Do you know what you've been saying?

> [HALLY *can't answer. He is rigid with shame.* SAM *speaks to him sternly.*]

No, Hally, you mustn't do it. Take back those words and ask for forgiveness! It's a terrible sin for a son to mock his father with jokes like that. You'll be punished if you carry on. Your father is your father, even if he is a . . . cripple man.

WILLIE. Yes, Master Hally. Is true what Sam say.

SAM. I understand how you are feeling, Hally, but even so . . .

HALLY. No, you don't!

SAM. I think I do.

HALLY. And I'm telling you you don't. Nobody does. [*Speaking carefully as his shame turns to rage at* SAM] It's your turn to be careful, Sam. Very careful! You're treading on dangerous ground. Leave me and my father alone.

SAM. I'm not the one who's been saying things about him.

HALLY. What goes on between me and my Dad is none of your business!

SAM. Then don't tell me about it. If that's all you've got to say about him, I don't want to hear.

> [*For a moment* HALLY *is at a loss for a response.*]

HALLY. Just get on with your bloody work and shut up.

SAM. Swearing at me won't help you.

HALLY. Yes, it does! Mind your own fucking business and shut up!

SAM. Okay. If that's the way you want it, I'll stop trying.

> [*He turns away. The infuriates* HALLY *even more.*]

HALLY. Good. Because what you've been trying to do is meddle in something you know nothing about. All that concerns you in here, Sam, is to try and do what you get paid for—keep the place clean and serve the customers. In plain words, just get on with your job. My mother is right. She's always warning me about allowing you to get too familiar. Well, this time you've gone too far. It's going to stop right now.

> [*No response from* SAM]

You're only a servant in here, and don't forget it.

> [*Still no response.* HALLY *is trying hard to get one.*]

And as far as my father is concerned, all you need to remember is that he is your boss.

SAM [*needled at last*]. No, he isn't. I get paid by your mother.

HALLY. Don't argue with me, Sam!

SAM. Then don't say he's my boss.

HALLY. He's a white man and that's good enough for you.

SAM. I'll try to forget you said that.

HALLY. Don't! Because you won't be doing me a favor if you do. I'm telling you to remember it.

> [*A pause.* SAM *pulls himself together and makes one last effort.*]

SAM. Hally, Hally . . . ! Come on now. Let's stop before it's too late. You're right. We *are* on dangerous ground. If we're not careful, somebody is going to get hurt.

HALLY. It won't be me.

SAM. Don't be so sure.

HALLY. I don't know what you're talking about, Sam.

SAM. Yes, you do.

HALLY [*furious*]. Jesus, I wish you would stop trying to tell me what I do and what I don't know.

> [SAM *gives up. He turns to* WILLIE.]

SAM. Let's finish up.

HALLY. Don't turn your back on me! I haven't finished talking.

[*He grabs* Sam *by the arm and tries to make him turn around.* Sam *reacts with a flash of anger.*]

Sam. Don't do that, Hally! [*facing the boy*] All right, I'm listening. Well? What do you want to say to me?

Hally [*pause as* Hally *looks for something to say*]. To begin with, why don't you also start calling me Master Harold, like Willie.

Sam. Do you mean that?

Hally. Why the hell do you think I said it?

Sam. And if I don't?

Hally. You might just lose your job.

Sam [*quietly and very carefully*]. If you make me say it once, I'll never call you anything else again.

Hally. So? [*The boy confronts the man*]. Is that meant to be a threat?

Sam. Just telling you what will happen if you make me do that. You must decide what it means to you.

Hally. Well, I have. It's good news. Because that is exactly what Master Harold wants from now on. Think of it as a little lesson in respect, Sam, that's long overdue, and I hope you remember it as well as you do your geography. I can tell you now that somebody who will be glad to hear I've finally given it to you will be my Dad. Yes! He agrees with my Mom. He's always going on about it as well. "You must teach the boys to show you more respect, my son."

Sam. So now you can stop complaining about going home. Everybody is going to be happy tonight.

Hally. That's perfectly correct. You see, you mustn't get the wrong idea about me and my Dad, Sam. We also have our good times together. Some bloody good laughs. He's got a marvelous sense of humor. Want to know what our favorite joke is? He gives out a big groan, you see, and says: "It's not fair, is it, Hally?" Then I have to ask: "What, chum?" And then he says: "A nigger's arse" . . . and we both have a good laugh.

[*The men stare at him with disbelief.*]

What's the matter, Willie? Don't you catch the joke? You always were a bit slow on the uptake. It's what is called a pun. You see, fair means both light in color and to be just and decent. [*He turns to* Sam] I thought *you* would catch it, Sam.

Sam. Oh ja, I catch it all right.

Hally. But it doesn't appeal to your sense of humor.

Sam. Do you really laugh?

Hally. Of course.

Sam. To please him? Make him feel good?

Hally. No, for heaven's sake! I laugh because I think it's a bloody good joke.

Sam. You're really trying hard to be ugly, aren't you? And why drag poor old Willie into it? He's done nothing to you except show you the respect you want so badly. That's also not being fair, you know . . . and *I* mean just or decent.

Willie. It's all right, Sam. Leave it now.

Sam. It's me you're after. You should just have said "Sam's arse" . . . be-

cause that's the one you're trying to kick. Anyway, how do you know it's not fair? You've never seen it. Do you want to? [*He drops his trousers and underpants and presents his backside for* HALLY's *inspection.*] Have a good look. A real Basuto[10] arse . . . which is about as nigger as they can come. Satisfied? [*trousers up*] Now you can make your Dad even happier when you go home tonight. Tell him I showed you my arse and he is quite right. It's not fair. And if it will give him an even better laugh next time, I'll also let *him* have a look. Come, Willie, let's finish up and go.

> [SAM *and* WILLIE *start to tidy up the tea room.* HALLY *doesn't move. He waits for a moment when* SAM *passes him.*]

HALLY. [*quietly*]. Sam . . .

> [SAM *stops and looks expectantly at the boy.* HALLY *spits in his face. A long and heartfelt groan from* WILLIE. *For a few seconds* SAM *doesn't move.*]

SAM [*taking out a handkerchief and wiping his face*]. It's all right, Willie.

> [*To* HALLY]

Ja, well, you've done it . . . Master Harold. Yes, I'll start calling you that from now on. It won't be difficult anymore. You've hurt yourself, Master Harold. I saw it coming. I warned you, but you wouldn't listen. You've just hurt yourself *bad*. And you're a coward, Master Harold. The face you should be spitting in is your father's . . . but you used mine, because you think you're safe inside your fair skin . . . and this time I don't mean just or decent. [*Pause, then moving violently towards* HALLY] Should I hit him, Willie?

WILLIE [*stopping* SAM]. No, Boet Sam.

SAM [*violently*]. Why not?

WILLIE. It won't help, Boet Sam.

SAM. I don't want to help! I want to hurt him.

WILLIE. You also hurt yourself.

SAM. And if he had done it to you, Willie?

WILLIE. Me? Spit at me like I was a dog? [*A thought that had not occurred to him before. He looks at* HALLY.] Ja. Then I want to hit him. I want to hit him hard! [*A dangerous few seconds as the men stand staring at the boy.* WILLIE *turns away, shaking his head.*] But maybe all I do is go cry at the back. He's little boy, Boet Sam. Little *white* boy. Long trousers now, but he's still little boy.

SAM [*his violence ebbing away into defeat as quickly as it flooded*]. You're right. So go on, then: groan again, Willie. You do it better than me. [*to* HALLY] You don't know all of what you've just done . . . Master Harold. It's not just that you've made me feel dirtier than I've ever been in my life . . . I mean, how do I wash off yours and your father's filth? . . . I've also failed. A long time ago I promised myself I was going to try and do something, but you've just shown me . . . Master Harold . . . that I've failed. [*pause*] I've also got a memory of a little white boy when he was still wearing short trousers and a black man, but they're not flying a kite.

[10] The Basutos are the people of Lesotho (formerly Basutoland), a small country completely surrounded by the Republic of South Africa.

It was the old Jubilee days, after dinner one night. I was in my room. You came in and just stood against the wall, looking down at the ground, and only after I'd asked you what you wanted, what was wrong, I don't know how many times, did you speak and even then so softly I almost didn't hear you. "Sam, please help me to go and fetch my Dad." Remember? He was dead drunk on the floor of the Central Hotel Bar. They'd phoned for your Mom, but you were the only one at home. And do you remember how we did it? You went in first by yourself to ask permission for me to go into the bar. Then I loaded him onto my back like a baby and carried him back to the boarding house with you following behind carrying his crutches. [*Shaking his head as he remembers*] A crowded Main Street with all the people watching a little white boy following his drunk father on a nigger's back! I felt for that little boy . . . Master Harold. I felt for him. After that we still had to clean him up, remember? He'd messed in his trousers, so we had to clean him up and get him into bed.

HALLY [*great pain*]. I love him, Sam.

SAM. I know you do. That's why I tried to stop you from saying these things about him. It would have been so simple if you could have just despised him for being a weak man. But he's your father. You love him and you're ashamed of him. You're ashamed of so much! . . . And now that's going to include yourself. That was the promise I made to myself: to try and stop that happening. [*pause*] After we got him to bed you came back with me to my room and sat in a corner and carried on just looking down at the ground. And for days after that! You hadn't done anything wrong, but you went around as if you owed the world an apology for being alive. I didn't like seeing that! That's not the way a boy grows up to be a man! . . . But the one person who should have been teaching you what that means was the cause of your shame. If you really want to know, that's why I made you that kite. I wanted you to look up, be proud of something, of yourself . . . [*bitter smile at the memory*] . . . and you certainly were that when I left you with it up there on the hill. Oh, ja . . . something else! . . . If you ever do write it as a short story, there *was* a twist in our ending. I couldn't sit down there and stay with you. It was a "Whites Only" bench. You were too young, too excited to notice then. But not anymore. If you're not careful . . . Master Harold . . . you're going to be sitting up there by yourself for a long time to come, and there won't be a kite in the sky. [SAM *has got nothing more to say. He exits into the kitchen, taking off his waiter's jacket.*]

WILLIE. Is bad. Is all all bad in here now.

HALLY [*books into his school case, raincoat on*]. Willie . . . [*It is difficult to speak.*] Will you lock up for me and look after the keys?

WILLIE. Okay.

> [SAM *returns.* HALLY *goes behind the counter and collects the few coins in the cash register. As he starts to leave . . .*]

SAM. Don't forget the comic books.

> [HALLY *returns to the counter and puts them in his case. He starts to leave again.*]

SAM [*to the retreating back of the boy*]. Stop . . . Hally . . .

[HALLY *stops, but doesn't turn to face him.*]

Hally . . . I've got no right to tell you what being a man means if I don't behave like one myself, and I'm not doing so well at that this afternoon. Should we try again, Hally?

HALLY. Try what?

SAM. Fly another kite, I suppose. It worked once, and this time I need it as much as you do.

HALLY. It's still raining, Sam. You can't fly kites on rainy days, remember.

SAM. So what do we do? Hope for better weather tomorrow?

HALLY [*helpless gesture*]. I don't know. I don't know anything anymore.

SAM. You sure of that, Hally? Because it would be pretty hopeless if that was true. It would mean nothing has been learnt in here this afternoon, and there was a hell of a lot of teaching going on . . . one way or the other. But anyway, I don't believe you. I reckon there's one thing you know. You don't *have* to sit up there by yourself. You know what that bench means now, and you can leave it any time you choose. All you've got to do is stand up and walk away from it.

[HALLY *leaves.* WILLIE *goes up quietly to* SAM.]

WILLIE. Is okay, Boet Sam. You see. Is . . . [*He can't find any better words.*] . . . *is* going to be okay tomorrow. [*changing his tone*] Hey, Boet Sam! [*He is trying hard.*] You right. I think about it and you right. To-night I find Hilda and say sorry. And make promise I won't beat her no more. You hear me, Boet Sam?

SAM. I hear you, Willie.

WILLIE. And when we practice I relax and romance with her from begin-ning to end. Non-stop! You watch! Two weeks' time: "First prize for promising newcomers: Mr. Willie Malopo and Miss Hilda Samuels." [*sudden impulse*] To hell with it! I walk home. [*He goes to the jukebox, puts in a coin and selects a record. The machine comes to life in the gray twilight, blushing its way through a spectrum of soft, romantic colors.*] How did you say it, Boet Sam? Let's dream. [WILLIE *sways with the music and gestures for* SAM *to dance.*] [*Sarah Vaughan sings.*]

"Little man you're crying,
I know why you're blue,
Someone took your kiddy car away;
Better go to sleep now,
Little man you've had a busy day." [*etc. etc.*]
 You lead. I follow.

[*The men dance together.*]

"Johnny won your marbles,
Tell you what we'll do;
Dad will get you new ones right away;
Better go to sleep now,
Little man you've had a busy day."

Joyce Carol Oates
(1938–)

In a *Newsweek* cover story he wrote about Joyce Carol Oates in December 1972, Walter Clemons said something about her that has often been quoted or repeated in slightly different words: that if, at a literary party, you met this "tall, pale young woman with enormous eyes and a timid, little-girl voice" and "failed to catch her name, it might be hard to imagine her reading, much less writing, the unflinching fiction that has made Joyce Carol Oates perhaps the most significant novelist to have emerged in the United States in the last decade." The surprise we might feel at this disparity would reflect less on Oates than on our naïveté in assuming that direct, literal experience rather than imagination is the crucible from which creative art must emerge. People who believe that the academic profession is especially divorced from the turmoil of life (including college students in the odd habit of contrasting college with what they call the "real world") would be especially baffled by the supposed paradox about Oates, since the outward data of her biography consist mainly of facts about her education, her career as a college teacher, and the publication of her works. In an age when many poets and novelists feel half-guilty and embarrassed about having to base themselves in university teaching jobs, Oates is a notable exception: a devouring reader, a dedicated teacher, a passionately committed intellectual unembarrassed by the debt she admits owing to writers and literary and philosophical traditions of the past. The really amazing thing about Oates and her writing is that *any* one person, little-girlish or big-boyish, cloistered or worldly, should have produced such work: not only unflinching in its treatment of obsessive love and violence but informed at all times by a comprehensive intelligence and visionary power that, after a quarter-century and some forty books of fiction, poems, plays, and literary criticism (not to mention hundreds of uncollected pieces), have never even briefly shown any sign of flagging.

Joyce Carol Oates was born in 1938 in the old Erie Canal town of Lockport, New York, a little north of Buffalo and east of Niagara Falls—a rural setting recognizable in several of her books. Oates has described her parents, Frederic and Caroline Oates, as inherently gifted people who were forced to leave school in childhood by the grim circumstances of the Depression. She grew up on the farm of her mother's parents. (Her rural, Catholic background, along with the bizarre subject matter and characters of certain of her novels and stories, has sometimes prompted comparisons of Oates with Flannery O'Connor, as exponents of, respectively, the "northern grotesque" and "southern grotesque.") After attending a one-room grade school, a junior high in Lockport, and a high school near Buffalo, she entered Syracuse University on scholarships—becoming the first college-educated member of her family. A star student of English and philosophy at Syracuse who would become the class of 1960 valedictorian, she did a considerable amount of creative writing there, regularly turning in stories to her teachers but also, once a semester or so, casually submitting a book-length manuscript. Oates has claimed to belong to a certain tradi-

tion of peasants-turned-thinkers: "Part of us is very intellectual, wanting to read all the books in the library—or even wanting to *write* all the books in the library. Then there's the other side of us, which is sheer silence, inarticulate—the silence of nature, of the sky, of pure being." In fact, the "peasant" side of Oates's imagination comes out in a less Wordsworthian vein, being best represented in her portraits of, say, tough and brassy middle-aged floozies, poignantly vulgar adolescents, and macho, shotgun-toting northern rednecks (as, for example, in her novels *Childwold,* 1976; *Son of the Morning,* 1978; and *Marya: A Life,* 1986). Oates is as comfortable with these types of characters as she is with sophisticated high-powered lawyers (*Do With Me What You Will,* 1973), medical doctors (*Wonderland,* 1971), neurotically introverted intellectuals (*The Assassins,* 1975; *Childwold*), and college professors (*The Hungry Ghosts,* 1974; *Unholy Loves,* 1979; *Marya: A Life*).

In 1960, Oates entered the graduate program in English at the University of Wisconsin, receiving her M.A. in 1961. There she met another graduate student, Raymond Smith, whom she married after a three-week courtship that Oates described as "very romantic." During the next year, while doing further graduate study in Texas at Rice University, she happened upon one of her own stories in the prestigious Martha Foley annual *Best American Short Stories* and decided suddenly to make creative writing her career. In 1962 she and her husband moved to Detroit (another favorite setting of her fiction, most notably the award-winning *them,* 1969, and *Do with Me What You Will*); he taught at Wayne State University and she at the University of Detroit. In 1966, they moved across the river to Canada, where they began teaching at the University of Windsor, Ontario. In 1978 Oates was appointed Writer-in-Residence at Princeton University.

Although "sex and violence"—the cynics' short-cuts to success in the entertainment industries—are rightfully recognized as hallmarks of Oates's writing, this reputation can be misleading. It is true that many of her novels and stories depict violence of the most horrifying and bizarre kind, and also true that many of her many love stories are powerfully erotic (the novel *them* includes one of the most remarkable sustained erotic episodes in recent fiction), but no intelligent reader of Oates could accuse her of gratuitous sensationalism or "sexploitation." On the contrary: as she writes in the Preface to her book on visionary literature, *New Heaven, New Earth,* 1974, "It is my belief that the serious artist insists on the sanctity of the world. . . . It may be that his role, his function, is to articulate the very worst, to force up into consciousness the most perverse and terrifying possibilities of the epoch, so that they can be dealt with and not simply feared; such artists are often denounced as vicious and disgusting when in fact they are . . . in the service of their epoch, attempting to locate images adequate to the unshaped, unconscious horrors they sense." She faces up to these leading motifs of the post-1960 world as she faces up to all aspects of contemporary culture, "high" and "low," as elements of an apocalyptic age that, she has sometimes suggested, may be on the verge of a transforming renewal.

The singling-out of sex and violence as characteristic of Oates is also misleading because, although she renders these things more powerfully than almost anyone else writing today, the true hallmark of her work is its comprehensiveness, variety, and versatility. It is characteristic of most un-

stintingly prolific writers that they work in a single vein for several books at a time—sometimes, indeed, for their entire careers. Nothing of the sort is true of Oates. At a time when she was barely into her fifties, she had written twenty-one novels and twelve volumes of short stories, and almost every one of these books attempts something fundamentally new, in subject or form. A master of documentary realism, as in *them,* which culminates with the Detroit riots of the late 1960's, Oates has also tried her hand at serious adaption of that fluffiest of genres, the gothic romance (for example, in the multigeneration saga *Bellefleur,* 1980, and *A Bloodsmoor Romance,* 1982). *Angel of Light,* 1981, is a retelling of the Orestes-Electra revenge story in the setting of the Washington politics-and-cocktails set. *Son of the Morning* relates, unironically and from the viewpoint of the protagonist, both the mundane and the mystical experiences of a spiritually obsessed evangelical preacher. *Unholy Loves* is a rarity: a serious, only faintly satirical novel about the academic profession. (Oates too can be satirical on the subject, however, as in the story-collection *The Hungry Ghosts.*) She can write with equally convincing authority about rural, urban, and suburban life, about the filthy rich and the grubby poor. At a time when male and female authors have become self-conscious about depicting the opposite sex or claiming to understand it, Oates has no qualms about attempting ambitiously conceived male characters, who, in fact, are as center-staged and fully realized as her women and girls. Some of Oates's works turn on fairly erudite issues of philosophy, theology, history, and esthetics; at the same time, she is capable of fully stocking a roadhouse juke box, the junk-foods section of a convenience grocery story, or the cosmetics counter at Woolworth's. She appears fairly frequently at scholarly symposia and has published important literary criticism on such writers as Franz Kafka, D. H. Lawrence (with whom she has a special affinity), and Sylvia Plath; she has also written a cover story on the program "Hill Street Blues" for *TV Guide.*

This comprehensiveness is more than the sign of an unusually wide-ranging mind: it is part of a program of inclusiveness Oates would seem to have assigned herself. She once remarked, "I have a laughably Balzacian ambition to get the whole world into a book." This statement is related to her discomfort with what she has called "the myth of the isolated artist" maintaining integrity in painful separation from the surrounding human and natural world. Oates believes that such egocentrism, inherited by the modern world from the Renaissance by way of the Romantic tradition, is the source of much great tragic literature but is perhaps in its death throes. The dualism implicit in the myth, as Joanne V. Creighton points out in a good book discussing these issues in Oates, can lead either to a lofty cerebralism, or to a deep withdrawal into a lonely subjective consciousness, or to a contrary rejection of mind and an implicit worship of the supposedly subhuman or nonhuman. Oates has sometimes suggested, with a radical optimism, that the spiritual dislocations of our time, the disorientations of personality and individual identity that are so prominent a part of the psychopathology of our age (and, one might add, so prominent in her own fiction) are preludes to a better new age in which human beings will no longer suffer from wasteful divisions within the psyche and separations in the seamless fabric of reality.

The omnivorous, inclusive quality of Oates's writing is related to her

rejection of such mutually exclusive dualisms. This rejection also helps explain what to many readers is the most unsettling thing about her fiction: its raw, unguided exposedness, the absence in it of explicit or implicit value-judgments about the characters or events she narrates. Exactly because Oates takes us so intimately into the minds of her characters, a fair number of whom are criminal or sinister or just plain unlikable, and exactly because the actions are so traumatic or controversial or incendiary, we reflexively look to the author for expressions of sympathy, or antipathy, or outrage, or approval. But we get no such judgments from Oates's narrative voice, except, of course, when the narrator is one of the characters. (This is the more notable in light of the passionate and polemical stands that Oates can take in her writing about other authors and the issues they raise.) Someone once remarked, half-admiringly and half-bemusedly, that you would not know from reading Oates's books whether the author was young or old, male or female, liberal or conservative. Her works are prime examples of literature that patently depends on a cooperative effort by the reader. This does not mean, however, that the reader is called on merely, or even primarily, to render value judgments. It may be that his or her first responsibility is more vital and elemental: to "articulate" and "force up into consciousness," to see rather than (at least immediately) to judge components of reality, to confront things fully before docketing them.

A good many readers believe that Joyce Carol Oates is at her best in her short stories. *The Wheel of Love*, when it appeared in 1970, was hailed by some reviewers as one of the best collections of short stories ever published in the United States. *Marriages and Infidelities*, which appeared two years later and included the story "Did You Ever Slip on Red Blood?", is of the same high order. Oates explained that the title of the collection was meant both literally and metaphorically, so as to include, besides actual marriages and adulteries, other kinds of commitment and betrayal. Both the literal and figurative senses apply to "Did You Ever Slip on Red Blood?", where various kinds of trust and suspicion are explored, as well as the complex relationship between violence and sex. One of many powerful evocations by Oates of the atmosphere and issues of the Vietnam era, the story also illustrates her peculiar combination of intimate, close-up revelation and authorial dispassionateness on emotionally loaded issues—a combination focused (almost literally) in the image of the telescopic rifle-sight and the image seen through it. The story addresses, among other themes, the ways in which identity and reality are defined in an era of trauma and mass technological culture: Severin sees himself, prospectively, on a movie or television screen at the moment when Oberon is seeing him, actually, through his rifle scope, while Marian will assert her own unique viewpoint on the harrowing event. As is often true in Oates's works, ideas are embodied in a peculiarly physical way—the idea, for example, of being "red-blooded." Above all, the story explores the Oatesian theme of the complex ways in which human personalities are dislocated and otherwise altered in the process of attempting, like authors, "to locate images adequate to the unshaped, unconscious horrors they sense."

FURTHER READING (*prepared by B. W.*): Since Joyce Carol Oates has been publishing a couple or so books every year, one good way to keep up with her, and opinion

about her, is simply to scan recent issues of journals that review books. Some good insights into Oates's mind and values, especially in light of her authorial self-efface-ment in her fiction, can be gleaned from her own literary criticism, especially *The Edge of Impossibility: Tragic Forms in Literature*, 1972; and *New Heaven, New Earth: The Visionary Experience in Literature*, 1974. Also illuminating is Oates's article "The Myth of the Isolated Artist" in *Psychology Today*, May 1973, pp. 74–75. For Oates's early life and background, and some of her early opinions about her craft, see Walter Clemons, "Joyce Carol Oates: Love and Violence," *Newsweek*, December 11, 1972, pp. 72–77. Other useful interviews with Oates are reported in Joe David Bellamy, "The Dark Lady of American Letters: An Interview with Joyce Carol Oates," *Atlantic*, Feb. 1972, pp. 63–67; and "Transformations of Self: An Interview with Joyce Carol Oates," *Ohio Review* 15 (1973), 51–53. See also *Conversations with Joyce Carol Oates*, 1989. The first chapter, "The Myth of the Isolated Artist," of Joanne V. Creighton's *Joyce Carol Oates*, 1979, is an excellent general introduction, discussing succinctly Oates's world-view and its relation to her art; readers who go on to read other works by Oates will find the rest of the book also lucid and penetrating. Other good general introductions for new readers of Oates appear in the opening chapters of book-length studies of her, including Mary Kathryn Grant's *The Tragic Vision of Joyce Carol Oates*, 1978, a book that elucidates Oates's attempt to foreshadow a new kind of consciousness; G. F. Waller's *Dreaming America: Obsession and Transcendence in the Fiction of Joyce Carol Oates*, 1979; and Ellen G. Friedman, *Joyce Carol Oates*, 1980. The Introduction by the editor, Linda W. Wagner, to *Critical Essays on Joyce Carol Oates*, 1979, is especially helpful on Oates's reputation, as are the reviews reprinted in the early part of this book; the latter part consists of more substantial critical essays. Harold Bloom has edited a volume on Oates, 1986, in the Modern Critical Views series. A thorough guide to criticism is Francine Lercangée's *Joyce Carol Oates: An Annotated Bibliography*, with a preface and annotations by Bruce Michelson, 1986.

DID YOU EVER SLIP ON RED BLOOD?

> *Did you?* she asked him repeatedly, angrily. *Did you ever? I mean did you ever slip on red blood yourself, do you know what it's like?*

She wept and brushed her hair back from her face, her eyes shut so that he could stare at her, starkly, closely, so that she hid nothing from him. Her nudeness made her radiant in the dim, coarse light of a winter afternoon. He felt how her nudeness was in her face, behind her eyes, in the pressure of her angry eyelids against her eyes. Everything about her was hard, smooth, stark, without deception.

"Nobody knows what we know," he said.

She said nothing. Her eyes were still closed.

The sheet had fallen away from her and she was shadowy in the dim light of this room he had rented for them. It did not look out onto the sky but across a terrible precipice to another building. The blinds were always closed; there was nothing to see. Here he had to see her with his hands, groping anxiously at her body with his hands. He could not believe in her except when they were together like this. She slipped from his mind, slipped out of focus. When they were together in this room she was brought up close to him, as if centered in the telescopic sight of a rifle.

They met like this for the first time in December. That was six weeks after the day they first had seen each other, at La Guardia Airport, and about nine months after the trial had ended out in Milwaukee—a trial Marian knew little about, involving four young men in their twenties indicted for conspiracy to advocate resistance to induction into the United States Army. Of the four young men only one was well known: the folk singer Jacob Appleman, who was sentenced to three years in jail. Two others were given similar sentences. The youngest of the defendants, Robert Severin, who was twenty-three at the time of the trial and also at the time of his death, had been acquitted. No one knew why.

Why was Severin acquitted? people asked. *Why Severin and no one else?*

Quick, weasellike, nervous, with something melancholic in his expression and in the thin mustache he had refused to shave off for the trial; with a habit of raising his hand to his mouth when he spoke, as if he distrusted his own words or was ashamed of them. "I'm not going to shave it off. I'm not going to misrepresent myself. I don't lie," he told his lawyer. He wouldn't remove the mustache and he wouldn't dress properly and he wouldn't meet anyone's eye, a lifelong habit of his, not even the eyes of his codefendants or of his lawyer, whom his father had retained for him. Severin was short, slender, dark, with a boyish frame and a shallow chest. As he sat, he twisted his body in small, uncoordinated movements, without seeming to know what he was doing. During the trial he had squirmed in his seat, his heart accelerating at strange times—especially during long dull periods in which nothing seemed to be happening. Severin feared that something was really happening at these times, but that no one knew. No one could guess. His heart had gradually increased its beat until it was pounding like mad during one forty-five minute period when an FBI agent, a stranger, talked about the size and colors and the texture of the paper and the type of print involved in a pamphlet written by the defendants and passed out to several thousand young men in Milwaukee at an antiwar meeting. Minutes and minutes passed as words were pronounced carefully by that man, that stranger, a courteous and handsome American in his thirties who spoke without any hatred or emphasis. . . . Listening to these simple, incredible words, Severin was afraid he would begin to scream.

But he never screamed so that anyone could hear.

The trial ended on the morning of March 6, after the jury returned its verdict. Severin walked out. He did not say good-by to his lawyer, or to his parents, who had spent the four weeks of the trial at a hotel in Milwaukee, or to the other defendants. He disappeared. He willed himself into disappearing. In his head for many days there had been a vision of himself disappearing, a fading image on a screen, a slow fade-out at the conclusion of a movie.

His mind flashed its thoughts like pictures on a screen, and one of the thoughts was Robert Severin. Always alone. Walking somewhere quickly, alone. Since his boyhood he had imagined himself as a character in a film, a figure pacing across a screen, blown up, enlarged, exaggerated. He could be gigantic sometimes. He knew this even if other people did not. At the age of fifteen he had reached his full growth: five feet seven inches. As if to show that he did not mind being this short, he often stood with his

weight balanced on one leg, the other leg bent indifferently. He did not walk with his shoulders back, he did not "observe" good posture. This was one of the things that annoyed his lawyer. "It might be better not to slouch in court," his lawyer said gently. His name was Morton Fisher and he was from New York, not Wisconsin, like the other attorneys; but still Severin did not trust him. He was a lawyer Severin's father had insisted upon. At first Severin had been eager to talk to Fisher, to explain his life, but it turned out that Fisher was not really interested in his life. "We have to concentrate on what is relevant to your case," Fisher kept saying. Finally Severin understood, with a shock, that this man did not like him. He was hurt. And then he was bewildered, for why shouldn't this man like him? Why shouldn't everyone like him? He wanted only to do good and to help others to do good. In the end, Severin hardly spoke to Fisher. He sat with his shoulders slumped, in a green-gray tweed suit with a vest, which he had bought especially for this trial. It was much too large for him, ill-cut, a parody of a suit. He had told the salesman in the discount department store that he wanted a baggy, old man's suit, "a joke of a suit," a proper outfit in which he might be tried by his government, which was displeased with him.

"Do you think that's funny, that suit?" his father asked him.

"Everything is funny," Severin said.

"Is that what you believe?"

"No. I believe that nothing is funny," Severin said in the same tone. "But we have to make certain pretenses."

Why was Severin acquitted and no one else? He could hear everyone ask this question. Making his way up the aisle of the courtroom, out where people stood around in the corridor, ducking when someone seemed to be swinging at him—it turned out to be a student waving a placard—his face darkening, heating; yet he had never screamed. Not out loud. He was free, freed. Time to disappear. *Robert Severin disappearing into the sky.*

When he shut his eyes he could see quite precisely a dark shape drawing into itself, withering, retreating into something that glowed fiercely, like the sun. Then it disappeared. That was peace, that disappearing, that nullity. He wouldn't even have to argue or explain himself. He would have no need for words.

It wasn't until several weeks later that the three others received their sentences; Severin read about it in a newspaper. By then he was in Montreal, where he knew no one. He stared at the photograph of Appleman—Appleman with his bushy hair and glum, sardonic expression and his career "just beginning to catch on," as people said—and Severin heard the voice in his head cry, *I don't know why Severin was acquitted, I don't know why Severin was acquitted, I don't know.* With these words he might have wanted to dissociate himself from Severin.

An incantation: *I don't know why.*

A litany: *I don't know why.*

And he did not know why. He did not understand. His brain replayed for him those hours of the trial, the testimony of FBI agents and the testimony of witnesses and the level, reasoned arguing of the defense lawyers, all of whom had the dark-rimmed, glowing eyes of men drowning for a good cause, and the occasional snorts and interruptions of the judge, whose terrible eyes Severin had never quite seen. He knew that he was

guilty, yet he had been found not guilty. He was as guilty as the others; they were as innocent as he. Yet it had not turned out that way.

He had tried to explain some of this to Marian Vernon, who had seemed to understand. "There was no difference between any of us," he told her. His voice had rattled, accelerating. He had not talked for many weeks and now he could not stop. She had nodded, yes, yes, she understood or seemed to understand, staring in prim panic into his face, their faces level, like brother and sister. "That was how I figured out they had me marked for something special," he told her angrily. "That's why I have to get out of the country. I don't have much time left. I'm going to explode if I don't get out." *Yes, yes,* she had said dumbly, but she had not really understood. Weeks and months after his death she went around saying she didn't understand, she didn't understand what he had wanted, why he had done it, why, why had it happened? "Jesus, if I could relive that hour," she said. She and Oberon talked about it all the time, talking about "it" as they embraced, closing their eyes upon a fast shocked image of Robert Severin's face. He was a stranger and yet they were close to him, intimate, knowing. He was always with them. His enlarged face followed them everywhere and excited them almost beyond endurance.

Sometimes she hated Oberon; her love shriveled into something bitter and white-hot and she hated him, she snapped at him, *You don't know what it's like to remember such a thing—did you ever slip on red blood yourself? You don't know what I know!*

And he would take her in his arms to quiet her.

Marian never had time for newspapers, never watched television, picked up important news and catastrophes from other people. Of course she had known nothing about the Milwaukee trial; the name Jacob Appleman was familiar to her, but she had never heard any of his records. She was a young woman of twenty-two, a stewardess with Pan American Airways. She had graduated with a Bachelor of Arts degree from the University of Oklahoma, which qualified her for teaching in the elementary schools of that state, but she had never really planned on teaching. The company of children, other teachers, the confinement of a room and a single building—these things frightened her. She wanted to live.

Her hair was a dark, wavy red, worn to her shoulders. Her face was lightly freckled, very healthy; her posture reflected health and enthusiasm; she had always been a happy child, a happy girl, arguing philosophically to herself that life was a wonderful adventure and that it should be faced with a constant smile. To a magazine reporter who had interviewed her in November she had confided, "That was how I got through that hour without cracking. I told myself that life is a wonderful adventure. I told myself that there is always a good, unexpected side to things, another arrangement we don't know about immediately."

"And did that turn out to be true?" the reporter asked.

She paused. She lowered her eyes, thinking of Oberon. She said finally, "I can't tell you about that."

Oberon had known about the trial, which was always referred to as the "Appleman Case," though three other men had been indicted. Oberon, who was interested in folk music, had followed Appleman's career since his

first record, in 1965, and he had been very disappointed at Appleman's political activities—the organization of a series of antiwar demonstrations in Chicago and Milwaukee. In his imagination he had even written Jacob Appleman a letter of warning. "My name is David Oberon and I am a stranger to you, yet believe me when I say that I wish you well. Why are you trying to destroy yourself? Why are you trying to corrupt hundreds of young Americans? Our country is engaged in a certain action in Southeast Asia and it is everyone's duty to support his country. . . ." But he did not dare type the letter. This was in the fall of 1969; Appleman had not been arrested yet, but Oberon knew the government was preparing a case against him. His letter might be confiscated. Even if he sent it anonymously, it might be confiscated and traced back to him.

Oberon had followed the case through the newspapers. He knew the names and a little of the facts concerning the other defendants, so the name Robert Severin was immediately familiar to him. Severin had been the only person acquitted and people had wondered about that. Oberon himself had not wondered, believing the jury had wanted to free someone, just to declare to the FBI and the Department of Justice that they could free a defendant who had probably been guilty of committing a crime against the United States government. It was a harmless act. He had heard, anyway, that Severin, the youngest of the four, had been indicted so that he could be acquitted—the government had had no interest in him, really.

He explained this to Marian, who was rosy, sunny, cheerful by nature, a young American woman with a personality simple as slides shown on a screen, one after another, and yet whose nature changed even as Oberon spoke to her, as if he were teasing her with his words about Severin, his superior knowledge of Severin, drawing her out of herself in a maddening way. "I don't know what you're doing to me," she laughed. "You're making me drunk. I feel drunk. Don't stop talking."

"What else do you want to know?" he asked her.

She hesitated. "What it was like."

"What it was like . . . ?"

"You know. What it felt like. To you. When it happened."

He had fallen helplessly in love with her.

He was fourteen years older than Marian Vernon, a tall, well-built man with brown hair, an amiable anonymous face, with something courteous and predictable in his smile. He was much taller than Robert Severin. If he had the occasion to stand beside him, he would have towered over him—poor Severin, with his girlish weasellike body, his narrow shoulders! If he had had the occasion to fight with him, he could have picked him up and thrown him down, knocking him senseless. Very deftly and courteously he could have pinned Severin's shoulders to the ground, holding him there safely until he could be arrested.

Oberon sometimes thought of that. He thought, while he lay with Marian, of holding Severin's squirming body down against the pavement. Once he told her about it. "Like this, and like this . . . like this . . . I would have held him down . . ." he whispered. They had lain together face to face, solemn, grieving, and then one of them had begun to laugh. Another time he hadn't told her what he was thinking of, but he sensed that she too

was thinking of Severin, always of Severin. "I love you, I love *you*," she had sobbed, as if arguing.

Seen up close like this, Marian was a stark, beautiful woman. Drained of superficial energy, the friendly charity of her kind of woman, which Oberon had always detested, she was hollow, hungry, almost unmanageable. Her love for him obviously frightened her. It was so violent, so intense, he almost sympathized with her dread of it. *What must a woman feel, to be convulsed like that, to suffer like that,* he thought. No one knew Marian Vernon except him. When she appeared in that Pan American Airways uniform— when she smiled her mechanical little smile—it was a joke, a horror! Only Oberon knew her.

She brushed her hair back from her damp face, impatiently. A strand of her hair stung his eye. He tried to listen to what she was saying: something about his wife. "What does she know? I saw her that evening. Her. She doesn't know. What do ordinary people know?"

"She can sense something. . . ."

"No. She can't. She would have to have been there, where I was. In my place. And she wasn't there, no one else was there except me. . . . You don't love her. Why do you stay with her?"

They stared at each other. He was perspiring, agitated, always he must stare at her in order to locate himself—his love for this woman, whom he hardly knew, whom he did not really like. There was something coarse about her boldness with him, her near-hysteria. She was younger than his wife, more beautiful than his wife, and he was sick with love for her and yet he did not want to think about divorce, remarriage, the routine intensity of married life.

"Do you love her?" Marian asked.

"No. It's another emotion."

"Another emotion, yes. It's ordinary. I don't want to hear about it. Ordinary people, ordinary ugly people . . . I don't want to hear about them."

As soon as he left her she began to slip out of focus. She began to fade back into that neat smiling little stewardess with the uniform, the short skirt, and tight-fitting, buttoned little jacket, with the hat perched cockily on her head. It frightened him, that he might lose her. That he might forget her. And yet he could not locate in his memory of her the passion he always felt in her presence. A kind of energy dominated them, gave them life; it did not belong to either of them.

Sometimes he went to stare at himself in a mirror, at home or anywhere, in a public rest room, but he saw only his public, unpersonal face, which was like Marian's uniform. It was like Marian's uniform. That face took him anywhere, flown in by helicopter to the airport, with his .308 Norma Magnum rifle. *What did it feel like?* Marian asked him, the first night they were together. *Did it have a kick? I felt the kick myself. I felt it. I felt you.* There was something anonymous and symmetrical about Oberon's face. As a younger man he had been annoyed when people were always coming up to him and calling him by the names of strangers—now it no longer bothered him. He could have grown a mustache, like Severin. But he never did. He thought of himself as belonging to a crowd, a crowd of American men as they might be imagined, or collected for a special photograph: not a real crowd of unruly and ugly people, but an ideal crowd of "average" American men,

fairly good-looking, of a certain height, in good health. Therefore he was six feet two inches tall, with short, wavy brown hair, a face that was almost handsome, with a strong clean nose and chin. His brown eyes looked ordinary and unalarming, but they were, in fact, extraordinary. His vision was perfect. He had always been proud of his eyesight. Eyes like muscles, tensing, erect, precise, fixing themselves on that stranger's face, adjusting themselves to the face, getting to know it closely, intimately. . . . The face had been framed by jumbled, spiky hair; it had been partly hidden by sunglasses; its skin was an eerie olive, pale and waxen and yet greasy, sagging with fatigue. The mustache had aged it.

Severin had bought the sunglasses in a drugstore north of Portland, Maine. It had rained all day and yet the sky glowed; it reminded him of the sky in Milwaukee, that soulless glowering that had pressed upon him for so many months. Swollen gray sky and lake, remote, bulbous, inescapable. . . . He wanted to break through to a place where the sun shone. He bought the sunglasses for $1.98 and they looked like aviators' glasses, with large lenses and wire frames. They were made of some synthetic material, not glass, a kind of plastic that did not break easily or even crack; they were thrown a dozen yards from his body, and yet they did not break.

Now for the approach: how to approach New York? He had family there, parents. He feared his father and his father's face. It wasn't enough, loving them and then not loving them; somehow they were mixed up with his childhood and the nation itself. Awake, unable to sleep, he began having little split-second dreams out on the highway—going crazy, eh, Severin?—and one of his visions was his father stretched out flat, the face stretched out like a big welcome mat, the bumpy hilly terrain of the United States, all someone's face. That could be. Wasn't there a movie about someone crawling across the faces at Mt. Rushmore? Or had Severin imagined that movie? Or was he an insect himself, crawling across the face of his father, not able to put the various parts of the face together into a whole?

His night dreams did not work. Did not function properly. That was because he couldn't sleep any more at night—why bother getting a motel room if he couldn't use the bed?—but even when he had been sleeping normally his dreams had not worked. How do dreams *work?* What is their *function?* "My dreams all dissolve and disappear," he told his lawyer, Mr. Fisher. He had no one else to talk to; by then he had quarreled with Appleman and the others, and their attorneys had quarreled with one another; it was not good. The government had already won. A story in *Look* magazine implied that Appleman was a saint, but Severin knew better than that, everyone knew better than that, it was just journalistic crap and yet you couldn't make your way through it: what would turn out to be true, what would turn out to be lies? "Jesus, I can't get myself straight; when I try to think about something it all dissolves. Even my dreams. . . . My dreams just disappear," he tried to explain to Fisher, who had pretended to be interested. "I don't dream like other people, only pieces of dreams like jigsaw puzzles. . . ."

After the verdict, Severin had walked away without saying good-by.

Not just his dreams but his bowels didn't work. Panic. Pain. Pain like fire. Sitting anxiously in the courtroom, fidgeting in his seat, he heard little

of the testimony and fixed his gaze upon sterile, empty space, trying not to show the pain he felt. Small rocks seemed to be passing through his intestines. Yet he had never screamed out loud. . . . *And now Severin will eradicate himself,* he thought as he walked out of the courtroom and out of the courthouse. *Severin walking fast, a comic figure. Almost running.* During those four winter weeks his weight had dropped from 145 to 128. His skin had grown so sensitive that he could not bear to be touched, and he could feel people breathing on him, he could feel the subtle but very abrasive touch of breath, air, against his skin. Appleman had a habit of gripping his arm, his elbow, as if to make sure Severin wouldn't get away. He hated Appleman's closeness, hated the feel of his breath. If he could get a table between them, good. He couldn't make sense of Appleman's nervous strategies, and after a while he stopped listening.

Anyway they were all guilty. That was one thing they had agreed upon.

So he sat through the weeks of the trial, sensing how words flowed about him, submerging him, threatening to suffocate him, and yet never quite touching him. How they talked, these adults . . . always talking, talking. . . . His lawyer wouldn't let him testify. None of the defendants was going to testify. All right, then, time would pass and nothing would matter, it was really completed; they were guilty and their punishment was beginning now, right now. That was why his bowels were turning to gas, poisonous rotting gas. That was why he couldn't sleep. In court, already a prisoner at the front of the courtroom, he stared at a certain space in the room, not a person or an object but a space, an invisible point in the air, and tried to hypnotize himself into calmness, silence, into nothing. Otherwise he might explode.

Grappling with the stewardess, the redhead, he had felt the danger of his body colliding with hers: a danger for her, not for himself.

"Don't make me kill you," he begged her.

She was his height, as full in the body as he, her face bleached out beneath her make-up.

As soon as the plane left the runway he stood, stood out in the aisle, and took the rolled-up towel out of his coat. She came toward him, a woman perfectly balanced as in a dream, while around her faces turned and chins creased and outside the windows the jumbled landscape of small houses fell backward and down, in silence. "Don't make me explode us all," he begged.

He had found the flare on a highway outside Montreal; he had laughed to see it so innocently left behind—it looked like a stick of dynamite! Walking in the perpetual drizzle, he had picked it up and hidden it in his jacket; you never knew when you might need dynamite, also you never knew when you might need a knife. He had bought a knife in a sporting goods store in a small town somewhere. He couldn't remember where, but probably someone had been watching him and knew. In grade school and high school he had never played with knives—you didn't "play with" knives in his family—but other boys had had knives and Severin had envied them. Now he had his own knife. And a flare that looked like dynamite. Maybe it *was* dynamite. It had a fuse that could be lit. The fuse was damp, but perhaps it could still be lit.

Outside Boston he took a motel room for a night, but he couldn't sleep. A waste of six dollars. He found a newspaper and looked up the weather

report: always raining. From Montreal down to New York: rain. He couldn't remember where he was exactly, but it was always raining, a cold steady drizzle, and yet the sky was light. The weather seemed to him very important. He had stopped thinking about everything in his past, and now he thought about the weather instead. There was a weather map of the United States and also a very helpful list of temperatures in cities around the world. He looked through the list several times and discovered that Algiers was missing. Why was it missing? The FBI had reasons for everything.

In Montreal he had been spied on; he knew the feeling and didn't question it. But he had not cared. He walked in the street, up and down the hilly streets, openly. It was a foreign country—Canada—and he was free here. In fact, he was free anywhere. Even in Milwaukee. He sent himself back to Milwaukee, that raw, freezing, ugly city, to the courtroom, to see if Robert Severin was still sitting there; yes, there he was, the size of a boy, pretending to listen while words flooded his head. Yes, he was guilty. Didn't he love his parents? Did he want to destroy his mother? Oh yes. No. Did he want to destroy himself? The first step was dropping out of law school—his father had pointed that out to him. The first step toward self-destruction. And this Appleman, who was Appleman? "Who is this Appleman, that you should follow him blindly?" his father demanded. The irony was that Appleman envied Severin and the others because they had gone to college while he, Appleman, so wealthy and so nervous, had barely managed to graduate from high school; but Severin didn't bother to tell his father that. Was he guilty of certain lies? Of avoiding certain statements? Guilty of a small unmanly body? The young man he had shared an apartment with near Columbia, a twenty-eight-year-old veteran of the Vietnam war and, like Severin, a law student, had flown out to Milwaukee to testify for him. *Very serious, very moral . . . a completely moral person. . . . We had little in common and we weren't friends, no, but I admired Bob for his honesty. . . .* Yet, when the courteous businesslike prosecutor had cross-examined him, he had faltered and said, *Yes, Bob is absolutely honest and he would never commit any crime, I mean any dishonest crime. . . .* Any dishonest crime! Severin himself had to laugh; by then he'd sat through one hundred hours of this crap and he knew what was what. Any dishonest crime! *It's a strange distinction for a young man entering the law,* the prosecutor had said gently, with a smile, as if a little embarrassed for the witness, *the division of crimes into honest and dishonest crimes. . . .*

Severin had stopped listening.

The jury spent ten hours discussing the case, and when they came back Severin stood for them, in honor of them, "at attention," in a parody of a young man in a green-gray tweed suit standing at attention in a courtroom, his face composed for a smirk and his bowels churning with flame and lava. Bastards! Bland faces and frank honest souls!

Mr. Foreman, how say you? Is Jacob Appleman, the defendant at the bar, guilty or not guilty?

Guilty.

Is John Harvey, the defendant at the bar, guilty or not guilty?

Guilty.

Is Russell Kurzon, the defendant at the bar, guilty or not guilty?

Guilty.

Is Robert Severin, the defendant at the bar, guilty or not guilty?
Not guilty.
Not guilty.

So he sent himself out of there, on a Greyhound bus up to Montreal. He was free. He had money. His father was always giving him money, for good nourishing food and for good hotel rooms. He tried to sleep on the bus but his skull seemed too large for his brain. His brain slipped wetly around inside the bone case, an unpleasant sensation. Were his thoughts dissolving, turning to poisonous intestinal vapors? They kept slipping, slithering, out of his grasp. He had to rely upon flashes of dreams in the daylight; that was where he got his best hunches. He telephoned home just once, collect, from a telephone booth that looked over and up to McGill University, buildings and grounds and university students so normal and handsome that he wanted to cry: his nose ran with envy and he could barely pay attention to his conversation with his father. . . . "Bob? Bob? Is that you, Bob? Are you all right, Bob?" his father had shouted across the distance. It was terrible to hear his voice. Severin changed his mind, he didn't want a father again, why hadn't he remembered what it was like? He hung up.

Anyway, the telephone was probably wiretapped.

"It is not necessary for the accused to have done anything," someone was explaining to the jury. It was the judge himself. He was the most adult of all the adults. "In a case like this, the prosecution has only to prove that they *agreed* to do something. The case rests entirely on intent and you must find the defendants guilty or not guilty according to their intent. . . ."

He intended now to blow up the country. He intended to fly up into the sun, to clean himself in the sun, to escape the rain of the East Coast. Why did it rain so often? And on clear days his head ached; he muttered in disgust, *Severin, you're going crazy.* Why else walk around with a fake stick of dynamite in your pocket, a kid's jackknife with three blades in your pocket? Oh it was a joke, like the green suit. People took him too seriously. Adults took him too seriously. Out in Milwaukee—maybe in the whole Midwest or the whole country—people thought the White House might be blown up just because Severin or someone with a mustache like his did not throw his shoulders back and blew his nose at the wrong time into a soiled Kleenex. The sunglasses helped his burning eyes but really they were part of the joke. You couldn't disguise yourself, of course. The FBI had cameras that x-rayed you antiseptically as you walked in the street. You couldn't hide from them; therefore, you joked with them in a mild and cavalier way.

"You don't joke with these people," Fisher had told him angrily, as if speaking to a child. "What do you think this is? A game?"

It turned out that all the defendants, when served with their indictments, had tried to joke nervously with the men who brought them. Tried to establish a quick jocular rapport with the low-level FBI men who questioned them, as if that would help. Wouldn't it help? A quick jocular alliance against the hierarchy, the Rulers. Wouldn't it help?

"No, you don't talk. You don't cooperate. You don't try to win their good favor. They are out to get you whether you can believe it or not. The government is out to get you. . . . Do you think that's a joke?"

It was so hard to believe, so hard to believe, that anyone wanted to hurt them, even the government that had dared to arrest them. The govern-

ment turned out to be men who looked like Severin's father and his lawyer: that is, good citizens, well dressed and polite. Of course, they hated the government and had accused the government of being fascistic, in their speeches, even in their televised speeches, but somehow it was hard to believe that these men, the FBI agents and their attorneys and the prosecutor, really wanted to hurt them. . . . Like most Americans, Severin believed he could make anyone like him if he tried. He had never been popular, in high school or college, but he had always cherished the belief that he could be popular if he worked at it.

The stewardess had smiled at him, her lipsticked lips baring her teeth in a slow numbed grimace, the two of them staring at each other levelly, the same height. He had felt like a brother to her. She was one of those pretty, sisterly girls so popular in high school, grinning hello to everyone in the halls, absolutely confident and shadowless. "I don't want to kill you," he had whispered. "Take me up front. Let me explain myself to the pilot. Let me explain and you can see how clear everything will be."

"Yes, I'll take you. Don't be upset," she said.

"I'm not upset. I'm not going to hurt you, or anyone, unless I have to. I'm very calm," Severin said.

Severin gripped her close. The pilot had a title: Captain. He was a man who resembled one of the other defense lawyers. Severin saw at once that this man was intelligent and would play no tricks on him: were the lives of fifty passengers worth any risk? No. It was logical. You read about it in the newspapers all the time. Yet something in the back of Severin's head told him, *What a joke this is, now, what a laugh! Are you really on this plane? Or still back in Montreal, dreaming a daylight dream?* "My destination is Algeria," Severin stated. "I am defecting. I am demanding diplomatic immunity."

But on the turnpike leaving Boston, he had walked slowly along for several hours before someone stopped. It was an FBI agent in an ordinary car. He joked with the man knowingly, delicately. That was the charm of it: you walked a kind of fence with them, teasing them. This man claimed to be a publisher's representative. Severin laughed and said, "Which publishers? Name one."

The man did give a familiar name. "I'm in the college department. Textbooks. Are you a college student?"

"Ha ha," Severin said. "Are you offering me a scholarship if I turn over all the evidence? I wouldn't mind going back to law school."

"I don't understand," the man said slowly.

"No, never mind. It's just a joke. I'm on my way out of the country, I'm just going to say good-by to my family."

"Where does your family live?"

Severin glanced at the man, sizing him up. A big man, like all of them. If it came to a fight, he'd have to use his elbows and feet to paralyze the bastard. He wouldn't want to use the knife; then it would be murder. Still, it would probably not come to a fight. They rarely touched you. Why should they?

"New York," Severin said. He felt helpless, telling the truth like this; but when they already knew the truth you had no choice but to say it.

He put on his sunglasses carefully, hooking them behind his ears. The

earpieces were made of wire and quite pliable. When Marian Vernon looked into his face for the first time—welcoming him frankly on board the plane—she did not see him. She did not remember seeing him. But after the take-off, when he stumbled to his feet and opened his oversized coat, she looked at him again and this time she saw him.

Out of his baggy green suit coat he drew a white towel, rolled up, and he unrolled it to show her a stick of dynamite. Mutely he raised it to her, his eyebrows arching. They walked together to the front of the plane. She felt his breath on the back of her neck, so close.

"I don't like violence. I don't like blood. I don't like knives and this is the first knife I ever bought," he told her earnestly. She glanced back to see that he had a knife in his hand. She went cold. *I went cold. The dynamite I couldn't believe in, it was so . . . so extreme. . . . But the knife was just the right size. . . . But he was very polite, very nice to me. . . . No. I wasn't afraid. I went cold, I was numb and like a robot, but I wasn't afraid. I would have been afraid to do what Mr. Oberon did. . . . that really took courage . . .*

"You don't resent the FBI risking your life then?" they asked her.

"Oh, no. No. I don't consider it that, that they risked my life. I mean, it was their job. It was Mr. Oberon's job. He was given orders. It was all done very carefully. I had faith in them. I prayed and I had faith in them. I wasn't afraid."

"How close did he stay to you?"

"Oh, very close. He held me from behind, my arm. His fingers were very tight around my arm, my upper arm, and he kept asking me if he was hurting me; he was very polite and didn't talk loud, he was sort of short, no taller than I was, and all along I could feel the knife in my back, like a fingernail, a man's fingernail. . . . He wanted to go to Algeria, he said. Something about the sun. He was tired of rain. The Captain told him, of course, this plane was headed for Cleveland and it wasn't a transatlantic plane and if he wanted that he would have to wait. . . ."

"And did he believe that?"

"Oh, yes, he believed that at once. He was very polite and apologetic about hurting me."

Why are you working with planes? Severin asked her. *This is no job for a woman. Planes explode in the sky all the time, disintegrate in the sky. . . .* She seemed to be listening to him intently. She nodded. He could see a droplet of perspiration on her forehead. She was a pretty young woman, like a sister, so pretty, so eager to please him, docile and not argumentative, as he had feared she might be. . . . *The sky is for men, it's dangerous. After this you should stay on the ground. Are you listening?*

Oh yes I'm listening, yes I'm listening. . . .

The other passengers had filed out. Severin stood with her just inside the door, at the top of the ramp, squinting out into the drizzle. Someone was speaking to him through a loudspeaker. But the loudspeaker did not work very well. "Where is that plane? That big plane? I'm waiting for it," he yelled out into the rain. He held the stewardess back against him, an embrace and yet not an embrace; it was an impersonal embrace. Minutes passed. He had the idea that an hour had passed and could not be retrieved. He saw a large jetliner being moved toward him, far away in the

rain, and then he wondered if he had seen correctly. Would they give him a pilot and a crew? All that expense, just for him?

"You might like Algeria yourself," he told the girl. "There, you could stay on the ground and forget about all this crap, this fooling around. You could stay there with me."

"You won't hurt me?"

"I don't want to hurt you."

"When will you let me go?"

"In Algeria."

They were calling to him: the plane is ready, the crew is ready. He saw the plane but it was some distance away.

"Closer, bring it closer! Don't you hear me?" he yelled.

The little knife, with one blade stuck out, pressed against the girl's back. Against the uniform. His face was hot from being so close to her hair. He breathed in and out, against the back of her neck. Her ear. He said, "I don't want to hurt you or kill you, I'm not in favor of violence or blood. . . . Tell them to bring that plane closer."

She cupped her hands to her mouth and tried to call to them, but she could not speak. He heard a sob from her. *I thought I would break down then, and that he would kill me, just slide the knife in me because he was disgusted. . . .* She sobbed, her shoulders shook; he relented and said, "All right, forget it, let's go. Let's go."

Stiffly he walked her down the ramp. She nearly slipped and he held her steady, his fingers tightening around her arm. She cried out with the surprise of it, the pain. He knew that people were watching him, from inside the hangars and from behind the steel fences; perhaps a camera crew was filming this. He imagined himself on film, on a television screen. An image of Robert Severin walking across a screen jerkily, streaks of rain on the camera lens. It would be so realistic. He could see his own figure, holding the stewardess tight against the front of him, walking her down the ramp carefully, stiffly, Robert Severin in his dirty, baggy suit wearing his aviator's sunglasses as if he were prepared for the sun of Algeria, his hair bunched and spiky from not having been washed for a month. *Robert Severin centered on a screen. Robert Severin centered in a telescopic sight.*

At the bottom of the ramp the girl slipped and stumbled two steps down, to the pavement. She turned as if to apologize to him and at that moment there was a shot. Severin jerked backward against the steps, away from her. Then another shot. His face exploded: she was looking up into his face when it exploded. It was as if something had been thrown against his face, an object stuffed with blood, and now the blood had burst out and was pouring from him. Did she hear him scream? Any sound at all? She caught the fullness of his weight as he fell, his body gone heavy, the blood gushing from him and onto her. She fell, she tried to get to her feet, screaming, but she slipped in his blood, she slipped to her knees and then pushed herself up, frantic to get away, to get away. . . .

I thought I was shot myself. I thought we were both shot.

Does this alter your plans?—your plans for a career?

Oh no. No.

You'll have something to tell your grandchildren, won't you?

Oh yes.
What do you think of the FBI man who did the shooting?
She studied the photographs in that evening's newspaper: a picture of herself, two microphones extended toward her, her face looking good enough, even her hair good enough; and a picture of the man at the steel wall, aiming his rifle. She stared. He had such dark hair, he held the gun so firmly, so certainly. . . . Other men stood below him, watching. They seemed such ordinary men. They watched him and he leaned over the wall, his back to them, aiming the rifle and peering through the scope, staring at her and Severin through the scope. . . . And yet neither she nor Severin had known about the rifle! She marveled at this, tracing with her forefinger her own face and then the outline of the FBI man's body and the rifle, aimed out of the picture, at that face of hers. Past her face. Over her shoulder and into Severin's face.

It was so confusing, so hard to think about. . . .

Powerfully, she felt the blow again: Severin slammed back from her, against the steps of the ramp. She had slipped on the wet steps. And then the shot, then the second shot. How she loved him! "Tell me what you felt," she said.

"I had the idea that the two of you could see me. Right back through the scope," he said.

"Did you? Did it seem as though I was watching you? What did I look like?"

"Very beautiful," he said.

"Was I beautiful? Was I? Even in the rain, even after that hour with him? Was I beautiful to you?"

"Yes, you were beautiful. . . . For fifteen minutes I was watching you, you and him. You. I had never seen a face like yours. . . ."

"Were you afraid?"

"No. I took my time. I knew how it would turn out. I had only to wait for the right moment in order to make it turn out that way. As soon as they flew me in, as soon as I got propped up on that wall, he was a dead man. But it took a while to kill him."

"Did you ever kill anyone before?"

"Never an American."

With his deer rifle he had shot the young man with the sunglasses, the first shot catching him squarely in the chest, the second shot squarely in the face. Excellent shots. For ten, fifteen minutes he had watched through the sight, hardly breathing, waiting patiently. He had been given his orders. Ah, that girl! That white, gasping face of hers!

The boy had bounced back. Blood had sprung out of his face like an exclamation.

One day Oberon sought her out, rang the doorbell to her apartment. He introduced himself. He heard her breathing inside the door, a few inches away. Silence. "You know who I am," he said. He was very excited; there was even an odor about him of intense excitement. The girl stood inside her door, which was latched with a safety lock, a chain, and he brought his smiling face to the crack in the door so that he could look at her. She was staring up at him.

"You know why I'm here," he said.

Alice Walker
(1944–)

In the title essay of her book *In Search of Our Mothers' Gardens*, Alice Walker has written of the gardens that her mother, a Georgia sharecropper, used to plant: "She planted ambitious gardens—and still does—with over fifty different varieties of plants that bloom profusely from early March until late November. Before she left home for the fields, she watered her flowers, chopped up the grass, and laid out new beds. When she returned from the fields she might divide clumps of bulbs, dig a cold pit, uproot and replant roses, or prune branches from her taller bushes or trees—until night came and it was too dark to see. Whatever she planted grew as if by magic, and her fame as a grower of flowers spread over three counties. Because of her creativity with her flowers, even my memories of poverty are seen through a screen of blooms—sunflowers, petunias, roses, dahlias, forsythia, spirea, delphiniums, verbena . . . and on and on." Elsewhere Walker has celebrated cooking and quilting as ways that impoverished women of color like her mother have expressed their otherwise thwarted creativity.

One does not have to read far in Alice Walker to realize that the humble arts of gardening, cooking, and quilting have served as powerful models for her own literary art. They link her metaphorically with earlier generations of anonymous, unsung female artists, even back to Africa: "And perhaps in Africa over two hundred years ago, there was just such a mother; perhaps she painted vivid and daring decorations in oranges and yellows and greens on the walls of her hut; perhaps she sang—in a voice like Roberta Flack's—*sweetly* over the compounds of her village; perhaps she wove the most stunning mats or told the most ingenious stories of all the village storytellers." But, more, they provide a loose formal model for her writing. Gardens, meals, and quilts do not have straightforwardly linear, narrative forms, but rather are organic, close to the simple patterns of everyday experience, expressing fairly directly the temperaments of those who create them. There could be worse descriptions of Walker's own writing.

Walker's search for her mothers' gardens is a search for the suppressed identity of black American women, the "mules of the world" (in Walker's phrase, quoting Zora Neale Hurston), doubly marginalized by racism and sexism. In her work, and in that of such other strong contemporary writers as Toni Morrison, Gwendolyn Brooks, Ntozake Shange, Toni Cade Bambara, and many others, the American black woman has found a tongue.

Walker was born in 1944 in Eatonton, Georgia, the eighth child of Willie Lee and Minnie Lou Grant Walker, sharecroppers. The story of how she escaped the material and spiritual poverty of rural Georgia is a curious one. When she was eight years old, one of her brothers accidentally shot her in the eye with a BB gun. She was blinded in that eye, and scar tissue covered the eye until the scar was removed in an operation when she was fourteen. She remembers that during this period, made an outsider by her disfigurement, she withdrew and became a close observer of relationships rather than an active participant. Ironically, too, her blindness qualified her for a

"rehabilitation scholarship" to Spelman College, America's oldest college for black women, in Atlanta. Spelman was a rather conservative institution, but while she was there (1961–63) Walker fell under the spell of the burgeoning civil rights movement. "Everyone was beautiful," she has written of this period, "because everyone was conquering fear by holding the hands of the person next to them." After two years at Spelman, Walker accepted a scholarship to finish her degree at Sarah Lawrence, the prestigious New York women's college. During the summer between her junior and senior year at Sarah Lawrence, Walker experienced a personal crisis that involved an accidental pregnancy, an abortion, and strong suicidal feelings. Out of this experience came her first book, a collection of poems called *Once*, which was published in 1968.

Following graduation from college in 1965, Walker worked in voter registration projects in Georgia and in the welfare department in New York City. In 1967, she married a white civil rights lawyer named Melvyn Rosenman Leventhal and moved to Mississippi with him. During the following seven years in the Deep South, Walker worked with Head Start programs and held appointments at Jackson State University and Tougaloo College. She also had a daughter, Rebecca Grant, and wrote her first novel, *The Third Life of Grange Copeland*, a rather brutal novel of three generations of a black sharecropping family which was published in 1970. *Revolutionary Petunias*, a second collection of poems, and *In Love and Trouble*, a collection of short stories, both appeared in 1973.

Walker and Leventhal moved back to New York in 1974, where Walker briefly worked for *Ms.* magazine. She published a second novel, *Meridian*, in 1976; it is the story of Meridian Hill, a young black woman involved in the civil rights movements and in a struggle for personal liberation. In the same year, Walker was divorced from Leventhal and moved to a farm outside San Francisco. Her third book of poems, *Good Night, Willie Lee, I'll See You in the Morning*, and an anthology of the work of Zora Neale Hurston, *I Love Myself When I'm Laughing . . . and Then Again When I Am Mean and Impressive*, both appeared in 1979. *You Can't Keep a Good Woman Down*, a second collection of stories, was published in 1981.

Walker won international fame in 1982 with the publication of *The Color Purple*, a novel in letters that tells the story of Celie, a young black woman in the south who is sexually abused by her stepfather and married off to an equally brutal husband. She gradually liberates herself with the aid of her sister Nettie and the strong, vital Shug Avery, a blues singer who has been Celie's husband's lover. The novel became a best-seller, won both the Pulitzer Prize and the American Book Award, and was made into a popular film by Steven Spielberg.

Since *The Color Purple*, Walker has remained prolific. *In Search of Our Mothers' Gardens*, a collection of essays, appeared in 1983; *Horses Make a Landscape Look More Beautiful*, a fourth collection of poems, in 1984; *Living by the Word*, another collection of essays, in 1988; and *The Temple of My Familiar*, a novel, in 1989. *The Temple of My Familiar*, which Walker has described as "a romance of the last 500,000 years," is centered around three contemporary marriages. But in the course of exploring them, it ranges back into the mythic past and out into visionary philosophy. It is perhaps less a novel in the ordinary sense than an encyclopedic philosophi-

cal allegory, and it was correspondingly received on publication with some puzzlement and disappointment from readers who had expected another *The Color Purple.*

The subtitle of *In Search of Our Mothers' Gardens* is "Womanist Prose," and much of Walker's quest for a black female identity has come to center around her concept of "womanism." The book begins with a parody of a dictionary entry giving four definitions of "womanist." The first is "A black feminist or feminist of color." This definition derives, Walker says, from the black folk expression of mothers to female children, " 'You acting womanish,' i.e., like a woman." So being a womanist is "Acting grown up. Being grown up . . . Responsible. In charge. *Serious.*" A second definition is "A woman who loves other women, sexually and/or nonsexually." But a womanist also "Sometimes loves individual men, sexually and/or nonsexually." A third definition says a womanist "Loves music. Loves dance. Loves the moon. *Loves* the Spirit. Loves love and food and round-ness. Loves struggle. *Loves* the Folk. Loves herself. *Regardless.*" The fourth definition is simple, "Womanist is to feminist as purple to lavender." The expression is humorous, but the content is quite serious. These are the materials for a black female identity: seriousness, self-acceptance, love, "purpleness," all qualities that characterize, not accidentally, Walker's own writing.

"To Hell with Dying" is from Walker's first short-story collection, *In Love and Trouble: Stories of Black Women.* The black woman is, of course, the narrator, and the story is a characteristic one for Walker of a journey over space and time, from a Massachusetts university to the rural south and from the present into a childhood past, spaces and times stitched together, quilt-like, by love.

FURTHER READING (*prepared by J. H.*): Critical response to Alice Walker has been quite voluminous for so comparatively young a writer, principally because of the various controversies provoked by *The Color Purple*: over her negative treatment of black men, her presumed "sentimentality" in her portrayal of black women, her treatment of lesbianism, and other such issues. Erma Davis Banks and Keith Byer-man, *Alice Walker: An Annotated Bibliography, 1968–1986*, 1989, is a reliable guide to all this commentary. One of the most thoughtful critics of Walker has been Barbara T. Christian. Her overview of Walker's career in the *Dictionary of Literary Biography* 33 is a good starting point. There are a number of good published interviews with Walker. One of the best appears in *Black Women Writers at Work*, ed. Claudia Tate, 1983. Barbara Christian places the narrator of "To Hell with Dying" in the context of Walker's other protagonists in "The Contrary Black Women of Alice Walker: A Study of Female Protagonists in *In Love and Trouble*," *Black Scholar*, 12 (1981).

TO HELL WITH DYING

"To hell with dying," my father would say. "These children want Mr. Sweet!"

Mr. Sweet was a diabetic and an alcoholic and a guitar player and lived down the road from us on a neglected cotton farm. My older brothers and

sisters got the most benefit from Mr. Sweet for when they were growing up he had quite a few years ahead of him and so was capable of being called back from the brink of death any number of times—whenever the voice of my father reached him as he lay expiring. "To hell with dying, man," my father would say, pushing the wife away from the bedside (in tears although she knew the death was not necessarily the last one unless Mr. Sweet really wanted it to be). "These children want Mr. Sweet!" And they did want him, for at a signal from Father they would come crowding around the bed and throw themselves on the covers, and whoever was the smallest at the time would kiss him all over his wrinkled brown face and begin to tickle him so that he would laugh all down in his stomach, and his moustache, which was long and sort of straggly, would shake like Spanish moss and was also that color.

Mr. Sweet had been ambitious as a boy, wanted to be a doctor or lawyer or sailor, only to find that black men fare better if they are not. Since he could become none of these things he turned to fishing as his only earnest career and playing the guitar as his only claim to doing anything extraordinarily well. His son, the only one that he and his wife, Miss Mary, had, was shiftless as the day is long and spent money as if he were trying to see the bottom of the mint, which Mr. Sweet would tell him was the clean brown palm of his hand. Miss Mary loved her "baby," however, and worked hard to get him the "li'l necessaries" of life, which turned out mostly to be women.

Mr. Sweet was a tall, thinnish man with thick kinky hair going dead white. He was dark brown, his eyes were very squinty and sort of bluish, and he chewed Brown Mule tobacco. He was constantly on the verge of being blind drunk, for he brewed his own liquor and was not in the least a stingy sort of man, and was always very melancholy and sad, though frequently when he was "feelin' good" he'd dance around the yard with us, usually keeling over just as my mother came to see what the commotion was.

Toward all of us children he was very kind, and had the grace to be shy with us, which is unusual in grown-ups. He had great respect for my mother for she never held his drunkenness against him and would let us play with him even when he was about to fall in the fireplace from drink. Although Mr. Sweet would sometimes lose complete or nearly complete control of his head and neck so that he would loll in his chair, his mind remained strangely acute and his speech not too affected. His ability to be drunk and sober at the same time made him an ideal playmate, for he was as weak as we were and we could usually best him in wrestling, all the while keeping a fairly coherent conversation going.

We never felt anything of Mr. Sweet's age when we played with him. We loved his wrinkles and would draw some on our brows to be like him, and his white hair was my special treasure and he knew it and would never come to visit us just after he had had his hair cut off at the barbershop. Once he came to our house for something, probably to see my father about fertilizer for his crops because, although he never paid the slightest attention to his crops, he liked to know what things would be best to use on them if he ever did. Anyhow, he had not come with his hair since he had just had it shaved off at the barbershop. He wore a huge straw hat to keep off the

sun and also to keep his head away from me. But as soon as I saw him I ran up and demanded that he take me up and kiss me with his funny beard which smelled so strongly of tobacco. Looking forward to burying my small fingers into his woolly hair I threw away his hat only to find he had done something to his hair, that it was no longer there! I let out a squall which made my mother think that Mr. Sweet had finally dropped me in the well or something and from that day I've been wary of men in hats. However, not long after, Mr. Sweet showed up with his hair grown out and just as white and kinky and impenetrable as it ever was.

Mr. Sweet used to call me his princess, and I believed it. He made me feel pretty at five and six, and simply outrageously devastating at the blazing age of eight and a half. When he came to our house with his guitar the whole family would stop whatever they were doing to sit around him and listen to him play. He liked to play "Sweet Georgia Brown," that was what he called me sometimes, and also he liked to play "Caldonia" and all sorts of sweet, sad, wonderful songs which he sometimes made up. It was from one of these songs that I learned that he had had to marry Miss Mary when he had in fact loved somebody else (now living in Chica-go, or De-stroy, Michigan). He was not sure that Joe Lee, her "baby," was also his baby. Sometimes he would cry and that was an indication that he was about to die again. And so we would all get prepared, for we were sure to be called upon.

I was seven the first time I remember actually participating in one of Mr. Sweet's "revivals"—my parents told me I had participated before, I had been the one chosen to kiss him and tickle him long before I knew the rite of Mr. Sweet's rehabilitation. He had come to our house, it was a few years after his wife's death, and was very sad, and also, typically, very drunk. He sat on the floor next to me and my older brother, the rest of the children were grown up and lived elsewhere, and began to play his guitar and cry. I held his woolly head in my arms and wished I could have been old enough to have been the woman he loved so much and that I had not been lost years and years ago.

When he was leaving, my mother said to us that we'd better sleep light that night for we'd probably have to go over to Mr. Sweet's before daylight. And we did. For soon after we had gone to bed one of the neighbors knocked on our door and called my father and said that Mr. Sweet was sinking fast and if he wanted to get in a word before the crossover he'd better shake a leg and get over to Mr. Sweet's house. All the neighbors knew to come to our house if something was wrong with Mr. Sweet, but they did not know how we always managed to make him well, or at least stop him from dying, when he was often so near death. As soon as we heard the cry we got up, my brother and I and my mother and father, and put on our clothes. We hurried out of the house and down the road for we were always afraid that we might someday be too late and Mr. Sweet would get tired of dallying.

When we got to the house, a very poor shack really, we found the front room full of neighbors and relatives and someone met us at the door and said that it was all very sad that old Mr. Sweet Little (for Little was his family name, although we mostly ignored it) was about to kick the bucket. My parents were advised not to take my brother and me into the "death room,"

seeing we were so young and all, but we were so much more accustomed to the death room than he that we ignored him and dashed in without giving his warning a second thought. I was almost in tears, for these deaths upset me fearfully, and the thought of how much depended on me and my brother (who was such a ham most of the time) made me very nervous.

The doctor was bending over the bed and turned back to tell us for at least the tenth time in the history of my family that, alas, old Mr. Sweet Little was dying and that the children had best not see the face of implacable death (I didn't know what "implacable" was, but whatever it was, Mr. Sweet was not!). My father pushed him rather abruptly out of the way saying, as he always did and very loudly for he was saying it to Mr. Sweet, "To hell with dying, man, these children want Mr. Sweet"—which was my cue to throw myself upon the bed and kiss Mr. Sweet all around the whiskers and under the eyes and around the collar of his nightshirt where he smelled so strongly of all sorts of things, mostly liniment.

I was very good at bringing him around, for as soon as I saw that he was struggling to open his eyes I knew he was going to be all right, and so could finish my revival sure of success. As soon as his eyes were open he would begin to smile and that way I knew that I had surely won. Once, though, I got a tremendous scare, for he could not open his eyes and later I learned that he had had a stroke and that one side of his face was stiff and hard to get into motion. When he began to smile I could tickle him in earnest because I was sure that nothing would get in the way of his laughter, although once he began to cough so hard that he almost threw me off his stomach, but that was when I was very small, little more than a baby, and my bushy hair had gotten in his nose.

When we were sure he would listen to us we would ask him why he was in bed and when he was coming to see us again and could we play with his guitar, which more than likely would be leaning against the bed. His eyes would get all misty and he would sometimes cry out loud, but we never let it embarrass us, for he knew that we loved him and that we sometimes cried too for no reason. My parents would leave the room to just the three of us; Mr. Sweet, by that time, would be propped up in bed with a number of pillows behind his head and with me sitting and lying on his shoulder and along his chest. Even when he had trouble breathing he would not ask me to get down. Looking into my eyes he would shake his white head and run a scratchy old finger all around my hairline, which was rather low down, nearly to my eyebrows, and made some people say I looked like a baby monkey.

My brother was very generous in all this, he let me do all the revivaling— he had done it for years before I was born and so was glad to be able to pass it on to someone new. What he would do while I talked to Mr. Sweet was pretend to play the guitar, in fact pretend that he was a young version of Mr. Sweet, and it always made Mr. Sweet glad to think that someone wanted to be like him—of course, we did not know this then, we played the thing by ear, and whatever he seemed to like, we did. We were desperately afraid that he was just going to take off one day and leave us.

It did not occur to us that we were doing anything special; we had not learned that death was final when it did come. We thought nothing of triumphing over it so many times, and in fact became a trifle contemptuous

of people who let themselves be carried away. It did not occur to us that if our own father had been dying we could not have stopped it, that Mr. Sweet was the only person over whom we had power.

When Mr. Sweet was in his eighties I was studying in the university many miles from home. I saw him whenever I went home, but he was never on the verge of dying that I could tell and I began to feel that my anxiety for his health and psychological well-being was unnecessary. By this time he not only had a moustache but a long flowing snow-white beard, which I loved and combed and braided for hours. He was very peaceful, fragile, gentle, and the only jarring note about him was his old steel guitar, which he still played in the old sad, sweet, down-home blues way.

On Mr. Sweet's ninetieth birthday I was finishing my doctorate in Massachusetts and had been making arrangements to go home for several weeks' rest. That morning I got a telegram telling me that Mr. Sweet was dying again and could I please drop everything and come home. Of course I could. My dissertation could wait and my teachers would understand when I explained to them when I got back. I ran to the phone, called the airport, and within four hours I was speeding along the dusty road to Mr. Sweet's.

The house was more dilapidated than when I was last there, barely a shack, but is was overgrown with yellow roses which my family had planted many years ago. The air was heavy and sweet and very peaceful. I felt strange walking through the gate and up the old rickety steps. But the strangeness left me as I caught sight of the long white beard I loved so well flowing down the thin body over the familiar quilt coverlet. Mr. Sweet!

His eyes were closed tight and his hands, crossed over his stomach, were thin and delicate, no longer scratchy. I remembered how always before I had run and jumped up on him just anywhere; now I knew he would not be able to support my weight. I looked around at my parents, and was surprised to see that my father and mother also looked old and frail. My father, his own hair very gray, leaned over the quietly sleeping old man, who, incidentally, smelled still of wine and tobacco, and said, as he'd done so many times, "To hell with dying, man! My daughter is home to see Mr. Sweet!" My brother had not been able to come as he was in the war in Asia. I bent down and gently stroked the closed eyes and gradually they began to open. The closed, wine-stained lips twitched a little, then parted in a warm, slightly embarrassed smile. Mr. Sweet could see me and he recognized me and his eyes looked very spry and twinkly for a moment. I put my head down on the pillow next to his and we just looked at each other for a long time. Then he began to trace my peculiar hairline with a thin, smooth finger. I closed my eyes when his finger halted above my ear (he used to rejoice at the dirt in my ears when I was little), his hand stayed cupped around my cheek. When I opened my eyes, sure that I had reached him in time, his were closed.

Even at twenty-four how could I believe that I had failed? that Mr. Sweet was really gone? He had never gone before. But when I looked up at my parents I saw that they were holding back tears. They had loved him dearly. He was like a piece of rare and delicate china which was always being saved from breaking and which finally fell. I looked long at the old face, the wrinkled forehead, the red lips, the hands that still reached out to

me. Soon I felt my father pushing something cool into my hands. It was Mr. Sweet's guitar. He had asked them months before to give it to me; he had known that even if I came next time he would not be able to respond in the old way. He did not want me to feel that my trip had been for nothing.

The old guitar! I plucked the strings, hummed "Sweet Georgia Brown." The magic of Mr. Sweet lingered still in the cool steel box. Through the window I could catch the fragrant delicate scent of tender yellow roses. The man on the high old-fashioned bed with the quilt coverlet and the flowing white beard had been my first love.

Chronology

Political and Social Events	Intellectual and Cultural Events

1620 Pilgrims land at Plymouth
Rock

1624 Franz Hals, *The Laughing Cavalier*
1628 William Harvey, *Essay on the Motion of the Heart and Blood*
1636 Harvard College founded
1637 René Descartes, *Discourse on Method*

1642–1660 English Civil War, Commonwealth, and Protectorate
1643 Louis XIV crowned King of France

1642 Rembrandt, *The Night Watch*

1653 Jean-Baptiste Lully becomes court composer at Paris

1669 Peter the Great begins reform and modernization of Russia

1669 Blaise Pascal, *Pensées*

1690 John Locke, *An Essay Concerning Human Understanding*

1692 Witchcraft trials at Salem, Massachusetts
1701–14 War of the Spanish Succession: a general European war over succession to the Spanish empire but more generally over the balance of power in Europe. It resulted in France's loss of much of its empire and the ascendancy of England
1714 George I of the German House of Hanover crowned King of England
1715 Louis XV crowned King of France. His rule, which extended to 1774, was corrupt and extravagant; it prepared the way for the French Revolution

1704 Johann Sebastian Bach's first cantatas composed
1709 First piano built
1710 George Berkeley, *Treatise Concerning the Principles of Human Knowledge*

1717 Jean Watteau, *Embarkation of Cythera*

1729 Johann Sebastian Bach, *St. Matthew Passion*
1738 Methodist Church founded by John Wesley and George Whitefield
1739 David Hume, *A Treatise of Human Nature*

1740 Maria Theresa Empress of Hapsburg lands; her succession precipitated the general European War of the Austrian Succession (1740–48)

Frederick II crowned King of Prussia (ruled until 1786)

1742 George Frederick Handel, *Messiah*

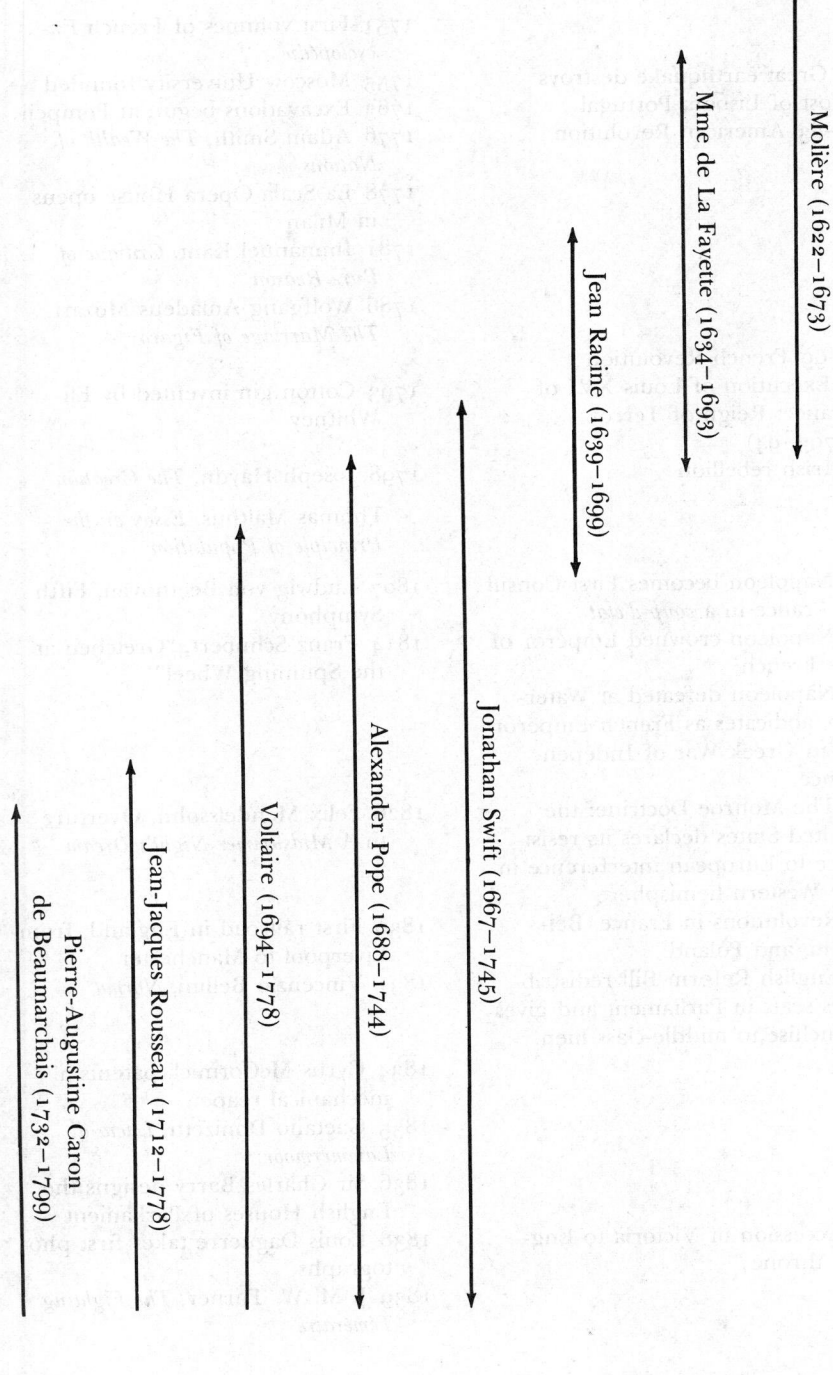

Molière (1622–1673)

Mme de La Fayette (1634–1693)

Jean Racine (1639–1699)

Jonathan Swift (1667–1745)

Alexander Pope (1688–1744)

Voltaire (1694–1778)

Jean-Jacques Rousseau (1712–1778)

Pierre-Augustine Caron
de Beaumarchais (1732–1799)

Political and Social Events	Intellectual and Cultural Events
	1751 First volumes of French *Encyclopédie*
1755 Great earthquake destroys most of Lisbon, Portugal	1755 Moscow University founded
1775–83 American Revolution	1763 Excavations begun at Pompeii
	1776 Adam Smith, *The Wealth of Nations*
	1778 La Scala Opera House opens in Milan
	1781 Immanuel Kant, *Critique of Pure Reason*
	1786 Wolfgang Amadeus Mozart, *The Marriage of Figaro*
1789–99 French Revolution	
1793 Execution of Louis XVI of France; Reign of Terror (1793–94)	1793 Cotton gin invented by Eli Whitney
1798 Irish rebellion	1798 Joseph Haydn, *The Creation*
	Thomas Malthus, *Essay on the Principle of Population*
1799 Napoleon becomes First Consul of France in a *coup d'état*	1807 Ludwig von Beethoven, Fifth Symphony
1804 Napoleon crowned Emperor of the French	1814 Franz Schubert, "Gretchen at the Spinning Wheel"
1815 Napoleon defeated at Waterloo, abdicates as French Emperor	
1821–29 Greek War of Independence	
1823 The Monroe Doctrine: the United States declares its resistance to European interference in the Western hemisphere	1826 Felix Mendelssohn, Overture to *A Midsummer Night's Dream*
1830 Revolutions in France, Belgium, and Poland	1830 First railroad in England, from Liverpool to Manchester
1832 English Reform Bill redistributes seats in Parliament and gives franchise to middle-class men.	1831 Vincenzio Bellini, *Norma*
	1834 Cyrus McCormick patents a mechanical reaper
	1835 Gaetano Donizetti, *Lucia di Lammermoor*
	1836 Sir Charles Barry designs the English Houses of Parliament
1837 Accession of Victoria to English throne	1838 Louis Daguerre takes first photographs
	1839 J. M. W. Turner, *The Fighting Téméraire*

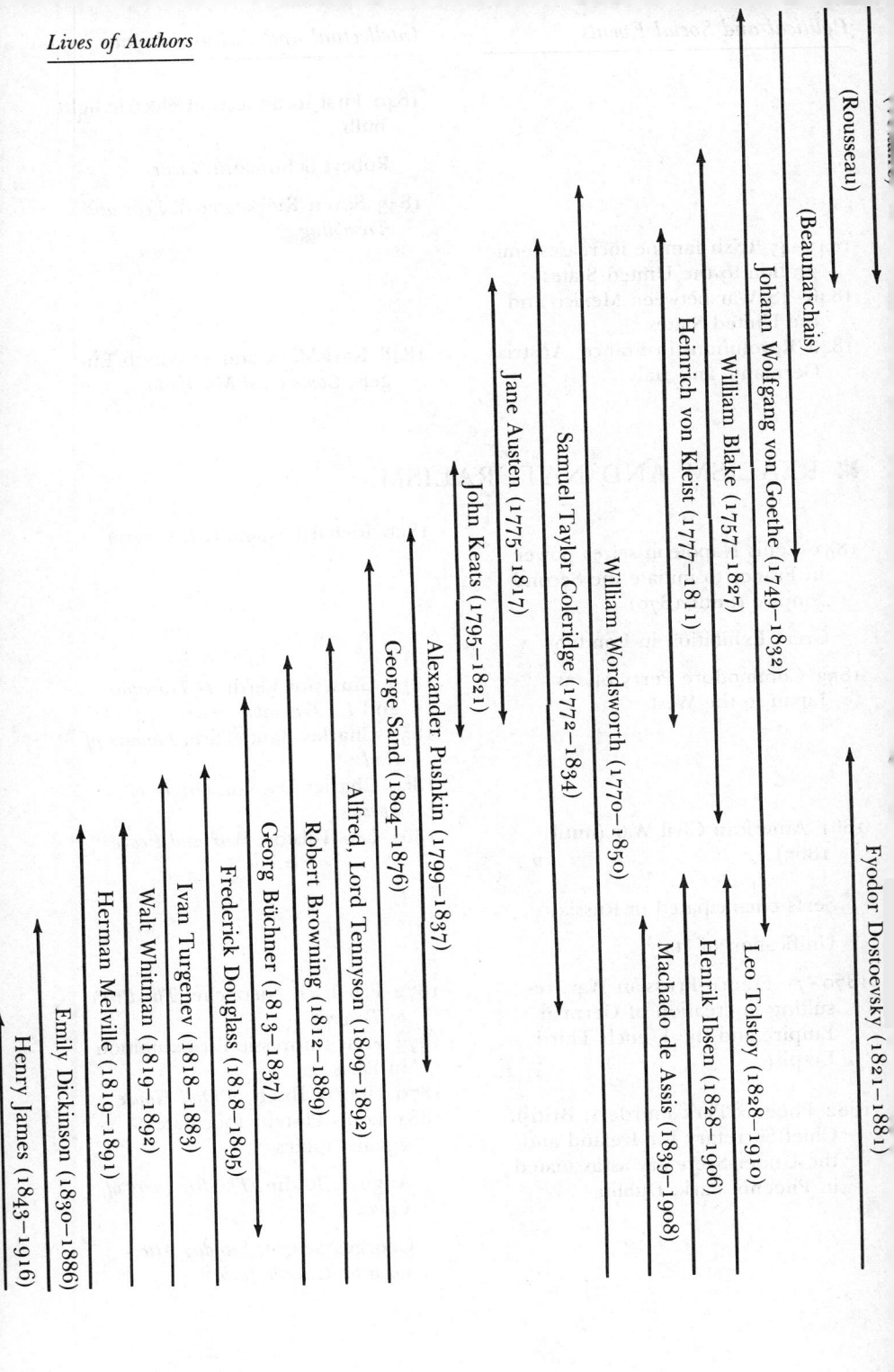

Political and Social Events	Intellectual and Cultural Events
	1840 First incandescent electric light bulb
	Robert Schumann, *Lieder*
	1843 Sören Kierkegaard, *Fear and Trembling*
1845–47 Irish famine increases emigration to the United States	
1846–48 War between Mexico and the United States	
1848 Revolutions in France, Austria, Germany, and Italy	1848 Karl Marx and Friedrich Engels, *Communist Manifesto*

❋ REALISM AND NATURALISM

Political and Social Events	Intellectual and Cultural Events
1851 Louis Napoleon seizes power in France to initiate the Second Empire (until 1870)	1850 Richard Wagner, *Lohengrin*
Great Exhibition in London	
1853 Commodore Perry opens Japan to the West	1853 Giuseppi Verdi, *Il Trovatore* and *La Traviata*
	1857 Charles Baudelaire, *Flowers of Evil*
	1859 Charles Darwin, *Origin of Species*
1861 American Civil War (until 1865)	1864 Leo Tolstoy, *War and Peace*
Serfs emancipated in Russia	
Unification of Italy	
1870–71 Franco-Prussian War, resulting in creation of German Empire and the French Third Empire	1872 Friedrich Nietzsche, *The Birth of Tragedy*
	1874 First Impressionist exhibition in Paris
	1879 Henrik Ibsen, *A Doll House*
1882 Phoenix Park murders: British Chief Secretary for Ireland and the Under-Secretary assassinated in Phoenix Park, Dublin	1884 Louis Pasteur inoculates against rabies
	Auguste Rodin, *The Burghers of Calais*
	Georges Seurat, *Sunday Afternoon on Grande Jatte*